# A NEW HISTC

UNDER THE AUSPICES OI
PLANNED AND ESTABLISHEₐ ₐ₁ ₁ₕₑ LATE T. W. MOODY

# I

# PREHISTORIC AND EARLY IRELAND

# A NEW HISTORY OF IRELAND

UNDER THE AUSPICES OF THE ROYAL IRISH ACADEMY
PLANNED AND ESTABLISHED BY THE LATE T. W. MOODY

*Already published

# A NEW HISTORY OF
# IRELAND

## I

## PREHISTORIC AND EARLY IRELAND

EDITED BY

## DÁIBHÍ Ó CRÓINÍN

**OXFORD**
UNIVERSITY PRESS

# OXFORD
## UNIVERSITY PRESS

Great Clarendon Street, Oxford OX2 6DP

Oxford University Press is a department of the University of Oxford.
It furthers the University's objective of excellence in research, scholarship,
and education by publishing worldwide in

Oxford New York

Auckland Cape Town Dar es Salaam Hong Kong Karachi Kuala Lumpur
Madrid Melbourne Mexico City Nairobi New Delhi Shanghai Taipei Toronto

With offices in

Argentina Austria Brazil Chile Czech Republic France Greece
Guatemala Hungary Italy Japan Poland Portugal
Singapore South Korea Switzerland Thailand Turkey Ukraine Vietnam

Oxford is a registered trade mark of Oxford University Press
in the UK and in certain other countries

Published in the United States
by Oxford University Press Inc., New York

British Library Cataloguing in Publication Data
Data available

Library of Congress Cataloging in Publication Data
Data available

ISBN 978-0-19-821737-4 (Hbk.)   978-0-19-922665-8 (Pbk.)

Typeset by SPI Publisher Services, Pondicherry, India
Printed in Great Britain
on acid-free paper by
Biddles Ltd.
King's Lynn, Norfolk

# PREFACE

THIS volume has been long awaited, and its appearance now reflects the development of studies in this area over the past twenty years. In the early years of the *New history*, scholars working in the period covered by this volume were relatively few, and contributors who had to withdraw or delay their work under pressure of other commitments were difficult to replace. The vigorous recent growth of scholarship in this period is shown not only in the bibliography (where stringent measures have been needed to keep within the space available) but in a scheme of chapters involving more scholars and a wider range of topics than our original plan. The chapters prepared by James Carney, Kathleen Hughes, and M. J. O'Kelly have proved to be of lasting value, requiring little more than annotation to take account of work appearing since their deaths. This volume has also, however, benefited from recent archaeological, linguistic, and historical research, and in some areas— notably music and numismatics—it amplifies and amends the accounts that appeared in earlier volumes of the *New history*.

In using forms of names, we have followed the guidelines in volume VIII (pp 4–5). Place-names have been given in their current English form (as used by the Ordnance Survey) except where obscure or unidentifiable.

Once again we acknowledge with gratitude the indispensable support of the late C. S. Andrews in setting the *New history* in motion; and the generous financial help provided by the late Dr John A. Mulcahy, of New York, and the directors of the American Irish Foundation, which enabled us to carry out much-needed research in the early stages of work on the project.

We take this opportunity of recording our debt to Dr Peter Harbison, whose energy and judgement in compiling the illustrations of this volume— as well as in his share of work on the bibliography—have been essential to its completion; and to our typist, Peggy Morgan, whose work for the *New history* to December 1994 completed over twenty-four years of invaluable service, including the typing of a substantial part of this volume.

Finally, we record with sorrow the death on 13 February 2000 of F. X. Martin, a member of the board of editors since the foundation of this project, and its chairman since 1984; the death on 31 December 2000 of William O'Sullivan; and the death on 5 June 2003 of Ann Hamlin, who revised the text written by Kathleen Hughes and contributed an introductory note.

F. J. BYRNE
W. E. VAUGHAN
ART COSGROVE
J. R. HILL
DÁIBHÍ Ó CRÓINÍN

*Royal Irish Academy*
*3 October 2003*

# CONTENTS

## BIBLIOGRAPHY

# CONTRIBUTORS

| | |
|---|---|
| John Harwood Andrews | M.A. (Dubl., Cantab.), M.Litt. (Dubl.), Ph.D. (Lond.); M.R.I.A.; fellow emeritus, Trinity College, Dublin |
| Ann Buckley | B.Mus., M.A. (N.U.I.), Doctoraal (Amsterdam), Ph.D. (Cantab.); research associate, Centre for Medieval and Renaissance Studies, Trinity College, Dublin; senior research fellow in music, National University of Ireland, Maynooth |
| Francis John Byrne | M.A. (N.U.I.); M.R.I.A.; professor emeritus, University College, Dublin |
| James Patrick Carney | B.A. (N.U.I.); M.R.I.A.; senior professor, School of Celtic Studies, Dublin Institute for Advanced Studies (died 7 July 1989) |
| Nancy Margaret Edwards | B.A. (Liverpool); Ph.D. (Dunelm.); reader in archaeology, department of history and Welsh history, University of Wales, Bangor |
| Thomas Mowbray Charles-Edwards | M.A., D.Phil.; F.R.H.S.; Jesus professor of Celtic, University of Oxford |
| Marie Therese Flanagan | B.A. (Deut. Akad. Austau.), M.A. (N.U.I.), D.Phil. (Oxon.); senior lecturer in modern history (medieval), Queen's University, Belfast |
| Ann Elizabeth Hamlin | M.A., Ph.D.; F.S.A.; M.R.I.A.; principal inspector of historic monuments, Northern Ireland (died 5 June 2003) |

| | |
|---|---|
| Peter Harbison | M.A. (N.U.I.), Dr Phil. (Marburg); F.S.A.; M.R.I.A.; honorary fellow of Trinity College, Dublin |
| Joseph Pedlow Haughton | M.A., M.Sc. (Dubl.); M.R.I.A.; fellow emeritus, Trinity College, Dublin |
| Kathleen Winifred Hughes | Ph.D. (Lond.); fellow of Newnham College, Cambridge; Nora Chadwick reader in Celtic Studies, University of Cambridge (died 20 Apr. 1977) |
| Michael Kenny | B.A., M.A. (N.U.I.); curator, art and industrial division, National Museum of Ireland |
| Donnchadh Ó Corráin | M.A., D.Litt. (N.U.I.); M.R.I.A.; associate professor of Irish history, University College, Cork |
| Dáibhí Ó Cróinín | M.Phil., Ph.D. (N.U.I.); M.R.I.A.; professor of history, National University of Ireland, Galway |
| Michael Joseph O'Kelly | M.A., D. Litt. (N.U.I.); F.S.A.; M.R.I.A.; professor of archaeology, University College, Cork (died 14 Oct. 1982) |
| William O'Sullivan | Ph.D. (N.U.I.); F.I.C.I.; M.R.I.A. (died 31 Dec. 2000) |
| Barry Raftery | M.A., Ph.D. (N.U.I.); M.R.I.A.; professor of Celtic archaeology, University College, Dublin |
| Hilary Hamilton Richardson | B.A., M.A. (Cantab.); M.A. (N.U.I.); former lecturer in archaeology, University College, Dublin |
| Paul Russell | M.A., M.Phil., D.Phil. (Oxon.); head of classics, Radley College, Abingdon (Oxon.); visiting lecturer in Celtic, University of Oxford |
| Alexander Brian Scott | D.Phil. (Oxon.); M.R.I.A.; emeritus professor of late Latin, Queen's University, Belfast |

Roger Andrew Stalley | M.A. (Lond.); F.S.A.; M.R.I.A.; M.R.I.A.I. (Hon.); fellow, and professor of the history of art, Trinity College, Dublin

Patrick Francis Wallace | Ph.D. (N.U.I.); F.S.A.; M.R.I.A.; director, National Museum of Ireland

Maps 1–8 have been drawn by Sarah Gearty, cartographic editor and project administrator of the Irish Historic Towns Atlas, Royal Irish Academy, in consultation with Mary Davies, B.A., cartographic adviser to this history.

The index is the work of Dr Helen Litton.

# MAPS

# PLATES

118   Horns and crotals from the late bronze-age (eighth–seventh century B.C.)
      hoard from Dowris, Co. Offaly (National Museum of Ireland)
119   Responsorial dialogue and preface with neumatic notation in the twelfth-
      century Drummond Missal (Pierpoint Morgan Library, New York, MS
      M.627, f. 37$^r$4)
120   Easter processional antiphon 'Dicant nunc Iudei', set for two voices in a
      twelfth- or thirteenth-century Irish gradual (Bodl., Rawl. MS C 892,
      ff 67–68$^r$)
121   Colophon set in three-part polyphony in an Irish psalter from the second half
      of the twelfth century (B.L., Add. MS 36929, f. 59$^r$)
122   The hymn 'Adest dies leticiae', in honour of St Brigid, in an Irish Divine
      Office antiphonal from the second half of the fifteenth century (T.C.D.,
      MS 78, f. 139$^v$)
123   Fragments of notation inscribed on one of four slates from Smarmore, Co.
      Louth, probably second half of the fifteenth century (National Museum of
      Ireland)
124   Detail from the shrine of the Stowe Missal ('shrine of St Maelruain's Gospel'),
      eleventh century, depicting a player of a three-stringed plucked lyre, seated
      between two clerics (National Museum of Ireland)
125   Breac Maedóic ('shrine of St Mogue'), eleventh century, bearing the earliest
      Irish illustration of a trilateral harp. This one appears to have eight strings,
      and may be an example of the *ocht-tédach* used by travelling clerics to
      accompany psalm-singing
126   Musicians on the east face of the Cross of Muiredach, Monasterboice, Co.
      Louth, early tenth century
127   Musicians on the south arm of the east face of the Cross of St Columba at
      Durrow, Co. Offaly, early tenth century
128   Reconstructed seating plan of Tech Midchúarda (the Hall of Tara) from the
      fourteenth-century Yellow Book of Lecan (T.C.D., MS 1318 (H.2.16), cols
      243–4 (facsimile ed., p. 418))
129   Among the names listed in the Dublin Guild Merchant roll (*c.*1190–1265) is
      that of Thomas le Harpur, accompanied by a sketch of a harp, in an entry
      for *c.*1200
130   Cross of the Scriptures, Clonmacnoise, Co. Offaly, showing a lyre-player
      (central panel, south side of shaft) and a player of the triple pipes
      (corresponding panel, north side), ninth or tenth century
131   Miracle of the loaves and fishes: figure with assymetrical lyre on the west face
      of the head of the ninth-century South Cross, or Cross of St Patrick and
      St Columba, Kells, Co. Meath
132   The only known medieval Irish representation of a bowed instrument is this
      twelfth-century carving of a lyre-player from St Finan's church, Lough
      Currane, Waterville, Co. Kerry
133   A harper at Solomon's court, on the west wall of Ardmore cathedral, Co.
      Waterford

134   Portrait of a musician from the Book of Kells, eighth or ninth century (T.C.D.,
      MS 58, f. 292$^r$): 'In principio' with a stylised seated figure (letter 'i') holding
      letter 'c' as a stringed instrument

135   Woodcut (plate 3) from John Derricke's *Image of Irelande* (1583), representing
      a harper and reciter (and possibly a pair of *crosáin* to the right) performing at
      Mac Suibhne's feast, 1581

136   A sword-dancing scene on a fifteenth- or sixteenth-century book-cover bearing
      the arms of one of the FitzGeralds of Desmond

137   (a) Fragment of a wooden bow; (b) detail of the terminal carved in the
      Ringerike style, excavated from a mid-eleventh-century site in Christchurch
      Place, Dublin (National Museum of Ireland)

138   Tuning pegs made of yew: (a) shorter examples, probably from lyres, fiddles,
      or psalteries; (b) a longer type, possibly from a harp (High Street; thirteenth
      century) (National Museum of Ireland)

139   Flutes and flute fragments from excavations of medieval Dublin, left to right:
      (a) bone flute with two fingerholes; (b) bone flute without fingerholes; and
      (c) mouthpiece fragment of a bone flute (all from High Street, thirteenth
      century) (National Museum of Ireland). Photos: National Museum of
      Ireland

140a  Fragments of a ceramic horn from Wood Quay, Dublin, thirteenth century
      (National Museum of Ireland)

140b  Horn of yew with bronze mounts, eighth or ninth century, from Lough Erne,
      Co. Fermanagh (Ulster Museum)

The originals of these illustrations were made available through the courtesy of the
following, and are published by their permission: Dúchas, The Heritage Service,
plates 1, 16, 67a, 73b, 87c, 88a, 88b, 89a, 89b, 90a, 91a, 92a, 92b, 97, 98, 101, 104,
106, 107, 111, 114, 115, 116, 130, 131, 132, 133; William O'Brien, plate 2; Cork
Public Museum, plate 3; National Museum of Ireland, plates 4, 25, 64a, 64b, 66a,
66b, 66c, 67b, 69b, 69c, 70d, 71a, 71b, 75a, 78, 79a, 82b, 85a, 85b, 86a, 86b, 87b, 93a,
93b, 94a, 94b, 96, 117, 118, 123, 124, 125, 136, 137, 138, 139, 140a; Cambridge
University Committee for Aerial Photography, plate 5 (Cambridge University
Collection of Air Photographs, plates 10, 11); Environment and Heritage Service,
Department of the Environment, Northern Ireland, plates 6, 7, 87a; Institute of Irish
Studies, Queen's University of Belfast, plate 8; Barrie Hartwell, plate 9; Peter
Harbison, plates 12, 15, 17, 100, 102, 126, 127; Liam Lyons, plate 13; Royal Irish
Academy, plates 14, 20, 22, 23, 59, 80a; Irish Tourist Board, plates 18, 103; the
Board of Trinity College, Dublin, plates 19, 33, 34, 35, 36, 42, 43, 44, 47, 55, 56, 61,
62, 65, 72, 74b, 75b, 76, 82a, 83, 84a, 84b, 99, 122, 128, 134, front cover; Würzburg
Universitätsbibliothek, plate 21; Biblioteca Ambrosiana, Milan, plates 24, 26, 27, 40;
Bibliothèque Nationale de France, plates 28, 31, 32; Augsburg,
Universitätsbibliothek, plate 29; Durham Cathedral Library, plate 30; British
Library, London, plates 37, 51, 52, 54, 68, 121; St Gallen, Stiftsbibliothek, plate 38;
Bodleian Library, Oxford, plates 39, 57, 58, 60, 84c, 120; Stadtsbibliothek,
Schaffhausen, plate 41; Lambeth Palace Library, London, plates 45, 46; Department
of Archives, University College, Dublin, plate 48; Cambridge University Library,

plate 49; Edinburgh University Library, plate 50; the Pierpoint Morgan Library, New York. plates 53, 119; the Françoise Henry Archive, plates 63, 69a, 70a, 70b, 73a, 73c, 74a, 79b, 79c; Ann Hamlin, plate 70c; Musée des Antiquités Nationales, Saint-Germain-en-Laye, plates 77a, 77b; Ulster Museum, Belfast, plates 77c, 79d, 80c, 140b; Museo Civico Medievale, Bologna, plate 80b; Victoria and Albert Museum, plate 81; Belzeaux, plate 83; Elinor Wiltshire, plates 87d, 91b; Österreichische Nationalbibliothek, plate 89c; Hilary Richardson, plates 90b, 93b; Oxford University Press, plates 95a, 95b; Roger Stalley, plates 105, 108, 109, 110, 112, 113; Dublin Corporation, plate 129

# LINE DRAWINGS AND TEXT FIGURES

# ABBREVIATIONS AND CONVENTIONS

Abbreviations and conventions used in this volume are listed below. They consist of (a) the relevant items from the list in *Irish Historical Studies*, supplement I ( Jan. 1968) and (b) abbreviations, on the same model, not included in the *Irish Historical Studies* list. Where an article is cited more than once in a chapter, an abbreviated form is used after the first full reference. Occasionally, however, the full reference is repeated for the convenience of the reader. Abbreviations that occur only within one chapter, where full details are given on first appearance, are not as a rule included in the following list.

| | |
|---|---|
| *a.* | *ante* (before) |
| *A.F.M.* | *Annala rioghachta Eireann: Annals of the kingdom of Ireland by the Four Masters from the earliest period to the year 1616,* ed. and trans. John O'Donovan (7 vols, Dublin, 1851; reprint New York, 1966) |
| *A.U.* | *Annála Uladh, Annals of Ulster; otherwise Annála Senait, Annals of Senat; a chronicle of Irish affairs, 431–1131, 1155–1541,* ed. W. M. Hennessy and B. MacCarthy (4 vols, Dublin, 1887–1901) |
| *A.U.* (1983) | Seán Mac Airt and Gearóid Mac Niocaill (ed.), *The Annals of Ulster to* A.D. 1311 (Dublin, 1983) |
| Allard, *Jean Scot écrivain* | G. H. Allard (ed.), *Jean Scot écrivain: actes du IVe Colloque International Montréal, 28 Aug.–2 Sept. 1983* (Montreal, 1986) |
| Almqvist, Ó Catháin, & Ó hÉalaí, *Heroic process* | Bo Almqvist, Séamas Ó Catháin, and Pádraig Ó hÉalaí (ed.), *The heroic process: form, function, and fantasy in folk epic* (Dublin, 1987) |
| *Anc. laws Ire.* | *Ancient laws and institutes of Ireland* (6 vols, Dublin, 1865–1901) |
| Anderson, *Adomnan's Life* | *Adomnan's Life of Columba,* ed. and trans. A. O. and M. O. Anderson (Edinburgh, 1961) |

| | |
|---|---|
| *Anal. Hib.* | *Analecta Hibernica, including the reports of the Irish Manuscripts Commission* (Dublin, 1930– ) |
| *Ann. Camb.* | 'Annales Cambriae', ed. E. Phillimore, in *Y Cymmrodor*, ix (1888) |
| *Ann. Clon.* | *The Annals of Clonmacnoise, being annals of Ireland from the earliest period to* A.D. *1408...*, ed. Denis Murphy (R.S.A.I., Dublin, 1896) |
| *Ann. Inisf.* | *The Annals of Inisfallen (MS Rawlinson B503)*, ed. and trans. Seán Mac Airt (Dublin Institute for Advanced Studies, 1951) |
| *Ann. Tig.* | 'The Annals of Tigernach', ed. Whitley Stokes, in *Rev. Celt.*, xvi–xviii (1896–7) |
| *Antiq. Jn.* | *The Antiquaries Journal* (London, 1921– ) |
| *Antiq. Soc. Scot. Proc.* | *Proceedings of the Society of Antiquaries of Scotland* (Edinburgh, 1851– ) |
| *Antiquity* | *Antiquity: quarterly review of archaeology* (Cambridge, 1927– ) |
| *Archaeology Ireland* | *Archaeology Ireland* (Dublin, 1987– ) |
| B.L. | British Library |
| B.L., Add. MS | —— Additional MS |
| B.L., Cott. MS | —— Cottonian MS |
| B.L., Eg. MS | —— Egerton MS |
| B.L., Harl. MS | —— Harleian MS |
| *Béaloideas* | *Béaloideas: the journal of the Folklore of Ireland Society* (Dublin, 1927– ) |
| Bede, *Hist. ecc.* (1969) | Bertram Colgrave and R. A. B. Mynors (ed. and trans.), *Bede's ecclesiastical history of the English people* (Oxford, 1969) |
| *Belfast Natur. Hist. Soc. Proc.* | *Proceedings and Reports of the Belfast Natural History and Philosophical Society* (Belfast, 1873– ) |
| Bibl. Nat. | Bibliothèque Nationale, Paris |
| Bieler, *Ir. penitentials* | Ludwig Bieler (ed. and trans.), *The Irish penitentials* (Scriptores Latini Hiberniae, v; Dublin, 1963) |

Bieler, *Patrician texts* — Ludwig Bieler (ed. and trans.), *Patrician texts in the Book of Armagh* (Scriptores Latini Hiberniae, x; Dublin, 1979)

*Bk Lec.* — *The Book of Lecan; Leabhar Mór Mhic Fhir Bhisigh Leacain*, with foreword by Eoin MacNeill and introduction by Kathleen Mulchrone (facsimile, I.M.C., Dublin, 1937)

*Bk Leinster* — *The Book of Leinster, formerly Lebar na Núachongbala*, ed. R. I. Best, Osborn Bergin, M. A. O'Brien, and Anne O'Sullivan (6 vols, Dublin Institute for Advanced Studies, 1954–83)

*Bk Rights*, ed. Dillon — *Lebor na Cert; The Book of Rights*, ed. Myles Dillon (Ir. Texts Soc., Dublin, 1962)

*Bk Uí Maine* — *The Book of Uí Maine, otherwise called 'The Book of the O'Kellys'*, with introduction by R. A. S. Macalister (collotype facsimile, I.M.C., Dublin, 1942)

Bodl. — Bodleian Library, Oxford

Bonner, *Famulus Christi* — Gerald Bonner (ed.), *Famulus Christi: essays in commemoration of the thirteenth centenary of the birth of the Venerable Bede* (London, 1976)

Bourke, *Isles of the north* — Cormac Bourke (ed.), *From the isles of the north: early medieval art in Ireland and Britain* (Belfast, 1995)

Bradley, *Settlement & society* — John Bradley (ed.), *Settlement and society in medieval Ireland: studies presented to F. X. Martin* (Kilkenny, 1988)

*Brit. Acad. Proc.* — *Proceedings of the British Academy* (London, 1903–   )

Brit. Arch. Reps — British Archaeological Reports

Byrne, *Ir. kings* — F. J. Byrne, *Irish kings and high-kings* (London, 1973; reprinted, 1987)

*c.* — *circa* (about)

*C.I.H.*

D. A. Binchy (ed.), *Corpus iuris Hibernici* (6 vols, Dublin, 1978)

CLA

*Codices Latini antiquiores: a guide to Latin manuscripts before A.D. 800* (12 vols, Oxford, 1934–71)

*Cal. Carew MSS, 1515–74* [etc.]

*Calendar of the Carew manuscripts preserved in the archiepiscopal library at Lambeth, 1515–74* [etc.] (6 vols, London, 1867–73)

*Cal. S. P. Ire., 1509–73* [etc.]

*Calendar of the state papers relating to Ireland, 1509–73* [etc.] (24 vols, London, 1860–1911)

*Camb. Med. Celt. Studies*

*Cambridge Medieval Celtic Studies* (Leamington Spa, 1981–93, 25 issues; continued as *Cambrian Medieval Celtic Studies*, Aberystwyth, 1993–   )

Carney, *Studies in Ir. lit.*

James Carney, *Studies in Irish literature and history* (Dublin, 1955)

*Celtica*

*Celtica* (Dublin, 1946–   )

Charlesworth, *Historical geology*

J. K. Charlesworth, *The geology of Ireland: an introduction* (Edinburgh, 1953)

*Chron. Scot.*

*Chronicum Scotorum: a chronicle of Irish affairs . . . to 1135, and supplement . . . 1141–1150,* ed. W. M. Hennessy (London, 1866)

Clarke & Brennan, *Columbanus*

H. B. Clarke and M. Brennan (ed.), *Columbanus and Merovingian monasticism* (Oxford, 1981)

Clarke & Simms, *Urban origins*

H. B. Clarke and Anngret Simms (ed.), *The comparative history of urban origins in non-Roman Europe* (Brit. Arch. Reps, International Series, cclv; 2 vols, Oxford, 1985)

Clarke, Ní Mhaonaigh, & Ó Floinn, *Ire. & Scandinavia*

H. B. Clarke, Máire Ní Mhaonaigh, and Raghnall Ó Floinn (ed.), *Ireland and Scandinavia in the early viking age* (Dublin, 1998)

*Clogher Rec.*

*Clogher Record* ([Monaghan], 1953–   )

| | |
|---|---|
| *Cog. Gaedhel* | *Cogadh Gaedhel re Gallaibh; the war of the Gaedhil with the Gaill*, ed. J. H. Todd (London, 1867) |
| Corish, *Ir. catholicism* | Patrick J. Corish (ed.), *A history of Irish catholicism* (16 fascs, Dublin and Melbourne, 1967–72) |
| *Cork Hist. Soc. Jn.* | *Journal of the Cork Historical and Archaeological Society* (Cork, 1892–   ) |
| d. | died |
| de Brún, Ó Coileáin, & Ó Riain, *Folia Gadelica* | Pádraig de Brún, Seán Ó Coileáin, and Pádraig Ó Riain (ed.), *Folia Gadelica: aistí ó iardhaltaí leis a bronnadh ar R. A. Breatnach* (Cork, 1983) |
| Dillon, *Ir. sagas* | Myles Dillon (ed.), *Irish sagas* (Cork, 1968) |
| Dopsch & Juffinger, *Virgil von Salzburg* | Heinz Dopsch and Roswitha Juffinger (ed.), *Virgil von Salzburg* (Salzburg, 1985) |
| Driscoll & Nieke, *Power & politics* | S. T. Driscoll and M. R. Nieke (ed.), *Power and politics in early medieval Britain and Ireland* (Edinburgh, 1988) |
| Dumville, *St Patrick* | David N. Dumville (ed.), *Saint Patrick A.D. 493–1993* (Woodbridge, 1993) |
| *E.H.R.* | *English Historical Review* (London, 1886–   ) |
| *Econ. Hist. Rev.* | *Economic History Review* (London, 1927–   ) |
| ed. | edited by, edition, editor(s) |
| Edwards, *Archaeology early med. Ire.* | Nancy Edwards, *The archaeology of early medieval Ireland* (London, 1990) |
| *Éigse* | *Éigse: a journal of Irish studies* (Dublin, 1939–   ) |
| *Emania* | *Emania: bulletin of the Navan Research Group* (Navan, 1986–   ) |
| Erichsen & Brockhoff, *Kilian* | Johannes Erichsen and Evamaria Brockhoff (ed.), *Kilian, Mönch aus Irland— aller Franken Patron: Aufsätze* (2 vols, Munich, 1989) |

| | |
|---|---|
| *Ériu* | *Ériu: founded as the journal of the School of Irish Learning* (Dublin, 1904– ) |
| *Études Celt.* | *Études Celtiques* (Paris, 1936– ) |
| Evans, Griffith, & Jope, *Proc. 7th Congress* | D. Ellis Evans, John G. Griffith, and E. M. Jope (ed.), *Proceedings of the Seventh International Congress of Celtic Studies, Oxford 1983* (Oxford, 1986) |
| *Facs nat. MSS Ire.* | *Facsimiles of the national manuscripts of Ireland*, ed. J. T. Gilbert (5 pts, Dublin, 1874–84) |
| *Féil-sgríbhinn Eoin Mhic Néill* | *Féil-sgríbhinn Eoin Mhic Néill: essays and studies presented to Professor Eoin Mac-Neill on the occasion of his seventieth birthday*, ed. John Ryan (Dublin, 1940) |
| *Fél. Oeng.* | Whitley Stokes (ed. and trans.), *Félire Oengusso Céli Dé: the martyrology of Oengus the Culdee* (London, 1905) |
| *fl.* | *floruit* (flourished) |
| Ford, *Celtic folklore* | Patrick K. Ford (ed), *Celtic folklore and Christianity* (Santa Barbara, 1983) |
| *Galway Arch. Soc. Jn.* | *Journal of the Galway Archaeological and Historical Society* (Galway, 1900– ) |
| *The Glynns* | *The Glynns: journal of the Glens of Antrim Historical Society* (Ballymena, 1983– ) |
| Gwynn & Hadcock, *Med. religious houses* | Aubrey Gwynn and R. Neville Hadcock, *Medieval religious houses: Ireland* (London, 1970) |
| H.C. | house of commons papers |
| Heist, *Vitae SS Hib.* | W. W. Heist (ed.), *Vitae sanctorum Hiberniae ex codice olim Salmanticensi nunc Bruxellensi* (Brussels, 1965) |
| Herbert, *Iona, Kells, & Derry* | Máire Herbert, *Iona, Kells, and Derry: the history and hagiography of the monastic familia of Columba* (Oxford, 1988; reprinted Dublin, 1996) |
| *Hermathena* | *Hermathena: a series of papers . . . by members of Trinity College, Dublin* (Dublin, 1874– ) |

| | |
|---|---|
| Herren, *Insular Latin studies* | Michael Herren (ed.), *Insular Latin studies: papers on Latin texts and manuscripts of the British Isles, 550–1066* (Toronto, 1981) |
| *Hist. Studies* | *Historical Studies: papers read before the Irish Conference of Historians* (1958– ) |
| Hughes, *Ch. in early Ir. soc.* | Kathleen Hughes, *The church in early Irish society* (London, 1966) |
| *I.E.R.* | *Irish Ecclesiastical Record* (171 vols, Dublin, 1864–1968) |
| *I.H.S.* | *Irish Historical Studies: the joint journal of the Irish Historical Society and the Ulster Society for Irish Historical Studies* (Dublin, 1938– ) |
| I.M.C. | Irish Manuscripts Commission |
| *Ir. Geneal.* | *The Irish Genealogist: official organ of the Irish Genealogical Research Society* (London, 1937– ) |
| *Ir. Geography* | *Irish Geography (bulletin of the Geographical Society of Ireland)* (vols i–iv, Dublin, 1944–63); continued as *The Geographical Society of Ireland, Irish Geography* (vol. v–, Dublin, 1964– ) |
| *Ir. Jurist* | *The Irish Jurist*, new series (Dublin, 1966– ) |
| *Ir. Monthly* | *Irish Monthly Magazine* [later entitled *Irish Monthly*] (London and Dublin, 1873–1954) |
| *Ir. Sword* | *The Irish Sword: the journal of the Military History Society of Ireland* (Dublin, [1949]– ) |
| *Ir. texts* | *Irish texts*, ed. J. Fraser, P. Grosjean, and J. G. O'Keeffe (5 fascs, London, 1931–4) |
| Ir. Texts Soc. | Irish Texts Society |
| *Irish University Review* | *Irish University Review: a journal of Irish studies* (Shannon, 1970– ) |

Karkov, Ryan, & Farrell, *Insular tradition*    Catherine E. Karkov, Michael Ryan, and Robert T. Farrell (ed.), *The insular tradition* (SUNY Series in Medieval Studies, ed. Paul E. Szarmach; Albany, N.Y., 1997)

Kenney, *Sources*    James F. Kenney, *The sources for the early history of Ireland, i : ecclesiastical* (New York, 1929; revised ed., Dublin, 1966)

*Kerry Arch. Soc. Jn.*    *Journal of the Kerry Archaeological and Historical Society* ([Tralee], 1968– )

*Kildare Arch. Soc. Jn.*    *Journal of the County Kildare Archaeological Society* (Dublin, 1891– )

*Léachtaí Cholm Cille*    *Léachtaí Cholm Cille* (Maynooth, 1970– )

Leask, *Churches*    H. G. Leask, *Irish churches and monastic buildings* (2 vols, Dundalk, 1955)

*Louth Arch. Soc. Jn.*    *Journal of the County Louth Archaeological Society* (Dundalk, 1904– )

Löwe, *Die Iren*    Heinz Löwe (ed.), *Die Iren und Europa im früheren Mittelalter* (2 vols, Stuttgart, 1982)

Macalister, *Corpus inscriptionum*    R. A. S. Macalister, *Corpus inscriptionum insularum Celticarum* (2 vols, Dublin, 1945)

Mac Conmara, *An léann eaglasta*    Máirtín Mac Conmara (ed.), *An léann eaglasta 1000–1200* (Dublin, 1982)

Mac Eoin, Ahlqvist, & Ó hAodha, *Proc. 6th Congress*    Gearóid Mac Eoin, Anders Ahlqvist, and Donncha Ó hAodha (ed.), *Proceedings of the Sixth International Congress of Celtic Studies held in University College, Galway, 4–13 July 1979* (Dublin, 1983)

MacLennan, *Proc. 1st N.A. Congress*    Gordon W. MacLennan (ed.), *Proceedings of the First North American Congress of Celtic Studies... 1986* (Ottawa, 1988)

Mac Niocaill & Wallace, *Keimelia*    Gearoid Mac Niocaill and P. F. Wallace (ed.), *Keimelia: studies in medieval archaeology and history in memory of Tom Delaney* (Galway, 1988)

Manning, *Beyond the Pale* — Conleth Manning (ed.), *Dublin and beyond the Pale: studies in honour of Patrick Healy* (Bray, 1998)

*Medieval Archaeology* — *Medieval Archaeology* (London, 1957– )

*Mitt. St.* — Bernhard Bischoff, *Mittelalterliche Studien: ausgewählte Aufsätze zur Schriftkunde und Literaturgeschichte* (3 vols, Stuttgart, 1966–7, 1981)

Monk & Sheehan, *Early med. Munster* — Michael A. Monk and John Sheehan (ed.), *Early medieval Munster: archaeology, history and society* (Cork, 1998)

n.d. — no date given

*N.H.I.* — *A new history of Ireland* (9 vols, Oxford, 1976–2005)

N.U.I. — National University of Ireland

*N. Munster Antiq. Jn.* — *North Munster Antiquarian Journal* (Limerick, 1936– )

Ní Chatháin & Richter, *Ire. & Christendom* — Próinséas Ní Chatháin and Michael Richter (ed.), *Irland und die Christenheit: Bibelstudien und Mission / Ireland and Christendom: the Bible and the missions* (Stuttgart, 1987)

Ní Chatháin & Richter, *Ire. & Europe* — Próinséas Ní Chatháin and Michael Richter (ed.), *Irland und Europa: die Kirche im Frühmittelalter / Ireland and Europe: the early church* (Stuttgart, 1984)

O'Brien, *Corpus geneal. Hib.* — M. A. O'Brien (ed.), *Corpus genealogiarum Hiberniae*, i (Dublin, 1962; reprint, 1976)

Ó Corráin, *Ir. antiquity* — Donnchadh Ó Corráin (ed.), *Irish antiquity: essays and studies presented to M. J. O'Kelly* (Cork, 1981)

Ó Corráin, Breatnach, & McCone, *Sages, saints, & storytellers* — Donnchadh Ó Corráin, Liam Breatnach, and Kim McCone (ed.), *Sages, saints, and storytellers: Celtic studies in honour of Professor James Carney* (Maynooth, 1989)

O'Grady, *Silva Gadelica*

Standish O'Grady, *Silva Gadelica* (2 vols, London, 1892; reprint, Dublin, 1935)

O'Meara & Baumann, *Latin script & letters*

J. J. O'Meara and Bernd Naumann (ed.). *Latin script and letters A.D. 400–900. Festchrift presented to Ludwig Bieler on the occasion of his 70th birthday* (Leyden, 1976)

O'Meara & Bieler,*Eriugena*

J. J. O'Meara and Ludwig Bieler (ed.), *The mind of Eriugena: papers of a colloquium* ... (Dublin, 1973)

O'Rahilly, *Early Ir. hist.*

T. F. O'Rahilly, *Early Irish history and mythology* (Dublin, 1946)

*p.*

*post* (after)

P.R.O.

Public Record Office, London

P.R.O.I.

Public Record Office of Ireland (part of National Archives of Ireland)

*Peritia*

*Peritia: journal of the Medieval Academy of Ireland* ([Cork], 1982–   )

Picard, *Ire. & northern France*

Jean-Michel Picard (ed.), *Ireland and northern France A.D. 600–850* (Dublin, 1991)

*P.L.*

*Patrologia Latina*, ed. J. P. Migne (221 vols, Paris, 1844–64)

Plummer, *Vitae SS Hib.*

Charles Plummer (ed.), *Vitae sanctorum Hiberniae, partim hactenus ineditae* ... (2 vols, Oxford, 1910)

*Prehist. Soc. Proc.*

*Proceedings of the Prehistoric Society* (Cambridge, 1935–   )

Q.U.B.

Queen's University of Belfast

R.I.A.

Royal Irish Academy

*R.I.A. Proc.*

*Proceedings of the Royal Irish Academy* (Dublin, 1836–   )

*R.I.A. Trans.*

*Transactions of the Royal Irish Academy* (33 vols, Dublin, 1786–1907)

R.S.A.I.

Royal Society of Antiquaries of Ireland

| | |
|---|---|
| *R.S.A.I. Jn.* | *Journal of the Royal Society of Antiquaries of Ireland* (Dublin, 1892–   ) |
| Raftery, *La Tène in Ire.* | Barry Raftery, *La Tène in Ireland: problems of origin and chronology* (Marburg, 1984) |
| *Rev. Celt.* | *Revue Celtique* (41 vols, Paris and London, 1870–1924) |
| *Ríocht na Midhe* | *Ríocht na Midhe: records of the Meath Archaeological and Historical Society* (Drogheda, [1955]–   ) |
| Ryan, *Ire. & insular art* | Michael Ryan (ed.), *Ireland and insular art A.D. 500–1200: proceedings of a conference at University College, Cork, 31 October–3 November 1985* (Dublin, 1987) |
| Rynne, *Figures from the past* | Etienne Rynne (ed.), *Figures from the past* (Dun Laoghaire, 1987) |
| Rynne, *N. Munster studies* | Etienne Rynne (ed.), *North Munster studies: essays in commemoration of Monsignor Michael Moloney* (Limerick, 1967) |
| *s.a.* | *sub anno* (under year) |
| *s.v.* | *sub verbo* (under word) |
| Schmidt, *Celts* | Karl Horst Schmidt (ed.), *History and culture of the Celts / Geschichte und Kultur der Kelten* (Heidelberg, 1986) |
| Scott, *Studies on early Ire.* | B. G. Scott (ed.), *Studies on early Ireland: essays in honour of M. V. Duignan* ([Belfast, 1981]) |
| *Seanchas Ardmhacha* | *Seanchas Ardmhacha: journal of the Armagh Diocesan Historical Society* ([Armagh], 1954–   ) (title appears as *Seanchas Ard Mhacha* from vol. v, no. 1 (1969)) |
| ser. | series |
| Script. Lat. Hib. | Scriptores Latini Hiberniae |
| Smyth, *Celtic Leinster* | Alfred P. Smyth, *Celtic Leinster: towards an historical geography of early Irish civilization A.D. 500–1600* (Dublin, 1982) |

Smyth, *Seanchas*  Alfred P. Smyth (ed.), *Seanchas: studies in early and medieval Irish archaeology, history and literature in honour of Francis J. Byrne* (Dublin, 2000)

Spearman & Higgitt, *Age of migrating ideas*  R. Michael Spearman and John Higgitt (ed.), *The age of migrating ideas: early medieval art in northern Britain and Ireland. Proceedings of the Second International Conference on Insular Art held in the National Museums of Scotland in Edinburgh, 3–6 January 1991* (Edinburgh, 1993)

*Speculum*  *Speculum: a journal of medieval studies* (Cambridge, Mass., 1926– )

*Studia Celt.*  *Studia Celtica* (Cardiff, 1966– )

*Studia Hib.*  *Studia Hibernica* (Dublin, 1961– )

*Studies in Ir. law*  Rudolf Thurneysen and others, *Studies in early Irish law* (R.I.A., Dublin, 1936)

T.C.D.  Trinity College, Dublin

*Thes. Pal.*  Whitley Stokes and John Strachan (ed. & trans.), *Thesaurus Palaeohibernicus* (2 vols, Cambridge, 1901–3, supplement by Whitley Stokes, Halle a/S, 1910; reprinted, 2 vols, Dublin, 1975))

trans.  translated (by)

*Trans. Phil. Soc.*  *Transactions of the Philological Society* (Oxford, 1855– )

Tranter & Tristram, *Early Ir. lit.*  Stephen N. Tranter and H. L. C. Tristram (ed.), *Early Irish literature: media and communication/ Mündlichkeit und Schriftlichkeit in der frühen irischen Literatur* (Tübingen ScriptOralia, x; Tübingen, 1989)

*Trip. life*, ed. Stokes  Whitley Stokes (ed. and trans.), *The tripartite life of Patrick* (2 vols, London, 1887)

*Trip. life*, ed. Mulchrone  Kathleen Mulchrone (ed.), *Bethu Phátraic: the tripartite life of Patrick* (Dublin, 1939)

U.C.D.  University College, Dublin

*U.J.A.*

*Ulster Journal of Archaeology* (Belfast, 3 series: 1853–62, 9 vols; 1895–1911, 17 vols; 1938–   )

Whitelock, McKitterick, & Dumville, *Ire. in early med. Europe*

Dorothy Whitelock, Rosamond McKitterick, and David N. Dumville (ed.), *Ireland in early mediaeval Europe: studies in memory of Kathleen Hughes* (Cambridge, 1982)

*Y Cymmrodor*

*Y Cymmrodor, embodying the transactions of the Cymmrodorion Society of London* (6 vols, London, 1877–83; continued as *Y Cymmrodor, the magazine of the Honourable Society of Cymmrodorion* (London, 1886–   ))

Youngs, '*Work of angels*'

Susan Youngs (ed.), '*The work of angels': masterpieces of Celtic metalwork, 6th–9th centuries* A.D. (London, 1989)

*Z.C.P*

*Zeitschrift für celtische Philologie* (Halle, 1896–1943, 23 vols; Tübingen, 1953–   )

The en rule (–   ), solidus (/), and saltire (×) are used in dates, as in the following examples:

678–80

denotes a process extending from the first to the second date.

678/80

denotes alternative dates for a specific event.

678 × 680

denotes the period within which a specific event, which cannot be more precisely dated, occurred.

Some footnotes give the full pagination of an article (or similar source) and also draw attention to specific pages within it. Instead of the words 'especially' or 'at', a colon is used; e.g. 'pp 157–75: 163–4'.

  Annals are frequently cited with reference to a date, rather than to pages in any particular edition of the text. In such cases the abbreviation appears in roman type; e.g. 'A.U.' instead of '*A.U.*' (a reference to the edition specified above).

INTRODUCTION

# Prehistoric and early Ireland

## T. M. CHARLES-EDWARDS

IRISH history from the first human settlement before 7000 B.C. to the Anglo-Norman invasion is the subject of this volume, a far longer period than those allocated to later volumes of *A new history of Ireland*.[1] It falls into two parts, distinguished since the early middle ages as pre- and post-Patrician. To make this division is not to assent to the picture of the apostle of the Irish, propagated at least since the seventh century, as the sole leading missionary in the island; the point is simply that, with Patrick, we begin to have texts written in Ireland. However informative may be external observers from the Graeco-Roman world or ogam inscriptions from within Ireland, some of which pre-date Patrick, his writings mark a new departure. They are, in terms of the inner man, among the most revealing texts of late antiquity. Different evidence now makes it possible to write a different kind of history: while archaeology plays a major role throughout the period of this volume—one need only cite the excavation of viking Dublin—written evidence only becomes important from the fifth century A.D. The period of Patrick's activity in Ireland, which many historians would now place in the second half of the fifth century, follows another date, 431, when the Christian community in Ireland received its first bishop, Palladius. By 431 at the latest, copying written texts must have been part of the culture of the early Christian community. As has often, and rightly, been said, Christianity was and is a religion in which books—preeminently those within the biblical canon—were essential authorities. By Patrick's time his writings, addressed to his Irish disciples as well as to his fellow-countrymen, the Britons, assumed that his readers would appreciate his many biblical references. By then, therefore, there was in Ireland a community united by reverence for, and understanding of, the Bible. Whatever the shifts of circumstance, that community was to endure in one shape or another throughout the rest of Irish history.

---

[1] I am grateful to Edel Bhreathnach and Raghnall Ó Floinn for their comments on a draft of this chapter.

The Irish settlements established in Britain in the late Roman period reveal an inescapable ambiguity in the approach taken by this volume: was it to be a history of Ireland or of the Irish? It necessarily begins as a history of Ireland, with a discussion of the physical environment and historical geography, since it is, as we shall see, quite uncertain at what point in prehistory it becomes legitimate to talk of 'the Irish'. Throughout the archaeological chapters up to and including the iron age we often read of influences coming into Ireland, rarely of influences going out. This archaeological Ireland is not so very different from Patrick's conception of his adopted country: a land on the western outskirts of the world, beyond which the ocean offered no home for men or women, no souls yet further removed from Jerusalem and still awaiting conversion. Patrick's Christianity, coming from the Mediterranean to the far north-west, followed a path already trodden by others.

Once Ireland had been converted to Christianity— which, as it happens, is approximately when the evidence enables one to speak of the Irish, a people, rather than just of Ireland, a country—the traffic in men and ideas was quite as much outwards as inwards. This expansive phase of Irish history had two layers just as it had two languages, Irish and Latin. What defined the people was a capacity to speak Irish, and thus those who settled in Britain were just as much Irish as those who remained in Ireland. Latin was the language of western Christianity, a bond between the Irish and their neighbours. There were Irish-speaking settlements from the Hebrides to Cornwall, yet much the most extensive outward-going influences were through the medium of Latin. As the Northumbrian Bede saw it, Latin was a language shared between the different peoples and languages of Britain, the Irish settlers among them.[2] In the last millennium covered by this book, therefore, the focus shifts a little, from the island to the people. One cannot say that Columbanus, who died in 615 at Bobbio, a monastery in the Apennines, is any less a part of Irish history than Ciarán, founder of Clonmacnoise on the banks of the Shannon. Even apart from issues of principle, Columbanus wrote works that have been preserved and that are excellent evidence for the culture of his native country.[3]

To introduce this period of some eight millennia I shall take four themes: the antiquity and thoroughness of the process by which the land was cleared and given a shape designed for human needs, as well as the fluctuations in the extent and intensity of agriculture; the origins of Celtic Ireland; the organisation of the church in the last half-millennium, A.D. 650–1150; and the relationship of the political order to the landscape. The third theme, the organisation of the church, has been chosen because Kathleen Hughes, who

[2] Bede, *Hist. ecc.*, i. 1 (B. Colgrave and R. A. Mynors (ed. and trans.), *Bede's ecclesiastical history of the English people* (Oxford, 1969), pp 16–17).
[3] *Sancti Columbani opera*, ed. and trans. G. S. M. Walker (Dublin, 1957); M. Lapidge (ed.), *Columbanus: studies on the Latin writings* (Woodbridge, 1997).

wrote the splendidly lucid chapters on the subject in this book, died in 1977. Her work and that of earlier scholars, notably J. F. Kenney, encouraged younger scholars to enter the field; it is appropriate to take note of this more recent research and thus of the stimulus to Irish ecclesiastical history which Hughes's work has given. In discussing these four themes, I shall not even attempt to give a comprehensive account of recent scholarship, but rather limit myself to giving indications of the direction that research has taken, together with enough bibliographical references so that topics can be pursued further.

IRISH archaeology has made rapid strides during the time in which this book has been in the making. The approach to the subject has shifted from a concentration on classifying objects to setting shifts in material culture within a framework supplied by broad conceptions of the relationship of social change to the landscape. The chronological range of intensive archaeological research has also extended far into the historical period; in this way bridges have been built with text-based history and with the history of art.[4] There have also been major changes in the techniques employed as well as dramatic individual discoveries. An outstanding example of such discoveries was the detection of early field systems beneath blanket bog in north-west Mayo (the Céide fields); this demonstrated that, in Ireland, a major reshaping of the landscape was undertaken by neolithic farmers.[5] Their investment of labour in clearance of the land and in the construction of boundaries was helped by a relatively warm climate, 1–2°C above present levels. The discovery also demonstrated that these farmers were permanently settled: they were no shifting cultivators, here one year, gone the next. The field systems of north-west Mayo have been preserved because a less favourable climate, and the consequent spread of blanket bog, preserved them undisturbed by later farmers. There is every reason to think that, in those parts of Ireland where cultivation has been continuous down to the modern period, the agricultural shaping of the landscape was at least as ancient.[6]

The implications for our understanding of prehistory are radical. A settled agriculture implies a shaping of the landscape and allows a higher density of

---

[4] Below, ch. VIII, pp 235–300, and Nancy Edwards, *The archaeology of early Christian Ireland* (London, 1990).

[5] Seamas Caulfield, 'Neolithic fields: the Irish evidence' in H. C. Bowen and P. J. Fowler (ed.), *Early land allotment* (Oxford, 1978), pp 137–44; idem, 'The neolithic settlement of north Connaught' in Terence Reeves-Smyth and Fred Hamond (ed.), *Landscape archaeology in Ireland* (Oxford, 1983), pp 195–215. For recent accounts, see Gabriel Cooney, *Landscapes of neolithic Ireland* (London, 2000); idem, 'Reading a landscape manuscript: a review of progress in prehistoric settlement studies in Ireland' in T. B. Barry (ed.), *A history of settlement in Ireland* (London, 2000), pp 1–49.

[6] For settlement in the historical period up to 1169 see the chapters by Charles Doherty, 'Settlement in early Ireland: a review', and Matthew Stout, 'Early Christian Ireland: settlement and environment' in Barry, *Settlement in Ireland*, pp 50–109.

population. Ireland appears to have been extensively and intensively in-habited since the neolithic period. Moreover, it comes as no surprise, once the implications of these discoveries have been considered, to find that there is no major break in the continuity of material culture throughout subsequent Irish prehistory. Any incoming influences had to reckon with an existing population that was large and well entrenched. This has an important bearing on, for example, the spread of the Irish language throughout the island before the first written evidence becomes available—our second theme.

Dramatic developments in technique include the construction of a se-quence of tree-ring dates for Irish oak and the analysis of pollen preserved in wet conditions so as to reveal changes in neighbouring flora.[7] Where oak was used in construction and enough of it survives, exact dates can be given for when an oak was cut down. Such accuracy is striking at any period, but once archaeology and history are harnessed together, as with viking Dublin, it becomes especially useful to be able sometimes to employ the same chron-ology for the material as for the textual evidence.[8] The pollen evidence has helped to show the antiquity of cultivation but it has also revealed that there were fluctuations in the extent and intensity of cultivation. The last down-turn within the period of this volume coincided approximately with the apogee of Roman power in the Mediterranean world, *c*.200 B.C.–A.D. 300. The revival of economic activity which followed this downturn prepared the way for early Christian Ireland, while the bronze age—which in Ireland lasted till *c*.500 B.C.—has left an impressive array of artefactual evidence. The two periods whose art dominate any record of Irish art before the twelfth century, bronze age and early Christian Ireland, thus sit either side of the more enigmatic iron age. For two reasons the Irish iron age is especially puzzling: first, the evidence for La Tène artefacts is extensive on the Contin-ent and in Britain, but not in Ireland; secondly, the relatively few artefacts surviving from the Irish iron age include pieces of the highest artistic quality, such as the so-called 'Petrie crown' and the Bann disc. How far this puzzle will resist further investigation is quite uncertain: the downturn suggested by the pollen evidence seems to occur rather earlier than the date of the last major structure at Navan Fort (shortly after 95 B.C., when the oak for the central pillar was cut down), and that date itself may be rather earlier than the corresponding ones for Knockaulin and for Tara.[9]

[7] An early statement is M. G. L. Baillie, 'Dendrochronology: the prospects for dating throughout Ireland' in Donnchadh Ó Corráin, *Irish antiquity* (Cork, 1981), pp 3–22; G. F. Mitchell, *The Irish landscape* (London, 1976); G. F. Mitchell and Michael Ryan, *Reading the Irish landscape* (Dublin, 1997).

[8] P. F. Wallace, below, pp 816–43.

[9] M. G. L. Baillie, 'The central post from Navan Fort: the first step towards a better understanding of the early iron age' in *Emania*, i (1986), pp 20–21; idem, 'The dating of the timbers from Navan Fort and the Dorsey, Co. Armagh' in *Emania*, iv (1988), pp 37–40; for the phase as a whole see D. M. Waterman, *Excavations at Navan Fort 1961–71*, completed and

Because of the limited evidence available, the relationship between Ireland and the Roman empire remains obscure. There are likely to have been what were called *emporia*, specialised trading centres, in Ireland; immediately prior to 360 there was a treaty between the Roman authorities and one or more Irish rulers; and this may have governed trade.[10] The odd burial is suggestive of individual immigration from the empire, while the general move towards inhumation with extended bodies may well be connected with similar developments in Roman Britain.[11] It would not be right, therefore, to claim that Ireland was isolated from the empire. Yet the most impressive examples of Roman influence come from the fourth and fifth centuries: the ogam inscriptions, most densely clustered in a belt across southern Munster and into central Leinster, from the Corkaguiney peninsula in west Kerry to County Carlow, commemorate named individuals on stone, a practice that is almost certainly imitated from Roman commemoration of the dead.[12] The ogam inscriptions are also of the highest importance because of the scarcity of other archaeological evidence for iron-age Munster. It has been said, with only modest exaggeration, that, if we could argue from silence, we might be tempted to doubt whether Munster was extensively inhabited in the iron age.[13] The ogam inscriptions, beginning in the fourth century at the end of the period, demonstrate that this impression is a matter of patchy evidence rather than patchy settlement. In the early Christian period, also, most of the evidence comes, just as it had in the previous period, from what is now northern Leinster and Ulster. There, too, it would be quite wrong to infer little activity in Munster or Connacht from little evidence.

The right policy, therefore, is to argue from the evidence that we have and, in general, to refrain from making any assertions based on gaps in the archaeological or textual record. What survives indicates that the late-prehistoric and early historic inhabitants of Ireland were just as able to manage the environment on land as they and their neighbours were to cope with the hazards of the sea. A striking example is the togher—a special type

ed. C. J. Lynn (Belfast, 1997), pp 159–71; Bernard Wailes, 'Dún Ailinne: a summary excavation report' in *Emania*, vii (1990), pp 10–21.

[10] Ammianus Marcellinus, *Res gestae*, ed. W. Seyfarth (Leipzig, 1978), xx. 1. 1. On Roman material in Ireland, see J. D. Bateson, 'Roman material from Ireland: a reconsideration' in *R.I.A. Proc.*, lxxiii (1973), sect. C, pp 21–97; idem, 'Further finds of Roman material from Ireland' in *R.I.A. Proc.*, lxxvi (1976), sect. C, pp 171–80; R. B. Warner, 'Some observations on the context and importation of exotic material in Ireland, from the first century B.C. to the second century A.D.', ibid., pp 267–92.

[11] Elizabeth O'Brien, 'Pagan and Christian burial in Ireland during the first millennium A.D.: continuity and change' in Nancy Edwards and Alan Lane (ed.), *The early church in Wales and the west* (Oxford, 1992), pp 130–62.

[12] Damian McManus, *A guide to ogam* (Maynooth, 1991); Catherine Swift, *Ogam stones and the earliest Irish Christians* (Maynooth, 1997).

[13] Barry Raftery, *Pagan Celtic Ireland: the enigma of the Irish iron age* (London, 1994), pp 226–8; see also the contributions on iron-age Munster by P. C. Woodman, Barry Raftery, and R. B. Warner to *Emania*, xvii (1998), pp 13–29.

of road constructed across a bog. An outstanding example was excavated
some years ago in Corlea Bog, County Longford, and dated by dendrochronology to 148 B.C.[14] In the seventh century A.D., Cogitosus, a scholar devoted
to the interests of the church of Kildare, wrote a Life of Brigit in which he
told a story which, quite incidentally, demonstrates that road-building might
be organised by a king of Leinster as a public obligation imposed on the
peoples of the whole province.[15] Different sections of the road were assigned
to different peoples, and then each section was again parcelled out among the
various kindreds. Brigit's people, the Fothairt, were relatively weak politically and so found themselves with an especially difficult stretch of road, one
that included stretches of bog and thus the building of a togher. The laws of
the eighth and ninth centuries include rules prescribing work on road-repair,
notably at the time of great assemblies. Very recently, also, evidence has been
found for a bridge across the Shannon by Clonmacnoise, which can be dated
by dendrochronology to the early ninth century.[16] Although much of the
neighbouring island of Britain benefited from Roman roads and Roman
bridges, their counterparts existed in Ireland and were maintained by public
authority.

    In Ireland the principal environmental problem was in managing the
drainage problems consequent on the glacial morphology of the central lowlands. Ireland is often compared to a dish: a rim of mountains surrounding
the low-lying lands of the interior. There is one major gap in this rim, on the
east coast between Dundalk and Dublin. From this part of the eastern coast
travellers could journey westward across the plains of Brega and Mide till
they reached the Shannon. In the early middle ages these were the kingdoms
of 'the Uí Néill from the Shannon to the sea'. The easternmost province of
Brega had the drier and better-drained soils, attractive to farmers since the
neolithic period, as the passage-tombs of the Boyne valley illustrate. Further
west, in Mide (now County Westmeath and parts of County Offaly), the
rainfall increased and drainage became more difficult. Yet from the 730s till
the twelfth century it was Mide that dominated Brega, and not vice versa.
On the north side of the central lowlands lay the drumlin belt, a zone in
which glacial action formed numerous small elliptical hills and lakes. The
drainage here is increasingly impeded as one goes west from County Down
in the drier east to Clew Bay, County Mayo, where the many islands are
drowned drumlins. The drumlin belt is also, however, the area in which the

---

[14] Barry Raftery, *Trackways through time* (Rush, 1991); idem, *Trackway excavations in the Mountdillon Bogs, Co. Longford, 1985–1991* (Dublin, 1996).
[15] Cogitosus, *Vita S. Brigitae*, c. 30, trans. Seán Connolly and J.-M. Picard in *R.S.A.I. Jn.*, cxvii (1987), pp 23–4; Fergus Kelly, *Early Irish farming* (Dublin, 1997), pp 392–3.
[16] Finbarr Moore, 'Ireland's oldest bridge—at Clonmacnoise' in *Archaeology Ireland*, x, no. iv (1996), pp 24–7; Aidan O'Sullivan and David Boland, 'Medieval Irish engineers conquer the River Shannon' in *Discovering Archaeology*, i, no. i (Jan./Feb. 1999), pp 33–7.

greatest concentration of crannógs is found, artificial islands constructed as secure homesteads and even as royal forts.[17] This type of site was in use in the bronze age, but it was most popular in the early Christian period in the drumlin belt, when it lasted from the seventh century to the end of the middle ages. Some, notably the royal fort of Lagore and Moynagh Lough in Brega, were even constructed in the drier eastern region south of Dundalk, well outside the drumlin belt. The crannóg illustrates the ability of people, both in the bronze age and in the early Christian period, to manage the environment of the wetlands.

A sound rule of thumb declares that the more delightful a landscape appears to the modern tourist the less attractive it was to the early farmer. This is not to say that all the western parts of Ireland were little settled. A recent study of the distribution of ringforts has shown, for example, a concentration in parts of County Sligo, while the valley of the River Moy in County Mayo was the basis of one of the most powerful kingdoms in Connacht.[18] On the other hand, the heartland of early-medieval Munster was the south of Tipperary, the east of County Limerick, and the north of County Cork—pleasant country but not quite such tourist attractions as west Kerry or Connemara. The part of Leinster that counted for most was west of the Wicklow Mountains, from the Liffey plain in the north over into the long Barrow valley running south towards Waterford, and also over to the Slaney valley running south-east towards Wexford. The lands east of the mountains, beautiful as they now are, and although they housed the great monastery of Glendalough set in its mountain valley, were the consolation prizes of failed dynasties. In Connacht the principal power usually lay in the east, in the drier soils of County Roscommon.

The early geography of Ireland suggested rather than imposed political boundaries. Although the crucial boundary between Munster and the Uí Néill lay approximately across Slieve Bloom in the centre of Ireland, even here the frontier was more political than natural. The major Munster monastery of Kinnitty, enjoying close connections with the Corkaguiney peninsula far off in west Munster, was next to the boundary, which thus appears to have followed the River Camcor; Kinnitty, however, was on the north side of Slieve Bloom and could be drawn into the politics of the Uí Néill, as shown by the ninth-century inscription on its high cross.[19] The whole area, with the

---

[17] Aidan O'Sullivan, *The archaeology of lake settlement in Ireland* (Dublin, 1998).
[18] Matthew Stout, *The Irish ringfort* (Dublin, 1997), pp 93–7.
[19] Liam de Paor, 'The High Crosses of Tech Theille (Tihilly), Kinnitty, and related sculpture' in Etienne Rynne, *Figures from the past* (Dún Laoghaire, 1987), pp 131–58; Domhnall Ó Murchadha and Giollamuire Ó Murchú, 'Fragmentary inscriptions from the West Cross at Durrow, the South Cross at Clonmacnois, and the Cross of Kinnitty' in *R.S.A.I. Jn.*, cxviii (1988), pp 53–66; *Corpus genealogiarum sanctorum Hiberniae*, ed. Pádraig Ó Riain (Dublin, 1985), § 665. 3; W. W. Heist (ed.), *Vitae sanctorum Hiberniae ex codice olim Salmanticensi nunc Bruxellensi* (Brussels, 1965), pp 153–60.

Uí Néill of Mide to the north, Munster to the south, Leinster to the east, and Connacht only a few miles away to the west, was the home of numerous major monasteries, such as Clonenagh, Clonfertmulloe, and Killeigh in Leinster, Aghaboe, Terryglas, and Lorrha in Munster, Birr, Rahan, Durrow, and Lynally in the Uí Néill client kingdom of Cenél Fiachach. Similarly, Clonmacnoise, on the east bank of the Shannon and thus in Mide, attained its greatest influence in Connacht to the west; hence the usefulness of the early ninth-century bridge. Early Christian Ireland was based in part on a political deal between the Uí Néill, the Éoganachta (rulers of Munster), and the Connachta. Their frontiers appear to have been planned as sacred zones where monasteries rather than warbands ruled the landscape; thus the kingdom of Cenél Fiachach just to the north of Slieve Bloom came to be known as Tír Cell, 'Church Land'.[20] The 'old order' of early Christian Ireland began to break down before the appearance of the first vikings, when armies were formed from the semi-lay client-farmers of these midland monasteries. These armies can be seen, in the second half of the eighth century, participating in the succession struggles of the kings of Mide and also, more damagingly, in warfare between the Uí Néill and Munster.[21] Instead of a security zone dominated by non-combatant monks, monastic armies now faced each other across the frontier. The logical consequence was the temporarily successful campaigning of the king of Munster in the 820s and 830s, Fedilmid mac Crimthainn, designed to conquer the border kingdoms of Tír Cell and Delbnae Bethra, and so to take control of the principal Uí Néill monasteries of the midlands.

It would be quite wrong to claim that there were no natural boundaries, yet the vast majority were capable of being redrawn. J. H. Andrews observes that the long east–west ridges characteristic of southern Munster are interrupted by the north–south ridge of high land known to the Elizabethans as Slieve Loughre, to the early Irish as Sliab Luachra. In the early Christian period this divided off the far west of Munster, Iarluachair, 'West of Luachair', where the greatest saint was St Brendan the Navigator, and where the kings of west Munster ruled from their royal seat at Lough Leane near Killarney. On the other hand, the east–west line of the Galty Mountains was in the middle of the leading Éoganacht dynasties, who were arranged around the mountains (called 'the Harps of Cliu') like feasters round a table.

Some apparently natural divisions were in reality man-made. The modern traveller from Dublin to Galway—one of the flattest roads in Ireland—must nevertheless go through 'passes': the Pass of Kilbride and Tyrrellspass. What these were is best shown by a text just beyond our period, the Norman-French poem 'The song of Dermot and the earl'. It includes a quite detailed account of fighting in 1169 at a pass well known to earlier sources from the

---

[20] A.U., *s.a.* 840.4.     [21] A.U., *s.a.* 764.6; 776.11.

seventh century onwards, the 'Pass of Gowran' (Belach Gabráin) between Leinster and Osraige.[22] Admittedly the Pass of Gowran does lie between Slieve Margy to the north and Freagh Hill to the south, yet the distance between the 500-ft contour lines is about six miles. What 'The song of Dermot and the earl' shows is that the effective pass was through forest, and that the gap left by the forest could be strengthened by man-made defences. The likely interpretation is that the high land on either side offered a possible boundary, and that, because the boundary lay across the Pass of Gowran, the forest was allowed to grow unhindered on either side of a narrow gap. This 'pass' had three elements: the hills, which were natural obstacles to settlement; the forest, which was extensive because it was politically convenient that it should be so; and temporary defences, which could be raised in the remaining gap. In examples such as Tyrrellspass (the boundary of 'Tyrrell's country'), there was no high land in the background: forest deliberately allowed to flourish, perhaps aided by bog, created these lowland passes.

ALTHOUGH notable excavated sites lie within the iron age, that period remains, as we have seen, perhaps the most enigmatic in Irish archaeology.[23] It is possible to write a survey of Irish prehistory in which all seems to progress harmoniously from one stage to another till a climax in the late bronze age, the Dowris period. Then, about 600 B.C., there is a gap till about 300 B.C. Again, after a brief period in which there is notable evidence, there is a further obscure stretch till the fourth century A.D. It is perhaps when the evidence is at its most unsatisfactory that the theoretical preferences of archaeologists become most clear. Recently many have preferred to favour continuity; but this standpoint faces perhaps its most difficult obstacles in the iron age.

This is not just because of insufficient evidence. Before the dawn of documentary history, and in circumstances that are difficult for the archaeologist to reconstruct, Celtic-speaking people succeeded in spreading their language throughout the island. Ireland was not just inhabited by people who, whatever their genetic background, now spoke Celtic, but it was one particular form of Celtic that prevailed.[24] Since language is one of the backbones of human culture, the spread of a single language throughout Ireland before Rome fell to the Goths gave a unity to the history of the island

[22] *The song of Dermot and the earl*, ed. and trans. G. H. Orpen (Oxford, 1892), pp 42–5; cf. pp 76–7. For the area of Belach Gabráin see Raghnall Ó Floinn, 'Freestone Hill, Co. Kilkenny: a reassessment' in A. P. Smyth (ed.), *Seanchas: studies...in honour of Francis J. Byrne* (Dublin, 2000), pp 12–29; A. P. Smyth, *Celtic Leinster* (Dublin, 1982), p. 11.

[23] See Raftery, *Pagan Celtic Ireland*, and his chapter below, pp 134–81.

[24] Paul Russell, below, 405–50; Kim McCone, Damian McManus, Cathal Ó Háinle, Nicholas Williams, and Liam Breatnach (ed.), *Stair na Gaeilge in ómós do Phádraig ó Fiannachta* (Maynooth, 1994), ch. 2.

that geography alone could not confer. It is one example of the many puzzles that continue to tease and to delight students of early Ireland that no one has yet found evidence that would determine when and how this change occurred.

Forty years ago the answer would have been sought by positing a theory of a Celtic invasion. A natural language does not exist except in a community of speakers; hence, it was not unreasonably supposed, for the Irish language to prevail throughout Ireland some group of speakers of that language must have entered the country and gained a political predominance. It is all too easy to construct an implausibly extreme version of this theory—to suggest that what was claimed was that a new population invaded and, by a series of wars directed towards 'ethnic cleansing', imposed themselves and their language on the entire island. In a reaction against such an idea, it has been argued that 'contacts between elite groups' or 'exchange networks' across the Irish Sea and between southern Ireland and continental Europe may have been the basis for cultural influence, and that this influence extended to the spread of a Celtic language to Ireland.[25] Ireland, in other words, may have acquired a single Celtic language, Irish, without any of the violence that accompanied the spread of, say, English in Ireland.

In the absence of good evidence to show when, let alone how, Ireland acquired a Celtic language, theories can have the field to themselves. It is, however, worth pointing out that, even when one thinks that a problem has been ejected, like some unwelcome visitor, through the front door, it may be inconsiderate enough to nip round and come in again through the back. The smaller one supposes the incoming linguistic community to be, the greater the transformation must be before the situation attested by the end of the iron age is reached—before, that is, Ireland is not just populated by Irish-speakers, but by Irish-speakers with a strongly linguistic sense of their identity as a people. That small body of Irish-speakers has to have induced the vast majority of the population to forsake whatever language or languages they may have spoken and to adopt instead the language of the small group of newcomers. The majority, moreover, were not hunter-gatherers but the heirs of millennia of settled agriculture, in which the landscape had been parcelled out, named, and made part of their culture. If, then, one supposes Irish to have been introduced to Ireland by merchants and craftsmen ('exchange networks'), rather than by political leaders with armies to sustain their authority, one has to explain how the language gained an exclusive dominance. Exchange networks may indeed spread a language, but something more is needed before it becomes the sole language of the inhabitants of the island.

---

[25] Gabriel Cooney and Eoin Grogan, *Irish prehistory: a social perspective* (revised ed., Dublin, 1997), p. 186.

Discussions of the issues by archaeologists and linguists suggest that distinctions need to be drawn.[26] The first introduction of a form of Celtic into the island should be separated from the final outcome, the complete dominance of Irish. These two dates may have been separated by many centuries. Secondly, although Irish is a Celtic language, whatever was introduced into Ireland was not necessarily a straightforward ancestor of Irish. More than one form of Celtic may have been brought into Ireland, and Irish may be the outcome of a complex interaction between them, and also between the incoming Celtic languages and the language or languages previously spoken in Ireland. I shall therefore distinguish between the introduction of some form or forms of Celtic at the start of the process and the final exclusive dominance of Irish. Secondly, by the end of the iron age the ogam inscriptions (especially the bilingual ones in Wales) suggest that Irishness was defined in terms of language, as it was in the early Christian period; nevertheless, language is by no means always the determinant of national identity. Sometimes aspects of material culture, such as clothing, personal adornments, styles of domestic goods, may be what is crucial; at others religion or social structure may be the dominant influence. By the end of the iron age there is a convenient congruence between the linguistic situation— the prevalence of Irish throughout the island—and ethnicity; but we cannot assume a similar congruence throughout what may have been the long and complex process of gaelicisation.

As well as these distinctions, certain limiting conditions need to govern any speculations. The first we have already met: there is no likelihood that Celtic could have been introduced into a thinly populated and only very partially settled island. The second is the absence of any sharp break in the material evidence. No such break can be associated with the first introduction of Celtic or the final exclusive dominance of Irish. The third constraint is the logical economy gained by supposing that the introduction of some form of Celtic was not very distant in time from the major expansion of Celtic speakers on the Continent in the first millennium B.C. The final constraint is that the form of Celtic that had prevailed by the end of the iron age was not that dominant in the neighbouring island, Britain.

The first limiting condition means that the introduction of Celtic can hardly have occurred through the immigration of a large community which from the start formed a major element in the population. Similarly, the second condition indicates that the prevalence of Irish was not associated

---

[26] J. P. Mallory, 'The origins of the Irish' in *Journal of Irish Archaeology*, ii (1984), pp 65–9; John Waddell, 'The question of the celticization of Ireland' in *Emania*, ix (1991), pp 5–16; J. T. Koch, 'Ériu, Alba and Letha: when was a language ancestral to Irish first spoken in Ireland?' ibid., pp 17–27; John Waddell, 'Celts, celticisation and the Irish bronze age' in John Waddell and Elizabeth Shee Twohig (ed.), *Ireland in the bronze age: proceedings of the Dublin Conference, April 1995* (Dublin, 1995), pp 158–69

with the prevalence of any material technology: there is no question of any simple equation of Celtic with iron, pre-Celtic with bronze. These considerations point towards positing a fairly long interval between the introduction of Celtic and the prevalence of Irish. They also push us towards assuming a distinction between Celtic- and non-Celtic-speakers based in non-material culture. The final constraint has implications for any theory that would associate the final dominance of Irish (as opposed to the initial introduction of some form or forms of Celtic) with exchange networks. Such networks across the Irish Sea have generally been crucial for Ireland; they have often led to the eastern part of Ireland having a more British-influenced character than the west; and similarly western parts of Britain have been more subject to influences from Ireland. Yet, however close these connections may have been, they did not have the result that one form of Celtic prevailed in the two islands.

If the final spread of that form of Celtic which we may already call Irish (or Gaelic) brought a cultural unity to the island, it also eventually came to link Ireland with Britain. Irish settlers found new homes from Scotland to Cornwall in the last years of the Roman empire. From the ninth to the twelfth century, Irish was the politically dominant language of a new Ireland beyond the sea, Scotia or Alba.[27] The relative success of the Irish settlement in northern Britain has much to do with the short distance, thirteen miles (21 km), from Fair Head to the Mull of Kintyre. Both Kintyre and northeast County Antrim were already, when Columba founded the monastery of Iona in 563, parts of a single kingdom, Dál Riata.[28] This political bridge across the North Channel is only one example of a theme that runs back to the beginning of human settlement in the island. The ships and seamanship that sustained Dál Riata and Iona had a long prehistory: the dangers of the northern seas had been conquered already in the neolithic period, as demonstrated most eloquently by the rich archaeology of the Orkneys.

If the dominance achieved by Irish was the effect of a long competition between Irish-speakers and others during the iron age, a partial parallel in

---

[27] For some recent views of the transition from Pictish to Scottish (Gaelic) identity, see Patrick Wormald, 'The emergence of the *Regnum Scottorum*: a Carolingian hegemony?' in B. E. Crawford (ed.), *Scotland in dark age Britain* (St Andrews, 1996), pp 131–60; Dauvit Broun, 'Pictish kings 761–839: integration with Dál Riata or separate development?' in S. M. Foster (ed.), *The St Andrews sarcophagus: a Pictish masterpiece and its international connections* (Dublin, 1998), pp 71–83; John Bannerman, 'The Scottish takeover of Pictland and the relics of Columba' in Dauvit Broun and T. O. Clancy (ed.), *Spes Scotorum, hope of Scots: Saint Columba, Iona and Scotland* (Edinburgh, 1999), pp 71–94.

[28] Ewan Campbell, *Saints and sea-kings: the first kingdom of the Scots* (Edinburgh, 1999), pp 11–15, argues that there is no archaeological evidence for Irish colonisation of Argyll in the post-Roman period; to the extent that he is right, it suggests that in the archaeological investigation of ethnicity the argument from silence is just as hazardous a business as it is elsewhere in early medieval studies, not that there was no colonisation. See also Richard Sharpe, 'The thriving of Dalriada' in Simon Taylor (ed.), *Kings, clerics and chronicles in Scotland, 500–1297* (Dublin, 2000), pp 47–50.

the early historic period is what happened to the Picts in north Britain. By the twelfth century there was no surviving Pictish identity and probably no surviving Pictish language; Picts were known only from the pages of Bede and from a handful of other records. The gaelicisation of what became Scotland north of Forth and Clyde may even have been a continuation of the gaelicisation of Ireland. As the former began in late antiquity, and thus at the end of the Irish iron age, and continued to the central middle ages, so the latter is likely to have been a similarly long process—one that may have ended not long before the arrival of Christianity. Moreover, one benefit of bearing in mind the historically attested phase of gaelicisation is to confirm again that a clear distinction has to be made between becoming a speaker of some form of Celtic and becoming Irish: the Picts spoke a Celtic language. Another benefit is that it indicates quite how complex the process is likely to have been, with religious influence, military conquest, and interference by third parties all playing a leading role at different stages. Finally, it demonstrates its ultimate effectiveness, even though no one supposes that there was any large-scale displacement of one population by another. Of the nations of Britain known to Bede in the eighth century—and which he defined in terms of language—the only non-survivor is the Pictish people. When the kings of the Scots ceased, in the eleventh and twelfth centuries, to pursue the gaelicisation of their new subjects in southern Scotland, they may have brought to an end a process that stretched back at least one and a half millennia far into prehistory.[29]

SINCE the chapters on the church were written in the 1970s, the views expressed so lucidly by Kathleen Hughes have been subject to major revision. A contribution by her to another volume, an admirably balanced account of the relationship between the Irish and British churches and the papacy, remains the standard account and is unlikely to be overturned.[30] That deserves to be noted, since the great controversies on this very issue initiated in the sixteenth century, and still rumbling on in the twentieth, have been laid to rest, at least in scholarly circles. It is now clear that the early Irish church recognised papal authority in the same way as did other western churches: Rome was a final court of appeal for great causes and a city peculiarly sanctified by the blood of many martyrs, from Peter and Paul onwards. The jurisdictional and bureaucratic edifice erected in the twelfth and thirteenth

---

[29] For the situation in the twelfth century, see G. W. S. Barrow, *The Anglo-Norman era in Scottish history* (Oxford, 1980), pp 145–68, and, for the continuing appeal to a Gaelic identity shared with Ireland, Dauvit Broun, *The Irish identity of the kingdom of the Scots* (Woodbridge, 1999).

[30] Kathleen Hughes, 'The Celtic church and the papacy' in C. H. Lawrence (ed.), *The English church and the papacy in the middle ages* (London, 1965), pp 1–28; reprinted in Kathleen Hughes, *Church and society in Ireland, A.D. 400–1200* (London, 1987), no. XV.

centuries, at the same time as other western governments were beginning to undergo similar changes, was not an issue in our period. Critics worried more about the temptations facing pilgrims than they did about ecclesiastical bureaucrats.

Hughes's view that an early episcopal church was replaced by one organised around great monasteries has been challenged. This concept of the development of the early Irish church goes back to the nineteenth century, and in the early twentieth it was accepted by Kenney in his invaluable survey of the sources.[31] Kathleen Hughes's contribution was to refine the chronology: many major monasteries, such as Clonard, Clonmacnoise, and Iona, were founded in the sixth century, but the triumph of a monastic organisation did not come till the eighth. The 'Collectio canonum Hibernensis', first compiled between 716 and 725, reflected both episcopal and monastic orderings of the church. The Roman party within the Irish church before 716 (when Iona was converted to the Roman Easter) favoured a more episcopal order; a more monastic one was revealed, according to Hughes, by the canons of the *Hibernenses*, the 'Hibernian' party. Whereas the Roman party triumphed on the questions of Easter and the tonsure, the ecclesiastical organisation favoured by the Hibernians prevailed.[32] For Hughes, as for Kenney, the ecclesiastical institution dominant from the eighth century to the twelfth was the monastic *paruchia*, by which she meant a federation of monasteries subject to the principal monastery of a founding saint, as Durrow and Derry were subject to Iona.[33] Hence the church order prevalent in Ireland till the reforms of the twelfth century was one in which the abbots of the great monasteries had supreme authority and bishops were essentially restricted to their sacramental function.

The development of views since Kathleen Hughes's death has been nourished by the introduction of a wider range of evidence into the debate. She herself had made a wider and more discerning use of Irish canon law; she was aware of, but did not closely analyse, a vernacular text that has played an important role in subsequent discussion, the Rule of Patrick (*Riagail Phátraic*).[34] The latter first became prominent in an article by Patrick Corish.[35]

---

[31] J. F. Kenney, *Sources for the early history of Ireland: ecclesiastical* (New York, 1929), pp 291–2; it remains an important theme in the recent survey by Dáibhí Ó Cróinín, *Early medieval Ireland, 400–1200* (London, 1995), ch. 6.

[32] Kathleen Hughes, *The church in early Irish society* (London, 1966), pp 125–8; eadem, *Early Christian Ireland: introduction to the sources* (London, 1972), pp 76–7.

[33] Máire Herbert, *Iona, Kells, and Derry: the history and hagiography of the monastic familia of Columba* (Oxford, 1988; reprinted Blackrock, 1996), pp 31–5.

[34] *Riagail Phátraic*, ed. and trans. J. G. O'Keeffe, 'The Rule of Patrick', *Ériu*, i (1904), pp 216–24; text also in *Corpus iuris Hibernici*, ed. D. A. Binchy (6 vols, Dublin, 1978), pp 2129.6–2130.37.

[35] P. J. Corish, 'The pastoral mission in the early Irish church' in *Léachtaí Cholm Cille*, ii (1971), pp 14–25; idem, 'The Christian mission' in P. J. Corish (ed.), *A history of Irish catholicism*, i, fasc. 3 (Dublin, 1972), p. 34.

More recently further evidence has been deployed by Colmán Etchingham, whose *Church organization in Ireland* makes effective use of a wider range of vernacular legal material than any previous scholar has deployed.[36] In between Corish's article and the book by Etchingham, Richard Sharpe wrote an article that offered, for the first time, a fundamental challenge to the accepted account of the early Irish church (and thus to some of the arguments advanced by Kathleen Hughes in this volume).[37] His argument had three main prongs: first, he claimed that bishops retained a pastoral authority even after the great monasteries had reached the peak of their power; secondly, he argued that the earliest Irish church was not tied to a regular assignment of one bishop to each minor kingdom (*tuath*); and, thirdly, he disputed the peculiarly monastic significance of the term *paruchia*. The first and last of the claims have been supported, with further evidence, by Etchingham; the second, bearing on the earliest period of the Irish church, was outside the chronological scope of his book.

We may take the terminological point first. *Paruchia* is a spelling of Latin *parochia*, a borrowing from Greek, where it was used for a dwelling in the neighbourhood of a major settlement. The normal contrast was between the city and settlement in the territory of the city. In Christian Latin the term usually retained the connection with the neighbourhood of a city, but did so in different ways. A rule proclaimed by the council of Nicaea prescribed that each city should have a bishop: henceforward, the episcopal status of a church and the urban status of a town were intimately related. In sixth-century Gaul, the *ecclesia* was the bishop's cathedral church within the walls of the city. Other churches were not *ecclesiae* but *basilicae* (if they were in the city or its suburbs) or *parochiae* if they were major churches within the territory of the city; smaller churches, such as those on private estates, could be called 'oratories'. A *parochia* was thus a church outside a city but subordinate to the episcopal *ecclesia* within the city. In Britain usage was different: there the entire territory attached to a city was the *parochia*—what, in modern terms, would be called the diocese (but not in-cluding the city itself).

In Ireland, the British terminology is sometimes found unchanged. The *parochia* (or *paruchia*) was then the territory subject to a bishop, a territory adjacent to his *civitas* (this Latin word, the source of our 'city', was used by Irish writers for a major church). Sometimes, however, the territory subject to a bishop did not lie in a single block; in a tenth-century annal noted by Etchingham, the 'heir of Féichíne' (the abbot of Fore in County Westmeath, the founder and patron saint of which was Féichíne) is described as 'bishop

---

[36] Colmán Etchingham, *Church organization in Ireland, A.D. 650 to 1000* (Maynooth, 1999).
[37] Richard Sharpe, 'Some problems concerning the organization of the church in early medieval Ireland' in *Peritia*, iii (1984), pp 23–70.

of the peoples of the Luigni'.[38] He was, that is, not just bishop of the Luigne of Mide, in whose territory Fore very probably lay, but also of the Luigne of Connacht, to whom Féichíne was himself believed to belong. This bishop's authority was divided between two territories in different provinces; what united them was that the Luigni, whether of Connacht or of Mide, constituted a single group whose identity was buttressed by the cult of their great saint, Féichíne. Yet a further shift came when *paruchia* was used for the sphere in which the authority of an abbot rather than of a bishop was exercised; this almost certainly did not constitute a single block of territory. The sense of *paruchia* by which it stood for a monastic federation was not, therefore, the normal meaning of the word; what usually expressed the unity of the churches subject to a great mother-church was *familia* (Irish *muinter*), 'household'. The mother-church was not necessarily a monastery: Armagh was an episcopal church first, a monastery second; yet that did not make it any the more difficult to speak either of a *familia* of St Patrick or of his *paruchia*.

Another particular characteristic of the British church by contrast with its Gallo-Roman and Frankish neighbour was that it did not maintain the fourth-century rule of one bishop to each city. The Dumnonii (who gave their name to Devon) were a single *civitas* with a capital at Exeter. According to the principle laid down at Nicaea, and almost always followed in Gaul, there should have been a single bishop for the Dumnonii with his see at Exeter; yet, by the late seventh century, Dumnonia, as it was then called, had more than one bishop; the same was true of Dyfed, in which there had been Irish settlements.[39] An Irish counterpart to Dumnonia or Dyfed would have been a province such as Brega or Ulster; but, by the seventh and eighth centuries, these, too, had more than one bishop.

Two further developments within Ireland shaped the episcopal organisation of the church. One of the principal characteristics of early Irish society was the multiplicity of hierarchies of status: there was one for the ordinary laity (headed by kings) and another for professional poets. In the church there were yet others: one for the ordinary clergy (headed by the bishop) and another for ecclesiastical scholars. Not only individual churchmen but also churches were caught up in this elaboration and multiplication of rank. A bishop had high rank by virtue of his consecration, but he also conferred, in a less formal way, prestige on his church; and the same was true of an eminent scholar and an anchorite. It was scarcely conceivable that a great church, such as Kildare, should be without one or more of these dignitaries. Indeed, it sometimes boasted of more than one bishop among its community,

---

[38] A.U., *s.a.* 993. 5; Etchingham, *Church organization*, pp 178–9 (who would, however, see the phrase 'peoples of the Luigne' as referring solely to the Luigne of Mide).
[39] Aldhelm, letter IV (Michael Lapidge and Michael Herren (ed. and trans.), *Aldhelm: the prose works* (Ipswich, 1979), pp 155, 158).

as in 875, when the Annals of Ulster recorded the death of two: Robartach mac na Cerda was bishop of Kildare, an excellent *scriba* (leading ecclesiastical scholar) and superior of the monastery of Killeigh in Uí Fhailgi; Lachtnán mac Mochtigirn was bishop of Kildare and superior of the monastery of Ferns in Uí Chennselaig. They are described by the annalist as 'bishops of Kildare', not just as resident in Kildare. Between them they extended the influence of the greatest church of Leinster into the north-west and the south-east of the province.

As bishops and leading scholars conferred prestige on their churches, so a major church conferred high rank on its head, even if his status was not elevated by personal attainments or consecration. The superior of a great church was the equal of a bishop. The ninth-century annals make explicit something that had probably been common earlier, namely that different sources of high status were often combined.[40] So Robartach mac na Cerda was bishop of Kildare, but he was also a leading scholar and the head of an important monastery, Killeigh. Any one of these qualifications would have given him high rank. Even in the ninth-century annals, Robartach might well have been described simply as 'Bishop Robartach, *scriba*, superior of Killeigh'. Bishops, because they had high rank by virtue of their consecration, were in a very different position from the head of a church who derived his high rank from his relationship to his church. Abbots and other superiors of churches (*principes*, *airchinnig*) were intrinsically tied to a church in a way that a bishop was not, which explains why the annals always link an abbot to a church but only sometimes do the same for a bishop. If one studies annalistic evidence for the headship of churches, it can seem as though abbots and other superiors were taking over authority earlier exercised by bishops; yet this is more a consequence of a growing preoccupation with ecclesiastical status on the part of the annalists than it is with any great shift of authority within the church.

When the annals associate a bishop with a place, it is almost always a particular church rather than a territory or people; his high rank, after all, elevated the standing of his church. A group of tenth-century annals studied by Etchingham are an exception to this rule.[41] In the Annals of Ulster, but not in the annals from the Clonmacnoise group, there are a few obits such as the following (A.D. 969): 'Eógan mac Cléirigh, bishop of the Connachta.' His authority was over an entire province and it is highly likely that there would have been other bishops of lesser authority within Connacht during his

---

[40] The possibility that such combinations were found earlier, though not recorded as such in the annals, is suggested by the guarantor-list in *Cáin Adomnáin*, ed. and trans. Kuno Meyer (Oxford, 1905), § 28; Máirín Ní Dhonnchadha, 'The guarantor-list of *Cáin Adomnáin*' in *Peritia*, i (1982), pp 185–6, where Flann Febla, described in his annalistic obit (A.U., *s.a.* 715.1) as abbot of Armagh, is here termed scholar-bishop (*suí-epscop*).

[41] Etchingham, *Church organization*, pp 177–86.

episcopacy; there are one or two earlier descriptions of bishops in the annals which suggest that this was not a new phenomenon.[42] Legal texts, both canonical and vernacular, sometimes distinguish different ranks of bishop: Eógan will have been a 'bishop of bishops'.[43] Yet even at the level of the *tuath*, the Rule of Patrick speaks of 'the chief bishop of a *tuath*', suggesting that more than one church within a single minor kingdom might have a bishop.[44] The annals bear out this implication: more than one church associated with Ciannacht Breg is known to have had a bishop, in particular Duleek and Monasterboice.[45] Yet because the annals often describe a bishop without saying to which church he was attached, we cannot decide whether such churches always had bishops. It is entirely possible that a bishop of Ciannacht Breg might sometimes have been located in Duleek, sometimes in Monasterboice.

The change in our understanding of the early Irish church since Kathleen Hughes wrote should not be exaggerated. The phenomenon she knew (following earlier scholars) as 'the monastic *paruchia*' existed and played a major role in the Irish church from the seventh century till the twelfth, only it was hardly ever termed *paruchia* but rather *familia* (or *congregatio* or *samad*— the choice of word may not be of great consequence). Those who made most use of the term *paruchia*—Kildare and Armagh—were making claims for an Ireland-wide jurisdiction for their sees, which they asserted were archbishoprics. The language in which they made these claims shows that *paruchia* was still contrasted with *civitas* as hinterland with city, and that the *paruchia*, the hinterland over which they claimed jurisdiction, was a larger version of the episcopal *paruchia* familiar since the earliest days of the Irish church. The traditional historians' use of *paruchia* was, therefore, at odds with the way the term was normally used in the seventh and eighth centuries.

If we leave aside the terminological point and concentrate on the organisation itself, the traditional conception appears oversimplified.[46] The authority of the heads of the great churches, whether they were abbots or merely bishops, extended over a wide variety of dependants: individual *manaig*, in the special sense of monastic clients (who might be married but were subject to regular discipline); whole kindreds of *manaig*, perhaps attached to a small local church; churches as such; and lastly monasteries. The classical type of dependence thought to characterise a *paruchia*, namely one monastery on another, such as Durrow on Iona, was only one variety. Moreover the degree of dependence varied from the 'unfree churches' obliged to pay tribute to

---

[42] A.U., 665.5; another possible example is 696.5.
[43] *Canones Hibernenses*, v. 9 (L. Bieler (ed.), *The Irish penitentials* (Dublin, 1963), p. 174).
[44] 'The Rule of Patrick', ed. and trans. O'Keeffe, § 1.
[45] A.U., *s.a.* 783.2; 837.1; 872.1; 885.7.
[46] Etchingham, *Church organization*, § 4.1.

largely nominal recognitions of superiority. Ecclesiastical lordship was ubiquitous and had developed numerous sub-forms to cater for special situations.[47]

In the seventh and eighth centuries the great churches were perceived in
different terms according to the context. When lordship and property was at
issue, the person concerned was the abbot or *princeps* (Irish *airchinnech*); this
overlapped with situations in which relationship to the patron saint (usually
the founder) was central, and the important person was then the heir of the
saint (*comarbae*, 'coarb'). Sometimes the church was a biblical 'city of refuge',
a sanctuary for those involved in a feud;[48] when cases were to be tried
according to canon law, the *scriba* was likely to be the judge; for pastoral care
the authority was the bishop. Sometimes one person was abbot (or *princeps*),
bishop, and *scriba*; sometimes these functions were separated. The great
churches were so successful because they had evolved a whole range of roles
for themselves.

For lack of evidence the ecclesiastical organisation of the fifth and sixth
centuries is much less well understood than that of the seventh and eighth.
Monasticism was probably more important for Patrick than used to be
thought.[49] As for the thesis that the *tuath* (in the sense of the minor kingdom) was taken as the unit for episcopal organisation, it has reasonably been
argued that things were hardly so tidy in the early years of conversion, but
the evidence remains very strong that it was the accepted rule once a mature
organisation was in place. Hughes contrasted an essentially episcopal church
in the early sixth century and one, already revealed by Cummian's Letter to
the abbot of Iona *c*.632, in which the 'heirs' of the great monastic saints had a
preponderant influence;[50] this has been much qualified but retains a considerable element of truth. The most important qualification is that bishops
retained their pastoral authority throughout the period. Episcopal power
could coexist with the *familiae* of the great churches because bishops often
worked from the mother-churches of those *familiae* and because ecclesiastical
lordship did not displace pastoral authority.

Different forms of authority (and high rank) coexisted most importantly
in the synod.[51] In the western church generally, those who had the right
to full participation in a synod were bishops. Others might be present, but
only bishops subscribed to the decrees. In Ireland, as in Wales, the official

[47] Thomas Charles-Edwards, *Early Christian Ireland* (Cambridge, 2000), pp 252–7.

[48] Charles Doherty, 'The monastic town in early medieval Ireland' in H. B. Clarke and
Anngret Simms (ed.), *The comparative study of urban origins in non-Roman Europe* (Oxford,
1985), pp 57–60.

[49] Michael Herren, 'Mission and monasticism in the *Confessio* of Patrick' in Donnchadh Ó
Corráin, Liam Breatnach, and Kim McCone (ed.) *Sages, saints and storytellers: Celtic studies in
honour of Professor James Carney* (Maynooth, 1989), pp 76–85.

[50] Cummian, *De controuersia paschali* (Maura Walsh and Dáibhí Ó Cróinín (ed.), *Cummian's
Letter De controuersia paschali and the De ratione computandi* (Toronto, 1988), pp 90–91).

[51] Charles-Edwards, *Early Christian Ireland*, pp 276–81; D. N. Dumville, *Councils and
synods of the Gaelic early and central middle ages* (Cambridge, 1997), pp 18–24.

membership of a synod was wider;[52] in Ireland it included all the highest
dignitaries of the church; and, as we have seen when considering status, high
rank could be attained by a scholar, an anchorite, and the head of a great
church; they were then the equals of a bishop and could sit in synod.[53] This
was crucial, since synods were the means by which great issues were settled.
For this reason, when the Irish church failed, in spite of meeting in more
than one synod, to agree a solution to the Easter dispute in the 630s, it split
into 'Roman' and 'Hibernian' synods.[54]

Disunity between synods encouraged some to look for other solutions. In
669 the arrival of Theodore of Tarsus from Rome introduced an authority
scarcely heard of in the west, that of the archbishop.[55] The eastern churches
acquired a threefold hierarchy of bishops: the patriarch or archbishop in
charge of a 'diocese' (Egypt, for example, was a late-Roman diocese, a form
of super-province within the empire); the metropolitan bishop in charge of a
normal province; and an ordinary bishop in charge of a city and its territory.
Britain had been a diocese in the fourth century, divided into three or four
provinces. By a decision of Pope Vitalian it was now to have an 'archbishop
of the island of Britain'. It can scarcely be an accident that it was in the
second half of the seventh century that first Kildare and then Armagh
claimed to be archbishoprics with an authority over the whole island of
Ireland. The derivative nature of these claims is further suggested by their
connection, as in Britain, with the Easter dispute, and by the attempt to
make the term *paruchia* (proper to a bishop) do service for the territorial
jurisdiction of an archbishop. The late-Roman diocese, hardly remembered
in north-western Europe, let alone Ireland, was not invoked.

Neither in Britain nor in Ireland would the conception of an island-wide
archbishopric survive. In 735 the English church reverted to the Gregorian
division into two provinces: both Canterbury and York would now be archbishoprics; and the title was thus detached from the diocese (of Britain) and
attached instead to the former metropolitan bishoprics of Canterbury and
York (based on provinces). In Ireland, Kildare's claim to an archbishopric
only had any strength as long as Armagh remained in the Hibernian camp.
But even when the Easter dispute was finally settled in 716, and two
scholars, one from Iona and the other from Munster, sat down to produce a
coherent guide to canon law, the 'Collectio canonum Hibernensis', an archbishopric of Armagh was no part of their proposals, even they often
recorded different ideas of how ecclesiastical life should be organised. What
remained was a primacy of Armagh: Emly, the principal church in Munster,

---

[52] For Wales, see Bede, *Hist. ecc.*, ii. 2 (ed. and trans. Colgrave & Mynors, pp 134–9).
[53] Bede, *Hist. ecc.*, ii. 19 (assuming that the pope-elect was replying to a letter from
members of a synod); Charles-Edwards, *Early Christian Ireland*, p. 277.
[54] Above, n. 32.
[55] Charles-Edwards, *Early Christian Ireland*, ch. 10.

had to express its authority in terms of a supposed agreement with Patrick.[56] In practice, the authority of Armagh fluctuated, as did the power of the kings of Tara. Armagh was aligned with Cenél nÉogain from the 730s and was thus stronger when a Cenél nÉogain ruler was king of Tara. At other times, the clergy of the midlands appear to have had a measure of independence.[57] Yet, whatever the fluctuations of its authority, Armagh remained the leading church in Ireland because its patron saint was now generally acknowledged to be the apostle of all the Irish, an apostle whose authority would extend even to the last days, and whose heir was therefore incontrovertibly the greatest churchman in Ireland.[58] This was crucial when several archbishoprics were established in Ireland in the twelfth century. By then Armagh was not just the see of Patrick and the primatial archbishopric but also the site of the leading school of Ireland and Scotland. The reforming synod at Clane in 1162 prescribed that 'no one should be a lector in a church in Ireland except an alumnus [dalta] of Armagh'; and on the eve of the English conquest in 1169, Ruaidrí Ua Conchobair, king of Ireland, endowed the lector of Armagh 'to give instruction to students of Ireland and Scotland'.[59] To judge by the participation of Scotland in the European movement to found universities, there was a good chance that Armagh would develop into the university of Ireland as well as its primatial see.

Armagh had, therefore, made a place for itself within the twelfth-century reform of the church. Yet that reform had harsh things to say about the old order, as is the habit of reform movements. Some scholars would, in essence, agree. Whatever their other disagreements, Hughes and Etchingham are united in expressing a gloomy view of the pastoral care provided by the pre-twelfth-century church for the general laity—those who were not dependants of the church.[60] On the other hand, Sharpe has argued that the church took its pastoral duties more seriously than Hughes (and Etchingham) would allow.[61] Partly this position is supported from prescriptive texts, such as the Rule of Patrick and the legal tract 'Córus Béscnai', partly from the impression given by admittedly patchy topographical studies into the density of pre-Norman Irish churches. Since Etchingham admits the existence of the prescriptive evidence but interprets it as ineffective aspiration, the most

---

[56] Vita S. Albei, cols 29–30 (Heist, Vitae SS Hib., p. 125); on the date of this text, see Richard Sharpe, Medieval Irish saints' Lives: an introduction to Vitae Sanctorum Hiberniae (Oxford, 1991), pp 297–339.

[57] A.U., s.a. 851.5.

[58] See the addition to Tírechán, c. 52 (Ludwig Bieler (ed.), The Patrician texts in the Book of Armagh (Dublin, 1979), p. 164).

[59] A.U., s.a. 1162, 1169.

[60] Hughes, below, ch. IX, pp 301–30; Etchingham, Church organization, pp 249–71.

[61] Richard Sharpe, 'Churches and communities in early Ireland: a preliminary enquiry' in John Blair and Richard Sharpe (ed.), Pastoral care before the parish (Leicester, 1992), pp 81–109.

promising way to resolve the disagreement is through studying the distribution of churches.[62]

IRELAND in the first millennium A.D. shows two leading characteristics: a strong sense of national identity and close ties with Europe.[63] Modern scholars have sometimes found it difficult to respond fully to both of these attributes, and this may lie behind the sometimes ill-tempered debate between 'nativists' and 'anti-nativists'. The strong sense of national identity was already present in the first written records, was almost certainly inherited from the iron age, and was strengthened still further by conversion to Christianity.

What has long been highly debatable is how far the Irish sense of identity was political. Among early Irish scholars it could be explained in different ways. According to one text, the 'Auraicept na nÉces' ('Scholar's primer'), composed probably early in the eighth century but remaining authoritative for centuries, the Irish were not one race but were of varied descent; what unified them was their language.[64] According to the Milesian legend, created no earlier than the seventh century but certainly widely disseminated by the ninth, the Irish were a race—that is, they were a people who shared the same ultimate ancestors.[65] Both sides were agreed, however, that the Irish were latecomers to Ireland. Modern historians have been similarly at odds on the question whether any political unity accompanied the single national identity; and their disagreements have sometimes echoed contemporary political issues. To the early twentieth-century debate between MacNeill and Orpen (respectively asserting and denying a pre-Norman kingship of Ireland) succeeded the sceptical arguments of Binchy (for whom the early kingship of Ireland was an aspiration of the Uí Néill, unrealised in practice and not accepted by the jurists).[66] Recently, however, strong evidence has been

---

[62] An example, which would suggest quite a high density, is Elizabeth O'Brien, 'Churches of south-east county Dublin, seventh to twelfth century' in Gearóid Mac Niocaill and P. F. Wallace (ed.), *Keimelia: studies... in memory of Tom Delaney* (Galway, 1988), pp 504–24.

[63] Donnchadh Ó Corráin, 'Nationality and kingship in pre-Norman Ireland' in T. W. Moody (ed.), *Nationality and the pursuit of national independence* (Belfast, 1978), pp 1–35. The theme of Ireland and Europe has stimulated a whole series of publications, notably Heinz Löwe (ed.), *Die Iren und Europa* (2 vols, Stuttgart, 1982); three volumes edited by Proinséas Ní Chatháin and Michael Richter: *Irland und Europa: die Kirche im Frühmittelalter/ Ireland and Europe: the early church* (Stuttgart, 1984); *Irland und die Christenheit: Bibelstudien und Mission* (Stuttgart, 1987); and *Irland und Europa im früheren Mittelalter: Bildung und Literatur/ Ireland and Europe in the early middle ages: learning and literature* (Stuttgart, 1996); and J.-M. Picard (ed.), *Ireland and northern France, A.D. 600–850* (Dublin, 1991).

[64] *Auraicept na nÉces* (Anders Ahlqvist (ed. and trans.), *The early Irish linguist: an edition of the canonical part of the Auraicept na nÉces* (Helsinki, 1983)).

[65] John Carey, *The Irish national origin-legend: synthetic pseudohistory* (Cambridge, 1994).

[66] G. H. Orpen, *Ireland under the Normans, 1169–1333* (4 vols, Oxford, 1911–20), i, 23–8; Eoin MacNeill, *Phases of Irish history* (Dublin, 1920), pp 244–8; D. A. Binchy, *Celtic and Anglo-Saxon kingship* (Oxford, 1970).

adduced to vindicate the essence of MacNeill's position: the kingship of Tara was recognised throughout Ireland.[67] In practice, the authority of individual kings of Tara varied greatly, but there was a political order embracing the entire island, at the summit of which the king of Tara was unquestionably placed.

This political order may have been established by violence, but its continuance was assured by narrative, *senchas*.[68] What had to be accepted as true was a complex of stories of how that order came to exist and how it developed up to the present, stories that presented a political and legal order as a necessary part of the very fabric of history. *Senchas* also embraced the principal written statement of the law, the 'Senchas Már' ('Great *Senchas*'), a compilation that was considered to express 'the *senchas* of the men of Ireland'; but this legal *senchas* had itself been brought within the wider body of traditions about the past by means of the Patrician legend.[69] The entire narrative—embracing stories about the past as well as laws that were themselves situated in the past—was not always consistent in detail; and it contained literature composed for aesthetic rather than political ends; but it was consistent and politically expedient in its central themes. It was, as a whole and not just in its legal part, normative. It encompassed the entire island and its history from the beginning: it was, that is to say, both spatially and chronologically all-embracing, allowing no room or time for an opposing narrative. In the process, significant places in the landscape had to be incorporated: the narrative extended its tentacles into each district. As a consequence, all across Ireland there were places that functioned as narrative prompts. There are few, if any, better examples in the whole range of medieval history to show how Max Weber's 'patrimonial' polity might have worked.

We may take a few examples to illustrate the seriousness of *senchas*. Two ninth-century Irish kings from the midlands were summarily punished for collaboration with the vikings, one by Máel Sechnaill mac Maíle Ruanaid and

---

[67] Edel Bhreathnach, 'Temoria: Caput Scottorum?' in *Ériu*, xlvii (1996), 67–88; see also eadem, *Tara: a select bibliography* (Dublin, 1995); and, for the site, Conor Newman, *Tara: an archaeological survey* (Dublin, 1997).

[68] F. J. Byrne, '*Seanchas*: the nature of Gaelic historical tradition' in J. G. Barry (ed.), *Historical Studies*, ix (Belfast, 1974), pp 137–59; Kathleen Hughes, *The early Celtic idea of history and the modern historian* (Cambridge, 1977), reprinted in Hughes, *Church and society in Ireland*, no. XIX; Donnchadh Ó Corráin, 'Irish origin legends and genealogy: recurrent aetiologies' in Tore Nyberg *et al.* (ed.), *History and heroic tale: a symposium* (Odense, 1985), pp 51–96; Katharine Simms, 'Charles Lynegar, the Ó Luinín family, and the study of Seanchas' in T. C. Barnard, Dáibhí Ó Cróinín, and Katharine Simms (ed.), *A miracle of learning: studies . . . in honour of William O'Sullivan* (Aldershot, 1998), pp 266–83.

[69] Kim McCone, 'Dubthach maccu Lugair and a matter of life and death in the pseudo-historical prologue to the *Senchas Már*' in *Peritia*, v (1986), pp 1–35; John Carey, 'The two laws in Dubthach's judgement' in *Camb. Med. Celt. Studies*, xix (summer 1990), pp 1–18; idem, 'An edition of the pseudo-historical prologue to the *Senchas Már*' in *Ériu*, xlv (1994), pp 1–32; and below, pp 337–42.

the other by Áed Findliath, both kings of Tara. In each case collaboration the one year was followed by punishment the next.[70] In 850 Cináed mac Conaing, king of Ciannacht Breg, allied with the vikings and rebelled against Máel Sechnaill. In the course of his rebellion 'he plundered the Uí Néill from the Shannon to the sea' and sacked the crannóg of his local rival and distant kinsman, Tigernach mac Fócartai, at Lagore 'so that it was level with the surface' of the lough. If the Irish were to keep the vikings at bay, it was crucial that client kings should maintain the allegiances inscribed in tradition—a tradition that excluded the Gaill, the Foreigners, namely vikings. When Máel Sechnaill's strength was fading, his successor as king of Tara, Áed Findliath, of the other dominant branch of the Uí Néill, Cenél nÉogain, allied with vikings to demonstrate his power and so enforce his succession.[71] Such an alliance did not challenge the established order, since it furthered established political practice; but for a client king on his own to ally with the vikings against his Irish overlord was a dangerous threat. It was hardly surprising that Cináed should be executed in spite of a guarantee of safe-conduct. In 863 'the kings of the Gaill' together with Lorcán mac Cathail, king of Mide, 'searched the cave of Achad Alddai and of Knowth, and the cave of Fert Boadán above Dowth, and the cave of the Wife of Angoba, something which had not been done before'. The next year Lorcán was blinded by Áed Findliath. The viking kings were presumably in pursuit of treasure, but they were also violating sites sanctified by ancient tradition; one of them, Knowth, was the royal seat of the Uí Néill king of the district (the successor of Cináed mac Conaing). These two offences may seem to us very different (do we punish persons using metal-detectors in pursuit of ancient treasure with blinding or death?), but they were not so very different in the ninth century. To violate known prehistoric monuments, and so to show contempt for a narrative implanted in the landscape, was to challenge the very basis of the political order. Talk of 'ritual landscapes' only embraces one element in a patiently constructed whole: a landscape that had been shaped over millennia was incorporated into narrative and so given a unified significance. A mark of the greater severity of 'the wars of the provincial kings' in the tenth and eleventh centuries was the practice of destroying the sacred tree (*bile*) of one's enemy; but, even then, there seem to have been limits on such ritual violence.

Scholars have often been more interested in the small inconsistencies and the necessary re-editing within the accepted narrative of Ireland than they have been in the significance of the whole enterprise. Yet the way in which stories could be adapted to cope with new developments (provided they were judged to be legitimate) shows the strength of the edifice as a whole. By any

[70] A.U., *s.a.* 850.3; 851.2; 863.4; 864.1.
[71] A.U., *s.a.* 861.1; 862.2.

reckoning conversion to Christianity was a huge innovation, yet through a reshaped St Patrick at the national level, as well as through numerous other saints in more local settings, this change could be brought within the tradition. The adaptation can be watched in the stories told by Tírechán at the end of the seventh century, and by later Patrician hagiographers, about the great circuit made by St Patrick around Ireland. To get Patrick to so many parts of the island in the course of a circuit redolent of kingly authority was not just to advance the interests of the Patrician community but to attach the districts he visited to a new theme in a wider narrative.

Particular shifts in political power could often be incorporated into tradition and so given legitimacy. The best-known example is the way Dál Cais sought to incorporate itself with the *senchas* of Munster, which had been framed in order to legitimise the authority of the rival Éoganachta. Less well-known are the efforts on behalf of the Uí Chonchobair, kings of the Connachta, to rewrite their relationship to the Uí Néill. In 1166, in the course of the events leading up to the Anglo-Norman invasion of 1169, the Annals of Tigernach (a source close to Ruaidrí Ua Conchobair) began a report of a campaign to subject Dublin, the king of the Airgialla, and others, as follows: 'A hosting by Ruaidrí Ua Conchobair together with the nobles of the Connachta, namely Tigernán Ua Ruairc and Diarmait Ua Máel Sechlainn...' What is startling about this annal is that Diarmait Ua Máel Sechlainn is described as a noble of the Connachta. With Tigernán Ua Ruairc there is no problem: his kingdom of Bréfne now extended far into the midlands, but at least he had a pedigree that purported to trace his descent from Brión mac Echach, eponymous ancestor of the Uí Briúin, of whom the Uí Chonchobair were currently the ruling branch. Diarmait Ua Máel Sechlainn, however, belonged to the Uí Néill, whose political supremacy had been proclaimed for centuries. Yet anyone who knew the first thing about the *senchas* of the men of Ireland knew that the Uí Néill were in origin a branch of the Connachta. He would also know that several crucial stories legitimating their kingship had been told about kings, such as Cormac mac Airt, acknowledged to be ancestors of the other Connachta as well as of the Uí Néill. The very text that ascribed Diarmait Ua Máel Sechlainn to the Connachta, the Annals of Tigernach, also contained one of the most complete records of the traditional pre-Patrician history of Ireland. The language used by the Annals of Tigernach might be startling, and it certainly suited the aspirations of Ruaidrí Ua Conchobair, but it required only a shift of perspective within the tradition, not some revolutionary rewriting.

To understand the political shape of early Christian Ireland, we need to study both the history of the landscape revealed by archaeology and the way it became the subject of narrative. We need both the landscape of archaeology and the landscape of *senchas*. One very good reason why they have to work together is that those portions of *senchas* that include the worst lies will often be the best evidence. It is important to know that Emain Macha was not a fortress and did not fall to the Uí Néill and their allies as late as the second, fourth, or fifth century A.D. but was deliberately destroyed early in the first century B.C.[72] Yet the reshaping of reality may help to explain what did happen at a later date. *Senchas* will be necessary to explain, for example, the name given to an entirely real king of the Airthir (the people around Armagh and Emain Macha) who died in 698 in battle in Fernmag (in Co. Monaghan), Conchobar Machae mac Maíle Dúin.[73] His first name, Conchobar, and the epithet, Machae, recalled the legendary king of the Ulstermen, whose capital was held to be at Emain Macha, Conchobar mac Nessa. This seventh-century king of the Airthir implicitly laid claim to *senchas* and thus to the ancient landscape of his own kingdom and died fighting in alliance with a king from the province of Ulster. Yet only a generation after his death, the Airgialla—of whom Conchobar Machae's people, the Airthir, were a part—were proclaiming that they had been principally responsible for destroying the ancient power of Ulster in a series of battles in the same Fernmag where Conchobar Machae met his death, an event that the experts in *senchas* accepted and placed in the third century A.D. In this sequence of events in the seventh and early eighth centuries, participants saw themselves and their kingdoms in terms of *senchas*, and a switch of political allegiance was proclaimed by means of a story.[74] Confronted by such a situation we need to appreciate the elements of both fiction and truth in the narrative—to clothe landscape and events in *senchas* as they did and yet to be able to stand outside the tradition and see it for what it was. It is evident that this can only be done by harnessing together different disciplines, history, archaeology, and the study of literature. What is implicit in this programme is that to understand history we need prehistory.

---

[72] Above, n. 9.    [73] A.U., *s.a.* 698.1.
[74] See Byrne, below, pp 656–79 (ch. XVIII).

CHAPTER I

# The geographical element
# in Irish history

J. H. ANDREWS

OF all geographical boundaries the seacoast is the most easily apprehended.
It is the one line that can be trusted to appear on even the oldest and crudest
of early maps; and as the antiquity of many insular names suggests, it is the
island, among all varieties of region recognised by geographers, that makes
the readiest psychological appeal. However closely Ireland resembled the
neighbouring countries, acre for acre, it was to be expected that insularity in
itself would create an impression of individual character or personality in the
mind of any commentator, at any historical period, who knew the country to
be enclosed by water. In the same way, the seas around Ireland would
be generally regarded as sufficient justification for the kind of unitary pan-
insular government that Irishmen in practice have not yet managed to
achieve; for the belief that a maritime boundary carries special political authority has lasted at least as long as Irish history. The same notion was
implicit in the Anglo-Saxon concept of a common 'world' linking Englishmen with the Celtic inhabitants of Britain,[1] as well as in the medieval belief
that islands possessed a distinctive political character by virtue of being at the
immediate disposal of the pope. And Giraldus Cambrensis was thinking
specifically of Ireland when he pronounced it unsafe for an island prince to
recognise any march or frontier but the sea itself.[2] Many Irishmen who
disagree with Giraldus about everything else would agree with him on this.
Even in the twentieth century, after the rise of nationalism had given a new
significance to purely ethnic boundaries, only a professional academic geographer would be subtle enough to deny that the sea is, in some sense or
other, a more natural frontier than the land.[3]

---

[1] Eric John, *Orbis Britanniae and other studies* (Leicester, 1968), pp 5–13.
[2] Thomas Wright (ed.), *The historical works of Giraldus Cambrensis* (London, 1863),
pp 174–5.
[3] Such a geographer is M. W. Heslinga in *The Irish border as a cultural divide* (Assen, 1962),
pp 10–12. For a modern Irish historian's endorsement of maritime natural frontiers see Oliver
MacDonagh, *States of mind: a study of Anglo-Irish conflict, 1780–1980* (London, 1983), p. 15.

Geographers of an older generation would have accepted the principle of maritime natural frontiers without demur. They might have tried to support it with the further claim that many islands derive their unity not just from a single enclosing border but also from certain characteristically insular qualities of life and culture. On this view, Ireland's acknowledged creativity in art, scholarship, and religion may come as a geographical surprise, for on grounds of simple probability a small area must be supposed less fertile in innovations than a large one, and more dependent on external sources for the substance of its history. By definition an island is smaller than a continent, and in islands the resulting lack of dynamism is accentuated by special difficulties of access. This was an idea for which Darwinian biologists could find statistical warrant by counting the number of species native to islands and continents respectively.[4] Under Darwin's inspiration it also seemed applicable (slightly modified to allow for the invention of the ship) to human societies, so that it was in no way untoward for one of Europe's offshore islands to have escaped several cataclysms of continental magnitude such as the Roman conquest and the post-Roman *Völkerwanderung*; or that such influences as did arrive should often have been distorted or attenuated in their passage. Islands thus figured in the anthropogeographer's textbook as repositories of archaism and cultural impoverishment.[5] Whatever its merits as a scientific law, this proposition had been anticipated in particular cases (including that of Ireland) by more than one staunchly empirical writer of the pre-Darwinian era: the now-familiar concept of a retarded Atlantic fringe, for example, is already implicit in Edmund Spenser's suggestion that certain culture-traits, formerly of wider extent, had by his time become confined to residual locations in Ireland and North Africa.[6]

Unlike physical insularity, anthropogeographic insularity is a relative concept, depending on the smallness of the insulated area and its remoteness from other land. Another geographic variable subject to continuous gradation is the difference between oceanic and continental. In this respect Ireland stands near the continental end of the scale. Its singularity is further compromised by close spatial relations with Great Britain, for archipelagos as well as individual islands make a strong appeal to the geographical intellect, and the idea of 'the British Isles' was already familiar to the geographers of the ancient world, who based it on putative similarities of climate, soil, race, and culture between the two islands, as well as on purely spatial links.[7] The

---

[4] A. R. Wallace, *Island life, or the phenomena and causes of insular faunas and floras* (2nd ed., London, 1892), p. 339.

[5] E. C. Semple, *Influences of geographic environment on the basis of Ratzel's system of anthropogeography* (New York, 1911), pp 409–72.

[6] Edmund Spenser, *A view of the present state of Ireland*, ed. W. L. Renwick (Oxford, 1970), p. 61.

[7] C. G. Stevens, 'Ancient writers on Britain' in *Antiquity*, i (1927), pp 189–90; J. F. Killeen, 'Ireland in the Greek and Roman writers' in *R.I.A. Proc.*, lxxvi (1976), sect. C, pp 207–15.

same idea found expression in the titles and sheet-lines chosen for their maps
of Britain and Ireland by sixteenth-century continental cartographers such as
Sebastian Münster and Abraham Ortelius,[8] though it was an Englishman
who conjured up the rather twisted image of Ireland as a 'buttress and a post
under England',[9] and another Englishman who drew the inference that the
two countries form, or ought to form, 'an entire empire in themselves'.[10]
The fact that the smaller island was shielded by the larger one from so many
possible continental embarkation-points no doubt gave greater plausibility to
this view.

Since they can be embraced within a single field of vision, the thirteen
miles (21 km) from Fair Head to Kintyre are too short a distance to be easily
tampered with by either the imagination or the intellect. Ireland's surface
area of 80,000 km² is less easily visualised and therefore more open to diverse
evaluations. Until the seventeenth century the country was generally
regarded as more extensive, in relation to Britain, than it actually is. Apart
from simple errors of geometrical estimation or measurement, the country
bulked larger in the geographical consciousness of western Europe than it
does today, and many writers made a point of giving it a high rank in this
respect, at least among the islands of the world.[11] Ireland was certainly too
large for a would-be conqueror to think of pacifying the whole of it by the
kind of mass extirpation or deportation that might be visited upon a single
tribe or town, and large enough to expose the invader to its own cultural
influences. Large enough, too, for some surprise to be caused among foreigners by the ease of communication among its native inhabitants: this at least is
one way of interpreting the auditory metaphor favoured by many English
writers, as when a part of Ireland is said to 'echo' the noise of some disturbance originating in another part.[12]

Having conquered Ireland, the English corrected (as it happened, over-
corrected) their exaggerated notions of its size. But Swift in 1725 could still
call it a 'great' kingdom.[13] His judgement becomes more comprehensible
when we remember that in terms of population, and doubtless of gross

[8] Denys Hay, 'The use of the term "Great Britain" in the middle ages' in *Antiq. Soc. Scot.
Proc.*, lxxxix (1955–6), pp 55–66: 63; R. W. Shirley, *Early printed maps of the British Isles,
1477–1650: a bibliography* (London, 1973).
[9] George Warner (ed.), *The libelle of Englysche polycye: a poem on the use of seapower, 1436*
(Oxford, 1926), p. 36.
[10] Francis Bacon, 'Certain articles or considerations touching the union of the kingdoms of
England and Scotland' in *The works of Francis Bacon*, ed. Basil Montagu (16 vols, London,
1825–36), v, 28.
[11] 'Ireland, next after England the greatest island of the known world...' (Abraham
Ortelius, *Theatrum orbis terrarum* (London, 1606), p. 14).
[12] J. T. Gilbert (ed.), *History of the Irish confederation and the war in Ireland, 1641–1643*
(7 vols, Dublin, 1882–91), i, 24.
[13] Jonathan Swift, *The drapier's letters to the people of Ireland against receiving Wood's half-
pence*, ed. Herbert Davis (Oxford, 1935), p. 153.

national product, the difference separating it from Britain had not yet been widened by the industrial revolution to anything like its later extent. But even if the density of people and economic activity in both countries had remained the same, Ireland would still have begun to cut a smaller figure as the scale of geographical thinking was transformed in the nineteenth century by the advent of the railway and the telegraph. This process of shrinkage came too late however to do much harm to Irish national aspirations, for with the growing influence of public opinion in world affairs the smallness of the underdog assumed an ideological value that Victorian *Realpolitik* had failed to take account of. Notwithstanding the continued progress of scale economies in the technology of the twentieth century, the average size of sovereign states has decreased, making the Irish Republic not less but more viable, in a political sense, with each decade of its existence.

HOWEVER incomplete its aloofness from the rest of the world in purely spatial terms, Ireland is both set apart and held together by certain features of its physical constitution, and particularly by a climate that, despite its regional variations, has almost always been treated, among non-climatologists at any rate, as an essentially national characteristic. And where national characteristics are concerned, the facts of nature in Ireland were rightly described by Frederick Engels as no less debatable than the facts of history.[14] It is not the meteorological conditions themselves that are in dispute—extremes of temperature are admitted to be rare throughout the country, and not even Ireland's harshest critics would deny that precipitation is abundant and well distributed—but rather the economic and political significance of these conditions. The belief so often expressed in the later nineteenth century that Ireland is more fit for grass than for corn is common to many periods of recorded geographical thought, including the earliest.[15] Yet it has not been quite unanimous: in Edward Wakefield's account of the Irish climate in 1812, one of the longest ever printed, this familiar proposition is never so much as hinted at.[16] The truth is that many Irish farms are physically capable of being either tilled or grazed, and there have been times, including that of Wakefield's visit, when the protection of distance, together with institutional barriers, has made corn-growing for export a profitable enterprise in almost every one of the thirty-two counties. Yet it cannot be denied that tillage has suffered hazards that have done a great deal, in combination or succession, to disturb the course of agrarian history. Many of Ireland's soils have proved liable to slow deterioration as a result of over-prolonged or unskilful cultiva-

[14] *Karl Marx and Frederick Engels on Ireland* (Moscow, 1971), p. 185.
[15] Eoin MacNeill, 'Greek and Latin writers on pre-Christian Ireland' in idem, *Phases of Irish history* (reprint, Dublin, 1968), p. 135.
[16] Edward Wakefield, *An account of Ireland, statistical and political* (London, 1812), pp 140–237.

tion, and this kind of ecological imbalance, as much as purely climatic change, has been held responsible by some investigators for the growth of peat bogs over much of the country's prehistoric corn land.[17] Short-term weather changes have left their mark as well, including as they do the kind of excessive rainfall that favoured the spread of the potato blight in 1845.[18] Biotic calamities apart, corn is known to have suffered more than livestock by being easily destroyed in time of war. In any case the bonanza conditions that prompted Wakefield's optimism were short-lived; nor were they likely to recur when the steamship and the railway had exposed the Irish wheat farmer to commercial attack from regions of lower production costs.

Through most of these vicissitudes some qualities of men and nature have remained constant. However permissive the Irish climate in an ecological sense, its economic influence has been governed by the fact that those of its properties conducive to livestock-raising are less widely distributed in the world at large, and therefore possess more scarcity value, than those that favour corn. Within Ireland the balance of economic advantage between tillage and grazing is strongly influenced by non-climatic factors—often to the detriment of corn-growing, for cattle can forage in many places that are too steep, too boggy, or too rocky for either plough or spade. Climate and physiography thus combine to encourage the Irish pastoralist. Irrespective of environmental influence, grazing carries more social weight than tillage. When the economies of the iron age and early Christian period are reconstructed by historians, it is the small farmer who grows most of the corn and the lord or freeman who keeps most of the animals. Ever since, the cattleman's life has remained a goal for ambitious Irish countrymen to aim at.[19]

Thus for several reasons livestock have flourished in Ireland when corn has failed. As an extensive rather than an intensive mode of land use, grass yields a rather low output of human food per unit area and supports a correspondingly low density of population. This makes large agglomerations of pastoral farmers difficult to sustain, and where water is widely available their habitations tend to be dispersed. Accordingly, most Irishmen of substance have chosen to live detached from other members of their own class—a habit exemplified in succession by the raths and cashels of the early Christian period, the tower houses of the middle ages, and the gentlemen's mansions of the landlord era. In the last of these periods, at any rate, the houses of the stronger tenantry have been scattered in much the same way. It is the humbler (and less well documented) farmsteads that appear to have been grouped

[17] Frank Mitchell, *The Shell guide to the Irish landscape* (London, 1986), p. 123.
[18] P. Austin Bourke, 'The impact of climatic fluctuations on European agriculture' in Herman Flohn and Roberta Fantechi (ed.), *The climate of Europe: past, present, and future* (Dordrecht, Boston, and Lancaster, 1984), pp 293–6.
[19] Estyn Evans, *Prehistoric and early Christian Ireland* (London, 1966), pp 25–6.

together beside their common arable fields.[20] But these clusters or 'cla-chans'[21] have usually been small, and deficient in the kind of community institution, whether church or inn, that has helped to give permanence and stability to the larger rural nucleations of other countries. It is true that Irish historical geographers have distinguished several kinds of 'village',[22] but these were generally too short-lived to affect the foregoing argument; few Anglo-Norman parochial or manorial centres withstood the trauma of being taken over by a minority church at the time of the reformation, while neither catholic chapels, textile mills, nor park entrances exerted much agglomerative effect on rural settlement until the eighteenth century or later.

Where villages are small, the same will be true of their appurtenant territories. The smallest units of community life have been variously designated in different parts of Ireland—balliboes, polls, tates, ploughlands, and so on[23]—but none of them was ever as large as the typical township of southern or middle England, at least if one can judge from the fact that their modern successors, the townlands of the Ordnance Survey map, average no more than 132 hectares (326 statute acres) in size. So fine a mesh of presumably ancient names and boundaries could never have been created by a nation of nomads. But pastoral habits do engender a disposition towards mobility, especially in a mild climate where accommodation for men and animals is inexpensive and easily replaced. In times of trouble, such as war or scarcity, Irishmen have travelled widely in their own country and abroad. Even in periods of normality foreign visitors have been struck by a certain air of rootlessness about the landscape. Thus through much of Ireland's history the main focus of exchange has been not the weekly market but the livestock fair, held at less frequent intervals and often drawing custom from longer distances but occupying sites that were devoid of urban amenities and perhaps without any kind of permanent building. In an economy whose chief prod-

---

[20] R. H. Buchanan, 'Field systems in Ireland' in A. R. H. Baker and R. A. Butlin (ed.), *Studies of field systems in the British Isles* (Cambridge, 1973), pp 614–15. For doubts about the antiquity of clachans see Matthew Stout, 'Ringforts in the south-west midlands of Ireland' in *R.I.A. Proc.*, xci (1991), sect. C., pp 201–43.

[21] The settlement term 'clachan', meaning a cluster of farmhouses, was introduced to Irish human geography by E. Estyn Evans ('Donegal survivals' in *Antiquity*, xiii (1939), pp 207–22; see also the same author's 'The Ulster landscape' in *Ulster Folklife*, iv (1959), pp 9–14:10) and popularised by his disciples. It was later criticised by Caoimhín Ó Danachair (*Ir. Geography*, v (1968), pp 494–5) and others on linguistic and methodological grounds, and is now less widely used.

[22] A survey of village-types applicable to many parts of Ireland is given in P. J. O'Connor, *Exploring Limerick's past: an historical geography of urban development in county and city* (Newcastle West, 1987).

[23] Thomas McErlean, 'The Irish townland system of landscape organisation' in T. Reeves-Smyth and F. Hamond (ed.), *Landscape archaeology in Ireland* (Oxford, 1983), pp 315–39. For the relation in Ireland between the townland unit and the English-style village, see Anngret Simms, 'Continuity and change: settlement and society in medieval Ireland, c.500–1500' in William Nolan (ed.), *The shaping of Ireland: the geographical perspective* (Cork, 1986), pp 55–7.

ucts were self-transporting, trade routes made little use of the harbours, river navigations and bridges that would have attracted settlement if inanimate material had needed to be stored and carried in large amounts. This helps to explain why hilltops retained their popularity as places of assembly for so much of the early historic period. The sites of many Celtic Christian monasteries were equally wanting in natural nodality; and although some of these ecclesiastical communities might have been urban in form and function to a degree unknown among earlier Irish settlements, in the last resort they were equally inessential to the everyday material life of the surrounding countryside.

In the absence of a firmly based native urban tradition, resistance to alien cultural pressure has been doomed for many centuries. But the lack of easy and decisive targets in the form of towns and villages also made the Irish a difficult people to conquer in a military sense, as they discovered for themselves without the aid of foreign invasions. Perhaps there was less motive for conquest in a lightly peopled country where the driving-off of cattle could be substituted for the acquisition of territory.[24] At any rate, among the numerous kingdoms and sub-kingdoms that shared the island in early historic times, and the numerous medieval 'countries' that succeeded them, the tendency towards political amalgamation and centralisation seemed weaker than in other parts of western Europe.[25] Two Irish problems thus confronted any foreigner who coveted land rather than cattle: military, arising from the elusiveness of his enemies in the field; and diplomatic, posed by the difficulty of getting more than a small proportion of them represented at the negotiating table on any one occasion.

These difficulties were exacerbated by the complexity of Ireland's regional geography, and especially by the intricate pattern of its mountains, bogs, and other natural barriers. William of Windsor, in the fourteenth century, is said to have admitted that despite having more experience of the Irish than any contemporary Englishman, he 'could never have access to understand and know their countries'.[26] Descending from the national to the regional scale, a modern geographer may well feel much the same. He certainly has little hope in Ireland that regions of similar soil or agricultural economy will match those defined by a common relationship to some internal or external focus; or that the regions delimited by his academic colleagues will be the same as those enshrined in popular consciousness. The first of these disharmonies is

[24] Katharine Simms, 'Warfare in the medieval Gaelic lordships' in *Ir. Sword*, xii (1976), pp 98–108.
[25] Proinsias Mac Cana, 'Notes on the early Irish concept of unity' in *The Crane Bag*, ii (1978), pp 57–71.
[26] John Davies, *A discoverie of the true causes why Ireland was never entirely subdued, nor brought under obedience of the crowne of England, until the beginning of his maiesties happie reigne*, ed. John Barry (Shannon, 1969), p. 37.

commonplace in geographical studies the world over; so is the tendency for adjacent geographical regions to merge or overlap. As an arena for debate between academic and non-academic regionality, Ireland poses its own problems. In a country where national unity has long been a burning issue, patriotic writers have naturally been reluctant to spend too much time contemplating internal divisions. It is true that some scholars credit the Irish in general with an unusually strong 'sense of place'—a theory for which they seek verification in the great wealth of Gaelic-based local names.[27] The wealth of names is undeniable, though to judge from modern Irish literature the feelings they evoke are stronger among those who have left their home district in early adult life than among those who have stayed to give that district its prevailing character. But localism is not the same as regionalism.

In all these circumstances geographers must proceed with care. They will doubtless agree that the most clearly defined of Ireland's 'vernacular' regions, such as Connemara, Fingal, or the Mackamores, are too small to encompass more than a minute share of the nation's historical experience, as also are the minor administrative areas known as baronies. Moreover, as with Ireland in general, though obviously to a lesser degree, regional individuality often seems attributable to the possession of maritime boundaries, so that when all the widely known examples have been itemised the interior of the country remains largely unaccounted for.[28] In this apparently hollow centre the only substitute for the geographer's natural region that has gained much currency in modern times as a unit of territorial thought among non-academics is the county. Counties, like other governmental areas, have the merit of being exhaustive in their spatial coverage, but they are comparatively recent creations without deep cultural roots, and once again it is only in the coastal examples that outside opinion shows much sign of recognising a definite personality.

At a higher level of integration Irish regionalism takes on a somewhat more positive character. The provinces of Leinster, Munster, Ulster, and Connacht (though not Meath) can still claim a degree of reality beyond the pretensions of, for example, the Anglo-Saxon heptarchy in present-day England. So many individual qualities have been attributed by tradition to the provinces (including comeliness, haughtiness, good manners, vehemence, and 'ale')[29] that it would be surprising if none of their peculiarities had survived into a more prosaic age. And long after having abandoned any aspirations to political sovereignty, the provinces were accorded official status

[27] Seán Ó Tuama, 'Stability and ambivalence: aspects of the sense of place and religion in Irish literature' in Joseph Lee (ed.), *Ireland: towards a sense of place* (Cork, 1985), pp 21–33.
[28] Pierre Flatrès, *Géographie rurale de quatre contrées celtiques: Irlande, Galles, Cornwall, et Man* (Rennes, 1957), p. 208.
[29] Alwyn Rees and Brinley Rees, *Celtic heritage: ancient tradition in Ireland and Wales* (London, 1961), pp 118–39.

in the Elizabethan institution of the presidency and later, by Irishmen themselves, in the parliamentary and military organs created by the confederation of Kilkenny. Even in the twentieth century it could be seriously suggested that separate political assemblies should be established for each of the four provinces. A possible weakness in any such political hypostatisation of the provinces would be its disregard for the rather different kind of regional pattern created in Ireland by certain social and economic forces that have come into prominence during the last three centuries. These newer patterns are by no means unrelated to the layout of the provinces, but the relationship is too loose for region and province to be treated as identical. The regions in question have about as good a title to reality as the historian would find acceptable for his conventional period divisions. Since some of them persist or recur from one period to another, their use as a supplementary framework for historical narrative or analysis may seem to offer some attractions. How far such a framework exposes historians to the kind of 'determinism' that eventually became so uncongenial to their geographical colleagues must remain an open question.

T HE central lowland is a latecomer to the Irish regional canon. As recently as the Tudor period, map-makers were still acting on Giraldus's opinion that the middle of the island is more mountainous than the coasts.[30] It was not until the canal era that the non-existence of these central mountains began to assume a positive quality of its own, and it was not until the carboniferous limestones of Ireland were mapped by Richard Griffith[31] that geological and physiographical taxonomies combined to establish the notion of the central lowland as taken for granted in the majority of modern textbooks. But Giraldus's mistake at least possessed a certain physical plausibility, and it was understandable for a Welshman to assume that the disjunctive character of the interior arose from the same causes in Ireland as in his own country.

In any case Giraldus got to the heart of the matter with his often-quoted reference to the ubiquity of pools and swamps in Ireland. North of the morainic ridges that stretch from Clare to Wexford, in particular, the hydrology of the central lowland is bewilderingly irregular. Lakes are numerous, and rivers sluggish and liable to flood, wide enough to obstruct the traveller but not sufficiently well patterned to form a system of navigable arteries and nodes. Even the largest, the Shannon, was cut off from its estuary, as are so many Irish rivers, by impassable rapids. Between the rivers the land is widely strewn with peat bogs, too wet for settlement without extensive drainage and

---

[30] *Works*, p. 20. A map of Henry VIII's time in which the interior of Ireland appears to be based on Giraldus's views is in B.L., Cott. MS, Aug. I, i, f. 9.

[31] R. J. Griffith, 'On the geological map of Ireland' in *Report of the fifth meeting of the British Association for the Advancement of Science* (Dublin, 1835), pt ii, *Notices of communications*, p. 56. I owe this reference to G. L. Herries Davies.

too barren for agriculture even then. Esker ridges provide some ancient
roadbeds between the bogs, but they too failed to make up a continuous
network and most of them run from east to west instead of helping to knit
the country together along its major axis. Apart from bogs and eskers, the
midlands are chiefly underlain by glacial drifts which for all their inherent
fertility were not easily cultivated with primitive implements. These soils are
likely to have supported a patchwork of forest for most of prehistoric times—
and for long afterwards in the drumlin belt that stretches from Dundalk to
Sligo Bay, where the pattern of river, lake, and bog is even more complex
than further south and the soils even less tractable.

It has long been recognised that Leinster, Munster, Ulster, and Connacht
are each grouped around one or more of the upland massifs that dominate
nearly all the coastline of Ireland except for some 80 km immediately to the
north of Dublin.[32] More recently it has been argued that this relationship
may be something more than an inevitable consequence of quartering a
basin-shaped surface, and that it was the thin, stony soils of the hill fringes,
easily cleared and dug by early farmers, that determined their role as prehistoric kernels of early kingdoms. Relevant to this hypothesis are the megalithic
tombs associated with some of Ireland's earliest farming communities of the
third and fourth millennia before Christ. Notably scarce in the midlands,
the tombs do show a corroborative preference for medium altitudes along the
margins of the coastal hills. They also exhibit some well-marked typological
differences—for instance between the court cairns of the north and the
wedge-shaped gallery graves of the south—which could be taken to imply
that the central lowland was separating the nuclear regions of different neolithic cultures as well as different concentrations of settlement. More recently
still, this theory has been disparaged on the ground that burials are only a
part, and perhaps an unrepresentative part, of neolithic culture as a whole;[33]
and no other pre-Christian archaeological distribution has been found to
throw much light on the issue. The early Christian era, in both artefacts and
literature, shows a remarkable consistency in lifestyle and settlement from
one end of the country to another; and it may be no accident that the advent
of the new religion seems to have accompanied the spread of new ploughs
and new crops and in consequence a more intensive occupation of the interior with a weakening of whatever separative power it may have exercised in
pagan times.[34]

Indeed, far from dividing early Christian Ireland on the cultural plane, the
midlands—or at any rate a part of them—could now claim to be acting as a

[32] E. E. Evans, *Irish folkways* (London, 1957), p. 17.
[33] Patrick O'Flanagan, 'The central lowlands of Ireland—an empty heart (land)?' in *Old
Athlone Society Journal*, i (1972–3), pp 127–32.
[34] G. F. Mitchell, 'Littleton Bog, Tipperary: an Irish agricultural record' in *R.S.A.I. Jn.*,
xcv (1965), pp 121–32: 129.

force for cultural unity, with monasteries insulated among the bogs of north Leinster contributing more to the art and scholarship of the British Isles between the seventh and ninth centuries than those of any other area of comparable extent.[35] In other spheres this kind of sub-regional core is harder to identify. In the complex and shifting political geography of the early Christian kingdoms, for example, the midland esker ridges repeatedly served as an east–west boundary between the *Leth Cuinn* and the *Leth Moga*;[36] and the Shannon was still dividing one kingdom from another for most of its course at the time of the Norman invasion. It would not have been in character for the Irish to anticipate their conquerors' thought-processes by transferring the theoretical centre of Ireland from a hill (Uisneagh) to a ford (Athlone) or to endow such a focal point, wherever it might be, with strategic as well as symbolic status. And when invaders from Britain lacked the strength to act on their own newly imported strategic judgement, it was not in the centre but on the margins of the country that the most dangerous anti-government power blocs showed most sign of coalescing. By 1642, when all parts of Ireland seemed finally to be joining in resistance to English rule, the essentially peripheral pattern of Ireland's larger towns had been established once and for all (mainly by settlers not averse to some kind of external allegiance) and Kilkenny, sixty miles (100 km) off centre, was apparently the only place in the interior with enough accommodation to serve the confederates as a modern-style capital.

The penetration of the midland bogs by artificial road surfaces and artificial waterways in the eighteenth century came too late to redress the balance between centre and periphery. No one answered George Semple's call in 1780 for a great axial road to join the north of Ireland with the south;[37] and when new routeways did create new junctions, as where the canals met the Shannon, hardly anything was done to take advantage of them. Another discovery of the canal period was that most of Ireland's coal resources lie outside the central lowland and away from navigable rivers;[38] but the resources in question are so small anyway that this has hardly been a factor of much importance.

The Irish of medieval and post-medieval times thus differed from some other nations, among them the French and the Czechs, in possessing no centrally placed and fertile river basin to provide a focus for national self-consciousness and a nucleus of geopolitical consolidation. It is the east and not the centre that comes nearest to the geographer's ideal of a nuclear zone. Nationality can exist without such physical aids, at any rate in its Celtic

---

[35] Alfred P. Smyth, *Celtic Leinster: towards an historical geography of early Irish civilisation* (Dublin, 1982), pp 94–5.
[36] Byrne, *Ir. kings*, p. 202.
[37] George Semple, *Hibernia's free trade* (Dublin, 1780), p. 177.
[38] Robert Kane, *The industrial resources of Ireland* (2nd ed., Dublin, 1845), p. 8.

forms: to judge from the present book, the literature of Irish self-defence and self-assertion has nothing whatever to say about the relation of politics to regional geography. But it cannot be an advantage for any country if the region best equipped to unify it has depended on foreigners for so much of its character—including for a long period its regional name. Admittedly two important geographical advantages had made their presence felt in eastern and south-eastern Ireland well before Englishmen had begun to speak of an English Pale: one a lowland corridor unusually free from bog, linking north and south along the River Barrow; the other, proximity to what was from an early date the more developed half of Britain. But without more knowledge of origins and provenances, it would be presumptuous to adduce phenomena as early as the Boyne valley tombs or the preeminence of the hill of Tara as a response to these physical conditions. Nor can much stress be laid on the fact that survivals of early Christian art and architecture are slightly more numerous in the south-east than in the rest of the country. Only in the ninth century does the geographic theorist begin to approach firm ground. The vikings are known to have approached Ireland from the north and yet to have chosen the south—and in three cases out of five the south-east—for all their major settlements. At Dublin the value they placed on cross-channel relationships was shown not only by their adoption of an estuarine site (which the Irish had been content to use as a political boundary) but by the association of this site with a large part of Britain in a single maritime Scandinavian kingdom.

For the Normans, working from a power base in southern England and south Wales, the south-east approach to Ireland was obviously the most inviting. Their originality lay not in underwriting the Scandinavian choice of town sites, but in attempting to combine several small foreigners' bridge-heads into a single large one. Strongbow's progress through Leinster to Dublin in 1170, especially after it had been followed a year later by Henry II's decision to retain the city and its surroundings as a royal demesne, must surely have been seen by contemporaries as a dramatic stroke, though it would perhaps be anachronistic to regard Dublin as a geopolitically 'forward' capital in relation to the settlement that followed. Under this settlement a link was forged between the two poles of Strongbow's enterprise in Waterford and Dublin, thus opposing the south-east of Ireland to the north-west along a frontier that in one form or another has been traceable ever since.[39]

By the treaty of Windsor in 1175 Leinster, Meath, and the kingdom of east Munster were brought under Norman influence, the rest of the country being left alone. As on many later occasions, a new settlement was fitted into

[39] For the qualifications necessary to any detailed application of the frontier thesis in Ireland see P. J. Duffy, 'The nature of the medieval frontier in Ireland' in *Studia Hib.*, xxii–xxiii (1982–3), pp 21–38. See also Robert Bartlett and Angus Mackay (ed.), *Medieval frontier societies* (Oxford, 1989).

old political boundaries—a reasonable course of action for an invader without boundary-making facilities of his own. It soon became clear, however, that the south-east of Ireland, no less than the rest of the country, presented the invader with two quite different kinds of terrain. First there were lands already under cultivation or capable of easily being brought under cultivation. When English chorographical descriptions of Ireland became common in the sixteenth century it was usual to describe such areas simply as 'plains'.[40] Many of these writings show surprise at the sparseness of the native population on such fertile land, and certainly medieval Englishmen had left a more vivid imprint on the plains of Ireland than any of their previous occupants. The colonists' buildings were stronger and larger than those of the Irish and more effectively nucleated into towns and villages. They were also better connected by roads, bridges, and navigable rivers, and served by a fringe of well-defended seaports. Moreover, unlike the ringforts and other native habitations that preceded them, these settlements were to prove adaptable with comparatively little modification to the needs of post-medieval society.

Small areas of waste land could be ingested by the Anglo-Norman organism and entirely removed from the landscape. But the larger tracts of forest and mountain in south-east Ireland constituted a second kind of terrain, and one on which, as in the midland bogs, the Irish proved better able to maintain their hold. Some of their hill land could be cropped on an 'outfield' system of occasional cultivation interrupted by long spells of fallow. The remainder gave summer grazing to cattle which, after harvest-time, were moved into the weeds and stubble of the more fertile and fully cultivated 'infield'. When winter and summer pastures lay far apart they could be linked by the practice of 'booleying', *an buaile*, in which both herds and herders spent the two seasons in alternate dwellings. This at least is how historical geographers would visualise medieval life in a region like west Wicklow, though most of the evidence for such practices comes from other periods and other places.[41] In eastern and central Ireland the earliest clear admission of the Anglo-Normans' economic inferiority outside the plains comes in a statute of 1297 distinguishing 'lands of peace' from places where the Irish could be found 'confiding in the thickness of the woods and the depth of the adjacent bogs'.[42]

The same distinction was evidently still valid when land quality, as well as defensibility, was cited by Edmund Campion (writing the history of the later

[40] Edmund Hogan (ed.), *The description of Ireland, and the state thereof as it is at this present, anno 1598* (Dublin and London, 1878), pp 14, 75, 150.
[41] The lack of readily accessible contemporary documentation for native field systems and related agrarian practices in medieval Ireland can be verified by following up the footnote references in the present work. See *N.H.I.*, ii, 211, 226–7, 331–2, 411–13, 468.
[42] *Statutes and ordinances, and acts of the parliament of Ireland, King John to Henry V*, ed. H. F. Berry (Dublin, 1907), p. 209.

middle ages) as a criterion for the definition of the English Pale.[43] Campion
raised a difficult question, however, when he described the Pale as the
'proper right' of the English, for this might be taken to imply that pre-
Norman juridical boundaries could be found to match his other criteria. It is
true that the Norman domain of 1175 was distinguished by possessing a
larger proportion of rich soil than the rest of Ireland, and that in some places,
such as the edge of the drumlin belt towards Monaghan and Cavan, the
physical and political limits coincided fairly well. It is also true that English
occupation within these limits had been intensive enough to blur the ancient
boundary between Leinster and Meath, and that Leinster (now including
Meath) emerged from the middle ages with the reputation of being more
easily governable than the other provinces. But even in the heart of Leinster
the edge of effective Anglo-Norman development followed a sinuous course,
with an upper margin not far from the 600-foot (180 m) contour. The largest
spreads of good soil in east and south-east Ireland were in Meath, Dublin,
Louth, and Kildare, a group of counties sometimes taken as synonymous
with the Pale. Further south there were other fertile strips along the rivers
that converge on Waterford Harbour to form the only major drainage system
in Ireland that can qualify as well articulated. Smaller patches of good land
occupied more isolated positions in south Wexford and east Cork. Altogether
the 'plains' of south-east Ireland formed an unwieldy assemblage. One threat
to regional unity was the great salient of midland bogs that pushed eastwards
to within about 30 km of Dublin. However offensive to modern geographical
scholarship, it was a sound geopolitical instinct to generalise these scattered
areas into the 'Bog of Allen',[44] especially at a time when much of the intervening firm ground was still wooded and when this whole extent of bog and
forest was buttressed by the high ground of the Slieve Margy, another barrier region with a well-established contemporary name later absorbed into the
textbook concept of the Castlecomer plateau.[45] Even nearer the coast lay the
wilderness of the Wicklow mountains and what were then their well-wooded
fringes in Carlow and the Duffry of north Wexford.[46] Between these two
native bastions there was only the narrow Barrow valley to complete the link
between the principal seaports of the Englishry at Dublin and Waterford. In
short, bog and mountain were so disposed that no compact area of more than
a few hundred square kilometres could be sure of excluding both. Certainly
no combination of pre-existing territories would suffice, not even the Pale in

[43] Edmund Campion, *A historie of Ireland written in the year 1571* (Dublin, 1809), p. 6.

[44] William Petty, 'The province of Leinster' in *Hiberniae delineatio* (London, 1685).

[45] William Nolan, *Fassadinin: land, settlement and society in south-east Ireland, 1600–1850*
(Dublin, 1979), pp 34, 39.

[46] For the regional name 'Duffry' see Billy Colfer, 'Anglo-Norman settlement in County
Wexford' in Kevin Whelan (ed.), *Wexford, history and society: interdisciplinary essays on the
history of an Irish county* (Dublin, 1987), pp 66–9.

its original mid-fifteenth-century sense of four counties. The nearest conceptual equivalent to this physiographic utopia was probably the 'Vale of
Dublin' as recognised by the early Anglo-Normans.[47]

By about 1500 the Pale had shrunk to a last ditch, defined, though probably never dug, to pass through Kells, Clane, Naas, and other towns even
closer to Dublin. Many smaller pockets of English influence remained outside, notably in the seaport towns. But it was not long before the government
of Henry VIII began to envisage a larger base, that would lie 'entire together
in one angle' (a word that may hint at a growing use of maps in Irish official
business) instead of being 'divided by quarters'.[48] Sometimes the Barrow was
proposed as a possible frontier for this south-eastern corner; sometimes,
more ambitiously, the Shannon. For the Pale, although an expression of
material weakness, provided a metaphor of great intellectual power and flexibility, transcending the fixed limits implied by ordinary geographical nomenclature with a prospect whose bounds could be set as near or as far as might
be practicable at any given time. It would be an oversimplification, however,
to treat the Elizabethan reconquest of Ireland as an extension of these
bounds. As a social region the Pale retained its individuality after 1603; forty
years later it was still capable of resurfacing as a political region.[49] And some
of its characteristics did not penetrate the rest of the country till after the
restoration of Charles II. One of these late-spreading wave-fronts was the
reinstatement of the shire as the largest unit of Irish local government when
the separate provincial administrations of Munster and Connacht were finally
abolished in 1672. Others were the Cromwellian network of new English
estates and proprietors, as endorsed by the restoration settlement, together
with various profound effects on the landscape—woodland clearance, town
foundation, road development—that followed the change of ownership. But
even after the whole country could be regarded as politically empaled,
Anglo-Irish landlordism never managed to level out the gradient between
north-west and south-east that had divided Ireland in the middle ages. It is a
gradient that reappears in modern maps of place-name elements (map 1),
vernacular house types,[50] and other aspects of folk life, where the frequency
of boundaries separating south-east from north-west has prompted the suggestion that in Irish as in British history a 'lowland zone' of superimposition
can be contrasted with a 'highland zone' of survival.[51] Some maps of physical

[47] *Calendar of documents relating to Ireland, 1171–1251* (London, 1875), p. 15.
[48] *State papers, Henry VIII* (11 vols, London, 1830–52), ii, pt 3, pp 298 (1536), 410 (1537).
[49] J. C. Beckett, 'The confederation of Kilkenny reviewed' in idem, *Confrontations* (London, 1972), p. 54.
[50] F. H. A. Aalen, *Man and the landscape in Ireland* (London, New York, and San Francisco, 1978), pp 244–68.
[51] Caoimhín Ó Danachair, 'Irish vernacular architecture in relation to the Irish Sea' in Donald Moore (ed.), *The Irish Sea province in archaeology and history* (Cardiff, 1970), pp 98–107:98.

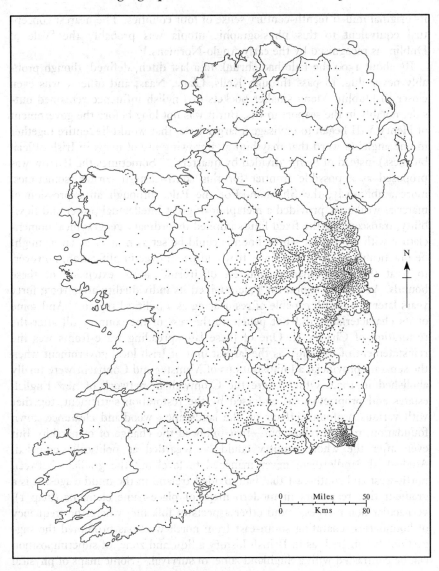

Map 1  Place-names with 'town' as suffix, by T. Jones Hughes

Redrawn from N. Stephens and R. E. Glasscock (ed.), *Irish geographical studies in honour of
E. Estyn Evans* (Belfast, 1970), figure 15.1.

anthropology show a similar pattern of residual and intrusive elements.[52]
Even the superstructure of the ubiquitous landed estate assumed a less com-

[52] W. E. R. Hackett, G. W. P. Dawson, and C. J. Dawson, 'The pattern of ABO blood
group frequencies in Ireland' in *Heredity*, x (1956), pp 69–84.

manding profile with increasing distance from the Irish Sea; east and south-east stand out in the nineteenth century as areas of fewer dwarf farms, a higher ratio of tillage to grass, a more complex class structure in both town and countryside, and a greater measure of social stability[53]—but not neces-sarily a keener sense of regional consciousness, as can perhaps be gathered from the disappearance of the term 'pale' except among historians. Some of the old regional contrasts between Irish and Anglo-Irish were strengthened or renewed by the events of the seventeenth century. By far the most suc-cessful English plantations of this period outside Ulster were those located furthest to the south-east, in Wicklow and north Wexford—almost a new English Pale in themselves, though much less effective in creating a homoge-neous community, as the rising of 1798 was to make clear.[54] This zone may be projected northwards into the streets of seventeenth-and eighteenth-century Dublin, where the import of commodities, people, ideas, and atti-tudes brought 'New Englishness' in all its forms to a pitch unequalled anywhere else in Ireland; sending fresh cultural ripples westwards as the city continued to polarise the national communications network, first with roads and later with canals and railways, until there seemed no chance of ever finding an alternative seat of government, not even in the twentieth century when such transfers had become a popular way of celebrating the independ-ence of new nation states.

WHEN Sir John Davies showed surprise in 1606 that some of the inhabitants of western Ireland should be as 'mere Irish' as those of Ulster,[55] he was voicing the usual contemporary attitude to what later came to be simplistic-ally considered the most British of the provinces. North of the Pale medieval English influence, such as it was, had been mainly concentrated east of the Bann in the region sometimes known as 'hither Ulster',[56] and even here it had left little lasting impression outside precarious footholds in the Ards and Lecale peninsulas. The survival of a native economy in Ulster, together with climatic theorising based on its northerly latitude, may be the reason why the agricultural possibilities of the province were so much undervalued by six-teenth- and early seventeenth-century writers.[57] In fact, far from being a natural wilderness, Ulster might persuasively be interpreted as a complete Ireland in miniature, with the Lagan valley as its Pale, the Mourne

---

[53] T. J. Hughes, 'Society and settlement in nineteenth-century Ireland' in *Ir. Geography*, v (1965), pp 79–96.

[54] L. M. Cullen, 'The cultural basis of Irish nationalism' in Rosalind Mitchison (ed.), *The roots of nationalism: studies in Northern Europe* (Edinburgh, 1980), pp 97–8.

[55] *Cal. S. P. Ire., 1603–6*, p. 470.

[56] Gerard Mercator and Jodocus Hondius, *Atlas, or a geographicke description of the regions, countries and kingdoms of the world* (2 vols, Amsterdam, 1636), i, 85.

[57] An example is the quit rents assigned to the four provinces—3d. per acre in Leinster, $2\frac{1}{4}$ d. in Munster, $1\frac{1}{2}$ d. in Connacht and 1d. in Ulster—in *The statutes of the realm* (12 vols, London, 1810–28), 16 Chas I, c. 33 (1641).

mountains as its Leinster Chain, the Bann as its Barrow or Shannon according to historical context, and with a reasonable amount of good land in each of its nine counties.

However 'mere Irish' its people, Ulster could hardly qualify as an Irish heartland in any geopolitical sense. On the contrary its cultural identity was largely due to the unusually strong geographical obstacles that divided it from Connacht and Leinster. In the west the River Erne and its lakes formed a barrier so effective that a supernatural explanation had to be found for it.[58] Cavan and Monaghan were dominated by the topographical chaos of the drumlin belt, here at its widest and most continuous. Further east the mountains of Slieve Gullion[59] and Cooley pierced the lowland drifts, confining much of the traffic between Meath and Ulster to what one Elizabethan administrator called the 'northern gap'.[60] These impediments filled most of the relatively narrow space between Sligo Bay and Carlingford Lough, which gives Ireland its nearest equivalent to the waist dividing England from Scotland. Ancient linear earthworks, collectively known to posterity as the Black Pig's Dyke, suggest that in the wars between Ulster and its southern neighbours the strategic possibilities of this border zone were being exploited as early as the first centuries after Christ, perhaps in conscious imitation of Hadrian's wall.[61]

As well as standing somewhat apart from the rest of Ireland, the north-east is exceptional in its proximity to the outside world. From mesolithic times onwards Scotsmen, Irishmen, and their predecessors have travelled freely and often to and from the western coasts of Scotland, and the very closeness of their contacts has helped to separate both parties to this essentially maritime relationship more sharply from their respective hinterlands. In the Celtic and Scandinavian periods the politics of the North Channel were much disturbed by flux and tension, but there was no commitment to unlimited territorial expansion from either east or west; and where Scots and Irish found themselves on the same side of the water, as often happened in the Glens and Route of Antrim, there were none of the cultural and economic contrasts that divided native and intruder further south.

This world of islands and sea-loughs may be seen as a late survival, its lifespan prolonged by the close proximity of its components, of something not unlike the historical geographer's 'medieval sea state', the kind of maritime association, once common along the European periphery, that was

---

[58] Abraham Ortelius, *Hiberniae Britannicae Insulae nova descriptio* (Antwerp, 1573). Ortelius was following a passage in Giraldus's 'Topography' that may have been intended for Lough Neagh. See J. J. O'Meara (ed.), *The first version of the topography of Ireland by Giraldus Cambrensis* (Dundalk, 1951), pp 47, 115.

[59] For an early use of this upland as a regional boundary marker see *Cal. S. P. Ire., 1586–8*, p. 248. See also *N.H.I.*, ii, 15.

[60] Sir John Perrot to Sir Francis Walsingham, 12 Nov. 1585, National Archives, S.P. 63/121/4.

[61] S. P. Ó Ríordáin, *Antiquities of the Irish countryside* (London, 1964), pp 14–15.

brought to an end by the rise of more powerful land-based monarchies.[62] For the Scots of Antrim and their neighbours, that end came rather suddenly with the belated appearance of one such new-style kingdom in the Scotland of James VI. Before succeeding to the English throne, James had already experimented with colonisation as a cure for the troubles of his own Celtic fringe in Lewis and Kintyre. In Ireland his advantage as a colonial impresario came not so much from ability or experience as from commanding resources of manpower superior in both quantity and quality to anything that English governments had been able to muster for earlier schemes of colonisation. To James's 'inland' Scots, as to the freelance highlanders who preceded them in Ireland, the main attraction of the Ulster plantation of 1610 was the shortness of the distance separating colony from colonist. In the same way it is distance, most elementary of geographical factors, that explains the collinearity of the Scots–English settlement boundary from one side of the North Channel to the other, with English influence relatively strong from south Down across to Fermanagh, and Scots characteristics more evident in north Down, Antrim, north Derry, north Tyrone, and Donegal.[63] Within this framework, simple proximity was also the reason why many settlers remained in hither Ulster instead of crossing the Bann into the escheated counties of the official plantation project. The result was that with increasing distance westwards and southwards from the ports of entry, the intensity of seventeenth-century British settlement fell off, leaving Leinster Palesmen and Ulster planters separated by a broad and sometimes troublesome zone of native survival bordering the line of the old provincial frontier through Cavan, Monaghan, and south Armagh.

It was not until the later seventeenth century that the Ulster plantation could be seen to have effected a more drastic change in Ireland's regional balance than any previous event in the country's written history. Unlike their Elizabethan predecessors further south, the Ulster planters included tenantry as well as gentry in large numbers. Supported by a flourishing linen industry they made the north-east into one of the most densely peopled parts of the island. And northerners were not only thicker on the ground than southerners but also better off, a notable achievement in an island where economic welfare and population density were tending to assume an inverse relationship. Even the old plantation ideal of 'civility' was realised to the extent that in 1841 Antrim, Down, and Londonderry were the only counties in Ireland where more than 70 per cent of the population were able to read or write. Whatever the origin and meaning of the expression 'black north' (it is at least

---

[62] H. C. Darby, 'The medieval sea state' in *Scottish Geographical Magazine*, xlviii (1932), pp 36–49.

[63] Philip Robinson, *The plantation of Ulster: British settlement in an Irish landscape, 1600–1670* (Dublin and New York, 1984), pp 94, 110.

as old as the mid-eighteenth century),[64] it carried no implication of economic backwardness.

Finally, the Ulster plantation created its own metropolis. In situation and mode of origin Belfast was not unlike the seaport towns already founded elsewhere in Ireland by the Danes, Normans, and English, but by the late nineteenth century it had become the only one of the outports to rival Dublin in size and energy, and to act as undisputed commercial capital for a whole province. Much of this growth was due to the survival of its industries, more than those of any southern town, into the factory era, in spite of having to look beyond Ireland for a large proportion of their raw materials and markets. External trade links provided a double illustration of Ulster's continuing detachment from the rest of the country, for they date from a time when Dubliners were blaming their own industrial failures partly on Ireland's poverty in native raw materials (or, in some versions, the government's refusal to exploit its wealth of native raw materials) and partly on the diminishing size of the Irish market as a result of emigration.

In the early days of the Ulster plantation there had been few illusions anywhere about the relative strength of the denominational and physical boundaries that divided mankind.

> Nothing, not bogs, not sands, not seas, not alps,
> Sep'rates the world so as the bishops' scalps.[65]

While Marvell's geographical or anti-geographical epigram was gradually becoming less applicable to the British context of his poem, Irishmen were continuing to cherish the hatreds associated with the reformation and counter-reformation, a proof in one respect of the anthropogeographical doctrine of insular archaism. Families of native and British origin remained distinguishable, generation by generation, particularly through differences of religion and later of politics. In Ulster these differences were reinforced by topography. The government in 1609 had intended to make a fairly even distribution of English, Scottish, and Irish communities throughout the six escheated counties, the details being settled by a lottery in which the English undertakers drew their share of difficult hill land. These intentions were soon to be frustrated, however, partly by the development of the broad regional gradients already mentioned and partly by a more complex pattern of local variation—not altogether different from that of medieval Leinster—in which protestants came to dominate the low ground of the Bann, Lagan, and Foyle valleys and the fringes of upper Lough Erne, while catholic majorities were largest in the Mournes, the Sperrins, the Glens of Antrim, and

---

[64] Richard Barton, *A dialogue, concerning some things of importance to Ireland: particularly to the county of Ardmagh* (Dublin, 1751), p. 25. For Barton, 'black' was a reference to the 'horrid mountains' of Newry and the Fews, as well as to 'other scenes of deformity'.

[65] E. S. Donno (ed.), *Andrew Marvell: the complete poems* (London, 1972), p. 186.

other upland areas (map 2). In the nineteenth century this balance was shifted by a large movement of catholics from country to town in search of industrial employment; but even in the physiographic neutrality of an urban environment the difference between mountain and lowland was reproduced by a still more sharply localised segregation dividing catholic streets from protestant streets.[66]

Until the present century the complexities of Ireland's denominational mosaic were of no more than local significance, and the word 'Ulster' could take turns as the name for either a block of nine counties or a dominant religious and political community. A serious geopolitical problem arose, however, when Northern Ireland came to be partitioned from the Irish Free State in 1921, for it was then discovered that there was no peaceful way, other than mass migration, of eliminating large minorities from one or both sides of the border between nationalists and unionists.[67] The problem was soluble only to the extent that some solutions to it were worse than others; but in the event all parties preferred to oversimplify the issue and Northern Ireland was left as the six parliamentary counties with the largest percentage of presumptive unionists, without anyone pausing to consider such niceties as whether a parliamentary county can be said to possess any territorial waters.

To a ship entering the Bay of Biscay from the south, Cork is almost as accessible as Cornwall, and the western coasts of the British Isles, being freer than the Saxon shore from entanglements with the north European continent, must sometimes have appeared the more attractive to the far-travelled adventurer. In the time of Tacitus, Ireland's harbours were well frequented by Roman traders; so much so that on his own mental map the country lay somewhere between Britain and Spain.[68] Tacitus also saw something arbitrary about the decision of his own countrymen to deny the Irish the benefits of empire; a view that gains colour from the close commercial and intellectual relationships connecting Ireland with Brittany, Spain, and even North Africa in the first few centuries of the post-Roman era.[69] Naturally these relationships affected the south of Ireland more than the north. More specifically, a zone of direct European influence roughly corresponding to the province of

---

[66] F. W. Boal, 'Territoriality on the Shankill–Falls divide' in *Ir. Geography*, vi (1969), pp 30–50.

[67] Statistical map of catholics and non-catholics by district electoral divisions, based on the population census of 1911, in Northeastern Boundary Bureau, *Handbook of the Ulster question* (Dublin, 1923).

[68] Harold Mattingly (ed.), *Tacitus on Britain and Germany* (London, 1948), p. 74.

[69] Charles Thomas, *Britain and Ireland in early Christian times, A.D. 400–800* (London, 1971), pp 86–90. See also Gearóid Mac Niocaill and M. A. G. Ó Tuathaigh, 'Ireland and Europe: the historical dimension' in P. J. Drudy and Dermot McAleese (ed.), *Ireland and the European community* (Cambridge, 1984), pp 13–19.

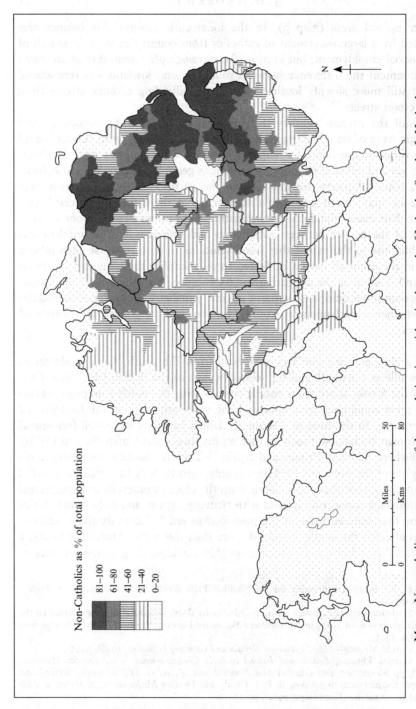

Map 2 Non-catholics as percentage of the population in parishes in the north of Ireland, 1835, by J. H. Andrews

*First report of the commissioners on public instruction, Ireland,* H.C. 1835, xxxiii.

Non-Catholics as % of total population

81–100
61–80
41–60
21–40
0–20

Munster can be related on the one hand to the continuing divisiveness of the central lowland, and on the other to the capacity of the harbours along the Waterford, Cork, and Kerry coastline compared with those of Wexford and Wicklow. The same impression is given by the geographical pattern of the inscribed ogam stones that mark the beginnings of literacy in Ireland.[70]

Considered in relation to Ulster, this view of Munster suggests a symmetrical picture of Ireland as a whole, and one that appealed on that account to several tidy-minded early historians: the north looking northwards for its external relations, the south southwards. A modern version of this theory places the country in 'the mainstream of coastwise diffusion'.[71] No doubt the Roman and early post-Roman links can be projected backwards, with the aid of archaeological taxonomy, into the iron and bronze ages and beyond. Forward extrapolation is not so easy. By Spenser's time, certainly, the desire of Irish antiquaries to 'fetch themselves from the Spaniards' was something of a curiosity,[72] which it is tempting to read more as a wish to dissociate oneself from Britain than as a dispassionate act of historical judgement. The next generation of Irishmen after Spenser had good reason to know that the Spaniards were about forty times as far away as the British, and that continental powers were now being excluded from Ireland by the same processes of political crystallisation that were drawing in the English and the Scots. Visits from Spanish fishing boats, merchantmen, even warships, were no substitute for an Ulster plantation.

The analogy between the two ends of Ireland is further weakened when one turns from external relations in general to relations with England in particular. From an Anglo-Norman vantage-point in Bannow Bay or Waterford Harbour, much of eastern and central Munster was as approachable as northern Leinster. The valley of the Suir is comparable in this respect with that of the Barrow, the coastal strip of Waterford with that of Wicklow. Of the remaining lowlands of east Munster, the Golden Vale[73] was accessible via the Suir Valley, while the corridors that meet the sea at Dungarvan, Youghal, and Cork are each made more accessible from Wales and the Bristol Channel by the diagonal trend of Ireland's southern coast. Several of these lowlands are wider, and the intervening ridges correspondingly lower, in the

---

[70] See E. G. Bowen, *Saints, seaways and settlements in the Celtic lands* (Cardiff, 1969) for distribution maps of ogam stones and a number of related subjects.

[71] Evans, *Prehistoric Ireland*, p. 5. See also the same author's 'The Atlantic ends of Europe' in *Advancement of Science*, xv (1958), pp 54–64, and 'Ireland and Atlantic Europe' in *Geographische Zeitschrift*, lii (1963), pp 224–41.

[72] Spenser, *View*, p. 43, and see *N.H.I.*, ii, 347.

[73] This regional name occurs as 'Goulden Valley' in 1681 (E. P. Shirley (ed.), 'Extracts from the journal of Thomas Dineley' in *R.S.A.I. Jn.*, iv (1856–7), p. 173). It is not known whether it derives from the Tipperary place-name Golden, which refers to a fork in the River Suir (P. W. Joyce, *The origin and history of Irish names of places (first series)* (4th ed., Dublin, 1875), p. 528) or whether it denotes wealth as in the Golden Vale of Herefordshire named on Christopher Saxton's map of that county in 1577.

east than in the west; and this may explain the unduly optimistic assessment of the province as a whole (as late as 1597 the 'most part' of it was recommended as 'limestone ground')[74] which helped to draw both medieval and Elizabethan Englishmen towards the more difficult country of Kerry and west Cork. Many of Munster's larger uplands could be outflanked by this process of westward movement, and it is interesting that the only hill-name to make much impression on English topographical reportage was 'Slieve Lougher' on the borders of Limerick and Kerry, by no means a spectacular massif but exceptional in running counter to the general east–west trend of both geography and history in this region.[75] In the end, the rough as well as the smooth parts of Munster's ridge and valley landscape had to be reckoned with, and the province was seen as less able than Leinster to give the plains-dwelling colonist a compact and defensible heartland. Its seaport towns came through the middle ages as a disconnected series of miniature English pales; and the Elizabethan and Jacobean plantations in Waterford, Cork, Kerry, and Limerick, even on the most generous view, 'cannot be said to have altered the province significantly from the rest of the country'.[76]

As the most fertile part of Ireland in which the British failed to make a lasting impact, the lowlands of the south-west offered the best prospect for a modernised version of the indigenous pastoral economy. It seems reasonable to cast the Munster dairying industry in this role (Map 3). Here, gradually maturing in the seventeenth and eighteenth centuries, was a system of husbandry that could support the tenant farmer, if not in high affluence, then at least in appreciable numbers—especially when compared with the kind of livestock ranching practised in certain other lowland areas, such as east Connacht, that had remained outside the orbit of both Pale and plantation. Some measure of regional economic success can be inferred from two nineteenth-century distribution patterns in which west Munster shows up differently from the remainder of western Ireland. First, unlike Ulster and Connacht, the province managed to absorb most of its seasonal labour surplus within its own borders.[77] Secondly, it escaped the problems associated with illicit distillation, partly for cultural reasons but also because even in remote areas butter could take the place of whiskey as a source of profit capable of absorbing transport costs without the aid of navigable water.[78]

Just as Ulster, on a non-political and non-administrative definition, was made smaller by eighteenth- and nineteenth-century forces, so Munster as a

---

[74] 'Platform for inhabiting Munster', 1597 (National Archives, M.3044).

[75] *Cal. S.P. Ire., 1574–85, passim.*

[76] Michael MacCarthy-Morrogh, *The Munster plantation: English migration to southern Ireland, 1583–1641* (Oxford, 1986), p. 285. See also Ralph Loeber, *The geography and practice of English colonisation in Ireland from 1534 to 1609* (Dublin, 1991).

[77] J. H. Johnson, 'Harvest migration from nineteenth-century Ireland' in *Transactions of the Institute of British Geographers*, xli (1967), pp 97–112.

[78] K. H. Connell, *Irish peasant society: four historical essays* (Oxford, 1968), p. 31.

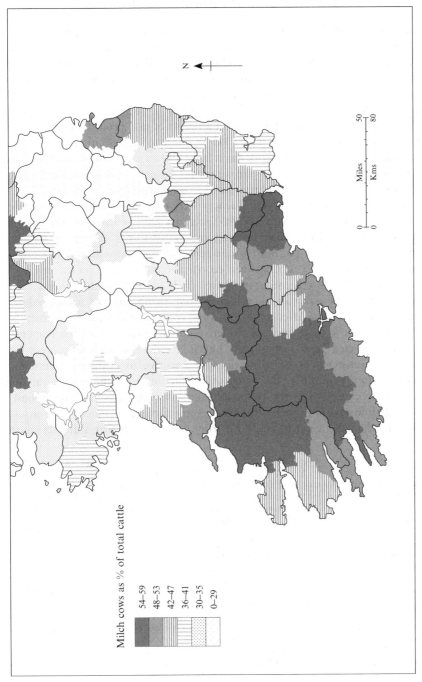

Milch cows as % of total cattle

54–59
48–53
42–47
36–41
30–35
0–29

Map 3  Milch cows as percentage of total cattle in Munster and adjacent areas, 1854, by poor law unions, by J. H. Andrews

Miles   0   50
Kms    0   80

social region may be said to have grown larger, capturing the south-east corner of the island from anything that might have been described as an English Pale. Perhaps the best index of this extended southern identity is the modernisation of the catholic church in Ireland and its growing influence on education, morality, and art—also on settlement patterns as represented by 'chapel villages' in the countryside and 'catholic quarters' in the towns.[79] In the end the church was to be equally dominant in all parts of non-protestant Ireland, but for a long time its greatest power lay in Munster and south Leinster. The foundation of this early success was a large and solidly catholic middle class, some of whose members were strong tenant farmers, others mercantile families in seaport towns that had continued to trade with catholic Europe.[80]

These socially conservative influences were only one element in a complex regional character. So many recent historians have written so much about violence in Ireland that their findings are almost impossible to digest,[81] but on one interpretation the most fundamental among many different kinds of post-medieval conflict was between economics and culture: on the one hand intrusive market forces encouraging free trade in land; on the other a belief in the right to be a farmer as springing from membership of some predetermined social group. After 1750 this view is supported by a propensity for disorder not in remote and unproductive outbacks (as with earlier responses to state-directed land forfeiture)[82] but in fertile and accessible areas like lowland Munster that were increasingly sensitive to changing commodity prices. More peacefully, the same dissatisfaction with the status quo was later to be expressed in the cooperative creamery movement of the 1890s.[83] By this time agrarian protest had also become familiar in much of Connacht. Perhaps the conclusion to be drawn from these facts is that although south-

---

[79] Kevin Whelan, 'The catholic parish, the catholic chapel and village development in Ireland' in *Ir. Geography*, xvi (1983), pp 1–16; also the same author's 'A geography of society and culture in Ireland since 1800' (Ph.D. thesis, N.U.I. (U.C.D.), 1981), pp 60–84.

[80] Kevin Whelan, 'The regional impact of Irish catholicism, 1700–1850' in W. J. Smyth and Kevin Whelan (ed.), *Common ground: essays on the historical geography of Ireland presented to Professor T. Jones Hughes* (Cork, 1988), pp 253–7.

[81] See especially T. D. Williams (ed.), *Secret societies in Ireland* (Dublin and New York, 1973); Samuel Clark, *Social origins of the Irish land war* (Princeton, 1979); J. J. Lee, 'Patterns of rural unrest in nineteenth-century Ireland: a preliminary survey' in L. M. Cullen and François Furet (ed.), *Ireland and France, 17th–20th centuries* (Paris, 1980), pp 223–37; Michael Beames, *The Whiteboy movements and their control in prefamine Ireland* (Brighton and New York, 1983); Paul Bew, *Conflict and conciliation in Ireland, 1890–1910* (Oxford, 1987); and Tom Garvin, *Nationalist revolutionaries in Ireland, 1858–1928* (Oxford, 1987). For a geographer's view of this historiographical trend see W. J. Smyth, 'Social geography of rural Ireland: inventory and prospect' in G. L. Herries Davies (ed.), *Irish Geography: the Geographical Society of Ireland golden jubilee 1934–1984* (Dublin, 1984), pp 223–6.

[82] S. J. Connolly, 'Violence and order in the eighteenth century' in Patrick O'Flanagan, Paul Ferguson, and Kevin Whelan (ed.), *Rural Ireland: modernisation and change, 1600–1900* (Cork, 1987), pp 42–8.

[83] Cormac Ó Gráda, 'The beginnings of the Irish creamery system, 1880–1914' in *Econ. Hist. Rev.*, xxx (1977), pp 284–305.

ern and south-western Ireland may lack the distinctiveness of the north-east, its loss of individuality is due not to any regional weakness but rather to the success of Munstermen's ideas in penetrating the rest of the country.

ANCIENT territories in Ireland have often been subdivided into east and west for purposes of geographical discussion, both by theorists and practical men, and the easterly bias that dominates such discussion appears in the frequency with which western areas are identified as 'further' or 'upper', both tendencies being also exemplified in the large number of sixteenth-century English maps of Ireland in which east appears at the bottom.[84] But such dispositions were partial and piecemeal. A general western identity was surprisingly slow to emerge, though today 'the west' would probably be accepted on its own level as the most meaningful of all Irish regional terms. In the aftermath of the Tudor reconquest, with the problems of Elizabeth's reign still fresh in the official mind, there were several proposals to reshape the political geography of Ireland—to turn the Pale inside out, as it were—by moving troublemakers to places where they would pose less threat to the seat of government; by moving them westwards, in other words. There was no coordination between the various projects of this period for transferring Leinstermen from Leix to Kerry, Ulstermen to Connacht and part of Munster, and Scottish borderers to Roscommon. It was left to the Cromwellian government, with the help of recent cartographic surveys, to systematise the idea of transplantation by choosing the Shannon as a border between its new intake of English settlers and what remained of the old Irish landlord class. The advantages of Connacht and Clare as an Irish ghetto lay in being clearly defined on the ground and on the map, easily isolated from the east, and on the seaward side protected to some degree by distance from the danger of foreign invasion. As an afterthought, the integrity of the provincial boundaries was further violated by the decision to exclude the transplantees from a continuous belt of land four miles (6.4 km) wide along the edges of their new reservation. (It was typical of Cromwellian administrative geography to flout tradition with an expedient of this kind, just as it was typical

[84] For 'low Leinster' see *Cal. S.P. Ire., 1574–85*, p. 428; R. Dudley Edwards (ed.), 'Letterbook of Sir Arthur Chichester, 1612–1614' in *Anal. Hib.*, no. 8 (1938), p. 37; and George O'Brien (ed.), *Advertisements for Ireland* (Dublin, 1923), pp 13, 52. 'Base Leinster' as applied to what is now east Wicklow (*Cal. Carew MSS, 1575–88*, p. 354) suggests a reference to position rather than to altitude. 'Nether Munster' in 1562 meant Munster excluding both Thomond and the Irishry of modern west Cork (*Cal. Carew MSS, 1515–74*, p. 336). The regional name Iar-Chonnacht (*angl.* west Connacht) was familiar to English writers in the early sixteenth century (*Cal. S.P. Ire., 1586–8*, p. 117). More confusingly, Sir Henry Sidney in 1576 distinguished Nether Connacht (Sligo and Mayo), Upper Connacht (Galway), and the Plains of Connacht (Roscommon) (*Cal. Carew MSS, 1575–88*, p. 48). For 'hither Ulster' see above, p. 17. For maps of Ireland with east at the bottom see J. H. Andrews, 'Colonial cartography in a European setting: the case of Tudor Ireland' in David Woodward (ed.), *The history of cartography*, iii (Chicago, forthcoming).

of Irish geographical thought to give a provincial interpretation to the same events with the slogan 'hell or Connacht'.) The device of the four-mile line shows space relations alone, and not the character of the soil, dictating the limits chosen in 1653. At any rate, in contemporary debate on the wisdom and justice of transplantation nobody seems to have suggested that the Irish had been deliberately given the worst land.

Although the Cromwellian idea of a native enclosure differed from the English Pale (as defined by Campion) in not including a reference to land quality, its boundaries showed the same propensity to withdraw by stages from the interior of Ireland towards the coast. It was not till the nineteenth century, however, that this process had gone far enough to give 'the west' its modern meaning. By that time much of lowland Connacht had been integrated with the rest of the country through the medium of a greatly improved road network. By that time, too, soil character had become the main influence here, as in eastern and northern Ireland, on the distribution of improved and unimproved landscapes. What distinguished the west, as it turned out, was the unusually close coincidence in its extremities between infertility and inaccessibility. Infertility was a function of heavy rainfall, poor drainage, high altitude, steep relief, or rocky terrain; often of several of these handicaps combined. Inaccessibility had two components: the distance of the whole region from Dublin, and the division of its parts by the turbulent waters of the Atlantic. This irregular pattern characterised the whole coastline from Inishowen southwards to the half-dozen prongs of Kerry and west Cork. Although not without their pockets of good soil, each of Ireland's Atlantic promontories was cut off from much of the prosperity which better communications had brought to the rest of the country in the course of the eighteenth century. At the same time it was in these areas, hitherto rather sparsely peopled, that potato-growing on small farms was now most effective among the complex mesh of determinants involved in Irish population increase.[85] Many western estates were owned by absentees; long leases to occupying tenants were less common than on richer soils and landlord supervision less rigorous, so that there was less check on the breaking up of tenements from one generation to the next; hence the rapid multiplication of smallholding families, most of them close to the border between poverty and starvation, that dominated the social structure of the Atlantic coastlands to a degree hardly known elsewhere (Map 4).

Official recognition of the administrative problems created by mass regional poverty in Ireland dates from the agricultural depressions that followed the Napoleonic wars. It owed something, no doubt, to the example of the Highland Roads and Bridges Board in Scotland. The union of 1801

---

[85] David Dickson, Cormac Ó Gráda, and Stuart Daultrey, 'Hearth tax, household size, and Irish population change, 1672–1821' in *R.I.A. Proc.*, lxxxii (1982), sect. C, pp 169–73.

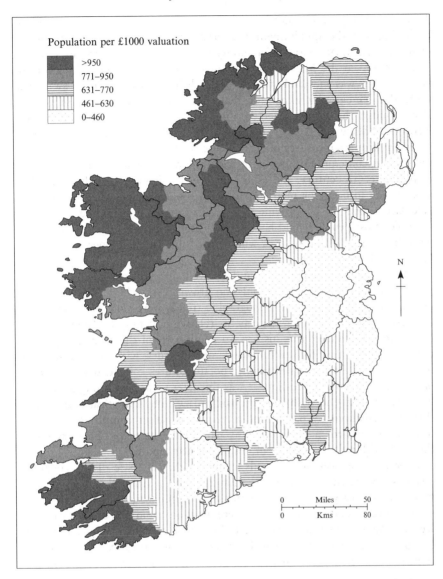

Population per £1000 valuation

>950
771–950
631–770
461–630
0–460

N

| 0 | Miles | 50 |
| 0 | Kms | 80 |

Map 4 Population per £1,000 valuation, 1841, by poor law unions, by J. H. Andrews
H.C. 1847, lvi.

had certainly made it easier for British public opinion to appreciate the
kind of affinity that was suggested by such phrases as 'the Irish Highlands'.[86]

[86] [H. Blake], *Letters from the Irish Highlands of Cunnemara* (London, 1825); Patrick Knight,
*Erris in the 'Irish Highlands' and the 'Atlantic railway'* (Dublin, 1836).

As in Scotland, communications were the first object of regional policy, beginning with the appointment of government engineers in 1822 to supplement the inadequate network of county roads in parts of Connacht and west Munster. Given the Malthusian state of the population living alongside the new roads, it was inevitable that some of their benefit should be swallowed up in the demographic expansion that culminated in the famine of 1846–8. For although the famine affected almost the whole of Ireland, its ravages were worst along the Atlantic margin, as the authorities had to recognise by applying stronger measures of relief in the west than the east. To judge from the titles of contemporary books, articles, and at least one poem, it was in the early nineteenth century, and especially after the famine, that the words 'the west' began to occur in an Irish context without explanatory definition.[87] If elucidation had to be provided, in addressing a non-Irish audience for example, most people would have agreed (though perhaps adding west Cork) with the French author of 1855 who defined the west as Donegal, Connacht, Clare, and Kerry.[88]

After the famine, emigration and delayed marriage assumed the role of preventive checks to further population growth everywhere in Ireland. Like other new tendencies, these demographic trends were slow to penetrate the far west; in this, as in other respects, its relative proximity to America having little direct influence on its history. In many parts of the region, population continued to increase for several post-famine decades, with renewed hardship in the 1870s and 1880s when further potato failures coincided with a period of general economic depression. It was this later crisis that brought the word 'congestion' into the Irish political vocabulary. The statistical definition of this term favoured by parliament in 1891 was rather complicated, and the districts so defined made a confusing pattern on the map, but every one of them fell within the western counties of popular repute.

Overcrowding was not the only common characteristic of the congested districts. Somewhat remote, as they remained, from the full force of nineteenth-century urban and commercial influences, they had also preserved several culture traits that were now in rapid retreat elsewhere in Ireland. Among these survivals were distinctive settlement types and forms of agrarian organisation, vernacular artefacts, and, historically most significant, the Irish language. Thomas Davis in 1843 had already recognised Irish

---

[87] Early examples from various media are W. H. Maxwell, *Wild sports of the west* (London, 1832); Thomas Davis, 'The west's asleep' in Thomas Wallis (ed.), *The poems of Thomas Davis* (Dublin, 1846), pp 9–10; *Papers relating to the aid afforded to the distressed unions in the west of Ireland* [1010], [1019], [1023], [1060], [1077], H.C. 1849, xlviii; S. G. Osborne, *Gleanings in the west of Ireland* (London, 1850); 'On emigration as affecting the west of Ireland' in *Royal Dublin Society: proceedings of the evening meetings*, Apr. 1853, pp 200–10; Henry Coulter, *The west of Ireland: its existing condition and prospects* (Dublin, 1862).

[88] Leonce de Lavergne, *Ensaio sobre a economia rural da Inglaterra, Escosia e Irlanda* (Lisbon, 1867), p. 312.

speech as an increasingly western phenomenon,[89] and his version of one of
the relevant boundaries, a line from Derry to Waterford, was confirmed by
the first official Irish linguistic census, held in 1851. Later censuses showed
how Gaelic, like Europe's other Celtic languages, was continuing to lose
ground in a strikingly literal sense.[90] By the middle of the twentieth century
its empire had shrunk from a continuous territory to a scatter of small and
insecure peninsulas and islands.

What might be called the residualism of western Ireland did not imply
that all its traits were necessarily of high antiquity, as the example of the
potato makes clear. Many of its farms and farm clusters are known or believed to be of comparatively modern origin; the same even applies, here and
there, to some of the racial strains in its population.[91] This lack of deep
historical roots, together with the irregular configuration of the land and the
poverty of its people, may help to explain why no distinctive western regional
consciousness evolved from within the region itself. Except in matters of
intimate local concern, such as the land war of the 1880s, it has generally
stood aside from the mainstream of Irish history. Its regional character, being
perceived from outside, has varied with the percipient. To Victorian public
servants of British background or outlook, the western cultural heritage was
simply an obstacle to progress. For tourists of similar provenance, the same
heritage offered the attractions of quaintness and apparent simplicity to add
to an aesthetically fashionable landscape. From the time of the Gaelic revival
onwards, the patriotic Irishman was in the difficult position of having to
combine elements from both these contradictory attitudes. On the one hand
he wished to bring economic relief to a people who deserved not only ordinary human sympathy but a special reward for linguistic good behaviour.
Such relief entailed an infusion of capital, technology, and managerial skill,
perhaps also a further decrease in population; whereas the other objective for
the west, the preservation of its cultural integrity, seemed unattainable except
by keeping these external influences at bay. Here was a dilemma of more
than regional significance, because for many Irishmen the west had now
become more than a region: it was a talisman of nationality, a charm to ward
off the evils of anglicisation, and in the last resort, like Atlantis or the
Fortunate Islands, a way of pretending that human insularity can be made
absolute and not just a matter of degree.

[89] Thomas Davis, 'Our national language' in *Literary and historical essays* (Dublin, 1846),
p. 181.
[90] Garret Fitzgerald, 'Estimates for baronies of minimum level of Irish-speaking amongst
successive decennial cohorts' in *R.I.A. Proc.*, lxxxiv (1984), sect. C, pp 117–55; cf. *N.H.I.*, vi,
385–91, 433–5.
[91] E. E. Evans, *The personality of Ireland: habitat, heritage, and history* (Cambridge, 1973),
p. 44. The alleged antiquity of the western cultural landscape is searchingly questioned in
Kevin Whelan, 'Settlement patterns in the west of Ireland in the pre-famine period' in Timothy Collins (ed.), *Decoding the landscape* (Galway, 1994), pp 60–78.

# CHAPTER II

# The physical environment

GEOGRAPHICALLY Ireland is part of the western fringe of Europe—a detached fragment of the continental mainland from which it is separated by shallow seas. It reaches farther west (10° 30') than any other part of Europe with the exception of Iceland, and shares the same latitude (51° to 56° N.) as Labrador, but its climate is tempered by the westerly winds that blow in from the warm waters of the Atlantic ocean, bringing relatively mild winter conditions not only to Ireland but to all the coastlands of north-west Europe. The island has a compact shape with a maximum length of 480 km (280 miles) from Malin Head in the north to Cape Clear in the south, and a maximum width of 300 km (190 miles) from Belmullet in Mayo to the Ards peninsula in County Down. Within its 84,400 km² (32,000 square miles) a variety of relief and soil conditions provide a wide range of physical environments. About 12 per cent of the total area is occupied by inhospitable, windswept hills and plateaus where rocky outcrops alternate with spreads of heather-covered peat. In contrast to this are the more sheltered lowlands with deep, well-drained soils of high agricultural potential. The latter are best developed in a triangular area that has as its base the coast between Dublin and Dundalk; and also in the 'Golden Vale' area of North Tipperary and Limerick. Intermediate in character are the poorly drained soils of the midlands; the coastlands and islands of the west where exposure to strong salt-laden winds may exclude all trees; and the hill slopes everywhere against which the soils thin out and where agriculture is attempted only in terms of dire need. The extensive raised bogs of the midlands, the result of active peat growth on areas of impeded drainage in historic times, are a feature of special interest. They have long been valuable as a source of fuel but are useless for settlement and have always been a serious barrier to communications.

Structurally Ireland is a continuation of the European mainland. A rising sea level in late glacial times flooded the lowlands that had linked it with Britain and the Continent (about 10,200 B.P.)[1] and interrupted the gradual

[1] There is considerable controversy about the nature of these land-links and when they were cut. See R. J. Devoy, 'The problem of a Late Quaternary landbridge between Britain and Ireland' in *Quaternary Science Review*, iv (1985).

recolonisation of Ireland by plants and animals that was taking place following the melting of the ice and the amelioration of the climate. This may be one of the reasons why the flora and fauna of Ireland are poorer than those of the neighbouring island and of the mainland. A fall in the present sea level of only 100 m would reestablish a land connection between Ireland and Wales and expose a broad lowland extending far to the south and west. The true edge of Europe lies between 100 and 400 km to the west of the present coastline,where the continental shelf drops steeply to the ocean deeps (map 5). Physically Ireland consists of a broad drift-covered lowland with many lakes and bogs scattered over its surface. This lowland is diversified by a number of hills and mountains and surrounded by a discontinuous rim of higher land (map 6). The streams that rise on the seaward slopes of the bordering mountains are short and rapid, but those whose sources lie on the inland side have low gradients with long devious courses and many lakes, the Shannon river being a typical example. The coastline, especially in the west, is so deeply indented that no part of the island lies more than 100 km from tidewater.

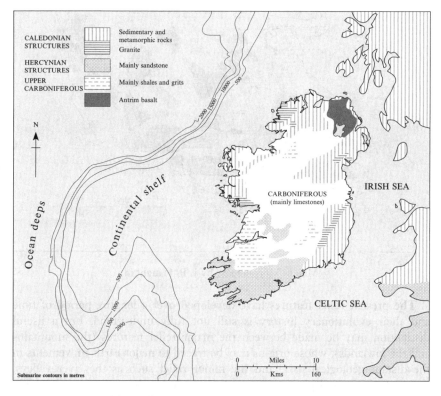

Map 5  Structural regions, by J. P. Haughton

# The physical environment

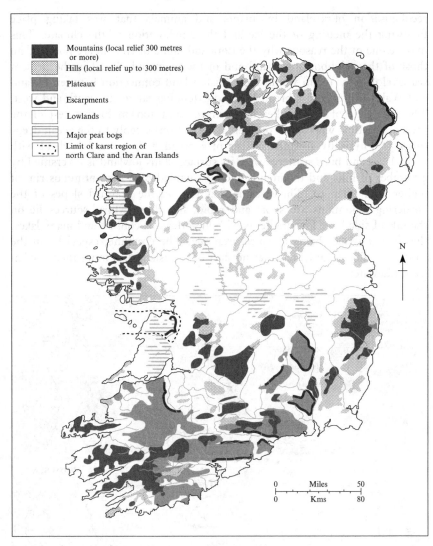

Map 6 Morphology, by J. P. Haughton

The present relief features have developed over a lengthy period of time and their evolutionary history is still not fully understood, but a useful distinction may be made between the major relief features (the mountains and the lowlands), whose origins may be traced to major earth-movements in the distant geological past, and the minor relief such as the river valleys, coastal features, and glacial topography, which are all more recent in origin and, in most cases, are still actively undergoing modification through the agents of erosion and deposition, and, to a lesser extent, through the activities of man himself.

Two of the great mountain systems of Europe converge westwards to meet and mingle in Ireland (map 5). The older (Caledonian) extends from Scandinavia through Scotland into north and west Ireland where it forms rugged mountainous country and has implanted a strong north-east to south-west trend to the countryside. Structures of a similar age are responsible for the Leinster chain and the Newry axis. The younger system (Hercynian) forms the mountains of central Europe north of the Alps and extends westwards through Brittany and south-west England to reappear in southern Ireland as a series of east–west-trending hills and valleys. Basically simpler than the Caledonian mountains, they are a series of anticlinal ridges separated by synclinal valleys with a drainage pattern that is imperfectly adjusted to this structure (map 7). Relatively isolated mountain ranges such as the Galtees, Slieve Aughty, the Silvermines, and the Slieve Blooms are similar in origin. They are islands of older rock protruding through the younger limestones of the lowland, but the simple east–west trend is modified by the proximity of pre-existing Caledonian structures. North-eastern Ireland, with its extensive basaltic lava flows of Eocene age, belongs to a young volcanic province, which embraces part of western Scotland and Iceland. This basalt caps the Antrim plateau, underlies the Lough Neagh basin, and rises again westwards to form the eastern part of the Sperrin mountains. An extensive lowland bounded by the Hercynian ranges in the south and by the Caledonian mountains to the north, west, and south-east is the most significant physical feature of the island. It is underlain mainly, though not entirely, by relatively undisturbed Carboniferous rocks and covered in many places by deep glacial drifts. It reaches the east coast for 80 km (50 miles) between the Dublin mountains and the Carlingford peninsula, giving access to the heart of Ireland from the Irish Sea along the valleys of the Boyne and Liffey. From the coast, this lowland rises gently inland to a height of between 100 m and 150 m where it forms the watershed between rivers flowing west and south to the Atlantic and eastwards to the Irish Sea. It sends broad corridors westward which meet the Atlantic ocean in Donegal Bay, Clew Bay, Galway Bay, and the Shannon estuary; and a north–eastern extension, underlain by basalt and deeply covered in drift deposits, forms the Lough Neagh depression and the Bann lowlands.

In discussing the minor relief features, especially those of the lowland, particular attention must be given to the effects of the ice age (Pleistocene Epoch), as it represents the last significant episode in the evolution of the physical landscape. At that time much of the country lay beneath a thick sheet of ice for a prolonged period but there were also occasions when the individual mountain masses were higher than the ice sheet and had independent ice-caps and valley glaciers. The effects on the uplands were mostly

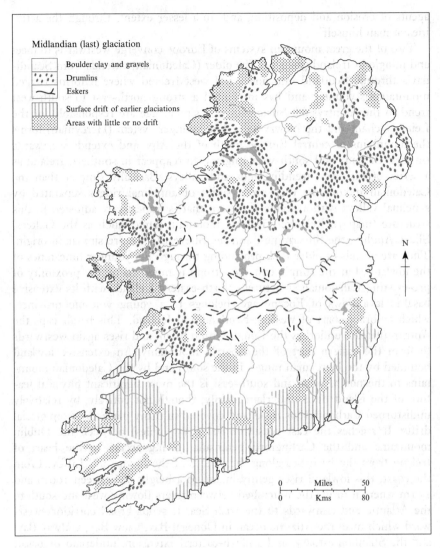

Midlandian (last) glaciation

    Boulder clay and gravels

    Drumlins

    Eskers

    Surface drift of earlier glaciations

    Areas with little or no drift

N

0     Miles     50

0     Kms     80

Map 7 Glacial landforms, by J. P. Haughton

Based on map 20, *Atlas of Ireland* (R.I.A., Dublin, 1979), compiled by F. M. Synge.

erosional, the most striking features being the deep cirques, many of them containing corrie lakes, which interrupt the otherwise smooth outline of many of the mountain crests, exemplified by Upper and Lower Lough Bray in the Wicklow mountains and Coumshingaun in the Comeraghs; and steep-sided valleys like that of Glendalough that penetrate deeply into the uplands. On

the lowlands there was largely deposition, so that the pre-glacial rock landscape may be completely hidden by a thick layer of unconsolidated material
left behind by the melting ice. It is on this drift surface that modern soil
development has taken place and, as most of the soil profiles are immature,
the composition of the drift has a strong influence on the nature of the
overlying soil type. There were two major advances of the ice. The earlier
and more extensive (equivalent to the Saale of northern Europe) covered
almost the whole country, and only a few of the higher parts of the south
and west were free from ice (map 8). During the decay of this ice-sheet,
meltwaters deposited sands and gravels and cut spillways in solid rock. Such
channels are well displayed on the east side of the Wicklow hills, where they
are now followed by the main north–south lines of communication. The
Glen of the Downs and the Scalp are striking examples. A return to colder
conditions heralded the beginning of another advance of the ice. Unlike
its predecessor, it covered only part of the country, and its southern limit is
clearly defined by a belt of hummocky morainic country extending from
the northern slopes of the Wicklow mountains south-westwards across the
lowlands to Tipperary and out to the sea at Kilkee, County Clare.
At approximately the same time, an independent ice cap developed in west
Cork and extended eastwards to Killumney and northwards to the Killarney
lowland, where its moraines partially block the outlet of the lower lake. The
topographic features left by this younger ice are fresh in appearance and have
been little affected by erosion or leaching. They include the steep-sided
drumlin hills of the north central lowlands and the sinuous esker ridges of
the midlands, all of which stand in marked contrast to the subdued relief
and leached soils on the deposits of the earlier glaciation. The decay of the
last ice sheet began by a regular recession of the ice margin in a north-
westerly direction leaving a mantle of boulder clay and gravel deposits on
the bedrock. Eskers, the long narrow gravel ridges, were formed by infilling
of the sub-glacial rivers that led to the ice margins. They are aligned roughly
in the direction of ice movement and were exposed after it had melted
back. Drumlins dominate the lowland north of a line running from Dundalk
to Kells, Longford, and Sligo, and also occur in the plains of Mayo and
in east Clare. They would appear to represent a change from an orderly
retreat to wholesale stagnation of the ice cap. This drumlin country, with
its hundreds of small steep-sided hills, ill-drained hollows, and a chaotic
drainage pattern, must always have been difficult for communication
and settlement, and, even today, has a distinctive pattern of small farms
associated with it.

After the dissolution of the ice there was a marine transgression in the
north-east. During this period Inishowen was an island, much of the Ards
peninsula was submerged, and Lough Neagh may have been part of a long
sea inlet. During this high sea level, meltwater from the remnants of the ice

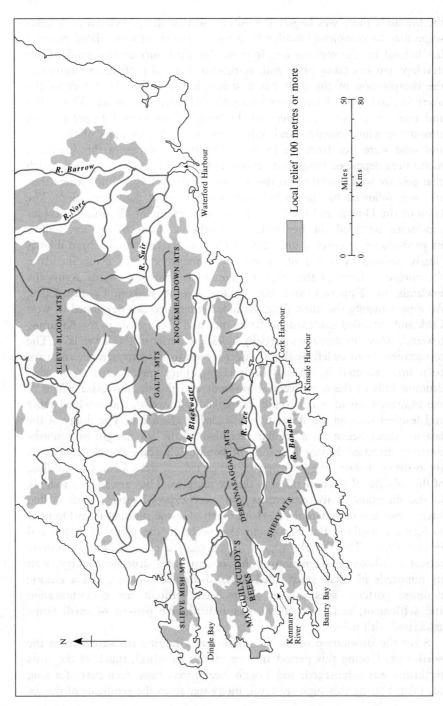

Map 8  River patterns in Hercynian Ireland, by J. P. Haughton

R. Barrow

R. Nore

R. Suir

SLIEVE BLOOM MTS

KNOCKMEALDOWN MTS

GALTY MTS

R. Blackwater

R. Lee

DERRYNASAGGART MTS

R. Bandon

SHEHY MTS

SLIEVE MISH MTS

MACGILLYCUDDY'S
REEKS

Waterford Harbour

Cork Harbour

Kinsale Harbour

Dingle Bay

Kenmare
River

Bantry Bay

N

Local relief 100 metres or more

Miles    0        50
Kms     0        80

sheet carried sand and gravel down to the valley of the Foyle and Faughan, forming the basis of the terraces that border these valleys today.

FOR the purposes of more detailed description Ireland may be divided into five physiographic regions (maps 1 & 2):

the Caledonian uplands of the north and west;
the Caledonian hills and lowlands of the east;
the east–west Hercynian ranges of the south;
the basaltic area of the north-east, including the Lough Neagh basin;
the central lowland with its residual plateau areas and isolated Hercynian
    hill masses.

Each of these divisions has its distinguishing relief features but also much topographic diversity. Everywhere the uplands are penetrated by river valleys that are followed by lines of settlement, and in the lowland the traveller is rarely out of sight of a hill or mountain range. There are also significant differences in drainage conditions leading to strong contrasts in land use.

FROM Malin Head in the north to Galway Bay in the west a high mountain barrier faces the Atlantic ocean. This rugged, rain-drenched terrain is fringed by a narrow, discontinuous coastal plain, and, to the east and south, interrupted by broad drift-covered valleys that provide the major areas for agriculture and settlement. Chief among these are the extensive Foyle–Swilly lowland; the lake-strewn valley of the Erne; the wide valley of the Moy; and the lowland leading to Clew Bay. With the exception of the Foyle–Swilly basin, these areas may be regarded as westward extensions of the central lowland.

In Donegal the barren and rugged character of the Irish highlands finds its most complete expression. A belt of ancient rocks, marked on the western side by granite intrusions, occupies a wide area in the counties of Donegal, Londonderry, and Tyrone. The present landscape is the result of the uplift and subsequent erosion of the roots of the ancient Caledonian mountain chain. The modern rivers, under the influence of the rock structure, have etched out a north-east to south-west grain in the country, which is strikingly seen in the Derryveagh mountains and in the orientation of the Foyle lowland. The highest plateau surface lies at approximately 400 m (1,200 feet) and forms broad areas of moorland, as, for example, east of the Rosses and to the south of the Bluestack mountains. A more widespread moorland surface occurs between 200 m and 260 m (600 and 800 feet) and another between 30 m and 100 m (100 and 300 feet). Above these level surfaces rise the great residual masses of resistant quartzite rock forming typical conical peaks such as Errigal (752 m) and Muckish (670 m). At a few places the higher mountains reach the sea, where they form fine coastal scenery. Most impressive of these are Slieve League (601 m) and Slieve Tooey (445 m) in the Inver peninsula, and Horn Head north of Dunfanaghy. The Foyle and Swilly lowlands, focus of life in the north-west, follow the Caledonian trend and represent a belt of weakness separating the mountains of Donegal from those of similar age and character in Londonderry and Tyrone.

THROUGHOUT the whole of north-west Ireland Pleistocene glaciation has left cirques on the higher mountains and modified the mountain valleys by steepening their sides and over-deepening their lower reaches so that the floors of some, like Lough Swilly, have fiordic characteristics. The flatter lowland areas, especially the Foyle valley and the head of Donegal Bay, are mantled by glacial moraines and outwash gravels, and these have always been the chief areas of cultivation and settlement.

To the south, the ancient rocks of the Donegal highlands fall in height towards the head of Donegal Bay, and along the Lough Erne depression where they disappear beneath a cover of nearly horizontal rocks of Carboniferous age. The latter forms an extensive and deeply dissected plateau surface with stepped edges, which end westwards in the great limestone promontory of Benbulbin (527 m) and southwards in the bleak shale and sandstone hills that flank Lough Allen. Manorhamilton lies at a focus of valleyways in the heart of this region. The Caledonian structures reappear from beneath these rocks close to Manorhamilton and form a narrow south-west-trending ridge which broadens into the Ox mountains of west Sligo. This ridge is breached by the Ballysodare river, and its narrow valley provides the main approach to the Sligo area from the south and east.

In west Connacht the mountains fall into a northern and southern group separated by a broad lowland, part of which has been submerged to form Clew Bay. Both mountain areas stand in contrast to the low-lying Carboniferous limestone that borders them on the east, where the junction between mountain and plain is marked by Loughs Conn, Mask, and Corrib. These lakes occupy basins that have been extended on their eastern sides through solution of the limestone by the acid waters from the hills. The northern group of mountains, though structurally similar to those of County Donegal, is less rugged in texture. Extensive areas of bare quartzite form a belt of high ground with summits above 600 m, extending from Achill Island through the Corraun peninsula to the Nephin Beg range. This high ground is continued northwards to the coast, where it forms a long line of cliffs in what is one of the most desolate areas of Ireland. An interesting topographical feature is a low-lying moorland surface situated to the east of these hills but draining westwards by the Owenmore river through a narrow gorge in the quartzite ridge which is followed by the main road to Belmullet. On the western flank of the range the mountains drop steeply to about 30 m and then slope more gradually to sea level. Most of this land is deeply covered in blanket bog and uninhabited. On the coast are broad estuaries choked with sand and alluvium.

South of Clew Bay and to the west of the Corrib–Mask lake chain, rugged, barren land again appears. The north-east to south-west Caledonian trend is here largely obscured, partly by the presence of the extensive granitic masses that occupy most of the southern half of the area, and partly by a series of east–west fracture lines that seem to be a major topographic control. Quartzite forms characteristic peaks in the Twelve Bens, the Maamturk mountains, and the isolated cone of Croagh Patrick, all over 600 m in height. A plateau-like area is widespread at about 600 m and is well represented in the Maamtrasna massif. The whole mountain mass is deeply dissected by narrow, glacially modified valleys, some of which are occupied by narrow ribbon lakes, while others, such as Killary harbour, have been flooded by the sea and are true fiords. South of an east–west line from Clifden to Oughterard, the high land gives way abruptly to a barren lake-strewn granitic lowland, interrupted here and there by hills reaching 200 m to 300 m above sea level. This is Connemara, a wilderness of bare rock, glacial erratics, water, and peat. Its western end is deeply penetrated by wide island-studded inlets of the sea; but its southern coastline on Galway Bay is straight and featureless.

EASTERN Ireland has two areas of Caledonian structure that differ markedly from each other. To the north the Newry axis is a roughly triangular area extending from Belfast Lough inland to the town of Longford, and thence eastwards to the sea near Drogheda. The north-west side of this triangle is probably a continuation of the boundary fault of the southern uplands of Scotland. The rocks are mainly slates, shales, and grits, but granite outcrops in Slieve Croob (532 m) in County Down and reappears again at the other end of the axis at Crossdoney, County Cavan, and, it is believed, lies elsewhere in depth. The area is largely rolling lowland and the geological boundaries and subsurface topography are blurred by the thick cover of glacial drift which has many drumlin features. Along its southern edge a change in the composition of the drift cover may be the only indication that the older rocks have given way to the younger limestones of the midlands. An alien element is introduced by occurrence of much more recent (Tertiary) igneous activity, which has left three striking groups of hills in the Slieve Gullion and Carlingford ring dykes and the great mass of granite that forms the Mourne mountains and culminates in Slieve Donard (850 m).

The second area of Caledonian structure in eastern Ireland is the Leinster mountain chain and the Wicklow–Wexford lowland. The mountains begin on the south side of Dublin Bay and extend south-westwards to the estuary of the Barrow. They form the most continuous area of high ground in Ireland and effectively isolate the south-east from the central lowland, thus strengthening the individuality of this part of the country which is also distinguished by its sunny climate, acid brown earth soils, and absence of peat development. The hills are the remnants of a great arch of sedimentary rocks into which granite was intruded in Devonian times. Long-continued denudation has exposed the granite core, which has weathered to form rounded peat-covered uplands. The granite is flanked by older shales and slates which have been altered to mica-schist along the line of contact, and in places (notably in the Glendalough–Glendasan area) this zone is strongly mineralised, giving rise to lodes of lead, silver, and zinc. The granite does not necessarily form high ground everywhere. On the south shore of Dublin Bay it rises to over 140 m in Killiney Hill and continues as a gently rolling surface between 65 m and 130 m before rising steeply to over 500 m in the Dublin mountains. From here southwards to the Slaney gap, a distance of 65 km, there are few passes through the mountains lower than 500 m. Croaghanmoira (665 m) is separated from the main range by a deep valley drained by the Aughrim and Shillelagh rivers. From the Slaney gap the chain is continued south-westwards as the Blackstairs–Mount Leinster group, its last prominent feature being Brandon Hill near Graiguenamanagh. Here, the upland is breached by the south-flowing River Barrow, giving the Carlow–Kilkenny lowland an important link southwards with New Ross and the Waterford estuary.

Throughout the Leinster chain there is a contrast in scenery between the rounded peat-covered granite domes and the more deeply dissected stratified deposits on either side. The granite–schist junction appears in many places as a belt of more resistant rock which tends to produce a distinct topographical feature, notably the summits of Knockree, Djouce, and Lugnagun. Streams such as the Glencree river and the King's river, which occupy wide valleys in the granite, are constricted as they cross this band. Outside the mica–schist belt there is a strong development of drainage parallel to the main axis, and evidence of much river capture. Thus the Liffey, rising on Kippure, at first flows westwards but then makes a right-angled bend southwards in the Blessington basin as a result of its capture by a tributary of the King's river. The combined waters of these streams continue the new direction before emerging on the central lowland through the Poulaphouca gorge, a youthful post-glacial cut in a slate ridge. Again, on the eastern slopes of the range, the waters from the deep, glacially modified valleys of Glendasan, Glendalough, and Glenmalure are drawn southwards as the Avonmore river, which follows the strike of the rocks for five miles before swinging south-east across the grain of the country to enter the sea at Arklow. The Slaney, which rises on the western slopes of Lugnaquilla, curves round to the south and crosses the axis of the mountains through a gorge at Bunclody, its lower course bearing little relationship to the underlying structure.

On the north-east flank of the mountains, ancient slates with interbedded sandstones form an impressive line of hills with typical quartzite peaks. The series begins with Howth Head on the north side of Dublin Bay and continues southwards as Carrickgolloghan, Bray Head, the Great and Little Sugarloaf, and Carrick Mountain near Wicklow. It reappears as a distinct topographical feature in Forth Mountain in south Wexford. The structural relationship of these rocks to those forming the main chain is obscure, but the rugged topography is clearly due to the greater resistance to weathering of the quartzite bands. In east Wicklow and Wexford the Ordovician slates and shales as well as older rocks underlie a maturely dissected lowland, which is diversified by small hills composed of volcanic material of the same age aligned along the Caledonian axis. Most of the area has a thin drift cover which is deeply weathered and gives rise to subdued surface forms. Towards the coast the drift cover thickens and may form clay cliffs 20 m high with a remarkably level upper surface. This flat surface rises gently inland to about 45 m above sea level. Just north of Wexford harbour there is a small area of fresher moraine with steep-sided hills and lake-filled hollows. This is a deposit from a tongue of ice that moved onshore from the Irish Sea basin during the last glaciation, and it has produced a landscape quite unlike any other in the south-east.

Most of the higher parts of the Wicklow mountains have been modified in detail by Pleistocene glaciation. Cirque formations on the north-east slopes break the otherwise mature skyline, and the corrie lakes that occupy them add greatly to the scenic interest. The larger valleys, the majority of which end blindly in the mountain mass (a feature that contributes to their isolation), show modification by local ice in their U-shape and terminal moraines, but they are also affected in the lower reaches by deposits from the lowland ice sheets that came across the lowland from the north. This drift has produced minor relief features, but more importantly has blocked river valleys and diverted drainage. It has been shown, for example, that the present course of the River Liffey through the Poulaphuca gorge is post-glacial, following the blocking of the old valley, which now lies buried in glacial drift about a mile north of the new cut. At one period meltwater was ponded between the retreating ice front and the mountains so that temporary lakes developed in Glencree, Glencullen, and the Bohernabreena and Blessington valleys. The waters escaped southwards on either flank of the mountains through a series of overflow channels which remain as youthful gorge-like features contrasting with the more mature relief around them. The road from Dublin to Wicklow passes through three such channels at the Scalp, Kilmacanogue, and the Glen of the Downs. On the western side of the hills, the waters from the ancient Lake Blessington scoured out the spectacular Hollywood glen. The economically important gravels that flank the Wicklow mountains are a legacy from this period.

SOUTHERN Ireland is composed of a series of alternating ridges and valleys oriented east–west but curving towards the south in west Cork and Kerry. In general, Devonian sandstones have resisted weathering to form higher ground, while the more easily eroded Carboniferous limestones and shales form the valleys (map 4). The bleak sandstone moorland of the Derrynasaggart mountains and the ridge of Shehy, with many summits above 500 m, form the modern boundary between Cork and Kerry and divide the area into two contrasting parts. West of this watershed, sandstone dominates in long, high mountain peninsulas separating straight sea inlets. To the east, on the other hand, the ridges are lower and communication between the valleys is easier; fertile land occurs on the wide areas of limestone or shale that floor the valleys of the Bandon, Lee, and Blackwater.

The most northerly of the western peninsulas is that of Dingle, where a number of summits exceed 600 m and Mount Brandon drops steeply from 953 m to the sea. At their western extremity the uncompromising sandstones give way to a pocket of older but more easily weathered shales, forming good soils, which have attracted settlement from Smerwick harbour to Dunquin. Eastwards the ridge disappears abruptly beneath the flat, alluvium-covered valley of the Main, which leads to the head of Dingle Bay and gives access southwards to the Killarney lowland.

South of Dingle Bay rise the massive sandstone group of Macgillycuddy's Reeks, which includes Carrauntoohil (1,041 m), the highest mountain in Ireland. The famous upper lake of Killarney lies within the north-eastern slopes of this range, whereas the larger Lough Leane below it is in an area of drift-covered Carboniferous limestone, which has potentially fertile soils. Between Kenmare and Bantry bays yet another outcrop of sandstone forms the Caha mountains and Slieve Miskish, the backbone of the remote Berehaven peninsula. In all these peninsulas glaciation has excavated cirques on the north-eastern slopes of the higher peaks; the hill slopes have been scraped bare of soil but glacial drift mantles the lower ground. The latter forms drumlin hills at the head of Bantry Bay and on Whiddy Island.

South of Bantry Bay the ridges are lower and they no longer exercise the control on drainage that they do farther north. Thus the Ilen river, after following the Ballinadee trough for some distance, turns abruptly southwards to breach a sandstone ridge before swinging west again towards the sea in the Skibbereen depression.

This stream pattern is repeated in the landscape of east Cork and Waterford, where the long east-flowing rivers may make sudden right-angled bends to flow southwards in narrow valleys through the ridges. It would appear that the main drainage was originally from north to south, but as erosion laid bare the east–west Hercynian structures, they deflected the drainage in this direction. This adjustment to structure, however, is still incomplete, and in places the Bandon, Lee, and Blackwater retain their ancient north–south courses as deep gorges through the sandstone ridges, thus forming important route links between neighbouring valleys. The intervening sandstone ridges only reach the dimensions of mountains in a few places; and in spite of the very acid soils derived from the sandstones, much of the land is of agricultural value. Extensive areas of almost flat land occur between 180 and 210 m and again at 60 to 120 m. The former, known as the 'South Ireland peneplain', is best preserved where it bevels the Devonian sandstones and grits in the broad interfluves. Its inner limits have been traced along the slopes of the Knockmealdowns, the Monavullaghs, the Comeraghs, and the south flank of Bagles's Mountain. The lower (60 m) surface, distinguished by its poorly developed drainage and the deep incision of the rivers towards its outer edge, fringes almost the entire south coast, where it terminates as a line of sea cliffs. A recent submergence has drowned the lower reaches of the river valleys, giving rise to complex sea inlets such as those of Waterford, Cork, and Kinsale. Though they are silting rapidly at their heads, these inlets are still fine natural harbours.

THE eastern part of County Antrim consists of a basaltic plateau sloping gently inland from heights of 300–450 m near the coast. Below this coastal escarpment an ancient beach, now raised above sea level, is followed by the Antrim coast road as far as Cushendall and has important mesolithic remains associated with it. Leading in from the coast are several deep glens that penetrate far into the plateau but, because they end abruptly within the hills, have always been rather isolated. The highest parts of the plateau lie some distance inland from the scarp face where Trostan (554 m) and Slieveanorra (513 m) are the chief summits. In the north, the isolated hill of Knocklayd behind the town of Ballycastle is a notable feature with the basalt capping white chalk; while in the south the conspicuous volcanic neck of Slemish (438 m) overlooks the Braid valley. To the south-west of the hills the broad north–south valley of the River Main is floored by well-drained glacial sands and gravels and has long been a favoured area for settlement and a focus for routes coming over the plateau from the glens. The drainage from this valley enters the north-east corner of Lough Neagh. Southwards the plateau presents a steep scarp face to the Lagan valley, in which the black basalt overlying the chalk is again strikingly seen. The uplands here are largely under grass and rough pasture, in contrast to north Antrim, where glacial moraines have disrupted the drainage and there are many peat bogs.

West of the Lower Bann the basalts reappear as a ridge running south from Downhill on the coast and reaching heights of 554 m in Mullaghmore and 527 m in Slieve Gallion, which is detached from the main range. The hills drop sharply to the west in a series of scarps overlooking the Roe valley and the Foyle lowland, but southwards the uplands are topographically continuous with the Sperrin mountains. These ancient schist mountains have rounded heather-covered summits, some of which rise above 650 m. South of this again an extensive plateau below 300 m is developed on Old Red

Sandstones; the acid nature of the rocks and the weak drainage on the almost level surfaces have given rise to deep bogs. Only where morainic ridges give better drainage is there good grazing, and farming is possible. At the extreme south the land falls to the moraine-covered limestone-floored Clogher valley, which acts as a routeway through to the lake-strewn Fermanagh lowland.

Lough Neagh and the Bann lowlands occupy an elongated depression in the basalts. The shores of Lough Neagh itself are low-lying and attractive only to fishermen; the Bann lowland is deeply covered by glacial deposits, some of which form drumlins, and there are some peat bogs, but there are also well drained sands and gravels well suited to agricultural activities. This whole lowland is open in the south-east to the Lagan corridor, a flat-floored valley about four miles wide trending from south-west to the north-east, where it is drowned by the sea to form Belfast Lough, a fine natural haven allowing easy communication with Scotland, which is only 40 km away on the other side of the North Channel. The valley floor is covered with glacial sands and gravels, so there is good drainage providing favourable sites for settlement.

THE heart of Ireland is a lowland which is monotonous in appearance when compared with the scenery of the bordering hill masses. However, it is not nearly so homogenous as a small-scale map might suggest, and there are significant differences in relief, drainage, and soils that make some parts attractive to settlement while other parts are hostile and difficult of access.

South of a line drawn from Dublin to Galway Bay, the drift-covered, relatively well drained lowland is fragmented by a number of substantial hill masses. Some of these hills are the result of folding, which has brought older resistant sandstones to the surface, where they form rounded heather-covered slopes with the crest lines broken by the occasional glacial corrie. They include the Slieve Bernagh and Arra mountains, which sit astride the Shannon where it begins its rapid fall to sea level, dividing this river into a placid, navigable upper section and a lower estuarine one. These hills are separated from the Silvermines and their continuation northwards, the Slieve Blooms, by a narrow corridor with Nenagh at its northern end, which is the main route link between the broad lowland surrounding the Shannon estuary and the midlands. The Silvermines and the Slieve Blooms form a waterparting between the Shannon and its tributaries, draining westwards to the Atlantic, and the Barrow, Suir, and Nore, which converge southwards to form Waterford Harbour. Farther south Slievenamon, the Galtees, and the Ballyhoura hills are of similar age and structure, and though standing in isolation they really belong to the Hercynian province of the south. In contrast to these ancient hill masses there are others which form low plateaus, and differ mainly from the lowland in their thin drift cover and acid, leached soils with poor drainage, often giving rise to blanket bog or reedy fields. The most westerly of these uplands and the least typical occurs in north Clare, where the scarped faces of Carboniferous limestone overlook Galway Bay. The limestone dips gently to the south, and much of it presents a surface of true karst with the bare rock forming great jointed slabs without surface drainage. Similar conditions occur in the Aran Islands in Galway Bay. Southwards the limestone disappears under deposits of shale and grits, and there is a striking change in the landscape. Bare limestone gives way to ill-drained, reed-covered fields; the houses are roofed with the local flagstones, and at the coast the plateau terminates in the cliffs of Moher, which rise vertically from the sea to form one of the most spectacular lines of cliff scenery in Europe. Towards the Shannon these rocks disappear under the glacial deposits, thick alluvium, and peat bogs of the estuary, but they reappear in the south as the Mullaghareirks, again an ill-drained peat-covered plateau rising to over 420 m. Its scarped edges, well seen in the vicinity of Newcastle West, form a sharp south-western limit to the Limerick lowland. The boundaries of Cork, Limerick, and Kerry meet within the bounds of this inhospitable upland.

Another extensive plateau area of similar structure and composition occurs to the west of the Barrow in Carlow, Kilkenny, and east Tipperary. It reaches 300 m in the northern part of the Castlecomer plateau, where it is coal-bearing. The River Nore cuts across its south-western flank, separating it from the Slieve Ardagh hills, which are similar in character. The Nore valley opens out southwards to form the small but important Kilkenny lowland, a major route focus.

North of the Dublin–Galway line the horizons open out and the main contrasts are between east and west. In the counties of Dublin, Kildare, Meath, and Louth there is some of the best agricultural land in the country. The bedrock is covered by thick morainic deposits largely derived from the underlying limestone rock; the soils are not greatly leached, owing to the relatively low rainfall, and drainage is good. Most of the streams, including the Liffey and the Boyne, are incised into the drift cover and are bordered by river terraces. Immediately to the north of the Boyne the underlying rocks are older, the topography rougher, and the soils poorer, but in spite of this the triangular area, with its base extending some 80 km from Dublin to Dundalk and its apex in the vicinity of Mullingar, is the real heart of lowland Ireland, but it is also the area most accessible to influences from the Irish Sea basin beyond.

West of Kildare the raised bogs appear. Wide areas of ill-drained land are interrupted by morainic mounds and eskers which provide the better-drained and usable land. A line of glacial gravel deposits can be traced across the country leading towards Athlone and these have always been an important routeway which has been loosely termed the Esker Riada.

The Shannon river, though navigable for about 160 km both above and below Athlone, is a barrier rather than a line of communication. In several places it widens into large lakes, as in Lough Ree and Lough Derg, and everywhere the bordering flood plains of the main river and its tributaries are liable to flooding and are avoided by settlement. The rapids at Athlone, where higher ground approaches both banks, gave the opportunity for a crossing place, and this has long been one of the main gateways to the west.

Beyond the Shannon the landscape changes again. The morainic cover is thinner and limestone outcrops over considerable areas. The soils are thin and leached. The hedgerows give way to stone walls and there is evidence of wind exposure in the vegetation. West of Galway town the limestone disappears, and though lowland continues it is underlain by ancient Caledonian structures and there is a wilderness of rocks and water—this is Connemara. To the north, however, in Clew Bay, the drift cover is thicker and there are numerous drumlins which form islands in the bay.

The northern part of the central lowland is covered by deep morainic drift heaped up into thousands of drumlins. These small hills alternate with hollows filled with peat, swamps, or open water connected by slow-flowing meandering streams well exemplified by the Erne lowland. This type of landscape extends in a broad arc from Donegal and Sligo bays eastwards through Fermanagh, Roscommon, Leitrim, Cavan, Monaghan, Armagh, and Down, with better drainage in the eastern half of the country. At its western extremity the belt is interrupted by a number of hill masses, the remnants of a deeply dissected plateau of nearly horizontal strata which has, as its most striking element, the flat-topped Benbulbin in Sligo (527 m); inland the Cuilcagh hills on the Cavan–Fermanagh border are over 600 m in height, while to the south Slieve Anierin, on one side of Lough Allen, and the Bralieve mountains, on the other, are composed of Carboniferous shales and sandstones giving rise to a heather-covered moorland that contrasts with the limestone slopes of Benbulbin and the dry Carraroe upland so rich in prehistoric remains. As a whole, the drumlin belt is an area of widely dispersed settlement and small farms. In the past, it has been a barrier to communication, especially where it crosses the wide corridor occupied by Cavan and Monaghan towns, which otherwise might have been a major routeway linking the central lowland with the Lough Neagh depression and the Lagan valley.

CHAPTER III

# Ireland before 3000 B.C. *

M. J. O'KELLY

Not much is known of the geological condition of Ireland in the tertiary era, but it is probable that it was already an island and that its main topographical features were much as they are today. During the succeeding era, the quaternary, which opened about two million years ago, Ireland, in common with the rest of Europe, experienced a great ice age. This was not a single extended period of severe glaciation, but rather consisted of alternating phases of extreme temperature change. Each major advance of the ice sheet was succeeded by a period of higher temperature when the ice melted and disappeared. These warm interglacial periods varied greatly in duration, as did the so-called interstadial periods when the ice was either stationary or in minor recession. There were localised fluctuations also in response to local topographical and other factors, which in turn gave rise to chain-reactions in

*REVISOR'S NOTE: M. J. O'Kelly submitted the first draft text of his contribution in 1971. He would undoubtedly have made changes and rewritten some sections in the light of more recent research. Unfortunately, his untimely death in 1982 prevented this. The task of the revisor, therefore, was to prepare the manuscript for publication with the twin aims of remaining as faithful as possible to the original text while at the same time incorporating new material and adding the most important new publications to the bibliography. The matter was not easy as there have been tremendous advances in Irish archaeology over the last two decades, and in some areas the state of knowledge current when O'Kelly was writing has been radically altered. It was decided, however, that the original text should be tampered with as little as possible in matters of interpretation, as this was O'Kelly's last statement on Irish archaeology. Significant changes have been made only in matters of fact, brought about by new discoveries, and this has been done most extensively in the case of the mesolithic, where there has been what can only be described as a revolution in our thinking over the last dozen or so years.

In his manuscript O'Kelly gave all radiocarbon dates as 'B.C.' dates. In the modern idiom this is used only for calibrated absolute dates. Accordingly, all radiocarbon dates are indicated in lower case (i.e. 'bc') which means that they are uncalibrated. However, where it is evident from O'Kelly's text that he was speaking in terms of absolute calendar years, the more conventional 'B.C.' is used. (For calibration, see M. Stuiver and G. W. Pearson, 'High precision of the calibration of the radiocarbon timescale, A.D. 1950–500 B.C.' in *Radiocarbon*, xxviii (1986), pp 805–38.)

Always trenchant in his views and unafraid of controversy, M. J. O'Kelly made a considerable contribution to the study of Irish archaeology. It is hoped that the text which follows retains something of his character and personality, and that his flowing literary style and human approach are not diminished by the work of revision.

BARRY RAFTERY

neighbouring areas. For these and other reasons, it is clear that further studies will ultimately show a much more complex picture of the events of the ice age than can be seen at present.

Early in the quaternary era, sea level was higher than now and wave action produced a striking feature along the Irish coast line. This is a platform and cliff that may be seen today at many places along the shoreline, especially in the south and east. The rock platform is remarkably level and is from five to ten feet (1.5–3 m) above high water. It is the oldest post-tertiary or pleistocene feature so far recognised in Ireland. The most notable exposure is at Courtmacsherry Bay, County Cork,[1] where the top of an extensive rock outcrop has been planed off by wave action. Where this surface meets the cliff it is covered by a beach deposit which is, in turn, overlain by a great mass of boulder clay deposited during the subsequent glaciations.

Two major advances of the ice sheet have been identified in Ireland, and it has been possible to correlate them to a greater or lesser extent with similar movements in Europe. In Alpine Europe at least four major advances are known to have taken place (Guntz, Mindel, Riss, and Wurm), while in northern Europe three are identified (Elster, Saale, and Weichsel). It is with the northern European rather than with the Alpine movements that the Irish and British ice-advances are best correlated. The influences exerted by the ice, whether advancing, stationary, or melting, were vast, not only climatically but also geologically and ecologically. Each advance of the ice had incorporated in it a mass of muds, clays, gravels, and large boulders, which it transported for substantial distances. For instance, granite boulders perhaps from Galway have been identified as far afield as east Cork,[2] and there are numerous other examples.

Although each ice-advance tended to obliterate the deposits of previous advances, enough has survived in certain areas to enable stratigraphical successions to be recognised, and these give valuable information as to direction and duration of the ice movement. Cores taken from the sea and ocean beds by drilling are also informative, as the deposition of sediments in the oceans was affected by the climatic conditions prevailing on land. It must also be appreciated that, as the ice advanced, more and more water was taken from the seas and oceans and stored away, occasioning an overall lowering of water level. Sea floors became dry land, shore lines became considerably altered, islands became joined to one another and often to neighbouring continents by land bridges. As the weight of the ice on the land increased, the downward pressure caused a lowering of land levels with an apparent compensatory rise in sea levels, thus permitting a partial return to their former positions and a partial restoration of some old shore lines. On the other

---

[1] G. F. Mitchell, 'The pleistocene epoch' in J. Meenan and D. A. Webb (ed.), *A view of Ireland* (Dublin, 1957), p. 33.
[2] Ibid.

hand, when the ice began to melt, vast quantities of water were released, bringing a real rise in sea levels; though, in accordance with the see-saw effect noted above, this was somewhat nullified by the lessening pressure on the land masses, which, thus relieved of the weight of ice, began to rise once more. The net relationship of land height to mean sea level is consequently a factor of two effects: lowering of sea levels and sinking of land as the ice advanced, and rising sea levels and rising land as the ice melted.

Efforts to ascertain the relationship between land height and sea level at any given time are complicated by the fact that local fluctuations of ice-advance or of melting, and local variations in the density of the ice, played a significant role, giving rise to localised variations. Where the ice was especially thick, the land sank to a greater degree in that particular area and formed basin-like depressions; conversely, when the ice melted in such areas bulges were formed. The result of this was that frequently the land move-ment was in the nature of a tilt, a feature of particular importance in our area of the northern hemisphere when the activities of early man come to be considered. Each time the ice melted, warmth returned with a consequent upsurge in vegetational growth and animal presence; regions of tundra with their attendant flora and fauna gave way to areas displaying conditions more consonant with those of the present day.

This alternation of glacial with temperate, or even warm, conditions, took place on a major scale in Ireland at least twice. It is usual to relate the earlier of these two major ice-advances to the Saale glaciation and the second to the Weichsel, both of northern Europe.[3] Evidence of a still earlier major Irish glaciation is beginning to emerge, however, and this may be equated with the Elster, also of northern Europe.[4] Between this earliest ice-advance (Elster) and the first of the two major advances, a long warm period, known as the great interglacial, ensued.

This has been interestingly documented in land deposits, notably near Gort, County Galway.[5] Many of the plants identified in the Gort deposits are representative of widely separated areas of Europe, the Caucasus, and even further east in Asia. Examples of these are the *Abies* (silver fir), *Picea* (spruce), and *Fagus* (beech) of central Europe; the *Buxus sempervirens* (box), *Rhododendron ponticum* (rhododendron) and *Lysimachia punctata* (loosestrife)

---

[3] Ibid., p. 32; G. F. Mitchell, 'The pleistocene history of the Irish Sea' in *Advancement of Science*, xvii (1960–61), p. 324.

[4] W. A. Watts, 'The interglacial deposits at Kilbeg and Newtown, Co. Waterford' in *R.I.A. Proc.*, lx (1959), sect. B, pp 79–134: 126; 'Interglacial deposits in Kildromin townland, near Herbertstown, Co. Limerick' in *R.I.A. Proc.*, lxv (1967), sect. B, pp 339–48: 344.

[5] Knud Jessen, S. T. Andersen, and Anthony Farrington, 'The interglacial deposit near Gort, Co. Galway, Ireland' in *R.I.A. Proc.*, lx (1959), sect. B, pp 1–78; G. F. Mitchell, 'Two interglacial deposits in south-eastern Ireland' in *R.I.A. Proc.*, lii (1948), sect. B, pp 1–14; and the two articles by W. A. Watts cited above, in *R.I.A. Proc.*, lx (1959), sect. B, pp 79–134, and lxv (1967), sect. B, pp 339–48.

of south-east Europe. North American flora is represented by *Eriocaulon septangulare* (pipewort). This record alone suggests a climate as warm as that of the present day and perhaps of a more oceanic character.

The first of the two major ice-advances in Ireland—the eastern general glaciation, corresponding to the Saale of northern Europe—succeeded the great interglacial. Ice formed first in the highlands of Cork, Kerry, and Donegal in the western half of the country, and in Antrim and Wicklow in the east. As conditions became more severe and as glaciers began to move out from these areas, local glaciations began to develop which augmented the initial ones. Furthermore, the eastern ice floes were augmented by a great mass of ice that came thrusting down from Scotland by way of what is now the Irish Sea. The movement of this eastern ice has been traced as far west as County Cork.[6] The ensuing interglacial period, centring on about 100,000 years ago, was (for a time, at any rate) warmer than any period since experienced.

The second major ice-advance—the midland general glaciation, corresponding to the Weichsel of northern Europe—was not as extensive as the previous one, and low-lying areas of Cork and Kerry were probably ice-free, though tundra conditions would have nonetheless prevailed. It is believed by some geologists that a similar, though somewhat lesser, strip of ground lying between Waterford and the Dingle peninsula (map 9) remained unglaciated during the previous (Saale) ice-advance also,[7] but this view is not accceptable to all.[8] Those in favour of the theory postulate that conditions in these areas would have been such that, despite the intense cold during maximum periods of glaciation, some elements of flora and fauna could have survived throughout and that with the onset of more favourable conditions regeneration would have taken place. At some periods cold was less severe, and since sea levels were low some animals entered the country by means of the land connections. One of these was the woolly mammoth (*Elephas primigenius*), whose teeth and bones have been found in the south in Counties Cork and Waterford,[9] and also in Antrim and Galway Bay.

Certain plants not native to Ireland, though found here at the present day, are thought by some to represent a survival in unglaciated regions, and the 'refuge' theory described above is adduced to account for it. American and so-called Lusitanian elements are prominent among these 'refuge' plants. The American species is again *Eriocaulon septangulare* while the Lusitanian elements are such species as *Daboecia cantabrica* (St Dabeoc's heath), *Erica*

---

[6] Mitchell, 'Pleistocene epoch', p. 32.
[7] Mitchell, 'Pleistocene epoch', p. 32.
[8] J. K. Charlesworth, *Historical geology of Ireland* (Edinburgh and London, 1963), pp 448–59.
[9] J. K. Charlesworth, *The geology of Ireland: an introduction* (Edinburgh, 1953), p. 207; H. L. Movius, *The Irish stone age* (Cambridge, 1942), pp 37–40.

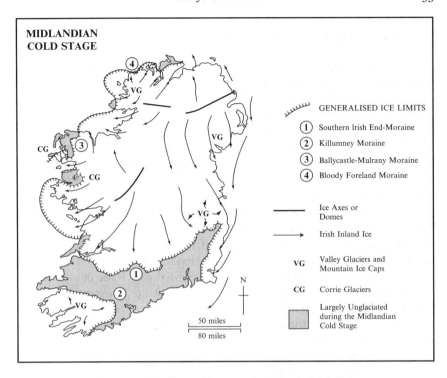

Map 9  Midlandian cold stage, after Marshall McCabe

The traditional model of the maximum limits of the last glaciation (Midlandian), after Marshall McCabe in K. J. Edwards and W. P. Warren (ed.), *The quaternary history of Ireland* (London, 1985). More recent research suggests that the ice-free areas may not have been as extensive as shown here. However, according to Peter Coxon (in C. Holland (ed.)), *The geology of Ireland* (Edinburgh, 2001)) the limits of the last glacial maximum are yet to be properly determined.

*ciliaris* (Dorset heath), *Erica scoparia* (pipewort), *Hymenophyllaceae* (filmy ferns), and *Hyocomium flagellare*. The American elements are found today in south-west Greenland and in Iceland, and the Lusitanian species exist chiefly in the mountainous interior of Iberia. These present-day locations are harsh, weatherwise, and are perhaps comparable to those that might have obtained near the margin of the Irish ice sheet in the past.

Does the 'refuge' theory account for the presence of these species, or are they late glacial immigrants that traversed the last remaining land connections between Ireland and Europe, or are they postglacial immigrants carried by water or by birds? While a good case has been made by exponents of the 'refuge' theory, the more orthodox view is that these plants (and animals) were reintroduced immediately following the last glaciation before land-connections were submerged, and before forest cover became dense. Some indeed think it is more remarkable that these elements survived the growth of forests than that they survived the ice.[10]

THE period from about 13,000 to 8500 B.C. is known as late glacial time, and during it more and more of the country became free of ice as the last glaciation, the midland general (corresponding to the Weichsel), melted. Broadly speaking, 10,000 B.C. marks the end of the ice age. Due to the pioneering studies of a Dane, Knud Jessen, a good deal of information on the flora of the period has been obtained though study of plant pollen trapped in muds and lake beds. These pollen grains are well-nigh indestructible, particularly when incorporated in such strata. As the pollen of each species differs from that of any other, identification of the grains establishes the tree and plant associations present in the area at the time the mud or peat deposits were laid down. A small sample suffices, and when the separate pollens are counted it is possible to calculate their percentage of frequency. This analysis enables the flora history of the area to be understood so that data on humidity, temperature, etc., can be inferred and synchronised with those of other areas. In this way the science of pollen analysis has built up an overall picture of late glacial time in Ireland.

Jessen distinguished three zones in late glacial time in this country.[11] In Zone I, 13,000 to 10,000 B.C., plant remains are naturally scanty and arctic in character since the country was then largely open tundra similar to that in present-day Iceland and south-west Greenland. In Zone II, the cold gave way to a more genial climate in which plants of sub-arctic character, various grasses, flowers such as the gentian and the mountain aven, and herbs of several varieties established themselves in open areas. Copses of birch trees also came into being. Fauna included the giant Irish deer (*Megaceros giganteus hibernicus*)—the so-called Irish elk—the bones of which have been recovered from peat bogs. The reindeer, bear, fox, wolf, banded lemming, and Irish hare are also known to have been present at this time. It is possible that the wild horse, the mammoth, and the Norwegian lemming were also present.[12] By the end of the period, c.9000 B.C., it is thought, the Irish deer had become extinct.

The pollen of Zone III shows a return to the climatic conditions of Zone I; that is to say, conditions akin to those of present-day northern Siberia. The plant remains are of a more northern type once again and forest is greatly reduced. It follows that there must have been a partial advance of the ice

---

[10] Charlesworth, *Historical geology*, p. 300; Mitchell, 'Pleistocene history of the Irish Sea', pp 324–5.
[11] Knud Jessen, 'Studies in late quaternary deposits and flora-history of Ireland' in *R.I.A. Proc.*, lii (1949), sect. B, pp 85–290.
[12] G. F. Mitchell and H. M. Parkes, 'The giant deer in Ireland' in *R.I.A. Proc.*, lii (1949), sect. B, pp 291–314.

during this time, 9000 to 8500 B.C., with consequent lowering of water levels and alterations of shore lines. Areas hitherto below water level became once more exposed so that partial land bridges were once again visible between this country and Britain—across the Irish Sea in the east and across the North Channel in the north-east. The same obtained for Britain, which in turn became connected with northern Europe across part of the North Sea as well, perhaps, as with France.[13]

THE period known as post-glacial time opened about 8000 B.C., with Zone IV, and lasted for somewhat more than 1,000 years. Once again the study of this period is largely based on pollen analysis, and the zonation system followed here is that of the late G. F. Mitchell,[14] who carried forward and developed Jessen's work. Zone IV is usually designated the pre-boreal period, and it immediately antedated the upsurge in forest growth that followed the complete melting of the ice. During Zone IV the low sea levels continued, so that overland connections between Ireland and Britain and the Continent continued to be maintained. Considerable improvement in climate encouraged the immigration of heat-loving plants, birch and pine woods expanded, and the wild boar and red deer became common.

Zone V commenced about 7000 B.C., by which time all ice had disappeared from Ireland. It and the succeeding Zone VI are together equated with the boreal period, which had a duration of about 1,500 years. In the beginning, sea levels were low and peat had begun to form on land that at the present time is below sea level. Some of this peat, on the North Sea floor for instance, is over 50 m below present mean sea level. The climate was of a continental type. Birch became still more plentiful and there was a notable increase of hazel in the early boreal period. Oak and elm appeared in Irish woods for the first time, having come via the still extant land bridges between this country and Britain, so that an extremely dense forest cover clothed Ireland, as indeed was the case also in Britain and on the Continent. Wild pig, wolf, and red deer were common animals. With the raising of temperatures there was a corresponding rise in water and land levels, but now the former outstripped the latter. As the extent of the seas increased, the climate was affected so that a more oceanic or so-called Atlantic phase began to supervene. Towards the end of the boreal period, the offshore peat deposits had become submerged and one-time bays and inlets became flooded.

Zone VII, the Atlantic period, began about 5500 B.C. The rise in sea level continued until it attained its maximum c.3000 B.C., at which stage a shore

[13] Jessen, 'Studies in late quaternary deposits'; Mitchell & Parkes, op. cit., p. 292; Mitchell, 'Studies in Irish quaternary deposits: no. 7' in R.I.A. Proc., liii (1951), sect. B, p. 111–206.
[14] G. F. Mitchell, 'Studies in Irish quaternary deposits: no. 7', p. 117; 'Post-boreal pollen diagrams from Irish raised bogs' in R.I.A. Proc., lvii (1954–6), sect. B, pp 186–9; 'Radiocarbon dates and pollen zones in Ireland' in R.S.A.I. Jn., lxxxviii (1958), p. 51.

line was formed. Subsequently the land-rise, which was slower to make itself felt, elevated this shore line or beach to a height of 7.6 m (25 ft) above present sea level in parts of the north-east of Ireland. This 25-foot raised beach, as it is now generally called, can be identified all along the north coast and also extending as far south as Sligo Bay in the north-west and Wexford Harbour in the south-east. Due to the tilt in the land already mentioned, the elevation diminishes as one progresses southwards to the fulcrum line that runs from Sligo to Wexford, until in the south the shore line is submerged. Hence it is that today, at exceptionally low tides, one can sometimes see, for instance at areas between Roscarbery in County Cork and Ardmore in County Waterford, the landward end of peat deposits that were formed before the tilt took place.[15] The raised beach of north-eastern Ireland is of especial interest, as much evidence of early man is connected with it. The submergence or virtual submergence of the beach in the southern half has effectively prevented us from ascertaining if similar remains of man were present there. Temperatures at this time were still about 2° C higher than at present and forests contained alder as well as oak, elm, and birch. At this time also the first raised and blanket bogs developed.

Zones VIII a and b, the sub-boreal and sub-Atlantic zones respectively, began at the time of maximum transgression of the sea on the land, c.3000 B.C. Pollen counts of these zones show a marked decline in the amounts of elm pollen together with a marked increase in pollens of such 'weeds of light' as *Plantago lanceolata* (common plantain) and others. This has been ascribed to the activities of man who, coming to realise that elm grows on good ground, began to clear it away by ring-barking and burning in order to cultivate cereals in its stead and to develop land for pasture. It is also possible that the elm was pruned of its young shoots for use as fodder for cattle, with a resultant decrease in the production of pollen.[16] Disease may also have accounted for some of the decline, though in general palaeobotanists incline to the belief that man's changeover from the food-collecting to the food-producing way of life was chiefly responsible.[17]

THE fact that land connections formerly existed between Ireland, Britain, and the Continent is held to account for the presence in the Irish flora of various European and Asiatic species such as the rhododendron, box, etc., as already

---

[15] Movius, *Ir. stone age*, p. 292.

[16] Mitchell, 'Post-boreal pollen diagrams', p. 242; 'Radiocarbon dates', p. 52.

[17] Recent thinking inclines to the view that elm disease may, in fact, have been a key factor in bringing about the decline in elm, and there are good grounds for believing that agriculture was already being practised in Ireland well before the phase of classic elm decline (e.g. W. Groenman-van Waateringe, 'The early agricultural utilization of the Irish landscape: the last word on the elm decline?' in *Landscape archaeology in Ireland* (Oxford, 1983), pp 217–32; K. Molloy and M. O'Connell, 'Neolithic agriculture—fresh evidence from Cleggan, Connemara' in *Archaeology Ireland*, ii (1988), pp 67–70.

noted. We have seen too that the mammoth was present in Ireland, having crossed presumably via these land connections. This was about 35,000 years ago. In Counties Cork and Waterford bones of mammoth have been found in natural caves in limestone country in areas which, as already mentioned, some geologists believe to have been ice-free at least during the last major ice advance. The caves in question are Shandon cave near Dungarvan, County Waterford, and Castlepook cave near Doneraile, County Cork. Other animals noted from these and similar caves in this area are cave hyena, arctic and Scandinavian lemming, giant Irish deer, reindeer, bear and arctic fox.[18] There is no record of man's presence.

If these animals reached Ireland in interglacial times, or even if they reached it towards the end of the second glaciation during a period of amelioration, there is no reason why old-stone-age man should not have followed in pursuit of the animals, particularly since his presence in Britain at this time is well documented. Acceptable evidence of his presence in Ireland, perhaps in the so-called refuge areas in the south, may yet come to light. A number of claims have been made for the presence of old-stone-age or palaeolithic man in various parts of Ireland but none of them is convincing nor has any been widely accepted. Three sites in particular may be mentioned from Sligo Bay on the north-west: Coney Island, Rosses Point, and Ballyconnell. Objects from these areas with alleged *levallois* features are almost certainly either of recent natural origin or are the result of modern activity by fishermen and others in the area.[19]

Claims were made for the presence of old-stone-age man in Kilgreaney cave near Dungarvan, County Waterford, when in 1928 the Bristol Spelaeological Society excavated the cave and found two skeletons, the lower of which was in the same horizon as bones of late glacial fauna. In 1932 Hallam Movius, of the Harvard archaeological mission to Ireland, reexcavated the cave and showed that the deposit was a disturbed one, that bones of ox and sheep occurred in the same horizon as those of extinct mammals, and that modern objects of iron, glass, pottery, etc., were similarly mixed through the deposits. Furthermore, he found that charcoal from a hearth in the same horizon as the alleged palaeolithic skeleton represented post-glacial woods such as hazel, oak, and ash. A radiocarbon date of 2630 ± 150 bc has since confirmed the date of the other skeleton, Kilgreaney A, and it is likely that the Kilgreaney B skeleton is of the same order of date.

The first securely dated mesolithic site in Ireland was investigated by G. F. Mitchell on the shore of Toome Bay in County Londonderry in 1951. His attention was brought to the site as some twenty years earlier, near the point where the lower Bann flows out of Lough Neagh, flint implements had

---

[18] Movius, *Ir. stone age*, p. 38.
[19] Ibid., pp 105–14.

been found lying apparently where dropped by their owners. It was possible
to show that the peat that had grown around the implements was of late
boreal date and that at least some of them were dropped before the growth of
the peat began. It thus seemed clear that man had been in the area before or
around 6000 bc. Mitchell's excavations were on a small scale and recovered
no more than a few fragments of worked timber and some further flint
artefacts, including a nosed scraper deemed to resemble European examples
of the aurignacian cultural phase.[20] No trace of a hut or other habitation was
discovered, though fires had been lighted at the then edge of the lake. Important, however, was the fact that charcoal from one of the pits on the site
yielded a carbon 14 date of 5730 ± 110 bc.

Scrapers were the principal tools present at Toome Bay, the working edges
having been achieved by a rather steep flaking technique, a method
that persisted in Ireland into neolithic times. These scrapers were used for
skinning animals and for scraping hides as parts of the curing process. The
hides must then have been sewn together to make clothing; objects such as
the flint perforators (fig. 1) were used to make the holes through which
threads made from sinews and gut were pulled. Scrapers must also have been
used for work on wood, bone, and antler, although such materials survive
only rarely in Irish mesolithic deposits. As well as scrapers, a few gravers and
chisel-like implements (burins) were found in the Toome area at various
times.[21]

The Toome investigations, though only limited in scope, had thus established a positive mesolithic dating for the earliest human presence in
the north-east of Ireland. This did not, however, come as a surprise at the
time, for it had long been accepted that the 8 m high raised-beach deposits
along the north-east coast, which had over the years been a prolific source
of water-rolled and abraded flints, were the remnants of a mesolithic or
middle-stone-age cultural horizon. In fact, extensive excavations there in the

Fig. 1 Flint perforators from Rough Island, Co. Down. After H. J. Movius, *The Irish
stone age* (Cambridge, 1942). Scale 2:3.

[20] G. F. Mitchell, 'The mesolithic site at Toome Bay, Co. Londonderry' in *U.J.A.*, 3rd ser.,
xviii (1955), p. 11; 'The Larnian culture: a minimal view' in *Prehist. Soc. Proc.*, xxxvii (1971),
p. 277.
[21] Movius, *Ir. stone age*, p. 118.

1930s by Hallam Movius had been the basis for an elaborate typological framework of the Irish mesolithic. Movius excavated five sites—Cushendun, Islandmagee, Glenarm, and Larne, all in County Antrim, and Rough Island, County Down. Larne was selected as the type-site and the earliest mesolithic inhabitants of north-east Ireland—as it was then believed—were named 'Larnians'.[22]

No remains other than flints have been recovered from these sites. At the time the 'Larnians' came, sea levels were rising, and it will be appreciated that as the sea transgressed more and more upon the land, those areas that had been occupied by man became gradually submerged. The inward-rolling waves tore up the land surface and destroyed the evidence of occupation. The postholes of houses and shelters, the rings of stones that may have weighted down the hide coverings of tent-like huts, the layers of ash and charcoal that would ordinarily have represented domestic hearths or cooking-places, were all washed away, together with the debris of living, such as animal bones. Artefacts in wood, bone, antler, flint, and stone, lost or dropped in and near the squatting places, were carried about by waves and long-shore currents until, in times of storm, they were flung with shingle and sand onto the storm beach at the head of the strand. In due course, as the sea encroached further, this storm beach was torn up again and the whole cycle repeated. None save the most indestructible materials could survive such violent treatment, and it is only flint and stone objects that have in fact been recovered, often with their cutting edges and arrises severely abraded and with their identifying features rounded off; none of them was in primary position. Large numbers have been recovered from the storm beach (the 8 m raised beach) formed at the time of the maximum transgression of the sea.

Movius's study of the 'Larnian' flints was detailed and comprehensive. At Larne, at a point near the southern end of a gravel spit known as 'the Curran', he dug a pit 5 m square and over 8 m deep and from it collected 5,515 worked flints. From a study of these he distinguished an early and a late phase, the early phase being common to Scotland also, since he believed that both countries were joined by land bridges. During the late phase, since the land connections had been severed, developments were different on both sides of the North Channel, an Obanian phase developing in Scotland, a late Larnian in Ireland. Doubt has, however, been cast on the whole of this thesis, and it is now argued that the separation of Ireland and Scotland had already been completed before 6000 bc. Mitchell,[23] using radiocarbon dates

[22] H. L. Movius, 'Report on stone-age excavation at Rough Island, Strangford Lough, Co. Down' in *R.S.A.I. Jn.*, lxx (1940), pp 111–42; 'An early post-glacial archaeological site at Cushendun, Co. Antrim' in *R.I.A. Proc.*, xlvi (1940), sect. C, pp 1–84; 'Curran Point, Larne, Co. Antrim: the type-site of the Irish mesolithic' in *R.I.A. Proc.*, lvi (1953), sect. C, pp 1–195.
[23] G. F. Mitchell, 'Some chronological implications of the Irish mesolithic' in *U.J.A.*, 3rd ser., xxxiii (1970), pp 3–14; 'The Larnian culture'.

then newly available, proposed a threefold chronological subdivision into Boreal Larnian (6000–5500 bc), represented by the finds from Cushendun and Toome; Atlantic Larnian (5500–3500 bc), represented by Islandmagee; and Ultimate Larnian (after 3500 bc), represented by several coastal and inland sites where there appears to be an overlap with the beginning of the new stone age, or neolithic. Some of the finds from the raised beach sites and from the midland lakes came into this category.

According to Movius the flints of the early Larnian period are small (fig. 2) and are made from carefully prepared cores. Blade implements predominate and were used as cutting tools, scrapers, and points. The forms of these vary from broad, oval, leaf-shaped points to narrow parallel-sided blades. There are some distinctive asymmetrical points (fig. 3). Size varies from 3 to 10 cm, but the majority centre on 6 cm in length. Many leaf-shaped points have their butt ends thinned and narrowed into an incipient tang (fig. 4). Similar points, but usually having a somewhat more developed tang, persist right through the Irish mesolithic and are sometimes found associated with

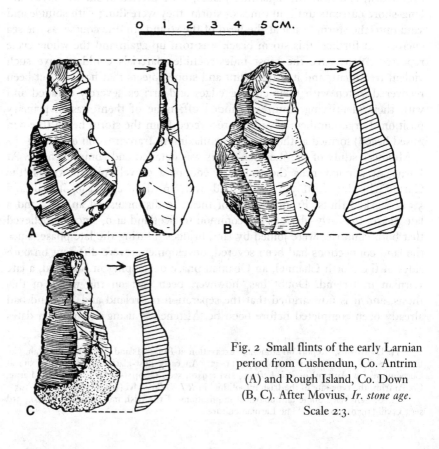

0  1  2  3  4  5 CM.

Fig. 2 Small flints of the early Larnian period from Cushendun, Co. Antrim (A) and Rough Island, Co. Down (B, C). After Movius, *Ir. stone age*. Scale 2:3.

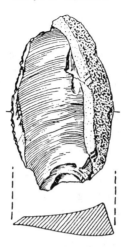

Fig. 3 Distinctive assymetrical points from Cushendun, Co. Antrim. After Movius, *Ir. stone age*. Scale 2:3.

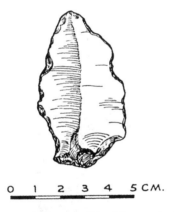

0   1   2   3   4   5 CM.

Fig. 4 Leaf-shaped point with the butt narrowed into an incipient tang, from Curran Point, Co. Antrim. After Movius, *Ir. stone age*. Scale 2:3.

deposits of the succeeding full neolithic age. This is true too of the parallel-sided blades, some of which, as well as the tanged points, have been found in a late phase of the deposits around the edge of the Newgrange tumulus, for instance. The fact that such blades and implements continued to be made virtually to an unchanged pattern for such a long time—they were first noted in the Toome deposits of *c*.6000 bc—shows that they were basic implements, which could satisfactorily be used for a variety of essential tasks. Mounted by fixing the tang into a short wooden handle or even by simply wrapping the butt in moss as in an example from the River Bann, now in the National

Museum of Ireland, they could effectively be used as knives; mounted on shafts, they became hunting spears; mounted in pairs or in groups on a suitably forked branch, they became multi-pronged fish spears. One piece of the timber found at Toome may have had a group of small flints fixed into it to produce a rough serrated knife or to act as barbs in a harpoon-like object. These multi-purpose flints, therefore, are not good subjects on which to hang a typology or a chronology and cannot be taken as characteristic of any particular phase of early man's activity.

Steep or core scrapers are common in the so-called early Larnian (fig. 5) and they persist into neolithic times. These somewhat coarse implements may have been used in woodworking. Notched scrapers (fig. 6), probably used like a spokeshave for shaping wooden arrow shafts, are few but also persist to become the remarkable hollow scrapers of the neolithic age. Perforators or awls occur as already noted, though they are not common. 'Larne picks' (fig. 7) which, properly speaking, were not implements at all but wasters resulting from core rejuvenation, were sometimes used because of their convenient natural shape and size for various kinds of rough working,

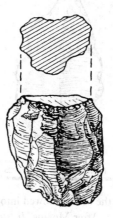

Fig. 5 Early Larnian core-scraper from Rough Island, Co. Down. After Movius, *Ir. stone age*. Scale 2:3.

Fig. 6 Notched scraper from Rough Island, Co. Down. After Movius, *Ir. stone age*. Scale 2:3.

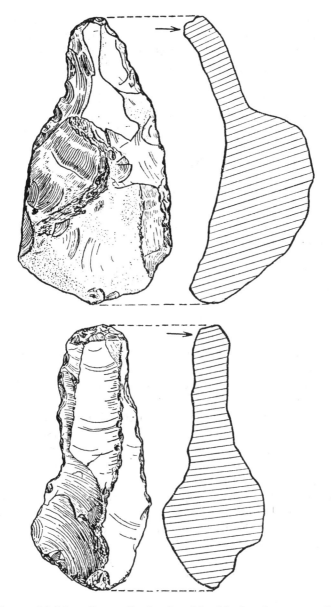

Fig. 7 'Larne picks' from Larne, Co. Antrim. After Movius, *Ir. stone age*. Scale 2:3.

perhaps for hacking down young trees or saplings, more by worrying through them than by cutting, so as to provide timber for the numerous purposes for which this material was needed and must have been used. Cores from which the flake implements were struck are common and usually display a plain striking platform.

All the early Larnian flint types persist into the late phase. Some large flake implements, used mainly as choppers, are found and leaf-shaped points now show a somewhat more developed tang. The notched scrapers, perforators, and awls of the earlier phase are here too. It is clear, therefore, that there is little development or change in the Larnian flintwork from first to last, and the concept of an early and a late phase is not a hard-and-fast one. As a result of observing a flint-knapping demonstration given by M. H. Newcomer to the members of the Quaternary Research Association at a meeting in London in 1971, Mitchell[24] put forward the view that many flints hitherto accepted as deliberately struck implements may in fact be no more than *debitage*. Many leaf-shaped points, simple triangular points, and some parallel-sided blades can therefore now be placed in this category. Chert was also used by mesolithic man. When the level of Lough Gara, a lake on the Sligo–Roscommon border, was reduced by drainage,[25] large numbers of implements in this material, mainly flakes and leaf-shaped points, were found lying on the newly exposed muds. Though chronologically late, they are in the same cultural phase as the flint implements already noted. Similar finds have been made along the banks of lakes in the midlands—such as Lough Kinale, Derravaragh, Iron, and Allen—and are also of late mesolithic age.[26]

More recent consideration of the so-called 'Larnian' horizon has cast serious doubt on its integrity as a genuine archaeological 'culture'. It is now generally held that most of the artefacts present are waste products left behind by flint-knapping activities and that the 'Larnian' is better viewed as representative of an industry rather than a culture. Moreover, it now appears that the Larnian material belongs to a late phase of the Irish mesolithic, which overlaps with the earliest appearance of the neolithic in the country.

Since the late 1970s our knowledge of the mesolithic culture in Ireland has changed dramatically, thanks to the discovery and early dating of a number of important occupation sites. In addition, the synthetic studies of the period carried out by Peter Woodman have very significantly advanced our understanding of the period.[27] It is now clear that the earliest occupation of Ireland

[24] 'The Larnian culture', p. 280.

[25] R. E. Cross, 'Lough Gara: a preliminary survey' in *R.S.A.I. Jn.*, lxxxiii (1953), pp 93–6.

[26] Mitchell, 'Some chronological implications'; 'The Larnian culture'.

[27] P. C. Woodman, 'The chronological position of the latest phases of the Larnian' in *R.I.A. Proc.*, lxxiv (1974), sect. C, pp 237–58; 'The Irish mesolithic/neolithic transition' in S. J. de Laet (ed.), *Acculturation and continuity in Atlantic Europe* (Bruges, 1976), pp 296–307; Woodman, *The mesolithic in Ireland* (Oxford, 1978), and *Excavations at Mount Sandel 1973–77, Co. Londonderry* (Belfast, 1985).

dates to the middle of the eighth millennium bc and that mesolithic settlement in the country was not confined to the north-east but extended to most
areas of the island, to the midlands, the west, and the far south. Today we
refer to an early mesolithic dating roughly from 7500 bc to 6000 bc and a
later mesolithic (which includes the 'Larnian') dating from about 5500 bc to
about 3200 bc.

Material of early mesolithic date has been found at eight or nine sites in
Ireland. The most significant of these are in Londonderry and Offaly, where
excavated sites have produced consistently early dates. The alleged early
dating of a site at Woodpark, County Sligo,[28] has, however, been called into
question by some scholars[29] because of the possibility that fossil wood might
have been used in the dating. Of the Londonderry sites, two at Mount
Sandel near Coleraine on the River Bann have yielded the best information
to date on the Irish mesolithic.[30] At the site known as Mount Sandel Upper,
excavations begun by Woodman in 1977 demonstrated the presence there of a
significant settlement of some permanence. In an artificially extended natural
hollow the remains of at least three roughly circular huts were found, each
about 6 m in diameter and each with traces of a central hearth. The huts,
which represented successive rebuilding on the site, were revealed as rings of
postholes without internal supports, indicating that the original constructions
were of very simple character. As well as the huts a large number of pits
were found at the site and it was possible to isolate specific areas where flint-
knapping had taken place.

The flint industry was dominated by narrow-bladed microliths, a form
unrepresented among the 'Larnian' industries. These are tiny blades, averaging 4 cm in length and generally less than 1 cm in width. Triangular forms
are also known, as well as a series of 'needle-points', micro-awls, and various
types of blades or bladelets. Some of these items might have come from
composite implements. A handful of ground stone axes also came to light
and artefacts of chert, a stone native to more southern areas of Ireland, were
also found.

Not only did Mount Sandel Upper reveal for the first time the house
types of the earliest inhabitants of Ireland, the site also produced important
organic remains, which amplify considerably our picture of their lifestyle.
The bones of wild pig and hare were found, but (significantly) there was no
evidence that the red deer had been hunted. Bird bones were also present but
large quantities of eel and salmon bones suggest that fish was a dominant
element in diet. A variety of seeds and hazelnut shells were also found. A
series of radiocarbon dates from the site ranged from 7010 ± 70 bc to

---

[28] G. Burenhult, *The archaeology of Carrowmore, Co. Sligo* (Stockholm, 1984), p. 64.
[29] E.g. Woodman, *Excavations at Mount Sandel*, p. 169.
[30] Woodman, *Excavations at Mount Sandel*.

6490 ± 65 bc[31] with a concentration in the first two centuries of this period.[32]

Mount Sandel Lower[33] had suffered extensive disturbance and the stratigraphy was greatly disturbed. Mesolithic remains from the site, however, resembled those from Mount Sandel Upper, though a greater quantity of axes occurred there. A section of the site that seems to have been undisturbed yielded a radiocarbon date of 6490 ± 200 bc.[34] A third Derry site, Castleroe, also on the Bann, provided a small amount of archaeological material, as well as hazelnuts and wood charcoal, which provided a radiocarbon date in the first half of the sixth millennium bc.[35]

Another mesolithic site of major importance was found sealed under the raised bog at Lough Boora, County Offaly, and was excavated by Michael Ryan in 1977.[36] There, on a peninsula jutting into the original lake (larger than the modern Lough Boora) a small settlement, which appears to have been a seasonal hunting camp, was discovered. No hut sites were found but hearths occurred. The lithic industry present resembled that at Mount Sandel Upper though the absence of flint in the region meant that chert was the dominant material used. As at Mount Sandel, it was clear that chert artefacts had been manufactured on the spot. The microliths, blades, and cores found at Boora compared closely with those from Mount Sandel and, like the latter, the Offaly site also produced ground stone axeheads.There were also a few scrapers of indifferent quality. Organic remains were also present at Lough Boora. The bones of wild pig, hare, and possibly dog were found and among the bird bones preliminary examination suggests that duck may be represented. Hazelnuts and various seeds were also present.

The close similarities in material culture between Boora and Mount Sandel Upper extends to the dating of the two sites. A series of radiocarbon dates from Boora range from 7030 ± 360 bc to 6525 ± 75 bc.[37] It thus seems evident that, contrary to popular opinion, the earliest inhabitants of Ireland were not confined to coastal regions but from the beginning penetrated deep into the heart of the country. It is likely that many more such early sites await discovery. The question of the origins of these early mesolithic groups remains a matter for debate and, indeed, it is not as yet fully clear to what extent they came to Ireland on foot or in boats. An immediate background for the Irish mesolithic somewhere in western Britain—perhaps southern

---

[31] UB-952; UB-2008.

[32] Woodman, *Excavations at Mount Sandel*, p. 148.

[33] A. E. P. Collins, 'Excavations at Mount Sandel, lower site, Co. Londonderry' in *U.J.A.*, 3rd ser., xlvi (1983), pp 1–22.

[34] UB-532.

[35] Woodman, *Excavations at Mount Sandel*.

[36] Michael Ryan, 'An early mesolithic site in the Irish midlands' in *Antiquity*, liv (1980), pp 46–7.

[37] UB-2268; UB-2199.

Scotland, England, or Wales—is likely and it is not impossible that the first inhabitants of what came to be the island of Ireland arrived by walking.

At the time of writing there is a gap in the archaeological record between the earlier and later mesolithic. The industry of the older period, characterised by fine microliths, is replaced by what is termed a heavy, broad-bladed industry dominated by flint axes, borers, and larger tools suitable for working wood. Sometimes the flakes, having been struck from the core, were employed without further working, but a characteristic feature of this industry is the practice of thinning and narrowing the butt end. At the end of the period one of the basic, recurring types is a leaf-shaped blade, most often of chert, trimmed and retouched at the base on both sides for hafting. This is called a 'Bann flake' and could have been used either as a knife or in a composite implement for spearing or pronging fish. Clearly recognisable projectile heads are absent. All in all the impression is that the late mesolithic culture in Ireland developed along its own insular lines, apparently in increasing isolation from contemporary developments abroad. Over a period of almost three millennia there are few indications of cultural or technological advance.

Numerous occupation sites belonging to the late mesolithic cultural horizon have by now been recognised in Ireland, especially along the eastern coast and on inland sites on Lough Derravaragh, Co. Westmeath, and Lough Kinale, Co. Longford.[38] Perhaps the best dated site of the period, however, is Newferry, County Antrim,[39] situated where the Lower Bann exits from Lough Neagh. Here a sequence of occupation levels has been excavated where they were preserved under thick deposits of diatomaceous soil and peat. These levels seem to represent the temporary, summer resting places of mesolithic fishermen. The occupation sequence, investigated by Woodman in 1970–71, was complex and some of the layers may well have been disturbed by water. The radiocarbon dates indicate, however, that habitation at the site began around or some time before the middle of the sixth millennum bc and continued well into the fourth millennum. Most of the principal types of late mesolithic flints were present.

The final stages of the mesolithic extend to the period when farming was already being introduced into Ireland in the fourth millennum bc. In some instances there is evidence of overlap between the traditional hunter-gatherer way of life of the mesolithic people and the cattle-rearing activities of the neolithic folk. Shell middens, dating to the period of maximum transgression of the sea, are found on the east coast at Rockmarshall, County Louth,[40] and

[38] Mitchell, 'Some chronological implications'; 'The Larnian culture'.
[39] P. C. Woodman, 'Recent excavations at Newferry, Co. Antrim' in *Prehist. Soc. Proc.*, xliii (1977), pp 155–99.
[40] G. F. Mitchell, 'An early kitchen-midden in Co. Louth' in *Louth Arch. Soc. Jn.*, xi (1947), pp 169–74; 'Further early kitchen-middens in Co. Louth', ibid., xii (1949), pp 14–20.

Sutton[41] and Dalkey Island,[42] County Dublin. At Rockmarshall broken flint pebbles and roughly struck flakes were found among the shells. At Sutton, as well as Bann flakes and other typically late mesolithic forms, some polished stone axes were found and at least one bone of a domesticated ox. Both these sites were dated by radiocarbon to around the middle of the fourth millennium bc. Neither produced any neolithic pottery. At Dalkey, however, as well as flints of mesolithic character, there were sherds of western neolithic pottery and some bones of domesticated animals. At this site there is evidence of continuity into the full neolithic. Recent investigations by Woodman on shell middens near Ballyferriter in County Kerry have revealed occupation debris, similar to that described above, which seems also to date to the transition between the middle and the new stone age.[43] The mesolithic culture in Ireland was thus a long-lived phenomenon, which spread in time to most areas of the country. There is evidence at some sites of gradual change to a farming economy. The extent to which the fully developed Irish neolithic culture was a product of immigrating population groups remains, however, a matter for debate.

[41] G. F. Mitchell, 'An early kitchen-midden at Sutton, Co. Dublin' in *R.S.A.I. Jn.*, lxxxvi (1956), pp 1–26; 'Further excavations of the early kitchen-midden at Sutton, Co. Dublin', ibid., cii (1972), pp 151–9.
[42] G. D. Liversage, 'Excavations at Dalkey Island, Co. Dublin, 1956–9' in *R.I.A. Proc.*, lxvi (1968), sect. C, pp 53–233.
[43] P. C. Woodman, M. A. Duggan, and A. McCarthy, 'Excavations at Ferriter's Cove: preliminary report' in *Kerry Arch. Soc. Jn.*, xvii (1984), pp 5–19.

CHAPTER IV

# Neolithic Ireland

M. J. O'KELLY

THE palaeobotanical evidence from pollen counts has already been mentioned, wherein elm pollen decreased and that of the weeds of light increased. Despite the fact that this is open to a number of interpretations[1] besides the straightforward ones that elm shoots may have been used as cattle fodder and that, since these trees usually grew on good ground, they were removed to provide pasture, the alteration in the hitherto prevailing ecological pattern must signify a corresponding change in man's behavioural pattern. These pollen changes antedate 3000 B.C. in many cases. Indeed, recent investigations at Ballyscullion, County Antrim,[2] Cashelkeelty, County Kerry,[3] and elsewhere indicate that agriculture was already being practised early in the fourth millennium B.C.

At Ballynagilly, County Tyrone, a site excavated between 1966 and 1971, elements were revealed of considerable interest and importance in the context of early neolithic activity in Ireland.[4] The focal point of the site was a rectangular house 6.5 m × 6 m, marked by foundation trenches and postholes. The trenches contained the burnt bases (20 cm high) of radially split oak planks which had formed the walls. A shallow pit may have provided the material for clay daub with which the wood may have been plastered. This was the first find of walls of this type in Ireland in a neolithic context, though they are well known in central Europe. Radiocarbon dates of 32l5 ± l25 bc[5] were obtained for the house. Older dates, the averages of which lie between 3700 and 3800 bc, were obtained from charcoal in hearths and pits in the habitation area. These are among the oldest dates so far obtained for neolithic material anywhere in these islands.

---

[1] Above, p. 56, notes 16, 17.
[2] A. G. Smith, 'Neolithic and bronze age landscape changes in Northern Ireland' in *The effect of man on the landscape: the highland zone* (London, 1975), pp 64–74.
[3] Ann Lynch, *Man and environment in south-west Ireland* (Oxford, 1981).
[4] A. M. ApSimon, 'An early neolithic house in Co. Tyrone' in *R.S.A.I. Jn.*, xcix (1969), pp 165–8; A. G. Smith, J. R. Pilcher, and G. W. Pearson, 'New radiocarbon dates from Ireland' in *Antiquity*, xlv (1971), pp 97–102.
[5] UB-199.

As a result of palaeobotanical studies carried out at Ballynagilly in conjunction with the excavations, it was ascertained that ribwort plantain appeared in the pollen record about 2900 bc. This plant is usually found in open grassland conditions; and since cereals do not appear to have been present at this time at Ballynagilly, it seems likely that the land was still being used for pasture. This activity lasted until about 2600 bc when the forest took over once more. About the year 2000 bc, however, the area was again settled with the arrival of Beaker people, who set up a mixed farming economy in which pastoralism was combined with grain cultivation. Two of the 'axe factories', which provided man with the means to tame the woodland, are known in the north-east of the country, at Tievebulliagh mountain in County Antrim and on Rathlin Island off the northern coast of the county.[6] They consist of sites where rough-outs of axes were made on the spot from pieces broken from the parent outcrop. At both these places, the rock is a close-textured porcellanite, blue-grey in colour with white or black specks, and is very suitable for axe manufacture. Thousands of rough-outs have been collected in areas from which the covering peat has become eroded. Many of them are flawed and broken, which is not surprising as the best specimens would no doubt have been taken away by the axe-makers for finishing at home by grinding and polishing with sand and water. Axes made from these outcrops of Antrim porcellanite are superior to those of flint because they are harder and less friable, and the cutting edges more lasting. Finished axes from these factories are well known not only in various parts of Ireland but in Britain also, at places as far apart as the south-east of England, the north of Scotland, and the outer Hebrides. The Irish factories have their counterparts at Mynydd Rhiw, Graig Lwyd, and Prescelly, all in Wales, at Great Langdale in Cumberland, and elsewhere. As the products of the British factories have also been identified in Ireland, the axe-trade must betoken widespread movement between the two countries, with all that this implies in the way of transference of culture and ideas.

Investigations at Tievebulliagh have shown that the rough-outs lie on clay in the base of a layer of peat that began to form over them at the beginning of the sub-boreal phase.[7] In Jessen's view there cannot have been a long interval between the deposition of the clay and the beginning of the growth of peat, so that a round figure date of 3000 bc is postulated. A like result has been obtained from Rathlin Island.[8] Here a settlement site marked by hearths

[6] E. M. Jope, 'Porcellanite axes from factories in north-east Ireland' in *U.J.A.*, 3rd ser., xv (1952), pp 31–60; Etienne Rynne, 'Two stone axeheads found near Beltany stone circle, Co. Donegal' in *R.S.A.I. Jn.*, xciii (1963), pp 193–6; P. R. Ritchie, 'The stone implement trade in third-millennium Scotland' in J. M. Coles and D. D. A. Simpson (ed.), *Studies in ancient Europe* (Leicester, 1968), pp 117–36.
[7] Knud Jessen, 'Studies in late quaternary deposits and flora-history of Ireland' in *R.I.A. Proc.*, lii (1949), sect. B, pp 142–3.
[8] Movius, *Ir. stone age*, p. 228.

and containing flints of late mesolithic form was excavated, not far from the porcellanite outcrop. A fragmentary, partly ground, and polished porcellanite axe was found in the same horizon, as was some pottery comparable to that already mentioned in connection with the sandhill sites and the Bann diatomite.[9]

WHAT activities marked this new way of life in its early stages? Man would first of all have begun hacking into the scrub and woodland with axes, making clearings or cutting access paths through it to less densely wooded areas where pasturage could be provided for his domesticated cattle, sheep, and goats. Wheat and barley are being sown, perhaps in the ash of deliberately fired undergrowth. The women are fashioning pottery vessels from clay found suitable for the purpose. It is refined by various treatments until round-bottomed bowls for use as containers and as cooking pots can be shaped by hand and fired. Whence came these new practices and skills?

It is generally assumed that this new way of life was introduced into Ireland entirely by newcomers to our shores, and that only after the passage of time were certain elements of it copied or acquired by the mesolithic people, who being hunters were, it is said, especially conservative. They are generally envisaged as beachcombers incapable of advancement, living in stagnant helplessness on the sea and lake shores. The mixtures of the old and the new that have been found in such places as the Bann diatomite and the sandhill settlements have been accredited to 'Larnians' who had, almost reluctantly as it were, adopted some things from invading or colonising neolithic people. While this may in some measure be true, it is probably a gross oversimplification. One could just as well argue that the evidence betokens neolithic people who had adopted the fishing expertise that the mesolithic people most certainly had developed. Late mesolithic man may have been travelling by boat to Britain and places further away to trade the good Antrim flint, Tievebulliagh axes, animal skins, smoked salmon, and other kinds of cured fish from Ireland. On his return, he may have put into practice some of what he had seen abroad, and this may account for the fact that there are so many differences of detail between the earliest Irish pottery,

[9] The effectiveness of neolithic land-clearance technique has been strikingly demonstrated in recent years by the discovery of an extensive system of field enclosures, sealed by blanket bog, at Behy/Glenulra in north-west Mayo (Seamus Caulfield, 'Belderg Bog, Co. Mayo' in T. G. Delaney (ed.), *Excavations 1973* (Belfast, 1973), pp 17–18; Caulfield, 'Neolithic fields: the Irish evidence' in *Early land allotment in the British Isles* (Oxford, 1978), pp 137–43; and Caulfield, 'The neolithic settlement of north Connaught' in *Landscape archaeology in Ireland* (Oxford, 1983), pp 196–215). The enclosures were formed of long parallel stone walls joined by cross walls to create fields of surprisingly large size. In the course of continuing investigations it has been shown that at least 250 hectares of land were so divided (Caulfield, personal communication), thus indicating the former presence in north Mayo of highly organised and socially cohesive cultural groupings. A number of neolithic settlement enclosures, clearly related to the fields, have also been found.

for instance, and those north British and continental ceramics with which, nevertheless, the Irish material must belong.[10]

There is no reason to think that he was not quick to realise the advantages of having control over a herd of tame animals that could be killed for food as needed. If he had observed such a practice abroad, why should he not have brought home a few calves to Ireland? It may be that it was in this way the bones of domesticated ox found their way into the upper levels of some of the raised beach deposits. If he once saw a grain crop grown, harvested, and brought into use as food, why should he not have brought home some seed corn to plant here himself? If, on the other hand, these practices were introduced by immigrant settlers, he would soon have joined forces with them in the production of extra supplies. Everything points to the immediate establishment of peaceful relationships between the late mesolithic folk and the small communities of neolithic foreigners who no doubt did come and settle here, some of them indeed invited or led there by travelling Irish hunter-gatherers. Almost everywhere that evidence of neolithic activity has been found, the mesolithic tanged points with thinned and narrowed butts, the parallel-sided blades, the steep scrapers, and the now perfected hollow scrapers, which had been developed from the cruder mesolithic prototypes, are also present. There is little doubt, however, that the seeds for the first corn crops grown in Ireland were imported, whether by native mesolithic people or neolithic newcomers. Likewise too, the first of our domesticated cattle, sheep, goats, and probably also pigs were brought into the country, though the latter could perhaps have been domesticated from the native wild pig.[11] The earliest neolithic of Ireland, particularly that of the north-east, appears to be closely connected with that of north Britain. Yorkshire provides the best parallels for the early shouldered-bowl pottery, and in turn there are connections from there across the North Sea to Europe.[12] It seems very likely, therefore, that the earliest neolithic immigrants came into northeast Ireland across the Irish Sea from north Britain, and the whole pattern of forest clearance and land taking (*landnam*) here must stem ultimately from a European background north of the Alps rather than from the western Mediterranean or south-west Europe via the supposed 'Atlantic seaways'.[13]

---

[10] H. J. Case, 'Foreign connections in the Irish neolithic' in *U.J.A.*, 3rd ser., xxvi (1963), pp 5, 12.

[11] Ibid., p. 5.

[12] H. J. Case, 'Irish neolithic pottery: distribution and sequence' in *Prehist. Soc. Proc.*, xxvii (1961), pp 174–233; 'Foreign connections'; and 'Neolithic explanations' in *Antiquity*, xliii (1969), pp 176–86.

[13] T. G. E. Powell, J. X. W. P. Corcoran, Frances Lynch, and J. G. Scott, *Megalithic enquiries in the west of Britain* (Liverpool, 1969), p. 247. The wide question of the origins of the Irish neolithic remains controversial. See, for example, John Waddell, 'The invasion hypothesis in Irish prehistory' in *Antiquity*, lii (1978), pp 121–8, and Michael Herity and George Eogan, *Ireland in prehistory* (London, 1977), for conflicting views.

FROM the shores of Lough Gur in the east of County Limerick comes the best evidence so far found of Irish houses built during the neolithic period. The Lough Gur landscape still embodies features that must have made it attractive to the early settlers. A small lake lies within a bowl of limestone hills covered with a light soil and divided up by sheltered valleys; the soil is warm even in winter, and when cleared of scrub would have been suitable for small-scale primitive tillage, and in due time would have supported a thriving cattle-raising economy even as it does today. During the course of several seasons of excavation S. P. Ó Ríordáin uncovered the remains of at least ten houses of neolithic age that had stood in ones and twos here and there in close proximity to the lake edge.[14] While variant house plans were recorded, the standard forms were circular and rectangular, and both types were being built and lived in contemporaneously (fig. 8).

Fig. 8 Reconstruction of round and rectangular houses from Knockadoon, Lough Gur, Co. Limerick (Cork Public Museum). After *Cork Public Museum guide*.

[14] S. P. Ó Ríordáin, 'Lough Gur excavations: neolithic and bronze age houses on Knockadoon' in *R.I.A. Proc.*, lvi (1954), sect. C, pp 297–459.

One of the rectangular houses had internal dimensions of 9.70 m × 6.1 m. The floor space had been divided into three aisles by two lines of posts running longitudinally. This may have meant that the centre aisle, which also contained the hearth, was used as the daytime living space, while the side aisles may have been for storage and sleeping quarters. The external walls were probably of mud with stone footings. Lines of posts stood just inside and outside the wall-footings and, together with the internal posts, must have supported the roof structure with its covering of thatch. Quite near this house the remains of another rectangular one was found, and just a little east of them were three circular houses. In two of these the mud wall had been built in the annular space between two concentric rings of wooden posts; in the third a single ring of posts supported the roof and the wall may have been constructed in wattle work, plastered inside and out with mud. Two of the houses had internal diameters of 5.20 m while the third was a little larger at 6.1 m. Where recognisable, the hearth was at or near the centre of the floor, and there were adjacent rubbish pits. Around about these houses were various irregular pits in the old ground surface, from which the mud had been taken for the building of the walls. Subsequently they were used as rubbish pits, and it is from them as well as from pits inside the houses that many of the small finds came.

Important among these objects are the large quantities of pottery sherds recovered. No vessel was found in a complete state, but it proved possible to assemble various individual groups of sherds so that several vessels were reconstructed (fig. 9). In the lowest layers of the refuse in the pits and in the house floors, the sherds belonged to large round-bottomed bowls with exaggerated T-shaped rims which were ornamented with incised patterns. The colour varies greatly from light brown to a very dark red. Some of them had a marked angular shoulder, a feature that concealed the fact that there was a joint in the wall of the pot at this point. The upper part of the vessel, consisting of rim and neck, was joined on to the bowl-shaped lower part at the shoulder. The fabric of these pots is remarkably good and shows that great care was taken in the preparation of the clay. Pieces of the clay found in the deposits show that it was refined until all grit had been removed; special types of grit were then deliberately added. A common material used at Lough Gur was crushed calcite, a white crystalline material available locally; sometimes, too, chopped grass was used in place of grit. Before firing, the pots were burnished with a smooth pebble or with a piece of bone so that well-preserved pieces exhibit polished surfaces. Experiments have shown that the clay itself, derived in some cases from volcanic ash, may have been obtained from a deposit about three miles away from Lough Gur. The vessels are similar in shape to those found in the sandhill settlement sites of north-east Ireland already mentioned.

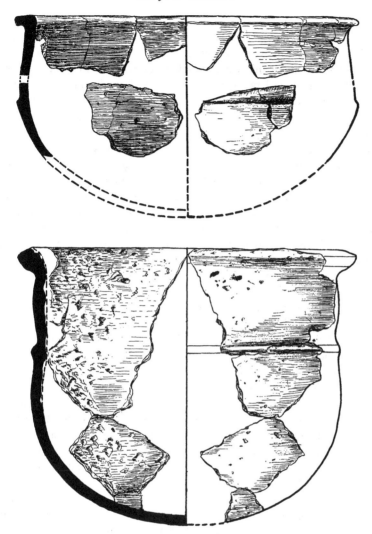

Fig. 9 Reconstructed drawings of Class I pots from Knockadoon, Lough Gur,
Co. Limerick. After S. P. Ó Ríordáin in *R.I.A. Proc.*, lvi, sect. C (1954). Scale 1:3.

Other houses at Lough Gur were found to have been surrounded by
circular enclosures, not for the purposes of defence against human enemies
but to keep the domestic animals out and perhaps prevent some of them—
goats for instance—from climbing on to the thatched roofs.[15] Excavation

[15] For modern publication of older excavations at Lough Gur see Eoin Grogan and George
Eogan, 'Lough Gur excavations by Seán P. Ó Ríordáin' in *R.I.A. Proc.*, lxxxvii (1987), sect. C,
pp 299–506.

revealed that the enclosing wall in these cases consisted of two concentric rings of low contiguous boulders or orthostats, the annular space between them being about 1 m wide. These acted as revetments inside and outside the base of an earthen bank which may have been about 1 m to 1.5 m high. In site K all the structural posts were set into rock-cut postholes. In this case the house was rectangular and the entrance through the circular enclosing bank had been fitted with a gate. Two C l4 dates (D-40 and D-41),which average at 2600 bc ± 240, are available for site L.[16]

The characteristic flint and chert leaf- and lozenge-shaped arrowheads, as well as some hollow-based types, are accompanied by Bann-type points with thinned and narrowed butts and by Larnian parallel-sided blades, so that here also we have a peaceful mesolithic–neolithic union. Bone is well preserved in the limestone soil of Lough Gur and numerous points and pins made from it are common on most of the excavated sites. Well preserved also were animal bones—food waste—of which large quantities were collected. The vast bulk of them were bones of domestic ox; small numbers of pig and sheep were present and there were a few dogs or wolves—it is not easy to distinguish between the bones of these two latter animals. Bones of bear and red deer show that a little hunting was still going on. A number of porcellanite axes from the Tievebulliagh factory have been found in the domestic deposits. As time went on at Lough Gur, the rims of the round-bottomed shouldered bowls became simpler and another type of ware appeared, flat-bottomed bucket-shaped pots which were coarsely and crudely made and sometimes have a crudely scratched ornament below the rim. There are some instances of encrustation (i.e., application of decorative bands of clay to the finished pots). These pots, made from various local clays, usually have large grits, of crushed chert, though some were still gritted with calcite. The colour is mostly a greyish black but there are some shades of brown also. This rough domestic ware eventually became the dominant pottery and the round-bottomed bowls disappeared from the record.

No other neolithic site in Ireland has given such a full picture as has been obtained at Lough Gur. Mention must be made, however, of two others, one in County Meath and one in County Antrim. At Slieve Breagh in County Meath a small group of circular houses has been excavated. In plan these were rather like the circular houses at Lough Gur and had hearths and rubbish pits within them also.[17] On the top of Lyles Hill near Belfast,[18] within a large earthen enclosure, great quantities of sherds of

---

[16] However, 'as both [dates] have very large standard deviations and as this area was one of intensive later activity, they are of limited value in dating the site' (ibid., p. 437).

[17] Liam de Paor and M. P. Ó hEochaidhe, 'Unusual group of earthworks at Slieve Breagh, Co. Meath' in *R.S.A.I. Jn.*, lxxxvi (1956), pp 97–101.

[18] E. E. Evans, *Lyles Hill, a late neolithic site in Co. Antrim* (Belfast, 1953): A. M. Gibson and D. D. A. Simpson, 'Lyles Hill, Co. Antrim' in *Archaeology Ireland*, i, no. 2 (1987), pp 6–10.

round-bottomed shouldered bowls, leaf- and lozenge-shaped flint arrow-heads, and hollow and round scrapers have been found, but no house plans were recovered. In the latest levels there too, the flat-bottomed coarse ware had come into use.[19]

SUCH information as we possess relating to earliest man in Ireland comes first from his weapons and tools and later from the utensils and dwellings he used during life; what happened to his body after death is virtually unknown. No cemetery of tombs or graves has been found for this early period. It is only when farming is well established, when domesticated animals are available for food, when cereal cultivation is a customary activity, that evidence is forthcoming for burial practices, and indeed one is in some measure a corollary of the other. Food production would need to be stabilised and organised before a community could undertake the elaborate structures that characterise some of the burial practices of the middle and later neolithic.[20]

Some 1,400 tombs built of large stones during the middle and late neolithic periods still survive in Ireland, and, having regard to the numbers destroyed in the past and in recent times also, hundreds more must once have existed. These, called megalithic tombs, have been divided into four main types for convenience of nomenclature and to facilitate study, but it must not be imagined that the different classes were mutually exclusive, or that each group was built in splendid isolation from another, or that there

[19] Our knowledge of neolithic house types in Ireland is now augmented by two important discoveries. At Ballyglass, Co. Mayo, the bedding trench for the timber posts of a rectangular house was found beneath the stones of a court tomb (Seán Ó Nualláin, 'A neolithic house at Ballyglass, near Ballycastle, Co. Mayo' in *R.S.A.I. Jn.*, cii (1972), pp 49–57). The house, which appears to have had internal divisions, had dimensions of 13 m × 6 m. Radiocarbon dates for charcoal from the wall slots ranged from 2730 ± 95 bc to 2530 ± 90 bc. More recently two house plans have been uncovered at Tankardstown South, Co. Limerick. House 1 (M. Gowen, 'Tankardstown, Co. Limerick: a neolithic house' in *Archaeology Ireland*, i, no. 1 (1987), pp 6–10, and *Three Irish gas pipelines: new archaeological evidence in Munster* (Dublin, 1988)) was rectangular in plan with dimensions of 7.40 m × 6.40 m. Its walls had been constructed of split oak planks and the roof had originally been supported by two internal posts. A series of radiocarbon dates for the house range between 3155 ± 45 bc and 2890 ± 80 bc. House 2, found some 20 m north-west of House 1, was similarly constructed but was larger with internal dimensions of 15 m × 7.50 m (M. Gowen and C. Tarbett, 'A third season at Tankardstown' in *Archaeology Ireland*, ii, no. 4 (1988), p. 156). It appears to have consisted of a single large room with a narrow annexe at each end. A further recent discovery of great importance for Irish neolithic settlement studies is the double-ditched hilltop enclosure at Donegore, not far from Lyles Hill in Co. Antrim (J. P. Mallory and R. Hartwell, 'Donegore' in *Current Archaeology*, xcii (1984), pp 271–5). The ditches, a few metres distant from one another, extend between the edges of a scarp around the summit of the hill to form an oval enclosure with a maximum internal width of 150 m. Although no house plans have as yet been discovered, large quantities of neolithic pottery and other domestic items have been recovered, indicating that this was a settlement site of some significance. The most interesting aspect of Donegore is, however, the fact that the ditches are interrupted along their length by a series of undug causeways. The enclosure is thus strikingly reminiscent of the well-known 'causeway camps' of the southern English neolithic.

[20] Case, 'Neolithic explanations'.

was no communication between their builders. Indeed the reverse was almost certainly the case as, if one lists the points of similarity rather than the differences, one can argue for a good deal of accord. The four main types were once listed as court cairns, portal dolmens, passage graves, and wedge-shaped gallery graves.[21] Today it is more customary to refer to court tombs, portal tombs, passage tombs, and wedge tombs.

Three hundred and seventy-three of the first are known at present, all of them, save for a half-dozen or so, lying in the northern third of Ireland, with the greatest concentrations in the coastal regions of Mayo, Sligo, and Donegal in the west, and a lesser one in Down and Louth in the east. There is, furthermore, a strong spread of tombs across mid-Ulster between the two areas. Related tombs are found in Scotland and on both sides of the Severn estuary in Britain. The older name 'court cairn' arises from the fact that the tomb chamber or chambers are covered by a cairn or mound of stones, and a court-like area bounded by standing stones or by stone-walling gives access to the tomb. The cairn is on average about 30 m in length and about 15 m wide at the front, narrowing to about half that at the rear. The long straight sides of this trapezoidal structure are usually marked by a revetment of orthostats, though dry-built walling may be present instead. The tomb gallery is situated along the long axis of the cairn and is built of orthostats. About 70 per cent of the tombs consist of two chambers divided from one another by jamb-stones or by jambs and sill-stones, but some three- and four-chambered tombs are also known. The roof was corbelled. In plan the court may be oval, circular, U-shaped, or semi-circular, the two latter being the commonest. Circular or oval courts, 'full courts', as they are sometimes called, are found in the western areas.[22] In the majority of cases the court and gallery are at the broad end of the cairn and face east. There are instances, however, of dual-court tombs, as at Cohaw, County Cavan,[23] and Audleystown, County Down,[24] where a court and tomb-gallery are present at each end of the cairn. Another variant is found where the court occupies a central position and galleries open from it longitudinally, as at Deerpark, County Sligo.

Only thirty-five of the almost 400 known tombs have been excavated and many of this number were only partially examined, so that evidence on the burial rite is, on the whole, unsatisfactory.[25] In the majority of the excavated

---

[21] Ruaidhrí de Valera and S. P. Ó Nualláin, *Survey of the megalithic tombs of Ireland, i: Co. Clare* (Dublin, 1961).

[22] Ruaidhrí de Valera and S. P. Ó Nualláin, *Survey of the megalithic tombs of Ireland, ii: Co. Mayo* (Dublin, 1964), p. 105.

[23] H. E. Kilbride-Jones, 'Double-horned cairn at Cohaw, Co. Cavan' in *R.I.A. Proc.*, liv (1951), sect. C, pp 75–88.

[24] A. E. P. Collins, 'The excavation of a double-horned cairn at Audleystown, Co. Down' in *U.J.A*, 5th ser., xvii (1954), pp 7–56; 'Further work at Audleystown long cairn, Co. Down' in *U.J.A.*, 3rd ser., xxii (1959), pp 21–7.

[25] Michael Herity, 'The finds from Irish court tombs' in *R.I.A. Proc.*, lxxxvii (1987), sect. C, pp 103–281.

sites one cremation only was found in the tomb, and in a number of cases this was a young male. Audleystown, however, one of the dual-court tombs mentioned above, contained thirty-four burials, of which only four were cremations, and Ballyalton, County Down,[26] had eight unburnt burials. Annaghmare, County Armagh,[27] had both burnt and unburnt burials representing possibly four individuals. In cases such as the above, where more than one person is present, it may be questioned whether the deposits were undisturbed. At Annaghmare, for instance, samples of charcoal taken from chambers 2 and 3 gave radiocarbon dates centred on early Christian times, while the forecourt gave a C 14 date of 2445 ± 55 bc.[28] While not proving that the burials in the chambers were late, it at least shows that unsuspected disturbance had taken place. A court tomb at Shalwy, County Donegal,[29] showed traces of early Christian occupation in the form of a hearth, pottery, metalwork, a bone comb, and a glass bead in addition to the customary court cairn assemblage. A charcoal sample from the chamber of a similar site at Shanballyedmond, County Tipperary, produced a radiocarbon date of 100 bc ± 130.[30] Until a demonstrably untouched court tomb is excavated, therefore, it is impossible to declare categorically that these tombs were primarily used for multiple burials. It is also becoming more and more apparent that many megalithic tombs are multi-period structures, and court tombs are no exceptions. Taking into account the subsidiary chambers that are found in the Annaghmare cairn, in the cairn of the very fine monument at Creevykeel, County Sligo, the cairn at Edenmore, County Down, and many others, one must see these as additions to the primary structure, though at which remove in time is not clear in most cases. Total excavation of a site will alone provide the answer, and it is this that has given such convincing results in Scotland, where the premise of multi-period court tombs has for long been accepted.[31]

One such total excavation carried out in Ireland was that of the Shanballyedmond court tomb, and though a multi-period structure was not revealed, several unique details of considerable interest came to light.[32] A funnel-shaped forecourt opened into a two-chamber gallery. The floors of both

[26] E. E. Evans and O. Davies, 'Excavation of a chambered horned cairn at Ballyalton, Co. Down' in *Belfast Natur. Hist. Soc. Proc.* (1933–4), pp 79–104.
[27] D. M. Waterman, 'The court cairn at Annaghmare, Co. Antrim' in *U.J.A.*, 3rd ser., xxviii (1965), pp 2–46; A. G. Smith, J. R. Pilcher, and G. W. Pearson, 'New radiocarbon dates from Ireland' in *Antiquity*, xlv (1971), pp 97–102.
[28] UB-241.
[29] L. N. W. Flanagan, 'The excavation ... of a two-chambered court-cairn in Shalwy townland' in *R.I.A. Proc.*, lxviii (1968), sect. C, pp 23–4.
[30] D-52.
[31] J. X. W. P. Corcoran, 'Multi-period construction and the origins of the chambered long cairn in western Britain and Ireland' in Frances Lynch and Colin Burgess (ed.), *Prehistoric man in Wales and the west: essays in honour of Lily F. Chitty* (Bath, 1972), pp 31–64.
[32] M. J. O'Kelly, 'A horned-cairn at Shanballyedmond, Co. Tipperary' in *Cork Hist. Soc. Jn.*, lxiii (1958), pp 37–72.

court and gallery were flagged. The gallery was surrounded by a U-shaped setting of non-contiguous standing stones joined to one another by dry-walling. Outside this post-and-panel type of revetment was a feature not found hitherto in any type of megalithic tomb in Ireland, namely a series of thirty-four postholes set in a U-shaped plan conforming to the U-shape of the post-and-panel revetment. The ends of this setting of postholes curved inward to connect with the outermost orthostats of the forecourt so as to form (on plan) an approximately flat façade at each side of the court entrance. There was a single cremation burial, that of a youth between 10 and 15 years of age. It lay in a partly stone-lined pit in the floor of the inner chamber. The finds at Shanballyedmond were characteristic of court tombs generally. These are round-bottomed bowls, with or without ornament; sometimes the pots are shouldered, sometimes not. Coarse flat-bottomed bucket-like ware is also present in some cases. The characteristic flints are leaf- and lozenge-shaped arrowheads and hollow scrapers, all of which are known at the habitation sites of Lyles Hill and Lough Gur, although only a single hollow scraper was found at the latter place.

It is argued by some that court tombs are the earliest of the megalithic tombs in Ireland and were introduced by the same immigrants that introduced farming. None of the excavated sites has so far upheld this theory, and such few meaningful radiocarbon dates as exist are of middle and late neolithic rather than early neolithic date. In a number of instances burnt areas, spreads of charcoal, stakeholes, and postholes have been found in the forecourts, and beneath the cairns also when sufficiently exhaustive investigations have taken place. In the past these have been interpreted as the preliminary clearing of the site by burning of the scrub and woodland before the work of erecting the tomb began; in other cases, they have been interpreted as evidence of ritual or as the site of the cremation pyre. These features can usually be better explained as being indications of pre-existing neolithic habitations, a point clearly demonstrated at Ballyglass, County Mayo, where the foundations of a timber house were found under a court tomb.[33] Until or unless radiocarbon dates and related evidence consonant with an early neolithic date are forthcoming, court tombs must be regarded as a burial practice originating in the middle neolithic.[34]

About 163 portal tombs are known in Ireland, and again, the majority are found in Ulster in much the same areas as the court tombs, though they are not so plentiful in the west.[35] Important numbers of them are found also

[33] Above, p. 77, n. 19.
[34] But see now Michael Herity, 'The finds from Irish court tombs' in *R.I.A. Proc.*, lxxxvii (1987), sect. C, pp 156–9.
[35] Ruaidhrí de Valera, 'The court cairns of Ireland' in *R.I.A. Proc.*, lx (1960), sect. C, pp 64–9; S. P. Ó Nualláin, 'Irish portal tombs: topography, siting, and distribution' in *R.S.A.I. Jn.*, cxiii (1983), pp 75–105.

along the eastern side of the country as far south as Waterford and along the western part as far south as County Clare. One example is known near Rosscarbery in County Cork. Similar tombs are known in Wales and Cornwall and perhaps also in the Cotswold–Severn region in England. The Irish Sea area of distribution is well documented by Frances Lynch.[36] The portal tomb has a straight-sided chamber, often narrowing towards the rear. The entrance is marked by a pair of tall stones or portals which are set inside the line of the side slabs. A single slab, often of enormous size, covers the chamber, resting on the high portal stones at the front and sloping steeply down towards the rear where it is supported either by the back stone of the chamber or, in some cases, by a second and lesser capstone which is in turn supported by the chamber orthostats. Usually a closing slab is recessed between the portals; sometimes it consists of a low sill or of a septal slab rising to the full height. The tombs tend to face east but not invariably so. The cairns are not well preserved as a rule, but there is evidence for both long and round forms. It has been demonstrated in Britain, however, that the long cairns are sometimes in the nature of additions to smaller round cairns, as at the portal dolman at Dyffryn Ardudwy in Wales.[37] Once again, only complete excavation will elicit the full story.

The evidence regarding the burials or the burial rite is not good, as few sites have been scientifically excavated.[38] An example excavated at Ballykeel, County Armagh,[39] produced typical portal tomb finds, that is, an assemblage much the same as that from court cairns—round-bottomed shouldered bowls plain or decorated, leaf-shaped arrowheads, and hollow scrapers.

Portal tombs, usually sited in low-lying positions, are impressive and striking to the eye, mainly because of the large capstone, poised high on the portal stones and sloping steeply back toward the rear of the tomb. Good examples such as that at Knockeen, County Waterford, or Leac an Scáil at Kilmogue in County Kilkenny, remind one when seen in profile of a great ship thrusting forward against the tide. Evans, like de Valera and Ó Nualláin, maintained that the portal tomb was an indigenous development, which began perhaps in central Ulster as a derivative of the court cairns. Archaeologists on the other side of the Irish Sea regard matters from a different angle and make a case for a starting-point in Cornwall, Ireland and Wales being on the receiving end of the movement. Frances Lynch, for instance, wrote: 'The presence of strikingly similar portal dolmens in both countries [Ireland and

[36] F. M. Lynch, 'The megalithic tombs of North Wales' in Powell, Corcoran, Lynch, & Scott, *Megalithic enquiries in the west of Britain*, p. 46.
[37] T. G. E. Powell, 'The chambered cairn at Dyffryn Ardudwy' in *Antiquity*, xxxvii (1963), pp 19–24.
[38] Michael Herity, 'The finds from the Irish portal dolmens' in *R.S.A.I.Jn.*, xciv (1964), pp 123–44.
[39] A. E. P. Collins, 'Ballykeel dolmen and cairn, Co. Armagh' in *U.J.A.*, 3rd ser., xxviii (1965), pp 47–70.

Wales] reveals that contact must have been close, whether it was a case of derivation one from the other, or of two parallel streams emanating from some common source as yet unidentified.'[40] Recent estimates[41] place the number of passage tombs somewhere between 150 and 300. They are mainly situated in the central east–west third of the country although examples occur both north and south of this area. Passage tombs differ from other types of megalithic tomb in that they tend to be situated on high ground and to be grouped in cemeteries. The four main cemeteries are in the Boyne Valley in County Meath; on the Loughcrew hills, also in County Meath; at Carrowkeel on the Bricklieve Mountains in County Sligo; and at Carrowmore, also in County Sligo.[42]

Probably the best known cemetery is that which lies within a bend of the River Boyne between Slane and Drogheda in County Meath. Here in an area 3 miles by 1 mile (5 km × 1.6 km) are the three great mounds of Newgrange,[43] Dowth,[44] and Knowth,[45] together with the numerous small mounds, most of which are likely to be passage tombs. The three great mounds, all of much the same dimensions (that is to say, covering about an acre (0.4 hectares) of ground and approximately 280 feet (85 m) in diameter), are strikingly situated on hilltops and can be seen in silhouette against the sky from many vantage-points in the neighbourhood. Knowth is about three-quarters of a mile (1.2 km) north-west of Newgrange, and Dowth is about the same distance to the east. If one stands on the top of any of the three one can see the other two therefrom. While as yet only one tomb is known in the Newgrange cairn, Knowth contains two and Dowth has two.

Immediately west of Newgrange on the shoulder of the same hill are two small mounds called K and L, both of which have been excavated. Mound L, though severely damaged more than a century ago by the insertion into it of a lime kiln, was found to contain a passage-tomb with a cruciform plan. A number of its decorated stones have survived, some from the chamber and some from the kerb, and these are now in the National Museum in Dublin as they could not be preserved satisfactorily on the site. Mound K was found to cover a simpler type of chamber, but the site as a whole had a very complex

[40] Lynch, 'Megalithic tombs of North Wales', p. 169.
[41] S. P. Ó Nualláin, 'The megalithic tombs of Ireland' in *Expedition*, xxi, no. 3 (1979), pp 6–15; George Eogan, *Knowth and the passage tombs of Ireland* (London, 1986), pp 24–5.
[42] Michael Herity, *Irish passage graves* (Dublin, 1974).
[43] M. J. O'Kelly, *Newgrange: archaeology, art, and legend* (London, 1982); M. J. O'Kelly, F. M. Lynch, and Claire O'Kelly, 'Three passage graves at Newgrange, Co. Meath' in *R.I.A. Proc.*, lxxviii (1978), sect. C, pp 249–352.
[44] M. J. O'Kelly and Claire O'Kelly, 'The tumulus at Dowth, Co. Meath' in *R.I.A. Proc.*, lxxxiii (1983), sect. C, pp 135–90.
[45] George Eogan, 'Excavations at Knowth, Co. Meath' in *R.I.A. Proc.*, lxvi (1968), sect. C, pp 299–400; 'Pins of the Irish late bronze age' in *R.S.A.I. Jn.*, civ (1974), pp 74–119; *Excavations at Knowth I* (Dublin, 1984); and *Knowth & passage tombs of Ire.*

building history of at least three phases. It also contained a number of carved stones.

As well as these, there are at least ten other sites worthy of investigation in the immediate vicinity of Newgrange, some of them passage tombs. There are a possible four passage tombs in the Dowth area, while about a mile and a half (2.4 km) to the north there is a small tumulus in Monknewtown and a passage tomb (site T) excavated by Eogan[46] which has been in the grounds of the Townley Hall estate. Immediately around the perimeter of Knowth, seventeen small mounds have been uncovered by excavation; all of them originally covered graves of passage-tomb type, some simple in plan, some cruciform; the plans of a few others were difficult to determine on account of damage.

There are two plain standing stones of large size on the edge of the river terrace to the south-east of Newgrange. In addition, two decorated stones from different locations in the Dowth townland have been brought in for safekeeping, one to the Newgrange Information Centre, and the other to the Newgrange enclosure.

Twenty-five miles (40 km) to the west of Newgrange, on the Loughcrew hills above Oldcastle, is another important cemetery where twenty-five tombs survive in various states of preservation. These tombs are magnificently situated and some of them can be seen from a long way off. All of them except cairns L and T are severely damaged, but twelve contain carved slabs. Cairns L and T, which contain important carvings, have had their damaged roofs restored.

In Sligo on the west coast of Ireland, there are two cemeteries, one on Bricklieve mountain, better known as Carrowkeel, where there are fourteen tombs, and the other at Carrowmore where thirty-four monuments now survive in various states of dilapidation out of an original sixty-five. The rock of Bricklieve mountain is horizontally bedded limestone, and the weathering-out of this into deep glens, with some remarkable vertical cliff features, provides most unusual topographical background for the tombs, some of which are dramatically situated on peaks with cliff sides. The cemetery lies in an area of great scenic beauty. Carrowmore, on the other hand, lies on a low-lying gravel ridge, though each individual monument in the group stands on its own little eminence. From here too the scenic views are extensive and a dominant feature of the landscape is Knocknarea mountain, also curiously shaped because of the horizontal bedding of its limestone and on top of which is a huge unopened cairn that may cover a passage tomb.

Apart from these great groups there are lesser concentrations and individual tombs elsewhere, the most northerly instances being in Donegal and

[46] George Eogan, 'A neolithic habitation site and megalithic tomb at Townleyhall townland, Co. Louth' in *R.S.A.I. Jn.*, xciii (1963), pp 37–81.

Antrim, the most southerly being in the east of County Limerick and in County Waterford. County Cork seems to have had one site; all that remains is a single decorated stone which is now preserved in the Cork Public Museum. The site was on the island of Cape Clear just off the south-west coast of the county.

The name 'passage tomb' comes from the nature of the tomb, which consists of a passage of varying length leading into a chamber which may be circular as at Dowth South; oval as at Fourknocks, County Meath; polygonal as at cairn G at Carrowkeel; trapezoidal or rectangular as at Listoghill in the Carrowmore cemetery. Often, two side cells and an end cell open off the chamber to give a cruciform plan to the whole as at Newgrange and Four-knocks. More complex plans also occur and these, and the cruciform ones, seem to be an Irish development of a practice that had already begun on the Continent where tombs with one or two side cells or pairs of transepts are known. The tombs are built of orthostats and the chambers are usually roofed in the corbel technique, though small chambers may have capstones laid directly on the orthostats. One excavated site, Fourknocks, which had an unusually large oval central chamber, was roofed partly in corbelled stone and finished in timber, this part having been supported on a centrally placed wooden post.[47]

Without exception, Irish passage tombs are found in circular cairns which vary in diameter from about 85 m in the largest to as little as 8 m (site W at Loughcrew) in the smallest examples. Many cairns are now much denuded, having been used as stone quarries in the past, but several are remarkably well preserved and a few remain to a height of 12 m or more. Most of them seem to have had massive orthostatic kerbs (plate 1). Among the exceptions to this are Fourknocks and the Mound of the Hostages at Tara, County Meath. Entrances to passage tombs face in all directions, but a preference was shown for an approximately south-east orientation.

The older excavations, of which there were about thirty, were unscientific and badly recorded, but the information from them and from a number of recent investigations gives some notion of the burial practice. Cremation seems to have been the normal rite in Ireland, though unburnt primary burials are also known. The skeletal material was placed in the side and end cells of the cruciform tombs, and on the floor of the passage and chamber in the less elaborate types. In about twelve tombs there are one or more shallow stone basins and the bones were presumably laid into these. The evidence from Fourknocks indicated that all the bones, representing at least twenty-four people, had been put into the tomb at one time—a single collective burial—after which it was closed. Similar evidence has come from the

---

[47] P.J. Hartnett, 'Excavation of a passage grave at Fourknocks, Co. Meath' in *R.I.A. Proc.*, lviii (1957), sect. C, pp 197–227; 'The excavation of two tumuli at Fourknocks (sites II and III), Co. Meath' in *R.I.A. Proc.*, lxxi (1971), sect. C, pp 35–89.

passage tomb known as the Mound of the Hostages at Tara. The most recent evidence is from Newgrange.[48] The cremated and unburnt bone fragments of a small number of people—perhaps four or five—were found embedded in the floor of the tomb chamber, but this may represent only a fraction of the original deposit, since the tomb has been open since 1699 and we do not know how much may have been removed as souvenirs or during cleaning-out operations in the interior.

A distinctive group of objects is found mixed through the masses of bone in Irish passage-tombs. The pottery, usually called Carrowkeel ware after the Sligo cemetery, is a coarsely made round-bottomed fabric of poor quality with much incised and jabbed ornament. Bone pins occur, some of them very long and made from deer antler, the best known of which are the 'mushroom' or 'poppy-head' types. Others have a herring-bone pattern carved on the shanks. Stone beads and pendants are also found, the pendants being particularly characteristic. These are hammer- or pestle-shaped, like those at Newgrange (fig. 10). Also noteworthy are the 'marbles', small spheroids made from Antrim chalk which is hard enough to take on a very smooth surface, amounting to a polish in some cases. As well as several of these chalk examples, Newgrange has produced two marbles made from serpentine. Among the small finds from passage tombs, however, perhaps the most spectacular item is the beautifully decorated macehead from Knowth.[49]

As in the case of the court cairns, there is clear evidence from some passage-tomb excavations that the sites on which they stand had already been habitation areas. At site T, at Townley Hall, County Louth, the tomb and its covering mound masked an intensively occupied area.[50] Mound L, just west of Newgrange, was built on a site previously inhabited by people using the

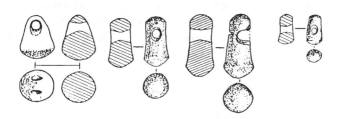

Fig. 10  Hammer-shaped pendants from Newgrange, Co. Meath. After
M. J. O'Kelly in G. Daniel and P. Kjaerum (ed.), *Megalithic graves and ritual*
(1973). Scale 1:2.

[48] The most comprehensive, up-to-date picture of passage-tomb culture comes from the extended and continuing excavations at Knowth, Co. Meath (above, p. 82, n. 45).
[49] George Eogan and Hilary Richardson, 'Two maceheads from Knowth, Co. Meath' in *R.S.A.I. Jn.*, cii (1982), pp 123–38; Eogan, *Knowth & passage tombs of Ire.*, pp 141–2, plate X.
[50] Above, p. 83, n. 46.

characteristic neolithic round-bottomed shouldered-bowl pottery. They had abandoned the site and the turf had grown over their debris before the passage tomb was built. The main Newgrange mound itself overlies pits connected with earlier activity on the hilltop. The Mound of the Hostages at Tara stands on a ditched enclosure already abandoned at the time the tomb was built.

It has frequently been suggested in the past that the background of the Irish passage tombs lies in Iberia where cemeteries of such tombs also occur, as for instance the very well known one at Los Millares in south-east Spain. Basin stones are known in a few Iberian tombs such as that at Castraz, Ciudad Rodrigo,[51] but the best is the rectangular example in the tomb at Matarubilia, Seville. This, perhaps, can be compared with the rectangular basin in the central chamber at Dowth North, County Meath. Furthermore, the poppy-head bone or antler pins, such as those from Carrowkeel, are best paralleled in Portugal.[52] But against this must be set evidence from France. The limestone pendants with helical groove from Cairn G, Carrowkeel,[53] seem to be closely paralleled by the numerous similar pendants from dolmens in the Hérault region of southern France.

In the absence of a sufficiency of radiocarbon dates for the Iberian tombs closest in form to the Irish examples, the derivation of the latter from Iberia cannot be conclusive for the present. On the other hand, in view of the very early C 14 dates obtained for some of the passage tombs in Brittany, *c.*3300 bc, or earlier, it may be that passage-tomb building had its origin there and spread southwards to Iberia and northwards to Ireland, Wales, Scotland, and Scandinavia. C 14 dates for the tomb structure at Newgrange centre on 2500 bc while those from the Mound of the Hostages centre on 2000 bc.[54]

Almost 400 wedge tombs have been recorded, and (while they are the most widespread of all types of megalithic tomb) their distribution has a marked southern bias,[55] 190 of them being in this part of the country, in the counties Cork, Kerry, Limerick, Clare, and Tipperary. The pattern is all the more worthy of note when it is realised that in the same five counties there are only

---

[51] G. and V. Leisner, *Die Megalithgräber der Iberischen Halbinsel; der Süden* (Berlin, 1943), p. 286.

[52] Eogan, *Knowth & passage tombs of Ire.*, pp 208–11.

[53] T. G. E. Powell, 'The problem of Iberian affinities in prehistoric archaeology around the Irish Sea' in Frances Lynch and Colin Burgess (ed.), *Prehistoric man in Wales and the west* (Bath, 1972), pp 93–106.

[54] Most of the radiocarbon dates from the Knowth tombs, like those from Newgrange, cluster around the middle of the third millennium bc (Eogan, *Knowth & passage tombs of Ire.*, pp 225–6). A series of early fourth-millennum bc dates from the Carrowmore, Co. Sligo, cemetery remain controversial (G. Burenhult, *The archaeological excavations at Carrowmore, Co. Sligo, Ireland, L977–9* (Stockholm, 1980); Burenhult, *The archaeology of Carrowmore, Co. Sligo* (Stockholm, 1984); Eogan, op. cit., p. 226; M. J. O'Kelly, *Early Ireland* (London, 1989), pp 107–9).

[55] De Valera & Ó Nualláin, *Survey of megalithic tombs*, i and iv.

four court tombs, five portal tombs, and two passage tombs. The remaining wedges are distributed throughout the areas in which the main concentrations of the other types of megalith occur. The name arises from the fact that the tomb is usually wedge-shaped both in plan and in longitudinal profile; that is, it is wider and higher at the end containing the entrance, usually the west or south-west. The wedges, therefore, are orientated in the opposite direction to that of the court cairns. The gallery is built of orthostats and roofed with slabs resting on them; corbelling proper does not occur.

It has been customary to divide the wedge tombs into two sub-groups, northern and southern wedges, so called at a time when it was thought the two sub-types had a mutually exclusive distribution, the one group in the northern part of Ireland, the other in the south.[56] It is now clear that this pattern is not correct, and in abandoning it some archaeologists have abandoned altogether the subdivision of the class. This, however, is to take up a position on the opposite extreme, because such a subdivision remains a valid concept even if the old names and patterns of spread are to be changed.

A good example of the northern type was excavated at Island, near Mallow, County Cork.[57] The tomb chamber consisted of a U-shaped orthostatic gallery wider at the entrance than at the east end, and it was entered between two tall portal stones. A second U-shaped setting of orthostats was placed outside the gallery at about a metre distant; the ends of its arms were joined with those of the tomb gallery by orthostats set so as to give a more or less flat façade to this part of the monument. Further settings of orthostats gave a more marked wedge shape to the western part of the monument. To close the spaces between the ends of these outermost lines of orthostats and the ends of the outer U, two further orthostats were added to the façade. Outside this again were the sockets of a setting of non-contiguous orthostats which would presumably have been joined to one another by dry-walling, and which would have formed a revetment to the edge of the covering cairn. This was round-heeled in plan and flat in front so as to conform with the flat façade of the tomb. In front of the façade, sockets for stones were found which would have marked off a semi-circular area in front of the entrance. The overall length of the monument was 11.5 m and the greatest width 9.5 m. A single non-structural stone stood near the southern portal, and the portico area itself was marked off from the chamber proper by a single jambstone standing forward of the north side of the gallery, and by a very low sill. In some northern wedges another chamber is formed at the east end of the gallery by means of a dividing slab. Sometimes, too, the façade is slightly curved. Average length is in general from 10 to 15 m.

---

[56] Ruaidhrí de Valera, 'A group of "horned cairns" near Ballycastle, Co. Mayo' in *R.S.A.I. Jn.*, lxxxi (1951), pp 178–9.

[57] M. J. O'Kelly, 'A wedge-shaped gallery grave at Island, Co. Cork' in *R.S.A.I. Jn.*, lxxxviii (1958), pp 1–23.

A southern wedge tomb is well exemplified at Baurnadomeeny, County Tipperary, where total excavation of the site was very rewarding.[58] The tomb gallery was in two parts, the portico at the west end being completely cut off from the chamber by a high septal slab. This is a customary feature of the southern wedge, and sometimes, too, there is a small closed cell at the east end of the gallery. The front edge of the portico was marked by a low sill and the roof was supported on two free-standing pillars set on the axial line. The chamber was well constructed of double walling, and a series of vertical buttresses stood against each side of the tomb. The closing stone at the east end of the tomb had not survived. It was roofed by means of capstones. The edge of the covering cairn had been marked by large slabs set in a circle, the tomb being centrally placed within it so that when complete it would have been completely hidden by the covering cairn. The tomb measured 7 m × 3.6 m and the cairn was 15 m in diameter.

From the above two examples it will be seen that similarities as well as differences exist between the two types. Unfortunately, despite being the most numerous class of megalithic monument, very few examples have been excavated, only twenty-five in all, and since some produced no finds it is difficult to be dogmatic about the finds or about the nature of the burial rite. Cremation appears to have predominated but unburnt burials have been found side by side with cremated examples. Six cremations are known from Baurnadomeeny, and the gallery at Island was closed after two or three cremations had been inserted. Of the excavated sites, no primary pottery is reported from seven, beaker pottery has been recorded from six, and in the case of ten other sites it is not possible to say how much of the pottery may be secondary.[59] Three tombs produced tanged-and-barbed arrowheads.

The coarse flat-bottomed ware of the court tombs and of Lough Gur and Lyles Hill is known from a number of wedges, as also are food vessels and urns, but these latter, like the beaker ware, are probably secondary insertions. Because of the occurrence of beaker there has been a tendency to think of the wedges as being the latest of the megalithic tombs, and for some the only radiocarbon date so far obtained for a wedge, 1160 bc ± 140[60] for Island, supports this view.[61] Nevertheless, the evidence as it stands at present is not sufficient to establish beakers as a primary element of wedges, let alone categorise them as monuments that 'belonged to a widespread and numerous beaker-using community'.[62]

---

[58] M. J. O'Kelly, 'A wedge-shaped gallery grave at Baurnadomeeny, Co. Tipperary' in *Cork Hist. Soc. Jn.*, lxv (1960), pp 85–115.
[59] De Valera & Ó Nualláin, *Survey of megalithic tombs*, i, 114.
[60] D-49.
[61] Two more recent radiocarbon determinations for samples from the same tomb are in keeping with this surprisingly late dating (O'Kelly, *Early Ire.*, p. 123).
[62] De Valera & Ó Nualláin, *Survey of megalithic tombs*, i, 116.

So far, no certain example of a wedge has been found in Britain; one must look elsewhere for related structures if it is not accepted that they are an indigenous development. De Valera and Ó Nualláin find prototypes for them in the Brittany region, seeing in the small antechambers and in the outer-walling of some of the *allées couvertes* of this area parallels to the porticos and the double walling of the Irish examples. They note also that beaker occurs in some of the Breton tombs, but here, however, its occurrence is generally regarded as secondary. When one compares small-scale plans of the monuments in both areas, close similarities certainly seem to exist, but in the field these are not nearly so compelling. In the view of some, the wedge tombs are an indigenous Irish development from the passage graves.[63]

How is all this tomb building activity to be related to what we already know of the neolithic period in Ireland? It is known that the megalithic tombs were built by communities practising stock-raising and cereal cultivation. Indeed some would have it that the court-tomb builders 'evidently came in sufficiently large numbers to establish the new traditions and appear to have brought both livestock and seed corn (wheat and barley)'.[64] As already stated, however, there is no dating evidence so far for the court tombs sufficiently early to warrant this proposition. As yet, no tomb in Ireland, of any type, has been dated as early as the beginning of farming, something that must now be envisaged perhaps at least as early as 3800 B.C., on the Ballynagilly evidence.[65] As a result of the Newgrange excavations it is known that cereal agriculture had already been introduced into the area before the tomb was built and that the surroundings were composed of woodland and open spaces. Even the very nature of the monument itself and of the neighbouring ones at Knowth and Dowth would seem to warrant, by their sheer size and elaborateness, the presence of a stable organised community able to provide a sizeable workforce.

Was tomb-building a normal part of the neolithic way of life from the beginning in Ireland or was it a cult practice that found ready adherents when its tenets had been promulgated? The cult, if such it was, is poorly represented at Lough Gur and not at all at Lyles Hill, two of the most prolific Irish settlements of the period. It would seem that megalithic tombs were not intended merely as repositories for the dead, but rather as houses in which the spirits of the dead would continue to live for a very long time, and so the most durable materials had to be used in order that the house should last for ever. Hence the great stone slabs in contradistinction to the ephemeral materials, wood and thatch, used for the houses of the living.

---

[63] E. A. Shee, 'Three decorated stones from Lough Crew, Co. Meath' in *R.S.A.I. Jn.*, cii (1972), pp 224–33.

[64] Ruaidhri de Valera, 'Neolithic' in *Encyclopedia of Ireland* (Dublin, 1968), p. 68.

[65] A. G. Smith, J. R. Pilcher, and G. W. Pearson, 'New radiocarbon dates from Ireland' in *Antiquity*, xlv (1971), p. 97.

It seems also that the tombs were built for special people only. The cult must have been practised over a long period of time, probably for 500 years or more. Ruaidhrí de Valera gave court tombs a life of 1,000 years, but this presupposed a beginning earlier than has so far been demonstrated by the C 14 dates. If one brings the number of tombs up from the surviving 1,400 to, say, 1,700 to allow for all those destroyed, and if these are spread over 500 years, this gives an average building rate of three or four per year.[66] One need not then see the tombs as the result of large colonising or invading forces but rather as a practice implanted here and there by a small group led by an accomplished preacher who addressed a mixed population of mesolithic and neolithic folk.[67]

This interpretation can also explain the difference in tomb types not only in Ireland but outside it as well. Once the missionary implanted the idea of the building of a house for the special dead people and had indicated the general form which, according to his sect, it should take, the details of construction were largely a matter for the builders. In this way local variations and exuberances easily came into being, and this must be why it is so difficult to find really close parallels for tombs as between one area or country and another. Passage tombs are known in Spain, Portugal, France, Britain, Ireland, and Scandinavia, and while a basic thread of recurrent features connects them all, not many tombs in Ireland are exactly or even closely paralleled in one of the other areas—each tomb was an individual effort. Nevertheless, passage tombs make the strongest claim to be regarded as the international tomb-type.

Court tombs as we know them in Ireland do not occur on the Continent, and while they are similar to tombs in Scotland and on both sides of the Severn estuary, there are important differences of detail. The strong coastal concentration of court tombs has given rise to arguments as to whether the builders arrived in force on the east coast of Ireland and spread westward or vice versa. But are such arguments legitimate? If a group of tombs is on or near the coast, does this necessarily mean that they were built by people who had lately come in from the sea? Is it not possible that such concentrations merely mean that coastal land was more amenable to settlement because, let us say, forest growth had been inhibited by the salt-laden winds from the sea?

The Sligo passage tombs have been said to be the degenerate offspring of tombs first built in Ireland by people who arrived by sea on the east coast and who gradually spread westward across Ireland. But surely this is a

---

[66] De Valera's original estimate seems today more realistic, and may, indeed, be conservative. This does not, however, detract from O'Kelly's central argument though, of course, we have no way of knowing how many tombs once existed in the country.

[67] See R. C. Reed, 'Irish court tombs: a minimum colonisation model' in *Journal of Irish Archaeology*, iv (1987–8), pp 1–6, for a recent discussion of this problem.

doubtful concept. There is nothing degenerate about the Carrowkeel tombs—indeed, their builders showed great expertise and resource. The fact that they are different in some details from some of those on the east and that they contain no art need not mean any more than that they were built by people who had a slightly different notion of how the house-for-the-dead idea should be carried into effect; and if the builders arrived by sea at all, they are as likely to have come in on the west as on the east, or indeed at several places at the same time.

One can now identify the remains of a single cruciform passage tomb in the Carrowmore cemetery. Otherwise, the tombs of this group are somewhat different from the rest of the Irish passage tombs, but this is not to say that they are degenerate or devolved structures. Indeed, the simplest of them bear some resemblances to the simplest passage tombs of Scandinavia, particularly to those of Denmark, but the more complex Carrowmore tombs differ in many respects from Danish monuments that at first sight might appear comparable. The superficial similarities are probably due to the fact that glacial boulders have been used at Carrowmore and in Denmark as building material.

Because some passage tombs occur in the Dublin–Wicklow mountains— the gold and copper-bearing area—and because some wedge tombs in the south-west are near the copper ore deposits, it has been argued that their builders were attracted to the particular areas by the presence of these minerals, but there is no evidence that this was so. No metal object of any kind has been found in a primary position in any Irish passage tomb and the same is true of the wedge tombs, because all of the supposed metal associations with them can be questioned. It should be remembered that the county that has the greatest number of wedges, Clare (over 100 of the tombs), has no known copper deposits.

Because the wedge tombs are found on hill slopes of medium height above the sea level up to levels above the present-day cultivation line, it has also been argued that their builders were herdsmen who occupied these levels because they provided sufficient grazing on which to winter their cattle.[68] It is difficult to prove or disprove this, for the presence of the tombs in such areas does not necessarily mean that the people who built them lived or herded animals anywhere near them. Obviously, the several issues raised by these megalithic structures will not be answered until many more of them have been fully excavated. There has been too much sampling of sites, too much find-seeking in the chambers, and not enough exploration of the cairns and what lies beneath them.

A number of non-megalithic single-grave burials are now known, which have in the past been regarded as dating to the late neolithic and as

---

[68] De Valera & Ó Nualláin, *Survey of megalithic tombs*, i, 11, 112, 116.

foreshadowing the single-grave rite of the early bronze age. These are known as Linkardstown-type burials.[69] One of the most recently discovered examples is that at Jerpoint West, County Kilkenny,[70] where a large polygonal cist stood at the centre of a tumulus composed of a central cairn of stones covered by a mound of turves. The cist contained the remains of two people, one burnt, the other unburnt, both placed in the grave at the same time. The finds included several pottery vessels, a bone pin, and a leaf-shaped arrowhead. One biconical vessel was round-bottomed and decorated with channelled ornament and had six lugs below the shoulder. A second vessel was an undecorated, round-bottomed shouldered bowl typical of the Irish neolithic.

The interesting group of burials found at Rathjordan, County Limerick,[71] may be grouped with the above as may those from Caherguillamore in the same county;[72] Drimnagh, County Dublin;[73] Norrismount, County Wexford;[74] Martinstown, County Meath;[75] and Rath, County Wicklow.[76] In recent times examples have been excavated in Wicklow,[77] Carlow,[78] and Tipperary.[79]

[69] So named after a classic example excavated in Co. Carlow (Joseph Raftery, 'A neolithic burial in Co. Carlow' in *R.S.A.I. Jn.*, lxxiv (1944), pp 61–2; S. P. Ó Ríordáin, 'Prehistory in Ireland, 1937–46' in *Prehist. Soc. Proc.*, xii (1946), pp 149, 158, pl. xi: 4). Almost all commentators have up to recently accepted these neolothic single burials as belonging to an advanced stage of the stone age (e.g. Barry Raftery, 'A prehistoric burial mound at Baunogenasraid, Co. Carlow' in *R.I.A. Proc.*, lxxiv (1974), sect. C, p. 311; Michael Herity, 'Irish decorated neolithic pottery' in *R.I.A. Proc.*, lxxxii (1982), sect. C, pp 283–5). However, on the basis of several new radiocarbon dates, which after calibration centre on the mid-fourth millennum bc, a far earlier dating for the group has been argued (A. Brindley, J. N. Lanting, and W. G. Nook, 'Radiocarbon dates from the neolithic burials at Ballintruermore, Co. Wicklow, and Ardcrony, Co. Tipperary' in *Journal of Irish Archaeology*, i (1983), pp 1–9). The matter remains controversial.
[70] M. F. Ryan, 'The excavation of a neolithic burial mound at Jerpoint West, Co. Kilkenny' in *R.I.A. Proc.*, lxxiii (1973), sect. C, pp 107–27.
[71] S. P. Ó Ríordáin, 'Excavation of a barrow at Rathjordan, Co. Limerick' in *Cork Hist. Soc. Jn.*, lii (1947), pp 1–4, and 'Further barrows at Rathjordan, Co. Limerick', ibid., liii (1948), pp 19–31.
[72] John Hunt, 'Prehistoric burials at Caherguillamore, Co. Limerick' in Etienne Rynne (ed.), *North Munster studies* (Limerick, 1957), pp 20–42.
[73] H. E. Kilbride-Jones, 'The excavation of a composite tumulus at Drimnagh, Co. Dublin' in *R.S.A.I. Jn.*, lxix (1939), pp 190–220.
[74] A. T. Lucas, 'Neolithic burial at Norrismount, Co. Wexford' in *R.S.A.I. Jn.*, lxxx (1950), pp 155–7.
[75] P. J. Hartnett, 'A neolithic burial from Martinstown, Kiltale, Co. Meath' in *R.S.A.I. Jn.*, lxxxi (1951), pp 1–5.
[76] E. Prendergast, 'Prehistoric burial at Rath, Co. Wicklow' in *R.S.A.I. Jn.*, lxxxix (1959), pp 17–29.
[77] Joseph Raftery, 'A neolithic burial mound at Ballintruermore, Co. Wicklow' in *R.S.A.I. Jn.*, ciii (1973), pp 214–19.
[78] Barry Raftery, 'A prehistoric burial mound at Baunogenasraid, Co. Carlow' in *R.I.A. Proc.*, lxxiv (1974), sect. C, pp 277–312.
[79] P. F. Wallace, 'A prehistoric burial mound at Ardcrony, Nenagh, Co. Tipperary' in *N. Munster Antiq. Jn.*, xix (1977), pp 3–20; Conleth Manning, 'A neolithic burial mound at Ashley Park, Co. Tipperary' in *R.I.A. Proc.*, lxxxv (1985), sect. C, pp 61–100.

Other megalithic monuments that undoubtedly began to be built in the late neolithic period and continued to be built and used in the succeeding metal age are standing stones and stone alignments. One or two very tall standing stones have had cist graves at their bases. In one case the 5.2 m high monolith in the Long Stone Rath at Furness, County Kildare, marked a cist-grave containing the fragmentary remains of two people. Unfortunately a few sherds of pottery found in the cist were of an indeterminate nature, but another object, a stone wrist-guard, may mean that this was a beaker interment.[80] The Punchestown Long Stone, County Kildare, also marked a cist grave, this one of bronze-age type, but there were no diagnostic grave goods.[81]

To the east-south-east of Newgrange, and visible from it, are two standing stones as already mentioned. The area around the base of the larger one, stone C in Coffey's survey, has been excavated,[82] and while some eighty pieces of flint were found, there were no diagnostic objects. Because the field had been tilled repeatedly in the past, it is not certain that any of these finds was directly associated with the standing stone, especially since similar flints can be picked up in any ploughed field in the area. The date and purpose of erection, therefore, remain indeterminate.

The alignments that are found in several parts of Ireland are often very remarkable monuments.[83] They usually consist of five or six tall orthostats set a couple of metres apart in a straight line lying approximately east and west and on the top of a ridge, so that from many points of vantage they are seen in silhouette against the sky. The tallest stone—examples 6 m high are known—is at the east end of the line, and the heights decrease gradually to the west end. No alignment has been excavated, and in the absence of other evidence it is assumed that they were ritual sites.[84]

AN aspect of megalithic tombs that has not so far been mentioned, although it is the one for which they are best known, is the presence in some passage tombs of carved motifs and patterns to which the name 'passage-tomb art' is given, though it may justly be argued that the word 'art' is a misnomer in a majority of cases since no organised design is perceptible or even perhaps intended. The motifs are picked, or occasionally, incised, on the structural stones by means of a sharp point, perhaps of quartz or flint. There is no

[80] R. A. S. Macalister, E. C. R. Armstrong, and R. Ll. Praeger, 'A bronze age interment near Naas' in *R.I.A. Proc.*, xxx (1913), sect. C, pp 351–60.
[81] H. G. Leask, 'The Long Stone, Punchestown, Co. Kildare' in *R.S.A.I. Jn.*, lxvii (1937), pp 250–52.
[82] E. A. Shee and D. M. Evans, 'A standing stone in the townland of Newgrange, Co. Meath' in *Cork Hist. Soc. Jn.*, lxx (1965), pp 124–30.
[83] Seán Ó Nualláin, 'Stone rows in the south of Ireland' in *R.I.A. Proc.*, lxxxviii (1988), sect. C, pp 179–256.
[84] Ann Lynch, *Man and environment in south-west Ireland* (Oxford, 1981), and 'Astronomy and stone alignments in south-west Ireland' in D. Heggi (ed.), *Archaeoastronomy in the Old World* (Cambridge, 1982), pp 205–13.

evidence from any Irish passage tomb that metal tools were known or employed.

The devices are geometrical in concept and non-representational, and while it is probable that they are symbolic, religious, or magical in content, it is unlikely that we will ever discover what any of them meant, since we cannot know the minds or the emotions of a people who did not know how to write and who are separated in time from us by more than four thousand years. Needless to say, speculations as to the meanings of various devices are many, but it must be remembered that the interpretations offered are not only purely personal, but are conditioned by the strength of the interpreter's imagination and by the climate of thought and psychology in which he has grown up. Recent studies of passage-tomb art in Ireland[85] have shown that there is a fairly restricted range of motifs that commonly occur. There is no means of knowing whether the carvings were meant to be art in our modern sense of the term or even whether they were thought of as ornament or decoration. In some instances, it is obvious that the carver was aware of the shape of the slab and that he laid out an overall pattern to fit the available space. The outstanding example of this is the entrance stone (K1) at Newgrange where an integrated pattern of lozenges, spirals, and concentric arcs was exactly fitted not only into the outline of the stone but also to its surface curvature. This carving is regarded as one of the great achievements of prehistoric art in western Europe. The kerbstone no. 52, which is diametrically opposite the entrance stone, has much of the same quality and may well have been carved by the same master hand. Other examples at Newgrange that bear patterns designed to fit the respective stones are the relief saltire on the leading edge of the lintel of the roof box, and the 'false relief' pattern of lozenges, triangles, and zigzags on a corbal in the western cell of the tomb. The entrance stone of the western tomb at Knowth has an organised pattern of boxed rectangles fitted to the shape of the stone,[86] and the Fourknocks stones lettered a, b, c, e, and f are other good examples.[87] For the rest, there are individual devices of high quality such as the S-spiral on kerbstone 67, or the three-spiral design in the end chamber at Newgrange,[88]

---

[85] Claire O'Kelly, 'Passage-grave art in the Boyne valley, Ireland' in *Prehist. Soc. Proc.*, xxxix (1973), pp 354–82; E. A. Shee, 'Some examples of rock-art from Co. Cork' in *Cork Hist. Soc. Jn.*, lxxiii (1968), pp 144–51; E. A. Shee-Twohig, *The megalithic art of western Europe* (Oxford, 1981); Michael Herity, *Irish passage graves* (Dublin, 1974), pp 89–116; Eogan, *Knowth & passage tombs of Ire.*, pp 146–76; M. O'Sullivan, 'Approaches to passage tomb art' in *R.S.A.I. Jn.*, cxvi (1986), pp 68–83, 'The art of the passage tomb at Knockroe, County Kilkenny' in *R.S.A.I. Jn.*, cxvii (1987), pp 84–95, and 'A stylistic revolution in the megalithic art of the Boyne valley' in *Archaeology Ireland*, iii, no. 4 (1989), pp 138–42.

[86] George Eogan, 'Excavations at Knowth, Co. Meath' in *R.I.A. Proc.*, lxvi (1968), sect. C, plate XXXIX.

[87] P. J. Hartnett, 'Excavation of a passage grave at Fourknocks, Co. Meath' in *R.I.A. Proc.*, lviii (1957), sect. C, pp 224–7.

[88] Claire O'Kelly, 'Passage-grave art in the Boyne valley', fig. 8.

the remarkable 'sundial' stone in the kerb at Knowth, the wheel-like motifs on a kerbstone at Dowth, or the rosette-like devices on stone 8 in the chamber of cairn T at Loughcrea; but as well as these, there are many items that can only be looked upon as doodles or graffiti executed by prentice hands in moments of idleness, so carelessly are they done in comparison with the best formal work described above.

In Ireland passage-tomb art is found in the Boyne cemetery, in the Loughrea cemetery, in Fourknocks, and in the Mound of the Hostages, all in County Meath; at Seefin and Baltinglass, both in County Wicklow; at Sess Kilgreen and Knockmany, both in County Tyrone; and at Carnanmore in County Antrim. In the Boyne valley at present, nineteen decorated tombs are known, comprising upwards of 300 decorated slabs. The greatest concentration is at Knowth, and since the work there is continuing, more decorated slabs will undoubtedly be forthcoming.

In addition to the above there are eight decorated slabs not now associated with any structure. Three of these have already been mentioned: the two slabs from Dowth townland and the one from Clear Island. Others are from Sess Kilgreen; King's Mountain, County Meath; Tournant, County Wicklow; Drumreagh, County Down; and Lyles Hill, County Antrim.[89] Decoration is not found at either of the two Sligo cemeteries, Carrowkeel and Carrowmore, though one site, Cloverhill, in the latter is often mentioned as an example of passage-tomb art. The structure itself is not a passage tomb and the devices do not resemble anything in the repertoire of passage-tomb art. They appear to be of the early iron age or of the early Christian period.

It is strange that none of the other Irish types of megalithic tomb have any comparable art work. One court tomb at Malinmore, County Donegal, has some picked designs on two structural stones, but like those on the Clover Hill structure at Carrowmore, County Sligo, these appear to be of the iron age or the early Christian period. A number of the wedge tombs have artificial cup-marks on some of their capstones, but there are no picked devices that would compare with those of the passage graves. In two instances, Baurnadomeeny, County Tipperary, and Scrahanard, County Cork, there are crudely incised criss-cross patterns on structural stones.[90] The Baurnadomeeny example is certainly ancient but there is some doubt about the other.

The inspiration for the art devices on Irish passage-tombs, no less than their *raison d'être* in the first place, is one of the most discussed questions in Irish archaeology. Two main continental sources are proposed, Brittany and Iberia, with a leaning towards the former because the early dates from Breton passage tombs are more in keeping with the 2500 B.C. date of Newgrange. A

---

[89] E. A. Shee, 'Three decorated stones from Lough Crew, Co. Meath' in *R.S.A.I. Jn.*, cii (1972), pp 224–33.

[90] M. J. O'Kelly, 'A wedge-shaped gallery grave at Baurnadomeeny, Co. Tipperary' in *Cork Hist. Soc. Jn.*, lxv (1960), p. 91.

few motifs such as circles, arcs, and zigzags are common to both Breton and Irish passage tombs; but spirals, for example, which are such a prominent feature of the Irish art and are so much to the fore at Newgrange, occur on one Breton tomb only, and an atypical one at that, on the island of Gavrinis in the Gulf of Morbihan; incidentally, they do not occur at all in Iberia. While the idea or cult may have come from these south-western European shores to Ireland, the evidence compels us to assume at this stage of our knowledge of the problem that the Irish art developed along its own lines and that it is therefore largely a native product.

COMPARABLE with some of the art of the passage-tombs is what is called 'rock art', so named because it is found on natural rock exposures and out-crops. The best and most prolific examples of it are found in the south-west of Ireland in the counties of Cork and Kerry[91]—where, incidentally, no passage tombs are known. Instances occur in at least sixteen other Irish counties also, and it is well known in the north of England and in Scotland. In rock art, as in the art of the passage tombs, the devices are picked in the majority of instances and probably with the same kinds of tools, flint and quartz points. There is some incised rock-art, but the status of this is not established and it is possible that some or all of the known instances are recent or modern graffiti.

In rock art, single circles and multiple concentric circles occur as in the passage-tomb repertoire. Cup-marks are very common in rock art and are present also, even if not frequently, in passage tombs. In Scotland some radial patterns, ovals, and spirals are found in rock art, but do not occur in the rock art of Ireland. It has been customary in Ireland to assign rock art to the bronze age mainly because of decorations that occur on the capstones of three cist graves. These have been found at Ballinvally, County Meath,[92] at Moylough, County Sligo,[93] and at Hempstown Commons, County Kildare.[94] These decorations are, however, more closely allied to passage-tomb art than to rock art.[95] Rock art has also been found on standing stones, and these have been thought of, again for no very good reason, as bronze-age monuments when in fact they may just as well be of neolithic date. Some of the art on the backs of kerb-stones at Newgrange and also on the upper surfaces of the passage roof slabs resembles some of the rock art. The resemblances between rock art and that of the passage tombs outside the Boyne valley, Loughcrew for instance, are as close, and it may well be that rock art derives from that of

[91] Eoin MacWhite, 'A new view on Irish bronze-age rock-scribings' in *R.S.A.I. Jn.*, lxxvi (1946), pp 59–80.
[92] John Waddell, 'Irish bronze age cists: a survey' in *R.S.A.I. Jn.*, c (1970), p. 126.
[93] H. Morris, 'Ancient graves in Sligo and Roscommon' in *R.S.A.I. Jn.*, lix (1929), p. 113.
[94] P. J. Hartnett, 'A crouched burial at Hempstown Commons, Co. Kildare' in *R.S.A.I.Jn.*, lxxx (1950), p. 193.
[95] Shee, 'Three decorated stones from Lough Crew, Co. Meath'.

the passage tombs, the rock artists concentrating on and developing particular motifs while ignoring others.[96] It has been argued too that Irish rock art had its immediate origin in the rock art of Galicia in north-west Spain, this in turn deriving from the Mediterranean. But the reverse may well be the case—Galician art may have been influenced from Ireland, because certain of the devices commonly found there seem more closely related to Irish rock art than to anything which precedes them in Iberia. A full corpus of the Irish material is needed before finality can be reached.

[96] E. A. Shee and M. J. O'Kelly, 'The Derrynablaha "shield" again' in *Cork Hist. Soc. Jn.*, lxxvi (1971), pp 72–6.

# CHAPTER V

# Bronze-age Ireland

## M. J. O'KELLY

THE clear-cut divisions of early times into stone age, bronze age, etc., that were once used in an attempt to categorise and catalogue early man's activities, require modification today. The more excavation and study that are undertaken, the more blurred become the dividing lines between one period and another. Although many scholars have discarded the old nomenclature, they have been forced to substitute other descriptive terms for them, so that in effect the divisions remain and only the names are altered. It is proposed here to retain the old divisions, employing the terms 'bronze age', etc., but in the knowledge that a good deal of so-called bronze-age activity actually took place before bronze was in use, just as neolithic activity took place in areas such as the shores of the River Bann, in the north of Ireland, before the implications of a neolithic way of life had fully dawned. It is proposed to deal first with some of the earliest signs of change in the neolithic way of life. One of these was the introduction at about 2000 B.C. of a type of pottery known as beaker ware. The best of these vessels were made to a high standard of quality. A fine clay was used, and though the pots were entirely hand-made the walls were thin and the firing was well done. Before firing, ornament was neatly put on by impressing a cord or comb stamp into the soft clay, the resulting geometrical patterns being arranged in horizontal zones in one type (B or bell beakers), and in panels in another (A or necked beakers) (fig. 11). The most recent classification of beakers is that proposed by D. L. Clarke,[1] which is based on a corpus of nearly 2,000 beaker finds in Britain and Ireland. He distinguishes seven beaker groups intrusive to Britain, and a number of locally evolved forms. Five of the intrusive groups reached Ireland through Britain.[2]

---

[1] D. L. Clarke, *The beaker pottery of Great Britain and Ireland* (Cambridge, 1970).
[2] A. M. ApSimon, 'An early neolithic house in Co. Tyrone' in *R.S.A.I. Jn.*, xcix (1969), pp 165–8; but see also J. N. Lanting and J. D. van der Waals, 'British beakers as seen from the Continent' in *Helinium*, xii (1972), pp 20–46.

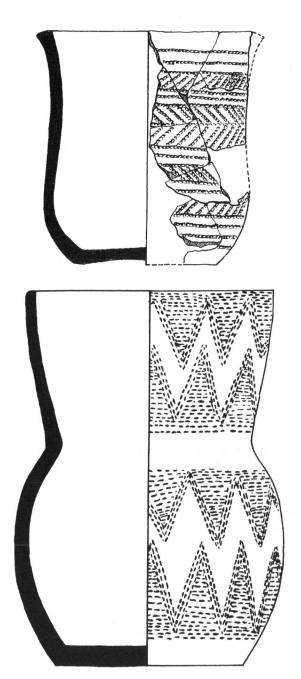

Fig. 11 Reconstruction drawing of a B or bell beaker from Moytirra West, Co. Sligo, after Cremin Madden, in *Kerry Arch. Soc. Jn.*, i (1968), and an A or necked beaker from Grange stone circle, Co. Limerick, after S. P. Ó Ríordáin in *R.I.A. Proc.*, liv, sect. C (1951–2). Scale 1:2.

The Beaker folk[3] had spread widely over much of Europe and Britain at about 2000 B.C., and some groups crossed from Britain to Ireland, to the northern half mainly, though there were those who found their way to Lough Gur in the south. While the neolithic inhabitants of that area were still making round-bottomed shouldered bowls and using flat-based coarse-ware cooking pots, the Beaker people came among them, peacefully it would seem. No specific Beaker house has been identified at Lough Gur. The beaker sherds are intermixed in the later neolithic strata and it must be assumed that the domestic arrangements of their makers did not differ appreciably from those of the native Lough Gur people. It has been suggested that Beaker people came to Ireland direct from the Continent also; from Brittany and the Rhine. Three groups of early bell beakers have been found near the Ballynagilly settlement, which appear to be related to the beakers of the north and middle Rhine;[4] and beaker sherds found at Moytirra, County Sligo, may be akin to certain beakers in north-west France.

Beaker males were bowmen who tipped their arrows with flint points of tanged-and-barbed form and used wrist-guards, carefully shaped rectangles of stone, perforated at the ends so that they could be tied to the wrist to protect it from the recoil of the bowstring. While the arrowheads are widely dispersed in Ireland, the wrist-guards are found in the northern half only.[5] An example from County Kildare has already been mentioned. Perhaps, too, they were the users of the flint objects usually called '*petit tranchet* derivative arrowheads'—in reality, tanged knives—and polished flint knives of discoidal form (fig. 12). These last two types of implement are known mainly in the north of Ireland as chance finds, but recently several of them have been found in the Beaker settlement that was set up around the edge of the Newgrange mound after it had fallen into disuse. Other objects that may have been introduced by the Beaker people are perforated stone hammers and stone axe-hammers or battleaxes. These occur as chance finds in various parts of Ireland (fig. 13), but in 1969 a perforated stone hammer was found in the Newgrange Beaker settlement.

The Beaker people are credited with having had close association with the knowledge of, and the search for, metal. Wherever they had gone in Europe

[3] The use of the term 'Beaker folk' has come under considerable scrutiny in recent times, and it is no longer clear to what extent the spread of Beaker cultural traditions across Europe reflects significant population movement (e.g. Colin Burgess, *The age of Stonehenge* (London, 1980), pp 62, 63). It would, however, be quite naive to deny that the dissemination of Beaker elements across wide areas of the Continent, and over the seas to Britain and Ireland, did not involve some migration, a point admitted even by D. L. Clarke ('The Beaker network—social and economic models' in *Glockenbecher Symposion, Oberried 1974* (Bussum and Haarlem, 1976), p. 474).

[4] ApSimon, art. cit.

[5] Peter Harbison, *Bracers and V-perforated buttons in the Beaker and food-vessel cultures of Ireland* (Bad Bramstedt, 1976).

Fig. 12 *Petit tranchet*-derivative arrowheads from Lough Eskragh. Co. Tyrone. After
A. E. P. Collins and W. A. Seaby in *U.J.A.*, xxiii (1960), p. 34. Scale 1:2.

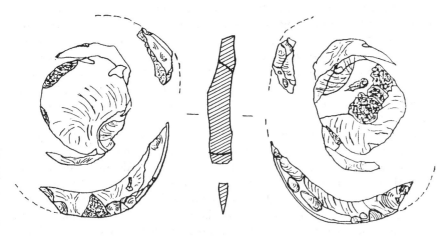

Fig. 13 Polished flint knife of discoidal form from Newgrange, Co. Meath. After
M. J. O'Kelly, *Newgrange* (London, 1982). Scale 3:4.

and Britain it is true that they appear to have been thus concerned, though
there is little direct evidence to show that they themselves were metallurgists.
In Britain they were among the early users of copper awls and knife daggers,
but even though these objects are found in Ireland the Beaker association is
lacking. The discovery of a thin-butted axe at the edge of the Newgrange
Beaker settlement is welcome evidence in this regard.[6] It has been suggested
that the Beaker folk came to Ireland as prospectors and miners looking for
suitable copper lodes to exploit. South-west Ireland, however, is the parent
area of the grey copper ores that most probably provided the metal for some
of the earliest Irish copper implements, but no single sherd of beaker has yet
been found in this region.

The Newgrange settlement consisted of a series of living floors (strung
around the edge of the passage-tomb cairn, which was already in collapse),

[6] M. J. O'Kelly and C. A. Shell, 'Stone objects and a bronze axe from Newgrange,
Co. Meath' in Michael Ryan (ed.), *The origins of metallurgy in Atlantic Europe* (Dublin, [1979]),
pp 127–44.

each with a hearth at the centre.[7] The hearths were usually rectangular in plan, one metre long by half a metre wide, and were outlined by carefully set stones. Each floor also had numerous pits and holes, some of them postholes, and though several such floors have now been exposed, it has not been possible to recover a house plan in any one case. The potsherds and the flints, as well as large quantities of animal bones, are concentrated on the floors and around the hearths. It appears, therefore, that these Beaker people were squatting in rather flimsy structures set up in the shelter of the high cairn of the passage tomb. Three separate radiocarbon dates which centre on 2000 B.C. have been obtained from charcoals from the settlement, and these agree well with the Ballynagilly Beaker settlement dates which also centre on 2000 B.C. The animal bones, the food waste of the squatters, are of special interest, for a study of them has revealed that for the most part they are those of domesticated cattle.[8] Sheep/goat and pig are also present in significant amounts, but there is little evidence that deer hunting was practised. Horses are also represented, but whether these were a wild or a domesticated species is not yet clear.

A similar type of squatting activity took place at Ballynagilly, County Tyrone, as already mentioned, and in a bog at Rockbarton, near Lough Gur, hearths with associated beaker and coarse-ware sherds were found.[9] At Knowth also, outside the main mound, evidence of Beaker settlement has also been found.[10] Even if direct evidence is lacking, it is legitimate to assume that houses similar to those of the neolithic period continued to be built after the advent of the Beaker people, about the time the metal age began to dawn.

In central Europe and in Britain, the Beaker folk followed a single-grave tradition of burial, while in the west, in Iberia and in Brittany, their pots are found as secondary intrusions in the megalithic tomb of the earlier collective burial tradition. Though our Beaker folk probably came to us from Britain, no certain Beaker burial in the single-grave manner has been found here as yet. Instead, apart from those already mentioned as having come from settlements, their pots are known from six wedge-shaped gallery graves, and one hesitates to attribute these monuments to the Beaker people on such slight evidence. The absence of specific Beaker single-grave burials also means that the associations of objects familiar in Britain are unknown here. On present evidence, at any rate, it looks as if the Beaker folk came here in groups and

---

[7] M. J. O'Kelly, R. M. O'Cleary, and D. Lehane, *Newgrange, Co. Meath, Ireland: the late neolithic/Beaker period settlement* (Oxford, 1983).

[8] L. H. van Wijngaarden-Baaker, 'The animal remains from the Beaker settlement at Newgrange, Co. Meath: first report' in *R.I.A. Proc.*, lxxiv (1974), sect. C, pp 313–83; '. . . final report', ibid., lxxxv (1986), sect. C, pp 17–111.

[9] G. F. Mitchell and S. P. Ó Ríordáin, 'Early bronze-age pottery from Rockbarton bog, Co. Limerick' in *R.I.A. Proc.*, xlviii (1942), sect. C, pp 255–72.

[10] George Eogan, *Excavations at Knowth I* (Dublin, 1984).

joined up with communities of neolithic people wherever they found them. This seems to have been the case at Newgrange, where beaker sherds are associated with various types of late neolithic pottery as well as with flints that exhibit a surviving Larnian/mesolithic tradition. A like situation obtained at Lough Gur,[11] as already noted, and the same has been revealed in excavations at Dalkey Island in Dublin Bay.[12]

Beaker ware has also been found in a stone circle at Grange, near Lough Gur, accompanied by a few of the tanged flint knives of the kind found at Newgrange. This Limerick monument, the most impressive of its type in Ireland, consists of a circle of contiguous standing stones, 45.7 m in diameter.[13] Some of the stones are very large, and one must weigh not less than fifty tons. Built against the stones on the outside is a broad bank of earth, 9 m wide and about 1.5 m high, through which there is an entrance passage flanked on each side by contiguous standing slabs. Since there is no external ditch, the material for the bank must have been scraped up from the surrounding area, and the same is true of a layer of soil, 60 cm thick, spread over the interior to conceal the packing stones in the sockets of the orthostats. Numerous sherds of pottery were found under this layer and in and around the orthostat sockets as well as under the external bank. These sherds represent the round-bottomed shouldered bowls and coarse flat-based pots with which we are already familiar, as well as beakers and 'food vessel' ware, a bronze-age ceramic which will be discussed below. One Beaker pot which it was possible to reconstruct from the surviving sherds is so closely similar to one from Wick Barrow, in Somerset, that both might have been made by the same hand. Some pieces of this pot had been thrown into the part-filled socket of one of the circle orthostats, so that when the filling was completed it was well covered. It seems certain, therefore, that some Beaker people were present at the building of the circle, and indeed the whole undertaking may have been inspired by them. If the Beaker folk were few in numbers, their influence must have been great, since evidently they were able to persuade the neolithic people living in the area to work with them or under their direction in the building of this remarkable monument. Large embanked enclosures known as henges seem also to belong to this neolithic/early bronze age transitional phase, as is demonstrated by the discovery of both neolithic and Beaker pottery at Monknewtown, County Meath.[14]

[11] S. P. Ó Ríordáin, 'Lough Gur excavations: neolithic and bronze age houses on Knockadoon' in *R.I.A. Proc.*, lvi (1954), sect. C, pp 297–459.

[12] G. D. Liversage, 'Excavations at Dalkey Island, Co. Dublin, 1956–9' in *R.I.A. Proc.*, lxvi (1968), sect. C, pp 53–233.

[13] S. P. Ó Ríordáin, 'Lough Gur excavations: the great stone circle (B) in Grange townland' in *R.I.A. Proc.*, liv (1951), sect. C, pp 37–74.

[14] P. D. Sweetman, 'An earthen enclosure at Monknewtown, Slane, Co. Meath' in *R.I.A. Proc.*, lxxvi (1976), sect. C, pp 25–73.

AT about the same time as the Beaker people introduced their distinctive ware to Ireland, or very soon afterwards, another pottery type appeared. It received the name 'food vessel' from the belief of early archaeologists that its purpose was to contain food and drink for the spirits of the dead. Although it seems indeed to have been principally used for funerary purposes and scarcely ever, if at all, for domestic use, no conclusive evidence has survived to show that it fulfilled the purpose ascribed to it by the early antiquaries. Sherds of food-vessel-type ware have, however, been found on some of the domestic sites at Lough Gur and on Dalkey Island; also on what appears to be a habitation site on Coney Island in Lough Neagh.[15]

Food vessels are as distinctive in their way as beaker, though by no means as widespread, being found in Ireland and Britain but not on the Continent. About 500 pots are known in Ireland. In general it is coarser, thicker, and heavier than beaker, and rougher to the touch because of the added grits. The ware is strong, hard, and well fired, and while there is a great variety of shapes, two predominate: a bowl and a vase, both flat-bottomed. Both have been found at least once in the same grave—Bishopstown, County Waterford.[16]

Ornament of geometrical type is profuse—an undecorated food vessel is rarely found—but a vase in point is the burial at Bishopstown just mentioned, where the vase is completely plain while the bowl is ornamented all over. Sherds of a third food vessel from the same grave are also from a vase, in this case ornamented all over. Some have comb-stamp ornament and have profiles reminiscent of beakers. It appears possible, therefore, that this type of pottery, and the single-grave form of burial with which it is associated, came quickly into being in Britain and Ireland under Beaker influence, though it is not easy to document this argument. It seems likely too that various late neolithic wares provided the basic stocks from which the different food vessel types evolved. The complex origins of the food vessel require much further study before they can be understood.[17] A small number of food vessels are associated with metal objects, e.g. a pot from Corkey, County Antrim, found with a dagger, and another from Carrickinab, County Down, found with a dagger and an awl. There is no direct evidence, however, that the makers of food vessels were directly connected with the making of metal objects.

We have seen that food-vessel pottery comes almost entirely from burials, the vast majority of them single graves or cists. These graves mark the final

[15] P. V. Addyman, 'Coney Island, Louth Neagh: prehistoric settlement, Anglo-Norman castle and Elizabethan native fortress' in *U.J.A.*, 3rd ser., xxviii (1965), pp 78–101.

[16] S. P. Ó Ríordáin, 'Burial with food-vessels at Bishopstown, Co. Waterford' in *Cork Hist. Soc. Jn.*, xliv (1939), pp 117–19.

[17] John Waddell, 'Cultural interaction in the insular early bronze age: some ceramic evidence' in S. J. de Laet (ed.), *Acculturation and continuity in Atlantic Europe* (Bruges, 1976), pp 284–95.

break with the collective burial practice of the megalithic tomb builders. Instead of setting up a great overground structure of stones which could contain the remains, cremated or unburnt, of many people, it became the custom to dig a small pit in the ground and line it with slabs of stone set on edge so as to make a rectangular box-like structure averaging about 80 cm long by 50 cm wide by about 50 cm deep. Sometimes the floor was flagged. The cist was so small that when the body was interred unburnt it had to be placed on its side with the knees drawn up to the chin and literally rammed into the grave. A single pot, exceptionally two or more, was placed near the head.

Cremations are also found in these cist graves—in fact in Ireland they probably predominate. The evidence, such as it is, suggests that cremation is about twice as common as inhumation. In these cases the fragments of burnt bone—twisted and distorted out of shape by the heat of the cremation fire— are found in a little heap on the floor of the cist, the pot standing close by, empty unless it has become filled with soil subsequently washed into the grave. In the later burials of this kind the food vessel pot may actually contain the cremated remains. The most recent account of cist-grave burials in Ireland lists 637 examples,[18] the majority of which are of the short form described above. But there is a small number of long and other forms which also belong to the bronze age.

When the burial ceremony had concluded, a capstone was laid over the grave, and the soil originally dug from the pit was filled back on top. Since not all the earth dug out would now go back because of the space occupied by the cist, the position of the grave must have been marked for a time by a slight mound that would have become less noticeable as the loose earth consolidated and would hardly have been visible at all once the vegetation had become reestablished. Or indeed, it may be that the surplus earth was scattered rather than mounded up over the grave. Thus, the majority of food-vessel cists were constructed as isolated graves and were for all practical purposes unmarked at the surface of the ground. The majority of them now known to us have been found by chance in the course of ploughing or other work on the land. Not all food-vessel burials are isolated cists. Forty-one instances have been listed by Waddell, in each of which a number of cists form a flat cemetery, as at Ballyenehan North, near Fermoy, County Cork, where at least seventeen graves were closely grouped on a gravel ridge.[19] There was no surface indication of their presence, and they came to notice only when a bulldozer was stripping the topsoil to expose the gravel.

---

[18] John Waddell, 'Irish bronze-age cists: a survey' in *R.S.A.I. Jn.*, c (1970), pp 91–139.
[19] E. M. Fahy, 'Bronze age cemetery at Ballynehan North, Co. Cork' in *Cork Hist. Soc. Jn.*, lix (1954), pp 42–9.

Another form of food vessel cemetery is that called a 'multiple cist cairn' of which thirty-six examples are known.[20] In this type of bronze-age monument, a circular cairn or mound, sometimes with orthostatic kerb, covers a number of cists. Sometimes one cist, centrally placed, is bigger than the others, and at Moneen, County Cork,[21] it was of megalithic proportions. The other cists are found on the south or south-west sides of the central cist. This type of monument may be a development of the arrangement found at Baurnadomeeny, County Tipperary, where a wedge-shaped gallery grave had a number of diminutive cists under the cairn base on the south side; these must have been put into place before the circular cairn was thrown up to cover both cists and tomb.

It has been suggested that the early makers of food vessels were the immediate descendants of the passage-tomb builders.[22] Evidence adduced in support of this is the occurrence in passage tombs of food-vessel burials as secondary intrustions. They are found in seven tombs, one of these being the Mound of the Hostages at Tara,[23] where some of the primary burials had been removed from the chamber to make room for them. In other cases, the secondary burials are found in the covering mounds of passage tombs, as at Fourknocks, County Meath. They are not generally found in other types of megalithic tomb. Another supporting factor for the above suggestion is that the capstones of three cist graves, Ballinvally, County Meath, Moylough, County Sligo, and Hempstown Common, County Kildare, bear decoration akin to passage-tomb art. Perhaps too, the Carrowkeel ware of the passage tombs contributed something to the development of the food vessel. Finally, the predominant rite in both food-vessel and passage-tomb burials was cremation, so that the likelihood of a relationship between the two peoples is strengthened, and it can be argued that food vessels began to be made soon after the period of passage-tomb building came to an end *c*. 2000 B.C.

ANOTHER category of pottery vessel associated with the early part of the bronze age is the urn. This, like the food vessel, was a funerary ware, although sherds have been found on a number of habitation sites near Downpatrick, County Down.[24] The urns are large vessels, often as much as 30 to 40 cm high. They have a large diameter at the rim or at the shoulder—25 to 30 cm—and a disproportionately small base, a fact that suggests that

[20] Waddell, 'Irish bronze age cists'.
[21] M. J. O'Kelly, 'Excavation of a cairn at Moneen, Co. Cork' in *R.I.A. Proc.*, liv (1952), sect. C, pp 121–59.
[22] Waddell, 'Irish bronze age cists', p. 104.
[23] Ruaidhrí de Valera, 'Excavation of the Mound of the Hostages: latest supplementary note, 1961' in S. P. Ó Ríordáin, *Tara: the monuments on the hill* (Dundalk, 1971), p. 278.
[24] A. J. Pollock and D. M. Waterman, 'A bronze age habitation site at Downpatrick' in *U.J.A.*, 3rd ser., xxvii (1964), pp 31–58; A. M. ApSimon, 'The earlier bronze age in the north of Ireland' in *U.J.A.*, 3rd ser., xxxii (1969), pp 28–72.

they were not meant to stand right way up. They are somewhat coarsely made; the walls are thick and gritty. Many are built up from rings of clay; consequently the pots tend to break along the lines of junction. Sometimes the finished pot was coated or slipped with a fine clay that was rubbed smooth before impressing it with twisted cord to form geometrical patterns.

The best-known Irish types are divided into collared, cordoned, and encrusted urns.[25] There is a number of variant types as well, some of which may be merely enlarged food vessels, and in fact all urns may have a background in the late neolithic flat-based coarsely made domestic pots, as well as in the beaker ware of the coarser type. The collared urn is so called because its 'overhanging' rim not only looks like a collar but was often achieved by applying a collar of clay to the top of the pot, as in an urn from Castlerichard, County Cork.[26] The cordoned urn has two parallel ribs or cordons of applied clay that encircle the vessel in its broad upper-middle part. Both collared and cordoned urns may be ornamented with geometrical patterns in the neck or rim area using impressed cord. A collared urn from Oatencake, near Midleton, County Cork,[27] has incised geometrical patterns. In the encrusted urn, ribs or bands of clay were applied in geometrical patterns to the finished vessel and luted down. Often these encrustations covered the whole vessel from rim to base, and some pots have encrusted rosettes set within the angles of an encrusted zigzag band just below the rim. The rosettes and bands were often further emphasised by 'herring-bone' incisions. Often too the internal slope of the rim has a number of parallel ridges and grooves marked with the same incisions. Some of the ornament may be skeuomorphic. The arrangement of applied vertical ribs may represent the poles bulging through the hide covering of a wigwam-like tent or hut, and some basketry patterns may likewise represent the wicker mats used in some forms of house construction. This in turn suggests perhaps that the mouth-downward urn was thought of as a hut or house for the dead rather than as a mere bone container—an idea that, as we saw above, may also have been in the minds of the builders of the passage tombs. Some urns have holes drilled near the rim. These might have been used in tying a skin or cloth cover over the mouth of the urn if the cremated bones had been put into the pot before inverting it in the gravepit, but they may also be 'soul-holes' through which the spirit of the dead could come and go.

[25] R. M. Kavanagh, 'The encrusted urn in Ireland' in *R.I.A. Proc.*, lxxiii, sect. C (1973), pp 507–617, and 'Collared and cordoned cinerary urns in Ireland', ibid., lxxvi (1976), sect. C, pp 293–403.
[26] M. J. O'Kelly and A. O'Connell, 'An urn burial at Castlerichard, Co. Cork' in *Cork Hist. Soc. Jn.*, lxxiii (1968), pp 48–51.
[27] M. J. O'Kelly, 'A cinerary urn from Oatencake, Midleton' in *Cork Hist. Soc. Jn.*, lii (1947), p. 126.

Some urn burials were placed in cist graves similar in character to those of the food-vessel users,[28] but often the burial was placed in a simple shallow pit with no stone protection. Most usually, the urn is found standing mouth downward over the cremated bones, and when it had been so placed in the pit the soil was back-filled around it. Initially there may have been a small, low mound of earth marking the position of the grave, but like food vessel burials, most urn graves in Ireland have been found by chance in ploughing or in the mechanical removal of topsoil from gravel deposits.

Urn burials are generally found in isolation, though some flat cemeteries containing a few graves, as at Keenoge, County Meath,[29] as well as 'cemetery cairns', are known. In the latter a low circular mound was thrown up to cover a group of burials, as at Knockast, County Westmeath,[30] or a pre-existing mound was used. The Mound of the Hostages at Tara is a case in point. Here several secondary urn burials were inserted into the top of the mound. Urn burials have also been found enclosed within shallow ring-ditches as at Urbalreagh, County Antrim,[31] or at Lissard, County Limerick.[32] But this too may be a continuance of a late neolithic tradition as found, for instance, at the Rathjordan, County Limerick, ring-barrow mentioned above.

These various forms of single-grave practice may have continued through the middle and into the late bronze age, but associations that would clearly establish this are not known. Indeed some hold that a change in funerary custom took place about 1400 B.C. when the practice of placing objects in the grave with the dead ceased.[33] In the absence of such objects it is difficult to place a particular burial in a datable horizon.

Sometimes urns are accompanied by pygmy cups, very small pottery vessels of various forms that may have had a ritual function.[34] Many have perforations in the side walls, a feature noted above in some urns. Some pygmy cups are in reality miniature food vessels, as at Ballynahow, County Cork,[35] but instances are also known of the occurrence of normal food vessels in the same graves with encrusted urns, as at Bealick, County

---

[28] Waddell, 'Irish bronze age cists'.

[29] Adolf Mahr, 'New aspects and problems in Irish prehistory' in *Prehist. Soc. Proc.*, iii (1937), p. 375.

[30] H. O'N. Hencken and H. L. Movius, 'The cemetery-cairn of Knockast' in *R.I.A. Proc.*, xli (1934), sect. C, pp 232–84.

[31] D. M. Waterman, 'Cordoned urn burials and ring-ditches at Urbalreagh, Co. Antrim' in *U.J.A.*, 3rd ser., xxxi (1968), pp 25–32.

[32] S. P. Ó Ríordáin, 'Excavations at Lissard, Co. Limerick, and other sites in the locality' in *R.S.A.I. Jn.*, lxvi (1936), pp 173–85.

[33] Colin Burgess, 'Chronology and terminology in the British bronze age' in *The Antiquaries Journal*, xlix (1949), pp 22–9.

[34] R. M. Kavanagh, 'Pygmy cups in Ireland' in *R.S.A.I. Jn.*, cvii (1977), pp 61–95.

[35] M. J. O'Kelly, 'Excavation of a cist-grant at Ballynahow, Fermoy, Co. Cork' in *Cork Hist. Soc. Jn.*, li (1946), pp 78–84.

Cork, mentioned below. Other urn associations in Ireland are stone axes, stone battleaxes, bronze razors, and faience beads.[36]

The exact relationship of the urns to food vessels is not altogether clear. In Britain there is evidence of a beaker–urn overlap and also of contemporaneity with food vessels.[37] At Labbamolaga, County Cork, an urn with encrusted basketry-decoration, placed in a simple pit grave, was stratigraphically later than a cist with vase-type food vessel which has an incised basketry-decoration.[38] At Bealick, County Cork, an encrusted urn and a vase food vessel were found together in a cist grave.[39]

The clearest picture comes from a sea coast site at Carrigillihy near the village of Unionhall in south-west Cork.[40] Here a well-built stone wall, 2.7 m thick, was constructed to an oval plan, the axes of which were 24.4 m and 21.3 m measured to the internal facings. Where best preserved, it stood to a height of 120 cm, but must have been somewhat higher originally. The entrance lay on the east side and faced the sea, an opening that had had carefully built jambs and a wooden post set against each of them to act as hanging- and meeting-stiles for a wooden gate. The holes in which these posts had stood were found. Inside this enclosure there had been an oval stone-built house of which only the foundations remained. Where best preserved, the wall-base remained to a height of nearly 60 cm and delineated a floor that measured 10 m × 6.7 m on its north-south and east-west axes. Strangely, no hearth site was found, but there were several postholes that gave some indication of the way in which the thatched roof may have been supported. The doorway was on the east side directly opposite the entrance to the enclosure. Against the jambs here also were the postholes of the door frame.

All over the floor of the house and spreading out through the door, as far as the enclosure wall and the entrance through it, was a layer of domestic refuse, blackened from the amount of finely fragmented charcoal mixed through it. The layer contained numerous fragments of coarse ware—flat-bottomed pots of the kind that were so prevalent in the later levels at Lough Gur and, as there, accompanied by pottery of the round-bottomed bowl type, though the amount of this at Carrigillihy was small. In the same horizon, however, there was found an awl—one of the earliest metal types known in

[36] A. B. Ó Ríordáin, 'Cordoned urn burial at Laheen, Co. Donegal' in *R.S.A.I. Jn.*, xcvii (1967), pp 39–44.

[37] I. H. Longworth, 'The origins and development of the primary series in the collared urn tradition in England and Wales' in *Prehist. Soc. Proc.*, xxvii (1961), p. 282; A. B. Ó Ríordáin, 'A prehistoric burial site at Gortnacargy, Co. Cavan' in *R.S.A.I. Jn.*, xcvii (1967), p. 63.

[38] M. J. O'Kelly, 'Two burials at Labbamolaga, Co. Cork' in *Cork Hist. Soc. Jn.*, lv (1950), pp 15–20.

[39] M. J. O'Kelly, 'Excavation of a cist-grave at Bealick, Macroom, Co. Cork' in *Cork Hist. Soc. Jn.*, xlix (1944), pp 116–21.

[40] M. J. O'Kelly, 'An early bronze age ring-fort at Carrigillihy, Co. Cork' in *Cork Hist. Soc. Jn.*, lvi (1951), pp 69–86.

these islands. One must conclude therefore that though neolithic-type pottery vessels were still in use, the metal age had already begun. In this connection it is important to note that there was no evidence of the Beaker people on the site.[41] Another early bronze-age domestic site on Coney Island in Lough Neagh produced some sherds of food-vessel-like ware contained within two rectangular structures, one measuring 2.7 × 6.1 m and the other 2.7 m × 3.3 m.[42] In layers overlying them were sherds of cord-ornamented pottery, almost certainly from cordoned urns. Another site is that near Downpatrick, County Down, where rescue excavations on a building site revealed what appear to be circular houses marked by foundation trenches within which was found pottery of undoubted cordoned urn type.[43]

Evidence is still wanting as to the domestic arrangements of the people of the middle bronze age—no informative settlement has as yet been found that can be shown to belong to this time. Site F on Knockadoon Hill, Lough Gur, is probably of this time. Here excavation revealed a house of roughly rectangular plan measuring 8.2 × 6.4 m built against a vertical rock face 1.8 m high, which formed one wall of the structure. Outside the house, but associated with it, was a hollow area containing a hearth in which several fragments of clay moulds and bronze casting-waste were found. With these materials and also within the house itself were numerous sherds of the well-known flat-based coarse ware, showing that this type of pottery continued in use to the middle bronze age, because where the mould fragments were big enough it could be seen that they were used for casting rapiers and socketed looped arrowheads. Presumably this was the house of a bronze-smith.[44]

MENTION has been made above of Beaker involvement in the building of the great ritual stone circle at Grange, Lough Gur. It is thought that Irish stone circles in general belong to the early part of the bronze age, though direct dating evidence is not good and it must be noted, moreover, that none of the excavated sites, other than Grange, produced beaker pottery. This is perhaps especially surprising in the case of two other excavated circles at Lough Gur, since so much beaker pottery has come from a great variety of

---

[41] The possibility of a date late rather than early in the bronze age for Carrigillihy has been put forward by a number of commentators, e.g. E. P. Kelly, 'A reassessment of the dating evidence for Knockadoon Class II pottery' in *Irish Archaeological Research Forum*, v (1978), pp 23–7.

[42] P. V. Addyman, 'Coney Island, Lough Neagh: prehistoric settlement, Anglo-Norman castle, and Elizabethan native fortress' in *U.J.A.*, 3rd ser., xxviii (1965), pp 78–101.

[43] A. J. Pollock and D. M. Waterman, 'A bronze age habitation site at Downpatrick' in *U.J.A.*, 3rd ser., xxvii (1964), pp 31–58.

[44] S. P. Ó Ríordáin, 'Lough Gur excavations: neolithic and bronze age houses on Knockadoon' in *R.I.A. Proc.*, lvi (1954), sect. C, p. 415.

sites there. The circles, lettered O and P in Windle's survey,[45] were quite different in construction from one another. Circle P, 10.7 m in diameter, consists of twenty-nine contiguous stones, which form a kerb around a platform of stones and earth. There was no entrance feature. Two cremation burials accompanied by large flat-based, coarsely made, unornamented pottery vessels were found below the base of the platform. It may be therefore that this monument is not a stone circle proper, but rather a burial tumulus of which only the kerb and basal portion of the mound now survive. The pottery vessels may be related to the flat-based domestic coarse ware so prevalent in the district.

Circle O, at 55 m in overall diameter, is a much larger structure. It consists of an outer earthen bank faced inside and out with large stone slabs. Within is a ditch which provided the earth fill for the bank. Concentrically placed within the ditch is an inner circle of contiguous orthostats. There is no clearly defined entrance and there were no diagnostic finds or burials.

In general, Irish circles are of non-contiguous stones and they vary greatly in diameter and in the number of stones used.[46] Several remarkable examples in the west of County Cork and in Kerry have a special feature not so far recorded in the rest of Ireland. Two adjacent orthostats are taller than the others, and diametrically opposite to them in the circumference is a recumbent stone, that is, one in which the long axis is horizontal instead of vertical. In two recently excavated examples the diameter, drawn centrally between the two tall stones and across the centre of the recumbent, when projected to the local horizon seems in one (Drombeg, near Glandore, County Cork)[47] to mark the point of sunset at the winter solstice, and in the other (Bohonagh, near Rosscarbery, County Cork)[48] to mark sunset at the time of the equinoxes. If this was deliberately arranged by the builders, the circles may have been used for some calendrical purpose. However, in a third instance in the same neighbourhood, Reenascreena,[49] the axis lay 24° to the south of the point of equinoctial sunset, and thus the calendrical explanation seems to fail here, unless the orientation is to a heavenly body other than the sun. Much discussion on this aspect of the stone circle problem has taken place in recent

[45] B. C. A. Windle, 'Megalithic remains surrounding Lough Gur, Co. Limerick' in *R.I.A. Proc.*, xxx (1912), sect. C, pp 302–4; Eoin Grogan and George Eogan, 'Lough Gur excavations by Seán P. Ó Ríordáin: further neolithic and Beaker habitations on Knockadoon' in *R.I.A. Proc.*, lxxxvii (1987), sect. C, pp 496–501.

[46] Seán Ó Nualláin, 'The stone circle complex of Cork and Kerry' in *R.S.A.I. Jn.*, cv (1975), pp 83–131; and 'A survey of stone circles in Cork and Kerry' in *R.I.A. Proc.*, lxxxiv (1984), sect. C, pp 1–77.

[47] E. M. Fahy, 'A recumbent-stone circle at Drombeg, Co. Cork' in *Cork Hist. Soc. Jn.*, lxiv (1959), pp 1–27.

[48] E. M. Fahy, 'A stone circle, hut, and dolmen at Bohonagh, Co. Cork' in *Cork Hist. Soc. Jn.*, lxvi (1961), pp 93–104.

[49] E. M. Fahy, 'A recumbent-stone circle at Reenascreena South, Co. Cork' in *Cork Hist. Soc. Jn.*, lxvii (1962), pp 59–69.

times in Britain, and some remarkable claims have been made for certain sites. There seems to be no doubt that orientation was important to neolithic and bronze age man, not alone in stone circles but also in megalithic tombs, but whether the more extravagant claims that have been made will ever be substantiated or not it is difficult to say in the present state of our knowledge.

Each of the three excavated west Cork sites was found to contain a single cremation burial, centrally placed at Drombeg and Bohonagh, but quite eccentrically placed at Reenascreena. At Drombeg the bones were contained in a pottery vessel, but there were no grave goods in the other two cases.The pottery compares well with the late neolithic/early bronze age flat-bottomed coarse ware from Lough Gur, but charcoal found with the bones has given a C 14 date of A.D. 600 ± 120.[50] This conflict of evidence has not been resolved.

The circles of Tyrone, Fermanagh, and Derry tend to be built of smaller stones than those of the Dublin–Wicklow, Lough Gur, or west Cork–Kerry groups. Often these circles may only come to light when peat that had grown over them is cut away. Peat cutting at Beaghmore in County Tyrone has revealed a most remarkable group of monuments[51] which includes several circles with tangential alignments and many small cairns and cists, the stones used in all these being quite small. One circle is completely filled with hundreds of small boulders carefully set upright. A small cairn on the circumference contained two cremated burials. A cairn 3 m in diameter, lying between two other closely adjacent circles, covered a cist in which was found a polished axe of porcellanite. It is not easy to understand or explain the various features of this site or to determine whether all the monuments are roughly contemporary or spread over a period of time. C 14 measurements place the whole complex within the date bracket 1535 ± 70 bc and 775 ± 55 bc,[52] and thus it is of the bronze age.[53] If it was a ritual or cult area, there is no evidence as to the nature of the rites practised. And this, alas, is true also of all other stone circles in Ireland.

STUDENTS of archaeology were satisfied not too many years ago to relate urn burials to the late bronze age in Ireland, but now that these have been updated to the early bronze age, we are left with only the scantiest information concerning burial rites in the Irish later bronze age.[54] Only a handful

[50] D-62.
[51] J. R. Pilcher, 'Archaeology, palaeontology, and 14C dating of the Beaghmore stone circle' in *U.J.A.*, 3rd ser., xxxii (1969), pp 73–91.
[52] UB-11; UB-163.
[53] A. G. Smith, J. R. Pilcher, and G. W. Pearson, 'New radiocarbon dates from Ireland' in *Antiquity*, xlv (1971), p. 99.
[54] Barry Raftery, 'Iron age burials in Ireland' in Donnchadh Ó Corráin (ed.), *Irish antiquity: essays and studies presented to M.J. O'Kelly* (Cork, 1981), pp 173–7.

of burial sites can be recognised that are likely to date to this period. Of these, Rathgall, County Wicklow, is the most important.[55] Here three cremation deposits in pits, one contained within an upright pot, were found inside an enclosure formed by a V-sectioned ditch. One of the cremations was at the centre of the enclosure and was surrounded by a large number of stake-holes of uncertain purpose. A comparable burial was found at Ballybeen, Dundonald, County Down.[56] At this site an unaccompanied cremation deposit in a pit occurred centrally placed within a small ring ditch. Two char-coal samples from the ditch yielded radiocarbon dates of 710 ± 70 bc[57] and 580 ± 70 bc.[58] Other cremation burials, possibly but less certainly later bronze age in date, are those at Mullaghmore, County Down,[59] and Lugg, County Dublin.[60] Cremation burials at Carnkenny, County Tyrone, may also belong to this period.[61] In general, however, it must be assumed that burials of the late bronze age were simple and unelaborate so that they scarcely impinge on the archaeological record. For the late bronze age, however, a number of sites are known, the majority being crannogs or lakeside settlements.[62] At Ballinderry Lough, County Offaly, a natural island had evidently been occupied for a short time over an area about 45 m long by 17 m wide. This was in the nature of a lakeside settlement rather than an artificial island or crannog.[63] At one end of the area the foundation planks of what may have been a house, 11.5 m square, were found. The walls of this had probably been of wattle construction plastered with mud. At the other end of the area were the bases of nine circular storage bins built also of wattles, and these too were originally plastered with mud. They varied in diameter between 1 m and 2 m and may have been used for storing grain.

The house occupants had used flat-bottomed coarse ware, not unlike the late neolithic ware of the same shape. In fact, one of the difficulties in regard to these coarse domestic wares is that when found by themselves (that is, unassociated with other datable objects) one cannot easily distinguish neolithic pots from those of the late bronze or iron ages. While this late coarse

[55] Barry Raftery, 'Rathgall: a late bronze age burial in Ireland' in *Antiquity*, xlvii (1973), pp 293–5, and 'Iron age burials', pp 171–204.

[56] J. P. Mallory, 'The Long Stone, Ballybeen, Dundonald, County Down' in *U.J.A.*, 3rd ser., xlvii (1984), pp 3, 4.

[57] UB-2640.

[58] UB-2641.

[59] J. M. Mogey and G. B. Thompson, 'Excavation of two ring-barrows in Mullaghmore townland, Co. Down' in *U.J.A.*, 3rd ser., xix (1956), pp 11–28.

[60] H. E. Kilbride-Jones, 'The excavation of a composite early iron age monument with "henge" features at Lugg, Co. Dublin' in *R.I.A. Proc.*, liii (1950), sect. C, pp 311–32.

[61] C. J. Lynn, 'The excavation of a ring-cairn in Carnkenny townland, Co. Tyrone' in *U.J.A.*, 3rd ser., xxxvi–xxxvii (1973–4), pp 17–31.

[62] George Eogan, 'The later bronze age in the light of recent research' in *Prehist. Soc. Proc.*, xxx (1964), p. 314.

[63] H. O'N. Hencken, 'Ballinderry crannog no. 2' in *R.I.A. Proc.*, xlvii (1942), sect. C, pp 1–76.

ware, as at Ballinderry, may be directly descended from the neolithic
coarse ware, some allow for the possibility that it was introduced into Ireland
at the end of the late bronze age. If this is admitted as a possibility, the
pottery may foreshadow the beginning of the iron age, if indeed it does not
belong actually to this new period, as we shall see has been argued for similar
pottery from the next site to be described below.

The inhabitants of Ballinderry kept cattle, pigs, sheep, and goats, and
these must have grazed on the land around the lake. Their meat was eaten,
and occasionally a red deer killed in the hunt provided some venison. The
bones of all these animals were found on the site. The wattle-and-daub grain
stores, if this is what they were, show that cereal crops were grown and stone
saddle querns and grain rubbers were used to grind it, more probably for use
as porridge than as flour for the making of bread. Bone and stone spindle-
whorls (the flywheel weights of hand-turned spindles) show that the sheep's
wool was spun into thread, and this probably was woven into cloth, though
there is no direct evidence of the presence of a loom. Some fragments of
leather may indicate that this material was also used for garments, and two
bronze awls may have been used as perforators to facilitate sewing the pieces
together. Two bronze pins are likely to have been used for fastening the
clothing. Ornaments worn by the womenfolk were amber beads and bracelets, armlets, or anklets made of shale and lignite (fossil wood), though some
of these were large enough to fit the men also. Various objects were made
from yew, ash, and hazel wood. These included a bowl, pins, and various
fragmentary objects, the purpose of which could not be determined. The
occupation was of short duration and was brought to an end by a rise in the
level of the lake. During this high-water period, the buildings decayed or
were swept away and the whole area of the settlement was covered by a layer
of chalk mud.

On a slight natural rise on the floor of Rossroe Lough, near Newmarket-
on-Fergus, County Clare, an artificial island, oval in shape and measuring
40 m by 20 m, was raised above the lake level to provide a naturally defended
area for a habitation. This had come to be known as Knocknalappa crannog,
named after the townland in which it lies. While there were objects of a
domestic nature—pottery, animal bones, and other things—there was no
evidence that houses or huts had been built. On the primary marl of the lake
bed was spread a thick layer of artificially deposited peat. Above this was a
layer of stones and over this an artificially deposited layer of marl. All this
was held in place by timber piles driven into the primary marl around the
edge of the artificial platform. Sherds from five or six pottery vessels were
found, one of which was capable of being restored. It had a slightly everted
neck above a swelling body that narrows downward to a flat base. The pot is
22 cm high, 16 cm in diameter at the rim, and the base is 10 cm in diameter.
This large vessel, dull black in colour, is similar to some of the pots from

Ballinderry as described above. The excavation also produced a fragment of a lignite armlet, some amber beads and a sunflower pin. The site had been brought to attention in the first instance by the finding on the surface of a bronze sword, a socketed bronze gouge, and a stone axe. The two bronze items clearly belong to the very end of the bronze age, and the excavator argued that the pottery already showed strong iron-age influence in its profile.[64]

Excavations at the crannog of Rathtinaun in Lough Gara, County Sligo, revealed a small late bronze-age settlement lying on a foundation of peat and brushwood held in place on the marl by wooden piles.[65] At the time the settlement was made, the surrounding area was a phragmites swamp. No house plan was recovered but there were several hearths and much domestic pottery of the kinds found at Ballinderry and Knocknalappa. This settlement was brought to an end by a rise in the water level of the swamp, during which time a layer of sand was laid down over it. In due time a second settlement was established on the spot, also mainly of the late bronze age, but iron objects were now present among the finds. No house plans survived, but several hearths similar to those of the first settlement were found. Again, large quantities of the coarse flat-based domestic pottery were present and there were fragmentary clay moulds and wooden objects including dishes. Beside the site a hoard of amber, bronze, gold, and tin ornaments was found. These included a tweezers, an ornamented pin, three gold-plated penannular rings, rings of various kinds and sizes in bronze and tin, an amber necklace of thirty-one beads, and five polished boar's tusks.[66] A series of radiocarbon dates for the late bronze-age activity at Rathtinaun centres on 200 B.C. If taken at face value this would suggest that a late bronze-age culture lasted on, in certain parts of the country at least, to the third or second century B.C., and must thus have overlapped with the beginning of the iron age.[67] The dates are today regarded with suspicion, however, and many, if not most, commentators would view them as archaeologically unacceptable.[68]

[64] Joseph Raftery, 'Knocknalappa crannog, Co. Clare' in *N. Munster Antiq. Jn.*, iii (1942–3), pp 53–72.
[65] Council for Old World Archaeology, *Survey 1 (Republic of Ireland)* (Cambridge, Mass., 1958), p. 11; Joseph Raftery, 'Iron age and Irish Sea: problems for research' in Charles Thomas (ed.), *The iron age in the Irish Sea province* (London, 1972), pp 2–3.
[66] George Eogan, 'The later bronze age in the light of recent research' in *Prehist. Soc. Proc.*, xxx (1964), pp 315, 347, and *Hoards of the Irish later bronze age* (Dublin, 1983), pp 151–2.
[67] Joseph Raftery, 'A matter of time' in *R.S.A.I. Jn.*, xciii (1963), pp 109–10.
[68] Other lake or lakeside settlements of likely late bronze-age date have been investigated at Lough Eskragh, Co. Tyrone (A. E. P. Collins and W. A. Seaby, 'Structures and small finds discovered at Lough Eskragh, Co. Tyrone' in *U.J.A.*, 3rd ser., xxiii (1960), pp 25–37; B. B. Williams, 'Excavations at Lough Eskragh, Co. Tyrone' in *U.J.A.*, 3rd ser., xli (1978), pp 37–48) and Moynagh, Co. Meath (John Bradley, 'Excavations at Moynagh Lough, Co. Meath' in *Ríocht na Midhe*, vii, no. 2 (1982–3), pp 12–32; no. 3 (1984), pp 86–93; no. 4 (1985–6), pp 79–92). Hilltop sites were also occupied during the later bronze age as, for example, at Downpatrick, Co. Down (V. B. Proudfoot, 'Excavations at the Cathedral Hill,

THE bronze age may have begun before 2000 B.C. with an initial copper phase, that is, a time during which unalloyed copper was used as raw material for the objects manufactured. Mainly on the basis of metal objects and, it must be stressed again, for convenience in their study rather than because of mutual exclusiveness, the bronze age is broadly divided into an early part, 2000–1400 B.C.; a middle, 1400–1200 B.C.; and a late, 1200–500 B.C. Apart from the appearance on the scene of new types of metal object and new forms of old types, there is no indication that conditions in Ireland during the middle bronze age were at all different from those of an earlier period. There was no outstanding technical advance nor, apart from a few to be mentioned below, was there any notable introduction of new tools, weapons, or ornaments. There is no evidence of a change in the way of life or in the method of burial, though evidence suggests that urn burials had ceased about 1400 B.C. About 1200 B.C., however, various innovations may be noted in the weapons of the period that betoken outside influences of north European origin.

Contact must already have existed between Ireland and south-western Europe during the neolithic period, since the same megalithic cult prevailed in both regions. As copper metallurgy had already begun in Iberia by 2500 B.C. it may be that the first metal objects came to Ireland from these areas.[69] On the other hand, it is difficult to point to any group of metal objects of the period in Ireland and show that they are unequivocally of Iberian provenance. The role of the Beaker folk in the spread of metal has already been mentioned, as has the fact that no unequivocal connection between them and metal-working is available for Ireland.[70] However and from wherever this country received its initiation into the mysteries of metallurgy, a flourishing

Downpatrick, Co. Down' in *U.J.A.*, 3rd ser., xvii (1954), pp 97–102, and 'Excavations at the cathedral, Downpatrick, Co. Down', ibid., xix (1956), pp 57–72), Navan Fort, Co. Armagh (C. J. Lynn, 'Navan Fort: a draft summary of D. M. Waterman's excavations' in *Emania*, i (1986), pp 11–19), Haughey's Fort, Co. Armagh (J. P. Mallory, 'Trial excavations at Haughey's Fort' in *Emania*, iv (1988), pp 5–20), and Rathgall, Co. Wicklow (Barry Raftery, 'Rathgall and Irish hillfort problems' in D. W. Harding (ed.), *Hillforts: later prehistoric earthworks in Britain and Ireland* (London, 1976), pp 339–57). It seems increasingly likely that hillforts began to be constructed at this time, but unequivocal proof of this remains elusive. A few small domestic enclosures of probable late bronze-age date have also been excavated. These include the ring-fort-like structures at Aughinish, Co. Limerick (E. P. Kelly, 'Aughinish Island, sites 1 and 2' in T. G. Delaney (ed.), *Excavations 1974* (Belfast, 1974), p. 21) and Ballyveelish and Curraghtoor, Co. Tipperary (M. G. Doody, 'Late bronze age settlement, Ballyveelish 2, Co. Tipperary' in R. M. Cleary, M. F. Hurley, and E. A. Twohig (ed.), *Archaeological excavations on the Cork–Dublin gas pipeline (1981–2)* (Cork, 1987), pp 22–35, and 'Late bronze age huts at Curraghtoor, Co. Tipperary', ibid., pp 36–42).

[69] Joseph Raftery, 'A matter of time', pp 107–8.
[70] See H. J. Case, 'Were Beaker-people the first metallurgists in Ireland?' in *Palaeohistoria*, xii (1966), pp 141–77; A. Sheridan, 'A reconsideration of the origins of Irish metallurgy' in *Journal of Irish Archaeology*, i (1983), pp 11–19. The recent discovery of what may be the marks of metal axes on timbers of a wooden trackway at Corlea in Co. Longford, for which a dendrochronological date of 2259 B.C. has been established, raises intriguing new questions about the origins of metallurgy in Ireland (Barry Raftery, *Trackways through time* (Dublin, 1990), p. 14).

industry in copper, bronze, and gold-working developed. It has been said
that the earliest metallurgists in Ireland were very highly skilled. Not only
could they select the right deposit, handpick, wash, and concentrate the ore;
they could control the roasting, smelting, and possibly refining processes in a
very competent way, and eventually alloy.[71] In the earliest period, in or even
before 2000 B.C., copper alone was used, but by 1700 B.C. tin bronzes were
being made, so that the bronze age proper may be said to begin about this
time. Important copper deposits are found in the counties of Cork, Kerry,
Tipperary, Waterford, and Wicklow and in lesser quantities in the counties
of Down, Dublin, Galway, Leitrim, Louth, Mayo, Meath, and Tyrone.
There is evidence of primitive mining in a number of these areas. Stone
mauls used as mining hammers have been found in the Rear Cross–Holyford
area of Tipperary; on Ross Island, Killarney; at Mount Gabriel, Derrycarhoon, and Ballyrisode, County Cork, and elsewhere. The commonest of these
hammers were made from beach cobbles of sizes convenient to the hand and
used, without hafts, as pounders. They were apparently selected for their
oval shape, and, when found at the mines, display at each end areas that have
become abraded in use. The more sophisticated examples have a chiselled
equatorial groove in which was placed a withy or pliable tree root, the two
ends of which were brought together and bound tightly to form a haft. In a
third variety the ends of the equatorial groove stop at each side of a carefully
made flat area. Experiment suggests that this type was hafted by butting a
wooden handle against the flat; the ends of the withy or flexible root were
then tightly bound to the handle and a wedge driven in between the handle
and the flat to take up any remaining slackness. Hafted in this way the maul
became a very serviceable tool (plate 2).

    The best evidence of mining activity has come from Mount Gabriel and
Derrycarhoon near Schull in south-west Cork. At Derrycarhoon in the last
century, when a 14 ft (4.3 m) thickness of peat had been cut away for fuel, six
old mine shafts were discovered and in them were found various objects used
in the mining process. Among these were a wood ladder, wooden shovels,
and stone mauls, of which only the mauls now survive. More recently,
twenty-five mines have been recognised on Mount Gabriel.[72] These appear
as small tunnels driven into rock scarps for varying distances up to 9 m.
Some of the mine-shaft walls show the characteristic spalling produced by
the technique of fire setting. The rock was heated by building a fire against it

---

[71] H. H. Coghlan and H. J. Case, 'Early metallurgy of copper in Ireland and Britain' in
*Prehist. Soc. Proc.*, xxiii (1957), p. 97.

[72] J. S. Jackson, 'Bronze age copper mines on Mount Gabriel, west Co. Cork, Ireland' in
*Archaeologia Austriaca*, xliii (1968), pp 92–114; 'Metallic ores in Irish prehistory: copper and
tin' in Michael Ryan (ed.), *The origins of metallurgy in Atlantic Europe* (Dublin, 1979),
pp 107–25; and 'The age of primitive copper mines on Mount Gabriel, west Co. Cork' in
*Journal of Irish Archaeology*, ii (1984), pp 41–50.

and then rapidly cooled by spilling water on it. This shattered the rock, which was then removed by pounding with the stone mauls, many of which, both broken and complete examples, have been found in the shafts and in the tip heaps outside their entrances. The copper-bearing rock thus obtained was brought from the mines and crushed by hammering to enable concentration to be done by handpicking and washing the richer material out of the gangue; it is this latter waste material that makes up the tip heaps outside each mine. As yet, no evidence of smelting has been found adjacent to the mines, and it must therefore be assumed that the ore concentrate was taken elsewhere, though not necessarily very far away, for further processing. Charcoal obtained from the tip-heaps outside mine no. 5 at Mount Gabriel has given a C 14 date of 1500 ± 120 bc,[73] showing that this particular mine is of early bronze-age date.

Since the ores are sulphides they must first have been roasted to remove the sulphur. This would have been done by interlayering the ore concentrate with wood charcoal and keeping the pile burning at a low temperature, perhaps for several days. Skill and experience were necessary to do this, for not only had the temperature to be controlled, but the pile had to be so constructed, maintained, and vented that there was free and even access of air to all its parts throughout the roast.[74] No direct evidence of the carrying-out of this process has so far been found in Ireland. The roasted ore was then smelted in a furnace, which also used charcoal as a fuel. Though no actual smeltery has been found, some of the cakes of raw copper produced are known and these give some indications of the nature of the furnace used. The cakes are 10 to 20 cm in diameter and about 1 cm thick and are known from Carrickshedoge, County Wexford, and Monastery, County Wicklow.

It is thought that the furnace was of the simple type in which the ore and charcoal were interlayered in, and mounded up over, a shallow circular bowl-shaped hollow dug in the ground and lined with clay. When a tuyere or clay funnel-shaped nozzle had been fixed on the side of the bowl and the charge had been fired, a clay dome-shaped cover was put on over the charge. There was a small vent at the top for the release of the furnace gases. A continuous controlled air blast was supplied through the tuyere from a pair of bellows. As the ore was reduced, the metal particles produced became molten, ran together, and passed down through the charcoal to the bottom of the furnace, there to be moulded to the form described above by the shape of the bottom of the furnace itself. Subsequently this cake or ingot, as it may be called, provided the metal from which axes and other objects were made. Pieces cut or broken from it were remelted in a clay crucible and poured into the requisite mould. If the alloying with tin had not been done during the

---

[73] VRI-66.
[74] Coghlan & Case, 'Early metallurgy of copper', p. 94.

smelting process, it could now be done in the crucible. Fragments of shallow dish-like crucibles believed to be of bronze-age date have been found on Dalkey Island in Dublin Bay.[75] Though these particular examples probably belong to the advanced bronze age, it is likely that they are not very different from those used earlier.

While the Irish craftsmen were using arsenical coppers, whether obtained by careful ore selection or by deliberate alloying, no problems other than those of a technical nature arose, for the raw materials were obtainable in Ireland. When it came to the making of tin bronze (approximately 90 per cent copper, 10 per cent tin) a new problem was immediately encountered— where to obtain the necessary tin ore or metallic tin. The presence of tin associated with alluvial gold in County Wicklow has long been known. This tin occurs as mineral tinstone or cassiterite ($SnO_2$) in the alluvial gravels along the Goldmines river and other streams in the area. Both the tinstone and the gold are confined to narrow strips of alluvium along a few streams, and the total workable area is very small. However, it is reasonable to assume that ancient man, attracted by the gold, might have recognised the coarse-grained tinstone. If he did recognise it, he would have been able to smelt it to obtain the tin, since he was already able to smelt copper ore. There is not as yet a satisfactory explanation of the ultimate source of the Wicklow tin, and research up to the present time has not revealed any other potential sources in Ireland. Spectroscopic tests have shown the presence of trace amounts of tin in the Allihies (County Cork) copper lodes, and minute traces have been detected in soils and peats, but no locality is recognised that might have been exploited even by the painstaking methods of the ancients.

Even if some tin had been obtained from the Wicklow alluvium, it is doubtful if it could have been enough to meet the developing demand, and so a trading or other arrangement must have been set up to obtain sufficient of the metal, probably from the Cornish mines, if not from somewhere further afield. This means that travel to and fro across the sea was taking place at this time, and that some materials were exported from Ireland in exchange for the tin, unless one envisages either that the Irish smith went to Cornwall to mine the ore, smelt it, and bring away enough metallic tin to supply his needs for a given length of time, or that there was a constant movement of itinerant smiths between Ireland and Britain, each one coming to Ireland with his stock-in-trade of tin.

Several stone moulds have been found in various parts of the country, and these were used for the casting of a variety of implements such as axes, knives, darts, spear-heads, sickles, etc. There are both single-valve and bi-valve moulds. The bivalve mould was in two parts so that, after casting, the

---

[75] G. D. Liversage, 'Excavations at Dalkey Island, Co. Dublin, 1956–9' in *R.I.A. Proc.*, lxvi (1968), sect. C, pp 89–91.

completely shaped object could be taken out by separating the two parts. The single-valve or open mould shaped only one face of the object being cast, and the other face had to be shaped by hammering and grinding. The open moulds for casting axes are probably among the earliest made and used in Ireland and technologically are of great interest. Of the ten known, the National Museum of Ireland possesses four good examples, the Ulster Museum, Belfast, one, and the Cork Public Museum one. Of the four in the National Museum, two are from County Cork (Doonour near Bantry and Kilcronat near Mogeeley) and one each from Counties Carlow and Leitrim. The Doonour mould[76] was found when a small field near the sea coast was being reclaimed by rotivation and the removal of stones. There was no evidence of a furnace or other associated structure. The object is a roughly rectangular block of grit measuring 31 × 22.5 × 14 cm in length, width, and thickness at the maximum points. Its form is partly natural and partly artificial. Parts of faces 1, 2, and 4, and all of 6, show clear evidence of shaping, the work having been done by percussion; the most likely implements for this were probably a pointed chisel used with a mallet. The stone was selected because it is a fine-grained freestone and therefore reasonably easy to carve. The source of the stone can be immediately local. There are matrices for five different sizes of axe and for two chisel-like implements. There is no evidence that any kind of lid was fitted to any of the matrices to convert them into closed moulds when they were being used. Hot metal was certainly poured into some of the matrices; and the colour change in, and the friable nature of, some of the internal surfaces indicate that the depth of the metal may have been about 8 cm.

As none of the opposing faces of the blocks are parallel, each matrix had to be set level before pouring so as to ensure that the metal would distribute properly in the matrix. In all cases the floor surfaces of the matrices are curved in two directions and the deepest parts are usually centred on the long axis but much nearer to the cutting-edge ends than to the butt ends. If therefore the matrix were set level and metal poured in to fill it to the requisite amount, the downward surface of the metal would have been moulded to the double curvature but the upper surface would have remained fairly flat. The cutting-edge end and the butt end would have been thick and blunt. In fact, the objects cast in such moulds can have been no more than rough-outs for axes to be finished by hammering and grinding.

In due time, bivalve moulds in both stone and clay were used, the stone now often being the easily carved steatite instead of the sandstones used for the open moulds. Evidence exists, too, that wooden models of objects were used on which to build up bivalve clay moulds for such things as spearheads

[76] M. J. O'Kelly, 'A stone mould for axeheads from Doonour, Bantry, Co. Cork' in *R.S.A.I. Jn.*, xcix (1969), pp 117–24.

and swords. Bivalve clay moulds were used with a core to make hollow castings such as socketed tools and weapons and the elegant curving trumpets or horns of the late bronze age. Many of these last exhibit clear evidence of having been cast in bivalve moulds that were probably made of clay. The cores were certainly of clay, as traces remain inside some horns. Very likely too, the 'lost wax' process of casting was employed, but evidence of this is not easy to find since the clay mould had to be broken to remove the newly made object. About 100 fragments of clay moulds, some of them for making rapiers and socketed looped spearheads, were found at house site F on Knockadoon, Lough Gur,[77] while at Dalkey Island, as well as the crucible fragments, fragments of clay moulds for socketed spearheads, knives, and perhaps an axe and a sword were found in the same area of the island. Large numbers of the metal objects made in such moulds have survived in Ireland. A recent count of the axes of the early part of the metal age shows that 2,000 have come down to us[78] and undoubtedly many more will be discovered in the course of time. This number does not include the socketed axes of the later bronze age. About 142 daggers and 150 halberds are known,[79] while a recent study[80] has listed 623 swords for the later bronze age. Apart from these implements and weapons, there are large numbers of diverse objects, tools, and ornaments.

The earliest of the axes are probably those with broad, thick butts, but they were soon replaced by a thin-butted variety with deeply curved and widely splayed cutting edges. Some examples of both types can be clearly seen to have been cast in open moulds such as the Doonour mould described above. These were presumably hafted, like the stone axes before them, by slotting into a wooden handle, and must have been maintained in place by a shrunk-on rawhide binding. This method proved unsatisfactory in use. The head soon began to work loose, especially if the haft was used as a lever to withdraw the axe when it became stuck, in the chopping of wood, for instance. Furthermore the head would have been forced back into the haft with every blow struck, eventually causing the slotted handle to split and the binding to burst.

To overcome these disabilities a new method of hafting was evolved. At first, very low flanges were hammered up along the sides of the axe and a

[77] S. P. Ó Ríordáin, 'Lough Gur excavations: neolithic and bronze age houses on Knockadoon' in R.I.A. Proc., lvi (1954), sect. C, p. 415. A large collection of clay mould fragments of late bronze-age date has been recovered at Rathgall, Co. Wicklow (Barry Raftery, 'Rathgall, Co. Wicklow: 1970 excavations' in Antiquity, xlv (1971), pp 296–8, and 'Rathgall and Irish hillfort problems' in D. W. Harding (ed.), Hillforts: later prehistoric earthworks in Britain and Ireland (London, 1976), p. 345).
[78] Peter Harbison, The axes of the early bronze age in Ireland (Munich, 1969), p. 1.
[79] Peter Harbison, The daggers and the halberds of the early bronze age in Ireland (Munich, 1969), pp 3, 35.
[80] George Eogan, Catalogue of Irish bronze swords (Dublin, 1965).

haft bent to an approximate right angle, a 'knee-haft', began to be used. The butt of the axe was thrust into a slot cut in the end of the knee, the flanges being tight against its sides to prevent lateral movement, and a binding held the axehead in place (fig. 14). By the end of the early bronze age or beginning of the middle bronze age, axes were cast with more pronounced flanges— haft-flanged axes as they are now called—but these still split their hafts in use. This defect was overcome by the introduction of the stop-ridge, a feature probably derived from the central thickening of some of the earlier flat axes. The ends of the knee-haft rested against the stop-ridges and thus backward movement was prevented. In the middle bronze age, flanges were drawn out and curved somewhat inward from each side so as to grip the ends of the knee more firmly, and in the later examples the metal of the septum was thinned so that the stop-ridge became a pronounced ledge-like feature. Sometimes, too, the ends of the flanges were continued downward on to the face of the blade to form a pointed ornamental feature. While it is possible that this type evolved into something like the 'west European' palstave or the corresponding British middle-bronze-age version, in which the flanges and

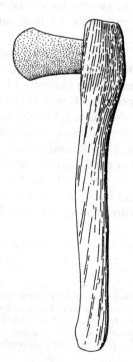

Fig. 14 Reconstruction of an early bronze age axe-head mounted in a club-shaped wooden shaft. After John Waddell, *The prehistoric archaeology of Ireland* (Galway, 1998).

stop-ridge coalesced to form haft pockets on each side of the septum, it is probable that the palstave was a fresh introduction into Ireland, here to be copied, though not extensively, by the Irish smiths.

Many of the flat- and low-flanged axes are ornamented in various ways (fig. 15) and some of them are so beautiful that one can hardly imagine them ever having been used for any kind of rough work. Many of the ornamental motifs are similar to those found on the food vessel pottery of the early bronze age, but it is not possible to say which copied which, if indeed there was any copying at all.

In his study of all the axes of the early part of the metal age in Ireland, Harbison[81] points out that 56 per cent of all the known examples are unprovenanced, and of the remaining 44 per cent about four-fifths have precise provenances. Almost 95 per cent of all the axes are isolated finds, and out of the thirty-seven associated finds only four included such items as halberds and daggers, and these four hoards (from Knocknague, County Galway;

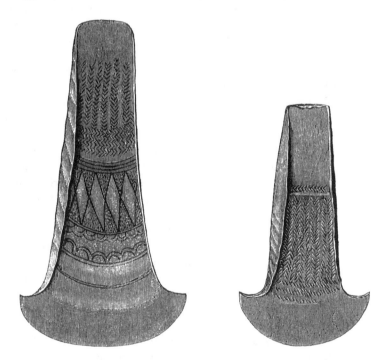

Fig. 15 Decorated bronze axeheads: that on the left without provenance; that on the right from Trim, Co. Meath. After John Evans, *The ancient bronze implements . . . of Great Britain and Ireland* (London, 1881). Scale 1:2.

[81] Harbison, *Axes*, p. 1.

Whitespots, County Down; Frankford, County Offaly; and Killaha East, County Kerry, respectively) provide the framework on which the chronological succession of axe types must be based.

The halberd has a sturdy blade with a strong midrib and was mounted at right angles to a long haft by means of rivets. In Ireland the haft seems always to have been of wood, while in central Europe some examples have tubular metal handles. Well preserved halberd blades show little evidence of wear or resharpening, and the points, which would have been very susceptible to damage, are remarkably perfect in many examples. It is not known whether it was used as an implement, as a weapon, or merely as a symbol of office or ceremonial object. The lightness of the riveted mounting and the absence of characteristic wear or damage from use suggest that it was not intended to be used in any strenuous activity.

Its distribution in Europe is widespread, from southern Italy to Scandinavia and from Hungary to Portugal; in addition, it is depicted in rock carvings, as for instance at Valcamonica in northern Italy. Its exact place of origin is not known nor has it been possible to determine its direction of spread. While Spanish and Italian origins have been suggested in the past, present opinion is hardening on central Germany. Because about 40 per cent of all the known halberds are concentrated in Ireland,[82] it has been argued that the object was invented and developed here and then distributed to Europe.[83] Ó Ríordáin divided the Irish halberds into six groups, which for him represented both a typological and chronological series, the earliest type being a translation into metal of an original flint implement. His type 4 was exported through Scotland to Scandinavia and central Germany. He dated the earliest Irish halberds to about 1800 B.C. and type 4 to about 1700 B.C., and assumed a halberd survival into the late bronze age. Disagreement with almost every point of Ó Ríordáin's thesis has, however, been expressed by various workers, the most recent of them being Harbison,[84] who conveniently summarises and gives the references to all the important discussions of the implement. He offers a classification into four types (fig. 16) and suggests 1700–1550 B.C. as the period during which the Irish halberds were made.

The most comprehensive work on Irish daggers has also been done by Harbison, and what follows is taken directly from his study.[85] The majority of the 142 early bronze-age daggers are single isolated finds discovered by chance in the course of peat cutting, river dredging, and suchlike works, and in many cases nothing is known of the circumstances in which they were found nor of their provenance. Only thirteen daggers have come from associ-

---

[82] Harbison, *Daggers & halberds*, p. 35.
[83] S. P. Ó Ríordáin, 'The halberd in bronze age Europe: a study in prehistoric origins, evolution, distribution and chronology' in *Archaeologia*, lxxxvi (1937), pp 195–321.
[84] Harbison, *Daggers & halberds*, pp 57–8.
[85] Ibid., pp 3–31.

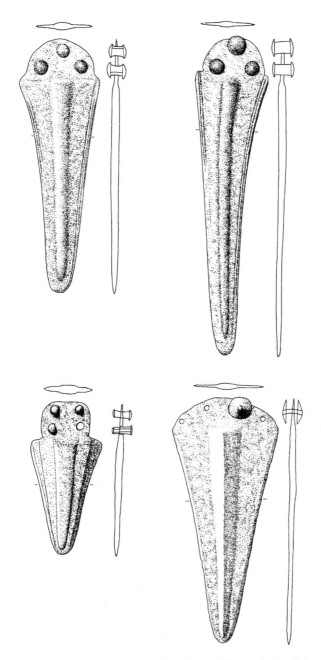

Fig. 16 Harbison's four types of halberd: Carn (from Hillswood, Co. Galway), Cotton (from the Hill of Allen, Co. Kildare), Clonard (from near Clonard, Co. Meath), and Breaghwy (from Breaghwy, Co. Mayo). After Peter Harbison, *The daggers and the halberds of the early bronze age in Ireland* (Munich, 1969). Scale 1:3.5.

ated finds—four from hoards, the rest all probably from graves. The hoards were chance finds, none of them scientifically excavated, found in bogs or hidden under stones. The graves containing daggers have, however, been excavated. These were usually inhumation burials in cists, sometimes with an accompanying pottery vessel. Some graves were isolated, some in small cemeteries and some were covered by a tumulus or cairn. Dagger graves are only a very small proportion of the known early bronze-age burials.

Irish daggers are diverse in style, dimensions and shape, and their classification is therefore very difficult; but, bearing this in mind, ten types covering eighty-three daggers are suggested by Harbison, leaving a miscellaneous residue of sixty-three daggers. He believes that all the daggers found in Ireland are of Irish manufacture. He says that there is no definite evidence that any of them was imported, though the idea of dagger-making and many of the dagger shapes did come from outside. The earliest Irish dagger—the tanged Knocknague type—has its nearest parallel in England and it was from there that the idea and the shape were introduced.

At the end of the early bronze age, if not at the beginning of the middle bronze age, some Irish daggers show a swing away from the English models, and the introduction of the 'Atlantic rapiers' indicates a new direction from which the Irish metal industry received fresh impulses. On the dagger evidence, this probably came from Brittany. French dirks and rapiers, or at least some knowledge of them, were now introduced into Ireland; and the dagger manufacturers, thus stimulated, embarked upon a series of local developments, some of which were very remarkable indeed, as for instance the rapier from Lissane, County Derry.[86] Razors, already present before the end of the early bronze age, became commoner and forty-one of them are now known from Ireland.[87]

The plain leaf-shaped spearhead with its socket extending into the blade probably came in at this time and the native smiths applied the hollow-casting technique embodied in it to the old tanged and part-socketed dagger-shaped spear, to produce the fully socketed spear with ribbed kite-shaped blade. This usually had loops on its socket for tying it to the shaft, and in due course the loops appeared also on the sockets of the leaf-shaped spears and eventually became incorporated into the bases of the blade-wings in some examples. The ribbed kite-shaped spears, and the stone moulds in which they were cast, are common in Ireland but are few in Britain. Throughout the period in question, 2000–1200 B.C., continuity in axe production is marked and the haft-flanged and wing-flanged types are straightforward developments from the early bronze-age flanged axe and were probably not at all influenced by the

[86] B. Trump, 'The origin and development of British middle bronze age rapiers' in *Prehist. Soc. Proc.*, xxviii (1962), p. 87; Peter Harbison, *Pre-Christian Ireland* (London, 1988), p. 129.

[87] E. Binchy, 'Irish razors and razor-knives of the middle bronze age' in Etienne Rynne (ed.), *North Munster studies* (Limerick, 1967), p. 43.

imported British or European palstaves. Technological continuity is also shown by the persisting use of stone moulds of various kinds, though these are now mainly of the bivalve type that replaced the earlier open moulds. They are of particular interest because several contain matrices for casting different types of object and in this way contemporaneity of some metal types is established. Here, following Eogan,[88] the middle bronze age has been tightly defined as the period from 1400 to 1200 B.C., even though it is likely that many of its features continued to a much later time, perhaps even down to 900 B.C., or later.[89] As already pointed out, 1200 B.C. is a convenient termination date for the middle period, as after this certain new influences, to be mentioned below, can be detected.

IT has been generally believed that the alluvial gold of County Wicklow was the metal used in the Irish gold ornaments of the bronze age. Recent research[90] has, however, thrown doubt on this assumption. In the 1960s, with the cooperation of the National Museum of Ireland, a programme of analysis of gold objects was initiated and at the same time nodules of Wicklow gold were examined, the whole work being done as part of a European study of the beginnings of metallurgy. In all, 1,425 European gold objects were studied, of which 507 were of Irish provenance. Dr Axel Hartmann, who carried out the analyses, argues that the majority of the Irish objects were not made from Wicklow gold and that metal must have been imported as raw material, or in some cases as manufactured objects. Only one group of sixty-six objects, made up of forty-one lunulae, fourteen sun discs, two foil earrings, a bracelet, and eight strips of gold foil, can plausibly be ascribed to a Wicklow source. He also suggests that this group is chronologically the earliest (1700–1400 B.C.). While these analytical results must now be taken into account in any discussion of Irish gold, many questions remain. It may be that there were sources other than Wicklow—for instance, the alluvial gold of Tyrone, Derry, Donegal, and Antrim. The finding of no less than forty-nine lunulae in the north and west of Ireland gives some substance to this suggestion.[91] Probably the earliest of our gold ornaments are the thin discs of various sizes from about 1 cm to 10 cm in diameter. A small plain disc, 11 mm diameter, with two perforations near the centre, was found in the excavation of the domestic

[88] George Eogan, 'The later bronze age in the light of recent research' in *Prehist. Soc. Proc.*, xxx (1964), pp 268–351.
[89] Colin Burgess, 'Chronology and terminology in the British bronze age' in *The Antiquaries Journal*, xlix (1969), p. 24.
[90] Axel Hartmann, *Prähistorische Goldfunde aus Europa: Studien zu den Anfängen der Metallurgie 3* (Berlin, 1970).
[91] J. J. Taylor, 'Lunulae reconsidered' in *Prehist. Soc. Proc.*, xxxvi (1970), pp 49, 64. There has been considerable discussion, and indeed criticism, of Hartmann's views regarding the allegedly non-native character of the Irish gold. See, for example, Joseph Raftery, 'Irish prehistoric objects: new light on the source of the metal' in *R.S.A.I. Jn.*, ci (1971), pp 101–5; Peter

settlement at Site D, Lough Gur,[92] in a horizon containing late neolithic flat-bottomed pottery and beaker sherds, as well as a number of objects in copper or bronze. The majority of the discs are ornamented with very low repoussé geometrical motifs arranged in cross-in-circle patterns or in concentric patterns of plain or zigzag lines. A few of the smaller discs of this type have beaker and early bronze-age associations in Britain. Apart from the Lough Gur example noted above, all the known Irish discs are chance finds, and little or nothing has been recorded of the circumstances in which they were found. It is known however that ten were found in pairs in different parts of the country. It has been assumed that these discs are the same sort of thing as the gold-plated bronze disc mounted on a little six-wheeled bronze waggon found at Trundholm Moss in Denmark.[93] A bronze figure of a horse stands on the front part of the waggon and the whole is thought to be a cult object representing a 'sun chariot'; hence, the Irish discs have been called 'sun discs'. The perforations at their centres suggest, however, that glued to a wooden or bone backing they were sewn on the clothing in pairs as ornaments or as ornamental buttons. Two discs from Roscommon are similar to a pair from Oviedo, Spain, and may indicate Irish–Iberian contact.[94]

One disc is different from all the rest. It is large, 12.1 cm in diameter, and has an all-over decoration made up of an elaborate pattern of concentric circles, triangles, and herring-bone devices. It was found in a peat bog at Latoon, County Cavan, with two gold bracelets and two dress fasteners, an association that indicates that it belongs to the Dowris or latest phase of the bronze age.[95] Also belonging to the early bronze age are the elongated basket-shaped earrings. The Irish examples are unlocalised, but three pairs were found in a bell beaker grave at Radley in Oxfordshire, England.[96] Another type of sheet gold earring has parallels in Portugal and may be further evidence of Irish–Iberian contact.[97] Penannular earrings of moulded, bar-

---

Harbison, 'Hartmann's gold analyses: a comment' in *R.S.A.I. Jn.*, ci (1971), pp 159–60; S. Briggs, J. Brennan, and G. Freeburn, 'Irish prehistoric gold-working: some geological and metallurgical considerations' in *Bulletin of the Historical Metallurgy Group*, vii, no. 2 (1973), pp 18–26; B. G. Scott, 'The occurrences of platinum as a trace element in Irish gold: comments on Hartmann's gold analyses' in *Irish Archaeological Research Forum*, iii, no. 2 (1976), pp 21–4; Axel Hartmann, 'Irish and British gold types and their west European counterparts' in Michael Ryan (ed.), *The origins of metallurgy in Atlantic Europe* (Dublin, 1980), pp 215–28.

[92] S. P. Ó Ríordáin, 'Lough Gur excavations: neolithic and bronze age houses on Knockadoon' in *R.I.A. Proc.*, lvi (1954), sect. C, p. 410.

[93] J. M. Coles and A. F. Harding, *The bronze age in Europe* (London, 1979), p. 314, pl. 12a; George Eogan, 'Gold discs of the Irish late bronze age' in Ó Corráin, *Ir. antiquity*, p. 157.

[94] J. J. Taylor, 'Early bronze age gold neck-rings in western Europe' in *Prehist. Soc. Proc.*, xxxiv (1968), p. 261.

[95] Eogan, 'Gold discs', pp 148–9, and *Hoards of the Irish later bronze age* (Dublin, 1983), pp 64–5.

[96] Stuart Piggott, *Ancient Europe from the beginnings of agriculture to classical antiquity* (Edinburgh, 1965), p. 101, fig. 55.

[97] Taylor, 'Early bronze age gold neck-rings', p. 261.

twisted, and flange-twisted forms are found in the middle period, thought to be inspired by eastern Mediterranean types. Hair or tress rings are also found, influenced by Egyptian wig-rings, if not actually imported from there.

The most characteristically Irish of the early bronze-age gold ornaments is the lunula, a crescentic collar made from thin sheet gold. While a few are completely unornamented, normally there is a finely incised pattern of triangles, lozenges, and chevrons near the points of the crescent and along the edges of the broad part of the plate. This ornamentation is so fine that it is visible only on close examination. When being worn, the lunula evidently relied for effect on its sheer expanse of glittering metal. Various prototypes have been suggested for it: namely, that it derived from the gold collars of Egypt, or from the crescentic jet necklaces found in Scotland and northern Ireland, but none is completely satisfying. The most complete study of the type[98] lists eighty-one lunulae as having been found in Ireland, and of these, forty-five are now in the National Museum of Ireland and four are in the Ulster Museum, Belfast. The United States has three, Canada has one, fourteen are in various museums in Britain, seven are in private collections, and seven are lost. Twenty-two have been found outside of Ireland: six in Scotland, four in England, one in Wales, nine in north-west France, and one each in Luxemburg and Germany. An Irish origin for the type as a whole is hardly disputable, and those lunulae found outside Ireland may be exports, or some of them may have been made abroad by travelling Irish craftsmen. Taylor compares the ornament on some of the Irish lunulae with motifs found on beaker pottery and considers this beaker influence on the collars to have taken place about 1700 B.C. This has led her to discount the supposed relationships of the lunulae ornament to that of the jet or amber necklace.

Who were the wearers of these collars, and were they men or women or both, and on what ceremonial occasions were the collars brought out? Since all are chance finds and for the most part unassociated with other diagnostic objects, one cannot be more specific than to say that the wearers were the descendants of the neolithic, beaker, food-vessel, and urn folk.

THE later bronze age is the period beginning about 1200 B.C. and continuing to the commencement of the iron age. Eogan has divided it into three phases, 1200–900 B.C., 900–700 B.C., and 700–200 B.C., the so-called Bishopsland, Roscommon, and Dowris phases respectively after three important hoards.[99] The Bishopsland phase is marked by the presence of new tools such as socketed axes, socketed hammers, punches, gravers, anvils, and the knobbed sickle, as well as ornaments, mainly of gold. Hoards are plentiful and contain much gold. The hoard discovered at Bishopsland, County Kildare, contained

---

[98] Taylor, 'Lunalae reconsidered'.
[99] George Eogan, 'The later bronze age in the light of recent research' in *Prehist. Soc. Proc.*, xxx (1964), pp 268–351.

the fine tools of a specialised craftsman. Before the end of the phase a new and important weapon had been introduced into Ireland, the bronze sword. Although the Roscommon phase covers approximately two centuries, the number of bronze finds that can be shown to belong to it is small. They include some hoards of scrap metal, such as the hoard that gives its name to the phase, and some swords of the flange-hilted or grip-tongue type.[100] The Dowris phase is marked by the presence of a considerable number of new types. The influences that brought about their development came from different regions and not only through southern Britain, as was largely the case during the Bishopsland and Roscommon phases.[101] Among the objects of the Dowris phase are swords, scabbard chapes, leaf-shaped spearheads with peg-holes in the sockets, socketed axes, knives of socketed and tanged forms, socketed sickles, socketed gouges, socketed and tanged chisels, trunnion chisels, socketed hammers, anvils, and flesh-hooks; and most of these had continued in being right through from the Bishopsland phase, as did also tweezers and bifid razors. Six shields made in bronze are now known,[102] and there are also examples in wood and leather from Cloonlara, County Mayo, Annandale, County Leitrim, and Clonbrin, County Longford. Two wooden shield moulds also occur. Buckets and cauldrons, made from sheet-bronze plates riveted together, are a feature of the Dowris phase and have a marked Irish distribution. The buckets, first imported from east-central Europe, were copied in Ireland, while the Irish-made cauldrons have an ultimate prototype in Greece.[103] There are also some wooden bowls, boxes, and the wooden cauldron-like object from Altartate, County Monaghan, which probably belong to the period.[104]

Bronze trumpets or horns are a marked feature of the Dowris phase, no fewer than twenty-four having been contained in the Dowris hoard itself. Over one hundred are known from Ireland, and apart from the twenty-four in the Dowris hoard they occur in two main concentrations, one in County Antrim and the other in south-west Ireland in the counties of Cork, Kerry,

---

[100] The integrity of this 'phase' as a genuine archaeological entity has in recent years come into question, not least by Eogan himself (*Hoards of Ir. later bronze age*, pp 7, 47, 49).

[101] Eogan, 'The later bronze age in the light of recent research', p. 293.

[102] J. M. Coles, 'European bronze age shields' in *Prehist. Soc. Proc.*, xxviii (1962), pp 156–90; Barry Raftery, 'Two recently discovered shields from the Shannon basin' in *R.S.A.I. Jn.*, cxii (1982), pp 5–17.

[103] This is the view most cogently and comprehensively argued in C. F. C. Hawkes and M. A. Smith, 'On some buckets and cauldrons of the bronze and early iron ages' in *The Antiquaries Journal*, xxxvii (1957), pp 131–98. More recently, however, S. Gerloff ('Bronze age class A cauldrons: typology, origins, and chronology' in *R.S.A.I. Jn.*, cxvi (1986), pp 84–115) has rejected the idea of a Mediterranean background for the insular cauldron series and has argued for a beginning for them in the last quarter of the second millennium B.C.

[104] Adolf Mahr, 'A wooden cauldron from Altartate, Co. Monaghan' in *R.I.A. Proc.*, xlii (1934), sect. C, pp 11–29; Barry Raftery, *La Tène in Ireland: problems of origin and chronology* (Marburg, 1984), pp 227–9. The date of this cauldron remains enigmatic. It could belong equally to the later bronze age or to the earlier part of the iron age.

and Clare. Coles, who has recently made a thorough study of them, shows that the sounds that could have been made with them were very simple indeed.[105]

Among the bronze ornaments were disc-headed and sunflower pins.[106] In the former the pin comes straight out of the centre of the back of the disc, while in the latter the pin is bent approximately at right angles just behind the disc. In both types the front of the disc usually has a central conical knob around which a group of close-set concentric circles is incised in the bronze. Between the outermost circle and the periphery there are often very lightly incised hatched triangles. These two pin types are derived from similar pins in Denmark and north Germany.

IN the Bishopsland phase gold was plentiful. At least thirty-one bar torcs are known from Ireland. They vary in size from those worn on the neck to the two very large ones found near the Rath of the Synods at Tara in 1810 which can be worn on the waist as girdles. The larger of the two is 122 cm long and the smaller is 120 cm long. Bar torcs in bronze came into Britain and Ireland from the west Baltic and were being made in gold in Ireland from about 1200 B.C. onward. Of the thirty-nine examples in Britain and the fourteen in France, some may be exports from Ireland.[107]

Presumably these various gold types continued to be worn during the Roscommon phase (900-700 B.C.) though evidence on this point is not good. During the succeeding and final part of the bronze age, the Dowris phase, beginning about 700 B.C. and continuing at least to the conventional round figure of 500 B.C.—probably much longer in most parts of Ireland—the number and variety of the gold ornaments in use was truly remarkable. These include sleeve- and dress-fasteners, hair-rings, lock-rings, bullae, bracelets of several kinds, gorgets, collars, neck-rings, boxes, hollow balls, beads, pins, strips, plates, rings, and various miscellaneous items.[108]

After the lunulae of the early bronze age, the gorgets of the late bronze age are probably the most spectacular items of Irish gold. These also are collars

[105] J. M. Coles, 'Irish bronze age horns and their relations with north Europe' in *Prehist. Soc. Proc.*, xxix (1963), pp 326–56; see also P. Holmes, 'The manufacturing technology of the Irish bronze age horns' in Ryan (ed.), *The origins of metallurgy*, pp 165–88.

[106] George Eogan, 'Report on the excavations of some passage graves, unprotected inhumation burials and a settlement site at Knowth, Co. Meath' in *R.I.A. Proc.*, lxxiv (1974), sect. C, pp 11–112.

[107] George Eogan, 'The associated finds of gold bar torcs' in *R.S.A.I. Jn.*, xcvii (1967), pp 129–75; see also M. Almagro Gorbea, 'The Bodonal de la Sierra gold find' in *R.S.A.I. Jn.*, civ (1974), pp 44–51.

[108] E. C. R. Armstrong, *Catalogue of Irish gold ornaments in the collection of the Royal Irish Academy* (Dublin, 1933); see also George Eogan, 'Lock-rings of the late bronze age' in *R.I.A. Proc.*, lxvii (1969), sect. C, pp 93–148, '"Sleeve-fasteners" of the late bronze age' in Frances Lynch and Colin Burgess (ed.), *Prehistoric man in Wales and the west* (Bath, 1972), pp 189–209, 'Gold discs of the Irish late bronze age' in Ó Corráin, *Ir. antiquity*, pp 147–62, 'The gold vessels of the bronze age in Ireland and beyond' in *R.I.A. Proc.*, lxxxi (1981), sect. C, pp 345–82, and *Hoards of Ir. later bronze age*.

of crescentic shape and nine of them are known. The crescent is decorated all over in rounded relief bands sometimes separated by rope mouldings, lines of dots, and other devices achieved by the repoussé technique, that is, by hammering up from the back. The ends of the crescent are affixed to discs ornamented in patterns of concentric circles and repoussé dots. One gorget only has been found in association with other objects and this is the example in the hoard found at Gorteenreagh in County Clare.[109] The other objects are a sleeve fastener, two lock rings, and two bracelets, which show that the period in question is the Dowris phase of the late bronze age.

The most remarkable hoard of gold ornaments ever found in Ireland, or indeed in western Europe, belongs to the late bronze age. It was discovered in March 1854 in the townland of Mooghaun North, County Clare, by men who were working on the construction of the West Clare railway.[110] The objects seem to have been contained within a stone setting of some kind, one stone of which protruded from the side of a cutting. When the stone was pulled out a cascade of gold ornaments followed. There was an immediate scramble for them and groups were sold at once in various places and apparently melted down. From contemporary accounts it is known, however, that the hoard contained at least 138 penannular bracelets, six collars, two neckrings, two lock-rings, and possibly two torcs, all of gold. Of these, thirteen items are in the National Museum of Ireland and thirteen or fourteen pieces are in the British Museum; a few may have survived in private collections but the rest have disappeared from the record.

Another old find of 1805 that one would like to know more about was also quickly dispersed. It is described as a kind of garment made of small oblong gold plates with herringbone decoration. The plates were held together by wires passing through holes and the garment lay over a skeleton found in a cave in east Cork. Beside the bones were several amber beads.[111] Armstrong, following Croker, gives Carrigacrump cave near Castlemartyr as the find place, but local tradition, strongly persisting even in 1945, insisted that the find was made in a cave on the roadside about one mile east of the village in the townland of Knockane.[112] The one surviving plate from this find is in the National Museum.

From a hoard at Derrinboy, County Offaly, comes an apparently unique necklet consisting of a leather core of cylindrical cross-section, 4 mm in diameter, made from a continuous thin strip, folded along its length and

[109] Joseph Raftery, 'The Gorteenreagh hoard' in Etienne Rynne (ed.), *North Munster studies* (Limerick, 1967), pp 61–71.
[110] E. C. R. Armstrong, 'The great Clare find of 1854' in *R.S.A.I. Jn.*, xlvii (1917), pp 21–36; Eogan, *Hoards of Ir. later bronze age*, pp 69–72.
[111] Thomas Crofton Croker, *Researches in the south of Ireland* (London, 1824), p. 253; Armstrong, *Catalogue of Ir. gold ornaments*, p. 92.
[112] M. J. O'Kelly, 'Some prehistoric monuments of Imokilly' in *Cork Hist. Soc. Jn.*, l (1945), p. 23.

sewn with gut. This was covered all over with a closely wound gold wire of D-section, 1 mm wide and half that in thickness. The full length of unbroken gold wire measures when uncoiled 15.25 m long. The two ends of the gold-covered leather were thrust into a gold cylinder or ferrule where they were held in place by a rivet, now lost.[113] The pair of ribbed cuff-like bracelets found with this necklet at Derrinboy has parallels in Britain and perhaps also in Scandinavia.[114] Other bracelets of this kind have come from the counties of Westmeath and Sligo.[115]

Six other hoards listed by Eogan[116] contain twisted, plain, and other forms of bracelet and ribbon and bar torcs, showing how plentiful gold was in the bronze age. There are now about 600 ounces of prehistoric gold in the National Museum of Ireland and there are various Irish pieces in other museums and private collections in this country and abroad. Add to this all the objects that are known to have been melted down or otherwise lost or destroyed, and it is not surprising that the period has been called Ireland's 'first golden age' in a literal as well as a metaphorical sense.

Mention has been made of the amber beads lying beside the gold-covered skeleton found near Castlemartyr, County Cork. Amber, presumably imported from the Baltic, was much used for decorative purposes during the bronze age, mainly in the form of necklaces of beads. While some amber undoubtedly belongs to the early and middle bronze age, most of it appears to belong to the Dowris phase of the late bronze age, particularly the elaborate necklaces of graduated beads. There are several such necklaces in the national collection and a fine one of 116 beads, from Garvagh, County Londonderry, is in the Cork Public Museum (pl. 3).[117] The multistringed example from Derrybrien, County Galway (pl. 4), originally had about 500 beads, of which 460 survive intact.[118] This was found at the base of a peat bog, in a layer that has a C 14 date of 150 ± 90 B.C.[119] A large collection of glass beads from the late bronze-age settlement at Rathgall, County Wicklow, indicates that this material too was already in use in the later stages of the bronze age.[120]

---

[113] Eogan, *Hoards of Ir. later bronze age*, pp 42–3.
[114] George Eogan, 'Some observations on the middle bronze age in Ireland' in *R.S.A.I. Jn.*, xcii (1962), p. 50.
[115] Armstrong, *Catalogue of Ir. gold ornaments*.
[116] Eogan, 'Some observations', p. 47.
[117] M. J. O'Kelly, 'Two burials at Labbamolaga, Co. Cork' in *Cork Hist. Soc. Jn.*, lv (1950), pp 15–20.
[118] E. Prendergast, 'Amber necklace from Co. Galway' in *R.S.A.I. Jn.*, xc (1960), p. 65.
[119] GrN-650.
[120] Barry Raftery and J. Henderson, 'Some glass beads of the later bronze age in Ireland' in *Marburger Studien zur Vor- und Frühgeschichte*, ix (1987), pp 39–53.

# CHAPTER VI

# Iron-age Ireland

## BARRY RAFTERY

IRELAND was still in a developing bronze age when iron was first used in Europe. Already in the seventeenth and sixteenth centuries B.C. there is evidence from Greece,[1] Slovakia,[2] and elsewhere that meteoric iron was cold-hammered to form rings and other small items, and it now seems that forged iron was already being produced on a small scale in western Europe soon after the middle of the same millennium.[3] The Hittite kingdom of Asia Minor was an important centre of iron-working from about the fourteenth century B.C. onwards, but seems not to have had a monopoly of industrial production as was once believed.[4] Towards the end of the millennium the knowledge began to spread across the west on a significant scale. The tenth century B.C. saw the extension of iron-smelting techniques to Greece, and Etruria followed not long afterwards.[5] Inspiration from one or other of these two areas, and perhaps both, must have been chiefly responsible for the rapid dissemination of the new metal technology across transalpine Europe. Influences from the east, carried by nomadic Cimmerian horsemen—themselves masters of iron-working from the ninth or eighth centuries B.C.—may also have contributed to the burgeoning middle European iron industry.[6]

Already in the late bronze age Urnfield culture iron objects of local fabrication began to appear north of the Alps. An iron sword from a late Urnfield grave at Singen-Hohentwiel in south-west Germany is a classic example of transitional technology.[7] The first large-scale exploitation of iron in transalpine Europe, however, was by the archaeologically named Hallstatt culture,

[1] G. Varoufakis, 'Investigation of some Minoan and Mycenaean iron objects' in H. Haefner and R. Pleiner (ed.), *Frühes Eisen in Europa* (Schaffhausen, 1981), pp 25–32.
[2] R. Pleiner, 'Die Wege des Eisens nach Europa', ibid., p. 115, Abb. 1.
[3] J. A. Charles, 'The middle bronze-age iron punch of south-east Drenthe' in *Palaeohistoria*, xxvi (1984), pp 95–9.
[4] J. C. Waldbaum, 'The first archaeological appearance of iron and the transition to the iron age' in T. A. Wertime and J. D. Muhly (ed.), *The coming of the age of iron* (Yale, 1980), pp 80–81.
[5] Pleiner, art. cit., p. 122.
[6] Ibid., p. 121.
[7] W. Kimmig, 'Ein Grabfund der jüngeren Urnenfelderzeit (Hallstatt B3) mit Eisenschwert von Singen am Hohentwiel' in Haefner & Pleiner, *Frühes Eisen*, pp 37–43.

the ethnic successors of the Urnfield groups. It was this culture that carried the knowledge westwards.

The spread was rapid. As early as the sixth, possibly even the seventh, century B.C. iron-smelting was known in England, as is suggested by the evidence of All Cannings Cross, Wiltshire, and elsewhere.[8] A west Alpine sword of iron found its way to Llyn Fawr in Wales hardly later than 600 B.C. and with it were found not only native bronzes, but also copies in iron of insular bronze types.[9] Thus it is clearly shown that a knowledge of iron-working had penetrated almost to the western fringe of Europe little more than a century after its appearance north of the Alps. But the earliest date for the introduction of iron technology to Ireland remains uncertain. During the seventh century B.C. and into the sixth, when Hallstatt cultural groupings were disseminating the new metal techniques across Europe, Ireland was reaching the undoubted climax of her bronze age.[10] By now there must have been considerable population density on the island, organised in tribal areas with a strong and prosperous ruling elite. A thriving metal industry existed, no doubt controlled and directed by this leading caste.

During these centuries the Irish metalworkers, heirs to a thousand years of knowledge and experimentation, achieved total mastery in the working of bronze and gold. In many areas of technology, especially in gold-working, they led Europe. Ireland, though geographically peripheral, was at this time in the mainstream of European technical advances, and the country enjoyed intimate contact with widely dispersed areas of the Continent. The country must surely have been a major destination in the network of bronze-age trade routes. Himilco, the intrepid Carthaginian sailor, travelled up the Irish Sea in the sixth century B.C., and he knew of Ireland.[11] His 'Periplous', a sailing manual, was intended for other voyagers following the same route. Himilco was thus not alone in making such lengthy voyages; some may have made landfall in Ireland.

Ireland could hardly have been unaffected by the changes sweeping Europe in the course of the seventh and sixth centuries B.C. It is only surprising how meagre is the extent of Hallstatt influence in the country. Swords of bronze, Hallstatt in form but of insular manufacture, appear,[12]

[8] J. Alexander, 'The coming of iron-using in Britain', ibid., p. 60.

[9] C. F. Fox and H. A. Hyde, 'A second cauldron and iron sword from the Llyn Fawr hoard, Rhiygos, Glamorganshire' in *Antiq. Jn.*, xix (1939), pp 369–404; H. Savory, *National museum of Wales: guide catalogue of the early iron age collections* (Cardiff, 1976), pp 46–7.

[10] George Eogan, 'The later bronze age in Ireland in the light of recent research' in *Prehist. Soc. Proc.*, xxx (1964), pp 268–351.

[11] James F. Kenney, *The sources for the early history of Ireland, i : ecclesiastical* (New York, 1929), pp 121–2; C. F. C. Hawkes, *Pytheas: Europe and the Greek explorers* (Oxford, 1977).

[12] The writer can see no reason to accept as a genuine Hallstatt sword the corroded and shapeless iron fragment from the River Shannon at Athlone (Etienne Rynne, 'A classification of pre-viking Irish iron swords' in B. G. Scott (ed.), *Studies on early Ireland: essays presented to M.V. Duignan* (Belfast, 1982), p. 93, fig. 2).

and these soon begin to influence the indigenous sword development.[13] There are also some winged chapes (a widespread Hallstatt C form) and a few bracelets,[14] dress-fasteners,[15] and other items of Hallstatt type have also been found in the country. Most of the Hallstatt objects are chance discoveries, predominantly riverine. Only rarely are they associated with native material. There is thus uncertainty as to the correct interpretation of this novel cultural presence in the country.[16] These artefacts, all of bronze, can hardly, on their own, be taken to represent an 'early iron age'. Equally, there is little in them that supports the concept of contemporary folk intrusion. The varied mechanisms of exchange, distribution, and stimulus diffusion would readily account for the scattered Hallstatt remains in Ireland.

There are, however, some further indications that suggest that Ireland may indeed have acquired a knowledge of iron-working, in certain pockets of the country at least, as early as the sixth century or so B.C.,[17] a knowledge not unrelated, perhaps, to the appearance in the land of these Hallstatt elements. The evidence is tentative and uncertain, but it is possible that an incipient iron age had emerged on the island before the middle of the last pre-Christian millennium. Two looped and socketed axeheads of iron, stray finds from County Antrim, seem in their form to embody bronze age traditions of axe manufacture, and they may represent a technologically transitional phase between bronze and iron.[18] A cauldron of riveted iron sheets from Drumlane, County Cavan—again an isolated find—could be similarly regarded.[19] But the value of such stray finds, unaccompanied and thus undated, in the context of such far-reaching hypotheses is questionable. The evidence from excavation is more telling.

At the Rathtinaun (County Sligo) crannog the second occupation level, following on a phase characterised only by material of late bronze-age type, contained similar late bronze-age artefacts but now with the significant add-

---

[13] George Eogan, *Catalogue of Irish bronze age swords* (Dublin, 1965), pp 12–13.

[14] E.g. Raftery, *La Tène in Ire.*, p. 10, fig. 2.

[15] E.g. E. M. Jope, 'Iron age brooches in Ireland: a summary' in *U.J.A.*, 3rd ser., xxiv–xxv (1961–2), pp 25–6; Raftery, *La Tène in Ire.*, p. 145, fig. 78. There can, of course, be no certainty that the Irish Hallstatt fibulae are genuine, ancient imports.

[16] See Colin Burgess, 'The bronze age' in Colin Renfrew (ed.), *British prehistory: a new outline* (n.p., 1974), p. 213.

[17] B. G. Scott, 'Some notes on the transition from bronze to iron in Ireland' in *Irish Archaeological Research Forum*, i, no. 1 (1974), pp 9–24; idem, 'The introductions of non-ferrous and ferrous metal technologies to Ireland: motives and mechanisms' in Michael Ryan (ed.), *The origins of metallurgy in Atlantic Europe* (Dublin, 1980), pp 189–204; idem, 'The origins and early development of iron use in Ireland as seen from the archaeological, linguistic and literary records' in Haefner & Pleiner, *Frühes Eisen*, pp 101–8; Barry Raftery, 'Dowris, Hallstatt and La Tène in Ireland: problems of the transition from bronze to iron' in S. J. de Laet (ed.), *Acculturation and continuity in Atlantic Europe* (n.p., 1976), pp 189–97.

[18] Scott, 'Some notes on the transition from bronze to iron', pp 10–16.

[19] Barry Raftery, 'Iron age cauldrons in Ireland' in *Archaeologia Atlantica*, iii (1980), p. 57 and references.

ition of a few objects of iron. These included a swan's-neck pin of Hallstatt form, an iron flesh-hook of bronze-age type, and a crudely forged shafthole axehead.[20] Conventional archaeological dating for this layer around, or before, the middle of the last millennium B.C. is at variance with the radio-carbon age-determinations, which suggest a date nearer the birth of Christ.[21] Taken at their face value these would indicate a late survival of bronze-age traditions in the country and a consequent late introduction of iron-working. Such a situation is, of course, eminently possible, for the bronze age could have lingered in places late into the last millennium B.C.[22] A question-mark must, however, hang over these dates; their accuracy must be considered doubtful. The second level at Rathtinaun may be anything up to four or five centuries older than is suggested by them.

Evidence from two other Irish occupation sites may also further support the notion of an early introduction of iron to Ireland. On Aughinish Island in the Shannon estuary, in County Limerick, two small stone enclosures produced a range of domestic material generally taken to be of late bronze-age type. Associated with this material within one of the enclosures was a corroded iron object which could be part of a horse-bit.[23] The initial settlement on Navan Fort (Emain Macha), County Armagh, a small, palisaded hilltop enclosure, clearly domestic in character, yielded a number of late bronze-age bronzes[24] in apparent association with portion of a Hallstatt C winged chape.[25] The eighth- or seventh-century B.C. radiocarbon age-determinations from the site are here wholly in keeping with the archaeological evidence.[26]

Navan Fort, Aughinish, and Rathtinaun appear, therefore, to indicate a bronze-age Ireland in touch, to varying degrees, with the world of iron. To these can be added a hoard of native bronzes from Kilmurry, County Kerry, which included an exotic, knob-ended bracelet of Hallstatt manufacture.[27] The iron axehead at Rathtinaun is likely to be of local manufacture, as may be the stray iron objects noted earlier, from Antrim and Cavan. Dating in the seventh or sixth century B.C. for these objects is possible. Thus it seems that before the middle of the last millennium B.C. Ireland was on the threshold of the iron age.

[20] Joseph Raftery, 'Iron age and Irish Sea: problems for research' in Charles Thomas (ed.), *The iron age in the Irish Sea province* (Cardiff, 1972), p. 3.

[21] *Radiocarbon*, iii (1961), pp 34–5 (D-53 to 61).

[22] B. Williams, 'Excavations at Kilsmullan, Co. Fermanagh' in *U.J.A.*, 3rd ser., xlvii (1984), pp 7–8.

[23] E. P. Kelly, 'Aughinish stoneforts' in Tom Delaney (ed.), *Excavations 1974* (n.p., n.d.), pp 20–21.

[24] A. Selkirk and D. M. Waterman, 'Navan Fort' in *Current Archaeology*, no. 22 (Sept. 1970), p. 306.

[25] Information from C. J. Lynn of the Archaeological Survey of Northern Ireland.

[26] C. J. Lynn, 'Navan Fort: a draft summary of D. M. Waterman's excavations' in *Emania*, i (1986), p. 16.

[27] George Eogan, *Hoards of the Irish later bronze age* (Dublin, 1983), pp 93–4, fig. 46B.

But round this time the archaeological record becomes obscure, and firm knowledge concerning social and cultural developments in the next few centuries is all but denied us. There can be little doubt, however, that significant changes were taking place, which were to play a major role in shaping the human geography of Ireland for many centuries to come. During this period the bronze age withered, mass-production in bronze and gold ceased, and Ireland appears to have withdrawn, for a time, into uncharacteristic insular isolation. The reasons for such changes are not clear. We do not know if the industries of the bronze age collapsed with cataclysmic suddenness (as is sometimes assumed), or died of slow strangulation. All we know is that when the fog partially clears in the last few centuries B.C. there is not the slightest trace of surviving late bronze-age influences. Climatic deterioration is frequently taken as contributing to the decline, and there may have been a significant expansion of bogland.[28] Reduction in living-space, combined with increasing population and consequent soil exhaustion, could have brought about pressure on living-space and subsequent political instability. Developments abroad could also have played a part. The rapid spread of a new social order across Europe, perhaps actively hostile to Irish interests, and the increasing obsolescence of bronze as a material for tools and weapons, might have had serious repercussions on an Irish export industry, thus further accelerating the momentum of economic recession.[29] The matter is speculative. It is clear, at any rate, that during these centuries there were no dramatic advances in the history of iron technology in Ireland.

THE social stagnation that seems to have beset Ireland around the middle of the last pre-Christian millennium contrasts with contemporary developments in Europe. Around 500 B.C. the late Hallstatt centres of eastern France and southern Germany had reached their greatest period of power and prosperity. Luxuries were demanded and could be readily afforded. Wine from the Mediterranean was traded northwards in enormous quantities and with it came goblets, flagons, strainers, mixing bowls, and many other exotic consumer goods to indulge the whims of an aristocratic élite, confident and secure in its wealth and its absolute authority. Influence from the Greek and Etruscan worlds reached deeply into late Hallstatt society. A wall of sundried mud bricks at the Heuneburg fort in southern Germany—a Greek replica, wholly unsuited to the damp middle-European climate—illustrates well the all-pervasive nature of classical influence.[30] So too do the imported

---

[28] See Stuart Piggott, 'A note on climatic deterioration in the first millennium B.C. in Britain' in *Scottish Archaeological Forum*, iv (1972), pp 109–13.

[29] See C. F. C. Hawkes and R. R. Clarke, 'Gahlsdorf and Caister-on-Sea: two finds of late bronze Irish gold' in Idris Foster and Leslie Alcock (ed.), *Culture and environment: essays in honour of Sir Cyril Fox* (London, 1963), pp 193–250.

[30] E. Gersbach, 'Ergebnisse der letzten Ausgrabungen auf der Heuneburg bei Hundersingen (Donau)' in *Arch. Korr.*, viii (1978), pp 301–11, and earlier literature.

gravegoods in the wagon-graves at Vix in eastern France[31] and Eberdingen-Hochdorf in southern Germany.[32] At the latter site in particular the presence of a unique wheeled settee underlines the almost reckless extravagance of the *nouveau riche* rulers.

But the spectacular climax was suddenly over: the Hallstatt strongholds declined rapidly. In the middle of the fifth century B.C. new foci of power emerged and a new culture appears in the archaeological record. This culture, representative of the second major phase of the European iron age, is referred to as the La Tène culture, so named after an important find-spot on Lake Neuchâtel in Switzerland. Now, for the first time, the evidence of archaeology is supported by the writings of classical authors, and now from the shadows of prehistory a Celtic-speaking people emerges, described collectively as Gauls or Galatians. These people, bearers across Europe of the La Tène culture, are those we most frequently term the Celts.

Wide-ranging folk movements from the early fourth century B.C. onwards—well documented both in history and archaeology—bring the La Tène Celts from their central European heartlands to Italy, Greece, the Balkans, and Asia Minor. They sacked Rome, burnt Delphi, treated with Alexander the Great; their impact on the classical world was considerable. An eloquent picture of them emerges from the contemporary accounts, stressing their warlike and belligerent personality, their vanity and love of pomp and ostentation, their head-hunting and feasting, their skilled use of chariots. There is much more besides and many of the details recur in the earliest Irish sagas.

Thousands of graves, richly bedecked with weapons, ornaments, and other paraphernalia, yield much information on the material culture of the Celts and confirm much of what the Greeks and Romans wrote. Warrior burials stand out, the dead most often accompanied by a heavy iron slashing sword, spears, and a long, oval shield. Chieftains in some areas were interred with a light, two-wheeled chariot. Women, too, were often sumptuously laid to rest with ornate jewellery, toilet implements, and other objects of personal adornment; they were in no way inferior to men, either in death or in life.

A major innovation in the material culture of the La Tène Celts is the appearance of an art form utterly divorced from the sterile geometry of the Hallstatt era. La Tène art is a curvilinear art, rooted ultimately in the foliate patterns of the Mediterranean, but developed from the beginning into abstract compositions of often astounding virtuosity. Palmettes, lyres, waves, spirals, S-scrolls, and leafy tendrils are the dominant motifs, writhing and flowing over the decorated surfaces in themes of great vigour and originality. This is art, not mere ornament, an art of tension and contrasts, where

[31] R. Joffroy, *Le trésor de Vix: histoire et portée d'une grande découverte* (Paris, 1962).
[32] J. Biel, 'Ein Fürstengrabhügel der späten Hallstattzeit bei Eberdingen-Hochdorf, Kr. Ludwigsburg Baden-Württemberg' in *Germania*, lx (1982), pp 61–104.

symmetry and asymmetry, discipline and indiscipline coexist with ease. There is mystery and illusion, fantasy and intrigue. Forms move and change, merging into one another to deceive the eye. Faces or suggested faces peer from the leafy background, undertones of the Netherworld are never far away. Poseidonius spoke of the Celtic delight in mystification. 'They speak in riddles,' he observed, 'hinting at things, leaving much to be understood.'[33] This is the essence of Celtic art. Through their art we can peer into the heart of the Celts, into their very soul.

The military hegemony of the Celts reached its zenith in the early third century B.C. but before that century had passed the tide had turned irrevocably: the slumbering Roman colossus was awake. At Telamon, in 225 B.C., a great Celtic confederation from both sides of the Alps suffered a disastrous reverse at the hands of the Romans, and the Celts ceased to be a force in Italy. From then on, with the inexorable advance of Rome, their world increasingly shrank. The year 51 B.C., a key date, saw the fall of Alesia to Caesar, and this signalled the collapse of Celtic independence in Europe.

The initial wave of La Tène expansion across Europe may have touched Britain but seems not to have reached Ireland. The 'dark age' continued. Pytheas, the Massaliote astronomer and geographer, followed the same route as Himilco up the Irish Sea in 325 B.C. In his later writings he referred to the 'Pretannic islands' and to Ireland by name—Ierne—but it is unlikely that he landed here.[34] He may have been acquainted with the rumours, current later, which regarded the country as a bleak and inhospitable place where unmentionable practices were everyday custom.[35]

But the earliest firm evidence of a continental La Tène presence in Ireland dates to the time of Pytheas. This is provided by the buffer-torc of gold, discovered in the nineteenth century with a ribbon-torc of the same metal at Clonmacnoise, not far from the Shannon in County Offaly.[36] The buffer-torc is a distinctive early La Tène type, the homeland of which is to be sought in the middle Rhine area. The accompanying ribbon-torc may, however, be of native manufacture.[37] We do not know how, or in what circumstances, the Clonmacnoise buffer-torc found its way to Ireland. It is a superbly fashioned example with fine ornament on the 'buffers' and on the nape portion, and was clearly a valuable object. It could have been a gift, a bribe, or maybe an offering for a successful voyage, or it might simply be an item of trade. At any rate it indicates direct contact with La Tène Europe around, or shortly

---

[33] J. J. Tierney, 'The Celtic ethnography of Posidonius' in *R.I.A. Proc.*, lx (1960), sect. C, pp 189–275.

[34] C. F. C. Hawkes, *Pytheas: Europe and the Greek explorers* (Oxford, 1977), p. 33.

[35] J. J. Tierney, 'The Greek geographic tradition and Ptolemy's evidence for Irish geography' in *R.I.A. Proc.*, lxxvi (1976), sect. C, pp 257–65.

[36] Barry Raftery, *A catalogue of Irish iron age antiquities* (Marburg, 1983), no. 451; *La Tène in Ire.*, pp 175–8.

[37] See Raftery, *La Tène in Ire.*, pp 178–81.

before, 300 B.C. But this isolated find can hardly be taken as demonstrating immigration to the west of Ireland from the European land-mass, nor indeed can it be seen as representing the beginnings in Ireland of a La Tène iron age. For this we must look to the north-east of the country, to County Antrim, the very region where the most extensive deposits of native iron ore are to be found. There, in the River Bann and in boggy land to the east, metal objects have been recovered that indicate for the first time in Ireland an established La Tène tradition.

County Antrim has produced the most important assemblage of La Tène artefacts from Ireland ever discovered. This was brought to light in the last decades of the nineteenth century in the course of turf-cutting activities at Lisnacrogher, about 16 km north-east of the town of Broughshane. The site appears once to have been a shallow lake. Unfortunately, though the find attracted widespread attention from contemporary collectors, there was no competent authority present to observe the discoveries or to make any first-hand record of the find contexts or of the structures revealed.

One of the earliest references to Lisnacrogher was by the Rev. William Greenwall, who published a note in 1869[38] on the discovery there, a year earlier, of a decorated scabbard-plate and six spearbutts. He noted that 'from the remains of piles and brushwood at the spot, it seems to have been the site of a crannoge'. The first extensive account of the discoveries was, however, given by W. F. Wakeman in a lecture at Armagh in August 1884, which he subsequently published.[39] He related that 'for some time during and preceding the two lately past summers, a number of men were employed in digging turf from the peat which had been bared by partial drainage of the loch'. He went on to note that 'oaken timbers', 'timbers and encircling stakes', and 'a very considerable quantity of rough, basket-like work' were reported to have been found. He then described and illustrated 'the array of antiquities which were found within and around it'. Further discoveries from Lisnacrogher were published by Wakeman in two later papers.[40]

Lisnacrogher gained rapid fame in archaeological and antiquarian circles and selections of the finds were widely illustrated. As early as 1881, for instance, Lindenschmit had figured a decorated scabbard from the site (the one published by Greenwell) in his famous *Altertümer*, though it is there wrongly provenanced to England.[41] Wood-Martin, too, paid special attention to Lisnacrogher in his monograph on the *Lake dwellings of Ireland*, but he

[38] W. Greenwell, note in *Proceedings of the Society of Antiquaries of London*, ii, no. 4 (1867–70), pp 256–7.
[39] W. F. Wakeman, 'Trouvaille of the bronze and iron age from crannog at Lisnacroghera, Co. Antrim' in *R.S.A.I. Jn.*, xvi (1883–4), pp 375–408.
[40] W. F. Wakeman, 'On the crannog and antiquities of Lisnacroghera, near Broughshane, Co. Antrim (second notice)' in *R.S.A.I. Jn.*, xix (1889), pp 96–106; third and fourth notices, ibid., xxi (1890–91), pp 542–5, 673–5.
[41] L. Lindenschmit, *Die Altertümer unserer heidnischen Vorzeit* (n.p., 1881), Taf. 3, 1a–c.

could add nothing to what Wakeman had written.[42] Robert Munro, the Scottish antiquary, visited the site in 1886 and observed 'irregularly disposed beams' and 'some remnants of oak beams, some showing the usual mortises'. He also referred to an 'undisturbed structure of stones just cropping through the turf'.[43] The final reference to Lisnacrogher is by Knowles, who stated in 1897 that 'it appears to be exhausted of its treasures now'.[44]

The exceptional importance of the material from Lisnacrogher is equalled by our ignorance of the nature of the site. The varying accounts of stakes, brushwood, and oaken beams are, of course, forcibly reminiscent of the crannogs which are well known throughout Ireland. Not surprisingly, therefore, the site is often referred to as a crannog of La Tène date. But this is far from certain. In Switzerland, at Cornaux[45] and at La Tène itself,[46] comparable metalwork assemblages have been found in association with constructions of timber, variously interpreted as having served as bridges or jetties. Such could also have existed at the Irish site. But even if the timbers at Lisnacrogher are accepted as the remains of a crannog, there is a further caveat, for the relationship of the La Tène artefacts with the timbers has not been positively established. In fact, Munro makes the specific point that 'as to the relics, there is no record of their association with the crannog beyond the fact of their being found in its vicinity'.[47] We do not know, therefore, if the La Tène metalwork complex from Lisnacrogher represents the debris of a settlement, of a workshop or trading centre, or a place of ritual deposition. Questions recently asked concerning the true character of La Tène—ritual or secular—apply also to a consideration of the function of the County Antrim site.[48]

There are between seventy and eighty surviving objects, mostly metal, which may reasonably be regarded as deriving from the primary, iron-age deposits at Lisnacrogher. Not all the artefacts, however, are contemporary, for the site was evidently in use over a number of generations. Weapons and decorated bronzes predominate. There are portions of four swords and four incomplete scabbards. Two iron spearheads were also found, some decorated cylindrical bronze ferrules and no fewer than twenty-two knobbed bronze

[42] W. G. Wood-Martin, *The lake dwellings of Ireland* (Dublin, 1886), p. 173.

[43] R. Munro, *The lake dwellings of Europe* (London, 1890), p. 380.

[44] W. J. Knowles, 'Portion of a harp and other objects found in the crannoge of Carncoagh, Co. Antrim' in *R.S.A.I. Jn.*, xxvii (1897), pp 114–15.

[45] H. Schwab, 'Entdeckung einer keltischen Brucke an der Zihl und ihre Bedeutung für La Tène' in *Arch. Korr.*, ii (1972), pp 289–94.

[46] J. M. de Navarro, *The finds from the site of La Tène, vol. I: scabbards and the swords found in them* (Oxford, 1972).

[47] Munro, *Lake dwellings of Europe*, p. 30.

[48] Schwab, art. cit.; A. Furger-Gunti, *Die Helvetier: Kulturgeschichte eines Keltenvolkes* (Zurich, 1984), pp 64–8.

spear-butts,[49] two still retaining a length of wooden shaft.[50] In one instance this was 1.80 m long. The site also produced two bronze pins, ringheaded and with gently curving shank, the head of each adorned with pinned-on studs of red enamel.[51] There were also bracelets from Lisnacrogher, mounts of bronze, and a variety of rings and other miscellaneous items of the same metal. A number of iron tools are said to have come from the deposits and a few items of wood are also preserved.

Archaeological attention has focused, to a very large extent, on the swords and the scabbards, which undoubtedly include the earliest remains from the site.[52] These are all surprisingly short, the blade lengths of the swords being, in every case, well below 60 cm. This is appreciably shorter than is the case with contemporary swords outside the country but is typical of all known Irish swords of the period; on some examples, indeed, the blades are less than 40 cm long. The organic hilt elements, probably of bone or horn, once present on the swords from Lisnacrogher have not survived, but the bronze fittings associated with grip, pommel, and hilt-guard are in several cases present. A feature that the Lisnacrogher swords share with other La Tène swords in the country is the quillon-plate, a curved bronze mount of hammered or cast bronze that fitted on to the tang and rested on top of the blade. Its profile is usually described as either 'bell-shaped', 'cocked-hat-shaped' or, more technically, 'campaniform'. Such quillion-plates are a diagnostic feature of the swords of early and middle La Tène Europe, especially the latter, and the Lisnacrogher specimens are classic examples of this European form. It is important also to note the finely wrought iron blades of these County Antrim swords, illustrated by the well-preserved specimen in the British Museum. Clearly of native fabrication, these blades display full command of the swordsmith's craft. Here at least there can be no uncertainty as to the existence in the country of a mature, developed, and non-experimental iron industry. But whether this represents a new beginning or a continuation of older, established traditions remains to be determined.

The scabbards that held the swords were made of two plates of bronze, bell-shaped at the top and with narrowed, cut-back tip to accommodate a slender, clinging, openwork chape. The plates were joined to form the scabbard by folding the edges of one around those of the other. A suspension-loop was riveted to the back, but this is never preserved in Ireland. Three of the Lisnacrogher plates are decorated from end to end with engraved

---

[49] Barry Raftery, 'Knobbed spearbutts of the Irish iron age' in Scott, *Studies in early Ireland*, pp 75–92; *La Tène in Ire.*, pp 110–15.

[50] Wakeman, 'Trouvaille...at Lisnacroghera', p. 395; Knowles, 'Portion of a keep', p. 115, fig. 3.

[51] W. A. Seaby, 'A ring-headed bronze pin from Ulster' in *U.J.A.*, ser., xxvii (1964), pp 67–72, fig. 1b, pl. X (4); Raftery, *La Tène in Ire.*, p. 161, fig. 86 (3, 4).

[52] Raftery, *La Tène in Ire.*, pp 62–107.

curvilinear ornament.[53] The designs share features with those on European La Tène scabbards but, like the swords, they are of undoubtedly local manufacture, a generation or so removed from their ultimate continental homeland. The patterns were executed with a hand-held tracer rocked gently from side to side to give a fine, zigzag line. S-motifs, running-waves, and tight, hairspring spirals are recurring themes, but a proliferation of micro-, even macro-designs fills the bodies of the principal decorative units and the spaces between them. For this dotting, minute spirals, leafy motifs, hatching, basketry, and other designs are employed; there is a palpable *horror vacui*.

To the Lisnacrogher swords and scabbards can be added four splendidly ornamented plates[54] and a sword fragment from the River Bann.[55] Taken with the Lisnacrogher objects, these weapons indicate the existence of an accomplished armoury in the north-east of the country perhaps as early as the third century B.C. but certainly no later than the early second. With these we can, for the first time, perceive in the country, however dimly, an 'iron age' of rather greater substance than anything hinted at for earlier periods. That this 'iron age' was introduced from outside is beyond question, but how and from where remains a matter for debate among scholars. Shared decorative details with some British bronzes have encouraged the view that it is in England that the origins of the earliest Irish La Tène iron age must lie.[56] This is improbable. The Irish scabbard style differs subtly from almost everything in Britain and there are details that can only be found on the Continent, in Gaul, in Switzerland, and even in Hungary.[57] The Irish openwork chapes, too, have their closest counterparts not in Britain but on the Continent in contexts dating to the end of the early La Tène and the beginning of the middle La Tène periods.[58] Conclusively confirming an early continental La Tène presence at Lisnacrogher are three hollow rings from the site, each made of two horizontally joined segments, the halves held together by two or three tiny rivets.[59] These rings were related to the belt, and seem in many cases to have been associated with the scabbard; they can only be paralleled in the graves of early and middle La Tène Europe.[60]

The number of outsiders who might have been involved in the introduction of the new metal-working techniques to north-east Ireland is, of course,

---

[53] E. M. Jope, 'An iron age decorated sword-scabbard from the River Bann at Toome' in *U.J.A.* , 3rd ser., xvii (1954), pp 81–91; Raftery, *La Tène in Ire.*, pp 79–87.

[54] Jope, art. cit.

[55] R. B. Warner, 'An early iron age sword from Toome, Co. Antrim' in *U.J.A.*, 3rd ser., xxx (1967), pp 41–3.

[56] Stuart Pigott, 'Swords and scabbards of the British early iron age' in *Prehist. Soc. Proc.*, xvi (1950), p. 16.

[57] Raftery, *La Tène in Ire.*, pp 99–195.

[58] Jope, art. cit., pp 87–8; Raftery, *La Tène in Ire.*, pp 104–5.

[59] Raftery, *La Tène in Ire.*, pp 105–6, and 'Three bronze rings of continental La Tène type from Ireland' in *Marburger Studien zur Vor- und Frühgeschichte*, vii (1986), pp 249–66.

[60] E.g. L . Pauli, *Der Durrnberg bei Hallein*, iii, pt 1 (Munich, 1978), pp 195–211.

speculative. There were probably not many, perhaps a handful of fighting men with their followers and their craftsmen. But apart from the hollow rings, which could be imports, the archaeological record can point only to objects of native manufacture. This illustrates well the recurring conundrum of Irish prehistory. Here we have something that is totally new in the country, yet rendered in a form that is different in detail from anything in the area of presumed origin. The human mechanism by which such a transformation takes place has yet to be convincingly explained.

THE continental background of the earliest Irish La Tène tradition, so clearly evident in the Clonmacnoise find and in the County Antrim scabbards, becomes less evident in the material of later centuries. That links with the European mainland continued, however, is shown by a sword from Ballyshannon Bay, County Donegal, which possesses a typical Gaulish anthropoid hilt of cast bronze. It was brought up from the seabed in a fishing-net and dates to about 100 B.C.[61] Late La Tène beads of continental type from eastern and north-eastern parts of the country may also represent imported items from the European land-mass in the last century B.C.[62] Increasingly, however, especially after the turn of the millennium, the surviving remains show contact with British craft traditions. In matters of art and technology there was mutual borrowing between the two islands and it is reasonable to suppose that small-scale movements between them were commonplace. But in everything the Irish craftsmen pursued a noticeably independent line, and everything produced here had the indelible stamp of Irish manufacture.

From the third or second century B.C., therefore, the archaeological evidence indicates the gradual adoption of La Tène forms in various parts of Ireland, and new types developed, wholly Irish in concept, but bearing local versions of the La Tène art style. But, quite apart from the indigenous aspect of most of the material, the quantity of objects scattered across the country that we can describe as 'La Tène' is small, so that we can scarcely speak of a great, sweeping change of population. Furthermore, it is not clear to what extent the La Tène artefacts are typical everyday objects or are representative only of a confined and exclusive section of late prehistoric Irish society. The material may be socially restricted; it is certainly restricted in area, for extensive regions of southern and south-western Ireland are virtually empty of La Tène remains. La Tène objects are confined in the main to eastern and central Ulster and to a broad discontinuous band from Meath across the central plain to Galway and Mayo in the west.

[61] R. R. Clarke and C. F. C. Hawkes, 'An iron anthropoid sword from Shouldham, Norfolk, with related continental and British weapons' in *Prehist. Soc. Proc.*, xxi (1955), p. 215; Raftery, *La Tène in Ire.*, p. 70, pl. 23.

[62] Barry Raftery, 'Some late La Tène glass beads from Ireland' in *R.S.A.I. Jn.*, cii (1972), pp 14–18.

The nature of contemporary society in the south of Ireland is not yet clearly defined. Recent attempts to fill the southern 'void' of the last centuries B.C. with a 'ringfort complex' deriving cultural influence from the Iberian peninsula are attractive, but suffer from a lack of hard evidence, not least of which is the absence of a precise chronology.[63]

The La Tène remains, limited though they are in extent, represent the clearest and most obvious manifestation of iron-age influences in the country. It is, however, readily apparent that the La Tène material constitutes only a single strand in a complex, many-faceted Irish iron age, but for the period immediately before the birth of Christ there seems little else of substance to go on. The picture provided is, of course, incomplete and much is missing. There are many problems of interpretation, problems compounded by the paucity of burials and the almost total absence of contemporary, excavated settlements.

THE emphasis on weaponry at Lisnacrogher has been noted, an emphasis in keeping with the known propensity for fighting and warfare among the La Tène Celts everywhere. But the fine scabbards and excellently wrought swords should not obscure the fact of their extreme scarcity in the country. Outside the north-east of Ireland there are only two known scabbard-chapes and the total number of swords of La Tène type for the whole country is scarcely two dozen. Even allowing for the poor preservative qualities of iron the lack is striking. Spearheads are even less frequent but in this instance the dearth is undoubtedly exaggerated by the near impossibility of dating isolated and unassociated specimens, a point confirmed by the relatively large number of bronze spearbutts known: of these there are over sixty examples. They are of various forms, short and knobbed as are common at Lisnacrogher,[64] long, tubular butts, cast or of hammered sheet-bronze,[65] or butts, always cast, of conical shape.[66] A few tanged iron butts could belong to the iron age.[67] The bow, unpopular throughout La Tène Europe, is not present in the contemporary archaeological record of Ireland; it is unlikely to have been used. The sling, on the other hand, equally absent from the surviving material, was probably widespread. The discovery of archaeological evidence for this would be entirely fortuitous.

[63] Seamus Caulfield, 'Celtic problems in the Irish iron age' in Ó Corráin, *Ir. antiquity*, p. 211.

[64] Barry Raftery, 'Knobbed spearbutts of the Irish iron age' in Scott, *Studies on early Ire.*, pp 75–92; *La Tène in Ire.*, pp 111–15.

[65] Joseph Raftery, *Prehistoric Ireland* (London, 1951), fig. 226 (1–4); Raftery, *La Tène in Ire.*, pp 115–17.

[66] E.g. John Waddell, 'A ringfort at Ballybrit, Co. Galway' in *Galway Arch. Soc. Jn.*, xxxii (1966–71), pp 78–9, fig. 4; Raftery, *La Tène in Ire.*, pp 117–18.

[67] E.g. Hugh O'Neill Hencken, 'Lagore crannog: an Irish royal residence of the 7th to 10th centuries A.D.' in *R.I.A. Proc.*, liii (1950), sect. C, p. 8, fig. 32; Raftery, *La Tène in Ire.*, p. 118.

Undoubtedly fortuitous was the finding of a complete shield of La Tène date during mechanical turf-cutting in Littleton Bog at Clonoura, County Tipperary.[68] This is the only example from the country, apart from the fragmentary bronze fittings from a late, imported shield recovered on Lambay Island, County Dublin,[69] and some possible iron binding-strips from Navan Fort, County Armagh.

The Clonoura shield, in contrast to the round shields of the bronze age, is rectangular in shape with rounded corners. It is small, only 55 cm by 35 cm. It is made of a wooden plank, gently convex to the front, with a sheet-leather covering on each face, tightly stretched and secured by stitched binding strips around the edges. A separately made wooden grip fits across a circular opening at the centre of the shield which is protected at the front by a domed wooden boss. This is also secured by a sheet-leather covering, stitched to the surface of the shield. Such light implements would have been effective and manageable in single combat at close quarters, the very combat that is suggested by the short, stabbing Irish swords. The Irish shield is quite different from the large, almost man-sized shields from continental La Tène graves, which would have been necessary against the heavy, slashing swords of the European Celts. That the Irish implement saw service in battle is vividly shown by the sword-cuts and probable spear-thrusts that scar its surface.

The chariot, eloquently described by the classical authors and well represented in the European archaeological record, is hardly present at all in the Irish material. The earliest Irish literature refers to 'chariots', but linguistic evidence suggests that these were a far cry from the light, sophisticated, two-wheeled vehicles of the Continent.[70] They may have been little more than simple carts. Indeed, if the heavy, cumbersome block-wheels from Doogary-more, County Roscommon (for which a date in the fifth or fourth century B.C. is suggested by radiocarbon age-determination), have any bearing on the nature of wheeled transport in late prehistoric Ireland[71] there can be little talk of war chariots such as are found on the Celtic coins[72] or depicted on a funeral stela from Padua.[73] Timber fragments from under an iron-age road at

---

[68] A. B. A. Ó Ríordáin, E. M. Prendergast, and Etienne Rynne, 'National Museum of Ireland: archaeological acquisitions in the year 1960' in *R.S.A.I. Jn.*, xcii (1962), p. 152, pl. XVIII (19); Raftery, *La Tène in Ire.*, p. 129.

[69] R. A. S. Macalister [1929, 243, no. 21, pl. XXIII (19)]; Etienne Rynne, 'The La Tène and Roman finds from Lambay, Co. Dublin; a reassessment' in *R.I.A. Proc.*, lxxvi (1976), sect. C, p. 236, pl. XXXIV (1); Raftery, *La Tène in Ire.*, p. 129.

[70] David Greene, 'The chariot as described in Irish literature' in Charles Thomas (ed.), *The iron age in the Irish Sea province* (Cardiff, 1972), pp 59–73.

[71] A. T. L. Lucas, 'Prehistoric block-wheels from Doogarymore, Co. Roscommon, and Timahoe East, Co. Kildare' in *R.S.A.I. Jn.*, cii (1972), pp 19–48.

[72] J. V. S. Megaw, *Art of the European iron age* (Bath, 1970), no. 103.

[73] Ibid., no. 102.

Corlea in Longford—if they are, as seems probable, part of a wheeled vehicle—are more likely to be from a farm cart than from a war chariot.[74]

A few bronze mounts are, however, preserved that suggest that chariots of more conventional type might occasionally have existed in the country. Two hollow bronze mounts from Lough Gur, County Limerick, for example, could have been chariot yoke mounts, and a British-made bronze terret (a loop through which the reins passed) from County Antrim is probably also from a chariot.[75] Otherwise, apart from a few wooden horse-yokes,[76] we can infer only indirectly from the evidence of horse-trappings that paired draught (and not necessarily for chariots) was known. Horse-bits of bronze, of which there are over 130 in the country, are occasionally found in pairs. The enigmatic Y-shaped objects of bronze (almost 100 are known) that fulfilled an unspecified role in the harness are also sometimes found in pairs. As well as this, asymmetric ornament on bits and on Y-shaped objects seems to infer original use in paired combinations.

But the preponderance of single, isolated specimens in the country strongly implies that travel on horseback was common in La Tène times. It is likely that by then a well-defined network of routeways existed and, in some areas at least, these must have been of some sophistication, especially if wheeled transport—of whatever kind—was in operation. A great corduroy trackway of huge riven oaks, crossing a bog at Corlea in County Longford, is a spectacular example of iron-age road building. Thanks to tree-ring analysis it has been precisely dated to 148 B.C.[77]

Celtic vanity and delight in bright colours and glittering ornaments are reflected, to an extent, in the Irish archaeological record. Of the gaudy clothing that must have been normal everyday dress, however, there is no trace. The only surviving textile from iron-age Ireland is a small fragment, fused to the back of a bronze locket, found on the shoulder of a female skeleton at Carrowbeg North, County Galway.[78] But dress-fasteners are known, generally of bronze, and these are sometimes finely adorned. They are, however, few in number. The safety-pin fibula, a basic type-fossil of the European La Tène culture, is represented in Ireland by a mere twenty-five

[74] See below; Barry Raftery, 'An iron age trackway in Ireland' in *Antiquity*, lx (1986), pp 51–4.

[75] Cyril Fox, 'Two Celtic bronzes from Lough Gur, Limerick, Ireland' in *Antiq. Jn.*, xxx (1950), pp 190–92; E. M. Jope, 'Chariotry and paired-draught in Ireland during the early iron age; the evidence of some horse-bridle bits' in *U.J.A.*, 3rd ser., xviii (1955), p. 37; Raftery, *La Tène in Ire.*, pp 57–61.

[76] Stuart Piggott, 'An iron age yoke from Northern Ireland' in *Prehist. Soc. Proc.*, xv (1949), pp 192–3, and 'Early iron age horn-caps and yokes' in *Antiq. Jn.*, xlix (1969), pp 378–81; Raftery, *La Tène in Ire.*, p. 61.

[77] Raftery, 'Iron age trackway'.

[78] G. F. Willmot, 'Two bronze age burials at Carrowbeg North, Belclare, Co. Galway' in *Galway Arch. Soc. Jn.*, xviii (1938–9), pl. 11b; Raftery, *La Tène in Ire.*, pp 205–6, pl. 64.

examples.[79] The number is paltry when set against the many thousands of such objects found in every area of La Tène Europe. But some, distinctively Irish in their treatment, display considerable virtuosity in their manufacture and decoration. Springs, tightly coiled for effective use, had to be hammered and annealed. Bows could be hammered or cast to either rod or leaf form. The foot is sometimes cast in the shape of a tiny bird's head as on a brooch from Lecarrow, County Sligo;[80] in one case the form represented on the foot seems to be that of a serpent.[81] An especially fine example is the well-preserved specimen from Clogher, County Tyrone, which, its arching bow embellished with thin elegantly curving trumpets and minute lentoids, is a minor masterpiece of fine casting in bronze.[82]

Ring-headed pins, an insular type,[83] were also worn in iron-age Ireland: there are about thirty examples known. We do not know if the distinction between them and the safety-pin fibulae was chronological or cultural. In some areas at any rate the two types are mutually exclusive in distribution. Ring-headed pins, following older traditions of dress-fastening, do not have a spring but are characterised by a straight or curving shank, a ring-head, and an angular shoulder to gather the cloth. The ring could be of simple, annular form[84] or it could be recessed for the retention of red enamel inlay as on the two examples from Lisnacrogher, County Antrim. More elaborate pins have cast ring-heads with raised, snail-shell coils[85] and there are also some pins with the head in the form of a stylised swan's neck, and often with sharply curving shank.[86]

A uniquely Irish type of dress-fastener appeared around the turn of the millennium, the Navan-type brooch, so called because two of the five known examples are said to have come from Navan Fort (Emain Macha), County Armagh.[87] These had an elaborately cast, openwork bow embellished with raised trumpets in profusion, set off, in the finest example (from Navan), by fine stippling.[88] The same Navan brooch had a stud of red enamel originally on the centre of its bow, while a comparable, but less fine, piece from Somerset, County Galway, was also adorned with enamel but in this instance

[79] C. F. C. Hawkes, 'The wearing of the brooch; early iron age dress among the Irish' in Scott, *Studies on early Ireland*, pp 51–73; Raftery, *La Tène in Ire.*, pp 144–53.
[80] E. M. Jope, 'Iron age brooches in Ireland: a summary' in *U.J.A.*, 3rd ser., xxiv–xxv (1961–2), pp 27–8, fig. 4(1), pl. 1; Raftery, *La Tène in Ire.*, p. 145, fig. 79 (a), pl. 47 (2).
[81] Jope, 'Iron age brooches', fig. 2 (7); Raftery, *La Tène in Ire.*, p. 147, fig. 80 (3), pl. 48 (2).
[82] Jope, 'Iron age brooches', pp 31–2, fig. 7; Raftery, *La Tène in Ire.*, p. 145, fig. 79 (8), pl. 45.
[83] G. C. Dunning, 'The swan's-neck and ring-headed pins of the early iron age in Britain' in *Archaeological Journal*, xci (1934), pp 269–95; Raftery, *La Tène in Ire.*, p. 145, fig. 79 (8), pl. 45.
[84] Raftery, *La Tène in Ire.*, p. 157, fig. 84.
[85] Ibid., p. 158, fig. 85 (1–6).
[86] Ibid., p. 162, fig. 85 (7–9).
[87] Jope, 'Iron age brooches', pp 34–7; Raftery, *La Tène in Ire.*, pp 153–7.
[88] P. M. Duval, *Les Celtes* (Paris, 1977), p. 228, pl. 239; Raftery, *La Tène in Ire.*, pl. 51 (1).

as champlevé inlay.[89] Four of the five Navan-type brooches had the pin attached to the back by means of a ball-socket mechanism. This appears to have been an Irish invention at this time and its presence underlines the originality and ingenuity of the Irish craftsmen.

There were other, less functional forms of personal ornament. Beads of glass and bone were worn on the neck, the wrists, and the ankles, and bracelets of a variety of materials were also known. We do not know if glass-working was carried on in iron-age Ireland but there is no reason why this should not have been so. There were also finger- and toe-rings, anklets, and, in one burial, a pair of possible ear-rings.[90] Belts are suggested by the three hollow bronze rings from Lisnacrogher referred to earlier, and the ring pairs from cremations at Carrowjames, County Mayo,[91] and Carbury Hill, County Kildare,[92] may also come from belts. A decorated strap-tag, probably also from a belt, was found at Rathgall, County Wicklow.[93]

Implements relating to the toilet are also recorded from Ireland, but these are infrequent and the majority are imports. Two mirrors are known, one from Ballymoney, County Antrim,[94] the other from the cemetery on Lambay;[95] a single iron-age tweezers comes from the exotic burial at 'Loughey', County Down.[96] Care for the hair is indicated by the single-edged bone combs from Lough Crew, County Meath,[97] and elsewhere, and the iron shears from Carbury Hill is likely to have been for trimming the hair.[98]

Without doubt, however, it is the neck ornaments of gold that stand apart as the most spectacular items of personal adornment from iron-age Ireland. The two torcs from Clonmacnoise, County Offaly, have already been considered.[99] Apart from this find there is only one major hoard of gold objects

[89] See below, p. 158; Joseph Raftery, 'A hoard of the early iron age' in *R.S.A.I. Jn.*, xc (1960), pp 2–5, pl. 1.

[90] Joseph Raftery, 'The Turoe stone and the rath of Feerwore' in *R.S.A.I. Jn.*, lxxiv (1944), p. 33.

[91] Joseph Raftery, 'The tumulus cemetery of Carrowjames, Co. Mayo, part II: Carrowjames II' in *Galway Arch. Soc. Jn.*, xix (1940–41), p. 31, pl. 1 (9, 11).

[92] G. F. Willmot, 'Three burial sites at Carbury, Co. Kildare' in *R.S.A.I. Jn.*, lxviii (1938), p. 136, fig. 4.

[93] Barry Raftery, 'A decorated strap-end from Rathgall, Co. Wicklow' in *R.S.A.I. Jn.*, c (1970), pp 200–11, and *La Tène in Ire.*, p. 207, fig. 103 (1), pl. 65.

[94] E. M. Jope, 'The Keshcarrigan bowl and a bronze mirror handle from Ballymoney' in *U.J.A.*, 3rd ser., xvii (1954), pp 92–6; Raftery, *La Tène in Ire.*, pp 208–10, fig. 104 (1), pl. 66.

[95] See below, pp 174–5; R. A. S. Macalister, 'On some antiquities discovered upon Lambay' in *R.I.A. Proc.*, xxxviii (1929), sect. C, p. 244, no. 34, pl. xxv (2); Etienne Rynne, 'The La Tène and Roman finds from Lambay, Co. Dublin: a reassessment' in *R.I.A. Proc.*, lxxvi (1976), sect. C, p. 238; Barry Raftery, *A catalogue of Irish iron age antiquities* (Marburg, 1983), no. 538.

[96] E. M. Jope and B. C. S. Wilson, 'A burial group of the first century A.D. from "Loughey" near Donaghadee' in *U.J.A.*, 3rd ser., xx (1957), p. 81, fig. 1, pl. V.

[97] See below, p. 158; Raftery, *La Tène in Ire.*, pp 210–13.

[98] Willmot, 'Three burial sites', p. 137, fig. 5.

[99] See above, p. 140.

from Ireland that is demonstrably iron-age in date, for gold of the period is rare, in sharp contrast to the astounding wealth of this metal during the later bronze age. The hoard is that from the townland of Broighter, near Limavady, County Londonderry, where seven objects were found during ploughing activities in 1896. These included five neck ornaments, a small hemispherical hanging bowl, and a model boat.[100]

There were two wire necklaces, one a single strand, the other composed of three strands (undoubtedly worn as a 'choker'), each made by skilfully interlocking hundreds of tiny gold loops to fashion chains of great strength and flexibility. The clasp mechanisms, one of which is adorned with granulation, are simple but ingenious. A little loop, projecting from one end, was inserted into an opening in the other end; a tiny, vertical bar was dropped through, thus securing the clasp. Two bar torcs (one fragmentary) also came from the hoard. These were closed by a simple hook-and-loop method. The final neck ornament from the collection is the famous buffer-torc, one of the finest examples of Irish iron-age metalwork.

This object is an elaborate piece,[101] far more ornate than the earlier Clonmacnoise specimen. It is now in two halves, each a hollow, semicircular tube with a separately made 'buffer' terminal at one end of each. Whatever attachment once existed at the nape portion is now missing. The tubular sections of the collar are adorned with repoussé ornament of almost baroque exuberance, but geometrically planned with rule and compass. Sinuous, foliate patterns, crisp lentoids, and raised scrolls are the dominant themes, arranged in deliberate, balanced asymmetry. For added relief a series of individually made snail-shell scrolls have been fitted into specially prepared openings in the collar. The relief decoration is set off by a background web of overlapping, compass-drawn arcs.

The terminals are in each case joined to the tubes by a pair of transverse gold bars that extend through the collar from one side to the other. One of the buffers retains the granulation (or simulated granulation) that originally adorned both. The clasp mechanism is clever. A T-shaped tenon, projecting from one face, fits into a corresponding rectangular slot in the opposing face; the junction is secured by a quarter-turn of the tubes.

---

[100] A. J. Evans, 'On a votive deposit of gold objects found on the north-west coast of Ireland' in *Archaeology*, lv (1897), pp 391–408; R. B. Warner, 'The Broighter hoard: a re-appraisal and the iconography of the collar' in Scott, *Studies on early Ireland*, pp 29–38; Raftery, *La Tène in Ire.*, pp 181–92.
[101] There is now a very extensive literature concerning this torc, and the object is frequently illustrated. The most important references (apart from those in the preceding note) are H. Maryon, 'The technical methods of the Irish smiths in the bronze and early iron ages' in *R.I.A. Proc.*, xliv, sect. C (1938), pp 210–11; R. R. Clarke, 'The early iron age treasure from Snettisham, Norfolk' in *Prehist. Soc. Proc.*, xx (1954), pp 41–2; J. U. S. Megaw, *Art of the European iron age* (Bath, 1970), no. 289; and P. M. Duval, *Les Celtes* (Paris, 1977), pp 200–02, pl. 1.

The torc belongs to a small but widely dispersed family of neck ornaments, which occur from eastern England as far as Switzerland and Italy.[102] Their date in the latter part of the last pre-Christian century is well-established. The present specimen is, however, of local manufacture, though a suggestion has been made that the terminals were imported and added in Ireland.[103] This may be so, but is scarcely provable. Other objects in the hoard are, however, certainly non-Irish. The wire necklaces, for example, are of Mediterranean, possibly Alexandrian origin.[104] The source of the remaining items in the hoard is less easy to establish.

The Broighter objects may have been placed in the ground for safe keeping, but it is not unreasonable to interpret the hoard as a votive deposit. The find-spot is isolated, well away from the main concentrations of La Tène metalwork. It is in a river valley close to the old coast of Lough Foyle. It is tempting to regard the presence of the boat in the hoard as indicating some ritual connection with the sea.[105]

This is, however, mere speculation. But the boat is important for it is the earliest rendering we have of an ocean-going vessel.[106] Elaborately equipped with mast and yard-arm, miniature oars and rowers' benches, steering oar, grappling hook, and other tools, it gives us a unique insight into the nature of deep-sea travel in the years around the birth of Christ. Eighteen oarsmen are implied, two more to man the steering oars. There would have been ample room in such a craft for passengers, provisions, and baggage besides. One detail escapes us, however, for we cannot say if the model was intended to represent a boat of hides or of timber.

The Broighter hoard, whether buried for reasons of ritual or of expediency, is far removed from the everyday needs and activities of the general populace. This silent majority finds little expression in the surviving archaeological remains. But the scattered artefacts do give us occasional glimpses of economy and daily life in La Tène Ireland.

A vital aspect of the daily economy was, of course, food production, and the widespread distribution of rotary querns emphasises this importance. In the northern two-thirds of the country the beehive variant was known, so called because the heavy, domed upper stone resembles somewhat a beehive in shape.[107] This stone, centrally perforated to receive the corn, was rotated

[102] See A. Furger-Gunti, 'Der "Goldfund von Saint-Louis" bei Basel und ähnliche keltische Schatzfunde' in *Zeitschrift für Schweizische Archäologie und Kunstgeschichte*, xxxix (1982), pp 1–14, for summary and recent references.
[103] E. M. Jope, 'The style of the Broighter collar and its significance' in *Irish Archaeological Research Forum*, ii, no. 2 (1975), p. 24.
[104] Evans, 'On a votive deposit', pp 396–8; Warner, 'Broighter hoard', p. 29.
[105] Warner, 'Broighter hoard', pp 35–6.
[106] A. W. Farrell and S. Penny, 'The Broighter boat: a reassessment' in *Irish Archaeological Research Forum*, ii, no. 2 (1975), pp 15–28.
[107] Seamus Caulfield, 'The beehive quern in Ireland' in *R.S.A.I. Jn.*, cvii (1977), pp 104–39.

by means of a detachable wooden handle on an iron spindle. This was more efficient and far less tiring to use than was the long-established saddle quern. The change was revolutionary. But soon the beehive quern itself was improved: the upper stone was reduced to a flat disc, similar to the lower, creating the so-called disc quern. This remained in use almost to modern times, so that individual specimens are not easy to date closely. The absence of beehive querns in the south of the country suggests that their place was taken, almost from the start, by the disc quern.

Inspiration from north-east England for the introduction of the beehive quern to Ireland has been postulated and it has been taken to indicate a folk movement to the country from that quarter.[108] But the appearance of a technological improvement of such striking and immediate relevance to the everyday life of the people would spread quickly once the idea was implanted and the principle understood. It seems hardly necessary to invoke significant population change to explain the development in the means of grinding corn.

It is not certain when the change took place, as no single beehive quern has ever been found in Ireland with another object. Decoration on some examples and the evidence of foreign analogies suggest that it may have been introduced to Ireland around the birth of Christ or a few centuries later. It may be, indeed, that the 'dramatic expansion in agriculture' evident in the pollen diagrams for Ireland 'at about 300 A.D.' is related to the appearance of the new means of grinding corn.[109]

Apart from the querns there is otherwise little in the surviving remains linked to agricultural pursuits. The only implement known that is directly linked to the harvest is an iron sickle from the Lisnacrogher deposit.[110] We can assume, however, that with widespread cultivation of the land, field systems must have evolved to a stage of some complexity and large areas of the country must have been enclosed. In a mixed economy with wandering domestic animals and the dangers of incursions by wild fauna, field boundaries were essential. We cannot point with certainty, however, to any field systems of demonstrably iron-age date from the country.[111]

Animal husbandry, which must have been at least equal to agriculture as a primary means of food production, is even less well represented in the archaeological remains than is agriculture. It may reasonably be assumed that cattle were a prime basis for wealth and, in consequence, cattle-rustling was probably endemic. Indeed, it has been suggested that the great 'travelling earthworks' that ran for kilometres across the country were a response to

[108] Ibid., pp 125–6.
[109] G. F. Mitchell, *The Irish landscape* (London, 1976), pp 134–8, 166.
[110] Wakeman, 'Trouvaille...at Lisnacroghera', pp 401–2. There is no proof that the fields at Cush, Co. Limerick, are contemporary with the iron-age burial mound there (*pace* Caulfield, 'Celtic problems', p. 209).
[111] Below, pp 263–4, 555–6.

large-scale cattle-rieving.[112] The *bóaire* of the early historic period had his roots, no doubt, in the pre-Christian iron age, and it should not be forgotten that the earliest Irish heroic saga, the Ulster cycle, revolves around an elaborate cattle raid.

Only two published excavations have yielded information on the nature of the faunal remains recovered: Feerwore, County Galway,[113] and Freestone Hill, County Kilkenny.[114] Bones of cattle, sheep/goat, pig, horse, and dog were present as well as those of red deer and a few smaller wild animals. The published statistics concerning relative percentages of the different animals are, however, suspect since they refer only to the relative bulk of the bones of individual species. Preliminary statements concerning the faunal remains at Navan Fort indicate a striking preponderance of pig-bones over those of cattle and sheep or goats.[115]

Otherwise the evidence is slight. A few sword hilts made of animal bones have survived (those of deer and sheep have been identified) and rib-bones of cattle were used for various purposes as at Lough Crew, County Meath,[116] and Freestone Hill. Animal bones were also used to make gaming pieces: the dice from a grave at Knowth[117] were made from the bones of a horse. As already noted, the frequency of horse-trappings underlines the popularity of the horse in Ireland.

We know virtually nothing of the house-types current in La Tène Ireland, so we can say little about their internal organisation and plenishings or the domestic activities that took place inside them. Any carvings, tapestries, or painted walls that might once have existed are lost to us. There are few domestic tools or implements preserved, apart from a few axeheads, an adze or two,[118] and an occasional knife.[119] Spinning and weaving are represented only by the alleged bone spindle-whorls from the late site on Freestone Hill.[120] There are no known loom-weights, which suggests that the horizontal rather than the vertical loom was in use. Bone scrapers from Freestone Hill may have been used in leather-curing,[121] and the expertly made Clonoura shield demonstrates skilled working in leather. The shield also shows

[112] Below, p. 170.
[113] Joseph Raftery, 'The Turoe stone', p. 49. A report by A. W. Stelfox states specifically: 'About 3 cwt of bones have been examined, divided into three lots...in which, respectively, the bones of ox amounted to about 75, 75, and 90 per cent of the bulk.'
[114] Barry Raftery, 'Freestone Hill: an iron age hillfort and bronze age cairn' in *R.I.A. Proc.*, lxviii (1969), sect. C, p. 104.
[115] C. J. Lynn, 'Navan Fort: a draft summary of D. M. Waterman's excavations' in *Emania*, i (1986), p. 16.
[116] Below, p. 159.
[117] Below, p. 155.
[118] Raftery, *La Tène in Ire.*, pp 238–41.
[119] E.g. Joseph Raftery, 'The Turoe stone', p. 34, fig. 4 (48).
[120] Barry Raftery, *La Tène in Ire.*, pp 49–50.
[121] Barry Raftery, 'Freestone hill', p. 50.

considerable competence in carpentry techniques and the same skills are evident in several of the carved wooden objects found under the trackway in Corlea bog, County Longford.[122] Domestic pottery was not used, as far as we can tell, in iron-age Ireland and wooden containers were probably widespread. Only a few survive, including two handled cups,[123] and there is at least one wooden cauldron, which may belong to an early stage of the Irish iron age.[124] Fragments of stave-built wooden vessels have been found under the trackway, earlier referred to, at Corlea. Metal containers also existed. Cauldrons of bronze were used, of globular and 'thick-bellied' form, but there are fewer than ten preserved from the whole country.[125] Again we are struck by the contrast with the situation in the preceding late bronze age, during which Ireland was a major western European centre of cauldron production.

Bronze drinking vessels, either bowls or handled cups, also exist. These are sometimes hammered, sometimes finished on a lathe after initial casting. They date around the birth of Christ. One particularly fine example, from Keshcarrigan, County Leitrim,[126] has a magnificently cast bird's-head handle with elegant, curving neck, upturned beak, and large staring eyes which were once filled with glass or enamel inlays. A comparable bird's-head handle was found with other metal objects at Somerset, County Galway.[127] We do not know what beverages were drunk from these vessels but the stave-built, wooden tankard from Carrickfergus, County Antrim—probably a first-century import from Wales—could have been for beer.[128] A pedestalled 'tazza' of sheet bronze from Edenderry, County Offaly (a roughly contemporary import)[129] might also have held the same beverage.

Drinking and feasting appear to have been important aspects of life among the Celts, which could have taken up much of their leisure time. There is little else to suggest periods of idleness. Games of chance, however, seem to be represented by the bone dice that sometimes occur in Irish iron-age contexts, and other 'gaming-pieces',[130] and there are also a few alleged 'counters' of stone.[131] A series of pegged bone objects from a grave at Knowth

[122] Barry Raftery, 'Iron age trackway', p. 52, pl. VII.
[123] Barry Raftery, *La Tène in Ire.*, p. 215, fig. 109.
[124] Adolf Mahr, 'A wooden cauldron from Altertate, Co. Monaghan' in *R.I.A. Proc.*, xlii (1934), sect. C, pp 11–29; Barry Raftery, 'Iron age cauldrons in Ireland' in *Archaeologia Atlantica*, iii (1980), p. 58, and *La Tène in Ire.*, pp 227–8, fig. 114.
[125] Raftery, 'Iron age cauldrons', and *La Tène in Ire.*, pp 226–36.
[126] E. M. Jope, 'The Keshcarrigan bowl and a bronze mirror handle from Ballymoney' in *U.J.A.*, 3rd ser., xvii (1954), pp 92–6; Raftery, *La Tène in Ire.*, p. 214, fig. 107 (1).
[127] Below, p. 157; Raftery, *La Tène in Ire.*, p. l24, fig.107 (2).
[128] Ibid., pp 223–4, fig. 112.
[129] Ibid., p. 226, fig. 113.
[130] Ibid., pp 247–50.
[131] E.g. George Eogan, 'Report on the excavation of some passage graves, unprotected inhumation burials, and a settlement site at Knowth, Co. Meath' in *R.I.A. Proc.*, lxxiv (1974), sect. C, pp 76–80, fig. 32.

appear to indicate the former existence of a board game.[132] There is no
evidence in the archaeological record for the vigorous games of hurling
which the young Cú Chulainn allegedly played at Emain Macha before pursuing his heroic and tragic destiny.

Cú Chulainn is a figure of legend and myth, but Emain Macha, the setting
for his greatest exploits, is a known hilltop site, now named Navan Fort,
some 6 km west of Armagh city.[133] At the foot of this hill, in boggy land,
once a lake, four great bronze trumpets were found in the townland of
Loughnashade in 1798 in apparent association with human remains.[134] Only
one survives.[135] Deposited in a lake close to a site of contemporary royal and,
it seems, ceremonial importance, it is difficult to escape the conclusion that
these four instruments came to their watery resting place in the course of
some votive activity.

Apart from the surviving trumpet from Loughnashade, there are several
other examples known, including a finely preserved specimen from Ardbrin,
County Down. The type is Irish and one was exported in ancient times to
Anglesey in north Wales where a fragment was found, significantly perhaps
in the presumed votive deposit at Llyn Cerrig Bach.[136]

These objects differ in every way from the cast trumpets of the bronze
age. Each of the two substantially complete iron-age examples is made of two
curved tubes joined to form a large arc which expands in width towards
the bell. The chord-length of the Ardbrin trumpet, the largest and best-
preserved piece, is no less than 1.42 m.[137] The tubes were made of prepared
strips of sheet bronze, hammered around a mandrel and curved to shape.
The junction of the precisely matching edges of each sheet was sealed by
riveting a narrow bronze strip along it on either the outer or inner surface.
On the exceptional Ardbrin trumpet, the internal sealing strip was secured
by no fewer than 1,094 tiny bronze rivets.[138] The outstanding technical

[132] Ibid., pp 76–80, fig. 3l.     [133] Below, pp 167–8.
[134] A. Browne, 'An account of some ancient trumpets dug up in a bog near Armagh' in
*R.I.A. Trans.*, viii (1802), pp 11–12; J. V. S. Megaw, *Art of the European iron age* (Bath, 1970),
no. 246; P.-M. Duval, *Les Celtes* (Paris, 1977), p. 161. fig. 166; Raftery, *La Tène in Ire.*, pp
134–43.
[135] See George Petrie, note in *Dublin Penny Journal*, ii (1833–4), pp 29–30; Barry Raftery,
'The Loughnashade horns' in *Emania*, ii (1987), pp 21–4.
[136] Cyril Fox, *A find of the early iron age from Llyn Cerrig Bach, Anglesey* (Cardiff, 1946), pp
44, 86, pls XII, XXXI; H. Savory, *National Museum of Wales: guide catalogue of the early iron
age collections* (Cardiff, l976), p. 58, fig. 23.
[137] James Stuart, *Historical memoirs of the city of Armagh* (n.p., 1819), pp 293–4; D. J.
Norreys, note in *R.S.A.I. Jn.*, xiv (1876–8), pp 277–9; R. F. Tylecote, *Metallurgy in archaeology* (London, 1962), pp 144–5; *An archaeological survey of County Down* (Belfast, 1966), p. 56,
fig. 33; Raftery, *La Tène in Ire.*, p. 135, fig. 72.
[138] There is confusion in the earlier accounts about the correct number of rivets. W. R.
Wilde (*A descriptive catalogue of the antiquities of animal materials and bronze in the museum of the
Royal Irish Academy* (Dublin, 1861), p. 625) gives 638, which is the correct number of rivets on
one half of the trumpet; the *Archaeological survey of County Down* follows this. Tylecote, op.
cit., gives 658.

excellence of such trumpets was further exanced in the case of the Loughnashade specimen by the addition of a bronze disc with ornate repoussé decoration around the bell.

These instruments, dating perhaps to the last century B.C., might have
sounded on ceremonial occasions or before battles, their deep, bass sounds
intended to intimidate and terrify the enemy. The Ardbrin trumpet, when
found in 1809, was immediately blown by a local bugler, its striking tones
startling the people of the surrounding region. The object can still be blown
today but gives only a limited range of notes.

The trumpets, especially that from Ardbrin, are particularly fine examples
of the skill and accomplishment of the Irish bronzesmith's craft at this time.
Indeed, repeatedly in the surviving remains it is the craft of the bronze-
worker that stands out. Flourishing centres must have existed, thriving and
well equipped workshops, and there were probably also travelling bronze-
smiths who carried out work akin to that of the tinkers of recent Irish
history. A wide range of specialist tools would have been used and an extensive network of contacts was also necessary, both immediately local and
distant, to provide the essential raw materials for the successful running of
the industry.

Yet archaeology reveals practically nothing of all this. Not a single metalworking tool is known, there are no moulds and no crucibles. In all these
things the bronze age tells us more.[139] But we can infer something from the
artefacts. There are unfinished objects, fresh from the mould, their casting
accretions not yet rubbed down. There are objects still retaining the marks of
the tools used on them. Thus we can recognise hammers, punches, chisels,
graving tools of various forms, drills, files, saws, compasses. Many others
must have existed: anvils of differing sizes, for instance, and tools of bone,
too, such as punches used in repoussé work and spatulae for the modelling of
*cire perdue* wax.

There is one hoard of objects that was clearly the property of a metalworker, that found in 1959 at Somerset, County Galway.[140] Ten objects
survive from the deposit: five bronze mounts, a gold ribbon torc, an openwork brooch of 'Navan-type',[141] a cup-handle in case bronze, shaped in the
form of a bird's head as on the Keshcarrigan cup,[142] an ingot, and a cake of
raw bronze. The cake has oblique hammer marks on it; perhaps a bowl
was to be made from it to which the handle was to be attached. There is a
mount too, which has had its original openwork ornament carefully

---

[139] See, for example, hoards of metalworker's tools from Bishopsland, Co. Kildare (George
Eogan, *Hoards of the later Irish bronze age* (Dublin, 1983), p. 36, no. 16) and Lusmagh, Co.
Offaly (ibid., p. 192, no. 22).

[140] Joseph Raftery, 'A hoard of the early iron age' in *R.S.A.I. Jn.*, xc (1960), pp 2–5; Barry
Raftery, *Catalogue of Irish iron age antiquities*, fig. 216.

[141] Above, p. 149.

[142] Above, p. 155.

removed—clearly showing that the bronzesmith was still at work on this object. The hoard, however, produced no tools, but the iron objects, found with the bronzes and subsequently lost, may have been such implements. It is tempting to regard the Somerset assemblage as the stock-in-trade of a travelling bronzesmith. We do not know, however, if a permanent workshop existed nearby.

Enamel-working is intimately associated with the bronzesmith's craft. This substance, essentially an opaque glass, is always red in colour during the earlier phases of the iron age. Sometimes it is pinned to the bronze in the form of preformed studs; sometimes it is applied in molten form to decorative panels sunk into the surface of the bronze to be adorned. The latter technique is called *champlevé*. In Ireland at least, there seems little chronological discrepancy between the two techniques, though outside the country the studs are earlier, following on the early La Tène custom of decorating bronzes with studs of coral. Several large blocks of red enamel have been found on the hill of Tara,[143] indicating the former existence of a bronze-working centre there. The high lead content of the enamel, as revealed by analysis, has been taken to suggest that the material was imported in bulk from the Mediterranean region, possibly Italy.[144] The implications of this, if true, in terms of social organisation at home and the extent of trading contacts abroad are considerable.

In seeking foci of metalworking in iron-age Ireland the unique assemblage of material found in the chambers of a neolithic passage grave at Lough Crew, County Meath, must be taken into account. First dug into in the 1860s,[145] later (in 1941) excavated scientifically,[146] the site produced a large collection of objects dating, in all probability, to the first century A.D.[147] The majority of the finds are fragmentary bone flakes, carefully polished and sometimes with compass-drawn ornament on them. Thirteen bone combs were also found, two small pins of the same material, beads of amber and glass, and some rings of amber and iron. A corroded iron object, allegedly the leg of a compass,[148] was found in the nineteenth-century investigations.

[143] Valerie Ball and Margaret Stokes, 'On a block of red glass enamel said to have been found at Tara Hill: with observations on the use of red enamel in Ireland' in *R.I.A. Trans.*, xxx (1892–6), pp 277–94 and pl. XIX; E. C. R. Armstrong, 'Note on the block of red enamel from Tara' in *R.S.A.I. Jn.*, xli (1911), pp 61–2.

[144] M. J. Hughes, 'A technical study of opaque red glass of the iron age in Britain' in *Prehist. Soc. Proc.*, xxxviii (1972), pp 98–107.

[145] E. A. Conwell, *Discovery of the tomb of Ollamh Fodhla* (Dublin, 1873).

[146] Joseph Raftery, 'Lough Crew, Co. Meath—ein Megalithgrab der La Tène Zeit' in E. Vogt (ed.), *Congrès international des sciences préhistoriques et protohistoriques, actes de la III^e session* (Zürich, 1953).

[147] H. S. Crawford, 'The engraved bone objects found at Lough Crew, Co. Meath, in 1865' in *R.S.A.I. Jn.*, lv (1925), pp 15–29; Raftery, *La Tène in Ire.*, pp 251–63.

[148] Crawford, op. cit., p. 15 and fig.; Barry Raftery, *Catalogue of Irish iron age antiquities*, no. 596.

This is now lost. Its relationship to the iron-age layer is unknown (it could be modern), nor is it certainly part of a compass.

Over 5,000 flake fragments were recovered, about 150 of which bear ornament. They are made from cattle rib-bones, generally ovoid or flattened-oval in shape, sometimes with one end pointed. Occasionally one end is pierced by a small, circular hole. Estimated original lengths vary between 5 cm and about 14 cm. The decoration consists most often of precisely conceived, compass-drawn compositions of considerable geometrical complexity. There are also examples, however, where the designs are unfinished, even botched, and some seem to represent no more than practice curves made without any intent at ornamentation. Only once is the compass left aside, in the awkward, crudely scratched stags present on one flake. But even here, the tiny circular eyes are mechanically produced.[149] The decorated flakes are often taken to be 'trial pieces' or 'pattern books', the work of a bronzesmith developing patterns in bone before committing them to the more permanent metal. The Lough Crew site is thus far regarded as a workshop. But the preponderance of blank flakes, each as carefully shaped and polished as those that are adorned, seems not to support this view. It should also be noted that none of the investigations there revealed positive evidence of metalworking. The presence of these objects within a passage grave, on a remote hilltop, hints rather at a non-utilitarian role for these enigmatic flakes, for it is evident that monuments such as Lough Crew were imbued with deep-seated supernatural undertones in indigenous Celtic mythology.

In terms of the native artistic development, the ornament on the Lough Crew flakes is important, for it represents a radical departure from the free-hand foliate patterns of the Ulster scabbards. Now there is a rigid dependence on the compass, and workshop links are not with Europe but with Britain, its south-west, but above all its north. Some of the Lough Crew designs, indeed, can otherwise only be matched in the latter area.[150] This Lough Crew school of decoration, along with the broadly contemporary Somerset, County Galway, material and its stylistic analogies, embodies a unified artistic tradition that found its way to all areas of La Tène influence in the country. In bronze, bone, stone, even gold, there is repeated overlap in stylistic emphasis and approach. There is a strong conservatism, an acceptance of stylistic norms, and an unwillingness to deviate from that which was held to be artistically appropriate and correct. The art on the flakes had ready parallels on the Broighter torc, on the so-called bronze 'spoons', on a 'gaming-piece' from Cush in County Limerick, and on horsebits as well. Unique bronzes such as the ornamental horns from Cork, the famous

[149] Raftery, *La Tène in Ire.*, p. 305, fig. 148 (4), pl. 111 (2).
[150] M. Simpson, 'Massive armlets in the north British iron age' in J. M. Coles and D. D. A. Simpson (ed.), *Studies in ancient Europe: essays presented to Stuart Pigott* (n.p., 1968), p. 250; Raftery, *La Tène in Ire.*, pp 261–3.

'Petrie crown', the large repoussé discs of 'Monasterevin-type', and the finely ornamented disc from Loughan Island on the Bann may all overlap in time with this Lough Crew school of craftsmanship. Most striking analogy of all for the art on the flakes is the ornament on a stone from Derrykeighan, County Antrim, which is so close to that on one of the flakes as almost to suggest that the sculptor had a decorated flake before him as he worked.[151]

The Derrykeighan stone is one of five decorated iron-age stones from Ireland, to which can probably be added a few undecorated monoliths, especially that known as the Lia Fáil at Tara. These are generally regarded as having had some cult significance. They vary considerably in their form and in their ornament. Some, such as Derrykeighan, are rectangular in section; others vary from a squat rounded profile (Castlestrange, County Roscommon)[152] to cylindrical shape with domed top (Turoe, County Galway).[153] The Turoe example is the finest. Made of granite and standing just over a metre above ground level (its total length is 1.68 m), the stone is lavishly ornamented with overall curvilinear designs, raised in false relief from the surface of the stone by chiselling the background voids. The design, not an 'asymmetric jungle' as one commentator suggested, has been carefully laid out in a quadripartite arrangement suggesting a four-faced prototype. Around the base there is a band of 'step' or 'maeandroid' ornament, incised in a manner noticeably less sophisticated than the ornament on the rest of the stone. Fragments of a similar monolith also stood in Killycluggin, County Cavan.[154]

The Turoe stone, like the others, is a native rendering and it dates to the last century B.C. Other stones could be slightly earlier or slightly later; one from Mullaghmast, County Kildare, dates around the middle of the first millennium A.D.[155] Stones of this type are unknown in Britain and find their best parallels in the Breton peninsula of France.[156] It is possible that impulses from there inspired native craftsmen to erect local versions. The Irish stones would thus reflect a widespread Celtic religious custom

---

[151] See Raftery, *La Tène in Ire.*, for full discussion and bibliography of above-mentioned parallels.

[152] George Coffey, 'Some monuments of the La Tène period recently discovered in Ireland' in *R.I.A. Proc.*, xxiv (1902–4), sect. C, pp 262–3, pl. XXI; see Raftery, *La Tène in Ire.*, pp 291–303, for discussion of Irish stones.

[153] Joseph Raftery, 'The Turoe stone', pp 42–6, fig. 5; M. V. Duignan, 'The Turoe stone: its place in insular La Tène art' in P.-M. Duval and C. F. C. Hawkes (ed.), *Celtic art in ancient Europe; five protohistoric centuries* (London, 1976), pp 201–18.

[154] R. A. S. Macalister, 'On a stone with La Tène decoration recently discovered in Co. Cavan' in *R.S.A.I. Jn.*, lii (1922), pp 113–16; Barry Raftery, 'Excavations at Killycluggin, Co. Cavan' in *U.J.A.*, 3rd ser., xli (1978), pp 49–54.

[155] Coffey, art. cit., pp 263–6, pl. XXII.

[156] P. R. Giot, 'Les stèles armoricaines de l'âge de fer' in *Congrès prehistorique de Monaco, XVIe session* (n.p., 1959), pp 578–85; and *Brittany* (London, 1960), pp 179–82.

extending to the Rhineland and ultimately to Etruria. The carved stone heads in Ireland,[157] along with the fine wooden carving from Ralaghan, County Cavan,[158] similarly reflect a pan-Celtic set of religious beliefs.

THE foregoing section represents a consideration of scattered material within the country described loosely as 'La Tène' because of the form of the objects concerned and because of their ornamentation. In Ireland the term has a rather different meaning from elsewhere because of the insularity and longevity of La Tène traditions in this country. Thus the cultural and chronological subdivisions of the La Tène that have been worked out for the Continent have only the most generalised validity for Ireland. For this country chronology is very imprecise: the objects involved belong to the centuries between 300 B.C. and A.D. 300.

The picture presented by the La Tène material is disjointed and incomplete and much remains uncertain, much eludes us. As already noted, the extent to which the surviving La Tène remains are representative of the ordinary people is unclear. Undoubtedly a significant part reflects the trappings of an aristocratic élite and, indeed, the very paucity of objects itself suggests that large sections of the contemporary population are unrepresented. But at least it can be said that the material of La Tène aspect, scarce though it is in the country, is indicative of a recognisable, innovative iron-age tradition in Ireland in the last centuries B.C., a tradition that continued for a time into the early centuries of the Christian era. In those southern areas of the country that lack a La Tène horizon, the task of recognising the nature of contemporary innovating iron-age influences remains problematical.

In all of this it is readily apparent that the key to our understanding of the full iron age in Ireland lies in the recognition and investigation of settlement sites of the period. For the La Tène horizon at least, our ignorance is almost total. Only at Feerwore, County Galway, can we point to a small, domestic settlement which produced material of clearly La Tène type.[159] There were no houses preserved, the debris consisting merely of broken scraps left behind after the settlement was abandoned. We do not know if the site was defended or not. Whatever may have existed was removed by the bank-and-ditch construction of the later ringfort there.

The ringfort is, of course, the settlement type *par excellence* during the early historic period in Ireland, and continued, along with the crannog, into medieval times. The extent to which the true ringfort belongs to the pagan iron age is, however, uncertain. None can be reliably dated before the birth

[157] Etienne Rynne, 'Celtic stone idols in Ireland' in Thomas, *Iron age in Ir. Sea province*, pp 79–98.
[158] Adolf Mahr, 'A wooden idol from Ireland' in *Antiquity*, iv (1930), p. 487; Raftery, *La Tène in Ire.*, p. 308, fig. 150 (1), pl. 112 (1).
[159] Joseph Raftery, 'The Turoe stone'.

of Christ; a few have produced what appear to be Roman and sub-Roman remains in association with native material.[160] In view of the known longevity of Roman forms in post-Roman contexts abroad, such occurrences should be treated with caution. It is nonetheless possible that ringfort building had begun in Ireland in the early centuries of the Christian era. With long-established indigenous roots it may well be that it is the ringfort that represents the basic ethnic substratum throughout late prehistoric Ireland, with the La Tène remains constituting a mere cultural overlay, confined in area and in social content. But the chronology of the earliest Irish ringforts remains tenuous.

There are other sites in the country, generally fortified and in strongly defensive situations, which are often regarded as belonging to the iron age. Excavation of these has not been extensive, so that close dating of individual structures is usually vague. Indeed discussion depends, for the most part, on a consideration of superficially observed surface features. Hillforts are one such group of monuments. Such structures, large defended hilltop enclosures, were a standard settlement from throughout Europe from at least the early part of the last millennium B.C., and continued through the whole of the iron age. In many areas of Britain too, especially in the south-east and in the Welsh marches, hillforts were major tribal centres. Hundreds of examples are known. The number of recognised sites in Ireland is small, for less than fifty have thus far been positively identified.[161] They are sometimes taken as synonymous with the presence of iron-age intruders but, on surface features alone, this is scarcely warranted. Structures similar to one another in design and intent can be widely separated in culture and time. The *pa*s of New Zealand teach us this.[162] Hillfort construction in Ireland may, in fact, have bronze-age roots, as is suggested by the evidence of Rathgall, County Wicklow.[163] At the same time, of course, some hillforts could reflect intrusive influences, for it would be folly to suggest that the hillfort phenomenon in Ireland reflects a single evolutionary line of development. Seen in the field today, hillforts present themselves as tumbled and ruinous mounds of rubble, sometimes grass- or heather-covered; encircling, contour-like, the summits of hills or cutting off the necks of steep-sided promontories. Often the ramparts are barely visible at ground level and can only be fully appreciated from the air. The identification of such sites is in many instances mere chance and it may be assumed that there are other, as yet undetected, examples.

[160] See Joseph Raftery, 'Iron age and Irish Sea: problems for research' in Thomas, *Iron age in Ir. Sea province*, pp 1–10; Barry Raftery, 'Irish hillforts', ibid., p. 53; Séamus Caulfield, 'Celtic problems in the Irish iron age' in Ó Corráin, *Ir. antiquity*, pp 208–9.

[161] Barry Raftery, 'Irish hillforts' in Thomas, *Iron age in Ir. Sea province*, pp 37–58.

[162] Cyril Fox, 'Two Celtic bronzes from Lough Gur, Limerick, Ireland' in *Antiq. Jn.*, xxx (1950), pp 190–92.

[163] Barry Raftery, 'Rathgall and Irish hillfort problems' in D. W. Harding (ed.), *Hillforts: later prehistoric earthworks in Britain and Ireland* (n.p., 1976), pp 339–57.

Strictly on the basis of morphology, hillforts in Ireland have been divided into three main types.[164] The first are those characterised by a single line of defence, which can cover an area of from under two hectares to about nine hectares. Brusselstown Ring, near Baltinglass, County Wicklow,[165] and Carn Tigherna, near Fermoy, County Cork,[166] are good examples. Hillforts with two or three ramparts widely spaced from one another form the second Irish category. Sites as large as 20 hectares in area are known.[167] These have a slight emphasis in their distribution to the south-west and west of Ireland. The great 12.5 hectare site at Mooghaun, near Newmarket-on-Fergus in County Clare, is the finest example of this hillfort-type in the country.[168] Cashel Fort, at Upton, County Cork, is another.[169] The third hillfort type, numerically limited, is the inland promontory fort. As the name implies, these occupy promontory situations where the natural slopes are sufficiently precipitous to necessitate the construction of artificial defences only across one end of the promontory. A feature of two of the finest examples, Lurigethen[170] and Knockdhu,[171] both not far from the coast in north Antrim, is the presence of a series of bank-and-ditch defences with no space between successive lines, i.e. closely spaced multivallation. This is a defensive concept fundamentally distinct from that implied by the widely spaced multivallation of Class 2 forts. Not all the inland promontory forts, however, are defended in this way. The site of Caherconree, situated some 630 m above sea level on Slieve Mish in County Kerry, has but a single line of defence.[172] The area defended at Caherconree is scarcely a hectare. The wall, well built of sandstone blocks, has internal terracing and still stands to a height in places of more than two metres. Also on the Dingle peninsula, on the eastern side of Mount Brandon in Benagh townland, is an even more extraordinary inland promontory fort.[173] Here two stone walls, about 100 m apart, cut off a narrow promontory some 762 m above sea level. We can only wonder as to the function, and indeed the date, of such spectacular fortresses.

[164] Raftery, 'Irish hillforts'.

[165] Ibid., p. 40, pl. 111.

[166] S. P. Ó Ríordáin, *Antiquities of the Irish countryside* (5th ed., revised by Ruaidhrí de Valera, London, 1979), p. 48.

[167] E. Cody, 'A hill-fort at Ballylin, County Limerick, with a note on Mooghaun, County Clare' in *R.S.A.I. Jn.*, cxi (1981), pp 70–80.

[168] Ibid.; Raftery, 'Irish hillforts', p. 45, fig. 15.

[169] Raftery, 'Irish hillforts', p. 45; S. P. Ó Ríordáin, in *Cork Hist. Soc. Jn.*, xl (1935), pp 40, 49; Raftery, 'Rathgall and Irish hillfort problems', pl. IX.

[170] E. E. Evans, *Prehistoric and early Christian Ireland: a guide* (London, 1966), p. 49; Raftery, 'Irish hillforts', pl. V.

[171] Evans, *Prehistoric & early Christian Ireland*, p. 49.

[172] P. J. Lynch, 'Caherconree, County Kerry' in *R.S.A.I. Jn.*, ix (1899), pp 5–17; Raftery, 'Irish hillforts', p. 47; J. Cuppage, *Archaeological survey of the Dingle peninsula* (Ballyferriter, 1986). p. 81.

[173] Stephen MacDonagh, *A visitor's guide to the Dingle peninsula* (Dingle, 1985); Cuppage, op. cit., p. 82.

*Iron-age Ireland*

Promontory situations on the coast were also exploited for defensive purposes, and these are far more frequent than the inland structures.[174] There
are over 200 examples around our coasts and they are found almost everywhere where a suitable tongue of land juts into the sea. Not infrequently they
offer closely spaced multivallate defences to the landward side in a manner
similar to that of the inland forts in Antrim. In the west of Ireland, too, there
are several stone forts, the widely spaced multivallate defences of which are
built up against a vertical cliff face for added protection. An inland site is
Cahercommaun, near Corrofin, County Clare.[175] On the Atlantic coast on
Inishmore, Aran, County Galway, is the mighty Dún Aengus, its formidable
ramparts and startling situation strengthened yet further by the *chevaux de
frise* around the second wall.[176] This last, a defensive device comprising
thousands of upright and outward-sloping stone spikes, close-set to form an
almost impenetrable obstacle around the fort, is found on three other western
Irish sites, two coastal promontory forts and the large stone cashel of Bally-
kinvarga, near Kilfenora, County Clare.[177]

Such are the fortified sites that have, from time to time, been considered
to belong to the iron age, and it may, indeed, be assumed that some at least
of the structures involved were important centres during this period. But
ultimately it is only the evidence from excavation that can demonstrate this
in individual cases.

Partial excavation in a few hillforts has revealed some information regarding
their period of occupation but little of substance about their initial construction. Late bronze-age beginnings have been hinted at for several sites, as
noted above, and occupation in the centuries immediately after the birth of
Christ has also been demonstrated.[178] The virtual absence of La Tène material from any excavated hillfort is striking. This distinction is further emphasised by the preponderance of major hillforts in the south of the country; the
greatest concentrations of large hillforts are in the very areas where La Tène
artefacts are virtually absent. It may thus be that in the future widespread
excavation of southern Irish hillforts will help us more fully to understand

[174] M. J. O'Kelly, 'Three promontory forts in Co. Cork' in *R.I.A. Proc.*, lv (1952), sect. C,
pp 25–59; V. B. Proudfoot and B. C. S. Wilson, 'Further excavations at Larrybane promontory
fort, Co. Antrim' in *U.J.A.*, 3rd ser., xxiv–xxv (1961–2), pp 91–115.

[175] Hugh O'Neill Hencken, *Cahercommaun: a stone fort in Co. Clare* (R.S.A.I. special edition, 1938).

[176] T. J. Westropp, 'The fort of Dun Aengus in Inishmore, Aran' in *R.I.A. Proc.*, xxviii
(1910), sect. B, pp 1–46; Peter Harbison, 'Wooden and stone *chevaux de frise* in central and
western Europe' in *Prehist. Soc. Proc.*, xxxvii (1971), pp 203–4.

[177] Harbison, art. cit., p. 203.

[178] E.g. Freestone Hill (Barry Raftery, 'Freestone Hill: an iron age hillfort and bronze age
cairn' in *R.I.A. Proc.*, lxviii (1969), sect. C, pp 1–108) and Clogher, Co. Tyrone (R. B. Warner,
'Some observations on the context and importation of exotic material in Ireland . . .' in *R.I.A.
Proc.*, lxxvi (1976), sect. C, p. 274, n. 16a).

the nature of social and cultural developments in these areas in the critical formative centuries around the birth of Christ.

Attempts, on the basis of structural evidence alone, to seek an external source for the Irish forts are less than satisfactory. Vague analogies for the widely spaced plan of some of the Irish sites exist in south-west England and in parts of Iberia,[179] but such analogies are unbuttressed by firm archaeological evidence. The possibility of an Iberian ingredient as one strand at least in the genesis of the Irish hillfort may well reward further consideration, for the use of *chevaux de frise* as at Dún Aengus and other western sites is an Iberian technique par excellence. Suggestions that the *chevaux de frise* in Ireland and Iberia are unrelated, deriving from a common timber prototype which reached Ireland through Britain, remain unsubstantiated.[180] We lack the evidence of excavation. A single, fragmentary bronze fibula of native La Tène type, allegedly from the inner enclosure at Dún Aengus,[181] tells us nothing of the fort's foundation.

Equally speculative is the dating of the promontory forts. These sites, distinct from the contour sites not merely in their situation but also by the not infrequent use of closely spaced multivallation, may well belong to a cultural horizon totally different from that of the contour hillforts. It is tempting to relate the coastal sites to closely similar forts in south-west England and north-west France, where they have been identified with a Gaulish tribe, the seafaring Veneti.[182] We may also recall the presence in Ireland of low, rounded monoliths of iron-age date,[183] a form especially concentrated in the territory of the Veneti.[184] Again, however, firm evidence to support the interesting possibilities raised by these analogies is lacking, and it must be accepted that promontory forts in Ireland and those outside could result from no more than a common response to a common defensive situation. It must also be borne in mind that promontory forts in Ireland had a long life, possibly into medieval times, so that the attempted dating of individual sites without excavation is futile.

During the period of their use these Irish forts would have been quite different in appearance from that which we observe today. There would have been high, vertically faced stone ramparts, stepped on the inside perhaps, or there could have been steeply sloping earthen mounds, strengthened by timbers and surmounted by wicker breastwork or wooden palisade. Narrow entrances with heavy swinging gates are likely to have existed, and who

[179] Raftery, 'Irish hillforts', p. 49.
[180] Harbison, 'Wooden and stone *chevaux de frise*', pp 216–21.
[181] Raftery, *La Tène in Ire.*, fig. 79 (7).
[182] R. E. M. Wheeler and K. M. Richardson, *Hillforts of northern France* (London, 1957), pp 17–22.
[183] See above, p. 162.
[184] P. R. Giot, *Brittany* (London, 1960); cf. figs 59, 67.

knows what guard-houses, gate structures, or other defensive constructions existed to intimidate the enemy without?

The nature of the inner areas of the forts is almost totally unknown, and indeed the purpose that these monuments served is often debated. Were they populous, bustling centres, the capitals of tribal regions? Were they empty for much of the year, used only by lowland peoples when danger threatened? Or did such sites serve only a ritual or ceremonial function?

Outside Ireland there is clear evidence to show that many hillforts were densely occupied and in use the year round. Equally, it is evident that some forts did serve merely as refuges. Either or both interpretations could apply to Ireland but it seems likely that the primary function was defensive, not ceremonial. Excavation to date has been insufficient to allow firm conclusions either way. It is, however, difficult to envisage lofty and exposed sites such as Caherconree and Benagh in County Kerry as in occupation during the winter months.

One thing seems certain. The effort involved in constructing the defences of a hillfort was considerable and involved significant numbers of people over an extended period of time. This, as well as the large areas enclosed, implies use by a large number of people. Whatever their precise function, it seems not unreasonable to see the hillforts as important focal points within the tribal area.

But not all the great hilltop enclosures of Ireland are so compellingly defensive in the appearance of their enclosing ramparts. There is in the country a small group of imposing sites that occupy commanding positions and are characterised by a rampart-and-ditch enclosure of substantial proportions, but may still have served a primary function other than the protection of the inhabitants. Distinguishing these, apart from their size and location, is the presence of a deep ditch running inside, rather than outside, the earthwork enclosure. Three major sites are included in this group: Navan Fort (Emain Macha), County Armagh; Dún Ailinne, County Kildare; and Ráth na Ríogh, Tara, County Meath.[185] A fourth site, at Carrowmably, near Dromore, County Sligo, spectacularly sited on a cliff edge overlooking the sea, also possesses a deep ditch around the inner perimeter of its well-preserved bank. In this instance, however, neither history nor archaeology provide the slightest clue as to its function or date.

The three enclosures initially listed above are all recognised royal centres prominent in the traditions and mythology of early Celtic Ireland.[186] Each is alleged to have been a provincial centre, important for inaugurations, ceremonies, and assemblies, and possibly even the seat of a royal household. These were clearly exceptional sites and this is given strong support by the

---

[185] Raftery, 'Irish hillforts', pp 42–3.
[186] Bernard Wailes, 'The Irish "royal sites" in history and archaeology' in *Camb. Med. Celt. Studies*, iii (1982), pp 1–29.

evidence of excavation at Navan Fort and Dún Ailinne. Oddly, a comparable earthwork enclosure is absent at Cruachan, the presumed contemporary capital of the ancient kingdom of Connacht.[187]

Tara, above all, figures prominently in the early literature.[188] Ráth na Ríogh, the 7-hectare internally ditched enclosure, dominates the ridge-top, but this monument is only one of an extensive complex of tumuli, ring-barrows, enclosures, and the enigmatic parallel ramparts known as the 'banqueting hall'. Additional sites have been revealed by aerial photography.[189] Few of these earthworks have been excavated. Each has a fanciful name deriving, for the most part, from the early medieval *Dindshenchas*,[190] but these are of no value in determining either the purpose or the date of any of the structures on the hill. Excavation has revealed activity from neolithic times[191] to the early centuries A.D.,[192] and individual unexcavated sites could belong anywhere within this extensive time-span. Some, such as the ringforts on the hilltop, could even be later. The majority of monuments at Tara are, however, likely to be of iron-age date.

Occupation on the summit of Navan Fort (Emain Macha) began, as noted earlier, in the seventh century B.C. during the later phase of the Irish bronze age.[193] At that time there is no evidence that the site was out of the ordinary, for there was only a single house which stood within a wooden stockade. Over many generations the plan of the settlement changed little, but the house was replaced on no fewer than eight occasions. A second house, twice rebuilt, was later erected on another site within the same palisaded enclosure. A third phase then followed, when the function changed radically and the hilltop may have acquired its ceremonial importance. It is possible that it was during this phase that the large, enclosing bank was raised, but this has not been demonstrated by excavation. Phase 3 involved the construction of a circular wall of horizontal timber planking, enclosing an area 40 m in diameter, within which were the five concentric rings of posts, 3 m apart, the posts of each ring 1.20 m to 1.80 m distant from one another. A single post-hole 2.30 m deep was found at the centre, within which was preserved the stump of an oak post 55 cm in diameter. Its original height could have been

[187] Michael Herity, 'A survey of the royal site of Cruachain in Connacht' in *R.S.A.I. Jn.*, cxii (1983), pp 121–42; cxiv (1984), pp 125–38.

[188] R. A. S. Macalister, *Tara: a pagan sanctuary of ancient Ireland* (London, 1931); S. P. Ó Ríordáin, *Tara: the monuments on the hill* (3rd ed., Drogheda, 1960).

[189] D. L. Swan, 'The hill of Tara, County Meath: the evidence of aerial photography' in *R.S.A.I. Jn.*, cviii (1978), pp 51–66.

[190] E. J. Gwynn (ed. and trans.), *The metrical Dindshenchas* (Dublin, 1903), pp 5–31.

[191] Michael Herity, *Irish passage graves* (Dublin, 1974), pp 252–3.

[192] Ó Ríordáin, *Tara*, p. 26; J. B. Bateson, 'Roman material from Ireland: a reconsideration' in *R.I.A. Proc.*, lxxiii (1973), sect. C, pp 71–2, fig. 1 (3–5).

[193] A. Selkirk and D. M. Waterman, 'Navan fort' in *Current Archaeology*, no. 22 (Sept. 1970), pp 304–8; C. J. Lynn, 'Navan fort: a draft summary of D. M. Waterman's excavations' in *Emania*, i (1986), pp 11–19.

as much as 13 m. From an entrance in the west there was an arrangement of postholes, interpreted by the excavator as an ambulatory, which led to the centre. After some restructuring the site seems to have been partially burnt, perhaps deliberately, before finally being sealed by a cairn some 46 m in diameter and 4.50 to 5 m high. Tree-ring analysis of the central post indicates a date just before 100 B.C. for the last major phase of activity at Navan Fort.[194]

The precise nature of the buildings that once stood at Navan is uncertain and it cannot be stated if the multi-ringed complex was ever roofed. This is possible. It is, however, difficult to avoid the conclusion that Navan Fort in its later stages served no ordinary practical purpose. This is especially emphasised by the final burning and monumental sealing of the structure. It is possible, at the same time, that secular occupation took place elsewhere on the hilltop. Much of the area within the enclosure remains unexcavated. Iron-age material recovered in the course of the excavation, such as a bone dice, a bone weaving-comb, and iron slag, all seem to indicate domestic activities. The discovery in one of the pre-cairn levels of a Barbary ape skull[195] is of outstanding importance, emphasising the singular importance of Navan Fort in late prehistoric times. It is not, however, clear to which phase the skull belongs.

Excavation on the summit of Dún Ailinne, County Kildare, uncovered a sequence of iron-age occupation as complex as that on Navan,[196] and as at the latter site the material remains associated with the hilltop activity are exclusively of La Tène and sub-Roman aspect. Initially, there were three successive circular, timber structures, each revealed as trenches in which a continuous series of upright posts had once stood. Phase 2 was made up of three concentric trenches gapped and with an annexe; Phase 3 had two concentric trenches enclosing an internal ring of large postholes, at the precise centre of which was a small, circular building. Then, in Phase 4, the outer and inner features were removed leaving only the ring of large free-standing posts. These in turn were later dismantled and the hilltop was used for a time as the site of intensive but sporadic open-air feasting. Carbon 14 age-determinations ranged from the third century B.C. to the fourth century A.D.

Navan Fort and Dún Ailinne, clearly overlapping culturally with the horizon that is otherwise represented only by the scattered La Tène artifacts, give us unique and important insights into aspects of contemporary society that the finds on their own can never give us. With these structures archae-

---

[194] M. G. L. Baillie, 'The central post from Navan Fort' in *Emania*, i (1986), pp 20–21.
[195] Lynn, 'Navan Fort', p. 16.
[196] Bernard Wailes, 'Dún Ailinne: an interim report' in D. W. Harding (ed.), *Hillforts: later prehistoric earthworks in Britain and Ireland* (London, 1976), pp 319–38, and 'Irish "royal sites"', pp 15–18.

ology, mythology, and even the first glimmerings of history are brought together. The great hostings of the 'Táin' can be dimly discerned as a backdrop to these extraordinary monuments, with warrior kings and queens, hemmed in by their onerous obligations and awesome taboos, presiding over the rituals vital for the prosperity and well-being of their people. The authority that such rulers could wield must have been considerable, to organise and co-ordinate the enormous labour that the construction of these great sites involved. A highly sophisticated social organisation is implied and a strong sense of community, allied perhaps also to powerful religious motivation, on the part of the workers who followed the directions of the leadership in the laborious project. We do not know, however, to what extent slave labour might also have been used.

The task was prodigious. Many men were needed and it must have taken months to complete. The digging of the ditch alone and the piling of the rubble below it, using the simplest of tools, was a great undertaking. But the timber structures on the hilltop required as much effort. Large numbers of trees had to be felled, trimmed, and then transported, who can say for how many kilometres, finally hauled uphill and erected in place. *In situ* they may have been carved or painted and there could have been extensive joinery work. And while all this was going on the work-force had to be fed, watered, and housed. It is thus likely that the whole community was preoccupied with this one project.

These internally ditched enclosures with their elaborate hilltop structures are not the only instances in iron-age Ireland of large-scale, corporate undertakings. The spectacular timber trackway at Corlea has earlier been referred to.[197] The 'linear' or 'travelling earthworks' too, which are found in northern and western areas of the country, are also contemporary physical manifestations of the same social phenomenon.[198] These earthworks appear now as discontinuous stretches of banks with a ditch between, sometimes a bank between two ditches, sometimes several banks and ditches; occasionally only a ditch is discernible. In boggy areas the line of the earthwork was often continued by well-constructed timber palisading. Where the bank is well preserved its basal width can be 10 m or more and its height in excess of 6 m. Individual stretches are sometimes several kilometres in length and these are best to be seen in Leitrim, Roscommon, Longford, Monaghan, Down, and south Armagh.

Inevitably, the precise purpose of these linear earthworks is uncertain. Vague correspondence with the alleged boundaries of early historic tribal areas has given rise to the suggestion that the earthworks originally formed a tribal frontier, continuous except where natural features mitigated the necessity for artificial ramparts. But we do not know if all the surviving stretches

---

[197] Above, p. 148.     [198] Lynn, 'Navan Fort' and references.

of earthworks are contemporary, nor indeed has it ever been shown that a continuous line ever existed. Legendary names from folk tradition such as the 'Dane's cast', the 'Black pig's dyke' and the 'worm ditch' serve only to deepen the mystery of these structures. More plausible are the interpretations that view the dykes as routeway defences or as attempts to hinder and forestall large-scale cattle-rustling. It is, however, hard to envisage these earthworks as ever having been permanently policed or manned.

Sometimes these cross-country ramparts are so located as to give the impression of enormous enclosures. At the Dún of Drumsna, for instance, on the Roscommon side of the Shannon at Drumsna, County Leitrim, a loop of the river is cut off by a great earthwork 30 m wide at its base, 4.50 m high and extending for a length of some 1.6 km.[199] Two lesser ramparts accompany the main one and there are two principal breaks, each 15 m wide, the opening flanked by the right-angled bends of the rampart ends. The size and situation are strikingly reminiscent of European late La Tène oppida, and these too are often characterised by inturned entrances. But the Drumsna 'entrances' are far too wide to have served as normal defended entries and, moreover, the returned ends run in the wrong direction if the area within the river loop is to be taken as a fortified enclosure. The suggestion that the earthwork may be related to attempts to control the river crossings here may have some merit.

Even more remarkable than the so-called Dún of Drumsna is the enigmatic enclosure in south Armagh known as the Dorsey.[200] Here an irregular, elongated area of about 125 hectares is enclosed by a discontinuous series of earthworks, which appear to pay no attention to any defensive advantages that the hilly topography might have offered. The earthworks, as substantial in places as those at Drumsna, comprise a main rampart between two ditches with a smaller rampart outside. Excavation has recently shown the nature of the timber constructions that continued the line of the earthworks across boggy areas. Clearest evidence was from the south-west corner of the enclosure, where the remains of a palisade were found made of reused, roughly squared oak posts, set continuously in a V-sectioned trench. These were held in place by adzed boards of oak wedged horizontally along the base of the trench on either side of the palisade. Charcoal associated with an initial phase of construction of the rampart indicated a date in the last quarter of the last millennium B.C., the first time a firm date had been established for a monument of this kind. Even more important, however, was the demonstration by dendrochronological methods that the timbers of the palisade in the bog had

[199] W. F. de Vismes Kane, 'The dun of Drumsna: a frontier fortification of the kingdoms of Aileagh and Cruaghan' in *R.I.A. Proc.*, xxiii (1915), sect. C, pp 324–32.
[200] Lynn, 'Navan Fort'.

been cut at precisely the same time as had the timbers of the last construction on the summit of Navan Fort.[201]

THE burial record, not only for the iron age, but also for almost the whole of the last pre-Christian millennium in Ireland, is meagre and the few known sites are generally uncertainly dated. For the later bronze age we can only point to two likely sites: Mullaghmore, County Down, where a ring-barrow produced cremations and coarse pottery,[202] and Rathgall, County Wicklow, where three cremation deposits were enclosed by a shallow ring-ditch.[203] At each site one of the burials was contained within a coarse upright pot. It must be assumed that the means of disposal of the dead during the late bronze age were such as to leave no obvious trace in the archaeological record. It may thus follow that the continued scarcity of burials in the iron age indicates the persistence into that period of those same conditions or customs that prevent us from recognising late bronze-age interments. This in itself hints at a strong measure of population stability throughout the millennium, and the surviving burial record, limited though it is, lends support to this impression. It is only around the turn of the millennium and into the beginning of the Christian era that a handful of clearly intrusive burials can be identified.

Though few in number, there is no small variety of iron-age burial customs in Ireland.[204] Both cremation and inhumation were practised, but there are some grounds to suggest that cremation may be the earlier. Cremation was, however, sporadically practised well into the first Christian millennium.[205] The dead were sometimes covered by mounds or ring-barrows, humble in size compared with the great sepulchral monuments of earlier eras. Sometimes older mounds were reused for burial deposits in the iron age, and occasionally burials were placed in the ground within simple embanked enclosures. Some unaccompanied cremations in pits may date to the iron age, and there are inhumations, unprotected and without covering mounds, sometimes in cemeteries, which may be of similar date. The burials of foreigners, recognisable by their exotic grave-goods, obviously stand apart from the Irish development, but these are rare.

[201] Ibid., pp 126–7.
[202] J. M. Mogey, 'Preliminary report on excavations in Mullaghmore townland, Co. Down' in *U.J.A.*, 3rd ser., xii (1949), pp 82–8; J. M. Mogey, G. B. Thompson, and V. B. Proudfoot, 'Excavations of two ring-barrows in Mullaghmore townland, Co. Down', ibid., xix (1956), pp 11–28.
[203] Barry Raftery, 'Rathgall, a late bronze age burial in Ireland' in *Antiquity*, xlvii (1973), pp 293–5.
[204] Barry Raftery, 'Iron age burials in Ireland' in Ó Corráin, *Ir. antiquity*, pp 173–204.
[205] Eoin Grogan, 'Excavation of an iron age burial mound at Furness' in *Kildare Arch. Soc. Jn.*, xvi (1983–4), pp 298–316.

It is possible, but not yet positively demonstrated, that ring-barrows belong to the earliest phase of Irish iron-age burials. These usually consist of a low, circular mound, hardly more than 1 m high, enclosed by a fosse with external bank which rarely exceeds 15 m in overall diameter. Cremation seems to have been the exclusive rite and individual mounds were used over a period of time, perhaps as family or tribal burial places. At Grannagh, County Galway, for instance, at least six interments took place, the earlier ones in the centre, the later ones in the silted fosse.[206] Grave-goods were simple, consisting mainly of bronze fibulae, glass beads, and a few other items.[207] At Carrowjames, County Mayo, no fewer than twenty-five burials had been deposited in the mound, concentrated towards the centre in three main phases of burial activity.[208] Only nine were accompanied, mainly by beads, metal rings, and some miscellaneous small objects of bronze. Tumulus II at Cush, County Limerick, represents a different type of burial.[209] This was a circular mound, 13.70 m in diameter and 2 m high, with shallow external fosse. On the old ground surface under the mound, sunk centrally in an area of fire-reddened soil (the probable site of the pyre), was a small pit which contained the burnt remains of a single individual. These were accompanied by a small, decorated bone plaque. Nearby stood a second, similar mound which might be contemporary and a third, certainly earlier, burial monument. A low mound (Site C), one of three burial sites on Carbury Hill, County Kildare, was just over 8 m in diameter but only 90 cm high. It covered an unaccompanied cremation deposit. The two other burial monuments on the hill, each formed by an enclosing bank with internal fosse (in one instance gapped at two opposed points on its circumference), probably also belong to the iron age, perhaps late within the period, but firm dating evidence is lacking. One enclosure was 25.90 m in diameter, the other about twice this. Two unaccompanied cremations came from one (Site A), the other yielded four cremations and fifteen inhumations. Nondescript grave-goods included an iron shears and some iron rings.[210]

At Kiltierney, County Fermanagh, a number of secondary cremations, associated with a bronze fibula and glass beads, had been placed in a large neolithic mound.[211] Four secondary inhumations were found in the silted ditch of a middle bronze-age mound at Carrowbeg North, County

[206] R. A. S. Macalister, 'A report on some excavations recently conducted in Co. Galway' in *R.I.A. Proc.*, xxxiii (1916–17), sect. C, pp 505–10; Raftery, 'Iron age burials', p. 180.

[207] See C. F. C. Hawkes, 'The wearing of the brooch: early iron age dress among the Irish' in Scott, *Studies on early Ireland*, pp 59–62.

[208] Joseph Raftery, 'Carrowjames II' (above, p. 150, n. 91).

[209] S. P. Ó Ríordáin, 'Excavations at Cush, Co. Limerick' in *R.I.A. Proc.*, xlv (1940), sect. C, pp 133–9, 154–6.

[210] G. F. Willmot, 'Three burial sites at Carbury, Co. Kildare' in *R.S.A.I. Jn.*, lxviii (1938), pp 130–42.

[211] Barry Raftery, 'Iron age burials', p. 187; Hawkes, 'The wearing of the brooch', pp 63–4.

Galway.[212] One of these, a female, had a bronze locket on her shoulder, to which traces of textile still adhered, and around one ankle she wore a string of bone beads. Simple, unaccompanied cremations are virtually undatable. Three from recent excavations at the Long Stone, Cullen, County Tipperary, may be iron-age.[213] That found in the mid-nineteenth century at 'Loughey' near Donaghadee, County Down, is certainly so, but is clearly non-native.[214]

Inhumations without associated material are also normally undatable, but again there are some in long stone cists that may belong to the iron age;[215] many, however, can be much later. An important cemetery of unprotected inhumations, twenty-seven in number, has recently been brought to light around the great mound of Knowth, County Meath.[216] The majority of skeletons were flexed, a few extended. One interesting double burial was that of two males, lying head to toe, each of whom appear to have been decapitated.[217] Beads of bone and glass, metal rings, bone dice, and other 'gaming pieces' were the main grave-goods. Dating for the Knowth burials within the first half-millennium A.D., perhaps within its second quarter, might be suggested.

The extent of our knowledge concerning the human remains from iron-age burials in Ireland is not great, but the limited pathological examination that has taken place has produced some interesting information. It is scarcely surprising to observe that life expectancy was not high, but the almost total absence of individuals of advanced age is, perhaps, worthy of note. Older skeletons are generally female: at Feerwore the female was 'over 30, probably over 40'.[218] At Carbury Hill (Site B, 11) the female was 'rather elderly'.[219] Average age of the deceased adults, however, where this could be determined, was between 20 and 30. Children, as might be expected, represent a significant percentage of the deceased individuals, and the remains of children often accompany those of adults. This is readily explicable when, as in Cremation 18 at Carrowjames, the remains of an unborn foetus accompanied

[212] G. F. W. Willmot, 'Two bronze age burials at Carrowbeg North, Belclare, Co. Galway' in *Galway Arch. Soc. Jn.*, xviii (1938–9), pp 121–40.

[213] Raftery, 'Iron age burials', p. 191; Michael Herity, 'Longstone, Co. Tipperary' in Brian de Breffny (ed.), *Ireland: a cultural encyclopaedia* (London, 1983), pp 142–3.

[214] E. M. Jope and B. C. S. Wilson, 'A burial group of the first century A.D. from "Loughey" near Donaghadee' in *U.J.A.*, 3rd ser., xx (1957), pp 73–94; E. M. Jope, 'The beads from the first century A.D. burial at "Loughey" near Donaghadee: supplementary note', ibid., xxiii (1960), p. 40.

[215] See Joseph Raftery, 'The Turoe stone', pp 28–30; Barry Raftery, 'Iron age burials', p. 194.

[216] George Eogan, 'Excavations at Knowth, Co. Meath, 1962–65' in *R.I.A. Proc.*, lxvi (1968), sect. C, pp 365–73, and 'Report on the excavation of some passage graves, unprotected inhumation burials and a settlement site at Knowth, Co. Meath' in *R.I.A. Proc.*, lxxiv (1974), sect. C, pp 68–87.

[217] Eogan, 'Report on the excavation', pp 73–5.

[218] Joseph Raftery, 'The Turoe stone', p. 46.

[219] Willmot, 'Three burial sites', p. 141.

an adult, presumed to be female.[220] But it is not clear why children varying from 5 to 9 years of age should have been buried with the remains of adults. In fact, at Carrowjames, apart from the unborn foetus, children were buried exclusively with adults, with the sole exception of a 6-year-old who was accompanied by tiny bones which may be those of a new-born infant. It is, no doubt, outlandish to ponder on the possibility of human sacrifice. But human sacrifice may have been practised in Ireland at this time if the embanked enclosure (Site 4) at the Curragh, County Kildare, dates to the iron age. Here, buried centrally within the enclosure, was the skeleton of a female whose strained and awkward position and unnaturally raised skull prompted the conclusion that she had, in all probability, been buried alive.[221] The bones thus far examined from Irish iron-age burials reveal little about contemporary disease or disability. Only occasionally has arthritic deformation of the joints been noted (e.g. Carrowjames, C. 17; Carbury Hill site 3, 1; Carrowbeg North, 13). Teeth are generally devoid of any traces of tooth decay (e.g. Carrowbeg, 12), but are often exceptionally worn. Where size could be estimated individuals were appreciably smaller than today. Females were under 5 feet (1.50 m), males 5 ft 8 in. (1.70 m), more or less.

There are some indications that suggest a gradual change during the second or third century A.D. from cremation to inhumation. Dating is of course at all times imprecise, but such a development could reflect contemporary change in Roman burial customs where, from the reign of Hadrian, inhumation became the dominant rite.[222] But this need not indicate any radical change in the population of Ireland, no more than the change in Rome itself involved such a change. Nonetheless it is evident that visitors from the Roman provinces did in fact find their way to Ireland from the beginning of the Christian era onwards.

At Lambay, an island off the coast of County Dublin, a group of settlers from what is now north-east England established themselves just after the middle of the first century A.D. and stayed long enough to die and be buried. By the second century the island was deserted, if Ptolemy's reference is taken as representing the contemporary situation.[223] The cemetery was never scientifically investigated and details concerning its nature or extent are scant.[224] All the burials, however, appear to have contained inhumed remains and one, at least, seems to have been that of a crouched skeleton. A range of

[220] Joseph Raftery, 'Carrowjames II'.

[221] S. P. Ó Ríordáin, 'Excavations of some earthworks on the Curragh, Co. Kildare' in *R.I.A. Proc.*, liii (1950), sect. C, pp 249–77.

[222] J. M. C. Toynbee, *Death and burial in the Roman world* (London, 1971), p. 40; R. G. Collingwood and I. A. Richmond, *The archaeology of Roman Britain* (London, 1969), p. 166.

[223] Warner, 'Some observations on the ... importation of exotic material', p. 278, n. 4.

[224] R. A. S. Macalister, 'On some antiquities discovered upon Lambay', in *R.I.A. Proc.*, xxxviii (1929), sect. C, pp 240–46; Etienne Rynne, 'The La Tène and Roman finds from Lambay, Co. Dublin: a reassessment' in *R.I.A. Proc.*, lxxvi (1976), sect. C, pp 231–44.

metal objects, almost all fragmentary, was recovered. From these it can be inferred that a warrior burial existed. This is represented by the remains of a long, heavy, iron sword (quite unlike any of the short native weapons), the decorative scabbard mounts, and a bronze shield boss. An iron mirror was also salvaged from the debris, five Roman bronze fibulae, a typically 'north-east English' beaded necklet of bronze, several rings, a lignite bracelet, and a substantial number of sheet bronze fragments. From these two decorated discs could be reconstructed, one circular, the other triangular. It is clear that the dead at Lambay were north Britons whose material culture was strongly influenced by Rome.

But Rome is more dramatically represented in Ireland by the second-century cremation from Stonyford, County Kilkenny.[225] Here, recovered in the early nineteenth century, was a classic Roman cist-burial, the burnt remains contained within a glass cinerary urn, sealed by a disc-mirror, and accompanied by a small glass bottle. Roman too, in all probability, were the inhumations in long stone cists found (and destroyed) on Bray Head, County Wicklow, in 1835. These were accompanied by second-century Roman coins.[226]

LAMBAY, Bray Head, and, above all, Stoneyford represent significant new cultural influences in the country emanating directly from the world of imperial Rome. The Lambay burials may, as has been suggested, represent a small band of fugitives, from north-east England, Brigantians perhaps, fleeing Roman occupation of their territory in the A.D. 70s at almost exactly the same time that Masada, at the other end of the empire, was also paying dearly for native revolt. The Bray Head cemetery could be the last resting place of a small colony of provincial Romans, traders, refugees again, or even shipwrecked sailors. We can only speculate. Most remarkable of all, however, is the cremation burial at Stoneyford, in every detail a typical Roman burial. How is this burial to be interpreted? Under what circumstances can we explain the presence in County Kilkenny of a delicate and fragile glass cinerary urn? It is difficult to envisage such an item as part of the normal cargo of a casual trading ship. The site of Stoneyford, as Warner has pointed out, is not far from an assumed crossing place on the River Nore, itself navigable to this point from the important harbour of Waterford to the south.[227] Clearly, Warner's suggestion that this burial indicates a Roman settlement of some permanence and stability must thus be seriously considered. The likelihood

[225] S. P. Ó Ríordáin, 'Roman material in Ireland' in *R.I.A. Proc.*, li (1950), sect. C, pp 249–77; J. D. Bateson, 'Roman material from Ireland: a reconsideration' in *R.I.A. Proc.*, lxxiii (1973), sect. C, pp 72–3; Barry Raftery, 'Iron age burials', p. 194, fig. 41 (1, 2).
[226] Bateson, 'Roman material', p. 45 and references.
[227] Warner, 'Importation of exotic material', p. 200.

that the remains are those of a female suggests further that a settlement more extensive than a temporary trading station existed.

The nature and extent of the Roman presence in Ireland has been the subject of considerable debate in recent times. There can be little doubt that the ports and coastal regions were tolerably well known to traders. Tacitus, for example, writing in the late first century A.D., noted that 'the interior parts are little known, but through commercial intercourse and the merchants there is better knowledge of the harbours and approaches'.[228] The late second-century map of Claudius Ptolemaeus, based on information from Marinus of Tyre of the earlier part of the century and possibly ultimately on material from the first-century Philemon,[229] gives much information concerning names of rivers, tribes, and possible tribal centres. Reasonable accuracy for the configuration of the country is achieved in northern, eastern, and southern areas but less so in the west. The work is obviously based on measurements and information from seafarers familiar with significant areas of the country.

It can be taken that merchants were not infrequent visitors to sheltered Irish ports, and they may have ventured inland on occasion seeking better markets for their merchandise. The stories that filtered back to the classical world concerning society in Ireland were often fabricated tales of savagery and barbarism, only to be expected of a nation living in wretched cold on the limit of the habitable world, as Strabo and others suggested.[230] More fanciful is the account of Pomponius Mela (perhaps following Strabo), who described the rich pastures as so succulent that the cattle, through overeating, were in danger of bursting![231] Tacitus, however, one of the few objective commentators, noted that 'the soil and climate, and the character and civilisation of the people, do not differ much from Britain'.[232]

That merchants came here is evident and that a Roman presence is clearly represented in the archaeological record is not in question. But there is no small amount of discussion whether a Roman military expedition might have landed in Ireland.[233] Agricola, as Tacitus tells us in an oft-quoted passage, felt that the country could be taken with 'one legion and a moderate number of auxiliaries',[234] and he plainly had the possibility of invasion in mind. An ambiguous statement in the same passage has been taken by some commentators as at least leaving open the possibility that such an invasion was

---

[228] *Agricola*, cap. XXIV; Kenney, *Sources*, p. 132.

[229] *N.H.I.*, ix, map 14 and note (pp 16, 98); J. J. Tierney, 'The Greek geographic tradition and Ptolemy's evidence for Irish geography' in *R.I.A. Proc.*, lxxvi (1976), sect. C, pp 259–65.

[230] Ibid., pp 259–60. It should be noted that Strabo was careful to add that he had no first-hand knowledge of such customs.

[231] Kenney, *Sources*, p. 134.

[232] Ibid., p. 132.

[233] See Killeen, 'Ireland in the Greek and Roman writers', pp 213–15, and Warner, 'Importation of exotic material', pp 180–81, for recent summaries.

[234] Kenney, *Sources*, p. 132.

attempted. Writing of Agricola's campaigns in Scotland Tacitus states that 'in the fifth campaign he crossed over in the first ship, and conquered hitherto unknown peoples, and fortified the coast of Britain facing Ireland, in hope rather than fear'. Killeen, who considered this passage, noted Pfitzner's query: 'having reached the narrow isthmus between the estuaries of Clyde and Forth and fortified it, where... could Agricola reasonably be said to have crossed by ship... except to Ireland?'[235] Even more intriguing is the oft-quoted reference in Juvenal, *Satire* 2, 159–163: 'We have taken our arms beyond the shores of Ireland and the recently conquered Orkneys, and Britain of the short nights.' The conquests of the Orkneys and Britain are historical fact; could there thus be truth in the reference to Ireland?[236]

Records for the relevant period are extremely scarce, and moreover it should be borne in mind that an unsuccessful military adventure to Ireland need not have been reported on in contemporary writings. But if a Roman military expedition was attempted in Ireland it was swallowed up in the Irish bogs: there is no trace of it in the archaeological record. Archaeological evidence for a Roman presence in the country is, however, far from insignificant. Scattered items of Roman manufacture have been recovered in native settlements and in hoards and as stray finds in various parts of Ireland.[237] Two main chronological groups have been noted, those objects dating to the first and second centuries A.D. and those that can be placed in the fourth or early fifth centuries. Artefacts of the third century are extremely scarce. Material of the earlier group is scattered around the eastern coastal lowlands and also along the northern coast of Antrim, Londonderry, and Donegal. This pattern is extended in the later phase by a broad inland spread of artefacts from the Shannon to Kilkenny. The commonest Roman objects in the country are coins, brooches, and pottery fragments.

There are sixteen reliably documented finds of Roman coinage from Ireland. These vary from isolated copper coins (such as that from the hillfort on Freestone Hill, County Kilkenny),[238] the gold coins from Newgrange, County Meath,[239] and the great hoards of silver coins from the north of Ireland.[240] The huge hoard from Ballinrees, County Londonderry, dated to the early fifth century A.D., contained no fewer than 1,701 silver coins as well as a quantity of ingots and pieces of plate.[241] About a dozen bronze

[235] Killeen, art. cit., p. 213.
[236] Ibid.
[237] See Bateson, 'Roman material', for extensive summary, and Warner, 'Importation of exotic material', for detailed discussion.
[238] Barry Raftery, 'Freestone Hill: an iron age hillfort and bronze age cairn' in *R.I.A. Proc.*, lxviii (1969), sect. C, pp 1–108.
[239] J. D. Bateson, 'The finding of Roman silver coins in the vicinity of the Giant's Causeway' in *U.J.A.*, xxxiv (1971), pp 50–57, and 'Roman material', pp 44–5.
[240] Herbert Mattingly and J. Pearce, 'The Coleraine hoard' in *Antiquity*, ii (1937), pp 39–45.
[241] Ibid.

178 _Iron-age Ireland_

brooches of varying Roman type are known from Ireland. These include the five from Lambay referred to above, a potentially important first-century example from near the 'holy well' at Randalstown, County Meath,[242] and other, isolated specimens. Two late Roman disc brooches from Newgrange,[243] a widespread late Roman type, are otherwise unknown in Ireland. The Newgrange excavations also produced a variety of other metal objects of probable Roman manufacture, including, in the nineteenth century, an important hoard of gold rings and neck ornaments.[244]

Sherds of Samian and Arretine ware have been recovered from a number of native Irish settlement sites. These distinctive pottery forms were widely manufactured and exported across the far-flung empire, and such vessels might, perhaps, have been highly prized in an aceramic society. The amount of such pottery in Ireland is, however, meagre when compared with almost any other region of contemporary Europe. It has, indeed, been argued that in many cases the Roman pottery fragments came to the country many centuries after their original manufacture, from long-abandoned villas of a vanished empire.[245] The point may be noted, but it is not proven.

There can be no doubt, however, that Roman pottery fragments from the major settlement at the Rath of the Synods, Tara, County Meath, came to the country in the early centuries of Christianity. This site also produced glass fragments, a Roman lead seal, and a varied collection of bronze and iron objects of the first few centuries A.D.[246] These reveal intimate contact with the Roman world and emphasise the wealth and importance of the community at Tara at this time.[247] There are other miscellaneous, scattered Roman imports. These include a bronze ladle from Bohermeen, County Meath,[248] a small handbell found with native bronzes at Kishawanny, County Kildare, and an interesting oculist's stamp from Goldenbridge, County Tipperary.[249] We should also not forget the gold-wire necklaces from the Broighter hoard, perhaps of Alexandrian manufacture, and the interesting possibilities that arise if the enamel blocks from Tara are accepted

[242] Hawkes, 'The wearing of the brooch', p. 65, fig. 11 (2).
[243] R. A. G. Carson and Claire O'Kelly, 'A catalogue of the Roman coins from Newgrange, Co. Meath, and notes on the coins and related finds' in _R.I.A. Proc._, lxxvii (1977), sect. C, pp 52, 53, pl. VIIA.
[244] C. Topp, 'The gold ornaments reputedly found near the entrance to Newgrange in 1842' in _Annual Report of the University of London Institute of Archaeology_, xii (1956), pp 53–62; Bateson, 'Roman material', pp 70–71; Carson & O'Kelly, 'Catalogue of Roman coins', pp 53–4.
[245] Contrast Warner, 'Importation of exotic material', pp 285–8, with Joseph Raftery, 'A matter of time' in _R.S.A.I. Jn._, xciii (1963), p. 112, and J. D. Bateson 'Further finds of Roman material from Ireland' in _R.I.A. Proc._, lxxvi (1976), sect. C, pp 171–80: 178–9.
[246] Bateson, 'Roman material', pp 71, 72, fig. 1 (3–5).
[247] S. P. Ó Ríordáin, 'Roman material in Ireland' in _R.I.A. Proc._, li (1947), sect. C, p. 61; Bateson, 'Roman material', p. 66.
[248] Raftery, _Catalogue of Irish iron age antiquities_, no. 593.
[249] Bateson, 'Roman material', p. 74.

as imported pieces from Italy.[250] Finally of note is the hoard of silver ingots and hacked plates from Balline, County Limerick, which date to the late fourth or early fifth century A.D.[251]

The significance of the Roman finds in Ireland is variously debated, and it is likely that no single explanation applies to the material as a whole.[252] Some must have come through trade, and a wine jar (*olla*) dredged from the Porcupine Bank, 450 km west of Galway, could be taken as evidence of a trading vessel, blown off course.[253] The Irish in return could have given foodstuffs, woollen garments, slaves, or Irish wolfhounds. Symmachus, a Roman noble writing in the last years of the fourth century, in fact referred to *Scotti canes* which were used for public amusements. In a letter to his brother Flavian he described 'seven Irish dogs' which 'so astonished Rome that it was thought they must have been brought in iron cages'.[254]

But trade will not account for all the Roman material in Ireland, and other interpretations must be sought. Refugees could have played a part, as Warner stressed, and this is a likely explanation for the Lambay settlement. Occasional adventurers and seekers of land must inevitably have come and settled, at least for a time. The Bray Head burials may be significant in this respect. Precious Roman material at Newgrange could have been brought there by provincial Roman tourists, pilgrims even, drawn by the reputation of the site as a place of great supernatural importance. The coins and the gold hoard might, in such a context, have been offerings.

Other mechanisms can also be surmised. Irish raiders, returning in the fourth and fifth centuries from their attacks on a crumbling empire, would have brought with them souvenirs and loot from plundered Roman villas. Copper coins, useless in a society ignorant of the benefits of currency, could thus be regarded as souvenirs of such forays. The silver hoards of Balline and Ballinrees, and the north of Ireland coin hoards, could also be plunder. But the possibility that these represent the pay of returned Irish mercenaries, on active service abroad under the Roman eagles, cannot be dismissed. Finally, Bateson's suggestion that the inland concentration of fourth- and fifth-century Roman material in the south of Ireland is related to the historic migration of the Déise to Romanised Wales at about this time, may well have merit.[255]

Just as the Roman material came to the country by various means, so it can be assumed that it had several different sources. Roman Britain must have been important, for in the early centuries A.D. native metal-workers in

[250] Hughes, 'Technical study of opaque red glass', p. 104.
[251] Ó Ríordáin, 'Roman material', pp 43–53; Bateson, 'Roman material', pp 73–4.
[252] See discussion in Bateson, 'Roman material', pp 29, 31, and Warner, 'Importation of exotic material', pp 276–82.
[253] Ó Ríordáin, 'Roman material', pp 65–6; Bateson, 'Roman material', p. 77.
[254] Epistola II; Kenney, *Sources*, p. 137.
[255] Bateson, 'Roman material', p. 37.

the two islands were in close touch. Objects of native British manufacture such as a heavy bronze armlet from Newry, County Down,[256] a terret from County Antrim, the Carrickfergus tankard,[257] and the Lambay bronzes were being imported to Ireland in the very centuries when the Roman items were appearing in the country. Migrations of Celtic groups on a small scale would have been part of a continuous process of cultural interaction between the two islands, and along with these could have come artefacts of Roman type. But Gaul too must have had direct links with Ireland in the early centuries A.D. The repeated classical descriptions of Ireland lying midway between Britain and Gaul should be borne in mind. If the virtual absence of third-century Roman material in the country reflects the political upheaval in Gaul during that century, then indirectly there is evidence of the importance of Gaulish contacts with Ireland during the Roman period.

THE Irish iron age thus emerges as a complex, multifaceted period without clear definition either in cultural or chronological terms. Like an unravelled tapestry there are pieces missing and many loose strands, some of which seem hopelessly tangled. One important strand, for instance, the La Tène material, can with difficulty be linked with the forts, which must also be part of this iron-age tapestry, while these in turn can scarcely be related to the burials. The missing strand of the southern iron age in the last centuries B.C. remains problematical, but it may be that the hillforts of the south will in time help to fill this major gap in our knowledge. After the turn of the millennium Roman imports add a significant new ingredient to the developing Irish iron age, and before the middle of the millennium the ringfort, rooted perhaps in earlier settlement forms, increasingly becomes the dominant feature of the Irish cultural landscape. Throughout the iron age Ireland received influence and inspiration from many external sources. Gaul was important but there were also contacts with the Rhineland, the east Mediterranean, and, possibly, Iberia. Britain too, over the centuries, provided much. But foreign impulses were always subjected to the strong island personality of Ireland and these, muted by environment and filtered by time, soon developed into a new synthesis which was wholly and recognisably Irish. We cannot say precisely when the Irish iron age ended. By the middle of the first Christian millennium La Tène influences had largely vanished, leaving in the material record little more than the art style as a reminder of past glories. Now the ringfort and the contemporary crannog were the standard settlement forms thoughout the land with an associated cultural assemblage reflecting little influence from the La Tène world. A new social order—the church—was an ever-increasing force in native cultural developments. But

---

[256] M. MacGregor, *Early Celtic art in north Britain* (Leicester, 1976), p. 233, pl. VIIb.

[257] E. M. Jope, 'Chariotry and paired-draught in Ireland during the early iron age: the evidence of some horse-bridle bits' in *U.J.A.*, 3rd ser., xviii (1955), p. 37.

throughout the millennium we can see in the archaeological record only slow social evolution unaccompanied by dramatic change, and many aspects of an archaic Irish iron-age tradition lasted well into medieval times. Some, perhaps, may be dimly discernible to the present day.

# CHAPTER VII

# Ireland, 400–800

## DÁIBHÍ Ó CRÓINÍN

FROM the eighth century onwards a succession of learned Irishmen devoted themselves to the task of reconstructing (or constructing, as the case may be) the history of their country in pre-Christian and early medieval times. One of them, possibly Cormac mac Cuillenáin, abbot of Cashel and king of Munster (902–8), chided his predecessors for their remissness in this task. In addition, he chastised the Irish people in general for what might nowadays be regarded as an uncharacteristic indifference to their own history:

Imprudens Scottorum gens, rerum suarum obliuiscens, acta quasi inaudita siue nullo modo facta uindicat, quoniam minus tribuere litteris aliquid operum quorum praecurat, et ob hoc genelogias Scottiae gentus litteris tribuam: primam Muminensium, secundam Laginensium, tertiam nepotum Neill, quartam Connachtorum.

(The foolish Irish race, forgetful of its history, boasts of incredible or completely fabulous deeds, since it has been careless about committing to writing any of its achievements. Therefore I propose to write down the genealogies of the Irish race: firstly that of the men of Munster, secondly that of the Leinstermen, thirdly that of the Uí Néill, and fourthly that of the men of Connacht.)[1]

In stating his purpose in this way, however, our author was in fact perpetuating a lie, for the scheme of things that he then goes on to relate represents a view of early Irish history that was of relatively recent date. The 'course of Irish history' as outlined in the corpus of genealogies and in the more ambitious 'Lebor Gabála Érenn' (the so-called 'Book of Invasions') was the result of efforts to harmonise different political and genealogical traditions and to weave the various strands into a unified whole. This version of events was then set in a framework of Irish protohistory, which sought to present the *status quo* of *c*.800 as the natural outcome of an evolutionary process whose beginnings could be traced back into the dawn of history.

---

[1] Text in M. A. O'Brien (ed.). *Corpus genealogiarum Hiberniae*, i (Dublin, 1962; repr. 1976), p. 192; though the version printed here is from Oxford, Bodl. MS Rawl. B 486 (with corrections of minor scribal errors) and reflects the Munster bias of the man who compiled that collection.

As a work of propaganda, this scheme was a *tour de force*. The political picture of an Ireland divided into two 'halves', one northern and one southern (rather than into 'fifths'), made a lasting impression on the learned of the period—whatever about their less literary compatriots—and together with the theory of proto-historic waves of invaders ('the Goidels and their predecessors', as one scholar termed them),[2] the mythical Firbolg, Fomorians, Tuatha Dé Danann, and Milesians, caught the imagination of scholars and laymen alike. We may judge its success by the fact that the whole towering schema has retained a hold on the minds of the Irish public to this day. The fact that the schema, in its prehistoric part, was entirely fictitious, and in the historical portion artificial (to say the least!), in no way diminished its attractiveness in the eyes of eighth-century contemporaries—although few of them can have been under any illusions about its authenticity. A few discordant voices may have been raised in protest against these 'unheard of and fabulous deeds', but they were rare, and despite such periodical scornful remarks, that picture of early Irish history held the stage for well over a thousand years.

With such an imposing unanimity of views among medieval writers (what the greatest of Irish historians of the period, Eoin MacNeill, called 'synthetic historians'),[3] the task facing the modern student of the period is difficult, sometimes impossible. The men who fashioned this edifice of early Irish history were learned and intelligent—*periti*, as they liked to describe themselves—well versed in the subtleties of their own craft of *senchas*, and being only too well aware of the deficiencies in their 'synthetic' history, they succeeded all too often in kicking over the traces of their patchwork. The writers of 'new history' should, however, think twice before condemning such earlier constructs. What follows in this account must, of necessity, be every bit as 'synthetic' as the history that was written a millennium ago; it is the best that can be offered in the face of a vast mountain of garbled and often incoherent information. Faced with what must have been already, by the seventh century, a bewildering array of disjointed and discordant texts, the 'synthetic historians' of that era did their best to harmonise and revise what must to them have seemed a very confused and confusing jumble of evidence. Some of them, doubtless, less scrupulous about the methods they were using, and less scrupulous again about their motives, tried to jettison the difficult material and substitute in its place the newer, self-perpetuating inventions that were calculated to please their political masters and legitimate the existing political *status quo*. The passage cited at the outset is a case in point, since the text is modified in the different versions to accord with the Munster, Leinster, Ulster, or Connacht bias of the writer, each one in turn placing his own

[2] Thomas F. O'Rahilly, 'The Goidels and their predecessors' in *Brit. Acad. Proc.*, xxi (1936), pp 323–72.
[3] Eoin MacNeill, *Celtic Ireland* (Dublin, 1921; reprint, 1981), ch. iii, pp 25–42: 'The Irish synthetic historians'.

people at the top of the list of important peoples in early Ireland.[4] One twelfth-century historian, Gilla in Choimded Ua Cormaic, offered an eloquent and pointed critique of such men, who practised six different techniques of rejigging the genealogies:

> Fuilet sé muid, sain mebair,
> cummaiscit cráeb ngenelaig:
> to-tinsma dáerchland ic dul
> i lloc sáerchland re slonnud.
> Torrchi mogad, mod mebla,
> ocus díbad tigerna,
> Serg na sáerchland, étig úath,
> la forbairt na n-athechthúath;
> Míscríbend do gné eolais
> do lucht ulc in aneólais,
> nó lucht ind eólais—ní ferr—
> gníit ar main míscríbend.

(There are six modes specially to be remembered which confound a genealogical table: a wholesale insertion of base-born folk, taking the place of nobles in surnames; multiplying serfs—a shameful mode—and extinction of lords; reducing the aristocracy—a hideous error—by increasing the rent-paying tribes; miswriting in the guise of learning by the evil folk of ignorance; or it is the learned—which is no better— who, for the sake of money, perpetrate the miswriting.)[5]

There is no reason to believe that such practices were any less prevalent in earlier centuries, and indeed the evidence of the genealogical corpus is eloquent testimony that they were prevalent.[6] Little that has come down to us from this period can be accepted as the haphazard record of a disinterested scholarship. Every text has its own tale to tell, and when the same text survives in several versions it is usually safe to conclude that there is good historical reason for the changes. As John V. Kelleher put it: 'In source materials of this age and kind, a good glaring contradiction is worth a square yard of smooth, question-begging consistency. A permanently unresolved problem over which many men have laboured unsuccessfully at different times, for varying reasons, is generally replete with information or suggestion.'[7]

---

[4] The text in some versions enumerates the races in terms of the three sons of Míl, adding their supposed cousin Lugaid Mac Ítha in order to make up the fourth group. The fact that the original scheme of things envisaged only *two* sons of Míl only serves to point up the irony!

[5] See Kuno Meyer, *Miscellanea Hibernica* (Chicago, 1916), p. 9.

[6] See the frequent references to *periti* and *imperiti*: 'Variant traditions which do not accord with the *senchas coitchenn* or accepted teaching of the schools are dismissed by ascription to *imperiti* (F. J. Byrne, 'Senchas: the nature of Gaelic historical tradition' in John Barry (ed.), *Hist. Studies*, ix (1974), pp 137–59: 139).

[7] John V. Kelleher, 'The pre-Norman Irish genealogies' in *I.H.S.*, xvi, no. 62 (Sept. 1968), p. 142.

In the course of their work on native historical traditions, the early *periti* did not all work hand in hand, of course, and so we have different and sometimes contradictory accounts. Their task was not made any easier by the fact that the Irish concept of 'history' (*senchas*) embodied, besides the data that might normally be included under such a heading, tribal lore and origin tales, topographical legends, and gobbets of law, in addition to genealogies and annals.[8] 'He is no poet who does not synchronise and adjust all the stories', was a dictum in Irish law,[9] and the law was followed to the letter. Only a counsel of despair could have led one synchronist to state that 'all the records of the Irish before Cimbáeth [d. 307 B.C.!] are uncertain' (*omnia monumenta Scottorum usque Cimbaeth incerta erant*).[10] It was the historians' task and duty to make a consecutive record out of the disparate materials of ancient Ireland. What revolutionised their approach was the introduction of Christianity, for with Christianity came a chronology of world history. What the Jewish people had in biblical tradition, and the Greek and Romans in classical tradition, was now to be supplied in the case of the Irish, and the result was a remarkable construction that sought to recreate the mythical protohistory of the early Irish and synchronise it with the great events of world history.[11] The historians concocted a list of prehistoric kings of Ireland, and added a similar tract for the Christian period entitled 'De flaithiusaib Érenn' ('On the rulers of Ireland'); this they appended to the 'Lebor Gabála' to produce an epic narrative comparable to that of the great empires of antiquity.

It can no longer be seriously maintained, however, that 'Lebor Gabála' preserves any genuine traditions of any kind, whether of prehistoric Celtic invasions or of anything else.[12] The story of Míl, progenitor of the 'Milesians', seems to have been cooked up in the eighth century, with his two sons Éremón and Éber being invented as ancestors of the Connachta/Uí Néill and Munster Eóganachta peoples respectively, 'in conformity with the theory that Ireland was divided into two spheres of influence, Leth Cuinn and Leth Moga'.[13] It was MacNeill who pointed out that Míl himself was nothing more than a misrepresentation of the Latin *miles Hispaniae* in Orosius's work 'Contra paganos', and the whole story nothing more than a learned fiction— 'an artificial product of the schools'—which tells us nothing about Irish

---

[8] For an excellent discussion of *senchas*, see Byrne, '*Senchas*'.

[9] E. J. Gwynn, 'An Old-Irish tract on the privileges and responsibilities of poets' in *Ériu*, xiii (1942), pp 1–53: 15, 220–36.

[10] Cited by MacNeill from the prehistoric section of the Annals of Tigernach (*Celtic Ire.*, p. 31).

[11] For the ultimate example of the genre, see Dáibhí Ó Cróinín (ed.), *The Irish Sex Aetates Mundi* (Dublin, 1983).

[12] The verdict also of Byrne, '*Senchas*', p. 143.

[13] Ibid., pp 143–4.

prehistory.[14] The passage cited above about the 'foolish Irish race' was probably composed as a sort of preface to the eighth-century compilation of genealogical lore, perhaps in Munster, since the source is alleged to have been the famous 'Psalter of Cashel', a collection of genealogical material.[15] By the time of its composition, however, the synchronists had been obliged to add to Míl's progeny posthumously: the Ulaid, the peoples of the ancient province of Ulster, did not belong genealogically to Leth Cuinn (Conn's Half) and never acknowledged the claims to sovereignty made by the Uí Néill, and hence they had to be fitted into the scheme by the addition of Ír son of Míl as their remote ancestor. Later again other dynasties, whose retrospective claims had to be accommodated, were grafted on to the scheme in their turn; the result was that Míl's posthumous sons proliferated from an 'original' two to a final count of eight!

If there ever was a popular native tradition concerning the origins of the Irish people, it did not survive. Instead, we have the multitude of medieval pseudohistorical theories about their origin 'in der Studienstube angekocht' ('cooked up in their studies'), as a great Swiss Celtic scholar put it.[16] They are the work of men such as Colmán mac Duach, 'son of the king of Connacht, professor and seer and sage of the *senchas* of the Gael, and a scholar of ecclesiastical learning, it was he who compiled the genealogies...'.[17] Learned in native tradition and well read in the historical literature of the church, these literati produced a seamless garment of early Irish history, which their modern successors must first unravel before attempting to refashion the threads into a new scheme that answers more closely the tests of modern scholarship. For this purpose the annals and genealogies represent the most important primary sources, for they contain, besides the material we have been speaking of, a considerable amount of valuable historical information, some of it of respectable antiquity. The poems preserved in the Leinster genealogies, and in some cases also in the Munster collections, date in part from the seventh century, and the painstaking accumulation of related fragments can, in fact, enable the reconstruction of our early history with at least some degree of confidence. Unfortunately, among this sea of names only one

[14] See Eoin MacNeill, *Phases of Irish history* (Dublin, 1920), pp 61–97, ch. iii: 'The pre-Celtic inhabitants of Ireland', esp. pp 90–95.

[15] F. J. Byrne has proposed to see the hand of Cormac Mac Cuilennáin in the text; see his review of O'Brien, *Corpus geneal. Hib.*, in *Z.C.P.*, xxix (1962–4), pp 381–5, esp. p. 384. Mac Neill thought that Columbanus's reference to the Irish as *Iberi* reflected a knowledge of the doctrine already *c.* A.D. 600, but the evidence is too slight to sustain such a view.

[16] Rudolf Thurneysen, 'Cóic Conara Fugill' in *Abhandl. Königl. Preuss. Akad. Wiss., Jahrg. 1925, philos.-hist. Kl.*, vii (Berlin, 1926), p. 13 (speaking of early Irish law; but the verdict is equally valid in our case).

[17] Text in Anne O'Sullivan (ed.), *The Book of Leinster, formerly Lebor na Nuachongbála*, vi (Dublin, 1983), 1470: '(Co)lman mac Duach mac rig Connacht ollam 7 faid 7 suí senchasa Gaedel 7 sui echnai is é ro thinóil genelaig...'; the entry is added in the margin of p. 336 of the MS.

or two can be reliably identified from other sources, and we must beware of arguing from too little evidence. The history of the Déisi in the seventh century, for example, has been misinterpreted on the basis of one mistaken identification, as we shall see.

MacNeill pointed out that the oldest 'fact' in Irish history was the existence, not of a bipartite division of the country, as the eighth-century literati had formulated it, but of the pentarchy, that division of Ireland into five provinces (*cóiceda*) that has left its mark even today in the use of the Modern Irish word *cúige* to denote a province.[18] The irony, however, is that at no time in the historical period did the political division represented by the word *cóiced*, 'a fifth', have a tangible existence. True, the political framework embodied in the pentarchy provides the backdrop for the events in the famous 'Táin' cycle of epic tales, but whatever form that scheme may have taken it was nothing more than a memory by the fifth century. The proof of this is in the fact that no document records the names or extents of the 'original' five provinces. The original division may have been Ulaid (Ulster) in the north (the present nine counties), Laigin (Leinster) in the south-east, Mumu (Munster) in the south, Connachta (Connacht) in the west, and Mide (Meath) in the centre. But we can only guess at the original extent of these kingdoms, and what their relationships to each other might have been. The great iron-age hillforts of Emain Macha (Navan Fort, County Armagh), Dún Ailinne (Knockaulin, County Kildare), and Cruachu (Rathcroghan, County Roscommon) are commonly regarded as the ancient capitals of these provinces, and Caisel (Cashel, County Tipperary)—though later in terms of its traditions—was likewise believed (perhaps wrongly) to have been the centre of the Munster kingdom. However, the best-known of these prehistoric royal sites, Temair (Tara, County Meath) was never situated in the ancient territory of Mide (which is the Irish word for 'middle') but possessed an aura that seemed to set it above the common status of the other provincial kingdoms. This was not just the work of later propagandists: the saga tales of the Ulster cycle in their oldest form show that Tara, not Cruachu, was the pivotal point in the alliance against the Ulstermen, while the kingship of Tara was still regarded in the seventh-century law text 'Bechbretha' ('Bee-laws') as the most important in Ireland. The archaic poems embedded in the Leinster genealogies record the claims of Laigin, Gáilióin, and Domnainn to be ancient kings of Leinster ruling from Dún Ailinne but also from Tara. The evidence of linguistics shows that there must have been some connection with the Dumnonii of Britain, and it is very likely that the Gáilióin/Domnainn were in origin a group of British (and ultimately Gaulish) invaders who occupied the eastern seaboard region in the remote past.

[18] MacNeill, *Phases of Irish history*, pp 98–132, ch. iv: 'The five fifths of Ireland'.

Between the faint echoes of ancient wars and the early historical period, however, there lies a vast and impenetrable wasteland. The dynasties that subsequently rose to power (whose records in some instances can be dated to the late sixth century, but hardly earlier) have their origin legends, but they tell us nothing about the ethnic roots of these people, nor could they: between the period of the pentarchy and the date of our earliest historical records there is a gap that cannot be filled; and between our period and that of the hypothetical prehistoric 'invasions' there is a hiatus of up to a thousand years. No traditions—however resilient—can survive that long.[19]

The most powerful of the early provinces may well have been Leinster (although one should be careful not to exaggerate the importance of Leinster claims from the relative abundance of their historical records). Dominated in the south-east by the upland massif that rises up from the coastline and in the west by the great midland bogs of County Offaly, the region boasted some of the best grasslands in the country, and the land around the River Liffey in County Kildare and further fertile strips along the rivers Barrow, Nore, and Suir that converge on Waterford Harbour offered rich pickings to the politically ambitious. By 800 Leinster was dominated by two great dynasties, the Uí Dúnlainge to the north and the Uí Cennselaig in the south. Our earliest records, however, paint a very different picture, and it is clear that these two groups were only the most recent to emerge from the maelstrom of the fifth and sixth centuries.

The earliest, cryptic references in the annals point to a prior supremacy of the Dál Messin Corb. The Annals of Ulster mention two battles in the late fifth century (485, 495)[20] in which the vanquished kings of Leinster belonged to the Dál Messin Corb (and more specifically, their principal sub-sept, the Uí Garrchon).[21] In the first entry, the Dál Messin Corb king Fincath is mentioned without patronymic or title, perhaps indicating a Leinster source for the information that required no elaboration.[22] His son Fráech mac Findchada, on the other hand, is termed *rí Laigen* ('king of Leinster') by the

---

[19] Paul Grosjean, S.J., the Belgian Bollandist scholar, remarked, apropos of oral memory in his own country, that 'local investigation has made it reasonably certain to me that in the vicinity of Waterloo *nobody knows anything* about the battle which was not either learned at school or picked up from a newspaper, a film, or a guide-book'; see 'An early fragment on Saint Patrick in Ui Briúin Breifne contained in the Life of Saint Benén (Benignus) of Armagh' in *Seanchas Ardmhacha*, i, pt. i (1954), pp 31–44: 44. The italics are Grosjean's.

[20] The Annals of Inisfallen and Tigernach have much the same data under different dates (cf. A.D. 493: Bellum Srotha, *Ann. Inisf.*); the record was clearly garbled.

[21] For their genealogies, see O'Brien, *Corpus geneal. Hib.*, pp 35 ff; for discussion, see Alfred P. Smyth, 'The Húi Néill and the Leinstermen in the Annals of Ulster, 131–516 A.D.' in *Études Celt.*, xiv (1974–5), pp 121–43; Smyth, *Celtic Leinster: towards an historical geography of early Irish civilization A.D. 500–1600* (Dublin, 1982).

[22] I follow the identification proposed by Smyth 'Húi Néill and the Leinstermen', p. 128, rather than that in Seán Mac Airt and Gearóid Mac Niocaill (ed.), *The Annals of Ulster to A.D. 1311* (Dublin, 1983), p. 53 n.

annalist. Both battles were against the Uí Néill, whose expansionary drive was to lead eventually to the annexation of extensive Leinster territories, and with it the effective elimination of the Dál Messin Corb as a political power. As so often in Irish tradition, however, the earlier supremacy of displaced dynasties is longer preserved in the ecclesiastical record than in the 'secular' annals. Thus the 'Vita Tripartita' (a tenth-century dossier of material relating to Patrick—some of it very early)[23] records that Patrick encountered an Uí Garrchon king Driccriu (otherwise unidentified), who was allied by marriage to the Uí Néill 'high-king' Lóeguire mac Néill;[24] although the meeting took place, according to the 'Vita', at Rath Inbir, the real location of the sept, to judge from the internal evidence of the saint's 'itinerary', was probably around Naas, County Kildare. The anecdote may serve to explain why Driccriu's line died out, for it states that he refused hospitality to the saint. Instead, Patrick was received by Cilline mac Rónáin, *quem Patricius bendixit* ('whom Patrick blessed'), as the genealogists put it,[25] while Cilline's son Marcán is described as 'the choicest herb, the best of the Uí Garrchon'.

The association of Lóeguire (the *bête noire* of Patrick in early tradition) with a Dál Messin Corb king is clearly anachronistic, for the annals—cryptic though they be—leave no doubt that the Uí Néill and the Dál Messin Corb were mortal enemies as the fifth century drew to a close. Smyth is undoubtedly correct in seeing the Dál Messin Corb as the principal defenders of Leinster against Uí Néill encroachments in the last quarter of the century, and their territories must have been in the front line of the conflict. Their later displacement and expulsion beyond the Wicklow mountains did not, however, erase all traces of an earlier period, when they held the richer flatlands of the Kildare plain—the traditional homeland of Leinster kings.[26] The genealogists provide ample evidence for the wider distribution of this people across north Leinster, while the saints that are claimed as descendant from another sub-sept, the Uí Náir, also provide corroborative testimony to a wider influence at an earlier date.[27] These include Kevin of Glendalough and Bishop Conláed of Kildare, contemporary of Brigit and her resident bishop, as well as Bishop Éitcheáin of Cluain Fota Báetáin Aba (Clonfad, County Westmeath). Smyth has revived a theory, first advanced by Shearman,[28] that Killeen Cormac (*Cell Fine Chormaic*), a few miles west of Castledermot, County Kildare, is to be identified with the *Cell fine* ('cell of the kindred') where according to the 'Vita Tripartita'[29] Palladius, 'first bishop of the Irish',

---

[23] *Trip. life*, ed. Mulchrone.
[24] Ibid., p. 113.
[25] O'Brien, *Corpus geneal. Hib.*, p. 39.
[26] The case is summarised in Smyth, 'Húi Néill and Leinstermen', pp 130–33.
[27] 'Brien, *Corpus geneal. Hib.*, p. 41.
[28] John F. Shearman. *Loca Patriciana: an identification of localities, chiefly in Leinster, visited by Saint Patrick* (Dublin, 1879), pp 38–54.
[29] *Trip. life*, ed. Mulchrone, p. 19.

left his books, together with a writing tablet and relics of Peter and Paul.[30] If there is any foundation for the belief that relics of the apostles were preserved at Killeen Cormac, then the site must certainly have been an important one, and if it were the *Cell fine* of Patrician tradition then this would certainly enhance any claim that the Uí Garrchon were the dominant political power in north Leinster until the end of the fifth century. The narrative in the 'Vita Tripartita' brings Patrick to the sites of Cell Usaile (Killashee, near Naas, County Kildare) and Cell Cuilinn (Old Kilcullen, County Kildare), both prominent early ecclesiastical sites associated with individuals who probably belonged to the mission of Palladius rather than of Patrick, and the implication seems to be that Christianity was introduced to those parts when the Uí Garrchon were in control of them. The original seat of their kingship was at Rath Inbir (not identified) but later tradition placed their territory within the modern County Wicklow. Hence their association with the Arklow area represents a later state in their history, after they had been ousted from the Leinster kingship.

The main rivals for control of the central plains in Leinster from the mid-seventh century on were, as we said above, the Uí Dúnlainge and the Uí Cennselaig; but the Uí Cennselaig, whose territories encompassed the present Counties Carlow and Wexford, were—like the Uí Dúnlainge—relatively late arrivals on the scene. The earlier position probably saw the Dál Cormaic (and particularly their main sub-group, the Uí Gabla) in that position, perhaps as rivals of the Dál Messin Corb. The annals for 498–502/3 record a series of battles in which the Leinstermen were worsted by the Uí Néill, beginning with the battle of Inis Mór 'in the territory of Uí Gabla' (*A.U.*, 498). The genealogies list the extent of their territories, which included parts of the present Counties Carlow, Kildare, Laois, and Offaly,[31] but their main concentration seems to have been in the area of the Kildare–Laois border. Pockets of them were to be found as far north as Monasterevin, where a branch was located along the Figile river (*Fid Gabla*, 'wood of the Uí Gabla').[32] The demise of one of their main branches, the Uí Gabla Roírenn, occurred in the first quarter of the eighth century, when they were obliterated by the rising Síl mBrain.[33] Their fortunes had been decided some time before that, however, and the annalists have no further record of them.

The Leinster regnal list for the archaic period, found fossilised in the early genealogies, is a good example of the manner in which the 'synchronists' sometimes preserved material that ran directly counter to their own

---

[30] Smyth, 'Húi Néill and Leinstermen', p. 133.

[31] O'Brien, *Corpus geneal. Hib.*, p. 34.

[32] Smyth, 'Húi Néill and Leinstermen', p. 136.

[33] O'Brien, *Corpus geneal. Hib.*, p. 74: '. . . Cellach mac Máel-Ottraich . . . is é dano ro-ort hUa Gabla Roírenn'.

doctrines.[34] They list the names of several provincial kings including Fiachu ba hAiccid (whose epithet preserves a unique archaism), Muiredach Mo-Ṡníthech, Móenach, Mac Caírthinn, and Nad Buidb; of these both Muiredach Mo-Ṡníthech and Móenach belonged to the Uí Bairrche and Nad Buidb to the Uí Dego, while Mac Caírthinn almost certainly belonged to the Uí Enechglaiss. All of these, then, were dynastic groups that had earlier enjoyed power but subsequently suffered a decline in their fortunes and were later subsumed into the genealogies of the parvenus Uí Dúnlainge and Uí Cennselaig. Their kings found no place in the later regnal lists, but their names were, as we have seen, preserved in the archaic material; some indeed were claimed as kings of Ireland (*Robo rí hÉrenn Muiredach Sníthe, ut Laidcenn dixit*, 'Muiredach Sníthe was king of Ireland, as [the poet] Laidcend stated', with reference to the archaic regnal list).[35] The name of Mac Caírthinn illustrates to an extraordinary degree how the flimsiest of surviving evidence can still suffice to show how the political landscape may have looked even in the fifth century—a 'lost century' otherwise in terms of our historical records.[36] This Mac Caírthinn, although not mentioned in any of the genealogical tracts, was tentatively (but plausibly) identified by Seán Mac Airt with the individual commemorated in an ogam inscription now located in the barony of Duleek (County Louth), near Slane: MAQI CAIRATINI AVI INEQUAGLASI, '[the stone] of Mac Caírthinn, grandson [or perhaps descendant] of Enechglass';[37] Mac Airt further identified this person with the Mac Caírthinn mac Cóelboth encountered by him in his editing of the Annals of Inisfallen at the year 447, where it is recorded that he fell in the battle of Mag Femin between the Laigin and the men of Munster. Here, as F. J. Byrne has pointed out,[38] 'the Munster annalist has probably confused the place-name "Femen" in Brega (the area where the inscription is cited) with the betterknown plain of that name around Cashel in Tipperary'. The ogam stone and the Annal entry fit much better into the traditions of warfare in the fifth century between the Uí Néill and the Laigin on the northern frontiers of Leinster, in Brega, and in the plains of Meath and Westmeath, and Mac Caírthinn's memorial is an eloquent proof that Leinster claims once extended as far north as there. The same annal adds the words *qui iecit genus Lagin* after Mac Caírthinn's name, and though the meaning is obscure it shows at least that the Uí Enechglaiss were regarded by some as legitimate claimants to the Leinster kingship in the fifth century.

---

[34] Ibid., pp 8–9: 'De regibus Lagenorum et de ordinibus eorum' ('On the kings of the Leinstermen and their sequence'.
[35] O'Brien, *Corpus geneal. Hib.*, p. 47.
[36] So described, in terms of the debate concerning St Patrick, by Seán Mac Airt, 'The churches founded by Saint Patrick', in John Ryan (ed.), *Saint Patrick* (Dublin, 1958), pp 67–80: 80.
[37] *Ann. Inisf.*, p. 589.
[38] Byrne, *Ir. kings*, p. 137.

The Uí Enechglaiss were, as we have seen, only one of several Leinster dynastic groups whose constant defensive warfare against the Uí Néill eventually ground them down. The demise of the Dál Messin Corb was followed by that of the Uí Máil, who had replaced them and the once powerful Uí Failgi as kings of Leinster by the end of the sixth century.[39] The genealogies of the Uí Failgi (whose memory has been preserved in the modern county name Offaly) are a confusing mass, which may reflect the weakness of their position *c*.600 or a deliberate attempt by later historians to obscure their former prominence.[40] An eighth-century poem records that they ruled from 'the fort over against the oakwood' at Rathangan (County Kildare) and lists each of their kings, back to Bruidge mac Nath Í.[41] Bruidge's death is recorded in the Annals of Ulster (579), and the assumption is that he died in battle against the Uí Néill.[42] Failge Berraide is recorded in the same annals (510) as victor in the battle of Fremu against the same foes, but the tide was already ebbing for the Uí Failgi; in the 'return' battle against the Uí Néill (516), Failge was defeated. The annalist adds ominously that 'thereafter the plain of Mide was taken from the Leinstermen', and so it was to be. The tributary tribes that occupied the buffer zone between the Leinstermen and their great rivals now fell under the control of the Uí Néill, but the Uí Failgi held out for some time in their heartland territories: a later dynast, Óengus Berraide, is said by the genealogists to have resided at Leccach (Lackagh parish in the barony of Offaly, County Kildare), indicating that the rich lands west of the monastery of Kildare were still in their hands despite that earlier setback, and in fact the Uí Failgi were to retain their hold on most of this area until the twelfth century.

The Uí Failgi, therefore, probably originally comprised the dominant political overlords in north Leinster up to the mid-sixth century, with territories centring on their royal seat of Brí Dam (north-east Offaly?) extending as far as the hill of Uisnech in the north-west.[43] The story in Patrician tradition that the ancient inauguration tree (*bile*) on the royal site was cursed by Patrick, and that Failge, the eponymous ancestor of the dynasty, died as a consequence (and went to hell!), was a later rationalisation of the dynasty's political misfortune.[44] In fact, however, the ever expanding Uí Néill had advanced their conquests to the very borders of Mide and Uí Failge and

---

[39] Smyth, 'Húi Néill and Leinstermen', p. 133.

[40] See O'Brien, *Corpus geneal. Hib.*, pp 56–9, and Alfred P. Smyth, 'Húi Failgi relations with the Húi Néill in the century after the loss of the plain of Mide' in *Études Celt.*, xiv (1974–5), pp 503–23.

[41] Text in O'Brien, *Corpus geneal. Hib.*, p. 58; another text, with translation, is in Kuno Meyer, *Learning in Ireland in the fifth century* (Dublin, 1913), p. 25.

[42] Smyth, 'Húi Failgi relations with the Húi Néill', p. 504.

[43] Ibid.

[44] *Trip. life*, ed. Mulchrone, pp 129–30; see also Smyth, 'Húi Failgi relations with the Húi Néill', p. 507.

threatened to strangle the Uí Failge and their power. They apparently tried to stave off the inevitable by allying with one of the rival septs of the midland Uí Néill, in the hopes, apparently, that internecine struggles among the old enemy would weaken them and grant a respite to the Leinstermen. In 604, according to the Annals of Ulster, Áed Rón, *rex nepotum Failgi*, was killed 'on the same day as Áed Sláine' (founder and king of the chief southern Uí Néill dynasty known subsequently as Síl nÁedo Sláine) of Brega. Áed Sláine was killed by Conall mac Suibni of a rival Uí Néill dynasty, the Clann Cholmáin Máir, and the death of Áed Rón on the same day doubtless means that the Uí Failgi king had taken the Síl nÁedo Sláine side, threatening a second front in the south against the Clann Cholmáin, already under pressure from their Brega cousins in the east. As it happened, the Mide kings were to turn the tables by allying with the rising power of the Uí Dúnlainge in north Leinster in the battle of Áth Goan (633), which saw the first consolidation of that dynasty in Leinster politics. That defeat, and the death not long thereafter (645?) of Tocca mac Áedo (misplaced in the Annals of Ulster, 477: *Mors Tocca m. Aedha regis Cualann*, 'king of Cualu') effectively sealed the fate of the Uí Máil as claimants to the kingship of Leinster. Cellach Cualann is termed *rex Lagen* at his death in 715, but his was the last Uí Máil bid for Leinster domination.

The only other serious claimants to Leinster kingship were the Uí Bairrche. As we saw above, an archaic regnal list buried in the Leinster genealogies preserved the name of two Uí Bairrche kings who had clearly exercised considerable power in the early sixth century, Muiredach Mo-Snithech and Móenach. They are listed in the genealogies as son and grandson of the eponymous ancestor Dáire Barrach, and great claims are made for them both. But neither figures in the annals, and we have no other means of assessing their claims. In fact the genealogists state that the kingship descended not through Muiredach but through Fiacc, another son of Dáire, and this would seem to have been the case.[45]

The most prominent of these later Uí Bairrche kings was undoubtedly Cormac mac Diarmata, whose reign occupied most of the second half of the sixth century. He figures prominently in the early Leinster hagiography, appearing both as patron and as enemy of saints in the various lives. He is presented as the principal rival to Uí Cennselaig ambitions: the Life of Fintan/Munnu of Tech Munnu (Taghmon, County Wexford) states that he was held captive by Cormac Camsrón of the Uí Cennselaig,[46] while the Life of Abbán (of the rival Dál Cormaic) depicts him as a harrier of that saint's foundations.[47] The most eloquent testimony to this king's power, however, is

---

[45] O'Brien, *Corpus geneal. Hib.*, p. 47; see also pp 10–11.
[46] Plummer, *Vitae SS Hib.*, ii, 102–3.
[47] Ibid., i, 23–4.

the fact that the biographers of the saints claim Cormac for the Uí Cennse-laig—despite the fact that the genealogies leave no doubt as to his Uí Bairrche affiliations! Clearly, Cormac mac Diarmata's impact was a formidable one, and not the least of his claims to fame is that he died peacefully, after retiring to the monastery of Bangor, County Down.[48] The choice of location for his retirement is surprising at first, but there are several early connections between Leinster and Ulster centring on the Uí Bairrche: Columbanus, the famous Irish missionary saint (d. 615), left his native Leinster for the monastery of Comgall at Bangor that Cormac mac Diarmata—an exact contemporary—also sought out, and in fact Bangor possessed extensive properties in Uí Bairrche territory allegedly granted to it by Cormac.[49] The later foundation of Dísert Diarmata (Castledermot, County Kildare) was regarded as a daughter-house of Bangor, and its founder, Diarmait ua Áedo Róin (d. 825) was the grandson of Áed Róin, Dál Fiatach king of Ulster (whose father in turn was called Bécc Bairrche). An actual alliance existed between the Ulaid and the Laigin in the eleventh century, during the reigns of Niall mac Eochada and Diarmait mac Maíl na mBó, and it is not beyond the bounds of possibility that such political and ecclesiastical connections existed long before then.[50]

Another early indication of Uí Bairrche importance in the political sphere is the fact that the dossier of materials relating to Patrick and early Christianity in Leinster that has been preserved in the Book of Armagh[51]—some of clearly very ancient origin indeed—preserves a tradition that the first bishop of Leinster was Fiacc of Slébte (Sletty, County Carlow), an Uí Bairrche saint. The tradition proved too strong to eradicate, and was preserved in the later 'Vita Tripartita', which also reflects the memory of Uí Bairrche and Uí Cennselaig rivalry when it records that Óengus mac Meicc Erca (a brother of the saint of Sletty) slew Crimthann mac Cennselaig (*A.U.*, 483) as vengeance for the exile of his people by the Uí Cennselaig.[52] Traditions of Uí Bairrche expulsion and exile are also to be found in the eighth-century tract known as 'The expulsion of the Déssi'.[53]

It is clear from what we have seen above that the classical scheme of Leinster politics in the early historic period, which presented a picture of north and south Leinster dominated, more or less, from time out of mind, by

---

[48] See Clare Stancliffe, 'Kings who opted out' in Patrick Wormald (ed.), *Ideal and reality in Frankish and Anglo-Saxon society: studies presented to J. M. Wallace-Hadrill* (Oxford, 1983), pp 154–76, especially pp 161, 165 (but without any detailed discussion).

[49] O'Brien, *Corpus geneal. Hib.*, p. 54.

[50] Byrne, *Ir. kings*, p. 146.

[51] See Ludwig Bieler (ed. and trans.), *Patrician texts in the Book of Armagh* (Dublin, 1979).

[52] *Trip. life*, ed. Mulchrone, pp 116–17; Smyth, 'Húi Failgi relations with the Húi Néill', p. 518.

[53] Kuno Meyer, 'The expulsion of the Dessi' in *Y Cymmrodor*, xiv (1901), pp 101–35, at p. 106; and in *Ériu*, iii (1907), pp 135–42: 137.

the rival Uí Dúnlainge and Uí Cennselaig dynasties, was in fact a great deal more convoluted. The claims made by the dominant dynasties of the seventh century and later to have ruled the province from ancient times is nowhere more clearly expressed than in the curious document known as 'Timna Cathaír Máir' ('The testament of Cathaír Már').[54] The 'Timna' purports to be the final bequest of Cathaír Már, ancestor of all the free peoples of Leinster, in which he distributes his inheritance among his sons, each of whom represents one of the tribes that later claimed descent from him. In its present form it was probably composed in the eighth century, though its style imitates the alliterative verse pattern of earlier compositions and some of the material in it may well date from the early seventh century or thereabouts.[55] The 'Timna' is puzzling, however, as a propaganda document, since it ignores the claims of the Uí Garrchon and Uí Máil while recognising the claims of the Uí Bairrche and Uí Enechglaiss—although these latter were just as formidable in their rivalry towards the now dominant Uí Dúnlainge and Uí Cennselaig. Most surprising of all, the 'Timna' gives pride of place to the Uí Failgi, bestowing on their ancestor Rus Failge the *ordan* (primacy), lordship, nobility, and cherished ancestral possessions:

> May he be head and king of the province,
> this festive Rus Failgech!...
> Victorious in battle on the frontier,
> he will stoutly conquer the plain of Tara...
> Cathaír, the torch of Ireland,
> his noble honoured father,
> has chosen him over his brothers...[56]

Second only to the Uí Failgi are the Uí Bairrchi. They are to have Cathaír's keen-edged weapons, and their role is clearly seen as that of defending the province against attack from the south. The only conceivable enemies in such a context are the Uí Cennselaig, whose ambitions were clearly to expand northwards from their ancestral site around Ráth Bile (Ravilly, County Carlow) past the western foothills of the Wicklow mountains and out on to the Liffey plain. They were thwarted in these plans, however, by the Uí Dúnlainge, but none of this is to be seen in the 'Timna Cathaír Máir'. There, after enumerating the fortunes of the other Leinster tribes, the text adds, as an obvious afterthought, a codicil concerning the 'inheritance' of Fiachu ba hAiccid, progenitor of the Síl Fiachach ba hAiccid (as the Uí Dúnlainge and Uí Cennselaig were to be known to the genealogists). Modelling itself clearly on the biblical story of Jacob's blessings on his sons (Gen. 49: 3–4, 15) the text pronounces:

[54] *Bk Rights*, ed. Dillon, pp 148–78; cf. Smyth, 'Húi Failgi relations with the Húi Néill', p. 515; Byrne, *Ir. kings*, pp 138–42.
[55] I accept the arguments for earlier strata advanced by Smyth.
[56] *Bk Rights*, ed. Dillon, pp 151–3.

His brethren will serve him.
He will seize pleasant Ailenn.
He will hold famous Carman.
He will rule venerable Almain.
He will strengthen Naas with splendour ...
He will seize Maistiu of the kings.[57]

This enumeration of all the chief royal sites of Leinster, the Hill of Alenn, the site of the fair of Carman, the ancient sites of Almu and Naas, and Maistiu (Mullaghmast, County Kildare), clearly presents Fiachu (and by implication his descendant) as the chosen one. But the rather transparent device of tacking on an additional section, favouring the most recent claimants to power, only serves to point up the fact that the original document presented a very different picture, one in which the Uí Dúnlainge and Uí Cennselaig had not yet established their ascendancy. The position represented by the 'Timna', therefore, probably reflects the political realities of the early seventh century; within a short space of time that position was to change drastically, and with the rise of the Uí Dúnlainge in north Leinster, and of the Uí Cennselaig in the south, the political map was to be redrawn along the lines that were to last until the coming of the Normans.

Early Uí Dúnlainge traditions claimed importance for two of their ancestors, Illann and Ailill. Bishop Tírechán, in his late seventh-century collectaneum on the subject of Patrick, tells how the saint's unflinching enemy Lóeguire, 'high-king of Tara', had refused baptism because his father Niall bade him 'to be buried in the ramparts of Tara ... face to face with the sons of Dúnlang, at Maistiu in the Liffey plain, in the manner of men at war, until the last day'.[58] There may be some truth in the claim, but the official doctrine that the Uí Dúnlainge had enjoyed a near monopoly of the kingship as far back as the fifth century is clearly spurious, and was supported by the later propagandists only through the expedient of converting their early genealogy into a supposed king-list. The true founder of the dynasty's fortunes is usually believed to have been Fáelán mac Colmáin (d. 666).[59] However, it may well be that his (elder?) brother Máel Umai has a greater title to that fame. He is stated by the genealogists to have attacked and routed Deichtire mac Findig, of the Uí Ercáin, *inna dún* ('in his fort') on the eve of the feast of Senach, 'and he took his treasure'.[60] Máel Umai's career is in marked contrast to his brother's early years, for Fáelán is said to have been fostered by

[57] Ibid., p. 167.

[58] Bieler, *Patrician texts*, p. 132, §12. There is a magnificent modern pastiche of this episode by John V. Kelleher: 'A dig at Tara' in *Too small for stovewood, too big for kindling* (Dublin, 1979), pp 42–7.

[59] See e.g. Byrne, *Ir. kings*, p. 151.

[60] O'Brien, *Corpus geneal. Hib.*, p. 339.

St Kevin of Glendalough.[61] The story may well be nothing more than a later invention, intended to highlight the close contacts between later Uí Dúnlainge kings and that monastery, but if there is any truth in it, it may suggest that the first moves towards Uí Dúnlainge expansion were made by Fáelán's brother, who may have been killed prematurely, making way for Fáelán.

There is, unfortunately, a great deal of obscurity about the Leinster regnal succession in the first thirty years or so of the seventh century. The annals record that Fáelán slew Crundmáel 'Bolg Luatha', a rival Uí Cennselaig king, in 628, and refer to Fáelán as *rex Laegen* (perhaps prematurely). The same Crundmael had been the subject of a siege (*obsessio*) by the Uí Néill two years previously, and the new Uí Néill 'high-king' Domnall, son of Áed mac Ainmerech, returned to the fray in 628, in what the annalist calls a 'devastation of Leinster' (*vastatio Lagen*). However, as we saw above, the same annals record the battle of Áth Goan in 633, in which Fáelán mac Colmáin fought in alliance with Conall mac Suibni of the Uí Néill and Fáilbe Fland, king of Munster, against the Uí Máil king of Leinster (*ri Lagenorum*) Crimthann mac Áedo. Hence the date of Fáelán's accession to the title of Leinster king is unclear, as indeed is the date of his demise. The Annals of Ulster do not record the date of his death, and the other annals offer different dates around 666. But since his Uí Cennselaig rival Crundmáel 'Erbuilc' mac Rónáin, who died ten years previously, is described as king of Leinster, it seems very likely that Fáelán's obit has been placed too late.[62]

We have seen how Fáelán's brother, Máel Umai, smashed the power of Deichtire mac Findig 'and took his treasure'. Deichtire was of the Uí Ercáin branch of the Uí Meic Cruaich, who were a sub-sept of the Fothairt. The Fothairt were the original population group around the site of Brigit's monastery at Kildare and the Uí Ercáin branch are remembered in the 'Vita Tripartita' as having been specially favoured by Patrick, who blessed them (*Dobert Pátraic bendachtain . . . for Uu hErcán huili*) and their king, Fergnae mac Cobthaig,[63] who is also mentioned in the life of Fintan/Munnu of Taghmon, where he encounters the saint *in campo Lyffi* ('in the Liffey plain').[64] This prestigious position, allied to the fact that the site now lay in the lands of the rival Uí Failgi, accounts for the ruthless determination to gain control of the church as a symbol of their overlordship, and there can be little doubt that this Uí Dúnlainge assault on the hapless Deichtire was the preliminary move in a bid to take over this most important ecclesiastical foundation. In fact, the Uí Dúnlainge were singularly successful in this, imposing their own nominees and maintaining a monopoly of the higher offices almost to the end of the seventh century. Fáelán's brother Áed Dub

[61] Plummer, *Vitae SS Hib.*, i, 250 ff.
[62] See the discussion in Byrne, *Ir. kings*, p. 151.
[63] *Trip. life*, ed. Mulchrone, p. 114.
[64] Plummer, *Vitae SS Hib.*, ii, 103.

(d. 638) was abbot and bishop of Kildare, and is described by the genealogists as 'royal bishop of Kildare and of all Leinster' (*ríg-epscop Cille Dara ocus Lagen uile*).[65] The same encomium goes on to describe Áed as a famous man of learning, and cites two verses that are perhaps the cleverest piece of political satire in the literature:

> Oh brother,
> If you follow faith,
> What right have you to compete with Áed,
> Unless indeed you have drunk henbane?
> Are yours the drinking-horns of the wild ox?
> And is yours the ale of Cualu?
> Is your land the Curragh of Liffey?
> Are you the descendant of fifty high-kings?
> Is Kildare your church?
> Is your companionship with Christ?[66]

These are pointed references to the *coirm Chualand*, 'ale of Cualu', and the plains around the Curragh of Kildare, traditional symbols of royal power in Leinster. They are found also in an early eighth-century poem in praise of Áed mac Diarmata, king of the Uí Muiredaig and would-be king of Leinster (d. 714?), 'a descendant... of the kings of the clans of Cualu... to whom lovely Liffey belongs'.[67] The closed shop that the dynasty operated in Kildare is good evidence for their hegemony in the region, which Fáelán sought to bolster by means of political marriage with Sárnat, daughter of Eochu mac Baíth of the Fothairt; a second marriage to Uasal, daughter of Suibne mac Commáin of the Déisi, suggests an equal concern with securing his south-western border (though it is worth remembering that one branch of the Fothairt, the Uí Brigti, also claimed a connection with Brigit).[68] The genealogists refer to Fáelán's son Conall laconically as 'the man who was not king' (*qui rex non fuit*),[69] though his descendants, the Uí Muiredaig, did in fact hold power after him. The genealogist interpreted the verses about Áed Dub as the utterance of his brother Áed Find, with the implication that he had been cheated of this plum job, and there may well have been some truth in the observation. As it happened, Áed Find's son Óngus did in fact succeed to the abbacy, which perhaps suggests that Fáelán's line failed to retain their hold.

The poem entitled 'Hail Brigit' by its first editor, Kuno Meyer, points a sombre contrast between the fortunes of all those Leinster kings down to

---

[65] Text in O'Brien, *Corpus geneal. Hib.*, p. 339.
[66] Based on the translation by Kuno Meyer.
[67] Text and translation in Whitley Stokes and John Strachan (ed. & trans.), *Thesaurus Palaeohibernicus* (2 vols, Cambridge, 1901–3), ii, 295.
[68] Byrne, *Ir. kings*, p. 155.
[69] O'Brien, *Corpus geneal. Hib.*, p. 341.

Conall mac Fáeláin's son Bran Mút (d. 693) who had supposedly occupied the great hillfort at Alenn, and the abiding glory of St Brigit. Its version of history, however, is the Uí Dúnlainge one, and Francis Byrne may be right in proposing as author the well-known Orthanach ua Cóellámae Cuirrig, bishop of Kildare (d. 840), 'a typical representative of the new school of synthetic historians'.[70] In fact, the later sources, particularly the genealogies, the interpolated annals, and the eleventh-and twelfth-century king-lists, conspire to present this classical picture of the political situation in early Leinster, 'and to create the impression that it had existed from time immemorial by some natural law'.[71] Despite claims to the contrary by their rivals the Uí Cennselaig, the Uí Dúnlainge could justly be said to have won the propaganda war, at any rate. As far back as the sixth century, in the person of their king Brandub mac Echach, the Uí Cennselaig had shown signs of emerging strength, and Brandub was victorious against the northern Uí Néill king Áed mac Ainmerech at the battle of Dún Bolg in 598. They could boast of greater success against the traditional enemy than their northern rivals, but despite vague references to 'seven blows against Brega' by Brandub, they failed to capitalise on their initial successes and never penetrated to the rich lands of Kildare. This may have been in part due to the effects of the great plagues of the 660s and 680s, which seem to have left the power of their chief Leinster rivals intact, while sapping their own. But the Uí Cennselaig revived to stage another bid for dominance in the early eighth century, only to fall victim yet again to the power of the Uí Néill.

The line of Crundmáel mac Rónáin, which claimed the kingship in the mid-seventh century, produced another claimant in Áed mac Colggen in the eighth. Áed expanded from the family's power base at Ard Ladrann (near Gorey, County Wexford) but his death at the battle of Áth Senaig (Ballyshannon, near Kilcullen, County Kildare) in 738 was the occasion for a remarkable account in the annals, which provides uncharacteristically detailed information about the alliances of the Leinster king.

The battle of Áth Senaig . . . between the Uí Néill and the Laigin was sternly fought, and the two kings respectively . . . i.e. Áed Allán (king of Tara) and Áed mac Colggen (king of Laigin) . . . Then the descendants of Conn [= Uí Néill] enjoyed a tremendous victory, when in extraordinary fashion they rout, trample, crush, overthrow, and destroy their Laigin adversaries, so much so that almost the entire enemy is well nigh annihilated, except for a few messengers to bring back the tidings. And men say that so many fell in this great battle that we find no comparable slaughter in a single onslaught and fierce conflict throughout all preceding ages. . . .

Áed mac Colggen was beheaded with a battle sword, and most of his allies died with him. They included Bran Bec mac Murchado of the Uí Dúnlainge;

[70] Byrne, *Ir. kings*, p. 156.
[71] F. J. Byrne, 'Tribes and tribalism in early Ireland' in *Ériu*, xxii (1971), pp 128–66: 154.

Fergus mac Móenaig and Dub-dá-Chrích mac aui Cellaig mec Triein, two kings of the Fothairt; Fiangalach hua Máele Aithchen of the Uí Briúin Cualann; Conall hua Aithechdai of the Uí Cennselaig; the four sons of Flann aui Congaile, probably of the Uí Failgi; and Éladach aui Máeluidir, as well as 'many others, omitted for the sake of brevity'. Though the later annotator of the annals sought to make Áed mac Colggen joint king with Bran Bec mac Murchado (and the regnal lists ignore him altogether, making Bran sole ruler), there is no doubt that Áed was king of Leinster, and he was therefore the last of the Uí Cennselaig to rule Leinster until the revival of their power in the eleventh century.

From 738 until 1042 the Leinster kingship remained a monopoly of the Uí Dúnlainge. Murchad son of Bran Mút produced four sons, each of whom headed a sub-dynasty of the family. The Uí Dúnchada, Uí Fáeláin, and Uí Muiredaig retained control of the kingship, alternating the title in a regular succession which was thought by no less a scholar than Eoin Mac Neill to represent a 'law' of dynastic succession. This was despite the fact that Bran Bec died alongside Áed mac Colggen at the battle of Áth Senaig, and his brother Fáelán (according to the same annal) died 'unexpectedly, at an early age' (*immature aetate ac inopinata morte*). There may be some confusion in the sources, but there is no denying that the Uí Dúnlainge presented a picture of formidable cohesion, and the four sons are listed as kings of Leinster in turn. From their dynastic bases at Maistiu (Mullaghmast) in south Kildare (the original seat of the Uí Dúnlainge) and further north at Naas, they controlled the plains as far north as Dublin.[72] It has been suggested that the Uí Dúnlainge were assisted in their ambitions by the Clann Cholmáin of Mide, anxious to fend off danger from their southern border by encouraging internal rivalries among the Leinstermen.[73] The first Clann Cholmáin high-king, Domnall Midi (d. 763), seems to have left them undisturbed throughout his twenty-year reign, while his successor Niall Frossach maintained the truce until his death in 770. The fact that hostilities ceased between the southern Uí Néill and their Leinster adversaries suggests that their perennial conflict had ceased to be a war of territorial conquest. By the early seventh century the Uí Néill had reached the limits of their expansion in the south midlands and were only too aware of the dangers that might face them if they overreached themselves.

When next the Uí Néill renewed their attacks it was as a result of a further bout of internal dynastic warfare within Leinster. Donnchad mac Domnaill Midi advanced and occupied the Hill of Alenn for a week and devastated the surrounding countryside; the process was repeated in 780 and again in the early 790s, when the new Uí Néill high-king Áed mac Néill of Ailech

[72] Byrne, *Ir. kings*, p. 150.   [73] Ibid., p. 156.

(County Donegal) asserted his new-found power. By 800, therefore, the subordinate position of Leinster was painfully obvious.

The political scene from the earliest period down to the eighth century and beyond is dominated by the Uí Néill. Their expansionary drive against Leinster provides a good deal of the subject-matter for the earliest annalists, and indeed John V. Kelleher even claimed at one point that the annals as we have them were wholly rewritten in the ninth century to advance the claim of Uí Néill sovereignty.[74] It is doubtful whether any scholar would subscribe to that view now; the bias that undoubtedly shows is a regional one, reflecting the different locations in which the various layers of the text were originally compiled. The bias in the Annals of Ulster is a northern one, but it is not a political bias in favour of the Uí Néill, any more than the other early annals can be said to represent anything other than their respective regional viewpoints. In fact, although the synthetic historians and saga writers succeeded admirably in conjuring up a view of their role that was ultimately to become standardised in the division of Ireland into two 'halves', the earliest annals are not at all clear about the origins of the Uí Néill or about their first kings.

The later geographical distribution of the Uí Néill in a band stretching northwestwards from the east coast to Donegal is usually taken as evidence for their ultimate origin in Connacht[75]—though this was disputed by scholars such as T. F. O'Rahilly and James Carney,[76] who argued instead for a westward expansion. John V. Kelleher has remarked that the Uí Néill emerge like cuttlefish from a black cloud of their own making, and there is more than a suspicion that what survives in the way of genealogical and pseudo-historical tradition about them has been doctored, if not concocted. When they are seen in the full glare of the eighth century they are dominant in the northern half of Ireland.[77] This spawned the 'traditional' division of the country into two 'halves', Leth Cuinn, 'Conn's half', and Leth Moga Nuadat, 'the half of the slave of Nuadu'. The term 'Conn's half' derives from the fact that the Uí Néill were seen as an offshoot of the Connachta, descendants of the legendary Conn of the Hundred Battles. The genealogists maintained, and the historical evidence confirms, that there were two main divisions: those of the north, claiming descent from Conall Gulban, Énda, and Eógan, three sons of Niall 'of the Nine Hostages', and the southern

---

[74] John V. Kelleher, 'Early Irish history and pseudo-history' in *Studia Hib.*, iii (1963), pp 113–27, at p. 122.

[75] Eoin MacNéill, 'Colonisation under the early kings of Tara' in *Galway Arch. Soc. Jn.*, xvi (1935), pp 101–24; F. J. Byrne, '*Senchas*: the nature of Gaelic historical tradition' in John Barry (ed.), *Hist. Studies*, ix (1974), pp 137–59: 143.

[76] T. F. O'Rahilly, *Early Irish history and mythology* (Dublin, 1946), pp 161–83, 193–208, 478, 489. I have heard James Carney express this view in a lecture, but have not seen a published text.

[77] For what follows, see especially F. J. Byrne, *The rise of the Uí Néill and the high-kingship of Ireland* (O'Donnell Lecture, Dublin, 1969).

branch, occupying the territories of Brega, Mide, and Tethbae, descended from Niall's other sons Coirpre, Lóeguire, Fiachu, Maine, and Conall Cremthainne. In the sagas these are the traditional enemies of the Ulstermen, and they are credited with the overthrow of that once powerful kingdom in the course of the fifth century. The confused legends about the death of Niall have led some to suggest that his dynasty's early prestige derived from raids that they carried out on sub-Roman Britain. However, the annals are hopelessly at sea in their dating of Niall, and their confusion is inextricably bound up with the daunting problems posed by the chronology of St Patrick.[78]

Although the earliest annals depict them engaged mostly against the Laigin, the Uí Néill's principal claim to fame was as conquerors of the great province of Ulster. Their traditions recorded the exploits of 'the three Collas', Conlae Uais, Conlae Menn, and Conlae Fochri, great-grand-sons of Cormac mac Airt, who met in seven great battles with Fergus Fogae, king of Emain (Navan Fort, County Armagh), and eventually stormed his citadel. The brothers then drove the Ulaid eastwards beyond the river Bann and settled the lands that they had won by the sword. From them were derived the Airgialla, a loose conglomeration of related tribes occupying the lands in a wide band across central Ulster and owing allegiance to the Uí Néill.[79] The medieval Irish historians placed these events in the early fourth century, but although the legend has an undoubted basis in fact, neither the chronology nor the details of the events have any call on our credulity.

The three Collas are nothing more than doublets of the three sons of Niall Noígiallach, whose epithet has been derived from the nine *tuatha* that supposedly made up the original Airgialla confederation.[80] Their name means 'those who give hostages'[81] and they were in all likelihood an old-established population that had once been tributaries of the Ulaid but now transferred that allegiance to their new conquerors. Their genealogies are confused and contradictory, and despite the claim that the Airgialla were 'closest to the Uí Néill after the Connachta' the artificiality of this scheme cannot have deceived anyone.[82] They were probably not settlers, planted by the Uí Néill as a buffer between themselves and the Ulaid, but indigenous tribes that had long acknowledged the overlordship of the kings at Emain. They were never,

[78] The best example of the problem is the chapter entitled 'Patrick and the kings' in James Carney, *Studies in Irish literature and history* (Dublin, 1955), pp 324–73.

[79] Michael A. O'Brien, 'The oldest account of the raid of the Collas (circa A.D. 330)' in *U.J.A.*, 3rd ser., ii (1939), pp 170–77.

[80] O'Rahilly, *Early Ir. hist.*, p. 233, n. 8.

[81] Michael A. O'Brien, 'The Old Irish Life of St Brigit' in *I.H.S.*, i, no. 2 (1938), pp 121–34: 131, correcting an earlier interpretation of the name as meaning 'the eastern hostages'.

[82] O'Rahilly, *Early Ir. hist.*, pp 225–33.

it seems, a coherent tribal or dynastic group, since each people had its own king, e.g. Ind Airthir, Uí Tuirtri, Uí Méith, and Uí Crimthainn; the title 'king of the Airgialla' (*rex na nAirgialla*), suggesting an overlordship of the group, first appears in the Annals of Ulster in the obit of Máel Fothartaig mac Máelduib (697).[83] Many of the northern Airgialla were later absorbed into the Cenél nEógain over-kingdom of Ailech, just as some of their south-ern cousins fell under the sway of the Mide and Brega kingdoms. The result was a blurring of the earlier state of affairs concerning their ultimate ancestry and their relationship with the Uí Néill.

There are some obscure and vague traces of the earlier scheme of things scattered throughout the genealogical collections and elsewhere. The archaic text known as the tract 'On the privileges and responsibilities of poets' lists the Laimne, Laigne, Luigne, Artraige, Daimne, Maigne, and Mugraige ap-parently as Uí Néill subject peoples.[84] There may be some truth in the statement, but the genealogies of the Luigni, and their close neighbours the Gailenga and Ciannachta, preserve archaic texts that seem to hint at an earlier and different state of affairs. The Ciannanchta Glinne Geimin, who formed a separate kingdom centred on Dungiven, in the barony that still preserves their name (Keenaght, County Londonderry), had related branches in Connacht and around the mouth of the Boyne in the east, and in both areas they were contiguous to the Gailenga and Luigne. The Gailenga Cor-ann (County Sligo) genealogies contain a very obscure passage, which seems to imply that the 'seven races' of the Gailenga once lived in Leinster (*in regionibus Tuatha Domnand ocus Tuatha Gáileóin*) along with (?) the Luigne (here represented by their eponymous ancestor, Lugnae Fer Trí).[85] The tract relates how Lugnae was received back from exile by a king named Nia Noí nGráinne (who must surely be Niall 'of the nine hostages') *in tempore Uolo-torum*, 'in the time of the Ulstermen'.[86] In subsequent versions of this mater-ial, Lugnae is the fosterer of Cormac mac Airt, ancestor of the Uí Néill and the man to whom they traced back their title to the kingship of Tara, and this important relationship then serves to explain why the Luigne enjoy 'most favoured nation' status with the Uí Néill.[87] The oldest recensions of this text, however, have nothing to say about Cormac or the Uí Néill origin legend attached to him, but preserve a version of the Luigne's origins 'older than the agreed genealogical fictions linking all the lineages of Ireland which

[83] O'Rahilly, ibid., p. 224, no. 4.
[84] Gwynn, 'Privileges and responsibilities of poets', p. 34.
[85] Text in Donnchadh Ó Corráin, 'An chléir agus an léann dúchais' in Pádraig Ó Fiannachta (ed.), *Léachtaí Cholm Cille*, xvi (1986), pp 71–86, at pp 75–7 (there is another version of the same tract, not noted by Ó Corráin, in the Book of Uí Maine, 89a 6 ff); see also Ó Corráin, 'Historical need and literary narrative' in D. Ellis-Evans and others (ed.), *Proceedings of the Seventh International Celtic Congress* (Oxford, 1986), pp 141–58: 150–51.
[86] The text is interpreted differently in Byrne, *Ir. kings*, p. 68.
[87] Ó Corráin, 'Historical need and literary narrative', p. 149.

were worked out, apparently, early in the seventh century'.[88] By the time the synthetic historians drew up their scheme of Irish history, this older version of events was conveniently forgotten, but traces were still to be found in the names they chose to represent the ultimate ancestors of the ruling dynasties. Thus in the prehistoric king-list we find that Éremón was succeeded by his three sons Muimne, Luigne, and Laigne, whose names are clearly eponyms of the Munstermen (Muimne), Leinstermen (Laigne), and the Uí Néill, traced back to Luigne Fer Trí (who may in fact have ultimately been the ancestor god of the Dál Cuinn or Connachta).[89] Evidently the Uí Néill had distanced themselves by the seventh century from the Luigne, Gailenga, Corcu Fer Trí and the other more obscure peoples with whom they were once closely associated, preferring to present these as tributary tribes that they had introduced as fighting men in the buffer lands between themselves and their great Ulster and Leinster foes.[90] By the time the Uí Néill had established their dominance in the midlands the earlier political context was rewritten, as in the saga of the battle of Crinna,[91] which purports to tell how Cormac mac Airt defeated the Ulaid with the help of Tadc mac Céin (ancestor of the Ciannachta), and by a clever fiction established the Ciannachta as a vassal kingdom of the Uí Néill around the area of the Boyne. By the mid-eighth century the Síl nÁedo Sláine kings of northern Brega were beginning to style themselves 'kings of Ciannacht', after they had apparently taken over Ciannachta lands following the battle of Imlech Pích in 688, but the older population retained some independence in the form of the Fir Ardda Ciannachta, whose autonomy survived into the ninth century.

   Although it is customary to use the term 'Uí Néill' to denote this group of families, there was no such implication of tribal descent as attached to similar names such as the Uí Bairrche or Uí Failgi of Leinster. 'The Uí Néill were neither a tribe nor a federation of tribes, but a dynasty which hived off from the parent tribal stem of the Connachta, and by so doing introduced a new force into the Irish polity which overlaid and eventually destroyed tribalism.'[92] Hence the term is an anachronistic one for the fifth century, since by that date the dynasty hardly comprised much more than the sons of Niall himself; in fact the earliest annals make no mention of them under that name, but refer to the sons individually. The date 440 given for Maine's death is the first of the annalistic obits for Niall's sons, and the earliest stratum of the annals—though always susceptible to later tampering—does offer the bare bones of a chronology for their rise to power.

---

[88] Ó Corráin, 'Historical need and literary narrative', p. 149.

[89] Kelleher, 'Pre-Norman Irish genealogies', p. 146.

[90] The theory that they were colonists and fighting men was first advanced by MacNéill, 'Colonization under the early kings of Tara', pp 102–24.

[91] O'Brien, *Corpus geneal. Hib.*, pp 403–5.

[92] Byrne, 'Tribes and tribalism in early Ireland' in *Ériu*, xx (1971), pp 128–66.

Much the best known—because immortalised by his role in Patrician saga—is Lóeguire mac Néill. As we saw above, Lóeguire is depicted in late seventh-century hagiography as the *bête noire* of the Irish Apostle, called by one of Patrick's biographers another Nebuchadnezzar who resided at Tara, 'their Babylon'.[93] Curiously enough, the topographical traditions incorporated in Bishop Tírechán's collectaneum concerning Patrick and his early foundations place the daughters of Lóeguire at Cruachu (Rathcroghan, County Roscommon), with the implication that Lóeguire himself ruled as king of Tara from Connacht. This Connacht origin for the sept is supported also by the fact that the Cenél Lóeguire genealogies locate one group of his descendants in the area west of Lough Erne.[94] The later expansion northwards and eastwards of the Uí Néill is usually attributed to the fact that they were 'more dynamic'.[95] How this was manifested in practical terms is difficult to see, but it does seem to be the case that they, more than their northern or southern rivals, organised their conquests on a strictly territorial and dynastic basis, distributing their newly won lordship among the sons of Niall over large areas, and in the process breaking down the older pattern of tribal kingships that had preceded their arrival.

The later 'Bóruma' tract, a propaganda piece allegedly explaining how the Uí Néill high-kings of prehistory had levied a huge cattle tribute from the Leinstermen, maintained that Lóeguire met his death while trying to impose this tribute on the Laigin. The story is pure saga, but the earliest annals do preserve a laconic record of fifth-century Uí Néill offensives southwards, beginning with the notice of a 'great slaughter of the Leinstermen' (*interfectio magna Lagenarum*) in 452, which is followed, perhaps significantly, by notice of Lóeguire's celebration of the 'feast' of Tara (*feis Temro*) two years later. On the whole, however, the meagre annalistic record suggests that Lóeguire's was not a very auspicious military career: a defeat at the hands of the Leinstermen is noted in 458 and his death in battle against them appears under 462. Even if we set little store by the exact chronology, there seems little doubt that Leinster resistance to Uí Néill was still strong up to the late fifth century, with the tide beginning to turn only during the reign of Niall's son Coirpre.

The first real Uí Néill successes were probably due to this Coirpre, rather than to Lóeguire. The text known as 'Buile Chuind' ('The vision of Conn'), in which Conn Cétchathach prophesies about the future kings of Tara,[96] is an archaic king-list, probably redacted towards the end of the seventh century, which, among other interesting features, includes Coirpre among the

[93] Muirchú, *Vita Sti Patricii*, i, 15; Bieler, *Patrician texts*, p. 84.
[94] See Eoin MacNeill, 'Topographical importance of the Vita Tripartita' in *Ériu*, xi (1930), pp 1–41; reprinted in MacNeill, *Saint Patrick* (Dublin, 1964), pp 179–220: 205.
[95] Byrne, 'Tribes and tribalism', p. 151.
[96] Gerard Murphy, 'Buile Chuind' in *Ériu*, xvi (1952), pp 146–51.

roll-call of high-kings. Considering that Coirpre's name was expunged entirely from all the later regnal lists, this fact is significant, and it finds support in another seventh-century work, Tírechán's 'Collectaneum'.[97] There Patrick encounters Coirpre at a royal feast held in Tailtiu (Teltown, County Meath), but Coirpre is hostile and Patrick curses him, saying that he would produce no kings but would serve his brothers forever. This story is reproduced in the later 'Vita Tripartita' and was intended originally to mean that the once powerful Cenél Cairpri still resided at Tailtu, where earlier Uí Néill kings had celebrated the famous *Oenach Tailten* (familiar in its modern guise as the Tailteann games). As MacNeill remarked, 'it is a commonplace, especially with Tírechán, to make Patrick's prophecies account for the ups and downs of the posterity of princes',[98] but in this instance Tírechán was blatantly ignoring the fact that three distinct sub-septs of the Cenél Cairpre were still powerful in his own time (*c.*700): the Cairpri Laigin whose name survives in the form of Carbury Hill (barony of Carbury, County Kildare) on the north-west frontier of Leinster, a second in the Cairpri Gabra (in the area of Granard, County Longford), and a third in the kingdom of Cairpri Dromma Cliab (around Drumcliff, County Sligo). Tírechán's political bias is exposed also by another detail preserved in the additamenta to the Patrician material in the Book of Armagh, where it is recorded that lands in the territory of the Cairpri Dromma Cliab were made over to Patrick by Coirpre himself (*regnum offerebat . . . Coirpre Patricio*).[99] Hence the topographical and historical evidence shows that Coirpre's territories extended at one point from Donegal Bay in the north-west in a broad band south-eastwards as far as the Leinster border. These territories were, however, cut into by the later rise of the midland Uí Néill dynasties descended from Diarmait mac Cerbaill, and all memories of the earlier political supremacy of Coirpre in the midlands were to be submerged in the mass of traditions centred on Lóeguire. Only one son, Eochu, is recorded for Coirpre, and he disappears without trace.

The other main Uí Néill protagonist of the early annalistic record is Muirchertach Mac Ercae, who may be identical with the Macc Ercae/Mac Ercéni of the 'Baile Chuind'. But the confusion in the Annals of Ulster about the form of his name, allied to the probable misplacement of his obit at 536 and the semi-legendary character of his reign, does not encourage confidence in the sources, and his 'conflate personality' may (as F. J. Byrne has suggested) be nothing but a later attempt by the Cenél nEógain branch of the northern Uí Néill to interpolate an early king of Tara into their ancestry.[100] Besides several victories over the Leinstermen (which by now had become

[97] *Collectaneum*, 9; Bieler, *Patrician texts*, p. 132.
[98] MacNeill, 'Topographical importance of the Vita Tripartita' in *St Patrick*, p. 192.
[99] *Additamenta*, 10; Bieler, *Patrician texts*, p. 174.
[100] Byrne, 'Tribes and tribalism', p. 149.

almost *de rigeur* for aspiring Uí Néill scions), the annals also record a victory by Muirchertach over Daui Tengae Umai, king of Connacht, at the battle of Segas in 502; following a series of battles laconically noted in the Annals of Ulster (498, 499, 500 (*bellum*, with no further elaboration!), 501), the victory at Segas may signal a westward shift in Muirchertach's ambitions. When next the Uí Néill advanced against the Leinstermen (510) they were led by Niall's son Fiachu, who was defeated by Failge Berraide of the Uí Failgi. However, as we saw above, Fiachu reversed this misfortune six years later (516) when he routed the Laigin at the battle of Druim Derge, as a result of which, according to the Annals of Ulster, the *campus Mide* was lost forever by the Leinstermen. By another curious twist Tírechán, who records an encounter between Patrick and a son of Fiachu (unnamed) at Uisnech, states that Fiachu's son killed members of the saint's party, evoking from him the customary prophecy of doom.[101] The Cenél Fiachach were, in fact, to slip on the political ladder (despite the fact that in the 'Vita Tripartita' Patrick's curse was averted from Fiachu and his brother Énda by the intervention of his assistant, Sechnall!), and the chief of their sept is given the lesser title *tigernae*, 'lord', not king, at the notice of his death in the Annals of Ulster (739).[102] The Cenél nÉndai, cursed along with their brothers, occupied a small kingdom around Raphoe, County Donegal, with another branch on the western shore of Lough Erne, and were apparently consigned to an early political obscurity.

These Uí Néill conquests led to the permanent annexation of the lands north of the present Kildare–Offaly border and with it the absorption of several small kingdoms that had been subject tribes of the Laigin. The Uí Néill occasionally adopted these older tribal names, with the result that it is often very difficult to make out their original affiliations. Thus groups such as the Fir Assail, Fir Bile, Fir Cell, and Fir Tulach were subsumed into the maze of Uí Néill sub-septs whose lands they occupied, circumstances that were represented by the rewriting of the genealogies to accommodate these changes. The Fir Tulach Midi, for example, claimed descent from the early seventh-century Uí Cennselaig king of Leinster Brandub mac Echach. The claim is probably spurious, since their land had probably fallen to the Uí Néill at least a century before Brandub's time. But despite their status as tributary people of the Uí Néill, their original affiliation with the Laigin is probably authentic.[103] In order to cover over the traces, however, the genealogists gave them a pedigree that derived them from a totally fictitious Fer Tulach, son of Niall. In the same way the Callraige of north Sligo and Leitrim, usually traced with the older branches of that people from Lugaid

[101] *Collectaneum*, 16; Bieler, *Patrician texts*, p. 136.
[102] MacNeill, 'Topographical importance of the Vita Tripartita' in *St Patrick*, p. 194.
[103] Paul Walsh, *The placenames of Westmeath* (Dublin, 1957), pp 162–5; Byrne, 'Tribes and tribalism', p. 147; Smyth, 'Húi Failgi relations with the Húi Néill', p. 505.

Cál, son of Dáire, are in a later tract given a spurious descent from an equally fictitious Cal, son of Coirpre mac Néill, simply because they occupied land in the Uí Néill territory of Cairpre Dromma Cliab.[104] Similar 'revisions' of the historical record could be listed for other peoples whose fate was that their lands straddled the frontiers between the great provincial rivals.

Niall's sons Coirpre, Lóeguire, Fiach, and Maine were the founders of the midland kingdoms of the southern Uí Néill in the ancient territories of Brega (Counties Meath, north Dublin, and south Louth), Mide (Counties West-meath and western Offaly), and Tethbae, later distinguished territorially as Tethbae Tuaiscirt and Tethnae Deiscirt—Tethbae north and south. Tethbae Deiscirt, centred on Ardagh and with its southern borders marked by the River Inny, was the kingdom of Maine, and a grandson of his, Áed mac Bréndain meic Maine, is noticed in the Annals of Ulster at 588 as *rex Tethba*; a later annotator states that it was he who granted to Colum Cille the land on which the monastery of Durrow was founded. The genealogies preserve the names of several other kings of the same line (Bécc mac Conlai, *rí Tethbae*, 771; his son Diarmait, *rex Tethbae*, 791; Conaing mac Congail, *rex Tethbae*, 823; and others, down to the close of the ninth century).[105] North-ern Tethbae was the territory of Cairpre, centred on Granard, and various sub-septs, under the designations Cenél Cairpri, Cairpre Mór, and Cairpre Gabra, figure in the Annals of Ulster during the seventh, eighth, and ninth centuries. The Cenél Fiachach occupied the lands of Mide between Birr (County Offaly) and Uisnech, while the Cenél Lóeguire were situated around Trim (County Meath), though a branch seems to have been located farther west, on Lough Erne.

But all these families were to be overshadowed by the more powerful dynasts of the southern Uí Néill descended from the sons of Diarmait mac Cerrbail: the Clann Cholmáin Máir of Mide and the Síl nÁedo Sláine, whose kingdom centred on Brega in the east and encompassed Tara itself in the west. The grandsons of Áed Sláine were contemporaries of Tírechán; one of them, Fínsnechtae Fledach (d. 695) is the last name mentioned in the archaic king-list 'Baile Chuind'. It is curious that these two great southern Uí Néill dynasties derived their origin, not directly from Niall, but from his great-grandson Diarmait, since Diarmait's career is obscure and has given rise to some scholarly scepticism about his true ancestry.[106] His grandfather Conall Eirr Breg ('chariot-rider of Brega') was also known as Conall Cremthainne (probably signifying—as MacNeill suggested—that he was fostered by the sept of Cremthainne).[107] He figures in Tírechán's account of Patrick's itiner-

[104] Donnchadh Ó Corráin, 'Lugaid Cál and the Callraige' in *Éigse*, xiii (1970), pp 225–6.
[105] Kuno Meyer, 'The Laud genealogies and tribal histories' in *Z.C.P.*, viii (1912), pp 291–338, at p. 324, 'De genealogia Fer Tathba .i. Claindi Maine'; MacNeill, *St Patrick*, p. 195.
[106] Byrne, *Ir. kings*, p. 90.
[107] MacNeill, *St Patrick*, p. 193.

ary, where he 'received him with great hospitality' (*cum gaudio magno*), eliciting the traditional blessing for him and his descendants.[108] A sub-sept of the family, Cenél nArdgail, traced their descent through a son of this Conall, and though they failed to capture the Uí Néill high-kingship they nevertheless retained their independence down to 837, when they disappear from the Annals of Ulster.[109]

The evidence for the crucial period of formation of the Uí Néill kingdoms is obscure and confused (perhaps deliberately so). It is, curiously enough, the less successful kindreds—Cenél Lóeguire, Cenél Maine (Tethbae), and Cenél Fiachach—that preserve the fullest genealogies. Where one would expect that the descendants of Conall Cremthainne, especially Síl nÁedo Sláine and Clann Cholmáin Máir, who monopolised the southern high-kingship, would provide the greater bulk of the historical record, the opposite is in fact the case. Their genealogical records are disappointingly meagre, fragmentary, and confused.[110] The Clann Cholmáin, for example, have no pedigree other than that of Flann Sinna mac Máel Sechnaill (king of Tara 879–916); the earlier period has to be pieced together from stray entries in the annals and other sources.

In the process, however, we cannot fail to note that much essential information has been deliberately suppressed, that the suppression seems to affect every possibly competing line within the descent from Diarmait mac Cerbaill (d. 565), and that for the sixth and early seventh centuries the annals seem to have been largely cleared of entries relating to the other southern Uí Néill tribes.[111]

The later synthetic historians liked to portray their rise in terms of their taking possession of the kingship of Tara, of which they claimed a virtual monopoly. Tírechán's exact contemporary, Abbot Adomnán of Iona (d. 704), in his Life of St Columba refers to Diarmait mac Cerbaill as the king 'ordained by God as ruler of all Ireland' (*totius Scotiae regnatorem deo auctore ordinatum*), and though the regnal lists acknowledge that before the time of Diarmait's ancestor Niall the kingship of Tara was not the sole prerogative of the Connachta, from Diarmait's time the term *rí Temro*, 'king of Tara', was understood—by Uí Néill propagandists, at any rate—to mean 'king of Ireland'.[112] The Uí Néill campaigns against the Laigin seem to have been part of their efforts to realise that claim, though they may also be a tacit acknowledgement that the Laigin had made such claims themselves in earlier

[108] *Collectaneum*, 10; Bieler, *Patrician texts*, p. 132.

[109] MacNeill notes that their pedigrees come down to *c*.850 (*St Patrick*, p. 194).

[110] John V. Kelleher, 'The pre-Norman Irish genealogies' in *I.H.S.*, xvi, no. 62 (1968), pp 138–53: 149.

[111] Ibid., p. 150.

[112] A. O. and M. O. Anderson (ed. and trans.), *Adomnan's Life of Columba* (Edinburgh, 1961), p. 280.

times.[113] Diarmait himself had a less than conspicuous military career, and the last few years of his reign were marked by a series of defeats (Cúl Dreimne (561), allegedly instigated by Colum Cille; Cúil Uinsen (562), where he fled the battle against Áed mac Brénaind of Tethbae; and his death at the hands of Áed Dub mac Suibne, this latter noted also by Adomnán in his 'Vita Columbae').[114] But like Lóeguire mac Néill before him, the subsequent success of his descendants was enough to ensure his fame.

The regnal lists and the annals display considerable confusion in the matter of who succeeded Diarmait in the high-kingship. The 'Baile Chuind', composed, as we have seen, during the reign of Fínsnechtae Fledach (d. 695), implies that Diarmait had no immediate successors, and in fact his son Áed Sláine seems to have been overshadowed by his northern cousin Colmán Rímid mac Báetáin (d. 604), king of Cenél nEógain and maternal grandfather of the Northumbrian king Aldfrith (685–704), and possibly also a brother of Bishop Fínán of Lindisfarne. It was not in fact until the joint reign of Áed Sláine's sons Diarmait and Blathmac (658–65) that the midland dynasty was firmly established.[115]

By the end of the seventh century, it is clear, the Uí Néill were the dominant power in the northern half of the country. According to the 'official' regnal lists from the eighth century and later, most of the so-called high-kings came from the Cenél Conaill and Cenél nEógain in the north and the Síl nÁedo Sláine and Clann Cholmáin in the south. Lóeguire mac Néill and his son Lugaid were also included, along with Tuathal Máelgarb, grandson of Coirpre mac Néill, but none of the other branches was accommodated in the scheme. The later doctrine was that these had acknowledged the superiority of the main septs, who monopolised the kingship. The southern Uí Néill held most of the fertile lands in the midlands, while their northern cousins straddled the strategic territories across the north-west to the sea. After the initial setback that had been marked by the defeat of Áed mac Ainmerech by Brandub mac Echach of Leinster at the battle of Dún Bolg in 598, his son Domnall mac Áedo apparently restored the situation on the southern frontier, while a further victory in 637 against the Ulaid at the battle of Mag Roth set the seal on his successful career. The annals term him *rex Hiberniae* on his death in 642/3—the only man to receive the title in the seventh century.

Domnall's grandson Loingsech mac Óengusso (d. 704) is only the second Uí Néill king to be accorded the title 'king of Ireland' by the annalists before the ninth century, but in fact the beginning of the eighth century was to see a period of intense internal rivalry among the Uí Néill themselves, culminat-

---

[113] See the comments on Muiredach Mo-Śníthech and Móenach of the Uí Bairrche, above, pp 191, 193.

[114] Adomnán, *Vita Columbae*, i, 36; Anderson, *Adomnan's Life*, pp 278–82.

[115] Byrne, *Ir. kings*, pp 104–5.

ing in the disastrous defeat of the northern high-king Fergal mac Máele Dúin at the hands of the Laigin in the battle of Almu (Allen, County Kildare) in 722. Their fortunes were restored, however, with the accession of Áed Allán of Cenél nEógain (734–43). Whether by coincidence or as the result of a mutual agreement, the title of high-king alternated regularly from 734 between the Cenél nEógain of Ailech and the Clann Cholmáin in Mide. During Áed Allán's reign the Cenél nEógain expanded from their stronghold at Ailech in the Inishowen peninsula into the northern Airgialla territories of Londonderry and Tyrone, and by their absorption of the northern Uí moccu Uais they succeeded in dealing a strategic blow to their Cenél Conaill rivals of Donegal, who were now cut off from access to the midlands to the south of them. This may in fact explain the otherwise unusual attempt by Loingsech mac Óengusso (penultimate Cenél Conaill claimant to the Tara kingship) to drive southwards into Connacht, where he met his end—'along with many other leaders'—in the battle of Corann (County Sligo).[116] Having asserted the dominance of his own dynasty against Loingsech's son and successor Flaithbertach, Áed Allán consolidated the Cenél nEógain supremacy in the north, adding the church of Armagh to his other gains, while in the south the Clann Cholmáin emerged from comparative obscurity as the dominant political force in the midlands, encroaching in their turn on the southern Airgialla territories of Uí moccu Uais Midi, Uí moccu Uais Breg, and the Mugdornai Breg.

Despite a litany of successes during the eighth century, which saw them establish effective hegemony over Leinster and an uneasy stand-off against the Ulaid, the Uí Néill had reached the peak of their power by c.800. It is difficult to say why they had enjoyed such phenomenal success, but it may be that the territorialisation of power that was their hallmark gave them an advantage over their rivals. Thus, for instance, by the mid-eighth century the descendants of Congalach mac Conaing, who ruled the kingdom of northern Brega centred on the ancient royal tumulus at Knowth, are termed kings of Ciannachta (as we saw above): they simply took over the tribal name of their newly acquired lands. 'Such a geographical application of a population name, and in particular its usurpation by outsiders, would scarcely have been possible in the earlier, more purely tribal, stage of Irish society.'[117] But the emergence of the northern and southern Uí Néill as separate power blocs was to prove their undoing in the decades to follow. Where in the sixth and seventh centuries there had still been some unity of purpose between the northern and southern branches, and a genuine feeling of ancestral solidarity, the Cenél nEógain and Clann Cholmáin were alienated from one another and each faced the new challenges of the tenth century on their own.

[116] Byrne, *Rise of the Uí Néill*, p. 20.
[117] F. J. Byrne, 'Historical note on Cnogba (Knowth)' in George Eogan, 'Excavations at Knowth, Co. Meath, 1962–65' in *R.I.A. Proc.*, lxvi, (1968) sect. C, pp 299–400: 397.

The saga material embodied in the stories of the Ulster cycle, centred on the famous 'Táin Bó Cuailnge', record the memories of long-distant wars between the Connachta and the Ulaid. The story of the fall of Emain Macha, prefaced to the genealogies of the Airgialla, placed that event in the early fourth century, but this date can be shown to be a fabrication of the later pseudo-historians, and in fact it is now doubted whether the downfall of the Ulster kingdom can be set so early. The collapse of the Ulaid was not total, nor did they themselves regard their defeat at the hands of the Uí Néill as anything but a temporary setback; as late as the seventh century—when the Uí Néill were claiming a monopoly of the high-kingship—one of their kings was described in a law tract as *rí Temro*, 'king of Tara'.[118] By the dawn of the documentary period the ancient provincial 'fifth' of Ulster was certainly no more, but the Ulaid were still independent and ruled over an extensive kingdom in the east of their ancient territory, while affecting a dignified superiority to their upstart Uí Néill supplanters.

The political boundaries of the Ulster kingdom from *c*.600 were every bit as fluid as those of the other kingdoms whose territories formed the object of Uí Néill ambitions. Nevertheless, it can be shown that the Ulaid still retained claims—whether realistic or not—to lands as far south as the Boyne. Thus in the archaic tract on the privileges and responsibilities of poets that is preserved in the law text known as 'Bretha Nemed' ('Judgements of privileged persons') the Ulster poet Aithirne laments the death of his client Borur, killed on a raid into Connacht (*a crich Connacht*) with the words 'Woe to the Ulstermen if they be beyond the Boyne' (*mairg d'Ulltaibh madh ala Boinn beid*).[119] The text preserves the memory of a period when the lands south of Ulster were occupied by the Connachta (before the rise of the Uí Néill), and when Ulster itself was at its greatest extent. The Ulaid, as the leading power in the north, gave their name to the province, which extended from the River Drowes (which separates County Leitrim from County Donegal) to the mouth of the Boyne (including present-day County Louth, which was still reckoned to be part of Ulster down to the seventeenth century).[120]

In historical documents (though not in the literary sources) the Ulaid are always identified as the population group whose ruling dynasty were the Dál Fiatach, who occupied most of the present south and east County Down.[121] Thus the title *rí Ulad* had a double signification: it could mean 'king of the Ulaid [i.e. Dál Fiatach]' and also 'over-king of Ulster'. More numerous and powerful in the archaic period, however, were the peoples known as Cruthin or Cruithni, later represented by the ruling dynasties of the Dál nAraidi

---

[118] Fergus Kelly and Thomas Charles-Edwards (ed. and trans.), *Bechbretha: an Old Irish law-tract on bee-keeping* (Dublin, 1983), p. 68, § 32.

[119] Gwynn, 'Privileges and responsibilities of poets', p. 20.

[120] O'Rahilly, *Early Ir. hist.*, p. 347.

[121] For what follows see especially ibid., pp 341–52.

(south County Antrim) and the Uí Echach Cobo (west County Down). In the sixth century these peoples still controlled parts of County Londonderry as well, and the great saga tale 'Táin Bó Cuailnge' preserves the distinction between them and the Ulaid. The annals too acknowledge the distinction: the Annals of Ulster, for instance, record in 668 the battle of Belfast (*Bellum Fertsi*) between the Ulaid and the Cruthin (*inter Ultu et Cruitne*), and this distinction is found also in other seventh-century writings, such as Muirchú's Life of St Patrick.[122] In the earliest sources the name 'Cruithni' is usually applied to the Dál nAraidi: Adomnán in his 'Vita Columbae' refers to them as *Cruithini* and *Cruthin populi*, while in the annals the term is used of them down to 773 (*Flathruae mac Fiachrach, rex Cruithne, moritur*), after which it is dropped in favour of the term 'Dál nAraidi'. This abandonment of 'Cruthni' may have something to do with the fact that the term is a Q-Celtic borrowing of '\*Priteni', the name of the oldest recorded inhabitants of the British Isles, better known under their Latin nickname 'Picti'. Irish authors writing in Latin, such as Adomnán, invariably used the term 'Picti' to denote the Picts of Scotland, but in Irish the term 'Cruthin' was used of both the Picts and their Irish cousins, and though the 'origin legend' of the Picts is relatively late in date we can assume with a reasonable degree of certainty that the connection that it presupposes was still a folk memory in the historical period. From the eighth century, however, the name 'Cruthin' was apparently dropped as 'savouring too much of a foreign "Pictish" origin',[123] and the genealogists attempted to cover over the traces by asserting that the Dál nAraidi were the 'true Ulaid' (*na fir Ulaid*) of antiquity, while conceding that the name 'Ulaid' applied to the Dál Fiatach 'today'—this even after the decline of Dál nAraidi power again in the tenth century, after which the rival Dál Fiatach reasserted their ancient position. In fact, the name 'Ulaid' continued to apply to the Dál Fiatach until the Anglo-Normans finally put an end to their power, thus illustrating how artificial and contrived were the doctrines of the genealogists at times.

The expansion of the Uí Néill doubtless had its impact on the political fortunes of other, lesser-known Ulster peoples in the early historical period, as it did in Leinster, and the later emergence of the Dál Fiatach and Dál nAraidi may well conceal the earlier supremacy of other tribes. The Annals of Ulster at 456 record the death of one Énnae mac Cathbotha, alias Énda Rogaillnech, ancestor of the Uí Echach dynasty of Ards,[124] and the subsequent Dál Fiatach domination of the monastery of Bangor may have resulted from their expulsion of the Uí Echach into the isolated Ards peninsula.

---

[122] Muirchú, *Vita Sti Patricii*, i, 11; Bieler, *Patrician texts*, p. 78.

[123] F. J. Byrne, 'The Ireland of St Columba' in *Hist. Studies*, v (1965), pp 37–58: 43; cf. O'Rahilly, *Early Ir. hist.*, p. 344.

[124] For the identification, see F. J. Byrne's review of O'Brien's *Corpus geneal. Hib.* in *Z.C.P.*, xxix (1962–4), pp 381–5: 382.

Another branch of the same tribe, the Uí Echach Cobo, which supplied occasional over-kings of Ulster, may likewise have been cut off from their Dál nAraidi allies to the north by Dál Fiatach expansion westwards to Lough Neagh. The Annals of Ulster have the enigmatic entry *expugnatio Duin Lethglaisi*, 'the storming of Downpatrick', at 496 (duplicated 498), which may well signify an important victory—though whether for or against the Dál Fiatach it is difficult to say. The former seems more likely, since the Dál Fiatach ruled Ulster from their royal seat at Downpatrick (Dún dá Lethglass) for centuries, and the site also had important ecclesiastical connections. The evidence of Patrician hagiography preserves traces of a connection between this site and the missionary church of St Patrick; indeed, some traditions remembered the site as that of Patrick's burial place.[125] The later ecclesiastical site seems to have grown out of an island hermitage, Cranny Island (Crannach Dúin Lethglaisse), which is recorded as having associations with the monastery of Bangor as early as *c.*600.[126] It is a curious fact that Bangor seems to replace Downpatrick as the centre of Dál Fiatach ecclesiastical influence; the shift does, however, indicate a northwards expansion into south Antrim.

The rival Dál nAraidi, whose kings resided at Ráth Mór east of Antrim town, may likewise have supplanted other lineages, but they seem to have borne the brunt of the conflict with the Uí Néill, and suffered losses in the mid sixth century from which they never really recovered. This was in spite of earlier successes against the same enemy, notably the defeat of the high-king Diarmait mac Cerbaill at the hands of the notorious Áed Dub mac Suibni, 'a very bloody man and slayer of many' (according to Adomnán, who was related to the high-king).[127] The victory became the subject of legend, 'which wove around it a magic aura suggestive of a ritual threefold slaying'.[128] According to this tradition, Diarmait was slain at Ráth Bec near the Dál nAraidi royal seat of Ráth Mór Maige Line, while making a royal 'circuit' of Ulster. The story is impossible, since no Uí Néill king of the time would have dared set foot inside Ulster, but that Diarmait fell at the hands of a Cruthin king is significant enough. Diarmait's son, Colmán Mór, also fell at the hands of another Cruthin king, Dubsloit hua Tréna, doubtless attempting to avenge his father's death.

The year 563 marked the decisive turn in Cruthin fortunes; the battle of Móin Dairi Lothair was won by a northern Uí Néill alliance against a combination of Cruthin kings, seven of whom are supposed to have fallen in the

---

[125] Richard Sharpe, 'St Patrick and the see of Armagh' in *Camb. Med. Celt. Studies*, iv (winter 1982), pp 33–59: 42–3.
[126] See Dáibhí Ó Cróinín, 'Mo-Sinu maccu Min and the computus at Bangor' in *Peritia*, i (1982), pp 281–95.
[127] Adomnán, *Vita Columbae*, i, 36; Anderson, *Adomnan's Life*, p. 280.
[128] Byrne, 'Ireland of St Columba', p. 44.

conflict. The rather garbled account in the Annals of Ulster seems to imply that the immediate cause was an internal struggle in which one Báetán mac Cinn (otherwise unknown; *lege* moccu Cruind—descendant of Cruind ba druí?) enlisted the Uí Néill against his Cruthin cousins, promising them the Lee and Ard Eólairgg (Magilligan Point) as reward (*mercede*). The battle was also remembered by Adomnán, who mentions a Cruthin king, Eochaid Laíb, who escaped from the slaughter in his chariot (*uictus currui insedens euaserit*);[129] Eochaid's name is not to be found in the annals or genealogies, though his son Eugan is commemorated at 611. The account of the battle is interesting confirmation of the fact that the territory of the Fir Lee, west of the river Bann, between the lands of the Ciannachta and the Bann, and north of the Moyola river (Mag Dola, in south-east Londonderry) became subject to the Ailech kings only in the years following 563—long after the date when, according to Uí Néill tradition, the kingdom of Ulster had collapsed. Between the Bann, which separated the Fir Lee from the small kingdom of Eilne, and the River Bush (the farthest western limit of the Dál Riata kingdom) the Uí Néill settled their Airgialla allies.

The loose confederation of Cruthin tribes that had taken the field against the Uí Néill regrouped after 563 in the area east of the lower Bann and consolidated around the remnants of the Dál nAraidi. Adomnán in another passage represents Columba of Iona, the patron saint of the Uí Néill, and Comgall of Bangor, patron of the Dál nAraidi, as the best of friends, jointly lamenting the antagonism between their respective peoples, and Columba prophesied that they would clash again at the battle of Dún Ceithirnn.[130] The battle was duly fought in 629, and the Dál nAraidi under Congal Cláen were routed, Congal escaping with his life. In fact, as late as 681 the Dál nAraidi under Dúngal Eilni were still resisting the Uí Néill in these parts in alliance with the Ciannachta of Derry; on that occasion Dúngal and his ally Cenn Fáelad were killed in his fortress in what the annalist called 'the burning of the kings at Dún Cethirnn' (*combustio regum i nDun Ceithirnn*).

Of the sixty-two names in the later Ulster king-lists, however, only ten belonged to the Dál nAraidi; the rest were kings of Dál Fiatach.[131] Much the most successful of these was Báetán mac Cairill: in a short reign of just nine years (572–*c*.581) Báetán did much to restore the military power of the Dál Fiatach and the prestige of the Ulaid. A poem that advances his claim to high-kingship asserts that he exacted hostages from Munster (whose centre, interestingly, is placed at Emly (*Imblech Ibair*), not the traditional Cashel), and that he received tribute from Ireland and Scotland at his fortress in Lethet.[132] The same genealogical tract also says that he 'cleared' the Isle of

---

[129] Adomnán, *Vita Columbae*, i, 7; Anderson, *Adomnan's Life*, pp 224–6.
[130] Adomnán, *Vita Columbae*, i, 49; Anderson, *Adomnan's Life*, pp 344–6.
[131] O'Rahilly, *Early Ir. hist.*, p. 347.
[132] O'Brien, *Corpus geneal. Hib.*, p. 406.

Man (*et is leis glanta Manand*), perhaps a reference to the expulsion of the
Conailli Muirtheimne, who seem to have occupied the island previously (and
one of whose grandees appears to be commemorated in an ogam inscription
there).[133] Báetán also took advantage of the colonisation of western Scotland
by the Dál Riata, whose kingdom straddled the territories on both sides of
the sea. The Ulster genealogical tract states that the Dál Riata king Áedán
mac Gabráin paid homage to Báetán at Ros na Ríg in Seimne (Islandmagee,
County Antrim). There is a hint of these events in the cryptic references of
the Annals of Ulster to an expedition (*periculum*) to the Isle of Man in 577 by
the Ulaid, followed by their retreat (*reuersio*) the following year; the same
annals record a victory by Áedán mac Gabráin in the battle of Man (*bellum
Manonn*) in 582, the year of Báetán's death. The genealogies say that Man
was evacuated by the Irish (*Gaídil*) two years after Baetán's death, and this
doubtless signals the first resurgence of Dál Riata independence after the
demise of their principal foe.

The sixth and seventh centuries saw considerable political activity between
the north of Ireland and Britain, and Báetán's campaigns are symptomatic of
a wide perspective. These Irish contacts are with all the peoples of north
Britain—Picts, Britons, and Angles. The Annals of Ulster record a joint
expedition to the Western Isles (*Iardoman*) by Colmán Bec (d. 587), son of
Diarmait mac Cerbaill of the southern Uí Néill, and Conall mac Comgaill,
Áedán mac Gabráin's predecessor as king of Dál Riata and the man who
granted the site of Iona to Colum Cille, while a northern Uí Néill prince,
Máel Umai mac Báetáin, fought in Áedan's army at the battle of Degsastan
in 603 (and lived to tell the tale; he died in 610). The Ulster tracts make
elaborate claims for Báetán mac Cairill, but even the later compilers were
forced to acknowledge his influence; they admit him alongside Brian Bóruma
as exceptions to the 'rule' that all high-kings of the historical period had
belonged to the Uí Néill and Connachta (but with the caveat that 'others do
not reckon Báetán among the great kings').[134] His wife seems to have
belonged to the Uí Tuirtre, who occupied the territories around Magherafelt,
Moneymore, Cookstown, and Stewartstown bordering on Lough Neagh,[135]
which may suggest a political alliance with this crucial buffer kingdom. His
death may have been premature, cutting off a promising career, but the
annals do not say. His path may have been smoothed by his brother Demmán, whose death in 572 may likewise have cut off an auspicious reign. The
genealogies state that he was fostered by Domangart mac Predae (Dál Riata?
a Pict?) with whom he fought against his dynastic rivals the Uí Ibdaig in
alliance with the Uí Echach Ulad and destroyed them at the battle of Dún

---

[133] Byrne, 'Ireland of St Columba', p. 56, n. 56.
[134] O'Brien, *Corpus geneal. Hib.*, p. 123.
[135] Ibid., p. 409.

Cleithe in 533, where, according to the genealogist, seven Uí Ibdaig princes fell. As things happened, it was Demmán's progeny who were to carry the torch for the Dál Fiatach in subsequent years. Báetán's sons were killed in internecine strife by their uncle Máel Dúin mac Fiachnai (whose own ambitions came to nothing).[136]

Báetán's successes are best seen in the effect they had on his enemies, particularly the Uí Néill and Dál Riata. Áedán mac Gabráin made alliance with the Uí Néill in order to establish a 'second front' against the encroaching Dál Fiatach; this alliance was, according to tradition, forged through the good offices of Colum Cille, whose cousin was the northern Uí Néill high-king, and was sealed at the famous convention of Druim Cett (County Londonderry) in 575 (where the saint is supposed to have saved the poets of Ireland from expulsion!). This saw a gathering of Áed mac Ainmerech, of the northern Uí Néill, and Áedán mac Gabráin, with Colum Cille and others in attendance. The annals are singularly uninformative about the event, and Adomnán, who mentions it in his 'Vita Columbae', is significantly silent about the purpose of the conference, not even mentioning the Dál Fiatach kings. It can hardly be doubted, however, that the convention settled the question of the relationship between the Dál Riata and the Uí Néill high-king, with the mainland branch of Dál Riata acknowledging the suzerainty of the Uí Néill high-kings; as a *quid pro quo* it may be assumed also that the position of the Iona federation of monasteries in Scottish Dál Riata territory was likewise guaranteed. As with every other place and period, these activities also had their ecclesiastical side.[137]

Colum Cille's earliest biographer, Cumméne Find (Cummeneus Albus), seventh abbot of Iona (657–69), reports that the saint strictly warned Áedán mac Gabráin against breaking this alliance with the Uí Néill, and in fact the arrangement was continued in joint hostility to the Ulaid for many years. In 627 they slew Fiachnae mac Demmáin of Dál Fiatach, nephew of Báetán mac Cairill and ancestor of all subsequent Dál Fiatach kings, who had just gained the over-kingship of Ulster. The Dál Riata suffered defeat, however, two years later in the battle of Fid Eóin at the hands of the Cruthin, where their king Conaid Cerr fell together with two grandsons of Áedán mac Gabráin, and two princes of the Northumbrian kingdom of Bernicia.[138] By this date a shift in Dál Riata policy seems to have taken place, and a reversal of their previous hostility towards the Ulaid. They now joined in alliance with them against the Uí Néill—despite the solemn warning given by Colum Cille to their ancestor Áedán—with disastrous consequences. The great battle of

[136] Ibid.
[137] See Marjorie O. Anderson, 'Columba and other Irish saints in Scotland' in *Hist. Studies*, v (1965), pp 26–36.
[138] See Hermann Moisl, 'The Bernician royal dynasty and the Irish in the seventh century' in *Peritia*, ii (1983), pp 103–26.

Mag Roth (Moira, County Down) in 637, between Domnall mac Áedo meic Ainmirig (the only seventh-century king to be accorded the title *rex Hiberniae* in the Annals of Ulster) and the combined forces of the Cruthin king Congal Clóen and Domnall Brecc of Dál Riata, was to become the stuff of later saga. It marked a turning point for the Ulaid, who had never given up hope of finally overthrowing their Uí Néill enemies and restoring the ancient prestige of the great province of old. The battle of Mag Roth put an end to these grandiose dreams and established the effective supremacy of the Uí Néill in the north—though the Ulaid never formally acknowledged such a position.

Thus the efforts by Báetán mac Cairill and others, to counter the Uí Néill conquests in the north by building up Ulster power beyond the sea, were foiled. A successor as over-king of Ulster, Fiachnae mac Báetáin of Dál Riata, also campaigned in Scotland, and a lost saga recounted the details of his expedition to Dún Guaire (the Irish name for the Northumbrian royal citadel at Bamborough). This may be the event recorded by the Annals of Ulster *s.a.* 623: *expugnatio Ratho Guali*, 'the storming of Ráth Guali'.[139] Fiachna was replaced by a namesake, Fiachnae mac Demmáin of the Dál Fiatach, in 626, who fell himself the following year in the battle of Ard Corann against the Dál Riata. The following years saw a further contraction of Ulaid power, with the occupation of Man by the Northumbrian king Edwin (616–32). There are some indications, however, that the Dál Fiatach retained their hold in Louth as far south as the Boyne even after these setbacks of the early seventh century, where they ruled over the ancient population group of Conailli Muirthemne (perhaps a scattered branch of the Corcu Temne or Temenrige who were also located around Castlebar, County Mayo). This region was the setting for the events of the famous 'Táin Bó Cuailnge' and also boasted a number of important early ecclesiastical sites, including Cill Slébe (Killeevy, County Louth), whose founder Moninne (alias Darerca) is stated by an obscure genealogy to have been daughter of an Ulster king (*rex Oueahulud; lege rex Ua Echach Ulad?*).[140] The foundation preserved an extraordinarily detailed list of its abbesses, which shows that several were of the Conailli. Uarcride ua Osséni, ancestor of the Conailli royal dynasty, is mentioned among the slain at the battle of Imlech Pích (688), which was an episode in an internal feud, not of the Ulaid, but of the southern Uí Néill. Arising from this battle the Ciannachta lost their independence south of the Boyne and fell under the sway of the Síl nÁedo Sláine, while the Conailli were doubtless also squeezed between the Uí Néill and their own northern overlords. The Dál Fiatach genealogies have a number of

---

[139] Byrne, 'Ireland of St Columba', p. 47.
[140] Mario Esposito, 'The sources of Conchubranus's Life of St Monenna' in *E.H.R.*, xxxv (1920), pp 71–8: 75.

curious details concerning the internal rivalries of the different sub-septs during the sixth and seventh centuries, and their impact in the Muirthemne area.[141] The ancestor of the dynasty is named as Muiredach Muinderg, *quem benedixit Patricius, ut alii dicunt, in regnum Hiberniae* ('whom Patrick blessed in the kingship of Ireland, as others say').[142] His descendants had their seat of power at Óchtar Cuillche (or Colland) *i nDruimnib Breg* (Collon, south of Ardee, County Louth). The tract then goes on to say that these divided their inheritance at this spot, at some date in the early sixth century. Dealing with events of the early seventh century the same tract states that Máel Dúin mac Fiachnai was slain by his own brother Dúnchad (d. *c.*644) at Óenach Deiscirt Maige, which was probably in the south of Muirthemne.[143] MacNeill drew from all this that the Dál Fiatach still ruled as overlords in Louth as late as the early eighth century, and that the Conailli first emerged as an independent kingdom following the defeat of Áed Róin mac Beicc Bairrche, a Dál Fiatach king, by the Uí Néill high-king Áed Allán in a battle *in regionibus Murtheimne* (735). The Annals of Ulster record the death in 741 of Amalgaid *rex Conaille* and of his successor Foidmiu mac Fallaig *rex Conaile Muirteimhne* in 752; this latter provided two daughters as abbesses of Killeevy.[144] By the eighth century, therefore, the Conailli Muirthemne were 'of Ulaid but not in it';[145] and in the timeworn fashion the medieval historians produced an 'origin legend' for them that 'explained' how this had come about, projecting these events onto a characteristically mythological plane. The Uí Néill, for their part, recast their traditions in a similar vein, resulting in the story of the Three Collas and their expulsion of the Ulaid eastwards across the Bann, and the vast edifice of the Uí Néill propaganda that sought to place these momentous events in the far distant past. The annals and genealogies tell an altogether different tale, and show quite clearly that the Ulaid were still a force to be reckoned with well into the seventh century (when Congal Clóen, of the Dál nAraidi, even claimed to be king of Tara), and in some parts of their old kingdom even into the eighth.

In 735, as we have seen,[146] the Uí Néill high-king Áed Allán mac Fergaile inflicted a severe defeat on the Ulaid in the battle of Fochairt (Faughart, near Dundalk, County Louth); the Dál Fiatach king Áed Róin and Conchad mac Cuanach of the Uí Echach Cobo were slain. The battle 'determined the political shape of County Louth until the end of the eleventh

[141] Eoin MacNeill, 'Oenach Deiscirt Maige' in *R.S.A.I. Jn.*, lvii (1927), pp 155–8; Byrne, 'Ireland of St Columba', pp 49–50.
[142] O'Brien, *Corpus geneal. Hib.*, p. 408.
[143] Byrne, 'Ireland of St Columba', p. 58, n. 89, points out that a sub-sept of the Conailli were known as Fir Tuaisceirt Maige.
[144] Esposito, 'Life of St Monenna', pp 75–6.
[145] Donnchadh Ó Corráin, 'Irish origin legends and genealogy: recurrent aetiologies' in Hans Bekker Nielsen and others (ed.), *History and heroic tale* (Odense, 1985), pp 51–96: 83.
[146] Above, p. 211.

century'.[147] Áed Allán himself was to meet his end in 743, when he and his allies the Airthir, Uí Cremthainn, and Uí moccu Uais were defeated by the southern Uí Néill claimant to the high-kingship, Domnall Midi mac Murchada. Dál Fiatach fortunes were restored by the reign of Fiachnae mac Áedo Róin (750–89), in which they succeeded in consolidating their power and driving northwards to the shores of Lough Neagh, thus cutting off the Dál nAraidi from their Uí Echach Cobo cousins. The old connection that had existed between Leinster and the monastery of Bangor (County Down) was renewed in his time, and in fact a son of his, Diarmait ua Áedo Róin, founded the monastery of Dísert Diarmata (Castledermot, County Kildare), later to become a centre of the so-called *céli Dé* reform. Fiachnae himself seems to have favoured Bangor, despite its earlier Cruthin connections, perhaps because the traditional Dál Fiatach royal monastery at Downpatrick was coming more and more under the influence of a rival branch of the dynasty. Royal patronage was to be transferred permanently to Bangor at the end of the ninth century, but before then Fiachnae's branch retained control, and a son of his, Loingsech mac Fiachnai, was abbot there at his death in 800.[148]

Between the Ulaid and their perennial enemies the Uí Néill, there lay the buffer kingdoms of the Airgialla and other small tribes. The Uí Tuirtre to the west (who may have been allied to the Dál Fiatach in Báetán mac Cairill's time)[149] were located west of the Bann and south of the Moyola river in the seventh century, to judge from Tírechán's account; he has Patrick crossing the Bann at Toome (*per Doim*) into the Uí Tuirtre territory.[150] Subsequently, however, the kings of Uí Tuirtre displaced the northern Dál nAraidi east of the Bann and north of Lough Neagh, as they themselves were displaced by the encroachment of the Cenél nEógain kings of Ailech. Dál nAraidi power was critically weakened by these developments. The same expansion of the Cenél nEógain also saw them absorb the petty kingdoms of the Airgialla: their nine tribes, the Uí Meic Caírthinn south of Lough Foyle, Uí Fiachrach Arda Sratha (Ardstraw) and the Uí Tuirtre west and east of the Sperrin Mountains (together known as Uí moccu Uais), the Fir Chraíbe and Fir Lí west of the Bann, the Airthir around Armagh, the Uí Cremthainn (earlier 'Cremthainne', which shows the singular form of the collective) in southern and western Monaghan, the Clogher district of County Tyrone, and between there and Lough Erne, and the Uí Meith and Mugdorna of County Monaghan, all now became tributary peoples of the Cenél nEógain. Other lesser and possibly related peoples, such as the Fir Rois, partly in County Monaghan and extending eastwards into Louth as far as Dunleer, and the Fir Cúli (Uí Segáin) in the northern angle of County Meath, who once controlled the

[147] Byrne, *Ir. kings*, p. 118.
[148] Ibid., p. 124.
[149] Above, p. 216.
[150] Tírechán, 'Collectaneum', 50; Bieler, *Patrician texts*, p. 162.

monasteries of Lann Léire (Dunleer) and Druim Ing (Drominn) and who were closely connected with the church of Armagh, were still under the Ulaid kings up to 735, but subsequently succumbed to the advances of the southern Uí Néill kingdoms of Mide and Brega.[151] By 800, therefore, the ancient kingdom of Ulster was a much contracted rump, surrounded on all sides by implacable enemies.

Sources for the early history of Munster are more sparing and less reliable than for Leinster or Ulster, although there are some Munster annals and a small collection of genealogical material. The Eóganachta, the dominant dynasty in Munster until the tenth century, claimed to be descendants of Eógan Már, and their rise to power can be traced back to the fifth century, parallel with (though not related to) the rise of the Uí Néill in the north. As in the case of the Uí Néill, however, the earliest references to the later Eóganachta tribes did not refer to them by that name,[152] and in fact only those lineages that were descended from Conall Corc, legendary founder of their 'capital' Cashel (County Tipperary), were really acknowledged to be 'true' Eóganachta. This excluded such other well-known tribes as the Uí Liatháin and Uí Fidgeinte (sometimes called Eóganacht Ua Liatháin and Eóganacht Ua Fidgeinte) and others such as the Uí Dedaid and Uí Chathbad (the latter allegedly descended from a mythical brother of Corc's, Cathub).[153] In the 'Vita Tripartita' Patrick encounters Ailill mac Cathboth, a son of this Cathub, at Óchtar Cuillend in Uí Cuanach (Cullen, on the Limerick-Tipperary border) and blesses him and his progeny.[154] The identification of the Uí Chathbad in the 'Vita Tripartita' with the Eóganacht Airthir Cliach is quite unhistorical, however, since the latter sept did not exist then; it probably masks an earlier humbler origin.[155]

By the eighth century the Eóganachta had their scattered branches ruling throughout Munster, occupying the best lands and located strategically among probably older tribal kingdoms such as the Múscraige who formed a broad band extending from the north to the south-west of the province. The earlier state of political affairs can be teased out slightly by reference to the traditions concerning those septs which claimed descent from the sons of Corc of Cashel.[156] These were Mac Iair, ancestor of the Uí Meicc Iair; Mac Brócc, ancestor of the Uí Meicc Brócc; Daig, ancestor of the Uí Muiredaig (named after a grandson of Daig); Coirpre, ancestor of Uí Choirpri Luachra—Eóganacht Locha Léin; Mac Cas, ancestor of Uí Echach Muman—Eóganacht Raithlind; and Nad Froích, from whose son Ailill were

---

[151] For the Uí Segáin see Byrne, 'Ireland of St Columba', p. 57, n. 84.
[152] David Sproule, 'Origins of the Eóganachta' in *Ériu*, xxv (1984), pp 31–7: 33.
[153] See Donnchadh Ó Corráin's review of Byrne, *Ir. kings* in *Celtica*, xiii (1980), pp 150–68: 161.
[154] *Trip. life*, ed. Mulchrone, pp 119–21.
[155] Ó Corráin, rev. cit.
[156] Text in O'Brien, *Corpus geneal. Hib.*, pp 195–6.

descended the Uí Éndai Áine—Eóganacht Áine, and from another son, Óengus, the Eóganacht Chaisil, Eóganacht Airthir Chliach, and Eóganacht Glendamnach.

In a remarkable aetiological piece, 'which probably dates in its origins
from the seventh century',[157] the geographical distribution of the various
branches of the Eóganachta is explained in terms of a dream that Aímend,
wife of Conall Corc, experienced on her first night in Cashel: she saw four
pups bathed in liquids, Nad Froích (ancestor of all the eastern Eóganachta)
in wine (the drink of sovereignty); Mac Cas (ancestor of the Eóganacht
Raithlind) in ale (also associated with rule); Mac Brócc in milk; and the
fourth, Mac Iair, in water. A fifth pup, Coirpre (ancestor of the Eóganacht
Locha Léin) entered Aímend's bed 'from outside' (*dianechtair*) and was
washed in blood.[158] The tract is intended to explain how the eastern Eóganachta and, to a lesser degree, the Eóganacht Raithlind were entitled to hold
the kingship of Munster, while the Eóganacht Locha Léin of Killarney, who
ruled the sub-kingdom of Iarmumu or West Munster, are regarded as bloody
intruders. The Uí Maic Iair, Uí Maic Brócc, and Uí Muiredaig all have brief
pedigrees extending down to the eighth century, but almost all trace of their
earlier position has been erased, and the medieval historians emphasised this
loss of political importance by associating their ancestors with milk and
water, rather than the twin drinks of sovereignty, wine and ale. However, as
Donnchadh Ó Corráin pointed out,[159] these were liquids symbolising the
religious life, and in fact the earlier power of these peoples is reflected in the
fact that Suibne mac Máele Umai (d. 682), *princeps* of Cork and the earliest
recorded cleric of that monastery, belonged to the Uí Maic Brócc, as most
probably did his successor, Roisséne (d. 686/7), while the Uí Maic Iair too
provided a number of clerics, including the later hereditary abbots of Cork,
the Uí Selbaig.[160]

The rise of Cork may perhaps have been a counter-balance to the influence of Imblech Ibair (Emly, County Tipperary), whose alternative designation *Medón Mairtine*, 'the centre of the Mairtine', is an echo of a once
important and widely scattered branch of the Érainn[161] who were perhaps
pushed out by the rise of the Eóganachta. The founder Ailbe is classed as
one of the so-called 'pre-Patrician' saints, though the information concerning
him is dubious in the extreme. His successor is numbered among the abbots

[157] Ó Corráin, rev. cit., p. 162.
[158] O'Brien, *Corpus geneal. Hib.*, p. 196.
[159] Ó Corráin, rev. cit., p. 162.
[160] As pointed out by Liam Ó Buachalla, 'Contributions towards the political history of
Munster, 450–800 A.D.' in *Cork Hist. Soc. Jn.*, lvii (1952), pp 67–86: 67, n. 8.
[161] O'Brien, *Corpus geneal. Hib.*, p. 377; in the unpublished genealogies in the Book of
Lecan, 269 (124rb 15 f.), corresponding to O'Brien, ibid., p. 280, they are said to have been
expelled from Leth Cuinn and settled in the territory later known as In Déis Tuaisceirt (and
later still as Dál Cais).

and men of learning called to attend the synod of Mag Léne (*c*.630) in order
to discuss the vexed Easter question.[162] Emly was the seat of historical learning according to the Triads (*Senchas hÉrenn Imblech Ibair*, 'the lore of Ireland
in Emly'), and it is significant that the collection known as the Annals of
Inisfallen is closely connected with that monastery, where in fact our extant
copy was probably written. Emly in fact retained an important place in the
ecclesiastical politics of Munster down to the eighth century and beyond.

   Another old population group later displaced by the Eóganachta were
the Múscraige, settled in various scattered branches across Munster, from
Múscraige Mittine in the valley of the River Lee (Muskerry, west Cork) to the
Múscraige Tíre around Nenagh in the north of County Tipperary. The earliest entry in the annals relating to Munster may refer to one of their kings,
*filius Coerthin filii Coelboth*, who fell at the battle of Femen in 446. The
annalist was clearly at a loss to identify this individual, remarking that 'some
say he was of the Cruthin'. But Ó Buachalla may have been right in seeing
him as Mac Cáirthinn, ancestor of the Múscraige Femen, and the battle may
be a vague memory of a setback to Múscraige fortunes in the fifth century.[163]
The synthetic historians present the Múscraige, Ciarraige, Corcu Baiscind,
Corcu Duibne, and Fir Maige Féne as vassal peoples of the Eóganachta,
connecting them by a genealogical fiction to the dominant dynasty of their
own times, and treating them as fighting men planted by their Eóganacht
overlords. The genealogies, however, claim that the Múscraige Tíre were
blessed by Patrick—a tradition to be found already in the Patrician texts in
the Book of Armagh, and subsequently incorporated into the 'Vita Tripartita'.[164] 'Genealogical fabrication is as common in Munster as elsewhere', as
Donnchadh Ó Corráin has pointed out,[165] and the almost total absence of
early references in the annals to events in Munster makes the task of evaluat-
ing them so much more difficult. Between the notice of the death of Óengus
mac Nad Froích (ancestor of most of the Eóganachta) in the battle of Cenn
Loenada (490) and that of his grandson Coirpre Crom (579/80) the annals are
a complete blank.[166] Coirpre is reported to have defeated Colmán mac Diarmata of the southern Uí Néill in the battle of Femen in 573, an early indication of Uí Néill ambitions in the south. At his death, the Annals of Inisfallen
describe Coirpre as *rí Caisil*, 'king of Cashel', but the title need have no more
than local significance at this time. The next entry of interest is found under
583 in the Chronicon Scotorum: *iugulatio Fergusa Sgandail, righ Mumhan*,

[162] Maura Walsh and Dáibhí Ó Cróinín (ed. and trans.), *Cummian's letter 'De controuersia paschali'* (Toronto, 1988).
[163] See, however, the alternative interpretation of this entry above, p. 191.
[164] For discussion, see Bartholomew Mac Carthy, 'The Tripartite Life: new textual studies' in *R.I.A. Trans.*, xxi (1889), pp 183–205, at pp 186–92; Donnchadh Ó Corráin, 'An chléir agus an léann dúchais annallód: an ginealas' in *Léachtai Cholm Cille*, xvi (1986), pp 71–86: 80–84.
[165] Ó Corráin, rev. cit., p. 161.
[166] For what follows see Ó Buachalla, 'Political history of Munster', pp 74 ff.

'slaying of Fergus mac Scandail, king of Munster'. This Fergus was of the Eóganacht Airthir Chliach, centred around the site of the present Tipperary town, and the violent death implicit in the annal is confirmed by references in the genealogies to an *éric* (fine for homicide) in the form of certain lands (Corcu Ele, Corcu Tened, Corcu Mo-Druad Alta) that were paid as compensation to his people.[167] Further evidence of internecine rivalry between the various branches of the Eóganachta is to be found in the subsequent annalistic notices of Munster kings: 590, Fedlimid mac Tigernaig of the Uí Echach branch of the Eóganacht Raithlind; 619, Fingen mac Áedo of Eóganacht Chaisil; 628, Cathal mac Áedo of Eóganacht Glendamnach; 637, Fáilbe Fland Feimin of the Eóganacht Chaisil. This Failbe had defeated the Connacht king Guaire Aidni in the battle of Carn Feradaig (Cahernarry, County Limerick) in 627/9, and in fact the Eóganacht settled some of their Déisi vassals in south Connacht, while themselves establishing a colony, the Eóganacht Ninussa, in the Burren area of north County Clare; they even established a foothold on the Aran Islands, where Onaght on Inis Mór preserves their name.[168] At 641 the Annals of Inisfallen record the death of Cuan mac Amalgaid of the Eóganacht Áine. Thereafter the succession revolves between the branches of the eastern Eóganachta, principally those of Glendamain and Cashel.

Some information regarding the political geography of west Munster can be gleaned from the tract known as the 'west Munster synod', probably written in its present form during the ninth century, but containing details relating to the earlier period.[169] The gist of the text is that the lesser west Munster peoples claimed independence from their Eóganacht Locha Léin overlord as a result of a 'conference' presided over by Macc Ardae mac Fidaig, king of Ciarraige Luachra, and attended by ecclesiastical representatives of all the west Munster tributary kingdoms. The tract concludes with an enumeration of the services and dues that were to be exchanged between the Ciarraige and the Eóganachta, and claims in fact a 'most favoured nation' status for the Ciarraige. The kingdom of Iarmumu envisaged in the tract was clearly larger than the area west of Sliabh Luachra, the mountains separating Cork, Kerry, and Limerick; it includes the lands of the Corcu Mo-Druad in the Burren region, and the Corcu Baiscind (also in Clare) together with those of the Uí Fidgeinte and their offshoots in County Limerick, in addition to their overlords of the Eóganacht Raithlind. Notable by their absence are the Déis Tuaiscirt or Dál Cais, but their rise to power only began in the mid-eighth century: the Annals of Ulster for 744 record the 'annihilation'

---

[167] Toirdhealbhach Ó Raithbheartaigh (ed.), *Genealogical tracts* (Dublin, 1932), p. 138, § 19 (from the Book of Lecan).

[168] O'Rahilly, *Early Ir. hist.*, p. 223, n. 1; F. J. Byrne, 'Eóganacht Ninussa' in *Éigse*, ix (1958), pp 18–19.

[169] *Z.C.P.*, viii (1912), pp 315–17; discussion in Ó Buachalla, 'Political history of Munster', pp 78–81; Byrne, *Ir. kings*, pp 216–20; Ó Corráin, rev. cit., p. 163.

(*foirddbe*) of the Corcu Mo-Druad by the Déis. Their conquest of 'the rough land of Lugaid' (County Clare) was doubtless facilitated by the weakening of the Eóganacht in those parts and by the eighth-century decline of the south Connacht kingdom of Uí Fiachrach Aidne.[170]

The alliance of the western tributary peoples with the Eóganacht Chaisil proved an insufficient basis, however, on which to build a provincial kingship to rival the power of the Uí Néill. The looseness of the Eóganacht hegemony over Munster has often been remarked,[171] but as Ó Corráin pointed out, the 'synod' shows a remarkable development of kingship among the Eóganacht over-kings and a concentration of power in their hands that belies their apparent weakness.[172] The fatal crack in their make-up appears to have been the emergence in the mid-eighth century of the west Munster Eóganachta as serious rivals to the monopoly of their eastern cousins. The evidence of the annals, together with the 'west Munster synod', suggests that the eastern branches of the Eóganachta were reluctant—to say the least—to admit the claims of their western cousins of Eóganacht Locha Léin ever to be high-kings of all Munster. For a century and a half before that time the over-kingship of Cashel had been the exclusive preserve of the Eóganacht of east Munster, mainly those of Glendamain and Cashel. With the appearance of Máel Dúin mac Áedo Bennáin, however, the tripartite alternation was broken. Prior to his accession the annals record the deaths of Eterscél mac Máele Umai (713–21), who was succeeded by the powerful Cathal mac Finguine (721–42)—the first Munster king to advance any serious claim to the high-kingship of Ireland. Cathussach mac Eterscélai succeeded his father in the Eóganacht Áine kingship, but neither the annals nor the king-lists have any record of him, and his claims to Munster overlordship are therefore dubious. In fact the annals implicitly reveal the real state of affairs when they fail to mention the names of any of the eastern Eóganachta as kings of Munster from the death of Cathal mac Finguine (742) to that of Máel Dúin (786), a period of forty-four years. However, defeat at the hands of the Uí Fidgeinte and the Arada Cliach in 766, and indications of further unrest in the years 793 and 803 (clashes with the Corcu Duibne and the Ciarraige), explain why the greatness of the Eóganacht Locha Léin was shortlived. The last of their line to bear the title *rí Iarmuman* ('king of West Munster') was Cú Chongelt mac Coirpri (d. 791); subsequent kings are merely styled *rí Locha Léin* (though the Annals of Ulster continue the older usage).[173] Máel Dúin was to be the only king of Eóganacht Irluachra to hold the high-kingship of Munster, and the later propagandists did their best to ignore the intrusion by omitting him from the regnal lists.

[170] Byrne, *Ir. kings*, p. 218.
[171] E.g. Donncha Ó Corráin, *Ireland before the Normans* (Dublin, 1972), p. 8.
[172] Ó Corráin, rev. cit., p. 163.
[173] Byrne, *Ir. kings*, p. 218.

Between Máel Dúin and the notice in 793 of the next king of Munster, Artrí mac Cathail of the Eóganacht Glendamnach, there is a curious gap. The Annals of Ulster at 796 mention Ólchobar mac Flaind, *rex Mumhen*, among a list of ecclesiastics who died in that year. He was of the Uí Fidgeinte, his father Flann mac Eircc (d. 763) having been king before him, and his brother Scandlán likewise until his death in 786. It is possible that Ólchobar's reign was a compromise one, and that he retired in favour of Artrí mac Cathail.[174] An alternative explanation offers perhaps a better solution to the problem: the Annals of Ulster may have confused him with one or other of two Eóganacht princes of the same name, Ólchobar mac Duib Indrecht (d. 805), *rígdamna Muman* (royal heir of Munster), or the later Ólchobar mac Cináedo, of the Eóganacht Locha Léin (or Eóganacht Áine), king and abbot of Emly (d. 851).[175]

An early law tract states that *ollam uas rígaib rí Muman*, 'supreme among kings is the king of Munster'. The dictum bespeaks a self-assurance that is reflected to a certain extent also in the annals. The men of Munster seem to have given little thought to events taking place beyond their borders, and do not appear to have set much store by the activities of the Uí Néill until forced to by Uí Néill encroachments on their territories. This perhaps explains the impression that some sources give, that the Munster kings had developed more rapidly in the area of royal power and the direct rule of kings. As early as the seventh century, apparently, the kings of Cashel enjoyed a special legal position as mesne overlords of Munster, and the law tract 'Críth Gablach' (*c*.700?) refers to a king's right of *rechtgae ríg*, 'special ordinance', 'as in the case of the *rechtgae* of the king of Cashel'.[176] The so-called 'west Munster synod' exhibits these over-kings exacting levies from their subject kingdoms, and it may be no coincidence that the earliest text of the 'Mirror of princes' type, the 'De duodecim abusivis' ('On the twelve abuses [*inter alia* of kingship]'), written probably in the mid-seventh century, is probably of Munster provenance.[177] That these rights and dues of Munster over-kings had been more or less formalised at a relatively early date is suggested also by the evidence of the texts called 'Frithfolud ríg Caisil' ('The reciprocal rights and dues of the king of Cashel').[178] These relate in their present form to the political circumstances of the ninth and tenth centuries,

---

[174] Ó Buachalla, 'Political history of Munster', p. 76. Ólchobar's date of death is given as 797 below, ix, 204.

[175] Byrne, *Ir. kings*, p. 213.

[176] D. A. Binchy (ed.), *Crith Gablach* (Dublin, 1941), p. 21, § 38.

[177] The most recent and comprehensive discussion is in Hans Hubert Anton, 'De duodecim...abusivis saeculi und sein Einfluss auf den Kontinent, insbesondere auf die karolingischen Fürstenspiegel' in Löwe, *Die Iren*, ii, 568–617.

[178] J. G. O'Keeffe, 'Frithfolaith Chaisil' in *Ir. texts*, i (1934), pp 19–21. For discussion, see Ó Buachalla, 'Political history of Munster', pp 81–6; Byrne, *Ir. kings*, pp 196–9; and Ó Corráin, rev. cit., pp 162–3.

but one recension appears to depict an earlier state of affairs, in which tribes such as the Uí Liatháin and the Corcu Loígde were more prominent than in subsequent centuries. Though falling short of a strictly 'constitutional' arrangement among the respective kingdoms, the tracts do indicate a greater degree of formal relationship between them than is to be found in any of the other provinces. But despite such superficial unanimity of purpose, the Munster kings were, in fact, unable to stem the rising tide of Uí Néill ambitions in the eighth century. Initial successes in skirmishes against the Uí Néill in the midlands seemed to augur well for Cathal mac Finguine (d. 742) but, though he ranged northwards as far as Tailtiu, he was beaten off and suffered a series of defeats (732, 735) that set him back again. The annals refer to a *dáil* (meeting) between him and the Uí Néill high-king Áed Allán at Terryglass (County Tipperary) in 737, but no details are given of what transpired. The entry immediately following reads 'Lex Patricii tenuit Hiberniam' ('the law of Patrick was enforced throughout Ireland'), and there has been an assumption that the two entries indicate a stand-off between the Uí Néill in the north and the Eóganachta in the south. But any illusions that Cathal mac Finguine may have had were in fact soon to be shattered by the Uí Néill, and not until the reign of Fedelmid mac Crimthainn in the next century did the Munster kingdom establish a serious claim to the high-kingship of Ireland.

If the sources for the early history of Munster are meagre, those for Connacht in the period before 800 are almost non-existent. The genealogies have only fragmentary texts for the Uí Briúin, Uí Fiachrach, Uí Maine, and Uí Ailella, while the evidence for the doings of lesser people such as the Callraige, Delbnae, Gaillenga, Grecraige, Luigne, and Sogain can only be guessed at from the few scattered remarks concerning them in texts that give no context for their activities. The sparsity of information does not, however, mean that Connacht in the early medieval period was a wasteland, cut off from the rest of the country and of no importance for the political developments of the fifth century and beyond. After all, some of the earliest traditions associated with the mission of St Patrick are set in Connacht, and in fact the dossier of texts concerning the saint does preserve early material relating to the province.

Alone among the provinces, however, Connacht lacks any strong tradition of an over-kingship. True, an early law tract, 'Miadslechta' ('Passages concerned with rank'), compares the king of Connacht with the highest rank of poet (*ollam*), and quotes as an example of this usage an archaic line of verse, *Ní hollam nad cóiced nAilello maic Máta móra*, 'he is no ollam who does not magnify the fifth of Ailill mac Máta'.[179] But even the genealogies point out that Ailill was in fact a Leinsterman, whose name 'mac Máta' derived from

---

[179] Cited by Byrne, *Ir. kings*, pp 175–6.

his mother, a Connacht woman who had married into Leinster. Hence Medb
and the Connacht men brought him 'home' to reclaim his *máthre* (inheritance
through the distaff side).[180] There is perhaps some echo of this early Leinster
connection in the fact that the area around Erris (County Mayo) was called
'Irrus Domnann', from the Fir Domnann who occupied it; these may have
been related to the Domnainn, one of the oldest population groups of ancient
Leinster. This may also explain why the earliest traditions relating to the
'Táin' presume a Tara origin for the campaign against Ulster, and why they
depict Medb, Ailill's queen consort, as having been intensely jealous of the
battalion of Leinster Gáileóin that bore the brunt of the fighting. Bishop
Tírechán, in his account of Patrick's mission in Connacht, names no over-
king for that province in the saint's time. This is particularly surprising since
Tírechán was a descendant of Amolngid, whose name survives in *Tír Amoln-
godo* (the barony of Tirawley, County Mayo) and whose sons feature prominently in the account of the saint's activities around 'the plain of Domnann'
(*de campo Domnon*), which was supposedly the location of Patrick's vision.[181]
Tírechán was himself probably a native of these parts, and would have been
thoroughly familiar with the local historical traditions, and those of Cruachu
(Rathcroghan, County Roscommon) to the south-east. Hence it is remarkable
that his account had the daughters of King Lóeguire resident at Cruachu,
implying that Lóeguire, while residing at Tara as 'high-king', was at the
same time king of Connacht.[182] The earliest claimant with any semblance of
historicity would be Dauí Tengae Umai who fell in the battle of Segais (502)
against Muirchertach mac Ercae of the Uí Néill. A later annotator of the
Annals of Ulster styles him *rí Connacht*, and he may possibly have been the
first Uí Briúin king to stake such a claim. However, Tírechán makes no
mention of a Dauí mac Briúin (nor indeed does he figure in the 'Vita Tripartita'). The omission would be strange had Tírechán in fact known of such a
king of Connacht; his narrative merely recalls that Patrick visited Selca, 'a
place where there were the halls of the sons of Brión' (near Tulsk, County
Roscommon), and he left them with his blessing.[183] Tírechán's own affiliations with the Uí Fiachrach may perhaps account for the silence.[184]

It would be rash to treat Tírechán's collection of materials as an accurate
picture of the fifth-century political map of Connacht, but for the seventh
century he is almost the only detailed source for peoples and places in his
own native north Connacht. The Uí Briúin were to emerge by the eighth
century as the most powerful dynasty in the province, but the rival

[180] O'Brien, *Corpus geneal. Hib.*, pp 22–3.
[181] Tírechán, *Collectaneum*, 14; Bieler, *Patrician texts*, pp 134–6.
[182] Tírechán, *Collectaneum*, 26; Bieler, *Patrician texts*, pp 142–4; see MacNeill, *St Patrick*, p.
205; Byrne, *Ir. kings*, p. 232.
[183] Tírechán, *Collectaneum*, 30; Bieler, *Patrician texts*, pp 146–8.
[184] See Byrne, *Ir. kings*, p. 245.

Uí Fiachrach (to which Tírechán belonged) were influential in north Connacht in the seventh century. They ruled in the territory around the estuary of the River Moy, east of Tirawley, in the district called Muiresc Sam—whence the name of Ailill's mother, presumably, and whence the later name *crích Ua Fiachrach la muir* (the coastal territory of Uí Fiachrach), O'Dowd's country of Tireragh (*tír Fhiachrach*) in the later middle ages.[185] The regnal lists claim a king of this line, Máel Cothaid mac Máele Umai, as king of Connacht, though the Annals of Ulster accord him no more exalted title than *rex nepotum Fiachrach*, 'king of Ua Fiachrach', in their notice of the battle of Echros (Augris Head, County Sligo) in 603, when the Uí Fiachrach were defeated by the Cenél Coirpri on the border between Connacht and the lands of the northern Uí Néill. A collateral branch were to acquire the kingship, represented first by Dúnchad Muirisci mac Máelduib (d. 683), 'killed by his own people', according to the regnal list. The same annals record a year previously the death of Cenn Fáelad mac Colggen of the Uí Briúin Seóla and style him *rex Connacht*. He is perhaps the first serious claimant from that dynasty to the over-kingship of Connacht, and his reign marks the beginning of Uí Briúin domination in north Connacht and in the province as a whole. Their emergence coincided with the disappearance of the Uí Ailello; after the eighth century they disappear entirely from the annals and genealogies.

As we noted above, some of the earliest annalistic references to Connacht concern the activities of their kings in the face of Uí Néill encroachment. In the seventh century the fact that the Uí Néill were an offshoot of the Connachta was still clearly recognised, and the oldest texts made a distinction between their ancestral territories, which were formerly in Connacht, and the lands that they acquired by conquest.[186] Hence the area of Cairpre Droma Cliab might be regarded as belonging to the Uí Néill group of lands, since it was ruled by the sept of Coirpre, son of Niall. It was here (around Drumcliff, County Sligo) that the battle of Cúl Dreimne was fought (probably in 561) by the northern Uí Néill, in alliance with Áed mac Echach, the Uí Briúin Aí king of Connacht, against Diarmait mac Cerbaill. The battle is mentioned by Adomnán in his 'Vita Columbae' as having taken place two years before Columba's departure from Ireland.[187] From time immemorial the northern border of Connacht was marked by the River Drowes (*Drobés*), which is north-west of Drumcliff. Tírechán still thinks of the area west of this as Connacht, and in fact in later centuries, when Connacht power was again resurgent and when the expanding Uí Briúin Bréifne had cut off this northern portion of the Cairpre kingdom from its southern half in County Longford, the territory was again claimed for Connacht. But the ties of kinship were still strong enough in the sixth century for the Cairpre to align them-

[185] For this and what follows, see Byrne, *Ir. kings*, pp 238–40.
[186] MacNeill, *St Patrick*, p. 206.
[187] Adomnán, *Vita Columbae*, second preface, and i, 7; Anderson, *Adomnan's Life* pp 186, 224.

selves with their Uí Néill kinsfolk at Cúl Dreime against the king of Connacht.

The best-known Uí Fiachrach king of Connacht, however, was undoubtedly Guaire Aidni mac Colmáin (655–63), later known as Guaire 'of the bounty' (*an Oinigh*). He was the central character in a cycle of saga tales and boasted an impressive array of natural and uterine brothers.[188] The career of Guaire is so thickly encrusted with legend, however, that even the best efforts of modern historians to separate the wheat of truth from the chaff of propaganda have been defeated. There is no doubt, on the other hand, that it was during his reign that the Uí Fiachrach Aidne reached the height of their power in Connacht. Indeed, it has been suggested that their influence may have extended also into north Munster in the early seventh century.[189] This region had been conquered by the Eóganachta probably in the sixth century when they had settled colonists in the Burren and on the Aran Islands,[190] and the emergence towards the end of the eighth century of the Dál Cais in this precise area undoubtedly has more to do with the decline of their Eóganachta masters in Munster, and a parallel decline of the Uí Fiachrach Aidne in south Connacht, than with their own 'conquest' of these lands.

The earliest Uí Briúin claimant to the provincial kingship, however, is Rogallach mac Uatach (622–49), who had been proposed as the true founder of that dynasty's fortunes.[191] On the other hand, the details of his death are redolent of saga, and have been justly described as suspicious.[192] The Annals of Ulster record his violent end (*guin*) and the Annals of Tigernach add that it was at the hands of Máel Brigte mac Mothlachán and the Corcu Cullu (a tributary people of the Ciarraige; the name 'Mothlachán' occurs only in the Ciarraige genealogies).[193] The reference to the Corcu Cullu is found also in a king-list, which states that Rogallach fell in the battle of Corann (704) against the Uí Néill high-king Diarmait mac Áedo Sláine. There is clearly confusion (or deliberate distortion) here, since the high-king involved in the battle of Corann was the northern Uí Néill Loingsech mac Óengusso, who is said by the annals to have fallen at the hands of Cellach mac Rogallaig, king of Uí Briúin Aí. The annalistic account of Corann lists among the slain 'two sons of Colgu' (*duo filii Colgen*), who may perhaps have been two sons of Colgu mac Áedo, king of Uí Briúin Seola, and it may be that they were brothers of the Cenn Fáelad mac Colggen whose violent death is also recorded at 682. The whole sequence is very confused, and the annals have

---

[188] See especially Sean Ó Coileáin, 'The structure of a literary cycle' in *Ériu*, xxv (1974), pp 88–125; Ó Coileáin, 'Some problems of story and history' in *Ériu*, xxxii (1981), pp 115–36.

[189] Ó Corráin, rev. cit., p. 165.

[190] Above, p. 224.

[191] Byrne, *Ir. kings*, p. 239.

[192] The death-tale is in Standish O'Grady, *Silva Gadelica* (2 vols, London, 1892), i, 394–6; for comment, see Ó Corráin, rev. cit., pp 165–6.

[193] See O'Brien, *Corpus geneal. Hib.*, p. 305 (Cland Findchada); Byrne, *Ir. kings*, p. 246.

been interpolated in places with propaganda inspired by the later success of the Uí Briúin; but if the 'two sons of Colgu' were in fact Uí Briúin Seóla princes in alliance with the Uí Néill against their Uí Briúin Aí rivals, there may be some truth in the picture of Cellach mac Rogallaig and Cenn Fáelad mac Colggen's brothers disputing for the over-kingship.[194] However, it is clear that 'the Uí Briúin, whatever the doubts about their early history, had emerged by the closing years of the eighth century not only as the dominant dynasty in Connacht but as a power to be reckoned with in Ireland as a whole'.[195] Indeed, the kingdom of Uí Briúin Bréifne, whose expansion from the eighth century onwards was to drive a fatal wedge between the northern Uí Néill and their southern cousins, was carved out from territory that was not originally reckoned as belonging to Connacht at all (as is clear, for instance, from Tírechán's narrative). Their defeat of the Conmaicne in 766 marked their consolidation east of the Shannon.

The evidence of Tírechán and the genealogies and annals implies that all the northern part of County Leitrim, before its occupation by the Uí Briúin Bréifne, was Calraige territory. The first mention in the Annals of a king of Bréifne is in 792, with the obit of Cormac mac Duib-dá-Chrích, but the Calraige were a much older people, an *aithechthuath* of the Uí Néill who were always regarded as separate from the Connachta. Their own traditions linked them with the related Calraige who had been subsumed into the southern Uí Néill territories in the counties of Longford, around Sliab Calraige (Slieve Golry; cf. Glencolry, County Mayo), and Westmeath; later Uí Néill propaganda, on the other hand, forged a spurious link with their own descent, through a fictitious 'Cal son of Coirpre mac Néill' in the case of the northern branch (simply because they occupied territory in the Uí Néill kingdom of Cairpre Droma Cliab) and through Maine mac Néill in the case of the southern branch (because they were ruled by the Cenél Maine).[196] The Book of Armagh contains a very interesting tract concerning the church of Druim Léas (Drumlease, at the eastern end of Lough Gill, about two miles (3.5 km) north of Dromahair, County Leitrim) which casts valuable light on the early regulation of abbatial succession.[197] It is quite clear from this evidence that the Calraige were still a force to be reckoned with in the seventh century.

Tírechán also makes a brief reference to the Uí Maine, where Patrick allegedly founded the church of Fidarta (Fuerty, County Roscommon). The kingdom must have been very extensive, stretching through all of east Galway and all of County Roscommon bounding on Galway. From an early

---

[194] For a different interpretation, see Ó Corráin, rev. cit., pp 165–6.
[195] Ibid.
[196] Donnchadh Ó Corráin, 'Lugaid Cál and the Callraige' in *Éigse*, xiii (1970), pp 225–6; Byrne, 'Tribes and tribalism', pp 147–8.
[197] Additamenta, vi (4), 9; Bieler, *Patrician texts*, p. 172.

period the kings both of southern Uí Néill Tethbae and of Uí Maine were buried at Clonmacnoise (originally in the territory of Delbna Bethra; the related sept of Delbna Nuadat west of the Shannon were under the rule of the Uí Maine), and from Tírechán's account it is quite clear that Clonmacnoise was an active and successful rival of Armagh in the greater part of Uí Maine territory and throughout south Connacht generally. Tírechán has a vituperative passage about those 'who hate Patrick's territorial jurisdiction' *(paruchia)* and who dispute Armagh's territorial claims in these parts; he was prevented from collecting material there for that reason.[198]

It may well be that the Uí Néill kingdom of Cenél Maine was merely an offshoot of the western Uí Maine that disguised its origins by means of a later forged affinity with the Uí Néill. Such evidence as there is suggests that there had once existed a single over-kingdom of Uí Maine straddling the Shannon, which was only fragmented when the Uí Néill in the sixth century began to emerge as a separate dynasty and carve out new lands for themselves.[199] The parting of the ways between the Uí Néill and the Connachta then led to the total separation of the Uí Maine and the Cenél Maine. The earliest annalistic reference to the Uí Maine in Connacht is at 538, where the battle of Clóenloch (possibly Coole Loch near Gort, County Galway) saw the defeat of Maine mac Cerbaill (a brother of Diarmait mac Cerbaill) while 'contending for the hostages of Uí Maine Connacht'.[200] The annals show that the Uí Fiachrach Aidne (who were victorious) were still dominant in this area. The Uí Néill failed to assert their suzerainty, but the annals make clear that domination of Uí Maine was essential for any successful claimant to the overkingship of Connacht, and the various references to battles, e.g. at Carn Feradaig (627/9) and Airthir Seola (653), mark episodes in the dynastic rivalries between Uí Briúin and Uí Fiachrach kings to control the strategic lands of Uí Maine. Tírechán, in one of his curious episodes, proceeds from the territory of the Uí Maine to Cruachu, heartland of the Uí Briúin Aí, then into the lands of the Grecraige (around Coolavin, County Sligo) and thence into the territories of the Cenél Macc Ercae, where the sons of Mac Ercae are cursed for stealing Patrick's horses. The prophecy is intended to explain how, in Tírechán's time, they had fallen under the sway of other septs, but the later 'Vita Tripartita'—which otherwise follows Tírechán's account closely—says of them that 'the race of Mac Ercae is the mightiest and strongest among the Connachta, but they do not rule like over-kings'. This reflects their later reemergence under the name Uí Briúin Sinna, a subsept of the Uí Briúin Aí.[201]

---

[198] Tírechán, *Collectaneum*, 18; Bieler, *Patrician texts*, p. 138.

[199] Byrne, 'Tribes and tribalism', pp 148–9, and *Ir. kings*, pp 92–3.

[200] See especially John V. Kelleher, 'Uí Maine in the annals and genealogies to 1225' in *Celtica*, ix (1971), pp 61–112.

[201] Byrne, *Ir. kings*, p. 232.

The years from 700 to 723 saw the consolidation of Uí Briúin power in Connacht.[202] The rival Uí Fiachrach supplied only three kings of Connacht in the eighth century, and their former domination was gradually eroded by Uí Briúin inroads into the lands of their lesser subject peoples. The defeat in 704 of Loingsech mac Óengusso, northern Uí Néill king, at the hands of Cellach mac Rogallaig in the battle of Corann marked the turning-point in Uí Briúin fortunes, as indeed it did also for the Cenél Conaill and Loingsech's line.[203] The reign of his successor Indrechtach mac Dúnchado Muirisci of the Uí Fiachrach Muaide (the Moy) (who may have forced Cellach into retirement: he died in 705 *post clericatum*, 'after entering clerical life') was short; he was slain in 707 in a 'return bout' with the Uí Néill—still smarting from their defeat at Corann. The annals call this Indrechtach *rí teora Connacht*, 'king of the three [divisions of] Connacht', apparently the earliest reference to a threefold alternation of kingship among the Uí Briúin, Uí Fiachrach, and Uí Ailello (it may be compared to the term *dux na tri sloinnte* (709), referring to the three divisions of the Luigni).[204] The Uí Briúin, however, as we saw, ousted the Uí Ailello at around this time and eventually occupied the central plains of Connacht from their prehistoric capital at Cruachu.

The reign of Indrechtach mac Muiredaig (707–23) established the Uí Briúin Aí firmly in the ascendant, despite sporadic victories of the rival Uí Ailello against their recalcitrant tributary tribes, the Calraige, Gailenga, Grecraige, and Luigni. The annals record that the Uí Ailello were overthrown (*prostrati sunt*) at the battle of Ard Maicc Rime (792) and they disappear from the record thereafter. The Uí Briúin Aí had doubtless looked on with some satisfaction at the discomfiture of their rivals in clashes among themselves, but their expansion was not without occasional difficulties: Ailill Medraige mac Indrechtaig, of the rival Uí Fiachrach Muaide, defeated them in 758 at Druim Robaig (Dromrovay, County Mayo) in territory ruled by the Fir Chera (formerly the *regiones maicc Ercae* of Tírechán's account). The genealogies state that 'their land was wide, i.e. the territory of Cera, until the sons of Brion took it from them as *éric* for Brión, who fell by Fiachra at the battle of Damchluain'.[205] The site of the battle therefore indicates that it was the Uí Briúin who were on the offensive.[206]

After Ailill Medraige's death in 764 the Uí Briúin regained their hold on the kingship, which thereafter was contested between rival branches of their line. Having established themselves securely in the heartlands of Connacht they turned their attentions next to the Uí Maine in the south-east. Two decades of sustained aggression reduced the Uí Maine and every other potential rival to submission, and by the 780s the final acceptance of the

---

[202] For what follows see ibid., pp 248–53.
[203] See above, p. 211.
[204] O'Rahilly, *Early Ir. hist.*, pp 405–8.
[205] MacNeill, *St Patrick*, p. 201.
[206] Byrne, *Ir. kings*, p. 249.

Uí Briúin as natural heirs to the kingship of Connacht was marked by the visit of Dub-dá-Lethe, abbot of Armagh, to promulgate the Law of Patrick in the province (783). In the closing years of the eighth century Connacht stood on the threshold of becoming a power to be reckoned with in national politics.

# CHAPTER VIII

# The archaeology of early medieval Ireland, *c*.400–1169: settlement and economy

## NANCY EDWARDS

IN contrast with the iron age, the archaeological evidence for early medieval Ireland is rich, plentiful, and varied. It is still possible to trace great numbers of sites, both secular and ecclesiastical, in the landscape, some with substantial upstanding remains. For example, it is estimated that as many as 45,000 ringforts are still identifiable.[1] Only a tiny fraction of the sites known has been sampled by excavation, but where conditions of survival are favourable, notably those caused by waterlogging, it has proved possible to learn an increasing amount about the way in which the early medieval Irish lived, their houses, and a range of other structures, such as souterrains and water-mills. Artefacts from excavations and chance finds, together with environmental evidence, including animal bones and seeds, can shed light upon exploitation of the landscape, the farming economy, and all kinds of craft activity, and can sometimes suggest mechanisms of exchange and trade. Archaeological evidence is therefore playing an increasingly important role in our understanding of early medieval Ireland and can also be used in conjunction with the evidence of other disciplines, not only the documentary sources, but also language and place-name studies, art history, and vegetation history, to build up a broader picture of this formative period between the dawn of Christianity and the Anglo-Norman intervention.

This chapter will begin with a brief consideration of the major developments in the archaeological study of the settlement and economy of early medieval Ireland. It will then focus on the archaeological evidence for settlement, paying particular attention to native secular sites. This will be followed by an examination of what the archaeological evidence reveals about the economy: farming and other exploitation of the landscape, craft, exchange, and trade. Finally, the archaeological evidence will be placed within a

---

[1] Matthew Stout, *The Irish ringfort* (Dublin, 1997), p. 53.

chronological framework in order to trace the evolution of settlement and the economy *c.*400–1169.

THE first breakthroughs in the archaeological study of early medieval Ireland occurred in the 1830s and 1840s, centred on George Petrie and John O'Donovan and their circle. This period saw the earliest recording of many ringforts and ecclesiastical sites by the Ordnance Survey (1830–42) and the acquisition of early Christian metalwork and manuscripts by the Royal Irish Academy.[2] These laid the foundations for the future. Sir William Wilde was the first to recognise the archaeological potential of crannogs, and was responsible for the discovery of Lagore, County Meath, in 1839.[3] Many other crannogs came to light as a result of drainage operations, and the wealth of material from them, both structural and artefactual, was meticulously published by W. G. Wood-Martin in 1886.[4] At the turn of the century T. J. Westropp's surveys of ringforts in western Ireland led to an increasing awareness of their number and variety.[5]

Archaeological excavation first came to the fore during the 1930s and 1940s with the work of Hugh O'Neill Hencken and S. P. Ó Ríordáin. Hencken excavated the stone fort of Cahercommaun, County Clare, and the crannogs at Lagore, Ballinderry 1, County Westmeath, and Ballinderry 2, County Offaly. In the excavation report on Lagore, where an exceedingly rich array of artefacts had been uncovered, Hencken linked the stratigraphy of the site with documentary references to Lough Gabhair in the annals, which identified it as a residence of the kings of southern Brega.[6] This link with the documentary sources was formative in the identification of a characteristic artefactual assemblage approximately datable to the seventh to tenth centuries. This suggested that where similar artefacts were found on other sites they too could be dated to the same period. S. P. Ó Ríordáin excavated several ringforts, including multivallate raths at Garranes and Ballycatteen, County Cork, and a group of sites around Lough Gur, County Limerick.[7]

---

[2] Jeanne Sheehy, *The rediscovery of Ireland's past: the Celtic revival 1830–1930* (London, 1980), pp 17–27; William Stokes, *Life and labours in art and archaeology of George Petrie* (London, 1868); Patricia Byrne, *John O'Donovan (1806–1861) a biography* (Kilkenny, 1987), pp 8–79.

[3] Hugh Hencken, 'Lagore crannog: an Irish royal residence of the 7th to 10th centuries A.D.' in *R.I.A. Proc.*, liii (1950), sect. C, pp. 36–7.

[4] W. G. Wood-Martin, *The lake dwellings of Ireland* (Dublin, 1886).

[5] E.g., T. J. Westropp, 'The ancient forts of Ireland' in *R.I.A. Trans.*, xxxi (1901), pp 579–726.

[6] Hugh Hencken, *Cahercommaun, a stone fort in Co. Clare* (R.S.A.I. special vol., 1938); 'Ballinderry crannog , no. 1' in *R.I.A. Proc.*, xliii (1936), sect. C, pp 103–239; 'Ballinderry crannog, no. 2' in *R.I.A. Proc.*, xlvii (1942), sect. C, pp 1–76; 'Lagore', pp 3–7.

[7] S. P. Ó Ríordáin, 'The excavation of a large earthen ring-fort at Garranes, Co. Cork' in *R.I.A. Proc.*, xlvii (1942), sect. C, pp 77–150; and P. J. Harnett, 'The excavation at Ballycatteen fort, Co. Cork' in *R.I.A. Proc.*, xlix (1943), sect. C, pp 1–43; 'Lough Gur excavations; Carraig Aille and the "Spectacles"' in *R.I.A. Proc.*, lii (1949), sect. C, pp 39–111.

During the 1950s and 1960s a programme of exploratory excavation of settlement sites was initiated in the north. This included several very ordinary ringforts, revealing much about their typology. In the 1970s and 1980s excavation continued to be focused in the north with a number of significant rescue digs, including raised raths at Rathmullan, County Down, and Deer Park Farms, County Antrim.[8] In the south rescue excavation (apart from urban contexts, notably viking Dublin) has, till recently, played a less significant role, and research excavations have continued to be of greater significance: for example, the early medieval settlements at Knowth and Moynagh Lough crannog, County Meath, and the raths Lisleagh 1 and 2, County Cork.[9]

Since the 1960s improvements in techniques, particularly the introduction of area excavations and the ability to cope with complex waterlogged sites, have greatly enhanced our understanding of the archaeological evidence. During the same period, developments in science have revolutionised archaeology. Radiocarbon dating, though not used extensively in Ireland till the 1970s, made it possible to confirm the broad dating of ringforts and crannogs to the early medieval period, as suggested by Hencken's dating of the artefacts at Lagore. However, the pioneering development of dendrochronology in Ireland during the 1970s and 1980s has been of greater importance, because it has enabled the precise dating of waterlogged sites incorporating large oak timbers.[10] Other significant scientific advances have been made in environmental archaeology, especially in their application to waterlogged sites. The study of animal bones has greatly increased our understanding of animal husbandry in early medieval Ireland, while research on insect remains can tell us about living conditions and disease. Investigation of plant remains, such as pollen and seeds, has revealed an increasing amount about land clearance, crops, and their processing, thereby revealing evidence for diet. The scientific study of artefacts and their manufacturing debris also has the potential to tell us more about early technology.

The importance of air photography for revealing, not just sites and their contexts, but complete archaeological landscapes, was first recognised in Ireland in the 1950s and 1960s[11] and continues to play a major role. Indeed, the

[8] Archaeological Survey of Northern Ireland, *An archaeological survey of County Down* (Belfast, 1966); C. J. Lynn, 'The excavation of Rathmullan, a raised rath and motte in Co. Down' in *U.J.A.*, xliv–xlv (1981–2), pp 65–171; 'Deer Park Farms' in *Current Archaeology*, cxiii (1989), pp 193–8.

[9] George Eogan, 'The iron age—early Christian settlement at Knowth, Co. Meath, Ireland' in Vladimir Markotic (ed.), *Ancient Europe and the Mediterranean: studies presented in honour of Hugh Hencken* (Warminster, 1977), pp 69–76; John Bradley, 'Excavations at Moynagh Lough, County Meath' in *R.S.A.I. Jn.*, cxxi (1991), pp 5–26; Mick Monk, 'A tale of two ringforts: Lisleagh I and II' in *Cork Hist. Soc. Jn.*, c (1995), pp 105–16.

[10] M. G. L. Baillie, *Tree-ring dating and archaeology* (London and Canberra, 1982), pp 175–96; *A slice through time* (London, 1995), pp 58–62, 70–2.

[11] E. R. Norman and J. K. S. St Joseph, *The early development of Irish society: the evidence of aerial photography* (Cambridge, 1969).

value of archaeological survey for extending our understanding of the numbers, context, distribution, and typology of early medieval sites such as ringforts, as well as aiding their conservation, is clearly evident. The publication of *An archaeological survey of County Down* in 1966 was ground-breaking, and in the 1980s and 1990s a considerable number of archaeological inventories and surveys have been completed in the Republic.[12] Computer databases, in the form of sites and monuments records, are now playing an expanding role.

Therefore, over the last half-century, there has been a dramatic increase in our knowledge and understanding of early medieval Ireland as a result of an expanding archaeological database. There has also been recent recognition of how the modern history of Ireland has affected the interpretation of this data in the past.[13]

The settlement pattern of early medieval Ireland, apart from some of the larger monastic sites and the intrusive viking towns (see pp 814–41), was entirely dispersed and rural and largely dependent upon a farming economy. Therefore settlement distribution is bound to have been affected by the availability of suitable land for grazing and tillage and other natural resources. Details of the form and evolution of settlement types are also likely to have varied from region to region, and the choice of building materials would likewise have been affected by the environment. While hazel for wattles would have been plentiful in most areas, dendrochronological evidence suggests a dwindling supply of mature oak timbers available for construction.[14] In rockier environments, such as Donegal and Kerry, drystone structures are a characteristic feature, but in Down such structures are largely limited to the slopes of the Mournes and in Meath, apart from souterrains, they are rare.

Ringforts (pls 5, 6, 8) are enclosed homesteads predominantly associated with a farming economy. They are by far the most characteristic early medieval Irish settlement type; indeed, they are the commonest archaeological field monuments in Ireland.[15] The term 'ringfort' is not entirely satisfactory; they are not forts in the military sense. Nevertheless it is a useful term, because it encompasses a variety of very broadly contemporary enclosed

[12] *Archaeological survey, County Down*; the most useful other surveys are: Brian Lacy, *Archaeological survey of County Donegal* (Lifford, 1983); G. T. Stout, *Archaeological survey of the barony of Ikerrin* (Roscrea, 1984); Judith Cuppage, *Archaeological survey of the Dingle Peninsula* (Ballyferriter, 1986); V. M. Buckley and P. D. Sweetman, *Archaeological survey of County Louth* (Dublin, 1991); Caroline Toal, *North Kerry archaeological survey* (Dingle, 1995); Ann O'Sullivan and John Sheehan, *The Iveragh Peninsula: an archaeological survey of South Kerry* (Cork, 1996).

[13] Jerry O'Sullivan, 'Nationalists, archaeologists and the myth of the Golden Age' in Michael A. Monk and John Sheehan (ed.), *Early medieval Munster: archaeology, history and society* (Cork, 1998), pp 178–89.

[14] Baillie, *Slice through time*, pp 125–7.

[15] S. P. Ó Ríordáin, *Antiquities of the Irish countryside* (5th ed., London, 1979), p. 29.

homestead sites which otherwise vary in size, complexity, and construction materials. Place-names and references in the documentary sources indicate some of these differences. The term *ráth* refers to a ringfort with one or more enclosing earth banks and *líos* to the enclosed space within. *Caiseal* and *cathair* are regional terms for a stone-walled ringfort. However, *dún* implies a site of some importance, such as Duneight, County Antrim, but does not only refer to ringforts: the bronze-age stone fort of Dún Aonghusa on Inis Mór and the viking town of Dublin are both termed *dún*.[16]

Ringforts are found throughout Ireland, but in some areas they are more densely distributed than in others. The highest density has been identified in Counties Sligo, north Roscommon, and north-east Mayo, an area where little research or excavation of ringforts has been conducted. Ringforts are generally found in areas with good-quality soils; the shortage of hospitable farmland therefore accounts for low densities in County Donegal and west County Mayo. However, the comparatively low densities found in much of south-east Ireland, areas of predominantly fertile farmland, are more difficult to understand.[17] It is likely, however, that farming, and particularly agriculture, which is concentrated in this area, has caused widespread destruction, perhaps compounded by the fact that this was also the area of most intensive Anglo-Norman settlement.

In contrast with many ecclesiastical sites, which hug the river valleys, ringforts are generally sited on slightly higher ground. The summits and slopes of small hills and drumlins, which provided a good view of the surrounding countryside, were especially favoured, but higher altitudes were avoided because of their unsuitability for farming.[18] For example, in the barony of Ikerrin, County Tipperary, 76 per cent of ringforts are sited between 91.5 m (300 ft) and 214.5 m (700 ft); on the Iveragh peninsula, County Kerry, 93 per cent are located below the 152 m (500 ft) contour, and in Counties Down and Louth only a handful are found above 183 m (600 ft).[19] Those at higher altitudes are more likely to be stone-built.

The defining feature of the ringfort is its enclosure. The most common type is the univallate earthen ringfort or rath. This consists of an area enclosed by a circular, oval, or pear-shaped bank with an outer ditch and sometimes traces of a counterscarp bank. The size of the area enclosed normally ranges between 15 m and 35 m (50 ft and 115 ft) in diameter, and there is a distinct cluster around the 30 m (100 ft) mark. A typical example is Killyliss, County Tyrone (fig. 17 A), the central area of which is approximately 30 m

[16] M. J. O'Kelly, 'Problems of Irish ring-forts' in Donald Moore (ed.), *The Irish Sea Province in archaeology and history* (Cardiff, 1970), pp 50–51; D. M. Waterman, 'Excavations at Duneight, Co. Down' in *U.J.A.*, xxvi (1963), pp 76–7; see P. F. Wallace, below, p. 817.

[17] Stout, *Irish ringfort*, pp 48–109.

[18] Ibid., pp 100, 106–7.

[19] Stout, *Ikerrin*, p. 29; O'Sullivan & Sheehan, *Iveragh Peninsula*, p. 136; *County Down*, fig. 72.1; Buckley & Sweetman, *County Louth*, fig. 153.

(100 ft) in diameter and surrounded by an earthen bank and outer ditch with traces of a counterscarp bank.[20] Bivallate earthen ringforts—those with two substantial banks with a ditch between them and sometimes a second, outer ditch—are much less common. In the adjacent baronies of Ikerrin, County Tipperary, and Clonlisk, County Offaly, they form 19 per cent of the total, and 24 per cent of the total on the Iveragh peninsula, County Kerry.[21] Some bivallate raths have internal diameters no larger than the average univallate example, but in many instances the area enclosed is more than 35 m (115 ft) in diameter and can rise to 50 m (165 ft) or more. Lisnageeha (Ballycrine 5), County Tipperary, is a characteristic example (fig. 17 B) with two banks and an intervening ditch enclosing a circular area 31 m (102 ft) in diameter. Lisnarahardin, Reenboy, County Kerry, is similar but larger, with a diameter of 43.5 m (143 ft), and is sited to take advantage of the natural topography so the interior is slightly raised.[22] Trivallate earthen ringforts are comparatively rare: for example, there are only two recorded from County Louth.[23] Again, some have interior diameters no larger than univallate raths: for example, Lisnagallaun, Shanacloon, County Kerry, before destruction measured only 30 m (100 ft) in diameter, but Rathdrumin, County Louth, is more typical with an internal diameter of 52 m (171 ft). Garranes, County Cork (fig. 17 C), is particularly impressive with an internal diameter of 67 m (220 ft).[24]

Raised and platform raths are further variations. These are more difficult to categorise without excavation, but in the north-west midlands they have been identified as representing 13 per cent of the total, and in County Louth 15 per cent. However, none has been recognised in south Donegal, probably because the topography is unsuitable.[25] Excavation has demonstrated that with a raised rath the interior has been heightened artificially, often in several stages over a period of prolonged occupation, so in the end the interior has the appearance of a flattish-topped mound. The summit, which is sometimes approached via a ramp, may be surrounded by a bank or a stone wall. There is a ditch round the base of the mound and sometimes further banks and ditches outside. Partial excavation of Rathmullan, County Down (fig. 17 D), revealed that in phase 1 it was a conventional univallate ringfort which, before the construction of phase 2, had been artificially built up by dumping

[20] Richard Ivens, 'Killyliss Rath, County Tyrone' in *U.J.A.*, xlvii (1984), p. 9.

[21] Matthew Stout, 'Ringforts in the south-west midlands of Ireland' in *R.I.A. Proc.*, xci (1991), sect. C, pp 207–10; O'Sullivan & Sheehan, *Iveragh Peninsula*, p. 135.

[22] Stout, *Ikerrin*, p. 35; Cuppage, *Dingle Peninsula*, pp 181–2, fig. 107.

[23] Buckley & Sweetman, *County Louth*, pp 182–3, fig. 154.

[24] O'Sullivan & Sheehan, *Iveragh Peninsula*, pp 204–5; Buckley & Sweetman, *County Louth*, p. 182, pl. 81; Ó Ríordáin, 'Garranes', p. 79.

[25] Stout, *Ikerrin*, p. 26; Buckley & Sweetman, *County Louth*, p. 152; G. F. Barrett, 'A field survey and morphological study of ring-forts in southern Co. Donegal' in *U.J.A.*, xliii (1980), p. 43.

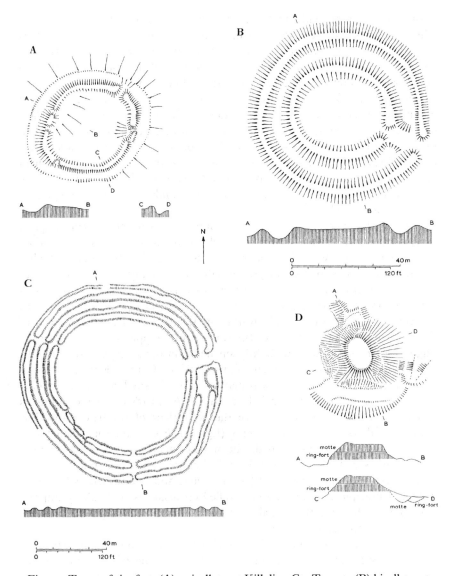

Fig. 17 Types of ringfort: (A) univallate, at Killyliss, Co. Tyrone; (B) bivallate, at Lisnageeha, Co. Tipperary; (C) multivallate, at Garranes, Co. Cork; and (D) raised, at Rathmullan, Co. Down. After Edwards, *Archaeology early med. Ire.*

0.6 m (2 ft) of earth, with further gradual build-up during phases 3 and 4.[26] The raised rath at Deer Park Farms, County Antrim, survived as a flat-topped mound approximately 25 m (82 ft) in diameter and 6 m (20 ft) high. On excavation it was found to consist of a gradual build-up of occupation debris with several phases of rebuilding; the lower levels were waterlogged. In contrast, at Big Glebe, County Londonderry, a substantial artificial mound had been constructed with a ramp to give access prior to the earliest phase of occupation. In the case of platform raths, a natural hillock is utilised to provide the raised interior. At Gransha, County Down, for example, a low bank and external ditch were constructed around the lower slopes of a small gravel ridge about 4.5 m (14 ft 9 in) high.[27] At Knowth, the mound of the main neolithic passage grave was utilised in a similar way by the digging of two concentric ditches.[28]

Stone-walled ringforts or cashels are similar to their earthen counterparts except that instead of banks they are enclosed by drystone walls and seldom have ditches. Because of the topography, cashels tend to be found in higher numbers in the west of Ireland. About half the surviving ringforts in County Donegal are cashels; in County Kerry, cashels on the Iveragh peninsula represent about 38 per cent of the total, but on the Dingle peninsula only 19 per cent. However they barely feature in the flatter rolling landscapes of County Louth and the barony of Ikerrin, County Tipperary.[29] Those with a single wall enclosing an area slightly smaller than the average univallate rath are the most common. Cahergal, Kimego West, County Kerry, a typical well-preserved and recently excavated example, is sited on the crest of a slight ridge and has an internal diameter of 26.2 m (89 ft). Some examples also have outer enclosures and are the equivalent of bivallate raths. For example, Cahersavane, County Kerry (fig. 18), has an internal diameter of only 23 m (75 ft 6 in), but outside the walled enclosure and separated by a wide berm is a ditch and outer bank.[30] Cahercommaun, County Clare, is slightly larger, about 30 m (100 ft) in diameter, and is unusually sited over-looking a precipice. Its main, stone-walled enclosure is particularly impressive, but it also has the remains of two outer, much slighter, drystone enclosures on the landward side.[31]

To what extent are ringforts defensive? The siting of most so as to provide a good view resulted in some protection both for the inhabitants, and for their cattle and crops in the surrounding countryside. This would have been

[26] Lynn, 'Rathmullan', p. 78, fig. 3.
[27] Ann Hamlin and Chris Lynn (ed.), *Pieces of the past* (Belfast, 1988), pp 38–47.
[28] Eogan, 'Knowth', pp 69–70, fig. 1.
[29] Lacy, *County Donegal*, pp 119–54; O'Sullivan & Sheehan, *Iveragh Peninsula*, p. 135; Cuppage, *Dingle Peninsula*, p. 99; Buckley & Sweetman, *County Louth*, pp 152–87; Stout, *Ikerrin*, pp 26–82.
[30] O'Sullivan & Sheehan, *Iveragh Peninsula*, pp 173–4, 187–9, figs 119, 124, pls 50, 54, XIb.
[31] Hencken, *Cahercommaun*, pp 5–7, pls II–III.

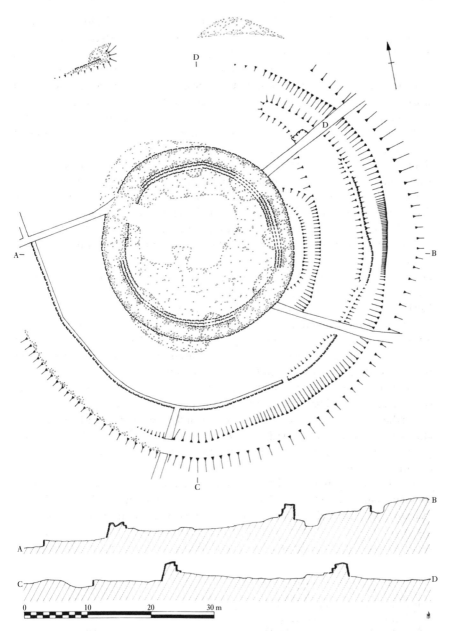

Fig. 18 Plan of a cashel at Cahersavane, Co. Kerry (after A. O'Sullivan and
J. Sheehan, *Archaeological survey of the Iveragh peninsula* (Cork, 1996)), by kind
permission of the Cork University Press.

enhanced by the fact that ringforts are often intervisible.[32] However, some, such as Lisleagh 1 and 2, County Cork,[33] are also overlooked by higher ground, which would have rendered them defenceless in a more prolonged attack. Strategic siting is rare and is only likely to have been a factor in the most important sites. For example, Garranes, a probable royal site associated with the Uí Eachach, is located with reference to the route across the hills connecting the Bandon valley with those of the Bride and the Lee.[34]

The banks of earthen ringforts were primarily constructed out of upcast from the ditches. At Killyliss, for example, a typical univallate rath, the dumped earth bank survived to the height of approximatly 1 m (3 ft 3 in), while the flat-bottomed ditch was approximately 2.4 m (8 ft) wide and up to 1.6 m (5 ft 3 in) deep. The ditch was waterlogged, and wattle fragments were discovered which were interpreted as a lining to prevent the sides of the ditch from slipping.[35] Internal and external timber revetments to consolidate the dump construction and prevent the bank from slipping into the ditch would probably have been relatively common, though usually the only evidence is a slot or row of postholes along the base of the bank. Stone revetments are also commonly found, as, for example, at Garryduff 1, County Cork.[36] The heightening of the bank with a hedge or fence along the top was probably also a characteristic feature, thereby making it more imposing. At Killyliss part of a fence of split-oak posts and wattles had fallen into the ditch and was therefore preserved, while at Lisleagh 1 evidence of a trench-set palisade with uprights *c*.80 mm (3.25 in) in diameter was found on the crown of the bank; it was also noted that the earth on the interior side was heavily compacted by walking,[37] which implies the need for a look-out.

Earthen ringfort entrances usually face roughly eastwards, with slight variations to north or south, with a causeway across the ditch and an entrance passage through the bank which would have been closed by one or occasionally more wooden gates.[38]

The lack of a ditch round many stone-walled ringforts is compensated for by a substantial drystone wall with masonry façades and a rubble infill. For example, at Cahergal the wall is 5.5 m (18 ft) wide at the base, tapering to 3.5 m (11 ft 6 in) at the top, and is up to 4 m (13 ft) high. On the internal face there are two terraces linked by several flights of steps, again allowing for

---

[32]   Stout, *Irish ringfort*, fig. 1.
[33]   Monk, 'A tale of two ringforts', p. 114.
[34]   Ó Ríordáin, 'Garranes', pp 77–8, 145–50.
[35]   Ivens, 'Killyliss', pp 15–22, 31.
[36]   Nancy Edwards, *The archaeology of early medieval Ireland* (London, 1990), p. 20; M. J. O'Kelly, 'The excavation of two earthen ringforts at Garryduff, Co. Cork' in *R.I.A. Proc.*, lxiii (1963), sect. C, pp 18–20, 22.
[37]   Ivens, 'Killyliss', pp 20–21, 31–2; Mick Monk, 'Excavations at Lisleagh ringfort, north County Cork' in *Archaeology Ireland*, ii, no. 2 (summer 1988), p. 58.
[38]   Edwards, *Archaeology early med. Ire.*, pp 21–2.

surveillance of the surrounding country. The entrance passage has two portal slabs projecting from the sides, indicating the position of the gate.[39]

The primary aim of these enclosures was to impress, and such an obvious outward expression of status is in keeping with the hierarchical structure of early medieval Irish society depicted in law texts such as 'Críth Gablach'.[40] The upper echelons of society, as for example at Garranes, would therefore have required more impressive enclosures to express their higher status and as an indication of their power over their clients and the subservient work-force who constructed them, as well as to protect their greater wealth. But the imposing appearance of these enclosed homesteads would also have served as a deterrent to would-be marauders and cattle-thieves, although they would not have been able to withstand a concerted attack.

Improvements in archaeological excavation mean we now know much more about the internal structures of ringforts than twenty-five years ago. In earthen ringforts wood was the usual building material and the earliest houses were round. At Deer Park Farms, evidence for about forty round houses between 4.7 m (15 ft 5 in) and 7 m (23 ft) in diameter was uncovered (pl. 7) in the gradual build-up of the raised rath. The lower levels were waterlogged, revealing a wealth of information about how they were constructed, their internal layout and functions. One phase of late seventh- or early eighth-century date was particularly well preserved. The main house was located towards the centre of the ringfort. It consisted of two conjoined round houses, with the doorway of the larger facing east towards the ringfort entrance. There was a similar figure-of-eight structure to the north-west and a single round house to the south-west, both approached by paths from the entrance. The round house walls were built of two concentric rings of hazel wattles with an insulating layer of straw, moss, grass, and heather between them. The inner wall was strongly constructed by driving over 100 uprights c.1 m (3 ft 3 in) high into the ground. Horizontals were then tightly woven between the uprights using a spiralling basketry technique. New verticals were driven into the walling once the tops of the first uprights were reached, and the horizontal wattling continued to the required level, in one case almost 3 m (10 ft) high. Construction of the outer wall, which was similar but less sturdy, began after the inner wall had commenced. There is no evidence of daub, but one house had a thatch of reeds woven into the wattle walling. The roof structure is still not well understood—it may simply have been an extension of the wattle walls which gradually bent inwards towards the centre—but it is more likely that the wattles that made up the framework of the roof were mounted on the tops of the walls, which would have been strong enough to withstand the full weight of the roof. The roof would have

[39] O'Sullivan & Sheehan, *Iveragh Peninsula*, pp 187–9, fig. 124, pl. XIb.
[40] Eoin MacNeill, 'Ancient Irish law: the law of status and franchise' in *R.I.A. Proc.*, xxxvi (1923), sect. C, pp 265–311.

been completed by weaving in further horizontal wattles and covering the structure with a thatch of reeds or straw.[41] The substantial oak door-frame from the main house survived and was dated by dendrochronology to A.D. 648, but high-precision radiocarbon dates from the wattles suggest the house was constructed sometime after A.D. 670, and therefore the timbers of the door frame had been reused.[42] Inside the house was a central stone-kerbed hearth, and against the walls were two curved brushwood platforms covered with plant material which functioned as beds and seating. The inner round house had a central hearth and a trough but no platforms. Humic silt from another house contained insects, a fact that suggested that the floor had been strewn with damp or waterside vegetation; the inhabitants suffered from both human fleas and lice, and domestic animal lice were also present.[43]

The discoveries at Deer Park Farms allow us to make considerably more sense of the structures found on sites that were not waterlogged. At Garranes, the original excavators recovered post-holes but no coherent house plans. In recent excavations, however, the burnt walls of a round house were uncovered.[44] At Dressogagh rath, County Armagh (fig. 19 A), two conjoined round houses were excavated, and more than one phase may be represented. The larger house was delineated by two concentric slots indicating post-and-wattle walling and beyond were two drip gullies; the smaller structure had no traces of walling, simply a curvilinear drip gully.[45] At Lisleagh 1 several phases of round houses were excavated and some had annexes added at a later date to form the characteristic figure-of-eight plans. A variety of construction techniques were used including single and double wattle-walling, denoted by stake-holes. One structure subject to subsidence was first rebuilt using more substantial rectangular and semi-circular uprights set into a trench, and finally with timber uprights morticed into sill beams with an outer wattle wall. Four large post-holes indicated that the roof had been supported by substantial posts.[46]

The excavated evidence also clarifies the descriptions of houses in 'Críth Gablach' and identifies them as round. *Aircha* ('back house') may well refer

[41] Lynn, 'Deer Park Farms'; C. J. Lynn and J. A. McDowell, 'A note on the excavation of an early Christian period settlement in Deer Park Farms, Glenarm, 1984–1987' in *The Glynns*, xvi (1988), pp 8–9, 11–16. For a reconstruction of a round house with the roof resting on the walls see Lynn, 'Rathmullan', p. 84, pl. 4.

[42] Baillie, *Slice through time*, pp 71–2.

[43] H. K. Kenward and E. P. Allison, 'A preliminary view of the insect assemblages from the early Christian rath site at Deer Park Farms, Northern Ireland' in James Rackham (ed.), *Environment and economy in Anglo-Saxon England* (Council for British Archaeology, Research Report 89, 1994), pp 93–6.

[44] Ó Ríordáin, 'Garranes', p. 84; M. G. O'Donnell, 'Lisnacaheragh, Garranes' in Isabel Bennett (ed.), *Excavations 1991*, p. 6.

[45] A. E. P. Collins, 'Excavations at Dressogagh rath, Co. Armagh' in *U.J.A.*, xxix (1966), pp 119–22, fig. 3.

[46] Monk, 'Lisleagh ringfort', pp 57–60.

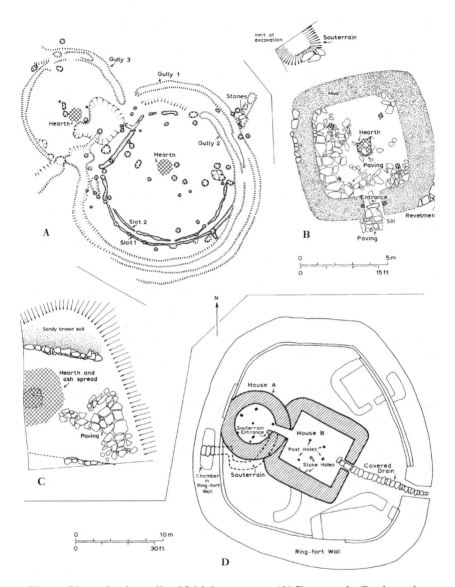

Fig. 19 Plans of early medieval Irish house-types. (A) Dressogagh, Co. Armagh;
(B) Whitefort, Co. Down; (C) Rathmullan, Co. Down; (D) Lecanbuile, Co. Cork.
After Edwards, *Archaeology early med. Ire.*

to the smaller component of the figure-of-eight house, while *imdai* is used to describe the bed platforms.[47]

The buildings associated with cashels are also characteristically round and of a similar size to those in raths, but are usually constructed of stone. They are therefore much more likely to be preserved than their wattle counterparts, though there has been comparatively little excavation of them. Sometimes there is a single central round house, as at Cahergall, or a figure-of-eight structure, as at Cathair Fionnúrach, Ballynavenooragh, County Kerry (pl. 10), but several round houses are not uncommon: at Caherdorgan North, County Kerry, there are six altogether, with four conjoined.[48] Many of these structures probably underwent a series of alterations and rebuildings, but without meticulous excavation these are difficult to detect. Such drystone round houses are frequently termed *clocháns*. Sometimes they have a broader kerb of stones at the base and slabs projecting from the walls, suggesting the former presence of an external layer of stacked turves to keep out the wind. Many round houses incorporate corbelling, including stone roofs. As an alternative the roofs were constructed of poles which rested on or slotted into the tops of the walls, perhaps with a framework of woven wattles which was then thatched or even covered with turves. Excavation, as at Cahergall and Cathair Fionnúrach, is now beginning to reveal the internal arrangements of these houses including central hearths and very large numbers of stake-holes which indicate the presence of bed platforms and possibly wattle partitions.[49]

Excavation of the raised rath at Rathmullan, County Down, uncovered four successive layers of occupation, the first two with wattle round houses, the third and fourth with rectangular buildings (fig. 19 C).[50] This resulted in the realisation that around the ninth century, on the basis of artefactual dating, round houses were being replaced by rectangular ones. The cause of this is unclear, though the influence of church buildings may well have played a part.[51] This change has also been recognised on a significant number of other sites elsewhere in Ireland, for example Carraig Aille 2, County Limerick, and Leacanabuaile, County Kerry (fig. 19 D).[52]

We know much less about rectangular houses built of wood compared with round ones because fewer have been excavated and none has been

---

[47] C. J. Lynn, 'Houses in rural Ireland, A.D. 500–1000' in *U.J.A.*, lvii (1994), pp 82, 87–8; McNeill, 'Ancient Irish law', paras 79, 87, 90.

[48] O'Sullivan & Sheehan, *Iveragh Peninsula*, p. 189, fig. 124, pl. 54; Cuppage, *Dingle Peninsula*, pp 192, 195, figs 113, 116, pl. VIIIb.

[49] Erin Gibbons, personal communication; 'Cathair Fionnúrach, Ballnavenoragh' in Isabel Bennett (ed.), *Excavations 1994*, pp 42–3.

[50] Lynn, 'Rathmullan', pp 71–95, figs 4, 5, 7, 11.

[51] C. J. Lynn, 'Early Christian Period domestic structures: a change from round to rectangular plans?' in *Irish Archaeological Research Forum*, v (1978), pp 37–8.

[52] Ó Ríordáin, 'Lough Gur excavations', pp 44–7, pl. 1; O'Sullivan & Sheehan, *Iveragh Peninsula*, pp 184–7, fig. 122.

preserved by waterlogging. However, the house excavated at Whitefort cashel, Drumaroad, County Down, is a particularly good example (fig. 19 B). In its second phase it consisted of a stone revetted platform on top of which had been built a thick mud-walled structure *c*.8 m (26 ft) square. The interior of the building was delineated by paving, as was the entrance, and two post-holes showed the position of the door.[53] It is difficult to speculate on the superstructure, but it seems likely that the low mud walls would have sup-ported a timber structure, most likely incorporating morticed sill beams and planks, although the use of wattles is also possible. At Carraig Aille 2 there were rectangular buildings indicated by paving and low stone walls,[54] very likely the foundations for sill beams, which would have been less likely to rot, thus creating more permanent structures.

In County Kerry the change from round to rectangular buildings is less clear, and both types appear to have been in use contemporaneously. Recent excavations at Loher fort revealed a circular drystone house and a rectangular drystone building which had been constructed at a later date, overlying a wattle round house. The walls of the rectangular building, which measured 7.55 m × 6.3 m (24 ft 9 in × 20 ft 8 in) internally, survived to a height of 1.2 m (3 ft 11 in) and had been constructed with an inner and outer façade and a rubble infill.[55]

SOUTERRAINS in the form of underground or semi-subterranean passages and chambers are a characteristic feature of the later phases of ringfort occu-pation. At Rathmullan (fig. 20 A), for example, the souterrain is associated with the rectangular house in phase 3,[56] and in north-east Ireland they are generally associated with rectangular buildings. However, in County Kerry they are also associated with round houses, though at Loher the souterrain was clearly later than the round house.

Souterrains are not confined to ringforts and are found on a variety of other secular and ecclesiastical settlements all over Ireland. However, there are notable concentrations, for example west of Dundalk, County Louth,[57] and County Cork, but these clusters may be misleading since construction techniques vary with the regional geology and some types leave behind more evidence than others. In much of the north the technique employed was to dig an open trench in the ground, or in the bank or make-up of a ringfort, revet the sides with drystone walling, and then place lintels over the passage to form a roof which was then hidden by a covering of earth. The

[53] D. M. Waterman, 'The excavation of a house and souterrain at Whitefort, Drumaroad, Co. Antrim' in *U.J.A.*, xix (1956), pp 76–83.

[54] Ó Ríordáin, 'Lough Gur excavations', pp 45–52, pl. 1.

[55] O'Sullivan & Sheehan, *Iveragh Peninsula*, pp 191–2, pl. 55.

[56] Lynn, 'Rathmullan', pp 86–91.

[57] Buckley & Sweetman, *County Louth*, pp 100–50.

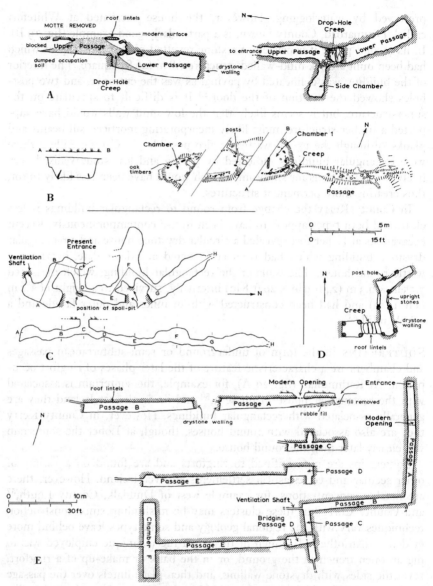

Fig. 20 Types of souterrain. (A) Rathmullan, Co., Down; (B) Cooleran,
Co. Fermanagh; (C) Keelnameela, Co. Cork; (D) Ballycatteen, Co. Cork;
(E) Donaghmore, Co. Louth. After Edwards, *Archaeology early med. Ire.*

passage often has one or more chambers off it made of drystone walling with
corbelled roofs, and passages which are sometimes built at more than one
level and linked by constricting drop-hole creeps. Most souterrains, as at

Rathmullan, have one or two passages and chambers but some, such as Donaghmore, County Louth (fig. 20 E), which has several interlinking passages, would have required considerable engineering skill to construct. Other features found in souterrains of this type include ventilation shafts, drains, a variety of creeps to restrict movement from one part of the souterrain to another which were sometimes closed off by wooden doors, and even cupboards, shelves, and benches.[58]

In some areas, where fewer souterrains have been found, this may be because they were constructed of wood, and therefore have not normally survived. Waterlogging resulted in the discovery of a wooden souterrain in the univallate rath at Coolcran, County Fermanagh (fig. 20 B). It consisted of an earth-cut trench 6.5 m (21 ft 4 in) long which led via a creep to a large sub-rectangular, flat-bottomed pit 9 m (29 ft 6 in) long by 3.5 m (11 ft 6 in) wide. The remains suggested that the pit was divided into two chambers lined with post-and-wattle walling; dendrochronology provided a felling date for the oak posts of A.D. 829 ± 9.[59]

In some areas, however, souterrains were more simply constructed by tunnelling into the clay or soft rock and removing the spoil through the entrance. Most consist of one or two short passages and chambers but there are also some more complex examples. In West Cork, souterrains with several chambers and creeps have been discovered which were constructed by digging large pits and then tunnelling horizontally; the spoil was then removed through the pits, which were filled in on completion (fig. 20 C).[60]

In the past there has been some discussion[61] concerning the functions of souterrains, but it now seems certain that they primarily acted as temporary hiding places which could be resorted to if the settlement was attacked. One documentary reference describes viking raiders digging into a souterrain in order to capture the occupants,[62] who may then have been sold into slavery. The fact that souterrains were hidden would have made their discovery more difficult, and the creeps would have made them easier to defend. Some even have 'sally-ports' beyond the ringfort enclosure, offering a means of escape and counter-attack.[63] However, some also had an ancilliary use for storage. They were safe places to hide valuables: for example, a bell was found

---

[58] Richard Warner, 'The Irish souterrains and their background' in H. Crawford (ed.), *Subterranean Britain* (London, 1979), pp 103–11.

[59] B. B. Williams, 'Excavation of a rath at Coolcran, Co. Fermanagh' in *U.J.A.*, xlviii (1985), pp 75–7.

[60] Warner, 'Irish souterrains', 101–5; J. P. McCarthy, 'Summary of a study of County Cork souterrains' in *Cork Hist. Soc. Jn.*, lxxxviii (1983), 100–05; D. C. Twohig, 'Recent souterrain research in County Cork' in *Cork Hist. Soc. Jn.*, lxxxi (1976), pp 19–38.

[61] Charles Thomas, 'Souterrains in the Irish Sea province' in Charles Thomas (ed.), *The iron age in the Irish Sea province* (London, 1972), pp 75–8; Warner, 'Irish souterrains', pp 128–34.

[62] A. T. Lucas, 'Souterrains: the literary evidence' in *Béaloideas*, xxxix–xli (1971–3), pp 165–91.

[63] E.g., Hencken, *Cahercommaun*, pp 20–22.

concealed under the floor of a souterrain at Oldcourt, County Cork, and an imported glass vessel was found in a souterrain at Mullaroe, County Sligo.[64] The discovery of fragmentary barrel hoops at Balrenny, County Meath,[65] suggests food storage, though it is possible that, like modern cellars, it had simply become filled with clutter.

The buildings inside the average ringfort would usually have consisted of up to six structures at any one time. Round houses are more common, but there are often rectangular buildings and souterrains in the later phases. Houses with hearths and bed platforms would have been the dwellings, probably of a small extended family (fig. 21). Other structures would have served for storage or as shelters for animals such as pigs;[66] it is likely that some structures would have been built for human habitation but later transfered to animals as they began to deteriorate. At Killyliss a latrine pit with a wooden superstructure was found set against the ringfort bank.[67] We should imagine the open spaces of the ringfort interior as fullfilling the functions of a farmyard with all the corresponding activities. The excavations at Deer Park Farms certainly suggest this, with the identification of middens and insect assemblages indicative of dung heaps. Dogs, pigs, and chickens would have rooted amongst the rubbish for food. Grain could be milled with a rotary quern, and essential craft activities, such as blacksmithing, could have been carried out. It has been argued that cattle were also driven into the ringfort overnight to protect them from raids,[68] but this seems unlikely except in an emergency, since space would have been limited and in wet weather they would have churned the farmyard into a mire. It is more likely that at night they would have been herded into a nearby pound or *lías*, sometimes a substantial enclosure surrounded by a bank and ditch, as at Garryduff 2,[69] but more often a wattlework corral. The problem is that there has been little excavation beyond the ringfort enclosure which might have brought evidence for such a structure to light. However it seems likely that many other activities, such as crop-processing, would have been carried on in the vicinity of the ringfort, where there might also have been a variety of outhouses and animal pens. At Duneight, County Down, for example, there was clear evidence of activity beyond the outer ditch in the form of post-holes, pits, and burning.[70] There has been much less excavation of larger

---

[64] C. Ó Cuileanáin and T. F. Murphy, 'A ring-fort at Oldcourt, Co. Cork' in *Cork Hist. Soc. Jn.*, lxvi (1961), p. 83; Edward Bourke, 'Glass vessels of the first nine centuries A.D. in Ireland' in *R.S.A.I. Jn.*, cxxiv (1994), pp 169, 205, pl. C2.

[65] George Eogan and John Bradley, 'A souterrain at Balrenny, near Slane, County Meath' in *R.S.A.I. Jn.*, cvii (1977), pp 102–3.

[66] Kenward & Allison, 'Insect assemblages at Deer Park Farms', pp 95–6.

[67] Ivens, 'Killyliss', pp 22–3.

[68] Finbar McCormick, 'Cows, ringforts and the origins of Early Christian Ireland' in *Emania*, xiii (1995), pp 34–5.

[69] O'Kelly, 'Exacavation of two earthen ringforts', pp 120–25.

[70] Waterman, 'Excavations at Duneight', p. 69.

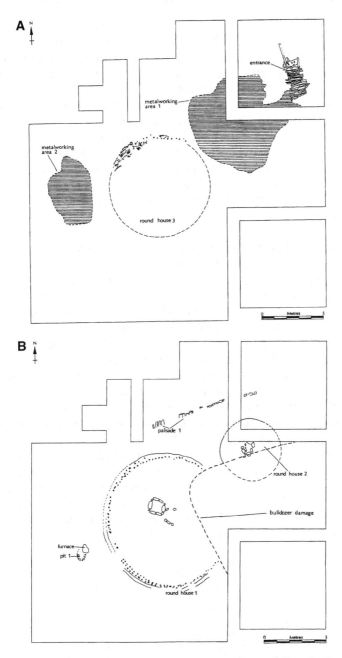

Fig. 21 (A) Phase X of the early medieval crannog at Moynagh Lough, Co. Meath.
By kind permission of John Bradley. (B) Phase Y of the early medieval crannog at
Moynagh Lough, Co. Meath. By kind permission of John Bradley.

254 The archaeology of early medieval Ireland, c.400–1169

multivallate ringforts like Garranes, but clearly the area enclosed implies more buildings which would have housed, not only the household, but also their retinue and hangers-on, and may have provided a location for larger gatherings. It would also have provided the space for a range of craft activities, including ornamental metalworking.[71]

Ringforts are often found in groups of two or three, as at Lisleagh, County Cork, and Ballypalady, County Antrim, or sometimes larger groups, such as Cush, County Limerick.[72] In some instances, as at Garryduff, a difference in function is implied between the ringforts, but at Lisleagh the relationship is more complex since it is thought that, although Lisleagh 1 preceded Lisleagh 2, they were both used for human habitation and were occupied contemporaneously, although Lisleagh 1 became the focus of ironworking in its later stages.[73]

SOME 200 coastal promontory forts are currently known in Ireland, mainly in the west, but remarkably few have been excavated. Their construction probably began in the late bronze age and, although there is less certain evidence of iron-age occupation, extensive activity has now been recognised at Drumanagh, Loughshinny, County Dublin, which may have served as a focus for trade with Roman merchants in the early centuries A.D.[74] Promontory forts were also occupied in the early middle ages and most are likely to have fulfilled a similar role to ringforts, except that there was a need for enclosure only on the landward approach. Some were certainly high-status sites. Although little now remains at Dunseverick, located on a spectacular rock-stack on the north coast of County Antrim (pl. 9), except a later castle, it was a royal stronghold associated with the Dalriada and was raided by the vikings in 870 and 934.[75] A promontory on Dalkey Island may have functioned in a similar way to Drumanagh. There was activity on the site at various times in prehistory and it was then reoccupied in the fifth and sixth centuries A.D., as evidenced by sherds of imported B-ware amphorae, but the dump contruction bank and external ditch across the promontory, together with a midden, hearth, and possible house within, were only built around the seventh century, as indicated by the presence of Type E imported pottery.[76]

[71] Ó Ríordáin, 'Garranes', pp 84–8.
[72] D. M. Waterman, 'A group of raths at Ballypalady, Co. Antrim' in *U.J.A.*, xxxv (1972), pp 29–36; S. P. Ó Ríordáin, 'Excavations at Cush, Co. Limerick' in *R.I.A. Proc.*, xlv (1940), sect. C, pp 83–181.
[73] Monk, 'Tale of two ringforts', p. 113.
[74] Barry Raftery, *Pagan Celtic Ireland* (London, 1994), p. 48; 'Drumanagh and Roman Ireland' in *Archaeology Ireland*, x, no. 1 (spring 1996), pp 17–19.
[75] Lord Killanin and Michael V. Duignan, *The Shell guide to Ireland* (London, 1967), pp 129–30; J. P. Mallory and T. E. McNeill, *The archaeology of Ulster from colonisation to plantation* (Belfast, 1991), p. 198.
[76] G. D. Liversage, 'Excavations at Dalkey Island, Co. Dublin 1956–59' in *R.I.A. Proc.*, lxvi (1968), sect. C, pp 53–223.

The economy of the promontory fort at Larrybane, County Antrim, has been described as similar to a small ringfort.[77] The rampart across the promontory, enclosing an area approximately 35 m (115 ft) across, consisted of a low clay bank up to 5.18 m (17 ft) wide with a drystone wall on top. There was evidence for at least four phases of occupation with rectangular buildings in the final phase. The small promontory of Dunbeg, County Kerry, was first occupied in the late bronze age. The exact sequence of defences, which consist of a large stone rampart with terracing on the inner face and a defended entrance, four outer earth banks, and five interspersed ditches, has proved difficult to determine. However, a radiocarbon date from ditch 1, which had been recut, indicates early medieval activity (cal. A.D. 680–1020). The large, stone-walled round house within the defences was also of probable early medieval date (cal. A.D. 870–1260). In addition, there was a souterrain which projected beyond the stone rampart so as to form a sallyport.[78]

A CRANNOG is a lake settlement. The word 'crannog' is derived from the Irish *cranu* ('tree') but only comes into use in the sources after the twelfth century. Before this, a lake settlement was either termed *inis* or *oileán*, which both mean 'island'.[79] However, archaeologists use the word 'crannog' to describe early medieval island settlements that are wholly or partially artificial, being constructed variously of timber and brushwood, peat, stones, soil, and other organic material built up into layers and retained by a timber palisade.[80] Other lacustrine settlements include stone-walled ringforts constructed on natural islands and promontory sites jutting out into the water.

In the region of 2,000 crannogs have now been identified in Ireland. They are mainly found in a broad band stretching across the northern half of the country from Mayo to Antrim, but there are particular concentrations in the small lakes of Cavan, Fermanagh, Leitrim, Monaghan, and Roscommon. They are usually built in shallow water not far from the lake edge, but some are found on natural islands in deeper water, and occasionally in rivers or coastal wetlands. Many are visible above the water as small, tree-covered islands; others are completely submerged and have only come to light as a result of land reclamation, where they may be recognised as hummocks covered in grass and trees.[81] Most are undated, but phases of early medieval

---

[77] V. B. Proudfoot and B. C. S. Wilson, 'Further excavations at Larrybane promontory fort' in *U.J.A.*, xxiv–xxv (1961–2), p. 107.

[78] T. B. Barry, 'Archaeological excavations at Dunbeg promontory fort, Co. Kerry' in *R.I.A. Proc.*, lxxxi (1981), sect. C, pp 295–330.

[79] Aidan O'Sullivan, *The archaeology of lake settlement in Ireland* (Discovery Programme Monographs 4, 1998), p. 152.

[80] C. J. Lynn, 'Some 'early' ring-forts and crannogs' in *Journal of Irish Archaeology*, i (1983), pp 50–51.

[81] Edwards, *Archaeology early med. Ire.*, pp 37–8; O'Sullivan, *Archaeology of lake settlement*, pp 32, 104–5, fig. 23.

occupation have been recognised on some by the recovery of artefacts, or more recently through dendrochronological sampling.[82] Only a handful, however, have been extensively excavated, and Moynagh Lough (fig. 21) is the only example in recent times. This is due in part to the difficulty of digging these often complex sites, but where excavation has taken place, the rewards have been great: if they are still waterlogged, much organic material will survive, not just the crannog make-up and structures, but also a range of artefacts, including wood, leather, and textiles and a great variety of environmental evidence which can shed light on the everyday lives of the inhabitants.

Crannogs would have required access to extensive resources, especially timber, and would have taken considerable labour to construct. Excavation has shown that early medieval crannog-builders quite often returned to sites that had been used in prehistory, perhaps because earlier occupation demonstrated their suitability, or to lessen the construction work involved. For example, both Ballinderry 2, County Offaly, and Rathtinaun, Lough Gara, County Sligo, were inhabited in the bronze age, and Moynagh Lough was occupied in both the mesolithic and the bronze age.[83]

It is possible to gain some idea of how crannogs were built by examining Ballinderry 1, a completely artificial island. The foundation of the crannog consisted of a raft of enormous split-oak timbers placed side by side on the lake bed and held in place with pegs and stakes. The crannog was then built up using radially-set timbers, many reused, with layers of brushwood, peat, and organic matter in between, the entire structure being retained by a plank palisade with an outer ring of piles.[84] Over time the crannog material would have compacted and sunk, making rebuilding necessary; this is clearly the case at Lagore, where a whole series of construction and occupation levels have now been recognised.[85] At Ballinderry 2 (fig. 22) the crannog structure was less substantial because it was built on a natural island and on top of the bronze-age settlement. It consisted of an oval area approximately 35 m (115 ft) in diameter, wholly or partially enclosed by a palisade; the centre was consolidated with piles, timber, and brushwood.[86] In rockier areas, such as County Donegal, timber was less readily available and therefore crannogs were constructed largely of stones built up into cairns.[87]

[82] B. A. Crone, 'Crannogs and chronologies' in *Antiq. Soc. Scot. Proc.*, cxxiii (1993), pp 249–50.

[83] Hencken, 'Ballinderry crannog no. 2, pp 6–27; O'Sullivan, *Archaeology of lake settlement*, pp 8, 89–90, pl. 19; Bradley, 'Excavations at Moynagh Lough', pp 7–12; 'Living at the water's edge' in *Archaeology Ireland*, x, no. 1 (spring 1996), pp 24–6.

[84] Hencken, 'Ballinderry crannog, no. 1', pp 107–18; O'Sullivan, *Archaeology of lake settlement*, p. 123.

[85] Hencken, 'Lagore', pp 47–54; C. J. Lynn, 'Lagore, County Meath, and Ballinderry No. 1, County Westmeath, some possible structural reinterpretations' in *Journal of Irish Archaeology*, iii (1985–6), pp 69–72.

[86] Hencken, 'Ballinderry crannog no. 2', pp 30–32, pl. IX.

[87] Lacy, *Archaeological survey of County Donegal*, pp 104–6.

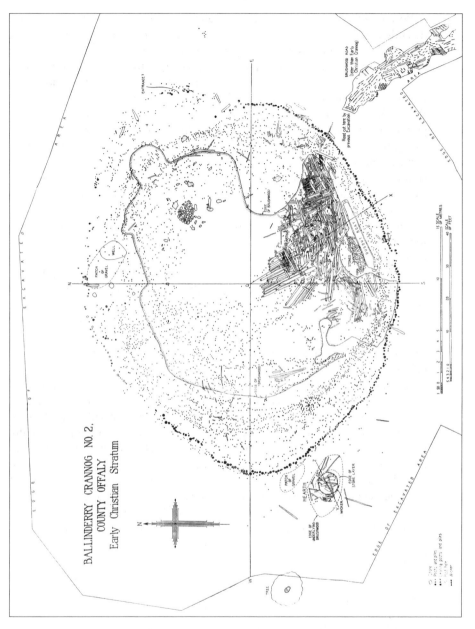

Fig. 22 Plan of the early medieval level of Ballinderry crannog no. 2, Co. Offaly.
After H. O'Neill Hencken in *R.I.A. Proc.*, xlvii, sect. C (1941–2).

Because of their location, access to crannogs is difficult and they are clearly defended monuments, though they would have been unable to withstand a sustained attack. For some the only approach was by boat, and dugouts have been found reused in the crannog make-up; jetties and landing-stages have also been identified.[88] For others direct access from the shore was possible via a stone causeway, brushwood road, or wooden gangway raised above the water on stilts. The perimeter palisade enclosing the crannog provided a further line of defence. It might consist of a close-set fence of substantial roundwood posts or a more complex structure of uprights with vertical mortice grooves into which horizontal planks were slotted.[89] As the crannog structure compacted and needed to be rebuilt, so did the palisade. At Moynagh Lough, for example, a palisade of oak planks with a dendro-chronological felling date of A.D. 748 was replaced by one of mainly oak saplings interwoven with wattles, which may indicate that larger oak timbers were no longer available in the neighbourhood.[90] Sometimes vertical piles have been traced outside the palisade, which would have further deterred hostile boats. We know much less about crannog entrances, though they generally face the shore and where possible were oriented eastwards. The best preserved so far was excavated in the early eighth-century phase at Moynagh Lough. It consisted simply of a wooden trackway partially set on runners, and incorporated some reused timbers. But there are hints of more complex superstructures: at Cuilmore Lough 2, County Mayo, four substantial posts could have supported a gate-tower.[91]

Excavations at Moynagh Lough, combined with those on ringforts (see above), have greatly increased our understanding of crannog buildings (fig. 21). The upper levels at Moynagh Lough are only partially waterlogged, but evidence for two wattle round houses was uncovered. One was unusually large (diameter 11.2 m; 36 ft 9 in) and consisted of a double wall of stake-holes with a large number of interior stake-holes around the walls, indicative of bedding areas, and a central stone hearth.[92] This discovery makes sense of the fragmentary wattle structures excavated at Lagore. These were not, as Hencken thought, the temporary shelters of the crannog-builders,[93] but rather permanent houses, which would have been replaced as they needed repair and the crannog structure needed to be rebuilt. At Ballinderry 1 the large areas of planking, originally identified as two phases of houses, have now been reinterpreted as successive phases of crannog structure, the earlier

[88] Hencken, 'Ballinderry crannog no. 2', pp 38, 60, pl. XI; 'Ballinderry crannog no. 1' pp 119–20.

[89] Hencken, 'Ballinderry crannog no. 2', pp 30–31; 'Lagore', pp 42–5.

[90] Bradley, 'Excavations at Moynagh Lough', pp 13–15.

[91] Etienne Rynne and Gearóid Mac Eoin, 'The Craggaunowen crannog: gangway and gate-tower' in *N. Munster Antiq. Jn.*, xx (1978), p. 51, fig. 3.

[92] Bradley, 'Excavations at Moynagh Lough', pp 15–16.

[93] Hencken, 'Lagore', pp 41–2.

with a central house, the latter with two rectangular houses near the perimeter.[94] There is no evidence to support the idea of large circular houses covering the majority of the crannog surface.[95]

Substantial evidence for craftworking, including luxury metalworking, is a feature of crannog sites. In the early eighth century at Moynagh Lough crannog there were two metalworking areas where both smelting and casting were taking place (fig. 21 A).[96] At the ninth-century crannog of Bofeenaun, County Mayo, no evidence for houses was found; instead the site was apparently utilised exclusively for ironworking.[97] This suggests that crannogs fulfilled a variety of functions. Some are identifiable in the annals as royal sites and this is supported by the richness of the artefacts. Lagore is *Lough Gabhair*, a residence of the kings of Southern Brega from the seventh to tenth centuries, while it has been suggested that Moynagh Lough could be *Loch Dé Mundech*, which is associated with the *Mugdorne* during the seventh and eighth centuries.[98] However, not all were year-round habitations; kings and their retinues may have resorted to them at certain times of year, to engage in fishing and fowling, for example, or used them as bolt-holes when danger threatened. An unusually large quantity of weapons was found at Lagore, and the discovery of skulls—with evidence that the individuals had met with violent deaths—suggests that a massacre had taken place on the site.[99] Cró Inis in Lough Ennell is where, according to the annals, King Máelsechnaill II of the Southern Uí Néill died in 1022. The crannog has recently been located and its identification as Cró Inis is supported by radiocarbon and dendrochronological dating. But it would be wrong to view the crannog in isolation, since it seems to have functioned as an adjunct to the main habitation, the raised rath of Dún na Sgiath on the nearby shore.[100] Indeed, there has been a growing realisation that crannogs should not be viewed in isolation from their hinterlands where the animals were kept and crops grown (pl. 11). Several ringforts and other enclosures have been identified in the neighbourhood of Moynagh Lough crannog, as well as the ecclesiatical site at Nobber.[101]

ARCHAEOLOGICAL investigations have concentrated on ringforts and crannogs because they stand out in the landscape. Habitations without obvious

---

[94] Hencken, 'Ballinderry crannog, no. 1' pp 114–25; Lynn, 'Lagore, County Meath', pp 72–3; O'Sullivan, *Archaeology of lake settlement*, p. 124.

[95] *Pace* R. B. Warner, 'On crannogs and kings' in *U.J.A.*, lvii (1997), p. 65.

[96] Phase Y, Bradley, 'Moynagh Lough crannog', pp 18–22.

[97] O'Sullivan, *Archaeology of lake settlement*, pp 121–3.

[98] Liam Price, 'The history of Lagore, from the annals and other sources' in Hencken, 'Lagore', pp 18–34; Edel Bhreathnach, 'Topographical note: Moynagh Lough, Nobber, Co. Meath' in *Ríocht na Midhe*, ix, no. 4 (1998), pp 16–19.

[99] Hencken, 'Lagore', pp 88–98, 199–203.

[100] Warner, 'On crannogs and kings', pp 62–3; C. E. Karkov and John Ruffing, 'The Southern Uí Néill and the political landscape of Lough Ennell' in *Peritia*, xi (1997), pp 337–9.

[101] O'Sullivan, *Archaeology of lake settlement*, p. 108, fig 25.

enclosures have received much less attention, and this has resulted in the erroneous view that their numbers were probably insignificant.[102] Many of those identified have survived because of their location in specialised environments such as unimproved uplands or coastal sand-dunes. For example, in such landscapes in County Kerry stone-walled huts still abound, and though they are difficult to date, at least those with souterrains may be identified as early medieval. In areas of improved farmland, as, for example, in the northeast, the chance discovery of souterrains has likewise provided a key to the identification of rectangular wooden houses, often set in small groups.

In County Kerry a variety of unenclosed stone round houses with souterrains may be identified. For example, at Ballynavenooragh on the lower slopes of Mount Brandon (60–90 m; 200–300 ft above sea level) is a cashel (see above) with three pairs of round houses located in the fields nearby. Without excavation it is impossible to tell whether they were occupied simultaneously, but one pair of conjoined round houses has a small associated souterrain. Likewise at a similar height on the southern slopes of Mount Eagle is Caherdadurras, Glenfahan, a group of three conjoined round houses of corbelled construction with a souterrain.[103] Similar round houses were a feature of coastal settlement. For example, at Canroe on the island of Beginish, County Kerry, a settlement of eight houses with several animal shelters and other structures, set in a network of small fields, has been investigated and two phases of early medieval occupation were identified. The first included a stone round house and the second a similar but better-preserved round house, both of which were fully excavated. Because of its exposed position the latter had been dug right into the ground and was approached by a lintel-covered passage. The sides of the pit had been lined with drystone walling which continued above ground level, and sockets in the top of the wall would have held the roof timbers. A runestone and other characteristic artefacts suggest the second phase was Hiberno-Norse.[104]

Few stone-walled open settlements have been investigated in other parts of Ireland. One exception is a site known as the 'Spectacles', located on a shelf of land overlooking Lough Gur, County Limerick. Situated in a group of small rectangular fields it included a stone-walled round house with a paved porch and a rectangular stone-walled building similar to some of the houses at the nearby cashel, Carraig Aille 1.[105]

In County Kerry occasional stake-holes and other evidence for wattle round houses have been found underlying stone ones,[106] suggesting that,

[102] Stout, *Irish ringfort*, p. 117.

[103] Cuppage, *Dingle Peninsula*, p. 396, pl. 52, fig 228, p. 407, fig 231, pl. XXIVb.

[104] M. J. O'Kelly, 'An island settlement at Beginish, Co. Kerry' in *R.I.A. Proc.*, lvii (1956), sect. C, pp 159–64; O'Sullivan & Sheehan, *Iveragh Peninsula*, pp 385–7, pls XXIIIa–b.

[105] Ó Ríordáin, 'Lough Gur excavations', pp 57–62.

[106] O'Sullivan & Sheehan, *Iveragh Peninsula*, pp 191, 382; M. J. O'Kelly, 'Church Island, near Valentia, Co. Kerry' in *R.I.A. Proc.*, lix (1958), sect. C, pp 59–61.

where suitable materials were available, homesteads constructed of wood, either unenclosed or surrounded by a palisade or fence, may have been relatively common. This is also likely to have been so elsewhere in Ireland where building in wood was the norm. Although such flimsy archaeological evidence is difficult to detect and is easily destroyed, occasional traces of open settlements with round houses or homesteads surrounded by a fence or palisade have come to light under ringforts.[107]

In County Antrim, examples of rectangular wooden houses, perhaps datable to the ninth century onwards, have been discovered because of their association with souterrains. For example, at Craig Hill a rectangular timber-framed house approximately 8 m (26 ft 3 in) in length, and delineated by post-holes, had been built on a terrace dug into the slope with a stone-lined drain on the uphill side. It had a paved porch at the eastern end, a central hearth, and a souterrain at the western end was probably entered directly from the house. At Ballywee (fig. 23) a partially enclosed settlement consisted of at least two rectangular houses with associated souterrains as well as outbuildings.[108]

Some of these settlements would have been occupied contemporaneously with ringforts (see below). They would therefore seem to be the dwellings of the lower echelons of society who had neither the power nor the wealth to construct anything more impressive. However, from the ninth century onwards, and with the gradual demise of the ringfort, it may be suggested that open settlements became more common.

TILL recently there has been a tendency to view early medieval settlements in isolation from each other and from the evolving landscape in which they were located. This is a mistake only now beginning to be rectified by more comprehensive regional surveys. The distribution pattern and varying morphology of ringforts has recently come under scrutiny for what it might reveal about the relationship between sites and the different grades of early Irish society evidenced in 'Críth Gablach'.[109] However, without excavation such an approach is flawed since it only takes account of the visible remains. Instead, detailed study of a locality, backed up by carefully targeted excavation, is likely to be much more profitable. Such an approach has been adopted at Lisleagh, County Cork, where, in addition to excavation of two ringforts (see above), other possible early medieval settlements, including a likely ecclesiastical site at Killeagh, have been plotted in relation to the local topography and artificial features such as routeways (fig. 24). The potential

---

[107] Edwards, *Archaeology early med. Ire.*, p. 18.

[108] D. M. Waterman, 'An excavatioin of a house and souterrain at Craig Hill, Co. Antrim' in *U.J.A.*, xix (1956), pp 87–91; C. J. Lynn, 'Ballywee' in *Excavations*, v (1984), pp 4–6.

[109] Matthew Stout, 'Ring-forts in the south-west Midlands of Ireland' in *R.I.A. Proc.*, xci (1991), sect. C, pp 229–41.

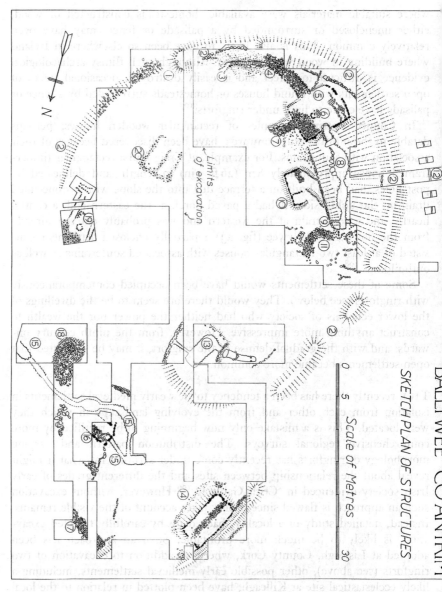

Fig. 23 A partially enclosed settlement with rectangular houses and souterrains at
Ballywee, Co. Antrim. By courtesy of Chris Lynn.

can also be seen in a similar project focussed on the Ferta valley, County
Kerry, where the important ecclesiastical site of Caherlehillan has been excavated and studied in relation to an adjacent possible high-status cashel on

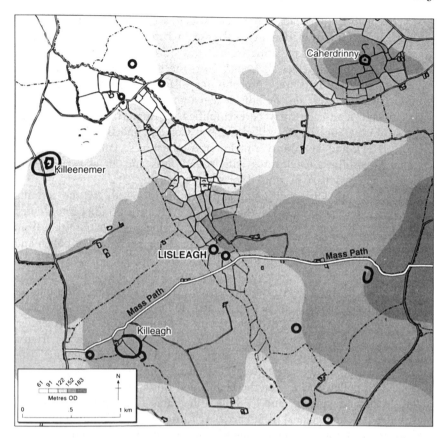

Fig. 24 Early medieval settlements in the landscape: the ringforts at Lisleagh, Co.
Cork, and other probable early medieval sites in the area. After Monk & Sheehan,
*Early med. Munster*, by kind permission of the Cork University Press.

the edge of good agricultural land and unenclosed huts on the pastureland
above.[110]

D ESPITE the growing interest in landscape archaeology, there has been very
little archaeological investigation of early medieval field systems. These
seldom survive in the more fertile lowlands because of their intensive use for
modern farming; but on more marginal land, and in areas that have escaped
land improvement, whole relict landscapes have been recorded by aerial
photography. Although there has been almost no excavation, where fields are

---

[110] Michael A. Monk, 'Early medieval secular and ecclesiastical settlement in Munster' in
Monk & Sheehan, *Early medieval Munster*, pp 35–40.

associated with ringforts an early medieval date seems likely. A rare lowland survival is at Rathlogan, County Kilkenny, where a probable multivallate ringfort has small fields radiating from it with further curvilinear enclosures nearby.[111] At the 'Spectacles', Lough Gur, the four small rectilinear fields associated with the huts were probably for tillage, while larger fields and a semi-circular enclosure on the hillside above may have been for livestock.[112] Relict upland landscapes may be exemplified by ringforts, huts, and a palimpsest of curvilinear stone-walled fields at Corrofin and Ballybaun, County Clare (pl. 11), and in County Antrim at Aughnabrack, Ballyutoag, by two conjoined curvilinear enclosures with round huts and an associated field system which may have been used for summer grazing.[113]

Palynology provides a different approach to the study of the farming landscape. Most important is the growing volume of radiocarbon-dated pollen diagrams from different parts of Ireland which demonstrate that from around the third century A.D. there was a steady decrease in tree pollen and a corresponding increase in field-weed and cereal pollen, which suggests a major expansion in both pastoral farming and tillage, the latter coinciding with a climatic upturn. At Loughnashade, County Armagh, clearance of woodland began as early as A.D. 150–200, followed by a dramatic rise in cereal pollen which transformed the area into an open landscape.[114] A similar pattern is repeated at Essexford Lough, County Louth, where, apart from a slight glitch in the mid-seventh century, when there was a temporary increase in hazel scrub, agricultural expansion continued throughout the period. The pollen species for the eighth and ninth centuries suggest both arable fields and grazing land.[115] Pollen diagrams from further south and west indicate some regional differences. At Littleton Bog, County Tipperary, agricultural expansion happened slightly later during the fifth and sixth centuries, and on more marginal land in the Burren, at the ringfort of Lislarheenmore, a clearance of woodland for grazing is indicated around the end of the sixth century immediately after the construction of the ringfort.[116]

I T used to be thought that livestock, particularly cattle, were the mainspring of early medieval Irish farming, partly because of the emphasis on the ownership of cattle as an indication of wealth and status in the documentary sources, but also because the evidence for agriculture was comparatively

[111] Frank Mitchell and Michael Ryan, *Reading the Irish landscape* (Dublin, 1997), col. 41.
[112] Ó Ríordáin, 'Lough Gur excavations' pp 61–2.
[113] Edwards, *Archaeology early med. Ire.*, p. 53, illustrations 20–21; B. B. Williams, 'Excavations at Ballyutoag, Co. Antrim' in *U.J.A.*, xlvii (1984), pp 37–49.
[114] D. A. Weir, 'Dark Ages and the pollen record' in *Emania*, xi (1997), 21–30.
[115] D. A. Weir, 'A palynological study of landscape and agricultural development in County Louth from the second millennium B.C. to the first millennium A.D.' in *Discovery Programme Reports*, ii (1995), pp 96–7.
[116] Stout, *Irish ringfort*, pp 39–47.

sparse. However many of the pollen diagrams, by demonstrating the increasing amount of field weeds and cereal, indicate the importance of a mixed farming economy and this is backed up by a range of other archaeological evidence.

The study of domestic animal bones, especially those from modern excavations where methods of collection and sampling are more reliable, has greatly increased our understanding of animal husbandry and provided a range of evidence for comparison with the documentary record (see below, pp 569–74). As might be expected from their importance in the literature,[117] the percentage of cattle exceeds that of either pigs or sheep in most bone samples, and further research to establish the sex and age of slaughter-patterns in cattle has convincingly demonstrated the vital role of dairying in the early medieval Irish farming economy and the secondary importance of beef production. Dairying was also facilitated by the mild, wet climate, encouraging the speedy growth of pasture, which meant that cattle could be grazed outside all year round without the need for hay. It has recently been suggested that, because there is no evidence for dairying in Ireland until the early centuries A.D., it was only introduced as a result of contact with the Roman world. Dairy products would certainly have provided an important new source of protein and fat in the diet, which would have had a beneficial effect on the health of the population.[118]

Early medieval cattle would have looked similar to the modern Kerry breed.[119] The study of bones from a variety of early medieval settlement sites, including Moynagh Lough crannog and the later settlements at Knowth and Marshes Upper 3, shows that the majority of cattle were slaughtered between 12 and 24 months old. These were the surplus male calves which were not required for traction or breeding and were therefore killed for their meat. In contrast, the bones of the mature beasts are generally female, demonstrating that they were kept as dairy cows which would have produced an annual calf and were only slaughtered when they were past their prime. In addition it can sometimes be shown that beef was being supplied to sites which were not themselves producers. At the monastery of Armagh the bones suggest that the inhabitants were consuming prime joints from older cattle, while a sample from Fishamble Street, Dublin, indicates adaptation to an urban market with older, less high-quality cattle, both male and female, being brought into town on the hoof.[120] It should also be remembered that, although cattle were kept primarily for dairying and secondarily for their

---

[117] Fergus Kelly, *Early Irish farming* (Dublin, 1997), pp 26–66.
[118] Finbar McCormick, 'Cows, ringforts and the origins of early Christian Ireland' in *Emania*, xiii (1995), pp 35–6.
[119] Kelly, *Early Irish farming*, pp 30–31.
[120] Finbar McCormick, 'Dairying and beef production in early Christian Ireland' in Terrence Reeves-Smyth and Fred Hamond (ed.), *Landscape archaeology in Ireland* (Oxford, 1983), pp 254–64.

meat, the carcass would have supplied a variety of other materials: leather, bone, horn, sinew, and tallow (see below).[121]

Although their skins and bones were also utilised, pigs were mainly kept for their meat, which was highly regarded and either eaten fresh or preserved by salting and smoking.[122] The animals would have been small, long-legged, and hairy. Osteological samples have shown that the number of pigs from a settlement site is usually less than the number of cattle. The pig bones from Moynagh Lough show that they were usually killed between 18 and 24 months old; at Rathmullan they were killed between 18 and 36 months old, and the fact that several were slaughtered at once may indicate that the surplus was preserved for use over the winter, or was donated as food render, or was destined for wider distribution to non-primary producers.[123] At Armagh, for example, there was a significantly higher-than-usual concentration of good meat bones and skulls, which had probably been utilised for offal, which suggests they had been brought to the site from estate farms for consumption.[124]

Sheep were primarily kept for their wool; their meat, skins, and milk were of secondary importance. Some goats were also kept, but their bones are difficult to distinguish from those of sheep. Sheep bones are common in the osteological record, though usually less numerous than pig, but in some instances, such as the promontory fort at Larrybane, they were much more important because the well-drained chalk headland provided ideal grazing.[125] The bones suggest that there was more than one breed: a small, primitive sheep similar to the Soay, and a larger, more modern variety.[126] Little detailed research on age of slaughter has been carried out, but at Rathmullan sheep were kept so as to maximise their wool, meat, and skin production. In phase 2 most were killed between 30 and 36 months old and only after they had been shorn for the first time; the rest, presumably the breeding ewes, survived beyond this.[127]

A variety of other domestic animal bones appear in the osteological record. Ponies were highly valued for riding, racing, drawing light carts, and farm-work, but they were very seldom eaten. Dogs were used in hunting and herding as well as to guard the settlement and as pets. A few cat bones are also sometimes found. They too were pets, and would also have kept the vermin at bay.[128]

---

[121]  Kelly, *Early Irish farming*, pp 54–7.

[122]  Ibid., pp 84–6.

[123]  Ibid., p. 85; Lynn, 'Rathmullan', pp 157–8.

[124]  Cynthia Gaskell Brown and A. E. T. Harper, 'Excavations on Cathedral Hill, Armagh' in *U.J.A.*, xlvii (1984), p. 156.

[125]  Proudfoot & Wilson, 'Further excavations at Larrybane', pp 105–6.

[126]  Kelly, *Early Irish farming*, pp 74–5.

[127]  Lynn, 'Rathmullan', p. 158.

[128]  Kelly, *Early Irish farming*, pp 88–121, 114–24; Finbar McCormick, 'The domesticated cat in early Christian and medieval Ireland' in Gearóid Mac Niocaill and P. F. Wallace (ed.), *Keimelia: studies in medieval archaeology and history in memory of Tom Delaney* (Galway, 1988), pp 221–4.

Domestic fowl produced down and feathers in addition to eggs and meat. The majority of the evidence is for hens, but some geese were also kept and there are occasional documentary references to ducks. The Romans were responsible for bringing domestic fowl to Britain, and they were probably introduced into Ireland shortly afterwards. As yet very little research has been done on bird bones, with the result that their significance in the early medieval Irish farming economy is unclear. A few domestic fowl bones have been recovered from a variety of sites including Boho, Larrybane, and the monastery at Armagh; there were both chicken and goose bones at Rathmullan.[129]

COMPARED with livestock-rearing, there is much less documentary evidence for tillage in early medieval Ireland. Nevertheless, archaeology is playing an increasing role in our understanding of the significance of crop husbandry. On modern excavations of early medieval sites the flotation and sieving of soil samples has resulted in the recovery of an increasing volume of archaeobotanical material, including charred grain and seeds. Together with pollen this can shed valuable light on what plants were grown and can be used in conjunction with evidence for agricultural equipment and structures used in crop-processing to help reconstruct the various stages of cultivation.

As already indicated, the pollen evidence shows a steady increase in cereal production after c. A.D. 200. Various types of grain were cultivated and provided an important element in the diet in the form of bread, gruel, porridge, and beer,[130] as well as animal feed. The eighth-century law text 'Bretha Déin Chécht' lists eight types of cereal in order of rank: bread-wheat, rye, spelt-wheat (?), two-row barley (?), emmer wheat (?), six-row barley, and the common oat.[131] Wheat was clearly considered a luxury. While it can be grown reasonably successfully in the south and east where there is more sunshine, less rain, and better soils, in the west its production would have been severely limited. It is therefore not surprising that wheat has a low incidence in early medieval grain samples. Wheat straw has been identified at the royal crannog of Lagore,[132] which may serve to underline the high status of the site; small amounts of charred wheat have also been identified on several more ordinary ringforts,[133] where it is possible that a proportion was

[129] Kelly, *Early Irish farming*, pp 102–7; Margaret McCarthy, 'Archaeozoological studies and early medieval Munster' in Monk & Sheehan, *Early medieval Munster*, p. 62; V. B. Proudfoot, 'Exacavations at the rath at Boho, Co. Fermanagh' in *U.J.A.*, xvi (1953), p. 52; Proudfoot & Wilson, 'Further excavations at Larrybane', p. 106; Gaskell Brown & Harper, 'Cathedral Hill, Armagh', pp 154–6; Lynn, 'Rathmullan', p. 154.

[130] Kelly, *Early Irish farming*, pp 316–59; Regina Sexton, 'Porridges, gruels and breads: the cereal foodstuffs of early medieval Ireland' in Monk & Sheehan, *Early medieval Munster*, pp 76–86; D. A. Binchy, 'Brewing in the eighth century' in B. G. Scott (ed.), *Studies in early Ireland* (Belfast, 1981), pp 3–6.

[131] Kelly, *Early Irish farming*, p. 219.

[132] Hencken, 'Lagore', p. 242.

[133] M. A. Monk, John Tierney, and Martha Hannon, 'Archaeobotanical studies in early medieval Munster' in Monk & Sheehan, *Early medieval Munster*, pp 65–75.

grown for food render. Rye is also found in small quantities on most sites. It served a useful role because it can be grown more successfully than wheat in cooler climates and on poorer soils. Although rye grains are present on some prehistoric sites, it has been suggested that, since the Old Irish word for rye (*secal*) is derived from Latin, new strains may have been introduced at the beginning of the period. Barley (mainly hardier six-row but sometimes less coarse two-row) was the most common cereal, closely followed by oats, because both are well suited to the climate and soils. The fact that they were so common is presumably why they were less valued in the law text.[134]

The steady increase in cereal production was largely made possible by the introduction of new technology from the Roman world, either during the Roman period, or in the following centuries most probably as a result of monastic contacts abroad. This is supported by the fact that a number of words connected with agriculture, such as *sorn* for 'grain-drying oven' and *muilean* for 'mill', entered Old Irish from Latin.[135] It is also borne out by the archaeological evidence.

Apart from rye, which might be sown in the autumn, spring ploughing and sowing were the norm. The prehistoric wooden ard with its iron-tipped ploughshare scratched a shallow furrow, using the cross-ploughing technique, and was only effective on light, well-drained soils. It is unclear when the heavier coulter plough was first introduced into Ireland. It has been argued that it was brought over from Roman Britain, where such ploughs were in use in the fourth century, and resulted in the cultivation of a much wider range of soils, including clays, and that this innovation was an important factor in the steady increase in cereal pollen after A.D. *c.*200. It has also been suggested that a rise in mugwort (*artemisia*) detectable in a number of pollen diagrams from *c.*600 onwards could indicate the introduction of the mouldboard plough, which made the turning of the sod possible.[136] However, these hypotheses have recently been questioned. First, there is no mention of the coulter plough in the earlier documents such as 'Críth Gablach'. Secondly, what archaeological evidence there is also tends to support the theory that the coulter plough reached Ireland later, perhaps around the tenth century, the same time that it came to be used extensively in Anglo-Saxon England and on the Continent.[137] Lastly, there is at present no archaeological or documentary evidence for a mouldboard plough,[138] and the

---

[134] Ibid. Kelly, *Early Irish farming*, pp 219–28; M. A. Monk, 'Evidence of macroscopic plant remains for crop husbandry in prehistoric and early historic Ireland' in *Journal of Irish Archaeology*, iii (1985–6), pp 33–4.

[135] Kelly, *Early Irish farming*, p. 222, n. 18.

[136] Frank Mitchell, *The Irish landscape* (London, 1976), pp 171–2.

[137] Niall Brady, 'Reconstructing a medieval Irish plough' in *I Jornados Internacionales sobre Tecnologia Agraia Tradicionale Museo Nacionale de Pueblo Español* (Madrid, 1993), pp 31–44.

[138] Kelly, *Early Irish farming*, p. 471.

rise in mugwort has instead been recently attributed to the introduction of fallow years to replenish the nutrients in the soil which would have allowed the weeds to grow unchecked.[139]

The coulter plough consisted of a wooden frame drawn by a team of four oxen yoked abreast, with an iron knife or coulter mounted in front of the iron-clad ploughshare (fig. 25). Its function was to cut through the ground, thereby clearing a way for the share, which formed the furrow. The archaeological evidence is meagre, but three types of iron ploughshare have so far been identified on early medieval settlements. From Carraig Aille 2 there is a small triangular example (length 83 mm; 3.25 in) from an eighth-century context; its size suggests that it was associated with an ard. There is a slightly longer type, with a flat rather than crescentic roof, from a seventh- or eighth-century context at Ballyfounder, County Down. Only the third, arrow-shaped type, which is considerably larger (length 228 mm; 9 in), can definitely be associated with a coulter, since the two were found together in a twelfth-century context on Lough Kinale crannog, County Longford. Both long-handled coulters, such as that from Whitefort (fig. 25 I), and short-handled examples, such as those from Lough Kinale and Ballinderry 1, are known. It has also been suggested that the coulter would have been mounted at 45° immediately in front of the ploughshare, and that the plough may have been of a one-handled type similar to those from Orkney.[140]

When the grain came to be harvested in September it was cut near the top of the stem with an iron socketed or tanged reaping-hook,[141] and was probably stacked in a rick in the farmyard.[142] The grain would then have been threshed and dried in a kiln. Examples of corn-drying kilns have been excavated on several sites. One at Killederdadrum, County Tipperary, was cut into the enclosure ditch, and consisted of a pit-like feature which contained a layer of carbonised oats with some barley and rye.[143] After drying, the grain would have been winnowed. There is little archaeological evidence for its subsequent storage. The Latin word for barn has been transfered into old Irish as *sabal*, and barns are sometimes mentioned in the documents, but so far only one likely example has been excavated at Ballywee, County Antrim (fig. 23). This was a rectangular structure 4 m × 8 m (13 ft 2 in × 26 ft 4 in), with an entrance in one of the narrow ends and a central path running the length of the interior with a row of post-holes on either side.[144]

[139] Weir, 'A palynological study', p. 109.
[140] Brady, 'Medieval Irish plough'.
[141] Hencken, 'Lagore', pp 106–7, fig. 39; S. P. Ó Ríordáin and J. B. Foy, 'The excavation of Leacanabuaile stone fort, near Caherciveen, Co. Kerry' in *Cork Hist. Soc. Jn.*, xlvi (1941), p. 93, fig. 1.
[142] Kelly, *Early Irish farming*, p. 239.
[143] Conleth Manning, 'The excavation of the early Christian enclosure of Killederdadrum in Lackenavorna, Co. Tipperary' in *R.I.A. Proc.*, lxxxiv (1984), sect. C, pp 242, 266.
[144] Kelly, *Early Irish farming*, pp 222, n. 18, 120–23, 480–82; Lynn, 'Ballywee', p. 6.

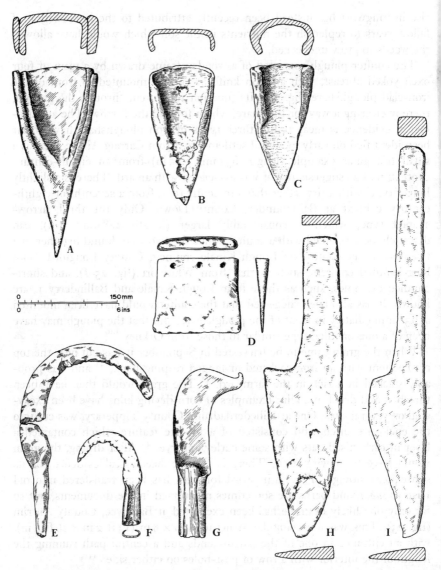

Fig. 25 Agricultural implements, including ploughshares (A–C), spade (D), reaping hooks (E–F), bill-hook (G), and plough coulters (H, I). After Edwards, *Archaeology early med. Ire.*

In the sixth or early seventh century both horizontal and vertical water-mills were introduced into Ireland from Europe. These enabled large quantities of corn to be ground and were used in secular and ecclesiastical contexts alike. Over the last twenty years we have learned a great deal about these from the archaeological evidence, because they were constructed from substantial oak timbers which have survived in millstreams and similar waterlogged conditions, though stone might be partially used for construction if timber was scarce. Not only do they demonstrate the considerable skills of early medieval Irish millwrights in both carpentry and engineering, but it is also possible to date the timbers precisely using dendrochronology. Horizontal mills are comparatively common and have been found throughout Ireland. They were usually small, two-storey wooden structures set astride the millstream with the millstones on the upper floor linked to the wheel below. Water from the millstream controlled by sluice gates, was conducted down a wooden chute, or flume, and flowed onto the dished paddles of the horizontal waterwheel, causing it to turn on a stone gudgeon. The wheel was connected to the upper millstone above which also turned, thereby grinding the corn. At Drumard, County Derry, for example, some of the timbers of the lower wheelhouse were discovered and dated dendrochronologically to A.D. 782, together with the flume, one of the mill-wheel paddles, and the lower millstone.

An efficient water supply was essential and evidence has also been found for its management. At Mashanaglas, County Cork, a mill dam was excavated and at High Island, County Galway, there was a complicated system which included an extended mill-pond, a feeder pond, and leats. At Little Island, County Cork, a particularly complex tidal mill (fig. 26) dated dendrochronologically to A.D. 630 has recently come to light, with evidence for two flumes and two horizontal waterwheels. Adjacent to it, and contemporary, was a vertical watermill, and a second example, dated dendrochronologically to A.D. 710, is known from Morrett, County Laois. With vertical watermills the two-storey millhouse was located adjacent to the stream. The water flowed along the wooden chute and the wheel was turned by water falling on to the paddles, which in turn rotated a cogwheel in the lower storey of the millhouse which turned the millstone above. At Morrett the V-shaped inlet chute was lined with planks with a sluice gate at the inner end and was connected to a wooden channel over which the wheel would have been mounted; the water exited via a second wooden chute. Some 27 mills have now been dated to the period, mostly by dendrochronology or sometimes by radiocarbon: the earliest is a tidal mill at Nendrum, Co. Down, dating to A.D. 619–21; the latest is from Clonlonan, County Westmeath, and is dated to c.1145, though this is currently the only example dated to the eleventh or twelfth centuries.[145]

[145] Baillie, *Tree-ring dating*, pp 177–95; Colin Rynne, 'The introduction of the vertical waterwheel into Ireland: some recent archaeological evidence' in *Medieval Archaeology*, xxxiii (1989), pp 21–31; 'Milling in the seventh century—Europe's earliest tidal mills' in *Archaeology Ireland*, vi, no. 2 (summer 1992), pp 22–4; 'The craft of the millwright in early medieval

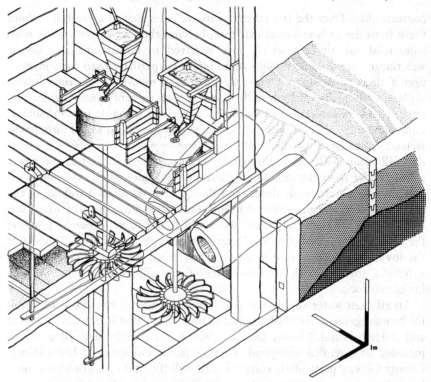

Fig. 26 Conjectural reconstruction of a double tidal horizontal mill at Little Island,
Co. Cork. By kind permission of Colin Rynne.

Although watermills were clearly an important feature in the landscape,
rotary querns with flat, disc-shaped upper stones are a common find on
settlement sites, where they would have been used to grind small quantities
of grain for household use. At Lisleagh 1, for example, charred barley, oats,
and rye were found close to rotary-quern fragments.[146] Rotary querns were
probably introduced into Ireland in the later iron age, replacing the more
primitive saddle quern.[147]

In addition to cereals, a variety of other plants were cultivated. Flax,
grown to make linen, was probably introduced into Ireland from Roman

Munster' in Monk & Sheehan, *Early medieval Munster*, pp 87–101; Colin Rynne, Grenlan
Rourke, and Jenny White-Marshall, 'An early medieval monastic watermill on High Island' in
*Archaeology Ireland*, x, no. 3 (autumn 1998), pp 24–7; Thomas McErlean, 'Tidal power in the
seventh and eighth centuries A.D.' in *Archaeology Ireland*, xv. no. 2 (summer 2001), pp 10–14.

[146] Monk, 'Excavations at Lisleagh ringfort', p. 60.
[147] Séamas Caulfield, 'The beehive quern in Ireland' in *R.S.A.I. Jn.*, cvii (1977), p. 126;
Raftery, *Pagan Celtic Ireland*, p. 124.

Britain. The seeds are a fairly common find as, for example, from Carraig Aille 1 and Deer Park Farms, where pod fragments of the dye plant woad were also discovered;[148] madder seeds were found at Boho, County Fermanagh.[149] We know from the documentary sources that pulses, such as peas and beans; vegetables, including onions, cabbage, and carrots; fruits, such as apples and plums; and herbs, such as chives, were all grown; some plants were specifically cultivated, especially in monastic gardens, for their medicinal qualities. These have yet to be discovered in archaeological deposits, though plum stones have been found in early eleventh-century levels in Hiberno-Norse Dublin.[150]

HUNTING was an aristocratic pastime but the osteological evidence does not suggest that game played a significant part in the daily diet. Red deer were the most common prey and were either pursued by hounds or trapped. Deer hunts were frequently carved on the stone crosses, and the late eighth- or early ninth-century shaft from Banagher, County Offaly, shows a stag with its leg caught in a trap. However deer bones, though often found on settlement sites, form only 1 or 2 per cent of the total.[151] It used to be thought that mounds of burnt stone with associated wooden troughs known as *fulachta fiadh* ('the cooking places of deer') were early medieval, but radiocarbon dating has now shown that in fact they are bronze age.[152] Other animals hunted include boar and hare, which are both shown in the hunting scene on the base of the South Cross, Castledermot, County Kildare.[153] It is not possible to distinguish the bones of a wild boar from those of a domestic pig, but hare bones have occasionally been found, as, for example, at Lagore. The freshwater location of crannogs was ideal for fowling and the bird bones from Lagore include several varieties of wild goose and duck. In coastal districts seabirds may have been hunted and their eggs gathered.[154]

The documentary record emphasises freshwater fishing rather than sea fishing in early medieval Ireland, although the significance of the latter

---

[148] M. A. Monk, 'The archaeological evidence for field crop plants in early historic Ireland', in J. M. Renfrew (ed.), *New light on early farming. Recent developments in palaeobotany* (Edinburgh, 1991), pp 316, 320; Kenwood & Allison, 'Insect assemblages at Deer Park Farms', p. 93.

[149] Proudfoot, 'Boho', p. 54; Monk, 'Evidence of macroscopic plant remains', p. 34; Kelly, *Early Irish farming*, pp 264–70.

[150] Ibid., pp 248–63.

[151] Ibid., pp 272–81.

[152] M. J. O'Kelly, 'Excavations and experiments in ancient Irish cooking places' in *R.S.A.I. Jn.*, lxxxiv (1954), pp 105–55; A. L. Brindley, J. N. Lanting, and W. G. Mook, 'Radiocarbon dates from Irish fulachta fiadh and other burnt mounds' in *Journal of Irish Archaeology*, v (1989–90), pp 25–33.

[153] Kelly, *Early Irish farming*, fig. 15.

[154] Hencken, 'Lagore', pp 225, 229–30; Kelly, *Early Irish farming*, pp 298–304; Proudfoot & Wilson, 'Further excavations at Larrybane', p. 106; O'Kelly, 'An island settlement at Beginish', p. 193.

probably increased towards the end of the period under viking influence.[155] Fishbones are fragile and can usually only be detected with the aid of sieving; as a result they have been little researched except in the viking towns. A large collection of fishbones from the ecclesiastical site at Drumcliffe, County Sligo, included scad, herring, and salmon; and in a shell-midden at Ought-ymore, County Derry, salmon trout, eel, plaice or flounder, cod, and had-dock have all been identified, demonstrating that the inhabitants probably practised both coastal and estuarine fishing.[156] The most common method of estuarine fishing was to construct a head weir which would entrap the fish on the ebb tide, making them easy to catch with a basket, net, spear, or gaff.[157] An intertidal survey of the Fergus estuary, County Clare, recovered a line of upright, roundwood posts interwoven with horizontal wattles which was identified as one side of a V-shaped head weir and dated by radiocarbon to cal. A.D. 534–646.[158] Three later examples, radiocarbon dated to the end of the first millennium, have been preserved in Strangford Lough, where a series of possibly later stone fish weirs have also been recorded.[159] Artefacts associated with fishing have also sometimes been found, notably fish spears, as, for example, from the Lagore and Strokestown crannogs.[160] Whales were not hunted at sea, but if they were washed up onshore they provided a welcome source of food, and whalebone was highly prized. Their bones have occasionally been found on settlement sites including the ringforts at Rath-mullan and Raheens, County Cork. Other marine mammals such as seal were also hunted.[161]

Shellfish were considered a low-status food and are therefore hardly men-tioned in the documents,[162] though the archaeological evidence suggests that they were more widely exploited. Small quantities of shellfish are a fairly common find on settlement sites as, for example, at Rathmullan, where a considerable number of mussels, as well as smaller quantities of oysters and limpets, were recovered.[163] Furthermore coastal shell-middens have the po-tential to tell us a lot more about this resource; but so far Oughtymore on the

[155] Kelly, *Early Irish farming*, pp 285–98.

[156] McCarthy, 'Archaeozoological studies', pp 61–2; J. P. Mallory and P. C. Woodman, 'Oughtymore: an early Christian shell midden' in *U.J.A.*, xlvii (1984), p. 55.

[157] Kelly, *Early Irish farming*, pp 287–9; A. E. J. Went, 'Irish fishing weirs' in *R.S.A.I. Jn.*, lxxvi (1946), pp 176–94.

[158] Aidan O'Sullivan, 'Intertidal survey on the Fergus estuary and the Shannon estuary' in *Discovery Programme Reports*, iii (1993), p. 63, fig. 39; 'Harvesting the waters' in *Archaeology Ireland*, viii, no. 1 (spring 1994), p. 10.

[159] Brian Williams, 'Intertidal archaeology in Strangford Lough' in *Archaeology Ireland*, x, no. 3 (autumn 1996), p. 16.

[160] Edwards, *Archaeology early med. Ire.*, p. 66; A. E. J. Went, 'Irish fishing spears' in *R.S.A.I. Jn.*, lxxxii (1952), pp 114, 124.

[161] Kelly, *Early Irish farming*, pp 284–5; Lynn, 'Rathmullan', pp 81, 154–5; McCarthy, 'Archaeozoological studies', p. 62; Edwards, *Archaeology early med. Ire.*, p. 65.

[162] Kelly, *Early Irish farming*, p. 298.

[163] Lynn, 'Rathmullan', pp 157–8.

Magilligan Peninsula is the only example to have been studied in any detail. Here winkles, cockles, and possibly mussels were systematically collected; oysters, whelks, and limpets were of secondary importance.[164]

Seasonal nuts and berries would also have been collected for consumption as well as other wild plants and seaweed.[165] Hazelnuts have been found on many sites including Lagore, Rathmullan, and the upland settlement of Ballyutoag. At Deer Park Farms hazelnuts, together with the seeds of blackberry, raspberry, and sloe have been identified. Wild cherry stones were also recovered from Ballinderry 1 crannog, and elderberry seeds from Armagh.[166] Wild plants gathered for consumption are more difficult to identify because many are also common weeds: the edible field weeds at Deer Park Farms were chickweed, fat-hen, and stinging nettle. In viking Dublin there is indisputable evidence that fat-hen was eaten.[167]

It is therefore clear that, although comparatively little research has so far been published, environmental archaeology is playing a rapidly increasing role in our understanding of the farming economy and what food was eaten in early medieval Ireland. It has demonstrated the steady expansion of both livestock farming and tillage from the early centuries A.D., aided by new technology, new farming methods, and probably the introduction of new crop strains and animal breeds, as well as by an upturn in the climate. It has also added greatly to our understanding of the importance of a mixed farming economy based predominantly on dairying and cereals with such foods as meat, fish, vegetables, fruits, and nuts adding not only nutrients but also variety to the diet. Although much of the food was seasonal, and poor harvests and animal disease could undoubtedly cause famine, overall it was a healthy diet which would support the idea of an increasing population.[168] Although the documentary evidence suggests that most farming communities were broadly self-sufficient in food, surpluses were clearly produced, partly for food render, but also in payment for a wide variety of more specialised goods and services, the purchase of agricultural equipment, for example. Some regional variation is also suggested by variations in climate and soils. This is also hinted at in the archaeological evidence, as well as the need to provide for non-primary producers, notably the major ecclesiastical foundations and later the viking towns.

[164] Mallory & Woodman, 'Oughtymore', pp 55–6.
[165] Kelly, *Early Irish farming*, pp 304–15.
[166] Hencken, 'Lagore', p. 41; Lynn, 'Rathmullan', p. 88; Williams, 'Ballyutoag', p. 45; Kenwood & Allison, 'Insect assemblages at Deer Park Farms', p. 93; Hencken, 'Ballinderry no. 1', p. 121; Ann Hamlin, 'The archaeology of the Irish church in the eighth century' in *Peritia*, iv (1985), p. 279.
[167] Kenwood & Allison, 'Insect assemblages at Deer Park Farms', p. 93; Siobhán Garaughty, *Viking Dublin: botanical evidence from Fishamble Street* (Medieval Dublin Excavations 1962–81, series C, ii, 1996), pp 29, 37.
[168] Kelly, *Early Irish farming*, pp 192–209, 316–59.

THE study of artefacts from all types of secular and ecclesiastical settlement, as well as more specialised sites and stray finds, can add enormously to our understanding of crafts and how these contributed to the economy. The investigation of waterlogged sites is particularly rewarding because of the preservation of organic materials. The modern excavation of craft-working areas as, for example, at Moynagh Lough crannog and the monasteries at Armagh and Clonmacnoise,[169] together with the reassessment of those from older excavations, such as Lagore and Garranes, can help to explain the processes of manufacture, since tools and equipment may be found alongside raw materials, debris, and unfinished products. There is also an increasing interest in how the natural environment was exploited to produce many of the raw materials used. It is equally important to examine the artefacts themselves, visually, microscopically, and scientifically, for what they may reveal about the technology of the period. On modern excavations artefacts are much more likely to be recorded in well-stratified contexts capable of being scientifically dated, and this is gradually leading to the establishment of more closely dated typological sequences. Archaeological evidence can also shed valuable light on the role of craftspeople and trade-and-exchange mechanisms, and how they developed over the period.

Woodland was of enormous economic importance in early medieval Ireland. It provided large construction timbers, smaller saplings, coppiced rods for wattling and basketry, firewood, charcoal for metalworking, evergreen leaves for winter grazing, fruits and nuts, including acorns for pigs, and bark for tanning. As we have seen, pollen diagrams suggest that from c. A.D. 200 the clearance of woodland accelerated resulting in increased areas of open farmland. Most woods therefore became concentrated on more marginal land and do not appear to have been very extensive.[170] The importance of this diminishing resource also meant there was a need for careful management, and there is increasing evidence for this in the archaeological record. The most valuable tree was the oak.[171] Large oaks seem to have been plentiful in the sixth to eighth centuries, as indicated by the construction of both crannogs and watermills, but dendrochronological research has suggested that by the ninth century they were scarcer and a period of woodland regeneration became necessary.[172] In areas of plentiful woodland oak uprights and hazel horizontals might be preferred for wattling, but where trees were less plentiful, such as Ballynavenooragh, County Kerry, there are hints that a wider variety,

[169] John Bradley, 'Moynagh Lough: an insular workshop of the second quarter of the 8th century' in R. M. Spearman and John Higgitt (ed.), *The age of migrating ideas* (Edinburgh and Stroud, 1993), pp 74–81; Gaskell Brown & Harper, 'Cathedral Hill, Armagh', pp 123–51; Heather King, 'Excavations at Clonmacnoise' in *Archaeology Ireland*, vi, no. 3 (autumn 1992), pp 12–14.
[170] Kelly, *Early Irish farming*, p. 379.
[171] Ibid., pp 380–82.
[172] Baillie, *Tree-ring dating*, pp 215–17.

including alder and willow, were exploited. Indeed, it has been estimated that one acre of managed woodland would have been required to provide sufficient hazel rods to construct a single double-walled round house.[173]

Axes and billhooks used for woodland clearance were regarded as important possessions. Examples have been found at Lagore, together with a variety of carpentry tools,[174] and there is increasing evidence that the early medieval Irish were skilled carpenters.[175] For example, the recent discovery of the waterlogged remains of a bridge over the Shannon at Clonmacnoise, one phase of which has been dated by dendrochronology to A.D. 804, has revealed a good deal about how it was constructed. Large vertical posts and beams were squared using axes, smaller beams were split using wedges, and mallets and planks may have been sawn with rip saws. The bridge was in the form of a raised walkway with the horizontal beams joined with the aid of bridle joints and half lap joints to vertical posts set in the riverbed. Dugout canoes were also found near the bridge, one of which contained an early medieval axehead and whetstone.[176]

Apart from luxury imports and native souterrain-ware pottery, which was confined to the north-east, Ireland was almost entirely aceramic throughout the period. Therefore wooden containers, including barrels, tubs, bowls, and platters, as well as baskets, would have been in daily use (fig. 27). Coopering was an important and specialist craft, evidence of which has been found at Moynagh Lough crannog.[177] Stave-built vessels were constructed from a variety of woods, though yew was particularly favoured, and the hoops which held the staves together were either made of split rods fastened with iron clamps or fashioned from thin iron bars. A particularly well-preserved yew bucket was found on Ballinderry 1 crannog, and an oak butterchurn was recovered from Lissue. Lathe-turning was another skill used in the manufacture of tableware including bowls, beakers, and platters, and lathe-turning waste has been found at Lissue as well as Lagore and Moynagh Lough crannogs.[178] An analysis of the forms and decoration of the bowls and beakers has suggested that earlier examples imitated luxury ceramic imports from the Mediterranean and France, while likely later ones show no such link. Other vessels, such as two wooden troughs from Ballinderry 2, were hollowed out manually.[179]

[173] John Tierney, 'Wood and woodlands in early medieval Munster' in Monk & Sheehan, *Early medieval Munster*, pp 55, 57.
[174] Kelly, *Early Irish farming*, pp 482–92; Hencken, 'Lagore', pp 105–10; Edwards, *Archaeology early med. Ire.*, p. 75.
[175] Kelly, *Early Irish farming*, pp 61–2.
[176] Finnbarr Moore, 'Ireland's oldest bridge—at Clonmacnoise' in *Archaeology Ireland*, x, no. 4 (winter 1996), pp 24–7.
[177] Bradley, 'Moynagh Lough crannog', p. 24.
[178] Edwards, *Archaeology early med. Ire.*, pp 76–7, fig. 30.
[179] Caroline Earwood, 'Turned wooden vessels of the early historic period from Ireland and western Scotland' in *U.J.A.*, liv–lv (1991–2), pp 154–9; Hencken, 'Ballinderry no. 2', p. 58.

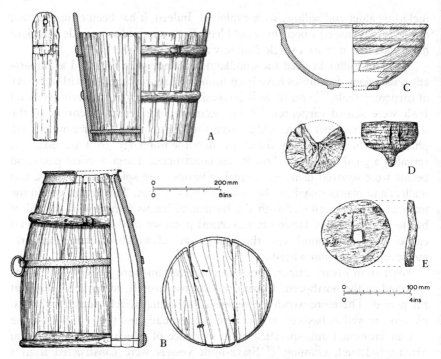

Fig. 27  Wooden containers: (A) stave-built bucket from Ballinderry Crannog no. 1,
Co. Westmeath; (B) stave-built butter-churn; (C) lathe-turned bowl; (D) and
(E) lathe-turning waste, all from the rath at Lissue, Co. Antrim. After Edwards,
*Archaeology early med. Ire.*

Many other artefacts were also made from wood but no major examples of
native rather than Hiberno-Norse wood-carving[180] have so far come to light.
However, more elaborate wooden objects, such as the Clonard bucket,[181]
were often decorated with ornamental metalwork.

IN areas where wood was less plentiful, drystone construction provided
a ready alternative to posts, wattles, and planks. However, from the late
seventh century some churches were built of masonry,[182] and from
the eighth large blocks of stone were quarried and transported to monasteries
where they were fashioned into carved crosses. This indicates the presence
of skilled masons, but archaeology has yet to shed light on the quarrying
process.

[180] James Lang, *Viking-age decorated wood: a study of its ornament and style* (Dublin, 1988).
[181] Susan Youngs (ed.), '*The work of angels': masterpieces of Celtic metalwork, 6th–9th
centuries A.D.* (London, 1989), no. 119.
[182] See Stalley, below, p. 725.

Many everyday artefacts were also made from stone. Querns, for example, were being manufactured at Moynagh Lough crannog and Ballyegan cashel, County Kerry.[183] Whetstones are a particularly common find and were used for sharpening the blades of knives, weapons, and agricultural tools, as well as for finishing metal objects cast in moulds. Most are rectangular in section, sometimes with shaped terminals and smoothed or polished surfaces. Small finely worked examples with a perforation at the top, so they could be hung from the belt, were probably a viking innovation.[184] In addition lignite, jet, and shale were used to make bracelets, rings, beads, and gaming pieces, some of which were produced on a lathe. Evidence for manufacture has been found at Oldcourt ringfort, County Cork, and at the monastery of Armagh.[185]

PERHAPS the most important by-product of animal husbandry was leather. A variety of animal skins were utilised, but oxhides and calf-skins were the most common. Although artefacts such as scabbards and bags were also made, the most common leather objects found on waterlogged sites are shoes (fig. 28). At Deer Park Farms both the manufacture and repair of shoes were taking place. A wooden shoe-last was found with tiny holes on the underside for tacks, which would have kept the leather in position during the shaping process. Leather fragments were reused till they wore out, suggesting that it was a valuable commodity which could not be wasted. Two different kinds of shoe have been identified in early medieval Ireland. The first was made of a single piece of leather fashioned into a simple wrap-round shoe or a more elaborate shaped slipper, sometimes with a decorated tongue. This is an indigenous type but was also adopted by the Hiberno-Norse. The second was a composite turn-shoe consisting of a sole, upper, and back made of two 'quarters'. It had been thought that these were a viking introduction, and they are commonly found in Dublin, but at Deer Park Farms they were found in earlier levels where there were fragments of shoes with pointed tongues, and ankle boots with laces, as well as children's shoes.[186]

A further specialist product was vellum for manuscripts. This was not tanned like leather but salted, soaked in lime water, scraped, and stretched upon a frame to dry. The skins of very young or fetal calves were essential to obtain smooth, light-coloured vellum. It would therefore have been very

[183] John Bradley, 'Excavations at Moynagh Lough crannog, Co. Meath 1980–81: interim report' in *Riocht na Midhe*, vii, no. 2 (1982–3), p. 28; M. E. Byrne, 'Ballyegan' in *Excavations 1991*, Isabel Bennett (ed.), no. 65, p. 23.
[184] Lil O'Connor, 'Iron age and early Christian whetstones' in *R.S.A.I. Jn.*, cxxi (1991), pp 45–76.
[185] Edwards, *Archaeology early med. Ire.*, pp 95–6.
[186] A. T. Lucas, 'Footwear in Ireland' in *Louth Arch. Soc. Jn.*, xiii (1956), pp 366–88; Marie Neill, 'A lost last' in *Archaeology Ireland*, v, no. 2 (summer 1991), pp 14–15; Daire O'Rourke, 'First steps in medieval footwear' in *Archaeology Ireland*, v, no. 1 (spring 1991), pp 22–3.

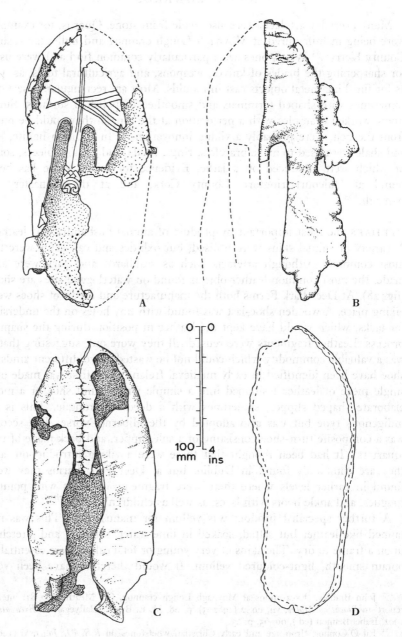

Fig. 28  Leather shoes from crannogs at Ballinderry no. 2, Co. Offaly (A–B),
Lagore, Co. Meath (C) and the ringfort at Killyliss, Co. Tyrone (D). After Edwards,
*Archaeology early med. Ire.*

expensive to produce, since large numbers of calf-skins were required to make a single volume.[187]

Bone and horn were also significant by-products of livestock farming. Red-deer antlers were collected in the woods after shedding in the late winter or early spring. Horn seldom survives, but waste material indicates that bone- and antler-working were frequently carried out on the same site, usually by professional craftsmen, since the materials would have taken considerable skill to prepare and work.[188] For example, bone and antler combs (fig. 29) were valuable possessions and could be highly ornamented, and their complexity clearly demonstrates the expertise of their makers. At the beginning of the period, small one-piece single-edged combs with high backs were used but the most characteristic pre-viking types were composite, being made up of several carved teeth plates held in position by rivetted side plates. These combs were fairly short and were either single- or double-edged with ornamental crests and decorated side plates. In the viking period Scandinavian types were introduced. These were much longer and thinner single-edge composite combs which were normally made of antler. They were mass-produced in Dublin and it is likely that some of the examples found on native sites, such as Lagore and Knowth, were the products of local trade with the Hiberno-Norse.[189]

Many other objects were also crafted from skeletal materials. These include bone pins, which range from the crude pig-fibula type and simple stick pins, to examples with elaborately carved heads, knife handles, and drinking horns which were decorated with ornamental metalwork.[190]

OVER the last twenty years significant numbers of textile fragments have been recovered from waterlogged levels in the viking towns, but finds from native sites, apart from Lagore, and more recently Deer Park Farms, remain extremely sparse. Wool and linen textiles were clearly the most important, though goat's hair was also sometimes used; there is as yet no evidence that the exotic silk imported into viking towns reached native sites.

Textile production was an important and time-consuming domestic craft, primarily associated with women, and various pieces of equipment used in the manufacture of cloth are commonly found on settlement sites. Spindle whorls, usually made of stone or bone, are almost ubiquitous finds. Other equipment includes wooden spindles, hand-held distaffs, which were

[187] Kathleen Ryan, 'Holes and flaws in medieval Irish manuscripts' in *Peritia*, vi–vii (1987–8), pp 243–64.
[188] Arthur MacGregor, *Bone antler ivory and horn* (London, 1985), pp 55–72; Edwards, *Archaeology early med. Ire.*, pp 83–4; Kelly, *Early Irish farming*, p. 63.
[189] Hencken, 'Lagore', pp 184–90; Mairead Dunleavy, 'A classification of early Irish combs' in *R.I.A. Proc.*, lxxxviii (1988), sect. C, pp 341–422.
[190] Hencken, 'Lagore', pp 190–98; Gaskell Brown & Harper, Cathedral Hill, Armagh', pp 125–8; Youngs, *'Work of angels'*, nos 53–4.

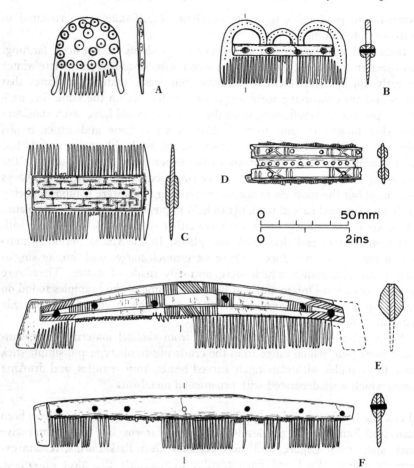

Fig. 29  Antler combs from (A–D) Lagore, Co. Meath; (E–F) Knowth, Co. Meath.
After Edwards, *Archaeology early med. Ire.*

regarded as significant female possessions in the laws,[191] and weaving swords;
there are also occasional discoveries of stone loom-weights, indicating the use
of vertical warp-weighted looms, and stone linen-smoothers. Many textiles
would have been dyed: evidence for both madder and woad have been found,
as well as the dye extracted from the dog whelk.[192]

An examination of textile fragments from Lagore indicates that nearly all
were of a simple tabby weave, though one fragment had a complex diagonal
weave and may therefore have been of viking manufacture. The cloth varied

[191]  Dunleavy, 'Classification of early Irish combs', p. 373.
[192]  Edwards, *Archaeology early med. Ire.*, pp 81–3.

according to the fineness and regularity of the yarn and how closely it was woven; the hem of one fragment had been sewn with decorative stitching, and fragments of tablet-woven braids, which were used to decorate the hems of garments, were also found.[193]

IRON, copper, tin, zinc, silver, gold, and mercury (used in gilding) were all employed in early medieval Irish metalworking. Iron ores, both from bogs and elsewhere, are plentiful in Ireland, though their quality is variable, and evidence for their exploitation has been found on several sites including Garryduff 1, County Cork.[194] Copper ores were also being extracted, as has recently been made clear by the early medieval radiocarbon dates from smelting furnaces in the vicinity of the bronze-age copper mines at Ross Island, County Kerry.[195] Tin would, however, have been imported from Cornwall, or possibly Brittany, since there were no native supplies. Sources for the other metals are all available in Ireland, but there is no definite evidence as to whether they were exploited, though the extraction of gold and silver seems likely.[196] Alternatively, metals could be recycled. Silver, for example, entered Ireland at the beginning of the period in the form of Roman hoards of coin, ingots, and scrap metal; supplies greatly increased during the viking period with imports of both bullion and coin.[197]

Iron was the primary industrial metal and was used for the production of a wide variety of everyday tools and artefacts ranging from knives, spears, and agricultural equipment to padlocks, keys, and nails, as well as higher-status objects such as swords, sheet iron ecclesiastical bells, and the highly ornamented wrought-iron slave collar from Lagore.[198] Limited metallurgical analysis has revealed that, although the range of manufacturing techniques in the period before the vikings was largely the same as those used in the iron age, there was some innovation, notably the utilisation of medium- or high-carbon steel cutting edges, but overall the standards of production were variable and lagged behind those on the Continent. The Irish were more influenced by external artefact types (for example, the introduction of

---

[193] Hencken, 'Lagore', pp 203–24.

[194] P. T. Craddock, 'Metalworking techniques' in Youngs, '*Work of angels*', p. 70; B. G. Scott, *Early Irish ironworking* (Belfast, 1990), pp 151–4.

[195] William O'Brien, 'Ross Island' in Isabel Bennett (ed.), *Excavations 1995*, no. 39, p. 42; Michelle Comber, 'Lagore crannóg and non-ferrous metalworking in early medieval Ireland' in *Journal of Irish Archaeology*, viii (1997), pp 105, 106.

[196] Niamh Whitfield, 'The sources of gold in early Christian Ireland' in *Archaeology Ireland*, vii, no. 4 (winter 1993), pp 21–3; Michael Ryan, 'Some archaeological comments on the occurrence and use of silver in pre-viking Ireland' in Scott, *Studies in early Ireland*, pp 45–50.

[197] J. D. Bateson, 'Roman material from Ireland: a re-consideration' in *R.I.A. Proc.*, lxxiii (1973), sect. C, pp 42–3, 63–4, 73–4; James Graham-Campbell, 'The viking age silver hoards of Ireland' in Bo Almqvist and David Greene (ed.), *Proceedings of the Seventh Viking Congress* (Dundalk, 1976), pp 39–74; Marilyn Gerriets, 'Money among the Irish: coin hoards in viking age Ireland' in *R.S.A.I. Jn.*, cxv (1985), pp 121–9.

[198] Edwards, *Archaeology early med. Ire.*, pp 88–90.

Roman sword types) than they were by the technology; for example, the Anglo-Saxon pattern-welded sword was not adopted. However, the viking settlement certainly led to an influx of superior know-how, which is clearly evidenced in the rapid adoption of viking swords.[199]

Some ironworking is evidenced on most settlement sites. However, the ringforts at Lisleagh have so far produced 800 kg of slag, suggesting that here ironworking was a major occupation in addition to farming.[200] Small-scale smithing may have been carried out by part-time blacksmiths in the farming communities. However, ironworking is highly skilled and there is definite evidence in the laws for professional ironworkers, which is supported by the archaeological evidence. Many smiths may have been peripatetic, travelling from farm to farm smithing tools, or employed under the patronage of royal masters as, for example, at Lagore and Clogher. There is also some evidence to suggest specialist ironworking sites at Ballyvollen, County Antrim, and Bofeenaun crannog, County Mayo, where a short-lived occupation (dated by dendrochronology to the beginning of the ninth century) produced large amounts of smelting and smithing slag, furnace fragments, and stones used to crush the ore prior to smelting.[201]

The analysis of ironworking debris from modern excavations is beginning to shed more light on the technology employed. Evidence for smelting includes small, shallow hollows in the ground, sometimes lined with clay, identifiable as the bases of furnaces, distinctive slags and fragments of clay cone-shaped tuyères that protected the nozzle of the bellows from the heat. In the past it was believed that the shallow depressions in the ground were the remains of simple, open 'bowl' furnaces. However, it is now recognised that a superstructure would have been essential for efficient functioning.[202] The form of this is unclear, but one of the furnaces excavated within a disused stone round house at the small ecclesiastical site of Reask, County Kerry, had a ring of charcoal in the upper fill which enclosed a layer of burnt clay, which, in the light of recent iron-age discoveries in north Wales, might be interpreted as the burnt remains of a substantial wattle-and-clay superstructure.[203] A piece of tap slag from Bofeenaun

---

[199] Scott, *Early Irish ironworking*; M. E. Hall, 'Iron working from some early medieval Irish sites' in *Peritia*, ix (1995), pp 221–33; Hencken, 'Lagore', pp 94–9; Etienne Rynne, 'A classification of pre-viking Irish iron swords' in Scott, *Studies in early Ireland*, pp 93–7.

[200] Scott, *Early Irish ironworking*, p. 158.

[201] Brian Williams, 'Excavations at Ballyvollen townland, Co. Antrim' in *U.J.A.*, xlviii (1985), pp 91–102; M. Keane, 'Lough More, Co. Mayo: the crannog' in *Irish Archaeological Wetland Unit Transactions*, iv (1995), pp 167–82.

[202] Scott, *Early Irish ironworking*, pp 159–60.

[203] Thomas Fanning, 'Excavation of an early Christian cemetery and settlement at Reask, Co. Kerry' in *R.I.A. Proc.*, lxxxi (1981), sect. C, pp 106–7; Scott, *Early Irish ironworking*, p. 167; Peter Crew, 'The experimental production of prehistoric bar iron' in *Journal of Historic Metallurgy*, xxv, no. 1 (1991), pp 21–36.

crannog suggests the introduction of more advanced shaft furnaces into Ireland by c.800.[204]

Smithing was often carried out on the same site as smelting, sometimes using dismantled furnaces as smithing hearths. At Clogher, for example, a smelting and smithing area radiocarbon dated to cal. A.D. 390–620 was excavated in the lee of a ditch. It consisted of two furnaces, together with a stone-built, clay-lined hearth with an adjacent boulder for an anvil and a scatter of small lumps of slag, indicative of bloom smithing. The hot iron would have been manipulated with tongs, which may be exemplified by those from Garranes.[205]

Copper-alloys, usually in the form of bronze, were employed in ornamental metalworking to make cast objects such as ringed pins, penannular brooches, and horse-harness mounts; sheet bronze was beaten out to form bowls and bucket plates. Copper-alloy was also used as the basis for the manufacture of complex composite objects such as the 'Tara' brooch, which was cast and then gilded and inlaid with gold filigree, silver, glass, and amber. Apart from the two smelting furnaces excavated at the copper-mining site at Ross Island, evidence for ornamental metalworking is almost entirely confined to important secular and ecclesiastical sites, where there was the wealth and patronage to foster the skills of highly trained craftworkers. For example, at Moynagh Lough two metalworking areas (fig. 21 A) dated to the second quarter of the eighth century have been excavated. The second consisted of an area 5.3 × 5 m (17 ft 5 in × 16 ft 5 in) of peaty clay and ash spreads in which was located a furnace, an area of burnt clay delimited by stones, a compacted pebble spread, and a dump containing metalworking debris. The furnace has been interpreted as most likely for smelting copper ore (because of the presence of slag) or possibly for the melting down of copper ingots, and had been used repeatedly. The clay area, which may have been sheltered from the wind by a wattle screen, was probably used for casting objects, which were then finished off on the pebble spread, before the debris was discarded on the dump. This included fragments of tuyères, clay crucibles, heating trays, and over 600 pieces of mould (fig. 30). The crucibles were used to hold the molten copper, which could then be mixed and alloyed, the resulting metal being poured into the moulds. A simple stone mould for casting ingots was found, together with clay fragments which were the remains of two-piece moulds that had been used to cast decorated penannular brooches, mounts, and studs. Amber chips used for inlays, tiny fragments of gold filigree, a bronze ingot, an iron stake used for beating out sheet metal, and several motif pieces used to try out designs, have also been found

[204] Keane, 'Lough More', pp 178–9.
[205] Scott, Early Irish ironworking, pp 160, 167; Ó Ríordáin, 'Garranes', p. 102, fig. 7.

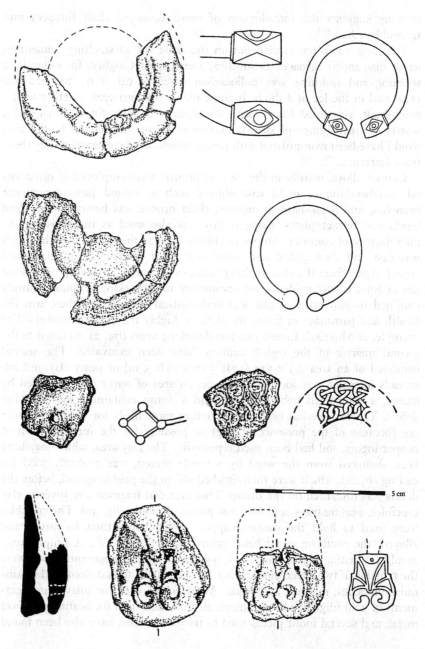

5 cm

Fig. 30 Clay moulds from the crannog at Moynagh Lough, Co. Meath. Drawing by courtesy of John Bradley. At the top, details of the penannular brooch terminals are shown in the centre at a scale of 2:1.

on the crannog.[206] At the monastic site of Armagh a similar range of debris had been dumped in the enclosure ditch, including evidence for glass- and enamel-working.[207]

To date no evidence of silver-working has come to light, though beaten silver objects, such as the Derrynaflan paten and chalice, cast silver penannular brooches, foils, gilding, and wire indicate the techniques employed. Gold was used very sparingly. The discovery of a tiny crucible with a gold droplet still adhering to it from the royal site at Clogher, County Tyrone, and gold wire from Moynagh Lough provide rare evidence for gold-working.[208]

Glass- and enamel-working were closely linked to ornamental metalworking: they were frequently carried out on the same sites; the equipment, including industrial hearths and crucibles, was similar, and the craftworkers are likely to have been the same people. Millefiori glass consists of different-coloured glass rods, arranged to form patterns in cross-section, which are then fused and drawn out before being cut into thin slices for use. In the early part of the period the multi-coloured millefiori rods were imported from the east Mediterranean, and objects such as pins and penannular brooches were decorated with slivers of millefiori set in fields of red enamel. In the late seventh and eighth centuries Irish glass workers developed more complex techniques, including the production of their own millefiori in the form of simpler chequerboard rods and blue-and-white millefiori insets, as well as the manufacture of glass studs, some of which were decorated with metal foils. Yellow enamel was also employed for the first time. These techniques were used to decorate complex pieces of ornamental metalwork such as the Moylough belt shrine and the Derrynaflan paten. Around the same time glass was also used for making a variety of blue, white, and yellow beads, frequently decorated with cabling, trails, and spirals, and predominantly blue glass bangles ornamented with white cables and dots, which may have been used as pendants or hair ornaments. A large number of beads and bangles were found at Lagore, and it has been suggested that the kingdom of Brega was a major centre for their production.[209] In the course of the ninth century enamel and millefiori went out of fashion, though they were revived in a different form at the end of the eleventh century.

---

[206] Bradley, 'Excavations at Moynagh Lough, 1982–3', p. 91; 'Moynagh Lough: an insular workshop', pp 76–80; Comber, 'Lagore crannóg and non-ferrous metalworking', p. 106; Youngs, *'Work of angels'*, pp 178–84.

[207] Gaskell Brown & Harper, 'Cathedral Hill, Armagh', pp 123–51.

[208] Youngs, *'Work of angels'*, pp 209–10.

[209] Judith Carroll, 'Millefiori in the development of early Irish enamelling' in Cormac Bourke (ed.), *From the isles of the North: early medieval art in Ireland and Britain* (Belfast, 1995), pp 49–57; 'Glass bangles as a regional development in early medieval Ireland' in M. Redknap et al. (ed.), *Pattern and purpose in insular art* (Oxford, 2001), pp 101–14; Hencken, 'Lagore', pp 127–50.

Glass in this period was of the soda–lime–silica type, and there is currently some debate as to whether some was actually made in Ireland from the raw materials or whether it was all brought in and reworked. Important evidence from the probable monastic site at Dunmisk, County Tyrone, has been interpreted as denoting glass-making as well as glass-working. Here an industrial area was excavated which included millefiori and glass rod fragments, a glass stud, a partly manufactured bead, and crucibles. Analysis of one of the crucibles suggested that glass-making was taking place on the site,[210] but this is yet to be replicated elsewhere. Some glass was definitely brought in and may have been recycled. Luxury glass vessels were imported from the Continent between the fifth and ninth centuries, and when these broke the resulting cullet may have been reused, though there is currently little unequivocal evidence to support this.[211] Glass rods for bead-making were probably also brought in from the Continent,[212] as were some millefiori rods from the eastern Mediterranean, though others were locally made. In general glass-working was concentrated on high-status secular sites, such as Garranes and Lagore, and major monasteries, such as Armagh and Movilla Abbey, County Down.[213]

As already indicated, early medieval Ireland was largely aceramic. The only major native pottery production was centered on north-east Ulster, the area of the kingdom of the Ulaid. This pottery is known as souterrain ware (fig. 31) and is commonly found on a wide variety of sites, demonstrating that it was regarded as low-status. This is supported by the simplicity of its technology, since it was hand-made, using coils, and probably fired in a bonfire kiln. As yet it is not known whether its production was based within the household—perhaps it was made by women—or whether it was manufactured by craftworkers who marketed their products locally. Some sherds have also been found on Iona and in viking Dublin, indicating the potential for wider distribution. Souterrain ware probably came into use around the eighth century, as indicated on the well-stratified sites of Rathmullan and Gransha, where it was found in later layers than imported E-ware pottery which was concentrated during the late sixth and seventh. It could have

---

[210] Julian Henderson, 'The nature of the early Christian glass industry in Ireland: some evidence from Dunmisk fort' in *U.J.A.*, li (1988), pp 115–26.

[211] Ewan Campbell, 'The archaeological evidence for external contacts: imports, trade and economy in Celtic Britain and Ireland A.D. 400–800' in K. R. Dark (ed.), *External contacts and the economy of late Roman and post-Roman Britain* (Woodbridge, 1996), pp 90, 93; Bourke, 'Glass vessels', p. 180.

[212] Youngs, '*Work of angels*', no. 205, p. 204.

[213] Ó Ríordáin, 'Garranes', pp 116–21; Hencken, 'Lagore', pp 129–32; Gaskell Brown & Harper, 'Cathedral Hill, Armagh', pp 135–6; Richard Ivens, 'Movilla Abbey, Newtownards, County Down: excavations 1981', in *U.J.A.*, xliv (1984), pp 98–102.

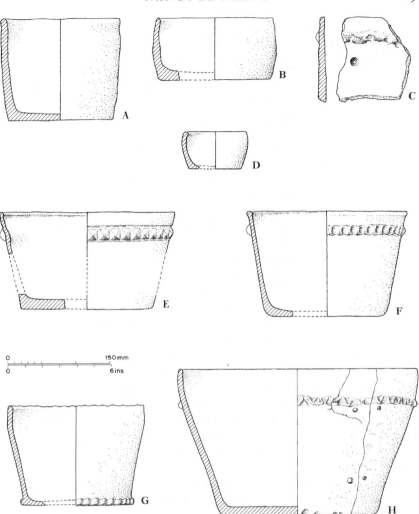

Fig. 31 Souterrain pottery from (A) Dundrum Sandhills, Co. Down; (B) Lough Faughan, Co. Down; (C) Nendrum, Co. Down; (D) Moylarg, Co. Antrim; (E–F) Ballymacash, Co. Antrim; (G) Lissue, Co. Antrim; and (H) Hillsborough Fort, Co. Down. After Edwards, *Archaeology early med. Ire.*

continued to the end of the period, when native potters began to manufacture everted-rim cooking-pots as a response to Anglo-Norman production.

The fabric of souterrain-ware pots, which ranges in colour from greys and buffs to reddish browns and black, is coarse and includes considerable amounts of grit as temper. Pots sometimes have the imprint of vegetation, usually on their bases, which indicates that they were placed on a bed of cut grass or leaves during manufacture to facilitate rotation. The forms are simple, ranging from small cups, dishes, and platters used as tableware, to cooking-pots, with soot and carbonised material still adhering to them, and large storage vessels. There are some indications, as, for example, at Lissue and Rathmullan, that the earliest pots were unornamented, but at some point plain cordons below the rim were introduced and later these were decorated with finger-tipping and incised ornament.[214]

So far we have examined the archaeological evidence for food production, exploitation of the landscape, and the full range of crafts, both domestic and those pursued by professional craftworkers. But what can archaeology tell us about the mechanisms of exchange and trade?

For the period before the viking incursions, archaeology can shed valuable light on long-distance trade. The most easily identifiable imports are pottery and glass. In the last quarter of the fifth century and first half of the sixth, pottery was being imported from the eastern Mediterranean via Byzantium (map 10). Different kinds of amphorae known as B ware were the most common, Bi originating in southern Greece, Bii from the north-west Mediterranean, and Biv which is not found in Ireland. These would have brought luxury commodities, such as wine and olive oil, by sea, mainly to south-west Britain, though Ireland also benefited, either directly or indirectly. Luxury red-slip bowls, known as Phocaean red slipware (PRS), from west Turkey, were part of the same cargoes. Additional products may have included millefiori glass rods, but many others, which do not survive in the archaeological record, may equally have come by this means. This trade-route would also have provided a vital link with Christian centres in the Mediterranean world.[215] Other imports were from the Carthage area of North Africa: Bv amphorae and African red slipware bowls, though the latter are not found in Ireland.

During the later sixth and seventh centuries the trade in imported pottery switched to Gaul and was under the control of Merovingian merchants. E-ware pottery consisted mainly of wheel-made jars and bowls, some with lids, which suggests that they were originally containers for luxury commodities such as madder dye and exotic foodstuffs. Wine in wooden casks and salt probably arrived by the same route.[216] Fine glass vessels—bowls, flasks, and beakers—mainly for wine-drinking, were also being imported. These are

[214] Edwards, *Archaeology early med. Ire.*, pp 72–5.

[215] Charles Thomas, *A provisional list of imported pottery in post-Roman western Britain and Ireland* (Redruth, 1981); Campbell, 'Archaeological evidence for external sea contacts', pp 84–9.

[216] Campbell, 'Archaeological evidence', pp 90–94; Charles Thomas, '"Gallici nautae de Galliarum provinciis"—a sixth/seventh century trade with Gaul, reconsidered' in *Medieval Archaeology*, xxxiv (1990), pp 1–26.

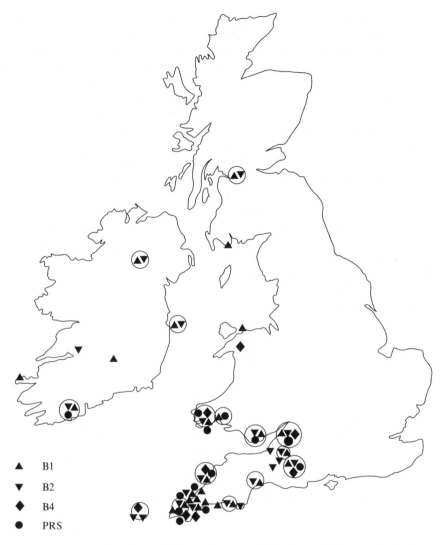

Map 10 Distribution of Bi, Bii, Biv amphorae and Phocaean red slipware bowls from
the eastern Mediterranean in western Britain and Ireland. By kind permission of
Ewan Campbell.

most likely products of the glass industry in western France during the sixth
and seventh centuries.[217]

In Ireland the distribution of A and B wares and Frankish glass is sparse,
being concentrated on relatively few, high-status, often identifiably royal
sites, such as Garranes and Clogher, but small quantities have also been

[217] Bourke, 'Glass vessels'; Campbell, 'Archaeological evidence', pp 90–91, 93.

found on ecclesiastical sites such as Reask. Equally, Bv amphorae have only been found on three Irish sites. However, E ware is found on a greater number and a broader range of sites (map 11), not only high-status examples such as Garranes, Clogher, Lagore, and Moynagh Lough, and the major monastery of Armagh, but also less wealthy ringforts such as Rathmullan. The distribution of imported glass in Ireland is similar (map 12). It is thought that coastal sites such as Dalkey Island in Dublin Bay may have acted as 'gateway communities'[218] for the importation of such luxury goods, which were then redistributed to the interior.

Trade with Britain in this period is archaeologically much more difficult to identify, because of the similarity in the material culture on either side of the Irish Sea. This was fostered by continued links between Irish settlers and their descendants who had migrated to western Scotland, north and south Wales, Devon, and Cornwall at the end of the Roman period, and their homeland, which must have resulted in trade and exchange, though specific artefact types are wanting. However, technology did spread from sub-Roman Britain to Ireland via these routes, as, for example, in ornamental metalworking, which is suggested by the introduction of the penannular brooch to Ireland, probably in the fifth century. More surprisingly, trade contacts with Anglo-Saxon England in the pre-viking period are equally difficult to identify. Probable trade with Scandinavia is evidenced in the eighth century by the importation of amber for metalwork inlays, and ornamental metalwork could have been exported in return, as, for example, the hanging bowl in the Oseberg ship burial. But in general Irish exports in this period are likely to have been raw materials such as leather, wool, and feathers, which leave no trace in the archaeological record.[219]

The archaeological evidence suggests that in the pre-viking period wealth was concentrated mainly in the hands of the many royal families and their kin. On sites such as Lagore and Moynagh Lough the ruling families had considerable excess wealth, which on the one hand they could afford to lavish on luxury imports, and on the other enabled them to act as patrons to a variety of professional craftworkers producing items such as weapons, ornamental metalwork, combs, and glass beads. The wealth was acquired in the form of land and its produce, payments for cattle held by clients, and food render, but might also include the spoils of cattle-raiding and warfare. In this period the concepts of gift-giving and reciprocity[220] bound society together, so lords feasted their retinues and passed on luxury goods such as penannular

---

[218] Campbell, 'Archaeological evidence', p. 95; Richard Hodges, *Dark age economics* (London, 1982), pp 50–51, 67.

[219] Mary A. Valente, 'Reassessing the Irish 'monastic town' in *I.H.S.*, xxxi, no. 121 (May 1998), p. 10.

[220] Charles Doherty, 'Exchange and trade in early medieval Ireland' in *R.S.A.I. Jn.*, cx (1980), pp 72–6.

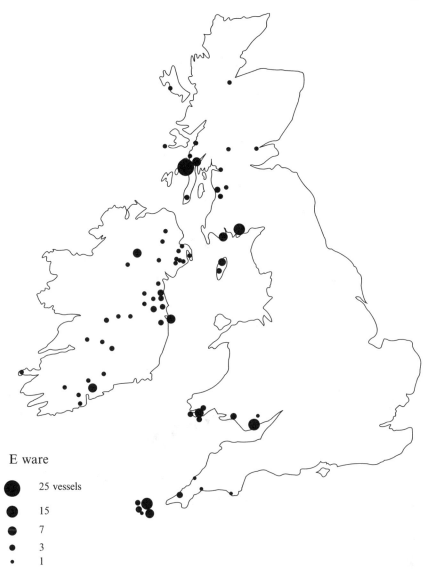

E ware

●      25 vessels

●      15

●      7

•      3

·      1

Map 11 Distribution of E-ware pottery in western Britain and Ireland. By kind
permission of Ewan Campbell.

brooches to their clients. The church was also a significant beneficiary, since
kings were important patrons who donated land and objects, such as altar
plate and reliquaries, to churches in their orbit of influence. The growing

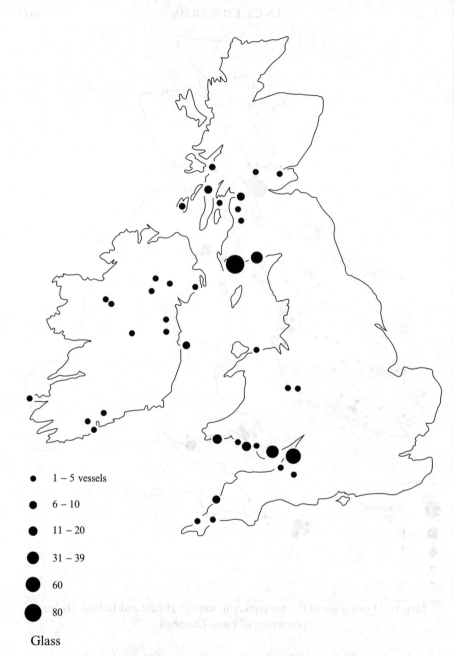

1 – 5 vessels

6 – 10

11 – 20

31 – 39

60

80

Glass

Map 12 Distribution of imported glass vessels in western Britain and Ireland. By
kind permission of Ewan Campbell.

wealth of the major monasteries meant that they were increasingly able to patronise luxury craftworkers themselves.

The extent of an internal market economy in the pre-viking period remains difficult to gauge. However, the idea that Ireland at this time was made up of completely self-sufficient farming communities based on the kin and client system is outmoded. Surpluses needed to be produced, not only to supply food render, but also for the payment of vital specialist craftworkers such as blacksmiths. There may also have been some specialisation within the local economy, as is suggested by the considerable evidence for ironworking at Lisleagh. In the early part of the period the tribal *óenach* or fair acted as a periodic focus for exchange and trade as well as for ceremonial gift-giving and religious activities. But as the period advanced the major monasteries may have begun to acquire some of these roles. The gatherings of pilgrims at such sites on holy days offered potentially lucrative opportunities for the exchange of goods.[221]

The advent of the vikings at the end of the eighth century was ultimately to have a profound effect upon the economy. Viking raids on wealthy monasteries and other sites were bound to be disruptive and have an impact on the native economy. The concentration of identifiable evidence for luxury craftworking at Lagore in the period before the viking raids and settlement, for example, could suggest that in the ninth century excess wealth was no longer used to oil the wheels of the hierarchical, client-based social system. Instead it was diverted into recovery and warfare, and became concentrated in the hands of a dwindling number of ruling elites. But the viking settlement and the growth of viking towns during the tenth century was ultimately to transform the market economy (see below, pp 836–41). The vikings brought Ireland into a regular network of international trade, which is clearly evidenced in the archaeological record. At a local level the townspeople needed food and other raw materials from the hinterland; professional craftworkers were attracted by the opportunities the towns afforded; and finished goods, such as pins and combs, were traded back to the countryside. The vikings also encouraged a movement towards a silver-based economy to facilitate trade. This is clearly evidenced in the deposition of viking silver hoards, especially during the tenth century. This eventually led to the minting of silver pennies for the first time in Dublin *c*.997 and the advent of a limited monetary economy that lasted into the twelfth century. Silver hoards were made up of bullion in the form of ingots, ornaments, and hack silver, and sometimes

---

[221] Ibid., p. 81; Charles Doherty, 'The monastic town in early medieval Ireland' in H. B. Clarke and A. Simms (ed.), *The comparative history of urban origins in non-Roman Europe* (2 vols, Oxford, 1985), pp 66–7. For an alternative view see Valente, 'Reassessing the Irish "monastic town"', pp 11–15.

coins. Their distribution beyond the areas of viking settlement, especially to the kingdoms of west Meath, north Brega, and mid- to north Leinster, testifies to wealth reaching the native interior as a result of trade and tribute as well as hostilities.[222] The increased availability of silver also signals the end of an economy where cattle-ownership was the major measure of wealth.

In the countryside large monasteries became the foci of markets for trade and exchange and may have taken on some urban functions. In the eleventh and twelfth centuries, it has been argued, Killaloe, County Clare, developed into a new urban settlement under the aegis of the kings of Munster. It consisted of their major fortified residence, the *dún* of Ceann Coradh, and the nearby monastery and cathedral of St Flannán; the archaeological evidence suggests a cosmopolitan Hiberno-Norse population engaged in craft and trade.[223]

UP to now the archaeological evidence for settlement and economy *c*.400–1169 has been treated largely thematically. However, over the last twenty-five years our understanding of the chronological framework has greatly increased as a result of radiocarbon and dendrochronological dating, combined with the excavation of well-stratified sites using modern techniques, more research on artefacts, and the use of documentary sources in conjunction with the archaeological evidence. In this concluding discussion the various strands will be brought together to try and paint a broader picture of some of the major developments in secular settlement and the economy over the period. Some of the interpretations are necessarily speculative. The archaeological data for early medieval Ireland is expanding steadily and will allow an increasingly sophisticated interpretation in the future.

With favourable climatic conditions, from *c*.200 onwards and beginning in the north-east, the pollen evidence indicates increasing woodland clearance and a major expansion in both pastoral farming and tillage. This suggests a rising population. This is likely to have been the result of a better diet indicative of farming improvements, probably coming from Roman Britain, which may have included the introduction of dairying, new types of domestic animal, new crop strains, and new technology. In the fourth and fifth centuries the rising population may have resulted in increasing economic pressures, which are likely to have been one of the factors that led to the emergence of the Uí Néill in Connacht and their expansion into the more fertile areas of Meath, as well as the emigration of population groups to northern and western Britain, where they took advantage of the vacuum created by the Roman withdrawal.

[222] Graham-Campbell, 'Viking age silver hoards', pp 39–74; Gerriets, 'Money among the Irish', pp 121–39.

[223] John Bradley, 'Killaloe: a pre-Norman borough?' in *Peritia*, viii (1994), pp 170–79.

Radiocarbon dating suggests that ringforts emerge as the predominant settlement type during the course of the fifth and sixth centuries.[224] However, their origins are still not well understood. Although outside influences are possible—for example, the enclosed homesteads of western Britain during the Roman period—it seems more likely that they may have had native iron-age antecedents[225] but were primarily a response to the emergence of a hierarchical, kin-based society pursuing a mixed farming economy, an idealised version of which is depicted in the seventh- and eighth-century laws. The numbers, size, and scale of the ringfort enclosures, as well as the varying wealth of the excavated examples, in general reflects a stratified society where there was a need to express status in the form of the settlement enclosure as well as to deter attack. However, the round houses within the enclosures were broadly similar whatever the wealth of the site. Promontory forts were simply an adaptation of ringforts, which took advantage of the topography.

Both dendrochronological dates and the artefactual assemblages suggest that crannogs came into vogue among the upper echelons of society at a slightly later date than ringforts in the late sixth and early seventh centuries. The origins of such sites are a matter of current debate. It has been argued, on the basis of radiocarbon-dated sites, that crannogs with substantial artificial make-ups and palisades originated in Scotland at the end of the bronze age and continued during the iron age and first half of the Roman period, re-emerging in the fourth century A.D. It has been suggested that the fashion was transferred from the Scottish kingdom of Dalriada to Ireland. However, the recent discovery of crannogs in Lough Gara, County Sligo, dated to the early iron age by radiocarbon, may indicate an alternative explanation involving a similar tradition of phases of crannog-building on either side of the Irish Sea.[226] The locations of crannogs were defensive, but they were also a tangible expression of status since they required considerable resources and labour to build.

However, the lowest levels of society are unlikely to have had the resources to build ringforts, and it may be suggested that they continued to live, as their forebears probably had done, in open or palisaded settlements of round houses which, if they were constructed of posts and wattles rather than stone, have left little trace in the archaeological record.

In the pre-viking period environmental and artefactual evidence from excavated sites is shedding more light on the mixed farming economy and on

---

[224] Stout, *Irish ringfort*, p. 131.

[225] Darren Limbert, 'Irish ringforts: a review of their origins' in *Archaeological Journal*, cliii (1996), pp 243–89; Gerry Walsh, 'Iron age settlement in County Mayo' in *Archaeology Ireland*, ix, no. 2 (summer 1995), pp 7–8.

[226] Crone, 'Crannogs and chronologies', pp 245–54; Christina Fredengren, 'Iron age crannogs in Lough Gara' in *Archaeology Ireland*, xiv, no. 2 (summer 2000), pp 26–8.

how the landscape was exploited. It is clear that the majority of the population was engaged in food production and that ringforts were essentially enclosed farmsteads, with their surrounding fields, pasture, and woodland. Archaeological evidence supports the legal texts concerning the importance of cattle, and particularly dairy-farming, in the economy, but also indicates the role of pigs, sheep, and other domestic animals. Archaeology has also confirmed the significance of cereal in the diet and the importance of the introduction from the Roman world (possibly via monastic contacts) of new technology, such as horizontal and vertical watermills, which are evidenced from the early seventh century. Technological improvements such as these would have made it practical to grow larger amounts to feed a growing population, although there may have been temporary setbacks, as for example in the mid-seventh century when there was a serious outbreak of plague.[227] It is also clear that we are not dealing with purely subsistence farming. The farming economy also supported those with specialist skills. Furthermore, via the client system, wealth became increasingly concentrated among the highest echelons of society, who may have had a monopoly on exotic imports and the patronage of professional craftworkers producing luxury goods. The ownership of these commodities again enhanced status and was made visible in such items as ornamental metalwork, clothing, and swords, as well as in conspicuous consumption through feasting and drinking and in generous gift-giving to both clients and the church.

It is unrealistic to see all ringforts as being occupied contemporaneously; some would have been abandoned and others constructed as the need arose. However, it is possible to highlight certain changes. During the eighth century some sites, such as Rathmullan and Deer Park Farms, start to be built up into raised raths. Around the ninth century the introduction of rectangular houses commences in the north-east. During the same period souterrains also begin to be constructed, most likely as a response to unsettled conditions. It has recently been argued[228] that a rising population would have put increasing pressure on the hierarchical, client-based society, which reached its apogee around the eighth century, and the lower strata may have found it increasingly difficult to fulfil their obligations. This would have been exacerbated if the wealth was concentrated in a contracting number of elites. Such a situation would have been made worse by the viking incursions, causing further instability and for some an irreversible loss of goods and status. General instability may also be reflected in the construction of new crannogs, such as Ballinderry 1, during the period.

The pattern of settlement from the tenth to the twelfth centuries is more difficult to determine. There are also hints of regional differences in

---

[227] Baillie, *A slice through time*, pp 127–30.
[228] Monk, 'Early medieval secular and ecclesiastical settlement', pp 46–7.

settlement evolution, with the west remaining more conservative. Radiocarbon dates suggest that the heyday of the ringfort lasted till about the tenth century.[229] Although there is currently a lack of evidence for the construction of new ringforts after this time, some certainly remained in occupation. In the north-east, Rathmullan, for example, continued to be inhabited during the eleventh and possibly the twelfth century. Likewise in the west, coin evidence indicates that the ringfort of Beal Boru, County Clare, which was possibly associated with the Dál Cais, was occupied during the late eleventh century.[230] It has recently been demonstrated that in the west some cashels functioned as important native strongholds in the later middle ages.[231] In some instances, however, while occupation of the ringfort site continued, the role of the enclosures became less important. At Carraig Aille 2, for example, during the ninth or tenth centuries the wall of the cashel was breached and, while occupation continued within the enclosure, rectangular houses and yards were also built outside; other rectangular houses were built over the ruinous enclosure wall. Likewise, at the royal site of Knowth from the ninth century onwards, rectangular houses with souterrains were built over the remains of the ditches of the earlier enclosed settlement on the passage-grave mound.[232]

The occupation of crannogs as high-status settlements continued during the tenth to twelfth centuries, and indeed, throughout the later middle ages.[233] For example, at Cró Inis, where King Maelsechnaill II of the Uí Néill died in 1022, a new palisade was constructed in the first half of the twelfth century.[234]

Although the occupation of some ringforts and crannogs continued, there is also a detectable shift towards more open settlements from the ninth century onwards. This is most clearly evidenced in the north-east in settlements with rectangular houses and souterrains, such as Ballywee and Craig Hill. In County Cork a considerable number of isolated souterrains have been located which appear to be associated not with ringforts or ecclesiastical sites, but with open settlements, though the plans of the houses, which were presumably constructed of wood, have yet to be recovered. In County Kerry the change from round to rectangular structures is less evident: some unenclosed round houses are sometimes associated with souterrains; others without souterrains were still being built towards the end of the period.[235]

[229] Stout, *Irish ringfort*, pp 24–9.
[230] Lynn, 'Rathmullan', p. 148; M. J. O'Kelly, 'Beal Boru, Co. Clare' in *Cork Hist. Soc. Jn.*, lxvii (1962), pp 1, 5–7, 27.
[231] Kieran Denis O'Connor, *The archaeology of medieval rural settlement in Ireland* (Dublin, 1998), p. 85.
[232] O Ríordáin, 'Lough Gur excavations', pp 108–9; Eogan, 'Knowth', pp 69–76.
[233] O'Connor, *Archaeology of medieval rural settlement*, pp 79–84.
[234] E. P. Kelly, 'Observations on Irish lake dwellings' in Catherine Karkov and Robert Farrell (ed.), *Studies in Insular art and archaeology* (Oxford, Ohio, 1991), pp 89–92.
[235] Monk, 'Early medieval secular and ecclesiastical settlement', p. 37; Cuppage, *Dingle peninsula*, no 1146, pp 396–7; O'Sullivan & Sheehan, *Iveragh Peninsula*, pp 385–6, no. 1208, p. 398.

It may be suggested that the partial eclipse of the ringfort during the tenth century was also linked to changes in society. During this period the hierarchical society idealised in the laws and symbolised by the ringfort was passing away. Minor ruling houses were losing their royal status; gradually wealth became concentrated amongst a handful of increasingly powerful dynasties such as the Uí Néill and the Dál Cáis. Many clients lost their free status and there was an increasing number of people among the lower grades of society.[236] The archaeological evidence seems to suggest that those who belonged to the powerful elites frequently continued to live on defended sites, ringforts, crannogs, and *dúns*. Such settlements were necessary both to provide protection and to demonstrate status and power. The continued occupation of some sites such as Knowth over many generations might serve to signify the long-held rights of a ruling elite or the legitimacy of a new dynasty. It is likely that some freemen also continued to occupy ringforts. However, it is possible that those who had lost their free status may also have lost their right to live in such enclosed homesteads; or they may have lacked the resources to maintain them.

Our knowledge of changes in the farming economy and the exploitation of the landscape during the tenth to twelfth centuries remains sketchy. There are hints of the over-exploitation of some natural resources. For example, dendrochronology has shown that large oaks had become scarce by the beginning of the tenth century, and there followed a period of regeneration which lasted about 100 years.[237] Technological and other farming improvements are less apparent than earlier, although it has been argued that the coulter plough could have been introduced as late as the tenth century.[238] The most detectable changes are in the markets for livestock and agricultural produce since, with the establishment of the viking towns and the growth in size of some of the major monasteries, an increasing number of people were non-producers and were therefore largely reliant on obtaining food from the farms in the surrounding countryside. There is evidence, for example, that cattle were being bred especially for these markets. Indeed, the development of the viking towns, with their mixed Hiberno-Norse populations, brought profound economic change with an expanding market economy and increasing international trade, which also had an impact on the population of the countryside and acted as a stimulus to regional trade and exchange. The elites may have lost their virtual monopoly of professional craftworkers making luxury goods, who instead moved to the monasteries and viking towns to ply their trades to a wider market requiring more mass-produced goods.[239]

[236] Donncha Ó Corráin, *Ireland before the Normans* (Dublin, 1972), pp 43–4.
[237] Baillie, *Tree-ring dating*, pp 216–17; *Slice through time*, fig. 8.3.
[238] Brady, 'Reconstructing a medieval Irish plough', p. 37.
[239] I would like to thank Huw Pryce and Mick Monk for their help with this article and the editor for his patience.

CHAPTER IX

# The church in Irish society,
# 400–800*

KATHLEEN HUGHES

W HEN Christianity reached Ireland in the fifth century it came from different sources, from Britain and from the Continent. Both were very different
from Ireland. Gaul lay at the end of a very long and thorough period of
romanisation. The barbarians were moving into Gaul in the fourth century,
but they were barbarians who had lived for some time on the fringes of the
Roman world and who were anxious to be assimilated into it. The church in
Gaul was identified with some aspects of the culture of the empire: most of
her bishops spoke and wrote good Latin; they presided in judicial disputes;
they had taken over the administration of some cities, organising their provi-
sioning and even their defence. Clergy had to be educated, so bishops were

*EDITOR'S NOTE: Kathleen Hughes wrote these two chapters in 1974, and when she died
suddenly in 1977 they were in the form in which they are published here. However, after such
a long delay, during which the study of the early Irish church has naturally advanced, it is
inevitable that the text will appear in some respects to be 'old-fashioned'. Yet this was the work
of the most distinguished early Irish church historian of her generation, and it has been
heralded as forthcoming in several publications since her death. The editors therefore felt that
it was only right to print the chapters as she wrote them; Dr Ann Hamlin, a friend of Kathleen
Hughes, kindly undertook to complete the footnote references and to update them where
necessary. (initially to 1990, but with a few later additions).

It is important, however, to emphasise that, while some recent work has taken issue with
some of Kathleen Hughes's views, the scholarly activity in the years since 1977 has been
profoundly influenced by her teaching and writing. Her first book, *The church in early Irish
society* (1966), "liberated" the subject from earlier stereotypes and helped to set it on a new
course, while her own use of source materials and her *Early Christian Ireland: introduction to the
sources* (1972) pointed the way to further advances. The years since her death have seen the
publication of editions of primary sources, as well as a number of monographs and a stream of
important articles in the Klett-Cotta *Ireland and Europe* series initiated by Heinz Löwe's *Die
Iren und Europa im früheren Mittelalter* (2 vols, 1982), in the volumes of *Peritia*, and elsewhere.
How Kathleen Hughes would have delighted in the lively activity in the field that she had
made her own!

A collection of previously printed articles by her appeared as *Church and society in Ireland
A.D. 400–1200*, ed. D. N. Dumville (1987), and a previously unpublished essay, 'The Celtic
church: is this a valid concept?', appeared in *Cambridge Medieval Celtic Studies*, i (summer
1981), pp 1–20. These chapters in *A new history of Ireland* are, therefore, the last things to
appear in print from her pen.

setting up their own schools; some were writing about the spiritual life in a way that showed their debt to classical philosophy. They were aristocratic leaders of a world heavily indebted to the Roman past.

Cassian of Marseilles and Honoratus (of Lérins) made a considerable impact on the Irish church of the sixth century, so it may be worth while to look briefly at some of the characteristics of the church of southern Gaul. Here monasticism started early. It was a monasticism individual in form, with a stress on asceticism and contemplation. Cassian urged the monk towards *spiritualis scientia*, meditation on the scriptures, which was to lead him to contemplative prayer in which the mind is possessed by God. Not far from Marseilles, on the island of Lérins, Honoratus encouraged the ascetic life with grace, consideration, and good manners. St Hilary says in his *Vita* that his insistence had an authority that was like a caress. 'What barbarian ways did he not tame?' In Hilary's portrait Honoratus appears as the most civilised possible being.

In northern Gaul, Tours and Auxerre most influenced the Irish church. Martin of Tours was uneducated, but his *acta* were written up and popularised by Sulpicius Severus, an Aquitanian noble who had won a reputation at the bar before retiring from the world. The writing is easy, attractive, amusing, undemanding. At Auxerre there was a flourishing school, and the Life of St Germanus shows a bishop active in the ecclesiastical affairs of northern Europe, helping to put down the Pelagian heresy in Britain. Germanus had been given a liberal education in Gaul and had studied law in Rome; then he held military office, before the clergy, nobility, and people united to make him bishop. He adopted the ascetic life with enthusiasm, but combined it with responsible care for public government. It was traditions of Auxerre that were strong enough to enter Muirchú's Life of Patrick.

It cannot be maintained with certainty, but it seems very likely that Palladius, the first bishop of the Irish, was connected with Auxerre. Prosper in his Chronicle under the year 429 says it was at the instigation of the deacon Palladius that Pope Celestine I sent Germanus to combat the Pelagian heresy in Britain. The most natural explanation is that Palladius was a deacon at Auxerre and that Germanus sent him to Rome. A cleric of Auxerre would be a very suitable candidate for the first Irish bishop in 431. Prosper says he came as bishop 'to the Irish believing in Christ'. The linguistic evidence proves that Christians were already living in Ireland, and that the first stratum of Christian loanwords was already established when the first Christian bishop (*epscop*) was sent.[1]

[1] D. A. Binchy, 'Patrick and his biographers' in *Studia Hib.*, ii (1962), pp 7–173: 166. Dáibhí Ó Cróinín has suggested that an Easter table ascribed to Patrick in a seventh-century source should rather be attributed to Palladius ('New light on Palladius' in *Peritia*, v (1986), pp 276–83).

It seems very likely that Palladius came to the southern half or central plain of Ireland and that Cashel was the capital of a Christian dynasty from the start, that is from the beginning of the fifth century.[2] As Binchy points out, 'Cashel' is an old loanword from Latin *castellum*, which suggests that its founders were already in contact with Roman civilisation.[3] No pagan inauguration rite (*feis*) is mentioned for Cashel, and when the poet of the 'Martyrology of Óengus' triumphs over the downfall of paganism at Tara, Emain, Cruachu, and Ailech, he omits Cashel. It is possible that Christianity was established here before it came to the north.

There are late legends about a number of pre-Patrician saints. Their *Vitae* do not inspire confidence,[4] but it is significant that all the saints who are supposed to have taught Christianity before the coming of Patrick are from the southern half of Ireland. Declan of Ardmore on the south coast, Ailbe of Emly in Munster, and Ciarán of Saigir in Osraige, are all supposed to have been older contemporaries of Patrick. Some traditions made Ibar, of Beg Éri in Wexford Harbour, a pre-Patrician saint. It seems likely that Christianity first came in via the south.

Patrick came from Roman Britain, though his own education was interrupted and his command of Latin exiguous.[5] Nevertheless, the Britain from which he came was firmly grounded in Roman government and administration. By the early fifth century conditions throughout Roman Britain were varying locally. Villas and towns had been interrelated phenomena, forming connected parts of the same economic system. A. L. F. Rivet's distribution map[6] shows the villas grouped round towns and along roads because they had to have access to markets. Villas were farms: not subsistence-economy farms, but farms that sold their surplus produce for capital gain. When the British economy was buoyant in the late third and early fourth century there was a period of rebuilding and extension, with elaborately heated rooms and mosaics. Coastal defences were then also in good order. But in the later fourth century the villas were more open to barbarian attack. Some villas went out of use, and where they continued they often did so with a much lower and simpler standard of life. Bath-houses were abandoned; rooms went out of use; some buildings were converted to industrial and agricultural uses. In finds from this period fewer coins are found and coarser pottery is more common. The residents must have had less money and fewer luxuries,

[2] D. A. Binchy, *Celtic and Anglo-Saxon kingship* (Oxford, 1970), pp 38–43.
[3] The study of Latin loanwords has been active in recent years; see, for example, Damian McManus, 'A chronology of the Latin loan-words in early Irish' in *Ériu*, xxxiv (1983), pp 21–71.
[4] Richard Sharpe argues that there is no early evidence that these saints preceded Patrick; see his 'Quatuor sanctissimi episcopi: Irish saints before St Patrick' in Donnchadh Ó Corráin, Liam Breatnach, and Kim McCone (ed.), *Sages, saints, and storytellers* (Maynooth, 1989), pp 376–99.
[5] Below, pp 305–6.
[6] A. L. F. Rivet, *The Roman villa in Britain* (London, 1969), p. 178.

though some villas went on as simple, sometimes subsistence-economy, farms well into the fifth century.

Urban life seems to have varied considerably between different towns. At Verulamium, for instance, it seems to have continued on something like the old lines. There was new building, and a gravity-fed pipe implies a functioning aqueduct and 'the survival of engineering craftsmanship'. This also implies sophisticated urban institutions, since there has to be some organisation to provide freshwater fountains inside a walled town.[7] But whereas towns such as Verulamium, Silchester,[8] and Carlisle[9] show continuity of urban life and organisation, the majority of Romano-British towns show a marked deterioration of standards in the fifth century. At York, for instance, there was a worsening of building technique: baths were no longer used as baths, hypocausts were blocked; part of a great sewer became filled with human excrement.[10] Other towns went right out of occupation. At Winchester urban life came to an end during the fifth century, and recent intensive excavation, now [to 1973] extending over a period of eleven years, has failed to produce any finds for the 200 years following *c*.450. The regular maintenance of streets ceased after over three centuries of unbroken attention.[11] So we have to imagine conditions varying locally in Roman Britain during the late fourth and early fifth century.[12]

Nevertheless, Christianity had taken root there. We know that British bishops attended the council of Arles in 314, and that there were three British bishops at the council of Ariminum in 359 who were poor, and were offered free transport home by the imperial posting service. They were presumably based in towns, but Romano-British towns have provided less evidence of Christianity than the villas. Some of the villa owners were certainly Christian, as we can see from the Hinton St Mary pavement or the Lullingstone frescoes.[13] At Canterbury, St Martin's, built 'while the Romans yet

[7] S. S. Frere, 'Verulamium, three Roman cities' in *Antiquity*, xxxviii (1964), pp 103–12; *Britannia* (London, 1967), p. 376.

[8] B. H. St John O'Neil, 'The Silchester region in the fifth and sixth centuries' in *Antiquity*, xviii (1944), pp 113–22; G. C. Boon, 'The latest objects from Silchester, Hants.' in *Medieval Archaeology*, iii (1959), pp 79–88.

[9] For the survival of engineering for a public water supply see the anonymous 'Life of Cuthbert', iv, 8, in Bertram Colgrave (ed. and trans.), *Two lives of Saint Cuthbert* (Cambridge, 1940), p. 122.

[10] H. G. Ramm, 'The end of Roman York' in R. M. Butler (ed.), *Soldier and civilian in Roman Yorkshire* (Leicester, 1971), pp 179–99.

[11] Martin Biddle, 'Winchester: the development of an early capital' in Herbert Jankuhn, Walter Schlesinger, and Heiko Steuer, *Vor- und Frühformen der europäischen Stadt im Mittelalter* (2 vols, Göttingen, 1973–4), i, 229–61.

[12] The archaeology of Roman Britain is a rapidly advancing field, and there has clearly been much progress since 1973. For a recent account of the fourth and fifth centuries see A. S. Esmonde Cleary, *The ending of Roman Britain* (London, 1989).

[13] Jocelyn M. C. Toynbee, 'Pagan motifs and practices in Christian art and ritual in Roman Britain' in M. W. Barley and R. P. C. Hanson (ed.), *Christianity in Britain 300–700* (Leicester, 1968), pp 177–92. Also Kenneth Painter in G. de G. Sieveking (ed.), *Prehistoric and Roman studies* (London, 1971), pp 156–71.

inhabited Britain', was still serviceable in Anglo-Saxon times, and Augustine was allowed to build *and repair* churches. Kenneth Cameron's work on *eccles* place-names shows these names surviving mainly in England west of the Pennines, north of the Bristol Avon, and south of Morecambe Bay.[14] They must imply the existence of some sort of British population-centres with organised worship. Since those names were adopted into English, it seems likely that British Christianity did not entirely die out here before the Saxon conversion.[15]

The Pelagian controversy shows us a body of educated Christians in Britain in the first half of the fifth century. Pelagius himself was a Briton. He spent a great deal of his adult life on the Continent, but it is reasonable to assume that he had received at least a part of his education in Britain. And his writings show that his education was first-class. He had some knowledge of classical literature: Lucretius, Virgil, Horace and Juvenal, Terence, Cicero, Sallust, perhaps Ovid. He knew something of classical philosophy. He was familiar with Christian writers in Latin and Greek, including Ambrosiaster, Jerome, Augustine, Rufinus, Chrysostum, and almost certainly Theodore of Mopsuestia. He has a sound and exhaustive knowledge of the Bible.[16] The vitality of a theological controversy presupposes a body of Christians with some education. When Germanus and Lupus came over to Britain in 429, they held a public debate with the Pelagian *rhetoria*. The debate was in Latin, and a crowd 'of vast proportions' turned up to listen and to judge the 'floods of eloquence' and the 'empty arguments'.[17]

Patrick's own education was very different from Pelagius'. His Latin was not that of the educated reader, but a colloquial and ecclesiastical Latin.[18] He spoke quite justifiably of his own *rusticitas*. He knew the Bible, and when its vocabulary was suited to what he has to say he is able to convey his meaning; but where he is relating everyday facts his style is so clumsy that his

---

[14] Kenneth Cameron, 'Eccles in English place-names' in Barley & Hanson, *Christianity in Britain*, pp 87–92.

[15] The evidence for Christianity in Roman Britain is discussed by Charles Thomas in *Christianity in Roman Britain to A.D. 500* (London, 1981).

[16] John Ferguson, *Pelagius: a historical and theological study* (Cambridge, 1956), pp 41–4.

[17] Constantius, *Vita S. Germani*, ch. xii. See also E. A. Thompson, *St Germanus of Auxerre and the end of Roman Britain* (Woodbridge, 1984).

[18] See Christine Mohrmann, *The Latin of Saint Patrick:* (Dublin, 1961). Continuing detailed analysis of Patrick's writing is building up a different picture from Christine Mohrmann's, which has been so influential. In 'St Patrick's reading' in *Camb. Med. Celt. Studies*, i (1981), pp 22–38, Peter Dronke demonstrates the clear influence of St Augustine's 'Confessions', acquaintance with other writers, 'theological literacy', and 'Patrick's power of selecting and combining what suited his purpose at that moment, and of discarding what did not'. David Howlett suggests that Mark 1: 1–15 was a source 'not only for the words and phrases which he pervasively quotes, but also for the structure of his thought and the manner of implying more than he seems to say'; see his 'Ex saliva scripturae meae' in Ó Corráin, Breatnach, & McCone, *Sages, saints, & storytellers*, pp 86–101. For a review of 'The beginnings of literacy in Ireland', see Jane Stevenson in *R.I.A. Proc.*, lxxxix (1989), sect. C, pp 127–65. This is an area of very active and lively debate.

meaning is often very difficult to grasp. Latin must have been his second language as a boy, but his captivity between the ages of 15 and 22 seriously weakened his command of Latin. He was a man of one book, and there are no traces in the 'Confession' or 'Epistle' of quotations or borrowings from any book other than the Bible. He was aware of the Pelagian heresy and opposed to it, but he does not enlarge on points of doctrine.

Our records say that Palladius had come to the Irish believing in Christ before Patrick's arrival, but if so it must have been to a different part of Ireland and his mission must have had limited influence, for Patrick found no Christian Latin tradition. 'Everything in Patrick's Latin', says Mohrmann, 'points to beginning and to isolation.' The church he reflects is more or less apostolic. He uses no word for church-building. Christians are called *plebs, fideles, credentes, timentes Deum, famuli Dei, sancti*. He speaks of the sacraments of baptism, confirmation, and ordination, and of the work of preaching. His language is that of an infant church with bishops and priests and deacons, and an organisation like that of early Christian days. There are practically no monastic terms. This proves conclusively that the Irish church had not yet developed its monastic character, and that in Patrick's day it had no close relationship with southern Gaul, where monasticism was firmly established.

We have already seen that the most likely area for Palladius's activity was the south. Patrick's own writings name no centre for his mission, but tradition locates it in the north at Armagh. This is almost certainly right. Armagh is two miles from Emain Macha, the capital of Ulster, and its foundation must pre-date the contraction of Ulster. The unsettled political history of this area in the later fifth and sixth centuries may well explain why Patrick drops out of Irish records until the seventh century.[19]

The annals give a variety of different dates for Patrick's floruit. The Annals of Ulster at 457 give *Quies senis Patricii ut alii libri dicunt*, and again at 461 *hic alii quietem Patricii dicunt*. The Annals of Inisfallen put his death at 496, but say *anno 432 a passione Domini*, and the Annals of Ulster give it again at 491 and 492: at 491 *dicunt Scoiti hic Patricium archiepiscopum defunctum*, and at 492 that he died in the 120th year of his age, on 17 March, sixty years after coming to Ireland. If we are to have any opinion on the validity of these entries we need first to discuss the way in which the fifth- and sixth-century annal entries were put together.

---

[19] There is no early evidence for where Patrick worked, or for Armagh having been founded by him. Rival claims were made by seventh-century writers for the Saul/Downpatrick area and for Armagh, and Armagh's case prevailed. See Byrne, *Ir. kings*, pp 78–82; Liam de Paor, 'The aggrandisement of Armagh' in T. D. Williams (ed.), *Hist. Studies*, viii (Dublin, 1968), pp 95–110, and Richard Sharpe, 'St Patrick and the see of Armagh' in *Camb. Med. Celt. Studies*, iv (1982), pp 33–59. See also Charles Doherty, 'The cult of St Patrick and the politics of Armagh in the seventh century' in Picard, *Ire. & northern France*, pp 53–93.

All the manuscripts of the Irish annals are late. The earliest is of the Annals of Innisfallen, in contemporary hands from the end of the eleventh century down to 1321. The Annals of Ulster have been transmitted in copies of the fifteenth and sixteenth centuries. The Annals of Ulster and the Annals of Tigernach go back to a similar text, to which the Annals of Inisfallen are related. After about 590 the sequence of events of all three is very similar; before 590, there are more discrepancies. It looks as if from c.590 onwards there was a set of Annals on which all the extant recensions drew. Before this date if we look at the Annals of Ulster and Annals of Tigernach less than half of the total entries are common; otherwise each set of Annals adds independently, arranging its entries in different order.

The chronology of the Annals seems to be roughly consistent for the sixth century. There are references to the grandsons of Niall Noígiallach between 507 and 522, to his great-grandsons between 536 and 565, to his great-great-grandsons between 554 and 604. But when we go back into the fifth century there is something badly wrong with the dating of the Irish Annals. Niall himself dies in the Annals of Inisfallen before 382, in 'Chronicum Scotorum' at 411, in the Four Masters at 405, but the sons of Niall are active between 429 and 516, and the brother of his alleged slayer dies c.483/5. This means that Niall's sons and associates have an absurdly long time-span. The reasonable events of the later fifth century have been extended backwards.

There was clearly no contemporary record for the fifth century, but later, perhaps in the seventh century, historians had an oral tradition to which they had to attach a chronology. Genealogy and tradition provided a roughly reliable record backwards until the late fifth century; beyond this chronological sequence in native affairs was extremely vague. Later historians had one fixed date, 431, when Palladius was sent as first bishop to the Irish believing in Christ. Native tradition emphasised Patrick as the Irish apostle, so Patrick had to come as soon as possible after this. Historians 'knew' that he came in the fourth year of Lóeguire, so that provided a date for Lóeguire's reign. But most of Niall's associates belong to the second half of the fifth century, and it might quite well be argued that Niall himself must have died not before the middle of the fifth century.[20]

The genealogical tracts say that Emain Macha fell to the three Collas, cousins of Niall's father, but it was Niall and his sons who finally broke up the 'fifth' of Ulster. It is almost certain that the foundation of the Christian centre of Armagh must belong to the period before the final collapse of Ulster.[21] If we date the death of Niall and the *floruit* of his sons to the second

---

[20] This, with many other Patrician problems, is discussed by D. A. Binchy, 'Patrick and his biographers' in *Studia Hib.*, ii (1962), pp 7–173.

[21] For a recent, balanced account of early Ulster history see Charles Doherty, 'Ulster before the Normans: ancient myth and early history' in Ciaran Brady, Mary O'Dowd, and Brian M. Walker (ed.), *Ulster: an illustrated history* (London, 1989), pp 13–43.

half of the fifth century we can accept the period of approximately 461–92 as a likely one for Patrick.[22]

This means we need to think of Christianity filtering in probably from the beginning of the fifth century, Palladius arriving in the southern half of Ireland in 431. Christianity penetrated slowly northwards. Auxilius and Iserninus, who are said to have died in 459 and 468, should perhaps be associated with the continental phase of the mission. Iserninus is supposed to have founded Aghade in Carlow and Kilcullen in Kildare, Auxilius Kilashee near Naas. The conversion of the north came with Patrick, probably in the second half of the century. It is impossible to be exact about dates, but the genealogies of kings and the deaths of associates accommodate a floruit of *c*.461–92 better than any other.[23]

The 'Epistle' and 'Confession' show a first-generation missionary church. The love of Christ had given Patrick to the Irish people, so that he was committed to serve them for the duration of his life. His position was insecure; he gave his free birth for the benefit of the Irish, suffering bonds. He speaks specifically of two periods of captivity, once for two months, when he was delivered on the sixtieth night, once in irons when he was delivered on the fourteenth day. He has preached constantly in the extremities of the world: 'We are witnesses that the gospel has been preached unto those parts beyond which there lives nobody.'[24] He has baptised thousands and confirmed many, and clerics have been ordained for them everywhere. He repeats these claims more than once: of many baptisms, confirmations, and the installation of priests to minister to the converts.

How was Patrick's mission financed? This is a problem that his own writings do not solve. He has refused gifts from pious women, and taken nothing for all his baptisms and ordinations. He says 'I have no wealth'; yet he has travelled everywhere dispensing generous patronage. He constantly gave presents to kings and paid fees to the kings' sons who formed his entourage. He has made gifts—in all the price of fifteen men—to those who

---

[22] R. P. C. Hanson, *St Patrick, his origins and career* (Oxford, 1968), argues for the arrival of Patrick in Ireland between 425 and 435 and his death about 460, but I have not found his arguments convincing. See my review in *E.H.R.*, lxxxv (1970), pp 348–50.

[23] The volume of writing about Patrick (including his dates) has, of course, continued to grow. Publications since this chapter was written include R. H. M. Dolley, 'Roman coins from Ireland and the date of St Patrick' in *R.I.A. Proc.*, lxxvi (1976), sect. C, pp 181–90; A. E. B. Hood, *St Patrick: his writings and Muirchú's life* (Chichester, 1978); P. A. Wilson, 'St Patrick and Irish Christian origins' in *Studia Celt.*, xiv–xv (1979–80), pp 344–79; Charles Thomas, op. cit., chs 13–14; R. P. C. Hanson, *The life and writings of the historical St Patrick* (New York, 1983); and see R. P. C. Hanson, 'A new star in the Patrician sky' in *Peritia*, v (1986), pp 419–22, for details of two books in Italian by Elena Malaspina (1984 and 1985). E. A. Thompson's *Who was Saint Patrick?* (Woodbridge, 1985) was reprinted in 1999, and David N. Dumville's *Saint Patrick A.D. 493–1993* appeared in 1993.

[24] *The works of St Patrick*, ed. Ludwig Bieler (London, 1953), p. 31.

administered justice.[25] Undoubtedly this behaviour would raise his prestige, but where the resources came from is not anywhere indicated.

It was not a monastic church, yet there were converts living an ascetic and celibate life. 'The sons and daughters of the kings of the Irish are seen to be monks and virgins of Christ.'[26] The number of virgins was increasing, though parents objected to the practice of virginity.

This is the picture of an active missionary church, successfully making converts, spreading its clergy; a church following a socially aristocratic routine, with a bishop accompanied by princes and distributing largesse. Patrick's own teaching must have been grounded on the scriptures, but probably on little else. He said himself: 'I have not studied like the others',[27] and it is difficult to believe that he could have had any substantial period of training at Auxerre or any comparable centre. The 'Epistle' and 'Confession' give only a vague idea of ecclesiastical administration.

But when we come to the canons of the first synod of Patrick, Auxilius, and Iserninus, we have a much more clearly defined picture of the way the church was organised. There is a hierarchy of clergy from ostiary to bishops. The church is divided into independent units, each under the control of its own bishop. Every cleric has to be recognised as part of the official body of clergy: there are to be no vagrant clerics, every new cleric needs the bishop's permission to minister, and British clergy need letters of introduction. The bishop has to consecrate newly built churches in his diocese. He visits and exercises jurisdiction in his own diocese, but he may not interfere in the diocese of another. This is a well-developed church which has proceeded beyond the unconventional missionary stage of the Patrician writings.

Yet the church of these canons of the first synod has not yet received a formal position in secular society. It is still a private organisation. Its clergy do not hold their honour-price according to their ecclesiastical order, as seventh-century clerics do. In these early canons their honour-price is unaffected by their clerical grade, so that a cleric who has the necesssary status may go surety, or he may be a man under yoke of slavery. Whereas in the seventh-century canons ecclesiastical judgements are supported with physical penalties, here, when the canons of the first synod define the sins that a Christian may commit, such as murder, theft, adultery, failure to pay debts, and so on, the only action taken against the sinning Christian is his excommunication. A Christian is specifically forbidden to call one who has wronged

---

[25] Ibid., p. 38.

[26] Ibid., p. 34. Michael Herren emphasises the importance of these ascetic converts as a 'spiritual vanguard' in Patrick's missionary work and sees the background as Gaulish, in 'Mission and monasticism in the *Confessio* of Patrick' in Ó Corráin, Breatnach, & McCone, *Sages, saints, & storytellers*, pp 76–85. This element in the very early Irish church must have been important for the growth of 'institutional' monasticism in the sixth century.

[27] *Works*, ed. Bieler, p. 23. This diffidence cloaks a solid grounding in theology and accomplishment in Latin; see above, n. 18.

him to the secular courts; disputes have to be dealt with within the church. The church is a community within a still-pagan society and is to hold itself separate from the world. The alms of pagans are not to be accepted. These are aspects of a church that had not yet been accepted by the secular law, as had the church of the seventh-century canons.[28]

There are other rulings that also suggest a church still in a fairly primitive state. The clerics of the diocese form a kind of college, who have to turn up at matins and vespers; yet they may be married. The church is served by bishops, priests, deacons, lectors, psalmists, ostiaries, but monks and virgins exist. These are probably people under vows of asceticism and celibacy, but we see them travelling about and they do not seem to be entirely withdrawn from ordinary life.

It seems to me that these canons must belong to the pre-monastic church. They were moreover issued by a church that had not yet been legally accepted by society, where the clergy do not yet hold an honour-price as clergy. On the other hand the church has a fully developed hierarchy of clergy; it has developed a number of separate dioceses, each under its own bishop, each recognising the independence of the others. The church of the first synod must therefore be later than the missionary church of Patrick's letters, but earlier than the monastic phase of the second half of the sixth century. Possibly they should be dated to the first half of the sixth century.[29]

The first stage of Irish Christianity lasts, then, from about 400 to 500. Christianity first arrived probably in the south of Ireland. Palladius, probably a cleric of Auxerre, arrived in 431 as the first bishop to the Irish Christians who had already established themselves. Christianity filtered north, and Auxilius and Iserninus were remembered church leaders. Probably in the second half of the century Patrick the Briton came to Ulster and a church was set up at Armagh near the old capital of Ulster. Emain Macha subsequently fell to the Uí Néill, the borders of Ulster were pushed eastwards, and Patrick disappeared from Irish tradition for 150 years. Stories put Patrick's arrival in the fourth year of Lóeguire son of Niall, and most of Niall's sons belong to the second half of the fifth century. Later historians wanted to put Patrick as soon as possible after the arrival of Palladius, and thus Lóeguire's reign was put back. Serious Irish chronology seems to start in the later fifth century.[30]

[28] See Hughes, *Ch. in early Ir. soc.*, pp 44–53.
[29] The date of the canons of the first synod of Patrick, Auxilius, and Iserninus remains a subject of debate. Different scholars favour the fifth, sixth, and seventh centuries. A new edition and discussion of the text is found in M. J. Farris (ed. and trans.), *The bishops' synod ('The first synod of St Patrick')* (Liverpool, 1976), which includes photographs of the manuscript. The text is translated in Liam de Paor, *Saint Patrick's world* (Blackrock, 1993), pp 135–8.
[30] A cautious view would now be that 'serious Irish chronology' begins only with seventh-century sources, or at least not until after the serious plagues in the mid-sixth century. See F. J. Byrne, 'A note on Trim and Sletty' in *Peritia*, iii (1984), pp 316–19, for two illuminating cases of how early records of churches were lost, or deliberately suppressed for dynastic reasons.

Probably by the early sixth century the church had considerably developed. There were separate dioceses, served by bishops and clergy, though clerical celibacy had not yet been introduced. But society was still largely pagan, and the church had not yet been recognised by secular law. The clergy held whatever status they had as private individuals, and their status was not affected by their ecclesiastical order. Christians were encouraged to settle disputes within the church and not to take them to the secular courts. There were ascetics and celibates, but they had not yet a dominant position in the church. This was the state of affairs when the monastic movement began to gain strength in the middle of the sixth century.[31]

THERE were monks and virgins in the fifth- and early sixth-century church, but the men who led the church were non-monastic bishops and clergy. Then, about the middle of the sixth century, the most influential people in the church took up the monastic life. If we are to believe the hagiographical tradition the vast majority of these early abbots belonged to the aristocracy. Some were bishops, many but not all were in priests' orders, and all were celibate.

Why did monasticism gain influence just at this time? It has been argued that monasticism came in from Britain, but it seems to have developed in Britain and Ireland at about the same period. Gildas wrote his 'De excidio Britanniae' perhaps about 530–40, and his church was led by secular clergy with married bishops, though it contained monks.[32] Some of the earliest monastic founders, Finnian of Clonard and Ciarán of Clonmacnoise, were founding houses in the 540s and died in the great plague of 548/9. It may be

---

[31] In what follows, Kathleen Hughes is outlining the view of church development that is fully argued in her *Ch. in early Ir. soc.* She saw the monastic church as largely replacing a non-monastic organisation. Since her death, and building on the foundation she laid, scholars have been developing a new 'model', seeing a more complicated pattern of the coexistence of the secular and monastic elements. The ascetic tradition, prominent in the Irish church since Patrick's time, clearly contributed to the growth of monasticism from the sixth century onwards, and abbots controlled not simply monks and monasteries but also landed estates and their inhabitants. At the same time bishops retained their supreme authority in spiritual matters, administered the sacraments, and supervised the non-monastic, pastoral clergy. This pattern of diversity embraces large and small establishments, episcopal seats, monasteries, 'mother churches' (probably early missionary centres), tribal and family churches, hermitages, and retreats. See especially Donnchadh Ó Corráin, 'The early Irish churches: some aspects of organization' in Ó Corráin, *Ir. antiquity*, pp 327–41, and Richard Sharpe, 'Some problems concerning the organization of the church in early medieval Ireland' in *Peritia*, iii (1984), pp 230–70. Also important is Patrick J. Corish's work on the pastoral ministry of the church: 'The pastoral mission in the early Irish church' in *Léachtaí Cholm Cille*, ii (Maynooth, 1971) pp 14–25, and 'The Christian mission' in Corish, *Ir. catholicism*, i, fasc. 3 (1972). An important recent contribution to the debate is Colmán Etchingham, *Church organisation in Ireland A.D. 650 to 1000* (Maynooth, 1999).

[32] Michael Winterbottom has published a new edition and translation of the 'De excidio' in *Gildas: the Ruin of Britain and other works* (Chichester, 1978). There is also a substantial volume of essays: Michael Lapidge and David Dumville (ed.), *Gildas: new approaches* (Woodbridge, 1984).

that the traumatic experience of plague encouraged a popular movement towards asceticism.

At first the abbot was responsible for the government of the monastery and for the spiritual welfare of the monks. As time went on he became more and more involved in general administration, and other priests in the monastery acted as confessors or 'soul-friends'. Other monastic houses and churches were founded, which became part of the *paruchia*. These houses might be widely scattered, not in a contiguous territory, and it was the abbot's duty to visit them. In the annals we find the abbot of Iona going *ad Hiberniam* to visit his houses there, Derry and Durrow, and in Adomnán's Life of Columba we see the saint in touch with the priors of his sub-houses in Scotland.[33]

The abbot was the *comarba*, or heir, of the founder. This meant that the property was legally vested in him, and he had ultimate decisions over the land and farming. In Adomnán's Life of Columba we get a first-hand picture of the activities and competence of an early abbot and his community. We see the monks working in the fields, milking, threshing the grain, fetching wattle, towing timbers over the island, carrying farm loads, building enclosures, constructing buildings. The abbot leads the services unless a bishop is present, writes, prays alone, receives visitors, goes to watch the brothers at work, checks the monastery's supplies, visits the sub-houses, baptises the laity, preaches and prophesies, buries in the monastic graveyard.

The organisation of the monastery was very different from that of the older episcopal church. The diocese had been coterminous with the *plebs* or *tuath*, and the clergy of one diocese were not to intrude on the territory of another. The monastic *paruchia* had no limits. There might be houses on both sides of the Irish Sea. The boundaries were elastic, so that the *paruchia* of a powerful saint might expand freely, and his property and wealth grow. Nor was the clerical community the same. The bishop's clergy had all been in orders of some kind, though they might be married and living with their wives. The monks were not all in orders, but they all lived a celibate, religious life.

We should not think of the episcopal church turning monastic. If this was all that happened, the manner of religious life would have changed, but the *paruchia* would probably still have remained much the same. The monastic *paruchia* seems to be a completely independent system. How can we account for this developing so differently? I suspect that it had something to do with the property endowment of bishoprics and monasteries.

---

[33] Richard Sharpe ('Some problems', pp 243–7) points out that 'the positive evidence for the existence of federations of monasteries ... is less secure than has generally been noted', and further that *paruchia* is a jurisdictional term, 'referring to the proprietary control of a mother-church over its dependencies ... There is nothing notably "monastic" ... about the *paruchia* at all'. See also Colmán Etchingham, 'The implications of *paruchia*' in *Ériu*, xliv (1993), pp 136–62.

If an early bishopric was sited very near a royal capital, it was almost certainly under the patronage of the king. And this meant that the bishopric would be coterminous with the kingdom. Armagh is two miles from Emain Macha, capital of ancient Ulster; Killashee, the church of Auxilius, is near the royal fort of Naas in North Leinster.[34] It is possible, also, that some early churches were endowed with property that had previously been used for the upkeep of pagan sites. St Brigit's church of Kildare and Kilcullen, the church of Iserninus, were both near the pagan site of Knockaulin; Saigir, founded by Ciarán, 'first born of the saints of Ireland', had a sacred fire. It may be that lands used for pagan sanctuaries were turned over to the early church.

Monasteries, on the other hand, seem to have been private foundations, on family land.[35] In the seventh-century Life of Samson of Dol we see the family making over its property to found the monastery. Samson's father, Amon, says to his wife: 'Nor not only I and you serve God, as is right and proper, but let us link together all our children in the service of God and let all that is ours become wholly God's.' Amon's brother, his wife, and three sons did similarly. We see another family monastery in Adomnán's Life of Columba, where the sons of Daiméne and their sister Maugin live together in religion at Clogher.[36] Communities founded like this could be attached to a saint, and so a widespread *paruchia* might grow up, with the succeeding abbot recognised as the founder's heir.

Family conversion may also explain why *manaig* existed from the very early days of monasticism. They are certainly present in the seventh-century canons. The word means 'monks'. Yet the *manaig* were married. They were the church clients who did the farm work, yet they had legal rights in the monastery. Their eldest sons were educated by the church, they had some rights in the selection of an abbot. Moreover they were submitted to a regime of severe sexual abstinence during fast periods, which could not have been imposed on the ordinary laity. They must be the *áes lánamnassa dligthig*, the 'folk in lawful wedlock', those in *matrimonio legitimo* who are required to abstain from their wives for the three forty-day fast periods in each year, and between three and five nights in each week in addition. The

---

[34] Charles Doherty discusses seventh-century evidence for the importance of Baslick, Co. Roscommon, near Cruachu, in the fifth century as a likely centre for the evangelising of Connacht, in 'The basilica in early Ireland' in *Peritia*, iii (1984), pp 303–15. For the juxtaposition of the church of Clogher, Co. Tyrone, and the likely royal capital of the Uí Chremthainn, see Richard B. Warner, 'The archaeology of early historic kingship in Ireland' in Stephen T. Driscoll and Margaret R. Nieke (ed.), *Power and politics in early medieval Britain and Ireland* (Edinburgh, 1988), pp 47–68.

[35] See Ó Corráin, 'The early Irish churches' for examples of 'private foundations on family land' which were not monastic churches; see also Thomas Charles-Edwards, 'The church and settlement' in Ní Chatháin & Richter, *Ire. & Europe*, pp 167–75, for family churches and ecclesiastical tenants.

[36] Anderson, *Adomnan's Life*, p. 336.

regulations vary slightly according to the text, but they are all of the same order of magnitude. It would surely be impossible to impose these restrictions on the laity as a whole, and the secular law tracts in any case show that the laity might have relations with more than one woman, with an *adaltrach* or with concubines as well as a chief wife. Such men could not be 'the folk in lawful wedlock' to whom the texts refer, but the description applies perfectly to the *manaig*.

It seems likely that if a whole kin group went over to monasticism some men did not separate from their wives but were willing to continue work while their brothers led a religious life. Though married, they remained part of the legal corporation of the monastery. These married monks and their families clearly lived under religious discipline. We hear of them attending church regularly each Sunday, going to confession, receiving communion, and the Rule of Patrick says that baptism, communion, and the singing of intercession are to be provided by the church for its *manaig*. But how much preaching in the country at large did the monks effect? Once the monastic system was imposed what happens to the work of evangelisation?

Our best evidence here is in the popular literature, both ecclesiastical and secular, the hagiography and the sagas. It is affected less than one would expect by Christian morality. Patrick's own writings give us an impression of complete honesty. He tells us plainly of his difficulties: he is 'the least of all the faithful, and utterly despised by many', rejected by one section of the British church, beaten and imprisoned in Ireland.[37] By the time Muirchú writes his Life in the seventh century Patrick is winning a series of exciting encounters with a king's druid. It is through the power of God that he does so, but the stress now has to be on Patrick's victories, not his difficulties. By 900, when we come to the 'Vita Tripartita', Patrick is still winning contests, but this time it is with an angel. The saint is browbeating the angel with better terms from God. Which of the other saints will not get that privilege? he asks, insisting on more favourable conditions, and sulking until he obtains his requests. It is an amusing story, but it has little relation to Christian morality. The hagiographer is showing his audience the saint's power, very little concerned with imparting Christian teaching.

This is the motive of much of the later hagiography. In the Life of Findchú of Brigown, when the king of Munster is attacked, his nobles advise him: 'let us send to the slaughterous warrior to the south of us, even to Findchú of Brigown', and Findchú comes with his crosier, which was named *Cenn-chathach* ('head-battler'). When the king wants to borrow Cenn-chathach the saint will not give it up, so that 'on himself might be the glory of routing the foe'.[38] As entertainment this is one of the most successful of Irish saints'

---

[37] *Works*, ed. Bieler, p. 21.

[38] Whitley Stokes (ed.), *Lives of saints from the Book of Lismore* (Oxford, 1890), pp 92–3, 239–40.

Lives, probably because the writer has borrowed with such little reserve from the secular tales. These Lives are aiming at glorifying the saint, and the manner of his glorification shows that public morality was not really determined by Christian values.

The secular tales may have been written down by churchmen, but they were composed by the *filid* for a lay audience. And they reflect a traditional secular morality. The monastic rules enjoin 'shunning of contention, gentle speech'. The religious is to eschew 'conceit of mind without abusement, haughty speech without subordination... accusations without compassion, reproaches without reflection, contumely without restraint'.[39] But the stories are full of violence, brains spattered by a well-aimed stone, heads severed, bodies split from head to navel (though whether this would in fact have been possible with a two-foot Irish sword is another matter). They are full of boasting and vengeance. In 'Fingal Rónáin' the heroic values are pushed to extremes. There is immediate recourse to violence without waiting for explanations, and the audience thoroughly understood the necessity of vengeance. The morality of these stories is in direct contradiction to some of the monastic rules, but they must have commanded the sympathy and delight of the audience.

Both tales and laws show a sexual morality different from that approved by the church. In the laws a man might have a chief wife and a subordinate wife. The usual word for her is *adaltrach*, and she was probably taken to provide sons if the chief wife had none. There are also concubines living in at least semi-permanent relationships. The ecclesiastical legislation insists on monogamy, but secular law recognises various classes of union with different degrees of liability and different rights of inheritance. One lawyer tries to justify native practice by appealing to biblical history: 'There is a dispute in Irish law as to which is more proper, whether many sexual unions or a single one: for the chosen [people] of God lived in plurality of unions, so that it is not easier to condemn it than to praise it.'[40] It is clear from the laws that monogamy as expounded by the canonists was not universally accepted by society at large.

It looks to me as if, for the first 250 years of its life in Ireland, Christianity made steady inroads. By 700 the position had stabilised. It is clear that by this time Ireland was nominally Christian; there were scores of monasteries, which must have been serving a considerable part of the country, providing baptism and Christian burial. But it is also clear that by about 700 the church

---

[39] David Greene (ed.), *Fingal Rónáin and other stories* (Dublin, 1955); and in *Irish sagas*, ed. Myles Dillon (Dublin, 1959), pp 167–77. Thomas Charles-Edwards looks at these themes in *Fingal Rónáin* in 'Honour and status in some Irish and Welsh prose tales' in *Ériu*, xxix (1978), pp 123–41.

[40] D. A. Binchy , 'Bretha Crólige' in *Ériu*, xii (1934), p. 45.

had adjusted itself to the secular law.[41] When the canons of the first synod of Patrick, Auxilius, and Iserninus were drawn up (as I think towards the mid sixth century) Christians were being encouraged to keep clear of secular courts and solve their disputes within the community of the Christian church. By the time the 'Collectio canonum Hibernensis'[42] was published in the early eighth century the situation had changed. These canons provide rulings on the law of evidence, on surety, on inheritance.[43] They reflect principles of the secular law, and show how the church, which had been a Roman institution, has now been brought into line with native legal practices. The 'Senchas Már' explains that there are many things in Irish customary law that are not mentioned in the scriptures. 'Dubthach showed these to Patrick. What did not disagree with the word of God in the written law, and with the consciences of the believers, was retained in the brehon code by the church and the *fili*'.[44] The native law had its own justification and was recognised, and to a considerable extent adopted, by the church.

By the eighth century the life of the monks had considerably changed. In the sixth century people had entered monasticism in search of spiritual perfection to lead a life of ascetic religion. Two hundred years later there were still such men in Irish monasteries, but they were probably a minority. The canons show that monasteries are now centres of population, markets, schools, prisons. The abbot is not merely the spiritual father of his monks; he is the *princeps*, the ruler of the community, and the *comarba*, the heir to the property. If he is heir, it is not surprising to see that in some monasteries there seems to have been family succession in the abbacy. At Lusk the annals allow us to trace six abbots extending over three and four generations,[45] while other monasteries show fathers and sons and sometimes grandsons succeeding.[46]

---

[41] Since D. A. Binchy's publication of the *Corpus Iuris Hibernici* in 1978 there has been a flowering of research based on the laws, much of it demonstrating the coming together of secular and ecclesiastical law—see, for example, Donnchadh Ó Corráin, Liam Breatnach, and Aidan Breen, 'The laws of the Irish' in *Peritia*, iii (1984), pp 382–438; Kim McCone, 'Dubthach maccu Lugair and a matter of life and death in the pseudo-historical prologue to the Senchas Már' in *Peritia*, v (1986), pp 1–35; and Donnchadh Ó Corráin, 'Irish vernacular law and the Old Testament' in Próinséas Ní Chatháin and Michael Richter (ed.), *Ireland and Christendom: the Bible and the missions* (Stuttgart, 1987), pp 284–307.

[42] Hermann Wasserschleben (ed.), *Die irische Kanonensammlung* (Leipzig, 1885).

[43] Hughes, *Ch. in early Ir. soc.*, pp 126–30.

[44] *Anc. laws Ire.*, iii, 30–32. *Anc. laws Ire.* has obviously been replaced by D. A. Binchy's *Corpus iuris hibernici* (1978), but see Binchy's paper 'The pseudo-historical prologue to the Senchas Már' in *Studia Celt.*, x–xi (1975–6), pp 15–28. See also Fergus Kelly, *A guide to early Irish law* (Dublin, 1988).

[45] Hughes, op. cit., p. 162.

[46] Ibid., p. 163. As Donnchadh Ó Corráin emphasises and demonstrates, 'the dynastic and hereditary factor lay at the heart of Irish church life' ('Early Irish churches', p. 330 and *passim*). Máire Herbert traces the family relationships of the abbots of Iona (Cenél Conaill genealogical tables, pp 310–11) in *Iona, Kells, and Derry: the history and hagiography of the monastic familia of Columba* (Oxford, 1988). See also the succession lists of clergy below, *N.H.I.*, ix, 237–63.

There is also evidence that by the eighth century not all abbots were in major orders. One canon of the 'Collectio canonum Hibernensis' distinguishes between 'the abbot' and 'the abbot who is a priest', making arrangements about how the property is to be divided between the abbot and monastery when the abbot leaves.[47] The 'Additions to Tírechán' lay down the succession to the abbacy of Druim Lias. This seems to be saying that the family of the donor, Feth Fio, should provide a candidate if a suitable one could be found; if not, then succession was to rest with the religious community (*di muintir*) or with its married monastic tenants (*no diamanchib*). Failing these a pilgrim of the household of Patrick is to take the abbacy.[48] Here the member of Feth Fio's family, or the monk of the religious community, might have been celibate and in major orders, but the *manach* would not have been.

With the increasing secularisation of the monasteries in the eighth century we find monasteries sometimes going to war with each other and engaging in pitched battles. In 760 there was war between the households of Clonmacnoise and Birr, and four years later a major battle between Clonmacnoise and Durrow, in which 200 men of the *familia* of Durrow fell and Clonmacnoise was victorious. Sometimes monasteries were involved in secular wars. In 759 there was a battle at Emain Macha between the Ulstermen and the Northern Uí Néill. The Annals of Tigernach say that the battle was caused by Airechtach priest of Armagh, through discord with Abbot Fer dá Chrích. This battle came at the beginning of Fer dá Chrích's abbacy, and Airechtach is probably the man of that name who died as abbot in 794. So he may have been disappointed at Fer dá Chrích's appointment, and have tried to stir up trouble.[49] In 757 the *princeps* of Mungret near Limerick was killed in a fight between the Munstermen. Words like *muintir* and *familia* to indicate the fighting forces, and the deaths of abbots and monastic officials, suggest that the monks were themselves involved in the battles. In any case the abbot must be responsible for the decision to go to war.

Armagh in the late eighth and early ninth centuries experienced strife between various factions for the abbacy. Armagh was in the sub-kingdom of Airthir, and the kingship of Airthir alternated between the members of a few ruling families.[50] The Uí Bresail, the Uí Nialláin, and the Uí Echdach were the most notable of these. It is therefore not surprising to find these families

---

Etchingham, *Church organisation*, clarifies the distinctions between the abbot, the *princeps*, and the bishop.

[47] *Collectio*, xliii, 6. See Hughes, op. cit., pp 158–60. Ó Corráin argues that canon law was based on the secular law of divorce ('Irish law and canon law' in Ní Chatháin & Richter, *Ire. & Europe*, especially pp 161–4).

[48] *Thes. Pal.*, ii, 239, emending *décrad di muintir Pátricc* to *deórad* (see E. J. Gwynn, 'Irish notes' in *Hermathena*, xvi (1911), pp 384–5). Hughes, op. cit., p. 160.

[49] Hughes, op. cit., p. 170.

[50] See Tomás Ó Fiaich, 'The church of Armagh under lay control' in *Seanchas Ardmhacha*, v (1969–70), pp 75–127.

supplying some of the main ecclesiastical officials of Armagh, the Uí Nialláin many of the stewards (*economi*) and the Uí Echdach some of the most notable abbots. Dub dá Leithe and his son Condmach[51] ruled at Armagh from about 775 till 807, and were opposed by rival claimants. Dub dá Leithe gained help from the Cenél nEógain king in opposing Fóendelach,[52] and another man, Gormgal, was a candidate of the Uí Chremthainn, a neighbouring sub-kingdom to the west of Airthir. In 793 Dub dá Leithe died and there seems to have been a dispute over the abbacy, for we hear that Fóendelach was violated and outraged (*sarugad*) by Gormgal, of the Uí Chremthainn, and that the Uí Chremthainn preyed and spoiled Armagh and killed a man there.[53] This looks as if Gormgal, with the help of the Uí Chremthainn, was trying to secure control of Armagh on Dub dá Leithe's death; but he did not succeed, for Fóendelach was received again. After Fóendelach's death in 795 Gormgal seems to have been once more in control, for it was he who imposed the *lex Patricii* over Connacht in 799. However, the Uí Chremthainn were disturbed by internal troubles in 804, and in that year it was Condmach son of Dub dá Leithe who, as abbot of Armagh, led a *congressio senatorum* of the Uí Néill in Dun Cuair. Two years later Gormgal died. He is called abbot of Armagh and Clones, so that his attention would not have been exclusively concentrated on Armagh. It seems very likely that Condmach son of Dub dá Leithe exercised power there at least from 804 until his death in 807.

This shows a disturbed period in the history of the abbacy of Armagh,[54] but the fertility of the annals suggests an active scriptorium there during this period. An abbacy important enough to attract rivalry may well indicate a flourishing house. Armagh is better documented than most churches and we can see rivalry here particularly clearly.

Monasticism in Ireland between 550 and 800 was by no means identical in its features throughout that period. It began in a burst of ascetic enthusiasm, was taken up by family groups, and spread over the country, so in many instances some of the early episcopal foundations seem to have declined in importance. It has been suggested that since Gaul was the worst source of infection in the plague of the mid sixth century, the churches in contact with Gaul would have been most badly affected by the pestilence. This may explain the decline or disappearance of many of the earliest churches,[55] though plague, once introduced, must surely have spread rapidly throughout the country.

[51] Of the Clann Sínaig, a branch of the Uí Echdach.
[52] See Hughes, op. cit., p. 171.
[53] A. U., 793.
[54] Kim McCone examines these rivalries and disturbances in 'Clones and her neighbours in the early period: hints from some Airgialla saints' lives' in *Clogher Rec.*, xi (1984), pp 305–25.
[55] De Paor, 'The aggrandisement of Armagh', p. 99.

Armagh does not disappear; on the contrary, in the seventh century the legend of Patrick develops and claims to primacy are put forward. But Armagh became not only the chief church in Ireland, but the chief monastery. As early as the 'Liber Angeli',[56] some version of which may have been in existence by the end of the seventh century, the church of Armagh appears as both episcopal and monastic. This tract shows the church being absorbed into the Irish legal system, and the seventh-century canons demonstrate a church that is accepting many of the conventions of Irish law, whereas the earlier canons had tried to hold the church separate.[57]

One of the tendencies of Irish law and tradition was to make all benefices hereditary within certain family groups,[58] so it is not surprising that many abbacies and offices within the monastery remained within family groups. Even in a church like Iona, where the early abbots were all priests, they are nearly all connected to each other, often distantly, by ties of blood.[59] In secularised monasteries, where abbots married, they almost inevitably passed on their offices to their sons. This was the state of affairs that had been reached in some churches by the eighth century.

At this time there were still ascetics in the church who were respected and honoured, and in the second half of the eighth century there was a revival of asceticism. This in itself shows that Irish monasticism had not lost its spiritual vigour. Early in the century there had been individual ascetics in, or attached to, monasteries. Now groups of ascetics banded together to found reformed houses, of which the best-known are Finglas and Tallaght near Dublin. They called themselves *céli Dé* (culdees), clients or vassals of God, for the culdee entered into a contract of vassalage with God as his lord.[60]

Their attitude to sexual sins was severe. A priest who had sinned against chastity lost his priest's orders and was never able to recover them, even though he repented and did penance. The reformers regarded women with great suspicion, and in the later Life of Máel Ruain of Tallaght woman is spoken of as man's 'guardian devil'. Samthann advises Máel Ruain to 'bestow no friendship or confidence on womankind'. We may see here the reaction

---

[56] It is edited by John Gwynn in *The Book of Armagh* (Dublin and London, 1913), ff 20$^r$–22$^r$, translated in Hughes, op. cit., pp 175–81. Richard Sharpe argues for a date in the 640s for the 'Liber Angeli' in 'Armagh and Rome in the seventh century' in Ní Chatháin & Richter, *Ire. & Europe*, pp 58–72. He sees its composition as an element in Armagh's attempt to claim primacy in the mid seventh century. See also Doherty, 'The cult of Saint Patrick', pp 61–70.

[57] Hughes, op. cit., pp 123–33, 44–53.

[58] Ó Fiaich, op. cit., p. 77.

[59] There is a family tree in William Reeves's edition of *Adomnan's Life of St Columba* (Dublin, 1857), opposite p. 342. For Iona see now Herbert, *Iona, Kells, & Derry* and also Richard Sharpe (trans.), *Adomnán of Iona: Life of St Columba* (London, 1995).

[60] On the culdees, see Peter O Dwyer, *Céli Dé: spiritual reform in Ireland 750–900* (Dublin, 1981). Etchingham, *Church organisation*, argues that there was continuity rather than a revival of asceticism at this time (pp 347–55).

against the laxity of the contemporary church with its lay abbots and married clergy and monks.

The reformers strictly observed the canonical hours, and two monks remained in church all night between the offices keeping up a round of prayer. Private prayer was encouraged, and the culdees remembered with enthusiasm the saints, drawing up the martyrologies of Óengus and Tallaght[61] for private observance. Sunday was strictly observed, with no travelling, no work, not even the gathering or preparation of food. The number of men in orders in culdee communities must have substantially increased, so it is not surprising to find more stress on the *opus dei* and on private prayer.

The other aspect of life that the ascetics emphasised was learning. In addition to the new communities of ascetics, the numbers of ascetics attached to old monasteries increased. In these monasteries the head of the scriptorium was often an ascetic, for the annals describe many people as *scriba et anchorita*. The rule of the *céli Dé* regards learning as a most excellent labour of piety, and declares that 'the kingdom of heaven is granted to him who directs studies, and to him who studies, and to him who supports the pupil who is studying.'[62]

The ascetic reform in Ireland has aspects in common with Carolingian monastic reform—the stress on the observance of the *opus dei*, on learning and writing, on a stricter regime. But no new constitutional measures were introduced, and once the period of enthusiasm has passed we find the new 'anchorites' following many of the old patterns of life, having sons who succeed them in office. But the interest in learning remained even when other standards were relaxed.

The first hundred years or so of the church in Ireland was a period of missionary effort, when princes and people were gradually converted by clergy trying to hold themselves separate from the world. Then came the great plague of the mid sixth century and the development of monasticism. Families set up their own monastic houses in a system quite different from the episcopal system of the early church. This constitution came into closer contact with secular men of learning, and ecclesiastical and secular law cohered, so that the church was fully integrated into secular life. The increasing secularisation of monasticism led to a revival of ascetic religion in the later eighth century. By 800 the Irish church was in a very healthy condition, rich and respected, with ascetics leading the spiritual life of the country and among Ireland's finest representatives of learning.

---

[61] Kathleen Hughes, *Early Christian Ireland: introduction to the sources* (London, 1972), pp 205–9. See also Pádraig Ó Riain, 'The Tallaght martyrologies redated' in *Camb. Med. Celt. Studies*, xx (1990), pp 21–38.
[62] E. J. Gwynn, in *Hermathena*, 2nd supp. vol. (Dublin, 1927), p. 63.

THERE is a basic spirituality common to all forms of Christianity, but different branches of the church at different periods of their history have laid varied emphases on various aspects of the spiritual life. For Ireland in the fifth century we cannot do better than start with evangelism. This comes out strongly in the writings of Patrick. His 'Confession' breathes the joy of the good news that he is propagating to the pagan Irish. 'I cannot be silent...about the great benefits and the great grace which the Lord has deigned to bestow upon me in the land of my captivity.' He and his converts are sons of God and joint heirs with Christ. Patrick rejoices in the fact that he is 'a letter of Christ for salvation unto the utmost part of the earth'. God has used him, lifted him out of the mire, and placed him on top of the wall, so he ought to cry aloud and render thanks for his great benefits. He has humbly and faithfully served the people whom the love of Christ gave over to him for the duration of his life. God has chosen him as his helper. His work is to spread everywhere the name of God, to care and labour for the salvation of others. It is holy and wonderful work for which God has constantly strengthened him, made good his many weaknesses and deficiencies. He is the debtor of God, who gave him grace so that many were reborn in God through him and afterwards confirmed, and clerics ordained everywhere for a people just coming to the faith whom the Lord took from the uttermost parts of the earth. He cannot leave Ireland, for God has brought him there and bade him stay for the rest of his life to preach the word. He has cast himself upon God, so though he may anticipate murder or captivity he does not fear it. 'May God never permit it to happen to me that I should lose his people which he purchased.'[63]

These sentences are all taken from the 'Confession', which is a perfect example of an evangelist's document, striving for and rejoicing in the salvation of the people. This quality of evangelism must have continued, for the conversion went on at a good pace. A hundred years after Patrick's death there were churches spread widely over Ireland. The last *feis Temro*, the pagan royal inauguration ceremony, was in 558. The canons of the first synod of Patrick refer to private Christians, separate from the world, not protected by secular law, but by the time the seventh-century canons were drawn up Christianity had been fully integrated into society and had a defined place in its legal structure. By the seventh century the first Christian advance was over and Ireland was formally Christian.

After this, evangelism went on abroad. Northumbria was the most obvious area. King Oswald (633–41) sent to Iona for missionaries to the pagan English. The first envoy was unsuccessful, but Aidan rapidly converted the Northumbrians. On the Continent evangelism seems to have been almost coincidental, for what sent the Irish abroad was the desire for pilgrimage,

[63] *Works*, ed. Bieler, pp 21–2, 24, 39, and *passim*.

one of the specifically Irish aspects of asceticism. Many leading Irish Christians were aristocrats, and in their own *tuatha* they commanded high status. One's status was of immense importance. If they went overseas their status disappeared; they were cast entirely upon God, with no protection from secular law. For the pilgrim life was a roadway, where, as Columbanus says, the pilgrim must travel as a guest of the world.[64]

Sometimes pilgrimage did not involve evangelism. Cormac made his three voyages from Iona, seeking a solitude in the ocean.[65] At the end of the eighth century there were Irish hermits in Iceland.[66] In places like this there can have been little opportunity for evangelistic enterprise. But on the Continent, though Christianity had never died out and Gaul was nominally Christian, Jonas (Columbanus's biographer) says that few people understood what Christianity meant, and the writings of Gregory of Tours show a society in which barbaric qualities were dominant. Irish pilgrims fitted well into the uncertainties and insecurities of this society. They asked nothing. They did not need solid buildings, the patronage of court or nobility; they were prepared to live in isolation, on starvation diet. Everything depended on the individual, so a disorganised political society did not matter, and spiritual life was unaffected by it.[67]

Irish pilgrims sought to cast themselves entirely on God. What the Christian seeks, said Columbanus, is to dwell in God as one of his living members. To achieve this demands a strenuous activity, 'to clean the field of our heart . . . to root out the vices and plant the virtues'. All the world's material goods are without value. The ascetic must cast out transitory things to gain the eternal: 'the whole world is foreign to you who are born and buried bare'. *Nudus natus nudus sepeliris* well sums up the ascetic's life. We do not pass from security to security, says Columbanus, but will obtain eternal joy. 'Live in Christ that Christ may live in you.'[68]

Columbanus frequently uses images about the pilgrim life. On life's roadway the pilgrim must be satisfied with no more than the poverty of a sort of travelling allowance; yet those who serve God shall eat and drink and leap for joy. Pilgrims must look ever towards their destinations, love the homeland not the roadway, live 'as travellers, as pilgrims, as guests of the world, entangled with no lists, longing with no earthly desires'. We live in foreign lands, he says, where even our life is not our own, where the pilgrim's aim must be sought by toil and maintained by enthusiasm, an effort requiring great vio-

---

[64] G. S. M. Walker (ed.), *Sancti Columbani opera* (Dublin, 1957), pp 96–7.
[65] Anderson, *Adomnan's Life*, pp 222–5, 440–47.
[66] J. J. Tierney (ed. and trans.), *Dicuili Liber de mensura orbis terrae* (Dublin, 1967), p. 76.
[67] Thomas Charles-Edwards throws new light on what sent the Irish abroad by looking at the social background at home, and tracing the changing status of pilgrims, in 'The social background to Irish *peregrinatio*' in *Celtica*, xi (1976), pp 43–59.
[68] Walker, *Sancti Columbani opera*, pp 102–3, and *passim*. See also M. Lapidge (ed.), *Columbanus: studies on the Latin writings* (Woodbridge, 1997).

lence. It is a life of total committal. There should be nothing free in the slaves of Christ, nothing proud in Christ's humility, yet though the pilgrim has nothing he has everything. For 'love is no trouble; love is more pleasant, more healthful, more saving to the heart'.[69]

It was this ascetic pilgrimage that drove Columbanus to Gaul. Yet he also went, as his early biographer Jonas says, to sow the seeds of salvation. After he had been some time in Gaul converts flocked to him, so that his monastery at Luxeuil was not sufficient for the brethren and he had to found another at Fontaines. Theuderic, king of Burgundy, at one stage of his life came to visit Columbanus and seek his spiritual advice. Later King Theuderic turned to hostility, and banished Columbanus to Besançon. There the holy man heard of a prison full of condemned men awaiting the death penalty, and went to preach to them. Theuderic's rival, Chlotar of Neustria, received Columbanus as a gift from heaven, and Columbanus called his attention to the abuses 'such as could hardly fail to exist at a king's court'. On the way to Italy he preached to the Swabians and destroyed an offering to Woden. In Lombardy he was welcomed by King Agilulf, and settled at Bobbio, where he died a year later. So Columbanus combined evangelism and ascetic pilgrimage, two of the characteristics of the spiritual life of the Irish church.

The ascetic life was both active and contemplative. The literature is full of active ascetic exercises: fasting, cross vigil, sleeping on nutshells or nettles, even sleeping in tombs. Prayer must be constant: 'Persist without hindrance in prayer and meditation of the Holy Trinity', says Íte;[70] and Samthann, when she is asked whether it is best to pray lying or sitting or standing, answers: 'One must pray in all positions.'[71]

But the contemplative aspects of prayer also appear frequently in the sources. The natural world is God's revelation. 'Understand the creation, if you wish to know the Creator', said Columbanus,[72] and a ninth-century poem conveys the same attitude: 'Let us adore the Lord, maker of wondrous works, great bright Heaven with its angels, the white-waved sea on earth.'[73] A poem of the viking age speaks of the necessity for the constant presence of Christ's cross 'over me as I sit...over me as I lie. Christ's cross be all my strength till we reach the King of Heaven.'[74] A ninth-century poem describes a severe ascetic discipline, a cold fearsome bed, an unpalatable meagre diet, but all with a purpose:

I should love to have Christ Son of God visiting me, my Creator, my King,
And that my mind should resort to Him
In the kingdom where he dwells.[75]

[69] Walker, pp 110–11.     [70] Plummer, *Vitae SS Hib.*, ii, 119.
[71] Ibid., p. 259.     [72] Walker, *Sancti Columbani opera*, pp 64–5.
[73] Gerard Murphy (ed.), *Early Irish lyrics* (Oxford, 1956), pp 4–5.
[74] Ibid., pp 34–5.
[75] Ibid., pp 22–3.

One of the loveliest of early Irish poems is that which tells how Jesus came as a baby to be nursed by St Íte, 'Jesus with Heaven's inhabitants is against my heart every night'.[76] The practice of the presence of God was the purpose of Irish prayer.

Another of the religious exercises that distinguished the Irish was penitential discipline. Monastic teaching stressed the inner life, the development of the spirit, man's moral reform, and the growth of the individual soul, and it went hand in hand with the birth of private penance. This is a system that stresses individual motivation and varying individual conditions. 'This is to be carefully observed in all penance', writes Cummean, 'the length of time anyone remains in his faults; what learning he has received; by which passion he is assailed; how great is his strength; with what intensity of weeping he is afflicted; with what oppression he has been driven to sin. For Almighty God who knows the hearts of all and has bestowed diverse natures will not weigh the weights of sins in an equal scale of penance.'[77] Vinnian, the author of the earliest penitential, legislates not only for sins of action which a man has committed, but also for sins of intention. There are deliberate sins and sins of inadvertence, there are sins of the flesh and sins of the spirit. 'If a cleric is wrathful or envious or backbiting or gloomy or greedy, great and capital sins are these ... But there is this penance for them.'[78] The spiritual involvement of monastic life comes across very clearly in Vinnian's penitential; he writes compelled by love *suis visceralibus filiis,* by the grace of love and in the interest of religion.

Penance was the 'medicine for souls'. Sin inflicted damage on the sinner as well as on his victim, and the 'soul-friend' (for the confessor is called *anmcharae* in Irish) had to diagnose and prescribe the remedy. 'For doctors of the body also compound their medicine in diverse kinds; thus they heal wounds in one manner, sicknesses in another, boils in another, bruises in another, festering sores in another, eye diseases in another, fractures in another, burns in another. So also should spiritual doctors treat with diverse kinds of cures the wounds of souls, their sicknesses, pains, ailments and infirmities.'[79] The penitentials were designed to help the soul-friend. They are detailed tariffs of penance for specific sins committed by people of different character under various provocation. Large monasteries had colonies of penitents. Sometimes the penitentials combine penance and composition according to the secular law.[80]

[76] Gerard Murphy (ed.), *Early Irish lyrics* (Oxford, 1956), pp 26–7.
[77] Ludwig Bieler, *The Irish penitentials* (Dublin, 1963), pp 132–3.
[78] Ibid., pp 84–5.
[79] Ibid., pp 98–9 (Penitential of Columbanus).
[80] Ludwig Bieler, 'The Irish penitentials: their religious and social background' in *Studia Patristica*, viii (1966), pp 329–39.

The system of private penance is essentially that practised by the church today, but it was not that of the early church. There the penance was public. 'Confess your sins to one another and pray for one another that ye may be healed' is one of many similar New Testament injunctions. Who first introduced private penance is a matter of dispute, but certainly the Irish, and perhaps the British, popularised it. And the system of commutation was Irish in origin, for the word *arreum*, used in the Latin 'Canones Hibernenses' for 'commutation', comes from the Irish *arre*, 'handing over on behalf of another', 'paying over something in place of something else'. Penance, one of the specific features of Irish spiritual life, had a widespread influence on Christianity.

Until the seventh century the Irish system of calculating Easter differed from that of the rest of Europe. There was no universally received method of calculation, but the Nicene council of 325 had said that the churches should follow a uniform practice, and during the later sixth and seventh centuries the Victorian and Dionysian methods of calculation that were widely used in Europe led to a high degree of uniformity, while Irish calculations showed marked differences.[81] Thus there was some truth in Cummian's claim that the Irish, a pimple on the outermost edge of the world, held out against the combined usages of Christendom.

The *Hibernenses* and the *Romani* seem to have regarded the dating of Easter very differently. The *Hibernenses* saw it as a matter of ritual, and on ritual different branches of the church might legitimately differ. 'Let Gaul, I beg,' writes Columbanus to the Frankish clergy, 'contain us side by side, whom the kingdom of Heaven shall contain.'[82] When an Irish synod was held at Mag nAilbe round about 630 to discuss the Easter question, the Irish spokesman Fintan (Munnu) pleaded for toleration: 'Let each of us do what he believes, and as seems to him right.'[83] The *Romani*[84] on the other hand regarded the date of Easter not as a matter of ritual but as a matter of belief. Wilfrid at the synod of Whitby in 664 claimed that the church everywhere except in the Celtic west followed the same practice, the one observed at Rome and derived from St Peter, and that catholics everywhere were obliged to conform. 'If you and your fellows', he says to the Irishman Colmán, who led the Hibernian party, 'having heard the decrees of the apostolic see, nay of the universal church, confirmed as they are by sacred scriptures, if you scorn to follow them, without any doubt, you sin.'[85] Cummian the Irishman,

---

[81] Hughes, *Ch. in early Ir. soc.*, pp 103–7.

[82] Walker, *Sancti Columbani opera*, pp 16–17.

[83] W. W. Heist (ed.), *Vitae sanctorum Hiberniae ex codice olim Salmanticensi nunc Bruxellensi* (Brussels, 1965), p. 207.

[84] For the *Romani*, see two papers in Ní Chatháin & Richter, *Ire. & Europe*: Richard Sharpe, 'Armagh and Rome in the seventh century', pp 58–72, and Pádraig Ó Néill, '*Romani* influences on seventh-century Hiberno-Latin literature', pp 280–90.

[85] Bede, *Hist. ecc.*, iii, 25; the wording quoted is from Charles Plummer's edition (2 vols, Oxford, 1896).

writing shortly after an Irish mission of enquiry had been sent to Rome in 631, speaks of a text 'excommunicating and expelling from the church and anathematising those who come against the canonical statutes of the four apostolic sees when these agree on the unity of Easter'.[86] Cummian fears to be cut off from the church, which has the power of binding and loosing. Both he and Wilfrid seem to have viewed nonconformity as heresy.

A synod was held at Mag Léne near Durrow about 630, attended by a number of clergy, mainly from southern churches. These agreed to conform with the date of Easter generally practised on the Continent. But afterwards a 'certain whited wall', who seems to have been the abbot of Clonmacnoise, withdrew from the agreement and caused dissension. A mission of enquiry was then sent to Rome, in accordance with the synodical decree that disputed cases were to be referred to Rome. It was there in 631, when the Irish date differed from that of Rome by a whole month, and on returning to Ireland its members reported that everywhere throughout the world except in the Celtic west the observance was the same. The conformity of the south of Ireland was now confirmed, but the northern churches held out until the end of the century. Armagh seems to have conformed before 688,[87] but Iona was not won over to the Roman Easter until 716 by the Anglo-Saxon Ecgbert, who had spent his adult life among the Irish and the Picts. The most troublesome peculiarity of the Irish church was thus resolved.

Ireland belonged spiritually and intellectually to the western church, but it had its differences of emphasis. The Irish church was an archaic church. Christianity reached Ireland in the very early stages of the Frankish invasion of Gaul and before the Anglo-Saxons came to Britain. Patrick truly called himself unlearned, and the Latin he brought to Ireland was a very elementary colloquial Latin, based on the living language of the fifth century.[88] Possibly the Latin of Palladius and other continental missionaries was different, for Columbanus at the end of the sixth and the beginning of the seventh century was using a Latin akin to that of fifth-century Gaul. It has, says Mohrmann, 'the appearance of a product of the Gaul of Sidonius Apollinaris dropped into the Gaul of Gregory of Tours'. He could not have learned this in contemporary Merovingian Gaul, so he must be writing the Latin he learned and taught as a young man at Bangor. It is a mannered style, varying to suit the character of his different works: florid and rhetorical for the letters, simpler for the sermons, more legalistic for the Rules. His vocabulary shows a liking for unusual, rare, poetical and archaic words. Apart from this it is a

---

[86] *P.L.*, lxxxv, ii, col. 972 B.C. See Maura Walsh and Dáibhí Ó Cróinín (ed.), *Cummian's letter De controversia paschali and the De ratione conputandi* (Toronto, 1988), and Maura Walsh, 'Some remarks on Cummian's paschal letter and the commentary on Mark ascribed to Cummian' in Ní Chatháin & Richter, *Ire. & Christendom*, pp 216–29.

[87] Hughes, *Ch. in early Ir. soc.*, p. 116.

[88] Mohrmann, *The Latin of St Patrick*. For Patrick's Latin learning see above, n. 18.

mixture of classical late Latin and very idiomatic Christian elements which reflect a very old tradition.[89]

Latin grammar was an indispensable preliminary to the biblical studies that were the core of ecclesiastical learning in the pre-viking age. The Irish took their Latin seriously. They composed treatises on Latin grammar, such as the 'Anonymus ad Cuimnanum' or the 'Ars Malsachani'.[90] They glossed the texts they used for teaching, the Pauline epistles, the psalms, and Priscian.[91] They also annotated these manuscripts with a series of construe marks to assist them in teaching, showing how to link the various elements in the strangely constructed Latin sentence.[92] At a time when Virgil was comparatively neglected on the Continent he was known to writers such as Adomnán and Muirchú. Unlike the writers of the Carolingian period, pre-Carolingian writers of Latin in Ireland did not establish a tradition of *belles-lettres*.[93] Nevertheless their Latin compares favourably with that of Merovingian Gaul and they tackled it as a foreign language, but in a workmanlike way.

The Irish spent a lot of time on biblical commentary.[94] Their exegesis was firmly rooted in the late patristic tradition. Most of it belongs to the Alexandrian school, which commented by an allegorical method. The Turin commentary on St Mark's gospel provides good illustrations. Bischoff thinks this may have been written by the Cummian who argued for the Roman Easter *c*.632,[95] though Clare Stancliffe has questioned this identification.[96]

[89] Christine Mohrmann, 'The earliest continental Irish Latin' in *Vigiliae Christianae*, xvi (1962), pp 216–33. Michael Lapidge argues that one of the hymns in the antiphony of Bangor, 'Precamur patrem', is by Columbanus, that it was written before he left Bangor (in about 590), that 'it reveals knowledge of a substantial number of Latin authors and competence in a scheme of versification as yet imperfectly understood, and attests to intellectual contact of some kind between Gaul and Bangor' ('Columbanus and the "Antiphonary of Bangor"' in *Peritia*, iv (1985), pp 104–16). See also Lapidge, *Columbanus: studies*, n. 68.

[90] Bengt Löfstedt, *Der hiberno-lateinische Grammatiker Malsachanus* (Uppsala, 1965). On grammatical treatises see Vivien Law, 'Malsachanus reconsidered' in *Camb. Med. Celt. Studies*, i (1981), pp 83–93; also her lengthier study, *The Insular Latin grammarians* (Woodbridge, 1982). Louis Holtz and Michael Herren comment on this book in *Peritia*, ii (1983), pp 170–84, 312–16.

[91] *Thes. Pal.*, i, 499–712; ii, 49–232.

[92] Maartje Draak, 'Construe marks in Hiberno-Latin manuscripts' in *Mededelingen der Koninklijke Nederlandse Akademie van Watenschappen afd. Letterkunde* (Nieuwe Reeks xx, nr. 10, 1957), pp 261–82; 'The higher teaching of Latin grammar in Ireland during the ninth century', ibid., xxx (1967), pp 109–44.

[93] Ludwig Bieler, 'The classics in Celtic Ireland' in R. R. Bolgar (ed.), *Classical influences on European culture A.D. 500–1500* (Cambridge, 1971), pp 45–9.

[94] Bernhard Bischoff, 'Il monachesimo irlandese nei suoi rapporti col continente' in *Settimane di Studio del Centro Italiano di Studi sull' alto medioevo*, iv (1956), p. 127.

[95] Bernhard Bischoff, 'Wendepunkte in der Geschichte der lateinischen Exegese in Frühmittelalter' in *Sacris Erudiri*, vi (1954), pp 189–281. The paper was reprinted in Bischoff, *Mittelalterliche Studien* (3 vols, Stuttgart, 1966–7, 1982). Martin McNamara (ed.), *Biblical studies: the medieval Irish contribution* (Dublin, 1976), includes a translation of Bischoff's important article (pp 74–160). The commentary is No. 27 in Bischoff's catalogue.

[96] Clare Stancliffe, 'Early "Irish" biblical exegesis' in *Studia Patristica*, xii (1975), pp 361–70; on Cummian, see above, n. 86.

The glosses, which are undoubtedly Irish, being written in Old Irish, elaborate the Alexandrian method further. The commentator, writing about 'the voice crying in the wilderness', meditates on the desert and says: 'Where the devil conquered he is conquered, where man fell there he rose.' The Irish gloss expands: 'In the desert of Paradise he has vanquished Adam; in the desert of the world Christ has vanquished him. In the desert of Paradise Adam has fallen; in the desert of the world, however, Christ has arisen.'[97] A little further on we come to the phrase: 'Preaching the baptism of penitence for the remission of sins', and the glossator adds: 'As catechumens are at first taught by a priest and are baptised and as they are then anointed by a bishop, so then John had begun to teach men and to baptise them at first, and they have then been anointed by Christ, i.e. the work which John had begun has been perfected by Christ and has been completed.'[98] The glosses go on in this style and examples of the allegorical method might be multiplied.

Sometimes the commentator follows the Antiochan method, concentrating on the literal and historical interpretation of the text. This is particularly marked in exegesis on the psalter, for there Theodore of Mopsuestia, who belonged to the Antiochan school, was a major influence on Irish commentary.[99] The Old Irish treatise on the psalter[100] divides interpretation into four, the first and second *stoir* (that is, the history that puts the psalms into their literal context), the *siens*, and the *morolus* (the mystical and moral interpretations). The Milan commentary (in Amb. C.301 inf.) writes, 'it is the history that is most desirable for us to understand'.[101] An early writer *de mirabilibus sanctae scripturae* says: 'In this work we have tried to explain the reason and order of actual events, excluding, at this stage, allegorical interpretations.'[102] The Antiochene method, rather rare in England and the Continent in the early middle ages, had considerable use in early Ireland.

Though these commentaries are conventional and in accordance with accepted ideas, they occasionally show traces of critical judgement. The Lambeth commentary on the Sermon on the Mount, which its editors date *c.*725,[103] commenting on Matthew 5: 21–4, says: 'Now we think it surprising what we see here, that is, in that there is the same punishment for murder as for anger, for it is *iudicium* that he gives for both of them.' And he goes on to explain to himself and his students the apparent anomaly: 'That is not likely:

---

[97] *Thes. Pal.*, i, 485.

[98] Ibid., p. 487.

[99] Martin McNamara, 'Psalter text and psalter study in the early Irish church (A.D. 600–1200)' in *R.I.A. Proc.*, lxxiii (1973), sect. C, pp 201–98.

[100] Kuno Meyer (ed.), *Anecdota Oxoniensia* (Oxford, 1894).

[101] *Thes. Pal.*, i, 13, quoted in McNamara, op. cit., p. 257.

[102] *P.L.*, xxxv, col. 2151–2. Cf. Mario Esposito, 'On the pseudo-Augustinian treatise, "De mirabilibus Sanctae Scripturae" written in Ireland in the year 655' in *R.I.A. Proc.*, xxxv (1920), sect. C, pp 189–207.

[103] Ludwig Bieler and James Carney, 'The Lambeth commentary' in *Ériu*, xxiii (1972), pp 1–55.

each of them is a different judgement. The first (for murder) is a human judgement, the last (for anger) is divine.' On the next verse he says again: 'Now we wonder at another thing we see here. He says here that he who says *racha* to his brother will be in danger of the council.' Then he goes on to discuss the different interpretations of this passage.[104]

The Irish knew patristic and some classical authors, though their libraries were probably scrappy and incomplete and they were sometimes attempting to acquire better texts. From the ninth century on they were adapting classical stories into Irish.[105] In the seventh and eighth centuries one of the most popular writers was Isidore of Seville. His works reached Ireland from Spain remarkably quickly.[106] Contacts with Spain in the seventh century are well confirmed. One of the most striking of many examples is the appearance on a cross slab at Fahan Mura of a peculiarly worded doxology sanctioned at the fourth council of Toledo in 633. This reappears in an Irish table of penitential commutations drawn up about 800.[107] The encyclopaedic, fantastic quality of Isidore's 'Etymologiae' especially appealed to Irish scholars, and strongly influenced their own views as to Irish prehistory.

Fantastic elaboration and detail are found in some of the apocryphal literature with which Ireland abounded. David Dumville has suggested that some of this came in from Spain, where texts with Priscillianist affiliations made frequent use of apocrypha.[108] 'The early Irish seemed to have allowed themselves a remarkable freedom to use the apocrypha and appear generally to have held such works in a high regard which would have been impermissible elsewhere.'[109] The Book of Armagh includes in its copy of the New Testament an apocryphal Pauline epistle to the Laodiceans, and comments laconically 'Incipit aepistola ad Laudicenses sed hirunimus eam negat esse Pauli.'

---

[104] On biblical exegesis, see Ní Chatháin & Richter, *Ire. & Christendom, passim*, including Gerard MacGinty, 'The Irish Augustine: *De mirabilis sacrae scripturae*', pp 70–83. See also Aidan Breen (ed.), *Ailerani interpretatio mystica et moralis progenitorum Domini Iesu Christi* (Blackrock, 1995), for the 'remarkable breadth' of scholarship shown.

[105] W. B. Stanford, 'Towards a history of classical influences in Ireland' in *R.I.A. Proc.*, lxx (1970), sect. C, p. 33, note 69, quoting James Carney.

[106] J. N. Hillgarth, 'Visigothic Spain and early Christian Ireland' in *R.I.A. Proc.*, lxii (1962), sect. C, pp 167–94; 'The east, Visigothic Spain and the Irish' in *Studia Patristica*, iv (1961), pp 442–56; 'Ireland and Spain in the seventh century' in *Peritia*, iii (1984), pp 1–16. Michael W. Herren's edition of *The Hisperica Famina: I The A-text* (Toronto, 1974) makes available an important seventh-century text, which is strongly influenced by Isidore of Seville. Kathleen Hughes included a note on this text, expressing her view that it comes from a monastic school, in Kathleen Hughes and Ann Hamlin, *The modern traveller to the early Irish church* (London, 1977), pp 52–3.

[107] See Hughes, *Ch. in early Ir. soc.*, pp 95–6.

[108] D. N. Dumville, 'Biblical apocrypha and the early Irish: a preliminary investigation' in *R.I.A. Proc.*, lxxiii (1973), sect. C, pp 299–338.

[109] D. N. Dumville, 'Biblical apocrypha and the early Irish: a preliminary investigation' in *R.I.A. Proc.*, lxxiii (1973), sect. C, p. 336.

This 'reveals no great sense of urgency or concern about the establishment of the scriptural canon'.[110]

One of the most delightful of these apocryphal stories is the poem on the gospel of Thomas, written about 700.[111] This begins with the story of the 5-year-old child Jesus making birds of clay on the Sabbath and blessing them so that they flew away, and continues with other boyhood miracles. Similar qualities of imagination show occasionally in the saints' Lives. Brigit hangs her cloak on a sunbeam, Columcille turns back the Loch Ness monster or restores to health a bird that arrives exhausted on Iona. Ireland had many saints—the number is clear from the Martyrology of Tallaght—and the multitude of stories about them are apparent in the allusions of the Martyrology of Óengus.

The church in Ireland in the pre-viking age was part of the church elsewhere in western Europe. It was orthodox, but not entirely conventional.[112] Its ideas about pilgrimage and penance had a profound effect on the church elsewhere. Its intellectual life was lively. It made a serious study of Latin grammar and spent much energy on biblical exegesis. The imagination that was so evident in Irish secular literature appeared in some of her religious literature, so that Irish spiritual and intellectual life in the pre-Carolingian period is a subject that well repays study.

[110] Ibid., p. 332. Pádraig Ó Néill argues that 'diligence about scriptural canonicity' was one of the characteristics of a group of seventh-century *Romani* texts, in Ní Chatháin & Richter, *Ire. & Europe*, p. 288.

[111] James Carney (ed. and trans.), *The poems of Blathmac son of Cú Brettan* (Ir. Texts Soc., xlvi; Dublin, 1974).

[112] In a sensitive and perceptive lecture, intended as a contribution to the memorial volume for Kathleen Hughes (but published posthumously as 'The originality of the early Irish church' in *R.S.A.I. Jn.*, cxi (1981), pp 36–49), D. L. T. Bethell develops the distinction between the northern church, of which Ireland was part, and the southern, Mediterranean church. In the north, Latin and not the vernacular was the sacred language, there was considerable emphasis on gesture and ritual in worship, and monasticism was important. Because of a social background broadly similar to the rest of northern Europe, Irish churchmen were influential as missionaries and scholars throughout the whole period to the twelfth century.

# CHAPTER X

# Early Irish law

T. M. CHARLES-EDWARDS

EARLY Irish vernacular law is the richest source of information about Irish society in the seventh and eighth centuries.[1] Yet my concern will not be with its value as a source, but rather with the history of the law itself—why law was written at all, what kind of law was written, what kind of law was not written, what kind of lawyer might have practised such law, what intellectual climate it reveals.[2] Although the surviving written texts must be our evidence, they are not identical with the subject to be investigated. The great bulk of legal activity was oral, and on this the written sources often shed only an indirect light. In spite of this difficulty, however, we must be concerned with the totality, both written and unwritten, since otherwise explanation will be impossible. It will also be necessary to examine the principal Irish text of canon law, the 'Collectio canonum Hibernensis'. I shall refer to the vernacular texts as native Irish law or as secular Irish law. This is without prejudice to questions such as the extent of clerical participation in the writing of the vernacular texts;[3] it reflects the lawyers' perception of their own tradition as distinctively Irish, and their recognition that there was another tradition of law within Ireland, distinct from the law they were concerned to expound, the law of the church.

The first distinction to be made is between the primary texts and the glosses and commentaries.[4] All the main primary texts, but only some of the glosses and commentaries, belong to the pre-Norman period. Moreover, all but a few of the primary texts were written down in a very short period, possibly no more than the century between 650 and 750, whereas the glosses and commentaries range from the ninth to the sixteenth

---

[1] See below, ch. XV. This chapter owes much to the criticisms of Robin Chapman Stacey.

[2] For an authoritative discussion of the contents of the texts, see Fergus Kelly, *A guide to early Irish law* (Dublin, 1988).

[3] This issue is discussed below.

[4] When the primary text is glossed it is written in a large script whereas the glosses and commentaries are written in a smaller script. For an example see R. I. Best and Rudolf Thurneysen, *The oldest fragments of the Senchas Már from MS. H. 2. 15 in the library of Trinity College* (I.M.C., Dublin, 1931).

century.[5] The contrast between a short primary period of legal writing and a long secondary period is one of the main problems to be confronted by the historian of Irish law.

Another is the scarcity of surviving legislation. The law that came to be written down consisted almost entirely of tracts on particular topics, such as fosterage or status, composed to instruct aspirant lawyers, as suggested by the use of such phrases as 'if you would be a judge, you should know . . .'. These tracts were the written expression of the legal tradition, not an account of royal legislation, and still less the instrument of such legislation. The tracts are anonymous and undated: they purport to declare the law of the Irish as it has been handed down from the immemorial past, not the opinions of a particular jurist.[6] Since they affect an air of timelessness, they rarely admit to any change in the substance of the law. Such texts are thus at the opposite remove from a document such as the capitulary of the Frankish king Childebert II which begins: 'To men of distinction. Since, in the name of God, we discussed certain decrees with our magnates on the 1st of March, we wish them to come to everyone's attention. And so, by the grace of God, it was agreed on the 1st of March in the twentieth year of our reign, at Andernach, that . . .'[7] With one or two possible exceptions, if the Irish law tracts name kings or judges, they are legendary.[8]

That is not to say that Irish kings did not legislate. On the contrary, the nearest approach among the Irish laws to a text on kingship lays some stress on their legislation.[9] What may create the impression that Irish kings had little or nothing to do with the law is partly that royal legislation was usually not written down, and partly that Irish lawyers regarded royal edicts as reinforcing existing law rather than enacting new law.[10] Neither of these reasons for the absence of surviving legislation is in the least surprising once Irish law is put into a European setting. Even the capitularies of a Charlemagne were essentially oral legislation deriving their authority from

---

[5] Liam Breatnach (ed. and trans.), *Uraicecht na ríar* (Dublin, 1987), p. 77, dates that text to the second half of the eighth century; Thomas Charles-Edwards and Fergus Kelly (ed. and trans.), *Bechbretha: an Old Irish law tract on bee-keeping* (Dublin, 1983), pp 12–14 for the date of the main text and pp 14–24 for the glosses; also Michael Dolley, 'The date of some glosses in *Bretha Déin Chécht*' in *Celtica*, viii (1968), pp 167–73.

[6] D. A. Binchy, 'The linguistic and historical value of the Irish law tracts' in *Brit. Acad. Proc.*, xxix (1943), pp 195–227: 214–15, reprinted in Dafydd Jenkins (ed.), *Celtic law papers introductory to Welsh medieval law and government* (Brussels, 1973), pp 92–4.

[7] Karl August Eckhardt (ed.), *Pactus Legis Salicae* (Hannover, 1962), p. 267.

[8] E.g., D. A. Binchy (ed.), *Corpus iuris Hibernici* (6 vols, Dublin, 1978), pp 583.30; 908.4–6. A partial exception to prove the rule is the reference in *Míadslechta*, C.I.H., p. 588.6, to a tract on the orders of the church attributed to Augustine, perhaps an Irish canonical work; but this tract is not said to be an authority on Irish law.

[9] D. A. Binchy (ed.), *Críth Gablach* (Dublin, 1941), pp 18–24, esp. lines 514–24.

[10] *Críth Gablach*, lines 515–6.

the 'word of the king', in other words, solemn promulgation by the king before an assembly of magnates.[11] Many edicts, admittedly, came to be written down, but writing did not confer an authority superior to that of 'the word of the king'; the survival of written texts was due as much to private effort as to preservation in a royal archive.[12] If kings sponsored the production of written codes, such as the Burgundian 'Lex Gundobada', they often did so in order to place themselves within, or perhaps even sometimes in competition with, a Roman tradition of written legislation.[13] One of the greatest of all Germanic legislators, the Lombard king Rothari, promulgated his laws in the year of a great campaign to conquer Roman Liguria;[14] Liutprand, some eighty years later, expressly permits the use of both Roman and Lombard law but suggests that the latter is to be preferred as being well known to all.[15] In Ireland, however, there was no continuing Roman imperial tradition to imitate or to rival.[16]

There was, however, a vigorous tradition of written law in the church. The importance of writing in legal processes was stressed by the *Romani*— the party in the Irish church (and its Pictish and English offshoots) that favoured Roman custom not only on the date of Easter but in other matters also.[17] Connections with northern Italy, in particular with Bobbio, would have acquainted some Irishmen with a society in which written legal instruments were common. The importance of writing is occasionally accepted in Irish secular law, often enough to show that the concerns of the *Romani* found an echo outside the church; but, in general, written law was perceived

[11] François L. Ganshof, *Was waren die Kapitularien?* (Weimar, 1961), pp 35–40.

[12] Ibid., pp 107–12; Rosamond McKitterick, 'Literacy in Carolingian government' in R. McKitterick (ed.), *The uses of literacy in early medieval Europe* (Cambridge, 1990), pp 283–4.

[13] J. M. Wallace-Hadrill, *Early Germanic kingship in England and on the continent* (Oxford, 1971), pp 32–7; Patrick Wormald, '*Lex scripta* and *Verbum regis*: legislation and Germanic kingship, from Euric to Cnut' in P. H. Sawyer and Ian N. Wood (ed.), *Early medieval kingship* (Leeds, 1977), pp 125–30.

[14] G. P. Bognetti, *L'età longobarda* (Milan, 1968), ii, 313–14; iv, 128–35.

[15] Fritz Beyerle (ed.), *Leges Langobardorum, 643–866* (2nd ed., Witzenhausen, 1962), p. 143 (cap. 91).

[16] Contemporaries were perhaps sometimes aware of this: Columbanus, *Epistolae*, III 3, V. 11, ed. and trans. G. S. M. Walker, *Sancti Columbani opera*. (Dublin, 1957), pp 24–5, 48–9. Among the Irish colonies in Britain, Scottish Dál Ríata, outside the empire, survived, whereas in Dyfed, within the late-Roman diocese of Britain, the Irish were probably assimilated to the Britons by the seventh century. By the time that the Irish laws were written, connections with the former imperial Rome were thus weaker than they had been.

[17] Kathleen Hughes, *Early Christian Ireland: an introduction to the sources* (London, 1972), p. 76; on the other hand, Wendy Davies, 'The Latin charter-tradition in western Britain, Brittany and Ireland in the early medieval period' in Dorothy Whitelock, Rosamond McKitterick, and David N. Dumville (ed.), *Ireland in early mediaeval Europe: studies in memory of Kathleen Hughes* (Cambridge, 1982), pp 258–80, p. 268, interprets the phrase *more Romanorum* without reference to the Roman party in the Irish church, apparently on the basis of an early dating for the second synod of St Patrick.

as church law while the secular law lived in 'the joint memory of the old men, the chanting of seers, transmission from one ear to another'.[18]

The way in which church law was made did not encourage the writing down of royal legislation. Late Roman law was perceived by barbarian and citizen alike as, in the sixth-century British writer Gildas's phrase, 'the edicts of the Romans', namely of 'the kings of the Romans'.[19] The association between law, legislation, and the king was natural and influential. But in Ireland the law of the church was a law made by synods and by learned men, not by a centralised supreme authority, in spite of the aspirations of Armagh.[20]

It would be going too far to assert baldly that royal legislation was never written down. The survival of early vernacular material depended upon the interest of later lawyers and they may have had more reason to preserve professional manuals of instruction than royal edicts. The latter had authority, in the first place, only within the territory of the king.[21] Whatever the element of truth in the claims advanced by and for kings of Tara to be kings of Ireland, there was no one king who could legislate for the whole country; but the legal tradition was common to the entire island. In the nature of things, therefore, an edict which did in fact pass into the general law would not do so because of its authority as the edict of a particular king, but rather because the content of that edict became generally accepted. Since, therefore, the authority of the law extended over a wider area than the territory of any king, the lawyer had no particular reason to record royal edicts as such.

A partial exception to this generalisation is the ecclesiastical *cáin* or *lex* which seems to have been promulgated by assemblies composed of both ecclesiastics and laymen. For the promulgation of his *lex* in 697 Adomnán, the abbot of Iona, went to immense trouble to secure the assent, and often perhaps the physical presence, of all the leading kings of Ireland or their heirs-apparent, before the law was promulgated at an assembly at Birr.[22] Indeed, the author of 'Críth Gablach' (*c.*A.D. 700) has no difficulty in perceiving it both as *recht Adomnáin*, 'the Law of Adomnán', and as an example

---

[18] *C.I.H.*, p. 596.30 = 751.5-6, etc.; 1376.16; cf. also p. 753.40, which disallows alienation of kin-land by means of a charter.

[19] Gildas, *De excidio Britanniae*, cap. 5 (ed. and trans. Michael Winterbottom, *Gildas: The ruin of Britain* (Chichester, 1978), pp 17–18.

[20] Compare the *Liber Angeli*, capp 28–9, with *Collectio canonum Hibernensis* (hereafter *Hib.*), XX, *De provincia*, ed. Hermann Wasserschleben, *Die irische Kanonensammlung* (2nd ed., Leipzig, 1885), pp 60–62; the latter, as might be expected with a document drawn up in part by a monk of Iona, implicitly denies the claims of Armagh: the Irish church ought to have a provincial structure corresponding to such regions as Dessmumu, 'South Munster' (capp 1–2); a province is to have a metropolitan (cap. 3); appeals are to be to a synod, apparently a synod at the level of a province such as Leinster and Munster, and then to Rome (cap. 5).

[21] Cf. *rechtgae ríg Caisil la Mumain*, *Críth Gablach*, lines 520–21.

[22] Máirín Ní Dhonnchadha, 'The guarantor list of Cáin Adomnáin' in *Peritia*, i (1982), pp 178–215. The text is edited by Kuno Meyer, *Cáin Adamnáin* (Oxford, 1905).

of a *rechtgae ríg*, 'royal edict'.[23] The context helps to explain what happened. Birr lay on the frontier between the southern Uí Néill and Munster. Meetings on or near the frontier are reasonably well attested in the annals; and they can be clearly distinguished from the normal assemblies of a given kingdom.[24] A *rígdál*, 'meeting of kings', was a grander affair than an ordinary *óenach* or *dál*. The guarantors of the Law of Adomnán were listed, first the clergy, headed by the bishop of Armagh, and second the lay rulers, headed by the king of Tara and kinsman of Adomnán, Loingsech mac Óengussa. Adomnán's achievement was to concert the whole power of Ireland, and indeed of the Picts, with a law from which kings and churches might profit financially and which the major institutions and rulers had backed in person or by representative.

The Law of Adomnán was exceptional. More typical examples are offered by annalistic entries on royal or royal-cum-ecclesiastical edicts for the Connachta. Two are of particular interest. In 783 the Law of Patrick was promulgated in Cruachain by Dub dá Leithi, abbot of Armagh, and by Tipraite mac Taidgg, king of the Connachta; in 814 the Law of Cíarán was enacted by Muirgus mac Tommaltaig, king of the Connachta, 'over Cruachain'. In the latter entry the usual way of saying who was subject to the law—namely that the law was 'over such-and-such a people'—is replaced by a statement that it was 'over Cruachain'. Cruachain, however, was the traditional 'seat of kingship' of the province and the site of an *óenach* accounted as one of the three principal assemblies of its kind in Ireland.[25] It is perhaps not too bold to see the phrase as shorthand for saying that the law was promulgated by Muirgus at an *óenach* of the Connachta at Cruachain. The legal evidence, moreover, would lead one to expect precisely this conjunction of *óenach* and edict. Such occasions were the Irish counterparts to the edicts promulgated by Childebert II at Andernach, Cologne, and elsewhere.

Parallels for the grander occasions, such as the Law of Adomnán, are the legislation of Chlothar II at Paris in 614, and the seventh-century Visigothic tradition of conciliar legislation. It is not impossible, given other evidence of links between Ireland and both Francia and Spain in the period, that written decrees of Frankish and Visigothic councils served as a model for their Irish

---

[23] *Críth Gablach*, lines 514–24: of the four types of *rechtge* in lines 515–21 the last, the *rechtge ríg*, seems to include the further triad in lines 521–4.

[24] A.U. 737, where the meeting between Áed Allán and Cathal mac Findguini at Terryglass, a few miles into Munster, appears to have led to the promulgation of the Law of Patrick in Munster as well as in Leth Cuinn, and also, perhaps, to an alliance against Leinster; 784, 838 (interestingly, close to the frontier between the Uí Néill and Leinster), 859 (Rahugh was just into Uí Néill territory, but Áed mac Bricc's Life shows that the community had strong interests in northern Munster). A much earlier example is the meeting at Druim Cete, A.U. 575, but probably nearer 590: Richard Sharpe, *Adomnán of Iona: Life of St Columba* (Harmondsworth, 1995), n. 204.

[25] Kuno Meyer (ed. and trans.), *The triads of Ireland* (Dublin, 1906), no. 35.

counterparts.[26] The dates of the earliest written *cánai*, 'Cáin Fuithirbe' (678–83) and 'Cáin Adamnáin' (697), are consistent with such a hypothesis.[27] They also lie within what I shall argue to be the main period of written law in Ireland and are part and parcel of that phenomenon, for though they were made with the authority of synods, they employed the language and the enforcement mechanisms of the native law.[28] Alternatively, they may be seen as a native development, in which the normal royal *cáin*, promulgated at an *óenach*, was extended to the whole country, just as different provincial synods occasionally came together.[29] A possible early example of joint meetings of church synods is the one that met in Mag Léne *c*.630 to discuss the Easter question. Mag Léne either included or was close to Durrow; at any event, it was within southern Uí Néill territory, but within a few miles of both Leinster and Munster.[30] The evidence of Cummian's letter to Ségéne of Iona and the hermit Béccán suggests that churchmen from Munster, Connacht, and Leinster may have been involved.[31] The synod of Mag nAilbe, however, that met at about the same time, recorded in the Life of Munnu, appears to have been a specifically Leinster synod.[32] The acceptance that different provincial synods might sometimes combine together could have provided the model for such events as the great assembly at Birr in 697.

The annalistic evidence for the *cáin* suggests that it may have been linked with the Féni, a name sometimes applied to all the Irish, but also referring to the Uí Néill, the Connachta, the Éoganachta, and their principal client-peoples. The *cánai* in the annals fall into two groups: there are those promulgated to the whole of Ireland, as was 'Cáin Adomnáin'; then there are the provincial *cánai*, such as that promulgated by Muirgus mac Tommaltaig for

[26] The main periods of Visigothic royal interest in conciliar legislation were the 630s and the 680s: see Roger Collins, *Early medieval Spain: unity in diversity* (London, 1983), pp 116–20. Given the date of *Cáin Fuirthirbe*, the second period in the 680s is slightly too late to be relevant. The Columbanian monasteries in Francia were deeply concerned by Chlothar II's display of his triumph over the heirs of his royal kinsman, Theuderic II of Burgundy, and the queen-mother, Brunhild.

[27] D. A. Binchy, 'The date and provenance of Uraicecht Becc' in *Ériu*, xviii (1958), pp 51–4; Liam Breatnach, 'The ecclesiastical element in the Old-Irish legal tract *Cáin Fhuithirbe*' in *Peritia*, v (1986), pp 35–50.

[28] In *Cáin Adomnáin* there is, apparently already standard, a technical vocabulary and a form appropriate to *cánai*, for example the term *for-tá*. It is likely that some at least of this standard form derived from earlier secular *cánai* made by *brithemain* for kings, as stated in a mid eighth-century gloss on the Würzburg MS of the Pauline Epistles, Wb 28 a 1 (*Thes. Pal.*, i, 679).

[29] A.U. 780. In A.U. 804 the synods that met at Dún Cuair (probably Rathcore, in Mide, but close to the Leinster border) appear to have been of the southern and northern Uí Néill (cf. 851).

[30] Ann. Tig., 1020; *Ann. Clon.*, p. 59.

[31] Maura Walsh and Dáibhí Ó Cróinín (ed. and trans.), *Cummian's letter De controversia paschali and the De ratione conputandi* (Toronto, 1988), lines 259–80.

[32] *Vita I S. Fintani seu Munnu*, capp 29–30, ed. Heist, *Vitae SS Hib.*, p. 207. Although the Life describes this as a *magnum consilium populorum Hybernie*, the named participants were all from Leinster. The Life also assumed that kings might participate, but this may be anachronistic (i.e., refer to a meeting such as that at Birr).

the Connachta. The annals offer quite numerous examples of the latter in the eighth and early ninth centuries; they appear to have come to an end once the disruptive wars between Munster and the Uí Néill and with the vikings gathered pace in the ninth century. Once these provincial *cánai* are collected, a striking picture emerges: there are *cánai* for Munster, for the Connachta, and for the Uí Néill, but none for Leinster or for the Ulaid. This is unlikely to be a consequence of the annalists' geographical limitations, since they preserved more information about Leinster and the Ulaid than about Munster. A possible explanation is that the Uí Néill had achieved sufficiently clear a domination over the Ulaid and Leinstermen as to prevent them from issuing independent legislation of this kind, whereas the Connachta and Éoganachta, as traditional allies and fellow-Féni, had legislative independence.

Even when legislation was sponsored by both churchmen and lay rulers, its chances of survival remained poor. The Law of Adomnán survives because it suited the church of Raphoe, some centuries later, to produce a new version in which colourful legend, more favourable to the interests of the church of Raphoe than to the reputation of its founder, Adomnán, was superimposed on the sober legal text of the original edict.[33] The argument from silence is always doubtful when applied to Irish law, whether lay or ecclesiastical: the major canonical text, the 'Collectio Canonum Hibernensis', though known to scholars simply as the 'Hibernensis', did not survive in any Irish manuscript. The main secular lawbook, the 'Senchas Már', survives only in fragments, most of which would probably have perished if it had not been for the industry of the Welsh scholar Edward Lhuyd.[34] What survives is doubly unrepresentative: though a remarkable quantity of Irish law has come down from the early middle ages, much was never written, and much that was written failed to survive. The texts which exist today cannot be assumed to be representative of the whole. What survives must therefore be examined for clues as to the nature of what did not survive or was never written, for only then can a rounded picture of early Irish law be given.

A CONSIDERABLE proportion of surviving Irish secular law consists of tracts or fragments of tracts belonging to the lawbook called 'Senchas Már', literally 'the great antiquity'; in other words, 'the great collection of ancient tradition'. It comprises a short introduction and a series of tracts on particular topics. In the manuscripts these tracts appear in a fixed order. One of the many contributions to the study of the laws by the greatest of Celtic scholars, Rudolf Thurneysen, was a discussion of the contents and date of the

---

[33] Hence §§ 1–27 of the existing text, ed. Meyer, *Cáin Adamnáin*, pp 2–14.

[34] Anne and William O'Sullivan, 'Edward Lluyd's collection of Irish manuscripts' in *Transactions of the Honourable Society of Cymmrodorion* (1962), pp 57–76; Charles Plummer, 'On the fragmentary state of the text of the Brehon Laws' in *Z.C.P.*, xvii (1928), pp 157–68.

'Senchas Már'.[35] His arguments are of fundamental importance and must therefore be appraised before we can go on to discuss the nature of the lawbook. Thurneysen himself changed his opinions on some aspects more than once and his results are certainly not to be treated with unquestioning reverence. We shall see, however, that the most important are also the most soundly based.

The contents of the 'Senchas Már' can be established from four categories of evidence. First, the Introduction itself names or refers to several tracts;[36] secondly, a number of manuscripts preserve parts of the 'Senchas Már', either complete or in the form of short extracts to which glosses and commentaries are appended;[37] thirdly, extracts are sometimes cited by late medieval or early modern scribes as belonging to one of the 'thirds' of the 'Senchas Már';[38] fourthly, the late Old Irish glossary ascribed to Cormac mac Cuilennáin quotes phrases or sentences which it ascribes to the 'Senchas Már', while the early modern glossary known as 'O'Davoren's glossary' has numerous extracts in the order of the text.[39] A reconstruction of the first two of the thirds of the 'Senchas Már' is as follows:[40]

First third
1. Introduction
2. *Di chethairshlicht athgabála* (Concerning the four kinds of distraint)
3. *Di gnímaib gíall* (On the functions of hostages)
4. *Cáin Íarraith* (The regulation of fosterage)
5. *Cáin sóerraith* (The regulation of a free fief)
6. *Cáin aicillne* (The regulation of base clientship)
7. *Cáin lánamna* (The regulation of a complete pairing) (mainly on the property consequences of the ending of a sexual relationship)
8. *Córus béscnai* (The lawful arrangement of customary behaviour) (on the relationship between church and laity)

[35] Rudolf Thurneysen, 'Aus dem irischen Recht, IV. 6. Zu den bisherigen Ausgaben der irischen Rechtstexte. 1. Ancient Laws of Ireland und Senchas Mar' in Z.C.P., xvi (1926), pp 167–96; cf. his 'Aus dem irischen Recht, V. 8. Zum ursprünglichen Umfang des *Senchas Már*' in Z.C.P., xviii (1930), pp 356–64.
[36] See Thurneysen's edition, 'Aus dem irischen Recht, IV', p. 176, §§ 5–9 (= C.I.H., pp 350.13–351.10).
[37] Thurneysen, ibid., pp 172–3; utilised and extended, with new evidence, by Liam Breatnach, 'On the original extent of the *Senchas Már*' in Ériu, xlvii (1996), pp 6–19.
[38] Listed by Liam Breatnach, 'On the original extent of the *Senchas Már*', pp 1–3.
[39] Kuno Meyer (ed. and trans.), *Sanas Cormaic: the Glossary of Cormac* in O. J. Bergin, R. I. Best, K. Meyer and J. G. O'Keeffe (ed.), *Anecdota from Irish manuscripts*, iv (Halle and Dublin, 1912), nos. 50, 575, 584, 693, 970, 975 (on nos 693 and 975 see Breatnach, 'On the original extent of the *Senchas Már*', p. 3 and n. 12). For the extracts in O'Davoren, see Breatnach, ibid., pp 10–14.
[40] This follows Liam Breatnach, 'On the original extent of the *Senchas Már*', pp 20–28, who also gives a list of the contents of the last third.

Second third

9. *Sechtae* (Heptads)

10. *Bretha comaithchesa* (Judgements on neighbourhood)

11. *Din techtugud* (On taking possession) (a text on *tellach*, 'entry', a procedure by which land could be claimed)

12. *Tosach béscnai* (Beginning of custom) (mainly consisting of a poem on kinship and women)

13. *Recholl breth* (Shroud of judgements) (or perhaps *Rocholl Breth*, 'The utter destruction of judgements')

14. *Di astad chirt and dligid* (On the establishment of right and entitlement) (a collection of triads and tetrads)

15. *Di thúaslucud rudrad* (On the dissolution of prescriptions)

16. *Fuidir* tract (on a category of half-freeman)

17. *Di fodlaib cenéoil thúaithe* (On the divisions of a lay kindred) (or *Fodlai Fine*, 'Divisions of the kindred')[41]

18. *Di dligiud raith ocus somoíne la flaith* (On the law of a fief and a lord's revenue)

19. *Díre* (Honour-price)

20. *Bandíre* (Women's honour-price)

21. *Bechbretha* (Bee-judgements)

22. *Coibnes uisci thairidne* (Kinship of conducted water) (on watermills)

23. *Bretha im fuillemu gell* (Judgements about fees for pledges)

24. *Bretha im gatta* (Judgements about thefts)

'Bretha im gatta' appears have been the last tract of the middle third, as Thurneysen was inclined to suppose. Of the tracts thought to belong to the last third, the only ones to be preserved in full are those concerning sick-maintenance, 'blood-lying', and injuries ('Slicht othrusa', 'Bretha crólige', and 'Bretha Déin Chécht'). A recent discussion by Breatnach, however, attributes twenty-three tracts to this last third.[42] In effect, therefore, the last third is almost lost to us although fragments of text enable us to have some notion of its contents. Yet there is some consolation. Since much of the evidence on the contents of the first two thirds of the 'Senchas Már' overlaps, we can be that much more certain that the tracts listed above did belong to the 'Senchas Már' and that they occurred in a fixed order. Even though our knowledge may be irritatingly limited, it is all the more securely founded. Moreover, what we do know is enough to provide some notion of the general character of the lawbook.

It is not easy to classify the texts contained in the 'Senchas Már' according to subject-matter. The usual categories of modern law (often derived from

---

[41] The title given in the marginal note uses the word *cenél*, but *fine* is used throughout the tract itself.

[42] Breatnach, 'On the original extent of the *Senchas Már*', pp 7–10, 13–19, 28–37.

Roman law) are not always appropriate. The following classification is only one way of dealing with material which often comes under more than one heading.[43]

A.  Legal activity: including process in court, the creation of legal obligation by contract or prescription, methods of pacifying parties in dispute.
    'Di chethairslicht athgabála'
    'Di gnímaib gíall'
    'Din techtugud'
    'Bretha im fuillemu gell'
    'Di thúaslucad rudrad'

B.  The law of social institutions, such as the church, lordship, kinship and status.
    'Cáin íarraith'
    'Cáin sóerraith'
    'Cáin aicillne'
    'Cáin lánamna'
    'Díre' and 'Bandíre'
    'Córus béscnai'
    'Maccslechta' (in the last third)
    'Fodlai Fine'
    The 'Kinship poem' in 'Tosach Béscnai'
    'Fuidir' (tract)
    'Di dligiud raith ocus somoíne la flaith'

C.  The law of things (including animals): land, buildings, and movables.
    'Bechbretha'
    'Coibnius uisci thairidne'
    More tracts on the law of things were contained in the last third: examples are:
    'Bretha for conslechtaib' (Judgements on categories of dog)
    'Bretha for catslechtaib' (Judgements on categories of cat)

D.  Heterogeneous text: for example, triads and heptads.
    Heptads
    'Di astad chirt ocus dligid'

The crucial distinction here is between A and B. Behind the distinction is a desire to do justice to two clear connections in the texts themselves. First,

---

[43] The classification in Fergus Kelly, *A guide to early Irish law*, appendix 1, is somewhat different.

there is the link between the tract on distraint and that on 'entry' (*tellach, techtugad*). These tracts are not juxtaposed in the 'Senchas Már', but nevertheless both deal with procedures by which claimants may seek to recover their rights and both refer, in much the same way, to the same legendary jurists, Senchae and Brig.[44] The pronouncements of these jurists are along the same lines in the two tracts. There is thus a basis in the texts for category A. Secondly, there are the 'Four *cánai*' (four regulations). These are juxtaposed in the 'Senchas Már', but, more importantly, all four deal with one-to-one relationships (usually relationships in which one of the two parties has authority over the other). In 'Cáin iarraith' we have the relationship of foster-parent and foster-child; in 'Cáin sóerraith' of lord and free client; in 'Cáin aicillne' of lord and base client; in 'Cáin lánamna' of man and woman in a sexual union. The connection between the four *cánai* is explicit and it must be taken seriously as a conscious legal classification by a contemporary lawyer. The third category, the law of things, covers tracts whose centre of interest lies rather in the law affecting material objects than in social institutions or in legal activities. The line is not easy to draw: a tract on watermills is also concerned with the relationships of neighbours. The fourth category, however, is straightforward: collections of triads and heptads covering a miscellaneous series of topics in no coherent order.

Once the classification has been done it reveals one striking fact about the 'Senchas Már'. It is very rich in material on social institutions. If we leave aside the Introduction to the 'Senchas Már', nearly two-thirds of the tracts assigned to the collection are concerned primarily with social organisation. This preoccupation explains why Irish law is such an important source for the history of early Irish society. It is not just a consequence of the inclusion of the four *cánai*, for, even if they were removed, this category would still be the largest. The 'Senchas Már', therefore, is concerned mainly with the legal shape of society and with the remedies and legal activities of ordinary people. It is a law of self-help in which individuals and groups of individuals occupy the foreground rather than the king, courts, lawyers, and officials. It is for this reason that notions of judging are applied very widely: in the tract on base clientship, 'Cáin aicillne', lords who have kept their side of the bargain have the right, indeed the obligation, to judge their clients.[45]

This does not imply for a moment that there were no courts or that kings and their officers played no part in the processes of law. A tract on the *airecht* demonstrates that some cases were heard in open-air courts presided over by a provincial king, accompanied by a bishop and 'the expert in every legal

[44] *C.I.H.*, p. 209. 12–23, transl. (by Binchy) in Calvert Watkins, 'Indo-European metrics and archaic Irish verse' in *Celtica*, vi (1963), pp 227–8; 377.24–8; 380.14–22. On this see D. A. Binchy, 'Distraint in Irish law' in *Celtica*, x (1973), p. 37.
[45] *Cáin Aicillne*, ed. Thurneysen, §§ 53 (contrast 54), 55 (contrast 58).

language with the rank of master'.[46] Such courts did not merely focus the legal expertise, the sureties, and witnesses necessary to settle issues, but also the political prestige and power necessary to give effect to decisions; and since the proceedings were conducted in full publicity, often perhaps at an *óenach*, the communal memory of a society was brought into play so as to ensure that any secondary dispute about the case could be settled. The *airecht* thus had three functions: to arrive at a judicial solution, to assemble the power to enforce the judgement, and to bring together representatives of a community to remember the judgement. In other cases, however, the parties would merely come to the house of the judge, where their case would be settled without any such power and publicity as was deployed by the *airecht*.[47] The categories of case that came straight to a judge and not to an *airecht* included, for example, disputes between neighbours over trespass. Such disputes were probably settled by a judge in relative privacy, because local social networks could usually be relied on to give adequate backing to his judgement.[48]

The focus of early Germanic written law, but probably not its local practice, was different. Most laws consisted of authoritative statements addressed to judges. 'Lex Salica', for example, begins: 'If anyone has been summoned to the *mallus* [local court] according to the king's laws and has not come, if no legal excuse detained him let him be judged at the *mallus*-hill to be guilty of *reaptena* [neglect], that is, liable to pay 600 *denarii* which make 15 *solidi*.'[49] Here we have laws which are king's laws, *leges dominicae*. A law defines an offence and prescribes a penalty; the court obeys. It is, therefore, a law prescribed by a legislator who seeks to control courts and legal process, a law concerned with particular offences and with their punishment rather than with the legal shape of social institutions. It aspired to be a law of the state.

The 'Senchas Már' is not easy to date. Many of the tracts are likely to have existed before they were incorporated into a lawbook. Their dates, in so far as they are known, are thus only useful as steps towards a *terminus post quem*. The probability is that the latest tracts to be incorporated into the 'Senchas Már' date from the first half of the eighth century.[50] The 'Senchas

---

[46] Fergus Kelly, 'An Old Irish text on court procedure' in *Peritia*, v (1986), pp 74–106 (the quoted passage is on p. 85); on the king see also Marilyn Gerriets, 'The king as judge in early Ireland' in *Celtica*, xx (1988), pp 29–52.

[47] *C.I.H.*, ed. Binchy, p. 2202, lines 33–4 = *Cóic Conara Fugill*, ed. R. Thurneysen, *Abhandl. Preuss. Akad. Wiss., Jahrgang 1925, phil.-hist. Klasse*, no. 7 (Berlin, 1926), p. 25 of the *Einzelausgabe*.

[48] Cf. Richard Sharpe, 'Dispute settlement in medieval Ireland: a preliminary enquiry' in Wendy Davies and Paul Fouracre (ed.), *The settlement of disputes in early medieval Europe* (Cambridge, 1986), esp. pp 174–6 (on a case in Tírechán), and 181–7 (on the role of the *brithem*); Robin Chapman Stacey, *The road to judgment: from custom to court in medieval Ireland and Wales* (Pennsylvania, 1994), pp 125–31.

[49] *Pactus Legis Salicae*, ed. Eckhardt, § 1.

[50] T. M. Charles-Edwards, 'The *Corpus Iuris Hibernici*' in *Studia Hib.*, xx (1980), pp 147–55.

Már' itself cannot, therefore, be earlier than *c.*700. A *terminus ante quem* is given first of all by references to the 'Senchas Már' in Cormac's Glossary (*c.*900), by 'the pseudo-historical prologue' to the 'Senchas Már' and by the existence of a collection of glosses in T.C.D., MS H.3.18, both of which have been dated to the ninth century.[51] From this one may conclude that the 'Senchas Már' belongs to the eighth or ninth century. To obtain any more precise date, however, is not so easy.

One approach is to date the language of the introduction. Unfortunately, it is too short for definite results to be attainable. Since the text was transmitted in late manuscripts it is difficult to determine the linguistic state of the original. Thurneysen's careful discussion suggested that it was somewhat earlier than the main body of the Würzburg glosses, themselves dated to *c.*750, but a clearer result depended upon a plausible but uncertain emendation of a single word.[52]

Thurneysen was too good a philologist to wish to rely solely on linguistic evidence in such unfavourable circumstances, and he also suggested a historical argument to reinforce the idea of a date in the first half of the eighth century. In an earlier article he had proposed a convincing reconstruction of a scribal note in a Breton manuscript of the 'Collectio canonum Hibernensis'.[53] This identified two scholars who had participated in the preparation of the 'Hibernensis', Rubin of Dairinis (d. 725) and Cú Chuimne of Iona (d. 747). The 'Hibernensis', however, survives in two recensions, A and B. Thurneysen suggested, therefore, that the earlier of the two scholars, Rubin, was responsible for what he believed, following Hellmann,[54] to be the earlier recension, B, and that Cú Chuimne was responsible for the later one, the A recension. From this one might conclude that the first recension belonged to the first quarter of the eighth century and the second one to the second quarter. In other words, the first half of the eighth century would have been a period of compilatory activity in the history of Irish canon law. On this basis Thurneysen went on to argue that 'it is not probable that the two great collections of ecclesiastical and secular law arose entirely independently of each other; one of them, the ecclesiastical, provided the stimulus for the other, the "Senchas Már".[55] This argument is strengthened by evident connections between the subject-matter of the two collections: some of the material incorporated into the 'Hibernensis' is Irish law in Latin dress; some of the tracts in the 'Senchas Már', notably 'Córus Béscnai', show a clear awareness of canon law.[56] The introduction itself betrays a sensitivity to the

[51] John Carey, 'An edition of the pseudo-historical prologue to the *Senchas Már*' in *Ériu*, xlv (1994), pp 1–32; D. A. Binchy, 'A text on the forms of distraint' in *Celtica*, x (1973), p. 72.
[52] R. Thurneysen, 'Aus dem irischen Recht, IV', pp 177–8, n. 1, p. 186.
[53] R. Thurneysen, 'Zur irischen Kanonensammlung' in *Z.C.P.*, vi (1908), pp 1–5.
[54] Siegmund Hellmann, *Sedulius Scottus* (Munich, 1906), pp 141–3.
[55] R. Thurneysen, 'Aus dem irischen Recht, IV', pp 186–7.
[56] Notably in the passages on first fruits, firstlings etc., *C.I.H.*, pp 530.32–531.24.

relationship of the two legal traditions: it perceives the 'Senchas Már' as secular and oral while canon law is written, but it also declares that the 'Senchas Már' should borrow material from canon law.[57] All this would be natural, on Thurneysen's view, if the compiler of the 'Senchas Már' was also working in the first half of the eighth century.

The argument is attractive but not conclusive. The scribal note referring to Rubin and Cú Chuimne offers no support to the notion that they were responsible for two different recensions. It is appended to a manuscript of the A recension and would more naturally be taken to suggest that the two scholars had been responsible only for that version.[58] Admittedly, the view that the 'Senchas Már' is posterior to the 'Hibernensis' has the smell of truth. The former is the written expression of an oral tradition while the latter is perceived as written from the start: it is *recht litre*, 'the law of the letter'. One would expect, therefore, that a project to make a major written collection of law would be first undertaken by those lawyers for whom writing was of the essence of their tradition, namely the canonists. So far so good, but this only establishes the priority of the 'Hibernensis', whereas Thurneysen proposed that both collections belonged to the same half-century. On his view, they were virtually contemporaneous. This may well be true—it is not uncommon to have short periods of intense activity in lawmaking—but it cannot be regarded as conclusively demonstrated.

On the other hand, subsequent work has all tended to strengthen Thurneysen's arguments. In the first place, the important tract on status, 'Críth Gablach', which did not belong to the 'Senchas Már', has been firmly dated to the first half of the eighth century for a mixture of historical and linguistic reasons.[59] Indeed it is one of the most securely dated of all texts in Old Irish. Fortunately, there are clear stylistic resemblances between it and the latest group among the tracts incorporated into the 'Senchas Már'.

To appreciate the argument it is necessary to consider this question of style. The issue is complex, for we would like to date a lawbook, the 'Senchas Már', through stylistic arguments which bear in the first place only on pieces of text; and yet a tract may include text of different dates and a lawbook includes tracts which are also of different dates. The argument must therefore proceed like this: the date of a tract will be that of the latest stratum of text within it, and the date of the lawbook is likely to be close to that of the latest tracts. We must, then, begin with the dating of text. The following classification derives as far as possible from the tracts themselves:[60]

---

[57] R. Thurneysen, 'Aus dem irischen Recht, IV', p. 175, § 1 (= *C.I.H.*, pp 344.24–347.17); cf. *C.I.H.*, p. 245.1–2.

[58] Cf. Maurice Sheehy, 'The Collectio Canonum Hibernensis—a Celtic phenomenon' in Löwe, *Die Iren*, ii, 534.

[59] *Crith Gablach*, pp xiii–xvi.

[60] Charles-Edwards, 'The *Corpus Iuris Hibernici*', pp 154–5.

A. Text written in forms deriving from the oral tradition of Irish law (*Féne-chas*):

    1. *Roscad* (verse in traditional metres).

    2. *Fásach* (legal maxim: e.g., *ní fognai lám láim* 'hand does not serve hand').[61]

    3. Rhetorical prose (e.g., the last part of 'Bretha Crólige').[62]

    4. Instruction by a sage to his pupil.[63]

    5. Triads, tetrads (but the status of heptads is uncertain).[64]

B. Material composed in styles which had solely a written background:

    1. Text not affected by stylistic devices deriving from elementary Latin grammar.[65]

    2. Text which is affected by such devices (question and answer, especially when it includes the stock formula *ní anse* 'it is not difficult'; enumeration other than the traditional triads, tetrads, and possibly heptads; etymology).[66]

The relationship between A and B is a difficult matter. It is not the same for texts of different provenance: the 'Bretha Nemed' group of tracts, the 'Senchas Már', and such tracts as 'Críth Gablach' or 'Berrad Airechta'. For the 'Senchas Már', there is no evidence that text belonging to any of the categories listed under A was composed to be written; on the contrary, it appears to have been quoted by the authors of written texts from oral tradition and it thus had a life quite separate from the written text.[67] For the 'Bretha Nemed', however, there is evidence that some text composed as *Fénechas* was from the start written; here, therefore, the relationship between oral and written forms was quite different.[68]

---

[61] *C.I.H.*, p. 400.13; cf. D. A. Binchy, 'Distraint in early Irish Law', p. 53, who observes that the *fásach* is hardly relevant to the context to which it is applied.

[62] D. A. Binchy, '*Bretha Crólige*' in *Ériu*, xii, pt 1 (1934), pp 1–77 (§§ 58–66).

[63] *C.I.H.*, p. 210.

[64] The heptads appear to reflect the seventh-century Irish interest in 'sevens': cf. Roger E. Reynolds, 'At "sixes and sevens"—and eights and nines: the sacred mathematics of sacred orders in the early middle ages' in *Speculum*, liv (1979), pp 669–84. In the laws it appears to antedate A.D. 700. For examples of triads and tetrads see *C.I.H.*, pp 219.29–234.8.

[65] Examples would be 'Bechbretha', 'Coibnius uisci thairdne', and 'Di dligiud raith ocus somaíne'.

[66] Cf. Charles-Edwards, 'The *Corpus Iuris Hibernici*', pp 147–51.

[67] The 'Senchas Már' quotes *Fénechas* but without introducing it with such phrases as *amal arin-chain Fénechas* (e.g., *C.I.H.*, pp 353.26–354.14 (= D. A. Binchy, *Ériu*, xvi (1952), p. 46). The introductory phrases are characteristic of texts outside the 'Senchas Már': 'Berrad airechta', §§ 10, 12, 59, 60, 79 (= *C.I.H.*, pp 591.34; 592.6; 596.6, 19; 599.17) and 'Críth Gablach', lines 21–2, 272–6, 462–5; in 'Bretha Nemed Toísech', the exx. at *C.I.H.*, pp 2212.3; 2221.32; 2222.19, 33 appear similar, but at 2211.2 *aracan feinechus* introduces a passage in 'textbook' style.

[68] Liam Breatnach, 'Canon law and secular law in early Ireland: the significance of *Bretha Nemed*' in *Peritia*, iii (1984), pp 439–59: 458.

The relationship between the two forms listed as B1 and B2 is easier. For linguistic reasons it is likely that text belonging to category B1 began to be composed no later than *c*.650, whereas text of category B2 seems to begin about 700.[69] 'Críth Gablach' contains a considerable amount of text belonging to B2. For the 'Senchas Már', therefore, a plausible theory would run as follows: up to *c*.650 the tradition was purely oral; from that date tracts began to be composed as written texts, in a form quite distinct from those current in the oral tradition; from *c*.700 stylistic forms derived from elementary Latin grammar, notably Donatus' 'Ars Minor', began to make themselves felt; these only affected the latest stratum of text and thus the latest tracts; on the assumption that the compilation of the 'Senchas Már' was the culmination of a period of activity in legal writing which reached its peak in the early eighth century, one may conclude that there was no great chronological gap between the latest tracts and the compilation of the lawbook; the 'Senchas Már', therefore, should not be dated much later than 700 and a date in the first half of the eighth century thus appears likely. If one accepts the priority of the 'Hibernensis', a date in the second quarter of the eighth century is probable.

Further support for Thurneysen comes from work done on the 'Bretha Nemed' ('Judgements on [or by] privileged persons'). In glossaries, in particular that of Cormac, quotations are taken from two main legal sources, the 'Senchas Már' and the 'Bretha Nemed'.[70] This suggests already that the 'Bretha Nemed' were a collection of tracts, a lawbook on something like the scale of the 'Senchas Már'. Several of these quotations have been traced to two sources: the first is a text entitled in the manuscript (BL, Cotton MS Nero A. 7) 'Córus Breatha Neimead', but in medieval glosses 'Bretha Nemed Toísech' ('the first Bretha Nemed'); the second is from a manuscript written by Dubhaltach Mac Firbhisigh (T.C.D., MS H.2.15B), but it was known to medieval glossators as 'Bretha Nemed Déidenach' ('the posterior Bretha Nemed').[71] These two must therefore be regarded either as constituting part of, or deriving from, the 'Bretha Nemed'. The next stage of the argument was to establish, on the basis of these two texts, the characteristics of the 'Bretha Nemed', in terms of style, choice of subject-matter, and use of technical terms. The main ones were a high proportion of verse (*roscad*) and of rhetorical prose, a preoccupation with the status and function of the *filid*, 'poet-seers', and a use of the term *nemed*, 'privileged person' to embrace not only the king, bishop, and chief poet and their equals, but all freemen.

---

[69] 'Bechbretha', pp 25–7.

[70] For the 'Senchas Már', see above n. 31; for the 'Bretha Nemed', see *Sanas Cormaic*, nos 142 (= *C.I.H.*, p. 2223.21), 430 (= *C.I.H.*, p. 2217.27), 689 (= *C.I.H.*, p. 2214.2), 877 (*C.I.H.*, p. 2217.41). In general see D. A. Binchy, 'Bretha Nemed' in *Ériu*, xvii (1955), pp 4–6.

[71] It was first edited by Edward Gwynn and hence is sometimes known as the Gwynn text: E. J. Gwynn, 'A text on the privileges and responsibilities of poets' in *Ériu*, xiii (1942), pp 1–60, 220–36 (= *C.I.H.*, pp 1111–38).

The usefulness of these characteristics as criteria by which one might judge whether a text belonged to the 'Bretha Nemed' was shown by Binchy's discussion of the tract on status entitled 'Uraicecht Becc' ('the small primer').[72] Though it did not contain verse or rhetorical prose, it was unusually concerned with the *filid* and other 'men of art' and it did use the term *nemed* in the wider sense found in the Nero and Gwynn texts. Moreover, it also exhibited close textual links with the opening section of the Nero text. The ascription of 'Uraicecht Becc' to the 'Bretha Nemed' collection was a result of the highest importance. Up to that point the status of the 'Bretha Nemed' was unclear in that the Gwynn and Nero texts certainly touch on a wide range of legal topics, but, apart from the *filid*, they lack the more systematic treatments characteristic of many tracts in the 'Senchas Már'. 'Uraicecht Becc', however, was a tract comparable to any of the tracts of the other collection. It also has a further importance in that it is almost certainly of Munster origin. This is not shown simply by the claim that the king of Munster is supreme above other kings, but by references to the important Munster monasteries of Emly and Cork.[73] More recently, Breatnach has advanced evidence indicating that the Nero text, 'Bretha Nemed Toísech', was compiled in Munster between 721 and 742 by three kinsmen— three descendants of Buirechán—Forannán, a bishop, Máel Tuile, a poet, and Báethgalach, a lawyer.[74] The evidence is too late to amount to anything like proof and the offices of the three supposed compilers perhaps all too faithfully reflect the structure of the text itself; none the less, a reasonable presumption has been established that the Nero text belongs to Munster and is of the first half of the eighth century.

These arguments have a bearing not just on the dating, but also on the place of origin of the 'Senchas Már'. Both the 'Senchas Már' and the 'Bretha Nemed' appear to have originated from the territories of the Féni, namely much of Munster, Connacht, the midlands from the Shannon to the Irish Sea, and all the north apart from the Ulaid and the Cruithni in the north-east.[75] It seems likely that the 'Senchas Már' did not stem from Munster; Leinster is excluded if it derives from the lands of the Féni; this leaves the northern half of the country but excluding the lands to the east of the Bann.

It would, however, be premature to claim that the 'Bretha Nemed' are simply the Munster counterpart of the 'Senchas Már'. Though further texts have been ascribed to the 'Bretha Nemed', notably 'Cóic Conara Fugill' and

---

[72] D. A. Binchy, 'The date and provenance of Uraicecht Becc' in *Ériu*, xviii (1958), pp 44–54.

[73] *C.I.H.*, pp 2282.12; 1618.8.

[74] Breatnach, 'The significance of *Bretha Nemed*', pp 439–44.

[75] *C.I.H.*, pp 365.5; 367.6; 377.10; 380.16; 2219.6; 2222.3; 2224.36; 2225.13, 15; 2227.20. This is also true of 'Críth Gablach' and 'Berrad airechta'.

'Cáin Fuithirbe', the evidence so far advanced is slender.[76] There is nothing corresponding to the introduction to the 'Senchas Már' to show that there was a definite compilation of a lawbook, as opposed to a mere accumulation of texts belonging to the same tradition and perhaps the same law-school. Nor is there anything to show that the 'Bretha Nemed' ever attained the same width of coverage as the 'Senchas Már'. On the contrary, much of what survives suggests that there were considerable differences between the two collections.[77]

The problems are clearly shown by comparing two arguments, both of which have been advanced by Binchy. On the one hand he has maintained that the 'Senchas Már' was at first only the product of a single law-school.[78] It had evidently attained the position of the leading legal collection by the time of Cormac's glossary (*c*.900), for, in spite of the Munster origins of the glossary, the 'Senchas Már' is extensively quoted. It retained this pre-eminence till the end of the Gaelic order. In Binchy's view, therefore, the story of the 'Senchas Már' is one of modest beginnings in one school followed by a rapid reception into other schools. On the other hand, he has argued that, if a legal text had Munster origins, that was in itself evidence that it formed part of the 'Nemed' collection;[79] yet this can only be the case if the 'Bretha Nemed' had from the beginning such a pre-eminence in Munster as to exclude the likelihood of any texts deriving from other sources. In other words, the 'Bretha Nemed' are conceded a position in Munster which is denied to the 'Senchas Már' in the northern half of the island.

Arguments may be advanced for seeing the 'Senchas Már' as the product of more than one legal centre. Binchy's view that the 'Senchas Már' 'originated...in a particular school and had at first purely local significance', and that it was only subsequently 'owing to its imposing proportions, and perhaps also to its intrinsic superiority' that it was received into other law-schools, sits uneasily with Thurneysen's picture of a 'Senchas Már' conceived on the grand scale as a counterpart for Fénechas of what the 'Hibernensis' had achieved for 'the law of the letter'.[80] The latter implies that the pre-eminence of the 'Senchas Már' was planned from the start rather than being a subsequent development. Indeed the introduction to the 'Senchas

---

[76] Binchy, 'Bretha Nemed', p. 6; idem, 'The date and provenance of Uraicecht Becc', pp 51–4. Cf. the difficulty met by Binchy in deciding whether 'Bretha Crólige' and 'Bretha Déin Chécht' belonged to either of the two great lawbooks: *Ériu*, xii (1934), pp 1–2; 'Bretha Déin Chécht' in *Ériu*, xx (1966), pp 2–3.

[77] As suggested by Breatnach, 'Canon law and secular law in early Ireland', pp 439–59.

[78] Binchy, 'The linguistic and historical value of the Irish law tracts', p. 208 (= *Celtic law papers*, p. 87); idem, 'Bretha Nemed', p. 5.

[79] Binchy, 'The date and provenance of Uraicecht Becc', pp 48–54.

[80] D. A. Binchy, as n. 64 above; R. Thurneysen, 'Aus dem irischen Recht IV', pp 186–7.

Már' itself appears to make claims which make it unlikely that its compilers thought of it as having only local significance.[81] Recent work has also attempted to show that groups of tracts exist within the 'Senchas Már' and that these groups are not just the work of different men but probably stem from different schools. Many years ago Thurneysen saw that the 'four Cánai' were the work of a single compiler or set of compilers.[82] The same has more recently been argued for other tracts, and in particular it has been maintained that it is possible to draw a distinction between a group of tracts due to a single compiler or set of compilers on the one hand, and a group due to redaction within a single law-school even though they were the work of different men.[83] This investigation is only in its infancy, so that no final verdict can be given, but it may be noted that this is just what the comparison with the 'Hibernensis' would lead us to expect. The latter was produced by the collaboration of scholars from opposite ends of the Irish world and attempted to embrace the hitherto rival traditions of the *Romani* and the *Hibernenses*. It would be surprising if the vernacular counterpart were the work of a single school.

The basis on which one may assign a text to one school rather than another or say that a collection of texts derives from several schools is uncertain and requires fine discrimination. By 'school' I mean a place in which professional training was to be obtained. The texts show that there was a professional hierarchy of lawyers and that within this hierarchy status depended upon knowledge of the law and skill in pleading and judgement.[84] The tracts purport to provide just such knowledge. The practice of the law was undoubtedly decentralised, for each king of a *túath* was expected to have his own *brithem*.[85] The tradition, however, appears to have been much less decentralised than the practice: Irish law is a single overall tradition with several sub-traditions. On the one hand, there are clear differences of detail, enough to suggest that professional training was to be had at several centres;[86] on the other hand, the close resemblances in legal doctrine, notably between the 'Senchas Már' and the 'Bretha Nemed', demonstrate a community of outlook, a common technical vocabulary and, by and large, adherence to the same rules of law. The degree to which the 'Bretha Nemed'

---

[81] R. Thurneysen, 'Aus dem irischen Recht IV', p. 175 (§§ 1 and 3 = C.I.H., pp 344.24–347.17; 348.10–11).

[82] *Cáin Lánamna*, ed. R. Thurneysen in D. A. Binchy (ed.), *Studies in early Irish law* (Dublin, 1936), p. 4.

[83] Breatnach, 'On the original extent of the *Senchas Már*', pp 38–40; *Bechbretha*, pp 27–30.

[84] C.I.H., pp 2278.15–2279.13. Cf. 896.19–41 and D. A. Binchy, '*Féchem, fethem, aigne*' in *Celtica*, xi (1976), pp 26–30.

[85] *Críth Gablach*, l. 537.

[86] For example the differences between the texts on status, 'Críth Gablach', 'Uraicecht Becc', and 'Míadslechta' or the differences discussed in *Bechbretha*, p. 90.

shared the interest of the 'Senchas Már' in the ancestor kings of the Connachta and Uí Néill as well as in the traditions of the Ulster cycle of tales is remarkable: references to Cormac mac Airt and to Conchobar mac Nessa far exceed any references to Munster kings.[87] There are one or two cases in which connections between different centres are shown in the text, notably the citation of 'Críth Gablach' in 'Bretha Nemed Toísech'.[88] There is also the analogy of the late medieval schools of law: though there were several centres associated with different legal families, members of one legal family might travel to another school for part or the whole of their training.[89] The character of the early texts suggests that a similar situation already existed in the seventh and eighth centuries.

WRITTEN Irish law is the result of a revolutionary change, the conversion of Ireland to Christianity. Writing itself is identified with Christianity: in legal matters, a book is a book of canon law or a penitential.[90] The changes, however, extended much further than the introduction of writing. It is likely that, before the triumph of Christianity, the pagan priest, the druid, had a role in the transmission and enforcement of the law. In the first synod of St Patrick, it is the druid who administers the oath in legal proceedings: the Christian must be commanded not to swear before him.[91] Such an oath was probably sworn by invoking a pagan god.[92]

On the other hand, there may already have been a multiplicity of different learned professions. In the legal texts of the seventh and eighth centuries there are distinct hierarchies for the *fili* 'poet-seer' and the *ecnae* 'ecclesiastical scholar' as well as the ordinary hierarchy of the church.[93] In most texts the druid is as if he had been forgotten, but some take the trouble to exclude him explicitly from the ranks of those who enjoy high status through their craft.[94] The *brithem* 'judge' has a separate hierarchy but at a somewhat

---

[87] E.g., *C.I.H.*, pp 1126.5, 27; 2217.28.

[88] *C.I.H.*, p. 2213.29-30, on which see Breatnach, 'Canon law and secular law in early Ireland', pp 456-7.

[89] Standish H. O'Grady, *Catalogue of Irish manuscripts in the British Museum*, i (London, 1926), pp 112, 125.

[90] *Bretha Crólige*, § 5 (p. 8).

[91] *Synodus I S. Patricii*, cap. 14, in Bieler, *Ir. penitentials*, p. 56 (on the assumption that the *(h)aruspex* is the druid; M. J. Faris (ed. and trans.), *The bishops' synod ('The first synod of St. Patrick')* (Liverpool, 1976), p. 4 and n. on pp 44-5, prefer 'soothsayer').

[92] Ruairí Ó hUiginn, 'Tongu do dia toinges mo thuath and related expressions' in Donnchadh Ó Corráin, Kim McCone, and Liam Breatnach (ed.), *Sages, saints, and storytellers* (Maynooth, 1989), pp 332-41, on such examples as *tongu do dia toinges mo thúath (toingte Ulaid)*, *Táin Bó Cúailnge*, recension I, ed. Cecile O'Rahilly (Dublin, 1976), lines 736, 794-5, 808 etc. (but note also *artung-sa déu*, l. 1150); Ó hUiginn argues that the phrase was invented by Christians and that it only sometimes refers to pagan gods.

[93] *C.I.H.*, pp 585.34-587.20; 2270.25-2272.23 (supplying DON ANRUTH after FICHE SED in p. 2272.21), 2279.16-1.

[94] *Bretha Crólige*, § 51 (p. 40).

lower level than either the *fili* or the *ecnae*.[95] He was attached to a particular kingdom; therefore, unlike poets, he did not have the right to go on circuit around other kingdoms.[96] Indeed, the *brithem* of a *túath* was one of the few persons without whom a king could not exist even in the busiest agricultural seasons of the year.[97] There is direct evidence that some major churches had a *brithem*.[98] Light on one of these churches, Slane, is offered by an addition to the 'Tripartite Life' of St Patrick, in which Erc, the patron-saint of Slane, is listed as the *brithem* in Patrick's household, in which the range of officers is evidently modelled on royal households.[99] This may be linked with an addition made to the text of one of the 'Senchas Már' tracts, *Córus béscnai*, highlighting the role of Erc as the one who first submitted to Patrick.[100] Similarly, the role of Cairnech, patron-saint of Dulane just to the north of Kells, in the ninth-century pseudo-historical prologue to the 'Senchas Már' suggested another claim: Cairnech was said to have been a leading light in the committee, headed by St Patrick, that produced the 'Senchas Már'; that this committee did not include Erc of Slane suggests conscious rivalries.[101] In this case also, if the legend was being advanced to buttress Dulane's claims to legal expertise in the ninth century, the claim must have been to a legal expertise in Irish vernacular law—the law contained in the 'Senchas Már'—and not just in canon law. On the other hand, if Dulane had a leading hand in the composition of the pseudo-historical prologue, the theological sophistication it exhibits may be attributed to that church.[102]

To some extent this social order, in which the trained *brithem* had a privileged status, may continue the situation which confronted Patrick and his fellow missionaries. In Patrick's 'Confessio' the judge appears as a person enjoying great power and high status.[103] There is also quite a lot of scattered

[95] *C.I.H.*, pp 2278.15–2279.13; Liam Breatnach, 'Lawyers in early Ireland', in D. Hogan and W. N. Osborough (ed.), *Brehons, serjeants and attorneys: studies in the history of the Irish legal profession* (Dublin, 1990), pp 1–13: 7.

[96] *C.I.H.*, pp 1268.75–1269.20; ed. and transl. Breatnach, 'Lawyers in early Ireland', p. 8.

[97] *Crith Gablach*, line 537.

[98] Meyer, *Triads of Ireland*, nos. 12 (Cloyne), 16 (Cork), 21 (Slane).

[99] *Trip. life*, ed. Mulchrone, p. 155 (this section is not in Bodl. Rawlinson MS B 512, and appears to be a Middle Irish addition).

[100] *C.I.H.* p. 528. 3–4 (probably an addition; it is not glossed).

[101] Carey, 'The pseudo-historical prologue to the *Senchas Már*', § 8 (= *C.I.H.*, p. 342.15).

[102] Kim McCone, 'Dubthach maccu Lugair and a matter of life and death in the pseudo-historical prologue to the *Senchas Már*' in *Peritia*, v (1986), pp 1–35, esp. pp 11–18; Damien Bracken, 'Immortality and capital punishment: patristic concepts in Irish law' in *Peritia*, ix (1995), pp 167–86; idem, 'Latin passages in Irish vernacular law: notes on sources' in *Peritia*, ix (1995), pp 187–96.

[103] *Confessio*, cap. 53, ed. Ludwig Bieler, *Libri epistolarum Sancti Patricii episcopi* (I.M.C., 2 vols, Dublin, 1952; reprinted Dublin, 1993), pp 86–7. In his commentary on this passage Bieler claims that Patrick was referring to 'local chieftains' (comparing the judges of the Old Testament Book of Judges) rather than to judges in the normal sense. This, however, is made unlikely by the phrase used, *qui iudicabant per omnes regiones*. *Iudicabant* is here intransitive, whereas according to the standard usage of the Bible, when a more general political power is in

evidence to show that the principal—and powerful—enemy of the Christian missionary was the druid.[104]

Several uncertainties, however, make it impossible to reconstruct the hierarchies of the pre-Christian period, in particular the relationships of the *fili* to the druid and of the *brithem* to both *fili* and druid.[105] If one were to argue by the analogy of the post-conversion situation, the likelihood would be that these were distinct hierarchies but that they were also closely bound together by ties of kinship and by the possibility that the one man might hold two offices. In the early eighth century it was relatively easy for a man who belonged by birth to one hierarchy, let us say that of the *filid*, to enter another, for example that of the church.[106] As a result it may have been common for members of the one kindred to belong to distinct professional hierarchies. The tract 'Bretha Nemed Toísech' was, if Breatnach is right, produced as a result of just such a family grouping, the Uí Buirecháin.[107] Binchy argued that the lawyers who produced the 'Bretha Nemed' were also *filid*, or at least that the one school was concerned both with *filidecht* and with the law.[108] The opening section of 'Bretha Nemed Toísech', regarded as the latest part of the text by Binchy, is argued by Breatnach to demonstrate that the authors of the tract also included churchmen.[109] On the other hand, the 'Hibernensis' warns a 'secular scholar' from presuming to judge ecclesiastical cases;[110] it thus implies a distinction between secular and ecclesiastical judge. The nature of the links between various learned professions may well have varied from place to place, but they were, to a greater or lesser extent, allied. As a result, the outlook of one was likely to affect that of the others; and likewise the interests of the one were likely to be maintained by the others.

The earlier involvement of the druid in the law suggests that the same community of outlook and interest obtained before conversion to Christianity.[111] If this is accepted, it will follow that conversion was not simply a

question, *iudicare* is transitive: *iudicare Israel.* The best parallels are 2 Chr. 19: 5 and Deut. 16: 18. The latter undoubtedly and the former very probably refer to appointed judges, as is shown by the reference in Deuteronomy to the gates: R. de Vaux, *Ancient Israel: its life and institutions* (London, 1961), pp 152–5, esp. p. 153.

[104] E.g., Adomnán, *Vita Columbae*, ii. 11, 34 (Anderson, *Adomnan's Life* (2nd ed., Oxford, 1991), pp 108–10, 144–6), perceives Columba's attempts to convert the Picts as implying a conflict with the druids, *magi*. In Ireland, he only has to defeat a *maleficus*, ii, 17 (pp 116–18). It is thus not only the Armagh writers who have inherited a pattern whereby the missionary must overcome the druid.

[105] There is a detailed discussion by Hermann Moisl in 'Some aspects of the relationship between secular and ecclesiastical learning in Ireland and England in the early post-conversion period' (D.Phil. thesis, Oxford, 1979), pp 147–79.

[106] Charles-Edwards, 'The *Corpus Iuris Hibernici*', pp 161–2.

[107] Breatnach, 'Canon law and secular law in early Ireland', pp 439–44.

[108] Binchy, 'Bretha Nemed', pp 5–6.

[109] Breatnach, 'Canon law and secular law in early Ireland', *passim*.

[110] *Hib.* (above, n. 20) XXI. 26*b*, and cf. the corollary in XXI. 27*b*.

[111] *Synodus I S. Patricii*, cap. 14 (above, n. 91).

matter of the replacement of the druid by the Christian cleric. For one thing, conversion brought not just one hierarchy of privilege, the ordinary clergy from doorkeeper to bishop, but also the ecclesiastical scholar, *ecnae*, and the *peregrinus*, *deorad Dé*.[112] For another, the change will have been profound for those professions which survived, the *fili* and the *brithem*, for their outlook and traditions were obliged to accommodate themselves to the new dispensation.

For the law there was a particular problem. It is evident from the first synod of St Patrick that in the sixth century the Christian church formed a partially separate community within a pagan *túath*. A Christian was prohibited from acting as binding-surety (*naidm*), an office central to the creation of most contractual obligations and thus to the fabric of society itself.[113] He was also discouraged from having recourse to the *brithem*.[114] A look at the 'Collectio canonum Hibernensis' shows the consequence of such a policy, for the 'Hibernensis' is more than a text of canon law: it is an attempt to create a Christian law for a Christian society. Its scope makes this obvious: it does not confine itself to strictly ecclesiastical issues but also covers such matters as inheritance and the law of contract.[115] It was able to deal with such topics because it borrowed so heavily from Mosaic law and because it interpreted the Old Testament texts in a creative way.[116] Admittedly it also borrowed from native Irish law, but this only made its challenge the more dangerous, by extending its scope and reinforcing its links with native custom.

There was a yet further danger posed by the conversion. It is likely that the druid and the *fili* were both much involved in the enforcement of the law. This was still claimed for the *fili* in 'Bretha Nemed Déidenach': the *filid* are said to have used the fear of satire and the consequent loss of honourprice to enforce a *cáin enech* 'rule of honour' throughout Ireland.[117] It is likely that similarly the druid gave a religious authority to the law. This is explicitly stated by Caesar for Celtic Gaul;[118] the community of outlook and interest between the Irish learned professions, together with the involvement of the druid in the processes of the law, led MacNeill to suggest that the explanation why *nemed* 'sacred' could be used in the eighth-century Munster text, 'Uraicecht Becc', for any person of free status, lay in Caesar's remarks:

---

[112] *C.I.H.*, pp 585.34–586.29; T. M. Charles-Edwards, 'The social background to Irish *peregrinatio*' in *Celtica*, xi (1976), pp 43–59, p. 53.

[113] *Synodus I S. Patricii*, cap. 8, in Bieler, *Ir. penitentials*, p. 54.

[114] Ibid., cap. 21 (p. 56).

[115] *Hib.*, XXXII–XXXIV.

[116] Raymund Kottje, *Studien zum Einfluss des alten Testaments auf Recht und Liturgie des frühen Mittelalters* (Bonn, 1964; 2nd ed., 1970), esp. pp 44–83; Paul Fournier, 'Le Liber ex lege Moysi et les tendances bibliques du droit canonique irlandais' in *Rev. Celt.*, xxx (1909), pp 221–34; Maurice Sheehy, 'The Bible and the *Collectio Canonum Hibernensis*' in Ní Chatháin & Richter, *Ire. & Christendom*, pp 277–83.

[117] *C.I.H.*, p. 1111.12–18.

[118] *De Bello Gallico*, vi, 13.

someone who was *nemed* could attend a major *óenach*, a combination of fair, assembly, party, and horse-races, and an occasion, as we have seen, on which kings might promulgate edicts.[119] The suggestion was a leap in the dark— Caesar is only the most indirect and uncertain evidence for early medieval Ireland—but it may well be correct. Conversion to Christianity posed, therefore, one major problem for Irish law—the rivalry of a different system of law—and may have posed another, the weakening of the authority behind the enforcement of its own rules.

The seventh- and eighth-century texts show the later stages of this upheaval. The weakness of the native legal system when compared to 'the law of the letter' was that its theoretical authority was in the nature of things inferior. Canon law was the law of scripture, the law of prophets and of apostles, a law dictated by God.[120] Columbanus showed very well the strength of Irish canon law when he claimed to the bishops of Gaul that the law by which he and his fellow *peregrini* lived was nothing other than the commands of the gospel: *hi sunt nostri canones, dominica et apostolica mandata*.[121] He was indeed asserting the New Testament basis of the monastic life, but his identification of *canones* with the rules found in the Bible was also the underlying theme of much of Irish canon law. The identification carried over into Hiberno-Latin: for Columbanus, as for others, *canon* may signify scriptural text, just as *canóin* does in Old Irish.[122] Columbanus's claim was not, therefore, special pleading but only what any Irishman might have said.

The native law required much more deliberate defence. It was claimed that the *fili* Dubthach moccu Lugair had explained to St Patrick the law of the Irish, and that everything obnoxious to Christianity had been expunged.[123] By implication, what remained had the authority of Patrick himself. It was also suggested that the native law derived part of its contents from the law of nature or even that it could be identified with the law of nature.[124] It was argued that the sages of the remote past, to whose authority Irish law sometimes appealed, had prophesied the Incarnation of Christ.[125] On this basis it could be suggested that their teaching had an authority analogous to that of the prophets of the Old

---

[119] Eoin MacNeill, 'Ancient Irish law: the Irish law of status or franchise' in *R.I.A. Proc.*, xxxvi (1923), sect. C, pp 265–315: 266.

[120] *C.I.H.*, pp 47.2; 240.22; 2261.18–27; cf. p. 528.16–20 which claims the authority of the law of prophets and the law of nature for the Irish legal tradition before the coming of Christianity. The native law is there attempting to gain some of the prestige belonging to canon law.

[121] *Ep.* II, 6, ed. Walker, *Sancti Columbani opera*, p. 16.

[122] E.g., *Ep.* V, 3 (ed. Walker, p. 38, line 22); cf. R.I.A., *Dictionary of the Irish language, s.v.* canóin.

[123] *C.I.H.*, p. 529.1–5.

[124] *C.I.H.*, pp 347.7; 527.14–15, 20; 528.18; 529.3.

[125] *C I.H.*, p. 528.19–20.

Testament.[126] It is symptomatic of the situation that the native law makes very little appeal to the authority of custom, for such an appeal would have cut little ice with canon lawyers who knew perfectly well that the moral habits of the Irish called out for reform.[127] What the native law does appeal to is an ancient tradition purged by Christianity, and, what is more, a tradition which is specifically Irish: it is the *senchas fer nÉrenn*, 'the ancient tradition of the men of Ireland'.[128] This appeal had its clear counterpart within the church in the defence made of their practices in the matter of the timing of Easter, and other details such as the tonsure, by the traditionalist Irish party in the seventh century, the *Hibernenses* or 'Hibernians', and it has its clear answer in the arguments of the *Romani* such as Cummian: what did it matter if the practices of the Irish were supported by native tradition, when they were not in accord with the universal church?[129]

The problem for the native lawyers was therefore acute. Their law had lost whatever religious backing it may once have enjoyed from the druid; religious authority was now possessed in a particularly dangerous form by a rival system of law, that of the canonists. Part of its defence against its critics was cast in terms which associated it with that party within the Irish church which was to lose its last stronghold on Iona in 716, shortly before the compilation of the 'Senchas Már'. In principle, then, one might suppose that the native law might have developed in one of two ways: if it wished to retain its close association with religion it might become a vernacular application of the principles maintained in the canon law; on the other hand, if it wished to remain faithful as far as possible to tradition, and also, perhaps, in closer accord with native custom, it might be secularized. In that case it would be a law for the laity, for the *túath*, while the canon law remained a law for the church and for those under its immediate lordship, *manaig*.

It is possible that native law did not respond to the challenge of Christianity in the same way in all parts of Ireland. The 'Senchas Már' tended to take the second path, that of secularization: even the tract which is most closely associated with the church, 'Córus Béscnai', is concerned to defend the rights of both the laity and the church.[130] There are clear cases where the 'Senchas

---

[126] *C.I.H.*, p. 528.16–20.

[127] T. M. Charles-Edwards, 'Custom in early Irish law' in *Recueils de la Société Jean Bodin pour l'histoire comparative des institutions*, lii, *La Coutume*, pt 2, *Europe occidentale médiévale et moderne* (Brussels, 1990), pp 435–43.

[128] *C.I.H.*, p. 344. 24.

[129] Columbanus, *Ep.* II, 5 (ed. Walker, pp 14–16); cf. Bede, *Hist. ecc.*, iii, 25; Cummian, *De controversia paschali*, ed. Walsh & Ó Cróinín, lines 114–20, 271.

[130] The primary concern of the tract is with *comúaim ecalsa fri túaith* (*C.I.H.*, p. 529.4) 'the linking together of the church with the laity'. Its version of the Patrician legend has been seen, rightly in my opinion, as having been framed so as to defend *Fénechas* against ecclesiastical critics: see D. A. Binchy, 'The pseudo-historical prologue to the *Senchas Már*' in *Studia Celt.*, x–xi (1975–6), pp 15–28, 24–5; a different analysis is given by Kim McCone, *Pagan past and Christian present* (Maynooth, 1990), pp 92–6. Its account of bequests and donations to the

Már' adopts a rule found in canon law, as with clerical marriage, and it explicitly acknowledges the authority of canon law. Similarly, it is entirely capable of defending the social practices of lay society by appealing to biblical precedent;[131] the standpoint adopted may nonetheless be quite different from that of the 'Hibernensis'.[132] The general tenor of the 'Senchas Már' is Christian rather than pagan but secular rather than ecclesiastical.[133] The Munster tract 'Bretha Nemed Toísech', on the other hand, as has been argued recently, had a strong ecclesiastical element.[134]

A rather different contrast appears in the way they reacted to the use of writing, a skill associated with the canon law, the 'law of the letter'. As I have argued above, the tracts included in the 'Senchas Már' contain different strata of text. The great preponderance of text composed by men accustomed to writing suggests that the legal schools behind the 'Senchas Már' went over to such forms of composition by *c*.650 and that the quotations and longer passages of oral material to be found in the 'Senchas Már' derive from an earlier oral tradition. The same cannot be said of 'Bretha Nemed Toísech'. Liam Breatnach has shown that it includes material translated from the 'Hibernensis'; moreover, this material appears not in the text composed in the written mode, but in text in the *roscad* style of the traditional *Fénechas*.[135] This appears to have been a matter of deliberate choice, for 'Bretha Nemed Toísech' included text in the latest of the styles distinguished earlier, that which shows the influence of elementary Latin grammar.[136] In other words, the one tract contained, side by side, and of the same date, text in a style which betrays its bookish and Latinate origins and text composed in a style purporting to belong to the oral *Fénechas*. In the 'Senchas Már' lawyers seem to quote the *Fénechas*; in the 'Bretha Nemed' they still compose it.

Church (*C.I.H.*, pp 532.1–535.31) may be compared with *Hib.*, XVII, 'De oblationibus'. Their principal concerns are quite different: for the 'Hibernensis', the chief aim is to protect the property rights of the church; for 'Córus Béscnai', the main objective is to support claims of the church arising principally from Old Testament law while also guarding the interests of secular kindreds.

[131] Binchy, '*Bretha Crólige*', § 57.

[132] *Hib.*, XLVI, 14–15 is wholly inconsistent with 'Bretha Crólige' (previous n.). A different view is taken by McCone, *Pagan past and Christian present*, p. 85.

[133] Cf. Binchy, 'The linguistic and historical value of the Irish law tracts', pp 218–20 (= *Celtic law papers*, pp 97–9); an example is the treatment of *díre* in *Bretha Crólige*, §§ 4–5, where the text contrasts its proper concern, *díre* in the native law, with what canon law may have to say, on which it does not elaborate.

[134] Breatnach, 'The significance of *Bretha Nemed*', *passim*.

[135] Breatnach, ibid., pp 445–52. The first two texts, both versions of the triad also found in Latin in the *Hib.*, book XLII, 2, are inconclusive, since it has not been shown that the original source of the triad was the 'Hibernensis', and moreover, such a proof, with triadic material, would be very difficult. But the third text (corresponding to *Hib.*, XLII, 4) is convincing evidence; once that is accepted the argument for the first two texts is greatly strengthened since they relate to the same book of the 'Hibernensis'.

[136] *C.I.H.*, pp 2210.1–11, 27; 2213. 3 (all in the opening section on the church).

Why the 'Bretha Nemed' retained the two styles side by side is not entirely clear. Provisionally, it may be argued that it uses the style derived from
Latin grammar (what may be called 'textbook style') for elementary instruction, as in 'Uraicecht Becc', whereas it retains the *Fénechas* style for everything else.[137] If this is so, there may be a link with the use of consciously
elevated Latin in the so-called Hisperic style, for the latter seems to have
been used as proof of the superior linguistic skills of the writer or speaker,
often in competition with rivals.[138] The *Fénechas* style, as practised in
the 'Bretha Nemed', included the occasional borrowing of just that sort of
arcane Latin vocabulary which was employed in Hisperic Latin.[139] Both,
therefore, may be seen as consciously literary and elevated in a way which
the more mundane tracts of the 'Senchas Már' usually avoid. The likely
reason for the difference between the 'Bretha Nemed' and the 'Senchas Már'
is the close connection posited by Binchy between law and *filidecht* in the
school or schools that produced the 'Bretha Nemed'.[140] The *roscad* was
the medium associated with the *filid* in 'Uraicecht Becc';[141] even in the
'Senchas Már', *Fénechas* is thought to be transmitted by the *filid*.[142] Breatnach posits a family link between lawyer, *fili*, and churchman behind 'Bretha
Nemed Tóisech'. The further implications for the relationship between the
law and Christianity remain uncertain. The 'Hisperica Famina' have been
seen as notably secular in outlook, and yet they must be the product of
ecclesiastical scholars, *ecnai*.[143] On the other hand, the 'Bretha Nemed' are
less secular than the 'Senchas Már'. Many problems therefore remain and
the full picture of the accommodation of native law to Christianity can, as
yet, only be seen in outline, and even then much remains the province of
conjecture.

To make the position a little clearer, I shall take one example of the influence of canon law on the 'Senchas Már' and discuss it in more detail.

In Irish law there are two forms of lordship over freemen, known to
modern scholars as free clientship and base clientship.[144] In this context,
freedom and servility are relative terms: free clientship is a freer relationship
for both parties than is base clientship; but, though base clientship is thought
to carry a taint of servility, it appears to have been normal for non-noble
freemen to be base clients. Base clientship was not, therefore, incompatible

---

[137] As suggested by Liam Breatnach, *Uraicecht na ríar*, pp 79–80.

[138] Liam Breatnach, 'The ecclesiastical element in . . . *Cáin Fhuithirbe*' in *Peritia*, v (1986),
pp 38–9.

[139] Michael Winterbottom, 'On the *Hisperica Famina*' in *Celtica*, viii (1968), pp 126–39:
129–36.

[140] Binchy, 'Bretha Nemed', pp 5–6.

[141] *C.I.H.*, p. 2256.25.

[142] *C.I.H.*, p. 346.25.

[143] Michael W. Herren (ed.), *The Hisperica Famina: I. The A-Text* (Toronto, 1974), p. 39.

[144] R. Thurneysen, 'Aus dem irischen Recht I. Das Unfrei-Lehen' in *Z.C.P.*, xiv (1923),
pp 336–94; 'Aus dem irischen Recht II. 2. Das Frei-Lehen' in *Z.C.P.*, xv (1925), pp 238–60.

with free status. The economic basis of the two clientships was quite different. The base client probably derived most of his cattle from a grant made by the lord at the beginning of the relationship. This grant of livestock assured to the lord the payment of fixed annual food-renders as long as the relationship lasted, that is to say, normally until the lord's death. If the client predeceased the lord, his heirs inherited the clientship. The base client also owed hospitality to his lord (together with the company that the latter was entitled to bring with him). The most important hospitality was due in the season between Christmas and the beginning of Lent, *aimser chue* 'the coshering season', a period when the proportion of meat in the diet was at its highest. This, together with the considerable element of meat in the annual food-render and the consumption needs of the client's own household, gradually reduced the client's herd. As a result, his heirs were obliged to begin the cycle all over again by receiving cattle from a new lord (who was, no doubt, often the heir of the previous lord).

The free client was in a quite different position. The value of the grant of cattle which he received from his lord was probably much less; he could terminate the relationship at will by returning the livestock granted; in any event free clientship came to an end in the seventh year when the livestock was returned to the lord. The proportionate value of the food-render was, however, much greater—one third of the value of the original grant was due each year—but if the grant was of low value, so also in absolute terms was the render. In effect, it seems that the free client derived no economic benefit from the grant, but that the resources he was obliged to devote to managing the cattle granted to him were only of marginal significance.

'Cáin sóerraith' ('the law of a free fief') describes the end of free clientship in the seventh year as follows: 'For one [animal] does not grow from another after seven years, for that [the seventh year] is the jubilee of freedom which annuls any claim to the revenue due from his chattels, apart from restitution.'[145] The implication appears to be that after seven years the client will not be receiving any profit in the form of calves, and therefore milk, from the cattle granted to him at the beginning. Part of the basis for the period of seven years is, therefore, the expected life-cycle of the cow. On the other hand, the term 'jubilee of freedom', *iubaile sóire*, comes—via some creative reinterpretation—from the 'sabbatical year' of Mosaic law. According to the latter, in every seventh year there was to be a general freeing of all Hebrew slaves.[146] The sabbatical year was modelled on the seventh day of rest in the work of creation: as all Jews should rest from servile labour on the day of rest, so should all native slaves be freed from their servile labour in the

---

[145] Thurneysen, 'Aus dem irischen Recht II. 2', p. 240 (but for *in tuilledh* read, with the MS, *ni tuilli*).
[146] De Vaux, *Ancient Israel*, pp 173–5.

seventh year. This emancipation, it should be noted, did not extend to foreign slaves.

A number of steps in a process of reinterpretation led from the Mosaic sabbatical year to the Irish lawyers' *iubaile soíre*. In the Mosaic law the sabbatical year is closely linked to another provision, the jubilee proper.[147] In effect the jubilee year is a sabbatical year of especial solemnity which recurs every fifty years, namely after seven times seven years. In the jubilee year there was a general cancellation of debts; since the slavery of native Jews was assumed to derive from undischarged debt, the jubilee was also a year in which Jewish slaves were emancipated. The first thing to notice about the Irish *iubaile soíre* is that it does not correspond to the jubilee of the canonists: for the latter, as in the Old Testament, the jubilee year recurred only every fifty years, not every seven. Thus the second synod of St Patrick speaks of the *lex iubelei, hoc est quinquagissimi anni*.[148] The transfer of the name *iubaile* 'jubilee' to the sabbatical year has apparently taken place in the native law, not in Irish canon law.

Secondly, the freedom promised in the seventh year is to be enjoyed not by slaves, native or otherwise, not even by base clients, but by free clients only. It has been transferred from the lowest form of dependence to the highest. This is a much more remarkable reinterpretation than the use of the term jubilee for the sabbatical year. In the latter case, there was already in the Mosaic law a very real connection between the two. The transference of the jubilee to the free client, however, completely changes the whole character of the institution. Moreover, it does so in a way which would probably not have found favour with the canonists. The freeing of slaves was perceived by the early Irish church as one of the most important of the works of mercy, and this was an attitude that the Irish carried with them to England.[149] The sabbatical year may have been important to churchmen in another way. For many serious sins the period of penance is seven years, a period which will free the penitent from the worst servility, subjection to the Devil.[150] For churchmen, therefore, the Old Testament provisions and their contemporary analogues referred to servility and could not be reinterpreted as applying only to the comparatively exalted dependence of the free client.

It is only possible to make a guess at the basis of the reinterpretation of the jubilee made by the secular lawyers. It will be remembered that the emancipation of slaves, whether in the sabbatical year or in the jubilee, applied only to native Jews, not to aliens. It may have been this which provided the opportunity for the lawyers to redirect the provision towards the free client. In the genealogies and origin legends it is sometimes suggested that the

---

[147] Ibid., pp 175–7.

[148] Bieler, *Ir. penitentials*, p. 196.

[149] *C.I.H.*, p. 528.5–6; Bede, *Hist. ecc.*, iii, 5 (1969), p. 228.

[150] E.g., Penitential of Cummean, ii, 2, 8, 9, 17 (ed. Bieler, *Ir. penitentials*, pp 112–14).

subjection of one kingdom to another took two forms, a more exalted form
which corresponded to free clientship and a less exalted form which corresponded to base clientship.[151] In the more exalted form the ruling dynasty of
the subject kingdom is thought to be native to the province of which the
kingdom forms part, whereas in the less exalted there has been an immigration from another province.[152] Similarly, it is often assumed that if a subject
kingdom is in the more exalted form of dependence and is thus a *sóerthúath*
'free people', the dynasty of that kingdom will be related to the ruling dynasty
of the province.[153] This association between free clientship and the dependence of a native as opposed to that of an alien seems to be the only route by
which the lawyers' reinterpretation of the jubilee year can have been carried
out. The *iubaile* could thus be perceived as offering its *sóire* to the native
client, just as the sabbatical year and the jubilee freed the native slave.

The implications of the native lawyers' use of the jubilee are important.
First, it shows, as do a number of other texts from the 'Senchas Már', a
readiness to use the Bible as a source of law.[154] It depends, however, on
a redirection of the original rule to a quite different situation from that envisaged in the Old Testament. We thus have a curious conjunction in the
lawyer's reasoning: on the one hand there is the life-cycle of the cow, on
the other (suitably reinterpreted) the Mosaic jubilee and sabbatical year. The
real basis of the institution may be the former, but it seems to be important to
give it a biblical dress. Secondly, the native lawyer's use of the jubilee is not
that of the Irish canonist. Indeed, it is by implication opposed to that policy of
emancipating slaves which the lawyers themselves saw as a distinctive social
programme of the Christian church, for it removes the obvious Old Testament basis of that programme. This accords with other evidence that the
native lawyers saw a general policy of emancipation as disruptive of society.[155]
The scriptural learning shown by the use of the jubilee and sabbatical year in
'Cáin sóerraith' must derive from ecclesiastical scholarship, but the use to
which this learning was put was not that favoured by the church.

It may be possible to suggest a context in which this kind of intellectual
operation could have taken place. On the one hand, we may assume a legal

---

[151] O'Brien, *Corpus geneal. Hib.*, pp 93–4, 137 (fol. 140 a 52 ff, 140 b 27 ff).
[152] Ibid., p. 138 (but contrast p. 278, fol. 157, 15 ff.).
[153] O'Brien, *Corpus geneal. Hib.*, p. 137 (as n. 124). Cf. the claim of the Airgialla to kinship
with the Uí Néill, ibid., p. 147, and their claim to be free clients, Máirín O Daly, 'A poem on
the Airgialla' in *Ériu*, xvi (1952), pp 179–88: 180, stanza 10, 181–4, stanzas 23–49 (transl.
pp 185–8). These forms of dependence between kingdoms are not simply modelled on free and
base clientship; in some respects the patterning works in the opposite way. Thus the usual
names of base clientship, *gíallnae* and *aicillne*, 'hostageship', are likely to derive from the political
dependence of a kingdom which is obliged to give hostages to guarantee its submission.
[154] *C.I.H.*, pp 351.27–8; 530.32–531.24; and see Donnchadh Ó Corráin, 'Irish vernacular
law and the Old Testament' in Ní Chatháin & Richter, *Ire. & Christendom*, pp 284–307.
[155] *C.I.H.*, pp 347.27–8; 348.10–11; cf. pp 527.27–8; 528.5–6 (the druid prophesies that
Patrick will subvert social hierarchy; contrast p. 525.1–28).

profession conscious of its role as preserver of Irish tradition, distinct from any ecclesiastical hierarchy, whether that of the scholar, the *suí litre* or *ecnae*, or of the ordinary churchman. 'Uraicecht Becc' gives a hierarchy for the *brithem* which is quite different from that of the *ecnae* or the *eclais*.[156] The canon lawyer, however, is likely to have been an *ecnae*: the Ailill mac Cormaic, abbot of Slane, whose death is recorded by the Annals of Ulster in 802, was *sapiens et iudex optimus*.[157] The evidence cited above concerning the aspirations of Slane to be a centre of legal studies suggests that he acted as a *brithem* as well as a *iudex* of canon law and an *ecnae* (*sapiens*); indeed the hereditary families that gained control of Slane from the mid-eighth century may have included *brithemain*.[158] In general, however, the *brithem* can hardly be identified with the *ecnae* for he is clearly of inferior status.[159] On the other hand, we must assume links between the *brithem* and the *ecnae* on such a scale as to sustain the writing of law in forms derived from Latin grammar as well as important borrowings from Mosaic law. Much of the intellectual climate of the native law points to the dominating influence of the *ecnae*. All this is only possible if we accept not merely that canon law, as the law of Scripture, was widely regarded as having an authority superior to that of the native law, but also that personal links between the *brithemain* and the *ecnai* were numerous. We must assume that links of kinship were common, such as those of the Uí Buirecháin, who were arguably responsible for 'Bretha Nemed Toísech'. We may also suppose that in a number of cases one man wore two hats: on the one hand, he was a trained *brithem* and, on the other, he was an *ecnae*, just as Colmán mac Lenéni was first a *fili* and then a monk, and, more importantly, did not abandon *filidecht* when he became a monk.[160] Even if we must suppose that the judge of canon law practised what was essentially a different law from that professed by the *brithem*, the one man may sometimes have practised both.

SOME scholars would go further and maintain that there was no clear distinction between the ecclesiastical *iudex* and the secular *brithem*.[161] They would

---

[156] *C.I.H.*, pp 2278.15–2279.13.

[157] Cf. Donnchadh Ó Corráin, 'Nationality and kingship in pre-Norman Ireland' in T. W. Moody (ed.), *Nationality and the pursuit of national independence* (*Hist. Studies*, xi; Belfast, 1978), pp 1–35, p. 14.

[158] For these families see Hughes, *Ch. in early Ir. soc.*, pp 162–3.

[159] 'The *brithem* of three languages', which included canon law, had the status of an *aire tuísea* (*C.I.H.*, p. 2279.12–13) and was thus only equal to an *ócsuí* (*C.I.H.*, p. 2279.22–3), the ecclesiastical scholar who ranked third after the *suí litre* and the *tánaise suad*; this suggests a lesser training in biblical law.

[160] R. Thurneysen, 'Colmán mac Lenéni und Senchán Torpéist' in *Z.C.P.*, xix (1932), pp 193–207.

[161] Ó Corráin, 'Nationality and kingship in pre-Norman Ireland', pp 13–16; Kim McCone, 'Notes on the text and authorship of the early Irish Bee-laws' in *Camb. Med. Celt. Studies*, viii (1984), pp 45–50; D. Ó Corráin, L. Breatnach, and A. Breen, 'The laws of the Irish' in *Peritia*, iii (1984), pp 382–438; Breatnach, 'The significance of *Bretha Nemed*', ibid., pp 439–59.

argue that the claims of the church to judicial authority had so far prevailed that native law continued only as one tradition employed by clerical lawyers alongside canon law. On this view the existence of written texts of Irish law is a consequence of this ecclesiastical takeover of the native legal tradition.

There are, however, serious difficulties in the way of such a view. In the first place, the 'Hibernensis' was put together in a way quite unlike the 'Senchas Már'. This is a matter less of its formal organization into books and chapters than of its intellectual modes of operation. The 'Hibernensis' has, roughly speaking, two such modes: a systematic mode and a dialectical mode. The early books on the grades of the church, heavily indebted to Isidore's 'De officiis', are relatively consistent and systematic. There is an underlying structure and a coherent set of ideas and rules.[162] Elsewhere, however, the dialectical mode is often uppermost. We may take as an example the first half of Book XVIII, 'De iure sepulturae'.[163] There are two conflicting principles in play. On the one hand, there is the rule that someone should be buried in their paternal cemetery. On the other, there is the belief that certain fundamental changes of personal condition, such as the marriage of a woman or entry into monastic life, so unite a person to a spouse or monastery as the case may be that their place of burial should now be determined by the new bond, not by paternity. Book XVIII begins, therefore, with a chapter whose title is 'That husbands and wives should be buried in a single burial ground'. The proposed rule is thus stated in the title, while the body of the chapter consists of supporting evidence (the two major categories of evidence deployed in the 'Hibernensis' are *testimonia* (texts) and *exempla* (instances, taken from the Bible or ecclesiastical history, that can be interpreted as illustrating a general rule). The second chapter, however, is headed 'That one should be buried in the paternal place of burial'; this rule, too, is supported by *testimonia*, including one from a synod of the *Romani*, and *exempla*. The third chapter reverts to the thesis that the claims of paternity can be set aside, only now in relation to monks; the supporting evidence here is solely from a synod or synods of the *Hibernenses*. The fourth chapter is a counter to the first, claiming that as a wife is free to go elsewhere after the death of her husband, so she should enjoy a corresponding freedom in relation to the place of her burial. In the long run such conflicts of authorities—of biblical quotations and *exempla*, patristic exegesis and synodal legislation—would lead to scholastic methods of distinguishing issues and the meanings of concepts. In early eighth-century Ireland, however, we are often left with two opposed principles and no clear resolution of the conflict.[164] The effect must have been to allow the widest discretion to judges.

---

[162] Most clearly seen in book IV, *De subdiacono*.

[163] *Hib.*, XVIII, 1–4 (ed. Wasserschleben, pp 55–7).

[164] For the approach, compare Julian of Toledo, 'Antikeimenon' in J. P. Migne (ed.), *P.L.*, xcvi, cols 595–704 (a reference I owe to Dr Thomas O'Loughlin).

One reason for this situation is that the law of the 'Hibernensis' was largely made by scholars rather than by synods; even when native synods are cited, their decisions are not always consistent, as in the above example when the *Romani* favoured the claims of paternity while the *Hibernenses* opposed them. The scholarly character of the 'Hibernensis' is demonstrated by its arrangement, built around chapter, *testimonia*, and *exempla*. Though there may be, as we have seen, conflict within a book, there is none within the chapter, for the chapter assembles the evidence to back up a single rule. Most of this evidence consists of passages from the Bible and from commentary on the Bible; sometimes a scriptural passage is immediately followed by the relevant exegesis.[165] The substance of much of the 'Hibernensis' is thus the application of biblical text to Christian living. Moreover this application does not stop short at issues which can be decided by courts. There is an entire book entitled 'De veritate' which consists in the main of scriptural quotations in praise of truthfulness; it even includes a chapter-heading 'Concerning the fact that truth is not loved', itself supported by a battery of authorities, both scriptural and non-scriptural.[166] This is moral reflection, not law.

Faced with such passages one might be tempted to argue that the 'Hibernensis' was less a collection of law than a moral treatise. Yet this would be to miss the point. The typical ecclesiastical judge is not always the bishop; he may be the *scriba*, and the latter is not a scribe in the modern sense but the pre-eminent biblical scholar in a given church.[167] In the book 'De iudicio' we are told that the *scriba* is a person fit to be a judge.[168] The text continues: 'Let the bishop summon together the elders and the *scriba*; let the *scriba* enquire of Scripture; hence Faustinus says: "I have searched and I have enquired and I have passed judgement."' Ecclesiastical judgements, in such cases, at least purported to be the outcome of biblical exegesis. Also one may strongly suspect that there was no sharp dividing-line between ecclesiastical judgement and spritual guidance: the one shaded into the other. If private individuals approached a *scriba* to resolve some issue in which there was no public dispute such as would naturally come before a court of law, they were treating him as a spiritual director, a soul-friend. On the other hand, the 'Rule of Patrick', a text of the eighth or early ninth century, defends

---

[165] E.g., XLII, 4.*c* is Pelagius's commentary on the passage cited in book XLII, 4.*b*.

[166] *Hib.*, XXII, 3 (ed. Wasserschleben, p. 74).

[167] E.g., A.U., 697.11; 730.5, 9 etc.; usually *scribae*, unlike *sapientes*, were attached to a church in their annalistic obits; a partial exception is 725.4, where Rubin, one of the compilers of the 'Hibernensis', is termed *scriba Mumhan* and *magister bonus euangelii Christi*, suggesting that he was not just recognised as the leading exegete in Munster but also had a role as a teacher. To judge by A.U., the position of *scriba* was thus generally an office, whereas *sapiens* signified a status. The analysis of these terms in Kathleen Hughes, 'The distribution of Irish scriptoria and centres of learning from 730 to 1111' in N. K. Chadwick (ed.), *Studies in the early British church* (Cambridge, 1958), pp 247–8, needs revision.

[168] *Hib.*, XXI, 1 (ed. Wasserschleben, p. 62).

the authority of a bishop by insisting on his right to act as soul-friend to all the clergy and laity of his diocese.[169] Here spiritual direction is an aspect of public authority. The same conclusion can be drawn from a consideration of the sanctions behind the rules given in the 'Hibernensis'. Sanctions of any kind will seem remarkably rare to anyone accustomed to Germanic laws or the decrees of Merovingian councils; but, among those that are given, although excommunication is attested as a general penalty, and although degradation is important as a punishment for clerics, penance is the commonest sanction for the generality of the laity.[170] Canon law and the penitentials worked in harness. There are thus clear practical reasons why law and morality should not have been kept apart in the 'Hibernensis'.

In the 'Senchas Már', too, there are many statements that are not rules enforceable by courts. Yet there is nothing comparable to the dialectical mode of the Hibernensis nor to the chapter headings which state a rule while the chapter itself assembles the authorities. In a tract on contracts, 'Di astud chor' ('On the making fast of contracts'), which was not part of the 'Senchas Már', there is at first sight something similar to the dialectical mode of the 'Hibernensis', but on closer examination the differences become more striking.[171] There, also, the problem is one of a conflict of principles: on the one hand, promises should be kept, and all the more so when they are made in public before witnesses and buttressed by sureties; on the other hand, some contracts are unfair and it is the business of the law to rectify injustice. The first part of the tract thus concentrates on the necessity of promise-keeping while the second part turns to the claims of justice. One might expect a third part resolving the conflict between the rival principles, but, just as in the statements of the 'Hibernensis' on burial, the judge is left to find his own solution; the text does not do it for him. Yet, in 'Di astud chor', there is no assembling of written authorities in support of the rival principles and there is no clear parallel to be drawn between it and Book XXXIII of the 'Hibernensis', 'De debitis et pignoribus et usuris'.[172] The latter is concerned with the problem of the poor man who cannot pay rather than with the valid but unfair contract. Neither in terms of substance nor in terms of logical structure can 'Di astud chor' be placed alongside the 'Hiber-

---

[169] *C.I.H.*, pp 2219 6–2130. 1 (ed. James G. O'Keeffe, 'The Rule of Patrick' in *Ériu*, i (1904), pp 216–24).

[170] E.g., penance: *Hib.*, I.22. a; II.25. a & b; XI.1.b; 2–6; XVI.13.d; XVII.5; XXVIII.5, 10; XXIX.8 etc. Degradation or deposition: I 8.b; 9.b; 13; II.27; X. *passim*; XI.1. a; 3; XVII.3.i. Invocation of the secular arm: I.22.b; cf. XXVII.4. Excommunication: I.22.a; ; X.i,t; XI.1.b; XVI.13.e; XVII.3.d, f; 6; XXI.26.c; XXVIII.11. Death: II.12. *Peregrinatio*, XVI.13.d; XVII.3.e. Multiple restitution: XXIX.3–5. Book XXVII is a collection of penalties from scripture; of course, there is no evidence that they were all in use in the Irish church.

[171] *C.I.H.*, pp 985.24–10002.3; 1194.10–1198.20; 1348.21–1359.25; 1962.27–1963.35; 2040.28–2045.30; 2046.34–2050.32; see now Neil McLeod (ed. and trans.), *Early Irish contract law* (Sydney, 1995).

[172] Ed. Wasserschleben, pp 118–22.

nensis'. The true explanation of the dialectical structure of 'Di astud chor' may lie in the tract 'Cóic conara fugill' ('The five paths to judgement').[173] This text distinguishes five types of action primarily according to the type of security required from the litigant, and, secondarily, according to subject-matter. In bringing an action, one had to choose one's 'path' and there was a penalty for any change. Cases concerning contracts belonged to two 'paths': if someone were bringing an action alleging a broken promise, he had to choose the path entitled *dliged*, 'entitlement' or 'obligation'; if he were bringing an action claiming that he had been cheated or had been unfairly disadvantaged by a contract (itself validly made), he had to choose the path called *cert* 'fairness'.[174] The two parts of 'Di astud chor' are therefore likely to be distinct because they relate to different 'paths to judgement'. They are certainly not distinct because a *scriba* has found opposing texts in the Bible, in the Fathers, or in synodal legislation and has assembled them under rival chapter headings. Indeed, the vernacular law tracts do not often stoop to justifying their rules at all; and, when they do so, they adduce general principles, oral tradition, and even legal practicalities rather than written authorities.[175]

In form and approach the ties between the native law-tracts and Latin grammatical treatises are closer than those between the law-tracts and the 'Hibernensis'.[176] The similarities between the latest stratum of texts (B2 above) and elementary Latin grammars are sufficient to demonstrate a conscious borrowing by the lawyers. Yet this does not invalidate Thurneysen's view that the 'Hibernensis' stimulated the compilation of the 'Senchas Már'. The stimulus was not so much through borrowing as through rivalry. The 'Senchas Már' and the 'Hibernensis' were the expressions of two legal traditions different in modes of thought, in attitudes to literacy, and in conceptions of authority. While the two traditions certainly borrowed from each other, they also sometimes adopted diametrically opposed solutions. For example, the native law had a simple rule for the division of land and other assets: the inferior party made the division and then each party made its choice in order of status. Thus the youngest son would divide the patrimony and the eldest would choose first.[177] The same principle is found in Welsh

---

[173] For a different explanation see R. Chapman Stacey, *The road to judgment*, pp 115–25, 131–2, and n. 35 on p. 272.

[174] Ed. R. Thurneysen, '*Cóic Conara Fugill*: die Fünf Wege zum Urteil' in *Abhandl. Preuss. Akad.Wiss., Jahrgang 1925*, no. 7 (1926), pp 18–20.

[175] *Bechbretha*, pp 35–6; e.g., *C.I.H.*, pp 591.33–7; 592.6–9, 22–31; 593.35–8.

[176] Charles-Edwards, 'The *Corpus Iuris Hibernici*', pp 147–51; Anders Ahlqvist (ed. and trans.), *The early Irish linguist: an edition of the canonical part of the Auraicept na nÉces* (Helsinki, 1982), pp 11–14; good examples of biblical commentary with stylistic affinities to some vernacular law are the short texts edited by Robert E. McNally, *Scriptores Hiberniae Minores*, i (Turnhout, 1973), pp 209–30.

[177] *C.I.H.*, p. 1289. 11; cf. Charles Plummer, 'Notes on some passages in the Brehon Laws, II' in *Ériu*, ix (1921–3), pp 31–42, 109–17, p. 31.

law, making it likely that the method is native and of great antiquity.[178] The 'Hibernensis', however, reverses the process on scriptural authority, making the senior divide and the junior choose.[179] Out of such rivalry came the 'Senchas Már'.

THE native law, therefore, remained a distinct legal tradition from that of the canonists, and the two were maintained by distinct, though overlapping, groups of men. Indeed, the different professions of secular lawyer, of *scriba*, and of *fili* all overlapped: the connections between native and canon law are shown by borrowings in both directions; those between the lawyer, the *fili*, and the grammarian are shown, among other things, by considerations of form and style in the law-tracts. Only such connections could explain the emergence of law-tracts composed as written text. Yet they remained distinct professions. The native law-tracts were written by men trained in the native legal tradition, for they wrote with the authority of lawyers entitled to instruct other lawyers in the ways of their ancestors. In spite of their belief in the oral nature of their tradition, lawyers themselves wrote the great majority of the tracts: they were not transcribed by churchmen from oral tradition.[180]

The comparison between the aims of the native lawyer and those of the canonist is as profitable as the comparison of form and structure. As we have already seen, the sanction behind the rule of the canonist and that of the native lawyer is different. Irish canon law was enforced by the ecclesiastical discipline set out in the penitentials. The penance is indeed quite often mentioned in the canon law proper, but it seems generally to be presupposed.[181] The authority behind the canon law is, therefore, as much the soul-friend as the *iudex*.[182] The *canones* and the *leges penitentiae* are two parts of a single system of law and moral instruction. If we turn to the 'Senchas Már', we find a law conceived in large part as a system of rights and obligations protected by compensation payments; and these, in their turn, are enforced partly by the power of lords, including that of the king, partly by the threat of vengeance, partly by the threat of satire and dishonour. Variants on *dligid ní* and *dlegar ní dó*, 'he is entitled to something' and 'he is obliged to do something', are notably more prevalent in the secular law than are any equivalents in the canon law. The normal response of the secular lawyer to any offence or injustice is that compensation should be paid. Much of the

---

[178] E.g., A. Rh. Wiliam (ed.), *Llyfr Iorwerth* (Cardiff, 1960), § 15, lines 40–42; § 82, lines 12–18.

[179] *Hib.*, XLII, 23 (ed. Wasserschleben, p. 168).

[180] Charles-Edwards, 'The *Corpus Iuris Hibernici*', pp 153–6.

[181] Cf. n. 140 above.

[182] Cf. the importance for the disciplinary authority of the bishop of his role as soul-friend in *Ríagail Phátraic*, *C.I.H.*, p. 2129.37–9.

skill of the *brithem* thus seems to consist in adjudicating on questions of compensation.

On the other hand, Irish law is far from being merely a system of rights protected by the duty to compensate. One function of the law is to provide remedies to use against the man who will not concede the justice of a claim or will not provide compensation. Though the provision of such remedies is much less prominent in the 'Senchas Már' than it is, for example, in the early common law, considerable attention is paid to distraint and to the method of claiming land by 'entry', *tellach*.[183] These remedies show, by the numerous delays which characterise their procedure, that the lawyers were anxious to allow the defendant every opportunity to concede the claim or to go to arbitration. It is as if the procedure put a high premium on legal tact, on saving face. The delicacy with which a claim must be enforced is not surprising. These remedies were essentially private, so that even though many claimants may have sought the patronage of the king or a powerful lord before beginning proceedings, such patronage was informal and not part of the legal procedure itself.[184]

Apart from remedies, the law provides legal tools, ways in which a person may give legal validity to something which he wishes to do. He may, for example, not have any children and wish to perpetuate his line of descent by adoption. The law will tell him how to give effect to his wishes.[185] He may wonder how to make a contract which has some chance of holding firm even if the other party subsequently wishes to flout his obligations: the law provides a way.[186]

Though the law may often be concerned with *dliged*, right and entitlement, there are also many cases in which it seeks *cocertad*, the balancing of one man's rights as against another's, or even *logad*, remission and conciliation.[187] A contract may be manifestly unfair, in which case the *brithem* should attempt to redress the balance. The law sometimes shows a desire to protect those who cannot protect themselves: it may, in particular, seek to prevent others from saddling the legally incompetent with obligations.

Some texts, notably 'Críth Gablach' in the matter of status, extend their scope beyond the realm of rights and rules to what is only appropriate or even merely what is in some sense tidy. A *mruigfer* has twenty cows and therefore he ought to have twenty sheep and twenty pigs, even though the

---

[183] *C.I.H.*, pp 205.22–213.17; 352.25–422.36.
[184] E.g., a man's lord might well have acted as his witness in *tellach*, but a witness did not have to be a lord.
[185] T. M. Charles-Edwards, *Early Irish and Welsh kinship* (Oxford, 1993), pp 73–8.
[186] *Berrad Airechta*, *C.I.H.*, pp 591.8–599.38; transl. and partially ed. by R. Thurneysen, 'Die Bürgschaft im irischen Recht' in *Abhandl.Preuss. Akad.Wiss.*, *Jahrgang 1928*, nr 2 (Berlin, 1928); transl. R. C. Stacey in *Lawyers and laymen: studies in the history of law presented to Professor Dafydd Jenkins* (Cardiff, 1986), pp 210–33.
[187] *Críth Gablach*, line 544; *C.I.H.*, p. 2256.35; *Cóic Conara Fugill*, p. 19.

archaeologist can tell us that cattle were far more common than pigs and sheep in eighth-century Ireland.[188] Part of the reason for this concern for what seems appropriate may be that, to be effective, the law must persuade for it can rarely compel. When a lawyer addresses his fellows, he will thus be concerned to present something which has an internal consistency, and this may easily lead to the false tidiness, the 'schematism' of parts of 'Críth Gablach'. Some of the modes of argument used by lawyers could have the same result. Though a lawyer might wish to base his case on *roscad*, the traditional verses in which *Fénechas* was preserved, or on a *fásach*, a legal maxim handed down from the past, he might have to rely on *cosmailius*, similarity or analogy, just as the canon lawyer used *similitudo*.[189] From some surviving examples we can see that sometimes these analogies were far-fetched or were pushed too far and so led to dispute.[190]

When discussing the value of law as a source, historians sometimes get entangled in a snare of their own making. They may, consciously or unconsciously, construe law as a system of commands expressing the will of some legislator. If they do so, they are necessarily uncomfortable with all early medieval law, for the limitations on the capacity of the legislator to see that his will was carried out are only too apparent. Even when law is at its most imperative in form, as in the capitularies of a Charlemagne, this is itself a device of persuasion; hence the frequent necessity of repeating such rules. Their discomfort must be increased a hundredfold when dealing with such a legal system as that of the Irish, in which any legislator, let alone one with extensive powers, is hard to come by. Historians think that they require from law a mirror of society, and that, since law is command, it can only give them this mirror if they can be sure that the commands are regularly obeyed. Yet, even if any law can be seen as a system of commands, early Irish law manifestly cannot. It is not so much a mirror of society as a part of it; it provides both an understanding, from inside, of some of the workings of society and also a range of devices for securing justice and the reconciliation of disputants. When it is descriptive, therefore, it is the description given by participants; and when it initiates action, it does so, not from outside, but by enabling ordinary men to act in their own interests.

THE age of written law in Ireland was a short one. The main texts were written by *c.*800. After that date the period of the glossator and the commentator begins. There are perhaps three main reasons why the fertile period

[188] Fergus Kelly, *Early Irish farming* (Dublin, 1997), p. 27; Michael V. Duignan, 'Irish agriculture in early historic times' in *R.S.A.I. Jn.*, lxxiv (1944), pp 141–2.

[189] *C.I.H.*, pp 377.10; 400.12–15; 1122.32; 1139.22–3; 1253.6–7; 2221.12; 2222.9; 2256.25; *Hib.*, XXI, 6.

[190] *Bechbretha*, pp 92–3; but see Rolf Baumgarten, 'The kinship metaphors in "Bechbretha" and "Coibnes Uisci Thairidne" in *Peritia*, iv (1985), pp 307–27.

from *c*.650 to *c*.750 did not initiate an enduring tradition of written law. In the first place, the native law remained in essence an oral tradition. This is what the texts themselves tell us, and we have no reason to doubt their testimony. Even for the authors of written tracts, the oral tradition has the supreme authority on all questions of native law; authoritative books were the perquisite of the canonist. Furthermore, the literate *brithem* may well have been the exception. No doubt tracts were written not just to be read by the literate, but to be read aloud to the illiterate, but even so the older oral modes by which the legal tradition was imparted to the aspirant lawyer are likely to have been more generally appropriate.[191]

Secondly, in so far as the native lawyer regarded his own books as worth bothering about, he treated them as he had been trained to do by the *ecnae*, the ecclesiastical scholar, and he in turn inherited his intellectual procedures from the schools of late antiquity. The *ecnae* would proceed by taking his text, *canóin*, and commenting on it, word by word, phrase by phrase, giving etymologies or proposing alternative explanations.[192] Once, therefore, our lawyer had his text, the intellectual tradition, to which he remained all too faithful, instructed him to gloss and to comment upon what he already had, rather than to compose anything new.

Thirdly, written Irish law is the product of a particular historical moment. It was the outcome of conversion to Christianity, of the authority of written texts within the new religion, of the existence of a rival system of law, that of the canonists. It was also the result of the persistence of part of the old, pre-Christian, learned classes, the *filid* and the *brithemain*. Their situation is most clearly expressed in the 'Auraicept na nÉces', a grammar of Old Irish. Just as the Introduction to the 'Senchas Már' perceives oral transmission as the business of the *filid*, so does the 'Auraicept' see their language as Irish, something to be cultivated and honoured as the *Laitneóir* preserved and respected Latin.[193] Therefore, even though the business of the *fili* is vernacular and oral, he too must have a grammar, just as Charlemagne was fascinated by Augustine's 'De civitate Dei' and the astronomical learning of Alcuin, and yet also sought to preserve in writing *barbara et antiquissima carmina* and to have his scholars write a grammar of his native language.[194] The writing of vernacular laws is part of the same movement as the writing of a vernacular grammar: as in the Carolingian renaissance, the emergence of the vernacular is an effect of a flourishing period in Latin learning, coupled with a pride in native tradition. Finally, the production of the 'Senchas Már' and the tracts

---

[191] Cf. the opening words of the *Senchas Már*, ed. Thurneysen, 'Aus dem irischen Recht IV', p. 175; Charles-Edwards, 'The *Corpus Iuris Hibernici*', pp 155–6.
[192] Henri-Irénée Marrou, *A history of education in antiquity* (London, 1956), pp 279–80; idem, *Saint Augustin et la fin de la culture antique* (4th ed., Paris, 1958), pp 126–8.
[193] Ahlqvist, *The early Irish linguist*, pp 19, 48 (1, 13–14).
[194] Einhard, *Vita Karoli*, cap. 29, ed. Oswald Holder-Egger (Hanover, 1911), p. 33.

of the 'Bretha Nemed' tradition may have been a cultural expression given to a political hegemony: although lawyers often treated the name *Féni* as embracing the Irish as a whole, it was also used for one *cenél* 'race' that included the Uí Néill and their allies, the Éoganachta and Connachta, as well as their principal client-peoples. *Fénechas*, 'the traditional law of the Féni', may have been a deliberately ambiguous term signifying the law that should govern all the Irish because it was a law belonging primarily to the alliance of the dominant peoples and dynasties. When that alliance began to crumble in the late eighth century, the political conditions propitious to large-scale definitions of law were probably past.

CHAPTER XI

# Hiberno-Latin literature
# to 1169

DÁIBHÍ Ó CRÓINÍN

THE formal introduction of Christianity to Ireland in the early fifth century marked the beginning of a new era in many ways. It meant the arrival of a new law to compare and eventually to vie with native legal practices; a new religion that was eventually to replace the old one of Ireland's pagan past; a new institution—the church—whose structure and personnel offered a challenge to the Irish learned orders. Above all, though, Christianity transformed Irish society by its introduction of a new language, church Latin, whose history and literature were markedly different from anything hitherto known in Ireland. The history of Hiberno-Latin learning and literature in the period following the missions of Patrick and Palladius is the story of how the Irish came to terms, first of all, with this new language and its traditions, and how they subsequently assimilated them to the point where Irish Latin writers were indistinguishable, either in style or in language, from their continental counterparts.[1] There were no dialectal differences, in the true sense, between the Latin written (and spoken) in Ireland and the lingua franca of Europe;[2] and the vernacular influence on Irish Latin, which is sometimes claimed as substantial, never in fact amounted to much.[3] The distinctiveness of Hiberno-Latin literature lies in the extent to which it flourished in times and in circumstances that must often have seemed inimical, and in the

[1] See Ludwig Bieler, 'Hibernian Latin' in *Studies*, xliii (1954), pp 92–5; idem, 'Das hiberno-lateinische und seine Erforschung' in *Wiener Studien, N.F.*, ix (1975), pp 216–29.
[2] See Jean-Michel Picard, 'Une préfiguration du latin carolingien: la syntaxe de la *Vita Columbae* d'Adomnán, auteur irlandais du VIIᵉ siècle' in *Romanobarbarica*, vi (1981–2), pp 235–83; idem, 'The Schaffhausen Adomnán: a unique witness to Hiberno-Latin' in *Peritia*, i (1982), pp 216–49. The notion that Hiberno-Latin is characterised by 'bizarre exuberance' is common but unfounded.
[3] Bengt Löfstedt, 'Some linguistic remarks on Hiberno-Latin' in *Studia Hib.*, xix (1979), pp 161–9; Michael Herren, 'Sprachliche Eigentümlichkeiten in den hibernolateinischen Texten des 7. und 8. Jahrhunderts' in Löwe, *Die Iren*, i, 425–33. The only thing approaching a systematic study of the material is in William G. Most, *The syntax of the Vitae Sanctorum Hiberniae* (Washington, D.C., 1946).

remarkable way in which it acquired and passed on to later generations ancient texts and fragments otherwise unknown or lost.[4]

The historical circumstances behind the missions of Palladius and Patrick have been discussed at great length,[5] though the 'problem of St Patrick' can still be said to bar the very portals of early Irish history.[6] The question is a minor one, however, from the point of view of our subject, inasmuch as neither figure could be accurately described as a 'Hiberno-Latin' writer. But the roles that their respective missions played in the establishment of Christianity are clearly of fundamental importance for the history of Latin learning in Ireland.[7] There is no doubt about the authenticity of Patrick's two surviving works, the 'Confession' and the 'Letter to Coroticus',[8] but scholars are generally agreed that neither text played any role in establishing a pattern for later Irish writers.[9] The background of Palladius's mission, on the other hand, was of a kind that one would expect to find reflected in later Hiberno-Latin writing; but no known work of his has survived, unless the Easter table (with accompanying prologue) referred to in seventh-century texts under the name of Patricius is, in fact, Palladius's.[10]

The letter of Mochta (Maucteus), a British disciple of Patrick, which is briefly quoted in the Irish Annals,[11] has unfortunately perished save for its introductory salutation, so that this potential piece of evidence too is lost. The only other item of Patrician literature with any claim to authenticity, the

---

[4] See Blanche B. Boyer, 'Insular contribution to medieval literary tradition on the Continent' in *Classical Philology*, xlii (1947), pp 209–22; xliii (1948), pp 31–9; C. H. Beeson, 'The text history of the Corpus Caesarianum' in *Classical Philology*, xxxv (1940), pp 113–25; C. W. Jones, 'Bede and Vegetius' in *Classical Review*, xlvi (1932), pp 248–9 (argues for Irish transmission of Vegetius, 'De re militari'); Fidel Rädle, 'Die Kenntnis der antiken lateinischen Literatur bei den Iren in der Heimat und auf dem Kontinent' in Löwe, *Die Iren*, i, 484–500; Virginia Brown, 'The "Insular intermediary" in the tradition of Lucretius' in *Harvard Studies in Classical Philology*, lxxii (1968), pp 301–8 (denies any Irish influence in the text transmission).

[5] See esp. D. A. Binchy, 'Patrick and his biographers, ancient and modern' in *Studia Hib.*, ii (1962), pp 7–173; a bibliography of writings on the Patrician problem is planned as an ancillary volume of the R.I.A.'s *Dictionary of medieval Latin*.

[6] The phrase is F. J. Byrne's in *Ir. kings*, p. 12.

[7] See esp. Eoin MacNeill, 'The beginnings of Latin culture in Ireland' in *Studies*, xx (1931), pp 39–48, 449–60; T. F. O'Rahilly, *The two Patricks* (Dublin, 1942); K. H. Jackson, *Language and history in early Britain* (Edinburgh, 1953); Damien MacManus, 'A chronology of the Latin loan-words in early Irish' in *Ériu*, xxxiv (1983), pp 21–71.

[8] The most recent edition is by D. R. Howlett (ed. and trans.), *The book of letters of Saint Patrick the bishop* (Dublin, 1994).

[9] Patrick and his works seem to have been almost unknown in Ireland till the seventh century.

[10] See Dáibhí Ó Cróinín, 'New light on Palladius?' in *Peritia*, iv (1986), pp 276–83. The technical details of the prologue preclude Patrick's authorship; on the other hand, the evident antiquity of the text, the reverence for it shown by Cummian (see below, p. 378), and the same technical evidence combine to suggest Palladian authorship or association.

[11] A.U., *s.a.* 534 (= 535).

hymn of Secundinus in praise of Patrick,[12] is now no longer regarded as a genuine product of the fifth century but is dated by recent writers to the sixth or seventh. After the initial phase of conversion and consolidation, therefore, Latin learning seems to have wavered in its development, if it did not indeed wither.[13] We have to wait until the mid-sixth century before picking up the trail again, and the texts that appear from that date indicate that the hundred years or so of silence concealed important developments in the organisation and structure of the Irish churches, changes that are reflected in the new genres of writing that emerge in this second phase.[14]

Distinctive of this second phase in Hiberno-Latin is the overwhelming monastic influence. The selection of themes is strictly utilitarian and vocational: monastic rules; handbooks of penance (penitentials) for spiritual confessors; canon law—these are the types of text that initially appear, first under influence from British monastic writers, but then from native Irish monastic founders and writers.[15] Although the rules that governed the monasteries of Columba on Iona and Comgall at Bangor have not, apparently, survived, they were in circulation in the ninth century,[16] along with a 'rule of the Irish brothers' (regula fratrum Hibernensium) likewise unfortunately lost. The regime at Bangor can, however, be reconstructed on the basis of Columbanus's rule for Luxeuil and its related foundations.[17] This reveals a harsh existence for the monks, with no concessions to the frailty of either body or soul. There is disappointingly little evidence here for scholarly pursuit, and no hint in Columbanus's regula of the astonishing grasp of language and style that make his letters such a pleasure to read.[18] Nor is there any hint in the

[12] Ludwig Bieler (ed.), 'The hymn of St. Secundinus' in R.I.A. Proc., lv (1953), sect. C, pp 117–27. A convincing case for its authorship by Colmán Alo (Lynally, Co. Westmeath; d. 612) was made by James Carney, The problem of St Patrick (Dublin, 1961), pp 40–46.

[13] Strong arguments for continuity have been advanced by David Howlett, The Celtic Latin tradition of biblical style (Dublin, 1995).

[14] For detailed catalogues of the works to follow, see esp. Kenney, Sources, pp 186 ff; Max Manitius, Geschichte der lateinischen Literatur des Mittelalters (3 vols, Munich, 1911–31), i, 107 ff; Mario Esposito, 'The Latin writers of mediaeval Ireland' in Hermathena, xiv (l907), pp 519–29; xv (1909), pp 353–64; 'Notes on mediaeval Hiberno-Latin and Hiberno-French literature' in Hermathena, xvi (1910–11), pp 58–72; 'Notes on Latin learning and literature in mediaeval Ireland' in Hermathena, xx (1930), pp 225–60; xxii (1932), pp 253–71; xxiii (1933), pp 221–49; xxiv (1935), pp 120–65 all reprinted in Esposito's collected papers (ed. Michael Lapidge), Latin learning in medieval Ireland (Aldershot, 1988); Franz Brunhölzl, Geschichte der lateinischen Literatur des Mittelalters, i (Munich, 1975), pp 156–99; Michael Herren, 'Classical and secular learning among the Irish before the Carolingian renaissance' in Florilegium [Toronto], iii (1981), pp 118–57.

[15] There is, unfortunately, no good modern study of Irish relations with the British churches in this period.

[16] All three are mentioned in a ninth-century Fulda catalogue; see Paul Lehmann, 'Fuldaer Studien' in Sitzungsb. d. Bay. Akad. d. Wiss., phil.-hist. Kl., 1925, iii (Munich, 1925), pp 1–53: 51.

[17] G. S. M. Walker (ed. and trans.), Sancti Columbani opera, ii (Dublin, 1957).

[18] Apart from the Latin original, Walker's translation has real literary merit, as Esposito pointed out in his review, 'On the new edition of the Opera Sancti Columbani' in Classica & Medievalia, xxi (l961), pp 184–203: 199.

stark formlessness of the penitentials that Irish writers were soon to prove themselves every bit as skilled as their European counterparts (with the possible exception of Spain). The penitential ascribed to Uuiniaus/Finnian (of Moville, County Down?),[19] while probably the oldest of the group, is probably also the work of a Welsh Briton (or Breton), to judge by the name,[20] and is therefore not strictly relevant to our purpose except as a possible model. Finnian's work was known to Columbanus, who states that he had also read a tract by the most important sixth-century Welsh writer, Gildas, written in response to some queries from Finnian.[21] Gildas's influence on Columbanus has been claimed as strong,[22] but it is not at all clear how much of his work was available in Ireland, nor how widespread was its use.[23] It has been demonstrated beyond a doubt, however, that Columbanus's style was strongly marked by his reading of St Jerome, and indeed much in the way of classical 'polish' in his writings has been traced to the same source.[24] Columbanus of course has been claimed as the first great Irish man of letters,[25] on the basis principally of the poems traditionally attached to his name. The classical reminiscences and, in some cases, direct quotations are found exclusively in his verse, and the theory of Columban authorship for these has been questioned.[26] While the alternative attributions of some of the poems may not have found favour with some scholars,[27] the old belief in Columbanus's authorship of all of them appears in need of revision.[28]

Columbanus ranks as a first-rate writer: his five surviving genuine letters (at least four others are lost)[29] are evidence that the Irish schools, even before

[19] Bieler, *Ir. penitentials*, pp 74–95.

[20] See Léon Fleuriot, 'Le "saint" breton *Winniau* et le pénitentiel dit "de Finnian"?' in *Études Celt.*, xv, no. 2 (1978), pp 607–26: 607–14.

[21] *Ep.* 1 § 7; Walker, p. 8.

[22] Michael Winterbottom, 'Columbanus and Gildas' in *Vigiliae Christianae*, xxx (1976), pp 310–17.

[23] See now Michael Lapidge and D. N. Dumville (ed.), *Gildas: new approaches* (Woodbridge, 1984).

[24] Johannes W. Smit, *Studies in the language and style of Columba the Younger (Columbanus)* (Amsterdam, 1971).

[25] See esp. Ludwig Bieler, 'The humanism of St Columbanus' in *Mélanges Columbaniens* (Paris, 1950), pp 95–102; Bieler, 'The island of scholars' in *Revue du Moyen Âge Latin*, viii (1954), pp 213–34.

[26] The most recent serious reexamination was begun by Smit, *Studies*, 209–53; the question was taken up again at length by Michael Lapidge, 'The authorship of the Adonic verses "Ad Fidolium" attributed to Columbanus' in *Studi Medievali*, 3rd ser., xviii, no. 2 (1977), pp 249–314, and more recently by David Howlett, 'Insular Latin writers' rhythms' in *Peritia*, xi (1997), pp 53–116.

[27] Some of Lapidge's historical arguments were attacked by Heinz Löwe, 'Columbanus und Fidolius' in *Deutsches Archiv*, xxxvii (1981), pp 1–19; his general thesis has been questioned by Peter Jacobsen, 'Carmina Columbani' in Löwe, *Die Iren*, i, 434–67.

[28] Howlett, 'Insular Latin writers' rhythms', p. 87, has concluded: 'The supposition that pre-Carolingian scholars in Ireland were ignorant, unable either to scan or to compose quantitative verse, may be due for revision, if not outright rejection'.

[29] Walker, *Epp* I–V. In his *Ep.* II Columbanus speaks of having sent three tomes on the subject of Easter to Pope Gregory I, and another *breuis libellus* on the same subject to Bishop Arigius of Lyons. None of these has yet been rediscovered.

the close of the sixth century, were already set in a firm pattern of study: Latin grammar, biblical study, and the ecclesiastical calendar (computus) were the three pillars of the curriculum and were to remain so at least until the ninth century.

Besides the usual texts that one would expect to find in a monastic library at the time (Bible, scriptural commentary, Jerome's 'De viris illustribus', and Eusebius's 'Ecclesiastical history'), Columbanus had access also to technical tracts on the computus such as Victorius of Aquitaine's paschal tables and the mysterious work of Anatolius, 'De Pascha'.[30] An unpublished fragment from another paschal tract, ascribed in the manuscripts to 'Palumbus' (a pen-name of his) is perhaps further evidence for Columbanus's involvement with questions of the calendar.[31] His position as master of the school at Bangor before his departure in 590 x 591, and his biographer's loud praise of his intellectual talents,[32] add further to the likelihood of his interest in such matters, and that impression is strengthened by the knowledge that his own teacher in Bangor, Sinilis (Mo-Sinu maccu Min, d. 610), was also remembered for his computistical studies.[33] The fact that Columbanus believed the Anatolian tract to be a genuine work of the third-century bishop of Laodicea clearly implies that it was in circulation for some time.[34] It is one of a number of such tracts, referred to by modern scholars—wrongly, as it happens—as 'Irish forgeries': Pseudo-Athanasius, Pseudo-Cyril (*Epistola*), Pseudo-Morinus, and Pseudo-Theophilus (the spurious 'Acts of the council of Caesaraea').[35] They bear witness to an intensity of study in this field and a variety of sources not equalled in any other western European country at that time.

Columbanus was clearly the product of an intensive schooling, one that had effectively mastered the techniques of language-teaching and textual analysis. He is perhaps not typical of the average Irish monastic student, but if he is typical of the average teacher, then sixth-century Irish schools had

---

[30] See Bruno Krusch, *Studien zur christlich-mittelalterlichen Chronologie* [1]: *die 84-jährige Ostercyklus und seine Quellen* (Leipzig, 1880); commentary in C. W. Jones (ed.), *Bedae opera de temporibus* (Cambridge, Mass. 1943), pp 82–8. See now D. P. McCarthy, 'Easter principles and a fifth-century lunar cycle used in the British Isles' in *Journal of the History of Astronomy*, xxiv (1993), pp 204–24, and idem, 'The origin of the *latercus* paschal cycle of the Insular Celtic churches' in *Camb. Med. Celt. Studies*, xxviii (winter 1994), pp 25–49; idem, 'The lunar and paschal tables of *De ratione paschali* attrinuted to Anatolius of Laodicea' in *Archives for History of the Exact Sciences*, xlix, no. 4 (1996), pp 285–320.

[31] See Dáibhí Ó Cróinín, 'A seventh-century Irish computus from the circle of Cummianus' in *R.I.A. Proc.*, lxxxii (1982), sect. C, pp 405–30: 426–7; Maura Walsh and Dáibhí Ó Cróinín (ed. and trans.), *Cummian's Letter 'De controuersia Paschali' together with a related Irish computistical tract 'De ratione conputandi'* (Toronto, 1988), pp 113–213.

[32] See Kenney, *Sources*, p. 201, for references.

[33] See Dáibhí Ó Cróinín, 'Mo-Sinu maccu Min and the computus at Bangor' in *Peritia*, i (1982), pp 281–95.

[34] McCarthy (see n. 30 above) has established a fifth-century Gallican authorship for the work; Esposito ('On the new edition of the Opera Columbani', p. 186) thought that its early circulation in Ireland implied British authorship.

[35] Krusch, *Studien*, i, 303–10 (Pseudo-Theophilus); pp 328–36 (Pseudo-Athanasius); pp 344–9 (Ep. Cyrilli).

every reason for the pride and self-confidence that are mirrored in his letters. The achievement is all the more remarkable when it is remembered that Latin was always a foreign tongue to the Irish, who never became citizens of the Roman empire. When the time came for them to give allegiance to Rome it was, as Columbanus himself phrased it, the Rome of the apostles Peter and Paul.[36]

The adoption of Latin as the everyday language of the church in Ireland (as it was elsewhere in the west) involved the Irish in practical problems that their fellow-Christians on the Continent never had to face, principally that of acquiring this new language from scratch. Faced with the task of introducing pupils to the very basics of Latin, Irish teachers rapidly realised that the standard grammars of late antiquity (Donatus and the like) were too elaborate for their needs, and they were forced to devise their own techniques of elementary instruction.[37] Hence the proliferation of noun- and verb-lists, extended paradigms to be learnt by rote, and long collections of excerpts, strung together without comment, from the ancient grammarians.[38] Parallel to this was the development of syntactical notation, by the use of which teachers were able to demonstrate, with a variety of signs and symbols, the relationships of words to each other within the Latin sentence.[39] Thus the mysteries of Latin syntax and sentence structure could be graphically unravelled, adding to the effectiveness of oral instruction.

Initial instruction in Latin grammar may have been the work of British monks in sixth-century Ireland, though one should not discount the possibility of a continuous tradition from the schools of the fifth-century missions. In a brilliant study, Louis Holtz has shown, by working back from our knowledge of seventh-century Latin grammars, how at least one such sixth-century work can be identified: the commentary on Donatus ascribed to Asperius.[40] Holtz has emphasised the starkly functional tone of the work, with its monastic milieu clearly to be seen in its list of classical examples

[36] *Ep.* V; Walker, 38: 'Nos enim sanctorum Petri et Pauli et omnium discipulorum divinum canonem spiritu sancto scribentium discipuli sumus.'

[37] See Maartje Draak 'Construe-marks in Hiberno-Latin manuscripts' in *Meded. d. Koninkl. Med. Akad. v. Wetensch. afd. Letterkunde*, xx (1957), pp 261–82; Draak, 'The higher teaching of Latin grammar in Ireland during the ninth century', ibid., xxx (1967), pp 109–44.

[38] Vivien Law, *The Insular Latin grammarians* (Woodbridge, 1982); see, however, the severely critical reviews of this book by Michael Herren in *Peritia*, ii (1983), pp 312–16, and by Anders Ahlqvist in *Camb. Med. Celt. Studies*, vi (winter 1983), pp 100–01; P. A. Breatnach in *Celtica*, xvi (1984), pp 182–6; and Dáibhí Ó Cróinín in *Studia Hib.*, xxii–iii (1982–3), pp 149–56; see also the review article by Louis Holtz, 'Les grammairiens hiberno-latins: étaient-ils des Anglo-Saxons?' in *Peritia*, ii (1983), pp 170–84.

[39] See esp. Draak, 'Construe-marks', *passim*.

[40] For what follows the indispensable work of reference now is his *Donat et la tradition de l'enseignement grammatical* (Paris, 1982). For Asporius, see pp 272–83 and the summary account in Holtz, 'Irish grammarians and the continent in the seventh century' in H. B. Clarke and Mary Brennan (ed.), *Columbanus and Merovingian monasticism* (Oxford, 1981), pp 135–52; Law, *Insular Latin grammarians*, pp 35–41.

filled out by inclusion of everyday Christian terms. Unfortunately, the text is anonymous, although trace of the original dedication seems to have survived in another, seventh-century Hiberno-Latin grammar.[41] The 'Ars Asperii' is the only known sixth-century Irish grammar to have come down to us, but there must have been many more like it. These texts, however, were still at the experimental level; the real flowering of Hiberno-Latin grammatical studies was to begin first in the seventh century, when the Irish gained access to a whole new range of grammars from late antiquity.[42]

In assessing the extent and quality of Latin learning in Ireland at the dawn of the seventh century it is important to guard against the modern trend towards compartmentalisation, which sees exegesis, grammar, and computus as separate disciplines each practised by different teachers. Columbanus—our best example—handled computus and exegesis with equal facility, and could express himself in a vigorous and forceful Latin of varying styles to suit the occasion. His biographer Jonas says that he composed a commentary on the psalms and *carmina* for instructional purposes (computistical verses?).[43] There is no reason to assume that he was an exception in this breadth of scholarship; our seventh-century evidence all suggests that Irish schools, north and south, pursued the same range of interests. Almost unheralded, the seventh century opens with a flourish. The famous paschal letter of Cummian[44] (possibly bishop or *fer légind* of Clonfert Brendan, County Galway)[45] is evidence for a quite remarkable number and variety of texts available in a typical southern Irish monastery of the time. In a work only five manuscript folios in length, there are quotations from the Bible (Vulgate and Vetus Latina) and patristic commentary by Augustine, Jerome, Cyprian, Origen, Ambrosiaster, and Gregory the Great, as well as some pseudo-patristic works. Reference is also made to canon law, ecclesiastical history, and synodal decrees (including those from the councils of Nicaea and Arles in their original, uncontaminated form), and a decretum that enjoined on the Irish that, if all else failed, they should take their grave problems to Rome.[46]

[41] Bernhard Bischoff and Bengt Löfstedt (ed.), *Anonymus ad Cuimnanum, Expossitio Latinitatis* (Turnhout, 1992). Asper wrote his grammar at the request of a certain 'Britus' ('Britone postulante'), possibly to be identified with Fergnae Brit, abbot of Iona (605–23).

[42] Holtz, *Donat*, pp 284 ff.

[43] Bruno Krusch (ed.), *Ionae vitae sanctorum Columbani, Vedastis, Iohannis* (Hanover and Leipzig, 1905), p. 158 (*Vita Columbani*, i, 3): 'multaque alia, quae vel ad cantum digna vel ad docendum utilia, condidit dicta'. See also Michael Lapidge, 'Columbanus and the Antiphonary of Bangor' in *Peritia*, iv (1985), pp 104–16.

[44] First edited by James Ussher, *Veterum epistularum Hibernicarum sylloge* (Dublin, 1632), pp 24–35, no. XI; reprinted in *P.L.*, lxxxvii, 969–78. See now the new edition, Walsh & Ó Cróinín, *Cummian's Letter* (n. 31 above).

[45] See Kenney, *Sources*, pp 220–21. The evidence for Cummian's localisation is examined in Walsh & Ó Cróinín, *Cummian's Letter*, pp 7–15.

[46] See J. E. L. Oulton, 'On a synod referred to in the "De controversia Paschali" of Cummian' in *Hermathena*, xlix (1935), pp 88–93. Oulton, however, was mistaken about the source of the decretal. See Walsh & Ó Cróinín, *Cummian's Letter*, pp 47–9.

Besides these, Cummian had to hand a collection of no fewer than ten paschal tracts, including one that he attributed to *sanctus Patricius, papa noster*: over forty separate texts in all, including perhaps a letter of Pelagius.[47] The range of texts in Cummian's letter is striking illustration of the threefold pattern of study in the Irish schools, and it is no surprise that Cummian should also be suggested by some as the possible author of a computistical manual[48] and a commentary on the gospel of Mark.[49] He is the first in time of a group of scholars based in schools in the south midlands area of the country, whose intense activity, particularly in the exegetical field, has long been known.[50] While it is not possible to speak of a 'school' of exegesis, there can be little doubt that they all knew of one another's work, and indeed they refer at times to the opinions of others in matters of scriptural interpretation.

Best-known of these, Cummian's contemporaries, is Laidcend mac Baíth Bandaig (d. 661),[51] who is known principally for his epitome of Gregory the Great's 'Moralia in Iob'[52] and a *lorica* (prayer).[53] He was a scholar at Cluain Ferta Mo-Lua (Clonfert-Mulloe townland of Kyle, County Laois) but may have been of the Uí Conairrge in origin, a minor sept of the Alltraige located around Ballyconry, County Kerry.[54] His name occurs in the form of a 'pet-name', Mo-Lagae, in an interesting unpublished tract, 'De fabulis Connacht i Mumain et de ratione na n-ires' ('On the tales concerning Connacht tribal groups in Munster, and on the reckoning of the histories'), whose unusual title is illustration of the interest early Irish scholars took in their own prehistory as well as in the technical subjects of the Latin tradition.[55] This juxtaposition of vernacular and Latin learning is a constant theme running through early Irish scholarship. Cummianus Longus (probably to be identified with the author of the paschal letter) is known both for his composition

---

[47] He uses the words 'Grandis labor est' in the doxology; this is possibly derived from Pelagius's letter to Demetriada (*P.L.*, xxx, col. 42D = *P.L.*, xxxiii, col. 1119). If so, this would be the earliest dateable Irish use of Pelagius's works in Ireland.

[48] See Ó Cróinín, 'A seventh-century Irish computus', *passim*.

[49] See Bernhard Bischoff, 'Wendepunkte in der Geschichte der lateinischen Exegese im Frühmittelalter' in *Sacris Erudiri*, vi (1954), pp 189–279; rev. ed. in Bischoff, *Mittelalterliche Studien: Ausgewählte Aufsätze zur Schriftkunde und Literaturgeschichte* (3 vols, Stuttgart, 1966–7, 1981), i, 205–73, 213–15, 257–9. The commentary has been recently re-edited by Michael Cahill, *Expositio evangelii secundum Marcum* (Turnhout, 1997). Cahill doubts the ascription to Cummian.

[50] See Kenney, *Sources*, pp 275–80; Paul Grosjean, 'Sur quelques exégètes irlandais du VIIᵉ siècle' in *Sacris Erudiri*, vii (1955), pp 67–98.

[51] See Louis Gougaud, 'Les témoignages des manuscrits sur l'oeuvre littéraire du moine Lathcen' in *Rev. Celt.*, xxx (1909), pp 37–46.

[52] Marc Adriaen (ed.), *Ecloga quam scripsit Lathcen filius Baith de Moralibus Iob quas Gregorius fecit* (Turnhout, 1969).

[53] Michael Herren, 'The authorship, date of composition and provenance of the so-called *Lorica Gildae*' in *Ériu*, xxiv (1973), pp 35–51.

[54] See Donnchadh Ó Corráin, 'Studies in West Munster history II: Alltraighe' in *Kerry Arch. Soc. Jn.*, ii (1969), pp 27–37.

[55] I have an edition of this text in preparation.

of a penitential and a hymn on the apostles;[56] he may also be the author of a descriptive list of the apostles that is found in both Irish and Latin versions.[57] Likewise, the 'Beccanus solitarius' to whom Cummian addressed his letter is probably identical with Béccán mac Luigdech, author of two extant Old Irish poems in praise of Colum Cille.[58] Writing in the vernacular was certainly established by c.600,[59] and Irish scholars (with just a few exceptions)[60] seem to have encouraged its use alongside the more universal language. The best example from the seventh century is the 'Cambrai homily',[61] but there is a general proliferation of Irish glosses in Latin manuscripts of the period, with Irish indeed by no means always the poor relation. The practice of making entries in texts (usually to explain a word or phrase, much as modern schoolgoers annotate their textbooks) seems to have begun at an early date, for many such glosses are written in dry-point on the text of the 'Ussher gospels', one of our oldest biblical manuscripts (c.600).[62] The comments are sometimes intended as teaching aids, sometimes merely the casual remark of a scholar as he broods on his text. Sometimes indeed the gloss might have nothing at all to do with the text but simply record the passing whim of the reader: 'magnus poeta Virgilius fuit', remarked the grammarian, twice—to which the Irish reader responded: 'and he's not easy, either!';[63] the scribe of the Book of Armagh (f. 78rb) remarked at the foot of the page that he had completed that column of writing with just three dips of the quill.[64] Another Irishman, exasperated by the grammarian Priscian's longwindedness, greeted the close of one exposition with the brusque comment: 'he's made his point at last!'[65] Most of the early glossing and commentary, however, is brief and concise, and seldom does more than translate or explain single Latin words. The Reichenau (now Karlsruhe) manuscript that preserves the only copy of a seventh-century Hiberno-Latin commentary on the

[56] J. H. Bernard and R. Atkinson (ed.), *The Irish Liber hymnorum* (2 vols, London, 1897–8), i, 16–21; ii, 108–12; penitential in Bieler *Ir. penitentials*, pp 108–35.
[57] See Dáibhí Ó Cróinín, 'Cummianus Longus and the iconography of the Apostles in early Irish literature' in Ó Corráin, Breatnach, & McCone, *Sages, saints & storytellers*, pp 268–79.
[58] Fergus Kelly, 'A poem in praise of Columb Cille' in *Ériu*, xxiv (1973), pp 1–34, Kelly, 'Tiughraind Bhécáin' in *Ériu*, xxvi (1975), pp 66–98.
[59] See David Greene, 'Archaic Irish', in K. H. Schmidt (ed.), *Indogermanisch und Celtisch* (Wiesbaden, 1977), pp 11–33.
[60] The author of the seventh-century (?) 'Additamenta' to Patrick's Life by Tírechán apologises for using so many Irish words; see Bieler, *Patrician texts*, p. 178; see also below, pp 398, 400.
[61] See Pádraig Ó Néill, 'The background to the Cambrai homily' in *Ériu*, xxxii (1981), pp 137–47. The text is in need of a re-edition.
[62] Bischoff, 'Wendepunkte' in *Mitt. St.*, i, 211.
[63] *Thes. Pal.*, ii, 224: 'ni réid chene.'
[64] *Thes. Pal.*, i, 495: 'tri tuimthea in lethraim.' At that rate of production, the whole MS would have required c.666 dips of the pen!
[65] *Thes. Pal.*, ii, 136: 'a airdérgud leiss fudeud hic.'

Catholic epistles (the oldest surviving commentary on that biblical book)[66] has a couple of such glosses, introduced at that point in the text where mention is made of Laidcend. Three others are mentioned by name: Brecannus, Banbanus, and Bercanus 'filius Aedo'.[67] These clearly formed one circle of scholarship with Laidcend and Cummian, with the unknown author of the 'De mirabilibus sacrae scripturae' ('On the miraculous things in sacred scripture'),[68] and with others that he in turn mentions: his teachers Manchianus and Eusebius, and the monks of 'Carthage' (the monastery of Carthagus/ Carthach/Mo-Chuta of Lismore, County Waterford).[69] Of all these the anonymous author of the 'De mirabilibus' is the most daring, for his tract is in marked contrast to the standard allegorising exposition in the other commentaries.[70] Far more original than Laidcend, his approach to the miracles in the Bible is rigorously naturalistic (it would be misleading to describe it as rationalistic): How explain the seemingly miraculous transformation of Lot's wife into a pillar of salt? He observes that salt is present in every human body (as tears amply testify); God did no more than accelerate its production to the point where the original microscopic element eventually overwhelmed the whole body! There was no new creation (which ended on the sixth day), nothing truly miraculous, simply a manifestation of God's working through previous creation.[71]

The way in which these masters combined the various disciplines is nicely illustrated by Pseudo-Augustine's explanation of the incident in the Book of Joshua (10: 12–13) when Joshua commanded the sun to stand still while the Israelites contended with their enemies. This 'miracle' was no miracle in fact, for there was no dislocation of the celestial movements: sun and moon stood still for the duration of the battle and resumed their courses in perfect equilibrium as before. The proof is in the constant recurrence of the luni-solar paschal cycles, which began at creation and continue, in periods of 532 years, up to the author's own time (*c*.655).[72] The Irish writer expounds the theory of cycles with perfect clarity—a master of the calendar as well as of exegesis and Latin. But his style of biblical exposition did not find general

---

[66] Robert E. McNally (ed.), *Scriptores Hiberniae minores* (Turnhout, 1968).
[67] Grosjean, 'Quelques exégètes', pp 76 ff.; Alfred Holder, 'Altirische Namen im Reichenauer Codex CCXXXIII' in *Archiv für celt. Lexikographie*, iii (1907), pp 266–7.
[68] *P.L.*, xxxv, cols 2149–200; see Kenney, *Sources*, pp 275–7; William Reeves, 'On Augustin, an Irish writer of the seventh century' in *R.I.A. Proc.*, vii (1861), pp 514–22; Mario Esposito, 'On the pseudo-Augustinian treatise *De mirabilibus sacrae scripturae*' in *R.I.A. Proc.*, xxxv (1919), sect. C, pp 189–207.
[68] The connection with Carthach's monastery at Lismore was first made by John Lanigan in *An ecclesiastical history of Ireland*, iii (Dublin, 1822), 31, n. 81.
[70] A new edition, by Dom Gerard McGinty, O.S.B., is to appear in the series Corpus Christianorum Series Latina (C.C.S.L.).
[71] *P.L.*, xxxv, col. 2149.
[72] Below, p. 400.

favour in Ireland, and his commentary is unusual as much for its methodological uniqueness as for its originality of thought.

Some reflection of current controversies and alignments is evident among
seventh-century writers, most notably on the subject of the Easter controversy.[73] The rivalry that marked off the two groups of *Hiberni* and *Romani*
seems, however, to have hinged rather on questions of organisation than of
doctrine or belief.[74] And yet there are occasional references to particular
interpretations of scripture that were being proposed by the *Romani*, sufficient to suggest that the rift ran deeper than is sometimes believed.[75] There
is a letter extant (probably seventh-century) from one Colmán to a confrère
named Feradach,[76] in which Colmán remarks almost casually that he has a
better text of Caelius Sedulius's 'Carmen paschale' than Feradach, and that
he got it from the *Romani*; Feradach's manuscript, on the other hand, was
wanting some five pages.[77] We do not know if Colmán was on the Continent
when he wrote; it is possible, but it need not have been the case. Cummian's
letter is usually regarded as a prime witness for the 'Romanist' cause, but it is
clear from his statements that harsh words were being tossed about even
before 632. The Colmán letter, therefore, could just as easily have been
written in Ireland as abroad. If it is seventh-century, it shows a remarkable
grasp of the *cursus* and a very creditable interest on the part of the two
correspondents in the technicalities of Latin metrical study.

There is no need to presume that the 'Carmen paschale' was a particularly
rare work in Ireland at this time,[78] although we cannot be sure about any
statement of this kind without first compiling a thorough index of books
known to the Irish. The epoch-making publication of Bernhard Bischoff's
'Turning-points in the history of Latin exegesis in the early middle ages'[79]
made known for the first time a whole range of Hiberno-Latin commentaries
hitherto unnoticed by scholars. Bischoff's careful source-analysis of these

---

[73] The question is one that still needs detailed examination.

[74] See Martin McNamara, 'Tradition and creativity in early Irish psalter study' in Michael
Richter and Proinséas Ní Chatháin (ed.), *Ireland and Europe in the early middle ages* (2 vols,
Stuttgart, 1984), ii, 283–328, and Pádraig Ó Néill, 'The *Romani* influence on seventh-century
Hiberno-Latin literature', ibid., ii, 280–90.

[75] See Hughes, *Ch. in early Ir. soc.*, pp 46 ff, 105 ff, 130 ff.

[76] Bibliothèque Royale (Brussels), MS 5665X, ff. 186ʳ–187; see Bischoff, 'Il monachesimo
irlandese nei suoi rapporti col continente' in *Mitt. St.*, i, 195–205, at p. 199; Bischoff, 'Die
europaische Verbreitung der Werke Isidors von Sevilla' in *Mitt. St.*, i, 171–94. The text has
been recently edited by Richard Sharpe, 'An Irish textual critic and the Carmen paschale of
Sedulius: Colmán's letter to Feradach' in *Journal of Medieval Latin*, ii (1992), pp 44–54.

[77] 'Quinque ferme paginas a librariis inuenimus pretermissas' (not 'tres', as Bischoff and
Sharpe have it, *Mitt. St.*, i, 181).

[78] Above, n. 49.

[79] Ibid. The recent attempted refutation of Bischoff's work in Michael Gorman, 'A
critique of Bischoff's theory of Irish exegesis: the commentary on Genesis in Munich
Clm 6302' in *Journal of Medieval Latin*, vii (1997), pp 178–233, appears to me to be wholly
misguided.

texts has revealed an Irish familiarity with most of the standard patristic commentaries and an interest in expounding on all the biblical books. Even the gospel of Mark, rarely commented on by patristic writers, received full treatment in an extensive work falsely transmitted under the name of Jerome but ascribed by Bischoff to an unidentified Comianus, perhaps Cummian, author of the paschal letter.[80] This commentary, and others like it, owed their survival to the fact that medieval copyists thought them to be works of the Fathers. Hence the proliferation of pseudonymous authors such as Pseudo-Augustine, Pseudo-Cyril, and Pseudo-Cyprian. Sometimes the Irish origins of a work were plain to see: thus Pseudo-Augustine's 'De mirabilibus' makes explicit reference to Ireland and even preserves a list of its wild animals.[81] Pseudo-Jerome's interesting tract on Mark, on the other hand, is not so readily localised and scholars are not unanimous in accepting Cummian's authorship.[82]

It is the quirks of style and the sources used that enabled Bischoff often to suggest Irish authorship for a text: the question-and-answer technique, with answer prefaced by the exclamation *non difficile* (Old Irish *ní ansae*); frequent use of the so-called 'three sacred languages' formula, whereby particular words were given in their Greek, Latin, and Hebrew forms (with Greek often and Hebrew occasionally being entirely fictitious!); a triadic pattern too appears characteristic,[83] as does the tendency to connect related passages of biblical text with the word *haeret* ('this belongs to . . .'). None of these usages alone guarantees Irish authorship of an anonymous text, but their frequent use, especially in combination, does argue strongly for such a provenance. In the area of sources used, of course the Irish drew on the same range of texts as their continental counterparts: besides the Fathers they cite Caelius Sedulius, Junilius, Juvencus, Prudentius, and so on. Where the Irish often differ is in their penchant for biblical apocrypha and commentaries (such as that of Pelagius) that were long since anathematised by the rest of the church.[84]

The use of Pelagius is a case in point: the survival of his commentary on the Pauline epistles is due almost entirely to its popularity with Irish writers,[85] and he retained that popularity from the seventh till the twelfth century.[86]

---

[80] Above, p. 377.

[81] See D'Arcy Wentworth Thompson, 'Sesquivolus, squirrel, and the *Liber de mirabilibus s. scripturae*' in *Hermathena*, lxv (1945), pp 1–7.

[82] See Clare Stancliffe, 'Early "Irish" biblical exegesis' in *Studia Patristica*, xii (Texte u. Untersuchungen, cxv; Berlin, 1975), pp 361–70, at p. 83; Cahill, *Expositio*, pp 116*–22*, is sceptical.

[83] Patrick Sims-Williams, 'Thought, word and deed: an Irish triad' in *Ériu*, xxix (1978), pp 78–111.

[84] See Martin McNamara, *The apocrypha in the Irish church* (Dublin, 1975).

[85] The most recent discussion is by Joseph F. Kelly, 'Pelagius, Pelagianism and the early Christian Irish' in *Medievalia*, iv (1978), pp 99–124.

[86] He is cited by Maél Brigte Ua Maéluanaig of Armagh in his commentary on Matthew (1138); see below, p. 403.

The earliest known author to cite his work is Cummian,[87] but evidence for widespread use is available only from the eighth century on.[88] The accusation of Pelagian practices contained in the letter of 640 from the pope-elect John IV to the northern Irish churches has unfortunately been misunderstood by modern commentators; the letter in fact has nothing to do with Pelagius's ideas but arose out of Roman misinterpretations of Irish practice in the matter of Easter observance.[89]

Such was the reputation of the Irish schools in the seventh century, says Bede,[90] that they attracted visiting students not only from Britain but also from Francia. He mentions one by name, Acgilberct, who—before spending some years as bishop of Wessex and then transferring to Northumbria and eventually back to Paris—spent many years in Ireland in order to study scripture.[91] Irish sources preserve the names of other such visitors[92] and Bede lists no fewer than twelve who were associated with the Anglo-Saxon monastery at Ráth Melsigi.[93] He reports them as having sometimes seated themselves behind the shoulder of their Irish masters and studied their scripture with them; books and board were provided free. This may be the background to one of the most curious of Hiberno-Latin texts, the 'Hisperica Famina'.[94] These 'western sayings' have long puzzled scholars, most of whom have tended to see in them the 'culture-fungus of decay'.[95] Composed in a bizarre and tortuous Latin, they seem to be the party-pieces of a group of dotty students whose days are spent trying to outdo one another in verbosity. Where a hard word can be substituted for a simple one the scholars never fail to do so, and if perchance they appear to slip into plain vocabulary it frequently transpires that theirs is not the normal usage of such words. They move about apparently begging from the local population for their sustenance, for which purpose they must relinquish the bonds of Latin and resort to Irish.[96] The implication in the text seems to be that the group is not Irish, and indeed the evidence of the manuscripts might appear to argue for a Breton origin for the group.[97] But the 'Hisperic style' certainly found favour

---

[87] Above, p. 377.

[88] See Kenney, *Sources*, pp 635–6.

[89] See Dáibhí Ó Cróinín, "New heresy for old"—Pelagianism in Ireland and the papal letter of 640' in *Speculum*, lx (1985), pp 505–16.

[90] *Ecc. hist.*, iii, 27; Plummer, i, 192; *Ecc. hist.* (1969), p. 312.

[91] *Ecc. hist.*, iii, 7; Plummer, i, 140; *Ecc. hist.* (1969), p. 234.

[92] The 'Martyrology of Oéngus' (*c.*800) names Ichtbricht, Berchert, Cuthbert, and others.

[93] See Dáibhí Ó Cróinín, 'Rath Melsigi, Willibrord, and the earliest Echternach manuscripts' in *Peritia*, iii (1984), pp 17–49.

[94] Michael Herren (ed. and trans.), *The Hisperica Famina* (2 vols, Toronto, 1974, 1987).

[95] The description is Eoin MacNeill's: 'Beginnings of Latin culture in Ireland' in *Studies*, xx (1931), p. 457.

[96] Herren, *Hisperica Famina*, i, 82–4.

[97] The evidence of the manuscripts (and particularly the Breton glosses in some) was perhaps not sufficiently taken into account by the text's most recent editor.

with the Irish, and seventh-century texts are peppered with exotic words of Greek or Hebrew derivation, and often too with 'sense neologisms' in the use of commonplace Latin words. Sometimes even Irish words creep in—though they are not common at any stage in the history of Hiberno-Latin literature, except when native personal or place-names are used. The seventh-century (?) grammarian Malsachanus (or his source) coined the verb *orgo* (from Irish *orgaim* 'to kill');[98] Adomnán, the biographer of Columba,[99] uses *tollus* (from Irish *tólae* 'flood') in his book on the Holy Lands, and this recurs as the only word of Irish derivation in the writings of Johannes Scottus Eriugena.[100] Adomnán has a few other terms such as *currucus* ('currach') and *tigernus* (Irish *tigern* 'lord') but they are infrequent in what is, by any standard, remarkably pure and polished Latin.[101] His writings date from the last quarter of the century, but the earlier writers are no more given to calques from the Irish than he. They may differ in style and accomplishment but they all maintain a relatively pure language; Latin is not a problem for them.

The new genre that emerges in the seventh century is hagiography, the writing of saints' Lives. The earliest in date is probably Cogitosus's Life of Brigit, founder of the monastery of Kildare.[102] It is one of three such biographies that date from this period, the other two being ascribed to Ultán (d. 657), bishop of Ardbraccan, County Meath, and to Ailerán 'the wise' (d. 665), a scholar of Clonard, also in Meath.[103] These two works were long believed to have perished but recent research has suggested that they may have survived as the underlying material of the so-called 'first Life' ('Vita prima Brigitae').[104] A reference by Muirchú moccu Machtheni, one of Patrick's biographers, seems to imply that Cogitosus served as his spiritual and literary mentor and that Cogitosus's Life was the first attempt by any Irish writer to compose a work of hagiography.[105] Unfortunately, neither his nor the other

---

[98] See Bengt Löfstedt (ed.), *Der hibernolateinische Grammatiker Malsachanus* (Uppsala, 1965).

[99] Kenney, *Sources*, pp 429–33; Denis Meehan (ed. and trans.), *Adomnan's De locis sanctis* (Dublin, 1958).

[100] Information kindly supplied by P. Édouard Jeauneau.

[101] See J.-M. Picard's papers cited above, n. 2.

[102] See Mario Esposito, 'On the earliest Latin life of St Brigid of Kildare' in *R.I.A. Proc.*, xxx (1912), sect. C, pp 307–26; Richard Sharpe, 'Vitae S. Brigitae: the oldest texts' in *Peritia*, i (1982), pp 81–106.

[103] Kenney, *Sources*, pp 279–81. Ailerán was also the author of an 'Interpretatio mystica progenitorum domini Iesu Christi' and of the verses 'Quam in primo speciosa quadriga' on the Eusebian canons of the Gospels. His poem is important as being the earliest Irish evidence for the so-called 'beast canon tables', which were to become such a characteristic of Insular illuminated gospel manuscripts. See Nancy Netzer, *Cultural interplay in the eighth century* (Cambridge, 1996), and Aidan Breen (ed. and trans.), *Ailerani Interpretatio mystica progenitorum Iesu Christi* (Dublin, 1996).

[104] Kim McCone, 'Brigit in the seventh century: a saint with three lives' in *Peritia*, i (1982), pp 107–45. Note that McCone's paper directly contradicts some of the arguments in Sharpe's paper, which immediately precedes it.

[105] Esposito, 'On the early Latin lives of St Brigid of Kildare' in *Hermathena*, xxiv (1935), pp 120–65.

two lives of Brigit tell us anything substantial either about the saint herself or about Kildare. The political circumstances in Cogitosus's time (*c*.650?) were dominated by the rise to power of the Uí Dúnlainge dynasty under their forceful king Fáelán mac Colmáin. The emergence of his dynasty in political terms had its reflection in the imposition of his brother, Áed Dub, as bishop of Kildare 'and of all Leinster',[106] and Uí Dúnlainge clerics dominated the monastery for some generations thereafter.[107] None of this, however, emerges from the narrative of Cogitosus, or any other Brigit life. They are merely catalogues of miracles designed, it would seem, to boost Brigit's reputation as a wonder-worker and therefore a suitable candidate for veneration.[108] The only hint of current political influence is the reference to Kildare as a 'metropolitan city' and the principal monastery in Ireland, where royal treasure was kept.[109] There were, however, undoubted political motivations behind the sudden interest in saints in the seventh century, and the emergence of rival monastic *paruchiae* in the period clearly had for a result the necessity for a 'propaganda war' for or against the claims of various churches.[110] The early claims of Kildare to a position of primacy, not only in Leinster but throughout the country, brought forth it seems a response from the *paruchia* of Patrick, and the church of Armagh in particular.[111] These ambitions on the part of Patrick's heirs are best exemplified in the 'Liber angeli' ('Book of the angel')—a bombastic manifesto of Armagh claims to primacy, allegedly bequeathed to Patrick by an angel.[112] The striking legal language used in the document, stating that Armagh 'overswears' its rivals and cannot be considered subject to the usual arbitration of casting lots, clearly shows that the Patrician group was advancing a legal case for its claims and was not relying merely on sentiment.[113] The 'agreement' attached at a later date to the 'Liber angeli',[114] whereby Armagh and Kildare allegedly came to terms, marked the triumph of the Armagh campaign.[115] But this came about only after that church had commissioned a full-scale biography of Patrick by Muirchú and a catalogue of properties claimed for him by Tírechán, a former student of Ultán's at Ardbraccan.[116] Besides being of

---

[106] Byrne, *Ir. kings*, pp 151–2.

[107] Félim Ó Briain, 'The hagiography of Leinster' in John Ryan (ed.), *Féil-sgríbhinn Eóin Mhic Néill* (Dublin, 1940), pp 454–64: 460–61.

[108] See Esposito's scathing (but amusing) comments in 'On the early Latin lives', pp 161–3.

[109] See the English translation in Liam de Paor, 'The viking towns of Ireland' in David Greene and Bo Almqvist (ed.), *Proceedings of the Seventh Viking Conference* (Dublin, 1976), pp 29–37: 29.

[110] McCone, 'Brigit in the seventh century', pp 138–44.

[111] Liam de Paor, 'The aggrandisement of Armagh' in *Hist. Studies*, viii (1971), pp 95–110.

[112] Translation and discussion in Hughes, *Ch. in early Ir. soc.*, pp 275–81.

[113] See D. A. Binchy, 'St Patrick's "First synod" in *Studia Hib.*, viii (1968), pp 49–59.

[114] McCone, 'Brigit in the seventh century', dates the agreement to after 800; Sharpe, 'Vitae S. Brigitae', argues for a much earlier date.

[115] McCone, p. 144.

[116] Bieler , *Patrician texts*.

interest for the history of the literature, these two works are valuable historical documents, and Tírechán's in particular is a mine of information. Pride
of place among Irish hagiographers, however, must go to Adomnán, ninth
abbot of Iona (d. 704). His biography of Columba is written in three books,
the first devoted to the saint's prophecies, the second to his angelic and other
visitations, and the third to his miracles.[117] Though the work suffers from
many of the basic traits that disfigure medieval hagiography in the eyes of
the modern reader, Adomnán's 'Vita Columbae' far surpasses all the other
seventh-century lives in its value as an authentic picture of its subject.
Adomnán, though not a contemporary of the saint, consulted many who had
known his closest disciples, and he was scrupulous in his use of evidence and
hearsay. There is no more touching story in all medieval literature than that
about Columba's horse that shed tears, knowing of his master's approaching
death.[118] Some of Adomnán's incidental narratives cast valuable light on the
everyday aspects of community life in his own time,[119] while his information
concerning political affairs is extremely useful.[120] In Adomnán's story of Iona
in the sixth century there is none of the bitter rivalry and rancour that so
disfigured monastic politics in the centuries to follow; Columba, Comgall of
Bangor, and Ciarán of Clonmacnoise are all seen in amicable contact, receiving and visiting one another regularly.[121] By Adomnán's time, however, the
primary position of Iona among the churches of northern Ireland and Scotland had come under challenge as a result of the Easter controversy, but
doubtless for political reasons as well. As a result there was a need to restate
the claims of Columba and his successors and to remind people in both
islands of the seminal role played by the monks of Iona both in the Irish
church and also, of course, in the establishment of Christianity in northern
Britain.[122] The Columban *paruchia* was being edged out of its once powerful
position (particularly in the north) by the emergent claims of Armagh. The
twin Lives of Patrick by Tírechán and Muirchú at the end of the century
staked out these claims in no uncertain manner. Tírechán, in the course of
his *itinerarium*, utters a vitriolic blast against the usurping expansionism of
Clonmacnoise. Were they to wish it, Tírechán boasts, Patrick's heirs could
reclaim their God-given prerogative of primacy throughout the whole of the
country.[123] The alleged historical basis for this primacy is described by

[117] Anderson, *Adomnan's Life* .
[118] *Vita Columbae*, iii, 23; Anderson, *Adomnan's Life*, pp 522–4.
[119] See the Andersons' discussion, pp 105–24.
[120] Dorbbéne, the scribe of the oldest surviving copy of the *Vita*, also had access to an
earlier life by Cummeneus Albus (d. 669), seventh abbot of Iona, which likewise preserves
invaluable historical information; see Kenney, *Sources*, pp 428–9.
[121] *Vita Columbae*, iii, 17; Anderson, *Adomnan's Life*, p. 500.
[122] See Jean-Michel Picard, 'The purpose of Adomnán's *Vita Columbae*' in *Peritia*, i (1982),
pp 160–77.
[123] Bieler, *Patrician texts*, p. 138.

Muirchú in a narrative that is every bit as racy and entertaining as the best modern fiction—and his account lacks nothing in fiction![124] As a supposed record of Patrick's achievement, however, Muirchú's *Vita* is a travesty of the man and his true sanctity. He seems to have known very little about his hero, and cared less about the facts concerning him. He was following in the footsteps of Cogitosus, his *pater*, and all the worst elements in that writer's work were shamelessly aped. Muirchú's Life of Patrick, and the Lives of Brigit, are sometimes fine literature, but they are not history.

The hagiographical writings were never more than occasional pieces, composed to suit a certain set of circumstances, and then only for a few saints. The real seventh-century blossoming took place in the three main subjects of the curriculum: exegesis, computus, and grammar. Grammar especially witnessed the production of a string of texts that paved the way for the remarkable contribution by Irish scholars to the Carolingian and post-Carolingian learning of Europe.[125] The impetus for this flourishing study seems to have derived from the Irish discovery of new grammars from late antiquity; hitherto reliant almost entirely on Donatus, they now had access to Priscian, Charisius (under the byname 'Comminianus'), Consentius, Diomedes, Probus, Servius, and Papirinus.[126] As well as these, they received anonymous texts from Spain on figures and tropes and another on the faults of speech.[127] This new *embarras de richesses* transformed tbe Irish schools and revolutionised the format of the standard Hiberno-Latin grammars. A study of the three principal manuals of the period, 'Anonymus ad Cuimnanum', 'Ars Ambrosiana', and 'Congregatio Salcani filli de uerbo',[128] shows the transition from a period when Donatus's 'Ars minor' was the basic tool, to a new era in which the teacher can now assume that his students know the text by heart and therefore it need be cited only in snippets. The bulk of the text is now made up of commentary in which the teacher not only treats of Donatus's

[124] Ludwig Bieler, 'Tírechán als Erzähhler' in *Sitzungsb. d. Bay. Akad. d. Wiss., phil.-hist. Kl.*, vi (Munich, 1974); idem, 'Muirchú's Life of St Patrick as a work of literature' in *Medium Aevum*, xliii (1974), pp 219–33.

[125] Holtz, *Donat*, pp 319–22.

[126] Vivien Law (*Insular Latin grammarians*, p. 29) says that only Virgilius Maro *grammaticus* and the English writer Aldhelm used Priscian's 'Institutiones' in the seventh century, but she has ignored some important Irish evidence that disproves her case; see the reviews of her book cited in n. 38 above.

[127] See the brilliant paper by Ulrich Schindel, 'Die lateinischen Figurenlehren des 5. bis 7. Jahrhunderts und Donats Vergilkommentar' in *Abh. d. Akad. d. Wiss. Göttingen, phil.-hist.Kl., iii, N. Folge*, Nr ix (1975). On the manuscript, see Herrad Spilling, 'Irische Handschriften-Überlieferung aus Fulda, Würzburg und Mainz' in Löwe, *Die Iren*, ii, 876–902: 893–9.

[128] On the Anonymus see Holtz, *Donat*, pp 267–70, 284–94; Law, *Insular Latin grammarians*, pp 87–90 (arguing for English authorship). On the Ambrosiana see Bengt Löfstedt (ed.), *Ars Ambrosiana e codice Mediolan. Bibl. Ambros. L.22.Sup.* (Turnhout, 1982); Holtz, *Donat*, pp 284–94; Law, *Insular Latin grammarians*, pp 93–7. For the *Congregatio Salcani Filii* see Law, 'Malsachanus reconsidered' in *Camb. Med. Celt. Studies*, i (summer 1981), pp 83–97 (which argues that only Malsachanus's source, not the writer himself, was of the seventh century).

rules but compares them with those of other grammarians, frequently criticising one or more of them.[129] The author who addressed his anonymous
commentary to the unidentified Cuimnanus[130] not only elaborates a sophisticated technique of exposition but prefaces the whole work with a remarkable
apologia for the study of Latin grammar as an end in itself.[131] Mindful of the
outburst against Donatus made by Pope Gregory I,[132] the anonymous author
took care to defend his position by reference to Jerome (a pupil of Donatus!).
That he should have felt it necessary to defend himself at all has been
interpreted as indicating that Irish schools in the late sixth century had
perhaps witnessed a struggle between those who would rid the curriculum of
these grammars (with their profane quotations from the pagan classical
authors) and have only strict functional instruction, and those on the other
side (like the 'Anonymus') who saw in the study of the ancient authors a
means to advance in their pursuit of scriptural knowledge, which, after all,
was also written in Latin. The eighth and ninth centuries clearly prove that
the victory had gone to the more enlightened party, though not without a
struggle. Some still resented the all-encompassing rules of the grammarians,
like the computist who burst out against the pedant that said the word *feria*
had no plural;[133] he doubtless had many sympathisers. Indeed, the pedantry
was such that it brought forth a glorious pastiche in the writings of Virgilius
Maro *grammaticus*.[134] Scholars do not quite know what to make of Virgil. Is
he just a dotty professor—like many of themselves, and therefore not to be
entirely dismissed? Or is he a comedian, sending up the inane pedantries of
the schoolmasters?[135] There is no doubt that some of his statements have
raised the eyes as well as the eyebrows of many a modern reader. What is
one to make of his doctrine of twelve kinds of Latin; or the many bizarre
etymologies with which he pads out his discourse? And what of his gallery of
grammatical 'greats' like Terrentius and Galbungus, who went at one another
hammer and tongs for fourteen days and as many nights about whether the

---

[129] Holtz, *Donat*, p. 286.

[130] Law (*Insular Latin grammarians*, p. 87) suggests that although the recipient was undoubtedly Irish the anonymous author may in fact have been English.

[131] Holtz, *Donat*, pp 267–9; Bischoff, 'Eine verschollene Einteilung der Wissenschaften' in
*Mitt. St.*, i, 273–88.

[132] 'Quia indignum uehementer existimo, ut uerba caelestis oraculi restringam sub regulis
Donati' (cited in Holtz, *Donat*, p. 254, n. 2).

[133] In the mainly Irish *Liber de computo*, *P.L.*, cxxix, cols 1275–372.

[134] Latest and best edition by Giovanni Polara (ed. and trans.), *Virgilio Marone Grammatico
Epitomi ed Epostole* (Naples, 1979); Holtz, *Donat*, pp 315–18; Michael Herren, 'Some new light
on the life of Virgilius Maro Grammaticus' in *R.I.A. Proc.*, lxxix (1979), sect. C, pp 27–71;
Dáibhí Ó Cróinín, 'The date, provenance, and earliest use of the works of Virgilius Maro
Grammaticus' in G. Bernt, F. Rädle and G. Silagi (ed.), *Tradition und Wertung: Festschrift
Franz Brunhölzl* (Sigmaringen, 1989), pp 13–22.

[135] See Paul Lehmann, *Die Parodie im Mittelalter* (Munich, 1923), pp 9–10; Vivien Law,
*Wisdom, grammar and authority in the seventh century* (Oxford, 1997); Martha Bayless, *Parody in
the middle ages: the Latin tradition* (Ann Arbor, 1996).

word *ego* had a vocative case or not?[136] Nor is the brush restricted to grammar alone; the computists get a rub of it as well when Virgil gives his 'secret code' of letters that have numerical values.[137] Such word-games were in fact played in the elementary schools to teach the youngsters their alphabets and their numbers together; but Virgil's scheme has neither rhyme nor reason to it and seems nothing more than spoof. He was undoubtedly poking fun at contemporaries who made their students do all kinds of abstruse mathematical calculations—like working out the number of moments Jonah spent in the belly of the whale![138] Virgil knew his curriculum and when he pokes fun at the schools it is clear that he had been through them himself. The most charitable judgement of him might be that he was a good teacher who knew full well that large doses of Donatus needed to be washed down with humour;[139] a little like teaching Latin in a pub. I have little doubt that Virgil's students liked him, and there is certainly more entertaining stuff in a page of his 'Epitomae' or 'Epistolae' than in all the other grammars put together. His style seems to have caught on too: an unpublished grammar purports to explain—in the three sacred languages, of course!—the names for the strokes in each letter of the alphabet: 'In Hebrew the letter "a" is *abst*, *ebst*, *ubst*, in Greek *albs*, *elbs*, *ulbs*; in Latin two oblique strokes and a horizontal one above'![140] Farther than this one cannot go, unless it be to the Chaldaean 'explanation' of the word *gloria* that is found in a slightly later text.[141] 'In the works of Virgil', Holtz has remarked, 'it is as though in the culture of scholarly Latin one still knew the tune but had forgotten the words.'[142] And yet the classics were not entirely forgotten. There still survives a commentary on Virgil culled from the (lost) treatises of Gaudentius, Iunilius, and Filargirius and which mentions in passing the comment of Adomnán on a line of the epic.[143] This may be the same Adomnán who composed the life of Columba, but we have no sure way of knowing.[144] The

---

[136] *Ep.* 2, 4; Polara, *Virgilio*, p. 210.

[137] *Ep.* 3, 2; Polara, *Virgilio*, pp 14–16.

[138] So the author of the seventh-century Irish computus came up with the figure 'II.dccclxxx. momentorum Ionas in medio coeti'.

[139] The verdict is Michael Herren's, given in conversation.

[140] See Bengt Löfstedt, 'Zur grammatischen Schwindelliteratur' in 'Miscellanea grammatica 3' in *Rivista di cultura classica e medioevale*, xxiii (1982), pp 156–64, at pp 162–4.

[141] Löfstedt, 'Schwindelliteratur', p. 163: 'Interpretatio gloriae apud Chaldaeos: Gloria est terra laudat creatorem, glori est terra magnificat, glor est terra miratur, glo est terra tremit in laudem, gl est terra tibi dei exultat, g est terra.'

[142] Holtz, *Donat*, p. 316.

[143] Georg Thilo, 'Beiträge zur Kritik der Scholiasten des Virgilius' in *Rheinisches Museum*, xv (1860), pp 119–52, esp. pp 132–3; Maurice Roger, *L'enseignement des lettres classiques d'Ausone à Alcuin* (Paris, 1908), p. 262; G. Funaioli, *Esegesi Virgiliana antica* (Milan, 1930); C. H. Beeson, 'Insular symptoms in the commentaries on Vergil' in *Studi Medievali*, 3rd ser., v (1932), pp 81–100.

[144] Adomnán's role as commentator/compiler is doubted by Donald Bullough, 'Columba, Adomnan, and the achievement of Iona I, II' in *Scottish Historical Review*, xlii (1963),

name, however, is undoubtedly Irish and the commentary therefore very likely a witness to Irish interests. It is one of those instances in which the Irish preserved texts otherwise lost. They use a text of Diomedes apparently better than any that has come down to us,[145] and Malsachanus (or his source) had citations from the poetical works of Accius no longer extant.[146]

The Irish seem to have some of these texts from of old. Others they had acquired more recently. One of the reasons for the radical transformation of Hiberno-Latin studies in the seventh century—besides their discovery of the new corpus of grammars—was the arrival from Spain of the works of Isidore of Seville (d. 636).[147] By mid-century his most important writings, the 'Etymologiae' and the 'De natura rerum' ('On the nature of things') were in general use with Irish authors,[148] and by the end of the century all but one of his texts had arrived. Isidore's etymologies especially were a revelation to the Irish, for his encyclopaedic descriptions of anything and everything that formed part of the classical Roman civilisation opened up whole new vistas to the Irish, who knew nothing of the empire and whose experience of classical Latin literature derived almost solely from the tags quoted by grammarians. In the same way, Isidore's treatise on the nature of things provided the Irish for the first time with a compendium of scientific and cosmographical facts not previously known. These two works were particularly beloved of the computists, and no Irish tract of the period fails to quote Isidore at length. So popular did he become in fact, and so esteemed were the 'Etymologies' especially, that the Irish referred to him affectionately as *Issidir in chulmin* ('Isidore of the summit', i.e. of the summit of learning).[149] In fact, tradition had it that the Irish literati were unable to recover the great native saga-tale 'Táin Bó Cuailnge' in its entirety because someone had swapped it for the Spanish Father's work!

The striking advances in computistical studies in this same period were also due to the Spanish connection, for besides the Isidorian texts the Irish also received patristic and post-patristic works such as the letters of Theophilus and Proterius of Alexandria, the letter of Bishop Pascasinus on the Easter question of 455, and a variety of others (some pseudepigraphical).[150]

---

pp 111–30; xliii (1964), pp 17–33: 24–6. On Virgil in Irish literature see Gerard Murphy, 'Vergilian influence upon the vernacular literature of medieval Ireland' in *Studi Medievali*, v (1932), pp 372–81.

[145] See Bischoff's evidence in A. Klotz, *Scaenicorum Romanorum fragmenta*, I: *tragicorum fragmenta* (Munich, 1953), p. 4 ff.

[146] Löfstedt, *Malsachanus*, p. 51.

[147] For the most recent discussion, with full bibliography, see J. N. Hillgarth, 'Visigothic Spain and Ireland in the seventh century' in *Peritia*, iii (1984), pp 1–16.

[148] See Michael Herren, 'On the earliest Irish acquaintance with the works of Isidore of Seville' in Edward James (ed.), *Visigothic Spain: new approaches* (Oxford, 1980), pp 243–50.

[149] James Carney, *Studies in Irish literature and history* (Dublin, 1955), pp 165–88.

[150] See Ó Cróinín, 'A seventh-century Irish computus', p. 407.

Some of these were ultimately of African origin, and Irish computistical collections of the seventh century represent a remarkable continuity of study from the fifth century up to their own time. They are important as providing the raw material without which the great English scholar Bede could not have achieved what he did.[151]

The other distinctive feature of Hiberno-Latin literature in the seventh century is the flowering of composition in verse. There is a large corpus of poems, on a variety of subjects: devotional, hagiographical, computistic, and lyrical, some of which may even date from the early years of the century.[152] The so-called hymn of Secundinus, 'Audite omnes amantes', in honour of St Patrick, is probably seventh-century rather than sixth, though a more precise dating is hardly possible.[153] The 'Altus prosator' traditionally ascribed to St Columba (d. 597) is probably not by him,[154] and some (but perhaps not all) of the so-called 'Columbanus poems' are probably inauthentic as well. From the mid-seventh century we have the synchronistic verses 'Deus a quo facta fuit', on the six ages of the world, which are internally dated to 645,[155] while the collection in the famous Bangor antiphonary was probably put together before 692.[156] There are many more preserved in the late 'Liber hymnorum' and others in scattered sources now preserved mainly in European libraries. An example is Ailerán's 'Quam in primo speciosa quadriga', on the subject of the Eusebian gospel canons, which is interesting both for its early date (before 665) and for the fact that it is the earliest known reference to the 'beast' canon tables that became such a distinctive feature of Insular gospel manuscripts, such as the Book of Kells.[157]

It is hardly surprising that the eighth century, in its initial phase at least, should have been a period of compilation rather than innovation. The 'Collectio canonum Hibernensis' ('Irish collection of canon law')[158] is perhaps the best example of the trend. Here in one great compendium are gathered together the canon law and synodal decrees of over two centuries, ranging in date from the so-called dicta of St Patrick to decisions of the compilatory period itself, c.725. The two compilers, Ruben of Dairinis and Cú Chuimne of Iona (d. 747)[159] drew on a wide variety of texts, not just ecclesiastical

---

[151] Ó Cróinín, 'The Irish provenance of Bede's computus' in *Peritia*, ii (1983), pp 229–47.

[152] The most convenient collection is Clemens Blume (ed.), *Hymnodia Hiberno-Celtica* (Leipzig, 1908).

[153] Above, pp 372–3.

[154] See David Howlett, 'Seven studies in seventh-century texts' in *Peritia*, x (1996), pp 1–70: 54–7.

[155] See Dáibhí Ó Cróinín, 'Early Irish annals from Easter-tables: a case restated' in *Peritia*, ii (1983), pp 74–86: 79–81.

[156] F. E. Warren (ed.), *The Antiphonary of Bangor* (2 vols, London, 1892, 1895).

[157] Above, p. 384, n. 103.

[158] Hermann Wasserschleben (ed.), *Die irische Kanonensammlung* (Leipzig, 1885).

[159] On the colophon in the Bibl. Nat. (Paris) MS 12021 that preserves the names, see Kenney, *Sources*, pp 247–50.

They cite, for example, a definition of Virgil the grammarian[160] and the computistical tract known as Pseudo-Theophilus, or the spurious 'Acts of the council of Caesarea'.[161] The collection is remarkable, if for no other reason than the fact that it quotes from every single work of Isidore's, bar one.[162]

Whatever about Ruben, his collaborator Cú Chuimne certainly seems to have said more than his prayers, if the words of the poet are anything to go by:

> Cú Chuimne in youth
> Read his way through half the truth.
> He let the other half lie
> While he gave women a try.
>
> Well for him in old age.
> He became a holy sage.
> He gave women the laugh.
> He read the other half.[163]

We are not told which he preferred. It was doubtless someone like him who had seen enough of the world to know that 'a peck is not the same as a kiss'.[164] A contemporary of Cú Chuimne's glossed 2 Cor. 12: 7, 'datus est mihi stimulus carnis meae (angelus Satanae)' with the comment: 'headache.'[165] That morning-after feeling seems commoner in these texts than before, though this is doubtless due to the vagaries of transmission; on the other hand, we have not yet reached the irascibility of the ninth century.[166]

Cú Chuimne, for his part, did not idle away all his time in a misspent youth; we have from his pen the poem 'Cantemus in omni die' ('Let us sing every day') in honour of the Virgin Mary, the oldest extant hymn on this theme.[167] It follows in the tradition of Hiberno-Latin versification, along with the poems of the Bangor antiphonary and the collection in the 'Liber hymnorum', and besides its importance for the history of Mariology it demonstrates the continuity of literary form in the Irish schools. Strikingly different, however, is the poem by an unknown Colmán to a confrère of the

---

[160] See Aidan Breen, 'Some seventh-century Hiberno-Latin texts and their relationships' in *Peritia*, iii (1984), pp 204–14.

[161] 'Teophilus episcopus dicit ad senes: Probate quod dicitis'; Wasserschleben, *Kanonensammlung*, p. 68 (xxi, 17).

[162] See the discussion in Hillgarth, 'Visigothic Spain' (n. 147 above).

[163] Old Irish text in Annals of Ulster, *s.a.* 747; the brilliant translation is by John V. Kelleher, *Too small for stovewood, too big for kindling* (Dublin, 1979), p. 12.

[164] *Thes. Pal.*, ii, 100: 'sain póc 7 pócnat.'

[165] Ibid., i, 616.

[166] Below, pp 394–5.

[167] 'It is considered to be the finest example extant of Hiberno-Latin versification', Kenney, *Sources*, p. 270, citing the relevant literature. See also Howlett, 'Five experiments in textual reconstruction and analysis' in *Peritia*, ix (1995), pp 1–50: 19–30.

same name, wishing him a safe journey home to Ireland.[168] This is a veritable
cento of lines from Virgil, skilfully wrought and touching as well.[169] It is one
of the earliest texts we have that bear witness to a genuine knowledge of the
classics and not just the hand-me-down tags of the grammarians. Earlier in
the eighth century Cellanus, Irish abbot of Péronne in Picardy and pen-
friend of the English scholar Aldhelm,[170] knew enough of Virgil's panegyric
verses to be able to model his own in honour of St Patrick on the earlier
work. He had the verses (and others, possibly also of his own composition)[171]
inscribed on the walls of a basilica at Péronne dedicated to Patrick. From
about the same period come the verses penned by the scribe (probably Irish)
of the Augsburg (formerly Harburg/Maihingen) Gospels in honour of Laurentius, scribe and companion of Willibrord at Echternach.[172] His colleague
and fellow-scribe Vergilius has also left us some stray verses.[173]

The traditional subjects of the curriculum were still being taught, of
course. From the eighth century, probably, are the commentary on the four
gospels of Pseudo-Jerome and the Würzburg commentary on Matthew.[174]
Moreover, the bilingualism of the Irish schools is best illustrated from this
period by the famous Würzburg codex with glossed letters of St Paul.[175] The
Latin text is very heavily glossed and commented on in the margin, in both
Irish and Latin, and reference is made to a wide variety of secondary authors,
including Pelagius (over 1,300 times). The glossators clearly knew their
grammar[176] and their computus as well.[177] Other Irish manuscripts of the
period preserve Latin and Old Irish glosses on Bede's computistical tracts,[178]

[168] Kuno Meyer 'Colman's farewell to Colman' in *Ériu*, iii (1907), pp 186–9; see Fidel Rädle, *Die Iren*, i, 465–7.
[169] 'So, in this charming way, the poem proceeds, gathering Virgilian flowers and breathing Virgilian fragrance' (F. J. E. Raby, 'Some notes on Virgil, mainly in English authors, in the middle ages' in *Studi Medievali*, v (1932), pp 359–71: 262).
[170] A letter of his to Aldhelm survives and is edited by James Ussher in *Sylloge*, 35–7, no. XII. See now Howlett, 'Insular Latin writers' rhythms' in *Peritia*, xi (1997), pp 53–116: 82–4.
[171] See Ludwig Traube, 'Perrona Scottorum, ein Beitrag zur Überlieferungsgeschichte und zur Palaeographie des Mittelalters' in *Sitzungsber. d. Bay. Akad. d. Wiss., philos-hist. Kl.* (Munich, 1900), pp 469–537; reprinted in Samuel Brandt (ed.), *Vorlesungen und Abhandlungen*, iii: *Kleine Schriften* (Munich, 1920), pp 95–119: 105–9; see also Michael Lapidge, 'Some remnants of Bede's lost Liber epigrammatum' in *E.H.R.*, xc (1975), pp 798–820: 804–5.
[172] Colour microfiche facsimile in Dáibhí Ó Cróinín (ed.), *Evangeliarium Epternacense (Universitätsbibliothek Augsburg, Cod. I. 2. 4° 2)* (Munich, 1988).
[173] E. A. Lowe, *Codices Latini antiquiores* (11 vols. Oxford, 1934–66), v.
[174] Bischoff, 'Wendepunkte', nos 11a and 22. For others of this date see *Mitt. St.*, i, 223 and further below.
[175] Ludwig Chr. Stern (ed.), *Epistolae beati Pauli glosatae glosa interlineali* (Halle, 1910). The Irish glosses are edited in *Thes. Pal.*, i, 499–712. For a bilingual commentary on Matthew, see James Carney and Ludwig Bieler, 'The Lambeth commentary' in *Ériu*, xxiii (1972), pp 1–55 . Perhaps the best example of all is the 'Vita Tripartita' of St Patrick; see *Trip. life*, ed. Mulchrone.
[176] *Thes. Pal.*, i, 585, gl. 24; p. 508, gl. 21 (quoting Consentius to the effect that the verb *induere* is passive whether it ends in *-o* or in *-r*); also *Thes. Pal.*, ii, 10, gl. 4.
[177] Ibid., i, 625, gll 13–15 (glossing Gal. 4: 10: 'Dies obseruetis, et menses, et tempora, et annos').
[178] Ibid., ii, 10–41.

while one of the largest of all known Hiberno–Latin grammatical collections probably dates from this time as well.[179] Another Würzburg codex preserves a set of vellum slips with glosses and commentary (some in Irish) on the gospel of Matthew, one of which contains a precious record of the computistical curriculum at Bangor, probably in Columbanus's own time.[180] One of the most curious texts of the period is the tract on the Irish monastic cursus, which purports to trace the origins of Irish practices back to St Mark.[181] Most impressive of all, however, is the massive Reference Bible (*c*.800),[182] which attempted to bring together commentaries on all the books of the Old and New Testaments in one volume. The list of sources is indicative of its range: Josephus, Pseudo-Clemens Romanus, Origen, Pseudo-Abdias, Efrem, Gregory of Nazianzen, Eucherius, Ambrose, Jerome, Augustine, Orosius, Sulpicius Severus, John Cassian, Gregory the Great, and Isidore. There is little here that is new, but there are some things that might have raised a flutter in continental circles,[183] for the Irish were still using apocrypha and pseudepigrapha long since lost or forgotten in Europe. But since originality in exegesis was never a virtue much practised in the early middle ages, the Reference Bible is hardly to be faulted on that score. However, things were changing and this massive commentary can be said to mark a turning-point in the history of medieval Latin exegesis.[184] After 800 Irish methods of biblical exposition were to lose favour and Irish scholars in Europe began to feel a harsher wind blowing against their kind of learning. The writing was perhaps already on the wall in the comment of a chronologist at Rome who wrote that 'all are agreed that the Lord will have appeared at the end of 6,000 years, although the Irish don't agree—they who believe themselves to have wisdom but who have lost knowledge'.[185] But the overall view of the Irish was still favourable in the Carolingian period. They figured in all the areas of contemporary scholarship: the court grammarian Clemens, a part at least of whose work still survives;[186] Dicuil, author of a remarkable cosmography, 'De mensura orbis terrarum' ('On the measurement of the earth'), as well as

[179] *Ars anonyma Bernensis*; see Holtz, *Donat*, pp 301–5, 320; Law, *Insular Latin grammarians*, p. 26 (denying Irish authorship).
[180] For the commentary see Bischoff, 'Wendepunkte', no. 22. For the note, see Dáibhí Ó Cróinín, 'Mo-Sinu maccu Min' in *Peritia*, i (1982), pp 281–95; David Howlett, 'Insular Latin writers' rhythms', pp 59–60.
[181] See W. Legg, 'Ratio decursus' in *Miscellanea Ceriani* (Milan, 1910), pp 149–67.
[182] Bischoff, 'Wendepunkte', no. 1.
[183] Bischoff, 'Wendepunkte', *Mitt. St.*, i, 232.
[184] Bischoff's description; and the title of his paper.
[185] Theodor Mommsen (ed.), *Laterculus imperatorum Romanorum Malalianus ad a. DLXXIII* (Berlin, 1884), pp 424–37, at p. 427. See now Jane Stevenson (ed.), *The 'Latercus Malalianus' and the school of Archbishop Theodore* (Cambridge 1997) (but see also the severe critique of this edition by Michael Winterbottom, *Notes and Queries*, new ser., xliii, pt 4 (Dec. 1996), pp 457–9.
[186] Kenney, *Sources*, pp 537–8; Law, 'Malsachanus reconsidered' in *Camb. Med. Celt. Studies*, i (1981), pp 85–9.

several short works on grammar and a computistical treatise in prose and verse that is one of the most interesting of all such texts.[187] The cosmography tells of voyages by Irish monks beyond the northernmost islands of Britain to a region where the sea turned to ice; Irish solitaries were the first to establish Christianity in Iceland, and their adventures may perhaps have provided inspiration for some of the Brendan legends. Though Dicuil is more interesting and original than most writers of his time, it has been remarked by one eminent scholar that his value would have increased a hundredfold had he only put aside the classical authorities like Pliny and Solinus, whose descriptions of natural phenomena he preferred to give rather than his own.[188] His computus, on the other hand, is remarkably original in a field where one does not expect to find such innovation in either content or form. His ideas did not always meet with a welcome response, however, and the Englishman Alcuin for one felt it necessary to complain sourly about the Irish teachers and their 'Egyptian boys'.[189] But Alcuin was mild by comparison with the formidable Visigothic bishop of Orléans, Theodulf. He inveighed against an unfortunate Scot whose offerings in the area of exegesis stretched the Spaniard's patience to the limit.[190] Another court poet— doubtlessa disciple of Theodulf—fired a second broadside across the Irishman's bows, this time conveniently identifying him as one Cadac-Andreas.[191] This anonymous bard poured scorn on all those worst features of Irish pedagogy: a fascination with etymologies (however fanciful) in the three sacred languages, a passion for numerical symbolism and pondering who was the first person to do certain things in the Bible, a pedantic interest in terminology, and so on; all these are mercilessly parodied by the poet. But his request to Charlemagne that the oaf be dismissed from the court seems to have fallen on deaf ears; Cadac was subsequently 'pensioned off' with a bishopric!

He was the exception, though, among Irishmen on the Continent at that time. Men such as Dungal of St Denis and Bobbio, later bishop of Pavia,[192]

---

[187] J. J. Tierney (ed. and trans.), *Dicuili 'Liber de mensura orbis terrae'* (Dublin, 1967). The title was taken over from Pliny's 'Historia naturalis'. On the computus see Mario Esposito, 'An unpublished astronomical treatise by the Irish monk Dicuil' in *R.I.A. Proc.*, xxvi (1907), sect. C, pp 378–445; see also André van de Vyver, 'Dicuil et Micon de Saint-Riquier' in *Revue Belge de Philologie et d'Histoire*, xiv (1935), pp 25–47; Werner Bergmann, 'Dicuil' in Paul Butzer and Dietrich Lohrmann (ed.), *Science in western and eastern civilization in Carolingian times* (Basel, 1993), pp 525–37.
[188] M. L. W. Laistner, *Thought and letters in western Europe*, A.D. 500 to 900 (Ithaca, N.Y., 1966), p. 285.
[189] See Dietrich Lohrmann, 'Alcuins Korrespondenz mit Karl dem Groaen über Kalender und Astronomie' in Butzer & Lohrmann, *Science*, pp 79–114: 90.
[190] Bernhard Bischoff, 'Theodulf und der Ire Cadac-Andreas' in *Mitt. St.*, ii, 19–25.
[191] Bischoff, *Mitt. St.*, ii, 21.
[192] See Mirella Ferrari, 'In Papia conveniant ad Dungalum' in *Italia Medioevale e Umanistica*, xv (1972), pp 1–52; Claudio Leonardi, 'Gli irlandesi in Italia: Dungal e la controversia iconoclastica' in Löwe, *Die Iren*, ii, 746–57.

and Donatus of Fiesole,[193] Clemens, and Duncaht[194] all enjoyed good reputations as scholars. Indeed such was the fame of the Irish for learning that one poor pilgrim, passing through Laon on his return from Rome, was forced to couch his plea for shoes and sustenance in the most abject terms of apology, for he was, he said, no grammarian.[195] On the other hand, the 'Anglo-Saxon Chronicle' reports the arrival in Britain in the year 891 of three Irishmen, Dubsláine, Mac Bethad, and Maél Inmuin, on the Wessex coast in a currach. They had set out to sea without oar or rudder, following wherever the Lord's will would take them. When they landed they headed directly for Alfred the Great's court.[196] They were doubtless of the same kind as the Irish group that landed on the coast of Gaul and took themselves off to the local market, there to announce (like Oscar Wilde) that they had nothing to declare but their genius.[197]

There were many other such wandering Irish scholars, but not all of them joined the 'brain drain'. Alcuin wrote to one Colcu, a teacher perhaps at Clonmacnoise, singing the praises of his student Joseph[198] (a eulogy he hardly deserved, according to one modern scholar, though the most recent research suggests otherwise).[199] We have another letter home from a group of men who left for Europe and, travelling via Wales, were entertained on the way by King Merfyn Frych (d. 844). At Merfyn's court they were met, however, by a strange reception: another Irishman who had gone before them, Dubthach by name, had left behind him a riddling text, which he urged the king to use as a test of any would-be scholar's worth.[200] The Irish group (Caínchobrach, Fergus, Dominnach, and Suadbar), undaunted by their countryman's cunning challenge, referred to their computistical manual (which, of course, they had brought with them) and promptly decoded the message: 'Conchenn salutes Merfyn the king!' Warning was sent back to their teacher Colgu, and direction given to coach any future travellers in the

---

[193] His 'Vita metrica Brigitae' is edited by Noel Kissane in *R.I.A. Proc.*, lxxvii (1977), sect. C, pp 57–192. In the metrical farewell that he addressed to his brothers before his death (*Acta SS*, 9 Oct., p. 661) he quoted the famous line from Virgil's fourth eclogue: 'Qui sancto nostras mundane baptismate culpas/*Iam noua progenies celo dimittitur alto*, / Noxia qui uetiti dissoluit prandia poni.' The borrowing might be at second hand, though, from Pseudo-Augustine's 'Sermo de natale domini', *P.L.*, xlii, col. 1123 ff.

[194] See Kenney, *Sources*, pp 573–4.

[195] 'Non sum grammaticus neque sermone Latino peritus'; see Kenney, *Sources*, p. 601.

[196] See the English translation in Simon Keynes and Michael Lapidge, *Alfred the Great* (Harmondsworth, 1982), pp 113–14.

[197] See Lewis Thorpe (trans.), *Einhard and Notker the Stammerer: two Lives of Charlemagne* (Harmondsworth, 1969), pp 93–4 (Notker, i, 1).

[198] Kenney, *Sources*.

[199] See Joseph F. Kelly, 'The originality of Josephus Scottus's commentary on Isaiah' in *Manuscripta*, xxiv (1980), pp 176–80. For an example of the pyrotechnics of which he was capable, see D. R. Howlett, *British books in biblical style* (Dublin, 1996).

[200] Dáibhí Ó Cróinín, 'The Irish as mediators of antique culture on the continent' in Butzer & Lohrmann, *Science*, pp 41–52.

intricacies of computus. These four were doubtless able men, but above all else the quality of their generation of Irish scholars in Europe is the best proof that good instruction was still to be had at home.

The ninth century is, of course, the age of Sedulius and Iohannes Scottus, the high point of achievement and reputation in Hiberno-Latin scholarship. But there were others. It is curious, therefore, that some recent writing has seemed to suggest that the Irish exported all their best teachers and went to seed at home; and furthermore, that the continental Irish learned all they knew abroad.[201] Louis Holtz, however, has brilliantly demonstrated how one of these *peregrini*, a man who modestly styled himself Murethach *doctissimus plebis* ('most learned of the people'), lies behind three generations of grammatical and biblical study at Auxerre, and how he in fact introduced the techniques of textual analysis that were once thought to be the hallmark of the later (eleventh- and twelfth-century) scholastic period.[202] His compatriots in the Carolingian and post-Carolingian period were hardly less important. A close study of their sources has shown that Sedulius, Murethach, and another anonymous Irish grammarian of the time all used the same underlying text of Donatus whose uniquely Irish format had been established already before their departure from Ireland.[203] Far from being the products of a 'nebulous Hiberno-Latin grammatical tradition',[204] these men and their writings bear clear witness to the lengthy period of development that had fashioned the Irish schools. Unfortunately, we do not know whence these great scholars came. The supposed Kildare origin of Sedulius and his circle has little or nothing in the way of evidence to support it.[205] On the other hand, there is clear implication, in a poem added in the margin of a ninth-century Augustine manuscript once on Reichenau,[206] that another member of this group, *magister* Fergus, belonged to Clonard, for he is lauded there as one of the three pillars of that monastery along with its founder Finnian and the illustrious seventh-century scholar Ailerán. The poem is interesting also in that it is based on Lucan's 'Pharsalia', which it quotes verbatim.[207] It is a pity, in the circumstances, that Fergus should be the man whose work we know least

---

[201] See the wryly pertinent title of Louis Holtz's paper, 'Les grammairiens Hiberno-Latins, étaient-ils des Anglo-Saxons?' in *Peritia*, ii (1983), pp 170–84.

[202] 'Grammairiens irlandais au temps de Jean Scot, quelques aspects de leur pédagogie' in *Jean Scot Érigène et l'histoire de la philosophie* (Paris, 1977), pp 69–78; see also Louis Holtz (ed.), *Murethach (Muridac), Ars grammatica* (Turnhout, 1977).

[203] Holtz, 'Grammairiens irlandais', p. 71.

[204] The verdict of Vivien Law (*Insular Latin grammarians*, p. 74).

[205] The only statement of any length in favour of the Kildare localisation is Robin Flower, *The Irish tradition* (Oxford, 1978), pp 38–9. A Clonard provenance appears preferable.

[206] 'Felix famosus Heleranus, Finnia, Fergi'; Karl Strecker (ed.), *M.G.H., Poet. lat. aev. carol.*, iv, pt iii (Berlin, 1896), p. 1124.

[207] 'Unde uenit Tytan et nox ubi sidera condit / Quoque dies medius flagrantibus aestuat horis.' There is, however, the possibility (pointed out to me by J. F. Killeen) that this knowledge was secondhand, from a commentary like that in Hermann Usener (ed.), *M. Annaei Lucani commenta Bernensia* (Leipzig, 1869), p. 11 (on 'Pharsalia', i, 15–16).

about.[208] He is one of a host of characters who flit across the ninth-century stage in walk-on parts, before disappearing again without a trace.

The Irish group at the court of Merfyn Frych in Wales is one of the most interesting, for their footsteps can be traced right across Europe. The Dubthach who set them the riddle went one better, it seems, for he penned a computistical poem in a Leiden manuscript of Priscian's grammar, in which he calculated the time of writing as precisely 3 o'clock, 14 April 838—a Thursday.[209] It may be the same Dubthach who is mentioned in the Annals of Ulster for 869: 'Dubthach mac Maél Tuile, doctissimus Latinorum totius Europae, in Christo dormiuit' ('D., most learned Latinist in all Europe, rested in Christ'). His combination of computus and grammar would have provoked no comment from contemporaries; the four Irish scholars Caíncho-brac, Dominnach, Fergus, and Suadbar—whom we met before when they wrote back to their teacher warning of the pitfalls that faced Irish travellers through Wales—combined the same disciplines, and their names recur time and again in the margins of manuscripts from the 'circle of Sedulius': bilingual Latin-Greek psalters, the poems of Horace, Priscian's grammar in Karlsruhe, Leyden, and St Gallen, and several others.[210] One of these perhaps is the author of the earliest known Irish 'aisling' or vision poem, which survives in a single, acephalous copy;[211] it and the poem by Donatus of Fiesole that begins 'Finibus occiduis describitur optima tellus' are Hiberno-Latin precursors of the genre that, in the Irish language, was to become such a characteristic form of expression for Irish political aspirations in the seventeenth century.

Sedulius (who probably adopted a Roman name in place of his native one, Suadbar) by his own admission liked nothing more than to read and teach.[212] But he knew how to enjoy himself as well and was not averse to prodding his patron, Bishop Hartgar of Liège, whenever the drink ran out.[213] The verses he composed mourning the loss of a ram, promised to him by Hartgar but cut short in life by a pack of dogs, are among the cleverest things ever

---

[208] For a summary of what is known about him see Bischoff, *Mitt. St.*, ii, 267.

[209] Ludwig Traube (ed), *M.G.H., Poet. lat. aev. carol.*, iii (Berlin, 1896), p. 685; see Bartholomew MacCarthy, *The codex Palatino-Vaticanus no. 830* (Dublin, 1892), p. 351.

[210] For the importance of the bilingual Greek–Latin biblical manuscripts associated with this Irish circle, see Bruce Metzger, *The text of the New Testament* (Oxford, 1973).

[211] Traube (ed.), *M.G.H., Poet. lat. aev. carol.*, iii (Berlin, 1896), pp 238-40. The poem by Donatus of Fiesole that begins 'Finibus occiduis describitur optima tellus' was rendered into Irish by Aogán Ó Rathaille as 'Inis fá réim i gcéin san iarthar tá'; see P. S. Dinneen and T. O'Donoghue (ed.), *Dánta Aodhagáin Uí Rathaille* (London, 1909 [1911]), p. 34. The editors doubt Aogán's authorship, though hardly with adequate reason.

[212] 'Aut lego uel scribo, doceo scrutorue sophiam'; cf. Bede, *Ecc. hist.*, Epil. (Plummer, i, 357): 'semper aut discere, aut docere, aut scribere dulce habui.' On Sedulius in general see Reinhard Düchting, *Sedulius Scottus, seine Dichtung* (Munich, 1968) and Kenney, *Sources*, pp 553-69.

[213] There is an English translation (by James Carney) in Ludwig Bieler, *Ireland, harbinger of the middle ages* (London, 1963), p. 124.

written.[214] The range of scholarship, however, is what marks out Sedulius:
he produced a grammar, a *collectaneum* of rare Greek and Latin works, and a
commentary on Matthew, as well as several glittering verses. Besides these,
and an interest in Greek and the Greek Bible, he also wrote 'De rectoribus
Christianis', a 'mirror of princes'; all in all, a formidable achievement. Small
wonder, therefore, that after that scholars find themselves at a loss to adequately describe Johannes Scottus Eriugena ('Irish-born'). The towering
intellect of the early middle ages, John burst upon the European scene like a
comet and disappeared again 'trailing clouds of glory', never to be heard of
again. Of his early background and associations we know nothing, and his
first appearance came unannounced. The circumstances arose out of the
troubled fortunes of Gottschalk, friend of Walafrid Strabo and reluctant
monk of Fulda, 'condemned for life to the order of St Benedict'.[215]
Gottschalk sought the only means of escape open to him, in his books, and
the result was a theory of predestination that pushed Augustine's interpretation to its logical limits: he boldly claimed that men were predestined not
only to good but to evil as well. In the ensuing uproar scholars across Europe
took sides, some for, some against. Faced with the prospect of victory for
heterodoxy, Archbishop Hincmar of Reims called in the heavy artillery, and
John the Scot was commissioned to refute the errant Gottschalk's heresies.
The result was a Pyrrhic victory: John came up with the idea (borrowed from
Greek neo-Platonic philosophy) of the non-existence of evil. For the orthodox bishops—to whom Gottschalk was proof enough of its existence—John's
treatise 'De praedestinatione' was a dangerous boomerang, and John himself
now became the subject of vilification almost equal to that of Gottschalk.
Prudentius of Troyes jeered in mock awe at this wonder from the west,
before whose coming nothing was clear but who now had set them all
aright.[216] John however seems to have survived the battle with only minor
scars—though his patron may have wondered about his continued usefulness. There followed a series of writings, a commentary on Luke, poems in
Greek and Latin,[217] a commentary on Martianus Capella and extracts from
Macrobius, as well as the great 'Periphyseon' ('On the nature of things'),[218] a
startling philosophical tract on the nature of creation that marked a radical
and unprecedented departure from all previous exegetical thinking in the
west. Like Sedulius though, John could also find time for less strenuous

[214] See James Carney, *Medieval Irish lyrics* (Dublin, 1967), pp 53–5.
[215] There is an evocative account in Helen Waddell, *The wandering scholars* (London, 1927),
pp 55–8.
[216] The standard account of John the Scot is Maieul Cappuyns, *Jean Scot Érigène: sa vie, son
oeuvre, sa pensée* (Louvain, 1933). See also Dermot Moran, *The philosophy of John Scottus
Eriugena: a study of idealism in the middle ages* (Cambridge, 1989).
[217] Michael Herren (ed. and trans.), *Iohannis Scotti Eriugenae carmina* (Dublin, 1993).
[218] Edited by I. P. Sheldon-Williams, *Iohannis Scotti Eriugenae Periphyseon (De diuisione
naturae)* (Dublin, 1968–  ).

pursuits; he is credited with having coined one of the best drinking jokes of the middle age while seated across the table from Charles the Bald, who seems to have been rash enough to engage in a drinking bout with the Irishman. The king asked blandly what was there between a sot and a Scot, to which John replied: 'The table.'[219] One manuscript catalogue even claims for him an interest in dogs and ascribes to him a work 'De compoto et natura canum' ('On reckoning, and on the nature of dogs').[220] Modern scholars have alluded learnedly to the touching picture of Odysseus, returned from his wanderings and recognised only by his faithful dog Argos (who promptly expired). But alas! Though John was not the first Irishman to evince an interest in man's best friend (and certainly not the last), he must be denied this frugal pleasure; his dogs (like those of St Patrick before him) must be put down, though in the gentlest manner possible: textual emendation. The catalogued work (if it really was by John) must surely have been 'De compoto et de nature *rerum*'. His computistical skill is evident from some remarks on the paschal cycle in his commentary on the 'De nuptiis Philologiae et Mercurii' of Martianus Capella, and such an interest in the calendar would fit well with the picture of Irish scholarship that we have from other sources. For we know that Martin Hiberniensis, friend of John's and teacher at the cathedral school of Laon, glossed Bede's computistical works heavily and with the practised hand of one who knew the subject well.[221] We have also the evidence of the Karlsruhe codex of Bede's tract 'On time', copiously glossed in Latin and Old Irish, and (according to its editor) the best surviving copy of that work.[222] John was himself compiler of a bilingual biblical glossary with a few difficult words given their Irish equivalents—doubtless as a helpmate for his students.[223] His pupils seem to have found him inspiring, for his name is mentioned seventy-seven times in the margins of the Berne codex of Horace.[224] He is mentioned in another work as the authority for a particular pronunciation of a Latin word,[225] and the Karlsruhe Priscian has a gloss on the text 'nisi si dicamus helenismo usum esse poetam' that says 'ón

---

[219] 'Quid distat inter sottum et Scottum? Tabula tantum' (Kenney, *Sources*, p. 589). An American scholar rather spoiled the fun by 'proving' that John never in fact used the phrase 'Quid distat inter', but always 'Quid inter est inter'!

[220] Becker, p. 68, no. 192: 'Iohannes Scottus de compoto et nature canum'; even so careful a scholar as Traube took the reference seriously (see *M.G.H., Poet. lat. aev. carol.*, iii, 757.

[221] See the fine study by John J. Contreni, *The cathedral school of Laon, its manuscripts and masters* (Munich, 1978), pp 126–8; C. W. Jones, 'Bede in medieval schools' in G. Bonner (ed.), *Famulus Christi* (London, 1976), pp 261–85.

[222] C. W. Jones, *Bedae opera de temporibus*, p. 146. See now Stephen B. Killion, 'The Old-Irish and Hiberno-Latin glosses on Bede's *De temporum ratione*' (forthcoming).

[223] See now John Contreni and Pádraig Ó Néill (ed. and trans.), *Glossae divinae historiae: the biblical glosses of John Scottus Eriugena* (Florence, 1997).

[224] John J. Contreni, 'The Irish in the western Carolingian empire (according to James F. Kenney and Bern, Burgerbibliothek, 363)' in Löwe, *Die Iren*, ii, 758–98: 769.

[225] *Thes. Pal.*, ii, 227.

nGrécdacht de libro Greco Iohannis';[226] what John's 'Greek book' was we do not, unfortunately, know. He may have penned a life of the poet Virgil[227] and maybe also some verses dedicatory for a chapel of Charles the Bald.[228]

All in all, though, despite his formidable intellectual powers, John comes across as a maddeningly enigmatic figure; despite having left so much in the way of literary achievement and despite the fame he obviously enjoyed in his lifetime, we know nothing about him, not even the date of his death. Perhaps soured by his experiences in the Gottschalk affair, he seems to have fallen out eventually with his patron Hincmar. He is credited with a biting epitaph on the archbishop that marked Hincmar's supposed departure from this life:

> Here lies Hincmar, a vicious and avaricious thief—
> The only noble thing he did was to die.[229]

John's own end is recorded by William of Malmesbury, and is doubtless apocryphal. William says that John was stabbed to death by his pupils with their metal styluses 'because he forced them to think'![230] After his departure the Irish star inevitably began to wane in the firmament of European scholarship. It was too much to expect that John's genius could be excelled, or even matched, and the history of Hiberno-Latin learning in subsequent years is less impressive.

The tenth century knows only a few Irish names of note, the best-known perhaps being Israel Scottus, one-time teacher and confidant of Archbishop Bruno of Cologne, brother to the emperor Otto the Great. Recent research has shown that Israel too taught Latin grammar in the time-honoured tradition of Irishmen abroad.[231] Édouard Jeauneau also discovered two new tracts by him, 'De anima' and 'De trinitate'.[232] Is he perhaps the same Israel whose name is associated with the fascinating board-game *alea evangelii* ('Gospel dice') in Oxford? This tenth-century 'Monopoly' seems to have been devised

---

[226] Ibid.

[227] See *Vita Gudiana I* in J. Brummer (ed.), *Vitae Virgilianae* (Leipzig, 1912), p. 62: 'set Iohannes Scottus has breuiter scripsit periochas dicens . . .'; see Brummer, 'Zur Überlieferungsgeschichte der sogenannten Donatischen Vita des Virgil' in *Philologus*, lxxii (1913), pp 289, 297.

[228] See Paul Dutton and Édouard Jeauneau, 'The verses of the Codex Aureus of Saint-Emmeram' in *Studi Medievali*, 3rd ser., xxiv, no. 1 (1983), pp 75–120.

[229] 'Hic iacet Hincmarus, cleptes uehementer auarus; / hoc solum nobile gessit, quod periit' (Kenney, *Sources*, p. 587).

[230] Prudentius tells the same story of Cassianus of Immola, who was likewise stabbed by his students.

[231] Colette Jeudy, 'Israël le grammairien et la tradition manuscrite du commentaire de Rémi d'Auxerre à l'*Ars minor* de Donat' in *Studi Medievali*, 3rd ser., xviii, no. 2 (1977), pp 187–248. For arguments in favour of a British (rather than Irish) origin for Israel, see Michael Lapidge, 'Israel the grammarian in Anglo-Saxon England' in Haijo Westra (ed.), *From Athens to Chartres: neoplatonism in medieval thought* (Leiden, 1992), pp 97–114.

[232] Édouard Jeauneau, 'Pour le dossier d'Israël Scot' in *Archives d'histoire doctrinale et littérature du moyen âge*, xxxiv, pt 5 (1986), pp 7–71.

with a view to teaching students how to master the Eusebian canon tables, or concordance to the gospels. It is a great pity that the playing instructions have not been preserved, but the layout of the pieces and some of the game's terminology have been faithfully copied, together with a note that says it was learned at the court of King Æthelstan of Wessex (924/5–939) by Dub Innse, bishop of Bangor (d. 953). He acquired the rules from a certain Frank and 'a learned Roman, i.e. Israel'.[233] Irish connections with Athelstan's court are known from other references,[234] so the presence of Israel there at some time should not be ruled out. He has been proposed also as the possible author of the 'Navigatio Brendani',[235] though it must be said that little solid evidence exists that would support the notion. There is, on the other hand, no doubting the success of that work; it took on the stature almost of a European epic and enjoys an undying popularity to this day.

Not till the end of the eleventh century do we encounter any other Hiberno-Latin writers of note. Perhaps the best-known is Marianus Scottus of Mainz, who was banished from his monastery of Moville, County Down, and spent the remainder of his years in Germany.[236] His chronicle of world history is one of the most important examples of a genre popular at that time and was very influential among both continental and English writers.[237] Marianus did not accept the Venerable Bede's calculation of the mundane era for Christ's advent, and composed an elaborate treatise in which he proposed his own date for the event. The chronicle thus follows closely in the long-established Irish tradition of computistical studies, and indeed Marianus preserves good recensions of some of the very early Irish pseudonymous tracts on the subject.[238] The bilingualism of the Irish tradition is also evidenced by the many Irish verses added in the margins of his autograph.[239] His namesake and contemporary Marianus of Ratisbon (in Bavaria) had the

---

[233] 'Alea euangelii quam Dubinsi episcopus Bennchorensis detulit a rege Anglorum, id est a domu Adalstani regis Anglorum, depicta a quodam Francone et a Romano sapiente, id est Israel', Corpus Christi College MS 122 (written at Bangor, Co. Down, some time after 1140). There is a facsimile in *Facs nat. MSS Ire.*, ii, pl. xlvii; cf. Kenney, *Sources*, p. 647.

[234] See Michael Lapidge, 'Some Latin poems as evidence for the reign of Æthelstan' in *Anglo-Saxon England*, ix (1981), pp 61–98. See, in general, J. Armitage Robinson, *The times of Saint Dunstan* (Oxford, 1923) and R. W. Runt (ed.), *Saint Dunstan's 'classbook' from Glastonbury (Oxford, Bodleian Library, MS Auct.F.4/32)* (Leyden, 1961). The codex bristles with Irish texts and symptoms.

[235] Carl Selmer, 'Israel, ein unbekannter Schotte des 10. Jahrhunderts' in *Studien u. Mitteilungen z. Gesch. d. Benediktinerordens*, lxii (1950), pp 69–86. See also his edition of the work, *Navigatio Sancti Brendani abbatis* (Notre Dame, 1956).

[236] Bartholomew Mac Carthy, *Codex Palatino-Vaticanus*, pp 3–7.

[237] Anna Dorothee von den Brinken, 'Marianus Scottus. Unter besonderer Berücksichtigung der nicht veröffentlichten Teile seiner Chronik' in *Deutsches Archiv*, xvii (1961), pp 191–238; Max Manitius, *Geschichte d. lat. Lit. d. M.A.*, ii (Munich, 1923), pp 388–94.

[238] Not all of them identified by Von den Brinken.

[239] Mac Carthy, *Codex Palatino-Vaticanus*, pp 20–28. See also Brian Ó Cuív, 'The Irish marginalia in Codex Palatino-Vaticanus No. 830' in *Éigse*, xxiv (1990), pp 45–67.

Irish name of Muredach Mac Robartaig and came probably of Donegal stock. With two companions, Iohannes and Candidus, he set out on pilgrimage to Rome in 1067, but on their way they were persuaded by another Irishman, Murchertach, to remain permanently at Ratisbon. Marianus's biography gives a very detailed and valuable picture of Irish–German connections at the time, and the Bavarian Schottenklöster were to remain important till the sixteenth century.[240] The *Vita* extols Marianus's scribal and scholastic skills, and we have still a glossed copy of the Pauline epistles from his hand.[241] The accompanying commentary is evidence for his wide reading in patristic and medieval exegesis. With the close of the eleventh century almost the last has been heard of Hiberno-Latin scholarship in Europe. Some evidence from native manuscripts indicates that the traditional subjects were still being taught and studied: Glendalough fragments of Clemens Scottus's 'Ars grammatica' and of Bede's 'De temporibus',[242] together with versions of John the Scot's 'Periphyseon' (possibly from the County Louth area),[243] and a copy of the 'De ratione metrorum' of Lupus of Ferrières.[244] But whereas it was for a long time believed to be the case that no trace of any influence whatever from the schools of scholastic theology in France is to be found in Ireland, nor of the ideas that were emerging from the writings of Peter Abelard and his contemporaries, recent discoveries have changed that picture. The glosses of Bernard of Chartres on Plato were recently discovered in a sensational find by Paul Edward Dutton, in the same manuscript with the Periphyseon texts just mentioned.[245] On the other hand, the gospel commentary of Maél Brigte Ua Maéluanaig (d. 1138) has recently been shown to derive entirely from the earlier Irish exegetical tradition, combining patristic and seventh-century Hiberno-Latin commentary material only; no sources later than Bede seem to have been used.[246] Similarly, the tract 'De statu ecclesiae' by Bishop Gilli Brigte (Gilbertus) of Limerick (*c*.1111), far from being a contemporary blueprint for structural reform in the Irish church, in fact derives almost entirely from earlier Frankish models.[247] Another recent study has shown that at least one of the Irish saints' Lives from the twelfth century may be the work of a

---

[240] See Pádraig A. Breatnach (ed.), *Libellus de fundacione ecclesiae consecrati Petri. Die Regensburger Schottenlegende* (Munich, 1977).

[241] Ibid., pp 618–19.

[242] Bernhard Bischoff and Ludwig Bieler, 'Fragmente zweier mittelalterlichen Schulbücher aus Glendalough' in *Celtica*, iii (1955), pp 216–20.

[243] I. P. Sheldon-Williams, 'An epitome of Irish provenance of Eriugena's *De diuisione naturae*' in *R.I.A. Proc.*, lviii, sect. C (1956), pp 1–20.

[244] Hans P. A. Oskamp, 'A schoolteacher's hand in a Florentine manuscript' in *Scriptorium*, xxxi (1977), pp 191–7.

[245] Paul Edward Dutton, 'The uncovering of the *Glosae super Platonem* of Bernard of Chartres' in *Medieval Studies*, xlvi (1984), pp 192–221.

[246] Jean Rittmueller, 'The Gospel commentary of Maél Brigte Ua Maél-uanaig and its Hiberno-Latin background' in *Peritia*, ii (1983), pp 185–214.

[247] Kenney, *Sources*, pp 763–4.

returned exile, a man who had been through the continental schools and who liked to show it.[248] But all in all, the twelfth century was a sad end to a once great and vibrant tradition. The 'crowded hour of glorious life' that was Irish scholarship in Europe during the second half of the ninth century was now 'an age without a name'. The likes of Sedulius and Iohannes Scottus were not to be seen again.

[248] Donnchadh Ó Corráin, 'Foreign connections and domestic politics: Killaloe and the Uí Briain in twelfth-century hagiography' in Whitelock, McKitterick, & Dumville, *Ire. in early med. Europe*, pp 213–31.

# CHAPTER XII

# 'What was best of every language': the early history of the Irish language

PAUL RUSSELL

TEN years after the dispersal of the languages from the Tower of Babel (Nimrod's Tower), Fénius Farsaid was asked by the school in Egypt to abstract a language from the many languages then in existence. That language was assigned to Goídel mac Aingin meic Glúinfind meic Láimfind meic Agnumain of the Greeks and was thus called *Goídelc* 'Irish'. It was constructed in the following way: *a mba ferr íarum do cach bérlu ⁊ a mba leithiu ⁊ a mba caímu, is ed do·repedh isin nGoídilc* 'then what was best of every language and what was widest and finest was cut out into Irish';[1] Irish was, therefore, sometimes called the *bérla tóbaide* (or *bérla teipide*) 'the selected language' (lit. 'the cut out language').[2] Thus, the 'Auraicept na nÉces' ('The poets' primer'), the central core of which dates from perhaps the late seventh century,[3] sees Irish as arising from a deliberate selection of all the best features of other languages. It may not be the language of Paradise but it comes a close second. A slightly different version of events is preserved in the 'Lebor Gabála Érenn' ('Book of Invasions'), compiled in the eleventh century: Goídel Glas, the son of Scotta, daughter of the Pharaoh (hence the Gaels are also known as Scots), created *Goídelc* from the seventy-two languages dispersed from the tower of Babel.[4] While the 'Lebor Gabála'

---

[1] Anders Ahlqvist (ed. & trans.), *The early Irish linguist: an edition of the canonical part of Auraicept na n-Éces* (Helsinki, 1983), p. 48 (§ 1, 13); George Calder (ed. & trans.), *Auraicept na n-Éces* (Edinburgh, 1917) p. 80 (lines 1053–5) = p. 225 (ll 4008–11).

[2] See Damian McManus, *A guide to ogam* (Maynooth, 1991), pp 148–9; Calvert Watkins, 'Language of gods and language of men: remarks on some Indo-European metalinguistic traditions' in Jan Puhvel (ed.), *Myth and law among the Indo-Europeans* (Berkeley, 1970), pp 1–17: 12; Victor Kalyguine, *La langue de la poésie irlandaise archaïque* (Hamburg, 1993), pp 73–4.

[3] Ahlqvist, *Early Irish linguist*, p. 36.

[4] For the text, see R. A. S. Macalister (ed. & trans.), *Lebor Gabála Érenn* (5 vols, Dublin, 1938–56), ii, 12–13 (§ 107). For a translation, see John Koch and John Carey (ed.), *The Celtic heroic age: literary sources for ancient Celtic Europe and early Ireland and Wales* (3rd ed., Oakville,

tradition is primarily concerned with tracing the Irish back to a single ancestor, the 'Auraicept' sees language as the crucial bond, and one particular
language at that, namely Irish. The aim of the work is to raise Irish to the
same level as the *tres linguae sacrae* of Latin, Greek, and Hebrew, and to
show that it had a structure of at least the same level as Latin. One important
step in that enterprise was to show that Irish was a language created by
choice and that it was not a product of the pride of Babel; hence, probably
the earliest documented case of language-planning.

A consequence of such a view is that it precluded identification of genetic
links between Irish and other languages, and *a fortiori* between Irish and
other Celtic languages; as far as the early Irish were concerned, other languages were merely products of Babel. The Irish and their language
were descended from Goídel, while the Welsh, according to the 'Historia
Brittonum', traced their descent from either Britto or Brutus, the latter
version deriving perhaps from Isidore.[5] The Irish did nevertheless recognise
the similarities between Irish and British and could come up with rules to
account for systematic correspondences between them, but they tended to
explain them in terms of language contact, borrowing, and 'corruption'
rather than by parallel genetic developments from a common ancestor. This
is particularly clear from the treatment of loanwords in Cormac's Glossary
('Sanas Cormaic'), probably compiled towards the end of the ninth century
in Munster under the auspices of Cormac mac Cuillenáin (d. 908), where
there is no difference in the treatment of British loanwords from that of
words borrowed from Latin, Greek, Hebrew, Old Norse, or even Pictish.[6]

Largely due to the popularity of the 'Lebor Gabála', such a view of the
origins of Irish prevailed throughout the medieval period. It was only with
the renaissance and the growth in knowledge of Greek and Hebrew and other

Conn., and Aberystwyth, 2000), pp 229–30 (§§ 16–18). For a general introduction, see John Carey, *The Irish national origin-legend. Synthetic pseudohistory* (Cambridge, 1994). See also the review by Thomas Charles-Edwards in *Camb. Med. Celt. Studies*, xxxi (summer 1996), pp 89–90.

[5] John Morris (ed.), *Nennius: British history and the Welsh annals* (London and Chichester, 1980), pp 60–63 (§§ 10–18). See also Francis J. Byrne, '*Senchas*: the nature of Gaelic historical tradition' in J. G. Barry (ed.), *Hist. Studies*, ix (Belfast, 1974), pp 137–59; Kim McCone, 'Prehistoric, Old and Middle Irish' in K. McCone and K. Simms (ed.), *Progress in Irish studies* (Maynooth, 1996), pp 7–53: 7–8. Cf. W. M. Lindsay (ed.), *Isidori Hispalensis Episcopi etymolo-giarum sive originum libri xx* (2 vols, Oxford, 1911), IX.ii.102: *Brittones quidam Latine nominatos suspicantur, eo quod bruti sint.*

[6] See Paul Russell, 'Brittonic words in Irish glossaries', in J. F. Eska, R. G. Gruffydd, and N. Jacobs (ed.). *Hispano-Gallo-Brittonica: essays in honour of Professor D. Ellis Evans on the occasion of his sixty-fifth birthday* (Cardiff, 1995), pp 166–82: 169–70; the phrasing of Cormac's Glossary (Kuno Meyer (ed.), 'Sanas Cormaic' in *Anecdota from Irish manuscripts*, iv (Halle, 1912)), § 853 *mid .i. Combrec rotrúaillned and .i. med* 'mid (mead), i.e. Welsh has been corrupted in it, i.e. *med*', may be compared with § 852 *máthair quasi mater, is ed rotrúailned and* '*máthair* (mother) as if *mater*; there has been corruption in it'. Cf. also Thomas Charles-Edwards, 'Language and society among the insular Celts A.D. 400–1000' in Miranda J. Green (ed.), *The Celtic world* (London, 1995), pp 703–36: 710. On Cormac generally, see Paul Russell, 'Sounds of a silence: the growth of Cormac's Glossary' in *Camb. Med. Celt. Studies*, xv (1988), pp 1–30.

further-flung languages that the view began to change. Edward Lhuyd's *Archaeologia Britannica* of 1707 was an important milestone in that it was the first to posit a genetic relationship between the individual Celtic languages, and also between them and the other languages of Europe.[7] The development of the Indo-European hypothesis and its refinement under the Neogrammarians firmly established the Celtic languages within the Indo-European group.[8]

The present essay attempts to give an overview of the Irish language over the time-span covered by the volume. The period in question approximately matches the span of Old and Middle Irish. It is conventional to divide the early history of Irish into the following periods: Primitive Irish (otherwise termed Archaic Irish) from the break-up of insular Celtic up to syncope; Early Old Irish (mid-sixth century to the end of the seventh); Classical Old Irish (eighth and ninth centuries); Middle Irish (tenth to twelfth centuries). This essay begins by considering general issues, such as the names for the language and geographical spread. Then the available sources are discussed along with the various orthographical systems employed to write the language. After a brief overview of the linguistic developments prior to the emergence of an identifiable Irish language, the basic phonological, morphological, and syntactic developments are considered. There is no intention, nor indeed space, to go into great detail; there are now several works available where such details may be sought.[9] The chapter ends with consideration of some important broader issues, such as questions of dialects and register in early Irish.

ACCORDING to the medieval view of the origin of Irish, O.Ir. *Goídelc* (-*ā* f.) (> Mod.Ir. *Gaeilge*, Sc.G. *Gaidhlig*) was so called because of the activities of one Goídel. However, as is often the case in origin legends, horses and carts tend

---

[7] Brinley F. Roberts, 'Edward Lhuyd and Celtic linguistics' in D. E. Evans, J. G. Griffith, and E. M. Jope (ed.), *Proceedings of the Seventh International Congress of Celtic Studies, Oxford 1983* (Oxford, 1986), pp 1–9.

[8] For a useful summary of the historical scholarship, see McCone, 'Prehistoric, Old and Middle Irish', pp 8–18. On the Celtic languages generally, see Paul Russell, *Introduction to the Celtic languages* (London and New York, 1995), and the collections of essays in Martin Ball and James Fife (ed.), *The Celtic languages* (London, 1993), and Donald MacAulay, *The Celtic languages* (Cambridge, 1992); see also Patrick Sims-Williams, 'The Celtic languages' in A. G. and P. Ramat (ed.), *The Indo-European languages* (London and New York, 1998), pp 345–79.

[9] See, for example, Rudolf Thurneysen, *A grammar of Old Irish* (2nd ed., revised and translated by D. A. Binchy and O. J. Bergin; Dublin, 1946); the collection of essays in Kim McCone, Damian McManus, Cathal Ó hÁinle, Nicholas Williams, and Liam Breatnach (ed.). *Stair na Gaeilge in ómós do Phádraig Ó Fiannachta* (Maynooth, 1994), especially Ahlqvist, 'Litriú na Gaeilge', pp 23–59, McCone, 'An tSean-Ghaeilge agus a Réamhstair', pp 61–219, and Breatnach, 'An Mheán-Ghaeilge', pp 221–333; on the phonology of early Irish, see Kim McCone, *Towards a relative chronology of ancient and medieval Celtic sound change* (Maynooth, 1996); on the verb, idem, *The early Irish verb* (2nd ed., revised with index; Maynooth, 1997). See also Gearóid Mac Eoin, 'Irish' in Ball & Fife, *The Celtic languages*, pp 101–44. Cathair Ó Dochartaigh, 'The Irish language' in MacAulay, *The Celtic languages*, pp 11–99.

to become rearranged. Both the term for the language, *Goídelc*, and the term for the people, *Goídel*, were borrowed from British, the modern forms in Welsh being *Gwyddeleg* 'the Irish language' and *Gwyddel* 'an Irishman'.[10] The borrowing must have taken place after the Welsh change of initial /w/- to /gw/-, the date of which is subject to some debate.[11] Within Welsh it is customary to relate the form to the adjective *gŵydd* 'wild', although the suffix *-el* is far from clear.[12] The suffix *-eg* (< *-ikā*) in *Gwyddeleg* is well established in Welsh as the suffix marking names for languages.[13] The Welsh origin of the term was not apparent or known to the compilers of the late Old Irish and Middle Irish glossaries, who either simply related it to the eponymous *Goídel* or analysed it as *guth Elg* 'the voice (of) Ireland', where *Elg* is another term for Ireland.[14] In addition to the common term *Goídelc*, the term *Scoitic* < Latin *Scotticus* (via British Latin /skotig/) is also attested and, in its Latin form *Scot(t)ice*, *Scotica* is regularly found beside *Hibernice* in early Irish glossaries when it is necessary to mark out Irish words from Latin, Greek, or Hebrew ones.[15]

Leaving aside issues of early migrations and movements, whether historical or mythological, in the historical period Irish was spoken not only in Ireland but also in Scotland from the fifth century onwards and for several centuries, between the sixth and ninth, in south-west Wales and the Lleyn peninsula. Linguistic evidence for the former is provided by the continued

[10] See David Greene, *The Irish language* (Dublin, 1966), p. 11; Charles-Edwards, 'Language and society', p. 723; Proinsias Mac Cana, 'Y trefedigaethau Gwyddelig ym Mhrydain' in G. Bowen (ed.), *Y Gwareiddiad Celtaidd* (Llandysul, 1987), pp 153–81: 168–9; Joseph Loth, 'Féni et Góidil' in *Rev. Celt.*, xli (1924), pp 350–52. John Koch has suggested that the avenue of transmission was from Strathclyde to Iona: see John T. Koch, *The Gododdin of Aneirin: text and context from dark-age North Britain* (Cardiff, 1997), p. xxvii (I am grateful to John Koch for allowing me to read a forthcoming paper on these terms). Although the basic idea is probably correct, the details remain unclear, particularly the dating of the loan.

[11] See Kenneth Jackson, *Language and history in early Britain* (Edinburgh, 1953; reprinted Dublin, 1994, with new introduction by William Gillies), pp 389–91; Patrick Sims-Williams, 'The emergence of Old Welsh, Cornish and Breton orthography, 600–800: the evidence of archaic Welsh' in *Bulletin of the Board of Celtic Studies*, xxxviii (1991), pp 20–86: 27, n. 4, 71-2; idem, 'Dating the transition to neo-Brittonic: phonology and history, 400–600' in Alfred Bammesberger and Alfred Wollmann (ed.), *Britain 400–600: language and history* (Heidelberg, 1990), pp 217–61: 222, 234, n. 59; John T. Koch, 'When was Welsh literature first written down?' in *Studia Celt.*, xx–xxi (1985–6), pp 43–66: 46; id. 'Further to Indo-Eurpean *g^{wh} in Celtic', in Eska *et al.*, *Hispano-Gallo-Brittonica*, pp 79–95: 91.

[12] See Eric P. Hamp, '*Goídil, Féni, Gŵynedd*' in *Proc. Harvard Celt. Coll.*, xii (1992), pp 43–50.

[13] See Paul Russell, *Celtic word-formation. The velar suffixes* (Dublin, 1990), pp 66–76. The uncomplimentary nature of the term, based on an adjective 'wild', seems to be reinforced by the use in Welsh of the plural form *Gwyddelod* 'Irishmen', where *-od* is the regular plural suffix used with animal names.

[14] For the *Goídel* analysis, see Whitley Stokes (ed.), 'O'Mulconry's Glossary', in *Archiv für celtische Lexicographie*, i (1900), pp 232–324 (§ 667); for *guth Elg*, see Meyer, 'Sanas Cormaic', § 713.

[15] E.g., Meyer, 'Sanas Cormaic', §§ 206, 850; Stokes, 'O'Mulconry's Glossary', pp 232–324 (§ 860).

presence of speakers of a Goidelic language, Scottish Gaelic, in Scotland and the clear dialectal links between that and northern dialects of Irish.[16] For the latter, the occurrence of a large number of bilingual inscriptions in Latin and Ogam Irish together with the detailed historical evidence leave us in no doubt of a long-term Irish presence.[17] In Ireland itself, Irish was by no means the only language of communication; Latin seems to have been used from the fourth century onwards at the latest and, to judge from the earliest loanwords, as a spoken language, though probably with a British accent.[18] The influx of Welsh ecclesiastics indicates that Welsh was also spoken. Its impact was not just lexical but also affected the morphology of the language;[19] for example, the suffix -(e)óc (and perhaps also -uc) found commonly in ecclesiastical names, and also in common nouns in a lower register of the language, derives from W. -[ɔ:g] which gave M.W. -awc, and Mod.W. -og.[20] Likewise, from the late Old Irish period onwards, Old Norse was spoken at least in the viking centres of Dublin, Limerick, Waterford, etc., and the lexical input into Irish from this contact was considerable.[21] Some indication of the language contact, in the Munster area at least, can be gained by consideration of the loanwords in Cormac's Glossary (late ninth century). Apart from the Latin, Greek, and Hebrew input which derives from learned sources, words are identified as British (*Combrec* or *isin Bretnais*), which may mean Welsh but could refer to one of the other Brittonic languages in particular contexts, as Old Norse (*lingua Galleorum*), as Old English (*Saxanbérla*), and even in one instance as Pictish

[16] On Scottish Gaelic, see William Gillies, 'Scottish Gaelic' in Ball & Fife, *The Celtic languages*, pp 145–227, and Donald MacAulay, 'The Scottish Gaelic language' in MacAulay, *The Celtic languages*, pp 137–248. On the dialect situation, see the references in Russell, *Introduction*, p. 66, n. 8; see in particular Kenneth Jackson, 'Common Gaelic' in *Brit. Acad. Proc.*, xxxvii (1951), pp 71–97; Brendan Ó Buachalla, 'Ní and cha in Ulster Irish' in *Ériu*, xxviii (1977), pp 92–41; Cathair Ó Dochartaigh, 'Cha and ní in the Irish of Ulster' in *Éigse*, xvi (1976), pp 317–36.

[17] See Kuno Meyer, 'The expulsion of the Déssi' in *Y Cymmrodor*, xiv (1901), pp 104–35; Tomás Ó Cathasaigh, 'The Déissi and Dyfed' in *Éigse*, xx (1984), pp 1–33; Melville Richards, 'Irish settlements in south-west Wales: a topographical approach' in *R.S.A.I. Jn.*, xc (1960), pp 133–62; Proinsias Mac Cana, 'Y trefedigaethau Gwyddelig'; Thomas Charles-Edwards, 'Language and society', pp 708–10; idem, *Early Christian Ireland* (Cambridge, 2000), pp 158–63; Myles Dillon, 'The Irish settlements in Wales' in *Celtica*, xii (1977), pp 1–11; Charles Thomas, *And shall these mute stones speak? Post-Roman inscriptions in western Britain* (Cardiff, 1994); Patrick Sims-Williams, *The Celtic inscriptions of Britain: phonology and chronology, c. 400–1200* (Oxford, 2003).

[18] See below, pp 436–8; for a useful collection of evidence, see Jane Stevenson, 'The beginnings of literacy in Ireland' in *R.I.A. Proc.*, lxxxix (1989) sect. C, pp 127–65; Michael Richter, 'The introduction of alphabetic writing to Ireland: implications and consequences' in K. Klar, E. E. Sweetser, and C. Thomas (ed.), *A Celtic florilegium: studies in memory of Brendan Ó Hehir* (Lawrence, Ma. 1996), pp 152–64; T. M. Charles-Edwards, 'The context and uses of literacy in early Christian Ireland' in Huw Pryce (ed.), *Literacy in medieval Celtic societies* (Cambridge, 1998), pp 62–82; see also the other essays in the same volume.

[19] For lexical borrowings, see Russell, 'Brittonic words'.

[20] Russell, *Celtic word-formation*, pp 108–16.

[21] See below, p. 438. For a discussion of Old Norse loanwords in Irish, see Carl Marstrander, *Bidtrag til det Norske sprogs historie i Irland* (Kristiana, 1915).

(*Cruithnech*).[22] Although much of the material in the glossary derives from pre-existing glossary collections, as opposed to direct culling from texts, nevertheless the identification of the languages seems to have been ongoing during the editorial process in that earlier versions of the glossary do not identify all the loanwords.[23]

The evidence for the Irish language before the introduction of Latin-based writing systems into Ireland is naturally sparse, and it would not be surprising if there was none. Despite Ireland's isolation from the civilisations of the Mediterranean basin, the island did figure on Ptolemy's map of the world and was named Ἰουερνία. The names given there seem to be largely coastal landmarks, river- and tribal names; many are obscure but some can be equated with later names, e.g. Βουουίνδα /bu:winda/ corresponding to Old Irish *Boänd* (modern Boyne), Αὐτεινοί /auteinoi/ (or perhaps/o:ti:noi/) to Old Irish *Úaithni*, etc.[24] There is, however, a surprising lack of correspondence between Ptolemy's names and those attested later in Old Irish sources. There may be an element of textual corruption involved in Ptolemy's text, but this discrepancy may also be indicative of substantial tribal movements and changes in the balance of power in the intervening period.

In one of the longer entries in Cormac's Glossary the following tale is recounted of Finn and Lomnae, his fool.[25] While Finn is away, Lomnae discovers that Finn's wife is having an affair with Coirpre. Unwilling to make a direct accusation, he hands the returning Finn a four-sided rod on which an obscure message is written in Ogam. Finn understands the oblique implications and reproaches his wife. But she, realising that it is Lomnae who has betrayed her, arranges for Coirpre to kill him. This is one of a number of references in early Irish literature and law to the use of Ogam on

[22] Meyer, 'Sanas Cormaic', §§ 110, 124, 206, 211, 239, 311, 327, 450, 568, 675, 853, 883, 1157 (British); 138, 523, 739, 1040 (Old Norse); 812, 845 (Old English); 301 (Pictish). See Russell, 'Brittonic words'; on *Combrec*, see also Charles-Edwards, 'Language and society', pp 710–23.
[23] See Paul Russell, '*Dúil Dromma Cetta* and Cormac's Glossary' in *Études Celt.*, xxxii (1996), pp 115–42; idem, 'Brittonic words'.
[24] For a discussion with illustration, see A. L. F. Rivet and C. Smith, *The place-names of Roman Britain* (London, 1979), p. 107; see also O'Rahilly, *Early Ir. hist.*, pp 1–46, which should be used with care. For an edition of the text, see C. Müller and C. T. Fischer (ed.), *Claudii Ptolemaei Geographia*, books i–v (Paris, 1883–1901), ii, 2; K. F. A. Nobbe (ed.), *Claudii Ptolemaei Geographia* (Leipzig, 1966). On Ptolemy, see now the essays in D. N. Parsons and P. Sims-Williams (ed.), *Ptolemy: towards a linguistic analysis of the earliest Celtic place-names of Europe* (Aberystwyth, 2000); especially cf. Gregory Toner, 'Identifying Ptolemy's Irish places and tribes', ibid., pp 73–82; on problems with the editions, see Paul Russell, 'On reading Ptolemy: some methodological considerations', ibid., pp 179–88.
[25] Meyer, 'Sanas Cormaic', § 1018; cf. Myles Dillon, 'Stories from the law-tracts' in *Ériu*, xi (1932), pp 42–65: 48–50; D. A. Binchy (ed.), *Corpus iuris Hibernici* (6 vols, Dublin, 1987), vi, 2230.3–5; see also McManus, *Guide*, pp 158–9, and Thomas Clancy, 'Fools and adultery in some early Irish texts' in *Ériu*, xliv (1993), pp 105–24.

perishable items, usually wood.[26] Indeed, the technical language of Ogam suggests that this may have been the more usual medium: *feda* 'letters' (plural of *fid* 'wood'), *flesc* 'stroke' (lit. 'twig'), etc., though the terminology may have as much to do with the appearance of the script.[27] Predictably, no Ogam inscriptions have survived on perishable materials. Dating from the fifth to sixth centuries, perhaps even from the late fourth, Ogam inscriptions on stone are found in a broad band running across southern Ireland and southern Wales.[28] The majority of the Welsh stones are bilingual Irish (Ogam script) /Latin (Roman script), while the ones from Ireland are simply written in Irish using Ogam. Essentially, the letters of Ogam were lines or notches cut in particular directions in relation to a stem line. On stone inscriptions the stem line was usually the vertical arris of the stone and the signs were incised either side of it starting at the bottom left-hand side and running up, across the top, and down the right-hand side. A corresponding Latin inscription (in Wales) would be on the facing surface. The origin of the system has been much debated over the years, but it is now generally accepted that the distribution of letters in the system derives from the classi-fication of letters found in Latin grammarians of the first to fourth centuries A.D.[29] That said, it was clearly not a slavish copy, since it reflects the sound system of Irish; for example, there is no sign for /p/ until the later manu-script versions of Ogam. The orthodox Ogam inscriptions constitute the earliest evidence for continuous phrases of Irish. Most are memorial inscrip-tions and tend to have a pattern like '(memorial/tomb) of A, son/descendant of B', e.g. GRILAGNI MAQI SCILAGNI.[30] The evidence of the Ogam inscrip-tions is crucial for our understanding of early Irish phonology and morph-ology, though the restricted syntactic range reduces their utility for morphology; they span the period of fundamental changes in the language, changes which turned Irish from a language structurally similar to Latin or Greek into one not dissimilar to the modern language.

---

[26] For a collection and discussion, see McManus, *A guide*, pp 153–66; the fullest collection still remains Macalister, *Corpus inscriptionum*; see also Sabine Ziegler, *Die Sprache der altirischen Ogam-Inschriften* (Göttingen, 1994); on the manuscript versions of Ogam, see McManus, *Guide*, pp 128–46; Patrick Sims-Williams, 'Some problems in deciphering the early Irish Ogam alphabet' in *Trans. Phil. Soc.*, xci (1993), pp 133–80; idem, 'The additional letters of the Ogam alphabet' in *Camb. Med. Celt. Studies*, xxiii (1992), pp 29–75. For general discussion, see Charles-Edwards, *Early Christian Ireland*, pp 163–76.

[27] That many of the letter names are names of plants and trees is probably a red-herring in this respect; see McManus, *Guide*, pp 35–43; idem, 'Irish letter-names and their kennings' in *Ériu*, xxxix (1988), pp 127–68.

[28] For distribution maps, see McManus, *Guide*, pp 46 (Ireland), 48 (Wales). On the Welsh inscriptions, the fullest collection is still V. E. Nash-Williams, *The early Christian monuments of Wales* (Cardiff, 1950); for the inscriptions of south-west Britain, see Elizabeth Okasha, *Corpus of early Christian inscribed stones of south-west Britain* (Leicester, 1993); Charles Thomas, *And shall these mute stones speak?*; Sims-Williams, *Celtic inscriptions of Britain*.

[29] McManus, *Guide*, p. 27.

[30] For a list of formulae and examples, see McManus, *Guide*, p. 52.

Given the attention usually devoted to Old Irish, the sources for the language are surprisingly thin, if our attention is to be restricted to texts written in the period from 700 to 900 and surviving in contemporary manuscripts.[31] They amount to short passages in Old Irish in the Book of Armagh, the Cambrai Homily (both dating to the early eighth century), and the three main collections of glosses on Latin biblical and grammatical texts: the Würzburg (Wb.) glosses (c.750) on the Pauline epistles; the Milan (Ml.) glosses on a commentary to the Psalms (c.800); and the St Gall (Sg.) glosses on Priscian (c.850, though probably containing different strata of material).[32] Thurneysen's grammar was based almost entirely on this material.[33] The glosses can range from single word translations or comments to relatively long commentaries that go far beyond the text and often go off at a tangent from it; the glossing on Romans 11: 33 (*O altitudo divitiarum sapientiae et scientiae Dei...*) provides a good example: there is a concise gloss *nís·fitir nech* 'no one knows them' (Wb. 5c15) on *investigabiles* and also a long discussion in the adjacent margin on the whole verse (Wb. 5c16).[34] The St Gall glosses on Priscian are particularly interesting in providing commentary on a grammatical text: the glossator was forced to think about linguistic terminology in Old Irish. It is not clear how familiar he was with the terminology of the 'Auraicept'; but he was certainly capable of producing his own set of neologisms.[35] Recent approaches have emphasised the importance of considering the glosses in relation to the manuscript tradition of the texts in which they are found.[36]

In addition, there is a vast amount of material preserved in later manuscripts, the originals of which have for one reason or another been attributed to the Old Irish period. The attribution may be on linguistic grounds; that is, among later linguistic forms the text in question contains forms which were current in the Old Irish period. It is then assumed that the later forms are scribal modernisations and that there was an underlying Old Irish original

---

[31] Most of it is collected in *Thes. Pal.*

[32] For a new edition of all the glosses in the first five books of the St Gall Priscian, see Rijcklof Hofman (ed.), *The Sankt Gall Priscian commentary, part 1* (2 vols, Münster, 1996). There are also glosses scattered in other manuscripts; see *Thes. pal.*, i, 1–6, 484–94, 713–14, ii, 1–48, 225–37; see also Dáibhí Ó Cróinín, 'Early Echternach manuscript fragments with Old Irish glosses' in Georg Kiesel and Jean Schroeder (ed.), *Willibrord. Apostel der Niederlande Gründer der Abtei Echternach* (Echternach, 1989), pp 135–43.

[33] Thurneysen, *Grammar of Old Irish*; see esp. pp 4–8 on the sources.

[34] *Thes. Pal.*, i, 530.

[35] On grammatical terminology, see Patricia Kelly, 'Variation in early Irish linguistic terminology' in Anders Ahlqvist and Vera Čapková (ed.), *Dán do Oide: essays in memory of Conn R. Ó Cléirigh 1927–1995* (Dublin, 1997), pp 243–6; Brían Ó Cuív, 'Linguistic terminology in the medieval bardic tracts' in *Trans. Phil. Soc.*, 64 (1965), 141–64. See also Russell, *Celtic word-formation*, pp 89–90. For examples from the St Gall glosses, see below, pp 438–9.

[36] See Hofman, *The Sankt Gall Priscian commentary*.

which has not survived in an unadulterated form.[37] One editorial approach to such texts is to attempt to normalise the text to a notional original, but there are difficulties; for example, the target language is not as uniform as might appear from an initial perusal of Thurneysen's *Grammar*: both the Würzburg and Milan glosses contain forms that might better be described as Middle Irish, and thus there is a danger that the original text is made more Old Irish than it ever was originally.[38] Moreover, more and more evidence is emerging that scribes were capable of writing in 'archaising' registers and of thus creating good Old Irish forms well into the Middle Irish period.[39] Where verse is concerned, metrical considerations, especially rhyme, may have the effect of anchoring a text more firmly in its period; for example, a rhyme that shows /a/ only rhyming with /a/ and not with /e/ or /i/, demonstrating that final vowels were still distinct, is usually regarded as belonging to the Old Irish period, though the ability to control such rhymes seems to have still been alive as late as the first quarter of the tenth century.[40]

The sources for Middle Irish are far more substantial than for Old Irish, even if we apply the rule of contemporaneous manuscripts. The most important collections of material are those preserved in the main manuscripts of the twelfth century, 'Lebor na hUidhre' (Oxford, Bodl. MS, Rawl. B 502), and the Book of Leinster.[41] The dating of Middle Irish texts has been a long-standing problem.[42] Few texts can be firmly dated: 'Saltair na Rann' was probably written in 988.[43] 'Cogad Gáedel re Gallaib' has been recently dated to 1103–13.[44] Another approach is to consider the *corpora* of poets whose obits fall within this period, such as Fland Mainistrech (d. 1056).[45] But, in general terms, analysis of linguistic features is better at giving us a relative chronology of the texts than anything absolute; for example, studies of verbal systems or declensional forms may allow us to decide that the language of

[37] For reservations about this kind of editorial procedure, see McCone, 'Prehistoric, Old and Middle Irish', pp 27–37.
[38] Kim McCone, 'The Würzburg and Milan glosses: our earliest sources of "Middle Irish"' in *Ériu*, xxxvi (1985), pp 85–106.
[39] For further discussion, see below, pp 445–6.
[40] M. A. O'Brien (ed.), 'A Middle Irish poem on the Christian kings of Leinster' in *Ériu*, xvii (1955), pp 35–51. The poem is in two parts: the first dateable to 915–40, the second to 1024–36; only in the first part is the quality of unaccented short vowels in final syllables still recognized for rhyming purposes.
[41] Breatnach, 'An Mheán-Ghaeilge', is based on a representative selection of texts from these manuscripts.
[42] See Gearóid Mac Eoin, 'On the dating of Middle Irish texts' in *Brit. Acad. Proc.*, lxviii (1982), pp 109–39; Kenneth Jackson (ed.), *Aislinge Meic Con Glinne* (Dublin, 1990), pp xx–xxvi.
[43] Jackson, *Aislinge*, p. xx.
[44] Máire Ní Mhaonaigh, '*Cogad Gáedel re Gallaib*: some dating considerations' in *Peritia*, ix (1995), pp 354–57.
[45] Liam Breatnach, 'Poets and poetry' in McCone & Simms, *Progress*, pp 65–77.

one text is more evolved in a particular direction than another but not necessarily when it was composed.[46]

BEFORE moving on to the distinctive linguistic characteristics of the various stages of Irish, it may be useful to consider the development of its orthography.[47] Apart from the names in the Greek script on Ptolemy's map, the earliest evidence for continuous Irish is written in Ogam.[48] It seems likely that the Ogam script was created in the late fourth or early fifth century. The fifth and sixth centuries witnessed most of the major phonological changes in the language, such as the phonemicisation of lenition and palatalisation following the loss of most final syllables. Some but not all of these changes are indicated in the Ogam spelling system, which continues in some respects to present a picture of the language before these changes took place. Thus we may compare Ogam LUGUDECCAS with the O.Ir. *Luigdech* /ˈluɣˈðˈəχ/ and CATUVIR with the O.Ir. genitive *Caithir* /ˈkaθˈərˈ/, where the later forms show the effects of lenition, loss of final syllables and syncope.[49] On the other hand, gradual changes, such as the loss of most final syllables, are reflected in the inscriptions; for example, the development of the feminine genitive singular ending *-iās* can be exemplified from the Ogam inscriptions as follows: -/iya(:)s/ (MAQI ERCIAS) > -/eyas/ or -/e(y)ah/ (MAQI RITEAS) > -/e(y)a/ (MAQI ESEA) > -/e/ (MAQI RITE) corresponding to Old Irish *Maic Reithe*.[50] However, it does not follow that the inscriptions from which these examples derive can be placed in chronological order on the basis of these forms. The writers of these inscriptions were capable of both maintaining more or less conservative orthographies and making errors that betray contemporary usage. Within one inscription it is

---

[46] For such analyses, see John Strachan, 'Contributions to the history of the deponent verb in Irish' in *Trans. Phil. Soc.*, xxii (1891–4), pp 444–568; idem, 'The verbal system of *Saltair na Rann*' in *Trans. Phil. Soc.*, xxiii (1895–8), pp 1–76; idem, 'Contributions to the history of Irish declension' in *Trans. Phil. Soc.*, xxv (1903–6), pp 202–46; Máirín O Daly, 'The verbal system of the LL-*Táin*' in *Ériu*, xiv (1943), pp 31–139; Máire Ní Mhaonaigh, 'Einige Bemerkungen zu den Verbalstammbildungen in *Cogad Gáedel re Gallaib*' in M. Rockel and St. Zimmer (ed.), *Akten des ersten Symposiums deutschsprachiger Keltologen* (Tübingen, 1993), pp 161–82; Alf Sommerfelt, 'Le système verbal dans *In cath catharda*' in *Rev. Celt.*, xxxvi (1915), pp 24–62, 295–334; xxxvii (1917–19), pp 230–46; xxxviii (1920–21), pp 25–47; xl (1923), pp 157–69; Uáitéar Mac Gearailt, 'The language of some late Middle Irish texts in the Book of Leinster' in *Studia Hib.*, xxvi (1991–2), pp 167–216; Gearóid Mac Eoin, 'Das Verbalsystem von *Togail Troí* (H.2.17)' in *Z.C.P.*, xxix (1962–4), pp 325–78. For a wide-ranging study of Middle Irish verbal formations, see McCone, *Early Irish verb*, pp 163–241.

[47] See Russell, *Introduction*, pp 208–11 and 223–7; McCone, *Towards a relative chronology*, pp 22–35; Ahlqvist, 'Litriú'.

[48] See McManus, *Guide*; Ziegler, *Die Sprache*. For a brief description of the system, see above, pp 410–11.

[49] Note that ' denotes a palatal consonant. The phonetic symbols in this chapter are those of the international phonetic alphabet.

[50] For the phonological developments exemplified in the inscriptions, see Ziegler, *Die Sprache*, pp 38–52.

possible to find forms that apparently reflect different chronological stages of the language: in MAQI-TTAL MAQI VORGOS MAQI MUCOI TOICAC, we may contrast the loss of -I in -TTAL and TOICAC with its preservation in other words.[51] In broad terms, then, Ogam was originally used to write a language that had final case endings, no phonemic lenition of intervocalic consonants, and no syncope; thus, Ogam $T$ and $D$ respectively correspond to Old Irish /t/ and /d/ in absolute initial position but to /θ/ and /ð/ in intervocalic position; thus RITTECC (or perhaps *recte* RETTECC): Old Irish *Rethech* /'R'eθəχ/.[52] The doubling of consonants seems to be haphazard; a possible bias towards duplicated stops corresponding to later non-lenited stops has been suggested but, if there is anything to it, the conditions have yet to be fully established.[53]

The presence of Ogam inscriptions in Britain is linked to the Irish colonisation of parts of Britain in the fifth and sixth centuries. The bilingual (Ogam/Latin) inscriptions, where the Irish form of the name is clearly independent of the Latin, show Irish to have been a spoken language in these areas. It has been assumed that the Ogam script was brought to Wales with the Irish. However, certain aspects of the situation may give pause for thought. The origin of the Ogam script seems to lie in a Latinate milieu; for example, the arrangement of letters seems to be based on Latin grammatical teaching.[54] Moreover, in Britain Latin was written in capitals (and later in half-uncials) and it may have been the incentive to produce an equivalent written medium for Irish that led to the creation of Ogam. The presence of a monumental script for Latin in Britain may have supplied the right environment and it is possible that Ogam was invented in Britain, and possibly south Wales, rather than in Ireland itself.[55]

While Ogam inscriptions continued to be produced, from about the beginning of the seventh century onwards Irish began to be written in an insular version of the Latin script. By this point Irish had undergone the major sound changes of the preceding centuries, particularly in this case the phonemicisation of lenition whereby /p t k/ > /f θ χ/ and /b d g/ > /v ð γ/ in intervocalic position and which had been phonemicised by the loss of final syllables and other changes.[56] In practice, such wholesale phonological changes do not necessarily entail major orthographical modification. In

---

[51] Macalister, *Corpus*, § 200; McManus, *Guide*, p. 82. See now also Andrew Garnett, 'On the prosodic phonology of Ogam Irish' in *Ériu*, l (1999), pp 139–60.

[52] See McManus, *Guide*, pp 103, 104 (for the suggested correction, see p. 8).

[53] See Anthony Harvey, 'The Ogam inscriptions and their geminate consonants' in *Ériu*, xxxviii (1987), pp 45–71; see also McManus, *Guide*, p. 125; Ziegler, *Die Sprache*, pp 4–5, 304–10; McCone, *Towards a relative chronology*, p. 25.

[54] McManus, *Guide*, pp 27–30.

[55] See Jackson, *Language and history*, p. 156; Charles-Edwards, 'Language and society', pp 722–3.

[56] For details, see below, pp 424–6.

Ogam T C B D G originally represented /t k b d g/ respectively in all positions and, as the phonological changes occurred, there would have been no need to modify the spelling system since no confusion would arise: T C B D G would continue to represent /t k b d g/ in absolute initial position but would now represent /θ χ v ð γ/ in internal post-vocalic position. Thus it is that we cannot tell whether the engraver who carved the Ogam spelling RITUVVECAS actually said /Rituwekas/ or /Riθuweχ(ah)/ or even /ˈReθəχ/ (: O.Ir. *Rethech*).[57]

This system was maintained sporadically into the earliest manuscripts written in a Latin script. The orthography of the *prima manus* (first scribe) of the Würzburg glosses shows some of the same Ogam-like spellings, thus *roslogeth* (: O.Ir. *ro·sluiced*), *adobrogart* (: O.Ir. *atob·rogart*), with g for /g/ and d for /d/ (relevant letters marked in bold).[58] Though there are traces of continuity between Ogam and the Latin orthographies of early Irish, this system was rapidly superseded by a spelling system based on the pronunciation of Latin in Britain.[59] In fifth-and sixth-century Britain both Latin and British (as well as Irish) were spoken languages, and the lenition that affected post-vocalic stops in British, i.e. /p t k/ > /b d g/ and /b d g/ > /v ð γ/, also affected the pronunciation of Latin; thus they pronounced *caper, locus, medicus, agō* as /kaber, loguh, meðiguh, aγu:/, even though they spelt them as above. Therefore, it would follow that *p t c* represent /p t k/ in non-leniting position but /b d g/ in leniting position, and similarly *b d g* had two values depending on their position in the word, namely /b d g/ in non-leniting position or /v ð γ/ elsewhere.[60] The well documented influence of British ecclesiastics and the regular contact between Britain and Ireland seem to have led to the adoption of this British Latin correspondence between sound and symbol in the spelling of Old Irish; that is, it reflected the British pronunciation of Latin with British lenition patterns in place. Thus, O.Ir. *tocad* /togəð/ 'luck', *cét* /keːd/ 'hundred', *ben* /ben/ 'woman', *slíab* /sliav/ show initial *t*, *c* and *b* for /t k b/ but post-vocalically they represent /g d v/. However, in Irish /p t k/ were lenited to /f θ χ/ (not to /b d g/ as in British). Now in Ogam, and in the Würzburg *prima manus* system, there was no problem since *p t c* could be used for /f θ χ/, while /b d g/ was spelt with *b d g*. But under the British system matters were more complicated as *p t c* were used post-vocalically to represent /b d g/, and given that this

---

[57] Ziegler, *Die Sprache*, p. 226.

[58] See *Thes. pal.*, i, p. xxiv, for further examples; see also James Carney, 'Aspects of archaic Irish' in *Éigse*, xvii (1978–9), pp 417–35; Anthony Harvey, 'Some significant points of early insular orthography' in Ó Corráin, Breatnach, & McCone, *Sages, saints & storytellers*, pp 56–66: 58.

[59] For discussion of lenition, see below, pp 424–6; at this point the issue of whether the voicing of /p t k/ and the spirantisation of /b d g/ were contemporaneous or separate events is of no concern.

[60] For the development of this system, see Russell, *Introduction*, pp 211–23; McCone, *Towards a relative chronology*, pp 17–22.

was the position where /f θ χ/ occurred in Irish, *p t c* could hardly each be used to represent two different sounds in the same position. Another complicating factor in the development of a satisfactory spelling system for Old Irish was the rise of post-vocalic (leniting position) voiceless stops from geminates or from secondary clusters arising after syncope. The solution was to adopt the practice of spelling /f θ χ/ as digraphs of the basic forms plus *h*, thus *ph*, *th*, *ch*. In practice full digraphs are relatively rare in the early manuscripts; usually scribes preferred to use a diacritic *spiritus asper* written over the letter to represent the fricative pronunciation. Whether the use of *h* or the *spiritus asper* arose out of a deliberate spelling reform, either in Irish or in British, or arose in both independently is unclear.[61] In favour of the latter is the clear evidence for wide experimentation in Old Welsh orthography with regard to the voiceless fricatives which would be unexpected if a consistent spelling had been taken over from Old Irish.[62] Moreover, the Cambrai Homily, written in the seventh century, shows some variation in the spelling of /k χ g/, e.g. *din cenelu* (: standard O.Ir. *din chenélu*), *i chomus* /i gomus/ (: standard *i com(m)us*), *loch* /log/ (: standard *loc(c)*).[63] In part this variation may have been inherited from Latin spelling systems where, for example, both *t* and *th* could represent /t/, etc.

There may be one case that suggests that this British spelling system was also used in Ogam. The example comes from the damaged bilingual inscription from Eglwys Nynnid near Margam in Wales on which we find Ogam P[O]P[IA.] corresponding to the Latin name PUMPEIUS (for *Pompeius*).[64] In Irish, clusters of /nt/ and /nk/ gave /d/ and /g/ respectively, with or without compensatory lengthening of the preceding vowel, and this is already found in Ogam, e.g. DECCEDAS /deχe:dah/ (< *dekantos* (gen. sg.)), TOGIT-TAC /togiθaχ/ (< *tonketakī*) = O.Ir. *Toicthig* (nom. *Toicthech*).[65] If so, /mp/ in an early loan word would have given /b/, and so the first three signs of P[O]P[IA.] should probably be understood as representing /pob/-. If so, the Ogam spelling is surprising since it suggests that a 'British'-type spelling is being used with P for /b/ in intervocalic position, while in Ogam we would normally expect B. The Ogam sign for P in this case seems to be a six-pointed star to the right of the line, though much of it has been damaged

[61] For the former view, see Anthony Harvey, 'Some significant points'; for the latter, McCone, *Towards a relative chronology*, pp 29–30. Cf. also the use of *ch* for /χ/ and *th* for /θ/ in Frankish Gaul; see Russell, *Introduction*, p. 224.

[62] See Russell, *Introduction*, pp 215–17.

[63] For the Cambrai Homily, see *Thes. pal.*, ii, 244–7; for the examples, see McCone, *Towards a relative chronology*, p. 29.

[64] Nash-Williams, *Early Christian monuments of Wales*, § 198; *Royal Commission on Ancient and Historical Monuments in Wales, Glamorgan, i: pt 3, The early Christian period*, p. 38 (+ plate 2 a and b); Charles-Edwards, *Early Christian Ireland*, pp 170–71; Sims-Williams, *Celtic inscriptions of Britain*, p. 54.

[65] See McCone, *Towards a relative chronology*, pp 106–8. For a parallel to the spelling of Latin /mp/ with Ogam P, cf. Latin *INGENVI* corresponding to Ogam IGENAVI (Macalister, *Corpus*, §446 (Lewannick, Cornwall)).

apart from the ends of the three strokes.[66] One difficulty is that some of the various P signs may also be interpreted as BB or even BBB. If so, the internal star-like sign could be interpreted as B(B) rather than as P but, if that was the case, it is still strange that the sign for B was not used. The important point, however, is that the same sign was used initially and internally to represent /p/ and /b/ respectively. If so, the implications are striking; for, while it is accepted that Ogam-style spellings carried over into manuscript Irish, it seems that in the Irish of Wales at least the converse also occurred. It is at least possible, then, that the British spelling of stops which became the norm in Ireland was first adopted into the spelling of Irish in Wales and was carried to Ireland by speakers and writers of Irish.

The Ogam spelling system, like the Latin system, did not distinguish vowel length; for example, both /a/ and /a:/ were spelt *A*. The early manuscript orthography experimented with doubling the vowel to indicate length, e.g. in the Cambrai Homily *baan* /ba:n/ 'white' (: standard O.Ir. *bán*), *is ee* /is e:/ 'it is', etc.[67] However, the system which predominated was one which seems to have been optional for a long period, of marking length by a superscript diacritic, conventionally transliterated as an acute accent, though often it looks more like a macron. The latter system gradully took over, though it is common to find compromise spellings, e.g. *láam* (: *lám*), *cúursagad* (: *cúrsagad*), *gabáal* (: *gabál*), etc.[68] However, the haphazard use of the diacritic sometimes to mark length, but on occasions simply to mark vowels, suggests that for many scribes of the Old Irish period and later orthographical marking of length was not high on their list of priorities.[69]

In addition to the basic consonant phonemes mentioned above, early Irish developed a set of palatal consonants, namely /p′ t′ k′ b′ d′ g′/, etc.[70] The alternation of palatal and non-palatal consonants carried grammatical information, e.g. O.Ir. *lám* /la:ṽ/ 'hand' (nom. sg.) : *láim* /la:ṽ′/ 'hand' (acc. sg.). The palatal nature of the consonant was marked by the writing of a glide vowel before or after the consonant in question;[71] thus, in the above example the *i* of *láim* marks the *m* as palatal, namely -/ṽ′/. Palatalisation

---

[66] Sims-Williams, 'The additional letters of the Ogam alphabet', pp 41–2, 44. Another possible example is suggested by Sims-Williams, ibid., pp 49–50: in Macalister, *Corpus*, § 7 (Corrower, Co. Mayo) he reads CETAIMIN and interprets it as 'first', cognate with Welsh *cysefin*. Other features suggest that this is a relatively late inscription (seventh century?) but nevertheless might indicate 'leakage' from manuscript orthography into Ogam. See also McManus, *Guide*, pp 123–4.

[67] See Russell, *Introduction*, p. 225; McCone, *Towards a relative chronology*, pp 28–9; Thurneysen, *Grammar of Old Irish*, p. 26.

[68] Thurneysen, *Grammar*, pp 20–21.

[69] The modern editorial convention is to mark long vowels with an acute accent. Diphthongs containing /i/ are indicated by an accent on the second element, e.g. *ai*, etc., in order to distinguish them from a long vowel followed by a glide vowel, e.g. *ái*.

[70] For their development, see below, pp 426–8.

[71] On glide vowels, see Russell, *Introduction*, pp 225–6; Thurneysen, *Grammar*, pp 32–4; Ahlqvist, 'Litriú', p. 30.

first became phonemic (that is, it carried grammatical information or indeed distinguished words) after final -/a/ affection; for example, in *[bodina] the /i/ palatalised the preceding consonant before it was raised to [e] under the influence of the following [a], thus /bud′ena/ (> O.Ir. *buiden* 'army' /buð′ən/). At that point, the palatal nature of the dental /d′/ was no longer conditioned by the following vowel . The subsequent loss of most final syllables brought about the complete phonemicisation of palatalisation in all environments. Ogam does not show palatalisation since at the period of its invention palatalisation was phonetic, not phonemic.

Essentially, then, in the original phonetic situation palatal consonants arose next to front vowels, /i(:) e(:)/, and non-palatal with back vowels, /a(:) o(:) u(:)/. But if or when the conditioning vowels were lost, the palatalisation of the consonant was retained and became phonemic, that is, it ceased to be related to the quality of the following vowel. Where the match between the quality of the consonant and vowel remained, the spelling was not problematic, e.g. *rún* /Ru:n/ 'secret', *tech* /t′eχ/ 'house', *síl* /s′i:l/ 'seed', *cruth* /kruθ/ 'shape', etc. But where there was a mismatch between the point of articulation of the consonant and that of the flanking vowels, a glide vowel was written; in monosyllables they were written from the earliest manuscripts onwards in cases such as *maic* /mak′/ 'son' (gen. sg.), *cruich* /kruχ′/ 'cross' (acc. sg.), *slóig* /slo:γ′/ 'host' (gen. sg.). They were far less commonly written in the early evidence before internal consonants, e.g. *túathe/túaithe* /tuaθ′e/ 'people' (gen. sg.), *mathi/maithi* /maθ′i/ 'good' (pl.). Presumably, the presence of the following front vowel was felt to be sufficient indication of the palatal nature of the consonant.

The writing of a back glide vowel between a front vowel and a non-palatal consonant, e.g. *sleachta* (O.Ir. *slechta*) /s′L′eχtə/ 'cutting' (gen. sg.), *fear* (O.Ir. *fer*) /f′er/ 'man', is a later feature and does not occur until the late Old Irish or early Middle Irish period. In such forms within Middle Irish a shift in syllable centre seems to have occurred so that the original glide vowel became the nucleus of the syllable; we may compare O.Ir. *fer* /f′er/, phonetically [f′eᵃr] with Mod.Ir. *fear* /f′ar/, O.Ir. *guide* /guð′e/ 'prayer' with Mod. Ir. *guí* (*guidhe*) /gi:/ or /giyə/.[72]

So far we have been considering on-glide vowels, those written in front of a consonant to indicate its palatal or non-palatal nature. Off-glide vowels were also written after consonants in non-initial, unaccented syllables. Unstressed vowels in internal syllables have been reduced to /ə/ before the eighth century and were thus spelt differently depending on the quality of the flanking consonants: as *a* between non-palatal consonants, e.g. *as·berat* /əs′b′erəd/ 'they say'; as *e* between a palatal and a non-palatal consonant, e.g. *ní·epret* /ni:′eb′r′əd/ 'they do not say'; as *i* between two palatals, e.g. *berit*

[72] See McCone, *Towards a relative chronology*, pp 140–41. See also below, pp 426–8.

/b'er'əd'/ 'they carry'.[73] Between a non-palatal and a palatal consonant the vowel is spelt (*a*)*i* with an optional off-glide, e.g. *ní·tab*(*a*)*ir* /niːtavər'/ 'he does not give'. After a palatal consonant an off-glide *i* is usual before /u/, e.g. *teilciud* /t'el'g'uð/ 'throwing'. Glide vowels also occur before final vowels where there is a mismatch, e.g. *doirseo* /dor's'o/ 'door' (gen. sg.), etc.

IRISH belongs to the Goidelic branch of the Celtic languages. The Celtic languages themselves are a sub-group of the vast Indo-European group of languages to which belong most of the languages of Europe and many of the languages of Asia as far east as India. The relationship can be simply exemplified by correspondences such as the following: Ir. *máthir* 'mother', Gaulish *matir*, Latin *mater*, Greek μήτηρ, Sanskrit *matir*; Ir. *deich* 'ten', W. *deg*, Latin *decem*, Greek δέκα, Sanskrit *daśam*; O.Ir. -*aib* /əv'/ (dat. pl. ending), Gaulish -*bi*: Latin -*ibus*, Greek -φi, Sanskrit -*bhis*, etc. The statements made in the last few sentences cover a multitude of possible relationships and beg numerous questions, not all of which will be discussed here.[74] The Celtic languages consist of two groups, which are geographically distinguished as insular and continental, the former attested in the British Isles (apart from Breton, a late returner to the Continent) and the latter in western continental Europe. The continental languages, Gaulish (attested in Gaul and in northern Italy), Lepontic (northern Italy), and Celtiberian (Spain) did not, as far as we can tell, survive the expansion of the Roman empire. Most of the insular languages, on the other hand, which are classified as either Goidelic (Irish, Scottish Gaelic, and Manx) or as Brittonic (Welsh, Cornish, Breton, and Cumbrian) have survived to the present day, except for Cornish and Cumbrian. Breton is closely related to Cornish, and its presence in Brittany is due to sixth- and seventh-century migrations from the south-west peninsula rather than its being a survival of Gaulish.[75] The significance of the insular /continental distinction has been much debated, and views on the interrelationship of the Celtic languages depend very much on what features are taken to be significant. For example, the commonly quoted 'P/Q' distinction, whereby the insular languages can be divided into 'P Celtic'

---

[73] In the Cambrai Homily (mid-seventh century) the 3rd plural ending was still spelt -*ot* and this is usually taken to reflect an unreduced vowel; on the other hand, orthographical conservatism cannot be ruled out.

[74] On Indo-European generally, see Oswald Szemerényi, *Introduction to Indo-European Linguistics* (Oxford, 1999) (translation of *Einführung in die vergleichende Sprachwissenschaft* (4th ed., Darmstadt, 1990)) on Greek and Latin, see Andrew L. Sihler, *New comparative grammar of Greek and Latin* (Oxford, 1995). For Celtic, see Holger Pedersen, *Vergleichende Grammatik der keltischen Sprachen* (2 vols, Göttingen, 1909–13); Henry Lewis and Holger Pedersen, *A concise comparative Celtic grammar* (2nd ed., Göttingen, 1961). For the question of Italo-Celtic, which is not discussed here, see Russell, *Introduction*, pp 18–20 (and references).

[75] On views to the contrary, see Kenneth Jackson, *A historical phonology of Breton* (Dublin, 1967), pp 25–35; Russell, *Introduction*, pp 128–9.

(Brittonic) and 'Q Celtic' (Goidelic) on the basic of the reflexes of I-E. /k$^w$/ which gave Brittonic /p/ but Irish /k$^w$/ and later /k/ (e.g. Ir. *cethair*, W. *pedwar* 'four' < *$kwetwor$-(cf. Latin *quattuor*, Greek τέσσαρες)) can also be applied to the continental languages; some forms in Gaulish and Lepontic share the /p/ reflex with Brittonic, e.g. Gaulish *petru*-'four', Lepontic -*pe* 'and' (< *-$k^we$; cf. Latin -*que*), while Celtiberian, like Irish, retained /k$^w$/, e.g. -*Cue*, *neCue* 'and, neither' (cf. Latin *neque*). It is, therefore, tempting to conclude that Celtiberian was related to Goidelic, and Gaulish and Lepontic to Brittonic.[76] The logical extension of this view, with the inclusion of other evidence, produces the Gallo-Brittonic hypothesis, whereby Brittonic and Gaulish share a close genetic relationship.[77] However, as has been observed, the 'P/Q' distinction is fundamentally trivial; the labial reflex (/k$^w$/ > /p/) occurs in many other languages, such as Osco-Umbrian (related to Latin where it does not occur), Greek (in certain environments), and Roumanian. As such it is a weak basis of linguistic classification.[78] To a large extent, the classification of the insular group does not rest on phonological criteria but on aspects of verbal morphology which are shared by the insular languages but which are absent from the continental languages.[79] This is not the place to explore these issues in greater detail, and in what follows a basic insular Celtic model will be assumed. Nevertheless, one observation on these arguments may be relevant which has to do with the attestation dates of these languages. The latest attestations of the continental languages are from the Roman period. On the other hand, apart from Ptolemy's names and British names in classical authors, our earliest systematic evidence for the insular languages are the fifth-century (perhaps some are late fourth) Ogam inscriptions, and our earliest textual evidence is at best late sixth-century. There is, then, a chronological gap between the two sub-groups which can at the very least prove methodologically inconvenient. An example may make the point: as was noted above, the notion of 'insular Celtic' as a genetic node was predicated largely on the basis of verbal morphology, more specifically on the basis of the complex absolute and conjunct inflection most fully attested

[76] Thus Karl Horst Schmidt, 'Insular Celtic: P and Q Celtic' in Ball & Fife, *The Celtic languages*, pp 64–98; idem, 'On the Celtic languages of continental Europe' in *Bulletin of the Board of Celtic Studies*, xxix (1980–82), pp 256–68; idem, 'On the reconstruction of Proto-Celtic' in Gordon W. MacLennan (ed.), *Proceedings of the First North American Congress of Celtic Studies* (Ottawa, 1988), pp 231–48.

[77] For the arguments, see John T. Koch, ' "Gallo-Brittonic" vs. "Insular Celtic": the inter-relationships of the Celtic languages reconsidered' in G. le Menn (ed.), *Bretagne et pays celtiques: langue, histoire, civilisation. Mélanges offerts à la memoire de Léon Fleuriot* (Saint-Brieuc and Rennes, 1992), pp 471–95; D. Ellis Evans, 'Insular Celtic and the emergence of the Welsh language' in Bammesberger & Wollmann, *Britain 400–600*, pp 149–77; and also Peter Schrijver, *Studies in British Celtic historical phonology* (Amsterdam and Atlanta, 1995), p. 464 for criticism, and McCone, *Towards a relative chronology*, pp 79–81.

[78] See McCone, *Towards a relative chronology*, pp 67–81, where the other evidence is also discussed, notably the reflexes of /m̥/ and /n̥/; see also Russell, *Introduction*, 15–18.

[79] See McCone, *Towards a relative chronology*, pp 98–104.

in Old Irish and residually in Brittonic languages.[80] The claim is that the verbal morphology of the continental languages shows no trace of this pattern; but in other respects it does show the same kind of patterning of compounding, e.g. Celtiberian *amPi-TiseTi* '?builds around' (consisting of a preverb *amPi-*and a verbal stem + ending).[81] However, we might reasonably ask whether continental forms, such as *to-med-eclai* (or *to-me-declai*), *to-so-kote*, *tio-in-uoru*, all of which seem to contain elements between preverb and verb, are significantly different from the reconstructed forms underlying the Old Irish paradigms.[82] The point may be not so much that the insular languages share an isogloss to the exclusion of the continental languages, but that the latter never survived long enough to generate the comparable forms. In other words, it is not entirely clear that verbal morphology is as weighty an argument as it appears.

The Celtic language as a group can be distinguished from other Indo-European languages on phonological grounds; that is, there is a number of sound changes which must belong to the Proto-Celtic period as they are evidenced in all the Celtic languages. Two broad areas may be considered: long vowels, together with the diphthongs, and the consonant system. Proto-Celtic inherited a system of five long vowels, /a: e: i: o: u:/, and six diphthongs, /ai ei oi/ and /au eu ou/. This system was re-adjusted within Proto-Celtic in such a way as to maintain the full complement of long vowels but to reduce the number of diphthongs. First, a series of mergers took place among the long vowels: /e:/ merged with /i:/, e.g. I-E. *\*rēks* 'king' (cf. Latin *rēx*) > Pr-C. *\*rīks* > Gaulish -*rix*, O.Ir. *ri*, M.W. *rhi*;[83] /o:/ merged with /a:/ in internal syllables, e.g. I-E. *\*mōros* 'big' (cf. Greek -μωρος) > Pr-C. *\*māros* > Gaulish -*marus*, O.Ir. *már*, W. *mawr*, but final -/o:/ > /u:/, e.g. I-E. *\*kwō(n)* 'dog' (cf. Greek κύων) > Pr-C. *\*kwū* > Ir. *cú*. The effect of these changes was to allow some of the diphthongs to simplify to long vowels and fill the gaps in the system; thus, /ei/ became /e:/, e.g. I-E. *\*deiwo-* (cf. Latin *dīvus*) > Pr-C. *\*dēwo-* > Gaulish *devo-*, O.Ir. *día* (gen. sg. *dé*), and /ou/, and /eu/ which had already merged with /ou/, became /o:/, e.g. I-E. *teuta* > Pr-C. *touta* (cf. Oscan *touto*) > *tōta* > O.Ir. *túath* 'tribe, people', W. *tud*. The latter change of /ou/ to /o:/ may not belong to the period of Proto-

---

[80] See below, pp 431–3.

[81] How exact the correspondence is partly depends on whether the final vowel of *amPi-TiseTi* is thought to have any phonetic reality or to be simply a product of the syllabic spelling system.

[82] On the forms, see Pierre-Yves Lambert, *La langue gauloise* (Paris, 1994), pp 67–8. On the segmentation *to-me-declai*; see Joseph Eska and Michael Weiss, 'Segmenting Gaul. *tomedeclai*' in *Studia Celt.*, xxx (1996), pp 289–92. Contrast the view of Schrijver that Gaulish at least out of the continental languages may have developed beyond the stage of verb-initial compound verbs to permitting such forms elsewhere in the clause; see Peter Schrijver, *Studies in the history of celtic pronouns and particles* (Maynooth, 1997), pp 177–82.

[83] On the possibility that I-E. *rēks* may be a secondary development, see Kim McCone, ' "King" and "Queen" in Celtic and Indo-European' in *Ériu*, xlix (1998), pp 1–12.

Celtic since Gaulish retains diphthongs, e.g. TOUTAS, etc.[84] On the other hand, /au/ seems to have survived into the separate languages.[85]

The Indo-European consonant system in the period immediately preceding Proto-Celtic seems to have had three sets of stops, voiceless, voiced, and voiced aspirates, and four points of articulation, labial /p b bh/, dental /t d dh/, velar /k g gh/, and labio-velar /k$^w$ g$^w$ g$^w$h/; of these /b/ seems to have been very rare.[86] Within Proto-Celtic this system was reduced to a seven-stop system: first, /g$^w$/ was labialised to /b/ thus filling the virtual gap in the labial group, e.g. I-E. *g$^w$ou-'cow' (cf. Sanskrit *gaus*, Greek βοῦς), Celtiberian *bou-*, O.Ir. *bó*, M.W. *bu-*. Secondly, the voiced aspirate series fell together with the voiced series; for example, the dentals in O.Ir. *rúad* /ruað/ 'red' and *cride* /kriðe/ 'heart' can be traced back to /dh/ and /d/ respectively, namely Pr-C. *roudh-* (cf. Greek ἐρυθρός, Lithuanian *raũdas*) and *krid-* (Greek κραδίη, Latin *cord-*). The final development was the loss of /p/, a change which is regarded as pre-eminently characteristic of Celtic languages, e.g. O.Ir. *athir* 'father' < *patēr* (cf. Latin *patēr*, Gothic *fadar*, etc.). However, it occurred relatively late in the history of Proto-Celtic as it left traces behind; for example, -/pt/- clearly gave -/χt/- before the /p/ was lost, e.g. Ir. *secht* 'seven' < *sept-*, *necht* 'niece' < *nept-* (cf. Sanskrit *napti*, etc.); again before the loss of /p/ a succession of /p...k$^w$/ assimilated to /k$^w$...k$^w$/, e.g. Ir. *cóic* 'five' < *kwenk$^w$e* < *penk$^w$e* (cf. Greek πέντε, Sanskrit *pañca*).[87]

Just as it is possible to identify diagnostic features that mark out a Celtic language from other Indo-European languages, so within Celtic we can identify features that separate Goidelic from Brittonic languages. Again chronology has to be borne in mind; the earliest systematic attestation of a Goidelic language (that is, not single words out of context or names) pre-dates the equivalent Brittonic material by some two centuries or more. Brittonic languages tend on the whole in morphological terms to be far less

[84] McCone, *Towards a relative chronology*, p. 63.

[85] Pierre-Yves Lambert, 'Welsh *Caswallawn*: the fate of British *au* in Bammesberger and Wollmann, *Britain 400–600*, pp 203–15.

[86] For the Indo-European situation, see the summaries in Kim McCone, 'The PIE stops and syllabic nasals in Celtic' in *Studia Celt. Jap.*, iv (1991), pp 37–69; idem, *Towards a relative chronology*, pp 37–8; and in greater detail, see Sihler, *A new comparative grammar*, pp 135–65. Among the Celtic consonants, the development of /g$^w$h/ has been regarded as most controversial; see Warren Cowgill, 'The etymology of Irish *guidid* and the outcome of *g$^w$h* in Celtic' in M. Mayrhofer, M. Peters, and O. E. Pfeiffer (ed.), *Lautgeschichte und Etymologie. Akten der VI. Fachtagung der Indogermanischen Gesellschaft* (Wiesbaden, 1980), pp 49–78; Patrick Sims-Williams, 'The development of the Indo-European voiced labiovelars in Celtic' in *Bulletin of the Board of Celtic Studies*, xxix (1981), pp 201–29, 690; idem, 'Indo-European *g$^w$h* in Celtic, 1894–1994' in Eska *et al.*, *Hispano-Gallo-Brittonica*, pp 196–218; John T. Koch, 'Gallo-Brittonic *Tasc(i)ouanos* "badger-slayer" and the reflex of Indo-European *g$^w$h* in *Journal of Celtic Linguistics*, i (1992), pp 101–18; idem, 'Further to Indo-European *g$^w$h* in Celtic' in Eska *et al.*, *Hispano-Gallo-Brittonica*, pp 79–95; McCone, 'The PIE stops'.

[87] See McCone, *Towards a relative chronology*, pp 43–5.

conservative than Goidelic; for example, even by the earliest evidence of Old Welsh and Old Breton there is no evidence for a functioning nominal declension, while in Irish declension has been maintained more or less up to the modern language. In phonological terms two features may be used to distinguish Goidelic from Brittonic. The first is the notorious 'P/Q' distinction discussed above; /p/ was lost in Proto-Celtic, but in the Brittonic languages /kʷ/ was labialised to give /p/, while in Goidelic it survived long enough to give $Q$ in Ogam but eventually fell together with /k/.[88] Secondly, there is the question of stress patterns: in Irish accented words are stressed on the first syllable, while in Brittonic the stress was on the penultimate syllable (and subsequently retracted to the original antepenultimate after the loss of final syllables).[89] The phonological effects of the Irish initial stress on word and phrase structure were far-reaching, being responsible *inter alia* for the syncope patterns which radically reduced the syllable structure of Irish, and for the reduction in the articulation of vowels and consonants in unstressed syllables.

The period of Primitive Irish, which post-dates the break-up of the insular languages and pre-dates the earliest manuscript evidence, witnessed major changes.[90] A full catalogue of these changes is not attempted here; instead, a number of the major developments are considered approximately in chronological order, though this is less easy in some cases where the changes took place in stages.[91] All the insular Celtic languages were subject to a weakening of the articulation of intervocalic consonants, irrespective of whether they were in the same word or not; thus, an initial consonant could weaken if preceded by a word with a final vowel, especially if the words were in close syntactic connection.[92] This weakening of articulation, termed lenition, was originally simply a phonetic phenomenon, and remained as such as long as the conditioning factors remained in place. A number of different factors seems to have brought about the phonemicisation of lenition. The most important of these was the loss of final syllables. But before then, the internal syncope of some syllables and the rise of geminates would have triggered a phonemicisation in certain environments. Moreover, in early Old Irish lenition of initial consonants only occurs within prosodic and syntactic groups, e.g. definite article + noun + adjective, preverb + infixed element + verb; later in Old Irish lenition of direct objects occurs after verbs. But in a phrase

[88] See above, pp 420–21.

[89] See Jackson, *Language and history*, pp 265–7. For evidence that Brittonic inherited an initial stress accent, which was preserved in Irish but not in Brittonic, see Schrijver, *Studies in British Celtic historical phonology*, pp 16–22; Joe Salmons, *Accentual change and language contact* (London, 1992), pp 152–61.

[90] John T. Koch, 'The conversion and the transition from Primitive to Old Irish' in *Emania*, xiii (1995), pp 39–50.

[91] See McCone, *Towards a relative chronology*. For a list of changes in relative chronological order, see Sims-Williams, *Celtic inscriptions of Britain*, pp 296–301.

[92] Russell, *Introduction*, pp 231–57; McCone, *Towards a relative chronology*, pp 81–98.

such as *ina thúaith cretid Coirpre 'in his túath Coirpre believes', there is no
lenition of the verb cretid nor of the subject Coirpre, even though at an earlier
period they would have been in a phonetically leniting position, namely [in
esyo θο:θi kredeθi korbreyas], since the preceding words ended in vowels at
this stage and thus the initial consonants of cretid and Coirpre were intervocalic. It would seem then on syntactic grounds that either lenition was
already phonemic before the loss of final syllables, since it had syntactical
significance as a phrase marker (and this may be borne out by the phonemi-
cising effects of syncope and the rise of geminates), or (alternatively but less
likely) there was a wholesale rearrangement of the marking of categories after
the loss of final syllables.[93]

In Irish lenition had the effect of reducing original voiced stops [b d g]
to voiced fricatives [v ð γ] and the voiceless stops [t k] to voiceless fricatives
[θ χ], e.g. *[bereti] > *[bereθi] (> O.Ir. beirid 'he carries', *[ga:bitus] >
[ga:viθuh] (> O.Ir. gábud 'danger'), etc. The Brittonic languages shared the
former change affecting voiced stops but not the latter change to voiceless
stops which were lenited to [b d g]. There has been considerable discussion
as to what extent continental Celtic shared these changes. The traditional
view was that they did not in any systematic way and that lenition was an
insular phenomenon. One view has been that all the Celtic languages shared
in this weakening of articulation at a phonetic level but that it was only
marginally indicated in the orthography of the Celtic languages.[94] For
example, recent analyses of Celtiberian have suggested that it has undergone
the phonetic lenition of voiced stops to [v ð γ ].[95] This fits with recent views
that the insular lenition is to be viewed as a gradual process with the reduction of articulation of voiced stops occurring in Proto-Celtic and that of
voiceless stops being a later development after the break-up of insular Celtic,
hence the variation between Brittonic and Goidelic.[96] It is important to bear
in mind that throughout this period lenition was an allophonic, phonetic
alternation which had no grammatical or morphophonemic ramifications
and, as such, it is hardly surprising that it was barely represented in the
orthographies of continental Celtic.

The final stage of the grammaticalisation of lenition came with the loss of
final syllables; for example, in Primitive Irish the collocation of the possessive

---

[93] See Russell, Introduction, pp 232–6.

[94] See André Martinet, 'La lénition en celtique et les consonnes du roman occidental' in
A. Martinet (ed.), Economie des changements phonétiques (Berne, 1955), pp 257–96; John T.
Koch, '*Cothairche, Esposito's theory and neo-Celtic lenition' in Bammesberger and Wollmann,
Britain 400–600, pp 179–202.

[95] Francisco Villar, Estudios de celtibérico y de toponimia prerromana (Salamanca, 1995),
pp 17–82.

[96] Sims-Williams, 'Dating the transition to neo-Brittonic'; Peter Wynn Thomas, 'The Bry-
thonic consonant shift and the development of consonant mutation' in Bulletin of the Board of
Celtic Studies, xxxvii (1990), pp 1–42; McCone, Towards a relative chronology, pp 81–98.

pronouns */esyo/ 'his' (lit. 'of him') and */esya:s/ 'her' with the noun */to:θa/ 'tribe' would phonetically have been as follows: [esyo θo:θa] 'his tribe' and [esy:as to:θa] 'her tribe'. Following the masculine pronoun the initial [t] was intervocalic and thus lenited to [θ], but this did not occur after the feminine pronoun; the lenition is caused by the intervocalic position of the consonant. With the loss of final syllables we end up in early Old Irish with /a θo:θ/ 'his tribe' and /a to:θ/ 'her tribe', and thus later Old Irish *a thúath* and *a túath* respectively. Here the loss of final syllables in both noun and pronoun has removed the conditioning factors and thus /t/ and /θ/ have become contrastive and are the only markers of the gender of the pronoun. However, the loss of final syllables was not a single catastrophic event, nor indeed did it affect all final syllables; final liquids and unlenited stops seem to have protected the preceding vowel from loss, e.g. O.Ir. *bráthir* /bra:θir/ 'brother' < Pr-C. */bra:te:r/ (cf. Latin *frater*, etc.), O.Ir. *berat* '(they) carry, let them carry' < */berod/ (*/beront/). In essence, the vowels that were lost were final short vowels unprotected by a liquid or unlenited stops; other final syllables survived.[97] The development of the following Primitive Irish noun forms may be used to illustrate the processes, */su:lih/ (< Pr-C. */su:lis/) 'eye', */weran/ (< Pr-C. */wiron/) 'man' (acc. sg.), */wiru:/ 'man' (dat. sg.), */wiru:h/ (< Pr-C. */wiro:s/) 'men' (acc. pl.), */ma:θi:r/ 'mother': (a) all absolutely final long vowels were shortened, thus */wiru/ (but cf. */wiru:h/); (b) in syntactically close groups the syllable boundary shifted so that final /Vh#/ and -/Vn#/ became -/V#h/- and -/V#n/- (# = word boundary), thus */su:li#h/-, */wera#h/-, */wiru:#h/- (the result being nasalisation of a following word or the prefixing of *h-* to an initial vowel); (c) all short vowels in final position were lost, thus /su:l'/, /wer$^n$/, /wiur/, but long vowels survived, thus /wiru:/, */ma:θi:r/; (d) finally all surviving long vowels in final syllables were shortened in the absence of any contrast of length with short vowels, thus /wiru/, */ma:θir/. The Old Irish outcome of the series was thus *súil*, *fer*$^N$ (acc. sg.), *fiuN* (dat. sg.), *firu* (acc. pl.), *máthair*. The loss of final syllables was, therefore, a piecemeal process culminating in the loss of short final vowels at stage (c) above. Irish, however, unlike Brittonic, continued a full functioning case system despite the loss of the crucial final syllable.[98]

A vital factor was the development of a set of palatalised (slender) consonants side by side with the basic (broad) set; thus beside /p t k b d g/, etc. developed /p' t' k' b' d' g'/, etc. which arose before a front vowel which in some environments either then disappeared or was modified. The distinction between palatal and non-palatal consonants thereby became in certain

---

[97] Kim McCone, 'Further to absolute and conjunct' in *Ériu*, xxxiii (1982), pp 1–29: 24–5; Russell, *Introduction*, pp 39–40 (incl. tables 2.7 and 2.8).

[98] On Brittonic, see John T. Koch, 'The loss of final syllables and loss of declension in Brittonic' in *Bulletin of the Board of Celtic Studies*, xxx (1982-3), pp 201–33.

instances grammatically crucial, e.g. O.Ir. /berəd'/ *berait* 'they carry' :
/berəd/ *berat* 'let them carry', /eχ/ *ech* 'horse' (nom. sg.) : /eχ'/ *eich* 'of a
horse' (gen. sg.) or 'horses' (nom. pl.). Phonetic palatalisation is widespread
in many languages; for example, we may compare English *coop* with [k]-and
*keep* with [k']-. It is far less common, however, for the distinction to become
phonemicised as it did in Irish. As with the loss of final syllables, the distinctions observable in Old Irish were the outcome of a staged development, two
stages of which took place before the loss of final syllables and one after.[99]
An important principle in what follows concerns the relative palatalising
power of the front vowels involved: in some instances both /e(:)/ and /i(:)/
can palatalise, in others only /i(:)/ is effective; in addition, it would appear
that syncopated and apocopated vowels (i.e. those lost in internal and final
syllables) seem to have a greater palatalising effect than those which survive.[100] The first stage seems to have occurred after the reduction of unstressed long vowels and after vowel affection in stressed syllables but before
vowel affection in unstressed syllables, the last of which separates the first
and second stages of palatalisation. The first stage was very sensitive to
context, being dependent not only on the quality of the flanking vowels but
also on the type of consonant involved. In short, if the flanking vowels were
both front, then the intervening consonant was palatalised, e.g. O.Ir. *beirid*
/ber'əð'/ 'he carries' (< *[ber'eθ'i]). But, if the preceding vowel was not a
front vowel, then the following vowel had to be /i(:)/, e.g. O.Ir. *gaibid*
/gav'əð'/ 'he takes' (< *[gav'iθ'i]), but *calad* /kaləð/ 'hard' (< *[kaleθah]).[101]
Where the preceding vowel was round, the consonant dental, and the
following vowel /i(:)/, then palalalisation occurred, e.g. O.Ir. *buiden* /buð'ən/
'army' (< *[buð'ena] < *[bud'ina]), *túaithe* /tuaθ'ə/ 'tribe' (gen. sg.)
(< *[to:θ'iyah]), but not if the consonant was labial or guttural, e.g. O.Ir. *tugae*
/tuχa/ 'roof' (< *[tugiya]), *úammae* /uaMə/ (< *[o:Miyah]). After the
lowering of /i/ to /e/ under the influence of /a(:)/ in the following syllable
and the consequent removal of the phonetic environment, this 'first'

---

[99] The following account is based on David Greene, 'The growth of palatalization in Irish'
in *Trans. Phil. Soc.*, lxxii (1973), pp 127–36; note also the modifications suggested by Kim
McCone, 'A note on palatalisation and the present inflection of *i*-verbs' in Ahlqvist & Čapková,
*Dán do Oide*, pp 303–13.

[100] The phonetics of this seem not to have been clarified. In descriptive terms, it would
appear that, while a vowel which survived retained its own distinctive features, the distinctive
features of a lost vowel moved backwards onto the preceding segment.

[101] The issue of a preceding /a:/ is more complicated; O.Ir. *ráithe* 'quarter (of a year)'
/raθ'e/ (< *[ra:θiya]), fits the pattern, but it is possible that voiced dentals were more resistant
to palatalisation; for example, within the paradigm of *ráidid* 'says' /ra:ð'ið'/ forms like the 3rd
pl. *rádat* /ra:ðad/, etc. suggest that /a:ð'i(:)/ were not palatalised and that subsequent palatalisation was due to paradigmatic pressure (see McCone, *Towards a relative chronology*, p. 117;
idem, 'A note on palatalisation'; idem, 'Zum Ablaut der keltischen *r*-Stämme' in J. E. Rasmussen (ed.), *In honorem Holger Pedersen. Kolloquium der Indogermanischen Gesellschaft von 26. bis
28. Marz 1993 in Kopenhagen* (Wiesbaden, 1994), pp 275–84). However, this depends on the
analysis of the direction of analogical pressure in the paradigm of these verbs.

palatalisation became phonemicised; for example, in *[al'iyah] (> O.Ir. *aile* 'other') the palatal [l'] was conditioned by the following [i], but after the lowering to /al'eyah/, the palatal consonant was no longer conditioned but contrasted with, for example, */kaleθah/ (> O.Ir. *calad* 'hard'); the phonetic conditions are the same but one has /l/, the other /l'/. A second stage of palatalisation occurred at this point and before the loss of final syllables, namely the palatalisation of initial consonants before /e(:)/ and /i(:)/, e.g. O.Ir. *beirid* /b'er'əð'/ (< */b'er'eθ'i/), *mligid* /m'l'iɣəð'/ (<*m'l'iɣθ'i)[102] Following the loss of final syllables, the pressure of the initial stress accent had the effect of reducing polysyllabic words by the syncope of the second syllable, and of the fourth syllable in a five- or six-syllable word.[103] The quality of the resulting consonant cluster was determined by the syncopated vowel. It would appear that vowels in such syllables had been reduced either to a front vowel /I/ or a back vowel /A/, the former leaving palatalisation behind when it was syncopated, the latter not, e.g. O.Ir. *toirthech* /tor'θ'əχ/ 'fruitful' (< */tor'Iθaχ / < *toret-āko-) beside *debthach* /d'evθəχ/'contentious' (< */d'evAθaχ / < *debut-āko-). This constitutes the last systematic stage of palatalisation, but the palatal form of a consonant has continued to be the marked variant even up to the modern language; for example, from Middle Irish onwards there has been a tendency to use palatalisation to mark the feminine gender.[104] Syncope was a relatively mechanical process determined by the strong initial stress; however, the resulting patterns were exploited within the history of Irish to make grammatical distinctions; for example, the Old Irish 3rd sg. deponent ending *-aigedar* and the passive *-aigther* arose from a common source, a deponent ending containing the element *-sag-* which was subject to different syncope patterns depending on the syllable structure of the stem; for example, a verb based on a disyllabic stem such as the noun *fogur* 'noise' produced a form *fograigedar*, but a verb based on a monosyllable such as *cruth* 'shape' produced *cruthaigther*.[105] The

---

[102] See McCone, *Towards a relative chronology*, p. 118. How far palatalisation spread through initial clusters at this stage is unclear. For example, even in the modern language initial labials are rarely phonetically palatal; e.g. *binn* 'peak' /biN'/ is often phonetically [bwiN'] and in some dialects *scél* 'story' is /sk'e:l/ rather than /s'k'e:l/ (phonetically [Ske:l]) (see Russell, *Introduction*, pp 80–81).

[103] For a schematic illustration, see Russell, *Introduction*, p. 31.

[104] See Russell, *Introduction*, pp 37–8, 82–4. For a discussion of the alternation of /f/ and /f'/ in the Old Irish *f*-future, see Jerzy Kuryłowicz, 'Morphophonological palatalization in Old Irish' in *Travaux linguistiques de Prague*, iv (1971), pp 67–73 (repr. in J. Kuryłowicz (ed.), *Esquisses linguistiques* (2 vols, Munich, 1973–5), pp 323–9).

[105] On the *-sag-* formant, see Lionel Joseph, 'The origin of the Celtic denominatives in *-sag-*' in Calvert Watkins (ed.), *Studies in memory of Warren Cowgill (1929–1985): papers from the East Coast Indo-European Conference, Cornell University, June 6–9, 1985* (Berlin, 1987), pp 113–59; Paul Russell, 'Agent suffixes in Welsh: native and non-native' in *Bulletin of the Board of Celtic Studies*, xxxvi (1989), pp 30–42: 38–9; idem, '"Verdunkelte Komposita" in Celtic' in *Studia Celt.*, xxx (1996), pp 113–25: 118–19; Conchubhar Ó Crualaoich, 'Syncope patterns in denominative verbs' in *Ériu*, xlviii (1997), pp 239–64.

two endings, -*aigedar* and -*aigther*, then became distinguished functionally as deponent and passive respectively.[106]

The developments discussed above constitute the most significant phonological changes between the break-up of insular Celtic and the emergence of attested manuscript Old Irish. In comparison, the developments within Old and Middle Irish were far less catastrophic, though in part they may have been concealed behind a consistent and conservative orthography. Most of the changes involved reductions in the articulation of pre-tonic elements and in post-tonic syllables in reaction to the intitial stress-accent.[107] The most important consonantal development was the late-seventh-century voicing of consonants on the word boundary next to an unaccented vowel. This affected both proclitics (thus *to·* > *do·*, etc.) and final consonants, e.g. -/θ/ >-/ð/, early O.Ir. *ro·slogeth* 'was swallowed' > O.Ir. *ro·slocad*, *díltuth* 'denying' > *díltud*; most of the evidence centres on the dental fricatives, but it also affected other consonants, e.g. ·*léicfea* 'will let': ·*léiciub* 'I shall let'; among the gutturals, palatal /χ'/ seemed prone to reduce to /γ'/, e.g. *pecthach*: *pecthaig* 'sinner(s)'.

As we have seen, there was also a progressive reduction of vowel distinctions in unaccented syllables.[108] With the apparent exception of /u/, internal vowels seem to have been reduced to /ə/ by the Classical Old Irish period, and their spelling then determined by the quality of the flanking consonants.[109] Apart from the merger of /a/ and /o/, final vowels, where it was important to maintain the distinctions for as long as possible, seem to have survived as distinct entities into the early Middle Irish period, when they fell together as /ə/. The consequences for nominal declensions where the grammatical distinctions were carried by final vowels were potentially catastrophic;[110] for example, among the declensional forms of *céile* 'companion', *céile* (nom., acc., gen. pl.), *céili* (gen. sg., nom. pl.), *céliu* (dat. sg., acc. pl.) were all pronounced /k'e:l'ə/. Within Old Irish, the maintenance of these distinctions seems to be confirmed by the accuracy of the rhyming patterns in verse which indicate that the vowels were still kept apart. On the other hand, evidence collected from the Old Irish glosses suggests that confusion was relatively common especially in the Milan and St Gall glosses.[111] Similarly, with internal vowels, confusion over /u/ is attested. This raises the

[106] McCone, 'Further to absolute and conjunct', pp 5–6; Warren Cowgill, 'On the prehistory of the Celtic passive and deponent inflection' in *Ériu*, xxxiv (1983), pp 73–111. For other effects of syncope, such as the resolution of consonant clusters and the development of epenthetic vowels, see McCone, *Towards a relative chronology*, pp 127–30.

[107] McCone, *Towards a relative chronology*, pp 134–7.

[108] For a summary, see McCone, *Towards a relative chronology*, p. 142.

[109] See above, pp 419–20.

[110] McCone, *Towards a relative chronology*, pp 142–3; Breatnach, 'An Mheán-Ghaeilge', p. 230. On the consequent development of new plural forms, see David Greene, 'Distinctive plural forms in Old and Middle Irish' in *Ériu*, xxv (1974), pp 190–99.

[111] McCone, 'The Würzburg and Milan glosses', pp 86–8.

question of when these reductions took place in the spoken language. It is possible that these changes took place as early as the eighth century in the spoken language, even though the distinctions may have been maintained in higher registers.[112]

The above account of the phonology of Old and Middle Irish has been highly selective but has focused on the main developments. It goes without saying that they had a massive effect on the morphology of the language. Two aspects are considered here: the nominal declension and the absolute and conjunct distinctions in the verb.

Irish inherited a series of nominal declensions corresponding to those attested in other Indo-European languages.[113] A glance at, for example, Latin or Greek will indicate how reliant those languages were on the distinctions carried by the final syllables of words. Given that Irish lost its final syllables, it might reasonably be asked how it succeeded in maintaining a declensional system, particularly when the Brittonic languages in a similar situation lost theirs.[114] A number of features seem to have come together to provide a sufficient number of distinctions for a case system to be maintained. For example, to take a relatively simple case, the declension of *fer* 'man' contains forms which display the effects of vowel affection and palatalisation and also cause different mutations of following closely associated words: *fer* (nom. sg.), *fer*[N] (acc. sg.), *fir*[L] (gen. sg.), *fiur*[L] (dat. sg.), *fir*[L] (nom. pl.), *firu* (acc. pl.), *fer*[N] (gen. pl.), *feraib* (dat. pl.). Added to these distinctions was a relatively fixed word order. The standard ordering of elements in Old Irish was V(erb)–S(ubject)–O(bject); genitives followed the noun which they modified. The combination of these syntactic and morphological features thus maintained enough distinctions for a case system to survive. However, the system was finely balanced and a change, such as the reduction of final vowels to -/ə/, as discussed above, was potentially very damaging. What emerges from a consideration of Middle Irish nominal development is that the main preoccupation was avoidance of homophony, especially between singular and plural;[115] accusatives and genitives could probably be distinguished by word-order patterns, and datives were by now almost entirely governed by prepositions, but distinctions of number were crucial. This was not a new problem; in Old Irish the nominative plural of neuter *o*-stem nouns had already been problematic in that they were often identical to the

---

[112] On different registers, see below, pp 448–9.

[113] For the details, see McCone, 'An tSean-Ghaeilge', pp 92–118; Breatnach, 'An Mheán-Ghaeilge', pp 239–51. For a detailed study of one declensional class, see Karin Stüber, *The historical morphology of n-stems in Celtic* (Maynooth, 1998).

[114] Koch, 'The loss of final syllables'; see also Eric P. Hamp, 'Miscellanea Celtica, I. The transformation of British inflexion' in *Studia Celt.*, x–xi (1975–6), pp 54–8.

[115] Greene, 'Distinctive plural forms'; Strachan, 'Contributions to the history of Irish declension'; Raymond Hickey, 'Reduction of allomorphy and the plural in Irish' in *Ériu*, xxxvi (1985), pp 143–62.

singular (the inherited ending was *-/a/ and so did not cause palatalisation like the masculine nominative plural). A longer ending in -*a* probably deriving in origin from the feminine nominative plural, e.g. *túatha*, spread to the neuters, and tended to occur if there was no other plural marker, such as a numeral or the article.[116] In Middle Irish this went further, and vowel final nouns tended to acquire plural endings from consonant stem nouns, especially from the lenited dental stem nouns, e.g. O.Ir. *céile* (nom. sg.): *céili* (nom. pl.) M. Ir. *céile* /k'e:l'ə/ : *céileda* /k'e:l'əðə/, etc.[117]

The verbal system of early Irish provides a full system of tenses, moods, and voices.[118] The feature that is unique to the insular Celtic languages and is most fully realised in Old Irish is the double system of 'absolute' and 'conjunct' verbal inflection. The system operated essentially as follows: when a simple verb was used in a declarative sentence with no negative or interrogative particle or conjunction, it went in first position in the sentence and took the 'absolute' form, e.g. *léicid* /'L'e:g'əð'/ 'he leaves', but if it was preceded by a particle of any sort it took the 'conjunct' form, e.g. *ní·léici* /n'i·'L'e:g'i/ 'he does not leave', *in·léici?* /in'L'e:g'i/ 'does he leave?', etc. In both cases the stress was on the first syllable of the verbal element. Compound verbs worked in a similar way except that the preverb took the place of the particle; thus, *do·léici* 'he throws' had the same stress pattern as *ní·léici*. But when the compound required another verbal particle, a negative or an interrogative, the preverb was amalgamated with the verb, e.g. *ní·teilci* /n'i·t'el'g'i/ 'he does not throw'. Thus simple verbs have a double system of inflection, but the stem remains unchanged. Compound verbs have a double stem formation, conventionally known as 'deuterotonic' and 'prototonic' respectively, e.g. *do·beir/ taibr-* 'give', *as·beir/ ep(e)r-*'say', *do·gní/ dén-* 'do', *im·soí/ impai* 'turn', etc. The pretonic particles, whether preverbs or grammatical particles, also carried enclitic, infixed pronouns. In early Old Irish a pronoun was suffixed to a simple verb, e.g. *sástum* 'it feeds me' (-*um* 1st sg. pronoun), *léicthi* '(he) leaves it', *bertius* 'he carried them', but infixed into a compound verb, e.g. *dom·beir* /dom'v'er'/ 'he gives me' : *do·beir* 'he gives',

---

[116] McCone, 'An tSean-Ghaeilge', p. 95.

[117] Breatnach, 'An Mheán-Ghaeilge', p. 246; Strachan, 'Contributions to the history of Irish declension', pp 2–24. With the reduction of /ð/ to /y/ or /γ/ the later language has had to look elsewhere for its plural formants, to guttural and nasal elements, e.g. -*acha(í)*, -*anna(í)* (Russell, *Introduction*, pp 84–5 and references).

[118] For general discussion, see Thurneysen, *Grammar of Old Irish*, pp 326–494; McCone, *Early Irish verb*; Pedersen, *Vergleichende Grammatik*, ii, 261–658 (= Lewis and Pedersen, *A concise comparative Celtic grammar*, pp 245–403); McCone, 'An tSean-Ghaeilge', pp 132–86; Breatnach, 'An Mheán-Ghaeilge', pp 278–325. For specific historical discussions, see Calvert Watkins, *The Indo-European origins of the Celtic verb: I, the sigmatic aorist* (Dublin, 1962); Kim McCone, 'From Indo-European to Old Irish: conservation and innovation in the verbal system' in Evans *et al.*, *Proceedings*, pp 222–66; idem, *The Indo-European origins of the Old Irish nasal presents, subjunctives and futures* (Innsbruck, 1991); Warren Cowgill, 'The origins of the insular Celtic conjunct and absolute verbal endings' in H. Rix (ed.), *Flexion und Wortbildung* (Wiesbaden, 1975), pp 40–70.

etc.[119] But by late Old Irish the infixed pronoun had been generalised as the standard pattern; with a simple verb a 'dummy' perverb *no* (probably in origin a sentence connective) was used, e.g. *nos·bert* 'he carried them', *nom·sása* 'it feeds me', etc.

The origin of these patterns has been much debated.[120] There are several issues here about word order (why is the verb initial and so closely bound up with pronouns?), lenition (why is there no lenition in, for example, *do·beir* /do͝b′er′/?), and the morphology of the endings (why do the absolute endings seem in origin to be a syllable longer than their conjunct counterparts?). It has been generally assumed that these questions are interrelated and that a coherent account should be able to explain them all. A view that still has many adherents was that a particle, which subsequently disappeared, was responsible for the lack of lenition and the longer absolute form; for example, a particle *\*es*, to take a case which has been argued at some length, would give O.Ir. *beirid* < *\*bereti-es*, and *do·beir* < *\*to-es beret*. In the compound it vanished but prevented lenition; in the simplex its presence prevented the loss of final -/i/, thus preserving the dental ending.[121] More recent explanations have rejected the particle and allotted greater weight to the personal pronoun, but they do salvage some aspects of this account, notably the use of an element, namely the personal pronoun, to block the loss of -/i/ in, for example, *\*bereti*. The account runs like this: beside *\*beret(i)* > O.Ir. *·beir*, the suffixed pronoun prevented the loss of -/i/, e.g. *\*bereti-em* > O.Ir. *beirthium* '(he) carries me'. In compounds the pronoun was in second position, *\*to-me-beret(i)* (> O.Ir. *dom·beir*). Subsequent developments presuppose a certain view of Indo-European word order, but the upshot is that out of the complexes of verb and pronoun new analogical verbal forms were extracted: from *\*bereti-em* a simple *\*bereti* arose (> O.Ir. *beirid*) and from *\*to-me-bereti* a compound *\*to beret(i)* (> O.Ir. *do·beir*).[122] Some recent accounts have been more

[119] On suffixed pronouns, see Liam Breatnach, 'The suffixed pronouns in early Irish' in *Celtica*, xii (1977), pp 75–107.

[120] Kim McCone, 'Pretonic preverbs and the absolute verbal endings in Old Irish' in *Ériu*, xxx (1979), pp 1–34; idem, 'Further to absolute and conjunct' in *Ériu*, xxxiii (1982), pp 1–29; idem, 'An tSean-Ghaeilge', pp 176–81; Cowgill, 'The origins'; Patrick Sims-Williams, 'The double system of verbal inflexion in Old Irish' in *Trans. Phil. Soc.*, lxxxii (1984), pp 138–201; Graham Isaac, 'Non-lenition in the neo-Celtic verbal complex' in *Bulletin of the Board of Celtic Studies*, xxxviii (1991), pp 93–7; idem, 'Issues in the reconstruction and analysis of insular Celtic syntax and phonology' in *Ériu*, xliv (1993), pp 1–32; John T. Koch, 'Prosody and the old Celtic verbal complex' in *Ériu*, xxxviii (1987), pp 143–76. Peter Schrijver, 'The etymology of the Celtic adverbs for "against" and "with" and related matters' in *Ériu*, xlv (1994), pp 151–89; idem, *Studies*, pp 147–58.

[121] Cowgill, 'The origins'.

[122] Calvert Watkins, 'Preliminaries to the historical and comparative analysis of the syntax of the Old Irish verb' in *Celtica*, vi (1963), pp 11–49; idem, 'Preliminaries to the reconstruction of the Indo-European sentence structure' in H. G. Lunt (ed.), *Proceedings of the Ninth International Congress of Linguists* (The Hague, 1964), pp 1035–42; see also Paul Russell, 'Preverbs, prepositions and adverbs: sigmatic and asigmatic' in *Trans. Phil. Soc.*, lxxxvi (1988), pp 144–72.

interested in single aspects of the question and less in trying to account for all the issues in one overarching theory. For example, it has been suggested that the non-lenition of the second element in a deuterotonic compound can be explained more simply as a normal phonological development, and we need not be so reliant on analogical developments.[123] Another aspect that has come in for scrutiny is the pattern of word-order reconstructed from Old Irish and the vestigial but supporting evidence from Brittonic. The issue is how to account for the change from an Indo-European word-order pattern where the verb is final (S(ubject), O(bject), V(erb)), or at least after the subject and object, to the Insular Celtic pattern of an initial verbal phrase (VSO). It has long been thought that enclitic particles were the key; in Indo-European they regularly came in second position (Wackernagel's Law) and Celtic seems to have developed a secondary restriction (Vendryes's Restriction) which associated these elements with the verb, hence the migration of the verb towards the front of the sentence. Until recently, this has been recognised but more often acknowledged than explained.[124]

Middle Irish witnessed some wholesale redevelopments of the verbal system.[125] The loss of neuter gender together with the reduction of unstressed vowels to /ə/ reduced the series of infixed pronouns to chaos, out of which arose the modern system of independent, stressed object pronouns. The breakdown of the infixed pronoun system was one factor in the erosion of the absolute/conjunct system (though it was preserved to a greater degree in Scottish Gaelic and Manx), since there was less need for pretonic preverbs in which to infix pronouns. The most frequent development was the creation of new simple verbs based on the prototonic forms of compound verbs, such as verbal nouns and imperatives, e.g. O.Ir. *do·léici*: ·*teilci* ⇒ M.Ir. *teilcid* 'throws', *do·sluindi*: ·*díltai* ⇒ M.Ir. *díltaid* 'denies', etc.[126] The paradigm was further clarified by the development of clear single sets of endings, notably 3rd sg. -*enn*/-*ann*.[127] The complex patterns of tense formations dependent on the class of verb was also ripe for simplification.[128] For example, depending on the stem class of the verb, the Old Irish future was marked by an *f*-suffix, reduplication of the initial of the verbal stem (with or without an *s*-suffix), or by a lengthened stem vowel, e.g. *léicfid* 'he will leave': *léicid* 'he

---

[123] Whether by assuming an original enclitic verb and accented preverb (Koch, 'Prosody and the old Celtic verbal complex') or by a process of 'non-intraphrasal juncture, across which neither early sandhi nor later mutations operated' (Isaac, 'Issues in the reconstruction and analysis of insular Celtic syntax and phonology', p. 27).

[124] For a recent study with important typological parallels, see Joseph Eska, 'On the crossroads of phonology and syntax: remarks on the origin of Vendryes' Restriction and related matters' in *Studia Celt.*, xxviii (1994), pp 39–62.

[125] McCone, *Early Irish verb*, pp 176–266; Breatnach, 'An Mheán-Ghaeilge', pp 278–325.

[126] McCone, *Early Irish verb*, pp 207–9.

[127] Ibid., pp 224–7.

[128] For a brief summary, see Russell, *Introduction*, p. 47 (table 2.13); see also McCone, *Early Irish verb*, pp 28–66.

leaves', *bebaid* 'he will die' : *báid* 'he dies', *memais* 'he will break' : *maidid* 'he breaks', *·béra* 'he will carry' : *beirid* 'he carries'.[129] Middle Irish displays a confused situation where each type seems to be being generalised at the expense of the others.[130]

THE lexicon of any language consists of words of different origins. By far and away the largest constituent will be the inherited vocabulary, which is constantly being expanded by the derivational and compositional resources of the language itself. The second important element consists of loanwords from other languages with which the speakers of our target language have come into contact; they provide evidence of social contact and can often provide a different approach to the question of absolute and relative chronologies. Thirdly, in certain contexts another type of borrowing occurs whereby words are not borrowed *per se* but their elements are translated or 'calqued'; this frequently occurs in the acquisition of learned or technical terminology.

All three types can be fully exemplified from early Irish. Old Irish had a fully established system of derivational morphology, i.e. of suffixes and prefixes by which nouns could be turned into adjectives, adjectives into nouns, nouns and adjectives into verbs, common nouns into abstract nouns, etc.[131] In addition Celtic languages continued a productive tradition of compound formations, i.e. formations of noun plus noun, etc., where, unlike a derivative formation, both elements were attested independently in the language.[132] Both types may be exemplified by consideration of the derivatives and compounds of O.Ir. *mac(c)* 'son, boy'.[133] In the following examples two strands of meaning are discernible, the specific genetic sense of 'son' and a broader sense of 'boy, young person'. Both productive adjectival formations are attested with an apparent difference in meaning, *maccach* 'son-bearing' and

[129] See Thurneysen, *Grammar*, pp 404–5.

[130] McCone, *Early Irish verb*, pp 241–50; Breatnach, 'An Mheán-Ghaeilge', pp 314–20; Brendan Ó Buachalla, 'The *f*-future in Modern Irish: a re-assessment' in *R.I.A. Proc.*, lxxxv (1985) sect. C, pp 1–36.

[131] See Patrizia de Bernardo Stempel, *Nominale Wortbildung des älteren Irischen: Stammbildung und Derivation* (Tübingen, 1999); for an overview, see Pedersen, *Vergleichende Grammatik*, ii, 1–63; see also Russell, *Celtic word-formation*; Dagmar Wodtko, *Sekundäradjektive in den altirischen Glossen* (Innsbruck, 1995); for modern Irish, see Aidan Doyle and Edmund Gussmann, *A reverse dictionary of modern Irish* (Lublin, 1996); cf. also Stefan Zimmer, *Studies in Welsh word-formation* (Dublin, 2000).

[132] On compound names and nouns, see Pedersen, *Vergleichende Grammatik*, ii, 1–15; Jürgen Uhlich, *Die Morphologie der komponierten Personennamen des Altirischen* (Witterschlick and Bonn, 1993); idem, 'Verbal governing compounds (synthetics) in early Irish and other Celtic languages' in *Trans. Phil. Soc.*, l (2002), pp 403–33.

[133] See E. G. Quin *et al.*, *(Contributions to a) Dictionary of the Irish language based mainly on Old and Middle Irish materials* (Dublin, 1913–76), *M*, cols 5–15; dates of attestation of examples may stray beyond 1169, but this is necessary to gain the full picture.

*macthae* 'pertaining to a boy, juvenile'.[134] A third adjectival derivative is *macamail* 'like a son, filial'; the 'suffix' here is in origin the adjective *samail* 'like, similar to', and it is arguable whether such forms are to be treated as derivatives or as compounds.[135] It is clear that in later Irish it develops into a suffix -/uːlʲ/ (in modern spelling *-úil*), but the status of the Old Irish examples is ambiguous.[136] Such formations come under the heading of 'verdunkelte Komposita';[137] for semantic or phonological reasons the second element is moving from being an independent element towards being a suffix and, as such, they occupy the grey area between derivatives and compounds. Nominal derivatives can have different senses: hypocoristic or familiar, e.g. *maccán*, *maccucán* 'dear little son' (the latter often used of Christ), collective *macrad* 'sons, boys, youths', abstract *macc(d)acht* 'childhood', *maccacht* 'position of being the king's son'.[138] These primary derivatives can themselves form the base for secondary derivatives, e.g. *maccánta* 'youthful, gentle' (: *maccán*) which is itself the base for the abstract noun *maccántacht* and *maccántas* 'youth, gentleness'. Similarly, *macrad* is the base for an Old Irish hypocoristic *macradán*. The latter examples illustrate the productivity and vitality of these derivational processes.

In addition to derivatives, *macc* also had an important role in compound formations where again it more usually has the more general sense of 'boy' or 'child' and even more generally, almost as a prefix, 'young —' (when it can even lose its gender specific sense), e.g. *maccléirech* 'young cleric', *maccaillech* 'young nun', *macloc* 'womb' (lit. 'child-place'), *macless* 'juvenile feat', *macgním* 'a boyhood deed'. Compounds can also be used to indicate a different relationship between the elements, e.g. *macslechta* 'sections of law about children'. *Mac* can also have a more metaphorical sense of a product of something, e.g. *maclebar* 'a book copied from another', a usage which is closer to the use of *mac* with a genitive in kennings, such as *mac tíre* 'wolf' (lit. 'son of a land'), *mac alla* 'echo' (lit. 'son of a cliff'), *mac snáma* 'large fish' (lit. 'son of swimming'). Of these compounds, *maccoím* 'boy, lad' (*macc* + *coím* 'fair') seems to be one of the

---

[134] For *-ach* and *-dae*, see the discussion in Russell, *Celtic word-formation*, pp 131–5, where no clear conclusion is reached. The examples here apparently show a distinction of 'qualitative' v. 'relative' meaning (*Celtic word-formation*, p. 123), but comparison is always difficult, as neither is frequently attested.

[135] See Wodtko, *Sekundäradjektive*, pp 312–16; Pedersen, *Vergleichende Grammatik*, ii, 14.

[136] On *-úil*, see Doyle and Gussmann, *Reverse dictionary*, pp 252–6.

[137] For the term, see Pedersen, *Vergleichende Grammatik*, ii, 13–15; for a discussion, see Russell, ' "Verdunkelte Komposita" '.

[138] On *-rad*, see Russell, ' "Verdunkelte Komposita" ', pp 121–3. On *macc(d)acht*, see Joseph Vendryes *et al.*, *Lexique étymologique de l'irlandais ancien* (Dublin and Paris, 1960), M-3; it may not be based on *mac* but, if not, it was influenced by it; it was borrowed into Welsh as *machdeith*. *Maccucán* is a secondary derivative in *-án* based on a derivative containing the borrowed suffix *-uc* (perhaps an early form of *-óc*; see Russell, *Celtic word-formation*, pp 115–16); idem, 'Patterns of hypocorism in early Irish hagiography' in J. Carey, M. Herbert, and P. Ó Riain (ed.), *Studies in Irish hagiography: saints and scholars* (Dublin, 2001), pp 237–49).

earliest and most deeply embedded in the language not only in that it has generated its own series of derivatives (always a useful diagnostic indicator), e.g. adjective *maccoímda* 'boyish, youthful', abstract nouns *maccoímdacht, maccoímnacht* 'youthful vigour', but also because it was borrowed into early Welsh as *mackwy(f)*.

The second area of the lexicon is that of loanwords, of which the Latin loanwords constitute the largest and most important group. Their significance is not simply cultural, though the context of loans is important; for they have major linguistic implications for the absolute chronology of the sound changes of early Irish.[139] The important point is that, when loanwords are absorbed into a language, they undergo all subsequent phonological changes as if they were native words, but do not reflect sound changes that occurred before their arrival in the language. Latin words borrowed into early Irish, therefore, can take on more than one form, depending on the date of their arrival; for example, Latin /p/ could appear as *c* or *p*, depending on whether it was borrowed before or after Irish had developed its own /p/ (Celtic /p/ had been lost), e.g. Latin *Patricius* > O.Ir. *Cothriche* or *Pátraic* (the most famous loanword of all); Latin intervocalic /t/ and /k/ appeared as *th* /θ/ and *ch* /χ/ or as *t* /d/ and *c* /g/, e.g. Latin *puteus* 'well' > O.Ir. *cuithe*, Latin *Natalicia* 'Christmas' > O.Ir. *Notlaic*, etc.[140] Words with Irish /k/ and /θ/ for Latin /p/ and /t/ must have been borrowed at the time before Irish had developed /p/ and before the lenition of /t/ to /θ/; on the other hand, forms with Irish *t* /d/ and *c* /g/ corresponding to Latin *t* /t/ and *c* /k/ came into Irish via British Latin and show the effect of British sound changes, especially the British lenition of /t/ to /d/, etc. The notion that the loanwords into Irish arrived in two groups has now largely been replaced by the view that there was a continual influx of words which can be dated relatively in terms of the sound changes which they have or have not undergone.[141] The fixed chronology centres on the connection (or lack of one) between the earlier representation of *Patricius* as *Cothriche* and St Patrick's mission to Ireland; in part that will depend on how frequently the name *Patricius* occurs as a name separately from the saint's

---

[139] The main studies are Jackson, *Language and history*, pp 122–45; Damian McManus, 'A chronology of the Latin loanwords in early Irish' in *Ériu*, xxxiv (1983), pp 21–72; idem, 'On final syllables in Latin loanwords in early Irish' in *Ériu*, xxxv (1984), pp 137–46. On dating, see also Sims-Williams, 'Dating the transition to neo-Brittonic'; Koch, '\*Cothairche, Esposito's theory and neo-Celtic lenition'; Anthony Harvey, 'The significance of Cothraige' in *Ériu*, xxxvi (1985), pp 1–9; idem, 'Latin, literacy and the Celtic vernaculars around the year A.D. 500' in C. J. Byrne, M. Harry, and P. Ó Siadhail (ed.), *Celtic languages and Celtic people: proceedings of the Second North American Congress of Celtic Studies (Halifax, August 16–19, 1989)* (Halifax, 1992), pp 15–26.

[140] See McManus, 'A chronology', pp 21–7; Jackson, *Language and history*, p. 126; Russell, *Introduction*, p. 43 (table 2.11).

[141] For the former, see Jackson, *Language and history*, pp 122–45; the latter has been advocated by McManus, 'A chronology'.

name.[142] The modern trend is for contacts between Latin and Irish to be pushed further and further back well into the pre-Patrician period. As we have seen, the creation of Ogam seems to be dependent on knowledge of Latin.[143] Even though Agricola's ambition, as he stood on the Rhinns of Galloway, to take Ireland with one legion was never realised, trading contacts between the Roman empire and Ireland were well established, particularly in the area to the north of the Liffey and in the north.[144] It is presumably in this context that the first loanwords were transmitted, words associated with trade and the military, such as *ór* (Latin *aurum*) 'gold', *fín* (*vīnum*) 'wine', *corcur* (*purpur-*) 'purple', *míl* (*mīles*) 'soldier', *trebun* (*tribūnus*) 'tribune', *arm* (*arma*) 'arms', *long* ((*navis*) *longa*) 'ship', *múr* (*mūrus*) 'wall', *drauc* (*dracō*) 'dragon', *leo* (*leō*) 'lion', etc.[145] The Christian loanwords may well have been somewhat later, but it is important to note that even among the linguistically earliest loanwords there is a selection that must derive from a Christian context, e.g. *axal* (< *apostolus*), *cásc* (< *Pāscha*), *cruimther* (< *\*prebiter/ \*premiter* (< *presbyter*)), and arguably *Cothriche* himself.[146] It is reasonable to assume that most of the Latin words borrowed into Irish in the early period were transmitted orally, in that they reflect sound-changes in Irish subsequent to their arrival. However, the bulk of Latin loanwords seem to have entered the language from early Old Irish onwards; and here the relative stability of the language (in contrast to the huge changes of the previous centuries) makes it difficult to establish a chronology. Moreover, in general terms the later the loanword, the more learned in character it is likely to be.[147] That said, they may be literary but often they reflect their Vulgar Latin origins, particularly in their vowel quantities, whereby length was associated with stress and originally long unstressed vowels were shortened, e.g. O.Ir. *bináir* (< *bīnārius* : Classical Latin *bīnārius*), *Enáir* (< *Jēnārius* : *Jēnārius*), *oróit* (< *orātio* : *ōrātio*), etc.[148] Another occasional feature of learned borrowings was their retention of the Latin ending,

---

[142] For Sims-Williams, 'Dating the transition to neo-Brittonic', p. 229, the name was very common and could have arrived in Ireland independently of the saint; for Koch, '*Cothairche*, Esposito's theory and neo-Celtic lenition', pp 185–6, the name was unique to the saint and he arrived earlier.

[143] See Stevenson, 'The beginnings of literacy'; Anthony Harvey, 'Latin, literacy and the Celtic vernaculars'; idem, 'Early literacy in Ireland: the evidence from Ogam' in *Camb. Med. Celt. Studies*, xiv (winter 1987), pp 1–15.

[144] Tacitus, 'Agricola', xxiv.3; Charles-Edwards, *Early Christian Ireland*, pp 155–7. See above, pp 174–7.

[145] See James Carney, 'Three Old-Irish accentual poems' in *Ériu*, xxii (1971), pp 23–80: pp 69–70; McManus, 'A chronology', pp 42–3. However, there is nothing inherent in the phonology of these words that makes them particularly early loanwords.

[146] McManus, 'A chronology', p. 48; for *cruimther*, see ibid., p. 46, n. 60; cf. Harvey, 'The significance of *Cothraige*', who does not accept this.

[147] McManus, 'A chronology', pp 66–9.

[148] Ibid., p. 68.

e.g. O.Ir. *augtartás* (< *auctoritas*), *mem(m)rum(m)* (< *membrum*), *súabais* (< *suāvis*).[149]

From the ninth century onwards Irish also received a substantial influx of loanwords from the viking settlers in Ireland.[150] Unlike Latin loanwords, in this instance they are all non-learned, practical terms associated with shipping, buildings, warfare, and commerce, e.g. M.Ir. *bát* 'boat' (< O.N. *bátr*), *ciúil* 'ship' (< *kjóll*), *cnarr* 'ship' (< *knorr*), *fuindeog* 'window' (< *vindauga*), *meirge* 'standard' (< *merki*), *boga* 'bow' (< *bogi*), *margad* 'market' (< *markaðr*), etc. The earliest examples occur in Cormac's Glossary where they are described as deriving from *lingua Normannica* or *lingua Galleorum*, but the majority of them derive from the Middle Irish saga texts.[151]

The third element of the lexicon is related to the second in that it involves input from another language, but instead of foreign words being borrowed wholesale they are analysed and the elements translated into the target language. These 'calques' are a feature of the learned and literary level of the language, in that they usually have to do with complex words.[152] Two types are attested in Irish. The first involves morphemic translation (*Lehnübersetzung*), e.g. *soiscél* (*so-* + *scél*) 'gospel' < Latin *evangelium* (= Greek εὖ 'good, well' +ἀγγέλιον 'message'), *locdatu* < Latin *localitas* (where *loc-da* (adj. suffix) *-tu* (abstract suffix) matches the morphemic structure of the source word exactly), *guthdae* 'vowel' ⇐ *vocalis*, *ranngabáil* 'participle' < *participium* (*rann-* 'part' + *gabáil* = *-cip-* 'taking'), etc.[153] The calquing is particularly prevalent in grammatical terminology where the Irish were keen to show that they had a native terminological system; simple borrowing, therefore, would not do. The following examples were generated by the Irish glossator on the St Gall Priscian and show the piecemeal nature of the translation: *dígabthach* 'diminutive' ⇐ *diminutiva*, *úadairbertach* 'pejoratively' ⇐ *abusive*, *remfuirmedach* 'preposition' ⇐ *praepositivae*, *foillsigthech* 'demonstrative' ⇐ *demonstrativa*.[154] The terminology of the case terms is another clear case: *ainmnid* 'nominative' ⇐ *nominativus*, *áinsid* 'accusative' ⇐ *accusativus*, etc., where the Latin terms are calqued by the agent noun suffix *-(a)id*. The Latin

---

[149] McManus, 'On final syllables', p. 161.

[150] Marstrander, *Bidtrag*; Alexander Bugge, 'Norse loans in Irish' in O. J. Bergin and C. Marstrander (ed.), *Miscellany presented to Kuno Meyer* (Halle, 1912), pp 291–306; Richard Sharpe, 'ME *falding*, MIr *fallaing*: Irish mantles in medieval England' in *Anglia*, cvii (1989), pp 416–29. For borrowings from Irish into Norse, see Gary Holland and John Lindow, 'Irish poetry and Norse *dróttkvætt*', in Klar *et al.*, *A Celtic florilegium*, pp 54–62: pp 59–60.

[151] Meyer, *Sanas Cormaic*, §§ 138 (*in lingua Galleorum*), 523, 739, 1040 (*nor(t)manica lingua*).

[152] Enrico Campanile, 'Calchi irlandese di voci latine' in *Studi e saggi linguistici*, x (1970), pp 5–13; D. A. Binchy, 'Semantic influence of Latin in the Old Irish glosses' in J. J. O'Meara and B. Naumann (ed.), *Latin script and letters A.D. 450–900. Festschrift presented to Ludwig Bieler on the occasion of his 70th birthday* (Leyden, 1970) pp 103–12; McManus, 'On final syllables', pp 135–45.

[153] Examples are taken from McManus, 'On final syllables', p. 141.

[154] For details, see Russell, *Celtic word-formation*, pp 89–90. On later grammatical calquing, see Ó Cuív, 'Linguistic terminology'.

terms are themselves calqued on the Greek terms and *accusativus* is a false rendering of Greek αἰτιατικὴ (πτῶσις 'case') which should be rendered as *causativus* (and is in Priscian, where it is calqued as *cóisid* in the St Gall glosses (Sg. 77a3)).[155] In a similar way the calquing could go astray in other cases too: for example, *airdegnúisigud* (Sg. 77a6) containing *airde* 'sign' and *gnúis* 'face' looks like an interpretation of *significatio* as containing *signum* and *facies*.[156] The distinction between borrowing and calque is not always clear; the following contain borrowed first elements but Irish suffixation: *mandáil* < *mandātum*, *cáilidecht* ⇐ *quālitas*, *caindigecht* ⇐ *quantitas*, etc.[157]

The second type of calque is in some ways more pervasive and at the same time harder to identify. They are termed 'semantic loans' or *Lehnprägungen*.[158] There is no structural or morphemic imitation of a foreign original but an existing native term is expanded to include a range of meanings belonging to its presumed Latin equivalent; for example, O.Ir. *dliged* 'right, obligation, etc.' was equated with Latin *ratio* and extended its meaning to include other senses of *ratio* such as 'principle, theory'; similarly, *folud* 'material' took on the abstract senses of Latin *substantia*;[159] O.Ir. *commám* 'joint union, wedlock' (lit. 'joint yoke') also acquired the sense of 'wife' on the semantic analogy of Latin *coniunx*;[160] likewise, *duille* 'leaf, page' may well have acquired the latter sense on the analogy of the range of meanings of Latin *folium*. Again, grammatical terminology was a fertile area: *aimser* 'point of time' ⇒ 'tense' (Latin *tempus*), *cenél* 'race, kindred' ⇒ 'gender' (*genus*), *césad* 'suffering' ⇒ 'passive' (*passivus*), *tuisel* 'fall' ⇒ 'case' (*cāsus*), etc.[161]

So far the discussion of early Irish has only briefly touched upon the idea of different registers and, more generally, of variation within the language. It has long been recognised that Old Irish was remarkably free of evidence for dialectal variation.[162] Given the multiplicity of small kingdoms, the relative difficulty of travel, and the geographical spread of the language, it is inconceivable that there were not dialects of Irish in the seventh and eighth centuries. A tantalising glimpse is offered by an entry in Cormac's Glossary where it is suggested that the word *naire*, otherwise designated *senbérla* 'archaic language', is claimed to be the current form (*gnáthbérla*) in west

---

[155] McManus, 'On final syllables', p. 142, n. 12.
[156] Binchy, 'Semantic influence', p. 171; McManus, 'On final syllables', p. 142, n. 11.
[157] McManus, 'On final syllables', p. 143.
[158] Binchy, 'Semantic influence', p. 171; McManus, 'On final syllables', p. 143.
[159] On *dliged* and *folud*, see Binchy, 'Semantic influence', pp 171, 173.
[160] McManus, 'On final syllables', p. 144.
[161] Ibid., p. 144.
[162] See Charles-Edwards, 'Language and society', pp 727–8.

Munster corresponding to *éicin* 'indeed'.[163] The implication seems to be that in the environs of Cashel *éicin* is usual and *naire* is regarded as old-fashioned, but further west *naire* was still in use. If so, this example provides a rare insight into localised dialectal variation in Munster. Such examples are very rare. But even if we are convinced that there must have been dialects, it is far from clear how we can make progress. Essentially we have the evidence of three corpora of glosses with which to work, but they are not contemporaneous with each other:[164] The Würzburg glosses are usually dated to *c*.750, Milan to *c*.800, and St Gall to *c*.850 (but the last is almost certainly a stratified collection with earlier material incorporated).[165] Milan seems to show a more evolved form of the language than Würzburg, but also seems to be more careless, especially with orthography. How, then, are we to assess the variation between them? How do we distinguish chronological variation from variation of register from differences due to the varying regional origins of the glossators? Some variation in register may betray regional origins but it need not do so; it may reflect, for example, a more or less poetical or rhetorical register.

Certain features of the language have been canvassed as perhaps showing signs of dialectal variation.[166] Thurneysen discussed a range of features of varying significance, though it is difficult to resist the conclusion that he used dialectal variation 'as a sort of pis-aller, to describe phenomena for which he had no other explanation'.[167] Methodological difficulties intervene if there is no check on the evidence by reference to the later language.[168] For example, Thurneysen's claim that the double superlative ending *-imem*, found only in Milan, the preference for the demonstrative *són* in St Gall but for *ón* in Würzburg and Milan, and the variation in the prefix *ar-/er-/air-/*

---

[163] Meyer, *Sanas Cormaic*, § 972. For *senbérla* and *gnáthbérla*, see below, pp 448–9.
[164] For details, see above, p. 412.
[165] See Hofman, *The Sankt Gall Priscian commentary*.
[166] Anders Ahlqvist, 'Remarks on the question of dialects in Old Irish' in J. Fisiak (ed.), *Historical dialectology: regional and social* (Berlin, New York, and Amsterdam, 1988), pp 23–38; Patricia Kelly, 'Dialekte im Altirischen?' in Wolfgang Meid, H. Ölberg, and H. Schmeja (ed.), *Sprachwissenschaft in Innsbruck* (Innsbruck, 1982), pp 85–9; Kim McCone, 'Zur Frage der Register im frühen Irischen' in Stephen N. Tranter and Hildegard L. C. Tristram (ed.), *Early Irish literature—media and communication/Mündlichkeit und Schriftlichkeit in der frühen irischen Literatur* (Tübingen, 1989), pp 57–97: 79–80.
[167] Ahlqvist, 'Remarks on the question of dialects', p. 26. For Thurneysen's comments on dialects, see *Grammar*, pp 12, 104, 306.
[168] Contrast the interesting progress made in tracing Middle Welsh dialectal variation over admittedly a small number of features; see Peter Wynn Thomas, 'In search of Middle Welsh dialects' in Byrne *et al.*, *Celtic languages and Celtic people*, pp 287–303; idem, 'Middle Welsh dialects: problems and perspectives' in *Bulletin of the Board of Celtic Studies*, xxxvii (1993), pp 1–42. Things are significantly easier in Middle Welsh, where there are a reasonable number of manuscripts which are approximately datable and locatable. There are, however, dangers as well: it is all too easy to map modern dialect distributions back into the medieval period and to assume that the boundaries have not shifted.

*aur-*, are all manifestations of dialectal variation is unprovable on the grounds that none of these features shows dialectal variation in the later language.[169] A converse example is equally unhelpful: the negative particles, *ní* and *cha*, are distinguished geographically in the modern languages, the former current in most of Ireland, the latter in Scotland, and both in Ulster Irish.[170] They derive from the Old Irish forms *ní* and *nícon*, the latter giving Middle Irish *nocho* and subsequently *nocha*, whence *cha*; in Old Irish there may have been some stylistic distinction but by Middle and Early Modern Irish *ní* and *nocho* seem to have been in free variation.[171] Thus, rather than being a dialectal variant in Old Irish, the *ní / cha* alternation seems to have arisen later, and so we cannot map the modern distribution back beyond late Middle Irish at the earliest.

Variation in the syntax of relative clauses may provide an earlier example.[172] The standard Old Irish prepositional relative clause was formed by means of a preposition + (*s*)*a* and a nasalised verb, e.g. *forsa·mmitter* (Wb. 6b22) 'on whom you pass judgement'.[173] However, even in Old Irish there are a few examples of a competing formation with the usual subject/object relative form of the verb with a resumptive conjugated preposition in the relative clause, e.g. *nech suidigther loc daingen dó* (Ml. 87a15) 'anyone that a strong place is assigned to' (lit. 'anyone which a strong place is assigned to him').[174] The standard pattern has been continued into present-day Scottish Gaelic and in literary Irish, while the prepositional type is the norm in spoken Irish. It is tempting to conclude, therefore, that the standard pattern was northern and the prepositional type southern. A similar analysis is prompted by the alternation of a palatal and non-palatal initial consonant in Old Irish *tech/tig* /t′eχ/ (nom.) 'house': the usual genitive and dative are *tige* /t′iγ′ə/ and *tig* /t′iγ′/ respectively, but sporadically in Würzburg and St Gall the forms *taige* /tiγ′ə/ and *taig* /tiγ′/ are attested with a non-palatal initial; etymological considerations indicate that the latter forms are innovations. Comparison with the modern dialect forms shows that Scottish Gaelic and Manx regularly have the /t/- forms, Irish dialects have /t′/-, but Ulster Irish has a mixed pattern. If, therefore, we accept the modern distribution as an indicator of the earlier situation, it would suggest

---

[169] On Thurneysen's other features, *cuicce* 'to her' in Wb. but *cucae* in Sg., *cadessin/ fadessin*, see Ahlqvist, 'Remarks on the question of dialects', p. 26. On *cadessin/fadessin*, see Schrijver, *Studies*, pp 72–83. Similarly, McManus, 'A chronology', pp 70–71, has suggested that the variation between older *spiurt* (gen. sg. *spiurto*) and later *spirut* (gen. sg. *spiruto/spirito*) may be due to dialect or at least to 'regional delay' in adopting the later standard form.

[170] See Ó Buachalla, '*Ní* and *cha*'; Ó Dochartaigh, '*Cha* and *ní*'.

[171] Ó Buachalla, '*Ní* and *cha*', p. 131; Heinrich Wagner, 'Das negative altir. Präverb *nícon* "non"' in *Z.C.P.*, xxxii (1972), pp 18–35.

[172] See McCone, 'The Würzburg and Milan glosses', pp 96–7.

[173] Thurneysen, *A grammar of Old Irish*, pp 312–13.

[174] Cf. Brittonic relative clause patterns; see Russell, *Introduction*, pp 188–9.

that the Würzburg glosses may have had some input from a northern source.[175]

Another approach to the issue is through the lexicon. For example, in Old Irish there tends to be a standard range of animal terms, e.g. *bó* 'cow, ox', *mucc* 'pig', *cáera* 'sheep', *sinnach* 'fox', etc. and beside them apparently non-standard terms, e.g. *ferb* 'cow', *feis* 'pig', *cethnat* 'sheep', *crimthann* 'fox', etc. which have in some sense been marginalised in the lexicon, either by use in a different register, such as verse, or by use as a personal name, e.g. *Crimthann*.[176] Some of this variation may possibly be due to regional preferences for different terms. It has also been suggested that the preservation of some of these terms together with loanwords from Welsh in Cormac's Glossary, compiled probably in the late ninth century in Munster, may again show a preference for local terms.[177] However, the processes of the compilation of Cormac's Glossary were very complex and seem to have involved amalgamation and re-editing material from a range of sources.[178] It is true that some are relatively local; for example, among the law tracts used in Cormac the Munster-based 'Bretha Nemed' material is significantly more common than material from the northern 'Senchas Már'.[179] But the entry on at least one of the words mentioned, *ferb* 'cow', clearly derives from the opening lines of the legal text 'Cetharslicht Athgabála', the first main text of the 'Senchas Már'.[180]

The upshot of this brief consideration of the evidence for dialect distinctions in Old Irish is that, while there are tantalising indications, little of it can be matched to modern dialect distributions, not least because it is unclear how far one can map modern dialectal patterns back onto the linguistic situation of early Ireland. Two points, however, do emerge. First, the more one tries to pin down any traces of dialectal variation, the more one is struck by the overwhelmingly uniform nature of the language. On the other hand, in the rare cases where one can get some grip on the variation and relate it to modern distributions, the standard features seem to correspond to what is

[175] Similarly, we might expect the language of the Milan glosses to be northern, given the Bangor/Bobbio link. Ahlqvist, 'Remarks on the question of dialects', pp 29–30 (he also discusses initial mutation in Old Irish relative forms and the form of the verb after adverbs in cleft sentences); see also Heinrich Wagner, 'Studies in the history of Gaelic dialects, Part 1' in *Z.C.P.*, xxxix (1983), pp 96–116.

[176] See Kelly, 'Dialekte im Altirischen?'; idem, 'The earliest words for "horse" in the Celtic languages' in Sioned Davies and Nerys A. Jones (ed.), *The horse in Celtic culture: medieval Welsh perspectives* (Cardiff, 1997), pp 43–63; R. A. S. Macalister, *The secret languages of Ireland* (Cambridge, 1937), pp 225–54.

[177] Kelly, 'Dialekte im Altirischen?'

[178] On glossaries in general, see Russell, 'Sounds of a silence'; idem, '*Dúil Dromma Cetta*'; on Welsh words, see idem, 'Brittonic words'.

[179] See Paul Russell, 'Laws, glossaries and legal glossaries in early Ireland' in *Z.C.P.*, li (1999), pp 85–115.

[180] Binchy, *Corpus*, ii, 352.26. See Fergus Kelly, *A guide to early Irish law* (Dublin, 1988), pp 279–80; Liam Breatnach, 'On the original extent of the *Senchas Már*' in *Ériu*, xlvii (1996), pp 1–43: 20.

found in Scottish Gaelic and Ulster Irish, while the marginal features are more southern.[181]

A register of standard non-dialectal language can be established in a number of ways.[182] Even though, as we have seen, the 'Auraicept' version of the origin of Irish has it being 'cut out' from other languages, standard non-dialectal Old Irish does not seem to have been like standard Classical Modern Irish into which different dialectal forms were admitted;[183] if that were so, we would expect to be able to perceive forms that could be related to different dialects and they would point to different dialects at the same time.[184] The dialect evidence, meagre as it is, points more to the rise in status of a single dialect, such as we see in standard late Old English or Castilian Spanish. Moreover, the orthographical variation suggests that it was not simply a *Schriftsprache* but rather an elite register spoken by the nobility as well as poets, churchmen, and judges, and presumably also by those who aspired to high status. As such, it was a language that was presumably representative of normal speech of an earlier period, but had been modified at a slower pace because of the braking effects of education and literacy.[185]

The Old Irish glosses, notably Milan, are not, however, perfect representatives of the standard language, and their departures from the standard provide some of the most revealing glimpses of the linguistic situation of eighth-century Ireland;[186] for the departures are not haphazard but rather foreshadow many of the developments by which a century or so later we would wish to characterise Middle Irish. We may take three examples of verbal morphology as illustrations.[187] In Old Irish the formation of a preterite with a stem final -s- was a feature of weak verbs; strong verbs formed their preterites in other ways, such as reduplication of an initial consonant or a long stem vowel.[188] In Middle Irish there was a tendency for weak verb patterns to spread at the expense of the less predictable strong verb forma-

[181] Both McCone, 'The Würzburg and Milan glosses', p. 96, and Patricia Kelly, 'Dialekte im Altirischen?', p. 89, make the same suggestion that it is perhaps possible to relate this to the rise of the northern Uí Néill in the seventh and eighth centuries and the relative decline in the fortunes of Munster in this period; see also Charles-Edwards, *Early Christian Ireland*, pp 569–85: 583. What this does not help us with is what regional varieties might have predominated at other periods, or indeed whether they did.

[182] Charles-Edwards, 'Language and society', pp 728–9.

[183] See above, pp 405–6. On Classical Modern Irish, see Brian Ó Cuív, 'The linguistic training of the medieval Irish poet' in *Celtica*, x (1973), pp 114–40.

[184] This point is tentatively suggested by McManus, *Guide*, pp 149–50, on the basis of an analysis of *bérla tóbaide/teipide* as a 'form of Irish "selected" or "abstracted"' from regional varieties of the spoken language'.

[185] McCone, 'The Würzburg and Milan glosses', pp 102–3; idem, 'Zur Frage der Register'. Charles-Edwards, 'Language and society', pp 728–9, sees the social range as wider, going beyond the church and the *áes dána*.

[186] McCone, 'The Würzburg and Milan glosses'.

[187] See McCone, *Early Irish verb*; Breatnach, 'An Mheán-Ghaeilge', pp 278–325; Jackson, *Aislinge*, pp 102–39.

[188] Thurneysen, *Grammar*, pp 415–37.

tions. In Old Irish, therefore, we would expect and find forms such as *foraithmenair* (Ml. 24c8) 'he has remembered', 3rd sg. suffixless preterite to the stem ·*moinethar*, but a 3rd pl. *s*-preterite, *forur·aithminset* (Ml. 135a1) 'that they have remembered' is less expected. Similarly, within a few lines of each other we find both *niru·frescachtar* (Ml. 34d17) 'they have not hoped', a reduplicated preterite to *fris·acci* 'hope', and *niru·frescisset* (Ml. 34c11), a 3rd pl. *s*-preterite.[189] Likewise, in the future tense *f*-forms, originally restricted to the weak verb, were spreading at the expense of other future formants;[190] thus, corresponding to the present *do·eim* 'protect' we find a regular and expected long vowel future, *du·éma* (Ml. 67c5), and an *f*-future, *do·emfea* (Ml. 128c8).[191] The third and most striking case has to do with hypercorrection, the phenomenon whereby speakers overgeneralise a rule. In standard Old Irish deuterotonic compound verbs had a prototonic variant used before negatives and other preverbal particles, thus *do·fócaib* 'he raises' /do͈ fo:gəv'/ but the negative *ní·tócaib* /ni:͈to:gəv'/. In early Middle Irish the prototonic forms, also found in imperatives and verbal nouns, began to be used as the stem of new simple verbs, thus M. Ir. *tócbaid* 'he raises'.[192] In Old Irish, therefore, the simple verb *tongid* 'he swears' would reasonably be supposed to be well behaved; thus we find, for example, a 3rd sg. imperfect *no·thongad* (Ml. 36a20) 'he used to swear' used, but in the next gloss, *nech dod·fongad* (Ml. 36a21) 'anyone who used to swear it'; the simple verb has been dismantled into a compound verb *\*do·fong* carrying an infixed pronoun, rather than the expected *\*nod·thongad*. The context of such hypercorrect reanalyses must be one where a speaker has more than one register: the one where he uses simple verbs and the other where compound verbs are used; *tongid* is, therefore, viewed in the same way as *tócbaid* and so in the higher registers resolved into a compound verb. For this glossator at least, then, the simple verbs were in some sense primary and in certain contexts capable of being broken down into compounds. While the language of the Old Irish glosses gives us a sample of a middling to high register of non-dialectal language, the deviations from it in Milan 'should give us a rough idea of everyday Irish in the eighth century, and the picture emerges of a language which was already well advanced on the road to what we know as Early Middle Irish'.[193] On the other hand, we would not expect glosses to be in a very high register of language, and even the non-deviant language of the glosses would not have been as high as registers of Old Irish could get;

---

[189] Ibid., p. 416.

[190] Ibid., pp 396–415.

[191] Ibid., p. 396. For the Middle Irish and later developments, see McCone, *Early Irish verb*, pp 241–50; O Buachalla, 'The *f*-future in Modern Irish'.

[192] McCone, *Early Irish verb*, pp 207–9; Russell, *Introduction*, p. 60.

[193] McCone, 'The Würzburg and Milan glosses', p. 102; see also Charles-Edwards, 'Language and society', p. 729.

the regular use of periphrastic constructions, for example, and indeed the whole context of the activity of glossing as producing a set of notes for private study, would suggest that the language of the glosses might well be more colloquial than it would be in a highly polished literary creation.

Moreover, it has emerged from recent work that registers of Old Irish which have usually been regarded as historically differentiated (i.e. one reflects an earlier stage of the language than another) may have to be distinguished stylistically rather than (or perhaps as well as) chronologically.[194] The study in question involves Old Irish translations, both in prose and in *rosc*, of sections of the 'Collectio canonum Hibernensis'.[195] Three types of *rosc* may be distinguished: syllabically regular lines with fixed cadence and alliteration but no rhyme; lines of a regular number of stressed words per line and alliteration; and lines with no clear syllabic or stress pattern but heavy alliteration.[196] They are to be distinguished, on the one hand, from prose and on the other from rhyming syllabic verse; another way of looking at it is to see a continuum of increasingly high registers, each of which shares features with its immediately neighbouring registers. Among other things, *roscada* contain a series of linguistic features that have traditionally been held to be 'archaic', such as preposed genitives (dependent genitives preceding rather than following the governing noun), tmesis, and Bergin's law formations, etc. which are characteristic of the earliest stratum of extant Old Irish texts. Although the dating of the 'Hibernensis' has been much debated, the earlier version cannot be dated earlier than 716; the latest authors quoted are Theodore (d. 690) in the A recension and Adomnán (d. 704) in the B recension. The compilers were Ruben of Dairinis (d. 725) and Cú Cuimne of Iona (d. 747). The Old Irish versions of sections of this text are to be found in the British Library MS, Nero A vii recension of the 'Bretha Nemed', which, it has been suggested, may have been written in Munster in the reign of Cathal mac Finguine (721–42).[197] In other words, in the first half of the eighth century it would appear that they were capable of operating in high style registers of apparently archaising Old Irish. Just as we have seen examples of *roscada* beside prose, at a later period the 'Amra Senáin', perhaps

---

[194] See Liam Breatnach, 'Canon law and secular law in early Ireland: the significance of the *Bretha Nemed*' in *Peritia*, iii (1984), 439–59; idem, 'Zur Frage der *Roscada* im Irischen' in Hildegard L. C. Tristram (ed.), *Metrik und Medienwechsel—Metrics and media* (Tübingen, 1991), pp 197–205. On 'archaic' Irish, see David Greene, 'Archaic Irish' in Karl Horst Schmidt (ed.), *Indogermanisch und Keltisch* (Wiesbaden, 1977), pp 11–33; D. A. Binchy, '*Bretha Déin Checht*' in *Ériu*, xx (1966), pp 1–65: 3–5; idem, 'Bergin's law' in *Studia Celt.*, xiv–xv (1979–80), pp 34–53; Heinrich Wagner, 'Zur unregelmässigen Wortstellung in der altirischen Alliterationsdichtung' in Wolfgang Meid (ed.), *Beiträge zur Indogermanistik und Keltologie* (Innsbruck, 1967), pp 289–314.

[195] Hermann Wasserschleben (ed.), *Die irische Kanonensammlung* (2nd ed., Leipzig, 1885).

[196] See Breatnach, 'Canon law and secular law', pp 452–3.

[197] Ibid., pp 439–44; idem, 'The first third of the *Bretha Nemed Toísech*' in *Ériu*, xl (1989), pp 1–40.

composed by Cormac mac Cuillenáin (d. 908), contains in the same composition *rosc* and rhyming syllabic verse.[198] Likewise, the 'Cauldron of poesy' and 'Bretha Déin Chécht' both contain prose, *rosc*, and rhyming syllabic verse.[199]

The effect of this work is to bring into sharper focus ideas on register as opposed to attributing all variation of this type to different chronological layers of texts. None of this necessarily rules out the possibility that some of the forms and structures attested in this high literary register reflect archaic patterns of word order or phrase structure; after all, even the standard Old Irish register presumably reflected the everyday colloquial speech of an earlier period. Indeed, the very notion of an 'archaising' register (as opposed to 'archaic') implies reference back to some original form of the language.[200] On the other hand, it is possible to take the view that these structures, rather than being 'archaising', are 'artifical'.[201] Even so, it is difficult to see how they could be conjured out of nothing, however artificial they might be; all this approach does, therefore, is open the search for another model. One candidate that has been canvassed recently is Latin verse and rhetorical style.[202] The advantage of this approach is that it does not deny the Indo-European input but rather presents a context in which archaic patterns might be artificially sustained in a high literary register through the influence of late Latin metrical patterns. Such an approach could not only help to explain, for example, the preservation of tmesis patterns and preposed genitives but also the historically inexplicable cases of tmesis and hyperbaton, such as *lécit mára meic Uí Chuind co noí mílib machta* 'the sons of the Uí Chuind leave with nine thousand men great slaughters behind', where the separation of *mára... machta* 'great... slaughters' may be compared with, for example, the separation of *una... disciplina* in the Rule of St Benedict, *una praebeatur in*

[198] Liam Breatnach, 'An edition of *Amra Senáin*' in Ó Corráin, Breatnach, & McCone, *Sages, saints & storytellers*, pp 7–31.
[199] Liam Breatnach, 'The caldron of poesy' in *Ériu*, xxxi (1981), pp 45–93; Binchy, '*Bretha Déin Checht*'.
[200] See, for example, Osborn Bergin, 'On the syntax of the verb in Old Irish' in *Ériu*, xii (1938), pp 197–214; Watkins, 'Preliminaries to the historical and comparative analysis of the syntax of the Old Irish verb'; idem, 'Preliminaries to the reconstructions'; cf. also Russell, 'Preverbs, prepositions and adverbs', pp 160–64.
[201] For this view, see Wagner, 'Zur unregelmässigen Wortstellung'. Breatnach, 'Poets and poetry', p. 73, hedges his bets: 'archaising or artificial.' See also Kalyguine, *La langue de la poésie irlandaise archaïque*, pp 128–44.
[202] Johan Corthals, 'Early Irish *retoirics* and their late antique background' in *Camb. Med. Celt. Studies*, xxxi (summer 1996), pp 17–36; idem, 'Some observations on the versification of the rhymeless "Leinster Poems"' in *Celtica*, xxi (1990), pp 113–25; idem, 'Zur Frage des mündlichen oder schriftlichen Ursprungs der Sagen *roscada*' in Tranter and Tristram, *Early Irish literature*, pp 201–20; idem, 'Zur Entstehung der archaischen irischen Metrik und Syntax' in H. Eichner and H. Ch. Luschützky (ed.), *Compositiones Indogermaniae in memoriam Jochem Schinler* (Prague, 1999), pp 19–45.

*omnibus secundum merita disciplina* 'let one rule be applied to all things according to merit'.[203]

Such influences presuppose a high level of functional bilingualism in Old Irish and Latin. This is not the place for a full-scale analysis of the relationship between the two languages at different periods, but it may be helpful to consider some instances where Irish and Latin come into contact with one another, and where we can chart the changing relationship between the two.[204] It has often been asserted that the earlier the text, the greater the proportion of Latin can be found in it.[205] That may well be the case when one is dealing with the development of one genre of text over a lengthy period of time, but it does not follow that any text containing a high proportion of Latin is therefore older than any other text containing less Latin; for the comparison to be valid, we have to be clear that the texts are comparable in terms of genre and type. For example, in the Annals of Ulster, though there is some short-term variation in the use of Irish as opposed to Latin at certain periods which may reflect the inclinations of particular annalists, there is a gradual but steady increase in the use of Irish in entries from about the middle of the eighth century onwards, but even so they do not predominate till the middle of the tenth century or later; there is then a marked shift to the vernacular in the entries from 939 onwards.[206] A similar pattern emerges in early Irish glossaries. Both the earliest stratum of O'Mulconry's Glossary (perhaps seventh-century) and the earliest versions of Cormac's Glossary contain a high proportion of entries where the technical framework is Latinate even though the words under discussion are Irish.[207] But in the later versions of Cormac the Latinate terminology is either glossed in Irish or replaced by Irish equivalents, e.g. *ab eo quod est* ⇒ *dindí as, óndí as, diminutivum* ⇒ *dispecad.*[208] Likewise, in the later versions passages in Latin are glossed in Irish, e.g *Ainne .i. cúairt. Veteres, [.i. na sendaíne], enim ponebant an pro circum, unde dicitur annus [.i. blíadain .i. fa chúairt bís an blíadain]* 'Ainne (ring), i.e. circle. For the ancients, [i.e. the old people], used to put *an*-in place of *circum*, thus annus (year) is said, [i.e. "year", i.e. because of the circuit which the year is]' (the text in square brackets is only

---

[203] Corthals, 'Early Irish *retoirics*', p. 36; idem, 'Some observations', p. 123.

[204] For a discussion, see McCone, 'Zur Frage der Register', pp 76–80; what follows here only touches on certain aspects of the broader question. See also Charles-Edwards, *Early Christian Ireland*, p. 592; Dáibhí Ó Cróinín, *Early medieval Ireland 400–1200* (London and New York, 1995), pp 189–95.

[205] See, for example, Kim McCone, *Pagan past and christian present* (Maynooth, 1990), p. 35.

[206] David Dumville, 'Latin and Irish in the *Annals of Ulster*, A.D. 431–1050' in Whitelock, McKitterick, & Dumville, *Ire. in early med. Europe*, pp 320–41: 328–30.

[207] See Stokes, 'O'Mulconry's Glossary'; Meyer, *Sanas Cormaic*; on the different versions of Cormac, see Russell, 'Sounds of a silence', pp 2–4.

[208] For examples of the former, see Meyer, *Sanas Cormaic*, §§ 64 (Latin), 32 (Irish); for examples of the latter, see §§ 2, 26.

found in the Y version).[209] However, consideration of other types of text
suggests that to look at only one or two genres of text may lead to oversimplification. In contrast to the Annals of Ulster and the glossaries, the texts
written in Irish in the Book of Armagh, the 'Additamenta' and the 'Notulae',
suggest that a different approach from a simple linear analysis may be appropriate.[210] The use of the vernacular in these notes may indicate that at this
period it was not so much that Irish was not used, but that it was for writing
purposes restricted to certain contexts which might be regarded as lower
level writing activities. The use of Irish to gloss Latin texts, as in the great
collections of Old Irish glosses, may be a case in point, though Latin
and Irish were both used for glossing purposes; the real difficulty with
the glosses is working out whether the Latin and Irish glosses belong to the
same stratum of glosses or represent different periods of glossing.[211] The
increase of the use of the vernacular in the annals and in the glossaries may
indicate the rise in status of Irish in relation to Latin in these types of text.
In other words, it may not simply be the case that the use of Latin is
diagnostic of an early text, but rather that the kinds of texts where Irish was
used in the early Old Irish period, namely texts written in a lower-register
language, such as notes or glosses, have not survived in sufficient amounts to
redress the balance of our perception that the more Latin there is, the earlier
the text.

We may finally return to the question of register. The preceding discussion has concentrated on modern perceptions of register in early Irish. But
there is evidence to suggest that speakers of early Irish had some idea of
different types of language. To what extent they match our notion of register
is less clear. The central term seems to be *gnáthbérla* which refers to the
usual, everyday language; as the 'Auraicept' puts it, *gnáthbérla fo·gní do cháach*
'...which serves for all'.[212] Two sets of distinctions seem to be operating.
At the beginning of this essay we saw how, according to the doctrine of
the 'Auraicept na nÉces', *in bérla tóbaide*, namely Irish, was created by 'cutting out' what was best of the other languages. Later in the 'Auraicept' this
language is subdivided into five or six different types, which we might want
to call registers: in addition to *gnáthbérla* we have *bérla Féne* 'language of
the Irish', *bérla na filed* 'language of the poets' (also *fásaige na filed*
'sayings of the poets'), *bérla fortchide* (*na filed*) 'obscure language (of the
poets)', *íarmbérla* 'cryptic language', *bérla etarscartha* 'separated/divided

[209] Meyer, *Sanas Cormaic*, § 14. The Latin text is from Macrobius's *Saturnalia*, probably
derived from a seventh-century Irish epitome known to Bede as the 'Disputatio Cori et Prae-
textati'; see Maura Walsh and Dáibhí Ó Cróinín (ed.), *Cummian's letter* De controversia
paschale *and the* De ratione conputandi (Toronto, 1988), p. 137, n. 16.
[210] Bieler, *Patrician texts*, pp 166–83; cf. *Thes. pal.*, ii, 238–43.
[211] See, for example, on the St Gall glosses, Hofman, *The Sankt Gall Priscian commentary*, i,
40–48.
[212] Calder, *Auraicept*, p. 102 (line 1334) = p. 245 (line 4650).

language'.[213] The first, *bérla Féne*, seems to be the language of professionals, particularly jurists. It is not clear exactly what the distinction is between *bérla na filed* and *bérla fortchide* since the latter is described as the language *tríasa n-aigaillit cách díb a chéle* 'by which they (*sc.* poets) speak to each other'.[214] The final term, *bérla etarscartha*, is rather clearer in that it probably refers to the Isidorean technique of etymological analysis, widespread in glossaries and elsewhere, by which words are analysed by dividing them into their supposed elements in order to get closer to their real meaning.[215] On the other hand, in Cormac's glossary, in addition to some of the terms discussed above which have probably been carried from the 'Auraicept', another series of distinctions is made. A number of them occurs in the following entry: *cloch, trí anmann lé .i. onn a íarmbérla, cloch a gnáthbérla, cloech a bérla n-airberta ar inní chlóes cach raod* '*cloch* (stone), three names for it, i.e. *onn* the cryptic term for it, *cloch* the normal term for it, *cloech* the term of use for it because it blunts everything'.[216] Of these terms, *íarmbérla* is common to the 'Auraicept' material. On the other hand, *bérla n-airberta* is a different term which seems to be called 'of use' because it has been modified to make its perceived semantic relation to *chlóes* more perspicuous;[217] elsewhere in Cormac this type of modification of a word, in order to clarify its etymology, is often marked by the use of *quasi*.[218] Likewise, the word *naire* 'indeed' is regarded as *gnáthbérla* in west Munster but as *senbérla* in east Munster.[219] Altogether, the range of terms at least indicates that in this period they were aware of different types of Irish. In that they emanate from a learned context, they are unsurprisingly preoccupied with fine distinctions between different types of high-register learned language. The precise distinctions are almost impossible to discern at this distance, even if real distinctions are being made. *Senbérla* is the only one which suggests that they had a sense of historical depth. In general, they are less concerned with lower-level distinctions of the type we may be interested in, such as the language of glossing and that of more literary texts.

---

[213] Calder, *Auraicept*, pp 100–05 (lines 1302–39) = pp 244–5 (lines 4619–52); see also McManus, *A guide*, pp 148–9, 185, n. 7. The term *íarmbérla* seems to have two senses: 'cryptic language' (as above) but it is also used to refer to unaccented words (see Calder, *Auraicept*, pp 100–01 (line 1304) = p. 244 (line 4621). On these terms, see Kalyguine, *La langue de la poésie irlandaise archaïque*, pp 64–75.

[214] Calder, *Auraicept*, pp 100–02 (lines 1302–16) = pp 244–5 (lines 4619–52).

[215] For a discussion, see Russell, 'Sounds of a silence', pp 21–7.

[216] Meyer, *Sanas Cormaic*, § 213.

[217] In Quin *et al.*, *Dictionary of the Irish language*, *s.v. airbert*, it is interpreted as 'the language of pleading' but, as is also suggested in the dictionary, *s.v. airbert* (d), it is more likely to reflect the more basic sense of the verbal noun, 'use' or 'application'.

[218] On the use of *quasi*, see Rolf Baumgarten, 'A Hiberno-Isidorean etymology' in *Peritia*, ii (1983), pp 225–8.

[219] Meyer, *Sanas Cormaic*, § 972; see above, pp 439–40.

As the final section has suggested, discussion of linguistic variation in early Irish, whether regional or stylistic, has only recently begun to receive the attention it deserves, as the complexity and the wealth of the different types of language are fully appreciated, a complexity and wealth that was not lost on the 'Auraicept': *7 gach són fordocha gach bérla fofhrith ined doib isin Gaedelg ara forleith sech gach mbescna* 'and for every obscure sound of every language a place was found in Irish on account of its comprehensiveness beyond every speech'.[220]

---

[220] Calder, *Auraicept*, p. 2 (lines 11–13) = p. 171 (lines 1167–70). This growing appreciation is not least because only recently have some of the most difficult texts in Old Irish been receiving the attention they require and deserve; see in particular the work of Liam Breatnach, for example, 'An edition of *Amra Senáin*' in Ó Corráin, Breatnach, & McCone, *Sages, saints, & storytellers*, pp 7–31; 'The cauldron of poesy' in *Ériu*, xxxi (1981), pp 45–93; 'The first third of the *Bretha Nemed Toísech*' in *Ériu*, xl (1989), 1–40; 'Zur Frage der *Roscada* im Irischen' in Tristram, *Metrik und Medienwechsel*, pp 197–205; for a general survey, see also idem, 'Poets and poetry' in McCone & Simms, *Progress*, pp 65–77.

CHAPTER XIII

# Language and literature
# to 1169

JAMES CARNEY

THE Irish language, sometimes known as Goidelic (nowadays as Gaelic), was spoken in historic times over the whole of Ireland, in the Isle of Man, and in western Scotland. In the prehistoric period in Ireland all learning (including law and religion) was controlled by the druidic order. The druids were an institution of great antiquity and common to all the Celtic peoples; the earliest reference to them is that of Sotion of Alexandria (*c*.200 B.C.). Posidonius refers to three learned classes among the Celts: druids, seers, and bards; but it seems certain that 'seers' and 'bards' were, at least in some sense, druids.

The Celtic druid, the Hindu brahmin, and the Roman pontifex are all thought to derive from the 'divine' king-priest of Indo-European society. In early Christian Ireland, when documentation becomes copious, the 'native' learned classes consisted of poets (*filid*)[1] and jurists (*breithemain*); the bard (*bard*) was one of the several grades through which the *fili* went, before achieving the highest, that of *ollam* ('greatest'). It is easiest to think of the functions of the *fili* and the *breithem* as being originally exercised by a single functionary, the *druí*, who was priest, prophet, jurist, and praiser in solemn rhythmic language of gods, kings, and powerful men. But the stages in which the various functions were distributed are not quite clear. With the coming of Christianity the *druí*, at least under that name, fell into disrepute; the last king to be associated with one was Diarmait mac Cerbaill (d. 561), during whose reign there may have been a brief revival, or rather a 'last stand', of paganism. In Latin writing, *druí* is translated *magus*, and his role is that of necromancer and watcher of the heavens. In so far as the *druí* survived in his ancient role of priest and possessor of all knowledge relevant to his society, he did so in the person of the *fili*. Like the druids, the *filid* were an order. All *filid* had similar training, met in great numbers at conventions, and,

---

[1] For a useful account of the evolution of the *filid*, see J. E. Caerwyn Williams, 'The court poet in medieval Ireland' in *Brit. Acad. Proc.*, lvii (1971), pp 85–135.

irrespective of political boundaries, could function anywhere in the Gaelic world from Kerry to the Hebrides. Ever the same essentially, but changing subtly with the political scene, the *filid* survived in Ireland until the end of the seventeenth century, and struggled on in Scotland until well into the eighteenth. Eleanor Knott, in her edition of the poems of the sixteenth-century Tadhg Dall Ó hUiginn, has this to say: 'the bardic profession was built upon the ruins of—or perhaps we might say was a protective metamorphosis of— the ancient druidic order, and was always a craft with its own dues, privileges, and prerogatives, decided by itself.'[2] Osborn Bergin defined the poet's place in society more closely, but with special reference to the later poet:

He was, in fact, a professor of literature and a man of letters, highly trained in the use of a polished literary medium, belonging to a hereditary caste in an aristocratic society, holding an official position by virtue of his training, his learning, his knowledge of the history and traditions of his country and his clan. He discharged, as O'Donovan pointed out many years ago, the functions of the modern journalist. He was not a songwriter. He was often a public official, a chronicler, a political essayist, a keen and satirical observer of his fellow countrymen.[3]

Traces of the original 'sanctity' of his office remained. His words had power—could produce, it was thought, a physical effect on the person to whom or against whom they were spoken. He could rhyme rats and mice to death, a faculty that had somehow come to Shakespeare's knowledge, as he shows in *As you like it*, III. ii, when he makes Rosalind say: 'I was never so berhymed since Pythagoras' time, that I was an Irish rat, which I can hardly remember.' The poet's person was generally sacred, and an outrage committed against him was likely to be followed by a *fiurt filed*, 'a poet's miracle', avenging the deed. Indeed, the sanctity of the person of the poet, inherited, as we assume, from that of the druid, probably explains why there were no martyrs for the faith in early Ireland: the Christian missionaries were regarded as foreign druids, and accorded the conventional courtesies.

Despite the general sanctity of the person of the poet or druid, it seems probable that even in pre-Christian times the order met with opposition: they wielded power, their numbers constituted a heavy economic burden, and the thinking or cynical prince must have sometimes questioned the value of their product. It is difficult, even impossible, to make an accurate estimate of the numerical strength of the poetic order at any given period. They were part of the fabric of society, and in the literature we read of important poets travelling with retinues of from fifty to 150 lesser practitioners, together with their

---

[2] Eleanor Knott (ed. and trans.), *The bardic poems of Tadhg Dall Ó Huiginn* (London, 1922), p. xli.
[3] Osborn Bergin, 'Bardic poetry' in *Journal of the Ivernian Society*, v (1912–13), pp 153–66, 203–19, at p. 154; reprinted in David Greene and Fergus Kelly (ed.), *Irish bardic poetry* (Dublin, 1970), pp 3–22: 4.

wives and dependants. A conservative estimate might put the strength of the order at 1,000 in the pagan period and at half that number when the church took over part of their former functions. In Leinster in the fifth century a dynast, Eochu son of Énda Censelach, is shown as slaying the poet Bécc, son of Lethdergáin, together with a company of 150 other poets. The same prince also slew another poet, Brí, son of Bairchid. In the course of the late fifth and sixth centuries the poets were christianised, at least superficially. According to a tradition later associated with Colum Cille, their whole position was called into question at the assembly of Druimm Cett (575): it was decided—we are told—that the poets should continue, but that their numbers should be reduced. About 597 (A.U.; 600 A.I.) the 'poetic company' (*in dám*) was 'destroyed' or 'slain' (*orgain*) in Leinster by the king, Brandub son of Eochu; the event is referred to in the early pseudo-prophetic text *Baile in Scáil* ('the phantom's vision'): *iurait Laigin a ndáma*, 'the Laigin will slay (destroy) their poetic companies.'[4] In the centuries to come, 'native' poets were certainly not unknown in Leinster, but they seem to have been thinner on the ground than in the other provinces. Despite such occasional incidents, the poets continued to be valued as long as their order lasted. The highest-ranking poet, the *ollam*, could theoretically have a dignity equal to that of a king; and a king of a tuath, an *ollam*, and a bishop all had an equal wergeld or honour-price. But, in fact, down through the ages, at least since the coming of Christianity, the poets had to fight hard to maintain something of their traditional influence and prestige. They constantly tell of the generosity of princes to them, but it was, of course, in their interest to exaggerate this.

In early Ireland a woman could apparently be an official poet. There are frequent references in the earliest literature to the *bancháinte*; and though this is usually translated 'female satirist' it is not clear that this was a depreciative term, nor that the function was restricted to satire. A saga generally assigned to the ninth century tells of the love of Liadan, a female poet of Corcu Duibne, County Kerry, for Cuirithir, a poet from Connacht.[5] The characters seem to belong to the seventh century. Irrespective of its historicity, the fact remains that a writer in the ninth century could expect his audience to believe that a woman poet (*banéces*) could travel around the country on a 'poetical circuit' (*cuairt filidechta*) in exactly the same manner as a man. Obits of poets enter tardily into the annals, and the deaths of poets of considerable renown often go unrecorded. But among those that appear is that of Uallach, daughter of Muimnechán (or Muinechán), described as *banfile Érenn*, 'poetess of Ireland', who died c.934.[6] It may perhaps be supposed

[4] Kuno Meyer (ed.), 'Mitteilungen aus irischen Handschriften' in *Z.C.P.*, iii (1901), pp 457–66: 465; cf. O'Rahilly, *Early Ir. hist.*, pp 283–85.
[5] See Gerard Murphy (ed. and trans.), *Early Irish lyrics, eighth to twelfth century* (Oxford, 1956), pp 82–5.
[6] *Ann. Inisf.*, p. 150.

that since poetry was a hereditary craft, a young girl might occasionally receive training, either because she showed exceptional talent at an early age, or because there was no male issue in the family.

With the introduction of Christianity, the church took over to a great degree the former functions of the druidic order: the ministry of religion, the teaching of the young, and the regulation of the calendar. In the first century or so of Christianity, it seems certain that the church drew heavily on the native learned class for the new ministry. In an early, but doubtless somewhat fictionalised, account of the establishment of the church in Leinster, Patrick is shown as seeking from Dubthach moccu Lugair (described by Muirchú as *poeta optimus*) one of his pupils to become a bishop in Leinster. He wishes for a man of good family, without physical defect or blemish, not poor, not rich, preferably a man with one wife, and to whom had been borne only one child. Dubthach had only one pupil who fitted this description, Fécc, an *adulescens poeta*, and he was thus the first bishop ordained in Leinster. In the next century we meet the poet Colmán mac Lénéni, who under the influence of St Brendan of Clonfert (County Galway) became a monk, founded the monastery of Cluain Uama (Cloyne, County Cork), and continued to practice the art of poetry.[7] Under these circumstances it is not strange that churchmen in Ireland became in part the guardians of the history and traditions of Ireland and cultivators of Irish language and poetry. Thus the church and the official poets were rivals even in this field, and like any commercial or cultural rivals they reacted on each other continuously.

The great mass of Irish poetry that survives from the period *c.*500–1200 derives from either churchmen or official poets. Frequently it may be known from attribution or subject-matter whether a poem comes from one group or the other. But there are a number of poems, often the more interesting, that are difficult to classify. Some, indeed, may have been written by people who were neither churchmen nor official poets, and there are attributions to individuals outside these classes. Literacy in early Ireland was more widespread than in other European societies. Furthermore, it would seem that a reputation for good conversation, whether in man or woman, would involve the ability to compose verse: a well-turned pungent quatrain, delivered extempore, could clinch an argument and annihilate an opponent. Indeed, this respect for formal or cleverly phrased language, involving sometimes the victory of rhetoric over logic, has lasted, even at the lower economic levels of Irish society, down to the present time.

The earliest Irish verse is written in various kinds of stressed metres. The commonest basic line had four stresses; the line was divided into two parts by a *caesura*, and there is alliterative linking between the two parts of the

---

[7] See Rudolf Thurneysen, 'Colmán mac Lénéni und Senchán Torpéist' in *Z.C.P.*, xix (1933), pp 193–207.

line. Furthermore, the lines and quatrains are similarly linked by alliteration; and the last word or words of a poem should echo the opening, so that the whole is a mnemonic unit. As an example of early alliterative verse may be quoted the first stanza of a poem attributed, perhaps correctly, to Colum Cille (d. 597):

> Sét no tíag    téiti Críst,
> crích i mbéo    bith cen tríst.

(The path I walk, Christ walks it; the land where I am, may it be without malediction.)[8]

Here there are two rhyming lines, each with a *caesura* and alliterative linking. The stanza is joined to the next by alliteration, and so throughout the poem. There are four stresses in each line.

Much of the oldest verse—unlike the example quoted above—is without rhyme. Rhyme as an essential feature of verse has been commonly held to be of medieval Latin origin. This view, however, may no longer be tenable, since rhyme is found in certain of the most archaic types of verse where we can hardly suppose ecclesiastical influence. It seems more likely that rhyme came into being independently in Ireland, and was at first used as a substitute for alliteration and as an occasional ornament. Once discovered, it proved irresistible, and eventually drove out alliteration as an important functional element in verse.

The earliest Irish alliterative verse corresponds closely in form to primitive Germanic verse. The correspondence is, in fact, so close that one is inclined to think in terms of a primitive Celtic-Germanic metric, dating from the period when Celts and Germans lived as close neighbours on the Continent. In the early seventh century this type of alliterative stressed verse became outmoded. The metres were remade, the length of line depending now on a syllable count rather than on stress. This new type of verse may be illustrated here by a single quatrain written in the course of the ninth century, when the Vikings were ravaging the coasts of Ireland:

> Is acher in gáith in-nocht,
> fu-fúasna fairrgae findfolt
> ní ágor réimm mora minn
> dond láechraid laind úa Lothlind.

(The wind is fierce tonight, it tosses the tresses of the sea; I do not fear the crossing of a quiet sea by the fierce warriors from Norway.)[9]

The poet's point is the paradoxical one that a rough sea connotes safety, and a quiet sea danger. In form it will be noticed that the lines are rhyming, that

---

[8] James Carney, 'Three Old Irish accentual poems' in *Ériu*, xxii (1971), pp 23–80: 23–9.
[9] Text and translation in *Thes. Pal.*, ii, 290.

there are seven syllables in each, and that alliteration, while present in three of the four lines, has merely an ornamental function. Kuno Meyer, in the introduction to his *Selections from ancient Irish poetry* (1911), made a classic statement:

In nature poetry the Gaelic muse may vie with that of any other nation. Indeed, these poems occupy a unique position in the literature of the world. To seek out and watch and love nature, in its tiniest phenomena as in its grandest, was given to no people so early and so fully as to the Celt. Many hundreds of Gaelic and Welsh poems testify to this fact. It is a characteristic of these poems that in none of them do we get an elaborate or sustained description of any scene or scenery, but rather a succession of pictures and images, which the poet, like an impressionist, calls up before us by light and skilful touches. Like the Japanese, the Celts were always quick to take an artistic hint; they avoid the obvious and the commonplace; the half-said thing to them is dearest.

An early Irish lyric may result from any situation in human experience. At best it will have immediacy and universality. The language, for obvious reasons, may present difficulties. But when this barrier has been crossed, it will be found that there is no ancient heroic or medieval veil between the reader and the poem. The poet's experience will, at least potentially, be the reader's. In the early period a poem will not normally be a conventional imitation of other similar poems: there is an immediate and fresh emergence from a universal human situation in a statement that can be as relevant today as it was a thousand or more years ago. In the best of this poetry there is always an inner tension where vitality and freshness strain at, but rarely—if ever—break the bonds of form and discipline.

A poem may result from such varied circumstances as watching the flight of a bee, feeling the cold, listening to birdsong, contemplating the sea, or, in mocking vein, reflecting on the death of a goose. There is the well-known ninth-century poem by a monk who, watching his pet cat, Pangur, devoting his life to hunting mice, humorously compares himself with it: he spends his life chasing words, and has a joy analogous to the cat's when he discovers a new one.[10] Poems could be written in delicate metaphorical terms, and scholars, reluctant to concede such sophistication to the early poets, tend at times to undervalue them by not going beyond the superficial literal interpretation. Such a poem is 'A maccucáin sruith in tíag' ('Young lad, venerable is the satchel'),[11] attributed (perhaps correctly) to Adomnán, abbot of Iona (d. 704), where he addresses a student on the contents of the satchel that he carries on his back. The literary contents are conceived of as relics, which could save one from any hazard on land or sea. The poem comes near

---

[10] Text and translation in *Thes. Pal.*, ii, 293.
[11] Ed. Lucius Gwynn, 'The reliquary of Adomnán' in *Archiv. Hib.*, iv (1915), pp 199–214; cf. James Carney, 'The dating of early Irish verse texts' in *Éigse*, xix, pt 2 (1983), pp 177–216.

to being a catalogue of the religious reading-matter of a young ecclesiastical student in the late seventh century. Another poem, 'An Crínóc',[12] probably of the eleventh century, is similar in that it deals with a book, but with a sexual imagery that for long obscured the poet's meaning and gave rise to bizarre sociological conclusions. The poet in old age discovered Crínóc ('dear little old thing') and addressed her as a lost lover with whom he had first slept at the age of 7. Since that time she had slept with four others; though outwardly ravaged her body is still undefiled; her music fills 'the pathways of the world', and if we followed her teaching we would go straight to God. In fact 'Crínóc' was a copy of the psalms, which in Irish monastic training was the first lesson book from which a boy of 7 began simultaneously to learn Latin, music, and correct religious attitudes.

Most enigmatic, however, is a poem, apparently of the eighth century, put into the mouth of a woman who, in the course of the poem, identifies herself as (or compares herself with) the ancient mythological character, the *Caillech* (*Sentuinne*) *Bérri*, 'the hag of Beare'.[13] This woman had spent her life as a courtesan, enjoying the favours of kings. She had enjoyed the spring and summer of her life, and autumn had not been bad. But now the first days of winter were upon her; instead of drinking wine with kings she supped whey in a convent with other old hags. She observed the ebb and flow of the sea, the ripening and cutting of the crops, and then the next year's growth. There is constant renewal in nature, but none for her; in turn she accepts and rebels, but rebellion is dominant. This poem is perhaps the greatest lyric in early Irish literature, and many poets in modern Ireland have attempted to translate it or to restate it. The poem reflects real experience. It can be held, but hardly with certainty, that the persona is a male poet who has served kings during a long life; he outlives his patrons and seeks some kind of consolation in religion. This poem illustrates one of the primary characteristics of the best of early Irish verse: Irish poets tend to avoid philosophical abstractions. When they have some comment to make on life, they prefer to dramatise their themes and to state their universals in terms of a particular person, time, and place. Hence, in writing on the subject of human mortality, a poet expresses his ideas in the person of St Ciarán, who died c.544 at the age of 33. The saint is shown as protesting to God against unripe death, and pleading for an adequate lifespan. Similarly, in another poem, the question of original sin and its consequences are stated by putting four self-accusing quatrains into the mouth of Eve.

A very important aspect of this is that since prehistoric times we must assume in Ireland and Gaelic Scotland a standardised language used by the poets and received at least by their upper-class patrons. Hence, while the

[12] See Kuno Meyer, 'Mitteilungen aus irischen Handschriften' in *Z.C.P.*, vi (1904), p. 266.
[13] See Murphy, *Early Irish lyrics*, pp 74–82.

poetic order lasted, problems of dialect could be ignored. The church quite naturally took over this standardised language, and thus, in contrast with Anglo-Saxon England, there are no linguistic clues as to the area in which any given text originated.

It is probable that only a small part of the immense production of poems was ever written down. Assuming a numerical strength of about 500 poets, and that with births, deaths, marriages, and other occasions in important families a poet would compose a minimum of ten poems in the year, this would connote the production of about half a million poems in a century, and some 5 million in the millennium 400–1400. It would be the normal fate of any poem, composed for a special occasion, to die on the lips of the reciter.[14] Of those that, for one reason or another, were committed to writing, only a very small part has survived, but the survivals enable us to make a fair judgement as to the nature and quality of this verse, even in the pre-Christian period.

The earliest surviving verses are those pieces, mostly mere fragments, found in the Leinster genealogies; these are in primitive accentual metres, and some may date from as early as the fifth century.[15] This earliest surviving stratum looks out on a Roman world and has non-ecclesiastical borrowings of such Latin words as *tribunus, miles, legio, murus, puteus, draco, leo, barca, (navis) longa, (dies) Mercurii*. In this poetry, oversea raiding of the type that brought St Patrick to Ireland as a slave is still a living memory. The longest fragment to survive consists of over fifty stanzas from a poem written about 500 A.D. to a Leinster dynast, Nad Buidb, son of Erc. The poet alludes to many of the subject's ancestors who have been kings of Tara, implying that this is also his right. He lays special emphasis on those of Nad Buidb's predecessors who have been renowned as sea-raiders. Speaking of one such, Fergus Fairrge, 'Fergus of the sea', he says:

> Cruth ná tabair tonn do thír tascnam
> tórann fairrge a fán fri ardd n-ascnam.

(In a manner in which the sea does not come over the land [he went over the sea so that] the sea's horizon is his gentle hill-slope in striving after the heights.)[16]

This stanza is imaginative, compressed, and dramatic, and with the convoluted expressions typical of the *filid*. Apart from the archaic character of the language, such verse could have been composed at any time up to the final dissolution of the poetic order in the seventeenth century.

---

[14] See, e.g., the anecdote in Adomnán's *Vita Columbae* (i, 42) concerning the saint and the poet Crónán; Richard Sharpe, *Adomnán of Iona, Life of St Columba* (Harmondsworth, 1995), pp 144–5.

[15] See O'Brien, *Corpus geneal. Hib.*

[16] Ibid., p. 2.

A poem on the coming of summer, 'Cétamon cain ré' ('Wonderful season of May'),[17] composed in archaic metrical style, perhaps about A.D. 600 or somewhat earlier, shows by its imagery, and perhaps by its metre, that it was composed by a member of the poetic order. It is the finest nature poem in early Irish, and, like certain other early poems of this type, is completely unaffected by Christian thought. Such poems give an idea of the poetic potentiality of pre-Christian Ireland, and suggest that we are not, generally speaking, to look for external models even for the religious lyric poetry of the Christian period; rather are we to see in that poetry the application of an ancient and well-established technique to the new Christian circumstances.

Closely allied with nature poetry are the poems called *dindshenchus*, 'place-name lore', which were cultivated, largely by the official poets, from the earliest times until the eleventh century. Much of the official poetry in pre-Norman times centred about the district of Brega, which included Tara; Muirchú, in the late seventh century, refers to a *dindshenchus*-type poem on Ferti Fer Féicc, 'the graves of the men of Fécc' (on the hill of Slane), written by one Ferchertne, who, as he tells us, was 'one of the nine druid-poets of Brega'. A poem that may be comparable in age to that quoted by Muirchú is 'Dind Ríg ruad tuam tenbath' ('Dind Ríg, red ridge of death by fire'); this poem purports to give the origin of the name Dind Ríg, 'fortress of kings', a Leinster royal residence on the River Barrow in County Wexford.[18] In the eleventh century, a great compilation of such poems was made, consisting mainly of compositions of the tenth and eleventh centuries.[19] In this collection we find poems written for or dedicated to such kings as Congalach, son of Máel Mithig (d. 956), and Máel Sechlainn Mór (d. 1022). Among prominent poets represented are Flann mac Lonáin (d. 896) and Cináed Ó hArtucáin (d. 975).

Apart from such poems, many official compositions survive, of which a few samples may be mentioned. In a ninth-century ecclesiastical manuscript we find a poem, possibly of the eighth century, 'Áed oll fri ándud n-áne' ('Áed great at kindling of brilliance'), written in praise of a Leinster dynast from Maistiu (Mullaghmast, County Laois);[20] in a seventeenth-century manuscript written by Micheál Ó Cléirigh there is preserved a fine poem, 'Uasalepscop Éirenn Áed' ('Áed is leading bishop of Ireland'), written in praise of Áed Ua Foirréid, bishop at Armagh, between 1032 and 1046;[21] in a

---

[17] Murphy, *Early Irish lyrics*, pp 156–9; see also Carney, 'Three Old Irish accentual poems', pp 23–80: 30–51.

[18] See Heinrich Wagner, 'The archaic *Dind Ríg* poem and related problems' in *Ériu*, xxviii (1977), pp 1–16.

[19] See E. J. Gwynn (ed.), *The metrical dinnshenchas* (5 vols, Dublin, 1903–35).

[20] See *Thes. Pal.*, ii, 295.

[21] See Gerard Murphy, 'A poem in praise of Aodh Úa Foirréidh, bishop of Armagh (1032–1056)' in Sylvester O'Brien, O.F.M. (ed.), *Measgra i gcuimhne Mhichíl Uí Chléirigh* (Dublin, 1944), pp 140–64.

fourteenth-century manuscript written by Ádhamh Ó Cianáin, there is a lament for Máel Sechlainn Mór written by an otherwise unknown poet, Flann file Ó Rónán, otherwise known as Flann na Marb ('Flann of the elegies'); the composition of this poem may be dated precisely to Sunday, 2 September 1022.[22] The tenuousness of the written tradition of these poems is underlined by the fact that each is preserved in a single manuscript only, and is thus an accidental survival.

From the earliest times there existed sagas in which the poet figured as 'hero'. In these sagas the poet performed deeds of prowess or merit analogous to those of the dynastic or military hero, but the exploits are concerned with the word rather than with the sword. One of these tales, the birth of Aí mac Ollaman, is a mythological 'charter' for the rights, privileges, and status of poets. In 'Immaccaldam in dá Thuarad' ('The colloquy of the two sages')[23] Néide, who like Cú Chulainn is a 'beardless boy', contests the chair of poetry at Emain Machae with his older rival Ferchertne. The love story of Liadan and Cuirithir is the equivalent in the poetic milieu of the stories of the 'heroic' lovers Deirdre and Naísiu, Diarmait and Gráinne. One of the most interesting of such tales, as yet untranslated, 'Airec menman Iraird meic Coisse' ('The entertainment of Irard mac Coisse'),[24] deals with the relationship between Domnall Ua Néill, king of Tara (d. 980) and the contemporary poet Irard mac Coisse; it could be held that the poet himself was the author of the saga.[25]

WITH the coming of Christianity it would have been a matter of immediate necessity to reconcile whatever ideas the Irish had of their remote origins with the book of Genesis. The book of Genesis had quite naturally a very strong impact on the Irish secular mind: it was a new, but incontrovertible, 'origin tale', the ultimate basis of all genealogical knowledge. It opened the eyes of the Irish to mankind and, with some imaginative research, made the whole world their traceable kin. One of the earliest results of the impact of the Bible on Ireland was 'Lebor Gabála', or, to give its longer title, 'Lebor Gabála Érenn' ('The book of the taking of Ireland').[26] There is uncertainty as to the date when a specific work with this title came into being. It remains, however, a convenient title for the traditions of the invasion of Ireland by the sons of Míl, which certainly existed in the seventh century or earlier, and the linking of such traditions with biblical history. Some of the ideas incorpor-

---

[22] See James Carney, 'The Ó Cianáin Miscellany' in *Ériu*, xxi (1969), pp 122–47: 142–7.
[23] See Whitley Stokes, 'The colloquy of the two sages' in *Rev. Celt.*, xxvi (1905), pp 4–64.
[24] Ed. Kuno Meyer, in *Anecdota from Irish manuscripts*, ii (Halle, 1908), pp 42–76.
[25] For references to other stories of the poets see below, pp 467–8.
[26] See [Eoin MacNeill and] R. A. S. Macalister (ed. and trans.), *Lebor Gabála Érenn, The Book of the Taking of Ireland* (5 vols, Dublin, 1938–56).

ated in this work remained constant down through the centuries. In a sense it provided a charter for the survival of primitive Irish tradition into the Christian period: the implicit terms were that any traditional being might be written of, but only when presented as a demon or as a descendant of Adam. The text of 'Lebor Gabála', which has come down in a large number of medieval manuscript copies, has not survived in its original form. Here we draw upon the specific recension represented by the twelfth-century Book of Leinster, and the closely related fourteenth-century copy in the hand of Ádhamh Ó Cianáin (d. 1373).

According to the 'Lebor Gabála', before the invasion of the sons of Míl— which is the main subject of the book—Ireland was successively inhabited by four groups. First came Cessair, daughter of Bith, son of Noah, with fifty maidens and three men, her father, Ladru, and Fintan, son of Bóchra. All died, except Fintan, who lived on miraculously for ages after the Flood to tell the tale. After this, Ireland was deserted for 300 or 'more correctly' 312 years, when it was occupied by Partholón, son of Sera, son of Srú, who fought a battle with Cichol Gricenchos, a leader of the Fomairi. All the people of Partholón died of plague except his brother's son Tuan, who survived 'in various forms' and was reborn in the sixth century as Tuan mac Cairill; he was thus able to tell the early history of Ireland to Finnian of Moville (d. 579 ) and Colum Cille (d. 597).

The third invasion was that of Nemed, son of Agnoman, 'of the Greeks of Scythia', who fought against Gend and Sengand, two kings of the Fomairi. After Nemed's death his people were oppressed by the Fomairi. Some fled to the Hebrides; another group fled to Greece where they multiplied, and were enslaved by the Greeks. Finally, as a company of 5,000, they made boats out of their bags (*builg*), set sail, and reconquered Ireland. These are the Irish Fir Bolg, and their leaders were five (Gand, Genand, Rúdraige, Sengand, and Sláine); hence came the division of Ireland into five provinces. Also belonging to this group were the Domnainn and the Gálióin, the ancestors of the Leinstermen. One of this group, Fergus Lethderg, accompanied by his son Británn, conquered Anglesey, and from there the whole island of Britain, where their descendants ruled until Hengist and Horsa defeated them, banishing them to the borders of the island.

The fourth invasion was that of the Tuatha Dea or Tuatha Dé Danann. These, the gods of the primitive Irish, are presented as a group who, like the Fir Bolg, were descended from Nemed. Having learned the arts of magic in the northern world, they invaded Ireland and defeated the Fir Bolg in the first battle of Mag Tuired. Their leaders were Nuadu Argatlám, Dian Cécht (otherwise In Scál Balb, 'the dumb phantom'), Ogma, and Lug. They fought the Fomairi in the second battle of Mag Tuired, and Lug slew their leader Balar, and became king of Ireland for forty years. He was succeeded by In Dagda.

The most important invasion in this schema was, of course, that of the Goídil. Their history, in brief, was as follows. They were descended from Gomer, son of Japheth. A descendant of Gomer, Fénius (*Fóenius Farsaid*), was at the Tower of Babel, and in his time the *Bérla Féne*, the Irish language, came into being. It was not one of the languages emerging from the confusion, but was made artificially by selecting the best elements from all of them.[27] Fénius's son Nél was called to Egypt by Pharaoh because of his knowledge of languages. Goídel, the ancestor from whom the Irish take their name, was a son of Nél and Pharaoh's daughter Scotta, whence the name *Scotti*. This group left Egypt when Pharaoh was drowned in the Red Sea, and their leader Éber Scott, a grandson of Goídel, took the kingship of Scythia to which he was entitled by descent. His descendants Agnoman and Agnoman's son, Lámfind, were banished from Scythia, and their offspring wandered around the world, finally conquering Spain. There, in the city of Brigantia, Bregon son of Bráth built a tower from which Ireland was seen one winter evening by Íth, son of Bregon. Íth set out for Ireland, landed in Kerry, and proceeded to Ailech in County Donegal, where he gave counsel to the kings of the Tuatha Dea and, apparently, the Fomairi. When he left he was followed and killed, and his body was brought back to Spain by his followers. Then came the successful invasion of Ireland by the sons of Míl. Ireland was divided into a northern and southern half, the halves being allotted respectively to Míl's sons, Éremón and Éber.

As noted above, the earliest extant manuscript copy of 'Lebor Gabála' is of the twelfth century. But the material in general, though not necessarily in particulars, is many centuries earlier. Míl, his son Éremón, the ancestors Goídel Glas, Fénius Farsaid, and all the others up to Adam, are referred to in portions of the Leinster poems that, with likelihood, may be regarded as early seventh-century. There was an earlier version of 'Lebor Gabála' in the eighth-century collection called 'Cín Dromma Snechtai' ('the Book of Drumsnat') and a version was used by the so-called Nennius (*c.*800) in compiling his 'Historia Britonum'.[28] When biblical texts are quoted, the influence of the Old Latin version is marked. The book is referred to as 'Gabála Érenn' ('the invasions of Ireland') in Cormac's Glossary (*c.*900). On the whole, therefore, it would seem safe to say that 'Lebor Gabála', in some form, or in various forms, was already in existence in the early seventh century, and its developed teaching dominated the study of early Irish history virtually until the nineteenth. Although its primary purpose was theological, it also had the political effect of giving all the Irish a common ancestry and of eliminating ethnic differences.

---

[27] See the discussion by Paul Russell, above, pp 405–6.
[28] See D. N. Dumville, '"Nennius" and the *Historia Brittonum*' in *Studia Celt.*, x–xi (1975–76), pp 78–95.

In considering the invasions of Ireland, we may dismiss as comparatively unimportant those of Cessair and Partholón. From the nature of the Tuatha Dé Danann it is clear that their invasion is fictional. This leaves us with an underlying tradition of two main elements in Ireland: the Goídil, the dominant race, and the descendants of Nemed, a subject people consisting of the Fir Bolg, the Domnainn, and the Gálióin. Perhaps significantly, the subject group is regarded as closely related to the British.

The question arises: who were the Fomairi? It will be noticed above that they never invade: they are just there. T. F. O'Rahilly believed that there was no original distinction between the Fomairi and the Tuatha Dé Danann. The name 'Tuatha Dé Danann' was, according to him, an invention of the author or authors of 'Lebor Gabála', as was the distinction drawn between them and the Fomairi. Another Celtic scholar, Gerard Murphy, remained unconvinced, and regarded the two as separate groups of mythological beings, the one resembling the Greek Olympians, the other the Titans. Murphy may well be right, or at least it can be said that there are some difficulties in the way of O'Rahilly's view.[29] In the Leinster poems, portions of which may be regarded as pre-'Lebor Gabála', we encounter Lug, who is spoken of favourably as a *scál finn*, 'fair phantom'. A Leinster dynast, one Art son of Mess-Delman, is spoken of as follows:

> Mál ad-rúalaid iatha marb,
> macc soer Sétni,
> selaig srathu Fomaire
> fo doíne domnaib.

(A prince who visited the lands of the dead, the noble son of Sétne; he smote the meadow-lands of the Fomairi, under the worlds of human beings.)

It would seem to be apparent from this material that the Fomairi represented an antagonistic spirit world, whereas Lug of the Tuatha Dé is a favourable figure. It may also be noted that, like the Tuatha Dé, the Fomairi inhabit a world that is located under ours. They bear 'barbarous' names, and in genealogical tradition are made to descend from Ham, son of Noah. This is apparently a reformed version of an earlier heterodox view that they were descended from Cain, son of Adam. On the other hand, as will be seen in the section on the mythological tales, the Tuatha Dé and the Fomairi intermarry, and the latter, as well as the former, function as culture heroes.

ACCORDING to Caesar the Gauls believed that they were descended from a god whom he names as Dis Pater. One would expect some similar view as to their own descent among the Irish, and, in name at least, In Dagda, 'the good god'

---

[29] O'Rahilly, *Early Ir. hist.*, pp 482–3; Gerard Murphy, 'Notes on Cath Maige Tuired' in *Éigse*, vii (1953–5), pp 197–8.

(otherwise Eochaid Ollathair, 'Eochaid the great father'), fits into the pattern of a general ancestor deity. Genealogy, in a very practical and immediate sense, was central to the whole Irish social and governmental system, and the ultimate origin of the Irish people or peoples would certainly have formed a not unimportant part of druidic teaching. As has been noted in the preceding section, an effort was made in early Christian Ireland to conceal the character of the ancient Irish gods. This was done through euhemerisation and censorship, but was only partially successful. In Cormac's Glossary (§159) there is reference to In Dagda, 'the good god'. He is shown as having three daughters (all apparently aspects of one divinity): Brigit Bé nÉxe, 'Brigit the lady of poetry' (also described as *dea poetarum*); Brigit Bé Legis, 'Brigit the lady of healing'; and Brigit Bé Goibne, 'Brigit the lady of smithcraft'. One Anu is described in the same source (§31) as *mater deorum Hibernensium*, and her name is seen in *Dá chích nAnund*, 'the two breasts of Anu', the name given in Irish to the Paps mountains in County Kerry. Reference is also made to Manannán mac Lir, 'Manannán son of the sea [*ler*]'. He was—the Glossary says in a brave euhemeristic effort—a renowned merchant who lived in the Isle of Man, the finest navigator in the western world, who, by inspecting the heavens, could predict the weather; 'hence the Irish and British called him the god of the sea, and said that he was the son of the sea' (§896).

Nothing approaching a comprehensive work on Irish mythology exists; the material is scattered over the entire corpus of early literature, notably in 'Immram Brain',[30] the Finn mac Cumaill tales, the large medieval collections of place-name lore (*dindshenchus*) and the early genealogies: it follows that theorising is somewhat hazardous.

Among the tales dealing with the early Irish deities,the former exclusively, the latter mainly, are 'Cath Maige Tuired' ('The battle of Moyturra')[31] and 'Tochmarc Étaíne' ('The wooing of Étaín').[32] The early version of 'Cath Maige Tuired'—although surviving only in a sixteenth-century manuscript—is the most important Irish mythological tale.[33] The text probably derives from the early Old Irish period, but in the course of transmission has been subjected to partial rewriting and possibly interpolation; for example, it has Norse loanwords and refers to the Hebrides as *Innsi Gall*, 'the islands of the northmen'. The tale is referred to in Cormac's Glossary and in a poem by Flannacán mac Cellaig, king of Brega (d. 896).

---

[30] See below, pp 502–6.

[31] Elizabeth Gray (ed. and trans.), *Cath Maige Tuired, the second battle of Mag Tuired* (London, 1982). See also John Carey, 'Myth and mythography in Cath Maige Tuired' in *Studia Celt.*, xxiv–xxv (1989–90), pp 53–69.

[32] Ed. Osborn Bergin and R. I. Best, 'Tochmarc Étaine' in *Ériu*, xii (1938), pp 137–96.

[33] Ed. John Fraser, 'The first battle of Moytura' in *Ériu*, viii (1915), pp 1–63. A much later version with points of considerable interest is found in a seventeenth-century manuscript, and has been editedby Brian Ó Cuív: *Cath Muighe Tuireadh* (Dublin, 1945). The points of contact with the earlier tale and with the folk tradition are discussed in the introduction.

In the tradition of 'Lebor Gabála', the Tuatha Dé Danann fought two battles at Mag Tuired, the first against the Fir Bolg, the second against the Fomairi. The second battle is the main subject of the mythological tale, but a brief account of the first is also included. O'Rahilly held that there was originally only one battle, that against the Fir Bolg, and that the tale of the second battle was a derivative of a primitive version of the first. Murphy took a directly contrary view: he held that references to the 'first' battle could not be traced beyond the eleventh century: the 'second' battle was the only one that was old and traditional.[34] Although Murphy's criticism of O'Rahilly may have some justification, his case is overstated. Too much depends on a dubious translation of *cétna fecht* as 'to begin with' in the poem of Flannacán son of Cellach referred to above. The phrase can only mean 'the first time', and involves an implicit comparison of the two battles, thus tending to prove the contrary of what Murphy intended, that is, that an account of the first battle existed before 896. The saga of the first battle, published by Fraser, is hardly, in its extant form, earlier than the eleventh century. It is fairly uniform in style, and there are no linguistic signs that, as a tale, it has undergone a long period of development from the Old Irish period onwards.

'Cath Maige Tuired', in its early version, is not merely an account of the battle against the Fomairi; in fact, the actual battle occupies quite a small portion of the text. The tale has an additional title: 'and the birth of Bress son of Elatha and his reign.' The tale in its extant form is, indeed, a dramatic history of Ireland in 'Lebor Gabála' terms from the invasion of the Tuatha Dé Danann to the defeat of the Fomairi. It is a well-composed story having the freshness, vigour, speed, and good dialogue associated with early narrative. It presents what must be a large part of the Irish pantheon, and the gods are assigned roles that doubtless reflect something of their pre-Christian character. The Dagda is a *ráth*-builder, and wields great power. He has a prodigious appetite, a natural consequence of his immense size, which may be gauged from the detail that lovers could lie in his ladle. Quite fittingly, his wife or paramour, the Mórrígu, daughter of Ernmass, is so gigantic that as she awaits her divine lover one foot is in a townland south of a river, the other in a townland to the north of it. Ogma is a strong man, a kind of Hercules. Dian Cécht and his son Miach are leeches, and his daughter Airmed is a herbalist. Lug is the *samildánach*, the god of all crafts, and invites comparison with the Gaulish god (probably his namesake), whom Caesar equates with Mercury and describes as *inventor omnium artium*. Despite the ultimate divinity of its characters, 'Cath Maige Tuired', more than any other tale, presents us with a panoramic view of early Irish society: kings, queens, druids, judges, poets, bards, satirists, storytellers, historians, leeches, herbalists, sorcerers, witches, harpers, pipers, horn-blowers, jugglers, fools, smiths,

---

[34] Murphy, 'Notes on Cath Maige Tuired' in *Éigse*, vii (1953–5), pp 191 ff.

wrights, *ráth*-builders, braziers, hospitallers, athletes, warriors, charioteers, and cupbearers. Their dress is magnificent in the manner of the characters in 'Táin Bó Cuailnge'. They eat beef, swine, sheep, and goats, porridge (*líte*), and small cakes. They drink ale and milk. Their entertainments are music, *fidchell* ('chess'), storytelling, swordplay, dog-and horse-racing.

'Tochmarc Étaíne' was known only in a fragmentary form until its publication in 1938.[35] The text is regarded as ninth-century, but since the tale existed in some form in the 'Cín Dromma Snechtai' we may assume the existence of some kind of written version in the seventh or eighth century.

'Tochmarc Étaíne' tells of the surreptitious begetting of Óengus, son of In Dagda, on Boand, wife of Elcmar of Bruig na Bóinne (now New Grange, County Meath); and of how by trickery, and with the collusion of In Dagda, he deprived Elcmar of the lordship of the Bruig. The central character of the tale is, however, not Óengus but his foster-father, Midir of Brí Léith (near Ardagh, County Longford). He sought to marry the most beautiful maiden in Ireland, Étaín, daughter of Ailill, king of north-eastern Ireland. In return for getting Ailill's daughter Midir had to perform certain great labours: the clearing of twelve plains, the provision of twelve rivers to water them, and the stocking of the rivers with fish from the sea. These labours would appear to be an ancient aetiological element. Having accomplished his labours, Midir took Étaín to wife, and lived with her for a year. But his first wife Fuamnach changed her into a pool of water; then she became a worm, and afterwards a purple fly of great beauty. The fly was always in Midir's company, and he was happy, knowing it was Étaín. But Fuamnach drove her off. Finally, after years of misery, she fell into a cup in the house of Étar of Inber Cíchmaine; she was swallowed by Étar's wife, and was reborn as his daughter. As Étar's daughter, Étaín married Eochaid Airem, king of Ireland, but eventually Midir gained possession of her by a trick, and Midir and Étaín flew away in the shape of swans. Eochaid Airem, seeking his wife, dug up the otherworld mounds of Ireland, and when he came to Brí Léith, Midir promised to restore Étaín. Eochaid picked out his wife, as he thought, from fifty identical women from the mounds. He brought her home, and she became pregnant by him. At this point, having bound peace on Eochaid, Midir revealed that the woman whom Eochaid had picked out was not Étaín, his wife, but his daughter, for Étaín was pregnant by Eochaid when Midir abducted her.

The child of the union of Eochaid and his daughter was exposed as the offspring of an incestuous union. Left in a dog-kennel, she was rescued and secretly reared by a herdsman, and grew up beautiful and accomplished. She was seen by the king Etarscéla and he made her his wife. Her name was Mess

---

[35] From the newly discovered nine leaves of the Yellow Book of Lecan previously in the famous Phillipps collection.

Buachalla, and she became the mother of Conaire mac Etarscéla, the doomed king in the saga 'Togail Bruidne Da Derga'.

This tale is well integrated and told in fine prose. It is in a sense an 'origin' tale, dealing with the history of the Leinster king Conaire mac Etarscéla (Etarscél being thought to have lived about the time of the birth of Christ).[36] The great Swiss Celtic scholar Rudolf Thurneysen commented on the monastic nature of the language as exemplified in such phrases as *ata-cobair in Dagda a cairdes collaidi*, 'the Dagda desired her in carnal friendship'.[37] One may also note the precision in dating: we are told that 1,012 years elapsed between Étaín's birth as daughter of Ailill and her rebirth to Étar's wife. This would leave, in the saga writer's mind, just over a thousand years between Tuatha Dé Danann domination and the early years of the Christian era. It would appear that a high degree of credibility was extended to such tales in medieval Ireland, even by professed Christians. The tale implicitly teaches that the powers of the otherworld are tricky, and that we must be careful in our dealings with them; dire consequences may follow interference with otherworld dwellings, a belief that has survived in some degree down to the twentieth century.

It would seem probable that uncensored oral traditions of the ancient gods continued strongly among the secular poets for many centuries after Christianisation, and that the tales and traditions that we possess are but the tip of the pagan iceberg. This may be illustrated by reference to a story told concerning the poet Flann mac Lonáin (d. 895).[38] Flann and his company of poets found themselves in a house without food. The weather was excessively bad, and it was impossible to leave. Suddenly they saw approaching them a monstrous, evil-looking being with a bill-hook in one hand and an ox in the other. He promised them that he would sell them the carcass in return for a cow he would himself choose. They assented, so he killed the beast, cooked it, and served it to them. A year later he returned with five others like himself. They behaved badly and said they would never leave unless they got an ever-yielding cow (*bó bithblicht*). Flann asked him his name and he answered: 'Fidbadach son of Fid Rúscach'. The poet made a long poem about his plight, incorporating this curious name (the poem may well be a genuine production of Flann). The evil-looking being then revealed himself. 'That', he said, 'is the cow I sought, for poetic art is ever-yielding and I am Óengus, in Macc Óc, who has come to you.'[39] In another tale of much earlier

---

[36] O'Brien, *Corpus geneal. Hib.*, i, 120, 24.

[37] *Z.C.P.*, xxii (1941), p. 4.

[38] Transcribed by Osborn Bergin in *Anecdota from Irish manuscripts*, i (Halle, 1912), pp 45–50.

[39] This incident, told of a poet, is the 'poetic' analogy to the 'heroic' version of the theme, the beheading incident in 'Fled Bricrend' and other related material. For this type of analogy, see p. 460 above.

date the sixth- or seventh-century poet Senchán Torpéist shows kindness to an evil-looking leper. The leper finally reveals himself as a beautiful youth, 'the spirit of poetry', who, as in the other tale, is probably intended to be Óengus, son of the Dagda. The leper who reveals himself as the spirit of poetry is the 'poetic' equivalent of heroic or dynastic tales where a loathsome hag, on being treated with unexpected sexual consideration, reveals herself as a beautiful maiden, who has the disposition of sovereignty. These tales suggest that the secular poets continued to remember and to cultivate some, at least, of the pagan gods, and did not worry very much about reconciling belief in them with their professed Christianity. One of the key figures in the history of letters in Ireland was this poet Senchán Torpéist (*fl. c.*580–*c.*650). He compiled a work on Irish families called the 'Cocangab Már', which, though it has not survived as a separate work, has probably been incorporated in the genealogies. He is shown in tradition as 'collecting' the central saga of Irish tradition, 'Táin Bó Cuailnge', from various poets, none of whom knew the complete tale. It is reasonable to accept the connection of Senchán with the 'Táin', and to regard him as symbolising the reaction of the native *literati* to the new conditions, a reaction that ensured that the Irish laws were committed to writing as early as the sixth or seventh century, and that Irish historical tradition was to achieve written form at this date, and during the coming centuries.

In the full historic period, the beginning of which may, in a general sense, be dated to the second half of the fifth century, Ireland appears to have just emerged from a period of political convulsion. Emain Machae, the capital of the great kingdom of the Ulaid, had recently fallen to the group whom O'Rahilly called the 'midland Goidels'. Ulster had now in effect shrunk to an area corresponding roughly to the present counties of Antrim and Down, and the ancient capital was thus in subject territory. Similarly Tara, the sacral capital of the Leinstermen, was now under the same control, that of the 'descendants of Conn'; these included the powerful mid-fifth-century dynast, Niall mac Echach, otherwise known as Niall Noígiallach ('Niall of the Nine Hostages'). This group dominated the midlands, Connacht, and the greater part of the historic province of Ulster, and claimed tribute from Leinster.

The Ulster–Connacht tales show a pre-Christian Ireland in which Ulster, with its capital at Emain Machae (Navan Fort, County Armagh), is threatened by a combination of Connacht, Leinster, and Munster. The combination is dominated by Ailill and Medb, king and queen of Connacht. Medb, according to genealogical tradition, was a daughter of Eochu Feidlech, king of Tara, who had suppressed the earlier Connacht dynasties, bestowing that kingdom on his daughter. Medb, now queen of Connacht in her own right, married Ailill, son of Ross Ruad of Leinster and his Connacht wife

Máta (or Mágu) Muirisce. The contemporary king of Ulster was Conchobar mac Nessa.

The society presented in these tales is one that seems basically similar to those of pre-Roman Britain and Gaul. We have thus, as it were, a picture of Celtic society from the inside. That the picture is generally authentic is confirmed by the fact that it corresponds remarkably well to the observations on Celtic society made by classical authors or historians, notably Diodorus Siculus, Caesar, Strabo, and Posidonius.[40] The central tale, which comes close to epic stature, is 'Táin Bó Cuailnge' ('The driving of the cattle of Cuailnge'); it exists in a number of versions, the most important being that found principally in 'Leabhar na hUidhre' (c.1100) and the fourteenth-century Yellow Book of Lecan. This version approximates in length to an average modern novel; its very length makes it unique, for apart from trans-lation literature and 'Acallam na Senórach' ('The colloquy of the ancient men'), there is hardly a tale in early Irish that cannot be read in under half an hour.

Just as the 'Táin' is the lengthiest and most important of the present group of tales, it is also the most unsatisfactory in its extant form. It begins imperfectly, and although the narrative has a clear line, its literary impact is lessened by reason of accretions, rewritten episodes, 'doublets' (incidents told more than once), and explicit references to the tradition of 'other books'. Thus the earliest extant form of the tale is a secondary compilation, mainly eighth- or ninth-century in language, but still at some remove from the first written recording. As to the date of the first recording, it is now generally agreed that this is to be attributed to the seventh century, but the stages of growth and change between then and the eleventh are by no means clear.

According to Irish tradition, the 'Táin' was first given written form in the seventh century, possibly by Senchán Torpéist, who is represented as collect-ing the material from the tradition of contemporary poets.[41] This written version gained oral currency and was again recorded from oral tradition in two independent versions in the ninth century. These versions, we are to assume, were very close, but in some minor respects had grown apart. The double recording has led to the appearance of 'doublets' in the surviving account. An eleventh-century compiler made a mechanical conflation of

[40] On this question see Kenneth Jackson, *The oldest Irish tradition: a window on the iron age* (Cambridge, 1964).
[41] The definitive modern edition is by Cecile O'Rahilly, *Táin Bó Cuailnge from the Book of Leinster* (Dublin, 1970). The best discussion is still Rudolf Thurneysen, *Die irische Helden- und Königsage*, i (Berlin, 1921), an outstanding work, though in many ways now out of date. In an important article in Z.C.P., xix, 209 ('Colmán mac Lénéni und Senchán Torpéist') Thurneysen reaches the following conclusions: 'Aus dem Vorhergehenden ergibt sich, dass ich der freilich sagenhaften Überlieferung, Senchán Torpéist habe die Táin Bó Cuailnge zusammengefügt, nicht mehr dasselbe Misstrauen entgegenbringe wie Ir. Helden-und Königsage I, iii' ('From the foregoing discussion it follows that I should now be less sceptical about the (clearly mythical) tradition concerning S. T.'s having brought T.B.C. together').

them and also used some *roscada* (statements by the characters of the saga in highly archaic poetic language), of which he had early written versions.

The events of the 'Táin' may be summarised as follows: Ailill and Medb gathered all their forces at Cruachu (Rathcroghan, County Roscommon) in Connacht in readiness for an attack on Ulster. These included allies from Leinster and Munster and a number of Ulster exiles, among them Cormac Condlongas, son of Conchobar, and Fergus mac Róich, who is the pivotal figure in the narrative. The immediate object of the attack (which is not stated here, but is referred to in other early sources such as 'Táin Bó Froích' ('The driving of Froích's cattle') is *do tháin inna mbó a Cuailnge*, 'to drive the cattle from Cooley' and to gain possession of a magnificent brown bull, the *Donn Cuailnge*, which rivals one possessed by Ailill (the *Findbennach*, 'white horned', of Mag Aí). These were no ordinary bulls; they were respectively the swineherds of Bodb, king of the otherworld mounds of Munster, and of Ochall, king of the otherworld mounds of Connacht: after a series of metamorphoses they had been reborn as bulls, for 'like Mongán mac Fiachnai' they had the power of shape-changing.[42] The men of Ulster within the borders of Ulster (thus excluding the Ulster exiles) were subject to a stupor or prostration called the *cess noínden*, which affected all men of military age, and lasted for the three months of winter. Cú Chulainn and his earthly father Sualtam were, however, immune. The attack on Ulster was strategically timed for the period of the *cess*, but the precise day was fixed, after a wait of fourteen days, by the auguries of druids. The march began on the Monday after the feast of Samain (approximately 1 November); the date is of some importance, because the army was to encounter severe winter conditions. As soon as they started, they met Fedelm, a woman-seer of Connacht who had been studying druidry in Britain, and at Medb's request she performed an augury as to how the expedition would fare. Her prophecies were ominous, but Medb insisted on interpreting them favourably and the march continued.

At the very beginning of the expedition Medb observed the efficiency and superiority of the Gálióin or Leinstermen, and did not like it, for two reasons: the credit for the victory would go to them, and they could not be trusted not to 'seize our land against us'. She proposed that they be slain. Ailill and Fergus opposed this, and the compromise achieved was that the Gálióin should not be allowed to exist as a single unit; they were divided among the rest of the army.

When, after some adventures, the army reached Áth nGabla ('Fork-ford'), they were confronted with the sight of the heads of four of their advance guard spitted on the forked branches of a tree-trunk that had been cut and

---

[42] Their origin is recounted in the saga *De Chophur in dá Muccado*, ed. Ernst Windisch, *Irische Texte*, iii (Leipzig, 1891), pp 230–78: 235 ff. Engl. transl. in Kuno Meyer and Alfred Nutt (ed. and trans.), *The voyage of Bran son of Febal* (2 vols, London, 1895), ii, 58–65, 65–6. See also Thurneysen, *Heldensage*, pp 275 ff.

planted in the middle of the ford that they must cross. Fergus is questioned and tells them that Cú Chulainn has done this deed. The army settles down for the night, and, in sight of the four spitted heads, the events of Cú Chulainn's youth are recounted by some of the Ulster exiles who had known him, principally by Fergus—a pathetic note, for Fergus had been Cú Chulainn's *aite* or foster-father. The narration of Cú Chulainn's boyhood deeds is one of the most effective pieces of early Irish narrative: its positioning in the saga, the *mise en scène*, with cold winter night, snowy landscape, spitted heads, the army resting after the preparation of food; the diversity achieved by having several narrators, who tell of the past but are all the time conscious of the immediate scene.

From here on the saga consists largely of a series of single combats by which Cú Chulainn impedes the advance of the allies; these culminate in his encounter with his former companion Ferdiad. The latter incident possibly figured in primitive material, but the written form in which it has survived is a highly romanticised version of the eleventh century; the presentation and style has something in common with the story of the fall of Troy, which was popular in translated form at the same period.

Attention may be called to some other aspects of the saga. During the course of his defence of Ulster, Cú Chulainn has comfort and some aid from his divine father Lug, and encounters the enmity of the Irish war-goddess, the Mórrígu. He is also helped by the River Crond, which rises against the enemy. Findabair, the daughter of Ailill and Medb (who figures prominently in 'Táin Bó Froích') is offered in turn to various warriors in return for undertaking single combat with Cú Chulainn. There is a love-affair between Fergus and Medb, and Cuillius, Ailill's charioteer, is set by Ailill to spy upon the pair. As Medb and Fergus lie together he steals Fergus's sword and brings it back to Ailill as a proof of betrayal. Fergus, finding his sword gone, goes into a wood and makes a wooden one, apparently to conceal his shameful loss. Ailill comforts himself with the thought that Medb's infidelity was due to her desire to have Fergus's help on the expedition. The whole matter is subsequently discussed by Ailill, Medb, and Fergus in *roscada*. The dialogue is continued over a game of *fidchell* between the two men, and the game in some way is related to the triangular situation. The obscure language bars the modern reader from full understanding, but one is left with the impression of a somewhat bitter and cynical humour. Medb's infidelity, however, causes no serious breach between Ailill and Fergus; this is apparently part of the characterisation of Ailill, who (as we know from other sources) is a man *cen ét cen omun*, 'without jealousy, without fear'. Fergus's sword is not returned to him until the final battle between the armies of Ulster and the allies. Fergus's position as an Ulsterman in the Connacht camp is always dubious, and he is under some suspicion from his newly found allies.

The allied army suffer great losses through Cú Chulainn, and are finally
defeated. Yet there is some ambiguity here, for the cattle of Cooley are
actually driven away. In the saga as it survives, the allies take away the Donn
Cuailnge, who meets Medb's Findbennach in combat in Connacht. The
Donn Cuailnge is victorious; the Connachtmen are about to slay him, but
Fergus intervenes, saying that he should be allowed to go where he would.
He sets out for his own land, leaving marks (and place-names) in the course
of his journey. He finally dies at Druim Tairb ('bull's ridge'), 'between
Ulster and Uí Echach ["Iveagh"]'. Ailill and Medb now make peace with the
Ulstermen and Cú Chulainn. Findabair is given to Cú Chulainn; the Con-
nachtmen return to Connacht and the Ulstermen to Emain Machae, and the
peace lasts for seven years.

The 'Táin' is the firm centrepiece of the Ulster cycle. Around it there are
gathered a number of tales telling of preceding events and of the subsequent
deaths of the participants. Foremost among these tales is 'Longas mac nUislenn' ('The exile of the sons of Uisliu').[43] This is the story of the love of
Deirdre and Noíse, and it seems to belong to a complex of love stories of
which the best-known internationally concerns Tristan and Isolde. It is a well
told and moving tale. Within the complex of the Ulster cycle its purpose is to
explain how it came about that Fergus mac Róich and other Ulstermen were
on the Connacht side during the 'Táin'. It seems to be a new composition,
perhaps of the eighth century; in the general cycle it has displaced a tale of
which only some lines survive, 'Fochunn Loingse Fergusa maic Róich' ('The
reason for the exile of Fergus mac Róich'). Other well-told associated tales
are 'Scéla Mucce maic Dathó' ('The happenings concerning Mac Dathó's
pig'),[44] and 'Fled Bricrend' ('Bricriu's feast').[45] A number of the pre-tales to
'Táin Bó Cuailnge' also bear the title 'Táin' with specific definition: 'Táin
Bó Froích', 'Táin Bó Regamno', 'Táin Bó Dartada', and others.[46] These all
tell of the efforts of Ailill and Medb to obtain allies before undertaking war
against Ulster. The most interesting is 'Táin Bó Froích': it has been maintained that this tale, belonging to the early Old Irish period, is essentially a
new composition made from traditional material combined with hints, suggestions, and incidents taken from the new monastic culture.[47] It has points
of similarity in both style and presentation to another archaic piece, 'Aislinge
Óengusso' ('The dream of Óengus'):[48] in this latter—and to a lesser degree

[43] Vernam Hull (ed.), *Longes mac nUislenn, the exile of the sons of Uisliu* (Cambridge, Mass.,
1954).
[44] Rudolf Thurneysen (ed.), *Scéla mucce maic Dathó* (Dublin, 1935).
[45] George Henderson (ed. and trans.), *Fled Bricrend: the feast of Bricriu* (London, 1899).
[46] Ed. Ernst Windisch, 'Vier kleine Táin' in *Irische Texte*, 2nd ser., pt 2 (Leipzig, 1887),
pp 185–256.
[47] Carney, *Studies in Ir. lit.*, pp 1–65. For an edition of the text, see Wolfgang Meid (ed.),
*Táin Bó Fraích* (Dublin, 1967).
[48] Francis Shaw (ed.), *The dream of Óengus: Aislinge Óengusso* (Brussels, 1936).

in 'Táin Bó Froích'—Ailill and Medb mix freely with otherworld figures such as In Dagda and his son Óengus. This feature distinguishes these two tales from 'Táin Bó Cuailnge' and certain other tales of the cycle, which by comparison are 'realistic' in that supernatural figures are presented as very rare visitants from a different sphere of existence. In 'Táin Bó Cuailnge' two mythological characters play an important role: Lug, who is Cú Chulainn's *athair a sídaib*, 'father from the (otherworld) mounds', and the Mórrígu, 'phantom queen', who is his enemy. But these are supernatural visitants, and do not interfere seriously with the general realistic character of the tale. In 'Táin Bó Froích', the hero Froích is a son to Bé Find 'from the (otherworld) mounds'. This tale furthermore contains an interesting passage on the origin of the three types of music, *Goltraiges*, *Gentraiges*, and *Suantraiges*, 'music of weeping', 'music of smiling', and 'music of sleep'; these were three sons fathered upon Boand 'from the (otherworld) mounds' by Uaithne, the Dagda's harper. 'Aislinge Óengusso', a seventh- or eighth-century tale, tells of the love-sickness of one of the most popular figures in Irish mythology, Óengus (In Macc Oac), son of In Dagda.

'Táin Bó Cuailnge' is some ten times as long as the average tale in early Irish. Thurneysen held that it was inspired by the 'Aeneid', from which it borrowed not only a reference to the fury Alecto but, more basically, the flashback technique used in the narration of Cú Chulainn's youthful deeds. But it seems unlikely that such a literary work, in its complete form, should rejoin the general stream of Irish oral tradition. It seems even less likely that, had this happened, it should then be recorded some two centuries later in two independent recordings, and with the comparatively slight degree of divergence that Thurneysen's theory suggests. The events of the Ulster cycle are presented as historical, and in their main lines were generally accepted as such. Present-day tendencies are to regard such characters as Conchobar, Medb, and Cú Chulainn as humanised deities (following O'Rahilly) or as fictional characters (following Jackson). A case might, however, be made for regarding most of such characters as essentially historic.

The society presented in these tales is very different socially and politically from that of Ireland in the seventh and subsequent centuries, when these tales were given something approaching their present literary form. One problem among many is to explain how, in the seventh to the ninth centuries, Irish writers could give such a good and convincing picture of the customs and institutions of such a remote date. Some scholars, notably Kenneth Jackson, have answered this by bringing the social and political scene of 'Táin Bó Cuailnge' and its associated tales virtually to the eve of the Christian period. It is not to be questioned that archaic institutions, discontinued elsewhere in the Celtic world, survived in Ireland until the coming of Christianity, and even beyond; it seems certain that in the sixth century an Irish poet would be capable of visualising a social and political scene that would be true for the early fifth century, and perhaps for many centuries before that date. But the question still remains: by what reasoning did the early Irish equate the year of Conchobar's death with A.D. 20? Jackson's view that the dating emerges from an equation of the year of Conchobar's death with that of Christ in the saga 'Aided Conchobair' ('The tragic death of Conchobar')[49] is hardly convincing. The general position in the genealogies (involving the whole country) implies a gap of several hundred years between the characters of 'Táin Bó Cuailnge' and Christianity. The genealogies cannot, of course, be relied upon in detail. But neither can we assume that they were subjected to a general revision in order to bring them into conformity with a minor saga, which in its extant, and here most relevant, form cannot have come into being before the eighth century.[50]

There are considerable difficulties in assessing the relationship of the 'Táin' and its satellite tales to primitive oral tradition, and this is a much-discussed problem. That in a general sense these tales reflect and derive from a primitive oral tradition is ground common to all commentators.[51] But it is difficult to regard them as simply recordings of oral narrative; some allowance (its extent will vary from commentator to commentator) must be made for changes made in the course of transferring material from the oral to the literary plane. There is also, of course, the possibility of religious and political censorship. It is important, in making comparisons with other oral cultures, to remember that early Irish material derives in general not from the tradition of simple people, nor from the local tradition of a small area, nor even of a province: it derives from a nationally based learned class, part of whose function was to perpetuate and maintain the historical tradition of Ireland as a whole. We may suppose that political censorship and distortion of material in the interests of this dynasty or that did sometimes happen.[52] But the fact that the poetic order was a national institution must necessarily have put a severe brake on intentional self-interested distortion: a new historical lie (such as the descent of the Irish from Míl) could gain universal currency only by consensus.

The Irish tradition that associates the collection of 'Táin'-related material with Senchán Torpéist—despite certain extravagances—is, as Thurneysen recognised, worthy of respect. The implication of the tradition is that when Senchán set about recording the material it was imperfectly known and was patched together from the various bits and pieces that had survived in the

[49] Ed. Kuno Meyer, 'Der Tod König Conchobars' in *Z.C.P.*, xiii (1919), p. 7.

[50] On the question of the equating of the deaths of Conchobar and of Christ, see Szöverffy in *Z.C.P.*, xxv (1956), pp 200 ff, and Carney, *Studies in Ir. lit.*, pp 295–8.

[51] See now, however, the views of Kim McCone, *Pagan past and Christian present* (Maynooth, 1989).

[52] See, e.g., the remarks of Gilla in Choimded Ua Cormaic, a twelfth-century scholar, on the subject of manipulating genealogies, in Kuno Meyer, *Miscellanea Hibernica* (Chicago, 1916), p. 9.

repertoire of a number of poets. Acceptance of this view of Senchán and his activity would be in line with another conclusion of Thurneysen's: that after the first shaping of a tradition in literature its subsequent life and development were on a literary plane, and there was no continuing influence of oral tradition. The earliest extant text of 'Táin Bó Cuailnge' would then be the result of a long period of literary remoulding, involving various hands up to the eleventh century. Then again, in the eleventh century the early version was used as a basis for the form of the tale found in the Book of Leinster, and in slightly varying forms in later manuscripts. The literary nature of this version is not in dispute.

O'Rahilly put forward a highly interesting view of the Ulster cycle. He conjectured that, since the midland Goidels were descendants of Conn, the name of their province or 'fifth' was *Cóiced Connacht*, and that this area would include Tara. Some time after what O'Rahilly regarded as the western and northern expansion of the midland Goidels, the most powerful element among them became known as the Uí Néill, and the designation *Connachta* came to be used exclusively of the western territory, which heretofore had been called *Cóiced Ol nÉcmacht*. In general support of this view, it is to be noted that in the poems of Béccán mac Luigdech (first half of the seventh century) the term *Connachta* is applied to the descendants of Niall, and has no necessary reference to the western province. O'Rahilly continues:

The genuine tradition of the Ulaid, before it became conventionalised in the literature, must have recognised quite well that their enemies in ancient times were the men of Tara on their southern border; but the literati judged it more diplomatic to represent the struggle as one between two provinces, and not between the Ulaid and the king of Ireland, for in their day the king of Tara would inevitably be regarded as king of Ireland. Accordingly Medb, the goddess who typifies the sovereignty of Tara, is made to reign, not in Tara, but in Cruachain, together with her husband Ailill mac Máta; and so in 'Táin Bó Cualnge' the narrator has first to bring Medb and her forces rapidly from the Cruachain to the Tara district before they can march northwards against the Ulaid.[53]

Some of the details of O'Rahilly's view may not command general agreement today, but there are a number of facts that give support to a view that the attack on south-east Ulster was originally made from Meath. In the summary given above, we saw that Medb succeeded in having the Gálióin divided, among other reasons so that they could not eventually claim credit for the victory. Behind this could lie a tradition that the surviving version of the saga had to deny: that it was the Gálióin and not the Connachta who had played the leading part in driving the cattle from Cooley. The (tenth-century?) compiler of the genealogies had access to a version of the 'Táin' that was different from, and in some respects more archaic, than our earliest surviving

[53] O'Rahilly, *Early Ir. hist.*, p. 176.

text. In this version Cú Chulainn's first exploit as a boy was a raid upon 'the land of Cairpre' (Leinster), which he undertook with his charioteer Ibor; this incident was presented in realistic terms, and lacked the fantasy of the surviving account.[54] In this early version there is confirmation of the suspicion voiced above that in the earliest tradition the Gáilióin were given the main credit for the expedition: it is said of Ailill *conid Ailill iarum do-acht Táin Bó Cuailnge cona tríchait cét Galéan* ('so that it is Ailill who thereafter drove the driving of the cattle of Cooley with his thirty hundreds of Gáilióin').

From this, a number of things are clear: Ailill was of the Gáilióin and was leader of the expedition; the breaking-up of the Leinster forces in the surviving tale is part of a deliberate revision of the tradition. This is confirmed even in the surviving saga, where the subsequent narrative ignores the supposed breaking-up of this force. Furthermore, in one of the difficult passages containing *roscada*, Ailill laughs at Fergus; Fergus refers to the laughter as 'the laughter of Gáilióin'. We are hardly, however, to conclude (as does O'Rahilly) that Ailill did not rule in Cruachu. In the earliest written tradition, that of the Leinster poems, which may be regarded as sixth-century, Ailill, son of a king of Leinster, rules and dies in Cruachu.

O'Rahilly's view that the expedition, in the original tradition, set out from Tara would appear to be only approximately correct. Ailill ruled at Cruachu. If he were to assemble an army from Leinster, Munster, and Connacht to invade Cooley he would not first bring them all to Cruachu: he would arrange a venue at a suitable strategic spot, to which he would first march himself. This strategic spot was apparently Cenandas na Ríg (Kells, County Meath). This emerges from a consideration of the incident concerning the prophetess Fedelm (which is one of Thurneysen's 'doublets'). In any great tale of a military expedition, the logical place for a prophecy of its outcome would be at the beginning. In the extant saga the army sets out from Cruachu and the prophecy is made as they begin to move. However, according to one of the 'other books', Fedelm's prophecy was given at a place called Slechtai ('Cuttings'); the onomastic basis of this version would seem to mark it as old and genuine. Slechtai was located beside Cúil Sibrille in the neighbourhood of Cenandas. There is considerable corroboration of this detail. Cenandas na Ríg ('Cenandas of the kings') was, by the testimony of its name, a seat of kingship. Furthermore, by the evidence of the Leinster poems and genealogies, it was the seat of Conn: we are told that Catháer Már of Leinster ruled in Tara while Conn ruled in Cenandas, and there was peace between them. Similarly in the partly archaic saga 'Esnada tige Buchet' ('The songs of Buchet's house'),[55] we are told that Cormac mac Airt was in Cenandas before he became king of Tara; Cenandas was 'the residence of the kings'. From all

[54] See O'Brien, *Corpus geneal. Hib.*, i, 281. The editor printed the word *Ibor* with a lowercase initial, not recognising it as a personal name.
[55] David Greene (ed.), *Fingal Rónáin and other stories* (Dublin, 1955), pp 27–41.

this we may perhaps conclude that O'Rahilly's 'midland Goidels' originally ruled at Kells. They spread out at a very early date to Connacht, and later conquered the greater part of Ulster. They were constantly at war with the Lagin, and their levying of a *bóruma* or tribute of cows was an assertion that their possession of Tara made them the legitimate over-kings of the whole province.

In considering the question of the nature and antiquity of 'Táin Bó Cuailnge' there are a number of pertinent facts. The first is the basic onomastic character of the greater part of the saga. Irish tales lay stress on onomastic details. But this is true in an exceptionally high degree of the 'Táin': it is largely built up on a series of onomastically based incidents involving the areas of Meath and south-east Ulster. The second fact concerns the dating of the earliest traceable written traditions concerning 'Táin Bó Cuailnge' and its associated tales. The *roscada* in the saga are of great importance. They are part of the earliest writing of the saga; being in metrical or quasi-metrical form, they were perhaps badly transcribed, but not rewritten. We may reasonably assume that they were written down in the seventh century, and may have had before that a lengthy existence in oral narrative. Two poems in the oldest known Irish metrical form are also of considerable importance. One of these was preserved in the eighth-century 'Cín Dromma Snechtai' and was also incorporated in the saga 'Tochmarc Emire' ('The wooing of Emer').[56] Even more important is the poem 'Conailla Medb míchuru' ('Medb had counselled evil contracts') by Luccreth moccu Chiara, a poet from Kerry who may be conceived of as having lived and composed towards the end of the sixth century. This poem, which is found among the genealogies in the fifteenth-century Oxford, Bodleian Library, MS Laud Misc. 610, has never been translated, and has been ignored by most commentators.[57] It tells how Medb seduced Fergus from his proper loyalty, how he went into exile, how his son Fiacc remained loyal to Conchobar and fought against his father's battalions. There is also there material relevant to the saga 'Aided Fergusa' ('The death of Fergus')[58] and to 'Táin Bó Froích' (the connections with the latter suggestive of a link with the Germanic myth of the death of Baldar). During the course of his poem Luccreth refers to the material he presents as *sen-eolas*; in other words it is traditional material that he had from his predecessors. From this we may at a minimum conclude that the story of the seduction of Fergus by Medb and their war against Conchobar was known, perhaps in Kerry, fully a century before Luccreth, that is, in

[56] This has been printed in editions of the saga, and in its *Cín Dromma Snechtai* form by Meyer under its title 'Verba Scáthaige fri Coin Culaind' ('The words of Scáthach to Cú Chulainn') in *Anecdota from Irish manuscripts*, v (Halle, 1913), pp 29–30.
[57] See Kuno Meyer, 'The Laud genealogies and tribal histories' in *Z.C.P.*, viii (1912), pp 292–338.
[58] See Vernam Hull, 'The death of Fergus mac Róig' in *Z.C.P.*, xviii (1930), p. 304.

the late fifth century. The province of Connacht is not mentioned. Tara is regarded as a seat of power, and the exiles who left Ulster, led by Fergus mac Róich, congregated there—a very striking corroboration of O'Rahilly's theory concerning the original form of 'Táin Bó Cuailnge'. Later in the poem, and in the accompanying prose, we read of Solchenn son of Cethern: he and his people were expelled from Ulster on account of the killing of Fiacc, son of Fergus. After a stay of unspecified length under the protection of Tara, the descendants of this group, in the time of Niall mac Echach (mid-fifth century), left the region of Tethba, crossed the River Inny, and were well received in Munster by Óengus, grandson of Conall Corc (d. *c*.494).

From surviving archaic material something can be learned of how these traditions were conserved, and some conclusions may be suggested. Poems such as 'Verba Scáthaige' and 'Conailla Medb míchuru' are to be taken as marking the end of a vigorous tradition, although unfortunately for the modern investigator they must function as the beginning. The poem by Luccreth is not quite like those introduced into later sagas and put into the mouths of one or other of the characters: it is full narrative, in the course of which the actors may be made to speak. The material of 'Táin Bó Cuailnge'—and indeed the whole cycle—contains elements that are obviously mythic, such as the origin of the bulls and their final conflict. Historically the tales are based on the opposition of the group whose sacral capital was at Tara, and the Ulster group whose capital was Emain Machae; Connacht was involved as an extension of the Tara power. The firm onomastic basis of 'Táin Bó Cuailnge' suggests that at some point in the conflict the cattle of Cooley were captured and driven away by a midland force. This event, if historic, must have taken place at some period well before the introduction of Christianity. But while we cannot assign dates to characters such as Medb, Ailill, and Fergus, it is perhaps easier to believe that they existed rather than that they are 'fictional' or 'mythic'.

THE involvement of Ulster in Irish literature is not confined to stories of the 'Táin' period, and there are broadly speaking two cycles of tales touching on eastern Ulster and the Dalriadic kingdom of Scotland. The first cycle concerns Mongán (d. 625) and his father Fiachnae Lurgan, king of the Ulaid (d. 626). The birth of Mongán is also part of the matter of 'Immram Brain'.[59] This material has survived through the medium of the lost eighth-century 'Cín Dromma Snechtai', and it has been suggested that the monastery of Bangor may have been closely involved in the first writing of these traditions.[60]

The second cycle of tales dealing with this historic period centres about the battle of Roth and includes 'Fled Dúin na nGéd' ('The feast of the Fort

---

[59] Meyer, *The voyage of Bran*. See below, pp 491, 502.
[60] Proinsias Mac Cana, 'Mongán mac Fiachna and *Immram Brain*' in *Ériu*, xxiii (1972), pp 102–42; idem, 'On the "prehistory" of *Immram Brain*' in *Ériu*, xxvi (1975), pp 33–52.

of the Geese'),[61] 'Cath Maige Rath' ('The battle of Mag Roth'),[62] and 'Buile Suibne' ('The madness of Suibne').[63] All these sagas belong to the Middle Irish period but incorporate older material: in the older strata the central battle was called *Cath Roth*, in the later *Cath Maige Rath*. Most interesting is the story of Suibne. He is fictitiously represented as a king of Dál nAraidi who went mad at the sight of carnage and fled from the battlefield. The tale has been the subject of much comment, and has affinity with the 'Vita Merlini' of Geoffrey of Monmouth. The depicting of the various stages of Suibne's madness makes this saga unique in Irish literature.[64]

THE historical traditions of the Lagin or Gálióin (Leinstermen) are in a sense the oldest written Irish traditions that exist: a considerable amount of verse fragments in the Leinster genealogies seem to date from the early sixth century, some perhaps even from the fifth. Apart from the poetic material, the genealogies of Leinster—as well as those of the rest of the country— show linguistic signs of having been recorded at latest in the early part of the seventh century. The material so recorded was not based on the haphazard memory of individuals: it depends on school material, learned by rote in verse or in rhythmic, formulaic language and passed on by the oral method from generation to generation. A tradition of this type could be expected to have something approaching the stability of a written text. The fact that the *filid*, the traditors of this material, were a national institution would limit the extent to which even powerful dynasties might interfere with it in their own interest. However, it would seem in this regard that by constant pressure over centuries the descendants of Niall Noígiallach succeeded in securing a fairly general acceptance of the idea that their remote ancestors had held the kingship of Tara; the dynasty had a very intimate connection with the poetic order from at least A.D. 600 onwards.

In oral tradition the genealogies, even in the pagan period, must have been heightened by stories and traditions of the more important characters. When this type of material came to be written it was sometimes known as *scél-shenchus*, which may be translated 'ancient tradition in narrative [prose] form'. Such material may be regarded as dramatised or fictionalised history; its primary purpose was usually not entertainment but instruction, and even the most obviously fictional elements may carry a didactic message. The didactic intent, the emphasis on 'history', has as a result that this type of material rarely achieves a satisfactory literary form: the 'facts' are primary,

[61] Ruth Lehmann (ed.), *Fled Dúin na nGéd* (Dublin, 1964).
[62] John O'Donovan (ed.), *The banquet of Dun na n-Gedh and the battle of Magh Rath* (Irish Archaeological Society, Dublin, 1842).
[63] J. G. O'Keeffe (ed.), *Buile Suibne* (Dublin, 1931).
[64] For studies of this tale, see Kenneth Jackson in *Féil-sgríbhinn Eoin Mhic Néill*, pp 535–50; Carney, *Studies in Ir. lit.*, pp 129–64, 385–93; Pádraig Ó Riain in *Éigse*, xiv (1972), pp 179–206.

the form secondary. The converse also appears to hold true. In the ninth- or tenth-century tale 'Fingal Ronáin',[65] telling how a supposed seventh-century king of Leinster slew his son through jealous suspicion, we have a spurious *scélshenchus* form, but a well-told tale. Here the 'history' is of minor importance; the emphasis is on the central psychological theme, good dialogue, and the verse that the characters speak at highly charged points in the narrative.

The historic reality behind *scélshenchus* is difficult to assess, particularly so since there has been a strong tendency in contemporary scholarship to regard many of the actors as having been originally gods. Among those 'deified', notably by O'Rahilly, are Medb, Conn Cétchathach, Cormac mac Airt, and Catháer Már. With 'deification' such characters are removed from the historical scene and regarded as 'timeless'. The methods by which scholars 'deify' characters who are presented in Irish tradition as politically active human beings are not always convincing. A protest against such excessive mythologising was made by Myles Dillon: 'It seems to me likely ... that the historians of the future will discover that Conn of the Hundred Battles and Eogan Mór and Cathaer Már, king of Leinster, and the famous Cormac mac Airt were historical persons, and that a fairly reliable historical tradition can be established from as early a time as the second century of the Christian era.'[66]

VIRTUALLY the whole of Leinster and midland *scélshenchus* concerns the kingship of Tara. Historically Tara was the sacral capital of the Leinstermen. But it lay within the territory held by the midland Goidels, and it would seem that in the period preceding Christianity both groups laid constant claim to the kingship. The matter was, it would appear, resolved about the middle of the fifth century by the supposed success of Niall Noígiallach, who (in the propaganda of his descendants) established himself as king of Tara with such effect that the kingship was held exclusively by his descendants and close collaterals until the Norman invasion. By virtue of being kings of Tara, the midland Goidels claimed a *bóruma* or cattle-tribute fron Leinster. The *bóruma* dispute—a subject of *scélshenchus*—continued until the eighth century. As late as the seventeenth the dominant group could regard the Leinstermen as *aithigh* or 'unfree'.

A very important item in the *scélshenchus* of Leinster and the midlands is 'Orgain Denda Ríg' ('The destruction of Dind Ríg').[67] This tale is told from a Leinster rather than a midland point of view. The hero is Labraid Loingsech, 'Labraid the sea-traveller [or exile]', otherwise known as Labraid Móen, son of Áine, son of Lóegaire Lorc. The date assigned to Labraid by a late eighth-century poet, Orthanach ua Cóellamae, is 500 B.C. This date could

[65] Greene, *Fingal Rónáin*, pp 1–14.
[66] Myles Dillon, *The cycles of the kings* (London, 1946), p. 118.
[67] See Wagner, 'The archaic *Dind Ríg* poem' (n. 14 above).

have been arrived at by counting generations in the received genealogies back from any dateable Leinster king and allowing about three generations to a century. The saga shows Labraid as having been born in Ireland and exiled from it; his subsequent conquest is a triumphant return with foreign allies. The early poetic material, however, suggests that he was regarded as an invader coming from the Continent. His people were the Gálióin; they carried a particular type of spear (*lágen*) from which they became known as *Lagin*—a typically spurious learned etymology. He 'slew the sons of renowned Ugaine' (*oirt maccu áin Úgaini*) and 'seized the lordship of the Goídil' (*flaithi Goídel, gabsus*). The 'invasion', like that of the Normans, was through Wexford, and at Dind Ríg, on the River Barrow, Labraid slew Cobthach Coíl Breg and thirty subordinate kings. The epithet of the king in possession when Labraid landed, that is Breg ('of Brega'), is significant. Cobthach Coíl Breg is regarded as an ancestor of the midland Goidels (Conn Cétchathach, Cormac mac Airt, Niall Noígiallach, and the rest). Labraid is the ancestor of the enemies of this group. We know from archaic Leinster verse that the tale in something like its extant form was known in the sixth century, and possibly for many centuries before. It is impossible to estimate what literal truth might lie behind such a tradition, but at a minimum it has a symbolic truth, illustrating as it does the constant struggle between the Gálióin and the Bregians.

The saga tradition of the midland Goidels depicts the rise of the Bregian dynasty at the expense of Leinster and Munster, and the extension of its power over Connacht and large areas of Ulster. The association with Connacht is a constant feature of the tradition. This is already evident in 'Táin Bó Cuailnge',[68] in which an alliance of the rest of Ireland, led by Ailill and Medb, king and queen of Connacht, is engaged in an attack on Ulster. According to the genealogical tradition, Ailill is of the Gálióin, a descendant of Labraid Loingsech; and his brother Cairpre, as king of Leinster, reigns in Tara. His wife, Medb of Cruachu, is a daughter of Eochu Feidlech, a descendant of Cobthach Coíl Breg, and thus a 'Bregian' and not a 'Gálióin' claimant. Ailill is king of Connacht not by any right of his own, but by virtue of his marriage to Medb. Medb is shown as being highly antagonistic to the Gálióin contingent in the allied army, and Ailill is their defender. The motivation behind Medb's antagonism to the Gálióin is not explicit in any version of the saga, but would not be missed by a medieval reader of the tale.

In world literature the story commonly called 'The birth of the hero' is usually applied to founders of dynasties or great innovators. The most basic element is that the hero, from obscure or unpromising beginnings, achieves his great destiny. This tale is told in varying forms of a number of figures in

[68] Above, p. 475.

the Bregian line: 'Cath Maige Muccrama' ('The battle of Mag Muccrama')[69] tells how Cormac mac Airt achieved kingship; 'Esnada Tige Buchet' ('The songs of Buchet's house'),[70] a very fine dramatic tale, exceeding the usual limitations of *scélshenchus*, applies the same formula to Cormac's son Cairpre Lifechair; in 'Echtrai mac nEchach' ('The adventures of the sons of Eochaid')[71] Niall, the son of a slave-girl, becomes king and the most renowned of his family. More remotely this theme is applied to an early ancestor (or alleged ancestor), Tuathal Techtmar. The constant use of this theme in connection with members of the midland dynasty suggests that their power, based on the kingship of Tara, was relatively new, and there are indications[72] that their original seat was at Cenandas (Kells, County Meath).

*Scélshenchus* referring to the period between Cormac mac Airt and Niall Noígiallach shows a clearing of peoples from the rich midlands. 'Tairered [Tochomlad] na nDésse' ('The wandering-out/expulsion of the Déssi')[73] is a saga existing in variant forms, and calling for deeper study. It shows the Déssi being expelled from Mag mBreg in the time of Cormac. Genealogically the rulers of the Déssi are presented as descendants of Fiachu Suigde, a brother of Conn Cétchathach, and thus 'Bregian' collaterals. According to the implied chronological indications in the material, the expulsion would lie in the early part of the fifth century, say *c*.430—a much later date than that usually assigned to Cormac (third century) in the synchronistic material of the historians. The archaic verse in the Leinster genealogies gives some support to such a late date: Cormac's son Cairpre Lifechair is presented as an opponent of the Leinster king Bressal Bélach, whose annalistic obit is given *c*.436. The Déssi were given land in Leinster by Fiachu Baccid, son of Catháer Már, and some of them crossed to Dyfed (*Demetia*) in Wales. About thirty years later they were expelled from Leinster and given land in the Decies (*Déssi*, County Waterford), by the Eóganacht king Óengus mac Nad Froích (d. *c*.494). According to O'Rahilly, all this material 'can be shown to be a fabrication'.[74]

Another, and a closely analogical, clearance of this area is referred to in the poem 'Conailla Medb míchuru', composed (as we saw above) by Luccreth moccu Chiara *c*.580. The pattern of fifth-century clearance, coincident with the rise of the 'Bregian' dynasty, and involving the Eóganacht king Óengus son of Nad Froích, cannot, it would appear, be dismissed lightly.

[69] Ed. Máirín O Daly, *Cath Maige Mucrama, The battle of Mag Mucrama* (Dublin, 1975); see also Tomás Ó Cathasaigh, *The heroic biography of Cormac mac Airt* (Dublin, 1977).
[70] See n. 50 above.
[71] Whitley Stokes, 'The death of Crimthann son of Fidach, and the adventures of the sons of Eochaid Muigmedón' in *Rev. Celt.*, xxiv (1903), pp 190–207.
[72] Above, pp 476–7.
[73] Kuno Meyer, 'The expulsion of the Dessi' in *Y Cymmrodor*, xiv (1901), pp 101–35.
[74] O'Rahilly, *Early Ir. hist.*, p. 64. O'Rahilly's judgement in this matter is, at least to some extent, conditioned by his 'deification' of certain characters in the saga.

It could be maintained that the finest saga of the early period, not excluding 'Táin Bó Cuailnge', is 'Togail Bruidne Da Derga' ('The destruction of
Da Derga's hostel').[75] Like the former, it has not been preserved as a satisfactory unified structure: the text is basically Old Irish, but is already to
some degree composite, apparently as a result of a complicated manuscript
tradition. This tale is 'Bregian', and the fine saga 'Tochmarc Étaíne' is a pre-
tale (*rémscél*) to it;[76] it tells of the origin and birth of Conaire Mór, son of
Etarscél, his achievement of kingship, and his death. The earliest reference to
the direct background of 'Togail Bruidne Da Derga' is in a Leinster poem of
*c*.500, where we are told that Nuadu Necht slew Etarscéla moccu Iair.[77] The
historic scene is usually set shortly after the 'Táin'. In the general tradition
Conaire avenged his father's death by slaying Nuadu, and he was himself
slain by In Trí Ruadchind, 'the three red-heads' of Leinster. A version or a
précis existed in the eighth-century 'Cín Dromma Snechtai', and the circumstances of Conaire's death were known in some form to the eighth-century
poet Orthanach ua Cóellamae. The theme is one of doom, in which the
central character is kingship itself; that the tragedy is worked out in the
person of Conaire is of secondary importance. The saga cannot be regarded
as what has been defined above as *scélshenchus*: the form is of paramount
importance, and the result of a fully conscious creative act.

'Togail Bruidne Da Derga' is, of course, like most early Irish tales, recounted in prose. But the prose is greatly heightened by poetic diction; the
dialogue is dramatic, poetic, and with sonorous formulaic repetition;
the tragic events in which the story ends are 'seen' and described before
they occur, a poetic device that underlines the fact that the final tragedy is
predetermined and inescapable. Substantial portions of the text, performed
by a skilful actor, would fall on the ears of the listener with the effect of
poetry rather than of prose. It represents an art form, fully valid in its own
right and in its own time, which, given suitable conditions, might have
evolved into poetic drama. This halfway stage between 'prose' and 'poetry',
between realism and fantasy, is found in many other Irish sagas (e.g. 'Esnada
Tige Buchet', 'Mesca Ulad'), but in none other is a calculated effect achieved
with such mastery and consistency. Eleanor Knott has made the following
comment:

Modern scholarship is vigorously opposed to the conception of Celtic literature
inspired by Matthew Arnold, but the reaction, justified as it is, need not drive us to
deny that we meet, here and there, as Whitley Stokes recognised, touches of 'that
magic of Celtic romance, which Matthew Arnold loved and praised'. Two Celtic
stories have it beyond all others—the Irish 'Togail Bruidne da Derga' and the Welsh

---

[75] Eleanor Knott (ed.), *Togail bruidne Da Derga* (Dublin, 1936).
[76] Above, pp 464, 466.
[77] O'Brien, *Corpus geneal. Hib.*, i, 1–4.

'Branwen verch Lyr', stories which have moreover some remarkable traits in common.[78]

Conaire, as a son of Etarscéla, was a legitimate heir to the kingdom of Tara. But, like many other heroes, he is represented as being of divine parentage: his father had come to his mother Mess Buachalla in bird-shape, and she was already pregnant on her marriage to Etarscéla. On the death of Etarscéla, Conaire gained kingship through the favour of the Otherworld, as revealed in a divinatory act. As king he was subjected to a number of mysterious *gessa* or taboos. Some of these may have been related to his office; most, however, concerned his person, and some may be simply anticipations of events in a traditional account of his life: he was not to go right-hand-wise around Tara, or left-hand-wise around Brega; he must not hunt the *cláenmíla* (lit. 'bending beasts') of Cernae;[79] he must not spend a period of nine days outside Tara; he must not sleep in a house if the light of a fire outside is visible within after sunset, or if a fire within is visible outside; three 'reds' must not precede him to the house of a 'red'; there must be no marauding in his kingship; he must not have the company of a single woman or a single man in his house after sunset; he must not settle a dispute between two serfs.

Conaire's reign represented the Irish ideal of kingship: good trade, good weather, good omens, such abundance of goodwill that nobody slew another, and to everyone in Ireland 'the voice of the other was as sweet as harpstrings'. This harmony was brought to an end: his three foster-brothers, the three sons of Donn Désa, whom he loved dearly, violated Conaire's *gessa* by acts of plunder. Conaire, on account of his affection for them (like Catháer Már in the case of his sons in 'Esnada Tige Buchet') bent the law in their favour. Not merely had Conaire's *gessa* been violated, but he knew himself that his doom was at hand because of delivering a false judgement: 'The judgement I have given is no lengthening of life to me.' One after another his *gessa* were violated until he eventually found himself following three red men (*deirg*) to the house of Da Derga where he and his followers were to meet death by fire and sword. The tragedy fully accomplished, the story ends on a strong note. Conall Cernach escaped from the hostel and met his father Amargein in front of his house in Tailtiu. 'What news of Da Derga's hostel?', asked Amargein. 'Is your lord alive?' 'He is not', said Conall. 'I swear by the god by whom my people swear, cowardly is the man who escapes alive, leaving his lord in death with his enemies.' 'My wounds are not white, old warrior', said Conall, showing his wounded arms, one of which was barely held by sinews to the body. 'That

[78] Knott, *Togail bruidne Da Derga*, pp ix–x.
[79] It is not clear what exactly were the 'bending beasts' of Cernae (Carnes, near Duleek, Co. Meath). One might, however, consider associating them with the *géssi Cernai*, 'the swans of Cernae'. These were regarded as sacred birds (*eonu Maic Dé bí*, 'birds of the Son of the living God'); they were hunted by Cano, son of Gartnán (see *Scéla Cano meic Gartnáin*, ed. Binchy (Dublin, 1963), p. 6).

arm fought all tonight, dear son, and was fought against', said Amargein. 'True, old warrior', said Conall, 'many are there who were given a drink of death tonight before the hostel.'

THERE are four main streams in early Irish tradition: the traditions of Ulster, of Leinster, of the midlands and Connacht, and of Munster. Those of Munster are linguistically as old as the traditions of the other areas, but are less substantial in volume. The earliest Munster historical saga tends to be presented somewhat artlessly, and there is little striving after style or dramatic effect. Among the more important saga traditions are—as one would expect—those concerning Cashel, the origin of the Éoganacht dynasty, and its descent from Conall Corc. Francis John Byrne has stressed the marked difference in Munster tradition:

The saga traditions of Conall Corc and the finding of Cashel present several features worthy of notice. There are no myths or legends concerning the rock of Cashel relating to pagan prehistory: we are told that the site (despite its obvious prominence in the Munster landscape) was found accidentally or revealed miraculously, and the story has a strong Christian coloration, even in its most archaic versions... The eighth-century collection of Munster genealogies tells the story of Conall Corc in a version which contains many folk motifs. Every Irish heroic saga usually prefers more exalted characters such as druids to be the intermediaries of the supernatural, but here we have references to witches and to palmistry which typify the different nature of the Munster tradition.[80]

This Munster 'difference' is a matter of some interest, which calls for closer investigation. It is also noteworthy that Munster tends to look northwards to Tara and to Ulster. It has already been pointed out that the sixth-century poet from west Munster, Luccreth moccu Chiara, was aware of the traditions of Ulster, and saw a number of peoples in Munster as being of remote Ulster origin. Similarly the saga 'Tairered na nDéisse' ('The expulsion of the Déssi') in its various forms tells that the Déssi of the present County Waterford were a population group originating in the region around Tara. The historical tract 'De Síl Chonairi Móir' ('Concerning the race of Conaire Mór'),[81] tells of the origin of certain Munster tribes in the region of Mag mBreg. It may be noted also in this regard that the sixth-century Munster poet Colmán mac Lénéni directed at least a part of his art towards kings of Tara, Domnall (d. 566) and Áed Sláine (d. 603).

An important part of Munster saga tradition centres around Mór Muman (d. 632), daughter of Áed Bennán of the Eóganacht of Loch Léin. In the saga material she is shown as being rescued from squalor and poverty in her

---

[80] Byrne, *Ir. kings*, p. 184. It is to be noted, however, that Corc is associated with a poet Gruibne (Cormac's Glossary, §§ 598, 688).
[81] Ed. Lucius Gwynn, 'De Síl Chonairi Móir' in *Ériu*, vi, 130–43.

youth, and finally attaining such happiness and success that she became a symbol with whom poets might compare the noblest and best-endowed women of Ireland. Mac Cana would see her as a local reflection of an Irish goddess of sovereignty.[82]

THE most remarkable Irish scholar of the earlier period was Cormac mac Cuilennáin, king-bishop of Cashel (d. 908). He is credited as the compiler of the Psalter of Cashel, a work that survives in part in the fifteenth-century collection Laud Misc. 610. It has also been suggested that he was the compiler of the great collection of the genealogies of Ireland that exists in a number of manuscripts (including Laud 610).[83] The opening sentence of the compilation, by placing the descendants of Éber before those of Éremón, betrays its Munster origin:

Imprudens Scottorum gens, rerum suarum obliuiscens, acta quasi inaudita sive nullo modo facta uindicat, quoniam minus tribuere litteris aliquid operum quorum prae-curat, et ab hoc genealogias Scotigenae gentis litteris tribuam primo gentis Ebir, secundo gentis Herimon, tertio gentis Hir, quarto gentis Lugdach meic Itha.

(The foolish Irish nation, forgetful of its history, asserts the historicity of unheard-of or completely fabulous deeds, because it is careless about committing to writing any of its achievements. Therefore I shall commit to writing the genealogies of the Irish race: firstly the race of Éber, secondly the race of Érimón, thirdly the race of Ír, and fourthly the race of Lugaid son of Íth.)[84]

The work by which Cormac mac Cuilennáin is most generally known is 'Sanas Cormaic' ('Cormac's Glossary').[85] This might be described as an 'etymo-logical' glossary, mainly of difficult Irish words. It is, however, more than a mere glossary, since the author draws extensively on early material for anec-dotes and illustrations. In addition to Irish, the author had a good knowledge of Latin, and could also quote Greek, Hebrew, British, Pictish, English (*Sax-anbérla*), and Norse (*lingua Galleorum*). He quotes 'Gabála Éirenn' ('The Irish invasions'), a number of Irish law-tracts, and sagas. In etymologising *caise*, 'cheese'(§ 312), he quotes a line of Virgil. A thorough edition of this text is still lacking.

Another Munster production, 'Aislinge meic Con Glinne' ('The vision of Mac Con Glinne')[86] is also 'different'. The text is thought to have been

---

[82] Proinsias Mac Cana, *Études Celt.*, vii (1955–6), pp 76 ff.

[83] O'Brien published his edition without any introduction or commentary. This is partially rectified by reviews of the work by F. J. Byrne in *Z.C.P.*, xxix (1962–4), pp 381–5, and by John V. Kelleher, 'The pre-Norman Irish genealogies' in *I.H.S.*, xvi, no. 62 (1968), pp 138–53.

[84] Byrne, art. cit., p. 381.

[85] Kuno Meyer (ed.), *Sanas Cormaic: Cormac's Glossary* (Halle, 1913). For detailed studies of the text, see Paul Russell, 'The sounds of a silence: the growth of Cormac's Glossary' in *Camb. Med. Celt. Studies*, xv (summer 1988), pp 1–30.

[86] Ed. Kuno Meyer, *Aislinge Meic Conglinne: the vision of Mac Conglinne* (London, 1892); K. H. Jackson (ed.), *Aislinge Meic Con Glinne* (Dublin, 1990).

composed in the twelfth century, and has been preserved in two versions: one in a seventeenth-century portion of the T.C.D. MS H.3.18 (H), the other in the fourteenth-century 'Leabhar Breac' (B). The relation between the versions is complex, but B is the lengthier and more interesting text. The scene is the reign of Cathal mac Finguine, king of Munster (d. 742). Central to the tale is a simple folk belief that a person may become possessed of a demon of gluttony; the cure is to bind him, to starve him, and to place before him the most delicious of foods. The demon will eventually be forced to leave his body to get at the foods. Building on this simple theme, the author satirises the church, the poets, the style of various types of Irish narrative, and, indeed, the historical methods in vogue by which silly verses are used as proof of important historical events. This composition reaches a high level of sophistication.

Two other Munster compositions may be mentioned: 'Cocad Goídel re Gallaib' ('The war of the Irish with the Northmen')[87] and 'Caithréim Cellacháin Chaisil' ('The victorious career of Cellachán of Cashel').[88] The first text was written in 'saga' style in the reign of Muirchertach (d. 1119), grandson of Brian Bóruma. It is based on annalistic material, and on other historical sources. Its purpose was to glorify Brian and his descendants. The second text deals with an earlier period, the reign of the Eóganacht king Cellachán Caisil (d. 954). It is a somewhat later composition than the other, and was apparently written by 'some scholar under MacCarthy (or O'Callaghan) patronage'.[89]

THE Ulster cycle of tales is centred mainly around Emain Machae and Cruachu, and their supposed period is the beginning of the Christian era. On the other hand, Finn, according to the earliest evidence, was of the Gálioin or Leinstermen; when he comes to be placed in time by the historians he is assigned to a much later period, the reign of Cormac mac Airt, which was thought to have been in the third century A.D. The cycles contrast in mood and style; also in the fact that in the early period of Irish writing the Ulster cycle is vigorous in manuscript whereas the Finn cycle is not. There is, however, sufficient evidence to show that Finn and his hunter-warrior bands (*fiana*) enjoyed a popularity that contrasts strongly with their meagre representation in material that is linguistically early; it is also clear that this popularity involved the whole of Ireland (doubtless too Gaelic Scotland), and not

[87] James Henthorn Todd (ed.), *Cogadh Gaedheal re Gallaibh* (Dublin, 1867); see Donnchadh Ó Corráin, 'Dál Cais—church and dynasty' in *Ériu*, xxiv (1973), pp 52–63.
[88] Alexander S. Bugge (ed.), *Caithréim Ceallacháin Chaisil* (Christiania, 1905); see John Ryan, 'The historical content of Caithréim Ceallacháin Chaisil' in *R.S.A.I. Jn.*, lxxi (1941), pp 89–100; Donnchadh Ó Corráin, '*Caithréim Chellacháin Chaisil*: history or propaganda?' in *Ériu*, xxv (1974), pp 1–69.
[89] So Brian Ó Cuív in 'Literary creation and Irish historical tradition' (Sir John Rhys memorial lecture, British Academy, 1963), pp 233–62: 241.

just the area with which Finn was associated historically. After the tenth century the Ulster tales are clearly declining, but Finn tales continue down to modern times. For as long as the Irish language survives in its rural setting, Finn and the *fiana* remain part of the folk consciousness, nor has the break been absolute even in the areas where Irish has disappeared. Paradoxically it could be almost said that the Finn cycle is dying in undiminished vigour. The cycles differ in other ways. The Ulster cycle presents a picture of a warrior society, living in heroic aristocratic splendour, with chariots, tents, fine clothes, rich equipment, servants, and luxurious dwelling places. Finn, on the other hand, is the leader of a *fian*, a small group of hunter-warriors, who use neither horse nor chariot, but go about on foot. They have few if any servants, and they cook their own food. Their opponents are frequently of the Otherworld, and the tales are strongly motivated by magic. The main characters are Finn (Fionn) son of Umall (or Cumall); his son Oiséne (Oisín); the latter's son Oscar; Finn's enemy Goll mac Morna; Diarmait, grandson of Duibne; and Gráinne and Ailbe, daughters of Cormac mac Airt.

Much has been written on the famous Macpherson controversy concerning 'Ossian'; it will suffice here to quote Murphy:

Cú Chulainn's fame has until recently been confined to Ireland. The names of Fionn, however (under the altered form Fingal), of his son Ossian (in Irish Oisín), and of his grandson Oscar, had by the nineteenth century become household words wherever the romantic literary movement had taken root. For this we have to thank the Scottish James Macpherson, who, in 1762 and 1753, published his *Fingal* and *Temora*, supposed to have been translated from epic poems written by Ossian in the third or fourth century of our era. James Macpherson's epics were mainly a figment of his own imagination, but the names of their heroes, and some of the incidents described, were based on genuine Gaelic balladry about Fionn, Oisín, Oscar, and the other Fianna. Men such as Napoleon in France and Goethe in Germany loved to read Macpherson's work, which was translated into many European languages and helped to awaken that interest in Celtic studies which has resulted not alone in the disproval of Macpherson's claim to be nothing more than a translator, but also in the better knowledge which men of learning all over Europe today have concerning Irish literature and the true nature of 'Ossianic' balladry.[90]

According to Murphy, Find (in primitive Celtic *Uindos*) was a central figure in the Celtic pantheon, and was identical with the god Lug. 'Lug... was the fighter of battles with otherworld beings, and had for his chief opponent the one-eyed Balar, whose eye used to burn up whatever it looked upon directly.'[91] Once the identity of Lug and Finn is accepted, the former can be used to build up the primitive Celtic picture of the latter. O'Rahilly's views

[90] Gerard Murphy, *The Ossianic lore and romantic tales of medieval Ireland* (Dublin, 1955), p. 6.
[91] Ibid., p. 8.

on this matter, while differing in detail, are broadly on the same lines as Murphy's, and Mac Cana[92] is well disposed towards this view. However, the views of Meyer—implicitly rejected by the later scholars referred to—should not be forgotten:

Many of those who have written on the origin and development of the Ossianic cycle have based their investigations almost exclusively on the tradition of the twelfth and the following centuries, quite forgetting or ignoring the fact that the later phase is preceded by centuries of gradual growth from small and obscure beginnings, in which Finn and his *fiana* do not play the part assigned to them by the later and modern legend. The figure of Finn, who in popular imagination early superseded Cú Chulainn and all the heroes of the Red Branch, has attracted to itself, from century to century, folklore of the most varied character. The whole history of Ireland has left its deposit in the formation of the new cycle of which he became the centre, while at the same time it absorbed much of the legendary lore of the older cycles. When Finn is once fully established in popular favour, all Ireland claims him as her own; pedigrees are invented for him that bring him into relation with almost all the provinces, with the most famous royal dynasties, and with Tara, until at last he becomes a national hero, and his *fiana* the *fiana Érenn*.[93]

Meyer's assumption that the Finn cycle is a 'new cycle', and that the popularity of tales concerning Finn is adequately represented in the early period by the surviving manuscript tradition, may be justly criticised. He may, however, be on firmer ground in regarding the Finn cycle as a tradition of such popularity that it could attract to itself the most heterogenous matter. Here it must suffice to point out that material concerning Finn has a close relevance to literatures outside Irish, where there has, however, been historic contact. The tale of the love of Diarmait and Gráinne is the closest known affinity to the British–Continental Tristan and Isolde; 'Macgnímartha Finn' ('The boyhood deeds of Finn') is closely related to the Eddic lay telling how Sigurd, by eating the dragon's heart, gained knowledge intended for his master; similarly a very strong case has been made, mainly by Max von Sydow and Gerard Murphy, for the relevance of Finn material to the Grendel episode in the Anglo-Saxon epic, 'Beowulf'.[94]

The most important tale in this cycle is 'Acallam na Senórach' ('The colloquy of the ancient men'), composed in or around 1200, but incorporating earlier matter. This, a frame-story in the same sense as the 'Arabian nights', is the lengthiest literary composition in early Irish; it is, however, incomplete, the end being missing in all manuscripts. The theme is as follows. The *fiana* have all died, with the exception of two: Oisín, son of Finn, and Caílte, who survive into the fifth century. They meet St Patrick and travel with him around Ireland; he interrogates them about every place

[92] Proinsias Mac Cana, *Celtic mythology* (London, 1970), p. 110.
[93] Kuno Meyer, *Fianaigecht* (Dublin, 1910), p. xv.
[94] Gerard Murphy, *Duanaire Finn*, iii (London, 1953), pp 184–8.

through which they travel, thus giving the author an opportunity to present something over 200 anecdotes, incorporating much nature and *dindshenchus* verse. A single anecdote may give an idea of the whole: Caílte was asked by Patrick to find for him a well to baptise the people of Brega, Mide, and Uisnech. He brings Patrick to Tráig dá Ban ('the strand of two women'), and speaks the poem:

> Well of Tráig dá Ban,
> lovely your pure-tipped watercress;
> since your verdure has become neglected
> no growth has been allowed to your brook-lime.
>
> Your trout out by your banks,
> your wild swine in your wilderness,
> fine for hunting the deer of your crags,
> your dappled, red-bellied fawns.
>
> Your mast on the tip of your trees,
> your fish in the mouths of your streams,
> lovely the colour of your arum-lily,
> green brook in the wooded hollow.

The poem, with its references to fish and game, reminds Patrick of food. He turns to Bishop Secundinus and asks: 'Are our dinner and provisions ready yet?' 'Yes', says Secundinus. 'Distribute it,' says Patrick, 'and give a half of it to those nine tall warriors, the survivors of the *fiana*.' Then his bishops and psalmodists bless the meat, 'and of both meat and liquor they had their fill, yet in such a manner as to serve the good of their souls'.

There follows the after-dinner conversation. Patrick asks: 'Was he a good lord with whom you were, that is Finn, son of Cumhall?' Caílte answers with a verse:

> Were but the brown leaf
> which the wood sheds gold,
> were but the white wave silver,
> Finn would give it all away.

Patrick then makes an enquiry, natural for a cleric, as to the ethical basis of the *fiana*: 'Who or what was it that maintained you so in your lives?' The answer is humanistic: 'Truth was in our hearts, strength in our arms, and fulfilment on our tongues.'

The 'Acallam' has not been subjected to a thorough examination from a literary point of view, but certain aspects of it are fairly clear. It is a fusion of 'native' and ecclesiastical tradition, and sufficiently sophisticated to show a romantic bias in favour of the old pagan days. The author was anything but a strict traditionalist: on occasion he took suitable bardic poems or poems from the ecclesiastical tradition of a century or more before his time, cast them back into the pagan period, put them into the mouth of a 'fenian' character, and wove about them newly created incidents.[95]

After the 'Acallam' the most extensive and important item in the Finn tradition is 'Duanaire Finn' ('The poem-book of Fionn').[96] This work, containing sixty-nine poems concerning Finn or the *fiana*, was compiled in the year 1627 in Ostend: the scribe was one Aodh Ó Dochartaigh, and his manuscript was for the use of Captain Sorley MacDonnell, an officer of the Spanish army in the Netherlands. The work is a collection of poems composed at various dates between 1100 and 1500.

THE Christian literature of early Ireland consists mainly of glosses and commentaries, for the most part on Latin biblical, exegetical, and grammatical texts; hagiographical material; verse or prose texts based on the scriptures and apocrypha, or dealing with some aspect of the Christian life; annalistic material, poems, and tracts dealing with world history, synchronising external with native events; imaginative literature of the 'vision' (*fís*) and 'expedition' (*echtrae*) type, and voyage tales (*immrama*)—some of the latter group, such as 'Immram Brain' ('The voyage of Bran'), are partly, at least, of pagan origin, but all reflect the Christian experience in a greater or lesser degree. Adaptations of classical and post-classical texts may also be included, since they would appear to be ultimately of monastic inspiration; in presentation, however, they owe much to 'native' sagas and style of writing.

The glosses (that is, marginal and interlinear explanations of Latin words or sentences, in Irish or in a mixture of Irish and Latin) are among the most important sources for the reconstruction of Old Irish, the language as it existed before A.D. 900. A gloss may consist of a single word, a sentence, or a lengthy paragraph. In sentences and lengthier passages the glossator may pass from Irish to Latin and back again to Irish, giving the impression that he can handle both languages equally well, and is not always conscious of which he is writing. Manuscripts containing glosses have survived mainly on the Continent, where they had been brought by Irish monks in the eighth and ninth centuries; they remained virtually unused in later centuries when the insular script ceased to be easily understood. In all, the total number of glosses has been estimated by the Italian Celtic scholar Ascoli at 16,300. Of these approximately 8,400 are in the Milan codex (Biblioteca Ambrosiana, MS C 130 inf., *c*.800), which contains a Latin commentary on the psalms

[95] For his procedure see Máirín O Daly, 'Úar in Lathe do Lum Laine' in James Carney and David Greene (ed.), *Celtic studies: essays in memory of Angus Matheson* (London, 1968), pp 22–32.

[96] The *Duanaire* has been published in three volumes of the Irish Texts Society. The first (vii), ed. Eoin MacNeill, appeared in 1908 and contained about half the poems; the second volume (xxviii), completing the textual matter, was published by Gerard Murphy in 1933. Finally in 1953 Murphy produced the third volume (xliii), containing introduction, notes, and glossary. See also Alan Bruford, *Gaelic folktales and mediaeval romances* (*Béaloideas*, xxxiv (1968)). This latter volume is the most comprehensive examination of the Finn tradition in existence.

with Irish glosses; some 3,500 are in the Würzburg codex (Würzburg, Universitätsbibl., MS M.p.th.f. 12, *c*.750), containing a glossed Latin text of the Pauline epistles; some 3,500 are found in a manuscript of Priscian's grammar preserved at St Gall (Stiftsbibl., MS 904, *c*.845); other sources contain the remaining 900.[97] Since this estimate was first made by Ascoli in the late nineteenth century some further glosses have come to light.[98]

The oldest piece of continuous Irish prose in an early source is the 'Cambrai homily' written in a manuscript preserved at Cambrai in northern France in the late eighth century, but copied from an older exemplar (probably seventh-century) by a continental scribe who was apparently ignorant of Irish.[99] The so-called 'Stowe Missal', the major portion of which was written at the monastery of Tallaght, County Dublin, shortly after 792,[100] contains, as well as some Irish charms, a tract on the mass, which is of some liturgical importance and was probably composed in the eighth century. The Book of Armagh, written in the early ninth century, contains, as well as occasional glosses, important notes in Irish appended to Bishop Tírechán's collection of material on the life of St Patrick.[101] Mention may also be made of the 'Lambeth commentary', a substantial fragment in mixed Irish and Latin of an eighth-century commentary on the gospel of St Matthew. This fragment came to light in recent years in the binding of a twelfth-century manuscript preserved in Lambeth Palace, London.[102] Somewhat similar material of early date is occasionally found in later Irish manuscripts, as for instance the substantial fragment of a treatise on the psalter, edited and restored to its eighth-century form by Kuno Meyer.[103]

MUCH of the older hagiographical material is in Latin: Muirchú's Life of St Patrick (*c*.700); Bishop Tírechán's notes on the same saint (late seventh century), Adomnán's 'Vita Columbae' (*c*.700),[104] and the 'Vita Brigitae' by Cogitosus (seventh century).[105] But early hagiographical material in Irish has

---

[97] See R. I. Best, *The commentary on the psalms* (Dublin, 1936), p. ix.

[98] The oldest known ink glosses were published by Dáibhí Ó Cróinín, 'Early Echternach fragments with Old Irish glosses' in Georges Kiesel and Jean Schroeder (ed.), *Willibrord, Apostel der Niederlande* (Echternach, 1989), pp 135–43.

[99] There is an edition in Rudolf Thurneysen, *Old Irish reader* (Dublin, 1946), pp 35–6; see also Pádraig Ó Néill, 'The background to the Cambrai homily' in *Ériu*, xxxii (1981), pp 137–47.

[100] George F. Warner (ed.), *The Stowe Missal.* (London, 1906, 1915); see also T. F. O'Rahilly, 'The history of the Stowe Missal' in *Ériu*, x (1926–8), pp 95–109.

[101] Bieler, *Patrician texts.*

[102] Ed. James Carney in *Ériu*, xxiii (1972), pp 1–55.

[103] *Hibernica minora, being a fragment of an Old-Irish treatise on the psalter* (Oxford, 1894). See also Pádraig Ó Néill, 'The Old-Irish treatise on the psalter and its Hiberno-Latin background' in *Ériu*, xxx (1979), pp 148–64.

[104] Anderson, *Adomnán's Life.*

[105] See Richard Sharpe, '*Vitae S Brigidae*: the oldest text' in *Peritia*, i (1982), pp 81–106; Kim McCone, 'Brigit in the seventh century: a saint with three lives?' ibid., pp 107–45.

survived, particularly in regard to these three saints. The 'Amra Choluim Chille',[106] a lengthy poetical composition in praise of Colum Cille, is generally accepted as having been composed on the occasion of or shortly after the saint's death in 597. Two highly interesting poems on Colum Cille, written perhaps about half a century after 597, are attributed, doubtless correctly, to his kinsman Béccán mac Luigdech.[107] A poem on St Brigit, preserved in the twelfth-century 'Irish Liber hymnorum',[108] presents biographical and legendary material, and is ascribed to the seventh-century St Broccán. Another, and perhaps an earlier, poem on the saint in the same source is attributed to the same Broccán; but there are other attributions, among them one to St Brendan the Navigator. The primitive Irish Life of the saint is probably of the eighth century.[109] Two compositions relating to St Patrick are in archaic metrical style and are of early date: the poem 'Atom-riug indiu' ('I bind myself today'), usually called 'St Patrick's breastplate', and ascribed to the saint himself; and Nínine's prayer 'Ad-muinemmar nóeb Pátraic' ('we invoke the holy Patrick'). Both are preserved in the 'Liber hymnorum'. The most ambitious hagiographical effort in the Irish language is the ninth-century 'Vita Tripartita',[110] based largely on the earlier Latin material. Kathleen Hughes has written about this text:

The 'Vita Tripartita' was almost certainly intended for preaching to the public on the three days of Patrick's festival. It was not to teach Christian behaviour but to build up revenue, to assert rights, to frighten the non-cooperative. Much of it is entertaining stuff, told with considerable zest. It seems to have set a fashion in saints' Lives, for many of those compiled later show similar characteristics. They stress the saint's property rights and the power of his relics (another aspect of the same thing); they have considerable entertainment value. As saints' Lives became more popular, characteristics of the secular saga become more noticeable.[111]

THE second half of the seventh century was a period of considerable hagiographical activity, partly for the reason that the lives of the great founder saints were relevant to contemporary monastic claims. Bishop Tírechán's notes on St Patrick, no less than Adomnán's Life of Colum Cille, have special interest in showing that the author had some idea of correct historical method. The bishop travelled over a wide area collecting information from

[106] Whitley Stokes, 'The Bodleian Amra Choluimb Chille' in *Rev. Celt.*, xx (1899), pp 31–55, 132–83, 248–89, 400–37, with corrections and additions, ibid., xxi (1900), pp 133–6.
[107] Fergus Kelly, 'A poem in praise of Columb Cille' in *Ériu*, xxiv (1973), pp 1–23; idem, 'Tiughraind Bhécáin' in *Ériu*, xxvi (1975), pp 66–98.
[108] J. H. Bernard and R. Atkinson (ed.), *The Irish Liber Hymnorum* (2 vols, London, 1898).
[109] See C. Plummer, J. Fraser, and P. Grosjean, 'Vita Brigitae' in *Ir. Texts*, i (London, 1931), pp 2–16, and M. A. O'Brien, 'The Old Irish Life of St Brigit' in *I.H.S.*, i (1938–9), pp 121–34, 343–53; Donncha Ó hAodha (ed.), *Bethu Brigte* (Dublin, 1978).
[110] Whitley Stokes (ed. & trans.), *The Tripartite Life of Patrick* (2 vols, London, 1887); *Trip. life*, ed. Mulchrone.
[111] *Early Christian Ireland: introduction to the sources* (London, 1972), p. 241.

Patrician foundations, examining inscriptions, observing archaeological remains, and laying some stress on things he had seen 'with my own eyes'. The production of Lives continued from this period at least to the twelfth century. Every individual Life is a special problem, for the Life that survives is frequently the end-result of a process of writing and rewriting that had gone on for centuries, involving translation from Irish to Latin, and then back again to Irish, and other possible variations of this process, The Lives reached heights of great extravagance, especially in later centuries. To the twelfth century, possibly shortly after 1122, may be assigned the Irish Life of Colmán mac Luacháin of Lann, County Westmeath.[112] This Life is so extravagant that it is something approaching a satire on the genre, thus having affinity with the more or less contemporary 'Aislinge Meic Conglinne' ('The vision of Mac Con Glinne').[113] The Life of Colmán gives no impression of being a representation of earlier material. There is an evenness of style, and it seems clear that the dramatic poems with which the narrative is interspersed are all by the same author, which is doubtless that of the writer of the prose. The hagiographical clichés, such as the use of 'etymological' deduction as historical evidence, reach an extreme of absurdity; every 'miracle' and act of smug piety leaves the saint richer and more influential than before.

The most important social document of a hagiographical nature is that edited under the title 'The monastery of Tallaght'.[114] This text is preserved in a late manuscript, but, in the opinion of the editors, was composed in the early ninth century, between 831 and 840. It is an account of the ascetic life in the monastery of Tallaght, County Dublin, during the lifetime of the founder Máel Ruain (d. 792) and in Terryglass during the lifetime of his pupil Máel Díthruib, 'anchorite and sage of Terryglass' (d. 840). There are also in this document anecdotes concerning the views and practices of other contemporary ascetics, and of some from an earlier period.

The current view of the authorship of 'The monastery of Tallaght' is that it was written by a monk who had been an inmate of that monastery during the lifetime of Máel Ruain.[115] This author knew Máel Díthruib and wrote during the latter's lifetime but added a single item after his death. Whatever about the details of this view, it is at least certain that the personality of Máel Díthruib is central to the document. This text brings the reader into immediate contact with life in the monastery, the prayers, hymns, and ascetic practices. When urged by another abbot to relax his total ban on beer on some of the chief festivals, Máel Ruain answered: 'As long as I shall give

---

[112] Kuno Meyer (ed.), *Betha Colmáin maic Lúacháin: Life of Colmán son of Lúachán* (Dublin, 1911).

[113] See n. 82 above.

[114] E. J. Gwynn and W. J. Purton, 'The monastery of Tallaght' in *R.I.A. Proc.*, xxix (1911–12), sect. C , pp 115–79.

[115] See now Peter O'Dwyer, *Céli Dé: spiritual reform in Ireland 750–900* (Dublin, 1981).

rules and as long as my injunctions are observed in this place, the liquor that causes forgetfulness of God shall not be drunk here' (§ 6). When he rejected the offer of a piper (*cuislennach*), who was also an anchorite, to play a tune for him as a thanks-offering for many gifts, Máel Ruain refused, saying 'these ears are not lent to earthly music that they may be lent to the music of heaven' (§ 10).

Sacred texts were being imported from abroad and studied at Tallaght. Máel Díthruib came to Tallaght, having previously belonged to what he regarded as a less worthy community. He was received with some reluctance by Máel Ruain, who had no wish to poach on the preserves of other abbots. Among the reasons Máel Díthruib gave for wishing to leave his old community and join that of Tallaght was his belief that Tallaght was in closer intellectual communion with the outside world. He says that in coming 'my first wish was to read and cast my mind over whatever sacred reading had come into the country' (§ 25). But while Máel Ruain clearly welcomed the importation of sacred knowledge, he opposed those who would go abroad in search of it. He quotes the 'elders' on the habit of 'deserting the land': 'Anyone who deserts his country, except to go from the east to the west, and from the north to the south, is a denier of Patrick in heaven and of the faith in Erin' (§ 17). This is an important statement, made in pre-viking times, on the religious, cultural, and intellectual unity of Ireland; it is hardly to be supposed, however—indeed, the contrary is implicit in the document—that this injunction would exclude travelling to the Gaelic areas of Scotland, which were, at least indirectly, 'Patrician' territory through the agency of Colum Cille.

The Tallaght document is probably unique in the history of western Christianity. There is an absence of the exaggeration and extravagance that characterise most Irish hagiographical work. What at first sight might appear as harshness or excessive puritanism can be modified by good sense. A certain Mac Óige of Lismore was approached by a student with a question as to what clerical attribute he should best acquire. Mac Óige answered that he should acquire that virtue with which fault had never been found. If one acquires charity it could be said that he was over-charitable; if he is humble he could be criticised for excessive humility; similarly asceticism could go too far. 'I have never heard, however,' said he, 'of anyone of whom it was said "This man is too steady"' (§ 76).

IN early Irish there is a great quantity of verse dealing with scriptural or ecclesiastical themes. Three compositions are of major importance as ambitious literary productions and as linguistic monuments: the poems of Blathmac,[116] son of Cú Brettan of the Fir Roiss, c. 750; the 'Félire Óengusso'[117]

---

[116] James Carney, *The poems of Blathmac* (Dublin, 1964).     [117] *Fél. Oeng.*

('The calendar of Óengus'), *c.*800; and 'Saltair na Rann' ('The psalter of quatrains'),[118] written by one Óengus who describes himself as *céle Dé* ('servant of God'). The 'Saltair', by reason of a somewhat problematic dating passage, is usually regarded as having been composed in 988; it has, however, been suggested that the dating passage should be rejected, and the work assigned to the second half of the ninth century. These three works mark the growing importance in ecclesiastical circles of the Irish vernacular from the mid-eighth century onwards.

The poems of Blathmac, only partly preserved, are known solely from a single imperfect seventeenth-century manuscript. The edition consists of 259 quatrains, and fragments of some twenty-five at the end of the manuscript are as yet unpublished. There are two poems: the first has 149 quatrains, the second (counting fragments) about 135. The second refers back to the first, so the poems constitute a unity. It has been suggested that there may originally have been three poems, each containing the mystical number of 150 quatrains, the number of psalms in the psalter.

Blathmac came of a minor ruling family, the Fir Roiss, who occupied a part of County Monaghan and extended into County Louth. According to saga tradition his father, Cú Brettan, son of Óengus, had taken part in the battle of Allen, which the annals date to 718. Cú Brettan died in 740 and a son of his, Blathmac's brother, was slain in the battle of Emain in 759. Blathmac was not an old man when he wrote, for he prayed to live to old age (§139). He was a monk, and the poems, in their phraseology and content, reflect an intellectual background of the type met with in the Milan and Würzburg glosses. Blathmac does not call himself *céle Dé*, 'servant of God', or *céle Críst*, 'servant of Christ', but he would have accepted such descriptions. He uses the latter variant once in reference to those who, from early Christian times, have suffered under kings (§ 254). In the unpublished fragments, apparently addressing Christ, he refers to himself as *bar mbochtán fessin* ('your own devotee of poverty'), a periphrasis for *bochtán Críst* or *pauper Christi*. His description of himself, implicit and explicit, is virtually identical with the terms that Óengus, the author of the 'Félire', uses of himself.

In using the terms *céle* and its abstract *célsine* ('clientship'), Blathmac sees the relationship between God or Christ and the devotee in terms of an Irish secular institution involving reciprocal obligations. In fact, the whole biblical scene is visualised in Irish terms. The idea of *célsine* is heavily underlined. The Jews were, it is implied, *céli Dé*, 'servants of God'; by reason of their *célsine* God had endowed them richly, but they had violated their 'counter obligations' (§ 106); opposing Christ was 'opposing a spear-point to [justly imposed] subjection' and was 'a denial after recognition', that is, a

[118] Whitley Stokes (ed.), *Saltair na Rann* (Oxford, 1883).

breach of contract (§ 99). The crime of the Jews was all the worse since, Mary being Jewish, the killing of Christ was *fingal*, 'kin-slaying' (§ 103). As a result of this deed the Jews are dispersed and have no kingdom, they are reviled by all, and hell is their destiny (§§ 117–18).

The existence of a specific type of monk called a *céle Dé* or 'culdee' could not be proved from the poems of Blathmac. There are, in his view, two kinds of people: the *céli Críst* and their antithesis, the *muintir diabuil*, 'the people of the devil' (§ 242). The former are not servants bound by evil oaths (§ 256). The latter include *ind ríg cloín*, 'the perverse kings', who are the *céli* of a bad lord, that is, of the devil; they will show a poor aspect on Judgement Day, for the lord whom they followed will be powerless (§ 244).

Blathmac's narrative extends from the Annunciation to the Ascension, drawing occasionally on the Old Testament. By describing the gospel of John as 'no heretical tale…the mystic utterance is to be believed' (§ 187) he implies a distinction between the canonical scriptures and apocryphal material. Nevertheless he draws to some slight extent on apocrypha, notably the popular 'Harrowing of Hell'; he tells also of the piercing of Christ's side by a Roman soldier called Longinus, and states that at the death of Christ all the trees of the world shed blood, an idea that has so far been paralleled in medieval literature only in the poems of the Anglo-Saxon Cynewulf.

Blathmac is an experienced poet, and, quite clearly, the inheritor of a long tradition. His narrative is good, often enlivened by striking images, and interspersed with lyrical passages. It is hardly likely that he was a trained poet in the sense that, at some time in his career, he had attended a native school of poetry. But he would have had at least a receiver's knowledge of such verse, and represents the fusion of the 'native' tradition with Latin ecclesiastical learning. He is the earliest poet of this type of whose verse a substantial portion has survived. But he is not the originator of the phenomenon of fusion; this antedates him by some two centuries, and can already be seen in the surviving fragments of the poems of Colmán mac Lénéni (d. 604). His poem has a dramatic framework. In the beginning he calls on Mary to come to him so that together they may keen for the dead Christ. The second poem, still addressed to Mary, is a celebration of the joyful aspects of the New Testament and the glories of the Christian martyrs. Like any poet in the 'native' tradition he asks for payment for his poem. His fee is that he should live to be old. He also demands salvation for those who use his poem as a prayer, and he stands as guarantor that Mary will see these promises are fulfilled.

The metrical 'Félire' of Óengus is at once a work of religious devotion and of scholarship. It was composed about 800 by one Óengus, son of Oengoba son of Oíbleán, an anchorite and bishop at Dísert Óengusa near the monastery of Cluain Eidnech (Clonenagh) in the present County Leix. The body of the poem consists of 365 quatrains; each mentions the events or persons,

Irish and foreign, commemorated liturgically on every day of the year. To this have been added a prologue and epilogue of 35 and 141 quatrains respectively. From the work itself we gather that Óengus regarded Máel Ruain of Tallaght as his mentor (*aite*), and that, at the time of writing, Máel Ruain was dead. He describes himself twice periphrastically as a *céle Críst* (*a Chríst dianda chéle*, 'O Christ, whose servant I am', Ep. 307, 426); similarly, addressing Christ, the poet says *ol is duit am céle*, 'for I am a servant of Thine' (Ep. 554). He further describes himself in varying terms as a devotee of poverty: *bochtán, dedblén truag, in pauperán truagsa, déorudán lobur*, all terms denoting wretchedness and misery endured for spiritual reasons. The saints and committed Christians are *rígrad Críst*, 'the king-folk of Christ', *tuath Dé*, 'the people of God', *mílid Íssu*, 'soldiers of Jesus', *amsáin ísil Íssu*, 'humble mercenaries of Jesus'. He rejoices in the passing of pagan splendour, Roman and Irish, and in the glorification of the humble devotees of Christ; visiting the grave of Donnchad, lately king of Tara, gives him no consolation; but at the grave of Máel Ruain 'is healed the sigh of every heart' (Prol. 221–8).

Apart from what can be gathered from the 'Félire', there is an amount of traditional biographical information in later prefaces. Some time after Óengus's death his grave at Cluain Eidnech was visited by another monk and poet called Óengus, who wrote a short poem expressing his devotion to his namesake, and giving a brief account of his life.[119] The later Óengus in this poem shows his earlier namesake as a saint for whom, during his life, miracles were wrought. While mentioning a sojourn at Tallaght he emphasises the connection with Cluain Eidnech: 'It is in Cluain Eidnech he was reared, in Cluain Eidnech he was buried; in Cluain Eidnech of the many crosses he studied his psalms at first'. A poem in the Book of Leinster[120] mentions twenty-four 'saints' who were buried at Cluain Eidnech. Óengus ua Oíbleán is among them, and also mentioned is *int Óengus eile* ('the other Oengus'), who is possibly the author of the short poem (and not impossibly of 'Saltair na Rann').

'Saltair na Rann', 'the psalter of quatrains', is a composition consisting of 150 poems of varying length covering in narrative form a number of events in the Old and, very sketchily, in the New Testament.[121] This, the 'body of "Saltair na Rann"' (*corp Saltrach na Rann*), contains almost 8,000 lines. To this have been added twelve substantial poems, presumably by the same author, one on repentance, one on man's fundamental ignorance of God and his creation, and ten poems on the events of each day in the period immedi-

---

[119] For this poem, *Aibind suide sund amne* ('Delightful to sit here thus'), see Stokes, op. cit., pp xxiv–vi.

[120] See Pádraig Ó Riain (ed.), *Corpus genealogiarum sanctorum Hiberniae* (Dublin, 1988), pp 92–3.

[121] For the Old Testament section, see David Greene and Fergus Kelly (ed.), *The Irish Adam and Eve story from Saltair na Rann*, i (Dublin, 1976).

ately preceding the Monday of the Last Judgement. In the poem on man's ignorance the poet names himself in the words *is mé Óengus, céle Dé* ('I am Óengus, servant of God'). The coincidence that the two longest poems in the early period should each have been written by a monk called Óengus has been heightened by scholars who gave the title *céle Dé* to both authors, and assumed that the term was in each case specific, connoting membership of a special type of reformed monastery. Lines 2,333–4 seem to date the poem to the year 988, but the passage is in many ways unsatisfactory, and it has been suggested that there has been interpolation, and that the 'Saltair' is of ninth-century date. This matter may be regarded as still undecided. The text has not yet been translated, and the edition of Stokes is not altogether adequate.

These three lengthy works are important sources, among other things, for the history of the use of extra-canonical biblical material in the early Irish church.[122] In this matter two other works may be mentioned. About 700 an Irish poet made a versified account of the 'Infancy Gospel of Thomas'.[123] The Thomas Gospel appears to have been a product of the second century, and was used by various heretical sects. The Irish poet seems to have used a Latin version no longer extant, and most closely related to a surviving version in Syriac. The second work is the text called 'In tenga bithnua' ('The ever-new tongue');[124] this appears to be partly based on a Latin apocalypse of Philip, of which no other trace has come to light outside Ireland. The text—if it is a rendering of such a work—is hardly a translation in any direct sense. It has rather the appearance of a mixture of adaptation and invention, and the narrative has often a distinctly Irish flavour. It has been dated to the tenth century, but there are difficulties in accepting such a comparatively late date. The lexical content, as well as many of the verbal forms, suggest that it is an eighth-century text which in the course of transmission has undergone partial modernisation.

A consideration of the apocryphal material found in early Ireland has led some scholars to look towards Spain as an important source for pre-Carolingian learning in Ireland. Not merely could Spain supply Ireland with 'the linguistic and literary goods of Latin Christianity', but this was also the Christian area that could best account for 'the warts and peculiarities' of Irish ecclesiastical learning'.[125]

---

[122] See Martin McNamara, *The apocrypha in the Irish Church* (Dublin, 1975); D. N. Dumville, 'Biblical apocrypha and the early Irish: a preliminary investigation' in *R.I.A. Proc.*, lxxiii (1973), sect. C, pp 299–338.

[123] Carney, *Poems of Blathmac*, pp 90–105.

[124] Whitley Stokes, 'The Evernew Tongue' in *Rev. Celt.*, ii (1905), pp 96–162; ibid., iii (1907), pp 34–5; Úna Nic Énri and Gearóid Mac Niocaill, 'The second recension of the Ever-new Tongue' in *Celtica*, ix (1971), pp 1–59; Engl. trans. only in Máire Herbert and Martin McNamara (ed.), *Irish biblical apocrypha* (Edinburgh, 1989), pp 109–19. See McNamara, *Apocrypha*, pp 115–18.

[125] Dumville, 'Biblical apocrypha', p. 330; see also Edmund Bishop, *Liturgica historica: papers on the liturgy and religious life of the western church* (Oxford, 1918), pp 165–202.

THREE Irish tale-types have a particularly close association: the *echtrae*, 'expedition'; the *fís*, 'vision'; and the *immram*, 'voyage'. The *echtrae* is in origin a native tale-type telling how a human hero made an expedition to the Otherworld of Irish pagan belief. This Otherworld was normally located under the land or under river, lake, or sea; it may also be located in distant islands, but it could perhaps be held that this is due to contamination with voyage tales. The earliest reference to such a tale is found in an archaic poem, possibly sixth-century or earlier, quoted in the Leinster genealogies: this tells how a hero, 'the noble son of Sétne', visited the 'lands of the dead' and fought battles against the supernatural Fomairi.[126] A typical example of this genre is 'Echtrae Loíguiri maic Crimthain co Mag Mell' ('The expedition of Loíguire son of Crimthan to the Plain of Delights');[127] here the hero goes to the Plain of Delights to assist one Otherworld chieftain against another, and obtains the love of a woman as a reward. A similar situation is found in 'Serglige Con Culainn' ('The sick-bed of Cú Chulainn').[128] The same idea, with certain appropriate adjustments, has persisted into the oral tradition of modern times: a man living in Boyle, County Roscommon, was asked to take part in a hurley match played by the fairies of Ireland against those of Scotland; the latter group had also acquired a human champion; the Irishman brought victory to his side, and was rewarded with a beautiful girl as a wife, and a cow.[129]

The earliest and best-known example of the *echtrae* is 'Echtrai Condli' ('The expedition of Condle the Fair').[130] Deriving as it does from the version in the eighth-century 'Cín Dromma Snechtai', it may be dated to about 700, or slightly earlier. The tale is short and well composed, with deep pathos, a high poetic quality, and skilfully arranged dialogue. It is an outstanding example of the short story, and (though dealing with an ancient historio-mythical scene) would seem to have symbolic relevance to Irish Christian society in the seventh century. A summary of the tale is as follows. Conn Cétchathach, the ancestor of the greatest ruling dynasties in Ireland, was one day walking with his son Condle on the hill of Uisnech in County Westmeath. Suddenly a woman from the Otherworld appeared. She spoke to Condle, asking him to come to the 'Lands of the Living', where there is neither death nor sin nor transgression, where all live in peace, and consume everlasting feasts. Only Condle could see the woman, though all could hear her voice. Conn called upon his druid Corán to help him in face of the

[126] Above, p. 463.
[127] Ed. K. H. Jackson in *Speculum*, xvii (1942), pp 377–89.
[128] Myles Dillon (ed.), *Serglige Con Culainn* (Dublin, 1953).
[129] Carney, *Studies in Ir. lit.*, p. 294.
[130] H. P. A. Oskamp, 'Echtra Condla' in *Études Celt.*, xiv (1974), pp 207–28. See James Carney, 'The deeper level of Irish literature' in *Capuchin Annual 1969*, pp 162–5. [Editor's note: the author appears to have revised his opinion of this text in the 1976 article cited below, n. 150].

invisible being that was trying to steal his son. The druid chanted a spell against the woman, which forced her to depart. But before going she threw an apple to Condle. He spent a month taking no food but the apple, which never diminished. Meanwhile he longed constantly for the woman. After a month she came back and renewed her supplications. Conn called his druid to banish her again. But she addressed Conn, telling him to give no honour to druidry, and she prophesied the advent of Christianity: in a short time a just man would come with many wonderful households; his law would destroy the spells of druids, despite the evil magic-working devil. Conn turned to his son and asked: 'Has what the woman says touched your heart?' Condle answered: 'It is not easy for me. I love my people beyond all. But I have been seized by a loneliness for the woman.' The woman tells him (in verse) that he is struggling against his love of home in order that he might go in her crystal boat to the Otherworld dwelling of Boadag. The latter, as she had said elsewhere, is 'the eternal Boadag' (victorious one) who has had 'no weeping or woe in his land since he took sovereignty'. 'It is the land', she continues, 'that rejoices the mind of all who walk about it. There is no race there but women and maidens.' Condle leapt into the boat. As it disappeared from sight his brother Art was seen approaching. 'Art is alone today,' said Conn, 'for he has no brother'. 'You have spoken a word of power', said Corán. 'That shall be his name till Doom: Art, the Lone' (Art Óenfer).

The author of this tale has synthesised three disparate elements: the Irish conception of the *áes síde* (the fairies or Otherworld folk of ancient Irish tradition); the Christian idea of the voluntary renunciation of the world for the sake of salvation; and an onomastic tale telling how Art Óenfer came to be so called. The third element exists in 'Cóir Anmann' ('Fitness of names'),[131] in what is, in all likelihood, its simple, original, and uncontaminated form: Conn had three sons, Art, Condle, and Crinda. Condle and Crinda were slain by Eochaid Find Fuath nAirt and thereafter Art was called Art Óenfer.[132] That the Irish Otherworld is known, at least in one of its aspects, as 'the land of women' is doubtless a primitive Irish concept, one that is encountered again in 'Immram Brain' and evidenced in the place-name Sliabh na mBan 'mountain of the (Otherworld) women' (Slievenamon, in County Tipperary); similarly Cnoc Áine (Knockaney, County Limerick) is presided over by a goddess. 'Echtrae Condli' is then explicitly an *echtrae*, an account of an expedition to the Otherworld, but it cannot be a representative example of the genre, since the tale ends when the *echtrae* proper begins. It also has an important element of didacticism and allegory, which is relevant to the cultural and religious scene at the time of composition. Some elements are explicitly Christian. But a folk motif (or a common literary one) may

[131] Whitley Stokes and Ernst Windisch (ed.), *Cóir Anmann* (Leipzig, 1897).
[132] *Cóir Anmann*, §§ 112, 167.

possibly have an allegorical Christian significance when seen in the general context of the tale. Such perhaps is the apple that, though constantly eaten, never diminishes. It may be taken as a promise of the eternal, thus quite simply symbolising the eucharist. Or—what amounts to the same thing—the apple may be taken as *justitia quae est Jesus Christus* of which it is said in the Lambeth commentary *ni bí sáithech di intí las mbí* ('he who is wont to have it is never satiated').[133] This tale has a function in the teaching of traditional history. In this regard it could be called a 'replacement tale'. For while seeking to oust earlier traditional matter, it retains the essence and fulfils exactly the same function, explaining as it does why Art should be called 'Art, the lone'.

The *fís* (Lat. *visio*) is a vision of the Christian heaven and hell, such as 'Fís Adomnáin' ('The vision of Adomnán').[134] This genre is represented in Latin by the 'Visio Tnugdali' ('The vision of Tnúthgal'), written in Ratisbon, in Bavaria, by an Irish monk called Marcus in 1149.[135] Marcus was from Munster, a friend and associate of Cormac mac Carthaig, king of Cashel. He states that his work was translated from Irish, but this is hardly true in a literal sense. Another important twelfth-century Hiberno-Latin vision is 'The vision of the knight Owen in St Patrick's Purgatory'. Through these two Latin texts Irish material entered the mainstream of European literature: the second, with Juan Perez de Montalvan as intermediary, forming the basis of one of Calderón's most popular plays, 'El purgatorio de San Patricio'.[136]

The subject of voyage tales bristles with difficulties with regard to date and interrelationship. The voyage tales are 'Immram Brain maic Febail' ('The voyage of Bran son of Febal');[137] 'Navigatio Sancti Brendani' (Latin);[138] 'Immram curaig Máele Dúin' ('The voyage of the curragh of Máel Dúin');[139] 'Immram Snédgusa ocus Maic Riagla' ('The voyage of Snédgus and Mac Riagla'); and 'Immram curaig Úa Corra' ('The voyage of the

---

[133] *Ériu*, xxiii (1972), p. 28, l. 119.

[134] Bergin & Best, *Lebor na hUidre*, pp 27–31. See Whitley Stokes (ed.), *Adamnáin Slicht Libair na Huidre: Adamnán's vision* (Simla, 1870); Herbert & McNamara, *Irish biblical apocrypha*, pp 137–48. C. S. Boswell, *An Irish precursor of Dante* (London, 1908).

[135] O. Schade (ed.), *Visio Tnugdali* (Halle, 1869); trans. J.-M. Picard, *The Vision of Tnugdal* (Dublin, 1989).

[136] The most comprehensive treatment of 'vision' literature and its relationship to the *immram* and the *echtrae* is in St John D. Seymour's *Irish visions of the Other-world* (London, 1930); from the same author comes *St Patrick's Purgatory* (Dundalk, 1918). For more recent discussion, see Michael Haren and Yolande de Pontfarcy (ed.), *Studies on Saint Patrick's Purgatory* (Dublin, 1996).

[137] Meyer & Nutt, *The voyage of Bran*. See also Séamus Mac Mathúna (ed.), *Immram Brain: the voyage of Bran to the Land of Women* (Tübingen, 1985).

[138] Carl Selmer (ed.), *Navigatio Sancti Brendani Abbatis* (Notre Dame, 1959). For some comments on this edition see the review by Carney in *Medium Aevum*, xxxii (1963), pp 37–44.

[139] A. G. van Hamel (ed.), *Immrama* (Dublin, 1941), pp 20–77; see also H. P. A. Oskamp (ed.), *The voyage of Máel Dúin* (Groningen, 1970), an edition and translation of the text combined with a general study of voyage literature.

curragh of the Uí Chorra').[140] Here it is possible to mention only the general features of the subject.

'Immram Brain maic Febail', in its extant form, belongs probably to the late seventh century, and this is one of the few points on which there is virtual consensus.[141] It has a relationship with the other voyage tales, but somewhat distant.[142] A summary of the tale is as follows: Bran, son of Febal, found near his house, Dún Brain, a silver branch with white flowers and brought it into the house. This was an action involving some risk—it was obviously a 'fairy' flower. In modern Irish folk-belief neither hawthorn nor wild woodbine should be brought into a house. When all were assembled there, a woman in strange attire[143] appeared among them, although all doors were closed. She sang a poem to Bran, describing a utopian Otherworld in a mixture of concepts, some perhaps primitive Irish or Celtic modified by Christianity, others perhaps Christian modified by native ideas. There is an island supported by four feet of white bronze (*findruine*) where there is a great flowering tree on which the birds sing the hours. There is no mourning, treachery, sorrow, or gloom; no rough voice but music striking upon the ear. There is eternal music and no knowledge of death or decay. It is a land of 'many thousands of variegated [Otherworld] women' (*ilmíli brecc mban*). In the ocean to the west there are three fifties of islands, each one twice or three times the size of Ireland. She then prophesies the birth of a man from a virgin, a man who will exercise sovereignty over many thousands. He will be a lord without beginning or end and he has created the whole world. He has made the heavens. Happy the one who cherishes him. He will cleanse hosts by pure water; he will cure the plagues of the people. Let Bran listen to her wisdom; let him not lie on a bed of sloth, let him not be overcome by drunkenness, let him start to voyage over the clear sea that perchance he may reach the 'land of Otherworld women'.

The woman vanishes, and Bran sets out to sea as the leader of a company of 'three nines', a conventional warrior grouping. On the third day at sea he meets the Irish sea-god Manannán son of Ler, who drives over the sea in a chariot. Manannán chants to him a lay of somewhat similar character to that of the Otherworld woman. What seems like ocean to Bran is to Manannán 'the plain of delights' (Mag Mell): its waves are shrubs, its salmon are leaping calves and lambs; although Bran does not know it, his boat is sailing over a populous kingdom. In this kingdom men and gentle women lie under a bush 'without sin, without transgression'. They have existed since the beginning

---

[140] Van Hamel, *Immrama*, pp 93–111. Also to be mentioned are the chapters on 'The adventures', 'The voyages', and 'The visions' in Myles Dillon's *Early Irish literature* (Chicago, 1948).

[141] See Carney, *Studies in Ir. lit.*, pp 280–95.

[142] Dillon, op. cit., p. 104, classified it as an *echtrae* rather than as an *immram*.

[143] Phrases such as 'in strange attire' or 'in a green mantle' almost always imply the supernatural. Hence, even today, there is a prejudice against green.

of creation, without age, or burial, for the Transgression (that is, of Adam and Eve) did not touch them. It was a bad day that the serpent came to the Ancestor in his dwelling and brought suffering into the world. It is an act of pride in this world to adore the elements and to deny God. But a noble salvation would come from the king who created the elements. Manannán then juxtaposes his prophecy of the incarnation with an analogous incident in which he would play a part. He, Manannán, would lie with Caintigirn, wife of Fíachna, and of this union would be born a wonderful son who would have god-like characteristics, that is, Mongán son of Fíachna. He prophesies Mongán's death at the age of 50. In the last stanza he encourages Bran to sail off to Emne, the land of women, which he will reach before nightfall.

Bran sailed on until he came to an island inhabited by people who laughed and grimaced. He sent one of his company ashore, and he became exactly like the rest of the islanders, so they must perforce sail without him. The name of that island was 'the island of happiness' (*Inis Subai*). Then they reached the land of women. The leader of the women called out a welcome, but Bran did not dare to land. She threw him a ball of thread, and when he caught it, it clove to his hand. She held the thread and pulled the boat ashore. They came into a mansion with twenty-seven couches, one for each couple. The meal that was served never diminished. They seemed to be a year there, but in fact many years had passed.

One of them, Nechtán mac Ala-Brain, was seized with homesickness. His kindred besought Bran to return to Ireland, and Bran was persuaded. The leader of the women warned him that none of them should set foot on land or they would regret it. They came eventually to Srúb Brain in Lough Foyle and were questioned by an assembly there as to the identity of those who had come over the sea. 'I am Bran son of Febal', said Bran. 'We do not know that man', said they; 'the voyage of Bran is in our ancient lore.' Nechtán was put ashore and he immediately turned to ashes as if he had been in the earth for many centuries. Bran then told his adventures from the boat and wrote the verses in ogam. He then said farewell, and nothing further is known of him.

No attempt will be made here to summarise the various opinions advanced in regard to this tale. As mentioned above, there is a fair consensus that it was written in the late seventh century. But the poetry could possibly be earlier still. It may be noted—for what it is worth—that the saga implies this when it says that the verses were written down in ogam. In some Irish compositions involving a mixture of prose and verse, the verse can often be shown to have been created by a different (and sometimes superior) mind to that of the prose writer, and such may well be the case in the present instance.[144]

[144] See James Carney, 'Two poems from Acallam na Senórach' in James Carney and David Greene, *Celtic studies ... in memory of Angus Matheson* (London, 1968), pp 22–32.

The poem, dealing partly with Mongán and his origin, could well have been written some short time after Mongán's death (629). That Mongán was begotten by Manannán, and that the sea-god was also his tutor, may be simple poetic hyperbole indicating Mongán's prowess at sea. Such a view might go a long way towards explaining the astonishing—and to a fully orthodox Christian society quite tasteless, even blasphemous—comparison of the Incarnation and the conception of Mongán. The description of an Otherworld folk, living in peace and harmony, and knowing no sin or death because they had not been touched by the Transgression, is, in the early Irish Christian scene, virtually orthodox. Scholars such as Dillon, in an effort to maintain the authentic paganism of the greater part of the verse, speak loosely of the Christian portions as 'interpolations'.[145] It is difficult to sustain this approach: the alliterative linking between stanzas in the first poem bind 'Christian' and 'pagan' elements together and suggest that the 'Christian' portions are an integral part of the composition.

The Bran story may be regarded (like 'Echtrai Condli')[146] as a product of Irish Christianity. The general moral would seem to be: strive hard, avoid sloth and drunkenness, levity and laughter, and you will gain eternity. Mac Cana has seen 'Immram Brain' and 'Echtrai Condli' as originating in the environment of the monastery of Bangor, County Down.[147] That rowing should be regarded as symbolic of striving towards eternal life is also instanced in a Latin hymn by Columbanus, who had a Bangor background: 'En, silvis caesa fluctu meat acta carina'.[148] But 'Immram Brain' is not a well-integrated allegory where every main action has an underlying symbolism.

Due consideration has not been given to one of the earliest and most important texts relevant to the history of Bran. It follows that previous comments must be revised or extended in the light of this material. The text in question consists of a mere eight quatrains, spoken by Bran and by a *banfáith*, a poetess or prophetess: 'Immaccaldam in druad Brain maic Febail ocus inna banfátho ós Loch Febail' ('The dialogue of the druid Bran son of Febal and the prophetess above Lough Foyle').[149]

In 'Immram Brain' no idea is given of the date of Bran or of his historical character or function: it can merely be deduced that the events took place before the birth of Christ. The dialogue of Bran and the prophetess, however, gives some help. It is a composition of considerable antiquity, and its

[145] Dillon, *Early Irish literature*, p. 104.

[146] Julius Pokorny, 'Conle's Abenteuerliche Fahrt' in *Z.C.P.*, xvii (1927), pp 193–205.

[147] Proinsias Mac Cana, 'Mongán mac Fiachna and *Immram Brain*' in *Ériu*, xxiii (1972), pp 102–42: 104.

[148] G. S. M. Walker (ed.), *Sancti Columbani opera* (Dublin, 1957), pp 190–92; Carney, *Medieval Irish lyrics* (Dublin, 1967), p. 8.

[149] Ed. Kuno Meyer in *Z.C.P.*, ix (1913), pp 339–40; cf. Paul Grosjean, 'S. Columbae Hiensis cum Mongano heroe colloquium' in *Analecta Bollandiana*, xlv (1927), pp 75–83.

occurrence in certain manuscripts suggests that it derives from the 'Cín Dromma Snechtai', and probably preceded 'Immram Brain' in that manuscript. While every word in these stanzas is not immediately clear, the following can be gathered. Loch Febail (Lough Foyle) was at one time Mag Febail, 'the plain of Febal', a great and prosperous kingdom. Its king was Febal. Bran, a druid or wise man, was his son, and the prophetess or poetess was the king's lover. One day, when Bran was in his dwelling among a group of people, his mind 'went to the high clouds', a phrase apparently implying that he had a mystic vision. There was revealed to him a well in which was a land of (Otherworld) women possessing jewellery that would enrich the man who found it. We are not told explicitly in the 'Dialogue' that Bran went to seek this land of bejewelled women, but we are to assume it. (This expedition to the netherworld would probably be the story referred to in the tale-lists as 'Echtrae Brain maic Febail'.)[150] The outcome of the adventure seems clear. Bran was defeated in a contest (*immarec*), and instead of being a wise druid he became a *fer fesso bic*, 'a man of little knowledge'. Through this disaster, and doubtless as a result of the vengeance of the Otherworld women, we are to assume the bursting of the well so that the kingdom of Febal became Loch Febail, and a once 'flowery plain' became 'a stony sea'. Presumably, as in the somewhat analogous story of the origin of Lough Neagh, only a few escaped to tell the tale, among them Bran and the prophetess. The role of the prophetess would probably have been that of Cassandra, or of the prophet Midend (Midiu?) in the Lough Neagh story as told in the poem 'Ba mol Midend midlaige'.[151]

The story behind the 'Dialogue' is a not uncommon type of aetiological tale. It is referred to in the ninth-century world history in annalistic form which records 'Tomaidm Locha Febail' ('The bursting-forth of Loch Febail') in the fourth age of the world.[152] The 'Dialogue' gives a convincing origin for the land of women in 'Immram Brain' and 'Echtrai Condli', and for the heavily underlined contrast between Bran's vision of the sea as water and Manannan's vision of it as 'a flowery plain'. It can reasonably be held that part of the Christianising process in 'Immram Brain' was to change an *echtrae* into an *immram*, and to make the land of women something close to a symbol of the Christian heaven.

Two of the other *immrama*, 'Immram Snédgusa ocus Maic Riagla' (of which there is a poetic version and a prose derivative) and 'Immram curaig Ua Corra', are purely monastic productions. The latter text is, in part, a moral tale with warnings against adultery, theft, dishonesty among smiths

---

[150] See James Carney, 'The earliest Bran material' in John J. O'Meara and Bernd Naumann (ed.), *Latin script and letters, A.D. 400–900. Festschrift presented to Ludwig Bieler on the occasion of his 70th birthday* (Leiden, 1976), pp 174–93.
[151] Meyer, *Z.C.P.*, viii (1912), p. 308.
[152] *Ann. Inisf.*, p. 14.

and craftsmen, and breaches of Sunday observance. In as much as it shows the punishment in the next world for these sins, it belongs in some degree to the *fís* category.

It is probable that in pagan and early Christian Ireland traditions of over-sea raiding would have given rise to the *immram*. Indeed, there are probably reflections of this in such references as those to Fergus Fairrge ('Fergus of the sea') in the Leinster poems: it may be also noted that the term *immram mara* ('rowing upon the sea') is used in the same source. But the earlier lost *immrama* may have gone under the title *longas*, a term that came to mean 'exile' but originally was a collective meaning 'fleet'. One of the Ulster tales, 'Fled Bricrend ocus loinges mac nDuíl Dermait' ('The feast of Bricriu and the exile [*loinges*] of the sons of Doel Dermait', has some of the characteristics of the *immram*.[153] After 'Immram Brain' the most important example of the genre is 'Immram curaig Máele Dúin'. This tale exists in two versions, one prose and one verse. The verse is somewhat later than the prose, and is based on it. In the introductory note to his edition of these texts, van Hamel says: 'From the language it is clear that the text of the Voyage of Máel Dúin was first written down in the earlier part of the Old-Irish period (eighth or ninth century), but it can only be dated approximately, since even our oldest available recension cannot be regarded as a faithful reproduction of the archetype.'[154] Since the date of this text has an important bearing on the history of 'Navigatio Brendani', a tentative view will be taken here that this 'Voyage' was first composed in the ninth century.

The 'Voyage of the curragh of Máel Dúin' is one of the rare prose tales from early Irish where there is a statement regarding authorship and purpose of writing: 'Ro córuig immorro Áed Find, ardecnaid Érenn, in scél sain amal atá sund. Combad airgairdiugud menman do rígaib agus do doínib Érenn é ina diaid' (Áed Find, chief sage of Ireland, arranged that story as it is here so that it might give mental pleasure to the kings and people of Ireland after him). This is found only in a single manuscript, but may be old since there is a corresponding colophon in the poetic version. (There is disagreement among scholars as to whether the colophon belonged originally to the prose or to the later poetic version). Áed Find has not been identified, but despite Thurneysen's view to the contrary, it is unlikely that he is mythical. The statement on authorship might suggest that before Áed Find's time the adventures of Máel Dúin existed in some form. The 'arrangement' (*córugad*) was made to give the story a stable form in which it would be read to or by the people of Ireland of high and low status.

Unlike many Irish stories this has a logical beginning, middle, and end. It opens with a formulaic account of 'the birth of the hero'. Ailill Ochair Ága was lord of the Eóganacht Ninussa, a sept inhabiting the Aran islands, and

[153] Henderson, *Fled Bricrend*.    [154] Van Hamel, *Immrama*, p. 24.

owing allegiance to his distant kinsman, the Eóganacht king of Cashel. While on a military expedition with his overlord, Ailill left his encampment at midnight and entered the church of Kildare where he found a nun ringing the bell for matins. Ailill raped her. After the act, she protested, saying that their predicament was difficult for it was her period for conception (an interesting phrase, suggesting that the Irish had some knowledge of 'safe' and 'unsafe' periods). Shortly afterwards Ailill was slain by brigands. His son, Máel Dúin, was born to the nun, and committed by her to the queen of the territory; he grew up in ignorance of his parentage. One day when the young men of the court were at their games a certain youth, envious of Máel Dúin, taunted him on his lack of knowledge of his parents. Máel Dúin immediately went to the queen and threatened not to eat or drink until she told him his origin. Having met his mother and heard the truth from her, he went to his father's territory where he was well received. One day in the churchyard where his father Ailill had been slain, Máel Dúin and a number of companions were playing the game of throwing the stone. A foul-tongued youth called Briccne (Briccriu) (apparently modelled on Briccriu of the Ulster cycle) who was watching the game commented: 'It would better become you to avenge the man who was burned here than to throw stones over his bare, burnt bones.' Through the conversation that followed Máel Dúin discovered who were the murderers of his father, and that they still pursued the occupation of sea-rovers.

He then went to Corcumruad to the druid Nucca to seek his advice about building a ship and to ask for a charm to protect him while building it and while sailing on the sea. He built his ship and was told to take no more and no less than a company of seventeen ('or sixty according to others', says the storyteller) As soon as he set sail three of his foster-brothers swam out and threatened to drown themselves unless they were taken aboard. Máel Dúin yielded reluctantly, thus violating Nucca's instructions. After little more than thirty-six hours sailing they came upon the island where Ailill's murderers lived. But a storm arose, and they were driven out upon the ocean. Máel Dúin blamed their failure on his three foster-brothers.

There now follows the voyage proper, which consists of over thirty separate adventures, before they finally rediscover the island of Ailill's murderers. In an anticlimactic manner, but in keeping with the Christian origins of the story, Máel Dúin makes peace with them. He relates his adventures according to the word of the 'prophet' (Virgil) who said 'Haec olim meminisse iuvabit' (*Aen.* i, 203). Máel Dúin returned home and one of the company went to Armagh and laid five half-ounces of gold, which they had acquired during an adventure, on the altar there.

'Immram curaig Máele Dúin' is the finest of the Irish *immrama*. It was written solely for the purpose of entertainment, and if the author wishes to inculcate a Christian virtue or two, he does it with a light hand. The view is taken here that the tale has borrowed incidents from earlier *immrama*, particularly from the 'Navigatio Brendani'. Whitley Stokes, the first editor of the text,[155] was in no doubt about this and stated that this tale had the 'Navigatio' as one of its main sources. This, however, has not been the opinion of Zimmer, of Thurneysen, nor of the most recent editor, Oskamp. The matter of the dating of the 'Navigatio' is crucial. The story of the 'Navigatio' may have had a prehistory in Ireland before the emergence of the fine literary composition edited by Selmer. Máel Dúin shares with Brendan a Munster, indeed a specifically Eóganacht background, and we may take it as probable that the explicitly religious Latin text and the secular Irish text are of Munster origin. Some kind of account of a voyage or voyages of Brendan must have been in existence in the seventh century. From the poem 'A maccucáin sruith in tiag' (late seventh century)[156] we can gather that among the reading-matter of a young monastic student there would be 'a lay that Brendan had made upon the sea' (*fil and laíd do-dergéni Brénainn forsin muir*).

THERE are in Irish renderings of a number of classical and post-classical texts that are earlier by several centuries than kindred material in any European vernacular.[157] These are referred to by Stanford as 'remarkably idiosyncratic Irish retellings and free translations of classical stories'.[158] The main texts are first 'Togail Troí' ('The spoiling of Troy'),[159] based on the sixth-century 'Historia de excidio Troiae', supposedly by Dares Phrygius. This, more than any other heroic classical tale, gripped the imagination of the Irish. There are three interrelated versions, one as yet unpublished, and a poetic summary attributed to Flann Mainistrech (d. 1056). Secondly, 'Imthechta Aeniasa' ('The adventures of Aeneas'),[160] an adaptation in story form of Virgil's 'Aeneid'. Thirdly, 'Merugud Uilix maic Leirtis' ('The wandering of Ulysses, son of Laertes'),[161] a curious prose abbreviation of Homer's 'Odyssey'. Fourthly, 'Togail na Tebe' ('The spoiling of Thebes'),[162] a prose version of the 'Thebaid' of Statius. The unfinished 'Achilleid' by Statius is used to present the *macgnímartha Aichil* ('the boyhood deeds of Achilles'), incorporated in a version of 'Togail Troí'.[163] Fifthly, 'The history of Alexander the Great'.[164] Here may be added the pseudo-correspondence between

---

[155] *Rev. Celt.*, ix (1888), pp 447–96.
[156] Ed. Lucius Gwynn in *Archiv. Hib.*, iv (1915), pp 199–214.
[157] See W. B. Stanford, 'Towards a history of classical influences in Ireland' in *R.I.A. Proc.*, lxx (1970), sect. C, pp 13–91, esp. pp 33–8.
[158] Ibid., p. 33.
[159] R. I. Best and M. A. O'Brien (ed.), *Togail Troí* (Dublin, 1966).
[160] George Calder (ed. and trans.), *Imtheachta Aeniasa: the Irish Aeneid* (London, 1907).
[161] Robert T. Meyer (ed.), *Merugud Uilix maic Leirtis* (Dublin, 1958).
[162] George Calder (ed. and trans.), *Togail na Tebe: the Thebaid of Statius* (Cambridge, 1922).
[163] There is also a poetic version based on the prose in N.L.I., MS G 3; it was copied by Ádhamh Ó Cianáin (d. 1371) from the Book of Glendalough.
[164] Ed. Erik Peters in *Z.C.P.*, xxx (1967), pp 71–264.

Alexander and Dindymus based upon 'De more Brachmannorum', attributed to St Ambrose.[165] Sixthly, 'In cath catharda' ('The civil war'), based upon Lucan's 'Pharsalia'.[166]

The whole matter of adaptations of classical texts in Ireland deserves investigation[167] and may be important for a study of the textual history of the classical texts themselves. Stanford writes: 'A question that deserves further consideration from classical scholars is that of the texts used by these Irish translators. One recent editor of Lucan's "Civil war" has touched on it briefly, and cites a few notable variant readings implied in the Irish version.'[168] As to the date of these adaptations, Mac Eoin suggests that 'Togail Troí' was adapted into Irish in the tenth century, and that from this all our extant versions derive.[169] Similarly Erik Peters, in his edition of the 'Alexandersage', suggests that the archetype dates, at latest, from the tenth century. A matter worth investigating also is the provenance of the surviving manuscripts of such texts. The general tendency is for such tales to exist in manuscripts from the Leinster area, on the one hand, and from north Connacht and south-west Ulster on the other. The Alexander story is typical. It is found in the fourteenth-century 'Leabhar Breac', into which it was copied from the Book of Berchán of Cluain Sost, a manuscript from the monastery of Clonsast in County Offaly. Otherwise it is preserved in the north Connacht manuscript, the Book of Ballymote, where it is found in association with 'Togail Troí', 'Merugud Uilix', 'Imthechta Aeniasa', and the correspondence between Alexander and Dindymus. It may be suggested here that the northern tradition came into being from the migration northwards of certain Leinster families, such as the family of Ó Duibhgeannáin, as a result of the reform of the church or normanisation in the twelfth century.

---

[165] Ed. Kuno Meyer, *Anecdota from Irish manuscripts*, v (Halle, 1913), pp 1–8.

[166] Standish H. O'Grady (ed.), 'The war of Pompey and Caesar: a fragment' in idem (ed. and trans.), *Caithréim Thoirdhealbhaigh* (2 vols, London, 1928–9), i, 193–224; ii, 202–40.

[167] See now Neasa Ní Shéaghdha, 'Translations and adaptations into Irish' in *Celtica*, xvi (1984), pp 107–24.

[168] Stanford, 'Classical influences', p. 38; the reference is to K. J. Getly, *M. Annaei Lucani de bello civili: liber I* (Cambridge, 1940), pp xiii–xiv.

[169] *Z.C.P.*, xxvii (1960–61), pp 201–2.

CHAPTER XIV

# Manuscripts
# and palaeography

WILLIAM O'SULLIVAN

NOTHING is more crucial for the history of a culture than the accurate dating of texts, and for this scholars naturally turn to palaeography, whose primary function is to date and place manuscripts. Unhappily, even in the hands of the leading practitioners of the art—for science it is not—Ludwig Traube, E. A. Lowe, or T. J. Brown—the study of Irish script is still far from fulfilling this function. However, although general agreement has not been reached, there have been considerable advances from the early part of the twentieth century, when the Book of Kells could be placed in the seventh century. A great deal of the work has been done by linguists and art histor-ians, and—as we shall see in the case of the Book of Durrow—it is time palaeographers cried halt and started to put their own house in order. While recognising the importance of the art historians' contribution, we need to be aware of the dangers of their methods, especially placing objects in sequence and then labelling them chronologically in a semi-mechanical way, which seems to make little allowance for likely cultural and geographical diversity. The end-product—subsequently taken too literally, particularly by workers in related fields—inevitably leads to confusing results.

Ireland, because of its troubled history, has lost almost all of its earlier manuscripts. Apart from a few preserved in Ireland as relics of saints, most of the survivors are to be found outside the country, some of the most important being now in England. Because the Irish taught the English to write, this has led to very considerable confusion and controversy as to which hands are Irish and which Anglo-Saxon. To the ninth-century librar-ian at St Gallen, in Switzerland, such manuscripts were simply *libri Scottice scripti* ('books written in the Irish fashion').[1] When the father of the study of palaeography, Jean Mabillon, published his *De re diplomatica* in 1681, he distinguished two types of script, literary and documentary, and five regional

---

[1] St Gallen, Stiftsbibliothek, MS 728, in Gustav Becker, *Catalogi bibliothecarum antiqui* (Bonn, 1885), no. xxii, p. 43; Johannes Duft and Peter Meyer, *The Irish miniatures in the cathedral library of St Gall* (Berne, 1954), pp 40–41.

varieties, one being *Saxonica*, none *Scottica*.[2] The Italian palaeographer, Scipione Maffei, emphasised the essential unity of all Latin writing, but introduced the threefold division—still in use—of majuscule, minuscule, and cursive.[3] Mabillon's *Saxonica* included only what we now call 'insular minuscule'. The recognition of the regional character of the majuscule came in 1705 from Humfrey Wanley, Robert Harley's librarian and the first English scholar of script, who labelled it Anglo-Saxon.[4] The Rev. Charles O'Conor in 1814 riposted with a list of Irish manuscripts that included the Lindisfarne Gospels, and even today these scripts remain a battlefield.[5]

Ludwig Traube first proposed the very simple solution, which is now generally accepted, of calling the scripts 'insular', but that did not still the combat.[6] W. M. Lindsay (who will be ever remembered for his pioneering work in the study and regionalisation of abbreviations) continued the struggle to find a touchstone that would distinguish Irish from early Anglo-Saxon script, and came up with a version of the *-tur* abbreviation as a sure mark of the latter.[7] To rely on this alone, however, would be to ignore the very great likelihood that a scribe readily takes over such things from his exemplar.[8] Another test was the scribe's name, where (perhaps following an Irish tradition) it was available, but to rely on this alone might be to ignore the important matter of his upbringing; besides, the name too might have been taken over from the exemplar. The presence of glosses in Irish or Anglo-Saxon is also useful, but is sometimes employed without establishing their status (e.g., whether or not in the scribe's hand and therefore likely to have belonged to the exemplar). Thus the Vatican manuscript Palatinus Latinus 68 can be described as employing an Irish style of writing and decoration, although it has the particular type of *-tur* symbol classified by Lindsay as English, and Anglo-Saxon glosses. These, and the scribe's name, Edilberict filius Berectfridi, probably belonged to the exemplar.[9] Similarly, the glossed Epistles of St Paul in Cambridge, Trinity College MS B.10.5, which also have the 'tell-tale' *-tur* symbol, are described (by Lowe) as being the work of

[2] Jean Mabillon, *De re diplomatica* (Paris, 1709 [1st ed., Paris, 1681]), pp 49, 52, 351.

[3] Scipione Maffei, *Istoria diplomatica che serve d'introduzione all' arte critica in tal materia* (Padua, 1727).

[4] Humfrey Wanley, *Librorum veterum septentrionalium . . . catalogus* (Oxford, 1705), sig. c$^v$–c2$^r$, pp 81–2.

[5] Charles O'Conor, *Rerum Hibernicarum scriptores veteres* (4 vols, Buckingham, 1814–26), i, pp cxxix–ccxxxvii.

[6] Ludwig Traube, *Vorlesungen und Abhandlungen*, ed. Franz Boll (3 vols, Munich, 1909–20), i, 95–100.

[7] W. M. Lindsay, *Notae Latinae: an account of abbreviations in Latin MSS of the early minuscule period (ca. 700–850)* (Cambridge, 1915), pp 373, 378–9.

[8] An illustration of this danger is provided (*Hermathena*, xl (1910), pp 44–5) when John Gwynn, worried by the presence of Old Latin passages in the Garland of Howth (see below) consulted Lindsay, who, without seeing the manuscript again, judged that the abbreviations indicated that it could not be later than the eighth century.

[9] Vatican City, Biblioteca Apostolica, MS Pal. Lat. 68; CLA (see n. 12), i, 78.

an Irishman, because the script is closest to that of the Milan Commentary on the Psalms (which is heavily glossed in Irish), but as written in Northumbria, because it contains a local Anglo-Saxon gloss, and the book was later in the library of Durham cathedral.[10] However, if the local gloss had been simply taken over from the exemplar, an Irishman could have written it anywhere.[11] E. A. Lowe, the twelve volumes of whose *Codices Latini antiquiores* are the essential tool for any judgement on Latin writing before 800, played a crucial role in the controversy.[12] Because Willibrord (the founder of Echternach) was a Northumbrian, Lowe thought the scripts associated with that monastery could be labelled Anglo-Saxon,[13] forgetting that the mission was based on Rath Melsigi in Ireland,[14] where the saint had spent the previous twelve years before his departure on the Frisian mission (A.D. 690), and that the scribes who accompanied him, young men judging by the quality of the scripts, were most likely to have been Irish. Most recently, Julian Brown, who did more splendid work in the insular field in recent years than any other man, struggled in vain to establish a clear path through the thicket.[15] He had early been an admirer of François Masai, pre-war keeper of manuscripts in the Bibliothèque Royale in Brussels, who, from a prison cell in wartime Belgium, elaborated the notion that all the great majuscule manuscripts were the product of northern England. Brown's career would—though unconsciously—seem to have been dedicated to the glory of Northumbria, particularly his creation of the Lindisfarne scriptorium, and also, to a degree, to the Italianising influence—as he saw it—of Wearmouth–Jarrow. Despite this, his groundwork is solid and perspicacity acute, even if some of his conclusions may not abide. This would seem to be the case with his terminology for the scripts, and the chronology of his proposed sequence of phases of insular, worked out for what he thought could be regarded as Anglo-Saxon examples, only to find those phases apparently contemporaneous in his Irish examples.[16]

---

[10] Cambridge, Trinity College, MS B.10.5; CLA (see n. 12), ii, 133.

[11] Próinséas Ní Chatháin, 'Notes on the Würzburg glosses' in Ní Chatháin & Richter, *Ire. & Christendom*, pp 190–202: 192–4.

[12] *Codices Latini antiquiores: a guide to Latin manuscripts before* A.D. *800* (12 vols, Oxford, 1934–71), cited below as CLA followed by the volume-number in roman numerals and the plate number of the manuscript in arabic. Addenda with plates will be found in Virginia Brown and Bernhard Bischoff, 'Addenda to CLA' in *Medieval Studies*, xlvii (1985), pp 317–66.

[13] CLA ii, pp xvi–xviii.

[14] Dáibhí Ó Cróinín, 'Rath Melsigi, Willibrord, and the earliest Echternach manuscripts' in *Peritia*, iii (1984), pp 17–49.

[15] Particularly in two articles: 'The Irish element in the insular system of scripts' in Löwe, *Die Iren*, i, 101–19, and 'The oldest Irish manuscripts and their late antique background' in Ní Chatháin & Richter, *Ire. & Europe*, pp 311–27, cited hereafter as 'The insular system of scripts' and 'The oldest Irish manuscripts' (reprinted in Janet Bately, Michelle B. Brown, and Jane Roberts (ed.), *A palaeographer's view: selected writings of Julian Brown* (London, 1993), pp 201–41).

[16] 'The insular system of scripts', p. 111.

Apart from Brown's work, the most important recent contributions to the study of the problem have been two articles by Malcolm Parkes on St Boniface's hand and on the Wearmouth–Jarrow scriptorium. A number of related annotating hands have been ascribed to Boniface (who would have learned to write in the last quarter of the seventh century), and Parkes narrows them down to a few examples; but when it comes to deciding whether the scribe was Irish or English, he is particularly influenced by the southern English background accepted for Oxford, Bodl. MS Douce 140 (a continental-style half-uncial manuscript with annotations in the Boniface hand),[16a] by Lindsay's judgement of the abbreviations, and by the use of runes for reference marks, which he believes, in the present state of our knowledge, makes it more likely that the annotator was English rather than Irish. Naturally, his decision in favour of Boniface rather than another had to be determined by the theological content of the annotations.[17] The minuscule hand, which was presumably introduced to southern England by Irish missionaries, is also found in a letter written c.704 by Wealdhere, bishop of London.[18] The Irish were still using this style of script at the begining of the ninth century, when a monk at Reichenau wrote the well-known Old Irish poem about the cat, Pangur Bán, in a manuscript now at St Paul in Carinthia.[19]

In his second and more important article, Parkes established the manner and criteria by which the scriptorium of Wearmouth–Jarrow bred out of the insular minuscule, common up to this point to both the English and the Irish, a variety of script that can properly be labelled Anglo-Saxon. This was to develop independently and to persist until the English reception of the Caroline script in the tenth century. Parkes demonstrated the development brilliantly, from a single manuscript, the Leningrad (now St Petersburg) Bede,[20] written by four scribes, the oldest closest to the Irish style, the younger showing the characteristic Anglo-Saxon compression and lengthening of the descenders under Merovingian influence, *f*, *p*, *r*, and *s* being written cursively, with the stems tending to split. Especially notable is

---

[16a] CLA, ii, 237.

[17] M. B. Parkes, 'The handwriting of St Boniface: a reassessment of the problems' in *Beiträge zur Geschichte der deutschen Sprache und Literatur*, xcviii (1976), pp 161–79 (reprinted in Parkes, *Scribes, scripts and readers: studies in the communication, presentation and dissemination of medieval texts* (London, 1991), pp 121–42). Since the Book of Armagh (A.D. 807) is the most securely dated example of the script, the possibility remains that the Boniface hand was written about 800 and that the letter in the same script written by Wealdhere, bishop of London, may be a later copy; see next note.

[18] Pierre Chaplais, 'The letter from Bishop Wealdhere...' in M. B. Parkes and A. G. Watson (ed.), *Medieval scribes, manuscripts and libraries: essays presented to N. R. Ker* (London, 1978). Such hands cannot at present be distinguished as Irish or Anglo-Saxon.

[19] St Paul in Kärnten, Benediktinerstift, MS sec. xxv. d. 86, f. 1$^v$.

[20] St Petersburg Public Library, Cod. Q.V.I. 18; CLA, xi, 1612; M. B. Parkes, *The scriptorium of Wearmouth–Jarrow*. Jarrow Lecture, 1982 (reprinted in Parkes, *Scribes, scripts & readers*, pp 93–120).

the long half-uncial *r*, the first stroke of which descends scarcely at all in Irish minuscule before the eleventh century. While the genesis of the Anglo-Saxon minuscule and its separation from the Irish can thus be placed in Northumbria (and perhaps towards the middle of the eighth century), the pace of its conquest of the whole of England has still to be measured.

The earliest surviving Irish manuscripts, like 'Usserianus Primus' (pl. 19),[21] probably dating from the sixth century, or the Cathach (pl. 20), probably from the seventh, are, unlike their continental counterparts, written on calfskin.[22] In 'Usserianus', however, the hair-side is very lightly scraped, leaving a strong colour contrast between the two sides, as is the case with contemporary continental sheepskins. The Irish economy was, uniquely in western Europe, a cattle-rearing one, and in consequence the scribes naturally turned to vellum made from calfskin instead of parchment made from sheepskin, which was the norm elsewhere. In time, the vellum-makers learned to scrape the skin so thoroughly that often it is difficult to tell the hair-side from the flesh-side with the naked eye. This was easier too because the skin is structurally homogeneous, unlike sheepskin, which is layered, and the surface layer is readily broken through, a matter of regular occurrence when corrections are made to a text. Apart from this, however, the insular scriptorium seems to have been a museum of codicological practices abandoned on the Continent, some as early as the fourth century.

The roll is the oldest form of book, and *liber* still meant 'roll' in the middle of the third century. The papyrologist Sir Eric Turner, studying the problems connected with the triumph of the codex over the roll, successfully established the priority of the papyrus over the parchment codex.[23] Papyrus was widely available throughout the empire, and the normal medium of book production. In fact, it was still available for that purpose at Luxeuil at the end of the eighth century, and continued in use at the papal chancery into the eleventh century.[24] Large papyrus codices appear early, whereas early parchment codices are small or intermediate in size. The splendid later ones were, Turner believes, consciously modelled on the large papyrus codices, but were intended to surpass them in elegance and durability. Papyrus is made by hammering together two layers of the papyrus reed, one vertical the other horizontal, so that on the two sides of the leaf the fibres lie in different directions. Exactly the same problem was to be posed by the hair- and flesh-sides of the parchment leaf. Quaternions, or sections of four bifolia, were

---

[21] T.C.D. MS 55 (A.4.15); CLA, ii, 271.

[22] My former belief that they were sheepskin has been corrected by Anthony Cains, director of the conservation laboratory, T.C.D. (see *Peritia*, iii (1985), p. 353).

[23] E. G. Turner, *The typology of the early codex* (Philadelphia, 1977).

[24] Bernhard Bischoff, *Latin palaeography: antiquity and the middle ages*, translated by Dáibhí Ó Cróinín and David Ganz (Cambridge, 1990), pp 8, 35, cited below as Bischoff, *Latin palaeography*. The first edition (Berlin, 1979) was entitled *Paläographie des römischen Altertums und des abendländischen Mittelalters*.

pretty standard for Latin codices from the fourth century, but this was less so with Greek codices, which tended to favour the quinion, or section of five bifolia. Just as the quaternion became the norm for Latin codices, so also did the regular succession of hair facing hair and flesh facing flesh. Strangely, Irish scribal practice does not follow the Latin west in a number of striking ways, but seems rather to echo the experience of the early papyrus codex. Thus the quaternion was never adopted as standard, and the Irish, if they favoured any number of leaves for a section, preferred the quinion, giving the name *cín* for 'book' in Old Irish—whence it passed into Anglo-Saxon as *cine*—but normally the number of leaves varied from section to section. Julian Brown wrote of the quinion being the rule in the Book of Kells, but the great majority of gatherings in that manuscript are, in fact, irregular.[25] Similarly, the Irish were generally indifferent to hair facing hair and flesh facing flesh within the codex, as had become standard on the Continent, but effective scraping prevented a serious colour contrast. It is not altogether fanciful to see the descendants of that most clumsy papyrus form, the primitive single-section codex, in the Books of Mulling (pl. 43) and Dimma (pl. 42), or in the Cadmug Gospels in Fulda, where most of the individual gospels are written as single sections. When it was new, the papyrus codex was regarded as second class. Fine manuscripts continued to be written on rolls, and the finer they were the narrower were the columns, whereas the early codex was written as a single column, in long lines. Later, the finest vellum codices were written in two or more columns. Here again the Irish scribes diverged, and some of their finest manuscripts, like the Books of Durrow and Kells, are in long lines.

An explanation for such anomalies can best be found in the history of the Irish church. Christianity reached Ireland perhaps partly from Gaul but mainly from Britain from the fourth century onwards. During the fifth century the barbarian invasions must have reduced contact with the Mediterranean world, but not, however, before the newest religious development, monasticism, had a chance to take root in the country. Irish society was rural. There were no cities where diocesan administration could be based, as in the parts of Europe that had belonged to the Roman empire, so the church came to be organized in monastic *paruchiae* or hegemonies. The monk-bishops played no part in administration, which was in the hands of abbots. By the middle of the sixth century, when more regular contact with the Continent was resumed in a wave of missionary activity, the Irish clergy

[25] T. J. Brown, 'Northumbria and the Book of Kells' in *Anglo-Saxon England*, i (1972), pp 219–46 (reprinted in Janet Bately, Michelle B. Brown, and Jane Roberts (ed.), *A palaeographer's view: selected writings of Julian Brown* (London, 1993), pp 97–124); cf. Roger Powell, 'The Book of Kells, the Book of Durrow: comments on the vellum, the make-up and other aspects' in *Scriptorium*, x (1956), pp 3–21; Bernard Meehan, 'The division of hands in the Book of Kells...' in Peter Fox (ed.), *The Book of Kells* (Lucerne, 1990), pp 249–56.

were found to be preserving not only a strange codicology but other unusual ecclesiastical practices, like the form of tonsure and the way of calculating the date of Easter. These preferences they are known to have shared with their British neighbours (not unnaturally, considering the source of Irish Christianity), and the Welsh held to them even more tenaciously. Britain must, equally naturally, be seen as the source of Irish script.

The British climate—unlike the Egyptian—does not preserve papyrus, so that it looked as if it would never be known how the Romans in Britain and the Romano-British wrote. Thanks, however, to the remarkable discoveries of Robin Birley, excavating at Vindolanda (a military station on Hadrian's wall) in 1973, we now know that they wrote just like their contemporaries in Egypt. Birley unearthed a quantity of what looked like oily wood-shavings, which turned out to be letters and documents written with ink on shavings of birch and alder wood, but generally legible now only in infra-red photographs.[26] The documents were written around the year A.D. 100, and display two types of handwriting: a formal script (rustic capitals), and an informal one (ancient Roman cursive).

In the course of the third century the latter script gave way to 'new Roman cursive', and although no local examples have yet been found, this must have been the informal script written by St Patrick, since it was current throughout the empire. By the fifth century, when the Romans withdrew from Britain, rustic had given way to uncial and to a somewhat less formal script, half-uncial, for book-work. All of these scripts could have been current in fifth-century Britain and available for transmission to Ireland by the missionaries. St Kilian's gospel-book (pl. 21) has been proposed as an example of Irish uncial.[27] Though the case is not generally regarded as a strong one, there are decorative connections with the psalter called the Cathach (pl. 20), particularly the spade-shaped horns on the initial *s*.[28] These two manuscripts also share the curious dissected *s* where the three strokes forming the letter are not joined together. This also occurs in early uncial manuscripts. Traditionally, this sixth-century gospel-book is believed to have been found with Kilian's body, though it would have been about a hundred years old in his day. Later additions in Merovingian script, roughly contemporary with the saint, have led palaeographers to claim that the manuscript was written in France. It might perhaps be considered as a sample of the sort of uncial that inspired the creation of insular majuscule. The decoration with

[26] A. K. Bowman and J. D. Thomas, *Vindolanda: the Latin writing-tablets* (London, 1983).
[27] Würzburg, Universitätsbibliothek, MS M.p.th.q.1a; CLA, ix, 1429; E. M. Thompson, *Handbook of Greek and Latin palaeography* (Oxford, 1912), p. 372.
[28] R.I.A., MS 12.R.33; CLA, ii, 266; Françoise Henry, 'Les débuts de la miniature irlandaise' in *Gazette des Beaux-Arts*, xxvi (1944), pp 34–44 (reprinted in F. Henry and Geneviève Marsh-Micheli, *Studies in early Christian and medieval art* (3 vols, London, 1983–5), ii, 25–7; all citations below are from this second volume of Henry, *Studies*).

spades and spirals, and the size of some of the initials—in one case half the width of the column[29]—might perhaps argue for the presence of some such manuscript in sixth-century Ireland. Brown claimed that the book-trade in late Roman Britain was not so organised that it could produce fine books in formal script, and perhaps uncial may not have been found in the fifth-century missionary's baggage. However, I do not believe that he could have managed without, at the very least, half-uncial script for gospels and service books, given the lighting conditions that must have prevailed: flickering lamps in dark churches and such small windows as there were, presumably covered with skins. The pocket-gospels, such as the Books of Mulling[30] and Dimma,[31] or indeed the Book of Armagh (pl. 44),[32] were personal, not liturgical books, and it is notable in the volume known as the Stowe Missal[33]—which combines a missal (pl. 22) with a pocket copy of part of St John's gospel (pl. 23)—that only the former is in large formal script.

Half-uncial was known to the Irish as the African script[34]—a witness perhaps to its fourth-century origins in North Africa, then the intellectual centre of the empire. However, the strongest evidence for the transmission of the half-uncial script to Ireland is the survival of two manuscripts, 'Usserianus Primus' and the 'Milan Basilius' (pl. 24), and the Springmount set of waxed tablets (pl. 25). From the damage the first has suffered, it was clearly enshrined as the relic of some saint. It contains a copy of the four gospels in the Old Latin version, which would have been in course of being superseded by the Vulgate in Ireland in the second half of the sixth century.[35] The 'Basilius' was a Bobbio manuscript, and could have been brought there by the founder, Columbanus, in 613.[36] This would seem to be a most significant survival, considering the reputation for learning enjoyed by the Irish monks, that Basil was a pioneer in the education of his monks, and that Columbanus himself was a very learned man. Judging by the other surviving half-uncial manuscripts, the script of these two, with flat-headed *g* and *t*, is quite unlike anything being written elsewhere at that time. This is not surprising, when the relative isolation of the Irish church since the fifth century is remembered. The waxed tablets, found in a bog in County Antrim, are described by

[29] Würzburg, MS M.p.th.q.1a, f. 252.
[30] T.C.D., MS 60 (A.1.15); CLA, ii, 276–7. For a detailed study of the 'pocket' gospels, see Patrick McGurk, 'The Irish pocket gospel book' in *Sacris Erudiri*, viii (1956), pp 249–70.
[31] T.C.D., MS 59 (A.4.23); CLA, ii, 275.
[32] T.C.D., MS 52; CLA, ii, 270.
[33] R.I.A., MS D.II.3; CLA, ii, 267–8.
[34] Bischoff, *Latin palaeography*, pp 76, 86, 211 n.
[35] T.C.D., MS 55 (A. 4.15); for a study of the palaeography, see William O'Sullivan, 'The palaeographical background to the Book of Kells' in Felicity O'Mahony (ed.), *The Book of Kells: proceedings of a conference at Trinity College Dublin, 6–9 Sept. 1992* (Aldershot, 1994), pp 175–82; T. K. Abbott (ed.), *Evangeliorum versio antehieronymiana ex codice Usseriano* (2 vols, Dublin, 1884).
[36] Milan, Biblioteca Ambrosiana, MS C 26 sup.; CLA, ii, 312.

Lowe as early Irish minuscule, but their angularities are clearly due to the stylus, not the script, which is the formal script of 'Usserianus'. Bella Schauman, who has made the closest study of the tablets, has also been misled into seeing vestiges there of 'ancient common writing', which went out of use in the Roman world in the third century.[37]

The colophon in 'Usserianus', marking the end of Luke's gospel and the beginning of Mark's, alone of these three examples includes uncial *d*, *n*, *r*, and *s*. This would suggest a deliberate attempt to write the colophon in another (and higher) script, a feature of early manuscripts.[38] Such oddities in this formal script as the frequent use of the tall *e* in ligature point to early sources, when the canon of half-uncial was still fluid.[39] The *et* ligature, which is such a noticeable feature of Irish script (and which became the basis on which the artists of the Book of Kells built some of their most ingenious designs) disappears from continental script after the fifth century.[40] 'Usserianus' was written by two scribes: one writing the first two gospels, Matthew and John, and the other, Luke and Mark. It is most instructive to see the differences in their ways of handling the same problems. The second man favours the early *li* ligature and the *s*-shaped *g* in ligature, which goes back to the fifth century but continues to prevail in insular for several centuries. Both the 'Usserianus' and 'Basilius' scribes include minuscule *n* as an alternative, but, apart from the colophon in the former noticed above, uncial *d* occurs only in corrections.

Perhaps in some ways the most significant difference between the 'Usserianus' and the 'Basilius' is the tucked-in tail of the *g* in the former, which will be transmitted to the insular majuscule. This *g* seems to involve a fourth stroke and is characteristic of the heyday of the majuscule, disappearing in the course of the ninth century to be replaced by a round-bottomed *g* like the early half-uncial type. Another symptom pointing to early sources is the first 'Usserianus' scribe's use of red for the opening words of text divisions. The second in the same places occasionally uses red dots on the black opening letters. The 'Basilius' uses red for the headings and occasionally red dots on the rare small initials. The approach stroke, which produces thickening of the ascenders (a feature of early half-uncial), sometimes opens deceptively

[37] Dublin, National Museum of Ireland, 1914:2; CLA, ii, 1684; E. C. R. Armstrong and R. A. S. Macalister, 'Wooden box with leaves indented and waxed found near Springmount Bog, Co. Antrim' in *R.S.A.I. Jn.*, l (1920), pp 160–66; D. H. Wright, 'The tablets from Springmount Bog: a key to early Irish palaeography' in *American Journal of Archaeology*, lxvii (1963), p. 219; Bella Schauman, 'The emergence and progress of Irish script to the year 700' (Ph.D. dissertation, Toronto, 1974), pp 329–69. Schauman provides a most thorough palaeographical analysis of the hands of the Cathach and the tablets.

[38] Bischoff, *Latin palaeography*, pp 78–9.

[39] Tall *e* was to persist in Irish script into the nineteenth century, but not necessarily for ligatures.

[40] CLA, ii, 271 (n. 21), f. 149ᵛ; T.C.D. MS 58 (A.1.6); E. H. Alton and P. Meyer (ed.), *Evangeliorum quattuor Codex Cennanensis* (3 vols (i–ii facsimile, iii commentary), Berne, 1950).

like a loop in 'Usserianus', and as a hook-shaped serif in the 'Basilius'. The tablets contain parts of Psalms 30–32 and were clearly the work of a practised scribe, writing rapidly and employing a well-established canon. The *a* is usually made in two strokes, often left open; the ascenders can have either a very slight loop or a hook.

These three examples altogether lack the characteristics of developed insular script: the triangular wedge-shaped serifs, the inclusion as alternatives of the uncial forms of *d*, *r* and *s*, and punctuation by the developed use of initials and diminuendo, where the letters following an enlarged initial gradually diminish to text size.[41]

A palimpsest half-uncial manuscript from Bobbio (pl. 28) dating from before 622 (and perhaps from Columbanus's own day) provides a useful contrast with this native half-uncial. Bella Schauman, who has made a close study of it, is inclined to label certain of the hands as Irish.[42] She is certainly right in seeing Irish influence in the decoration (as Françoise Henry had done before her),[43] and in the diminuendo. The script however—though some of the writers may have been Irish, as she says—is at the very most Franco-Irish, as easy local legibility would have required, and such as one might expect to emerge from a mixed community like Luxeuil or Bobbio, with the continental aspects, such as the hooked tops to the *g* and *t*, predominating. The long-standing dispute over the location of the Luxeuil script, whether in that house or in northern Italy, must be connected with the Columbanus heritage in both. Columbanus was educated in the middle of the sixth century and was already in his forties when he set out for Gaul. This would seem to suggest that the explosion of learning in the Irish monasteries, and the consequent need for the multiplication of books, must predate his departure. The end of the relative isolation of the Irish church would then have provided suitable conditions for the development of a new script. Traube (and after him Lowe) saw the origins of insular in a variety of half-uncial they called 'quarter-uncial', which Bischoff preferred to call 'cursive half-uncial' and Brown, more recently, 'literary cursive'.[44] It is characterised by the mixed alphabetical forms that were later to be standard in insular majuscule. The few surviving whole books written in the script (generally found only as an annotating hand in early uncial manuscripts) are

---

[41] The considerable part played by the Irish in the development of punctuation is splendidly outlined by M. B. Parkes, 'The contribution of insular scribes of the 7th and 8th centuries to the "grammar of legibility"' in A. Maieru (ed.), *Grafia e interpunzione del latino nel medioevo: Seminario Internazionale Roma, 27–29 Settembre 1984* (Rome, 1987), pp 15–30 (revised ed. in Parkes, *Scribes, scripts & readers*, pp 1–18).

[42] Milan, Biblioteca Ambrosiana, MS S 45 sup.; CLA, iii, 365; Bella Schauman, 'The Irish script of the MS Milan, Biblioteca Ambrosiana, S.45 sup. (ante ca. 625)' in *Scriptorium*, xxxii (1978), pp 3–18.

[43] Henry, 'Débuts de la miniature irlandaise'.

[44] 'The insular system of scripts', p. 103.

mostly grammatical—a particular interest of the Irish, who had to learn their Latin from scratch. These books date from the fifth century and seem to have come down through the Bobbio library.[45] An example of what Lowe saw as a related script, an offset of four pages of Arator, 'De actibus aposto-lorum', was found by Neil Ker on the wooden boards of the fifteenth-century binding of a twelfth-century English manuscript. He published it jointly with Lowe, who, although he claimed to find the nearest parallel in the fifth-century primary script of the palimpsested part of the Bobbio Missal, dated it to the seventh century, perhaps because its alphabet is somewhat different, and word division, which was introduced by the Irish, more advanced. It is in fact not far from the Basilius, though much less formal and with the tendency to hook the tops of *g* and *t*, as in continental half-uncial.[46] For the place of writing he suggested north Italy or France, but something of the kind must have been available in sixth-century Ireland, though this particular piece is not likely to have had a Welsh or Irish origin.

The little psalter known as the Cathach (from its having been regarded as a relic of St Columba and frequently carried into battle to bring victory) is generally accepted as the earliest surviving example of the insular majuscule script (pl. 20), in Lowe's term. David Wright, however, prefers to see the Milan Orosius (pl. 27)[47] in that position, and it certainly has a more tentative air, lacking the assurance of the Cathach, but this may be the scribe's fault. The flat-topped *t* would, however, seem to make his proposal that the script originated at Bobbio most unlikely. Françoise Henry remarked the striking decorative parallel between the opening of the Orosius and the opening of a late-seventh-century Luxeuil manuscript, with the implication that the style had survived in that house from the sixth-century Irish mission.[48] Earlier the script of these manuscripts had been called 'Irish half-uncial', and Julian Brown revived this name, rejecting Lowe's wisdom in choosing a neutral term with no very strict prior meaning, and now (as we have seen above) there is, in the script of 'Usserianus', a better candidate for this title.[49] The current theory is that the inventors of the majuscule were inspired by the sight of uncial manuscripts.[50] The shrinking of ascenders and descenders to produce a solid bar of text across the page would certainly seem to ape one of the most striking characteristics of Roman uncial. There must have been a

[45] Naples, Biblioteca Nazionale, MS Lat.2; CLA, iii, 397a, 398.

[46] N. R. Ker, E. A. Lowe, and A. P. McKinlay, 'A new fragment of Arator in the Bodleian' in *Speculum*, xix (1944), pp 351–2 (reprinted in E. A. Lowe, *Palaeographical papers* (2 vols, Oxford, 1972), i, 345–7); Parkes, *Pause and effect*, p. 23.

[47] Milan, Biblioteca Ambrosiana, MS D 23 sup.; CLA, iii, 328; Alban Dold and Leo Eizenhöfer (ed.), *Das irische Palimpsestsakramentar im Clm 14429 der Staatsbibliothek München* (Beuron, 1964), p. 36.

[48] 'Débuts de la miniature irlandaise', p. 33 (reprinted in Henry, *Studies*, p. 27).

[49] CLA, iv, p. vi.

[50] 'The insular system of scripts', p. 105.

clearly felt need for a more solemn script for liturgical purposes than the native half-uncial. However, rather than imitate the uncial—as the English were to do at Wearmouth–Jarrow at the end of the seventh century—or the contemporary continental half-uncial—as the southern English may have done at about the same time—the Irish preferred to upgrade an existing informal script, the cursive half-uncial. This would be in keeping with the confident expansive character of the Irish church in the second half of the sixth century. Timothy O'Neill—himself a calligrapher—considers that the Cathach was written rapidly, the whole psalter taking no longer than seventy-two hours to complete,[51] and this might serve to reinforce the notion that the insular majuscule was already well established as a script style and that its invention ought to be placed in the second half of the sixth century at latest. As Brown pointed out, two of the elements of the decoration of the Cathach, the fish and the cross on a dais, reflect the style of a Roman uncial manuscript now at Troyes, a copy of Pope Gregory's 'Pastoral care' dating from the lifetime of the author.[52] This conceivably may be the very copy that Gregory sent to Columbanus at Luxeuil in 594.[53] The emperor Tiberius II (578–82) introduced the cross on a dais on the reverse of his coins,[54] so if Columba wrote the Cathach it must have been towards the very end of his life.

Stanley Morison felt that the initial acceptance of the triangular serif, which was to remain the most abiding feature of insular script, would have required the weight of great authority behind it, such as its use by some very renowned scribe.[55] Ireland had many famous scribes, but none more revered than Columba. F. J. Byrne believes that the oldest surviving example of the insular majuscule is to be found in the inscription on a pillar stone on Inchagoill Island in Lough Corrib (County Galway), which can be dated by its language to the sixth century.[56] It is not certain, however, that the insular serif is used on the stone.

The north of England was to be the scene of the extension of Columba's Iona-based mission to Scotland, which had begun in 563, when St Aidan founded a daughter house of Iona on the island of Lindisfarne in 635, and here Wilfrid was educated. He in turn is credited with the education of

---

[51] Timothy P. O'Neill, *The Irish hand* (Dublin, 1984), p. 61.

[52] Troyes, Bibliothèque Municipale, MS 504; CLA, vi, 838; Brown, *A palaeographer's view* (London, 1993), p. 193. Brown is, however, unduly generous in ascribing his own discovery to Carl Nordenfalk, who, in 'Before the Book of Durrow' in *Acta Archaeologica*, xviii (1947), pp 141–74: 156, refers to a less striking parallel in another late-sixth-century Italian manuscript.

[53] G. S. M. Walker (ed. and trans.), *Sancti Columbani opera* (Dublin, 1957), p. 11.

[54] Stanley Morison, *Politics and script* (Oxford, 1972), p. 99.

[55] Ibid., p. 147.

[56] *The Irish hand*, introduction by F. J. Byrne, p. xii. The absence of triangular serifs (judging from the photographs kindly supplied by the Office of Public Works) might suggest that it predates the invention of the majuscule, but inscriptions cut in stone tend to vary in this matter. However, J. G. Higgins shows some in his drawing of this stone, *The early Christian cross slabs, pillar stones and related monuments of County Galway, Ireland* (Oxford, 1987), ii, fig. 31A.

Willibrord, during his time in charge of the monastery of Ripon.[57] Willibrord's handwriting survives in a marginal note in his Calendar (pl. 30).[58] Although the note has suffered restoration, it retains enough early features (like open *a* and tall *c* in medial and final positions) to inspire some confidence that its original type can still be identified. The Calendar probably dates from the first decade of the eighth century, but Willibrord's hand would have been formed in the middle of the seventh, and the origins of insular minuscule, a description that fits Willibrord''s writing, must be placed at latest in the first half of that century.

In time, the minuscule was to replace the majuscule as the normal Irish formal script, characterized by the use of a pointed as opposed to a more rounded *a*. One of the earliest surviving books in a large 'set' minuscule—as Brown terms it[59]—is the Echternach Gospels, called after the monastery founded by Willibrord in what is now Luxembourg. A colophon indicates that the exemplar was in southern Italy in the sixth century. The Rev. Martin McNamara has found that the primary text of Echternach is closest to an Armagh manuscript, the ninth-century MacDurnan Gospels,[60] suggesting that this text may have been available in Ireland before the mission to Frisia, or alternatively, that Echternach served as an entrepôt for the transmission of biblical texts to Ireland, including even possibly the so-called 'Irish text' of the gospels. The Frisian mission was based on Rath Melsigi (now Clonmelsh, County Carlow),[61] but it is unlikely that the Echternach Gospels were written in Ireland, because the non-insular character of the vellum argues strongly for a continental origin, most likely Echternach itself.[62] The main text is in a splendid set minuscule, preliminaries in a script mixing majuscule and minuscule forms, while the first page is in pure majuscule. To Julian Brown we owe the very significant discovery of the close relationship between this script and that of the Durham Gospels (pl. 30).[63] The evidence

---

[57] Wilhelm Levison, *England and the Continent in the eighth century* (Oxford, 1946), pp 53–69.

[58] Bibl. Nat., MS lat. 10837, ff 34–41; CLA, v, 605; H. A. Wilson (ed.), *The Calendar of St Willibrord* (London, 1918), f. 39ᵛ, cited hereafter as *Calendar*.

[59] Bibl. Nat., MS lat. 9389, CLA, v, 578; Brown, 'The insular system of scripts', p. 109.

[60] Martin McNamara, *Studies on texts of early Irish Latin gospels* (Steenbrugge, 1990), pp 102–11; London, Lambeth Palace, MS 1370; B.L., Harl. MS 1802. Patrick McGurk has noticed a rubric common to Harl. 1802 and Echternach in 'The Gospel book in Celtic lands: contents and arrangement' in Ní Chatháin & Richter, *Ire. & Christendom*, pp 165–89: 171, n. 25.

[61] See Ó Cróinín, 'Rath Melsigi, Willibrord, and the earliest Echternach manuscripts' in *Peritia*, iii (1984), pp 17–49.

[62] A survey by a team from the Patologia del Libro in Rome has identified it as goatskin; see A. Di Majo, C. Federici, and M. Palma, 'Indagine sulla pergamena insulare' in *Scriptorium*, xlii (1988), p. 138.

[63] Durham, Cathedral Library MS A.II.17.; CLA, ii, 149; T. D. Kendrick, R. Bruce-Mitford, and T. J. Brown (ed.), *Evangeliorum quattuor codex Lindisfarnensis* (2 vols, Olten and Lausanne, 1956, 1960), ii, 100, cited hereafter as *Cod. Lindisfarn.*; C. D. Verey and T. J. Brown (ed.), *The Durham Gospels* (Copenhagen, 1980).

that would make them identical, as he proposed, cannot be conclusive, but the scribes must have been trained at the same place at about the same time, given the sort of scriptorium discipline found in manuscripts like the Book of Kells. Brown himself noticed that the two manuscripts used different forms of uncial *g*. Ecgbert, an English monk, the inspirer of the Frisian mission, who had been received into the community of Rath Melsigi as a young man after the synod of Whitby, moved to Iona in 716,[64] and he might perhaps be seen as the link between the two manuscripts—though not likely to have been the scribe of either. Durham's text of John's gospel was available to the Iona scriptorium when the Book of Kells came to be written. In these manuscripts we have examples of the scripts practised in Ireland at this time. Durham might have been written at Rath Melsigi or at Iona, whence it would later have been taken south to Wearmouth–Jarrow, which would have provided the added punctuation *per cola et commata*, as well as the uncial fragment that was later to be bound with it. We know that Adomnán's 'De locis sanctis' followed this route,[65] and the Durham library—judging by the survivors—seems to have fallen heir to Wearmouth–Jarrow manuscripts rather more than to those of Lindisfarne.[66]

The protean character of insular as it had already developed in seventh-century Ireland is nowhere better illustrated than in the first few decades of the mission at Echternach. As we have seen, there are three hands in the Gospels.[67] Willibrord's own rough hand appears in the margin of his Calendar, which is in a quite different but very fine majuscule, whose scribe seems to turn up again in the Augsburg Gospels (pl. 29).[68] The script is clearly related to that of the gospel-book now divided between Cambridge, Corpus Christi College, MS 197b, B. L. MS Cotton Otho C.V, and Royal MS 7.C.XII, ff 2–3, whose decoration is strikingly close to that of the Echternach Gospels. Still more intriguing is the close and, so far as is known, unique structural relationship between the canon tables of Kells and those of the Royal fragment.[69] Nothing is known of the medieval provenance of this manuscript, but before the dismemberment it belonged to Cardinal Wolsey, and so might more conveniently be referred to as the Wolsey Gospels. The dismemberment would have taken place after it reached the Royal Library, where it fell prey to the later collectors, Archbishop Parker and Sir Robert

---

[64] Levison, *England and the Continent*, pp 52, 271 n., 278 n.

[65] Denis Meehan (ed. and trans.), *Adamnan's De locis sanctis* (Dublin, 1958), pp 4–5.

[66] CLA, ii, 148a–c, 153.

[67] Four, if the colophon is included; *Cod. Lindisfarn.*, ii, 96–7.

[68] CLA, v, 605; Augsburg (formerly successively Maihingen and Harburg) Gospels, Universitätsbibliothek, Cod.1.2.4° 2; CLA, ix, 1215; for a microfiche facsimile, see Dáibhí Ó Cróinín, *Evangeliarium Epternacense (Universitätsbibliothek-Augsburg, Cod. I.2.4°2), Evangelistarium (Erzbischöfliches Priesterseminar St. Peter, Cod. ms. 25)* (Munich, 1988).

[69] CLA, ii, 125; P. McGurk, 'Two notes on the Book of Kells and its relation to other insular gospel books' in *Scriptorium*, ix (1955), pp 155–7.

Cotton. However, as in the case of the Durham Gospels, the connection with the Iona scriptorium is very striking. The Echternach book of the Prophets (pl. 33) provides other forms of insular script, written in part by Virgilius (a name that may already equate with the Irish Fergil, as it does later), who wrote charters for the monastery between 709 and 722.[70]

The Maeseyck Gospels—most likely a product of Echternach with a so-called 'Irish text'—uses still another insular script. Thomas, the scribe of the insular majuscule portion of the Trier Gospels, using a similar text, also probably worked at Echternach, writing a lively if somewhat lighter hand.[71] Willibrord's Calendar was preserved at Trier until the seventeenth century.[72] A very formalised, not to say imitative, version of this majuscule appears in the Lindisfarne Gospels, which is attributed by a tenth-century colophon to Eadfrith, bishop of Lindisfarne (d. 721).[73] Laurentius (perhaps already used as the Latin equivalent of the Irish name Lorcán) wrote the Echternach martyrology in minuscule, but this version of the script is very remote from that of the Echternach Gospels.[74] Laurentius too wrote charters for Echternach between 704 and 722.[75] Such a variety of scripts could only be characteristic of a new monastery, before the establishment of a house style, where the scribes accompanying the missionaries were trained in several different scriptoria and must have been drawn from more Irish houses than Rath Melsigi. They provide an apt illustration of the proliferation of the insular script that accompanied the well-attested expansion of Irish learning in the seventh century.

Such a variety of scripts, all more or less contemporary, must alert us again to the dangers and difficulties of trying to use insular script for dating, even in the early days of the script. The Book of Durrow (pl. 33), because of its connections at several points with the decoration of the Echternach group, is probably best seen as an example of the contemporary majuscule script as practised at Iona, and perhaps throughout the Columban communion.[76] Particularly striking in its decoration is the extraordinary evangelist symbol of the lion, which is peculiar to Durrow and Trier (almost more boar than lion). The lightly decorated Echternach Calendar has a simple space-filler—two

[70] Bibl. Nat., MS lat. 9382; CLA, v, 577; Carl Nordenfalk, 'On the age of the earliest Echternach manuscripts' in *Acta Archaeologica*, iii (1932), pp 57–62: 59, 61.

[71] Trier, Domschatz, MS 61; CLA, ix, 1364; J. J. G. Alexander, *Insular manuscripts 6th to 9th century* (London, 1978), p. 53, pl. 125; cited below as Alexander, *Insular manuscripts*.

[72] *Calendar*, p. ix.

[73] B.L., Cott. MS Nero D.IV.O; CLA, ii, 187; Alexander, *Insular manuscripts*, pp 39–40. Julian Brown characterised the script as 'the most elaborate and difficult formal hand ever used and the doggedly even quality...should command respect' (*Cod. Lindisfarn.*, ii, 93).

[74] Bibl. Nat., MS lat. 10837, ff 2–33; CLA, v, 604.

[75] Nordenfalk, 'The earliest Echternach manuscripts', pp 59, 61.

[76] Ibid., pp 59–60; T.C.D. MS 57 (A.4.5.); CLA, ii, 273; A. A. Luce, G. O. Simms, P. Meyer, and L. Bieler (ed.), *Evangeliorum quattuor Codex Durmachensis* (2 vols (i facsimile, ii commentary), Olten, 1960), cited hereafter as *Cod. Durmach.*

horizontal lines connected by a zigzag line—which reappears in the Lucan glossary of Durrow (f. 124ʳ) and in the Augsburg Gospels (f. 128ʳ).[77]

The Book of Durrow, because it has been dated—probably mistakenly—to the seventh century, is regarded as the decorative prototype of all the great insular gospel-books, evangelist portraits alone of the main motifs being absent. The manuscript begins with a page of design based on a double-armed cross with square terminals. This will reappear in Kells, but with circular terminals, and there it precedes and probably originally faced (being inverted) the opening of the Matthean nativity story.[78] After this in Durrow comes a page in which the four evangelical symbols are arranged around a cross. This turns up in the Trier, Lichfield, and Armagh Gospels and is a major element of the architecture of Kells. In Durrow it is followed by a page of abstract design based on Celtic ornament, the first of five so-called 'carpet'-pages, one of which originally faced the opening of each gospel. This one, facing the opening of St Jerome's letter to Pope Damasus, displays the first of the series of elaborate initial designs that culminate in the opening of St John's gospel, where the initial occupies the whole height of the page. After the letter comes the Matthean glossary of Hebrew names and the Eusebian canon tables. The prefaces, which serve to introduce each evangelist, and the *breves causae*, or chapter-headings, come next (but in an odd order, being completed at the end of the book). Each gospel is introduced with a whole page devoted to a framed evangelist symbol. This is paralleled in the Echternach and Wolsey (Royal) Gospels, but in most of the other insular books, like Kells, it is replaced by the evangelist's portrait. This serves to reinforce my belief that Durrow is contemporary with these manuscripts.

Current scholarship, however, dates Durrow at about 670, but this is largely to allow for a hypothetical script development that would permit the placing of the Lindisfarne Gospels at 698, in the belief that the free variable script of Durrow must necessarily be a near stage on the road to the tightly controlled script of Lindisfarne.[79] Much closer to Lindisfarne (as we have seen) is the type of majuscule found among some Echternach manuscripts, though few now accept Brown's suggestion that the single scribe—as he saw it—of the Durham and Echternach Gospels was an older contemporary of Eadfrith at Lindisfarne.[80] As I have suggested above, Rath Melsigi-Iona might provide a more likely background for the Durham Gospels. Françoise

---

[77] See Dáibhí Ó Cróinín, 'Is the Augsburg gospel codex a Northumbrian manuscript?' in Gerald Bonner, David Rollason, and Clare Stancliffe (ed.), *St Cuthbert, his cult and his community to A.D. 1200* (Woodbridge, 1989), pp 189–201: 196, n. 30.

[78] The main decorative pages of Kells are on single leaves and could be readily misplaced in the course of rebinding.

[79] 'The insular system of scripts', p. 108.

[80] Ibid.; William O'Sullivan, 'The Lindisfarne scriptorium: for and against' in *Peritia*, viii (1994), pp 80–94: 84–5.

Henry, who played a large part in establishing the accepted sequence of manuscripts, had some second thoughts about this question, and as long ago as 1963, in reviewing the commentary volume accompanying the Lindisfarne facsimile, warned that Durrow might not be in the direct line of ascent.[81] The discovery of some unpalimpsested leaves of the Turin Gospels in the National Library there has underlined her wisdom, because they show a hand so like that of Durrow that it could only be the work of a man trained at the same time in the same scriptorium.[82] Julian Brown suggested that a single scribe wrote the Durrow and Turin Gospels, but the evidence of the hands does not seem to warrant this conclusion. Both manuscripts employ *diminuendo*. This is a prominent feature of the oldest manuscripts in insular script, like the Cathach, but not of the still older Irish half-uncial Usserianus. In later books, like Kells, only the letter immediately after the initial is usually enlarged. *Diminuendo*, however, occasionally reappears in later manuscripts, like the Garland of Howth (pl. 35), where the scribe is probably copying from an early exemplar.

The Turin Gospels book, which was palimpsested at Bobbio in the fifteenth century, was destroyed in the fire in the National Library in 1904, leaving (it was thought) only some badly damaged leaves, including four full pages of illumination and some photographs. The palimpsesting, curiously, spared large initials and illuminations. The character of the decoration suggested to Françoise Henry a relationship with the St Gall Gospels (which she placed in the middle of the eighth century), but perhaps fifty years later.[83] It is hard to see how a headlong collision between palaeographers and art historians can be avoided in this situation. Zimmermann had tried to divide the Turin illuminated pages between the eighth and the tenth centuries, but Henry showed that this was not possible.[84] If Durrow was not written at the place from which it takes its name, then it must have been at some other house of the Columban communion, which was spread widely over Ireland and Scotland. The notion that it was Northumbrian initially arose from a mistaken belief that its text, which is a relatively pure Vulgate, was close to that in the Amiatine Bible from Wearmouth–Jarrow. On closer examination,

---

[81] *Antiquity*, xxxvii (1963), p. 105 (reprinted in Henry, *Studies*, p. 46).

[82] This most important discovery was announced by Mirella Ferrari, 'Spigolature Bobbiesi' in *Italia Medioevale e Humanistica*, xvi (1973), pp 9–12. Her view that the newly discovered leaves belong to the Turin Gospels has been rejected, but unconvincingly, by C. S. Montel, *I manoscritti miniati della Biblioteca Nazionale di Torino*, i (Turin, 1980), pp 12–13.

[83] Turin, Biblioteca Nazionale, MS O. 4. 20.; CLA, iv, 466; Ferrari, 'Spigolature Bobbiese', plate iii; Brown, 'The insular system of scripts', p. 106; Françoise Henry, *Irish art in the early Christian period (to 800 A.D.)* (London, 1940), p. 196; Henry, *Irish art during the viking invasions (800–1020 A.D.)* (London, 1967), pp 96–7; cited hereafter as Henry, *Ir. art*, i, ii. Durrow seems to reach the pinnacle of its worldly power in the middle of the eighth century, when the annals show it waging war against Clonmacnoise and supplying troops for the high-king's invasion of Munster (A.F.M., 764, 776).

[84] Henry, *Ir. art*, i, 150.

however, this was found not to be so; but meanwhile, as a result of the Sutton Hoo excavations, a new reason for making it Northumbrian was discovered in its decorative use of a little formalised Germanic-style animal found in Anglo-Saxon jewellery. Much of the Durrow artist's inspiration is based on Celtic jewellery, none of it necessarily new, and considering the portable nature of such jewellery, and its capacity for survival, the weight the Anglo-Saxon jewellery has been allowed to carry seems scarcely credible, especially in the matter of dating.[85] The manuscript has two colophons, the first of which may have been taken over from the exemplar, but has suffered alteration. In it Columba claims to have written the gospel-book in twelve days, and asks a blessing of Patrick. Such a dual invocation reflects the political reality of the early ninth century, when the Iona community took refuge in Ireland, at Kells, and is repeated on the Cross of the Tower, erected there at that time.[86] In the seventh century, Columba's may have been the most prestigious *paruchia*, but by the ninth it was eclipsed by Patrick's.

The Book of Durrow (or a copy of it) must have provided the model for the bizarre order of the preliminaries found in the Book of Kells.[87] In Durrow the scribe seems initially to have omitted the *breves causae*, or chapter-headings of Luke and John, and then added them in at the end of the gospels. Although they are all placed at the beginning of Kells, they follow the same order. The gospel texts are very different. Where Durrow has a reasonably pure Vulgate, Kells, like the Book of Armagh, has a so-called 'Irish' text, a Vulgate contaminated with Old Latin readings (now known to be Italian in origin). The oldest surviving example, the seventh-century gospels at Split, in Dalmatia, was probably written in Italy.[88] The earliest insular examples of this version would seem to be of Echternach provenance, like the Augsburg Gospels (as we have seen above). There is no sign of the 'Irish' text in Adomnán's 'Vita Columbae'.[89] The text of John in Kells is, however (as we have already seen), so close to that in the Durham Gospels as to suggest dependence, serving to reinforce the suggestion above that the Durham Gospels have a connection with Ecgbert's transfer to Iona. If

---

[85] In 1985 Uta Roth placed it shortly after 600; see Michael F. Ryan (ed.), *Ireland and insular art A.D. 500–1200* (Dublin, 1987), p. 28. G. L. [Marsh-]Micheli, *L'enluminure du haut moyen âge et les influences irlandaises* (Brussels, 1939), p. 15, credits the Irish with introducing the use of jewellery designs for the decoration of manuscripts.

[86] Henry, *Ir. art*, ii, 138.

[87] *Cod. Durmachensis*, ii, 33; but see now Patrick McGurk, 'The texts at the opening of the Book of Kells' in P. K. Fox (ed.), *The Book of Kells* (Lucerne, 1990), ii, 37–58.

[88] Martin McNamara, 'The text of the Latin Bible in the early Irish church: some data and desiderata' in Ní Chatháin & Richter, *Ire. & Christendom*, p. 29. The Augsburg Gospels may contain the earliest insular version of this text (see Ó Cróinín, *Evangeliarium Epternacense*, p.31), but it is also used for the corrected readings in the Echternach Gospels.

[89] Jean-Michel Picard, 'The Bible used by Adomnán' in Ní Chatháin & Richter, *Ire. & Christendom*, pp 246–57.

Durrow must be placed with Turin in the first half of the eighth century, then Kells—as Julian Brown proposed—is unlikely to be there too.[90]

The most noticeable change in the majuscule between Durrow and Kells is in the proportions of the letters, the more rounded letters like *a* and *o* in Durrow being taller in proportion to their width in Kells, Lichfield, and in the later Irish examples. The decoration of Kells has very complicated relationships, but one of the most striking is with the Corbie Psalter, now at Amiens. The artist of the man and animal initials in Kells seems to have adapted into the insular medium something very close to the initials found in this late eighth-century French psalter.[91] The beast canon tables too have some still undefined relationship with those in Carolingian gospel-books. The lavish scale and expensive pigments indicate that Kells could only have been produced in such an extremely wealthy monastery as the mother house of the Columban communion. Whether this was before or after the scriptorium moved from Iona to Kells in the early ninth century is still debated; few follow Julian Brown's suggestion that it may be the product of an unknown house in eastern Pictland, or that the scribe must have been trained at Lindisfarne.[92] The vikings first attacked Iona in 802, and the community was massacred there in 806. A decision was taken to transfer to Kells, in County Meath, and the building of the new monastery began in 807. The church was complete by 814 and the Cross of the Tower, dedicated jointly to Columba and Patrick, in its decoration carried on aspects of the Iona series of crosses.[93] The abbot is still called abbot of Iona, and later the successor of Columba. There is no reference to an abbot of Kells, as such, before the eleventh century, the two houses forming a single entity. The vikings' control of the sea lanes, and settlement on the Scottish islands, would have made it necessary for the abbot and community to be normally resident at Kells from the early ninth century, though a presence was maintained on Iona. References in the annals to the movement of relics backwards and forwards across the sea would have been connected with the levying of dues.[94]

Brown calls the Kells script 'display' because the bottoms of verticals are slightly splayed, and finished with a horizontal stroke. However, his distinction between half-uncial, display half-uncial, and hybrid minuscule does not seem to me to bear useful fruit.[95] It is true that the base of verticals in Kells

---

[90] T. J. Brown, 'Northumbria and the Book of Kells', p. 234 (reprinted in *A palaeographer's view*, pp 97–122).

[91] Françoise Henry, *The Book of Kells* (London, 1974), pp 125–6; Bernard Meehan, 'The Book of Kells and the Corbie Psalter' in T. C. Barnard, Dáibhí Ó Cróinín, and Katharine Simms (ed.), *'A miracle of learning': essays for William O'Sullivan* (Aldershot, 1998), pp 29–39.

[92] 'Northumbria and the Book of Kells', p. 243; 'The insular system of scripts', p. 109.

[93] Henry, *Ir. art*, pp 18–20.

[94] For a different view, see Herbert, *Iona, Kells, & Derry*, ch. 5, and George Henderson, *From Durrow to Kells* (London, 1987), ch. 6.

[95] 'The insular system of scripts', pp 108–9. Its unhelpfulness is well illustrated by Nancy Netzer, who has clearly struggled hard with the system in her *Cultural interplay in the eighth*

is squared by a horizontal finishing stroke, but so are those of Lindisfarne—as his own plate 15 makes clear.[96] The Cathach does not have this stroke, but the base of the verticals often ends in a slight curl to the right as the pen lifts, just as it does in the Orosius. There Brown calls it a foot-serif, and curiously labels the script hybrid minuscule in consequence. But it is also found in Durrow, which he calls half-uncial. Such a finish is already present in Usserianus, which we have found to be a pre-insular half-uncial. Brown's nomenclature, based as it is on the way the pen is cut or held (rather than on the shape of the letters) is not acceptable. Kells is the product of a highly disciplined scriptorium (pl. 34), so that it is not generally possible to be sure where the hand of one man ends and another begins. There are obvious differences throughout the manuscript, some lengthy spirited passages interspersed with others more pedestrian. Françoise Henry has outlined the three main styles, which she has labelled A, B, C (following the order of the book), and more recently Bernard Meehan (using the evidence of the decoration) has further divided C, distinguishing a fourth hand D.[97] In the order of writing, the synoptic gospels would surely have been first (styles C and D), followed by St John's gospel and the opening of the preliminaries (style A), and lastly the brilliant calligrapher (style B), whose job it was to finish the work—not only the preliminaries but other areas, like the end of St Matthew's gospel and the verso of the initial page of Luke. His work may have followed a considerable time-gap, as it is accompanied by a different choice of pigments. This scribe writes supremely well, not only the splendidly solemn monumental script of the gospels, clearly chosen for its solidity, but—as if to show off—a variety of other types as well, some with a minuscule emphasis. This is especially the case with the later preliminaries, which are also characterised by constant switching of ink colour (red, purple and faded yellow), but also black carbon ink, which in itself would argue against an early date for Kells. That was the normal ink of antiquity but had given way before the gall ink, which is the norm in northern European and, of course, insular manuscripts. Usually brownish-black in colour, this bites into the skin and is permanent, whereas

*century: the Trier Gospels and the making of a scriptorium at Echternach* (Cambridge, 1994). She writes (p. 35) of Brown's categories that his 'first phase distinctions between hybrid minuscule are sometimes blurred', and (p. 38) of the scribe of the insular portions of the manuscript: 'Thomas did not completely understand phase II half-uncial as developed at Lindisfarne' (p. 88). For a serious critique of Brown's system, see Ian Doyle, 'A fragment of a Northumbrian service book' in Michael Korhammer, Karl Reichl, and Hans Sauer (ed.), *Words, texts and manuscripts* (Cambridge, 1992), pp 17–18.

[96] *Cod. Lindisfarn.*
[97] Henry, *Book of Kells*, pp 154–7; Fox, *The Book of Kells*, ii, 249–56. This is the second volume, the first being a complete colour facsimile of the whole manuscript. See also Elizabeth Eisenlohr, 'The puzzle of the scribes...' in O'Mahony, *The Book of Kells Proceedings*, pp 196–208.

carbon ink is inclined eventually to flake off, especially on the smoother flesh side of continental parchment. So well prepared is the vellum of Kells that it flakes off indifferently on both sides. The play with ink colours connects Kells with the Stockholm gospel-book, the Codex Aureus, a product of the mid-eighth-century Canterbury school. It is similar with the lettering on coloured bands decorated with plant and animal motifs, particularly areas written by B, like the opening of the Lucan *breves causae* (f. 9ᵛ) or *Uespere autem* (f. 127ᵛ), which also links up with the late eighth-century Barberini Gospels and the ninth-century Book of Cerne, most probably written in southern England.[98] The later history of insular majuscule in Ireland does not reach the heights of Kells in the surviving manuscripts, but the gospel-book which Giraldus Cambrensis described seeing at Kildare must have been a worthy rival.[99]

The fragmentary Dublin gospel-book known as the Garland of Howth (pl. 35)[100] takes its odd name from the medieval English corruption of the Irish for 'four books', *ceithre leabhair*. It came from the monastery on Ireland's Eye, spending the later middle ages in the parish church of Howth. It was clearly written against what, judging especially by the vellum, must have been a relatively impoverished background, an index perhaps of the still-pagan vikings' control of the area in the late ninth or early tenth century. Two decorated pages survive, uniquely combining portraits with the elaborate initials of gospel-openings, one for the Matthean Nativity story with which the manuscript now begins, and the other for Mark (perhaps inspired by some of the great Kells openings, where large human figures form part of the elaborate design). Much of St Matthew's gospel is in the Old Latin version.[101] The Garland was the work of a number of different scribes, some of the script being decidedly artificial in character, none of the first class. Very close in style is the script of the fragmentary service book in Turin on similar vellum, formerly dated to the seventh century and thought to be older than the Antiphonary of Bangor, but which must be roughly coeval with the Garland.[102] It is characterised by much use of tall uncial *a*, little uncial *d*, and uncommonly short descenders, so that even the tail of *g* seems to sit on the line, and, as in the case of the Garland of Howth, occasional use of *diminuendo* (by then long out of fashion), suggesting early exemplars in the case of both manuscripts.

[98] Vatican City, Biblioteca Apostolica, MS Barberini Lat. 570; Cambridge, University Library, MS L.R.I.10. See Michelle Brown, *The Book of Cerne* (London, 1996).

[99] J. F. Dimock (ed.), *Topographia Hiberniae*, ch. xxxviii (London, 1867), pp 123–4.

[100] T.C.D. MS 56 (A.4.6); CLA, ii, 272.

[101] H. C. Hoskier (ed.), *The text of Codex Usserianus 2.r 2 ('Garland of Howth')* (London, 1919).

[102] Turin, Biblioteca Nazionale, MS F.iv.1, fasc. ix; CLA, iv, 454; Kenney, *Sources*, pp 712–13.

This artificiality persists in two of the tenth-century psalters studied by Françoise Henry: the Cotton Psalter, which seems to be a product of Monasterboice, and the Southampton Psalter at St John's College, Cambridge.[103] The proportions of the rounded letters, such as *a*, *d*, and *o*, reflect the earliest majuscule, but with little use of the alternative half-uncial forms of *d*, *r*, and *s*. In both manuscripts the three strokes forming the *s* are inclined to separate, as in the Cathach, and the first stroke of the uncial *R* goes below the line, another early device. This last is found to a still greater degree in the St Ouen double-psalter, where the other descenders are also longer.[104] It includes the half-uncial forms of *d* and *s*, and is altogether more lively and without the artificial air of the script of the other two psalters. Closer in spirit to the majuscule of Kells in its proportions is the Gallicanum part of the fragment of another roughly contemporary double-psalter in T.C.D (pl. 36), where the Hebraicum on facing pages is in minuscule.[105] This play with contrasting scripts is used again in the Trinity 'Liber Hymnorum' (pl. 47), with the Latin hymns in majuscule and the Irish in minuscule.[106] The majuscule there is close to that of the Trinity double-psalter, but somewhat heavier. For dating we have to turn to the art historian, who places it in the late eleventh century. The Psalter of St Caimin (pl. 48), thought to be earlier, has somewhat similar proportions, but more contrast of thick and thin strokes, with the first stroke of uncial *R* going below the line.[107] Perhaps ultimately used only for service books, the majuscule naturally became desiccated with time and lost the ability to renew itself that characterised the ordinary bookhand, the minuscule.

The latest surviving example of the use of the majuscule for a whole book, the Cormac Psalter (pl. 37), dates from after the twelfth century reform of the Irish church, when the continental religious orders were already supplanting the old monasteries, but before the Anglo-Norman introduction of gothic script.[108] The presence of St Bernard's absolution suggests a Cistercian provenance, which is confirmed by some musical staves added later. Oddly, the opening page of the text is in minuscule and, as one would expect, so are the headings to each psalm. The script shows little variation

[103] B.L. MS Cotton Vitellius F.XI; Françoise Henry, 'Remarks on the decoration of three Irish psalters' in *R.I.A. Proc.*, lxi (1960), sect. C, pp 23–40 (reprinted in Henry, *Studies*, pp 143–80); Anne O'Sullivan, 'The colophon of the Cotton Psalter (Vitellius F.XI)' in *R.S.A.I.Jn.*, xcvi (1966), pp 179–80.

[104] Henry, *Studies*, ibid.; Rouen, Bibliothèque Municipale, MS 24.

[105] T.C.D., MS 1337 (H.3.18), [ff ii–iii$^v$]. Ed. Ludwig Bieler and Gearóid Mac Niocaill, 'Fragment of an Irish double-psalter with glosses in the Library of Trinity College Dublin' in *Celtica*, v (1960), pp 28–39.

[106] T.C.D., MS 1441 (E.4.2).

[107] Killiney, Franciscan Library, MS A 1; Françoise Henry and Geneviève L. Marsh-Micheli, 'A century of Irish illumination (1070–1170)' in *R.I.A. Proc.*, lxii (1962), sect. C, pp 101–64: 117–19; cited hereafter as Henry, 'Century' (reprinted in Henry, *Studies*, pp 199–201).

[108] B.L., Add. MS 36929; Henry, *Studies*, pp 243–6.

between thick and thin strokes, and avoids the alternative half-uncial letter forms. It is most brilliantly decorated with all the colours of the rainbow, a fitting close to the splendid career of the insular majuscule. As it was acquired in Munich, the psalter probably spent the later middle ages in some well-appointed continental library, sheltered from the troubles that destroyed its fellows in Ireland. The scribe signs and asks our prayers: *Cormacus scripsit hoc psalterium ora pro eo* ('Cormac wrote this psalter, pray for him').

Among the varieties of the majuscule there is one particularly striking subdivision, which substitutes compressed rectangularity for roundness. Three examples are known to me: the Stowe Missal,[109] usually dated to around 800; the St Gall Gospels (pl. 38), dated by Françoise Henry to the middle of the eighth century;[110] and the monastic customary fragment believed to come from Reichenau, a monastery with strong Irish associations.[111] Decoratively, the St Gall Gospels share a crucifixion design with the Durham Gospels, and the theme of the Last Judgment (but not the design) with the Turin Gospels. The St Gall manuscripts may have been the gift of the Irish bishop Marcus, who settled in St Gall with his nephew, Móengal or Marcellus, who came to head the abbey school in the middle of the ninth century.[112] The gospel of St John bound with the Stowe Missal (pl. 23) is written in a minuscule very close to that of St John's gospel in the Book of Dimma (which comes from Roscrea), and as the missal spent the later middle ages at Lorrha, in the same area, this curious rectangular majuscule may be a local style. However, the important majuscule gospel-book from the same general area, written by Mac Regol (who died as abbot of Birr in 822), has a very different script (pl. 39), a lively personalised version of the standard majuscule.[113]

The Springmount tablets (pl. 25) have been frequently regarded as minuscule, but are better seen as an example of the Irish half-uncial that pre-dated the invention of the insular script. The fragment of Isidore's 'Etymologiae' at St Gall is more generally considered to be the earliest surviving example of the insular minuscule, dating from around the middle of the seventh century (but perhaps it might also be regarded as a majuscule, though written so rapidly that it is well on its way to being a minuscule).[114] It presents many abbreviations, fully developed triangular serifs, sometimes not filled with ink, and the alternative letters (*d, n, r, s*) of the insular alphabet. *Diminuendo*, as with the Cathach, is a most striking feature of the manuscript.

---

[109] R.I.A., MS Stowe D.II.3; CLA, ii, 268; G. F. Warner (ed.), *The Stowe Missal* (2 vols, London, 1906 [facsimile], 1915 [text]).

[110] St Gallen, Stiftsbibliothek, Cod. 51; CLA, vii, 901; Henry, *Ir. art*, i, 196–8.

[111] Karlsruhe, Badische Landesbibliothek, Cod. Aug. CCXXIII, now Fragmentum Augiense 20; CLA, viii, 1118; Gearóid Mac Niocaill, 'Fragments d'un coutumier monastique irlandais du VIIᵉ–IXᵉ siècle' in *Scriptorium*, xv (1961), pp 228–33.

[112] Kenney, *Sources*, pp 596–7.

[113] Bodl., MS Auct. D.2.19; CLA, ii, 231.

[114] Kenney, *Sources*, pp 285–328; St Gallen, Stiftsbibliothek, Cod.1399a 1; CLA, vii, 995.

The first satisfactorily dateable example of the minuscule is the Antiphonary of Bangor (pl. 40), which contains a poem listing the abbots of Bangor down to Crónán (d. 691).[115] The vellum is yellowed by the presence of light brown hair follicles, and not of good quality, and the manuscript must have been personal rather than a service-book proper. In keeping with its minuscule character, *a* is made in two strokes, uncial forms of *r* and *s* rarely occur. Uncial *d* is normal, but not exclusive. There is an occasional use of uncial *g* and of the early *s*-shaped *g* in ligature with *n*. One short section in majuscule (f. 35) may be a later addition.

The next important landmark in the development of the insular minuscule is the manuscript of the Life of St Columba by Adomnán (pl. 43), written by Dorbbéne, the abbot of Iona who died in 713.[116] Still at Reichenau in the early seventeenth century, when it first became known to Irish historians, it is now at Schaffhausen, in Switzerland. Here the script has already reached the angularity that is to characterise the Irish minuscule to its latest days. This was achieved (the calligrapher Timothy O'Neill tells us) by a sharper pen angle, thirty degrees to the writing line.[117] The *a* is made in three strokes, but with a pointed top; uncial *d* is normal, but a half-uncial form, inclined to be open, also occurs; the top stroke of the *g* is waved; the open bowl of the *p* is finished by a serif to the right; the *q* is very much like the *a* with an added tail. Compared to the minuscule of the Echternach Gospels,[118] perhaps a generation later, it is heavier and somewhat lacking in elegance, but the scripts are basically the same (though the intentions are very different: one a straightforward library book, the other a great work of art for use in church). Neither script is cursive and the deliberate separation of the letters is particularly striking in the Adomnán. More comparable with it is the Echternach Martyrology, written by Laurentius in the first quarter of the eighth century, which is equally plain but less angular.[119] All of these scripts lack the compression of even the oldest of the four hands in the St Petersburg (Leningrad) Bede, which (as we have seen above) has been studied by Malcolm Parkes.[120]

With the minuscule of the 'pocket' Gospels, which were first seen as a distinct category by Patrick McGurk,[121] we are again in the less formal world of personal books, with script often verging on cursive; but decoration

---

[115] Milan, Biblioteca Ambrosiana, MS C 5 inf.; CLA, iii, 311; F. E. Warren (ed.), *The Antiphonary of Bangor* (2 vols, London, 1893 [facsimile], 1895 [text]).

[116] Schaffhausen, Stadtbibliothek, MS Gen.1; CLA, vii, 998; William Reeves (ed.), *The life of St. Columba... by Adamnan* (Dublin, 1857); Anderson, *Adomnan's Life*.

[117] O'Neill, *The Irish hand*, p. 62.

[118] Bibl. Nat., MS lat. 9389; CLA, v, 578.

[119] Bibl. Nat., MS lat. 10837, ff 2–33; CLA, v, 605.

[120] See n. 20.

[121] Patrick McGurk, 'The Irish pocket gospel books' in *Sacris Erudiri*, viii (1956), pp 249–70.

is not forgotten, and the evangelist portraits and the opening pages echo the designs of their greater relatives. The Mark portrait in the Book of Dimma[122] is obviously closely related to that of the Matthew symbol in the Echternach Gospels, which, although written abroad, must have drawn on a model already present in Ireland at the beginning of the eighth century, or carried there before the end of that century. The decoration has been used by Françoise Henry to date several of these little books to the latter time.[123]

The styles of writing vary not only between the books but also within them. Thus the Book of Mulling (pl. 43)[124] employs three different hands: one for the preliminaries (formerly dated later than the others, when the gospels, following the colophon attribution to Mulling, who died in 696, were thought to be seventh-century, a notion now abandoned). The second hand wrote the synoptic gospels, the script being close to the three mostly grammatical manuscripts now at Naples (formerly at Bobbio), redated, perhaps unwisely, to the seventh/eighth century by Brown against Lowe's eighth-/ninth-century dating.[125] Lowe was influenced by their closeness to the Book of Armagh, which is thought to be securely dated around 807. The third hand is that of St John's gospel, using the open *a* and the tall *c* of early types, but presumably contemporary here, in the Irish way that so baffled Julian Brown when attempting a chronology of the scripts.[126]

The Book of Dimma[126a] also uses three scripts. The first, in what was probably imagined to be an impressive style, may have been the work of the illuminator, perhaps a distant reminiscence of the fashion that led to the opening of the minuscule Echternach Gospels with a page in majuscule. The scribe of the synoptic gospels—because this is a personal book—revels in abbreviations, which are almost entirely absent from the great gospel-books like Durrow and Kells. He is responsible for the main style of these gospels (pl. 42), using reversed *e*, open *q* and *a* sometimes like half-uncial *d*. The script of John is very different, bold yet neat and regular, and the decoration, with evangelist portraits facing framed opening pages of the other gospels, here gives way to a striking evangelist symbol facing an equally striking and vigorous initial design. The book takes its name from the scribe Dimma, whose name appears in the colophons to the gospels. He is known from the Life of St Crónán, the founder of the monastery of Roscrea (Co. Tipperary), as the writer of a famous gospel-book. The name, however, is

[122] See n. 126.
[123] Françoise Henry, 'An Irish manuscript in the British Museum (Add. 40618)' in *R.S.A.I. Jn.*, lxxxvii (1957), pp 147–66.
[124] T.C.D. MS 60 (A.1.15); CLA, ii, 276–7.
[125] Naples, Biblioteca Nazionale, MS Lat.1 (CLA, iii, 388–90); Lat. 2 (CLA, iii, 391–7b); IV.A.8 (CLA, iii, 400–04); Brown, 'The insular system of scripts', p. 114.
[126] Brown, ibid., pp 111, 113.
[126a] T.C.D. MS 59 (A.4.23); CLA, ii, 275; R. I. Best 'On the *subscriptiones* in the Book of Dimma' in *Hermathena*, xx (1926), pp 84–100.

written over an erasure in each case. The name of the man for whom it was made survives at the end of Luke: Dianchride.[127] Another of these pocket gospels, now in the British Library (Add. 40618), was heavily restored in England in the twelfth century, but it still retains one portrait, which is very close to the one preceding St Mark's gospel in the Book of Mulling.[128] The script is very tiny, and in more than one hand. The first uses open half-uncial *d* and short descenders, and the hand beginning on f. 51 uses uncial d and r and longer descenders. The initials, now restored in gold, are set far out in the left margin, even when they belong to a word in the middle of the line.

Often grouped with these little gospels, because of its small size, is the Book of Armagh (pl. 44), a 'pocket' New Testament with, in addition, St Patrick's Confession and two seventh-century accounts of the saint (by Tírechán and Muirchú), as well as Sulpicius Severus's Life of St Martin of Tours.[129] One of the scribes, Ferdomnach, tells us that he was writing for Torbach, *comarba* or abbot of Armagh, which allows us to date the manuscript around 807. The script is a more refined version of that used by Dorbbéne for Adomnán's Life of Columba, sometimes close to the script attributed to St Boniface, and to that of the scribe of the synoptic gospels in the Book of Mulling (but much more elegant, as befits the scriptorium of a primatial centre). It can also be full of fancies and flourishes. The Latin 'Pater Noster' is written with Greek letters and on one page the text is arranged so that the centre is in the shape of a diamond (f. 160[v]). Ferdomnach has decorated the gospels with splendid uncoloured drawings of the evangelist symbols and elaborate opening initials. Françoise Henry has pointed out the likeness of these initials to those of the Book of Kells, suggesting contemporaneity with the latter. Another scribe seems to be responsible for the Pauline epistles (perhaps Torbach himself at an earlier time), and here the initials are coloured, but less inventive. A third hand is responsible for the Patrician texts and the opening of the Life of Martin. Ferdomnach appears in the character of a finisher, providing an appendix for the first and completing the latter. His inscriptions were later scrubbed out and the manuscript attributed to the hand of St Patrick. As such, it was enshrined in 937.[130] It then became part of the abbatial (and later episcopal) insignia, with its own hereditary keeper.

When Ferdomnach died he was noticed like many another in the annals as a scribe.[131] This word was not, however, used simply to denote a copier of

[127] To Pádraig Ó Riain I owe a reference to this rare name in the Uí Corcráin genealogy in the Book of Ballymote.
[128] B.L., Add. MS 40618; CLA, ii, 179.
[129] T.C.D. MS 52; CLA, ii, 270; John Gwynn (ed.), *Liber Ardmachanus. the Book of Armagh* (Dublin, 1913); E. J. Gwynn (ed.), *The Book of Armagh: the Patrician documents* (facsimile, Dublin, 1937).
[130] A.F.M., 937.
[131] A.U., 845.

books, but implied a man of great learning, especially in Old Testament studies. Bella Schauman records that the Annals of Ulster name eighty-six scribes between the eighth and the eleventh centuries.[132] On such entries Kathleen Hughes has based her account of the distribution of Irish scriptoria, and in so far as great scholars tend to flourish in the wealthy centres, where alone great scriptoria can be maintained, it is not misleading. However, she did not, perhaps, sufficiently allow for the partial nature of the annals in their geographical interests, and their haphazard survival.[133]

The MacDurnan Gospels (pl. 45), the latest in the pocket format, was presented to Christ Church, Canterbury, by Æthelstan (924–39), but the inscription recording the gift also tells us of its earlier connection with Máel Brigte mac Tornáin, abbot of Armagh (888–927).[134] The book is splendidly decorated in a sort of linear pattern in brilliant colours, after the traditional manner, with a cross page, evangelist portraits, and elaborate opening pages for each gospel. As frequently happens, there are two opening pages in Matthew's gospel, one for the genealogies and a grander one for the nativity narrative.[135] The script, presumably dating from the end of the ninth century, shows the continuance of the Ferdomnach style at Armagh. The manuscript is in excellent condition, having spent the middle ages in the comfort of a well-appointed English library.

PRISCIAN'S grammar, composed in Constantinople c.500, was particularly popular with the Irish, and three of their copies (and a fragment of a fourth) survive, dating from the first half or middle of the ninth century. Two, the St Gall MS 904 and Leyden MS 67, are decorated with initials in the Armagh style, and the script too is similar to Ferdomnach's, but more robust, as befits the larger format of these books. Both manuscripts contain a mass of Irish glosses, and the St Gall copy contains the two well-known Old Irish poems of the scholar writing in the open air beneath the trees, and the poet rejoicing in the wild weather that will keep the Norsemen away.[136] Several scribes contributed to the writing and tell us their names: Máel Pátricc, Coirbbre, Finguine, and Donngus.

While the split descenders of the letters *f*, *p*, and *s* were confined to the initials in the Book of Armagh, here they have invaded the text. The Leyden copy was partly written by Dubthach, who dated it 11 April 838.[137] He was probably the man, *doctissimus Latinorum totius Europae*, whose death is

[132] Bella Schauman, 'Early Irish manuscripts: the art of the scribes' in *Expedition: University of Pennsylvania Magazine of Archaeology and Anthropology*, xxi, no. 3 (1979), pp 33–47: 33.
[133] Kathleen Hughes, 'The distribution of Irish scriptoria and centres of learning' in N. K. Chadwick (ed.), *Studies in the early British church* (Cambridge, 1958), pp 243–72.
[134] London, Lambeth Palace, MS 1370; Alexander, *Insular manuscripts*, p. 86.
[135] P. McGurk, 'The gospel book in Celtic lands', p. 168.
[136] *Thes. Pal.*, ii, 290.
[137] Kenney, *Sources*, p. 557.

recorded in the Annals of Ulster in 869. He seems to have been writing on the Continent and has been identified with one of the circle of Sedulius Scottus, the Irish expatriate poet and man of letters who was based in Liège from about 848. Sedulius knew Greek, and two Greek psalters with interlinear Latin translation in an Irish hand are associated with him: Paris, Bibl. de l'Arsenal, MS 8407, and Basel, Stadtbibl., MS A. vii.3—the latter being in a hand like those of St. Gall 48 and the Dresden Codex Boernerianus—all from the second half of the ninth century.[138]

Three manuscripts from Reichenau (but perhaps written at Péronne) and now at Karlsruhe, share a single Irish scribe, among others. One of these manuscripts is a Priscian, another various texts of St Augustine, and the third Bede's 'De temporum ratione'. The script is much more rapid and cursive than the Priscians discussed above, and Lindsay noted that the scribe is inclined to tie the *m* suspension stroke to the previous letter.[139] The prominence of Irishmen in the intellectual life of the Continent reached its peak in the ninth century, perhaps at least partly because of the difficulties that may have beset study at home as a result of the warfare intensified by the viking invasion and settlement. Most of these scholars seem to have dropped the insular hands of their upbringing, choosing instead to use—presumably for easier legibility—the Caroline minuscule of their continental colleagues. Among them was Martin, who was in charge of the palace school at Laon, and who wrote Laon, Bibl. Munic., MS 444 in the middle of the ninth century.[140]

The following century continued to be disturbed politically, but it saw the carving of the most splendid of the high crosses and the enshrining of manuscripts like the Book of Durrow (916) and the Book of Armagh (937). Such was the destruction of libraries in Ireland throughout the centuries that only books enshrined because of their supposed association with saints were to survive at home. The process was, however, very hard on the manuscripts. They were pierced with nails, like the Book of Durrow or Bodl. MS Rawlinson G 167. They rattled about, like 'Usserianus Primus', until the front and back leaves were reduced to the size of postage stamps. They were stained with green from the copper plates of the shrine, like the Books of Armagh and Mulling—though this, by inhibiting moulds, may have helped

[138] Ibid., pp 554–69; Ludwig Bieler, *Ireland, harbinger of the middle ages* (London, 1963), pp 120–25.
[139] Kenney, *Sources*, pp 670–71. The binding of the Bede contained fragments of an eighth-century Irish majuscule sacramentary, which seems to be related textually to the Stowe Missal (ibid., pp 701–2); W. M. Lindsay, *Early Irish minuscule script* (Oxford, 1910), pp 54–7.
[140] Bieler, *Harbinger*, pp 126–34; Kenney, *Sources*, pp 569–91. Could this have some bearing on Bischoff's finding that most of the oldest Irish texts in Latin were transmitted in Carolingian copies? Cf. Martin McNamara (ed.), *Proceedings of the Irish Biblical Association*, x (1986), p. 90. Eriugena seems, however, to have retained the insular script of his youth; cf. T. A. M. Bishop, 'Autographa of John the Scot' in R. Roques (ed.), *Jean Scot Érigène et l'histoire de la philosophie* (Paris, 1977), pp 88–94.

in their preservation, since the close atmosphere inside the shrine in the prevailing dampness could readily turn the vellum to slime. Little in the way of script seems to survive from the tenth century, apart from the Howth Gospels, the two majuscule psalters, and the Trinity fragment of a double-psalter noticed above. The last, however, writes the Hebraicum in a large and handsome set minuscule, evidence of what we have lost from this century. The glosses of the St Ouen Psalter provide small quantities of tenth-century minuscule, and the 'Lambeth Commentary' (found as part of the binding of a twelfth-century Llanthony manuscript, which would indicate a Duleek provenance), a fine continuous specimen (pl. 46).[141] Another candidate for this century would seem to be the binding-fragment from Oxford, Bodl. MS Lat. th. d. 7, displaying three very distinct hands, only one of which looks towards the greater standardisation that was to follow. These hands are clearly on the earlier side of the watershed that seems to develop at this point in the history of the script. The *a* is frequently not sharply pointed; half-uncial *d* is still present; the first stroke of the *r* does not descend below the line. Despite these factors, the Lambeth fragment is, in general appearance, already close to the hands of the later medieval scribes. Something very like it must have served as a model for the hand of Fáelán in the Book of Uí Maine.

The twelfth-century historians, especially those of the O'Brien camp, looked back to the late tenth century as a period of renaissance under Brian Boru. Certainly, it saw the decay of the old literary language, which in itself suggests a very serious loss of continuity and the infiltration of outsiders into the learned caste. At the same time, Irish—though it did not replace Latin—assumed a prominent role in liturgy. The change became more clearly visible in the eleventh century, when more surviving manuscripts again become available. Pádraig Ó Riain, following Conell Mageoghagan, in his introduction to the Annals of Clonmacnoise, sees the famous lost 'Psalter of Cashel' (a great compendium of genealogical and historical lore) as having been produced under the aegis of Brian.[142] Recent research casting doubt on the antiquity of the (lost) 'Cín Droma Snechtae' (formerly seen as an eighth-century prototype of such compendia of Irish traditional learning), would reinforce the likelihood that, in origin, they are a late-tenth-century phenomenon.[143] Translations from the Latin classics, like the Aeneid and Statius, also belong to this time, though many of the texts are now available only in much later copies.

The insular scripts continued in use for both Latin and Irish at a time when they were being rapidly abandoned in England. Even the majuscule (as

[141] London, Lambeth Palace, MS fragments 1229; Ludwig Bieler and James Carney, 'The Lambeth commentary' in *Ériu*, xxiii (1972), pp 1–55; William O'Sullivan, 'Medieval Meath manuscripts' in *Ríocht na Midhe*, vii, no. 4 (1985–6), pp 3–21: 17.

[142] Pádraig Ó Riain, 'The Psalter of Cashel: a list of contents' in *Éigse*, xxiii (1989), pp 126–8.

[143] Séamus Mac Mathúna (ed. and trans.), *Immram Brain* (Tübingen, 1985), pp 421–69.

we have seen) survived the introduction of the continental religious orders. The minuscule of the eleventh and twelfth centuries is clearly based on the Armagh script of the ninth, though sharpened and standardised to a degree. The *r* has already assumed its final form, with lengthened descender and widely splayed base. This is the script that was to be revived by the learned families in the fourteenth century, after the traumatic collapse of learning that followed the Anglo-Norman conquest. It is not easy to be sure of regional differences in Irish script, but the dominant position of Armagh in the religious and intellectual life of the country is well attested, and eventually was to be recognised in a mid-twelfth-century synodal decree confining the teaching profession to those who had been through the Armagh schools.[144] Perhaps because of this uniformity it is rarely possible to date these eleventh-/twelfth-century manuscripts by their script alone, and dating has usually been left to the art historians and the linguists, in the absence of other internal evidence. There is, however, a great variety of degrees of formality and many very individual hands.[145] At the most formal end comes the minuscule of the Trinity 'Liber Hymnorum' (pl. 47), placed by art historians and linguists in the late eleventh century; its more elegant fellow (belonging to the Irish Franciscans), may be a little later (pl. 48).[146] These are church books, judging by the splendid initials and large size of the script, and despite the amount of commentary in small glossing hands. More than any other manuscripts, they bring home the degree to which the liturgy had come to be naturalized in Ireland. Decoratively less complex but similar in script is the Gallican psalter in the Vatican.[147]

The Welsh Ricemarch Psalter, so called because it includes a poem by Ricemarcus (Rhigyfarch), was written by his brother Ithael in the late eleventh century. They were the sons of Sulien, bishop of St David's, who had studied in Ireland in the middle of the century and established a school at Llanbadarn Fawr, outside Aberystwyth. Françoise Henry saw the decoration as reflecting that of the tenth-century Irish psalters, and even in some measure that of the Book of Armagh.[148] The script is scarcely distinguishable

---

[144] A.F.M., 1162.

[145] Right at the beginning comes the inscription in the Book of Armagh entered by Caluus Perennis (Mael Suthain) in the presence of Brian Bóruma during his visit to Armagh in 1004. This already shows the characteristic pointed *a*, dominance of uncial *d*, and the first stroke of the half-uncial *r* descending as far as the *s* or *p*. The second part of the inscription seems to have been rather heavily restored.

[146] T.C.D., MS 1441 (E.4.2) and Killiney, Franciscan Library, MS A.2; J. H. Bernard and R. Atkinson (ed.), *The Irish Liber Hymnorum* (2 vols, London, 1897); Henry, 'Century', pp 129–34 (repr. Henry, *Studies*, pp 211–16).

[147] Vat. Lat. 12910; see 'A Gallican psalter in Irish script' in Ludwig Bieler, *Ireland and the culture of early medieval Europe*, ed. Richard Sharpe (London, 1987), no. XIX.

[148] T.C.D. MS 50 (A.4.20); H. J. Lawlor (ed.), *The psalter and martyrology of Ricemarch* (2 vols, London, 1914). See now Nancy Edwards, 'Eleventh-century Welsh illuminated manuscripts: the nature of the Irish connection' in Cormac Bourke (ed.), *From the isles of the north* (Belfast, 1995), pp 147–55.

from Irish examples, but while remote from any of the scripts in the ninth-/
tenth-century Welsh marginalia of the Lichfield Gospels,[149] it does probably
show some English influence, as the decoration of the major openings certainly does.

Scotland was a different case, as the Gaelic areas continued to belong to
the Irish script province until the end of the middle ages. Unhappily very
little survives for our period. The oldest manuscript would seem to be the
strange gospel-book known as the Book of Deer (pl. 49),[150] which, although
written in minuscule, belongs decoratively (but perhaps with an added
whimsical dimension) to the world of the tenth-century Irish majuscule psalters considered above. One of them, the sadly damaged Cotton Psalter (B.L.
MS Cotton Vitellius F. XI), from Monasterboice, seems to share the curious
tendency for the body of the $t$ in the $et$-ligature to be reduced to a simple
perpendicular. The Edinburgh Psalter (pl. 50), placed by Françoise Henry in
the early eleventh century, is small in size, with the very individual informal
air of having been written rapidly but skilfully with much use of open $a$.[151] It
is a personal book, unlike the Coupar Angus (Perthshire) Psalter, which is
large with large script, very much in the more standard style of the twelfth-
century Irish missals, and clearly intended for church use.[152]

The Irish missionary impulse of the seventh century was renewed in the
tenth, and the eleventh century saw the *Schottenklöster* movement flourishing
in Germany. Again the missionaries adopted the continental script, judging
by the copy of St Paul's epistles made by Marianus Scottus (Muiredach macc
Robartaig), abbot of Ratisbon, in 1079,[153] and the corrections added by the
other Marianus Scottus (but in Irish Móel Brigte), the *inclusus* at Mainz, to
his own chronicle. The body of this was, however, written in fine Irish
minuscule by a young man newly arrived on the Continent in 1072.[154]
Manuscripts like the eleventh-century Irish liturgical calendar in Turin,
which is bound with a copy of Gregory the Great's 'Pastoral care' in twelfth-
century English or French script, would have been written in Ireland, in
this case probably in Duleek.[155] Traffic the other way, perhaps from a

---

[149] Lichfield Cathedral Library, MS s.n.; for a plate see Dafydd Jenkyns and Morfydd
Owen, 'The Welsh marginalia in the Lichfield Gospels, part 1' in *Camb. Med. Celt. Studies*,
v (1983), pp 37–66.
[150] Cambridge University Library, MS Ii. 6.32; for facsimiles see John Stuart (ed.), *The
Book of Deer* (Edinburgh, 1869), and Alexander, *Insular manuscripts*, plates 329–32.
[151] Edinburgh University Library, MS 56; C. P. Finlayson (ed.), *Celtic Psalter* (Edinburgh,
1962) (facsimile).
[152] Vatican City, Biblioteca Apostolica, MS Palatinus Lat. 65; Henry, 'Century', pp 157–9
(repr. Henry, *Studies*, pp 239–41).
[153] Vienna, Österreichische Nationalbibliothek, MS lat. 1247; Kenney, *Sources*, pp 618–19.
[154] Vatican City, Biblioteca Apostolica, MS Pal. Lat. 830; Kenney, *Sources*, pp 614–15.
[155] Turin, Biblioteca Nazionale, MS D.IV.18; A. V. Brovarone and Fiorenza Granucci, 'Il
calendario Irlandese del codice D.IV.18...' in *Archivio Glottologico Italiano*, lxvi (1981),
pp 33–69. Pádraig Ó Riain is working on a new edition of the calendar.

*Schottenkloster*, is suggested by the presence in Ireland of an eleventh-century gospels written and decorated in the current German style.[156] Other examples of formal minuscule hands from this period are the gospels and missal at Corpus Christi College, Oxford, the two Harleian gospels (pls 51, 52) in the British Library (MSS 1023, 1802), the Drummond Missal (pl. 53), now in the Pierpont Morgan Library in New York, and the Rosslyn Missal, in the National Library of Scotland.[157] Only one of them (Harl. 1802) is dated and signed, and this was written by Máelbrigte hua Máeluanaig in Armagh in 1138. Working from the decoration, Françoise Henry and G. M. Marsh-Micheli—in a most brilliant article—managed to put the others in a chronological order, a *tour de force* that is, however, subject to dispute by scholars in other fields.

All three missals have the same proto-Sarum type of text, Roman in origin (and believed by Aubrey Gwynn to have been introduced about the time of Brian Bóruma). Henry dated the Corpus Missal to the early twelfth century and placed it in the west of Ireland, when Toirdelbach Ua Conchobair was king, but Gwynn preferred to place it in the monastery of SS Peter and Paul in Armagh, and believed it was written during the archbishopric of his grandson Tomaltach (1181–1201).[158] The first seven folios containing the canon are in a clumsy majuscule[159] (presumably a gesture to a sense of hierarchy in scripts), but the remainder employs a large but skilful minuscule with lively decoration in brilliant colours.

The Rosslyn Missal is a cathedral book and has been plausibly placed by Lawlor at Downpatrick, after the establishment of the diocesan system (but not in the late thirteenth/fourteenth century, as he suggests). Henry quite properly dates it to the middle or late twelfth century. In doing so, she would relate it to the Corpus Gospels, which she describes as written in a 'very regular and compact' minuscule, showing some continental influence, probably introduced by St Malachy at Bangor or Armagh.[160] However, later provenance—the Gospels were the gift to Corpus of Henry Parry, many of whose manuscripts came from Llanthony—suggests Duleek, which was granted to Llanthony by Hugh de Lacy around 1180.[161] A poem concerning St Kevin allows us to place the Drummond Missal fairly firmly at Glenda-

[156] T.C.D. MS 61 (A.4.14).

[157] Oxford, Corpus Christi College, MSS 122, 282; B.L., Harl. MSS 1023, 1802; New York, Pierpont Morgan Library, MS 627; Edinburgh, National Library of Scotland, MS 18.5.19 (A.6.12).

[158] Henry, 'Century', pp 137–40 (reprinted in Henry, *Studies*, pp 219–22); Aubrey Gwynn, 'Tomaltach Ua Conchobair, coarb of Patrick' in *Seanchas Ardmhacha*, viii (1979), pp 260–68.

[159] Ibid., first plate.

[160] H. J. Lawlor (ed.), *The Rosslyn Missal* (London, 1899); Henry, 'Century', pp 155–7 (repr. Henry, *Studies*, ii, 237–9).

[161] William O'Sullivan, 'Medieval Meath manuscripts' in *Ríocht na Midhe*, vii (1985–6), p. 17.

lough, but while Henry would date it on art-historical grounds to the late eleventh/early twelfth century, Gwynn believed it to belong to the time when St Laurence O'Toole was abbot there (but not yet archbishop of Dublin): 1153–62. Most recently, Pádraig Ó Riain has placed it in St Laurence's newly founded house for Augustinian canons, St Saviour's at Glendalough.[162] Hans Oskamp, who made a palaeographical study of the manuscript, noted that it is the work of two main scribes with later additions, some of which he would place as late as the fourteenth century; but this is unacceptable, as the addition in gothic script clearly dates from around 1150, and the inscriptions in Irish hands, from their placing, must have been written still earlier.

Two other manuscripts can be attributed to Glendalough, both in quite different hands. They are the second part of Oxford, Bodleian Library, MS Rawl. B 502, now recognised to be the lost Book of Glendalough[163] (one of the three great compilations of Irish traditional scholarship surviving from before the Anglo-Norman invasion), and two 'schoolbook' fragments (pl. 54) in B.L. MS Egerton 3323, ff 16, 18. The latter provide examples in Irish minuscule of texts that indicate the degree to which the twelfth-century clergy were in touch with the contemporary intellectual life of the Continent. The first fragment is part of the 'Ars grammatica' of the ninth-century expatriate Irishman Clemens Scottus; the second is a fragment of the 'De abaco' of Gerbert of Aurillac, the tenth-century abbot of Bobbio, who became Pope Silvester II. The hands of the fragments are quite distinct and they have been analysed by Ludwig Bieler and Bernhard Bischoff, who thought they saw in the second a ductus for writing Irish rather than Latin. It is certainly closer to most of the later medieval hands, though not to all.[164] A striking feature of the first fragment is the extension upwards of the left-hand stroke of the *a*, which is frequently found in later manuscripts and is such a noticeable feature of the fifteenth-century Book of the White Earl.[165] The first fragment contains the inscription which places the scribe in Glendalough and dates it to 1106, when Abbot Tuathal died, though the name may be too common for absolute certainty.

A fine copy of Boethius, 'De consolatione philosophiae', in the Laurentian Library in Florence, written in a clear hand with many interlinear and

---

[162] Gwynn was working on this at the time of his death, but did not, I think, publish it. Pádraig Ó Riain, 'Some bogus Irish saints' in *Ainm*, iii (1988), p. 2; H. P. A. Oskamp, 'The Irish quatrains and salutation in the Drummond Missal' in *Ériu*, xxviii (1977), pp 82–91.

[163] Pádraig Ó Riain, 'The Book of Glendalough or Rawlinson B 502' in *Eigse*, xviii (1981), pp 161–76 id., 'Rawlinson B 502 alias Lebar Glinne Dá Locha: a restatement of the case' in *Z.C.P.*, li (1999), pp 130–47.

[164] Ludwig Bieler and Bernhard Bischoff, 'Fragmente zweier frühmittelalterlicher Schulbücher aus Glendalough' in *Celtica*, iii (1956), pp 211–20.

[165] Anne and William O'Sullivan, 'Three notes on Laud Misc. 610 (or the Book of Pottlerath)' in *Celtica*, ix (1971), pp 135–7.

marginal glosses, is placed by Françoise Henry in conjunction with the Corpus Missal, which she dates between 1120 and 1130.[166] Chapters 19–34 of Boethius' 'De arithmetica' survive in T.C.D. MS 1442 (pl. 57), in an eleventh-/twelfth-century hand, rapid and businesslike with numerous abbreviations. In the same library, MS 1316, pp 98–90, is a fragment of Stephen of Tournai's 'Summa super decretum Gratiani' (pl. 56), probably copied during the author's lifetime, in a very different hand, less compressed and broader in character with short descenders.

Nothing gives so strong a sense of our great losses in this field of scholarly texts in Latin as the Bodleian manuscript Auct. F.3.15 (pl. 57), which opens with the Calcidius translation of Plato's 'Timaeus', in a fine large minuscule with pointed bases to the minims and well-formed serifs, but without much contrast of thick and thin strokes, the work of a scribe named Salmon. Francis John Byrne has identified the main, much smaller and more scholarly, hand of the rest of the book as that of the teacher Tuilecnad mentioned in a gloss. This name (in the form Tuileagna) was to be common in the later middle ages in the learned family of Ó Maolchonaire.[167] The hand is a rapid and very variable one, with open *a* sloping strongly to the left, and frequently *v* for *u*. It is remarkable how a manuscript like this seems to be echoed in some of the legal hands of the sixteenth century. The final text consists of extracts from the 'Periphyseon' of John Scotus Eriugena. Part of the manuscript is palimpsest over a decorated insular service book of the eighth century, presumably from Armagh.

Bodleian MS Laud Misc. 460 (pl. 58), Gregory's 'Moralia in Iob', was written for a Máel Brigte during the twelfth century in a number of different hands in Armagh. The quotations from Job are in majuscule, the commentary in minuscule, but the script has a curiously artificial air. The book still retains its medieval binding of white leather over wooden boards. Earlier Irish bindings are extremely scarce. The boards of the Book of Armagh, covered with pink leather decorated with blind stamps, survive, and the holes that carried the cords enabled Berthe van Regemorter to diagnose it as Carolingian, and so contemporary with the manuscript.[168] Later it was to be covered over in brown leather decorated with silver nails, in a style she called Armenian (from having met with it on the Armenian manuscripts in Venice). This might have been provided by John de Courcy after the battle of Down in 1178, when the book had to be recovered from the dead body of its

---

[166] Florence, Biblioteca Medicea-Laurenziana, MS LXXVIII, 19; Henry, 'Century', pp 140–41 (reprinted in Henry, *Studies*, ii, 222–3).

[167] Bodl. MS Auct. F.3.15; F. J. Byrne, *A thousand years of Irish script: an exhibition of Irish manuscripts in Oxford libraries* (Oxford, 1979), pp 14–15.

[168] Berthe van Regemorter, 'Évolution de la technique de la reliure du viiie au xiie siècle' in *Scriptorium*, ii (1948), pp 275–85. Anthony Cains, director of the conservation laboratory in the library of T.C.D., is currently engaged in a study of the Armagh binding.

hereditary keeper.[169] When Sir William Betham opened the shrine of the Cathach he found 'a thin piece of board covered with red leather, very like that with which eastern manuscripts are bound'.[170] The back board of the St Gall Priscian also carries Carolingian-type holes, and is probably part of the original binding of this manuscript. Perhaps under the present covering of the Stowe Missal there may likewise be early boards.

THE Latin works mentioned above are, however, part of the world of international scholarship, and can be easily paralleled in other countries. It is quite otherwise with the native learning in Irish. The first surviving specimen of continuous Irish prose—as opposed to glosses—written in insular is found in the Book of Armagh; the somewhat earlier text known as the Cambrai Homily is in continental script.[171] Probably from the late tenth or eleventh century (as we have seen above), it became fashionable to collect such material into large compendious volumes, but only three—all fragmentary, though substantial—have been preserved from before the Anglo-Norman period. Clearly, a great deal more was available up to the seventeenth century, and fortunately the late medieval antiquaries were assiduous copyists.

Leabhar na hUidhre (pl. 59), the oldest of the survivors, is thought by the linguists to date from the late eleventh or early twelfth century. It was written by two main scribes and a later interpolator. One of the scribes, who wrote his name in a pen-trial, was identified in a fourteenth-century colophon as the Máel Muire who was slain at Clonmacnoise in 1106. Richard Best thought the reference was to the second hand in the manuscript, the original scribe of the page on which the pen-trial occurs, but Tomás Ó Concheanainn believes it refers to the interpolator, who also intervenes on the same page.[172] This naturally makes some difference to the dating of the original manuscript, which was fragmentary when the latter scribe was working. The first scribe wrote a fine formal minuscule, the second is much less formal, but still careful, while the interpolator wrote rapidly, like a scholar intent rather on content than style. The fourteenth-century restorer seems to have cut the bifolia into single leaves, which he then made up with artificial joints into new sections of twenty-seven, marking each with the signatures A–I, K–U, X–Z, and [= et], est, amen, which must have been as clumsy in binding as the eighth-century pocket-gospel books. The hand of the interpolator turns up again, adding material to the fragment of the 'Irish World Chronicle' or the so-called 'Annals of Tigernach' (pl. 60) in Bodl. MS

[169] Séamus Ó hInnse (ed. and trans.), *Miscellaneous Irish annals* (Dublin, 1947), p. 67.

[170] Sir William Betham, *Irish antiquarian researches* (Dublin, 1826), p. 110.

[171] Cambrai, Bibliothèque Municipale, MS 619; *Thes. pal.*, ii, p. xxvi.

[172] R.I.A. MS 1229 (23.E.25); R. I. Best and O. Bergin (ed.), *Lebor na hUidre: the Book of the Dun Cow* (Dublin, 1929); Tomás Ó Concheanainn, 'The reviser of Leabhar na hUidre' in *Éigse*, xv (1973–4), pp 277–88; H. P. A. Oskamp, 'Mael Muire: compiler or reviser?' in *Éigse*, xvi (1975–6), pp 177–82.

Rawl. B 502, ff 1–12 (generally dated to the late eleventh or early twelfth century, and one of only two annalistic manuscripts to survive from before the Anglo-Norman arrival). The interpolator's additions were not carried into the main text of these annals, which dates from the fifteenth century.[173]

Rawl. B 502, ff 19–89, is all that remains of the Book of Glendalough, which, like Clonmacnoise (the provenance of the two last manuscripts), was one of the greatest of the Irish monasteries, and its book one of the most prestigious of sources for the late medieval scribes.[174] Françoise Henry made a detailed study of the lively decoration in this manuscript and agreed with the linguists and historians in dating it to about 1120.[175] It is the work of a single scribe using a narrow pen, which provides little contrast in the thickness of the strokes. The annals and the Book were bound together in the seventeenth century by their owner, the antiquary Sir James Ware.

The third of the great compendia of vernacular Irish texts is the so-called Book of Leinster (pl. 61), more properly known by its medieval name, 'Lebar na Nuachongbála' (after Oughaval, Co. Leix, the place where it was kept, a rectory belonging to the priory of Great Connell, Co. Kildare).[176] Oughaval is close to Dunamase, the greatest of the midland castles, which was in O'Moore hands in the later middle ages, and when their lands were expropriated they took the manuscript with them to Ballyna, County Kildare. The Book was compiled over a long period in the second half of the twelfth century (after 1151 and before 1198), in a number of hands showing varying degrees of formality, but basically similar. The three chief hands are those of Aed Ua Crimthainn, coarb of Terryglass (County Tipperary), who claims to have written it, compiling it from many books; the second is a strong, rounded, but not fine hand, with little contrast of thick and thin strokes; a grand calligraphic hand (F) showing good contrast and careful spacing; and a rough and careless hand (T), sharing the copying of the text of the 'Táin' with scribe F. He was also probably the assembler of the fragments of Aed's legacy, and so the architect of the Book as it survives today.

Palaeographically, the most potentially interesting for dating purposes of these few surviving early manuscripts in Irish is that of the Annals of Inisfallen. It was originally copied in 1095 for the use of Lismore (County Waterford), one of the greatest of the southern monasteries, from a text provided by the once greater house of Emly (County Tipperary), and it finally reached

[173] Bodl. MS Rawl. B 502, ff 1–12; R. I. Best, 'Palaeographical notes 1, the Rawlinson B 502 Tigernach' in *Ériu*, vii (1913), pp 114–20; H. P. A. Oskamp, 'The first twelve folia of Rawlinson B 502' in *Ériu*, xxiii (1972), pp 56–72.

[174] See n. 162.

[175] Henry, 'Century', pp 134–6 (reprinted in Henry, *Studies*, ii, 216–18).

[176] T.C.D. MS 1339 (H.2.18); Robert Atkinson (ed.), *The Book of Leinster* (Dublin, 1880) (lithographic facsimile); R. I. Best, O. Bergin, M. A. O'Brien, and A. O'Sullivan (ed.), *The Book of Leinster* (6 vols, Dublin, 1954–83) (diplomatic ed.); William O'Sullivan, 'Notes on the scripts and make-up of the Book of Leinster' in *Celtica*, vii (1966), pp 1–31.

Innisfallen after 1130, subsequently being added to until the fourteenth century. It was extensively studied by Richard Best and Seán Mac Airt, who identified twenty-eight successive insular hands between 1095 and 1214.[177] The last of these has, in its broadness, a superficial resemblance to the latest of the Latin text-hands noticed above, the Stephen of Tournai fragment. It is not yet possible to use the hands of these Annals for dating purposes, but perhaps further study may change that situation.

It is a similar case with the Irish charters entered on blank pages in the Book of Kells (pl. 62), of which seven survive and a further five, lost from the Book, are known from seventeenth-century copies.[178] The existence of these charters, compared with others from Wales and Brittany, has allowed Wendy Davies to draw very interesting conclusions about the nature of charters in the Celtic-speaking countries in early Christian times.[179] The Kells charters are thought to have been entered during the critical period of the reform of the Irish church, in the middle and second half of the twelfth century, when the property of the old monasteries was being redistributed. The seven charters still surviving in the Book of Kells display six different hands. The first to be entered were the four spread over ff 6ᵛ–7, by four scribes, probably in their present sequence. The first three can be dated textually to the late eleventh century, the fourth to around 1133. Following this come two charters from a single scribe, writing the most calligraphic hand: that begining on f. 6ᵛ (dated 11 November 1133) and that on the top of f. 27 (dated to 1161), both probably entered about the latter time. Very close to this hand is the single charter entered in the Book of Durrow, whose text seems to date from the end of the eleventh century.[180] The final charter, that at the bottom of f. 27, has a text datable to the second decade of the twelfth century. Best remarked the resemblance of this excessively sharp hand (with strong beaks to the bowls of *d* and *g*) to hand 21 in the Annals of Inisfallen, which covers the years 1159–74.

For the time being we have an outline of the development of Irish script, not all of it solid and much still subject to dispute. The Irish learned their

[177] Bodl. MS Rawlinson B 503; R. I. Best and E. MacNeill (ed.), *The Annals of Inisfallen* (facsimile, Dublin, 1933); Seán Mac Airt (ed. and trans.), *The Annals of Inisfallen* (Dublin, 1951).

[178] *Cod. Cennanensis*, ff 5ᵛ–7, 27; Gearóid Mac Niocaill, 'The Irish charters' in Fox, *The Book of Kells*, pp 153–65. For a historical but non-palaeographical study of the charters, see Máire Herbert, 'Charter material from Kells', ibid., pp 60–77. Many of the most important decorated pages are on single leaves, which are readily lost when the binding is shaken. Four seem to have been lost since Archbishop Ussher counted them in 1621; cf. Bernard Meehan, 'Dimensions and original number of leaves', ibid., pp 175–6.

[179] Wendy Davies, 'The Latin charter tradition in western Britain, Brittany, and Ireland in the early medieval period' in Whitelock, McKitterick, & Dumville, *Ire. in early med. Europe*, pp 258–80. See now Dauvit Broun, *The charters of Gaelic Scotland and Ireland in the early and central middle ages* (Cambridge, 1995).

[180] R. I. Best, 'An early monastic grant in the Book of Durrow' in *Ériu*, x (1928), pp 135–42.

letters—beginning perhaps as early as the fourth century—for the most part from British missionaries. The scripts included an early half-uncial, pre-dating the development of the canonical Italian half-uncial of the early sixth century, as well as some more cursive forms. Largely isolated from the current continental fashions, they continued to use these scripts into the second half of the sixth century, when, perhaps inspired by the desire to emulate uncial, they created out of the quarter- or cursive half-uncial the splendid insular majuscule, suitable for the most solemn purposes, particularly the writing of books for display in church. It is likely that this happened as part of the general growth of learning in the Irish monasteries, of which Columbanus is an index. Once established, it came to be written more quickly and cursively, and so produced the minuscule, which became standard for ordinary books. Both scripts were fully fledged before the middle of the seventh century, whence the first surviving specimens of the minuscule seem to date. The troubled history of Ireland worked against the survival of books at home, so we have to look to England and the Continent to find examples of the sequence of scripts for the whole of our period. To add to the complications, the English disciples of the Irish missionaries took to writing in the Irish style, because they lacked a tradition of their own. This did not happen to any appreciable extent on the Continent, where there was such a tradition. The thorniest of all problems is that of distinguishing English handwriting from Irish—or, as Leonard Boyle has formulated it, Anglo-insular from Hiberno-insular script.[181] Concentration on this question has, however, served to throw light on many other important aspects, and helped to clarify the whole sequence of the scripts, which may now—thanks to the work of Malcolm Parkes—be seen to diverge in the second quarter of the eighth century in the north of England, but perhaps later in the south. The next great watershed in the development of Irish script falls around the year 1000, coinciding with a turning-point in the history of the culture. This was to be the final flowering of the script; the fourteenth-century revival, although it was responsible for much fine writing, remained antiquarian in intention as well as in fact.

[181] Leonard P. Boyle, *Medieval Latin palaeography: a bibliographical introduction* (Toronto, 1984).

# CHAPTER XV

# Ireland *c.*800: aspects of society[1]

## DONNCHADH Ó CORRÁIN

In Ireland of the eighth and ninth centuries and before, there were expanses of upland wood, and great bogs covered large areas of the country. The woodlands were not stable: they advanced and retreated in response to human activity, prehistoric and historic. Most woods were privately owned, managed for large timbers, and coppiced and pollarded for small ones. They provided many products: timbers of many kinds (for buildings, carpentry, basketry, and domestic vessels), pannage and rough grazing for animals, wild fruit and nuts for human consumption.[2] The bogs were used for peat[3] and summer pasture. Literary and legal sources convey the impression that large woods were scarce. Scots pine may have been harvested to virtual extinction. Great clearances had taken place in the fourth, fifth, and sixth centuries, and a growing population led to extensive colonisation and a remarkable extension of arable farming in the very early medieval period.[4] Irish saga and mythological literature written down from the seventh century onwards preserves vivid memories of the lowland clearances and the breaking-in of new lands; and monastic writings contain references to the colonisation of wood-

---

[1] This chapter was submitted to the editors in early 1978. It was revised in part and the references were updated as far as possible, given constraints of time, in Aug. 1999.

[2] *C.I.H.*, pp 78–9, 202, 582, 2183; Fergus Kelly, *Early Irish farming: a study based mainly on the law-texts of the 7th and 8th centuries A.D.* (Dublin, 1997), pp 83–4, 379–90.

[3] A. T. Lucas, 'Notes on the history of turf as fuel in Ireland to 1700 A.D.' in *Ulster Folklife*, xvi (1970), pp 172–202.

[4] Frank Mitchell, *The Irish landscape* (London, 1976), p. 3; for literary evidence of enclosure, not there cited by Mitchell, see R.I. Best and O.J. Bergin (ed.), *Lebor na hUidre* (Dublin, 1929), p. 320; John Colgan, *Triadis thaumaturgae ... acta* (Louvain, 1647; repr. Dublin, 1997), p. 534a; Plummer, *Vitae SS Hib.*, ii, 112–13; *Thes. Pal.*; Osborn J. Bergin and R. I. Best (ed. and trans.), 'Tochmarc Étaíne' in *Ériu*, xii (1938), pp 137–96: 176–8; for palynological evidence, David A. Weir, 'Dark ages and the pollen record' in *Emania*, xi (1993), pp 21–30; idem, 'The environment of Emain Macha' in J. P. Mallory and Gerard Stockman (ed.), *Ulidia: proceedings of the first international conference on the Ulster cycle of tales* (Belfast, 1995), 171–9; Barry Raftery, *Pagan Celtic Ireland: the enigma of the Irish iron age* (London, 1994), pp 121–8; Edwards, *Archaeology early med. Ire.*, p. 52; Harold Mytum, *The origins of early Christian Ireland* (London, 1992), pp 199–201.

land. It is not easy to form a general picture of the landscape and rural economy *c.*800, since archaeological excavations are far too few to be representative, Irish palynological research is not yet well developed, and much of the literary evidence has yet to be sifted and analysed critically. Further, in the present state of knowledge it is difficult, sometimes impossible, to distinguish regional and local variations, and many unavoidable generalisations made here must be taken to refer to part of the country only. Any treatment of settlement and material culture is therefore impressionistic and incomplete.

ECCLESIASTICAL foundations and monastic towns of varying sizes dotted the countryside. Some were tiny, in remote and barren parts of the country, on islands and headlands, while others were small churches in settled farming areas, each with its lands and circular enclosure, and little different in outward appearance from secular settlements. In the rich lowlands and rivervalleys there were large monastic towns such as Trim and Lismore, while other houses, great and small, occupied the fertile islands of the central bogland. The settlements of farmers were scattered thickly where land was at all suitable for cow or plough. In one area of Cavan, for example, there is evidence for an early Irish farming settlement for every hundred hectares; in other areas, settlement was twice or three times as dense. The remains of some 40,000 ringforts, roughly contemporary with one another, still dot the landscape, and archaeologists are agreed that the vast bulk of them are the farm enclosures of the well-to-do of early medieval Ireland.[5] Since many have been obliterated by centuries of land use and now come to light only in air photography the total may have been 50,000 or more.[6]

The great hillforts of the iron age and the impressive neolithic sites had long been abandoned as centres of leadership and defence; by the tenth century they were the object of antiquarian speculation, by the twelfth their purpose had been forgotten. The greater kings had moved to new residences, larger and more impressive versions of the ordinary farm settlements, and some had begun to live in the monastic towns. The establishments of petty kings and greater lords were distinguished from those of commoners by size and by a corvée rampart (*drécht gíalnai*) or two, but in plan they were little different from those of the richer farmers. But the lifestyle was different: kings were conspicuous consumers of luxuries.

The circular earthen rath or ringfort (Irish *ráith*), which averages about thirty metres in diameter, was the farmyard of the better class of self-sufficient farmer. Its distribution is uneven and one may posit regional

[5] Matthew Stout, 'Ringforts in the south-west midlands of Ireland', in *R.I.A. Proc.*, xci (1991), sect. C, pp 201–43; idem, *The Irish ringfort* (Dublin 1997).
[6] E. R. Norman and J. K. S. St Joseph, *The early development of Irish society: the evidence of aerial photography* (Cambridge, 1969).

cultural differences, particularly since the many place-names that derive from these features vary notably from province to province. These structures vary greatly in size and materials—univallate and multivallate, revetted with timber or stone, with or without a palisade, with or without a raised interior—and reflect the different standards of wealth and class of their owners. In rocky areas where building materials in stone are plentiful and ditch-digging difficult, and especially in the west, stone-built ring-enclosures (Irish *cathair*, *caisel*) are common. In lakeland and marsh, similarly sized enclosures (Irish *crannóg*) were constructed of timber or stone and clay on islands in lakes, natural and artificial, and surrounded with a defensive palisade. There may have been over 2,000 of these, many of them built in the late sixth and early seventh centuries, but sometimes occupied into the later middle ages. Most of these served the same purpose: each was a well-fenced farmyard for ordinary agricultural purposes and offered minimal defence against thieves and raiders in more disturbed times.[7] Some, like Cróinis on Lough Ennell and Lagore, were great royal sites and yield luxury items, such as fine metalwork.[8]

Most ringforts had souterrains, and about 2,000 of these are known. These were underground chambers, laboriously constructed by open trenching, rock-cutting, or tunnelling. Some are constructed using dry-stone masonry, and may be corbelled in part, and roofed with slabs. They were used for the storage of valuables, food (including dairy produce), and perhaps essential seed, and for refuge in times of attack. Souterrains have also been found in association with unenclosed houses. They seem to belong to the second half of the first millennium.[9]

Within the enclosure were lean-to and free-standing houses and sheds. The *les* or enclosed area was a farmyard in every sense of the word, with squawking hens, dogs, and pet pigs, and none too clean, as we know from the story of Bricriu and his queen who fell from their *grianán* as Cú Chulainn tore their *dún* apart, 'and wound up in the dunghill in the middle of the *les* among the dogs'.[10] The Laws speak of the 'dog of the four doors', specified in the 'Canones Hibernenses' as the master's house, the sheep pen, the calf pen, and the cattle pen.[11] The commentary on the fragmentary 'Conslechtai' ('Tract on dogs') speaks of different kinds of dogs and the compensation for

[7] V. B. Proudfoot, 'The economy of the Irish rath' in *Medieval Archaeology*, v (1961), pp 94–121; idem, 'Irish raths and cashels; some notes on chronology, origin and survival' in *U.J.A.*, xxxiii (1970), pp 37–48; Matthew Stout, 'Ringforts in the south-west midlands of Ireland', pp 201–43; idem, *The Irish ringfort*.
[8] Frank Mitchell and Michael Ryan, *Reading the Irish landscape* (revised ed., Dublin, 1990), pp 254–81.
[9] A. T. Lucas, 'Souterrains: the literary evidence', in *Béaloideas*, xxxix–xli (1971–3), pp 165–91; Mitchell & Ryan, *Irish landscape*, pp 264–81.
[10] *Lebor na hUidre*, p. 255 ('Fled Bricrend').
[11] *C.I.H.*, pp 2216, line 37; 2287, line 17 ('Bretha Nemed'); Bieler, *Ir. penitentials*, pp 174–5.

killing them: 'the dog of the four doors ... the herding dog ... and the dog of the dunghill, that is the dog of the worm-mound', namely, well-rotted farmyard manure.[12] The free-standing houses, as archaeologists have shown, were generally round, rectangular, or sub-rectangular in shape, and in area they range from 2 to 55 square metres. Proudfoot states that on archaeological evidence it is rarely possible to determine how many buildings were in use simultaneously, and he tends to the view that only one family dwelling-house could have been occupied at any one time.[13] However, there is archaeological evidence for three or more houses within the enclosure, and it is quite clear from early texts that more than one family lived in houses within a single enclosure. In one admittedly aristocratic context there are five inhabited houses within the *les*.[14] The materials used in house-building varied: some houses had stone-faced walls filled with rubble and were thatched; others were built of hazel wattles and daub, and had cavity walls filled with insulating moss, straw, or heather.[15] Many were flimsy and were frequently rebuilt. According to 'Críth Gablach' (*c.*700), farmers' houses ranged in size from 6 m to 8 m, but only one dimension is given. However, whether round or rectangular (and the balance of opinion is that the measurement is one of length) these dimensions accord well with those established by excavation for the houses of ordinary to prosperous farmers at Carraigaille, Cush, and Leacanabuaile.[16] With few notable exceptions, excavation has been confined in each case to the enclosure itself, and the surrounding area has been neglected. This is to be regretted, become some of the important farm buildings lay outside the enclosure, as we know from the laws. Corn-drying kilns, barns, and mills are specifically mentioned as buildings which might lie outside the *les*.[17] The *macha* or milking yard also lay outside, and in some cases dwelling-houses stood in the fields nearby. At Carraigaille Ó Ríordáin found house-sites and yards in the area between the two stone forts, and

---

[12] Liam Breatnach, 'On the glossing of early Irish law texts, fragmentary texts, and some aspects of laws relating to dogs', A. Ahlqvist and others (ed.), *Celtica helsingiensia: proceedings from a symposium in Celtic Studies* (Helsinki, 1996), pp 11–20: 18; for the text, see *C.I.H.*, p. 1107; for other references to *cú crumduma*, see Cormac's Glossary, § 314 (Kuno Meyer (ed.), 'Sanas Cormaic', Osborn J. Bergin and others (ed.), *Anecdota from Irish manuscripts*, iv (Halle, 1912), p. 27); *O'Dav.* (see n. 28), § 368 = *C.I.H.*, p. 1479, lines 36–7; *C.I.H.*, p. 111, lines 6–7; p. 1386, lines 25–7; cf. p. 1390, lines 7–9.

[13] Proudfoot, 'Economy', p. 103.

[14] *Ériu*, ii (1905), pp 206–26; *C.I.H.*, p. 5 = *Anc. laws Ire.*, v, 134 (comm.); D. A. Binchy (ed.), *Scéla Cano meic Gartnáin* (Dublin, 1963), p. 4; Mitchell & Ryan, *Irish landscape*, pp 259–60.

[15] Mitchell & Ryan, *Irish landscape*, 259–60 (reporting Dr Chris Lynn's remarkable findings at Deer Park Farms).

[16] S. P. Ó Ríordáin, 'Excavation at Cush, Co. Limerick' in *R.I.A. Proc.*, xlv (1940), sect. C, pp. 83–181; idem, 'Lough Gur excavations: Carraig Aille and the Spectacles' in *R.I.A. Proc.*, lii (1949), sect. C., pp 39–111; S. P. Ó Ríordáin and J. B. Foy, 'The excavation of Leacanabuaile stone fort, near Caherciveen' in *Cork Hist. Soc. Jn.*, xlvi (1941), pp 85–9.

[17] *C.I.H.*, pp 74, 196 = *Anc. laws Ire.*, iv, 116, 118 (comm.).

there were less definite indications of houses on the gentler southern slopes of the ridge on which the forts stood. Elsewhere unprotected houses, similar to those found within ringforts, have been discovered and these too have souterrains.[18] The impression one gets from the literary sources is that the houses of many small farmers, cottiers, and lesser tenantry were unenclosed and stood unprotected in the fields.

In the seventh and eighth centuries land was owned and farmed by the *derbfine*, a four-generation agnatic lineage-group which was the family for legal purposes. Each adult male member of this group took an equal share of the family land (*fintiu*) and this land was clearly delimited and marked off from that of others by mearing stones and fences.[19] Land was owned jointly by the members of the *derbfine* and inheritance was partible. When the paterfamilias died, the heirs divided the estate *per capita* and set up dividing fences about their portions.[20] However, it is not at all clear from the law tracts whether partition was obligatory at this point and, besides, minor adjustments to a member's share of kinland could take place from time to time. Coparceners enjoy the benefit of survivorship, and on occasion it is to the profit of some to prolong their membership of the group and delay partition. On other occasions, family disputes probably led to earlier divisions. In the case of division, and in the case of land inherited from more remote kindred which had become extinct, the greatest care was taken to apportion the land equally, quality as well as quantity was taken into account, and the implication is that land of all kinds, arable and pasture, good and bad, was included in each man's portion; and if inequity became evident after a few years of land use, redistribution followed.[21] The *derbfine* functioned as a joint-farming co-operative, and joint ploughing and pasturage were usually matters for arrangement among kinsmen. It would seem from the system of partible inheritance and joint-farming and from the land law, especially that of trespass and the insistence of the lawyers that all animals should be herded by day and enclosed by night, that the farming system was of the rundale or run-rig type. Human as distinct from animal trespasses are also listed.[22] Land was divided into three categories: arable infield tilled in strips, fenced pasture (probably tilled on occasion), and commonage in wood, upland, and bog used by the local community as a whole. However, a great deal of woodland was in private ownership perhaps as early as the seventh century, and the land law goes into considerable detail on the fines and penalties for

[18] A. E. P. Collins, 'Settlement in Ulster, o–1100 A.D.' in *U.J.A.*, xxi (1968), p. 53.
[19] D. A. Binchy (ed. and trans.), 'An archaic legal poem' in *Celtica*, ix (1971), pp 152–68; T. M. Charles-Edwards, *Early Irish and Welsh kinship* (Oxford, 1993), pp 61–88, 415–30.
[20] *C.I.H.*, p. 64 = *Anc. laws Ire.*, iv, 68 ('Bretha Comaithchesa').
[21] Rudolf Thurneysen (ed. and trans.), *Cóic Conara Fugill*, in *Abhandlungen d. Preuss. Akad. d. Wissenschaften, Jhg. 1925, phil.-hist. Kl.*, Nr. 7 (Berlin, 1926), pp 42–3 = R. Thurneysen, *Gesammelte Schriften* (3 vols, Tübingen, 1991), iii, 387; *Studies in Ir. law*, p. 140.
[22] *C.I.H.*, pp 191–4, 202–5 = *Anc. laws Ire.*, iv, 98, 150–54.

theft and damage in privately owned woods.[23] Trees are classified in the laws according to their economic value: the nobles of the wood (*airig fedo*) are oak, hazel, holly, yew, ash, Scots pine, and apple. Oak was valued for its mast and the quality of its wood; hazel for its fruit and its pliable rods for basketry and house-building; holly for cart-shafts, cooking-spits, and winter fodder; yew for high-quality woodcraft, including domestic and dairy vessels; Scots pine (which may have become very scarce) for its resin and its beams; and apple for its fruit. Damage to these trees was severely punished: the penalty fine was the equivalent of five heifers and, besides, the perpetrator had to compensate the owner for the damage.[24] These rules indicate that good timbers were scarce in the seventh and eighth centuries, and therefore highly valued.

Not all land was kin-land: some land (we have no idea how much, but it was substantial) was privately owned by individuals who could dispose of it much as they wished, by sale, grant, or testamentary disposition, and there was a market in land.[25] Some land was held by written title, and this kind of title was not confined to church land.[26]

Effective fences, between kindred sharing ownership of common kin-lands and between kin and non-kin, were vital for good management of mixed farming and for good relationships between neighbours, and the laws, especially 'Bretha Comaithchesa', which dates from the second half of the seventh century, preserve valuable information. Four kinds of ordinary fences that inheriting kindred erect about their portions of the kin-land are distinguished: a ditch-and-dyke (*clas*), a stone fence (*cora*), and oak fence (*dairime*), and fence of post and wattles (*felmae* or *nochtaile*). The tools for making them are listed for each: a spade (*ráma*) for a ditch-and-dyke, a ploughshare (*soc*) for a stone fence, an axe (*biail*) for an oak fence, and a billhook (*fidbae*) for a

---

[23] Binchy, 'Archaic legal poem', pp 157–8; *C.I.H.*, pp 202–4 = *Anc. laws Ire.*, iv, 146–54 ('Bretha Comaithchesa').

[24] Fergus Kelly, 'The Old Irish tree-list' in *Celtica*, xi (1976), pp 107–24; idem, *Irish farming*, pp 379–90; Mitchell & Ryan, *Irish landscape*, pp 284–5.

[25] For examples of sales and grants of land: ten in the *additamenta* in the Book of Armagh, dated to *c.* 700 (*Thes. Pal.*, ii, 337–41 = *Trip. life*, ed. Stokes, ii, 238–43 = Bieler, *Patrician texts*, pp 166–79); R. I. Best, 'An early monastic grant in the Book of Durrow' in *Ériu*, x (1926–8), pp 135–42 (witnessed by Muirchertach Ua Briain, and dated 1103 × 1116); Gearóid Mac Niocaill (ed), *Notitiæ as Leabhar Cheanannais, 1033–1161* (Dublin, 1961) contains twelve eleventh- and twelfth-century records of grants or sales; Wendy Davies, 'The Latin charter-tradition in western Britain, Brittany and Ireland in the early mediaeval period' in Whitelock, McKitterick, & Dumville, *Ire. in early med. Europe*, pp 258–80. According to 'Córus Bésgnai', a man may acquire land by purchase and may bequeath it to whom he wishes, provided he leaves to his kindred what is their due (*C.I.H.*, pp 532–4 = *Anc. laws Ire.*, iii, 42–4; Charles-Edwards, *Irish and Welsh kinship*, pp 67–8).

[26] *C.I.H.*, p. 748, lines 35–7 (*senscribinn deód(h)a eclasa ł tuaithe cona coimet téchta* 'a godly ancient document of church or lay community with its appropriate keeping', i.e. kept in an appropriate place by an appropriate custodian); cf. *C.I.H.*, p. 751, line 1 = p. 596, line 29 = p. 1376, line 1 = *Anc. laws Ire.*, v, 368; *C.I.H.*, p. 231, lines 7–10 (*comscribeann deoda* 'joint godly document', i.e. a document of grant drawn up by both parties).

post-and-wattle fence. All these are obvious fencing tools except for the ploughshare: this was used to strike out the line of the stone fence and the topsoil was ploughed aside to give it a firmer foundation in the subsoil. Glossators explain that the ditch and stone fence were used in the bare plain (the arable), the oak fence in the wood, and the post-and-wattle fence in the *leth-machaire* (perhaps pastureland occasionally fenced). All are specified as being 180 cm high (in the case of the ditch-and-dyke this is the measurement from the bottom of the ditch to the top of the dyke). The stone fence is made of three courses of stone and is 90 cm in thickness. The post-and-wattle fence has three courses of wattling binding together the posts, which must be smooth on top to prevent possible damage to overleaping animals. The posts are set in firmly about 20 cm apart and a crest of woven blackthorn is put on top to prevent animals jumping over the fence. The oak fence was used in private woodland. It was made by cutting a line of trees low in the trunk. However, the trunks were not cut through, and when felled they formed an unbroken line that gave a quick fence that thickened naturally with the passage of time. It had to be 180 cm high so that large animals could not overleap it, and dense enough to prevent small animals getting through.[27] The evidence for fencing, in field and wood, points to sedentary agricultural-ists who carefully managed the resources of their environment.

The arable lay in fenced fields near the farmyards (the *gort faithche* of the law tracts). In some cases, perhaps the majority, it was farmed in strips or *immairi* (a term that is latinised *jugerum* and glossed 'a day's ploughing') rather than in blocks.[28] These strips may have been separated by shallow ditches.[29] Since considerations of absolute equality of share were a major preoccupation, it is likely that these were scattered widely throughout the infield in order to take different qualities of soil into account. Beyond lay the fenced pasture-lands (perhaps the equivalent of the *gort gabála* of later literary texts) some of which were preserved for winter (*etham*) while others were grazed in spring and again in autumn. On some occasions at least, these fields were not owned as a block but were dispersed among those of other kinsmen, for the laws make detailed provisions for the driving of cattle over other men's land where

[27] *C.I.H.*, pp 73, 195–6 = *Anc. laws Ire.*, iv, 112; *C.I.H.*, pp 1855, 2133; *Collectio Canonum Hibernensis*, liii, 9 = Hermann Wasserschleben (ed.), *Die irische Kanonensammlung* (Leipzig, 1885, reprinted Aalen, 1966), p. 215 (hereafter cited as *Hib.*): fencing of cornfields, vineyards and gardens against trespass by hens; D. Ó Corráin, 'Some legal references to fences and fencing in early historic Ireland' in T. Reeves-Smyth and F. Hammond (ed.), *Landscape archaeology in Ireland* (Oxford, 1983), pp 247–51; Kelly, *Irish farming*, pp 372–6; Ó Ríordáin, 'Cush', p. 141.

[28] *Thes. Pal.*, ii, 298; Plummer, *Vitae SS Hib.*, ii, 113; Charles Plummer, *Miscellanea hagiographica hibernica* (Brussels, 1925), pp 16–17; Whitley Stokes (ed.), 'O'Davoren's glossary' in *Archiv für celtische Lexikographie*, ii (Halle, 1904), §§ 1075, 1121 (hereafter cited as *O'Dav.*); *Trip. life*, ed. Mulchrone, p. 116; *Ériu*, ix (1921–3), pp 157–8; *Críth Gab.*, p. 9.

[29] Kuno Meyer (ed.), 'Sanas Cormaic', p. 43, § 516; Whitley Stokes (ed.), 'O'Mulconry's glossary' in *Archiv für celtische Lexikographie*, i (Halle, 1889), p. 257, § 478.

there are no roads or droving lanes.[30] One of the law-tracts specifies that droving lanes must be provided, and it is likely that a network of such lanes ran through family lands as they did in more recent examples of the rundale system. Farmers usually had access to commonage in the form of rough grazing on bog, upland, or in woodland.[31] Milch cows, often tended by women, were grazed in these seasonal pastures and stores of dairy products were laid down for the winter.[32] Arrangements for common pasturing were, it seems, made by groups of partners (kin or non-kin) of differing status who held farms of unequal size. Partnership of this kind supplemented some of the functions of kinship. Each contributed his own amount of privately owned pasture land to the common pool and was entitled to put a proportionate number of cattle in the common herd that grazed the fenced pasture and harvested arable in turn, an arrangement that was to the partners' advantage since grazed fields take time to regenerate.[33] One cannot say to what degree this system of partnership between smaller kinship groups and individuals may have served to alter the rundale system, nor indeed can one show whether the rundale system was itself universal or merely limited to certain areas. Successive subdivision among joint heirs leads relatively rapidly to extensive fragmentation when family numbers increase; but, given the disturbed demographic conditions of the late seventh and early eighth centuries, it is likely that fragmentation and consolidation balanced each other within small kinship groups, though there is some evidence in the law tracts of persons losing status because their inheritance has become too small through subdivision to provide them with the necessary qualifications in property. It is likely that large, isolated, individually owned farmsteads (*Einzelhöfe*) also existed (perhaps among the lordly class); but, as the geographers have shown, there is no necessary polarity between these and the rundale farms. Given partible inheritance and the contingencies of family increase and decrease, the one can develop into the other in the course of a few generations.[34]

---

[30] *C.I.H.*, p. 205 = *Anc. laws Ire.*, iv, 156 ('Bretha Comaithchesa'); *Ériu*, xiii (1940–42), p. 33 ('Bretha Nemed').

[31] *Ériu*, xiii (1940–02), p. 33 ('Bretha Nemed').

[32] John Fraser and others (ed.), *Irish texts*, i (London, 1931), p. 4, § 12 ('Vita Brigitae'); p. 34, 5 ('Story of Maelruain'); *Thes. Pal.*, ii, 328; Whitley Stokes (ed.), *Lives of the saints from the Book of Lismore* (Oxford, 1890), p. 57; Charles Plummer (ed.), *Bethada náem nÉrenn* (2 vols, Oxford, 1922), i, 157; Pádraig Ó Moghráin, 'Some Mayo traditions of the buaile' in *Béaloideas*, xiii (1943), pp 161–71, 292; idem, 'More notes on the *buaile*' in *Béaloideas*, xiv (1944), pp 45–52; J. M. Graham, 'Transhumance in Ireland' in *Advancement of Science*, x, no. 37 (1953), pp 74–9; Caoimhín Ó Danachair, 'Summer pasture in Ireland' in *Folk Life*, xxii (1983–4), 36–54; A. T. Lucas, *Cattle in ancient Ireland* (Kilkenny, 1989), pp 41–67.

[33] T. M. Charles-Edwards, 'On common farming' in Kathleen Hughes, *Early Christian Ireland: introduction to the sources* (London, 1972), pp 61–4.

[34] Desmond McCourt, 'The dynamic quality of Irish rural settlement' in R. Buchanan and others (ed.), *Man and his habitat* (London, 1971), pp 126–64; R. H. Buchanan, 'Field systems of Ireland' in A. R. H. Baker and R. A. Butlin (ed.), *Studies of field systems in the British Isles* (Cambridge, 1973), pp 580–618.

Ó Ríordáin's excavations at Cush give us some idea of the size and general economy of a prosperous cattle-raising and grain-growing community of farmers in the early medieval period, perhaps in the seventh or eighth centuries. The site, which commands a fine view, is on a northward extension of the Ballyhoura hills, between the 700-ft and 800-ft contour, on the borders of arable and rough pasture. There are two groups of conjointed or closely associated ringforts, one of six with a large enclosure beside them and occupying in all 1.2 hectares, and another to the north of five. The first is an example of expansion from one to four and finally to six ringforts, and the large enclosure was added later. The ringforts of the second group appear to be coeval with each other. Most of them contained houses and elaborate souterrains, while two other houses stood in the southern enclosure and another in the fields to the west. The finds point to a peaceful and prosperous community which was not rich in ornaments or metals, though some glass beads and a few bronze items did occur. Some iron-working was carried on: an iron sickle-blade, a spearhead, iron knives and nails, and some eight kilogrammes of iron slag indicate that what metal the occupants had was for strictly utilitarian purposes. Stone whorls and loom weights are evidence for domestic spinning and weaving. The very large number of querns—twenty-six stones and fragments were recovered from one ringfort alone—points to the importance of grain-growing in their economy. The associated fields to the east and running uphill are contemporary with the ringforts. They are very large—two are about five hectares and two others are a little over two hectares—and are the fields of graziers. Other smaller fields, probably the arable, nestle close to the southern cluster of ringforts.[35]

Cultivation by spade, a simple wooden implement with an iron sheath, went on side by side with ploughing over large areas of the country and among the poorer classes everywhere. However, the normal preparation of land for cereal-growing was by ploughing and harrowing. In this context, it has to be stressed that the extent of cultivation and the economic importance of cereals in early medieval Ireland have been underestimated. The laws preserve a great deal of information on agriculture, and archaeological excavation is slowly filling in the picture. Ploughing was done with oxen, though in exceptional circumstances a horse could take the place of an ox in the team. The plough was drawn by four, less usually six, oxen harnessed to the plough with head-yokes or withers-yokes. Both kinds were in use in Ireland and there is some slight evidence to indicate that the first type was considered the earlier. Only very prosperous farmers (for example the *mruigfer*) and monastic establishments possessed a full ploughing-team; even well-off farmers owned only a half or a quarter of a plough and ploughing-team, and

---

[35] Ó Ríordáin, 'Cush', pp 83–181.

pooled their resources for joint ploughing.[36] Not much is known about the types of plough in use in early medieval Ireland. The usual early plough was a coulterless ard: it broke up the soil but did not turn the sod. This meant that cross-ploughing and ground preparation with spades and mattocks was still necessary. Substantial coulters and shares, which have been excavated, indicate fairly well-developed farming equipment[37] but their date is uncertain. According to Hencken, a coulter found at Lagore is descended from La Tène and Roman types and indicates a big plough and big team suitable perhaps for wet and heavy soils,[38] and Mitchell has argued that the mouldboard plough was introduced about A.D. 600.[39] However, recent research shows that coultered ploughs, more commonly with short-tanged coulters and heavy shares, first appeared in Ireland in the tenth century, in line with changing practice in the north-western Atlantic coastal regions, and the plough of the early middle ages was an ard with a small iron share.[40] Harrowing, which is notably poorly evidenced elsewhere in early medieval Europe, is mentioned in 'Críth Gablach' (*c.*700) and in a number of early sources.[41] In Ireland as elsewhere the harrow was drawn by horses; speed is necessary to break the clods and oxen are too slow for the purpose. From the term *cliath fuirside* we may infer that the harrow was a wooden implement, perhaps with iron teeth.

Manure (*gert, tuar, fual, miaslach, ailech*) was relatively scarce because of the pattern of summer grazing and the lack of an extensive system of winter housing and foddering. What was available was highly valued. Manure was carted to the fields in autumn and land for barley was manured before the winter: *cuna thuar dligthech air i foghmur* ('with its lawful manuring in autumn').[42] The dung of a milch cow or an ox was worth a scruple, that of other cattle half a scruple.[43] The sources, mostly commentary on the laws, preserve little detail. Cattle were run on the harvested arable in autumn, and this may have done something to enrich the soil. It is implied in hagiographical texts that systematic manuring was part of the ordinary process of culti-

[36] A. T. Lucas, 'Irish ploughing practices' in *Tools and tillage*, ii (1972-5), pp 52–62, 67–83, 149–60, 195–210: 53–62; Kelly, *Irish farming*, 468–78.

[37] Michael Duignan, 'Irish agriculture in early historic times' in *R.S.A.I. Jn.*, lxxiv (1944), pp. 128–38.

[38] H. O'N. Hencken, 'Lagore crannog: an Irish royal residence of the 7th to 10th centuries A.D.' in *R.I.A. Proc.*, liii (1950), sect. C, pp 7–8.

[39] Mitchell, *Irish landscape*, pp 173–4.

[40] Niall Brady, 'Reconstructing a medieval Irish plough' in Dirección General de Bellas (ed.), *1 Jornadas internacionales sobre tecnologia agraria tradicional* (Museo Nacional del Pueblo Espagnol, Madrid, 1993 [= 1994]), pp 31–44.

[41] *Críth Gab.*, p. 16 (*dá chapall do foirtsiud* 'two horses for harrowing'); *C.I.H.*, p. 750; A.U., s.a. 1013 (for the meaning of this entry, see *Éigse*, xiv, no. 1 (summer 1973), p. 23); R.I.A., *Dictionary of the Irish language, s.vv* cliath (d), daintech.

[42] *C.I.H.*, pp 480–81 = *Anc. laws Ire.*, ii, 238, 240 ('Cáin Aigillne' and gloss).

[43] *C.I.H.*, p. 1772 = *Anc. laws Ire.*, ii, 200, 218, 220; *Z.C.P.*, xiv (1923), p. 350; Plummer, *Vitae SS Hib.*, ii, 245; Heist, *Vitae SS Hib.*, p. 163.

vation: that the monks should be able to work the land and have abundant produce without any manuring (*sine ulla stercorum cultura*) is represented as a miracle. The same texts indicate that dung from the sheepfold was also used as manure.[44]

Ploughing was done in March and the corn was sown in the same month, ideally at any rate.[45] It was harvested in September, or perhaps earlier, depending on the weather. Corn was usually grown in narrow ridges as in classical times.[46] Ridge cultivation is explicitly mentioned in a twelfth-century praise-poem of the king of Uí Echach Cobo: *A fir flatha fo dero/tóla n-etho ar gach indra* ('His princely righteousness is the cause of an abundance of corn on each ridge').[47] Given the heavy rainfall, this method is particularly suitable for field drainage and is well attested in Ireland in modern times, from the sixteenth to the nineteenth centuries. The cultivated cereals in order of importance were oats, barley, rye, and wheat, though it is likely that this order varied from place to place (and from time to time given micro-climatic shifts) because of differences of soil and rainfall.

There are difficulties in regard to the types of cereals grown in early medieval Ireland. Archaeobotanical research is in its early stages—materials from less than thirty sites have been analysed—and the literary evidence is limited. What follows is based mainly on the pioneering work of Jessen and Helbaek and on the researches of Monk and Kelly.[48] Some varieties of wheat—spelt (*T. monococcum*), emmer (*T. diococcum*), and possibly bread wheat (*T. aestivum*)—were brought into Ireland by the neolithic farmers. Whatever its origins, bread wheat was well established in the early medieval period, especially on monastic farms, though not at all as widespread as barley or oats. The Irish words for wheat, *cruithnecht* and the rarer *tuirenn*, are of uncertain origin: O'Brien suggests that *cruithnecht* is an internal compound of Irish *cruth* 'shape', and *necht* 'cleansed', meaning 'winnowed, purified'; and he believes that *tuirenn* goes back to the Indo-European root that

---

[44] Plummer, *Vitae SS Hib.*, ii, 245 14, 248 17; Heist, *Vitae SS Hib.*, p. 163 11, 165 12.

[45] *C.I.H.*, p. 1516 = O'Dav., p. 417 1249; *C.I.H.*, pp 480–81 = *Anc. laws Ire.*, ii, 238, 240 ('Cáin Aigillne' and gloss) = R. Thurneysen, 'Aus dem irischen Recht I: Das Unfrei-Lehen' in *Z.C.P.*, xiv (1923), pp 335–94: 348–50.

[46] John O'Loan, 'A history of early Irish farming' in *Éire: Department of Agriculture, Journal*, lxi (1964), pp 242–84: 252–7; lxii (1965), pp 131–97.

[47] K. Meyer (ed. and trans.), 'Ein mittelirische Lobgedicht auf die Uí Echach von Ulster' in *Sitz-Ber. Kgl. Preuss. Akad. Wiss., phil.-hist. Kl., 1919*, pp 89–100: 93 23; Meyer's date, 993–1004, is based on a mistaken identity.

[48] Knud Jessen and Hans Helbaek, 'Cereals in Great Britain and Ireland in prehistoric times' in *Kongelige Danske Videnskabernes Selskab, Biologiske Skrifter*, iii, no. 2 (1944), pp 1–68; M. A. Monk, 'Evidence from macroscopic plant remains for crop husbandry in prehistoric and early historic Ireland: a review' in *Irish Archaeological Journal*, iii (1985–6), pp 31–6; idem, 'The archaeobotanical evidence for field crop plants in early historic Ireland' in J. Renfrew (ed.), *New light on early farming: recent developments in paleoethnobotany* (Edinburgh, 1991), pp 315–28; Kelly, *Irish farming*, pp 219–28.

give Latin *triticum* 'wheat'.[49] At Lagore, the excavator found straw that corresponded in size and structure to modern farm wheat and indicated large and well-grown domestic wheat.[50] *Rúadán*, which is mentioned occasionally in early texts, has been variously understood. Mitchell suggested that *rúadán* referred to the polygonaceae in general and that these were grown as a deliberate crop and not simply gleaned off the fallows.[51] However, *rúadán* is identified with wheat in O'Davoren's glossary and glossed *cruithnecht ruad .i. mael-cruithnecht*,[52] which may point to an identification with emmer, which can have a reddish stalk. Wheat was very highly esteemed: indeed, the turning of lesser cereals into wheat is a stock miracle in the lives of the saints.[53] It is likely that the return was low: one may suppose that the yield in Ireland was no higher than that of Carolingian Francia, where the reported return was 2 : 1 or 2.5 : 1. Wheaten bread was a luxury in early Ireland, the bread of festivals and the food of kings and nobles, and as such it is frequently mentioned in the sagas and hagiography.[54] Amongst the renders of a base client to his lord is *míach cruithnechta cruaid inbíd*, 'a bushel of hard [probably kiln-dried] wheat, suitable for food'.[55]

Barley (Irish *éornae*, Latin *hordeum*) was of great importance in Ireland as it was in continental Europe, where the Merovingian kings took most of their tribute from Germany in it. It is the dominant cereal in archaeobotanical samples recovered from early medieval sites. Two types of barley—two-row and six-row—occur in early medieval Ireland, though the second is the more common. Rents and renders were very often paid in prime malted barley, and much of the crop was used to produce ale.[56] It was also used for bread-making, but if we may judge from its frequent prescription as a penitential diet it was regarded as no luxury. Its importance as a crop stretches back to the bronze age, for 75 per cent of the bronze-age evidence for cereals in Britain and Ireland points to barley.[57] Excavators have found it at Lough Gara crannog (*c*.200 B.C.) and at much later sites at Lough Faughan and Lissachiggel.[58]

---

[49] Micheál Ó Briain [= M. A. O'Brien], 'Hibernica' in *Z.C.P.*, xiv (1923), pp 309–34: 319.

[50] Hencken, 'Lagore crannog', p. 242.

[51] Breandán Ó Ríordáin, 'Excavations at High Street and Winetavern Street, Dublin' in *Medieval Archaeology*, xv (1977), p. 77; see also *Medieval Archaeology*, xvii (1973), pp 151–2; Mitchell, *Irish landscape*, p. 180.

[52] *O'Dav.*, p. 439, § 1369.

[53] Plummer, *Vitae SS Hib.*, ii, 214, § 26; Heist, *Vitae SS Hib.*, p. 137, § 295 (Molua); Stokes, *Lis. Lives* (see n. 32), p. 124, lines 4164–9 (Ciarán of Clonmacnoise).

[54] A. T. Lucas, 'Irish food before the potato' in *Gwerin*, iii, no. 2 (1960), p. 5; Stokes, *Lis. Lives*, p. 81, lines 2734–7 (Finnian of Clonard); ibid., p. 124, ll 4164–69 (Ciarán of Clonmacnoise); ibid., p. 313.

[55] Thurneysen, 'Aus dem irischen Recht I: das Unfrei-Lehen' in *Z.C.P.*, xiv, (1923), pp 335–94: 355.

[56] D. A. Binchy, 'Brewing in eighth-century Ireland' in B. G. Scott (ed.), *Studies on early Ireland: essays in honour of M. V. Duignan* (Belfast, 1981), pp 3–6.

[57] *Z.C.P.*, xiv (1923), p. 250; *Prehist. Soc. Proc.*, xviii (1952), p. 205.

[58] *Louth Arch. Soc. Jn.*, ix (1939), pp. 209–43; *U.J.A.*, xviii (1955), pp. 45–81.

Oats (Irish *corcae*, Latin *avena*), the richest of the cereals in proteins and fats, came into Europe as a weed mixed with wheat and first appears in Ireland in the iron age. It has been found in excavation at Ballingarry Downs, Lough Faughan crannog, Church Island, and elsewhere. The oat grows well in the damp, cool conditions of the west and north. It has a far lower sale value than barley: a bushel of oats has half the value of a bushel of barley. *Serbán* and what may be a variant form of the same word, *serbann*, is explicitly mentioned as being milled as grain and may be a variety of oats, *Avena strigosa*, bristle-pointed oats, also called pilcorn or black oats, which grows well on very poor land. Oats and barley were the cereals of the peasantry: as the commentator on 'Bretha Comaithchesa' observes: *tri bairgina coirci and, and an cetna d'eornain, uair is amhlaid icthar meich in comaithchesa* ('three oaten loaves for it and the same number of barley loaves, for it is thus that the bushels [of corn] are paid within a neighbourhood group')—and the *comaithches* is made up of ordinary farmers.[59] Oats appear to have been widely grown, were eaten in various forms of porridge and gruel, and provided the bread of the masses in Ireland down to the nineteenth century.[60]

Rye (*Secale cereale*) occurs very widely in early medieval sites though less frequently than oats. It was a crop of very considerable importance. There is a hagiographical legend that St Déclán of Ardmore first brought it to Ireland. However, rye had reached Ireland in the bronze age, and the story may merely enshrine a vague memory that different varieties of rye came with the monastic farmers. Significantly, the Irish term for rye, *secal*, is a late Latin borrowing and no earlier term appears to survive. There is a little literary evidence from the twelfth century for the growing of winter rye: a furious impatient approach is compared to *ag n-allaid do gebbad guirt gem-shecoil a mís Mitheman*, 'a wild deer to the cropping of a field of winter-rye in the month of June'.[61] Rye-bread was eaten, but not by the best people: a poisonous satirical fragment that describes its victim as having a pig's eye and the bulbous snout of a cur depicts him as eating rye-bread and butter.[62]

Corn was reaped with sickles, and it has been concluded from their size and shape that the straw was cut high up on the stalk as it was in medieval Europe generally.[63] The remaining stubble, after the cattle had grazed and trampled it, was ploughed back into the ground as fertiliser. Threshing was

---

[59] *C.I.H.*, pp 73–4 = *Anc. laws Ire.*, iv, 118.
[60] *R.I.A. Proc.*, lv (1953), sect. C, p. 245; *U.J.A.*, xviii (1955), pp 75–6; *R.I.A. Proc.*, lix (1958), sect. C, p. 130; David Greene (ed.), *Fingal Rónáin and other stories* (Dublin, 1955), pp 48, 55.
[61] Kenneth H. Jackson (ed.), *Aislinge meic Con Glinne* (Dublin, 1990), p. 33, line 1014 = Kuno Meyer (ed. and trans.), *Aislinge meic Conglinne* (London, 1892), p. 85.
[62] Rudolf Thurneysen (ed.), *Mittelirische Verslehren*, in Whitley Stokes and E. Windisch (ed.), *Irische Texte*, series iii, 1 (Leipzig, 1891), pp 1–182: 91, § 26 = *Gesammelte Schriften*, ii, 430.
[63] Duignan, 'Irish agriculture', p. 140.

done with the flail, which probably originated in Roman Gaul in the fifth century, but the date of its introduction to Ireland is uncertain. The Old Irish word for the flail, *súst*, is a borrowing of the Latin *fustis* 'beating stick' and the term was applied by the Irish both to the more primitive beating stick and to the flail proper, but an indigenous term *flesc* 'rod' is attested in the laws.[64] Both means of threshing continued in use till recent times. Threshing was done in kiln-houses in the case of the well-to-do, but in the case of the poor and not-so-poor farmers it was done on any paved or suitably dry area, probably on hides or other covering, as weather permitted.[65] Winnowing was also carried out in corn kilns but this may have been done from time to time as grain was required, for it is likely that grain and chaff were stored together. If we may trust some high-flown references, winnowing was done by slaves, at any rate when such were available in royal households.[66]

Because of Ireland's heavy rainfall, corn was artificially dried either before threshing or before milling, and specially constructed kilns were built for this purpose. Kilns like the early medieval ones were commonplace in the countryside till recently. It was a structure consisting of a lower room or bowl, tapering towards the base, into which led a flue some six or more feet in length. Hurdles were laid over the top and covered with matted straw. The grain was placed on the matting, and heat rising from red peat coals, placed in the outer end of the flue, dried the grain. The structure was usually covered with a conical thatched roof. In early Ireland, much larger kiln-houses (Irish *áith*, Latin *canaba*) were built by craftsmen. It is likely that the flue was absent and fire was therefore a hazard, as the law tracts clearly indicate. Woven wattling may have taken the place of straw matting. Threshing by flail was also carried out in these larger kiln houses,[67] but there is a good deal of evidence that the corn was dried in the ear, as it was in the Faroes and Hebrides till recently.[68] One of the saints' Lives explicitly describes this process as 'the custom of the westerners, of Britain and Ireland'. Corn for renders and dues was already kiln-dried when paid to lords.[69] It is

---

[64] Ó Danachair, loc. cit.; Latin *flagellum* had already been borrowed in its primary meaning, 'scourge'; Kelly, *Irish farming*, 481–2.

[65] Heist, *Vitae SS Hib.*, p. 191; *C.I.H.*, p. 273 = *Anc. laws Ire.*, iii, 220.

[66] Kuno Meyer, *Fianaigecht* (Dublin, 1910), p. 86; *Cogadh Gaedhel re Gallaibh; the war of the Gaedhil with the Gaill*, ed. J. H. Todd (London, 1867), p. 116.

[67] Heist, *Vitae SS Hib.*, p. 191, § 35.

[68] *Vita Columbae*, i, 45 (William Reeves (ed.), *The life of St Columba... by Adamnan* (Dublin, 1857), p. 88 = Anderson, *Adomnan's Life*, p. 82 = Richard Sharpe (trans.), *Adomnán of Iona: Life of St Columba* (Harmondsworth, 1995), p. 148, and Sharpe's note 195 on *canaba*, pp 308–9); Plummer, *Vitae SS Hib.*, i, 204 (Ciarán of Clonmacnoise); Heist, *Vitae SS Hib.*, p. 191 (Cainnech). Alan Gailey, 'Irish corn-drying kilns' in *Ulster Folklife*, xv–xvi (1970), pp 52–71; M. A. Monk, 'Post-Roman drying kilns and the problem of function: a preliminary statement' in Ó Corráin, *Ir. antiquity*, pp 216–30.

[69] *Z.C.P.*, xiv (1923), pp 352–3; *Críth Gab.*, pp 5–6.

evident from the law tracts that only the monastic houses and the better-off farmers owned their own kilns. The *óc-aire*, for example, shared one with his neighbours.[70] The poorer classes either had access to a kiln with the owner's permission (for a price) or used the much more primitive method of scorching the grain in the straw and scutching it ('graddaning'), which combined drying, threshing, and winnowing. This method remained in use in Ireland at least until the nineteenth century and appears to be a survival of an archaic practice once widespread among early cultivators.[71]

The safe storage of grain, whether it was threshed in bulk or, as seems likely, simply stored in stacks, presented serious problems for the early farmer, for corn had to be guarded from the elements and protected from marauders as well. The burning of corn, either in the field or in storage, was a standard practice of warfare down to the seventeenth century. Quite apart from that, the enemy forces lived off the country, and while cattle could be driven off to a place of safety (*port éicne*) the grain harvest lay at their mercy. When, for example, Niall mac Áeda, king of Ailech, raided Meath in December 914, he sent out a very large foraging troop to provide his camp with corn. Again, when Diarmait mac Maíl na mBó invaded Munster about 1 November 1061 he burned the houses and the stored corn of the plain of Munster (*go ro loisc machaire na Mumhan ettir thigibh and arbhar*). It is likely that essential seedcorn was stored in souterrains for safety and that bulk corn may have been placed in them in times of war and want.[72] Grain was stored in barns by the well-off: the *bó-aire* and the monastic farms had their own barns, the *óc-aire* had a share in one.[73] We are at a loss to know how the great bulk of the tillers of the soil stored their grain, but it is likely that they had no barns at all, as was the case with their successors from the seventeenth to the nineteenth centuries. Grain may have been stored in the ear in stacks in the haggard and used as required. Threshed grain may have been placed in sealed pits, as it was in the iron age. It is very likely that the seemingly archaic straw-rope granary, attested in south-west Munster (*fóir, fóirín, síogóg, síogán*), served the purpose of a barn for the ordinary farmer. It is first attested for the sixteenth century: in 1579 the sons of the earl of Desmond pursued scorched-earth tactics and destroyed *gach tigh, gach teghdhais, gach síocc, gach stáca* ('every house, every habitation, every *síocc*, every stack of corn').[74] *Síocc*, earlier *síc*, appears to mean two separate things: a strip or

---

[70] *Críth Gab.*, pp 4, 6, 8, 10.

[71] Gailey, loc. cit., p. 69; A. T. Lucas, '*An fhóir*: a straw-rope granary' in *Gwerin*, i, no. 1 (1956), pp 1–20; ii, no. 2 (1959), pp 58–67: i, 14; Caoimhín Ó Danachair, 'The flail and other threshing methods' in *Cork Hist. Soc. Jn.*, lx, no. 191 (1955), pp 6–14.

[72] Lucas, 'Souterrains', pp 165–91; *Z.C.P.*, viii (1912), p. 132; *U.J.A.*, xvii (1954), p. 98.

[73] *Saball*, the normal Old Irish word for a barn, is a Latin borrowing; *scioból*, the modern term, is unattested in the early literature and according to O'Rahilly may be a British loan-word.

[74] Lucas, '*An fhóir*: a straw-rope granary'; A.F.M., *s.a.* 1579.

stripe and a straw-rope granary. Structures like these leave no distinct material traces and, since they were used by humbler peasants, they are not likely to enter the literary record except by chance.

Corn was ground by quern and in horizontal watermills, and both methods continued in use side by side until modern times. Grinding by quern was heavy labour, and in aristocratic households it was often considered to be the work of slaves. This is illustrated in the legend about the introduction of watermills. King Cormac made his quern-maid Ciarnat pregnant. He took pity on her, and to save her the heavy work of grinding his corn he sent overseas for a millwright who built the first watermill in Ireland.[75] According to a ninth-century Life, when St Ciarán was enslaved by the king his work was 'turning the quern each day to make flour', and other references indicate that this was the work of slaves, occasionally captive vikings, down to the twelfth century.[76] Grinding with the quern was one of the regular if less exalted duties of the ordinary commoner's wife, and if the daughters of the aristocrats learned sewing, cutting-out, and embroidery, the daughters of the *óc-aire* were taught the use of the quern, kneading-trough, and sieve.[77]

The horizontal mill, which has been used for some two millennia, has a distribution stretching along the Atlantic coast of Europe from Spain to Scandinavia. Elsewhere the Vitruvian mill with a vertical wheel was usual. However, the Irish millwrights were also familiar with the vertical mill: there is a notable tidal example from Little Island, Co. Cork, that is dated to *c*.A.D. 630. The horizontal mill was a rectangular two-storey building, usually made of wood, masonry, or both. On the lower floor there was an upright mill-shaft (tentering shaft) and waterwheel with dished paddles or vanes set in a stone gudgeon. The upper floor, usually at ground level, housed the millstones. Water was brought by a specially constructed mill-race, stored in a dam or pond and released by chute or flume (and some mills were twin-flumed and twin-wheeled) as a jet against the paddles, which turned clockwise. The mill was turned on and off by a sluice-gate which controlled the supply of water. The millshaft passed up through the floor, through the stationary lower millstone (the bedstone), and was firmly fitted to a rynd (power socket) in the upper stone (runner stone). There was no gearing and each turn of the shaft produced a turn of the millstone. The mill did not usually have a hopper and needed constant manual feeding. A notable variant is the tidal mill.[78] The

[75] Edward Gwynn, *The metrical Dindsenchas* (5 vols, Dublin, 1903–35), i, 20, 22; Kuno Meyer, *Otia merseiana*, ii (1901), p. 75; *Revue archéologique*, xiv (1921), pp 263–74.

[76] Plummer, *Vitae SS Hib.*, i, 203; Heist, *Vitae SS Hib.*, pp 79–80; *Cog. Gáedhel*, p. 116; *C.I.H.*, p. 467, lines 31–4 = *Anc. laws Ire.*, v, 394, lines 1–4 ('Bretha im Fuillema Gell'); John Strachan and J. G. O'Keeffe (ed.), *Táin bó Cuailgne* (Dublin, 1912), p. 43, lines 1131–5.

[77] *C.I.H.*, p. 1760, lines 21–2; p. 174, line 21 = *Anc. laws Ire.*, ii, 152, lines 10–12; 410, lines 16–17; *Studies in Ir. law*, pp 34, 190.

[78] Colin Rynne, 'Milling in the 7th century—Europe's earliest tide mills' in *Archaeology Ireland*, vi, no. 2 (1992), pp 22–3.

most strikingly sophisticated example, recently discovered and dated to 787, belongs to the monastery of Nendrum on Strangford Lough. It is a two-storey stone-built structure, housing a horizontal mill. The incoming tide flowed twice daily beneath it into a walled dam, 2 m deep, 25 m wide, and 150 m long, and the water was trapped by a sluice gate. When the tide ebbed, the water was released through the flume to drive a millwheel with twenty-four paddles and turn a millstone a little under a metre in diameter. Horizontal mills were of an excellent standard of construction and were usually built by specialised millwrights of high social standing.[79] Currently, the earliest datable examples belong to the seventh century (the evidence comes from texts and from dendrochronology) and there are others from the eighth, ninth, and later centuries. Milling technology is likely to have reached Ireland from mainland Europe in the very early medieval period, perhaps towards the end of the sixth century.[80]

Mills and monasteries are often mentioned together, and they provide the occasion of many stock miracles in hagiography. This association is confirmed by archaeology. Clonmacnoise in the tenth century had a number of mills within the *termann*, and Giraldus Cambrensis has reference to monastic mills with miraculous qualities.[81] A seventh-century law tract, 'Coibnes Uisci Thairidne', deals with the rules governing the ownership and use of mills and the construction of a mill-race—and incidentally provides the earliest European vernacular technical terms for the parts of a horizontal mill. Mills could be owned in severalty or jointly. In the first case, the mill-owner erects the mill on his own estate; where the mill-race must be conducted over his neighbours' land they may not normally refuse passage, but they must be compensated either by a single payment to the value of the land breached or by a day's free grinding at the mill at fixed intervals. Only monasteries, nobles, and the highest grade of commoner owned mills in severalty. The normal substantial farmer (*óc-aire*, *bó-aire febsa*) shared ownership of a mill with his neighbours and used it in rotation with his partners. Others—no doubt the majority—could grind at the mill with the owner's permission and for a consideration, usually paid in grain. Use of a mill without permission

[79] E. Cecil Curwen, 'The problem of early watermills' in *Antiquity*, xviii (1944), pp 130–46; A. T. Lucas, 'The horizontal watermill in Ireland' in *R.S.A.I. Jn.*, lxxxiii (1953), pp 1–36; Edward M. Fahy, 'A horizontal mill at Mashanaglass, Co. Cork' in *Cork Hist. Soc. Jn.*, lxi (1956), pp 13–57; Gearóid S. Mac Eoin, 'The early Irish vocabulary of mills and milling' in B. G. Scott (ed.), *Studies on early Ireland: essays in honour of M. V. Duignan* (Belfast, 1982), pp 13–19; Colin Rynne, 'The early Irish watermill and its continental affinities', in *Medieval Europe 1992: technology and innovation*, iii (York, 1992), pp 21–25; idem, 'The craft of the millwright in early medieval Munster' in M. A. Monk and John Sheehan (ed.), *Early Munster: archaeology, history and society* (Cork, 1998), pp 87–101.
[80] Rynne, 'The craft of the millwright in early medieval Munster', p. 95; Kelly, *Irish farming*, pp 482–5.
[81] A.U., *s.a.* 959 = A.F.M., *s.a.* 957 (=959); John O'Meara, *The first version of the topography of Ireland by Giraldus Cambrensis* (Dundalk, 1951), pp 73–4.

entailed severe penalties, especially if any damage were done, intentionally or through neglect.[82] Given the frequent references to mills in the literature, the detailed provisions of the law tracts, the extent of investment in structures and mill-races, it is evident that mills were one of the important and common features of the Irish landscape, and cereal-growing was a crucial aspects of the agricultural economy in the early middle ages.

Vegetables were grown on a small scale, certainly outside the monastic farms. Some varieties of onion were grown in ridges in small vegetable plots within the *les* or nearby. The most common term for these is *cainnenn*, sometimes wrongly translated 'garlic'. In fact, it may be a generic term for a number of types of onion, and since the texts refer to *ingni* or cloves of *cainnenn*, it may also include varieties like the Welsh onion. It was eaten with its greens and bulbs. A *bó-aire* grew six ridges of it, and it formed part of the food-rent of a base client.[83] *Fírchainnenn* means fresh onions (with their foliage)—and their odour was appreciated—as distinct from pickled onions.[84] Fresh and pickled, they were eaten as condiment, very likely with bread. Another vegetable of the same group, *borrlus*, I take from its etymology to be the ordinary leek with its characteristic fleshy root, rather than garlic, as it is often translated. These various types were eaten fresh and pickled as relish with bread and were also used as seasoning to give butter a 'high' taste. They formed part of the peasant's usual render to his lord and were a normal part of his diet.[85] Another member of the *allium* family, *foltchép*, is certainly to be identified with the chive (*Allium schoenoprasum*). It derives from Irish *folt* 'hair of the head', and Latin *cepa* 'onion'; it is said to resemble rushes in appearance, and it is cut to the ground with a sharp knife. These details make it certain that *foltchép* is identical with chives.[86] Chives were known in Roman Britain, and their cultivation in Ireland was no doubt due to the monasteries and they were probably common in monastic gardens, perhaps rare outside. It is not clear that garlic was cultivated but extensive use was made of *crem* or wild garlic (*A. ursinum*). Reference is made to *crem allda*

---

[82] D. A. Binchy, 'Irish law-tracts re-edited I; *Coibnes Uisci Thairidni*' in *Ériu*, xvii (1955), pp 52–85; *Críth Gab.*, pp 4, 6, 8–10; *C.I.H.*, p. 287 = *Anc. laws Ire.*, iii, 280–82 (text and commentary); Heist, *Vitae SS Hib.*, p. 133.

[83] *C.I.H.*, p. 644, lines 6–7; *C.I.H.*, p. 479, lines 23–4 = Rudolf Thurneysen, 'Aus dem irischen Recht III' in *Z.C.P.*, xv (1925), pp 302–76: 371; *C.I.H.*, p. 1611, l. 42 = *Anc. laws Ire.*, v, 90, l. 14; *Críth Gab.*, p. 3.

[84] *Críth Gab.*, 7; Kuno Meyer (ed. and trans.), 'Comad Manchín Léith' in *Ériu*, i (1904), pp 38–40: 39, § 10 = Gerard Murphy, *Early Irish lyrics* (Oxford, 1956), p. 30, § 10. The expression *fírchainnenn chumra* should be translated 'fresh fragrant onion'.

[85] *C.I.H.*, p. 1599, lines 34–5 = *Anc. laws Ire.*, v, 40, lines 10–14; *R.I.A. Proc.*, xxxvi (1923), sect. C, p. 274; *Rev. Celt.*, xx (1899), p. 284; *O'Dav.*, §§ 288, 909, 1074, 1138; Kuno Meyer, *Anecdota oxoniensia: Hibernica minora* (Oxford, 1894), p. 47; *Críth Gab.*, pp 3, 7; Meyer, *Aislinge meic Conglinne*, pp 39, 89; *Ériu*, i (1904), p. 139.

[86] *Trip. life*, ed. Stokes, i, 200–01 = *Trip. life*, ed. Mulchrone, pp 120–21, 124; *L.U.*, p. 261 ('Fled Bricrend'). It is glossed *barr uindiun* 'onion top' in *Archiv für celtische Lexikographie*, iii, 28.

'wild garlic' in the laws, and this may imply that a cultivated variety existed.[87] However, most literary references are to wild garlic. It was an important if seasonal salading and relish and gave its name to a period of the year called *crimmes* 'garlic feast', a time of short rations at the end of spring and the beginning of summer, when winter stores were nearly exhausted and summer milk not yet plentiful.

Other vegetables are mentioned in the literature, but they pose serious problems of identification. *Imus* is frequently referred to in the laws as a cultivar grown, like *cainnenn*, on ridges but in smaller quantities, and an unlimited amount of it is prescribed as medicinal food for the sick.[88] It is equated with Latin *apium* in later medical manuscripts and identified as celery or smallage. However, wild celery (*A. graveolens*) is poisonous, and the modern cultivar, the product of selective breeding, did not come into use as a vegetable in Europe till relatively recent times. Some suggest parsley, but this is only a guess. Some tap-roots (*meacain*) were cultivated, but the term probably includes all edible roots. It is likely that the parsnip, which was known to Pliny and which was in general use all over Europe, was among them. Little or nothing is known of the types of *brassica* that formed an important part of monastic diet. Charlock was apparently cultivated as a vegetable in the neolithic and its use may have continued. It is likely that various types of kale were grown, but heading cabbage as we know it is a product of the later middle ages and was not known in Ireland till the seventeenth century.[89]

Beans and peas are mentioned more rarely. The term for the bean is *seib*, a borrowing through Brittonic of Latin *faba*.[90] The type in question is the broad bean (*Vicia faba*) and was probably introduced to Ireland by early monks. It is not a heavy cropper. It is mentioned on a few occasions in legal contexts, and one early source indicates that the growing of beans was women's work.[91] The impression one gets is that it was a crop of little importance. With the coming of the vikings the Irish borrowed a new word for beans, *pónair* from Old Norse *baunir*, and this in itself would suggest that the Irish no longer or indeed had never cultivated beans on any wide scale and perhaps that the vikings introduced a new variety.[92] References to peas are even scarcer.

[87] *C.I.H.*, p. 241, line 19 = *Anc. laws Ire.*, v, 482, line 23.

[88] D. A. Binchy (ed. and trans.), 'Bretha Crólige' in *Ériu*, xii (1934), pp 36, 70.

[89] *Éire, Department of Agriculture, Journal*, lxi (1964), 260; A. T. Lucas, 'Nettles and charlock as famine food' in *Bréifne*, i, no. 2 (1959), pp 137–46: 142–4; *Gwerin*, iii, no. 2 (1960), p. 24.

[90] Rudolf Thurneysen, *Grammar of Old Irish* (Dublin, 1946), p. 571, § 921.

[91] *Ériu*, xx (1966), p. 22; Kuno Meyer (ed. and trans.), *Cáin Adamnáin: an Old Irish treatise on the law of Adamnan* (Oxford, 1905), p. 32, § 52.

[92] David Greene, 'The influence of Scandinavian on Irish' in Bo Almqvist and David Greene (ed.), *Proceedings of the Seventh Viking Conference* (Dublin, 1976), p. 79; Kelly, *Irish farming*, pp 248–9.

The only other crop of importance for which ploughing was done was flax (*Linum usitatissimum*), Irish *lín*, from Latin *linum*, and thus very likely introduced from Roman Britain. The laws and archaeological finds leave us in no doubt about the domestic importance of linen production. Spinning and weaving were among the activities of the ordinary housewife, and this implies that a patch of flax was normally grown by the farmer.[93]

Of the fruit, only apples were cultivated. They were highly regarded and formed an important component in the diet. They were grown in or near the settlement, and there is clear evidence from the ninth and tenth centuries for fenced orchards, particularly in monasteries. Monks of the stricter sabbatarian observance were not allowed to pick apples or even lift one fallen apple from the ground on Sundays.[94] In the laws there are references to the planting of apple trees and to penalties for damage done to them, and domestic apples are clearly distinguished from wild apples and crabs.[95] While excavation results are indecisive, the literary evidence for the cultivation of apple trees and for enclosed orchards is overwhelming in the period from the tenth to the twelfth centuries, though Giraldus Cambrensis comments sourly on the few kinds of apples available here and on the laziness of the cultivators who were unwilling to plant the foreign varieties.[96]

WHATEVER the importance of arable farming (and this varied with soil, situation, and resources), all the evidence, literary and archaeological alike, points to the dominant position of stock-raising and of dairying in particular. Taxes and renders, fines and penalties, the honour-prices of lords and commoners were calculated in terms of milch cows or fractions of their value, again expressed in terms of cattle and calves, though lesser values were accounted in bushels (*miach*) of oats and barley. Land itself was estimated in terms of the number of cows it could feed. The typical self-sufficient farmer was the *bó-aire* 'cow-man', because the customary due (*bés tige*) he rendered his lord was a cow and her accompaniments (subsidiary payments, usually in bacon, grain, and vegetables). And cows rather than land formed the normal fief granted by the lord to his client. Cattle-raiding was the typical act of war, and the readiest means for young nobles to win a reputation and a following.

---

[93] *C.I.H.*, p. 379, lines 4–12 = *Anc. laws Ire.*, i, 150 ('Athgabáil'); *Studies in Ir. law*, pp 15–16; Monk, 'Archaeobotanical evidence', p. 320; Kelly, *Irish farming*, 269–70.

[94] E. J. Gwynn and W. J. Purton (ed. and trans.), 'The monastery of Tallaght' in *R.I.A. Proc.*, xxix (1911), sect. C, p. 49 (hereafter cited as *Mon. Tall.*).

[95] *C.I.H.*, p. 239, 1876 = *Anc. laws Ire.*, v, 474, 500 (comm.).

[96] *R.I.A. Proc.*, liii (1950), sect. C, p. 242; *Bk Leinster*, v, 1138, lines 33516–7 ('Tochmarc Ferbae'); John O'Donovan, *The annals of Ireland: three fragments* (Dublin, 1860), p. 202; Whitley Stokes (ed. and trans.), 'Acallam na Senórach' in Whitley Stokes and Ernst Windisch (ed.), *Irische Texte* (Leipzig, 1900), line 6204; George Calder (ed.), *Auraicept na n-éces* (Edinburgh, 1917), line 1153; Meyer, *Aislinge meic Conglinne*, p. 5; Ann. Inisf., *s.a.* 1109; Ann. Tig., *s.a.* 1157; O'Meara, *Topog. Ire.*, p. 86.

Kings engaged in inaugural forays (*crech ríg*) to prove their prowess, and these took the form of a grand cattle-raid.[97] Such activities were so much accepted and taken for granted by society as a whole that the monasteries insisted on their right to a share in the spoils.[98] Indeed in the case of the monasteries, where it is likely agriculture was more intensively practised than elsewhere, cattle-raising was of the greatest importance. In the Lives of the saints, most of which were written up between the eighth and the twelfth centuries, very many of the stock miracles have to do with herding and dairying, and the writers unconsciously reflect the monastic economy of their own time. Apart from the herds of their own extensive farms, the monasteries claimed tithes of stock and received most of their offerings from the faithful in cattle. The annalists of the tenth and eleventh centuries record raids on monasteries in which great preys of cattle were taken. In 951, for example, the Dublin vikings raided Kells and took 'a very large prey of cows and horses, gold and silver', and a second large cattle prey was taken by the vikings and the Leinstermen in 970.[99] The Airgialla and their allies took 2,000 cows from Armagh in 996, and it was again raided for cattle by the Ulaid in 1015.[100] Such details are not to be found in the sparer reports of the earlier annalists, but there is no reason to believe that cattle were less important in the monastic economy in the eighth and ninth centuries, and many of the ninth- and tenth-century viking raids on monasteries were really cattle raids. In secular society, numbers taken in raids are reckoned in hundreds and thousands, and though medieval figures are quite likely to be inaccurate in detail the broad pattern is reliable enough. Archaeological excavation, in cases where faunal remains are preserved, tells the same story and indicates that beef formed the greater part of what meat was eaten by the upper classes. At Ballinderry I cattle bones made up 70 per cent of the remains, at Ballinderry II 70 to 90 per cent, at Lough Faughan 63 per cent, at Cahercommaun 97 per cent, and at Lagore between 72 per cent and 84 per cent, varying according to periods, in so far as these can be determined.[101]

The bulk of the cattle were milch cows and only a small number of male animals were raised for breeding and draught. The laws point to the same conclusion.[102] Irish cattle were of the ordinary variable domesticated type

[97] D. Ó Corráin, *Ireland before the Normans* (Dublin, 1972), p. 37; Pádraig Ó Riain, 'The "crech ríg" or "royal prey"' in *Éigse*, xv, no. 1 (1973), pp 23–30.
[98] A. T. Lucas, 'Cattle in ancient and medieval Ireland' in *The O'Connell School Union Record* (Dublin, 1958), pp 75–87.
[99] A.U., *s.a.* 951, 970.
[100] A.U., *s.a.* 996; Chron. Scot., *s.a.* 1013 (= 1015).
[101] Duignan, 'Agriculture', pp 141–2; *U.J.A.*, xviii (1955), pp 45–81; *R.I.A. Proc.*, xlvii (1942), sect. C, p. 68; Finbarr McCormick, 'Dairying and beef production in Early Christian Ireland' in T. Reeves-Smyth and F. Hammond (ed.), *Landscape archaeology in Ireland* (Oxford, 1983), pp 253–68.
[102] A. T. Lucas, 'Irish food before the potato'; *C.I.H.*, 192 = *Anc. laws Ire.*, iv, 100 ('Comingaire').

(*Bos longifrons*), common to Ireland and Britain, and similar in size to the modern Kerry cow. Cattle were mostly black, but browns, reds, brindles, duns and occasional whites also occurred.[103] In Irish literature there are frequent references to white cows with red ears, which were considered superior. It was long believed that these were fairy or magical animals of Celtic story, but Bergin has shown that such cattle exist and reference is made to them in the Welsh laws and elsewhere.[104]

Cattle were grazed on fenced and unfenced pastures, on the harvested arable, and transhumance was practised in the summer months.[105] In these cases, constant daylight herding of cattle and other animals was necessary; it is insisted on in the law tracts, and is also evident from the Lives of the saints which refer from time to time to the monastic herdsman (*armentarius*).[106] At night, cattle were put in a cattle enclosure (*bódaingen, buaile*). Evidence for the housing of animals in winter is poor. It is very probable that at least some cows were kept in the dwelling-house in winter, a custom found all over northern Europe, and there is some eleventh-century annalistic evidence for this.[107] It is well attested for Ireland from the sixteenth to the nineteenth centuries, and we can assume that it was practised in the early middle ages. The warmth of the house and a little additional hand-feeding would have kept a few animals from the herd in good condition and may have provided a minimal supply of milk from a few cows that had not gone in calf or were bulled only in autumn, so that they went in calf late and milked late. However, this is uncertain, since the lactation period of medieval cattle may well have been shorter. The commentator of 'Córus Bésgnai' states that cows calved in the dwelling-house,[108] where they could be supervised, helped if needed, and protected from exposure to bad weather. Keeping newly dropped calves in the house was common enough in rural Ireland till recent times. While there are some literary references to housing for cattle (presumably in winter),[109] it is evident that the vast bulk of the herds wintered out. Adequate cover seems never to have been provided for cattle and sheep, nor is there any archaeological evidence of extensive animal houses. It is notable, for example, that no byre is listed among the usual 'legal' buildings of the *bó-aire*, though a calf-fold, sheepfold, and pigsty are

---

[103] Proudfoot, 'Economy of the Irish rath', p. 110; Duignan, 'Agriculture', pp 142–3; Lucas, *Cattle in ancient Ireland*, 239–45; Kelly, *Irish farming*, pp 29–36.

[104] O. J. Bergin, 'White red-eared cows' in *Ériu*, xiv (1946), p. 70; Lucas, loc. cit.

[105] Lucas, *Cattle in ancient Ireland*, 58–67.

[106] *C.I.H.*, p. 72 = *Anc. laws Ire.*, iv, 96 ('Bretha Comaithchesa'); Plummer, *Vitae SS Hib.*, i, xcvi–xcvii; Lucas, 'Cattle', p. 79.

[107] Ann. Inisf., *s.a.* 1028, 1040.

[108] *C.I.H.*, p. 1814, lines 26–32 = *Anc. laws Ire*, iii, 40, lines 15–22.

[109] *Rev. Celt.*, xiv (1893), p. 430, § 56; *The Book of Ballymote*, ed. Robert Atkinsòn (Dublin, 1887) (cited below as *B.B.*) 397b2.

listed[110]—calves, pigs, and shorn sheep are much more vulnerable to low temperatures than mature cattle.[111] There is plenty of evidence for the winter housing of calves; and it is likely that young animals were reared in the dwelling-house, another common northern European custom which survived in Ireland till recent times.[112] Outdoor animal shelters have been noted by archaeologists, but these are small and unroofed. Experimental work shows that in the Irish climate there is no significant difference between outwintered and inwintered cattle in weight gain and general health, if they are properly fed.[113]

The Irish did not save hay, and winter fodder was consequently scarce. There are occasional references to the stall-feeding of cattle and to the stall-fattening of table animals on grass, corn, and milk, but these are exceptional. So also was the hand-feeding of sheep, which is rarely mentioned.[114] Pigs, on the other hand, had the run of the woods for pannage but were housed, tended, and fed on corn and milk by the housewife, and the annals make it clear that mast was collected and stored as pig-feed.[115] *Caisearbhán* (*Endivia sylvestris*) was collected by women as food for pigs till recent times and the Old Irish name of the plant, *serbán mucc*, suggests that this may well have been the custom in the earlier period. However, it is possible that hand-feeding was largely confined to the fattening time, and herds of pigs may have been left to forage for themselves in winter. This supposition is supported by annalistic reports of the loss of pigs through exposure—and pigs are vulnerable to low temperatures.[116]

The non-provision of winter fodder was due to climatic conditions, not agricultural backwardness. Ireland's high rainfall and relatively mild winter conditions make for a long growing season, and cattle can be wintered on foggage which, again because of the absence of severe frosts, maintains much of its nutritive value. The only other winter grazing available was rough grass on bogland and hill and the undergrowth of the woods. All types were reserved as specific winter grazing, though of course the most valuable was foggage on prime pasture (*etham díguin*). The modern median date for the beginning of the grass-growing season for the greater part of Ireland is before mid-March and it does not stop till the beginning of December.[117] This is

---

[110] *Crith Gab.*, p. 6; the *caule ouium et vitulorum et bouum* mentioned in 'Canones Hiberneses' (Bieler, *Ir. penitentials*, pp 174–5) should be translated literally as a fenced enclosure (that is to say, a pen) for the animals concerned rather than a byre as Bieler (loc. cit.) and others translate it.

[111] T. Keane (ed.), *Climate, weather and Irish agriculture* (Dublin, 1986), pp 182–92.

[112] *Rev. Celt.*, xiv (1893), p. 455; xv (1894), pp 308, 468; xxii (1901), p. 19.

[113] Keane, op. cit., pp 191–3.

[114] *Z.C.P.*, vii (1910), p. 303, 8; *Lebor na hUidre*, p. 248 ('Fled Bricrend'); Eleanor Knott, 'Bó thúir' in *Ériu*, vii (1913), p. 26; *Leabhar Breac* (Dublin, 1872–6), 114a23.

[115] *C.I.H.*, p. 509 = *Anc. laws Ire.*, ii, 366–8, 412–14 (comm.); *Studies in Ir. law*, pp 35–5; A.F.M., s.a. 967 (= 969); Ann. Inisf., s.a. 985; A.F.M., s.a. 1031; A.U., s.a. 1097.

[116] e.g. Ann. Inisf., s.a. 1105; cf. Keane, op. cit., p. 186.

[117] Irish National Committee for Geography, *Atlas of Ireland* (Dublin, 1979), p. 31.

reflected in the laws: the winter itself and the first two months of spring when growth is poor were usually classed as winter-time from the grazier's point of view, and the fines for trespass were double those of summer.[118] This system worked well in good years, though there were frequent stock losses in the critical month, February, and cattle were still weak in March, when grass growth began in average years, but as we shall see it was disastrous in bad conditions.[119]

Finbar McCormick has recently argued that systematic dairying, absent in Britain and Ireland before the iron age, was introduced from Roman Britain, with the coming of Christianity, or possibly somewhat earlier. Dairying, as against beef-farming, leads to a fourfold increase in food output from the same resources in land. This dramatic rise in food production would lead to an increased population and the kind of expansion of agriculture that is evident in early medieval Ireland,[120] but linguistic evidence undermines this bold hypothesis. To judge from the literary texts of the seventh and later centuries, milk and its products (*bán-bíd*), especially in summer, were of the greatest importance, and milk was to keep its primacy in the national diet till the seventeenth century. It was consumed as liquid milk, curd, butter, and cheese, and all these were prepared in many different ways. The laws and the general literature indicate that the management of milk production was the work of women.[121] A great deal of liquid milk was drunk in various forms: soured, thickened, mixed with whey and with buttermilk. *Tremanta*, englished in the seventeenth century as 'troander', was made by boiling sweet milk and adding sour buttermilk, and this light acid mixture was considered a pleasant summer drink. Whey on its own, or mixed with water or milk, is frequently mentioned as the drink of penitents and ascetics.

Milk was conserved in the form of butter and cheese. Butter-making was done in dash churns and in swing churns, and both probably continued in use side by side. The oak churn found at Lissue, stave-built to a high standard with a circular base and an oval top, may well have been a swing churn.[122] Many kinds and sizes of dairy vessels are mentioned in the texts, and these were usually made of wood, yew and oak being preferred. Skin-covered vessels were used to transport liquid milk on horseback. Butter-making, probably more than any other farming activity, has magical associations and has always been surrounded by an aura of superstition which

---

[118] *C.I.H.*, pp 66, 69–70; 67 = *Anc. laws Ire.*, iv, 78, 88, 90, 92; 80, 82 (comm.).

[119] *Todd Lecture Series*, iv (Dublin, 1892), p. 10 ('Cath Ruis na Ríg').

[120] Finbarr McCormick, 'Cows, ringforts and the origins of early Christian Ireland' in *Emania*, xiii (1995), pp 33–7. McCormick further argues that the ringforts were protected farmsteads, originally devised to protect valuable dairy herds from rustlers.

[121] *Studies in Ir. law*, pp 31–2.

[122] Gerhard Bersu, 'The rath in the townland of Lissue, Co. Antrim' in *U.J.A.*, x (1947), pp 30–48.

may not yet have quite disappeared. It is not surprising, then, that Goibniu, the artificer-god of pagan times, was still invoked by the butter-makers in the ninth and tenth centuries, and many other pagan beliefs about the 'turn' and the 'luck of the butter' survived till the cooperative creameries took butter-making out of the hands of the farmers.[123] Buttermilk (*bláthach*, so named from the fragrant volatile substances of ripened cream released in the churning) was widely drunk and buttermilk curds were used for cheese-making. There were two main types of butter: fresh butter (*im úr*), which was unsalted or lightly salted for immediate consumption, and *gruiten*, heavily salted butter incorporating 5 per cent or more of coarse, unrefined salt for long-term storage. Fresh butter was much more highly regarded than the salted kind, which was considered suitable for the lower classes but scarcely good enough for the sons of comfortable farmers. It was stored in wicker hampers, bark containers, and stave-built firkins, some very large, and was occasionally buried in bogs, where cool antiseptic conditions prevented it going rancid and allowed it to be kept for long periods without heavy salting.

Curd was much eaten as a summer food but a great deal of it was preserved as cheese. There are considerable difficulties in the way of identifying the various types made. Cheese generally became standardised in quality and type only in recent times in response to a market economy; similar types go by different names; and the references to cheeses in the early texts give no details about the processes used in manufacturing them. The generic term is *cáise*, a borrowing of Latin *caseum*, and this is taken to mean a pressed cheese. *Tanach*, glossed *formella* and derived from *tana* 'thin', was a skim-milk cheese pressed hard in moulds and bulging in shape. *Fáiscri grotha*, literally 'pressings of curd', were obviously pressed-curd cheeses, but we know nothing about their consistency. These cheeses must have been small, for a woman could carry several in the fold of her cloak. *Máethal*, a term which is applied in modern times to cooked beestings, was a large, soft-bodied, smooth-textured cheese which was round in shape. *Mulchán* has been taken to be a firm buttermilk cheese, but the term probably covered a wide range of different types. There seem to have been two cooked cheeses. In the case of *táth*, a sour-curd cheese, the curds were probably heated and stirred till they coagulated. *Millsén*, as the name indicates, was a sweet-curd cheese made with rennet, cooked with butter, and perhaps flavoured with honey. It probably remained flocculent and was stored in vessels in semi-liquid condition (like the *mel i mato* of the Pyrenees). It must have been quite common, for it was part of the food render of base clients.[124] Foreign

[123] H. d'Arbois de Jubainville (ed. and trans.), 'Mélanges' in *Rev. Celt.*, xii (1891), pp 154–5.
[124] *Z.C.P.*, xiv (1924), pp 154–5.

observers of the sixteenth and seventeenth centuries were surprised again and again at the large part that milk and its products played in the Irish diet. Had they been travellers of the eighth century, their observations would have differed little whether they were travellers in Ireland or in many other parts of the British Isles.[125]

Pigs probably came a poor second to cows in sheer numbers but they were of great importance in the economy.[126] If we may trust the statistics from excavations, however, that importance varied greatly from place to place and from class to class. In the prosperous cattle-raising communities of Leacana-buaile and Cahercommaun, pig bones form a tiny percentage of the faunal remains. In the royal settlement of Lagore, they account for 8 to 10 per cent of the remains, and elsewhere they vary from 10 to 24 per cent.[127] However, the excavated sites are those of the well-off classes, and even there the sample is too small to be reliable. The decline in cattle remains and the increase in pig and sheep bones in the later strata at Lagore and Ballinderry have been interpreted as a real decline in prosperity; and this inference may be correct, for pig-meat, fresh or salted, seems to have been the meat generally eaten by the lower classes, in so far as they ate meat in any quantity. The provisions of the laws, and the frequent annalistic references to meat, indicate that pigs were raised in large numbers. Carcasses of pork and sides of bacon formed a normal part of the peasants' customary render to the lords, and this may well be the source of the faunal remains of swine at royal sites.[128] And it is evident that pigs were slaughtered quite young, even when sucklings.

Sheep were raised principally for their wool and seem to have been the responsibility of the women who processed the wool. However, sheep (and especially fat wethers) provide meat, and in some cases mutton formed part of the peasant's render to his lord. This is evident from faunal remains and from the legal tract on clientship.[129] In Ireland as elsewhere, sheep were important as milk-producers down to modern times and may have provided a good deal of the milk and butter of the poorer classes, especially in areas unsuitable for cattle.[130]

Survival depended on a delicate balance of factors: there was never abundance for all. Famine and its concomitants, disease, fever, and social disor-

[125] Micheál Ó Sé, 'Old Irish cheeses and other milk products' in *Cork Hist Soc. Jn.*, liii (1948), pp 83–7; idem, 'Old Irish buttermaking', ibid., liv (1949), pp 61–7; Lucas, 'Irish food', pp 12–14.
[126] Kelly, *Irish farming*, 79–88.
[127] *R.I.A. Proc.*, xlvii (1942), sect. C, p. 71; *U.J.A.*, xviii (1958), p. 78; *Cork Hist. Soc. Jn.*, xlvi (1941), p. 95.
[128] *Críth Gab.*, p. 5; *Z.C.P.*, xiv (1923), pp 348–57.
[129] *Z.C.P.*, loc. cit.
[130] Meyer, *Aislinge meic Conglinne*, p. 33; *Ériu*, xx (1968), p. 64; *Cork Hist. Soc. Jn*, lvi (1951), pp 123–5; T. F. O'Rahilly (ed.), *Gadelica* (Dublin, 1912–13), p. 38; Lucas, 'Irish food', pp 22–3; Kelly, *Irish farming*, 67–76.

ganisation, were feared with good reason, for they were matters of common experience. Even the monks of the stricter observance in Tallaght and Terryglass, whose rule forbade meat, took a particle of flesh at Easter as a good-luck token to guard against scarcity and hunger in the following year.[131] The food supply depended on the two major activities of the rural economy, cereal-growing and animal husbandry, and of course there was little or no long-distance trade in basic foodstuffs to cushion the population against shortfalls. There are occasional references, it is true, to the sale of corn in times of want, but trade can have done little to alleviate general misery.[132] The failure of one or the other resulted in severe hardship; the failure of both brought inevitable disaster in a society that had little surplus for the most part. Despite the climatic optimum of 750–1200,[133] cereal-growing in Ireland remained hazardous. Heavy and protracted spring snow and ice (as in 764–5, 780, 789, 855, 965), which either delayed sowing till it was too late to have an adequate growing season or damaged the sown seed after germination, led to poor yields and scarcity. Heavy rains in late summer and autumn were dangerous, too. In 1109, people engaged in fasts, abstinences, and prayers for the banishment of heavy summer and autumn rains that threatened the harvest. The careful detail and chronological accuracy with which these climatic situations are recorded by the annalists is itself evidence of their crucial importance. The wet summer of 759, for example, was followed by famine in 760, though this may have been caused in part by probable cattle losses due to heavy snow in the beginning of spring. Similar harvest failures are specifically recorded for 777, 912, 975, 1012, 1050, 1094, and 1107, and we can be sure that such failures occurred quite frequently. There were other hazards. An extremely dry and hot summer could also cause the loss of the grain harvest, as it did in 773 and, to a degree, in 760. High winds or heavy rainfall or a combination of both could be dangerous. The annalist describes the autumn of 858 as 'rainy and most ruinous for crops', while in 1077 and 1093 famine (and what in the latter case may be famine-fever) followed the destruction of the grain harvest by high winds.

It is clear even from the annalistic evidence that stock-raising and dairying were an even more important part of the rural economy, and losses of stock on a large scale had more serious consequences and led to far greater upset and misery in society at large. Animal husbandry was subject to two main hazards: epidemics of disease of cattle, and shortage of winter fodder in bad years. In 700 cattle plague spread from England to Ireland, where it broke out in early spring and continued throughout the following year. It seems to

---

[131] E. J. Gwynn and W. V. Purton, 'The monastery of Tallaght' in *R.I.A. Proc*, xxix (1911), sect. C, p. 132, § 12, p. 146, § 51. This custom is rationalised as an additional penitential discipline.

[132] *Ann. Clon.*, *s.a.* 1009 (= 1116).

[133] E. Le Roy Ladurie, *Times of feast, times of famine* (London, 1972), pp 244–308.

have remained quiescent for a few years, for the same plague reached epidemic proportions again in 708. There was another outbreak of cattle plague between 776 and 779: this was followed by famine, disease, and the usual concomitant disorders. There are no records of such large-scale plagues for the ninth century, but livestock epidemics are reported twice in the tenth century (909, 987) and four times in the eleventh.

Much more common, if less spectacular, were heavy losses of cattle and other animals due to exposure and lack of winter fodder in adverse weather conditions. Cattle were usually wintered out on foggage and rough grazing. This worked well in the usual mild winters, but brought about disastrous losses of stock and subsequent dearth when winter frosts and snows were prolonged into the spring. Again, the detail with which the annalists record spring frosts is evidence of their critical importance.[134] In 748 an extraordinary snowfall 'destroyed almost all the cattle of Ireland'. In 764 heavy snow cover, which lasted almost three months, led to great want and famine. Again in 917, snow and frost and unusual cold led to heavy losses in cattle.[135] Exposure and lack of fodder made cattle less resistant to disease, a fact noted by the annalists in 960–61.[136] Pigs and sheep were also lost because of exposure. The vulnerability of the herds must be stressed. A snowfall of a day and a night on 13 March 1107, when the cattle were weakest, led to heavy losses of stock throughout Ireland. And it takes a number of years to bring stock numbers back to their former size.

The combination of cereal failure and stock losses, due either to epidemic or exposure, led to immediate and terrible famine. In 700 the cattle plague that had affected England broke out in the Irish midlands, and the epidemic continued into 701. The winter of 700 was long and so extremely cold that rivers and parts of the sea were frozen, and this may have delayed or destroyed spring sowing. The result was a major famine which lasted three years. It was accompanied by epidemic diseases, most probably famine fever and a recrudescence of the plague of 683–4, and no doubt by endemic diseases which attacked a population whose resistance was lowered by malnutrition. The misery was so great that there was cannibalism. Cannibalism occurred again as a result of the plague and famine of 1113–16, and it did not disappear from famine-stricken Europe until the close of the middle ages. The same combination of factors in 964–5 led to what the annalist calls 'a great and insufferable famine' in which men sold their sons and daughters into slavery in return for food. The custom of selling children is referred to again in 1116, and according to a hagiographical text they were usually sold

---

[134] A.U., *s.a.* 760, 789, 918, 848, 855, 856, 1008.

[135] It is to be noted that the term used by the annalists (*bó-ár*) does not always imply cattle plague or murrain. It can also be used of serious cattle losses due to hunger of exposure. This second meaning is not clearly given in the dictionary.

[136] Chron. Scot., *s.a.* 959 (= 960); Ann. Clon., *s.a.* 955 (= 961).

into remote territories. It is possible that the monasteries acquired the type of monastic base clients called *dáermanaig núna*, 'base monastic clients of famine', from among farmers ruined by crop failure and cattle losses, who commended themselves and their lands to the church in return for maintenance.[137]

More general disorders resulted from famine in this vulnerable economy. Cattle plagues had a direct effect on the grades of society and on the reciprocal relationships of a lord and his clients. According to the laws, the status of the substantial commoners depended directly on their property qualifications: 'what is lacking from the property qualification of a *bó-aire* is lacking from his honour-price.'[138] When men lost their property, most of it in herds (and land without herds is not worth much), they lost status and slipped downwards in the social scale. Much of the lords' incomes were in food-renders consumed on circuit of their clients,[139] and these of course fell off in times of shortage, bringing confusion and conflict into the complicated mutual relationships of lords and clients. Lords no longer had the surplus stock to offer in fiefs to clients and dependants, and without clients a noble lost his status and his influence. A late example of this exact occurrence is recorded in the annals for 1085 when, as a result of a plague in men and cattle, some of the rich (read nobles) were reduced to becoming working occupiers of the soil.[140] In short, where status depended to a large degree on property and negotiable property was principally in herds, and where the nexus of lord and client was inextricably linked with exchanges of property and service, cattle-plagues and major cattle losses played havoc with the ordering of the social hierarchy and the inter-relationships of its parts.

There were two major effects of shortage: internal migration and a general rise in the level of violence, especially towards the churches. Internal migration in the face of local plague and famine is to be expected, though the annalists record no instance of it prior to the eleventh century, and they then record what can only have been very large-scale migration. In 1006 the Ulaid spread throughout Ireland because of shortage, and again in 1047 they migrated to Leinster for the same reason. Because of famine, a pestilence that emptied churches, farmsteads, and whole areas, and disturbed political conditions, the Leinstermen dispersed throughout Ireland in 1116, and some of them went overseas. Again in 1137 the Connachtmen moved to the west of the province because of famine, and in 1152 the annalists record the temporary migration of Munster peasants because of famine brought about by warfare between Uí Briain and Meic Carthaig. It is likely that similar migrations

---

[137] *C.I.H.*, p. 522, lines 6–7 = *Anc. laws Ire.*, iii, 10 (comm.).
[138] *Críth Gab.*, pp 5–6.
[139] D. A. Binchy, 'Aimser chue' in *Féil-sgríbhinn Eoin Mhic Néill*, pp 18–22.
[140] *A.F.M., s.a.* 1085.

took place at an earlier period, bringing disorder among the migrants and their hosts and putting strain on the social institutions.

Famine brought about a rise in the general level of violence, and much of this was directed against the churches. The monastic towns, with their extensive farms, income from the faithful, and trade, were among the few places that could accumulate a surplus, though even they were sometimes abandoned, as were Emly and many of the churches of Munster in 1015, on occasions of scarcity and protracted warfare. In the earlier instances, the annals are not explicit about the connections between the plundering and burning of monastic towns and the outbreak of famine, though the connection is to be inferred from the annalistic record as a whole. Following the large cattle losses of 748, Clonfert and Kilmore (near Armagh) were burned in 749, Fore and Domnach Pátraic in 750. Again, in the disturbed conditions of 774–9, when the population was ravaged by famine, smallpox, and dysentery, and its food supply ruined by cattle plague and cereal losses, Clonmacnoise, Armagh, Kildare, Kildalkey, Clonburren, Clonmore, and other monasteries were attacked. Only in the eleventh and twelfth centuries do the annalists expressly link the two phenomena. In 1050 there was a famine, 'so that there grew up dishonesty among all, so that neither church nor *dún* nor gossip nor covenant was spared'. Donnchad mac Briain, king of Munster, and the Munster magnates enacted a law restraining such attacks. None the less, Kildare (with its church and oratory), Emly, and Duleek were burned and Clonmacnoise, Dunleer, Inis Clothrann, and many other monasteries were ransacked. Immediately following the famine of 1094–5, again due to cereal failure and cattle losses, Kells, Durrow, Ardstraw, Fore, Glendalough, Lismore, Clonbroney, Clones, and Clonmacnoise were attacked and burned. Again, in the famine and plague of 1113–16, Fore, Clonard, Cong, Kilcullen, Cork, Emly, Lismore, Kildare, and other monasteries were attacked. The Annals of Inisfallen patriotically attribute 'these evils: battles and fights, raids and murders, violations of churches and holy places throughout Ireland, both of laity and clergy' to the sudden illness of Muirchertach Ua Briain, king of Munster, but we can be sure that famine and want caused the attacks. A succinct entry of 1077 expresses the connection directly: 'a great scarcity in this year and the ravaging of churches.'[141]

F OR many people life was short and inevitably harsh and, as in nearly all early medieval populations, the average life-expectancy was probably no more than 40 for the great majority. There is some doubt about figures derived from skeletal assemblies, but they do give some indication of vital statistics. Figures from Francia in the fifth and sixth centuries, referring to a peaceful community, give 40 as the average expectation of life, while Anglo-Saxon

---

[141] A.F.M., *s.a.* 1077.

statistics indicate that some 57 per cent were dead at the age of 30, and 82 per cent at the age of 40.[142] Life-expectancy may not have been any higher in Ireland. An examination of skeletal remains at Castleknock, dated between 850 and 1050, showed that 23 per cent died between birth and 15, 6.5 per cent between 16 and 20, 68.1 per cent between 20 and 50. That is to say, 97.6 per cent were dead by the age of 50.[143] Skeletal remains at an ecclesiastical site at Gallen yielded somewhat different results. The size of the sample was 127. The excavator found that 13.3 per cent died between 21 and 35, 59.1 per cent between 36 and 55, 26.8 per cent between 56 and 75. This was a monastic community and therefore the range of ages is to a degree preselected, and early medieval and late medieval skeletons can scarcely be separated.[144] This may account to a degree for the differences in the figures from Gallen and Castleknock, and there may be other variables quite unknown to us. Examples of longevity are of course recorded in the annals, but these (if they are correct, and they may not be), refer to the most privileged and of course best-fed class in the population, the leading clerics and dominant kings.[145] In the case of the majority, chronic malnutrition, especially in childhood, impaired health, and (as the medical historians have shown and contemporary observation proves) multiple pathology is characteristic of deficiency diseases.

Major epidemics struck every generation of the Irish population in the second half of the seventh century, throughout the eighth, and in the first quarter of the ninth. Some major changes must have taken place in Irish society in this period, in the churches and in secular society (if we can separate the two) as a result of this remarkable series of disasters, but we can only guess what they were. The epidemics may have played a part in the emergence of great monastic federations—that is to say, the strong grew stronger and took over smaller churches and lesser monasteries depopulated by plague. In the case of secular society, it is hardly a coincidence that the dynasties that were to dominate Irish politics until the twelfth century rose to power, for the most part, in the period of the plagues and their aftermath.

No further major epidemics—with the possible exception of 907, when the *annus mortalitatis* was probably due to famine—are again reported till the middle of the tenth century. In the second half of that century epidemic diseases strike again. However, the annalistic record is vague, especially as to their nature, and apart from the epidemic among the vikings of Dublin in 951 most of the deaths could equally be caused by malnutrition and deficiency

---

[142] Calvin Wells, *Bones, bodies and disease* (London, 1964), pp 176–80.

[143] *U.J.A.*, xx (1957), pp 4–7.

[144] W. W. Howells, 'The early Christian Irish: the skeletons at Gallen priory' in *R.I.A. Proc.*, xlvi (1941), sect. C, pp 103–219.

[145] For some examples of early medieval longevity see Bart Jaski, 'Druim Cett revisted' in *Peritia*, xii (1998), pp 340–50: 343–4.

diseases. Reports of famine and shortage, or of conditions which almost inevitably lead to such, are frequent for the middle third of the ninth century but relatively rare for the remainder of the period. Again, the population apparently escaped lightly in the first half of the eleventh century. Epidemics were localised, largely confined to towns such as Armagh and the viking ports, and there are few reports of famine. However, in the second half of the century, there were epidemics on a national scale and according to the Annals of Tigernach the plague of 1084–5 killed a quarter of the population.

The general pattern is one shared with contemporary Europe and common to societies in a comparable stage of development. Life was hard; famine occurred with harsh inevitability generation after generation; and apart from the privileged few, want and hunger were the common, even the familiar, lot of most people. In Europe, the starving peasants of the countryside migrated to the cities and towns looking for food; in Ireland, the lords plundered the monastic towns for food and valuables. According to 'Cáin Adomnáin' the punishment for robbing a church is death, but hunger knew no law. Famine brought migration and disease, and the one helped to spread the other. And the plagues cut swathe after swathe through a society suffering from chronic malnutrition. It is likely that the population stood at about half a million or a little less; estimates from similar contemporary societies are about the same, but it probably fluctuated considerably in the short term, here as elsewhere. Increases and decreases alternated and compensated for each other. All the evidence indicates that the population increased in the fifth and sixth centuries, an era of colonisation at home and abroad, and the Irish retained a curiously tenacious memory of overpopulation in the early seventh century. The plagues restored the balance, and recurrent epidemics and famines trimmed back each successive increase.

Some of these epidemic diseases can be identified with some probability from the annalistic account, especially in the early period. Yet uncertainty remains; diseases have their evolutionary history, mutations which can occur rapidly change their nature, symptoms, and virulence, and much of their effect depends on the circumstances of the population in which they occur. What seems to have been an outbreak of bubonic plague occurred in 664, though medical historians are far from being agreed about it. The plague is transmitted to man by the fleas of the black rat (*Rattus rattus*), and it has been argued that since the black rat was absent from Ireland, so also was bubonic plague. However, some evidence has been advanced that there were rats in Ireland,[146] and MacArthur has confidently identified the epidemic as bubonic plague.[147] It broke out on 1 August of a warm summer and autumn

---

[146] Kelly, *Irish farming*, pp 243–4, cites some evidence for the presence of the black rat.

[147] W. P. MacArthur, 'The identification of some pestilences recorded in the Irish annals' in *I.H.S.*, vi, no. 23 (1949), pp 170–81. It is possible that the annalistic entries (Chron. Scot., *s.a.* 1013 (= 1015): *plag lochad ic Galloib and is Laignip*, and A.F.M., *s.a.* 1109: *lochaidh ag ithe na*

(conditions ideally suited for its spread), continued into 665, and broke out with renewed virulence in 667–8. It seems to have been quiescent for the next decade and a half, but it flared up again in 683–4, when it is described as *mortalitas puerorum* ('death of boys') because of the heavy death toll among children and adolescents who had developed no resistance by previous contact with it. If bubonic plague was in question in this case, it is appallingly virulent, causes panic and terror throughout the population, and some 80 to 90 per cent of those who become infected die of it. Its ravages were long remembered in Irish learned tradition. In 680 and again in 742, 769, and 779 there were recurrent outbreaks of *lepra*, which has been identified with smallpox. This disease, noted by Gregory of Tours in 580, was widely disseminated by the Arab invasions and thereafter became endemic in Europe, where as late as 1775 97 per cent of the entire population was affected, and 14 per cent of those affected died of it. In its earlier forms it is likely that it was much more virulent than it was subsequently, and this supposition is borne out by the record of fourteen abbatial and royal deaths for 780 alone. In 709, a population already weakened by protracted famine and deficiency diseases in 700–03 was struck by a new epidemic called *baccach*. From the description of it in Irish sources it is may be identical with the 'colic disease' described by Paulus of Aegina (625–90), which occurred as an epidemic and left paralysis of the limbs, which regressed in the course of a few months. It is very likely that this was poliomyelitis or a closely related viral infection of the nervous system.[148] From 764 to 778 an epidemic of dysentery or cholera type, called *fluxus sanguinis* by the annalists, first swept the country and then flared up again with recurrent virulence.[149] It was accompanied by smallpox, famine fever, and many other diseases, among which was rabies, which attacked the dogs in 776 and no doubt spread to other domestic animals and to man.[150] Finally in 783 and again in 786 a disease called *scamach*, clearly pulmonary in character and probably to be identified with influenzal or streptococcic pneumonia, caused widespread death and apparently attacked livestock as well.[151] There were further outbreaks in 806, 814, and 825.

Reeling from famine and malnutrition and ravaged by disease, the population was seized by terror and despair bordering on mass hysteria, like

---

*ngort uile in arailibh tiribh i nErinn*) may refer to rats rather than to mice, but other rodents (e.g. voles) may be in question. Calvin Wells, op. cit., p. 89 and Jean-Noël Biraben and Jacques Le Goff, 'La peste dans le haut moyen âge' in *Annales E.S.C.*, xxiv (1969), pp 1484–510, categorically deny that bubonic plague reached these islands before the later middle ages.

[148] A.U., *s.a.* 709; P. A. Janssens, *Palaeopathology: diseases and injuries of prehistoric man* (London, 1970), p. 111.

[149] It was accompanied by diarrhoea, A.U., *s.a.* 709. *Colera rubea* is glossed *lir* in the Carlsruhe Bede (*Thes. Pal.*, ii, 24).

[150] A.U., *s.a.* 776; see R.I.A., *Dictionary of the Irish language, s.v. confa(i)d*; *Peritia*, xiv (2000), p. 254.

[151] *Anecdota from Irish manuscripts*, iii, 6.

the strange seizures during and after the Black Death. 'The fair of the hand-clapping in which there was thunder and lightning like the day of judgement' is probably an example of such hysteria, and as a result of this the Irish fasted 'for fear of the fire'.[152] The usually sober pages of the annalists reflect the popular terror. In 725, and again in 753 and 807, they report that the moon was bloody. In 763 the sun was darkened in the third hour of the day, though we know that no eclipse was visible from Ireland. In 745, in the wake of an epidemic of smallpox, and again in 765, in the course of another epidemic, 'a horrible and wondrous sign was seen in the stars at night'.[153] Dragons were seen in the sky in 735 and 746; and in 786, at the height of an epidemic called *scamach*, 'a frightful vision was seen at Clonmacnoise and there was great penitence throughout all Ireland'. In 826 a warning of forthcoming plague by a Munster cleric caused 'great terror in Ireland'. Some of the meteorological phenomena are attested in foreign chronicles and may have been real, but this is not the relevant consideration. Their true importance lies in the fact that they appeared as symbols and portents of disaster to a terrified population. The feeling of utter helplessness is apparent in the entries of the later annalists, who see the ravages of the plague as the work of demons. According to the Annals of Tigernach the epidemic of 987 was 'caused by demons which inflicted a slaughter on people and they were clearly visible before men's eyes'—an account reminiscent of Procopius's description of the plague of Justinian, where those doomed to die were struck by phantoms in human shape or visited by them in their dreams.[154] The plague of 1084, which according to the annalist killed a quarter of the population, was also seen to be the work of 'demons which came from the northern isles of the world, three battalions of them and there were three thousand in each battalion... This is the way they were seen by Mac Gilla Lugáin: wherever their heat and their fury reached, there their poison was taken, for there was a sword of fire in the throat of each of them and each of them was as high as the clouds of the sky.' Even more interesting, the annalist goes on to state that it was the pagan god, Óengus Óc, son of the Dagda, who revealed the cause of the plague to Mac Gilla Lugáin, who frequented the *síd* (elf-mound) every Hallowe'en. The reaction of the population in the eighth and ninth centuries can hardly have been much different, and if the educated and literate could look to demons and pagan gods to explain the ravages of the plague, how much wilder and more terror-stricken must have been the feelings and reactions of the ignorant masses?

RECOURSE was had to more orthodox religion. 'Cáin Domnaig', a sabbatarian tract of the first half of the eighth century, seems to reflect the general gloom of the times: 'any pestilence that God has brought on the races of mankind

---

[152] A.U., *s.a.* 772.        [153] A.U., *s.aa* 745, 765.        [154] *De bello persico*, xxxii.

from the beginning of the world' shall be visited on those who break the law of the sabbath.[155] This threat would have struck home to the people with terrifying immediacy. An Old Irish hymn, attributed to Colmán moccu Chluasaig (d. *c.*661) and added to significantly in the early ninth century by the abbot of Armagh, is a prayer beseeching the saints of the Old Testament and the New for protection against plague and famine.[156] Relics of the saints were carried on circuit to give the people more palpable encouragement and consolation: those of Trian of Kildalkey in 743 to protect people against the smallpox; those of Erc of Slane and Finnian of Clonard in 776 during what may have been a typhoid epidemic; those of Tola and Trian in 793–4 in the course of a prolonged outbreak of *scamach* and smallpox.[157]

It is against this background of social upset and disorder that we must in large measure consider the development of the ecclesiastical *leges* or *cána* which in Thurneysen's words 'shot up like mushrooms in the eighth century'.[158] Famine and plague brought disorder and upset, and even the rich and populous monastic towns were among the sufferers. Social order may have tended to break down in general, and the *leges* may be an attempt at public law (enforced with the help of the kings) at a time when the secular rulers alone and customary law were incapable of dealing with what amounted to social disaster

The movement began with *Cáin Adomnáin* (697, renewed 727) a *lex innocentium* aimed at protecting non-combatants and church property from violence.[159] Armagh took it up in 734 with the *Lex Patricii*, a law protecting clerics from violence, and was soon followed by *leges* from Rahan, Clonmacnoise, Clonfert, Emly, and other monasteries. The monastic towns were animated by a genuine concern for the good ordering of society. All but six of the twenty-nine instances of the promulgation of the 'law' of a saint or the going on circuit with his relics between 721 and 806 are directly linked with a recorded outbreak of plague or famine and its consequent disorders. One of the laws deals with a matter of general rather than narrow ecclesiastical concern. In 810, *Bóshlechtae* (also called *Cáin Dar Í*), a law against the stealing and killing of cattle, was promulgated in Munster by Aduar mac

---

[155] Vernam Hull (ed. and trans.), 'Cáin Domnaig' in *Ériu*, xx (1966), p. 170.

[156] *Thes. Pal.*, ii, 298–301; Kenney, *Sources*, pp 726–7.

[157] For further examples, see Hughes, *Ch. in early Ir. soc.*, pp 168–9.

[158] Rudolf Thurneysen, 'Aus dem irischen Recht v. Nachträge zur Bürgschaft' in *Z.C.P.*, xviii (1930), pp 375–96; Kathleen Hughes, 'The church and the world in early Christian Ireland' in *I.H.S.*, xiii, no. 50 (Sept. 1962), pp 101–4.

[159] Meyer, *Cáin Adamnáin*; Máirín Ní Dhonnchadha, 'The guarantor list of *Cáin Adomnáin*, 697' in *Peritia*, i (1982), pp 178–215; eadem, 'The *Lex innocentium*: Adomnán's Law for women, clerics and youths, 697 A.D.' in Mary O'Dowd and Sabine Wichert (ed.), *Chattel, servant or citizen: women's status in church, state and society* (*Hist. Studies*, xix; Belfast, 1995), pp 58–69.

Echin, a cleric of Ossory later revered as a saint.[160] It was promulgated in Connacht in 812, in the Uí Néill lands in 813, and in Connacht for a second time in 826, the year following a major famine and outbreak of plague and clearly a time of great disorder.

The promulgation of these laws, with the full panoply of church ceremony, by the abbots of great monastic towns and their clergy, bearing the relics of popularly venerated founders and accompanied, as they often were, by the secular rulers, must have made a powerful impact on the population at large. Of course, there were motives of gain and monasteries as well as their royal supporters profited from the offerings of the people and from the fines for the infringement of the laws. Armagh was to the fore in this as in other things, and it is likely that the *leges* were soon to serve the greed of monks and kings alike. Nonetheless, historians have been too cynical about the motives of the churches and too reluctant to credit them with a genuine concern for order and for the consolation of the people in times of great hardship.

The church of the eighth and ninth centuries was rich, comfortable, and powerful. By now, clerical and lay society had become so intermeshed that any attempt to distinguish the traditional categories of church and state does some violence to the evidence. The self-confidence, not to say arrogance, of the church is evident from a number of documents. The prologue to the Martyrology of Óengus, written about 828 × 833,[161] far from being revolutionary or reformist, gives full voice to the Christian triumphalism of the establishment—an attitude perhaps already foreshadowed by Muirchú's work on St Patrick. Significantly, Óengus's basic metaphor is the kingship of the Christian saints, seen here of course as the representatives of their earthly foundations, the greater churches and monastic federations of his contemporaries. His is the exultant voice of a powerful and influential church rather than the expression of simple joy at the passing of heathenism. 'Tara's mighty burgh perished with the passing of her princes; with a host of venerable champions great Armagh abides. Rathcroaghan has vanished with Ailill's victorious offspring; fair the sovranty over princes in the city of Clonmacnoise. The famous kings have been stifled; the Domnalls have been plagued; the Ciaráns have been enkinged; the Crónáns have been magnified'.[162] It is

---

[160] Pádraig Ó Riain, 'A misunderstood annal: a hitherto unnoticed cáin' in *Celtica*, xxi (1990), pp 561–6; for the genealogy of Aduar, see Paul Walsh, *Genealogiae regum et sanctorum Hiberniae* (Maynooth, 1917), p. 93 (where the genealogy is syncopated); Ó Riain, *Corpus genealogiarum sanctorum Hiberniae* (Dublin, 1985), p. 31, § 186, p. 45 277; O'Brien, *Corpus geneal. Hib.*, 105; on the Laws themselves, see Thurneysen, op. cit.; *C.I.H.*, p. 254 = *Anc. laws Ire.*, iii, 110 (comm.).

[161] Pádraig Ó Riain, 'The Tallaght martyrologies redated' in *Camb. Med. Celt. Studies*, xx (1990), pp 21–38.

[162] *Fél. Oeng.*, pp 23–7; David Greene and Frank O'Connor (ed. and trans.), *A golden treasury of Irish poetry*, A.D. 600–1200 (London, 1967), pp 61–6.

noteworthy that Óengus refers not to what historians have considered to be the spiritual powerhouses of the *céli Dé* to whom he has traditionally been supposed to belong, but to the church in general and to the older, richer, and more powerful establishments. Nor is Óengus alone in these attitudes. Another poem, attributed to Orthanach ua Cóellamae (d. 840), bishop of Kildare and highly skilled poet, makes the same pointed comparison between the transience of earthly kings, however splendid, and the abiding glory of the churches: 'Brigit in the land I behold, where each in his turn has lived; your fame has proved greater than that of the king; you are superior to them.'[163]

When we examine the role of the church in society at large, and especially in its upper echelons, we see good reason for the triumphalism of Óengus and his peers. Armagh and the Uí Néill kings were working in tandem, each (it would seem) content to boost the pretensions of the other. In Leinster, the monastic town of Kildare was a dynastic capital in the ninth century, though of course its connections with the dynasty that was to dominate Leinster were intimate even in the seventh century, when Cogitosus, the biographer of the foundress, describes Kildare as the keeper of the royal treasury.[164] In fact, it is quite likely that he was writing when a member of the Uí Dúnlainge, the royal dynasty of Leinster, held office as abbot. In the case of Emly, its first explicit documented connection with the kingship of Munster was the simultaneous proclamation of the law of its founder and the 'ordination' of the king of Munster (793), and two, perhaps three, of its abbots held the kingship of Munster in the ninth century. A Munster king-list, edited at Emly, stresses the participation in the kingship of Munster of the dynastic stock that dominated its area and supplied many of its abbots.[165]

As a general principle the great hereditary clerical families were usually discard segments of royal lineages, pushed out of the political struggle and forced to reprise themselves in the church. Once established there, they proved extremely tenacious and were displaced only with great difficulty by later royal segments or by new and expansive dynasties.[166] Here were good grounds for conflict, which might more conventionally be interpreted as conflict between church and state. Some examples may be useful. Lann Léire (Dunleer) was ruled from the eighth to the tenth centuries by a segment of the locally ruling Fir Rois. Another lineage of the same dynasty later

---

[163] Kuno Meyer (ed. and trans.), *Hail Brigit* (Halle, 1912); Greene & O'Connor, *A golden treasury of Irish poetry* (from whom the translation is cited). Carney's reservations about the identity of Orthanach (*Ériu*, xxii (1971), p. 58) are unfounded.
[164] *P.L.*, lxxii, col. 778, translated in Seán Connolly and Jean-Michel Picard, 'Cogitosus's Life of St Brigit: content and value' in *R.S.A.I. Jn.*, cxvii (1987) 5–27; Kuno Meyer, 'Aed Dub mac Colmáin, bishop-abbot of Kildare' in *Z.C.P.*, xi (1913), pp 458–60.
[165] This king-list in the Laud Synchronisms (*Z.C.P.*, ix (1913), pp 478–9, 482) was edited at Emly, as the additions show, and note that some of the additions have become misplaced.
[166] D. Ó Corráin, 'Dál Cais—church and dynasty' in *Ériu*, xxiv (1973), pp 52–63.

held the office of hereditary priest at Armagh.[167] Some branches of the Éoganacht Áine held power in Emly and from them derived the hereditary abbatial family, Uí Laígenán.[168] Uí Meicc Brócc, an early discard segment of the Éoganacht, held abbatial office in Cork in the second half of the seventh century, while the genealogy of their kinsmen, Uí Meicc Iair, a similar lineage, is full of clerical names. The later hereditary abbots of Cork, Uí Selbaig, claimed descent from Uí Meicc Iair (however historically sound that descent may be), and were ousted from office only in the twelfth century.[169]

Their tenacity was remarkable. A branch of the Ciannachta, settled about Portrane and Lusk, dominated the monastery of Lusk from the late seventh to the early ninth century while their secular kinsmen succumbed to Uí Néill power in the early eighth century. Another branch of the Ciannachta, who apparently went under to Uí Néill attack in the early ninth century, held out as abbots and clergy at Monasterboice till the twelfth century and produced many scholars, among whom the historian, Flann Mainistrech (d. 1056), is the best-known.[170] Despite the collapse of Southern Uí Fiachrach power in the seventh century, clerical lineages of that dynasty supplied some eight of the fourteen abbots of Tuaim Gréne between 752 and 1100 in the teeth of the expanding power of Dál Cais.[171] Most remarkable of all, despite the power of the great Leinster royal families, the splintered and declining Fotharta, who claimed Brigit herself as their own and whose archaic poem states that they would hold Leinster as long as they were loyal to her, continued to supply leading clergy to Kildare. To Uí Chúlduib, one of their branches, belonged the two abbesses, Muirenn (d. 918) and Eithne (d. 1016); to the obscure Fothairt Airbrech belonged the earlier abbess, Sebdann (d. 732), and another Kildare ecclesiastic (d. 750); while two further abbesses, Coblaith (d. 916) and Muirenn (d. 964), belonged to an ecclesiastical branch of Fothairt Fea. And it is highly probable that many other Kildare clerics, whose origins cannot be established with certainty, belonged to Fotharta.[172]

The monastery of Trim, on which there is more information than most, may be taken as an example of hereditary succession, though how typical it was is difficult to judge. It was ruled from the early eighth century to the middle of the ninth by the descendants of Colmán mac Duib Dúin, a discard segment, according to its own records, of the ruling dynasty of the petty

---

[167] *Bk Lec.*, 79ᵛa–c = *B.B.*, 114b–aa5c; Tomás Ó Fiaich, 'The church of Armagh under lay control' in *Seanchas Ardmhacha*, v (1969), pp 75–127.

[168] *Bk Lec.*, 214ra = *B.B.*, 178d.

[169] O'Brien, *Corpus geneal. Hib.*, pp 213–15.

[170] Ibid., pp 168–9; Hughes, *Ch. in early Ir. soc.*, p. 162 (where however the abbatial list is incomplete and the relationship with the dynasty not shown); O'Brien, *Corpus geneal. Hib.*, pp 247–8; M. E. Dobbs, 'The pedigree and family of Flann Mainistrech' in *Louth Arch. Soc. Jn.*, v, no. 3 (Dec. 1923), pp 149–53.

[171] Ó Corráin, 'Dál Cais', p. 55.

[172] O'Brien, *Corpus geneal. Hib.*, pp 80–86.

kingdom of Lóegaire in which Trim lay. According to a claim that goes back at least to the seventh century, Trim was founded by St Lommán, a disciple of Patrick, and by St Fortchern, son of one Feidlimid, a leading early prince of the dynasty. This claim was well known to the abbots of Trim in the ninth century, who, if we may judge from the genealogies of the saints and from an entry in the Martyrology of Tallaght taken from the records of Trim itself, looked on themselves as the heirs of St Lommán and his disciples. The same genealogies list a formidable group of some thirty-seven saints of Lóegaire, some of whom, like the eighth- and ninth-century abbots, are represented as married men and themselves ancestors of other saints. The hereditary clergy of Trim clearly saw the past in terms of their own present and their own institutions, and they seem to have acted quite unselfconsciously as an ecclesiastical dynasty. In a matter-of-fact way, they record in the genealogies of Lóegaire (which were kept at Trim) their own marriages to the daughters of aristocratic and royal families, though they preserve no such details for the kings of Lóegaire. These marriages are highly informative, for they used marriage to establish contacts with leading aristocratic families and also to extend their connections with neighbouring monasteries. For instance, Báethchellach, abbot of Trim (d. 756), was married to the daughter of Feradach, king of Lóegaire (d. 704): this is recorded in the genealogies and in the later martyrologies, which account Báethchellach a saint. Other members of the family were married to the daughters of the local aristocracy. Still others established an alliance by marriage with the ecclesiastical family of Cell Duma Glind (Kilglyn, some kilometres to the south-east of Trim). This church is said to have been founded by St Mugenóc, brother of St Lommán, founder of Trim; and, an interesting parallel, the abbots of Trim considered themselves to be dynastically related to the monastic family of Cell Duma Glind, Uí Chuanna, who lived there and also held Telach Ard, a minor ecclesiastical foundation a little over 3 kilometres to the north of Trim.[173] This relationship was cemented by two marriage alliances. Colmán, the family founder, married Fínnechta, daughter of Máel Fithrig of Cell Duma Glind. His great-grandson Móenach chose one of his wives from the same family, Nath Í, his third and fourth cousin. The family of Trim tried to expand into the great monastery of Clonard, about 25 km to the south-west. Two abbots of Trim, Suibne (d. 796) and Cenn Fáelad (d. 821) held offices there as *tánaise abbad* 'deputy abbot', and though Suibne's son Cormac died as abbot of Clonard in 830, they did not succeed, despite a great deal of effort, in bringing it under their control.[174]

---

[173] *Bk Lec.*, 62ᵛc4 = *B.B.*, 87a17 (Uí Chuanna).
[174] *B.B.* 87d26–eb24; *Bk Lec.*, 46ʳd12 (descendants of Colmán mac Dub Dúin); for obits of clergy descended from Colmán, see A.U., *s.a.* 747, 796, 821, 830, 838, 846; R. I. Best and H. J. Lawlor (ed.), *Martyrology of Tallaght* (London, 1931), p. 17 (17 Feb.).

The Uí Chrítáin, hereditary clergy at Druim Inesclainn, who were claimed as remote collaterals of Lóegaire, shared some of the characteristics of their better-known cousins. Here the patron was St Rónán mac Beraig who died in the great plague of 665 and whose relics were enshrined in 801. Uí Chrítáin ruled Druim Inesclainn without an apparent break from the mid-ninth century to 978. Like other families, they created a suitable background for themselves: they claimed to be descendants of Lóegaire, and quite impossibly identified their eponym, Crítán, with the grandfather of St Rónán. Further, they claimed five saints of their lineage, one being St Colum Cúile, their direct ancestor.[175] Such legend-building was widespread, and one must suspect that the genealogies of the saints, most of which were put together in the eighth century, primarily served the needs of such clerical dynasties.[176]

There were of course factors that ran counter to the general relationship of church and dynasty. Some monasteries kept up close contact with the homeland of the founder, often from a different part of Ireland. Lismore, founded by Mochutu of the Ciarraige Lúachra, is a case in point. There is good evidence of hereditary succession by clergy of unknown origin in the ninth century, and the local dynasty took a hand in ruling it in the tenth century. However, one of the most famous of its abbots, Flann mac Fairchellaig (814–25), *céle Dé* and saint, belonged to Ciarraige Luachra, as did Cináed ua Conmind, bishop of Lismore (d. 958).[177] Monasteries on the borders of powerful kingdoms were pushed and pulled between rival dynasties, and often got a great deal of their own way as a result. Uí Maine and Múscraige, for example, provided clergy on different occasions to Terryglass, and when Dál Cais became powerful they intruded their own clerical lineages. Clonmacnoise, another such monastery, despite the claims that have been made on its behalf, was quite untypical in its choice of early abbots.[178] The building-up of monastic federations, which was advanced to the point of confrontation by the late seventh century, if we may judge by Tírechán's embittered comments, also tended to cut across dynastic lines.[179] Great monastic families, at the head of their federations, generated an ambition and momentum of their own, and this is frequently expressed as grand pluralism in the eighth century and in less edifying inter-monastic warfare, even though the lesser churches, as we shall see, made a stand for their independence.

---

[175] *B.B.* 88b6–20 (Uí Chrítáin of Druim Inesclaind); for obits of Uí Chrítáin clergy, see A.U., *s.a.* 879, 891, 912; A.F.M., *s.a.* 976 [= 978]; for the five saints of the lineage, see Ó Riain, *Corpus,* p. 52 325, p. 127 690.7, 690.15.

[176] Ó Riain, *Corpus*, pp i–liv.

[177] Flann mac Fairchellaig: *Bk Lec.*, 121ʳa5 = *B.B.* 159b6 (Uí Flannáin of Uí Thorna, Ciarraige genealogies); Walsh, *Genealogiae*, p. 108 = Ó Riain, *Corpus*, p. 53, 329. Cináed Ua Conmind: *Bk Lec.*, 120ʳb51 = *B. B.*, 158b36 (Ciarraige genealogies), Ann. Inisf., *s.a.* 958.

[178] John Ryan, 'The abbatial succession at Clonmacnoise' in *Féil-sgríbhinn Eoin Mhic Néill*, pp 490–507.

[179] Bieler, *Patrician texts*, p. 130, § 7; p. 138, § 18; p. 140, § 22; p. 142, § 25; p. 160, § 47.

None the less, the dynastic hereditary factor lay at the heart of Irish church life. A telling point in favour of this view is that the greater part of the surviving genealogical corpus, far from being the work of secular men of learning, is the product of the dynastically minded clergy.[180] For example, the core of the Airgialla genealogies derives from Armagh, where it was preserved by the clerical lineages of the dynasty.[181] The terminal names in the Ciannachta genealogies are those of the early twelfth-century hereditary abbots of Monasterboice, and it is probably they, themselves men with a reputation for learning, who preserved the record.[182] The Múscraige genealogies were kept at the monastery of Lothra. These explicitly quote from 'Lebor Sochair Lothra' (which must date from the period 750–800), list the Múscraige families associated with some dozen local ecclesiastical foundations, and record the genealogy of the *fer léigind* (head of the monastic school), perhaps the compiler of the text itself. It is interesting to note that the Múscraige genealogies have come under the influence of the greatest of ecclesiastical legends, the Patrician story, and quote extensively from the 'Vita Tripartita' of St Patrick.[183] To the monastery of Glenn Uissen we owe the Uí Bairrche genealogies with their detailed listing of churches and church families.[184] Books cited in the genealogical tracts—'Saltair Caisil', 'Lebor Sochair Lothra', 'Lebor Inse Dúine', and 'Lebor Dromma Sailech'[185]—also point to clerical compilation, and the author of such dynastic origin-legends as 'Do bunad imthechta Éoganachta' (which models itself directly on the scriptural story of Joseph) and 'Timna Chathaír' (which is based on Jacob's blessing of his sons) can only have come from an ecclesiastical environment.[186] In some aspects the genealogies are none other than the files of an aristocratically minded hereditary clergy, documents that justify their offices and possessions

---

[180] D. Ó Corráin, 'Creating the past' in *Peritia*, xii (1998), pp 177–208.

[181] Z.C.P., viii (1912), pp 317–24; *Corpus geneal. Hib.*, pp 139–53, 181–5.

[182] O'Brien, *Corpus geneal. Hib.*, pp 168–69; A.U., *s.a.* 702, 722, 731, 736, 778, 783, 784, 787, 791, 796, 804, 804 (Ciannachta Mide); O'Brien, *Corpus geneal. Hib.*, p. 247; A.U., *s.a.* 855, 1005, 1056, 1104; A.F.M., *s.a.* 1117, 1122 (Ciannachta Breg).

[183] T.C.D, MS H. 2. 7, 98b = *Bk Lec.*, 104 Rb, 110 Rd = *B.B.*, 141b13; a defective copy of this tract (from *Bk Leinster*) is printed in O'Brien, *Corpus geneal. Hib.*, pp 367–75; D. Ó Corráin, 'An chléir agus an léann dúchais anallód: an ginealas' in Pádraig Ó Fiannachta (ed.), *Léann na cléire* (*Léachtaí Cholm Cille*, xvi, 1986), pp 71–86.

[184] O'Brien, *Corpus geneal. Hib.*, pp 46–54.

[185] Pádraig Ó Riain, 'The Psalter of Cashel: a provisional list of contents' in *Éigse*, xxiii (1989), pp 107–30; for Lebor Sochair Lothra see *Bk Lec.*, 111ᵛb7, 15 = *B.B.*, 199b37, 44; Lebor Sochair Lothra is probably identical with Lebor Lothra Ruadáin, cited in the genealogies in *Bk Lec.*, 113ʳa32 = *B.B.*, 201ac33 = *Bk Uí Maine*, 34ᵛb32; for Lebor Ailéin Inse Dúine see *Bk Lec.*, 111ᵛb15 = *B.B.*, 199b44; for Lebor Dromma Sailech (said to be a source for the Callraige genealogies) see *B.B.*, 200a38–9 = *Bk Uí Maine*, 34ʳb19 = John O'Donovan (ed. and trans.), *Miscellany of the Celtic Society* (Dublin, 1849), p. 28.

[186] Z.C.P., viii (1912), pp 312–13; Myles Dillon (ed. and trans.), *Lebor na cert: the Book of rights* (Ir. Texts Soc., xlvi; Dublin, 1962), pp 148–78; D. Ó Corráin, 'Irish origin-legends and genealogy: recurrent aetiologies' in Tore Nyberg, Iørn Piø, *et al.* (ed.), *History and heroic tale: a symposium* (Odense, 1985), pp 51–96: 53–4.

by right of descent, and the proper exploitation of these sources may yet throw more light on the organisation of the early Irish churches.

CHURCHES and churchmen had early found an honoured place for themselves in Irish society—how early is difficult to know, but they had achieved it by the seventh century, when the laws were being written, very largely by clerics or by those trained in clerical schools.[187] The impression one gets is that the churches were deeply concerned with law from the beginning and had a large part in moulding it. Seventh- and eighth-century texts from the *Nemed* school of law[188] lay particular stress on the dignity and importance of the ecclesiastical scholar, the *saí litre* who practises *ecne*, here largely understood as canon law and the law of scripture, no doubt the mix of scriptural, canon, and secular law best represented in the 'Hibernensis', most of which was in existence at the beginning of the eighth century.[189] Texts that went into the making of the 'Hibernensis' are translated into Old Irish in 'Bretha Nemed', the first third of which is almost entirely a canon-law tract.[190] 'Bretha Nemed', citing the earlier 'Comperta breth Fíthil', places scholar and churchman (elsewhere in the tract defined as bishop and abbot), king and poet on the same level; none of them may be sued against because they are beyond the capacity of ordinary individuals and protected by privilege. The same text states that nobody is a scholar who cannot arbitrate correctly according to scriptural and canon law.[191]

In another text from the same school, 'Uraicecht Becc', the seven ecclesiastical orders are listed and are said to correspond to the secular grades of society.[192] However, most of the orders are subsequently ignored in the text, which chiefly concerns itself with important bishops, abbots, and monastic literati. The highest grade of bishop and the abbots of great monastic cities, such as Emly and Cork, are equated in dignity with the king of Munster. In the case of the *brithem*, the highest status is accorded only to those who can

---

[187] D. Ó Corráin, 'Irish law and canon law' in Ní Chatháin & Richter, *Ire. & Europe*, pp 157–66; D. Ó Corráin, Liam Breatnach, and Aidan Breen, 'The laws of the Irish' in *Peritia*, iii (1984), pp 382–438; D. Ó Corráin, 'Irish vernacular law and the Old Testament' in Ní Chatháin & Richter, *Ire. & Christendom*, pp 284–310.

[188] D. A. Binchy, 'Bretha Nemed' in *Ériu*, xvii (1955), pp 4–6; idem, 'The date and provenance of Uraicecht Becc' in *Ériu*, xviii (1958), pp 44–54; Liam Breatnach (ed. and trans.), 'The first third of *Bretha nemed*' in *Ériu*, xl (1989), pp 1–40; idem, 'Canon law and secular law in early Ireland: the significance of *Bretha nemed*' in *Peritia*, iii (1984), pp 439–59.

[189] Wasserschleben, *Die irische Kanonensammlung*.

[190] Breatnach, 'Canon law and secular law', 445–52; idem, 'The first third of *Bretha nemed*', p. 8, § 3; pp 12–14, § 12; pp 16–18, § 22.

[191] E. J. Gwynn (ed.), 'An Old Irish tract on the privileges and responsibilities of poets' in *Ériu*, xiii (1940–42), pp 30–31.

[192] The number and nature of the ecclesiastical orders was a concern of Irish scholars; see Roger E. Reynolds, 'At sixes and sevens—and eights and nines: the sacred mathematics of sacred orders in the early middle ages' in *Speculum*, liv (1979), pp 669–84; *Críth Gab.*, p. 1, ll 7–9, states that the grades of secular society are formed by analogy with the ecclesiastical grades.

handle canon law as well as customary law and the law of the poets. Here again there is particular stress on the *saí litre*, and the various grades of the office are given separate categorisation. The drift of the text, from its initial arguments on the foundations of law to the status awarded the clergy, argues for clerical compilation at Cork or Emly by a *saí litre* or ecclesiastical scholar.[193] Another tract on status, which dates to the first half of the eighth century, is so close in the parts that deal with the wounding or outraging of a bishop to the canon-law tract, 'Sinodus Hibernensis', that one must argue that the Irish is a translation of the Latin or both are based, in part at least, on the same text.[194] The same material from 'Sinodus Hibernensis' on the wounding of a bishop appears in the eighth-century 'Bretha Déin Chécht', in the section in high diction attributed to Laidcend mac Ercaid.[195] The compiler of 'Críth Gablach' (*c.*700), one of the principal tracts on status and probably compiled at a law-school in Meath, had as one of his sources a monastic tract dealing with the grades of *manaig*, similar to other law tracts on the status.[196] The prefatory matter to the legal collections, early and late, draws heavily on a legend that Irish law was revised in the light of Christian revelation and drew its inspiration from it—in reality, an argument in defence of Irish law and of its practice by the clerical scholars.[197] These indications, together with the presence of Irish legal technical terms (in Latin translation or adaptation) in the earliest canon law—and increasingly in the later[198]—must lead us to believe that churchmen had a large part in the shaping of Irish law and practised as secular as well as canon lawyers. There is solid annalistic evidence for this from the ninth to the twelfth centuries,[199] and equally good

[193] *C.I.H.*, pp 1590–1618 = *Anc. laws Ire.*, v, 2–114, translated by Eoin Mac Neill in *R.I.A. Proc.*, xxxvi (1923), sect. C, pp 272–81.

[194] *C.I.H.*, pp 588–89 = *Anc. laws Ire.*, iv, 362–8; Bieler, *Ir. penitentials*, p. 170; cf. in particular, *C.I.H.*, p. 588, lines 17–23 and 'Sinodus Hibernensis', p. 170, §§ 1–6.

[195] D. A. Binchy (ed. and trans.), 'Bretha Déin Chécht' in *Ériu*, xx (1966), pp 1–66: 40, § 31; D. Ó Corráin, 'Irish law and canon law', pp 164–6.

[196] *Críth Gab.*, pp 6–7 (*aithech baitside, bóaire gensa* are terms for church tenantry); see also *C.I.H.*, pp 582, 584, 585 = *Anc. laws Ire.*, iv, 344, 350, 352. There are occasional references to 'Cáin Manach' (e.g. *C.I.H.*, p. 1378, lines 8–9 = *Anc. laws Ire.*, v, 364, lines 6–7), an apparently lost tract on *manaig*.

[197] D. A. Binchy, 'The pseudo-historical prologue to the Senchas Már' in *Studia Celt.*, x–xi (1975–6), pp 15–28; Ó Corráin, Breatnach, & Breen, 'Laws of the Irish', pp 384–91; K. R. McCone, 'Dubthach moccu Lugair and a matter of life and death in the pseudo-historical prologue to the Senchas Már' in *Peritia*, v (1986), pp 1–35; John Carey, 'The two laws in Dubthach's judgment' in *Camb. Med. Celtic Studies*, xix (1990), pp 1–18; Damian Bracken, 'Immortality and punishment in Irish law' in *Peritia*, ix (1995), pp 167–86.

[198] D. A. Binchy, 'St Patrick's "first synod"' in *Studia Hib.*, viii (1968), pp 49–59; Hughes, *Ch. in early Ir. soc.*, pp 44–53; Maurice P. Sheehy, 'Influence of ancient Irish law on the "Collectio hibernensis"' in *Proceedings of the 3rd International Congress on Medieval Canon Law* (Vatican City, 1971), pp 31–42.

[199] D. Ó Corráin, 'Nationality and kingship in pre-Norman Ireland' in T. W. Moody (ed.), *Nationality and the pursuit of national independence* (*Hist. Studies*, xi; Belfast, 1978) pp 1–35: 14–15; to the examples there cited add *Fer Fughaill epscop Cluana Dolcain*, 'Man of Judgement [i.e. the Judge], bishop of Clondalkin' (A.U., *s.a.* 789 = *A.F.M.*, *s.a.* 784 [= 789]).

evidence for the study of Irish law in Slane, Cork, Cloyne, Glendalough, and other monastic towns in the same period. There was of course no centralised ecclesiastical authority: practice differed no doubt from place to place, and differing customs and standards were tolerated among the churches. Nonetheless, we can take it that the Irish law tracts, taken as a whole, fairly represent in a general way the church establishment of the late seventh and eighth centuries, its attitudes, and its place in society.

In the tracts of all the schools, early and late, the principal ecclesiastics are equated in status with the local king, and the masters of the privileged professions and the lesser orders with the appropriate secular grades; and, though there are differences in detail and interpretation in the various tracts, the broad classification is the same in all. The privileges of the *fili* and *brithem* are extended to the clergy. For example, a bishop, like a king or *fili*, is not responsible for the liabilities of his son.[200] The familial element is equally if less explicitly present in canon law. The church is not liable for the delicts of others—fugitive monks, wicked pilgrims, or those whom it has expelled—in the same way, the canonist argues, as God and his angels are not responsible for the delicts of the devil. Much more important, the church (read churchmen) is not responsible for the liabilities of its lay kindred, a rule that takes on a great deal more significance when we understand how close was the relationship—in blood and politics—between the lay aristocracy and the clerical families. On the other hand, canon law lays great stress on the kindred responsibility of laymen in offences against the church; in close parallel with the vernacular laws, it lists the widening circle of persons answerable for another's crime; and finally (a significant addition), if a person has offended the church and none can be found to bear liability, recourse is to be had to the king of the province (*rex maximus provinciae*) in which the church is situated.[201] Here we find the churches making an appeal to the larger kingships that had arisen and giving them their blessing, and over-kings of the eighth and ninth centuries did avenge attacks on churches within their province.

The church, then, enjoyed the special protection of the law and the patronage of the rich and powerful, and fitted cosily into society. Its canon law took over many of the inherited basic concepts of the vernacular law and shared many rules in matters of detail. For example, those excluded from the right to contract independently are essentially identical in both legal systems, and the vernacular law explicitly recognised that the *manach* (earlier 'monk', later 'monastic client') may not contract independently of his abbot.[202] In the

---

[200] *C.I.H.*, pp 31, 1045, 1841 = *Anc. laws Ire.*, v, 234 (heptad xxxv).

[201] *Hib.*, xlii, 29-31; *C.I.H.*, pp 2011–12 = *Anc. laws Ire.*, iv, 240–42. The expression *rex maximus provinciae* is a translation of *rí ruirech, rí cóicid*. The text of the vernacular laws do not specify the over-king, but the later glossator does.

[202] *Hib.*, xvii 9–10; xxxiv, 3; xxv 5 (h); *C.I.H.*, pp 522, 536 = *Anc. laws Ire.*, iii, 10, 58; *C.I.H.*, p. 2136.

matter of the law of succession to property, canon law fits well with secular custom and, while teaching the usual Christian norms at least as an ideal, quietly recognises the pragmatics of secular polygamic marriage.[203] The father is bound in canon law to divide his property in equal shares between sons, while he reserves a like share for himself, which he grants to the eldest. This appears to be the extra share of the son who has the duty of maintaining his parents in their old age, and this fell on the eldest.[204] The custom of assignment by lot is supported by scriptural citation[205] while the rules governing the disposition of estates in the absence of sons are those of vernacular law. Indeed, canon law concerns itself in detail with the problems of heiresses in a patrilineal society and adopts many of the rulings of vernacular law. They must give sureties that they will not alienate family estates; they have a life interest in them, but the estates must eventually be returned to their father's nearest male relatives. They may make bequests from the estate to the church, provided such bequests are not contested by the ultimate heirs. It is envisaged that they should marry men of their paternal kindred and thus pass the property to their male relatives while giving their children an interest in the estate, a provision supported by scriptural citation (Num. 36: 8) and one that runs quite counter to the earlier romanising ruling which forbids marriage between those not separated by four degrees (second cousins or more remote kin).[206] More remarkable still, the property relationship of the abbot who is a locum tenens with his church and his *manaig* is explicitly based on the same principles as that of a lord with his clients, and as the contractual relationship of a man and his wife in marriage. And when such an abbot parts with his church, willingly or unwillingly, the arrangements for the disposition of property and the categories of property involved are strikingly similar in concept and terminology to those in use in the law governing divorce.[207] The rules vary in detail but the principles are clear. What

[203] *Hib.*, xxxi, 18; xxxii, 3, 11 (note that these canons refer to Deut. 21: 15–17, which deals with inheritance by sons of different wives); cf. *Hib.*, xxxii, 11.

[204] *Hib.*, xxxi, 18; xxxii, 4; *C.I.H.*, p. 591; Rudolf Thurneysen, 'Die Bürgschaft im irischen Recht' in *Abh. d. preuss. Akademie d. Wissenschaften, phil.-hist. Kl., Jhg 1928* (Berlin, 1928), p. 7 = *Gesammelte Schriften*, iii, 90–174: 94; Anderson, *Adomnán's Life*, pp 154–62 (ii, 39); Robin Chapman Stacey, '*Berrad airechta*: an Old Irish tract on suretyship' in T. M. Charles-Edwards and D. B. Walters (ed.), *Lawyers and laymen: studies in the history of law presented to Professor Dafydd Jenkins* (Cardiff, 1986), pp 210–33: 211; *Studies in Ir. law*, p. 134; D. A. Binchy, 'Some Celtic legal terms' in *Celtica*, iii (1956), pp 221–31: 228–31; Peter Schrijver, 'OIr. *gor* "pious, dutiful", meaning and etymology' in *Ériu*, xlvii (1996), pp 193–204.

[205] *Hib.*, xxxii, 8; *Z.C.P.*, xv (1925), pp 136–7 ('Gúbretha Caratniad'); Thurneysen, *Cóic Conara Fugill*, §§ 64–6.

[206] *Hib.*, xxxii, 17–20 (inheriting females); *Studies in Ir. law*, pp 129–79; T. M. Charles-Edwards, *Early Irish and Welsh kinship* (Oxford, 1993), pp 516–19; Bieler, *Ir. penitentials*, p. 196, § xxix; D. Ó Corráin, 'Women and the law in early Ireland' in O'Dowd & Wichert, *Chattel, servant, or citizen*, pp 45–57: 52–6.

[207] *C.I.H.*, pp 502–4 = *Studies in Ir. law*, pp 2–3, §§ 1–3 ('Cáin Lánamna'); *Hib.*, xliii, 6; xliv, 20 note (o).

property the abbot brought with him to the office, he takes in full; what was given him as part of the office he leaves intact, except that the necessary expenses of office may be deducted from it; the offerings of the faithful during tenure and the ordinary increase and profits of the monastic herds are divided in two between the abbot and the church. This is close enough to the rules governing divorce by mutual consent.[208] If, however, the abbot were a priest, the rules are different and identify his interests more closely with those of the church.

The church, then, at its lowest as well as at its highest levels, in its canon law as well as in its personnel, was fully integrated with Irish society as a whole and deeply imbued with its values. This was the case by the late seventh and early eighth centuries: there is no reason to believe that the nexus changed significantly in the following centuries.

THE relationship of church and people was conceived in terms of a legal contract involving mutual obligations (*folud* and *frithfolud*), a basic concept in Irish law. The church provides religious rites and services—baptism, communion, requiems, mass on Sundays and on the chief festival days—in return for which the people pay the church its dues for the maintenance of the clergy. In this regard, we know most about the *manaig*, the clients of the church, that is to say, those who farmed church land and whose landlord was the superior of the church or monastery. Though the word *manach* is derived from Latin *monachus* 'monk', the *manaig* were not monks, and this use of the word to describe a class of monastic tenants is very old: it is attested in 'Aipgitir Chrábaid' (*c.*600), which carefully distinguishes the monk (*bráthair*) from the *manach*: among the things a proper monk must avoid are: *fáitbe mbráithre...comairb do manchaib* 'derision of brethren [i.e. fellow monks]...strife with *manaig*'.[209] The *manaig* are often seen as occupying an intermediate position between clergy and laity. Usually they were clients of the church, tenantry of church lands, or at least bound to render certain services to the church. They lived in lawful wedlock (this means canonical marriage with all that it entails) and, ideally at least, observed a notably strict sexual regime.[210] Looked at from another point of view, they

---

[208] Ibid.; even the technical term *semen in pecoribus* (*Hib.*, xliii, 6) is a close translation of *indoth* (*Studies in Ir. law*, p. 28). Note, however, that these rules seem reminiscent of those laid down in the *acta* of the ninth council of Toledo in 655 (J. Vives (ed.), *Concilios visgóticos e hispano-romanos* (Barcelona and Madrid, 1963), pp 299–300, § 4: 'Quae de conquistis rebus inter ecclesiam et sacerdotis haeredes divisio fiat') and the Irish may have had access to that text.

[209] Vernam E. Hull (ed. and trans.), '*Apgitir Chrábaid*: the alphabet of piety' in *Celtica*, viii (1968), pp 44–89: 62 (my interpretation of the text differs from Hull's); idem, 'The date of *Aipgitir crábaid*'in *Z.C.P.*, xxv (1956), pp 88–90. Most texts are inherently ambiguous because *monachus* and *manach* can be used for both kinds of person.

[210] *Hib.*, xlvi, 11; Bieler, *Ir. penitentials*, p. 222, § 9 ('Bigotian Penitential'); p. 265, § 36 ('Old-Irish penitential').

are the parishioners of the church, but more than parishoners because of the property nexus and other privileges. There is early evidence that they attended church regularly and were entitled to spiritual guidance and a monastic education for at least some of their sons. According to 'Ríagail Phátraic', a text of c.800, a superior forfeited his right to rule over his *manaig* and the church was not entitled to its income from them—tithes, heriots, labour services, and bequests—unless an ordained cleric was provided to carry out religious services for them, and this will indicate that *manaig* may have lived on properties some distances from the main church and served by a dependent church. The priest who ministered was entitled to take certain legal steps to ensure proper payment for his service—proof, if any were needed, that dues were hard to collect—and the *manaig* in turn maintained him with their labour.[211] The vernacular law tract 'Córus Bésgnai' deals extensively with the relationship of the church and the laity in general, and again the nexus is seen as a contractual one. Clergy and laity belong to two separate but related jurisdictions: 'Clerics and nuns are bound by the church under the authority of a confessor, by law and rule, by a vow until it is broken, by a pledge thereafter, in accordance with the laws of the church, under the rule of an abbot and a proper confessor. Gentlemen, gentlewomen, and the ordinary people of the lay community are controlled by their lord.'[212] The lords give pledges for the payment of tithes, first fruits, and firstlings by those subject to them, and their subjects must redeem those pledges by paying their dues. The lay community 'is entitled to its prerogatives from the church, i.e. baptism, communion, requiem, and mass are required of each church to all as a right of faith, together with the preaching of the word of God to all those who listen to and comply with it'. In return, the church is entitled to 'their offering, their tithes, their first fruits, their firstlings, their legacy at the point of death, and their bequest'. The church must maintain proper order within its own jurisdiction, and only a church that does so is entitled to payments. Firstlings include animals as well as humans. The firstborn child of lawful wedlock is to be given to the church, but he is not cut off from his family. He receives his share in his inheritance as do other sons and lives on his own farm, but he is educated by the church and is under certain obligations of service to it as a *manach*. First fruits are defined as the first of every crop, big and small, and each first lamb and first calf born in the year.[213] It is uncertain how far these ambitious provisions could be applied to the population at large. Some regard them as a cleric's ideal, while

---

[211] *C.I.H.*, pp 2129–30 = J. G. O'Keeffe (ed. and trans.), 'The rule of Patrick' in *Ériu*, i (1904), pp 216–24; E. G. Gwynn, *The rule of Tallaght*, in *Hermathena*, xliv, second supplemental volume (Dublin, 1927), pp 78–87.
[212] *C.I.H.*, p. 523 = *Anc. laws Ire.*, iii, 14–16.
[213] *C.I.H.*, pp 526–31 = *Anc. laws Ire.*, iii, 24–42 ('Córus Bésgnai'); Bieler, *Ir. penitentials*, 166–8; Ó Corráin, Breatnach, & Breen, 'Laws of the Irish', pp 384–7, 406–12.

others may consider them a fully worked-out system of pastoral care and material support for the church.

Indeed, the whole area of pastoral care is problematical and much remains uncertain.[214] In the first place, it has been traditionally seen in the terms of a church dominated by monasticism since the late sixth or early seventh century, and thus what pastoral care there was came from monastic houses. That global interpretation has recently been shown to be mistaken.[215] What emerges from this is that ministry to the people was carried out by a mixture of clergy, some secular, some monastic (and the difference between these is not at all clear cut), under the supervision of the bishop whose powers were jurisdictional and sacramental. There were very many churches—so much is clear from Tírechán—and they were of different origins. Tírechán (§18) speaks of *omnes primitiuae aeclessiae Hiberniae* 'all the early churches of Ireland'. Sharpe thinks these may be the first founded churches, the mother churches.[216] 'Liber Angeli', which dates to 640 × 650, lists three types: *aeclessia libera* 'free church', a *ciuitas* founded by a bishop, and a *dominicum*.[217] Tírechán knew that churches with the element *domnach* (< Latin *dominicum*) in their names were long-established, and they have been taken to be ancient parish churches.[218] Some churches were local churches founded by a monastery and some originated as hermits' cells. Many others (as we shall see later) were privately owned by the local lord or lordly family, bore the dynastic name, and very likely had a parochial jurisdiction coextensive with the *túath* ruled over by that family. In some ways, this latter situation seems to be the one envisaged by 'Córus Bésgnai'. The *túath* (Latin *plebs*) was the smallest secular political community and was in reality a local lordship, and of course it varied in size. There are some references to the *cléirech tuaithe* 'cleric of the *túath*', who is called in Latin *clericus plebilis* or *clericus plebis*, and who is not a monk.[219] This is the parish priest, and very likely in many instances the *túath*

---

[214] Patrick J. Corish, 'The Christian mission' in Corish, *Ir. catholicism*, i, fasc. 3, pp 7–11, 32–41, 53–7; T. M. Charles-Edwards, 'The pastoral role of the church in the early Irish laws' in John Blair and Richard Sharpe (ed.), *Pastoral care before the parish* (Leicester, 1992), pp 63–80; Richard Sharpe, 'Churches and communities in early medieval Ireland', ibid., pp 81–109.

[215] Richard Sharpe, 'Some problems concerning the organization of the church in early medieval Ireland' in *Peritia*, iii (1984), pp 230–70; idem, 'Churches and communities', pp 98–109.

[216] Sharpe, 'Churches and communities', pp 93–4.

[217] Bieler, *Patrician texts*, p. 188; David Howlett, 'The structure of the Liber Angeli' in *Peritia*, xii (1998), pp 254–70: 257.

[218] Deirdre Flanagan, 'The Christian impact on early Ireland; place-names' in Ní Chatháin & Richter, *Ire. & Europe*, pp 25–51; Seán Mac Airt, 'The churches founded by St Patrick' in John Ryan (ed.), *St Patrick* (Dublin, 1958), pp 67–80: 79.

[219] E. J. Gwynn (ed. and trans.), 'An Irish penitential' in *Ériu*, vii (1914), pp 121–95: 170; revised translation by D. A. Binchy, 'The Old-Irish penitential' in Bieler, *Ir. penitentials*, pp 258–77: 273, § 17; *Bigotian Penitential*, iv, 6, 4 (Bieler, op. cit., p. 230); *Canones Hibernenses*, i, 28–9 (ibid., p. 162).

corresponds to the parish. People belonged to their parish: for example, a woman who marries outside her parish does not end her obligations to her natal church, and she must continue to pay her dues to it.[220] Every *túath* had a church: 'Bretha Nemed' states: *Ni ba tuath tuath gan egna gan egluis gan filidh gan righ...Ni ba heagluis eagluis gan oifreann* ('a *túath* is not a *túath* without a scholar, a church, a poet, and a king...a church is not a church unless mass is offered in it').[221] Saying mass and administering the sacraments are the duty of the priest: he may absent himself from his church for a day; if he is absent for more than that he must do penance, particularly if a corpse is brought to the church while he is away; if he is absent on a Sunday he must do penance on bread and water for twenty days, and if he is missing for two or three Sundays, he is degraded.[222] These rules reflect a keen consciousness of pastoral needs, especially Sunday mass. 'Ríagail Phátraic' expresses the same concerns. The priests were supervised by the bishop, but what was his area of jurisdiction? Binchy thought 'the original episcopal *paruchia* was certainly the *túath*',[223] but this is uncertain and anyway it may have changed over time. In some cases, at least, a bishop ruled over a number of *túatha*. 'Ríagail Phátraic' speaks of the bishop as one who rules over *túatha* and churches.[224] According to the 'Old Irish penitential', a fallen cleric must be reconsecrated before he can resume his ministry and be confirmed by an *epscop túath* 'a bishop of *túatha*'.[225] This means an ordinary bishop who ruled over *túatha*, not some kind of 'archbishop' and not a *chorepiscopus*, described as *vicarii episcoporum vel unius plebis* 'vicars of the bishops or of one *plebs*'.[226] It is reasonable to conclude that a *túath* was served by a parish priest or sometimes by a chorepiscopus, but a bishop's area of jurisdiction was wider. It appears that bishops lived at larger church sites that may have had more than one church and perhaps a monastery or priory of monks, and they went on their epicopal circuits from these. The very many small churches depended on the bigger centres for clergy and training, but were able to draw on their own resources for material support. Churches were very numerous: historical sources and the landscape itself preserve a record of about 4,000 of them. These 'bear witness to what in its time was one of the most comprehensive pastoral organisations in northern Europe'.[227] Superimposed

---

[220] *Studies in Ir. law*, pp 42–3, § 20 ('Cáin Lánamna').

[221] E. J. Gwynn (ed), 'An Old-Irish treatise on the privileges and responsibilities of poets' in *Ériu*, xiii (1942), pp 1–60: 31, lines 7–14 = *C.I.H.*, p. 1123, lines 30–35.

[222] *Hib.*, ii, 25.

[223] *Studia Hib.*, vii (1967), p. 219.

[224] O'Keeffe, 'The rule of Patrick', p. 219, § 6: *nach epscop tra soertha tuatha 7 eclaisi* 'whom *túatha* and churches ennoble', i.e. who holds the dignity of bishop by ruling over *túatha* and churches. The meaning of this statement is not brought out in O'Keeffe's translation.

[225] Gwynn, 'Old-Irish penitential', p. 142; trans. Binchy, in Bieler, op. cit., p. 263. The expression is mistranslated by both Gwynn and Binchy.

[226] *Hib.*, p. 5, note (i), a citation from the copy of *Hib.* in Paris, BN lat. 3182.

[227] Sharpe, 'Church and communities', p. 109.

on this basic system was a hierarchy of churches that had proprietary interests in the churches beneath them, and at the top, and several tiers up, were
the small number of major churches, the obits and doings of whose clergy fill
the pages of the annals.[228]

IN the seventh century, great monastic federations (these are called *paruchiae*
by Irish historians) had come into being, led by foundations of growing
power and influence, such as Clonmacnoise. Their extensive lands and services from their clients and dependants, the offerings of the faithful, bequests, burial dues, and income from relic circuits made these churches
prosperous. Already in the seventh century monasteries were becoming
towns. The early life of St Munnu represents his monastery (*civitas*) as
containing seven places marked with crosses where the principal buildings
were erected,[229] and the corporate personality of the institution was given
explicit physical expression. Cogitosus, writing in the mid seventh century,
describes Kildare:

And what words are capable of setting forth the very great beauty of this church, and
the countless wonders of that monastery which we may call a city [*civitas*], if it is
possible to call a city that which is enclosed by no circle of walls? However, since
numberless people congregate within it and since a city acquires its name from the
assembly in it of many, this is a very great city and the seat of a metropolitan. No
human foe nor enemy onset is feared in its *suburbana*, the clear boundaries of which
holy Brigit herself marked out. But it (together with all its church lands throughout
the whole of Ireland) is the most secure city of refuge for all fugitives. The treasures
of the kings are kept there . . . [230]

Cogitosus had been thinking seriously about the nature of cities in general
and what an ecclesiastical *civitas* should be. Kildare was, one can assume,
surrounded by an enclosing ditch-and-dyke, but clearly this was not, in
Cogitosus's view, the equivalent of the city walls of antiquity and especially
of Scripture (Num. 25: 3–4), and so he echoes a useful passage in Augustine
to surmount that difficulty.[231] In drawing up the regulations concerning the
precincts of monastic towns, the canonists of the seventh century quote the
extensive measurements for holy places from Ezekiel 45 and speak of large
areas of sanctuary, surrounded by their suburbs, and identify the clergy with
the well-endowed Levites of the scriptural text. Again, in describing the
divisions of the monastery into areas that are holy, holier, and holiest, they
speak of the second as an area 'into the streets of which we allow to enter the
crowds of rustics not much given to wickedness'. And beyond this again is an
area of the monastery not forbidden to sinners.[232]

[228] Sharpe, 'Church and communities', pp 106–7.
[229] Heist, *Vitae SS Hib.*, p. 203.          [230] *Acta SS*, Feb. I, p. 141 (viii, 39).
[231] Augustine, *Epistola 138*, 10 (*P.L.*, xxxiii, col. 529); but cf. Isidore, *Etymol.*, XV, ii, 1–8.
[232] *Hib.*, xliv, 2, 5, note (e).

Monastic sites could be very large, and had become towns.[233] Aerial photography has revealed what has been called 'the incredible extent of Clonard', and even monastic sites little known from the historical record have areas of between 1.6 and 2.4 hectares within their enclosing walls.[234] We know from the annals of the eleventh and twelfth centuries that there were extensive streets of houses and workshops within monastic towns, and it is not unlikely that this was the case in some monasteries as early as the seventh and eighth centuries. In the absence of detailed surveys, however, it is difficult to form any estimate of the probable population of the monastic towns. The ninth- and tenth-century annals do give some indication of the possible population, but these are inferences from uncertain data. In 764, for example, Durrow and Clonmacnoise fought a pitched battle in the course of which 200 of the men of Durrow fell. It is not likely that more than one-third of the troops of Durrow was slain and certainly not more than a half. In that case, Durrow fielded an army of between 400 and 600 men, and it is likely that a total population (counting all heads) of between 1,500 and 2,000 would be required to put that number of men in the field. In 869 Armagh was raided by the vikings and 1,000 people were either killed or taken prisoner; in a subsequent raid in 895, some 710 people were captured, and there is no suggestion in the annals that Armagh closed down temporarily as a result. On the contrary, life continued as usual. In these instances, it is not likely that the numbers given by the annalists are wildly inaccurate, even if they are inexact. We are justified in concluding that very large numbers of people were involved in these incidents, but who were they? Most likely the lay and clerical

---

[233] Whether or not monasteries became towns has given rise to a lively debate. See D. Ó Corráin, *Ireland before the Normans* (Dublin, 1972), pp 72–3, 86–8; Charles Doherty, 'Exchange and trade in early medieval Ireland' in *R.S.A.I. Jn.*, cx (1980), pp 67–89; idem, 'The monastic town in early medieval Ireland' in H. B. Clarke and Anngret Simms (ed.), *'The comparative history of urban origins in non-Roman Europe: Ireland, Wales, Denmark, Germany, Poland and Russia from the ninth to the thirteenth century* (Oxford, 1985), pp 45–75; Brian J. Graham, 'Urban genesis in early medieval Ireland' in *Hist. Geog. Jn.*, xiii (1987), pp 3–16; idem, 'Urbanization in medieval Ireland, ca. A.D. 900 to ca. A.D. 1300' in *Urban Hist Jn.*, xiii (1987), pp 169–96; John Bradley, 'Recent archaeological research on the Irish town' in Helmut Jäger (ed.), *Stadtkernforschung* (Cologne and Vienna, 1987), pp 321–70; idem, 'The role of town-plan analysis in the study of the medieval Irish town' in T. R. Slater (ed.), *The built form of western cities: essays for M. R. G. Conzen on the occasion of his eightieth birthday* (Leicester and London, 1990), pp 39–59; Brian J. Graham, 'Early medieval Ireland: settlement as an indicator of social and economic transformation, c.500–1100 A.D.' in Brian J. Graham and L. J. Proudfoot (ed.), *An historical geography of Ireland* (London, 1993), pp 19–57; Przemysław Urbańczyk, 'The origins of Irish towns' in A. Buko (ed.), *Studia z dziejów cywilizacji* (Warsaw, 1998), pp 233–9; Mary A. Valante, 'Reassessing the Irish "monastic town"' in *I.H.S.*, xxxi, no. 121 (May 1998), pp 1–18: 8–9.
[234] E. R. Norman and K. St Joseph, *The early development of Irish society* (Cambridge, 1969), pp 90–121; D. L. Swan, 'Enclosed ecclesiastical sites and their relevance to settlement patterns in the first millennium A.D.' in Reeves-Smyth & Hamond, *Landscape archaeology in Ireland*, pp 269–94; idem, 'Monastic proto-towns in early medieval Ireland: the evidence of aerial photography' in Clarke & Simms, *The comparative history of urban origins*, pp 77–102.

population of the monastery and the *termann*, the surrounding area under its jurisdiction and governed by the monastic superior.

Power and riches led to ambition and to the burgeoning of monastic *paruchiae*, and there seems to have been a steady build-up of this kind of organisation in the seventh and eighth centuries. Proprietary consciousness was highly developed among the federations of the late seventh century. So much we know from Tírechán who reports adversely on the expansionism of Clonmacnoise. It is equally reflected in the hagiography, early and late. The great Patrician federation at Armagh stretched its tentacles southwards into Munster. In the tenth century, it was strong enough to negotiate with the king of Munster and, using a change of dynasty to its advantage, cut into the territory of the powerful monastery of Emly. Cork claimed most of the churches in its hinterland and soon came into conflict with Cloyne in the east and Ross on the west, and even did battle with more distant Clonfert. Clonard claimed extensive properties in the midlands, but also held lands and churches in Connacht and Munster.[235] The patchwork-quilt political map of Ireland is simplicity itself compared with the complicated network of ecclesiastical ownership, loyalties, conflicts, claims, and counter-claims which extended throughout the entire country and even overseas. Involvements in secular politics and dynastic loyalties—and disloyalties—made the ecclesiastical situation even more complex. The records are scattered through different sources, especially in those dossiers of monastic claims, the Lives of the saints, but historians have yet only begun to unravel the tangled skein.

Wealth led to rivalry, and the invective of Tírechán in the seventh century becomes the armed conflict of the eighth. In 760 Clonmacnoise and Birr were at war, a hostility reflected in the Life of St Ciarán.[236] Four years later, there was a major battle between Clonmacnoise and Durrow, and Bressal mac Murchada, who led Clonmacnoise to victory on that occasion, was murdered shortly afterwards. In 807 there was a battle between Cork and Clonfert in which there was 'a countless slaughter of the ecclesiastics and of the noblest of the community of Cork'—evidence that the clergy themselves took part in the fighting. Kildare plundered the *céle Dé* monastery of Tallaght in 824, and in 842 Kinnitty and Clonmacnoise were at war. Of course the annals note only the major conflicts, and countless local scuffles and skirmishes between rival monastic interests have escaped the record. These struggles bear witness to the rapid consolidation of monastic property and political interests, and when they die out (as they seem to do) in the late ninth century, perhaps the *paruchiae* had reached the limits of expansion and

---

[235] Kathleen Hughes, 'The historical value of the lives of St Finnian of Clonard' in *E.H.R.*, lxix (1954), pp 353–72; eadem, 'The cult of St Finnian at Clonard' in *I.H.S.*, ix, no. 33 (Mar. 1954), pp 13–27.

[236] A.U., *s.a.* 760; Whitley Stokes, *Lives of the saints from the Book of Lismore* (Oxford, 1890), pp 126–7.

a relatively stable situation had come about. In any case, it is probably mistaken to attribute this change to any feeling of solidarity in the face of the vikings' attack.

The wealth and power of the great monasteries and their close dynastic connections brought violence and warfare in their train. The three battles at Ferns between 769 and 817, for example, were part of a segmentary struggle for supremacy in the area, in which the monasteries were participants as well as victims. Ferns lost 400 men, lay and cleric, at the hands of Cathal mac Dúnlainge, king of Uí Chennselaig, and his ally, the monastery of Taghmon. The killings at Kilclonfert in 789 were really part of a dynastic struggle between two leaders of Uí Failge, the local dynasty. The kings tried to gain control of the monastic towns and draw on their resources in their own struggles. And these resources were extensive. Bodbgal, abbot of Mungret, had sufficient forces to engage the king of Uí Fidgente, the local overking, in battle in 752, and the Uí Néill drew heavily and successfully on the military support of Durrow in 776. No attacker could afford to ignore the monastic town of his enemy, frequently that enemy's ally, bound to him by dynastic ties and, on occasion, his principal residence. And so the churches, quite apart from being victims in times of famine, were drawn into the general pattern of secular warfare. The viking raiders fell on no innocent monkdom but on populous centres and towns with a long history of violence. It is no surprise, then, that Taghmon should join forces with the king of Uí Chenn-selaig in driving off viking raiders in 828, that forces from Armagh should be the aggressors in an attack on the vikings at Carlingford Lough in 831, or that the abbot of Terryglass and Clonenagh and the vice-abbot of Kildare should fall fighting the vikings at the head of their monastic contingents at Dunamase.

If the heads of great monastic towns such as Cork and Emly could be equated in dignity with the king of the province, at least in clerical eyes, and if the rulers of Armagh, Kildare, Clonard, Clonmacnoise, and other towns could be ranked among the great political figures of the land, the priests or pastorally active monks of the hundreds of tiny churches scattered through-out the countryside could have no such pretensions, and rarely if ever appear in the records of the great and powerful, the annals. These small churches and monastic houses that served local populations were more plentiful than parish churches now are, and they must have been altogether different from busy and bustling towns like Lismore or Trim, which, after all, were as distant from most men's lives as cities were from the medieval countryman.

Many of these small churches were private or proprietary churches owned by an ecclesiastical branch of the local aristocratic families. Hundreds of entries in the genealogies record their existence and that of the families who owned them. The following is an example of such records chosen at random from the genealogies of the Lóichsi:

Lugnae mac Eógain had seven sons: Ruadán, Garbán, Nisse, Laignech, Ercc, Columb, Comgall. Ruadán, Garbán, and Columb: their land is Ráith Ruadán and Caílle Coluimb and Cell Meithne and Ard mBruchas. Nisse: his inheritance is Bile Methes and Cluain Meic Nisse. Laignech son of Lugnae, from which descend Uí Báeth and Uí Brócáin: his inheritance is Loch Laignich and Cluain Connaid. Ercc son of Lugnae, from whom descend Uí Diamráin and Do Deccae and Uí Forandla and Uí Cormaic: his land is Tech Décláin and Domnach Findchon and Cóelbóthur and Cluain Dá Fiach and Cluain Dartada and the inheritance which Uí Forandla occupy.[237]

In this aetiological piece, six or more churches (another text adds a seventh, Cell Garbán)[238] occur in the inheritance of a group of families, and this descent group is seen as the owner of both secular and ecclesiastical property. Amongst the Múscraige, the aristocratic family Uí Raibne owned Cell Cére (Kilkeary), allegedly founded by St Ciar, one of their own lineage, while their cousins held the nearby churches of Druim Inbir (Dromineer), Tóm in Baird (Toomyvara) and Cell Ua Máel Lachtna (Kilaughnane), all in the rich farmlands on the east shore of Lough Derg. Other aristocratic branches of the same family held other smaller foundations and some of them were settled at the great monastery of Birr. Uí Daigre, another branch of the Múscraige, held the church of Letracha Odráin (Latteragh) and claimed that Odrán, its founder, was one of them. Uí Léiníne were a family of Uí Daigre, and as late as 1074 the annals record the death of Gilla Brénainn Ua Léiníne, superior (*airchinnech*) of Letracha Odráin.[239]

These churches were of different origins. Some were early episcopal foundations and many such are mentioned in the genealogies. Domnach Findchon of the Lóichsi, cited above, may be one. Mag nAirthir of Ciarraige Luachra, the eighth-century genealogists tell us, was the foundation of one Bishop Fáelán of the local ruling family: it reappears as the parish church of Murher in the later middle ages.[240] Others were the churches of small early communities (some of which disappeared or were overrun at a very early period) and bore the name of the community or of the dynasty that ruled it—Cell Lámraige, Domnach Sairigi, Cell Tídill (church of Dál Tidill), Cell Cnámraige are examples. Cell Cnámraige must have been the church of Cnámraige, a community that barely leaves a trace in the records. It and another parcel of land are described in a text of *c.*900 as the inheritance of Cendlachán mac Muindig of the ruling family among the Múscraige.[241] Others may have been anchorites' cells. Whatever their ultimate origin, the most of them appear to be proprietary churches, owned, as ordinary estates

[237] O'Brien, *Corpus geneal. Hib.*, pp 89–90.
[238] T.C.D., MS H.3.17, 802.
[239] O'Brien, *Corpus geneal. Hib.*, p. 368 = H. 2. 7., 99b14 = *Bk Lec.*, 104$^r$d4 = *B.B.*, 141c24; Ó Riain, *Corpus*, p. 109, § 665.
[240] D. Ó Corráin, 'Alltraighe' in *Kerry Arch. Soc. Jn.*, ii (1969), pp 29, 34.
[241] O'Brien, *Corpus geneal. Hib.*, p. 369.

were owned, by aristocratic families or by monasteries, but claiming freedom from secular imposts and other privileges usually claimed by churches. Some were so closely associated with such families that the families themselves took their name from the church: Aicme Cille Cúile of the Déisi were named from their church of Cell Cúile (Kilcooley) and there are other examples of this practice.[242]

Such churches are mentioned in ecclesiastical documents. 'Ríaguil Phátraic' speaks of a lord who does not impose the duty of providing religious services on his own church (*a eclais saindíles*), and one provision of canon law in regard to bequests to the church by female heirs may also refer to family-owned churches.[243] One may suspect that some churches were merely family estates, which were turned into church establishments by their owners with little change either in function or appearance, apart from a little church and graveyard and the ministrations of a priest if he were available.[244]

Others may have been early foundations, the ecclesiastically privileged lands of which were farmed as a secular holding, except that a minimal religious function was maintained. Church Island, near Valentia, may have been such a family church. Its occupation has been divided into two phases. In the first there is a tiny wooden church with thirty-three associated burials and a circular wooden hut; in the second, a stone oratory twice as large as the original church, a large round stone house and, considerably later, a rectangular stone house was added and the island enclosed. Everything points to a small community (perhaps a few families), and the finds reflect a mixed fishing, herding, and small-time grain-growing economy which was that of the coast community generally.[245]

It is hard to know whether many of these were churches or monasteries in any real sense, and it may be wrong to think that they were. Some no doubt kept up their religious function, but with great difficulty. Firstly, there seems to have been a chronic shortage of ordained clergy. Early synods laid down that a fallen cleric should depart his cure and serve under an abbot elsewhere, but the ruling *c*.700 allowed a rehabilitated cleric to minister explicitly because of the shortage of priests.[246] The late and rigorist 'Second vision of

---

[242] Ibid., p. 162.

[243] *Ériu*, i (1904), p. 219, § 5; 'si ecclesiae habuerint partem (vl. si ecclesiam paternam habuerint), dabunt ei de sua hereditate (vl. dabunt ei partem de hereditate sua)' in *Hib.*, xxxii, 20, and the text cited in note (k); cf. *Studies in Ir. law*, pp 177–8.

[244] Cf. Charles Plummer (ed.), *Baedae opera historica*, i (Oxford, 1896), pp 414–17, where Bede inveighs against fraudulent monasteries of this type in Northumbria; Eric John, *Orbis Britanniae* (Leicester, 1966), pp 80–81, 170–72.

[245] M. J. O'Kelly, 'Church Island near Valencia, Co. Kerry' in *R.I.A. Proc.*, lix (1958), sect. C, pp 57–136; idem, 'An island settlement at Beginish, Co. Kerry' in *R.I.A. Proc.*, lvii (1956), sect. C, pp 159–94.

[246] *Hib.*, xi, 3: 'causa paucitatis (vl. raritatis) sacerdotum'; *Old-Irish penitential*, ii, 10 (Gwynn, 'An Irish penitential', pp 121–95: 170; D. A. Binchy (trans.), 'The Old-Irish penitential' in Bieler, *Ir. penitentials*, pp 258–77: 26, § 10).

Adamnán' insists that there should be two ordained clergy in each church for baptisms, communion, and requiem masses, but this is a counsel of perfection.[247] Much more realistically, 'Ríaguil Phátraic' allows one priest to minister to three or four churches when ordained clergy are scarce. It also refers explicitly to 'the little churches of the community [*túath*]' and lays down that when there is a priest serving in one of them he is entitled to the reward of his order—a house and enclosure and his rations, a milch cow every quarter, a sack of grain with its condiment, and food on festival days.[248] Very often, the abbot was not in major orders in the eighth century and earlier,[249] and it is likely that there were churches and monasteries which had no ordained clergy at all and rarely saw a priest. The law tracts speak of the church that has lost its right to ecclesiastical privilege—the church that has become a den of thieves or a place of sin, the church ruled by a layman unreproved by an abbot or by a backslider who has failed to honour his vow of chastity, the church from which bell and psalm have departed, the church that does not observe the canonical hours, and the derelict church[250]—and echo faithfully the strictly ecclesiastical documents. These are called unlawful churches and are excluded from privilege, though in fairness some larger churches should have lost their status if these rules had been enforced to the full. It is likely that there were many churches of this kind in the eighth and ninth centuries, and that in some ecclesiastical discipline had grown slack.

The greater monasteries encroached ruthlessly on these lesser churches. The early strata of the Life of Bairre shows the monastery of Cork swallowing up the church of Éolang at Aithbe Bolg (the new position is justified with great skill by the hagiographer) and a dozen other independent foundations.[251] The increase of pluralism (clerical double-jobbing) among the abbots and lesser clergy of the great monasteries in the late eighth and ninth centuries is strong evidence for this type of consolidation, and it likely that the same thing was happening lower down on the scale. Often the surviving Lives of the greater saints are mostly dossiers of claims to smaller churches and collections of aetiological miracles, covenants, and agreements justifying these claims. And the motives of the expanding churches were as mercenary as those of the kings: dependent churches paid rents and dues. In the twelfth century, the community of Lann, for example, absorbed the nearby Cell Bechrachán and then granted it to a family called Uí Scoil in return for services and rent (*manchine*).[252] In fact, Cell Bechrachán and its lands were

---

[247] *Rev. Celt.*, xii (1891), p. 428, § 18.
[248] *Ériu*, i (1904), p. 220, §§ 11, 13.
[249] *Hib.*, xliii, 6; xliv, 20, note (o); Hughes, *Ch. in early Ir. soc.*, pp 158–60.
[250] *C.I.H.*, pp 1–3, 1881–2 = *Anc. laws Ire.*, v, 118 (heptad 1).
[251] Plummer, *Vitae SS Hib.*, i, 65–74; idem, *Bethada náem nÉrenn*, i, 11–22; Pádraig Ó Riain (ed. and trans.), *Beatha Bharra: St Finbarr of Cork; the complete Life* (London, 1993 [1994]), pp 78–80, 150–56.
[252] Kuno Meyer, *Betha Colmáin maic Lúacháin* (Dublin, 1911), p. 100.

treated as a fief, but it is difficult to establish how old or how representative this practice was. It is clear that the expanding *paruchiae* had to overcome deeply entrenched localism, and this is perhaps best shown by the rules governing succession to an abbacy. The family of the founder has first right to provide an abbot 'even if there is only a psalm-singer among them'. Failing that, the donor's kin come next, and if none of them is suitable, the *manaig* may supply an abbot. Only when all these fail may an abbot be chosen from the community of the head church of the *paruchia*. And the sense of family right is so strong that when a better candidate from the founder's family becomes available, the abbot drawn from any other category must resign in his favour.[253] These rules seem to apply to all monasteries, but it is likely that the little churches, where often the founder's and the donor's kindred were the same, made use of them to assert what independence they could. However, given their remoteness and often isolation, the shortage of ordained clergy, the pressure from greater houses which used them for their own purposes, the vicissitudes of the rise and fall of the aristocratic families that owned them, and the likelihood that these took more interest in property than in church matters, it is likely that their survival as churches in any real sense was a matter of chance. On the other hand, since a church that had ceased to function as a church lost its status at law and thus its income and its value as an asset, its owners had good reason to to see that it carried out its pastoral functions.

Within the broad area of the church establishment there was a wide range of practice and ample tolerance of differing opinions and approaches—'In my father's house there are many mansions'. Practice ranged from the extremes of asceticism—such as that practised by the anchorite Colcu, who was attached to the monastic town of Slane and who gave away most of his food to the poor because he was worried about the purity of the monks who provided it[254]—to the lifestyles of worldly and opulent prince-abbots of the great monastic towns and their aristocratic wives. Yet even the great administrators and political clerics showed real religious feeling, at least on occasion. Diarmait ua Tigernáin (d. 852), one of the most political of all the abbots of Armagh, added a few devout if trite lines to the Old Irish hymn attributed to Colmán moccu Chluasaig, and Mug Róin (d. 980), the busy head of the entire Columban federation in Ireland and Scotland, added a few more.[255] Three other religious pieces are attributed to Mug Róin; one, a litany on the Trinity, shows considerable devotion, while another, on the cross, is full of religious feeling.[256]

---

[253] *C.I.H.*, pp. 1820–21 = *Anc. laws Ire.*, iii, 72–8; cf. *Thes. Pal.*, ii, 239.
[254] Gwynn & Purton, 'The monastery of Tallaght', p. 159, § 77.
[255] *Thes. Pal.*, ii, 305–6.
[256] Charles Plummer (ed. and trans.), *Irish litanies* (London, 1925), pp xxi, 78–84; Gerard Murphy, *Early Irish lyrics* (Oxford, 1956), pp 32–4.

The sixth- and early seventh-century tradition of asceticism never died, and the annals preserve the names of some who were attached to the greater houses—Áedán of Bangor (d. 610), Áed of Sletty (d. 700), Echaid mac Colggan (d. 731) and Do Chummai Bolgan (d. 733) of Armagh—but there must have been many others who had no such connections to preserve their memory. The ascetic tradition was highly respected, and on occasions greater abbots—for example, Nuadu (d. 812), abbot of Armagh, or Bishop Cenn Fáeled (d. 821), abbot of Trim—are described as anchorites. In this context, we must place the growing prominence in the records of the anchorite and scribal movement of the late eighth and early ninth centuries, which some have described as the *céle Dé* reform.[257] The term *céle Dé*, literally 'client of God', is a purely indigenous one and means a man who took God for his lord and recognised no other lord, secular or ecclesiastical, but God. It indicates a highly individualistic approach to personal sanctification and is the very antithesis of community life or organised reformation. The movement was very prolific: to it we owe the Martyrologies of Tallaght and perhaps of Óengus, the Stowe Missal, the Old Irish Penitential and Table of Penitential Commutations, the text called the 'Monastery of Tallaght' and the Rule of Tallaght, and some other pieces,[258] and the extent of this literary activity tends to lend it a misleading appearance of homogeneity as a reform movement. True, in some of the ascetic texts there are disparaging references to 'the people of the old churches' whose rule of life was inadequate, and to 'the lax folk', but these must be taken in the more general context of the Irish church establishment, into which the anchoritic movement fitted more readily than might at first be imagined. Óengus, as we have seen, celebrates the power and prestige of the great monastic towns—Armagh, Glendalough, and others—while the compiler of the Martyrology of Tallaght took over without question the list of traditional saints celebrated at Trim, a well-known hereditary monastery and a good example of 'laxity'. Later martyrological texts, the sources of which may well derive from the anchorite movement, more generously saint some of the hereditary eighth-century abbots of the monastery. In other respects, too, the anchorites were deeply traditional; the strict sabbatarianism of their texts is in evidence already in the early eighth century, a generation before their rise to

---

[257] Robin Flower, 'The two eyes of Ireland: religion and literature in Ireland in the eighth and ninth centuries' in William Bell and N. D. Emerson (ed.), *The Church of Ireland, A.D. 432–1932* (Dublin, 1932), pp 67–75; Hughes, *Ch. in early Ir. soc.*, pp 173–93.

[258] R. I. Best and H. J. Lawlor (ed.), *The martyrology of Tallaght* (London, 1931); *Fél. Oeng.*; George F. Warner (ed.), *The Stowe Missal* (London, 1906); T. F. O'Rahilly, 'The history of the Stowe Missal' in *Ériu*, x (1926–8), pp 95–109; E. J. Gwynn (ed.), 'An Irish penitential'; idem, *The rule of Tallaght*; Gwynn & Purton, 'The monastery of Tallaght'; Kuno Meyer (ed. and trans.), 'The Old-Irish treatise *De arreis*' in *Rev. Celt.*, xxv (1895), pp 485–98; D. A. Binchy (trans.), 'The Old-Irish table of commutations' in Bieler, *Ir. penitentials*, pp 277–83; William Reeves, *The culdees of the British islands* (Dublin, 1864, reprinted Felinfach, 1994).

prominence,[259] and the notion of penitential commutation (arre), so often associated with them, is fully developed in the *De arreis*[260] (which draws on a seventh-century source), and may well represent an early practice of the Irish church.[261] Again, their puritan attitudes to sexuality and their strict regime for married people under their spiritual guidance (a certain morbidity apart) merely reflect the views of earlier ascetics. Within the texts themselves, there is ample evidence of differing attitudes—Máel Ruain's monks may not drink, those of Dublitter of Finglas may, while Clemens mac Nuadat (d. 802) of Terryglass is given to tippling and is regarded as none the worse for it.[262] Máel Ruain and Hilary of Roscrea differ as to the order in which prayers should be recited, Cornán the piper may be an anchorite but Máel Ruain has no time for his earthly music, and opinions differ on the acceptance of gifts from lay people. Each has to determine his own standard of asceticism, and such freedom is characteristic of the Irish churches as a whole. The people whose opinions are cited in the texts of the ascetic movement, apart from famous earlier saints such as Colum Cille, Comgall, Adomnán, and others, are their own leading representatives and the ascetics of the previous generation. They see themselves as a continuity. Like many puritans, they showed little or no missionary zeal and were reluctant to offer spiritual guidance, certainly to lay people, and their attitude to the laity in general was at best élitist, at worst dismissive. As one would expect, they made no attempt at any general constitutional change within the church. Some new houses were founded. Such was Tallaght, which had its lands and servants and tithes as other monasteries and was expansive enough to be sacked by Kildare in 824, but in general the anchorites remained attached to older houses, where they sometimes, as formerly, held high office and where generous provision was made for their upkeep.

The church, then, was richly endowed and powerful. Its organisation is not clear to us: instead of single hierarchical order there was a marked diversity of structures, institutions, and jurisdictions, but we must not interpret this as anarchy. One cannot postulate disorder because order breaks down periodically—for example, in the inter-monastic battles of the eighth century. High achievement is not the product of anarchy. On the contrary, one must assume capable government in the case of churches and monasteries (such as Armagh, Clonmacnoise, Clonard, Cork, and many others) that survived without a

---

[259] Kuno Meyer (ed.), 'Göttliche Bestrafung der Sonntagsübertretung' in 'Mitteilungen aus irischen Handschriften' in *Z.C.P.*, iii (1901), pp 226–63: 228; J. G. O'Keeffe (ed. and trans.), 'Cáin Domnaig, I. The epistle concerning Sunday' in *Ériu*, ii (1905), pp 189–214; Vernam Hull, '*Cáin Domnaig*'; Máire Herbert, 'Dlithe an domhnaigh in Éirinn 600–750 A.D.' in Máirtín Mac Conmara and Éilís Ní Thiarnaigh (ed.), *Cothú an dúchais: aistí in ómós don athair Diarmuid Ó Laoghaoire S.J.* (Dublin, 1997) 60–69.
[260] Bieler, *Ir. penitentials*, pp 162–6.
[261] Binchy, 'Penitential commutations', pp 53–4.
[262] Gwynn & Purton, 'Monastery of Tallaght', pp 128–30, 143.

break over half a millennium, in changing and often difficult circumstances (for example, the viking wars), and not only survived but functioned to extraordinary effect as bearers and makers of a most remarkable early medieval culture. Hereditary succession to church office, and especially to the rule of great monasteries, had begun at least by the seventh century. 'Evil and adulterous' such superiors may appear in the eyes of St Bernard, but hereditary succession does not necessarily make for bad government, bad morals, or bad Christian scholarship; and clerical marriage and piety are not necessarily strangers to one another. Celibacy remained the ideal: the celibate bishop 'who had all the qualifications required of him' had the highest honour-price of all clerics;[263] but other bishops and priests who were content to admire rather than practise such virtue were held in the highest regard in contemporary society, and provided the churches with their cadres of administrators, heads of schools, savants, and writers. These churchmen played a major role in society: as lawmakers (in Latin and in the vernacular), theologians, biblical scholars, creators of a fine literary culture (in Irish and in Latin), patrons of the arts, and as advisors of kings and proponents of a theory of Christian kingship that was influential far outside Ireland.[264] One must continually bear in mind that, at the top levels of society, clergy and laity shaded imperceptibly into each other, and it is wrongheaded and quite anachronistic to draw a sharp line of demarcation that was not perceived by contemporaries. In our terms, there was laicisation of the church and clericalisation of kingship and society, but such concepts were largely foreign to the society in which these very processes were taking place. Only conscious reformers—and these were late—saw the categories as quite distinct.

[263] *C.I.H.*, p. 588 = *Anc. laws Ire.*, iv 362 (*Miadslechta*).
[264] Siegmund Hellmann (ed.), *Ps-Cyprianus De XII abusiuis saeculi* (Leipzig, 1909); Hans Hubert Anton, 'Pseudo-Cyprian: *De duodecim abusivis saeculi* und sein Einfluß auf dem Kontinent, inbesondere auf die karolingishen Fürstenspiegel' in Löwe, *Die Iren*, pp 586–617; idem, *Fürstenspiegel und Herrscherethos in der Karolingerzeit* (Bonn, 1968), pp 261–82; Lunedd M. Davies, 'Sedulius Scottus: *Liber de rectoribus christianis*, a Carolingian or Hibernian Mirror for princes?' in *Studia Celt.*, xxvi–xxvii (1991/2), pp 34–50; Michael Edward Moore, 'La monarchie carolingienne et les ancien modèles irlandais' in *Ann. ESC*, li (1996), pp 307–24.

# CHAPTER XVI

# The viking age

## F. J. BYRNE

THE monks who wrote the Irish annals were no timid cloistered clerics unaware of the realities of the outside world. Contrary to the picture painted by too many modern historians, the Irish annalistic notices of viking attacks are not coloured by any undue shock or rhetoric. They are quite coldly matter-of-fact. The figures they give are not exaggerated, and so, when an act of particular atrocity is recorded, we may have some confidence in its historicity.[1] Nothing in the contemporary Irish sources equals the ferocity of the Norse literary evidence, some of which, it is too often forgotten, was composed in the viking period by pre-literate skalds. A healthy scepticism as to the absolute historicity of the Icelandic sagas and other medieval Nordic sources, combined perhaps with the fact that most recent work on the vikings has been dominated by the archaeological evidence, has led to a neglect of the skaldic evidence and of the runic material which demonstrates the folly of regarding the Scandinavians as totally illiterate.

THE 'pagans' (*gentiles*) burst on the horizon in 794 with their devastation of 'all the islands of Britain', and their burning of Rechru (Rathlin or Lambay) and laying waste of Skye the following year brought them into the direct sphere of interest of the annalists. Their first incursion on to the Irish mainland occurred in 798, when they not merely burned Inis Pátraic off the Brega coast but made a cattle-raid and broke the shrine of St Do-Chonna, making 'great incursions between Ireland and Britain'. No divine portents of doom accompany these raids, and no fiery dragons are seen in the sky. The annalist devotes far more space to the natural disaster that occurred on the eve of St Patrick's Day 804 off the coast of Clare, when a great storm divided the island of Fita into three parts and covered the land with sand, occasioning the loss of 1,010 lives. The vikings' appearance off the Connacht coast in

---

[1] That the same is true of the Frankish annals has been shown by J. M. Wallace-Hadrill, 'The vikings in Francia' in idem, *Early medieval history* (Oxford, 1975), pp 217–36.

807, with the burning of Inishmurray off Sligo and Roscam in Galway Bay,[2] was their furthest venture so far, and only their second recorded exploit in Ireland.[3] They were to find Connacht inhospitable enough: in 812 a party of them were slaughtered by the Fir Umaill of Clew Bay, though they inflicted similar damage on the Conmaicne of Connemara. In future years the Norse were to make no permanent settlement there, though the Tripartite Life, in the first of its two passing references to the 'pagans', mentions their occupation of Killaspugbrone on the southern peninsula of Sligo Bay.[4] So, although Old Norse does have the name Konnakstír for Connacht, it has not passed into English along with the names of the other provinces.[5]

It may have been the same vikings, reconnoitering the western seaboard, who met with disaster again in 812 when they were defeated in Kerry by Cobthach mac Máele Dúin, king of Loch Léin. Another attack in western Connacht resulted in the first notable Irish casualties of the viking wars: Coscrach mac Flannabrat and Dúnadach king of Umall fell at their hands in 813. In 811 the Irish annals record a slaughter of the pagans by the Ulaid laconically enough, but it was considered significant by the annalists of Charlemagne's court, who enter a victory of the Irish over the Northmen under the year 812.

It was not until 821 that vikings made their next appearance, raiding Howth and taking a great prey, not of cattle but of women. This too was the year when they occupied the islands in Wexford Harbour, an event referred to in the Tripartite Life. In 823 and again in 824 they invaded Bangor, destroyed the wooden church, shook the relics of Comgall from their shrine, and according to the Annals of Inisfallen, put the scholars and bishops to the

---

[2] The H MS of A.U. reads 'Roscomm' which the modern editors, following the precedent of Hennessy's edition, have expanded to 'Ros Commáin', and so rendered in their translation. *Chron. Scot.* reads quite clearly 'Roiss Caim' (p. 126). The misidentification with Roscommon is in A.F.M., *s.a.* 802 [= 807].

[3] However, Ann. Inisf. at the kalend corresponding to [795] record the plundering of Iona, Inismurray and Inishboffin, and the presence of the *geinte* in Ireland the following year; these entries are probably conflated and misplaced.

[4] *Trip. life*, ed. Stokes, i, 140 (= *Trip. life*, ed. Mulchrone, pp 86–7); the other reference is to the removal to Sletty of the relics of Erdit and Agustín from the 'lesser island' in Wexford Harbour since that had been occupied by them (*Trip. life*, ed. Stokes, p. 192 = *Trip. life*, ed. Mulchrone, pp 116–17); the plundering of Begerin and Dairinis Cáemáin is recorded in A.F.M., *s.a.* 819 [= 821].

[5] Ulster comes from Old Norse (O.N.) *Ulaðstír, Ulaztír*, which is well attested; the O.N. forms behind Leinster and Munster must be inferred from the medieval French and Middle and Modern English names. *Konnakstír* occurs both in the 'Njálssaga' as the site of Brian's palace of *Kankaraborg* (Kincora) and in the saga of Magnus Barelegs as the home province of Brian's great-grandson Moriartak (Muirchertach Ua Briain). While inaccurate, it may well reflect knowledge of the Dál Cais tradition that Co. Clare had been conquered by them in the distant past from Connacht, or of the counter-claims made by Toirrdelbach Ua Conchobair in the 1120s (for which see Donnchadh Ó Corráin, 'Historical need and literary narrative' in D. Ellis Evans, J. G. Griffith, and E. M. Jope (ed.), *Proceedings of the 7th International Congress of Celtic Studies* (Oxford, 1986), pp 141–58: 146.

sword.[6] A quatrain appended to the Annals of Ulster records a prophecy of Comgall's that his bones would be brought safely to Bangor's daughter house at Antrim.[7] These entries are by far the most circumstantial to date: the danger had struck nearer to the heart and home of the annalist. While some may feel that it is too harsh to label the vikings as murderous psychopaths, this is perhaps because the mist of centuries has cast a romantic glow over their activities. It is possible that some will be more disturbed by their attitude to books and shrines, in which they displayed an attitude that gave their distant relatives the Vandals a perhaps undeservedly bad name. The annalist is less concerned about the fate of the women taken from Howth, but one fears that the object of this exploit may have been coldly commercial, the first taste of the economic benefits that the vikings are alleged by their apologists to have brought. Yet it is hard to conceive of any possible motive of gain or glory that led some vikings in the same year to raid the Skelligs, abduct the resident hermit Étgal, and leave him to starve of hunger and thirst. However, it was in 824 too that the ecclesiastical army of Kildare took the trouble to plunder what one might have assumed to have been the impecunious, if somewhat offensively pious, community of Tallaght.

B Y now, however, the viking presence could no longer be ignored. The second phase of their activity in Ireland had already begun in 837 when two fleets of *Nordmanni*, each of sixty ships, arrived on the Boyne and Liffey estuaries. This operation had evidently been planned on a large scale, and had been preceded by a reconnoitring raid on southern Brega the previous year in the course of which many prisoners were taken from Dairmag na mBretan (a church whose precise location has not been determined); many had been killed and many taken off into captivity. The two fleets that came in 837 were coordinated and were no mere raiding party. They must have comprised an army of between 3,000 and 4,000 men. In the words of the annalist: 'Those two forces plundered the Liffey plain and the plain of Brega, churches and fortresses and homesteads. The men of Brega routed the

[6] A.U.'s entry for 823 is brief and in Latin: 'Gentiles inuaserunt Bennchur Mor.' That for 824 is longer and in Irish: 'Orggain Benncair ac Airtiu [= at the Ards] o gentibh 7 coscradh a derthaigi 7 reilgi Comghaill do crothadh asa scrin'. The Annals of Inisfallen has an entry at 823: 'Indred Bennchoir o gentib 7 scrín Chomgaill do brissiud doib 7 a suíd 7 a hepscoip do thecht fo gin claidib;' and a second at 824 which records also the plundering of Moville: 'Mag mBile 7 Bennchor do orgain do gentib'.

[7] Compare the removal of the relics of Erdit and Augustín to Sletty above. This may be the appropriate point to note that all the marginalia and interlinear glosses in the H MS of A.U. that are marked in the Mac Airt and Mac Niocaill edition by the siglum $H^1$ are not, as stated in the introduction at p. viii, by a later interpolator, but are in the *prima manus*, that of Ruaidhrí Ó Luinín: this applies to nearly all the quatrains, most of which Ó Luinín omits in the R MS. It would appear that Mac Airt originally meant to indicate such additions in the *prima manus* by the siglum *H* and did do so for the first few pages of the edition. The quatrain on the foundation of Kells at A.U. 804 is, however, an interpolation and signalled as such by $H^2$(?) in the edition.

foreigners [*Gaill*] at Deóninne in Mugdorna Breg, and six score of them fell.'
The pagans (*geinnti*) won a battle at Inber na mBarc against the Uí Néill
'from the Shannon to the sea', in which an uncounted number were slaughtered, though the principal kings escaped (*sed primi reges euasserunt*).

Deóninne must have been somewhere north of Slane, while Inber na
mBarc is the Boyne estuary. The phrase 'from the Shannon to the sea' is
descriptive, however, of the realms of the Southern Uí Néill, rather than of
the area devastated. But later the leader of the great army (*toísech na nGall*)
had been killed by the Ciannachta. His name is given as Saxolb (Old Norse
*Saxulfr*), which suggests a Danish origin. He has the distinction of being
the first viking known by name to the Irish, after forty years of raids and the
same period of Norwegian settlement in the Isles. At last the Irish and Norse
were on speaking terms. Perhaps more: Murchad mac Máele Dúin, the deposed king of Ailech, had apparently cooperated with Niall mac Áeda in 833
when they both defeated a force of vikings at Derry, and the genealogists
credit him with a son Erulb. While this may represent an Anglo-Saxon Here-
wulf, an Old Norse *Herulfr* seems more likely, considering that his son bore
the unmistakeably Norse name Olaf or Anleif, gaelicised as Amlaíb, and that
other members of the Ua hEruilb family in the tenth and eleventh centuires
bore the name Thorir (gaelicised as Tomrair); another son of Erulb was called
Suartdubdae, an homonymous hybrid of Norse *svart* and Irish *dubdae*, both
meaning 'black'. If the pedigrees of the Muinter Eruilb are genuine, then this
would be the earliest recorded marriage alliance between Irish and Norse.[8]

Meanwhile other, probably quite independent, forces plundered Iniscealtra
on Lough Derg and destroyed all the churches on Lough Erne, notably
Devenish and Clones. The latter site is not on Lough Erne, but well within
striking distance: that the vikings should have made for it demonstrates their
increasing knowledge of the geography of power. The Norse were beginning
to extend their raids into the interior. These attacks demonstrated their exploitation of the internal waterways as well as their awareness of potentially
rich targets. But already in 836 an overland raid had been made on Kildare
from a pirate base at Arklow, which must have involved the use of horses
commandeered locally. The city had already suffered the humiliation of
an attack by the Munster claimant to the high-kingship, Fedlimid mac
Crimthainn, the same year; on this occasion we are told that half of the church
was burned, but the major casualties occurred at Clonmore, which was
attacked on Christmas Eve, where many were killed and even more
taken captive. A shrewd acquaintance with the Christian calendar and the

---

[8] The Muinter Eruilb are mentioned in the genealogies as descended from Murchad (see
O'Brien, *Corpus geneal. Hib.*, p. 135) and a Niall ua hEruilb features in the annals for 949, 958,
and 964, but only the unpublished genealogies in H. 2. 7, f. 23a, give his parentage ('mac
Amlaim m. Eruilb') along with the pedigree of his great-grandson Máel Coluim and of 'Tomrar
mac Gilla Muire m. Tomrair m. Sartdobdai'.

possibilities that major feasts (attended by large crowds of pilgrims and sight-seers) afforded to slave-traders is also exemplified by the raid on Roscrea in 845 on the occasion of the feast of Peter and Paul, 'when the fair had assembled', though this resulted in a battle in which the Norse jarl 'Onphile' was killed.[9] The years 836 and 837 saw havoc in all the lands of the Connachta, a slaughter of the Déis Tuaisceirt (later known to fame as the Dál Cais) who commanded the Shannon rapids above Kincora, and a major royal casualty when Muirgius mac Muirgiusa, brother of Cathal king of Connacht, was slain in battle.

Events in Ireland were closely paralleled in Britain and on the Continent. Nowhere had the Christian kingdoms been able to organise any form of defence against viking raids, and the Carolingian empire had depended largely on diplomacy to keep the Danes in check. But equally, nowhere had the long generation of piracy from the north seriously disrupted the course of political history. But now, in the thirties of the century, a real threat to all the countries of north-western Europe arose.

Serious attacks on Francia begin in 834 with the disputes between Louis the Pious and his sons. Frisia, part of which had been ceded to the Danish king Hrorik by Louis, was now totally overrun, and the important trading centre of Dorestad destroyed. Much further south, at the mouth of the Loire, the island monastery of Noirmoutier, for long a victim of viking raids, was finally abandoned in 836. In 841 Asgeir sailed up the Seine and sacked Rouen, while the following year a fleet swept across the English Channel after an attack on London to sack Quentovic and back again to Rochester. The sack of Nantes in 843 by vikings from Vestfold in Norway was accompanied by frightful slaughter, and a base-camp was set up at Noirmoutier from which the regions of the Loire and Aquitaine were to be attacked. The most famous exploit was the siege of Paris in 845 by Reginhere, who may or may not have been the Ragnarr Loðbrók of saga and the father of the leaders of the great army that was to conquer Northumbria in 867. For the rest of the century Francia was not to be free of the vikings.

Meanwhile in England a great fleet of 'heathen men' descended on the isle of Sheppey in Kent in 835. Egbert, king of the Gewissi of Wessex and overlord of the previously independent kingdoms of Kent, Sussex, Surrey, and Essex, was defeated in 836 by a fleet of 'Danish men', thirty-five ships strong, at Carhampton (Charmouth) on the Bristol Channel, but the following year the 'Westwealas' of Cornwall, who had been at war with

[9] The raid on Kildare is in A.U., that on Clonmore in Chron. Scot. (it may be the same occasion as the raid there and on Ferns recorded the previous year in A.U.), while the battle at Roscrea is recorded only in the 'Cocad Gáedel re Gallaib', which was probably drawing on Munster annals now lost: it is dated there to the year of Forindán's capture (845). Cogitosus' seventh-century Life of Brigit is the *locus classicus* for the attraction of crowds to Kildare on the major festivals; A. P. Smyth was the first to observe the significance of such dates as the occasion of viking raids.

Egbert for thirteen years, joined forces with the vikings and were defeated at the battle of Hingston Down. This first alliance between Christian and heathen led to the end of Cornish independence, the incorporation of the last remnant of the Celtic kingdom of Dumnonia into that of Wessex, and the subjection of their churches to the authority of Canterbury. However, some local autonomy survived, and the death by drowning of the last Celtic sub-king of Cornwall, Dungarth rex Cerniu, is recorded by the 'Annales Cambriae' in 875. Those whom the Wessex chroniclers termed the *Norðwealas*, the Welsh of Wales, seem to have been spared attacks till 850, when the 'Annales Cambriae' notes the death at the hands of the 'Gentiles' of an unknown Cyngen: three years later Anglesey, the most fertile part of Gwynedd, was ravaged by the 'Black Gentiles'.[10]

In England further attacks on London, Rochester, and Portsmouth and battles with varying fortunes between Danes and local ealdormen occurred in the 840s, as well as the killing of King Rædwulf of Northumbria in 844. A second battle of Charmouth is recorded in almost identical terms by the 'Anglo-Saxon Chronicle' at 843, where Egbert's son and successor Æthelwulf was defeated, but in 851 at the unidentified site of Aclea he defeated a huge host of 350 ships that had ravaged London and Canterbury. His reign culminated in a prolonged pilgrimage to Rome in 855 and marriage to Judith, daughter of Charles the Bald. The Annals of Ulster record his obit as 'Adulf rex Saxan' in 858, while the victory of the Saxons over the *Normainni* noticed in the Fragmentary Annals—though somewhat dislocated chronologically—may well refer to the battle of Aclea. His more famous father and even more famous son, Alfred the Great, find no place in the Irish annals.[11]

MÁEL Sechnaill, the new high-king, already famous for his capture of Turgéis in 845, and apparently none the worse for his defeat in 846 at the hands of Tigernach of Lagore (an occasion on which Máel Sechnaill was in alliance with Ruarc mac Brain, king of Leinster), rooted out a pirate band of Luigni and Gailenga who had established themselves on an island on Loch Ramor and were imitating the viking way of life.[12] Four notable victories over the

---

[10] 'Mon uastata est a gentilibus nigris', Ann. Camb., s.a.; cf. Egerton Phillimore (ed.), 'The *Annales Cambriae* and Old Welsh genealogies' in *Y Cymmrodor*, ix (1888), pp 152–69.

[11] Cenwulf, king of Mercia, who was pursuing a vigorous campaign against the Welsh both in Dyfed and Gwynedd, merits an obit in A.U. 821: 'Comulf [= Coinulf] rex Saxonum moritur.' His predecessor, the great Offa, received a more curious tribute from the Irish: not merely do the annals style him 'Offa rex bonus Anglorum' (A.U. 796), but his coinage was remembered in the Old Irish word *affaing* 'a penny', attested in the saga of Cano mac Gartnait as well as in Cormac's Glossary (where the Bodl. copy has the older form *ofing*); Cormac actually regarded it as a native Irish unit, 'the scripulus of the Gaels'! ; see D. A. Binchy (ed.), *Scéla Cano meic Gartnáin* (Dublin, 1963), pp 22 ff.

[12] In 837 the Four Masters record the murder by the Gailenga of Écnech, bishop of Kildalkey, and in 827 they had revolted against Máel Sechnaill's uncle, the high-king Conchobar mac Donnchada, at the Óenach Tailten.

vikings occurred in the year 848, which were reported to the emperor and recorded in the 'Annales Bertiniani', where the king of the Irish is said to have requested safe passage for a proposed pilgrimage to Rome. The embassy may well have been that which brought Sedulius Scottus and his companions to Liége, and as there is reason to believe that they came from Dísert Diarmata, the king on whose behalf they spoke was probably not Máel Sechnaill but Ólchobar, king of Cashel, who together with Lorcán mac Cellaig, king of Leinster, had routed a viking force at Sciath Nechtain beside that monastery with the reported slaughter of 12,000; the same king was probably involved in the victory of the Éoganacht Caisil at Dún Máele Tuili, where 500 were killed. In Leth Cuinn the high-king slew 700 at Forach near Skreen, and his erstwhile enemy Tigernach boasted twelve-score or 1,200 dead at Daire Dísirt Do-Chonna.[13]

These events mark the real beginning of the viking wars in Ireland as the Norse came no longer as mere marauders, but in larger hosts under powerful jarls with political and, no doubt, territorial ambitions. Their very size, however, and the fact that they made fortified encampments, meant that they were more easily targeted by the Irish. In 845 the Dublin Norse had made an encampment at the monastic site of Cluain Andobair on the banks of the upper Barrow, from which they raided as far west as Killeigh. It was probably also from this base (later named Dunrally after Rodulf who arrived there around 855 and proceeded to ravage Ossory before his forces were routed by Cerball mac Dúnlainge) that they raided the ancient fortress of Dún Masc and slew two eminent ecclesiastics, Áed mac Duib dá Chrích, abbot of Terryglass and Clonenagh, and Ceithernach mac Con Dínaisc, *secnap* of Kildare; Dún Masc was the centre of the Uí Chremthannáin, whose hereditary monastery was Terryglass (though situated, in fact, in Munster).

Rodulf remained in the vicinity however, for he attacked Leighlin about 861, taking many hostages, and was again defeated by Cerball at Slievemargy. In 862 his fleet was again defeated by Cerball and his ally Cennétig mac Gáethíne of the Loíges; although the 'Fragmentary Annals' say that the fleet had recently arrived from 'Lochlann' they may too have come from Carlingford, since among the slain in the viking host were two men with Irish names, Conall Ultach (the Ulsterman) and Luirgnén. Whether it was remnants of this fleet that were slaughtered at Fertagh by Cerball in 863 is not stated.

But the fortifications at Dunrally remain and have recently been excavated. Eighty years later they were apparently reoccupied, for the Four Masters record the 'martyrdom' of Flann Ua Cathail in 940 at the hands of the Norse of Cluain Andobair. He may have been of the Uí Fhailge; at any

---

[13] This site remains unidentified, but was near the coast in South Brega and had been an early victim of viking raids.

rate in the same year Coibdenach, abbot of Killeigh, was drowned at Dalkey, where he had apparently been held prisoner. The names Flann, Cathal, and Coibdenach are all characteristic of the Uí Fhailge, and Killeigh was one of their chief churches, situated on their far western border. The Annals of Ulster note a defeat of the Dublin Norse by the Uí Fhailge under the year 942, but with a note to the effect that this had actually occurred the year before. Cluain Andobair was on the borders of Uí Fháeláin and Uí Fhailge: the monastic site east of the Barrow in Uí Fháeláin and the Norse fortress west of the river in Uí Fhailge. It is noteworthy how well the raiders, as early as 845, had become acquainted with the local geography: having established a base at Cluain Andobair they made straight for Killeigh.

Political intentions were made evident by the arrival in 849 of a fleet of 140 ships *di muinntir ríg Gall* (of the people of the king of the foreigners) to impose royal authority over all the Norse who had settled in the country. These new arrivals 'disturbed all Ireland afterwards', say the Annals of Ulster. Máel Bressail mac Cernaig, a former king of Mugdorna who had entered a monastery, was slain and the high-king laid siege to the invaders at Crufait on the Boyne.

Political ambitions also gave rise to the possibility of alliances with some of the natives, and the first of such came in 850 when the king of North Brega, Cináed mac Conaing of Knowth, kinsman and rival of Tigernach, revolted and ravaged the lands of the Southern Uí Néill together with the Norse, and razed Tigernach's island fortress of Lagore. The allies did not spare ecclesiastical property: among the churches attacked was Trevet. Most serious was the fact that they did not spare the innermost sanctuary, but burned the oratory with the 260 who had sought refuge there. Vengeance was condign and swift, the high-king Máel Sechnaill and Tigernach showing themselves more vindictive than the ecclesiastical authorities. In the terse language of the Annals of Ulster (851): 'Cináed mac Conaing, king of Ciannachta, was cruelly drowned in a pool by Máel Sechnaill and Tigernach, in spite of the guarantees of the nobles of Ireland, and the successor of Patrick in particular.'[14]

A more picturesque account is in the Fragmentary Annals, which emphasise the indignity that Cináed was drowned in 'a dirty stream' (the Nanny) after the high-king had arranged a parley. The punishment no doubt fitted the crime, as drowning was a Norse form of execution. The very idea of the execution of a king was a novelty, as opposed to death in battle or the all too frequent assassination, and Cináed's fate did not fail to arouse sympathy from those loyal to him.

[14] 'Cináed mac Conaing, rex Ciannachta, demersus est in lacu crudeli morte ó Maelsechnaill 7 ó Tigernach, di fhoesmaib deg-doíne nÉrenn 7 comarbbai Pátraic specialiter.' This sentence was mistranslated in Hennessy's edition of A.U. The correct meaning was first shown by Binchy and has been adopted in the new edition by Mac Airt and Mac Niocaill.

Other events of the highest importance took place this year. Indeed the Fragmentary Annals claim that Máel Sechnaill's pretext for the parley with Cináed was the arrival of the Black Gentiles in Dublin. The *Dub-geinti* arrived at Dublin and slaughtered the *Finn-Gaill*, destroying their *longphort*, plundering all its wealth—a significant detail—and slaughtering many. They suffered heavy losses themselves, however, in an attack on the Norse encampment at Annagassan. The absence of any references to viking raids in 854 and 855 lends support to the statement of the Fragmentary Annals that Olaf left Dublin after organising the colony there, perhaps to go to Man and the Hebrides. In 855 Áed mac Néill unsuccessfully raided Ulaid, losing many of his men, including two princes of Cenél nEogain. There were severe winters in 855 and 856: snow at the end of April in 855, and lakes and rivers frozen from November 855 till January 856.

Máel Sechnaill's last few years were troubled by opposition within the Uí Néill dynasty. In 860 he led a great hosting with the forces of Leinster, Munster, Connacht, and the Southern Uí Néill to In Fochla, camped near Armagh and successfully repulsed a night attack by Áed mac Néill and his nephew Fland mac Conaing of North Brega (brother of Cináed). The following year Áed allied with the Norse to raid Mide. He is said to have given his daughter to Olaf, who also married the daughter of Cináed mac Ailpín (d. 857); the half-Christian son of Olaf and Áed's daughter was Helgi. In 862 Áed led a renewed invasion of Mide with the kings of the Gaill and Fland mac Conaing, probably to ensure his own succession.

So Máel Sechnaill's unprecedented success in achieving the high-kingship of all Ireland was marred by the chronic complaint of Irish politics: having united the Ulaid, Munster, Osraige, Connacht, and Leinster, he was attacked at the end of his reign by a combination of Uí Néill kings.

WERE the Norse who raided Ireland in the ninth century pirates or merchants? In some ways it is a distinction without a difference. As the Belgian historian Henri Pirenne has said, 'piracy is the first stage of commerce'.[15] In the saga of Egil Skallagrímsson we are told that 'Björn was a great venturer, was sometimes out raiding, and sometimes on trading voyages [*stundum í víking enn stundum í kaupferðum*]'. But when, after abducting a bride from the Fjord province, he asks his father for a warship, Brynjolf replies: 'You cannot expect me to give you a warship and a big crew when I am not sure that you wouldn't get up to all sorts of things that I would disapprove of completely. After all you have caused quite enough trouble as it is. I will provide you with a merchant ship, and the cargo along with it. Go south

---

[15] Henri Pirenne, *Economic and social history of medieval Europe* (New York, 1937), p. 21. For a critique of Pirenne's views, see Richard Hodges and David Whitehouse, *Mohammed, Charlemagne, and the origins of Europe: archaeology and the Pirenne thesis* (London, 1983).

*The viking age*

then to Dublin. That is the most popular route.'[16] The saga is set in the tenth century and may reflect a contemporary Norwegian view of Dublin, but it is well to remember that the actual author was most probably Snorri Sturlason, in thirteenth-century Iceland.

The etymology of the word 'viking' has been much debated.[17] The term occurs only in western Europe, in contrast to the peaceful connotations of the Varangians (*Væringjar*) in the east, where the Swedes in Russia were able to exploit and develop already existing trade-routes to the rich markets of Central Asia and Constantinople. *Væringjar* (Slavic *Varjag*) were seafarers who concluded truces with the natives in order to trade. From those of Russia and the Ukraine, but also later from the ranks of Anglo-Saxon nobility displaced by the Normans, were recruited the Varangian guard of the Byzantine emperors. But even in the west 'viking' is rarely found in the contemporary chronicles, which usually refer to the raiders as Northmen or Gentiles.

In 'Egilssaga' the jarl sends a messenger to the vikings to ask if they come as plunderers, and a similar situation occurs in the well-known 'coastguard scene' in the famous Old English epic poem, 'Beowulf'. But the unfortunate reeve of Wessex made a fatal mistake when he assumed that the Danish ships that arrived in 789 were merchant vessels, and neglected the necessary courtesies: 'In this year King Brihtric married Offa's daughter Eadburh. And in his days there came for the first time three ships of Northmen[18] and then the reeve rode to them and wished to force them to the king's residence, for he did not know what they were; and they slew him. Those were the first ships of Danish men which came to the land of the English.'[19]

IN Ireland, after the first generation of sporadic raids on individual monasteries, viking settlement began on a permanent basis as camps in strategic

---

[16] Christine Fell (trans.), *Egils Saga* (London, 1975), p. 47.

[17] The word is older than the viking age proper, for it occurs in Old English in the eighth century, where *uuicingsceade* is found with the meaning 'pirate' (*uitsing* in Old Frisian), and in Old High German of the same period *Wiching* is found as a personal name. It is from such a name—rather than from the common noun—that Wicklow (*Vikingaló* 'viking's meadow') is derived, as well as the Irish name *Uiginn*. The interpretation *vík-king* 'king of the fjords' is impossible: the Old Norse for 'king' is *konungr*; and furthermore, not all vikings were 'sea-kings'. The idea that it comes from the Vík (Oslo Fjord in southern Norway) is likewise linguistically discredited: Oslo Fjord was 'the Vík' *par excellence*, but the word cannot mean a native of this region, for the suffix *-ing* is never attached to a monosyllable: whereas the inhabitants of Húsavík or Súðavík may be *Húsvíkingar* or *Súðvíkingar*, those of the Vík are always known as *Víkverjar*, and it seems more likely to come from the verb *víkja* 'to turn, to turn aside, to deviate' (the nautical command *lát víkja* is the opposite of *halda svá fram* 'keep straight ahead'). The viking was thus one who sails, not to a definite destination, as does the merchant, but according to whim, an explorer seeking the chance to turn warrior and reap profit from his venture.

[18] Some MSS add 'from Horthaland'.

[19] Dorothy Whitelock (trans.), *The Anglo-Saxon Chronicle* (London, 1961), p. 35. However, the wording of this entry makes it rather suspect: it may record an actual event, but it is hardly a contemporary annal.

positions, then gradually assumed the character of towns, which soon became important commercial centres appreciated by the natives. Indeed, by the eleventh and twelfth centuries, when the Norse no longer presented a serious military or political threat, Irish kings proved anxious to gain control of their towns—not, be it stressed, in order to expel the 'foreigners', but so as to exploit their wealth: the later Ua Briain kings actually took up residence in Limerick.

It has been suggested in fact that the very situations of these towns—Dublin, Wexford, Waterford, Cork, and Limerick—show that the Norse were not primarily interested in Ireland for itself, but merely regarded it as a jumping-off point from which to reach the Continent. The so-called 'western route' (vestrvegr) led from Norway via the Hebrides and Ireland to Normandy, and Rollo, founder of the Norman duchy, may have had connections with the Norse of Limerick and the Hebrides. In the first half of the tenth century the rulers of Dublin and Waterford concentrated their attention on winning the kingdom of York, and both Irish and Arabic sources imply contacts between Dublin and Moslem Spain.

Nevertheless, the absence of Norse towns from the north of Ireland is not to be attributed solely to a lack of interest in that area on the part of the vikings—as a glance at the ninth-century annals will show; it was rather the result of the tough resistance put up by both the Northern Uí Néill and their hereditary foes the Ulaid. The latter were among the few peoples, not only in Ireland, but in north-west Europe generally, who ventured to meet the vikings in their own element and engaged them successfully in naval warfare.

There can be little doubt that the Norse would have colonised Ireland, as they did the islands to the north and as the Danes did in England and Normandy, had they not met with effective resistance. For the annals show that when pinned down to a pitched battle the vikings were more often than not defeated. Their strength lay in surprise: hit-and-run raids before local forces could be assembled. The Norse settlements on Lough Neagh and at Annagassan, Dublin, Waterford, and Limerick, were significantly situated at chinks in the Irish defensive armour, on the borders of provinces or over-kingdoms; on the other hand, an attempt to settle at Drogheda failed, since the Boyne estuary lay in the centre of the kingdom of Brega.

It can, however, scarcely be denied that piratical activities were more in evidence in Ireland than commercial ones, at least before the tenth century. The reason may be the rural nature of the economy. There were no great towns or markets in Ireland or Britain. The only localities approaching the nature of towns were the larger monasteries, which in fact are termed civi-tates in Irish Latin. These were storehouses of treasure, unguarded and practically waiting to be looted. Apart from these the only commodities Ireland had to offer were probably slaves and hides, though the importance of the latter to the Scandinavians, whose own countries were unsuitable for grazing, should not be underestimated. The land itself was rich, and if the Norse did not succeed in conquering large tracts, it was well capable of keeping their settlements provisioned and thus enabled a town such as Dublin to become large and prosperous as an emporium of trade between Iceland and Norway, on the one hand, and the Continent on the other.

It has often occasioned surprise that the 'barbarian' vikings should have introduced 'urban civilisation' to Ireland. Misplaced patriotism has sought evidence to prove that Ireland owes nothing to the Norse and that Dublin existed before the vikings.[20] Similar indignation was manifested by Soviet historians and archaeologists, who argued against the 'Normannist' theories of the origins of the Russian state. But the facts cannot be so explained away, nor is there any need to. The paradox is only apparent, and is not due to any inherent superiority of 'Nordic' over 'Celtic' culture, but simply to the economic circumstances of the period.

The native Scandinavian civilisation had much in common with the Irish, though the standard of culture in Ireland had, of course, been greatly heightened by the introduction of Christianity four centuries previously. But on a material and politico-social level there was little to choose between the two, and Scandinavia had the advantage in iron-working and ship-building. Politically also the Scandinavians had manifested a democratic tradition, not always incompatible with kingship, and Iceland was a republic. Society was perhaps less stratified and hierarchical than in Ireland, and the Thing was a primitive parliament and high court, an essential element of every Norse settlement. In origin it resembled the Irish *óenach* or assembly, though apparently with greater powers. Neither Scandinavia nor Ireland had come under the influence of the Roman empire that had overlaid primitive western societal patterns, and to which even the Germanic conquerors of the *Völkerwanderung* had succumbed. To Scandinavia, no less than to Ireland, the urban civilisation of the Mediterranean world was strange. The Far Northern and the Far Western civilisations (in Toynbee's terminology) were rural. Towns arose in the North only within the viking age and as a result of it. Birka in Sweden, Hedeby in Denmark, Grobin in Latvia, Novgorod in Russia were all built as merchant colonies (at first perhaps temporary, or only for seasonal use) and were directly due to the new flow of trade caused by the shift in the centre of gravity in Europe from the Mediterranean to western Germany and the Rhineland, the changeover from the old Roman gold currency to one of silver, and the flow of that commodity from Central Asia via the Russian waterways to Gotland and Sweden. So, when the vikings built fortified ship-camps (which the Irish called *longphort*—a new word for a new phenomenon, though formed from two pre-existing words in the Irish language, both

---

[20] The recent Temple Bar excavations in Dublin are another instance of such thinking. A preliminary report suggested that the earliest traces of urban settlement there are, in fact, Anglo-Saxon in type.

borrowed much earlier from Latin) they were really introducing something that was as new to them as it was to the Irish. Their lack of success in conquering any major territory in Ireland also made it necessary for them to fortify their toeholds on the coast. The Danes who settled the greater part of northern and eastern England built no towns, though they occupied York and made strenuous attempts to capture London, the two capitals of the Roman provinces of Britain which had managed to maintain an attenuated existence through the Anglo-Saxon period. In the Faroes, Shetland, the Orkneys, Sutherland, the Hebrides, and in Iceland itself, where they settled desert or conquered inhabited lands, no towns arose. Significantly, however, there was a market town at the monastic site of Iona.

Jordanes, in the sixth century, called Scandinavia an *officina gentium*, the cradle of the Germanic peoples of the *Völkerwanderung*, though recent scholars are somewhat sceptical of his ethnological geography.[21] Jordanes's Goths and their allies belonged to the East Germanic linguistic group, which is now extinct, though it left its literary mark in Wulfila's Old Gothic biblical translations. The Germans of Caesar and Tacitus were of the West Germanic group, and they too participated in the *Völkerwanderung*: the Franks, the Frisians, the Saxons and the Angles (though the last-named had their home in southern Denmark). Whether the Goths are really to be identified with the Geats who remained at home in southern Sweden (Gautland), and whether the Vandals came from Vendel in southern Uppland, and the Burgundians from Bornholm, is uncertain, although antiquarianism at the height of Swedish ascendancy under Gustavus Adolphus inspired his official title of 'king of the Swedes, Goths, and Vandals'. But in any event, the Scandinavians, who did not participate in such adventures until they burst upon an unsuspecting western world at the end of the eighth century, belonged to the North Germanic linguistic group. Nevertheless, the exploits of the leaders of the earlier Germanic invasions, such as Ermanaric, ruler of the Gothic empire that had stretched from the Baltic to the Black Sea, and who committed suicide after the eruption of the Huns in A.D. 375, were remembered both in the Icelandic Edda and in fragments of Old English epic. The Anglo-Saxons of the seventh and eighth centuries celebrated Beowulf of the Geats and his uncle Hygelac, who had been killed by the Merovingian Franks in a raid on Frisia in the early sixth century, as well as Ingjald of the Heathobards and the Offa of the Angles who had built the Danevirke (just as their own Offa of the Mercian Angles had built the dyke that still demarcates England from Wales), while the ship-burial of Sutton Hoo demonstrates cultural contacts and very possibly dynastic affiliations between East Anglia and Vendel in the Swedish Uppland.

---

[21] See, e.g., Walter Goffart, *The narrators of barbarian history* (A.D. 550–800) (Princeton, 1988), pp 20–111.

Before the viking age proper the Swedes had been active in the eastern Baltic, and archaeological finds at Grobin in Latvia attest to the presence of immigrants from the island of Gotland. The Danes too had interests on the Wendish coasts. Between them these ventures led to the opening up of the trade routes through Slavic lands on the Vistula and Dvina to meet the great Russian river system. The Finns called the Swedes *Ruotsi*, from the eastern coastal province of Rothrsland (whence the Slavic word *Rus'*, and Greek ρως), who reached the Black Sea and the Caspian to meet up with the Byzantines and the Arabs. The latter had conquered Persia and discovered silver-mines in Central Asia. The far eastern trade now no longer flowed to Constantinople from Persia, or via the Khazars of the Lower Volga and Caucasus, but the imperial city was bypassed by a new trade-route along the Russian rivers to northern Europe. Arab demand for furs and slaves could hitherto only be satisfied at second hand through the Byzantine or Carolingian empires, but now the Swedes established direct contact, and silver from Samarkand and Tashkent began to flow to Gotland and Birka. The first hoards of Kufic coins in Gotland appear towards the end of the seventh century, a hundred years before the vikings began to raid in the west. Chinese silk has been found at Birka, and a bronze statuette of a Buddha at Helgö on Lake Mälaren. So numerous were the trading settlements, which became the centres of principalities, along the Russian waterways—Novgorod (*Holmgarðr*), Smolensk, and of course Kiev—that the Old Norse name for this huge area was *Garðaríki* 'the land of towns'. The Rus' even threatened Constantinople itself, but were beaten back by superior naval power and the famous Greek fire, just as in the far west the Moors were able to prevent serious encroachments by Irish and other vikings on Spain. By contrast, the unwieldy and precociously united Carolingian empire had not the economic or social infrastructure to afford protection to the Christian peoples of western Europe: in the ninth century it had to contend also with Arab assaults from the Mediterranean, and the break-up of the empire was to be followed in the tenth century by a new threat from the pagan Magyars in the east.

At this time the richest of the Scandinavian territories was that of the Svear or Swedes of Uppland (*Svithjóð*) with its sacral monarchy of the Yngling kings at Uppsala and trading centres such as Birka on Lake Mälaren. By the eighth century the Swedes seem to have come to an arrangement with Gotland that gave them a base for their eastward expansion into Finland and the eastern Baltic. While Scania (*Skåne*) was to remain until the seventeenth century outside the Swedish realm, the land of the Geats was assimilated by the Svear, although it retained its own legal code. The very name *Sveariki* ('kingdom of the Svear') indicates the relative stability of their state. They alone of the historical peoples of Scandinavia are recognisable in the pages of Tacitus as the *Suiones*.

Denmark consisted of Skåne or *Skáney* (regarded as an island by the ancients, whence the name Scandinavia or more correctly *Scadinavia* <*Skaðin-aujô*) together with Seeland with the royal seat of Lejre, and the neighbouring islands and also Jutland, whence the Jutes had accompanied their southern neighbours the Angles to colonise eastern Britain in the fifth century. The name *Danmørk* stresses the character of the 'marcher land of the Danes' (Old Norse *Danir*), just as Anglian Mercia does that of the English march with the *Northwealas* or Welsh. The natural border against the western Germans formed by the extensive swamps of Schleswig established a permanent division between the Northern and West Germanic tongues and was reinforced by the Danevirke. This eighth-century landmark was reinforced by the Danish king Godred in 808 to protect the trade of Hedeby. In the course of the ninth century the Danes too were to create a powerful kingdom, and one which was in the closest contact with Carolingian Europe. Thus the name of Dane was often applied to all Scandinavians by the Christian inhabitants of western Europe, while writers learned in Latin sometimes misused the classical term *Daci* (originally that of a Thracian nation) to describe them. One chronicler even derives the Danes from the Hebrew tribe of Dan, and their neighbours the Jutes from the *Judaei*! But the Norse themselves often called their common language *dansk tunga* 'the Danish tongue', even though it already showed distinct dialect divisions: East Norse in Denmark and Sweden and West Norse in the fjords of Norway, and hence in the settlements of Faroe and Iceland. The term *norrøna* was also used indifferently for both. Snorri Sturluson, in the preface to the 'Heimskringla', says that he intends to write the history of all the kings of those peoples who spoke the 'Danish tongue', but later on he cites as his major authorities poems and writings in the *Norrøn mál*. By the ninth century the dialects were sufficiently differentiated for us to distinguish Danish from Norwegian elements in place-names and loanwords of Scandinavian origin in Britain and Ireland.

The name Norse properly refers to the people and language of Norway, the poorest and least developed of the Scandinavian lands. The inhabitants are called *Norðmenn* by Swedes and Danes, but *Austmenn* 'Easterners' by the Icelanders, Faroese, and Hebrideans (hence Ostmen as the term for the Hiberno-Norse in twelfth-century Ireland—though somewhat confusingly, if quite logically, the term is used of the Swedes by the Norwegians). Until the late ninth century it was a conglomeration of petty kingdoms and chieftaincies. Its name does not denote a political unit but a trade route: *Norðvegr* 'the Northern way' (though the name *Norðmannaland* is also found). But Danish influence was always strong in the south, particularly around the Vík, and during much of the viking period considerable regions of Norway were under direct or indirect Danish control. Whereas much of Danish viking activity, particularly from the late ninth century onwards, can be construed as overtly political, and by the beginning of the eleventh century was definitely expansionist (culminating in the empire of Svein Forkbeard and his son Cnút over Denmark, Norway, and England), the Norse who took the western way to the Atlantic and down into the Irish Sea were primarily individualistic adventurers. Indeed, when political unity was finally imposed on the Norwegian jarls by Harald Fairhair towards the end of the ninth century, it contributed to the colonisation of Iceland and perhaps (though much more doubtfully) to the settlement of Normandy by Norse aristocrats unwilling to submit to his yoke, and in no way wishing to further any imperial ambitions that he or his successors of the Westfold line might have had over the viking settlements in the west. In order to further their ambitions, these claimed descent from the sacral Yngling kings of Uppsala—this is the purpose of the tenth-century skaldic poem, the 'Ynglingatál', used by Snorri (and subjected by him to historicist rationalisation) as the basis for his 'Ynglingasaga'.

Though starting off on their adventures much later than the Swedes, the Norse rivalled their achievements by their western voyages across the uncharted ocean. Their very own 'North way' led to the White Sea, a route described in detail by Ohthere to King Alfred, while their settlement of the Faroes is mentioned already by Dícuil, the Irish geographer at the court of Charlemagne. Dícuil knew too that Irish monks had reached Ultima Thule (Iceland),[22] but two generations later the Norwegians colonised it for the first time, acknowledging the previous Irish presence in the names of the Vestmannaeyar and Papeyar, but proceeding even further to Greenland (where their colony was doomed to disappear in the fifteenth century) and discovering the American continental coast at Vinland.

SHIP-building was the craft that gave the vikings their terrifying power and enabled them to span a quarter of the globe with an ease unparalleled until modern times. A Swedish rune-stone from Högby in Östergötland commemorates the fate of such a family of adventurers:

| | |
|---|---|
| Gulle, a good husbandman, | begat five sons: |
| Ásmund fell at Fyris[23] | a warrior unafraid, |
| Azurr met his end | east in Greekland. |
| Halfdan was slain | on Bornholm |
| and Kári at Dundee; | Búe too is dead. |

The long sea-voyages, and especially the transatlantic explorations, were made not in the famous longship (*langskipr*) but in the rounder merchant vessel (*knörr*, whence Irish *cnairr*), and mainly by sail. But the longship was propelled mainly by oar, was light, and could sail up rivers and be carried across portages. The Gokstad ship of the late ninth century had sixteen pairs

---

[22] J. J. Tierney (ed. and trans.), *Dicuili Liber de mensura orbis terrae* (Dublin, 1967).
[23] The river that flows by Uppsala.

of oars, and it is estimated that the larger viking ships carried crews of forty or sixty men, while later, in the eleventh century, royal ships—such as those of Cnút, or the Great Serpent of Olaf Tryggvason—held a hundred men. A replica of the Gokstad ship has been sailed across the Atlantic, but its free-board was very low and it was intended for local raids along the coasts and fjords of Norway, while the Oseberg ship is more in the nature of a yacht. The five ships found in recent times in the fjord of Roskilde in Denmark represent a cross-section of the vessels available in the mid eleventh century: a small ferry or skiff, a coastal trader, a magnificent 'Greenland merchant vessel', and two warships, one rather patched together for the compulsory *leiðingr* or naval levy imposed by the king on all communtities, and the other the largest longship ever found, built perhaps in Dublin of Irish oak in 1060.

O F particular interest to the historian of Ireland in the rich literature of Old Norse is the history of the kings of Norway compiled by the thirteenth-century Icelandic scholar and politician Snorri Sturlason: the 'Heimskringla', or 'Orbit of the Earth', so called after its opening words. His contemporary Saxo Grammaticus wrote a 'History of the Danish kings', but in Latin. Snorri also composed the mythological work known as the Prose Edda. The anonymous Poetic Edda, with its many poems and fragments of varying age from the ninth to the fourteenth century, is of greater artistic worth. But the longest and best of the Icelandic family sagas is the 'Njálssaga', or 'Saga of Burnt Njál'. This contains an account of the battle of Clontarf, which differs markedly in tone from the rest of the work and is thought to have been taken from an older independent saga on King Brján (Brian Bóruma).

Old Norse literature, as with the society that produced it, shares many features with that of early Irish. The official praise-poetry, with its artificially heightened language and kennings, is common to skalds and bards, and some metrical devices in Icelandic may show Irish influence. In narrative, Irish and Norse are unusual among early literatures in preferring prose to verse, but there the resemblance ends. Irish sagas display two very different styles: that of Old Irish being stark, spare and sometimes impressively laconic, sharing with the lyrics (as opposed to the verse of the learned) an impressionist talent of creating vivid pictorial effects, which is replaced in Middle Irish by a bombastic alliterative prose, exemplified by the 'Cocad Gáedel re Gallaib', the chief literary source for the Norse period of Irish history. Common to both styles, however, is an element of mythological and decorative fancy, which shields us from accepting the narrative as literal truth. Many Icelandic sagas have the art that conceals art to the extent that scholars have, till recently, thought that their matter-of-fact sober style guaranteed historical accuracy. Conscious literary works of art composed some centuries after the viking age, they cannot be trusted to present a true picture of the viking ethos. But the 'Heimskringla', in particular, contains many fragments of genuine skaldic verse, which, on occasion, afford a more accurate view. Axel Olrik, contrasting the death-lay of Ragnar Loðbrok in the late saga that bears his name with the genuine poem of Hákon the Good after his defeat in battle in 961, comments that 'the army that was to achieve Valhalla was not a cheerful army. They were much more inclined to offer Odin the souls of their enemies than their own.' More realistic than heroic are the maxims of the 'Hávamál'. But this text too has room for repute after death:

> Deyr fé, deyja frændr,
> deyr sjálfr it sama;
> ek veit einn at aldri deyr:
> dómr um dauðan hvern.

(Wealth dies, kinsmen die, man himself dies too; I know one thing that never dies: the repute of each after death.)

HOW stands now the reputation of the vikings? 'One thing that doesn't die', as Oxenstierna remarks,[24] is the dispute about the historical judgement to be passed on their activities. The opinion of their contemporaries was quite clear: *A furore Normannorum libera nos Domine!* As the author of an invocation in a vellum fragment found in the binding of an early ninth-century Reichenau manuscript (the Carlsruhe Bede) expressed it: *Dithólu æchtrann et námat et geinte ·et fochide diphlágaib tened et nóine et gorte et galræ nile nécsamle* (From a flood of foreigners and foes and pagans and tribulations: from plagues of fire and famine and hunger and many diverse diseases [protect us]).[25]

The fragment has another invocation at the top of the page: *sancte trinitatis et sancti cronáni filii lugædon*, showing that it was written at Clondalkin, a monastery that was raided 'by the gentiles' in 833, and where Olaf of Dublin built a fortress that was burnt by the Irish in 867.[26] Better known perhaps are the verses from the St Gall Priscian:

> Is acher in gáeth innocht
> fu·fúasna fairggæ findfolt
> ni-ágor réimm mora minn
> dond láechraid lainn úa Lothlind.

(The wind is fierce tonight: it ruffles the ocean's fair mane; I do not fear the wild warriors of Lothlind sailing on a quiet sea.)[27]

[24] Eric Oxenstierna, *The world of the Norsemen* (London, 1957).
[25] *Thes. Pal.*, ii, 256.
[26] A.U. 833: Orggain Cluana Dolcan o Ghenntibh; A.U. 867: Loscadh Duine Amhlaim oc Cluain Dolcain la m. nGaithini 7 la Mæl Ciaran m. Ronain 7 ár .c. cenn di airechaibh Gall in eodem die apud duces predictos in confinio Cluana Dolcain.
[27] *Thes. Pal.*, ii, p. xxx.

Among the Anglo-Saxons, Alcuin of York, in several letters home from his abbacy of Tours to Ethelred, king of Northumbria, Higbald, bishop of Lindisfarne (whose church had been the first in Britain to suffer in 793), and others, cites the words of the prophet Jeremiah: 'From the north shall an evil break forth upon all the inhabitants of the land. For behold I will call together all the families of the north, saith the Lord.' Such comments have been discounted by modern writers as emanating from 'monkish' sources with a bias against healthy heathen men. But their authors did not live sheltered lives: they were often worldly enough and no strangers to either violence or cupidity. The chroniclers (as we remarked at the outset) are quite matter-of-fact in recording viking activity. Horror stories come, not from the sober if monastic annals, but from sermons and saints' Lives, from much later political propaganda, such as the twelfth-century 'Cocad Gáedel re Gallaib' and its imitators, and most notably from the Scandinavian sources themselves, whether from the perfervid outpourings of contemporary skalds, lauding the ferocity of their patrons, or from the medieval Icelandic sagas, whose authors seem often to glory in atavistic nostalgia for the good old pagan times. The romantic view of the vikings is relatively modern and was fostered by poets and historians such as Bishop Tegnér, who hoped, by harking back to the days of their ancestors, to put an end to the traditional animosity between Danes and Swedes. The movement was eagerly taken up in England, with the revival of Anglo-Saxon studies, and by German romantic nationalism.

But it is an error to speak, as we often do, of 'the viking nations'. Few even of those Scandinavians who 'went a-viking' spent the best part of their lives on such ventures. The free farmer or *bondi* was industrious, sober, pessimistic, and intensely conservative, especially in matters of religion. He had little time for the exaggerated heroics of the berserks, and his philosophy is expressed in the 'Hávamál', which stands in relation to the other Eddic poems as Hesiod to Homer:

> In the evening can the day be praised
> and when she's dead a wife;
> a sword when you've made trial of it,
> a maiden when she's married.
> Praise ice when you've got over it,
> and beer when it's drunk.

One should always look carefully behind the door when one enters a house: one never knows where enemies may be lying in wait.

A living man is always worth more than a lifeless one ... the lame man can ride on a horse ... the blind man is better than one who has been burnt; a dead man is no use to anyone.

They can fight, but not from bravado, but for the simple reason that:

The coward thinks he will live for ever
if only he keeps clear of fights;
but old age will give him no truce
even if weapons do.

This is very different from the viking ideal pictured in 'Egilssaga', where a
jarl's daughter refuses to sit beside a young man whom she accuses of never
having been embroiled in slaughter: in fact Egil had burnt down a farmhouse
in Kurland and massacred the townspeople of Lund, and successfully vindi-
cates his right to a place on the ale-bench. The best commentary on all this is
that, till the romantic revival, the word *viking* was used in Scandinavia in
ordinary speech in the sense of 'blackguard'. And it was not the wild ravaging viking but the stay-at-home farmer who resisted most stubbornly the
advance of Christianity in the North. The viking did not burn churches out
of hatred for Christianity, but because they were storehouses of wealth,
centres of population, and, in Ireland, often situated for his convenience on
islands or coastal sites. But closer contact with Christians resulted in surprisingly early conversions: the two Olafs who pressed the new religion on a
reluctant community in Norway were vikings. Sweden, on the other hand,
did not succumb until the twelfth century.

THE older Scandinavian religion was centred on Frey and the sacred king, as
revealed in the ninth-century 'Ynglingatál' (as distinct from Snorri's rationalised interpretation of it in his 'Ynglingasaga'). Odin was the god of skalds
and berserks, associated with sinister magic and traits of shamanism. He was
undomesticated: not the god of a people or territory but of the *Männerbund*,
the secret society of young men outside tribal law (as in Celtic mythology
Finn was of the *fíanna*). Thor was friendlier but clumsier, and seems to have
been a favourite of the Irish vikings: his sacred grove outside Dublin was
desecrated by Brian Bóruma in the year 1000 and his ring (fixed to the door
of his temple and a talisman by which solemn oaths were sworn) had been a
spoil of war when Máel Sechnaill captured the city five years earlier. The
idea of a warrior's paradise in Odin's Valhalla is not found in the oldest
fragments of Norse literature, but was a development of the viking age. The
Swedish kings of Uppsala were sacrificed to Frey and went to Hel, the
goddess who is the death-aspect of Freya, the love-goddess (*Venus Libi-
tina*)—there is no suggestion in the 'Ynglingatál' that only cowards went to
her abode. It was essential that the king should sacrifice 'for peace and a
good year' (*til árs ok friðar*): the Christian Hákon the Good was forced to eat
horse-flesh before he was accepted as king of Norway. Frey—'the Swedish
god'—and his shrine at Uppsala were described by Adam of Bremen as still
flourishing as late as the 1060s. Warriors often exchanged the worship of
Thor for that of the more powerful Odin, or might even assert self-reliant

atheism, but the farmers of the fertile Swedish Uppland were too conservative to jeopardise well-tried methods of ensuring fertility. The tradition of
the king-sacrifice survived into the Christian era in the patron martyr kings
Olaf, Cnút, and Erik. The evidence of the 'Njálssaga' even suggests an
attempt by Icelanders (or perhaps by the people of Man and the Isles) to
find such a royal saint in the person of Brian Bóruma.

# APPENDIX

## OLD NORSE BORROWINGS INTO IRISH

Whereas in English the influence of Old Norse (or rather Old Danish), does not merely consist of loanwords but almost amounts to a symbiosis of the two closely related languages in some respects, the number of Norse words that have come into Irish is relatively small, and by no means all have survived into the modern period. The Norwegian Celtic scholar Magne Oftedal has said: 'In the majority of Scandinavian loanwords in Irish (including names) there is nothing to tell us whether the loans are of Danish or Norwegian origin. But in a certain number of loans—Marstrander enumerates about forty—there are features either of vocabulary or of phonetic development which could only be Norwegian and more specifically south-west Norwegian, while there are no features that point unambiguously to Denmark.'[28] These relate mainly to commerce, shipping, fishing, warfare, and dress. The most notable are: *accaire* 'anchor' < *akkeri* (from Latin *anchora* which had earlier been borrowed into Irish as *ingor*); *ármann* 'officer' (not a word that survived) < *ármaðr* 'royal steward'; *att* 'hat, hood, helmet' < *hattr*; *bát* 'boat' < *bátr*; *beoir* 'beer' < *bjórr*; *bog, boga* 'bow' (a weapon not used by the Irish, although a word for it, *fidboc*, existed); *cairling* 'hag' < *kerling*; *cnapp* 'button' < *knappr*; *cnairr* < *knörr* 'merchant-ship'; *Danair* 'Danes' < *Danir*; Mod.Ir. *dorgha* < *dorg* 'a trailing-line for small fish'; *gagar, gadar* 'hound, beagle' < *gagarr* 'dog'; *garda* 'garth, yard, garden' < *garða*; Mod.Ir. *geadas* 'pike (the fish)' < *gedda*; *íarla* 'jarl, earl' < *jarl* (the earlier form *erll* is found as *erell* in *A.U.* 848); *Lagmann* (mainly as a proper name, though the Annals of the Four Masters refer to the 'Lagmainn' and the 'Lagmainn of the Isles' *s.a.* 960, 972 (= 962, 974) < *lögumaðr* 'lawspeaker' (rendered in Irish as *aurlabraid* 'spokesman' in the Annals of Tigernach and the *Chronicum Scotorum* at 980); *laídeng* 'ship, vessel' < *leiðangr* 'ship levy; war tax'; *margad* 'market' < *markaðr*; *mattal* 'cloak' < *mattall* (ultimately from Latin *mantella*); *meirgg* 'banner' < *merki* 'mark, token, sign, banner'; *?penning* 'penny' may derive from Old Norse *penningr* but is probably taken direct from Anglo-Saxon (Old Irish uniquely has preserved in the word *afaing* the name of the coinage of the eighth-century Mercian king Offa); *?scatán* 'herring' (etymology unknown but possibly Old Norse: the English word *skad* is first attested in Cornwall); *sgeir* < *sker* (gen.pl. *skerja*) 'a rock in the sea'; *sciggire* 'giggler, buffoon, derider' < *skeggiar*; *scibbad* 'snatching, sweeping away' < *skipa* 'arrange, put in order'; *scúta* 'a cutter (ship)' < *skúta* 'skiff'; *?serrcenn* 'galley' (probably < *serr* 'sickle' + *cenn* 'head'; but Marstrander thought from *serpens* 'snake', a calque on *snekkja* 'swift sailing-ship'); *sníding* 'villain; apostate' < *níðingr* (not really a loanword, for it occurs only in the course of a dialogue in the 'Cocad Gáedel re Gallaib'); *Somarlaide* < *sumarliði* 'summer sailor' (only as a personal name, except for a reference in the Scottish 'Chronicle of the Kings' referring to a raid on Buchan at some date during

[28] Magne Oftedal, 'Scandinavian place-names in Ireland' in Bo Almqvist and David Greene (ed.), *Proceedings of the 7th Viking Congress* (London, 1976), pp 125–34.

the reign of Indulf between 954 and 962); *stiúir* 'rudder' < *stri*; *stiúrad* 'to steer' < - *stýra*; *stiúrasmann* 'helmsman' < *strimaðr*; *suaittrech, suairtlech* 'mercenary' < *svartle- ggja* 'black-handled axe; billetted soldier'; *targa* 'targe, shield' < *targa*; *trosc* 'cod' < *thorskr*. The longest-lasting vocabulary consists of words (not all listed above) connected with sea-fishing; this was an occupation apparently introduced by the Norse, for in Old Irish sources salmon and trout are the only fish regarded with any esteem.

In the Gaelic of Scotland, however, both loanwords and place-names of Norse origin are far more numerous. It was not for nothing that the Hebrides (anciently the *Ebudae* and in early Irish *Innse Iboth*) came to be known to the Irish as *Innse Gall*, the Isles of the Norsemen. But the Orkneys and Shetland retained their older names in Irish: *Innse Orc* and *Innse Cat*.

Some well-known Irish place-names are of Norse origin, though most survive only in English, many having been borrowed into that language no doubt through trading contacts a century or more before the Anglo-Normans arrived in Ireland:[29]

Arklow, first attested in the 'Gesta regis Henrici II' as *Herkelou, Herkete- lou*, is derived by Price from the personal name *Arnkell, Arnketill*[30] (though Oftedal denies that the element *ló* 'meadow' is found with a personal name).

Carlingford is probably Old Norse *Kerlingafjorðr* 'fjord of the hags' from the mountain stacks known as the 'Three Nuns', or from a proper name.

Dalkey: Old Norse *Dálkøy* 'cloak-pin island' or 'dagger island'; Old Norse *dálkr* is itself a borrowing from Old Irish *delg*.

Dunrally is *Longphort Rothlaíb* a Norse fortress recorded in the annals at 862, on the site of the monastery of Cluain Andobair, at Dunrally Bridge, County Laois, just across the River Barrow from Cloney, where a viking presence is attested as early as 845. It derives its name from a leader Rodolb < *Hróthleifr* or *Hróðúlfr*.

Dursey: the sixteenth-century spellings *Dorsees, Dorsies* render unlikely a deriv- ation from Old Norse *dýr*, 'deer', whence one would also expect a name without the genitive *s*. But the name must be Norse.

Fingal is not Norse but the Irish term for their territory (*Fine Gall*).

Gaultier (the Norse territory adjoining Waterford) shows similar Irish elements recomposed in Norse pattern: genitive plural *Gall + tír*.

Helvick is Old Norse *heilvík* 'safe inlet'.

Howth may not be simply Old Norse *høfuð* 'head' as this is never found without a compound as in *Uxahøfuð Krhøfuð*. Oftedal thinks it is Old Norse *høfði* 'rocky headland' (often connected to the mainland by a narrow neck).

Ireland's Eye is *Írlands øy* 'Ireland's island'.

Lambay is Old Norse *lambøy* 'lamb's island' or *lambaøy*, with genitive plural.

Leixlip may be from *laxhlaup* 'salmon leap', but as this word is not attested in Old Norse, Marstrander was probably correct in deriving the name from *laxhløypr* 'salmon's leaping place', although this is also unattested elsewhere. Marstrander's

[29] Oftedal, loc. cit.; he does not discuss the names Arklow, Gaultier, Helvick.
[30] Liam Price, *The placenames of County Wicklow* (7 pts, Dublin, 1945–67), pt vii, p. 477.

other phonological doubts were unwarranted, as the name went straight from Old Norse into English, without any Irish intermediary stage.

Longford is not a Norse place-name but the Irish word *longphort* 'military camp'; this word is, however, of relevance here since it first came into use as a term for the Norse phenomenon of fortified beach-heads. Derived from two Irish words (both old borrowings from Latin) *long* 'ship' and *port* 'port', it soon came to mean any camp, not necessarily one for the protection of a fleet.

Saltee is Old Norse *Saltøy*, 'salt island'.

Skellig is not Norse, but Irish *Sceilg*: Oftedal wished to derive it from Old Norse, in spite of its attestation in *A.U.* 823. He based his hypothesis that Old Norse words could be borrowed so early on the mention by the Annals of the Four Masters of an Irishman with the Norse name of Gofraid (*Guðfriðr*) who went to Scotland *c*.835, but this is an entirely bogus annal invented to justify the later medieval claim of the Norsemen of the Isles to descent from the Airgialla.

Skerries is not discussed by Oftedal, but he mentions the loanword *sgeir* in discussing the place-name *Sgeir nan Sgarbh* 'skerry of the cormorants', while denying Sommerfelt's contention that this is a translation of Old Norse *Skarfasker*: Gaelic *sgarbh* is borrowed from Old Norse *skarfr*, but the name is Gaelic (though composed of two loan-words).

Smerwick is Old Norse *Smjørvík* 'butter bay'. There are many Norwegian place-names with this 'butter' element: Iceland has a *Smjörfjall* 'butter mountain' and a *Smjörsund* 'butter sound'; there is also a Gaelic *Smeircleit* in South Uist (Old Norse *Smjørklettr* 'butter crag').

Strangford is Old Norse *Strangfjørðr* 'rough or rapid fjord', with reference to its notorious tidal currents.

Ulster < Old Norse *Ulaðstír, Ulaztír*. Sommerfelt has shown that this derives from the Old Irish genitive *Ulad* + Old Norse genitive element *s* + Old Irish *tír* 'land'. This form passed from Old Norse into Anglo-Norman and English (as must have Leinster and Munster).

Oftedal does not discuss Old Norse *Kunnak(s)tír* for Connacht, which occurs in the *Heimskringla* and the *Njálssaga*, but which did not pass into English. Sommerfelt[31] pointed out the opposite development in *Briggethorfinn* in north-west England, where Norse elements are combined according to Irish rules.

Waterford (in Middle English *Vadrefiord*) derives from an Old Norse *Veðra(r)fjørðr* 'ram fjord' or 'windy fjord'. Oftedal does not discuss the Irish form Port Láirge, which is an exception to the general non-acceptance of Norse names in Irish: it derives from the early viking settler Láraic < Old Norse *Hlárekkr*.

Wexford (Middle English *Weisford*) is probably < Old Norse *Veigsfjørðr* 'fjord of Veig'; the meaning of *veig* is uncertain: perhaps 'waterlogged island or piece of land'.

Wicklow is first attested as *Wikingelo* by the late-twelfth-century Anglo-Norman writer Giraldus Cambrensis, then in Middle English as *Wykynlo*. Oftedal doubts whether it commemorates 'vikings' as such, but his argument seems rather weak. He says that *víkingr* is rare in place-names and prefers a derivation from a personal name *Víkingr*, or from an unattested weak form *Víkingi*, but he admits that *Víkingavatn* in

[31] Alf Sommerfelt, 'The Norse influence on Irish and Scottish Gaelic' in *Proceedings of the [First] International Congress of Celtic Studies* (Dublin, 1962), p. 75.

Iceland probably does contain the genitive plural. The element *ló* (cognate with English *lea*, 'meadow'), frequent in Norway and found also in Sweden and Denmark, is unknown in Iceland or the Hebrides and is never combined with a personal name (unless we except Oslo < *Ás-ló* from *áss* 'god').

Wulfrichsford is now obsolete, but was common throughout the medieval period and is first attested in Anglo-Norman sources in 1210, and as Old Norse *Ulfreksfjorðr* in *Ólafs saga hins helga*. This name, as though that of a fjord named after a viking Ulfrekr, is more probably a Norse *Volksetymologie* from the Irish *Inber Ollarba*, the mouth of the River Ollarba. In modern times the Old Irish population name *Latharna* has reasserted itself for the name of the port of Larne (County Antrim).

In all there are not more than fifteen or sixteen certain examples of Norse place-names in Ireland and, with the exception of Helvick, none of these has been adopted into the Irish language (though Port Láirge and Dunrally commemorate individual vikings). The situation is similar in Wales: Anglesey, Bardsey, and Swansea retain their native names in Welsh, as do Benn Étair (Howth), Loch Cuan (Strangford Lough), and Loch Garman (Wexford) in Irish (the last-named is also found in its Irish form in the Welsh 'Hanes Gruffudd ap Cynan'). Scotland, however, is differ-ent, in that many Gaelic place-names are of Norse origin. Of these the following are attested in Middle Irish sources:

Lewis (Gaelic *Leodhus*) < Old Norse *Ljóðus*.
Uist (Gaelic *Uidhist*) < Old Norse *Ívist*, attested in *Magnussaga hins Bárfóta*. In addition we may note *Sciggire*, the Faroe Islands < Old Norse *Skeggjar*.

In Oftedal's opinion 'the majority of Scandinavian place-names in Ireland are Norwegian . . . one must keep one's mind open to the possibility that some names were originally given by speakers of Danish, but among the names I have examined there are none that show any particularly Danish features'. Names like *Ballygunnar, Ballytruckle, Ballyfermot*, which may contain Old Norse *Gunnar, Thórkell, Thór-mundr*, are Irish in structure and hardly earlier than *c*.1150 (when *baile* names first become common). Oftedal disagreed with Sommerfelt,[32] who thought *Ballygunnar* to be an Irish translation of pre-existing *Gunnarsbr* or *Gunnarsbor* (like Lincolnshire *Gunnersby*). These names came into English through the mediation of Irish. As they are relatively late, there is not even evidence that the eponyms were Norse, rather than Irishmen who bore names of Norse origin (a common phenomenon by the eleventh century). But Rathturtle in County Wicklow shows a combination of the Old Irish *ráith* with the Hiberno-Norse personal name Torcall (*Thórkell*). The *ráith* element here suggests an early date of formation, rather than a later hibernicisation of a Norse form, since the combination of this word with a personal name is characteris-tic of Old rather than Middle Irish. Whether the reference in *A.U.* 867 to the burning by the Irish of 'Dún Amlaím' at Clondalkin should be taken as evidence of a place-name in the proper sense is doubtful: it probably means no more than 'Olaf's fortification'. Therefore, there would seem to be no purely Old Norse settlement

[32] Alf Sommerfelt, 'The English forms of the main provinces of Ireland' in *Lochlann*, i (1958), pp 223–7.

names in Ireland. On the other hand, there is documentary evidence that the form *Ostmannsby* (with the characteristically Danish rather than Norwegian *-bý*) existed alongside and presumably before Oxmanstown: the Lord John's charter of 15 May 1192 to Dublin, and his confirmation of same as king on 7 November 1200, refers to it as 'Houstemanebi'.[33] This is a useful warning against too sweeping a denial of the existence of similar Danish place-names: the apparent absence from Ireland of names in *-by* may be deceptive. It is also notable that the name 'Ostmen' must have been used by the Hiberno-Norse of themselves, since it does not occur in Gaelic Irish sources, while the nomenclature *Ostamanneby* must pre-date the Anglo-Norman settlement of Dublin.

---

[33] Gearóid Mac Niocaill, *Na buirgéisí* (2 vols, Dublin, 1964), i, 78, 82.

CHAPTER XVII

# The Irish church, 800–*c*.1050

KATHLEEN HUGHES*

IRELAND at the beginning of the ninth century was a stable society, and the church was well established. The country had absorbed one major foreign element, Christianity, and integrated it with her own legal structure and to some extent with her own culture. Churches had been set up all over Ireland, living off the land like the raths of secular lords, the major monasteries having churches within their *paruchiae* much as a *rí ruirech* had his sub-kings. By 800 these churches were centres of population.[1] They had clerics performing the *opus dei*, ascetics leading a very strict religious life, *manaig* living with their wives and families and farming the land, but attending church on Sundays and under some circumstances even electing the succeeding abbot. There were also penitents attached to a big church, some of whom had committed major crimes against society. There was a school with a man of learning in charge, teaching grammar to the boys, superintending the copying and illumination of books; the students here were mainly future clerics, but some laymen also seem to have sent their sons to monastic schools. A large monastery either had metalworkers of its own or, more probably, sometimes employed jewellers and skilled craftsmen. Travellers came for hospitality, merchants brought their wares, poets and clerics from a distance might stay on their journeys. The church was thus a major centre of population. There was coming and going and contact with the outside world.

*See above, p. 301.
[1] Charles Doherty explores the 'urban' aspects of major monasteries, as centres of population, places of refuge, meeting- and trading-places, especially from the ninth century onwards, in 'Exchange and trade in early medieval Ireland' in *R.S.A.I. Jn.*, cx (1980), pp 67–89, and 'The monastic town in early medieval Ireland' in H. B. Clarke and Anngret Simms (ed.), *The comparative history of urban origins in non-Roman Europe* (2 vols, Oxford, 1985), i, 45–76. He has a more recent survey of the evidence in Howard B. Clarke, Máire Ní Mhaonaigh, and Raghnall Ó Floinn (ed.), *Ireland and Scandinavia in the early viking age* (Dublin 1998), pp 288–330. See also Leo Swan, 'The early Christian ecclesiastical sites of County Westmeath' in John Bradley (ed.), *Settlement & society in medieval Ireland: studies presented to F. X. Martin* (Kilkenny, 1988), pp 3–31, and Michael Ryan, 'Fine metalworking and early Irish monasteries: the archaeological evidence', ibid., pp 33–48. Howard Clarke has a comparative survey in 'Proto-towns and towns in Ireland and Britain in the ninth and tenth centuries' in Clarke, Ní Mhaonaigh, & Ó Floinn, *Ire. & Scandinavia*, pp 331–80. For a more recent (and sceptical) review of the evidence, see Mary Valante, 'Reassessing the Irish "monastic town"' in *I.H.S.*, xxi (1998–9), pp 1–18.

Monasteries did not all conform to one set pattern. We see this most clearly in the election of abbots and, since the abbot's office was fairly auto-cratic, the kind of abbot a monastery had must have considerably influenced the kind of life its community led. There were some abbots who led a strict religious life, ascetic and celibate: these are described in the annals as abbot (sometimes also *episcopus*) and *anchorita*. But we also hear of occasions when the *manaig* elected the abbot, and they may well have chosen one of more secular life. Certainly the eighth- and ninth-century annals (and the seventh-century canons) show us married abbots. Sometimes their sons succeeded them in high office in the monastery, as abbot or *economus*. Succession of son to father in the abbacy was usually not direct, but at one or even two removes, rather like the succession to the office of kingship.

Sometimes in the pre-viking age monasteries were attacked by laymen. Usually we do not know why this was.[2] For example, in 757 Kilmore was burned by the Uí Chremthainn, and in 776 Durrow, a border monastery, was involved in fighting between the Uí Néill and the Munstermen. If families fought for the abbatial succession they may sometimes have obtained secular support: for example, a poem on the list of coarbs of Patrick says that Dub dá Leithe, abbot of Armagh, 'is at hand with kings from the north'.[3] But we need to grasp just how limited was this sort of 'war' in secular Irish society. Kings were constantly going to war with each other. Occasionally there were big battles between over-kings, but usually, in the battles between petty kings, the numbers involved were fairly small and warfare drew on only one class of society. Raths were not usually burned down, and the common people got out of the way. The prize was not the capture and annexation of land, for when the battle was over the victors withdrew, taking with them cattle. Then the other kingdom might initiate another 'war' to recap-ture cattle. In fact war was generally a kind of sport for the aristocracy, in which rules of honour were maintained, a sport that raised prestige and also brought an economic boost. The nearest parallel I can think of is medieval hunting in England, which was also sport and a source of food supply. Irish 'war' was more savage, probably more closely related to honour. The parallel is not exact, but early Irish war and medieval hunting have strong similar-ities.

So when kings attacked a monastery, as they occasionally did in the pre-viking age,[4] the disturbance seems to have been only temporary. Ecclesias-tical society and civilisation were not damaged by such occasions. Sometimes

---

[2] Donnchadh Ó Corráin sees 'good grounds for conflict' between tenacious clerical families and lay members of their own or 'new and expansive dynasties', and he illustrates examples in 'The early Irish churches: some aspects of organization' in Ó Corráin, *Ir. antiquity*, pp 328–30.

[3] H. J. Lawlor and R. I. Best (ed.), 'The ancient list of the coarbs of Patrick' in *R.I.A. Proc.*, xxxv (1919), sect. C, pp 316–62: 322.

[4] See Kathleen Hughes, *Early Christian Ireland: introduction to the sources* (London, 1972), pp 148–59, for the controversy about this.

the attack was in pursuit of an individual: probably the entry in 735 (Ann. Tig.), when Áed Róin was taken out of the 'oratory' of Faughart to be killed, is such an occasion. When sanctuary was violated, monasteries secured compensation,[5] or they might curse the offender.[6] There are only five recorded occasions in the Annals of Ulster, Inisfallen, and Tigernach for the period before 831 (that is, before the period of viking settlement) when the plundering of monasteries by Irishmen could compare in damage with a viking attack. Two of these were by Fedelmid, king of Cashel, who burned Gailinne and Fore in 822 and 830. Fedelmid's actions are so far an unsolved puzzle. He was a cleric, a scribe and anchorite, as well as a king, and may have feared ecclesiastical vengeance less than the ordinary layman. It has been suggested, rather implausibly, that his attacks were part of a policy of reform.

The viking conception of war was quite different from that of the Irishman. They were driven more implacably by the need for economic survival, and their warfare was far more wholesale and more savage. It is probable that in times of trouble the Irish population in the countryside brought their goods into the monastic enclosure for safety, and the vikings may well have raided to secure them.[7] But the two contemporary sources that we have, archaeology and the annals, show very clearly that the vikings also took a different kind of plunder. By the ninth century the monasteries were centres of valuable metalwork. There were altar-vessels and book-covers and shrines, while the church must have had a small bank of objects, such as brooches, which could be given as pledges in legal agreements. Such objects have been found in ninth-century Norwegian graves.[8] We know also that the vikings were slave-traders, and the annals show that they took prisoners from centres of population. We read of 'a great prey of women' taken from Howth in 821; great numbers of the family of Armagh taken captive in 831; many captives carried off from southern Brega in 836; bishops, priests, and scholars taken on a raid in 840. The annals usually only mention the ecclesiastical aristocracy, but presumably other people were seized as well. The emphasis on captives goes on right through the period. Sometimes numbers are given: in 869 a thousand lost at Armagh between captives and slain; in 895, 710 persons carried away from Armagh into captivity. In 871 we hear of the

---

[5] As Tallaght did in 811.

[6] The family of Columcille went to Tara to curse King Áed in 818 after the killing of the abbot of *Rath Both*.

[7] This has been suggested by A. T. Lucas: 'The plundering and burning of churches in Ireland, 7th to 16th century' in Étienne Rynne (ed.), *North Munster studies* (Limerick, 1967), pp 172–229; and 'Irish–Norse relations: time for a reappraisal?' in *Cork Hist. Soc. Jn.*, lxxi (1966), pp 62–75. See now Colmán Etchingham, *Viking raids on Irish church settlements in the ninth century* (Maynooth, 1996), and Charles Doherty, 'The vikings in Ireland: a review of the evidence' in Clarke, Ní Mhaonaigh, & Ó Floinn, *Ire. & Scandinavia*, pp 288–330.

[8] Recent finds of insular metalwork from Norway are discussed and mapped by Egon Wamers in 'Some ecclesiastical and secular insular metalwork found in Norwegian graves' in *Peritia*, ii (1983), pp 277–306, with an update in *Ire. & Scandinavia*, pp 37–72.

vikings bringing 'a great prey of men into captivity' from Scotland to Dublin; they name English, Britons, and Picts. In 881 Norsemen took 'its full of people' (*a lán di dhoínibh*) from the church of Duleek. The annals show us, without any doubt, numbers of people carried off from the churches. It is agreed that these entries are not fictitious, even if numbers may be exaggerated. The problem lies in how to assess the effects of viking violence.

The vikings had a clear objective. They wanted plunder. But their methods of warfare were quite different from Irish methods. Those whom they did not carry off they often killed. When the vikings attacked Iona in 825 some of the community fled, but Blathmac and others remained behind to receive martyrdom. In 836, when the vikings attacked southern Brega they not only carried off a great many captives, they also killed a great many; in 840 when they took captive bishops and priests and *sapientes* from Louth they put others to death; in 869 Armagh was plundered with a great loss of captives and also of slain. This sort of attack must have had a devastating effect on the monastic population. Moreover, when the vikings had looted a monastery they set fire to it. Most of the buildings in the eastern half of Ireland would have been wood and thatch in the ninth century, and they burned easily. We read in the annals of eighty-three plunderings and burnings by the Norse between 830 and 880,[9] and constant captures and killings. Viking warfare was far more destructive and savage than Irish war had been. The old war as a violent sport had been replaced by a total attack.[10]

It has recently been suggested that the Irish were just as responsible for attacking churches as were the Norse.[11] But a closer consideration of the figures shows that, though Irish kings attacked monasteries occasionally in the ninth century, the Norse attacks were far more frequent. Between 830 and 880, when Norse raids were very heavy, there were ten attacks by Irishmen and three Hiberno-Norse attacks, as against the eighty-three attacks by the Norse; in the period 881–919, when Norse pressure decreased, there were six attacks by Irishmen and twenty-seven by the Norse. The annals for this period are contemporary records. They do not show us ninth-century history as a war of the Irish against the Foreigners. There were occasions when Irish allied with vikings against Irish, or when vikings fought vikings, and many times when Irish fought Irish. All the same, the annals leave no doubt at all that far more damage was done to churchmen and church property in the ninth century by the vikings than by the native Irish.[12]

---

[9] For tables see Hughes, *Sources*, p. 157; Etchingham, *Viking raids, passim*.

[10] It appears from the annals that Irish warfare became increasingly large-scale and total in the ninth century. See T.M. Charles-Edwards, 'Irish warfare before 1100' in Thomas Bartlett and Keith Jeffery (ed.), *A military history of Ireland* (Cambridge, 1996), pp 26–51.

[11] Lucas, 'Plundering and burning'.

[12] Hughes, *Sources*, pp 148–59.

We must not, however, exaggerate the effect of these viking attacks. Irish annalists were used to small-scale 'wars', and viking attacks seemed to them phenomenal. Yet when we look at the annals we see that few of the houses were extinguished. Here my evidence is from the Annals of Ulster; the Annals of Tigernach are missing their entries for the ninth century. For this period the Annals of Ulster are fairly well informed about the houses of the central east. It seems that Armagh was then having a crucial influence on the form of the record,[13] and Armagh may have had some interest in the affairs of Brega. In 888 an abbot of Trevet died who was '*máer* ['steward'] of the household of Patrick to the south of the mountain', and another *máer* for this area died in 894. The mountain seems to be Sliab Breg, i.e. the heights north of Drogheda. Moreover, Slane, which is just to the south of Sliab Breg, has an unusually full succession of entries: in the viking period it is mentioned at 834, 838, 839, 845, 849, 856, 869, 877, and 890. No other house in the area has quite so complete a history at this time. Bishop Erc, patron of Slane, was Patrick's judge.[14] There may have been some special link between Slane and Armagh in the ninth century, which led to the recording of its affairs.

If we look at the churches that would have been most affected by the vikings on the eastern seaboard, the evidence is not at all easy to assess. A number of houses have only one or two entries, and it needs a sequence of entries to draw any conclusions about the effects of the viking raids. In some cases it looks as if there was some serious dislocation in the first generation of viking settlement. We know that the most severe period of viking attack was from 832 until about 865, so it is interesting to see which monasteries appear in the annals during that time. Bangor, situated on the north Down coast, plundered by vikings in 823–4, is mentioned in 839 and 849, then not again till 871. Tallaght, on the outskirts of Dublin, appears at 825 and 827, then no more till the entries recommence in 868. Louth, about eight miles from the sea and uncomfortably near to the viking centre of Annagassan, appears four times in the first three decades of the century; then the house was attacked in 832, 840, 864, and 873, and is not mentioned again during the ninth century.[15] These entries might suggest a generation of acute disturbance during the first period of the viking settlement.

But this is not the picture we get for other houses. There could hardly be a monastery in a more exposed position than Lusk, a short distance from the coast, with Lambay Island just opposite. But there is a steady sequence of

[13] Ibid., pp 129–35.
[14] *Trip. life*, ed. Stokes, i, 265. He comes third in the list of Patrick's household found in 'Leabhar Breac' and appended to the B.L. Egerton MS of the 'Vita Tripartita'.
[15] For other houses there are not sufficient entries to suggest dislocation between 832 and 865, though the entries could be read this way; e.g. Finglas, 812, 825, 838, 867; Fennor, 829, 834, 838; Killashee, 829, 872.

ecclesiastical officials here, at 836, 839, 853, 875, 881, 883, 891, though the 'oratory' was burned by the Norsemen in 856. Monasterboice is seven or eight miles from the coast; but the death of an abbot is recorded at 846, the drowning of another abbot in 855, then entries at 878, 884, and 891. Duleek has an entry in the bad period at 849, before a sequence beginning in 868.[16] It is therefore clear that viking proximity, plundering and burning, and the seizure of monastic population did not necessarily mean discontinuity. The monastery went on functioning. What then did it mean? The annalists insist on the shock and horror that the viking attacks caused. And the entries that they record suggest that the period saw certain modifications in the legal and institutional position of the church, some of which seem to be directly due to the effects of viking pressure. First, the series of *cána* that began in 697 ended in 842. These 'laws' seem to have been mainly aimed at protecting non-combatants and church property from violence. A gloss on Colmán's hymn describes 'the four chief laws of Ireland', as follows: 'the law of Patrick and of Dáire and of Adomnán and of Sunday. The law of Patrick, now, not to slay clerics; the law of Dáire, not to steal cattle; of Adomnán, not to slay women; of Sunday, not to travel.'[17]

Our most illuminating treatise here is the Law of Adomnán, preserved in a composite text of which the oldest part goes back to the end of the seventh or eighth century.[18] The Law was said to have been first promulgated in 697 at the synod of Birr. Its aim was to protect 'clerics and women and innocent children until they are capable of slaying a man'. The *cána* were promulgated by an abbot together with a provincial king (this much is clear from the annals); one secular law tract, 'Críth Gablach', cites the Law of Adomnán as one of the three kinds of government that an overking binds on his people.[19] Fines were imposed for the violation of the law, and officials were appointed to collect them, so that the *cána* brought financial advantages, and these may have become their chief purpose. *Cáin* has, in fact, a double sense, and means 'tribute' as well as 'law'.

The administration of the *cána* followed the normal usages of Irish law, enforced by pledges and sureties. But the concept of this kind of law was something new, for whereas secular law was based on custom, the *cána* were partly based on will. The law of Patrick extended the church's right of sanctuary, and other traditional laws provided ecclesiastical protection. So, if we recognise the battering that churches took from the vikings in the

---

[16] Other houses with entries in the bad period are Trevet at 839 and 850, Lann Léire at 845 and 850, Ardbraccan at 849, Dunshaughlin at 851.

[17] *Thes. Pal.*, ii, 306.

[18] Ed. Kuno Meyer (Oxford, 1905); critical discussion by John Ryan in *Studies in Ir. law*, pp 269–76. See also Hughes, *Sources*, pp 80–82; Máirín Ní Dhonnchadha, 'The guarantor list of *Cáin Adomnáin*, 697' in *Peritia*, i (1982), pp 178–215; and Herbert, *Iona, Kells, & Derry*, pp 50–51 and elsewhere.

[19] D. A. Binchy (ed.), *Críth Gablach* (Dublin, 1941; 2nd ed., 1970), lines 521–4.

generation following 832, it is not surprising to find that the *cána* ceased in 842. Their promulgation and practice needed conditions of stability, and these no longer existed. It must have been very difficult to secure the alliance of provincial kings, to perform the circuit, to send out officials to collect taxes. Viking pressure provides the best explanation for the cessation of the *cána* in 842.

The annals show us other modifications in the administration of the church, which were certainly not caused, but may have been encouraged, by the effects of viking settlement. There had been occasions in the eighth century when the same man had held an ecclesiastical appointment in two or more churches.[20] There are a number of these entries between 773 and 807, then the entries become infrequent. But between 863 and 900 in the Annals of Ulster there are fourteen recorded instances: typical examples are Tuathal son of Feradach, abbot of Rechru (Lambay Island) and Durrow (850); Muirchertach son of Niall, abbot of Derry *et aliarum civitatum* (882); Cellach son of Ailill, abbot of Kildare and Iona (865). Usually it is abbacies that are held jointly; occasionally a man is *economus* (steward) in one house and *princeps* (abbot) in another, or *secnap* (chosen successor in the abbacy) in one and *princeps* elsewhere, or even bishop and scribe in one and *princeps* in another. I think these offices must have been held conjointly, and not in succession. If one were reading an academic obituary notice today the first sentence would say 'John Smith of Oxford', even though further down the column in the elaboration of the dead man's career, we should be told he first held an academic appointment in Manchester, then became head of a department in London before he was elected to a chair at Oxford. The Irish annals are laconic, and I doubt if so brief a record would do more than give the offices the man held at his death. Moreover there is the use of the word *antea* in an entry of 848: 'Fínsnechtae of Limerick, *ancorita et rex Connact antea mortuus est*'. Here the annalist definitely intends to say that, although Fínsnechtae died an anchorite, he had been king of Connacht before. This formula is not used in the records of ecclesiastical pluralities.

Pluralism is not new in the last four decades of the ninth century, but the practice seems substantially to increase. Is it just a fashion in recording? There is a little spurt of these entries in the 770s, 780s, and 790s, perhaps one annalist's lifetime. The practice starts up again in considerable numbers in the 860s. But it does not die out completely in the intervening period, so it does not look to me like the whim of an annalist. Pluralism may be explained by various hypotheses. It may be caused by a shortage of suitable candidates; if we believe the annalist's account of captures and killings in the generation following 832—and surely we must—this is a possible explanation. Or it may

---

[20] Hughes, *Ch. in early Ir. soc.*, pp 164–6.

be caused by the need to combine livings to make a more economically profitable appointment. It may well be that the wealth of churches declined under the viking impact, so that ambitious men wanted to secure the resources of more than one house. The combination was personal and temporary. The abbacies were often relatively near, but not always. Terryglass and Clonfert, Clonard and Duleek, Kildare and Killeigh are within fairly easy reach, while 'Louth and other churches', 'Kildalkey and other churches' may have been in each others' vicinity; but Kildare and Iona are not. The vikings did not cause pluralism in the Irish church, but by carrying off churchmen and, even more, by destroying church wealth, they may well have created the conditions that favoured its growth.[21]

Another practice that had begun before the period of viking settlement[22] is found occasionally recorded in the ninth century. This is when a king combines his royal office with a monastic appointment. Cathal son of Dúnlaing, king of Uí Chennselaig, made war on Ferns in 817, and when he died in 819 it was as king of Uí Chennselaig and *secnap* of Ferns. Was the community of Ferns compelled to appoint him? In 836 Fedelmid, king of Cashel, entered into the abbacy of Cork,[23] and the same year Dúnlaing, abbot of Cork, died without communion in Cashel; those entries seem to be related. Muiredach son of Máelduín, who died in 863, was not only king of Airthir but also *secnap* of Armagh, which lay within his kingdom. Muiredach, king of Leinster (d. 885), was also abbot of Kildare, the most important monastery within his overlordship.

This may indicate the secularisation of the church, but if so it had started before the real effects of the vikings could have been felt. Similarly the inheritance of abbatial office from father to son may be seen in the eighth-century annals, and it continued in the ninth century.[24] Slane, Trevet, Dunshaughlin, Kilmoone, Killeshin, Lann Léire, Clondalkin, and probably Lusk, Emly, Monasterboice, and Kildalkey are all places where the annals show family inheritance.

One other practice known in the pre-viking age, however, seems to change. Although monastic communities were still occasionally attacked by Irish kings, Irish monasteries after 840 stopped fighting major battles against

---

[21] Donnchadh Ó Corráin, on the other hand, sees a high degree of continuity during this period. Characteristics of a church that was intimately bound up with secular society were well established before the viking period; they persisted during that period, and beyond. See his *Ireland before the Normans* (Dublin, 1972), pp 82–9; 'The early Irish churches' in Ó Corráin, *Ir. antiquity*, pp 327–41; and in R. F. Foster (ed.), *The Oxford illustrated history of Ireland* (Oxford, 1989), pp 31–8.

[22] Hughes, *Ch. in early Ir. soc.*, pp 211–14.

[23] Ann. Inisf., s.a. 836.

[24] Hughes, *Ch. in early Ir. soc.*, pp 163, 189, 210–11. Ailbhe Séamus Mac Shamhráin, in *Church and polity in pre-Norman Ireland: the case of Glendalough* (Maynooth, 1996), traces the close links between secular rulers and Glendalough, and finds many examples of officeholding within families.

each other such as they had fought in the eighth and early ninth centuries;[25] indeed, for a time they stopped fighting altogether. It looks as if the damage and defeat that they suffered from the vikings put a stop to their own warlike tastes.

We have to conclude that, in the period between 832 and about 865, the population and wealth of vulnerable monasteries were both badly hit. But the church as an institution changed very little. The 'secularisation' that used to be seen as the result of the viking pressure had certainly begun well before the vikings arrived. And if we now turn to look at the obits of anchorites in the annals, we shall see that the numbers remain fairly constant during the thirty-five years of severest attack (830–65) and the thirty-five years of diminishing disturbance (866–900). It is possible that anchorites in 900 may not have been quite so ascetic as anchorites a century earlier, but they certainly existed, and were being supported by churches. There is no evidence here that the vikings caused a decline in the spiritual life of the Irish church.

What of its intellectual life? Scriptoria in the areas vulnerable to the vikings may have been less active between 832 and 865. If we take the Annals of Ulster (which are especially interested in the central east, where the vikings were very active), we have sixteen scribes' obits for the period 800–31, eight for the period 832–65, and twenty-two for the period 866–900. This may indicate a regression during the period of severe viking pressure, and a subsequent revival. Or maybe it means that news was coming in more regularly and consistently to the annalist after about 865. But if so, surely this is itself significant, for it would indicate an increasing stability again during the last decades of the ninth century, after the generation when the disturbance was worst.

Some ninth-century Irish scholars were undoubtedly going to the Continent to share in the Carolingian renaissance. Murphy argued that the exodus was at least encouraged by the horrors of conditions at home; that the cruel northern storm that flung Sedulius on the hospitality of Bishop Hartgar of Liège was the rushing north wind of the vikings.[26] This sounds likely, though we have to remember that Irishmen had been going to the Continent for centuries.[27] There seems, however, to have been a change in the overriding character of pilgrimage at about this time.[28] The sixth- and

---

[25] Hughes, *Ch. in early Ir. Soc.*, pp 169–70, 207. Donnchadh Ó Corráin suggests that perhaps 'the *paruchiae* had reached the limits of expansion and that a relatively stable situation had come about, rather than attribute the change to any feeling of solidarity in the face of the threat from the vikings' ('The early Irish churches' in Ó Corráin, *Ir. antiquity*, p. 336).

[26] Gerard Murphy, 'Scotti peregrini' in *Studies*, xvii (1928), pp 39–50, 229–44, especially p. 45: 'Namque volans Aquilo non ulli parcit honori crudeli rostro nos laniando suo' (For the rushing north wind spares no persons, lacerating us with his cruel beak).

[27] Above, p. 322.

[28] See Kathleen Hughes, 'The changing theory and practice of Irish pilgrimage' in *Journal of Ecclesiastical History*, xi (1960), pp 143–51.

seventh-century pilgrims had been ascetic exiles for Christ. No doubt such still continued in the ninth century, but the ones who now dominated the scene were scholars looking for patronage.

> Vescor, poto libens, rithmizans invoco Musas,
> dormisco stertens: oro deum vigilans.
>
> (I eat and freely drink, I make my rhymes,
> And snoring sleep, or vigil keep and pray.)[29]

Sedulius's devotions do not get in the way of good living. It is, however, not the vikings who bring about this changing emphasis, but the different conditions created by the Carolingian renaissance. Ambitious latinists could find jobs and prestige and good company on the Continent, at a time when life at home was particularly difficult.

One other very important change can be seen in ninth-century Irish scriptoria. The language of scholarship was changing. In the Annals of Ulster the early entries are in Latin. There are quite frequently words in Irish, sometimes whole sentences of Irish, but Latin is the predominant language. As we reach the ninth century the amount of Irish increases a little, substantially so in the 830s. By the mid 830s most of the obituary notices are in Latin, but most of the other entries are in Irish, and this goes on throughout the century. This is a change that begins well before the era of viking settlement, but it grows rapidly as the less conventional entries about viking devastation increase.

In the pre-viking age most ecclesiastical scholarship had been for monks. The grammar and exegesis had been for churchmen; even the saints' Lives read as if they were intended mainly for ecclesiastics. But changing the language from Latin into the vernacular widens the whole possibility of communication. We may now expect a much broader range of subject, more borrowing from vernacular ideas into ecclesiastical literature. This begins in the ninth century, but it is far clearer in the tenth; so we may defer its discussion until our next section.

What effect did the vikings have on the church in the ninth century? Churches were damaged, church property was stolen and destroyed; but the churches usually recovered fairly quickly from the raids.[30] Clerics were carried off and killed, but monastic life usually went on. The *cána* ceased, and the vikings seem to be the cause of that termination, for church property and non-combatants could no longer be protected. Certain practices of the eighth-century church revived with renewed force, viz. pluralism and the

---

[29] 'Apologia pro vita sua' in Helen Waddell (ed. and trans.), *Medieval Latin lyrics* (London, 1929), pp 122–3, from which the English version is taken; other poems by Sedulius appear on pp 118–21, 124–5.

[30] Present conditions in the north of Ireland—conditions of shock, disturbance, yet continuity—may provide a parallel. [Editor's note: This was written in the early 1970s.]

inheritance of church office within a family; but churches stopped going to war against each other. Spiritual life went on with its old vitality. Irish scriptoria may have suffered some dislocation in the period 832–65, but if so the dislocation was not long-lived, and the scriptoria show renewed activity in the later part of the century. The language of scholarship had started to change before the vikings settled, and the change progressed during the century, with all the possibilities of development that implied. All in all, the churches took a battering from the vikings far more severe than they had suffered till then in native wars; yet the church as an institution remained much as it had been in the pre-viking age.

B Y the tenth century the viking pressure on the Irish church was lessening. We still hear of attacks. In 948 the abbot of Slane was taken prisoner and died in gentile hands. In 950 the bell-tower of Slane was burned, together with a particularly fine bell and the crosier of the patron saint, and the lector and many people were burned; probably they had taken refuge with the monastery's valuables in the tower. In 951 Godfrey (Godfrid) with the Foreigners of Dublin plundered Kells, Donaghpatrick (Domnach Pátraic), Ardbraccan, Dulane, and Kilskeer and other churches, and took a great number of captives (the annals say 3,000) and booty of cows and horses, gold and silver. All the same, if we add up the total number of attacks by vikings that are mentioned, there are fewer than in the ninth century. The overkings were gaining power and were able to respond with major victories, as in 980 when Máel Sechnaill mac Domnaill won the battle of Tara, or in 989 when he won the battle of Dublin, or 999 when he and Brian won the battle of Glenn Máma. But, probably most significant, the viking kingdom had become firmly established and part of the Irish political scene. Irishmen were constantly using the Foreigners as allies against other Irish kings, so that Dublin became one more kingdom among the other Irish kingdoms.

We can see the mutual influence of Irish and vikings. By the later tenth century the vikings were Christian. This was probably so by 921, for when Godfrid of Dublin plundered Armagh in that year he spared the ecclesiastical buildings and the *céli Dé*. After the battle of Tara in 980 the defeated king Olaf Cuarán (Amlaíb, Anlaf) of Dublin retired to Iona: 'Amlaíb son of Sitric, high-king of the Foreigners of Dublin, went to Iona on pilgrimage and died after sanctification and penance.' We find also that viking chiefs were giving their sons the names of Christian saints, such as Gilla Pátraic, son of Ivar of Waterford,[31] or Gilla Ciaráin, son of Glún Iairn of Dublin, who fell in the battle of Clontarf.[32] Christianity must have filtered through, perhaps via captives or, more probably, through friendly contacts with the Irish aristocracy.

---

[31] A.U., *s.a.* 983.        [32] A.U., *s.a.* 1014.

Viking methods of warfare were increasingly adopted by Irish kings. This must have been inevitable, since they frequently fought as allies. Ecclesiastical sanctuary was less often respected. In 939 and 940 Donnchad, on hostings into Brega, destroyed Fennor and Dunleer, actually killing a priest in the church at Fennor. In 953 the men of Munster joined with the Foreigners to plunder Clonmacnoise. In 971 Domnall went on a hosting into Meath and spoiled all its churches and forts. It looks as if churches were more and more regarded, like any secular centres, as places from which troops might be collected for retaliatory raids and as sources of plunder. In 995 the men of Fernmag and Airgialla plundered Armagh and carried off 2,000 cows, burning the monastery's *fid-nemed*.[33] Monastic 'cities' were sometimes battle-grounds for opposing factions: for the Uí Echach and the Uí Nialláin at Armagh in 986, for the kings of Fernmag and Cenél nEógain at Armagh in 988, for Máel Sechnaill of Meath and the king of Luigne at Donaghpatrick in 993. We hear more about Patrician houses because of the nature of the annals, but similar battles were probably happening elsewhere. Monastic sanctuary was being violated, taboos on violence within the monastic 'city' were being broken by Irishmen as well as by foreigners. The monastery was becoming yet another fort.

Sometimes the saint exacted vengeance or compensation for infringements of his rights. When the three sons of Cerball plundered the *termann* of Cóemgen in 983 three of the band were killed before night. When Máel Sechnaill carried off the shrine of Patrick from Ardee to Áth Sige in 985, he had afterwards to perform the 'decision' (*ríar*), the legal award, of Patrick.[33a] But often it must have seemed that the saint was leaving the monastery to protect itself. The church had lost some of the privileges it had once enjoyed.

Monasteries themselves joined in wars. We find records of abbots participating in battles. This presumably means that the monastery had a warband which accompanied the abbot, similar to that of a petty king. In 901 Dubcuilind, abbot (*princeps*) of Ros Ech, died in a battle against the Luigne; in 908 there was a battle between Munster and the North, in which the abbots of Cork and Kinnity were killed, and in 917 Máel Máedóc, scholar and bishop (*suí et episcopus princeps*) of Leinster, fought in the battle of Cenn Fuait when the viking leader Sitric gained a victory. Abbots and bishops often came from the same class as the secular nobility, were indeed of the same kin, so that there must have been a strong community of interest between ecclesiastical and secular lords.

Study of the annals suggests that a number of minor houses are being mentioned less frequently in the tenth century, and that major houses were emerging into increasingly dominant positions. This may be due to the way the annals were being kept at this time, but it seems more probable that it

---

[33] *Ann. Tig.*, p. 350.     [33a] *Ann. Tig.*, pp 344–5.

represents a real change in ecclesiastical affairs. This is a period when the power of overlords was growing at the expense of minor kings, a development that had begun before the viking age, but must have been urged on by ninth-century conditions.[34] Men needed a powerful lord to protect them. A tendency to build up overlordships, clearly recognisable in the world, may also have been followed by the church.

It is most obvious in the case of Armagh. In the pre-viking age the *cána* had been exercised by a number of different abbots. In the tenth-century annals we hear only of circuits by the abbot of Armagh. As in the ninth century, Armagh had her *máer* in Brega. He is mentioned in the Annals of Ulster at 922 (the abbot of Dunleer), in 924 (the abbot of Monasterboice), and in 929 (the bishop of Duleek and Lusk). But we see from the appendix to the 'Vita Tripartita' that in the time of Joseph, abbot and bishop of Armagh (d. 936), Patrick had a 'unity' of twenty-four who were said to have been at the king of Cashel's table from the time of Fedelmid mac Crimthainn (d. 847), while in 973 the annals tell that Abbot Dub dá Leithe went on a circuit (*for cuairt*) of Munster to collect his tax (*ríar*).[35] A similar right to tribute was being exercised in Cenél nEógain. In 947 a bell-full of silver was given by the Cenél nEógain to Patrick.[36] Abbot Muirecán went on a circuit of the Cenél nEógain in 993, when he conferred the degree of king (*co ro erlegh gradh righ*) on Áed mac Domnaill in the presence of Patrick's congregation. Thereafter he made a great circuit of the north of Ireland. It appears from this that the abbot of Armagh had established his rights in Munster, supported by the king of Cashel, and that his superiority was recognised throughout the north. His association with the kings of Cenél nEógain seems to have been particularly close.[37] Brian was the first king to control the forces of south and north. When he made his circuit of all Ireland in 1006 he recognised the claims of Patrick's successor (*co tarait oighreir samhtha Patraic ocus a comharbai*), and the scribe, Móel Suthain, recorded them in the Book of Armagh in the presence of Brian *imperator Scotorum*.[38]

For periods in the tenth century the abbot of Armagh had secured control of the *paruchia* of Columcille. Máel Brigte died in 927 as coarb of both Patrick and Columcille.[39] And towards the end of the century, in 989, Dub dá Leithe, abbot of Armagh, took the coarbship of Columcille, 'by the counsel of the

---

[34] See Byrne, *Ir. kings*, pp 254–74.

[35] He obtained his 'decision' or 'award'.

[36] The full of Patrick's *finnfaidhech* ('sweet-sounding').

[37] See Tomás Ó Fiaich, 'The church of Armagh under lay control' in *Seanchas Ardmhacha*, v (1969), pp 75–127, at pp 84–5. The *rígdomna* of the Cenél nEógain was buried *in cimiterio regum* at Armagh in 935.

[38] Arm. f. 16ᵛ b *Trip. life*, ed. Stokes, ii, 336.

[39] Máire Herbert discusses the context and importance of these joint appointments in *Iona, Kells, & Derry*, chs 5 and 6.

men of Ireland and Scotland'.[40] This union was not permanent. But the tenth century shows Armagh building up her power throughout Ireland, extending her claims to tribute in both south and north with the support of the major overlords.

It appears from the annals as if pluralism fell sharply after the 950s. This may be due to annalistic convention; but it seems likely that, as prosperity increased in the latter part of the century, the need to combine offices decreased.

Throughout the tenth century some of the dividing lines between church and secular society were becoming blurred.[41] We have seen Irishmen as well as vikings invading sanctuary, raiding 'churches and forts' as if there was little difference between the two. In some monasteries, for which we have detailed abbatial lists, we can see a principle of hereditary succession being adopted very much as if the abbacy were a secular kingship.[42] In the second half of the tenth century the Clann Sínaig family came back into power in Armagh.[43] This kin-group was a branch of the Uí Echdach, one of the leading peoples of Airgialla, the territory in which Armagh lay. Dub dá Leithe began to hold office in 965. After a comparatively short intermission his nephew Máel Muire succeeded in 1001. After this the family held the abbacy until 1137, often succeeding in the collateral branch. It seems that these abbots were not married priests but laymen. They often controlled other important offices in the monastery, that of *fosairchinnech*,[44] master of the schools and head of the guest-house. Another Airgialla kin group, the Uí Bresail, frequently filled the position of *secnap*.[45]

The position at Clonmacnoise was somewhat similar. Here we find the kin of Mac Cuinn na mBocht, in the mid ninth century, appearing as anchorites, scribes, and *airchinnaig* of Eclais Bec. Then in 955 Dúnadach died, a bishop of the same kin. His brother was *airchinnech* of Eclais Bec and his son head of the schools. His grandson died as *anmchara* in 1024, and Conn na mBocht, the famous ecclesiastic whose sons dominated Clonmacnoise in the second half of the eleventh century, was directly descended from him.[46] Some at least of these men were definitely in orders, but had sons who succeeded them.

---

[40] A.U., *s.a.* 989.

[41] Recent work, especially following the publication of *Corpus Iuris Hibernici*, shows that these lines were never very clear. Several of the publications referred to in earlier notes bear on this question.

[42] Ó Fiaich, art. cit., p. 88. For succession lists of major churches, see *N.H.I.*, ix, 237–63.

[43] Dub dá Leithe and his son Condmach of the Clann Sínaig had been abbots from about 775 to 807. See Ó Fiaich's genealogical tree, art. cit., p. 124.

[44] See Ó Fiaich for table, art. cit., pp 90, 125.

[45] Ó Fiaich, genealogical tree, art. cit., p. 126.

[46] See genealogical tree by John V. Kelleher, 'The *Táin* and the annals' in *Ériu*, xxii (1971), pp 107–27, opposite p. 126.

By the second half of the tenth century, probably much earlier, it seems to have made very little difference whether or not the abbot was in orders. The monastery had a bishop or priest for spiritual requirements. The abbot was an administrative, legal, social figure who went on circuit to maintain and extend rights, acted as guarantor in legal agreements, negotiated with kings, even sometimes apparently led a warband. In some of the more prosperous foundations, major offices in the church came into the hands of particular kin-groups. The practice probably increased security, and made the ties between ecclesiastical and secular nobility even closer.

By the tenth century the main language of the monastic schools was Irish. By now *scriba* is a very rare title in the annals: it has given way to *fer léigind* (man of learning), which probably in many cases denotes the head of the monastic school. Learned ecclesiastics in the pre-viking age usually (though certainly not always) wrote in Latin; now they usually wrote in Irish. Texts written in Latin must have been read by a very limited group of educated clerics, while texts written in Irish could appeal to a much wider audience, so it is not surprising to find that in this period the content of ecclesiastical learning has changed. The fusion of church and secular society that we have seen in abbatial succession is nowhere clearer than in the literature.

Of course some of the literature written by clerics in Irish was written primarily, perhaps solely, for themselves, not for a lay audience. The metre of the lyric poetry suggests that it was written by churchmen, by men familiar with the rhymed syllabic metres of Hiberno-Latin hymns. Some of it is religious in content.

> Ísucán,
> alar lium im dísiurtán;
> cía beith cléirech co lín sét
> is bréc uile acht Ísucán.

(It is little Jesus who is nursed by me in my little hermitage. Though a cleric have great wealth, it is all deceitful save Jesukin.)[47]

This poem, so often (perhaps rather falsely) admired for its tenderness and charm, is, rather, in keeping with the religious feeling of the tenth century. Íte, who speaks, has pride in her lord, rich, generous, a lord on whom she may completely rely: 'my eternal fortune, he bestows and does not default'. He is better than all the princes' sons who come to her; she expects no advantage from them. She fosters a nobler babe, the king of heaven.

Some of the lyrics belong to the group known as 'nature' poetry. Here is one that David Greene describes as 'an extraordinarily ingenious little

---

[47] Gerard Murphy, *Early Irish lyrics* (Oxford, 1970), pp 26–7. There is a detailed analysis of this poem by E. G. Quin in *Camb. Med. Celt. Studies*, i (1981), pp 39–52. Quin regards the poem as 'for all practical purposes Old Irish'. He demonstrates that it is full of legal terms and that it is 'a far from simple poem' (p. 40).

poem ... the last word in wit and sophistication'. It has alliteration, internal rhyme, and end rhyme.

> Tánic sam slán sóer
> dia mbí clóen caill chíar;
> lingid ag seng snéid
> dia mbí réid rón rían.

(Summer's come, healthy, free, that bows down the dark wood; the slim, spry deer jumps and the seal's path is smooth.)[48]

At a very early period we can see Irish monks delighting in the created world. Now in the viking age they are doing it again with a new skill. The clerics who wrote these nature poems were joyously aware of the bird's song, the salmon's leap, the deer's cry, the wind in the branchy wood.[49]

Scholarly literature was also still being written with a clerical audience in mind. 'Saltair na Rann', dating from 985, a collection of poems which put biblical history, mainly Old Testament history, into verse, was probably enjoyed by learned clerics, by the sort of men who appreciated the skill that lay behind the metrical pattern and already knew the stories quite well. This poet sees the Old Testament narrative through Irish eyes, adding details of his own which make the stories fit the social and legal assumptions of his people;[50] he brings the ancestor of all the Gaels to graze flocks in Egypt, makes Adam fast against God to win forgiveness, or David demand legal sureties from Saul before he goes to fight Goliath. Thus the Bible narrative is given in an Irish rendering, but probably still a rendering for clerics.

Such men were keenly interested in the Irish past. Human history began when God created Adam, and the tradition (*senchus*) of pre-Christian Ireland had to be fitted in to God's time-scheme. That scheme scholars knew (and accepted literally) as it was recorded in the Old and New Testaments. Their own *scél nó shenchus*, what Carney calls 'ancient tradition in narrative form', 'fictionalised history', has much in common with some of the Old Testament. The story in the 'Lebar Gabála', the 'Book of the invasions of Ireland' in pre-Christian times, must, like some of the Old Testament history, have been a vernacular tradition before it was written down. It was

[48] Frank O'Connor and David Greene (ed. and trans.), *A golden treasury of Irish poetry* (London, 1967), p. 103.
[49] Donnchadh Ó Corráin argues that 'these are not the ingenuous products of the primary emotions and experiences of the hermit life, a spiritual autobiography in verse. Here, rather, religious life is seen through the conceits and tropes of cultivated and scholarly men writing to meet the needs and tastes of a cultured elite' ('Early Irish hermit poetry?' in Ó Corráin, Breatnach, & McCone, *Sages, saints, and storytellers*, pp 251–67). Even if they are poems of the scriptorium rather than the hazel grove, however, it is difficult to disagree that the world of nature was close and a source of joy to the clerical writers and their audience.
[50] This is discussed and these examples cited, by David Greene in 'The religious epic' in James Carney (ed.), *Early Irish poetry* (Cork, 1965), pp 79–83.

recorded in various versions, for the reference in Nennius[51] is different from the Irish account.

The clerics of the ninth and tenth centuries were busy accommodating native tradition to biblical history. For instance the death of the great hero Conchobar of Ulster is made to synchronise with the death of Christ. Conchobar had received a severe wound in battle, when the ball made of the brains of his enemy Mes Gegra lodged in his head. His doctors sewed up the wound, leaving the brain-ball in his head, and warned him to take life very quietly. So he lived gently for seven years. But at the time when Christ was crucified a great trembling came on the earth, and Conchobar asked his druid what monstrous deed was being done to cause such a phenomenon. The druid, with his sight, told the king that the Son of God was being crucified, and that he had been born on earth on the same day (though not in the same year) as Conchobar himself. Then Conchobar rushed out to attack the forest, crying, 'Thus would I avenge Christ', and with his fury the brain of Mes Gegra sprang from his head and he died of it. Our Irish historian regarded Conchobar's blood as his baptism. So Conchobar was fitted into the divine plan of Christian history.[52] The old gods were denied by the Christian scholar, but the heroes had a firm place in his mind and heart.

One of the main activities of the Irish 'historian' had for long been the preparation of genealogies. The Psalter of Cashel, a lost manuscript that seems to have been compiled about 900, and which can be partly reconstructed from the fifteenth-century Bodleian Library MS Laud Misc. 610,[53] contained genealogies fitted into a chronological sequence. The Laud MS gives parallel lists of the kings of Assyria, Judaea, and prehistoric Ireland, then a parallel list of Roman emperors, popes, and Irish kings, putting Tuathal Techtmar alongside the emperor Hadrian and Lóeguire mac Néill alongside the emperor Theodosius. The Books of Lecan and Ballymote ascribe to the Psalter of Cashel a Latin passage which F. J. Byrne suggests[54] may have come from the original compiler. Byrne translates: 'The foolish Irish nation, forgetful of its history, asserts the historicity of unheard-of or completely fabulous deeds, because it is careless about committing to writing any of its achievements. Therefore I shall commit to writing the genealogies of the Irish race.' It seems an unjust accusation. The scholars of the viking age (and of the earlier period as well) were keenly aware of their history. King-lists and genealogies were one aspect of it, though much of the material

---

[51] Theodore Mommsen (ed.), *Historia Britonum* (Berlin, 1894), p. 154 (§ 13).

[52] Kuno Meyer (ed. and trans.), *The death tales of the Ulster heroes* (Dublin, 1906), pp 4–10. Kenneth Jackson translates this in *A Celtic miscellany* (London, 1951), no. 8, and dates it '?ninth century'.

[53] Kuno Meyer (ed.), 'The Laud synchronisms' in *Z.C.P.*, ix (1913), pp 471–85. See also F.J. Byrne, *A thousand years of Irish script* (Oxford, 1979), pp 25–7.

[54] In his review of O'Brien, *Corpus geneal. Hib.*, in *Z.C.P.*, xxix (1962–4), p. 384. The passage is in O'Brien, op. cit., p. 192.

here is fabulous. The history of contemporary times was being recorded by the monastic annalists.[55]

Antiquarian tradition held an enormous attraction for erudite Irish clerics. It can be seen in the 'Sanas Cormaic',[56] an etymological glossary attributed to King Cormac, who died in 908. '*Catar*, the gospels *a quatuor libris*', and '*cingciges*, Whitsuntide, i.e. *quinquagesimus die a pascha*' are typical of some of its shorter and simpler entries. The man who wrote this glossary was definitely a cleric. He could write Latin, and he knew words of Greek and Hebrew. He was also familiar with the Scriptures. When he is commenting on *cruimther* ('priest') he can finish with a reference to Psalm 22: 6;[57] or he explains *crand-caingel* as *cranncliath*, 'a beam hurdle', 'the hurdle in the beam between laymen and clerics after the likeness of the veil of the temple'.[58] This is the sort of analogy that would only occur to someone with a classical education. He puts Irish 'history' into the context of biblical history, as in the reference to Cáel Cáenbrethach, who was brehon at the time of the expulsion of the sons of Míl,[59] and who went to the children of Israel to learn Hebrew; or he makes Cú Chulainn prophesy the advent of Christ. This is typical of the clerical learning we have already seen.

But there are comparatively few ecclesiastical allusions in Cormac's Glossary. The compiler is steeped in secular native tradition and in myth, for there are allusions to Dian Cécht, the god of health, to Banba, Macha, Bríg, the Dagda, and others. He quotes stories about the heroes: about well-known heroes such as Cú Chulainn and Conchobar, as well as less famous ones like Mol, doorkeeper of Tara. There are illuminating references to legal practices and customs: here the notes on agricultural customs, about which we know little, are especially valuable.[60] Topography and legends about places (*dindshenchas*) frequently come in: most interesting are the references to *Coire Breccáin*, the whirlpool off the north coast of Ireland which got its name from Breccán, son of Niall of the Nine Hostages, who was swallowed up here

---

[55] See below, ch. XIX.

[56] Ed. Kuno Meyer, *Anecdota from Irish manuscripts*, iv (Halle, 1912); trans. John O'Donovan, ed. Whitley Stokes (Calcutta, 1868). Paul Russell offers 'a very brief survey' of Cormac's and other Irish glossaries in 'The sounds of a silence: the growth of Cormac's Glossary' in *Camb. Med. Celt. Stud.*, xv (1988), pp 1–30.

[57] No. 211: 'I am a worm (*cruim*) and no man.'

[58] We know some Irish churches were arranged like this from the description at the end of Cogitosus's 'Vita Brigitae'. See the recent translations by S. Connolly and J.-M. Picard in *R.S.A.I. Jn.*, cxvii (1987), pp 11–27: 25–6.

[59] The immediate predecessors of the Goídil in Ireland.

[60] E.g. Meyer, *Sanas Cormaic*, p. 82, on *gelistar*, where the land round the ford is fenced in for the pasturage of cattle and there is common passage to it; or p. 65, *etarce*, the furrow between two ridges, which may imply some kind of open-field farming; or p. 84, on *gall*, 'They are not neighbours until [their] properties are [provided] with boundaries [?] of pillar-stones'; or p. 141, *rot* 'a great path ... Every neighbour whose land reaches it is bound to cleanse it'. See now Fergus Kelly, *Early Irish farming* (Dublin, 1988), which gives a very full picture of agriculture, based mainly on the laws.

with his fifty trading curraghs; or to the Irish settlements in Britain, Dinn Tradui, Glastonbury of the Gael, and Dinn map Lethain[61] in the lands of the Cornish Britons. There are constant references to the *filid*, to their grades and their special speech, and anecdotes about particularly distinguished ones such as Senchán Torpéist and Ferches.[62] There is the occasional grammatical jingle which shows that correct Irish was very important and that the compiler took an interest in archaic aspects of the language.[63] There are references to Irish texts that a student would be expected to know: for example, *Lege Gabála Érend si vis plenius scire* (read the 'Book of Invasions' if you want fuller knowledge). The glossary is a mine of information, which badly needs further discussion and comment.

Probably most fascinating of all are the references to pagan practices: to the driving of cattle at Beltaine between the two great fires that druids had made with incantations, in order to protect the beasts against disease; to the aspen rod that was kept in heathen cemeteries and used for cursing; to the ritual that the poet followed that he might see and prophesy (which Patrick is said to have abolished). This Christian cleric knew Irish *senchas* from the beginning, pagan, heroic, and Christian, gods and heroes, druids and *filid* and saints. It was proper for a cleric to have amassed such knowledge, and to write about it.

The *immrama* or voyage tales are another kind of literature in which Christian and secular elements become inextricably interwoven, Here native traditions of the Other World, of an island or under the sea, become fused with the Christian idea of Paradise. Classical tales also contribute. If we go back into the pre-viking period we can see that this fusion had already begun. The pre-viking 'Voyage of Bran'[64] was written by a monk in a Christian society,[65] but the secular elements are clear to see: Bran is invited to the Other World by a fairy woman; he meets the sea god Manannán Mac Lir; the goal is the Land of Women.

There were stories circulating about voyaging saints in the pre-viking age.[66] But *immrama* continue vigorously in the viking age. This is the period, in the ninth or tenth century, when the Latin 'Navigatio Brendani' was composed,[67] a text that is undoubtedly meant for clerics. It is structured round the monastic day and the monastic year, the voyage is a *peregrinatio*

[61] Presumably the Uí Liatháin who belonged to the central south coast of Ireland.

[62] See Meyer, p. 102, for what was surely meant as a funny story.

[63] E.g. on the three words for 'stone', masculine, feminine, and neuter. The neuter gender was obsolete by the tenth century.

[64] Kuno Meyer and Alfred Nutt (ed. and trans.), *The voyage of Bran* (2 vols, London, 1895, 1897). There is a more recent edition of the 'Voyage of Bran', by Séamus Mac Mathúna: *Immram Brain: Bran's journey to the Land of Women* (Tübingen, 1985).

[65] Carney, *Studies in Ir. lit.*, p. 280.

[66] Cormac's voyages in Adomnán's 'Life of Columba'. See also H. P. A. Oskamp, *The voyage of Máel Dúin* (Groningen, 1970), pp 36–8.

[67] Carl Selmer (ed. and trans.), *Navigatio Sancti Brendani abbatis* (Indiana, 1959).

*pro Christo* in search of the Land of Promise of the saints, Brendan and his company meet holy ascetics, they see Judas crouched on a rock in brief respite from his eternal torment. The Irish 'Immram curaig Máele Dúin' is probably ninth-century. This also was written by a cleric, and draws on Christian, Irish secular, and probably classical material, and on fantasy. The ecclesiastical and secular traditions here converge, and the author 'has lost touch both with the magic-pagan character behind several of the secular motifs, and with the holy ideals of asceticism behind the *peregrinatio*',[68] so that he produces a new and original work of art.

We see the combination of religious and secular elements probably nowhere better than in the saints' Lives. The 'Vita Tripartita'[69] of Patrick was written at the very end of the ninth century. It was to be preached on the saint's festival, and its message was meant for the lay public. It starts with a text: 'The people that walked in darkness have seen a great light.' The beginning is entirely conventional. There is a note on the prophet Isaiah. Then the preacher takes the literal, historical interpretation of the text, and discusses its *persona*, *tempus*, and *locus*. After that he turns to the spiritual, allegorical interpretation, portraying the *umbra mortis* as the darkness and gloom of heathendom in which the Irish walked aforetimes, and the 'great light' as the light of Christ. The apostles were as lamps lighted by Christ. So we come to Patrick.

The tone of the rest of the Life is lively and aggressive. Patrick is shown not only as a great miracle-worker; he has to be recognised as a greater saint than any other, able to worst even the angel and win better and better terms from a reluctant God. There are parts of this Life that are a travesty of Christian teaching. The author has to prove Patrick's power. The saint fasts against God and the angel offers him the power to rescue seven people from hell every Saturday until Doom, but Patrick demands twelve. The angel promises that no Saxons shall dwell in Ireland. He offers relief for the souls who sing Patrick's hymn, but Patrick protests that it is long and difficult, and the angel agrees that the passage from *Christus illum* to the end will suffice. The angel offers Patrick a soul from hell for every hair on his chasuble, but Patrick protests: 'Which of the other saints who labour for God will not bring that into heaven?' and the angel promises him seven persons per hair. So the bargaining goes on, until at last Patrick obtains that he is to be judge of the men and women of Ireland at Doomsday. This sermon must have been entertaining listening, and an unsophisticated audience might have been cheering on its saint, but such a passage shows how confused was the morality behind the saint's popular power.

[68] Oskamp, op. cit., p. 75.
[69] *Trip. life*, ed. Stokes, pt ii, and *Trip. life*, ed. Mulchrone. The dating of the 'Tripartite Life' is not secure: see 'The dating of the Tripartite Life of St Patrick' in Dumville, *St Patrick*, pp 255–8.

During the tenth and early eleventh century the church regained some of its wealth and authority. The church of Armagh in particular gained a position of preeminence. But the separateness of the church was diminished, her abbots sometimes married and not in orders. The churches were attacked more readily and themselves sometimes went to war. Spiritual life was by no means dead—the nature poetry and a text such as the 'Vision of Adomnán' prove this—but it must sometimes have gone on in monasteries where most of the clergy were very well integrated with secular life. There was enthusiasm for scholarship, and the specialist in Irish 'history' and antiquities commanded high prestige. Whereas in the sixth century there had been a great void between the cleric and the *filid*, by the eleventh century the gap had almost disappeared. The close contact between Latin and vernacular learning was a source of strength to the church. Without it the voyages and visions and much of the historical material of early Ireland would never have been written. But the secularisation of the church that resulted led to a need for reform. That was to come in the later eleventh and twelfth centuries.[70]

[70] In his paper 'Some problems concerning the organization of the church in early medieval Ireland' in *Peritia*, iii (1984), pp 230–70, Richard Sharpe emphasises continuity rather than a pattern of decline and reform: 'instead of a series of reactions—decline and reform, decline and reform—one should look out for the element of continuity. During this whole period there is quiet and continuous development' (p. 267). Colmán Etchingham also emphasises continuity: 'there are many pointers, not to major change and reaction, but to a large measure of continuity' (*Church organisation*, p. 456).

CHAPTER XVIII

# Church and politics,
# c.750–c.1100

F. J. BYRNE

WHILE copying the text of the gospel of Mark into the manuscript known
as the Book of Armagh (T.C.D. MS 58) at Armagh, a young scribe added in
the margin the name 'Kellakh'. He used the fanciful mixture of Greek and
Latin script that he had employed previously, when completing the gospel of
Matthew 'in feria Matthi'—on the evangelist's own feast-day. He used this
decorative script again to record his own name, Ferdomnach, and that of
Torbach, the heir of Patrick at whose dictate he and his two companions
were compiling a book that was to contain the New Testament, the Life of
St Martin, and the Epistles of Patrick himself (St Martin's nephew, as some
thought, and certainly his emulator), and all the Patrick-related documents
that the diligence of his coarbs ('successors') had collected through the centuries: the Book of the Angel, which laid down the privileges that Armagh
propagandists claimed for this apostolic see of the Irish, the city of Armagh;
the canons; the hagiographical writings, then a century old, of Muirchú from
Ulster and Tírechán from Connacht, together with some anecdotes written
in Irish as well as in Latin. Some scraps of information had been gleaned in
Ferdomnach's time from Constans, the anchorite of Eóinis on Lough Erne
(now deserted), a cousin of Nuadu, one of the seniors of Armagh, which
Constans had picked up on his journeys in Gaul. Certainly the most important texts were those written by Patrick himself, and these Torbach may have
brought with him from Louth, the monastery of Mochta, Patrick's own
British priest and disciple, and more recently of the visionary Fursu, who
had travelled to England and further to northern Francia, where his foundation at Péronne in Picardy still venerated the cult of Patrick and welcomed
Irish pilgrims.[1]

---

[1] See Charles Doherty, 'The cult of St Patrick and the politics of Armagh in the seventh
century' in Jean-Michel Picard (ed.), *Ireland and northern France AD 600–850* (Dublin, 1991),
pp 53–94; Michael Richter, *Ireland and her neighbours in the seventh century* (Dublin, 1999),
pp 126–33.

Ferdomnach wrote the name of Cellach, probably the abbot of Iona who had fled from the murdering pagans. Cellach had sought refuge in Ireland in these last days, when, according to the annals, 'pestilence stalked the land and the moon had turned to blood'. If his humiliation was the cause of some grim satisfaction at Armagh, whose primacy had been threatened by Iona's rival claims, the religiously minded in the community had little reason to feel complacent. Their own abbot had just met a sudden if unexplained death: he was Condmach son of Dub dá Leithe the son of Sínach—'the son succeeding his father', one of the signs of Doom as foretold by the legendary prophet Bec mac Dé—after a generation of violence in which abbots, some not in sacerdotal orders, were seeking to replace the bishop of Armagh as effective heirs of Patrick. The high-king Áed mac Néill once again proclaimed the Law of Patrick throughout Ireland as his uncle Áed Allán had done many years before, in 734, after his meeting with Cathal mac Finguine, king of Cashel, at Terryglass. Armagh's supremacy seemed secure, with royal support at home and the destruction of Iona.

The reign of the high-king Áed Oirdnide mac Néill from 797 to 819 marked a significant step in the advance of the Cenél nEogain to power in the North, and hegemony over a large segment of Ireland. Its course represents a continuum with the previous history of the Uí Néill, rather than any response to viking raids. Áed became high-king in 797 no less than fifty-four years after the death of his uncle, Áed Allán. He had succeeded his first cousin Máel Dúin mac Áedo Alláin as king of Ailech in 788. Máel Dúin himself had displaced Domnall mac Áeda Muindeirg of Cenél Conaill in 787 and Domnall attempted to recover the kingship but was defeated by Áed at the battle of Cloitech (Clady on the southern bank of the River Finn) in 789. Domnall is still styled *rí ind Fochlai*, 'king of the North', at his obit in 804, which shows that his dynasty were still very much in competition with the Cenél nEogain for the title. Both the Cenél Conaill and the Clann Cholmáin of Mide, represented by the high-king Donnchad mac Domnaill who died in 797, had supported the Columban church (Donnchad and Bressal, abbot of Iona, had proclaimed the Law of Colum Cille in 778). Áed Allán was probably responsible for the proclamation of the Law of Patrick in conjunction with the king of Cashel in 737; though the annals do not specifically associate this proclamation with the meeting between the two kings at Terryglass that year, it seems a fair inference. Áed Allán too had welded together the various sub-kingdoms of the Airgialla into a federation under Uí Néill overlordship on the terms set out in the 'Charter poem':[2] when he was killed by the first of the Clann Cholmáin high-kings Domnall mac Murchada at Seredmag in 743 kings of three major branches of the Airgialla, the Airthir of Armagh, the Uí Chremthainn to the west of them, and the Uí Thuirtri to the north, fell

[2] Máirín O Daly, 'A poem on the Airgialla' in *Ériu*, xvi (1952), pp 179–88.

with him (the Mugdorna to the south seem to have avoided falling under the hegemony of the Cenél nEogain until the eleventh century and their fortunes remained linked with those of their overlords, the Síl nÁedo Sláine of Brega). In his turn Áed Oirdnide was supported by Cathal mac Echdach, king of Uí Chremthainn, and the leaders of the two other main branches of that dynasty who were killed in 791 when Áed attacked Donnchad at Tailtiu, the site of the óenach of the kings of Tara, but was overthrown and his forces routed to Carn Maic Caírthinn, which has not been identified. The annals call him not Áed 'the Ordained', but Áed Ingor ('the Unfilial'), and D. A. Binchy thought that this referred to his conduct towards the high-king. Such an epithet rather implies unfilial behaviour towards his father, the notoriously religious Niall Frossach, rather than political opposition to a very distant relative whose father had killed his uncle Áed Allán. It is true that Donnchad was his father-in-law: his wife Euginis ingen Donnchada, 'queen of the king of Tara', died in 802. But Áed lost no time in killing Donnchad's brothers at the battle of Druim Ríg immediately after Donnchad's death. The battle of Seredmag had not been forgotten or forgiven in 797 nor indeed as late as 915, as verses in the annals attest.[3] The same annals ominously record after the battle: 'The devastation of Mide by Áed mac Néill and the beginning of his reign.'

The battle of Druim Ríg took place beside Dunshaughlin in the Síl nÁedo Sláine kingdom of Southern Brega. The late high-king had pursued a consistent war (significantly termed *cocad* in the annals) against the northern branches of that dynasty, which itself was notoriously riven by internal feuds, the *fingal Síl Áedo Sláine* or 'kinslaying of the Seed of Áed Slaine', the *parricidium* that Adomnán had foretold a century earlier would result in their loss of the high-kingship.[4] Áed was able to ally himself with the Knowth branch, who would certainly have supported his championship of Armagh's claims to primacy. They had been foiled in their attempt to install Airechtach ua Fáeláin of the Uí Bressail of Airthir as coarb of Patrick in 759, though he was briefly to succeed another Airthir abbot, Dub dá Leithe mac Sínaig of the Uí Echdach, from 793 to 794.

The Clann Cholmáin high-king from Mide, Domnall who had killed and displaced Áed Allán in 743, had proclaimed the Law of Colum Cille in Ireland in 753, and his son Donnchad did the same in 778, and while the Law of Patrick had been proclaimed again in 767, during the reign of Niall Frossach, father of the present high-king, Niall himself had retired to Iona,

---

[3] See A.U. 797 and 915; the regnal list in *The Book of Leinster*, ed. Robert Atkinson (facsmile, Dublin, 1880), 25b wrongly states that the high-king Donnchad was himself slain at Druim Ríg; cf. *Bk Leinster*, i, 97. The same list has a somewhat similar error concerning the circumstances of Áed's own death in 819.

[4] Adomnán's 'Vita Columbae', I, 14. The warning is put in the mouth of Colum Cille, but proved truly prophetic, since the Síl nÁedo Sláine effectively lost their hegemony over the Southern Uí Néill within a generation of Adomnán's death.

not to Armagh, to spend the last seven years of his life; the Life of Samthann of Clonbroney, whose staff had been made into a relic by him, shows that the nuns of the monastery ignored its foundation by Patrick and had connections with Iona. Munster had broken away from allegiance to Patrick when the Law of Ailbe of Emly, the central cult-site of the Eóganacht dynasties, was proclaimed there in 782 (admittedly at a time when the kingship of the province was claimed by Máel Dúin mac Áedo of the western kingdom of Loch Léin, a region over which not even the most assiduous of Armagh's research scholars had been able to provide convincing evidence for any cult of Patrick), but evidently with the connivance of Dúngalach mac Fáelguso, king of the Eóganacht of Cashel. At this date the early Life of Ailbe was composed. Now once again this pre-Patrician saint (or Christianised pagan deity) had been exalted with the formal 'ordination' of Artrí, son of Cathal mac Finguine, as king over Munster in 793, a year in which Armagh's moral authority was at a low ebb.

It was in 793 that Dub dá Leithe mac Sínaig, progenitor of a family that was in later years to exercise a monopoly over the abbacy of Armagh, had died, having held the abbacy for twenty years or more. In that year too the bishop, Fóendelach, was 'violated' by Gormgal mac Dindnotaig, abbot of Clones, supported by the Uí Chemthainn who invaded and ravaged the city with the loss of at least one life. Fóendelach was received again into Armagh but died 'a sudden death' two years later, while yet a third claimant, the priest Airechtach ua Fáeláin, who had failed to win office thirty-five years before, is given the title abbot in his obit at 794. Airechtach is accorded a year in the primacy in the official list of the heirs of Patrick preserved in the diptychs on the altar of Armagh, and Fóendelach three. The annotations to the earliest copy of this list, in the twelfth-century Book of Leinster, say that Fóendelach fell in a conflict at Ros Bodba, at the hands of Dub dá Leithe, who was supported by 'kings from the north'. This is not in accordance with the chronology of the annals, but may reflect an earlier violent expulsion combined with a rumour that Fóendelach's death owed something to Dub dá Leithe's son and successor Condmach. Condmach, at any rate, was supported by the Cenél nEógain in the person of Áed Oirdnide mac Néill, who became high-king in 797, while Gormgal is expressly excluded from the record as one of 'the three *airchinnig* who seized the abbacy by force and who are not commemorated at mass'. The two others are Eógan Mainistrech, who was installed by Áed mac Néill's son Niall Caille at the battle of Leth Cam in 827, and the colourful Fland Roí mac Cummascaig who 'yelled out of the chariot' at the hounds. Since Dub dá Leithe's predecessor, Cú Dínaisc mac Conássaig, died in 791, but is accorded a term of office of only four (or seven) years in the list, it is possible that he too had been ousted by Dub dá Leithe as early as 772 or 775. The first certain records of Dub dá Leithe and his son Condmach actually holding office occur in the annals for 783 and 804 respectively. Dub dá Leithe belonged to the Airthir sept of Uí Echdach. The more aristocratic Fland Roí, son and grandson of Uí Bresail kings of Airthir (his father Cummascach mac Conchobair Machae had fallen at the side of Áed Allán at the battle of Seredmag beside Kells in 743) may, however, have set his hounds on one of the claimants from western Airgialla who did not enjoy the favour of the kings of the North, perhaps Cú Dínaisc or Gormgal. Neither his activities nor his death are recorded in the annals.

In Connacht too, now emerging as a united province of the Three Connachta, the Law of Patrick was rivalled by those of Brendan of Clonfert, Commán and Áedán of Roscommon, and most threateningly by that of Ciarán of Clonmacnoise. The ambitions of Clonmacnoise had been denounced more than a hundred years earlier by the Armagh propagandist, Bishop Tírechán, whose account of Patrick's missionary journeys was transcribed by Ferdomnach into the Book of Armagh—not, we may be sure, in a merely antiquarian spirit, but to be supplemented by further *notitiae* of Armagh's claims to properties, churches, and ecclesiastical jurisdiction in the west.[5] It was Tipraite mac Taidg who established the supremacy of the Uí Briúin dynasty of Mag nAí over the other Connachta, and on his accession to sole power in 783 he and Dub dá Leithe had proclaimed the Law of Patrick at the ancient royal site of Cruachain. He was succeeded by his cousin's son Muirgius mac Tommaltaig, whose reign from 789 to 815 briefly made the western province a force to be reckoned with, and who established a dynasty that was to hold the kingship of Connacht in an almost unbroken line until the thirteenth century. Gormgal mac Dindnotaig travelled to Connacht in 799 to proclaim the Law again, but as his own claim to primacy was challenged in Armagh itself, the efficacy of this action must remain dubious. In the fateful year 793 Muirgius and Aildobur, abbot of Roscommon, proclaimed the Law of Commán over the Three Connachta.

Clonmacnoise had shown no timidity in reinforcing its spiritual claims by secular means. The author of the Old Irish 'Tripartite Life' echoes Tírechán's denunciations in even more forcible terms by the use of the verb *for-cuirethar* 'rape' in describing some of Ciarán's conquests.[6] In 760 the monastery had raised a fighting force to attack the border church of Birr in Munster, for causes that are unknown to us, and in 764 there was a bloody battle with the great Columban church of Durrow. As in this affray Diarmait

---

[5] Law of Brendan 744; Laws of Commán and Áedán in 772, 780, 793; Law of Ciarán in 744, 775, 788. The Book of Armagh is the sole surviving manuscript of Tírechán's text, though considerable elements of it were incorporated into the later Latin and Irish Lives of Patrick, most notably the Tripartite Life.

[6] The significance of this usage was pointed out by MacNeill (see *Saint Patrick* (2nd ed., Dublin, 1964), p. 168); it is not brought out in *Trip. life*, ed. Stokes.

mac Domnaill fell and Bresal mac Murchada is named as leader of the victorious Clonmacnoise host, it is possible that the matter at issue was the burial of the high-king Domnall mac Murchada at Durrow the previous year: besides proclaiming the Law of Colum Cille he had retired at least twice during his career to religious retirement in that monastery, and the battle may have been fought between his son and his uncle.[7]

These were to be the first of a series of unedifying ecclesiastical battles that straddle the pages of the Irish annals over a period of nearly a hundred years bisected by the first ravages of the pagan vikings. The clash between Cork and Clonfert recorded in the annals at 807 may seem more surprising than most because of the distance between the two churches. But Clonfert, though situated in Connacht, was the chief church of Saint Brendan, patron of the Ciarraige, and one to which the Munster annals, sparse as they are for this period, devote more than usual attention (no doubt because they derive from Lismore, itself a church of the Ciarraige saint Mo-Chutu), so the battle, wherever it took place, most probably concerned a dispute over jurisdiction in west Munster, and may well have been connected with the revolt of the Ciarraige against their Loch Léin overlords in 803. In 828 the community of Cork were again involved in what the Annals of Inisfallen describe as a *baccrad* or 'threat' in the territory of Múscraige Mittine, where fell Éladach mac Dúnlainge and 170 others. Undeterred, they again assembled the Uí Echach Muman and the Corco Loígde for an expedition that proved equally unsuccessful, losing 200 men. The abbot at the time was Dúnlaing mac Cathasaig, and both he and Éladach were almost certainly princes of the Uí Echach. In the same year Coirpre mac Cathail, king of Uí Chennselaig, led an army from the monastery of Taghmon to defeat a force of vikings. But his father Cathal mac Dúnlainge had led the same community in battle against Ferns in 817, slaying 400, and died in 819 as king of Uí Chennselaig and *secnap* ('vice-abbot') of the conquered monastery. This was possibly the same Cathal who, as *oeconomus*, had engaged the abbot Fiannachtach in battle as early as 783. It is apparent that from the eighth century the office of *oeconomus* in major churches had often fallen into the hands of secular dynasts or of their clerical relations, and that this position was often combined with that of *secnap* (also called *secundus abbas* or *tánaise abbad*), and a consequent claim to the abbatial succession.

Dub dá Leithe was not the first heir of Patrick to have been the son of another: Fer dá Chrích, the bishop whose succession had been unsuccessfully challenged on the field of battle by the priest Airechtach ua Fáeláin in 759, was son of Suibne, bishop from 715 to 730, and the bishop Congus, who as a

---

[7] A.U. 764: 'Bellum Argamain inter familiam Cluana moccu Nois 7 Dermaighi ubi ceciderunt Diarmait Dub m. Domnaill 7 Dighlach m. Duib Liss 7 .cc. uiri de familia Dermaige. Bresal m. Murchada uictor exstetit cum familia Cluana.' Ann. Tig. (764): 'Cathargain inter familiam Cluana mc. Nois 7 Durmuig ubi cecidit Diarmuit mac Domnuill.'

'scribe' was an authority on the law and the scriptures, had, when he died in 750, left behind a family, the 'fruit of Congus's pen' as one wit put it. But neither had so blatantly passed on their office to a son as Dub dá Leithe had. He was also the first heir of Patrick not to have held episcopal orders, as we learn from the obit in 794 of Affiath, bishop of Armagh but not head of that church. In Lismore the writer of the Annals of Inisfallen seems to darkly hint at the presage of Doom involved in Condmach's succession to his father's office in the cryptic entry for 794: 'Violation of the Rule of Lismore in the reign of Áedán Derg.' Áedán Derg ('the Red') might well be a hint at the less benevolent side of Áed Oirdnide ('the Ordained'), who, as we have seen, is called Áed Ingor ('the Unfilial') by the northern annalist in 791, when he revolted against his father-in-law, the high-king Donnchad, at Tailtiu (no doubt on the occasion of the annual *óenach*) and was put to an ignominious flight in which several of his Airgiallan vassals fell, including the king of Uí Chremthainn, Cathal mac Echdach. More ominously, the reign of Áedán Derg features in the prophecy of Bec mac Dé.

If the last days are full of dread—whether we learn of them from the gospels or Apocalypse, or from the less reputable prophecies of a half-pagan sixth-century Irish *vates*—they also herald the building of the New Jerusalem, the heavenly city. It is not clear whether Ferdomnach's reference to Cellach of Iona is sympathetic or condemnatory. When he came to write the text of the Book of Revelations into the Book of Armagh, however, Ferdomnach excelled himself in his depiction of the heavenly city with a whole page of decoration.[8] The Book of Armagh, unlike its famous contemporary, the Book of Kells (brought probably to Ireland in this very year), is modest in size and has no comparable full-scale coloured illumination. It is not an evangeliary, for display rather than use, as are the great codices of the Hiberno-Northumbrian school. It is nevertheless a sacred book, the charter of Patrick's heirs, the only surviving complete copy of the New Testament from early Ireland. As the 'Canóin Phátraic' it came to rank with Patrick's crosier, the Bachall Ísa, and St Patrick's Bell among the *vexilla* or insignia and battle-standards of Patrick's heirs, the physical presence and possession of which were essential to their authority (as St Malachy was to find in his struggle to obtain recognition in the twelfth century). The Book might have been contained in the *armarium* that Nuadu, bishop of Armagh, took with him on the occasion of his visit to enforce the Law over Connacht in 811. The Book is a jewel of calligraphy: here Ferdomnach raises the Irish cursive script (regarded as inferior to the great majuscule half-uncials of the gospel-books) to the level of a book-hand of great beauty and versatility. Nevertheless, as a practical work, he does not disdain to somewhat disfigure it with his jottings, the so-called 'Notulae', a draft index to a projected Life similar to

---

[8] I am indebted to Charles Doherty for this interpretation.

the 'Vita Tripartita'. The value of the Book of Armagh to the linguist and historian is immeasurably enhanced by the care with which Ferdomnach and his colleagues set down their copy, carefully noting with a marginal *Z* every crux they encountered in the text. But beside the script, which occasionally breaks out into quite arabesque flourishes at appropriate points, the Book has some exquisite pen-and-ink drawings. In this respect it resembles the St Gall Priscian, written about half-a-century later, probably at Castledermot in Kildare. The best-known of the drawings are those of the evangelist symbols at the head of each gospel. But the apocalyptic page of the New Jerusalem expresses a concept dear to the heart of Irish canon lawyers and monastic town-planners, who drew both on the Book of Revelations and on its Old Testament model in Ezekiel.

And a new city was built in 807. It was at Kells in Meath (*Cenondas*), a royal site in the possession of Armagh. According to some the name Cenondas (later Cenannas) was particularly applied to sites which were the residences of heirs to the kingship: it was at Kells in Meath, for instance, that Cormac mac Airt had lived before he could gain admittance to Tara and recognition as high-king. Was Kells for Cellach and his community to be a final halting-place on their heavenly journey? It would have been perfectly possible for them to have established residence at the already long-established Columban houses at Derry or Durrow. There may have been personal or political reasons behind such a refusal, perhaps a feeling that such a move would imply renunciation of their jurisdiction in Scotland. At any rate, a *nova civitas* was what Cellach felt the need to build, and, once completed, he resigned office in 814, to die the following year. The foundation marked the resolution of any remaining rivalry between the Columban and Patrician churches and the accord is commemorated in the inscription on one of the high crosses at Kells: CRVX PATRICII ET COLVMBAE. As the eleventh-century historian, Gilla Cóemáin mac Gilla Samthainne, put it in his poem 'Annálad anall ille' 'the granting of Kells without battle to musical Colum Cille', and if *cen chath* was put in merely as a rhyming cheville, it is nevertheless, given the circumstances, appropriate enough.[9] This verse is interpolated into the margin of the Annals of Ulster by a secondary hand at 804. There is no valid reason to accept this rather than 807 as the real date of the foundation of Kells. Máire Herbert has pointed out that the date 804 is inferred from the forty-one years that elapse in Gilla Cóemáin's poem between the death of Domnall Midi in 763 and the foundation of Kells.[10] But, of course, Gilla Cóemáin was himself using an archetype of our annals, and as Herbert noted, it is interesting that the date 804 is that of the assembly of Dún Cuair, an appropriate occasion for the 'synods' of the Uí Néill, Áed mac Néill, and

[9] 'Tabairt Cenandsa cen chath do Cholum Chille cheolach': see *Bk Leinster*, iii, 501.
[10] Herbert, *Iona, Kells, & Derry*, p. 69.

Condmach of Armagh to have discussed the grant of the site, prompted by the first raids on Iona in 795 and 802. Herbert also discussed plausible reasons why the previous high-king, Donnchad, might have favoured the grant before his death in 797, as a move against the Síl nÁedo Sláine in whose sphere of influence it lay. And the new high-king, Áed mac Néill, could have had a similar ulterior motive in granting away a site that Donnchad's dynasty of Clann Cholmáin might have found prestigious. It was, after all, at Seredmag beside Kells that his uncle Áed Allán had been killed by Donnchad's father in 743, and though that was long ago, its memory clearly rankled.[11] A more edifying motive might indeed be sought in the memory of that event: Cellach may have sought to sanctify a spot too closely associated with both the pagan and the recent past, and, by building a New City, establish the Columban community as not either favouring or appearing dependent upon either the Northern Uí Néill of Derry or the Southern Uí Néill at Durrow. An earlier abbot of Iona, Cilléne Droichthech (726–52), descended from a relatively obscure family of the Southern Uí Néill, had come to Ireland in 727 to make peace between the Cenél Conaill and Cenél nEógain.

The hypothesis that Columban clerics might have been planning a new city at Kells before Donnchad's death gains some support from an anecdote in the Tallaght Memorandum concerning the revered authority Colcu ua Duinechda (d. 796), author of the 'Scúap Crábaid', who hindered Diarmait, abbot of Iona (the title must on this theory be proleptic), and Blathmac (the monk who was martyred at Iona in 825) from celebrating mass because they had been polluted by their presence at the deathbed of a certain Cú Roí who, it has been suggested, may be the Cú Roí mac Óengusso, king of Lóegaire, who died in 797.[12] Dr Herbert is sceptical of Armagh's involvement in the grant of Kells, though she notes the mention in Tírechán of Áth dá Loarcc beside Cenondas.[13] But Tírechán does not mention sites without a reason, and the purpose behind his whole work is the extension of Armagh's claims

---

[11] See above, p. 658.

[12] Peter O'Dwyer, *Céli Dé: spiritual reform in Ireland 750–900* (Dublin, 1981), pp 50 ff, where the chronological difficulties regarding the proposed identification of this Colcu with Alcuin's correspondent (d. 794 according to Simeon of Durham, with an obit at 796 in the Frankish annals) and with Colcu ua Duinechda of Clonmacnoise (d. 796), alleged author of the 'Scúap Crábaid', are discussed. The duplicate obit at A.F.M. *s.a.*791 (= 794) is, I suggest, due to a desire to equate the obit with that given by Simeon of Durham, due perhaps to Colgan's identification of that other friend of Alcuin and Colcu, Joseph, with the abbot Ioseph ua Cerrnae of Clonmacnoise who also died in 794. Dorothy Whitelock suggests in *English historical documents*, i (Oxford, 1955), p. 84, that Colcu (who was almost certainly in Britain when Alcuin wrote to him in 790) was abbot of Inishbofin in Mayo, citing the obit of Blathmac *daltae Colggen* (foster-son or pupil of Colcu) abbot of that monastery given at A.U. 813 (= 814). This raises the further question as to whether the author of the Tallaght Memorandum (who was clearly writing at least a generation after Máel Ruain's floruit) may not have confused Blathmac of Inishboffin with the martyr of Iona.

[13] Herbert, *Iona, Kells, & Derry*, p. 70.

to all churches of ancient foundation.[14] This particular case forms part of a specific programme to incorporate the *paruchia* of the fifth-century bishop Caethiacus, who had founded churches in Mag nAí in Roscommon and among the Uí Ailello in Tirerill to the north of that region. Tírechán claims that Caethiacus was of the Uí Ailello but that his maternal kin was of the Corcu Sai: he used to celebrate Easter at their church of Domnach Sairigi beside Duleek, but Low Sunday at the church of his nun Cáemgella beside Kells.[15]

That Kells itself should have been a royal site affords a striking parallel to the apparently contemporaneous foundation of a safer inland metropolis for the Columban community in Scotland at Dunkeld. Dún Caillden was a secular fortress preserving the name of the ancient Caledonians of Agricola's campaigns in the first century. The death of Conall mac Taidg noted above in the annals for 807 is entered in the Annals of Inisfallen as well as in the Annals of Ulster (though corruptly as 'Congal' and without reference to his killer). He appears in the Scottish regnal lists with a reign of two years, following upon that of a Domnall, who allegedly had reigned for twenty-four, but who is not mentioned in the annals—unless he be identical with the rather oddly named Donn Corci 'rex Dail Riatai' whose obit occurs in 791. Nor do the annals give the obit of Conall mac Áedáin, to whom the lists attribute a reign of four years. They do, however, record a battle between Causantín and Conall in 789 (with a variant dating under 790): a battle between the Picts, in whch Conall mac Taidg escaped and Causantín was victor. 'Conaul filius Tarl' or 'filius Tang' also occurs in the Pictish king-list with a reign of five years (in list P but not in list Q). To Causantín is attributed the foundation of Dunkeld, but the transference there of the relics of Colum Cille is said to have occurred in the sixth year of the reign of Cináed mac Ailpín, that is to say in 849.[16]

Since the end of serious viking threats, there had been attempts to revive the role of Iona as head of a united Columban church in Ireland and Scotland. This had been briefly achieved in the person of Mugrón, abbot and bishop of Iona and coarb of Colum Cille in Ireland and Scotland from 978 till 980 or 981. His predecessor as abbot or erenagh of Iona, but not coarb of Colum Cille (the title that denoted headship of the Columban group of

---

[14] But Cathy Swift ('Tírechán's motives in compiling the *Collectanea*: an alternative interpretation' in *Ériu*, xlv (1994), pp 53–82) has suggested, with some plausibility, that his primary aim was an appeal to the Southern Uí Néill kings of Síl nAedo Sláine to assert their authority over Connacht; this, of course, is not in conflict with his interest in Kells and the churches of Mag nAí.

[15] Bieler, *Patrician texts*, p. 147, where the translation of *pasca secundo* is to be amended as above.

[16] See Marjorie O. Anderson, *Kings and kingship in early Scotland* (Edinburgh, 1988), pp 41, 91, and John Bannerman, '*Comarba Coluim Chille* and the relics of Columba' in *Innes Review*, xliv, no. 1 (spring 1993), pp 14–47.

churches), was Fiachra Ua hArtacáin, possibly a brother or cousin of the poet Cináed ua hArtacáin, whose royal patron Olaf Cuarán, king of Dublin, retired there to die a year after his signal defeat at the battle of Tara in 980. But the sudden appearance in the Isles of a new group of pagan Danes, the sons of Harald, had resulted in the martyrdom of his successor Máel Ciarán ua Maigne on Christmas Eve 986. Furthermore, just as Kells had been established in 807 as a New City for the Columban church in Ireland after the first viking destruction of Iona, so too the kings of the Dál Riata Scots, having moved east into the old Pictish region of Fortriu, had set up Dunkeld as the centre of a Scottish Columban church. Malcolm II may have had a vested interest in maintaining this 'national' institution: at any rate he married his daughter to Crínán, the abbot of Dunkeld. Crínán himself died a warrior's death, leading an army in 1045 to avenge his son's murder on MacBeth. Whether MacBeth had any special attachment to Iona we do not know; the statement in the Chronicle of the Picts and Scots that he was buried there has no such implications, for the same is said of most of the kings, including Malcolm II and even Duncan. In 1034, the year of Malcolm's death, Macnia Ua hUchtáin, *fer légind* of Kells and a relative of the current coarb of Colum Cille, Máel Muire Ua hUchtáin, abbot of Kells and Raphoe from 1025 to 1040, was drowned coming from Scotland, and one of the chief relics, the *culebad* or flabellum of Colum Cille, was lost with him. It must have been replaced, for it was brought south to Kells from Tír Conaill by Óengus Ua Domnalláin in 1090, together with other relics, a bell and two gospel books, and 140 ounces of silver. It must have been on this occasion that Cathbarr Ua Domnaill, king of Cenél Lugdach, and Domnall mac Robartaig, abbot of Kells, had the Cathach enshrined. Óengus Ua Domnalláin is found as coarb of the Culdee hermitage of Kells in a charter dated to between 1087 and 1094, by which time Domnall mac Robartaig had been replaced as abbot by Ferdomnach Ua Clucáin; the hermitage itself had been founded by a charter dated most probably between 1073 and 1080. Domnall mac Robartaig, whose family were to be hereditary keepers (*máer*) of the Cathach until the sixteenth century, died in retirement or exile from Kells in 1094, and his successor Ua Clucáin died in 1114; but contemporaneous with them was an abbot of Iona, Donnchad Mac meic Móenaig, who died in 1099, but who is not accorded the title of coarb of Colum Cille. That became the prerogative of the abbots of Kells, and remained so until the sweeping winds of the twelfth-century reform raised Kells to the status of a diocesan see and brought about a reorganisation of the Columban churches under Derry and its abbot Flaithbertach Ua Brolcháin.

It is not clear whether Robartach mac Ferdomnaig, the abbot of Kells and coarb of Colum Cille who died in 1057, would have supported a return to Iona: he may have been a son of Máel Sechnaill's appointee of 1008, and so committed to the Southern rather than the Northern Uí Néill. But there were tensions and even violence during or before his tenure of office. Muirchertach mac Loingsig Ua Maíl Sechlainn, styled 'coarb of Finnian and Colum Cille', fought a pitched battle against Dub dá Lethe, abbot of Armagh, at Martry (Martarthech, 'the house of relics' between Navan and Kells). Muirchertach had just succeeded Tuathal Ua Falloman, of the Clann Cholmáin Bic, as abbot of Clonard, a title he still held at his death in 1092; his father, Loingsech *sapiens*, died in 1042 as *fer légind* of that monastery (the family were distantly related to the kings of Mide, and he had killed Áed Ua Con Fhiacla, king of Tethba in 1043). His claim to be coarb of Colum Cille is unclear: was it based on his tenure of Kells or of Durrow? If the former, then he would have succeeded in 1040 on the death of Máel Muire Ua hUchtáin, which seems unlikely in view of the date of his death. In any case his claim did not survive his defeat by Dub dá Lethe, armed as he was with the Bachall Ísu, the crosier of St Patrick. Another violent incident occurred in 1076, during Domnall mac Robartaig's abbacy. Murchad mac Flainn Ua Maíl Sechlainn, 'king of Tara for three nights' the annals say (probably after his assassination in 1073 of the last significant king of Mide, his uncle Conchobar, 'despite the protection of the Bachall Ísu, and while the Crosier was in their presence'), vainly sought refuge in the round tower at Kells, where he was killed by the local sub-king of Gailenga, Mac meic Máeláin.

Three years earlier the abbot of Iona, apparently a Scot named Mac meic Báethéne, had been killed, not by Danes, but by the son of the previous abbot. Like several recorded abbots of Iona in the tenth and eleventh centuries, he is not styled coarb of Colum Cille. But his predecessor was 'coarb of Colum Cille in Ireland and Scotland'; he was Gilla Críst Ua Maíl Doraid, of the royal line of Cenél Conaill, who died in 1062. He may have been installed in Iona some years before he could assume the office of coarb on the death of Robartach, coincidentally in the very year that MacBeth was killed.

We can see why Conall mac Taidg's celibacy should have merited mention in his 807 obituary, but his successor Ailill mac Cormaic was, like him, given the title *sapiens* and also *iudex optimus*. This, and the obit of Condmach of the Connacht Uí Briúin in 806, are the first annalistic references to judges, and we may suspect that they were brehons as well as canon lawyers. Bishop Erc of Slane, Patrick's first convert after the famous lighting of the paschal fire, came to be regarded as pre-eminent in law; he was assigned the role of brehon in Patrick's legendary household, and Slane is regarded in the ninth-century Triads of Ireland as the seat of *Fénechus*, or brehon law. We do not know what, if any, was the relationship between the two families that controlled Slane[17] for the best part of a century, nor if either of them retained power there later, but they may well have been of the Mugdornai, a minor

---

[17] See Hughes, *Ch. in early Ir. soc.*, pp 162–3.

power in the area of central and south Monaghan and parts of northern Meath. By the eighth century, at any rate, they were counted as a constituent kingdom of the Airgialla, but later split into two entities, the northern and apparently larger (the Mugdorna Maigen, with its ecclesiastical centre of Donaghmoyne) coming with the rest of the Airgialla into the orbit of the Cenél nÉogain, while the southern (the Mugdorna Breg, with their church of Donaghmore) remained under the overlordship of the Síl nÁeda Sláine. The somewhat more plebeian Fir Rois, whose territory extended across to Ardee in Louth, may have formed a wedge between them, as they first appear as a separate kingdom in the ninth century. Colmán na mBretan features in the Book of Armagh Additamenta together with Éladach lord of Cremthainne, of the Síl nAedo Sláine.

Torbach of Louth was certainly of the Mugdornai, as was probably his scribe Ferdomnach. The first recorded *scriba* of Armagh was also named Ferdomnach; he died in 732, and was probably of the Uí moccu Uais. Ferdomnach, abbot of Clonmacnoise from 869 till 872, was also of the Mugdornai, while Conaing mac Ferdomnaig, abbot of Donaghpatrick, might have been a son of the scribe of the Book of Armagh; both died in the same year, 846. Both Torbach's father Gormán and his son Áeducán were abbots of Louth, but died on pilgrimage at Clonmacnoise, the former in 758 and the latter in 835. Later, when his descendants attained an unassailable position at Clonmacnoise, they were to claim a more aristocratic ancestry, from the Síl nÁeda Sláine of Brega: while false (at least patrilinearly), the new pedigree suggests that Torbach was indeed related to some of the abbots of Slane. From the tenth to the twelfth century strong literary and other connections were built up between Louth, Slane, Monasterboice, and Clonmanoise, which are reflected most clearly in the Book of the Dun Cow (*Leabhar na hUidhre*), one of whose scribes, Máel Muire mac Célechair, slain by marauders in 1106, was a direct descendant of Torbach.[18]

Louth itself was in the territory of the Conaille Muirtheimne, and therefore technically part of the province (the *cóiced* or 'fifth') of Ulster. But although we have a complete dossier of the abbots from the middle of the seventh century, we cannot tell if any of them came from the ruling dynasty of the Conaille: several of the abbesses of Killeevy were, while Colmán mac Ailella (d. 926), abbot of Clonard since 888 and of Clonmacnoise since 904, was of the Conaille, whose chief church was Drumiskin, itself controlled by a family which claimed descent from the fifth-century high-king Lóeguire mac Néill.[19] Colmán mac Ailella played an important part in the transmission of annalistic writing. It is during his abbacy of Clonmacnoise that the annals

[18] For the offices held by this family at Clonmacnoise see *N.H.I.*, ix, 246–50.
[19] For Dromiskin, see Donnchadh Ó Corráin, 'The early Irish churches: some aspects of organisation' in Ó Corráin, *Ir. antiquity*, pp 327–41: 330.

associated with that school become independent of the parent corpus. It has been suggested with some plausibility that Clonard received and then continued the basic Iona text that arrived in Ireland in or around 740. In that case Colmán mac Ailella is the obvious carrier of the tradition. Another copy certainly was continued either at Armagh itself or at a house with a lively interest in its affairs.

The involvement of monastic families with lay dynasties had been common for generations, but took many different forms. The desire of the Uí Chrítáin of Dromiskin to associate themselves with Lóeguire may have been no more than harmless snobbery—as most certainly was the claim of the Clonmacnoise family of Conn na mBocht to descent from Áed Sláine—but it may also have been part of a process of empire-building by the family of Trim, who also attempted to gain a footing at Clonard, the prestigious border monastery that had passed from Leinster control into that of the Southern Uí Néill in the last quarter of the eighth century. Rumann the poet (who was claimed to be to Ireland what Homer had been to the Greeks and Virgil to the Romans) was brother, father, and grandfather to abbots and bishops of Trim. He is termed *poeta optimus* at his obit in 747, a term which may reflect the Irish word *ollam*, and he is the first secular poet to be mentioned in the annals. Though an Irish metre was named after him, we have no certain remains of his works apart from a quatrain on the death of Fergal mac Máele Dúin at the battle of Allen in 722, and another on the battle of Kildalkey in 724, as well as what Greene and O'Connor have rightly called a 'marvellous poem' on a storm at sea, allegedly composed for the Norse of Dublin while he was drunk.[20] The quatrain on the death of Fergal is written in a variety of the metre named after Rumann. The metre of the poem on the storm is unique, and although Rumann cannot have written it for the Norse, the poem itself is almost certainly earlier than the eleventh century (the date assigned by the editor and translator), since it is quoted in the ninth-century metrical tracts. The saga of the battle of Allen also ascribes quatrains on that occasion to a survivor, Cú Brettan mac Congusso, described (perhaps anachronistically) as king of Fir Rois. Cú Brettan died in 740 and was of the Uí Ségáin, a branch of the Uí Chruinn of the Airthir who held the church of Dunleer and later were to provide hereditary priests to the church of Armagh. His son Donn Bó also appears in the saga, though depicted unhistorically as the son of a poor widow of Fir Rois who entertains the army with his poems and royal tales. His decapitated head laments the fallen king after the battle, but he is resuscitated and returned safely to his mother

[20] Pádraig Ó Riain (ed.), *Cath Almaine* (Dublin, 1978), p. 29; Radner, *Fragmentary annals of Ireland* (Dublin, 1978), p. 80; Gerard Murphy, *Early Irish metrics* (Dublin, 1961), p. 51; David Greene and Frank O'Connor (ed.), *A golden treasury of Irish poetry* (London, 1967), pp 126–9. That the word *optimus* may have a technical sense in Hiberno-Latin has been suggested to me by Professor Michael Richter.

through the miracles of Colum Cille. In fact, Donn Bó killed Congal mac Éicnig, king of Airthir, at Ráith Esclai near Dunleer in 748, and his own career ended dramatically enough at the battle of Emain Machae in 759, together with Dúngal mac Conaing of the Síl nÁedo Sláine, attempting to win the abbacy of Armagh for Airechtach the priest against the incumbent bishop Fer dá Chrích. In the quatrains cited in the Annals of Ulster on the battle, Donn Bó seems to be styled king, and may well have held the kingship of Fir Rois, though the annals do not specifically mention kings of that people before the ninth century. No doubt because of the sacerdotal position held by the Uí Chruinn at Armagh, elaborate pedigrees have been preserved in the later genealogical manuscripts. Neither these nor the annals, however, mention the most remarkable member of the family, Blathmac mac Con Brettan, whose poems to the Blessed Virgin lay undiscovered in a seventeenth-century manuscript till published by James Carney in what is arguably the most important contribution made this century to our knowledge of Old Irish literature.[21]

The commonest paradigm used by recent historians to account for the secular dominance over so many churches is that it served a useful function by which the 'discard segments' of dynasties could be compensated for loss of political power. But abbots were more likely to live to enjoy the company of their grandchildren than their politically successful cousins. They certainly were in a position to employ their wealth more profitably: most of the major works of art in the early Irish period are the product of their patronage. Such secularisation of the church had already produced an ascetic reaction in the movement which modern scholars have labelled the Culdee reform, associated particularly with the names of Máel Ruain of Tallaght (d. 792) and Dublittir of Finglas (d. 796). The term *céle Dé* or 'vassal of God', however, was older than this: it is a rendering of the common Latin monastic metaphor of *miles Christi* (the term actually used in the annalistic obit of Máel Ruain in A.U.), and adherents of this way of life were to be found within the most worldly of monasteries. Colcu, an anchorite attached to the church of Slane, wanted to join Máel Ruain's community because he had scruples about receiving food from a tainted source, but Máel Ruain rebuked him and sent

---

[21] James Carney (ed. and trans.), *The poems of Blathmac son of Cú Brettan* (Dublin, 1964). It is a curious coincidence that the importance of the Uí Chruinn and Uí Shégáin was discovered about the same time by Tomás Ó Fiaich: see his articles, 'Uí Cruinn: a lost Louth sept' in *Louth Arch. Soc. Jn.*, xii (1951), pp 105–12, and 'The church of Armagh under lay control' in *Seanchas Ardmhacha*, iii, pt 1 (1969), pp 75–127; in 'Cérbh é Niníne Éigeas' in *Seanchas Ardmhacha*, i (1961–2), pp 95–100, Ó Fiaich uncovered from the same genealogical sources in the Books of Lecan and Ballymote the identity of the legendary Ninníne Éces, author of the earliest vernacular hymn to St Patrick. He probably lived in the early eighth century and was affiliated by the genealogists to the Uí Echdach, who provided the later kings of Airthir and the Clann Sínaig abbots of Armagh; he was allegedly great-great-grandfather of the abbot and bishop Féthgna mac Nechtain (852–78).

him back, advising him to give the surplus to the poor.[22] Louth, though an 'old church', was in close touch with the reform movement. Echu ua Tuathail, abbot from 818 till his death in 822, was also a bishop and anchorite; he had consulted Dublittir of Finglas concerning the soul of a murdered layman of the Mugdornai, who, with his wife, had lived under his spiritual direction. Cuanu, abbot of the same church, is styled bishop and *sapiens* at his obit in 825; Máel Cánaig of Louth, who died in 815, was an anchorite of such reputation that the death of the high-king Áed in 819 was attributed to the power of his maledictions.

Óengus ua hOibléin of Clonenagh and Tallaght proved quite triumphalist in his celebration of the power of the great monastic cities, which the stricter *céli Dé* regarded as the corrupt 'old churches.' The community of Roscrea reacted to the reform of Elair (Hilarius), who had re-established the ascetic site of the founder saint Crónán on the island of Loch Cré (Monahincha), by claiming that the saint had quite deliberately abandoned that site out of charity, so that he could offer hospitality to the poor travellers on the royal road, the *Slige Dála*, where he built a great monastery which grew into the famous city of Roscrea (although his timorous monks begged him to stay in the security of his original cell).

The most blatant example of political control of the church, however, is demonstrated by the history of Kildare, control of which was essential to any king of Leinster. Fínsnechtae Cetharderc mac Cellaig had in 803 procured by treachery the killing of Óengus mac Mugróin, king of Uí Failgi, in whose territory the site of Kildare lay, but was expelled by the high-king Áed Oirdnide in 804. His return to the kingship of Leinster (mentioned in the annals for 806) is, significantly, followed by the assassination of the new king of Uí Failgi, Flaithniae mac Cináeda, at Rathangan. Fínsnechtae set the pattern for a monopoly of office in the church by his own family, the Uí Dúnchada, which was to last for over a century and a half. He had begun his royal career in 795 by burning his predecessor Bran mac Muiredaig, together with his wife Eithne, daughter of the high-king Donnchad Midi, at the church of Cell Cúile Dumai, near Stradbally. Bran had been allied with the kings of Uí Failgi, and his marriage had temporarily ended the century-old strife between the Uí Néill and the Laigin, to the extent that Donnchad had entered Leinster in 794 to aid the Laigin against a threatened attack from the newly 'ordained' Artrí, king of Cashel. The alliance had probably been negotiated at the synod of Tara presided over by the Culdee leader Dublittir in 780, following on a thorough devastation of all Leinster, including church property, by Donnchad. If Bran had been installed on that occasion, he was ousted by Ruaidrí mac Fáelán, Donnchad's enemy in 782; but on Ruaidrí's death in 785 he did succeed. The new alliance seems to have been the

---

[22] O'Dwyer, *Céli Dé*, p. 69.

occasion of a somewhat obscure poem on the history of the conflicts between the Uí Néill and Laigin composed by Orthanach ua Cáeláma Cuirrig, author of other historical poems, including the well-known 'Hail Brigit', and who was to be bishop of Kildare from 834 until his death in 840. The poem 'Masu de chlaind Echdach aird' ('If you are of the family of Echaid Ard') has complimentary references to Donnchad Midi and to the cult of Patrick which led James Carney to attribute it to another Orthanach, the abbot of Kilbrew south of Slane who died in 814. This might well be true, in which case the attribution in the sole manuscript, the Book of Leinster, would be due to confusion with the better-known bishop of Kildare; this would not mean that the Brigit poem, 'Slán seiss a Brigit co mbuaid', or the historical survey of Leinster history, 'A chóicid cain Cairpri chruaid', were not by the latter. But Carney must be correct in thinking that the stylistic peculiarities mark out all three as being by the same author. The difficulty he had with regard to the Kildare authorship of the first poem is not insuperable: Orthanach could well have been writing poetry before 797, the date of Donnchad's death (or indeed before the burning of Bran in 795), and still have become bishop of Kildare in 834; he may not even have been resident in Leinster at the time of composition, hence the apparent reference to his living north of that province. But the epithet of his grandfather shows that he was associated with the Curragh of Kildare, and the poem seems to present itself as a dialogue between two bards, one a spokesperson of the Uí Néill, who is a devotee of Patrick, and another, Orthanach himself, descendant of Echaid, that is to say a member of the Fothairt to whom Brigit and many of her successors at Kildare belonged. Donnchadh Ó Corráin has enumerated the following abbesses who belonged to various branches of the Fothairt: Muirenn ingen Suairt (d. 26 May 918) and Eithne ingen Suairt (d. 1016) of the Uí Chúlduib; Sebdann ingen Cuirc (d. 732) of the Fothairt Airbrech (the 'aue Cuirc' whose obit is recorded in 750 was no doubt her nephew or cousin, but we do not know what office he held); Coblaith ingen Dub Dúin (d. 916) and Muirenn ingen Flannacáin m. Colmáin (d. 964) of the Fothairt Fea.[23] Coblaith was probably a sister of the abbot Dubán (d. 906). To these we may add Tuilelaith ingen Uargalaig (d. 885) of the Uí Ercáin; her family from around Norragh (Forrach Pátraic) are blessed by Patrick (but without any reference to Kildare!) in the Tripartite Life in an episode anticipated already in the Book of Armagh Notulae. Accommodation between Armagh and Kildare is expressed in an addendum to the 'Liber Angueli' in the Book of Armagh made probably in the eighth century, and the 'Vita Quarta' of Patrick, based also on an eighth-century original, places the boundary between the two

---

[23] Ó Corráin, 'The early Irish churches', p. 328. But the Bodl. MS Rawl. B 502, f. 126a, seems to assign these to the Fothairt Maige Itha; cf. O'Brien, *Corpus geneal. Hib.*, p. 85.

*paruchiae* at the Lia Ailbe, the sacred standing stone of Brega at Clonalvey in County Meath.[24]

Fínsnechtae's savage reassertion of Leinster independence was followed in 798 by the installation of his brother as abbot of Kildare. This brother, Fáelán mac Cellaig, was to be succeeded in turn by two others, Muiredach (804–23) and Áed (823–8), while their sister Muirenn became abbess in 805. It was in Kildare that Fínsnechtae died peacefully—if painfully—of an anal fistula a year after he had been restored to power. Despite the frequency with which members of the Uí Dúnlainge held office as abbots between 639 and 967, only two abbesses can be identified as belonging to this dynasty: Condál ingen Murchado (773–97) probably, and Muirenn ingen Cellaig (805–31) certainly. It is likely that Muirenn ingen Congalaig (d. 979) was daughter of Congalach Cnogba. Her succession to office in 964 after the exceptionally long tenure of Muirenn ingen Flannacáin (918–64) coincided apparently with that of her brother-in-law Conchobar mac Find to the kingship of Uí Failge. Lann ingen meic Selbacháin (1016–47) might possibly have been of the Osraige. With the death of Dub Dil (1047–72), whose affiliations are unknown, the office of abbess becomes once again blatantly political, contested by the Uí Chennselaig, Uí Fáeláin, and Uí Failge dynasties.

One early Kildare abbot who was a rank outsider, Lóchéne Mend *sapiens*, of the Mugdornai, was murdered in 696, as was the penultimate abbot Cuilén mac Cellaig (922–55); his antecedents are unknown, though his predecessor, Flannacán ua Riacáin (905–22), *rígdamna Laigen*, was probably grandson of Riacán mac Echthigirn, king of Uí Chennselaig (876–93). Muiredach mac Fáeláin restored the abbacy to the Uí Dúnchada in 955, but was murdered in 966. Thereafter the office of abbot lapses, and the Uí Dúnchada shift their activities westwards to Cualu, soon ceasing to contend the kingship of Leinster. The office of bishop continues, and seems rarely to have been held by a Leinster dynast, except in the case of Áed Dub mac Colmáin at the very start of that dynasty's accession to power. The genealogist makes a point of stressing his virginity and learning. His brother Áed Find was father of the abbot Óengus (dates unknown) and ancestor of the Uí Máele Caích of Naas. A remote cousin, Brandub mac Fiachrach, was also abbot: he was of the same generation as Óengus but we do not know the order of their succession, as we have no annalistic dates for office-holders between the obit of Áed Dub in 639 and the obits of the abbess Gnáthnat and the abbot Lóchéne Mend in 690 and 696 respectively. It is perhaps worthy of note that both had northern connections: Gnáthnat was also abbess of Killeevy, and may have been of northern stock, while Lóchéne's Mend's obit in A.U. is accompanied by that of another member of the Mugdornai (Cumméne Mugdorne); Lóchéne was

[24] F. J. Byrne and Pádraig Francis, 'Two Lives of Saint Patrick: *Vita Secunda* and *Vita Quarta*' in *R.S.A.I. Jn.*, cxxiv (1994), pp 5–117.

assassinated, though the genealogists call him *optimus scriba Scottorum*. He and the anchorite Do-Dímmóc (d. 748), abbot of Clonard since 745, are the only two abbots of Kildare to have interrupted a straight succession of Uí Dúnlainge abbots from before 639 to 787; the antecedents of Eódus ua Dícolla (d. 798) are unknown. Bishop Tuathchar, the scribe, had a northern mother, from Uí Echach Cobo, and may have had a hand in the recension of one of the Lives of Monenna of Killeevy, but we do not know his father's name or origins. One bishop of the Uí Dúnchado was Suibne ua Fínsnechtai (875–81); his predecessors Robartach mac na Cerddae (870–5) and Lachtnán mac Mochthigirn (d. 875) were pluralists, Robartach being scribe and abbot of Killeigh (an Uí Failge church), while Lachtnán, whose episcopate lasted less than a year—unless (which is possible) they were two rival bishops, representing Uí Failgi and Uí Chennselaig interests—had been abbot of Ferns since 870. The obit of Bishop Scandal is given in A.U., together with that of Abbess Tuilelaith in 885 as the first entry for the year, which is also marked by a solar eclipse (16 June), and by the (peaceful!) death of Muiredach mac Brain, abbot since 870 and king of Leinster for a year. A.U. also records a 'secret murder' (*dunetathe*) in Kildare in the entry immediately following Muiredach's obit. In spite of the more sacral nature of the office, one bishop, Eóthigern, was murdered in 762 by the priest of Kildare. Lergus mac Cruinnén was killed in battle against the vikings in 888, when Flann Sinna was defeated and the king of Connacht and the abbot of Kildalkey were also slain. In the previous year Kildare had been plundered by the Norse: 280 prisoners were taken, including the *secnap* ('vice-abbot') Suibne mac Duib dá Boirenn.

The abbacy of Cellach mac Ailello (852–?865) apparently interrupted an Uí Dúnchado succession after the three brothers of Fínsnechtae Cetharderc mac Cellaig: Fáelán (798–804), Muiredach (804–23), and Áed (823–8) and their close relative Artrí mac Fáeláin (830–52), and before Cobthach mac Muiredaig (?a. 865–70) and Muiredach mac Brain (870–85). Cobthach was, however, *sapiens et doctor* according to the Fragmentary Annals and the Four Masters, which cite quatrains on his death that are also found in the Leabhar Breac. These mention his learning, while the Four Masters' quatrain on Muiredach mac Brain stresses his kingly rather than ecclesiastical character. Síadal mac Feradaig, of unknown ancestry, was abbot from 828 to 830. Cáenchomrac mac Siadail, *equonimus Cille Daro* (d. 835) may have been of Uí Bairrche. Cellach mac Ailello's name suggests Leinster dynastic affiliation too, but he was abbot of Iona since the pilgrimage of Indrechtach in or before the year of his 'martyrdom' in 854, and he died in Pictland in 865. He may well have been the author of the Pictish 'Chronicle', which was certainly composed at Abernethy and alleges that that church was founded by Dar Lugdach, immediate sucessor of Brigit. Indrechtach was grandson or descendant of a Fínsnechtae and had been abbot of Iona apparently since the

resignation of Diarmait daltae Daigri in 831. Was he too of the Uí Dúnchado? He visited Ireland in 849.[25] Does the abbacy of Cellach mac Ailello,
coinciding partly with that of the abbess Tuilelaith ingen Úargalaig (855–85),
and the bishopric of Áedgen Britt, 'scribe and anchorite' (840–64), indicate a
temporary 'reform' of the Kildare community? But Áedgen was allegedly a
centenarian when he died, so that he may have actually been in retirement
for some time, and have exercised office much earlier in his life.

The desire to avoid similar blatant dynastic control by the Cenél nÉogain
might explain the development at Armagh of hereditary clergy drawn from
the ranks of the local Airthir. Amidst this turmoil of the age, the achievement
of the Clann Sínaig abbots of Armagh is remarkable.

> Sirsan duit a chléirchén chochlaich
> as náridir nathraich
> t'étan friad bodbae ndochraid
> do chúl frisin chathraich
>
> Do leithne fri Locha Eirne
> éraim duit i Mide
> ocus do leithne alaile
> fri Glenn roglach Rige.
>
> (Well done, cowled little cleric,
> as modest as a snake!
> your face to your hateful foe,
> your back to the city.
>
> Your flank to the lakes of Erne
> as you course into Meath,
> and your other flank
> to strife-torn Glenree.)[26]

This 'generation of vipers', as St Bernard of Clairvaux was to unkindly call
them in his Life of St Malachy, needed the wisdom of the serpent. And even
the censorious Cistercian had to admit that they were men of learning. To
them we owe the Annals of Ulster; but the independent Clonmacnoise and
Munster annals amply demonstrate that they were able to command respect
throughout the country. They were not mere lay-abbots, robber barons who
had seized control of a monastery, a charge that might be levelled against
most of the Uí Dúnchada abbots of Kildare in the ninth and tenth centuries.
Rather, they saved their church from subordination to blatant political inter-

---

[25] Herbert's scepticism as to the Kildare connections of Cellach mac Ailello (*Iona, Kells, &
Derry*, p. 73, n. 24: 'since Cell Daro is not an unusual or unique compound' (!)) is, of course,
unwarranted.

[26] A.U., 759: the verses refer to the battle of Emain Macha in which the king of Ulster
defeated an attempt to oust the abbot Fer dá Chrích. Lough Erne and Glenree formed the
western and eastern boundaries of Airgialla.

ests. In this respect their record compares favourably with that of the papacy between 896 and 1046.

In the year 1001 Muirecán was deposed from the abbacy of Armagh by Máel Muire of the Clann Sínaig; he died in 1005. The 'Chronicon Scotorum' calls him *Muirecán Bocht*, which implies that he held the office of 'head of the poor', as did Cummascach Ua hErudáin, who also briefly interrupted the Clann Sínaig monopoly between 1060 and 1063; he was of the Airthir sept of Uí Bresail, whereas Muirecán was of the Ciannachta. Since he was acting as coarb in 993 he must have displaced Dub dá Lethe II, the uncle of Máel Muire. Dub dá Lethe died in 998 at the age of 83, and had become coarb of Colum Cille in 989; there is no statement that he had been deposed from his office at Armagh. He had deposed the previous coarb of Patrick, Muiredach mac Fergusa, in 965. Muiredach died in 966 and is said in a gloss in A.U. (and also in the Book of Leinster list of coarbs) to have been from Sleivegullion, so had probably been associated with Killevy. The Book of Leinster says further that he was from Glenn Airinn, which is unidentified. None of the Clann Sínaig had held office at Armagh since the death of Abbot Condmach son of Dub dá Lethe I in 807.

Despite the violent episodes that punctuated their rule, they were to prove acceptable mediators between the hostile Cenél nÉogain and Ulaid, and between the former and the Dál Cais of Munster. In fact, they created the most stable ecclesiastical dynasty, not merely in the north, but in the whole of Ireland. They appear to have instituted a new office, that of *fosairchinnech*, 'serving-' or 'resident erenagh', perhaps to replace that of *oeconomus*; and they kept this within their own close family. However, an *oeconomus* (probably of the Uí Nialláin) may be mentioned in the poem 'Uasal-epscop Érenn Áed'.

This was composed in 1042 for Bishop Áed Ua Forréid, who held office from 1032 till his death at the age of 74 in 1056.[27] It paints a pleasing, if complacent, picture of a clerical coterie. The learned, chaste, holy, and above all hospitable bishop Áed mac Cróngilla, descendant of Tigernach (son of Muiredach son of Éogan) and of Daui (great-grandson of Tigernach), the Moses of Cenél nÉogain, 'a nail through the heart of Antichrist':

> Tempul ecnai Érenn Áed
> táeb re légenn cretrai is chín
> ól 'na thig threbraid co trén
> mór ro lég do lebraib ríg.
>
> (The temple of Ireland's wisdom is Áed,
> addicted to sacred lore and books;

[27] Gerard Murphy, 'A poem in praise of Aodh Úa Foirréidh, bishop of Armagh (1032–1056)' in Sylvester O'Brien (ed.), *Measgra i gcuimhne Mhíchíl Uí Chléirigh* (Dublin, 1944), pp 140–64.

heavy drinking in his ornate house;
much has he read of the books of kings.)

The bishop turns his face to God and his back to womankind (but had not always been celibate, for the genealogies give us the pedigree of his great-grandson Gilla Ailbe). In a somewhat incongruous blend of the bard's own interests and those of his subject, Áed is declared to be the archbishop of Ireland who has studied deeply and whose talk is pleasant in drink; austerely devout, music is with him always as he prays, horns are drunk to him in splendid houses. Outside he has founded a great school; angels visit him behind the chancel screen, but the poet is allowed into his mansion, where malt is brewed. The poet has his eye on a particularly elaborate drinking-horn whose variegated hues are echoed in the alliteration of his verse, and he is not shy in demanding it as his reward. He also praises the youthful horse-loving abbot Amalgaid; the *oeconomus* Echnertach mac Cernaig, distributing beer from his vats to the poets; the stern Scotsman, Dubthach the confessor and anchorite; Cummascach Ua hErudáin, 'head of a thousand poor'; the aged lector Máel Pátraic Ua Bileóce, 'an angel who wrote a volume beside the cross'; the priest and preacher Doiligén mac Gilla Chríst of the Uí Chruinn of Dunleer. The guest-master, Mac Gilla Chiaráin Ua Brol-cháin, is mentioned and four honoured guests: the generous Muiredach, abbot of Dromiskin (perhaps identical with the abbot of Duleek who died in 1045); Flann from Monasterboice, 'Ireland's ultimate scholar'; Eochucán, who never imputes blame, who was a scribe, abbot of Slane and lector of Swords; and finally the mass-priest who appreciates good poetry, Ua Ruad-rach, abbot of Termonfeckin. Abbot Amalgaid's brother Dub dá Lethe is not mentioned: he had not yet achieved high office. The darker side of the picture is understandably not hinted at. Ua Bileóce's predecessor as lector, Máel Petair Ua hÁilecáin, had been murdered by the Fir Fernmaige in the very year in which this poem was recited. Dub dá Lethe, when abbot, would fight a pitched battle against an Ua Maíl Sechnaill pretender to the coarbship of Colum Cille in 1055, and be involved in a 'great war' in Armagh itself in 1060, when he was temporarily ousted from the abbacy by Cummascach Ua hErudáin.

Dub dá Lethe III became lector on Ua Bileóce's death in 1046, and abbot on his brother Amalgaid's death in 1049, whereupon Bishop Áed took up the lectorship. His grandmother belonged to the Cenél nEógain family of Ua Brolcháin. His grandfather Eochaid Ua Flannacáin (d. 1004) had also been lector of Armagh and a famous historian, and was nephew of Dub dá Lethe II, abbot of Armagh from 965 to 998 and coarb of Colum Cille from 989. Eochaid's son Máel Muire was abbot from 998 to 1020, and was succeeded by his two sons, Amalgaid and Dub dá Lethe. Dub dá Lethe was succeeded in turn by his nephews, Amalgaid's sons Máel Ísu (1064–91) and Domnall

(1091–1105). Máel Ísu's grandson, Cellach mac Áeda, was to institute the reform of the church of Armagh when he had himself ordained priest and consecrated bishop on his accession in 1105. His designated successor, Máel Máedóc (St Malachy) who completed the process, was not of the family, and met with opposition from Domnall's son Muirchertach, who died as abbot and 'coarb of Patrick' in 1134, and from Cellach's brother Niall, who clung to office until 1137, as well as from the Cenél mBinnig of Tullaghogue.

But Máel Máedóc himself was son of a lector of Armagh, Mugrón Ua Morgair (or Mongair, probably an anagram of Gormáin), and nephew of the 'Ulster bishop' Óengus Ua Gormáin, abbot of Bangor. His nomination by Cellach to succeed him as primate was canonically irregular, and like the reforming pope Gregory VII ninety years before, he had to resort to simony to acquire from Niall the primatial insignia: the Crosier of Jesus, the Bell of the Testament, and the 'Canon of Patrick' or Book of Armagh. When Niall resigned the abbacy, Malachy resigned the archbishopric, reverting to his former status as bishop of Down. They were succeeded by a candidate acceptable to traditionalists and reformers alike in the person of Gilla Meic Liac, the Columban abbot of Derry.

ON the other hand, family influence could be consistent with celibacy, as is shown by the succession at Iona, the majority of whose abbots came from the 'founder's kin' of Colum Cille himself, the Cenél Conaill. At Bangor two different trends are in evidence: abbots and *secnap*s or *oeconomi* of the Cruthin dynastic families, such as Cenn Fáelad ua Áedo Bricc (d. 705), Conall mac intSaír (d. 778) and his son Airmedach mac Conaill (d. 800), whose brother Fer dá Chrích was *secnap*, Robartach (d. 805), Máel Tuili mac Donngaile (d. 820), whose kinsman Máel Pátraic mac Céléne (d. 929) was to be *secnap* as well as *airchinnech* of Glenavy, Ferchar mac Congusso, great-nephew of Airmedach (d. 881), and the *secnap* Ultán mac Áedán (d. 782), alternate throughout the eighth and ninth centuries with abbots of unknown pedigree and apparent Culdee affiliations, such as Augistín (d. 780), Sírne (d. 791), Tómas (d. 794), Mac Óige (d. 802), and the scholar Máel Gaimrid (d. 839), while later abbots, such as Móenach mac Síadail (d. 921) and Céle Dabaill mac Scannail (d. 929), enjoyed a reputation of sanctity. Literary activity of a secular kind congenial to the tastes of aristocratic abbots seems attested for eighth-century Bangor by the texts associated with the lost manuscript, the 'Cín Dromma Snechtai'; Druim Snechtai itself (Drumsnat, County Monaghan), was in some sense a daughter-house of Bangor, founded by the west Munster saint Lugaid moccu Óchae, or Mo-Lua: it does not feature in the annalistic records, and seems to have disappeared, its place being taken by Mo-Lua's later foundation of Clonfertmulloe, on the southern slopes of Slievebloom among the Loíges of Leinster.

In the seventh century Bangor also had possessions in southern Leinster, in the Uí Bairrche kingdoms of Carlow and Wexford, but these too declined with the rise to power of the Uí Chennselaig in those areas. This loss was later compensated for by the foundation in 812 of Dísert Diarmata (Castledermot, County Kildare) by a representative of the Culdee tradition, Diarmait ua Áedo Róin (d. 825), nephew and grandson of kings of Ulster. His uncle, Fiachnae mac Áedo Róin, had restored the fortunes of the Ulaid during his reign from 750 to 789, had successfully intervened in the Armagh sucession dispute of 759, and had begun Dál Fiatach patronage of the Cruthin manstery of Bangor. In contrast to Diarmait's foundation of Castledermot, Down was occupied by his non-celibate cousin, Loingsech mac Fíachnai (d. 800), brother of the kings Eochaid (d. 810) and Cairell (d. 819); the families descended from Loingsech and Cairell remained prominent at Down, and in the 880s their dynasty were involved in a blood-feud with the Uí Thrichim (the ecclesiastical family that claimed descent from St Patrick's first Ulster convert, Díchu), and took a 'third' of the city from them. The establishment of a monastery at Down may well date only from the eighth century (the first abbatial obit is that of a certain Scandlán in 753), and have been a ploy by the ruling branch of the Dál Fiatach dynasty to retain the ancient capital in their own hands as they moved their centre north towards the lands between Belfast Lough and Lough Neagh, while their cousins remained in the south and even attained separate royal status as kings of Leth Cathail (whence the name Lecale).

Clonmacnoise prided itself on the plebeian origins of its founder, and the abbatial succession appears to demonstrate this. The majority of abbots came from the subject peoples of Mide and Connacht. However, examination of the succession reveals that many of them held office for a short time only, which suggests that the abbacy normally passed to the eldest member of the community, whereas other important offices were hereditary, and hostility to Munster radically qualified their ecumenism. The most notable ecclesiastical family to hold office at Clonmacnoise was that of Conn na mBocht, the head of the Culdees who died in 1059 or 1060, which claimed descent from Torbach of Louth, abbot of Armagh: from the beginning of the ninth century they supplied bishops, anchorites and scribes, including Máel Muire mac Céilechair, one of the scribes of Leabhar na hUidhre, who was killed by marauders in 1106, but none of them seems to have attained the abbacy. However, since we have not as detailed a dossier for most churches as we have for Armagh and Clonmacnoise, generalisations are dangerous.

# CHAPTER XIX

# Visual arts and society

HILARY RICHARDSON

IRISH art has a singular beauty and fantasy of its own. It reached its most creative period during the centuries following the conversion of the country to Christianity, traditionally associated with the arrival of St Patrick in 432 A.D. From then onwards the golden age of art in Ireland began to unfold. It was a time when Irish craftsmen reached a point of excellence never surpassed in the history of the island. Works produced then, such as the Tara brooch (pl. 64) or the Book of Kells (pl. 65), are of world-wide renown, themselves the hallmark of what is generally identified as Irish art.

Between the seventh and the twelfth centuries the full range of Irish art was at its best. It was a period of astonishing activity. There is no doubt that this span of time included a phase so brilliant that it equates in Irish terms with the Florence of the renaissance, or the Paris of more recent days. What caused a flowering of such luxuriance? To understand Irish art one must return to the very roots of its origin. There is no other course. Its subtle character is inextricably bound up with its past.

First of all, the people possessed 'a fine artistic instinct', to quote Margaret Stokes, the nineteenth-century scholar who pioneered the study of early Irish art.[1] There was more to it than that, though. Several specific reasons brought about the golden age. The particular conditions of Ireland in the world at that precise moment were so favourable that for once the natural artistic gifts of the people could flourish freely without hindrance. A number of propitious circumstances converged on Ireland in the early part of the first millennium, which encouraged Irish culture to thrive independently within its own idiom. The visual arts were able to develop and go on from strength to strength until an astonishing level of accomplishment was reached in the eighth century. Inevitably we have a somewhat limited knowledge of the fabric of society then, but the various elements that remain are of such a quality that they support the tradition of contemporary Ireland as the land not only of saints and scholars but of artists and poets also. For Irish lyric poetry, based on an intimate knowledge and love of nature, is another aspect

[1] Margaret Stokes, *Early Christian art in Ireland* (London, 1887), p. 142.

of the same background, marking the originality and refinement of intellectual life at the time.

Geographical and historical factors combined to set the conditions that promoted this development. The extreme western location had a great deal to do with it. Down through the centuries Ireland's westerly situation, perched on the very periphery of Europe, was a controlling force. 'For all we Irish, inhabitants of the world's edge' was how St Columbanus put it in a letter that he wrote to the pope from Milan in 613. The geographical position and the state of being an island were of crucial significance in the moulding of Irish culture, affecting art, religion, language, and people. From time to time external pressures from the outside world exerted influences for change, but during intervals of comparative peace Ireland was able to develop quietly along its own lines. A fairly stable situation existed till the time of the viking onslaughts in the ninth century. An abstract art of distinction had flourished for centuries among the Celts under pagan patronage, and the same germ that had come to maturity in pagan Celtic art went on to produce fresh growth in Christian surroundings. The period of relative calm was conducive to the growth of an Irish style both in inspiration and skills. It was vital to the survival of the Celtic genius, which would otherwise have been stifled by more powerful outside forces. Elsewhere, particularly in places dominated by the Roman empire, the imaginative spirit of the Celts languished or faded away altogether.

Effectively there was no fundamental change till the coming of the vikings. Marauders descended on the Irish coasts around 800 and brought instability and oppression for many years. In the meantime there was the rise of the Carolingian empire with its high level of Christian art. The course of tradition in Ireland was broken at last. Radical innovations were made, especially in sculpture with the advent of narrative scenes and well modelled figures. The high crosses (pl. 63) of the ninth and tenth centuries are the most impressive and important monuments of their age in the west. Then from the middle of the eleventh century in more peaceful times again, like an Indian summer, a second phase favoured the work of craftsmen. But the end was near. With the coming of the Normans the vitality of native Irish art finally departed.

CHRISTIAN Irish art was the product of the Celtic temperament wedded to the new religion, Christianity. It had a unique character because the vision of Irish artists sprang from prehistoric roots. In this respect Ireland was exceptional in Europe. The wealth of a pagan culture was successfully rechannelled to advance the objectives of the Christian church. It is hard to find another instance where a prehistoric style was adapted with verve and invention to proclaim the Christian message. The success of the adaptation is astonishing.

It was the Celts who provided the social structure on which this art developed. Unlike her neighbours, Ireland had remained untouched by major formative influences, escaping not only the barbarian invasions but also occupation by the Roman legions. Over a hundred years ago Douglas Hyde, later to become the first president of Ireland, gave a dynamic lecture entitled 'The necessity of de-anglicising Ireland' (1892). He noted the special place of Irish culture and its freedom from domination by 'the victorious eagles of Rome. We alone of the nations of western Europe escaped the claws of those birds of prey; we alone developed ourselves naturally upon our own lines outside of and free from all Roman influence; we alone were thus able to produce an early art and literature, *our* antiquities can best throw light upon the pre-Romanised inhabitants of half Europe and—we are our fathers' sons'.[2] Irish society was never crushed under provincial Roman culture. The free independent spirit of the heroic age of the Celts, as depicted in their epic sagas such as 'Táin Bó Cuailnge', survived. Their distinctive iron-age style associated with the name of La Tène, the famous site on Lake Neuchâtel, survived also. It had been devised to suit the taste of warrior chieftains, and we know it mainly from its superb metalwork. The origins of prehistoric Celtic art are to be found during the fifth century B.C. in the Rhineland and eastern France. It was the La Tène conception of design that dominated later art in Britain and Ireland. At one time what one might call the 'empire' of the Celts was of vast extent, stretching right across Europe into Asia Minor. But with the ascendancy of Rome, and as Roman provincial civilisation progressively gained sway over Europe, Celtic culture was pushed further and further towards the west. Eventually the art style that had been developed in central Europe, to please native princes and warriors, continued to flourish only in the British Isles and Ireland. The complete absence of Roman rule in Ireland and the continuation of a Celtic way of life without interruption meant that Ireland was left as a place apart, with a tradition spreading back into antiquity. It was in this milieu that Christianity took root in such an original and vital way.

No direct connection has been established between the art of the earlier pre-Celtic-speaking communities in Ireland and that of the Celts. The megalith-builders, for instance, already possessed an impressive personal art style, witnessed particularly in the monuments of the Boyne valley. The Celts had a gift for assimilating anything that came to hand for their own purposes, and they must surely have been conscious of the remarkable remains of former prehistoric people, which are even today such a striking feature in the landscape. Whether any link bridged the gap between them is as yet an unresolved problem.

---

[2] Douglas Hyde, *Language, lore and lyrics*, ed. Breandán Ó Conaire (Dublin, 1986), p. 156.

Thus already by the third millennium B.C. Ireland possessed art of unusual quality. The setting-up of imposing megalithic monuments involved
communal efforts on a large scale. The surface of stones was shallowly carved
with recurrent motifs, such as lozenges, triangles, chevron patterns, and
spirals (pl. 67a). The spiral indeed is emphasised throughout Irish art as a
whole. In passage graves it occurs in over a quarter of the decorated surfaces,
rising to a higher percentage in the case of the Boyne valley.[3] Nowhere else
in megalithic contexts does it figure on this scale. Were the spirals of the iron
age lineally descended from these much earlier spirals? It is impossible to be
certain of any relationship. One point of contact existed at Lough Crew,
County Meath (pl. 66b), where there is evidence that Cairn H was occupied,
perhaps as a workshop, in the first centuries A.D. If so, craftsmen at this site
were plying their trade in surroundings covered with the engravings of the
passage-grave people.

The Celts used and elaborated the spiral within their own system of design
(pl. 67b). It was a favourite in iron-age work in Ireland, often coiled into a
hairspring (fig. 32). It does not feature in continental La Tène art to any
great extent. In Ireland many years later the spiral survived as one of the
chief components of ornament, appearing in abundance in illuminated manuscripts and enamelwork.

The problem of any sequence from megalithic art has taken on a new
dimension with the discovery in 1982, in the current excavation at Knowth,
of a carved ceremonial macehead of pale flint.[4] All four sides of the macehead
are ornamented with designs in low relief, while the narrow ends are covered
with a mesh of lozenge shapes, laboriously hollowed out by grinding. These
interlocking lozenges find their counterpart in a few early maceheads in
Britain, but the winding spirals on two sides and the C-shaped motif on one
face show a sense of form and design that is completely unexpected. The
C-shaped curve or pelta is found in La Tène work, continuing on many well
known pieces into early Christian times. It is a major surprise to find it on
the Knowth macehead. It suggests that later Irish artists were more indebted
to their predecessors of megalithic times than has been hitherto admitted
(fig. 33).

THE Celtic chieftains on the Continent liked subtle abstract decoration to
embellish weapons and jewellery. Their fashions gravitated with the Celtic
tribes to Britain and Ireland. When the advancement of the Roman empire
undermined native Celtic life, the style prospered without restriction on the
western seaboard of Europe, just as the Celtic languages had been pushed to
the western extremities. In the iron age, Celtic artists evolved ways of seeing

---

[3] Muiris O'Sullivan, 'The megalithic art of site I at Knowth and its context in Ireland'
(M.A. thesis, N.U.I. (U.C.D.), 1981), i, 169.
[4] George Eogan, *Knowth and the passage-tombs of Ireland* (London, 1986), colour plate X.

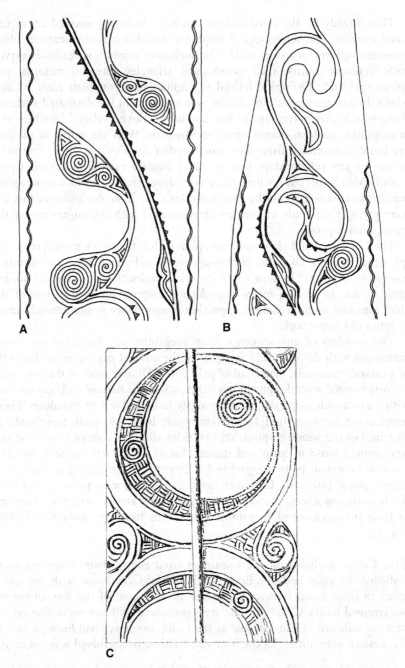

Fig. 32 Details of decorated bronze scabbards from Lisnacrogher, Co. Antrim. All line drawings in this chapter are by Hilary Richardson..

Fig. 33 Extended drawing of ornament on four sides of macehead from Knowth,
Co. Meath.

and methods of decoration that were handed on without interruption to later generations of artists. This long continuity of methods and ideas, from pre-historic to historic times, is perhaps the most notable feature of Irish art.

The La Tène heritage certainly forms the core of Irish art. Celtic design made use of long-established semi-geometric principles. Grids and compasses were employed to build up running patterns of curves to give a feeling of life and movement. This art was linear, largely covering surfaces, and the strict methods of construction achieved ungeometric flowing effects (pls 66a, 66c). The style is ever changing, exploring new curvilinear ideas, hard to pin down. The essence of La Tène art is the curve, with harmonious schemes worked out with care. It is characterised by a wonderfully free, uninhibited use of linear ornament. Repetition and obvious groupings are avoided to make sure that nothing bores the eye. Shapes are suggested rather than stated. Faces seem to lurk in a few floating indications. There is no attempt at realism in the treatment of figures. Cult heads and deities (pl. 70) reflect the religious dimension, especially in stone-carving. In the formation of their style the Celts on the Continent had turned a blind eye to the lifelike figures of classical art. They treasured painted Attic ware among their possessions, yet chose to borrow only Greek plant motifs, while ignoring realistic figure scenes. Even then, the plant motifs became an excuse for pattern-making in running curves.

The grammar of the style stayed fundamentally unchanged in Ireland up to medieval times.[5] No shocks or incursions upset the system. It suited the temperament and outlook of early Irish society and must have satisfied a wide general taste. Artists continued unreservedly to work within this tradition. As they came in contact with new influences and new neighbours, they assimilated an occasional addition into their repertoire. Techniques such as chipcarving in metalwork were borrowed from the Saxons. Motifs such as interlace were introduced. Animal themes were acquired through Germanic sources. But although Irish artists were adaptive, their way of thinking remained constant.

When Christianity arrived in Ireland these sophisticated traditional methods of seeing, symbolising, and constructing still held sway. The same mechanism for laying out designs can be seen in pagan and Christian work; in the surface ornament on metalwork or stone, and in the decoration of gospel books. Using compass-drawn curves, flowing arrangements were produced. It required skill and practice to work out different combinations. The final effect could appear to be spontaneous but in fact this was far from being the case.

Marks of compass points sometimes indicate the procedure that was used to carry out compositions. In the elaborate pages (pl. 70) of the Lindisfarne Gospels (c.700) Bruce-Mitford found that the compasses or dividers employed 'must have been remarkable implements, capable of describing accurate circles as small as 0.75 mm in radius'.[6] In manuscripts the points may pierce the vellum, revealing intricate schemes carried out to perfection. Plans can be traced elsewhere in other media also. Trial-pieces (or motif-pieces, as they are called according to more recent terminology) fit in this context. Compass-drawn patterns, like rough drafts to explore the various combinations of arcs, or technical drawings for designs on finished objects, occur on some of the bone plaques discovered in the cairn at Lough Crew (pl. 66b), previously mentioned. Also recorded there in

[5] Below, ii, 737–80.
[6] R. L. S. Bruce-Mitford et al., *Evangeliorum quattuor codex Lindisfarnensis* (2 vols, Olten–Lausanne–Fribourg, 1960), commentary, p. 226.

the nineteenth century were fragments of iron, including one leg of a pair of compasses. The gold Broighter torc (pl. 66a) from County Londonderry has a raised running design closely paralleled by one of these curvilinear engravings on bone.

Information in addition may occasionally be gleaned from designs that have been left unfinished, where the underlying framework is exposed to view like a skeleton. An example can be seen on one face of the stone from Mullaghmast, County Kildare (pl. 69b), now in the National Museum of Ireland. Here guidelines have been carefully engraved for a design of circular bosses linked by curves. Similar patterns, which have been completed, are found in stone (pl. 69a) and metal. A scheme of linked raised spirals appears on the Moylough belt-shrine (pl. 69c) from County Sligo. Its die-stamped rectangular silver panels were planned from a draft like that made by the Mullaghmast sculptor, but in miniature.

A fascinating description, which throws further light on these methods, was found by O'Curry in an early Irish saga. It recounts how a design had to be invented for Cú Chulainn's shield. A new device was needed, following a law that all the Ulstermen should have their own individual emblems blazoned on their shields. The armourer was unable to work out an original composition for Cú Chulainn, who threatened him with death. Then, at the last moment, a supernatural being suddenly arrived in the workshop and drew a design of arcs with a 'fork' with two prongs projecting from it, like a pair of compasses. The surface he used was of ashes, which had been specially laid down on the floor for that purpose. A device was thereby created that met Cú Chulainn's requirements. The ashes provided a ground for sketching, more ephemeral than the bone-slips but fulfilling the same practical function.[7]

Although mechanical means prepared the groundwork of compositions, it is rarely possible to analyse the structure at a brief glance. The forms are so carefully integrated that time is needed to unravel the way that they have been put together. Geometric art elsewhere can often be clear-cut, making a direct statement. The explicit open designs of Anglo-Saxon garnet brooches or the complex geometric construction of Islamic art are a world apart from these elusive Irish designs, where the eye is led on without rest. The quality of elusion is a special feature of Celtic art. Obviousness and rigidity are avoided at all costs. It is a balancing act between the abstract and the concrete. At the same time, ambiguity was favoured. Shapes could imply several meanings, changing and disappearing, adding to the general richness. The story about Cú Chulainn's shield demonstrates the premium that was set on originality and variety. It was plainly a difficult task to invent a new formula that was not derivative.

[7] R. A. S. Macalister, *The archaeology of Ireland* (London, 1928), pp 145–8.

THIS unusual and successful abstract approach to decoration, evolved by the Celts during the La Tène era, went on thriving in Ireland with the same rules governing the layout of design. The new faith was the next vital element to set the scene for the golden age. Christianity was able to avail of the native artistic heritage. The long unbroken tradition of visual skills, enriched by outside contacts, was unexpectedly powered by a new all-compelling patron in the shape of the church. It was a recipe for extraordinary creative activity. The expertise of artists was now matched only by their dedication.

The big change in patronage was beneficial for craftsmen. They had an enormous new field of enterprise. Previously they had worked for warlords and chieftains, when objects of fine metalwork were commissioned by a warrior class. Many descriptions in the epic sagas show the prestige and importance of such wealth. No doubt this demand continued, but now patronage centred on the church. There was no clash of opposition but a gentle adaptation of the age-old methods to an altogether grander sphere of operation, both on a material and a spiritual level. Christianity fitted easily into Irish society. Monasticism, following the eastern model, was particularly congenial. Just as the life of a monk was one of prayer and devotion, so much of the skilled craftsmanship was now dedicated to the service of God. Frequently the two callings of artist and religious were combined in the one person, since monastic centres were the powerhouses of early Irish culture.

It took a little time for Christian art to come to its full potential. There was a period of adjustment till about the mid seventh century, when the various strands merged in unified vigour. Some aspects were quite foreign and had to be learned, such as writing and the illumination of books. Other techniques in metal were long in use, but were now exploited to adorn sacred vessels and shrines. Carving and stone-cutting came into their own, although much of the treatment of stone remained a surface decoration (pl. 72c). The mainstream of native art continued, while new influences from outside were selected, absorbed, and given an Irish identity. Adaptability was an ever-present trait.

At the beginning our knowledge of designs largely comes from metalwork, from personal ornaments—brooches, dress-fasteners, such as the objects called latchets, and handpins (fig. 34). These were made in cast bronze which was decorated with champlevé enamel, normally in red. Their ornamental motifs, derived from La Tène, were ready at hand when artists were first confronted with the task of painting and copying texts on vellum for religious books. The same fund of patterns is found on early stonework also. Metalwork was well in advance of manuscripts and stonecarving, and therefore provided the principal source of inspiration. Of course we are dependent on materials that have been able to surivive the rigours of centuries, so that inevitably the picture is fragmentary.

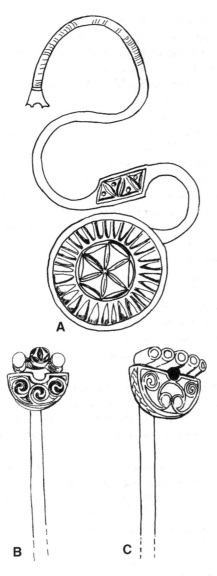

Fig. 34  Latchet from Newry, Co. Down, and two handpins.

Dating for much of the earlier period is conjectural. Later on we are on surer ground when certain shrines and book covers have inscriptions naming craftsmen or donors. These make a network linking less well documented items. Many of the finest objects dating from before 800 have been found in isolation with no archaeological background or historical connections. Any information must be gleaned from the works themselves. Dating in such cases depends on internal evidence, on patterns and techniques, and on parallels to be found in other media that have a better chronological basis. The extraordinary correspondence of designs in a range of differing materials sometimes helps to bridge difficulties of dating and origin. The stock of motifs is much the same on everything, and is fairly small, but the ingenuity and exuberance of the artists disguise their rather limited repertoire. Frequently an exact detail in a manuscript can be paralleled on a cast bronze object or in sculpture. The designs of enamelled discs or of squares of millefiori glass are imitated both in painting and in stone-carving (pls 74a, 74b, 76, 77c). Owing to viking raids and the plundering of valuables, a large proportion of the precious metalwork has been lost. Many fragments survive in Scandinavian museums. On the other hand, the abundance of contemporary literary and historical sources makes it certain that some sites, where there is little visible on the ground today, were once important monastic centres, quite able to sustain the conditions necessary for the production of the finest manuscripts and other works of art. The immense heritage of early Irish texts is only partially tapped at present. Its extent is often not appreciated, especially outside Ireland, for it presents an extraordinary body of written sources for this early date.

The whole emphasis now was on work for the church. From the beginning we hear that 'Assicus, the holy bishop, was a coppersmith, in the service of Patrick, making altar patens.' Tírechán reports how 'Patrick took with him across the Shannon fifty bells, fifty patens, fifty chalices, altar stones, books of law, books of the gospels' and left them in new foundations.[8] The classes of poets, bards, and craftsmen in the tribal pattern of Celtic society went on with their work but in newly orientated roles, so that there was a minimum of upheaval.

The early centuries of Christianity were imbued with a deep spirituality. There was a direct, immediate response to the gospels, with the church as the mainspring of existence. All aspects of life fell into place within a cosmic plan, seen to be of God's creating. Medieval thinking throughout Christendom was pervaded by mystical symbolism, used to explain and expound the scriptures. This elaborate system took hold in Ireland more or less at the same time as the conversion of the country. It reached a climax in the writings of the great philosopher Johannes Scottus Eriugena (*c*.810–77), but is in evidence much earlier, for example in the acrostic hymn 'Altus Prosator' composed by St Colum Cille of Iona (d. 597).[9] Ireland had never been subjected to the Roman empire or the Roman pantheon, so could embrace the ideas of the Neoplatonists and their followers without any conflict. Helen

---

[8] Bieler, *Patrician texts*, pp 141, 123.
[9] John MacQueen, *Numerology* (Edinburgh, 1985), pp 51–5.

Waddell noted the special feeling of early Irish scholars for classical literature with 'their handling, sensitive and fearless, of paganism'.[10] In a similar way, themes of Celtic mythology were not rejected; instead, they could be transformed by a Christian meaning. The voyage tales, the *immrama* of the *filid*, reappeared as the wanderings of early saints such as St Brendan. For *peregrinatio* was itself part of the ascetic character of Irish monasticism. The same mixture of values may be seen in Irish art. Celtic pagan ideas were adapted to Christianity, while on the other hand numerology and medieval mystical philosophy had a strong appeal. These influences appear in artistic design. The symbolic association of numbers and measurements for a theological purpose was attractive to the Celtic turn of mind. The richness of imagery gave multiple interpretations and layerings of meanings. Of course it is impossible to prove conclusively the exact intentions of an artist, yet there is no doubt that theories of the harmony of numbers and similar concepts were uppermost in contemporary thought and permeate art as well. The composition of a carpet page or the design of a chalice may enclose meanings that go unrecognised or have been completely forgotten. In spite of this, the beauty of the object can be appreciated at other more obvious levels of colour, texture, or shape. A phrase often repeated by early Irish writers is 'to see with the eyes of the heart' or the 'eyes of the mind', and it is a good metaphor for understanding something of the aims of artists at this time. Early Christian art in Ireland was full of spiritual meaning. It was liturgical rather than religious; an art constructed to aid contemplation and prayer.

It has been customary to group surviving work under broad headings of manuscripts, metalwork, and stone. Building, however, depended on wood, clay, and wattles for many centuries, and wherever wood was plentiful it must have been the normal material for carving. Occasional items of wood have been preserved, like the stylish gaming-board of yew-wood (pl. 70d) of the tenth century from the crannog at Ballinderry no. 1 (Westmeath). Recently a large boss carved with interlace was found in the Dublin excavations at Fishamble Street; it probably formed the centre of a wooden cross. The finials (the carved beams projecting above the line of the roof) in the illustration of Solomon's temple in the 'Temptation of Christ' in the Book of Kells (*c*.800), show the elaborate treatment that may well have been the norm in carving wood (fig. 35).

We know paintings existed, but none have survived. The Venerable Bede (d. 735), the great English historian, records how the church at Wearmouth was furnished with pictures of biblical subjects that had been brought back from the Continent by Benedict Biscop; and Cogitosus's description (*c*.650) of the church at Kildare mentions similar paintings. 'One wall, covered with linen curtains and decorated with paintings, traverses the

---

[10] Helen Waddell, *The wandering scholars* (London, 1927), p. 36.

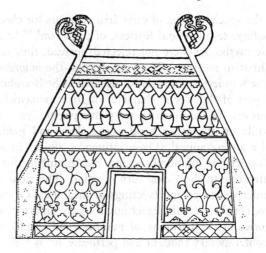

Fig. 35 Book of Kells (T.C.D., MS 58), f. 202ᵛ: Solomon's temple.

eastern part of the church from one side to the other.'[11] These paintings
must have been like icons. Illustrations on vellum, such as the Book of
Kells's 'Virgin and child with angels' (pl. 72), probably reflect the type of
work done on wood or linen. In some instances also an outline is lightly
engraved on a stone slab, and one may imagine that colour was applied to the
flat surface, again suggesting icon-painting. These artists were accustomed to
a large scale, judging by the crucifixion scenes depicted on slabs at Duvillaun
(pl. 73c) and Inishkea North, islands off the Mayo coast where there were
early monasteries. A smaller example is the bust of a monk, holding a cross,
on the pillar at Killeen Cormac, County Kildare (fig. 36).

Early stone churches tended to be simple and rather dark, as the windows
let in little light. Most of the craftsmanship was concentrated on portable
objects—on chalices, patens, liturgical vessels, hand-bells, precious covers
for books, and lamps. While the buildings were insignificant, the furnishings
in contrast were colourful and rich. Of vestments and fabrics we know little,
but in metalwork some of the techniques were devised to add brilliance and
sparkle to the dim interior. The materials were bright in themselves—gold,
gilt-bronze, and silver—and to them were added crystals, amber, glass, and
many decorative devices. Chipcarving was a metalworking technique
borrowed from Germanic contacts and widely used from the time of its
introduction because it made the most of metal. Usually in cast bronze, the
surface was designed in a myriad of sharply angled facets which reflected

[11] Ludwig Bieler, *Ireland: harbinger of the middle ages* (London, 1963), p. 28.

Fig. 36 Figure engraved on a pillar at Killeen Cormac, Co. Kildare.

light from all sides. When this was gilded, as on the stem of the Ardagh chalice (pl. 71), the effect was spectacular.

Enamel was used with a freedom not encountered before. The same champlevé method continued in favour, but was no longer confined to red. Combinations of colours glowed from decorated studs and plaques. Sometimes tiny pieces of millefiori glass in minute chequerboard or floral designs, in a further range of colours, were fused to the enamel or set in small frames. It is not clear how or why millefiori became so popular in Ireland. It was a technique, like gold filigree, that had been introduced from the Roman world. It had largely disappeared elsewhere, but was very much the fashion in Ireland, especially in the sixth and seventh centuries. Actual sticks of millefiori glass, from which the craftsman removed tiny horizontal slices for decoration, have been found in workshops on some excavated sites, such as the ring fort at Garranes, County Cork, and Lagore crannog, County Meath.[12] The finest of the bronze zoomorphic penannular brooches, the large brooch from Ballinderry crannog no. 2 (pl. 75a), has altogether six different patterns in the platelets of millefiori that lie in a field of red enamel filling the terminals.

These brooches are basically a moveable pin on an open ring (pl. 73a). The ring terminates at either end in an animal's head, the snout facing towards

---

[12] S. P. Ó Ríordáin, 'The excavation of a large earthen ring-fort at Garranes, Co. Cork' in *R.I.A. Proc.*, xlvii (1942), sect. C, pp 77–150; H. O'Neill Hencken, 'Lagore crannog: an Irish royal residence of the 7th to 10th centuries A.D.' in *R.I.A. Proc.*, liii (1950–51), sect. C, pp 1–247.

the ring, almost biting it. The break in the ring is of the utmost importance for the function of the brooch. The pin can swing between the terminals and locks the brooch in position on the wearer, fastening the two sides of a cloak together. Brooches worn in this way are clearly depicted on figures carved on the high crosses, in the scene of the baptism of Christ on the Broken Cross at Kells for example, or the Ecce Homo or arrest of Christ on the Cross of Muiredach at Monasterboice (pl. 73b). Originally penannular brooches were practical dress-fasteners, rather plain and utilitarian. Then the terminals began to expand and flatten out, as the possibilities of enamel decoration were explored. The early patterns had been a narrow line of red in curves and spirals against the bronze. Now the area of colour versus metal was reversed, and it was the metal that left a threadlike design against the enamel. Although they remain a constant feature, the animal heads are sometimes stylised to an unrecognisable degree. The descriptive analysis of their evolution in the pioneering work of Kilbride-Jones remains valuable. These brooches remained in fashion till about 700, when a more opulent style came into vogue with the use of silver and gold. But the ring-shaped brooch was long characteristic of Irish apparel, and prestige was attached to the wearing of these splendid objects.

It was not easy to combine curvilinear patterns in bronze with the insertion of millefiori glass, which tended to be rectangular in shape. A change in the aspect of enamelwork in the seventh century may in part be due to this but also to the proximity of Anglo-Saxon jewellers and acquaintance with their methods. Cloisonné, for enamel and the setting of glass and gem-stones, was the technique favoured by the Germanic peoples as a whole. In Anglo-Saxon work outstanding examples can be seen in Kentish jewellery and in the royal equipment at Sutton Hoo, which was newly made at the time of the ship-burial (*c*.625). The appearance of cloisonné was adopted by Irish craftsmen, though not the actual method. Enamel now was arranged in angular compartments, often L- and T-shapes of red and yellow, interspersed with plaques of millefiori. This type of work may be seen on the Moylough belt-shrine (pl. 69c), which is one of the few objects to which a technical study has been devoted. The small human figures that adorn the Myklebostad hanging bowl (pl. 74a) are striking examples of the same style. This Irish bronze bowl, buried in a viking grave of the ninth century in Norway, has the shape of a small bearded man in three escutcheons, or mounts for suspension. The impressive head in cast bronze remains in the Celtic tradition, while the body, simplified to a cube, is bright with squares and angular shapes of enamel and millefiori.

Hanging bowls have been and continue to be the subject of much discussion, but it seems reasonable to argue that they functioned as lamps, although the term certainly covers a wide range of vessels. Many were valuable and highly ornate; they may well have been used for the lighting of churches or

for the liturgical washing of hands. A few escutcheons have been found in
Ireland but the distribution is predominantly in pagan Saxon and viking
contexts, probably the result of either looting or trade. One group of bowls
have round escutcheons enamelled in curvilinear and trumpet patterns in the
Irish manner.[13] These designs are repeated in an astonishing way in a magnificent painted carpet page in the Book of Durrow (c.650) (pl. 75b). From
this and from the style of enamelling and use of millefiori, Françoise Henry
maintained that the bowls were of Irish manufacture.[14] It is more generally
agreed that they come from a Celtic or western background. In recent years
evidence of the actual making of hanging bowls in a Pictish workshop was
discovered at Craig Phadrig in Inverness. Further north again, at the brough
of Birsay in Orkney, a lead disc was found, which could be used directly as a
die or as a master pattern for an escutcheon (Fig. 37).[15] But the most elaborate bowl of all, the largest of the Sutton Hoo hanging bowls, certainly
appears to have been made in Ireland. It had been beautifully repaired,
patched in silver, by a Saxon craftsman, and was clearly a revered heirloom
at the time of its burial, so that it dates back to 600 or even earlier. The
enamelling and millefiori come from a similar background to the Ballinderry
brooch, while the ornament on the frames of the escutcheons has exact

Fig. 37 Decorated disc from the brough of Birsay, Orkney.

[13] The literature on hanging bowls is extensive. For a useful source of reference, see Jane
Brenan, *Hanging bowls and their contexts* (BAR British Series, 200; Oxford, 1991).
[14] Françoise Henry, *Studies in early Christian and medieval Irish art, i: enamels and metalwork*
(London, 1983), plate XXXII, p. 153.
[15] C. L. Curle, 'An engraved lead disc from the brough of Birsay, Orkney' in *Antiq. Soc.
Scot. Proc.*, cv (1972–4), pp 301–6.

parallels in contemporary Irish metalworking. Hanging bowls, treasured in their own time, leave many questions unanswered. With more finds amassing over the years and almost a hundred bowls listed so far, research should bring further clarification.

The cult of relics became important in Ireland, and craftsmen devoted much of their skill to the making of shrines.[16] Tradition centred on the local saint or founder of a church. His most treasured possessions were enshrined, often in elaborate metal casings at a later date, and revered for centuries. The erenach or hereditary keeper was granted certain rights or privileges in return for the guardianship of the relics, which sometimes remained in the keeping of one family in the same region for generations, right up to the nineteenth century or later in some cases. In Ireland the three attributes commonly associated with a holy man were his bell, book, and walking staff (pl. 79a). These were the stock in trade of the religious life and are sometimes depicted in carvings of ecclesiastics, such as the little monk carrying a bell on the Killadeas pillar (County Fermanagh) or the White Island figures (pl. 79b, 79c). Gospel-books were needed for the spread of the faith from the beginning, while psalters were particularly used for study and teaching. The bells were small iron or bronze handbells (pl. 79d), and the crosiers were the walking sticks of these early saints. Shrines were made of all these, and are characteristic of the early church in Ireland and Scotland.

Elaborate metal casings were made to protect these precious belongings, and fresh decoration was added from time to time, perhaps when repairs were necessary. Sometimes shrines were hung around the neck or worn as breast plates. Fittings for the attachment of straps were common, as shrines might be carried in procession or used for special ceremonies. The casings were often arranged in small gilt or silver panels and frequently fragments have been preserved on this account, because viking raiders easily broke them up into separate units, which could be adapted to make brooches or ornaments. A great amount of social history, about local families and genealogies, has accumulated around individual reliquaries. Some shrines were used for the swearing of oaths, others for testing the truth and similar functions, so that signs of wear may be visible. Book shrines or *cumdachs* were simply rectangular boxes of wood, covered with metal plates, made to fit the manuscript to be enclosed. The shrine of the Cathach ('the battler'), the late sixth- or early seventh-century psalter traditionally believed to have been copied by St Colum Cille himself, was constructed in the eleventh century for Cathbarr O'Donnell, chief of the princely family to which the saint had belonged. It was reputed to have the power of ensuring victory in warfare. A beautiful case for a large gospel-book was found in 1986 on the

---

[16] Charles Doherty, 'The use of relics in Ireland' in Ní Chatháin & Richter, *Ire. & Europe*, pp 89–101.

bed of Lough Kinale, County Longford, and is the earliest as the workmanship appears to be of the eighth century. The ornament, arranged in a cross
with raised metal bosses in high relief, is quite outstanding.

Of all the bells the most venerated is that of St Patrick (pl. 78), a bronze-
coated iron bell with a splendid shrine made in Armagh at the end of the
eleventh century by Cú Dúilig Ó hInmainén and his sons, according to the
inscription. The Annals of Ulster record that St Patrick's relics were treasured by St Colum Cille, who gave the bell to Armagh. Most of the crosiers
were enshrined in the later period also.

The Moylough belt-shrine, on the other hand, probably dates to the end
of the seventh century. The name of the saint whom it commemorates has
been lost, since it was discovered by accident during turf-cutting in County
Sligo. A whole series of miscellaneous articles, such as purses or shoes, were
enshrined but this is the only surviving belt-shrine, although others are
mentioned in lives of the saints. It is a hinged girdle of metal casing, once
colourful with shining panels of embossed silver, blue and white millefiori
glass, and red and yellow enamel borders. The acid conditions of the bog
have dulled its visual impact, but inside the casing is the real treasure: the
remains of the leather belt, which formerly belonged to a much venerated
holy man.

A special group of shrines, characteristic of Ireland and Scotland, are the
tiny house-shaped shrines: portable reliquaries in the shape of a sarcophagus
or small church building. There are roughly a dozen of these, from Ireland,
Scotland, and places abroad close to Irish centres. They usually consist of a
wooden box and lid, generally of yew hollowed from the solid, encased in
decorated metal plates with fittings on the end walls for carrying-straps. The
roofs are hipped and steeply pitched. A ridge pole along the top ends in
animal-headed finials, of the type already seen in the illustration of Solomon's temple in the Book of Kells. Often a small oratory or church shape is
repeated in the centre of a ridge pole, while the Lough Erne shrine (National
Museum) contained a second miniature shrine. A considerable number of
component parts from shrines survive. Sometimes they have been broken off
as plunder, for their value, or in other cases they have turned up in the stock
of a metalworker, such as the important recently discovered hoard from the
River Blackwater at Shanmullagh, County Armagh, which was assembled
near the end of the ninth century. Also from the Blackwater is the Clonmore
shrine (Ulster Museum), represented by tiny tinned bronze plates forming
the back and front walls (pl. 8oc). It is considered to be the earliest reliquary,
largely because its beautiful curvilinear decoration draws on the La Tène
repertoire, without any of the later, acquired motifs. It makes a strong
contrast to the Saint-Germain objects (pls 77a, 77b), two finials from a shrine
of considerable dimensions, designed in a spirit close to the Book of Kells and
magnificently cast in bronze. Some house-shaped shrines came from viking

graves, but the best preserved, even with the carrying chain in good order, though lacking a wooden interior, is the Bologna shrine (pl. 80b), which for many years went unrecognised. Just as some of the earliest Irish manuscripts once in the monastery library at Bobbio, St Columbanus's foundation, are now in Milan, so the Bologna shrine will have had a similar history.

Iona occupied a key position in the seventh and eighth centuries, radiating outwards to Northumberland, Pictland, and further afield, while keeping in touch with Ireland. The provenance of the house-shaped shrines, as well as the present location of early manuscripts, shows the extent of the Irish province. Irish monastic training had a widespread influence. In France, Switzerland, and Italy, a chain of monasteries founded by St Columbanus (d. 615) and his followers extended the Irish mission further. The travelling monk typified the period. In the middle ages the Irish were known as *Scotti*. It is still a practical term to cover Irish, Scottish, and Northumbrian elements, which together formed a cultural milieu at this time. St Aidan, summoned from Iona by the Northumbrian king, had settled at Lindisfarne, Holy Island, in 635. Northumbria was the meeting point not only for western and northern traditions, but for traditions from the south stemming from St Augustine's mission to the Anglo-Saxons in 597. Further Mediterranean influences followed with the arrival of Theodore of Tarsus and his retinue at Canterbury, where he held the see for over twenty years. Foreign craftsmen, brought from the Continent, were employed in the construction of the famous monasteries at Monkwearmouth and Jarrow, while pilgrimages to Rome and the Holy Land introduced fresh trends from abroad. All these strains went into the making of Northumbrian art. Anglo-Saxon, Celtic, Pictish, Mediterranean, and Byzantine elements mingled. The Lindisfarne gospels epitomise a conglomeration of different influences. Irish methods of design formed a sizeable part of the mixture because many northern monasteries, like Lindisfarne itself, were originally Irish foundations. Even after the synod of Whitby, the Irish training remained a forceful presence; manuscript decoration, for example, still used compass-drawn compositions in the La Tène manner.

THE illumination of manuscripts is the most renowned aspect of Irish art. But it is in book decoration that the interchange of influences within the cultural province of the Irish mission is most clearly seen. Insular art, accordingly, is an acceptable term to use when exact origins of manuscripts are often in doubt. The great insular gospel-books were unrivalled in Europe and must still be regarded with awe and amazement. Their almost miraculous intricacy of design and detail appears incredible today. It is only possible to understand such work in its spiritual context.

In Ireland writing had been introduced at the same time as Christianity for the specific purpose of spreading the gospel. The early lives of St Patrick refer to the alphabet tables he made for people as he journeyed around the country. All literary pursuits were bound up with the church initially, and the occupation of scribe was of considerable importance. Mac Riagoil (d. 822) was abbot of Birr, County Offaly, but in the annals his title of scribe takes precedence over his other titles. In the Annals of Ulster the number of entries naming scribes and anchorites suddenly increases in the eighth century, coming to a notable climax between eight hundred and nine hundred. Robin Flower understood the statistics to relate to the *céli Dé*, the Culdees or servants of God, who brought a new movement of asceticism and reform to the church.[17] The luxury gospel-books rose to great heights from the mid seventh century to the early ninth century, but their production was short-lived. The best known examples are the Book of Durrow (mid seventh century), ascribed to County Offaly or Northumbria, the Lindisfarne gospels (*c.*700), written at Lindisfarne itself, and the Book of Kells (*c.*800), begun on Iona and probably completed at Kells, County Meath, though a small group of manuscripts, now in varying stages of fragility, were equally splendid in their day. The Lichfield gospels, the Echternach gospels, the Turin gospels (from Bobbio), the Durham gospels (MS A.II.17), the St Gall gospels (Codex 51), and others belong to a class of extravagantly planned and magnificently ornamented books created for ceremonial use. Manuscript art came into being for the sake of the scriptures, in something like the way calligraphy, or beautiful writing, had a spiritual purpose in Islamic art, where the text of the Koran itself is sacred. It is in this light that the illumination of insular books must be regarded.

Illumination of the text is already present even in the Cathach (pl. 80a), mentioned above. Now in the keeping of the Royal Irish Academy, it was discovered in the nineteenth century, hidden away inside its *cumdach*. Each psalm opens with a decorated capital, and the initial letters gradually diminish in size to enter the main body of the script. Outline dotting in red surrounds the enlarged letters. These characteristics remain constant throughout Irish illumination. As the beginning and end of the psalter are lost, one cannot tell if there was a decorated title page or illustrations. The Cathach is of particular interest at this early date (possibly prior to 600), because it was written at a time before interlace was included in the repertoire, yet already has a distinctive Irish capital script. Interlace begins to take a prominent role in gospel-books of the seventh century, such as Durham Cathedral Library MS A.II.10 and the Book of Durrow. The latter not only has borders of broad ribbons throughout the decorated pages, but has one carpet page at the opening of St John's Gospel that includes panels of animal interlace, a favourite in Germanic work (pl. 75b). From now on interlace, whether

---

[17] Robin Flower, ' "The two eyes of Ireland": religion and literature in Ireland in the eighth and ninth centuries' in William Bell and N. D. Emerson (ed.), *The Church of Ireland, A.D. 432–1932* (Dublin, 1932), pp 66–75.

zoomorphic, plain, or with small human figures, becomes the leitmotiv of Irish art. That interlace was in use in Coptic manuscripts around 500 is demonstrated by the *crux ansata* page of the Glazier Codex. The carpet page, a carpet-like spread of decoration covering the page, is a speciality of insular work, where it takes the place of the painted cross-page found in some eastern manuscripts. Indeed, the design of many carpet pages, on analysis, is seen to be cross-based.

Decoration plays an ever more important part. The opening text of the gospels displays massive initials, closely interwoven with designs, while the facing page often has a brilliant carpet of ornament. At the beginning of each gospel there is a page carrying the symbol or portrait of the evangelist (pl. 81). A peak of dazzling luxuriance is reached in the Book of Kells, where a single initial is able to stretch the limits of the page, filled with designs of unsurpassed complexity and ingenuity. There is a surprising combination of strong, spacious compositions and microscopic intricate ornament sweeping across the vellum. A wealth of mystical meaning and symbolism lies in the designs. Some may be interpreted: for example the *chi-rho* page (pl. 83), the page devoted to the sacred monogram of Christ, unites images of Christ, the resurrection, and the eucharist. Not only that, but a lively feeling for nature appears here and there. Sporadically throughout the text small episodes occur, such as a cock and some hens (fig. 38), a greyhound hunting, or an otter catching a fish. The essence of each creature is accurately caught. Always they fulfil a function, whether as illustration, as symbol, or even as an aid to guide the reader.

The script of these manuscripts is one of their most beautiful features. It is a stately rounded majuscule, going right across the page in the case of the Book of Kells (pl. 84a) and the Lichfield gospels, which have perhaps the finest hands. In a few instances we know the name of the scribe. Mac Riagoil, abbot of Birr, previously mentioned, was both painter and scribe of the large, colourful gospels (Bodl. MS Auct. D.2.19) that bear his name (fig. 39). The writing, strong and rhythmical, is clearly that of an expert. The Book of Armagh (pl. 82a) is securely dated to 807, and the scribe, Ferdomnach, whose death is entered in the Annals of Ulster in 845, was a virtuoso penman. His cursive script has a striking elegance and his vivid line drawings emphasise the evangelists' symbols, treating them in the same fashion as those in the Book of Kells (fig. 40). Irish pocket books, such as the eighth-century Book of Dimma (pl. 84b), should also be mentioned. These are small, compact gospels, which were in the possession of one individual. The future development of book production lay in the same direction, with emphasis on small, personally owned books for private use. Travelling monks carried their books in leather satchels, but only a few ornamented examples of the latter survive, even though leather-workers had attained a high degree of skill at an early date.

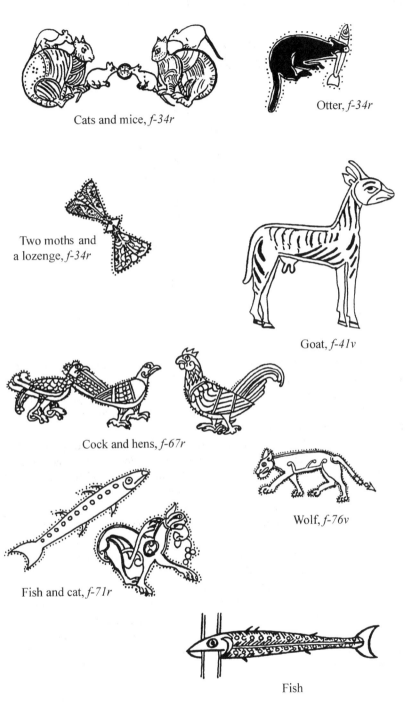

Cats and mice, *f-34r*

Otter, *f-34r*

Two moths and
a lozenge, *f-34r*

Goat, *f-41v*

Cock and hens, *f-67r*

Wolf, *f-76v*

Fish and cat, *f-71r*

Fish

Fig. 38 Book of Kells (T.C.D., MS 58): details of animals and fish.

Fig. 39  Book of MacRegol (Bodl., MS Auct. D.2.19): details of f. 127.

The Stowe Missal, a pocket book of *c*.800, is an important manuscript, despite its small size. It is the only early missal to come down to us intact. It includes a short treatise in Old Irish on the actions and symbolism of the mass, which is of special interest because it throws light on liturgical plate and contemporary custom.[18]

The Ardagh chalice (pl. 71) was discovered in a hoard with four brooches and a small plain chalice in County Limerick in 1868. Its superlative quality was perceived at once. Then in 1980 the major find of the Derrynavlan treasure (pl. 85) vastly increased our knowledge of sacred vessels for the altar. From an early monastic site associated with the Culdees, not far from Cashel, the ancient seat of the kings of Munster, the Derrynavlan hoard consists of a silver chalice, a silver paten and stand, a strainer of gilt-bronze, and a bronze bowl. It is therefore an altar service, though the chalice appears to be of ninth-century work, whereas the paten and strainer are eighth-century like the Ardagh chalice. Just as the gospel-books are supreme for their time, so the church metalwork is of an excellence that was never equalled again. These liturgical vessels are among the finest in the whole early Christian world. They have a robust design of a type only found in Ireland, yet the technical detail in the case of the paten and the Ardagh chalice is of extraordinary refinement and delicacy. The large size of the

---

[18] F. E. Warren, *Liturgy and ritual of the Celtic church* (Oxford, 1881).

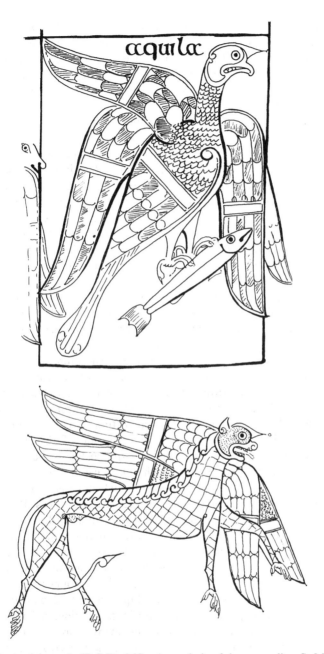

Fig. 40 Book of Armagh (T.C.D., MS 52): symbols of the evangelists St Mark and St John.

paten may be accounted for by the complex division of the bread, the *fractio panis*, described in the Stowe Missal.[19] The Ardagh chalice has a fuller, more pleasing shape than the Derrynavlan chalice, but they are both capacious. It is thought that these two-handled chalices were used for giving communion to the people. Their richness and sumptuous decoration suggests that they were royal gifts originally.

The silver is set off by applied decoration in gold filigree and other brilliant materials. The Derrynavlan chalice depends to a large extent on amber as an extra effect, but the paten and the Ardagh chalice between them have a profusion of ornament and colour, finely balanced against the polished silver. During valuable conservation work in the British Museum laboratories it was possible to analyse the methods used by Irish goldsmiths over a thousand years ago. For example, the gold filigree, on a minute scale, is sometimes three wires in depth in order to achieve a desired result. Openwork patterns of filigree in interlace, animal interlace, or even little human figures, were soldered on to backplates of metal or gold foil in a technique skilfully devised by these artists.

The programme of the applied decoration of these vessels is founded on Christian numerology and symbolism. The treatise in Old Irish in the Stowe Missal links numbers to mystical meanings in the eucharist, but this whole system of medieval mysticism was endemic to the time. A simple example is the number twelve, which has an obvious association with the apostles, whose names are engraved in beautiful insular script around the Ardagh chalice just beneath the girdle of ornament that runs through the handles (pl. 71). The girdle is designed to hold twelve polychrome studs and twelve filigree panels. Eight symbolised the resurrection. It is the number emphasised in the brilliant decoration on the underside of the Ardagh chalice (fig. 41), completely hidden from view till the chalice is elevated, and it is the number emphasised right through the Derrynavlan chalice, as the radiograph demonstrates. The interpretation of such designs is as yet in its infancy, and demands a thorough study of the written sources. But number is important also in sculpture, involving measurement as well.

The same technical perfection in metalwork may be seen in the brooches of this period. The famous Tara brooch (pl. 64) is not the largest by any means. It is covered on both faces with a vast range of designs, minutely executed. These include gossamer-thin spirals in copper against gold or silver grounds, bird processions in gilt chipcarving, long-bodied animals in filigree with joints in spirals or picked out in granulation, red and blue studs with silver inset grills, amber borders, and many more. Each surface is as complex as a detail in the Book of Kells and it is virtually impossible to

---

[19] Peter O'Dwyer, *Célí Dé: spiritual reform in Ireland 750–900* (Dublin, 1981), pp 155–8.

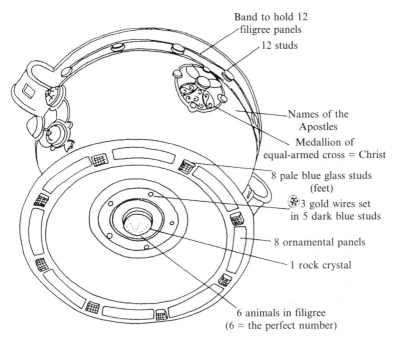

Band to hold 12
filigree panels

12 studs

Names of the
Apostles

Medallion of
equal-armed cross = Christ

8 pale blue glass studs
(feet)

3 gold wires set
in 5 dark blue studs

8 ornamental panels

1 rock crystal

6 animals in filigree
(6 = the perfect number)

Fig. 41 Diagram showing the use of numbers in the design of the Ardagh chalice.

appreciate the delicacy without the aid of a magnifying glass. The eighth-
and ninth-century brooches are derived from the earlier penannular brooches
but are now generally of silver or silver gilt. Now the terminals are linked to
form a crescent-shaped plate with the ring up to 5 in. (12.8 cm) in diameter,
and the pins are so long as to be dagger-like in some cases. They are objects
of prestige and rather less practical to wear because there is no break in the
ring through which the pin can swivel to lock the brooch easily in position.
The motifs on the pinhead and terminals carry through a theme and variations for each individual brooch, so that every one of the major brooches is a
*tour de force* in its own right with a personality of its own. Some of the finest
are the Cavan brooch (pl. 86b), the Roscrea brooch, the Tipperary brooch,
the Killamery brooch (pl. 86a), and the brooches in the Ardagh hoard.

In recent years there has been an upsurge in information about metalwork
and many new finds; some of these are quite spectacular, such as the eighth-
century cast bronze decorated door-handle from Donore, County Meath
(pl. 82b), and the elaborately designed fittings that accompanied it. The
sudden development comes about partly as a result of modern technology,
but also through changes in land usage and farming methods, as well as
through excavations such as Moynagh Lough, County Meath, where the

crannog settlement included a workshop active in the first half of the eighth century.

In turning to carvings of this period, the influence of metalwork can still be seen. There was no native tradition of building in cut stone, so that when the high crosses appear in the eighth century, they represent an entirely new aspect of Irish art. Prehistoric monuments and early cross-inscribed pillars did not change the natural shape of the stone, and carving was confined to surface decoration. The first free-standing cross seems to be at Carndonagh in the far north-west in County Donegal (pl. 88b), with Fahan Mura nearby, where the large upright slab (pl. 88a) in the graveyard bears the only early inscription in Greek in Ireland and has on either face crosses of broad inter-lace in the Book of Durrow style, skilfully carved in low relief. These are best dated to the mid-seventh century, though a much later context has also been argued for them. There is no absolute dating for many stone carvings around the countryside. However, the type of site on which slabs and cross-stones occur often indicates an early date. They were set up around early monasteries, perhaps where no remains of buildings exist now or just a few ruins. A large proportion are found along the west coast or on islands that were suitable places for retreat or for hermitages. The crosses (pls 87a, 87b, 87c) carved or engraved on pillars are of a wide variety: sometimes a Greek cross inscribed in a circle, a Latin cross with wedge-shaped terminals, or with the arms curling into spirals. Recumbent grave slabs survive in large numbers at Clonmacnoise (pl. 87d) and other important monasteries. They are flat grave-markers, and their pleasing cross designs are attractively matched by engraved inscriptions that use formalised prayers along with the name of the deceased. It has been possible in some cases to identify the person commemorated from entries recorded in the Annals from the early eighth century onwards.[20] The high cross is clearly a separate conception from any of these.

The crosses of Ireland and Britain are unique in western Europe in the early middle ages. They are the most impressive monuments of their time, and occupy a quite exceptional position in the history of western sculp-ture. The Irish high crosses, along with their offshoots in western Scotland, form a distinctive series of their own, characterised by a ring of stone that connects the arms to the upright, thereby creating the familiar outline of a Celtic cross. A number of different explanations for the origin of the ring have been put forward, some symbolic, some functional. The source may well have come from the Roman world, where the victor's laurel wreath was used to celebrate a triumph. An association with ancient sun-worship is another suggestion, while a further solution is that the ring is simply a halo

[20] Françoise Henry, 'List of dated inscriptions with the corresponding entries in the annals', appendix to Padraig Lionard, 'Early Irish graveslabs', ed. Françoise Henry in *R.I.A. Proc.*, lxi (1960–61), sect. C, pp 157–69.

around the cross, which represents Christ. A functional view maintains that the ring came from a wooden prototype, where diagonal braces strengthened the cross and these in turn were changed from straight pieces into the curves of a circle for aesthetic reasons. Whatever the reason, the structure shows that Irish artists continued to work within their own idiom. Hence the Celtic cross has come to be the embodiment of Irish art.

The high crosses belong to a period stretching from the eighth to the twelfth centuries. Remains of some three hundred crosses survive, of which over a hundred have carved decoration. There are several local schools of sculpture, but the broad plan of the cross is much the same (fig. 42). A stone shaft, like a pillar, is carved on four sides in low relief, often in panels. It is set in a separate base of cubic or pyramid form. The upper part of the shaft terminates in a cross, and a capstone on top completes the monument. The capstone usually is carved in the shape of a small oratory or church, and is normally made from a separate block, like the base. Crosses range in height from about 3 m to 6 m (10 ft to almost 22 ft) and several may be found at one location. They were erected in the precincts of monasteries, where they had a

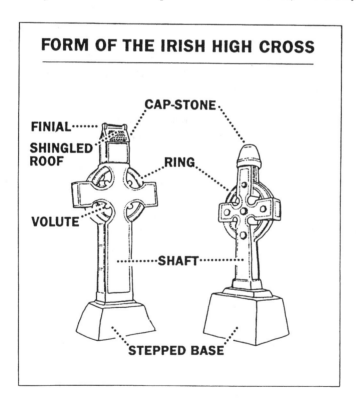

Fig. 42 Form of the Irish high cross.

protective significance and probably served as points of assembly for religious ceremonies. Recent research on their iconography suggests that they had a special place in the liturgy. The votive character of some crosses is also borne out by inscriptions. The south cross at Kells, County Meath (pls 89a, 89b), is called the 'Cross of Patrick and Columba' in its inscription. Its erection is thought to mark the arrival there of monks fleeing from Iona in the first decade of the ninth century. A diagram in the eighth-century Book of Mulling shows a plan of a monastery with its circular enclosure. A number of crosses, dedicated to the prophets and evangelists, are indicated outside the ramparts, while other named crosses are situated within the sanctuary. It is known that Iona once possessed many crosses, and names are preserved for St Martin's Cross and St John's Cross, among those that remain.

The high crosses present a remarkable advance in sculpture. They are complex works, carefully measured and organised in three dimensions. The earliest group, of which the North Cross at Ahenny (pl. 90a) is a fine example, dates from the eighth or more probably the ninth century and is found in a very restricted area in County Tipperary and County Kilkenny, close to Slievenamon. Although they are carved in stone, they imitate wooden crosses covered with metal plates, riveted together and decorated with elaborate bosses. The hatched moulding around the edges copies a metal binding. These crosses have the stepped base that represents the actual site at Golgotha. They have sparse figure carving on the cross itself, which is mainly devoted to ornament, in designs typical of contemporary metalwork in gilt chipcarving.

It seems probable that this treatment of pseudo-metalwork is linked to events that happened in Jerusalem from the time of Constantine, such as the finding of the true cross, the large ornate cross set up at Golgotha, described by Adomnán in his 'De locis sanctis', and the triumphant restoration of the relic of the true cross in 630 after its capture by the Persians. The attention of early Christendom was focused on these happenings. It is significant that the best account in the seventh century of the city of Jerusalem is that of Bishop Arculf, who sketched plans of the holy sites he had visited on a waxed tablet for Adomnán and the community at Iona about 683. A mid-ninth-century manuscript of Adomnán's text (pl. 89c) is illustrated with a number of these sketches.[21]

A change in the balance between ornament and figure-carving on the crosses is contemporary with the *céli Dé* movement and may have been due to its influence with its new emphasis on spiritual reform. Biblical subjects become increasingly important. The network of spirals, interlacings, and fret patterns on the crosses at Ahenny, Kilkieran, Kilrea, and Killamery, gives

[21] Vienna Cod. 458; Denis Meehan (ed. and trans.), *Adamnan's De locis sanctis* (Dublin, 1958).

way to figured scenes on the main surfaces of the cross. Patterns persist, but are relegated to panels on the narrow sides or less prominent places.

A big group of crosses, over thirty in number, widely scattered from the far north to County Carlow, are heavily panelled with figure carvings. These are sometimes known as scripture crosses, after the *Cros na screaptra*, the Cross of the Scriptures at Clonmacnoise (pl. 91b), mentioned in the annals in 1060. They may be dated between the ninth and the first part of the tenth centuries, and show a transformation in Irish sculpture. Now Irish artists radically departed from the traditional vision of the Celts. They chose to depict narrative subjects, realistically represented. Perhaps the historical situation, with the need to assert Christian values in the face of the viking incursions, may explain this change. Biblical stories are told with a vivid directness and the figures are modelled in relief, which marks a further development. The new style of figure-carving must have had some model. In all probability there was contact with Carolingian work, where ivory book-covers portray similar biblical subjects.

The iconography of the biblical scenes on the crosses is of great interest. There is repetition of a fairly limited range of themes from both Old and New Testaments that continue a programme found in the earliest Christian art in the catacombs and on sculptured sarcophagi. The Old Testament subjects come originally from Jewish prayers for salvation, the 'Help of God', and include scenes such as Daniel in the lions' den and Noah (pl. 91a). To these subjects further Old Testament scenes were added prefiguring the life of Christ, and scenes from the New Testament, especially miracles such as the multiplication of the loaves and fishes. Irish poems and hymns of the early ninth century, such as the hymn of St Colmán moccu Chlúasaig, follow the same sort of formulas. The biblical scenes have symbolic reference to salvation and the eucharist, which is also the meaning implied in panels depicting episodes in the lives of St Paul and St Antony, the hermits of the Egyptian desert, who were the founders of monasticism. Their appearance reinforces the importance of an eastern original as the inspiration for Irish monastic practice. The Last Judgement is the climax of the scenes on the crosses. The biblical subjects make a fairly readable scheme of redemption, from the fall of man to the second coming. On the scripture crosses, the cross-head is often carved with a crucifixion on the west face, balanced by a Last Judgement or Christ in glory in the corresponding position on the reverse.

It is not always possible to interpret the subjects of some panels with any certainty. A few scenes relate to historical persons. Even mythological explanations have been offered in some cases. Enigmatic hunting scenes or processions of horsemen still occur, as they did on the earlier crosses.

Two crosses seem to mark a transition towards the panelled organisation of the scripture crosses. These are the South Cross at Clonmacnoise, and the

Cross of Patrick and Columba at Kells (pl. 89a, b). The Cross of Patrick and Columba appears to date to the first viking raids on Iona, with the exodus of the monks to Kells early in the ninth century as we have seen. It is interesting that both these crosses have connections with Iona. The South Cross at Clonmacnoise bears a strong resemblance to the Ahenny group, but it also has a representation of the crucifixion on the west face. The ornamental bosses stand out in bold relief and are now semi-spherical. This is the striking treatment found on the Iona crosses, where the entire east face of St Martin's Cross (pl. 90b) is an interlocking orchestration of raised bosses and serpents. The roundel at the centre of the west face of the cross-head shows the Virgin and Child enthroned with angels. The Child, seated on the Virgin's knee, is in profile, like the Christ child in the Book of Kells illustration of the same subject. On Islay nearby, the cross at Kildalton also includes this scene, which is not found on any of the Irish high crosses. There are clear links between the carvings that remain at Iona and the Book of Kells, as well as further links between the crosses at Kells and the Book of Kells itself. The Cross of Patrick and Columba, although rather small in size, has an attraction of its own, with subjects freely rendered and full of movement. Alone of all the crosses, it has the same emphasis on the symbols of the evangelists that is so significant in the Book of Kells.

As a result of new work on inscriptions, considerable advance has been made in the dating of the high crosses in recent years. The chronology of a number of crosses is reasonably secure. There are more inscriptions extant than had been recognised. Many crosses were designed with a plain panel at the bottom of the shaft to take lettering. However, in the case of the Cross of Muiredach at Monasterboice, the finest of all the scripture crosses, it seems that the inscription was added as an afterthought because it weaves behind the sculptured cats, carved almost in the round, on the foot of the shaft. This cross was erected in the early tenth century by the abbot of Monasterboice who died in 923. It belongs to the same workshop as the Cross of the Scriptures erected at Clonmacnoise for Flann Sinna, king of Ireland, in the first years of the tenth century. The cross at Kinnity, County Offaly, was put up by Flann's father, Máel Sechnaill mac Máele Ruanaid, who reigned from 846 to 862. From rubbings it has been possible to read inscriptions on the north and south faces. The south face, in translation, reads: 'A prayer for King Máel Sechnaill son of Máel Ruanaid. A prayer for the king of Ireland'. Máel Sechnaill established himself as king of all Ireland in 859. A good measure of wealth is reflected in the magnificence of the crosses. Patronage of vision and substance was necessary. The crosses were commissioned by kings and abbots, just as the luxury gospel-books bear evidence of the prosperity of the monasteries in whose scriptoria they were illuminated.

Even though the figure carving at Monasterboice is naturalistic, yet the abstract character of Irish work can still be felt. Françoise Henry noted that the Cross of Muiredach seemed to be composed on the theme of the semi-spherical spiral. Such spirals are used to decorate the ring and also the side panels, and from a distance they seem to cover the two arms of the cross. But on examination this 'ornament' is discovered to be figures of the blessed and the damned on either side of the judgement throne. It is remarkable that the Last Judgement here, with St Michael weighing the souls, was carved soon after 900, some two centuries before the same scene filled the tympana of Romanesque churches on the Continent.

This figurative art comes to an end very suddenly. The crosses of the eleventh and first half of the twelfth centuries are quite different. They show a diversity, from St Patrick's Cross at Cashel (pl. 92b) with strange pillarlike supports at either side, the imposing cross at Dysert O'Dea (pl. 92a), and other crosses of County Clare, carved from the local grey limestone, and the large Tuam cross erected by King Toirrdelbach Ua Conchobair (1106–56). These now show archaic tendencies, and ornament again takes a prominent place. Spirals have begun to disappear while animal interlacings with marked Scandinavian features predominate. On one side of these crosses there is always a representation of the crucifixion in very bold relief. With the first ornamental crosses the shape of the cross itself, raised against the sky, was all-important; it stood for both the symbol and the person of Christ. Later an elaborate theological commentary was spread in panels over the surface of the monument. Lastly the cross developed into a huge crucifix. It is interesting to note that during the period when viking raiders ravaged the country the growth of crosses reached a very high point.

The effect on art of the viking incursions is hard to evaluate. Treasures and books were certainly lost in the early Norse raids, but native warfare also accounted for much damage. Scholars tend to take differing views about Scandinavian influences, though there can be no doubt that silver became much more prominent in fine metalworking as a direct result of the 'foreign-ers'. Brooches are large and return to the genuine penannular form with a break in the ring. They have simpler designs than the Tara type of brooch, and plain silver is favoured with characteristic decoration of hemispherical bosses of burnished silver. It is not till the eleventh and twelfth centuries that Scandinavian art styles are current in Irish work. However, it seems rather strange that stone crosses of the late ninth and early tenth centuries should reach their peak of accomplishment during troubled years and show little sign of a viking presence. A. Kingsley Porter reasoned that Irish sculptors were loath to take over artistic ideas from people whom they saw as barbaric enemies.

Many valuable manuscripts were destroyed then; not that they were plundered for themselves, but rather for their precious casings of metal and jewels. An example of this is the Book of Kells. The first mention of this great work is generally believed to be the entry in the annals for the year 1007, telling how 'the chief relic of the western world' was stolen from the sacristy of the stone church at Kells. Later the manuscript was found fairly complete but stripped of its golden shrine. Intervals of respite allowed for activity, but for over sixty years from 920 the onslaughts had a devastating effect on ordinary life. The eleventh and twelfth centuries brought renewed stability, and the splendid art of the metalworkers of that age has come down to us in a sequence of objects, well preserved. Cultural life now began to thrive again. Scholastic work flourished in the monasteries, where important collections of texts in Irish were assembled.

Eleventh- and twelfth-century art represents a particular strain of Romanesque art, with an individuality all its own. With the integration of viking settlers and with connections on the Continent, it brought together many elements of diverse origin. Nevertheless it was still charged, for the time being at least, with some of the old Celtic power. Motifs were employed in slightly different ways, foliage ornament was now in favour, and new processes were used. Many reliquaries were made at this time, most notably a range of magnificent crosiers (pl. 93b), and also book shrines, such as the shrine of the Stowe missal (pl. 94a) and the shrine of the Cathach. The shrine of St Lachtin's arm (pl. 93a) was made for the kings of Munster about 1120, to house the relic of the sixth-century saint, patron of Freshford, County Kilkenny, and Donaghmore, County Cork. Although it is covered with ornament, there is an artlessness in its direct, almost severe, design. Like most of the shrines, it consists of a wooden frame encased in bronze plates elaborately patterned, mainly with animal interlace. The inscription is placed on the vertical strips that cover the joints of the metal plates. A plant scroll decorates the palm of the hand, covered in a sheet of gilt silver. The restraint and elegance of this shrine is typical of Irish art in the twelfth century. The Cross of Cong (pl. 96), made on the order of Toirrdelbach Ua Conchobair to enshrine a small piece of the true cross, is beautifully designed in the same manner with strong outlines and an abundance of Scandinavian Urnes interlacing animals in gilt bronze. Perhaps the most remarkable shrine is that known as the shrine of St Manchan, which is still preserved in the neighbourhood of the monastery at Lemanaghan in County Offaly. Originally as colourful as the Cross of Cong, with brilliant enamels and the same mesh of animal interlace, it also has a series (now incomplete) of Romanesque figures in cast bronze, highly stylised, almost to the point of caricature.

Manuscript illuminators used animal and foliage interlace like the metalwork, with the same mixture of Irish and Norse elements. But the manuscripts that follow the period of Scandinavian supremacy are far less imposing and without figurative illustrations. They still maintain some of the charm of earlier decorated initials. The Corpus Gospels (MS 122) have initial letters formed by animals, picked out in blue and purple, and surrounded by knotwork against a vermilion ground. Similarly, the capitals of the Corpus Missal (MS 282) are often of elongated beasts, entwined with snakes (pls 95a, 95b).

If illumination in Ireland was just a shadow of its former glory, nevertheless insular models had widespread influence on the painting of manuscripts abroad. Some scholars have even seen the style as a motivating force in the rise of Romanesque sculpture. In the end the distinctive character of art in Ireland, which sprang from its prehistoric past, had to succumb to a more general European mould. With the coming of the Normans the pressure was too great for native originality to survive.

Early Irish art is perhaps the most successful of all abstract styles of decoration. The artistic traditions of the pagan Celts had been brilliantly adapted to a spiritual art in the early Christian period. The Irish were able to retain a unique vision, the heritage of their Celtic past, up to the twelfth century. Today we are fortunate to have at least a partial understanding of the minds of sculptors, painters, and jewellers who lived at a remote date, yet whose work can still have an immediate impact. In their search for fresh approaches, modern artists in the twentieth century have helped to create a new interest in this art. From their study and that of various other disciplines, it seems that we are slowly drawing closer to the deep sources of early Irish art and the people who produced it.

# CHAPTER XX

# Ecclesiastical architecture before 1169

## ROGER STALLEY

THE austere ideals of the Irish church were more fully reflected in the character of its buildings than in any other artistic sphere. Until the twelfth century, ecclesiastical architecture retained a simplicity that forms a puzzling contrast to the intricate skills encountered in metalwork, manuscript illumination, and stone sculpture. For reasons that have never been satisfactorily explained, the Irish clergy were reluctant to erect the type of imposing buildings that many of them must have seen abroad. The story of Irish architecture thus centres on the simple stone oratories that survive in great numbers throughout the country, often in remote locations of great natural beauty.[1] More adventurous in structural terms were the detached bell towers, the graceful campaniles that represent Ireland's most distinctive contribution to the architecture of the early middle ages.

One immediate difficulty confronting the historian is the fact that the churches and towers that can be seen today are not representative of Irish architecture as a whole. Most belong to the era after $c$.900, and it is difficult to form a reliable picture of the first four or five centuries of Christian building. We have only a hazy idea, for instance, of the appearance of the churches erected by St Patrick and his followers. Moreover, apart from the clocháns or beehive huts, few if any of the domestic dwellings of the monks survive intact. To gain a more complete picture it is necessary to turn to documentary sources, particularly to the annals, to the ancient laws, and to the Lives of the saints, the latter providing some useful hints about architectural practice at a

---

[1] The major works of reference for the study of early church architecture are George Petrie, *The ecclesiastical architecture of Ireland anterior to the Anglo-Norman invasion, comprising an essay on the origin and uses of the round towers of Ireland* (Dublin, 1845); Arthur C. Champneys, *Irish ecclesiastical architecture* (London, 1910); Harold G. Leask, *Irish churches and monastic buildings* (Dundalk, 1955); Peter Harbison, 'Early Irish churches' in Löwe, *Die Iren*, pp 618–29; Maurice Craig, *The architecture of Ireland from the earliest times to 1880* (London, 1982), pp 25–48; Ann Hamlin, 'The study of early Irish churches' in Ní Chatháin & Richter, *Ire. & Europe*, pp 117–26. The comments and conclusions of C. A. Ralegh Radford, 'The earliest Irish churches' in *U.J.A.*, xl (1977), pp 1–11, need to be treated with caution in the light of recent research.

time when virtually all churches were constructed of wood. These sources can be supplemented by the fruits of archaeological investigation. The history of Church Island, a remote hermitage in County Kerry, was thoroughly explored by M. J. O'Kelly in the 1950s, and at Reask (also in County Kerry) an early church site, complete with its enclosing walls, was excavated by Thomas Fanning in the 1970s.[2] In the same decade exciting finds were made by the late Liam de Paor at Inishcealtra (County Clare) which included a rectangular oratory made of earth and wattle. This discovery was especially interesting, since the methods of construction appear to be similar to those credited to St Patrick at Foirrga, where a lack of suitable wood encouraged the saint to build 'a quadrangular church of moist earth'.[3] Regrettably, the potential for arch-aeological research has frequently been compromised by the continued use of monastic ruins as places of burial, a problem especially acute at such major monasteries as Glendalough, Clonmacnoise, Kells, and Monasterboice. More-over, the ruined condition of most Irish churches means that there is far less chance of discovering traces of constructional timber—floors, joists, scaffold-ing posts, etc.—the sort of evidence that has dramatically altered our under-standing of Anglo-Saxon architecture in England.[4]

Most ecclesiastical buildings in early medieval Ireland were constructed of wood, in the form of logs, planks, or wattlework, materials that have long since decayed. It is important to appreciate that the famous stone-roofed houses and oratories, found in eremetic sites along the west coast, as at Skellig Michael or Inishmurray (County Sligo), were not typical of Irish monasteries as a whole (pls 16, 97). This was a region where good timber was in short supply and where exposure to Atlantic gales made stone con-struction a more durable proposition. It is also important to remember that the populous monastic 'cities' of the ninth and tenth centuries, with their numerous houses, streets, and public spaces, must have differed enormously in appearance—in density of building if nothing else—from the ascetic com-munities of an earlier age. Ecclesiastical sites differed considerably in status, function, and wealth, and many of them were not necessarily monastic. General comments about church architecture must therefore be tempered by an awareness of the different types of community that existed over a period of 700 years and by the fact that, despite the force of tradition, architectural

[2] M. J. O'Kelly, 'Church Island near Valencia, Co. Kerry' in *R.I.A. Proc.*, lix (1958), sect. C, pp 57–136; Thomas Fanning, 'Excavations of an early Christian cemetery and settlement at Reask (Co. Kerry)' in *R.I.A. Proc.*, lxxxi (1981), sect. C, pp 67–172.
[3] Harbison, 'Early Irish churches', pp 628–9. Excavations in 1994 at Illaunloughan near Portmagee, Co. Kerry, have revealed further evidence for sod-built oratories; see Jacqueline O'Brien and Peter Harbison, *Ancient Ireland from prehistory to the middle ages* (London, 1996), p. 60.
[4] Warwick Rodwell, 'Anglo-Saxon church building: aspects of design and construction' in L. A. S. Butler and R. K. Morris (ed.), *The Anglo-Saxon church: papers on history, architecture and archaeology in honour of Dr H. M. Taylor* (London, 1986), pp 156–75.

design was far from static. The most radical changes in the period took place in the twelfth century, when traditional building practices were transformed by the introduction of the Romanesque style from abroad.

In 1162 one of the most ambitious clerics of the Romanesque era, Flaith-bertach Ó Brolcháin, abbot of Derry, constructed a new wall around his monastery, allegedly to separate the church (or churches) from the neigh-bouring town. This was a substantial operation which involved the demoli-tion of over eighty houses. An enclosing wall was a feature characteristic of the early monasteries and the monks of Derry were following a tradition that had existed from at least the sixth century. What made their wall remarkable was that it was built of stone, a clear indication of the status to which Derry aspired as head of the Columban church. Away from the west coast, enclos-ing walls usually consisted of an earthen rampart with a ditch or vallum outside, the top of the bank being surmounted by a hedge or perhaps a wooden fence.[5] Digging ditches and building walls was one of the first tasks undertaken at the foundation of a new monastery, a symbolic ritual that defined the sacred precinct or *termann*. St Enda, for example, is said to have used his own hands to dig deep ditches around his monastery, 'pulling out poisonous herbs and thorns' in the process.[6] Although the remains of these ecclesiastical enclosures are difficult to spot on the ground, several hundred have been detected in recent years through the use of aerial photography. Whether they were all monastic sites continues to be a matter of debate. The enclosures usually have a circular or sub-circular plan, with a diameter ranging from 90 to 120 m, considerably larger than the contemporary raths.[7] At major sites, like Kells, Glendalough, or Armagh, there were additional, concentric, walls, defining an inner and outer sanctum. In a few places, as at Seirkieran (County Offaly) and at Glendalough, enough survives to appreci-ate the enormity of the ecclesiastical earthworks. The Glendalough enclosure was approached through a stone gatehouse of eleventh- or twelfth-century date, two arches of which remain.[8] There must have been many monasteries

[5] There were, of courses, exceptions, like the stone enclosure around St Mella's cell at Lemanaghan (Co. Offaly); see now Elizabeth Fitzpatrick and Conor O'Brien, *Medieval churches of Offaly* (Dublin, 1998), ch. 1.

[6] Plummer, *Vitae SS Hib.*, ii, 62. In some cases local chiefs provided assistance in building the enclosures. The Life of St Mochuda tells how Constantine, the son of Fergus king of Alba, helped Mochuda build the monastery at Rahan, Co. Offaly: 'It was he who marked out the church of Rahan and dug the mound of it and cultivated "Constantine's Plot" to the south of Rahan' (ibid., ii, 291).

[7] Leo Swan, 'Enclosed ecclesiastical sites and their relevance to settlement patterns of the first millenium A.D.' in T. Reeves-Smyth and F. Hammond (ed.), *Landscape archaeology in Ireland* (Oxford, 1983), pp 269–73. Swan has noted at least nine sites with an inner and outer enclosure, including Duleek, Lusk, Tuam, Glendalough and Killala. He regards the majority of these sites as secular settlements with an ecclesiastical presence, whereas Hamlin prefers to see most of them as monastic; Ann Hamlin, 'The archaeology of the early Irish church in the eighth century' in *Peritia*, iv (1985), pp 279–99: 282.

[8] Contrary to prevailing opinion, there is no evidence that the arched gateway at Glenda-lough was surmounted by a tower.

where an impressive gateway, built either of timber or stone, was the first piece of architecture encountered by the visitor.[9]

In coastal regions, particularly in the west, where thin soils made ditch-digging impossible and where suitable stone was abundant, the monasteries were surrounded by dry-stone walls, as in the forts or 'cashels' of the region. The most impressive example is to be found at Inishmurray (pl. 97), where the masonry, almost 5 metres thick in places, describes a roughly oval shape, measuring 41 by 53 m. There are several points of entry through this power-ful rampart, each covered by stone lintels, and, once inside, open staircases give access to the top of the walls. Lesser walls divide the enclosure into different areas; within the various sections are three stone churches along with a (rebuilt) *clochán*. The walls at Inishmurray are unusually substantial and they may in fact pre-date the monastery. There are a number of docu-mented cases where local kings handed over existing raths or forts to the church, and in such cases the monastic communities no doubt retained the existing defences. The three concentric walls of dry-stone masonry that sur-round the monastery at Nendrum (County Down) have sometimes been interpreted in this way.

In secular sites, the purpose of stone walls and earthen banks was self-evidently defensive, but why did the monasteries require such fortifications? There were certainly occasions when monastic communities felt a similar need for protection, and an impressive circuit of walls might at least deter wolves, thieves, and casual raiders. In most cases, however, the walls would not have offered much of a barrier to a determined enemy. At Church Island the masonry was less than 2 metres high, and M. J. O'Kelly concluded it was designed more for protection against the weather than against any human threat. The chief function of the walls and ramparts was to establish religious and legal boundaries. They defined the sacred area or *termann* of the monas-tery (often rendered as 'termon' in place-names), separating the religious activities of the monks from the secular world outside, emphasising the area where the abbot's authority was paramount. When the wall of Derry was finished in 1162, malediction was 'pronounced upon him who should come over it for ever'. The termon was hallowed territory, marked out by crosses, pillar stones, and other Christian emblems. The concept of 'enclosure' is fundamental to monasticism and many of the earliest monasteries in the East had an impressive circuit of walls. Clear boundaries encouraged concentra-tion on spiritual affairs, as Bede implies in his account of St Cuthbert's hermitage on the Farne Islands, which was surrounded by an earthen mound so high that the saint 'could from thence see nothing but heaven'.[10] By

---

[9] Leask suggested that decorated stones at Inchcleraun belonged to a gateway, but there is no certainty that the stones to which he referred in fact belonged to a gate; Leask, *Churches*, p. 13.

[10] Bede, *Hist. ecc.* (1969), iv, 28.

discouraging monks from wandering abroad, the walls also made it easier to enforce monastic discipline.

Within the outer walls or vallum, a remote hermitage or religious settlement might contain a simple oratory with one or two domestic dwellings, like those excavated at Reask and Church Island. In larger monastic settlements there was a plethora of separate buildings, which could include a number of churches.[11] There was a need for a refectory and kitchen, as well as one or more houses for sleeping. At Iona the monks evidently resided together in a single building or 'great house' (there is little evidence to support the popular impression of rows of individual cells); an equivalent structure at Durrow was circular in form, though this seems to have been unusual, most monastic buildings being rectilinear in plan.[12] The abbot usually had his own lodgings. These could be quite impressive structures, to judge from an example at Armagh, which was described as 'the great house of the abbots' (it was destroyed by fire in 1116). St Columba made use of two separate buildings at Iona, his private lodgings or sleeping quarters (which had lockable doors provided with keyholes), and a wooden hut or writing house, which was elevated above the ground in some way. To accommodate visitors, each monastery had a guest house or *hospitium* and the picture was completed by various utility buildings, a scriptorium perhaps, along with workshops, storehouses, barns, and animal sheds.[13] A barn used for storing grain lay close to the monastic vallum at Iona and a *teach screaptra* or 'house of writings' is recorded at Armagh in 1020. To judge from the written sources, building methods followed traditional, local patterns, with little to distinguish monastic dwellings from those in the secular world. Solid timber was used for the 'great house' at Iona, whereas wattle, collected by the monks from the field of a neighbouring layman, was employed for the guest house.[14]

Although there is no indication that the domestic buildings were linked together in any formal way, the layout of the monasteries was not as arbitrary as previous writers assumed.[15] By the ninth and tenth centuries, if not before, there is evidence of a more structured approach, with regular patterns tending to emerge. When St Máedóc founded the monastery of Druim Lethan he is said to have arranged its ramparts and cemeteries, measured and marked out temples, churches, and round towers; although this is a

---

[11] The literary evidence for domestic architecture is summarised in John Ryan, *Irish monasticism* (Dublin, 1931), pp 285–94. See also Hamlin, 'Archaeology of the Irish church', pp 286–7.

[12] A. D. S. MacDonald, 'Aspects of the monastery and monastic life in Adomnán's Life of Columba' in *Peritia*, iii (1984), pp 271–302: 284–6.

[13] Anderson, *Adomnan's Life*, pp 495, 221, 271, 359–60.

[14] Ibid., pp 453, 329. It remains an open question whether the 'great house' was a church or a large domestic building.

[15] Hamlin, 'Archaeology of the early Irish church', p. 297; Michael Herity, 'The layout of Irish early Christian monasteries' in Ní Chatháin & Richter, *Ire. & Europe*, pp 105–16.

fictional description as far as the sixth century is concerned, it shows what was taken for granted in the eleventh or twelfth century.[16] The monastic enclosure was subdivided into separate areas, an arrangement clearly visible at places like Reask and Inishmurray where the dividing walls were made of stone. Access to the most sacred area around the main church or the saint's shrine was in normal circumstances out of bounds to the laity. The written sources contain occasional references to pathways, streets, and courtyards (*platea* or *plateola*) and in some major monasteries there is evidence for a formally defined space in front of the main church: this is very obvious at Clonmacnoise (pl. 98), where the cross of the scriptures was placed opposite the west door of the cathedral, presumably in the centre of a courtyard. When round towers were added to the monastic precincts (from the tenth century onwards) their location appears to have been chosen with care. Many lie a short distance to the north-west or south-west of the main church, with their doors facing the church, implying that there were no structures between, an arrangement apparent at both Glendalough and Clonmacnoise. A recent study of Armagh has gone further, arguing that, far from being an arbitrary collection of buildings, the monastery was deliberately laid out as an image of the heavenly Jerusalem.[17] The circular enclosure invites comparisons with the cosmos, suggesting a tangible link between this world and the next. Notwithstanding this concern for order, the Irish approach to ecclesiastical planning was fundamentally distinct from the systematic arrangements found in the Benedictine monasteries of the Carolingian empire, reflected most notably in the famous plan of St Gall (*c.*830). Not until the arrival of foreign monastic orders in the twelfth century did the Irish church accept the concept of the cloister and the classical principles of planning which it implied.

A distinctive feature of the larger monasteries was the presence of numerous small churches rather than one large structure.[18] At Glendalough, for example, there are at least eight stone oratories of various dates scattered along the valley, several outside the main enclosure. This appears anomalous, particularly when the tiny Irish churches are compared with the great basilicas erected in the monasteries of the Carolingian world. In fact the Irish custom was far more widespread in the early middle ages than is sometimes appreciated. Between the sixth and ninth centuries most of the major Christian sites of Europe included several different churches, the group of seventh-century churches at Canterbury being among the best-known. The

---

[16] Lisa Bitel, *Isle of the saints: monastic settlement and Christian community in early Ireland* (Ithaca, N.Y., 1990), p. 62.

[17] N. B. Aitchison, *Armagh and the royal centres in early medieval Ireland: monuments, cosmology, and the past* (Woodbridge, 1994), ch. 4.

[18] By the seventh century there is evidence that monasteries contained more than one church; Hamlin, 'Archaeology of the Irish church', p. 283.

Carolingian renaissance encouraged a trend towards integrating the main liturgical activities of a monastery or cathedral into a single large building, usually a basilican structure containing many different altars. This process had no impact in Ireland, where the clergy proudly adhered to their fragmented approach. The well-known incident that took place at Bangor in 1140 neatly illustrates the clash of the two traditions. The reforming prelate, Malachy of Armagh, had begun to build a great church on European lines, but he was hotly opposed by one local inhabitant, who insisted that this was a needless frivolity, proclaiming 'we are Irish not Gauls'.[19] The protester was in fact defending a custom that went back to the earliest years of Christianity in northern Europe.

Exactly how the various churches were used is far from clear, for we know little about the way in which religious rituals related to their architectural setting.[20] Various words were used to describe the early churches—*oratorium, templum, basilica, ecclesia* or *eclais, cell, erdam*—but the precise meanings of the words in an Irish context is not well understood. Did services take place in different churches at the same time or were some buildings reserved for special ceremonies? There is evidence to show that one of the oratories was usually associated with the founding saint, marking his place of burial or containing relics. As Lisa Bitel has remarked, 'monastic architecture, like hagiography, advertised the eternal presence of the saints in their relics'.[21] Thus there was a 'house of St Patrick' (*tig Patraic*) at Armagh, and a small structure at Clonmacnoise is traditionally linked with St Ciarán.[22] At Devenish the ruins of a Romanesque church mark the site of 'St Molaise's house', a twelfth-century reconstruction of a wooden building evidently destroyed in the fire of 1157. These buildings tend to be small in scale, and in some cases there may have been a deliberate attempt to reproduce the form of the saint's original oratory or domestic dwelling. Such buildings functioned as commemorative shrines and places of pilgrimage, rather than for congregational worship. At Armagh in the seventh century there were at least two substantial churches. The seventh-century 'Liber Angeli' explains that the laity were allowed 'to hear the word of preaching in the church of the northern district' on Sundays, whereas in the southern basilica 'bishops and priests and anchorites and the other religious offer pleasing praises'.[23] Armagh had a precious collection of relics, some associ-

---

[19] H. J. Lawlor (trans.), *St Bernard of Clairvaux's life of St Malachy of Armagh* (London, 1920), p. 110.
[20] Aitchison, *Royal centres*, pp 267–8, is one of the few authors to address this issue.
[21] Bitel, *Isle of the saints*, p. 57.
[22] *Trip. life*, ed. Stokes, i, 236–7. Radiocarbon dating of mortar has suggested a date between 660 and 980 for Teampull Chiaráin, which would place it amongst the earliest stone churches with mortar in Ireland; Rainer Berger, 'Radiocarbon dating of early medieval Irish monuments' in *R.I.A. Proc.*, xcv (1995), sect. C, pp 169–70.
[23] Aitchison, *Royal centres*, p. 240.

ated with St Patrick, others with the martyrs of Rome. The latter were housed in the southern church, and the 'Liber Angeli' describes a procession that took place each Sunday to this 'shrine of the martyrs'. In most cases there was one church of particular importance, the 'great church' as it is often called. It was from the *erdam* (sacristy?) of the 'great church' at Kells that the great gospel-book of Colum Cille, now known as the Book of Kells, was stolen in 1007. In some instances specific oratories were reserved for women—this seems to have been the case with St Mary's church at Glenda-lough—and there are instances where churches were occupied by independ-ent groups of ascetics. By 920 the *céli Dé* had their own church at Armagh.

Throughout the early middle ages, Irish craftsmen were famed for their skill at carpentry. There are many references to this expertise, the best-known being Bede's description of the church that Bishop Finán erected at Lindisfarne in 652, which was erected after the manner of the Irish, 'not of stone, but of hewn oak'.[24] The lives of the saints are filled with tales of 'wondrous workmanship', many associated with the mythical craftsman the Gobbán Sáer,[25] giving the impression that timber churches were far more than simple utilitarian structures. The tradition of building wooden churches survived well into the twelfth century. St Bernard of Clairvaux described how Malachy of Armagh built an oratory at Bangor, made 'of smoothed logs...fitly and strongly woven together, rather beautiful work in the Irish fashion'.[26]

Although not a single wooden church survives, there is considerable information about their design. Some were clearly quite large, as indicated by a grim entry in the Annals of Ulster for 850, which records the burning of 260 people in a wooden church at Trevet in County Meath. Even if the victims were squashed together, this must have measured at least 12 by 8 metres, and probably much more. The most sophisticated church known is that which served the double monastery of St Brigit in Kildare, described at length by the monk Cogitosus in the seventh century. This was a spacious building 'of awesome height', and, since the church served both monks and nuns, the main body was divided down the centre by a wooden partition. The chancel was separated off by a further screen, providing three distinct spaces within the building. The church was splendidly decorated, the parti-tions 'painted with pictures and covered with wall hangings'. There is also a suggestion that one of the doorways was embellished with carving. What is most surprising in an Irish context is the subdivision of the interior, so that, as Cogitosus explained, 'in one vast basilica, a large congregation of people of varying status, rank, sex, and local origin' could worship together under one

[24] Bede, *Hist. ecc.*, iii, 25.
[25] The achievements of the Gobbán Sáer are discussed by Plummer in *Vitae SS Hib.*, i, pp clxiii–iv.
[26] Lawlor, *Life of St Malachy*, p. 32.

roof.[27] The church at Kildare may have been exceptional: unlike early stone churches there were many windows and the chancel as a separate space has no known parallels until at least the eleventh century.[28] An ambiguous and less reliable description of a wooden church, evidently square in plan, is found in the 'Hisperica Famina'. Here the author describes an elaborate building with 'an ornamented roof', surmounted by four pinnacles or towers. It had a west doorway and an 'extensive portico'.[29] The oratory was 'fashioned out of candle-shaped beams', presumably akin to the 'smoothed logs' used by Malachy at Bangor. Most of the wooden churches mentioned in the written sources appear to have been made with solid timber, without the use of wattle, a point reflected in the term *derthech* or 'oak house', frequently employed to describe them.[30] Their inherent strength is confirmed by various tales in the lives of the saints. The Gobbán Sáer managed to turn one upside-down without dislodging a single plank, and St Samthann is credited with moving an oratory to a new site without dismantling it.[31] Derthechs were also blown over in high winds, apparently without disintegrating.[32]

Further clues about the appearance of wooden oratories can be gleaned from painting and sculpture. The temple depicted on folio 202$^v$ in the Book of Kells shows a church with an ornate roof of shingles (wooden tiles), emphatic 'barge-boards' (defining the edge of the roof), and carved finials on the top of the gables. Similar features can be seen on the capstone of Muiredach's cross at Monasterboice, which takes the form of a miniature oratory or shrine, the shingled roof in this case being very precisely depicted (pls 99, 100). The general picture of the derthech that emerges from all these sources is of a gabled building with strong corner-posts, the walls built with planks or planed logs. The buildings were evidently rectangular in plan, sometimes with a side chamber or portico attached to the walls.[33] The steeply pitched roofs were usually covered with shingles, though there were occasions when sheets of lead were used.[34] There are suggestions that the

---

[27] Seán Connolly and Jean-Michel Picard, 'Cogitosus: Life of Saint Brigit' in *R.S.A.I. Jn.*, cxvii (1987), pp 25–7.

[28] Cogitosus does not explicitly state that the church at Kildare was made of wood, though most authorities have assumed it was.

[29] Harbison, 'Early Irish churches', p. 626.

[30] Variously spelt *duirtheach*, *dairtech*, or *duirtech*.

[31] *Vitae SS Hib.*, ii, 257.

[32] As happened on St Martin's day 892 (A.U.).

[33] At Iona Adomnán describes *exedra, quae oratorii adhaerebat parieti* (Anderson, *Adomnan's Life*, p. 505), which has been variously interpreted as a chamber, portico, or chapel. The word *erdam*, apparently referring to some sort of sacristy or chapel, is often encountered in the written sources. On occasions it seems to be used as a synonym for an independent building; Petrie, *Round towers*, pp 438–44; MacDonald, 'Aspects of the monastery', pp 283–4.

[34] At Lindisfarne Bishop's Finán's wooden church in the Irish style was originally covered with reeds later replaced with lead by Bishop Eadbert; Bede, *Hist. ecc.*, iii, 25. A church roofed with sheets of lead at Mayo was burnt by Turgesius between 831 and 845; John Lynch (ed.), *Cambrensis eversus* (3 vols, Dublin, 1848, 1852), ii, 191.

shingles were sometimes cut in decorative patterns and ornamental finials embellished the tops of the gables. Inside there were wooden floors, evidently fashioned out of boards.[35] Some of these features were deliberately repeated in later stone churches, presumably to demonstrate continuity with the buildings of the past. The projecting 'antae' that became a feature of the gable walls of many stone churches can be seen as a reflection of the corner-posts of timber buildings, and there are many churches that have (or had) decorated finials. More intriguing are the roofs of the church on St Mac-Dara's Island, County Galway (pl. 101), and of St Molaise's House at Devenish, where the stones were cut to simulate wooden shingles.[36] At Labba Molaga (County Cork) the portal of a much-ruined oratory is fashioned from three pieces of stone, a direct copy, as Maurice Craig has observed, of a post-and-lintel doorway of timber.[37] Like the Doric order of the Greeks, wooden elements were evidently transformed into stone with the intention of providing permanent and supposedly indestructible versions of ancient buildings. The same phenomenon can be observed in Anglo-Saxon England, where the stone churches include a number of features taken from timber architecture.[38]

The Lives of the saints tell us more about the difficulties of building wooden churches than about their appearance. Finding suitable timber was one problem; another was transporting it to the site. It was often easier to float heavy timbers down rivers or across the sea than to drag them overland. Adomnán describes how oak timbers were towed by a flotilla of boats some distance across the sea to Iona, and at St Mullins, in County Carlow, workmen found it impossible to shift timber needed for the construction of a church: in this instance they were saved by a storm, which miraculously swept the material down the River Barrow to the gates of the monastery.[39] When a church was under construction at Lorrha, timber could not be brought from the forest on account of a lack of horses and manpower; St Máedóc intervened and a band of angels miraculously came to the rescue in the middle of the night.[40]

Once trees were felled, the timber could be used either as logs or split into planks, the latter practice accounting for the description of 'a church of a

[35] The Penitential of Cummean, in Bieler, *Ir. penitentials*, n. 19, 1. 188., par. 34; H. Murray, 'Documentary evidence for domestic buildings in Ireland *c*.400–1200 in the light of archaeology' in *Medieval Archaeology*, xxiii (1979), pp 81–97: 85.

[36] J. E. McKenna, *Devenish: its history, antiquities and traditions* (2nd ed., Enniskillen, 1931), pp 25–32. The church on St MacDara's Island also appears to belong to the twelfth century; Harbison, 'Early Irish churches', pp 621–2.

[37] Craig, *Architecture of Ireland*, pp 30–31.

[38] Rodwell, 'Anglo-Saxon church building', pp 171–4.

[39] Anderson, *Adomnan's Life*, pp 453–5; Plummer, *Vitae SS Hib.*, ii, 194–5.

[40] Charles Plummer, *Lives of Irish saints* (2 vols, Oxford, 1922), ii, 230–31. In the hard winter of 818 materials for building an oratory were carried across the frozen waters of upper and lower Lough Erne.

thousand boards' at Rahan (County Offaly) in 747. If a substantial labour force was available, there is no reason why wooden oratories could not have been built rapidly, perhaps in a matter of weeks, or even days. At St Mullins oak trees sufficient for a wooden building were cut down in a single day.[41] Decent equipment was obviously essential: saws, axes, hatchets, augers, adzes, chisels, as well as ropes; a few examples of such tools (albeit of poor quality) were recovered from the crannóg at Lagore in County Meath.[42] The alternative to solid timber was wattle, usually made of branches of hazel from which the bark was peeled off, and thus described as 'white rods' in the literature. St Brigit on one occasion managed to secure a hundred horseloads of such rods for building a house at Kildare.[43]

Archaeological investigation has yet to add much information to the history of the derthech. Although traces of wooden churches have been discovered in the form of post-holes, timber uprights, and pieces of wattle, they offer little information about the visual appearance of the structures.[44] So far ecclesiastical archaeology has nothing to compare with the well-preserved wooden buildings found in the urban excavations of Dublin and Waterford. Non-monastic sites have, nonetheless, provided confirmation of the much-vaunted skills of Irish craftsmen. Timbers with a sophisticated system of pegs and holes were reused by late-tenth-century builders in the crannóg at Ballinderry (County Meath), and the carved woodwork discovered in the Dublin excavations suggest that the 'wondrous carvings and brave ornaments' attributed to craftsmen like the Gobbán Sáer may not be entirely fictional.[45]

One of the most fundamental changes that took place in Irish church architecture was the introduction of stone, a development frequently regarded as a response to the devastation wrought by the vikings. Despite its popularity, such a view has little basis in fact. The development of stone architecture was a slow process, extending over several centuries, and it cannot be regarded as a swift response to the dangers posed by the

---

[41] Ibid., ii, 194–5.

[42] The equipment required by craftsmen is mentioned in the laws; see Eoin MacNeill, 'The law of status or franchise' in *R.I.A. Proc.* (1923), sect. C, pp 291–2.

[43] Murray, 'Documentary evidence', p. 84.

[44] Post-holes have been found beneath simple stone oratories at Reask and Church Island, as well as beneath a medieval church at Carnsore, Co. Wexford. Liam de Paor uncovered traces of wooden buildings at both Ardagh in Co. Longford and at Inishcaltra. Dudley Waterman found a timber structure underneath the stone church at White Island, Co. Fermanagh. For these discoveries and others, see Hamlin, 'Archaeology of the Irish church' pp 285–8; Hamlin, 'The study of early Irish churches', p. 123; Harbison, 'Early Irish churches', pp 627–9. Recent excavations in Waterford uncovered a series of post-holes under the later stone church of St Peter's (Maurice Hurley, C. Walsh and O. Scully, 'Waterford in the late viking age' in Michael Ryan (ed.), *Irish archaeology illustrated* (Dublin, 1994), pp 160–63: 161).

[45] Hugh O'N. Hencken, 'Ballinderry crannóg no. 1' in *R.I.A. Proc.*, xliii (1936), sect. C, pp. 110–11; Plummer, *Lives of Irish saints*, ii, 182.

Northmen. Contrary to the prevailing impression, the stone church (or *daimhliag*) was not fireproof, since such buildings were generally covered by timber-framed roofs. The occasional stone church existed in the pre-viking period: there was one at Duleek in the seventh century and another at Armagh in 789, when a man was murdered in the doorway.[46] Outside major centres like Kells and Armagh, however, they remained rare until the tenth century, long after the initial impact of the vikings was over. It may be significant that the first stone church recorded in the annals was built at Armagh, the monastery that claimed to be the centre of Christian Ireland. The development of stone building probably had more to do with status than with the vikings.

A more puzzling question is why it took so long for stone churches to become the norm. Timber was extensively used for church building in Europe, but for major monastic or cathedral churches it was seen as a temporary expedient. Thus a wooden church constructed at York in 627 was quickly replaced in stone.[47] Timber had some obvious disadvantages: it was vulnerable to fire and lightning, as the annals frequently testify; over thirty wooden churches were burnt between 612 and 795 either through accident or malevolence.[48] Even if safe from hostile action, rot and natural decay took their toll. Bede recounts how St Cuthbert's oratory on the Farne Islands became dilapidated with age, so that gaps between the planks had to be stuffed with hay and clay to keep out the wind.[49] Masonry was more durable and afforded better protection for relics and other precious items. Stone was also the Roman way of building, and as such conveyed a degree of prestige. So why was the change resisted in Ireland? Reverence for the simple structures associated with the saints may have been a factor, so too perhaps the ancient veneration for the oak tree, as one scholar has recently suggested.[50] Such beliefs may lie behind an enigmatic comment in the 'Hisperica Famina':

> Do you hew the sacred oak with axes
> in order to fashion square chapels with thick beams?

There were also practical reasons: in most regions of Ireland timber was in plentiful supply, making wooden oratories quick and easy to build. It took a

<hr/>

[46] Hamlin, 'The study of early Irish churches', p. 118. Long has pointed out that the period 800–850 sees a sharp rise in references to *derthech*s in the annals, which may not be giving a balanced impression of the quantity of stone and timber churches, especially before 800; W. H. Long, 'Medieval Glendalough: an interdisciplinary study' (Ph.D. thesis, University of Dublin, 1997), pp 121–4.
[47] Bede, *Hist. ecc.*, ii, 14.
[48] A. T. Lucas, 'The plundering and burning of churches in Ireland, 7th to 16th century' in Etienne Rynne (ed.), *North Munster studies: essays in commemoration of Monsignor Michael Moloney* (Limerick, 1967), pp 172–229: 174.
[49] *Two lives of St Cuthbert*, ed. and trans. Bertram Colgrave (Cambridge, 1940; reprinted 1985), ch. xvli.
[50] Long, *Medieval Glendalough*, p. 124.

year and a half to complete a stone church at Duleek, many times longer than the average wooden oratory.[51] Even if destroyed, a derthech could be replaced within a matter of weeks.

The character and development of stone architecture have been the subject of much debate. Traditionally it has been assumed that the earliest buildings in stone are the remarkable series of dry-stone huts or clocháns found predominantly along the south-west coast, where they were used as living accommodation in many of the exposed hermitages and Christian settlements.[52] The corbelled method of construction has a long history, from prehistoric tombs to twentieth-century farm buildings. No mortar is used, and as each stone is placed in the circular wall, it is made to project slightly inward over the stone below, forming a pointed dome. Such methods are encountered in various parts of Europe and are not unique to Ireland; there are particular concentrations in Provence and Apulia. The best collection of clocháns can be seen on Skellig Michael (pl. 16), perched on terraces almost 200 metres above the Atlantic waves. There were originally six huts, five of which survive. Entered through doorways with stone lintels and inclined jambs, they are surprisingly spacious inside: some are over 5 m in height, sufficient for an intermediate floor. The clocháns at Skellig are difficult to date, but they probably existed in 823 when the rock was plundered by the vikings.

A rectangular version of the clochán, the boat-shaped oratory, was developed to serve as a Christian oratory. There were two such oratories on Skellig Michael, and the remains of at least thirty of them have been identified along the west and south-west coasts. In structural terms the boat-shaped oratory is not as sound as a clochán, for if the building reaches any size there is a tendency for the roof to sag midway along its length. The oratories on Skellig were rather loosely constructed, but the most famous example, Gallarus oratory near Kilmalkedar in County Kerry (pl. 102), has masonry impeccably fitted together. Measuring 4.65 by 3.10 m (internally), it is entered at the west end through a lintelled doorway. There is a small round-headed window in the opposite wall. The craftsmanship is so accomplished that it is tempting to regard Gallarus as the culmination of a tradition that was already several centuries old. Opinions about its date vary from the sixth to the twelfth century.[53] Although most scholars favour a date towards

---

[51] Despite the length of time needed to build a stone church, the well-known commentary on the laws relating to charges states that a *daimhliag* cost the same as the *derthech* if they were both covered by shingles (Petrie, *Round towers*, p. 365). The Annals of Ulster (1164) state that a great stone church at Derry, over 90 ft in length, was completed in the space of forty days, though the fact that the time was mentioned suggests this was exceptional. The forty days may not have included dressing stone, which could have been prepared in advance.

[52] Françoise Henry, 'Early monasteries, beehive huts, and dry-stone houses in the neighbourhood of Cahirciveen and Waterville, Co. Kerry' in *R.I.A. Proc.*, lviii (1957), sect. C, pp 45–166.

[53] Peter Harbison, 'How old is Gallarus oratory? A reappraisal of the role of Gallarus oratory in early Irish architecture' in *Medieval Archaeology*, xiv (1970), pp 34–59.

the end of this range, boat-shaped oratories certainly go back to the eighth century if not earlier. The remains of an oratory at Illaunloughan, County Kerry, have recently been dated on scientific grounds to between 640 and 790.[54]

Corbelled roofs were also applied to a small group of churches with upright walls, as an alternative to thatch, shingles, or lead sheets. These roofs have straight-sided triangular cross-sections, instead of the curved profile found at Gallarus. A late example can be found on St MacDara's Island (pl. 101) off the coast of County Galway, where the ancient roof was rebuilt in 1975. The original roof was evidently reinforced with mortar and it has been suggested that wooden cross-struts may have been employed to prevent internal sagging, though no physical evidence of this has been found. A similar roof was erected over the small oratory on Friars' Island in the Shannon (moved to Killaloe in County Clare when the Ardnacrusha hydroelectric scheme flooded the island in 1929). These churches were small, and to prevent collapse in larger buildings some form of internal support was essential. This came with the introduction of barrel vaulting, the outward forces of the vault neatly countering the inward forces of the roof. There are several buildings that take this form, including St Columba's 'House' at Kells (pl. 103), St Kevin's church at Glendalough, and St Flannan's church at Killaloe. In both cases a tiny croft was fitted between the vault and the stone roof, accessible only by ladder through a hole in the vault. Built of rubble masonry, these buildings lack any form of adornment, but as architectural structures they were strong and logically designed, representing one of Ireland's most original contributions to early medieval architecture. None of the buildings is easy to date. St Columba's House has been linked with a church mentioned in the annals in 814, but the presence of a barrel vault makes this unlikely, as such vaulting was not widely used in Europe till the eleventh century.[55] St Flannan's definitely belongs to the early years of the twelfth century. The finest-looking corbelled roof was that erected over Cormac's Chapel (pl. 111) at Cashel (c. 1132–4), where the roof is made of ashlar, cut from local sandstone. Although impressive in appearance, the structural components were not as well integrated as in some of the earlier examples: the barrel vault was too low to support the roof, which instead had to be reinforced by a pointed vault immediately under the external masonry. High-quality ashlar was also used for the corbelled roof on St Molaise's

[54] On the basis of radiocarbon analysis of the mortar, reported in O'Brien & Harbison, *Ancient Ire.*, p. 60.

[55] Scientific dating based on the radiocarbon analysis of mortars has assigned a date in the range 1000–1280 for St Kevin's Church at Glendalough, and a range of 690–980 for the much rougher roof of Teach Molaise on Inismurray. Two samples analysed from St Columba's House at Kells provided dates in the range 540–1020 and 610–980; Berger, 'Radiocarbon dating', pp 159–74.

House at Devenish (1157), a much smaller building, which had no interior vault or support.

In the past some historians have tended to look at the stone-roofed buildings in a Darwinian manner, organising and assessing them in evolutionary terms. Thus Leask believed that there was a natural development from clocháns to beehive huts and on to corbelled roofs at places like Kells and Glendalough. Such an interpretation places too much emphasis on the stone buildings of the west coast. As Peter Harbison has pointed out, stone oratories like those at Gallarus 'may well be a local variant confined to the west coast of Ireland and divorced from the mainstream of structural development in Irish architecture'.[56] Outside the south-west, stone-roofed oratories were exceptional, for most of the stone churches elsewhere had roofs of timber.

Although a large body of stone churches survive from pre-Romanesque Ireland, there are few that can be dated on the basis of documentary evidence. Even when the annals record the construction of churches, as at Clonmacnoise in 908 or Tuamgraney in 964, there is no certainty that the references refer to the present buildings. Various alternative approaches have been attempted—dating by the quality of the masonry, by the presence or absence of mortar, or by the proportions of the plan—but all are open to objections. Within the last few years the radiocarbon dating of mortars has offered an alternative aid to chronology, a technique that may eventually transform our understanding of architectural development.[57] As the general simplicity of church design does not lend itself to sequences based on style, it is safer at the moment to consider all pre-Romanesque churches together, without attempting too much chronological precision.

Early stone churches have a number of common characteristics. They are single-cell structures, often with a length-to-breadth ratio of 3:2. A law tract, which mentions the payment for churches measuring 15 by 10 ft (4.5 by 3 m), suggests that this ratio represented some sort of official norm.[58] The north and south walls frequently continue slightly beyond the corners to form antae, one of the best-known features of early Irish architecture. These supported the roof timbers which overhung the gable wall.[59] In a few cases antae were replaced by corbels, a cheaper and more economical arrangement, seen at two of the churches at Glendalough (Reefert and Trinity). The most common form of roof was made of shingles, fitted over a timber frame; thus in 1125 the annals report that the shingled roof of the 'great stone church' of

[56] Harbison, 'Gallarus oratory', p. 58.

[57] Berger, art. cit.

[58] Petrie, *Round towers*, pp 364–6, citing T.C.D. MS H.3.17.; Harbison, 'Early Irish churches', p. 625.

[59] It is significant that all but two of the stone-roofed churches do not have antae, confirming the impression that antae were intended to support the overhanging beams of a wooden roof.

Armagh was renewed and provided with a 'protecting ridge' at the top (perhaps some form of decorated crest?). The west wall of the early churches invariably contained a lintelled doorway with inclined jambs, framed in some cases by an 'architrave' band projecting from the surface in thin relief, as at Tuamgraney. Though deceptively simple in form, the doorways are built of well-dressed stone, robust and imposing in appearance. Windows tend to be very small, their heads either triangular or round-headed. In the latter case they are often cut from a single stone, rather than constructed as a genuine arch. There is no evidence, either from documentary or archaeological evidence, for the use of glass, but, given its use in Anglo-Saxon England, it is hard to believe that it was unknown in Ireland. At the very least wooden shutters must have been essential in adverse weather. On many occasions services were conducted in semi-darkness, the gloom pierced by flickering candles, with the exiguous light glinting perhaps on the polished surfaces of a chalice or a reliquary.

Churches furnished with antae and lintelled doorways are widely distributed across the country, from Temple McDuach on Aranmore to St Begnet's on Dalkey Island. They vary considerably in size and some, like Temple Diarmait on Inchcleraun, are less than 3 metres long. But irrespective of size, there is a striking lack of variation in design: most stone churches of the pre-Romanesque age must have looked remarkably similar. A typical example is the church of St Fechín at Fore (County Westmeath), which was originally a single-cell structure, measuring 11.29 m by 7.21 m (internally), dimensions close to the popular 3:2 ratio. The walls of St Fechín's (pl. 104) are about 1 metre thick, sufficient to support a roof of thatch or shingles, but not of stone. The west façade contains an impressive lintelled doorway, the lintel stone itself having an estimated weight of two-and-a-half tons, smoothly dressed on the outer and lower faces. Above the door is a raised panel with a simple cross-inscribed circle.

Among the largest pre-Romanesque churches were the cathedrals at Clonfert, Clonmacnoise, and Glendalough. The cathedral at Clonmacnoise (pls 18, 98) was reduced in width in the later middle ages, and it remains an open question whether the original structure corresponds to that erected by King Flann and Abbot Colmán about the year 908 or to Flaithbertach Ó Loingsig's 'great church' of c.1100. The cathedral at Glendalough is slightly smaller, measuring 14.71 by 9.05 m, sufficiently close to a ratio of 1:1.618 to suggest that in this case the golden section was employed, as Con Manning has pointed out. While constructing the cathedral, the builders made use of materials salvaged from a smaller, earlier structure.[60] The antae are too narrow for a building of this scale and the lintelled doorway has been crudely

---

[60] Conleth Manning, 'The nave of Glendalough cathedral' in *Bulletin of the Irish Association of Professional Archaeologists*, no. 22 (spring 1996), p. 6.

heightened to suit its new location. The builders also recovered some large, well-shaped blocks of stone, which were incorporated into the lower walls.[61] The fabric of Glendalough cathedral provides a useful demonstration of the fact that the buildings we see today were not necessarily the earliest structures on the site.

Many pre-Romanesque churches, including the cathedral at Glendalough, now have chancels attached at the east end, but on close inspection these generally turn out to be additions to the original fabric. The chief architectural challenge posed by a chancel was the need to construct a chancel arch. The earliest-known cases in which nave and chancel were built together can be found in two churches at Glendalough, Reefert and Trinity (pl. 105), buildings that most scholars assign to the eleventh or early twelfth century. Here the voussoirs which form the chancel arches are made of large, precisely cut blocks of stone. This type of construction was an inheritance from the Roman world and it has been suggested that, without Roman monuments in front of them, Irish builders were slow to master the principles of the arch. However, the technology involved is not that sophisticated; if separate chancels were required it is hard to believe they could not have been built. The introduction of the chancel as a separately defined space probably had more to do with changes in liturgical practice and the need to separate the congregation from the officiating clergy, a development perhaps associated with the onset of the reform movement in the later eleventh century.[62]

The quality of the rubble masonry found in the early churches is often very high. When stones of different colour and texture are neatly fitted together, as in the so-called 'Men's Church' on Inishmurray, the visual effect can be highly attractive. The joints between the stones are often so precise, like 'carefully fitted crazy paving', that a certain amount of dressing must have been involved.[63] The actual character of the masonry varies a great deal, in part reflecting local geological circumstances. When granite was used, its intractable nature called for the use of spawls, small stones fitted into the joints. In the limestone areas of the west, oblong blocks were easily extracted from the quarry face, the results of which are splendidly evident at places like Kiltiernan, County Galway. In parts of Kerry a vibrant red sandstone

---

[61] It has often been supposed that there was a chancel at Glendalough from the start, on the basis of three D-shaped stones reused in the wall of the nave. Conleth Manning has demonstrated the fallacy of this, arguing that the stones come from tympana over doors or windows of the earlier building.

[62] The nature of the chancel in the early Irish church remains a problem. There is a reference to a chancel in the 'Additamenta' of Tírechán, which refers to a declaration at Druim Lías being made 'between the chancel and the altar' (Charles Doherty, 'The basilica in early Ireland' in *Peritia*, iii (1984), pp 303–15: 311–12). In this context the chancel (*crochaingel*) may refer to some sort of screen or dividing arch. The Rule of Tallaght contains an ambiguous statement that 'it was not customary for them to pass between the altar and the transverse choir which is in front of the altar' (Hamlin, 'The study of early Irish churches', p. 119).

[63] The description comes from Craig, *Architecture of Ireland*, p. 28.

was used, incongruously combined with grey limestone in the church at Ratass. There are many examples of what is termed 'Cyclopean masonry', which appears to consist of blocks of immense size. In fact this is an illusion, as the technique consisted of setting relatively thin stones on edge, leaving an unbonded rubble fill in the centre of the wall. The lower courses of Glendalough cathedral are constructed in this way; and at Temple Benen, on Aranmore (pl. 106), a single stone occupies about a third of one wall. How much of this masonry was actually visible is an open question. There is some evidence that the walls of early churches were covered by lime plaster, traces of which have been discovered at Clonmacnoise cathedral.

The varied character of early Irish stonework is also visible in the round towers (pl. 107), the most dramatic architectural innovation of the early middle ages, which even today give an identity to ancient monastic sites. Over sixty survive, many of them still substantially intact. The towers—or at least those that are complete—range in height from 23 to 34 m (75 to 111 ft), the tallest being that at Kilmacduagh (County Galway).[64] Unlike most medieval towers, they have a a pronounced batter: at Rattoo in County Kerry, for example, the diameter diminishes from 4.60 m at the base to 3.50 m at the cap. While this reduction may have been based on some structural rationale, it adds considerably to the elegance of the towers. The interiors were divided by wooden floors into several storeys (in some cases reinstated) and the topmost chamber usually had at least four substantial windows. The towers were surmounted by conical caps, built of stone on the corbelled principle. Doorways were generally raised well off the ground, accessible only by an external staircase or a ladder, giving the impression that defence was a primary consideration.

Among the early antiquarians, the function of the round towers was the subject of extravagant speculation, and it was not till George Petrie appeared on the scene that their religious purpose was firmly established. In a famous essay of 1833 Petrie demonstrated that the towers were monastic buildings, serving as belfries and places of refuge. The first documented reference to a round tower (or *cloictech*) comes in 950 when the tower at Slane 'was burned by the foreigners with its full of relics and distinguished persons together with Caineachair, lector of Slane, and the crosier of the patron saint, and a bell the best of bells'. There are in fact six references in the annals to people being killed or massacred in the towers as they tried to escape from an enemy.[65] A round tower was clearly a good place to store the valuables of a

---

[64] The dimensions quoted are all taken from G. L. Barrow, *The round towers of Ireland* (Dublin, 1979). See now Brian Lalor, *The Irish round tower: origins and architecture explored* (Dublin, 1999).

[65] Documentary references have been collected together in Michael Hare and Ann Hamlin, 'The study of early church architecture in Ireland: an Anglo-Saxon viewpoint, with an appendix on the documentary evidence for round towers' in L. A. S. Butler and R. K. Morris, *Papers... in honour of H. M. Taylor*, pp 140–42.

monastery and a good place to hide in an emergency. But despite popular views to the contrary, it is unlikely that the towers were designed with defence in mind. The word *cloictech* means bell-house and their main purpose was to contain a bell (or bells). It is important to remember that the routine of every monastery depended on the regular sounding of the bell, as we are reminded by an early verse:

> The clear-voiced bell
> On chill wild night God's hour doth tell.[66]

Punctuality was crucial and to maintain discipline the bell had to be audible. Indeed, the penitentials make it clear that those who arrived late at the daily offices were liable to be punished.[67] As monastic settlements developed into urban centres, hearing the bell may have become a problem: a tower extended the range of bell, while at the same time asserting the importance of regular observance. The popular view that they were a response to viking aggression should be treated with scepticism. The towers appeared in the Irish landscape over a century after monastic communities experienced their first taste of pagan violence.

It is generally assumed that several times a day the *aistreoir*, the official charged with timekeeping, climbed to the top of the tower and rang a handbell out of each of the four windows. While perfectly feasible, this would have been a tiring and time-consuming occupation. Alternatively a larger bell installed in the upper chamber may have been rung by means of a bell-rope, as was the practice elsewhere in Europe.[67a]

The idea of a belfry tower was not in itself unusual. What makes the Irish towers distinctive is that they were circular and free-standing. During the so-called 'first Romanesque' era, detached campaniles were quite common along the Mediterranean seaboard, but the vast majority of these were square in plan. The best parallels for the circular form are to be found at Ravenna, where there is a cluster of free-standing brick towers. Although the examples at Ravenna are built like elongated cylinders and lack both the distinctive batter and the stone caps, they seem to provide the most convincing background for the Irish belfries.[68] This is disputed, however, and some scholars argue for a derivation from the stair turrets of Carolingian churches. It would be interesting to know which monastery was responsible for introducing the

---

[66] Robin Flower, *The Irish tradition* (Oxford, 1947), p. 49.

[67] Otto Seebass (ed.), 'Regula coenobialis S. Columbani Abbatis' in *Zeitschrift für Kirchengeschichte*, xvii (1897), pt 12, p. 230: *Et qui audierit sonitus orationum, XII psalmos.* For references in the penitentials along the same lines see Bieler, *Ir. penitentials*, pp 55, 63, 107, 127.

[67a] Roger Stalley, 'Sex, symbol and myth: some observations on the Irish round towers' in C. Hourihane (ed.), *From Ireland coming: Irish art from the early Christian to the late Gothic period and its European context* (Princeton, 2001), pp 27–47: 39–43.

[68] Hector McDonnell, 'Margaret Stokes and the Irish round tower: a reappraisal' in *U.J.A.*, lvii (1994), pp 70–80.

round tower to Ireland. The consistency of design over the centuries suggests that a prestigious exemplar existed in one of the major monasteries, at Kildare, Clonmacnoise, Kells, or perhaps Armagh. The construction of the first belfry, close to 100 ft high, must have been a momentous occasion, a gesture which would have accorded well with Armagh's claims to jurisdiction over the churches of Ireland.[69]

A high proportion of the remaining towers belong to the twelfth century and several of these may be 'second generation' buildings. A few metres from the impressive Romanesque example at Devenish are the foundations of an earlier tower, perhaps damaged in the fire that afflicted the monastery in 1157. The annals record a number of catastrophes involving round towers, some of which were the responsibility of the builders. Several were built over graves, leading to differential settlement, a problem obvious at Kilmacduagh, where the tower leans a few degrees out of the vertical. This type of error may have caused the collapse reported in 1039, when 'the steeple of Clonard fell down to the earth'.[70] Foundations are often less than a metre in depth, dangerously shallow for such tall structures. The height and isolation of the towers also made them vulnerable to lightning; in 1135, for example, 'lightning struck off the head of the *cloictech* of Clonmacnoise and pierced the *cloictech* of Roscrea'.[71]

The annals carry references to round towers over a period of almost 300 years, from 950 to 1238, the latter date relating to the construction of a tower at Annaghdown (County Galway). Those constructed in the twelfth century are relatively easy to distinguish, on account of their ashlar masonry and Romanesque ornament. At Devenish, for example, the round tower has a decorated string course, embellished with grotesque masks, and at Timahoe (County Laois) there is an elaborate Romanesque doorway, carried out by masons who worked on the neighbouring church at Killeshin (County Laois). One of the finest towers is the late-twelfth-century example at Ardmore (County Waterford), where the ashlar is very precisely cut and external string courses define the location of the various floor levels (pl. 116). The pre-Romanesque towers are more difficult to date and there is considerable variation in the character of their stonework. Some are built of relatively well-coursed rubble; others like Kilmacduagh contain examples of 'Cyclopean masonry'.

In view of the lack of any previous tradition of tall building, the round towers were an adventurous undertaking on the part of Irish masons. The

---

[69] Although there have been suggestions that the round towers were preceded by wooden belfries, there is no archaeological or documentary evidence to support this. There is no reference to wooden towers (unlike wooden churches) in the legal tract relating to payment of craftsmen; Petrie, *Round towers*, pp 364–6.

[70] Ann. Clon., *s.a.* 1039.

[71] A.F.M., *s.a.* 1135.

gentle taper was executed with considerable skill (a batter as subtle as 1 : 77 has been discerned at Glendalough), and in many examples the stones are discretely shaped to match the curve of the circumference. There were problems associated with the sheer height of the towers. Stones had to be lifted to a greater height than in any previous building, requiring a reliable system of cranes, jibs, and pulleys, the latter presumably mounted on external scaffolds (at Roscam near Galway there is a set of putlog holes marking the position of the scaffolding timbers). Given the problems associated with tall buildings, it is hard to understand why the towers had to be so high. Even at 50 ft, the sound of a bell would have carried a good distance. Those towers that are complete—or almost complete—have an average height of 29.53 m (97 English feet) and it is possible that there was a belief, perhaps grounded in symbolic thinking, that the ideal tower should be 100 ft above the ground. The average circumference is 15.63 m (51 English feet), which suggests the employment of a 2 : 1 ratio between height and circumference. While most towers deviate from the average (some quite considerably), it is interesting to note that the tower at Glendalough (pl. 107) is 100 ft tall, with a circumference of 50 ft 2 in. This is unlikely to be a coincidence.

The problems associated with the construction of round towers brings us to the question of who actually erected monastic buildings. The Lives of the saints imply that constructional tasks were sometimes performed by the monks themselves, and this was certainly the case in the sixth century. Adomnán describes a vision in which St Columba saw his deputy at Durrow, Laisrén, working the monks beyond their strength on an icy winter's day.[72] At Bobbio St Columbanus is said to have joined in building work, although he was over 70 years of age. But the monks often received assistance from the laity, as in 664 when the local chief and neighbouring inhabitants helped Colman to build his monastery at Mayo; in 868 we are told that Queen Flann had 'many carpenters in the wood felling and cutting timber' prior to building a church at Kildare.[73] As time progressed, ecclesiastical building became increasingly professional, a point confirmed by passages in the laws. Although building was not necessarily a full-time occupation (master builders might find themselves making boats or chariots, carving crosses, or constructing stepping-stones), experienced craftsman, such as the wright of an oak house or a master of yew-carving, were men of status who were accorded a high honour price.[74] Such individuals were free to travel and work in any kingdom.

[72] Anderson, *Adomnan's Life*, p. 265.
[73] John O'Donovan (ed. and trans.), *Three fragments copied from ancient sources by Dubhaltach Mac Firbisigh* (Dublin, 1860), pp 178–9; see also Joan Newlon Radner (ed. and trans.), *Fragmentary Irish annals* (Dublin, 1978), p. 133.
[74] *Anc. laws Ire.*, v, 93–5.

A rather convoluted legal text outlines the charges that might be imposed for the construction of both wood and stone churches, as well as round towers. Costs varied according to the size of the building and the quality of the materials. A *derthech* measuring 15 by 10 ft was worth the equivalent of ten heifers, but if the roof was made of shingles rather than rushes, it was twice the cost, being the equivalent of ten cows. The text also explains how the charges were allocated: 'a third of it for trade [i.e., profit for the builder ?], a third for materials, and a third for diet, and for workmanship, and for smiths.'[75] Although the text may have been written down as late as the thirteenth century, it seems to reflect the practices of an earlier age, demonstrating that building was a complex professional business, which needed regulation. The complexities no doubt increased with the development of stone building, which added to the range of skills required, calling for professional teams of quarriers, masons, and layers.

The isolation of Ireland from European architectural developments gradually waned during the twelfth century and, long before the Norman invasion, Irish builders had adopted many of the techniques associated with the Romanesque style. This was a direct consequence of the church reform movement, stemming from the activities of men like Malachy of Armagh and Malchus of Lismore. The reorganisation of the Irish church created an environment that was far more open to architectural change than before. It is nonetheless remarkable that for almost half a century Irish builders remained immune to the massive building programmes that followed the Norman conquest of England, and it was not till the second quarter of the twelfth century that external influences began to have a serious impact. The most noticeable innovations came with the arrival of Cistercian monks in 1142, whose churches must have seemed enormous to the native Irish; it is no coincidence that the first Cistercian foundation at Mellifont was known as *an Mainistir Mór*, the Great Monastery. For the first time conventual buildings were systematically grouped around a cloister garth, with covered walkways giving access to the various chambers and offices. The architectural innovations, however, had little impact on the ancient foundations, which continued to erect churches that were tiny in comparison with those of the Cistercians. As Françoise Henry noted, 'it is disconcerting still to be faced with such indifference to the articulation of the various parts of a building and the play of masses, at a time when architects in Europe were ceaselessly experimenting with new formulae'.[76] Instead the local response was to furnish doors, arches, and occasionally windows, with intricate ornament. The contrast between the small but exquisitely decorated buildings of the ancient

---

[75] Petrie, *Round towers*, pp 364–6; the passages have been examined at length by Long, *Medieval Glendalough*, ch. 5.

[76] Françoise Henry, *Irish art in the Romanesque period 1020–1170* A.D. (London, 1970), p. 148.

monasteries and the massively austere churches of the Cistercians could not be more explicit.

These alternative approaches to ecclesiastical architecture developed alongside each other, often with the same patrons involved. Derbforgaill, benefactor of Mellifont, later founded the Nun's Church at Clonmacnoise, one of the most characteristic monuments of the Hiberno-Romanesque style. Diarmait MacMurrough, king of Leinster, founded the Cistercian monastery at Baltinglass (County Wicklow), and was also involved in the Romanesque church at Killeshin.[77] There has been a tendency in the past to treat Hiberno-Romanesque and Cistercian architecture as if they belonged to separate epochs, but by the time the masons began to cut the stone for the portals at Clonfert or Killaloe, at least a dozen Cistercian houses were either complete or under construction.[78] Confronted by Cistercian asceticism, the older monasteries flaunted their artistic traditions, an ornate portal being one way of asserting the status of a monastery and its sacred associations. Thus Flaithbertach Ó Brolcháin, the colourful abbot of Derry, made a new portal for his church in 1155, at the time when he was energetically promoting Derry as head of the Columban church.[79] At Roscrea (pl. 108) and Ardfert the churches were rebuilt with arcaded façades, a useful way of enhancing local claims for cathedral status. Art and politics were closely linked in twelfth-century Ireland, when arguments over the choice and location of episcopal sees encouraged monasteries to take a greater interest in the physical appearance of their churches. As an international style, Romanesque was bound up with the expansion of the Latin church to the periphery of Christian Europe; Ireland was not the only country where architectural changes followed in the wake of religious reform.

Another misconception is the notion that the Norman invasion of 1169 destroyed the Hiberno-Romanesque style. In fact, Romanesque ornament survived longer in Ireland than in most countries of Europe, particularly west of the Shannon. As late as 1216–25 the abbey church at Ballintober (County Mayo) was decorated with Romanesque carvings, giving the style a chronological span from *c*.1100 to at least *c*.1225.[80] It is not easy to follow the development of architecture during this period, as many crucial buildings have been lost—at Lismore, Cork, Derry, Armagh, Bangor, and pre-Norman Dublin, to name just a few. The annals proudly state that a new church erected at Derry in 1164 was 90 ft in length, far longer than most Hiberno-

---

[77] Roger Stalley, *The Cistercian monasteries of Ireland* (London and New Haven, 1987), pp 13, 242, 248; idem, 'Hiberno-Romanesque and the sculpture of Killeshin' in P. G. Lane and William Nolan (ed.), *Laois: history and society* (Dublin, 1999) 89–122: 91–5.

[78] Leask, *Churches, passim*.

[79] Herbert, *Iona, Kells, & Derry*, pp 113–15.

[80] R. A. Stalley, *Architecture and sculpture in Ireland, 1150–1350* (Dublin, 1971), pp 110–16; T. Garton, 'A Romanesque doorway at Killaloe' in *Brit. Arch. Ass. Jn.*, cxxxiv (1981), pp 31–57: 55–6.

Romanesque monuments. In this case Abbot Ó Brolcháin's building activities were backed by the high king, Muirchertach Mac Lochlainn, underlining the relationship between building and royal patronage that was especially notice-able in the twelfth century. One royal centre that retains its Hiberno-Roman-esque cathedral is Tuam, the home base of the O' Connor kings of Connacht. Here the church was reconstructed shortly after 1184, its chancel embellished with a diverse array of sculpture (pls 109, 110) which includes some of the most imaginative animal ornament found in Irish art.[81]

The inclusion of a chancel was one of the few developments that took place in the overall structure of the buildings. A more radical innovation occurred at Cashel, where square towers were incorporated at the east end of the nave (pl. 111), presenting a new architectural model for the Irish church (fig. 43). Paired towers, flanking the chancel or the apse, were a feature of many churches within the German empire, and it has long been assumed that those at Cashel were derived from St James at Regensburg or one of the other *Schottenkirchen*.[82] But eastern towers and turrets were also a

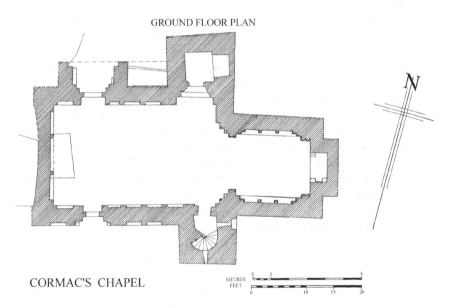

Fig. 43 Plan of Cormac's Chapel, Cashel, as surveyed by Richard Stapleton. Illustration by courtesy of Dúchas, The Heritage Service.

[81] R. A. Stalley, 'The Romanesque sculpture of Tuam' in A. Borg and A. Martindale (ed.), *The vanishing past: studies of medieval art, liturgy, and metrology presented to Christopher Hohler* (Oxford, 1981), pp 179–95.

[82] Roger Stalley, 'Three Irish buildings with West Country origins' in P. Draper and N. Coldstream (ed.), *Medieval art and architecture at Wells and Glastonbury* (British Architectural Association Conference Transactions for the year 1978; London, 1981), pp 62–5.

feature of Norman churches in England, so the background may be closer to home.[83] It was not just the presence of the towers that was novel, but the fact that they were square rather than round in plan. The southern one housed a spiral staircase (the first in Ireland?), the other evidently contained a tiny chapel. Although the twin towers of Cashel advertised the new international outlook on the part of the church in Munster, the architectural formula was not repeated. Elsewhere the incorporation of towers and turrets was handled in a very different manner. At Clonmacnoise (Teampull Finghín) a miniature version of the traditional *cloictech* was neatly placed between the nave and chancel and at both Ferns and Glendalough (Trinity church) a circular tower was added at the west end of church (that at Glendalough was blown down in a gale in 1818). A more bizarre scheme had earlier been tried at St Kevin's church at Glendalough, where a circular bell-turret projects from the roof like a chimney, giving rise to its nickname 'St Kevin's kitchen'.

The most important development of the Romanesque era was the construction of arches in recessed orders, each order having its own base, column, and capital. The system is well illustrated at Killeshin (pls 112, 113), where four concentric orders embellish the west portal. The actual opening measures a mere 85 cm, but the expanding width of the orders gives the impression of an enormous doorway. The effect is to draw the eye inwards, as if anticipating movement into the church. It is easy to take these arrangements for granted and to forget that they were unknown in Ireland before about 1100. In England a solid tympanum was usually placed inside the innermost arch, but this was rarely the case in Ireland, where the structure of the portals has more in common with those in Spain and western France. At Killeshin the engaged columns are in fact little more than pseudo-shafts, carved on the angle of the square jamb, a technique favoured in Hiberno-Romanesque. The most striking features of the portal is the steep 'tangent' gable, one of seven examples found in Irish architecture. In some cases these mark the outer edge of a stone porch, but at Killeshin and Clonfert, they are little more than a decorative or symbolical adjunct. There has been considerable debate over their origin and meaning. 'Tangent' gables are known to have been a feature of the screens that formed the entrance to the chancel in some churches of the Mediterranean world, and it is possible that the Romanesque examples may echo liturgical arrangements found in earlier Irish churches. They have also been seen as reflections of the gabled façades of ancient churches, as if the ancient *derthech* or *daimliag* was being reproduced at a reduced scale. Although the tangent gables and ornamental

[83] M. G. Jarrett and H. Mason, 'Greater and more splendid: some aspects of Romanesque Durham cathedral' in *The Antiquaries Journal*, lxxv (1995), pp 212–22; Eric Fernie, *The architecture of Norman England* (Oxford, 2000), pp 263–4.

arches of the Hiberno-Romanesque era mark a radical break from the austere lintelled doorways of previous centuries, one memory of the past was retained. This was the inward lean of the jambs, anomalous in the context of Romanesque, but characteristically Irish in its identity.

While it is not too difficult to recognise the local ingredients in Hiberno-Romanesque, there has been considerable debate about the imported elements. German, French, Spanish, and English sources have all been cited in connection with specific features. The wine trade has been used to explain contacts with western France, and the pilgrimage to Santiago de Compostela may have opened the eyes of at least some Irish patrons.[84] More important were the contacts between the twelfth-century reformers and institutions in England, which seem to have brought masons with English experience to Cashel and other sites in Munster. Cormac's Chapel (pl. 111) was among the first Irish buildings to be embellished with sculpture, and as such is thought to mark the birth of Hiberno-Romanesque, providing an early injection of foreign techniques, which within a few years were integrated into Irish practice.[85] It is unlikely, however, to have been the first building to introduce Romanesque techniques. There are other potential candidates in Munster, and there is also the church of St Peter and St Paul in Armagh, consecrated in 1126.[86]

Although both the scale of Cormac's Chapel, and its corbelled roof, are consistent with Irish traditions, the building is, in the words of Leask, an exotic import. Here are many of the familiar characteristics of European Romanesque: ashlar masonry, portals with recessed orders, barrel vaulting with transverse ribs, and walls enlivened with string courses and arcades. Everywhere there is sculptural adornment—carved capitals and corbels, along with geometric patterns on the interior arcades (pl. 114). Searching for the origin of these features has become a fashionable pastime for art historians. Much of the evidence points to south-west England, where there are links with the parish churches of Dorset and Somerset, as well with the choir of Old Sarum cathedral, a monument built by the justiciar of England, Bishop Roger of Salisbury.[87] Both the elaborate north portal and the smaller southern doorway contain sculptured tympana, decorated in an English manner with grotesque beasts. In seeking to explain these connections, it should be remembered that Malchus of Lismore, one of Cormac's advisors, had formerly been a monk at Winchester. Although the labour force at Cashel may have included English craftsmen, some of the sculptured heads have an Irish flavour, indi-

---

[84] Henry, *Irish art in the Romanesque period*, pp 148–89.

[85] Liam de Paor, 'Cormac's Chapel, the beginnings of Irish Romanesque' in Rynne, *N. Munster studies*, pp 133–45.

[86] For the Munster churches and a revised view of the arrival of Romanesque in Ireland see Tadhg O'Keefe, 'Lismore and Cashel: reflections on the beginnings of Romanesque architecture in Munster' in *R.S.A.I. Jn.*, cxxiv (1994), pp 118–51.

[87] Henry, *Irish art in the Romanesque period*, pp 169–75; Stalley, 'Three Irish buildings', pp 62–5.

cating that local masons were present in what must have been a thoroughly eclectic workshop. The same team was also employed at Gill abbey, the Augustinian Abbey in Cork.[88]

The prominence given in the annals to the consecration of Cormac's Chapel in 1134 suggests that the novelties of the building were widely appreciated, which makes it curious that the architecture did not have a greater influence. The artistic splendour was enhanced by painted decoration, remnants of which survive in the chancel, where a cycle devoted to the Infancy of Christ was painted on the surface of the vault. The finest remains come from a scene depicting the three Magi before Herod.[89] The paintings, which were executed about forty years after the consecration of the chapel, made use of costly materials, including lapis lazuli, vermilion, and gold leaf. The quality of the paintings underlines the importance of the chapel in twelfth-century Ireland, though its original function has never been satisfactorily explained. There is a strong possibility that it was intended as a private chapel for the kings of Munster, a burial place perhaps for Cormac himself. The nave now houses a magnificent twelfth-century sarcophagus, decorated with juicy-looking snakes in the Irish-Urnes style; its dimensions, however, indicate that this cannot have been designed for the chapel.[90]

Although the decoration of Cormac's Chapel had some influence in Munster, it was only one of the routes by which foreign ideas entered the country. The portals at Dysert O'Dea and Clonfert (pl. 115) include a curious scalloped ornament, the ultimate origin of which lies in the art of Islamic Spain. Arcades that decorate the west façades of the churches at Ardmore, Roscrea (pls 116, 108), and Ardfert have been compared with examples in western France[91] and at Ardfert the arcades are filled with a form of *opus reticulatum* which must have been copied from some building on the Continent.[92] There are also parallels abroad for arches decorated with human and animal heads. At Clonfert, Clonmacnoise, and Dysert O'Dea there is a delightful variation in which grotesque beasts bite the mouldings of the arch. Although this technique is thought to have spread from western France, the biting beast

[88] John Bradley and Heather King, 'Romanesque voussoirs at St Fin Barre's cathedral, Cork' in *R.S.A.I. Jn.*, cxv (1985), pp 146–51.

[89] Mark Perry, 'The Romanesque frescoes in Cormac's Chapel, Cashel' in *Ireland of the Welcomes*, xliv, no. 2 (1995), pp 16–19; Roger Stalley, 'Solving a mystery at Cashel: the Romanesque painting in Cormac's Chapel' in *Irish Arts Review Yearbook*, xviii (2002), pp 25–9. The only parallel for painted decoration in a Romanesque context is to be found at Lismore; O'Keefe, 'Lismore and Cashel', pp 126–7.

[90] John Bradley, 'The sarcophagus at Cormac's Chapel, Cashel, Co. Tipperary' in *N. Munster Antiq. Jn.*, xxvi (1984), pp 14–35.

[91] Tadhg O'Keefe, 'La façade romane en Irlande' in *Cahiers de civilisation médiévale*, xxxiv (1991), pp 357–65.

[92] This type of masonry, which is Roman in derivation, occurs in Carolingian buildings and it reappears in Romanesque architecture in Saintonge and Poitou: see, for example, Aulnay, Rioux, Pont l'Abbé and especially Échillais; also St Génereux.

has a long history in Irish art, so that its use in Hiberno-Romanesque may not be quite so straightforward.[93] Recent archaeological discoveries have demonstrated that beast heads gripping a ring had been used for the handles of early church doorways.[94] Indeed, the delight of Hiberno-Romanesque lies in the fusion of native and foreign components; imported elements were rarely employed without some local modification.

This is certainly true of chevron ornament, the zigzag patterns found almost everywhere. Recent studies have shown that Irish chevron, although inspired by English art, is far from being a tame derivative. Hiberno-Romanesque sculptors loved to embellish the zigzags with additional ornament, in the form of foliage patterns, monster heads, or tiny animals; there are spectacular examples at Killeshin (pls 112, 113), Clonmacnoise, and Dysert O'Dea. The most remarkable instance occurs in a rebuilt window at Annaghdown (County Galway), where the chevrons meet on an arris roll that takes the form of an elongated beast, its feet on one side of the arch, its twisting head on the other, the whole treatment evoking memories of borders in the Book of Kells. The introduction of amusing or unexpected details is part of the charm of twelfth-century architecture, from which the Cistercians in their sober monastic environment were not immune: at Corcomroe Abbey in county Clare (c.1200), fierce dragons can be seen sliding down the cornerstones of the chancel.

A striking feature of Hiberno-Romanesque portals, particularly in Leinster, are the human heads used to decorate capitals and arch stones. There are eleven such heads at Killeshin, some with deep pointed chins and curious moustaches. Human heads in various guises are found in the Romanesque sculpture of almost every country in Europe, a practice that has been ascribed to a mixture of Roman and Celtic influences. In Ireland they are usually employed quite prominently on the angle of a capital. What they meant to the medieval spectator is an open question. In the past there has been a tendency to dismiss them as a whim of the sculptor, but the ten heads lining the entrance to the church at Killeshin suggest a more profound intention. At Clonfert five of the disembodied heads in the gable are fitted under decorated arches, leaving space for their bodies to be added in paint. As Françoise Henry observed, this reproduces a technique found in continental enamelwork, in which only the heads were cast in full relief.[95] The

[93] George Zarnecki and Françoise Henry, 'Romanesque arches decorated with human and animal heads' in *Brit. Arch. Ass. Jn.*, xx–xxi (1957), pp 1–35.
[94] Michael Ryan, 'The Donore hoard: early medieval metalwork from Moynalty near Kells, Ireland' in *Antiquity*, lxi (1987), pp 57–63.
[95] Henry, *Irish art in the Romanesque period*, p. 161. By 1007 the main church at Clonmacnoise possessed a gold or gilded antependium which was purchased from elsewhere, providing a local precedent for the importation of liturgical furnishings; see Raghnall Ó Floinn, 'Clonmacnoise: art and patronage in the early medieval period' in Cormac Bourke (ed.), *From the isles of the north* (Belfast, 1995), pp 255–6.

scheme was evidently copied from an imported shrine or altar frontal and there can be little doubt that the sculptured figures were intended to have a Christian meaning, the elect in heaven perhaps, looking down on the world below. Above the arcade, further heads peep out of triangular 'windows' in a manner reminiscent of depictions of the Heavenly Jerusalem found in Romanesque art. Despite the popularity of the disembodied head, figural sculpture in Hiberno-Romanesque is relatively rare. In Ulster there are lintels (or friezes) decorated with New Testament subjects and at Ardmore the west gable includes a motley collection of figures, some evidently relating to the Last Judgement.[96] Given the prominence of scriptural subjects on the high-crosses of the ninth and tenth century, it is a surprise that figure sculpture played such a marginal role.

Part of the explanation for this is that the imagination of Romanesque masons was fired by contemporary metalwork, rather than by the sculpture of the ancient crosses. Indeed, the favourite design of twelfth-century metal-workers, the so-called Irish-Urnes style, is encountered regularly in stone carving. A synthesis of Irish and viking forms, it usually comprises two large beasts, often arranged diagonally, enmeshed in a web of snakes or ribbons. Before it was exploited by the stone-carvers, it had been employed on such works as the cross of Cong or the shrine of St Lachtin's arm. Good examples can be seen at Killeshin, Clonfert, and Clonmacnoise, and unusual variations of the style are represented on the windows at Tuam Cathedral. The sculpture at Tuam is organised in narrow panels, as if copied directly from metal-work; there are even small bosses, corresponding to metal rivets in the original (pl. 110).

Romanesque masons created dazzling, often complex, patterns of orna-ment, which in the case of the portals furnished magnificent entrances to the small, shrine-like churches. When highlighted in colour, the effects must have been stunning. The fact that paint was employed often comes as a surprise, but it helps to explain two of the more unusual features of Hiberno-Romanesque, the shallow nature of the carving and the preoccupa-tion with detail. In many instances the carving is so thinly incised on the surface of the stone that the designs would have been scarcely visible without the use of colour. The carving thus provided a guide for the painters as well as adding a three-dimensional element. The flat, graphic approach of Irish sculptors underlines their dependence on two-dimensional models in

---

[96] Susan McNab, 'The Romanesque figure sculpture at Maghera, Co. Derry and Raphoe, Co. Donegal' in J. Fenlon, N. Figgis, and C. Marshall (ed.), *New perspectives: studies in art history in honour of Anne Crookshank* (Blackrock [Dublin], 1987), pp 19–33; Susan McNab, 'The Romanesque sculptures of Ardmore cathedral, Co. Waterford' in *R.S.A.I. Jn.*, cxvii (1987), pp 50–68; Tadhg O'Keefe, 'Romanesque architecture and sculpture at Ardmore' in William Nolan and Thomas P. Power (ed.), *Waterford: history and society* (Dublin, 1992), pp 73–104.

metalwork and manuscript illumination. As for the cult of the minute, this had been a feature of Irish art for many centuries, a tradition inherited from the early Christian metalworkers. For Irish patrons diminutive scale was deemed to be a mark of quality, imbuing works of art with an unreal, mysterious appearance, an aesthetic attitude encapsulated by Giraldus Cambrensis, when he described an Irish gospel-book as the work 'not of men but of angels'. The delight in intricate and subtle forms, whether expressed in interlace, elongated animals, or geometric ornament, is fully revealed in Hiberno-Romanesque, nowhere more so than on the seven densely carved orders of the portal at Clonfert. While ready to take motifs from abroad, the masons and the clergy who gave them instructions were equally prepared to exploit the artistic resources of their own monasteries. Romanesque is generally defined as a pan-European style coloured by strong regional accents; a definition beautifully illustrated in Ireland, where the twelfth-century churches could never be mistaken for buildings in any other country.

# CHAPTER XXI

# Music in Ireland to *c*.1500

ANN BUCKLEY

BEFORE proceeding to discuss the question of music in prehistoric Ireland, it may be helpful to consider how the evidence is identified and assessed. Two requirements for the investigation of prehistoric music cultures are archaeological excavation and a broad range of comparative data. The former is essential, since the only evidence we can hope for is that of material survivals. We have no written records; thus objects which would have been used for producing sound, and depictions of these objects, or of music-making situations (e.g., dance), are our only sources. Comparative data are usually a *sine qua non*, for the range of sound-producing objects is, in theory, unlimited. If little is known about the musical behaviour of a particular society, how are we to recognise the tools that may have been used for intentional sound-production? By building up evidence for the kinds of occasions and purposes for which organised sound may have been used, according to particular types of social requirements and patterns of behaviour, we begin to build more realistic theories and hence assist in the identification of relevant artefacts.

At the most general level, any hard object is a potential sound-producing tool, since rhythm can be produced by beating it. A tube can be blown to produce a pitch; a stretched membrane can be struck (as in a drum), and gut may be plucked (using as a resonator the mouth, a hollowed-out gourd, or a soundboard). Objects retrieved from prehistoric sites are made of stone, bone, clay, and metal. Wood and other organic materials, such as membrane, are not robust enough to survive the ravages of time, therefore the nature of the substance has limited our prospects of recovering information. Paleolithic and neolithic sound tools that survive in various parts of Europe include rocks which, when struck, sound like bells (instances are documented in western Scotland, Scandinavia, and the Canary Islands); bone flutes, bullroarers, and scrapers in Scandinavia, Germany, France, and central Europe. From the central and west European bronze and iron ages we have metal rattles, jingles, and bells, and a range of bone objects. Ceramic pots have been recovered from Roman sites in Germany and from iron-age Scandinavia, with holes pierced around the neck, sometimes with traces of organic deposit. This is suggestive of a stretched skin which, when tied down under tension, could be struck like a drum.

The critical factor in building a theoretical construct is a plausible social model: to consider likely uses of organised sound, it is necessary to have some idea of the type of society being investigated, and from there to suggest a possible soundscape. For example, in a hunter-gatherer society, animal calls would be likely on a range of whistles, serving several functions, including that of decoys in trapping birds and animals, and calling to other hunters. The need to signal over long distances might be served by wood, bone, or metal wind instruments in addition to vocal cries.

While it is thought that the first Celtic immigrants arrived in these islands during the fifth century B.C., we have not inherited contemporary accounts concerning the way of life of British and Irish settlers. Writing is found very late in the Celtic period and is limited to memorial and boundary stones in a form known as Ogam, consisting of straight lines in various combinations of vertical and diagonal, which, despite its esoteric appearance, is based on the Roman alphabet.[1]

The observations of classical writers on the music of continental Celts merit our attention as we attempt to assemble an admittedly diffuse picture. Diodorus Siculus (born during the reign of Caesar Augustus, 27 B.C.– A.D.14), writing in Greek, derived his information from the Greek writer Poseidonios who, c.80 B.C., referred to the 'barbaric' nature and 'harsh' sounds of the Celtic war-trumpets, which he termed *salpinges*.[2] The Greek historian Polybius (b. Arcadia c.200 B.C., d. after 118 B.C.), in his account of the battle of Telamon (225 B.C.), described the terrifying effect on the Roman army of the din and clamour created by large numbers of Celtic trumpeters and horn-blowers, and by the war-cries of the entire Celtic army. He also referred to the fear inspired by the appearance and gestures of the finely built naked warriors in the front lines and by their leaders, who were richly adorned with gold torcs and armlets.[3] Diodorus Siculus wrote also of the lyric poets of the Celts who sang of heroic deeds 'to the accompaniment of instruments resembling lyres, sometimes a eulogy and sometimes a satire' (V.§31.2). Lyre-players are depicted on seventh-century B.C. Hallstatt urns

---

[1] Modern Celtic scholars have painstakingly addressed the problems of deciphering this script (also found in Wales, in those parts of Pembrokeshire settled by immigrants from Munster, the Dési), in contrast to a number of romantics who have insisted that a cryptic system of musical notation was intended; some have even postulated that Celtic interlace patterns comprise musical notation when a five-line stave is superimposed, with pitches designated at points of intersection. Apart from this being a wholly unfounded hypothesis, staff notation had not even been invented at this time.

[2] J. J. Tierney, 'The Celtic ethnography of Posidonius' in *R.I.A. Proc.*, lx (1960), sect. C, pp 189–275, 228, V. § 30.3, and 251.

[3] Polybius, *The histories*, trans. W. R. Paton (6 vols, London and Cambridge, Mass., 1967), i, 313–15.

from Sopron (in present-day Hungary) as well as on Gaulish and British coins of some six centuries later. The *carnyx* or animal-headed horn associated with the Celts is featured on coins also, as well as on the Gundestrup silver cauldron found in Denmark (but probably of Danubian origin), which dates to 100 B.C.[4]

Bronze-age Ireland has bequeathed an impressive quantity of horns. A total of ninety complete examples survive, as well as some fragments (plate 1a). It is difficult to date them precisely, but they are generally assigned to a period stretching from the late eighth to perhaps the second century B.C. They involved skilled craftsmanship and sophisticated engineering, and were evidently instruments of high status. Distinctive variations in construction detail and decoration point to the existence of several foundries across the country, and their quantity and distribution permit the study of significant technical developments over a long period of time. There is evidence for two types, in the north-east and south-west of Ireland, respectively, with both types occurring in the midlands.[5] Many of the horns were found in pairs, one side-blown, the other end-blown; the former are otherwise extremely rare in prehistoric Europe, and may represent an indigenous Irish development. Several theories have been advanced for the likely social function and musical possibilities of these impressive finds. An experiment was carried out in March 1857 by Robert Ball of Dublin (1802–57) on an instrument in the National Museum of Ireland, during which he attempted to produce high pitches of trumpet-like quality—assuming the instrument to have been used in this manner.[6] The repeated efforts resulted in a burst blood-vessel, which caused his premature death.

Holmes[7] provides a detailed account of construction techniques and performance capabilities.[8] His analysis of the mouthpieces indicates that the horns are not suited to calls at high pitches, yet they respond controllably when a player employs gentler wind pressure with flaccid embouchure, produ-

---

[4] A photograph of this depiction may be seen in Ian Finlay, *Celtic art: an introduction* (London, 1973), p. 59, pl. 21. It affords a rare glimpse of instruments in use: the scene depicts a figure, possibly a king, being sacrificed by drowning in a cauldron, attended by warriors bearing shields and holding a tree aloft on the points of their spears; behind this are three figures blowing horns.

[5] See distribution map in John Coles, 'Irish bronze age horns and their relations with northern Europe' in *Prehist. Soc. Proc.*, xxix (1963), pp 326–56: 331; also ibid., pp 349–56, for a catalogue of Irish wind instrument materials from the bronze age. Similar instruments have been identified from late bronze-age Denmark and southern Sweden.

[6] Ball had distinguished himself in geological and zoological science and had supervised the restoration of the historic harp in the museum of T.C.D., where he was curator.

[7] Peter Holmes, 'The manufacturing technology of the Irish bronze age horns' in Michael Ryan (ed.), *The origins of metallurgy in Atlantic Europe* (Dublin, 1979), pp 165–81.

[8] Experimental sound recordings have been made of some of the Irish horns; see Simon O'Dwyer, *Coirn na hÉireann. Horns of ancient Ireland* (cassette), CNE 001 (Blackrock [Dublin], 1994).

cing a low, penetrating drone rather like that of the Australian didjeridu. If they were used thus, we can only speculate as to the nature of any interaction between pairs or larger groups. Holmes's research suggests that pitch and precision of timbre were not critical factors—the bore of the instruments being left in a rough state. This cannot be interpreted as carelessness or incompetence on the part of the manufacturers, since in all other respects a high standard of engineering and casting technique is manifest. The horns may have functioned as signalling instruments. We should also be mindful of their possible use before and during battle to terrify the enemy by contributing to the clamour and tumult. Their combined sound, some perhaps used as voice enhancers, might have presented a daunting challenge to the fiercest of warriors, particularly when—as the evidence suggests—they symbolised power, status, and wealth. It is possible that they also had a role in corporate music-making, perhaps with a religious or other ritual function. The late bronze-age Dowris hoard from County Offaly consists of twenty-seven horns, forty-eight crotals (metal rattles), and seven metal vessels (plate 118). Coles has suggested that they may have been used in rituals connected with a bull cult.[9]

While detailed description is not afforded by early medieval Irish literary sources, two terms are encountered for wind instruments: *corn*, meaning a horn, and *stoc*, a wind instrument (horn or trumpet) of war. The practice of inspiring fear in the enemy by producing a war-cry with a deep rasping drone is well attested in the tales of Fionn Mac Cumhaill and his Fianna warriors (and documented as an Irish practice as late as 1581 in John Derricke's *Image of Irelande*).[10] The entire army is said to have made a loud noise called *dord-fhian* or 'Fianna drone', which had the reputation of overwhelming opponents.

In spite of the impressive nature and size of the horn deposits, the range of finds of Irish prehistoric sound-tools as a whole is meagre. This is no doubt due as much to the difficulties of identification as to the extent of materials requiring examination. A reassessment of museum holdings is timely in the light of continuing revision of interpretation and new work in the expanding field of music archaeology.

MOVING to the historic period, before the arrival of the Normans in large numbers Gaelic Irish society was led by lordly landowners on whom entire

[9] John M. Coles, 'The archaeological evidence for a "bull cult" in late bronze age Europe' in *Antiquity*, xxxix (1965), pp 217–19.
[10] John Derricke, *The image of Irelande; with a discoverie of woodkerne (1581)*, repr. with introduction, transliteration and glossary by David B. Quinn (Belfast, 1985). See Ann Buckley, 'Representations of musicians in John Derricke's *The image of Irelande*' in Vjera Katalinić and Zdravko Blažeković (ed.), *Festschrift Koraljka Kos* (Croatian Musicological Society; Zagreb, 1999), pp 77–91: 88.

communities depended. The country was divided into about 150 units of government called *tuatha*, each ruled by its *rí* ('king'). Larger units, comprising several of these *tuatha*, were built up by stronger chieftains whose families maintained ascendancy, so that only some thirty existed by the early twelfth century.

It was the custom to employ an official court poet or *fili*, whose duty it was to compose poetry in praise of his patron and to be the oral repository of historical events, presented in a way that would uphold the excellence of the king's line of descent. A *fili* often combined these duties with the office of *brithem*, or judge. He held the highest position at court next to the king and was also an *ollam*, one who had pursued an approved course of training in a particular discipline such as law or poetry. In the performance of court poetry the poem made by the *fili* was recited, probably in a declamatory fashion, by a functionary known as *reacaire*, accompanied by a musician, or *oirfidech*, who was usually a *cruit(t)*, a player of a stringed instrument. This musician enjoyed professional standing which was sometimes recognised in law as equivalent to the highest grade of independent commoner or freeman, that of a superior *bó-aire* (i.e. entitled to an 'honour-price'—the fine levied on anyone who insulted or injured him—of four cows). In some tracts it is allowed that he enjoyed this status whether or not in the employ of a court, and that he was free to travel about as he wished. Other craftsmen and entertainers, while having the status of freemen, had an honour-price only when officially attached to a patron. Within the feudal social system an individual with unfree status might acquire franchise by practising a skilled trade. Therefore, not only *cruit*-players but also smiths and physicians were classified as freemen according to the maxim of law, *is ferr fer a chiniud*—'a man is better than his birth'.[11] Chieftains' courts provided open house to travelling musicians and poets who received hospitality and gifts in return for their services of entertainment. The subject of a poem was often, not surprisingly, that of praise for the host. Where a collection of such praise-poetry was committed to writing it was called a *duanaire*, or 'poem-book'.[12]

The narrative literature of early Ireland is ostensibly mythological. Tales were recited for leisure and entertainment, and their content and style inform us greatly about the mentalities of their reciters and patrons. Exaggeration in accounts of personal valour or misfortune was an important convention. Detailed descriptions of superhuman deeds and heroic attitudes indicate the social codes of the time. And there are numerous references to music. The most common characteristics alluded to are the triad of weeping music (*gol-traige*), laughing music (*geantraige*), and sleeping music (*suantraige*), classifi-

---

[11] Byrne, *Ir. kings*, p. 175, taken from the 'Uraiccecht Bec' ('Small primer'), an eighth-century legal text from Munster, dealing with rank and status.

[12] See Brian Ó Cuív, *The Irish bardic duanaire or poem-book* (Dublin, 1983).

cations of great antiquity which have been observed in disparate cultures and civilisations. The functions of music include assisting in the casting of spells, tricking enemies, praising gods. There are numerous references to stringed instruments with golden tuning-pegs and silver strings. Whether these details can be relied on as accurate accounts of general practice is doubtful, but they contain significant information as to meaningful concepts among those for whom the tales were recited.

Similarly, when examining praise-poetry and genealogies, it should be borne in mind that the first task of the *reacaire* and of the *oirfidech* was to please the king, the chief patron, on whom board and lodging as well as future employment depended. Thus an impressive lineage, traced through a noble series of heroes as far back as Moses and Adam, is clearly not historically reliable, to say the least, but it demonstrates what was important to the distinguished personage being praised, as well as the nature of the tasks confronting the poets and reciters. Furthermore, the references to music underline, as in other areas, the importance of the tales as model-setting or exemplary exercises.[13]

From the numerous descriptions in Irish literature of lavishly decorated instruments and sweet-sounding music, we may form some idea as to the importance attached to this art at the courts, but the kind of music it was, stylistically or structurally, and the precise nature of the instruments, elude us, for no accounts are sufficiently detailed. We are thus heavily dependent on comparative information from British and continental sources for suggestions and implications as to possible instrumental types. Although likely, it is impossible conclusively to establish whether there were characteristically Irish instruments in existence during the early middle ages. However, examination of iconographic sources does suggest some possibilities; these are discussed below.

Irish sources provide many names for musical instruments. Primary among them are *cruit* or *crot*, and *timpán*, both stringed instruments. Others are *cuisle ciúil*, *feadán*, *píopaí*, different kinds of pipes and whistles, *crotal* (rattles), *corn* (a horn), *stoc* (a war-trumpet), *orgán*, a general term for a musical instrument, and *crann chiúil*. The last term has been used to denote both *cruit* and *timpán*. Literally, it means 'tree of music', probably because of the association of the wood from which they were fashioned; and with their sound often compared to birdsong, they were poetically considered as 'musical trees'. A similar term, but with other association, is *craeb chiúil* or 'musical branch'—a wooden staff with bells, carried about by poets, which

---

[13] See Ann Buckley, ' "And his voice swelled like a terrible thunderstorm ...": music as symbolic sound in medieval Irish society' in Gerard Gillen and Harry White (ed.), *Irish Musical Studies*, iii (1995), p. 34 ff., and eadem, 'Music and manners: readings of medieval Irish literature' in *Bullán*, iii, pt 1 (1997), pp 33–43.

functioned both as a symbol of office and as a means of summoning an audience to attention.

A *cruit* was probably a lyre, the earliest dating for which in Irish practice is difficult to assess. The most we can observe at present is that a player's legal status was incorporated in the earliest surviving version of the brehon law tracts, the oldest example of which dates from the sixth/seventh century A.D., though preserved in a twelfth-century manuscript. The laws determined a *cruit*-player's 'honour-price' as four cows, in addition to other payment. The tracts are silent on details of the instrument, as the only matters in need of definition were duties and compensations, reflecting feudal hierarchies and obligations. Older forms of *cruit*, in its meaning of lyre, were superseded some time during the late tenth or eleventh century by the trilateral harp, to which the name was then transferred.

A *timpán* (*tiompán* in modern Irish) appears to have been a plucked lyre, which came to be bowed around the eleventh or twelfth century, when it is thought the bow was adopted in western Europe. The plucked *timpán* was sounded with the fingernails, as was the *cruit*. But we observe a twelfth-century comment on the brehon law tracts where it is stated that a *timpán* player who suffered a blow and lost his nail 'from the black upwards' was entitled to a compensatory 'wing nail' (presumably a quill plectrum, or perhaps a false nail fashioned from quill), while his assailant was fined.

The earliest reference to a *timpán* is found in a source dating from the ninth or tenth century, whence a trail of comments leads through to the seventeenth; presumably this indicates that the instrument was obsolete by that time.[14] Lyres were long established in the Germanic lands, as well as in England and Wales, where they were termed *crowd* and *crwth* respectively. The Irish *timpán* was generally described as a three-stringed instrument in the earlier literature, but the bowed *crwth* that survived in Wales until the early nineteenth century was a six-stringed double-coursed instrument, i.e., with two strings to each pitch. The *crowd* seems to have been obsolete in England by the early sixteenth century; *crowder* became a term of abuse for an incompetent or unworthy fiddler.

Scant references to other instruments in the early sources should most probably be understood as an indication that they did not feature prominently in court life. There is, however, evidence of travelling musicians and poets, players of *cruit* and *timpán* as well as jesters and buffoons (*crosáin*). *Cruit*-players were more often attached to a chieftain's household than were *timpán*-players, the latter being employed usually in the absence of

---

[14] For a full discussion, see Ann Buckley, 'What was the tiompán? A problem in ethnohistorical organology: evidence in Irish literature' in *Jahrbuch für musikalische Volks-und Völkerkunde*, ix (1978), pp 53–88.

a more prestigious *cruit*-player, perhaps a comment on the status of the household.

THE question of ranking and social function of musical instruments is central to any investigation into medieval European music history. At the English and French courts, as well as within the German-speaking principalities, trumpeters commanded the highest status, probably because the performance of their office affirmed the authority and presence of the ruler (whether indoors at ceremonial occasions or outdoors). Players of stringed instruments, such as various forms of lute and harp, were often accorded the status of second rank, being members of the courtly retinue who were required to provide music for indoor convivial gatherings, such as banquets, or for more private occasions, such as the diversion or consolation of an individual in chambers. At a lower level were various other unattached minstrels, some of whom occasionally gained access to courtly audiences but otherwise entertained at fairs, at weddings for the lower orders, and at outdoor spectacles or tournaments. Consistently, the most reviled group were beggars, who often performed on hurdy-gurdies, accompanied dancing bears, and otherwise performed feats of acrobatics and juggling wherever they were tolerated.

The scribes of both the twelfth-century Book of Leinster and the late fourteenth-century Yellow Book of Lecan drew an imaginary sketch of the great banqueting hall at Tara as it might have been in the days of the mythological king Cormac mac Airt. Although the later manuscript provides greater detail, both contain depictions of seating arrangements and portions of meat due to all those present at the king's table, according to rank.

In the centre aisle are three hearths, a cauldron, a candlestick, and a lantern; the long tables are arranged two deep on either side of this group; a number of musicians are included. In the older manuscript[15] we observe *cruit*-players seated between horsemen and judges; all are served pigs' shoulders, as are deer-stalkers, fifth-grade poets, champions, master wrights, and their successors. Horn- and trumpet-players (*cornairí* and *buinnirí*) are at the same table, nearer to the door, between builders and wrights on one side and engravers on the other. These musicians are due the 'middle portion', apparently on a par with the cooks. Pipers (*cuislinnaigh*) are seated at the left-hand inner table at the end, next to the schoolteachers; this group eat the shin portions, as do *airi désa* (fourth-grade nobility), chess-players, soothsayers, and druids. Of the musicians only *cruit*-players were freemen, yet all are placed in positions superior to jesters and conjurors (who are entitled to

---

[15] Seating plan of Tech Midchúarda (the Hall of Tara) from the Book of Leinster in *Bk Leinster*, i, 116.

shinbones), king's fools (who are due backbones), and satirists and cordwainers (who receive mere shoulder fat).

The version in the Yellow Book of Lecan (plate 128)[16] is almost identical except that *timpánaich*, *timpán*-players, are seated with the *cruit*-players. Is this inclusion perhaps an indication that the instrument was more commonly known at court in the fourteenth century? While the sketch is, of course, an imaginary reconstruction of a prehistoric past, it is likely to be realistic as an account of social hierarchy, since an eighth-century law tract, the Críth Gablach, similarly describes seating arrangements appropriate to the hall of a petty chief.[17] This is the earliest surviving source of the seating protocol.

We may also draw useful observations from an eleventh-century poem on the Fair of Carman, a large-scale event of commercial, political, and festive importance, which took in the period down to the seventh century. Written between 1033 and 1079, the text provides references to trumpets, harpers, *tiompán*-players, fiddlers, horns, pipes, shriekers, shouters, pipers, story-telling, riddles, proverbs, and 'bonemen' (possibly playing the bones in the same way as spoons are used nowadays). The poem is thus highly informative regarding codes of reference, as well as providing substantial accounts of travelling performers and reciters. In particular, we find the first known mention of fiddles in an Irish manuscript, a discovery that should not lead anyone to claim that this type of instrument (even less its post-sixteenth-century version) was well established in Ireland by the time of writing. As the fair was an occasion of commerce, it is feasible that the instrument was newly in circulation and noteworthy for that. Or, together with the reference to 'foreign Greeks', this may be an instance of inclusion topical to the eleventh century, consequent upon the settling and integration of the vikings. Doubtless, this latter sequence of events generated fresh patterns of trade, with exotic goods on offer, or otherwise in evidence.

References in both the narrative literature and iconographic sources attest also to the realistic nature of these craftsmen and performers. Players of flutes and whistles are frequently referred to as providers of entertainment, often in the company of string-players. For example, in what is probably a late twelfth-century version of the battle of Mag Roth (637), which also provides an exceptionally detailed account of the technique of *tiompán*-playing,[18] there occurs a passage describing the music played on the eve of battle to put Congal Cláen, prince of Ulster, to sleep:

---

[16] The texts and drawings from both MSS are discussed in George Petrie, 'On the history and antiquities of Tara Hill' in *R.I.A. Trans.*, xviii (1839), pp 196–212. Included are line drawings of the schemes from both MSS (the Book of Leinster version opposite p. 205, that of the Yellow Book of Lecan opposite p. 207).
[17] Cf. Byrne, *Ir. kings*, p. 33, and D. A. Binchy (ed.), *Críth Gablach* (Dublin, 1941).
[18] See Buckley, 'What was the tiompán?', p. 62 ff, for fuller discussion of this topic.

Ocus ro chodail Congal iar sin re ciuin-fhogar na cuisleann ciuil, ocus re foscad faídemhail, fuasaídech, fir-truag na téd ocus na timpán ga tadall d'aigthib ocus d'form-nadaib eand ocus ingen na duas 'gá sar-sheinm.

(And after that Congal slept to the quiet sound of the musical pipes and the proph-etic ominous truly sad shadows of the strings and tiompáns being touched by the fronts [i.e. front surface of the fingers], sides [of the knuckles], [finger-] tips and nails of the performers who played so well on them.)

Thus wind instruments were not only instruments of war and court ceremo-nial. In 'Táin Bó Froích' there is an account of magical horns. Froích, the human son of an Otherworld woman, went on a mission to woo Findabair, daugher of Ailill and Medb, monarchs of Connacht. His hosts caused him a severe illness by inducing him to enter a pool where he was attacked by a water-monster. His horn-players (a chornairi) went ahead to the fort, where-upon the melting plaintiveness of their music caused thirty of Ailill's dearest friends to die of rapture. It may reasonably be assumed that here something more elaborate than signalling instruments was in question. We shall see sub-sequently how their symbolic importance was also transferred to a Christian religious context.[19]

In Froích's retinue were also other professional entertainers whose duty it presumably was to provide services while camped for the night. They in-cluded three buffoons (druith) wearing coronets; seven horn-players (cornaire) with instruments of gold and silver, wearing many-coloured clothes and white shirts; and three cruit-players, each with the appearance of a king from the style of his dress, his arms, and his steed.

This description is one of the most elaborate in terms of detail. The instruments referred to as cruit were carried in bags of otterskin, ornamented with coral over which was more ornamentation of gold and silver. The bags were lined on the inside with white roebuck skins, these in turn overlaid with black-grey strips of skin.[20] White linen cloths were wrapped around the strings. The frames of the instruments were decorated in gold, silver, and findruine ('white bronze'), with figures of serpents, birds, and greyhounds. As the strings vibrated, these figures 'went around the men', in other words, appeared to move and dance with the movement of the instruments and of the strings. The musicians played the three strains of weeping, laughing, and sleeping music, just as they had done when Froích's mother was in labour, reflecting the sequence of her emotions of pain, joy, and rest, supporting and comforting her in the process.

[19] See Buckley, ' "And his voice swelled" ', pp 40–41, for details of sources.
[20] For a recent study of harp bags, see Martin van Schaik, 'The harp bag in the middle ages: an iconographical study' in The historical harp: proceedings of the International Harp Symposium, Utrecht 1992 (Utrecht, 1994), pp 3–11.

There is a dearth of information to hand on most matters of existence outside of the Irish courts. Nor is there any clear evidence that non-professionals were engaged in singing and dancing for their own entertainment. None the less, we may assume only that such concerns were beneath the notice of learned officials and monkish scribes, the chroniclers of events and duties. And it is also likely that they disapproved (at least officially) of such behaviour, as it was contrary to Christian ideology. Dancing was suppressed by the early Christian church, which regarded it as devilish and immoral. As a result, there is no evidence for its existence as a professional and court activity between the late Roman empire and the early fourteenth century. However, it was hardly the case that Celts, vikings, and Anglo-Saxons never moved to music, but that more modern concepts and fashions of courtly step and formalised gesture would not have applied till later with the development of more elaborate court societies.[21] No specific word for dancing can be found in Old or Middle Irish. In modern Irish the words *damhsa* and *rince* are used, derived respectively from Old French and Scandinavian. The English word *dance* is derived from French, like its modern Irish counterpart. Examining an early Irish treatment of the dance of Salome before Herod, a tenth-century poem includes the words *clessaigecht*, acrobatics, *lémenda*, leaping about, and *opairecht*, dexterity, or perhaps 'skill in activity'. Old and Middle English (and Latin) sources reveal similar concepts; leaping and acrobatics seem to include dancing.

There is insufficient space to deal more fully with many related practices: some of them have been merely outlined above; others must await another occasion. Certain well-known topics are widely attested and need to be developed, ideally, within a more comprehensive sociological framework. A survey along those lines would include all uses of organised sound as a marker of circular and linear time. Circular time, the repetitive acts of day, week, month, season, and year, was ordered, for example, by the use of bells to signal moments in the daily cycle of work, prayer, eating, and relaxation; the chanting of the office symbolically marked the course of the twenty-four-hour day; day- and night-time activities, seasonal labour, etc., were symbolised by animal bells, calls, songs, cries, and other rituals associated with craftsmen such as smiths, builders, masons, agricultural labourers, hunters, fishermen; traders; travelling clerics and pilgrims; seasonal festivities for spring and harvest, and for the summer and winter solstices (later subsumed within the Christian calendar, though retaining pre-Christian elements); saints' and other liturgical feasts; processions; pilgrimages. Fairs, including kings' royal assemblies (political meetings) as well as days of public festivity, were

---

[21] See Walter Salmen, *Der Tanzmeister: Geschichte und Profile eines Berufes vom 14. bis 19. Jahrhundert. Mit einem Anhang, 'Der Tanzmeister in der Literatur'* (Hildesheim, Zürich, and New York, 1997), pp 5–7.

attended by stringed and wind instruments to mark certain occasions and their associated rituals of hospitality and entertainment. Linear time includes life-cycle rituals: birth (as in the tale of the three kinds of music performed for Fraích's mother while she was giving birth), initiation, betrothal, death; age-group rituals such as the activities of members of the Fían; initiation rites for kings accompanied by music on *corn* and *stoc*, followed by court entertainment; elaborate lamentations for the dead, particularly that of warriors and kings, and on occasion of loss in battle.

A Latin song from *c*.600 attributed to Columbanus is very suggestive of actual singing of worksongs. Although Carney may be correct in proposing that it represents a metaphoric exhortation to his monks to persevere in their Christian faith, like men steering a boat in rough weather,[22] it would seem unreasonable not to regard it as modelled on such a song from real life, given its use of the refrain, *Heia viri! nostrum reboans echo sonet heia!* ('Heave, men! And let resounding echo sound our "heave"!') in the first four stanzas, changing to *Vestra, viri, Christum memorans mens personet heia!* ('You men! remember Christ with mind still sounding "heave"!') for stanzas five to eight.[23] The lament tradition is well attested in the vernacular mythological literature, and reflected *inter alia* in the (?late sixth-century) 'Amra Choluim Chille' ('Lament for Colum Cille') and in the eleventh-century 'Eve's lament', 'Mé Éba'.[24] And it rightly forms part of the study of the history of Latin and vernacular *planctus* in the wider European tradition. The following lines from the probably seventh-century elegy (*marbnad*) on the death of Cummian, attributed to Colmán moccu Cluasaig, may well be suggestive of oral-tradition *caoine* which would certainly have existed side by side with the ritual compositions of official poets: 'A heart does not break, even if it painfully laments a dead man, no matter whom its lamentation concerns, if the ears of the living westwards from Cliu are not shattered by the lamentations for Cummine'.[25] There are many other references to weeping and lamentations on the occasion of death and burial. Not all of them may be assumed to have taken the form of a *caoine*, but they would probably have included this aspect. Examples may be seen in the Life of St Molua,

[22] James Carney, *Medieval Irish lyrics* (Portlaoise, 1967), p. xvi.

[23] See ibid., pp 8–10. The authorship of this song has been disputed by some scholars. Lapidge & Sharpe (*Bibliography*, p. 172, no. 654) locate it in the Carolingian period, attributing it to another Columbanus, abbot of Saint-Trond (*fl. c*.780 × *c*.815). This publication also contains further bibliographic references for the use of *celeuma* (organised rhythmic activity in groups) in Christian Latin poetry.

[24] Carney, *Medieval Irish lyrics*, pp 72–5.

[25] Fleischmann & Gleeson, 'Music in ancient Munster', p. 86. Cf. R. Thurneysen, *Die Irischen Helden- und Königsagen* (1921), p. 84.

who brought Croin back to life. Croin's sisters were described as weeping in a circle round her (*flentes circa eam*).[26] And in 'Betha Shenáin', in an account of the saint's having restored a chieftain's only son to life, when Senán arrived with his tutor, Notál, at Cell Mór Arad Tíre, he saw a great multitude wailing and sorrowing (*oc caíne agus oc toinsi*).[27]

The existence of formal laments may also provide valuable insights into questions of identity and patronage of musicians, as in the case of the lament for Conchubhar Mac Conghalaigh, harper to Domhnall Ó Donnabháin, who was chief of Clann Chathail from 1584 to 1639.[28]

THERE has been been little attention accorded the subject of women's music in medieval Ireland, that is, music performed by women for the purpose of entertainment and leisure. Clearly women were associated with lamenting the dead. What other evidence there is is not extensive, because the usual context for it is the sphere of private life and informal household activities. It is worth mentioning the *grianán* where women sat and did handiwork, such as embroidery, to the accompaniment of a sweet-stringed *timpán*. There are also occasional references to individual women musicians, whether professional or amateur, for example, the fairy musician in 'Aislinge Óengusso' who played a *timpán* to which Oengus slept.[29] Interestingly, I have not come across references to women performing on other instruments, not even a *cruit*. However, the paucity of information makes any speculation unwise. The 'Fragmentary annals' contain an entry for the year 689 concerning the slaying of Diarmait of Mide about which a woman satirist (*bancháinte*) is said to have sung at the Fair of Tailtiu—clearly a reference to a professional performer.[30] It is likely that more information will be brought to light in future research.[31]

---

[26] Plummer, *Vitae SS Hib.*, ii, 220, § 19.

[27] See Whitley Stokes (ed.), *Lives of the saints from the Book of Lismore* (Oxford, 1890), p. 61, l. 2105. Cf. the reference below (p. 763) to Gerald of Wales's comment on the practice of wailing at funerals among the Irish and the Spanish.

[28] See the study by Seán Ua Súilleabháin and Seán Donnelly, '"Music has ended": the death of a harper' in *Celtica*, xxii (1991), pp 165–75. See also Rachel Bromwich, 'The keen for Art O'Leary, its background and its place in the tradition of Gaelic keening' in *Éigse*, v (1945–7), pp 236–52; Breandán Ó Madagáin, 'Irish vocal music and syllabic verse' in Robert O'Driscoll (ed.), *The Celtic consciousness* (Toronto, 1981), pp 311–32; Angela Partridge, 'Wild men and wailing women' in *Éigse*, xviii (1980–81), pp 25–37.

[29] Francis Shaw (ed.), *Aislinge Óengusso: the dream of Oengus* (Dublin, 1934); see Buckley, 'What was the tiompán?', p. 56 ff., for further discussion.

[30] Buckley, '"And his voice swelled"', p. 52.

[31] See, for example, the useful survey by Ruth P. M. Lehmann, 'Women's songs in Irish, 800–1500' in John F. Plummer (ed.), *Vox feminae: studies in medieval women's songs* (Kalamazoo, 1981), pp 111–34, who discusses woman's voice in medieval Irish lyric. Her focus is not on authorship or professional performers, however, but rather on how the female voice or persona is presented and given expression.

IMPORTANT sources of historical information concerning the identities of musicians are the extensive collections of annals dating from the late medieval to the early modern periods, e.g., the Annals of Ulster (fifteenth century), the Annals of Connacht (fifteenth century), Dowling's Annals of Ireland (sixteenth century), the Annals of Clonmacnoise (English translation 1627, the original is lost), and the Annals of the Four Masters (seventeenth century).[32] They contain accounts of local events, genealogies of well-known personages, and obituaries. Identical information sometimes appears in two or more collections, indicating that scribes copied from a common earlier source. There are several references to musicians who were attached to particular chieftains. Usually in the form of obituaries, these musicians are referred to as *ollamh* or *saí* (modern Irish *saoi*, a wise or learned person), and both *cruit* and *tiompán* players are included. In all, fourteen professional musicians are recorded in the annals. The following example is taken from the Annals of Connacht: '1361 Gilla-na-Naem h. Conmaig ollam Tuadmuman re seinm mortuus est' ('In the year 1361 Gilla-na-Náem ua Conmaig, *ollamh* of Thomond in instrumental music, died'). This indicates that he was chief musician to the leading family of Thomond, the O'Briens.

Similarly, the next reference from the Annals of the Four Masters: '1361 Mac Raith ua Find ollamh Sil Muireadaigh i seinm agus i tiompánacht decc' ('In the year 1361 Mac Rath ua Find, *ollamh* to the Síl Muireadaigh in instrumental music and *tiompán*-playing, died'). The reference to the *tiompán* may simply qualify the kind of instrumental music which he played, although the distinction, *seinm/tiompánacht*, may indicate that he also performed on other instruments. An example of how accounts may vary is the following quotation from the Annals of Ulster: '1361 Gilla-na-Naem Ó Conmaid, ollam Tuad-Muman, idon re timpánacht, d'ég' ('In the year 1361 Gilla-na-Náem Ó Conmaid, *ollamh* of Thomond, that is, in *tiompán*-playing, died'). This is the same musician as mentioned above in the Annals of Connacht, but without the distinction between instrumental music in general and the more particular *tiompán* reference. Sometimes too there are discrepancies in the dates given for events, and differences of opinion as to whether a particular instrumentalist was a player of *cruit* or *tiompán*. These are small points which do not obscure our view of the social status of the musicians in question or of their attachment to specific households, and probably indicate only that those who recorded the information were not concerned with such technicalities.

---

[32] Full bibliographic details for these and the quotations that follow may be found in Buckley, 'What was the tiompán?', p. 78 ff.

There are two references to *tiompán*-players whose patrons are mentioned. Although only one of these players is specifically stated to have been an *ollamh*, it goes without saying that the other, Maelruanaid Ó Cerbaill, also had this status. The latter was one of the victims in an assault on Sir Seán Mac Feorais (Sir John Bermingham, Anglo-Norman earl of Louth), described in the Annals of Connacht as 'the most energetic and last baron in the country'. An account of the slaughter is provided in Clyn's Annals of Ireland, dated to 1329:

In ista strage et eodem die Cam O'Kayrwll, famosus ille tympanista et cytharista, in arte sua fenix, ea pollens prerogativa et virtute, cum aliis tympanistis discipulis ejus circiter 20 ibidem occubuit. Iste...vocatus Cam O'Kayrwill, quia luscus erat nec habebat oculus rectos, sed oblique respiciens, et si non fuerat artis musice cordalis primus inventor, omnium tamen predecessorum et precedentium ipsum ac contemporaneorum, corrector, doctor et director extitit.

(In that slaughter and on the same day, Cam O'Kayrwill, that famous *tiompán*-player and harper, a phoenix in his art, excelling in this beyond all others, and in merit, died along with twenty other *tiompán*-players who were students of his. He...was called Cam O'Kayrwill, because he was blind in one eye, nor did he have straight eyes but looked sideways [i.e. he was squint-eyed]. And if he was not the original inventor of string music, of all his predecessors and contemporaries he was the corrector, teacher, and director.)

This is of special importance, as it contains the only known reference to a school of *tiompán*-players, and to a particular teacher. However, it is undoubtedly suggestive of more widespread practice.

An unusual account is found in Dowling's Annals of Ireland (late sixteenth century) for the year 1137. Often cited as evidence for antiquity and continuity of a noble tradition, as also for the presumed superiority of Irish stringplayers, the text was officially invoked in sixteenth-century Wales during a meeting of Welsh bards concerned to protect their profession by establishing a musicians' guild:

Griffith ap Conan, princeps Northwallie, natus in Hibernia, ex muliere Hibernica, filia regis Eblane, aliter Dublin, duxit secum ex Hibernia lyras, tympanas, cruttas, cytharas, cytharizantes.

(Grufydd ap Cynan, prince of North Wales, born in Ireland of an Irishwoman, daughter of the king of Eblana, otherwise Dublin, brought with him from Ireland *lyrae*, *tympanae*, *cruttae*, *cytharae*, and players of *cytharae*.)

THAT Ireland had an established reputation for instrumental music during the middle ages is indicated by several writers, including Gerald of Wales. And so it has sometimes been claimed that these musicians were brought to Wales specifically for the purpose of training Welsh players, in order that authority and pedigree might subsequently be claimed for the guild in the fifteenth century. Corroborative evidence from Welsh sources indicates the likely truth of this, and of close intercourse in general between Wales and Ireland in political, ecclesiastical, and artistic matters during the twelfth century.[33] Only the issue of precise dating seems in doubt here, since 1137 is in fact the year of Grufydd's death. It seems likely therefore that the reference is an incomplete copy of an obit taken from an earlier source (or from oral tradition), in which some of Grufydd's accomplishments were recorded.

A more substantial source of information is the account by Giraldus Cambrensis (Gerald of Wales), a Norman-Welsh cleric who first visited Ireland in 1183. Through his maternal grandmother, Gerald was related to all of the influential Norman families of Ireland. He made his journey with his brother Philip, in order to reclaim title to lands lost over the years. Two much-debated works flowed from Gerald's pen on matters Irish (he also wrote accounts of travels in Wales and numerous discourses on religious and ethical topics): 'Topographia Hibernica' ('The Irish topography'),[34] and 'Expugnatio Hibernica' ('The conquest of Ireland').[35] It is the former that concerns us here, as it presents much provocative information on music-making, as well as on people and manners. It is true that both works contain remarks that are unsympathetic to Irish inhabitants: Gerald failed to make allowances for the fact that his own view of the world reflected very different cultural norms. He was accustomed to life among the wealthy and influential in the cities of continental Europe, and had a fine regard for social degree and etiquette. An exception to his displeasure was Irish music, particularly harping, which he praised repeatedly.

Gerald's travels were confined to the south-east of Ireland, while his observations imply knowledge of a much wider area and draw on material that is clearly secondary. Perhaps his Irish relatives provided him with further accounts; it is clear that he was an avid collector of didactic tales. Much of his writing was done during his second trip to the country in 1185; he accompanied Prince John, newly appointed 'lord of Ireland'. It is possible that impressions gathered during his first trip were enhanced by several other writers' accounts and included in his presentation. And he may have (silently) incorporated fables and opinions derived from people he met.

---

[33] See Sally Harper, 'So how many Irishmen went to Glyn Achlach? Early accounts of the formation of *Cerdd Dant*' (paper presented at the Fifth Conference of the Centre for Advanced Welsh Music Studies, University of Wales, Bangor, July 1999).

[34] J. F. Dimock (ed.), *Topographia Hibernica et Expugnatio Hibernica* (8 vols, London, 1861–91), v. See also J. J. O'Meara (ed.), 'Giraldus Cambrensis in Topographia Hibernicae. Text of the first recension' in *R.I.A. Proc.*, lii (1948–50), sect. C, pp 113–78; idem (trans.), *The first version of the Topography of Ireland* (Dundalk, 1951).

[35] See A. B. Scott and F. X. Martin (ed. and trans.), *Expugnatio Hibernica: the conquest of Ireland, by Giraldus Cambrensis* (Dublin, 1978).

The many copies of 'Topographia' attest to its wide popularity during Gerald's time and after. Those currently available emanate from a period spanning 400 years (from the twelfth to the sixteenth century) and are now found in the holdings of the National Library of Ireland, Westminster abbey, the British Library, Cambridge University Library, Corpus Christi College, Cambridge, and the Bodleian Library, Oxford. Despite elaborate disputes on what Gerald saw and wrote about, there is as yet no scholarly account in which a detailed comparative survey is presented of various versions of the text. It would be invaluable to review the points of concordance and disparity in accretion, omission, and the use of illustrations. These latter, not found in all surviving copies, depict people (including musicians), animals, and plants.

Three manuscripts contain a rich variety of illustrations which include instruments: MS 700 (f. 42$^r$) in the National Library of Ireland (possibly a late twelfth- or early thirteenth-century source), MS Royal 13 B VIII in the British Library (late twelfth- or early thirteenth-century), and MS Ff.1.27 in Cambridge University Library (late thirteenth- or early fourteenth-century) include depictions of monks blowing animal horns. The Dublin manuscript depicts a harper tuning his instrument with a tuning key (f. 36$^r$); the British Library version illustrates a female figure playing a psaltery with two beaters (f. 26$^r$). The Cambridge source includes both harper (f. 39$^v$) and psaltery player (f. 40$^r$—the latter also tuning her instrument (with a tuning key), while plucking a string with a plectrum in her left hand. Both harp representations are of low-headed instruments, typical medieval harps. In all of the above instances of decoration the text is as follows:[36]

In musicis solum instrumentis commendabilem invenio genti istius diligentiam. In quibus, prae omni natione quam vidimus, incomparabiliter instructa est. Non enim in his, sicut in Britannicis quibus assueti sumus instrumentis, tarda et morosa est modulatio verum velox et praeceps, suavis tamen et jocunda sonoritas. Mirum quod, in tanta tam praecepiti digitorum rapacitate, musica servatur proportio; et arte per omnia indemni, inter crispatos modulos, organaque multipliciter intricata, tam suavi velocitate, tam dispari paritate, tam discordi concordia, consona redditur et completur melodia.

(It is only in the case of musical instruments that I find any commendable diligence among these people; on them they are incomparably more skilled than any people we have seen. The manner of playing is not as on British instruments to which we are accustomed, slow and solemn, but truly quick and joyous, while the sound is sweet and pleasant. It is remarkable how, with such rapid fingerwork, the rhythm of the music is maintained; and with unimpaired art throughout, against the ornate measures [divisions? extemporisations?] and the extremely intricate organa [imitative tex-

---

[36] *Distinctio*, III, cap. 11. Cf. Dimock, pp 153–4.

tures? suggestions of polyphony?], with such smooth rapidity, such sharing of the material between the parts, such concord achieved through [rapidly shifting?] discord, the melodic line is preserved and complete.)

Seu diatesseron, seu diapente chordae concrepent, semper tamen a B molli incipiunt, et in idem redunt, ut cuncta sub jocundae sonoritatis dulcedine compleantur.

(Whether the strings strike together the intervals of a fourth or a fifth [the players] always begin on a B flat and return to the same, so that everything is concluded with the sweetness of joyous sounds.)

Tam subtiliter modulos intrant et exeunt; sicque, sub obtuso grossioris chordae sonitu, gracilium tinnitus licentius ludunt, latentius delectant, lasciviusque demulcent, ut pars artis maxima videatur artem velare, tanquam. 'Si lateat, prosit ars deprensa pudorem.' Hinc accidit ut ea, quae subtilius intuentibus, et artis arcana acute discernentibus, internas et ineffabiles comparant animi delicias, ea non attendentibus, sed quasi videndo non videntibus, et audiendo non intelligentibus, aures potius onerent quam delectent; et tanquam confuso inordinatoque strepitu, invitis auditoribus fastidia pariant taediosa.

(So subtly do they approach and leave their rhythmic patterns; they freely play the tinkling sounds [on the thinner strings] above the more sustained tone of the thicker strings, they take such secret delight and caress [the strings] so sensuously that the most important element in their art appears to be in veiling it, as if 'it were the better for being hidden; art revealed brings shame'.[37] Hence it happens that those things which afford personal delight to people of subtle perception and acute discernment of the secrets of the art, burden rather than delight the ears of those who have no such appreciation; looking, they see not; hearing, they understand not; to unwilling hearers fastidious things appear tedious and have a confused and disordered sound.)

Notandum vero quod Scotia et Wallia, haec propagationis, illa commeationis et affinitatis gratia, Hiberniam in modulis aemula imitari nituntur disciplina. Hibernia quidem tantum duobus utitur et delectatur instrumentis; cithara scilicet, et tympano. Scotia tribus; cithara, tympano, et choro. Wallia vero cithara, tibiis, et choro.

(It is truly to be noted that both Scotland and Wales, the former by virtue of affinity and intercourse, the latter by virtue of propagation, use teaching to imitate and rival Ireland in musical style. Ireland uses and delights in two instruments only, the *cithara*, namely, and the *timpanum*. Scotland uses three, the *cithara*, the *timpanum*, and the *chorus*. Wales, in truth, uses the *cithara*, the *tibiae* and the *chorus*.)

Aeneis quoque utuntur chordis, non de corio factis. Multorum autem opinione hodie Scotia non tantum magistram aequiparavit Hiberniam, verum etiam in musica peritia longe praevalet et praecellit. Unde et ibi quasi fontem artis requierunt.

(They also use strings made of brass, not of leather [i.e., animal gut]. In the opinion of many, however, Scotland today not only equals her Irish mistress but truly even

---

[37] A paraphrase from Ovid, 'Ars amatoria', II. 313.

far outdoes and surpasses her in musical skill. Hence people look there now as though to the source of the art.)

While Gerald did not comment in sufficient detail for us to be certain as to the forms of the instrumental types enumerated, it is probable that *cithara* referred to harp, *timpanum* to *timpán* or lyre, *tibiae* to pipes of some kind, and *chorus* to either bagpipes or double pipes. A particular aspect of this passage has given rise to extensive speculation in musicological and historical writing. It hinges upon the references to B flat and the implications of polyphony.

The above passage is found in the earliest and all later copies of the 'Topographia'. Further discourse on music appears only in extended versions. The following extract concerns the ascribed benefits of music to mankind:

Unde et animosis animositates, et religiosis pias fovet et promovet intentiones. Hinc accidit ut episcopi et abbates, et sancti in Hibernia viri, citharas circumferre et in eis modulando pie delectari consueverint. Quapropter et Sancti Keivini cithara ab indigenis in reverentia non modica, et pro reliquiis virtuosis et magnis, usque in hodiernum habetur.

(Hence it inspires courage in brave men and it promotes good intentions in the religious. Thus it was that bishops and abbots and holy men in Ireland carried their citharae [lyres? harps?] about and delighted in playing pious music upon them. Because of this, Saint Kevin's *cithara* is held in no mean reverence by the natives and until this day is regarded as a great and sacred relic.)

Praeterea bellica tuba cum strepitu clangoris musicam effert, consonantiam; quatinus et clangor altisonus congrediendi signum cunctis indicat, et consona sonoritas animosis audaciam altius infigat.[38]

(Furthermore, the war trumpet with its strong sound shows the corresponding effect of music; when its loud alarm gives the battle signal, its strong sound raises the spirit of the brave to the highest.)

There is likely to be an essence of truth in the account of St Kevin's instrument, the reverence accorded it, and the recognition of the aesthetic and ceremonial function of such portable instruments when used in worship.

Two versions of what is evidently the same tale in a Welsh setting concern a horn associated with a saint. In the 'Topographia' a poor Irish mendicant is described as carrying St Patrick's bronze horn around his neck as a relic. He held it out to the crowd to be kissed (an Irish custom, according to Gerald). A priest named Bernard snatched and blew it, only to be struck with a double sickness within the hour: he became tongue-tied and lost his memory.

---

[38] *Distinctio*, III, cap. 12. Cf. Dimock, p. 155.

Gerald claims to have met the priest some days later, and testifies that he no longer knew the psalms and required assistance with elementary literacy, in contrast to his previous skills.

The version in 'Itinerarium Cambriae' begins with a statement that St Patrick's horn was a source of wonder. It was brought to Wales 'recently from Spain' and was made of bronze, not gold. Gerald then refers to his Irish account but relates the event to a funeral at which one of the bearers has about his neck a horn, supposedly owned by St Patrick. Out of respect for the saint no one dared blow it. As above, the relic was held out to be kissed and Bernard blew it, suffering the same fate immediately. The afflicted priest then travelled to Ireland to visit St Patrick. His health mended. Clearly we are in the realms of folklore, to which Gerald evidently was a willing contributor (St Patrick died some 700 years earlier!). There are points, however, which need to be noted. The importance of relics in medieval society is widely attested, and while we know of no other source which associates horns with saints, there are many reports of saints' bells' being invested with powers to bless and curse. Gerald himself comments on the reverence and fear accorded bells and staffs, noting St Kevin's *cithara* also in this context.

A further comment concerning Irish musical practice should be noted here, although it is not found within the earliest version and, like the above, was probably derived from secondary sources:[39]

Est itaque tanquam convertibilis musica naturae. Hujus enim opera, animum si intendis; si remittis, amitis. Unde et gens Hibernica et Hispanica, aliaeque nationes nonnullae, inter lugubres funebrum planctus musicas efferunt lamentationes: quatinus vel dolorem instantem augeant et recentem, vel forte ut minuant jam remissum.

(Thus it is that music has many aspects; when used to intensify feelings, it inflames; when to calm them, it soothes. Hence both the Irish and Spanish people, and other nations, mix plaintive music with their funereal wailings: giving sympathetic expression to their present grief so that they may alleviate what has passed.)

It is reasonable to regard the accounts of funeral practices as valid, to judge from other literary sources (such as are indicated above). However, from so late a copy, was the inclusion approved by Gerald? Interestingly he announced his intention to discuss the benefits of music to mankind, as in the passages just cited, in the preamble to his earliest versions (he listed the topic immediately prior to the passage on harpers and their music), but no such discussion was included till the much later versions were penned. To what extent the additional entry reflected Gerald's intentions is impossible to say.

---

[39] *Distinctio*, III, cap. 12. Cf. Dimock, p. 157.

The final puzzle for this tentative appraisal of Gerald's information lies within 'Descriptio Cambriae', where he praises Welsh harping and remarks on its prevalence within every household and the readiness with which visitors were entertained by young girls. He cannot find words enough to convey his appreciation of such excellence, and thus leads himself to repeat the account of Irish harping given in 'Topographia', incorporating the long passage concerning combined melodies, the prominence of B flat, and the desirability of restraint, and subtle concealment of art. Gerald concludes by listing again the three instruments, *cithara*, *tibia*, *chorus*, as pertaining to the Welsh. Are we justified in assuming similarity in style and idiom between the two societies? Gerald obviously has no doubts that his Irish account suited his new purpose as he repeats it '... to save time'.[40]

FOLLOWING the formal establishment of English administration in Ireland under Henry II, rather than Ireland becoming anglicised in any uniform or totalising way, the new French- and English-speaking settlers engaged in patronage of Gaelic harpers and poets, just like the longer-established chieftains. However, they also introduced other types of artistic expression, particularly in the form of English rites, to the new ecclesiastical centres that they established (such as the cathedrals in Dublin). And so alongside the use of Sarum, establishment of cathedral choir schools, and Corpus Christi processions in urban centres, the culture of the old Gaelic courts continued to flourish, among the existing Gaelic lords as well as under the patronage of the new settlers.

Whether our concern is with liturgical or secular practices, it seems wise to redirect attention to processes of social behaviour rather than seeking isolates and treating them out of context. The range of this topic is extremely far-reaching and all aspects must be taken into account. Two major processes of (internal) acculturation have been overlooked; they merit separate treatment, and work has barely commenced.

First of all, the Scandinavian influence in the towns and cities of Ireland needs to be addressed. Entertainers from Iceland were said to have visited the court of the Hiberno-Norse kings in Dublin in the tenth century. Similarly, Irish poets and storytellers were said to have been welcomed by the Scandinavian settlers.[41] There are also finds of musical instruments and

[40] An analysis of the reception history of Gerald's commentary on music may be found in Paul Nixon, 'Giraldus Cambrensis on music: how reliable are his historiographers?' in Ann Buckley (ed.), *Proceedings of the First British–Swedish Conference on Musicology: Medieval Studies (11–15 May 1988)* (Stockholm, 1992), pp 264–89. It serves as the basis for the above account. See also Shai Burstyn, 'Is Gerald of Wales a credible musical witness?' in *Musical Quarterly*, no. 72 (1986), pp 155–69.

[41] Fleischmann & Gleeson, 'Music in ancient Munster', p. 93.

associated fragments from Scandinavian and Hiberno-Norman Irish urban centres (presented in futher detail below).

Secondly, the Anglo-Normans introduced French- and eventually English-speakers into Ireland in large numbers. All of these demographic movements will undoubtedly have included the importation and assimilation of new repertories of singing and dancing. As we shall see, liturgical manuscripts representing the new accommodation are relatively late, while Irish music-related manuscripts of secular association are very few in number. None contains notation, though their poems would have have been sung, as is suggested from their forms and styles.

Two Anglo-Norman romances survive in Irish sources. One, 'The song of Dermot and the earl' (now in the Carew collection of Lambeth Palace library, London, MS 596), concerns events surrounding the arrival of the Normans in Ireland. Long suggests that the author received the account at first hand from Morice Regan, secretary to Diarmait Mac Murchada (King Dermot), which would date it to the late twelfth century.[42] The other is a thirteenth-century poem on the walling of New Ross (County Wexford) in 1265, included in a collection of poems in English, French, and Latin usually referred to as 'the Kildare poems'.[43] They belonged to a Franciscan House in the Waterford or Wexford region and are now preserved in B.L. MS Harley 913. Another important collection is contained in the Red Book of Ossory, now MS D 11/1/1 in the Representative Church Body Library, Dublin. This is a set of Latin songs (*cantilenae*) by Richard Ledrede, bishop of Ossory from 1317 to *c*.1360.[44] With the aim of diverting his clergy's attention away from profane delights and frivolities, these devotional texts were intended to replace the singing of popular songs, the first lines of which are given in the rubrics to indicate the appropriate melodies.[45] Unfortunately these are no longer recoverable, since no other sources are known.

---

[42] See Joseph Long, 'Dermot and the earl: who wrote "the Song"?' in *R.I.A. Proc.*, lxxv (1975), sect. C, pp 263–72; Alan J. Bliss and Joseph Long, 'Literature in Norman French and English' in *N.H.I.*, ii, 715–36.

[43] See W. Heuser, *Die Kildare-Gedichte* (Bonn, 1904), for an edition of the English poems; also Hugh Shields, 'Carolling at New Ross, 1265' in *Ceol*, iv, pt 2 (1973), pp 34–6; idem, 'The walling of New Ross: a thirteenth-century poem in French' in *Long Room*, xii–xiii (1975–6), pp 24–33.

[44] See Edmund Colledge (ed.), *The Latin poems of Richard Ledrede, O.F.M., bishop of Ossory, 1317–1360* (Toronto, 1974).

[45] A fuller discussion of all of these is found in Bliss & Long, 'Literature in Norman French and English', together with bibliographies; see also Long, 'Dermot and the earl'. The Kildare poems and those in the Red Book of Ossory are also referred to by Scott in the present volume (below, pp 976–80). Shields considers the attribution of this poem to 'Brother Michael' to be unfounded ('The walling', p. 27, n. 12), and believes that it was in fact written in England (p. 26). For a discussion on references to music in the poem, see idem, 'Carolling at New Ross'.

The likelihood of residence in Ireland of English harpers, i.e. harpers in an Anglo-Norman tradition, should not be overlooked either, as witness some seven entries in the Dublin Guild Merchant roll (*c.*1190–1265).[46] Their profession is further underlined by the addition of an outline sketch of a harp in the case of one of them, Thomas le Harpur, in an entry for *c.*1200 (pl. 129).[47] Other Irish walled towns are likely also to have housed instrumentalists—the practice of composing *chansons de geste* in Hiberno-Norman settlements further attests to the likelihood of the presence of professional performers, although we have so far uncovered no specific information or surviving instruments. And the cross-over of musicians between native Irish and Anglo-Norman (later Hiberno-Norman) settlers has yet to be examined in detail.[48]

The account roll of Holy Trinity includes two references to the engagement of musicians on the occasion of a visit of the justices to dinner at the priory in 1338 when payments were made to the justices' trumpeters, and to 'a certain little harper' (*quidam parvo cittheratori*).[49] We cannot know from this whether they may have been of Irish, Anglo-Norman, or (for that matter) Norman-Welsh extraction. However, there are references in the Red Book of Ormond to Anglo-Norman harpers (e.g., Roberto Fil David Citheratore), and the 'Calendar of Ormond deeds' lists a number of individuals with the name 'Le Harpur' *c.*1300, at which time (as in the case of Thomas in the Dublin source) such a reference can still be assumed to be linked to a profession.[50]

The equally sparse documentation on liturgical and secular dramatic performance should not blind us to the likelihood of a wide range of activities. A hint occurs in the statutes of Kilkenny (1366), of which the seventh decree declares a prohibition on the holding of games and spectacles in cemeteries.[51] And a medieval English morality play is recorded uniquely on some pages left blank in the account roll of Holy Trinity cathedral priory for 1337–46. It is not clear whether it was written during this period, but is probably not of

---

[46] Now Dublin City Archives MS G-1/1. m.11d/A.

[47] See Philomena Connolly and Geoffrey Martin (ed.), *The Dublin Guild Merchant Roll, c.1190–1265* (Dublin, 1992), p. 41, and frontispiece, where the sketch is reproduced.

[48] Keith Sanger has identified what may well be the grave slab of an Irish harper at Heysham, near Lancaster; see idem, 'An Irish harper in an English graveyard?' in *Harpa*, xxi (spring 1996), p. 17. It may be that of William Dodmore, who was in the service of Thomas of Lancaster (later duke of Clarence, d. 1421); Thomas became king's lieutenant in Ireland in 1400.

[49] See James Mills (ed.), *Account roll of the priory of Holy Trinity, Dublin* (Dublin, 1890–91); reprint, with introductions by James Lydon and Alan J. Fletcher (Dublin, 1996), p. 19.

[50] For further discussion, see Sanger, 'An Irish harper … ?'

[51] This is, of course, in keeping with similar injunctions elsewhere, e.g., Scotland (1225), Exeter (1287), Winton (1308), York (1367), London (1603). For further discussion on Ireland, see Aubrey Gwynn, 'Anglo-Irish church life, fourteenth and fifteenth centuries' in Corish, *Ir. catholicism*, ii (1968), p. 51.

much later date. Mills, who edited the text (entitling it 'The pride of life'), was of the opinion that it was English in origin. Since this version was obviously written down by one of the community, it is likely to have been performed for the entertainment and instruction of members of the priory. Its clerical context is underlined by the fact that, although the play itself is in the vernacular, both rubrics (in the form of 'stage instructions') and *dramatis personae* are given in Latin.[52] We have no information on the role of music in performances of this play, though the presence of musicians is likely. However, there are references from 1542 to payments having been made for 'singing the Passion' and 'playing the Resurrection' at Holy Trinity,[53] while in 1528 the prior cooperated with the priors of two other Dublin monasteries (St John of Jerusalem, and All Hallows) to produce a play on the Passion and one on the deaths of the Apostles.[54] These performances took place in Hoggen Green, a common in the area of present-day College Green.

Detailed documentation survives of the protocol for the elaborate annual pageants in celebration of the feast of Corpus Christi and St George's day, from the late fifteenth and mid sixteenth centuries, respectively. Both were celebrated as important civic and religious occasions in Dublin.[55] For the Corpus Christi pageants, the city guilds each had an assigned function: the bakers, the cordwainers, the butchers, etc. Sometimes there are references to the hiring of musicians: for example, four trumpeters were required for the St George's day pageant. The first city waits were appointed in 1465, though it is likely that the office is at least a century older.[56]

DEPICTIONS of musical instruments are found on Irish high crosses of the eighth to tenth centuries which mark the sites of early monastic settlements. The representations are mainly of stringed instruments in a variety of shapes and (implied) sizes. Images in stone cannot be relied upon for accuracy of detail owing to the intrinsic difficulties of the medium—translating

---

[52] The same manuscript also contains eight lines of Old French verse, immediately preceding the Old English morality. Mills gave an account of the play to the R.I.A. at its meeting on Monday, 13 Apr. 1891, on the occasion of his election as a member. The notice appears in the minutes of the meeting included in *R.I.A. Proc.*, ii (1891–3), sect: C; the paper, however, appears to have remained unpublished. See the reprinted edition in Mills, *Account roll of Holy Trinity*, pp 126–42, and introduction, p. xxiii.

[53] See Barra Boydell, *Music at Christ Church*, pp 26, 40–41 (an illustration of the 1542 document is reproduced on p. 40).

[54] See the new introduction by Alan Fletcher in Mills, *Account roll of Holy Trinity*, p. xxxiii.

[55] Details may be found in J. Warburton, J. Whitelaw, and Robert Walsh, *History of the city of Dublin from the earliest accounts to the present time* (2 vols, London, 1818), pp 108–9, and in Charles Davidson, *Studies in the English mystery plays* (Yale, 1892), pp 90, 98. For the most recent account, see Alan J. Fletcher, *Drama, performance, and polity in pre-Cromwellian Ireland* (Cork, 2000), pp 82 ff, 90 ff, 138 ff.

[56] Fletcher, *Drama*, pp 148 ff. Fletcher's book represents the most comprehensive survey of this and related topics, which, both chronologically and in terms of content, exceed the remit of the present account, whence the abbreviated summary above.

three-dimensional objects and figures into two-dimensional representations—and the problems of weathering.[57]

As a rule, realistically portrayed instruments tend to be lyres rather than
harps on Irish monuments. Such instruments occur in three forms: (i) with
one curved and one straight arm; (ii) round-topped; and (iii) oblique. Their
strings are fitted in both parallel and fan formation except for type (iii),
which has only fan formation. Type (i) occurs on the crosses at Ullard and
Graiguenamanagh (ninth/tenth century). Examples of the second are found
on the Cross of the Scriptures, Clonmacnoise, County Offaly (early tenth
century; pl. 130), on the West Cross at Kells, County Meath, and on the
Cross at Castletown and Glinsk, County Offaly. Oblique lyres may be seen
on the Cross of Muireadach, Monasterboice (also early tenth century, pl.
126), and on the South Cross at Kells (pl. 131). Parallel strings occur on
Ullard; a fan disposition is evident on Clonmacnoise (pl. 130) and Durrow
(pl. 127). The latter shows a six-stringed example particularly clearly: the
strings are attached at the top of the curved arm, pass over a bridge, and
converge at the base. A bridge is also visible on the Clonmacnoise lyre.

A unique manuscript depiction of a plucked lyre exists in the Irish psalter,
B.L. MS Cott. Vitellius F. XI, f. 52$^r$.[58] Both the instrument and the seating
position of the player are close in style to that on the shaft of the Clonmacnoise cross—an observation made long ago by Françoise Henry.[59] On the
basis of this and other details she suggested that the manuscript is more or
less contemporary with the (early tenth-century) crosses at Clonmacnoise
and Monasterboice.

Other sources of iconographic information are reliquaries and metal
shrines. A panel on the shrine of the Stowe Missal (also known as the shrine
of St Maelruain's Gospel, pl. 124) depicts a small figure crouched between
two clerics, plucking a lyre similar in shape to that on the Durrow cross,
though with only three strings where Durrow has six. Of the two clerics on
the shrine, one holds a bell, the other a crosier, suggestive of episcopal authority. The shrine was manufactured between 1026 and 1033 and refurbished in
1381; the panel in question is believed to date to the earlier period.[60]

---

[57] The discussion that follows is a summary only. For a complete survey of Irish music
iconographic sources, see Buckley, 'Music-related imagery on early Christian insular sculpture:
identification, context, function' in *Imago Musicae: International Yearbook of Musical Iconography*, viii (1991) [1995], pp 135–99; and for some questions of interpretation, eadem, ' "A
lesson for the people": reflections on image and habitus in medieval insular iconography' in
*RIdIM/RCMI Newsletter*, xx, pt 1 (spring 1995), pp 3–9.
[58] The Cotton manuscripts were badly damaged in a fire, but the detail of this image may
still be observed in the original source.
[59] Françoise Henry, 'Remarks on the decoration of three Irish psalters' in *R.I.A. Proc.*, lxi
(1960), pp 23–40, p. 32. A facsimile of the MS figure may be found in plates IV and VI, with a
photograph of the figure on the Clonmacnoise cross shaft on plate V. See also Buckley, 'Music-
related imagery', fig. 34, for a particularly clear reproduction.
[60] Pádraig Ó Riain, 'Dating the Stowe Missal shrine' in *Archaeology Ireland*, v, no. 1 (spring
1991), pp 14–15.

The round-topped, six-stringed lyre was the commonest court instrument of north-west Europe from at least the fifth to the tenth century (the early seventh-century Anglo-Saxon instrument from Sutton Hoo being perhaps the best-known example). Hence we can be reasonably confident that these Irish carvings are based on local knowledge. And whereas no west-European material evidence is known to exist for oblique lyres, the consistency of this form in Irish iconography is significant, and perhaps realistic in local terms.

Lyres appear to have predominated in north-west Europe till *c.*1000, when harps began to replace them, eventually becoming the leading aristocratic instrument of the central middle ages. Lyres did not become extinct, however. Though of lower status than harps, they continued in use up to at least the fourteenth or fifteenth century in England, possibly the sixteenth in Ireland, and as late as the nineteenth century in Wales and Scandinavia.

Little is known about harps in this greater region prior to *c.*1000. They are found in ninth-century continental sources such as the Utrecht Psalter, and on Pictish stone carvings of the eighth, ninth, and tenth centuries. The earliest Irish image is found on the eleventh-century Breac Máedóic (pl. 125). It has about eight strings but twelve tuning pins, and is thus somewhat inaccurate. The instrument is large in proportion to the player; a bird hovering nearby probably represents the Holy Spirit inspiring the singing of the chant. Another harp occurs on the shrine of St Patrick's tooth (*Fiacail Phádraig*), *c.*1100, dating to the time of its refurbishment *c.*1376; the harp dates from the latter period).[61] Both instruments have a distinctly lighter frame than the 'Brian Boru' harp now preserved in the Library of Trinity College, Dublin, which dates from the fourteenth or fifteenth century.[62] This latter type is nowadays generally regarded as the 'Irish harp', and is distinguished by a heavy, monoxylous soundbox, deep-curved neck, and sturdy rounded forepillar (often with zoomorphic carving). But there may well have been a variety of lighter-framed instruments in use before, and indeed during, this time.

The regional history of bowed instruments is similarly obscure. A unique carving of a bowed lyre survives among the ruins of St Finan's church, Lough Currane, Waterville (County Kerry) on a loose stone which was set into the church wall probably in recent times (pl. 132). The church is thought to have been built *c.*1127 by St Malachy, and the carving appears to be contemporaneous. Six strings are discernible. A ridge over the soundbox

[61] See the illustration in Ann Buckley, 'Musical instruments in Ireland 9th–14th centuries: a review of the organological evidence' in Gerard Gillen and Harry White (ed.), *Irish Musical Studies*, i (1990), pp 13–57, fig. XVII.

[62] This is the approximate date suggested by organologists, but it has been questioned by Raghnall Ó Floinn, who suggests the fifteenth or sixteenth century as the period of its manufacture, and also expresses the view that it is not possible conclusively to establish whether it was produced in Ireland or Scotland. See *Treasures of Ireland: Irish art 3000 B.C.–1500 A.D.* (Dublin, 1983), p. 180.

represents the stringholder or tailpiece, and the player's left hand can be seen stopping the strings on the fingerboard through a hole in the lower frame of the instrument. The unmistakeable curved bow held in the player's right hand is typical of many fiddle bows of the period.

Depictions of wind instruments are few when compared with the relatively rich variety of stringed examples. This is most likely a reflection of their social function rather than of the extent of their use in medieval Irish society. Stringed instruments were superior, belonging to the highest-ranking musicians, who played at court and for religious rituals. It is undoubtedly because of their latter association that they appear so often on crosses, reliquaries, and shrines. Wind instruments were in all probability very common in secular life, and not necessarily confined to professional use. But we should not ignore the repeated pattern of chordophone and aerophone players together on the same scene, as in our examples from Monasterboice, as also on the Last Judgement scenes of Durrow, though there association might be with the Last Trump, whereas in Monasterboice the player seems very much part of the choral performance.

Players of triple pipes are seen on Muireadach's Cross, to the left of Christ in Judgement (pl. 126), and on the shaft of the Cross of the Scriptures, Clonmacnoise (pl. 130) without specific association. Both carvings suggest the performance of multi-part music: the instruments have three conical pipes of unequal length, that to the player's left being considerably longer than the other two, and with a bell-shaped terminal; it probably served as a drone while the melody was played on the two shorter pipes—perhaps at an interval of a third or a fifth, in view of the difference in length.[63]

INTERPRETING images of musicians on stone monuments is not always straightforward. Musician figures are placed either in panels alone or in group scenes. Crucifixion scenes with a string-player in a neighbouring panel are found on several Irish crosses. For example, the high cross at Ullard, County Kilkenny, has a lyre-player to the left of the head of the cross. At the centre is Christ crucified, on the right the sacrifice of Isaac, and underneath is a scene of the fall of Adam and Eve. The same four scenes occur on other crosses of the so-called Barrow valley group: the Castledermot North and South Crosses, and the Graiguenamanagh cross. In the case of Castledermot North Cross, the Adam and Eve scene is at the centre on the west face—the same side as the string-player and the sacrifice of Isaac—while the crucifixion is placed on the opposite side. What have these portraits of musicians to do with the neighbouring scenes? Perhaps nothing. But on the other hand, a lone musician is not a narrative in itself, unless set in some kind of context.

---

[63] Such an instrument is played in Sicily (called *launeddas*)—the only part of Europe where it is now to be found. Perhaps it enjoyed wider use in the early middle ages, but adequate evidence is lacking today.

Perhaps it is a comment on David as the prefigurer of Christ; possibly it represents a court musician performing a lament, another way of pointing to the scene at the centre of the cross.

Illustrations of the Last Judgement/Christ in Glory usually have musicians on the left arm, to the right of Christ, the side of the just. Here we might expect angels blowing trumpets or singing in choirs, according to conventional description. However, apart from one angelic figure on the Durrow Cross (pl. 127; the feathered wing is visible) the musicians are cloaked in monastic habits, play lyres or wind instruments, and usually form part of a group. The musicians' group *par excellence* is undoubtedly that on the Cross of Muireadach (pl. 126), where a choir of monks is accompanied by a lyre- and a horn-player, behind whom one of their number holds a book—perhaps a psalter or a hymnal.

And withal, it has commonly been assumed that representations of music-making were based solely on biblical scenes. Yet it would be difficult to see all of these as first-level David iconography, even if David is implicitly the typological model for pious music-making, and even if, in strict terms, some of these musicians were copied in whole or in part as Davidic iconography: they have been deployed on the crosses in a very different and striking way, and it would be impossible not to view them as having a local application. Indeed, on closer examination, one can discern a number of instances where there is no obvious connection with any biblical text.

The first example has been interpreted as an account of the miracle of the loaves and fishes, on the ninth-century Cross of Patrick and Columba at Kells (pl. 131). Two figures are seated face to face: to the left, a musician plays a lyre; the figure on the right appears to be holding a round object which resembles a loaf of bread; several more loaves are placed between them. Below the two figures, a pair of fish overlap in the familiar shape of an 'X' (the Greek letter 'chi'). In the background above, human heads seem to represent a crowd of onlookers.

The second example occurs on the twelfth-century tympanum of Ardmore cathedral, though the carvings may be older, as they are thought to have been taken from another monument on the site. In the upper panel of the right-hand arch is a scene representing the judgement of Solomon (pl. 133). Solomon is seated at the left; before him, to the right, are the two women who claim to be mother of the same child. This child is held up to view by the woman nearest Solomon, who gestures towards them with his hand. At the far right of this group is a seated harper. Is this David? If so, does he belong apart, representing a totally other scene, as it were?[64]

---

[64] For discussion of Kells, see Peter Harbison, *The high crosses of Ireland: an iconographical and photographic survey* (3 vols, Bonn, 1992), i, 212; and for Ardmore, idem, 'Architectural sculpture from the twelfth century at Ardmore' in *Irish Arts Review*, xi (1995), pp 96–103, pp 97–8. Harbison regards this Kells image as representing David before Saul; and interprets the representations of Solomon and the harper as belonging to two separate scenes.

David was no longer living when Solomon made his judgement; and he certainly was not around in New Testament times to assist at the miracle of the loaves and fishes. However, the role of the musician could be a way of representing a performance of the narrative. And it hardly needs pointing out that, based on local norms, an Irish onlooker would have expected to see a musician in attendance at a royal court. By the same token, no feast would have been complete without the presence of musicians to entertain and to recite genealogies and praise-poetry in honour of the host. To that extent Solomon, and Christ, are here identified as would be a local king or high dignitary, always attended by a bard. But before we continue along this vein, let us look at a few other examples of insular representation, this time not for biblical narrative as such, but to examine the way in which certain aspects of the musicians are pointed up.

Details of representation can also reveal important information of a purely local character. The performers we have examined up to now are invariably seated on chairs or thrones, which accords with representations elsewhere in European (and Byzantine) Christian art. Some of the furniture is decorated with animal-like carvings, but in many cases the details are now badly weathered and can no longer be seen. Unlike the throne of more formal Davids, the king in Carolingian iconography, some insular monuments show the musician figure seated on the ground with legs outstretched, or knees drawn up. The lack of contemporary models elsewhere suggests that this too may represent actual practice at local level.

The oldest such image is from the eighth-century Book of Kells (pl. 134), where the figure, facing to the left, plays a stylised chordophone in the shape of the letter 'C'; he is seated on the ground with his left knee drawn up along the side of the instrument. Four carvings, with wider geographical distribution, show a string-player seated on the ground with outstretched legs. These occur on the North Pillar at Carndonagh (ninth/tenth century), on the late eighth-century St Martin's Cross and St Oran's Cross fragment, both from Iona, and on a tenth-century carving at Kirk Michael, Isle of Man.[65]

Most interestingly, a relatively late source, Derricke's *Image of Irelande* (1581), shows a harper sitting on the ground next to a *reacaire* (reciter) who is performing in an animated way, with his arms outstretched. Derricke himself mentioned that performers (and other members of Irish chieftains' courts) did not use furniture but rather sat on the ground on a tuft of grass, which does lend considerable weight to the hypothesis that the older carvings are in this respect credible scenes of the time (see pl. 135).[66]

[65] See Buckley, 'Music-related imagery', figs 1, 16, 17, 20. For further discussion of the issues, see eadem, ' "A lesson for the people" '.

[66] See Buckley, ' "A lesson for the people" ' and eadem, 'Representations of musicians in John Derricke's *The image of Irelande* (above, n. 10), and 'Representations of musicians

Apart from Derricke, there is little iconographic account of secular contexts for music-making from the Irish middle ages. A bone book-cover discovered in a private house in Donabate (County Dublin) in 1850[67] bears a unique carving of a sword-dancing scene (pl. 136). It has been dated to the fifteenth/sixteenth centuries and is believed to come from Munster.[68] At the centre of the scene, a group of four men face each other with raised swords; to the left a fifth figure beats an object resembling a small frame-drum (or *bodhrán*, as it would be termed nowadays). Above the central scene a boar is depicted on its side, and at the top, a knight on a charger lances a dragon. The upper portion of the cover bears the arms of one of the Desmond Fitzgeralds. Nothing is known of the source of this object, but such dances were widely known throughout western Europe—the last vestiges still surviving in mummers' performances. The significance of the boar is not clear. In manuscript illustrations the animal is sometimes portrayed playing a set of bagpipes—which may be intended as humorous, or as a fanciful comment on the structure of the instrument. However, in this particular context of sword-dancing, it may refer to characters assumed by the performers, who dressed up as animals for their plays and pageants, and for seasonal rituals.

A hunting scene on the top west-face panel of the high cross at Old Kilcullen (County Kildare) includes a figure blowing a horn. Here too the context explains the musical reference.[69] A much later example of a hunting scene with a horn-blower is barely to be discerned on a fifteenth-century wall painting at Holy Cross abbey (County Tipperary). Horn-players are depicted on the thirteenth-century matrices of the seal of the lord mayor of Dublin, where their function as another kind of signal is clearly intended: that of warning the citizens of oncoming danger in the harbour.[70]

THE contribution of excavation to research in Irish music archaeology has been especially significant in recent years. Urban archaeology, most notably in Dublin, Cork, and Waterford, has yielded objects for which no other evidence exists.[71] And needless to say, the nature of the societies represented by these excavations is reflected in the kinds of objects recovered, being

in medieval Christian iconography of Ireland and Scotland as local cultural expression' in Katherine McIver (ed.), *Art and music in the early modern period: essays in honor of Franca Trinchieri Camiz* (Aldershot, 2003), pp 217–31.

[67] Now in the collection of the National Museum of Ireland, Dublin.

[68] This is the assessment of Helen Roe, recorded on the information card accompanying the book-cover at the National Museum.

[69] See Buckley, 'Musical instruments in Ireland', fig. XIX; eadem, 'Music-related imagery', fig. 43.

[70] See E. C. R. Armstrong, *Irish seal matrices and seals* (Dublin, 1913), p. 125. An engraving of both matrices is published in *Rental of the estates of the right honorable the lord mayor, aldermen, and burgesses of Dublin* (Dublin, 1884), pl. XVIII.

[71] Full details may be consulted in Buckley, 'Musical instruments from medieval Dublin—a preliminary survey' in E. Hickmann and D. Hughes (ed.), *The archaeology of early music*

different from the materials in ecclesiastical iconography. On the other hand, these urban excavations, while they have produced a valuable array of artefacts, give us little or no contextual information on musical activity as human behaviour. All of the objects recovered were discarded in their own time and have survived in rubbish dumps, hearths, and underneath the foundations of houses—the empty shells of long-dead cultures. One disadvantage, therefore, is the impossibility of making any kind of comparative assessment on an institutional (e.g. monastic, court, peasant, artisan) or regional basis, since the various categories of evidence rarely belong to the same chronological period, nor have they survived in sufficient quantity or detail.

None of the instruments found in archaeological excavations can be said to be peculiar to Ireland: on the contrary, they underline the cultural kinship that existed among the populations of north-west Europe. However, one artefact from the excavation of medieval Dublin has been the cause of some considerable excitement. Out of the rubble behind the hearth of a house in Christchurch Place has emerged a bow made of dogwood, dating to the early or mid eleventh century (pl. 137a). It is not possible to ascertain whether such a bow was used to play a lyre, a psaltery, or a fiddle, though it is tempting to link it with a lyre. It is broken off at the end where it would have been held by the player, but is complete at its tip (where the other end of the hair was attached), which features an animal-head carving in Ringerike style, typical of this period when Dublin was a Hiberno-Scandinavian city and Irish art had become a fusion of the older Celtic and Hiberno-Saxon styles with those of the new settlers. This object is unique not only for Irish music archaeology, it is also unprecedented in European terms: no bow has been found anywhere else from so early a date.

Unlike the excavations at York (a viking city rivalled in importance only by Dublin) and at other medieval sites in England, Germany, and Scandinavia, Dublin has not produced any lyre bridges or bodies of instruments. But other chordophone-related materials were found in the form of tuning pegs from eleventh- and thirteenth-century sites in Dublin (pl. 138), thirteenth-century levels in Cork, and both eleventh-/twelfth- and thirteenth-century levels in Waterford. The majority are made of yew wood and average *c*.6 cm in length, hence would have been used in fiddles, lyres, or psalteries. Some longer examples, including one from Cork made of bone, and two from Waterford (10.7 cm and 11.4 cm respectively), probably came from thicker-framed harps. The Irish pegs include some with a recessed terminal, to facilitate a thumb-and-forefinger grip for tuning purposes, and also some with a square head, which would have required the use of a tuning key.

*cultures* (Bonn, 1988), and eadem, 'Musical instruments in Ireland', and 'Sound tools from the Waterford excavations' (unpublished, 1991).

For both quantity and variety, aerophones (wind instruments) represent the richest category. There are flutes and flute-fragments made of birdbone and elderwood. There are flutes both with and without fingerholes, although in some cases it is not possible to assess this feature because of damage. A total of six flutes and flute-fragments have emerged from the sites at Christchurch Place (c.1200), High Street (thirteenth century; see pl. 139), Winetavern Street (thirteenth century), and John's Lane, off Fishamble Street (thirteenth century). A three-holed bird-bone flute and a whistle were found in Waterford, both at twelfth-/thirteenth-century levels. There is no certain indication of how they may have been sounded, but the likelihood is that they were block-and-duct or fipple flutes, with a piece of cork or wood inserted in the mouthpiece to direct the channel of air through the window or blowhole. Blocks do not easily survive, being made of soft organic materials. Other simpler aerophones include perforated bones of various kinds such as may have been used as 'buzzbones' and as whistles for amusement, or as animal decoys.

Fragments of ceramic horns of Saintonge ware were recovered from a thirteenth-century rubbish dump by the River Liffey, Dublin, and from Waterford. They are identifiable by their narrowing mouthpieces, and by the presence of perforations for the insertion of carrying straps (pl. 140a). Such objects were well known all over western Europe, serving both as signalling instruments (for hunting, keeping watch, etc.) and pilgrim's horns, purchased as souvenirs at pilgrimage centres. Other horns or trumpets now preserved in the National Museum of Ireland include a straight horn made from two pieces of hollowed-out willow bound together by a ribbon of copper alloy. It was found in a bog in the west of Ireland in 1791 and is thought to date from the early ninth century. Another horn, dating to the eighth/ninth century, was recovered from the bed of the River Erne close to two ancient monastic sites. It is made of two pieces of yew (a sacred wood) lapped together with bronze fittings (pl. 140b), and bears decoration similar to that found on bells and (liturgical) buckets of the period.[72] The horns depicted on the crosses at Monasterboice, Durrow, and Clonmacnoise may be examples of this type.[73]

Over seventy medieval ecclesiastical bells have been recovered. More than half of them are of sheet iron, the remainder of cast bronze.[74] Their survival rate is high because of the importance attached to them as sacred relics and as symbols of office. They were the essential prerequisites of a church: a large bell in the tower, handbells for summoning the monks to prayer, etc. Bells are depicted on stone-carvings and metalwork, usually in the hand of an

---

[72] For further discussion, see Buckley, 'Musical instruments in Ireland', p. 177 ff.
[73] Cf. the discussion about the possible liturgical associations of horns, below, p. 805.
[74] Cf. Cormac Bourke, 'Early Irish hand bells'.

ecclesiastic, and accompanied by other religious accoutrements, such as a book and a crosier on the north pillor at Carndonagh,[75] and a crosier and lyre on the Stowe Missal Shrine (pl. 124). It is often stated that bells were introduced to Ireland by Christian missionaries, and this may well hold true for religious bells. But there is every reason to suppose that bells were used in Ireland, also before the arrival of Christianity, in association with farming and herding. There are two harness bells in the National Museum of Ireland which probably belonged to this sphere of activity. Such objects do not easily withstand the ravages of time, eventually disintegrating from rust, or perhaps smelted down and reused for other purposes.

Hiberno-Scandinavian sites have not yielded any jew's harps. These instruments emerged elsewhere in Ireland from the thirteenth/fourteenth centuries, as in other parts of western Europe. A total of thirty-three have been recovered, dating between this period and the late nineteenth century, the majority from the sixteenth and seventeenth centuries. They are usually made of iron, and appear to have been as popular in Ireland as they were in England. They were listed for sales taxation in the first *Boke of Rates* published for Ireland (Dublin, 1608), indicating that they were probably originally imported.[76]

Our investigation is limited by the nature of the artefacts recovered. We nevertheless glean some information of a cultural nature from examining the styles and the typology. We do not recover the sounds, however, and we have few written records to help explain the uses to which such materials were put. Insight into deeper-structure musical mentality is thus rare, though we should not underrate the significance of any of the objects. Together, they form an important corpus of evidence for culture contact, methods of sound production, and the types and contexts of at least some of the materials once in use. It is only in collaborative international (and interdisciplinary) teamwork that we can most usefully assess them, coordinating local information in the service of the greater, longer-term aim of assembling a historical map of European orally transmitted musical practices.

THE liturgical practices of the Celtic churches have been referred to as the 'Celtic rite' since the late nineteenth century. The term is to some extent a misconception, fostered at a time of antiquarianism. Churches in Celtic-language areas were not as unified in administration or as uniform in practice

---

[75] See Buckley, 'Musical instruments in Ireland', fig. V; eadem, 'Music-related imagery', fig. 1. And for material finds see Cormac Bourke, 'A crozier and bell from Inishmurray and their place in ninth-century Irish archaeology' in *R.I.A. Proc.*, lxxxv (1985), sect. C, pp 145–68.

[76] See Ann Buckley, 'A note on the history and archaeology of jew's harps in Ireland' in *N. Munster Antiq. Jn.*, xxv (1983), pp 30–36: 32–3; eadem, 'Jew's harps in Irish archaeology' in Cajsa S. Lund (ed.), *Second Conference of the ICTM Study Group on Music Archaeology* (Stockholm, 1986), pp 145–62: 151.

as the church of Rome aspired to be. Nor were they separate and free of interaction with their continental neighbours.

The term 'Celtic rite' is best understood as a complex of regionally distinct, and locally varied, liturgical practices which admitted fusions of Egyptian, Gallican, Spanish, Roman, Irish, Scottish, Welsh, and Breton elements, as opposed to concepts of unvarying and separate worship, putatively brought to an untimely end by secular politics and hostility to indigenous expression. Ireland was the last of the Celtic-speaking regions to have been brought into line with the Roman church, through the synod of Cashel in 1172, preceded by Wales (which submitted to Canterbury with the election of Bernard, a Norman, to the see of St David's in 1115); Scotland, with the reforms of Queen Margaret (d. 1093), and Brittany, with the imposition of central authority on the monks of Landévennec in 818 by Charlemagne's son, Louis the Pious. However, these were not the first of the romanising reforms, and at no time could it be said that any of the Celtic churches were set completely apart from international clerical networks. The Roman canon of the mass was introduced shortly after 800 (as indicated by additions to the Stowe Missal). But already in the seventh century, Gertrude, daughter of Pepin, mayor of the imperial palace, and abbess (626–?659) of Nivelles in Brabant, is said to have invited St Foíllán and St Ultán, brothers of St Fursa, to instruct her nuns in the liturgy.[77] She sent to Rome for the books, as she was known to be an admirer of Roman customs. Irish monks could not have been employed for this purpose if they were not competent in Roman practices. A particularly explicit reference is found in a seventh-century Life of St Brigid, by Ailerán the Wise of Clonard, to the replacement of the old Roman mass by the Gregorian.[78] From the late eighth century onwards, there was considerable contact with the Roman church through monks, scholars, and pilgrims who journeyed frequently between Ireland, Britain, and the Continent.

It is sometimes also overlooked that the second wave of viking immigrants was in the process of being christianised during the tenth century. As the vikings had been christianised by Anglo-Saxon missionaries to Scandinavia, they had long looked to Canterbury (which see had observed the Roman rite since St Augustine's mission and the synod of Whitby, 664) as their centre of ecclesiastical authority. Hence, Anglo-Roman rites of liturgy would have been known to some people for over a hundred years prior to the establishment of the Normans in Ireland in 1172.

---

[77] Lester K. Little, *Benedictine maledictions: liturgical cursing in Romanesque France* (Ithaca, N.Y., and London, 1993), p. 178.

[78] Bruno Stäblein, 'Zwei Melodien der altirischen Liturgie' in Heinrich Hüschen (ed.), *Musicae Scientiae Collectanea: Festschrift für Karl Gustav Fellerer zum 70. Geburtstag* (Cologne, 1973), pp 590–97: 594, n. 22.

The diocesan system was introduced in Dublin as early as 1042, Waterford in 1086, and Limerick in 1107. Several of Dublin's first bishops swore allegiance to Canterbury.[79] Furthermore, Malachy was introducing reforms with papal approval during his period as archbishop of Armagh (1134–48), and Laurence O'Toole, after his appointment as archbishop of Dublin in 1162, introduced the Augustinian canons regular to the Cathedral of the Holy Trinity (Christ Church) and was said to have been actively involved in chant reform.[80] The Arroasian rule, which he encouraged, was adopted thereafter in many other Irish cathedrals and churches.[81]

The customs that the Anglo-Normans brought with them to Dublin and beyond reflect a number of regional entities and have connections with Wales, with western England (in particular Gloucester, Chester, and Bristol), and indirectly with Normandy. This can be seen not only from rituals and manuscript stemma, but also from the devotion to saints as exemplified in Irish sources, for instance, Saints Cadoc and David (Wales), Ouen (from Rouen, Normandy—anglicised 'Audoen'), to whom churches were dedicated in Bristol and Dublin, Werburgh (Chester and Bristol), and Osyth (Bristol), as well as several Anglo-Saxon saints not included in the Salisbury (or Sarum) rite. Similarly elsewhere, late evidence for the tenacity of local practices is afforded by various Scottish manuscripts (up to and including items in the Aberdeen Breviary published in 1529) which reveal the honouring of regional saints. Interestingly, Gerald of Wales (c.1146–c.1223), in his 'Topographia Hibernica', commented on meeting a monk of the Roman rite in Ireland, as if the incident were noteworthy, even after the synod of Cashel.

The existence of post-twelfth-century Irish notated manuscripts has been well known since the late nineteenth century, but their study has been seriously neglected. For example, Frank Harrison stated: 'As far as is at present known, the music of the Celtic rite has sunk without leaving any trace',[82] and in this he has been followed by Bruno Stäblein: 'With the loss of political independence, the Old Irish liturgy also came to an end. The later liturgical books from Ireland which contain melodies can be passed over; they do not differ in any respect from the generality of manuscripts written in the West' (my translation).[83] Aloys Fleischmann's article on 'Music of the Celtic rite' for the 1980 edition of the *New Grove dictionary* draws a veil over any

---

[79] For further details, see Aubrey Gwynn, 'The first bishops of Dublin' in *Reportorium Novum*, i (1955–6), pp 1–26; reprinted in Howard Clarke (ed.), *Medieval Dublin: the living city* (Dublin, 1990), pp 37–61.

[80] Thomas Messingham, *Florilegium insulae sanctorum* (Paris, 1624), pp 384–5.

[81] Aloys Fleischmann and Ryta Gleeson, 'Music in ancient Munster and monastic Cork' in *Cork Hist. Soc. Jn.*, lxx (1965), pp 79–98: 95.

[82] Frank Harrison, 'Polyphony in medieval Ireland' in E. M. Ruhnke (ed.), *Festschrift Bruno Stäblein* (Kassel, 1967), pp 74–9: 75.

[83] Stäblein, 'Zwei Melodien der altirischen Liturgie', p. 591, n. 12.

consideration of Irish sources after the establishment of Anglo-Norman rule in 1172, which, he states, 'effectively put an end to insular practices'.[84]

In an attempt to establish whether there are some features by which Irish Sarum manuscripts may be identified as regionally distinctive, Patrick Brannon has observed that while, for example, Saints Patrick and Brigid are listed in English Sarum Kalendars, proper texts and music notation for these saints are not normally included in English Sarum sources.[85] The Sarum printed breviary usually contains some short readings and prayers for Brigid, but no text or melodies for Patrick. However, in the Irish manuscripts proper materials are included for saints such as Patrick, Brigid, Canice, and Brendan, suggesting established local practice. There are some thirty pre-eleventh-century Irish liturgical manuscripts known to exist, of which only one, the late eighth-century Stowe Missal,[86] is found in Irish holdings. This figure excludes psalters, gospel-books, manuscripts containing hymns and non-liturgical prayers,[87] while there are also numerous fragments in flyleaves, bindings, and palimpsests in thirteen different libraries over five different countries, on which much primary work remains to be done.[88] Apart from occasionally informing us on local practices, Irish manuscripts can also provide a missing link for liturgical rituals elsewhere, especially Gaul, since so little survives from there because of the imposition of the Roman rite through the Carolingian reform movement already in the ninth century. Equally, manuscripts such as the late seventh-century 'Antiphonary' of Bangor[89] provide evidence of oriental influence (in particular from Palestinian and Egyptian Christian observance), most of which would have reached Ireland also via Gaul. Thus we are conscious, in the case of these older manuscripts, of the potential of such sources not only for uncovering information about Irish use, but also as a contribution towards international scholarly endeavours to reconstitute other parts of the west European liturgical map of the early middle ages.

[84] Aloys Fleischmann, 'Music of the Celtic rite' in Stanley Sadie (ed.), *The new Grove dictionary of music and musicians*, iv (London, 1980), p. 53.

[85] Patrick Brannon, 'The search for the Celtic rite: the T.C.D. Sarum Divine Office manuscripts reassessed' in Gerard Gillen and Harry White (ed.), *Irish musical studies*, ii (Blackrock [Dublin], 1993), pp 13–40: 16.

[86] Dublin, R.I.A. MS D.II.3. See George F. Warner (ed.), *The Stowe Missal, MS D.II.3 in the Library of the Royal Irish Academy, Dublin* (2 vols, London, 1906, 1916); cf. also Bartholomew Mac Carthy, 'On the Stowe Missal' in *R.I.A. Trans.*, xxvii (1886), pp 135–268.

[87] These are listed in Michael Lapidge and Richard Sharpe (ed.), *A bibliography of Celtic Latin literature 400–1200* (Dublin, 1985), under 'Liturgy'.

[88] See Marc Schneiders, 'The origins of the early Irish liturgy' in Próinséas Ní Chatháin and Michael Richter (ed.), *Ireland and Europe in the early middle ages: learning and literature* (Stuttgart, 1996) pp 76–98: 76, n. 1, for further bibliographical details.

[89] Milan, Bibl. Ambrosiana, MS C.5 inf. See F. E. Warren (ed.), *The Antiphonary of Bangor* (2 vols, London 1893, 1899); Michael Curran, *The Antiphonary of Bangor* (Blackrock [Dublin], 1984).

Where actual repertories are concerned, Hiberno-Latin hymns represent the largest body of material from any of the Celtic-speaking regions. They attest to a new fusion between Latin poetry and indigenous Irish verse forms, of which the chief characteristics are short lines with extensive use of alliteration, internal rhyme, and assonance. By contrast, no examples survive from neighbouring regions, apart from two late Breton hymns.[90] The use of hymns in liturgical services seems to have been particularly cultivated in Ireland. Gallican practice also reveals a strong interest in hymnody, whereas it was not permitted in the Roman rite until the twelfth century.[91]

The Hiberno-Latin hymn repertory is evidently influenced by, but nonetheless quite distinct from, other collections of western hymns. It includes, in particular, hymns from Gaulish sources as well as registering the influence of early Christian Roman authors. But it also displays a great deal of creativity in the composition of new hymns. Colum Cille (Columba) was said by his biographer Adomnán to have written a book of hymns for the week (*hymnorum liber septimaniorum*), which suggests a weekly *cursus* of hymns on Iona, paralleling Caesarius of Arles's *cursus hymnorum*. This idea is supported also by the preface to the hymn 'Altus prosator' in the T.C.D. copy of the Irish 'Liber hymnorum', where it is related that Gregory the Great (d. 604) sent Colum Cille a cross and *immain na sechtmaine*, 'hymns of the week'.[92]

There are two main sources for Irish hymns: the late seventh-century Antiphonary of Bangor, which also contains canticles and collects, and the Irish 'Liber hymnorum', which survives in two late eleventh-/early twelfth-century manuscripts, T.C.D. MS 1441 (*olim* E.4.2) and O.F.M.–U.C.D., MS A (formerly Franciscan Library, Killiney, MS A.2).[93] The Bangor Antiphonary is supported by the Turin fragment, which includes two of its hymns, 'Hymnum dicat' and 'Spiritus divinae lucis'.[94] Very few of these hymns are rubricated, hence their liturgical function is unclear; nor is it always certain whether they were intended for liturgical use or for private devotion.

In addition to the Antiphonary of Bangor and the Irish 'Liber hymnorum', texts of Irish hymns may be found also in English and continental manuscripts, where numerous Irish saints' cults grew up in the religious houses of Francia. The extant liturgical calendars of Frankish Gaul provide evidence

[90] Lapidge & Sharpe, *Bibliography*, nos 983 and 984 (twelfth and eleventh centuries, respectively).
[91] Jane Stevenson, 'Hiberno-Latin hymns: learning and literature' in Ní Chatháin & Richter, *Ire. & Europe* (1996), pp 99–135: 103, and n. 22 (quoting Louis Duchesne).
[92] See Thomas Owen Clancy and Gilbert Márkus, *Iona: the earliest poetry of a Celtic monastery* (Edinburgh, 1997), pp 93, 238, n. 40.
[93] See J. H. Bernard and Robert Atkinson (ed. and trans.), *The Irish Liber Hymnorum* (2 vols, London, 1898).
[94] See Kuno Meyer, 'Das turiner Bruchstück der ältesten irischen Liturgie' in *Nachrichten v.d. königl. Gesellsch. d. Wissensch. zu Göttingen, phil.-hist. Kl.* (Göttingen, 1903), pp 163–214.

for the cults of over forty Irish saints. For example, the feast of St Brigid was celebrated at Rebais, Meaux, Nivelles, Senlis, Corbie, Marchiennes, Saint-Amand, and Saint-Vaast.[95] Both Brigid and Patrick were widely venerated; while a ninth-century Bavarian litany includes invocations to Columbanus, Fursey, Patrick, Colum Cille, Comgall, Adomnán, Brigid, Kilian, Íte, and Samthann.[96]

The oldest recorded hymns are the 'Gloria', 'Te Deum' (of which the Bangor Antiphonary represents the earliest manuscript tradition), and 'Precamur patrem', which was probably written by Columbanus at Bangor c.580. Among the sources, there are not only prose hymns but also rhythmical hymns and even rhythmical collects (a feature that occurred only in Ireland, apparently, and not in Gaul). Metrical forms and poetry abound, though the question of performance and performance-contexts is not always clear. Curran has suggested that hymns and rhythmical collects reflect an Irish tendency to use verse for every occasion which merited a special composition.[97]

FIVE of the hymns in the Bangor Antiphonary bear rubrics indicating their liturgical function (AB items 8, 9, 10, 11, and 12). Of these, the hymn 'Sancti venite' (AB 8) is the oldest recorded communion hymn. Bangor contains eight *unica*, and ten that were certainly intended for liturgical use. Some of them are related to saints' cults, e.g., Irish saints such as Patrick, Comgall, and Camelac, as well as 'international' figures who were particularly venerated in Ireland, such as Martin and the Virgin Mary. For example, 'Cantemus in omni die', attributed to the Ionan monk Cú Chuimne (d. 747), is the oldest known Latin hymn to the Virgin, while the eighth-/ninth-century Book of Kells contains one of the oldest images of the Madonna and Child in these islands of which we are aware.[98] While it is important to remember that this is not an especially Celtic devotion, but rather a reflection of the international Christian world of the time, following the formal establishment of Mary's four great feasts in the church calendar by Pope Sergius (d. 701), it is notable that her veneration was observed early in the insular churches.[99]

[95] See Little, *Benedictine maledictions*, pp 180–81.

[96] Maurice Coens, 'Les litanies bavaroises du *Libellus precum* dit de Fleury (Orléans MS 184)' in *Analecta Bollandiana*, lxxvii (1959), pp 373–91: 379–80, 383.

[97] Curran, *Antiphonary of Bangor*, p. 85.

[98] T.C.D. MS 58, f. 7ᵛ; along with two eighth-century crosses from Iona (Clancy & Márkus, *Iona*, pp 33–4).

[99] Compare also the vernacular Marian poetry of Blathmac (c.750–70), ed. James Carney, *The poems of Blathmac son of Cú Brettan* (London, 1964). From the music-historical point of view also, there is undoubtedly common ground to be explored between Hiberno-Latin and vernacular hymnody. However, this topic exceeds the scope of the present discussion. For a more thoroughgoing discussion of Latin hymns in Ireland, see Jane Stevenson, 'Irish hymns, Venantius Fortunatus and Poitiers' in Jean-Michel Picard (ed.), *Aquitaine and Ireland in the middle ages* (Blackrock [Dublin], 1995), pp 81–110, and eadem, 'Hiberno-Latin hymns', *passim*.

The importance attached to hymns is made clear in a number of Irish literary tales, and in references contained in liturgical books. They were a source of indulgence and grace, and in this connection, the singing of the last three stanzas was considered sufficient to earn a spiritual reward. Hymns also served the function of a protective charm, as did certain prayers, indicating an absorption of Christian doctrine within local beliefs of longer standing. In his discussion of the poetry of Blathmac, James Carney noted that this poet 'has a reverent perception of the mystery, the awesomeness, and the power of the chanted word', and that these and other religious texts 'are conceived of as a breastplate and helmet against evil powers'.[100]

While some of the hymns in Irish manuscripts are unique, others belong to the realm of international Christian worship and are widely attested elsewhere. However, without corroborating evidence, this does not mean that the one group were 'Irish' and the other 'foreign' compositions. Irish Latin hymnody bears the characteristics of both Latin and Gaelic verse, sometimes separate, sometimes resulting in a fusion of the two. It is thus not always useful to speak in terms of 'Irish' composition as though it were something wholly separate, since Irish monks also composed verse according to classical and other metres. A more realistic appraisal of hymns, or of any other aspect of Irish cultural production, would thus be to take account of everything that was part of the repertory at a particular time and place, and on that basis to attempt to account for its existence. For example, 'Hymnum dicat' (attributed to Hilary of Poitiers) is found only in insular manuscripts and so had been assumed by several scholars to be Irish. Irish 'origin' is perhaps less useful a criterion than the question of Irish use and practice. None the less, this does not, and should not, preclude the search for an explanation of particular forms and styles as resulting from either local or international influences. As anyone who studies oral tradition will know, things may be absorbed from over a wide area, but may yet be given specific characteristics according to who uses them and in what context(s).

ALL surviving Irish liturgical manuscripts with music notation are late in date when compared with English and continental materials,[101] but are greater in both quantity and chronological span than the sum total of surviving pre-reformation sources for both Scotland and Wales. They range from the twelfth to the fifteenth centuries and include six missals; one gradual; one breviary; two psalters; five antiphonals; one troper; two processionals; and two sources with fragments of polyphonic singing lessons.

---

[100] For references and further discussion, see Ann Buckley, ' "And his voice swelled like a terrible thunderstorm..." ': music as symbolic sound in medieval Irish society' in Gerard Gillen and Harry White (ed.), *Irish Musical Studies*, iii (1995), pp 11–74: 42 ff.

[101] Full details are given in abbreviated form in appendices I (type) and II (libraries).

Of these, eight are Sarum-rite sources, including a missal, a troper and consuetudinary, four divine office manuscripts, and two processionals. In addition there are sources connected with particular religious orders: a missal of the Victorine canons regular, an Augustinian psalter, a Carmelite missal, a Franciscan antiphonal, and a gradual from a cathedral to which a Benedictine house was attached. Systematic studies of the provenances, contents, and history of these sources are in progress. The discussion that follows is therefore necessarily of a preliminary nature, and deals in the main with specifically Irish aspects such as the veneration of local saints.

THE oldest is the Drummond Missal (New York, Pierpont Morgan Library, MS M. 627),[102] from the early twelfth century, one of a group of three Irish missals which register various stages in the reform movement. It shares features with the eighth-/ninth-century Stowe Missal, as well as incorporating later developments.[103] It is thought that this missal was compiled during the period of reforms set in train by Malachy, and that some of the material, including the chants, may have been copied in part from an older exemplar, perhaps from as early as the tenth century, thus linking directly to a period when 'Celtic' chant was flourishing. The Corpus (or Clones) Missal (Oxford, Corpus Christi College MS 282),[104] also from the twelfth century, and the thirteenth- or fourteenth-century Rosslyn Missal (Edinburgh, National Library of Scotland, Advocates MS 18.5.19),[105] show even greater evidence of the growing influence of continental or English forms of the liturgy, but with particular elements that belong to their Irish context. The Corpus Missal may pre-date the arrival of the Normans in Ireland. It is thought also to reflect the reforms being instituted by Malachy and his followers, although it may be a copy of an early eleventh-century exemplar.[106] The Rosslyn Missal is based on an older English exemplar.

Both the Corpus and Rosslyn Missals contain inflection marks to serve as a guide in the declamation of the orations and lections, but are without

---

[102] See G. H. Forbes (ed.), *Missale Drummondiense: the ancient Irish missal in the possession of the Baroness Willoughby de Eresby* (Burntisland, 1882). See also H. P. A. Oskamp, 'The Irish quatrains and salutations in the Drummond Missal' in *Ériu*, lxxvii (1977), pp 82–91.

[103] For a recent account, see Sara G. Casey, 'The Drummond Missal: a preliminary investigation into its historical, liturgical, and musicological significance in pre-Norman Ireland' (M.A. thesis, University of Pittsburgh, 1995).

[104] F. E. Warren (ed.), *The manuscript Irish missal belonging to the president and fellows of Corpus Christi College, Oxford* (London, 1879).

[105] H. J. Lawlor (ed.), *The Rosslyn Missal: an Irish manuscript in the Advocates' Library* (Edinburgh and London, 1899).

[106] See the full discussion of the MS in Aubrey Gwynn, 'The Irish Missal of Corpus Christi College, Oxford' in *Studies in Church History*, i (1964), pp 47–68; repr. in Gwynn, *The Irish church in the eleventh and twelfth centuries* (Blackrock [Dublin], 1992), pp 17–33. See also William O'Sullivan, above, ch. XIV.

notation.[107] However, sections of the Drummond Missal (mainly preface and Sanctus chants) are provided with unheighted (or non-diastematic) neumes, i.e., they are on one horizontal plane and thus do not show the rise and fall of the melodic line (pl. 121). Most closely resembling the St Gall type of notation, they have until lately been considered indecipherable.[108] However, a new study indicates that the Drummond neumes are indeed readable, making possible hypothetical reconstructions of intervallic relationships, melodic patterns—including distinctive melismas (i.e., ornamental passages)—and text–melody relationships.[109]

A notated fragment, bound in with T.C.D. MS 1305 (ff 19ʳ–20ᵛ), is the only surviving part of the earliest example of an Irish Sarum missal. The use of green and yellow initials, in addition to the usual red, is striking, as is the use of 'b *quadratum*' (nowadays referred to as 'b natural') as a clef—a feature of other Irish sources also (see below). Its relatively early date (twelfth-/ thirteenth-century) makes it also one of the very earliest texts of the Sarum Missal.

The other missals are somewhat later, and their notation is standard square (or 'plainsong') notation on four lines, hence it may still be easily read nowadays. The oldest of these (now B.L. Add. MS 24198) dates from the early fourteenth century, and comes from the Victorine abbey of St Thomas the Martyr, Dublin. It has also received scholarly attention because of the inclusion of six polyphonic motets on its flyleaves, of which four represent items not found in any other source. All are considered to be of English provenance, but only three of the six are complete.[110]

A partially noted missal in London, Lambeth Palace Archiepiscopal Library MS 213, dates from the early fifteenth century. It contains proper materials for Brigid (f. 180ᵛb), Patrick (ff 185ʳb–186ʳa) and Finian (ff 230ʳa–b), indicating use in Ireland.[111] However, none of these is provided with music notation (which is confined mainly to preface chants).

Two missals date from the fifteenth century. The Kilcormac Missal (T.C.D. MS 82, ff 1ʳ–154ᵛ) originally belonged to the Carmelite monastery

[107] See further Aloys Fleischmann, 'The neumes in Irish liturgical manuscripts' (M.A. dissertation, N.U.I. (U.C.C.), 1932), pp 38–42.

[108] Cf. Fleischmann, 'Celtic rite', p. 53.

[109] See Casey, 'The Drummond Missal'; eadem, 'The Sanctus chant of the Drummond Missal: a semiotic study' (unpublished TS, 1996); eadem, ' "Through a glass, darkly": steps towards reconstructing Irish chant from the neumes of the Drummond Missal' in *Early Music*, xxviii, no. 2 (May 2000), pp 205–15.

[110] Frank Harrison (ed.), *Motets of English provenance* (Monaco, 1980), nos 15, 16, and 17, and ibid., fragments 23, 26, and 29 respectively. Cf. RISM [*Répertoire international des sources musicales*] B IV¹, 513–15.

[111] Frere does not refer to any of these Irish saints in his list of Lambeth Palace sources; see Walter H. Frere, *Bibliotheca musico-liturgica*, I.1.2 (London, 1894; reprint, Hildesheim, 1967), while the library catalogue records Finnian only: see M. R. James and C. Jenkins, *A descriptive catalogue of the manuscripts in the library of Lambeth Palace* (Cambridge, 1932), pp 341–2.

at Kilcormac (now Frankford, County Offaly).[112] Obits of important personages from the region are included in the Kalendar, and the manuscript is distinguished by being the only Carmelite missal to survive from any house in Britain or Ireland. It contains very little notation, and none for the Sanctorale, which includes Brigid (f. 105[r]b), Patrick (ff 105[v]a–106[r]a) and Brendan (f. 109[v]). It is now bound with a fragment of sixteen folios from a Sarum antiphonal (see *infra*). The other missal is B.L. Egerton MS 2677, which is also a Sarum manuscript adapted to Irish use, as indicated by materials for Irish saints (only a few sections of the proper are provided with music notation—but not those for Irish saints).[113]

A fragment of another missal was included in the Red Book of the Exchequer. The Red Book, unfortunately destroyed in the Dublin Public Record Office fire of 1922, belonged to the court of the exchequer in Dublin.[114] It dates from the thirteenth century, with additions continuing up to the seventeenth. According to Flood, the missal, which was richly illuminated, largely followed the Use of Sarum. He reported that the book also contained a 'transcript of the Gregorian modes', a hymn for the feast of the Ascension, another to St Nicholas, a copy of the hymn 'Ut queant laxis', and a church calendar with various notices (for the period 1264–1524). 'Ut queant laxis' is a hymn from the Second Vespers for the feast of John the Baptist.[115]

Frere's account largely agrees with Flood's. He lists a Sarum Kalendar (May–April) adapted to Irish Dominican use (p. 37), votive masses with Ordinary and Canon (p. 48), the four gospels (p. 62), and sections with notation for parts of the services for the Ascension, and the feastdays of St John the Baptist and St Nicholas. He dated all of these materials to the

---

[112] According to the colophon on f. 154 it was written in 1458 by Dermot O'Flanagan, a brother of the Carmelite Priory at Loughrea, for Edward Higgins, prior of Kilcormac. The only study remains that of H. J. Lawlor, 'The Kilcormick Missal—a manuscript in the Library of Trinity College, Dublin' in *R.I.A. Trans.*, xxxi (1896–1901), pp 393–430, though Fleischmann ('The neumes', pp 65–8 and plates IX–XI) discusses certain aspects, particularly the music palaeography.

[113] An anonymous handwritten note entered in the B.L. copy of the *Catalogue of additions* (1968) describes this source as: 'Dublin use (many modifications from Sarum use)'.

[114] Frere, *Bibliotheca musico-liturgica*, II.1.2 (1932; reprint, Hildesheim, 1967), p. 75. Cf. William H. Grattan Flood, *A history of Irish music* (Dublin, 1905), pp 135–6. A fuller account of the contents of the entire book may be found in James Frederick Ferguson, 'Calendar of the contents of the Red Book of the Irish exchequer' in *R.S.A.I. Jn.*, iii (1854–5), pp 35–52. I am obliged to Dr Harold Clarke for this reference.

[115] This hymn is famous for having been used throughout the middle ages as a method for teaching the hexachord, the first six degrees of the diatonic scale, and for learning to sing at sight. Each phrase begins on a successively higher note, with the first syllable of every line (UT queant laxis, REsonare fibris, etc.) providing the name of the so-called 'solmisation' syllables (ut, re, mi, fa, sol, la). This system was devised by Guido of Arezzo (*c*.991/2–*p*. 1033), who may have composed the melody (or adapted an existing one). The text is much older and is commonly attributed to Paul Warnefrid (d. 799), also known as 'Paul the Deacon'.

thirteenth century. Frere also itemised the hymn 'Eterne rex', which is undoubtedly the Ascension hymn to which Grattan Flood referred.

The notated materials, interspersed with Latin prayers, appear to represent ceremonies held regularly at the court of the exchequer. According to the rubrics, the second remembrancer (one of the principal officers of the court) should commence the singing of 'Eterne rex' (Ferguson (1856), p. 51). The ceremonies may have been linked to those in which the choir of Christ Church cathedral participated. From some time after 1547 the choir used to sing there four times a year at the end of each term. This custom arose following the suppression of the choral foundation at St Patrick's cathedral in 1547, when six of its priests and two boys were redeployed to Christ Church, funded by a royal grant from the exchequer. The first documented record may be one dated 9 August 1589.[116] According to Ferguson (1854–5, p. 51), whenever this ceremony was performed, an entry was made in one of the rule-books of the court to the effect that 'the chantour of Christ Church brought into court the vicars choralls and performed theire accustomed service and homage due to his majestie, by singing an antheme and saying certain collects and prayers, which being done they had warrant under the barons hands directed to the vice treasurer for receiveing their wonted fee of ten shillings sterling.' Unfortunately Ferguson supplies no dates for these entries, but in his account (pp 50–51) he suggests that the ceremonies may have been entered into the book during the reign of Henry VI (1422–61, 1470–71), thus around a century before the presumed involvement of Christ Church. However, in the absence of the original documents, the question must remain open, including the possibility that they may be even as old as the thirteenth century, the date supplied by Frere.

Finally, another missal was described by Grattan Flood as having been written in the fifteenth century by a member of the Franciscan friary at Enniscorthy and to be 'still in existence' (i.e. at the time of writing—Flood's book was published in 1898). Around the same time, Lawlor, in a brief discussion of medieval Irish missals, understood that it was '. . . some time ago in the hands of Cardinal Moran'. No trace of it can now be found, nor is there any surviving record (such as Frere) to indicate whether it contained notation; this therefore seems unlikely.[117]

The gradual, Oxford, Bodl. MS Rawl. C 892, dates from the second half of the twelfth century and hails from an Irish cathedral to which a Benedictine monastery was attached (Downpatrick is thought the most likely). Prayers for both Brigid (f. 102ᵛ) and Patrick (f. 106ʳ) are included in the

---

[116] Alan J. Fletcher, *Drama, performance, and polity in pre-Cromwellian Ireland* (Cork, 2000), p. 388, n. 115; also pp 256–7 and 436–7, n. 228.

[117] See Grattan Flood, *History of Enniscorthy* (Enniscorthy, 1898), p. 195; Lawlor, 'Kilcormick Missal', p. 393, n. 1.

Fig. 44 Two-part setting 'Dicant nunc of the Easter antiphon 'Christus resurgens'
(Bodl., Rawl. MS C 892, ff 67ᵛ–68ʳ).

(a)

Be - ne - di - ca - mus Do - mi - no

(b)

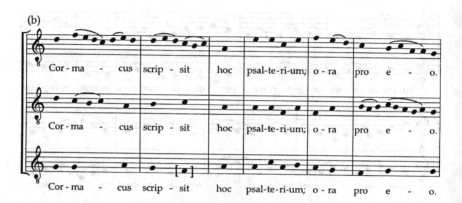

Cor - ma - cus scrip - sit hoc psal-te-ri-um; o - ra pro e - o.

Cor - ma - cus scrip - sit hoc psal-te-ri-um; o - ra pro e - o.

Cor - ma - cus scrip - sit hoc psal-te-ri-um; o - ra pro e - o.

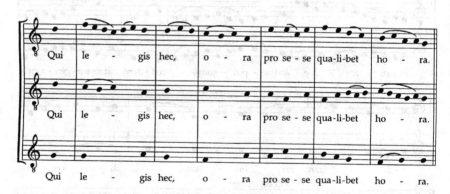

Qui le - gis hec, o - ra pro se - se qua-li-bet ho - ra.

Qui le - gis hec, o - ra pro se - se qua-li-bet ho - ra.

Qui le - gis hec, o - ra pro se - se qua-li-bet ho - ra.

Fig. 45 (a) Sarum 'Bendicamus Domino', after Salisbury Cathedral Library MS 175, f. 135ᵛ. (b) Colophon in three-part polyphony in an Irish psalter, second half of the twelfth century (B.L., Add. MS 36929, f. 59ʳ). The reconstruction is conjectural: the voices are not precisely aligned in the manuscript, and text is supplied only for the tenor.

Sanctorale, and Brigid is mentioned in the introit 'Gaudeamus' for the Common of Virgins (f. 143ᵛ). A few words in Irish are recorded in the lower margin of f. 144ʳ, and some Latin in Irish lettering on f. 131ᵛ. It has received particular attention because it contains a two-part polyphonic arrangement of

the verse 'Dicant nunc Iudei' (ff 67$^v$–68$^r$) from the Sarum processional antiphon 'Christus resurgens', which was sung at the beginning of the Easter
morning service (pl. 120 and figure 44). Although 'Dicant nunc' itself—and
other aspects of this manuscript—reveal close connections with Winchester,
the only concordance for a polyphonic setting is found in a manuscript from
Chartres (Cathedral Library, MS 109, f. 75, *c*.1100), a centre important in the
pre-Notre Dame history of polyphony. Indeed, it remains the only polyphonic
item from before the Notre Dame epoch (twelfth century) for which a musical
concordance has been identified.[118] This raises questions as to the possible
wider existence of multi-part liturgical singing in Ireland (as do the few surviving examples from Chartres for French practices outside of Paris).

There are particular music-palaeographical features in this manuscript that
are unusual. For example, the presence of green staff lines on f. 37$^r$,
and purple and brown on f. 26$^v$ (in place of the more usual red or black); the
use of double clefs, and of b-*quadratum* ('B natural')—both of which
appear to be common features of Irish scribal practice.[119] We shall return
below to the question of clefs and the related question of Irish music palaeography.

T.C.D. MS 80 is an early fifteenth-century noted breviary which was used at
Kilmoone, County Meath. In addition to the regular Sarum materials, it
contains offices for both Patrick (ff 122$^r$–124$^v$)[120] and Brigid (ff 114$^v$–117$^r$) in
its Sanctorale.

THE Christ Church psalter is a fourteenth-century codex from the Cathedral
of the Holy Trinity, Dublin (called Christ Church after the reformation),
now in the Bodleian Library, Oxford (MS Rawl. G 185). Written
between 1350 and 1380, perhaps in East Anglia, it contains richly illuminated
capitals and miniatures, with some particularly striking representations
of instruments and singing monks. Many of the psalms are provided with
reciting tones, and the antiphons are notated also. Stephen of Derby,
who was prior of Christ Church 1347–?1382, is acknowledged as the
commissioner of the collection; later additions on the front flyleaves and
end folios comprise memoranda relating to the priory from 1374 to 1409,
together with some prayers and a form of absolution. No Irish saints are

---

[118] See Marion S. Gushee, 'The polyphonic music of the medieval monastery, cathedral and
university' in James McKinnon (ed.), *Antiquity and the middle ages: from ancient Greece to the
fifteenth century* (Man and Music; Basingstoke and London, 1990), pp 143–69: 151.

[119] Cf. Stäblein, *Schriftbild*, n. 14, who points to these features, as does E. Nicholson, *Early
Bodleian music*, iii (Oxford, 1913), pp lxxxiv–lxxxv and plate LXIV. Nicholson suggested a
Waterford provenance for the MS. The MS has not been published in facsimile but a photograph of f. 69$^r$ is given in Bruno Stäblein, *Schriftbild der einstimmigen Musik* (Leipzig, 1975),
pl. 12, accompanied by a brief discussion of the source on p. 120. See also RISM BIV$^1$, p. 573

[120] The beginning of the Patrick Office is wanting in this source.

celebrated in liturgical services, but the Kalendar is particularly rich in such references.[121]

Another Irish psalter, B.L. Add. MS 36929, dating to the middle or second half of the twelfth century, is remarkable for its inclusion of a fragment of polyphony (on f. 59[r]) in the form of a colophon written by its Irish scribe, Cormac, but is otherwise without notation (pl. 121, fig. 45b). This will be discussed below.

THE antiphonals include three Sarum Divine Office manuscripts, T.C.D. MSS 77, 78, 79, as also MS 82,[122] a Sarum antiphonal (c.1300) which is bound together with the Kilcormac Missal, and T.C.D. MS 109, a late fifteenth-century antiphonal of Irish Franciscan Roman use. MS 77 (dating probably to between 1416 and c.1450) contains numerous references to Armagh, and was used by the *céli Dé* of Armagh cathedral. Its psalter has a number of unusual characteristics, among them three antiphons with music notation for the feast of St Patrick, found in the section for the Little Hours, following Psalm 118 on f. 74[r]. These items, 'Iubilemus puro cor de Christo' (f. 75[r]), 'Ut nos Deus in tuo adventum' (f. 78[r]), and 'Laus et honor resonet' (f. 80[r]) are concordant with the same items in MSS 79 and 80. MS 78 (late fifteenth century) reveals a particularly strong Irish element, including some saints not found elsewhere. They represent a wide range of Irish localities, in particular Ossory, as well as including several English saints not found in the Sarum rite.[123] In the Sanctorale of this source there occur notated offices for Brigid (ff 139[v]–141[v]; cf. pl. 122), Patrick (ff 150[r]–151[v]), and Canice (ff 168[r]–170[v]), as well as prayers and references to Mokyn and Kieran in the rubrics of the Sanctorale. The Canice material is unique to this source, and includes antiphons, verses, responses, an invitatory, and a hymn.

MS 79 (dating to probably between 1431 and 1435) was associated with the parish church of St John the Evangelist in Dublin. It was begun in the fifteenth century, when feasts of seven Irish saints were listed; later additions during the course of the fifteenth and early sixteenth centuries include

---

[121] See Geoffrey Hand, 'The psalter of Christ Church, Dublin (Bodleian MS Rawlinson G 185)' in *Reportorium Novum*, i, pt 2 (1956), pp 311–22.

[122] For detailed discussion of the Irish Sarum Divine Office sources (T.C.D., MSS 77–80), and their inclusion of liturgical celebration of Irish saints, see Brannon, 'Four notated Sarum Divine Office MSS', pp 160–98, and with respect to chants in particular, pp 262–302. Brannon, 'The search for the Celtic rite', contains a summary of these findings. Cf. also idem, 'Medieval Ireland: music in cathedral, church and cloister' in *Early Music*, xxviii, no. 2 (May 2000), pp 193–202. See also Andrew Hughes, 'British rhymed offices' in Susan Rankin and David Hiley (ed.), *Music in the medieval English liturgy* (Plainsong and Medieval Music Society Centennial Essays; Oxford, 1993), pp 239–84.

[123] Discussed in W. Hawkes, 'The liturgy in Dublin 1200–1500: manuscript sources' in *Reportorium Novum*, ii, pt 1 (1958), pp 33–67: 44–6 and 46–9, respectively.

twenty more. It contains a notated office for Patrick in the Sanctorale (ff 160$^r$–162$^v$). MS 82 (*c*.1300) is a fragment only, and probably representative of Irish Sarum use. It is now bound with the Kilcormac Missal (on ff 156$^r$–168$^v$, 170$^r$–171$^v$, 169$^{r-v}$)[124] but once formed part of a separate codex. MS 109 (late fifteenth century) contains texts and chant for Lauds for the office of St Patrick (ff 95$^r$–99$^r$), as well as unnotated text for matins.

THE so-called 'Dublin Troper' (in fact a troper-proser) has been widely studied, and reproduced in facsimile, with an edition of some of its contents.[125] It was in use at St Patrick's cathedral, Dublin, *c*.1360. An important source on several counts, it is unique in containing a separate proser devoted exclusively to the Virgin; almost half of the proses (or sequences) contained therein appear to have been composed in Dublin—at least this manuscript is the only known source. A number of items from the liturgical proser may also be original compositions, including the texts of two St Patrick sequences (and the melody of one of them).

The melody of 'Laeta lux' is an *unicum*, but another copy of the text exists in T.C.D. MS 83 (*olim* B.3.4.), a fifteenth-century missal of the Use of York.[126] The other sequence, 'Laetabundus decantet', is found also in B.L. Egerton MS 2677 on f. 254$^r$. With its most usual text (generally referred to as 'Laetabundus'), this melody is used in a Christmas sequence, the oldest sources of which date to eleventh-century France (where it is thought to have originated) and Germany, spreading to England in the twelfth century.[127] Numerous texts have been set to this melody, including sequences in honour of other Irish saints, e.g., for the Translation of Patrick, Brigid, and Columba;[128] the feast of Colman,[129] and the Anglo-Norman drinking song 'Or hi parra'. The codex also contains three copies of the famous song, 'Angelus ad Virginem', one monophonic, one in three parts (incomplete), and a complete version in three parts (this time without words),[130] as also

[124] The current sequence of folio numbers is a result of misbinding (see Colker, *T.C.D. catalogue*, i, 148).

[125] René-Jean Hesbert (ed.), *Le Tropaire-Prosaire de Dublin: MS Add. 710 de l'Université de Cambridge (vers 1360)* (Rouen, 1966). See RISM B V$^1$, pp 151–2.

[126] G. M. Dreves, Clemens Blume, and H. M. Bannister (ed.), *Analecta hymnica medii aevi* (58 vols, Leipzig 1886–1922), xl, no. 303, pp 261–2.

[127] Ibid., pp 302, 260–61. Cf. Geoffrey Hand, 'Cambridge University [*sic*] Additional Manuscript 710' in *Reportorium Novum*, ii, no. 1 (1958), pp 17–32: 28.

[128] Cf. *Analecta hymnica*, xl, no. 304, p. 262.

[129] Ibid., xli, no. 6, pp 94–5.

[130] The three-part version is unique to the Dublin MS. For further details, see E. J. Dobson and Frank Ll. Harrison, *Medieval English songs* (London, 1979), p. 303 ff; also John Stevens, 'Angelus ad Virginem: the history of a medieval song' in P. L. Heyworth (ed.), *Medieval studies for J. A. W. Bennett aetatis suae lxx* (Oxford, 1981), pp 297–328: 299.

the Latin *lai*, 'The song of the Flood', 'Omnis caro'—one of only three notated sources for this extended narrative piece.[131]

THE two Sarum processionals, dating to *c.*1400, belonged to the parish church of St John the Evangelist, Dublin, at least by the second half of the fifteenth century. This church, originally dedicated to St John the Baptist and built in the shadow of Christ Church cathedral, was served by the members of the cathedral from *c.*1230, following a directive from the archbishop. The manuscripts, now Oxford, Bodl. MS Rawl. Liturg.d.4, and Dublin, Marsh's Library, MS Z.4.2.20,[132] contain dramatic ceremonies for Easter, including the ceremony of the Burial of the Cross and the Host on Good Friday and their retrieval on Easter morning ('Depositio crucis et hostiae', 'Elevatio crucis et hostiae'), and the 'Visitatio Sepulchri' play, representing the three Marys arriving at the empty tomb on Easter morning. While it remains unclear where these manuscripts were written, it is likely that the Marsh's manuscript, and perhaps both, were executed in Dublin,[133] perhaps at Christ Church itself, given other evidence for the performance of liturgical drama by the Augustinian canons at that cathedral. The Marsh's manuscript has additional proper chants for Patrick (ff 104$^v$–105$^v$) and Columba (ff 107$^v$–108$^v$), while one of its three litanies (ff 130$^v$–133$^r$) includes the names of four Irish saints: Patrick, Columbanus, Columba, and Brigid. The Bodley codex contains chants for the feasts of Patrick (ff 188$^r$–190$^r$) and Audoen (f. 190$^{r-v}$, incomplete), and includes the same four Irish saints in the litanies.

There is other extant evidence for the enactment of liturgical drama in Dublin, as we have indicated above (p. 768). Meantime, it is of relevance to mention a much older source which suggests the use of drama in the early medieval Irish church and centres that came under its influence. It occurs in the Northumbrian Book of Cerne (Cambridge University Library, MS Ll.1.10, written in Mercia at the beginning of the ninth century) which,

---

[131] For further details see John Stevens, *Words and music in the middle ages: song, narrative, dance and drama, 1050–1350* (Cambridge, 1986) 144ff. Cf. also Hesbert, *Le Tropaire-Prosaire de Dublin*, pp 97–105 (edition) and 184–6 (facsimile).

[132] The Oxford MS contains the 'Depositio', ff 68$^v$–70$^r$, two versions of the 'Elevatio', ff 85$^v$–86$^r$ (short), and 127$^v$–130$^r$ (long), and the 'Visitatio sepulchri' play on ff 130$^r$–132$^r$; the Marsh's Library MS has two versions of the 'Elevatio crucis et hostie', on ff 58$^v$–59$^r$ (short) followed by the 'Visitatio sepulchri' play on ff 59$^v$–61$^r$, with the long version of the 'Elevatio' on ff 138$^v$–140$^r$.

[133] Notices appeared in Hawkes (1958, 38ff), and Dolan (1975, 148ff) who discusses the historical problems in detail and includes photographs of ff 59$^r$–61$^r$ of the Marsh's Library source. Lipphardt gives a summary in vi, 256, 358–9, based on both previous studies. For the most recent study of dating, provenance, and contents of these sources, see Máire Egan-Buffet and Alan V. Fletcher, 'The Dublin *Visitatio Sepulchri* play' in *R.I.A. Proc.*, xc (1990), sect. c, pp 159–241. This publication also contains an edition of the plays, with photographs from both manuscripts.

along with a breviate psalter, prayers, and hymns, contains the text of the play on the 'Harrowing of Hell'. David Dumville, noting the Irish metrical structure of the hymns, the Irish nature of the breviate psalter, and evidence in the prayers of Spanish-Irish as well as Roman-Gallican influence, has put forward the hypothesis that the manuscript is a copy of an older exemplar which, if not of direct Irish provenance, was in all probability introduced to Northumbria by Irish missionary monks in the eighth century during the episcopate of Æðiluald of Lindisfarne (721/4–740).[134] Thus the text itself may be older, perhaps dating to eighth-century Lindisfarne, which would render it likely to have come originally from an Irish milieu. Such evidence for the existence of dramatic representation would thus pre-date by a full century the earliest continental source for liturgical drama, from St Martial de Limoges. Dumville goes so far as to suggest that Ireland may have thereby been the 'original home' for this genre,[135] but this is somewhat rash in view of the variety of possible ways in which such lessons may have been performed, represented, or 'dramatised' throughout western Europe in order to illustrate forms of sermons or other instruction, or to enhance important church feasts. Such a 'play', and others like it, may well have existed over a wider area and a much longer period of time, but our knowledge is limited by lack of further written evidence.

Another important topic currently under investigation concerns liturgical materials from continental Irish houses, and those subject to Irish influence.[136] In addition to sources for Patrick, Brigid, and Colum Cille, we have identified proper chants for Brendan, Columbanus, Findan, Fridolin, Fursey, Gall, Kilian, Laurence O'Toole, Maglorius, and Malachy, and non-notated materials for many more.[137]

---

[134] David Dumville, 'Liturgical drama and panegyric responsory from the eighth century? A re-examination of the origin and contents of the ninth-century section of the Book of Cerne' in *Journal of Theological Studies*, new ser., xxiii (1972), pp 374–406: 384–5, 393–4, 396. For a more recent detailed study of the manuscript, see Michelle P. Brown, *The Book of Cerne* (London, 1997), especially pp 145–6, 150–51, where she takes up some of Dumville's observations.

[135] Dumville, 'Liturgical drama', p. 381.

[136] This forms part of the long-term research programme of the International Research Group for Music of Medieval Celtic Regions, and includes an in-progress publication by Ann Buckley and Sara Casey, *Liturgical sources for the veneration of Irish saints: an annotated checklist* (2 vols). This work, which will cover all of the source materials, both insular and continental, involves a complete revision and extension of Dreves, Blume & Bannister, *Analecta hymnica* [AH], now long out of date, but which contains material for almost forty Irish saints in a survey of some 300 manuscripts.

[137] See, for example, Jean Leclercq, 'Documents on the cult of St Malachy' in *Seanchas Ardmhacha*, iii (1959), pp 318–36: 327–32, and plate II; also David Hiley, 'Rouen, Bibliothèque Municipale, MS 249 (A.280) and the early Paris repertory of ordinary of mass chants and sequences' in *Music & Letters*, lxx, pt 4 (1989), pp 463–82: 471–2, 481–2, for a source of sequences in honour of St Laurence O'Toole from the collegiate church of St Laurent at Eu, where the saint died in 1180; Theodore Karp, 'A serendipitous encounter with St Kilian' in *Early Music*, xxviii, no. 2 (May 2000), pp 226–37.

A large collection of fragments dating to the twelfth and thirteenth centuries, most of them with music notation, was recently discovered at the Irish foundation in Vienna, the Schottenstift.[138] The Schottenabtei, or 'Irish monastery', was the first such foundation to be established in Vienna when, in 1155, Irish monks arrived from the Irish community of St Jakob in Regensburg. Hence, items dating from the earlier part of the twelfth century are likely to have been brought from Regensburg by the founding monks. Among their contents are materials for the veneration of Irish saints (Patrick, Brigid, Columba, Kilian, Báethgen), including a copy of the vespers hymn for the office of St Patrick, 'Ecce fulget clarissima' (without notation; see below). The fragments represent five or six antiphonals, one troper, two graduals, one breviary, one sacramentary, and one manuscript containing chants for both daily mass and the divine office. They are mostly in plainsong notation, and were written by Irish or Irish-trained scribes. Characteristic is the use of clef letters 'b' (i.e. B flat), 'D', and 'h' (i.e., '*b quadratum*' or B natural), as well as double clefs (i.e., combining two letter-clefs on different lines or spaces). They bear a resemblance to some of the palaeographic features of the Downpatrick Gradual already discussed (above, pp 788–90). In addition, they display a striking use of the colours blue and green, associated also with other Irish manuscripts.

ALTHOUGH there are no Irish manuscripts with music notation dating prior to the twelfth century, this may not preclude the possibility of recovering the melodies of pre-twelfth-century Irish liturgical repertories from later sources, among them two antiphons preserved in a thirteenth-century breviary (of the use of Bayeux) from the collegiate church of Saint-Sépulcre, Caen.[139] The first is a setting of 'Ibunt sancti', which was said to have been sung on his deathbed by Theudoaldus, a monk of Columbanus's community in Bobbio, after he had received the last rites. The account is by Jonas, Columbanus's biographer, writing between 639 and 642.[140] Another reference to 'Ibunt

[138] See László Mezey, 'Fragmentforschung im Schottenstift 1982–1983' in *Codices manuscripti: Zeitschrift für Handschriftenkunde*, 2/10 (1984), pp 60–71. For commentary (by Walter Pass) and selected illustrations, see *Musik im mittelalterlichen Wien* (Historisches Museum der Stadt Wien, 103. Sonderausstellung, 18 Dezember 1986 bis 8. März 1987), pp 39, 54 ff. Since these publications appeared, more fragments have been identified, and the shelf numbers of the entire collection have been revised. See Martin Czernin, 'Fragments of liturgical chant from medieval Irish monasteries in continental Europe' in *Early Music*, xxviii, no. 2 (May 2000), pp 217–24. A complete facsimile edition is shortly due for publication, with contributions from an interdisciplinary team of specialists. See Martin Czernin (ed.), *Die Musik der irischen Benediktiner in Wien* (Graz, forthcoming 2003).
[139] Now Paris, Bibliothèque de l'Arsenal, MS 279, f. 214ᵛ. See Stäblein, 'Zwei Melodien', *passim*.
[140] Bruno Krusch (ed.), *Ionae vitae sanctorum Columbani, Vedastis, Iohannis* (Hanover and Leipzig, 1905), p. 292; see Stäblein, 'Zwei melodien', pp 593–4.

Fig. 46 The antiphon 'Ibunt sancti', adapted from the thirteenth-century Caen Breviary, Paris, Bibliothèque de l'Arsenal, MS 279, f. 241ᵛ, after Stäblein, 'Zwei Melodien' (1973), p. 593.

sancti' occurs in the 'Navigatio Brendani',[141] where it is described as being sung continuously by three choirs in turn on the island where Brendan and his companions landed.

The Caen manuscript is the unique source of this text with its melody which, however, departs from Jonas's version of the words in the second line by substituting a series of *alleluias*. Stäblein reconstructed the original which conforms exactly to the surviving melody (reproduced here as fig. 46). The text features the common Irish characteristics of assonance and alliteration; its melody is formed from two simple motifs in ABA form for the first line, repeated exactly in the second. This parallel structure is not a characteristic of Roman chant and is found elsewhere only in the more elaborate structure of the liturgical sequence. Similarly the repetition of the cell within the melodic line is un-Roman.

The other antiphon, 'Crucem sanctam', follows on the same folio in this manuscript but, unlike 'Ibunt sancti', it is widely attested in sources from England, northern France, Italy, Spain, and Switzerland. The four phrases are grouped in pairs, each with a different incipit (A, B, C, D) followed alternately by 'x' (with a half close) and 'x¹' (with a full close; see fig. 47).[142] The upper and middle voices of the polyphonic piece 'Cormacus scripsit' consist of two phrases repeated exactly in sequence, in which respect it too resembles the form of 'Ibunt sancti' (pl. 121 and fig. 45b). And the hymn 'Mediae noctis tempus est', found with its melody in a central- or south-Italian hymnar from the first half of the thirteenth century,[143] reveals textual and melodic characteristics similar to those of the antiphons from Caen (see fig. 48). It is in origin a continental hymn, perhaps from Poitiers, with a text dating to at least the sixth century; its use in Ireland is attested as far back as the Antiphonary of Bangor.[144]

[141] Carl Selmer (ed.), *Navigatio Sancti Brendani abbatis* (Notre Dame, Ind., 1956), p. 50; see also Curran, *Antiphonary of Bangor*, pp 170–71.
[142] For details cf. Stäblein, 'Zwei Melodien', pp 592, 595 ff.
[143] Berlin, Staatsbibliothek Preußischer Kulturbesitz, MS Hamilton 688; the hymn is found on ff 33–4 with the slightly different incipit, 'Mediae noctis tempore'.
[144] See Stevenson, 'Irish hymns', pp 105–6.

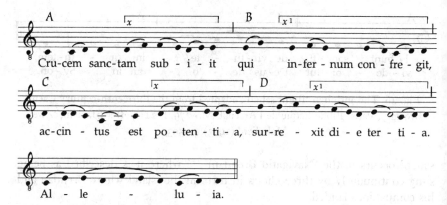

Fig. 47 The antiphon 'Crucem sanctam', Paris, Bibliothèque de l'Arsenal, MS 279, f. 214ᵛ, after Stäblein, 'Zwei Melodien' (1973), p. 596.

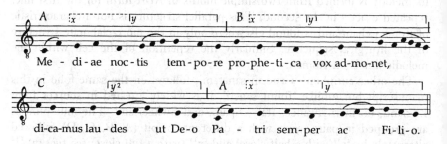

Fig. 48 First strophe of the hymn 'Mediae noctis tempore', adapted from a central or south Italian hymnal of the first half of the thirteenth century, Berlin, Staatsbibliothek, MS Hamilton 688, ff 33–4, after Fleischmann, 'Celtic rite' (1980), p. 53.

Another item of relevance to this discussion is 'Ductu angelico', a matins responsory for the feast of St Patrick which occurs in T.C.D. MSS 79 (ff 161ᵛ–162ʳ) and 80 (f. 124ʳ). It is distinguished by a particularly melismatic style formed from a small group of melodic cells which recur throughout the piece (fig. 49). The same cellular construction occurs in a number of chants for the office of Columba (Colum Cille) which survive in fragmentary form in a fourteenth-century antiphonal (Edinburgh University Library, MS 211.iv) believed to have come from Inchcolm abbey, an Augustinian foundation dedicated to Colum Cille, and situated on Inchcolm Island in the Firth

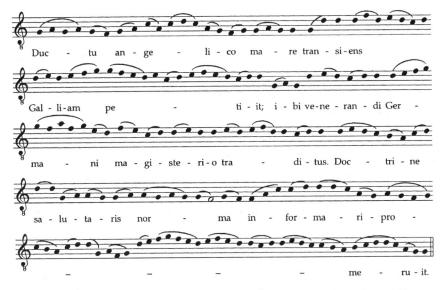

Fig. 49 Transcription of 'Ductu angelico', in honour of St Patrick T.C.D., MS 79, ff 161ᵛ–162ʳ.

of Forth, Scotland.[145] In 849 the relics of Colum Cille were brought by King Kenneth I from Iona to Dunkeld, and there is an indirect link between Inchcolm and Iona, since the bishops of Dunkeld were protectors of Inchcolm priory (later abbey) from the time of its foundation, c.1123, until at least the thirteenth century. Thus the Inchcolm material may well represent long-term continuity of practice—in this case, from the mid ninth century (perhaps even back to the Columban church itself)—and it certainly indicates that similar practices obtained in both Ireland and Scotland. In addition to those melodies, other chants included in the Inchcolm fragments represent continental (Gregorian) and Sarum repertories, providing evidence that all three styles were used in tandem. This distinction therefore suggests that the cellular, repetitive structure may have been a more widespread feature of older practice, and one which continued as an element of Scottish liturgy, as in Irish, for several centuries after the English reforms.

A more direct link with pre-Norman Ireland is found in the vespers hymn 'Ecce fulget clarissima' (fig. 50), in honour of St Patrick. It survives with notation in T.C.D. MS 80 (f. 122), but most significantly, a concordance is found also with the text contained in the T.C.D. copy of the Irish 'Liber Hymnorum' (MS 1441, f. 29), dating from the late eleventh century. Al-

[145] See Isobel Woods, ' "Our awin Scottis Use": chant usage in medieval Scotland' in *Journal of the Royal Music Association*, cxii, pt 1 (1987), pp 21–37.

Fig. 50 Transcription of the hymn 'Ecce fulget', in honour of St Patrick, T.C.D., MS 80, f. 122ʳ.

though attested in several modern compilations, there are no earlier sources for the melody, according to the present state of knowledge. It is therefore impossible to ascertain whether it too dates from an earlier period, whether it was newly composed, or whether indeed it was imported from elsewhere. It shares characteristics with hymns in honour of other Irish saints which are not found in the Sarum repertoire. On the basis of his study of the T.C.D. Sarum Divine Office manuscripts, Patrick Brannon has suggested a link with the Germanic sphere of influence.[146] Given the concentration of Irish *pere-grini* in that part of continental Europe, this is perhaps no surprise. And while it may not be possible to establish in which direction the influence was moving, further work of a comparative and systematic nature can only help to shed light on such questions.

While research on insular manuscripts is as yet at an early stage, there are some signs of a stylistically distinctive kind of melodic structure in both Irish and Scottish sources, which suggests that some older elements may have survived the eleventh- and twelfth-century reforms. However, whether we can classify them specifically as Celtic chant—i.e. regionally distinctive— must remain open until more information emerges.[147]

HYMN texts and religious poetry, together with literary references to chant and hymn-singing in saints' Lives and in secular tales, attest to an enormous

[146] Patrick Brannon, 'A contextual study of the four notated Sarum Divine Office manu- scripts from Anglo-Norman Ireland' (Ph.D. diss., Washington University, Seattle, 1990; Uni- versity Microfilms International, no. 9103125 (Ann Arbor, Michigan, 1994)), p. 283, and idem, 'The search for the Celtic rite', p. 35, also p. 19 and n. 24 for a list of concordant melodies.

[147] For further discussion of these issues, see Ann Buckley, 'Celtic chant' in *The new Grove dictionary of music and musicians*, ed. Stanley Sadie, v (London, 2001), pp 341–9. For sound recordings, cf. The Schola Cantorum of St Peter's in the Loop (director J. Michael Thompson), *In honor of St Patrick: chant for his feast* (The Order of St Benedict, Collegeville, Minnesota, 1998). Selected items from the offices of Patrick, Brigid, Colum Cille, Gall, and Kilian have been reconstructed from Irish, Scottish, Swiss, and Austrian sources by the Altramar Medieval Music Ensemble and recorded on two CDs entitled *Crossroads of the Celts: medieval music of Ireland, Brittany, Scotland and Wales* (Dorian, New York, 1999), DOR-93177; and *Celtic wanderers: the pilgrim's road* (Dorian, New York, 2000), DOR-93213. These programmes are not confined to liturgical music but also include musical settings of religious and secular poetry and narrative.

body of devotional material. It is clear from literary sources that chant was preeminent in the Irish church. The psalter was the single most studied book, in the Gallican version, in which the 150 psalms were grouped into 'three fifties'. According to the Rule of Columbanus, psalms formed the main component of the divine office and were sung in threes: the first two straight through, the third antiphonally, i.e., with the singers divided into two groups, one intoning the psalm, the other the response. In a tantalising reference by Jonas, Columbanus's biographer, the saint was reported to have set out instructions for the performance of chant.[148] Unfortunately, no record of this has survived. The Luxeuil legislator commented on singing of the psalms responsorially with the insertion of a refrain after each individual or group of psalms.[149] Unison singing seems to have been the practice on Iona, whence it reached Northumbria. Stephanus's 'Vita Wilfridi' contains a reference to the introduction of (previously unknown) antiphonal singing into Northumbria.[150]

Apart from the obvious relevance here of hymns as sung poetry, some of their texts contain information on ways in which they may have been performed. In the opening lines of 'Cantemus in omni die', attributed to Cú Chuimne of Iona (d. 747), the word *varie* in the first line is glossed as *inter duos choros*, while the third line refers explicitly to antiphonal singing:

Cantemus in omni die        concinentes varie
conclamantes deo dignum     ymnum sanctae Mariae

bis per chordum hic et inde  collaudemus Mariam

and the following from stanza 9 of 'Ecce fulget clarissima' (discussed above in another context), in which reference is made to alternating voices and to stringed instruments:

Psallemus Christo cordibus       alternantes et vocibus

Similarly, the structure of Comgall's hymn 'Recordemur iustitiae' (preserved in the Antiphonary of Bangor) implies the use of two choirs and a subdivision of the congregation into two, providing a refrain for each of the choirs. Each alphabetic stanza is followed, respectively, by the first and second two lines of the refrain.[151]

---

[148] Krusch, *Columbae, Ionae et Vedastis vitae*, p. 158.
[149] Louis Gougaud, 'Celtic (Liturgies)' in *The catholic encyclopaedia*, iii (New York, 1908), cols 2969–3032: col. 3018.
[150] Stevenson in F. E. Warren, *Liturgy and ritual of the Celtic church* (Oxford, 1881; reprint, Woodbridge, 1987), pp lxxvii–lxxviii.
[151] Much more research is needed on this topic. For earlier discussion of some of these questions, see Gougaud, 'Celtic (liturgies)', col. 3018; Fleischmann & Gleeson, 'Music in ancient Munster', p. 87 and *passim*, and Stevenson, 'Hiberno-Latin hymns', pp 113–15.

'Precamur patrem' (composed probably by Columbanus, and also preserved in the Antiphonary of Bangor) has an *alleluia* after the first and last stanzas, perhaps indicating reponsorial singing by the congregation after each one. The matins hymn 'Spiritus divinae lucis' (in the same collection) has a one-line refrain following each stanza, as does the (?) seventh-century 'Celebra Iuda', with an *alleluia* following each pair of lines. Similarly, the canticle from Exodus, 'Audite caeli quae loquor', in the Antiphonary contains repetitions of the first verse at intervals, suggesting that it was used as a response, or possibly a refrain, sung by the congregation.

All of these features imply the presence of a trained choir or a soloist who took responsibility for the longer and more complex parts. Hymns without refrain are either short or confined to their last three stanzas, probably implying *cantus directaneus*, i.e., with the congregation singing straight through without subdivision of the choir or addition of refrains.

EVIDENCE for the liturgical use of polphony in Ireland, though not extensive, is nonetheless suggestive of wider practice from at least the twelfth century. In 1228, Stephen of Lexington was sent by the abbot of Clairvaux to undertake a visitation of Irish Cistercian houses. A large collection of letters has survived from this visit, of which some provide insights into the performance of church music. Among the injunctions forwarded to each monastery following the conclusion of his tour was the requirement that nobody should attempt to sing 'with duplicated tones against the simplicity of the Order', under pain of flogging and a diet of bread and water.[152] This term is given as *vocibus duplicatis*, which is likely to mean 'doubling' at another pitch; in other words, probably *organum*.

The polyphonic fragment in Cormac's Psalter (pl. 121 and fig. 45b) holds especial interest for musicologists. While the actual psalms and canticles are without any trace of notation, a personal fingerprint so beloved of medieval scribes is found in the form of a colophon which follows the concluding canticles to the first group of fifty psalms. It is set for three voices—remarkable for so early a date—using as tenor (or lowest voice) an adaptation of a Sarum 'Benedicamus Domino',[153] and the text in the scribe's own name. This item has no known concordance.

---

[152] See Barry O'Dwyer (trans.), *Stephen of Lexington: Letters from Ireland, 1228–1229* (Kalamazoo, 1982), p. 167, and discussion in Brannon, 'Four notated ... manuscripts from Anglo-Norman Ireland', p. 30.

[153] See Françoise Henry and Geneviève Marsh-Micheli, 'A century of Irish illumination' in *R.I.A. Proc.*, lxi (1962), sect. C, pp 101–66, who first referred to this in print; a facsimile is included in plate XLII. The fragment is edited in Harrison, 'Polyphony in medieval Ireland', pp 76–7, and in David Howlett, 'The polyphonic colophon to Cormac's Psalter' in *Peritia*, ix (1995), pp 81–91. Both contain slight errors. An emended version is included here as fig. 45b.

Another example of polyphony in an Irish manuscript is the verse 'Dicant nunc', set for two voices in a gradual, thought to come from the Benedictine community at Downpatrick cathedral (Oxford, Bodl. MS Rawl. C 892; see pl. 120 and fig. 44). The Irish gradual, reveals links with Winchester, which may be especially significant here since materials from this centre are among the most important for the early history of *organum*—i.e. largely 'note against note', rather than with independent voices.[154] Both of these instances raise questions about the possible wider use of polyphony in medieval Ireland, which as in England was probably well established in practice but not usually committed to writing.[155] The use of thirds and sixths (regarded as discords in continental polyphonic practice) was typical of English polyphony of the thirteenth and fourteenth centuries. They represent the continuity of an older custom of embellishing plainchant with improvised polyphony or 'descant'. For example, thirds may be seen in the series of three notes for the setting of '-cant nunc' (fig. 44, opening); on the first and third syllables of 'sepulcrum' (fig. 44, second system). In the Cormac piece (fig. 45b), thirds occur between the three voices on the first syllable of 'scripsit' and between the tenor (lowest) and duplum (middle) voice setting of the first syllable of 'ora', while there is an interval of a sixth between the tenor and the triplum (upper voice). Among the three versions of 'Angelus ad virginem' in the mid fourteenth-century Dublin Troper, two are arranged in three-part polyphony, where the voices are set at intervals of thirds and sixths.[156]

A polyphonic choir was established at St Patrick's cathedral, Dublin, in 1431, and from the late fifteenth century the Smarmore fragments attest to the teaching of polyphony also in a locality away from the cathedral cities. A set of four pieces of slate which contain singing exercises in three-part polyphony was found in an excavation at Smarmore (County Louth) in 1961, and is now housed in the National Museum of Ireland (pl. 123). Transcriptions of those portions that could be deciphered were published by Harrison.[157] The fragments belong to a larger collection of other schoolwork activity, in English (medical and veterinary texts) and Latin (mainly ecclesiastical).[158]

[154] For a recent survey of the topic, see Susan Rankin, 'The early theory and practice of organum' in Susan Rankin and David Hiley (ed.), *Music in the medieval English liturgy* (Oxford, 1993), pp 59–99.

[155] Ibid., p. 99.

[156] See Dobson & Harrison, *Medieval English songs*, p. 305; also pp 266–8 for a transcription. A more recent study by Stevens, '*Angelus ad virginem*', examines the entire MS tradition of this song.

[157] Harrison, 'Polyphony in medieval Ireland', p. 78, ex. 2; facsimile on p. 79.

[158] For a full report on the slates see Alan J. Bliss, 'The inscribed slates at Smarmore' in *R.I.A. Proc.*, lxiv (1965), sect. C, pp 33–60, who includes a transcription of the fragment on slate 24 by Thurston Dart on p. 42, fig 1, and its facsimile in plate IIIb. Dart dated them to the second quarter, Harrison to the second half, of the fifteenth century. Such objects are rare but not unique. Music notation has also been found on a set of slates from Somerset, now in the

Overall, one may conclude that, in spite of sparse evidence, there is sufficient to indicate that liturgical polyphony was practised in Ireland as elsewhere in these islands. There is nothing in the sources to indicate that the nature of multi-voice singing was different from anywhere else.[159] The question whether *organum* itself was originally an insular practice, which was exported to the Continent through missionary activity, remains a possibility, given the fact that the oldest theoretical sources for this practice (discussed in the next section) come from a part of northern France in which there was a concentration of British and Irish teachers. But with lack of firm evidence from before the ninth century, this must remain a matter of speculation.[160]

WITH regard to the use of musical instruments, an Irish explanatory tract on the psalms in the form of a series of questions and answers, contains a reference to antiphonal singing based on the commentaries of Cassiodorus. Preserved in the fifteenth-century Bodl. MS Rawl. B 512, it has been cited variously as a reference to harp accompaniment of psalm-singing in an Irish context:[161]

This is what David did in his last days. He selected four thousand chosen men of the sons of Israel to sing and practise the psalms always without cessation. One-third of them for the choir, one-third for the *crot*, one-third for the choir and the *crot*. The word *psalmus* applies to what was invented for the *crot* and is practised on it. *Canticum* applies to what is practised by the choir and is sung with the *crot*. *Psalmus cantici* applies to what is taken from the *crot* to the choir. *Canticum psalmi* applies to what is taken from the choir to the *crot*.

City Museum, Wells. Cf. R. S. Bates, 'Musical slates', and comment by Rev. S. H. A. Hervey, in *Notes & Queries for Somerset and Dorset*, ed. G. W. Saunders and Joseph Fowler, xxii, pt 190 (Sept. 1936), item no. 49, pp 50–51.

[159] Howlett ('Polyphonic colophon', p. 84 ff) suggests that Gerald of Wales's discussion of the multi-voice practices of Irish harpers (see above, p. 761) may well be an indication that Cormac's composition would have been far from unusual in twelfth-century Ireland. However, apart from the fact that Gerald's vivid account concerns secular instrumental polyphony, it is hardly necessary to refer to this to explain what appears to be part of widespread insular practice. Once again, it is its very survival, and perhaps even the fact that it was ever committed to writing, that make Cormac's piece remarkable, rather than the detail of its content and structure.

[160] Cf. Michel Huglo, 'L'organum à Landévennec au IXe siècle' in *Études Celt.*, xxiii (1986), pp 187–92, and his exploration of the question whether it might be linked to an earlier period of insular ascendancy, or to the time of the Carolingian reform movement and the earliest theoretical attestation of this type of singing. Owing to a lack of historical source materials for Brittany at this time, he has (not unreasonably) left the question open.

[161] See Fleischmann, 'References to chant in early Irish manuscripts' in Seamus Pender (ed.), *Féilscríbhinn Torna* (Cork, 1952), pp 43–9: 47, and idem, 'Celtic rite', p. 53; Fergal J. McGrath, *Education in ancient and medieval Ireland* (Dublin, 1979), p. 230. The text is edited by Kuno Meyer, *An Old-Irish treatise on the psalter* (Oxford, 1894), pp 8–9, 31, n. 275, 89, n. 285. The reference is on f. 46'a in the Bodley codex.

The discussion of terminology is a paraphrase of Cassiodorus's *In psalmos*, caps V–VIII,[162] in which the scribe has used the Irish term *crot* for Cassiodorus' *instrumentum musicum*. While the primary text is addressed to Old Testament practice, it is likely that its interpretation and accompanying commentary also had local significance. Michel Huglo has highlighted references in the 'Musica enchiriadis' to the organal voice joining with instruments,[163] and to different instruments being used in octave doubling.[164] Both the 'Scolica enchiriadis' and the 'Musica enchiriadis' (which probably developed in an Insular milieu in northern France in the ninth century) contain numerous citations of the 'Te Deum', which occupied a special place in Celtic liturgies. Accompanied singing of sacred songs is well attested elsewhere also; for example, in the case of Tuotilo in ninth-century St Gall, who composed and performed tropes to the accompaniment of a *rotta* (presumably here a Latin translation of the Irish *crot*, a lyre),[165] and Patrick, second bishop of Dublin (1074–84), who referred in a poem to a woman who had taught him to play a six-stringed lyre (*cithara chordis que sex resonare solebat*),[166] perhaps while in training in Worcester. This may be a reference to one of the muses, but it could equally be a human female.

Huglo has noted references by Isidore of Seville to the presence of a stringed instrument alternating with the singing of psalmody in Hispanic liturgies, as well as more general references in continental sources to the use of instruments in the course of the office, for psalmody, the singing of tropes, textless alleluiatic sequences, and subsequent proses (but not for the choral offices).[167] It was also an established teaching method to use a stringed instrument in the training of choirs. Hucbald of St Amand, in his treatise 'De musica' (*c.*800), mentioned that a six-stringed *cithara* (probably a lyre) was adapted for the purpose of teaching chant.[168] Hence, as in other instances, we are led to view the Celtic world not as a thing apart, but rather sharing common ground with practices elsewhere.

From a number of sources it is clear that increasing clerical resistance to 'histrionic abuses' led to the gradual banishment of all instruments save

---

[162] *P. L.*, lxx, cols 15–16.

[163] M. Gerbert (ed.), *Scriptores ecclesiastici de musica sacra potissimum* (3 vols, St Blasien, 1784; reprint, Hildesheim, 1963), i, 166b. See Michel Huglo, 'Les instruments de musique chez Hucbald' in Guy Cambier (ed.), *Hommages à André Boutemy* (Paris, 1976), pp 178–96: 193.

[164] Gerbert, *Scriptores*, p. 161b. Cf. Eriugena's reference to *organicum melos* in 'De divisione naturae' (*c.*870) which Huglo, 'L'organum à Landévennec', p. 191, interprets as instrumental accompaniment rather than the usual reference to organal singing, or vocal organum.

[165] Ekkehardt IV, *Casus Sancti Galli*, ch. 46: MGH, Scriptores rerum Sangallensium II, p. 101.

[166] Aubrey Gwynn (ed. and trans.), *The writings of Bishop Patrick, 1074–1084* (Dublin, 1955), pp 90–91.

[167] Huglo, 'L'organum à Landévennec', p. 192.

[168] Ibid., p. 189.

the organ by the twelfth century in parts of continental Europe.[169] However, we should not draw conclusions in this respect as far as Ireland is concerned, or indeed many other places situated far from large urban centres where the excesses (and consequent controls) are more likely to have been concentrated. We have evidence in Ireland from as late as Turlough O'Carolan (late seventeenth/early eighteenth century) that harpers performed during mass,[170] and this raises numerous questions which we are not yet in a position to answer. On the other hand, it needs to be pointed out that we have little information on the use of organs in Irish liturgical services in the medieval or pre-reformation period.[171] Grattan Flood stated that there were organs at Christ Church in 1358, in both of the Dublin cathedrals in 1450, and that a new organ was built in Christ Church in 1470. But like much else about this author's tantalising accounts, he provides no documentary evidence.[172] The first apparently authenticated reference to an organ in Ireland concerns an instrument in St Thomas's abbey, Dublin, in the 1450s.[173] Archbishop Tregury bequeathed his pair of organs to the Lady Chapel at St Patrick's cathedral in 1471 for use in the celebration of the divine office,[174] and there are records of payments to organists at that establishment during the following two centuries.[175]

---

[169] Michel Huglo, 'Organologie et iconographie médiévales' in *Annales d'Histoire et d'Arts et d'Archéologie*, iii (1981), pp 110–11.

[170] See, e.g., Charles O'Conor, *Memoirs of the life and writings of the late Charles O'Conor of Belanagare* (Dublin, 1796), pp 162–4; further references in Fleischmann, 'References to chant', p. 48, and n. 57.

[171] Unfortunately, an erroneous report concerning the presumed destruction of organs at the Irish church of Cluain Cremha in the ninth century still sometimes reappears in the scholarly literature. The original source is an entry for the year 814 in the Annals of Ulster. Fleischmann, 'References to chant', p. 48, noted that the reference, *orgain Cluain Cremha*, was glossed *direptio* in the margin, a correct translation of the Irish term *orgain* ('destruction'), but one that has been misconstrued as referring to organs by a number of writers ever since. The Old and Middle Irish term *organ* can refer to a musical instrument or to some kind of organised sound in one or, usually, more parts (like the Latin term *organum* from which it is derived); but clearly not in this case. It is regrettable that Warren's study was republished, in its original 1881 version (1987, p. 126 and n. 4), without correction of this error. But it also underlines the critical importance of checking the original source and having due regard, in particular, for the complexities of medieval Irish (and other) terminology. See also full discussion in Buckley, '"And his voice swelled"', p. 56, and p. 69, n. 143.

[172] William H. Grattan Flood, 'Irish organ-builders from the eighth to the close of the eighteenth century' in *R.S.A.I. Jn.*, xl (1910), pp 229–34.

[173] John Holmes, 'The organ in Ireland' (unpublished pamphlet, 1984), p. 1.

[174] H. F. Berry, *Register of wills and inventories of the diocese of Dublin in the time of Archbishops Tregury and Walton 1457–1483* (Dublin, 1898), 26.

[175] W. H. Grindle, *Irish cathedral music: a history of music at the cathedrals of the Church of Ireland* (Belfast, 1989), pp 133–4. For further discussion, see Brian Boydell, 'Music before 1700' in *N.H.I.*, iv, 548 ff, and Denise M. Neary, 'Organ-building in seventeenth- and eighteenth-century Dublin, and its English connections' in *The British Institute of Organ Studies: BIOS Journal*, xxxii (1997), pp 20–27. Since the present chapter went to press, new information has been assembled on the pre-reformation history of organs in Ireland, suggesting that the instrument was probably well established in areas far from Dublin by at least the fifteenth century.

But to return to stringed instruments, there are numerous references in Irish narrative literature to travelling clerics who sang to the accompaniment of a small stringed instrument described as *ocht-tédach* ('eight-stringed one'—undoubtedly a lyre, perhaps later a small harp), which they carried about with them attached to their girdle. Gerald of Wales also referred to travelling clerics' use of a *cithara*, which he stated was commonly carried about by bishops and abbots and holy men in Ireland who delighted in playing pious music on it. Because of this, St Kevin's instrument was held in no mean reverence in Ireland, and was regarded as a great and sacred relic even in Gerald's day.

The iconographic record also attests to a clerical context for string-playing. Examples may be seen on the shrine of the Stowe Missal (mid eleventh century), where a player of a three-stringed lyre is seated between two ecclesiastics, one (to the left) holding a bell, the other a crosier. Above the group an angel hovers (pl. 124). On the *Breac Máedóic* (the shrine of St Mogue, eleventh century), a cleric is seen performing on a trilateral harp which appears to have eight strings (pl. 125). The Last Judgement scene on Muiredach's Cross at Monasterboice (early tenth century) provides a particularly detailed example in which a choir of monks is led by two monks playing a lyre and some kind of wind instrument (perhaps a straight horn), respectively (pl. 126). The combination of horn- and string-player may also be seen on the Durrow Cross (pl. 127), while on the Cross of the Scriptures at Clonmacnoise, a horn-player alone leads the group at the scene of the Last Judgement.

It is possible in some of these instances that the sounding of the Last Trump by St Michael is being evoked, but we should not overlook the fact that the use of horns in Irish liturgical practice is also suggested by the contexts of archaeological finds—a hypothesis further attested by annalistic references to horns with metal fittings and precious stones which were the property of the monasteries of Clonmacnoise and Derry. There are also references to such objects being included among church treasure in twelfth-century Ireland, although these may well be symbolic ritual objects, perhaps drinking-horns, rather than blast horns. Gerald of Wales refers to the use of sounding horns as saints' relics. And more generally the symbolic power of horns (expressive of the political power of their owners) is well attested in

Kilkenny appears to have been an important centre for organ-building at that time. Actual instruments are documented for the Dominican abbey at Athenry (1479); Duiske abbey, whose organ was confiscated at its dissolution in 1576; and the cathedral at Limerick, whose instrument was reportedly destroyed during the Elizabethan wars. For full details see Ann Buckley, 'The musical instruments in the paintings' in P. Gosling, C. Manning, and J. Waddell (ed.), *New survey of Clare Island: the abbey* (Dublin; in press). Among the wall paintings in the abbey (which are believed to date from *c*. 1420–50) are illustrations of a positive organ, a lyre, and a harp.

the narrative literature; hence it is possible that these instruments were deliberately taken over by clerics from pre-Christian practice, and adapted to their new ritual purposes.[176]

Bells were a particularly common clerical accoutrement, and were important objects of veneration as well as symbols of saintly power in Ireland, Scotland, Wales, and Brittany. They were used to bless and to heal, to cast out devils, and to inflict curses on those who displeased or thwarted their owners, but there is no evidence that they were used as musical instruments in the narrow sense, i.e., to provide rhythmic or melodic accompaniment to the singing of the liturgy. Distinctive types of bells and bell-shrines survive to this day.[177]

REGARDING music education, much may reasonably be assumed, but little of substance can be addressed owing to a lack of primary information. Instruction in liturgical chant (*musica practica*) and in music theory (*musica theoretica* or *speculativa*) undoubtedly followed the established traditions of the monastic schools and, later, university curricula. Chant was traditionally taught by rote, and with the increasing use of manuscripts copied or variously acquired from other houses, repertories, and undoubtedly some aspects of singing style, became more uniform. Music was one of the important subjects in the liberal arts. A set of six early seventh-century wooden tablets was found in Springmount Bog, County Antrim. One of the tablets contains extracts from the psalter and is suggestive of more general practice. They were probably used as an *aide-mémoire* in teaching, and perhaps also for instruction in calligraphy.[178]

An ordinale from the Cistercian abbey of Rosglas (Rosse Walle, Monasterevin, County Kildare), now Oxford, Bodl. MS Rawl. C 32 (which dates to 1501), holds musicological interest because of the presence of notation of singing exercises on its flyleaves, as well as marginal illustrations of bagpipe

[176] See Buckley, ' "And his voice swelled" ', pp 43–4, for further discussion.

[177] For a complete survey of all surviving examples, see Cormac Bourke, 'Early Irish hand bells' in *R.S.A.I. Jn.*, cx (1980), pp 52–66, and idem, 'A crozier and bell from Inishmurray and their place in ninth-century Irish archaeology' in *R.I.A. Proc.*, lxxxv (1985), sect. C, pp 145–68, and idem, 'Les cloches à main de la Bretagne primitive' in *Bulletin de la Société Archéologique du Finistère*, xc (1982), pp 339–53, and 'The hand-bells of the early Scottish church' in *Antiq. Soc. Scot. Proc.*, cxiii (1983), pp 464–8, for information on the wider distribution of Celtic bells and their implications as evidence for communication between the Irish, Scottish, and Breton churches. For fuller disscussion of use of symbolic sound in medieval Ireland to express supernatural power, see Buckley, ' "And his voice swelled" ', p. 43 ff and *passim*.

[178] The tablets are housed in the National Museum of Ireland, Dublin, no. S.A. 1914:2. See Martin McNamara, 'Psalter text and psalter study in the early Irish church' in *R.I.A. Proc.*, lxxiii (1973), sect. C, pp 201–80: 206–7, 213–14, and the edition of the text by Maurice P. Sheehy *apud* McNamara (appendix I, pp 277–80). Cf. also T. J. Brown, 'The earliest Irish manuscripts and their late antique background' in Ní Chatháin & Richter, *Ire. & Europe* (1984), pp 311–37: 312.

and horn players (on ff 31ᵛ and 37ʳ, respectively). This former represents the earliest known Irish depiction of bagpipes. The copyist and illustrator was Donatus Okhellay, a monk of that monastery.

Only two manuscripts containing music-theoretical texts are thought to have Irish associations; both are well post-Norman. One, an anonymous 'Tractatus de musica', is found in MS 1 (ff 59–70) in the GPA–Bolton (formerly Cashel Diocesan) Library at Cashel. It is in origin an English manuscript from the first half of the thirteenth century, and was apparently intended as a textbook for the young.[179] There is no record of how it found its way to Ireland. However, Hawkes believed that another Cashel manuscript, MS 2,[180] may have originated in the Augustinian priory at Darley, or its dependent hospital in Derby town, perhaps with a link to St Mary's Osney (in Oxford) which had associations with Cashel. And so, although there is no evidence to prove it, this could be one possible route for the arrival of MS 1 in Ireland. The other theoretical source is Fitzwilliam (Milton) Irish MS 71, now in the Northamptonshire Record Office, Northampton. It is a fragment of the 'Metrologus' preserved on a flyleaf from the beginning of the fourteenth century, and its Irish origin is uncertain.[181]

CHARTING the history of music in Ireland of any period is a multi-layered task. To account adequately for the full range of cultural expression at any one time, it is necessary to identify both those aspects that were characteristically local and those shared with international European culture. While its particular regional characteristics are indisputable, theories of cultural remoteness and unchanging tradition dissolve in an examination of the evidence. Native traditions established through centuries of continuous activity represent distinctive threads in a complex weave, which also includes innovations introduced from outside through the agency of ecclesiastical and secular administrators, travelling musicians, pilgrims, merchants, etc. Documentation is scant in proportion to the enormous amount of institutional activity—a result of the vicissitudes of decay and destruction, but also a consequence of

---

[179] Notes from Marvin Colker's description of the MS were kindly supplied by Stuart Ó Seanóir, assistant librarian, manuscripts department, T.C.D. library. The full text, edited by Charles Burnett and Michael W. Lundell, has since been published on the T.M.L. (*Thesaurus musicarum latinarum*) website at Indiana University, Bloomington, Ind.

[180] A twelfth-/thirteenth-century codex containing a psalter, missal, breviary, and some extracts from a *Manuale*. See W. Hawkes, 'Cashel MS 2: a thirteenth-century liturgical document in Dublin' in *Reportorium Novum*, iii, pt 1 (1962), pp 83–93, and notes by Colker held in the T.C.D. manuscripts department.

[181] The 'Metrologus' is one of four major commentaries on the theoretical music treatise, 'Micrologus', by one of the most famous music pedagogues of the middle ages, Guido d'Arezzo (*c*.991/2–*p*. 1033). Confined to the elementary part of the older work, it is believed to have been written by an Englishman in the thirteenth century for the purpose of introducing pupils to the principles of music study; see also RISM [*Répertoire international des sources musicales*], BIIIᵃ, p. 99.

oral-traditional practices of which only contemporaneous commentary could have preserved a glimpse. For this reason we are indebted to the writings of Gerald of Wales and the fortuitous twist of fate that led him to document his observations. In our own time, Grattan Flood has left us with tantalising hints, but little that is open to further scrutiny, since he overlooked the primary obligation of detailing his sources. Most of these cannot now be traced, owing to the burning of the Public Record Office in 1922, *inter alia*. Nevertheless, in spite of relatively sparse primary sources, Irish liturgical manuscripts that do survive with music notation can occasionally shed light on local practices. And even in sources without notation, rubrics and wider comparative study of relevant texts can contribute substantial information, if not on melodies *per se*, then on the role of music in Irish Christian worship, and its wider cultural links.

Literary references to music provide a veritable *embarras de richesse* for enquiry on topics such as terminology, social occasions of performance, patronage, roles and status of musicians, types of instruments, perceptions of the power and effects of music, and the overall role of symbolic sound as means and expression of social cohesion and emotional orientation. Through transmission and adaptation of images, the considerable repositories of music-iconographic data, in particular on ecclesiastical stone sculpture and metalwork, reveal much about the symbolic meanings, and probably about realistic situations, of music-making in medieval Ireland. Material culture, such as the yields of musical instruments from archaeological sites, helps in a particularly reliable way to locate musical activities in Ireland within their wider British and European contexts.

And finally, there is some need for caution when Irish sources are found to be unique. They may or may not indicate regional variants or 'chthonic invention', and in some cases they may represent part of a wider pattern for which evidence no longer exists elsewhere. With that in mind, we can deploy them not only in reconstructing the history of music in Ireland but also in an attempt to fill certain critical gaps in the history of music of the greater European area.

# APPENDIX I

## IRISH MEDIEVAL MANUSCRIPTS CONTAINING MUSIC NOTATION

### Missals

1 New York, Pierpont Morgan Library, MS M. 627 (the Drummond Missal, first half of the twelfth century)
2 Dublin, T.C.D., MS 1305 (fragments, twelfth/thirteenth century)
3 London, B.L., Add. MS 24198 (early fourteenth century)
4 London, Lambeth Palace, MS 213 (early fifteenth century)
5 Dublin, T.C.D., MS 82, ff 1$^r$–154$^v$ (1458)
6 London, B.L., MS Egerton 2677 (fifteenth century)

### Gradual

Oxford, Bodl. MS Rawl. C 892 (second half of the twelfth century)

### Breviary

Dublin, T.C.D., MS 80 (early fifteenth century)

### Psalters

1 London, B.L., Add. MS 36929 (mid or second half of twelfth century)
2 Oxford, Bodl., MS Rawl. G 185 (fourteenth century)

### Antiphonals

1 Dublin, T.C.D., MS 77 (probably between 1416 and c. 1450)
2 Dublin, T.C.D., MS 78 (probably between 1488 and 1500)
3 Dublin, T.C.D., MS 79 (probably between 1431 and 1435)
4 Dublin, T.C.D., MS 82, ff 156$^r$–168$^v$, 170$^r$–171$^v$, 169$^{r–v}$ (c. 1300)
5 Dublin, T.C.D., MS 109 (late fifteenth century)

## Troper and sequentiary

Cambridge, U.L., MS Add. 710 (*c.* 1360)

## Processionals

1  Dublin, Marsh's Library, MS Z.4.2.20 (*c.* 1400)
2  Oxford, Bodleian Library, MS Rawl. Liturg. d.4 (*c.* 1400)

## Miscellaneous

1  Oxford, Bod. MS Rawl. C. 32 (Cistercian ordinale with singing lessons on fly-leaves, 1501)
2  Dublin, National Museum of Ireland, 1961:12, 24, 34, and 41 (slates with singing lessons, probably second half of fifteenth century)

# APPENDIX II

## INDEX OF LIBRARIES

### Cambridge

#### University Library

*1    MS Add. 710. The 'Dublin Troper'.*

Sarum consuetudinary, troper, and sequentiary. Contains sequences in honour of St Patrick.

### Dublin

#### Marsh's Library

*2    MS Z.4.2.20.*

Sarum processional. Formerly belonging to the church of St John the Evangelist, Dublin. Contains liturgical drama, 'Visitatio sepulchri', and proper processions for Patrick, Columba, and Stephen. Patrick, Brigid, Columba, and Columbanus are included in one of the litanies.

#### National Museum of Ireland

*3    1961:12, :24, :34, :41. The Smarmore tablets.*

Fragments of polyphonic singing lessons.

#### Trinity College

*4    MS 77 [olim B.1.1.]. 'Antiphonary of Armagh'.*

Divine Office MS, formerly belonging to the *céli Dé* (vicars choral) of Armagh cathedral. Includes notated chants for Patrick.

---

*Dates are included in appendix I, to which reference may be made under the typological headings.

### 5    *MS 78 [olim B.1.3.].*

Divine Office antiphonal designed for use at St Canice's cathedral, Kilkenny. Contains offices for Brigid, Patrick, and Canice. Obits and added feasts indicate use at Clondalkin during the mid sixteenth century. The psalter is noted in part.

### 6    *MS 79 [olim B.1.4.].*

Divine Office antiphonal, formerly belonging to the church of St John the Evangelist, Dublin; contains notated office for Patrick, and numerous references to Dublin.

### 7    *MS 80 [olim B.1.5.].*

Divine Office breviary used at Kilmoone; contains notated offices for Brigid and Patrick.

### 8    *MS 82 [olim B.3.1.]. The Kilcormac Missal and Sarum Antiphonal.*

The missal, formerly belonging to the Carmelite priory of Kilcormac, County Offaly, contains unnotated services for Brigid, Patrick, and Brendan. The antiphonal, a separate source now bound with the missal (ff 156$^r$–168$^v$, 170$^r$–171$^v$, 169$^{r-v}$), is probably Irish Use of Sarum.

### 9    *MS 109 [olim B.1.2.].*

Antiphonal. Irish Franciscan Roman use (partially notated).

### 10    *MS 1305.*

Fragment of noted Missal (ff 19$^r$–20$^v$ only). Irish Use of Sarum. One of the earliest surviving texts of the Sarum Missal.

## London

## The British Library

### 11    *Add. MS 36929.*

Psalter containing three-part polyphonic autograph, 'Cormacus scripsit'.

### 12    *Add. MS 24198.*

Missal from the abbey of St Thomas the Martyr, Dublin.

### 13    *MS Eg. 2677.*

Missal of the Sarum rite adapted for Dublin practice (partially noted, but not in the case of materials for Irish saints).

Lambeth Palace Archiepiscopal Library

*14   MS 213.*

Missal of the Sarum Rite (partially notated). Includes Proper masses for Brigid, Patrick, and Finian (without notation).

## New York

Pierpont Morgan Library

*15   MS M. 627.*

The Drummond Missal. Partially noted in non-diastematic neumes.

## Oxford

Bodleian Library

*16   MS Rawl. C 32.*

Missal from Cistercian abbey of St Mary of Rosse Walle (Monasterevan, County Kildare). Notation for singing lessons is found on one of the flyleaves. The missal itself is not noted.

*17   MS Rawl. C 892 [12726].*

Gradual from Downpatrick Benedictine house. Includes a three-part setting of the processional antiphon 'Dicant nunc Iudei'. Reference to Brigid in the Common of Virgins; prayers for Brigid and Patrick in the sanctorale.

*18   MS Rawl. G 185.*

Augustinian psalter from cathedral of the Holy Trinity (Christ Church), Dublin.

*19   MS Rawl. Liturg. d. 4.*

Processional. Formerly belonging to the church of St John the Evangelist, Dublin. Contains liturgical drama, 'Visitatio sepulchri', materials for the feasts of Patrick and Audoen; Patrick, Brigid, and Columba are included in the litanies.

CHAPTER XXII

# The archaeology of Ireland's viking-age towns

PATRICK F. WALLACE

THANKS in the main to the prolific results of the large archaeological excavations that have been carried out in our various towns over the past quarter of a century, great advances have been made in the understanding of the physical character of the towns of the later viking age as well as of the contemporary crafts and occupations and commercial contact.[1] Summaries of the excavations undertaken at Waterford, Wexford, and Limerick, as well as the publication of the first half-dozen or so volumes of reports of the National Museum of Ireland's excavations in Dublin, have already appeared. An interim report appeared on one of the Wexford sites as well as a valuable synthesis for Waterford, and relevant documentary references have been assembled in the case of Cork. Most recently, a general comparison of the physical attributes that survive in the archaeological record—location, layout, defences, and building types—shows that the later viking-age towns shared many traits, that there was such a thing as the Hiberno-Norse town, and that the Dublin excavations, impressive though they are, need no longer be studied in isolation. The recent publication of Scully's and Hurley's report on the prolific Waterford sites allows of even greater comparison with the Dublin results.

A general exercise such as this is made difficult by the different amounts of excavation that have been undertaken in the various towns, the variety of the nature and location of the sites, the different degrees of preservation, and the lack of synthesis on the results of the excavations. It should be noted that while the evidence for layout, defences, and buildings in Dublin is good from the early tenth century, the comparative evidence from the other towns tends to be late and to come mainly from the later tenth and eleventh centuries, so that topographical comparisons are reliable only for the later viking age

---

[1] For sources relating to this period, see sections IV C1 (c) and (d) of the bibliography, below, pp 1064–77.

or Hiberno-Norse period. Despite considerable work on the documentary evidence by Charles Doherty, it is unfortunate that archaeological knowledge of contemporary native, non-urban settlement in Ireland is relatively poor when compared with the results from Dublin, Waterford, Limerick, Wexford, and possibly Cork, which are probably best studied by comparison with one another and with so-called later viking-age towns abroad. A great deal more work has to be done on the nature and chronology of native (including monastic) sites to allow the search for comparisons with the archaeology of Norse towns in the broader Irish scene to proceed.

DESPITE the writer's best intention to incorporate the most up-to-date and complete information on all the towns, Dublin is unavoidably accorded undue prominence because of the writer's greater familiarity with its archaeology and because of the relative amount of historical research that has focused on the capital for the period in question. The early discovery of the viking burials at Islandbridge/Kilmainham, and their publication by Wilde and republication by Coffey and Armstrong as well as by Boe, and the historical treatments of Dublin's viking-age history by Haliday, Curtis, and Ryan means that Dublin was much better studied than the other towns even before the modern excavations began in 1961. Arising from the national museum's twenty-year excavation campaign, a whole series of essays on Dublin's origins, topography, hinterland, commerce, artefacts, art, and coins, as well as recent monographs on the buildings, carved wood, and ship timbers in the joint National Museum/Royal Irish Academy series of reports means that viking Dublin is now widely known. Apart from the museum's excavations at High Street, Winetavern Street, Christchurch Place, and Fishamble Street/Wood Quay, the Office of Public Works (O.P.W.) has undertaken excavations in Dublin Castle and, more recently, there have been excavations by contract archaeologists at High Street, Castle Street, Ross Road, and Parliament Street.

DUBLIN was founded twice over by the vikings: first as a *longphort* or permanent trading-cum-piratical base in the 840s, and secondly from about 917 as a defended town, or *dún*, as it is later referred to by the Irish annalists. The first settlement appears to have ended about 902 when the Irish Norse were exiled mainly to northern England, where, it has been suggested, they learned about urbanisation before political and military circumstances combined to allow their return to Ireland about the middle of the second decade of the tenth century when Dublin was re-established, and when Waterford as well as probably Limerick, and possibly Wexford and Cork, were established. The vikings may be regarded as catalysts through whom the idea of urbanisation was transferred from England to Ireland, where they then uniquely expressed it having digested it elsewhere, and where also, thanks to the monasteries, several elements of the town were already in place. The development of Hedeby/Haithabu and Kaupang in the ninth century shows that some vikings were already familiar with the 'trading settlement' species of proto-town.

No definite archaeological evidence for either the location or character of the ninth century *longphort* has yet come to light. It is possible that it resembled the large circular defended enclosure that overlooks the present village of Annagassan, County Louth, a location that is historically documented as the other mid-ninth-century *longphort*. It is possible that the ninth-century viking settlement at Dublin was located upstream, also on the south bank of the River Liffey but in the Islandbridge/Kilmainham area, where one of the largest viking-age cemeteries was discovered during the mid-nineteenth-century construction of the Great Southern & Western railway and in the 1920s during the construction of the First World War memorial park.

By analogy with ninth-century townships in Scandinavia, a cemetery would normally be located in the vicinity of a settlement. The *longphort* was almost certainly of more pure Scandinavian inspiration and character than the later town of the tenth century, and may well have been an undefended *portus* with an attached fortified citadel on the lines of Birka or Hedeby/Haithabu. Alternative possibilities for the location of the enigmatic *longphort* include the possibility of a situation near the confluence of the Liffey and the Poddle in an unexcavated area of the old town, or in the old town where the ninth-century levels may have left little or no trace.

Notwithstanding the problems of location and topography, history records that the Dublin vikings were defeated and exiled in 902 by a successful alliance of Irish kings. It is not certain whether the *longphort* was abandoned altogether at this time or whether the associated farming community that probably inhabited the hinterland also went into exile. A great number of Irish Norse who poured into Wales and north-western England in the early tenth century undoubtedly included many from the *longphort*. The great silver hoard at Cuerdale, near Preston, was probably assembled in Dublin and is possibly their most tangible physical legacy. In this period also the Irish Norse expanded their imperial designs on York and supplied many of its kings. They became involved in the politics and warfare of Mercia, opposed Æthelflæd's forces in several battles, and laid siege to Chester. The military tide turned against them early in the second decade of the tenth century when Ireland became the focus of their attention once more.

The political and military reverses suffered by the vikings in England in the early tenth century seem crucial to the timing of the refoundation of Dublin. The successes of the Mercians against the Irish-Norse, the general effectiveness of the defended Alfredian and west Saxon *byrig*, and the vikings' failure at the siege of Chester, as well as their difficulties regarding the retention of York, probably decided some of them to return to Ireland, where a changed balance of power (after the battle of Belach Mugna in 908) also probably contributed to their decision. That their earliest campaigns on their return were concentrated in the south where their other principal towns—Limerick and Waterford, and possibly Cork and Wexford—were founded shows the extent to which they exploited political situations to further economic ends.

The Dublin of the resettlement soon became an enclosed town with an intensive network of streets, plots, pathways, and houses. It is uncertain whether it was fully planned from the very beginning of the foundation, since the archaeological evidence in Fishamble Street is somewhat equivocal at the lowest layers and especially as H. B. Clarke informs me that the term *dún* comes into use only in the late 930s after the initial Irish attack on the settlement, as if it was only then that it was established and wealthy enough to be worth raiding. It is not possible to show clearly how the enclosing bank and plots related to one another in Dublin as they did in some of the Anglo-Saxon towns. On present indications, however, it is possible to say that a new settlement, which very soon became a full town, was founded on an apparently fresh site of the south bank of the Liffey without regard to either any native or Scandinavian settlement that proceeded it.

It is significant that during the decade and a half of their exile in England the Irish-Norse would have been exposed to an 'urban revolution' in the building of new towns and royal *byrig* and the redefending of old Roman settlements. It is also significant, in regard to urban origins, that Irish historians and archaeologists are now attributing quasi-urban functions and character to the indigenous large monastic and secular settlements, and a fresh examination is being undertaken of the historical and archaeological sources. Why should semi-hibernicised Scandinavians not have drawn on relevant local influences when they existed? This discussion will only be advanced by further archaeological information on the nature and location of the layout of the *longphort* as well as on that of other settlements of both native and Scandinavian origin and of Anglo-Scandinavian and European towns in general in the late ninth and tenth centuries.

Waterford appears to have been founded by the vikings about 914. Excavation started in 1982 when substantial parts of the thirteenth-century defences were unearthed. The more recent Arundel Square/Peter Street excavations have shed light on the buildings, plots, churches, and streets, and the remains of over one hundred buildings are now known, in addition to those of an apsed church of about 1100. In contrast to Dublin, there are but few historical references to the vikings in Waterford. While the settlement is said to have been founded in 853 by Sitricus, the year 914 is more generally accepted and it is recorded that 'a great fleet of Norwegians landed at Port Láirge and they plundered northern Osraige and brought great spoils and many cows and livestock in their ships'. To date, the excavated evidence from Waterford appears to relate more to the eleventh century and later, and there is an absence of built evidence from the period of the apparent foundation and slow evolutionary growth during the tenth.

Wexford probably also dates from the early tenth century, although there are only a few historical references to it. There are mentions of the 'foreigners' of Loch Garman in 888, 933, and 1088. The Bride Street excavations were most productive and yielded a building sequence from about 1000 to 1300 as well as evidence for property boundaries and changes in town layout.

Although well documented historically, viking-age Limerick has not been as archaeologically productive as either Dublin or Waterford. Excavations at John's Castle, which, along with St Mary's cathedral, the other main focal point of the old English town area (believed to correspond to the Hiberno-Norse town), must be built on the site of the viking settlement, yielded evidence for buildings in the defences. Although there are several references to a ninth-century settlement, Limerick appears to have been founded in 922 by Tamar Mac Ailche, 'king of an immense fleet', who established a *long-phort*. It was dominated by the Dublin vikings between 936 and 967 and captured by the Ua Briain after the battle of Sulchóid in 967. Toirrdelbach Ua Briain, king of Munster (1063–86), made Limerick his capital. During his reign and his successor Muircherteach's, at the height of the so-called Hiberno-Norse period, Limerick really flourished and had its first bishop consecrated in 1107. Medieval topographical descriptions of viking-age Limerick are relatively good, and in one twelfth-century description the town is depicted as a fortified stronghold with a gate, houses, and towers. The 'Chronicon Scotorum' mentions the burning in 1015 of the 'fortress and all the houses that were from the fortress outwards'.

The viking presence in Cork is thought to date from the mid-ninth century when there appears to have been a *dún*. Nothing is known of the nature of this settlement. Maurice Hurley, the Cork city archaeologist, believes that the historical and topographical evidence points to the south island, i.e. the area defined by the present South Main Street, as the possible Hiberno-Norse area of settlement, a view supported by Bradley and Halpin but yet to be confirmed by excavation. There are references to the Norse plundering of the monastery of Cork in 915, which has been seen as a prelude to a renewed occupation at a time when a large viking expedition appears to have resulted in the establishment of Waterford and, in 917, to the refoundation of Dublin.

IRISH viking-age towns seem to be located on relatively high ground overlooking the confluences of tidal river estuaries and their tributaries. This is not only a feature of Irish viking-age towns: it is also typical of viking-age towns in general. Dublin was established in the tenth century on the south bank of a then fast-flowing Liffey on high ground above its confluence with its tributary the Poddle, the east bank of which had probably already had a Gaelic settlement called 'Dubhlinn'. Waterford appears also to have been established in the early tenth century in a triangular promontory bounded on the north by the River Suir and on the south east by marshy ground on either side of the St John's river. This promontory would also have been easily defended by the construction of an earthwork across the western side, the only landward approach. 'Waterford' is one of the few Scandinavian place-names in Ireland and appears to be derived from the Old Norse words for 'ram fjord' or 'windy fjord'. The modern name 'Port Láirge' is thought to commemorate Láraig, an early viking leader. Wexford was also built on the confluence of an estuary and a tributary— the Slaney and the Bishopswater rivers respectively. Limerick was probably established in the later 'Englishtown', north of the confluence of the Shannon and its tributary, the Abbey river. As has been noted, the viking settlement in Cork is thought to have been located on the south island in the River Lee.

Access to boats and the sea seems to have been paramount both for the ninth-century *longphorts* and for the proto-towns of the early tenth century. Significance was also attached to the location of towns at estuaries of great rivers, which gave access often to rich interiors. The siting of towns at points where tributaries fed into main rivers, and the apparent preference for high ground, appear to be no more than taking maximum advantage of natural defensive features and minimising the effort necessary to defend such settlements. Such choices of location are different from those found at the sites of the great monasteries, which were often selected for their territorial position in or between kingdoms or for their rich agricultural potential. The choice of Irish viking town sites differs from contemporary English choice of settlement location, in which apparent influences such as river mouths, estuary positions, proximity of tributaries, and ease of defence do not apparently figure so prominently. Most existing English towns stood on or near Roman sites. Locating towns at estuarine river-mouths near tributaries and capitalising on natural defences may have been the most original viking contribution to Irish urbanisation. In some cases, the choices made on these grounds may have made difficult the subsequent development of street and town layout on the relevant sites. Indeed, the very location of Dublin itself at a position suitable for the beaching of viking longships (which only require a relatively shallow draft of water) made for difficulties in the thirteenth century and later, when the draft of water at Dublin was found so inadequate that Dalkey had to become the deep-sea port for Dublin.

THE idea of defending towns within earthen embankments, the predecessors of medieval town walls, was widespread in different parts of northern Europe from the late ninth and early tenth centuries. Some embankments, like those in England, completely encircled the settlements they defended, while others, especially those in Scandinavia, defended their settlements only on the landward sides. The latter embanked crescents were often open on the waterfront side, which was sometimes protected by stakes or piles driven into the water or by deliberately sunken ships. Roskilde harbour in Denmark was protected in this way at a later date with ships that included a warship made in Dublin in the mid-eleventh century. When the Dublin banks are viewed against this background, it is clear that they fit more into the English pattern than into the Scandinavian. It should also be remembered that the scale and plan of the banks as found at Fishamble Street and more recently at Ross Road are in keeping with those of the better-defended contemporary Irish farmstead, the ringfort or rath. Possibly even more relevant in the relation to urban origins are the defences of the larger monastic settlements such as Kells, County Meath, and Armagh. On present evidence it seems best to regard the early tenth-century embankments of Dublin as part of a general northern European development. As far as Dublin is concerned, the idea of enclosing a town within banks, even the very idea of the town itself, was probably derived from contact with England, where towns were developed earlier and where the Irish Norse had learned much about urbanisation.

Evidence for town defences has been found at Dublin, Waterford, and Limerick. The Dublin evidence is the earliest and the most complete to date. Dublin was enclosed by an earthen bank in the tenth century, with a second larger bank built outside it and around it in the eleventh century. These banks, as recent excavations at Ross Road and Dublin castle confirm, completely encircled the town. Banks were enlarged in the course of the eleventh century by the addition of layers of estuarine mud. The enlarged bank had a stone revetment placed in front of it and it seems that in places this wall was more than a façade and was a full free-standing town wall. Both Dublin and Waterford were enclosed by such walls in the Hiberno-Norse period. Limerick's bank may have been stone-faced; Wexford appears to have been defended by a stone wall at the time of the Norman invasion.

To date, the most extensive series of defences has been excavated at Fishamble Street, Dublin, where a succession of nine waterfronts along the south bank of the River Liffey were uncovered. These waterfronts include two possible flood banks and two definitely defensive embankments from the viking period, as well as the stone wall, already referred to, which was built around 1100. The earliest embankments were low and non-defensive and were probably located above the contemporary high-water line. They were not more than a metre high and do not appear to have been palisaded. It is not clear how much of the settlement they encircled. Their primary function was to keep dry the properties on the sloping ground above the foreshore, where there is some evidence for the accumulation of possible yard detritus before the construction of the embankments. Some time later in the tenth century, an extensive embankment was erected along the high-water line. This was built in a number of sections, although probably conceived of as a unit and probably erected by royal or civic authority. It is built on top of dumped organic refuse and was stabilised at the top by a pre-existing fence. The bank was bonded in estuarine mud, and its location on a naturally rising slope made its external aspect higher than its internal. It was protected from the erosive action of the tidal river by a breakwater secured in a channel cut into the rocky foreshore. A short stretch of cobblestoned intramural pathway existed inside and parallel to the bank along its eastern stretch towards Fish-amble Street. A ditch 1.6 m deep and 2 m wide was cut into the natural limestone immediately outside part of a bank. A series of planks were set edge to edge on the outer slope of this part of the bank, each with a large mortice through which they were probably originally pegged to the bank. The planks appear to have been intended to provide a smooth beaching or docking slipway for ships, or, less likely, they may have been the surviving lowest part of a palisade erected on the forward slope of the bank. This first viking defence seems to have encircled the whole town, because it was also represented in the Dublin castle and Ross Road excavations.

Not much time elapsed between the abandonment of this bank and the construction of a successor, which in places incorporated the earlier struc-ture. This larger bank was built in at least four different stages and erected at the riverward side of the predecessor, probably around the year 1000. Gravel, stones, and earth were used in the construction, the dumped layers being reinforced by discarded post-and-wattle screens as well as by layers of brush-wood. At one stage in its history this bank was crowned by a post-and-wattle palisade; later, when the bank was heightened, a more robust stave wall, which was anchored from the back, was placed on top. In its final phase this bank was covered over with estuarine mud brought from the bed of the river; this dried out and formed a hard surface. There is little doubt that this second defensive embankment encircled the whole town; it was represented at Ross Road as well as at two sides of Dublin castle: the Powder Tower, where the eastern ramparts of the viking-age town were unearthed, and along a short southern stretch immediately west of the later Birmingham Tower. An even higher bank was erected before the construction of the stone wall. It is likely that for a large part of the Hiberno-Norse period Dublin was encir-cled by the earthen embankments just described.

Probably towards the end of the eleventh century a stone wall of about 1.5 m in width and possibly as much as 3.5 m in original height was built outside the embankments just described. The average surviving height of the wall is about 2 m along Wood Quay, across which over 100 m of the wall was uncovered. The wall was composed of a rubble fill with mortared stone facings. A number of splits in the coursing on the inner face of the wall indicate that the outer face may have been built first and then completed on the inside. It seems that the wall was not meant to be completely free-standing, and that its lowest part may have been a revetment or quay wall that fronted a bank of organic mud layers dumped behind. The recent discovery of a long stretch of the wall at Ross Road in the southern part of the Hiberno-Norse town strongly suggests that the wall encircled the whole town and that it was probably almost entirely free-standing. It is possible that the reason the *dún* of Dublin was marvelled at as one of the wonders of Ireland in a poem of about 1120 in the Book of Leinster was because this stone wall was a relatively new feature at that time.

Waterford's defences seem to parallel the development of those at Dublin. It was only, however, after the expansion of the town that embankments were added, and this was well into the eleventh century. About 35 m of the eleventh-century earthen bank have been exposed. This bank was accompanied by a ditch 8.5 m wide at the top and 2.5 m at the base, which varied in depth between 2 m and 2.5 m. The bank is described as 'substantial', was made of turves, and was up to 4 m in width, the original height being in excess of 3 m. Maurice Hurley believes that the bank was built in sections by gangs of workmen under the control of some administrative authority, rather as I believe to have been the case in Dublin. Interestingly, oak beams may have formed some sort of superstructure on the bank. These have been dated to 1070–90. The banks of the front face of the first defensive bank at Fishamble Street, Dublin, present a possible earlier parallel. The Waterford bank was demolished in the second quarter of the twelfth century; the ditch was backfilled to accommodate a substantial wall of which 22 m survived to a maximum height of 1.65 m, i.e. eight courses of construction. The wall was built as a revetment against the eastern half of the bank, and according to the excavator was never entirely free-standing. Like the Hiberno-Norse wall around Dublin, it had a projecting footing and was slightly battered. It had a rubble core and was built in different sections with vertical joints appearing between these section; all of this finds parallels in the Dublin wall. There was also a cobble pathway or berm outside the wall, a feature that may be paralleled at Limerick.

The Waterford excavations also produced evidence for a pre-Norman gateway, which to date is unique in the Irish archaeological record. This was at Peter Street, where the outer face of a 1.72 m gateway in the town wall was exposed. It consisted of 'two ashlar-built jambs . . . above projecting plinths', which survived to a height of about three or four courses.

The King John's Castle site at Limerick produced what was described as a 10.1 m stretch of a 'clay bank revetted by a limestone wall'. This had a maximum surviving height of 1.7 m and a pathway 1 m wide on a berm at the base, beyond which was a ditch 2.8 m deep. It is thought that these features represent the south side 'of a massive stone-revetted earthen rampart which, from the associated finds, may date to the twelfth century'. That this 'earlier structure was utilised in the normal defences for a limited duration' was confirmed by the discovery of its being bonded to the later, mortared east curtain wall of Limerick castle.

There is no archaeological confirmation as yet for the viking-age defensive embankment proposed for Wexford by Hadden. Neither the Bride Street excavations nor the earlier investigations by Roseanne Meahan of the south end of the town reveal any trace of a bank. The absence of banks from the relatively closely located Bride Street and Oyster Lane excavations could mean that Wexford was not defended by a bank along its eleventh-century waterfront. The surviving walls of Wexford suggest a much later date. Giraldus Cambrenis uses the term *murum* for Wexford's defences, a term he also uses for the town walls of Dublin, Waterford, and Limerick, which implies that the towns in question were each defended before the coming of the Anglo-Normans.

HIBERNO-NORSE towns were divided by streets and laneways, from which post-and-wattle boundary fences sometimes radiated to further subdivide them into plots or yards. It is likely that some streets and lanes expanded into open public spaces where markets and fairs were located. It is also likely that some markets were centred outside the main town gates, where produce from the hinterland would have been brought. Street lines tended to follow the natural contours. A length of about 16 m of the original surface of Peter Street, Waterford, was uncovered in the course of excavation. Its maximum excavated width was 3.6 m and it had 'a metal surface ... with closely set small stones and gravel'. This is the only actual Hiberno-Norse street excavated to date, and it led to a gateway in the town wall. Gravel and stone pathways have been found in Dublin, where to date no street has been uncovered.

It may be assumed that many of the early streets lie under their present much widened successors. Some laneways have been found in Dublin, including, as we have seen, an intramural example located inside one of the earthen embankments at Fishamble Street. Analysis of the boundaries and the pathways that gave access to the yards suggests the existence of a street on the line of the later Fishamble Street in the viking and Hiberno-Norse periods.

The excavations at Fishamble Street show that that part of the town was divided into yards at a comparatively early date in its existence, probably from about 940. Coin evidence shows that some of the earliest occupation levels in Dublin were along the waterfront area in Fishamble Street. This sector developed early with its fenced-off yards and may not be entirely typical of tenth- and eleventh-century Dublin. The recently discovered silver coin and ornament hoard at Castle Street, which has a deposition date of about 995, was found near the earliest occupation level in that area and warns against acceptance of maximum active occupation at too early a date. Not all of Dublin need have been subdivided into yards as early as the first half of the tenth century.

The boundary fences dividing the Fishamble Street yards were of post-and-wattle and generally succeeded one another on the same line. Even where boundary defences did not survive or were never used, the boundaries were heightened by posts driven into the waste that was constantly piling up in the yards. In many cases, walls of houses were deliberately coincided with boundary lines and acted as fences. In the recent Castle Street excavations, a wattle panel that was found in a gap in a boundary fence has been interpreted as a gate, which suggests that access across yards may sometimes have been agreed by yard owners. Generally, though, the Fishamble Street evidence indicates that access was through the yards, where often a series of pathways zigzagged their way around the buildings, control of access presumably being vested in the hands of the yard owner. Such control may have applied particularly in yards where the building nearest the street straddled the entire width, whereby persons wishing to get to the back of the yard would have had to pass through the house at the front.

The only major shift in the Fishamble Street yard divisions appears to have been related to the erection of the larger defensive embankment. The general layout of the yards remained unchanged over two centuries and even left its imprint on the post-medieval layout. Although the lines of the yard boundaries often remain constant, the position of houses, outhouses, pens (?), pathways, and pits often changed with each succeeding building phase. Successive buildings were often built in different places to different sizes while the boundaries tended to remain the same.

Yard areas varied greatly in size in the Fishamble Street part of Dublin. While lengths probably depended on the position of the two assumed determinants, the street and the waterfront, it is impossible to be absolutely certain about this because (with the exception of two yards) neither the front or backs turned up in the area available for excavation. There is no doubt about the variety of the yard widths. The trapezoidal, rather than rectangular, shape of many of the Fishamble Street yards make their respective areas difficult to measure. It is assumed that the trapezoidal shape of the yards derives from the sinuous line of the original Fishamble Street. The most northerly or riverward of the yards had their wide ends towards the street and the narrow ends towards the waterfront, in contrast with the more southerly or uphill yards, in which the positions of the respective widths were reversed.

Buildings were situated end-on rather than broadside to the street in Fish-amble Street, where pathways usually led (apparently from the street) to the front end of the main buildings. Pathways are defined as radiating back into the yards from the street's edge. It appears from the relative lengths of the pathways that the Dublin buildings were set back several metres from the streets in about the tenth or eleventh centuries. Each of the Fishamble Street plots had an individual pathway linking the plot and the 'front' end of the main building with the presumed main street. The pathways are about 1.5 m wide and mostly consisted of elongated wattle mats laid on top of one another. Sometimes, however, pathways consisted of round or half-round logs laid on longitudinal runners. Most rarely they were of gravel or paving-stones. Interestingly, in Dublin at least, quality carpentry construction was occasionally applied to pathway surfaces and rails, after its introduction to the town about the middle of the eleventh century. While Dublin's public lanes and pathways were relatively narrow, it is likely that its streets were wide, if the Hiberno-Norse street discovered at Waterford is anything to go by. It is likely that the main streets of the Hiberno-Norse towns were wide enough to accommodate busy pedestrian and possibly packhorse traffic, as well as the odd street market or small fair. There is not enough evidence to say whether vehicular traffic, flocks of sheep, or herds of cattle were driven through parts of the town. The relative absence of calf bones from the Dublin excavations suggest that cattle were not kept in the towns and were most likely slaughtered near the cattle fairs outside the walls.

Murray's work on the Dublin excavations directed by Brendan O'Riordan up to 1976 shows that the Fishamble Street layout evidence is not entirely typical of either viking or Hiberno-Norse Dublin. She shows the relative growth in occupation in High Street during the eleventh century, and the boundaries and pathway positions were already in place before more inten-sive use of the area got under way after the expansion of the town from the presumed Fishamble Street/Castle Street nucleus westwards along High Street.

Murray also suggests that there could have been different approaches to layout at the various sites: whereas High Street appears to have been an area with large yards and small buildings (in the leather-working area), there were larger buildings with greater potential in Christchurch Place, where the buildings were set slightly back from the streets or lane and often had an individual pathway leading to the entrance, as was found in Fishamble Street. Murray likened the layout of Winetavern Street to High Street 'with small buildings on either side of a pathway leading down the hillside' in what was a relatively congested layout. The Fishamble Street buildings and yards give the impression of a consistently better-off and more established environ-ment. The relatively high incidence of coin discovery in the latter area could mean that it was a merchant's quarter.

It is difficult to prove from purely archaeological evidence the existence of an urban authority that might have controlled property layout and the continuity of boundary positions. There is no doubt, however, that much if not all of Hiberno-Norse Dublin was divided into plots or yards, although it probably took some time for this development to be complete. The Winetavern Street (and to some extent the Christchurch Place yard) evidence shows that not all yards were as large as those discovered at Fishamble Street. Matters were different at Waterford, where yards were not always evident, although Waterford also has evidence for the continuity of yard boundaries and of yard orientation over the centuries.

Literary evidence suggests the acceptance even by native annalists of Dublin's plots and, by inference, an organised urban authority. As early as 944, there is a reference to the construction of Dublin with 'houses, divisions [*airbeadha*], ships, and other structures'. The earliest dated use of *garrdha* in the annals is under the year 989 when the king, Máel Sechnaill, imposed a tax of an ounce of gold on every *garrdha* or yard in Dublin. This practise continued in the eleventh century. The idea of levying a single cess on individual yards suggests that they were owned by the equivalent of the later medieval burgess. F. J. Byrne believes that when tenth- and eleventh-century writers came to ascribe imaginary glory to the then long-deserted Tara they may well have had Dublin in mind, especially when they assigned special quarters to craftsmen such as cobblers and comb-makers. To date, our excavations suggest that Dublin's comb-makers were concentrated in High Street, the metalworkers in Christchurch Place, the cobblers in High Street, the amber-workers and possibly the woodcarvers and merchants in Fishamble Street, with some other craftsmen, possibly including blacksmiths and boat-builders, outside the defences. The annals indicate that as early as 1015 Dublin was no longer contained within its banks because in that year houses both within and 'outside the *dún*' were burned. It may well have been to protect the latter area that the town defences appear to have been extended in the course of the eleventh century.

There is also evidence in Waterford for contiguous houses in parallel alignment as at Fishamble Street, Dublin. At least fourteen plots were aligned roughly on to Peter's Street, Waterford, from the eleventh century onward for a length of over 90 m. Maurice Hurley has shown that type 2 houses occurred behind those of type 1, as at Dublin, and also that the narrow axis of the yards fronted on to the streets, which was a common experience in Dublin. Rather different from Dublin was the discovery at Waterford of several houses at the centre of 'blocks of ground' with no apparent access by pathway or street and the discovery of three sunken-featured structures at considerable distances from the streets. Waterford produced evidence of back yards; common storage pits, barrels, and animal pens made of wattle and brushwood were found with type 2 houses of the rare type 1s which were near the street frontage. Like Dublin, Waterford also had substantial pathways leading from the back doors of the type 1 houses. These were either plank, wattles, gravel, stone slabs, or cobbles. Paths extended as long as 12 m through the back yards. Wattle fences delimiting long rectangular yards did not exist at each level, and a regular alignment, although relatively standard, was not universally adhered to; and, in at least five cases at Waterford, boundary fence locations were changed significantly. Plots or yards apparently laid out when houses were built do not appear to have been a 'constant feature' at Waterford as they were at Fishamble Street.

Edward Bourke's excavations at Bride Street, Wexford, demonstrated the continuity of yard boundaries over eight levels from the eleventh to the thirteenth and fourteenth centuries. These levels show the adjoining parts of two yards which were separated by a succession of boundary fences, and other divisions on more or less the same lines over several centuries. The yards in question were aligned on the present Main Street. Bourke also took the regularity of layout to be an argument for the existence of a pre-Norman authority, which also appears to be the case in Dublin and Waterford. Even more intriguing in Wexford is the discovery that the three lowest levels were not aligned on the main street but had a pattern of yard boundaries that appears to belong to an earlier layout. It is thus possible that the layout of tenth- and early eleventh-century Wexford was redrawn in the middle to late eleventh century in this part of the town, possibly because of an expansion from an earlier core area in the Slaney/Bishopswater river confluence.

There is no evidence as yet for Limerick's Hiberno-Norse subdivision into yards, although it is likely that yards existed there as in the other towns. There are historical references as early as the 960s that show that Limerick had streets, as we know references to the taking of the 'fort' by the Dál gCais, who slaughtered the vikings 'on the streets and in the houses'.

The single most important result of the Dublin excavations is the evidence they have used for town layout, particularly the division of the town into plots or yards that were separated from their neighbour by boundary fences, often located in the same place in successive levels over the centuries; this clearly indicates that the yards were the product of an ordered society in which urban property was respected and its regulation possibly controlled. The continuity of property positions and of house types, over the two centuries or so for which we have archaeological evidence in viking-age Dublin, shows that this was not an emergent urban community but rather had a developed urban sense and belonged to a deeply rooted and unchanging tradition. This brings us back to the origins of the various traditions, both urban and architectural, that culminated in the entity that we know from our tenth-century archaeology. The great challenge must be to find and identify the probable origins of these physical urban traits in the *longphort*.

W HILE five main building types have been proposed for viking-age Dublin, it now appears that there may have been be as many as seven different types of building in our viking-age towns. These include the almost ubiquitous type 1, which has turned up everywhere except Limerick, and appears to have been on the decline from the twelfth century. Type 1 comprises over 75 per cent of all the buildings found to date in Dublin; it is the only one found on all sites and at all levels and may truly be described as the Dublin and indeed the Hiberno-Norse urban building type *par excellence*. In its classic expression, this building had low post-and-wattle walls and roofs supported by two pairs of large posts (or groups of posts) situated well in from the side- and end-walls and on either side of a centrally located, stone-kerbed hearth, which was positioned on a line between the end walls, both of which usually had a doorway. The longitudinal floor strip that ran between the end-wall doorways was flanked on either side by built-up bedding/bench areas that backed onto the side walls. These areas were fronted by low post-and-wattle or stave-built revetments that ran between the roof supports. While in some of the wider buildings of this type it was probably possible to walk into such side areas, their more usual narrow character, coupled with the apparent lowness of the side walls and the raised character of the bedding/benches, probably meant that they were only beds/seats and were not meant to be walked on. The average floor area of these buildings in Dublin was 40 m$^2$. Smaller versions of the type are comparatively rare, the most popular size (30–40 m$^2$) occurring at eleven different building levels at Fishamble Street, the medium to large size (40–50 m$^2$) also occurring at many different levels. Fishamble Street also yielded three type 1 buildings about 60 m$^2$ in area; to this group a very large (66 m$^2$) building from the recent Castle Street excavations may also be added.

Thirty-six type 1 buildings with fifty-four different floor levels were distinguished in Peter Street, Waterford. The well-preserved type 1 houses at Arundel Square in general appear to have wider central aisles than those from Dublin, as well as thinner and wider door jambs. Generally, though, they were very like the Dublin type 1 houses with built-up organic seats along the side walls, double lines of post-and-wattle in the walls, entrances at both ends, well-constructed pathways leading to the thresholds, undressed timbers thrown down to make reinforcement rafts in the soft ground, and timbers laid flat as retainers.

Ten type 1 buildings were found in the Bride Street excavations in Wexford, where Edward Bourke attests the longevity of the type 1 into the thirteenth century and possibly beyond. The relative similarities of form, layout, and scale between the type 1 buildings at Dublin, Waterford, and Wexford means that this was the building type *par excellence* in Irish towns of the eleventh century. Its discovery at the lowest or earliest levels in Dublin, where the evidence is much earlier than presently available for the other towns, shows that the type was already part of an established tradition at the time of the refoundation of Dublin in the second decade of the tenth century. Its longevity is best attested at Wexford, where it continued after the Norman invasion and into the thirteenth century, if not later.

Type 2 buildings have turned up only in the more large-scale excavations at Dublin and Waterford. However, because they have been found in both towns and in the same ancillary context to the type 1 and apparently fulfilling the same function, they may be regarded as a Hiberno-Norse type that may yet turn up at the other towns. The type 2s are of sub-rectangular plan with markedly rounded corners, are smaller than the type 1, were not divided into aisles, and seldom appear to have had formal fireplaces. They usually had a solitary doorway in a side wall and their floors were often completely covered in woven wattle mats. Less than 6 per cent of the Dublin buildings were of this type; the floor areas varied between 6.2 m² and 22.15 m²; however, the five specimens measured averaged more than 16 m².

Type 3 buildings appear to occur only in Dublin, where they have a localised distribution in the Fishamble Street area. They may have been deliberately evolved to fit the relatively unusually narrow east end of the relevant plots. In some ways, they appear to be slimmed down and shortened versions of the type 1, but lack the threefold subdivision of the floor space and the related pairs of roof supports characteristic of the latter. Sometimes they have a doorway in each end wall despite their small size. Slightly more than 6 per cent of all the Dublin buildings conform to this type; they have an average floor area of 14.46 m². It is their relative longevity as well as the roof support system that separates them from type 2 and emphasises their case for acceptance as a distinct type.

Sunken-floored buildings, or type 4, are the second most widely distributed Hiberno-Norse building type. They are found at Waterford, Limerick, and Dublin, although not as yet at Wexford. The relative nearness of the Bride Street site in Wexford to the waterfront probably ruled out the use of buildings of this type in an area that was possibly not embanked, and which anyway was liable to flooding. The type was well evolved by the eleventh century, where similar versions existed at Waterford and Limerick. This group features stone-lined entrance walls widening towards single doorways with strong wall posts and sill beams. In the absence of fireplaces, Maurice Hurley (probably properly) reconstructs buildings of the Waterford/ Limerick type as having upper floors in contrast with the Dublin group which are earlier, smaller, less sturdily built, and lacking the formality of the stone entrances. Hurley believes that two separate sunken-floor building traditions may be represented: an older, in which the main floor was sunken with earthen walls backed up around the sides under a probably relatively low roof; and a later, more urban, 'cellared' tradition, in which the principal floor was located over a sunken cellar with wooden walls supporting an above-ground storey.

Type 5 describes the seven or so small sub-rectangular huts and pens that mainly turned up at the west ends of the long Fishamble Street yards. It is possible that one of the thirteenth-century outbuildings in Wexford also belongs to this type. Pending full analysis of the surviving floor deposits, it is likely that these buildings included toolsheds, farrowing pens, and privies.

The introduction of improved carpentry techniques to Dublin and Waterford in the course of the eleventh century appears to have resulted in the construction in Waterford of what Hurley describes as 'sill-beam houses'. These buildings had walls of load-bearing potential and appear also to have dispensed with the aisled subdivision of the floor spaces. They also appear to have been substantially longer than type 1. Buildings of sill-beam construction first appear in the early to mid twelfth century in Waterford; their closest relatives, so far, in Dublin are the timber-framed cellars that were dated to 'between the end of the twelfth and the early fourteenth century'. They were recently designated Hiberno-Norse building type 6, and they may well be related in plan, if not in wall construction, to what was designated as Hiberno-Norse type 7 in which, again at Waterford, was found a building with load-bearing stone walls and a well-preserved wooden floor laid on joists and with uprights against the outer wall, possibly 'to support a cantilevered superstructure'. This specimen was dated to about the time of the coming of the Normans. The likelihood is that secular stone building dates from possibly the late eleventh century onwards in the towns.

There are sufficient similarities and overlaps of physical evidence between the various eleventh-century Irish towns to say that there was such a thing as a Hiberno-Norse town and that it had common distinguishing physical characteristics. Archaeologically, the towns may be regarded as a group. It is important to realise that, apart from Dublin, most of our town evidence comes a full four centuries after the first beginnings of the town in the post-Roman world among the trading settlements of the North Sea, as evidenced at places such as Ribe in Denmark, and a full two centuries after the first viking-age urban *floruit* at Hedeby/Haithabu and Birka. It is also about two centuries later than the viking *longphorts* at Dublin and Annagassan, and a century after the reestablished settlement at Dublin. Of English towns, only York's archaeological evidence presents a range of parallels to the Irish towns. York's viking-age settlement was located in the elbow between the Ouse and the Foss; its defensive embankment at Hungate conforms to the scale used in Irish towns; its sunken-featured structures and early buildings find parallels here, and historical references link it to Dublin, with which until the mid-tenth century it was ruled by a common dynasty. The numbers of stone and carpented buildings in English towns would probably have been different from the contemporary Hiberno-Norse town, where the majority of buildings were wattle-walled, thatched, and of low, single-storey stature. The Anglo-Saxon pattern with its grid layout, large enclosing embankments, and buildings with load-bearing walls, which was the English norm before and indeed throughout the viking age, was different to that of the Irish towns.

The popularity of *laft* or horizontal log walls in the houses of the Baltic and Scandinavian areas by the mid eleventh century shows how differently the physical nature of the built town had developed there from the contemporary Hiberno-Norse town. The excavations of the eleventh- and twelfth-century towns of Oslo, Trondheim, and Tonsberg show how different were the buildings, defences, and yard layout in Norway from those of the Hiberno-Norse towns of the same period.

Finally, in social, historical, and visual terms it is important to emphasise that all Irish town buildings were of rectangular plan and nearly all had side- and end-walls of post-and-wattle, with rounded corners. The walls were low, almost inconsequential, skins demarcating the floor areas. The roofs were probably hipped and relatively steeply pitched. Buildings were thatched with straw, probably on a sod or turf underlayer to which the thatch was fixed with pointed wooden pins or scallops (*scailb*). The thatch probably oversailed the eaves as generously as the often narrow space between neighbouring buildings would allow. There was a marked absence of daub, at least in Dublin, where conditions for its survival in burnt form were favourable. It is possible that houses were not daubed but that cow dung was applied to the walls as an insulation that did not survive in the archaeological record.

The Dublin buildings are unlikely to have had windows, although types 6 and 7 could have been so provided. It is also likely that smoke was channelled through smoke-holes in the roofs. Often separately walled-off corner compartments were deliberately floored with paving stones or dismembered barrel staves as if to achieve a level surface on which to stand a container of some kind (perhaps containing water, milk, beer, or even wine).

O UR impression of the crafts in viking-age Dublin is coloured by what has been found in the excavations. However, this is only a partial picture, because there were many crafts and occupations of which no physical record survives. For instance, the brewers and the bakers have left nothing behind, and the sail-, rope-, and net-makers are only poorly represented. Not all the objects that turned up in the excavations were produced by specialist craftsmen. Every household probably had its own handyman, someone who could put a handle on an axe, sickle, hammer, or knife or maybe carve a bone whistle or toy boat for a child or make a rough jewel box for a woman, twist a straw or hair rope, or produce a tool chest for himself. The blacksmith made tools for many other craftsmen, and some craftsmen probably made their own tools. Spindles, whorls, weaving tablets, needles, and weaver swords were all part of the textile-worker's gear and could have been made by the relevant craftsman himself. Similarly, wooden net floats and stone net-sinkers were probably made by the craftsmen who used them. It is not too difficult to imagine fishermen making and mending their own nets.

Wood was a raw material in which many different craftsmen worked. These include shipbuilders, who made and repaired ships of all sizes. Dublin probably had its own shipyard, to judge from the large mid-eleventh-century warship from Roskilde, which has been dendrochronologically assigned to the Irish Sea area and probably to Dublin. In addition to oars, large planks, blocks for mast-steps, and other fittings, thousands of iron nails were also required by shipbuilders. Builders and carpenters worked in cooperation with wall- and fence-makers, whose skills resembled those of the basket-weaver. Apart from weaving fences, pathways, bed bases, floor-mats, screens, and door panels, they also made baskets of all shapes and sizes. Coopers and turners also worked in wood; coopers made staves, bases, hoops, and lids of barrels, kegs, buckets, and churns, all of which have been found in the excavations. Wooden bowls, trays, lossets, troughs, cups, dishes, ladles, and spoons were made by the turner. Bowls and even gaming-pieces were made in groups and only finally detached from one another when they were nearly finished. Wooden shovels and spades were also produced. Some of the shovels were fitted with iron blades.

Although knobs, finials, and other parts of chairs have turned up, it is unlikely that there were any specialist furniture makers. The simple three- and four-legged stools that were common could have been made by any handyman. It is unclear whether the ropes and tethers that were made from tree roots and withies were made by specialists or by ropemakers, whose raw materials would also have included hay, straw, and possibly linen fibre.

Comb-making was one of the commonest activities. The antler of the red deer was used mostly, although cattle horn was another material that was used. Much of the materials used by the combmaker have come to light—sawn-off antler burrs and tines and other waste and offcuts, discarded antler tips, blanks, tooth-plates, side-plates, and rivets—as well as a whole range of finished combs. These were both single- and double-sided. Comb cases, into which the combs were fitted in order to protect their teeth, were also made mainly of antler. Other bone and antler artefacts—spindle-whorls, spindles, pins, needles, spools, caulking spades, handles, whistles, casket panels, buckets, strap ends, weaving tablets, buzz-discs, bone-marrow scoops, gaming-pieces, ice-skates, clamps, and vices—are commonly found. Cattle bones were used for most of the smaller items; walrus ivory for gaming-pieces; horse leg-bones for skates; whalebones for clamps and spatulae; pig bones for marrow scoops, buzz-discs, and toggles. The leg-bones of birds were favoured for whistles. Bone motif and trial pieces, which are the equivalent of headline copybooks for viking-age artists, were also found in large numbers.

Dublin's blacksmiths must have been among the most numerous and valued of the craftsmen. Not only did they make and repair weapons of war, they also made nails and washers for ships as well as tools for virtually every other craftsman. They made implements for farmers and fishermen. The great fires that were so essential for the smith and his forge almost certainly meant that they had to be located at some distance from the town.

Personal ornaments, brooches, and smaller metal objects were usually made by metalsmiths who worked principally in copper alloy, lead alloy, silver, and gold. Among the items commonly made by the non-ferrous smiths were tweezers, pans, beams and chains for weighing scales, needle-cases, and toilet sets. Personal ornaments include stick-pins, ringed-pins, strap-tags, buckles, finger rings, and bracelets. Artefacts connected with the production of such objects, including moulds, crucibles, ingots, and heating trays, have all been found.

The plaited gold and silver rings and bracelets that have been excavated are exactly similar to copper-alloy versions. The discovery of so many blobs of melted lead on the floors of many of the houses, where rubbish often stuck to the lead, probably testifies to its common use by non-specialist craftsmen.

The excavations have also yielded information on the production of tex-tiles. Not only have several examples of cloth and spools of thread survived, the implements of their production have also been found. Spindles of wood and metal, and whorls of bone, stone, and clay, are commonly found. Weavers' swords were made in wood and in different sizes. Weaving tablets were mostly of antler and bone, although wooden specimens have also turned up. Not surprisingly, needles of all shapes and sizes, mostly in copper alloy and bone, have been discovered in great numbers.

One of the most convincing workshops to have been identified at Fish-amble Street was that of an amber-worker. Although evidence for his imple-ments is lacking, hundreds of flakes and broken, cast-off, or unfinished rings, pendants, earrings, and beads amply testify to the local presence of this craft. Jet was also worked and even glass beads were made, probably principally from recycled broken glass vessels. Stone was used for building and for moulds used by metalworkers. It was the raw material from which sharpening-stones, lamps, whorls, grindstones, loom-net weights, and quern-stones were produced. The tiny stone discs that were sometimes used in necklaces were probably locally made, while large soapstone bowls and pipkins were imported from the Scottish islands.

Although hundreds of leather items have been found in the excavations, apart from cobblers' waste there is little evidence for the leatherworker's craft. Shoes have been found in great numbers, also scabbards, knife-sheaths, and satchels. Awls, needles, scorers, punches, and a last are all that survive of one of the town's busiest crafts.

THE importance of the hinterland to the town has to be emphasised. From the farms around Dublin the cattle were driven to the town to be slaughtered; sheep appear to have been raised for their fleeces at this time. Bread was always the staple diet, and it was from the hinterland that ground corn was brought to the town. The comparative rarity of quernstones from the excavations suggest that corn was already milled into flour in the countryside before being brought in.

The area around the town also produced timber, wattles, straw, and other building materials. The raw materials for craft industries, including bone and antler, timber, lead, and copper, all originated in the countryside. A visitor at a landward gate to the late tenth-century town would have witnessed some of this traffic from the hinterland. Cattle, sheep, cereals, and other foodstuffs, possibly coppiced wattles, and turves would have been produced for regular supply to the town. Fruits, berries, and nuts available in the wild, as well as mosses (which were collected for use as 'toilet paper') and shed antler for the use of the comb industry, were probably all picked up by professional scavengers. Transporting lead and copper was a more long-distance chore: it was probably in the hands of men who travelled long distances on packhorses to trade silver with the native population beyond the hinterland. Finished products such as combs, brooches, exotic spices, wine, and beer, as well as clothes, shoes, and otherwise unobtainable weapons, implements, and gadgets, were traded back to the hinterland in return for agricultural produce and raw materials. The tribute of iron, shoes, gloves, and combs paid by the inhabitants of Dublin to the archbishop of Armagh, according to Jocelyn's Life of St Patrick, can be accepted in evidence for the movement of Dublin's industrial products to centres beyond the hinterland. In this context it is possible that items such as these were traded, sold, or exchanged in rural centres such as Knowth, where artefacts that appear to have originated in Dublin have been found.

The exchange or trading of goods should not, however, be confused with the transmission of ideas and beliefs. For example, the coiled wooden snake pendant from Fishamble Street is probably no more than a wooden version of a type represented elsewhere in the viking world in jet. It represents the transmission of an idea or a fashion, rather than the actual import of an artefact. In much the same way, the late Thomas Fanning demonstrated that the occurrence of bronze ringed pins of Irish type on viking sites in the north Atlantic colonial area reflects the transmission of an Irish fashion along the

Atlantic trade routes. That is not to say that Dublin did not mass-produce fashion and dress items such as small kite-shaped brooches, zoomorphic headed strap-tags, and plaited wire rings, which made their way across the same north Atlantic world of the Norse.

THE discovery of native or 'souterrain' pottery of the eleventh and twelfth centuries represents one of the few tangible archaeological examples of Irish trade in Hiberno-Norse Dublin. It appears that Ireland was aceramic until the Anglo-Norman period, except for the north-east, from which the Dublin 'souterrain' vessels were probably brought. Evidence for more long-distance imports from the excavations is better. These imports range from finished articles such as cloth, glass, pottery, soapstone vessels, and walrus-pieces to raw materials, which were brought in bulk to be manufactured locally. Amber and lignite are especially conspicuous in the latter category; it is also possible that broken glass fragments were imported to Dublin to supply the local bead-making industry.

The exotic nature of the imports testifies to the wealth of tenth- to eleventh-century Dublin. High-quality worsted fabrics have been identified; these include some with diamond twills that could have been locally woven; silk lappings for edging, probably from Byzantium or some Islamic centre, patterned compound silks from either Byzantium or Persia, and gold braids that could have originated in Central Asia. Such discoveries recall the description of the loot taken from Limerick by the Limerick vikings after the battle of Sulchóid, which mentions 'their beautifully woven clothes of all colours and of all kinds, their satins and silken cloth, pleasing and variegated, both scarlet and green and also some cloths in light colours'. In 999 'many and various cloths of all colours' were taken from Dublin by Brian Bóruma who also 'seized the greatest quantities of gold, silver, bronze, precious stones, gems, horns, and beautiful goblets'. The appeal of these materials for the Irish may be implicit in the 'saddles beautiful and foreign' and 'the jewels and best property . . . gold and silver' taken from Limerick in 968. There is even an Arabic account of the wealth of the viking towns of Ireland from the eleventh century! That the Hiberno-Norse towns were regarded by the Irish as repositories of treasure in the tenth and eleventh centuries, in much the same way as the vikings earlier regarded the monasteries as the equivalent of the 'modern bank stronghold', is evident from Congalach's capture of 'jewels, treasures and [?]' in Dublin as early as 944.

The bulk of Dublin's apparently considerable imports of late Saxon pottery came from England, especially from the Cheshire region, probably from the port of Chester. England probably supplied Dublin with the bulk of its pottery in the succeeding Saxo-Norman period in the eleventh century, although there is growing evidence for the importation of Norman red-painted and glazed Andennes after the Norman conquest of England.

Soapstone vessels seem to have included typical large bowls and handled pipkins, which were imported in a finished state from Shetland. The large quantities of amber that have been recovered from the Dublin excavations are thought to have originated either along the east coast of England or, more likely, in the Baltic region. Finished beads, rings, earrings, and pendants, as well as unworked lumps and discarded amber waste, have been found and an amber workshop has been identified. Lignite, which was being worked into bracelets in possibly the same workshops as the amber, was imported in considerable amounts, probably from Whitby in Yorkshire.

It may never be possible to identify genuine Irish exports such as hides among the archaeological remains of foreign settlements, but it is easy to demonstrate the presence of Irish-made souvenirs and Irish metal loot in the graves of the ninth-century vikings. Irish material is also represented among the artefacts recovered from the early Norse trading station at Kaupang. A number of merchants' graves, identified by the association of their occupants with weights, balances, and scales, were found in the ninth-century viking cemetery at Islandbridge/Kilmainham. The scales and weights underline the presence and importance of the merchant element in Dublin from an early date, even back to the *longphort* era of the ninth century.

Over a hundred silver hoards and 140 single finds of silver have been found in Ireland. Taken in association with the great gold hoard from Hare Island, County Westmeath, and the Cuerdale hoard, which was almost certainly assembled in Ireland, these enormous quantities of precious metal reflect the wealth of the island in the late ninth, tenth, and early eleventh centuries. There can be little doubt about the part played by the vikings in the distribution of this silver. Many of the silver hoards were recovered from native settlements of both secular and monastic character, which suggests that precious metal was in native hands probably because of the protection and ransom practices of native kings, among whom the Southern Uí Néill in the present County Westmeath area were the most successful. It is likely that much of the imported silver was mediated through the towns, especially Dublin.

Even allowing for exaggeration, there is no doubt that the early historic Irish sources associate great wealth with tenth- and eleventh-century Dublin. For example, in 989 a levy of 1 ounce of gold had to be paid by every garth and tenement in Dublin, while in 1023 Dublin is reported to have paid a ransom of 600 ounces of gold and 600 of silver, as well as 1,250 cows and 150 Welsh horses, for the return of Oláfr. Wine was shipped into the town in considerable quantities. A levy of 150 vats of wine a year had to be paid by Dublin to Brian Bóruma, who also claimed thirty-two gallons of wine every day from the town of Limerick. Gerald of Wales wrote of the abundance of wine in Ireland and of how it had to be paid for by the return to 'Poitou of hides and animals and skins of flocks and wild beasts'. There is literary evidence too, for the export of marten skins to Chester and for the import of salt from England. Alfred Smyth has argued for the relationship of Dublin's expanding wealth to the flourishing condition of the slave markets in the Iberian peninsula in the earlier part of the viking age. Slaves were shipped from Ireland to the Islamic centres of the middle east via Scandinavia and the Russian rivers. We even have the name of an enslaved Irish princess in a mid-tenth-century south-west Swedish slave market. Saxo-Grammaticus described viking Dublin as 'filled with the wealth of barbarians' and there are many references in the Scandinavian sagas that testify to the wealth of Dublin, the most famous port of the western Norse world by the end of the tenth century. The route out to Dublin was accounted 'the most famous' in 'Egil's saga', while in the 'Heimskringla' we are told that many were 'in the habit' of making a journey to Dublin.

The contrast in the numbers of silver hoards between Ireland and Scotland underlines the location of wealth; James Graham Campbell argues that 'it must be the towns which account for the presence in Ireland of such wealth'. The scarcity of coins, and the absence of towns from Scotland and its islands, support this hypothesis. Tangible proof of the wealth comes in the variety of the imported pottery and especially in the range and volume of the imported exotic cloths. The discovery of coins, silver ingots, and gold plaited-wire rings and, especially, of a pair of gold bracelets found in a late tenth/early eleventh-century context at High Street is further proof.

Nine lead balance weights, decorated by the incorporation in them of parts of insular reliquaries and other ornaments, were recovered from the Islandbridge graves. Two of these seem to equate with the Scandinavian *ore* as discussed by Skarre; they weighed 26.67 g and 24.9 g respectively. Generally, these weights tended to be slightly lighter than the 200 or so weights found in tenth- and eleventh-century Dublin excavation levels, in which the *ore* was about 26.5 g. Evidently a slight change in the system of weights occurred in the tenth century, possibly in conjunction with the variety of other changes that I would tentively ascribe to Anglo-Saxon influence. I have identified about twenty weight shapes in Dublin, and these can be grouped into weights to be placed on pans, and those for weighing heavier objects. The shapes have no bearing on the weights nor, apparently, do they relate either to the time or the find-spot of any particular weight. In addition to the weight pans, beams and suspension chains have also been found in the excavations.

Dublin's (indeed Ireland's) first mint was established probably in 997, although Anglo-Saxon coins had been hoarded before this by Dublin merchants, for use probably with Anglo-Saxon merchants who may possibly have been reluctant to accept handfuls of hack silver in return for their commodities because by then they dealt in controlled currencies. The Dublin coinage was based on the English Æthelræd II series and was introduced in order to facilitate trade around the Irish Sea, especially in Anglo-Saxon ports such as Chester. Dublin's silver pennies eventually found their way all over Europe. In the period between 997 and about 1040 they were found in hoards as far away as Iceland, the Faeroes, Norway, Denmark, Sweden, Finland, Russia, the Baltic States, northern Germany, and even Rome. Hoards such as those from Sylt in the Friesian Islands probably indicate direct links with Dublin because of the relatively high incidence in them of pennies with Dublin's mint signature. More usually, the relative paucity of Dublin coins indicates only an indirect contact.

The Fishamble Street excavations produces a fine series of Anglo-Saxon coins, including specimens minted at Oxford (925), Derby (*c.*930), Canterbury (*c.*935), Chester (two of *c.*950 and one of *c.*965–70), Norwich, and Lincoln (?) (957–73), as well as Æthelræd coins from Barnstaple (*c.*980), London (two of 991–7), and Exeter (one of 997–1003 and another of 1003–9). There was also a Cnút penny minted at Gloucester about 1025. At High Street and Christchurch Place, the earliest stratified coins were of Oláfr Sigtryggeson, struck at York in the 940s, and a coin of Oláfr Gotfrithason of *c.*940 struck at Derby and found in association with an Eadmond penny.

The numismatic evidence appears to be different at the two sides of the hill on which Dublin developed. For while the coins in the Fishamble Street or riverward side seem to indicate more Anglo-Saxon ties, especially those of Mercian origin, coins from the High Street/Christchurch Place sites appear to comprise relatively more of the Dublin series (but to include also a couple of early specimens from York, which were not paralleled at Fishamble Street). The Fishamble Street series definitely shows a high incidence of Anglo-Saxon coin hoarding before the initiation of the local series. It is interesting also to note the decline in the number of Irish coins after the 1030s and a falling-off in the number of English coins found in Dublin in the same period. It seems that during the reign of King Cnút Dublin coins were not as readily acceptable in England as before.

The discovery of coins at native sites must not necessarily be regarded as evidence for coin exchange between Irish and Scandinavian centres. Such discoveries indicate simply that tribute in silver was being paid in the currently acceptable medium. The decline in weight and legibility in the Dublin coins in the mid and late eleventh century means that the use of coins was then more confined to the locality. Although this could be interpreted as a relapse to non-coin exchange, it should be remembered that this is the time at which there is evidence for coin and minting at other Irish centres. It is also a time when Dublin's trading contacts seem to have been multiplying, to go by the surviving archaeological evidence. The discovery of two coin hoards near the lowest occupation levels in the recent Castle Street excavations show that large hoards were accumulated in Dublin on the eve of the setting-up of Dublin's own mint. Both hoards include Æthelræd II coins, and one also includes silver jewellery, underlining that it was the silver weight rather than the coins that mattered. The absence of coins from the other towns is noteworthy; while claims have been made for a mint at Waterford, these have not been successfully confirmed.

Ireland owed its importance in the viking trade network to its western location in the Atlantic, and Dublin its importance to its position on the western shore of the Irish Sea, through which the northern sea traffic passed from Scandinavia, Iceland, the Faeroes, the Scottish islands, south-western Britain, France, and Spain. It seems that the Atlantic traffic tended not to be directed along the western coasts of Ireland but rather through the Irish Sea via Dublin.

The absence on the western coast of towns north of Limerick, and the scarcity of silver finds in the north-west, shows that the vikings tended to navigate the more sheltered Irish Sea route, notwithstanding the burial at Eyrephort, County Galway, the finds with viking associations in Donegal, and the enigmatic Scandinavian presence at Beginish, County Kerry. Limerick was probably chosen for settlement as much for its relatively inland position and access to the Shannon and the centre of Ireland, with rich monasteries like Clonmacnoise, as for its position on the Atlantic, just as Waterford was probably chosen for the access it gave to the hinterland of the rivers Nore, Suir, and Barrow. The location of the early settlements at Dublin, Annagassan, and possibly Carlingford shows that the Irish Sea route was well chosen from the beginning. It continued in use throughout the extended viking period in Ireland.

The Irish Sea seems to have been a veritable 'viking lake' from the ninth to the eleventh centuries. It was dominated by Dublin, which looked eastwards to the Isle of Man, to north-western England, and across the Pennines to Northumbria and York. Dublin traded extensively with Chester on the far shore of the Irish Sea till about 980 when, according to the late Michael Dolley, trade with Chester declined and swung around to an emerging Bristol in the south-west. This tilt southwards in Dublin's main trade access could have had as much to do with the decline of direct Norse contact and of the trade routes to the north as with the political eclipse of Chester. The archaeological evidence at Dublin suggests an increasing shift southwards of the trade axis towards south-western Britain and France in the eleventh century, a trend that seems to be supported by the place-name evidence in Wales. The trade route between Dublin and south-western England (especially Bristol) and France was to prevail well into the twelfth and thirteenth centuries and later, and may well have been 'a contributory factor to the Norman conquest of Ireland'. The shift southwards of Dublin's trade access in the eleventh century could also explain the comparative absence of Hiberno-Norse coins in Scotland. There may have been little trade between

Dublin and Scotland after the battle of Clontarf and the defeat of Earl Sigurd of the Orkneys.

Despite Dublin's undoubted importance in the western and northern Atlantic routes, it probably did not forge direct trade links of its own with very many continental (including Scandinavian) towns. Dolley believed that the Dublin coins made their way to the Baltic by the English Channel and Denmark, and that even the Hiberno-Norse coins that arrived in Norway came by the English Channel and possibly Hedeby/Haithabu, although whether the latter was long-lived enough to have been involved in their transmission is questionable. This pattern also suggests that 'coinlessness' and 'townlessness' went together, as appears to have been the case in Scotland until comparatively late. David Wilson has underlined the signifi-cance of Dublin as an entrepôt from which 'wines, silver, wool, and other goods readily obtainable in the markets of England and the Continent were traded northwards to Iceland and Norway and to which ivory, furs, amber, resins, and slaves were shipped southwards'.

The surest evidence we have for the wealth and importance of Hiberno-Norse Dublin lies in the increasing interest attached to it by the Irish kings who competed to control it. The most conspicuous of these was Diarmait mac Maíl na mBó, who gained control of Waterford in 1037 and captured Dublin in 1052, when he left his son as his permanent representative in charge of the town. Diarmait was in close contact with the Anglo-Scandinavian Godwinsons, from whom he may have learned the lesson of controlling towns and of having urban capitals in the contemporary European fashion. Such urban centres accompanied the development of centralised authority and the growth of national feeling in Ireland as elsewhere. The selection of Dublin as the archbishop's see in preference to the old ecclesi-astical capital, Kildare, shows how Dublin was regarded by Irish kings and ecclesiastics. By the late eleventh century the original Scandinavian founda-tion had become a wealthy Hiberno-Norse town and the most important centre of population in the country. It was already the unofficial capital of Ireland and would have to be controlled in any attempt by an Irish provincial king claiming to be high-king or an invading force wishing to subjugate Ireland. The capture of Dublin by the Anglo-Normans in 1170, the resulting siege of the town by the high-king Ruaidrí Ua Conchobair, and the subse-quent raising of the siege show how crucial the position of Dublin had become by then.

Unfortunately, the relationship between the various Hiberno-Norse towns remains relatively uncharted. Limerick appears to have been the first to have been subjected to the interests and ambitions of native kings, while Wexford and later Waterford and finally Dublin were only subjugated in the mid-eleventh century. Apart from their clearly shared physical character, which may owe a lot to local influence, they never had a common political purpose. Ongoing analysis of the craft traditions and evidence for imports from the results of excavations in the towns other than Dublin may, however, show that there was commercial and technical cooperation and interaction.

## CHAPTER XXIII

# Coins and coinage
# in pre-Norman Ireland

MICHAEL KENNY

THE history of coinage in Ireland, prior to the advent of the Normans, may be divided into three main periods. The first two are reasonably distinct and well defined. The third, apart from its starting-point, is considerably less so. The periods and approximate dates are as follows: first, the coinless period, until the end of the ninth century; second, the 'Anglo-Saxon' period, from the end of the ninth to the end of the tenth century; and third, the 'Hiberno-Norse' period, from the end of the tenth to the middle of the twelfth century. Although the third period has been traditionally referred to as 'Hiberno-Norse' in numismatic textbooks, it must be emphasised that this is largely for convenience purposes. The term, as signifying the coinage of an independent viking kingdom, becomes increasingly meaningless from the 1030s onwards, as Dublin comes more and more under the control of successive Irish kings. The period might reasonably be subdivided into an early Hiberno-Norse phase, *c*.995–*c*.1035; an 'anonymous Hiberno-Norse' phase, *c*.1035–*c*.1100; and the bracteate phase, *c*.1100–*c*.1150. The light, thin, and stylistically novel bracteate coins of the twelfth century have generally been referred to as Hiberno-Norse by numismatists, but since they differ so radically from the preceding issues, and may possibly have been struck under an Irish rather than a viking authority, the subdivision suggested here is reasonable.

PRE-CHRISTIAN Ireland was coinless, which is not in any way surprising, since there was no direct contact with the Roman empire. What is rather surprising is that this situation continued to obtain during the Christian era, when it is considered that there were strong religious and commercial links not only with England but also with Spain, France, and Italy. The most likely explanation is that those coins that found their way into the country were regarded merely as pieces of precious metal, to be melted down and used by craftsmen. Certainly there is no evidence that coins circulated as such or any suggestion that they had a monetary function. This holds true for Roman, Merovingian, and early Carolingian finds alike.

During the first century of mainly violent contact with the vikings, the situation remained largely unchanged, and ninth-century hoards are so few that it would be most unwise to suggest any geographical or chronological pattern. It is fairly clear from the historical and numismatic evidence that the early vikings were not themselves a coin-using people.[1] The point has also been made by modern historians that 'Danes' is a singularly inappropriate term to describe those vikings who came to dominate the Irish scene. These were, in the main, Norse vikings whose theatre of operations also included Scotland, the Hebrides, Wales, and north-west England—those areas of Britain that were furthest removed from the developing monetary economy of the Anglo-Saxon heartland. They were a flexible and versatile trading people; it can be assumed that they did not use coins simply because they did not find it necessary for their activities. Finally, it must be said that even if the vikings had begun to use coins at an earlier stage, one should not necessarily expect to see this trend reflected immediately in coin hoards, prior to the establishment of stable and permanent settlements.

With the advent of the tenth century the situation changed dramatically, and this is reflected by a greatly increased number of coin hoards. There were a number of causes. The economy of the Scandinavian homeland at this point was 'transformed, almost over night, by a new flood of Kufic dirhams ... and temporary though this was to be, it was not long before the tenth-century viking had acquired a taste for coin'.[2] Furthermore, the last decade of the ninth century witnessed the appearance of independent viking coinages in East Anglia and York.[3] The political and economic links with England, particularly along the Dublin–York axis, brought the Dublin vikings into contact with coin-using viking communities. These used whatever coins came to hand—Islamic dirhams from Central Asia, deniers from the Carolingian empire, their own coin issues, but above all, Anglo-Saxon pennies. These latter formed the largest element by far in the tenth-century Irish hoards,[4] hence the title suggested for this particular phase.

Why did the Dublin vikings not develop a coinage of their own? What effect did the advent of coinage have upon the Irish? Why have such a high

[1] Michael Dolley, *Sylloge of Hiberno-Norse coins in the British Museum* (London, 1966), pp 24–5; Philip Grierson and M. A. S. Blackburn, *Medieval European coinage*, i (Cambridge, 1986), p. 318.

[2] Dolley, *Sylloge*, p. 25.

[3] Christopher E. Blunt, 'The St Edmund memorial coinage' in *Proceedings of the Suffolk Institute of Archaeology*, xxxi (1969), pp 232–54; C. S. S. Lyon and B. H. I. H. Stewart, 'The Northumbrian viking coins in the Cuerdale hoard' in Michael Dolley (ed.), *Anglo-Saxon coins* (London, 1961), pp 96–121; Michael Dolley, *Viking coins of the Danelaw and Ireland* (Dublin, 1965).

[4] Richard Hall, 'A checklist of viking-age finds from Ireland' in *U.J.A.*, 3rd ser., xxxvi–xxxvii (1973–4), pp 71–86.

proportion of viking-age hoards been found in areas far from Dublin or indeed any viking settlement? Answers to these questions must be sought in the broader field of economic history rather than numismatics. With regard to Dublin's failure to emulate York and Lincoln, one possible reason may be that the Dubliners, and even more so their cousins in Limerick and Waterford, traded with and became part of an economic system that differed considerably from that experienced by the vikings in England. The point is underlined by the fact that Hiberno-Norse kings showed no reluctance to issue coins at York when in control there.[5] Whatever the reasons, the Hiberno-Norse remained satisfied with the coins of others until the very end of the century.

It is difficult to assess the impact of coinage on the Irish. Until fairly recently, the commonly held view was that they had little use for coin. This view, held by numismatists, historians, and archaeologists alike, was based in the main upon two arguments. First, it was held that since they lacked a market economy and were a pastoral, non-urbanised people, they simply had no need for coins. Secondly, it was perceived that coin-finds were strongly concentrated in the eastern half of the country and that hoards discovered in Irish areas merely represented loot. Recent historical research and a growing body of hoard evidence, however, suggest that the situation was rather more complex. It has now been accepted, for example, that Irish society was by no means static during the viking age. Indeed, many of the changes originally attributed to the vikings were already present and discernible in the eighth century.[6] Secondly, the growing towns were not the only commercial and trading points. The monastic cities were important 'redistributive centres' and the two types of settlement obviously did not exist in mutual isolation.[7] Thirdly, the majority of coin hoards have been found in Irish regions well removed from the viking towns or areas of influence. Many of them have turned up in the vicinity of the great monasteries, such as Glendalough, Kildare, Burrow, Rahan, Clonmacnoise, and Armagh.[8] Fourthly, it is highly unlikely that the Irish of Meath and north Leinster, for example, could have had commercial, political, and social contact with Dublin continuously throughout this period and yet remain totally unaffected by its trading practices.[9] While on this point it is worth noting that a

---

[5] Michael Dolley, 'The post-Brunanburgh viking coinage of York' in *Nordisk Numismatisk Arsskrift, 1957–8*, pp 13–85; 'The Anglo-Danish and Anglo-Norse coinages of York' in R. A. Hall (ed.), *Viking-age York and the north* (London, 1978), pp 26–31; J. J. North, *English hammered coinage* (2 vols, London, 1963), i, 16–18.

[6] Charles Doherty, 'Exchange and trade in early medieval Ireland' in *R.S.A.I. Jn.*, cx (1980), pp 67–89: 70–72.

[7] Ibid., p. 71.

[8] Michael Kenny, 'The geographical distribution of Irish viking-age coin hoards' in *R.I.A. Proc.*, lxxxvii (1987), sect. C, pp 514–17.

[9] Ibid., pp 516–17.

growing body of archaeological evidence, especially from the midlands, suggests that there was little difference in the material culture of the two civilisations by the tenth century.

All these factors must be borne in mind when assessing the use of coins in non-viking areas. The most interesting development, however, and the one that makes a revision of the traditional picture necessary, is the emerging pattern of hoard distribution. There is a noticeable concentration of finds in the Clann Cholmáin territory of west Meath and to a lesser extent in north Brega and north Leinster, the majority of which must have been deposited by Irish rather than viking hands.[10] Many of these cannot be correlated with recorded plunderings of Dublin, which weakens the 'booty theory' considerably. Many of them are so small—about 45 per cent of all recorded hoards are of thirty coins or less—that they are quite insignificant as bullion. Indeed the entire viking-age coin hoards of Ireland comprise only a small fraction of the silver wealth of the period. It is quite possible therefore that the numerous little finds of four, five, and six coins, so prevalent in the midlands, may reflect or represent a more general usage or at least a greater awareness of coins than hitherto believed. Admittedly we are straying somewhat here into an area that is properly the domain of the economic historians, but the evidence certainly suggests that the attitude towards coinage in non-viking areas was by no means totally negative. It is essential therefore that in teasing out those issues we should first dispense with rigid distinctions between 'coin-users' and 'non-coin-users' and with generalisations regarding 'Irish' and 'viking' economies. The economies and trading practices of those kingdoms most in contact with Dublin were obviously more permeated by its influence than were Connacht or Ulster. Coin-users and non-coin-users were not necessarily mutually exclusive groups. Since coins had a useful trading function they could be kept aside for use in trade with outsiders without being used in the monetary sense at home. The possibility of a hybrid or transitional stage between a bullion-based and a monetary economy in some parts of the country cannot lightly be dismissed, and the picture of a clean distinction between Irish and viking is at odds not only with the hoard evidence but with what is known of Irish–Norse contacts generally.

It is also possible, of course, to exaggerate the importance of coins among the vikings themselves. Limerick and Waterford, for example, do not appear to have had as much contact with coinage as Dublin and did not emulate the latter in developing independent issues of their own. Both were busy trading ports. Grierson's caveat that 'coinage is far from being the universally convenient device that economists believe it to have been'[11] is very pertinent

---

[10] Ibid., pp 511–16.
[11] Philip Grierson, *Numismatics* (London, 1975), p. 6.

here. The same author also makes the point that credit is not just characteristic of modern sophisticated societies, but can play an 'equally conspicuous role, however different in its details, in societies that have no coin at all'.[12] To complicate the picture further, there are numerous examples in medieval Europe of busy trading links that have left no numismatic evidence at all behind them.[13] As Heslip has so aptly put it, 'trade, at any level, was not dependent upon the availability of coin, although it provided a convenience'.[14] Coinage may be a useful indicator of economic activity or development. Its absence cannot be read as an indication of backwardness or stagnation.

IT is not proposed to describe in detail here the various Dublin-produced issues of the eleventh and twelfth centuries. The entire series was divided into seven principal phases by Dolley,[15] but the dates assigned to these are open to question. It is not clear to what extent each succeeding type overlapped, nor is it clear whether or not there was substantial reminting of earlier issues. What is fairly clear, however, is that after a century of using Anglo-Saxon pennies the Dublin vikings under Sitric III initiated a series of their own, sometime between 995 and 1000. The exact starting-date is not certain. The prototype was the Anglo-Saxon penny with which the Dubliners were so familiar, and which also provided the prototype for the Scandinavian coinages that emerged around the same time. Some of these early Dublin pennies were total imitations, in that they copied not only the design but also the actual legends of the contemporary Anglo-Saxon issues. Some, on the other hand, bear the name of Sitric and a Dublin mint signature. As if this were not confusing enough, many of the coins are hybrids, bearing the name Sitric and an English mint signature, or Æthelræd II of England and a Dublin mint signature.

The coins were, initially at any rate, of good weight and quality and were struck from literate dies. There are even examples of actual Anglo-Saxon dies being used in Dublin, which further complicates the picture.[16] Whether they were taken across by force, or as the result of some trading agreement, is unclear, but it must be presumed that with them came some knowledge of English minting technology and practice. Just why Sitric III chose to issue an

[12] Ibid., p. 2.
[13] Ibid., p. 4.
[14] Robert Heslip, 'Reflections on Hiberno-Norse coinage' in *U.J.A.*, 3rd ser., xlviii (1985), pp 25–30: 26.
[15] Dolley, *Sylloge*, pp 92–150.
[16] M. A. S. Blackburn, 'Hiberno-Norse imitations of Watchet long cross coins' in *Numismatic Chronicle*, 7th ser., xv (1975), pp 195–7, and 'Thoughts on imitations of the Anglo-Saxon coins' in *Seabys Coin and Medal Bulletin*, 1977, pp 344–50; W. A. Seaby, 'An Aethelraed/Sihtric Watchet die link' in *Seabys Coin and Medal Bulletin 1971*, pp 90–91. English dies were also brought to Scandinavia.

independent coinage at this juncture remains something of a mystery. He may have been spurred on by pride, ambition, economic considerations, or all three.[17] Dublin was of course a busy trading centre and entrepôt and a significant proportion of its trade was with England. The new development most certainly was not a reflection of growing viking political and military strength. On the contrary, the subjugation of Dublin by Máel Sechnaill II after the battle of Tara (980) had reduced its fortunes considerably. The issuing of coins could of course be interpreted as an attempt by Sitric to reassert his independence and strengthen his own grip on the throne, but how does one then explain why so many of his coins carry the name and title of Æthelræd II of England? If, on the other hand, one regards them as straightforward forgeries, struck intentionally to deceive, why then does Sitric's own name appear on so many of the pieces? Finally, whether the driving-force was deception or emulation, neither motive effectively explains those combinations such as Sitric/York or Æthelræd/Dublin, which do not really fit into either explanation. This brings us to the question of usage. For whom were the coins intended? It has been suggested that the 'Irish' types were intended for the home front and the 'English' types for use in trade with England,[18] but again this does not explain the combinations noted above. In all of this, it is well to remember that the great majority of those using coins are likely to have been illiterate and not particularly interested in legends or titles. What they were interested in were coins that would be acceptable in trade, without necessarily wishing to enforce the strict controls on weight and design that would have been necessary had they been intended to pass by tale.

Pennies based directly upon contemporary Anglo-Saxon types continued to be produced up to about 1020. The next phase (c.1020–35) saw the advent of a more independent coinage, in that the Dublin moneyers no longer sought to imitate Anglo-Saxon issues but went their own way, striking coins that were essentially based upon their own earlier imitations of the Anglo-Saxon long-cross penny. Initially the coins of this new phase were heavier than their immediate predecessors, but the weight soon deteriorated. From this point there is a noticeable falling-off in the incidence of Dublin coins in Scandinavian hoards, and it has been suggested that the lighter penny could not compete internationally. Its disappearance from Scandinavia has also been interpreted as signifying a weakening of the links between Dublin and the viking homeland. This may well be true. The international standing of the Hiberno-Norse penny is quite another matter. Archaeological evidence and historical research has shown that Dublin carried on a substantial business, including a flourishing slave trade, with Britain and Europe at this

---

[17] Michael Kenny, 'Hiberno-Norse coinage', awaiting publication.
[18] John D. Brand, *Periodic change of the type in the Anglo-Saxon and Norman period* (Rochester, 1984), p. 27.

time. The obvious conclusion must be that coin was by no means an essential element in such activities—a point that economists would do well to remember when discussing so-called 'monetary economies' in this period. The idea of coinage as a barometer of economic activity holds up poorly to critical examination.

During the 1030s the issues already described gave way to a new coinage of noticeably poorer stylistic and literary quality. The legends were by now largely garbled and meaningless. The increasingly anepigraphic nature of this and succeeding issues make it difficult to date the various types with any degree of precision. The earliest coins of this group were slightly heavier than the later coins of the preceding group, suggesting a reformation similar to that of *c*.1020. The basic model continued to be the long-cross penny but there was a growing use of symbolism, such as hands on the reverse and various devices around the stylised bust on the obverse. The chronological span of this particular group corresponds roughly to the period of dominance of Diarmait mac Máil na mBó, who subdued not only Dublin but also Wexford and Waterford, and whose son Murchad was described in the Annals as 'lord of the Norse'. The effectiveness of Diarmait's authority is hard to estimate and it is unclear what if any influence he may have exerted over the minting of coins. Certainly there is no evidence on the actual coins of any involvement on his part, nor even the slightest reference to his position or pretensions. It is also worth noting that there is no concentration of hoards in Diarmait's home territory of north Wexford comparable to that of west Meath in the previous century, when the Clann Cholmáin had sacked Dublin at regular intervals. Either Diarmait had no interest in monetary matters, or his attitude towards Dublin was more political than that of his predecessors.

In the 1050s a brief issue of coins struck from partly engraved rather than punched dies, appeared, but was soon replaced by yet another issue known as 'Dolley Phase V'.[19] The coins of this group, for which a date range of *c*.1065–95 has been suggested, present a most confusing array of styles and motifs, some harking back to the end of the previous century, some derived from Hiberno-Norse issues of the intervening period, and some quite obviously copied from contemporary Anglo-Saxon and Norman issues. In terms of the style, weight, and design these coins leave much to be desired. They turn up but rarely outside Ireland, which is interesting when one considers the busy overseas trade that Dublin conducted throughout this period.[20] Clearly, the city's economic activity was by no means dependent upon a well-ordered or centralised monetary system. It should

[19] Dolley, *Sylloge*, pp 134–9.
[20] Patrick F. Wallace, 'The English presence in viking Dublin' in M. A. S. Blackburn (ed.), *Anglo-Saxon monetary affairs* (Leicester, 1986), pp 208–13; Aubrey Gwynn, 'Medieval Bristol and Dublin' in *I.H.S.*, v, no. 20 (Sept. 1947), pp 275–86.

also be pointed out that late Anglo-Saxon and early Norman coins are rarely found in Ireland, reinforcing the point made earlier regarding coins and trading patterns. By this time the average weight of the silver penny was a mere 0.5 g—less than 40 per cent of the weight of Sitric's earliest coins. A final issue of light and extremely crude pieces brought to an end the 'reign' of the long-cross penny some time during the early decades of the twelfth century.

T HE relative paucity of hoard evidence for the last 'bracteate' phase of the pre-Norman coinage (there are only two substantial finds, one from County Down and one from County Cork) makes the numismatic history of this period even more obscure than previously. The coins, which were extremely light (the word 'bracteate' comes from the Latin *bractea*, a leaf), may be divided into two sub-groups, one composed of coins with an attempted design on both sides, the other with a design on one side only. The former are known as semi-bracteates, the latter as pure bracteates. Stylistically the coins are quite unlike the issues that preceded them, and it has been suggested that they may have been produced under Irish rather than viking authority. Toirrdelbach Ua Conchobair, in particular, has been mentioned in this regard, principally because of the claim made in *Cambrensis eversus*: 'argentumque postea Clonmacnoisiae signare jussit.'[21] The claim has not, however, been backed up by any coins attributable to Toirrdelbach or to Clonmacnoise. No hoards of bracteates have been found in the vicinity of Clonmacnoise, or indeed anywhere in Connacht. Toirrdelbach's own kingdom was the one where a coinage would have been least expected on economic grounds. If he did involve himself in the striking of coins, the most likely motivating force would have been the desire to make a political statement—something that could not be achieved by an anonymous coinage which carried neither the name nor title of the issuing authority. The bracteates, therefore, remain something of a mystery, although it must be stressed that their evolution was not solely an Irish phenomenon. The twelfth century saw the development of bracteate coinages in several parts of northern Europe, especially in Germany, Poland, and Scandinavia,[22] and it is within this wider context that one should view the Irish bracteates, rather than as an obscure postscript to the Hiberno-Norse series. Irish monetary history has traditionally been viewed in the context of what was taking place in England,

[21] John Lynch, *Cambrensis eversus*, ed. Matthew Kelly (3 vols, Dublin, 1848), ii, 60–61, where this passage appears in the English version as '[he] founded a royal mint at Clonmacnoise'.
[22] Arthur Engel and Raymond Serrure, *Traité de numismatique du moyen âge* (3 vols, Paris, 1894), ii, 848–72; R. A. G. Carson, *Coins, ancient, medieval, and modern* (London, 1962), pp 333–40, 389–94, 398–9.

and because that country did not develop a bracteate coinage there has been a tendency to regard its appearance in Ireland as a sign of decay and decline.

Who or what was the issuing authority? The question is just as pertinent for the 1050s as for the 1150s. The domination of Dublin by strong Irish kings pre-dates the bracteate phase by a full century, so that there could hardly have been a genuinely independent Hiberno-Norse coinage from the middle of the eleventh century onwards. The proliferation of designs, motifs, and styles suggests the absence of a strong centralised minting authority. Since the political and propaganda element is absent, there is a distinct possibility that the coins were actually struck by city merchants or traders and might more properly be designated as tokens.[23] One of the problems in this regard is that the political history of the period is rather unclear. What is fairly clear, however, is that kings such as Diarmait mac Máel na mBó of Leinster, Toirrdelbach Ua Briain of Munster, and Toirrdelbach Ua Conchobair of Connacht, who at different times controlled Dublin, have left no trace whatever on its coinage.

A GROWING body of evidence suggests that by the end of the tenth century the Irish, especially in Meath, were by no means ignorant of coin and its uses. It follows that distinctions between users and non-users of coin, if they have any validity at all, should be made on a regional basis, rather than in simple Irish-versus-viking terms. With regard to the vikings themselves, it must be stressed that coinage was but one element, and by no means the most significant one, in their trading activities. It formed but a small portion of the silver wealth of the period and one should be careful not to read too much into its absence from a given region, trade route, or excavation site.

On the question of the Hiberno-Norse coinages, there are a number of points to be kept in mind. The advent of a Dublin coinage in the 990s was not an isolated event, but part of a wider development in the viking world. It came at a time when, in the words of one numismatist, 'the Baltic was awash with silver in the form of both coin and bullion, and trade apparently thrived'.[24] The direction that it subsequently took, away from weight, parity, and stylistic similarity with the Anglo-Saxon prototype, was the result neither of political growth nor economic decline. The suggestion that the Dublin penny was unable to retain international acceptance begs the question: did it seek such acceptance? If it was intended essentially for local use,

[23] Kenny, 'Hiberno-Norse coinage'.

[24] M. A. S. Blackburn, 'An imitative workshop active during Aethelraed II's long cross issue' in C. J. Becker (ed.), *Studies in northern coinages of the eleventh century* (Copenhagen, 1981), p. 56. See also Kolbjorn Skaare, *Coins and coinage in viking-age Norway* (Oslo, 1976), and 'Mints in viking-age Scandinavia' in *Proceedings of the Eighth Viking Congress* (Odense, 1981), pp 37–42; B. Ahlstrom, B. F. Brekke, and B. Hemmingsson, *The coinage of Norway* (Stockholm, 1976), p. 12; Kirsten Bendixen, *Denmark's money* (Copenhagen, 1967), pp 17–23.

foreign acceptance was irrelevant. Analysis, too, has shown that, whereas the weight of the coinage decreased, the purity of the silver did not, or at least did so to a far lesser degree.[25] Heslip's observation on this point, that 'reduction in weight is more likely to be a declared devaluation, whereas debasement tends more to fraud',[26] is worth remembering. On the question of style and fabric there are numerous examples, from Athens in the fifth century B.C. to Florence in the fifteenth century A.D., where the coinage failed completely to reflect the economic or cultural preeminence of the issuing city.[27] For example, the silver denarius of Venice, one of the major political and economic powers of the Mediterranean world, weighed a mere 0.4 g by 1200 and contained only 25 per cent silver.

The anonymous nature of those Dublin issues that post-date Sitric III, and the absence of any political message, suggest that they may have been produced by a merchant oligarchy. If so, then perhaps we should be concentrating more on the basic question of use and function rather than design, fabric, or political content. The answers to many of the questions and contradictions are as likely to be provided by archaeological and historical study as by numismatics. Staying with numismatics, however, it must be said that the parallels between Dublin and the rest of the viking world throughout this period are indeed striking. The developments of the eleventh and twelfth centuries should be seen in this context rather than as mere steps on the road to decline and decay.

[25] Heslip, 'Reflections on Hiberno-Norse coinage', p. 29. The parallels with Scandinavia are worth noting. The Norwegian bracteates of the twelfth century, for example, reached a low of 0.1 g, while retaining a fineness of about 90 per cent silver (Ahlstrom, Brekke, & Hemmingsson, *Coinage of Norway*, pp 16–19).

[26] Heslip, 'Reflections on Hiberno-Norse coinage', p. 29.

[27] Grierson, *Numismatics*, pp 4–5.

# CHAPTER XXIV

# Ireland before the battle of Clontarf

F. J. BYRNE

IN the autumn of 913 a fleet of hungry vikings arrived in Munster.
The 'Anglo-Saxon Chronicle' tells us that they had come from Brittany to
the Bristol Channel earlier in the year, that they had raided all around the
Welsh coast, captured Cyfeiliog, bishop of Archenfield, who was ransomed
by King Edward for forty pounds of silver; that their subsequent attempts at
plundering further inland had been thwarted by the forces of Hereford and
Gloucester, and that they had finally been stranded starving on the island of
Steepholm off Barry, on the coast of south Wales, whence they moved to
Dyfed and Ireland. They were led by two jarls, Hroald and Ottar, and the
latter's arrival in Britain is mentioned briefly in the Welsh annals. Hroald
and Ottar's brother had been killed by the English, but the Irish annals take
up the story of Ottar himself.

That the fleet had come from Brittany is significant. A year or two earlier
the fateful cession of the neighbouring north-western coast of Francia by
Charles the Simple to the viking Hrolf the Ganger resulted in the eventual
settlement of these 'Northmen' to become the Christian and gallicised
'Normans' of Normandy. But determined efforts by other vikings to win
such concessions around the lower reaches of the Loire proved ultimately
unsuccessful. Over the previous century the viking attacks had proved
indirectly beneficial to the Bretons: they threw off the subjection to the
Carolingian empire that had been imposed by Louis the Pious, and between
857 and 874 Solomon was able to style himself an independent monarch:
*gratia Dei totius Britanniae rex* (by the grace of God, king of all Brittany).The
Breton church broke away from the archbishop of Tours and proclaimed
metropolitan status for the bishop of Dol, and the royal title was assumed
again by Alan the Great, count of Vannes, after his defeat of the vikings at
Questembert in 888. The independence of Brittany from Francia is even
recognised in the 'Anglo-Saxon Chronicle' at its notice of the accession of
Charles the Fat in 885: here and in their account of Ottar's fleet the term

used for Brittany is *Lidwiccas* or *Lioðwiccas*, corresponding to the Welsh *Llydaw*.[1]

But Hroald and Ottar had been too hasty in their retreat from Brittany, for in fact that country experienced the most devastating effects of viking warfare in the decades following Alan's death in 907. Both nobles and clergy fled to Francia and England, scattering abroad the relics of Breton saints and the products of Breton libraries (including the most important manuscripts of the Irish canon law collections). Even Nantes and the Loire were briefly ceded to viking control in 921 by Robert of Neustria (later Robert I of France). Alan's son-in-law, Matuédoi of Poher, died in exile at the court of Aethelstan in England, and it was with the support of that king that Matuédoi's son Alan Barbetorte was able to stage a reconquest in 937. Aethelstan, 'the Pierpont Morgan of his age',[2] was an avid collector of holy books and relics as well as a protector of foreign princes: among his collection was the Armagh evangeliary presented to him by Mac Durnan, abbot of Armagh and Iona. He was foster-father of Hákon the Good, first Christian king of Norway, and gave shelter to Louis d'Outremer, son of the ousted Charles the Simple.

Jarl Ottar (called *Oitir Dub*, 'Oitir the Black', by the 'Cocad Gáedel re Gallaib') proceeded to Munster and established himself at Waterford. The province seems to have been in disarray, without a king of Cashel, since the death of Cormac mac Cuilennáin at the battle of Belach Mugna in 908. The annals tell us that Flaithbertach mac Inmainén (Cormac's evil genius, according to the saga account) took the kingship in 914; but if he did this in response to the new viking threat, he seems to have been ineffective. The saga says that he had retired to his monastery of Inis Cathaig after the battle, but reemerged after a few years to assume the kingship, which he held for thirty-two years.[3] However, this seems to be a mere inference on the part of the writer from the meagre data in the Annals of Inisfallen, which say no more about him after 914 till his obit in 944. The Four Masters, however, record his abdication into religious retirement in 922 and his capture at the culdee retreat of Monahincha the following year by vikings who took him to Limerick. They also note that he was succeeded as king of Cashel by Lorcán mac Conlígáin, but this information they may have simply taken from the regnal lists. Neither these nor the annals give any information as to the length of Lorcán's reign or the date of his death. The genealogies inform us

---

[1] Old Welsh *Litau*, the Celtic and Latin *Letavia*; in Irish the same word occurs as *Lethae* but is most frequently used for the Continent in general: the otherwise loquacious Irish authorities seem to have had a blind spot as far as Brittany was concerned.

[2] Christopher Brooke, *The Anglo-Saxon and Norman kings* (London, 1963), p.132.

[3] That Flaithbertach (whose origin is totally obscure) was abbot of Inis Cathaig seems only to be recorded by Keating, but he was drawing on the saga of the battle of Belach Mugna, the beginning of which is missing from the 'Fragmentary Annals'.

that he was of the Cenél Conaill branch of the Éoganacht Caisil, and again the Four Masters record the killing of his father in 903 in revenge for his assassination of the deposed Cenn nGécáin (Cormac's predecessor) the previous year. No more is known of the kingship of Cashel until the appearance of Cellachán Caisil in a less than heroic role, when he led the Munstermen in an attack on Clonmacnoise in 936. He raided Clonenagh and Killeigh and plundered Mide as far as Clonard in 939, and repeated his attacks on Clonmacnoise in 951 and 953.

While the account of the total devastation of Munster by Ottar and his associates in the 'Cocad' is undoubtedly exaggerated (claiming that Munster suffered half of all the depredations in Ireland),[4] and is marred by chronological confusion, it is probably correct in stating that the Waterford vikings formed themselves into three bands, which proceeded to raid from Cork, from Iny in County Kerry, and from an unidentified Glaslinn (probably west of Kinsale). The contemporary annals for Munster are too sparse to confirm the details but they do record the arrival of a great fleet at Waterford in 914, reinforced by another the following year, and their devastation of Munster, including attacks on Cork, Lismore and right up the Nore as far as Aghaboe in the far north of Ossory. In 916 the Annals of Ulster record the killing of the king of Uaithne Cliach in north-east Limerick by the Waterford vikings, and again their devastation of both Munster and Leinster, while the Annals of Inisfallen add the death at their hands of another petty king, Gébennach of Uí Chonaill Gabra in west Limerick. The 'Cocad' is probably drawing on contemporary sources for other details, such as the invasion of Múscraige and Uí Chairpre and the deaths of Domnall mac Donnchada of Cashel and of Loingsech king of Uaithne Tíre.[5]

About the same time the Welsh annals record the ravaging of Ireland and an invasion of Anglesey. With the last notice we may possibly connect the naval battle off the Isle of Man in 914, which the Annals of Ulster mention just before the arrival of the fleet at Waterford. Here Ottar's son Barith was defeated and slain by a formidable rival, Ragnall the grandson of Ivar of the

---

[4] *Cog. Gaedhel*, pp 38–41: 'Imtusa imorro na Mumhan ocus Cloinne Imhair inister sunn coleicc, dóigh ro-fodaimsiot a n-aenar leth-dochair ocus dochraite re hErinn uile. Tanic dia Oitir Dubh iarla lucht .c. long co Port Lairge ocus ro-hindradh airther Muman ocus a deiscert ocus ro-thairbhir fo chain ocus fo gheillsine Gall uile iad ocus ro-thoccaibh a chios roghda forra. Do lionadh Mumha uile do thola eradbhail ocus do murbhrucht diaisneisi long ocus laidheng ocus cobhlach conach raibhe cuan na caladhphort no dún no daingen no dingna i Mumhain uile gan longeas Danmarccach ocus Allmurach.' ('We proceed now to relate here the history of the [men of] Mumhain and of the sons of Imar, for they alone sustained half the troubles and oppressions of all Erinn. The earl, Oiter Dubh, came with an hundred ships to Port Lairge, and the east of Mumhain was plundered by him, and its south; and he put all under tribute and service to the foreigners; and he levied his royal rent upon them. The whole of Mumhain became filled with immense floods, and countless sea-vomitings of ships, and boats, and fleets, so that then was not a harbour, nor a landing-port, nor a dún, nor a fortress, nor a fastness, in all Mumhain, without fleets of Danes and pirates.')

[5] Ibid., p. 30.

dynasty that had evacuated Dublin in 902.[6] Welcome or not, Ragnall appears to have proceeded to Waterford in 915 and taken control of operations.

The return of the grandsons of Ivar was recognised on all sides as marking a new and most unwelcome phase. None of our sources tells us whether Ivar, Ragnall, Gothfrith, and Sitric were brothers or cousins. While the Norse invariably used patronymics, these have not survived: the Irish, in their usual fashion, referred to them by the name of their most renowned ancestor, the 'king of the Northmen of all Ireland and Britain' who had died in 873, rather than by their less distinguished father or fathers.[7] This in itself is an indication of familiarity—if not necessarily of affection—on the part of the Irish.

The north of Ireland was more prepared both intellectually and militarily than Munster for the new turn of events. This may be an accidental impression due to the nature of our sources. Nevertheless, our main authority is still the Armagh annals, and the school there was better placed than usual to appreciate what was happening, for it had now close relations with Scotland. A revival of the Columban church in Ireland and Scotland may have been made possible by a relative quietude in the Isles, due to the conversion of a number of the settled Norse and the emigration of many of them to Iceland. A generation earlier in 878 the shrine and relics of Colum Cille had come to Ireland in flight before them. A union between Armagh and Iona had taken place in the person of Máel Brigte mac Tornáin, 'Máel Brigte edón na hoentad' (i.e., 'of the Unity),[8] who held office at Armagh from 883 and titularly at Iona from 891 till his death in 927. His successor, the bishop Joseph mac Fathaig (927–36), was of the Dál Riata, thus maintaining the Scottish connection.

The fact that Máel Brigte was installed as early as 883 may indicate that the union was contemplated beforehand, since he was the first abbot of Armagh to have come of the Cenél Conaill. He has achieved some fame as the donor of the fine illuminated manuscript 'Mac Durnan's Gospels' now at Lambeth Palace in London, which he presented as a gift to King Aethelstan. A note in the twelfth-century Corpus Gospels indicates the presence at Aethelstan's court of another noted Irish ecclesiastic (who may well have been Máel Brigte's envoy), Dub Innse bishop of Bangor, who learned there from 'a certain Frank and a learned Roman Jew' the intriguing game of *alea evangelii* ('Gospel dice').[9] Dub Innse died in 953 and seems to have been a

---

[6] It is just possible, but seems less likely, that Barith was son of the Jarl Ottar who was killed in Mercia in 911.

[7] Ragnall is the Irish form of a name which was probably Ragnar, like that of his reputed great-grandfather, but it could also represent another Norse name, Røgnvald, which seems to be indicated by the English and Scottish sources. On his coins he is called RAIENALT.

[8] See H. J. Lawlor and R. I. Best, 'The ancient list of the coarbs of Patrick' in *R.I.A. Proc.*, xxxv (1919), sect. C., pp 316–62: 327, 360.

[9] See Kuno Meyer, 'The Laud genealogies and tribal histories' in *Z.C.P.*, viii (1912), pp 292–338: 413.

member of the Ua Brolcháin family so prominent in Irish ecclesiastical affairs (particularly in Armagh and Derry, but also at Kildare and in Ossory) in the eleventh and twelfth centuries. He was grandfather of Máel Muire mac Eochada, the Clann Sínaig abbot of Armagh who died in 1020, and also of the famous religious poet Máel Ísu Ua Brolcháin, who died at Lismore in 1086 (the chronological discrepancy is by no means unparalleled in the Irish genealogical record: Máel Muire was born in 963 and Máel Ísu was evidently quite old at his death; his son died in 1095 and a pupil of his in 1091). Further connections of the Ua Brolcháin family with Bangor may be seen in the alleged blessing given to their remote ancestor Díchu (grandfather of Brolcháin) by Máel Rubai, coarb of Comgall and founder of Applecross in Scotland (he died in 722 at the age of 80)—like the Uí Brolcháin he was a member of the Cenél nÉogain (of the Cenél mBinnig), whereas they were of the Cenél Feradaig. An uncle of Dub Innse's bore the unusual name Máel Gaimrid, which was also that of the well-known abbot of Bangor who died in 839 and who is quoted as an authority in the Milan glosses on the psalms. The manifold ecclesiastical and political interests of the Ua Brolcháin family suggest that one of them (perhaps the Máel Brigte mac in tSaír who was bishop of Kildare from 1042 to 1097, and whose father was probably the *prím-sháer Érenn*, 'chief wright of Ireland' who died in 1029) was the compiler of the so-called 'Fragmentary Annals'. Mac Neill suggested that their family tree, uniquely preserved in Laud Misc. 610, may have been drawn up by Dub dá Leithe III, son of the abbot Máel Muire and himself firstly *fer léigind* and subsequently abbot of Armagh (1049–64); the lost Book of Dub dá Leithe is cited as an authority in the Annals of Ulster and in Rawl. B 512.

It was during Máel Brigte's tenure of office too that St Catroe of Metz, who may have been a Briton of Strathclyde, travelled from Scotland to Armagh to perfect his studies (though it may be noted that the wisdom he sought there was secular and not religious).

Máel Brigte travelled to Munster in 913 in order to redeem British captives. They were no doubt victims of the harrying of Strathclyde by the Norse which is recorded in the final sentence of the 'Fragmentary Annals': 'Æthelflæd through her own cleverness made peace with the men of Alba and with the Britons, so that whenever the same race should come to attack her, they would rise to help her... The king of the Lochlannaig came after that and ravaged Strathclyde and plundered the land. But the enemy was ineffectual against Strathclyde.' The passage occurs immediately after an acount of how great armies of the Dub-Gaill and Finn-Gaill came to attack England 'after Sitriuc ua Ímair had been made king' and how the queen defeated the pagans after their king had been taken ill and died in a forest beside the battle-ground, and Jarl Ottar had fled into the forest and been slaughtered with his followers. It is not clear whether the kingdom won by

Sitriuc ua hÍmair was that of Dublin, but the account sounds like a version of the defeat of the great Northumbrian force that had invaded Mercia in 911 and which, according to the 'Anglo-Saxon Chronicle', was defeated by Edward the Elder, brother of Æthelflæd, with the slaughter of two Norse kings, Healfdene and Eowils, the earl Ohtere, and nine other named notables. This apparently was after the battle of Tettenhall in the same year, after which we are told that Æthelflæd fortified *Bremesburg*. Due to the somewhat clumsy incorporation of the so-called 'Mercian Register' into some copies of the 'Anglo-Saxon Chronicle' at this period, the precise sequence of events is uncertain, and it is possible that duplication of the same event (the battle of Tettenhall) has occurred.

Niall Glúndub's mother was Máel Muire, daughter of Cináed mac Ailpín, and her death is noted in the Annals of Ulster under the year 913. It is not impossible that the Anglo-Saxon annalist of York was correct when he asserted that Niall was brother to the Sitric who slew him in 919, for Máel Muire may have been married also to a son of Ivar. Perhaps she was the 'daughter of Cináed' alleged in the 'Fragmentary Annals' to have been put aside by Olaf and desired by Auisli. At any rate, Áed Findliath had had Norse allies in his storming of Dún Sobairche in 871, and a marriage alliance had been made with some Norse settled on Lough Swilly or Lough Foyle under the leadership of Barith or his son Uathmarán—Barith (Barðr) had been king of Dublin and foster-father of Eystein son of Olaf.

DID the decline of Uí Néill power and the even more obvious collapse of their solidarity in the eleventh century actually aid the acceptance of the 'official doctrine' of their former supremacy? It is clear that the Cenél nEógain were quite ineffective outside their immediate sphere of influence from 1036 to 1080. That they were no more powerful than their rivals the Cenél Conaill is shown by references in the Annals of Inisfallen. These give us a fresh perspective: apart from the primacy of Armagh the North has become almost isolated from the rest of Ireland. The process had begun in 827 with the absorption of Airgialla (except for the Mugdorna) into the sphere of influence of the Cenél nEógain, and it was completed by the failure of Domnall ua Néill in 970 to establish himself as high-king of all Ireland by controlling Mide. The break between the Northern and Southern Uí Néill was confirmed by the refusal of the former to aid Máel Sechnaill against Brian Bóruma's ambitions.

Flaithbertach Ua Néill had moved in 1015 to help Máel Sechnaill reestablish his authority over Leinster, in the fond hope that he would succeed to the high-kingship in time-honoured fashion. But any solidarity that may once have existed among the Uí Néill had long since vanished. Flaithbertach's father Muirchertach Midech had been imposed by Domnall ua Néill as king of Mide in the previous century, which would not have endeared his son to the Southern Uí Néill. Furthermore, Flaithbertach did not win the support of his supposed vassals among the Airgialla. He was either unable to control his kinsmen when they made incursions into the territory of the Airthir in 1021 and 1024, or else he supported their aggression against them. Nor was there unity within the ruling dynasty, as is suggested by the dark hint, reported by Dub dá Lethe in the Annals of Ulster, that his uncle and predecessor Áed Ua Néill, victor over the Ulstermen at the battle of Cráeb Tulcha in 1004, had been slain in or after that battle by the Cenél nEógain themselves.

The far-flung lands of Cenél nEógain were divided by the Sperrins, and differences arose between Cenél nEógain na hInnse of Inishowen and Cenél nEógain Telcha Óc of Tullaghogue in Tyrone. The earliest mention of Tír Eógain as a political entity is in the Annals of Ulster 993 when Muirecán mac Ciarucáin from Bodoney, coarb of Patrick, 'conferred the degree of king' on Áed Ua Néill. However, in 1101 the Annals of Ulster employ the term Tír Eógain in the wider sense of the territory of Cenél nEógain, as the context shows. James Hogan suggested that Conaing mac Néill Glúnduib was the first to be associated with the move to Tullaghogue. His son or grandson Fergal succeeded Domnall in 980, but abdicated or was deposed in 989 or 993; he died in 1001. He is also called king of Ailech in 988, when he killed Laidcnén mac Cerbaill, king of Fernmag, at Armagh. Fergal's son Niall was killed *a genere suo* in 1015: the annals give him no title. Niall's sons Áed and Flaithbertach are both referred to as 'ua Fergail' and 'king of Tullaghogue' when they were killed, the first by the Fir Fernmaige in 1054 and the second by the Cenél mBinnig in 1068. They could have been called Ua Néill, since their ancestor Conaing was a son of Niall Glúndub. The hostility of the Fir Fernmaige is explicable in view of the killing of Laidcnén in 988, far back as that event was; that of the Cenél mBinnig perhaps by their loyalty to the Uí Néill, who had now virtually disappeared from the scene. All this suggests that Hogan's view may be mistaken, and that Fergal's descendants were supported by the Ailech over-kings against the 'true Ua Néill' grandsons of Flaithbertach. It is possible that Fergal had abdicated or been deposed by 993: if he was son rather than grandson of Conaing he would have been in his sixties. On the other hand, he might have held Ailech as a local title during the reign of Áed Ua Néill, though the latter is styled king of Ailech in his obit at 1004. There seems little reason to support Hogan in his view that the descendants of Niall Glúndub did not reside at Ailech: very possibly they did not, but they kept the title. Flaithbertach Ua Néill is 'high-king of Ailech' in his obit at 1036, and his son Áed 'king of Ailech and *rígdamna* of Ireland' in his at 1033. There is not much evidence for Hogan's theory that Conaing mac Néill Glúnduib established residence at Tullaghogue (Telach Óc), but it is likely that his base was in Tyrone, for in 933 he and his brother

Muirchertach were defeated at Mag Uatha (unidentified), by their cousin Fergal mac Domnaill, king of Ailech, and his half-Norse nephew Sichfraid mac Uathmarán (whose base would have been on Lough Foyle or Lough Swilly). Conaing's allies were killed: Máelgarb mac Garbíth, king of Derlas (the name does not occur in the Uí Thuirtre genealogies, but the editors of A.U. suggest that C. S. took the patronymic from the next entry, the obit of Célecán mac Garbíth king of Ind Airthir) and Conmál mac Bruaturáin king of Tuath Achaid (unidentified), who seems to have been of the Uí Echdach of Airthir.

In the same year Conaing, with the Norse of Lough Neagh, inflicted a defeat on the Ulaid at Ruba Con Congalt (also unidentified). Muirchertach's connections too were with the south: his mother was of the Conaille Muirtheimne. Muirchertach's son Domnall died at Armagh and relied during his high-kingship on his cousin Murchad Glún re Lár to be the local king in the North, and he enjoyed the title 'king of Ailech' in 970 and at his death in 974. Murchad was grandson of Flaithbertach son of Domnall mac Áeda. So the division between Inishowen and Tyrone seems to go back to the time of the brothers Domnall and Niall at the beginning of the tenth century.

THE events of 988 and 993 may foreshadow the later split between the dynasty which controlled the site of Ailech, and that (the O'Neills) which was based at Tullaghogue. The annals tell us that the Cenél nEógain themselves intervened to prevent a breach between the ancestors of these two branches, Domnall and his brother Niall in 905. They cooperated in a raid on Tlachtga in 908. Domnall's son Flann died in 906 and Domnall retired into religious life in 911; he himself died in 915.

But the most damaging blow to Ua Néill prestige came from an unexpected quarter. The Ulstermen, both Dál Fiatach and Dál nAraide, hereditary foes of the Uí Néill since the dawn of history, had been reduced to frantic disarray by the battle of Cráeb Tulcha in 1004. All of their kings and sub-kings had been killed in a slaughter that stretched from their inauguration site at Crew Hill to Dunbo and Duneight. The loss, not merely of kings, but of *rígdamnai*, or persons eligible to be king, was disastrous: the years 1006 to 1108 saw no fewer than four would-be kings eliminate each other. Only the death of the victor palliated the gloom. But Flaithbertach Ua Néill did not rest on his uncle's laurels. In 1011 he burnt Duneight, both fort and bailey (*dún* and *baile*—the earliest occurrence of this word in the sense of settlement or 'town'—it may well be the origin of the English word *bailey*, conventionally associated with the Normans, but not attested in English until the thirteenth century and without a convincing French etymon or cognate). He took guarantor hostages from the latest king to emerge from the Ulster turmoil, and the following year he plundered as far as the Ards of Ulster, bringing back untold numbers of cattle and captives. That humans as well as cows should form a large part of the prey illustrates an unpleasant and increasingly frequent feature of Irish warfare.

Within the year the humiliated king, Niall mac Duib Thuinne, was defeated in battle and deposed by his namesake and close kinsman, Niall mac Eochada. He fled north to Dál nAraide, whence he returned twice to regain his throne, in 1014 and again in 1016. On the second attempt he and his allies, Domnall Ua Loingsig, king of Dál nAraide, and Conchobar Ua Domnalláin, king of Uí Thuirtre, were killed. 'Niall', say the Annals of Ulster, 'was triumphant'. He remained triumphant for the rest of his life and reign until his peaceful death in 1063, his only disappointment the premature death of the son he had hopefully ordained as his successor. The relative silence of the annals about internal Ulster affairs indicates that he kept the province under control: he was able to rely on the loyalty of Conchobar Ua Loingsig, king of Dál nAraide, and it is worthy of notice that the few raids that the Cenél nEógain were able to make into Ulster (apart from one in 1027, and another into Uí Echach by Ua Néill in 1041) were across the Lower Bann into Dál nAraide: in 1030 they demolished Ua Loingsig's banqueting hall in Antrim; the Cenél mBinnig of Glenconkeine were no doubt the perpetrators, for he lost no time in slaying their *muire*, Máel Dúin mac Ciarmeic. When Conchobar was killed in 1046, it was by a member of his own family in Leinster, where the Ulster nobility had been forced to seek sustenance due to famine in their own land.

THE Clann Cholmáin of Mide fared no better: in contrast to the polyphiloprogenitive proclivities of the Cenél nEógain, they were represented only by the family of Ua Maíl Sechnaill, all descended from Flann Sinna, the great-grandfather of Máel Sechnaill II. As they did not proliferate into septs, so they did not expand their territories. Máel Sechnaill had effectively crushed the Síl nÁeda Sláine of Brega, and his rule theoretically extended from the Shannon to the sea. As Tara was now under his immediate control, he could use the title 'king of Tara' with some impunity: the Northern Uí Néill were no longer in a position to assert hegemony in the midlands. This was the purpose behind his revival of the Óenach Tailten in 1008, after his effective deposition from the high-kingship by Brian Bóruma. This was the claim made for him by his panegyrist Cuán ua Lothcháin. This too was his aim in replacing the Armagh coarb of Colum Cille by his own nominee, Ferdomnach, as abbot of Kells. The negative aspect was to be (since none of his successors were able to build upon his own previous exploits of bringing Dublin under his control, nor to extend their rule beyond their over-kingdom) that Tara was to become the appellation, not of the pretender to the high-kingship of all Ireland, but of the provincial king of a Meath that extended beyond the limits of ancient Mide to cover Brega to the east and

Tethba to the north. But when Áed Mac Crimthainn compiled his regnal lists in the Book of Leinster, he pointedly entitled them 'kings of Uisnech' after the mythological umbilical centre of Ireland that was the focus of ancient Mide. This title is never found in the contemporary annals; by using it, Áed wished to deny Ua Maíl Sechnaill whatever prestige still clung to the kingship of Tara.

# CHAPTER XXV

# Ireland and her neighbours, *c*.1014–*c*.1072

F. J. BYRNE

BRIAN Bóruma did not create a high-kingship of Ireland: he built on foundations that had been laid over the preceding centuries by the Uí Néill, north and south. His claim to be *imperator Scottorum*, inscribed by his notary Máel Suthain in the Book of Armagh on his visit there in 1005, may indeed have implied overlordship not merely of Ireland but also of the Gaelic realm in Britain, and such wider authority is implied in the unusually fulsome obituary accorded him by the Armagh annalist. It curiously anticipates Toynbee's concept of the 'abortive' north-western civilisation embracing Saxon, Celt, and Dane that was brought to an end by the Norman conquest of England: *Brian m. Cennetigh ard-rí Gaidhel Erenn 7 Gall 7 Bretan August iartair-tuaiscirt Eorpa uile...* ('Brian mac Cennétig high-king of the Gael of Ireland and of the Gaill and of the Britons and Augustus of the whole of north-western Europe...').

In 1014 Máel Muire, coarb of Patrick, 'went with the seniors and relics to Sord Coluim Cille (Swords) and brought thence the body of Brian king of Ireland and the body of Murchad his son and the head of Conaing and the head of Mothla, so that he was buried at Armagh in a new tomb. Twelve nights were the community of Patrick waking the bodies on account of the honour due to the king who was placed there'. In spite of this eulogy (not echoed in the Munster Annals of Inisfallen), and the elaborate obsequies at Swords and Armagh, Brian's pyrrhic victory of Clontarf had exposed the weakness of his high-kingship: he had been supported merely by the forces of Munster, southern Connacht, and some allies from Scotland against a revolt of Leinster and Dublin aided by Sigurd of Orkney; Máel Sechnaill, the former high-king and until now Brian's subordinate, held aloof, while both the Northern Uí Néill and their enemies of Ulster ignored the whole affair. As late as 1152, Bishop Find ua Cianáin of Kildare was to rank the battle of Clontarf among the victories of the Leinstermen in the verses he added to Cináed ua hArtacáin's poem 'Fiana batar i nEmain' in the Book of Leinster.

Yet perhaps the title 'Augustus' was not entirely a vain boast. Armagh appreciated Brian, if Irish kings and the clergy of Emly and Clonmacnoise did not. The Christian English core of Æthelstan's and Edgar's *imperium* of the Orbis Britanniae, for which Probus and perhaps St Dunstan had sought Armagh's approval and the patronage of St Patrick, had just been conquered by Svein Forkbeard, the pagan king of Denmark. Domnall mac Eimín, *mormáer* of Marr, had fallen on Brian's side. The last British kingdom north of Wales was about to be absorbed into Scotland, as was the northern half of English Bernicia. Wales was without a king of Deheubarth in the south (unless the probably Irish Aeddan map Blegywryd be counted as such), and if the annalist of St David's did not eulogise Brian he devoted a long entry to the battle. Even the cool Emly scribe said that it had resulted in 'a slaughter of the Norse of the western world', and it was long remembered in the northern world as 'Brian's battle', an event that marked an era in Scandinavian history. In this context we should discount the hagiography of Brian in the 'Njálssaga': this is taken from an originally separate saga devoted to Brian which agrees too closely with the Ua Briain view of history to be independent; its origin may be sought in the Western Isles at a period when Man was under their influence or direct rule.

The second half of Sitric Silkbeard's reign in Dublin, from Brian's death in 1014 till 1036, coincided with that of Cnút in England and Denmark, and his death (perhaps in exile) in 1042 with the end of the Anglo-Danish empire. The alliance between Sitric and Cnút found its legacy in the foundation of Christ Church cathedral and the establishment of a bishopric in Dublin dependent on the see of Canterbury. But after the deposition of Sitric's successor Echmarcach in 1052 by Diarmait of Leinster, Dublin ceased to be an independent power on the Irish political stage. Henceforth its not inconsiderable role was to be as a supplier of military and naval forces, either to its various Irish overlords or to foreign adventurers.

The most famous, because the most successful, of these was Gruffydd ap Cynan, born in exile of an Irish mother in the 'commote of Colum Cille' at Swords. His Welsh Life, the 'Hanes' or 'Historia Hen',[1] translated from a Latin original composed in the 1160s for his son and successor Owein, king of Gwynedd from 1137 to 1170, elaborates on his connections with the royal families of Dublin, Leinster, Ulster, and Munster. Some of this may be fabulous, but the author had good information about the Irish kings, and if there is forgery it is such as would only impress a twelfth-century audience. Waterford and Wexford are referred to in Welsh renderings of their Irish names as Porth Larg and Llwch Garmawn, and Munster is called 'two parts of Ireland' in accordance with the theory of the Book of Rights. Gruffydd's first attempt in 1075 succeeded and failed, but in 1081 he brought an Irish

---

[1] D. Simon Evans (ed.), *Historia Gruffud vab Kenan* (Cardiff, 1977).

fleet and troops to help Rhys ap Tewdwr, when they won the famous battle of Mynydd Carn; the previous year St David's had been pillaged, and the Annals of Inisfallen record a naval expedition of Diarmait Ua Briain to Wales, from which he returned with great plunder.

Had Gruffydd not persisted, he would no doubt have been dismissed as an Irish impostor, as was the man who 'would have himself called Rhain' and claimed to be son of Maredudd, the king of Deheubarth who had died in 999. Aeddan ap Blegywryd, to judge by his name if not his patronymic, may have been another Irish pretender, who was briefly successful (we do not know for how long or in which region of Wales), till killed with his four sons by Llywelyn ap Seisyll in 1018.

The gaelicised Norse found a new power base in the Isle of Man and Galloway (*Gall-Goídil*, the land of the 'foreign Gaels' or gaelicised Norse), whither Echmarcach of Dublin had retired. Murchad son of Diarmait pursued him there, and he himself went into exile to Rome in 1064; Marianus Scottus records his death in 1065 as *rex inna Renn* 'king of the Rhinns (of Galloway)'. But the kingdom he had founded was re-established some ten years later by Godred Crovan or Gofraid Méránach, a refugee from the battle of Stamford Bridge and briefly (1090–94) to be king of Dublin. During the minority of Godred's son Olaf till 1114 it was to fall under Ua Briain rule, but thenceforth the kingdom of Man and the Isles was to be an important player in the history of Ireland and Scotland.

The success of Sitric effectively stopped Máel Sechnaill and his heirs from repeating his exploits of the 980s and 990s against Dublin, and the Southern Uí Néill of Mide were never to extend their power effectively to the coast, despite their nominal suzerainty over Brega. By the middle of the century an alliance between Niall mac Eochada of Ulster and Diarmait of Leinster shut off the Irish Sea from Northern and Southern Uí Néill alike. Although Conchobar Ua Maíl Sechnaill succeeded in maintaining internal stability for more than forty years, his final triumph over Diarmait of Leinster at the battle of Odba in 1072, when he carried the offensive into the Dublin territory of Fine Gall, was negatived by his assassination the following year. The final bankruptcy of his dynasty was to become painfully apparent over the course of the next generation.

BRIAN'S successor, Donnchad, was in no position to assume his father's mantle, and (perhaps more surprisingly) the Uí Néill were unable to resume their former leading role. Máel Sechnaill indeed was able to maintain himself once more as high-king till his death in 1022, but Brian's career had been a shattering blow to Uí Néill prestige. Much more important, however, was the fact that since 970 the Northern and Southern Uí Néill were no longer merely rivals, but irreconcilable foes, and the *selad* or gentleman's agreement of alternate succession to the kingship of Tara was never to be restored. The scholar who glossed the late ninth-century list of the kings of Tara, 'Baile in Scáil' (most probably Dub dá Lethe, abbot of Armagh) identified one of the prophesied kings with Flaithbertach Ua Néill, king of Ailech from 1004 to 1036, but Flaithbertach proved unable even to control the north of Ireland.

Flann Mainistrech of Monasterboice was the leading light among the 'synthetic historians' who shaped what was to remain for native scholars the official history of Ireland till the seventeenth century and beyond. He had been preceded by such figures as Máel Muru Othna, who wrote for Flann Sinna in the 880s and put into verse the main scheme of the 'Lebor Gabála' or Book of Invasions, and Eochaid ua Flannacáin of Armagh, 'the key to the lock of Ireland's ignorance', who died in 1004. The latter may not be identical with Eochaid ua Flainn who wrote also in the tenth or eleventh centuries and elaborated the 'Lebor Gabála', for the latter refers to himself as being of the Luigne, whereas the Armagh scholar was nephew of the abbot Dub dá Lethe II and himself ancestor of all the subsequent Clann Sínaig abbots.

Flann belonged to the ancient royal line of Cianachta Breg (Fir Arda of Ferrard), who were now hereditary abbots of Monasterboice. He himself was not abbot but *fer légind* ('lector' or head of the school), as was his father; this was an office second only in prestige to the abbacy, at least at Kells, Derry, and Armagh. Dub dá Lethe of Armagh was *fer légind* before succeeding his brother as abbot, and on his promotion the bishop Áed ua Forréid did not consider it beneath him to assume the lectorship. Flann's son Echtigern was abbot, but wrote some poems continuing Flann's interests; one of these is dedicated to his exact contemporary, the Áed ua hUalgairg who had a brief spell in the kingship of the North. The last recorded abbot of Monasterboice was Flann's grandson, 'the erenagh and learned priest Fergna mac Echthigeirn', who died in 1122.

Flann suffered the fate of many famous poets, in that the verses of inferior men were foisted upon him by later scribes. A pedestrian list of Patrick's household addressed to Clothna mac Maíl Enaig, abbot of Emly from 1046 to 1048, who had evidently cast aspersions on the abbatial court at Armagh, is hardly worthy of Flann, though its author claims that name. A piece of historically inaccurate doggerel listing the kings of Cashel up to Donnchad mac Briain is attributed to a 'Fland' in the Book of Leinster, though not in the hand of Áed mac Crimthainn. Of two poems on the kings of Mide and Brega which follow on Flann's Cenél nEógain suite in the same manuscript, the first was ascribed to Flann in a scribal note that was subsequently erased; it is clear that neither is his work. All three regnal poems occur also in the earlier manuscript, Rawl. B 502, which names no author. Characteristically, the compiler of the Rawlinson manuscript, who was a competent versifier, brings the Cashel and Mide poems right up to date. The Cashel poem is continued to conclude with the current reign of Cormac Mac Carthaig (thus anterior to 1138), and the Mide poem, which originally ended with the death

of Conchobar Ua Maíl Shechnaill in 1073, has six additional quatrains enumerating five further kings of Mide down to Donnchad mac Murchada
(d. 1106): these may have been written before 1127. It may be noted that
Rawlinson's poem on the kings of Ulster, 'Ulaid uaisle inse Fáil', seems to
end with the year 1127, though an illegible quatrain may have carried the
tale a little further, and the poem on the kings of Dál nAraide, 'A chlann
Chóelbad meic Cruind cruaid', ends with Domnall Ua Loingsig, who reigned
from 1130 to 1141. More likely to be a genuine product of Flann's, though
poorly preserved in late manuscripts, is the poem 'Cruithnig cid dos-farclam'
on the origin of the Picts, their adventures in Ireland, and their eventual
settlement in Scotland. The penultimate quatrain adverts to the Scottish
kings of Dál Riata who displaced the Picts, and should read:

> Cóeca ríg céim crechach maráen do Shíl Echach
> ó Fhergus ro-fírad co Mac mbrígach mBethath.
>
> (Fifty kings, a plundering stride, together of the Seed of Echu
> since Fergus, it has been verified, until vigorous Mac Bethad.)

Flann Mainistrech's regnal poem on the Christian kings of Tara, 'Ríg
Themra tóebaige iar tain', was written before 1022, and records the restor-
ation of Máel Sechnaill *conid é Érenn óen-rí*, 'so that he is the only king of
Ireland', and ends with a 'Long live our high-king': *corop suthain ar n-ard-rí*!
It was largely on his authority that the official doctrine of the monopoly of
the high-kingship by the Uí Néill from the time of St Patrick to the usurpation of Brian became accepted, even by the Munster Annals of Inisfallen.
The poems of Gilla Cáemáin mac Gilla Samthainne and of Gilla Mo Dutu
Ua Casaide, written in 1072 and 1143 respectively, merely elaborate Flann's
history. Gilla Cáemáin's contribution was to add regnal years to Flann's lists
both of prehistoric and Christian high-kings: Flann's declared purpose had
been to describe the manner of their deaths (*aideda*). Gilla Mo Dutu acknowledges that both the Munstermen and those of Ulster claim to have produced
high-kings in the past, but this does not alter the overall picture of effective
Uí Néill dominance.

However, in the long poem 'Rédig dam, a Dé do nim',[2] on the Kings of
the World from prehistoric times to the emperor Leo III, based on the
Eusebian World Chronicle and Bede, and written in 1056, the last year of his
life, when Niall mac Máil Sechnaill was king of the North and Dub dá Lethe
primate of the Irish church, Flann does not know of any high-king of
Ireland: he enumerates the six or seven kings of the day:

> Conchobur clannmín, fo-chen!
> Áed, Gairbíth, Díarmait dúrgen,

---

[2] See Seán Mac Airt, 'Middle Irish poems on world kingship' in *Études Celt.*, viii (1958–9),
pp 98–119.

Donnchad, dá Níall cen sním snéid
ríg na ré sea co roréid.

(Smooth-haired Conchobar, welcome!
Áed, Garbíth, hardy Diarmait,
Donnchad, two Nialls without swift sorrow,
are very evidently the kings of this era.)

These are Conchobar Ua Maíl Shechnaill of Mide, Áed Ua Conchobair of Connacht, Garbíth Ua Cathassaig of Brega, Diarmait mac Maíl na mBó of Leinster, Donnchad mac Briain of Munster, and the two Nialls (mac Maíl Shechnaill of Ailech and mac Eochada of Ulster). The ambivalent epithet *dúrgen*, literally 'hard birth', perhaps 'dour, strict, unfeeling' or 'firm, hardy, resolute', is also applied to Diarmait by Gilla Cáemáin in the final quatrain of his annalistic poem, recording his death in 1072. It seems to have been his stock epithet, for we find it, almost certainly in a complimentary sense in the *dindshenchas* poem of the Fair of Carman, ascribed to Fulartach, but in additional verses composed for Diarmait. In the early tenth century Dallán mac Móre had applied it to an earlier Diarmait, the grandfather of his patron Cerball mac Muirecáin.

The lost Book of Dub dá Lethe contained a text of 'Baile in Scáil' as well as an early version of the Annals of Ulster. The manuscript of the Annals of Inisfallen was written in 1092, probably at Emly, and the regnal list which precedes the post-Patrician section derives from one drawn up during the contest for supremacy between Congalach Cnogba and Ruaidrí ua Canannáin in the mid tenth century; it thus ignores the reigns of Domnall ua Néill and Máel Sechnaill, but that of Brian and the last nine years of Máel Sechnaill conclude the list. The regnal years assigned to the earlier kings are probably the work of the scribe, not part of his exemplar. Not here, but in the text of the annals under the year 721, he claims that five kings of Cashel had been high-kings of Ireland. The scheme of the prehistoric section, a version of the World Chronicle contaminated by the 'Lebor Gabála', cites Flann Mainistrech's poetic version composed in 1056, but the compiler seems unaware of the author's identity and calls him a *poeta* and a *fili*, almost certainly not titles that an ecclesiastical *ecnaid* like Flann would have wanted to claim. There are only two other apparent instances of the application of *fili* to a cleric. Máel Muru Othna is so styled at his obit in 888, but there is no hint that he was attached to a church: at least one of his works is addressed to a king. His name suggests that he came from Fahan, but it could be interpreted simply as 'the devotee of St Muru of Fahan'. Flann mac Maíl Máedóc ended his life in 979 as *airchinnech* of Killeshin and belonged to the hereditary clergy of that monastery. But he did not attain that office till some date after 953, and at least one of his poems was composed before 944. A possible link in the transmission of Flann's 'official doctrine' from Monasterboice and

Armagh to the Annals of Inisfallen may be found in the obit of Cathal Ua Forréid, evidently a close kinsman of Bishop Áed of Armagh, at Emly in 1088.

Flann devoted a series of poems to the exploits of the Cenél nEógain,[3] and was apparently on intimate terms with Dub dá Lethe's successor as *fer légind*, Áed Ua Forréid,[4] bishop of Armagh and himself a member of the Cenél nEógain dynasty of Cenél Tigernaig, but expresses disagreement with the teaching of 'Baile in Scáil' in a matter of prehistory, and quite plainly did not see Flaithbertach or any of his successors as realistic claimants to the high-kingship.

Flann's primary allegiance should have been to the Síl nÁeda Sláine, and indeed he wrote on the miraculous birth of their ancestor, versifying a text composed in the reign of Congalach Cnogba, who was buried at Monaster-boice in 956. It may have galled him to introduce the name of their sup-planter Garbíth into his verse. This circumstance, together with the encroachments of 'Diarmait dúrgen' and Niall mac Eochada into Brega, may have induced him to turn to the Cenél nEógain for patronage. He composed his poems on the kings and exploits of the Cenél nEógain in the reign of Niall mac Maíl Shechnaill (1036–61). His *dinnshenchas* poem on Ailech opens with a graceful apology for plagiarism, borrowed from a ninth-century Irish commentary on the Psalms, but ultimately from an early Life of Virgil: *d'éis Echdach áin iss gait a chlaidim ó láim Ercoil*, 'after glorious Eochaid it is stealing his sword [Flann should have said club] from the hand of Hercules' to attempt to write on a subject that had been dealt with so well by Eochaid, Dub dá Lethe's grandfather. One of the poems was continued after Flann's death, bringing the history of Northern victories up to 1091, when Domnall ua Lochlainn killed Donn Slébe mac Eochada, king of Ulster, but it does not call him king of Ireland. And when enumerating those kings of the dynasty who had attained the kingship of all Ireland, Flann does not include Flaith-bertach's name. Nor indeed do the Armagh annalists acknowledge any king of Ailech as high-king of Ireland before Domnall ua Lochlainn, and then only in his obituary at 1121: *Domnall mac Ardgair meic Lochlainn ard-rí Érenn*. They had given the title 'king of Ireland' to his rival Muirchertach Ua Briain at his death two years earlier.

After 1022 the annals use the title 'king of Tara' no longer in a national sense, but merely for the king of Mide, who now was overlord of Brega and so had Tara within his domain. So too in the south the title 'king of Cashel' has a merely local significance, referring to the head of the Éoganacht Caisil, represented in the eleventh century by the descendants of Donnchad son of

---

[3] See Eoin MacNeill, 'Poems by Flann Mainistrech on the dynasties of Ailech, Mide and Brega' in *Archivium Hibernicum*, ii (1913), pp 37–99.

[4] Gerard Murphy, 'A poem in praise of Aodh Ua Foirréidh, bishop of Armagh (1032–1056)' in Sylvester O'Brien (ed.), *Measgra i gcuimhne Mhichíl Uí Chléirigh* (Dublin, 1944), pp 140–64.

Cellachán Caisil. The O'Briens reserved to themselves the title 'king of Munster', when not actually claiming to be high-kings of all Ireland. The term Éoganacht came to be applied particularly to those of Loch Léin in west Munster, just as in the North 'Uí Néill' on its own referred primarily to the Cenél nEógain, rather than to the greater dynastic group.

What distinguished the great interregnum of 1022–72 from other periods of Irish history is that is was recognised as such by contemporary observers, apart from Dub dá Lethe and the self-styled 'king of Ireland', Donnchad son of Brian Bóruma, and by those who wrote in the following century.

After the death of king Moyleseaghlin this kingdome was without a king for the space of twenty years: Dureing which time the Realme was gouerned by two learned men, the one called Cwan o'Lochan, a well learned temporall man and cheefe poet of Ireland, the other Corcrann Cleireagh a devout and holy man, that was anchorite of all Ireland, whose most abiding was at Lismor. The land was Governed like a free state, & not like a monarchy by them.

So wrote Conell Mageoghegan in 1627, rendering into English the Annals of Clonmacnoise. This picture of a 'Free State', an Irish commonwealth or republic, is an historiographical curiosity. It is taken, not from the original Clonmacnoise annals, but from the twelfth-century Book of Leinster. Mageoghegan has misunderstood the passage in which Áed Mac Crimthainn described a *comflathius* or joint-rule of provincial kings in place of a high-kingship, and summarised the chief events of the interregnum, including the obits of the poet Cuán ua Lothcháin in 1024 and that of Corcrán Clérech of Lismore in 1040:

Joint sovereignty over Ireland for 42 years. Cuán Ua Lothcháin. Corcrán Clérech. Great snow. Amalgaid coarb of Patrick. The battle of Sliab Crott. Niall mac Eochada. Niall mac Maíl Shechnaill. Diarmait mac Maíl na mBó was king of Ireland with opposition [*rí Érenn co fressabra*]. The kings with opposition are thus reckoned in the royal succession: i.e, if the king be from Leth Cuinn [the northern half of Ireland], and he have all Leth Cuinn and one province of Leth Moga [the southern half of Ireland], then that man is king of Tara and of Ireland with opposition. But if he be from Leth Moga he is not called king of Ireland until he have all Leth Moga and Tara with its districts and one of two provinces of Leth Cuinn as well. Thus Mac Maíl na mBó was king of Ireland, since he had all Leth Moga and the Connachtmen and the men of Meath and the Ulstermen and the Airgialla. It was by him that Brian's son was expelled overseas.

The term *rí Érenn co fressabra*, a staple of the history books from the twelfth century to the twentieth, was most probably an invention of Áed's, who was abbot of Terryglass and court historian (*fer légind*—an ecclesiastical term now pressed into royal service) to Diarmait Mac Murchada. It was taken up by later versions of the 'Lebor Gabála' and also by some legal commentaries. For Áed it justified the claims both of Diarmait and of his great-grandfather and namesake. It could be argued that the 'high-kings with opposition' met with opposition precisely because they tried to become kings of Ireland in a real sense. They were not less successful than their predecessors, but only seemed so in the light of the teaching of the schools.

Evidence for the continued and growing exercise of royal jurisdiction is the appearance now in the annals of the king's officials: the *rechtaire*, the *muire*, the *air-rí*, and the *máer*. However, the *máer* of Dál Cais, Cú Macha Ua Cléirchén, killed by Mac Lochlainn in 1053, was not a Munsterman, still less a representative of Donnchad mac Briain, but the steward of Armagh in Munster. The peaceful obit of another of the same family, Óengus, is recorded in 1108. A Muiredach Ua Sínacháin was *máer* of Munster at his death in 1052; Cormac Ua Clothacáin in 1073, and Gilla Críst Ua Longáin in 1072. This office became hereditary in the Uí Bressail family of Ua Longáin, and their headquarters were at Ardpatrick in the south of County Limerick. Diarmait Ua Longáin is styled *máer Muman* in the Armagh Annals of Ulster in 1113, but *airchinnech* or *comarba* of Ardpatrick in the Clonmacnoise 'Chronicon Scotorum' and the Emly Annals of Inisfallen. Áed Ua Longáin's obit as *máer* of Munster is recorded in 1141. From them descend the well-known family of scribes and poets of the eighteenth and nineteenth centuries, concluding with the last professional scribe, Joseph O'Longan, who made the lithographic transcript of the Book of Leinster for the Royal Irish Academy in 1880.

Before the end of the eleventh century *máer* (Latin *maior*) always denotes a steward of church revenues. Between 814 and 929 the annals record the names of several of Armagh's stewards in Brega, including the abbot Muiredach, who died in 924, and who is commemorated on the cross named for him at Monasterboice. Mageoghegan renders the title of the last of these, Tuathal mac Óenucáin, scribe and bishop of Duleek and Lusk, as 'sergeant of St Patrick'. Under the same year the Annals of the Four Masters note the obit of Cáencomrac mac Maíl Uidir, abbot and bishop of Derry and *máer* of the Cáin Adomnáin; he was responsible for collecting the revenues due for enforcement of Adomnán's 'Law of the Innocents', which guaranteed the protection of women and children. In later times the title of *máer* was also applied to the hereditary keepers of such important relics as the Bachall Ísu, the Book of Armagh, and the Cathach of Colum Cille.

It would seem that the Ua Brolcháin family provided stewards of the Columban church in Ossory. The introduction to the ancient elegy on the saint, the 'Amra Choluim Chille', in the version found in Rawl. B 502, a Killeshin manuscript written in 1130, claims that the dues of Ossory are to be paid to the Cenél Feradaig, i.e., Ua Brolcháin, and the poem detailing these anticipates the actual visitation of Ossory made for this purpose by the great abbot of Derry, Flaithbertach Ua Brolcháin, in 1161. It even goes so far as to assert that Dallán Forgaill, author of the elegy, was of the Cenél Feradaig.

Máel Brigte mac int Saír Ua Brolcháin was bishop of Kildare from 1042 to 1095, having gained office when the abbacy was occupied by Sadb, grand-daughter of Selbachán, who may have been of Ossory origin, for Donnchad mac Gilla Phátraic of Ossory was king of Leinster from 1033 to 1039. The Fragmentary Annals from the lost Book of Clonenagh may have been com-piled by a woman of the Uí Brolcháin in the middle of the twelfth century.

But by the twelfth century kings in Ireland and in Wales were giving the title of *máer* to bailiffs responsible for the rural settlements that had come to be called *baile*, and also to administrators of newly acquired territories. In later legal texts *máer* replaces *rechtaire* as the title of a royal tax-gatherer or law-enforcement officer. Perhaps the first example in the annals of a secular *máer* occurs at 1095 with the obit of Glún Iarnn Ua Coinnéin as *máer* of Ormond: his obit occurs in the Annals of Inisfallen among the laity who fell victim to the great plague of that year, and he apparently belonged to the same family as Cenn Fáelad, the lector of Tomgraney who died in 1010. Thus he was a Dál Cais official whom Ua Briain had put in charge of the former Múscraige kingdom of Ormond. Similarly, a member of the Síl Muiredaig of Connacht, Ua Fallomuin of Clann Uatach, is called *máer* of Uí Maine in 1169, and would have been Ua Conchobair's man in that kingdom. On the other hand, Máel Ísu Ua hAirtrí, the *máer* of Connacht who died in 1123, was steward of Armagh's interests in the province.

The Scottish *mórmáer* (perhaps a term of Pictish origin, though often rendered as 'great steward') was quite another and more exalted person, the equivalent of the Norse jarl or English earl; the *mórmáer* of Moray was regarded as a king by the Irish. But both in Ireland and Scotland the *máer* is subordinate to a high-king or a primate for a portion, not the whole, of the latter's dominion. There is one example of an Irish *mórmáer*: the title is applied in the Annals of the Four Masters to Ragnall mac Turcaill of Dublin, whom the other annals style 'king'. Mac Turcaill (Thorkellsson) was defeated and killed by Flaithbertach Ua Cathassaig of South Brega in 1146. Ragnall may have been subordinate to Ottar of the Isles, who obtained the kingdom of Dublin in 1142 and held it till his death in 1148; the Welsh annals mention both Ottar and Ragnall as leaders of an Irish fleet brought to Aber-menai by Cadwaladr, the rebel brother of Owain Gwynedd in 1144. The last Norse king of Dublin, Askulf Mac Turcaill, was Ragnall's son, and it was to the Isles and to Orkney that he looked for support on his expulsion by Diarmait Mac Murchada and the Normans in 1170. The eponymous ances-tor, Turcaill mac Eóla, was killed together with Rhys ap Tewdwr of South Wales by the Normans of Brycheiniog in 1093. His provenance is unknown, but Rhys had fled to Ireland in 1088 and there gathered a fleet of 'pirates, Scots and Irish', and in 1092 St David's had been destroyed by the men of the Isles. Turcaill may have been a brother of the Hamond 'filius Iole', the native Manx bishop of Man, and a son of the 'Iola' who joins Hamond in witnessing a charter of Godred Crovan. The mysterious *ecclesia filie Zole* mentioned in Diarmait Mac Murchada's grant of Baldoyle to All Hallows may preserve the name in disguise, if the initial *Z* be a misreading of an Old English 3 (the letter 'yogh' for J).

The Gaelic charters in the Book of Deer feature the *toísech* as well as the *mórmáer*, and show that in Scotland he had become a royal thane (Anglo-Saxon Þegn, 'servant of the king'), rather than an autonomous 'leader', 'chieftain', or 'petty king'. In Ireland the term becomes increasingly common in the eleventh and twelfth centuries. In the annals of the eighth and ninth centuries it occurs occasionally, and is often rendered in Latin as *dux*. In the letter sent to St Anselm, archbishop of Canterbury, by Muirchertach Ua Briain and the citizens of Waterford in 1096 requesting episcopal consecration for Máel Ísu ua hAinmere (Malchus), beside the signature of 'Murchertachus rex Hiberniae' appears that of his brother 'Dermeth dux frater regis'. Following upon his reconciliation with his brother in 1093, Diarmait may have been installed at Waterford; but when he died in 1118, after a more successful revolt, he was in Cork.

But a person who in one source might be described as *dux* or *toísech* may appear in another as *rí* or king of a *tuath*, a word which has such wide connotations that no one English equivalent is adequate. Primarily 'people', it has often been rendered 'tribe', but it also means 'the laity' or 'lay property', as opposed to clerics or churches. In the Old Irish period it meant particularly a political community, a kingdom ruled by a *rí*. By the eleventh century its political status had declined, and its head is usually termed *toísech*, which in origin was a military office, like that of the medieval *dux*, the Germanic *Herzog*. In 1101 the Annals of the Four Masters mention Ua hIndredáin as *toiseach teaghlaigh Uí Mhaoileachlainn*, or leader of Ua Maíl Shechnaill's household troops, the equivalent of the Welsh *teulu* or 'warband'. From other sources we know that Ua hIndredáin was 'king' of Corco Roíde. As in so many instances of kingship in this period, we cannot be sure whether he was the native 'tribal king' of a people who had apparently disappeared from the political scene in 810, or whether he was an administrator of the district (the barony of Corkaree just north of Ua Maíl Shechnaill's patrimonial lands in Westmeath). In 1013 the *lucht tige* or 'household company' of Máel Sechnaill allowed valour to get the better part of their discretion when they sallied out after drinking to repel a cattle-raid by Ua Ruairc and Ua Ciarda of Tethba.

The word *toísech* most frequently occurs in the northern annals in conjunction with *muinter* 'household', used as the definition of a sept within a dynasty. For example, the Muinter Birn were a family of the Cenél nEógain in Tyrone, but evidently not a 'kingdom', and the Muinter Eólais were a sub-group within the Conmaicne of Leitrim. Among the Cenél mBinnig of Cenél nEógain and also in Bréifne, the word *tellach* 'hearth' is found: this may imply the foundation of a new territorial unit. As the *muinter* prolifer-ated into new septs, the heads of these distinguished themselves by sur-names.

The *trícha cét*, literally 'thirty hundred', was also a military unit in origin. Its use as a territorial term does not pre-date the tenth century. By the twelfth it had replaced the *tuath* as the smallest effective political entity. The Normans had no difficulty in equating it with the Welsh cantred (*cantref* 'hundred homesteads'), and took it over as a going concern; it became a 'feudal' barony.

However, conservatism coexisted with innovation, and the title *rí* con-tinues to be given to many persons of very minor political importance. This was an embarrassment to the annalists of the seventeenth century, the Four Masters and Mageoghegan, who had exalted notions of monarchy. The so-called Four Masters (a term invented by Colgan) entitled their compilation 'Annála Ríoghachta Éireann' ('The Annals of the Kingdom of Ireland'). Roderick O'Flaherty in his *Ogygia*, published in 1685, with wider historical perspectives, had no objection to the term *rex* for petty kings, but he terms the high-king of Ireland *monarchus*. The Four Masters restricted the term *rí* to kings of the provinces of Ulster, Meath, Leinster, Munster, and Con-nacht, and degraded all others to the level of *tighearna* or 'lord'; occasionally they use *taoiseach* (for early Irish *toísech*). Mageoghegan a few years earlier had followed the same principle. Both sometimes refer to the 'high-kings of Ireland' as *an Rí* or 'the King' *tout court*, a usage never found in the earlier annals they were adapting or translating.

The *rechtaire* was an official attested in early sources, but not important enough to warrant mention in the annals before the eleventh century. He was the steward, revenue-collector, and to an undefined extent administrator of a king; in Old Irish the term is used to gloss the Latin *procurator regis*. According to the law tracts, both the *rechtaire* and the *techtaire* 'messenger' of a ruler (*flaith*) are entitle to half the sick-maintenance of their lord. The ninth-century 'Tripartite Life' has St Patrick bless the Uí Ercáin, a branch of the subordinate Fothairt in the south of Kildare, saying that they would never be subject to an outside king or *rechtaire*, and adds that they have their own *brithemnas*, capacity of judging and being judged, in their own territory. Their neighbours to the north, however, the branch of the Loíges that dwelt around Moone, would suffer oppression and be ruled by an external prince. In the ecclesiastical sphere the early 'Cáin Adomnáin' and the ninth-century sabbatarian 'Epistle of Jesus' mention *rechtairi* as officials appointed to en-force these laws; they may have been identical with the official prosecutors, *fir thobaig* or 'men of levying', referred to in the eighth-century 'Cáin Domnaig'.

The first occurrence of *rechtaire* in the annals is in 1018, when Cais Mide, Máel Sechnaill's *rechtaire*, was killed on a raid into Fir Chell in the south-west of Meath and Éle across the border in Munster. In 1133 Gilla na Náem Ua Birn, *toísech* of Tír Briúin na Sinna (on the shores of the Shannon in the east of Roscommon) is given the exalted title of *ríg-rechtaire Érenn*, 'royal steward of Ireland', in the Annals of Tigernach, a source which by then had assumed the character of a court chronicle of Ua Conchobair, probably written at Roscommon, and of course supporting Tairdelbach Ua Conchobair's claim to be high-king of Ireland. The same source records in 1172 the murder by Donn Slébe Ua hEochada, king of Ulster, of Mac Gilla Espuic, *toísech* of Clann Aílebra and *rechtaire* of the 'Cath Monach', which was immediately avenged by the nobles of Ulster putting the king to death. This is somewhat obscure, since the term 'the Monach battalion' is unique. Unlike the Monaig or Fir Manach of Lough Erne, the Monaig of Ulster maintained their local autonomy in various parts of County Down. They are mentioned in the annals from the tenth century and have a genealogical record which lists the Clann Aílebra as one of their leading *tuatha*. In the previous year Gilla Óengusa mac Gilla Espuic, who is probably the same person and has the title *rechtaire Monach*, aided Donn Slébe in the killing of his brother and predecessor in the kingship, the evil-living Magnus. An ecclesiastical *rechtaire* appears at Clonmacnoise in 1069: he was 'steward of the poor', in charge of the Culdee establishment known as the Ísel Ciaráin, and was killed by the son of the king of Meath, who was imposing a *trén-coinnmed* or excessive levy upon them. Compensation was awarded: in Mageoghegan's words, 'Murrogh m^cConnor o'Melaghlyn, prince of Meath, did so overcess the family of Moylekyeran m^cCon ne mBoght in Isillkyeran and the poore of that house, that the steward of that familie was slain by them, for which cause Moyvora was granted to the poore'.

These notices do not tell anything of the functions of the *rechtaire*. However, others display him in a position of command. Thus Ua hÓcáin of the Cenél Fergusa of Cenél nEógain is found as *rechtaire* of Tulach Óc (Tullaghogue in Tyrone), the power-base of Ua Néill, and in the later middle ages, at any rate, the O'Neill inauguration site. Gilla Muru mac Ócáin occupied that office in 1059, after the eclipse of the Ua Néill family, as did Ragnall Ua hÓcáin, killed by the Fir Maige Ítha in 1103, and Donn Slébe Ua hÓcáin, *toísech* of Cenél Fergusa, who died in 1122. At a much earlier date the Tripartite Life has a story to tell of Faillén, *rechtaire* of the royal fort of the king of Leinster at Naas, who feigned sleep in order to avoid giving hospitality to Patrick, and whose divine punishment, eternal sleep, gave rise to a proverb.

The Dál Cais kings of Munster had a strategic stronghold at Dún na Sciach (Donaskeagh, north-east of Tipperary town). This was demolished by Mac Gilla Phátraic, king of Ossory, when he invaded Munster in 1031, and its *rechtaire* was killed. Mac Gilla Phátraic burned the fort again in 1043, as did Domnall Ua Maíl Shechnaill in 1090. In 1095 one of the victims of the plague was Domnall mac Beólláin, called *flaith* 'prince' or 'ruler' of Dún na Sciach. And in 1108 Limerick was burned, by lightning not by enemy action, and coincidentally Ua Beoáin, *rechtaire Lumnig*, met an 'unfortunate' end— *infeliciter mortuus est*. The names Ua Beoáin and Ua Beólláin are distinct, but both families were of the Dál Cais. The former were of the Uí Blait: Donngal son of Beoán died as abbot of Tomgraney in 1003. The latter were more closely allied to Ua Briain, being descended from Mathgamain son of Tair-delbach, brother of St Flannán the royal saint and patron of Killaloe. One of the nobles (*optimi*) of Munster who were killed on a raid into Dál nAraide led by Muirchertach Ua Briain in the preliminaries to the disastrous battle of Mag Coba in 1103 rejoiced in the nickname of Petta Demain ('the devil's pet' or perhaps 'pet devil') Ua Beoáin: his name is correctly given in the Annals of Ulster and of Inisfallen, but confused with Ua Beólláin in the Clonmacnoise annals.

The *muire* is more elusive. The translation 'lord' is obviously inadequate, though he was a person of authority. The Four Masters no longer under-stand the word and usually replace it with *tighearna*. It is very early, and its derivative and apparent synonym *muiredach* 'a person capable of acting as *muire*' is common as a personal name from the sixth century onwards. It appears only rarely in the law-tracts and then in somewhat obscure passages. In the *Cáin Domnaig* the accused can exonerate himself by his own oath supported by the oaths of two close relatives or of his *muire* and two others. Furthermore, the same text allocates half of the fines collected to various lords and *muirig*. An early tract on the hostage-sureties needed to guarantee observance of a treaty gives the *muiredach* the status of an enforcing officer, empowered to imprison the hostage-surety if necessary. Each party to the treaty had such a *muiredach*. A fragmentary text dealing with the functions of a hostage also refers to the *muire*.[5] Because of the association of *muire* with hostages and their eventual custody later texts, such as the Middle Irish poem of advice to a prince, 'Diambad messe bad rí réil', seem to regard the term as merely a synonym for a king, who by nature of his office had to have hostages ('a king without hostages is a leaky vessel'). This is probably mis-taken, although in the eleventh century the *muire* might well be the head of his sept or 'king' of a small territory. A much later tract, one of the few from the Middle Irish period, speaks of the *muire rechtge* ('*muire* of royal ordin-ance') as one who brings hostage-sureties into the king's house and receives a third of the third due to them from the property of a person killed outside the *tuath* for whom they have obtained the blood-fine.

Other gnomic texts associate the *muire* with a definite territory or district, a *methas* or *mennat*. The prophecy of Bec mac Dé, detailing the moral

---

[5] On this difficult subject see R. Chapman Stacey, *The road to judgment* (Philadelphia, 1994), pp 84–95.

breakdown presaging the end of world, declares that individuals will take the law into their own hands: *muiredach cách a mennait*, 'each man a sheriff of his own district'. The suggestion is that the *muire* was the representative responsible to the king for good order within his territory or the representative, often but not necessarily the head, of an important aristocratic sept. If so, his function would correspond to that of the eighth-century *aire túise* as defined in 'Críth Gablach'.

In 1018 Gilla Críst mac Conaing, *muire* of the Clann Sínaig of Armagh, was killed on an expedition made by the Cenél nEógain into Brega; he was first cousin to the abbot Máel Muire. In 1059 another *muire* of Clann Sínaig was killed; he was Gilla Muire mac Airechtaig, but his relationship to the abbatial family is unknown. In the same year Tomaltach Ua Maíl Brénainn, *muire* of Síl Muiredaig, died; he was evidently not a member of the ruling Ua Conchobair family, nor does he seem related to any of the prominent septs of the dynasty. On the other hand, Áed mac Cennétig, *muire* of Clann Tairdelbaig in 1054 and 'the pre-eminence of Dál Cais', who was killed that year, was a second cousin of the king Donnchad mac Briain. Most of the other examples in the annals refer to the Cenél nEógain. Máel Dúin mac Ciarmeic was *muire* of a branch of the Cenél mBinnig in 1030; Áed ua hUalgairg, briefly king of Ailech, was merely *muire* of his own sept at his death in 1067; Mac Raith Ó hÓcáin was *muire* of Cenél Fergusa in 1081; another *muire* of Clann Sínaig, Gilla Mo Ninne Ua hEochada, was killed in battle in 1086. Two more Cenél nEógain *muirig*, Máel Ruanaid Ua Cairelláin of Clann Diarmata and Gilla Críst Ua Luinig of Cenél Maién, were killed 'by treachery on the same day' by their king Domnall Mac Lochlainn in 1090; the former belonged to the ruling family of his sept, the latter apparently did not. Another Ua hUalgairg, Gilla Ciaráin, *muire* of Uí Duib Indrecht, was killed in 1095, and in the same year Muirchertach Ua Cairre, *muire* of Cenél nÓengusa, died. Remarkably, Ua Cairre is also styled *rígdamna* of Ailech; the Annals of Inisfallen also notice his obit and call him *muire* of the Cenél nEógain of Tullaghogue. Another *muire* of the same sept, Amlaíb Mac Cana, 'pillar of valour and vigour of all Cenél nEógain' died in 1155. In 1100 Assíd Ua hAmráin (or Ua hAmradáin), *muire* of Dál Fiatach, died; Dál Fiatach was the name of the Ulaid proper (as distinct from the Cruthin), and of their territory, now the diocese of Down, so this was a very far-reaching title indeed. We do not know the relationship of this individual to any of the major families of the area, although the genealogical tracts, edited probably by Muirchertach Ua Cairill the judge, historian and erenagh of Downpatrick who died in 1083, are very detailed. But in 1099, on the occasion of the massive defeat of the Ulstermen at the hands of Domnall Mac Lochlainn, an unnamed Ua hAmráin, no doubt the head of the family, was a casualty when the cavalry were routed. A metaphorical use of the term occurs in the obituary of the noted ecclesiastic Máel Muire Ua Dúnáin in 1117: the Annals of

Ulster call him 'learned bishop of the Gael and head of the clerics of Ireland and *muire* of alms of the world'.

THE word *air-rí*, often translated 'sub-king' or 'under-king', properly means 'viceroy' and is so used in all the earliest occurrences in the literature. Thus in biblical history Joseph is the *air-rí* of Pharaoh in Egypt, and Pontius Pilate the *air-rí* of Caesar. It has the same meaning in the eleventh-century annals. The dictionary is misleading in restricting the meaning 'viceroy, governor' to foreign contexts, while giving 'tributary king, chieftain' as the primary meaning. While there is evidence from the ninth and tenth centuries to show that provincial kings and high-kings appointed or permitted close kinsmen to exercise royal authority at home while they pursued wider ambitions, the term *air-rí* first appears in the annals in 960. In this year Eógan mac Muiredaig, *er-rí Érenn*, was killed by the Uí Failge: his father was second cousin to the high-king Domnall ua Néill. Murchad Glún re Lár stood in the same relationship to Domnall and held the local title king of Ailech during Domnall's high-kingship, while Domnall put his own son Muirchertach into Meath (though neither of these is called *air-rí* in the annals). The 'Cogad Gáedel re Gallaib' mentions Tadc Ua Cernacháin *air-rí Bréfni* as having been slain by Máel Sechnaill in the episode involving the high-king's *lucht tige* in 1013. In 1032 Diarmait mac Echach, *air-rí* of Munster, died; his father, prince (*flaith*) of Clann Scandláin of Dál Cais, had fallen at Clontarf.

   Máel Sechnaill's court poet Cuán ua Lothcháin, in his poem on Tara, lays out his ideal polity of Ireland as consisting of seven kings: the kings of the ancient Five Fifths, the King of Ireland, and his viceroy—*rí Érenn is a hair-rí*. Cathal mac Labrada, *air-rí* of Meath, was killed by the rebellious sons of Donnchad Find and their ally, the king of Uí Méith, in 1003. We do not know his relationship to Máel Sechnaill. And on May day 1021, Branacán Ua Máeluidir, *air-rí* of Meath, was drowned in Lough Ennell; according to the Four Masters, Mac Conaillig, *prím-reachtaire Maolseachlainn*, shared his fate (this being only nine days after they had both plundered the shrine of St Ciarán). The last annalistic reference to an *air-rí* is the death at the battle of Mag Coba in 1103 of Muirchertach Ua Briain's *air-rí* of Leinster, the total outsider Ua Muiredaig king (or *rígdamna* according to the Munster annalist) of Ciarraige.

   Later in the middle ages Early Modern Irish *uirriogh* means sub-king or 'chieftain', a member of the overlord's *oireacht*. Already in a charter in the Book of Kells written between 1134 and 1136, Tigernán Ua Ruairc appears as *ri Brephni* 'king of Bréifne' and Gofraid Ua Ragallaig as *er-ri na Macairi ocus flaith muintir Mailmorda*, 'governor of the Machaire and prince of Muinter Maíl Mórda', whereas in another dated 1 November 1133, Ua Ragallaig is styled *ri Macairi Gaileng*, 'king of Machaire Gaileng' (whence the barony of Morgallion, County Meath). Here the transition from 'governor' to 'sub-king' appears to be taking place. Lughaidh Ó Cléirigh, in his 'Beatha Aodha Ruaidh',[6] appears to distinguish *air-ríogh* 'viceroy, governor, deputy' from *uirríogh* 'chieftain'. He had access to the Ó Cléirigh and other glossaries and makes full use of them to introduce archaisms into his biography of Red Hugh O'Donnell that have sometimes misled modern historians as to the nature of Gaelic society at the end of the sixteenth century. In this case he distinguished the two meanings of the same word by using the early and modern orthography.

A genealogical fragment in the Book of Lecan that may be as early as the twelfth century uses *uir-ríg* in the later sense: the Uí Duibne and Uí Chuinn were *uir-ríg* of Corco Fhir Thrí until displaced by Clann Taidc m. Céin (the Luigne and Gailenga). But a tract summarised by Mac Fir Bhisigh in the Introduction to his Book of Genealogies tells how Cormac mac Airt exercised *ainfíre flatha* 'a prince's injustice' upon the last representative of the old Gamanrad kings of Connacht when he put a governor (*ur-ríg*) over him and gave the viceroyalty of Connacht (*oirríghe Connacht*) to his own uterine brother and foster-brother, Nia mac Lugna, ancestor of the Corco Fhir Thrí. 'And Cormac was the first king of the kings of Ireland that ever put a viceroyalty over Connacht.' Nia mac Lugna oppressed the Gamanrad terribly because they had killed his father, but Cormac persisted and finally deposed Áed altogether.

The transition whereby the office of viceroy disappeared and the local kings and leaders usurped the title is somewhat analogous to the transformation of the Carolingian counts, officers of the king, into hereditary feudal lords. In the twelfth century many local 'petty kings' are seen to function primarily as military officers of the high-king, and this no doubt eased the transition. Alternatively, it may be viewed as merely a reversion to type. However, the later Gaelic *uir-riogh*, if not always a reliable vassal, did not have the dignity of the title 'king' enjoyed by his ancestors. He was primarily perceived as a member of his overlord's *oireacht*, so much so that this word came to be transferred to the territory ruled by the latter, as in Oireacht Uí Chonchobhair, Oireacht Uí Chatháin. Early Irish had many words for kings, over-kings, kings of over-kings, and high-kings; it had no word for a sub-king.

The Old Irish *airecht* was the assembly of the *airig*, the 'free' men, also a court presided over by the king. As the social structure simplified to the detriment of the 'free', the *airecht* developed into something more like the king's council. It seems to be in this sense that we find it used in the annals when, in 1023, Donnchad Ua Duinn, king of Brega, is seized by the Norse 'in his own court' and sent across the sea, or when three years later another king of Brega, Domnall Ua Cellaig, betrays and kills Muiredach Ua Céle in

[6] Paul Walsh (ed. and trans.), *Beatha Aodha Ruaidh Uí Dhomhnaill* (2 vols, Dublin, 1948).

his court. Similarly in 1053, Mac na hAidche ('son of the night') Ua Ruairc treacherously kills Cú Chiar Ua Maíle Dúin, king of Lurg in north Fermanagh, in the latter's own court. The sense of the later medieval *oireacht* appears in 1093 when Muirchertach Ua Briain invaded Connacht and the Síl Muiredaig 'came into his court', which did them little good, for he gave the kingship over them to his ally Ua hEidin of Aidne. And in 1114 Domnall Mac Lochlainn, hearing of Muirchertach's paralysis, mounted an expedition to Rathkenny in Meath, where Eochaid Ua Mathgamna and the Ulstermen 'came into his house' (the normal term for submission) together with the kings of Dál nAraide, Bréifne, and Meath; the combined forces proceeded across Athlone to Ballinasloe, where Toirrdelbach Ua Conchobair and the Connachtmen and Domnall's own son, with the Cenél Conaill, 'came into his court', before advancing into Thomond.

*C ÁIN* and *rechtge* again are terms from classical law denoting royal jurisdiction and ordinance: the early eighth-century 'Críth Gablach' singles out the *cáin* and *rechtge* exercised by the king of Cashel as exemplary. '*Cáin* is a "law" (*Regelung*) enacted by kings, the church, and, perhaps, other great personages, and by these alone, and enforced by suitable penalties. In the same way *rechtge* is the law in force under a prince.'[7] The Dál Cais kings of Munster proclaimed such measures from the time that Mathgamain seized the kingship of Cashel and expelled the Norse from Limerick in 972. In 1040 Brian Bóruma's son Donnchad enacted a *cáin* and *rechtge* 'such as was not enacted in Ireland since the time of Patrick', enforcing the *Cáin Domnaig* or Law of Sunday, forbidding servile work and the carrying of arms on Sunday; it also legislated against theft, with the result 'that no one should dare to fetch cattle within doors'. He is said to have enacted another 'great *cáin*' in 1050. In 1068 Tairdelbach ua Briain reenacted Donnchad's *cáin* and *rechtge* 'with the result that neither cow not horse was housed at night, but allowed to wander at will'. And the synod of Ráith Bressail in 1111, presided over by Muirchertach Ua Briain, is described as having 'enacted discipline and law [*smacht ocus recht*] better than any made in Ireland before their time'. The correlative of *cáin* was *cís*, the tax paid in return for such royal protection. Thus *cáin* itself comes to mean 'tax; rent; tribute': in 1061 the Annals of Tigernach record that the king of Dublin, Murchad son of Diarmait mac Maíl na mBó, went to the Isle of Man and exacted *cáin* from it.

MUCH has been made by historians of the 'decline' of the Uí Néill in the eleventh century. Perhaps this is a tribute to the success of their own

---

[7] John Ryan, 'The O'Briens in Munster after Clontarf' in *N. Munster Antiq. Jn.*, ii (1941), pp 141–52; iii (1942–3), pp 1–152, 189–202: ii, 143, n. 7, translating Thurneysen's definition from *Irisches Recht*.

propaganda. The fiction of the high-kingship of Ireland has tended to distract attention from the local achievements of the 'provincial' kings. Now they demand our full attention. If the Ireland of the 'interregnum' appears to be in chaos, it is largely because our gaze has been diverted by the chimera of national unity. The Uí Néill, north and south, had their own quite different problems: if the northerners suffered from internal faction it was in large part due to over-extension of their lordship; if the southerners failed it was for other reasons, and we must avoid the temptation to read back the later impotence of the Southern Uí Néill into this period.

Genuine members of the old stock of the Cenél nEógain, to name only two, were the Cenél Feradaig, who had lost the over-kingship in the seventh century, but were now moving south into the Airgiallan lands around Clogher. Their chief claim to fame, however, lies in the ecclesiastical branch of the family, Ua Brolcháin, who produced a distinguished line of clerics in both Armagh and Derry, the poles as it were of the Cenél nEógain dominion. The Cenél Fergusa were remarkable in that while one division, Ua Maíl Fhábaill, remained at home as kings of Carraic Brachaide in the east of Inishowen, another followed their overlords south to Tullaghogue, of which site Ua hÓcáin became the guardian, and in later centuries at any rate, the official who inaugurated the O'Neill. The first of the family mentioned is Gilla Muru mac Ócáin who was *rechtaire* of Tullaghogue at his death in 1056. Áed Ua Forréid, of the dubious Cenél Tigernaig, became bishop and *fer légind* ('lector' or head of the school) at Armagh, but neither he nor any Ua Brolcháin were able to control the abbacy, which now entailed the coarbship of St Patrick and primacy of honour, if not of jurisdiction, in the Irish church.

The Cenél nEógain may be said to have become victims of their own success. Their phenomenal expansion into Derry and Tyrone was accompanied by a no less extraordinary proliferation of septs. The genealogical record compiled in the middle of the eleventh century reveals a large number of petty kingdoms of whom there is little trace in the earlier records. Some of these we may believe to have been late affiliations to the ruling dynasty rather than the result of a normal biological process. It is true that the Cenél mBinnig, who established a number of settlements along the western shore of the Lower Bann, in Glenconkeine, and at Tullaghogue itself, are recognised as early as the ninth century in the Tripartite Life of Patrick as warrior sons of Éogan mac Néill, but the same source reveals, and the eleventh century genealogy hints, that the Cenél nEchdach of Tirkeeran were originally Uí Fhiachrach of Airgialla: the representatives of that people remained ensconced around Ardstraw and expanded their power briefly over Lurg in Fermanagh. Again, the pedigrees of Cenél Tigernaig are several generations too short. Furthermore, the peculiarly named Cenél Moain or Moén of Mag nÍtha south of Inishowen in north-east Donegal, were most probably the early race to whom Finten moccu Moie, St Fintan of Taghmon, belonged. Mag nÍtha was to be for a thousand years the crucial battleground between the Cenél nEógain and the Cenél Conaill, and it was vital for the former that it be held by loyal vassals or directly by members of the dynasty. Thus it comes about that the term 'Fir Maige Ítha' is exasperatingly ambiguous, varying as it does according to the actual power in the land. For much of the eleventh century the Clann Conchobair sept held the title, but by the 1070s they had conquered most of the lands of the Ciannachta of mid-Derry, and adopted the surname Ua Catháin. Confusingly, the surname of the Ciannachta kings themselves, who still held on to some territory, was Ua Conchobair. The Cenél Moain then emerged in Mag nÍtha under the ruling family of Ua Gairmledaig.

More urgently, the unloved cousins of Cenél Conaill were not to be neglected. Ruaidrí Ua Canannáin had made a nearly successful attempt to regain the high-kingship in the middle of the previous century; the Munster Annals of Inisfallen recognise his claim, but more significantly, they term Flaithbertach's exact contemporary, Domnall Ua Maíl Doraid, 'king of Cenél Conaill and Cenél nEógain' at his obit under the year 1033. Domnall had probably been killed the previous year; but when Flaithbertach Ua Néill was absent on his pilgrimage to Rome in 1030, his son and regent Áed had to face the threat from the west, and killed Domnall's predecessor, Ruaidrí Ua Canannáin. Although the official view was that Flaithbertach had taken up the kingship on his return in 1031, the southern annalist says that he only regained authority after the death of Ua Maíl Doraid.

The closely related families of Ua Canannáin and Ua Maíl Doraid were to be at each other's throats for the best part of three centuries, but this feud does not seem to have affected the potential of the Cenél Conaill as a whole. Like the Cenél nEógain they faced in two directions: Ua Maíl Doraid was based in the extreme south of his large territory, at Belleek and Ard Fothaid, claimed to exercise overlordship in the Uí Néill kingdom of Cairpre in north Sligo and Leitrim, and fostered ambitions to extend his hegemony over at least the northern parts of Connacht. Ua Canannáin too seems to have been based in the south. But it is significant that Domnall Ua Maíl Doraid was slain in the north, by the Clann Fhiangusa of Cenél Lugdach. The Clann Fhiangusa and their cousins the Clann Snédgaile occupied lands westwards from Letterkenny to the territory of another cousin, Ua Domnaill of Loughveigh and Kilmacrenan. These held the birthplace of Colum Cille himself, and also his battle talisman, the psalter known as the Cathach.

The ancestors of Ua Domnaill had made a brief appearance as kings of Cenél Conaill at the end of the ninth century when the balance of power had shifted from south to north to deal with viking activities on Lough Swilly and a dangerous alliance between some of these pirates and the Cenél nEógain; similar threats from Scots, Normans and some of the Cenél nEógain account for the eventual success of Ua Domnaill at the beginning of the thirteenth century. A poem in the persona of the late ninth-century Flann ua Lonáin, and reworked by Giolla Brighde Mac Con Midhe in the thirteenth century, purportedly in praise of the Éicnechán mac Dálaig, the king of Cenél Conaill who died in 906, was actually composed for his descendant Éicnechán Ua Domnaill, between 1202 and 1208. But even in the eleventh century the Cenél Lugdach were displacing the Cenél mBóguine of the Rosses as the second power in Tír Conaill; the axis had shifted from east–west to north–south. Furthermore, the Cenél Lugdach had apparently be-friended a forlorn Uí Néill dynasty that claimed descent from Énda mac Néill, and planted them around Adomnán's church of Raphoe, a rival Columban centre to Derry and a strategic point from which to attack Mag nÍtha.

Ua Néill's satellite states of Airgialla exhibit a picture of chaos in this period. The name is most often used now of the southern kingdoms. In the North the Uí Fhiachrach of Ardstraw were isolated from their former relatives and neighbours the Uí Thuirtre. These had lost their centre at Tullaghogue to Ua Néill and much of their other lands to the Cenél mBinnig, but had expanded eastwards into Ulster, occupying the northern parts of Dál nAraide (the ancient Eilne). Still keeping hold of Fir Lí west of the Bann and Loughinsholin west of Lough Neagh, they were for their Ulster lands apparently free of Uí Néill lordship.

So for many years no real power accrued to the Cenél nEógain from their overlordship of Airgialla. Perhaps the success of the Fir Fernmaige owed something to Ua Néill support. At the furthest remove from Tullaghogue, they were the less likely to be hostile. The northern Uí Chrimthainn, the Fir Lemna and Síl nDuibhthíre, and even more the Fir Manach were restless subjects and even dangerous neighbours; the Fir Fernmaige could be encour-aged to keep them in check and turn their own aggression southwards to the ultimate benefit of Ua Néill.

In Armagh the Airthir remained within the same bounds as in the seventh century, but feuding was endemic between their petty kingdoms of Uí Nial-láin, Uí Bressail, and Uí Echdach; the only novelty is the appearance of a fourth entity, that of Uí Dorthainn to the west. These were provided with a pedigree of their own, but came under the control of the Uí Bressail, thereby incurring the jealousy of the sons of Áed Ua Néill, as can be seen from the entries *A.U.* 1009, 1021 and 1024. The Uí Bressail indeed expanded in the eleventh century and gained territory at the expense of the Uí Nialláin. The office of *oeconomus* of Armagh, held by the Clann Chernaig of Uí Nialláin since the eighth century, appears to have lapsed after the death of Cummascach mac Ailello (whose name is commemorated on a fine bronze bell) in 909. The chief royal families were Ua Lorcáin and Ua hÁnluain.

But the Uí Bressail maintained control of the office of *secnap* of Armagh, which they had held for 200 years. The Ua Longáin stewards of Armagh in Munster at Ardpatrick were another of their families. However, Mac Árchon Ua Célecáin, king of Uí Bressail, slew his distant cousin, the *secnap* Gilla Pátraic Ua hErudáin in 1052: the position passed, first to Mac Árchon's uncle and then to the latter's son. The brother of the murdered Gilla Pátraic, Cummascach Ua hErudáin, 'head of the poor', succeeded in dislodging the Clann Sínaig abbot Dub dá Lethe for three years between 1060 and 1063. Mac Árchon fell together with Áed Ua Fergail of Tullaghogue at the hands of the Fir Fernmaige in 1054.

The Clann Sínaig abbots of Armagh were a branch of the Uí Echdach, but relations between them and the royal line were not always peaceful either. In 1038 Orc Allaid 'the Wild Boar' Ua Ruadacáin, king of Ui Echdach, was killed by the Clann Sínaig at Armagh in revenge for his killing of Eochaid, son of the abbot. It is not clear if this was a nickname for Muiredach Ua Ruadacáin, king of Ui Echdach, who defeated and slew the kings of Uí Bressail and Uí Nialláin the previous year on the River Callann. Muiredach's son Ruaidrí became king in 1055 and enjoyed a long reign till his death in 1099. He has a favourable obituary notice in the annals. Although he had killed Lethlobar Ua Laidcnén of Fernmag, who is called 'high-king of Airgialla', in 1078, his son fell a victim to the Fir Fernmaige in 1085, and it is painfully clear that no one was in a position to act as 'high-king' of all Airgialla.

More movement was to be seen among the Uí Chrimthainn: already by the end of the eighth century they had split into numerous sub-kingdoms covering a wide area. Now the senior branch was being pushed south and west from their ecclesiastical city and pre-Christian centre of Clogher by the Cenél Feradaig: it is even possible that they took their relic, the Domnach Argit evangeliary, and its shrine to Clones at the time of this expulsion. A king of Uí Chrimthainn in south Tyrone ruled over the Three Tuatha of Uí Chrimthainn, Fir Lemna, and Síl nDuibthíre. But the septs with a future were those that took the name of Fir Manach from the early peoples whose lands in eastern Fermanagh they occupied, and the Fir Fernmaige who took theirs from the 'alder plain' of Fernmag between Lough Ooney and Monaghan (in later times the name Farney followed their expansion much further south). In the process they displaced a once important group, the Uí Méith, one branch of whom seem to be already settled in Omeath in the Ulster peninsula of Cooley as early as the 1040s. Over the course of the century they began to take over the Mugdorna and Fir Rois.

The Mugdorna stretched over all the south of Monaghan and into northern Meath: although brought into the Airgiallan coalition in the eighth century, they had never come into the sphere of the Cenél nEógain, but had always remained loyal to the Síl nÁeda Sláne of Brega. As the power of the latter rose and fell, so did theirs. The plebeian Fir Rois had been raised to the status of a kingdom by the Cenél nEógain as a thorn in their side and that of the Brega dynasty, splitting the Mugdorna lands and extending as a buffer zone between Ulster and Brega; more important than their kings were the churchmen of Dunleer with their close links to Armagh. Under the brief renaissance of the dynasty of Knowth in the second half of the tenth century the Mugdornai regained their unity, but now they came under attack both from the men of Fernmag and from the Gailenga to the west. The Gailenga of eastern Cavan and their symbiotic neighbours the Luigne to the south of Kells were the sometimes unruly subjects of the Ua Maíl Sechlainn kings of Mide, but by the 1070s some of the Gailenga had fallen victim to Ua Ruairc of Bréifne: in a charter granted to Kells at this time Donnchad Ua Ruairc is somewhat grandiosely described as 'king of Connacht and Gailenga' and he seems to have granted the kingship of Gailenga to the twice-exiled Ua Briain prince Cennétig mac Lorcáin.

THE history of the eleventh century must be read on its own terms. In Munster, Brian's son Donnchad between 1026 and 1033 entertained vain hopes of emulating his father. That he could not do so does not detract from his success in consolidating Dál Cais rule over the whole province, and sometimes beyond; though not the ancestor of the later O'Briens, he laid the foundation for their success. In the west the Síl Muiredaig of Connacht were able to expand their rule over wider areas, while more fortunate than the Cenél nEógain in maintaining a dynastic solidarity that enabled them to fend off rivals. The emergence of the Irish Sea as a centre of political power was exploited not only by Sitric Silkbeard of Dublin, till 1036 in alliance with Cnút, king of Denmark and England, but by a resurgent Ulster under Niall mac Eochada from 1012 till 1063, and later by his ally Diarmait mac Maíl na mBó of Uí Chennselaig. Diarmait shifted the balance of power within Leinster from the Liffey plains to those of the Barrow and the Slaney; he was also the first Irish king to gain control of Dublin and extend his hegemony over the Isle of Man.

IF the year 1014 is traditionally viewed as marking the end of the viking era in Irish history, it must be remembered that it also saw the apogee of the Scandinavian period in the history of northern Europe. The viking way of life still had its attractions for many, but had become something of an anachronism; viking bands as such were no longer a political factor, rather it was the fleets of Scandinavian kings, or mercenary forces such as those of Dublin and Waterford, that were significant. The Danish conquest of England, begun by Svein Forkbeard in 1013, was completed after his death in 1014, and the brief restoration of Æthelræd the Unready and the even briefer reign of his son Edmund Ironside, with the accession of Cnút in

1016. The new Anglo-Danish realm lasted until 1042. Since 1000 Denmark had exercised suzerainty over Norway as well, interrupted by the reign of St Olaf, from 1016 until his expulsion in 1028. Cnút too was to claim authority over parts of Sweden.

The first decades of the eleventh century also witnessed the acceptance of the Scandinavian kingdoms into the household of western Christendom. The conversion of Denmark, begun by Harald Bluetooth in the 960s, had been interrupted by the career of his pagan son Svein. It was confirmed by Cnút: his enthusiastic adoption of the Christian traditions of England, his law-codes, and his famous pilgrimage to Rome to witness the coronation of the emperor Conrad II in 1026, enhanced his international prestige. He set the trend for forty years of visits to Rome by others, including several Irish kings.

The viking Olaf Tryggvason had converted Norway with more enthusiasm than tact in his brief but memorable reign from 995 to 1000, and contributed to the conversion of Iceland in the year 1000, when the new religion was formally adopted by the Althing there. But it was Olaf Haraldsson who was to be commemorated and canonised as the true founder of the Norwegian church, though he too was defeated and killed by a combination of local revolt and foreign intrigue at the battle of Stiklestad in 1030. Sigurd the Fat, jarl of Orkney, was 'converted' by Olaf Tryggvason, but allegedly still waved the raven banner when he fell at Clontarf. After some years of strife, his youngest son, Thorfinn the Mighty, established a Christian lordship over the Orkneys, Shetlands, and Western Isles which lasted till 1065; his rise to power had been aided at first by the goodwill of St Olaf, his nominal over-lord, but more importantly by that of his grandfather, Malcolm II of Scotland.

Also around the turn of the millennium, Olaf Skotkonung of Sweden had accepted baptism, but a pagan reaction was to set in seventy years later, and it was not until the next century that the pagan cult at Uppsala was finally replaced by a Christian cathedral. Further east again, the conversion of the Rus', whose princes claimed Swedish ancestry, was accomplished in 988, albeit to the Greek and not the Roman rite. Since the definitive break be-tween Rome and Constantinople had not yet come to pass, this did not prevent Yaroslav, originally of Novgorod, and then of Kiev (1016–54), forming an impressive array of marriage alliances for his daughters with the royal houses of England, France, Norway, Poland, Hungary, and Byzantium.

THE Byzantine empire under Basil the Bulgar-slayer (976–1025) achieved new heights, and under his successors was to attempt the reconquest of Sicily. While the Bulgars and most of the Balkan Slavs had been won to the Greek rite, the papacy made a notable acquisition with the crowning by Silvester II of Stephen of Hungary in the year 1001; two generations earlier the pagan Magyars had been as much a threat to central Europe, and even to Italy, as the vikings had been to the north and west, and the Muslims in the Mediterranean. Pope Silvester, the noted mathematician Gerbert of Aurillac, canon of Rheims and formerly abbot of Bobbio, in alliance with the precocious young German emperor Otto III, himself son of the Byzantine princess Theophano, also established independent status for the nascent Polish church. Boleslav was to be admitted to the comity of catholic kings in 1025, and in 1049 an Irish monk, Aaron of Cologne, became the first archbishop of Cracow when that see was raised (temporarily as it proved) to metropolitan status in the 1060s. A less fortunate Irish pilgrim, Colmán (Coloman or Kálmán), was to become a patron saint of Hungary; returning through that land from a pilgrimage to Jerusalem in 1016, he was killed on suspicion of being a spy. Further afield, among the pagan Wends of Mecklenburg, the martyrdom of an Irish missionary bishop Johannes is recorded in 1066 by Adalbert of Bremen, the metropolitan of Scandinavia.

The Irish prominent on the Continent in this period concentrate at first on the old Carolingian lands of Lotharingia: notably at Cologne, Toul, and Metz, and then into the territories of the newer imperial houses. There was no longer any great movement to the older centres of Irish influence in Western Francia. The route followed by the Irish seems to have been via Scotland or York to the Rhine. Marianus Scottus (Máel Brigte) left Moville in Ulster to be ordained priest at Cologne in 1056; he ventured further into Franconia, the headquarters of the Salian dynasty, where he became an *inclusus* at Mainz and wrote his chronicle. He kept in touch with events in Ireland and Scotland; he is a contemporary source for the reign of MacBeth. He also records the killing of Ua Mathgamna, king of Ulster, in the church of Bangor in 1065, and has many references to the Irish community at Cologne. His namesake, the calligrapher Marianus Scottus (Muiredach mac Robartaig), came from Tír Conaill and settled further east, at Regensburg, in 1070. He was founder of the Irish *Schottenkloster* there.

Irish monks at Cologne are mentioned as under the headship of Ailill from Mucknoe in 1042; Donnchad mac Gilla Mo Chonna, *sapientissimus Scotorum*, abbot of Dunshaughlin and brother of Gilla Sechnaill, king of South Brega, died there in 1027, as did the exiled and blinded Bróen mac Máel Mórda, king of Leinster in 1052. Marianus Scottus had been ordained priest there in 1056, before moving on to Mainz. The Irish community there evidently provided much of the foreign news that reached the Irish annalists, such as the death of the emperor Henry II and the succession of Conrad in 1024, the battle of Bar-le-Duc in 1037, when Lotharingia was finally saved from the ambitions of Eudes, count of Champagne, and the famine of 1045.

Notices of the papacy in the Irish annals are confined to the obits of John XIX, Clement II and Paschal II. The last, in the Annals of Ulster for 1118: *Paschalis comarba Petair seruus relegiosus cum dilexione Dei et proximi ad*

*Christum migrauit* ('Paschal, coarb of Peter, a religious servant with love of God and of his neighbour, departed to Christ'), is the only one with a tone of piety, no doubt because of that pope's interest in the reform of the Scottish church, begun by St Margaret and completed by Bishop Turgot. Indeed, he may have sent letters to Ireland, as we know he did to Scotland; the same annal records news brought by pilgrims of the disastrous earthquakes that had shaken Lombardy the previous year.

The first papal obit is entered under the year 1030 in the Annals of Tigernach (the correct year is 1032). John is called by his secular name Romanus; as count of Tusculum, *consul et dux* of Rome, he only took holy orders on his accession to the papal throne. It was he who crowned Conrad II emperor on 26 March 1027, the occasion of Cnút's visit there. The second obit occurs in the Annals of Ulster at 1048: 'The coarb of Peter and twelve of his courtiers perish along with him after drinking poison that the coarb who had previously been banished gave them.'

Of the three popes deposed by Henry III at the synod of Sutri in 1046, Benedict IX (Theophylact, count of Tusculum, d. 1055), nephew of Benedict VIII (d. 1024) and of John XIX, was to emerge again as anti-pope in 1048, Silvester III disappeared, and the reforming but technically simoniac Gregory VI (Pierleoni) was banished to Cologne, where he died. The German Graf Suitger, bishop of Bamberg, superseded them under the name of Clement II, and his death on 9 October 1047 was rumoured to be the work of Benedict IX.

No better paradigm of the panorama here presented could be found than the career of Harald Hardrada, king of Norway as related in Snorri Sturluson's 'Haraldssaga Hardráði'. At the age of 15 he fought in the army of his half-brother St Olaf at Stiklestad in 1030. Thence he fled, under the protection of Rognvald Brusason, nephew of Thorfinn the Mighty, to Yaroslav in Russia. Later he joined the Varangian guard at Constantinople, and saw distinguished service under George Maniakes, at first in the east and later in Sicily, amassing a considerable fortune, which he entrusted to Yaroslav. Falling foul of the authorities, he was imprisoned at Constantinople, but (according to his praise-poet) had the satisfaction of personally blinding the emperor (Michael V, not Constantine Monomachos, as the saga says), who was overthrown in a spectacular coup in 1042. Thence he returned to Novgorod, collected his treasure, and the hand of Yaroslav's daughter Elizabeth, and made his way to Sweden in 1045, where he joined forces with Svein Estridson, the nephew of Cnút.

Svein had been passed over for the kingship of Denmark on the death of Cnút's son Harthacnút in 1042: his father Ulf was not royal, but his mother was Cnút's sister and half-sister to Olaf, king of Sweden. Meanwhile Harald's nephew, Magnus the Good, son of St Olaf, had been accepted as king not only of Norway, but also of Denmark. After some warfare and an uneasy compromise, Harald succeeded to the sole kingship of Norway on the death of Magnus in 1047. He was not slow to take up Magnus's claims on Denmark in opposition to his erstwhile ally, Svein, and for most of the rest of his reign engaged in naval warfare against the Danes. A peace treaty was finally agreed in 1064.

Now, however, other ambitions lured him westwards. When Cnút died in 1035, he had left the kingdom of Denmark to his son Harthacnút, while another son, Harold, was left as regent in England. Magnus the Good had reasserted the independence of Norway, and in 1037 Harold, with the support of one faction of the English, led by his mother Ælfgifu of Northampton and Leofric earl of Mercia, took control of England, only to die in 1040. The Annals of Ulster note his death, giving him the title 'king of the Gewissi', the ancient name for the people of Wessex. Earl Godwin of Wessex, however, supported by Cnút's other widow, Emma sister of Duke Richard of Normandy and widow too of Æthelræd the Unready, supported Harthacnút's claims. Harthacnút had come to a peculiar and fateful arrangement with his rival Magnus of Norway, that if either should die without heirs, the other was to succeed to his kingdom, but Harthacnút probably did not (or could not) intend this agreement to apply to the kingdom of England, and seems to have been making arrangements for the recall of Edward, Emma's son by Æthelræd, from exile in Normandy, when he died in his cups in 1042. Magnus promptly took over the rule of Denmark with no little success; his claim to England failed, but was not to be forgotten by his uncle and successor Harald Hardrada.

Edward, to be known as 'the Confessor' and later canonised, came to England under better auspices than had his elder brother Alfred, who had been enticed thither on Cnút's death and murdered, as some thought, on the suggestion of Godwin. Nor was Edward the only Anglo-Saxon royal exile. The children of Edmund Ironside had been smuggled abroad as far away as Hungary: one of them, also named Edward, was recalled by the Confessor in 1057, possibly with the intention of making him his heir, but he too met his death in suspicious circumstances. His son, known as Edgar the Ætheling (the Irish would have termed him *rígdamna*, 'one fit to be king'), was indeed chosen by some of the Anglo-Saxons after the Norman invasion, but both he and they repented of their foolhardiness in the light of William's success, and he was lucky to be allowed to drift into a life of aimless and intermittent exile, as the last male representative of the line of Alfred the Great. The Ætheling's sister Margaret achieved greater fame as queen of Scotland, mother of kings, reformer of the church, and saint.

Edward the Confessor had first introduced Normans to England, placing many of the friends he had made in exile into prominent positions in church and state, notably Robert of Jumièges as bishop, first of London and then archbishop of Canterbury. The native resentment against these descendants of the vikings, who had now become more French than the French, and who were evidently regarded as more foreign than the Danes, was led by the ambitious Earl Godwin of Wessex, who sought to gain control of the king through marrying him to his daughter Edith. But he overplayed his hand and was forced into exile with his sons in 1051. Here Edward was helped by the jealousy Godwin had inspired among the other earls, notably Leofric of Mercia and his son Ælfgar of East Anglia. Two of Godwin's sons, Harold and Leofwine, fled to Ireland. The following year Godwin and Harold were back in favour, not without the use of force (Godwin from Flanders and Harold from Ireland), and Edward was forced to expel his Norman protégés, including the bishops, but he apparently had set his heart upon leaving the kingdom to Duke William of Normandy, although he allowed Harold Godwinson to succeed his father as earl of Wessex, and in 1055 appointed another son of Godwin, Tostig, to succeed Siward as earl of Northumbria.

Harold continued to support the king and contained the threat posed by Gruffydd ap Llewelyn, the first (and only) king of all Wales, carrying the campaign into Gwynedd in 1063; Gruffydd himself was slain within the year. Meanwhile, however, in a confusing turn of events, Ælfgar was expelled from his earldom of East Anglia in 1055. Following the example of Harold, and of Welsh princes or pretenders before him, he sought and found help in Ireland, and joined forces with Grufydd in a devastating attack on Hereford, then held by a Norman nephew of the king's, Ralph of the Vexin. He was successful in his primary aim of restoration to his earldom, and in his secondary aim of succeeding his father as earl of Mercia, which he did in 1057. But in the rearrangement of earldoms that followed, most of the rest of England was controlled by the sons of Godwin.

Ælfgar renewed his alliance with Gruffydd, was expelled yet again, but returned in force and was restored a second time. He apparently predeceased his ally, now father-in-law, Gruffydd. But what is remarkable about his second adventure was the participation, not merely of Irish mercenaries, but indirectly of Harald Hardrada, whose son Magnus led a fleet drawn from the Orkneys, the Western Isles, and Dublin; and according to the Annals of Tigernach it was only through divine providence that Magnus did not succeed in winning the kingdom of England on that occasion.

This episode is not mentioned in the 'Haraldssaga', but an earlier connection with Dublin is, albeit in a not altogether accurate account. We are told that Harald's sister's son, Guthorm Gunnhildarson, 'often went on viking expeditions and enjoyed asylum and permission to winter at Dublin and was on friendly terms with King Margad'. Guthorm and Margad went on a plundering expedition to Wales, but quarrelled over the vast silver hoard they amassed; in the ensuing fight in the Menai Straits on St Olaf's eve, Guthorm slew Margad and slaughtered all his followers, attributing his victory to a vow he had made to his sainted uncle to give his church a tenth of the spoils. The editors of the text have taken Margad to be Echmarcach, king of Dublin, who displaced Sitric Silkbeard in 1035, was himself displaced by Ivar Haraldsson in 1038, and ruled Dublin again from 1038 to 1052, to which year they assign this exploit. It is certain, however, that 'Margad' represents the Irish Murchad, eponym of the Mac Murroughs. He had been placed in Dublin in 1052 by his father Diarmait mac Maíl na mBó, king of Leinster, driving Echmarcach into exile in the Isle of Man. In the event neither he nor Echmarcach were killed in 1052, but the record in the Welsh annals for that year of the foundering of an Irish fleet off the coast of Deheubarth may have some connection with these events.

The expedition of 1058 indicates that Harald Hardrada was able to secure the cooperation both of Thorfinn the Mighty and Murchad of Dublin. It is also likely that the accession to the throne of Scotland of Malcolm Canmore, who later married Thorfinn's widow Ingibjorg, was a significant factor.

Another anecdote told by Snorri, not in the 'Haraldssaga', but in that of Olaf the Saint, tells how the 3-year-old Harald played with a fleet of wooden shavings on a pond, an indication to his half-brother of his future achievements. One of the chief reasons for his incessant warfare against the Danes may well have been the desire to secure access to oakwoods, which were not available in Norway; Olaf Tryggvason's famous 'Long Serpent' was built of pine. Even Denmark's timber resources were not inexhaustible: in 1047 and again in 1048 Svein had appealed to Edward the Confessor for a fleet of fifty ships to aid his war against Magnus and his successor Harald. The Mercian version of the 'Anglo-Saxon Chronicle' reports that the English (in effect Earl Leofric) refused to allow their king to acquiesce to the request.

In this context, the fact that the largest viking warship ever to be discovered is among the Skuldelev ships sunk at the entrance to Roskilde fjord in Denmark is highly suggestive, for it has been found to have been built at Dublin in 1060. Whether it had been commissioned by Harald or his enemy Svein, or brought to Denmark by the sons of Harold Godwinson in their exile after the battle of Hastings, it is evidence that Dublin was a major centre of ship-building in the eleventh century. The abundance of oak (of which the threatened wood at Coolattin, County Wicklow, is the remnant) in Diarmait mac Maíl na mBó's home territory of Uí Chennselaig was a factor in the rise of his dynasty to supreme power in Leinster. A sixteenth-century record in Hanmer's Chronicle tells that at the end of the century William Rufus imported Irish oak to roof his new palace of Westminster Hall. The combination of such a natural resource with control of Dublin made Diarmait a powerful force to be reckoned with throughout the north-western world. It is no surprise that Godwin's sons fled to him in 1051, nor Harold's sons in 1066, so that in 1068 Diarmait was able to present Toirrdelbach ua Briain with the banner of the king of England.

Harald Hardrada's last adventure was at the invitation of Tostig, earl of Northumbria, the disaffected brother of Harald Godwinson. Foreseeing the inevitable succession of either William the Bastard of Normandy or of his own brother to the English throne, he brought Harald a welcome reminder that there were those in England who would prefer a royal successor of Cnút to the leader of an English faction or a French duke. Harald and Tostig fell at Stamford Bridge in Yorkshire on 25 September 1066, and the victorious Harold Godwinson marched south to meet his doom at Hastings on 14 October. The Irish annals mention 'the battle of the English' in 1066, but it was the September battle that caught their attention. As Gilla Cáemáin, writing in 1072, puts it:

> Da bliadain ní bréc i ngliaid
> o éc Dondchaid meic Bríain;
> cath Saxan seol nglaine.
> i torchair rí Lochlainne.

(Two years, no falsehood in dissension, after the death of Brian's son Donnchad, the battle of the English (course of clarity) in which the king of Norway fell.)

The annals first mention the Normans in England when, in 1072, 'the French went into Scotland and took the son of the king of Scotland with them in hostage-suretyship'. William's conquest was not complete in 1066. Svein Estridson of Denmark had responded to a Northumbrian revolt in 1069 by sending a fleet of 240 ships, but, after William's notorious 'harrying of the North', made a peace-treaty in 1070. Edgar the Ætheling fled to his brother-in-law Malcolm, whereupon William invaded Scotland and forced the king to do homage at Abernethy and deliver up Duncan, his eldest son by Ingibjorg of Orkney. The Ætheling left for Flanders, though he did play a minor part in Scottish history later when he helped his nephew and namesake, Malcolm's son Edgar, to the throne in 1097. A final threat to the Norman conquest in 1085 collapsed when the Danes refused to finance the ambitions of their new king Cnút IV, son of Svein. Cnút was assassinated by his rebellious subjects the following year, and in 1100 Pope Paschal permitted his cultus as a martyr. Henceforth the Danes had to turn their faces eastwards to defend themselves against the still-pagan Wends.

THE new strength of Ulster established during the reign of Niall mac Eochada (1012–63) and signalled by his naval operations against Dublin in 1022 and later consolidated by his alliance with Diarmait mac Maíl na mBó from 1042 on must have contributed to dynastic weakness within Cenél nEógain and may have called forth an alliance with the Cenél Loairn of Moray, which was also to their advantage if it helped to reserve the ecclesiastical claims of Derry–Kells–Iona to preserve the unity of the Columban federation as against the Cenél nGabráin establishment of a separate

Columban church in Scotland under Dunkeld. The reign of Niall mac Eochada appears to have been remarkably free from opposition or internal disorder, in marked contrast to the state of affairs prevailing in the territories of the Cenél nEógain and Airgialla. He met with no trouble from Conchobar mac Loingsig of Dál nAraide, whose alliance with the Norwegian viking Eyvind Urarshorn, friend of St Olaf, against Einar jarl of Orkney, resulted in the sea-battle of Ulfreksfjord (Larne) in 1018. This event is not noted in the Irish annals, but only in the Norse sagas (the 'Orkneyingasaga' and the 'Óláfssaga hins helga', whose editors have hitherto failed to identify 'Konofogor' the Irish king. The battle forms a fitting prelude to Niall mac Eochada's own naval victory over Dublin in 1022, whereby he seems effectively to have foiled any attempt by Flaithbertach Ua Néill to retrieve the high-kingship. Twenty years later his alliance with Diarmait mac Máel na mBó of Leinster led to control of the whole of the Irish Sea coast by the traditional enemies of the Uí Néill, and was brought to a fitting conclusion with Diarmait's capture of Dublin in 1052. Diarmait thereupon took the novel step (to be followed in the next generation by his protégé Tairdelbach ua Briain and again by his son and successor Muirchertach) of putting in his own son Murchad (eponym of the Mac Murchada family) as king there, expelling Echmarcach, who fled to Man and Galloway. Murchad by 1061 had extended the power of Dublin over Man as well, and is certainly the 'Marga∂ king of Dublin' who features in the saga of Harald Hardrada. He was remembered also in Welsh tradition as 'Mwrthach', whose son 'Solor' (?) was one of the three great commanders of fleets of the island of Britain.

It might not have seemed obvious at the time, especially to the land-locked Ua Néill of Tír Eógain or Ua Maíl Shechlainn of Mide, but in an age when the Irish Sea became a political arena of the first importance, the revival of Ulster deprived the Northern Uí Néill of any hope of dominance in Ireland or influence abroad. The Southern Uí Néill, by their failure to follow up the successes of Máel Sechnaill against Dublin in the 980s and 990s, also found themselves excluded. A double seal was attached by the arrival of another old enemy refreshed for the fray, when in 1042 the province of Leinster acquired a new lord from the southern kingdom of Uí Chennselaig. Not only was Diarmait mac Maíl na mBó to gain control of Dublin, but he formed a close alliance with the Ulster king. From 1052 to 1063 the whole east coast of Ireland from Rathlin to Waterford was in their grip. These dates are in fact too restrictive: Niall had shown as early as 1022 that he could defeat Sitric Silkbeard with a fleet on the open sea. The same year he inflicted great losses on the Airgialla at Sliab Fuait. In 1026 he led a victorious expedition into Fine Gall. In 1031 he was bold enough to attack Tullaghogue itself, and on another raid into Uí Echach less gloriously attacked the church of Cell Chomair, killing clerics and taking captives. In 1034 he led another far inland into Mide. By the time he formed his alliance with Diarmait Brega was at their joint mercy. And after Niall's death Diarmait still held sway over Dublin, Fine Gall, and beyond through his son Murchad and for the last years of his life till he fell defending the territory in 1072. As for Ulster, in the light of Niall's career, his grandson Donn Slébe's attempt in 1084 to revive the ancient Fifth of Ulster with its prehistoric boundaries seems less foolhardy than it would appear.

In 1036 leadership of the North passed from Tullaghogue and the descendants of Niall to the descendants of Domnall in Inishowen. Flaithbertach's return from pilgrimage had been followed by the death of his son and heir designate Áed three years before his own. In this he shared a misfortune which was to befall both Niall of Ulster and Diarmait of Leinster. It is doubtful whether the attempt of these three kings to preempt the succession and introduce filiogeniture was modelled on the highly successful example of the Capetian kings of France. In fact it is unlikely that they were aware of these monarchs. The Irish annals know of the emperors, especially through their contacts with Cologne, but the only references to 'kings of France' or 'of the Franks' are in fact to the duke of Normandy in 1027 and to the count of Champagne in 1038; Rouen was known to the Irish, but not Paris (the Annals of Tigernach record 'famine in France, and great scarcity and poverty in Cologne and Rouen' in 1045). In the normal course of events, the direct succession of a son would not have caused much joy to the royal family, whose members would have been deprived of their turn in the kingship. The Annals of Ulster actually record as a divine punishment on Tadg ind Eich Gil, king of Connacht, the fact that only one of his sons, Áed in Gaí Bernaig, produced royal progeny. Filiogeniture indeed replaced the Irish mode of succession in Scotland in the twelfth century, and this has usually been explained by English or French influence; but it has been pointed out that it may have been due as much to biological accident as to policy, and in any case reversion to the Pictish matrilineal system was not out of the question there till the death of 'the son of Lulach's daughter' in 1130. But in all three of the Irish cases the premature death of the heir-designate, who sometimes at least was actually functioning as king, brought disruption and discontinuity, though not perhaps for the same reasons in each instance.

Flaithbertach, in fact, left two or three sons who survived him, two apparently called Muiredach, unless the text of the annals is corrupt: one Muiredach was killed by the Léthrenna or Uí Labrada of Uí Chrimthainn in 1039; Muirchertach was regarded as king of Cenél nEógain (though perhaps only of Tullaghogue) by the Munster annalists at his obit in 1045; he had raided Uí Echach in Ulster in 1041. However, the over-kingship and the title 'king of Ailech' had been seized by a surprisingly distant relative, Niall mac Maíl Shechnaill. It is uncertain whether Niall succeeded as early as 1036, as the schematised regnal lists would have it, but he held the title in 1044. In that year he raided Uí Méith and Cuailgne to avenge an alleged profanation of the Bell of the Testament (St Patrick's Bell); in emulation Muirchertach raided the Mugdorna in pursuit of the same offence. Hundreds of cows and 'a large number of captives' suffered transplantation and worse to satisfy royal rivalry or religious zeal. Muirchertach met a somewhat ignominious end the following year: while returning from a raid on Brega he was chased by the plebeian king of that kingdom, Garbíth Ua Cathassaig, trapped by a high tide at Annagassan, and killed. His brother the second Muiredach died in Iveagh in 1046, possibly as a fugitive from the débâcle at Annagassan: he and his host Aitid Ua hAitid, king of Uí Echach, were burned in Ua hAitid's house by the king of Uachtar Tíre, a sub-kingdom of Uí Echach in the south of the County Down.

Niall reigned till his death in 1061 but made little impact outside his own kingdom apart from raids into Brega in 1047 and into Dál nAraide in 1056. But his apparent inactivity, together with the good relations he enjoyed with his more vigorous nephew, Ardgar mac Lochlainn, suggests that he succeeded in bringing some stability to the North. The very fact of his accession without any recorded conflict shows that the majority of the Cenél nEógain favoured a break with the Ua Néill tradition.

After the death of Muirchertach Ua Néill in 1046, Niall installed his nephew, Ardgar mac Lochlainn, at Tullaghogue. Ardgar was expelled in 1051 and replaced by Áed Ua Fergail, who like Ua Néill was a descendant of Niall Glúndub (he was grandson of Fergal mac Conaing, who died in 1001, having been deposed from the kingship of Ailech by Áed Ua Néill sometime before 993). In revenge Ardgar attacked the Cenél mBinnig of Loch Drochit in 1053, taking cattle and prisoners and killing the *secnap* or vice-abbot of Clonfeacle and the 'steward' (*máer*) of Dál Cais.

In the event, Áed Ua Fergail was killed by the men of Fernmag in 1054, and Ardgar continued to be active, leading the Cenél nEógain into Dál nAraide in 1059, and succeeding his uncle Niall in 1061. Although he reigned only three years he twice invaded Connacht, well outside the normal Cenél nEógain sphere of influence, carrying off 6,000 cows in 1062 and imposing his troops on Tír Conaill and northern Connacht as far as the Moy in 1063; on this occasion Áed Ua Conchobair, his two Ua Ruairc rivals, and all the kings of Connacht 'came into his house'. Ardgar died triumphant at Tullaghogue, and was buried in the royal mausoleum at Armagh. In his short career he had shown some of the ability to be inherited by his son Domnall ua Lochlainn. Given his military success in the far west (which clearly demonstrated his ability to control Tír Conaill as well as Ailech and Tír Eógain), it seems that we may plausibly credit him with a diplomatic coup to the east in Ulster. He may well have intruded a 'stranger in sovereignty' upon the Ulaid on the death of Niall mac Eochada in 1063, in the person of Donnchad Ua Mathgamna from the favoured Fir Fernmaige of Airgialla. Donnchad was assassinated in sacred precincts of the church of Comgall at

Bangor in 1065, but members of his family continued to contest the kingship of Ulster with the descendants of Niall mac Eochada until the third decade of the twelfth century. Significantly, none of them except Donnchad is admitted by Áed Mac Crimthainn into his regnal lists.

There occurred a curious hiccup in the succession after Ardgar's death. A person only remotely connected with his immediate predecessors seized the kingship of Ailech. Áed Ua hUalgairg was of the obscure Clann Duibindrecht, and none of his ancestors had held the kingship since Niall Caille in the first half of the ninth century. They were not even petty kings: in 1026 Gilla Ciarán son of the eponymous Ualgarg is merely styled *toísech* of his sept, while Áed himself in his obituary notice in 1067 is similarly only *muire* of Uí Duibindrecht: the annals do not tell us how he lost the title of king in the two years since he seized power. Were it not for a poem on the famous convention of Druim Cett, probably composed by Echtigern abbot of Monasterboice, son of the leading historian Flann Mainistrech, and who shares the same brief obit with Áed in the Annals of Ulster, we would not know his father's name nor be able to guess at the territory his sept occupied. The poem calls Áed 'mac Flainn' and indicates that he ruled over Druim Cett in the Ciannacht lands of County Londonderry.

The next two kings of Tullaghogue, Muirchertach Ua Néill (presumably a grandson of Flaithbertach) and Flaithbertach brother of Áed Ua Fergail were murdered by the Uí Chrimthainn and the Cenél mBinnig respectively in 1064 and 1068, Muirchertach being the last of the name Ua Néill to appear in the annalistic record for a century. And then the new king of Ailech, Áed son of Niall Ua Maíl Shechnaill, hit on a revolutionary scheme to keep control of Tullaghogue while remaining himself based in Inishowen. In 1069 he placed the exiled Conchobar Ua Briain from Munster as king in Tullaghogue, and when he was inevitably slain by the Cenél mBinnig in 1078, Áed persisted in this policy, putting in Conchobar's brother Cennétig mac Lorcáin. The latter was either ungrateful or nervous, and found another proffered kingship more attractive. He accepted that of Gailenga in east Cavan and north Meath from the ambitious Donnchad Ua Ruairc, married his daughter Sadb to Donn Slébe mac Eochada, king of Ulster, as part of a planned coalition against Tairdelbach Ua Briain, and fell together with Ua Ruairc at the battle of Móin Cruinneóce in 1084. Thus ended a remarkable experiment.

THE poem of 'Advice to a prince', 'Cert cech ríg co réil', supposedly composed for Áed Oirdnide mac Néill by Fothad na Canóne of Fahan Mura in 804, is really addressed to Áed mac Néill meic Máel Shechlainn *c*.1070. The practice among poets of composing such 'forgeries' was quite common. It was no more than a dramatisation of the apologue normal in later bardic poetry. The distinction between apologue and impersonation is that between simile and metaphor. The pseudonymous poem of Flann ua Lonáin to Éicnechán is an example. So is the well-known 'Mór-thimchell Érenn uile', allegedly an eyewitness account by Cormacán Éces of the circuit of Ireland made by Muirchertach mac Néill 'of the Leather Cloaks' in 941, but composed for the high-king Muirchertach mac Néill Meic Lochlainn on the occasion of his circuit in 1157. In all three cases the person addressed has the same name as his supposed ancestor.

Linguistically 'Cert cech ríg co réil' is too late to have been written either for Áed Oirdnide or for his grandson, Áed Findliath mac Néill (864–79), and the starkly realistic and unheroic tone suit better the problems facing a Northern high-king in the eleventh century. His primary duty is to avoid being assassinated, defenceless in his hut. Many verses urge obedience to the churches and reverence for bells, shrines and relics. The clergy are to be freed from all secular impositions, but Áed must impose harsh rule against outlaws and criminals. The 'seven daughters of a king', who enforce his peace, are Fetter, Gallows, Pit, Prison, Water, Blade, and Fire. The Ulstermen indeed owe him hostages, but Armagh, Tara, and Cashel are exempt. Áed must first put his own house in order: *do thuatha fadéin / tuc dot réir ar tús*; many high-kings had been killed by their own followers; the Cenél nEógain in particular regard it as a glory to kill their kings and princes—*onóir cech fhir díb / marbad ríg nó fhlaith*; though his brothers and sons may seem honourable and obedient, he is to weld together them to be of his own faction—sensible advice, since Áed had killed his own brother and predecessor, the religious Domnall Bocht. Let him keep the Cenél Conaill and Cairpre on his right hand, the descendants of Colla Uais and of Cian (the Uí Thuirtre and Ciannachta) on his left, the lions of Clanna Éogain (evidently those of Tullaghogue) go into battle ahead of him. He can trust only his Gaill (his Norse mercenaries on the Swilly and Foyle) to be behind him. He is to look after the five territories of the descendants of Colla fo Chríth. These perhaps are the Airthir and the *trí tuatha* of the Uí Chrimthainn; or the three branches of the Airthir (Uí Bressail, Uí Echdach and Uí Nialláin) together with the Uí Méith and the Uí Chrimthainn; or the Fir Fernmaige, the Fir Manach, the Fir Lemna, the Uí Méith, and the Airthir. The third of the legendary Collas, Colla Mend, ancestor of the Mugdorna, is not mentioned. The Mugdorna were in decline, and in any case traditionally loyal to Brega, not to the North.

Áed's father, Niall mac Maíl Sechnaill, may have sought an alliance with MacBeth of Scotland. Mac Bethad mac Findlaích was son of the *mormáer* of Moray, and representative of the Dál Riata house of Cenél Loairn, which had in the seventh and eighth centuries contested the kingship with the Cenél nGabráin, to which Malcolm II—Máel Coluim mac Cináeda—belonged. On Malcolm's death in 1034 his daughter's son Duncan (Donnchad) had succeeded in defiance of the Gaelic rules of succession. If matriliny were to be accepted, MacBeth had claims too as grandson through his mother of Cináed mac Maíl Choluim, as did his stepson Lulach son of Gruoch, granddaughter of Cináed mac Duib. Lulach, who was briefly to succeed MacBeth in 1057 before being killed by Malcolm Canmore in 1058, was also of the Cenél Loairn on his father's side. In any case, Gaelic authorities regarded these mormáers as kings of Alba or at least of Moray. The Armagh annalists show a keen interest in the fortunes of this house from 1020 until its overthrow by David I in 1130. The Columban church at Deer in Aberdeenshire was favoured by their benefactions, as is shown by the remarkable series of charters in Middle Irish, which parallel those of the Irish Columban houses of Kells and Durrow. It is against the background of MacBeth's successful reign from 1040 to 1057 (interrupted by the now fashionable pilgrimage to Rome that he made in 1050, when, according to the Irish chronicler Máel Brigte or Marianus Scottus at Mainz, he scattered gold to the poor) that we can understand the genesis of the curious legend linking the Cenél Loairn and Cenél nEógain: Muirchertach, alias Mac Ercae, the legendary sixth-century king of Tara and ancestor of the ruling sept of the dynasty since 700, was said to have been the son of Eógan and the Scottish princess Erc daughter of Loarn. This was of course a deliberate misreading of the Old Irish masculine proper name Mac Ercae as a matronymic, but it served the purpose.

But there was more than one Scottish card to play. Malcolm II had married his other daughter to Sigurd the Fat, the jarl of Orkney who fell with his raven banner at Clontarf. Their son was to gain the name of Thorfinn the Mighty; at first confined to the mainland territories of Caithness and Sutherland, about 1035 he gained control of the whole *jarlsríki*, and extended his rule beyond this over the Hebrides and Man which he held until his death around 1065 or 1066. He is not mentioned in the Irish annals, but there can be no doubt that his presence was felt. While the account of his career in the 'Orkneyingasaga' may not be reliable, he cannot have been without an active interest in the dynastic changes among the Dublin Norse between 1036 and 1052. He must have tolerated and may have actively supported the Irish Sea policies of Niall mac Eochada and later of Diarmait mac Maíl na mBó. He certainly supported the claims of Malcolm Canmore against MacBeth, and in fact Malcolm's first wife was Thorfinn's daughter Ingibjorg, mother of his elder sons, including Duncan II. He must have cooperated with the Irish Sea expedition against England of Magnus, son of his nominal overlord Harald Hardrada of Norway. And of course the jarls of Orkney were the deadliest foes of the mormáers of Moray, the Cenél Loairn, and all MacBeth's kin. It cannot be an accident that Diarmait's poet forged a link between Brandub mac Echach, the Uí Chennselaig king of Leinster who had defeated the Northern Uí Néill, and Áedán mac Gabráin, ancestor of Malcolm Canmore.

IT was the end of an era. The new age of Norman chivalry was that of a uniform and self-confident west-European culture imbued with crusading and colonising spirit. The reform of the papacy resulted in the final breach with the Greeks, though the coining of the term 'Byzantine' as an insulting denial of Constantinople's Roman heritage appears to have been the work of an anti-papal Italian bishop anxious to assert the legitimacy of the German emperor. The old north-western world flared up in a spectacular last blaze in 1098, when Harald Hardrada's grandson Magnus Barelegs reestablished Norwegian authority over the Isles. He brought a great fleet to the Irish Sea, and almost inadvertently halted the Norman conquest of north Wales. He installed his young son Sigurd as king of Man, and married him to the daughter of Muirchertach Ua Briain in 1102. His death in a skirmish on the Ulster coast in August 1103 is the probable cause of the military disaster that Muirchertach suffered at Mag Coba, which put an end to his hopes of becoming king of all Ireland.

# CHAPTER XXVI

# High-kings with opposition, 1072–1166

MARIE THERESE FLANAGAN

FOLLOWING the death at the battle of Clontarf of Brian Bóruma and his son, Murchad, who had been associated with him in rulership, a disputed succession for the kingship of Dál Cais and Munster ensued between Brian's sons, Tadg and Donnchad, who were half-brothers, with an Eóganacht Caisil dynast, Tadg mac Muiredaig (d. 1024), also making a bid for the kingship of Cashel. This ensured that Brian Bóruma's immediate successors failed to match his achievements in pursuit of the high-kingship of Ireland. Tadg was slain at the instigation of Donnchad in 1023, but his removal did not terminate Dál Cais dynastic dissension since Tadg's son, Toirrdelbach, took over his father's ambition to be king of Munster. A decisive factor in the struggle between uncle and nephew was the alliance concluded between Toirrdelbach and Diarmait mac Maíl na mBó, king of Leinster (1042–72). In 1063 Toirrdelbach succeeded in deposing Donnchad, who was to die in exile in Rome in 1064. But although Toirrdelbach assumed the kingship of Munster, he faced opposition from Donnchad's son, Murchad an Sgéith Girr, who, not unnaturally, harboured ambitions to succeed his father as king. However, the killing of Murchad in 1068 removed Toirrdelbach's most serious rival for the kingship of Munster. In the same year he proclaimed a *cáin 7 rechtge*, a public assertion of his rule as king of Munster. His visit to the court of Diarmait mac Máel na mBó, king of Leinster, from which he returned, having received as a ceremonial gift, or *tuarastal*, the sword of his grandfather, Brian Bóruma, was an endorsement of his kingship. In the same year, Máel Ísu, *comarba Pátraic*, that is head of the church of Armagh (1064–91), undertook a circuit of Munster which may have affirmed Toirrdelbach's kingship of Munster, and possibly even encouraged his pursuit of the high-kingship in imitation of Brian Bóruma. The kings of Cenél nEógain had been the patrons of the church of Armagh since at least the ninth century, but dynastic tensions within the Cenél nEógain during the eleventh century may have persuaded the *comarba Pátraic* to endeavour to continue the link with the Dál Cais dynasty that had been so successfully promoted by Brian Bóruma.

The death of the Leinster king, Diarmait mac Maíl na mBó, in 1072 allowed Toirrdelbach greater freedom in his bid to reconstitute the Dál Cais overlordship of his grandfather, Brian Bóruma, while the assassination in 1073 of Conchobar Ua Máel Sechlainn, king of Mide, removed the legitimist Uí Néill candidate for the high-kingship. Toirrdelbach's transferral of Conchobar's head from its burial place in Clonmacnoise, and its public display at Kincora (reported in the Annals of Tigernach) may have been intended to underline his own aspiration to the high-kingship. From 1072 till his death in 1086, Toirrdelbach achieved a degree of acknowledgement from the kings of Leinster and Osraige and, unlike Brian Bóruma, he never had to face rebellion in Leinster on the scale that had occasioned the battle of Clontarf. He was able to exploit the regnal instability within the Uí Chennselaig dynasty that had followed on the death of Diarmait mac Maíl na mBó. In 1072 Gofraid, Hiberno-Norse king of Dublin, along with the kings of Leinster and Osraige, acknowledged Toirrdelbach's overlordship. He intensified his hold on Dublin in 1074 when he expelled Gofraid and installed his own son, Muirchertach, as king there. Not only was he associating his son with him in rulership, in the manner in which Brian Bóruma had promoted his son, Murchad, it also represented a significant restoration of Dál Cais influence within the city of Dublin, which had been compromised by the battle of Clontarf in 1014. Control of Dublin gave Toirrdelbach access to the movable wealth generated by the manufacturing and trading activities of the city, and to additional naval fleets that could be deployed in the pursuit of a wider overlordship, particularly in Leth Cuinn. For a good part of his reign, he also exerted some degree of influence in Connacht, Mide, Bréifne, and Ulaid. In Connacht he exploited rivalries between the competing lineages of the Uí Briúin Aí, in the person of Ruaidrí na Saide Buide Ua Conchobair, and the Uí Briúin Bréifne, in the person of Áed mac Airt Uí Ruairc: in 1074 Toirrdelbach intervened to promote Ruaidrí as king of Connacht at Áed's expense. In 1072, 1073, 1079, and 1080 he took hostages from Ua Máel Sechlainn, king of Mide. Military expeditions into Mide were aimed, not only at asserting lordship over its king, but also at curtailing expansion into the east Mide subkingdom of Gailenga by Donnchad Ua Ruairc, king of Bréifne, brother of Áed mac Airt Uí Ruairc, aspirant to the provincial kingship of Connacht. Donnchad Ua Ruairc's opposition to Toirrdelbach Ua Briain is evidenced by his association with the dissident Dál Cais dynast, Cennétig Ua Briain, son of Lorcán son of Donnchad (abd. 1063, d. 1064), son of Brian Bóruma, whom Ua Ruairc temporarily placed in the kingship of Gailenga in 1078. Toirrdelbach had taken hostages from Gailenga in 1073, but in 1078 Cennétig Ua Briain was installed as subordinate king under Donnchad Ua Ruairc. Evidently Cennétig had taken refuge with Donnchad Ua Ruairc as a prominent opponent of Toirrdelbach.

In 1075 Toirrdelbach mounted a major military expedition into the north; his army comprised, not only the men of Munster, but contingents from Leinster, Connacht, Osraige, and Mide as well as Hiberno-Norse fleets, indicating his widening sphere of influence. He was forestalled, however, at Ardee by a force from Airgialla, and obliged to retreat without any tangible gains. An alternative means of extending his influence in the north presented itself in 1078 when Donn Sléibe, king of Ulaid, repaired to Toirrdelbach's court at Kincora after he was deposed by a rival dynast, Áed Méránach.[1] By that act of submission, which he renewed in 1081, Donn Sléibe recovered the kingship. In 1084, however, he rejected Toirrdelbach's overlordship and concluded an alliance with Donnchad Ua Ruairc, king of Bréifne, offering *tuarastal* to Ua Ruairc at Drogheda in a vainglorious gesture intended to signify the restoration of the ancient kingdom of Ulaid, which formerly had extended as far as the River Boyne. This was a calculated insult to Toirrdelbach's pretensions to overlordship in that area, and Toirrdelbach responded by taking the army of Munster into Mide. In its absence from Munster Donnchad Ua Ruairc plundered in Dál Cais territory and then, with contingents recruited from east Connacht, Cairbre, and Gailenga, invaded Leinster, by way of provocation. On 19 October 1084, at Móin Cruinneoice (Monecronock near Leixlip, County Kildare), Ua Ruairc was engaged in battle by a Munster army led by Toirrdelbach's son, Muirchertach, which included contingents from Leinster, Osraige, and Dublin, indicating that the majority of Leinster kings, whether perforce or from choice, held to Toirrdelbach's side. Ua Ruairc was killed, and among the four thousand reputed to have fallen on the vanquished side was the dissident Cennétig Ua Briain and four other Ua Briain dynasts. Donnchad Ua Ruairc's head was taken for triumphant public display to Limerick. His defeat as the ringleader of an opposition party against Toirrdelbach's pretensions to a wider hegemony was a significant victory for Toirrdelbach. In the context of Dál Cais dynastic politics the battle of Móin Cruinneoice also signified the triumph of the line of Tadg mac Briain Bóruma over that of Donnchad mac Briain Bóruma: the heirs of Donnchad were to give no further trouble to either Toirrdelbach or his son, Muirchertach, when the latter succeeded his father in 1086.

By contrast with Brian Bóruma, Toirrdelbach made fewer attempts to assert lordship over the northern Uí Néill. For the greater part of his reign the Cenél nEógain were weakened by dynastic dissension between the Ua Néill and Mac Lochlainn lineages. During the eleventh century the descendants of Niall Glúndub (d. 919, *a quo* Ua Néill), whose power base lay south

---

[1] Niall mac Eochada, king of Ulaid 1016–63, had been in alliance with Diarmait mac Maíl na mBó, king of Leinster.

of the Sperrin mountains and was centred around the royal site of Telach Óc (Tullaghogue, County Tyrone), lost its hold on the overkingship of Cenél nEógain to more distant Mac (Ua) Lochlainn kinsmen, whose stronghold was located on the Inishowen peninsula (whence Cenél nEógain na hInnsi). In the manner of Donnchad Ua Ruairc, king of Bréifne, the Cenél nEógain na hInnsi attempted to deploy Dál Cais dissidents as a means of defying Toirrdelbach. In 1078 Áed mac Néill, king of Cenél nEógain (1068–83), installed the Dál Cais exile, Conchobar (brother of Cennétig Ua Briain), in the kingship of Telach Óc at the expense of the rival Ua Néill lineage, and following Conchobar's almost immediate assassination, replaced him with Cennétig, who was to move on to the kingship of Gailenga under the auspices of Donnchad Ua Ruairc, king of Bréifne (above, p. 900). The kingship of Cenél nEógain did not stabilise till the accession of Domnall Mac Lochlainn (1083–1121), and hence did not pose a significant threat to Toirrdelbach's pretensions to the high-kingship.

Toirrdelbach's assertion of overlordship was demonstrated, not merely by military force or the latent threat of it, but also by the attendance of subordinates at his court in Kincora or Limerick. Donn Sléibe, king of Ulaid, had visited Toirrdelbach's court at Kincora in 1078. In 1083 Donn Sléibe's rival, Áed Méránach, was drowned at Limerick; possibly he too had been prepared to offer voluntary submission to Toirrdelbach, which may account for Donn Sléibe's change of policy towards Toirrdelbach in 1084 (above, p. 901). In 1077 Donnchad Ua Flainn, king of Eóganacht Locha Léin, was killed as he was returning from Toirrdelbach's house at Kincora. In 1080 Máel Sechlainn Ua Máel Sechlainn, king of Mide, attended on Toirrdelbach at Limerick. The increasing political importance of such public ceremonial events is evidenced by their recording in the annals. In general, however, annalistic entries for Toirrdelbach's reign are sparse. There were just enough entries to enable James Hogan to piece together the association of Toirrdelbach's dynastic rivals, Cennétig and Conchobar Ua Briain, with his political enemies, Donnchad Ua Ruairc, king of Bréifne, and the Cenél nEógain na hInnsi.[2] A charter-text copied into the Book of Kells, recording a land transaction between 1073 and 1087, contains a tantalising reference to Donnchad mac Carthaig Uí Chellacháin, 'king of Cashel of the kings'.[3] While 'king of Cashel' in this instance almost certainly denoted king of Eóganacht Caisil, rather than king of Munster, it may be inferred that Donnchad mac Carthaig was an Eóganacht dissident, who, like Conchobar and Cennétig Ua Briain, pursued his political ambitions in association with Toirrdelbach's enemy, Donnchad Ua Ruairc, king of Bréifne, who in the same charter-text is styled

---

[2] James Hogan, 'The Uí Briain kingship in Telach Óc' in *Féil-Sgríbhinn Eóin Mhic Néill*, pp 406–44.

[3] Gearóid Mac Niocaill, *Notititae as Leabhar Cheanannais, 1033–1161* (Dublin, 1961), pp 14–15; 'The Irish charters' in *Kells commentary*, pp 153–65:155.

'king of Connacht and Gailenga'. Since Toirrdelbach had supported the accession of Ruaidrí Ua Conchobair to the provincial kingship of Connacht, Donnchad Ua Ruairc's titulature may be interpreted as a defiance of Toirrdelbach. Such cryptic clues hint at the ramifications beyond Munster of his pursuit of the high-kingship.

Of domestic politics within Dál Cais and Munster during Toirrdelbach's reign little is recorded in the annals, but the construction as public royal works of bridges across the Shannon at Killaloe and at Áth Caille (probably Athlunkard) in the space of a week is recorded in 1071 in the Annals of Inisfallen, an indication that Toirrdelbach could exact labour services from his subjects on a not insignificant scale and in an organised manner. His overlordship of Dublin from 1072 onwards would have necessitated an interest in overseas trade, which probably explains the visit in 1079 of five Jews bearing gifts to Toirrdelbach; possibly they came from the city of Rouen, which had one of the largest Jewish populations in western Europe at this period. It was also as a by-product of Toirrdelbach's overlordship of Dublin that his son, Diarmait, led a plundering fleet to Wales in 1080, since control of the Irish Sea province had a direct bearing on Dublin's trade.

A very important dimension of Toirrdelbach's pursuit of the high-kingship was his relations with the church. While the Dál Cais dynasty traditionally had aimed to control the key churches in Munster, Toirrdelbach's ecclesiastical policies ranged more widely. His involvement in the city of Dublin introduced an overseas dimension. The circumstances in which the Hiberno-Norse communities in Ireland converted to Christianity remain obscure, but by the early eleventh century the Christian population of Dublin was sufficiently large to warrant its own bishop. The death of the first known bishop of Dublin, Dúnán (Donatus) is recorded in 1074. The creation of his episcopal see is presumed to date from the reign of Sitric, Hiberno-Norse king of Dublin (acceded 981, deposed 1036, died 1042), who went on pilgrimage to Rome in 1028, and who, according to later medieval tradition, was the founder of Christ Church cathedral. There is no secure evidence as to where, or by whom, Dúnán was consecrated as bishop, but in 1074 Dúnán's successor, Gilla Pátraic (Patricius), sought consecration at the hands of the archbishop of Canterbury. Since the cathedral church of Dublin appears to have been founded under the auspices of King Sitric, and since in the aftermath of the battle of Clontarf (1014) the city was relieved for a time from the overlordship of Irish kings, and may have been drawn into the orbit of influence of the Anglo-Danish empire of King Cnút, who had conquered England in 1016, it has been postulated that Dúnán may have sought consecration at Canterbury. According to that view, it was a precedent set by Dúnán that determined that his successor, Gilla Pátraic, had recourse to Canterbury in 1074. There is, however, no conclusive evidence that Dúnán actually had been consecrated at Canterbury, and it is equally possible that

Gilla Pátraic was the first bishop of Dublin to seek consecration there. Before Gilla Pátraic's elevation to the see of Dublin in 1074 he had been a monk in the Benedictine community at Worcester. Its prior, Wulfstan, had been elected bishop of Worcester in 1062, and had chosen to be consecrated by Ealdred, archbishop of York (1062–9): although acknowledging that the see of Worcester was a suffragan of Canterbury and therefore owed obedience to its archbishop, Wulfstan had deliberately avoided consecration by the then archbishop of Canterbury, Stigand (1052–70 (dep.)), because Stigand's own consecration was uncanonical. Instead, Wulfstan sought consecration at York, without, however, making a profession of obedience to Ealdred in prejudice to that which Wulfstan believed was due to Canterbury. In August 1070, following the deposition of Stigand and the consecration of the Italian schoolman and reformer, Lanfranc, Wulfstan offered his profession of obedience to Lanfranc as canonically consecrated archbishop of Canterbury. Those circumstances are likely to have been known to Gilla Pátraic via his associations with Worcester, and may have determined his recourse in 1074 to Canterbury for episcopal consecration. Taking into account the chronology of contemporary developments in canon law, Gilla Pátraic's request for consecration by the archbishop of Canterbury is more readily explicable in his case than in that of his predecessor, Dúnán. Canon law required that a bishop-elect be consecrated by a plurality of bishops, and, although participation of a metropolitan archbishop was desirable, it did not have the same urgency during the period when Dúnán is presumed to have become bishop of Dublin (c.1028–36). By the time of Gilla Pátraic's consecration in 1074, however, circumstances had changed. Pope Leo IX (1048–54) had inaugurated his reform of ecclesiastical offices with an attack on simony at the council of Rheims (1049), which had the effect of highlighting procedures for the election and consecration of bishops. The reforming Cardinal Humbert, in his 'Adversus simoniacos libri tres' (1057) insisted on three stages: election by the clergy, request by the people, and consecration by the bishops of the province on the authority of the metropolitan. The eleventh-century Irish church, however, lacked a canonically acceptable metropolitan. The church of Armagh had enjoyed a traditional honorific preeminence, but its principal offices had been monopolised from the mid tenth century by the laicised Clann Sínaich family, whose members not only succeeded each other in hereditary succession, but had ceased to take holy orders. Consecration by a canonically valid metropolitan would have created difficulties for Gilla Pátraic and may explain his resort to Archbishop Lanfranc. It is posssible, therefore, that Gilla Pátraic's consecration by the archbishop of Canterbury was indeed the first such of an Irish bishop. This is suggested also by the fact that Lanfranc, who on his accession to Canterbury undertook a thorough investigation of the rights and privileges of his new see, made no mention of any precedent for consecration of a bishop of Dublin, or any other Irish

bishop, in the letters that he addressed in the wake of Gilla Pátraic's consecration to Toirrdelbach Ua Briain and to Gofraid, king of Dublin. But,
whatever way the link between the see of Dublin and Canterbury was established, certain it is that by 1074 Irish churchmen were brought into contact,
in the person of Lanfranc, with a commited advocate of the European church
reform movement. Lanfranc addressed Toirrdelbach as *magnificus Hiberniae
rex*, while he wrote to Gofraid, king of Dublin, as *gloriosius Hiberniae rex*,
the differing styles of address indicating that he understood Toirrdelbach to
be Gofraid's overlord, if not indeed 'king of Ireland'.[4] Lanfranc wrote, as he
said to Gofraid, *more antecessorum nostrorum* (in the manner of our predecessors). This may mean no more than that he was aware, as he would have
been from reading Bede's 'Ecclesiastical history', that Laurence, archbishop
of Canterbury (604–19), had written a 'letter of exhortation in conjunction
with his fellow bishops to the Irish' (*Hist. ecc.*, ii, 4). In his letter to Toirrdelbach, Lanfranc stated that he had heard much about Toirrdelbach from Gilla
Pátraic, and exhorted Toirrdelbach to order bishops and religious to convene
an assembly that he should attend in person with his chief advisers; in
particular, Lanfranc urged reforms relating to the consecration of bishops
and the abolition of simony; he also adverted, both in his letter to Toirrdelbach and to Gofraid, to the reprehensible practices, which he understood
were current in Ireland among the laity, of divorce and remarriage, and
concubinage. From Lanfranc's correspondence it is plain that Gilla Pátraic
must have had contact with Toirrdelbach prior to his journey to Canterbury
and had his approval to seek consecration there. After Gilla Pátraic's
drowning while crossing the Irish Sea in 1084 (additional evidence of the
overseas dimension of his career), his successor, Donngus (Donatus), was
consecrated in 1085 by Lanfranc 'at the request of the king, clergy, and
people of Ireland' (according to the 'Acta Lanfranci'). The annals of
St Mary's Abbey, Dublin (possibly drawing on a Worcester source), went
further in asserting that it was *petentibus atque eligentibus eum Terdyluaco
Hibernie rege et episcopis Hibernie regionis atque clero et populo prefate civitatis*.[5]
Donngus had been trained as a monk at Christ Church, Canterbury, and
after his consecration he too returned with letters of exhortation to the kings
and clergy of Ireland (no longer extant). From a subsequent letter of Lanfranc's successor, Archbishop Anselm, we learn that Lanfranc had also given
Donngus books, vestments, and ornaments for the church of Dublin.

It is difficult to gauge how the church of Armagh, which claimed a traditional preeminence within the Irish church, may have reacted to the consecrations of bishops of Dublin at Canterbury. In the seventh century Armagh

---

[4] *The letters of Lanfranc, archbishop of Canterbury*, ed. Helen Clover and Margaret Gibson
(Oxford, 1979), nos 9, 10.
[5] *Chartul. St Mary's, Dublin*, ii, 250.

had claimed metropolitan status and an appelate jurisdiction, but that emphasis had long since given way to asserting overlordship of a primarily fiscal character. In 1005 Brian Bóruma had secured endorsement for his high-kingship from the church of Armagh. In 1021 Amalgaid, *comarba Pátraic*, undertook a circuit of Munster and in 1026 celebrated Easter with Donnchad mac Briain Bóruma at his court in Kincora, indicating the continuity of the association.[6] In 1068 Máel Ísu, *comarba Pátraic*, had undertaken a circuit of Munster, presumably with the acquiesence of the new king, Toirrdelbach, and possibly in endorsement of his accession (above, p. 899). As far as is known, however, this was the only occasion during Máel Ísu's period in office (1064–91) on which he visited Munster (the next recorded circuit of a *comarba Pátraic* in Munster was that of Domnall mac Amalgada in 1094 (see below, p. 911). It remains uncertain, therefore, how far Toirrdelbach may have enjoyed the support of Máel Ísu after 1068. The long-standing association of the church of Armagh with the Cenál nEógain kings had undoubtedly been compromised by Armagh's endorsement of Brian Bóruma's high-kingship and by regnal instability in the kingship of Cenél nEógain during the eleventh century (above, pp 901–2), but it may have been restored after the accession of Áed mac Néill as king of Cenél nEógain (1068–83), which would have militated against a closer relationship between Toirrdelbach and the church of Armagh. Deteriorating relations with Armagh may have induced Toirrdelbach to allow the consecrations of Gilla Pátraic and Donngus at Canterbury; and he may well have felt that the wisdom of such action was affirmed by Lanfranc's letter addressing him as *magnificus Hiberniae rex*, which could be interpreted as an endorsement of his high-kingship. Toirrdelbach also received a letter from Pope Gregory VII (1073–85), styling him *inclitus rex Hiberniae*.[7] It is difficult to judge whether the pope wrote independently of Lanfranc, or at the latter's suggestion, since Gregory's letter lacks a secure date and it cannot be ascertained if it pre- or post-dates Lanfranc's contact with Toirrdelbach in 1074. Whether or not directly inspired by Gregory's and/or Lanfranc's admonitions, there is evidence of concern about doctrinal issues in Toirrdelbach's court circle. About 1080–81 Toirrdelbach's chief ecclesiastic, Bishop Domnall Ua hÉnna, notwithstanding that he belonged to a hereditary ecclesiastical family associated with the Dál Cais church of Killaloe, exhibited religious concerns by writing to Lanfranc querying whether infants in danger of death had to receive the eucharist as a prerequisite for eternal salvation. Lanfranc, horrified by the question, replied very firmly that neither the English nor the continental churches held such a view. Domnall also had the temerity to raise questions about secular learning to which Lanfranc's acid response was that his pastoral

---

[6] In 1073 Bébinn, daughter of Brian Bóruma, died at Armagh (A.U.).
[7] M. P. Sheehy (ed.), *Pontificia Hibernica* (2 vols, Dublin, 1962, 1965), i, no. 2.

responsibilities precluded him from dealing with them. At the very least, however, Domnall Ua hÉnna's letter reveals that Irish churchmen were becoming more conscious of differences and anomalies in Irish ecclesiastical discipline and organisation.

In 1085 Toirrdelbach Ua Briain succumbed to an illness from which he died on 14 July 1086. He was described as 'king of Ireland' in his death notice, not only in the partisan Munster Annals of Inisfallen, but also in the Annals of Ulster, and in 'Chronicon Scotorum', as 'king of the greater part of Ireland', an acknowledgement of his achievements in extending his overlordship beyond the southern half of Ireland. A regnal succession dispute ensued within the Dál Cais dynasty, with a compromise initially of a division of Munster between three of Toirrdelbach's sons, Muirchertach and Tadg, who were full brothers, and a half-brother, Diarmait. Tadg died almost immediately 'in his father's bed at Kincora' (which may be taken to indicate that he did so from natural causes), whereupon Diarmait was banished by Muirchertach, who became sole king of Munster. Since Muirchertach had been associated in rulership from 1075 as governor of Dublin, and probably also of Leinster, it may be assumed that he was his father's chosen successor-designate. However, it was to take till 1093 before he fully overcame his half-brother Diarmait's opposition, eventually reconciling him by delegating to Diarmait governorship of the Hiberno-Norse city of Waterford.

The first ten years of Muirchertach's reign were spent in sustaining and consolidating the overlordship beyond Munster which his father, Toirrdelbach, had achieved in Leinster, Dublin, Connacht, and Mide. Muirchertach campaigned in Leinster in 1087, 1088, 1089, 1091, and 1092. Initially, he faced collusion between his half-brother, Diarmait, and Donnchad mac Domnaill Remair, king of Leinster (1075–89), who also took control of Dublin for a time; however, at the battle of Ráith Étair (County Dublin) in 1087, Muirchertach inflicted a defeat on their combined forces, which probably also confirmed Muirchertach's overlordship of the city of Dublin. About 1091 Godred Crovan (Gofraid Méránach), king of Man since 1075/9, succeeded in intruding himself for a short period into Dublin, but he was expelled in 1094 and replaced by Muirchertach's own son, Domnall. Thereafter, Muirchertach's influence in the city was secure, and, generally he was acknowledged as overlord by all the major dynasts of Leinster, with the possible exception only of the north Leinster Ua Conchobair kings of Uí Failge.

In his bid for the high-kingship, Muirchertach's chief opponent was to be Domnall Mac Lochlainn, king of Cenél nEógain (1083–1121), whose reign broadly coincided chronologically with Muirchertach's as king of Munster (1086–1119). Muirchertach's attempts to assert overlordship in Connacht were challenged almost immediately by Mac Lochlainn, who took hostages in 1088 from Ruaidrí Ua Conchobair, king of Connacht, and obliged the Connacht king to participate in a marauding expedition into Munster, in the course of which the Dál Cais stronghold of Kincora was attacked and captives taken whom Muirchertach subsequently was obliged to ransom. Nevertheless, Muirchertach campaigned with increasing success in Connacht in 1089, 1092, 1093/2, 1094, and 1095. In much the same way as his father Toirrdelbach had done, he used a combination of military campaigns and strategic exploitation of internal dynastic dissension to extend and sustain his influence beyond Munster. In 1092, when the Uí Briúin Aí dynast, Ruaidrí na Saide Buide Ua Conchobair, king of Connacht since 1087, was blinded by Flaithbertach Ua Flaithbertaig of the Uí Briúin Seóla, who seized the kingship in his stead, Muirchertach, according to the Annals of Inisfallen, 'assumed the kingship of Connacht himself'. In 1093 he attempted to instal as king of Connacht Gilla na Nóeb Ua hEidin, king of Uí Fiachrach, a south Connacht sub-kingdom that bordered Dál Cais territory and was subject to intermittent Dál Cais influence. Annalistic entries for the reign of Muirchertach are more detailed than for that of his father, Toirrdelbach. Military campaigns, in particular, are described at greater length, reflecting their increasing importance in determining political developments and a growing diversity of tactics. Not only did Muirchertach make extensive use of fleets on the River Shannon and at sea, there is also evidence for his deployment of semi-permanent field armies, manned garrisons, contingents of cavalry, and siege warfare. In the Connacht campaign of 1095, for instance, he besieged Dún Tais (the name indicates a fortified stronghold), near Athlone, from 6 January till 21 November, and Mag Ua Fiachrach from 21 June till 29 September. At the same time he maintained a large fleet on Loch Ree. He thereby obtained the submission of Síl Muiredaig and Conmaicne and installed Domnall Ua Ruairc as king of Connacht (1098–1102), arrogating to himself lordship of the Connacht sub-kingdoms of Uí Fiachrach, Uí Maine, and Luigne. In 1106 he was to intervene again to determine the regnal succession in favour of Toirrdelbach mac Ruaidrí na Saide Buide Ua Conchobair, who was to enjoy an exceptionally long reign as king of Connacht (1106–56), and ironically to become a powerful rival to Dál Cais pretensions to the high-kingship.

Muirchertach's attempts to extend Dál Cais hegemony into the North met with implacable opposition from Domnall Mac Lochlainn, king of Cenél nEógain. In 1090 Muirchertach Ua Briain, on campaign in Mide, was forced to submit to Mac Lochlainn at Athboy; indeed, Muirchertach had to give Mac Lochlainn hostages in order to secure the safe passage of his army back to Munster. In 1094 Mac Lochlainn persuaded Domnall mac Flainn Uí Máel Sechlainn, king of Mide, who had voluntarily submitted to Muirchertach at Limerick in 1093, to join him and together they engaged Muirchertach's army, which comprised the forces of Munster, Leinster, and Osraige (and Dublin?) at Uachtar (Oughterard, County Dublin), a location significantly within Leth Mogha, that is Muirchertach's supposed sphere of influence. Mac Lochlainn inflicted a clear defeat on Muirchertach, from which, however, the northern king failed to make significant gains when his erstwhile allies refused to undertake further military action. Regaining the initiative, Muirchertach went on to expel Gofraid from the kingship of Dublin and to campaign in Mide, deposing Domnall mac Flainn Ua Máel Sechlainn, banishing him to the North, and appointing as king another Ua Máel Sechlainn dynast, Donnchad mac Murchada. Later in the same year, Muirchertach effected a partition of Mide between Donnchad mac Murchada and Conchobar mac Máel Sechlainn Ua Máel Sechlainn, the dynastic repercussions of which seriously weakened the Clann Cholmáin royal dynasty and precluded any effective opposition to Muirchertach's assertion of lordship over Mide. With dominance in Leinster, Dublin, Connacht, and Mide achieved, to the extent that neither the kings of Connacht nor Mide again opposed him, from 1097 onwards Muirchertach embarked on an extended series of campaigns to penetrate Domnall Mac Lochlainn's sphere of influence. With an army drawn from Munster, Leinster, Mide, and Connacht, he sought to advance into the North via Ulaid, but was forestalled by a truce arranged between himself and Mac Lochlainn under the auspices of Domnall mac Amalgada, *comarba Pátraic*. In 1098 Muirchertach tried to enter via Airgialla, and again in 1099, but yet another truce was negotiated between him and Mac Lochlainn. In 1100, approaching by the western route through Connacht, his progress was halted at Assaroe by Mac Lochlainn's subordinate, the king of Cenél Conaill, while a Dublin fleet, which had sailed north on Muirchertach's behalf, was destroyed by Mac Lochlainn himself, who engaged it off the Inishowen coast. Eventually in 1101, with an army drawn from Munster, Leinster, Osraige, and Connacht, Muirchertach penetrated Mac Lochlainn's sphere of influence via Cenél Conaill. Advancing into Cenél nEógain, he headed for, and reputedly destroyed, the fortress of Ailech as the symbol of Cenél nEógain power, and proceeded eastwards into Ulaid, where he took hostages. By this campaign he had effectively challenged Mac Lochlainn's hegemony in the north. According to the Annals of the Four Masters, Muirchertach's soldiers each brought a stone away from the fortress of Ailech in their knapsacks in revenge for Domnall Mac Lochlainn's attack on Kincora in 1088 (above, p. 908). Muirchertach's campaign of 1101, styled a *slóighedh tímchill* in the Annals of the Four Masters, was a clear challenge to Domnall Mac Lochlainn, who had elected not to engage Muirchertach in battle. But neither had Mac Lochlainn conceded hostages; indeed, while Muirchertach was on circuit in the north, a northern naval force attacked Dál Cais territory, plundering the church of Inis Cathaig (Scattery Island) in the Shannon estuary. In 1102 Muirchertach concluded a treaty with Magnus III (Barelegs), king of Norway (1093–1103), who had been operating in the Irish Sea province from 1098 in a bid to assert Norwegian supremacy in the Western Isles, Man, and Anglesey. Magnus's naval operations, particularly in relation to the Isle of Man, which had dynastic links with the Hiberno-Norse aristocracy in Dublin, would have been of concern to Muirchertach as overlord of Dublin. It was in Muirchertach's interest to control piracy and to protect trade in the Irish Sea province. Like Dublin, the Isle of Man could provide mercenary fleets for hire, including to such potential enemies as Domnall Mac Lochlainn. In concluding an alliance with King Magnus, which was formalised by the betrothal of Magnus's twelve-year old son, Sigurd, to Muirchertach's daughter, Ben Muman, Muirchertach may have aimed to enlist the aid of Magnus and his fleet in advance of Domnall Mac Lochlainn. and to use it as a means of extending his own influence in the north of Ireland.

Suzerainty over Ulaid now became the deciding factor in the struggle for supremacy in the North. In July 1103 Muirchertach, with the forces of Munster, Leinster, Osraige, Dublin, Connacht, and Mide, hosted to Armagh in support of Donnchad mac Duinn Sléibe, king of Ulaid. The Munster army besieged Armagh for a fortnight, while Domnall Mac Lochlainn took no action. In an act reminiscent of Brian Bóruma's benefaction on his visit to Armagh in 1005, Muirchertach made an offering of eight ounces of gold, and pledged a payment of 160 cows to the church of Armagh. He then divided his forces into three sections, permitting the Eóganacht contingents to return to Munster, and leaving a portion of the Munster army with contingents from Leinster and Osraige in Mag Coba (near Dromore, County Down), while he himself went on foray into Dál nAraide. Muirchertach's forces thus divided, Domnall Mac Lochlainn attacked, and at the battle of Mag Coba, fought on 5 August 1103, Muirchertach's army suffered a heavy defeat. Among those slain on his side were the king of Osraige, five Leinster dynasts, the Munster kings of Ciarraige, Corcu Duibne, and Déise, and three Hiberno-Norse leaders from Dublin. Muirchertach's royal tent (*pupall*) and many other valuables were captured. Later in the same month, on 23 or 24 August, King Magnus of Norway was killed in a skirmish in Ulaid, where he may have been intending to operate on Muirchertach's behalf. In 1104 Muirchertach campaigned in Mag Muirtheimne (County Louth), traditionally regarded as part of the overkingdom of Ulaid, and in 1105 and 1109 in Bréifne, with a view to curtailing the expansion of Ua Ruairc, king of Bréifne, into Mide. Only intervention by the *comarba Pátraic* and negotiation of a truce prevented hostilities between Muirchertach and Domnall Mac Lochlainn in 1109. When in 1113 Mac Lochlainn deposed Donnchad mac Duinn Sléibe from the kingship of Ulaid, divided Ulaid between Ua Mathgamna and sons of Donn Sléibe, and arrogated to himself lordship of Uí Echach Coba and Dál nAraide, Muirchertach mounted another expedition to Mag Coba in support of Donnchad mac Duinn Sléibe, but once again battle was avoided through the intervention of the *comarba Pátraic*.

About the same time as Muirchertach had concluded an alliance with King Magnus of Norway, another of Muirchertach's daughters, named as 'Lafracoth' by the Norman chronicler Orderic Vitalis, was betrothed to Arnulf de Montgomery, lord of Pembroke. The marriage-alliance was formed against the background of a rebellion by Arnulf's brother Robert, earl of Shrewsbury, against King Henry I of England (1100–35). Almost certainly Arnulf's primary intention was to secure for the de Montgomery brothers the neutrality of Muirchertach's ally, King Magnus, who in 1098, on a marauding expedition in north Wales, had killed Robert's elder brother, Hugh, the then earl of Shrewsbury. Additionally, the Montgomerys may have hoped to procure mercenaries from Muirchertach and King Magnus. In entering into alliance with rebellious subjects of King Henry I, and in supplying men for an expedition to Wales, Muirchertach incurred the hostility of Henry I, with the consequence (according to the English chronicler William of Malmesbury), that Henry placed an embargo on trade between Ireland and England. Such an embargo would adversely have affected Dublin and Waterford, and consequentially Muirchertach, as overlord of those towns. The situation was sufficiently grave for Muirchertach to seek the intercession of Anselm, archbishop of Canterbury, with Henry I on behalf of his son-in-law, Arnulf de Montgomery.

Muirchertach's recourse to Archbishop Anselm as mediator stemmed from continuing contacts between the sees of Canterbury and Dublin, while in 1096 a new link had been forged when Anselm consecrated the first bishop of Waterford. In December 1091 Domnall mac Amalgada had succeeded his brother, Máel Ísu, as head of the church of Armagh. During Máel Ísu's term of office (1064–91), he had, as far as is known, made only one visit to Munster, in 1068 (that is, before Toirrdelbach's bid for the high-kingship was launched in 1072). In 1093 Máel Ísu's successor visited Munster and played a part in the reconciliation between Muirchertach and his half-brother and rival, Diarmait, who had been exiled to Ulaid in 1092. In 1094 Domnall mac Amalgada made a circuit of Munster, exacting dues. He could hardly have done so without Muirchertach's acquiesence, and some form of rapprochement between Muirchertach and the new *comarba Pátraic* may perhaps be inferred. However, notwithstanding those contacts with Armagh, following the death of Donngus, bishop of Dublin, on 22 November 1095 (from the pestilence that afflicted Ireland in that year), his successor, Samuel Ua hÁingliu, who was also his nephew, was consecrated by Archbishop Anselm of Canterbury on 27 April 1096. Additionally, on 27 December Anselm consecrated Máel Ísu (Malchus) Ua hAinmire as the first bishop for the Hiberno-Norse city of Waterford. Both men had trained in England, Samuel in the Benedictine community of St Albans, while Máel Ísu had been a priest of Walkelin, bishop of Winchester (1070–92). The written request to Anselm for consecration of Máel Ísu Ua hAinmire, as preserved by Anselm's biographer, Eadmer, in his 'Historia Novorum', was subscribed by Muirchertach, *rex Hiberniae*, his brother, Diarmait, *dux frater regis* (as governor of Waterford), Bishop Domnall (Ua hÉnna, chief bishop in Munster), Máel Muire Ua Dúnáin, bishop of Mide, Samuel, bishop of Dublin, and Ferdomnach, 'bishop of the men of Leinster' (Eadmer stated that there were other signatories whose names he omitted).[8] The tenor of the letter—indeed, the very dispatch of a formal petition for consecration—indicates a desire to meet the canonical requirement that an episcopal candidate be chosen freely *ex clero et populo*. The letter also emphasised that the bishop-elect was a priest, properly instructed, who had progressed *in gradibus singulis*. Apostolic renewal of ecclesiastical office and conformity with canon law were main thrusts of the European church reform movement which had been promoted by successive popes from the mid eleventh century onwards, and the letter indicates that that concern had been taken on board by those Irish ecclesiastics who signed *huic decreto canonico*. Indeed the phrase suggests that a synod had been convened for the purpose of electing Máel Ísu. The titles accorded the Irish bishops in the letter of petition also indicate that a move towards territorially-defined episcopal sees was in train in those areas under Muirchertach Ua Briain's overlordship, possibly in response to Archbishop Lanfranc's earlier criticism, as expressed in his letter to Toirrdelbach Ua Briain, that bishops in Ireland were 'ordained to villages or small towns'. Shortly after Anselm's accession to the see of Canterbury in 1093, he had addressed a letter to Irish ecclesiastics, naming specifically *senior Domnaldus* (i.e., Bishop Domnall Ua hÉnna), and Donatus (i.e., Donngus, bishop of Dublin), and exhorting them to seek his advice if any matters arose which the Irish bishops were unable to resolve according to canon law. As Anselm would have been aware from the 'Acta Lanfranci', Domnall Ua hÉnna had previously sought guidance from Lanfranc (above, pp 906–7). In his letter Anselm accorded precedence to Domnall Ua hÉnna over Donngus, bishop of Dublin, who had made a profession of obedience to Lanfranc. This suggests that Anselm was not unduly concerned about giving precedence to Domnall, even though he had not been consecrated at Canterbury. It is noteworthy that the letter from Ireland, requesting the consecration of Máel Ísu as bishop of Waterford in 1096, simply addressed Anselm as *Anglorum archiepiscopus*, whereas in the professions of obedience sworn by Samuel Ua hÁingliu as bishop-elect of Dublin, and by Máel Ísu Ua hAinmire as bishop-elect of Waterford, Anselm was styled *sanctae Cantuariensis ecclesiae archiepiscopus et totius Britanniae primas* (archbishop of the holy church of Canterbury and primate of all Britain). That titulature, however, was not invented specifically for the Irish bishops-elect, since it had already been used in the profession of

---

[8] Eadmer, *Historia novorum*, ed. Martin Rule (Rolls Series, London, 1884), pp 76–7; Kenney, *Sources*, no. 640.

obedience made by Robert Bloet, bishop of Lincoln, to Anselm on 12 February 1094. While it might have been possible to interpret the 'island of Ireland' as falling within the wider ambit of the unspecific *Britanniae* over which both Lanfranc and Anselm claimed a primacy, the title used in the Waterford petition of *archiepiscopus Anglorum* 1096 unambiguously confined Anselm's jurisdiction as far as his Irish petitioners were concerned to England. This suggests that neither Muirchertach Ua Briain, nor the Irish ecclesiastics who were signatories to the petition, viewed consecration by Anselm as conceding a claim to primacy by the church of Canterbury in Ireland, and, indeed, Anselm's dealings with Ireland suggest that his primary interest was the promotion of church reform. About the time of his consecration of the bishops of Dublin and Waterford, Anselm addressed two exhortatory letters to Muirchertach, *gloriosus gratia Dei rex Hiberniae*, urging the king to promote canon law, particularly in respect of marriage practices and the canonical consecration of bishops. Anselm's letters echoed the earlier letter of Lanfranc to Toirrdelbach Ua Briain, and may have reinforced debate on those issues in Irish ecclesiastical circles. Neither Lanfranc nor Anselm directly made primatial claims for Canterbury in relation to the Irish church, though a number of their successors may be said to have done so, but arguably primarily as a means of bolstering their assertion of primacy over the see of York, and not because of a predatory or aggrandising interest in the Irish church.

Sometime after 1096 a change in relation to bishops-elect of the Hiberno-Norse cities seeking episcopal consecration at Canterbury occurred. Domnall mac Amalgada, as head of the church of Armagh, had already played an active role as a peace negotiator between kings, and, although still not in holy orders, he began also to take a greater public part in more religious matters. In 1095 a pestilence had raged in Ireland, and the fact that the feast of the decollation of John the Baptist (29 August) fell on a Friday in 1096 caused widespread consternation. The clergy of Ireland, with Domnall mac Amalgada at their head, decreed days of abstinence, almsgiving, and donations of land to churches from the laity, 'so that the men of Ireland were saved for that time from the fire of vengeance' (A.F.M.; cf. A.U.). This suggests that Armagh was now seeking to take a more leading role in the Irish church, perhaps to regain ground that it may have lost to reformist ecclesiastics. At the same time Armagh may have sought a closer relationship with Muirchertach Ua Briain as high-king. In 1101 an ecclesiastical synod was convened at Cashel under Muirchertach's auspices, one of the most significant outcomes of which was the donation of the former Eóganacht royal site of Cashel 'as an offering to St Patrick and to the Lord'. A grant in honour of Patrick implies a rapprochement with the church of Armagh. Such a move would have been at the expense of Domnall Mac Lochlainn. His accession in 1083 had brought to the fore a lineage within Cenél nEógain that was cultivating close relations with the Columban church of Derry (below, p. 930). Domnall's association with Derry (where he was to be buried at his death in 1121) may have been of concern to the church of Armagh, and may have persuaded the *comarba Pátraic* to recognise the high-kingship of Muirchertach Ua Briain.[9] The synod of Cashel (1101) was a public endorsement of Muirchertach's high-kingship. He had secured recognition from Armagh, the chief church in Ireland, in a manner analogous to Armagh's acknowledgement of Brian Bóruma's high-kingship in 1005. It may have led Muirchertach to abandon his approval of Irish bishops seeking episcopal consecration at Canterbury. While, in any event, probably a long-term aim of the reformist party in the Irish church, the timing may have been determined, in part, by Muirchertach's difficulties with King Henry I, arising from his association with the rebellious Arnulf de Montgomery. That a shift occurred in Muirchertach's ecclesiastical policy is reflected in the pseudo-historical 'Lebor na Cert', or Book of Rights, compiled about the time of his triumphal circuit of the north and the synod of Cashel.[10] The Book of Rights claimed that the king of Cashel was the supreme secular ruler of Ireland, just as the *comarba Pátraic* held the supreme ecclesiastical office. It quite anachronistically propounded an association between the city of Dublin and St Patrick, and detailed the tributes owed by Dubliners to the saint, an artificial attempt to create a venerable and ancient link between Dublin and the church of Armagh that took chronological precedence over more recent links forged with Canterbury. A reorientation in Muirchertach's ecclesiastical strategy may also be indicated by the fact that Samuel Ua hÁingliu, who had been consecrated for the bishopric of Dublin by Anselm in 1095, subsequently was reproved by Anselm for assuming metropolitan pretensions. Disengagement from Canterbury is further suggested by the fact that Gilla Espaic (Gilbertus), the first known bishop of Limerick, was not consecrated at Canterbury. This was probably facilitated by an important development in the church of Armagh. In August 1105, Domnall mac Amalgada was succeeded as *comarba Pátraic* by his nephew, Cellach mac Áeda. Although Cellach belonged to the hereditarily entrenched and laicised Clann Sínaich, he took sacerdotal orders on 23 September 1105. This was in accordance with the synod of Cashel (1101), which had legislated against laymen or laicised clerics holding or trafficking in ecclesiastical offices. When, in 1106, Cáenchomrac Ua Baigill, bishop of Armagh, died, it became possible for Cellach to unite in his person the coarbal and episcopal office, thereby providing a canonically valid metropolitan for the Irish

___

[9] Notwithstanding the donation by Domnall Mac Lochlainn of an elaborate new shrine for the bell of Patrick, commissioned (according to the inscription) during Domnall mac Amalgada's term of office (possibly following the pestilence of 1095), which undoubtedly was intended to curry favour with the church of Armagh.

[10] *Bk Rights*, ed. Dillon.

church, a significant step for the progress of the reform movement. During a visit to Munster in 1106 Cellach received episcopal orders and was acknowledged as primate of the Irish church. Recourse to Canterbury for consecration by a canonically acceptable metropolitan was no longer necessary. The circumstances of Gilla Espaic's consecration as the first bishop of Limerick are unknown, but it was probably Cellach who performed the ceremony. Gilla Espaic would have had a close association with Muirchertach Ua Briain, who retained a royal residence in the city of Limerick. Archbishop Anselm subsequently wrote to congratulate Gilla Espaic on his elevation to the see of Limerick, with no suggestion that the see of Canterbury had been slighted or ought to have been involved. This passing reference serves to highlight once again just how reliant historians are on the fitful information afforded by the Canterbury correspondence in tracing the early stages of the Irish church reform movement.

In 1111 another ecclesiastical assembly was convened under Muirchertach's auspices at Ráith Bressail (possibly to be identified with the earthen enclosure of that name in the townland of Fortgrady, parish of Dromtariff, barony of Duhallow, County Cork), which legislated for an islandwide diocesan hierarchy for the Irish church. Two metropolitan sees, one at Armagh, the other at Cashel, were set up, with precedence accorded to Armagh. Each archdiocese was to have twelve suffragan bishops, the boundaries of whose dioceses were defined by geographical landmarks and placenames. Máel Ísu Ua hAinmire, who had been consecrated as bishop of Waterford by Anselm in 1096, witnessed the decrees of the synod of Ráith Bressail as 'archbishop of Cashel', while the preexisting see of Waterford was silently incorporated into the newly created diocese of Lismore, and the preexisting see of Dublin into the newly created diocese of Glendalough. The diocesan boundaries delimited at Ráith Bressail reflect contemporary political divisions, and detailed analysis reveals much about the relative strengths of individual rulers. Muirchertach's predominance is evidenced in the boundaries of the dioceses of Killaloe and Limerick, which were coterminous with the Dál Cais heartland, while the diocese of Cashel reflected the more extended sphere of Dál Cais influence in North Munster. Cashel lay in the heart of an area that traditionally had been associated with the Eóganacht Caisil, but its diocesan boundaries were drawn at the expense both of the Eóganacht church of Emly, which had been the most important Munster church in the early Christian period, and which, although assigned an episcopal see, had attached to it a relatively small diocesan territory, and of the Eóganacht Caisil dynasty, which was losing control of its patrimonial heartland and being forced to move south-westwards into Uí Echach (Eóganacht Raithlinn) territory.

According to the mid-twelfth-century Life of St Malachy of Armagh written by St Bernard of Clairvaux, which, like the Canterbury correspondence,

constitutes another very important externally generated source for the Irish
church reform movement, Gilla Espaic, bishop of Limerick, was the first
native papal legate appointed to Ireland. The date and circumstances of Gilla
Espaic's appointment are unknown, but he may have undertaken a mission to
the pope with the consent, if not at the behest, of Muirchertach Ua Briain
(who would have been aware that his father had received a letter from Pope
Gregory VII (above, p. 906). Gilla Espaic may have visited Rome in
advance of the synod of Ráith Bressail. He was the author of a treatise, 'De
statu ecclesiae', outlining a schematic hierarchical episcopal structure, and
emphasising a clear distinction between secular and monastic clergy, which
possibly originated as a discussion document for the synod of Ráith Bressail.
Papal approval may also be inferred from Gilla Espaic's appointment as
native papal legate. Insofar as Muirchertach was acknowledged as paramount
king in Ireland, it was with the implacable opposition of the northern king,
Domnall Mac Lochlainn, but that limitation was to some extent offset by
Muirchertach's range of external contacts and the endorsement that he secured from the church of Armagh.

In addition to annalistic entries, which become less jejune and more
detailed and narrative in approach during Muirchertach's reign, there are
two important pseudo-historical sources emanating from his court circle that
throw light on his aims and aspirations: 'Cocad Gáedel re Gallaib'[11] is an
encomiastic biography of his illustrious ancestor, Brian Bóruma, partly modelled on Asser's Life of King Alfred of Wessex. Just as Asser portrays Alfred
as the saviour of the English against a viking take-over, so 'Cocad Gáedel re
Gallaib' depicts Brian Bóruma preserving Ireland from a similar fate. The
text indicates the extent to which Brian Bóruma served as an exemplary
model for Muirchertach's high-kingship. The composition of 'Lebor na
Cert', the Book of Rights, was probably occasioned by Muirchertach's na-
tionwide circuit of 1101. It detailed the reciprocal obligations between the
high-king of Ireland and his subordinates, adopting as paradigm that
the high-king would be a king of Cashel.

A protracted paralysing illness befell Muirchertach in 1114, which not only
put an end to further expansion and consolidation of his overlordship, but
was to undermine much of what he had achieved. By the time of his death on
13 March 1119, his overlordship had been repudiated in Leinster, Dublin,
Connacht, and Mide, while within Munster itself his brother, Diarmait, had
attempted to seize the kingship. Diarmait, in fact, predeceased Muirchertach
in 1118, but Diarmait's sons were to carry his ambitions into the next generation, and it was they, rather than Muirchertach's direct heirs, who took
the kingship of Munster after his death. The principal beneficiary of
Muirchertach's illness beyond Munster was to be not his old adversary,

[11] *Cog. Gaedheal.*

Domnall Mac Lochlainn, king of Cenél nEógain, whose career at the age of 67 was now drawing to a close, but the 27-year-old Toirrdelbach Ua Conchobair whom ironically Muirchertach had helped to instal in the kingship of Connacht in 1106 (above, p. 908). In 1118, with an army drawn from Connacht, Bréifne, and Mide, Toirrdelbach Ua Conchobair invaded Munster and effected a partition of the province: the northern half (Thomond, *Tuadmuma*), was apportioned to Conchobar and Toirrdelbach, sons of Diarmait, Muirchertach Ua Briain's brother and rival, while the southern half (Desmond, *Desmumu*) was assigned to Tadg Mac Carthaig of the Eóganacht Caisil, thereby reviving the main rival dynasty to the Dál Cais in Munster. Having taken hostages from the Uí Briain and Meic Carthaig dynasts, Toirrdelbach Ua Conchobair proceeded to Dublin, where he expelled Muirchertach's son, Domnall, and took control of the city himself; he also secured the submission of Énna Mac Murchada, king of Leinster, and of Mac Gilla Pátraic, king of Osraige. That a provincial king of Connacht was contesting for the first time the high-kingship of Ireland was signalled ceremonially by Toirrdelbach's celebration of the Óenach Tailten in 1118. The Óenach Tailten was associated with the Uí Néill overkingship of Tara, and, just as the title of 'king of Tara' had become synonomous with the high-kingship of Ireland, so the celebration of the Óenach Tailten was promoted by contemporary political ideologues as a prerogative of the high-kingship. Domnall Mac Lochlainn's reaction was to take an army to Athlone, where Toirrdelbach Ua Conchobair was obliged to sue for peace, but he preserved the integrity of Connacht by negotiating at its border. Mac Lochlainn died on 9 February 1121, and, in the aftermath of Muirchertach Ua Briain's death, there was indeed some justification for the title 'king of Ireland' accorded him, not only by the partisan Annals of Ulster, but also by the Munster Annals of Inisfallen.

Domnall Mac Lochlainn's death left Toirrdelbach Uí Conchobair as the main contender for the high-kingship of Ireland. Toirrdelbach's efforts to extend his influence beyond Connacht were concentrated, not unnaturally, in the first instance on Munster, which not only bordered directly on Connacht but had provided a series of formidable claimants to a non-Uí Néill high-kingship in the persons of Brian Bóruma (d. 1014), Toirrdelbach (d. 1086), and Muirchertach (d. 1119) Ua Briain. Toirrdelbach Ua Conchobair mounted a series of extended land and naval campaigns in Munster in 1119, 1121/2, 1122, 1123/4, 1125, 1126, 1127, 1131, and 1132, and factional tensions within the Dál Cais dynasty prevented it from curtailing his campaigns in Munster. His now paramount position in Ireland may be said to have secured some measure of external recognition when he obtained a fragment of the True Cross, brought on circuit to Ireland in 1123 in the wake of the first Lateran council, as a means of promoting Irish participation in the papally fostered crusading movement. That he was thus favoured was exploited, no doubt, by Toirrdelbach as an endorsement of his high-kingship.

The encasing of the relic in the highly elaborate processional Cross of Cong suggests that he may already have been seeking metropolitan status for an archbishopric of Connacht, eventually to be secured at the synod of Kells in 1152 (below, p. 927).

From 1123 onwards, Toirrdelbach's bid to assert overlordship over Munster was frustrated by the Eóganacht dynast, Cormac Mac Carthaig. The collapse of Muirchertach Ua Briain's authority consequent upon his illness, and the ensuing dynastic strife within the Dál Cais dynasty from 1114 onwards, had enabled the Eóganacht dynasty to stage a political come-back under Tadg Mac Carthaig (1118, dep. 1123, d. 1124) and his brother Cormac (1123–38). Cormac not only claimed the kingship of Munster, but was sufficiently powerful to play a role on a wider political stage, spearheading a revolt against Toirrdelbach Ua Conchobair in 1124. Cormac concluded an alliance with Murchad Ua Máel Sechlainn, king of Mide (who had made submission to Toirrdelbach Ua Conchhobair in 1118 and reaffirmed it in 1122), with Énna Mac Murchada, king of Leinster, and with Tigernán Ua Ruairc, king of Bréifne. Their combined forces attempted an incursion into Connacht, but Ua Conchobair successfully held the bridge of Athlone and prevented a Shannon crossing. Further, he retaliated by executing Cormac Mac Carthaig's son, Máel Sechlainn (his forename is suggestive of a marital alliance between Cormac and a daughter of Ua Máel Sechlainn, king of Mide), whom he held as a hostage, and by hosting into Osraige and taking hostages from Mac Gilla Pátraic, king of Osraige (who had given hostages to Tadg Mac Carthaig in 1120). In 1125 Toirrdelbach Ua Conchobair punished Murchad Ua Máel Sechlainn for his rebellion by deposing him from the kingship of Mide. Dividing Mide into four parts, Ua Conchobair allotted one portion to Tigernán Ua Ruairc, king of Bréifne, in return for his resubmission and alliance, the remainder being shared between three Ua Máel Sechlainn dynasts. When Énna Mac Murchada, king of Leinster, died early in 1126, Toirrdelbach Ua Conchobair seized the opportunity to host into Uí Chennselaig 'to constitute a king' (Ann. Tig.). His intervention there provoked a military response from Cormac Mac Carthaig, but Ua Conchobair inflicted a defeat on him in Osraige. Ua Conchobair went on temporarily to instal his own son, Conchobar, in the kingship of Leinster and Dublin. Recognising that Cormac Mac Carthaig was his most formidable opponent, in 1127 Toirrdelbach Ua Conchobair invaded Munster by land and sea, heading for Cormac's power-base at Cork. Cormac was obliged to seek temporary asylum in the church of Lismore, but was restored later in the same year with the support of the Dál Cais dynasts, Toirrdelbach and Conchobar Ua Briain. Their opposition to Toirrdelbach Ua Conchobair, arising largely from the latter's encroachments upon Dál Cais territory, persuaded them for a brief period to acknowledge Cormac Mac Carthaig as king of Munster. Cormac proved himself worthy of Dál Cais support when, in 1133, he organised a military and naval alliance against Toirrdelbach Ua Conchobair, which mustered not only the forces of Munster and Leinster, and the fleets of Cork, Dublin, Wexford, and Waterford, but also Ua Máel Sechlainn, king of Mide, and Tigernán Ua Ruairc, king of Bréifne. A coordinated land and naval invasion of Connacht was staged which succeeded in penetrating Connacht in spite of a ring of defensive structures erected by Toirrdelbach Ua Conchobair. Mac Carthaig and his allies are recorded in the annals to have destroyed the bridge and *dún* of Athlone, Dún Mugdhorn (Doon, County Mayo), and Dún Mór (Dunmore, County Galway). Collaboration with the Dál Cais, and Cormac's role as military coordinator of the forces of the southern half of Ireland during these campaigns against Connacht, are reflected in the pseudo-historical tract 'Caithréim Chellacháin Chaisil'.[12] The work, which depicts the tenth-century Eóganacht dynast, Cellachán, king of Cashel, as saving Ireland from the threat of a viking conquest, was composed as an Eóganacht riposte to the Dál Cais 'Cocad Gáedel re Gallaib', which had depicted the Dál Cais king Brian Bóruma in similar vein. It differs, however, in placing due emphasis on the fruitful collaboration of the Dál Cais and Eóganacht dynasties against a common foe, which, in place of the vikings, may be read as Toirrdelbach Ua Conchobair. When the allied forces regrouped and prepared to invade Connacht again, Ua Conchobair forestalled them by suing for a year's peace with Cormac Mac Carthaig and Conchobar Ua Briain. The treaty concluded at Abhall Ceithernaig, near Uisnech (County Westmeath), on behalf of the Connacht king by his chief ecclesiastic, Bishop Muiredach Ua Dubthaig, was a public acknowledgement of the strength of the opposition, and a serious setback to Toirrdelbach Ua Conchobair's bid for the high-kingship.

Cormac Mac Carthaig set out to present himself not just as king of Munster, but also as a candidate for the high-kingship of Ireland. His patronage of an elaborate ecclesiastical building programme on the rock of Cashel, which culminated in the consecration of the so-called Cormac's Chapel in 1134 in the presence of a large gathering of clergy and laity, marked the public return of Eóganacht influence to Cashel: an Eóganacht royal site which had been donated to the church by the Dál Cais king, Muirchertach Ua Briain in 1101 (above, p. 914) was so decisively reclaimed that Cormac's name is still associated with the church that he endowed.[13] Cormac's chapel also served to emphasise his assumption of the role of principal royal patron of the church reform movement in place of Muirchertach Ua Briain. Cormac secured support among influential reformist ecclesiastics, and notably from Máel Máedóc Ua Morgair, otherwise known as St Malachy. Although a

---

[12] See Donnchadh Ó Corráin, 'Caithréim Chellacháin Chaisil: history or propaganda?' in *Ériu*, xxv (1974), pp 1–25.

[13] The death of Cormac's brother, Tadg, in Cashel, recorded in 1124, indicates the return of Eóganacht influence to the Rock even before the accession of Cormac Mac Carthaig.

member of an hereditary laicised clerical family, Malachy had espoused the cause of reform when, as a youth, he came into contact with Cellach mac Áeda, *comarba Pátraic* and bishop of Armagh, who had been acknowledged as head of the Irish church at the synod of Ráith Bressail (1111). Malachy had inaugurated his own career as a reformer by restoring conventual life at the secularised monastic site of Bangor, with which his family had connections, and in 1124 had been consecrated by Cellach as bishop of Bangor. Because of local opposition, however, he was obliged to seek temporary refuge at Lismore, where he encountered Cormac Mac Carthaig, who, according to Malachy's biographer, Bernard of Clairvaux, formed a high regard for him. While on a visit to Munster in 1129, Cellach died at the ecclesiastical settlement of Ardpatrick (County Limerick), shortly before his death designating, according to Bernard of Clairvaux (*fecit quasi testamentum*), Malachy as his successor at Armagh 'and especially enjoining both kings of Munster and the elders of the land' to accept that decision. Cellach, therefore, envisaged support from the Munster kings for Malachy's candidacy at Armagh. However, a member of the Clann Sínaich, Muirchertach mac Domnaill, had moved immediately to take control of Armagh and the insignia of Patrick. It was not until 1132 that Malachy consented to be consecrated for Armagh, and then on the understanding that he would be allowed to resign when the Clann Sínaich monopoly had been broken. Muirchertach mac Domnaill's death on 17 September 1134 paved the way for Malachy's attempted installation, but he had to suffer yet another Clann Sínaich layman as rival, Niall mac Áeda, who refused to relinquish control of the temporalities of the church of Armagh. The Connacht Annals of Tigernach, which at this period function virtually as a house chronicle of the Ua Conchobair family, record that, shortly after the consecration of Cormac's Chapel at Cashel in 1134, Malachy 'entered into the seat [*cathaír*] of Patrick with the prayers of the men of Ireland'. This unusual expression indicates that Malachy was now acknowledged as head of the church of Armagh. The immediately preceding annalistic entry recounted the withdrawal from Cashel 'in displeasure' of the clerics of Connacht, while the 'Chronicon Scotorum' recorded 'the profanation of the reliquary [*cathach*] of Iarlaith' that is, of the patron of the church of Tuam. It is possible that in the interim between the death of Cellach in 1129 and the consecration of Malachy to the see of Armagh in 1132, that Muiredach Ua Dubthaig, styled 'bishop of Connacht' in the annals, had claimed leadership of the Irish church as a correlative of Toirrdelbach Ua Conchobair's claim to the high-kingship. The circumstances of Muiredach Ua Dubthaig's consecration are unknown, but he may have been consecrated by Cellach before the latter's death in 1129. Cellach certainly had contact with Toirrdelbach Ua Conchobair, for he had acted as a peace negotiator between him and the kings of Munster in 1128.[14] The Annals of Tigernach, in 1134, when

---

[14] A.U., A.F.M. The Annals of Tigernach record the theft in 1129 of a chalice given by Cellach to the church of Clonmacnoise.

recording Muiredach Ua Dubthaig's role as a peace negotiator between Toirrdelbach Ua Conchobair and the Munster kings, Cormac Mac Carthaig and Conchobar Ua Briain, style Ua Dubthaig *uasalespoc na hÉrenn*, and his death notice in 1150 in the same annals described him as *airdespoc Connacht 7 Érenn*. Whether or not Muiredach Ua Dubthaig had claimed primatial status, the recognition of Malachy as, in effect, head of the Irish church in 1134 may have caused dissatisfaction in Connacht: it is conceiveable that Toirrdelbach Ua Conchobair would have taken exception to Connacht ecclesiastics having to acknowledge the authority of an archbishop of Armagh who was so closely associated with his political opponent, Cormac Mac Carthaig. A circuit of Munster by Malachy as bishop of Armagh is recorded in 1134 and again in 1136 (none is recorded for Connacht).[15] The supposed successful siege and capture of Armagh from vikings by the Eóganacht king Cellachán, which figures so prominently in the pseudo-historical 'Caithréim Chellacháin Chaisil', while it undoubtedly was influenced by the portrayal in 'Cocad Gáedel re Gallaib' of Turgéis seizing the abbacy of Armagh, may also be a reflex of, and intended to emphasise, the cordial relations enjoyed by Cormac Mac Carthaig with Malachy, and his support for Malachy's installation at Armagh.[16] The approbation of the church reform party was a significant prop for Cormac Mac Carthaig's kingship, an advantage that Toirrdelbach Ua Conchobair neither appears, nor deserves, to have enjoyed, given the slower progress of ecclesiastical reform in Connacht during his reign. The assassination in 1138 of Cormac Mac Carthaig at the instigation of the Dál Cais *leth-rí*, Toirrdelbach Ua Briain, at Mag Tamnach (Mahoonagh, County Limerick) brought an end not only to Cormac's career but also to the revival of Eóganacht fortunes in Munster. The kingship of Munster dissolved again into the two divisions of Thomond and Desmond. Cormac Mac Carthaig may be said, however, to have achieved his aim of preventing Toirrdelbach Ua Conchobair's effective intervention in, and overlordship of, Munster, and thereby also of compromising his high-kingship.

The accession of a new king in Leinster, Diarmait Mac Murchada (at a date between 1126 and 1132) set in train a consolidation and expansion of that kingdom, which not only thwarted Toirrdelbach Ua Conchobair's ambitions to wield influence in Leinster, but also further impeded his efforts to assert overlordship in Munster. Already by 1134, when the Eóganacht–Dál Cais alliance collapsed, it was Diarmait Mac Murchada, rather than Toirrdelbach Ua Conchobair, who exploited it effectively, hosting into Osraige, seeking to detach the Hiberno-Norse city of Waterford from the

---

[15] By 1140, however (if not earlier), Malachy's successor at Armagh, Gilla meic Liac, had secured recognition from the province of Connacht, for he made a circuit of Connacht in that year and again in 1151.

[16] Malachy built the monastery of 'Ibracense' in Munster with Cormac Mac Carthaig's benefaction; its precise location remains unknown.

overlordship of Cormac Mac Carthaig and to extend Leinster influence into
the adjoining Munster subkingdom of Déise. By 1137 Conchobar Ua Briain,
*leth-rí* of Thomond, submitted to Diarmait Mac Murchada, and together
they besieged Waterford, Ua Briain soliciting recognition as overlord of
Desmond from Mac Murchada at the expense of Cormac Mac Carthaig. The
death of Conchobar Ua Briain in 1142 left his brother, Toirrdelbach, as sole
king of Thomond. Cormac Mac Carthaig's successor as king of Desmond,
his brother Donnchad (1138–43), initially defeated Toirrdelbach Ua Briain,
but was later captured and handed over to him, dying in captivity in 1144.
Toirrdelbach Ua Conchobair attempted to profit from the Eóganacht–Dál
Cais struggle for dominance in Munster by campaigning there in 1143, but
had to retreat without hostages or spoil. A peace treaty subsequently was
arranged between Toirrdelbach Ua Conchobair and Toirrdelbach Ua Briain
at Terryglass in 1144, but it failed to endure, and in 1145 and 1146 Toirrdel-
bach Ua Conchobair again campaigned in Munster without tangible gains.
Toirrdelbach Ua Briain actually took the offensive against Toirrdelbach Ua
Conchobair when in 1149 he invaded Connacht, and destroyed the fortress of
Galway. The struggle for control of Munster between Toirrdelbach Ua
Briain and the Meic Carthaig intensified dramatically in 1151. Diarmait Mac
Carthaig, king of Desmond since 1143, secured support from Toirrdelbach
Ua Conchobair, king of Connacht, and Diarmait Mac Murchada, king of
Leinster, and their combined forces inflicted a decisive defeat on Toirrdel-
bach Ua Briain at the battle of Móin Mór (County Cork) at which 7,000
reputedly were slain. Although, according to the partisan Annals of Tigernach, 'the king of Ireland' returned to Connacht with the hostages of
Munster and Leinster in his train, in reality Ua Conchobair's high-kingship
was facing challenges on too many other fronts for the victory to yield him
permanent advantage. His pursuit of the high-kingship was to be thwarted
also by the remarkable expansion of Bréifne and Airgialla under two able and
long-reigned kings who emerged almost simultaneously, Tigernán Ua
Ruairc, king of Bréifne (*a.* 1128–1171), and Donnchad Ua Cerbaill, king of
Airgialla (*a.* 1133–1168). Bréifne, which had been conquered and settled in
the course of the seventh and eighth centuries by a branch of the Uí Briúin
royal dynasty of Connacht, was classed as a satellite kingdom of Connacht.
During the eleventh century the Ua Ruairc kings of Bréifne had aspired to
the provincial kingship of Connacht, and Domnall Ua Ruairc, king of
Bréifne, who died in 1102, was styled 'king of Connacht' in his death notice.
His was the last attempt, however, by an Uí Briúin Bréifne dynast to bid for
the provincial kingship of Connacht. Thereafter, the Uí Ruairc concentrated
on territorial expansion into Mide, carving out a corridor between Connacht
and the northern Uí Néill sphere of influence. This impeded Toirrdelbach
Ua Conchobair in extending his influence northwards, and at a time when he
might otherwise have been able to take advantage of the regnal instability in

the kingship of Cenél nEógain that followed on the death of Domnall Mac Lochlainn in 1121. Although generally Tigernán Ua Ruairc was obliged to acknowledge the overlordship of Toirrdelbach Ua Conchobair, and then of his son and successor, Ruaidrí (1156–83), Ua Ruairc increasingly came to do so only by setting specific conditions, most graphically in 1167 when he was to insist that Ruaidrí Ua Conchobair exact compensation on his behalf from Diarmait Mac Murchada, king of Leinster, for the abduction of Ua Ruairc's wife, Derbforgaill, fourteen years previously in 1152. To the east of Bréifne, Donnchad Ua Cerbaill, king of Fernmag (the *caput* of which was located around Loch Uaithne near Clones, County Monaghan), set out to reconstitute the confederate overkingship of Airgialla, which had been dismantled by the Cenél nEógain king, Niall Caille (823–46) at the battle of Leth Cam (827). After Leth Cam, the northern and eastern portions of the former Airgiallan overkingship had been subjected to the dominance of the Cenél nEógain kings while the western Airgiallan kingdoms managed to retain a degree of autonomy from Cenél nEógain overlordship, although their territories on the northern frontier were gradually eroded by Cenél nEógain expansion southwards. By the early twelfth century, the most powerful western Airgiallan dynasty was that of the Uí Cerbaill, kings of Fernmag. Donnchad Ua Cerbaill, first mentioned as king of Fernmag in the annals in 1133, may be identified with the king, mentioned in Bernard of Clairvaux's life of St Malachy, who supported the installation of Malachy at Armagh in 1134, and opposed his Clann Sínaich rival, Niall mac Áeda. Donnchad Ua Cerbaill's support for Malachy is one indication of his determination to resist Cenél nEógain overlordship, for the Clann Sínaich monopoly of offices at Armagh typically had enjoyed the support of the Cenél nEógain kings. Airgiallan losses on their northern frontiers to the Cenél nEógain kings were more than offset by the extensive territorial gains made to the south and east by Donnchad Ua Cerbaill in the course of his long career. By 1130 the Ulaid sub-kingdom of Conaille Muirtheimne (in north County Louth) had been taken over, and by 1142 Donnchad Ua Cerbaill had gained control of the whole of the modern county of Louth. From his newly acquired territories near the banks of the River Boyne he donated land for the foundation of the first Irish Cistercian house at Mellifont in 1142, and also facilitated the introduction of the first Augustinian community of the Arrouaisian observance at the early church site of St Mochta, Louth. With Donnchad Ua Cerbaill's support and cooperation, St Malachy was able to use the kingdom of Airgialla as a trial ground for his reform strategies, and more particularly that portion which had been so recently annexed by Donnchad Ua Cerbaill. Malachy had encountered the Cistercian and Arrouasian monastic observances during his visit to the Continent in 1139–40, and had determined to introduce them as agencies of monastic reform into the Irish church. While Cormac Mac Carthaig till his death in 1138 had acted as

Malachy's principal royal patron in the southern half of Ireland, Donnchad Ua Cerbaill thereafter took over that role in the northern half of the country. In 1136 Malachy resigned the see of Armagh in favour of Gilla Meic Liac, abbot of Derry since 1121. This was a conciliatory gesture made in the expectation that Gilla Meic Liac would secure the support of Muirchertach Mac Lochlainn, who in the same year succeeded to the kingship of Cenél nEógain, and that a mutually beneficial relationship between the church of Armagh and the kings of Cenél nEógain, which Malachy had so conspicuously failed to secure, might be restored. In return for Donnchad Ua Cerbaill's support for his church reform programme, Malachy detached from the diocese of Armagh, as delimited by the synod of Ráith Bressail (1111), the area in County Louth into which Ua Cerbaill had expanded, and transferred it to the diocese of Airgialla, so as to make the enlarged diocese coterminous with Ua Cerbaill's expanded kingdom. In 1135 Malachy consecrated his own brother, Gilla Críst (Christianus), as bishop of Airgialla, the cathedral church of which moved from Clogher (which had been designated as the episcopal see at Ráith Bressail) to Louth, which also became the location of Donnchad Ua Cerbaill's newly established Arrouasian house of St Mary's abbey, Louth. The Arrouaisian canons introduced at Louth functioned also as the bishop's cathedral chapter. The property of the canons and the bishop was held in common, and while the bishop was the titular head of the monastic community, a prior was responsible for its routine administration. Malachy may have viewed such an arrangement, whereby the monastic community would also serve as cathedral chapter, as a means of ensuring canonical episcopal elections, free from the kind of secular interference which he had had to endure from the Clann Sínaich family at Armagh. In 1179 Gualterus, abbot of Arrouaise, recorded that Malachy had visited in the time of his predecessor, Abbot Gervase (1121–47), and had the customs of Arrouaise copied, regarding them as particularly suitable for the clergy of cathedral churches. Although Malachy had reached the Continent too late to attend the second Lateran council, which met 8–17 April 1139, he would have informed himself of its deliberations. The council had reiterated and reinforced the canons of the first Lateran council (1123) against lay investiture in ecclesiastical offices and had legislated for a role in episcopal elections by *viri religiosi*, that is monks, though without detailing how it was to operate. It had also enjoined that the goods of deceased bishops were not to be seized by any individual, but were to remain freely at the disposal of the clergy for the needs of the church and the succeeding incumbent. As Malachy himself had experienced all too painfully at Armagh, this was a pressing issue for the recently established Irish episcopate. It was in those circumstances that Malachy may have regarded the customs of Arrouaise as particularly suited to cathedral churches. And although no longer bishop of Armagh after 1136, Malachy's appointment as native papal legate by Pope

Innocent II in 1139 invested him with an overriding authority to drive the reform movement forward.

The territorial expansion of the kingdoms of Bréifne and Fernmag was made chiefly at the expense of Murchad Ua Máel Sechlainn, king of Mide (1106–53). Throughout the first half of the twelfth century Mide contracted steadily, not just on its northern frontier, but also on its southern borders, where both the kingdoms of Dublin and Leinster made gains at its expense. Furthermore, Mide experienced chronic regnal instability, with depositions, joint rules, and rival kings.[17] Yet, while many aspirants came and went, Murchad Ua Máel Sechlainn managed to enjoy an exceptionally long, if much interrupted, reign of forty-seven years, and to die of natural causes as king of Mide 'in his own bed' in Durrow in 1153. Mide had also had to contend with the intervention of successive would-be high-kings, first Toirrdelbach and Muirchertach Ua Briain and then Toirrdelbach Ua Conchobair. In 1125 Ua Conchobair partitioned Mide into eastern and western portions (above, p. 918). In 1143 he deposed Murchad Ua Máel Sechlainn and installed his own son, Conchobar, in the kingship of Mide, and when the latter, not surprisingly, was killed by the men of Mide in 1144, Toirrdelbach redivided Mide, giving the western portion to Donnchad Ua Máel Sechlainn and the eastern half jointly to Tigernán Ua Ruairc, king of Bréifne, and Diarmait Mac Murchada, king of Leinster, a circumstance that was greatly to exacerbate rivalries between the two. Mide was to suffer partition again in 1150, this time at the hands of Muirchertach Mac Lochlainn, king of Cenél nEógain (succeeded 1136, deposed 1143, restored 1145, died 1166). His intervention reflected the shift in the balance of power that had taken place between 1144 and 1150, which brought Muirchertach Mac Lochlainn to the fore as a formidable rival to Toirrdelbach Ua Conchobair's high-kingship.

In the early decades of his reign Toirrdelbach Ua Conchobair had concentrated on extending his influence into Munster, Leinster, and Mide and had made little attempt to intervene in the north. After 1145 he was precluded from doing so by the strengthening position of Muirchertach Mac Lochlainn, king of Cenél nEógain. The death of Domnall Mac Lochlainn in 1121 had been followed by a spate of dynastic conflict within Cenél nEógain between the Meic Lochlainn and the Uí Gairmledaig rulers of the Cenél nEógain sub-kingship of Cenél Móen and Mag nÍtha. In 1143 Domnall Ua Gairmledaig had succeeded temporarily in wresting the kingship of Cenél nEógain from Muirchertach Mac Lochlainn. In 1145, with the help of the Cenél Conaill, Muirchertach recovered the kingship and, having reasserted his position

---

[17] Mide was partitioned in 1094, 1125, 1143, 1144, 1150, 1151, 1152, 1161, 1162, 1163, and 1169 (Ann.Tig., 1094, 1161, 1162, 1163.; A.U., 1125; Chron. Scot., 1143; A.F.M., 1143, 1144, 1150, 1152, 1162, 1163, and 1169).

within Cenél nEógain, embarked on a series of campaigns to extend his power, both in the north of Ireland and beyond. Before a Cenél nEógain king could play a political role outside the north, it was important for him to exercise a secure lordship over Cenél Conaill on his western flank and Ulaid on his eastern flank. Some ground had already been laid by Domnall Mac Lochlainn (1083–1121), who had exploited his power-base on the Inishowen peninsula as a strategic location from which to dominate Cenél Conaill. At the synod of Ráith Bressail (1111), the Inishowen peninsula had been attached to the newly created diocese of Cenél Conaill, with Derry designated as its episcopal see. Derry was a Cenél Conaill church, but during the reign of Domnall Mac Lochlainn it came under Cenél nEógain control (the death of a Cenél nEógain *airchinnech* of Derry, Congalach mac Meic Conchaille, is recorded in 1112, A.U.). The unusual disposition made at Ráith Bressail almost certainly was intended to afford Domnall Mac Lochlainn a means of exerting influence in Cenél Conaill through the links which Derry had with that kingdom. On his death in 1121 Domnall Mac Lochlainn was buried in Derry, in contrast with previous kings of Cenél nEógain, who usually had been interred at Armagh. A further instance of Domnall Mac Lochlainn's concern to dominate Cenél Conaill was the installation of his son Niall in the kingship of Cenél Conaill in 1113. Suzerainty over the kingdom of Ulaid had been a factor in the struggle for supremacy between Domnall Mac Lochlainn and Muirchertach Ua Briain, but after the disastrous defeat suffered by Ua Briain at the battle of Mag Coba in 1103 (above, p. 910), the kings of Ulaid were left to reach an accommodation as best they could with the Cenél nEógain kings. In 1113 Domnall Mac Lochlainn took the high-handed action of deposing Donnchad mac Duinn Sléibe from the kingship of Ulaid, dividing it between two other dynasts, and of taking the Ulaid sub-kingships of Dál nAraide and Uí Echach under his direct rule. Such intervention in the internal politics of Ulaid was continued by Muirchertach Mac Lochlainn, who, in 1148, divided Ulaid between four kings. With control of Cenél Conaill and Ulaid secured, Muirchertach Mac Lochlainn embarked on the extension of his overlordship beyond the north. In 1149, on an expedition styled a *ríghthurus* ('royal circuit') by the Annals of the Four Masters, and intended to signal his bid for the high-kingship, Mac Lochlainn took hostages from Tigernán Ua Ruairc, king of Bréifne, Murchad Ua Máel Sechlainn, king of Mide, and the men of Tethba, and from Diarmait Mac Murchada, king of Leinster, as well as the Hiberno-Norse of Dublin— all of those submissions made at the expense of Toirrdelbach Ua Conchobair, king of Connacht. In 1150 Muirchertach Mac Lochlainn undertook another *rígthurus* southwards, where at Inismochta (Inismot, County Meath) he was joined by Donnchad Ua Cerbaill and Tigernán Ua Ruairc. In a preemptive move, Toirrdelbach Ua Conchobair sent hostages, obviously fearing an attack on Connacht. In 1151 Muirchertach Mac Lochlainn took immediate advantage from the depletion of Toirrdelbach Ua Conchobair's resources after the battle of Móin Mór (above, p. 922) by hosting to Connacht. Unwilling so soon again to expose his forces in open battle, Ua Conchobair was obliged to give him hostages, whereupon Mac Lochlainn also received hostages from Diarmait Mac Murchada, king of Leinster, who had fought alongside Toirrdelbach Ua Conchobair at Móin Mór. By 1151, therefore, it was clear that Muirchertach Mac Lochlainn had effectively challenged Toirrdelbach Ua Conchobair for the high-kingship: as the Annals of the Four Masters expressed it, Mac Lochlainn was now 'king of Ailech and Tara'.

The shift in the balance of power in favour of Muirchertach Mac Lochlainn is reflected in the decisions of the reforming synod convened by the papal legate, Cardinal John Paparo, at Kells in March 1152. Its main purpose was to give papal assent to the islandwide diocesan framework for the Irish church that had been first detailed at the synod of Ráith Bressail (1111). The papal legation was undertaken in response to an Irish request to Pope Eugenius III (1145–53) for *pallia*, the insignia of papal authorisation, for the Irish archbishops. In 1148 Malachy had embarked on a second journey to the Continent and prior to his departure had held a synod at Inis Pátraic (St Patrick's Island, off Skerries, County Dublin).[18] Ráith Bressail had approved two archbishoprics, Armagh and Cashel, with precedent status being accorded to Armagh. The synod of Kells, however, authorised four archdioceses, Armagh, Cashel, Dublin, and Tuam, with Armagh as the primatial see. The creation of the archdiocese of Tuam, coterminous with the provincial kingdom of Connacht, was a tribute to the standing of Toirrdelbach Ua Conchobair. But the fact that the dioceses of Bréifne and Ardagh (which corresponded to the Bréifne sub-kingdom of Conmaicne) were included in the province of Armagh, rather than Tuam, may be said to reflect the strength of Muirchertach Mac Lochlainn's position by 1152, for Bréifne traditionally had been reckoned within the orbit of the king of Connacht. The archdiocese of Armagh, as delimited at the synod of Kells, therefore reflected the dominance by that date of Muirchertach Mac Lochlainn. No doubt, it was to Mac Lochlainn's advantage that Cardinal Paparo, on arrival in Ireland, first visited Armagh and spent a week there with Archbishop Gilla Meic Liac, who subsequently set out on a visitation of Connacht. Muirchertach Mac Lochlainn's overriding influence at the synod of Kells is also demonstrated by the temporary deposition of Donnchad Ua Cerbaill from the kingship of Airgialla 'in revenge for the *comarba* of Patrick, whom he had wounded and violated some time before' (A.F.M.). The dispute between Gilla Meic Liac and Donnchad Ua Cerbaill almost

---

[18] The offshore location on the boundary between Leth Cuinn and Leth Mogha suggests tensions, perhaps over precedence or the extent of their provinces, between the archbishops of Armagh and Cashel.

certainly arose over diocesan boundaries: it is likely that Gilla Meic Liac had sought to overturn Malachy's transfer of the substantial southern portion of the diocese of Armagh to the diocese of Airgialla (above, p. 924).

In 1153 Muirchertach Mac Lochlainn demonstrated his ability to intervene in Munster affairs. In the wake of the battle of Móin Mór (above, p. 922), Toirrdelbach Ua Conchobair had deposed Toirrdelbach Ua Briain in favour of the latter's brother, Tadg, as king of Thomond. Toirrdelbach Ua Briain took refuge with Muirchertach Mac Lochlainn, who undertook a military campaign on his behalf and routed a Connacht army at Fardrum (County Westmeath). Mac Lochlainn went on to instal Máel Sechlainn Ua Máel Sechlainn in the kingship of Mide, and to take hostages from Tigernán Ua Ruairc, king of Bréifne, confirming that Bréifne and Mide were no longer within Toirrdelbach Ua Conchobair's sphere of influence. In 1154 Toirrdelbach Ua Conchobair tried a different tack: relying on the superiority of the naval forces that he had built up over decades, he sailed the Connacht fleet to the north. Muirchertach Mac Lochlainn was obliged to hire ships in the Isles of Scotland, but none the less was decisively defeated at sea. He immediately regained the initiative, however, when he led an army overland into the heartland of Connacht, and Toirrdelbach Ua Conchobair, once again, elected not to engage him in open battle. Mac Lochlainn moved on to Dublin, where the citizens accepted him as their overlord in return for a proffer of 1,200 cows. When Máel Sechlainn Ua Máel Sechlainn, whom he had installed as king of Mide in 1153, died early in 1155, Mac Lochlainn hosted into Mide, in advance of Toirrdelbach Ua Conchobair, once again to place his own nominee in the kingship. Toirrdelbach Ua Conchobair was in the process of organising an alliance against Muirchertach Mac Lochlainn when the Connacht king died in May 1156. Despite the glowing obituary 'king of all Ireland, and the Augustus of the west of Europe' accorded him in the partisan Connacht Annals of Tigernach, his claim to the title of high-king had been effectively negated by Mac Lochlainn. And although Toirrdelbach Ua Conchobair had achieved the creation of the archdiocese of Tuam at the synod of Kells (1152), one limitation of his pursuit of the high-kingship had been his apparent inability to exploit the church reform movement more effectively. By 1156 Cistercian monasteries had been founded by Donnchad Ua Cerbaill, king of Airgialla (Mellifont), by Diarmait Mac Murchada, king of Leinster (Baltinglass, Killenny), by Toirrdelbach Ua Briain, king of Thomond (Monasteranenagh, Inislounaght), and Ua Máel Sechlainn, king of Mide (Bective), often on contested lands which thereby were neutralised at the expense of political rivals or subordinates. The first Cistercian house in Connacht, the monastery of Grellechdinach (later moved to Boyle, Co. Roscommon), founded in 1148, owed its endowment to a subordinate king of Síl Muiredaig, Mac Diarmata, king of Mag Luirg, and apparently received no patronage from Toirrdelbach Ua Conchobair. He concentrated his ecclesiastical patronage on the long-established church sites of Tuam, which secured papally endorsed archiepiscopal status at the synod of Kells (1152), and on Clonmacnoise, where he was to be buried in 1156. He succeeded in drawing Clonmacnoise into the Connacht sphere of influence at the expense of the Ua Máel Sechlainn kings of Mide, but he did not win the degree of support from reform-minded clerics that benefited Cormac Mac Carthaig, king of Munster, Donnchad Ua Cerbaill, king of Airgialla, Muirchertach Mac Lochlainn, king of Cenél nEógain, and the Leinster king, Diarmait Mac Murchada.[19]

Muirchertach Mac Lochlainn skilfully garnered support for his high-kingship from both reformist and more conservative ecclesiastical circles. In 1157 he was present at the consecration of the newly completed church of Mellifont abbey, the mother-house of the Cistercian order in Ireland. The ceremony was attended by a large gathering of clergy and laity, including the first abbot of Mellifont, Gilla Críst Ua Connairche, now bishop of Lismore and native papal legate, and Archbishop Gilla Meic Liac of Armagh. Although Donnchad Ua Cerbaill had made available the original land grant for the foundation of Mellifont in 1142, situated as it by then was in both the kingdom and diocese of Airgialla, it was Muirchertach Mac Lochlainn as high-king who presided as benefactor at the consecration of Mellifont's church in 1157. Shortly after, he issued a confirmation charter to the Cistercian abbey of Newry (County Down), which had been founded as a daughter-house of Mellifont. It is indeed possible that, as in the case of Mellifont, it was Donnchad Ua Cerbaill who had given the original land grant for the foundation of Newry, for Ua Cerbaill had also been expanding into the southern area of the kingdom of Ulaid. In his charter of confirmation to Newry abbey, Muirchertach Mac Lochlainn styled himself *rex totius Hiberniae*, and, addressing *omnibusque et singulis Hiberniensibus*, claimed that any grants of land to Newry by the local kings or *duces* of Ulaid, Airgialla, or Uí Echach had to be made *dum liberam licentiam et voluntatem meam habeant ut sciam quid et quantum de terreno meo regno coelestis rex possideat ad opus pauperum suorum monachorum*, a very aggressive assertion of his overlordship.[20] In 1161 an insertion in Irish in the Book of Kells recorded that Muirchertach Mac Lochlainn, styled *ríg Érend*, confirmed immunity from secular exactions to the church of Ardbraccan in the Mide sub-kingdom of Lóegaire, a similar affirmation of overriding rights of overlordship. It also illustrates how his support for new reformist monastic communities was balanced by continuing concern for long-established churches. He enjoyed a fruitfully cooperative

[19] Diarmait Mac Murchada's career as king of Leinster is discussed in detail below, *N.H.I.*, ii, chs I and II.
[20] William Dugdale, *Monasticon Anglicanum*, ed. J. Caley et al. (6 vols in 8, London, 1817–30), vi, II, pp 1133–4; Charles O'Conor, *Rerum Hibernicarum scriptores* (4 vols, Buckingham, 1814–16), i, p. clviii.

relationship with Gilla Meic Liac, first as abbot of Derry and then as archbishop of Armagh, and with Flaithbertach Ua Brolcháin, abbot of Derry
from 1150. In 1158 a synod held at Brí Mhic Thaidc (County Meath),
presided over by Gilla Meic Liac in the presence of the papal legate, Gilla
Críst Ua Connairche, bishop of Lismore, and attended by twenty-five other
bishops, created a personal episcopal chair for Flaithbertach Ua Brolcháin.
This may have been partly by way of compensation for the loss of the
episcopal status of the church of Derry: although Derry had been designated
as the see for the diocese of Cenél Conaill at the synod of Ráith Bressail
(1111), by the time of the synod of Kells (1152) it had been replaced by the
church of Raphoe, while Derry and the Inishowen peninsula were now attached to the diocese of Cenél nEógain, an arrangement that more accurately
reflected the political spheres of Cenél nEógain and Cenél Conaill. The
synod of Kells confirmed Ráth Luraig (Maghera) as the cathedral church of
the diocese of Cenél nEógain. The titular episcopal dignity accorded to
Flaithbertach Ua Brolcháin in 1158 therefore offset Derry's loss of episcopal
status. At the same time he was confirmed as *comarba Colum Cille*, that is as
head of the Columban filiation of churches. In the late ninth century the
headship of the *familia* of Colum Cille had shifted from the abbey of Iona to
the monastery of Kells (County Meath). Since Derry was termed 'Daire
Colum Cille' for the first time in 1121 in the Annals of Ulster, when
recording the death of Domnall Mac Lochlainn, king of Cenél nEógain, it is
likely that it was Domnall who first attempted to have the headship transferred from Kells to Derry. The change certainly had been effected by the
time of the accession of Flaithbertach Ua Brolcháin in 1150, when he was
styled *comarba Colum Cille*, if not earlier, and may be presumed to have had
the approval of the primate and archbishop of Armagh (and former abbot of
Derry), Gilla Meic Liac, who in the same year undertook a circuit in Cenél
nEógain and received tribute from Muirchertach Mac Lochlainn. The close
links between the churches of Derry and Armagh at this period are epitom-
ised by Flaithbertach Ua Brolcháin, for he belonged to a Cenél nEógain
ecclesiastical family which had been prominent in the church of Armagh
from the eleventh century. The collection of dues by Flaithbertach Ua
Brolcháin as head of the Columban affiliation in Ulaid in 1153 may also be
presumed to have had the approval of Gilla Meic Liac.

   What prerogatives stemmed from the grant in 1158 to Flaithbertach
Ua Brolcháin, as *comarba Coluim Cille*, of 'a chair like that of every bishop' is
unclear, but in 1161 Muirchertach Mac Lochlainn presided over an assembly
of laity and clergy at Áth na Dairbrige (County Meath) at which 'the
churches of Colum Cille in Mide and Leinster were freed by the *comarba
Coluim Cille*, namely by Flaithbertach Ua Brolcháin, and their tribute and
jurisdiction were given to him, for they were subject before that'. This may
signify no more than that secular exactions formerly paid by those churches

were now to go to him, but it is just possible that exemption for Columban churches from the newly created episcopal jurisdictions was sought, by analogy with the immunity from local episcopal authority claimed by Cistercian houses. That Ua Brolcháin, as *comarba Coluim Cille*, exercised a direct relationship with Columban churches is indicated by the annalistic record in 1161 of a circuit made by him of Osraige, during which he received payments of tribute. In 1162 he and Muirchertach Mac Lochlainn together embarked on an ambitious building programme in Derry, possibly part-funded by those payments, which demarcated more clearly the ecclesiastical from the secular quarter (in which Muirchertach's royal seat may be presumed to have been located), while in 1164 Muirchertach was associated with the building by Flaithbertach Ua Brolcháin of the great church of Derry, which was eighty feet in length. Muirchertach's close links with Flaithbertach would have enabled him to claim royal patronage of the Columban *familia*. Such a role could have benefited his pursuit of the high-kingship by creating loyalist Columban centres of support for him in areas where he might have had little influence previously. It would, for instance, have been advantageous to Mac Lochlainn if the important Columban church of Durrow, which had such close links with the Mide royal family of Ua Máel Sechlainn and practically functioned by the twelfth century as their familial church, became directly subject to the jurisdiction of Flaithbertach Ua Brolcháin. Similarly, the Columban church of Moone (County Kildare), if directly subject to the *comarba* of Colum Cille, might provide Muirchertach Mac Lochlainn with a loyalist foothold in the heart of the kingdom of Leinster. Support for church restructuring, if not actually reform, could offer such tangible gains.

Just as Muirchertach Mac Lochlainn had checkmated Toirrdelbach Ua Conchobair's bid for the high-kingship, so Muirchertach Mac Lochlainn's high-kingship was to be compromised by Toirrdelbach's son, Ruaidrí, who had succeeded his father as king of Connacht in 1156. In 1159 Ruaidrí launched his bid for the high-kingship when, accompanied by a large Connacht army (which included a battalion from Munster), he gave battle to Muirchertach Mac Lochlainn near Ardee (County Louth), where, however, Ruaidrí suffered a decisive defeat. Later in the same year, Muirchertach Mac Lochlainn retaliated by hosting into Connacht with the armies of Cenél nEógain, Airgialla, Ulaid, and Cenél Conaill, yet, although much destruction was wrought, he was obliged to retreat without hostages. In 1161, following a hosting by Muirchertach Mac Lochlainn into Bréifne and Tethba, Ruaidrí Ua Conchobair crossed the Shannon and voluntarily made submission to Muirchertach Mac Lochlainn, offering hostages for Bréifne, Conmaicne, half of Munster, and half of Meath, 'and thereupon Mac Lochlainn gave his entire province [of Connacht] to him', in other words ceding him a delimited sphere of influence, an acknowledgement of the threat that Ruaidrí now posed. About the same time, Diarmait Mac Murchada, king of Leinster, renewed his submission to Mac Lochlainn. In the words of the Annals of the Four Masters, 'Muirchertach Mac Lochlainn was therefore on this occasion king of Ireland without opposition'. It was not to last. A revolt of Eochaid Mac Duinn Sléibe, king of Ulaid, against Muirchertach Mac Lochlainn in 1165 triggered his downfall. Initially, Mac Lochlainn reacted by removing Mac Duinn Sléibe from the kingship, but subsequently, in a settlement negotiated under the auspices of Archbishop Gilla Meic Liac at Armagh, agreed to his restoration. Mac Lochlainn received as hostages the sons of every *toísech* of Ulaid as well as Mac Duinn Sléibe's own daughter, the first known occurrence of a female being taken as a political hostage, presumably to preempt her father exploiting her marriage to constitute a new political alliance. Mac Duinn Sléibe was also obliged to cede the territory of Bairrche (barony of Mourne, County Down) to Mac Lochlainn, who reassigned it to Donnchad Ua Cerbaill, king of Airgialla. In 1166 Muirchertach Mac Lochlainn blinded Eochaid Mac Duinn Sléibe while a guest in his Easter house. That breach of hospitality and honour and violation of the solemn season of Easter afforded the pretext for a more general repudiation of Muirchertach Mac Lochlainn's high-kingship. A key figure was Donnchad Ua Cerbaill, who had gone surety for the agreement between Muirchertach Mac Lochlainn and Mac Duinn Sléibe in 1165, and now joined the opposition that had been gathering momentum around the leadership of Ruaidrí Ua Conchobair. Ua Conchobair took the Connacht army into Mide, where he received the submission of Ua Máel Sechlainn, king of Mide, and Tigernán Ua Ruairc, king of Bréifne. Their combined forces moved on to Dublin and took hostages from the Hiberno-Norse, who formally recognised Ruaidrí Ua Conchobair as high-king, in return for a proffer of 4,000 cows. Donnchad Ua Cerbaill, having first submitted to Ruaidrí Ua Conchobair, moved into Cenél nEógain, accompanied by battalions from Bréifne and Conmaicne, to attack Muirchertach Mac Lochlainn, who was killed in a minor skirmish. His death left the way clear for Ruaidrí Ua Conchobair to claim the high-kingship. Munster posed no immediate menace since in 1165 Muirchertach Ua Briain had seized the kingship of Thomond in rebellion against his father, Toirrdelbach, and sought an alliance with Ruaidrí Ua Conchobair, who brought a large army into Munster on his behalf and ravaged Desmond. It was Diarmait Mac Murchada, king of Leinster, who himself aspired to the high-kingship, who constituted the real threat, but Ruaidrí gained a key advantage by securing acknowledgement from the citizens of Dublin. The north-Leinster kings of Uí Fáeláin and Uí Failge and the king of Osraige submitted to Ua Conchobair, and Mac Murchada's support began to drain away in Leinster. In August 1166 the combined forces of Mide, Bréifne, and Dublin, under the command of Tigernán Ua Ruairc, king of Bréifne, acting as ally of Ruaidrí Ua Conchobair, attacked Mac Murchada's stronghold in Ferns, destroying his 'stone house' there. His capital destroyed, and his kingship rejected by the men of Leinster themselves, Diarmait Mac Murchada, now in late middle age, went into exile, but, unlike earlier royal exiles who had been content to go on pilgrimage, he determined to return and stage a bid not only for recovery of the kingship of Leinster, but also for the high-kingship. His appeal to Henry II, king of England, for military aid, and his recruitment of mercenaries within Henry's dominions, enabled him to recover the kingship of Leinster and to discredit the high-kingship of Ruaidrí Ua Conchobair, but its more momentous long-lasting effect was to be the onset of English rule in Ireland.

# CHAPTER XXVII

# Latin learning and literature in Ireland, 1169–1500

A. B. SCOTT

To attempt to give an account of the Latin writings of Irishmen, in Ireland or abroad, between the arrival of the Normans and the end of the middle ages is a truly hazardous, not to say foolhardy undertaking.[1] It may well be argued that there is nothing to survey; that writings in Latin among the Gaelic Irish had already become infrequent and quite devoid of any literary interest well before the establishment of the Anglo-Norman colony, and that Anglo-Norman society itself produced little that could be called literature. What survives is mostly philosophy and theology, with some canon law, annals, and hagiography. More important, none of this body of writings is united by having any Irish or Celtic characteristics. FitzRalph's 'Summa de questionibus Armenorum' or Thomas of Ireland's 'Manipulus florum' were written by members of the Anglo-Irish colony who had become part of the intellectual world that embraced England and western Europe. There is nothing specifically Irish about their work. It may well be argued that it is superficial and meaningless to link, say, Peter of Ireland, who taught Thomas Aquinas at Naples, with Richard FitzRalph or the Kilkenny friar John Clyn. In the earlier medieval period the distinctiveness of their Celtic background meant that, although the Irish were writing within different genres and at different periods, one can to some extent isolate their work and talk about 'Hiberno-Latin literature', even if that literature is not marked off by any distinctively Irish stylistic features. Not so with these *Hibernenses* of the later

---

[1] Anyone who writes on the Latin literature of late medieval Ireland must acknowledge a great debt to Mario Esposito, whose articles on Hiberno-Latin in *Hermathena* and elsewhere provide the basic framework without which authors might have been omitted from the account or wrong attributions made. See now the convenient *Variorum* reprints of these articles, brought together with a helpful preface by Michael Lapidge: Mario Esposito, *Latin learning in medieval Ireland*, and *Irish books and learning in medieval Europe* (2 vols, London, 1988, 1990). Dr Lapidge has retained the original pagination of the articles, so references to Esposito's articles in my notes may be followed up in the original place of publication or in the reprint. For biographical details, see Michael Gorman, 'Mario Esposito (1887–1975) and the study of the Latin literature of medieval Ireland' in *Filologia Mediolatina*, v (1998), pp 299–321.

middle ages. If Peter or Thomas were not called 'of Ireland', we would not
have guessed at their Irish origin. That origin is itself often a matter for
doubt. The only proof that some of these writers are Irish is the title *de
Hibernia* or *Hibernensis* added to their names in the manuscripts. Even when
there seems to be no doubt as to their Irish origin, as in the case of Thomas
of Ireland or Peter of Ireland, we know nothing whatever about their lives in
Ireland before their arrival in Britain or the Continent. So the only excuse
that can be made for writing this chapter is that it helps to indicate the links
that continued to exist between the two communities in Ireland and the
intellectual centres of Britain and the Continent. It also gives some idea of
the contribution made to the intellectual life of western Europe over a period
of three-and-a-half centuries by both the Gaelic Irish and the Anglo-Irish,
both those who remained in Ireland and those who left it never to return.

Most of the writers discussed will be from the Anglo-Irish rather than the
Gaelic tradition. Why should this be? The writing of Latin works seems to
peter out among the Gaelic Irish in the eleventh and twelfth centuries.
Writing in the vernacular begins earlier in Ireland than in many other western European countries. So, at quite an early stage Latin came to be reserved
for use in a limited range of genres. Even hagiography is not a monopoly of
Latin, while in the writing of history Latin is the exception rather than the
rule. Indeed some of the more literary and more interesting Latin works of
the period before 1169 are Latin texts written within genres in which the
general practice is to write in Irish—the 'Voyage of Brendan' is a good
example. It is possibly naive to blame the lack of Latin writings among the
Gaelic Irish on chaotic and warlike conditions in the post-viking period,
conditions that were perpetuated after the arrival of the Normans simply
because their conquest was incomplete, and there was continual warring
between Gael and Anglo-Irish, and indeed within the Gaelic community
itself. True, many of the monasteries that had been centres of Latin learning
had been destroyed by the vikings and, if refounded, were occupied by
orders introduced from the Continent in the reforming period of the twelfth
century. Irish traditional learning would have less place in a refounded
Bangor, or a newly founded Greyabbey. But we know that traditional Irish
learning survived even during the most disturbed periods of the middle ages,
and even under the far more adverse conditions of the sixteenth and seventeenth centuries.

The real reason for the decline of Latin learning in Gaelic Ireland in the
middle ages is a kind of cultural conservatism among the Irish. The kind of
learning that they had offered, first to Anglo-Saxon England and then to
Carolingian Europe, learning based on a thorough knowledge of the Bible
and the Latin grammarians, had been outstripped by more sophisticated
thought and learning as found in the cathedral schools of the twelfth century,
and then in their successors, the universities. By this later period the Irish

had much less to contribute to a western Europe that was rediscovering Aristotle, had a much better grip of ancient medicine transmitted to it through the Arabs, and was once more becoming familiar with Roman law. Individual Irishmen might go to the English or continental centres of learning. They might do very well there, and distinguish themselves. But they were drawing on the learning to be found there, not making any uniquely Irish contribution to it. In short the traditional Latin learning of the Irish was no longer in demand, as it had been in Carolingian Europe, and where it was noted at all, must have seemed quaint and outmoded.

Partly as a result of this, the perception that writers elsewhere had of the Irish was now very different from what it had been in the earlier middle ages. For Bede, Ireland was a place to which many English had resorted 'either for the sake of religious studies or to live a more ascetic life'.[2] Aldhelm has to admit grudgingly that 'the verdant country of Ireland is adorned with a browsing crowd of scholars'.[3] But by the twelfth century references to the Irish as backward barbarians are standard. Giraldus Cambrensis's anti-Irish prejudice is notorious.[4] St Bernard's emphasis on the barbarism of Irish society may be deliberate exaggeration with a view to making his subject, St Malachy, all the more saintly by comparison, or it may be the result of his having taken his information about Ireland from Irish Cistercian sources deeply committed to reform. After his experiences as visitor among those same Irish Cistercians, by now distinctly unreformed, a hundred years later, Stephen of Lexington might be excused for calling the Irish *gentes bestiales*.[5] But it is, perhaps, more significant that the historian William of Malmesbury, with no axe to grind, simply states as a fact that Ireland was an undeveloped land 'devoid of all products', and bred a race of unkempt peasants who, unlike the English and French, lived outside towns.[6] References to the Irish as simple, uninstructed peasants can be found in several papal documents, not just in *Laudabiliter*, where again one might suspect a deliberate exaggeration of Irish backwardness.[7]

The Anglo-Irish colony in the south and east of Ireland produced rather more writers than the areas that remained under Gaelic rule, but not many

---

[2] Bede, *Hist. ecc.* (1969), p. 136.

[3] Letter V, trans. Michael Lapidge and Michael Herren, *Aldhelm, the prose works* (Ipswich, 1979), p. 163.

[4] For Giraldus's many unflattering references to the Irish, see my comments in A. B. Scott and F. X. Martin (ed. and trans.), *Expugnatio Hibernica; the conquest of Ireland by Giraldus Cambrensis* (Dublin, 1978), introduction, pp xxv–xxvii.

[5] Stephen of Lexington, *Registrum*, ed. Bruno Griesser in *Analecta Ordinis Cisterciensis*, ii (1946), ch. 41.

[6] R.A.B. Mynors, R.M. Thomson, and M. Winterbottom (ed.), *Gesta regum Anglorum*, v, 409 (Oxford, 1998), pp 739–41.

[7] For instance, in the letters of Pope Alexander III to the kings of Ireland (Maurice P. Sheehy (ed.), *Pontificia Hibernica* (2 vols, Dublin, 1962, 1965), no. 7) or to King Henry II of England (ibid., no. 8).

more, and these mostly wrote after they had left Ireland, and settled in Oxford, Paris, or one of the Italian universities. From the fourteenth century the colony was in decline, and even places such as Carlow and Kilkenny were subject to attack by the Irish. The constant instability and the need to raise forces for its own defence meant that, after an initial period of prosperity, the colony remained poor. This, together with the geographical isolation that still handicaps higher education in Ireland, prevented any centre growing up that was remotely like Oxford, Paris, or even less important places of learning such as Lincoln or Salisbury. In particular the cathedrals were poor and there are few traces of any schools attached to them.[8] Above all, there was no *studium generale* or university in Ireland.

In 1310 John Lech, archbishop of Dublin, applied to Pope Clement V for authority to found a university in Dublin, and in 1312 the pope gave permission for such a foundation of a *scolarium universitas et in qualibet scientia et facultate licita . . . studium generale*, 'a corporation of scholars and a *studium generale* in all permitted branches of learning and faculties'. Lech's successor, that stormy petrel Alexander Bicknor, set up this university in 1320. The Annals of St Mary's, Dublin, give us the names of two masters, both friars, who incepted in theology, while the dean of St Patrick's incepted in canon law (incepting being the formal granting of a degree, enabling the recipient to teach). The dean also acted as chancellor, and a fourth teacher, also a friar, is named. Other evidence for the activities of this university is meagre,[9] but it may have continued for a period in a limited way and with no very great success. There is a grant of protection to the students 'at the said university', issued by Edward III in 1358.[10] But this sounds like a second attempt to found a failed university rather than an indication that the *studium* optimistically founded in 1320 had had a continuous existence until 1348. From 1363 we have a petition to the pope from Irish priests in which it is stated apologetically that they have no degrees because there is no university in Ireland.[11] So clearly, if there was a fresh attempt to start a *studium generale* in

---

[8] In his *Education in ancient and medieval Ireland* (Dublin, 1978) Fergal McGrath does his best with very meagre sources, but can only produce two pages on the cathedral schools, and they are full of phrases like 'it would be reasonable to suppose' and 'there are grounds for thinking'.

[9] Even the sources are contradictory. The annalist John Clyn's terse remark: 'A university started up at Dublin, but would that it had been a reality rather than just a name' (*Incepit universitas Dublinie quoad nomen, sed utinam quoad factum et rem*), ed. Richard Butler (Dublin, 1849), p. 14, would seem to indicate that he saw it—as did H. Rashdall in his *The universities of Europe in the middle ages*, rev. F. M. Powicke and A. B. Emden (Oxford, 1936), ii, 325–8—as a 'paper university'. Relevant documents are printed in E. B. FitzMaurice and A. G. Little, *Materials for the history of the Franciscan province of Ireland, A.D. 1230–1450* (Manchester, 1920), pp 107–9. Two more recent accounts are by F. McGrath, op. cit., pp 216–33, and Aubrey Gwynn, 'The medieval university of St Patrick's, Dublin' in *Studies*, xxvii (1938), pp 199–212, 437–54.

[10] See FitzMaurice & Little, loc. cit.

[11] McGrath, op. cit., p. 220.

1358, it too had foundered. Two further attempts to found universities, at Drogheda in 1465 and again in Dublin in 1475, seem not to have got off the ground at all.

The absence of a *studium generale* in Ireland had two consequences. First, there was no forum for intellectual discussion, which might result in philosophical, or more likely theological, writings. The Irish of both traditions who were concerned with intellectual debate—FitzRalph and Maurice O'Fihelly are examples—lived their intellectual life in Oxford or on the Continent, even though they may ultimately have returned to bishoprics in Ireland. It is this absence of an intellectual centre in Ireland, coupled with the fact that most of the written material we have from post-conquest Ireland takes the form of annals or legal documents, that gives us the impression that the typical Irish churchman is preoccupied with securing his own position, quite uninterested in matters of theology, and impervious to the whole world of abstract thought. Debates are concerned with rights and privileges, and are conducted in courts of law, or even on the streets with the aid of armed retainers. They are not concerned with abstruse points of doctrine. Where, as in the case of Bishop Ledred, accusations of heresy are bandied about, they are just that—accusations based on witchcraft or other malpractices, not a detailed, carefully worked-out attack on false doctrines.

The second consequence became clearer as the universities in Britain and the Continent began to evolve as a well-organised system, and were linked to the career structure in the church, so that it became almost the rule for a leading churchman, say an archdeacon or a bishop, to have attended a university. As Ireland had no university, anyone who wished to pursue a career in the part of the church that lay within the sphere of English influence would almost certainly have to spend time at a university, probably studying canon law or a combination of canon and civil law. For ambitious ecclesiastics living in the Gaelic-dominated regions of the north and west, university training was perhaps not so essential. Membership of an ecclesiastical family might be equally important. But many Gaelic Irish did go to the universities through the later middle ages.

One other path to higher education lay through the religious orders, and in particular the friars, who had their own arrangements for the education of their members. Both Dominicans and Franciscans had made provisions for lectors to teach theology in each of their houses. In the Dominican order these lectors were originally trained at the Paris convent, and then four *studia generalia* were created, one in each province, more being added later as new provinces were added. Like the original Paris *studium* these were linked to the universities, and friars staying there would attend the university courses and obtain university degrees. The teaching given within the order would count as equivalent to part of the degree. From 1314 the Irish Dominicans, who were part of the English province, had the right to send two students to Oxford, two to Cambridge, and one to Paris each year, and could share in any quota assigned to the English province for sending students to other European *studia*.[12] By the middle of the fourteenth century there were thirty-two Franciscan houses in Ireland. Unlike the Dominicans, the Irish Franciscans formed their own province. Most of their houses seemed to have had rectors most of the time, and E. B. FitzMaurice and A. G. Little have assembled a number of references to them,[13] which show that several had studied on the Continent. Clearly the Dublin house of the Franciscans was thought capable of providing the advanced teaching needed for the proposed university. According to Luke Wadding, Pope Eugenius IV suggested to the order that they should set up two advanced schools *distincta a studiis ordinariis theologiae* in Galway and Drogheda. Whether these materialised, or how long they survived, we do not know.[14] Franciscan friars were selected by the provincial chapter from the houses within each province to go to houses of the order in Oxford and other university towns and take their degree. But the system does not appear to have been as well defined as that of the Dominicans.

The Augustinians had a fully worked out system of educating their friars, which reflects the emphasis the order placed on learning. The upper tier of this system changed a good deal in the course of the fourteenth century, but basically it provided for the study of grammar as a first stage, followed by the study of logic. From that the student would move on to a provincial school, where he would spend at least three full years in the study of theology. After this the best students would be selected to go to a *studium generale* for five years or more, one student per year from each province being chosen to spend this further period of study in the most prestigious house of studies, at Paris. The number of university centres designated as *studia* for Augustinians fluctuated in the fourteenth century, but Paris, Oxford, and Cambridge were always included in their number.[15] As the order was always particularly strong in Italy, it seems likely that some Irish friars would have spent time in Italian houses of study. The number of friars of all kinds from Ireland listed in Emden's register of the University of Oxford is surprisingly small: seven Dominicans, thirteen Franciscans, and ten Augustinians, while there is a solitary Carmelite.[16] Many of the other Irish entries must be friars without our knowing it.

[12] See W. A. Hinnebusch, 'Foreign Dominican students and professors at the Oxford Blackfriars' in *Oxford studies presented to Daniel Callus* (Oxford, 1964), p. 114.

[13] FitzMaurice & Little, op. cit., p. xxviii.

[14] Ibid., p. 190.

[15] See Aubrey Gwynn, *The English Austin friars in the time of Wyclif* (Oxford, 1940), ch. iii: 'The organization of studies'.

[16] A. B. Emden, *A biographical register of the University of Oxford to A.D. 1500* (3 vols, Oxford, 1957–9). I am most grateful to Dr J. I. Catto, editor of the medieval volume of the *History of the University of Oxford*, for so readily making available to me the computer printout listing Irish students included in Emden's *Register*, and also to my colleague at Queen's University, Dr Evelyn Mullally, who has computerised the material in the *Register* to such good effect.

Among the monastic orders other than mendicants only the Cistercians seem to have sent students from Ireland to universities. Six names of Cistercians are recorded in Emden's *Register*. The Cistercians, in theory at least, had arrangements for educating their monks similar to those of the friars. In 1245 the general chapter had decreed that every monastery should have a *studium*, and that there should be a more advanced *studium theologicum* in each province. There were to be even more advanced *studia* in the great university centres, seven in all, and Irish monks were to go to the Oxford *studium*.[17] Given the long history of dissension within the Irish Cistercian monasteries, one might suppose that this blueprint was not fully carried out in the Irish province.

For the bright young friar or monk, then, the way to a higher education was through the houses of his order, ending up in all probability in Oxford, Cambridge, or some European university centre. The secular cleric who had ambitions would also go to university, with the support of his family or of a benefice previously obtained. Thus the universities provided the framework for the intellectual life of the later middle ages. Apart from annals and hagiography, so much of the writing to be discussed here originates in that intellectual life of the universities. So it seems not irrelevant to give a brief account of the part that both kinds of Irish played in the university world.

The majority of the Irish went to Oxford. Cambridge was a smaller university, was more remote geographically, and catered more for students from the eastern side of England. This preference of the Irish for Oxford has always been known, but we are now in a position to quantify it. The entries in Emden's *Register* have been computerised, so that we can break down and analyse the mass of information contained in it. As a result we have a listing of all students from Ireland included in the register. We have as yet no such analysis of his companion volume, the register of the University of Cambridge to 1500.[18] However, a comparison of the Gaelic Irish with names beginning with Mac or O' is instructive. The Oxford register has seventy-six Macs and O's, but the Cambridge register only one, Cornelius O'Mullally, subsequently bishop, in quick succession, of Clonfert, Emly, and Elphin.

In general, university documents lump together Anglo-Irish and Gaelic Irish students, though by the fifteenth century, when the Irish pressure on the Anglo-Irish colony began to cause the English government to regard the Gaelic Irish as an unnecessary security risk who should be sent back to Ireland, the distinction is made. In the period covered by Emden's *Register*,

---

[17] See Gearóid Mac Niocaill, *Na manaigh liatha in Éirinn* (Dublin, 1959), pp 217–22.
[18] A. B. Emden, *A biographical register of the University of Cambridge to 1500* (Cambridge, 1963).

between about 1150 and 1500, there are 304 graduates from Ireland. Trevor H. Aston, in his masterly article on Oxford's medieval alumni,[19] puts the number at 315, but on checking through the entries in Emden corresponding to the names isolated as belonging to Irish students on the computer print-out I have found several double entries, and a few where there is no evidence of their being Irish. Three hundred students, or thereabouts, over a period of 250 years may not seem many, but as Aston has pointed out, Emden's list represents only those alumni whose names chance to be recorded on some sort of document. He estimates that the 15,000 students listed by Emden may represent as little as 20 per cent of all students.

Of these 300 students, ninety appear to be Gaelic Irish, just over 200 Anglo-Irish. Most students would begin by taking the arts course, though this could be abbreviated for those going on to a law degree, especially towards the end of the medieval period, and friars could have study completed within their own convents accepted as equivalent to part of the arts course. Then the young cleric would go on to read law, civil or canon, or theology. Only one of the Irish students listed by Emden read medicine. In the case of forty-five of the Gaelic Irish students we do not know what courses they followed. Of the remaining forty-four, fifteen read canon law, four civil law, sixteen *utrumque ius* (the peculiarly Oxford combination of canon law with some civil law), and nine theology. Again we do not know what courses 137 out of the total of 214 Anglo-Irish students followed. Of the remaining seventy-seven, sixteen read canon law, twenty-six *utrumque ius*, twelve civil law, and twenty-three theology. So by far and away the greatest proportion in each group went to Oxford to read law: not the customary common law, a knowledge of which was acquired at the inns of court in London, but civil Roman and canon law, which would enable them to hold administrative positions in the church or in the courts of magnates, lay or clerical. These figures help put the Irish presence in Oxford and other universities in perspective. These are not wandering scholars blithely going from one university to another for the sake of learning. They are men preparing for a career in administration in church or state. Most of them will not have continued on to the doctorate, the highest point in their field of studies, but will have returned home equipped with a bachelor's degree in civil or in canon law. A minority of the Anglo-Irish stayed on in England and obtained benefices in the church there, but the majority of both Gaelic Irish and Anglo-Irish returned to Ireland, and one can see their subsequent careers in the entries in Emden.

Yet, though these students may not seem so attractive as the carefree wanderers through the Europe of Charlemagne and his successors, the length of the medieval university course did demand considerable commitment

[19] Trevor H. Aston, 'Oxford's medieval alumni' in *Past & Present*, lxxiv (1977), pp 3–37.

to learning on their part. Quite apart from the preliminary arts degree which, if not abbreviated, required seven years of study before the student could obtain the M.A.,[20] the bachelor of civil law took four years, the bachelor of canon law three. No one could begin the canon law course at Oxford unless he either had a B.C.L. or in lieu had studied civil law for three years. The complete doctoral course in civil law would take thirteen years for someone who already had an M.A., or fifteen for those who did not, a prospect that would hold little attraction for present-day grant-giving bodies. But the normal 'graduate in both laws' would have the B.C.L. and B.Cn.L., and would not proceed beyond these.[21] Most students who obtained the doctorate in theology would have taken nine years after their M.A.[22] We would not expect to find many writers or thinkers among the ranks of the lawyers. As Leonard Boyle puts it: 'The plain fact is that unlike the faculties of arts and theology, the faculty of canon law (and needless to say that of civil law) never amounted to much academically in the middle ages.' William of Drogheda is the only one of the authors considered in this chapter to have issued from the law faculties. All the others are university theologians—of course, by no means all of them Oxford men—or else they are friars.

In her *Making of Ireland and its undoing*,[23] Alice Stopford Green devotes a chapter to the Irish at Oxford. In line with the strongly tendentious views expressed throughout her book—she makes no secret of who she thinks is responsible for the 'undoing'—she depicts an Oxford thronged with the Irish, with an Irishman's Meadow, an Irishman's Street, and even an Irishman's Pool. She is, of course, trying to depict the Irish presence at the universities of the later middle ages as a return to the golden age of Irish intellectual preeminence in early medieval Europe. But, as I have tried to show, the circumstances in the thirteenth and fourteenth centuries were quite different from those that prevailed in the Carolingian period or the age of Bede. The figures derived from Emden's *Register* indicate exactly the place of the Irish at Oxford. They were the largest non-English group within the university, but roughly 300 out of a total of roughly 14,900 names is just over a fiftieth part of the whole. But the Irish did make their mark on Oxford. No other Irish Oxonian equalled Richard FitzRalph's achievement in becoming chancellor, but there were others, such as Henry Crumpe, Philip Norreys, John Whitehead, and the Augustinian friar Adam Payne, who went up through the Oxford system to become doctors of theology, and could argue and debate on equal terms with the brightest intellects of their

---

[20] See J. M. Fletcher, 'The Faculty of Arts', ch. 9 in *The history of the University of Oxford* (Oxford, 1984), i, esp. pp 374–88.
[21] See Leonard E. Boyle, 'Canon law before 1380', ibid., pp 541–7.
[22] See Catto, 'Theology and theologians 1220–1320', ibid., ch. 12, esp. p. 476.
[23] Alice Stopford Green, *The making of Ireland and its undoing, 1200–1600* (London, 1908).

day. A number of Irishmen were principals of university halls, which were in effect hostels or lodging houses, not fully collegiate establishments, but under the general supervision of the university. Two of these halls had especially strong Irish connections: Aristotle Hall and Spreadeagle or Eagle Hall.[24] Of the thirty-four Irish entries in Emden where membership of a hall is known, eleven belong to Aristotle Hall and five to Eagle Hall. Neither Beef Hall nor St Patrick's Hall, both mentioned as haunts of the Irish by Green, figure at all. In general, Aston's comment that, though few Irish found a place in any of the seventeen medieval colleges, 'they (and the Welsh) obtained reasonably ready accommodation in the halls'[25] seems to be justified. Many of the Irish would, of course, be accommodated in the house of their order, if they were friars, or members of an order, such as the Cistercians, that had an Oxford house.

Unlike Paris, the student body at Oxford was not formally divided into nations, each with its own rector and officials. But there was a very real and disruptive division into northerners and southerners, unofficial, but recognised by the university to the extent that it was a statutory requirement that one of the two proctors should be a northerner and one a southerner, while similar arrangements held good for other university offices. Several of the colleges had a distinct bias towards northern or southern students. As far as England was concerned the dividing-line seems to have been the Nene rather than the Trent.[26] Irish and Welsh students were counted as southerners, and those Scots who went to Oxford rather than Paris as northerners. This division between northerners and southerners was as frequent a cause of bloodshed as that between town and university.

In theory, then, the Irish and Welsh students would be involved in the north-versus-south rivalry, but as southerners rather than national minorities. There are, however, occasions when the Irish are singled out and specially mentioned. Thus in 1252 a meeting of Congregation solemnly ratified a treaty to end the *magna dissensio et discordia* that had arisen between northerners and Irish. A similar agreement was signed in 1267. On the first occasion twenty-eight arbitrators were chosen from each side, thus providing a useful source of names for Emden. A third agreement, made in 1274, was *inter Australes, Marchiones, Hybernienses, et Walenses ex una parte et Boriales et Scotos ex altera* (between southerners, marchers, Irish, and Welsh on one

[24] Aristotle Hall was in Kybald Street, near Merton College. A house with the same name is still to be found in the street. Irish principals of Aristotle Hall listed by Emden are ?Fynglas, James Porter, William Rathe, and John White; while David Haket was principal of Eagle Hall, Philip Norreys of Little University Hall, James Hedyan of Merston Hall and Mailler of Ireland of Ape Hall, Peter Paris was principal of Haberdash Hall, rented Little St Edmund Hall, and was keeper of one of the university chests.

[25] Aston, 'Oxford's medieval alumni', p. 23.

[26] See A. B. Emden, 'Northerners and Southerners in the organization of the university to 1509' in *Studies presented to Daniel Callus*, pp 1–30.

side, and northerners and Scots on the other).[27] Likewise Irish students were not singled out by townspeople for attack just because they were Irish, but they do seem 'just to have happened to be about' when one of the worst fights between town and gown broke out. The riot of 1238 began when the brother of the papal legate, who was staying at Oseney abbey, threw a cauldron of hot water over 'a poor Irish cleric who was begging for alms at the kitchen door'.[28] The brother was killed by students who saw what happened, the legate fled for his life and appealed to the king, the university was suspended, and students dispersed to Northampton and Salisbury. Among the list of clerks allegedly involved in this fracas sent by the king to the sheriff of Oxford, many Irish, Welsh, and Scots names appear;[29] and one of the ringleaders, who was put in the Tower for a period, was a lawyer, Odo of Kilkenny.[30]

Two of the main sources used by Emden are Oxford coroners' records, splendidly edited many years ago by H. E. Salter, and the records of the royal courts. So, inevitably, many of the Irish included in his *Register* have come to his attention because they have met a violent end, or committed a violent act for which they were punished. Thus John Burel was killed in a tavern brawl; William de Bangor drowned while bathing in the Thames; John de Falwath was arrested as an accomplice to murder; John Begus was sent down from the university for theft; Robert of Ireland was accused of burglary, while another Robert, in the mid fourteenth century, was accused of murder; Walter le Whit had attacked some footballers with a knife at the Eastgate, while Robert Pursell's chosen weapon was a fork. The only noted Irish lawyer, William of Drogheda, was stabbed to death by his servant. But for once we have to agree with Green that medieval universities were extremely violent places, and amid the constant brawling and bloodshed reflected in the Oxford coroners' records, the Irishmen do not particularly stand out as being either more accident-prone or more criminal than the rest.

In the first half of the fifteenth century a series of royal proclamations, issued in response to petitions in parliament, expressed a different attitude towards the Irish. Green predictably regarded these enactments as deliberate attempts to keep the Irish down by preventing them from obtaining

---

[27] References to the relevant documents are given in Rashdall, *The universities of Europe in the middle ages* (revised by Powicke & Emden), iii, 50.

[28] H. R. Luard (ed.), *Matthaei Parisiensis: Chronica majora* (7 vols, London, 1872–84), iii, 481.

[29] Two lists of clerks who had absconded or found sureties for good behaviour are in *Close rolls 22 Henry III (1238)*, membrane 12d, p. 136.

[30] Matthew Paris, loc. cit. (iii, 483), refers to a *magister Odo legista* as a ringleader, and the directive to the constable of the Tower to deliver Odo and others to the custody of the bishop of Lincoln and the bishop of London is in *Close rolls 22 Henry III (1238)*, membrane 14, p. 53. Odo's career seems to have suffered no hindrance from this episode, as we find him in the next year acting as advocate in the papal court for the chapter of Lincoln in a case against Bishop Grosseteste (Matthew Paris, op. cit., iii, 529).

qualifications for holding benefices or positions as legal advisors in church or state. She indignantly refutes the idea that the Irish could have been the troublemakers they are alleged to have been in the petitions. There were in fact several motives for this intermittent and partial banning of Irish students from the two universities and the inns of court. These motives are reflected in the texts of the proclamations. In 1413 all Irish clerks, except for graduates and sergeants at law with their apprentices, those with inherited possessions in England, and professed religious, were required to leave England.[31] Those with benefices in Ireland must stay there 'for the defence of the land of Ireland'. This is one reason for repeated demands that the Irish—in this case the Anglo-Irish—should return to Ireland. It was felt that the colony had been seriously denuded of potential defenders against the growing strength of the Gaelic Irish. But this is only one of the reasons given for this proclamation. The other is 'the peace and tranquillity of England'.

When the ban was renewed in slightly different terms in 1423,[32] this is made the main reason. The Irish have caused 'homicides, murders, rapes, felonies, robberies, riots, conspiracies, and other misdeeds' in the counties of Oxford, Berkshire, Wiltshire, and Buckinghamshire. Both Irish and Anglo-Irish are expressly mentioned this time: 'some of whom are liege subjects of our lord the king, while others are not liege subjects, but enemies... called wylde irisshmen'. There are many more exceptions allowed than in the first proclamation, and even students who are not graduates may remain if they can provide sureties and letters under the seal of the lieutenant or the justiciar in Ireland testifying to their loyalty. Here for the first time what may be the real reason for these bans emerges. During the first half of the fifteenth century the English, hard pressed abroad, suffered a bout of what may be called nervous xenophobia. Not just the Irish but all foreigners were under suspicion of being security risks.[33]

Yet when the matter is raised again in 1429[34] the apparent reason for the renewal of the ban is disorderly behaviour. Security is not given as an overt reason. This time the complaints against the Irish, as well as Scots and Welsh students, come from Cambridge. The royal response, though, is significant. The existing statutes are to be enforced against the Irish, but no action is to be taken against Scots or Welsh students till the king has taken advice on the matter. Again there is not a total ban, but Irish students must give sureties for their good behaviour. So the motives for these partial expulsions of the Irish appear to be mixed: the well-known fear that the Anglo-Irish colony within the Pale might become depleted and unable to defend

---

[31] *Rot. Parl. 1 Henry V (1413)*, p. 13, no. 39.
[32] *Rot. Parl. 1 Henry VI (1422)*, p. 190.
[33] For an excellent description of the forms taken by this xenophobia see Sylvia L. Thrupp, 'A survey of the alien population of England in 1440' in *Speculum*, xxxii (1957), pp 262–73.
[34] *Rot. Parl. 8 Henry VI (1429)*, p. 358.

itself; a suspicion of Gaelic Irish students as a security risk; and also, quite likely, a desire to make some money for the treasury from those students who purchased permission to stay on in England. But there must have been some reality behind that persistent charge of riotous behaviour by Irish students, for it to have been used so constantly as a excuse for their expulsion.

Clearly the Irish made their presence felt at Oxford, and to a lesser degree at Cambridge, for good or ill. But when we consider their presence in the continental universities it is clear that we are dealing not with large numbers of Irish students but with individuals. Before Oxford evolved as a university in the first decades of the thirteenth century, English students had gone to Paris, where they filled the ranks of the 'English nation' within the university. After Oxford had begun to flourish, the flow of English students to Paris almost dried up, and the records of the 'English nation' contain far fewer English names but a large number of Scots and Germans, so that eventually it became known as 'the German nation'. The Irish too seem to have been diverted from Paris to Oxford once Oxford became established. I can find only one reference to the Irish as a group at Paris. The moralist Servasanto de Faenza, criticising the loose life led by students at Paris, remarks: 'Drunks in particular act like this, as for instance many at Paris, and especially the Irish, who consume in one day of drinking whatever they earn in a whole week by copying.'[35] There are only a handful of Irish names in Glorieux's repertoires of thirteenth-century Paris arts and theology graduates, and fewer still in the records of the 'English nation' published by Denifle and Chatelain.[36] No other Irishman seems to have had such a lasting connection with the university as Thomas of Ireland, the compiler of the 'Manipulus florum', though Maurice of Ireland was procurator of the 'English nation' in 1275. Presumably a good many Irish friars spent time in their house at Paris, but the only one we know about is Thomas O'Colman, O.F.M., rector in the Franciscan convent at Armagh, who had studied at Oxford, Cambridge, and Paris.[37]

[35]   *Liber de virtutibus et vitiis*, dist. vii. 4 , cited from L. Oliger, 'Servasanto da Faenza e il suo *Liber de virtutibus et vitiis*' in *Miscellanea Francisco Ehrle* (Studi e Testi, xxxvii; 1924), pp 148–89, at p. 180, cited by C. H. Haskins, *Studies in mediaeval culture* (Cambridge, Mass., 1929), p. 64.

[36]   Phillipe Glorieux, *La Faculté des Arts et ses maîtres au xiii^e siècle* (Paris, 1971) gives eight Irish entries: Geoffrey of Waterford, the translator into French of the 'Secreta Secretorum' (no. 113); William of Ireland, M.A. in 1318 (no. 1766); John MacCarwill, or MacCarwell, later bishop of Meath (no. 1591); Maurice of Ireland (no. 1069); Patrick of Ireland, M.A. 1203 (no. 1203); another Patrick of Ireland (no. 328, see below, p. 961); Robert of Ireland, mentioned in a document of 1284 (no. 1237), and the well-known canonist William of Drogheda (no. 639). Apart from Thomas of Ireland (for whom see below, p. 958), there appear to be no Irish entries in Glorieux's companion volume, *Repertoire des maîtres en théologie de Paris au xiii^e siècle*. Likewise I have found no Irishmen among the lists given by Denifle and Chatelain in their edition of the 'Book of the procurators of the English Nation at Paris, 1333–1406' in *Auctarium Universitatis Parisiensis* (Paris, 1889), i.

[37]   See FitzMaurice & Little, *Materials*, p. 156, and Emden, *Register*, ii, 1387.

One has the feeling, perhaps totally unfounded, that more of the Irish, especially the friars, studied in Italy. Two of the authors discussed below taught in Italian universities, Peter of Ireland at Naples and Maurice O'Fihelly at Padua. Matthew Machegan, O.F.M., had also studied at Bologna, as had Raymond O'Flanagan.[38] Thomas O'Herlihy (O'Hurley or O'Heirlighy), bishop of Ross 1561–80, had been 'brought up in Italy', according to Holinshed, whatever that may mean. Whether David Duff, alias Fitzgerald, a civil lawyer whom Holinshed picturesquely records as having arrived at Pisa attired entirely in clothes woven by himself, stayed on to study there is not known.[39]

Some of the Irish entered the papal service at Rome or Avignon, while others attained eminence in their order or in the wider church. Thus James Stanton was in the service of Pope Urban VI when he died mysteriously in a wood near Tivoli in 1391. Matthew O'Gryffa spent some time at the curia, and may have been employed there rather than merely acting as procurator for some Irish or English suitor at the papal court.[40] Ralph O'Kelly was procurator-general of the Carmelites, and spent some years at the papal court at Avignon. Even after becoming archbishop of Cashel he was used more than once by the pope as a 'troubleshooter'. For instance, he investigated the complicated quarrels arising out of the troubled episcopate of Alexander Bicknor in Dublin in 1343, and again in 1347. Patrick Foxe, later to become bishop of Ossory (1417–21), was a member of the household of Henry de Minutelis in 1407, and attended the council of Constance, where he was head of the 'English nation' for a time, and represented it on the panel of judges that pronounced sentence on Pope John XXIII, on John Hus in 1415, and on Jerome of Prague in the following year.[41]

A few Irish, again mostly friars, studied in German-speaking lands. David Obuge, O. Carm., was sent to Trier by his order and studied there, and appears to have done some teaching before returning to Ireland as prior provincial of his order. Whether he really was, in the words of Holinshed, 'the gem and lantern of his country' we cannot know, as none of his works, listed by Ware, has survived.[42] The newly founded university of Vienna attracted Matthew O'Driscoll and Robert Hore.[43] We hear of three young

---

[38] For Malachy O'Quirk, see Emden, *Register*, ii, 1388, for Matthew Machegan see Fitz-Maurice & Little, *Materials*, p. 192; for Raymond O'Flanagan see Emden, *Register*, ii, 1392.

[39] Holinshed's scrappy two-page list of Irish writers and learned men, *Chronicles of England, Scotland and Ireland* (London, 1808), vi, 60–62, does not inspire confidence, yet is used surprisingly often as if it were itself an original source.

[40] For Stanton see Emden, *Register*, iii, 63, and for O'Gryffa, ibid., ii, 393.

[41] Emden's Cambridge register (above, p. 940, n.18), p. 239, and Aubrey Gwynn, 'Ireland and the English nation at the council of Constance' in *R.I.A. Proc.*, xlv (1940), sect. C, pp 214–16.

[42] These are sermons (Ware, *De scriptoribus Hiberniae* (Dublin, 1639), p. 67; a collection of thirty-two letters: 'propositions discussed' (*propositiones disputatae*); 'lectures given at Trier'; 'legal precepts'; 'Against Gerard of Bologna'; and unspecified biblical commentaries.

[43] Emden, *Register*, ii, 1394, and i, 962 in the Bodleian interleaved copy.

friars being sent from Askeaton to Cologne in 1441, presumably to the university.[44] A royal document of 1375 gives Marianus Curydany, O.F.M., permission to travel through England in order to take up his studies at Strasbourg.[45] There was no university at Strasbourg at this period, and indeed he is said to be going *ad scholas*, not *ad studium generale*, so presumably he was going to the house of his order at Strasbourg.

Richard FitzRalph must surely be the best-known of all those who went from Ireland to the schools of Oxford. Katherine Walsh has described him as 'the most significant personality linking Ireland with the intellectual world of continental Europe during the millennium between Columbanus and Luke Wadding'.[46] This is to underestimate Eriugena, who, though perhaps not so influential on later thought as was FitzRalph, was surely a deeper and more original thinker. But during the later middle ages no Irish or Anglo-Irish churchman had such a spectacularly successful career as FitzRalph, and none moved with equal ease in intellectual circles at Oxford and the cosmopolitan papal court at Avignon.

FitzRalph belonged to a well-off, but not aristocratic, burgess family of Dundalk. He was at Oxford by 1325, a regent master in theology by 1331/2 and, while not much more than 30 years of age, chancellor of the university by early 1332. As chancellor he was faced with the crisis caused by the famous secession of masters and students to Stamford. His handling of that crisis does not seem to have harmed his career, and may well have advanced it, for it may have been the cause of his first visit to the papal court at Avignon in the autumn of 1334. He was to spend a sizeable part of the rest of his life at Avignon, for he was there during the period 1337–44, and from 1349 to 1351, while his last visit lasted from 1357 till his death in 1360. He was dean of Lichfield from 1335 until he became archbishop of Armagh in 1346. Despite his long absence from Lichfield in Avignon between 1337 and 1344 he seems to have been a thoughtful and efficient administrator.

It was soon after his return from Avignon to Lichfield in 1344 that FitzRalph began to keep what is usually called his 'sermon diary',[47] containing notes of where he preached, summaries in Latin of sermons preached in the vernacular, and the full Latin text of his more learned sermons of theological

---

[44] Wadding, *Annales Ordinum Minorum*, xi, 144, as quoted in FitzMaurice & Little, *Materials*, p. 192. The phrase is *missi sunt ad studia generalia*.

[45] FitzMaurice & Little, *Materials*, p. 157.

[46] Katherine Walsh, *A fourteenth-century scholar and primate: Richard FitzRalph in Oxford, Avignon and Armagh* (Oxford, 1981), p. 465. For an excellent bibliography of FitzRalph, including editions of works cited here, see Richard Sharpe, *A handlist of the Latin writers of Great Britain and Ireland before 1540* (Turnhout, 1997), pp 478–81.

[47] Cf. Aubrey Gwynn, 'The sermon diary of Richard FitzRalph…' in *R.I.A. Proc.*, xliv (1937), sect. C, pp 1–57. See also T. P. Dolan, 'English and Latin versions of FitzRalph's sermons' in *Latin and vernacular: studies in late medieval texts and manuscripts* (Cambridge, 1989), pp 27–37.

content, preached mainly at Avignon. This fascinating document gives us a good idea of where FitzRalph was at any given time. The notes on the vernacular sermons in particular tell us much about his character, and his preoccupations with social problems of the day. FitzRalph preached twenty-nine sermons in Ireland to congregations of churchmen or of the English-speaking burgesses of the trading communities of Dundalk, Drogheda, and various places in Meath. He denounced the sharp practices among the traders. For instance, a sermon delivered at Drogheda in 1352 shows a knowledge that would do credit to a modern accountant of the various ways in which traders can avoid paying tithes. Even more interesting is his insistence, in sermons delivered to an Anglo-Irish audience, that the native Irish should be treated justly. It was not to be an excuse for the murder of Irishmen that 'they are all disloyal anyway', or that it was 'according to marcher law'. It was equally wrong to discriminate against the native Irish by refusing them entry into the craft guilds. There are denunciations of wasteful extravagance at guild functions, and the more usual castigation of laxity among the clergy to be found in the Latin sermons. All in all FitzRalph emerges as a severe but very fair and serious-minded pastor of his divided flock.

His tenure of the archiepiscopal throne was as difficult as had been his chancellorship at Oxford. There was a running battle with the Dublin archbishop for the right to be called primate; conditions even quite close to the coastal towns remained very unsettled; and it was during his time as archbishop that the black death ravaged Ireland. Yet he seems to have been as competent in Armagh as he had been in Oxford and Lichfield. The only matter in which he showed notable lack of judgement was his obsessive pursuit of the mendicant orders towards the end of his life, a pursuit that led him into a battle he could not possibly win.

FitzRalph was not an original thinker, but his years at Oxford had equipped him with a subtlety in argument that enabled him to take up and develop current ideas that suited his purpose. His earliest work, the commentary on Peter Lombard's 'Sentences', is very much a product of the Oxford schools of the first half of the fourteenth century. Its arguments are so carefully hedged around and qualified that they are often hard to follow, even by the standards of scholastic philosophy. But Katherine Walsh has shown that the commentary is not so conservative or remote from currents of contemporary thought as was previously imagined, and that it was also quoted and discussed extensively by his contemporaries at Oxford. In picking and choosing which parts of Lombard's work to comment on, he dealt with such topics as the concept of infinity, predestination and free will, the role of the will in perceiving the 'clear vision' of God, and the subordination of the will to the intellect. Unlike his two later and better-known works, the influence of the commentary on 'Sentences' was immediate rather than long-lasting. But all his contemporaries, even those who take issue with his views, speak of the work in respectful terms.

When FitzRalph arrived in Avignon from Lichfield in 1337 there was much interest in the eastern church. The work of Dominican missionary friars in greater Armenia had resulted in a Latinising party arising within the Armenian church, which favoured union with Rome, and two Armenian bishops who had followed this line fled to Avignon. Pope Benedict XII, beset by requests for help against Islam from the orthodox Armenian church on the one hand, and unfavourable accounts of the doctrines and practices of the same church from these Latinising bishops on the other, set up an inquiry into the Armenian church. FitzRalph, as a skilled Oxford theologian, was asked to participate, and it is this involvement in the inquiry that led to his writing the bulky 'Summa de questionibus Armenorum', in nineteen books. The 'Summa' is in the form of a dialogue between Ricardus and Johannes. The first ten books contain a rational defence of western theology against Armenian beliefs and practices, but the next four deal with the errors of the eastern churches as a whole, while the last five books discuss the basic problems of grace, free will, and predestination, and are a general defence of Christian belief. While not the most influential of FitzRalph's works, the 'Summa' contains much of interest to anyone concerned with the intellectual contacts between east and west, Christian orthodox, Jew, and Muslim; for FitzRalph not only had long discussions with the Armenians at the papal court, but also with the Calabrian Greek Barlaam of Seminaria, who taught Petrarch Greek, and a Jewish convert whom he mentions, but does not identify by name.

The work also reveals a very considerable shift in FitzRalph's methodology.[48] His commentary on the 'Sentences' had been the work of a schoolman. There he had applied the arguments of scholastic logic to support views subtly refined and discussed. Scholastic modes of argument would make no impression on eastern churchmen, nor would arguments based on western traditions of belief, or on the teaching of western theologians writing after the separation of the two churches became a reality. Curiously enough, Fitz-Ralph makes little use of patristic writers over whose views the two churches might have been in agreement. He tells us himself at the beginning of the *Summa* that his arguments would be based almost entirely on scripture. In the middle books (XV–XVII), where he is largely concerned with attacking 'modern' heresies, he reverts to scholastic methods of proof. But in general the 'Summa' marks a turning-point, and his later work is much more directly based on scripture, and less dependent on arguments based on scholastic logic. The 'Summa' is also a sign of things to come in that we already find

---

[48] FitzRalph's own view of this change in his method is best set out, with illustrative quotations, by Walsh, op. cit., p. 176.

there some of the views FitzRalph put forward in his final work, the 'De pauperie Salvatoris', notably the thesis of just lordship and jurisdiction.

It is unfortunate that what most people, from the late middle ages till the present, have remembered about FitzRalph has been the violent controversy with the mendicant orders that clouded the last ten years of his life. His formal attack on the friars began with a sermon preached before Pope Clement VI in Avignon in 1350, and clearly by the time of his death ten years later his antagonism had become an obsession. It has always seemed surprising that someone who, both at Oxford and Avignon, had been in close intellectual contact with the friars, should have come to be known throughout the church as their enemy *par excellence*. It seems most likely that in trying to administer his difficult Irish diocese he had felt thwarted by the presence there of religious exempt from his authority, who could in a sense cut out the secular clergy and provide an alternative ministry, and above all alternative confessors to the laity, and in return receive gifts and legacies that the diocese, struggling under an incubus of debt, could well have done with. In modern terms, the friars, better educated and organised than the diocesan clergy, could offer a better service.

Whatever the origins of FitzRalph's opposition to the friars, he attacked them on two fronts: the incompatibility of their present activities with the doctrine of poverty, and their engaging in pastoral work outside the parochial and diocesan structures. His most violent attacks on the friars were made in his later sermons, and in particular sermons delivered at St Paul's Cross in London in the summer of 1356 and the beginning of 1357. These sermons brought him into conflict with Edward III, who tried unsuccessfully to prevent him leaving England for Avignon. The friars issued an appeal to the papal court listing twenty-one alleged errors in the archbishop's teaching, while FitzRalph in turn petitioned for a commission of cardinals to hear his case against them. The case dragged on before the cardinals through the winter of 1357 and the spring of 1358. The response (*exceptiones*) of each side to the original charges of the opposing party were very bitter, and that of the mendicants descended to personal abuse. The wide circulation of his sermons against the friars after his death shows that FitzRalph had many tacit supporters among the seculars and monks, but tacit they remained. He had no financial resources to match those of the friars in feeing advocates, and his own grasp of canon law was shaky. The case was still apparently being debated, off and on, before the committee, when FitzRalph died in 1360. If he had lived, defeat would have been inevitable.

FitzRalph's last work, begotten by his controversy with the friars, was his 'De pauperie Salvatoris', again a dialogue in form. The first five books deal, not so much with poverty, but with the nature of such concepts as 'lordship', 'ownership', 'property', 'possession', and 'right of use'. He discusses the meaning of lordship or dominion, first in terms of God and the nature of his dominion over creation, and then considers the natural lordship enjoyed by Adam before the Fall, and how lordship, now much altered as a consequence of the Fall, is exercised through kings and princes. The third and fourth books try, not very successfully, to define the relationship between abstract lordship and actual possession and use of some power or property. It is in the fourth book that the proposition central to the whole work, and the one that most influenced Wyclif and other reformers, is enunciated in its fullest form. Lordship or dominion over goods and peoples only exists when it is justly based, and the lord or possessor is in a state of grace with God. Otherwise he may continue to possess in practical terms but, as a sinner, he does not enjoy true dominion over people or property. In book V FitzRalph reverts again to the lordship enjoyed by Adam before the Fall, while books VI and VII deal with the more immediately practical aspects of mendicant poverty. Book VIII, which was not part of the work as originally planned, is more closely concerned with the issues raised at the proceedings at Avignon, being a clarification of some of the points on which FitzRalph based his case there.

The 'De pauperie Salvatoris' is surely the most influential of FitzRalph's writings. Wyclif's development of this theory of just dominion in 'De dominio divino', and his frequent quotation from FitzRalph, left no doubt in the minds of his contemporaries who his mentor in this matter was. The influence of FitzRalph's writing on Wyclif, the Lollards, and the Czech reformers went further than this. Their attacks on the friars clearly owe much to his sermons, while their emphasis on the Bible text as the only valid criterion on which Christian beliefs may be based may owe something to FitzRalph's insistence on the primacy of the Scriptures, found first in the 'Summa de questionibus Armenorum'. But FitzRalph is not a reformer in the sense that they were, nor was he a precursor of reformers. He was an ambitious, successful, and sometimes vain churchman, who at several periods of his life held a plurality of livings. Only at the very end of his life was he accused of heresy, and that by the friars whom he was attacking. Although clearly his obdurate stance against the friars was embarrassing to the papal court, he never seems to have fallen out of favour there.

Katherine Walsh has rightly remarked on the curious fact that no fewer than three Anglo-Irish churchmen followed FitzRalph in attacking the friars, and has suggested that the problems caused by the mendicants were particularly acute in the Irish church.[49] Two of the three, Henry Crumpe and John Whitehead, were contemporaries, but Philip Norreys was active half a century later, which suggests that there were continuing local reasons that made the Anglo-Irish secular clergy particularly hostile to the friars.

---

[49] See also the comments of F. X. Martin in 'An Irish Augustinian disputes at Oxford: Adam Payne, 1402' in *Scientia Augustiniana: Festschrift Adolar Zumkeller* (Würzburg, 1975), p. 298.

Curiously enough Henry Crumpe, at least at the beginning of his Oxford career, was a violent opponent of Wyclif's views on dominion, though later on he was himself condemned for views on the sacrament that seemed too close to the Wycliffite position. He gives every impression of having been a more intemperate debater than FitzRalph, and reminds one of the sort of student who successfully sails close to the wind in his dealings with authority, and after many vicissitudes just about scrapes home in his finals. Crumpe preached a university sermon against Wyclif's 'De civili dominio', and in 1380 was one of the committee who condemned Wyclif's views on the eucharist. But Wyclif was not without his supporters in the university. Crumpe, who has been credited with being the first to apply the word 'Lollards' to Wyclif's followers, was suspended from all teaching and disputation in the university for a short period in 1382. He returned to Ireland soon afterwards, and there preached against the friars. Unfortunately for Crumpe, the bishop of Meath at this time was a Dominican, William Andrew. He delated Crumpe to the university on grounds of heresy in 1385. This charge does not seem to have stuck, but Crumpe did not return to Oxford from Ireland till about 1391. It did not take him long to get into trouble, this time necessitating an appearance before the king's council. He was condemned in May 1392 at Stamford by a commission that included the archbishops of York and Canterbury and nine other bishops, a considerable testimony to his importance. Once again he was suspended from teaching or disputing in the university. Once again he returned to Ireland. Once again he preached against the friars, and eventually, in 1401, was prohibited by the pope from preaching on this subject.

John Bale attributed to Crumpe a set of *determinaciones scholasticae*, the *determinacio* being a scholastic exercise that takes the form of a summing up and reasoned judgement on a subject under debate in the schools; and also two works, the 'Contra religiosos mendicantes' and 'Contra objecta', which seems a very likely by-product of Crumpe's pugnacious career. He also attributed to him a work on the foundation of monasteries in England.[50] No copies of any of these have as yet surfaced in manuscripts or catalogues of manuscript collections.

John Whitehead left Ireland to study at Oxford in 1349. By 1408 he is referred to as a doctor of theology, and from 1389 till at least 1415 was rector of Stabannon, County Louth. Two short works of his remain unprinted in a Bodleian manuscript: 'Determinacio in materia de mendicitate' ('assessment in the matter of mendicant poverty') and 'Determinacio de confessione et absolucione' ('assessment concerning confession and absolution').[51] Clearly Whitehead adopted the same two-pronged attack on the friars as did

---

[50] *Index scriptorum Britanniae*, ed. R. L. Poole (Oxford, 1902), p. 161.
[51] Bodl., MS Digby 98, ff 200 (*De mendicitate*) and 208 (*De confessione et absolutione*).

FitzRalph, on the theological front questioning whether their poverty was true poverty as understood by Christ, and on the pastoral front asserting that the friars were abusing their powers to act as confessors. Whitehead's sermons against the friars led to his being cited before the convocation of the province of Canterbury held at St Paul's, London, in February 1410. His at times vigorous and witty response is printed in Wilkins's *Concilia*.[52] In the previous year he had been sent to the council of Pisa as the proctor of Archbishop Fleming of Armagh. He was considered by the friars a formidable enough adversary for the Augustinian Adam Payne and the Franciscan John Cuock to have been sent by a joint meeting of the friars in England to counter any attack made on them by Whitehead at the council.[53] However, the controversies raised by Whitehead in England seem to have been allowed to lapse, unlike the tempest that was raging simultaneously in the university of Paris.

Compared with the running battles with the friars, which seem to have occupied most of the career of Philip Norreys, the lives of Crumpe and Whitehead must seem tranquil and trouble-free. Norreys, originally from the Dublin diocese, had a successful career in both university and church. Before going to Oxford he was vicar of Dundalk from 1427. He was a doctor of theology at Oxford by 1435, and subsequently a canon, prebendary, and later (1457) dean of St Patrick's, Dublin, and rector of Trim. But already by 1431 he had to be granted letters from the university protecting him against 'the hostility of those who are slandering him' (*calumpnancium invidiam*), which sounds as if he was already under attack from the friars. By 1437 he was cited to appear before the papal judge delegate, and subsequently before the bishop of Bath and Wells, because of attacks on the friars delivered in the course of university lectures. On this occasion the university supported him. The mendicants tried unsuccessfully to raise Norreys's attacks on them in the convocation of Canterbury, and then appealed to Rome, and after various vicissitudes, including a period in prison on the orders of Henry VI, a papal court declared Norreys guilty of heresy in 1443. However, this resilient controversialist appealed successfully to the council of Basel, his sentence of excommunication was revoked, and the friars were ordered by Calixtus III to leave him alone in future. He died in 1465. According to Bale,[54] Norreys wrote sermons, *declamationes* (whatever they may be), a book of scriptural commentary, and 'Contra mendicitatem validam', a curious title, perhaps to be translated 'Against mendicant poverty that is supported by force', the force maybe being the force of the law or the civil arm.

---

[52] D. Wilkins, *Concilia Magnae Britanniae et Hiberniae* (London, 1737), iii, 324–5.

[53] We must rely on the chronicle of Friar Nicholas Glasberger for the account of Whitehead's presence at Pisa. I feel rather more doubtful than does F. X. Martin (art. cit., p. 302) that Whitehead was such a central figure. He was one of many secular clergy mounting attacks on the friars at Pisa.

[54] *Index scriptorum Britanniae*, pp 246–7.

The careers of these three indicate that there was strong, though usually latent opposition to the friars, especially at the universities. But what is particularly interesting in the context of this chapter is that they all three illustrate equally the way in which Anglo-Irish clerics could rise through the university and, although there was no intellectual centre within the English colony in Ireland, could make the most of their Oxford training, and take leading parts in university controversies even at quite a rarified level. Oxford served as the intellectual centre that was lacking in Ireland. Although he was on the other side of the quarrel between the friars and the secular clerics and monks, the career of the Augustinian friar Adam Payne illustrates the point equally well. Like FitzRalph, Crumpe, and the others he belonged to the 'middle nation',[55] the Anglo-Irish, who, though they certainly did not identify with the Gaelic Irish, yet resented interference from 'across the water' in the affairs of the colony, including its ecclesiastical affairs. The first we hear of him is as the champion of the rights to a limited degree of independence of the Irish houses within the English province of the Augustinians. He was the youngest of three Anglo-Irish friars sent by the Irish houses to the general chapter of the order held at Würzburg in 1391. They were successful in having restored to the Irish houses their former privileges, and as part of the 'package' agreed Adam Payne was allowed to go to Oxford to study for the rectorate, though he had not fulfilled all the preliminary stages required by the order's regulations. We have a glimpse of Payne at the very end of his lengthy progress towards the doctorate in theology. The text has survived of a theological *quaestio* composed as a normal academic exercise by Payne when he had already incepted as doctor in theology, and was entitled to be styled as *doctor*.[56] This work covers but three sides of the printed page, and manages to discuss a wide range of subjects, from the procession of the Trinity and the Incarnation to ideas of divine justice, and the Immaculate Conception of Mary. So, clearly, it is written in a kind of scholastic shorthand—a glance at what has been called its 'angular' style will make that plain enough. Yet it is not without a certain arch, donnish humour, especially where Payne makes punning references to his opposing disputant. Some traces of Scotist influence, and perhaps also of ideas originating with William of Ockham, have been seen in the *quaestio* by F. X. Martin. Original ideas can hardly be expected in such a short and routine academic exercise. But it is surprising to find a friar who himself took part in the great debate in the church on the mendicant orders quoting FitzRalph as an authority, and urging oral confession 'duly made to one's priest, or another who has his permission' (*immo confessio vocalis rite facta proprio curato, vel alteri de eius licencia*).

Payne was obviously regarded as an able man by his order. He was chosen by the Oxford Augustinians as their custos, or advocate, and subsequently

---

[55] For Payne's career, see F. X. Martin, art. cit., pp 294–6.
[56] Printed in ibid., pp 319–22.

(1404) nominated as one of two Augustinian proctors in a case in which the order's Atherstone house was in dispute with local secular clergy. The apogee of his career was clearly the mission to the council of Pisa, together with the Franciscan John Cuock. Presumably he had a hand in, or at least signed, the manifesto of June 1410, in which the friars defended themselves against the attacks on them by their many enemies, including the university of Paris. But we have no firm information on his role at Pisa. Like FitzRalph he ended up in an Irish bishopric, becoming bishop of Cloyne in 1413. His final appearance on the ecclesiastical scene is as chief actor in one of those disputes that seem endemic in the Irish church in the late middle ages. In 1418 he renewed earlier attempts by his predecessors to have the diocese of Cloyne united with Cork, and raised the matter in the upper house of the Irish parliament, but without success, though the two dioceses were united on his resignation in 1429.

Geoffrey (Galfridus) Shale is another capable Augustinian who spent a part of his life in the Irish sub-province or 'limit' of his order, and may well have been Irish, or of Irish ancestry. It has been suggested that this seemingly rather Germanic name is an anglicised form of O'Sheil or O'Scahill.[57] On the other hand, 'Galfridus' is not an Irish name. Whatever his origins, Shale seems to have ended his life in the Dublin friary where, in 1421, he was made master regent 'whensoever and as often as he wishes', and was granted for life the room 'which had formerly belonged to Master John Holywood'.[58] In the next year he was named as vicar of the provincial chapter of the order held at Gorleston in Norfolk. Shale had attended the council of Constance, and preached several times before the university. The colophon of the manuscript that contains the sermon describes him as a doctor of theology of Cambridge.[59] Of his life before his Cambridge days, or indeed subsequent to his appearance at Gorleston, we know nothing.

Shale's sermon is simply constructed, and the subject developed under three headings. It is easier to follow than many of the elaborately structured 'thematic' sermons of the conciliar period. When he refers to his sermon as being *forma exilis et inculta*, Shale is not just being modest, but indicating a deliberate choice of the 'plain' or 'humble' style. The division of a subject into three parts is recommended by contemporary or near-contemporary writers of manuals for preachers,[60] and this tripartite division has had a long run for its money, being still popular with nonconformists and particularly

[57] F. X. Martin and A. de Meijer, 'Irish material in the Augustinian Archives, Rome, 1354–1624' in *Archivium Hibernicum*, xix (1956), pp 61–134.
[58] Art. cit., p. 79, quoting from the registers of the prior general of the order.
[59] The sermon is printed in A. Zumkeller, 'Unbekannte Konstanzer Konzilspredigten der Augustiner—Theologen Gottfried Shale und Dietrich Vrie' in *Analecta Augustiniana*, xxxiii (1970), pp 5–45.
[60] For example, Robert of Basevorn in his 'Forma praedicandi' ('Form of preaching'), trans. L. Krul in *Three medieval rhetorical arts*, ed. J. J. Murphy (Berkeley, 1971), p. 138.

presbyterian preachers. The theme in this case is an apposite one for a sermon delivered before the council of Constance, that of unity in the church, the text chosen being 'Unum corpus sumus in Christo' ('We are one body in Christ'). When announcing the triple division of his sermon at the outset, and again at the beginning and end of each division, Shale has short passages of rhymed, balanced clauses, which are a kind of free verse, and sum up that part of the overall theme. This again points to a preoccupation with clarity on the part of the preacher. This is an exhortatory rather than a teaching sermon, and there is little theological content. In fact a fair proportion of the text consists of quotation, mainly from Augustine. Yet it is a not unattractive work, mainly, I think, because it shows a sincere concern with the subject, namely unity in the church.

Shale's other work, the 'De modo sermocinandi', is as yet unedited, and so far only two manuscripts containing it are known.[61] The main problem facing any future editor of this text will be to work out how it fits into the *artes praedicandi* tradition. Shale, in his work, refers back to an anonymous treatise which precedes his in MS Gg VI. 20 in Cambridge University Library. This work seems to draw heavily on the 'De arte sermocinandi' of Thomas Penketh, O.S.A., which in turn owes much to the 'Ars componendi sermones' of Ranulph Higden.[62] One certainly has the impression that Shale's work, while not a mere résumé of earlier *artes praedicandi*, at least deals with a relatively selective range within the subject-matter discussed by practitioners such as Robert de Basevorn or Thomas Walys. After devoting only a few sentences to the ways in which a sermon may be introduced, and the theme divided, he then sets out the four scriptural senses according to which it may be interpreted. The second half of the work deals, in pretty succinct fashion, with the four ways of developing a theme (the *modus agendi*).[63]

All the writers mentioned above were what we would nowadays call 'Oxbridge' graduates. A smaller number, a mere handful, shone in the continental universities, and had their intellectual roots in Paris or Italy. No one

---

[61] Cambridge University Library, MS Gg. VI. 20 (s. xv), fol. 107–11 and Brno, University Library, MS A. 88 (s. xv), ff 103ᵛ–108ᵛ, formerly in the Augustinian friary in the town. See F. Roth, 'The English Austin friars, 1249–1538, I: History' in *Cassiciacum*, vi (1966), p. 569.

[62] Th.-M. Charland, *Artes praedicandi* (Paris and Ottawa, 1936), pp 76, 90.

[63] One literary 'ghost' among these controversialists of the conciliar period has to be laid. The attribution of a work 'Adversum Johannem Wiclefum' to 'William of Waterford' by Baxter, Willard, and Johnson, 'Index of British and Irish Latin writers' in *Archivum Latinitatis Medii Aevi*, vii (1932), p. 185, is simply wrong, though in this they are following Luke Wadding, *Scriptores Ordinis Minorum*, ix, 129. It is by the well-known adversary of Wyclif, William Woodford, and indeed is correctly attributed to him by the editor, E. Brown, in his *Fasciculus rerum expetendarum et fugiendarum* (London, 1690), p. 190. No doubt the variant spelling Wodeford has given rise to this wrong attribution to William of Waterford. The 'De religione' attributed to him by Ware, *De scriptoribus Hiberniae* (Dublin, 1639), p. 74, has not as yet been identified.

could have been more closely connected with the schools of Paris than Thomas of Ireland. He is the author of three short works on theology and biblical exegesis, but his real claim to fame is as the compiler of the 'Manipulus florum' ('A handful of flowers'), an anthology which by the standards of any age was a best-seller. This awesome collection of some 6,000 extracts from patristic and a few classical authors has been the subject of an equally awesome piece of scholarship by Richard and Mary Rouse.[64] If it were not for their work in setting him in his scholastic background, establishing the affiliations of his anthology with other, earlier compilations, and its relation to the fourteenth-century development of preaching, Thomas would be as shadowy a figure as many of the others discussed in this chapter.

As it is, even the Rouses have been unable to unearth any information that would cast light on his origins in Ireland. There are several references to him in Sorbonne documents, and there is extant his will in favour of the Sorbonne. In all of these he is explicitly cited as 'Thomas Hybernicus' or 'Thomas de Hibernia'. He is named as a fellow of the college in a Sorbonne document of 1295, and was then a master of arts, and thus probably about 20 years of age. He had ceased to be a fellow by 1306, since the earliest manuscripts of the 'Manipulus florum' refer to him as 'a former fellow' (*quondam socius*), and it was published in 1306. But he kept up his connection with the college. The 'Manipulus florum' is extracted from books which—again thanks to the work of the Rouses—we know were in the Sorbonne library, and at his death he bequeathed his books and sixteen pounds Parisian to the college. These books are described as being from his legacy in the 1338 Sorbonne catalogue, but he had almost certainly been dead for some years by the time this was compiled.

The 'Manipulus florum' survives in 190 manuscripts; the first printed copy is as early as 1483; it was printed twenty-six times in the sixteenth century, eleven times in the seventeenth, and even remained popular in the age of reason, with eighteenth-century editions at Vienna and Turin. Even as late as this the anthology was still felt to be answering a need of preachers and was reprinted as a practical tool for their use. It was even 'hijacked' by a Genevan printer who altered and pruned key entries to give the collection a Calvinist bias.

Why was Thomas's anthology so successful? Simply because it was more than just an anthology. It filled a growing need at a time in the middle ages when the church was beginning once more to put greater emphasis on preaching. Although Thomas himself was a secular, his anthology was well suited to the needs of the new mendicant preaching orders. Its users could, at a glance, locate quotations from patristic and classical authors relevant to

---

[64] Richard H. and Mary A. Rouse, *Preachers, florilegia and sermons: studies on the 'Manipulus florum' of Thomas of Ireland* (Toronto, 1979).

any subject they might wish to touch on in their sermons. The second half of the thirteenth and beginning of the fourteenth century saw the first appearance of the biblical concordance, and also the subject index appended to the book. The concept of alphabetical arrangement, though not totally unknown earlier, is more to the fore in this period. Thomas was among the pioneers in these techniques. In particular, he alphabetises more thoroughly than had previous makers of indexes. He includes cross-references to synonyms, e.g. *Scientia vide sapiencia* ('for knowledge see wisdom'), and his citations are concise and relevant to the topic they are meant to illustrate. Within each topic there is a consistent sequence of authors referred to. If they have a relevant quotation to contribute, Augustine, Ambrose, Jerome, and Gregory come first; then other, later Christian writers; and finally a select group of pagan authors including Seneca and Cicero. He provides a list of authors excerpted at the end of the collection. Thomas took over the majority of his extracts from existing anthologies, but about a third do come direct from original texts. In his selection, and in the various indexing techniques he invented or improved on, he reveals true originality and inventiveness.

Thomas wrote three short works as well as the 'Manipulus florum'. One of these, 'De tribus punctis religionis Christianae' ('On the three main points of the Christian religion'), is a kind of rule for secular priests setting out what should be their articles of faith, and what code should govern the way they lived their lives. This little work was incorporated into the first statutes of the Prague archdiocese, and in this form circulated quite widely in central Europe. His 'De tribus hierarchiis' ('On the three hierarchies') is a simplified presentation of some of the teachings of Pseudo-Dionysius the Areopagite. It is very short and survives only in eight manuscripts. The 'De tribus sensibus sacre Scripture' ('On the three senses of holy Scripture') was no best-seller. There are only three known manuscripts, and one of these is the copy Thomas presented to the Sorbonne. Thomas's claim to fame is as an anthologist rather than an original author.

Peter of Ireland went even further afield than Thomas. The two earliest lives of St Thomas Aquinas, by William of Tocco and Peter Calo, each independent from the other, agree that 'Petrus de Ibernia' taught the young Thomas Aquinas in the newly founded university of Naples.[65] This, the first *studium generale* to have been deliberately founded by a ruler to lend prestige to his kingdom and provide it with a nucleus of educated administrators, was initiated by the Hohenstaufen king of Sicily, Frederick II, in 1224. It was subsequently transferred to Salerno in 1252, before being brought back to Naples by Manfred in 1258. But it was during its first period in Naples that,

[65] For Thomas Aquinas's years in Naples, see Martin Grabmann, 'Magister Petrus von Hibernia der Jugendlehrer des hl. Thomas von Aquin' in idem, *Mittelalterliches Geistesleben* (Munich, 1926), i, 254; James A. Weisheipl, *Friar Thomas D'Aquino: his life, thought and works* (Oxford, 1975), pp 13–20.

between 1239 and 1244, Thomas Aquinas attended the lectures there. According to William of Tocco he was taught grammar and logic by Master Martin, and natural philosophy by Peter of Ireland. Peter Calo, on the other hand, tells us that having learned all he could about grammar from Master Martin, he went to Peter of Ireland for instruction in logic and natural philosophy. Till some of his writings were discovered in manuscripts by those giants in the field of medieval philosophy, Clemens Baeumker and Auguste Pelzer, that was all that was known about Peter.[66]

The first work to be discovered and published by Baeumker was a *determinatio magistralis* pronounced by Peter on the question whether the bodily organs have been created in order that they might carry out their functions, or the functions created for the benefit of the organs. The *determinatio magistralis* was the definitive judgement of a question in a university disputation, delivered by a *magister*. The choice of subject seems to reinforce the statement of both biographers that Peter's chosen field of study was natural philosophy, though (as M. J. Crowe has shown) Peter regarded this particular question as purely a metaphysical one. Other writings attributed to Peter, discovered by Pelzer in two Vatican manuscripts, are commentaries on Porphyry's 'Isagoge' and on the 'Perihermenias', both therefore logical works, and a commentary on Aristotle's 'De longitudine et brevitate vitae', which is an extract from the 'Parva Naturalia'. This commentary discusses physical questions on the nature of life, and the qualitative differences between the life of heavenly and material creatures, but also of necessity examines metaphysical questions, and in particular the nature of the efficient cause of life, and the various ways in which periods of life may be measured.

Clearly Peter had a good knowledge of a range of Aristotle's works. This is not surprising in someone writing in the middle of the thirteenth century in a south Italian milieu where Arab, Jewish, and Christian knowledge had been mingling for more than a century and a half. But more than that, Baeumker in his article on the *determinatio* showed that Peter had used Michael Scot's translation of Averroes's commentary on Aristotle. The *determinatio* dates from a period as much as twenty years after Aquinas had left the *studium* at

---

[66] The basic articles recounting the rediscovery of Peter's writings are Clemens Baeumker, 'Petrus von Hibernia der Jugendlehrer des Thomas von Aquino und seine Disputation vor König Manfred' in *Sitzungsber. d. Bay. Akad. d. Wissensch.* (Munich, 1920), pp 3–49; and Auguste Pelzer, 'Un cours inédit d'Albert le Grand sur la morale à Nicomaque' in *Revue neoscholastique de philosophie*, xxiv (1922), pp 333–61: 355–7, discuss Peter of Ireland. These discoveries were first analysed by Grabmann, op. cit., pp 249–65, and then by M. B. Crowe, 'Peter of Ireland, teacher of St Thomas Aquinas' in *Studies*, xlv (1956), pp 443–56; and 'Peter of Ireland's approach to metaphysics' in *Miscellanea Medievalia* (Veröffentlichungen des Thomas-Instituts an der Universität Köln, ii: *Die Metaphysik in Mittelalter* (Berlin, 1963), pp 154–60. See now James McEvoy, 'Maître Pierre d'Irlande, professeur *in naturalibus* à l'université de Naples' in J. Follon and J. J. McEvoy (ed.), *Actualité de la pensée médiévale* (Louvain, 1994), pp 146–58, and the brief survey by M. Gunne, *Hiberno-Latin Newsletter* 7 (1997/8), pp 3, 4. He attributes the commentary on the 'Isagoge' to Jean le Page.

Naples. Whether and to what degree Aquinas was influenced by Peter's Averroist slant is probably unanswerable, or at any rate unanswerable by those who are not versed in scholastic philosophy.

Philosophers of any age are not much inclined to giving autobiographical details in their works, and though we now know more about Peter's thought, and the influences that lie behind it, we are no wiser as to the details of his life. He must be considered to be 'of Ireland'—the two biographers of Aquinas, writing independently of each other, would hardly invent that. Crowe is probably right in guessing that someone called Peter would most likely be of Anglo-Irish stock. But where he gained his grounding in philosophy, in which university he graduated as *magister*, and by what route he arrived in Naples, remain a mystery. Even more mysterious is the Patrick of Ireland whose short 'Sophisma determinatum' is in two fourteenth-century manuscripts, in the Bavarian State Library, Munich, and the University Library, Basel. We know nothing of him other than that he was a Paris master.[67]

Maurice O'Fihely is the latest in time of the Irish who flourished in the medieval continental universities, and the only indisputable Gael among all the theologians mentioned above. He is a link between the late medieval and renaissance worlds. He devoted his life to Scotism, surely the quintessence of medieval philosophy, and yet had close links with the printers of Venice, one of the half-dozen most important centres of early printing, and indeed is not very far removed in time from the Irish scholars of the counter-reformation. His life is an excellent example of the way in which the intellectual world of late scholasticism could coexist quite happily with that of the fully developed renaissance.

Maurice is normally thought of as having been a native of west Cork, or even more precisely of Baltimore. True, west Cork is the home of the O'Fihely family, but there does not seem to be any real evidence that he was brought up there, or entered the Franciscan order at Sherkin friary.[68] Maurice often refers to himself on title pages as 'Mauritius de portu'. Wherever this port may have been, Baltimore can hardly have been dignified with the title of port as early as 1460. Ware in his account of Maurice is rightly cautious about his place of origin, and reports alternative claims for Galway, and even Downpatrick, as his birthplace.

There is no indication where Maurice first studied. Quite possibly he went from some internal Irish Franciscan studium straight to Italy, where he was

---

[67] The text, as seen by him in Clm 3852 (s. xiv), f. 47ᵛ, is described, but not printed, by Grabmann in 'Die Sophismataliteratur' in *Beitr. z. Gesch. d. Philos. d. Mittelalters*, xxxvi, pt. 1 (1940), p. 65. Patrick is listed as a Paris master in Glorieux, *La Faculté des Arts*, p. 268, no. 328. There is a recent ed. by H. Roos, 'Drei Sophismata zum Formproblem in der Hs. Uppsala C 604', in *Cahiers de l'Institut du Moyen Âge Grec et Latin*, xxiv (1978), pp 16–34.

[68] As stated, e.g., by Peter Somerville-Large in his *The coast of West Cork* (London, 1972), p. 72.

regent at the Franciscan schools at Milan in 1488. All his work on Scotist philosophy dates to the period beginning in 1491 during which he taught at the university of Padua. Though made archbishop of Tuam by Pope Julius II in 1506, he was still in Italy in 1512, as he was present at the Lateran council, and only left for his Connacht see in that year. He died in Galway in 1513. Perhaps the sudden transition from the urbane, sophisticated world of renaissance Padua and Venice to the remote fastnesses of Connacht was too much for him.

Maurice is often referred to by subsequent editors of Dun Scotus's works as his 'devoted disciple', and indeed more than once he speaks of Scotus in moving and reverential terms in the various prefaces to his commentaries and editions of the works of the *doctor subtilis*. Virtually all his work consists of commentaries on, or improved editions of, Scotus's works, together with one or two commentaries on the works of other Scotists. Both the commentaries and the editions are the result of his lecturing, or were produced with the express purpose of helping his students through the intricacies of Scotist reasoning. They were printed in the last decade of the fifteenth and the first of the sixteenth century, mostly at the Venice press of Bonetus Locatellus, for the publisher Octavianus Scottus (Ottaviano Scotto). Maurice and other Padua Scotists clearly found this partnership particularly suitable or sympathetic to their needs. But there seems to be no evidence that he was a proof-reader for either printer or publisher as has sometimes been stated.

Many of Maurice's commentaries were reprinted in the Lyons edition of Scotus' works, begun in 1636, in which Luke Wadding was assisted by fellow Irishmen.[69] There the editors have usually broken up the commentaries, and put the resulting sections after each chapter of the Scotist work on which they comment. Only a scholastic philosopher, skilled in the decoding of Scotist subtleties, could give an adequate assessment of Maurice's contribution to the better understanding of his hero. But a clear idea of his methods, particularly the way in which he set about editing the texts of Scotus, can be gleaned from his prefaces.

Probably Duns Scotus's most important work is his commentary on the four books of Peter Lombard's 'Sentences'. The textual tradition of this commentary is incredibly complex. Put in the simplest terms it goes back to one series of lectures on 'Sentences' given by Scotus at Oxford, and a further series given subsequently at Paris. Elements of both series are to be found in the *Ordinatio*, the revised 'official' form of the commentary. Maurice concerned himself only with this *Ordinatio*. Such was the interest in Scotus in fifteenth-century Italy that there had already been nine editions of the *Ordi-*

---

[69] For a fascinating account of the financial side of this enterprise, see Benignus Millett, 'Irish literature in Latin, 1550–1750' in *N.H.I.*, iii, 583.

*natio* printed at Venice before the one with which Maurice was associated, that of Simon de Lovere in 1506.[70] Maurice's work in editing the text was important enough to warrant his edition being included in the critical apparatus to the new Vatican edition. In his preface he tells us that he has restored to the text certain sections that had been added by Scotus to his original work, but had been omitted by subsequent editors. These he underlines. He has also, he claims, made some further additions in the light of recent advances in Scotist thought. The work is 'emended, its order corrected, adorned with notes, and now for the first time augmented with a number of additions'. This edition by Maurice was subsequently reprinted at Venice in 1514, and in Paris in 1513. In 1521/2, there was another Venice edition, put out by the heirs of Octavianus Scottus.

For Scotus's commentary on the traditional body of Aristotelian logic—Porphyry's 'Universalia', the 'Praedicamenta', 'Perihermenias', 'De interpretatione', and 'Elenchi'—Maurice provided both a full exposition and a revised text. The exposition incorporated his lectures, delivered at Padua, and written up by him in Ferrara in August 1499—we learn this from the colophon to the 1512 Venice edition. The revised text was printed, also in Venice in 1512, but separately.[71] Maurice included with his commentary the text of the grammatical work 'De modis significandi', which he thought was probably by Scotus, but which modern Scotists would reject. This he intended to lecture on 'soon' at Padua. He seems to have done little in the way of revising the text.

The 'Theoremata', which are really just short notes, may be by Scotus or by a pupil. In the 1497 Venice edition, printed by Bonetus Locatellus, Maurice edited the text, and added his own notes and preface. This edition also contains the 'De primo principio', a genuine work by Scotus, also with Maurice's notes and preface. Maurice provided a revised text of Scotus's 'Quaestiones super libros metaphysicorum' and a commentary. Both are printed in the 1497 Venice (Bonetus Locatellus) edition with two prefaces, to Pietro Barozzi, bishop of Padua, and to a fellow teacher at Padua, who subsequently became bishop of Urbino, Antonio Trombeta, or Trombete. Maurice's comments to Barozzi on the difficulty of understanding Scotus deserve to be quoted: 'Many things are discussed in these *quaestiones* which are difficult and rarefied and beyond human power to understand.' This from an expert who had devoted many years to the elucidation of Scotist conundrums!

The 'Quaestiones miscellaneae de formalitatibus', a work not now thought to be by Scotus, exercised the intellects of several of Maurice's

---

[70] See the *Elencus editionum* in *Johannis Duns Scoti opera omnia*, ed. C. Balić and others (Rome, Vatican, 1950–   ), i, 128–30.
[71] Both text and commentary may be conveniently found bound together in the Bodleian Library, printed book A. 2. 8 Art. Seld.

contemporaries, including Antonio Trombete. Maurice produced a tiny epit-
ome of the work, which occupies but a page in the 1514 Venice (Lucas
Antonius Junta) edition, and is also found in the collection of works relating
to the 'Formalitates' printed by A. Gothutio in his *Gymnasium speculativum*
(Paris, 1605). He also edited the commentary on the 'Formalitates' by
Stephen Brulifer, printed at Venice in 1501, and that by Antonius Sirectus.
The 1514 Venice edition of Sirectus's commentary contains 'new additions of
the most celebrated Archbishop Maurice and the most excellent doctor Antonio de Fantis of Treviso', but the extent to which each contributed is not
clear. Maurice's colleague in Padua, Trombete, also commented on the 'Formalitates'. Maurice edited the commentary on Aristotle's 'Metaphysics' by
Antonius Andreas, printed at Venice in 1501 by the Locatellus–Scottus partnership, and the commentary on 'Sentences' by Franciscus de Mayronis,
printed at Venice in 1507.[72]

The same Locatellus–Scottus partnership printed Maurice's own, original
*Enchyridion fidei* in 1509. It deals with predestination, divine foreknowledge
and contingent circumstances, inevitability, and free will. The work is laid
out in tabular form; thus will is divided up into divine will and created will,
which are in turn subdivided. There is much quotation, especially of Aristotle, Augustine, and Boethius, but the argument seems to be Maurice's own.
Perhaps the most interesting thing about this far from scintillating work is its
dedication to 'Geraldus' (Gearóid Mór), eighth earl of Kildare, the only
indication we have of any interest Maurice may have had in the power
politics of his native land. Maurice's outline sketch of the contents of Peter
Lombard's 'Sentences', written in hexameters, follows the *Enchyridion*, in the
Venice edition. Clearly, Maurice O'Fihely deserves to be remembered as a
commentator on and editor of the works of his idol Scotus, not as an original
writer. But he remains, like FitzRalph before him, a shining example of an
Irishman who integrated fully with the intellectual life of Europe at its
highest and most rarefied level.

One work that has, in the past, been wrongly attributed to Maurice is a
collection of biblical *distinctiones*, in other words an alphabetically arranged
repertory of biblical quotations with their allegorical interpretation, devised
for the use of preachers. Part of this was printed as Maurice's at Venice in
1603.[73] This work is in fact a thirteenth-century compilation, and though
some of the manuscripts give the author's name as 'Mauritius', none of those
listed by Stegmüller in his *Repertorium*[74] add that he is Irish or from Ireland.

---

[72] See Frederick Stegmüller, *Repertorium commentariorum in Sententias* (2 vols, Würzburg,
1947), i, 98–9, no. 218.

[73] *Dictionarium sacrae scripturae Mauritii Hybernici ... in Patavino gymnasio primum philoso-
phiam publice profitentis ... archiepiscopi Tuamensis ... universis concionatoribus apprime utile et
necessarium* (Venice, 1603). It contains sections A–E only.

[74] *Repertorium Biblicum Medii Aevi* (Madrid, 1940–80), iii, 556–7, no. 5566.

Pierre Bersuire quotes from the collection in his *Repertorium morale*,[75] but again gives the author's name simply as Mauritius.

IT may seem strange that, whereas the great majority of Irish of both races who attended the universities were lawyers, only two, whose Irishness indeed is somewhat in doubt, have left their mark on the legal literature of the period. But given the very vocational nature of the law courses, especially at Oxford, this is understandable. Almost all those who attended the medieval law schools went immediately afterwards into what we would recognise as administration, very often back in their own diocese. Only a very few, then as now, stayed on at the university to become academic lawyers, and even these would spend some of their time actually pleading in the church courts. This was the career chosen by William of Drogheda, probably the best known Oxford lawyer of the thirteenth century. Significantly, his single work, the 'Summa aurea', is entirely concerned with legal practice, and tells the budding ecclesiastical lawyer the procedure and forms of canon law to be gone through in presenting a case and 'making it stick'. No legal principles are enunciated, but many tips and artful dodges well calculated to win a case are imparted.

The great pre-war German canonist Hermann Kantorowicz wrote of William: 'His work, had he lived to publish the whole ... would have been one of the worst products of medieval literature and equally repugnant on account of its verbose and clumsy style as its juristic and moral level.'[76] This is far too severe a judgement, particularly in view of William's strictly practical aims. It is just as pointless to criticise this manual for not being literature as it would be to write an unfavourable review in the *Times Literary Supplement* of a similar modern text guiding solicitors in the proper forms to be used in conveyancing houses. In fact the style is far from pompous, for the *Summa* is written in a sort of legal shorthand, in which many sentences are unfinished, as the reader will know how the formula ends, just as he will immediately pick up cryptic references to the various parts of the Roman civil law.

Kantorowicz, and the others who have written about William,[77] have stressed the disorder and chaos of the subject-matter. The author's aim seems to have been to give a complete guide to every sort of action with which an ecclesiastical lawyer might have to deal. His work is highly incomplete, and appears to represent only the first book of the six that William

---

[75] (Venice, 1583), i, 248, under *benedicere*.

[76] Hermann Kantorowicz, *Bractonian problems* (Glasgow, 1941), pp 28–9.

[77] H. G. Richardson, 'Azo, Drogheda and Bracton' in *E.H.R.*, lix (1944), pp 22–47; F. de Zulueta, 'William of Drogheda' in *Mélanges de droit romain dediès a G. Cornil* (2 vols, Paris, 1926), ii, 639–65. The only edition of the *Summa Aurea* is by L. Wahrmund, in *Quellen zur Geschichte des römisch-kanonischen Prozesses im Mittelalter*, ii, pt 2 (Innsbruck, 1914). For an up-to-date account of the Oxford law school of William's day, see Leonard Boyle, 'Canon law before 1380' in *The History of the University of Oxford*, i (1984), ch. 14.

seems to have intended, from what he says in his preface. F. de Zulueta is probably right in thinking that the scale of the work defeated William, and that its incompleteness is due to his having given up, rather than to his sudden death. But though the work as it now stands treats of some only of the things a canon lawyer must know, the subjects which are treated are gone into very thoroughly, and in a very practical way. Besides, the 'Summa aurea' is not so chaotic as it has seemed to some. If one allows for the way in which the methods of argument used in theological and philosophical teaching, and writings derived from that teaching, invaded the more practical fields of medicine and law, then the work is less disordered than Kantorowicz or de Zulueta make out. William's method is to discuss each subject in general terms, beginning with a definition of it. He follows this with a long series of *cautelae*, cautionary tips, and handy hints for the practising advocate. After that, as in theological works of the day, a series of *quaestiones* discuss particular difficulties, with arguments for and against each solution proposed. Those modern scholars who have decried William's lack of plan have not thought fit to mention the little introductions of two or three sentences with which he prefaces each new section and dismisses the previous one. These make it clear that he was working to a definite plan.

William begins by setting out the precise forms to be used for citing someone to appear before an ecclesiastical court, and what is to be done if the defendant, the plaintiff, or even the judge fail to turn up. Who is liable for costs? Ought any of the three to be punished? Also in this section William discusses the proper way for judges and advocates to behave, penalties for bad behaviour, and the highly practical question of fees for advocates. His next main subject is the way in which the advocate is to proceed with his case. The *cautelae* in this section reveal many artful dodges for holding up the case or winning over the judges. For the general reader—if there are any—this is probably the most interesting part of the 'Summa'. There follows a long section on the appointment of proctors to present a case in ecclesiastical courts to which the advocate himself does not have access, in which William also defines the status of friends who undertake a case for someone else, advocates acting (as they must almost always have done) for a corporate body, arbiters, assessors, and judges generally.

The whole central part of the work is devoted to legal documents and the proper way of issuing them, but with special reference to *libelli* (writs), setting out all the various kinds of *libelli* to be met with in Roman civil and in canon law. William considers the various ambiguities or inaccurate definitions in *libelli* that can be turned to his advantage by the advocate, and there is a long list of *cavillationes* that can be entered against particular *libelli*. Much of this section is derived from the 'De libellis' of Roffredus of Benevento. There follows a short section on adjournments, and this leads to a discussion of the appointment of sub-delegates by judges delegate, highly technical and very boring. By contrast the section on papal rescripts, their validity, how their genuineness can be established, and how they can be falsified, contains much that must be of interest to students of curial forms at this stage of the thirteenth century. The final section, on *exceptiones*, discusses ways in which actions can be invalidated and cases brought to an untimely end, and particular emphasis is placed on ways of having a judge or opposing advocate rejected as being disqualified, for some personal reason or family interest, from acting in a case.

Particularly in the sections on citation and writs the 'Summa' is very much a formulary, and many documents are included as examples. Where names of places and persons are given these are all connected with Oxford and Oxfordshire, and many of the cases are described as having been heard in the university church of St Mary the Virgin. William several times mentions himself as 'regent in laws' at Oxford, and rector of the church of 'Petha', which Wahrmund and de Zulueta identified as Petham in Kent, and Emden as Pett in Sussex. William was also rector of Grafton Underwood in Northamptonshire by 1245. The only fact of William's life that the general reader may know is that he was murdered in his house in the High Street in Oxford. Matthew Paris describes him as dying 'in miserable circumstances' (*lugubriter*) in 1245, while engaged in an important case.[78] His murder is indeed recorded in the assize rolls for Oxford for 1247.[79] William's house, or rather the site of it, is next door to the lodgings of the warden of All Souls, in the High Street. It retained the name of Drawda Hall till 1985, when it was metamorphosed from a bookshop into a unisex hairdressing salon.

So one way and another we know quite a lot about William: who he was, roughly when he wrote, and even, unusually for a medieval writer, exactly where he lived. But what was his connection with Drogheda? He calls himself 'W. de Drokeda' more than once in the 'Summa', yet in a deed dated 8 January 1241/2, given under his seal, he grants that same Oxford house 'situated in the parish of St Peter [in the East] between the property of Walter Hinge and Alwin de Tornoor' to the abbey of Monk Sherborne in Hampshire, on condition that the monks will celebrate a daily mass 'in our church of Sherborne ... where my mother and father will lie after their death, and I along with them'.[80] Perhaps William's family had lived in Drogheda when he was young, but had long since removed 'back to the mainland' as we would put it nowadays, perhaps to property that had always been

---

[78] *Chronica Majora, s.a.* 1245., ed. Luard, iv, 423.

[79] The murderer has been variously described as his valet, apprentice, or squire. The deed that describes the killing is a presentment to the Oxfordshire eyre (assizes) of 1247, quoted by H. E. Salter, *Cartulary of the abbey of Eynsham* (Oxford, 1908), p. 174, n. l. The Latin word used to describe the murderer, Ralph de Boklande, is *armiger* 'squire'.

[80] Printed in Salter, op. cit., pp 174–5. Curiously enough, one of those subsequently detained on suspicion of having something to do with the murder was one 'Johannes de Schireburne'.

in the family. In that case his claim to be Irish or even Anglo-Irish must be on a level with that of Joyce Cary, Louis MacNeice, or those 'Irish' field-marshals who were so active in the second world war. Whatever their origins, their effective careers from early manhood were in England. Richardson in his article suggested that William might have got his name from having taught at Drogheda, which was indeed one of the few places in the English colony outside Dublin where we have any references to the existence of schools. But it would, I think, be unusual, though not unheard of in the middle ages, for someone to be named from the place in which he had taught rather than from his birthplace.

William of Drogheda's name is known to a few historians, though the issue-dates stamped on the copies of the 'Summa aurea' used by me in two different libraries suggest that there are few alive today who have actually dipped into it. But even historians of canon law, who must be well used to pursuing the neglected byways of medieval scholarship, regard John of Fintona as an obscure figure. The sixteenth-century Greco-Italian legal historian Tommaso Diplovataccio refers to him as *subtilissimus canonum doctor* ('a most subtle teacher of canon law'), and compiler of a fine commentary on the decretals.[81] But he devotes only five lines of text to his life, which is much shorter than usual for him, and quite clearly knows only the work, and has no information at all on the author's life, origin, or where he taught. The second part of John's name is found in several forms—Phintona, Fincona, Phitona, and even Sicona. The name is our only pointer to an Irish origin, and Gillmann, the only modern scholar to concern himself with John, raises the possibility that he is really 'of Finden', the village just south of Aberdeen, best known as the home of the finnan haddock.[82] It is indeed hard to come to grips with the concept that Fintona, County Tyrone, hitherto famous only for having the last functioning horse-tram in Ireland, should have produced a canon lawyer in the middle ages. Whatever his origins, John, unlike William, is of the European tradition in canon law rather than the Anglo-Norman *utriusque iuris* tradition of the Oxford schools. Considering the kind of work he produced, he must have been trained in Paris or more likely in the north Italian schools.

On examining several Vatican manuscripts and one Frankfurt manuscript of Gratian's 'Decretum' Gillman found that they contained glosses, running right through the text, and attributed to 'Jo. de Fi.', 'Jo. de Fiton.', and occasionally even 'Jo. de Fyntona'. These explanatory glosses, as well as John's analysis, by division, of each section of the text of the 'Decretum', were much used by the more famous canonist Guido de Baysio in his

---

[81] Thomas Diplovatatius, 'De claris iuris consultis', ed. G. Forschielli and A. M. Stickler in *Studia Gratiana*, x (Bologna, 1908), p. 126.

[82] F. Gillmann, 'Johannes von Phintona ein vergessener Kanonist des 13 Jahrhunderts' in *Archiv für katholisches Kirchenrecht*, cxvi (1936), pp 446–84.

'Rosarium', but are also quoted as John's by a few other canonists of the same period. Guido also used and quoted from, by name, a commentary of John's on the later canon law code, the 'Decretals', and also quoted views expressed by John in a set of 'Questions on the "Decretum"', but apart from his one quotation we have no other evidence for this last work. The 'Decretals' commentary is presumably that referred to by Diplovataccio. John's gloss on the 'Decretum' can be dated, though only within rather broad limits. Guido's work is usually dated to about 1300, while John in his commentary cites the commentary of Innocent IV on 'Decretals', a commentary that appeared in 1245. Thus John was writing some time in the second half of the thirteenth century.

The later middle ages abound in moral treatises. These are not so closely connected with the universities, their teaching, and controversies as the writings already mentioned, though of course in most cases they will have been written by men who had been to the schools, or spent some time in their order's house in a university town. One such work is the *Venenum* ('Poison'), attributed to Friar Malachy of Ireland, O.F.M., by Henry Stephanus, who printed the one and only edition in 1518.[83] In most of the medieval manuscripts that contain it, it is attributed to Robert Grosseteste. Only three of the forty-seven manuscripts listed by Harrison Thompson in his *Writings of Robert Grosseteste*[84] give Malachy as the author's name. But, as Thompson puts it, 'any ascription at all to a relatively obscure person... has great weight'. In other words it is all too likely that a work will get drawn into the orbit of a well-known figure such as Grosseteste, but very unlikely that a scribe will conjure up the name of Malachy out of the void. The other possibility, that scribes seeing some references to Ireland in the work should foist it on the well-known Malachy, the friend of St Bernard, cannot be ruled out, but seems a little unlikely so long after Malachy's lifetime. So there seems no reason why we should not trust the few against the many scribes, and accept that the author was a Malachy. Whether we can go further, with Mario Esposito,[85] and identify the author with the Franciscan Malachy of Limerick, who was an unsuccessful candidate for the archbishopric of Tuam in 1280, seems doubtful, despite his careful arguments in favour. All that we can say is that the work was written by an Irishman, probably a friar, for he quotes *beatus Franciscus* ('blessed Francis'), and says at the end that his book has been written 'for the instruction of simple men who have to teach the people'.

---

[83] *F. Malachie Hibernici ordinis minorum... Libellus... qui dicitur Venenum Malachie.* (Paris, 1518). The colophon gives the date of printing and the additional, unsubstantiated information that Malachy flourished around 1300.

[84] p. 269.

[85] 'Friar Malachy of Ireland' in *E.H.R.*, xxxiii (1918), pp 359–66.

'Malachy' takes the seven deadly sins in turn, and equates each with a poisonous snake, reptile, or insect, comparing each individual characteristic of each creature with a different facet of the sin he is discussing. Thus the chameleon is compared to the hypocrite 'who alters the complexion of his mind to suit his company', the salamander to the 'false religious', different kinds of envy to different species of asp, the various kinds of avarice to different species of spider. For the poison of each of these pests the writer gives first the approved medical antidote, and then the moral remedy against the equivalent sin. The physical descriptions of the reptiles and insects are drawn from Pliny and Isidore, with occasional references to the 'Bestiary'. He also quotes Aristotle's 'De animalibus', Avicenna, and Constantine the African. It is interesting, though not extraordinary, to find a fourteenth-century author citing these authorities. Clearly the writer had spent some time at the schools either in England or the Continent. For his moralisations of the physical attributes of the animals, and their equation with the virtues and vices, he draws on Gregory the Great's 'Moralia in Job'. In all cases he is scrupulous in acknowledging his debt to the various authorities.

Thus the *Venenum* tells us a little about the learning that could be acquired by one of the Irish clerics whose names appear in Emden's *Biographical register*, and of whose careers we have only the barest of outlines. There are, too, several references to Ireland, and to the state of Irish society. When discussing greed, the author has occasion to mention Crete, and notes that it is the same size as Ireland, or *Scotia major*, as he calls it. The Irish, he thinks, are descended fron the Greeks, and he goes on to make the traditional comment that Ireland contains no poisonous animal. Its human inhabitants, however, are not lacking in poison: 'But alas, that poison from which . . . God has kept that country free, he has permitted to hold sway in the characters of the people. For more than any other land it abounds in three forms of spider . . . understood in the moral sense.' There is, it seems, in Ireland a species of woolly spider, which the ingenious author equates with *histriones*, which may here mean something like 'men who put on an act', and flatterers. According to Malachy robbers are made so arrogant by listening to this flattery that they can never be persuaded to 'go straight'. This sounds like an oblique attack on the *filid* (poets) and genealogists of the native Irish tradition. Reverting to the Cretans, he reminds us of St Paul's quotation of Menander: 'the Cretans are always liars',[86] and invites us to make the implicit comparison. Other pests to be found in Ireland, and to be equated with a particular kind of spider, are the 'bailiffs and officials' who direct their venom against the 'poor and innocent'. He goes on to make a strange distinction between 'good' robbers, who share out the proceeds of their crimes, and those who are avaricious and hold on to their ill-gotten gains: 'I believe that this

---

[86] Titus, 1: 12.

generosity, though dispensed out of other men's substance, brings many [i.e. of the robbers] to a state of grace in Ireland, where thieves and robbers have been accustomed to be generous with other men's goods.' Is it too much to see this apparent acceptance of brigandage as a reflection of the ethos of the Pale and the march lands, with their incessant raiding by Gaelic and Anglo-Irish alike?

In his final section, on sexual vice (*luxuria*), the writer ponders on why Ireland, with its cold climate and cold food—he must surely have had some experience of Irish inns—has a population so given to fornication and adultery that neither threats of excommunication nor admonitions from the pulpit can persuade them to enter into the bonds of lawful wedlock. Lust is severely punished by God, hence, according to Malachy, the high-kingship of Ireland ended with Rory O'Connor, because he refused to give up his six wives.

All these references to Ireland give us tantalising glimpses of Malachy's views on Irish society. His name would lead one to assume that he is of Gaelic Irish stock. But as there are one or two Patricks among the Anglo-Irish, might an Anglo-Irish cleric not be given the name of the great twelfth-century reformer of the Irish church? Malachy once refers to flattery as holding sway among the *gens nativa*—'the native population'. Would a Gaelic Irish priest or friar, however censorious of his people, refer to them in this way? Malachy's ethnic affiliation, like his place in contemporary Irish society, remains a mystery, with just enough of his personal feelings seeping through into his work to tantalise us.

Another work which, like Malachy's *Venenum*, belongs to the category of moral literature is a collection of *exempla* compiled between 1270 and 1279 by an anonymous Franciscan, who had been brought up in Warwickshire but had clearly spent many years in Ireland.[87] An *exemplum* is a story, often centred round a miracle, which illustrates and reinforces some point of moral teaching or of—usually very elementary—theology. It is the sort of story, at once amusing, arresting, and edifying, that preachers still insist in bringing into their sermons. These stories were collected together for the use of preachers in the middle ages, and indeed such collections continued to appear well into the last century. Similar collections of anecdotes are even now being published for the benefit of after-dinner speakers. No doubt these stories were often collected and read for their own sake, for pure enjoyment, by those who had no intention of working them into sermons. They are a major channel by which folklore, particularly Jewish and Arab folklore, has come into the vernacular literatures of western Europe.

The compiler of this collection has drawn largely on the collections of stories that originate in Syrian and Egyptian asceticism of late antiquity,

---

[87] A. G. Little (ed.), *Liber exemplorum ad usum praedicantium* (Aberdeen, 1908).

such as the 'Verba seniorum', the 'Institutes' of John Cassian, and the 'Dialogues' of Gregory the Great. But he has also drawn his anecdotes from near-contemporary writers such as Hugh of St Victor and St Bernard, as well as from his own experience. He draws almost thirty stories, out of the collection of 213, from Giraldus Cambrensis's 'Gemma ecclesiastica', and appears to have had something to say about him in the preface, now lost. This prominence given to a work of the most famous of the de Barrys, together with the presence in the collection of two stories about a lady brewer, a tenant of David de Barry in Wales, and later at Carrigtohill, County Cork, suggests that the author was in some way connected with the de Barry family. The most interesting stories are those he has heard, rather than those he has read. His informants are quite often other friars—Nicholas of Wexford, O.F.M., Geoffrey Blund, O.P., Brother Bartholomew, O.P., Henry Foxon, O.F.M., and Tomás Ó Cuinn (Thomas O'Quinn), O.F.M., bishop of Clonmacnoise 1252–78. The inclusion among his informants of Dominicans and Gaelic Irish suggests that where a good story was concerned the writer was free from the sort of prejudice one would expect in an English Franciscan.

Unfortunately there are only seven stories with an Irish setting, and these do not tell us very much about the life of the Anglo-Irish colony. Perhaps the one exception is the account of the admittance to the Dublin friary of David de Burgh, and his kidnapping, or rescue, depending on one's point of view, by his brother Walter, earl of Ulster, though the account of the Drogheda housewife 'well known to the author', who was cured of cursing and swearing by a vision, has been known to raise a smile from a Latin tutorial on a wet Belfast winter's morning.

But in general the stories that the friar has himself heard in Paris, where he was a fellow student with Roger Bacon, or stories told him by visiting dignitaries of the order, are the most interesting. The best, perhaps, is the account of the Scandinavian practice of holding a 'hen party' at a house where there has been a recent birth, from which the women dance out into the street, with the straw effigy of a man, and 'debag' any male they chance to meet. The stories, which feature people known to the compiler back in his home area of Arden in Warwickshire, are positively racy, and give us an excellent idea of life in the rural midlands of England in the first half of the thirteenth century.[88]

The writer tells us that he was once rector at the Cork friary, and one can get some idea from this collection of the mental furniture of an average teacher in an Irish friary in the high middle ages. One cannot really see him as a deep thinker, though his mind is well stocked with at least anthology

---

[88] The compiler mentions as the source of several stories a collection of *exempla* made by one John of Kilkenny: 'This Brother John gave this account in his book, from which I have myself copied it out with my own hand.' 'His book' has not survived.

selections of patristic and medieval writers. But even the most profound thinker, when writing in this genre, would be reduced to displaying the credulity and naïvety that the genre demands. He does show a concern for accuracy, and a regard for the authenticity of his stories, worthy of a historian. He is also very meticulous in naming his sources, written or oral. Only a few stories are vaguely referred to as 'taken from an old sermon'. In many ways one feels that this anonymous friar wasted his talents on an inferior genre.

The uninventive or lazy preacher who resorted to collections of *exempla* may well have found a moral concordance (*concordantia moralis*) useful. The *exempla* collections provided a repertoire of colourful stories with which he could brighten up his sermons, while the moral concordance could provide him with a skeleton of appropriate biblical texts, which would lend the sermon an air of having been carefully prepared and constructed. This particular kind of concordance was what we would call conceptual, a subject concordance, rather than a mere list of places in the Bible where a particular word might be found. It is organised alphabetically by theme, and under each theme brings together scriptural passages from epistle, gospel, and Old Testament readings, so that a sermon appropriate to a saint's day or a particular occasion or audience can be constructed round those passages to form a coherent whole. Another simpler method of arrangement is to base the concordance on virtues and vices. In spite of the name under which they are known these moral concordances do not go in for the moralisation or allegorising of their themes.

The moral concordance attributed by its editor, Luke Wadding, to St Anthony of Padua[89] is probably the best-known example of the genre, and was even used by the Anglo-catholics of the nineteenth century in a version brought out by that great translator of medieval hymns, John Mason Neale.[90] Wadding included in his edition another concordance, which he called the 'Promptuarium morale', and which Neale also used in the second edition of his translation. In the title page of his edition, Wadding attributed the work to 'an anonymous Irish Franciscan'. Quite clearly the author is Irish, for among the feasts for which he provides suitable texts are those of SS Columba, Patrick, Brigid, Columbanus, Malachy, and Laurence O'Toole, while on 3 May he includes the feast of 'the translation of St Patrick's arm'. Equally clearly he was a Franciscan, for all the major feast days of the order are given, and he must have been writing after the canonisation of St Clare in 1254. On the other hand he mentions the Templars in a way that suggests that they had not yet been suppressed, and that event took place in 1312. He

---

[89] *Concordantiae morales S. Antoni Patavensis* (Rome, 1624).
[90] *The Moral Concordances of Saint Antony of Padua, translated, verified and adapted to modern use. With some additions from the Promptuarium Morale of Thomas Hibernicus* (London, 1867).

also brings together texts for a sermon to be delivered before a congregation of 'brothers of the sack', and this order was suppressed at the council of Lyons in 1274. So Kleinhans, the only modern scholar to have studied the 'Promptuarium', concluded that it was written between 1254 and 1274.[91]

As to the identity of the author, Wadding subsequently abandoned the wise caution of his earlier title page, and in his *Scriptores ordinis minorum*[92] attributed it to *Thomas Palmeranus ... dictus Thomas Hibernicus apud Kildarenses*. Kleinhans has found no reason for this attribution, and even less for attributing the work to Thomas the compiler of the 'Manipulus florum', which is in any case quite a different sort of concordance. His conclusion is that until further manuscript evidence appears—and the manuscript used by Wadding has not survived—we should keep an open mind as to the identity of the author.

The 'Promptuarium' is divided into three sections. The first two correspond to the usual divisions *de tempore* and *de sanctis* found in missals. First come texts grouped together to form the framework for sermons appropriate to the different seasons of the church's year. Then come themes for saints' days in the order of the liturgical calendar, while the third part, much the most interesting, consists of themes 'for all sorts and conditions of men', as the anonymous author puts it. In all these sections the texts chosen are given in full, and sometimes run to eight or nine verses of scripture. The third section, which is preceded by a little index, sets out a fascinating and very comprehensive list of those who were to be preached at: widows, Templars, guardians of orphans, rulers, teachers and scholars, farmers, and members of religious orders other than the Franciscans. One feels that it might be difficult to assemble a congregation consisting of some of the groups listed: 'those besieging a city' might be too busy with their siege, 'presumptuous preachers' too occupied in preaching elsewhere. It is hard to conceive of an audience of assembled anchorites, or, for rather different reasons, one of prostitutes, who, if they were ever corralled within the walls of a church, were to be assailed by a sermon based largely, it seems, upon the more severe moral pronouncements of the Pentateuch. All in all this third section provides the only light relief in a work that cannot by any stretch of the imagination be regarded as a piece of literature, but is a representative of a well-defined late medieval genre, and thus cannot be ignored in a survey of this kind.

Like 'Malachy', the Warwickshire collector of the *exempla* and the author of the 'Promptuarium', Richard Ledred, bishop of Ossory between 1317 and c.1360, was a Franciscan. There the resemblance ends. Difficult, jealous of

---

[91] A. Kleinhans, 'De concordantiis biblicis S. Antonio Patavino aliisque fratribus minoribus saeculi xiii attributis' in *Antonianum*, vi (1931), pp 273–326; pp 306–8 deal with the *Promptuarium*.

[92] Edition of 1650, p. 326b; ed. of 1806, p. 229a; ed. of 1906, p. 217.

his episcopal rights to the point of paranoia, and eccentric, though clearly gifted, he could have benefited from some of the advice on morals to be found in their writings. Yet the apologia for his conduct during his feud with powerful Anglo-Irish families is probably the most interesting piece of writing to have come from within the English colony in Ireland in the late middle ages.[93] Thanks to that account he is a real, if not lovable, character, who stands out among his shadowy fellow bishops.

This apologia is a skilful justification of the bishop's actions, written in sonorous Latin. The writer is particularly good at reporting conversation and the heated exchanges between the bishop and his enemies. Ledred wrote religious verse, and given that he had this literary bent, the apologist must surely be the bishop himself, rather than one of his clerks.

As an Englishman and a royal appointee coming into an area controlled by great Anglo-Irish families, Ledred was bound to have a rough ride, and his lack of diplomacy cannot have helped. The early part of his episcopate lay within a period when struggles between the Despensers and the Mortimers in England spilled over into the Irish colony, and in 1332 Ledred was implicated in a plot alleged to have been laid against Edward, son of the deposed Edward II.[94] This blew over, but he seems to have been at the centre of controversy to the very end of his episcopate, of which he spent twenty years, between 1329 and 1349, in exile. In particular he had a long-standing feud with his metropolitan, Alexander Bicknor, archbishop of Dublin, himself by no means a man of peace.

At first sight Ledred may seem to have been obsessed with heresy, as he accused Bicknor of harbouring heretics, and heresy (taking the particular form of witchcraft) was at the centre of the struggle with Alice Kyteler, the Power family, and their influential relatives. But heresy was very much a live issue in early fourteenth-century Ireland. In his encounters with the Powers, as related in the apologia, Ledred appears hard and unyielding, much inclined to stick to his rights, and to the letter of the law, but not a fool, still less eccentric or mad. For instance, when imprisoned by Arnold Power he is careful to get hold of and retain the warrant for his imprisonment as evidence of wrongful arrest. He seems to have seen himself as a sort of latter-day Thomas Becket, struggling against wickedness among the magnates of the colony. It is significant that his principal persecutor, William

---

[93] Thomas Wright (ed.), *A contemporary account of the proceedings against Dame Alice Kyteler* (London, 1843).

[94] The vicissitudes of Ledrede's tempestuous life are well set out in the introduction by E. Colledge to his edition, *The Latin poems of Richard Ledrede, O.F.M., bishop of Ossory, 1317–1360* (Toronto, 1974), pp xv–xxxiv. See also Ann Neary, 'Richard Ledrede, English Franciscan and bishop of Ossory, 1317–c.1360' in *Butler Society Journal*, ii (1984), pp 273–82, and eadem, 'The origins and character of the Kilkenny witchcraft case of 1324' in *R.I.A. Proc.*, lxxiii (1983), sect. C, pp 333–50.

Outlaw, was ultimately punished by being assigned a pilgrimage to Canterbury as a penance.

Ledred is now remembered mainly for his prosecution of Alice Kyteler on a charge of witchcraft, but the central figures in the struggle between the bishop and the local magnates are Alice's son—the said William Outlaw—and the seneschal of Kilkenny, Arnold Power. Ledred's efforts against Alice were unsuccessful, as she was protected by her influential relatives and escaped to obscurity in England. The unfortunate Petronella of Meath, who presumably lacked such useful connections, was indeed burned as a witch, and caught the attention of chroniclers as the first person to have been burned as a heretic in Ireland. Throughout, the writer of the apologia stresses how Ledred's enemies benefited from the support of those in high places, particularly Roger Outlaw, prior of the hospital of Kilmainham, and deputy treasurer of Ireland. Perhaps the most interesting aspect of the affair is that it represents the uphill struggle of an outsider to bring to book those who he believed, rightly or wrongly, were guilty of crimes against the church, but who had the support of the local establishment and were able to put infinite obstacles in his way.

Strong-willed and undiplomatic Ledred may have been, but there are two characteristics that he displays throughout his vicissitudes in Ossory: originality of mind bordering on eccentricity, and sincerely held convictions. So it is quite in character that he should have produced a collection of sacred songs for his clergy to sing, 'lest lips dedicated to God should be defiled by base worldly songs, worthy of the theatre' (*cantilenis teatralibus turpibus et secularibus*). Thus says the preface to the collection, which occupies a booklet in the Red Book of Ossory, which is still in Kilkenny, in the library of the Church of Ireland bishop of Cashel, Waterford, Lismore, Ossory, Ferns, and Leighlin. These are indeed *cantilenae*, songs, rather than hymns. They are nearly all written for Christmas or Easter. Half of them have refrains, and are in effect carols. The metres are complicated, but almost always lively, and some could have been danced to as well as sung. Examples are the first, a Christmas song, with refrain:

> *Verbum caro factum est*
> *de virgine Maria,*

or best of all, the ninth, with the splendid refrain:

> *Da da nobis nunc.*

Ledred prefaced ten of these Latin songs with the first line of a song in English. Presumably all he wished to do was to indicate some popular tune to which he wished his *cantilenae* to be sung. The interest of Middle English scholars in these tags has tended to overshadow the *cantilenae*, but now, with three editions of them appearing within two years, Ledred himself could not complain that his work has been neglected.[95]

Fr Colledge, whose introduction, translation, and notes make his the most useful of this trio of simultaneous editions, brings out well the way in which these songs reflect the ideas and vocabulary of earlier medieval hymns, and especially of verse with a Franciscan background. Ledred uses conceits that have a long history in devotional verse, such as the comparison of Christ, the living bread in Mary's womb, to bread baking in the oven. He used rhetoric. But he is restrained in his use of both rhetoric and conceit. He does not 'go over the top' in his use of a special devotional vocabulary, in the way that, say, St Bonaventure does. There is almost no allegory, and what there is is commonplace, as for instance the allegorisation of the three gifts of the magi in his Epiphany song (no. XXXVIII). These songs are, for the most part, simple narratives of the event they celebrate, in which Ledred recounts the events of the birth of Christ or the resurrection, and invites his clergy to meditate on them.

Ledred did not hesitate to borrow themes and images from the rich stock of earlier Christian devotional writings. More than that, he took over, cut, and edited large parts of a devotional meditation on the Blessed Virgin by Walter of Wimborne, and turned them into eight separate songs (nos XLVIII–LV). A. G. Rigg has shown with what care and originality this has been done,[96] and no one in the middle ages would have thought any the worse of Ledred for what we would regard as plagiarism. None of Ledred's songs have survived in any other manuscript, so far as we know, so they are not part of the common stock of western hymnody. Whether his clergy sang them we cannot know, but given the violent enmities he stirred up in his diocese, and the inclination of men simply to enjoy themselves at the great festivals, it seems pretty unlikely.

The medieval plays with which we are most familiar are the mysteries, miracle, or passion plays, acted in the streets, and in which the main parts were taken by the laity. This kind of drama may have existed in Dublin in the later middle ages.[97] Less spectacular dramatic scenes were enacted within the walls of cathedrals and collegiate churches throughout western Europe. These were in Latin rather than in the vernacular, and in them the roles were taken by the clergy, and the boys from the choir or the cathedral school. These little plays were much more closely linked with the celebration of the

---

[95] All three—that by Colledge cited above, another by R. L. Greene (Oxford, 1974), and a third by Theo Stemmler (Mannheim, 1975)—are reviewed, not without some wit, by A. G. Rigg in *Medium Aevum*, xlvi (1977), pp 269–78.

[96] A. G. Rigg (ed.), *The poems of Walter of Wimborne* (Toronto, 1978).

[97] See Aubrey Gwynn, 'The origins of the Anglo-Irish theatre', *Studies*, xxviii (1939), pp 260–74.

liturgy, and though individuals represented particular biblical characters, the simple scenery was usually provided by existing furnishings in the church, and the costume by liturgical vestments which most suited the role in question. The very large number of different texts, mainly Easter or Christmas plays, collected by Karl Young in his *Drama of the medieval church* gives the impression that they were put on in most cathedrals or collegiate churches.[98] It would therefore be strange if we did not have at least one example from Dublin. It is, however, surprising that the one example extant from there comes not from either of the two cathedrals, but from the not terribly important parish church of St John the Evangelist.

These short dramatic scenes had originally been inserted before the introit of mass on Easter day, but then gravitated to the end of matins, just before the 'Te Deum', which marks the end of that lengthy office. The kernel of the Easter drama was the question put by the angel at the empty tomb to the women who came seeking the body of Christ: 'Whom do you seek in the tomb, worshippers of Christ?' The women reply: 'Jesus of Nazareth, the crucified, dwellers in the sky', and the final response of the angel is: 'He is not here, he has risen as he foretold; go and announce that he has risen from the tomb.' Young shows in fatiguing detail how this original dialogue accumulated further elements, and how several kinds of Christmas playlets developed using the same question-and-answer formula as those associated with Easter. The development from these simple to more complex forms did not proceed everywhere at the same pace, and quite simple forms of the drama were still in use late enough to be incorporated in printed texts of some local service books. But there were, roughly speaking, three stages in the development of the Easter drama. The first has just one scene, the dialogue between the women at the tomb and the angel. In the second is added a very dramatic scene in which Peter and John are shown running up to the tomb, while in the most developed form a third scene is added in which Christ himself appears and reveals himself to Mary Magdalen, who at first mistakes him for the gardener.

The Dublin play belongs to the second stage, and in Young's view is outstanding within its group as 'exhibiting the most dramatic skill and literary finish'. The text is found in two fourteenth-century manuscripts.[99]

---

[98] Karl Young, *The drama of the medieval church* (2 vols, Oxford, 1962). Young is inclined to over-emphasise the importance of these para-liturgical plays. Richard Axton, in his *European drama of the early middle ages* (London, 1974), puts them in perspective and relates them to the other kinds of formal and informal popular drama of the middle ages.

[99] The text is printed by Young, *Drama*, i, 347–50. He also prints (pp 168–72) the text of the ceremonies of the burial of the cross and Host on Good Friday, and of their retrieval on Easter morning, taken from the same manuscript, and thus also probably used in the church of St John the Evangelist; see now the full edition, with analysis of the text and music, in Máire Egan-Buffet and Alan J. Fletcher, 'The Dublin *Visitatio Sepulchri* play' in *R.I.A. Proc.*, xc (1990), sect. C, pp 159–241.

Indeed the Dublin version of the Easter play has a highly lyrical element. The central dialogue between the women and the angel is preceded by very effective stanzas lamenting the death of Christ. The stage directions as to the actions of the characters are very explicit—the women are to enter the tomb 'lowering their heads and looking down into the tomb, and saying in a loud voice, as if rejoicing: "The Lord has risen"'. The costumes to be worn by the two apostles are given in similar detail. John is to wear a white tunic and carry a palm branch, Peter a red tunic, with a symbolic set of keys in his hand. There is nothing in the text to betray an Irish origin. Indeed the text has most likely been adapted from the usage of some English or continental church. But it gives us just a tiny glimpse of Dublin church life in the high middle ages, and such glimpses are all too few.[100]

Little Latin verse was written in this period in Ireland. Esposito discovered a versification in accentual metre of the 'De duodecim abusivis' in a T.C.D. manuscript. He also noted an account in seventeen lacklustre hexameters of a law case involving a parson's theft of an ox, written by a certain Simon of Ireland.[101] The Norman French and English verse in B.L. Harleian MS 913 have received some attention over the years, but the items in Latin have been neglected since some of the verse was printed by Thomas Wright and J. O. Halliwell in the last century.[102] The manuscript, dating to about 1330, is clearly of Franciscan provenance and Irish origin, written perhaps in Kildare, perhaps in the New Ross–Waterford area.

The Latin pieces in the anthology are either short extracts relating to St Francis and other early Franciscans, or else moral and satirical verse. There is a text of the well-known 'Drinkers' mass', preceded by 'Hours for the drowsy', and followed by 'Moral and medical precepts'. There is also a prophecy in verse concerning Scotland found, in a somewhat different version, in other contexts, including Walter Bower's *Scotichronicon*. But some of the verse items look as if they were composed by the author of the English verse in the manuscript. The most amusing is an account in forty-three

[100] Although we have no liturgical plays from the two Dublin cathedrals, the Dublin Troper gives some idea of the liturgy as celebrated at St Patrick's. See Brian Boydell, 'Music before 1700' in *N.H.I.*, iv, 542–67: 543. The MS is reproduced in facsimile by Dom Hesbert, *Le Tropaire-Prosaire de Dublin* (Rouen, 1966). See also Geoffrey Hand, 'Cambridge University Additional Manuscript 710' in *Reportorium Novum*, ii (1957), pp 17–32. See now also Barra Boydell, *Music at Christ Church before 1800: documents and selected anthems* (Dublin, 1998).

[101] 'Notes on Latin literature and learning in medieval Ireland' in *Hermathena*, xlviii (1933), pp 233, 248. For bibliography on the 'De duodecim abusivis', see Michael Lapidge and Richard Sharpe, *A bibliography of Celtic-Latin literature, 400–1200* (Dublin, 1985), pp 17–32. See now also Aidan Breen (ed.), *De Duodecim abusiuis* (Dublin, 1996).

[102] James O. Halliwell [-Phillipps] and Thomas Wright (ed.), *Reliquiae antiquae* (2 vols, London, 1841, 1843) and T. Wright, *The political songs of England from the reign of John to that of Edward II* (Camden Society; London, 1839). For the Norman French and English verse, see Alan Bliss and Joseph Long, 'Literature in Norman French and English' in *N.H.I.*, ii, 720–32. The manuscript was described, and most of the English and some of the Latin poems printed, by Wilhelm Heuser, *Die Kildare-Gedichte* (Bonn, 1904).

rhythmical stanzas of the drinking exploits of the abbot and prior of Gloucester, how they refused to share their wine with the rest of the community, got
sick, and were reported to the bishop. After a more severe punishment had
been mooted they were let off with a fine. The Latin is deliberately atrocious.
Thus *Ego semper stavi dorsum / inter rascalilia* seems to mean 'I always stood
behind among the rascals'. Although the piece is found in a good many
manuscripts not of Irish provenance, the Irish word *coirín* ('can') appears in
this, as it does in one of the English poems.

Two poems are found in both Latin and English versions. The subject of
the first is a gloomy one: the various meanings and implications of 'earth'
and mortal man's return to it after this life. There is also a Latin translation
of the English poem on the deceitfulness of this world: 'Lollai, lollai, litil
child, whi wepistou so sore?' It occurs at the very end of the collection,
separated from its English original. It looks as if these Latin pieces were
written by the composer or composers of the English ones. Much the most
substantial and sophisticated piece may not be of Irish provenance, as it
occurs in a good many other manuscripts and has no Irish allusions in the
text. This is a rhythmical satire in 144 verses, written in stanzas of unequal
length, against unjust judges:

> *Beati qui esuriunt*
> *et sitiunt et faciunt*
> *iusticiam,*
> *et oderunt et fugiunt*
> *iniurie nequiciam.*

The poem is influenced by Walter of Châtillon's *Propter Sion non tacebo*, but
is nevertheless original and lively. The Latin contents of this manuscript
ought to be looked at anew, especially now that we have Walther's *Alphabe-
tisches Verzeichnis* to enable us to see in what sort of context the pieces of
verse are found in other manuscript anthologies.[103]

ONE genre much practised in the middle ages, but hardly found at all in
classical Latin literature, is travel writing of various kinds. Most medieval
travelogues have their origin in pilgrimage. They are either accounts of
pilgrimages to Palestine, Rome, or Compostella, or else guides for prospect-

---

[103] 'The abbot of Gloucester', beg.: 'Quondam fuit factus festus'; cf. Hans Walther, *Alpha-
betisches Verzeichnis der Versanfängen mittellateinischer Dichtungen* (Göttingen, 1959), no. 16347,
is printed in Halliwell and Wright, *Reliquiae*, i, 140–44; the poem on earth, beg.: 'When erth
hath erth', and *Terram per iniuriam* (Walther, no.19238), is printed in Halliwell & Wright, ii,
216, and Heuser, pp 180–83; 'Lolla lolla parvole' (Walther, no. 10380), is printed in Heuser,
p. 175. The satire against judges (Walther, no. 2098), is printed in Wright, *Political songs*,
pp 224–30. For the prophecy about Scotland, beg.: 'Regnum Scotorum fuit inter cetera'
(Walther, no.16547), see Halliwell & Wright, ii, 245, 266. For an analysis of B.L., Harl. MS
913, see now D. Hadfield Moore, 'Paying the minstrel: a cultural study of B.L. MS Harley
913' (Ph.D. thesis, Q.U.B., 2001).

ive pilgrims. Others tell of journeys undertaken with a diplomatic end in view, such as Liudprand's hilarious account of his ill-starred embassy to the Byzantine emperor Nicephorus Phocas, or the story of the fascinating and highly courageous journeys of friars in Central Asia. An Irishman seems to have taken part in one of these latter. The commune of Udine, in Friuli in north-east Italy, voted a sum of money to a certain James of Ireland for his services as companion to their fellow citizen Odoric of Pordenone, who had travelled as far as Sumatra and China between 1316 and 1330.[104]

But the only Irishman to have left an account of a journey to the east is Symon Semeonis, a Franciscan, whose name Aubrey Gwynn was probably right in thinking should be anglicised, or rather normalised, as Simon Fitz-Simon.[105] The writer's companion on his journey—he died in Cairo—was *Hugo Illuminator*, 'Hugh the Illuminator'. Clearly both were of Anglo-Irish rather than of Gaelic stock. But Simon regards himself as Irish, for when he speaks of leaving Ireland he calls it his *solum nativum*, and more than once compares Arab with Irish customs. Thus horses in Egypt are swift and lively and very like those ridden by young lads in Ireland.

Simon begins his account with a striking ablative absolute: 'Having scorned the highest honour...I set out...', and goes on to tell us that he left Ireland immediately after the Franciscan provincial chapter at Clonmel in March 1323. What the honour was we cannot know. Presumably it was offered him in the course of the chapter. Simon's route through England was that followed by modern travellers from Ireland to London who entrust themselves to the vagaries of British railways: Caer Gybi (interestingly given its Welsh name rather than Holyhead), Chester, Stafford, and Lichfield. His comments on London, and later Paris and Genoa, contain a large number of superlatives, and suggest the naïvety of someone who had not hitherto travelled outside Ireland. But if this was so he rapidly adjusted to the experiences of travel, and his descriptions of various Mediterranean cities are shrewd and realistic.

He travelled across north-eastern France as far as Beaune, and then down the Saône and Rhône, and proceeded through Provence to Nice. Interestingly enough he was struck by the beauty of the 'Riparia', the Italian Riviera. En route for Venice he stopped off at Bobbio to visit the tomb of Columbanus, another interesting indication of his Irishness. From Venice to Egypt his

---

[104] For the reference to James see FitzMaurice & Little, *Materials*, p. 132. A convenient collection, in translation, of pre-crusade pilgrims' accounts of their journeys to the Holy Land is J. Wilkinson, *Jerusalem pilgrims before the crusades* (London, 1978). Translations of the accounts of Central Asian journeys can be found in H. Yule, *Cathay and the way thither* (Hakluyt Society; London, 1866) and Charles R. Beazley, *Texts and versions of John de Plano Carpini and William de Rubruquis* (Hakluyt Society; London, 1903).

[105] Note by him at p. 22 of the edition by Mario Esposito (ed. and trans.), *Itinerarium Symonis Semeonis ab Hybernia ad Terram Sanctam* (Dublin, 1960).

way lay through a string of Venetian possessions, so he is not very informative on the Byzantine world. But his descriptions of Durazzo, Ragusa, and other Venetian colonies give an interesting insight on the ethnic mix of their populations. Like most western travellers to the Arab world, especially after the crusades, Simon had to endure long delays and 'hassle' while customs men at Alexandria suspiciously examined his baggage, and he waited to obtain a permit from the authorities to allow him to travel further into Egypt. The customs men, when they came upon images of Christ, the Virgin, and St John in his baggage, contented themselves with spitting on them, but did not confiscate them, as their modern opposite numbers in some Marxist countries might well have done.

Simon spent some weeks in both Alexandria and Cairo and gives an interesting description of both. Much of what he says is found in other pilgrims' accounts. But he is particularly interested in dress, and his account of the various uniforms worn by Jews, Arabs, and Christians of different classes reminds us of how, in the middle ages, the way in which men dressed gave an immediate clue to the place they had in society. He also gives a very good account of the Coptic church and its beliefs, and shows more sympathy for it than for the Greek Orthodox church. Despite many indignities heaped on both Jews and Christians, certain Christian churches were open for worship, including one in Old Cairo where the Orthodox patriarch resided, and at least one which was made available to the communities of foreign merchants, the *fondacos*, for worship according to the Latin rite. It was here that Simon's companion Hugh the Illuminator was buried. Indeed Simon seems to have celebrated mass at more than one church in Cairo.

Having finally got his permit, Simon set off for Jerusalem, and we have a detailed account of his journey north through the Gaza desert. After just eight paragraphs of description of the Holy City the account breaks off. As this is the part of the journey most fully documented from other pilgrimage accounts it is perhaps no great loss. References in the earlier part of the work to Roman topography, and to the distance between Milan and Pavia, seem to indicate that Simon came back by a slightly different route, but we do not know whether he returned to Ireland or stopped off for a while in some English Franciscan house. Simon's journey was not so exciting as, for instance, that by William de Rubruquis in Central Asia, which follows it in Corpus Christi College (Cambridge) MS 407, the only manuscript text we have of the pilgrimage from Clonmel to the Holy Land. But he was a shrewd observer, far less naïve than most pilgrims who have left us accounts of their travels; and like his great predecessor in Egypt, Herodotus, he clearly has a real interest in the way of life and manners of the various peoples among whom he travelled.

Nowhere in Ireland could compare with Compostella, Rome, or the Holy Land as places of pilgrimage in the middle ages. Lough Derg, which in modern times is at least a national centre of pilgrimage for the Irish, was already from the middle of the twelfth century attracting a steady trickle of pilgrims. But it was a trickle, and curiously enough, all the accounts we have of the pilgrimage are by foreigners. No mention is made of Lough Derg pilgrimages in the Irish annals till 1492, when in its medieval form it was closed down by Pope Alexander VI. It seems to have been ignored by the native Irish.

The pilgrimage took a somewhat different form from that seen today. The pilgrim, after fifteen days of penitential living on bread and water, with constant prayer, was let down into a pit or cave, often referred to as the 'Purgatory of St Patrick', and spent twenty-four hours there. Those few who could afford to make their way across the Irish Sea and up through bogs and forests to a place still remote even today, came armed with letters of recommendation, usually from both the archbishop of Armagh and the bishop of Clogher. They were given a ritual warning about the dangers of entering the cave by the prior of the Augustinian canons who looked after the site and regulated the pilgrimage. According to popular tradition, some who entered the cave came out mad, while others never emerged at all. All the accounts we have relate visions seen by the pilgrims, so that in fact they belong rather to the genre of vision literature, so much of which in the middle ages seems to be influenced by Celtic ideas of the other world, and its links with our world through caves and openings in the ground. In fact these writers have disappointingly little to say about their journeys through Ireland to and from Lough Derg.

The Lough Derg pilgrimage really took off due to the immense success of the account of the visit of the knight Owein to the cave and the revelations he received there, written around 1185 by Henry, a Cistercian monk from Saltrey in the diocese of Lincoln. This was a best-seller, and its influence can be seen in all later accounts of visions experienced while in the cave, and can be traced all the way through European literature to Dante.[106] The writers of subsequent accounts are noblemen, which is due perhaps as much to the popularity of the Owein account among aristocratic circles as to the fact that only the well-to-do could afford to journey all the way to Lough Derg. We have the names of some eighteen pilgrims who made that journey between the thirteenth and the fifteenth century. Apart from those who have left accounts of the pilgrimage, we have for some letters of recommendation from the archbishop of Armagh or, in the case of Malatesta of Rimini and Niccolo de Beccaio, from the English king, while others are mentioned in the accounts as having met the writer on the way into or out of the cave. There are accounts in Catalan by Raymond, viscount of Perelhos,

<hr>

[106] See now the excellent translation with introduction by Jean-Michel Picard and Yolande de Pontfarcy, *St Patrick's Purgatory* (Dublin, 1985).

of which there is also a version in the *langue d'oc*; in Italian by Antonio Mannini; and in Middle English by William Staunton from the diocese of Durham.[107]

Three pilgrims wrote in Latin, or rather had their visionary adventures 'written up' for them. The earliest and most elaborate account is that of the Hungarian George Crissaphan.[108] It was read and used in the later accounts of Louis of Auxerre, Raymond of Perelhos, Antonio Mannini, and Laurenz de Pászthó. George was a young nobleman who had, while serving with King Louis of Hungary at the time when he was attempting to make good a claim to the kingdom of Naples, spent some time as royal governor of Trani in Apulia. In the course of his rule there he had, on his own admission, caused the deaths of over 350 people. In time he repented, visited the papal court, and was assigned the appropriate penance for his crimes. But feeling that he had not expiated his guilt he first visited Compostella and then, in 1353, set out for Lough Derg from Galicia, travelling on foot through the Basque country, Navarre, the length of France, and England, until eventually he reached the priory of Augustinian canons near Lough Derg. But he had not provided himself with the necessary letters from the archbishop and the bishop of Clogher, and so had to trail all the way back to find Richard FitzRalph somewhere in the neighbourhood of Dundalk or Drogheda. After he had reemerged from the cave he felt that he had to go back to FitzRalph to pass on a message he had been told to give him in the course of his visions.

The main body of the work consists of twenty-six of these visions, most of them highly complex—the last alone takes up sixty-eight pages of text. The sceptical reader, faced with the almost lyrical inventiveness of the young Hungarian, must suspect that either the canons of Lough Derg or the unknown cleric who compiled the text, as Katherine Walsh tactfully puts it, 'helped to formulate' George's recollections of what he had seen.[109] Hammerich showed that on stylistic and internal circumstantial grounds the account was written in or near Avignon by an Augustinian whose native speech

---

[107] A list of known visitors to Lough Derg was first given by Hippolyte Delehaye, 'Le pèlerinage de Laurent de Pászthó au purgatoire de S. Patrice' in *Analecta Bollandiana*, xxvii (1908), pp 35–64, and added to by L. L. Hammerich, 'Eine Pilgerfahrt des xiv Jahrhunderts nach dem Fegfeuer des h. Patrizius' in *Zeitschrift für deutsche Philologie*, liii (1928), pp 25–40. These lists are consolidated, and a full bibliography of accounts of the pilgrimage given, in Michael Haren and Yolande de Pontfarcy (ed.), *The medieval pilgrimage to St Patrick's Purgatory: Lough Derg and the European tradition* (Clogher Historical Society; Enniskillen, 1988). This does not entirely supersede Shane Leslie, *St Patrick's Purgatory* (London, 1932), which has a useful collection of lengthy extracts from most of the accounts.

[108] Ed. L. Hammerich, 'Visiones Georgii', *Det Kgl. Danske Videnskabernes Selskab* (Copenhagen, 1930).

[109] For her clear and witty account of George's travels in Ireland see Katherine Walsh, *Richard FitzRalph*, pp 308–18. Michael Haren, 'Two Hungarian pilgrims' in *The medieval pilgrimage to St Patrick's Purgatory*, pp 120–68, in his analysis of the reasons why George's visions took the form they did, broadly agrees with her. He also gives a helpful historical background to both Hungarian accounts, and a summary of the contents of each vision.

was the *langue d'oc*. The visions end with messages that George was to pass
on to FitzRalph, the pope, the French and English kings, and the 'sultan of
Babylon'. These read a bit like the more political utterances of the Delphic
oracle. The more 'visionary' parts of the visions, so to speak, seem to owe
much to Henry of Saltrey's account of Owein's vision.[110]

Another Hungarian nobleman, Laurenz de Pászthó, visited Lough Derg in
November 1411.[111] He is named in a recommendatory letter from Sigismund
I, king of Hungary and future German emperor, as his chief steward and
seneschal, and arrived in Ireland in some style, appearing in Dublin 'with all
the proper accoutrement of a knight, with his own herald and other servants'.
Encouraged by a favourable dream he set off for Lough Derg. He gives a
detailed description of the lough 'abounding in trout, salmon, and other
kinds of fish', the island on which was the cave, and the dimensions of the
cave and the chapel that enclosed it. He had but five visions there, and none
is recounted in such detail as George's. They also seem to the inexpert eye to
be less fanciful, more 'run of the mill': he routs two devils with the sign of
the cross; the devil in the guise of a pilgrim tries to persuade him that Christ
is not the son of God; and Laurenz is tempted by the inevitable lovely lady.
Here there are, I think, some echoes of the ethos of courtly love, for the devil
impersonates a lady whom Laurenz had longed for in the past, but without
being able to consummate his love. The phantom assures him that he can
now have his way with her. Laurenz, quick off the mark, spots that it is a
phantom and rejects the offer. St Michael appears and shows him the souls
of his relatives and friends being tormented in purgatory.

We know the identity of the person who put together this account, one
James Yonge, notary, of the city of Dublin. This Yonge tells us himself,[112]
adding that most of the material he has got by word of mouth from Laurenz,
but that the latter had also given him some notes, and so his account is based
on both kinds of material.

The account of the visit to Lough Derg by Louis of Auxerre, alias Louis
of France, was dictated to Fr Taddeo de Gualandis of Pisa, O.F.M.[113] Louis
had been infatuated by tournaments and had spent his time going from one
to another in France, Germany, and Italy. Feeling remorse for the part he
had played in wounding and killing others, he decided to go to Lough Derg
and, after getting the pope's blessing at Avignon, set out. He entered the
cave on 27 September 1368. About half-an-hour after he had been ushered

---

[110] For a partial analysis of George's sources see M. Voigt, *Beiträge zur Geschichte der
Visionenliteratur im Mittelalter* (Leipzig, 1924), pp 121–219.
[111] Ed. Delehaye, art. cit., pp 43–60.
[112] Ed. cit., p. 58.
[113] Ed. Karl Strecker at the end of Voigt's monograph, cited above. For possible sources of
this account in Italian folklore see now J.-M. Picard, 'The Italian pilgrims' in *The medieval
pilgrimage to Patrick's Purgatory*, p. 172, and Hugh Shields, 'The French accounts', ibid.,
pp 91–2.

in by the canons, the apparition of a venerable abbot appeared and gave him the password that would see him safely through the trials he was about to undergo: 'The Word was made flesh and dwelt among us. May God and the Holy Trinity be always with me.'

Louis's vision is divided into two parts. First he encounters a number of temptations, in all of which beautiful women figure. They offer themselves to Louis, but always, as he looks behind him, he sees monsters, which they threaten to unleash if he will not yield to their advances. On each occasion Louis saves himself by repeating the holy formula. Finally, having success-fully eluded a whole convent of handsome but lascivious nuns, he is con-fronted by three lovely lasses playing chess under a tree. They show him a narrow bridge across which he must travel over boiling waters full of mon-sters. The bridge is blocked by a fierce warrior on a red horse. With the help of his password he finally crosses this. This is his last test, and from there he is led through Purgatory to Paradise.

There he is guided by two vested bishops into a beautiful city, like the heavenly Jerusalem of Revelation, and into a lovely hall, where music is playing, and innumerable kings are sitting on thrones, then into another hall where queens are on their thrones, and finally into lovely gardens where the kings and queens come and mingle. He is then guided to another city, even more splendid, and outside it is a spring with seats all round where the kings and queens sit. There is an even more splendid garden, and in it a castle, which in a literal translation of the Latin 'put everything else in the shade'. There Louis sees the Trinity enthroned in splendour. Finally the bishops impart certain secrets to him, which he is never to divulge, and vanish. The venerable abbot reappears. He too imparts secrets and vanishes, and Louis comes to himself to find the canons coming in to release him from the cave.

Frati[114] analysed the vision of Louis as being about two-thirds derived from Henry of Saltrey while the rest was original. Max Voigt[115] felt, rightly I think, that the influence of Henry of Saltrey was much less, though not entirely absent, and that certain features, such as the bridge episode, were shared with the 'Visio Tnugdali'. In Voigt's view there is at least an indirect link between Louis's visions and those of George Crissaphan. Like Criss-aphan's they would repay a new analysis.

Compared with pilgrimages from Clonmel to Jerusalem and from Galicia to Lough Derg, Archbishop John Colton's nine-day journey around the diocese of Derry in October 1397 must seem somewhat of an anticlimax.[116]

---

[114] Luigi Frati, 'Tradizioni storiche del purgatorio de S. Patrizio' in *Giornale storico de la letteratura italiana*, xvii (1891), pp 46–79: 51.

[115] Op. cit., pp 221–3.

[116] Ed. William Reeves, *Acts of Archbishop Colton in his metropolitan visitation of the diocese of Derry* (Ir. Arch. Soc.; Dublin, 1850). For a recent analysis of Colton's career in Ireland and a perceptive account of his journey, see John A. Watt, 'John Colton, justiciar of Ireland...and

In its own way, though, it could have been just as hazardous, given that almost all archbishops of Armagh in the late middle ages were Anglo-Irishmen, who spent most of their time in the English-controlled area of the archdiocese around Drogheda and Dundalk, and seldom visited Armagh itself, never mind that majority of their suffragan dioceses which lay 'among the Irish'. But Colton's relations with the Ó Néill and other northern Irish kings were good, and indeed he was accompanied on his journey to Derry by Thomas O'Lucheran, a canon and later dean of Armagh, who had been Niall Óg Ó Néill's secretary and interpreter when he had made his submission to Richard II at Drogheda in 1395.

In 1397 the see of Derry had been vacant for over two years. Archbishop Colton's aim in coming into the diocese was to secure the primatial rights during a vacancy, in terms both of revenues and of jurisdiction. The account we have of his visit, drafted by his notary, Richard Kenmore, is a piece of propaganda intended to make his claims stick, to show what the primatial rights were in a vacant diocese, and particularly to record the concession of these rights by the wholly Gaelic Irish clergy. Emphasis is placed on the willing provision made for the archbishop's party by the erenaghs of individual churches of food, lodging, and horses. By willingly giving these they were recognising the archbishop's jurisdiction according both to western European church custom and to Gaelic Irish custom.

The archbishop entered the diocese at Cappagh, where the erenagh could give him food, but no bed for the night. He proceeded to Ardstraw, and then Urney and Leckpatrick, on opposite sides of Strabane. From there the bishop reached Derry, crossing the river by ferry. There was some resistance to his claims over the diocese in a vacancy. Fortunately he had the support of the dean, William McCawell. But the archdeacon and some other members of the cathedral chapter initially refused to meet him, were summoned by public proclamation, and when they still did not appear were declared contumacious and excommunicated. However next day they made peace overtures through the bishop of Raphoe and did in fact make their submission to Colton at Banagher three days later. During his short stay in Derry Colton investigated the affairs of the Augustinian canons, in whose monastery he was staying, and gave the community a set of decrees intended to bring about a thorough reform under a new abbot. These must surely have been drawn up in advance.

Richard Kenmore's account is at pains to show the bishop acting as diocesan ordinary and adjudicating over the normal disputes that might arise in any diocese. It records, in J. A. Watt's words, 'ten days in the life of a bishop

archbishop of Armagh' in James Lydon (ed.), *England and Ireland in the middle ages: essays in honour of Jocelyn Otway-Ruthven* (Dublin, 1981), pp 196–213. Watt rightly points out that technically Archbishop Colton's journey was not an official episcopal visitation, but his activities in Derry much resemble those of a bishop visiting his diocese.

of Derry': the reconsecration of churches that had been desecrated by the shedding of blood at Ardstraw, Clooney, and Dungiven; adjudication in a dispute over erenagh lands at Banagher, and in the tangled matrimonial affairs of two members of the Ó Catháin and the Mac Giollagáin families. It is this feeling that we are getting a glimpse of everyday routine in a fully Gaelic diocese that makes this account interesting, and separates it from merely factual documents such as are found in the surviving Armagh registers. The very names of the clergy and laity who appear before Colton— Ó Catháin, Ó Dochartaigh, and Mac Giollagáin—are the same as we see today in the columns of the *Derry Journal*. The account of the visit proper is followed by an episcopal edict forbidding the newly elected abbot of Derry, 'Odo' O'Doherty, from cohabiting with Caitlín O'Doherty or any other woman, and enjoining him to return all goods and revenues that he had alienated during his period as custos.

One cannot help feeling that this account has been carefully presented so as to give the impression of wider consent and goodwill towards Colton than may have existed in reality. Even so, the fact that he was able to move about so freely in a totally Gaelic diocese is very striking. Perhaps, as Watt as suggested, the coarb of Patrick was still a prestigious figure, even when he was an Anglo-Irishman.

In contrast to the well-known Irish annals, the annals written within the sphere of English influence in Ireland have been little studied. The texts in which we read them are unsatisfactory in various ways and the editions antiquated. These Anglo-Irish annals stand apart from their Gaelic Irish counterparts, but not altogether on linguistic grounds. They are, of course, all written in Latin. But anyone familiar with the Irish annals will know that Latin formulae recur there regularly and the Annals of Inisfallen are partly written in Latin. But, as Gearóid Mac Niocaill has felicitously put it,[117] the difference lies in their 'stance'. They are more interested in events in England than are the Irish annals, and have only a limited knowledge of and interest in events in Gaelic Ireland outside the colony.

Indeed Aubrey Gwynn's analysis of these chronicles, made many years ago,[118] sought to show that several of them have a common origin in annals imported into Ireland in the early twelfth century from Worcestershire. He pointed out that a brief and fragmentary chronicle in the Black Book of Christ Church shares its entries with entries for the same years in the so-called 'Chronicle of Multyfarnham'. The compilers of that chronicle, of the Annals of St Mary's abbey, Dublin, and of the later Pembridge's Annals all seemed to have used an earlier stage of the Christ Church Annals that we

---

[117] Gearóid Mac Niocaill lists these Anglo-Irish annals with a brief discussion in *The medieval Irish Annals* (Dublin, 1975), pp 37–41.
    [118] 'Some unpublished texts in the Black Book of Christ Church' in *Anal. Hib.*, no. 16 (1946), pp 281–337.

now have, in a fragmentary form, in the Black Book. Gwynn printed the surviving fragment, and also constructed the remaining section from 1171 down to 1273 by bringing together the entries for those years shared by the other chronicles mentioned.

The foundation year of Winchcombe abbey is included in the Christ Church Annals, and it is a fictitious date (797) rather than the real date (972). This led Gwynn and Robin Flower to pin down Winchcombe as the place of composition of the original annals from which all the above, including the Christ Church Annals themselves, derive. Considerable doubt has been thrown on all these claims by some brilliant work presented by Bernadette Williams in her as yet unpublished doctoral thesis.[119]

The only one of the Anglo-Irish chronicles that is at all well known is that written in the thirteenth century by John Clyn, a friar in the Franciscan house in Kilkenny.[120] Clyn was appointed guardian of the friary founded at Carrick-on-Suir in 1336, and thus was presumably a man of mature age by that date. So his editor, Butler, is probably right in putting the date of his birth slightly before the turn of the century. Before 1264 the chronicle entries are brief, but from then till 1349 they are much fuller, and constitute a real historical account rather than mere annalistic notes. The chronicle stops just after the account of the black death in Ireland. It is always assumed, though there is no clear evidence, that Clyn himself died in that plague.

Clyn has much more to tell us about events in Gaelic Ireland than the other Anglo-Irish chroniclers. He was writing in Kilkenny, at the centre of the great Butler lordship with its many links with the Gaelic parts of the country. He will often mention events in the nearer parts of Connacht and even Ulster. His account is full of detail, even down to his giving the length—'some fifty feet, some thirty'—of whales that had been stranded in Dublin Bay in 1331. Not only are there long lists of those killed in the innumerable minor battles and ambushes, but he will often give the price of a crannoc of corn, when mentioning food shortages. On reading Clyn one is reminded of stretches of Orderic Vitalis, where the seemingly endless accounts of feuds, killing, and burning end up by giving us a very clear account of a turbulent but lively society. At the end of his account he gives us the traditional reason for writing: 'lest acts that deserve to be noticed perish with the time in which they happened, and vanish from the memory of future generations.' But his serious purpose is underlined by his touching provision of parchment to enable the chronicle to be continued after his death: 'if any man should remain alive in future times, or anyone of the seed of Adam can escape this pestilence and continue the work.'

---

[119] Bernadette Williams, 'The Latin Franciscan Anglo-Irish annals of medieval Ireland' (Ph.D. thesis, University of Dublin, 1991).

[120] Ed. Richard Butler, *The Annals of Ireland by Friar John Clyn and Thady Dowling* (Dublin, 1849).

Alone of the annalists he gives us some idea of his own thoughts and opinions. He quite often comments on those whose actions or death he is recording. Thus Hoel de Bathe, archdeacon of Ossory (d. 1336) is 'a man of learning and generous' (*vir litteratus et largus*), while Lord James Butler, who died in the previous year, is 'generous and amiable' (*liberalis et amicabilis*). In this fairly frequent adding of two epithets after someone's name, summing up their character, one can perhaps see stylistic echoes of Giraldus Cambrensis, as one does in phrases such as 'with more reputation than real ability' (*plus nominis quam hominis habens*). Indeed Clyn is the only one of these writers who can be said to have a good Latin style. The other writers simply string out the events they are describing in an unadorned narrative.

The stylistically plainest and most unliterary of these chronicles is the so-called 'Kilkenny' chronicle, edited by Robin Flower from B.L. Cotton MS Vespasian N. XI.[121] From 1316 onwards these annals are identical with Clyn, almost word for word, but the earlier part is drawn from other sources. Bernadette Williams has shown that this text consists of three separate chronicles. The first was compiled by a Franciscan, probably in the friary at Castledermot. The second owes much to the Annals of Multyfarnham mentioned below, while the third is indeed closely linked to John Clyn's chronicle.

No one has yet explained satisfactorily why the Annals of Multyfarnham should be so called.[122] There is another puzzle in that the writer seems to be a Franciscan: there are references to elections of provincial ministers under the years 1266 and 1270 and to the death by drowning of the two friars who were sent from England to conduct a visitation of Irish Franciscan houses in 1273. On the other hand there is a reference to the burning of the Dominican friary at Roscommon in 1270. There are several references to the d'Exeter (*De Exonia*) family: the marriage of Richard d'Exeter in 1269; the birth of his son John in the next year; and his term as justiciar, also it seems in 1270. Under the year 1246 the birth of 'Brother Stephen d'Exeter' is recorded, while in 1263 'Brother Stephen d'Exeter took the habit' (*indutus est frater Stephanus de Exonia*). It looks as if Stephen d'Exeter was the compiler of this chronicle, but was he a Franciscan or a Dominican? Perhaps the answer can be found in the fact that the friary of Strade, on the River Moy, close to Lough Conn, had been founded as a Franciscan house by Jordan d'Exeter, but that he had subsequently, in 1252, given it to the Dominicans. The d'Exeters had come into east Mayo with the de Burgh settlement of Connacht in 1235. Their manor was Ballylahan, near Foxford, and just a few miles from Strade, and the MacJordain d'Exeters were still at Ballylahan as

---

[121] In *Anal. Hib.*, no. 2 (1931), pp 330–40.

[122] The most likely guess is that made by Aubrey Gwynn in *Anal. Hib.*, no. 16 (1946), p. 315, n. 4. Text ed. Aquila Smith, *Miscellany of the Irish Archaeological Society* (Dublin, 1842), pp 1–26.

late as 1585.[123] Like the de Burghs they became gaelicised at an early date. Even if the compiler of this chronicle is not himself a d'Exeter, his connection with that family, and the de Burghs—the death of Walter de Burgh in 1271 causes him to sigh 'Alas' (*pro dolor*)—means that the part of his work which is original, from about 1266 on, is an invaluable source of information on events in the Sligo–Roscommon–Mayo area till it breaks off in 1274.

The annals to which Sir James Ware, probably with good reason, gave the title 'Annals of St Mary's abbey, Dublin'[124] have large gaps in the thirteenth and early fourteenth century due to the loss of leaves in the manuscript. For instance, everything between 1221 and 1308 has gone. But enough remains to show us that the compiler, unlike the 'Multyfarnham' chronicler, has little knowledge of events in Gaelic Ireland. The entries consist mainly of obits of dignitaries in the Anglo-Irish part of the church, English kings, and chief governors of Ireland, and notes on the arrival in Ireland of newly appointed governors. In fact, apart from a burst of interest in Irish church affairs in the last quarter of the eleventh century, there is no mention of Irish affairs before 1155, and the more detailed section between 1169 and the turn of the century is a compressed text of Giraldus Cambrensis' 'Expugnatio Hibernica'. Political events in Ireland only seem to rate a mention when they involve the intervention of the English king, or some other notable figure from the mainland such as Edward Bruce. Nevertheless, though limited in its range, this text has always been useful to the historians of the period in helping them to confirm the chronological framework of their narrative.

Another set of annals, also printed by J. T. Gilbert in his *Cartularies of St Mary's abbey*, was attributed by Ware to a certain Pembridge. Robin Flower has tried to make this attribution stick, but as with all of these chronicles the exact identity of the author matters little. The way in which the annals are weighted and slanted can usually tell us a good deal about the likely background, and even the character of the compiler. 'Pembridge' is a man of some spirit. He includes several stories worthy of Giraldus: for example the vision seen by John de Courcy while in prison, John's exploits in splitting timber, or the deeds of John Huse, the torturer of Athenry. He gets very worked up over the execution of William de Bermingham in 1332, and his enmity against the justiciar Ralph d'Ufford, and considerable prejudice against the Irish—they are always described as 'robbers' (*latrones*)—are also reminiscent of Giraldus. For the late twelfth and early thirteenth century he does in fact use Giraldus, and throughout he makes occasional use of the Annals of St Mary's abbey, or perhaps shares a common source with them. For the later thirteenth century his material seems to derive in large part from a chronicle written in Britain, for he goes into events there in great

---

[123] G. H. Orpen, *Ireland under the Normans, 1169–1333* (4 vols, Oxford, 1911–20), iii, 198.
[124] Ed. John T. Gilbert, *Cartularies of St Mary's Abbey* (2 vols, Dublin, 1884), ii, 241–92.

detail, including the Welsh and Scots wars of Edward I, and occasionally ranges as far afield as Hungary. In the course of that century Irish events come more to the centre of the stage, but are still inserted into the middle of this detailed account of events in Britain. From about 1307 on the chronicler confines himself to matters Irish. His account of Edward Bruce's Irish wars is particularly detailed, and indeed gripping. The reader gets a clearer idea from his account than from Clyn of the devastation caused by the Bruce invasion, and the irreparable damage it did to the English colony in Ireland. Curiously, his account of the Alice Kyteler affair in Kilkenny is far more detailed, circumstantial, and lively than that of Clyn, 'the reporter on the ground'. Like Clyn, 'Pembridge' breaks off in 1347, but the chronicle is continued by a second annalist down to 1370.

The chronicle of Henry Marlborough, vicar of Balscaddan, covers the years 1133 to 1421.[125] For the twelfth, thirteenth, and fourteenth centuries Marlborough draws on some of the same material as 'Pembridge'. He is not directly dependent on him, though, for although his treatment is generally skimpier, and he skips years without an entry, yet every now and again he gives details that are not in 'Pembridge'. Thus under 1332 he explains that when Sir Walter de Bermingham was hanged, his son escaped because he was a cleric. 'Pembridge' merely says that he was set free, but does not say why. Marlborough also draws on the Annals of St Mary's abbey—the two chronicles often agree word for word. Beginning with the last years of the fourteenth century Marlborough's account becomes fuller, and there is an increasing emphasis on Dublin events. Reading the entries for the first twenty years of the fifteenth century, one senses very much the emergence of the Pale. Pointers to this are the vague way in which he refers to individual 'Irish enemies', his lack of any knowledge of events beyond the borders of Leinster, and the meticulous detail in which he chronicles marriages and deaths among the Anglo-Irish nobility of the Pale area.

In 1517 Philip Flattisbury of Johnstown near Naas, County Kildare, the compiler of the Red Book of Kildare, put together the Annals based on 'Pembridge', of which the text is to be found in T.C.D. MS 583. These have never been edited. A similar, but not identical set of annals is to be found in B.L. MS Cotton Domitian A XVIII, where it is attributed, in a hand other than the scribe's, to Philip Flattisbury. These Domitian annals are identical for long stretches with the annals attributed to 'James Grace of Kilkenny' by their editor, Richard Butler.[126] Another British Library manuscript, Add. MS 40674, contains an abridged text of 'Pembridge's' Annals, with the later part of the Annals of Marlborough added at the end, and then on the next page notes and sketchy annals for the years 1394 to 1513, these last in a hand

---

[125] Ed. and partly trans. by James Ware, *Chronicle of Ireland by Henry of Marleburrough* (Dublin, 1633).

[126] *Miscellany of the Irish Archaeological Society* (Dublin, 1842).

that Robin Flower identified as that of Flattisbury, as seen in the Red Book. Again, these agree closely with part of Grace's Annals. Any further discussion of Flattisbury's work will have to start from an examination of these three manuscripts. The relationship between the T.C.D. manuscript and the Domitian text will need to be worked out, and also the relationship of these two manuscripts on the one hand, and the printed Grace's Annals on the other. Both Robin Flower and Gearóid Mac Niocaill were inclined to believe that 'Grace' is a 'ghost writer', and that all the material in these three manuscripts, and in two other less important Cottonian manuscripts, represents successive stages of Flattisbury's reworking of his sources.

A churchman who is outside this annalistic tradition, but who clearly had an interest in history, was Philip of Slane O.P., rector of the Dublin convent of the Dominicans about 1309, and bishop of Cork from 1321 till his death in 1326. He made an abridged version of Giraldus Cambrensis's 'Topographia Hibernica' that survives in a single manuscript, B.L. Add. MS 19513, and was later translated into Provençal. Esposito believed that this might contain some material by Philip himself. But no analysis of the contents has as yet been made.[127]

Hagiography forms a considerable part of Hiberno-Latin literature of the earlier period of the middle ages.[128] The Lives of Columba by Adomnán, two Lives of Brigit, one anonymous and the other by Cogitosus, and the two very different Lives of Patrick by Muirchú and Tírechán, are probably the most attractive part of that literature. But after that there follows a period, from about 800 on, when Latin learning in Ireland was in somewhat of a decline, and saints' Lives began to be written in Irish. Richard Sharpe, who believes that nine more Latin lives may be dated to that earlier period already mentioned,[129] has suggested that the dominance of Irish in the ninth and tenth centuries makes it unlikely that any Latin Lives were composed between 850 and 1050. In the twelfth century two Lives of Irish saints circulated widely, but both were written on the Continent: the Life of St Malachy by his friend St Bernard, and that of Laurence O'Toole of Dublin by the canons of Eu in Normandy where he died.[130] The Lives of SS Flannan,

---

[127] For Philip see T. Kaeppeli, *Scriptores Ordinis Praedicatorum medii aevi* (Rome, 1980), iii, 275. For Esposito on Philip see 'Further notes on mediaeval Hiberno-Latin...' in *Hermathena*, xvi (1911), p. 327.

[128] Richard Sharpe, *Medieval Irish saints' Lives: an introduction to Vitae Sanctorum Hiberniae* (Oxford, 1989). I am greatly indebted to Prof. Sharpe for allowing me to read this work prior to publication. It is far and away the most significant treatment of the subject for a very long time.

[129] Ibid., pp 274–96.

[130] The Life of Malachy was ed. by Jean Leclercq and Aubrey Gwynn in *Opera S. Bernardi* (Rome, 1957–77), iii, 295–378, and trans. by H. J. Lawlor, *St Bernard of Clairvaux's Life of St Malachy of Armagh* (London, 1920). The Life of St Laurence O'Toole was ed. by Charles Plummer, 'Vie et miracles de S. Laurent, archevêque de Dublin' in *Analecta Bollandiana*, xxxiii (1914), pp 121–86. See now also the dissertation by Maurice F. Roche, 'The Latin Lives of St Laurence of Dublin' (2 vols, Ph.D. thesis, N.U.I. (U.C.D.), 1978).

Mochuille, and Lasrán (patron of Leighlin) can be dated to that same twelfth century, and suggest that there had been a revival in the writings of saints' lives in Ireland by then. But the real achievement of the late medieval period in hagiography is the compilation of three great collections of lives, which formed the basis of the work on Irish saints by seventeenth-century scholars like Colgan and Hugh Ward, and also of the modern editions by Plummer and Heist.

The first collection is found in two Dublin manuscripts that derive from the same original: Marsh's Library, MS Z 3.1.5, often referred to (probably wrongly) as 'Codex Kilkenniensis', written at the end of the fourteenth or beginning of the fifteenth century; and T.C.D. MS 175, written at the end of the fourteenth century. References to places and people in some of the Lives in the collection have suggested to Professor Sharpe that it was compiled in south Leinster. Both manuscripts have lost part of the collection, and so the whole has to be reconstructed from a comparison of both. It contained twenty-nine Lives in all.

The 'Codex Salmanticensis' is so called because it spent a brief period in the newly founded Irish College at Salamanca before being sent to Brussels to the Bollandists and eventually ending up in the Bibliothèque Royale in Brussels, where it is now MSS 7672–4. It was compiled in the late fourteenth century by someone who was probably writing in the part of Ireland under English influence, since the Irish names have given him considerable trouble. It contains just short of fifty Lives, which have been edited by William Heist.[131] The third collection is found in two Oxford manuscripts: Bodl. Rawlinson B 485, written in the early fourteenth century, and Rawl. B 505, written in the late fourteenth century, both in the Westmeath–Longford area. Charles Plummer edited nine Lives from this collection in his *Vitae sanctorum Hiberniae*.[132] To a greater or lesser degree the compilation of each of these collections is a work of literary creation; indeed, they could be seen as representing the most impressive Latin literature of the period under review. In the past, scholars such as Plummer have compared the text of a particular Life in one collection with that of the same Life in another, but such a comparison can have only a limited value unless we know the overall relationship of the collections to each other. One of Sharpe's aims in his thesis has been to establish this relationshop; no easy task, since a group of Lives within one collection may relate to Lives in another, while other Lives in that first collection do not. He has clearly shown that two of the collections—that represented by the two Dublin manuscripts, and that represented by the two Rawlinson ones—each have a real entity, as the compiler has imposed his own 'house style' on the diverse Lives that he has included in his compilation.

---

[131] Heist, *Vitae SS Hib.*      [132] Plummer, *Vitae SS Hib.*

The compiler of the Dublin collection seems to have had a strong interest in the period in Ireland just before and during St Patrick's mission, and in Irish history, genealogy, and topography. His use of certain words and phrases over and over again has imposed a uniformity of style on the Lives, which he has gathered from different sources. On the other hand, the compiler of the Oxford collection shows less interest in Irish geography or customs, and lays more emphasis on miracles and the saint's devout life. The tone is more pious and homiletic. The compiler of the 'codex Salmanticensis' is much more conservative in retaining the texts he included more or less unaltered. Consequently 'Salmanticensis' is a less uniform collection in its style and its treatment of the subject-matter. Each Life reflects the background and interests of its original composers to a greater degree in this collection.

Professor Sharpe's method of comparing a Life within one of the collections with a text of the same Life that is independent of the collection has very profound implications for the future study of the individual Lives. If the relationship between the three great collections which he has worked out on the basis of that comparison is accepted, it will make possible for the first time a proper survey of the Irish hagiography of the later middle ages.[133]

[133] See now, however, Pádraig Ó Riain, 'Codex Salmanticensis: a provenance *inter Anglos* or *inter Hibernos?*' in Toby Barnard, Dáibhí Ó Cróinín, and Katharine Simms (ed.), '*A miracle of learning*': *essays in honour of William O'Sullivan* (Aldershot, 1998), pp 91–100, and William O'Sullivan, 'A Waterford origin for the *Codex Salmanticensis*' in *Decies*, liv (1998), pp 17–24.

# BIBLIOGRAPHY

DÁIBHÍ Ó CRÓINÍN, F. J. BYRNE, AND PETER HARBISON

## INTRODUCTION

The compilation of a bibliography for this volume has presented peculiar difficulties, which have led to important departures from the standard bibliographical plan of the *New history*. The volume covers by far the longest period of any in the series, stretching from the first emergence of the island as a physical entity to the coming of the Anglo-Normans. Moreover, this period (more properly a group of periods) has long attracted interest as the source of fundamental traditions in Irish culture, and has been for over a century the subject of much scholarly activity in several disciplines: archaeology, genealogical and hagiographical studies, languages and literature, toponymy, numismatics, palaeography, and the visual arts. In recent decades work in these fields, as well as in others (notably social and economic history), has intensified and now involves an increasing number of scholars.

Our initial attempts at a bibliography of the period, therefore, though by no means fully comprehensive, produced a compilation nearly three times larger than any other bibliography in the *New history*, which would in itself have formed a volume of several hundred pages. Reducing it to a practicable size has entailed drastic expedients. Emphasis has been placed on section I, 'bibliographies and guides': the inclusion of published lists of the writings of such important and prolific scholars as Bieler, Carney, MacNeill, O'Kelly, and Thurneysen, has largely avoided the need to mention individual items from their work. A list of manuscript repositories has not been included, as the detailed coverage of manuscripts in sections II and III makes it less necessary. Our main economy of space, however, has been made by excluding works listed in recently published bibliographies of special subjects, such as those of Fergus Kelly on the laws, Michael Lapidge and Richard Sharpe on Celtic-Latin literature, John Waddell on prehistoric archaeology, and Martin Werner on insular art, and the bibliographies in books by Nancy Edwards and Dáibhí Ó Cróinín. Where this has been done, the reader is directed to these bibliographies by headnotes to the sections affected. Many older publications have been excluded, though some, of particular importance in the development of their area of study, are retained. In compensation, we have tried to ensure that all major work published since the appearance of these bibliographies, and up to the end of the year 2000, has been added. We have included some sources cited in the footnotes of this volume (itself the most heavily footnoted of the series), but not all. The notes to individual chapters, therefore, give further guidance to reading in those areas. Where a composite work, considered as a whole, merits entry under a particular heading, we have not entered its constituent articles separately, although exceptions have been made for articles deserving special attention.

We are grateful to the contributors of this volume, and to other scholars in several fields, for their advice and suggestions.

# CONTENTS

# I  BIBLIOGRAPHIES AND GUIDES

Ainsworth, John A. Manuscript collections in private keeping: reports in National Library of Ireland. In *Anal. Hib.*, no. 32 (1985), pp 27–33.

Andrews, J. H. Ireland in maps: a bibliographical postscript. In *Ir. Geography*, iv (1962), pp 234–43.

*Archaeological bibliography for Great Britain and Ireland, 1968.* London, 1970.

Baumgarten, Rolf. *Bibliography of Irish linguistics and literature 1942–71.* Dublin, 1986.

Baxter, J. H.; Johnson, C.; and Willard, J. F. An index of British and Irish Latin writers, 400–1520. In *Bulletin du Cange*, vii (1932), pp 110–219.

Best, Richard I. Bibliography of the publications of Whitley Stokes. In *Z.C.P.*, viii (1912), pp 351–406.

—— *Bibliography of Irish philology and of printed literature to 1912.* Dublin, 1913. 2nd reprint (with augmented indexes). Dublin, 1992.

—— Bibliography of the publications of Kuno Meyer. In *Z.C.P.*, xv (1925), pp 1–65.

—— *Bibliography of Irish philology and manuscript literature.* Dublin, 1942.

Bhreathnach, Edel. *Tara: a select bibliography*. Dublin, 1995. (Discovery Programme Reports, 3.)

Bieler, Ludwig. Patrician studies in the *Irish Ecclesiastical Record*. In *I.E.R.*, 5th ser., cii (1964), pp 359–66.

BIELER. O'Meara, John J., and Naumann, Bernd. Bibliography Ludwig Bieler. In id. (ed.), *Latin script and letters A.D. 400–900: Festschrift presented to Ludwig Bieler on the occasion of his 70th birthday* (Leyden, 1976), pp 1–18.

BINCHY. Baumgarten, Rolf. Professor D. A. Binchy: a bibliography. In *Peritia*, v (1986), pp 468–77.

Bollandiani, Socii. *Bibliotheca hagiographica latina antiquae et mediae aetatis.* 2 vols. Brussels, 1898–1901. Supplement: *Subsidia hagiographica, 12.* Brussels, 1911.

Bonser, Wilfrid. *An Anglo-Saxon and Celtic bibliography (450–1087).* 2 vols. Oxford, 1957.

Brady, Anna. *Women in Ireland: an annotated bibliography.* New York, 1988. (Bibliographies in Women's Studies, 6.)

Brennan, Mary. A bibliography of publications in the field of Eriugenian studies 1800–1975. In *Studi Medievali*, 3rd ser., xviii (1977), pp 401–47.

Bromwich, Rachel. *Medieval Celtic literature: a select bibliography.* Cambridge, 1974.

Brunhölzl, Franz. *Geschichte der lateinischen Literatur des Mittelalters.* 3 vols. Munich, 1975–92.

Byrne, F. J. Seventh-century documents. In *I.E.R.*, cviii (1967), pp 164–82. Reprinted in *Proceedings of the Irish Catholic Historical Committee, 1965–7* (1968), pp 5–23.

——Thirty years' work in Irish history (II): Ireland before the Norman invasion. In *I.H.S.*, xvi (1968), pp 1–14. Revised version in T. W. Moody (ed.), *Irish historiography 1936–70* (Dublin, 1971), pp 1–15.

BYRNE. Francis John Byrne: writings. In Smyth, *Seanchas*, pp vii–x.

Cabrol, Fernand, and Leclercq, Henri. *Dictionnaire d'archéologie chrétienne et de liturgie.* 4 vols. Paris, 1907–53.

*The Cambridge history of later Greek and early medieval philosophy.* Cambridge, 1967.

Canning, Joseph. A select bibliography relating to Armagh diocesan history. In *Seanchas Ardmhacha*, xiii (1988), pp 234–38.

Carney, James. De scriptoribus hibernicis. In *Celtica*, i, pt 1 (1946), pp 86–110.

CARNEY. Baumgarten, Rolf. James Carney: a bibliography. In Ó Corráin, Breatnach, & McCone, *Sages, saints, & storytellers*, pp 463–72.

Connolly, Philomena. List of Irish material in the class of Chancery files (Records) (c. 260) Public Record Office, London. In *Anal. Hib.*, no. 31 (1984), pp 1–18.

Cullen, Clara; Mac Keogh, Kay; and Breathnach, Proinsias. Recent geographical literature relating to Ireland. In *Ir. Geography*, xiv (1981), pp 117–25.

Dekkers, Eligius, and Gaar, Aemilius. *Clavis patrum latinorum seu propylaeum ad Corpus Christianorum.* Bruges, 1961.
Lists of editions, MSS, and critical studies of pre-Bedan Christian Latin authors, including Hiberno-Latin writers; reprinted from *Sacris Erudiri*, iii (1961).

DILLON. Baumgarten, Rolf. Myles Dillon (1900–1972), a bibliography. In *Celtica*, xi (1976), pp 1–14.

DOLLEY. Thompson, R. H. The published writings of Michael Dolley, 1944–1983. In M. A. S. Blackburn (ed.), *Anglo-Saxon monetary history* (Leicester, 1986), pp 315–60.

Donahue, Charles. Medieval Celtic literature. In J. H. Fisher (ed.), *The medieval literature of western Europe: a review of research* (New York, 1966), pp 381–98.

Edwards, John. *The Irish language: an annotated bibliography of sociolinguistic publications, 1772–1982.* New York and London, 1983.

ENGLISH. O'Brien, Gearóid. A bibliography of the writings of N. W. English. In Harman Murtagh (ed.), *Irish midland studies: essays in commemoration of N. W. English* (Athlone, 1980), pp 3–4.

ERIUGENA. Sheldon-Williams, I. P. A bibliography of the works of Johannes Scottus Eriugena. In *Journal of Ecclesiastical History*, x (1959–60), pp 198–224.

Esposito, Mario. *Latin learning in medieval Ireland.* Ed. Michael Lapidge. Aldershot, 1988.

——*Irish books and learning in medieval Europe.* Ed. Michael Lapidge. Aldershot, 1990.

Gougaud, Louis. Inventaire des règles monastiques irlandaises. In *Revue Bénédictine*, xxv (1908), pp 167–84, 321–33.

Gougaud, Louis. The remains of ancient Irish monastic libraries. In *Féil-sgríbhinn Eóin Mhic Néill*, pp 319–34.

Gwynn, Aubrey, and Hadcock, R. Neville. *Medieval religious houses: Ireland.* London, 1970.

GWYNN. Martin, F. X. The historical writings of Reverend Professor Aubrey Gwynn, S.J. In J. A. Watt, J. B. Morrall, and F. X. Martin, *Medieval studies presented to Aubrey Gwynn, S.J.* (Dublin, 1961), pp 502–9.

——Historical writings of Aubrey Gwynn: addendum. In Aubrey Gwynn, *The Irish church in the eleventh and twelfth centuries*, ed. Gerard O'Brien (Dublin, 1992), pp xiii–xiv.

Haenel, Gustavus. *Catalogi librorum MSS qui in bibliothecis Galliae, Helvetiae, Belgii, Britanniae M., Hispaniae, Lusitaniae asservantur.* Leipzig, 1830.

Hayes, Richard J. *Manuscript sources for the history of Irish civilisation.* 11 vols. Boston, Mass., 1965.

——*Sources for the history of Irish civilisation: articles in Irish periodicals.* 9 vols. Boston, Mass., 1970.

HEALY. Ireland, Aideen. Pádraig Ó hEailidhe/Patrick Healy: published and unpublished work. In Conleth Manning (ed.), *Dublin and beyond the Pale* (Bray, 1998), pp xiii–xv.

HENNIG. Severus, Emmanuel von, O.S.B. Bibliographie Dr.Phil. Dr.Phil.h.c. John Hennig 1932–1970. In *Archiv für Liturgiewissenschaft*, xiii (1971), pp 141–71; xix (1978), pp 98–105.

Updated by Angelus A. Häussling, O.S.B., ibid., xxviii, no. 2 (1986), pp 235–46.

HENRY. Richardson, Hilary. Bibliography of Dr Françoise Henry. In *Studies*, lxiv (1975), pp 313–25. Reprinted, with additions, in Françoise Henry, *Studies in early Christian and medieval Irish art, iii: architecture and sculpture* (London, 1985).

Herren, Michael. Celtic-Latin bibliography. In *Peritia*, v (1986), pp 422–6.

Hughes, Kathleen. *Early Christian Ireland: an introduction to the sources.* London, 1972.

HUGHES. Dumville, David N. Bibliography of the publications of Kathleen Hughes. In Whitelock, McKitterick, & Dumville, *Ire. in early med. Europe*, pp 13–18.

HUNT. Harbison, Peter. Published work of John Hunt. In *N. Munster Antiq. Jn.*, xx (1978), pp 81–3.

Kelly, Fergus. *A guide to early Irish law.* Dublin, 1988.

Bibliography of works on Irish law, pp 287–95.

——Early Irish law: the present state of research. In *Études Celt.*, xxix (1992), pp 15–22.

Kelly, Joseph. A catalogue of early medieval Hiberno-Latin biblical commentaries. In *Traditio*, xliv (1988), pp 537–71; xlv (1990), pp 393–434.

Supersedes his earlier 'Bibliography of Hiberno-Latin biblical texts' in Martin McNamara (ed.), *Biblical studies: the medieval Irish contribution* (Proceedings of the Irish Biblical Association, 1; Dublin, 1976), pp 161–4.

Kenney, James F. *The sources for the early history of Ireland, an introduction and guide, i: ecclesiastical.* New York, 1929. 2nd revised ed. by Ludwig Bieler. New York, 1966.

Ker, N. R. *Medieval libraries of Great Britain.* Oxford, 1941. 2nd ed. 1964. Supplement, Oxford, 1987.

Lapidge, Michael, and Sharpe, Richard. *A bibliography of Celtic-Latin literature 400–1200.* Dublin, 1985.

Lavell, C. *Handbook for British and Irish archaeology: sources and resources.* Edinburgh, 1998.

LEASK. Harold G. Leask: list of published works. In *R.S.A.I. Jn.*, xcvi (1966), pp 3–6.

Lester, Dee Gee. *Irish research: a guide to collections in North America, Ireland and Great Britain.* New York, 1987 (Bibliographies and Indexes in World History, 9).

Levison, Wilhelm. *Conspectus codicum hagiographicorum. Descriptio codicum* (M.G.H., Scriptores Rerum Merovingicarum, vii; Hanover, 1920), pp 551–706.

*Lexikon des Mittelalters.* Munich, 1977–98.

MACALISTER. Brennan, Mary Lou. Robert Alexander Stewart Macalister (1871–1950): a bibliography of his published works. In *R.S.A.I. Jn.*, ciii (1973), pp 167–76.

Additional items, compiled by Siobhán de hÓir, in *R.S.A.I. Jn.*, cxxiii (1993), p. 170.

McLaughlin, Joseph. Early Irish church history: a bibliography. In *Seanchas Ardmhacha*, xiv, no. 2 (1992), pp 236–42.

MACNEILL. Martin, F. X. The published writings of Eoin MacNeill. In F. X. Martin and F. J. Byrne, *The scholar revolutionary* (Shannon, 1973), pp 325–53.

Mac Niocaill, Gearóid. Gaelic Ireland to 1603. In Joseph Lee (ed.), *Irish historiography 1970–79* (Cork, 1981), pp 1–12.

Manitius, Max. *Geschichte der lateinischen Literatur des Mittelalters.* 3 vols. Munich, 1911–31.

Martin, F. X. Bibliography of Patrician literature. In Eoin MacNeill, *Saint Patrick* (2nd ed., ed. John Ryan), pp 221–4.

MOLONEY. de Nais, Roisín. Published work of the late Monsignor Michael Moloney. In Rynne, *N. Munster studies*, pp 5–7.

Moody, T. W.; Martin, F. X.; and Byrne, F. J. (ed.). *A chronology of Irish history to 1976: a companion to Irish history, part i.* Oxford, 1982. (A New History of Ireland, viii.)

——————*Maps, genealogies, lists: a companion to Irish history, part ii.* Oxford, 1984. (A New History of Ireland, ix.)

Ó Corráin, Donnchadh. A handlist of publications on early Irish history. In *Hist. Studies*, x (1976), pp 172–303.

ó HÉALAIDHE. See HEALY.

Ohlgren, Thomas H. *Insular and Anglo-Saxon illuminated manuscripts: an iconographic catalogue* c.A.D. *625 to 1100.* New York and London, 1986.

O'KELLY. Davis, Helen Moloney. Published work of Professor [M. J.] O'Kelly. In Ó Corráin, *Ir. antiquity*, pp 343–50.

O'Reilly, Edward. *A chronological account of nearly four hundred Irish writers with a descriptive catalogue of their works.* Transactions of the Iberno-Celtic Society, Dublin, 1821. Reprint with introduction by Gearóid S. Mac Eoin. Shannon, 1970.

Pender, Seamus. A guide to Irish genealogical collections. In *Anal. Hib.*, no. 7 (1935).

RAFTERY. The published works of Joseph Raftery. In Michael Ryan (ed.), *Irish antiquities: essays in memory of Joseph Raftery* (Bray, 1998), pp vii–xii.

REEVES. Garstin, John R. *Bibliography of the works of William Reeves, D.D.* Dublin, 1893.
    Separate print from Lady Ferguson, *Life of the Right Rev. William Reeves, D.D.* (Dublin, 1893), pp 196–206.

*Repertorium fontium historiae medii aevi.* . . . 8 vols. Rome, 1962–72. In progress.
    *Additamenta I: series collectionum continuata et aucta.* . . . Rome, 1977. (Istituto Storico Italiano per il Medio Evo.)

ROE. Haworth, Richard. The published works of Helen M. Roe. In Rynne, *Figures from the past*, pp 19–26.

Schneiders, Marc, and Veelenturf, Kees. *Celtic studies in the Netherlands: a bibliography.* Dublin, 1992.

Sharpe, Richard. *Handlist of Latin writers of Ireland and Britain, to A.D. 1541.* Turnhout, 1997.

Sigurdsson, Gisli. *Gaelic influence in Iceland: historical and literary contacts: a survey of research.* Reykjavik, 1988.

THURNEYSEN. Heiermeier, Anna. Bibliographie der wissenschaftlichen Veröffentlichungen Rudolf Thurneysens. In *Schriftenreihe der 'Deutschen Gesellschaft für keltischen Studien'*, x (1942).

Tyrell, J. G. Recent geographical literature relating to Ireland. In *Ir. Geography*, xv (1982), pp 125–9.

Waddell, John. *The prehistoric archaeology of Ireland.* Galway, 1998.
    Bibliography, pp 378–408.

Wallace, Patrick F. Dublin 840–1300: an archaeological bibliography. In id. (ed.), *Miscellanea I* (Medieval Dublin Excavations 1962–81, ser. B, ii; Dublin, 1988), pp 1–6.

WARREN. Flanagan, Marie-Therese. The writings of W. L. Warren. In *Peritia*, x (1996), pp 385–8.

Watts, Gareth O. *Bibliotheca Celtica: a register of publications relating to Wales and the Celtic peoples and languages.* National Library of Wales. Aberystwyth, 1974.
    Published annually, 1910–28; new ser. 1929–52; 3rd ser. 1953–  .

Werner, Martin. *Insular art: an annotated bibliography* [to 1979]. Boston, 1980.

Writings on Irish history, 1936–  . In progress. Lists for 1936–78 published annually in *I.H.S.*, 1938–79. Lists for 1979–83 (ed. R. V. Comerford) circulated in microfiche and typescript, 1982–5. Subsequent lists published as booklets issued with *I.H.S.*: *1984*, ed. J. R. Hill (1986); *1985–7*, ed. Clara Cullen (1987–91); *1988–94*, ed. Sarah Ward-Perkins (1994–9).

## II MANUSCRIPT SOURCES

### A GENERAL

As a general rule, items that appear in Martin Werner, *Insular art: an annotated bibliography* (Boston, 1980) are not listed below.

Alexander, J. J. G. *Insular manuscripts, sixth to ninth century: a survey of manuscripts illustrated in the British Isles, i.* London, 1978.

Brown, Michelle P. Embodying exegesis: depicting the evangelists in 'insular' manuscripts. In A. M. Luiselli Fada and É. Ó Carragáin (ed.), *Le isole britanniche e Roma in età Romanobarbarica* (Biblioteca di cultura Romanobarbarica, 1; Rome, 1998), pp 109–27.

Cronin, James. The evangelist symbols as pictorial exegesis. In Bourke, *Isles of the north*, pp 111–17.

Doan, James E. Mediterranean influences on insular manuscript illumination. In John T. Koch and Jean Rittmueller (ed.), *Proceedings of the Harvard Celtic Colloquium*, ii (1982), pp 31–8.

Dodwell, C. R. *The pictorial arts of the west, 800–1200.* New Haven and London, 1993.

Edwards, Nancy. 11th-century Welsh illuminated manuscripts: the nature of the Irish connection. In Bourke, *Isles of the north*, pp 147–55.

Farr, Carol. History and mnemonic in insular gospel book decoration. In Bourke, *Isles of the north*, pp 137–45.

Guilmain, Jacques. An analysis of some ornamental patterns in Hiberno–Saxon manuscript illumination in relation to their Mediterranean origins. In Spearman & Higgitt, *Age of migrating ideas*, pp 92–103.

Haseloff, Günther. Die insulare Buchmalerei. In Heinrich Beck, Herbert Jankuhn, Kurt Ranke, and Reinhard Wenskus (ed.), *Reallexikon der germanischen Altertumskunde* (Berlin, 1979), iv, 74–85.

——Irische Handschriften des 7. und frühen 8. Jahrhunderts. In Erichsen & Brockhoff, *Kilian*, pp 93–106.

Henderson, George. *From Durrow to Kells: the insular gospel-books, 650–800.* London, 1987.

Henry, Françoise. Remarks on the decoration of three Irish psalters. In *R.I.A. Proc.*, lxi (1960), sect. C, pp 23–40.

——*Studies in early Christian and medieval Irish art, ii: manuscript illumination.* London, 1984.

Marx, Susanne. Studies in insular animal ornament in late 7th-and 8th-century manuscripts. In Bourke, *Isles of the north*, pp 105–10.

——The miserable beasts—animal art in the Gospels of Lindisfarne, Lichfield and St Gallen. In *Peritia*, ix (1995), pp 234–45.

Meehan, Bernard. Irish manuscripts in the early middle ages. In Michael Ryan (ed.), *Treasures of Ireland* (Dublin, 1983), pp 48–55.

Mersmann, Wiltrud. Orientalische Einflüsse auf die insulare Kunst im Zeitalter des hl. Virgil. In Dopsch & Juffinger, *Virgil von Salzburg*, pp 216–28.

Nees, Lawrence. Ultán the scribe. In *Anglo-Saxon England*, xxii (1993), pp 127–46.

Netzer, Nancy. Willibrord's scriptorium at Echternach and its relationship to Ireland and Lindisfarne. In Gerald Bonner, David Rollason, and Clare Stancliffe (ed.), *St Cuthbert, his cult, and his community to A.D. 1200* (Woodbridge, 1989), pp 203–12.

Neuman de Vegvar, Carol L. *The Northumbrian renaissance: a study in the transmission of style.* Selinsgrove, 1987.

Nordenfalk, Carl. Book illumination. In André Grabar and Carl Nordenfalk, *Early medieval painting from the fourth to the eleventh century* (Lausanne, 1957), pp 89–218.

—— One hundred and fifty years of varying views on the early insular gospel books. In Ryan, *Ire. & insular art*, pp 1–6.

Ó Cróinín, Dáibhí. Is the Augsburg gospel-codex a Northumbrian manuscript? In G. Bonner, D. Rollason, and C. Stancliffe (ed.), *St Cuthbert, his cult and his community to A.D. 1200* (Woodbridge, 1989), pp 189–201.

O'Reilly, Jennifer. Patristic and insular traditions of the evangelists: exegesis and iconography. In A. M. Luiselli Fada and É. Ó Carragáin (ed.), *Le isole britanniche e Roma in età Romanobarbarica* (Biblioteca di cultura Romanobarbarica, 1; Rome, 1998), pp 49–94.

O'Sullivan, William. A finding list of Sir James Ware's manuscripts. In *R.I.A. Proc.*, xcvii (1997), sect. C, pp 69–99.

—— The Slane manuscript of the Annals of the Four Masters. In *Ríocht na Midhe*, x (1999), pp 78–85.

—— The manuscript collection of Dubhaltach Mac Fhirbhisigh. In Smyth, *Seanchas*, pp 439–47.

Pirotte, Emmanuelle. Ornament and script in early medieval insular and continental manuscripts. In Hourihane, *From Ire. coming*, pp 277–88.

Powell, Roger. The Book of Kells, the Book of Durrow: comments on the vellum, the make-up and other aspects. In *Scriptorium*, x (1956), pp 3–21.

Rickert, Margaret. *Painting in Britain: the middle ages*. Harmondsworth, 1954.

Simms, G. O. *Irish illuminated manuscripts*. Dublin, 1985. (Irish Heritage Series, xxix.)

—— Early Christian manuscripts. In *Treasures of the Library, T.C.D.* (Dublin, 1986), pp 38–56.

Spilling, Herrad. Irische Handschriftenüberlieferung in Fulda, Mainz und Würzburg. In Löwe, *Die Iren*, i, 876–902.

Stalley, Roger. The Book of Durrow and the Book of Kells. In *Actes du Colloque Littérature et Arts Visuels en Irlande* (Publications de la Société Française d'Études Irlandaises; Rennes, 1982), pp 13–20.

Stevick, Robert D. The Echternach Gospels' evangelist-symbol pages: forms from the 'true measure of geometry'. In *Peritia*, v (1986), pp 284–308.

—— *The earliest Irish and English book arts: visual and poetic forms before A.D. 1000*. Philadelphia, 1994.

Sweeney, James Johnson. *Miniatures irlandaises/ Irish illuminated manuscripts/ Irische Miniaturen/ Miniaturas Irlandesas*. Lausanne and Paris, 1970.

Wieder, Joachim. Betrachtungen zur irisch–angelsächsischen Buchmalerei: Forschungsprobleme und Forschungsergebnisse. In Otfried Weber (ed.), *Bibliothek und Buch in Geschichte und Gegenwart: Festgabe für Friedrich Adolf Schmidt-Künsemüller zum 65. Geburtstag am 30. Dez. 1975* (Munich, 1976), pp 13–44.

Wright, David H. Insular contributions to early Carolingian manuscript illumination. In A. A. Schmid (ed.), *Riforma religiosa e arti nell' epoca Carolingia* (Atti del XXIV Congresso Internazionale di Storia dell' Arte; Bologna, 1983), pp 89–91.

Youngs, Susan. Medium and motif: polychrome enamelling and early manuscript decoration in insular art. In Bourke, *Isles of the north*, pp 37–47.

## B INDIVIDUAL

### *1 The Book of Armagh*

Bieler, Ludwig. The Book of Armagh. In *Great books of Ireland* (Thomas Davis Lectures; Dublin, 1967), pp 51–63.

Meehan, Bernard. 'A melody of curves across the page': art and calligraphy in the Book of Armagh. In *Irish Arts Review Yearbook*, xiv (1998), pp 90–101.

### *2 The Cathach*

Herity, Michael. The return of the Cathach to Ireland: conflicting accounts of the repatriation of the Cathach from the Continent. In Smyth, *Seanchas*, pp 454–64.

Lawlor, H. J. The Cathach of St Columba. In *R.I.A. Proc.*, xxxiii (1916), sect. C, pp 241–443.

Ó Cochláin, R. S. The Cathach, battle book of the O'Donnells. In *Ir. Sword*, viii (1968), pp 157–77.

Simms, George Otto. *The psalms in the days of Saint Columba*. Dublin, 1963.

### *3 The Book of Durrow*

[Bruce-Mitford, Rupert.] The third great codex: the Book of Durrow's place in the Celtic world. In *Times Literary Supplement*, 22 Feb. 1963.

de Paor, Liam. The Book of Durrow. In *Great books of Ireland* (Thomas Davis Lectures; Dublin, 1967), pp 1–13.

Elbern, Victor H. Die Dreifaltigkeitsminiatur im Book of Durrow: eine Studie zur unfigürlichen Ikonographie im frühen Mittelalter. In *Wallraf-Richartz-Jahrbuch*, xvii (1955), pp 7–42.

Laing, Lloyd. The provenance of the Book of Durrow. In *Scottish Archaeological Review*, ix/x (1995), pp 115–24.

Meehan, Bernard. *The Book of Durrow: a medieval masterpiece at Trinity College, Dublin*. Dublin, 1996.

Rösner, Corinna. *Das Book of Durrow im Spiegel der Forschung zur hiberno-sächsischen Kunst*. Munich, 1985. (Schriften aus dem Institut für Kunstgeschichte der Univerität München, iii.)

Roth, Uta. Zur Datierung des Book of Durrow. In Otto-Herman Frey, Helmut Roth, and Claus Dobiat (ed.), *Gedenkschrift für Gero von Merhart zum 100. Geburtstag* (Marburger Studien zur Vor-und Frühgeschichte, vii; Marburg, 1986), pp 277–92.

——Early insular manuscripts: ornament and archaeology, with special reference to the dating of the Book of Durrow. In Ryan, *Ire. & insular art*, pp 23–9.

Shaw, Francis. Comments on the 'editio princeps' of the Book of Durrow. In *Éigse*, x (1963), pp 300–04.

Stevick, Robert D. The shapes of the Book of Durrow Evangelist-symbol pages. In *The Art Bulletin*, lxviii (1986), pp 182–94.

Werner, Martin. The four Evangelist symbols page in the Book of Durrow. In *Gesta*, viii (1969), pp 3–17.

——The Durrow four Evangelist symbols page once again. In *Gesta*, xx, no. 1 (1981), pp 23–33.

——The cross-carpet page in the Book of Durrow: the cult of the True Cross, Adomnan, and Iona. In *The Art Bulletin*, lxxii (1990), pp 174–223.

——The Book of Durrow and the question of programme. In *Anglo-Saxon England*, xxvi (1997), pp 23–39.

### 4   The Book of Kells

Battersby, William. *The Book of Kells*. Navan, 1995.

Bourke, Cormac. The Book of Kells: new light on the temptation scene. In Hourihane, *From Ire. coming*, pp 49–59.

Brown, Peter. *The Book of Kells: forty-eight pages and details in colour from the manuscript in Trinity College, Dublin, selected and introduced by Peter Brown*. London and New York, 1980.

Brown, T. Julian. *Northumbria and the Book of Kells*. Jarrow, 1972. (Jarrow Lecture 1971.) Reprinted in *Anglo-Saxon England*, i (1972), pp 219–46, and in Janet Bateley, Michelle P. Brown, and Jane Roberts (ed.), *A palaeographer's view: selected papers of Julian Brown* (London, 1993), pp 97–124.

de Paor, Liam. The world of the Book of Kells. In idem, *Ireland and early Europe* (Dublin, 1997), pp 147–59.

Farr, Carol. Liturgical influences on the decoration of the Book of Kells. In Catherine Karkov and Robert Farrell (ed.), *Studies in insular art and archaeology* (American Early Medieval Studies, i; Oxford, Ohio, 1991), pp 127–41.

——The Celtic hero and the Arrest scene in the Book of Kells. In Susan J. Ridyard and Robert G. Benson (ed.), *Minorities and barbarians in medieval life and thought* (Sewanee Mediaeval Studies, vii; Sewanee, Tenn., 1996), pp 235–48.

—— *The Book of Kells: its function and audience*. London and Toronto, 1997.

Friend, A. M. The canon tables of the Book of Kells. In Wilhelm R. W. Koehler (ed.), *Medieval studies in memory of Arthur Kingsley Porter* (Cambridge, Mass., 1939), ii, 611–41.

Guilmain, Jacques. The forgotten early medieval artist. In *Art Journal*, xxv, no. 1 (1965), pp 33–42.

Harbison, Peter. Three miniatures in the Book of Kells. In *R.I.A. Proc.*, lxxxv (1985), sect. C, pp 181–94.

Henderson, Isabel. Pictish art and the Book of Kells. In Whitelock, McKitterick, & Dumville, *Ire. in early med. Europe*, pp 79–105.

——The Book of Kells and the snake-boss motif on Pictish cross-slabs and the Iona crosses. In Ryan, *Ire. & insular art*, pp 56–65.

——Variations on an old theme: panelled zoomorphic ornament on Pictish sculpture at Nigg, Easter Ross, and St Andrews, Fife, and in the Book of Kells. In Karkov, Ryan, & Farrell, *Insular tradition*, pp 143–66.

Henry, Françoise. *The Book of Kells: reproductions from the manuscript in Trinity College, Dublin, with a study of the manuscript by Françoise Henry*. London and New York, 1974.

Lewis, Suzanne. Sacred calligraphy: the Chi Ro page in the Book of Kells. In *Traditio*, xxxvi (1980), pp 139–59.

Luce, A. A. The Book of Kells and the Gospels of Lindisfarne: a comparison. In *Hermathena*, lxxix (1952), pp 61–74; lxxx (1952), pp 12–25.

MacLean, Douglas. The Keills Cross in Knapdale, the Iona school and the Book of Kells. In John Higgitt (ed.), *Early medieval sculpture in Britain and Ireland* (Oxford, 1986), pp 175–97.

Meehan, Bernard. *The Book of Kells*. London, 1994.

—— The Book of Kells and the Corbie Psalter. In Toby Barnard, Dáibhí Ó Cróinín, and Katharine Simms (ed.), *'A miracle of learning': studies in manuscripts and Irish learning. Essays in honour of William O'Sullivan* (Aldershot, 1998), pp 29–39.

Meyvaert, Paul. The Book of Kells and Iona. In *The Art Bulletin*, lxxi (1989), pp 6–19.

Nordenfalk, Carl. The Book of Kells. In *Lexikon des Mittelalters*, ii (1981), col. 440.

—— Katz und Maus und andere Tiere im Book of Kells. In Helmuth Roth (ed.), *Zum Problem der Deutung frühmittelalterlicher Bildinhalte* (Veröffentlichungen des Vorgeschichtlichen Seminars der Philipps-Universität Marburg a. d. Lahn, Sonderband iv; Sigmaringen, 1986), pp 211–19.

O'Mahony, Felicity (ed.). *The Book of Kells: proceedings of a conference at Trinity College, Dublin, 6–9 September 1992*. Dublin and Aldershot, 1994.

O'Reilly, Jennifer. The Book of Kells, fol. 114r: a mystery revealed yet concealed. In Spearman & Higgitt, *Age of migrating ideas*, pp 106–15.

O'Sullivan, William. The Book of Kells. In *Great books of Ireland* (Thomas Davis Lectures; Dublin, 1967), pp 14–25.

Simms, George Otto. *Leaves from the Book of Kells, the great gospel-book of Colm-cille*. Dublin, 1962.

—— *Exploring the Book of Kells*. Dublin, 1988.

Werckmeister, O. K. Die Bedeutung der 'Chi' Initialseite im Book of Kells. In Kurt Böhner and others (ed.), *Das erste Jahrtausend: Kultur und Kunst im werdenden Abendland an Rhein und Ruhr* (2 vols, Düsseldorf, 1964), ii, 687–710.

Werner, Martin. The *Madonna and Child* miniature in the Book of Kells. In *The Art Bulletin*, liv (1972), pp 1–23, 129–39.

—— Three works on the Book of Kells. In *Peritia*, xi (1997), pp 250–326.

Whitfield, Niamh. Brooch or cross? The lozenge on the shoulder of the Virgin in the Book of Kells. In *Archaeology Ireland*, x, no. 1 (1996), pp 20–23.

## 5 The Book of Mulling

Lawlor, H. J. *Chapters on the Book of Mulling*. Edinburgh, 1897.

Nees, Lawrence. The colophon drawing in the Book of Mulling: a supposed Irish monastery plan and the tradition of terminal illustration in early medieval manuscripts. In *Camb. Med. Celt. Studies*, v (summer 1983), pp 67–91.

Stevick, Robert D. The plan of the Evangelist portrait pages in the *Book of Mulling*. In *R.S.A.I. Jn.*, cxxi (1991), pp 27–44.

## 6   *The St Gall manuscripts*

Duft, Johannes. Irische Handschriftenüberlieferung in St Gallen. In Löwe, *Die Iren*, ii, 916–37.

Micheli, Geneviève L. Recherches sur les manuscrits irlandais décorés de Saint-Gall et de Reichenau. In *Revue Archéologique*, 6th ser., vii (1936), pp 188–223; viii (1936), pp 54–79.

Nees, Lawrence. The Irish manuscripts at St Gall and their Continental affiliations. In James C. King (ed.), *Sangallensia in Washington: the arts and letters in medieval and baroque St Gall viewed from the late twentieth century* (New York, 1993), pp 95–132, 314–24.

Ochsenbein, Peter; Schmuki, Carl; and von Euw, Anton. *Irische Buchkunst: die irischen Handschriften der Stiftsbibliothek St Gallen und das Faksimile des Book of Kells*. St Gallen, 1990.

Stevick, Robert D. A geometer's art: the full-page illuminations in St Gallen Stiftsbibliothek Cod. Sang. 51, an insular gospel book of the VIIIth century. In *Scriptorium*, xliv, no. 2 (1990), pp 161–92.

## 7   *The Stowe Missal*

Byrne, F. J. The Stowe Missal. In *Great books of Ireland* (Thomas Davis Lectures; Dublin, 1967), pp 38–50.

Gwynn, Edward. The Stowe Missal. In *Irish Church Quarterly*, ix (1916), pp 119–33.

Mac Carthy, Bartholomew. On the Stowe Missal. In *R.I.A. Trans.*, xxvii (1877–86), pp 135–268.

O'Rahilly, T. F. The history of the Stowe missal. In *Ériu*, x (1926–8), pp 95–109.

Todd, J. H. On the ancient Irish missal and its silver box, described by Dr O'Conor in his catalogue of the Stowe MSS, and now the property of the earl of Ashburnham. In *R.I.A. Trans.*, xxiii (1856), Antiquities, pp 3–37.

### *Other manuscripts*

Bieler, Ludwig. A Gallican psalter in Irish script: Vaticanus Lat. 12910. In idem, *Ireland and the culture of early medieval Europe*, ed. Richard Sharpe (London, 1987), no. XIX.

Cochrane, Robert. The Garland of Howth. In *R.S.A.I. Jn.*, xxiii (1893), pp 404–7.

Contreni, John J. *Codex Laudunensis 468: a ninth-century guide to Virgil, Sedulius and the liberal arts*. Turnhout, 1984. (Armarium Codicum Insignium, iii.)

Dold, Alban, and Eizenhöfer, Leo (with Wright, David H.). *Das irische Palimpsestsakramentar im Clm 14429 der Staatsbibliothek München*. Beuron, 1964.

Hemphill, Samuel. The Gospels of Mac Regol of Birr; a study in Celtic illumination. In *R.I.A. Proc.*, xxix (1911–12), sect. C, pp 1–10.

O'Reilly, Jennifer. The Hiberno-Latin tradition of the evangelists and the Gospels of Mael Brigte. In *Peritia*, ix (1995), pp 290–309.

O'Sullivan, Anne. The colophon of the Cotton Psalter (Vitellius F XI). In *R.S.A.I. Jn.*, xcvi (1966), pp 179–80.

## III  PRINTED SOURCES

### *A  GENERAL*

#### *1  Manuscripts: facsimiles and diplomatic editions*

Alton, E. H.; Meyer, P.; and Simms, G. O. *Evangeliorum quattuor Codex Cenannensis.* 3 vols. Berne, 1950–51.

Atkinson, Robert. *The Book of Leinster.* Lithographic facsimile by Joseph O'Longan. Dublin, 1880.

—— *The Book of Ballymote.* Photographic facsimile. Dublin, 1887.

—— *The Yellow Book of Lecan.* Collotype facsimile. Dublin, 1896.

Bernard, J. H., and Atkinson, Robert. *The Irish Liber Hymnorum.* London, 1898. (Henry Bradshaw Society, xiii, xiv.)

Best, R. I. *The commentary on the psalms with glosses in Old Irish preserved in the Ambrosian Library (MS C 301 inf.).* Collotype facsimile. Dublin, 1936.

—— and Bergin, Osborn. *Lebor na hUidre: Book of the Dun Cow.* Dublin, 1929. Reprinted, 1972, 1992.

—— —— and O'Brien, M. A. *The Book of Leinster, formerly Lebar na Núachongbála,* i. Dublin, 1954.

—— and MacNeill, Eoin. *The Annals of Inisfallen reproduced in facsimile from the original manuscript (Rawl. B 503) in the Bodleian Library, Oxford.* Dublin and London, 1933.

—— and O'Brien, M. A. *The Book of Leinster, formerly Lebar na Núachongbála.* Vols ii–v. Dublin, 1956–67.

For vol. vi see O'Sullivan, Anne.

—— and Thurneysen, Rudolf. *Facsimiles in collotype of Irish manuscripts 1: the oldest fragments of the Senchas Már from MS H.2.15 in the library of Trinity College.* Dublin, 1931.

Bieler, Ludwig. *Psalterium Graeco-Latinum.* Codex Basiliensis A. vii. 3. Amsterdam, 1960. (Umbrae Codicum Occidentalium, v.)

Buchanan, E. S. *The four gospels from the Irish Codex Harleianus numbered Harley 1023 in the British Museum.* London, 1914.

*Der Codex Boernerianus: der Briefe des Apostels Paulus (Msc. Dresd. A.145b) in Lichtdruck nachgebildet.* Introduction by Alexander Reichardt. Leipzig, 1909.

Duft, Johannes, and Meyer, Peter. *Die irischen Miniaturen der Stiftsbibliothek St Gallen.* St Gall, 1953. English translation, *The Irish miniatures in the abbey library of St Gall.* Berne, Olten, and Lausanne, 1954.

Forbes, G. H. (ed.). *Missale Drummondiense: the ancient Irish missal in the possession of the Baroness Willoughby de Eresby.* Burntisland, 1882.

Fox, Peter (ed.). *The Book of Kells, MS 58, Trinity College Library, Dublin: with commentary.* Lucerne, 1990.

Gilbert, John T., and James, Henry. *Facsimiles of the national manuscripts of Ireland.* 5 pts. London, 1874–84.

——*Leabhar Breac.* Lithographic facsimile by Joseph O'Longan. Dublin, 1876.

Gwynn, Aubrey. The Irish missal of Corpus Christi College, Oxford. In *Studies in Church History,* i (1964), pp 47–68. Reprinted as 'An Irish missal of the eleventh or twelfth century' in Gerard O'Brien (ed.), *The Irish church in the eleventh and twelfth centuries: Aubrey Gwynn S.J.* (Dublin, 1992), pp 17–35.

Gwynn, John. *Liber Ardmachanus: the Book of Armagh.* Dublin, 1913.

Gwynn, E. J. *The Book of Armagh: the Patrician documents.* Collotype facsimile. Dublin, 1937.

Hagen, Hermann. *Augustinus, Beda, Horatius, Ovidius, Servius, alii Codex Bernensis 363.* Leyden, 1897. (Codices Graeci et Latini Photographice Depicti Duce Scatone de Vries, Bibliothecae Leidensis Praefecto, ii.)

Hunt, R. W. *Saint Dunstan's classbook from Glastonbury. (Bodl. Auct. F.4.32).* Amsterdam, 1961. (Umbrae Codicum Occidentalium, iv.)

Kendrick, T. D., and others. *Evangeliorum quattuor Codex Lindisfarnensis.* 2 vols. Lausanne and Freiburg, 1956, 1960.

Lawlor, Hugh Jackson. *The Rosslyn missal: an Irish manuscript in the Advocates' Library, Edinburgh.* London, 1899.

*Lebor na hUidre: Book of the Dun Cow.* Lithographic facsimile by Joseph O'Longan. Dublin, 1870.

Luce, A. A.; Simms, G. O.; Meyer, P.; and Bieler, Ludwig. *Evangeliorum quattuor Codex Durmachensis.* 2 vols. Lausanne and Freiburg, 1960.

Macalister, R. A. S. *The Book of Uí Maine.* Collotype facsimile. Dublin, 1941.

——*The Book of Lismore.* Collotype facsimile. Dublin, 1950.

Meyer, Kuno. *Rawlinson MS B 502—a facsimile edition.* Oxford, 1909.

Mulchrone, Kathleen. *The Book of Lecan.* Collotype facsimile. Dublin, 1937.

Munding, Samuel. *Die Kalendarien von St Gallen aus XXI Handschriften neuntes bis elftes Jahrhundert.* Beuron, 1948. (Texte und Arbeitungen herausgegeben von der Erzabtei Beuron i, 36.)

Ó Cróinín, Dáibhí. *Evangeliarium Epternacense (Universitätsbibl. Augsburg, Cod. I.2.40 2) + Evangelistarium (Erzbischöfliches Priesterseminar St. Peter, Cod. MS 25).* Munich, 1988. (Codices Illuminati Medii Aevi, ix.)

O'Sullivan, Anne. *The Book of Leinster, formerly Lebar na Núachongbála.* Vol. vi. Dublin, 1983.

Stern, L. Chr. *Epistolae beati Pauli glossatae glossa interlineali. Irisch-lateinischer Codex der Würzburger Universitätsbibliothek.* Collotype facsimile. Halle a/S., 1910.

Warner, G. F. *The Stowe Missal: MS D.ii.3 in the Library of the Royal Irish Academy, Dublin.* 2 vols. London, 1906, 1915. (Henry Bradshaw Society, xxxi, xxxii.)

Warren, F. E. *The manuscript Irish missal belonging to the president and fellows of Corpus Christi College, Oxford.* London, 1879.

——*The Antiphonary of Bangor.* 2 vols. London, 1893, 1895. (Henry Bradshaw Society, iv, ix.)

Wilson, H. A. *The Calendar of Willibrord from MS Paris Lat. 10837.* London, 1918. (Henry Bradshaw Society, lv.)

## 2 Texts

Anderson, A. O. *Early sources of Scottish history, A.D. 500–1286.* 2 vols. Edinburgh, 1922.

Bayless, Martha, and Lapidge, Michael. *Collectanea Pseudo-Bedae.* Dublin, 1998. (Script. Lat. Hib., xiv.)

Bergin, O. J.; Best, R. I.; Meyer, Kuno; and O'Keeffe, J. G. *Anecdota from Irish manuscripts,* i–v. Halle, 1907–13.

Bieler, Ludwig. *The Patrician texts in the Book of Armagh.* Dublin, 1979. (Script. Lat. Hib., x.)

Douglas, David C., and Greenaway, George W. *English historical documents, ii: 1042–1189.* London, 1953.

Doyle, Edward Gerard (ed.). *Sedulius Scottus: On Christian rulers and the poems.* Translated with introduction. Binghampton, N.Y., 1983.

Fraser, John; Grosjean, Paul; and O'Keeffe, J. G. *Irish texts.* 5 fascicles. London, 1931–3.

Haddan, A. W., and Stubbs, William. *Councils and ecclesiastical documents relating to Great Britain and Ireland.* 3 vols. Oxford, 1869–78.

Hofman, Rijcklof. *The Sankt Gall Priscian commentary.* 2 vols. Münster, 1996. (Studien und Texte zur Keltologie (hg. Erich Poppe).)

Jackson, Kenneth H. *A Celtic miscellany: translations from the Celtic literature.* London, 1951.

Löfstedt, Bengt. *Ars Laureshamensis (expositio in Donatum maiorem).* Turnhout, 1977. (Grammatici Hibernici Carolini aevi, ii. C.C.C.M., xlA.)

Mac Carthy, Bartholomew. *The Codex Palatino-Vaticanus, No. 830.* Dublin, 1902. (R.I.A. Todd Lecture Series, iii.)

Mac Giolla Léith, Caoimhín. *Oidheadh Chloinne hUisneach: the violent death of the children of Uisneach.* London, 1993. (Irish Texts Society, lvi.)

Matthews, John. *A Celtic reader: selections from Celtic legend, scholarship and story.* London, 1991.

Meyer, Kuno, and Stokes, Whitley. *Archiv für celtische Lexikographie.* 3 vols. Halle a/S, 1898–1907.

Sheehy, Maurice. *Pontificia Hibernica: medieval papal chancery documents concerning Ireland, 640–1261.* 2 vols. Dublin, 1962.

Stokes, Whitley, and Strachan, John. *Thesaurus Palaeohibernicus: a collection of Old-Irish glosses.* 2 vols. Cambridge, 1901–3. Supplement by Whitley Stokes, Halle a/S, 1910. Reprinted, Dublin, 1975.

Thurneysen, Rudolf. *Zu irischen Handschriften und Literaturdenkmälern.* Vols i, ii. Berlin, 1913. (Kgl. Gesellsch. der Wissensch. zu Göttingen. Abh. xiv, no. 3.)

Warren, F. E. *The liturgy and ritual of the Celtic church.* Oxford, 1881. Reprinted with a new introduction by Jane Stevenson. Woodbridge, 1988. (Studies in Celtic History.)

Whitelock, Dorothy. *English historical documents, i:* c. *500–1042.* London, 1955.

Windisch, Ernst, and Stokes, Whitley. *Irische Texte.* 4 vols. Leipzig, 1880–1909.

### 3 Secondary works

Ahlqvist, Anders. Latin grammar and native learning. In Ó Corráin, Breatnach, & McCone, *Sages, saints, & storytellers*, pp 1–6.

Bieler, Ludwig. The classics in Celtic Ireland. In R. R. Bolgar (ed.), *Classical influences on European culture A.D. 500–1500* (Cambridge, 1971), pp 45–9.

Bischoff, Bernhard. *Mittelalterliche Studien*. 3 vols. Stuttgart, 1966–81.

Carney, James. *Studies in early Irish literature and history*. Dublin, 1955.

——The earliest Bran material. In J. J. O'Meara and B. Naumann (ed.), *Latin script and letters* (Leyden, 1976), pp 167–73.

——The history of early Irish literature: the state of research. In Mac Eoin, Ahlqvist, & Ó hAodha, *Proc. 6th Congress*, pp 113–30.

Clancy, Thomas Owen, and Márkus, Gilbert. *Iona: the earliest poetry of a Celtic monastery*. Edinburgh, 1997.

Contreni, John J. *Carolingian learning, masters and manuscripts*. Hampshire, 1992. (Variorum Collected Studies Series.)

Dillon, Myles. *Early Irish literature*. Chicago, 1948.

——Laud Misc. 610. In *Celtica*, v (1960), pp 64–76; vi (1963), pp 135–55.

Dumville, David N. Biblical apocrypha and the early Irish: a preliminary investigation. In *R.I.A. Proc.*, lxxiii (1973), sect. C, pp 299–338.

——The textual history of 'Lebor Bretnach': a preliminary study. In *Éigse*, xvi (1975–7), pp 255–73.

Ford, Patrick K. The blind, the dumb, and the ugly: aspects of poets and their craft in early Ireland and Wales. In *Camb. Med. Celt. Studies*, xix (summer 1990), pp 27–40.

Gillies, William. Heroes and ancestors. In Almqvist, Ó Catháin, & Ó hEalaí, *Heroic process*, pp 57–73.

Hellmann, Siegmund. *Ausgewählte Abhandlungen zur Historiographie und Geistesgeschichte des Mittelalters*. Ed. H. Beumann. Munich, 1961.

Henry, P. L. *Saoithiúlacht na Sean-Ghaeilge*. Dublin, 1978.

——The Celtic literatures in the context of world literature. In Schmidt, *Celts*, pp 145–53.

Jennings, Rachel. A translation of the Tochmarc Treblainne. In *Emania*, xvi (1997), pp 73–8.

Mac Cana, Proinsias. *Celtic mythology*. London, 1970.

——*Fianaigecht* in the pre-Norman period. In Almqvist, Ó Catháin, & Ó hEalaí, *Heroic process*, pp 75–99.

——Early Irish ideology and the concept of unity. In Richard Kearney (ed.), *The Irish mind* (Dublin, 1985), pp 56–78.

——Notes on the combination of prose and verse in early Irish narrative. In Tranter & Tristram, *Early Ir. lit.*, pp 125–48.

McCone, Kim. *Pagan past and Christian present*. Maynooth, 1990. (Maynooth Monographs, iii.)

Mac Eoin, Gearóid. The Celticity of Celtic Ireland. In Schmidt, *Celts*, pp 161–74.

MacKillop, James. *Fionn Mac Cumhaill: Celtic myth in English literature*. Syracuse, N.Y., 1986.

McNamara, Martin. Psalter text and psalter study in the early Irish church (A.D. 600–1200). In *R.I.A. Proc.*, lxxiii (1973), pp 201–98.

—— *The Apocrypha in the Irish church.* Dublin, 1975.

—— *The psalms in the early Irish church.* Sheffield, 2000. (*Journal for the Study of the Old Testament*, Supplement Series 165.)

Nagy, J. F. *The wisdom of the outlaw: the boyhood deeds of Finn in Gaelic narrative tradition.* (Berkeley, Los Angeles, and London, 1985).

Ní Chatháin, Próinséas. Beobachtungen zur irischen und lateinischen Literatur des 8. Jahrhunderts in Irland. In Dopsch & Juffinger, *Virgil von Salzburg*, pp 130–34.

Ó Broin, Tomás. 'Craebruad': the spurious tradition. In *Éigse*, xv (1973), pp 103–13.

—— Lia Fáil: fact and fiction in the tradition. In *Celtica*, xxi (1990), pp 393–401.

Ó Cathasaigh, Tomás. The semantics of 'síd'. In *Éigse*, xvii (1977–8), pp 137–54.

—— Pagan survivals: the evidence of early Irish narrative. In Ní Chatháin & Richter, *Ire. & Europe*, pp 291–310.

—— The concept of the hero in Irish mythology. In Richard Kearney (ed.), *The Irish mind* (Dublin, 1985), pp 79–90.

—— The sister's son in early Irish literature. In *Peritia*, v (1986), pp 128–60.

Ó Coileáin, Seán. The structure of a literary cycle. In *Ériu*, xxv (1974), pp 88–125.

—— Some problems of story and history. In *Ériu*, xxxii (1981), pp 115–36.

—— The saint and the king. In P. de Brún, S. Ó Coileáin, and P. Ó Riain (ed.), *Folia Gadelica* (Cork, 1983) pp 36–46.

Ó Cuív, Brian. Literary creation and Irish historical tradition. In *Brit. Acad. Proc.*, xlix (1963), pp 233–62.

—— The motif of the three-fold death. In *Éigse*, xv (1973), pp 145–50.

—— Medieval Irish scholars and classical Latin literature. In *R.I.A. Proc.*, lxxxi (1981), sect. C, pp 239–48.

Olmsted, Garrett. The Gundestrup version of *Táin Bó Cuailnge*. In *Antiquity*, l (1976), pp 95–103.

O'Loughlin, Thomas. *Teachers and code-breakers: the Latin Genesis tradition, 430–800.* Turnhout, 1998.

Radner, Joan. The significance of the Threefold Death in Celtic tradition. In Ford, *Celtic folklore*, pp 180–200.

Reichl, Karl. Zur Frage des irischen Einflusses auf die altenglische weltliche Dichtung. In Löwe, *Die Iren*, pp 138–70.

Slotkin, Edgar M. Medieval Irish scribes and fixed texts. In *Éigse*, xvii (1978–9), pp 437–50.

Smit, Josef W. *Studies on the language and style of Columbanus the Younger.* Amsterdam, 1971.

Stanford, W. B. Monsters and Odyssean echoes in the early Hiberno-Latin and Irish hymns. In O'Meara & Naumann, *Latin script & letters*, pp 113–20.

Stevenson, Jane. L of the Patrician dossier in the Book of Armagh. In R. McKitterick (ed.), *The uses of literacy in early medieval Europe* (Cambridge, 1990), pp 11–35.

Toner, G. Emain Macha in the literature. In *Emania*, iv (1988), pp 32–5.

Tranter, Stephen N., and Tristram, H. L. C. Die Fragestellung: Problembereich und Spannungsbreite der Medialität im älteren irischen Schrifttum. In Tranter & Tristram, *Early Ir. lit.*, pp 13–38.

Travis, James. *Early Celtic versecraft: origin, development, diffusion.* Ithaca, N.Y., 1973.

Trindade, W. Ann. Irish Gormlaith as a sovereignty figure. In *Études Celt.*, xxiii (1986), pp 143–56.

Wagner, Heinrich. Origins of pagan Irish religion. In *Z.C.P.*, xxxviii (1981), pp 1–28.

—— The Celtic invasions of Ireland and Great Britain. In *Z.C.P.*, xlii (1987), pp 1–40.

Wais, Kurt. Volkssprachliche Erzähler Alt-Irlands im Rahmen der europäischen Literaturgeschichte. In Löwe, *Die Iren*, pp 639–85.

Wasserstein, David. The creation of Adam and the Apocrypha in early Ireland. In *R.I.A. Proc.*, lxxxviii (1988), pp 1–17.

Watson, Alden. The king, the poet and the sacred tree. In *Études Celt.*, xviii (1981), pp 165–80.

Sims-Williams, Patrick. The evidence for vernacular Irish literary influence on early mediaeval Welsh literature. In Whitelock, McKitterick, & Dumville, *Ire. in early med. Europe*, pp 235–57.

Wright, Charles D. Apocryphal lore and insular tradition in St Gall, Stiftsbibliothek MS 908. In Ní Chatháin & Richter, *Ire. & Christendom*, pp 124–45.

—— The Irish 'enumerative style' in Old English homiletic literature, especially Vercelli Homily IX. In *Camb. Med. Celt. Studies*, xviii (winter 1989), pp 27–74.

—— The three 'victories' of the wind: a hibernicism in the *Hisperica Famina*, *Collectanea Bedae*, and the Old English prose *Solomon and Saturn* Pater Noster dialogue. In *Ériu*, xli (1990), pp 13–25.

## B  PARTICULAR

### *1  Inscriptions*

See also below under 'High crosses' (pp 1089–95).

#### *(a) Primary texts*

Barnes, Michael P.; Hagland, Jan Ragnar; and Page, R. I. *The runic inscriptions of viking age Dublin.* Dublin, 1997. (Medieval Dublin Excavations, 1962–81, ser. B, v.)

Kermode, P. M. C. *Manx crosses, or the inscribed and sculptured monuments of the Isle of Man from about the end of the fifth to the beginning of the thirteenth century.* London, 1907.

Lionard, Pádraig. Early Irish grave slabs. In *R.I.A. Proc.*, lxi (1960–61), sect. C, pp 95–169.

Macalister, R. A. S. *The memorial slabs of Clonmacnois, King's County.* Dublin, 1909.

—— (ed.). *Corpus inscriptionum insularum Celticarum.* 2 vols. I.M.C., Dublin, 1945–9.

Nash-Williams, V. E. *The early Christian monuments of Wales.* Cardiff, 1950.

Okasha, Elizabeth. *Corpus of early Christian inscribed stones of south-west Britain.* Leicester, 1993. (Studies in the Early History of Britain.)

Petrie, George. *Christian inscriptions in the Irish language*. Ed. Margaret Stokes. 2 vols. Dublin, 1872, 1878.

*(b) Secondary works*

Brady, C. F. Some observations on the Ogham script. In *Teabhtha*, i (1983), pp 124–33.

Fulford, Michael, Handley, Mark, and Clarke, Amanda. An early date for Ogham: the Silchester Ogham stone rehabilitated. In *Medieval Archaeology*, xliv (2000), pp 1–23.

Harbison, Peter. Regal (and other) patronage in Irish inscriptions of the pre-Norman period. In *U.J.A.*, lviii (1999), pp 43–54.

Higgitt, John. Early medieval inscriptions in Britain and Ireland and their audiences. In David Henry (ed.), *The worm, the germ, and the thorn: Pictish and related studies presented to Isabel Henderson* (Balgavies, 1997), pp 67–78.

Macalister, R. A. S. *Studies in Irish epigraphy*. 3 vols. Dublin, 1897–1907.

McManus, Damian. *A guide to Ogam*. Maynooth, 1991 (Maynooth Monographs, 6).

MacWhite, Eóin. Contributions to a study of Ogam memorial stones. In *Z.C.P.*, xxviii (1960–61), pp 294–308.

Manning, Conleth, and Moore, Fionnbar. An ogham stone from Clonmacnoise. In *Archaeology Ireland*, v, no. 4 (1991), pp 10–11.

Michelli, P. E. The inscriptions on pre-Norman Irish reliquaries. In *R.I.A. Proc.*, xcvi (1996), sect. C, pp 1–48.

Moore, Fionnbarr. Munster ogham stones: siting, context and function. In Monk & Sheehan, *Early med. Munster*, pp 23–32.

Swift, Catherine. *Ogham stones and the earliest Irish Christians*. Maynooth, 1997. (Maynooth Monographs, Series Minor, 2.)

Thomas, Charles. *And shall these mute stones speak? Post-Roman inscriptions in western Britain*. Cardiff, 1994.

Warner, R. B. The Drumconwell ogham and its implications. In *Emania*, viii (1991), pp 43–50.

Sims-Williams, Patrick. *The Celtic inscriptions of Britain: phonology and chronology, c. 400–1200*. Oxford, 2003.

## 2   Annals

*(a) Primary texts*

ab Ithel, John Williams (ed.). *Annales Cambriae*. London, 1860. (Rolls Series.)

Best, R. I. The Leabhar Oiris. *Leabhar Oiris agus annála ar cogthaibh agus ar cathaibh Éireann annso síos* [979–1027]. In *Ériu*, i (1904), pp 74–112.

Broderick, George. *Chronicle of the kings of Mann and the Isles: Recortys reeaghyn Vannin as ny hEllanyn*. Part I. Latin transcription and English translation by George Broderick; Manx translation by Brian Stowell. Edinburgh, 1973.

Gleeson, Dermot, and Mac Airt, Seán (ed.) The Annals of Roscrea. In *R.I.A. Proc.*, lix (1958), sect. C, pp 137–80.

Hennessy, William (ed.) *Chronicum Scotorum: a chronicle of Irish affairs from the earliest times to A.D. 1135, with a supplement 1141–50*. London, 1866. Reprinted, Wiesbaden, 1964.

Hennessy, William (ed.) *The Annals of Loch Cé: a chronicle of Irish affairs, 1014–1590.* 2 vols. London, 1871. Reprinted in reflex facsimile. I.M.C., Dublin, 1939.

——and Mac Carthy, Bartholomew (ed.) *Annála Uladh: Annals of Ulster, otherwise Annála Senait, a chronicle of Irish affairs, 431–1131, 1155–1541.* 4 vols. Dublin, 1887–1901. Vol. i ed. Hennessy, vols ii–iv ed. Mac Carthy.

Jones, Thomas. *Brut y Tywysogion: Peniarth MS 20.* Cardiff, 1941.

——*Brut y Tywysogion: Peniarth MS 20 version; translated with introduction and notes* Cardiff, 1952.

Mac Airt, Seán (ed.). *The Annals of Inisfallen (MS Rawlinson B 503).* Dublin, 1951.

——and Mac Niocaill, Gearóid (ed.). *The Annals of Ulster (to 1131).* Part 1: text and translation. Dublin, 1983.

Mac Niocaill, Gearóid (ed.). Annála gearra as próibhínse Ard Macha. In *Seanchas Ardmhacha*, iii (1958/9), pp 337–40.

Martin Freeman, A. (ed.). The annals in Cotton MS Titus A xxv. In *Rev. Celt.*, xli (1924), pp 301–30; xlii (1925), pp 283–305; xliii (1926), pp 358–84; xliv (1927), pp 336–61.

Morris, John. *Nennius: British history and the Welsh annals.* London and Chichester, 1980. (Arthurian Period Sources, viii.)

Murphy, Denis (ed.). *The Annals of Clonmacnoise, being annals of Ireland from the earliest period to* A.D. *1408, translated into English,* A.D. *1627, by Conell Mageoghegan.* Dublin, 1896. Reprinted, Llanerch, 1993.

O'Donovan, John (ed.). *Annála ríoghachta Éireann: annals of the kingdom of Ireland by the Four Masters, from the earliest period to the year 1616.* 7 vols. Dublin, 1851. Reprinted, New York, 1966. 3rd reprint (with introduction by K. W. Nicholls), Dublin, 1990.

——*Annals of Ireland: three fragments copied from ancient sources by Dubhaltach Mac Firbhisigh.* Dublin, 1860.

Ó hInnse, Séamus (ed.). *Miscellaneous Irish Annals,* A.D. *1114–1437.* Dublin, 1947. Comprises 'Mac Carthaigh's Book' (1114–1437) from N.L.I. G 5–6; Connacht annals (1237–1314) and annals of Inis na Naomh on Lough Ree (1392–1407), both from Rawlinson B 488.

Phillimore, Egerton (ed.). The *Annales Cambriae* and Old-Welsh genealogies from Harleian MS 3859. In *Y Cymmrodor*, ix (1888), pp 141–83.

Radner, Joan (ed.). *Fragmentary annals of Ireland.* Dublin, 1978.

Stokes, Whitley (ed.). The Annals of Tigernach. In *Rev. Celt.*, xvi (1895), pp 374–419; xvii (1896), pp 6–33, 119–263, 337–420; xviii (1897), pp 9–59, 150–97, 267–303. Reprinted, Llanerch, 2 vols, 1993.

*(b) Secondary works*

Brunner, Karl. Auf den Spuren verlorener Traditionen. In *Peritia*, ii (1983), pp 1–22.

Dumville, David. Ulster heroes in the early Irish annals: a caveat. In *Éigse*, xvii (1977), pp 47–54.

——Latin and Irish in the *Annals of Ulster*, A.D. 431–1050. In Whitelock, McKitterick, & Dumville, *Ire. in early med. Europe*, pp 320–44.

——Some aspects of annalistic writing at Canterbury in the eleventh and twelfth centuries. In *Peritia*, ii (1983), pp 23–58.

——On editing and translating medieval Irish chronicles: the Annals of Ulster. In *Camb. Med. Celt. Studies*, x (winter 1985), pp 67–86.

——St Patrick, the *Annales Cambriae*, and St David. In Dumville, *St Patrick*, pp 279–88.

Grabowski, Kathryn, and Dumville, David. *Chronicles and annals of medieval Ireland and Wales*. Woodbridge, 1984.

Harrison, Kenneth. *The framework of Anglo-Saxon history to A.D. 900*. Cambridge, 1976.

——Episodes in the history of Easter cycles in Ireland. In Whitelock, McKitterick, & Dumville, *Ire. in early med. Europe*, pp 307–19.

Jaski, Bart. Additional notes to the Annals of Ulster. In *Ériu*, xlviii (1997), pp 103–52, 428–31.

Leach, R. H. *Cogadh Gaedhel re Gallaibh* and the Annals of Inisfallen. In *N. Munster Antiq. Jn.*, xi (1968), pp 13–21.

McCarthy, Daniel P. The chronology of the Irish annals. In *R.I.A. Proc.*, xcviii (1998), sect. C, pp 203–55.

——The status of the pre-Patrician Irish annals. In *Peritia*, xii (1998), pp 98–152.

MacDonald, Aidan. Notes on terminology in the Annals of Ulster, 650–1050. In *Peritia*, i (1982), pp 329–34.

MacNeill, Eoin. An Irish historical tract dated A.D. 721. In *R.I.A. Proc.*, xxviii (1910), sect. C, pp 123–48.

——The authorship and structure of the Annals of Tigernach. In *Ériu*, vii (1913), pp 30–113.

——On the reconstruction and date of the Laud synchronisms. In *Z.C.P.*, x (1915), pp 81–96.

Macalister, R. A. S. The sources of the Preface to the Annals of Tigernach. In *I.H.S.*, iv, no. 13 (Mar. 1944), pp 38–57.

Mallory, J. P. A provisional checklist of Emain Macha in the annals. In *Emania*, i (1986), pp 24–7.

——A provisional checklist of Cruachain in the annals. In *Emania*, v (1988), pp 24–6.

Maund, K. L. The second obit of St Patrick in the 'Annals of Boyle'. In Dumville, *St Patrick*, pp 35–8.

——Sources of the 'World Chronicle' in the Cottonian Annals. In *Peritia*, xii (1998), pp 153–76.

Miller, Molly. Matriliny by treaty: the Pictish foundation-legend. In Whitelock, McKitterick, & Dumville, *Ire. in early med. Europe*, pp 133–64.

——The chronological structure of the Sixth Age in the Rawlinson fragment of the 'Irish World-Chronicle'. In *Celtica*, xxii (1991), pp 79–111.

Ó Buachalla, Breandán. Annála Ríoghachta Éireann is Foras Feasa ar Éirinn: an comthéacs comhaimseartha. In *Studia Hib.*, xxi–xxiii (1982–3), pp 59–105.

Ó Buachalla, Liam. The construction of the Irish annals, 429–66. In *Cork Hist. Soc. Jn.*, lxiii (1958), pp 103–16.

Ó Buachalla, Liam. Notes on the early Irish annals, 467–550. In *Cork Hist. Soc. Jn.*, lxiv (1959), pp 73–81.

Ó Cróinín, Dáibhí. Early Irish annals from Easter-tables: a case restated. In *Peritia*, ii (1983), pp 74–86.

Ó Cuilleannáin, Cormac. The Dublin Annals of Inisfallen. In S. Pender (ed.), *Féil-sgríbhinn Torna* (Cork, 1947), pp 183–202.

Ó Riain-Raedel, Dagmar. Twelfth- and thirteenth-century Irish annals in Vienna. In *Peritia*, ii (1983), pp 125–34.

Radner, Joan N. Writing history: early Irish historiography and the significance of form. In *Celtica*, xxiii (1999), pp 322–5.

Sanderlin, Sarah. The manuscripts of the Annals of Clonmacnois. In *R.I.A. Proc.*, lxxxii (1982), sect. C, pp 111–23.

Smyth, A. P. The earliest Irish annals: their first contemporary entries, and the earliest centres of recording. In *R.I.A. Proc.*, lxxii (1972), sect. C, pp 1–48.

von den Brincken, Anna-Dorothee. *Studien zur lateinischen Weltchronistik bis in das Zeitalter Ottos von Freising*. Düsseldorf, 1957.

——Marianus Scottus als Universalhistoriker iuxta veritatem evangelii. In Löwe, *Die Iren*, pp 970–1012.

Walsh, Paul. The annals attributed to Tigernach. In *I.H.S.*, ii, no. 6 (Sept. 1940), pp 154–9. Reprinted in Walsh, *Irish men of learning* (Dublin, 1947), pp 219–55.

——The dating of the Irish annals. In *I.H.S.*, ii, no. 8 (Sept. 1941), pp 355–75.

### 3   Genealogies and origin legends

#### (a) Primary texts

Bannerman, John. Senchus Fer nAlban. In *Celtica*, vii (1966), pp 142–62; viii (1968), pp 90–111. Reprinted in idem, *Studies in the history of Dalriada* (Edinburgh, 1974), pp 27–118, with additional material to p. 156.

Boyle, Alexander. The Edinburgh synchronisms of Irish kings. In *Celtica*, ix (1971), pp 169–79.

Meyer, Kuno. The Laud genealogies and tribal histories. In *Z.C.P.*, viii (1912), pp 291–338.

——The Laud synchronisms. In *Z.C.P.*, ix (1913), pp 471–85.

O'Brien, Michael A. *Corpus genealogiarum Hiberniae*, i . Dublin, 1962. Reprinted with introduction by J. V. Kelleher, 1976.

Ó Donnchadha, Tadhg. *Leabhar Cloinne Aodha Buidhe*. Dublin, 1931.

——*An Leabhar Muimhneach*. Dublin, 1940.

O'Donovan, John. *The tribes and customs of Hy-Many, commonly called O'Kelly's country*. Dublin, 1843. New ed., Cork, 1976.

——*The tribes and customs of Hy-Fiachrach, commonly called O'Dowda's country*. Dublin, 1844.

Ó Raithbheartaigh, Toirdhealbhach. *Genealogical tracts*, i. Dublin, 1932.

Ó Riain, Pádraig. *Corpus genealogiarum sanctorum Hiberniae*. Dublin, 1985.

Pender, Séamus (ed.). *Déssi genealogies.* I.M.C., Dublin, 1937.
——(ed.) The O'Clery Book of genealogies. In *Anal. Hib.*, no. 18 (1951).
Walsh, Paul. *Genealogiae regum et sanctorum Hiberniae by the Four Masters.* Dublin, 1918.

*(b) Secondary works*

Byrne, F. J. *Senchas:* the nature of Gaelic historical tradition. In J. G. Barry (ed.), *Hist. Studies,* ix (Belfast, 1974), pp 137–59.
Byrne, Paul F. The ancestry of St Finnian of Clonard. In *Ríocht na Midhe,* vii, no. 3 (1984), pp 29–36.
Dumville, David N. Kingship, genealogies and regnal lists. In P. H. Sawyer and I. Wood (ed.), *Early medieval kingship* (Leeds, 1977), pp 72–104.
Ó Cathasaigh, Tomás. The Déisi and Dyfed. In *Éigse,* xx (1984), pp 1–33.
Ó Ceallaigh, Séamus. *Gleanings from Ulster history.* Cork, 1951. Reprint, compiled by Graham Mawhinney. Ballinascreen, 1994.
Ó Concheanainn, Tomás. Aided Nath Í and Uí Fhiachrach genealogies. In *Éigse,* xxv (1991), pp 1–27.
Ó Corráin, Donnchadh. The regnal succession in Ciarraighe Luachra. In *Kerry Arch. Soc. Jn.,* i (1968), pp 46–55.
——The Alltraighe. In *Kerry Arch. Soc. Jn.,* ii (1969), pp 27–37.
——A further note on the Alltraighe. In *Kerry Arch. Soc. Jn.,* iii (1970), pp 19–22.
——Dál Calathbuig. In *Éigse,* xiv (1971), pp 13–16.
——Corrigenda to the Lecan Miscellany. In *Éigse,* xvii (1978), pp 393–401.
——On the 'Aithechthúatha' tracts. In *Éigse,* xix (1982), pp 159–65.
——Irish origin legends and genealogy: recurrent aetiologies. In Tore Nyberg, Iørn Piø, P. M. Sørensen, and Aage Trommer (ed.), *History and heroic tale: a symposium. Proceedings of the Eighth International Symposium organized by the Centre for the Study of Vernacular Literature in the Middle Ages; held at Odense University on 21–22 November 1983* (Odense, 1985), pp 51–96.
——Celtic narrative tradition: historical need and literary narrative. In Evans, Griffith, & Jope, *Proc. 7th Congress,* pp 141–58.
——Creating the past: the early Irish genealogical tradition. In *Peritia,* xii (1998), pp 177–208.
Ó Doibhlin, E. O Neill's 'own country' and its families. In *Seanchas Ardmhacha,* vi (1971), pp 3–23.
Ó Riain, Pádraig. Two legends of the Uí Máille. In *Éigse,* xiv (1971), pp 1–12.
Sproule, David. Politics and pure narrative in the stories about Corc of Cashel. In *Ériu,* xxxvi (1985), pp 11–28.

## 4  Law

As a general rule, items listed in Fergus Kelly, *A guide to early Irish law* (Dublin, 1988) do not appear below. Exceptions have been made for important source material published earlier.

## (a) Primary texts

Bieler, Ludwig. *The Irish penitentials*. Dublin, 1963. (Script. Lat. Hib, v.)

Binchy, D. A. (ed.). *Corpus Iuris Hibernici*. 6 vols. Dublin, 1978.

Breatnach, Liam. *Uraicecht na Ríar: the poetic grades in early Irish law*. Dublin, 1987. (Early Irish Law Series, ii.)

——The first third of *Bretha Nemed Toísech*. In *Ériu*, xl (1989), pp 1–40.

Carey, John. An edition of the pseudo-historical prologue to the Senchas Már. In *Ériu*, xlv (1994), pp 1–32.

Charles-Edwards, T. M., and Kelly, Fergus. *Bechbretha: an Old Irish law-tract on bee-keeping*. Dublin, 1983. (Early Irish Law Series, i.)

Dillon, Myles. Stories from the law-tracts. In *Ériu*, xi (1932), pp 42–65.

——*Lebor na Cert: the Book of Rights*. Dublin, 1962. (Ir. Texts Soc., xlvi.)

Faris, M. J. (ed.). *The bishops' synod ('the first synod of St Patrick')*. Liverpool, 1976.

Hancock, W. N.; O'Mahony, Thaddeus; Richey, A. G.; and Atkinson, Robert (ed.). *The ancient laws of Ireland*. 6 vols. Dublin, 1865–1901.

Kelly, Fergus. *Audacht Moraind*. Dublin, 1976.

——An Old-Irish text on court procedure. In *Peritia*, v (1986), pp 74–106.

McLeod, Neil. *Early Irish contract law*. Sydney [1992]. (Sydney Series in Celtic Studies, i.)

Ní Dhonnchadha, Máirín. The *Lex innocentium*: Adomnán's law for women, clerics, and youths, 697 A.D. In Mary O'Dowd and Sabine Wichert (ed.), *Chattel, servant or citizen: women's status in church, state and society* (*Hist. Studies*, xix; Belfast, 1995), pp 58–69.

O'Donovan, John (ed.). *Leabhar na g-Ceart or The Book of Rights*. Dublin, 1847.

Poppe, Erich. A new edition of *Cáin Éimíne Báin*. In *Celtica*, xviii (1986), pp 35–52.

——The genealogy of Émín(e) in the Book of Leinster. In *Ériu*, xl (1989), pp 93–8.

Wasserschleben, F. W. H. *Die irische Kanonensammlung*. Leipzig, 1874. 2nd revised ed., 1885. Reprinted, Aalen, 1966.

## (b) Secondary works

Bieler, Ludwig. Towards an interpretation of the so-called 'Canones Wallici'. In J. Watt, J. B. Morrall, and F. X. Martin (ed.), *Medieval studies presented to Aubrey Gwynn, S.J.* (Dublin, 1961), pp 387–92.

——Patrick's synod: a revision. In *Mélanges offerts à Mlle Christine Mohrmann* (Utrecht, 1963), pp 96–102.

——Aspetti sociali del Penitenziale e della Regola di san Columbano. In *Atti del Congresso Internazionale di Studi Colombaniani* (Bobbio, 1965), pp 119–26.

——The Irish penitentials: their religious and social background. In *Studia Patristica*, viii (Texte und Untersuchungen, xciii; 1966), pp 329–39.

Binchy, D. A. MacNeill's study of the ancient laws of Ireland. In F. X. Martin and F. J. Byrne, *The scholar revolutionary* (Shannon, 1973), pp 37–48.

——Opening address. In Ní Chatháin & Richter, *Ire. & Europe*, pp 1–8.

Breatnach, Liam. Lawyers in early Ireland. In N. Hogan and W. N. Osborough (ed.), *Brehons, serjeants and attorneys: studies in the history of the Irish legal profession* (Dublin, 1990), pp 1–13.

——On the original extent of the *Senchas Már*. In *Ériu*, xlvii (1996), pp 1–43.

——Law. In Kim McCone and Katharine Simms (ed.), *Progress in medieval Irish studies* (Maynooth, 1996), pp 107–22.

Carey, John. The two laws in Dubthach's judgement. In *Camb. Med. Celt. Studies*, xix (summer 1990), pp 1–18.

——The testimony of the dead. In *Éigse*, xxvi (1992), pp 1–12.

Clancy, Finbarr G. The Irish penitentials. In *Milltown Studies*, xxi (1988), pp 87–109.

d'Arbois de Jubainville, Henri. *La famille celtique: étude de droit comparé*. Paris, 1905.

Davies, Wendy. The place of healing in early Irish society. In Ó Corráin, Breatnach, & McCone, *Sages, saints, & storytellers*, pp 43–55.

——The Latin charter-tradition in western Britain, Brittany and Ireland in the early medieval period. In Whitelock, McKitterick, & Dumville, *Ire. in early med. Europe*, pp 257–80.

Charles-Edwards, T. M. The pastoral role of the church in the early Irish laws. In John Blair and Richard Sharpe (ed.), *Pastoral care before the parish* (Leicester, 1992), pp 63–80.

——*Early Irish and Welsh kinship*. Oxford, 1993.

——A contract between king and people in early medieval Ireland? *Críth Gablach* on kingship. In *Peritia*, viii (1994), pp 107–19.

——The construction of the *Hibernensis*. In *Peritia*, xii (1998), pp 209–37.

Finnane, Rowena. *Late medieval Irish law manuscripts*. Sydney, 1995. (Sydney Series in Celtic Studies, iii.)

Flanagan, Marie Therese. The context and uses of the Latin charter in twelfth-century Ireland. In Pryce, *Literacy in medieval Celtic societies* (Cambridge, 1998), pp 113–30.

Gerriets, Marilyn. Theft, penitentials and the compilation of the early Irish laws. In *Celtica*, xxii (1991), pp 18–32.

Hamlin, Ann. Using mills on Sunday. In Scott, *Studies on early Ire.*, p. 11.

Henry, P. L. The cruces of *Audacht Morainn*. In *Z.C.P.*, xxxix (1982), pp 33–53.

——A note on the Brehon law tracts of procedure and status, *Cóic Conara Fugill* and *Uraicecht Becc*. In *Z.C.P.*, xlix–l (1997), pp 311–19.

Hughes, Kathleen. Synodus II S. Patricii. In O'Meara & Naumann, *Latin script & letters*, pp 141–7.

Jaski, Bart. Marriage laws in Ireland and on the Continent in the early middle ages. In C. E. Meek and M. K. Simms (ed.), *'The fragility of her sex'? Medieval Irish women in their European context* (Blackrock, 1996), pp 16–42.

Jenkins, Dafydd (ed.). *Celtic law papers*. Aberystwyth, 1971. Brussels, 1973. (Studies presented to the International Commission for the History of Representative and Parliamentary Institutions, xlii.)
Includes articles by D. A. Binchy, Eoin MacNeill, and Rudolf Thurneysen.

Kelly, Fergus. *A guide to early Irish law*. Dublin, 1988. (Dublin Institute for Advanced Studies: Early Irish Law Series, iii.)

Kohler, Josef. Das Recht der Kelten. I: Das irisch-keltische Recht. In *Zeitschrift für vergl. Rechtswissenschaft*, xxiii (1910), pp 213–49.

Kottje, Raymund. *Die Bußbücher Halitgars von Cambrai und des Hrabanus Maurus: ihre Überlieferung und ihre Quellen*. Berlin and New York, 1980. (Beiträge zur Geschichte und Quellenkunde des Mittelalters, viii.)

——Überlieferung und Rezeption der irischen Bußbücher auf dem Kontinent. In Löwe, *Die Iren*, pp 511–24.

——Der Liber ex lege Moysis. In Ní Chatháin & Richter, *Ire. & Christendom*, pp 59–69.

Lindeman, Fredrik Otto. A note on a difficult passage in Bretha Déin Chécht. In *Celtica*, xxi (1990), p. 252.

McLeod, Neil. Parallel and paradox: compensation in the legal systems of Celtic Ireland and Anglo-Saxon England. In *Studia Celt.*, xvi–xvii (1981–2), pp 36–9.

——The concept of law in ancient Irish jurisprudence. In *Ir. Jurist*, xvii (1982), pp 356–67.

MacNeill, Eoin. Kinship in Irish law. In *R.S.A.I. Jn.*, lvii (1927), pp 154–5.

——Celtic law. In *Encyclopaedia of the Social Sciences*, ix (1933), pp 246–9.

——*Early Irish laws and institutions*. Dublin, 1935.

Melia, Daniel F. The Irish church in the Irish laws. In S. Pearce (ed.), *The early church in western Britain and Ireland* (Oxford, 1982), pp 363–78.

——Law and the shaman saint. In Ford, *Celtic folklore*, pp 113–28.

Mori, Setsuko. Irish monasticism and the concept of inheritance: an examination of its legal aspects. In *Comparative aspects of Irish and Japanese economic and social history* (1993), pp 123–47.

Murray, Kevin. A Middle Irish tract on *cró* and *díbad*. In Smyth, *Seanchas*, pp 251–60.

Nagy, J. F. Sword as Audacht. In A. T. E. Matonis and Daniel F. Melia (ed.), *Celtic language, Celtic culture* (Van Nuys, Calif., 1990), pp 131–6.

Ní Dhonnchadha, Máirín. An address to a student of law. In Ó Corráin, Breatnach, & McCone, *Sages, saints, & storytellers*, pp 159–77.

Ó Corráin, Donnchadh. Some legal references to fences and fencing in early historic Ireland. In Terence Reeves-Smyth and Fred Hamond (ed.), *Landscape archaeology in Ireland* (Oxford, 1983), pp 247–52.

——Law and society—principles of classification. In Schmidt, *Celts*, pp 234–40.

——Irish vernacular law and the Old Testament. In Ní Chatháin & Richter, *Ire. & Christendom*, pp 284–310.

Ó Fiannachta, Pádraig. Cáin Adamnáin. In idem, *Na mná sa litríocht* (Maynooth, 1982), pp 93–111.

O'Leary, Philip. A farseeing driver of an old chariot: legal moderation in early Irish literature. In *Camb. Med. Celt. Studies*, xi (summer 1986), pp 1–6.

Ó Riain, Pádraig. A misunderstood annal: a hitherto unnoticed cáin. In *Celtica*, xxi (1990), pp 561–6.

Oakley, Thomas P. Celtic penance: its sources, affiliations and influence. In *I.E.R.*, 5th ser., lii (1938), pp 147–64, 581–601.

Paganini, Carlo. Presenze dei penitenziali irlandesi nel pensiero medievale. In *Studia et Documenta Historiae et Iuris*, xxxiii (1967), pp 359–65.

Patterson, Nerys T. Kinship law or number symbolism? Models of distributive justice in Old Irish law. In *Proceedings of the Harvard Celtic Colloquium*, v (1985), pp 49–86.

——*Early Irish kinship: the legal structure of the agnatic descent group*. Boston, 1988. (Irish Studies Program.)

——Brehon law in the late middle ages: 'antiquarian and obsolete' or 'traditional and functional'? In *Camb. Med. Celt. Studies*, xvii (summer 1989), pp 43–63.

——Patrilineal groups in early Irish society: the evidence from the Irish law texts. In *Bulletin of the Board of Celtic Studies*, xxxvii (1990), pp 133–65.

——Gaelic law and the Tudor conquest of Ireland: the social background of the sixteenth-century recensions of the pseudo-historical prologue to the Senchas Már. In *I.H.S.*, xxvii, no. 107 (May 1991), pp 193–215.

——*Cattle-lords and clansmen*. New York and London, 1991.

Poppe, Erich. The list of sureties in Cáin Éimíne. In *Celtica*, xxi (1990), pp 588–92.

Price, Huw. Early Irish canons and medieval Welsh law. In *Peritia*, v (1986), pp 107–27.

Reynolds, Roger. Unity and diversity in Carolingian canon law collections: the case of the Collectio Hibernensis and its derivatives. In U.-R. Blumenthal (ed.), *Carolingian essays* (Washington, 1983), pp 99–135.

Scott, B. G. An early Irish law tract on the blacksmith's forge. In *Journal of Irish Archaeology*, i (1983), pp 59–62.

Sharpe, Richard. Dispute settlement in medieval Ireland: a preliminary inquiry. In W. Davies and P. Fouracre, *The settlement of disputes in early medieval Europe* (Cambridge, 1986), pp 168–89.

Sheehy, Maurice. Influences of ancient Irish law on the Collectio Hibernensis. In S. Kuttner (ed.), *Proceedings of the Third International Congress of Medieval Canon Law* (Vatican City, 1971), pp 31–42.

——The Collectio Canonum Hibernensis—a Celtic phenomenon. In Löwe, *Die Iren*, i, 525–35.

——The Bible and the Collectio Canonum Hibernensis. In Ní Chatháin & Richter, *Ire. & Christendom*, pp 277–83.

Stacey, Robin Chapman. Ties that bind: immunities in Celtic law. In *Camb. Med. Celt. Studies*, xx (winter 1990), pp 39–60.

——Law and order in the very old west: England and Ireland in the early middle ages. In Benjamin T. Hudson and Vickie Ziegler (ed.), *Crossed paths: methodological approaches to the Celtic aspect of the European middle ages* (Lanham, Maryland, 1991), pp 39–60.

——*The road to judgement: from custom to court in medieval Ireland and Wales*. Philadelphia, 1994. (Middle Ages Series.)

Thurneysen, Rudolf. Ir. eneclann. In *Z.C.P.*, xx (1936), pp 205–12.

Walters, D. B. The general features of archaic European suretyship. In T. M. Charles-Edwards, M. Owen, and D. B. Walters (ed.), *Lawyers and laymen* (Cardiff, 1986), pp 92–118.

## 5   Hagiography

See also above (sect. I) for bibliographies compiled by R. I. Best and Rolf Baumgarten, and bibliographies of the published works of Ludwig Bieler, Daniel Binchy, and John Hennig.

### (a) Primary texts

Anderson, Alan O. and Marjorie O. *Adomnan's Life of Columba*. Edinburgh, 1961. 2nd ed., Oxford, 1990.

Bieler, Ludwig. Eine Patricksvita in Gloucester. In J. Autenrieth and F. Brunhölzl (ed.), *Festschrift Bernhard Bischoff* (Stuttgart, 1971), pp 346–63.

Breatnach, Liam. An edition of *Amra Senáin*. In Ó Corráin, Breatnach, & McCone, *Sages, saints, & storytellers*, pp 7–32.

Byrne, F. J., and Francis, Pádraig. Two Lives of St Patrick: 'Vita Secunda' and 'Vita Quarta'. In *R.S.A.I. Jn.*, cxxiv (1994), pp 5–117.

Connolly, Seán. Vita prima sanctae Brigitae: background and historical value. In *R.S.A.I. Jn.*, cxix (1989), pp 5–49.

——and Picard, J.-M. Cogitosus's Life of Saint Brigit: content and value. In *R.S.A.I. Jn.*, cvii (1987), pp 5–27.

Herbert, Máire. The Irish Life of Colum Cille. In Herbert, *Iona, Kells, & Derry*, pp 209–88.

——and Ó Riain, Pádraig. *Betha Adamnáin: the Irish Life of Adamnán*. London, 1988. (Ir. Texts Soc., liv.)

Hood, A. B. E. *St Patrick: his writings and Muirchu's Life*. London, 1978.

Lacey, Brian (ed.). *The life of Colum Cille by Manus O'Donnell*. Ed. Dublin, 1998.

Mac Eoin, Gearóid. A Life of Cumaine Fota. In B. Almqvist, B. Mac Aodha, and G. Mac Eoin (ed.), *Hereditas* (Dublin, 1975), pp 192–205.

Ó hAodha, Donncha. *Bethu Brigte*. Dublin, 1978.

O'Nolan, Kevin. Translation of 'Vita Findani' (Life of Findan of Rheinau) in Reidar Th. Christiansen, 'The people of the North' in *Lochlann*, ii (1962), pp 155–64. Text from Holder Egger's ed., pp 148–55.

Ó Riain, Pádraig (ed.). *Beatha Barra, Saint Finbarr of Cork: the complete life*. London, 1994.

Picard, Jean-Michel, and de Pontfarcy, Yolande. *The vision of Tnugdal*. Dublin, 1989.

Sharpe, Richard. *Adomnán of Iona: Life of St Columba*. Harmondsworth, 1995.

### (b) Secondary works

Berschin, Walter. *Biographie und Epochenstil im lateinischen Mittelalter. II. Merowingische Biographie: Italien, Spanien und die Inseln im frühen Mittelalter*. Stuttgart, 1988. 'Irland und England im frühen Mittelalter', pp 223–58.

Bieler, Ludwig. *Studies on the life and legend of St Patrick*. Ed. Richard Sharpe. London, 1986.

Binchy, D. A. Patrick and his biographers. In *Studia Hib.*, ii (1962), 17–173.

Binchy, D. A. A pre-Christian survival in mediaeval Irish hagiography. In Whitelock, McKitterick, & Dumville, *Ire. in early med. Europe*, pp 165–78.

Bowen, E. G. *Saints, seaways and settlements in the Celtic lands*. Cardiff, 1969.

—— The cult of St Brigit. In *Studia Celt.*, viii–ix (1973–4), pp 33–47.

Bray, Dorothy Ann. Motival derivations in the *Life of St Samthann*. In *Studia Celt.*, xx–xxi (1987), pp 78–86.

—— The image of St Brigit. In *Études Celt.*, xxiv (1987), pp 209–15.

—— Heroic tradition in the Lives of the early Irish saints: a study in hagio-biographical tradition. In MacLennan, *Proc. 1st N.A. Congress*, pp 261–71.

—— A list of motifs in the Lives of the early Irish saints. In *FF Communications*, cix, pt. 2, no. 252 (1992).

Breatnach, Pádraig. An inventory of Latin Lives of Irish saints from St Anthony's College, Louvain, *c.* 1643. In Smyth, *Seanchas*, pp 431–8.

Carney, James. *The problem of St Patrick*. Dublin, 1964.

Connolly, Seán. The authorship and manuscript tradition of the *Vita I S. Brigidae*. In *Manuscripta*, xvi (1972), pp 67–82.

—— Verbal usage in *Vita Prima Brigitae* and *Bethu Brigte*. In *Peritia*, i (1982), pp 268–72.

—— Some palaeographical and linguistic features in early *Lives of Brigit*. In Ní Chatháin & Richter, *Ire. & Europe*, pp 272–9.

—— The power motif and the use of Scripture in Cogitosus' Vita Brigitae. In J.-M. Picard (ed.), *Aquitaine and Ireland in the middle ages* (Dublin, 1995), pp 207–20.

Cross, J. E. The influence of Irish texts and traditions on the *Old English Martyrology*. In *R.I.A. Proc.*, lxxxi (1981), pp 173–92.

Davies, Oliver, and O'Loughlin, Thomas (ed.). *Celtic spirituality*. New York and Mahwah, 1999.

Doan, James. A structural approach to Celtic saints' lives. In Ford, *Celtic folklore*, pp 16–28.

Duft, Johannes. St Colomban dans les manuscrits liturgiques de la bibliothèque abbatiale de Saint-Gall. In Gabriel Le Bras and others (ed.), *Mélanges colombaniens: actes du congrès international de Luxeuil, 20–23 juillet 1950* (Paris, [1950]), pp 317–26.

Dumville, David N. St Finnian of Movilla: Briton, Gael, ghost? In Lindsay Proudfoot (ed.), *Down: history and society* (Dublin, 1997), pp 71–84.

—— (ed.), *Saint Patrick A.D. 493–1993*. Woodbridge, 1993.
Includes essays by Alicia Correâ and D. N. Dumville.

Charles-Edwards, T. M. The new edition of Adomnán's Life of Columba. In *Camb. Med. Celt. Studies*, xxvi (1993), pp 65–74.

Fontaine, Jacques. La question martinienne. In *Peritia*, iv (1985), pp 371–6.

Ford, Patrick K. Aspects of the Patrician legend. In Ford, *Celtic folklore*, pp 24–49.

Hennig, John. *Medieval Ireland, saints and martyrologies: selected studies*. Ed. Michael Richter. Northampton, 1989.

Herbert, Máire. The preface to *Amra Coluim Cille*. In Ó Corráin, Breatnach, & McCone, *Sages, saints & storytellers*, pp 67–75.

——*Iona, Kells, and Derry: the history and hagiography of the monastic* familia *of Columba*. Oxford, 1988.

——Hagiography. In Kim McCone and Katharine Simms (ed.), *Progress in medieval Irish studies* (Maynooth, 1996), pp 79–90.

Howlett, David. Vita I Sanctae Brigitae. In *Peritia*, xii (1998), pp 1–23.

Jackson, Kenneth H. The date of the Tripartite Life of St Patrick. In *Z.C.P.*, xli (1986), pp 5–45.

Kerlouégan, François. Les vies de saints bretons les plus anciennes dans leurs rapports avec les Iles brittaniques. In Herren, *Insular Latin studies*, pp 195–214.

Lapidge, Michael. The cult of St Indract at Glastonbury. In Whitelock, McKitterick, & Dumville, *Ire. in early med. Europe*, pp 179–212.

Laporte, R. P. D. Les sources de la biographie de saint Colomban. In Gabriel Le Bras and others (ed.), *Mélanges colombaniens: actes du congrès international de Luxeuil, 20–23 juillet 1950* (Paris, [1950]), pp 75–80.

McCone, Kim. Bríd Chill Dara. In P. Ó Fiannachta (ed.), *Na mná sa litríocht* (Maynooth, 1982), pp 30–92.

——Brigit in the seventh century: a saint with three lives? In *Peritia*, i (1982), pp 107–45.

——An introduction to early Irish saints' Lives. In *Maynooth Review*, xi (1984), pp 26–59.

——Clones and her neighbours in the early period: hints from some Airgialla saints' Lives. In *Clogher Rec.*, xi, no. 3 (1984), pp 305–25.

Mac Donncha, Frederic. Dáta Vita Tripartita Sancti Patricii. In *Éigse*, xviii (1980), pp 125–42; xix (1983) pp 354–72.

Ó Briain, Felim. Brigitana. Ed. Frederic Mac Donncha. In *Z.C.P.*, xxxvi (1977), pp 112–37.

Ó Caoimh, Tomás. Mocheallóc mac Uibhleáin of the Corco Dhuibhne: a saint of west Munster. In *Tuosist 6000* (Tuosist, 1999), pp 79–87.

Ó Coileáin, Seán. The saint and the king. In de Brún, Ó Coileáin & Ó Riain, *Folia Gadelica*, pp 36–46.

Ó Corráin, Donnchadh. Foreign connections and domestic politics: Killaloe and the Uí Briain in twelfth-century hagiography. In Whitelock, McKitterick, & Dumville, *Ire. in early med. Europe*, pp 213–34.

Ó Laoghaire, Diarmuid. St Virgil and his Irish background. In *Milltown Studies*, xiv (1984), pp 72–85.

O'Loughlin, Thomas. Muirchú's *Vita Patricii*: a note on an unidentified source. In *Ériu*, xlvii (1996), pp 89–93.

Ó Riain, Pádraig. Traces of Lug in early Irish hagiographical tradition. In *Z.C.P.*, xxxvi (1977), pp 138–56.

——The Irish element in Welsh hagiographical tradition. In Ó Corráin, *Ir. antiquity*, pp 291–303.

——Beathaí agus beathaí béil. In Mac Conmara, *An léann eaglasta*, pp 104–18.

——Towards a methodology in early Irish hagiography. In *Peritia*, i (1982), pp 146–59.

——Cainnech *alias* Colum Cille, patron of Ossory. In de Brún, Ó Coileáin, & Ó Riain, *Folia Gadelica*, pp 20–35.

—— Samson alias San(c)tán? In *Peritia*, iii (1984), pp 320–23.

—— Finnian or Winniau? In Ní Chatháin & Richter, *Ire. & Europe*, pp 52–7.

—— Les Vies de Saint Fursy: les sources irlandaises. In *Revue du Nord*, lxviii (1986), pp 405–13.

—— St Abbán: the genesis of an Irish Saint's Life. In Evans, Griffith, & Jope, *Proc. 7th Congress*, pp 159–70.

—— Celtic mythology and religion. In Schmidt, *Celts*, pp 241–51.

—— Sanctity and politics in Connacht *c.* 1100: the case of St Fursa. In *Camb. Med. Celt. Studies*, xvii (summer 1989), pp 1–14.

—— The saints and their amanuenses: early models and later issues. In Tranter & Tristram, *Early Ir. lit.*, pp 267–80.

—— The Tallaght martyrologies, redated. In *Camb. Med. Celt. Studies*, xx (winter 1990), pp 21–38.

—— Saints in the catalogue of bishops of the lost *Register of Clogher*. In *Clogher Rec.*, xiv, no. 2 (1992), pp 66–77.

—— The *Catalogus praecipuorum sanctorum Hiberniae*, sixty years on. In Smyth, *Seanchas*, pp 396–430.

Ó Riain-Raedel, Dagmar. Aspects of the promotion of Irish saints' cults in medieval Germany. In *Z.C.P.*, xxxix (1982), pp 220–34.

—— Kalendare und Legenden und ihre historische Auswertung. In Tranter & Tristram, *Early Ir. lit.*, pp 241–66.

—— The question of the 'pre-Patrician' saints of Munster. In Monk & Sheehan, *Early med. Munster*, pp 17–22.

—— Patrician documents in medieval Germany. In *Z.C.P.*, xlix–l (1997), pp 712–24.

Ó Súilleabháin, Pádraig. Beatha Cholaim Chille: an chóip atá i LS. A.8. In *Celtica*, xi (1976), pp 203–13.

Picard, Jean-Michel. The marvellous in Irish and continental saints' Lives of the Merovingian period. In Clarke & Brennan, *Columbanus*, pp 91–104.

—— The purpose of Adomnán's *Vita Columbae*. In *Peritia*, i (1982), pp 160–77.

—— Bede, Adomnán, and the writing of history. In *Peritia*, iii (1984), pp 50–70.

—— Structural patterns in early Hiberno-Latin hagiography. In *Peritia*, iv (1985), pp 67–82.

—— Les celticismes des hagiographes irlandais du vii siècle. In *Études Celt.*, xxix (1992), 355–73.

—— Adomnán's *Vita Columbae* and the cult of Colum Cille in continental Europe. In *R.I.A. Proc.*, xcviii (1998), sect. C, pp 1–23.

Powell, Timothy E. Christianity or solar monotheism: the early religious beliefs of St Patrick. In *Journal of Ecclesiastical History*, xliii (1992), pp 531–40.

Selmer, Carl. A study of the Latin manuscripts of the 'Navigatio Sancti Brendani'. In *Scriptorium*, iii (1949), pp 177–82.

Sharpe, Richard. Hiberno-Latin *laicus*, Irish *láech* and the devil's men. In *Ériu*, xxx (1979), pp 75–92.

—— *Vitae S. Brigitae:* the oldest texts. In *Peritia*, i (1982), pp 81–106.

—— The Patrician documents. In *Peritia*, i (1982), pp 363–9.

Sharpe, Richard. Quatuor sanctissimi episcopi: Irish saints before St Patrick. In Ó Corráin, Breatnach, & McCone, *Sages, saints, & storytellers*, pp 376–99.

—— Maghnus Ó Domhnaill's source for Adomnán's *Vita S. Columbae* and other *uitae*. In *Celtica*, xxi (1990), pp 604–7.

—— *Medieval Irish saints' lives: an introduction to Vitae Sanctorum Hiberniae*. Oxford, 1991.

Simms, George Otto. *St Patrick: the real story of Patrick who became Ireland's patron saint*. Dublin, 1991.

Sperber, Inger. The life of St Ciarán of Saigir. In William Nolan and Timothy P. O'Neill (ed.), *Offaly: history and society* (Dublin, 1998), pp 131–52.

Stancliffe, Clare. *St Martin and his biographer: history and miracle in Sulpicius Severus*. Oxford, 1983.

—— The miracle stories in seventh-century Irish saints' Lives. In Jacques Fontaine and J. N. Hillgarth (ed.), *Le septième siècle: changement et continuité. The seventh century: change and continuity. Proceedings of a joint French and British colloquium held at the Warburg Institute 8–9 July 1988* (Studies of the Warburg Institute; London, 1992), pp 87–115.

Strijsbosch, Clara The heathen giant in the Voyage of St Brendan. In *Celtica*, xxiii (1999), pp 369–407.

## 6 Latin prose

### (a) Primary texts

As a general rule, works published before Michael Lapidge and Richard Sharpe (ed.), *A bibliography of Celtic-Latin literature 400–1200* (Dublin, 1985), do not appear below.

Bayless, Martha, and Lapidge, Michael. *Collectanea Pseudo-Bedae*. Dublin, 1998. (Script. Lat. Hib., xiv.)

Berschin, Walter. Ich Patricius. Die Autobiographie des Apostels der Iren. In Löwe, *Die Iren*, i, 9–25.

Breatnach, Pádraig A. *Die Regensburger Schottenlegende: Libellus de fundacione ecclesie Consecrati Petri*. Munich, 1977. (Münchener Beiträge zur Mediävistik und Renaissance-Forschung, xxvii.)

Breen, Aidan. *Ailerani interpretatio mystica et moralis progenitorum Domini Iesu Christi*. Dublin, 1995.

Cahill, Michael. *Expositio evangelii secundum Marcum*. Turnhout, 1997. (C.C.S.L., lxxxii.)

Carracedo-Fraga, José. *Liber de ortu et obitu patriarcharum*. Turnhout, 1996. (C.C.S.L., cviiiE.)

Contreni, John J., and Ó Néill, Pádraig P. (ed.). *Glossae divinae historiae: the biblical glosses of John Scottus Eriugena*. Florence, 1997.

Dumville, David N. *The Historia Brittonum, iii: the 'Vatican' recension*. Woodbridge, 1985.

Fischer, Peter, and Ellis Davidson, Hilda. *Saxo Grammaticus. The history of the Danes*. 2 vols. Woodbridge, 1979.

Hanson, R. P. C. *The life and writings of the historical Saint Patrick.* New York, 1983.

Herren, Michael W. *The Hisperica Famina.* 2 vols. Toronto, 1974, 1987. (Pontifical Institute of Mediaeval Studies; Studies & Texts, xxi, lxxxv.)

Howlett, David R. *The book of letters of Saint Patrick the bishop.* Dublin, 1994.

——*Synodus prima Sancti Patricii*: an exercise in textual reconstruction. In *Peritia*, xii (1998), pp 238–53.

——The structure of the *Liber Angeli.* In *Peritia*, xii (1998), pp 254–70.

Jeauneau, Édouard. *Maximus Confessor, Ambigua ad Iohannem, latina interpretatio Ioannis Scotti Eriugenae.* Turnhout, 1988. (C.C.S.G., xviii.)

——*Iohannis Scotti Eriugenae Periphyseon (De diuisione naturae), Lib. IV.* With the assistance of Mark A. Zier and English translation by John J. O'Meara and I. P. Sheldon-Williams. Dublin, 1995. (Script. Lat. Hib., xiii.)

Laga, C., and Steel, C. *Maximus Confessor, quaestiones ad Thalassium, una cum latina interpretatione Ioannis Scotti Eriugenae.* 2 vols. Turnhout, 1980, 1990. (C.C.S.G., viii & xxii.)

Law, Vivien. Fragments from the lost portions of the *Epitomae* of Virgilius Maro Grammaticus. In *Camb. Med. Celt. Studies*, xxi (summer 1991), pp 113–25.

Lehner, Albert. *Florilegia. Florilegium Frisingense (Clm 6433). Testimonia divinae scripturae (et patrum).* Turnhout, 1987. (C.C.S.L. cviiiD.)

Löfstedt, Bengt, Holtz, L., and Kibre, A. *Smaragdus, Liber in partibus Donati.* Turnhout, 1986. (Corpus Christianorum, Continuatio Medievalis, lxviii.)

MacGinty, Gerard. *The Reference Bible, das Bibelwerk: inter Pauca problesmata de enigmatibus ex tomis canonicis, nunc prompta sunt praefatio et libri de Pentateucho Moysi.* Turnhout, 2000. (Corpus Christianorum, Continuatio Medievalis, clxxiii; Scriptores Celtigenae, iii.)

Martin, Lawrence T. *Homiliarium Veronense.* Turnhout, 2000. (Corpus Christianorum, Continuatio Medievalis, clxxxvi; Scriptores Celtigenae, iv.)

O'Loughlin, Thomas. *St Patrick.* Dublin, 1999.

Simpson, Dean. *Sedulius Scottus: Collectaneum miscellaneum.* Turnhout, 1988. (C.C.C.M., lxvii and supplement.)

*(b) Secondary works*

Anton, Hans Hubert. Pseudo-Cyprian De duodecim abusivis saeculi und sein Einfluß auf dem Kontinent, insbesondere auf die karolingischen Fürstenspiegel. In Löwe, *Die Iren*, i, 568–617.

Bammel, Caroline P. H. Das neue Rufinfragment in irischer Schrift und die Überlieferung der Rufin'schen Übersetzung der Kirchengeschichte Eusebs. In *Philologia Sacra. Biblische und patristische Studien für Hermann J. Frede und Walter Thiele zu ihrem siebzigsten Geburtstag*, ed. Roger Gryson (2 vols, Freiburg, 1993), ii, 483–513.

Bartlett, Robert. *Gerald of Wales, 1146–1223.* Oxford, 1982.

Bischoff, Bernhard. Wendepunkte in der Geschichte der lateinischen Exegese im Frühmittelalter. In *Sacris Erudiri*, vi (1954), pp 189–281. Reprinted in Bischoff, *Mittelalterliche Studien* (3 vols, Stuttgart, 1966–7, 1981), i, 205–73.

Translated as 'Turning-points in the history of Latin exegesis in the early middle ages' in Martin McNamara (ed.), *Biblical studies: the medieval Irish contribution* (Proceedings of the Irish Biblical Association, no. 1; Dublin, 1976), pp 74–160.

Breen, Aidan. Some seventh-century Hiberno-Latin texts and their relationships. In *Peritia*, iii (1984), pp 204–14.

—— The evidence of antique Irish exegesis in Pseudo-Cyprian, *De duodecim abusivis saeculi*. In *R.I.A. Proc.*, lxxxvii (1987), sect. C, pp 71–101.

—— Pseudo-Cyprian *De duodecim abusivis saeculi* and the Bible. In Ní Chatháin & Richter, *Ire. & Christendom*, pp 230–45.

—— The text of the Constantinopolitan creed in the Stowe missal. In *R.I.A. Proc.*, xc (1990), sect. C, pp 107–21.

—— The liturgical materials in MS Oxford, Bodleian Library, Auct.F.4./32. In *Archiv für Liturgie-Wissenschaft. Jahrgang 34*, Heft 1/2 (Maria Laach, 1992), pp 121–53.

—— The date, provenance and authorship of the Pseudo-Patrician canonical materials. In *Zeitschrift der Savigny-Stiftung für Rechtsgeschichte*, cxxc, Kanonistische Abteilung lxxxi (1995), pp 83–129.

Carey, John. The Irish 'Otherworld': Hiberno-Latin perspectives. In *Éigse*, xxv (1991), pp 154–9.

Conneely, Daniel. *St Patrick's letters: a study of their theological dimension*. Ed. Patrick Bastable and others. Maynooth, 1993.

de Pontfarcy, Yolande. Le *Tractatus de Purgatorio Sancti Patricii* de H. de Saltrey: sa date et ses sources. In *Peritia*, iii (1984), pp 460–81.

Herren, Michael W. The pseudonymous tradition in Hiberno-Latin: an introduction. In O'Meara & Naumann, *Latin script & letters*, pp 121–31.

—— Insular grammarians. In *Peritia*, ii (1983), pp 312–16.

—— Editing the *Hisperica Famina*: a reply. In *Camb. Med. Celt. Studies*, xvii (summer 1989), pp 65–8.

Holtz, Louis. Les grammairiens hiberno-latins étaient-ils des Anglo-Saxons? In *Peritia*, ii (1983), pp 169–84.

—— L'enseignement des maîtres irlandais dans l'Europe continentale du IX^e siècle. In Picard, *Ire. & northern France*, pp 143–56.

—— L'Ars Bernensis, essai de localisation et de datation. In J.-M. Picard (ed.), *Aquitaine and Ireland in the middle ages* (Dublin, 1995), pp 111–26.

Howlett, David. Ex saliva scripturae meae. In Ó Corráin, Breatnach, & McCone, *Sages, saints, & storytellers*, pp 86–101.

Kelly, Joseph F. T. Christianity and the Latin tradition in early medieval Ireland. In *John Rylands Library Bulletin*, lxxiii (1985–6), pp 410–33.

—— *Das Bibelwerk*: organization and *Quellenanalyse* of the New Testament section. In Ní Chatháin & Richter, *Ire. & Christendom*, pp 113–23.

Kerlouégan, François. Une mode stylistique dans la prose latine des pays celtiques. In *Études Celt.*, xiii (1972), pp 275–97.

—— Gildas. In *Peritia*, iv (1985), pp 380–82.

—— Un exemple de *metaphora reciproca* dans le *De excidio Britanniae*: Gildas et le 'Donat chrétien'. In *Peritia*, vi–vii (1987–8), pp 223–6.

Law, Vivien. When is Donatus not Donatus? Versions, variants and new texts. In *Peritia*, v (1986), pp 235–61.

Lewis, David J. G. A short Latin *Gospel of Nicodemus* written in Ireland. In *Peritia*, v (1986), pp 262–75.

Löfstedt, Bengt. Fregit bellum ante Cassibellaunum. In *Éigse*, xviii (1981), p. 181.

Löfstedt, Bengt. Eine wenig beachtete hibernolateinsche Grammatik. In Ní Chatháin & Richter, *Ire. & Christendom*, pp 272–6.

MacGinty, Gerard. The Irish Augustine: *De mirabilibus sacrae scripturae*. In Ní Chatháin & Richter, *Ire. & Christendom*, pp 70–83.

McNamara, Martin. *The Apocrypha in the Irish church*. Dublin, 1975.

——Tradition and creativity in early Irish psalter study. In Ní Chatháin & Richter, *Ire. & Europe*, pp 338–89.

——The inverted Eucharistic formula *Conversio corporis Christi in panem et sanguinis in vinum*: the exegetical and liturgical background in Irish usage. In *R.I.A. Proc.*, lxxxvii (1987), sect. C, pp 573–91.

——The text of the Latin Bible in the early Irish Church: some data and desiderata. In Ní Chatháin & Richter, *Ire. & Christendom*, pp 7–58.

——Plan and source analysis of *Das Bibelwerk*, Old Testament. In Ní Chatháin & Richter, *Ire. & Christendom*, pp 84–112.

——The Echternach and Mac Durnan Gospels: some common readings and their significance. In *Peritia*, vi–vii (1987–8), pp 217–22.

——The Irish affiliations of the *Catechesis Celtica*. In *Celtica*, xxi (1990), pp 291–334.

Malaspina, Elena. *Patrizio e l'acculturazione latina dell'Irlanda*. Rome, 1984.

——*Gli scritti di san Patrizio: alle origini del cristianesimo irlandese*. Rome, 1985.

O'Loughlin, Thomas. The exegetical purpose of Adomnán's *De locis sanctis*. In *Camb. Med. Celt. Studies*, xxiv (winter 1992), pp 37–53.

——An Irish (?) interpolation in Caesarius of Arles' *Sermo 84*. In *Milltown Studies* (spring 1993), pp 143–5.

——The library of Iona in the late seventh century: the evidence from Adomnán's *De locis sanctis*. In *Ériu*, xlv (1994), pp 33–52.

——Adomnán and *mira rotunditas*. In *Ériu*, xlvii (1996), pp 95–9.

——Adomnán's *De locis sanctis*: a textual emendation and an additional source identification. In *Ériu*, xlviii (1997), pp 37–40.

Ó Néill, Pádraig P. *Romani* influences on seventh-century Hiberno-Latin literature. In Ní Chatháin & Richter, *Ire. & Europe*, pp 280–90.

Orchard, A. P. McD. Some aspects of seventh-century Hiberno-Latin syntax: a statistical approach. In *Peritia*, vi–vii (1987–8), pp 158–201.

Picard, Jean-Michel. The Schaffhausen Adomnán—a unique witness to Hiberno-Latin. In *Peritia*, i (1982), pp 216–49.

——The metrical prose of Adomnán's *Vita Columbae*; an unusual system. In Ní Chatháin & Richter, *Ire. & Europe*, pp 258–71.

——Donatus Ortigraphus. In *Peritia*, v (1986), pp 427–32.

——The Bible used by Adomnán. In Ní Chatháin & Richter, *Ire. & Christendom*, pp 246–57.

——Eloquentiae exuberantia: words and forms in Adomnán's *Vita Columbae*. In *Peritia*, vi–vii (1987–8), pp 141–57.

Richter, Michael. Gilbert of Limerick revisited. In Smyth, *Seanchas*, pp 341–47.

Rittmueller, Jean. The Gospel commentary of Máel Brigte ua Máeluanaig and its Hiberno-Latin background. In *Peritia*, ii (1983), pp 185–214.

——Afterword: the Gospel of Máel Brigte. In *Peritia*, iii (1984), pp 215–18.

Sharpe, Richard. Gildas, a father of the church. In Michael Lapidge and David Dumville (ed.), *Gildas: new approaches* (Woodbridge, 1984), pp 193–205.

Simpson, Dean. The 'Proverbia Grecorum'. In *Traditio*, xliii (1987), pp 1–22.

——Sedulius Scottus and the Latin classics. In Benjamin T. Hudson and Vickie Ziegler (ed.), *Crossed paths: methodological approaches to the Celtic aspect of the European middle ages* (Lanham, Md., 1991), pp 25–38.

Stewart, James. Gleann na nGealt: a twelfth-century Latin account. In *Celtica*, xvii (1985), pp 105–11.

——*Topographia Hiberniæ*. In *Celtica*, xxi (1990), pp 642–57.

Swift, Catherine. Tírechán's motives in compiling the *Collectanea*: an alternative interpretation. In *Ériu*, xlv (1994), pp 53–82.

Walsh, Maura. Some remarks on Cummian's Paschal Letter and the Commentary on Mark ascribed to Cummian. In Ní Chatháin & Richter, *Ire. & Christendom*, pp 216–29.

Wasserstein, David. Semitica Hiberno-Latina. I: An unknown Jewish sect in four-teenth-century Egypt? II: An unidentified Arabic word in a fourteenth-century Hiberno-Latin writer. In *Peritia*, ii (1983), pp 215–24.

——Semitica Hiberno-Latina III: Symon Symeonis on the Sultan's slaves in Old Cairo. In *Peritia*, iii (1984), pp 219–21.

## 7   Latin poetry

### (a) Primary texts

Herren, Michael W. *The Hisperica Famina. II. Related poems.* Toronto, 1987.

——*Iohannis Scotti Eriugenae carmina.* Dublin, 1993. (Script. Lat. Hib., xii.)

Howlett, D. R. Rubisca: an edition, translation and commentary. In *Peritia*, x (1996), pp 71–90.

Lapidge, Michael. A new Hiberno-Latin hymn on St Martin. In *Celtica*, xxi (1990), pp 240–51.

### (b) Secondary works

Bulst, Walter. Hymnologica partim Hibernica. In O'Meara & Naumann, *Latin script & letters*, pp 83–100.

Byrne, F. J. Latin poetry in Ireland. In James Carney (ed.), *Early Irish poetry* (Cork, 1965), pp 29–44.

Curran, Michael. *The antiphonary of Bangor and the early Irish monastic liturgy.* Dublin, 1984.

Dronke, Peter. 'Ad deum meum convertere volo' and early Irish evidence for lyrical dialogues. In *Camb. Med. Celt. Studies*, xii (winter 1986), pp 23–32.

——Towards the interpretation of the Leiden love-spell. In *Camb. Med. Celt. Studies*, xvi (winter 1988), pp 61–76.

Dutton, Paul E. Eriugena the royal poet. In G.-H. Allard (ed.), *Jean Scot écrivain* (Montreal, 1986), pp 51–80.

Herren, Michael W. The stress systems in insular Latin octosyllabic verse. In *Camb. Med. Celt. Studies*, xv (summer 1988), pp 63–84.

Herren, Michael W. The stress system of the Hiberno-Latin hendecasyllable. In *Celtica*, xxi (1990), pp 223–30.

Hofman, Rijklof. Some new facts concerning the knowledge of Vergil in early medieval Ireland. In *Études Celt.*, xxv (1988), pp 189–212.

Howlett, D.R. The earliest Irish writers at home and abroad. In *Peritia*, viii (1994), pp 1–17.

——The Brigitine hymn *Xpistus in nostra insula*. In *Peritia*, xii (1998), pp 79–86.

Lapidge, Michael. Columbanus and the Antiphonary of Bangor. In *Peritia*, iv (1985), pp 104–6.

Stancliffe, Clare. Venantius Fortunatus, Ireland, Jerome: the evidence of *precamur patrem*. In *Peritia*, x (1996), pp 91–7.

Stevenson, Jane. The Antiphonary of Bangor. In *Peritia*, v (1986), pp 433–6.

——Bangor and the *Hisperica Famina*. In *Peritia*, vi–vii (1987–8), pp 202–16.

——Introduction to F. E. Warren, *Liturgy and ritual in the Celtic church* (2nd ed., Woodbridge, 1988).

——Irish hymns, Venantius Fortunatus and Poitiers. In J.-M. Picard (ed.), *Aquitaine and Ireland in the early middle ages* (Dublin, 1995), pp 81–110.

——Altus Prosator. In *Celtica*, xxiii (1999), pp 326–68.

Wesseling, Margaret. Structure and image in the *Altus prosator*: Columba's symmetrical universe. In *Proceedings of the Harvard Celtic Colloquium*, viii (1988), pp 46–57.

## 8   Irish prose

### (a) Primary texts

Ahlqvist, Anders. *The early Irish linguist: an edition of the canonical part of the Auraicept na nÉces*. Helsinki, 1983. (Commentationes Humanarum Litterarum, lxxiii.)

Breathnach, Pól. Scéla laí brátha. In T. de Róiste and others (ed.), *Mil na mBeach* (Dublin, n.d.), pp 62–8.

——Scéla na hEsérgi. Ibid., pp 69–78.

Breatnach, Liam. Tochmarc Luaine ocus Aided Athairne. In *Celtica*, xiii (1980), pp 1–31.

Breatnach, Máire. A new edition of Tochmarc Becfhola. In *Ériu*, xxxv (1984), pp 59–92.

Corthals, Johan. Die Trennung von Finn und Gráinne. In *Z.C.P.*, xlix–l (1997), pp 71–91.

Gray, Elizabeth A. *Cath Maige Tuired: the second battle of Mag Tuired*. London, 1982. (Ir. Texts Soc., lii.)

Jackson, Kenneth H. *Aislinge Meic Con Glinne*. Dublin, 1990.

Kinsella, Thomas. *The Táin*. Dublin, 1969.

Mac Gearailt, Uáitéar. The Edinburgh text of *Mesca Ulad*. In *Ériu*, xxxvii (1986), pp 133–80.

Mac Mathúna, Séamus. *Immram Brain: Bran's journey to the Land of the Women.* Tübingen, 1985.

Macalister, R. A. S. *Lebor Gabála Érenn*. 5 vols. Dublin, 1938–56.

—— and MacNeill, John. *Leabhar Gabhála: the Book of the Conquests of Ireland, I* (recension of Mícheál Ó Cléirigh). Dublin, 1916.

Ó Cathasaigh, Tomás. *The heroic biography of Cormac mac Airt*. Dublin, 1977.

Ó Cróinín, Dáibhí. *The Irish Sex Aetates Mundi*. Dublin, 1983.

Ó Cuív, Brian. Comram na Cloenferta. In *Celtica*, xi (1976), pp 168–79.

Ó Fiannachta, Pádraig. *Táin Bó Cuailgne*. Dublin, 1966.

O'Grady, S. H. *Silva Gadelica*. 2 vols. London, 1892. Reprint, Dublin, 1935.

O'Rahilly, Cecile. *The Stowe version of Táin Bó Cuailgne*. Dublin, 1961.

—— *Táin Bó Cuailgne from the Book of Leinster*. Dublin, 1967.

—— *Táin Bó Cuailgne: recension I*. Dublin, 1976.

—— Cathcharpat serda. In *Celtica*, xi (1976), pp 194–202.

Roider, Ulrike. *De chophur in dá muccida*. Innsbruck, 1979.

Todd, James H. *The Irish version of the Historia Britonum of Nennius*. Dublin, 1848.

—— *Cogadh Gaedhel re Gallaibh: the war of the Gaedhil with the Gaill, or the invasions of Ireland by the Danes and other Norsemen*. London, 1867.

Van Hamel, A. G. *Lebor Bretnach: the Irish version of the Historia Britonum ascribed to Nennius*. Dublin, n.d.

*(b) Secondary works*

Aitchison, N. B. The Ulster cycle: heroic image and historical reality. In *Journal of Medieval History*, xiii (1987), pp 87–116.

Backhaus, Norbert. The structure of the list of *Remscéla Tána Bó Cualngi* in the Book of Leinster. In *Camb. Med. Celt. Studies*, xix (summer 1990), pp 19–26.

Baumgarten, Rolf. Discourse markers in medieval Irish texts: *cs. cair, ni,* and similar features. In *Ériu*, xliii (1992), pp 1–37.

Borsje, Jacqueline. The *bruch* in the Irish version of the Sunday Letter. In *Ériu*, xlv (1994), pp 83–98.

Breatnach, Caoimhín. The historical context of Cath Fionntrágha. In *Éigse*, xxviii (1994–5), pp 138–55.

Bruford, Alan. Oral and literary Fenian tales. In Almqvist, Ó Catháin, & Ó hEalaí, *Heroic process*, pp 25–56.

Bryson, S. The tale of Deirdre. In *Emania*, v (1988), pp 42–7; vi (1989), pp 43–7; vii (1990), pp 54–8.

Buttimer, Cornelius J. *Un joc grossier* in *Orggain trí mac Diarmata*. In *Celtica*, xix (1987), pp 128–32.

—— *Longes Mac nUislenn* reconsidered. In *Éigse*, xxviii (1994–5), pp 1–41.

Campanile, E. Ein Element der weiblichen Schönheit in der keltischen Kultur. In *Z.C.P.*, xlvi (1994), pp 36–8.

Carey, John. Sequence and causation in *Echtra Nerai*. In *Ériu*, xxxix (1988), pp 67–74; xl (1989), p. 194.

——Eithne in Gubai. In *Éigse*, xxviii (1994–5), pp 160–4.

——On the interrelationships of some *Cín Dromma Snechtai* texts. In *Ériu*, xlvi (1995), pp 71–92.

——Native elements in Irish pseudohistory. In D. R. Edel (ed.) *Cultural identity and cultural integration* (Dublin, 1995), pp 45–60.

Carey, John. The rhetoric of *Echtrae Chonlai*. In *Camb. Med. Celt. Studies*, xxx (winter 1995), pp 41–65.

Clancy, Thomas Owen. Fools and adultery in some early Irish texts. In *Ériu*, xliv (1993), pp 105–24.

Connon, Anne. The *Banshenchas* and the Uí Néill queens of Tara. In Smyth, *Seanchas*, pp 98–108.

Cormier, Raymond J. Anonymity and oralism in the *Táin*. In *Studia Celt.*, xiv–xv (1979–80), pp 66–70.

——Pagan shame or Christian modesty? In *Celtica*, xiv (1981), pp 43–6.

Corthals, Johan. *Táin Bó Regamna: eine Vorerzählung zur Táin Bó Cúailnge*. Vienna, 1987. (Österreichische Akademie der Wissenschaften, Phil-Hist. Klasse. Sitzungsberichte 478; Veröffentlichungen der Keltischen Kommission, NR 5.)

——The retoiric in *Aided Chonchobuir*. In *Ériu*, xl (1989), pp 41–59.

——Zur Frage des mündlichen oder schriftlichen Ursprungs der Sagen*roscada*. In Tranter & Tristram, *Early Ir. lit.*, pp 201–20.

——A reference to the listener to early Irish prose tales? In *Camb. Med. Celt. Studies*, xxiii (summer 1992), pp 25–8.

Davies, Morgan T. Kings and clerics in some Leinster sagas. In *Ériu*, xlvii (1996), pp 45–65.

Dumville, David N. The textual history of 'Lebor Bretnach': a preliminary study. In *Éigse*, xvi (1975), pp 255–73.

——*Echtrae* and *Immram*: some problems of definition. In *Ériu*, xvii (1976), pp 73–94.

——Towards an interpretation of *Fís Adamnán*. In *Studia Celt.*, xii–xiii (1977–8), pp 62–77.

——The conclusion of Fingal Rónáin. In *Studia Celtica*, xiv–xv (1979–80), pp 71–3.

Edel, Doris. *Helden auf Freiersfüßen. 'Tochmarc Emire' und 'Mal y kavas Kulhwch Olwen'. Studien zur frühen inselkeltischen Erzähltradition*. Amsterdam, 1980.

——Die inselkeltische Erzähltradition zwischen Mündlichkeit und Schriftlichkeit. In Tranter & Tristram, *Early Ir. lit.*, pp 99–124.

——Caught between history and myth? The figures of Fergus and Medb in the Táin Bó Cúailnge and related matter. In *Z.C.P.*, xlix–l (1997), pp 143–69.

Gray, Elizabeth A. Cath Maige Tuired: myth and structure. In *Éigse*, xviii (1981), pp 183–209; xix (1982), pp 1–35; (1983), pp 230–62.

Gwara, Scott James. Gluttony, lust and penance in the B-text of *Aislinge Meic Conglinne*. In *Celtica*, xx (1988), pp 53–72.

Harrison, Alan. Séanadh Saighre. In *Éigse*, xx (1984), pp 136–48.

Henry, P. L. *Táin roscada*: discussion and edition. In *Z.C.P.*, xlvii (1995), pp 32–75.

Herbert, Máire. The Irish *Sex aetates mundi*: first editions. In *Camb. Med. Celt. Studies*, xi (summer 1986), pp 97–112.

—— Fled Dúin na nGéd: a reappraisal. In *Camb. Med. Celt. Studies*, xviii (winter 1989), pp 75–88.

—— Celtic heroine? The archaeology of the Deirdre story. In T. O'Brien Johnson, and D. Cairns, *Gender in Irish writing* (Philadelphia, 1991), pp 13–22.

—— The universe of male and female: a reading of the Deirdre story. In C. J. Byrne, M. Harry, and P. Ó Siadhail (ed.), *Proceedings of the Second North American Congress of Celtic Studies* (Halifax, Nova Scotia, 1992), pp 53–64.

—— Goddess and king: the sacred marriage in early Ireland. In L. O. Fradenburg (ed.), *Women and sovereignty* (Edinburgh, 1992), pp 264–75.

—— The death of Muirchertach Mac Erca: a twelfth-century tale. In Folke Josephson (ed.), *Celts and vikings* (Göteborg, 1997), pp 27–40.

—— Caithréim Cellaig: some literary and historical considerations. In *Z.C.P.*, xlix–l (1997), pp 320–32.

Herren, Michael. Classical and secular learning among the Irish before the Carolingian renaissance. In *Florilegium*, iii (1981), pp 118–57.

—— The sighting of the host in *Táin Bó Fraích* and the *Hisperica Famina*. In *Peritia*, v (1986), pp 397–9.

Jaski, Bart. Cú Chulainn, *gormac* and *dalta* and the Ulstermen. In *Camb. Med. Celt. Studies*, xxxvii (summer 1999), pp 1–31.

Jennings, Rachel. A translation of the Tochmarc Treblainne. In *Emania*, xvi (1997), pp 73–8.

Hollo, Kaarina. The feast of Bricriu and the exile of the sons of Dóel Dermait. In *Emania*, x (1992), pp 18–24.

—— Conchobar's 'sceptre': the growth of a literary topos. In *Camb. Med. Celt. Studies*, xxix (summer 1995), pp 11–25.

Kitson, Peter. The jewels and the bird *Hiruath* of the 'Ever-new tongue'. In *Ériu*, xxxv (1984), pp 113–36.

Mac an Bhaird, Alan. Varia II. Tadhg mac Céin and the badgers. In *Ériu*, xxxi (1980), pp 150–54.

Mac Cana, Proinsias. Mongán mac Fiachna and *Immram Brain*. In *Ériu*, xxiii (1972), pp 102–42.

—— On the 'prehistory' of *Immram Brain*. In *Ériu*, xxvi (1975), pp 33–52.

—— The sinless Otherworld of *Immram Brain*. In *Ériu*, xxvii (1976), pp 95–118.

—— Varia V. An instance of modified narrative repetition in *Fled Bricrenn*. In *Ériu*, xxviii (1977), pp 168–72.

—— *The learned tales of medieval Ireland*. Dublin, 1980.

McCone, Kim. *Aided Cheltchair maic Uithechair*: hounds, heroes and hospitallers in early Irish myth and story. In *Ériu*, xxxv (1984), pp 1–30.

—— A tale of two ditties: poet and satirist in *Cath Maige Tuired*. In Ó Corráin, Breatnach, & McCone, *Sages, saints, & storytellers*, pp 122–43.

—— and Ó Fiannachta, Pádraig. *Scéalaíochta ár sinsear*. Maynooth, 1991.

Mac Donncha, Frederic. Seanmóireacht i nÉirinn ó 1000 go 1200. In Mac Conmara, *An léann eaglasta, 1000–1200*, pp 77–95.

——*Do'n Tarmchrutta*—an 11th-century homily on the Transfiguration. In *Collect. Hib.*, xxv (1983), pp 7–11.

——*Imdibe Críst*—an 11th-century homily on the circumcision of Christ. In *Collect. Hib.*, xxvi (1984), pp 7–12.

Mac Eoin, Gearóid. Suithchern and Rónán Dícolla. In *Z.C.P.*, xxxvi (1977), pp 63–82.

——The death of the boys in the mill. *Celtica*, xv (1983), pp 60–64.

Mac Eoin, Gearóid. Orality and literacy in some Middle Irish king-tales. In Tranter & Tristram, *Early Ir. lit.*, pp 149–84.

Mac Gearailt, Uáitéar. On textual correspondences in early Irish heroic tales. In MacLennan, *Proc. 1st N.A. Congress*, pp 343–55.

——*Cath Ruis na Ríg* and twelfth-century literary and oral tradition. In *Z.C.P.*, xliv (1991), pp 128–53.

McNamara, Martin. The bird *Hiruath* of the 'Ever-new Tongue' and *Hirodius* of gloss on Ps. 103:17 in Vatican Codex Pal. Lat. 68. In *Ériu*, xxxix (1988), pp 87–94.

McTurk, Rory. An Irish analogue to the Kráka-episode of Ragnars Saga Loðbrókar. In *Éigse*, xvii (1978), pp 277–96.

Mallory, J. P. The sword of the Ulster cycle. In Scott, *Studies on early Ire.*, pp 99–114.

——Silver in the Ulster cycle of tales. In Evans, Griffith, & Jope, *Proc. 7th Congress*, pp 31–78.

——The career of Conall Cernach. In *Emania*, vi (1989), pp 22–8.

——(ed.). *Aspects of the Táin.* Belfast, 1992.

Includes articles by Patricia Kelly, J. P. Mallory, and Ruairí Ó hUiginn.

Meek, Donald E. *Táin Bó Fraích* and other 'Fráech' texts: a study in thematic relationships. In *Camb. Med. Celt. Studies*, vii (summer 1984), pp 1–38; viii (winter 1984), pp 65–86.

Meid, Wolfgang. Zur sprachlichen Form altirischer Texte, hauptsächlich am Beispiel der 'LU-Táin'. In Tranter & Tristram, *Early Ir. lit.*, pp 185–200.

Myrick, L. D. The stelographic transmission of prediluvian *scéla*: an apocryphal reference in the Irish *Lebor Gabála*. In *Z.C.P.*, xlvii (1995), pp 18–31.

Nagy, J. F. How the Táin was lost. In *Z.C.P.*, xlix–l (1997), pp 603–9.

Ní Bhrolcháin, Muireann. A possible source for Keating's Forus Feasa ar Éirinn. In *Éigse*, xix (1982), pp 61–81.

Ní Chatháin, Próinséas. Bede's *Ecclesiastical history* in Irish. In *Peritia*, iii (1984), pp 115–30.

——Notes on the Würzburg glosses. In Ní Chatháin & Richter, *Ire. & Christendom*, pp 190–202.

——A reading in the Cambrai Homily. In *Celtica*, xxi (1990), p. 417.

Nagy, J. F. Heroic destinies in the *Macgnímrada* of Finn and Cú Chulainn. In *Z.C.P.*, xl (1984), pp 23–39.

Ní Mhaonaigh, Máire. Bréifne bias in *Cogad Gáedel re Gallaib*. In *Ériu*, xliii (1992), pp 135–58.

——*Cogad Gáedel re Gallaib* and the annals: a comparison. In *Ériu*, xlvii (1996), pp 101–25.

Ní Mhaonaigh, Máire. Friend and foe: vikings in ninth- and tenth-century Irish literature. In Clarke, Ní Mhaonaigh, & Ó Floinn, *Ire. & Scandinavia*, pp 381–404.

Ó hÁinle, Cathal. Cogadh Gaedhel re Gallaibh. In *Léachtaí Cholm Cille*, xiii (1982),
pp 76–98.

Ó hAodha, Donnchadh. The Irish version of Statius' Achilleid. In *R.I.A. Proc.*, lxxix
(1979), sect. C, pp 83–138.

Ó Cathasaigh, Tomás. On the LU version of 'The expulsion of the Dési'. In *Celtica*,
xi (1976), pp 150–57.

——The theme of *lommrad* in *Cath Maige Mucrama*. In *Éigse*, xviii (1981),
pp 211–24.

——The theme of *ainmne* in *Scéla Cano Meic Gartnáin*. In *Celtica*, xv (1983),
pp 78–87.

——*Cath Maige Tuired* as exemplary myth. In de Brún, Ó Coileáin, & Ó Riain,
*Folia Gadelica*, pp 1–19.

——The rhetoric of *Fingal Rónáin*. In *Celtica*, xvii (1985), pp 123–44.

——Varia III. The trial of Mael Fhothartaig. In *Ériu*, xxxvi (1985), pp 177–80.

——The rhetoric of *Scéla Cano meic Gartnáin*. In Ó Corráin, Breatnach, & McCone,
*Sages, saints, & storytellers*, pp 233–50.

——Three notes on *Cath Maige Tuired*. In *Ériu*, xl (1989), pp 61–8.

——On the *Cín Dromma Snechta* version of *Togail Brudne Uí Dergae*. In *Ériu*, xli
(1990), pp 103–14.

Ó Coileáin, Seán. The making of *Tromdám Guaire*. In *Ériu*, xxviii (1977), pp 32–70.

——A crux in *Aislinge Óenguso*. In *Celtica*, xx (1988), pp 167–8.

——*Echtrae Nerai* and its analogues. In *Celtica*, xxi (1990), pp 427–40.

Ó Concheanainn, Tomás. The act of wounding in the death of Muirchertach Mac
Erca. In *Éigse*, xv (1973), pp 141–3.

——Notes on Togail Bruidne Da Derga. In *Celtica*, xvii (1985), pp 73–90.

——The textual tradition of *Compert Con Culainn*. In *Celtica*, xxi (1990), pp 441–55.

Ó Cuív, Brian. A passage in Aided Con Culainn. In *Éigse*, xv (1973), p. 140.

——*Is tre fhír flathemon*. In *Celtica*, xiii (1980), pp 146–9.

Ó Háinle, Cathal. The *Pater noster* in Irish: the pre-reformation period. In *Celtica*,
xxi (1990), pp 470–88.

O'Hehir, Brendan. The Christian revision of *Eachtra Airt meic Cuinn ocus Tochmarc
Delbchaíme ingine Morgain*. In Ford, *Celtic folklore*, pp 159–79.

Ó hUiginn, Ruairí. Rúraíocht agus Rómánsaíocht: ceisteanna faoi Fhorás an Traidi-
siúin. In *Éigse*, xxxii (2000), pp 77–87.

Olmsted, Garrett. The Aided Fraich episode of *Táin Bó Cuailnge*. In *Études Celt.*, xv
(1978), pp 537–47.

——Mórrígan's warning to Donn Cuailnge. In *Études Celt.*, xix (1982), pp 165–72.

Olsen, Karin. The cuckold's revenge: reconstructing six Irish roscada in *Táin Bó
Cúailnge*. In *Camb. Med. Celt. Studies*, xxviii (winter 1994), pp 51–70.

Ó Néill, Pádraig P. The Old-Irish treatise on the Psalter and its Hiberno-Latin back-
ground.In *Ériu*, xxx (1979), pp 148–64.

——The background to the *Cambrai homily*. In *Ériu*, xxxii (1981), pp 137–48.

——The date and authorship of *Apgitir Chrábaid*: some internal evidence. In Ní
Chatháin & Richter, *Ire. & Christendom*, pp 203–15.

—— The Latin colophon to the 'Táin Bó Cúailnge' in the Book of Leinster: A critical view of Old Irish literature. In *Celtica*, xxiii (1999), pp 269–75.

—— The Old Irish tract on the Mass in the Stowe Missal: some observations on its origins and textual history. In Smyth, *Seanchas*, pp 199–204.

O'Rahilly, Cecile. Repetition; a narrative device in T.B.C. In *Ériu*, xxx (1979), pp 67–74.

Ó Riain, Pádraig. The materials and provenance of 'Buile Shuibhne'. In *Éigse*, xv (1974), pp 173–88.

Poppe, Erich. Deception and self-deception in *Fingal Rónáin*. In *Ériu*, xlvii (1996), pp 137–51.

—— *Stair Nuadat Find Femin*: eine irische Romanze? In *Z.C.P.*, xlix–l (1997), pp 749–59.

—— Varia II. King Ahab, Boia, Mac Da Thó and Ailill. In *Ériu*, l (1999), pp 169–73.

Rekdal, Jan Erik. Parallels between the Norwegian legend of St Sunniva and Irish voyage tales. In Clarke, Ní Mhaonaigh, & Ó Floinn, *Ire. & Scandinavia*, pp 277–87.

Sadowska, Eva. 'Horses led by a mare': martial aspects of *Táin Bó Cuailnge*. In *Emania*, xvi (1997), pp 5–48.

Sayers, William. Varia IV. Three charioteering gifts in Táin Bó Cúailgne and Mesca Ulad: immorchor ndelend, foscul ndíriuch, léim dar boilg. In *Ériu*, xxxii (1981), pp 163–7.

—— Textual notes on descriptions of the old Irish chariot and team. In *Studia Celtica Japonica*, iv (1991), pp 15–36.

—— Contracting for combat: flyting and fighting in *Táin Bó Cuailnge*. In *Emania*, xvi (1997), pp 49–62.

Scowcroft, R. Mark. Some recent work on Irish mythology and literature. In *Camb. Med. Celt. Studies*, iv (1982), pp 86–9.

—— Miotas na Gabhála i *Leabhar Gabhála*. In *Léachtaí Cholm Cille*, xiii (1982), pp 41–72.

—— *Leabhar Gabhála* I: the growth of the text. In *Ériu*, xxxviii (1987), pp 81–142.

—— *Leabhar Gabhála* II: the growth of the tradition. In *Ériu*, xxxix (1988), pp 1–66.

Simms, Katharine. Propaganda use of the *Táin* in the later middle ages. In *Celtica*, xv (1983), pp 142–9.

Slotkin, Edgar M. The structure of *Fled Bricrenn* before and after the *Lebor na hUidre* interpolations. In *Ériu*, xxix (1978), pp 64–77.

Sproule, David. Politics and pure narrative in the stories about Corc of Cashel. In *Ériu*, xxxvi (1985), pp 11–28.

Swartz, D. Dilts. Balance in the Book of Leinster Táin Bó Cuailgne and in classical studies. In *Proceedings of the Harvard Celtic Colloquium*, vi (1986), pp 29–46.

—— The problem of classic influence in the *Táin Bó Cuailgne*: significant parallels with 12th-century neo-classical rhetoric. In *Proceedings of the Harvard Celtic Colloquium*, vii (1987), pp 96–125.

Thurneysen, Rudolf. *Die irischen Helden- und Königsage*. Halle, 1921.

Toner, Gregory. The transmission of *Tochmarc Emire*. In *Ériu*, xlix (1998), pp 71–88.

Toner, Gregory. Reconstructing the earliest Irish tale lists. In *Éigse*, xxxii (2000), pp 88–120.

Tristram, Hildegard L. C. *Tense and time in early Irish narrative*. Innsbruck, 1983.

—— *Studien zur Táin Bó Cuailgne*. Tübingen, 1993.

—— The 'Cattle-raid of Cuailgne' in tension and transition between the oral and the written, classical subtexts and narrative heritage. In D. R. Edel (ed.), *Cultural identity and cultural integration* (Dublin, 1995), pp 61–81.

—— Latin and Latin learning in the *Táin Bó Cúailnge*. In Z.C.P., xlix–l (1997), pp 847–77.

—— The 'Cattle-Raid of Cuailnge' between the oral and the written: a research report (SFB 321, Projekt A 5, 1986–96). In Z.C.P., li (1999), pp 125–9.

Tymokzo, Maria. Animal imagery in *Loinges mac nUislenn*. In *Studia Celt.*, xx–xxi (1985–6), pp 145–66.

Watson, Alden. A structural analysis of *Echtra Nerai*. In *Études Celt.*, xxiii (1986), pp 129–42.

West, Máire. Leabhar na hUidhre's position in the manuscript history of *Togail Bruidne Da Derga* and *Orgain Brudne Ui Dergae*. In *Camb. Med. Celt. Studies*, xx (winter 1990), pp 61–98.

—— The genesis of *Togail Bruidne da Derga*: a reappraisal of the 'two-source' theory. In *Celtica*, xxiii (1999), pp 413–35.

Sims-Williams, Patrick. Thought, word, and deed: an Irish triad. In *Ériu*, xxix (1978), pp 78–111.

## 9   Irish poetry

### (a) Primary texts

Boyle, Séamus. A poem on Cenél Énnai. In *Proceedings of the Harvard Celtic Colloquium*, i (1981), pp 9–20.

Breatnach, Liam. 'The caldron of poesy'. In *Ériu*, xxxii (1981), pp 45–94.

—— Addenda and corrigenda to 'The caldron of poesy'. In *Ériu*, xxxv (1984), pp 189–92.

—— An edition of *Amra Senáin*. In Ó Corráin, Breatnach, & McCone, *Sages, saints, & storytellers*, pp 7–32.

Byrne, F. J. The lament for Cummíne Foto. In *Ériu*, xxxi (1980), pp 111–22.

Carney, James. Three Old-Irish accentual poems. In *Ériu*, xxii (1971), pp 23–80.

—— *A maccucáin, sruith in tíag*. In *Celtica*, xv (1983), pp 25–41.

Dillon, Myles. A poem on the kings of the Eóganachta. In *Celtica*, x (1973), pp 9–14.

Greene, David, and Kelly, Fergus. *The Irish Adam and Eve story from Saltair na Rann*. Dublin, 1976.

Greene, David, and O'Connor, Frank (ed.). *A golden treasury of Irish poetry* A.D. 600 to 1200. London, 1967.

Gwynn, Edward J. *The metrical Dindshenchas*. 5 parts. Dublin, 1903–35. Reprinted, 1991. (R.I.A. Todd Lecture Series, viii–xii.)

Henry, P. L. The caldron of poesy. In *Studia Celt.*, xiv–xv (1979–80), pp 114–28.

—— *Verba Scáthaige*. In *Celtica*, xxi (1990), pp 191–207.

—— *Dánta Ban: poems of Irish women, early and modern*. Dublin, 1991.

Herbert, Máire. The seven journeys of the soul. In *Éigse*, xvii (1977), pp 1–11.

Hogan, Edmund I. *Mórthimchell Érenn uile*. Dublin, 1901.

Kelly, Fergus, A poem in praise of Columb Cille. In *Ériu*, xxiv (1973), pp 1–23.

——Tiughraind Bhécáin. In *Ériu*, xxvi (1975), pp 66–98.

Kennelly, Brendan. *The Penguin book of Irish verse*. Harmondsworth, 1970.

Kinsella, Thomas. *The new Oxford book of Irish verse*. Oxford, 1986.

Lehmann, Ruth. *A Marbáin, a díthrubaig*. In *Z.C.P.*, xxxvi (1977), pp 97–111.

Lehmann, Ruth. Poems from the *Death of Cú Chulainn*. In *Z.C.P.*, xlix–l (1997), pp 432–9.

Lucey, Seán. *Love poems of the Irish*. Cork, 1967.

Mac Eoin, Gearóid. The lament for Cummíne Fota. In *Ériu*, xxviii (1977), pp 17–31.

Montague, John. *The Faber book of Irish verse*. London, 1974.

Murdoch, Brian. *Saltair na Rann* xxv–xxxiv: from Abraham to Joseph. In *Ériu*, xlvi (1995), pp 93–120.

Ó hAodha, Donncha. The lament of the Old Woman of Beare. In Ó Corráin, Breatnach, & McCone, *Sages, saints, & storytellers*, pp 308–31.

Ó Cuív, Brian. A penitent's prayer. In *Éigse*, xiv (1971), pp 17–26.

——Mael Ísu Ua Brolcháin's prayer to St Michael. In *Éigse*, xiv (1971), p. 17.

——Two items from Irish apocryphal tradition. In *Celtica*, x (1973), pp 87–113.

——Three Middle Irish poems. In *Éigse*, xvi (1975), pp 1–17.

——A Middle-Irish poem on Leinster dynasties. In *Études Celt.*, xviii (1981), pp 141–50.

——Varia VII. The two herons of Druim Ceat. In *Ériu*, xxxvii (1986), pp 194–6.

——A poem of prophecy on Ua Conchobair kings of Connacht. In *Celtica*, xix (1987), pp 31–54.

——Two religious poems in Irish. In *Celtica*, xx (1988), pp 73–84.

——An item relating to the legend of Labraid Loingsech. In *Ériu*, xxxix (1988), pp 75–8.

——The Irish marginalia in Codex Palatino-Vaticanus no. 830. In *Éigse*, xxiv (1990), pp 45–67.

O'Donovan, John. The circuit of Ireland by Muircheartach mac Neill, prince of Aileach. In *Tracts relating to Ireland* (Irish Archaeological Society, Dublin, 1841), pp 3–65.

Ó Macháin, Pádraig. Ar bhás Chuinn Chéadchathaigh. In *Éigse*, xxi (1986), pp 53–65.

Ó Néill, Pádraig. Airbertach mac Cosse's poem on the psalter. In *Éigse*, xvii (1977), pp 19–46.

Oskamp, H. P. A. The Irish quatrains and salutation in the Drummond missal. In *Ériu*, xxviii (1977), pp 82–91.

Poppe, Erich. A Middle Irish poem on Éimíne's Bell. In *Celtica*, xvii (1985), pp 59–72.

Stokes, Whitley. *On the Calendar of Oengus*. Dublin, 1880. (*R.I.A. Trans.*, Irish Manuscripts Series, 1.)

*(b) Secondary works*

Bowen, Charles. A historical inventory to the Dindshenchas. In *Studia Celt.*, x–xi (1975–6), pp 113–37.

Breatnach, Liam. Poets and poetry. In Kim McCone and Katharine Simms (ed.), *Progress in medieval Irish studies* (Maynooth, 1996), pp 65–78.

Breatnach, Pádraig A. The chief's poet. In *R.I.A. Proc.*, lxxxiii (1983), pp 37–79.

Campanile, Enrico. Indogermanische Metrik und altirische Metrik. In *Z.C.P.*, xxxvii (1979), pp 174–202.

Carey, John. Cosmology in *Saltair na Rann*. In *Celtica*, xvii (1985), pp 33–52.

—— The heavenly city in *Saltair na Rann*. In *Celtica*, xviii (1986), pp 87–104.

—— A tract on the Creation. In *Éigse*, xxi (1986), pp 1–9.

—— Angelology in *Saltair na Rann*. In *Celtica*, xix (1987), pp 1–8.

—— The Irish vision of the Chinese. In *Ériu*, xxxviii (1987), pp 73–80.

—— *Visio Sancti Pauli* and the *Saltair*'s Hell. In *Éigse*, xxiii (1989), pp 39–44.

—— The three things required of a poet. In *Ériu*, xlviii (1997), pp 41–58.

—— Transmutations of immortality in 'The lament of the Old Woman of Beare'. In *Celtica*, xxiii (1999), pp 30–37.

Carney, James. Linking alliteration ('Fidrad Freccomail'). In *Éigse*, xviii (1981), pp 251–62.

—— The dating of early Irish verse texts. In *Éigse*, xix (1983), pp 177–216.

—— A girdle around the earth. In *Ireland of the Welcomes*, xxxv, no. 3 (May–June, 1986), pp 38–9.

—— The dating of archaic Irish verse. In Tranter & Tristram, *Early Ir. lit.*, pp 39–56.

Clancy, Thomas Owen. Mac Steléne and the eight in Armagh: identity and context. In *Éigse*, xxvi (1992), pp 80–91.

Corthals, Johan. Some observations of the versification of the rhymeless 'Leinster poems'. In *Celtica*, xxi (1990), pp 113–25.

Draak, Martje. 'Rindard'. In *Celtica*, xi (1976), p. 60.

Ford, Patrick K. The blind, the dumb, and the ugly: aspects of poets and their craft in early Ireland and Wales. In *Camb. Med. Celt. Studies*, xix (summer 1990), pp 27–40.

Gillies, William. The classical Irish poetic tradition. In Evans, Griffith, & Jope, *Proc. 7th Congress*, pp 108–20.

Harrison, Alan. Snéadhbhairdne. In *Éigse*, xvii (1977–8), pp 181–96.

Hollo, Kaarina. The alliterative structure of Mael Ísu ua Brolcháin's *A aingil, beir*. In *Ériu*, xli (1990), pp 77–80.

—— Cú Chulainn and Síd Truim. In *Ériu*, xlix (1998), pp 13–22.

Hull, Vernam. Varia linguistica Hibernica. In Wolfgang Meid (ed.), *Beiträge zur Indogermanistik und Keltologie Julius Pokorny zum 80. Geburtstag gewidmet* (Innsbruck, 1967), pp 175–8.

—— Four Old-Irish songs of summer and winter. In *Celtica*, ix (1971), pp 200–1.

Hull, Vernam. A note on Buile Shuibhne. In *Celtica*, ix (1971), p. 214.

Jacobs, Nicolas. The Green Knight: an unexplored Irish parallel. In *Camb. Med. Celt. Studies*, iv (winter 1982), pp 1–4.

Kelleher, John V. On a poem about Gormfhlaith [see Brian Ó Cuív in *Éigse*, xvi, 1–17]. In *Éigse*, xvi (1976), pp 251–4.

Lambkin, B. K. The structure of the Blathmac poems. In *Studia Celt.*, xx–xxi (1985–6), pp 67–77.

——Blathmac and the Céili Dé: a reappraisal. In *Celtica*, xxiii (1999), pp 132–54.

Lubotsky, Alexander. Varia IV. On the alliteration in 'The guesting of Athirne'. In *Ériu*, xxxiii (1982), pp 170–71.

Mac an Bhaird, Alan. Dán díreach agus ranna as na hAnnála 867–1134 A.D. In *Éigse*, xvii (1977–8), pp 157–68.

Mac Cana, Proinsias. The poet as spouse of his patron. In *Ériu*, xxxix (1988), pp 79–86.

McCaughey, Terence. The performing of dán. In *Ériu*, xxxv (1984), pp 39–58.

——Bards, beasts and men. In Ó Corráin, Breatnach, & McCone, *Sages, saints, & storytellers*, pp 102–43.

Mac Eoin, Gearóid. Observations on Saltair na Rann. In *Z.C.P.*, xxxix (1982), pp 1–28.

McManus, Damian. *Uaim do rinn*: linking alliteration or a lost *dúnad*? In *Ériu*, xlvi (1995), pp 59–64.

Meek, Donald E. Development and degeneration in Gaelic ballad texts. In Almqvist, Ó Catháin, & Ó hÉalaí, *Heroic process*, pp 131–60.

——The banners of the Fian in Gaelic ballad tradition. In *Camb. Med. Celt. Studies*, xi (summer 1986), pp 29–69.

Melia, Daniel F. Further speculation on marginal *.r.* In *Celtica*, xxi (1990), pp 362–7.

Murdoch, Brian. From the Flood to the Tower of Babel: some notes on *Saltair na Rann* xiii–xxiv. In *Ériu*, xl (1989), pp 69–92.

——In pursuit of the *Caillech Bérre*: an early Irish poem and the medievalist at large. In *Z.C.P.*, xliv (1991), pp 80–127.

Ní Bhrolcháin, Muireann. The manuscript tradition of the Banshenchas. In *Ériu*, xxxiii (1982), pp 109–35.

——An Banshenchas. In P. Ó Fiannachta (ed.), *Na mná sa litríocht* (Maynooth, 1982), pp 5–29.

——*Maol Íosa Ó Brolcháin*. Maynooth, 1986.

Ní Chatháin, Próinséas. Some early Irish hymn material. In Bonner, *Famulus Christi*, pp 229–38.

——Some themes in early Irish lyric poetry. In *Irish University Review*, xxii (1992), pp 3–12.

Ní Dhonnchadha, Máirín. Two female lovers. In *Ériu*, xlv (1994), pp 113–20.

——The poem beginning 'A Shláine inghean Fhlannagáin'. In *Ériu*, xlvi (1995), pp 65–70.

——On Gormfhlaith daughter of Flann Sinna and the lure of the sovereignty goddess. In Smyth, *Seanchas*, pp 225–37.

Ní Riain, Noirín. The female song in the Irish tradition. In E. Ní Chuilleanáin (ed.), *Irish women, image and achievement* (Dublin, 1985), pp 73–84.

Ní Shéaghdha, Nessa. The poems of Blathmac: the 'fragmentary quatrains'. In *Celtica*, xxiii (1999), pp 227–30.

Ó hAodha, Donncha. The first Middle Irish metrical tract. In H. L. C. Tristram (ed.), *Metrik und Medienwechsel: Metrics and media* (ScriptOralia, xxxv; Tübingen, 1991), pp 207–42.

Ó Baoill, Colm. Person-shifting in Gaelic verse. In *Celtica*, xxi (1990), pp 377–92.

Ó Cathasaigh, Tomás. Curse and satire. In *Éigse*, xxi (1986), pp 10–15.

Ó Concheanainn, Tomás. The three forms of Dinnshenchas Érenn. In *Journal of Celtic Studies*, iii (1981), pp 88–131.

——A pious redactor of Dinnshenchas Érenn. In *Ériu*, xxxiii (1982), pp 85–98.

——Smacht rí agus ruire. In *Celtica*, xvi (1984), p. 86.

Ó Corráin, Donnchadh. Early Irish hermit poetry? In Ó Corráin, Breatnach, & McCone, *Sages, saints, & storytellers*, pp 251–67.

Ó Cróinín, Dáibhí. Three weddings and a funeral: rewriting Irish political history in the tenth century. In Smyth, *Seanchas*, pp 212–24.

Ó Cuív, Brian. The linguistic training of the medieval Irish poet. In *Celtica*, x (1973), pp 114–40.

Ó Duinn, Seán. Maol Íosa Ó Brolcháin agus a chuid filíochta. In Mac Conmara, *An léann eaglasta*, pp 96–103.

Ó Fiannachta, Pádraig. The development of the debate between Pádraig and Oisín. In Almqvist, Ó Catháin, & Ó hÉalaí, *Heroic process*, pp 183–205.

Ó hAodha, Donncha. The first Middle Irish metrical tract. In H. L. C. Tristram (ed.), *Metrik und Medienwechsel: metrics and media* (ScriptOralia xxxv, Tübingen, 1991), pp 207–42.

——Rechtgal úa Síadail, a famous poet of the Old Irish period. In Smyth, *Seanchas*, pp 192–8.

Ó Néill, Pádraig P. Airbertach mac Cosse's poem on the Psalter. In *Éigse*, xvii (1977), pp 19–46.

Oskamp, Hans P. A. The Irish material in the St Paul Irish codex. In *Éigse*, xvii (1978), pp 385–91.

Poppe, Erich. Cormac's metrical testament: 'Mithig techt tar mo thimna'. In *Celtica*, xxiii (1999), pp 300–11.

Quin, E. G. The early Irish poem *Ísucán*. In *Camb. Med. Celt. Studies*, i (summer 1981), pp 39–52.

——Ochtfhoclach Choluim Chille. In *Celtica*, xiv (1981), pp 125–53; xv (1983), p. 141.

Schneiders, Marc. 'Pagan past and Christian present' in 'Félire Óengusso'. In D. R. Edel (ed.), *Cultural identity and cultural integration* (Dublin, 1995), pp 157–69.

Simms, Katharine. The poet as chieftain's widow: bardic elegies. In Ó Corráin, Breatnach, & McCone, *Sages, saints & storytellers*, pp 400–11.

——Images of warfare in bardic poetry. In *Celtica*, xxi (1990), pp 608–19.

Sproule, David. Complex alliteration in Gruibne's *roscad*. In *Ériu*, xxxiii (1982), pp 157–60.

——Complex alliteration, full and unstressed rhyme, and the origin of *deibide*. In *Ériu*, xxxviii (1987), pp 185–200.

Sveinsson, Einar Ólafur. An Old Irish verse-form roaming in the North. In B. Almqvist and D. Greene (ed.), *Proceedings of the Seventh Viking Congress* (London, 1976), pp 141–52.

Travis, James. *Early Celtic versecraft: origin, development, diffusion*. Cornell and Shannon, 1973.

Wagner, Heinrich. The archaic *Dind Ríg* poem and related problems. In *Ériu*, xviii (1977), pp 1–16.


## IV · SECONDARY WORKS

### *A GENERAL HISTORY*

Adamson, Ian. *The identity of Ulster: the land, the language and the people.* Belfast, 1982.

Aitchison, Nicholas. *Armagh and the royal centres in early medieval Ireland: monuments, cosmology and the past.* Woodbridge, 1994.

Bardon, Jonathan. *A history of Ulster.* Belfast, 1992.

Beckett, J. C. *A short history of Ireland.* London, 1973. 6th ed., 1986.

Bieler, Ludwig. *Irland, Wegbereiter des Mittelalters.* Olten, 1962. English version, *Ireland, harbinger of the middle ages.* Oxford, 1963.

——*Ireland and the culture of early medieval Europe.* Ed. Richard Sharpe. London, 1987.

Brady, Ciaran, and Gillespie, Raymond (ed.). *Natives and newcomers.* Dublin, 1986.

Buckley, Victor. From the darkness to the dawn: the later prehistoric and early Christian borderlands. In Raymond Gillespie and Harold O'Sullivan (ed.), *The borderlands: essays in the history of the Ulster–Leinster border* (Belfast, 1989), pp 23–40.

Byrne, F. J. Die keltischen Völker. In Theodor Schieder (ed.), *Handbuch der europäischen Geschichte*, i (Stuttgart, 1976; 3. Auflage, 1991), pp 449–92.

Graham-Campbell, James. The early viking age in the Irish Sea area. In Clarke, Ní Mhaonaigh, & Ó Floinn, *Ire. & Scandinavia*, pp 104–30.

Chadwick, Nora K. *Studies in the early British church.* Cambridge, 1958.

——*Celt and Saxon: studies in the early British border.* Cambridge, 1963.

——*Celtic Britain.* London, 1963.

——(ed.). *Studies in early British history.* Cambridge, 1954.

Culleton, Edward. *Celtic and early Christian Wexford, A.D. 400–1166.* Dublin, 1999.

Curtis, Edmund. *A history of medieval Ireland from 1110 to 1513.* London, 1923.

——*A history of Ireland.* Oxford, 1936.

Davies, R. R. *Historical perception: Celts and Saxons.* Cardiff, 1979.

——Presidential address: the peoples of Britain and Ireland, 1100–1400. In *Transactions of the Royal Historical Society*, 6th ser., iv (1994), pp 1–20.

de Breffny, Brian (ed.). *Ireland: a cultural encyclopaedia.* London, 1983.

de Paor, Liam. *The peoples of Ireland: from prehistory to modern times.* London, 1986.

——*St Patrick's world: the Christian culture of Ireland's apostolic age.* Dublin, 1993.

——*Ireland and early Europe: essays and occasional writings on art and culture.* Dublin, 1997.

——and de Paor, Máire. *Early Christian Ireland.* London, 1958. Reprinted 1964.

Dillon, Myles, and Chadwick, N. K. *The Celtic realms.* London, 1967.

Driscoll, Stephen T. The relationship between history and archaeology: artefacts, documents and history. In Driscoll & Nieke, *Power & politics*, pp 162–87.

Duval, Paul-Marie. *Les Celtes.* Paris, 1977.

Etchingham, Colmán. Early medieval Irish history. In Kim McCone and Katharine Simms (ed.), *Progress in medieval Irish studies* (Maynooth, 1996), pp 123–54.

Evans, D. Simon. The Welsh and the Irish before the Normans: contact or impact. In *Brit. Acad. Proc.*, lxxv (1989), pp 143–61. (Sir John Rhys memorial lecture.)

Foster, R. F. *An illustrated history of Ireland.* Oxford, 1989. 2nd ed., *The Oxford history of Ireland.* Oxford, 1992.

Frazer, T. B., and Jeffrey, Keith (ed.). *Men, women, and war.* Dublin, 1993. (*Hist. Studies*, xviii.)

Gougaud, Louis. *Les chrétientés celtiques.* Paris, 1911. English ed. (translated by Maud Joynt) published as *Christianity in Celtic lands* (London, 1932). Reprinted with introduction by J.-M. Picard (Dublin, 1992).

Green, Miranda. *The gods of the Celts.* Gloucester, 1986.

—— Celtic religion. In D. R. Edel (ed.), *Cultural identity and cultural integration* (Dublin, 1995), pp 129–44.

—— (ed.). *The Celtic world.* London and New York, 1995.

Greene, David. The coming of the Celts: the linguistic viewpoint. In Mac Eoin, Ahlqvist, & Ó hAodha, *Proc. 6th Congress*, pp 131–7.

Helle, Knut. The history of the early viking age in Norway. In Clarke, Ní Mhaonaigh, & Ó Floinn, *Ire. & Scandinavia*, pp 239–58.

Jones, Gwyn. *A history of the vikings.* Oxford, 1968.

Laing, Lloyd, and Laing, Jennifer. *Celtic Britain and Ireland A.D. 200–800: the myth of the dark ages.* Dublin, 1990.

Lydon, James. *The making of Ireland from ancient times to the present.* London and New York, 1998.

Mac Cana, Proinsias. The influence of the vikings on Celtic literature. In Brian Ó Cuív (ed.), *Proceedings of the* [First] *International Congress of Celtic Studies* (Dublin, 1962), pp 78–118.

—— *Celtic mythology.* London, 1970. Reprinted, 1996.

MacCurtain, Margaret, and Ó Corráin, Donnchadh (ed.). *Women in Irish society.* Westport, 1979.

McNally, Robert (ed.). *Old Ireland.* Dublin, 1965.
Includes articles by Ludwig Bieler, John Hennig, J. N. Hillgarth, Robert McNally, Diarmuid Ó Laoghaire, and Jeremiah O'Sullivan.

Mayr-Harting, Henry. *The coming of Christianity to Anglo-Saxon England.* London, 1972.

Morris, Christopher. Raiders, traders and settlers: the early viking age in Scotland. In Clarke, Ní Mhaonaigh, & Ó Floinn, *Ire. & Scandinavia*, pp 73–103.

Ó Corráin, Donnchadh. Prehistoric and early Christian Ireland. In R. F. Foster (ed.), *An illustrated history of Ireland* (Oxford, 1989), pp 1–52, and *The Oxford history of Ireland* (Oxford, 1992), pp 1–43.

—— Ireland, Scotland and Wales c.700 to the early eleventh century. In R. McKitterick (ed.), *The new Cambridge medieval history* (Cambridge, 1995), pp 43–63.

—— Ireland, Wales, Man and the Hebrides. In P. Sawyer (ed.), *The Oxford illustrated history of the vikings* (Oxford, 1997), pp 83–109.

Ó hÓgáin, Dáithí. *Myth, legend, and romance: an encyclopaedia of the Irish folk tradition.* Dublin, 1990.

O'Keeffe, Tadhg. *Medieval Ireland A.D. 1100–1600*. Stroud, 2000.

O'Loughlin, Thomas. *Celtic theology: humanity, world, and God in early Irish writings*. London, 2000.

Ó Murchadha, Seán. Diseart Tola and its environs. In *The Other Clare*, xvi (1992), pp 53–7.

Otway-Ruthven, A. J. *A history of medieval Ireland*. London, 1968. 2nd ed., 1980. Introductory chapter by Kathleen Hughes.

Piggott, Stuart. *The druids*. London, 1968.

Powell, T. G. E. *The Celts*. London, 1958.

Price, Glanville. *Ireland and the Celtic connection*. Gerrards Cross, 1987.

Raftery, Joseph. *The Celts*. Dublin, 1967.

Rees, Alwyn, and Rees, Brinley. *Celtic heritage: ancient tradition in Ireland and Wales*. London, 1961.

Richter, Michael. *Irland im Mittelalter: Kultur und Geschichte*. Stuttgart, 1983. English ed. (translated by Brian Stone and Adrian Keogh) published as *Medieval Ireland: the enduring tradition*. London and Dublin, 1988.

——Towards a methodology of historical sociolinguistics. In *Folia Linguistica Historica*, vi, no. 1 (1985), pp 41–61.

——*Ireland and her neighbours in the seventh century*. Dublin, 1999.

Ritchie, Anna. *Viking Scotland*. London, 1993.

Roesdahl, Else. *The vikings*. Copenhagen, 1987. English ed., translated by Susan M. Margeson and Kirsten Williams. Harmondsworth, 1991.

Ross, Anne. *Everyday life of the pagan Celts*. London, 1970.

——*Pagan Celtic Britain*. London, 1967. Revised ed., 1992.

Sawyer, Peter. *The age of the vikings*. 2nd ed., London, 1971.

——*Kings and vikings*. London, 1982.

Thompson, E. A. *Romans and barbarians*. Madison, 1982.

Tierney, J. J. The Celtic ethnography of Poseidonios. In *R.I.A. Proc.*, lx (1960), sect. C, pp 189–275.

Wagner, Heinrich. *Studies in the origins of the Celts and of early Celtic civilisation*. Belfast and Tübingen, 1971.

——Beiträge in Erinnerung an Julius Pokorny. In *Z.C.P.*, xxxii (1972), pp 1–89.

——Studies in the origins of early Celtic traditions. In *Ériu*, xvi (1975), pp 1–26.

——Origins of pagan Irish religion. In *Z.C.P.*, xxxviii (1981), pp 1–28.

——Zur Etymologie von keltisch *Nodons*, Ir. *Nuadu*, Kymr. *Nudd/Ludd*. In *Z.C.P.*, xli (1986), pp 188–213.

——The Celtic invasions of Ireland and Great Britain. In *Z.C.P.*, xlii (1987), pp 1–40.

Wilson, David. *The vikings and their origins*. London, 1970.

## B COMPOSITE WORKS

Composite works concerned with specific subjects are listed in the appropriate sections.

Almqvist, Bo, and Greene, David (ed.). *Proceedings of the Seventh Viking Congress, Dublin, 15–21 August, 1973.* London, 1976.

—— Ó Catháin, Séamas; and Ó Héalaí, Pádraig (ed.). *The heroic process: form, function and fantasy in folk epic.* Dún Laoghaire, Co. Dublin, 1987.

Barnard, T. C.; Ó Cróinín, Dáibhí; and Simms, Katharine (ed.). *'A miracle of learning': studies in manuscripts and Irish learning. Essays in honour of William O'Sullivan.* Aldershot, 1998.

Harper-Bill, C. (ed.) *Anglo-Norman Studies 20: Proceedings of the Battle Conference in Dublin, 1997.* Woodbridge, 1998.

Includes essays of Irish interest by Leslie Abrams, Mark Philpott, Seán Duffy, Pádraig Ó Néill, Judith Everard, John Gillingham, S. D. Church, M. T. Flanagan, and Yoko Wada.

Bonner, Gerald (ed.). *Famulus Christi: essays in commemoration of the thirteenth centenary of the birth of the Venerable Bede.* London, 1976.

Bourke, Cormac (ed.). *From the isles of the north: early medieval art in Ireland and Britain.* Belfast, 1995.

—— (ed.). *Studies in the cult of Saint Columba.* Dublin, 1997.

Bradley, John (ed.). *Settlement and society in medieval Ireland: studies presented to F. X. Martin.* Kilkenny, 1988.

Broun, Dauvit, and Clancy, T. O. (ed.). *Spes Scotorum, hope of Scots: St Columba, Iona and Scotland.* Edinburgh, 1999.

Byrne, C. J.; Harry, Margaret; and Ó Siadhail, Pádraig (ed.). *Celtic languages and Celtic people. Proceedings of the Second North American Congress of Celtic Studies (Halifax, August 16–19, 1989).* Halifax, Nova Scotia, 1992.

Carver, Martin (ed.). *The age of Sutton Hoo: the seventh century in north-western Europe.* Woodbridge, 1994.

Clarke, H. B., and Brennan, Mary (ed.). *Columbanus and Merovingian monasticism.* Oxford, 1981. (Brit. Arch. Reps, International Series, cxiii.)

Clarke, H. B., and Simms, Anngret (ed.). *The comparative history of urban origins in non-Roman Europe.* 2 vols. Oxford, 1985. (Brit. Arch. Reps, International Series, cclv.)

Clarke, H. B.; Ní Mhaonaigh, Máire; and Ó Floinn, Raghnall (ed.). *Ireland and Scandinavia in the early viking age.* Dublin, 1998.

Davies, Oliver, and O'Loughlin, Thomas (ed.). *Celtic spirituality.* New York and Mahwah, 1999.

de Brún, Pádraig; Ó Coileáin, Seán; and Ó Riain, Pádraig (ed.). *Folia Gadelica: aistí ó iardhaltaí leis a bronnadh ar R. A. Breatnach.* Cork, 1983.

[de Paor, Liam (ed.)]. *Great books of Ireland.* Dublin, 1967.

Dopsch, Heinz, and Juffinger, Roswitha (ed.). *Virgil von Salzburg, Missionar und Gelehrter: Beiträge des internationalen Symposiums von 21.–24. September in der Salzburger Residenz.* Salzburg, 1985.

Driscoll, S. T., and Nieke, M. R. (ed.). *Power and politics in early medieval Britain and Ireland.* Edinburgh, 1988.

Duffy, Seán (ed.). *Medieval Dublin I: Proceedings of the Friends of Medieval Dublin Symposium 1999.* Dublin, 2000.

Edel, D. R. (ed.) *Cultural identity and cultural integration: Ireland and Europe in the early middle ages*. Dublin, 1995.

Edel, D. R. (ed.) Gerritsen, W. P.; and Veelenturf, K. (ed.) *Monniken, ridders en zeevaarders*. Münster, 1988.

Erichsen, Johannes, and Brockhoff, Evamaria (ed.). *Kilian, Mönch aus Irland—aller Franken Patron*. 2 vols. Munich, 1989. (Veröffentlichungen zur Bayerischen Geschichte und Kultur, 1989.)

Evans, D. Ellis; Griffith, John G.; and Jope, E. M. (ed.). *Proceedings of the Seventh International Congress of Celtic Studies, Oxford 1983*. Oxford, 1986.

Ford, Patrick K. (ed). *Celtic folklore and Christianity*. Santa Barbara, 1983.

Herren, Michael (ed.). *Insular Latin studies: papers on Latin texts and manuscripts of the British Isles, 550–1066*. Toronto, 1981.

Hofman, Rijcklof; Smelik, B.; and Jongeling, K. (ed.). *Kelten van Spanje tot Ierland*. Münster, 1996.

Hourihane, Colm (ed.). *From Ireland coming: Irish art from the early Christian to the late Gothic period and its European context*. Princeton, 2001.

Josephson, Folke (ed.). *Celts and vikings: proceedings of the fourth symposium of Societas Celtologica Nordica*. Göteborg, 1997.

Karkov, Catherine; Farrell, Robert T.; and Ryan, Michael (ed.). *The insular tradition*. Albany, N.Y., 1997. (SUNY Series in Medieval Studies, ed. Paul E. Szarmach.)

Kearney, Richard (ed.). *The Irish mind: exploring intellectual traditions*. Dublin, 1985.

King, H. A. (ed.). *Clonmacnoise studies i*. Dublin, 1998.

Laing, Margaret, and Williamson, Keith (ed.) *Speaking in our tongues: proceedings of a colloquium on medieval dialectology and related disciplines*. Woodbridge, 1994.

Lapidge, Michael (ed.). *Columbanus: studies on the Latin writings*. Woodbridge, 1997.

Löwe, Heinz (ed.). *Die Iren und Europa im früheren Mittelalter*. 2 vols. Stuttgart, 1982.

Luisella Fadda, A. M., and Ó Carragáin, É. (ed.). *Le isole britanniche e Roma in età romanobarbarica*. Rome, 1998. (Biblioteca di Cultura Romanobarbarica, 1.)

McCone, Kim, and Simms, Katherine (ed.). *Progress in medieval Irish studies*. Maynooth, 1996.

Mac Eoin, Gearóid; Ahlqvist, Anders; and Ó hAodha, Donncha (ed.). *Proceedings of the Sixth International Congress of Celtic Studies held in University College, Galway, 4–13 July 1979*. Dublin, 1983.

McGrail, Seán (ed.). *Woodworking techniques before A.D. 1500: papers presented to a symposium at Greenwich in September 1980*. Oxford, 1982. (Brit. Arch. Reps, British Series, xxx.)

MacLennan, Gordon W. (ed.). *Proceedings of the First North American Congress of Celtic Studies... 1986*. Ottawa, 1988.

McNally, Robert (ed.). *Old Ireland*. Dublin, 1965.

Mac Niocaill, Gearóid, and Wallace, Patrick F. (ed.). *Keimelia: studies in medieval archaeology and history in memory of Tom Delaney*. Galway, 1988.

Martin, F. X., and Byrne, F. J. (ed.). *The scholar revolutionary: Eoin MacNeill, 1867–1945, and the making of the new Ireland*. Shannon, 1973.

Meyer, Marc Anthony (ed.). *The culture of Christendom: essays in medieval history in commemoration of Denis L. T. Bethell.* London and Rio Grande, 1993.

Monk, Michael A., and Sheehan, John (ed.). *Early medieval Munster: archaeology, history and society.* Cork, 1998.

Ní Chatháin, Próinséas, and Richter, Michael (ed.). *Irland und Europa: die Kirche im Frühmittelalter/Ireland and Europe: the early church.* Stuttgart, 1984.

————(ed.). *Irland und die Christenheit: Bibelstudien und Mission/Ireland and Christendom: the Bible and the missions.* Stuttgart, 1987.

————(ed.). *Irland und Europa im früheren Mittelalter: Bildung und Literatur/ Ireland and Europe in the earlier middle ages: learning and literature.* Stuttgart, 1996.

Ní Chuilleanáin, Eilean (ed.). *Irish women: image and achievement.* Dublin, 1985.

Nolan, William (ed.). *The shaping of Ireland: the geographical perspective.* Dublin, 1986.

Ó Corráin, Donnchadh (ed.). *Irish antiquity: essays and studies presented to Professor M. J. O'Kelly.* Cork, 1981.

——Breatnach, Liam; and McCone, Kim (ed.). *Sages, saints and storytellers: Celtic studies in honour of Professor James Carney.* Maynooth, 1989. (Maynooth Monographs, ii.)

O'Loughlin, Thomas (ed.). *The scriptures and early medieval Ireland: proceedings of the 1993 conference of the Society for Hiberno-Latin studies on early Irish exegesis and homiletics.* Steenbrugge and Turnhout, 1999.

O'Meara, John J., and Naumann, Bernd (ed.). *Latin script and letters A.D. 400–900: Festschrift presented to Ludwig Bieler on the occasion of his 70th birthday.* Leyden, 1976.

Pearce, Susan M. (ed.). *The early church in western Britain and Ireland: studies presented to C. A. Ralegh Radford arising from a conference organised in his honour by the Devon Archaeological Society and Exeter City Museum.* Oxford, 1982. (Brit. Arch. Reps, British Series, cii.)

Pender, Séamus (ed.). *Féilsgríbhinn Tórna: essays and studies presented to Tadhg Ua Donnchadha (Torna).* Cork, 1947.

Picard, Jean-Michel (ed.). *Ireland and northern France A.D. 600–850.* Dublin, 1991.

——*Ireland and Aquitaine in the middle ages.* Dublin, 1995.

Ryan, John (ed.). *Féil-sgríbhinn Eóin Mhic Néill: essays and studies presented to Professor Eóin MacNeill on the occasion of his seventieth birthday.* Dublin, 1940.

Rynne, Etienne (ed.). *North Munster studies: essays in commemoration of Monsignor Michael Moloney.* Limerick, 1967.

Sawyer, Peter, and Wood, I. N. (ed.). *Early medieval kingship.* Leeds, 1977.

Schmidt, Karl Horst (ed.). *History and culture of the Celts / Geschichte und Kultur der Kelten.* Heidelberg, 1986.

Scott, B. G. (ed.). *Studies on early Ireland: essays in honour of M. V. Duignan.* [Belfast, 1981].

Small, Alan (ed.). *Proceedings of the Fourth Viking Congress.* Aberdeen, 1965.

Smith, Brendan (ed.). *Britain and Ireland, 900–1300: insular responses to medieval European change.* Cambridge, 1999.

Smyth, A. P. (ed.). *Seanchas: studies in early and medieval Irish archaeology, history, and literature in honour of Francis J. Byrne*. Dublin, 2000.

Spearman, R. Michael, and Higgitt, John (ed.). *The age of migrating ideas: early medieval art in northern Britain and Ireland. Proceedings of the Second International Conference on Insular Art held in the National Museums of Scotland in Edinburgh, 3–6 January 1991*. Edinburgh, 1993.

Taylor, Simon (ed.). *Kings, clerics, and chronicles in Scotland 500–1297*. Dublin, 2000.

Thomas, Charles (ed.). *The iron age in the Irish Sea province*. London, 1972. (Council for British Archaeology, Research Report, ix.)

Tranter, Stephen N., and Tristram, H. L. C. (ed.). *Early Irish literature: media and communication / Mündlichkeit und Schriftlichkeit in der frühen irischen Literatur*. Tübingen, 1989. (ScriptOralia x.)

Tristram, H. L. C. (ed.). *Metrik und Medienwechsel: Metrics and media*. Tübingen, 1991. (ScriptOralia xxxv.)

—— (ed.). *Medialität und mittelalterliche insulare Literatur*. Tübingen, 1992. (ScriptOralia 43.)

Whitelock, Dorothy; McKitterick, Rosamond; and Dumville, David N. (ed.). *Ireland in early mediaeval Europe: studies in memory of Kathleen Hughes*. Cambridge, 1982.

Würzburger Diözesanverein (ed.). *Herbipolis Jubilans: 1200 Jahre Bistum Würzburg Festschrift zur Säkularfeier der Erhebung der Kiliansreliquien*. Würzburg, 1952.

# C    SPECIAL FIELDS AND TOPICS

## 1    Archaeology and material culture

With the exception of some archaeological inventories, most of the works listed below were published after the bibliographies in Nancy Edwards, *The archaeology of early medieval Ireland* (London, 1990), and John Waddell, *The prehistoric archaeology of Ireland* (Galway, 1998), to which the reader is referred for earlier material.

### (a) General works

Alcock, Olive; de hÓra, Kathy; and Gosling, Paul. *Archaeological inventory of County Galway, ii: north Galway*. Dublin, 1999. (Archaeological Survey of Ireland.)

Barrett, G. F. The reconstruction of proto-historic landscapes using aerial photographs: case studies in Co. Louth. In *Louth Arch. Soc. Jn.*, xx (1981–4), pp 215–36.

Barry, Terence. *The archaeology of medieval Ireland*. London, 1987.

Bennett, Isabel. Archaeological excavations in County Kerry, 1985–1993. *The Kerry Magazine*, v (1994), pp 19–22.

—— (ed.). *Excavations 1998: summary accounts of archaeological excavations in Ireland*. Bray, 2000.
The latest in a series of reports beginning in 1970.

Bradley, John. Excavations at Moynagh Lough, County Meath. In *R.S.A.I. Jn.*, cxxi (1991), pp 5–26.

Brindley, Anna. *Archaeological inventory of County Monaghan*. Dublin, 1986. (Archaeological Survey of Ireland.)

—— and Kilfeather, Annaba. *Archaeological inventory of County Carlow*. Dublin, 1993. (Archaeological Survey of Ireland.)

Buckley, Victor M. From the darkness to the dawn. In R. Gillespie and H. O'Sullivan (ed.), *The borderlands* (Belfast, 1989), pp 23–39.

—— *Archaeological inventory of County Louth*. Dublin, 1986. (Archaeological Survey of Ireland.)

—— and Sweetman, P. D. *Archaeological survey of County Louth*. Dublin, 1991.

Carroll, Frederick. Some finds on the Sillees river around Ross Lough, Co. Fermanagh. In *Clogher Rec.*, xiv, no. 2 (1992), pp 109–31.

Condit, Tom. *Ireland's archaeology from the air*. Dublin, 1997.

Cramp, Rosemary. Northumbria and Ireland. In Paul Szarmach (ed.), *Sources of Anglo-Saxon culture* (Kalamazoo, 1986), pp 185–201.

Cuppage, Judith. *Archaeological survey of the Dingle peninsula*. Ballyferriter, 1986.

Donnelly, Colm J. *Living places: archaeology, continuity and change at historic monuments in Northern Ireland*. Belfast, 1997.

Earwood, Caroline. Bog butter: a two thousand year history. In *Journal of Irish Archaeology*, viii (1997), pp 25–42.

Eogan, George. Irish antiquities of the bronze age, iron age and early Christian period in the National Museum of Denmark. In *R.I.A. Proc.*, xci (1991), sect. C, pp 133–76.

Flanagan, Laurence. *A dictionary of Irish archaeology*. Dublin, 1992.

Fry, Malcolm F. *Coití: logboats from Northern Ireland*. Belfast, 2000. (Northern Ireland Archaeological Monographs, no. 4.)

—— Ó Cathmhaoil, Stiofán, and Gilmour, Gillian. Where are they now? Locating the small finds from excavations conducted in Northern Ireland between 1950 and 1990: an inventory and database. In *U.J.A.*, lviii (1999), pp 114–33.

Gosling, Paul. *Archaeological inventory of County Galway, i: west Galway*. Dublin, 1993. (Archaeological Survey of Ireland.)

Grogan, Eoin, and Hillery, Tom. *A guide to the archaeology of County Wicklow*. Wicklow, 1993.

—— and Kilfeather, Annaba. *Archaeological inventory of County Wicklow*. Dublin, 1997. (Archaeological Survey of Ireland.)

Grose, Francis. *Antiquities of Ireland*. 2 vols. Ed. Edward Ledwich. London, 1791, 1795. Supplemented by Daniel Grose (*c.* 1766–1838), *The antiquities of Ireland*, ed. Roger Stalley (Dublin, 1991).

Hall, Valerie A. Ancient agricultural activity at Slieve Gullion, Co. Armagh: the palynological and documentary evidence. In *R.I.A. Proc.*, xc (1990), sect. C, pp 123–34.

Hamlin, Ann. *Historical monuments of Northern Ireland*. Belfast, 1983. (H.M.S.O., Department of Environment, N.I.)

Harbison, Peter. *Guide to the national and historic monuments of Ireland*. Dublin, 1992.

——*Ancient Irish monuments*. Dublin, 1997.

——*Beranger's Antique buildings of Ireland*. Dublin, 1998.

——(ed.). *Beranger's Views of Ireland* Dublin, 1992.

Herity, Michael. *Gleanncholmcille: a guide to 5,000 years of history in stone*. Togra Ghleanncholmcille Teo., 1990.

Johnstone, Paul.*The sea-craft of prehistory*. London, 1980.

Jope, E. M. The crafts and arts. In Schmidt, *Celts*, pp 121–215.

Killanin, Lord, and Duignan, Michael V. *The Shell guide to Ireland*. 3rd ed. London, 1989.

Lacey, Brian. *Archaeological survey of County Donegal*. Lifford, 1983.

——County Derry in the early historic period. In Gerard O'Brien (ed.), *Derry and Londonderry: history and society* (Dublin, 1999), pp 115–48.

Lamb, H. H. *Climate past present and future*, ii. London, 1977.

——Climate from 1000 B.C. to A.D. 1000. In M. E. Jones and G. Dimbleby (ed.), *Environment of man: the iron age to the Anglo-Saxon period* (Oxford, 1981), pp 53–65.

McDonald, Theresa. *Achill: 5000 B.C. to 1900 A.D.; archaeology, history, folklore*. [Dooagh, 1992?]

Mallory, J. P., and McNeill, T. E. *The archaeology of Ulster: from colonization to plantation*. Belfast, 1991.

——and Ó Donnabháin, Barra. The origins of the population of Ireland: a survey of putative immigrations in Irish prehistory and history. In *Emania*, xvii (1998), pp 47–81.

Mitchell, Frank G. Early settlements and society before 500 A.D. In W. Nolan (ed.), *The shaping of Ireland* (Dublin, 1986), pp 28–43.

——*The way that I followed*. Dublin, 1990.

——and Tuite, Breeda. The great bog of Ardee. In *Louth Arch. Soc. Jn.*, xxiii, no. 1 (1993), pp 7–96.

Moore, Michael J. *Archaeological inventory of County Meath*. Dublin, 1987. (Archaeological Survey of Ireland.)

——*Archaeological inventory of County Wexford*. Dublin, 1996. (Archaeological Survey of Ireland.)

——*Archaeological inventory of County Waterford*. Dublin, 1999. (Archaeological Survey of Ireland.)

Mytum, Harold C. *The origins of early Christian Ireland*. London, 1992.

Newman, Conor. *Tara: an archaeological survey*. Dublin, 1997. (Discovery Programme Monograph 2.) Includes articles by Joe Fenwick, Kieron Goucher, Thomas Cummins, Mark Noel, Peter O'Connor, Ralph W. Magee, and Elizabeth Anderson.

Norman, E. R., and St Joseph, J. K S. *The early development of Irish society: the evidence of aerial photography*. Cambridge, 1969.

O'Brien, Caimin, and Sweetman, P. David. *Archaeological inventory of County Offaly*. Dublin, 1997. (Archaeological Survey of Ireland.)

O'Brien, Elizabeth. Excavation of a multi-period burial site at Ballymacaward, Bally-shannon, Co. Donegal. In *Donegal Annual*, li (1999), pp 56–61.

O'Connell, Michael. Early land use in north-east County Mayo—the palaeoecological evidence. In *R.I.A. Proc.*, xc (1990), sect. B, pp 259–79.

O'Donnell, Mary G. Excavation of a section of the Rian Bó Phádraig near Ardfinnan. In *Tipperary Journal 1999*, pp 183–90.

O'Donovan, Patrick F. *Archaeological inventory of County Cavan.* Dublin, 1995. (Archaeological Survey of Ireland.)

O'Kelly, Michael J. *Early Ireland; an introduction to Irish prehistory.* Cambridge, 1989.

Ó Néill, John. A summary of investigations by the Lisheen Archaeological Project. In *Tipperary Historical Journal 2000*, pp 173–90.

Ó Ríordáin, Seán P. *Antiquities of the Irish countryside.* London, 1965. Revised ed. by Ruaidhrí de Valera. Dublin, 1975.

O'Sullivan, Aidan. *The archaeology of lake settlement in Ireland.* Dublin, 1998. (Discovery Programme Monograph, no. 4.)

—— *Crannogs: early Irish lake dwellings.* Dublin, 2000.

O'Sullivan, Ann, and Sheehan, John. *The Iveragh Peninsula: an archaeological survey of South Kerry.* Cork, 1996.

Piggott, Stuart. The coming of the Celts: the archaeological argument. In Mac Eoin, Ahlqvist, & Ó hAodha, *Proc. 6th Congress*, pp 139–40.

—— Horse and chariot: the price of prestige. In Evans, Griffith, & Jope, *Proc. 7th Congress*, pp 25–30.

—— Archaeological evidence: Britain and Ireland. First millennium B.C. to recent times. In Schmidt, *Celts*, pp 52–6.

Power, Denis, and others. *Archaeological inventory of County Cork.* Vol. i: *West Cork.* Dublin, 1993. Vol. ii: *East and south Cork.* Dublin, 1994. Vol. iii: *Mid Cork.* Dublin, 1997. (Archaeological Survey of Ireland.)

Raftery, Barry. Pre- and protohistoric Ireland: problems of continuity and change. In *Emania*, xiii (1995), pp 5–9.

Ryan, Michael. *The illustrated archaeology of Ireland.* Dublin, 1991. 2nd ed., entitled *Irish archaeology illustrated.* Dublin, 1994.

—— Archaeology. In Kim McCone and Katharine Simms (ed.), *Progress in medieval Irish studies* (Maynooth, 1996), pp 155–64.

—— and Cahill, M. *Gold aus Irland: Gold-, Silber-, und Bronzeschmuck dreier Jahrtausende.* Frankfurt-on-Main, 1981.

Rynne, C. *The archaeology of Cork city and harbour.* Cork, 1993.

Stout, Geraldine T. *Archaeological survey of the barony of Ikerrin.* Roscrea Heritage Society. Roscrea, 1984.

—— and Stout, Matthew. Problems in the past: County Dublin 5000 B.C.–1000 A.D. In F. H. A. Aalen and Kevin Whelan (ed.), *Dublin city and county from prehistory to present: studies in honour of J. H. Andrews* (Dublin, 1992), pp 5–41.

Sweetman, P. David, Alcock, Olive, and Moran, Bernie. *Archaeological inventory of County Laois.* Dublin, 1995. (Archaeological Survey of Ireland.)

Toal, Caroline. *North Kerry archaeological survey.* Dingle, 1995.

Waddell, John. The archaeology of the Aran Islands. In John Waddell, J. W. O'Connell, and Anne Korff (ed.), *The book of Aran: the Aran Islands, Co. Galway* (Kinvara, 1994), pp 75–135.
Wallace, Patrick F. *Guide to the National Museum of Ireland*. Dublin, 2000.
Weir, Anthony. *Early Ireland: a field guide*. Belfast, 1980.

*(b) Prehistoric period*

With few exceptions, this section includes only works that appeared after the mid-1997 completion of the bibliography in John Waddell, *The prehistoric archaeology of Ireland* (Galway, 1998), to which (and to the section on composite works, above) the reader is referred for earlier material.

Aitchison, Nick. Late bronze age ritual and Haughey's Fort: the evidence of the deposited cup-and-ring marked stone. In *Emania*, xvii (1998), pp 31–9.
Avery, Michael. The patterns of the Broighter torc. In *Journal of Irish Archaeology*, viii (1997), pp 73–89.
Baillie, M. G. L., and Brown, M. D. Further evidence confirms the twelfth-century B.C. dendro date from the inner ditch of Haughey's fort. In *Emania*, xvii (1998), pp 45–6.
Bergh, Stefan. Transforming Knocknarea—the archaeology of a mountain. In *Archaeology Ireland*, xiv, no. 2 (2000), pp 14–18.
Bracken, Gerry. Solar alignments in the west of Ireland. Were they synchronised? In *Archaeology Ireland*, xiii, no. 4 (winter 1999), pp 12–14.
Bradley, John. Archaeological excavations at Moynagh Lough, Co. Meath, 1995–6. In *Ríocht na Midhe*, ix, no. 3 (1997), pp 50–61.
Excavations 1997–8, ibid., x (1999), pp 1–17.
Bridgford, S. Mightier than the pen? An edgewise look at Irish bronze age swords. In J. Carman (ed.), *Material harm: archaeological studies of war and violence* (Glasgow, 1997), pp 95–115.
Brindley, A. L. Irish grooved ware. In R. Cleal and A. MacSween (ed.), *Grooved ware in Britain and Ireland* (Oxford, 1999), pp 23–35.
——and Lanting, J. N. Radiocarbon dating for Irish trackways. In *Journal of Irish Archaeology*, ix (1998), pp 45–68.
Buckley, Laureen. Bronze age backache. In *Archaeology Ireland*, xi, no. 1 (spring 1997), p. 13.
Byrnes, Emmet. Recent excavations at Richardstown, Co. Louth. In *Archaeology Ireland*, xiii, no. 4 (winter 1999), p. 33.
Cahill, Mary. Mooghaun bracelet re-discovered. In *Archaeology Ireland*, xii, no. 1 (spring 1998), pp 8–9.
——A gold dress-fastener from Clohernagh, Co. Tipperary, and a catalogue of related material. In Michael Ryan (ed.), *Irish antiquities: essays in memory of Joseph Raftery* (Bray, 1998), pp 27–78.
Casey, Markus. Excavation of a promontory fort at Doonamo, Aughernacalliagh, Co. Mayo. In *Galway Arch. Soc. Jn.*, li (1999), pp 65–76.

Caulfield, Seamas. 14C dating of a neolithic field system at Céide Fields, County Mayo, Ireland. In *Radiocarbon*, xl (1998), pp 629–40.

Cleary, Rose M. The potter's craft in prehistoric Ireland, with specific reference to Lough Gur, Co. Limerick. In Desmond, *New agendas*, pp 119–34.

Clinton, Mark. Porthole-slabs in souterrains in Ireland. In *R.S.A.I. Jn.*, cxxvii (1997), pp 5–17.

Cody, Eamon. Rock art at Magheestown, Co. Donegal. In *Donegal Annual*, l (1998), pp 109–12.

Coles, John. Prehistoric archaeology in Ireland: reflections and responses. In Desmond, *New agendas*, pp 225–31.

Condit, Tom. Connacht curiosities. In *Archaeology Ireland*, xii, no. 1 (spring 1998), pp 29–30.

——Discovering new perceptions of Tara. In *Archaeology Ireland*, xii, no. 2 (summer 1998), p. 33.

——Observations on aspects of the Baltinglass hillfort complex. In *Wicklow Archaeology and History*, i (1998), pp 9–25.

——and Buckley, Victor M. *The Doon of Drumsna*. Bray, 1998. (*Archaeology Ireland* Heritage Guide, no. 1.)

——and Cooney, Gabriel. Newgrange, Co. Meath. *Neolithic religion and the midwinter sunrise*. Bray, 1999. (*Archaeology Ireland* Heritage Guide, no. 8.)

——and Grogan, Eoin. Prehistoric and ritual enclosures in south-east Clare. In *The Other Clare*, xxii (1998), pp 30–33.

——and Lacy, Brian. *The Beltany stone circle*. Bray, 1998. (*Archaeology Ireland* Heritage Guide, no. 4.)

——and O'Sullivan, Aidan. *Magh Adhair, a ritual and inauguration complex in southeast Clare*. Bray, 1998. (*Archaeology Ireland* Heritage Guide, no. 2.)

————Landscapes of movement and control: interpreting prehistoric hillforts and fording-places on the River Shannon. In *Discovery Programme Reports 5* (Dublin, 1999), pp 25–39.

——and Simpson, D. Irish hengiform enclosures and related monuments: a review. In A. Gibson and D. Simpson (ed.), *Essays in honour of Aubrey Burl. Prehistoric ritual and religion* (Stroud, 1998), pp 45–6.

Connolly, Michael. Copper axes and ringbarrows—ritual deposition or coincidence? In *Archaeology Ireland*, xii, no. 2 (summer, 1998), pp 8–10.

——*Discovering the neolithic in County Kerry: a passage tomb at Ballycarty, Tralee.* Bray, 1999.

——and Condit, Tom. Ritual enclosures in the Lee valley, Co. Kerry. In *Archaeology Ireland*, xii, no. 4 (winter, 1998), pp 8–12.

Cooney, Gabriel. Excavation of the portal tomb site at Melkagh, Co. Longford. In *R.I.A. Proc.*, xcix (1997), sect. C, pp 195–244.

——Breaking stones, making places: the social landscape of axe production sites. In A. Gibson and D. Simpson (ed.), *Essays in honour of Aubrey Burl. Prehistoric ritual and religion* (Stroud, 1998), pp 108–18.

——Social landscapes in Irish prehistory. In P. J. Ucko and R. Layton (ed.), *The archaeology and anthropology of landscape* (London, 1999), pp 46–64.

——A boom in neolithic houses. In *Archaeology Ireland*, xiii, no. 1 (spring 1999), pp 13–16.

——*Landscapes of neolithic Ireland*. London, 2000.

——*Sliabh na Caillighe through time. Loughcrew, Co. Meath*. Bray, 2000. (*Archaeology Ireland* Heritage Guide 12.)

——Recognising regionality in the Irish neolithic. In Desmond, *New agendas*, pp 49–65.

Cooney, Gabriel. and Mandal, Stephen. *The Irish stone axe project: monograph 1*. Bray, 1998.

————and Byrnes, E. An Irish stone axe project report: non-porcellanite stone axes in Ulster. In *U.J.A.*, lviii (1999), pp 17–31.

——and others. *Brú na Bóinne*. Supplement to *Archaeology Ireland*, xi, no. 3 (autumn 1997).

Corlett, Christiaan. Prehistoric pilgrimage to Croagh Patrick. In *Archaeology Ireland*, xi, no. 2 (summer 1997), pp 8–11.

——A *fulacht fiadh* site at Moynagh Lough, County Meath. In *Ríocht na Midhe*, ix, no. 3 (1997), pp 46–9.

——A survey of the standing stone complex at Killadangan, Co. Mayo. In *Galway Arch. Soc. Jn.*, l (1998), pp 135–50.

——The prehistoric ritual landscape of Croagh Patrick, Co. Mayo. In *Journal of Irish Archaeology*, ix (1998), pp 9–26.

——The prehistoric ritual landscape of the Great Sugar Loaf. In *Wicklow Archaeology and History*, i (1998), pp 1–8.

——*Antiquities of old Rathdown: the archaeology of south County Dublin and north County Wicklow*. Bray, 1999.

——Rock art on Drumcoggy mountain, Co. Mayo. In *Galway Arch. Soc. Jn.*, li (1999), pp 43–64.

Crumlish, Richard. The excavation of a Fulacht Fiadh at Clonaddadoran townland, Co. Laois. In *Kildare Arch. Soc. Jn.*, xviii, no. 4 (1988–9), pp 456–72.

Desmond, Angela; Johnson, Gina; McCarthy, Margaret; Sheehan, John; and Shee Twohig, Elizabeth (ed.). *New agendas in Irish prehistory: papers in commemoration of Liz Anderson*. Bray, 2000.

Desmond, Sylvia. A tomb with a view. In *Archaeology Ireland*, xiv, no. 1 (spring 2000), pp 30–31.

Donaghy, Caroline, and Grogan, Eoin. Navel-gazing at Uisneach, Co. Westmeath. In *Archaeology Ireland*, xi, no. 4 (winter 1997), pp 24–6.

Doody, Martin. The Ballyhoura hills project: a survey of Carn Tigherna hillfort, Co. Cork. In *Discovery Programme Reports 5* (Dublin, 1999), pp 97–110.

——Bronze age houses in Ireland. In Desmond, *New agendas*, pp 135–59.

Duke, Seán. The Romano-Irish of Tara. In *Technology Ireland*, xxx, no. 3 (1998), pp 16–18.

Dunne, Laurence. Recent rock art discovery at Ventry. In *Archaeology Ireland*, xii, no. 1 (spring 1998), p. 6.

——Late iron age crematoria at Ballyvelly, Tralee. In *Archaeology Ireland*, xiii, no. 2 (summer 1999), pp 10–11.

Eogan, George. Pattern and place: a preliminary study of the decorated kerbstones at site 1, Knowth, Co. Meath, and their comparative setting. In J. L'Helgouac'h, C.-T. Le Roux, and J. Lecornec (ed.), *Art et symboles du megalithisme européen. Revue archéologique de l'Ouest*, supplément no. 8 (1996), pp 97–194.

——Symbolism, ritual and deposition in later bronze age Ireland. In Peter Schauer (ed.), *Archäologische Forschungen zum Kultgeschehen in der jüngeren Bronzezeit und frühen Eisenzeit Alteuropas* (Regensburger Beiträge zur prähistorischen Archäologie—2; Regensburg, 1996), pp 81–5.

——Cohesion and diversity: passage tombs of north-western Europe and their social and ritual fabric. In A. Rodríguez Casal (ed.), *O Neolitico Atlántico e as orixes do Megalitismo* (Santiago, 1997), pp 45–64.

——The earlier bronze age grave-group from Rahinashurock, Co. Westmeath, reviewed. In *Ríocht na Midhe*, ix, no. 3 (1997), pp 28–45.

——Overlays and underlays: aspects of megalithic art succession at Brugh na Bóinne, Ireland. In *Brigantium*, x (1997), pp 217–34.

——Further evidence for neolithic habitation at Knowth, Co. Meath. In *Ríocht na Midhe*, ix, no. 4 (1998), pp 1–9.

——Knowth before Knowth. In *Antiquity*, lxxii (1998), pp 162–72.

——Heart-shaped bullae of the Irish late bronze age. In Michael Ryan (ed.), *Irish antiquities: essays in memory of Joseph Raftery* (Bray, 1998), pp 17–26.

——Homes and homesteads in bronze age Ireland. In Bernhard Hänsel (ed.), *Mensch und Umwelt in der Bronzezeit Europas: Man and environment in the European bronze age* (Kiel, 1998), pp 307–26.

——Megalithic art and society. In *Prehist. Soc. Proc.*, lxv (1999), pp 415–46.

——A group of megalithic monuments at Kingsmountain–Clonasillagh, Co. Meath. In *Ríocht na Midhe*, xi (2000), pp 1–16.

——Aspects of passage tomb settlement in Ireland. In K. W. Beinhauer, G. Cooney, C. F. Giksch, and S. Kus (ed.), *Studien zur Megalithik-Forschungstand und ethnoarchäologische Perspektiven* (Weissbach and Mannheim, 2000), pp 347–60.

——and Ó Broin, Niamh. A decorated stone at Mullagharoy, Co. Meath. In *Ríocht na Midhe*, ix, no. 4 (1998), pp 10–11.

——and Roche, Helen. Further evidence for neolithic habitation at Knowth, Co. Meath. In *Ríocht na Midhe*, ix, no. 4 (1998), pp 1–9.

Eogan, James, and Finn, Damian. New light on late prehistoric ritual and burial in County Limerick. In *Archaeology Ireland*, xiv, no. 1 (spring 2000), pp 8–10.

Fenwick, Joe; Brennan, Yvonne; Barton, Kevin; and Waddell, John. The magnetic presence of Queen Medb (magnetic gradiometry at Rathcroghan, Co. Roscommon). In *Archaeology Ireland*, xiii, no. 1 (spring 1999), pp 8–11.

Fitzpatrick, Martin, and Crumlish, Richard. The excavation of three burnt mounds on the outskirts of Galway. In *Galway Arch. Soc. Jn.*, lii (2000), pp 135–43.

Flanagan, Lawrence. *Ancient Ireland: life before the Celts.* Dublin, 1998.

Foley, Claire, and MacDonagh, Michael. Copney stone circle—a County Tyrone enigma. In *Archaeology Ireland*, xii, no. 1 (spring 1998), pp 24–8.

Fraser, Shannon Marguerite. The public forum and the space between: the materiality of social strategy in the Irish neolithic. In *Prehist. Soc. Proc.*, lxiv (1998), pp 203–24.

Fredengren, Christina. Lough Gara through time. In *Archaeology Ireland*, xii, no. 1 (spring 1998), pp 31–3.

——Iron age crannogs in Lough Gara. In *Archaeology Ireland*, xiv, no. 2 (2000), pp 26–8.

Gahan, Audrey. A course on Irish prehistory—excavations at Castle Upton, Temple-patrick, Co. Antrim. In *Archaeology Ireland*, xi, no. 2 (summer 1997), pp 29–30.

Gibbons, Michael. A bridge too far. In *Archaeology Ireland*, xi, no. 2 (summer 1997), p. 35.

Gibson, A. Hindwell and the neolithic palisaded sites of Britain and Ireland. In A. Gibson and D. Simpson (ed.), *Essays in honour of Aubrey Burl. Prehistoric ritual and religion* (Stroud, 1998), pp 68–79.

——Circles and henges: reincarnations of past traditions. In *Archaeology Ireland*, xiv, no. 1 (spring 2000), pp 11–14.

——and Simpson, Derek. Prehistoric ritual and religion. In *Archaeology Ireland*, xii, no. 2 (summer 1998), p. 34.

Gowen, Margaret. Palaeoenvironment and archaeology—excavations at Derryville bog. In *Archaeology Ireland*, xi, no. 4 (winter 1997), pp 27–9.

Grogan, Eoin. Changing plans: settlement patterns in prehistory. In *The Other Clare*, xx (1996), pp 48–52.

——Excavations at Mooghaun South, 1995. Interim report. In *Discovery Programme Reports 5* (Dublin, 1999), pp 125–30.

—— *The late bronze age hillfort at Mooghaun*. Dublin, 1999.

——O'Sullivan, Aidan; O'Carroll, Finola; and Hagen, Ines. Knocknalappa, Co. Clare: a reappraisal. In *Discovery Programme Reports 5* (Dublin, 1999), pp 111–23.

——and Condit, Tom. The funerary landscape of Clare in space and time. In Ciarán Ó Murchadha (ed.), *County Clare studies: essays in memory of Gerald O'Connell, Seán Ó Murchadha, Thomas Coffey and Pat Flynn* (Ennis, 2000), pp 9–29.

Hartwell, B. The Ballynahatty complex. In A. Gibson and D. Simpson (ed.), *Essays in honour of Aubrey Burl. Prehistoric ritual and religion* (Stroud, 1998), pp 32–44.

Hayes, Thomas D. Using astronomy in archaeology, with a look at the Beaghmore alignments. In *U.J.A.*, lviii (1999), pp 32–42.

Hill, J. D. The pre-Roman iron age in Britain and Ireland (ca. 800 B.C. to A.D. 100): an overview. In *Journal of World Prehistory*, ix (1995), pp 47–98.

Johnston, Susan A. Three problematic rock art stones from Ireland. In *R.S.A.I. Jn.*, cxxvi (1996), pp 147–51.

Jones, Carleton. Final neolithic/early bronze age occupation of the Burren. In *The Other Clare*, xxi (1997), pp 36–9.

——The discovery and dating of the prehistoric landscape of Roughan Hill in Co. Clare. In *Journal of Irish Archaeology*, ix (1998), pp 27–44.

——Roughan Hill, a final neolithic/early bronze age landscape revealed. In *Archaeology Ireland*, xiii, no. 1 (spring 1999), pp 30–32.

——and Gilmer, Alix. First season's excavation at CL 153: a court tomb on Roughan Hill and the expansion of the settlement and field wall survey. In *The Other Clare*, xxiii (1999), pp 24–6.

Jones, Carleton, and Walsh, Paul. Recent discoveries on Roughan Hill, County Clare. In *R.S.A.I. Jn.*, cxxvi (1996), pp 86–107.

Kilbride-Jones, H. E. An unrecorded enclosure and megalithic chamber in Keeldrum, Co. Donegal. In *Journal of Irish Archaeology*, viii (1997), pp 1–23.

Kearns, Hugh. Newgrange and the lost sand solution. In *Archaeology Ireland*, xi, no. 4 (winter 1997), pp 15–17.

Keeley, Valerie. Archaeological excavation of a burial ground, Greenhills townland. In *Kildare Arch. Soc. Jn.*, xvii (1987–91), pp 180–201.

——Iron age discoveries at Ballydavis. In Pádraig G. Lane and William Nolan, *Laois: history and society* (Dublin, 1999), pp 25–34.

Kelly, Eamon P., and Condit, Tom. Limerick's Tara. In *Archaeology Ireland*, xii, no. 2 (summer 1998), pp 18–22.

Kimball, Michael J. Variation and context: ecology and social evolution in Ireland's later mesolithic. In Desmond, *New agendas*, pp 31–47.

King, Heather. *Armschutzplatten*, wristguards or bracers in early bronze age archery: a question of function and nomenclature. In *Archaeology Ireland*, xi, no. 4 (winter 1997), pp 12–14.

——Excavation on the Fourknocks Ridge, Co. Meath. In *R.I.A. Proc.*, xcix, sect. C (1999), pp 157–98.

Lanting, J. N., and Brindley, A. L. Dating cremated bone: the dawn of a new era. In *Journal of Irish Archaeology*, ix (1998), pp 1–8.

——Radiocarbon dates for Irish trackways. In *Journal of Irish Archeology*, ix (1998), pp 45–68.

——Reservoir effects and apparent 14C-ages. In *Journal of Irish Archeology*, ix (1998), pp 151–65.

Lawless, Christy. Discoveries at Breastagh, Rathfran, County Mayo: linear ditch, flint and chert implements and Fulachta Fiadh. In *Cathair na Mart*, xvii (1997), pp 29–48.

Lohan, Máire. Ceremonial monuments in Moytura, Co. Mayo. In *Galway Arch. Soc. Jn.*, li (1999), pp 77–108.

Lynch, A. Excavation of a stone row at Maughanasilly, Co. Cork. In *Cork Hist. Soc. Jn.*, civ (1999), pp 1–20.

McCartan, Sinéad. A shard of neolithic pottery from Sess Kilgreen passage tomb, Co. Tyrone. In *U.J.A.*, lviii (1999), p. 152.

——The utilisation of island environments in the Irish mesolithic: agendas from Rathlin Island. In Desmond, *New agendas*, pp 15–30.

McCarthy, Margaret. Hunting, fishing, and fowling in late prehistoric Ireland: the scarcity of the bone record. In Desmond, *New agendas*, pp 107–17.

McComb, A. M. G. The carbonised hazel nut shell fragments from Feature No. 283 at Haughey's Fort, Co. Armagh. In *Emania*, xvii (1998), pp 41–4.

McCourt, Anne. An unusual angular shaped axe head from the lower River Bann. In *U.J.A.*, lviii (1999), pp 148–9.

——and Simpson, Derek. The wild bunch: exploitation of the hazel in prehistoric Ireland. In *U.J.A.*, lviii (1999), pp 1–16.

McDermott, Conor. The prehistory of the Offaly peatlands. In William Nolan and Timothy P. O'Neill, *Offaly: history and society* (Dublin, 1998), pp 1–28.

McMorran, T. A locational analysis of Fulachta Fiadh on the Dingle peninsula. In M. Comber (ed.), *Association of Young Irish Archaeologists: proceedings of the Annual Conference 1998* (Galway, 1998), pp 51–6.

McNaught, Brian. Early mesolithic site discovered in Donegal. In *Donegal Annual*, l (1998), pp 64–5.

——The Drumhaggart early bronze age pit burial. In *Donegal Annual*, li (1999), pp 36–40.

Mac Uistin, Liam. *Explaining Newgrange*. Dublin, 1999.

Maher, Denise, and Sheehan, John. Different ages, varying perspectives: the phenomenon of hoarding. In Desmond, *New agendas*, pp 177–87.

Mallory, J. P.; Brown, D. M.; and Baillie, M. G. L. Dating Navan Fort. In *Antiquity*, lxxiii (1999), pp 427–31.

——and Hartwell, Barrie. Down in prehistory. In Lindsay Proudfoot (ed.), *Down: history and society* (Dublin, 1997), pp 1–32.

Masterson, Barry. A survey of Carn Tigherna hillfort, Co. Cork. In *Discovery Programme Reports 5* (Dublin, 1999), pp 101–10.

Meighan, I. G.; Fallick, A. E.; and Rogers, G. Isotopic provenancing of north Antrim porcellanites. In *U.J.A.*, lviii (1999), pp 150–51.

Monk, Michael. Seeds and soils of discontent: an environmental archaeological contribution to the nature of the early neolithic. In Desmond, *New agendas*, pp 67–87.

Moroney, Anna-Marie. Winter sunsets at Dowth. In *Archaeology Ireland*, xiii, no. 4 (winter 1999), pp 29–31.

——*Dowth: winter sunsets*. Drogheda, 1999.

Mount, Charles. Early bronze age burial in south-east Ireland in the light of recent research. In *R.I.A. Proc.*, xcvii (1997), sect. C, pp 101–93.

——Five early bronze age cemeteries at Brownstown, Granby West, Oldtown and Poopluck, County Kildare, and Strawhall, County Kildare. In *R.I.A. Proc.*, xcviii (1998), sect. C, pp 25–99.

——Ritual landscape and continuity in prehistoric County Sligo. In *Archaeology Ireland*, xii, no. 3 (autumn 1998), pp 18–21.

——Excavation and environmental analysis of a neolithic mound and iron age barrow cemetery at Rathdooney Beg, County Sligo, Ireland. In *Prehist. Soc. Proc.*, lxv (1999), pp 337–71.

Neill, Ken. Microliths, megaliths, beakers and bronze—the prehistoric archaeology of County Londonderry 7000–400 B.C. In Gerard O'Brien (ed.), *Derry and Londonderry: history and society* (Dublin, 1999), pp 29–68.

Newman, Conor. Ballinderry crannog no. 2: the later bronze age. In *Journal of Irish Archaeology*, viii (1997), pp 91–100.

——Reflections on the making of a 'royal site' in early Ireland. In *World Archaeology*, xxx, no. 1 (1998), pp 127–41.

——Notes on four cursus-like monuments in County Meath, Ireland. In A. Barclay and J. Harding (ed.), *Pathways and ceremonies: the cursus monuments of Britain and Ireland* (Oxford, 1999), pp 141–7.

O'Brien, William. Mount Gabriel and metal sourcing in the bronze age. In *Journal of the Historical Metallurgy Society*, xxxi, no. 1 (1997), pp 8–11.

O'Brien, William. New light on Beaker metallurgy in Ireland. In R. Harrison and others (ed.), *Bell beakers today: proceedings of the Riva del Garda conference, May 1998* (Trento, 1999), pp 144–60.

—— Resource availability and metal supply in the insular bronze age. In A. Hauptmann and others (ed.), *The beginnings of metallurgy: proceedings of the international conference 'The beginnings of metallurgy', Bochum 1995; der Anschnitt*, Beiheft 9 (1999), pp 227–35.

—— *Sacred ground: megalithic tombs in coastal south-west Ireland.* Galway, 1999. (Bronze Age Studies, 4.)

—— Megalithic tombs, metal resources, and territory in prehistoric south-west Ireland. In Desmond, *New agendas*, pp 161–76.

Ó Donnabháin, Barra. An appalling vista? The Celts and the archaeology of later prehistoric Ireland. In Desmond, *New agendas*, pp 189–96.

O'Dwyer, Simon. The Loughnashade trumpet—curved trumpet or carnyx? In *Archaeology Ireland*, xii, no. 2 (1998), pp 28–9.

Ó Faoláin, Simon, and Northover, J. P. The technology of late bronze age sword production in Ireland. In *Journal of Irish Archaeology*, ix (1998), pp 69–88.

Ó hÓgáin, Dáithí. *The sacred isle: belief and religion in pre-Christian Ireland.* Cork, 1999.

Ó Néill, John. A recently discovered wedge tomb in Shankill townland, Co. Dublin. In *Archaeology Ireland*, xiii, no. 3 (autumn 1999), pp 27–30.

—— and Stevens, Paul. New discoveries at Lisheen. In *Archaeology Ireland*, xii, no. 1 (spring 1998), p. 5.

Ó Nualláin, Seán. Excavation of the smaller court-tomb and associated hut sites at Ballyglass, County Mayo. In *R.I.A. Proc.*, xcviii (1998), sect. C, pp 125–75.

—— and Cody, Eamon. A re-examination of four sites in Grange townland, Lough Gur, Co. Limerick. In *N. Munster Antiq. Jn.*, xxxvii (1996), pp 3–14.

Ó Ríordáin, Breandán. A bronze age cemetery mound at Grange, Co. Roscommon. In *Journal of Irish Archaeology*, viii (1997), pp 43–72.

O'Sullivan, Aidan. Interpreting the archaeology of late bronze age lake settlement. In *Journal of Irish Archaeology*, viii (1997), pp 115–21.

—— Last foragers or first farmers? In *Archaeology Ireland*, xi, no. 2 (summer 1997), pp 14–16.

—— and Boland, Donal. *Clonmacnoise bridge.* Bray, 2000. (*Archaeology Ireland* Heritage Guide, no. 11.)

O'Sullivan, Muiris. Knockroe and the neolithic settlement of Munster. In *Group for the Study of Irish Historic Settlement Newsletter*, vi (1996), pp 1–5.

—— Megalithic art in Ireland and Brittany: divergence or convergence? In J. L'Helgouac'h and others (ed.), *Art et symboles du mégalithisme européen* (Actes du 2ᵉ Colloquium International sur l'art mégalithique, Nantes, juin 1995; *Revue archéologique de l'Ouest*, supplément no. 8 (1997)), pp 67–80.

Power, Denis. Archaeological survey in Cork and elsewhere: an update. In Desmond, *New agendas*, pp 197–207.

Raftery, Barry. Die Kelten in Irland. In T. Bader (ed.), *Die Welt der Kelten* (Eberdingen, 1997), pp 97–100.

——Kelten und Keltizismus in Irland: die archäologischen Belege. In A. Müller-Karpe, H. Brandt, H. Jöns, D. Krause, and A. Wigg (ed.), *Studien zur Archäologie der Kelten und Römer in Mittel-und Westeuropa* (Rahden, 1998), pp 465–76.

——Observations on the iron age in Munster. In *Emania*, xvii (1998), pp 21–4.

——Knobbed spearbutts revisited. In Michael Ryan (ed.), *Irish antiquities: essays in memory of Joseph Raftery* (Bray, 1998), pp 97–110.

——Paths, tracks, and roads in early Ireland: viewing the people rather than the trees. In A. F. Harding (ed.), *Experiment and design: archaeological studies in honour of John Coles* (Oxford, 1999), pp 170–82.

——The milling fields. In B. Coles, J. Coles, and M. Schou Jørgensen (ed.), *Bog bodies, sacred sites, and wetland archaeology* (WARP Occasional Paper 12; Exeter, 1999), pp 191–201.

——Une voie en bois de l'âge du fer irlandais. In B. Chaume, J.-P. Mohen, and P. Perin (ed.), *Archéologie des Celtes: mélanges à la memoire de René Joffroy* (Montagnac, 1999), pp 299–306.

——A bit too far: Ireland's Transylvanian link in the later iron age. In Smyth, *Seanchas*, pp 1–11.

Read, Christopher. Neolithic/bronze age cemetery site at Ballyconneely, Co. Clare. In *Archaeology Ireland*, xiv, no. 4 (2000), pp 28–9.

Redmond, Markus. A promontory fort at Rathfarnham, County Dublin. In *R.S.A.I. Jn.*, cxxvii (1997), pp 125–6.

Robinson, M. E.; Shinwell, D. W.; and Cribbin, G. Re-assessing the logboat from Lurgan townland, Co. Galway, Ireland. In *Antiquity*, lxxiii (1999), pp 903–8.

Roche, Helen. Late iron age activity at Tara, Co. Meath. In *Ríocht na Midhe*, x (1999), pp 18–30.

Ruggles, Clive. *Astronomy in prehistoric Britain and Ireland*. New Haven and London, 1999.

Shee Twohig, Elizabeth. A 'problem' solved: the location of the stone with rock-art from Mothel, County Waterford. In *R.S.A.I. Jn.*, cxxvii (1997), pp 127–8.

——Frameworks for the megalithic art of the Boyne valley. In Desmond, *New agendas*, pp 89–105.

Simpson, Derek, and Meighan, Ian. Pitchstone—a new trading material in neolithic Ireland. In *Archaeology Ireland*, xiii, no. 1 (spring 1999), pp 26–9.

Spaulding, Gary L., and others. Lithic material from the River Bann at Molloy's Ford, Glenone T[ownlan]d, Co. Londonderry. In *U.J.A.*, lviii (1999), pp 143–7.

Stanley, Michael. An Irish Star Carr? In *Archaeology Ireland*, xiv, no. 4 (2000), pp 30–32.

Stout, Geraldine. *The bend of the Boyne: an archaeological landscape*. Dublin, 1997.

Swan, Leo. *Teltown*. Bray, 1998. (*Archaeology Ireland* Heritage Guide, no. 3.)

——and Condit, Tom. New enclosure at Brú na Bóinne. In *Archaeology Ireland*, xiv, no. 4 (2000), pp 24–7.

Vonhof, Christa. More rock art discoveries in County Kerry. In *Archaeology Ireland*, xiii, no. 2 (summer 1999), pp 31–2.

Waddell, John. *The prehistoric archaeology of Ireland*. Galway, 1998.

Walsh, Paul. In praise of field-workers: some recent 'megalithic' discoveries in Cork and Kerry. In *Archaeology Ireland*, xi, no. 3 (autumn 1997), pp 8–12.

—— A 'most interesting set of stones' at Pluckanes North, Co. Cork. In *Cork Hist. Soc. Jn.*, ciii (1998), pp 141–51.

Warner, R. B. Is there an iron age in Munster? In *Emania*, xvii (1998), pp 25–9.

—— An iron age lead pin from County Donegal. In Michael Ryan (ed.), *Irish antiquities: essays in memory of Joseph Raftery* (Bray, 1998), pp 111–22.

—— The Broighter hoard—a question of ownership. In Gerard O'Brien (ed.), *Derry and Londonderry: history and society* (Dublin, 1999), pp 69–90.

Waterman, D. M. *Excavations at Navan Fort 1961–71*. Ed. C. J. Lynn. Belfast, 1997.

Westropp, T. J. *Archaeology of the Burren: prehistoric forts and dolmens in north Clare*. Ennis, 1999.

Whelan, S. Craft specialisation and the Irish smith in the late bronze age. In M. Comber (ed.), *Association of Young Irish Archaeologists: proceedings of the Annual Conference 1998* (Galway, 1998), pp 35–43.

Woodman, Peter. Rosses Point revisited. In *Antiquity*, lxxvii (1998), pp 562–70.

—— George Morant and the mesolithic of Ballyhoe Lough. In Michael Ryan (ed.), *Irish antiquities: essays in memory of Joseph Raftery* (Bray, 1998), pp 1–16.

—— The early iron age in south Munster: not so different after all. In *Emania*, xvii (1998), pp 13–19.

—— Hammers and shoeboxes: new agendas for prehistory. In Desmond, *New agendas*, pp 1–14.

—— Anderson, E.; and Finlay, N. *Excavations at Ferriter's Cove, 1983–95: last foragers, first farmers in the Dingle Peninsula*. Bray, 1999.

## (c) Early medieval period

Most of the items listed below appeared after the bibliographies in Nancy Edwards, *The archaeology of early medieval Ireland* (London, 1990), and T. B. Barry, *The archaeology of medieval Ireland* (London, 1987), to which the reader is referred for earlier material.

Ambrosiani, Björn. Ireland and Scandinavia in the early viking age: an archaeological response. In Clarke, Ní Mhaonaigh, & Ó Floinn, *Ire. & Scandinavia*, pp 405–20.

Avery, Michael. Caiseal na nDuini and Cashelreagan: two forts in Rosguill, Co. Donegal. In *U.J.A.*, liv–lv (1991–2), pp 120–28.

Baillie, M. G. L. Dark ages and dendrochronology. In *Emania*, xi (1993), pp 5–12.

Barton, Kenneth James. The medieval pottery of Dublin. In Mac Niocaill & Wallace, *Keimelia*, pp 271–324.

Bennett, Isabel. The settlement pattern of ring forts in County Wexford. In *R.S.A.I. Jn.*, cxix (1989), pp 50–61.

—— Excavations of clocháin in Glin North townland, Co. Kerry. In *Kerry Arch. Soc. Jn.*, xxvii (1994), pp 107–25.

Boland, David, and O'Sullivan, Aidan. Underwater excavations of an early medieval wooden bridge at Clonmacnoise, Co. Offaly. In Fraser Mitchell and Catherine Delaney (ed.), *The quaternary of the Irish midlands* (Irish Association for Quaternary Studies, Field Guide no. 21; Dublin, 1997), pp 55–63.

Bourke, Edward C. Two early eleventh century viking houses from Bride Street, Wexford, and the layout of properties on the site. In *Journal of the Wexford Historical Society*, xii (1988–9), pp 50–61.

——Life in the sunny south-east. Housing and domestic economy in viking and medieval Wexford. In *Archaeology Ireland*, ix, no. 3 (1995), pp 33–4.

Bradley, John. The interpretation of Scandinavian settlement in Ireland. In id. (ed.), *Settlement and society in medieval Ireland* (Kilkenny, 1988), pp 49–78.

——Excavations at Moynagh Lough, County Meath, 1985 and 1987. In *Ríocht na Midhe*, viii, no. 3 (1990/91), pp 21–35.

——The archaeology and history of Saint Patrick: a review article. In *N. Munster Antiq. Jn.*, xxxv (1993–4), pp 29–44.

——Scandinavian rural settlement in Ireland. In *Archaeology Ireland*, ix, no. 3 (1995), pp 10–12.

——and Halpin, Andrew. The topographical development of Scandinavian and Anglo-Norman Waterford city. In William Nolan and Thomas R. Power (ed.), *Waterford: history and society* (Dublin, 1992), pp 105–30.

————The topographical development of Scandinavian and Anglo-Norman Cork. In Patrick O'Flanagan and Cornelius Buttimer (ed.), *Cork: history and society* (Dublin, 1993), pp 15–44.

Brennan, James. Monastic sites in ancient Ossory: an archaeological view. In *Old Kilkenny Review*, xlvii (1995), pp 127–39.

Brindley, Anna L. Early ecclesiastical remains at Selloo and Kilnahalter, County Monaghan. In *U.J.A.*, li (1988), pp 49–53.

Byrne, Martin E., and Mullins, Clare. A report on the excavation of a cashel at Ballyegan, near Castleisland, Co. Kerry. In *Kerry Arch. Soc. Jn.*, xxiv (1991), pp 5–31.

Campbell, Ewan. The archaeological evidence for external contacts: imports, trade and economy in Celtic Britain A.D. 400–800. In K. R. Dark (ed.), *External contacts and the economy of Roman and post-Roman Britain* (Woodbridge, 1996), pp 83–96.

Cassidy, Beth. Digging at Dunbell Big. In *Archaeology Ireland*, v, no. 2 (1991), pp 18–20.

Clyne, Miriam. Interim report on the archaeological excavations at Moone Abbey, Co. Kildare, 1988. In *Kildare Arch. Soc. Jn.*, xviii, no. 4 (1998–9), pp 473–92.

Connolly, Michael, and Coyne, Frank. The underworld of the Lee valley. In *Archaeology Ireland*, xiv, no. 2 (2000), pp 8–12.

——Cloghermore cave: the Lee Valhalla. In *Archaeology Ireland*, xiv, no. 4 (2000), pp 16–19.

Corlett, Chris, and Shanahan, Brian. Evidence for a horizontal mill on the River Dee, near Nobber, County Meath. In *Ríocht na Midhe*, ix, no. 4 (1998), pp 20–27.

Cotter, Claire. Cahercommaun Fort, Co. Clare: a reassessment of its cultural context. In *Discovery Programme Reports 5* (Dublin, 1999), pp 25–39.

Crone, B. A. Crannogs and chronologies. In *Antiq. Soc. Scot. Proc.*, cxxiii (1993), pp 249–50.

Crothers, Norman. Excavations in Upper English Street, Armagh. In *U.J.A.*, lviii (1998), pp 55–80.

Doyle, Ian. The early medieval activity at Dalkey Island, Co. Dublin: a re-assessment. In *Journal of Irish Archaeology*, ix (1998), pp 89–104.

Duke, Sean. An ancient Irish bridge [Clonmacnoise]. In *Technology Ireland*, xxviii, no. 5 (1996), pp 31–2.

Edwards, Nancy. *The archaeology of early medieval Ireland*. London, 1990.

Eogan, George. Ballynee souterrains, County Meath. In *R.S.A.I. Jn.*, cxx (1990), pp 41–64.

——Prehistoric and early historic culture change at Brugh na Bóinne. In *R.I.A. Proc.*, xci (1991), sect. C, pp 105–32.

Farrell, Robert. The Crannóg Archaeology Project (CAP): archaeological field research on the lakes of the west midlands in Ireland. In Catherine Karkov and Robert Farrell (ed.), *Studies in insular art and archaeology* (American Early Medieval Studies 1; Oxford, Ohio, 1991), pp 99–110.

Fitzpatrick, Liz. An early Christian site at Curraclone, Co. Laois. In *Kildare Arch. Soc. Jn.*, xvii (1987–91), pp 213–15.

Foley, Claire. Excavations at a medieval settlement site in Jerpointchurch townland, County Kilkenny. In *R.I.A. Proc.*, lxxxix (1989), sect. C, pp 71–126.

Fry, Susan Leigh. *Burial in medieval Ireland 900–1500*. Dublin, 1999.

Geraghty, Siobhán. *Viking Dublin: botanical evidence from Fishamble Street*. Dublin, 1996. (Medieval Dublin Excavations, 1962–81, ser. C, ii.)

Gosling, Paul. The Burren in early historic times. In J. W. O'Connell and A. Korff (ed.), *The book of the Burren* (Kinvara, 1991), pp 77–91.

Gowen, Margaret. Excavation of two souterrain complexes at Marshes Upper, Dundalk, Co. Louth. In *R.I.A. Proc.*, xcii (1992), sect. C, pp 55–121.

Graham, B. J. Urban genesis in early medieval Ireland. In *Journal of Historical Geography*, xiii (1987), pp 3–16.

——Medieval timber and earthwork fortifications in western Ireland. In *Medieval Archaeology*, xxxii (1988), pp 110–29.

Harbison, Peter. *Pilgrimage in Ireland: the monuments and the people*. London, 1991.

——Early Irish pilgrimage archaeology in the Dingle peninsula. In *World Archaeology*, xxvi, no. 1 (1994), pp 90–103.

——An ancient pilgrimage 'relic-road' in North Clare? In *The Other Clare*, xxiv (2000), pp 55–9.

Hurl, Declan P. Houses of the holy: domestic architecture in early Christian Ireland. In *Archeomaterials*, vii, no. 1 (1993), pp 151–60.

Hurley, Maurice. Excavations at an early ecclesiastical enclosure at Kilkieran, County Kilkenny. In *R.S.A.I. Jn.*, cxviii (1988), pp 124–30.

——The vikings in Munster—evidence from Waterford and Cork. In *Archaeology Ireland*, ix, no. 3 (1995), pp 23–5.

——Viking age towns: archaeological evidence from Waterford and Cork. In Monk & Sheehan, *Early med. Munster*, pp 164–77.

——and Scully, Orla M. B., with McCutcheon, Sarah W. J. *Late viking age and medieval Waterford: excavations 1986–1992.* Waterford, [1997].

Ivens, R. J. The early Christian monastic enclosure at Tullylish, Co. Down. In *U.J.A.*, l (1987), pp 55–121.

Ivens, Richard. Dunmisk Fort, Carrickmore, Co. Tyrone: excavations 1984–1986. In *U.J.A.*, lii (1989), pp 17–110.

Johnson, Ruth. Ballinderry Crannóg No. 1: a reinterpretation. In *R.I.A. Proc.*, xcix (1999), sect. C, pp 23–71.

Jope, E. M., and Ivens, R. J. The rath at Ballymacash, County Antrim. In *R.I.A. Proc.*, xcviii (1998), sect. C, pp 101–23.

Karkov, Catherine, and Ruffing, John. The crannógs of Lough Ennell: a computer survey. In *Ríocht na Midhe*, viii, no. 3 (1990/91), pp 105–13.

——The settlement systems of Lough Ennell: the 1992 survey. In *Ríocht na Midhe*, viii, no. 4 (1992/3), pp 53–61.

Kelly, Eamonn P. Observations on Irish lake dwellings. In Catherine Karkov and Robert Farrell (ed.), *Studies in insular art and archaeology* (American Early Medieval Studies, 1; Oxford, Ohio, 1991), pp 81–98.

——Vikings on the Barrow. In *Archaeology Ireland*, ix, no. 3 (1995), pp 30–32.

——and O'Donovan, Edmond. A viking *longphort* near Athlunkard, Co. Clare. In *Archaeology Ireland*, xii, no. 4 (1998), pp 13–16.

Kenward, H. K., and Allison, E. P. A preliminary view of the insect assemblages from the early Christian rath site at Deer Park Farms, Northern Ireland. In James Rackham (ed.), *Environment and economy in Anglo-Saxon England* (Council for British Archaeology, Research Report 89, 1994), pp 89–107.

King, Heather. Excavations at Clonmacnoise. In *Archaeology Ireland*, vi, no. 3 (1992), pp 12–14.

Lawless, Christy. An ancient horizontal mill, Ballygarriff, Turlough, Co. Mayo. In *Cathair na Mart*, xviii (1998), pp 61–76.

——Ó Floinn, Raghnall; Baillie, Michael; and Brown, David. Levallinree crannóg: an early 7th-century lake-dwelling in Co. Mayo. In *Cathair na Mart*, ix, no. 1 (1989), pp 21–5.

Lennon, Anne-Marie. Excavation of a ringfort, Raheens 1, near Carrigaline, Co. Cork. In *Cork Hist. Soc. Jn.*, xcviii (1993), pp 75–81.

——Summary report on excavation of ringfort Raheens no. 2, near Carrigaline, Co. Cork. In *Cork Hist Soc. Jn.*, xcix (1994), pp 47–65.

Limbert, Darren. Irish ringforts: a review of their origins. In *Archaeological Journal*, cliii (1996 [1997]), pp 243–89.

Lynn, C. J. Excavations at 46–48 Scotch Street, Armagh, 1979–80. In *U.J.A.*, li (1988), pp 69–84.

——Houses in rural Ireland, A.D. 500–1000. In *U.J.A.*, lvii (1994), pp 81–94.

Lyttleton, James. Loughpark 'crannog' revisited. In *Galway Arch. Soc. Jn.*, l (1998), pp 151–83.

McCormick, Finbar. Cows, ringforts and the origins of early Christian Ireland. In *Emania*, xiii (1995), pp 33–7.

McDermott, Conor, and O'Carroll, Ellen. Recently identified archaeological sites in Lemanaghan works, Co. Offaly. In Fraser Mitchell and Catherine Delaney (ed.), *The quaternary of the Irish midlands* (Irish Association for Quaternary Studies, Field Guide no. 21; Dublin, 1997), pp 40–48.

McDowell, J. A. Excavations in an ecclesiastical enclosure at Doras, Co. Tyrone. In *U.J.A.*, l (1987), pp 137–54.

McGrail, Sean. Ships' timbers from Wood Quay, Dublin, and other medieval sites in Ireland. In *Bullán*, i, no. 1 (1994), pp 49–61.

McNeill, T. E. Excavations at Dunsilly, Co. Antrim. In *U.J.A.*, liv–lv (1991–2), pp 78–112.

Manning, Conleth. The stone-built ringfort entrance at Cahervagliair, Cappeen, Co. Cork. In *Journal of Irish Archaeology*, iv (1987/8), pp 37–54.

—— The earliest plans of Clonmacnoise. In *Archaeology Ireland*, viii, no. 1 (1994), pp 18–20.

—— Clonmacnoise monastery. In Fraser Mitchell and Catherine Delaney (ed.), *The quaternary of the Irish midlands* (Irish Association for Quaternary Studies, Field Guide no. 21; Dublin, 1997), pp 49–54.

—— The very earliest plan of Clonmacnoise. In *Archaeology Ireland*, xii, no. 1 (1998), pp 16–17.

—— *St Mullins*. Bray, 1999. (*Archaeology Ireland* Heritage Guide, no. 5.)

Marshall, Jenny White, and Rourke, Grellan D. *High Island: an Irish monastery in the Atlantic*. Dublin, 2000.

—— The secular origin of the monastic enclosure wall of High Island, Co. Galway. In *Archaeology Ireland*, xiv, no. 2 (2000), pp 30–34.

—— and Walsh, Claire. Illaunloughan: life and death on a small early monastic site. In *Archaeology Ireland*, viii, no. 4 (1994), pp 24–8.

—— Illaunloughan, Co. Kerry: an island hermitage. In Monk & Sheehan, *Early med. Munster*, pp 102–11.

Masterson, Rory. Some lesser-known ecclesiastical sites in Fore, Co. Westmeath. In *Ríocht na Midhe*, ix, no. 4 (1998), pp 40–48.

Medieval Britain and Ireland. Continuing series in *Medieval Archaeology*.

Mitchell, G. F., and Ryan, Michael. *Reading the Irish landscape*. Dublin, 1997.

Monk, Michael. A tale of two ringforts: Lisleagh I and II. In *Cork Hist. Soc. Jn.*, c (1995), pp 105–16.

—— and Sheehan, John (ed.). *Early medieval Munster: archaeology, history and society*. Cork, 1998.

Moore, Finbarr. Ireland's oldest bridge—at Clonmacnoise. In *Archaeology Ireland*, x, no. 4 (1996), pp 24–7.

Moore, Michael J. Irish cresset stones. In *R.S.A.I. Jn.*, cxiv (1984), pp 98–116.

Mount, Charles. Excavations at Killanully, County Cork. In *R.I.A. Proc.*, xcv (1995), sect. C, pp 119–57.

Murphy, Donald. Monasterboice: secrets from the air. In *Archaeology Ireland*, vii, no. 3 (1993), pp 15–17.

Mytum, Harold C. Across the Irish Sea: Romano-British and Irish settlements in Wales. In *Emania*, xiii (1995), pp 15–22.

O'Brien, Elizabeth. A re-assessment of the 'great sepulchral mound' containing a viking burial at Donnybrook, Dublin. In *Medieval Archaeology*, xxxvi (1992), pp 170–73.

——Contacts between Ireland and Anglo-Saxon England in the seventh century. In *Anglo-Saxon Studies in Archaeology and History*, vi (1993), pp 93–102.

——A tale of two cemeteries. In *Archaeology Ireland*, ix, no. 3 (1995), pp 13–15.

——The location and context of viking burials at Kilmainham and Islandbridge, Dublin. In Clarke, Ní Mhaonaigh, & Ó Floinn, *Ire. & Scandinavia*, pp 203–21.

Ó Floinn, Raghnall. Of silver, slaves, and secrets: the 'Viking age Ireland' exhibition at the National Museum. In *Archaeology Ireland*, ix, no. 3 (1995), pp 26–9.

——Two viking burials from Co. Wicklow. In *Wicklow Archaeology and History*, i (1998), pp 29–35.

——The archaeology of the early viking age in Ireland. In Clarke, Ní Mhaonaigh, & Ó Floinn, *Ire. & Scandinavia*, pp 131–65.

——Freestone Hill, Co. Kilkenny: a reassessment. In Smyth, *Seanchas*, pp 12–29.

O'Keeffe, Tadhg. Omey and the sands of time. In *Archaeology Ireland*, viii, no. 2 (1994), pp 14–17.

——*Medieval Ireland: an archaeology*. Stroud, 2000.

Ó Néill, John. A Norse settlement in rural County Dublin. In *Archaeology Ireland*, xiii, no. 4 (1999), pp 8–10.

Ó Ríordáin, Breandán. The High Street excavations. In Bo Almqvist and David Greene (ed.), *Proceedings of the Seventh Viking Congress, Dublin, 15–21 August, 1973* (London, 1976), pp 135–40.

O'Sullivan, Aidan. An early historic period fishweir on the Fergus estuary, Co. Clare. In *N. Munster Antiq. Jn.*, xxxv (1993–4), pp 52–61.

O'Sullivan, Jerry. The Lisnagun project. In *Archaeology Ireland*, iv, no. 3 (1990), pp 23–5.

——Hannon, Martha; and Tierney, John. Excavation of Lisnagun ringfort, Darrara, Co. Cork (1987–9). In *Cork Hist. Soc. Jn.*, ciii (1998), pp 31–66.

Redmond, Markus. A survey of the promontory forts of the Kerry peninsulas. In *Kerry Arch. Soc. Jn.*, xxviii (1995), pp 5–63.

Ryan, Michael. Furrows and browse: some archaeological thoughts on agriculture and population in early medieval Ireland. In Smyth, *Seanchas*, pp 30–36.

Rynne, Colin. Archaeology and the early Irish watermill. In *Archaeology Ireland*, iii (1989), pp 110–14.

——The introduction of the vertical watermill into Ireland: some recent archaeological evidence. In *Medieval Archaeology*, xxxiii (1989), pp 21–31.

——Some observations on the production of flour and meal in the early historic period. In *Cork Hist. Soc. Jn.*, xcv (1990), pp 20–29.

——Early medieval horizontal-wheeled milled penstocks from Co. Cork. In *Cork Hist. Soc. Jn.*, xcvii (1992), pp 54–68.

——Milling in the 7th century—Europe's earliest tide mills. In *Archaeology Ireland*, vi, no. 2 (1992), pp 22–4.

Rynne, Colin. The craft of the millwright in early medieval Munster. In Monk & Sheehan, *Early med. Munster*, pp 87–101.

——Rourke, Grellan; and Marshall, Jenny White. An early medieval monastic watermill on High Island. In *Archaeology Ireland*, x, no. 3 (1996), pp 24–7.

Scally, Georgina. The early monastery of High Island. In *Archaeology Ireland*, xiii, no. 1 (1999), pp 24–8.

Scott, B. G. *Early Irish ironworking*. Belfast, 1990.

Shee Twohig, Elizabeth. Excavation of a ringfort at Sluggary, Co. Limerick. In *N. Munster Antiq. Jn.*, xl (2000), pp 1–27.

Sheehan, John. Viking age hoards from Munster: a regional tradition? In Monk & Sheehan, *Early med. Munster*, pp 147–63.

——Early viking age silver hoards from Ireland and their Scandinavian elements. In Clarke, Ní Mhaonaigh, & Ó Floinn, *Ire. & Scandinavia*, pp 166–202.

——Viking age silver and gold from County Clare. In Ciarán Ó Murchadha (ed.), *County Clare studies: essays in memory of Gerald O'Connell, Seán Ó Murchadha, Thomas Coffey and Pat Flynn* (Ennis, 2000), pp 30–41.

Simpson, Linzi. Forty years a-digging: a preliminary synthesis of archaeological excavations in medieval Dublin. In Sean Duffy (ed.), *Medieval Dublin I: proceedings of the Friends of Medieval Dublin symposium 1999* (Dublin, 2000), pp 11–68.

Stout, Matthew. Ringforts in the south-west midlands of Ireland. In *R.I.A. Proc.*, xci (1991), sect. C, pp 201–43.

——Plans from plans: an analysis of the 1 : 2500 O.S. series as a source for ringfort morphology. In *R.I.A. Proc.*, xcii (1992), sect. C, pp 37–53.

—— *The Irish ringfort*. Dublin, 1997. (Irish Settlement Studies, no. 5.)

Swan, D. L. The churches, monasteries and burial grounds of the Burren. In J. W. O'Connell and A. Korff (ed.), *The book of the Burren* (Kinvara, 1991), pp 95–118.

——Excavations at Kilpatrick, Killucan, Co. Westmeath; evidence for bone, antler and iron working. In *Ríocht na Midhe*, ix, no. 1 (1994/5), pp 1–21.

Swan, Leo. Enclosed ecclesiastical sites and their relevance to settlement patterns of the first millennium A.D. In Terence Reeves-Smyth and Fred Hamond (ed.), *Landscape archaeology in Ireland* (Oxford, 1983), pp 269–94.

Swift, Catherine. Forts and fields: a study of 'monastic towns' in seventh- and eighth-century Ireland. In *Journal of Irish Archaeology*, ix (1998), pp 105–26.

Thomas, Charles. Cellular meanings, monastic beginnings. In *Emania*, xiii (1995), pp 51–67.

——Early medieval Munster: thoughts upon its primary Christian phase. In Monk & Sheehan, *Early med. Munster*, pp 9–16.

Twohig, Dermot C. Excavation of three ring-forts at Lisduggan, north County Cork. In *R.I.A. Proc.*, xc (1990), sect. C, pp 1–33.

Vince, Alan G. Early medieval English pottery in viking Dublin. In Mac Niocaill & Wallace, *Keimelia*, pp 254–70.

Waddell, John, and Clyne, Miriam. M. V. Duignan's excavations at Kiltiernan, Co. Galway, 1950–1953. In *Galway Arch. Soc. Jn.*, xlvii (1995), pp 149–204.

Wallace, Patrick F. The archaeological identity of the Hiberno-Norse town. In *R.S.A.I. Jn.*, cxxii (1992), pp 35–66.

——The viking age buildings of Dublin. 2 pts. Dublin, 1992. (Medieval Dublin Excavations 1962–81, ser. A, i.)

Wamers, Egon. Insular finds in viking age Scandinavia and the state-formation of Norway. In Clarke, Ní Mhaonaigh, & Ó Floinn, *Ire. & Scandinavia*, pp 37–72.

Warner, Richard. Tree-rings, catastrophes and culture in early Ireland: some comments. In *Emania*, xi (1993), pp 13–19.

——On crannogs and kings. In *U.J.A.*, lvii (1994), pp 61–9.

Weir, D. A. A palynological study of landscape and agricultural development in County Louth from the second millennium B.C. to the first millennium A.D. In *Discovery Programme Reports*, ii (1995), pp 77–126.

——Dark ages and the pollen record. In *Emania*, xi (1997), pp 21–30.

## (d) Early medieval building, architecture, and architectural sculpture

Most of the works listed below are not in the bibliographies in Nancy Edwards, *The archaeology of early medieval Ireland* (London, 1990) or Martin Werner, *Insular art: an annotated bibliography* (Boston, 1984), to which (and to section (e) below) the reader is referred for earlier material.

Aalen, F. H. A. Clochans as transhumance dwellings in the Dingle peninsula, Co. Kerry. In *R.S.A.I. Jn.*, xciv (1964), pp 39–45.

Barrow, G. L. *The round towers of Ireland: a study and gazetteer.* Dublin, 1979.

Berger, Rainer. 14C dating mortar in Ireland. In *Radiocarbon*, xxxiv, no. 3 (1992), pp 880–89.

——Radiocarbon dating of early medieval Irish monuments. In *R.I.A. Proc.*, xcv (1995), sect. C, pp 159–74.

Beuer-Szlechter, H. V. Les débuts de l'art cistercien en Irlande d'après les vestiges des abbayes de Mellifont (Louth) et de Baltinglass (Wicklow). In *Citeaux, Commentarii Cistercienses*, fasc. 3–4 (1970), pp 201–18.

Bhreathnach, Edel. Killeshin: an Irish monastery surveyed. In *Camb. Med. Celt. Studies*, xxvii (1994), pp 33–47.

Black, Lynn. The round towers of Ireland. In *The Glynns*, xxviii (2000), pp 11–24.

Bourke, Edward. Two early 11th-century viking houses from Bride Street, Wexford, and the layout of properties on the site. In *Wexford Hist. Soc. Jn.*, xii (1988–9), pp 50–61.

Bradley, John, and King, Heather A. Romanesque voussoirs at St Fin Barre's Cathedral, Cork. In *R.S.A.I. Jn.*, cxv (1985), pp 146–51.

Brady, Niall. *De oratorio: Hisperica famina* and church building. In *Peritia*, xi (1997), pp 327–35.

Brash, R. R. *The ecclesiastical architecture of Ireland to the close of the twelfth century.* Dublin, 1875.

Buckley, Victor M. Ulster and Oriel souterrains—an indicator of tribal areas? In *U.J.A.*, xlix (1986), pp 108–10.

Buckley, Victor M. Meath souterrains: some thoughts on early Christian distribution. In *Ríocht na Midhe*, viii, no. 2 (1988–9), pp 64–7.

Campbell, Ian Hannah. Some Irish religious houses. In *Archaeological Journal*, 2nd ser., lxxii (1915), pp 89–134.

——Irish cathedral churches. In *Archaeological Journal*, 2nd ser., lxxii (1915), pp 343–400.

Casey, Christine, and Rowan, Alistair. *North Leinster*. Harmondsworth, 1993. (The Buildings of Ireland.)

Champneys, Arthur C. *Irish ecclesiastical architecture,with some notice of similar or related work in England, Scotland, and elsewhere*. London and Dublin, 1910. Reprinted with introduction by Liam de Paor. Shannon, 1970.

Christe, Yves. Quelques portails romans et l'idée de théophanie selon Jean Scot Érigène. In O'Meara & Bieler, *Eriugena*, pp 182–9.

Clyne, Miriam. Romanesque carvings at Killodiernan, Co. Tipperary. In *N. Munster Antiq. Jn.*, xxvi (1984), pp 44–53.

Corlett, Christiaan. Interpretation of round towers: public appeal or professional opinion. In *Archaeology Ireland*, xii, no. 2 (1998), pp 24–7.

Craig, Maurice. *The architecture of Ireland from the earliest times to 1880*. London, 1982.

Crawford, H. S. The Romanesque doorway at Clonfert. In *R.S.A.I. Jn.*, xlii (1912), pp 1–7.

——and Leask, H. G. Killeshin church and its Romanesque ornament. In *R.S.A.I. Jn.*, lv (1925), pp 83–94.

Crotty, Gerard. A Romanesque fresco in Cormac's Chapel. In *Tipperary Historical Journal 1988*, pp 155–8.

de Paor, Liam. Cormac's Chapel: the beginnings of Irish romanesque. In Rynne, *N. Munster studies*, pp 133–45.

——*Inis Cealtra: report on archaeological and other investigations of the monuments on the island*. Privately printed. 3 vols. Dublin, 1997.

——and Glenn, Deirdre. St Caimin's, Inis Cealtra. Reconstruction of the doorway. In *N. Munster Antiq. Jn.*, xxxvi (1995), pp 87–103.

Dunraven, Edwin, 3rd earl. *Notes on Irish architecture*. Ed. Margaret Stokes. 2 vols. London, 1875, 1877.

Eogan, George. Ballynee souterrains, County Meath. In *R.S.A.I. Jn.*, cxx (1990), pp 41–64.

Fanning, Thomas. Some field monuments in the townlands of Clonmelsh and Garryhundon, Co. Carlow. In *Peritia*, iii (1984), pp 43–9.

Fitzpatrick, Elizabeth, and O'Brien, Caimin. *The medieval churches of County Offaly*. Dublin, 1998.

Galloway, Peter. *The cathedrals of Ireland*. Belfast, 1992.

Garton, Tessa. A Romanesque doorway at Killaloe. In *Journal of the British Archaeological Association*, cxxxiv (1981), pp 31–57.

——Masks and monsters: some recurring themes in Irish romanesque sculpture. In Hourihane, *From Ire. coming*, pp 121–40.

Graham, B. J. Twelfth- and thirteenth-century earthwork fortifications in Ireland. In *Ir. Sword*, xvii (1987–90), pp 225–43.

Harbison, Peter. Tipperary Romanesque. In W. J. Hayes (ed.), *Tipperary remembers* ([Tipperary], 1976), pp 52–60.

—— St Doulagh's church. In *Studies*, lxxi (1982), pp 27–42.

—— Two Romanesque carvings from Rath Blathmaic and Dysert O'Dea, Co. Clare. In *N. Munster Antiq. Jn.*, xxix (1987), pp 7–11.

—— The Romanesque Passion lintel at Raphoe, Co. Donegal. In Agnes Bernelle (ed.), *Decantations: a tribute to Maurice Craig* (Dublin, 1992), pp 72–7.

—— Architectural sculpture from the twelfth century at Ardmore. In *Irish Arts Review Yearbook*, xi (1995), pp 96–102.

—— A crucifixion plaque in stone? In *Archaeology Ireland*, ix, no. 2 (1995), pp 11–12.

—— The biblical iconography of Irish Romanesque architectural sculpture. In Bourke, *Isles of the north*, pp 271–80.

Haworth, Richard. The site of St Olave's Church, Dublin. In Bradley, *Settlement & society*, pp 177–92.

Henry, Françoise. *Studies in early Christian and medieval Irish art, iii: architecture and sculpture*. London, 1985.

Comprises reprints of articles not listed individually here.

—— Early Irish monasteries, boat-shaped oratories, and beehive huts. In *Louth Arch. Soc. Jn.*, xi (1948), pp 296–304.

—— and Zarnecki, George. Romanesque arches decorated with human and animal heads. In *Journal of the British Archaeological Association*, xx–xxi (1957–8), pp 1–34.

Herity, Michael. *Studies in the layout, building, and art in stone of early Irish monasteries*. London, 1995.

Comprises reprints of articles not listed individually here.

Hickey, Helen M. A Romanesque arch and font at Wicklow. In *R.S.A.I. Jn.*, cii (1972), pp 97–104.

Hill, Arthur. *Ancient Irish architecture. Ardfert cathedral, Co. Kerry*. Cork, 1870.

—— *Ancient Irish architecture. Kilmalkedar, Co. Kerry*. Cork, 1870.

—— *Ancient Irish architecture. Templenahoe, Ardfert*. Cork, 1870.

—— *Ancient Irish architecture: a monograph of Cormac's Chapel, Cashel, Co. Tipperary*. Cork, 1874.

Hodkinson, Brian. Excavations at Cormac's Chapel, Cashel, 1992 and 1993: a preliminary statement. In *Tipperary Historical Journal, 1994*, pp 167–74.

Horn, Walter; Marshall, J. W.; and Rourke, G. *The forgotten hermitage of Skellig Michael*. Berkeley, Los Angeles, and Oxford, 1990.

Hourihane, Colm. The mason and his craft in medieval Ireland. In *Bantry Historical and Archaeological Society Journal*, i (1991), pp 66–74.

Hunt, John. Heritage in stone. In *N. Munster Antiq. Jn.*, xx (1978), pp 63–79.

Johnson, David M. The Romanesque arch at Wicklow church. In *R.S.A.I. Jn.*, ciii (1973), pp 224–5.

Karkov, Catherine. The decoration of early wooden architecture in Ireland and Northumbria. In Catherine Karkov and Robert Farrell (ed.), *Studies in insular art and archaeology* (American Early Medieval Studies, 1: Oxford, Ohio, 1991), pp 27–48.

Lalor, Brian. *The Irish round tower: origins and architecture explored.* Dublin, 1999.

Leask, Harold G. Carved stones discovered at Kilteel, Co. Kildare. In *R.S.A.I. Jn.*, lxv (1935), pp 1–8.

—— El Románico Irlandés. In *Goya*, xliii–xlv (1961), pp 90–97.

—— *St Patrick's Rock, Cashel.* Dublin, n.d.

—— *Fore, Co. Westmeath: official historical and descriptive notes.* Dublin, n.d.

McCabe, Brian. A stone head from Lough Ramor, County Cavan. In *R.S.A.I. Jn.*, cxxvi (1996), p. 183.

McDonnell, Hector. Margaret Stokes and the Irish round tower: a reappraisal. In *U.J.A.*, 3rd ser., lvii (1994), pp 70–80.

McGrath, Mary. The wall paintings in Cormac's Chapel at Cashel. In *Studies*, lxiv, no. 256 (winter 1975), pp 327–32.

—— The materials and techniques of Irish medieval wall-paintings. In *R.S.A.I. Jn.*, cxvii (1987), pp 96–124.

McMahon, M. *Medieval church sites of North Dublin.* Dublin, 1991.

McNab, Susanne. The Romanesque figure sculpture at Maghera, Co. Derry, and Raphoe, Co. Donegal. In Jane Fenlon, Nicola Figgis, and Catherine Marshall (ed.), *New perspectives: studies in art history in honour of Anne Crookshank* (Blackrock, 1987), pp 19–33.

—— The Romanesque sculpture of Ardmore cathedral, Co. Waterford. In *R.S.A.I. Jn.*, cxvii (1987), pp 50–68.

McNeill, Charles, and Leask, Harold G. Monaincha, Co. Tipperary: historical and architectural notes. In *R.S.A.I. Jn.*, l (1920), pp 19–35.

Manning, Conleth. Excavation of Kilteel church, Co. Kildare. In *Kildare Arch. Soc. Jn.*, xvi, no. 3 (1981–2), pp 173–229.

—— St Buite, Mellifont and Toberboice. In *Peritia*, iii (1984), pp 324–5.

—— Archaeological excavations at two church sites on Inishmore, Aran Islands. In *R.S.A.I. Jn.*, cxv (1985), pp 96–120.

—— *Clonmacnoise.* Dublin, 1994.

—— Clonmacnoise cathedral: the oldest church in Ireland? In *Archaeology Ireland*, ix, no. 4 (1995), pp 30–33.

—— *Early Irish monasteries.* Dublin, 1995.

—— The nave of Glendalough cathedral. In *IAPA Newsletter. Bulletin of the Irish Association of Professional Archaeologists*, xxii (spring 1996), p. 6.

—— Kilteel revisited. In *Kildare Arch. Soc. Jn.*, xviii, no. 3 (1996–7), pp 296–300.

—— The date of the round tower at Clonmacnoise. In *Archaeology Ireland*, xi, no. 2 (1997), pp 12–13.

—— Clonmacnoise cathedral. In Heather A. King (ed.), *Clonmacnoise Studies, i: seminar papers 1994* (Dublin, 1998), pp 56–86.

—— Some notes on the early history and archaeology of Tullaherin. In *In the Shadow of a Steeple*, vi (1998), pp 19–39.

—— References to church buildings in the annals. In Smyth, *Seanchas*, pp 37–52.

Mytum, Harold C. *The archaeology of rural monasteries.* Oxford, 1989.

O'Brien, Elizabeth. Churches of south-east County Dublin, 7th to 12th century. In Mac Niocaill & Wallace, *Keimelia*, pp 504–24.

Ó Floinn, Raghnall. Some decorated stone sculptures from Liathmore, Co. Tipperary. In Manning, *Beyond the Pale*, pp 193–201.

O'Keeffe, Tadhg. La façade romane en Irlande. In *Cahiers de civilisation médiévale x^e–xii^e siècles*, xxxiv, nos 3–4 (Juillet–Décembre 1991), pp 357–65.

——Romanesque architecture and sculpture at Ardmore. In William Nolan and Thomas P. Power (ed.), *Waterford: history and society* (Dublin, 1992), pp 73–104.

——Lismore and Cashel: reflections on the beginnings of Romanesque architecture in Munster. In *R.S.A.I. Jn.*, cxxiv (1994), pp 118–52.

——Appendix I. The Romanesque portal. In Kenneth Hanley, Mairéad Weaver, and Judith Monk (ed.), *An archaeological survey of St Molagga's church, Aghacross, Mitchelstown, Co. Cork* (Cork, 1994), pp 24–7.

——The Romanesque portal at Clonfert cathedral and its iconography. In Bourke, *Isles of the north*, pp 261–9.

——Architectural traditions of the early medieval church in Munster. In Monk & Sheehan, *Early med. Munster*, pp 112–24.

——Diarmait Mac Murchada and Romanesque Leinster: four twelfth-century churches in context. In *R.S.A.I. Jn.*, cxxvii (1997), pp 52–79.

——The fortifications of western Ireland, A.D. 1100–1300, and their interpretation. In *Galway Arch. Soc. Jn.*, l (1998), pp 184–200.

——Romanesque as metaphor: architecture and reform in early twelfth-century Ireland. In Smyth, *Seanchas*, pp 313–22.

O'Reilly, Seán D. *Irish churches and monasteries: an historical and architectural guide.* Cork, 1997.

O'Sullivan, Marie. A history of the development of St Brendan's cathedral, Ardfert. In *Kerry Arch. Soc. Jn.*, xxi (1988), pp 148–65.

Perry, Mark. The Romanesque frescoes in Cormac's Chapel, Cashel. In *Ireland of the Welcomes*, xliv, no. 2 (Mar.–Apr. 1995), pp 16–19.

Petrie, George. *The ecclesiastical architecture of Ireland anterior to the Anglo-Norman invasion, comprising an essay on the origin and uses of the round towers of Ireland.* Dublin, 1845. Reprinted, with introduction by Liam de Paor. Shannon, 1970.

Originally published in *R.I.A. Trans.*, xx (1845), pp 1–521.

Phipps, C. B. The problem of dating ancient Irish buildings. In *Hermathena*, liv (1939), pp 54–92.

Roche, Helen. A souterrain at Nobber, County Meath. In *R.S.A.I. Jn.*, cxv (1985), pp 164–6.

Rowan, Alistair. *North-west Ulster.* Harmondsworth, 1979. (The Buildings of Ireland.)

Ryan, Gerrard. Pre-reformation church and monastic sites in the barony of Bunratty Lower, c.500 A.D.–1500 A.D. In *The Other Clare*, ix (1985), pp 44–50.

Rynne, Etienne. The round towers of Ireland: a review article. In *N. Munster Antiq. Jn.*, xxii (1980), pp 27–32.

——Evidence for a tympanum at Aghadoe, Co. Kerry. In *N. Munster Antiq. Jn.*, xxix (1987), pp 3–6.

Rynne, Etienne. The round tower, 'evil eye', and holy well at Balla, Co. Mayo. In Manning, *Beyond the Pale*, pp 177–84.

Sheehan, John. The early historical church-sites of North Clare. In *N. Munster Antiq. Jn.*, xxiv (1982), pp 29–47.

——and Moore, Fionnbar. An unrecorded ecclesiastical enclosure at Ballyallaban, Co. Clare. In *N. Munster Antiq. Jn.*, xxiii (1981), pp 5–8.

Silke, John J. Airgialla churches and churches in Donegal. In *Clogher Rec.*, xiii, no. 1 (1988), pp 85–9.

Smith, J. T. Ardmore cathedral. In *R.S.A.I. Jn.*, cii (1972), pp 1–13.

Stalley, R. A. *Architecture and sculpture in Ireland, 1150–1350*. Dublin and London, 1971.

——The architecture of the Cistercian churches of Ireland, 1142–1272. In Christopher Norton and David Park (ed.), *Cistercian art and architecture in the British Isles* (Cambridge, 1986), pp 117–38.

——*The Cistercian monasteries of Ireland*. London and New Haven, 1987.

——*Ireland and Europe in the middle ages: selected essays on architecture and sculpture*. London, 1994.

Comprises reprints of articles not listed individually here.

——In search of Romanesque sculpture. In *Archaeology Ireland*, viii, no. 4 (1994), pp 7–9.

——Saint Bernard, his views on architecture and the Irish dimension. In *Arte Medievale*, II serie, Anno VIII, n. 1, tomo secondo (1994), pp 13–20.

——Decorating the lavabo: late Romanesque sculpture from Mellifont abbey. In *R.I.A. Proc.*, xcvi, sect. C (1996), pp 237–64.

——Hiberno-Romanesque and the sculpture of Killeshin. In Pádraig Lane and William Nolan (ed.), *Laois: history and society* (Dublin, 1999), pp 89–122.

——*Irish round towers*. Dublin, 2000.

——Sex, symbol, and myth: some observations on the Irish round towers. In Hourihane, *From Ire. coming*, pp 27–47.

Stokes, Margaret. *Early Christian architecture in Ireland*. London, 1878.

Swan, Leo. Newcastle Lyons—the prehistoric and early Christian periods. In Peter O'Sullivan (ed.), *Newcastle Lyons* (Dublin, 1986), pp 1–10.

——The early Christian ecclesiastical sites of County Westmeath. In Bradley, *Settlement & society*, pp 3–31.

Sweetman, P. D. Archaeological excavations at Kilcash church, Co. Tipperary. In *N. Munster Antiq. Jn.*, xxvi (1984), pp 36–43.

Swift, Cathy. A 'square earthen church of clay' in seventh-century Mayo. In *Trowel*, iv, pt 1 (1993), pp 32–7.

Swinfen, Averil. *The forgotten stones*. Dublin, 1992.

Veelenturf, Kees. Vroege kerkelijke architectuur in Ierland: het materiaal in de geschreven bronnen. In D. R. Edel, W. P. Gerritsen, and K. Veelenturf (ed.), *Monniken, ridders en zeevaarders* (Amsterdam, 1988), pp 61–81.

Waddell, John. An archaeological survey of Temple Brecan, Aran. In *Galway Arch. Soc. Jn.*, xxxiii (1972–3), pp 7–27.

Wallace, Patrick F. Anglo-Norman Dublin: continuity and change. In Ó Corráin, *Ir. antiquity*, pp 247–68.

—— Irish early Christian 'wooden' oratories: a suggestion. In *N. Munster Antiq. Jn.*, xxiv (1982), pp 19–28.

—— Archaeology and the emergence of Dublin as the principal town of Ireland. In Bradley, *Settlement & society*, pp 123–60.

—— A viking Dublin perspective on Irish vernacular architecture studies. In Mac Niocaill & Wallace, *Keimelia*, pp 574–96.

—— *The viking age buildings of Dublin*. 2 pts. Dublin, 1992. (Medieval Dublin Excavations 1962–81, series A, i.)

Walsh, Gerry. Preliminary report on the archaeological excavations on the summit of Croagh Patrick. In *Cathair na Mart*, xiv (1994), pp 1–10.

—— Recent archaeological excavations in Mayo. In *Living Heritage*, xiii, no. 1 (summer 1996), pp 23–4.

Walsh, Paul. The monastic settlement on Rathlin O'Birn Island, County Donegal. In *R.S.A.I. Jn.*, cxiii (1983), pp 53–66.

—— The round tower at Nohaval Lower, County Cork. In *R.S.A.I. Jn.*, cxvii (1987), pp 144–6.

Warner, Richard. Irish souterrains and their background. In Harriet Crawford (ed.), *Subterranean Britain: aspects of underground archaeology* (London, 1979), pp 100–44.

Whyte, Eileen. Church property dumped in Limerick castle. In *Archaeology Ireland*, x, no. 1 (1996), pp 14–16.

## (e) Arts and crafts

### (i) General

Most material on this subject published before 1980 can be found in Martin Werner, *Insular art: an annotated bibliography* (Boston, 1984), and is therefore omitted here. Hence, this section concentrates largely on works that have appeared since then, and should be read in conjunction with items listed under sections (a)–(c) above.

Arnold, Bruce. *A concise history of Irish art*. London, 1969.

Bakka, Egil. Westeuropäische und nordische Tierornamentik des achten Jahrhunderts in überregionalen Stil III. In *Studien zur Sachsenforschung*, iv (1983), pp 1–56.

Berger, Pamela. The Ardagh chalice, numerology, and the Stowe Missal. In *Éire-Ireland*, xiv, no. 3 (1979), pp 6–16.

Bradley, John. Moynagh Lough: an insular workshop of the second quarter of the 8th century. In Spearman & Higgitt, *Age of migrating ideas*, pp 74–81.

Budny, Mildred. Deciphering the art of interlace. In Hourihane, *From Ire. coming*, pp 183–210.

Christensen, Arne-Emil. Ship graffiti and models. In P. F. Wallace (ed.), *Miscellanea I* (Medieval Dublin Excavations 1962–81, ser. B, ii; Dublin, 1988), pp 13–26.

Cone, Polly (ed.). *Treasures of early Irish art 1500 B.C.–1500 A.D.* New York, 1977. Contributors include Liam and Máire de Paor, Peter Harbison, G. Frank Mitchell, and Roger Stalley.

Cramp, Rosemary. Northumbria and Ireland. In Paul Szarmach (ed.), *Sources of Anglo-Saxon culture* (Kalamazoo, 1986), pp 185-201.

Elbern, V. H. Irische Kunst. In *Lexikon für Theologie und Kirche*, v (1960), pp 750–73.

Gerke, F. Die Anfänge der frühchristlichen Kunst in Irland. In *Kunst und Kirche*, xvi (1939), pp 104–8.

Graham-Campbell, James. Irish monastic art, 5th to 8th centuries. In *Monastic Studies* [Montreal], xiv (1983), pp 225–45.

Harbison, Peter. Early Irish reliquary-shrines in bronze and stone. In *Würzburger Diözesangeschichtsblätter*, li (1989), pp 37–50.

——The otherness of Irish art in the twelfth century. In Hourihane, *From Ire. coming*, pp 103–20.

——Potterton, Homan; and Sheehy, Jeanne. *Irish art and architecture*. London, 1978.

Haseloff, Günther. Keltische Stilzüge in der frühmittelalterlichen Kunst. In G. Grasmann, W. Janssen, and M. Brandt (ed.), *Keltische Numismatik und Archaeologie* (Brit. Arch. Reps, International Series, cc; Oxford, 1984), pp 98–118.

——Insular animal styles with special reference to Irish art in the early medieval period. In Ryan, *Ire. & insular art*, pp 44–55.

Henderson, Isabel. Françoise Henry and Helen Roe: fifty-five years' work on Irish art and archaeology. In *Camb. Med. Celt. Studies*, xvii (summer 1989), pp 69–74.

Henry, Françoise. Un domaine nouveau de l'histoire de l'art: l'art irlandais du VIII<sup>e</sup> siècle et ses origines. In *Gazette des beaux-arts*, 6<sup>me</sup> période, xvii (1937), pp 131–44.

Herity, Michael. Carpet pages and chi-rhos: some depictions in Irish early Christian manuscripts and stone carvings. In *Celtica*, xxi (1990), pp 208–22.

Hicks, Carola. *Animals in early medieval art*. Edinburgh, 1993.

Jansson, Ingmar, and others (ed.). *Irland den gåtfulla ön*. Stockholm, 1988.

Kilbride-Jones, H. E. On some origins in the ecclesiastical art of the early church in Celtic Ireland. In *Bulletin of the Board of Celtic Studies*, xxxix (1992), pp 299–314.

——Early Christian symbolism with particular reference to objects of Irish provenance: interpretation and application. In Bourke, *Isles of the north*, pp 9–16.

Kitzinger, Ernst. Interlace and icons: form and function in early insular art. In Spearman & Higgitt, *Age of migrating ideas*, pp 3–15.

Laing, Lloyd. *Later Celtic art in Britain and Ireland*. Aylesbury, 1987. (Shire Archaeology.)

——and Laing, Jennifer. *Celtic art in Britain and Ireland: art and society*. London, 1995.

Lang, James. Survival and revival in insular art: some principles. In Karkov, Ryan, & Farrell, *Insular tradition*, pp 63–77.

Le Clerc, Percy, and others. The exhibition of ancient Celtic art. In *Rosc '67* (Dublin, 1967), pp 123–89.

McNab, Susanne. Celtic antecedents to the treatment of the human figure in early Irish art. In Hourihane, *From Ire. coming*, pp 161–82.

Megaw, J. V. S., and Megaw, Ruth. *Early Celtic art in Britain and Ireland*. Aylesbury, 1986.

————*Celtic art from its beginnings to the Book of Kells*. London, 1989.

Nees, Lawrence. Art and architecture. In *New Cambridge medieval history, ii: c.700–c.900* (Cambridge, 1995), pp 809–44, 1029–39.

O'Brien, Jacqueline, and Harbison, Peter. *Ancient Ireland*. London, 1996.

Ó Floinn, Raghnall. Clonmacnoise: art and patronage in the early medieval period. In Bourke, *Isles of the north*, pp 251–60.

O'Neill, Henry. *The fine arts and civilisation of ancient Ireland*. London and Dublin, 1863.

Raftery, Joseph, and O'Sullivan, William. *Artists and craftsmen: Irish art treasures*. Dublin, 1980.

Richardson, Hilary. Number and symbol in early Christian Irish art. In *R.S.A.I. Jn.*, cxiv (1984), pp 28–47.

——Die Kunst in Irland im 8. Jahrhundert. In Dopsch & Juffinger, *Virgil von Salzburg*, pp 185–215.

——Observations on Christian art in early Ireland, Georgia, and Armenia. In Ryan, *Ire. & insular art*, pp 129–37.

——Celtic art. In James P. Mackey (ed.), *An introduction to Celtic Christianity* (Edinburgh, 1989), pp 359–85.

——Christian iconography in early Irish and Armenian art. In [B. L. Zekiyan (ed.),] *Atti del Quinto Simposio Internazionale di Arte Armena, 1988* (Venice, 1992), pp 575–93.

——Remarks on the liturgical fan, flabellum or rhipidion. In Spearman & Higgitt, *Age of migrating ideas*, pp 27–34.

——Lozenge and Logos. In *Archaeology Ireland*, x, no. 2 (1996), pp 24–5.

Ryan, Michael. *Early Ireland: culture and treasures*. Dublin, 1991.

——The Sutton Hoo ship burial and Ireland: some Celtic perspectives. In Robert Farrell and Carol Neuman de Vegvar (ed.), *Sutton Hoo: fifty years after* (American Early Medieval Studies 2; Oxford, Ohio, 1992), pp 83–116.

——(ed.). *Treasures of Ireland: Irish art 3000 B.C.–1500 A.D.* Dublin, 1983.

——(ed.). *Ireland and insular art A.D. 500–1200: proceedings of a conference at University College, Cork, 31 October–3 November 1985*. Dublin, 1987.

Rynne, Etienne (ed.). *Figures from the past: studies on figurative art in Christian Ireland in honour of Helen M. Roe*. Dublin, 1987.

Stalley, Roger. The long middle ages. From the twelfth century to the reformation. In Brian de Breffny (ed.), *The Irish world: the history and cultural achievements of the Irish people* (London, 1977), pp 71–98.

Stokes, Margaret. *Early Christian art in Ireland*. London, 1887. 2nd ed. 1894.

Thomas, Charles. The earliest Christian art in Ireland and Britain. In Ryan, *Ire. & insular art*, pp 7–11.

Toorians, Lauran. Is Isis Mary and Osiris the crucified? In Mat Immerzeel and others (ed.), *Essays on Christian art and culture in the middle east*, iii (Leiden, 2000), pp 29–39.

*Treasures of Celtic art: a European heritage*. Tokyo, 1998.

Wamers, Egon. Egg-and-dart derivatives in insular art. In Ryan, *Ire. & insular art*, pp 96–104.

——Insular art in Carolingian Europe: the reception of old ideas in a new empire. In Spearman & Higgitt, *Age of migrating ideas*, pp 35–44.

Wilson, David M. Scandinavian ornamental influence in the Irish Sea region in the viking age. In Tom Scott and Pat Starkey (ed.), *The middle ages in the north-west* (Oxford, 1995), pp 37–57.

Wright, David H. The Irish element in the formation of Hiberno-Saxon art: calligraphy and metalwork. In Löwe, *Die Iren*, i, 99–100.

## (ii) Metalwork and other crafts

See the note above at the beginning of section (e).

Armstrong, E. C. R. Four brooches preserved in the library of Trinity College, Dublin. In *R.I.A. Proc.*, xxxii (1915), sect. C, pp 243–8.

—— The bell shrine of St Senan, known as the Clogán Óir. In *R.S.A.I. Jn.*, xlix (1919), pp 132–5.

Bardon, Roisín. A possible slave-chain from Knowth, Co. Meath. In *Ríocht na Midhe*, xi (2000), pp 20–23.

Bierbrauer, Volker. Das sogenannte Rupertuskreuz aus Bischofshofen. In Dopsch & Juffinger, *Virgil von Salzburg*, pp 229-43.

Blindheim, Martin. A house-shaped Irish-Scots reliquary in Bologna, and its place among the other reliquaries. In *Acta Archaeologica*, lv (1984), pp 1–53.

Bourke, Cormac. Early Irish hand bells. In *R.S.A.I. Jn.*, cx (1980), pp 52–66.

—— Les cloches à main de la Bretagne primitive. In *Bulletin de la Société Archéologique du Finistère*, cx (1982), pp 339–53.

—— The hand-bells of the early Scottish church. In *Antiq. Soc. Scot. Proc.*, cxiii (1983), pp 464–68.

—— A crozier and bell from Inishmurray and their place in ninth-century Irish archaeology. In *R.I.A. Proc.*, lxxxv (1985), sect. C, pp 145–68.

—— Early Irish bells. In *Seanchas Dhroim Mor: journal of the Dromore Historical Society*, iv (1986), pp 27–38.

—— The Doras/Tullyniskan bell. In *U.J.A.*, l (1987), pp 155–6.

—— Irish croziers of the eighth and ninth centuries. In Ryan, *Ire. & insular art*, pp 166–73.

—— A ringed pin from Lough Ravel Crannog, Co. Antrim. In *U.J.A.*, li (1988), pp 55–60.

—— Three twelfth-century appliqué figures. In Mac Niocaill & Wallace, *Keimelia*, pp 112–26.

—— On a lost mount from the Cross of Cong. In *Archaeology Ireland*, iii, no. 1 (1989), pp 14–16.

—— Notes on the relics of St Patrick. In *Lecale Miscellany*, vii (1989), pp 5–10.

—— The Blackwater shrine. In *Dúiche Néill: journal of the O Neill Country Historical Society*, vi (1991), pp 103–6.

—— The Ballyrea brooch. In *Emania*, x (1992), pp 66–7.

—— *Patrick: the archaeology of a saint*. Belfast, 1993.

—— The chronology of Irish crucifixion plaques. In Spearman & Higgitt, *Age of migrating ideas*, pp 175–81.

——The hand-bells of the early western church. In Catherine Laurent and Helen Davis (ed.), *Irlande et Bretagne: vingt siècles d'histoire. Essais; Actes du Colloque de Rennes, 29–31 Mars 1993* (Rennes, 1994), pp 77–82.

——Further notes on the Clonmore shrine. In *Seanchas Ardmhacha*, xvi, no. 2 (1995), pp 27–32.

——A note on the Delg Aidechta. In Cormac Bourke (ed.), *Studies in the cult of St Columba* (Dublin, 1997), pp 184–92.

——Insignia Columbae II. Ibid., pp 162–83.

——Fine metalwork from the River Blackwater. In *Archaeology Ireland*, xii, no. 3 (1998), pp 30–31.

——The bells of Saints Caillín and Cuanu: two twelfth-century cups. In Smyth, *Seanchas*, pp 331–40.

——and Close-Brooks, Joanna. Five insular enamelled ornaments. In *Antiq. Soc. Scot. Proc.*, cxix (1989), pp 227–37.

——Fanning, Thomas; and Whitfield, Niamh. An insular brooch-fragment from Norway. In *Antiq. Jn.*, lxviii (1988), pp 90–98.

——and Warner, Richard. A seventh-century reliquary from Armagh. In *Archaeology Ireland*, v, no. 2 (1991), p. 16.

Bourke, Edward. Glass vessels of the first nine centuries A.D. in Ireland. In *R.S.A.I. Jn.*, cxxiv (1994), pp 163–209.

Bradley, John. Moynagh Lough: an insular workshop of the second quarter of the 8th century. In Spearman & Higgitt, *Age of migrating ideas*, pp 74–81.

——and Dunne, Noel. The findplace of the 'Athlone' crucifixion plaque. In *Organization of Irish Archaeologists Newsletter 8* (1989), pp 13–18.

Briggs, C. S., and Sheehan, John. A hoard of dispersed viking age arm-rings from 'the Liffeyside', County Dublin. In *Antiq. Jn.*, lxvii (1987), pp 351–2.

Brown, Michelle P. 'Paten and purpose': the Derrynaflan paten inscriptions. In Spearman & Higgitt, *Age of migrating ideas*, pp 162–7.

Bruce-Mitford, Rupert. Ireland and the hanging-bowls: a review. In Ryan, *Ire. & insular art*, pp 30–39.

Buckley, J. J. Some early ornamental leatherwork. In *R.S.A.I. Jn.*, xlv (1915), pp 300–9.

Cahill, Mary, and Ó Floinn, Raghnall. Two silver kite brooches from near Limerick city. In *N. Munster Antiq. Jn.*, xxxvi (1995), pp 65–82.

Graham-Campbell, James. The viking-age silver hoards of Ireland. In Bo Almqvist and David Greene (ed.), *Proceedings of the Seventh Viking Congress* (London, 1976), pp 39–74.

——Western British, Irish, and later Anglo-Saxon. In *Archaeological Journal*, cxxxiii (1976), pp 277–89.

——*Viking artefacts*. London, 1980.

——Some viking-age penannular brooches from Scotland and the origins of the 'thistle-brooch'. In Anne O'Connor and D. V. Clarke (ed.), *From the stone age to the 'Forty-five* (Edinburgh, 1983), pp 310–23.

——Western penannular brooches and their viking age copies in Norway: a new classification. In James E. Knirk (ed.), *Proceedings of the Tenth Viking Congress:*

*Larkollen, Norway, 1985* (Universitetets Oldsaksamlings Skrifter, Ny Rekke, ix; Oslo, 1987), pp 231–46.

Graham-Campbell, James. A lost zoomorphic penannular brooch from Kells, County Meath. In *R.S.A.I. Jn.*, cxvi (1987), pp 122–3.

——From Scandinavia to the Irish Sea: viking art reviewed. In Ryan, *Ire. & insular art*, pp 144–52.

——A viking-age silver hoard from near Raphoe, Co. Donegal. In Mac Niocaill & Wallace, *Keimelia*, pp 102–11.

——and Briggs, C. S. Some neglected viking-age silver hoards from near Athlone and Co. Cork. In *Peritia*, v (1986), pp 309–16.

Carroll, Judith. Millefiori in the development of early Irish enamelling. In Bourke, *Isles of the north*, pp 49–57.

Comber, Michelle. Lagore crannóg and non-ferrous metalworking in early historic Ireland. In *Journal of Irish Archaeology*, viii (1997), pp 101–14.

Connolly, Michael. An iron sickle from a previously unrecorded souterrain at Beaufort, Co. Kerry. In *Kerry Arch. Soc. Jn.*, xxv (1992), pp 20–36.

Cooke, Thomas Lalor. Description of the Barnaan Cuilawn, and some conjectures upon the original use thereof: together with an account of the superstitious purposes to which it was latterly applied. In *R.I.A. Trans.*, xiv (1825), Antiquities, pp 31–45.

de Paor, Liam. Irish belt-buckles and strap-mounts. In Gerhard Bersu (ed.), *Bericht über den V. internationalen Kongress für Vor- und Frühgeschichte, Hamburg, 1958* (Berlin, 1961), pp 649–53.

——The Derrynavlan hoard. In *Art About Ireland*, ii, no. 2 (June–July 1980), pp 8–12.

Dickinson, Tania M. Fowler's type G penannular brooches reconsidered. In *Medieval Archaeology*, xxvi (1982), pp 41–68.

Dooley, Joseph, and Rice, Gerard. Some objects found at Ervey Lake, Co. Meath. In *Riocht na Midhe*, x (1999), pp 31–51.

Dunlevy, Mairead. A classification of early Irish combs. In *R.I.A. Proc.*, lxxxviii (1988), sect. C, pp 341–422.

Dunraven, earl of. On an ancient chalice and brooches lately found at Ardagh, in the county of Limerick. In *R.I.A. Trans.*, xxiv (1874), pp 433–54.

Earwood, Caroline. *Domestic wooden artefacts in Britain and Ireland from neolithic to viking times.* Exeter, 1993.

Elbern, Victor H. Eine Gruppe insularer Kelche. In Ursula Schlegel and Claus Zoege von Manteuffel (ed.), *Festschrift für Peter Metz* (Berlin, 1965), pp 115–23.

——Kelche der Karolingerzeit. In Michael Ryan (ed.), *Irish antiquities: essays in memory of Joseph Raftery* (Bray, 1998), pp 123–40.

Fanning, Thomas. Some aspects of the bronze ringed pin in Scotland. In A. O'Connor and D. Clarke (ed.), *From the stone age to the 'Forty-five* (Edinburgh, 1983), pp 324–42.

——Three ringed pins from viking Dublin and their significance. In Bradley, *Settlement & society*, pp 161–75.

——Ringed pins, the Hiberno-Norse and the discovery of Vinland. In *Archeology Ireland*, vi, no. 1 (1992), pp 24–6.

——*Viking age ringed pins from Dublin*. Dublin, 1994. (Medieval Dublin Excavations, 1962–81, ser. B., iv.)

——and Crumlish, Richard. A bronze ringed pin from Ballintemple, Tullaghobegley, Co. Donegal. In *Donegal Annual*, xliv (1992), pp 83–7.

Fuglesang, S. H. *Some aspects of the Ringerike style: a phase of 11th-century Scandinavian art*. Odense, 1980. (Medieval Scandinavia Supplements, i.)

——Stylistic groups in late viking and early Romanesque art. In *Institutum Romanum Norvegiae: Acta ad Archaeologiam et Artium Historiam Pertinentia, serie altera in 8°*, i (1981), pp 79–125; ii (1982), pp 125–73.

Halpin, Andrew. A 'Winchester-style' bronze mount. In P. F. Wallace (ed.), *Miscellanea I* (Medieval Dublin Excavations 1962–81, ser. B, ii; Dublin, 1988), pp 7–12.

Hamlin, Ann, and Howarth, R. G. A crucifixion plaque reprovenanced. In *R.S.A.I. Jn.*, cxii (1982), pp 112–16.

Harbison, Peter. A lost crucifixion plaque of Clonmacnoise type found in Co. Mayo. In Harman Murtagh (ed.), *Irish midland studies* (Athlone, 1980), pp 24–38.

——The date of the Moylough belt shrine. In Ó Corráin, *Ir. antiquity*, pp 231–9.

——The bronze crucifixion plaque said to be from St John's (Rinnagan), near Athlone. In *Journal of Irish Archaeology*, ii (1984), pp 1–17.

——The Derrynaflan ladle: some parallels illustrated. In *Journal of Irish Archaeology*, iii (1985–6), pp 55–8.

Haseloff, Günther. *Email im frühen Mittelalter: frühchristliche Kunst von der Spätantike bis zu den Karolingern*. Marburg, 1990. (Marburger Studien zur Vor- und Frühgeschichte, Sonderband i.)

Henderson, Julian. The nature of the early Christian glass industry in Ireland: some evidence from Dunmisk fort, County Tyrone. In *U.J.A.*, li (1988), pp 115–26.

——and Ovens, Richard. Dunmisk and glass-making in early Christian Ireland. In *Antiquity*, lxvi, no. 250 (1992), pp 52–64.

Henry, Françoise. *Studies in early Christian and medieval Irish art, i: enamels and metalwork*. London, 1983.

Comprises reprints of articles not listed individually here.

Johnson, Ruth. On the dating of some early-medieval Irish croziers. In *Medieval Archaeology*, xliv (2000), pp 115–58.

Kilbride-Jones, H. E. *Zoomorphic penannular brooches*. London, 1980. (Reports of the Research Committee of the Society of Antiquaries of London, xxxix.)

——Metalworking practices in early Ireland. In *Archaeology Ireland*, viii, no. 3 (1994), pp 19–21.

Kelly, Dorothy. Crucifixion plaques. In *Irish Arts Review Yearbook 1990–91*, pp 204–9.

Kelly, Eamonn P. The Lough Kinale book-shrine. In Spearman & Higgitt, *Age of migrating ideas*, pp 168–74.

Kendrick, T. D., and Senior, Elizabeth. St Manchan's shrine. In *Archaeologia*, lxxxvi (1937), pp 105–18.

Lang, James T. Eleventh-century style in decorated wood from Dublin. In Ryan, *Ire.
    & insular art*, pp 174–8.
——*Viking-age decorated wood: a study of its ornament and style*. Dublin, 1988.
    (Medieval Dublin Excavations 1962–81, ser. B, i.)
La Niece, Susan, and Stapleton, Colleen. Niello and enamel on Irish metalwork. In
    *Antiq. Jn.*, lxxiii (1993), pp 148–51.
Mac Namidhe, Margaret. The 'Buddha bucket' from the Oseberg ship find. In *The
    GPA Irish Arts Review Yearbook 1989–90*, pp 77–82.
McRoberts, D. The ecclesiastical significance of the St Ninian's Isle treasure. In
    Alan Small (ed.), *Proceedings of the Fourth Viking Congress* (Aberdeen, 1965),
    pp 224–46.
Michelli, Perette E. Migrating ideas or migrating craftsmen? The case of the bossed
    penannular brooches. In Spearman & Higgitt, *Age of migrating ideas*, pp 182–7.
Mitchell, G. F. The cap of St Lachtin's arm. In *R.S.A.I. Jn.*, cxiv (1984), pp 139–40.
Mount, Charles, and Keeley, Valerie. An early medieval strap-tag from Balally,
    County Dublin. In *R.S.A.I. Jn.*, cxx (1990), pp 120–25.
Needham, Stuart. The development of embossed goldwork in bronze age Europe. In
    *Antiq. Jn.*, lxxx (2000), pp 27–65.
Newman, Conor. Fowler's type F3 early medieval penannular brooches. In *Medieval
    Archaeology*, xxxiii (1989), pp 7–20.
——Notes on some Irish hanging bowl escutcheons. In *Journal of Irish Archaeology*,
    v (1989–90), pp 45–8.
——Further notes on Fowler's type F3 penannular brooches. In *Medieval Archae-
    ology*, xxxiv (1990), pp 147–8.
——The iron age to early Christian transition: the evidence from dress fasteners. In
    Bourke, *Isles of the north*, pp 17–25.
Nieke, Margaret R. Penannular and related brooches: secular ornament or symbol in
    action? In Spearman & Higgitt, *Age of migrating ideas*, pp 128–34.
O'Carroll, Ellen. Ireland's earliest crozier? In *Archaeology Ireland*, xiv, no. 2 (2000),
    pp 24–5.
Ó Floinn, Raghnall. Viking and Romanesque influences 1000 A.D.–1169 A.D. In
    Michael Ryan (ed.), *Treasures of Ireland* (Dublin, 1983), pp 58–69.
——The shrine of the Book of Dimma. In *Éile: journal of the Roscrea Heritage
    Society*, i (1983), pp 25–39.
——A bronze shield grip of viking age date from the River Bann. In *U.J.A.*, xlix
    (1986), pp 106–8.
——Irish Romanesque crucifix figures. In Rynne, *Figures from the past*, pp 168–88.
——Schools of metalworking in eleventh- and twelfth-century Ireland. In Ryan, *Ire.
    & insular art*, pp 179–87.
——A Romanesque crucifix figure from Athgarrett. In *Kildare Arch. Soc. Jn.*, xvii
    (1987–91), pp 211–12.
——The Soiscél Molaisse. In *Clogher Rec.*, xiii, no. 2 (1989), pp 51–63.
——A fragmentary house-shaped shrine from Clonard, Co. Meath. In *Journal of
    Irish Archaeology*, v (1989–90), pp 49–55.
——Two ancient bronze bells from Rath Blathmach, Co. Clare. In *N. Munster
    Antiq. Jn.*, xxxii (1990), pp 19–31.

——The 'Tipperary brooch': a reprovenance. In *Tipperary Historical Journal, 1990*, pp 187–92.

——Ecclesiastical objects of the early medieval period from Co. Clare. In *The Other Clare*, xv (1991), pp 12–14.

——*Irish shrines and reliquaries of the middle ages.* Dublin, 1994.

——Sandhills, silver and shrines—fine metalwork of the medieval period from Donegal. In William Nolan, Liam Ronayne, and Mairead Dunlevy (ed.), *Donegal: history & society* (Dublin, 1995), pp 85–148.

——Insignia Columbae I. In Cormac Bourke (ed.), *Studies in the cult of Saint Columba* (Dublin, 1997), pp 136–61.

——Innovation and conservatism in Irish metalwork of the Romanesque period. In Karkov, Ryan, & Farrell, *Insular tradition*, pp 259–81.

O'Meadhra, Uaininn. *Early Christian, viking and Romanesque art: motif-pieces from Ireland, 2: a discussion on aspects of find-context and function.* Stockholm, 1987. (Theses and Papers in North-European Archaeology, xvii.)

——Irish, insular, Saxon, and Scandinavian elements in the motif-pieces from Ireland. In Ryan, *Ire. & insular art*, pp 159–65.

——Motif-pieces and other decorated bone and antler work. In Maurice F. Hurley and Orla M. B. Scully with Sarah W. J. McCutcheon (ed.), *Late viking age and medieval Waterford: excavations 1986–1992* (Waterford, 1997), pp 699–702.

Organ, Robert M. Examination of the Ardagh chalice: a case history. In William J. Young (ed.), *Application of science in examination of works of art* (Boston, 1973), pp 238–71.

O Rahilly, Celie. A classification of bronze stick-pins from the Dublin excavations 1967–72. In Manning, *Beyond the Pale*, pp 23–33.

Ó Riain, Pádraig. The shrine of the Stowe missal, redated. In *R.I.A. Proc.*, xci (1991), sect. C, pp 285–95.

Petrie, George. On the Cross of Cong. In *R.I.A. Proc.*, iv (1850), pp 572–85.

Prendergast, E. A viking sword from Harley Park. In *Old Kilkenny Review*, iv, no. 1 (1989), pp 815–19.

Reeves, William. *Five chromo-lithographic drawings representing an Irish ecclesiastical bell, which is supposed to have belonged to St Patrick.* Belfast, 1850.

——On the bell of St Patrick, called the Clog an Edachta. In *R.I.A. Trans.*, xxvii (1877–86), pp 1–30.

Rice, Gerard. An addition to the corpus of bronze open work plaques emanating from a Clonmacnoise workshop in the twelfth century. In *Ríocht na Midhe*, viii, no. 3 (1990–91), pp 114–17.

Ross, Martin Chauncey. An Irish cloisonné enamel. In *Journal of the Down & Connor Historical Society*, v (1933), pp 43–6.

Ryan, Michael. An early Christian hoard from Derrynaflan, Co. Tipperary. In *N. Munster Antiq. Jn.*, xxii (1980), pp 9–26.

——The Roscrea brooch. In *Éile: journal of the Roscrea Heritage Society*, i (1982), pp 5–23.

——Metalworking and style in the early Christian period, 7th–10th centuries A.D. In Michael Ryan (ed.), *Treasures of Ireland* (Dublin, 1983), pp 34–45.

Ryan, Michael. (ed.). *The Derrynaflan hoard I: a preliminary account.* Dublin, 1983.

—— The Derrynaflan hoard and other early Irish eucharistic chalices: some speculations. In Ní Chatháin & Richter, *Ire. & Europe*, pp 135–48.

—— Early Irish chalices. In *Irish Arts Review*, i, no. 1 (1984), pp 21–5.

—— An insular gilt-bronze object in the Royal Museums for Art and History. In *Musea*, lvi (1985), pp 57–60.

—— *Early Irish communion vessels: church treasures of the golden age.* Dublin, 1985. 2nd ed., 2000.

—— The horn-reliquary of Tongres/Tongeren: a 12th-century Irish object. In *Bulletin des Musées Royaux d'Art et d'Histoire*, lvi, no. 2 (1985), pp 43–55.

—— Some aspects of sequence and style in the metalwork of eighth- and ninth-century Ireland. In Ryan, *Ire. & insular art*, pp 66–74.

—— The Donore hoard: early medieval metalwork from Moynalty, near Kells, Ireland. In *Antiquity*, lxi, no. 231 (1987), pp 57–63.

—— A suggested origin for the figure representations on the Derrynaflan paten. In Rynne, *Figures from the past*, pp 62–72.

—— The Irish horn-reliquary of Tongres/Tongeren, Belgium. In Mac Niocaill & Wallace, *Keimelia*, pp 127–42.

—— Fine metalworking and early Irish monasteries: the archaeological evidence. In Bradley, *Settlement & society*, pp 33–48.

—— Frühe irische Metallarbeiten. In Johannes Erichsen and Evamaria Brockhoff (ed.), *Kilian, Mönch aus Irland* (2 vols, Munich, 1989), pp 75–83.

—— Derrynaflan ten years on, 1: the impact of the find on our heritage. In *Tipperary Historical Journal, 1990,* pp 153–8.

—— Decorated metalwork in the Museo dell' Abbazia, Bobbio, Italy. In *R.S.A.I. Jn.*, cxx (1990), pp 102–11.

—— The formal relationships of insular early medieval eucharistic chalices. In *R.I.A. Proc.*, xc (1990), sect. C, pp 281–356.

—— Decorated Irish metalwork in Bobbio, Italy. In *Archaeology Ireland*, v, no. 2 (1991), p. 17.

—— Links between Anglo-Saxon and Irish early medieval art: some evidence of metalwork. In Catherine Karkov and Robert Farrell (ed.), *Studies in insular art and archaeology* (American Early Medieval Studies, i; Oxford, Ohio, 1991), pp 117–26.

—— *Metal craftsmanship in early Ireland.* Dublin, 1993.

—— The menagerie of the Derrynaflan chalice. In Spearman & Higgitt, *Age of migrating ideas*, pp 151–61.

—— Ten years of early Irish metalwork. In *Irish Arts Review Yearbook*, x (1994), pp 153–6.

—— Early Christian metalwork: new evidence from Ireland. In Kenneth Painter (ed.), *'Churches built in ancient times': recent studies in early Christian archaeology* (London, 1994), pp 313–24.

—— The decoration of the Donore discs. In Bourke, *Isles of the north*, pp 27–35.

—— The menagerie of the Derrynaflan paten. In *Irish Arts Review Yearbook*, xi (1995), pp 82–7.

——The menagerie of the Derrynaflan paten. In Karkov, Ryan, & Farrell, *Insular tradition*, pp 245–57.

——The Derrynaflan hoard and early Irish art. In *Speculum*, lxxii (1997), pp 995–1017.

——A house-shaped shrine of probable Irish origin at Abbadia San Salvatore, province of Siena, Italy. In Michael Ryan (ed.), *Irish antiquity: essays in memory of Joseph Raftery* (Bray, 1998), pp 141–50.

——Ó Floinn, Raghnall; Lowick, Nicholas; Kenny, Michael; and Cazalet, Peter. Six silver finds of the viking period from the vicinity of Lough Ennell, Co. Westmeath. In *Peritia*, iii (1984), pp 334–81.

——and Kelly, Eamonn P. New finds at the National Museum of Ireland. In *Ireland of the Welcomes*, xxxvi, no. 5 (Sept.–Oct. 1987), pp 22–5.

Rynne, Etienne. The date of the Ardagh chalice. In Ryan, *Ire. & insular art*, pp 85–9.

——Gilt-bronze brooch from near Kilshanny, Co. Clare. In *N. Munster Antiq. Jn.*, xxx (1988), pp 52–4.

——The Kilshanny bell. In Ciarán Ó Murchadha (ed.), *County Clare studies: essays in memory of Gerald O'Connell, Seán Ó Murchadha, Thomas Coffey and Pat Flynn* (Ennis, 2000), pp 42–54.

Sheehan, John. A bronze bell-crest from the Rock of Cashel, Co. Tipperary. In *N. Munster Antiq. Jn.*, xxx (1988), pp 3–13.

——A pair of viking-age animal-headed arm-rings from Co. Cork. In *Cork Hist. Soc. Jn.*, xcv (1990), pp 41–54.

——A viking-age silver arm-ring from Portumna, Co. Galway. In *Galway Arch. Soc. Jn.*, xlii (1989–90), pp 125–30.

——Coiled armrings—an Hiberno-viking silver armring type. In *Journal of Irish Archaeology*, vi (1991–2), pp 41–53.

——The Rathmooley hoard and other viking age silver from Co. Tipperary. In *Tipperary Historical Journal, 1992*, pp 210–16.

——Silver and gold hoards: status, wealth and trade in the viking age. In *Archaeology Ireland*, ix, no. 3 (1995), pp 19–22.

Smith, Reginald A. Evolution of late-Keltic pins of the hand type. In *Proceedings of the Society of Antiquaries*, 2nd ser., xx (1903–5), pp 344–54.

——Note on thistle and other brooches. In *Proceedings of the Society of Antiquaries*, 2nd ser., xxi (1906–7), pp 63–71.

——The evolution of the hand-pin in Great Britain and Ireland. In *Opuscula Archaeologica Oscari Montelio Septuagenario Dicata D. IX M. Sept. A. MCMXIII* (Stockholm, 1913), pp 281–9.

Somerville, Orna. Kite-shaped brooches. In *R.S.A.I. Jn.*, cxxiii (1993), pp 59–101.

Stevenson, Robert B. K. Further notes on the Hunterston and 'Tara' brooches, Monymusk reliquary, and Blackness bracelet. In *Antiq. Soc. Scot. Proc.*, cxiii (1983), pp 469–77.

——Brooches and pins: some seventh- to ninth-century problems. In Ryan, *Ire. & insular art*, pp 90–95.

——The Celtic brooch from Westness, Orkney, and hinged-pins. In *Antiq. Soc. Scot. Proc.*, cxix (1989), pp 239–69.

Stevenson, Robert B. K. Further thoughts on some well known problems. In Spearman & Higgitt, *Age of migrating ideas*, pp 16–26.

Stokes, Margaret. *Notes on the Cross of Cong*. Dublin, 1895.

Swan, Leo. Fine metalwork from the early Christian site at Kilpatrick, Co. Westmeath. In Bourke, *Isles of the north*, pp 75–80.

Walsh, Aidan. A summary classification of viking age swords in Ireland. In Clarke, Ní Mhaonaigh, & Ó Floinn, *Ire. & Scandinavia*, pp 222–38.

Wamers, Egon. Some ecclesiastical and secular insular metalwork in Norwegian viking graves. In *Peritia*, ii (1983), pp 277–306.

—— *Insularer Metallschmuck in wikingerzeitlichen Gräbern Nordeuropas*. Neumünster, 1985.

Warner, Richard B. Ireland and the origins of escutcheon art. In Ryan, *Ire. & insular art*, pp 19–22.

Westropp, T. J. The Clog an Oir, or bell shrine of Scattery. In *R.S.A.I. Jn.*, xxx (1900), pp 237–44.

Whitfield, Niamh. Motifs and techniques of Celtic filigree: are they original? In Ryan, *Ire. & insular art*, pp 75–84.

—— Animal ornament on insular metalwork of the late 7th–8th centuries: its character and development. In *Medieval Europe 1992: art and symbolism, pre-printed papers 7*, pp 9–15.

—— The filigree of the Hunterston and 'Tara' brooches. In Spearman & Higgitt, *Age of migrating ideas*, pp 118–27.

—— Some new research on gold and gold filigree from early medieval Ireland and Scotland. In Christian Eluère (ed.), *Outils et ateliers d'orfèvres des temps anciens* (Antiquités Nationales, Mémoire ii; Saint-Germain-en-Laye, 1993), pp 125–36.

—— The sources of gold in early Christian Ireland. In *Archaeology Ireland*, vii, no. 4 (1993), pp 21–3.

—— Formal conventions in the depiction of animals on Celtic metalwork. In Bourke, *Isles of the north*, pp 89–104.

—— 'Corinthian bronze' and the 'Tara' brooch. In *Archaeology Ireland*, xi, no. 1 (spring 1997), pp 24–8.

—— The Waterford kite-brooch and its place in Irish metalwork. In Maurice F. Hurley, Orla M. B. Scully, and Sarah W. J. McCutcheon (ed.), *Late viking-age and medieval Waterford: excavations 1986–1992* (Waterford, 1997), pp 490–517.

—— Filigree animal ornament from Ireland and Scotland of the late-seventh to ninth centuries. In Karkov, Ryan, & Farrell, *Insular tradition*, pp 211–43.

—— Design and units of measure on the Hunterston brooch. In Jane Hawkes and Susan Mills (ed.), *Northumbria's golden age* (Stroud, 1999), pp 296–314.

—— The 'Tara' brooch: an Irish emblem of status in its European context. In Hourihane, *From Ire. coming*, 211–47.

—— and Graham-Campbell, James. A mount with Hiberno-Saxon chipcarved animal ornament from Rerrick, near Dundrennan, Kirkcudbrightshire, Scotland. In *Transactions of the Dumfriesshire and Galloway Natural History and Antiquarian Society*, 3rd ser., lxvii (1992), pp 9–27.

—— and Okasha, Elizabeth. The Killamery brooch: its stamped ornament and inscription. In *Journal of Irish Archaeology*, vi (1991–2), pp 55–60.

Wilson, David M. A group of penannular brooches of the viking period. In Kristján Eldjárn (ed.), *Third Viking Congress, Reykjavik 1956* (Reykjavik, 1958), pp 95–100.

—— An early representation of St Olaf. In D. A. Pearsall and R. A. Waldron (ed.), *Medieval literature and civilization: studies in memory of G. N. Garmonsway* (London, 1969), pp 141–5.

Youngs, Susan. Fine metalwork to *c.*A.D. 650. In Youngs, *'Work of angels'*, pp 20–23.

—— The Steeple Bumpstead boss. In Spearman & Higgitt, *Age of migrating ideas*, pp 143–50.

—— Two medieval Celtic enamelled buckles from Leicestershire. In *Leicestershire Archaeological and Historical Society*, lxvii (1993), pp 15–22.

—— A penannular brooch from near Calne, Wiltshire. In *Wiltshire Archaeology and Natural History Magazine*, lxxxviii (1995), pp 127–31.

—— Enamelling in early medieval Ireland. In *Irish Arts Review Yearbook*, xiii (1997), pp 43–51.

—— Recent finds of insular enameled buckles. In Karkov, Ryan, & Farrell, *Insular tradition*, pp 189–209.

—— 'From Ireland coming': fine Irish metalwork from the Medway, Kent, England. In Hourihane, *From Ire. coming*, pp 249–60.

—— (ed.) *'The work of angels': masterpieces of Celtic metalwork, 6th–9th centuries* A.D. London, 1989.
   Includes articles by Raghnall Ó Floinn and Michael Ryan.

*(iii) High crosses and other stonework*

Martin Werner, *Insular art: an annotated bibliography* (Boston, 1984) and the bibliography in Peter Harbison, *The high crosses of Ireland: an iconographical and photographic survey* (3 vols, Bonn, 1992), cover material up to 1991, which is therefore omitted here. This section concentrates largely on material that has appeared within the last decade.

Alexander, Shirley. Daniel themes on the Irish high crosses. In Karkov, Ryan, & Farrell, *Insular tradition*, pp 99–114.

Bailey, Richard N. An early Irish carved stone in northern England. In *R.S.A.I. Jn.*, cxx (1990), pp 126–8.

Bourke, Cormac. Notes on the cross of Downpatrick. In *Lecale Miscellany*, x (1992), pp 42–3.

—— Carved stones from Donagheary and Stewartstown. In *The Bell: journal of the Stewartstown and District Local History Society*, v (1995), pp 60–64.

Bradley, John. The sarcophagus at Cormac's Chapel, Cashel, County Tipperary. In *N. Munster Antiq. Jn.*, xxvi (1984), pp 14–35.

Brennan, Emma J. A cross-carved slab from Kildare cathedral. In *Camb. Med. Celt. Studies*, xiv (winter 1987), pp 53–60.

Bryce, Derek. *The symbolism of the Celtic cross.* Felinfach, 1989. 2nd ed., revised, 1992.

Cahill, Mary. Excavations at the base of St Patrick's Cross, Cashel. In *N. Munster Antiq. Jn.*, xxv (1983), pp 9–18.

Cleary, Rose M. Cross-inscribed slab from Bilboa, Co. Limerick. In *Tipperary Historical Journal 1992*, pp 203–5.

Corlett, Chris. Previously unrecorded cross-slab from Feenane in the barony of Murrisk, County Mayo. In *R.S.A.I. Jn.*, cxxiii (1993), pp 169–70.

Cronin, Rhoda. Late high crosses in Munster: tradition and novelty in twelfth-century Irish art. In Monk & Sheehan, *Early med. Munster*, pp 138–46.

de Paor, Liam. A grave-slab associated with the high cross at Durrow. In Manning, *Beyond the Pale*, pp 203–5.

Dolan, Ana. The high cross at Moone: report on conservation works to date. In *Kildare Arch. Soc. Jn.*, xviii, no. 4 (1998–9), pp 513–15.

Edwards, Nancy. Review article: The iconography of the Irish high crosses. Carolingian influence in Ireland in the ninth century. In *Early medieval Europe*, iii, no. 1 (1994), pp 63–71.

—— A group of shafts and related sculpture from Clonmacnoise and its environs. In Heather A. King (ed.), *Clonmacnoise Studies, vol. i: seminar papers 1994* (Dublin, 1998), pp 101–18.

—— The Irish connection. In Sally M. Foster (ed.), *The St Andrews sarcophagus: a Pictish masterpiece and its international connections* (Dublin, 1998), pp 227–39.

Eogan, George. High crosses in Brega. In *Ríocht na Midhe*, xii (2001), pp 17–24.

Fanning, Thomas. Excavation of an early Christian cemetery and settlement at Reask, County Kerry. In *R.I.A. Proc.*, lxxxi (1981), sect. C, pp 3–172.

Feehan, John. The nature and function of Irish exhibitionist figure sculpture: evidence from the south midlands. In *Éile*, i (1982), pp 45-52.

Fenwick, Joe. Cross-slab—Hill of Skreen. In *Ríocht na Midhe*, ix, no. 2 (1996), pp 46–7.

Fitzpatrick, Liz. The crowning hand of God. In *Archaeology Ireland*, xi, no. 1 (1997), pp 21–3.

Gelly, Mary Ann. The Irish high cross: methods of design. In Bourke, *Isles of the north*, pp 157–66.

Grant, Christine. New Leitrim high cross. In *Archaeology Ireland*, viii, no. 4 (1994), pp 16–17.

Hall, Mark E. Two early Christian slabs from Dysart, Thomastown, County Kilkenny. In *R.S.A.I. Jn.*, cxx (1990), pp 131–2.

Hamlin, Ann. Early Irish stone carving: content and context. In Susan M. Pearce (ed.), *The early church in western Britain and Ireland* (Oxford, 1982), pp 283–96.

—— Iona: a view from Ireland. In *Antiq. Soc. Scot. Proc.*, cxvii (1987), pp 17–22.

—— The Blackwater group of crosses. In Bourke, *Isles of the north*, pp 187–96.

Harbison, Peter. The date of the crucifixion slabs from Duvillaun More and Inishkea North, Co. Mayo. In Rynne, *Figures from the past*, pp 73–91.

—— Meath high-cross fragments—lost and found. In *Ríocht na Midhe*, vii, no. 3 (1990/91), pp 134–44.

—— *The high crosses of Ireland: an iconographical and photographic survey*. 3 vols. Bonn, 1992.

—— A high cross base from the Rock of Cashel and a historical reconsideration of the 'Ahenny group' of crosses. In *R.I.A. Proc.*, xciii (1993), sect. C, pp 1–20.

——The extent of royal patronage on Irish high crosses. In *Studia Celtica Japonica*, new ser., vi (1994), pp 77–105.

——*Irish high crosses with the figure sculptures explained*. Drogheda, 1994.

——A shaft-fragment from Slane, Co. Meath, and other recent high cross discoveries. In Manning, *Beyond the Pale*, pp 171–6.

——The holed high cross at Moone. In *Kildare Arch. Soc. Jn.*, xviii (1998–9), pp 493–512.

Hawkes, Jane. Columban Virgins: iconic images of the Virgin and Child in insular sculpture, In Cormac Bourke (ed.), *Studies in the cult of Saint Columba* (Dublin, 1997), pp 107–35.

——Old Testament heroes: iconographs of insular sculpture. In David Henry (ed.), *The worm, the germ, and the thorn: Pictish and related studies presented to Isabel Henderson* (Balgavies, 1997), pp 149–58.

——An iconography of identity? The cross-head from Mayo abbey. In Hourihane, *From Ire. coming*, pp 261–75.

Henderson, Isabel, and Okasha, Elisabeth. The early Christian inscribed and carved stones of Tullylease, Co. Cork. In *Camb. Med. Celt. Studies*, xxiv (winter 1992), pp 1–36.

Addendum, xxxiii (summer 1997), pp 9–17.

Henry, Françoise. *Studies in early Christian and medieval Irish art, iii: architecture and sculpture*. London, 1985.

Comprises reprints of articles not listed individually here.

Herity, Michael. Early Christian decorated slabs in Donegal: An Turas and the tomb of the founder saint. In William Nolan, Liam Ronayne, and Mairead Dunlevy (ed.), *Donegal: history and society* (Dublin, 1995), pp 25–50.

——Kelly, Dorothy; and Mattenberger, Ursula. List of early Christian cross-slabs in seven north-western counties. In *R.S.A.I. Jn.*, cxxvii (1997), pp 80–124.

Higgins, J. G. Some early Christian and medieval sculpture from Coolcashin, Co. Kilkenny. In *Old Kilkenny Review*, iv, no. 3 (1991), pp 599–610.

——An early Christian cross-slab from Roscam, Co. Galway. In *Galway Arch. Soc. Jn.*, xliv (1992), pp 209–12.

——A chi-ro decorated pebble from Kilcorban, County Galway. In *R.S.A.I. Jn.*, cxxiii (1993), pp 164–5.

——and Gibbons, Michael. Early Christian monuments at Kilgeever, Co. Mayo. In *Cathair na Mart*, xiii (1993), pp 32–44.

Higgitt, John. (ed.). *Early medieval sculpture in Britain and Ireland*. Oxford, 1986. (Brit. Arch. Reps, British Series, clii.)

Includes articles by Nancy Edwards, Peter Harbison, and Isabel Henderson.

Hon. Editor [Michael Herity]. Early Christian sculpture at Ahenny and other sites. In *R.S.A.I. Jn.*, cxxi (1991), pp 171–2.

Hourihane, Colum. *De camino ignis*: the iconography of the three children in the fiery furnace in ninth-century Ireland. In Hourihane, *From Ire. coming*, pp 61–82.

Trench-Jellicoe, Ross. Pictish and related harps: their form and decoration. In David Henry (ed.), *The worm, the germ, and the thorn: Pictish and related studies presented to Isabel Henderson* (Balgavies, 1997), pp 159–72.

Kilbride-Jones, H. E. Early ecclesiastical art in Corca Dhuibhne and its implications abroad. In *N. Munster Antiq. Jn.*, xxviii (1986), pp 7–15.

——On some instances of Celtic art patterns inscribed on grave-slabs discovered at Carrowntemple, Co. Sligo, Ireland. In *Bulletin of the Board of Celtic Studies*, xxxvi (1989), pp 230–38.

Karkov, Catherine. Adam and Eve on Muiredach's Cross: presence, absence, and audience. In Bourke, *Isles of the north*, pp 205–11.

Kelly, Dorothy. Cross-carved slabs from Latteragh, County Tipperary. In *R.S.A.I. Jn.*, cxviii (1988), pp 92–100.

——The heart of the matter: models for the Irish high crosses. In *R.S.A.I. Jn.*, cxxi (1991), pp 105–45.

——The high crosses of Ireland: a review article. In *R.S.A.I. Jn.*, cxxii (1992), pp 67–78.

——Some remains of high crosses in the west of Ireland. In *R.S.A.I. Jn.*, cxxiii (1993), pp 152–63; cxxiv (1994), pp 213–14.

——Cross at Ogulla, County Roscommon. In *R.S.A.I. Jn.*, cxxiv (1994), p. 213.

——The relationships of the crosses of Argyll: the evidence of form. In Spearman & Higgitt, *Age of migrating ideas*, pp 219–29.

——The Virgin and Child in Irish sculpture. In Bourke, *Isles of the north*, pp 197–204.

——A sense of proportion: the metrical and design characteristics of some Columban high Crosses. In *R.S.A.I. Jn.*, cxxvi (1996), pp 108–46.

——The crosses of Tory Island. In Smyth, *Seanchas*, pp 53–63.

King, Heather. The medieval and seventeenth-century carved stone collection in Kildare. In *Kildare Arch. Soc. Jn.*, xvii (1987–91), pp 59–95.

——Moving crosses. In *Archaeology Ireland*, vi, no. 4 (1992), pp 22–3.

——Prophets and evangelists (speaking from stone). In *Archaeology Ireland*, viii, no. 2 (1994), pp 9–10.

——Burials and high crosses at Clonmacnoise (Ireland). In Guy de Boe and Frans Verhaeghe (ed.), *Death and burial in medieval Europe: papers of the Medieval Europe Brugge 1997 conference*, ii (Bruges, 1997), pp 127–31.

Lang, James T. Some units of measurement in insular art. In Mac Niocaill & Wallace, *Keimelia*, pp 95–101.

Lanigan Wood, Helen, and Verling, Eithne. Stone sculpture in Donegal. In William Nolan, Liam Ronayne, and Mairead Dunlevy (ed.), *Donegal: history and society* (Dublin, 1995), pp 51–84.

Lowry-Corry, Lady Dorothy. The stones carved with human effigies on Boa Island and on Lustymore Island in lower Lough Erne. In *R.I.A. Proc.*, xli (1933), sect. C, pp 200–04.

——The sculptured stones at Killadeas. In *R.S.A.I. Jn.*, lxv (1935), pp 23–33.

Lynn, Chris. Muiredach's Cross: *dextra Dei* and divine bulls. In *Archaeology Ireland*, x, no. 4 (winter 1996), pp 18–19.

McAnallen, Brendan. Glenarb and its crosses. In *Dúiche Néill*, no. 5 (1990), pp 9–23.

MacLean, Douglas. Technique and contact: carpentry-constructed insular stone crosses. In Bourke, *Isles of the north*, pp 167–75.

——The status of the sculptor in old-Irish law and the evidence of the crosses. In *Peritia*, ix (1995), pp 125–55.

McNab, Susanne. Styles used in twelfth century Irish figure sculpture. In *Peritia*, vi–vii (1987–8), pp 265–97.

——A note on the reconstructed high cross at Roscrea, Co. Tipperary. In *N. Munster Antiq. Jn.*, xxxii (1990), pp 96–7.

——Early Irish sculpture. In *Irish Arts Review Yearbook 1990–1991*, pp 164–71.

——From Tomregan to Iniscealtra: Irish twelfth century sculpture. In *Irish Arts Review Yearbook*, xiii (1997), pp 32–4.

Manning, Conleth. Cross-slab at Ardamore. In *Kerry Arch. Soc. Jn.*, xiii (1980), pp 39–44.

——Cross-slabs from Clonenagh, Co. Laois. In Manning, *Beyond the Pale*, pp 185–92.

——Toureen Peakaun: three new inscribed slabs. In *Tipperary Historical Journal 1991*, pp 209–14.

——The base of the North Cross at Clonmacnoise. In *Archaeology Ireland*, vi, no. 2 (1992), pp 8–9.

——A cross-inscribed pillar stone on Tonelegee Mountain, Co. Wicklow. In *Wicklow Archaeology and History*, i (1998), pp 26–8.

Mason, Albert. Cross-inscribed slab in Archbold's Castle, Dalkey, County Dublin. In *R.S.A.I. Jn.*, cxiii (1983), pp 143–4.

Mulcahy, Michael. Stonework in Ardmore. In *Ardmore Journal*, iii (1986), pp 11–17.

Neuman de Vegvar, Carol. In the shadow of the sidhe. Arthur Kingsley Porter's vision of an exotic Ireland. In *Irish Arts Review Yearbook*, xvii (2001), 48–60.

Ní Ghabhláin, Sinéad. Carved stone head from Glencolumbkille, County Clare. In *R.S.A.I. Jn.*, cxviii (1988), pp 135–8.

O'Brien, Caimin. New finds from Co. Offaly. In *Archaeology Ireland*, viii, no. 1 (1994), pp 16–17.

Ó hÉailidhe, P. Early Christian grave slabs in the Dublin region. In *R.S.A.I. Jn.*, ciii (1973), pp 51–64.

——Three unrecorded early grave-slabs in County Dublin. In *R.S.A.I. Jn.*, cxii (1982), pp 139–41.

——Decorated stones at Kilgobbin, County Dublin. In *R.S.A.I. Jn.*, cxiv (1984), pp 142–4.

O'Farrell, Fergus. Carved stone at Rathmullen, County Donegal. In *R.S.A.I. Jn.*, cxiv (1984), pp 149–50.

——*Looking at high crosses*. Dublin, 1992.

Ó Floinn, Raghnall, and Fanning, Thomas. The evangelist slab at Athlone, and some additional cross-inscribed stones from Athlone and Lemanaghan. In *Old Athlone Soc. Jn.*, ii, no. 6 (1985), pp 116–23.

O'Meadhra, Uaininn. A medieval Dubliner's talismanic portrait? An incised profile cut-out head from Christchurch Place, Dublin. In *Camb. Med. Celt. Studies*, xxi (summer 1991), pp 39–54.

Richardson, Hilary. The jewelled cross and its canopy. In Bourke, *Isles of the north*, pp 177–86.

Roe, Helen M. The Roscrea pillar. In Rynne, *N. Munster studies*, pp 127–32.

Royal commission on the ancient and historical monuments of Scotland. *Argyll: an inventory of the monuments, vol. iv: Iona*. Edinburgh, 1982.

Rynne, Etienne. A pagan Celtic background for Sheela-na-Gigs? In Rynne, *Figures from the past*, pp 189–202.

—— The 'Luguaedon' pillar-stone. In *Galway Arch. Soc. Jn.*, xlvii (1995), pp 205–11.

—— Ireland's earliest 'Celtic' high crosses: the Ossory and related crosses. In Monk & Sheehan, *Early med. Munster*, pp 125–37.

Shee Twohig, Elizabeth. A cross-inscribed slab from Laheratanvally, Skibbereen, Co. Cork. In *Cork Hist. Soc. Jn.*, xcvii (1992), pp 120–23.

Sheehan, John. Some early historic cross-forms and related motifs from the Iveragh peninsula. In *Kerry Arch. Soc. Jn.*, xxiii (1990), pp 157–74.

—— A Merovingian background for the Ardmoneel stone? In *Cork Hist. Soc. Jn.*, xcix (1994), pp 23–31.

Siggins, Albert. Some early Christian slabs from Fuerty and Clontuskert. In *Journal of the Roscommon Historical and Archaeological Society*, ii (1988), pp 55–9.

Stalley, Roger A. *Irish high crosses*. Dublin, 1991. (Irish Heritage Series, lxix.) Reissued, 1996.

—— Scribe and mason: the Book of Kells and the Irish high crosses. In Felicity O'Mahony (ed.), *The Book of Kells: proceedings of a conference at Trinity College, Dublin, 6–9 September 1992* (Dublin and Aldershot, 1994), pp 257–65.

—— Sculptured stone figure. In Maurice F. Hurley, Orla M. B. Scully, and Sarah W. J. McCutcheon (ed.), *Late viking age and medieval Waterford: excavations 1986–1992* (Waterford, 1997), pp 400–03.

—— The Tower Cross at Kells. In Karkov, Ryan, & Farrell, *Insular tradition*, pp 115–41.

Stevick, Robert D. Shapes of early sculptured crosses of Ireland. In *Gesta*, xxxviii, no. 1 (1999), pp 3–21.

Swan, D. L. A carved stone head from Killaspuglonane, Co. Clare. In Rynne, *Figures from the past*, pp 159–67.

—— The Market Cross at Kells, Co. Meath. In *Ríocht na Midhe*, ix, no. 4 (1998), pp 49–55.

Swift, Cathy. Dating Irish grave slabs: the evidence of the annals. In Bourke, *Isles of the north*, pp 245–9.

—— Early medieval Irish grave slabs and their inscriptions. In *Durham Archaeological Journal*, xiv–xv (1999), pp 111–18.

Timoney, Martin A. Recently discovered high cross at Drumcliff, Co. Sligo. In *The Corran Herald*, 1999/2000, pp 41–3.

Van Hoek, M. A. M. Early Christian rock art at Cleghagh, Co. Donegal. In *U.J.A.*, lvi (1993), pp 139–47.

Veelenturf, Kees. Stenen raadsels: de hoogkruisen van Ierland. In *Millennium*, ix (1995), pp 46–61.

—— *Dia Brátha: eschatological theophanies and Irish high crosses*. Stichting Amsterdamse Historische Reeks, Amsterdam, 1997.

—— Irish high crosses and continental art: shades of iconographical ambiguity. In Hourihane, *From Ire. coming*, pp 83–101.

Verkerk, Dorothy Hoogland. Pilgrimage *ad limina apostolorum* in Rome: Irish high crosses and early Christian sarcophagi. In Hourihane, *From Ire. coming*, pp 9–26.

Wallace, P. F., and Timoney, M. A. Carrowntemple, Co. Sligo, and its inscribed slabs. In Rynne, *Figures from the past*, pp 43–61.

Webster, Leslie. Two Anglo-Saxon carved zoomorphic mounts from Dublin. In Mac Niocaill & Wallace, *Keimelia*, pp 162–7.

Werner, Martin. On the origin of the form of the Irish high cross. In *Gesta*, xxix, no. 1 (1990), pp 98–110.

Williams, Margaret M. Warrior kings and savvy abbots: the sacred, the secular, and the depiction of contemporary costume on the Cross of the Scriptures, Clonmacnois. In *Avista Forum Journal*, xii, no. 1 (1999), pp 4–11.

——Constructing the market cross at Tuam: the role of cultural patriotism in the study of Irish high crosses. In Hourihane, *From Ire. coming*, pp 141–60.

## (f) Writing and manuscripts

See also above, pp 1002–10.

Armstrong, E. C. R., and Macalister, R. A. S. Wooden book with leaves indented and waxed found near Springmount Bog, Co. Antrim. In *R.S.A.I. Jn.*, l (1920), pp 160–66.

Best, R. I. Palaeographical notes I. The Rawlinson B 502 Tigernach. In *Ériu*, vii (1914), pp 114–20.

——Palaeographical notes II. Lebor na Huidre. In *Ériu*, viii (1916), pp 117–19.

——Palaeographical notes III: the Book of Armagh. In *Ériu*, xviii (1958), pp 102–10.

Bischoff, Bernhard. *Die südostdeutschen Schreibschulen und Bibliotheken in der Karolingerzeit*. Vol. i, Leipzig, 1940; vol. ii, Wiesbaden, 1970.

——*Paläographie: deutsche Philologie im Aufriß*. Berlin, 1957.

——Irische Schreiber im Karolingerreich. In R. Roques (ed.), *Jean Scot Erigène et l'histoire de la philosophie* (Paris, 1977) pp 47–58.

——*Latin palaeography: antiquity and the middle ages*. Translated by Dáibhí Ó Cróinín and David Ganz. Cambridge, 1990.

Brady, C. F. Some observations on the Ogham script. In *Teabhtha*, i (1983), pp 124–33.

Brown, T. Julian. The Irish element in the insular system of scripts to circa A.D. 850. In Löwe, *Die Iren*, pp 101–19. Reprinted in Janet Bately, Michelle P. Brown, and Jane Roberts (ed.), *A palaeographer's view: selected papers of Julian Brown* (London, 1993), pp 201–20.

——The oldest Irish manuscripts and their late antique background. In Ní Chatháin & Richter, *Ire. & Europe*, pp 311–27. Reprinted in Janet Bately, Michelle P. Brown, and Jane Roberts (ed.), *A palaeographer's view: selected papers of Julian Brown* (London, 1993), pp 221–41.

Breen, Aidan. A new Irish fragment of the *Continuatio* to Rufinus–Eusebius *Historia ecclesiastica*. In *Scriptorium*, xli (1987), pp 185–200.

Bruun, Johannes. *An enquiry into the art of the illuminated manuscripts of the middle ages, i: Celtic illuminated manuscripts.* Stockholm, 1897.

Byrne, F. J. Introduction to Timothy O'Neill, *The Irish hand* (Portlaoise, 1984), pp xi–xxvii.

Calkins, Robert G. *Illuminated books of the middle ages.* London, 1983.

Carney, James. The invention of the Ogom cipher. In *Ériu*, xxvi (1975), pp 53–65.

Contreni, John J. À propos de quelques manuscrits de l'école de Laon au IX^e siècle: découvertes et problèmes. In *Le Moyen Âge*, lxxviii (1972), pp 15–26. Reprinted in idem, *The cathedral school of Laon from 850 to 930: its manuscripts and masters* (Münchener Beiträge zur Medievistik und Renaissance-Forschung, xxix; Munich, 1978).

Daniels, Peter T., and Bright, William. *The world's writing systems.* Oxford, 1996.

Dumville, David N. 'Scéla lái Brátha' and the collation of Leabhar na hUidhre. In *Éigse*, xvi (1975), pp 24–8.

——Motes and beams: two insular computistical manuscripts. In *Peritia*, ii (1983), pp 248–56.

Esposito, Mario. The so-called psalter of St Caimín. In *R.I.A. Proc.*, xxxii (1913), sect. C, pp 78–88.

Forstner, Karl. Das Salzburger Skriptorium unter Virgil und das Verbrüderungs-buch von St Peter. In Dopsch & Juffinger, *Virgil von Salzburg*, pp 135–40.

Hamp, Eric P. The ogam inscriptions and their geminate symbols. In *Ériu*, xxxviii (1987), pp 45–72.

Harvey, Anthony. The ogham inscriptions and the Roman alphabet: two traditions or one? In *Archaeology Ireland*, iv, no. 1 (spring 1990), pp 13–14.

Henry, Françoise. *Studies in early Christian and medieval Irish art, ii: manuscript illumination.* London, 1984.

Comprises reprints of articles not listed individually here.

Jeauneau, Édouard. Quisquiliae e Mazarinaeo codice 561 depromptae. In *Recherches de Théologie Ancienne et Médiévale*, xlv (1978), pp 79–129.

Lambert, Pierre-Yves. Les signes de renvois dans le Priscien de Saint-Gall. In *Études Celt.*, xxiv (1987), pp 214–28.

——Le vocabulaire du scribe irlandais. In Picard, *Ire. & northern France*, pp 157–68.

Lowe, E. A. *Codices Latini antiquiores.* 11 vols and supplement. Oxford, 1935–72. Vol. ii: Great Britain and Ireland (1935; 2nd. ed. 1972); vol. vii, Switzerland (1956).

——*Palaeographical papers.* 2 vols. Ed. Ludwig Bieler. Oxford, 1972.

McGurk, Patrick. The Irish pocket gospel-book. In *Sacris Erudiri*, viii (1956), pp 249–70.

——The Gospel Book in Celtic lands before A.D. 850: contents and arrangement. In Ní Chatháin & Richter, *Ire. & Christendom*, pp 165–89.

——*Latin gospel books from A.D. 400 to A.D. 800.* Paris, Brussels, Antwerp, and Amsterdam, 1961. (Les Publications de Scriptorium, v.)

McKitterick, Rosamund. The scriptoria of Merovingian Gaul: a survey of the evidence. In Clarke & Brennan, *Columbanus*, pp 173–208.

Mostert, Marco. Celtic, Anglo–Saxon, or insular? Some considerations on 'Irish' manuscript production and their implications for insular Latin culture *c.*A.D.

500–800. In Doris Edel (ed.), *Cultural identity and cultural integration: Ireland and Europe in the middle ages* (Dublin, 1995), pp 92–115.

Ó Concheanainn, Tomás. The scribe who wrote for the White Earl. In *Celtica*, x (1973), p. 210.

——The scribe of the Leabhar Breac. In *Ériu*, xxiv (1973), pp 64–79.

——The reviser of Leabhar na hUidhre. In *Ériu*, xxv (1974), pp 277–88.

——The scribe of John Beaton's 'Broad Book'. In *Ériu*, xvi (1975), pp 99–101.

——The YBL fragment of Táin Bó Flidais. In *Celtica*, xiii (1980), pp 56–7.

——The Book of Ballymote. In *Celtica*, xiv (1981), pp 15–25.

——The source of the YBL text of TBC. In *Ériu*, xxxiv (1983), pp 175–84.

——LL and the date of the reviser of LU. In *Éigse*, xx (1984), pp 212–25.

——The manuscript tradition of two Middle Irish Leinster tales. In *Celtica*, xviii (1986), pp 13–33.

——A personal reference by Giolla Íosa Mac Firbhisigh. In *Celtica*, xviii (1986), p. 34.

——The manuscript tradition of Mesca Ulad. In *Celtica*, xix (1987), pp 13–30.

——Scríobhaithe Leacáin Mhic Fhir Bhisigh. In *Celtica*, xix (1987), 141–75.

——A Connacht medieval literary heritage: texts derived from *Cín Dromma Snechtai* through Leabhar na hUidhre. In *Camb. Med. Celt. Studies*, xvi (winter 1988), pp 1–40.

——Aided Nath Í and Uí Fhiachrach genealogies. In *Éigse*, xxv (1991), pp 1–27.

Ó Corráin, Donnchadh. The education of Diarmait Mac Murchada. In *Ériu*, xxviii (1977), pp 71–81.

Ó Cróinín, Dáibhí. Pride and prejudice. In *Peritia*, i (1982), pp 352–62.

——Rath Melsigi, Willibrord, and the earliest Echternach manuscripts. In *Peritia*, iii (1984), pp 17–42.

——Cummianus Longus and the iconography of Christ and the apostles in early Irish literature. In Ó Corráin, Breatnach, & McCone, *Sages, saints, & storytellers*, pp 268–79.

——Merovingian politics and insular calligraphy: the historical background to the Book of Durrow and related manuscripts. In Ryan, *Ire. & insular art*, pp 40–43.

——Early Echternach manuscript fragments with Old Irish glosses. In Georges Kiesel and Jean Schroeder (ed.), *Willibrord, Apostel der Niederlande, Gründer der Abtei Echternach. Gedenkgabe zum 1250. Todestag des angelsächsischen Missionars* (Echternach, 1989), pp 135–43.

——The Old Irish and Old English glosses in the earliest Echternach manuscripts (with an appendix on the Old Breton glosses). In Michele Camillo Ferrari, Jean Schroeder, and Henri Trauffler (ed.), *Die Abtei Echternach* (Echternach, 1999), pp 85–95.

Ó Cuív, Brian. Irish words for 'alphabet'. In *Ériu*, xxxi (1980), pp 100–10.

——Observations on the Book of Lismore. In *R.I.A. Proc.*, lxxxiii (1983), pp 269–92.

Ó Muraíle, Nollaig. The autograph manuscripts of the Annals of the Four Masters. In *Celtica*, xix (1987), pp 75–95.

——Leabhar Ó Maine alias Leabhar Uí Dhubhagáin. In *Éigse*, xxiii (1989), pp 167–95.

Ó Muraíle, Nollaig. A page from Mac Fhir Bhisigh's 'Genealogies'. In *Celtica*, xxi (1990), pp 533–60.

O'Neill, Timothy. *The Irish hand: scribes and their manuscripts from the earliest times to the seventeenth century*. Portlaoise, 1984.

Ó Riain, Pádraig. The Book of Glendalough or Rawlinson B 502. In *Éigse*, xviii (1981), pp 161–76.

——The Psalter of Cashel: a provisional list of contents. In *Éigse*, xxiii (1989), pp 107–30.

——Rawlinson B 502 alias Lebar Glinne Dá Locha: a restatement of the case. In *Z.C.P.*, li (1999), pp 130–47.

Oskamp, Hans. P. A. Notes on the history of Lebor na hUidre. In *R.I.A. Proc.*, lxv (1967), sect. C, pp 117–37.

——The first twelve folia of Rawlinson B 502. In *Ériu*, xxii (1972), pp 56–72.

——On the collation of Lebor na hUidre. In *Ériu*, xxv (1974), pp 147–56.

——The Yellow Book of Lecan proper. In *Ériu*, xxvi (1975), pp 102–21.

——Mael Muire: compiler or reviser? In *Éigse*, xvi (1976), pp 177–82.

——The Irish quatrains and salutation in the Drummond missal. In *Ériu*, xxviii (1977), pp 82–91.

——A schoolteacher's hand in a Florentine manuscript. In *Scriptorium*, xxxi, 2 (1977), pp 191–7.

O'Sullivan, Anne, and O'Sullivan, William. Three notes on Laud Misc. 610. In *Celtica*, ix (1971), pp 135–51.

——and Herbert, Máire. The provenance of Laud Misc. 615. In *Celtica*, x (1973), pp 174–92.

O'Sullivan, William. Notes on the scripts and make-up of the Book of Leinster. In *Celtica*, vii (1966), pp 1–31.

——Ciothruadh's Yellow Book of Lecan. In *Éigse*, xviii (1981), pp 177–81.

——Insular palaeography: current state and problems. In *Peritia*, iv (1985), pp 346–59.

——Medieval Meath manuscripts. In *Ríocht na Midhe*, vii, no. 4 (1986), pp 3–21.

——Additional medieval Meath manuscripts. In *Ríocht na Midhe*, viii (1987), pp 68–70.

——The Book of Uí Maine formerly the Book of Ó Dubhagáin: scripts and structure. In *Éigse*, xxiii (1989), pp 151–66.

——The Lindisfarne scriptorium: for and against. In *Peritia*, viii (1993), pp 80–94.

——Notes on the Trinity *Liber Hymnorum*. In John L. Sharpe (ed.), *Roger Powell, the compleat binder* (Bibliologia, xiv; Elementa ad Librorum Studia Pertinentia; Turnhout, 1996), pp 130–35.

Plummer, Charles. On the colophons and marginalia of Irish scribes. In *Brit. Acad. Proc.*, xii (1926), pp 11–44.

Powell, Roger. Further notes on Lebor na hUidre. In *Ériu*, xxi (1969), pp 99–102.

Pralle, Ludwig. Ein keltisches Missale in der Fuldaer Klosterbibliothek. In *Fuldaer Geschichtsblätter*, xxxi (1955), pp 8–21.

Quigley, E. J. The Corpus missal. In *I.E.R.*, 5th ser., xvii (1921), pp 381–9, 496–503, 603–9.

Robinson, F. N. The Irish marginalia in the 'Drummond missal'. In U. T. Holmes and A. J. Denomy (ed.), *Medieval studies in honor of J. D. M. Ford* (Cambridge, Mass., 1948), pp 193–208.

Robinson, Stanford F. H. *Celtic illuminative art in the gospel books of Durrow, Lindisfarne and Kells.* Dublin, 1908.

Ryan, Kathleen. Holes and flaws in medieval Irish manuscripts. In *Peritia*, vi–vii (1987–8), pp 243–64.

Schauman, Bella. The Irish scripts of the Milan, Biblioteca Ambrosiana, S. 45 sup. (ante ca. 625). In *Scriptorium*, xxxii (1978), pp 3–18.

——Early Irish manuscripts: the art of the scribes. In *Expedition: the University* [of Pennsylvania] *Museum magazine of archaeology/ anthropology*, xxi, no. 3 (spring 1979), pp 33–47.

Schiaparelli, Luigi. Intorno all' origine e ad alcuni caratteri della scrittura e del sistema abbreviativo irlandese. In G. Cencetti (ed.), *Note paleografiche (1910–32)* (Rome, 1969), pp 189–314.

Wright, David H. The tablets from Springmount bog: a key to early Irish palaeography. In *American Journal of Archaeology*, lxvii, no. 2 (1963), p. 219.

## (g) Coinage

Blackburn, M. Hiberno-Norse imitations of Watchet long cross coins. In *Numismatic chronicle*, xv (1975), pp 195–7.

——Thoughts on imitations of the Anglo-Saxon coins. In *Seabys Coin and Medal Bulletin, 1977*, pp 344–50.

Blunt, Christopher E. The St Edmund memorial coinage. In *Proceedings of the Suffolk Institute of Archaeology*, xxxi (1969), pp 232–54.

Briggs, C. S., and Graham-Campbell, James. A lost hoard of viking-age silver from Magheralagan, Co. Down. In *U.J.A.*, xxxix (1976), pp 20–24.

Carson, R. A. G., and O'Kelly, Claire. A catalogue of the Roman coins from Newgrange, Co. Meath, and notes on the coins and related finds. In *R.I.A. Proc.*, lxxvii (1977), sect. C, pp 35–55.

Dolley, Michael. Some new light on the viking-age silver hoard from Mungret. In *N. Munster Antiq. Jn.*, viii (1960), pp 116–33.

——The 1843 (?) find of viking-age silver coins from Co. Tipperary. In *Cork Hist. Soc. Jn.*, lxvii (1962), pp 41–7.

——New light on the 1837 viking-age coin-hoard from Ballitore. In *R.S.A.I. Jn.*, xcii (1962), pp 175–86.

——The Dublin pennies in the name of Sitric Silkbeard in the Hermitage Museum at Leningrad. In *R.S.A.I. Jn.*, xciii (1963), pp 1–8.

——*Viking coins of the Danelaw and of Dublin.* London, 1965.

——*The Hiberno-Norse coins in the British Museum.* London, 1966. (Sylloge of Coins in the British Isles, Series B, i.)

——Two numismatic notes: 1. Some Hiberno-Norse coins of Dublin recently discovered on the Baltic island of Gotland; 2. The mythical Roman coin-hoard from Tara. In *R.S.A.I. Jn.*, xcviii (1968), pp 57–65.

——The Hiberno-Norse coins in the 1967 find from Immelunda parish, Gotland. In *R.S.A.I. Jn.*, xcviii (1968), pp 197–9.

Dolley, Michael. Some further light on the 1891 viking-age coin-hoard from Bally-castle. In *U.J.A.*, xxxvi–xxxvii (1973–4), pp 87–9.

—— Roman coins from Ireland and the date of St Patrick. In *R.I.A. Proc.*, lxxvi C (1976), sect. C, pp 181–90.

—— The Hiberno-Norse coins of Gotlands Fornsal, Visby. In *British Numismatic Journal*, xlviii (1978), pp 20–34.

Gerriets, Marilyn. Money in early Christian Ireland according to the Irish laws. In *Comparative studies in society and history*, xxvii (1985), pp 323–39.

—— Money among the Irish: coin hoards in viking age Ireland. In *R.S.A.I. Jn.*, cxv (1985), pp 121–39.

Grierson, Philip, and Blackburn, M. A. S. *Medieval European coinage, i: the early middle ages (5th to 10th centuries)*. Cambridge, 1986.

Hall, R. A check-list of viking-age coin-hoards from Ballycastle. In *U.J.A*, xxxvi–xxxvii (1973–4), pp 71–86.

Heaslip, Robert. Reflections on Hiberno-Norse coinage. In *U.J.A.*, 3rd ser., xlviii (1985), pp 25–30.

Kellner, H.-J. Die Forschungssituation zum Münzwesen der Kelten. In Schmidt, *Celts*, pp 216–33.

Kenny, Michael. A find of Anglo-Saxon pennies from Newtonlow, Co. Westmeath. In *Riocht na Midhe*, vii, no. 3 (1984), pp 37–43.

—— A small hoard of Anglo-Saxon and Hiberno-Norse coins from County Louth. In *Seaby Coin Medal Bulletin*, no. 801 (1985), pp 201–4.

—— A hoard of silver coins from Ellistown, Rathangan. In *Kildare Arch. Soc. Jn.*, xvi (1985–6), pp 438–40.

—— The geographical distribution of Irish viking-age coin hoards. In *R.I.A. Proc.*, lxxxvii (1987), sect. C, pp 507–25.

—— Coins and coinage in the Irish midlands during the viking age. In Catherine Karkov and Robert Farrell (ed.), *Studies in insular art and archaeology* (Oxford, Ohio, 1991), pp 111–16.

Lyon, C. S. S., and Stewart, B. H. I. H. The Northumbrian viking coins in the Cuerdale hoard. In Michael Dolley (ed.), *Anglo-Saxon coins* (London, 1961), pp 96–121.

McShane, James. Viking ingots found at Mungret, Co. Limerick. In *Irish Numismatics*, xiii (1980), pp 164–5.

Ó Cuív, Brian. A mark of gold. In *Éigse*, xv (1974), pp 312–13.

O'Sullivan, William. The earliest Irish coinage. In *R.S.A.I. Jn.*, lxxix (1949), pp 180–235.

Seaby, W. A. Die-links of an eleventh-century Dublin penny in the Isle of Man. In *Irish Numismatics*, xiii (1980), pp 61–4.

Shetelig, Haakon (ed.) *Viking antiquities in Great Britain and Ireland*. 5 parts. Oslo, 1940.

Smart, Veronica. Scandinavians, Celts, and Germans in Anglo-Saxon England: the evidence of moneyers' names. In M. A. S. Blackburn (ed.), *Anglo-Saxon monetary history* (Leicester, 1986), pp 171–84.

Wallace, Patrick F. The English presence in viking Dublin. Ibid., pp 208–13.

## 2   Geography and toponymy

For the many published works on the linguistic aspects of place-names, see Rolf Baumgarten, *Bibliography of Irish linguistics and literature 1942–71* (Dublin, 1986), and the journals *Dinnsheanchas*, *Ainm*, and *Ulster Placename Studies*.

Aalen, F. H. A. Perspectives on the Irish landscape in prehistory and history. In Terence Reeves-Smyth and Fred Hamond (ed.), *Landscape archaeology in Ireland* (Oxford, 1983), pp 357–72.

——Whelan, Kevin; and Stout, Matthew. *Atlas of the Irish rural landscape*. Cork, 1997.

Aldridge, R. B. The routes described in the story called *Táin Bó Flidhais*. In *Journal of the North Mayo Historical and Archaeological Society*, i, no. 5 (1987), pp 60–66.

Andrews, J. H. Maps and mapmakers. In W. Nolan (ed.), *The shaping of Ireland* (Dublin, 1986), pp 99–110.

Arbuthnot, Sharon. Short cuts to etymology: placenames in *Cóir Anmann*. In *Ériu*, l (1999), pp 79–86.

Barry, Terry. Rural settlement in Ireland in the middle ages: an overview. In *Ruralia I: Pamatky Archeologické; Supplementum 5* (Prague, 1996), pp 134–41.

——(ed.). *A history of settlement in Ireland*. London, 2000.
Includes essays by Gabriel Cooney, Charles Doherty, Anngret Simms, and Matthew Stout.

Baumgarten, Rolf. The geographical orientation of Ireland in Isidore and Orosius. In *Peritia*, iii (1984), pp 189–203.

——Place-names, etymology, and the structure of *Fianaigecht*. In Almqvist, Ó Catháin, & Ó hÉalaí, *Heroic process*, pp 1–24.

Bhreathnach, Edel. The documentary evidence for pre-Norman Skreen, Co. Meath. In *Ríocht na Midhe*, ix, no. 2 (1996), pp 37–45.

——Topographical note: Moynagh Lough, Nobber, Co. Meath. In *Ríocht na Midhe*, ix, no. 4 (1998), pp 16–19.

Bowen, Charles. A historical inventory to the Dindshenchas. In *Studia Celt.*, x–xi (1975–6), pp 113–37.

Bowen, E. G. *Britain and the western seaways*. London, 1972.

——The geography of early monasticism in Ireland. In *Studia Celt.*, vii (1972), pp 30–44.

Bradley, John. The topographical development of Scandinavian Dublin. In F. H. A. Aalen and Kevin Whelan, *Dublin, city and county* (1992), pp 43–56.

Bradley, John (ed.). *Viking Dublin exposed: the Wood Quay saga*. Dublin, 1984.

Buchanan, R. H. History in maps. In *Ulster Local Studies*, viii, no. 2 (1983), pp 18–22.

——Historical geography of Ireland pre-1700. In *Ir. Geography*, xvii (1984), pp 129–48.

——Man and the landscape. In *Ulster Local Studies*, ii, no. 2 (1989), pp 7–13.

Butlin, R. A. Historical geography and local studies in Ireland. In *Geographical Viewpoint*, i (1966), pp 141–54.

Carville, Geraldine. *The occupation of Celtic sites in Ireland by the canons regular of St Augustine and the Cistercians.* Kalamazoo, 1987.

Clarke, H. B. The mapping of medieval Dublin: a case-study in thematic cartography. In Clarke & Simms, *Urban origins*, pp 617–43.

Clinton, Mark. Settlement patterns in the early historic kingdom of Leinster (seventh–mid twelfth centuries). In Smyth, *Seanchas*, pp 275–98.

Cooney, Gabriel. Images of settlement and the landscape in the neolithic. In Peter Topping (ed.), *Neolithic landscapes* (Neolithic Studies Group seminar papers 2; Oxbow monographs 86; Oxford, 1997), pp 23–31.

de Val, Séamus. Logainmneacha Locha Garman. In Kevin Whelan (ed.), *Wexford: history and society* (Dublin, 1987), pp 40–64.

Dimier, M.-Anselme. Le mot locus employé dans le sens de monastère. In *Revue Mabillon*, lviii (1970), pp 133–54.

Dodgshon, Robert A. Symbolic classification and the development of early Celtic landscape. In *Cosmos: yearbook of the traditional cosmology society, i Duality* (Edinburgh, 1985), pp 61–83.

Duffy, P. J. The territorial organisation of Gaelic landownership and its transformation in County Monaghan. In *Ir. Geography*, xiv (1981), pp 1–23.

Duffy, Seán. *Atlas of Irish history.* Dublin, 1998.

Charles-Edwards, T. M. The church and settlement. In Ní Chatháin & Richter, *Ire. & Europe*, pp 167–78.

Etchingham, Colmán. Evidence of Scandinavian settlement in Wicklow. In Ken Hannigan (ed.), *Wicklow: history and society* (Dublin, 1994), pp 113–38.

Evans, E. Estyn. *The personality of Ireland: habitat, heritage and history.* London, 1973. Enlarged and revised ed., Belfast, 1981.

Fahy, Gerard. Geography and geographical education in Ireland from early Christian times to 1960. In *Geographical Viewpoint*, x (1981), pp 5–30.

Flanagan, Deirdre. Ecclesiastical nomenclature in Irish texts and place-names: a comparison. In H. H. Hewig (ed.), *Proceedings of the Tenth International Congress of Onomastic Sciences* (Vienna, 1969), pp 379–88.

—— The Christian impact on early Ireland: place-names evidence. In Ní Chatháin & Richter, *Ire. & Europe*, pp 25–42.

Foley, Clare. Prehistoric settlement in Tyrone. In Charles Dillon and Henry A. Jefferies (ed.), *Tyrone: history and society* (Dublin, 2000), pp 1–38.

Gibbons, Michael. The archaeology of early settlement in County Kilkenny. In William Nolan and Kevin Whelan (ed.), *Kilkenny: history and society* (Dublin, 1990), pp 1–32.

Graham, B. J. Medieval settlement in County Roscommon. In *R.I.A. Proc.*, lxxxviii (1988), pp 19–38.

—— Secular urban origins in early medieval Ireland. In *Ir. Econ. & Soc. Hist.*, xvi (1989), pp 5–22.

—— and Proudfoot, L. J. *An historical geography of Ireland.* London, 1993.

Hamp, Eric P. Varia. In *Scottish Gaelic Studies*, xvi (winter, 1990), pp 191–5. Includes criticism of Nicolaisen's proposed pre-Celtic origin of some Scottish place-names.

Hayes-McCoy, G. A. *Ulster and other Irish maps.* Dublin, 1964.

Herries Davies, Gordon L. The concept of Ireland. In W. Nolan (ed.), *The shaping of Ireland* (Dublin, 1986), pp 13–27.

Hickey, Elizabeth. Notes on the topography of early monastic Clonard. In *Seanchas Ardmhacha*, xvi, no. 2 (1995), pp 33–8.

Hogan, Edmund I. *Onomasticon Goedelicum locorum et tribuum Hiberniae et Scotiae. An index, with identifications, to the Gaelic names of places and tribes.* Dublin, 1910.

Hughes, A. J. The virgin St Duinsech and her three Ulster churches near Strangford Lough, County Down. In *Celtica*, xxiii (1999), pp 113–24.

Hurley, Maurice. Late viking age settlement in Waterford city. In William Nolan and Thomas P. Power (ed.) *Waterford: history and society* (Dublin, 1992), pp 49–72.

*Irish Historic Towns Atlas.* Ed. J. H. Andrews, Anngret Simms, H. B. Clarke, and Raymond Gillespie. Dublin, 1986–  . (R.I.A.) *I: Kildare.* By J. H. Andrews (1986). *II: Carrickfergus.* By Philip Robinson (1986). *III: Bandon.* By Patrick O'Flanagan (1988). *IV: Kells.* By Anngret Simms with Katherine Simms (1990). *V: Mullingar.* By J. H. Andrews with K. M. Davies (1992). *VI: Athlone.* By Harman Murtagh (1994). *VII: Maynooth.* By Arnold Horner (1995). *VIII: Downpatrick.* By R. H. Buchanan and Anthony Wilson (1997). *IX: Bray.* By K. M. Davies (1998). *X: Kilkenny.* By John Bradley (2000). I–IV ed. J. H Andrews and Anngret Simms; V ed. J. H. Andrews, Anngret Simms, and H. B. Clarke; VI ed. Anngret Simms and H. B. Clarke; VII–X ed. Anngret Simms, H. B. Clarke, and Raymond Gillespie.

Jäger, Helmut. Land use in medieval Ireland: a review of the documentary evidence. In *Irish Economic and Social History*, x (1983), pp 51–65.

——Medieval landscape terms of Ireland: the evidence of Latin and English documents. In Bradley, *Settlement & society*, pp 277–90.

Jefferies, Henry Alan. The history and topography of viking Cork. In *Camb. Med. Celt. Studies*, x (winter 1985), pp 14–26.

Joyce, Patrick W. *Irish names of places.* 3 vols. Dublin, 1869–1913.

Killeen, J. F. Ireland in the Greek and Roman writers. In *R.I.A. Proc.*, lxxvi (1976), sect. C, pp 207–15.

Lacey, Brian. Prehistoric and early historic settlement in Donegal. In William Nolan, Liam Ronayne, and Mairead Dunlevy (ed.), *Donegal: history and society* (Dublin, 1995), pp 1–24.

Mac Aodha, Breandán S. Clachán settlement in Iar-Chonnacht. In *Ir. Geography*, v, no. 2 (1965), pp 20–28.

——Riocht na háitainmníochta i nÉirinn. In *Ir. Geography*, xvii (1984), pp 167–85.

Mac Cana, Proinsias. Place-names and mythology in Irish tradition: places, pilgrimages and things. In MacLennan, *Proc. 1st N.A. Congress*, pp 319–41.

McCourt, Desmond, and McCourt, Camblin. The geographical setting. In Gerard O'Brien (ed.), *Derry and Londonderry: history and society* (Dublin, 1999), pp 1–28.

MacDonald, Aidan. Iona's style of government: the toponomastic evidence. In *Peritia*, iv (1985), pp 174–86.

McErlean, Thomas. The Irish townland system of landscape organisation. In Terence Reeves-Smyth and Fred Hamond, *Landscape archaeology in Ireland* (Oxford, 1983), pp 315–39.

Mac Giolla Easpaig, Dónall. Placenames and early settlement in Donegal. In William Nolan, Liam Ronayne, and Mairead Dunlevy (ed.), *Donegal: history and society* (Dublin, 1995), pp 149–82.

——Early ecclesiastical settlement names of County Galway. In Gerard Moran and Raymond Gillespie (ed.), *Galway: history and society* (Dublin, 1996), pp 795–816.

Mac Shamhráin, Ailbhe S. Placenames as indicators of settlement. In *Archeology Ireland*, v, no. 3 (1991), pp 19–21.

Mahon, William. Glasraige, Tóecraige and Araid: evidence from ogam. In *Proceedings of the Harvard Celtic Colloquium*, viii (1988), pp 11–30.

Mallory, J. P. The literary topography of Emain Macha. In *Emania*, ii (1987), pp 12–18.

Matley, Ian M. Elements of Celtic placenames. In *Names*, xiii (1965), pp 39–54.

Mitchell, G. F. *The Irish landscape*. London, 1976.

——and Ryan, Michael. *Reading the Irish landscape*. Dublin, 1997.

Monk, Michael A. Early medieval secular and ecclesiastical settlement in Munster. In Monk & Sheehan, *Early med. Munster*, pp 33–52.

Morris, Henry. Some places in the metrical Dindsenchus. In *R.S.A.I. Jn.*, lxix (1939), pp 179–89.

Murphy, Donald. The distribution of early Christian monastic sites and its implication for contemporary settlement in County Louth. In *Louth Arch. Soc. Jn.*, xxii, no. 4 (1992), pp 364–86.

Mytum, Harold. Early medieval settlement in western Britain and Ireland: cultural unity and diversity. In *Ruralia I: Pamatky Archeologické; Supplementum 5* (Prague, 1996), pp 124–33.

Nolan, William. Some civil and ecclesiastical territorial divisions and their geographical significance. In idem, *The shaping of Ireland* (Dublin, 1986), pp 66–83.

Ó Canann, Tomás G. Áth Uí Chanannáin and the toponymy of medieval Mide. In *Ríocht na Midhe*, viii, no. 4 (1992–3), pp 78–83.

Ó Cearbhaill, Pádraig. Cill Chaise nó Cill Chais? Logainm i gContae Thiobraid Árann. In *Éigse*, xxvii (1993), pp 89–97.

Ó Cíobháin, Breandán. *Toponomia Hiberniae*. 4 vols. Dublin, 1978–85.

Ó Coileáin, Seán. Mag Fuithirbe revisited. In *Éigse*, xxiii (1989), pp 27–38.

——Placenames: rivers and streams of North Cork. In *Mallow Field Club Journal*, no. 7 (1989), pp 119–37.

O'Flanagan, Patrick. Surveys, maps and the study of rural settlement development. In Ó Corráin, *Ir. antiquity*, pp 320–26.

——Placenames and change in the Irish landscape. In W. Nolan (ed.), *The shaping of Ireland* (Dublin, 1986), pp 111–22.

Oftedal, Magne. Scandinavian place-names in Ireland. In Bo Almqvist and David Greene (ed.), *Proceedings of the Seventh Viking Congress* (London, 1976), pp 125–33.

O'Keeffe, Tadhg. Rural settlement and cultural identity in Gaelic Ireland, 1000–1500. In *Ruralia I: Pamatky Archeologické; Supplementum 5* (Prague, 1996), pp 142–53.

O'Kelly, Owen. *The place-names of County Kilkenny*. Kilkenny, 1985.

O'Loughlin, Thomas. An early thirteenth-century map in Dublin: a window into the world of Giraldus Cambrensis. In *Imago Mundi*, li (1999), pp 24–38.

Ó Mórdha, Eoghan. The place-names in the Book of Cuanu. In Smyth, *Seanchas*, pp 189–91.

Ó Murchú, Séamas. Cill Mhura agus Sgreathan. In *Éigse*, xxvii (1993), p. 58.

Ó Muraíle, Nollaig. *Mayo places: their names and origins*. Dublin, 1985.

Ó Murchadha, Diarmuid. Odhbha and Navan. In *Ríocht na Midhe*, viii, no. 4 (1992–3), pp 112–23.

——Mag Cetne and Mag Ene. In *Éigse*, xxvii (1993), pp 35–46.

——Sódh i logainmneacha. In *Éigse*, xxviii (1994–5), pp 129–34.

——*The Annals of Tigernach: index of names*. 1997. (Irish Texts Society Subsidiary Series, 6.)

——Early history and settlements of the Laígis. In Pádraig G. Lane and William Nolan (ed.), *Laois: history and society* (Dublin, 1999), pp 35–62.

O'Rahilly, T. F. Notes on Irish place-names. In *Hermathena*, xxiii (1933), pp 196–220.

Ó Riain, Pádraig. 'To be named is to exist': the instructive case of Achadh Bolg (Aghabulloge). In Patrick O'Flanagan and Cornelius G. Buttimer (ed.) *Cork: history and society* (Dublin, 1993), pp 45–62.

Pokorny, Julius. *Die Geographie Irlands bei Ptolemaeus*. In *Z.C.P.*, xix (1953), pp 94–120.

Power, Patrick. *Logainmneacha na nDéise: the placenames of Decies*. Cork, 1952.

Price, Liam. *The placenames of County Wicklow*. 7 parts. Dublin, 1945–67.

Rackham, O. *Trees and woodland in the British landscape*. London, 1990.

Richards, Melville. Irish settlements in south-west Wales: a topographical approach. In *R.S.A.I. Jn.*, xc (1960), pp 133–62.

Rivet, A. L. F., and Smith, C. *The place-names of Roman Britain*. London, 1979.

Room, Adrian. *A dictionary of Irish place-names*. Belfast, 1986.

Shearman, John. *Loca Patriciana: an identification of localities, particularly in Leinster, visited by St Patrick*. Dublin, 1879.

Sheeran, Patrick F. *Sacred geography: the Irish dimension*. In *Éire-Ireland*, xxii, no. 4 (1988), pp 79–86.

Simms, Anngret. Irland: Überformung eines keltischen Siedlungsraumes am Rande Europas durch externe Kolonisationsbewegungen. In J. Hagedorn, J. Hövermann, and H. J. Nitz (ed.), *Gefügemuster der Erdoberfläche: Festschrift zum 42. deutschen Geographentag*. (Göttingen, 1979), pp 261–308.

——Frühe Entwicklungsstufen der europäischen Seehandelsstädte auf dem Hintergrund ethnischer Überlagerungen, dargestellt am Beispiel von Dublin in Irland. In *Lübecker Schriften zur Archäologie und Kulturgeschichte*, v (1981), pp 113–26.

——Frühformen der mittelalterlichen Stadt in Irland. In *Würzburger Geographische Arbeiten*, lx (1983), pp 27–19.

Simms, Anngret. Continuity and change: settlement and society in medieval Ireland, *c*.500–1500. In W. Nolan (ed.), *The shaping of Ireland* (Dublin, 1986), pp 44–65.

——Newcastle as a medieval settlement. In Peter O'Sullivan (ed.), *Newcastle Lyons: a parish of the Pale* (Dublin, 1986), pp 11–23.

——Core and periphery in medieval Europe: the Irish experience in a wider context. In W. J. Smyth and Kevin Whelan (ed.), *Common ground: essays on the historical geography of Ireland presented to T. Jones Hughes.* (Cork, 1988), pp 22–40.

Stout, Geraldine. Wicklow's prehistoric landscape. In Ken Hannigan (ed.), *Wicklow: history and society* (Dublin, 1994), pp 1–40.

Stout, Matthew. Early Christian settlement, society and economy in Offaly. In William Nolan and Timothy P. O'Neill (ed.), *Offaly: history and society* (Dublin, 1998), pp 29–92.

Tierney, J. J. The Greek geographic tradition and Ptolemy's evidence for Irish geography. In *R.I.A. Proc.*, lxxvi (1976), pp 257–65.

Von den Brincken, Anna-Dorothee. Mappa mundi und Chronographia. Studien zur *imago mundi* des abendländischen Mittelalters. In *Deutsches Archiv*, xxiv (1969), pp 118–86.

——Zur Universalkartographie des Mittelalters. In *Miscellanea medievalia*, vii (1970), pp 249–78.

Walsh, Paul. *The placenames of Westmeath.* Dublin, 1957.

Williams, B. B. Early Christian landscapes in County Down. In Terence Reeves-Smyth and Fred Hamond (ed.), *Landscape archaeology in Ireland* (Oxford, 1983), pp 233–46.

Sims-Williams, Patrick. The Irish geography of *Culhwch and Olwen.* In Ó Corráin, Breatnach, & McCone, *Sages, saints & storytellers*, pp 412–26.

## 3 Language and literature

### (a) Irish

Ahlqvist, Anders. *The early Irish linguist: an edition of the canonical part of Auraicept na n-Éces.* Helsinki, 1983. (Commentationes Humanarum Litterarum, lxxiii.)

——Remarks on the question of dialects in Old Irish. In J. Fisiak (ed.), *Historical dialectology. Regional and social.* (Trends in Linguistics: Studies and Monographs, xxxvii; Berlin, New York, and Amsterdam, 1988), pp 23–38.

——Sg. 199b 1. In *Z.C.P.*, xlix–l (1997), pp 28–30.

——(ed.). *Diversions of Galway: papers on the history of linguistics.* Amsterdam and Philadelphia, 1992.

——and Čapková, Vera (ed.). *Dán do oide. Essays in memory of Conn R. Ó Cléirigh 1927–1995.* Dublin, 1997.
Includes articles by Patricia Kelly and Kim McCone.

Armstrong, John. Phonological irregularity in compound verbs in the Würzburg glosses. In *Ériu*, xxvii (1976), pp 46–72.

Ball, Martin, and Fife, James (ed.). *The Celtic languages.* London, 1993. (Routledge Language Family Descriptions.)
Includes articles by William Gillies, Gearóid Mac Eoin, and K. H. Schmidt.

Bammesberger, Alfred. The etymology of Irish *áit* 'place'. In *Ériu*, xlix (1998), pp 41–44.

—— and Wollmann, Alfred (ed.). *Britain 400–600: language and history*. Heidelberg, 1990.

Includes articles by D. Ellis Evans, John T. Koch, and Patrick Sims-Williams.

Baumgarten, Rolf. A Hiberno-Isidorean etymology. In *Peritia*, ii (1983), pp 225–8.

—— Etymological aetiology in Irish tradition. In *Ériu*, xli (1990), pp 115–22.

—— 'Craide hé...' and the early Irish copula sentence. In *Ériu*, xlv (1994), pp 121–7.

Binchy, D. A. (ed.). Bergin's law. In *Studia Celt.*, xiv–xv (1979–80), pp 34–53.

—— Semantic influence of Latin in the Old Irish glosses. In O'Meara & Naumann, *Latin script & letters*, pp 103–12.

Borst, Arno. *Der Turmbau von Babel: Geschichte der Meinungen über Ursprung und Vielfalt der Sprachen und Völker*. 4 vols. Stuttgart, 1957–63.

Breatnach, Liam. The suffixed pronouns in early Irish. In *Celtica*, xii (1977), 75–107.

—— An edition of *Amra Senáin*. In Ó Corráin, Breatnach, & McCone, *Sages, saints, & storytellers*, pp 7–31.

—— An Mheán-Ghaeilge. In K. McCone and others (ed.), *Stair na Gaeilge*, pp 221–333.

—— Zur Frage der *Roscada* im Irischen. In H. L. C. Tristram (ed.), *Metrik und Medienwechsel—Metrics and media* (Tübingen, 1991), pp 197–205.

—— Varia II. 1. Irish geined and geinit, Gaulish geneta, Welsh geneth; 2. Prepositions with added vowel in relative compound verbs. In *Ériu*, xlv (1994), pp 195–8.

—— Poets and poetry. In *Ériu*, xlvii (1996), pp 65–77.

Breeze, Andrew. Varia V. Middle Irish *dordán* 'buzz, roar'; northern English *dirdum* 'uproar, din'. In *Ériu*, xlv (1994), pp 205–7.

—— *Deorc* 'bloody' in *The dream of the rood*: Old Irish *derg* 'red, bloody'. In *Éigse*, xxviii (1994–5), pp 165–8.

—— Irish *brat* 'cloak, cloth'; English *brat* 'child'. In *Z.C.P.*, xlvii (1995), pp 89–92.

Brown, Alan K. Old Irish *astal*, Old English *æstel*: the common etymology. In *Camb. Med. Celt. Studies*, xxiv (winter 1992), pp 75–92.

Byrne, F. J. *Dercu*: the feminine of *Mocu*. In *Éigse*, xxviii (1994–5), pp 42–70.

Campanile, Enrico. Calchi irlandese di voci latine. In *Studi e saggi linguistici*, x (1970), pp 5–13.

Carey, John. The name 'Tuatha Dé Danann'. In *Éigse*, xviii (1981), pp 291–4.

—— *Fir Bolg*: a native etymology revisited. In *Camb. Med. Celt. Studies*, xvi (1988), pp 77–84.

—— Vernacular Irish learning: three notes. In *Éigse*, xxiv (1990), pp 37–44.

—— *A new introduction to the* Lebor Gabála Érenn, *the Book of the Taking of Ireland*. Dublin, 1993.

—— *The Irish national origin-legend: synthetic pseudohistory*. Cambridge, 1994. (Quiggin Pamphlets on the Sources of Medieval Gaelic History, i.)

—— *King of mysteries: early Irish religious writings*. Dublin, 1998.

—— Varia I. *Ferp Cluche*. In *Ériu*, l (1999), pp 165–8.

Carney, James. Aspects of archaic Irish. In *Éigse*, xvii (1978–9), pp 417–35.

Charles-Edwards, Thomas. Language and society among the insular Celts A.D. 400–1000. In M. J. Green (ed.), *The Celtic world* (London, 1995), pp 703–36.
—— The context and uses of literacy in early Christian Ireland. In Huw Pryce (ed.), *Literacy in medieval Celtic societies* (Cambridge, 1998), pp 62–82.
Clancy, Thomas O. Fools and adultery in some early Irish texts. In *Ériu*, xliv (1993), pp 105–24.
Corthals, Johan. Early Irish *retoirics* and their late antique background. In *Camb. Med. Celt. Studies*, xxxi (summer 1996), pp 17–36.
—— Zur Frage des mündlichen oder schriftlichen Ursprungs der Sagen *roscada*. In Tranter & Tristram, *Early Ir. lit.*, pp 201–20.
—— Zur Entstehung der archaischen irischen Metrik und Syntax. In H. Eichner and H. Ch. Luschützky (ed.), *Gedenkschrift für Jochem Schindler* (forthcoming).
Cowgill, Warren. The origins of the insular Celtic conjunct and absolute verbal endings. In H. Rix (ed.), *Flexion und Wortbildung* (Wiesbaden, 1975), pp 40–70.
—— The etymology of Irish *guidid* and the outcome of *$g^wh$ in Celtic. In M. Mayrhofer, M. Peters, and O. E. Pfeiffer (ed.), *Lautgeschichte und Etymologie: Akten der VI. Fachtagung der Indogermanischen Gesellschaft* (Wiesbaden, 1980), pp 49–78.
—— On the prehistory of the Celtic passive and deponent inflection. In *Ériu*, xxxiv (1983), pp 73–111.
—— The distribution of infixed and suffixed pronouns in Old Irish. In *Camb. Med. Celt. Studies*, xiii (summer 1987), pp 1–6.
Dumville, David N. Latin and Irish in the *Annals of Ulster*, A.D. 431–1050. In Whitelock, McKitterick, & Dumville, *Ire. in early med. Europe*, pp 320–41.
—— Language, literature and law in medieval Ireland: some questions of transmission. In *Camb. Med. Celt. Studies*, ix (summer 1985), pp 91–9.
Elsie, Robert. *Dialect relationships in Goidelic: a study in Celtic dialectology*. Hamburg, 1987.
Eska, Joseph F. On the crossroads of phonology and syntax: remarks on the origin of Vendryes' Restriction and related matters. In *Studia Celt.*, xxviii (1994), pp 39–62.
Garrett, Andrew. On the prosodic phonology of Ogam Irish. In *Ériu*, l (1999), pp 139–60.
Greene, David. The growth of palatalization in Irish. In *Transactions of the Philological Society*, lxxii (1973), pp 127–36.
—— Distinctive plural forms in Old and Middle Irish. In *Ériu*, xxv (1974), pp 190–99.
—— The influence of Scandinavian on Irish. In Almqvist & Greene (ed.), *Proc. Seventh Viking Congress* (1976), pp 75–82.
—— Archaic Irish. In K. H. Schmidt (ed.), *Indogermanisch und Keltisch* (Wiesbaden, 1977), pp 11–33.
Hamp, Eric P. The significance of *Cothraige*. In *Ériu*, xxxvi (1985), pp 1–10.
—— *Goídil, Féni, Gŵynedd*. In *Proceedings of the Harvard Celtic Colloquium*, xii (1992), pp 43–50.
—— Tascio-. In *Z.C.P.*, xlvi (1994), p. 13.
—— Varia IV. *op(i) in Celtic. In *Ériu*, xlv (1994), pp 203–4.

——Varia II. 1. On the Old Irish dat. sg. in *+ mi; 2. 'yes' and 'no'; 3. Irish uirghe f.; 4. tene, ten masc. > fem. 'fire'; 5. teng, ting 'tongue'; 6. for·érig. In *Ériu*, xlvii (1996), pp 209–11.

——Varia I. tál. In *Ériu*, xlviii (1997), p. 265.

Harvey, Anthony. Aspects of lenition and spirantization. In *Camb. Med. Celt. Studies*, viii (winter 1984), pp 87–100.

——Early literacy in Ireland: the evidence from ogam. In *Camb. Med. Celt. Studies*, xiv (winter 1987), pp 1–15.

——Some significant points of early Insular Celtic orthography. In Ó Corráin, Breatnach, & McCone, *Sages, saints, & storytellers*, pp 56–66.

——Retrieving the pronunciation of early Insular Celtic scribes: towards a methodology. In *Celtica*, xxi (1990), pp 178–90.

——Retrieving the pronunciation of early Insular Celtic scribes: the case of Dorbbene. In *Celtica*, xxii (1991), pp 48–63.

——Latin, literacy and the Celtic vernaculars around the year A.D. 500. In C. J. Byrne, Margaret Harry, and Pádraig Ó Siadhail (ed.), *Celtic languages and Celtic people* (Halifax, Nova Scotia, 1992), pp 11–26.

——and Power, Jane. Varia IV. Hiberno-Latin scaltae. In *Ériu*, xlviii (1997), pp 277–9.

Herren, Michael. Old Irish lexical and semantic influences on Hiberno-Latin. In Ní Chatháin & Richter, *Ire. & Europe*, pp 197–209.

Hickey, Raymond. Reduction of allomorphy and the plural in Irish. In *Ériu*, xxxvi (1985), pp 143–62.

Hofman, Rijcklof (ed.). *The Sankt Gall Priscian commentary*. Pt. 1. 2 vols. Münster, 1996.

Holland, Gary, and Lindow, John. Irish poetry and Norse *dróttkvætt*. In K. Klar and others (ed.), *A Celtic florilegium* (Lawrence, Ma., 1996), pp 54–62.

Hughes, A. J. Some aspects of the salmon in Gaelic tradition past and present. In *Z.C.P.*, xlviii (1996), pp 17–28.

Isaac, G. R. Vocative plural of masculine *(y)o-stems in Old Irish. In *Z.C.P.*, xlix–l (1997), pp 333–40.

——Varia I. Deibide. In *Ériu*, xlix (1998), pp 161–4.

Isaacs, Graham. Issues in the reconstruction and analysis of insular Celtic syntax and phonology. In *Ériu*, xliv (1993), pp 1–32.

Jackson, Kenneth H. Some questions in dispute about early Welsh literature and language, II: Who taught whom to write Irish and Welsh? In *Studia Celt.*, viii–ix (1973–4), pp 18–32.

——The historical grammar of Irish: some actualities and some desiderata. In Mac Eoin, Ahlqvist, & Ó hAodha, *Proc. 6th Congress*, pp 1–18.

Jacobs, Nicholas. *The Seafarer* and the birds: a possible Irish parallel. In *Celtica*, xxiii (1999), pp 125–31.

O'Brien Johnson, T., and Cairns, D. (ed.). *Gender in Irish writing*. Philadelphia, 1991.

Joseph, Lionel. The origin of the Celtic denominatives in *-sag-. In C. Watkins (ed.), *Studies in memory of Warren Cowgill (1929–1985): papers from the East Coast Indo-European Conference, Cornell University. June 6–9, 1985* (Berlin, 1987), pp 113–59.

Kalygin, V. P. Indogermanische Dichtersprache und altirische mythopoetische Tradition. In *Z.C.P.*, xlvi (1994), pp 1–10.

—— [Kalyguine, Victor]. *La langue de la poésie irlandaise archaïque.* Hamburg, 1993.

—— Deux correspondances de vocabulaire mythologique entre les langues celtiques
et balto-slaves: 1. Irl. Balor—lit. Giltinė 'Göttin des Todtes'; 2. Irl. Macha—
slave Moskoš? In *Z.C.P.*, xlix–l (1997), pp 367–73.

Kelly, Fergus. Two notes on final-verb constructions. In *Celtica*, xviii (1986),
pp 1–12.

—— Varia III. Old Irish creccaire, Scottish Gaelic kreahkir. In *Ériu*, xxxvii (1986),
pp 185–6.

—— A note on Old Irish círmaire. In *Celtica*, xxi (1990), pp 231–3.

Kelly, Patricia. Dialekte im Altirischen? In W. Meid, H. Ölberg, and H. Schmeja
(ed.), *Sprachwissenschaft in Innsbruck* (Innsbrucker Beiträge zur Kulturwis-
senschaft, 50; Innsbruck, 1982), pp 85–9.

—— The earliest words for 'horse' in the Celtic languages. In S. Davies and N. A.
Jones (ed.), *The horse in Celtic culture: medieval Welsh perspectives* (Cardiff,
1997), pp 43–63.

—— Two relative clauses in Críth Gablach. In *Z.C.P.*, xlix–l (1997), pp 373–7.

Klar, Kathryn; Sweetser, Eve E.; and Thomas, Claire (ed.). *A Celtic florilegium:
studies in memory of Brendan O Hehir.* Lawrence, Ma. 1996.

Koch, John T. Further to Indo-European *$*g^{wh}$* in Celtic. In J. Eska, R. G. Gruffydd,
and Nicholas Jacobs (ed.), *Hispano-Gallo-Brittonica: essays in honour of Professor
D. Ellis Evans on the occasion of his sixty-fifth birthday* (Cardiff, 1995),
pp 79–95.

—— Gallo-Brittonic *Tasc(i)ouanos* 'badger-slayer' and the reflex of Indo-European
$g^{wh}$. In *Journal of Celtic Linguistics*, i (1992), pp 101–18.

—— Prosody and the old Celtic verbal complex. In *Ériu*, xxxviii (1987), pp
143–76.

—— The conversion and the transition from Primitive to Old Irish. In *Emania*, xiii
(1995), pp 39–50.

—— Ériu, Alba, and Letha: when was a language ancestral to Gaelic first spoken in
Ireland? In *Emania*, ix (1991), pp 17–27.

—— On the origins of the Old Irish terms *Goídil* and *Goídelc.* In Geraint Evans,
Bernard Martin, and Jonathon Wooding (ed.), *Proceedings of the First Australian
Conference of Celtic Studies* (Sydney, 1991), pp 3–16.

—— and Carey, John (ed.). *The Celtic heroic age: literary sources for ancient Celtic
Europe and early Ireland and Wales.* Malden, Ma., 1995.

Kuryłowicz, Jerzy. Morphophonological palatalization in Old Irish. In *Travaux linguistiques de Prague*, iv (1971), pp 67–73. Reprinted in J. Kuryłowicz (ed.),
*Esquisses linguistiques* (2 vols, Munich, 1973–5), pp 323–9.

Lambert, Pierre-Yves. Notes on Saint Gall glosses. In *Celtica*, xviii (1986),
pp 77–86.

—— Les gloses celtiques aux commentaires de Virgile. In *Études Celt.*, xxiii (1986),
pp 81–128.

—— Les différents strates de gloses dans le manuscrit de Saint-Gall, no 904. In P. Ní
Chatháin and M. Richter (ed.), *Irland und Europa im früheren Mittelalter: Bildung*

*und Literatur. Ireland and Europe in the earlier middle ages: learning and literature* (Stuttgart, 1996), pp 187–94.

Lindemann, Fredrik Otto. Varia I. Old Irish *ithid*. In *Ériu*, xlv (1994), pp 191–4.

——Varia I. On a possible Celtic–Greek etymological correspondence. In *Ériu*, xlvi (1995), pp 165–6.

——Varia II. On some Celtic compound verb forms. In *Ériu*, xlvi (1995), pp 167–70.

——Varia I. Notae Mediolanenses. In *Ériu*, xlvii (1996), pp 205–7.

——Varia II. Notae Mediolanenses. In *Ériu*, xlviii (1997), pp 267–72.

——Varia III. On the origin of Old Irish *\*fo-noí* 'cooks'. In *Ériu*, xlix (1998), pp 171–4.

——Varia V. On a possible Celto-Germanic etymological correspondence. In *Ériu*, l (1999), pp 179–82

——Varia VI. On the origin of the Celto-Germanic etymon *\*nent-*. In *Ériu*, l (1999), pp 183–4.

——Old Irish *inne*. In *Celtica*, xxiii (1999), pp 155–6.

Löfstedt, Bengt. Zur Grammatik in Paris, Bibl. nat. MS lat. 7491. In *Peritia*, xii (1998), pp 95–7.

Lucht, I. Doppelte Markierung des Akkusativs beim Transitivum im Altirischen. In *Z.C.P.*, xlvi (1994), pp 80–118.

MacAulay, Donald (ed.). *The Celtic languages*. Cambridge, 1992.

Mac Cana, Proinsias. Latin influence on British: the pluperfect. In O'Meara & Naumann, *Latin script & letters*, pp 194–206.

——Y trefedigaethau Gwyddelig ym Mhrydain. In G. Bowen (ed.), *Y Gwareiddiad Celtaidd* (Llandysul, 1987), pp 153–81.

Mac Cana, Proinsias. Word-order in Old Irish and Middle Welsh: an analogy. In A. T. E. Matonis and Daniel F. Melia (ed.), *Celtic language, Celtic culture* (Van Nuys, Cal., 1990), pp 253–60.

——The historical present and the verb 'to be'. In *Ériu*, xlv (1994), pp 127–50.

——Ir. *ba marb*, W. *bu farw* 'he died'. In *Z.C.P.*, xlix–l (1997), pp 469–81.

——Varia III. 1. Insula Fortium: Ynys y Kedeirn/Kedyrn. 2. Lethenach/leathanach 'page'. In *Ériu*, xlviii (1997), pp 273–6.

——The motif of trivial causes. In Smyth, *Seanchas*, pp 205–11.

——and Ó Baoill, Dónall P. On the extended use of *ag* before verbal nouns. In *Ériu*, xlvii (1996), pp 185–91.

Mac Cárthaigh, Eoin. Article + uile + noun and IGT II § 20. In *Ériu*, xlix (1998), pp 45–70.

McCone, Kim. Pretonic preverbs and the absolute verbal endings in Old Irish. In *Ériu*, xxx (1979), pp 1–34.

——Further to absolute and conjunct. In *Ériu*, xxxiii (1982), pp 1–29.

——The Würzburg and Milan glosses: our earliest sources of 'Middle Irish'. In *Ériu*, xxxvi (1985), pp 85–106.

——From Indo-European to Old Irish: conservation and innovation in the verbal system. In Evans, Griffith, & Jope, *Proc. 7th Congress*, pp 222–66.

——*The early Irish verb*. Maynooth, 1987.

McCone, Kim. Zur Frage der Register im frühen Irischen. In Tranter & Tristram, *Early Ir. lit.*, pp 57–97.

——*Pagan past and Christian present*. Maynooth, 1990.

——*The Indo-European origins of the Old Irish nasal presents, subjunctives and futures.* Innsbruck, 1991. (Innsbrucker Beiträge zur Sprachwissenschaft, lxvi.)

——Varia II. Old Irish *co*, *cucci* 'as far as (him, it)' and Latin *usque* 'as far as'. In *Ériu*, xliv (1993), pp 171–6.

——Zum Ablaut der keltischen *r*-Stämme. In J. E. Rasmussen (ed.), *In honorem Holger Pedersen. Kolloquium der Indogermanischen Gesellschaft von 26. bis 28. Marz 1993 in Kopenhagen* (Wiesbaden, 1994), pp 275–84.

——Old Irish *con-dieig* 'asks, seeks,' verbal noun *cuin(d)gid*: a problem of syncope and verbal composition. In *Éigse*, xxviii (1994–5), pp 156–9.

——OIr. *Senchae*, *senchaid* and preliminaries on agent noun formation in Celtic. In *Ériu*, xlvi (1995), pp 1–10.

——Prehistoric, Old and Middle Irish. In Kim McCone and Katharine Simms (ed.), *Progress in medieval Irish studies* (Maynooth, 1996), pp 7–53.

——*Towards a relative chronology of ancient and medieval Celtic sound change.* Maynooth, 1996. (Maynooth Studies in Celtic Linguistics, i.)

——'King' and 'queen' in Celtic and Indo-European. In *Ériu*, xlix (1998), pp 1–12.

——; McManus, Damian; Ó Háinle, Cathal; Williams, Nicholas; and Breatnach, Liam (ed.). *Stair na Gaeilge in ómós do Phádraig Ó Fiannachta*. Maynooth, 1994.

Mac Eoin, Gearóid. On the dating of Middle Irish texts. In *Brit. Acad. Proc.*, lxviii (1982), pp 109–39.

——Satire in Middle Irish literature. In Folke Josephson, *Celts and vikings* (Göteborg, 1997), pp 9–26.

——Old Irish *briugu* 'hospitaller' and connected words. In *Celtica*, xxiii (1999), pp 169–73.

Mac Gearailt, Uáitéar. Zum Irischen des 12. Jahrhunderts. In *Z.C.P.*, xliii (1989), pp 11–52.

——The language of some late Middle Irish texts in the Book of Leinster. In *Studia Hib.*, xxvi (1991–2), pp 167–216.

——Verbal particles and preverbs in Late Middle Irish. In *Ériu*, xlvii (1996), pp 153–83.

——Infixed and independent pronouns in the LL text of Táin Bó Cúailnge. In *Z.C.P.*, xlix–l (1997), pp 494–515.

Mac Giolla Easpaig, Dónal. Aspects of variant word order in early Irish. In *Ériu*, xxxi (1980), pp 28–38.

Mackey, J. P. Mythical past and political present: a case-study of the Irish myth of the Sovereignty. In *Z.C.P.*, li (1999), pp 66–84.

McManus, Damian. A chronology of the Latin loanwords in early Irish. In *Ériu*, xxxiv (1983), pp 21–72.

——On final syllables in the Latin loan-words in early Irish. In *Ériu*, xxxv (1984), pp 137–62.

—— *Linguarum diversitas:* Latin and the vernaculars in early medieval Britain. In *Peritia*, iii (1984), pp 151–88.

—— The so-called *Cothrige* and *Pátraic* strata of Latin loan words in early Irish. In Ní Chatháin & Richter, *Ire. & Europe*, pp 179–96.

—— Ogam: archaising orthography and the authenticity of the manuscript key to the alphabet. In *Ériu*, xxxvii (1986), pp 1–32.

—— Irish letter-names and their kennings. In *Ériu*, xxxix (1988), pp 127–68.

—— Runic and ogam letter-names: a parallelism. In Ó Corráin, Breatnach, & McCone, *Sages, saints, & storytellers*, pp 144–8.

—— Classical Modern Irish. In Kim McCone and Katharine Simms, *Progress in medieval Irish studies* (Maynooth, 1996), pp 165–88.

—— The Irish grammatical and syntactical tracts: a concordance of duplicated and identified citations. In *Ériu*, xlviii (1997), pp 83–102.

Mac Mathúna, Liam. Observations on Irish *lann* '(piece of) land; (church) building' and compounds. In *Ériu*, xlviii (1997), pp 153–60.

—— The Christianization of the early Irish cosmos?: *muir mas, nem nglas, talam cé* (Blathm. 258). In *Z.C.P.*, xlix–l (1997), pp 532–47.

McQuillan, Peter. On the semantics and pragmatics of *cía* in early Irish. In *Ériu*, xlix (1998), pp 89–120.

—— Complementation and the subjunctive in early Irish. In *Ériu*, l (1999), pp 87–132.

Matonis, A. T. E., and Melia, Daniel F. (ed.). *Celtic language, Celtic culture: a festschrift for Eric P. Hamp.* Van Nuys, Calif., 1990.
    Includes essays by P. de Bernardo Stempel, J. Eska, Patrick K. Ford, H. M. Hoenigswald, Proinsias Mac Cana, Daniel F. Melia, K. H. Schmidt, and Calvert Watkins.

Meid, Wolfgang. The Celtic languages. In Schmidt, *Celts*, pp 116–22.

Motta, Filippo. Contributi allo studio della lingua delle iscrizioni ogamiche (A–B). In *Studi e saggi linguistici*, xviii (1978), pp 257–333.

Muhr, Kay. Water imagery in early Irish. In *Celtica*, xxiii (1999), pp 193–210.

Murray, Kevin. Varia VII. *at(t)ba/éc at(t)bai.* In *Ériu*, l (1999), pp 185–8.

Nagy, J. F. *Conversing with angels and ancients: literary myths of medieval Ireland.* Dublin, 1997.

Ní Chatháin, Próinséas. A linguistic archaism in the *Dúil Laithe.* In *Z.C.P.*, xlix–l (1997), pp 610–14.

Ní Dhonnchadha, Máirín. *Caillech* and other terms for veiled women in medieval Irish texts. In *Éigse*, xxviii (1994–5), pp 71–96.

Nic Eoin, Máirín. *B'ait leo bean. Gnéithe den idé-eolaíocht inscne i dtraidisiúin liteartha na Gaeilge.* Dublin, 1998.

Ní Mhaonaigh, Máire. *Cogad Gáedel re Gallaib:* some dating considerations. In *Peritia*, ix (1995), pp 354–7.

—— Einige Bemerkungen zu den Verbalstammbildungen in *Cogad Gáedel re Gallaib.* In M. Rockel and S. Zimmer (ed.), *Akten des ersten Symposiums deutschsprachiger Keltologen* (Tübingen, 1993), pp 161–82.

—— Some Middle Irish declensional patterns in *Cogad Gáedel re Gallaib.* In *Z.C.P.*, xlix–l (1997), pp 615–28.

Ó Briain, M. A. Notes on Irish proper names. In *Celtica*, ix (1971), p. 212.

——Old Irish personal names. In *Celtica*, x (1973), pp 211–36.

Ó Cathasaigh, Tomás. Early Irish narrative literature. In Kim McCone and Katharine Simms (ed.), *Progress in medieval Irish studies* (Maynooth, 1996), pp 55–64.

Ó Coileáin, Seán. The structure of a literary cycle. In *Ériu*, xxv (1974), pp 88–125.

——Some problems of story and history. In *Ériu*, xxxii (1981), pp 115–36.

Ó Con Cheanainn, Tomás. *Ó Maoil Chonaire* agus sloinne Shean-Phádraig. In *Éigse*, xxxii (2000), pp 23–34.

Ó Corráin, Ailbhe. Spatial perception and the development of grammatical structures in Irish. In Folke Josephson (ed.), *Celts and vikings* (Göteborg, 1997), pp 89–102.

——On the syntax and semantics of expressions of being in Early Irish. In *Z.C.P.*, xlix–l (1997), pp 629–42.

Ó Corráin, Donnchadh; Breatnach, Liam; and McCone, Kim (ed.), *Sages, saints and storytellers: Celtic studies in honour of Professor James Carney*. Maynooth, 1989.

Ó Cróinín, Dáibhí. The oldest Irish names for the days of the week? In *Ériu*, xxxii (1981), pp 95–114.

——An Old-Irish gloss in the Munich computus. In *Éigse*, xviii (1980–81), pp 289–90.

Ó Crualaoich, Conchubhar. Syncope patterns in denominative verbs. In *Ériu*, xlviii (1997), pp 239–64.

Ó Cuív, Brían. The linguistic training of the medieval Irish poet. In *Celtica*, x (1973), pp 114–40.

——Irish words for 'alphabet'. In *Ériu*, xxxi (1980), pp 101–11.

——Aspects of Irish personal names. In *Ériu*, xxxi (1980), pp 151–84.

O Daly, Máirín. The verbal system of the LL-*Táin*. In *Ériu*, xiv (1943), 31–139.

Ó Dochartaigh, Cathair. *Cha* and *ní* in the Irish of Ulster. In *Éigse*, xvi (1976), pp 317–36.

——The Irish language. In D. MacAulay (ed.), *The Celtic languages* (Cambridge, 1992), pp 11–99.

Ó Flaithearta, M. Altirisch *tess, echtar* und die Frage der Konsonantengruppe-cst-im Keltischen. In *Z.C.P.*, xlix–l (1997), pp 653–63.

Ó hUiginn, Ruairí. On the Old Irish figura etymologica. In *Ériu*, xxxiv (1983), pp 123–34.

——Notes on Old Irish syntax. In *Ériu*, xxxviii (1987), pp 177–84.

——Tongu do dia toinges mo thuath and related expressions. In Ó Corráin, Breatnach, & McCone, *Sages, saints, & storytellers*, pp 332–41.

——Aspects of clause subordination in the Celtic languages. In Folke Josephson, *Celts and vikings* (Göteborg, 1997), pp 69–88.

——Complementation in early Irish: the verba dicendi. In *Ériu*, xlix (1998), pp 121–48.

O'Leary, Philip. Contention at feasts in early Irish literature. In *Éigse*, xx (1984), pp 115–27.

——A farseeing driver of an old chariot: legal moderation in early Irish literature. In *Camb. Med. Celt. Studies*, xi (summer 1986), pp 1–6.

——Verbal deceit in the Ulster cycle. In *Éigse*, xxi (1986), pp 16–26.

——The honour of women in early Irish literature. In *Ériu*, xxxviii (1987), pp 27–44.

——*Fír Fer:* an internalized ethical concept in early Irish literature? In *Éigse*, xxii (1987), pp 1–14.

——Honour-bound: the social context of early Irish *geis*. In *Celtica*, xx (1988), pp 85–197.

——Magnanimous conduct in Irish heroic literature. In *Éigse*, xxv (1991), pp 28–44.

——Jeers and judgments: laughter in early Irish literature. In *Camb. Med. Celt. Studies*, xxii (winter 1991), pp 15–29.

——Choice and consequence in Irish heroic literature. In *Camb. Med. Celt. Studies*, xxvii (summer 1994), pp 49–60.

Olmsted, Garrett. Luccreth's poem Conailla Medb Michuru and the origins of the *Táin*. In *The Mankind Quarterly*, xxix (1988), pp 3–72.

——The earliest narrative version of the *Táin*: seventh-century poetic references to *Táin Bó Cuailnge*. In *Emania*, x (1992), pp 5–17.

Ó Néill, Pádraig. The Old-Irish words in Eriugena's biblical glosses. In Allard, *Jean Scot écrivain*, pp 287–98.

——Welsh *anterth*, Old Irish *anteirt*. In *Ériu*, xli (1990), pp 1–11.

Ó Riain, Pádraig. Conservation in the vocabulary of the early Irish church. In Ó Corráin, Breatnach, & McCone, *Sages, saints, & storytellers*, pp 358–66.

——Early Irish literature. In Glanville Price (ed.), *The Celtic connection* (Gerrards Cross, 1992), pp 65–80.

——When and why was Cothraige first equated with Patricius? In *Z.C.P.*, xlix–l (1997), pp 698–711.

Pennaod, G. La désignation de l'année en celtique. In *Études Celt.*, xxiii (1986), pp 53–6.

Pryce, Huw (ed.). *Literacy in medieval Celtic societies.* Cambridge, 1998.

Quin, E. G. and others. (*Contributions to a*) *Dictionary of the Irish language based mainly on Old and Middle Irish materials.* Dublin, 1913–76. Now complete.

Rankin, D. *Bendacht dee agus andee fort, a ingen* (Táin Bó Cúalnge 2111, O'Rahilly). In *Z.C.P.*, li (1999), pp 116–24.

Richter, Michael. The introduction of alphabetic writing to Ireland: implications and consequences. In K. Klar and others (ed.), *A Celtic florilegium* (Lawrence, Ma., 1996), pp 152–64.

Roberts, Brinley F. Edward Lhuyd and Celtic linguistics. In Evans, Griffith, & Jope, *Proc. 7th Congress*, pp 1–9.

Rockel, Martin. *Grundzüge einer Geschichte der irischen Sprache.* Vienna, 1989.

——Das Verhältnis von Sprache und Literatur bei den keltischen Völkern. In *Z.C.P.*, xlix–l (1997), pp 778–83.

Russell, Paul. A footnote to spirantization. In *Camb. Med. Celt. Studies*, x (winter 1985), pp 53–6.

——Preverbs, prepositions and adverbs: sigmatic and asigmatic. In *Transactions of the Philological Society*, lxxxvi (1988), pp 144–72.

——The sounds of a silence: the growth of Cormac's Glossary. In *Camb. Med. Celt. Studies*, xv (summer 1988), pp 1–30.

——*Celtic word-formation: the velar suffixes.* Dublin, 1990.

Russell, Paul. *Introduction to the Celtic languages.* London and New York, 1995.

Russell, Paul. Notes on words in early Irish glossaries. In *Études Celt.*, xxxi (1995), pp 198–204.

——Brittonic words in early Irish glossaries. In Joseph F. Eska, R. G. Gruffydd, and Nicholas Jacobs (ed.), *Hispano-Gallo-Brittonica* (Cardiff, 1995), pp 166–82.

——*Dúil Dromma Cetta* and Cormac's Glossary. In *Études Celt.*, xxxii (1996), pp 115–42.

——'Verdunkelte Komposita' in Celtic. In *Studia Celt.*, xxx (1996), pp 113–25.

——Laws, glossaries, and legal glossaries in early Ireland. In *Z.C.P.*, li (1999), pp 85–115.

——Patterns of hypocorism in early Irish hagiography. In *Proceedings of the International Conference on Hagiography—Cork 1997* (forthcoming).

Sayers, William. Old Irish *fert* 'tie-pole', *fertas* 'swingle-tree', and the seeress Fedelm. In *Études Celt.*, xxi (1984), pp 171–83.

——'Mani maidi an nem...': ringing changes on a cosmic motif. In *Ériu*, xxxvii (1986), pp 99–118.

——Airdrech, sirite and other early Irish battlefield spirits. In *Éigse*, xxv (1991), pp 45–55.

Schmidt, Karl Horst. Zur Entwicklung einiger indogermanischer Verwandschafts-namen im Keltischen. In *Études Celt.*, xvi (1979), pp 117–22.

——The emergence of the Celtic languages: the Celtic languages in their European context. In Evans, Griffith, & Jope, *Proc. 7th Congress*, pp 199–221.

——On the reconstruction of Proto-Celtic. In MacLennan, *Proc. 1st N.A. Congress*, pp 231–48.

Schrijver, Peter. The Celtic adverbs for 'against' and 'with' and the early apocope of *-l. In *Ériu*, xlv (1994), pp 151–90.

——OIr. *gor* 'pious, dutiful': meaning and etymology. In *Ériu*, xlvii (1996), pp 193–203.

——On the nature and origin of word-initial h- in the Würzburg glosses. In *Ériu*, xlviii (1997), pp 105–228.

——Vowel rounding by Primitive Irish labiovelars. In *Ériu*, l (1999), pp 133–8.

Schumacher, Stefan. Old Irish *tucaid, tocad and Middle Welsh tynghaf, tynghet re-examined. In *Ériu*, xlvi (1995), pp 49–58.

——The preterite of ithid 'eats'. In *Ériu*, xlix (1998), pp 149–60.

Scowcroft, R. Mark. On liminality in the Fenian cycle. In *Camb. Med. Celt. Studies*, xiii (summer 1987), pp 97–100.

——Abstract narrative in Ireland. In *Ériu*, xlvi (1995), pp 121–58.

Sharpe, Richard. Hiberno-Latin *laicus*, Irish *láech* and the devil's men. In *Ériu*, xxx (1979), pp 75–92.

——Latin and Irish words for 'book-satchel'. In *Peritia*, iv (1985), pp 152–6.

——ME *falding*, MIr *fallaing*: Irish mantles in medieval England. In *Anglia*, cvii (1989), pp 416–29.

Shields, K. Old Irish *lín* 'numerus': another Indo-European/Near Eastern connection? In *Z.C.P.*, xlviii (1996), pp 287–90.

Sproule, David. Complex alliteration in Gruibne's *roscad*. In *Ériu*, xxxiii (1982), pp 157–60.

——Complex alliteration, full and unstressed rhyme, and the origin of *deibide*. In *Ériu*, xxxviii (1987), pp 185–200.

Stempel, P. de Bernardo. Spuren gemeinkeltischer Kultur im Wortschatz: 1. 'Tochter'; 2. bri(u)gu; 3. Vercelli; 5. Banassac; 6. Plumergat. In *Z.C.P.*, xlix–l (1997), pp 92–106.

Stevenson, Jane. The beginnings of literacy in Ireland. In *R.I.A. Proc.*, lxxxix (1989), sect. C, pp 127–65.

——Literacy in Ireland: the evidence of the Patrician dossier in the Book of Armagh. In Rosamond McKitterick (ed.), *The uses of literacy in early medieval Europe* (Cambridge, 1990), pp 11–35.

——Literacy and orality in early medieval Ireland. In D. R. Edel (ed.), *Ireland and Europe in the early middle ages* (Dublin, 1995), pp 11–22.

Strasser, Ingrid. Irisches im Althochdeutschen? In Löwe, *Die Iren*, pp 399–424.

Stüber, Karin. The inflection of masculine and feminine n-stems in Irish. In *Ériu*, xlviii (1997), pp 229–64.

Testen, David. Stem-final *-KK-* in Celtic terms for 'pig'. In *Ériu*, l (1999), pp 161–4.

Uhlich, Jürgen. *Die Morphologie der komponierten Personennamen des Altirischen*. Witterschlick and Bonn, 1993. (Beiträge zu Sprachwissenschaften, i.)

——On the fate of intervocalic *-u-in Old Irish, especially between neutral vowels. In *Ériu*, xlvi (1995), pp 11–48.

——Einige britannische Lehnnamen in Irischen: Brénainn (Brenden), Cathaír/ Catháer und Midir. In *Z.C.P.*, xlix–l (1997), pp 878–97.

Vallancey, Charles. *An essay on the antiquity of the Irish language, being a collation of the Irish with the Punic language*. Dublin, 1772.

Vallancey, Charles. *A grammar of the Iberno-Celtic, or Irish language*. Dublin, 1773.

Vendryes, Joseph; Bachellery, Edouard; and Lambert, Pierre-Yves. *Lexique étymologique de l'irlandais ancien*. Dublin and Paris, 1960 (M, N, O, P), 1974 (R, S), 1978 (T, U), 1981 (A, B), 1987 (C), 1996 (D).

Wagner, Heinrich. Das negative altir. Präverb *nícon* 'non'. In *Z.C.P.*, xxxii (1972), pp 18–35.

——Studies in the history of Gaelic dialects, pt 1. In *Z.C.P.*, xxxix (1983), pp 96–116.

——Zur unregelmässigen Wortstellung in der altirischen Alliterationsdichtung. In W. Meid (ed.), *Beiträge zur Indogermanistik und Keltologie* (Innsbruck, 1967), pp 289–314.

Watkins, Calvert. The etymology of Irish *dúan*. In *Celtica*, xi (1976), pp 270–77.

——Varia I. A Hittite–Celtic etymology. In *Ériu*, xxvii (1976), pp 119–22.

——Varia III. 1. OIr. *clí* and *cleth* 'house-post'. 2. '*In essar dam do á?*' In *Ériu*, xxix (1978), pp 155–65.

——*Is tre fhír flathemon;* marginalia to *Audacht Morainn*. In *Ériu*, xxx (1979), pp 181–98.

Sims-Williams, Patrick. Indo-European *$g^{wh}$* in Celtic, 1894–1994. In J. Eska, R. G. Gruffydd, and Nicholas Jacobs (ed.), *Hispano-Gallo-Brittonica: essays in honour of Professor D. Ellis Evans on the occasion of his sixty-fifth birthday* (Cardiff, 1995), pp 196–218.

Sims-Williams, Patrick. Some problems in deciphering the early Irish Ogam alphabet. In *Transactions of the Philological Society*, xci (1993), pp 133–80.
—— The additional letters of the Ogam alphabet. In *Camb. Med. Celt. Studies*, xxiii (summer 1992), pp 29–75.
—— The Celtic languages. In A. G. and P. Ramat (ed.), *The Indo-European languages* (London and New York, 1998), pp 345–79.
—— The development of the Indo-European voiced labiovelars in Celtic. In *Bulletin of the Board of Celtic Studies*, xxix (1981), pp 201–29, 690.
—— The double system of verbal inflexion in Old Irish. In *Transactions of the Philological Society*, lxxxii (1984), pp 138–201.
—— The emergence of Old Welsh, Cornish and Breton orthography, 600–800: the evidence of archaic Welsh. In *Bulletin of the Board of Celtic Studies*, xxxviii (1991), pp 20–86.
Wodtko, Dagmar S. *Sekundäradjektive in den altirischen Glossen.* Innsbruck, 1995. (Innsbrucker Beiträge zur Sprachwissenschaft, lxxxi.)
Ziegler, Sabine. *Die Sprache der altirischen Ogam-Inschriften.* Göttingen, 1994. (Historische Sprachforschung, Ergänzungheft xxxvi.)

## *(b) Hiberno-Latin*

As a general rule, works listed in Michael Lapidge and Richard Sharpe, *A bibliography of Celtic-Latin literature 400–1200* (Dublin, 1985), do not appear below. For works by Ludwig Bieler, see John J. O'Meara and Bernd Naumann, 'Bibliography Ludwig Bieler' in id. (ed.), *Latin script and letters A.D. 400–900: Festschrift presented to Ludwig Bieler on the occasion of his 70th birthday* (Leiden, 1976), pp 1–18.

Breen, Aidan. Iduma (Idouma). In *Celtica*, xxi (1990), pp 40–50.
Campanile, Enrico. Latino d'Irlanda o latino gallese? Un contributo alla storia degli Hisperica Famina. In *Annali della Scuola normale superiore di Pisa*, xxxii (1963), pp 189–209.
Cizek, Alexandru. Virgile le grammairien: un auteur hiberno-aquitain? In J.-M. Picard (ed.), *Aquitaine and Ireland in the middle ages* (Dublin, 1995), pp 127–36.
Dumville, David. An Irish idiom latinised. In *Éigse*, xvi (1975–6), pp 183–6.
Esposito, Mario. *Latin learning in medieval Ireland.* Ed. Michael Lapidge. Aldershot, 1988.
Gorman, Michael. A critique of Bischoff's theory of Irish exegesis: the commentary on Genesis in Munich Clm 6302. In *Journal of Medieval Latin*, vii (1997), pp 178–233.
Herren, Michael. Sprachliche Eigentümlichkeiten in den hibernolateinischen Texten des 7. und 8. Jahrhunderts. In Löwe, *Die Iren*, pp 425–33.
—— Insular Latin C(h)araxare (Craxare) and its derivatives. In *Peritia*, i (1982), pp 273–80.
—— Old Irish lexical and semantic influences on Hiberno-Latin. In Ní Chatháin & Richter, *Ire. & Europe*, pp 197–209.
—— *Latin letters in early Christian Ireland.* Aldershot, 1996.

——Scholarly contacts between the Irish and the southern English in the seventh century. In *Peritia*, xii (1998), pp 24–53.

Hofman, Rijcklof. The gender of Latin *Dies* (Day). In D. R. Edel (ed.), *Cultural identity and cultural integration* (Dublin, 1995), pp 82–91.

Howlett, David. Five experiments in textual reconstruction and analysis. In *Peritia*, ix (1995), pp 1–50.

——Seven studies in seventh-century texts. In *Peritia*, x (1996), pp 1–70.

——Insular Latin writers' rhythms. In *Peritia*, xi (1997), pp 53–116.

——Hellenic learning in Insular Latin: an essay on supported claims. In *Peritia*, xii (1998), pp 54–78.

Kobus, I. *Imtheachta Aeniasa: Aeneis*-Rezeption im irischen Mittelalter. In *Z.C.P.*, xlvii (1995), pp 76–86.

Law, Vivien. *The Insular Latin grammarians*. Woodbridge, 1982.

——*Wisdom, grammar, and authority in the seventh century*. Oxford, 1997.

Le Moine, Louis. Scrutari 'lire' et pingere 'écrire'. Note sur le colophon du Vatican Regina 296. In *Études Celt.*, xxv (1988), pp 233–6.

Lindeman, Fredrik Otto. Notes on two biblical glosses. In *Celtica*, xix (1987), pp 177–9.

——A note on the theological background of two Milan glosses. In *Celtica*, xix (1987), pp 179–81.

——Notes on two biblical glosses. In *Celtica*, xx (1988), pp 108–9.

Moran, Dermot. Review article: Expounding Eriugena. In *I.H.S.*, xxxi, no. 122 (Nov. 1998), pp 247–58.

Netzer, Nancy. *Cultural interplay in the eighth century*. Cambridge, 1996.

Ó Cróinín, Dáibhí. Hiberno-Latin *calcenterus*. In *Peritia*, i (1982), pp 296–7.

——Bischoff's Wendepunkte fifty years on. In *Revue Bénédictine*, cx, no. 3–4 (2000), pp 204–37.

O'Loughlin, Thomas. The Latin sources of medieval Irish culture. In Kim McCone and Katharine Simms (ed.), *Progress in medieval Irish studies* (Maynooth, 1996), pp 91–106.

Ó Néill, Pádraig. *Romani* influences on seventh-century Hiberno-Latin literature. In Ní Chatháin & Richter, *Ire. & Europe*, ii, 280–90.

Richter, Michael. Sprachliche Untersuchung der Kosmographie des Aethicus Ister. In Dopsch & Juffinger, *Virgil von Salzburg*, pp 147–53.

Sharpe, Richard. An Irish textual critic and the Carmen paschale of Sedulius: Colmán's letter to Feradach. In *Journal of Medieval Latin*, ii (1992), pp 44–54.

Silagi, Gabriel. Notwendige Bemerkungen zu Gormans 'Critique of Bischoff's theory of Irish exegesis'. In *Peritia*, xii (1998), pp 87–94.

Wright, Charles D. Bischoff's theory of Irish exegesis and the genesis commentary in Munich Clm 6302: a critique of a critique. In *Journal of Medieval Latin*, x (2000), pp 115–75.

*4  Early medieval history: political and ecclesiastical*

As a general rule, works that appear in the bibliography of Dáibhí Ó Cróinín, *Early medieval Ireland, 400–1200* (London and New York, 1995) are not listed below.

Aitchison, Nicholas B. Kingship, society and sacrality: rank, power and ideology in early medieval Ireland. In *Traditio*, xlix (1994), pp 45–75.

——*Armagh and the royal centres in early medieval Ireland: monuments, cosmology and the past.* Woodbridge, 1994.

Allen, W. E. D. *The poet and the spae-wife: an attempt to reconstruct Al-Ghazal's embassy to the vikings.* Dublin, 1960.

Anderson, Marjorie O. *Kings and kingship in early Scotland.* Edinburgh, 1973. 2nd ed., 1980.

——Dalriada and the creation of the kingdom of the Scots. In Whitelock, McKitterick, & Dumville, *Ire. in early med. Europe*, pp 106–32.

Baillie, M. G. L. Patrick, comets and Christianity. In *Emania*, xiii (1995), pp 69–77.

Bhreathnach, Edel. Killeshin. An Irish monastery surveyed. In *Camb. Med. Celt. Studies*, xxvii (summer 1994), pp 33–47.

——Caput, civitas, oppidum, borg: Tara, a renowned fortress. In *Seanchas Ardmhacha*, xvi, no. 2 (1995), pp 22–6.

——Temoria: caput Scotorum? In *Ériu*, xlvii (1996), pp 67–87.

——Saint Patrick, vikings and Inber Dée—longphort in the early Irish literary tradition. In *Wickow Archaeology and History*, i (1998), pp 36–40.

——The tech midchuarta, the 'house of the mead-circuit': feasting, royal circuits and the king's court in early Ireland. In *Archaeology Ireland*, xii, no. 4 (1998), pp 20–22.

——Authority and supremacy in Tara and its hinterland *c.* 950–1200. In *Discovery Programme Reports 5* (Dublin, 1999), pp 1–24.

——Kings, the kingship of Leinster and the regnal poems of laídshenchas Laigen: a reflection of dynastic politics in Leinster, 650–1150. In Smyth, *Seanchas*, pp 299–312.

Bitel, Lisa M. Women's donations to the churches in early Ireland. In *R.S.A.I. Jn.*, cxiv (1984), pp 5–23.

——Women's monastic enclosures in early Ireland: a study of female spirituality and male monastic mentalities. In *Journal of Medieval History*, xii (1986), pp 15–36.

Bradshaw, Brendan. The wild and woolly west: early Irish Christianity and Latin orthodoxy. In W. J. Sheils and Diana Wood (ed.), *The churches, Ireland and the Irish* (Studies in Church History, 25; Oxford, 1989), pp 1–23.

Byrne, F. J. King and commons in Gaelic Ireland. In Brian Farrell (ed.), *The Irish parliamentary tradition* (Dublin, 1973), pp 26–36.

——MacNeill the historian. In F. X. Martin and F. J. Byrne, *The scholar revolutionary* (Shannon, 1973), pp 15–36.

——A note on Trim and Sletty. In *Peritia*, iii (1984), pp 318–19.

——Irland in der europäischen Geisteswelt des 8. Jahrhundert. In Dopsch & Juffinger, *Virgil von Salzburg*, pp 45–51.

——The trembling sod: Ireland in 1169. In *N.H.I.*, ii, 1–42.

——Note on Old Kilcullen. Appendix to Herity in Rynne, *Figures from the past*, pp 127–9.

Byrne, Paul F. The community of Clonard from the sixth to the twelfth centuries. In *Peritia*, iv (1985), pp 157–73.

——Ciannachta Breg before Síl nÁeda Sláine. In Smyth, *Seanchas*, pp 121–6.

Byrnes, Michael. The Árd Ciannachta in Adomnán's *Vita Columbae*: a reflection of Iona's attitude to the Síl nÁeda Sláine in the late seventh century. In Smyth, *Seanchas*, pp 127–36.

Clarke, H. B. The bloodied eagle: the vikings and development of Dublin, 841–1014. In *Ir. Sword*, xviii (1991), pp 91–119.

——The vikings in Ireland: a historian's perspective. In *Archaeology Ireland*, ix, no. 3 (1995), pp 7–9.

Corish, Patrick J. The early Irish church in the western patriarchate. In Ní Chatháin & Richter, *Ire. & Europe*, pp 9–15.

Culleton, Edward. The rise and fall of Norse Wexford. In *Journal of the Wexford Historical Society*, xiv (1992–3), pp 151–9.

Curran, Michael. Cathedral and monastic office in Ireland. In *Milltown Studies*, ii (1978), pp 42–57.

Davies, R. R. *The age of conquest: Wales 1063–1415*. Oxford, 1987.

Davies, Wendy. Clerics as rulers: some implications of the terminology of ecclesiastical authority in early medieval Ireland. In N. Brooks (ed.), *Latin and the vernacular languages in early medieval Britain* (Leicester, 1982), pp 81–97.

Dempsey, G. T. Aldhelm of Malmesbury and the Irish. In *R.I.A. Proc.*, xcic (1999), sect. C, pp 1–22.

de Paor, Liam. The aggrandisement of Armagh. In *Historical Studies*, viii (Dublin, 1971), pp 95–110.

——The coming of Christianity. In idem (ed.), *The coming of Christianity* (Cork and Dublin, 1986; reprinted 1991), pp 20–30.

——The history of the monastic site of Inis Cealtra, Co. Clare. In *N. Munster Antiq. Jn.*, xxxvii (1996), pp 21–32.

de Pontfarcy, Yolande. A note on the two dates given for the foundation of Baltinglass. In *R.S.A.I.Jn.*, cxviii (1988), p. 163.

Doherty, Charles. The basilica in early Ireland. In *Peritia* iii (1984), pp 310–15.

——Ulster before the Normans: ancient myth and early history. In C. Brady, M. O'Dowd, and B. Walker (ed.), *Ulster: an illustrated history* (London, 1989), pp 13–43.

——Zur Struktur der frühen Kirche in Irland. In Johannes Erichsen and Evamaria Brockhoff (ed.), *Kilian, Mönch aus Irland, ü: Aufsätze* (Munich, 1989), pp 29–37.

——The vikings in Ireland: a review. In Clarke, Ní Mhaonaigh, & Ó Floinn, *Ire. & Scandinavia*, pp 288–330.

——Cluain Dolcáin: a brief note. In Smyth, *Seanchas*, pp 182–8.

Doyle, Ian. The foundation of the Cistercian abbey of Dunbrody, Co. Wexford, and its historical context. In *Journal of the Wexford Historical Society*, xiv (1992–3), pp 81–91.

Duffy, Seán. Irishmen and Islesmen in the kingdoms of Dublin and Man, 1052–1171. In *Ériu*, xliii (1992), pp 93–133.

——Pre-Norman Dublin: capital of Ireland? In *History Ireland*, i, no. 4 (winter 1993), pp 13–18.

Duffy, Seán. Ostmen, Irish and Welsh in the eleventh century. In *Peritia*, ix (1995), pp 378–96.

——*Ireland in the middle ages*. Dublin, 1997.

——Ireland and Scotland, 1014–1169: contacts and caveats. In Smyth, *Seanchas*, pp 348–56.

Dumville, David. An episode in Edmund Campion's 'Historie of Ireland'. In *Éigse*, xvi (1975–6), pp 131–2.

——Some British aspects of the earliest Irish Christianity. In Ní Chatháin & Richter, *Ire. & Europe*, pp 16–24.

——Two troublesome abbots. In *Celtica*, xxi (1990), pp 146–52.

——(ed.). *Saint Patrick A.D. 493–1993*. Woodbridge, 1993. Includes articles by Lesley Abrams, T. M. Charles-Edwards, Alicia Corrêa, K. R. Dark, and David Dumville.

——Derry, Iona, England and the governance of the Columban church. In Gerard O'Brien (ed.), *Derry and Londonderry: history and society* (Dublin, 1999), pp 91–114.

Duncan, Archibald. Bede, Iona, and the Picts. In R. R. C. Davis and J. M. Wallace-Hadrill (ed.), *The writing of history in the middle ages* (Oxford, 1981), pp 1–42.

Charles-Edwards, T. M. Bede, the Irish and the Britons. In *Celtica*, xv (1983), pp 42–52.

——'The continuation of Bede', *s.a.* 750: high-kings, kings of Tara and 'Bretwaldas'. In Smyth, *Seanchas*, pp 137–45.

——Geis, prophecy, omen and oath. In *Celtica*, xxiii (1999), pp 38–59.

——*Early Christian Ireland*. Cambridge, 2000.

Enright, Michael J. Royal succession and abbatial prerogative in Adomnán's *Vita Columbae*. In *Peritia*, iv (1985), pp 83–103.

——*Iona, Tara, and Soissons: the origin of the royal anointing ritual*. Berlin, 1985. (Arbeiten zur Frühmittelalterforschung, Bd. 17).

Etchingham, Colmán. The implications of *paruchia*. In *Ériu*, xliv (1993), pp 139–62.

——*Viking raids on Irish church settlements in the ninth century*. Maynooth, 1996. (Maynooth Monograph Series, I.)

——*Church organisation in Ireland A.D. 650 to 1000*. Maynooth, 1999.

——Bishops in Ireland and Wales in the early middle ages: some comparisons. In John R. Guy and W. E. Neely (ed.), *Contrasts and comparisons: studies in Irish and Welsh church history* (Llandysul, 1999), pp 7–25.

——Episcopal hierarchy in Connacht and Tairdelbach Ua Conchobair. In *Galway Arch. Soc. Jn.*, lii (2000), pp 13–29.

FitzPatrick, Elizabeth. Raiding and warring in monastic Ireland. In *History Ireland*, i, no. 3 (1993), pp 13–18.

——The inauguration of Tairdelbach Ó Conchobair at Áth an Termoinn. In *Peritia*, xii (1998), pp 351–8.

——The early church in Offaly. In William Nolan and Timothy P. O'Neill (ed.), *Offaly: history and society* (Dublin, 1998), pp 93–130.

Flanagan, M. T. Mac Dalbaig, a Leinster chieftain. In *R.S.A.I. Jn.*, cxi (1981), pp 5–13.

—— Strongbow, Henry II and Anglo-Norman intervention in Ireland. In John Gillingham and J. C. Holt (ed.), *War and government in the middle ages: essays in
honour of J. O. Prestwich* (Woodbridge, 1984), pp 62–77.

—— Henry II and the kingdom of Uí Fáeláin. In Bradley, *Settlement & society*,
pp 229–40.

—— *Historia Gruffud vab Kenan* and the origins of Balrothery, Co. Dublin. In *Camb.
Med. Celt. Studies*, xxviii (winter 1994), pp 71–94.

—— Irish and Anglo-Norman warfare in twelfth-century Ireland. In Thomas
Bartlett and Keith Jeffery (ed.), *A military history of Ireland* (Cambridge, 1996),
pp 52–75.

Fradenburg, L. O. (ed.). *Women and sovereignty*. Edinburgh, 1992.

Frame, Robin. *The political development of the British Isles, 1100–1400.* Oxford, 1990.

Geary, Patrick. Insular religion [review article]. In *Journal of British Studies*, xxxii,
no. 1 (1993), pp 71–6.

Gwynn, Aubrey. Some notes on the history of Ardmore. In *Ardmore Journal*,
x (1993), pp 13–16.

Hamlin, Ann. The early Irish church: problems of identification. In Nancy Edwards
and Alan Lane (ed.), *The early church in Wales and the west* (Oxford, 1992),
pp 138–44.

—— The early church in County Down to the twelfth century. In Lindsay Proudfoot (ed.), *Down: history and society* (Dublin, 1997), pp 47–70.

—— The early church in Tyrone to the twelfth century. In Charles Dillon
and Henry A. Jefferies (ed.), *Tyrone: history and society* (Dublin, 2000),
pp 85–126.

Hanson, R. P. C. *Saint Patrick: his origins and career.* Oxford, 1968.

—— The rule of faith of Victorinus and of Patrick. In O'Meara & Naumann, *Latin
script & letters*, pp 25–36.

—— Germanus and Britain. In *Peritia*, iv (1985), pp 377–9.

Harrison, Kenneth. Episodes in the history of Easter cycles in Ireland. In Whitelock,
McKitterick, & Dumville, *Ire. in early med. Europe*, pp 307–19.

Herbert, Máire. *Rí Érenn, rí Alban*: kingship and identity in the ninth and tenth
centuries. In Simon Taylor (ed.), *Kings, clerics and chronicles in Scotland: essays
in honour of Marjorie Ogilvie Anderson on the occasion of her ninetieth birthday*
(Dublin, 2000), pp 62–72.

Herren, Michael. Mission and monasticism in the Confessio of Patrick. In Ó Corráin,
Breatnach, & McCone, *Sages, saints, & storytellers*, pp 76–85.

Hickey, Elizabeth. *Clonard; the story of an early Irish monastery 520–1202.* Leixlip,
1998.

Hillgarth, J. N. *Christianity and paganism, 350–750: the conversion of western Europe.*
Philadelphia, 1986.

—— Modes of evangelization of western Europe in the seventh century. In Ní
Chatháin & Richter, *Ire. & Christendom*, pp 311–21.

Hudson, Benjamin. The family of Harold Godwinson and the Irish Sea province. In
*R.S.A.I. Jn.*, cix (1979), pp 92–100.

—— The viking and the Irishman. In *Medium Aevum*, lx (1991), pp 257–67.

Hudson, Benjamin. Gaelic princes and Gregorian reform. In Benjamin T. Hudson and Vickie Ziegler (ed.), *Crossed paths: methodological approaches to the Celtic aspect of the European middle ages* (Lanham, Md., 1991), pp 61–82.

——William the Conqueror and Ireland. In *I.H.S.*, xxix, no. 114 (Nov. 1994), pp 145–58.

——*Prophecy of Berchán: Irish and Scottish high-kings of the early middle ages.* Westport, Conn., 1996.

Hughes, Kathleen. The Celtic church: is this a valid concept? In *Camb. Med. Celt. Studies*, i (summer 1981), pp 1–20.

——and Hamlin, Ann. *The modern traveller to the early Irish church.* London, 1977.

James, Edward. Ireland and western Gaul in the Merovingian period. In Whitelock, McKitterick, & Dumville, *Ire. in early med. Europe*, pp 362–86.

——Bede and the tonsure question. In *Peritia*, iii (1984), pp 85–98.

Jaski, Bart. The vikings and the kingship of Tara. In *Peritia*, ix (1995), pp 310–51.

——Kings over overkings: propaganda for pre-eminence in early medieval Ireland. In M. Gosman, A. Vanderjagt, and J. Veentra (ed.), *The propagation of power in the medieval west* (Groningen, 1996), pp 163–76.

——Druim Cett revisited. In *Peritia*, xi (1997), pp 428–31; xii (1998), pp 340–50.

——Early medieval Irish kingship and the Old Testament. In *Early medieval Europe*, vii (1998), pp 329–44.

——*Early Irish kingship and succession.* Dublin, 2000.

Jefferies, Henry Alan. Desmond: the early years, and the career of Cormac Mac-Carthy. In *Cork Hist. Soc. Jn.*, lxxxviii (1983), pp 81–99.

Johnston, Elva. Timahoe and the Loígse: monasticism. In Pádraig G. Lane and William Nolan (ed.), *Laois: history and society* (Dublin, 1999), pp 25–34.

Joyce, Carmel; Hawkes, Jane; and Goldrick, Stephen. Mayo of the Saxons—an introduction to its history and archaeology. In Kevin Barton and Karen Molloy (ed.), *South central Mayo* (Irish Association for Quaternary Studies field guide no. 22; Dublin, 1998), pp 32–9.

Kehnel, Annette. *Clonmacnois—the church and laws of St Ciarán. Change and continuity in an Irish monastic foundation (6th to 16th century).* Münster, 1997. (Vita Regularis, Band 8.)

——Reform als institutionelle Krise: Überlegungen zur irischen Kirchenreform des 12. Jahrhunderts am Beispiel des Klosters Clonmacnois. In *Historisches Jahrbuch*, cxix (1999), pp 84–119.

Kelleher, John V. Uí Maine in the annals and genealogies. In *Celtica*, ix (1971), pp 61–112.

——On a poem about Gormfhlaith. In *Éigse*, xvi (1976), pp 251–4.

——The battle of Móin Mhór, 1151. In *Celtica*, xx (1988), pp 11–17.

Kelly, Eamonn P., and Maas, John. The vikings and the kingdom of Laois. In Pádraig G. Lane and William Nolan (ed.), *Laois: history and society* (Dublin, 1999), pp 123–60.

Lacey, Brian. *Colum Cille and the Columban tradition.* Dublin, 1997.

——County Derry in the early historic period. In Gerard O'Brien (ed.), *Derry and Londonderry: history and society* (Dublin, 1999), pp 115–48.

Mac an Ghallóglaigh, Domhnall. Breifne and its chieftains, 940–1300. In *Bréifne*, vii (1988), pp 523–55.

McCafferty, John. The Céli Dé: monastic reforms in 8th and 9th century Ireland. In *U.C.D. History Review*, iii (1989), pp 12–14.

McCarthy, Daniel, and Ó Cróinín, Dáibhí. The 'lost' Irish 84-year Easter table rediscovered. In *Peritia*, vi–vii (1987–8), pp 227–42.

McNamara, Martin. Monastic schools in Ireland and Northumbria before A.D. 750. In *Milltown Studies*, xxv (1990), pp 19–36.

Mac Niocaill, Gearóid. The background of the battle of Tarbga. In *Celtica*, xi (1976), pp 133–40.

——Die politische Szene Irlands im 8. Jahrhundert: Königtum und Herrschaft. In Dopsch & Juffinger, *Virgil von Salzburg*, pp 38–44.

Mac Shamhráin, Ailbhe S. Prosopographia Glindalachensis: the monastic church of Glendalough and its community, sixth to thirteenth centuries. In *R.S.A.I. Jn.*, cxix (1989), pp 79–97.

——The Uí Muiredaig and the abbacy of Glendalough in the eleventh to thirteenth centuries. In *Camb. Med. Celt. Studies*, xxv (summer 1993), pp 55–76.

——The 'unity' of Cóemgen and Ciarán: a convent between Glendalough and Clonmacnois in the tenth to eleventh centuries. In Ken Hannigan (ed.), *Wicklow: history and society* (Dublin, 1994), pp 139–50.

——*Church and polity in pre-Norman Ireland*. Maynooth, 1996.

——Notulae discutiuntur? The emergence of Clann Cholmáin, sixth–eighth centuries. In Smyth, *Seanchas*, pp 83–97.

——The making of Tír nEogain: Cenél nEogain and the Airgialla from the sixth to the eleventh centuries. In Charles Dillon and Henry A. Jefferies (ed.), *Tyrone: history and society* (Dublin, 2000), pp 55–84.

Milis, L. *L'ordre des chanoines réguliers d'Arrouaise*, i. Bruges, 1969.

Miller, Molly. Hiberni reversuri. In *Antiq. Soc. Scot. Proc.*, cx (1978–80), pp 305–27.

Millett, Benignus. Dioceses in Ireland up to the fifteenth century. In *Seanchas Ardmhacha*, xii (1986), pp 1–42.

Moisl, Hermann. Das Kloster Iona und seine Verbindungen mit dem Kontinent im siebenten und achten Jahrhundert. In Dopsch & Juffinger, *Virgil von Salzburg*, pp 27–37.

——The church and the native tradition of learning in early medieval Ireland. In Ní Chatháin & Richter, *Ire. & Christendom*, pp 258–71.

Nic Aongusa, Bairbre. The monastic hierarchy in twelfth-century Ireland: the case of Kells. In *Ríocht na Midhe*, viii, no. 3 (1990–91), pp 3–20.

Nicholls, K. W. The land of the Leinstermen. In *Peritia*, iii (1984), pp 535–58. Review of A. P. Smyth, *Celtic Leinster* (Dublin, 1982).

Ní Ghabhláin, Sinéad. Church and community in medieval Ireland: the diocese of Kilfenora. In *R.S.A.I. Jn.*, cxxv (1995), pp 61–84.

——The origin of medieval parishes in Gaelic Ireland: the evidence from Kilfenora. In *R.S.A.I. Jn.*, cxxvi (1996), pp 37–61.

Nieke, Margaret R., and Duncan, Holly B. Dalriada: the establishment and maintenance of an early historic kingdom in northern Britain. In Driscoll & Nieke, *Power & politics*, pp 6–21.

O'Carroll, Michael. Our Lady in early medieval Ireland. In Smyth, *Seanchas*, pp 178–81.

Ó Cíobháin, Breandán. Deoisí na hÉireann i ndiaidh Sionaid Cheanannais, 1152: Téacsanna [Texts]. In *Dinnsheanchas*, v (1972–3), pp 52–6. 'Foinsí éagsúla' (various sources), pp 71–85; 'Nótaí téacsa' (textual notes), pp 119–28.

——Liosta Deoisí ón 17ú céad. In *Dinnseanchas*, vi (1974–7), pp 121–3.

——Deoise Ard Mhacha sa Dara Chéad Déag. In *Seanchas Ardmhacha*, ix (1978), pp 51–69.

Ó Conchúir, Donncha. Thoughts on the early Christian church. In *Kerry Arch. Soc. Jn.*, xxvi (1993), pp 93–106.

Ó Corráin, Donnchadh. The career of Diarmait Mac Máel na mBó, king of Leinster. In *Journal of the Old Wexford Society*, iii (1970–71), pp 27–35; iv (1972–3), pp 17–24.

——Caithréim Chellacháin Chaisil: history or propaganda? In *Ériu*, xxv (1974), pp 1–69.

——The Uí Chennsalaig kingship of Leinster, 1072–1126. In *Journal of the Old Wexford Society*, v (1974–5), pp 26–31; vi (1976–7), pp 45–54; vii (1978–9), pp 46–9.

——The families of Corcomroe. In *N. Munster Antiq. Jn.*, xvii (1976[7]), pp 21–30.

——Mael Muire Ua Dúnáin (1040–1117), reformer. In P. de Brún, S. Ó Coileáin and P. Ó Riain (ed.), *Folia Gadelica* (Cork, 1983), pp 47–53.

——Res Celticae. In *Peritia*, iv (1985), pp 390–95; v (1986), pp 461–7.

——Brian Boru and the battle of Clontarf. In Liam de Paor (ed.), *Milestones in Irish history* (Cork, 1986), pp 31–40.

——Diarmait Mac Murrough (1110–71) and the coming of the Anglo-French. In Ciarán Brady (ed.), *Worsted in the game: losers in Irish history* (Dublin, 1989), pp 21–34.

——Early Ireland: directions and redirections. In *Bullán*, i, no. 2 (1994), pp 1–15.

——Viking Ireland—afterthoughts. In Clarke, Ní Mhaonaigh, & Ó Floinn, *Ire. & Scandinavia*, pp 421–52.

——The vikings in Scotland and Ireland in the ninth century. In *Peritia*, xii (1998), pp 296–339.

——Muirchertach Mac Lochlainn and the Circuit of Ireland. In Smyth, *Seanchas*, pp 238–50.

Ó Cróinín, Dáibhí. New light on Palladius? In *Peritia*, iv (1986), pp 276–83.

——*Early medieval Ireland, 400–1200.* London and New York, 1995.

Ó Cuív, Brian. Diarmaid na nGall. In *Éigse*, xvi (1975), pp 135–44.

Ó Duibhir, Peadar. Lorcán Ó Tuathail agus a ré. In Mac Conmara, *An léann eaglasta*, pp 11–18.

——An Mhaighdean Mhuire agus an nua-spioradáltacht. Ibid., pp 70–76.

O'Dwyer, Peter. *Célí Dé: spiritual reform in Ireland, 750–900.* Dublin, 1981.

——The Céli Dé reform. In Ní Chatháin & Richter, *Ire. & Europe*, pp 83–8.

——*Mary: a history of devotion in Ireland.* Dublin, 1988.

Ó Fiaich, Tomás. The early period. In Réamonn Ó Muirí (ed.), *Irish church history today* (Armagh, [1991?]), pp 1–12.

Ó Laoghaire, Diarmuid. An spioradáltacht: an Naomhshacraimint, oilithreachtaí. In Mac Conmara, *An léann eaglasta*, pp 52–69.

——Irish spirituality. In Ní Chatháin & Richter, *Ire. & Europe*, pp 73–82.

——Irish elements in the Catechesis Celtica. In Ní Chatháin & Richter, *Ire. & Christendom*, pp 146–64.

Ó Mordha, P. The medieval kingdom of Mugdorna. In *Clogher Rec.*, vii (1971–2), pp 432–46.

Ó Muraíle, Nollaig. Doire na bhFlann alias Doire Eidhneach: an historical and onomastic survey. In *Studia Hib.*, xx (1980), pp 111–39.

——Some early Connacht population-groups. In Smyth, *Seanchas*, pp 161–77.

O'Rahilly, T. F. Cúán Ua Lothcháin and Corcrán Clérech. In *Celtica*, i, no. 2 (1950), pp 313–17.

Ó Raifeartaigh, T. A rationale for the censuring of Saint Patrick by the *Seniores*. In *Celtica*, xvi (1984), pp 13–33.

Ó Riain, Pádraig. Battle-site and territorial extent in early Ireland. In *Z.C.P.*, xxxiii (1974), pp 67–80.

——Sanctity and politics in Connacht *c.* 1100: the case of St Fursa. In *Camb. Med. Celt. Studies*, xviii (summer 1989), pp 1–14.

——Pagan example and Christian practice: a reconsideration. In D. R. Edel (ed.), *Cultural identity and cultural integration* (Dublin, 1995), pp 144–56.

O'Sullivan, Anne. Saint Brecán of Clare. In *Celtica*, xv (1983), pp 128–39.

Picard, Jean-Michel. The strange death of Guaire mac Áedáin. In Ó Corráin, Breatnach, & McCone, *Sages, saints, & storytellers*, pp 367–75.

——Church and politics in the seventh century: the Irish exile of King Dagobert II. In Picard, *Ire. & northern France*, pp 27–52.

——Princeps and principatus in the early Irish church: a reassessment. In Smyth, *Seanchas*, pp 146–60.

Ó Riain-Raedel, Dagmar. Diarmaid Mac Carthaigh, king of Cork (d. 1185). In *Cork Hist. Soc. Jn.*, xc (1985), pp 26–30.

——German influence on Munster: church and kings in the twelfth century. In Smyth, *Seanchas*, pp 323–30.

Richter, Michael. Irland und Europa: die Kirche im Frühmittelalter. In Ní Chatháin & Richter, *Ire. & Europe*, pp 409–32.

——The interpretation of medieval Irish history. In *I.H.S.*, xxix, no. 95 (May 1985), pp 289–98.

——The European dimension of Irish history in the eleventh and twelfth centuries. In *Peritia*, iv (1985), pp 328–45.

——Practical aspects of the conversion of the Anglo-Saxons. In Ní Chatháin & Richter, *Ire. & Christendom*, pp 362–76.

——Models of conversion in the early middle ages. In D. R. Edel (ed.), *Cultural identity and cultural integration* (Dublin, 1995), pp 116–28.

Ryan, John. *Toirdelbach Ó Conchubair*. Dublin, 1967. (O'Donnell Lecture, N.U.I.)

Sanderlin, Sally. The monastery of Lismore, A.D. 638–1111. In William Nolan and Thomas P. Power (ed.), *Waterford: history and society* (Dublin, 1992), pp 27–48.

Sawyer, Peter. The vikings and Ireland. In Whitelock, McKitterick, & Dumville, *Ire. in early med. Europe*, pp 345–61.

Scherman, Katharine. *The flowering of Ireland: saints, scholars and kings*. Boston and Toronto, 1981.

Schlegel, Donald M. The origin of the Three Collas and the fall of Emain. In *Clogher Rec.*, xvi, no. 2 (1998), pp 159–81.

Scott, B. G. 'Tribes' and 'tribalism' in early Ireland. In *Ogam*, xxii–xxv (1970–73), pp 197–205.

Sharpe, Richard. Churches and communities in early medieval Ireland: towards a pastoral model. In John Blair and Richard Sharpe (ed.), *Pastoral care before the parish* (Leicester, 1992), pp 81–109.

—— The thriving of Dalriada. In Simon Taylor (ed.), *Kings, clerics and chronicles in Scotland: essays in honour of Marjorie Ogilvie Anderson on the occasion of her ninetieth birthday* (Dublin, 2000), pp 47–61.

Silke, John J. Some notes on early Christianity in Co. Donegal. In *Donegal Annual*, xxxix (1987), pp 4–16.

—— *Two saints*. Dublin, 1998.

Smyth, A. P. The Black Foreigners of York and the White Foreigners of Dublin. In *Saga-Book Viking Society*, xix (1972–6), pp 111–17.

—— *Scandinavian kings in the British Isles 850–880*. Oxford, 1977.

Sproule, David. Origins of the Éoganachta. In *Ériu*, xxxv (1984), pp 31–8.

Swift, Cathy. Christian communities in fifth- and sixth-century Ireland. In *Trowel*, vii (1996), pp 11–19.

—— The local context of *Óenach Tailten*. In *Ríocht na Midhe*, xi (2000), pp 24–50.

Thompson, E. A. *St Germanus of Auxerre and the end of Roman Britain*. Woodbridge, 1988.

Thornton, David E. Early medieval Louth: the kingdom of Conaille Muirtheimne. In *Louth Arch. Soc. Jn.*, xxiv, no. 1 (1997), pp 139–50.

Warner, Richard B. The archaeology of early historic Irish kingship. In Driscoll & Nieke, *Power & politics*, pp 47–68.

Whitelock, Dorothy. Bishop Ecgred, Pehtred and Niall. In Whitelock, McKitterick, & Dumville, *Ire. in early med. Europe*, pp 47–68.

Wilson, P. A. St Patrick and Irish Christian origins. In *Studia Celt.*, xiv/xv (1979–80), pp 344–79.

Wormald, Patrick. Celtic and Anglo-Saxon kingship: some further thoughts. In P. Szarmach (ed.), *Sources of Anglo-Saxon culture* (Studies in Medieval Culture, xx; Kalamazoo, 1986), pp 151–83.

5   *Social, cultural, and economic history*

Bernier, G. Les navires celtiques du haut moyen âge. In *Études Celt.*, xvi (1979), pp 287–91.

Binchy, D. A. Brewing in eighth-century Ireland. In Scott, *Studies on early Ire.*, pp 3–6.

Bradley, John. The early development of the medieval town of Kilkenny. In William Nolan and Kevin Whelan (ed.), *Kilkenny: history and society* (Dublin, 1990), pp 63–74.

—— Killaloe: a pre-Norman borough? In *Peritia*, viii (1994), pp 170–79.

Clarke, H. B. Proto-towns and towns in Ireland and Britain in the ninth and tenth centuries. In Clarke, Ní Mhaonaigh, & Ó Floinn, *Ire. & Scandinavia*, pp 331–80.

—— (ed.). *Medieval Dublin: the living city*. Dublin, 1990.

—— (ed.). *Medieval Dublin: the making of a metropolis*. Dublin, 1990.

Danaher, Kevin. Irish folk tradition and the Celtic calendar. In R. O'Driscoll (ed.), *Celtic consciousness* (Toronto, 1982), pp 217–42.

Davies, Wendy. Unciae: Land measurement in the Liber Landavanesis. In *Agricultural History Review*, xxii (1973), pp 111–21.

—— Celtic women in the early middle ages. In B. Cameron and A. Kuhrt (ed.), *Images of women in antiquity* (London and Canberra, 1983), pp 145–66.

de Búrca, Seán. Gobbán saer, the craft artificer. In W. Meid (ed.), *Beiträge zur Indogermanistik und Keltologie* (Innsbruck, 1967), pp 145–6.

de Paor, Liam. The viking towns of Ireland. In Bo Almqvist and David Greene, *Proceedings of the Seventh Viking Congress* (Dublin, 1976), pp 29–37.

Doherty, Charles. Exchange and trade in early medieval Ireland. In *R.S.A.I. Jn.*, cx (1980), pp 67–89.

—— Some aspects of hagiography as a source for Irish economic history. In *Peritia*, i (1980), pp 300–28.

—— The use of relics in early Ireland. In Ní Chatháin & Richter, *Ire. & Europe*, pp 89–101.

—— The monastic town in early medieval Ireland. In Clarke & Simms, *Urban origins*, pp 45–75.

Charles-Edwards, T. M. Irish warfare before 1100. In Thomas Bartlett and Keith Jeffery (ed.), *A military history of Ireland* (Cambridge, 1996), pp 26–51.

Eogan, George. Life and living at Lagore. In Smyth, *Seanchas*, pp 64–82.

Finlay, Nyree. Outside of life: traditions of infant burial in Ireland from cillín to cist. In *World Archaeology*, xxxi, no. 3 (2000), pp 407–22.

Finney, Jon. Warfare in late pagan and early Christian Ireland *c.*500 A.D. to *c.*750. In *Medieval Life*, ix (1998), pp 3–10.

Fox, J. R. Kinship and land tenure on Tory Island. In *Ulster Folklife*, xii (1966), pp 1–17.

Gerriets, Marilyn. The organization of exchange in early Christian Ireland. In *Journal of Economic History*, xli (1981), pp 171–6.

—— Kingship and exchange in pre-viking Ireland. In *Camb. Med. Celt. Studies*, xiii (summer 1987), pp 39–72.

Graham, B. J. Secular urban origins in early medieval Ireland. In *Irish Economic and Social History*, xvi (1989), pp 5–22.

Heckett, Elizabeth. Some Hiberno-Norse headcoverings from Fishamble Street and St John's Lane, Dublin. In *Textile History*, xviii (1987), pp 157–74.

Holm, Poul. The slave trade of Dublin, ninth to twelfth centuries. In *Peritia*, v (1986), pp 317–45.

Jankuhn, Herbert. Trade and settlement in central and northern Europe up to and during the viking period. In *In R.S.A.I. Jn.*, cxii (1982), pp 18–50.

Jesch, Judith. *Women in the viking age*. Woodbridge, 1994.

Kavanagh, Rhoda. The horse in viking Ireland: some observations. In Bradley, *Settlement & society*, pp 89–122.

Kelly, Fergus. *Early Irish farming*. Dublin, 1997.

Killeen, J. F. Fear an énais. In *Celtica*, ix (1971), pp 202–4.

Kristjánsson, Jónas. Ireland and the Irish in Icelandic tradition. In Clarke, Ní Mhaonaigh, & Ó Floinn, *Ire. & Scandinavia*, pp 259–76.

Lanigan Wood, Helen. Women in myths and early depictions. In E. Ní Chuileannáin (ed.), *Irish women* (Dublin, 1985), pp 13–34.

Lucas, A. T. The social role of relics and reliquaries in ancient Ireland. In *R.S.A.I. Jn.*, cxvi (1986), pp 5–37.

——Cattle in ancient Ireland. Kilkenny, 1989. (Studies in Irish Archaeology and History.)

Lysaght, Patricia. The supernatural woman. In E. Ní Chuilleanáin (ed.), *Irish women* (Dublin, 1985), pp 25–36.

——The Banshee: the Irish supernatural death-messenger. Dublin, 1986.

Mac Cana, Proinsias. The *topos* of the single sandal in Irish tradition. In *Celtica*, x (1973), pp 160–66.

McCone, Kim. Werewolves, cyclops, *díberga* and *fíanna:* juvenile delinquency in early Ireland. In *Camb. Med. Celt. Studies*, xii (winter 1986), pp 1–22.

MacCurtain, Margaret. The historical image. In E. Ní Chuilleanáin (ed.), *Irish women* (Dublin, 1985), pp 37–50.

Mac Eoin, Gearóid. The *briugu* in early Irish society. In *Z.C.P.*, xlix–l (1997), pp 482–93.

Mac Mathúna, Liam. 'Geilt' sa chiall 'Duine lomnocht'. In *Éigse*, xviii (1980), pp 39–42.

Mac Niocaill, Gearóid. Investment in early Irish agriculture. In Scott, *Studies on early Ire.*, pp 7–9.

Mitchell, G. F. *Archaeology and environment in early Dublin*. R.I.A., Dublin, 1987. (Medieval Dublin Excavations, Series C, i.)

Morris, Carole A. Early medieval separate-bladed shovels from Ireland. In *R.S.A.I. Jn.*, cxi (1981), pp 50–69.

Ní Chatháin, Próinséas. Swineherds, seers, and druids. In *Studia Celt.*, xiv–xv (1979–80), pp 200–11.

——Traces of the cult of the horse in early Irish tradition. In *Journal of Indo-European Studies*, xix (1991), pp 123–31.

——Aquitaine in early Irish sources. In J.-M. Picard (ed), *Aquitaine and Ireland in the middle ages* (Dublin, 1995), pp 137–46.

Ní Dhonnchadha, Máirín. The *Lex Innocentium*: Adomnán's law for women, clerics and youths. In M. O'Dowd and S. Wichert (ed.), *Chattel, servant or citizen: women's status in church, state and society* (Belfast, 1995), pp 58–69.

O'Brien, A. F. Commercial relations between Aquitaine and Ireland c.1000 to c.1550. In J.-M. Picard (ed), *Aquitaine and Ireland in the middle ages* (Dublin, 1995), pp 31–80.

Ó Corráin, Donnchadh. Corcu Loígde: land and families. In Patrick O'Flanagan and Cornelius Buttimer (ed.), *Cork: history and society* (Dublin, 1993), pp 63–81.

Ó Crualaoich, Gearóid. Continuity and adaptation in legends of Cailleach Bhéarra. In *Béaloideas*, lvi (1988), pp 153–78.

Ó Cuív, Brian. The surname *Ó Caiside*. In *Ériu*, xxxvii (1986), p. 176.

——Personal names as an indicator of relations between native Irish and settlers in the viking period. In Bradley, *Settlement & society*, pp 79–88.

Ohkuma, Keishiro. Kingship in ancient Ireland. In *Journal of Indo-European Studies*, xiv (1986), pp 231–45.

Partridge, Angela. Wild men and wailing women. In *Éigse*, xviii (1980), pp 25–37.

Powell, Timothy E. The idea of the three orders of society and social stratification in early medieval Ireland. In *I.H.S.*, xxix, no. 116 (Nov. 1995), pp 475–89.

Sayers, William. Early Irish attitudes toward hair and beards, baldness and tonsure. In *Z.C.P.*, xliv (1991), pp 154–89.

——Varia VII. The deficient ruler as avian exile: Nebuchadnezzar and Suibhne Geilt. In *Ériu*, xliii (1992), pp 217–20.

Scott, B. G. Varia II. 1 Early Irish *cáer*; 2 *Iarn aithlegtha*; 3 *crédumae*. In *Ériu*, xxxii (1981), pp 153–7.

——Goldworking terms in early Irish writings. In *Z.C.P.*, xxviii (1981), pp 242–54.

Spears, Arthur. 'An scuab as Fánaid' and the XIth century pandemonium. In *Donegal Annual*, xxxv (1983), pp 5–20.

Swift, Catherine. Pagan monuments and Christian legal centres in early Meath. In *Ríocht na Midhe*, ix, no. 2 (1996), pp 1–26.

——The local context of Óenach Tailten. In *Ríocht na Midhe*, xi (2000), pp 24–50.

——Óenach Tailten, the Blackwater Valley and the Uí Néill kings of Tara. In Smyth, *Seanchas*, pp 109–20.

Thornton, David E. Clann Eruilb: Irish or Scandinavian? In *I.H.S.*, xxx, no. 118 (Nov. 1996), pp 161–6.

Valante, Mary A. Reassessing the Irish 'monastic town'. In *I.H.S.*, xxxi, no. 121 (May 1998), pp 1–18.

——Dublin's economic relations with hinterland and periphery in the later viking age. In Seán Duffy (ed.), *Medieval Dublin I: proceedings of the Friends of Medieval Dublin Symposium 1999* (Dublin, 2000), pp 69–83.

Wallace, Patrick F. *Garrda* and *airbeada*: the plot thickens in viking Dublin. In Smyth, *Seanchas*, pp 261–74.

## 6  The Irish peregrinatio

Angenendt, Arnold. Die irische Peregrinatio und ihre Auswirkungen auf dem Kontinent vor dem Jahre 800. In Löwe, *Die Iren*, i, 52–79.

Autenrieth, Johanne. Irische Handschriftenüberlieferung auf der Reichenau. In Löwe, *Die Iren*, ii, 903–15.

Binchy, D. A. The Irish Benedictine congregation in medieval Germany. In *Studies*, xviii (1929), pp 194–210.

Blanke, Friedrich. Neue Beobachtungen zum Missionswerk Columbans des Jüngeren. In *Evangel. Missions-Magazin*, xcv (1951), pp 164–79; xcvi (1952), pp 172–86; xcvi (1953), pp 165–80.

Bowen, E. G. *Saints, seaways, and settlements in the Celtic lands*. Cardiff, 1969.

Boyer, Blanche B. The insular contribution to medieval literary tradition on the Continent. In *Classical Philology*, xlii (1947), pp 209–22; xliii (1948), pp 31–9.

Breatnach, Pádraig A. The origins of the Irish monastic tradition at Ratisbon (Regensburg). In *Celtica*, xiii (1980), pp 58–77.

——Über Beginn und Eigenart der irischen Mission auf dem Kontinent einschließlich der irischen Missionare in Bayern. In Dopsch & Juffinger, *Virgil von Salzburg*, pp 84–91.

——Irish churchmen in pre-Carolingian Europe. In *Seanchas Ardmhacha*, xi (1985), pp 319–30.

Brunner, Karl. Auf den Spuren verlorener Traditionen. In *Peritia*, ii (1983), pp 1–22.

Bullough, Donald A. Columba, Adomnan and Iona. In *Scottish Historical Review*, xliii (1964), pp 111–30; xliv (1965), pp 17–33.

——The missions to the English and Picts and their heritage (to *c*.800). In Löwe, *Die Iren*, pp 80–89.

——The career of Columbanus. In M. Lapidge (ed.), *Columbanus: studies on the Latin writings*. Woodbridge, 1997.

Bulst, Neithard. Irisches Mönchtum und cluniazensische Klosterreform. In Löwe, *Die Iren*, ii, 958–69.

Campbell, James. The debt of the early English church to Ireland. In Ní Chatháin & Richter, *Ire. & Christendom*, pp 332–46.

Chute, Desmond. On St Columban of Bobbio. In *Downside Review*, lxvii (1949), pp 170–82, 304–14.

*Colombano, pioniere di civilizzazione cristiana europea; atti del Convegno Internationale di Studi Colombaniani, Bobbio 1965*. Bobbio, 1973.

Contreni, John J. The Irish colony at Laon during the time of John Scotus. In *Jean Scot Erigène et l'histoire de la philosophie* (Colloques internationaux du Centre National de la Recherche Scientifique, dlxi; Paris, 1977), pp 59–67. Reprinted in idem, *The cathedral school of Laon from 850 to 930, its manuscripts and masters*. Munich, 1978. (Münchener Beiträge zur Mediävistik und Renaissance-Forschung, xxix.)

Contreni, John J. Inharmonious harmony: education in the Carolingian world. In *Annals of Scholarship: metastudies in the humanities and social sciences*, i (1980), pp 81–96.

——John Scottus, Martin Hibernensis, the liberal arts, and teaching. In Herren, *Insular Latin studies*, pp 23–44.

——The Irish in western Carolingian Europe (according to James F. Kenney and Bern, Burgerbibliothek 363). In Löwe, *Die Iren*, ii, 758–98.

——Carolingian biblical studies. In U. R. Blumenthal (ed.), *Carolingian essays* (Washington, 1983), pp 71–98.

——The Carolingian renaissance. In W. T. Treadgold (ed.), *Renaissances before the renaissance* (Stanford, 1984), pp 69–74.

——Sedulius on grammar. In *Peritia*, iv (1985), pp 387–94.

——The Irish contribution to the European classroom. In Evans, Griffith, & Jope, *Proc. 7th Congress*, pp 79–90.

Cross, J. E. The influence of Irish texts and traditions on the Old English Martyrology. In *R.I.A. Proc.*, lxxxi (1981), sect. C, pp 173–92.

Dienemann, Joachim. *Der Kult des heiligen Kilian im 8. und 9. Jahrhundert: Beiträge zur geistigen und politischen Entwicklung der Karolingerzeit.* Würzburg, 1955.

Dopsch, Heinz. Die Salzburger Slawenmission im 8./9. Jahrhundert und der Anteil der Iren. In Ní Chatháin & Richter, *Ire. & Christendom*, pp 421–44.

Düchting, Reinhard. Sedulius Scottus—ein 'Heiliger Drei König mehr' aus dem Abendland. In Löwe, *Die Iren*, ii, 866–75.

Duft, Johannes. Iromanie-Irophobie. Fragen um die frühmittelalterliche Irenmission exemplifiziert an St Gallen und Alemannien. In *Zeitschrift für Schweizerische Kirchengeschichte*, i (1956), pp 241–62.

——Irische Handschriftenüberlieferung in St. Gallen. In Löwe, *Die Iren*, ii, 916–40.

Dunleavy, Gareth. Old Ireland, Scotland and Northumbria. In R. McNally (ed.), *Old Ireland* (Dublin, 1965), pp 173–99.

Eberl, Immo. Das Iren-Kloster Honau und seine Regel. In Löwe, *Die Iren*, i, 219–38.

Charles-Edwards, T. M. The social background to Irish *peregrinatio*. In *Celtica*, xi (1976), pp 43–59.

——Bede, the Irish and the Britons. In *Celtica*, xv (1983), pp 42–52.

Flachenecker, Helmut. *Schottenklöster: Irische Benediktinerkonvente in hochmittelalterlichen Deutschland.* Paderborn, 1994. (Quellen und Forschungen aus dem Gebiet der Geschichte, neue Folge 18.)

Forstner, Karl. Das Salzburger Skriptorium unter Virgil und das Verbrüderungsbuch von St Peter. In Dopsch & Juffinger, *Virgil von Salzburg*, pp 135–40.

Fowkes, R. A. Irish and Germans on the Continent in the middle ages. In *Z.C.P.*, xlix–l (1997), pp 204–12.

Gamber, Klaus. Irische Liturgiebücher und ihre Verbreitung auf dem Kontinent. In Löwe, *Die Iren*, pp 536–48.

Ganz, David. Codex Laudenensis 468. In *Peritia*, iv (1985), pp 360–70.

——The Luxeuil Prophets and Merovingian missionary strategies. In *Beinecke Studies in Early Manuscripts* (*Yale University Library Gazette*, lxvi (1991)), pp 105–17.

Gibson, M., and Nelson, J., with Ganz, D. (ed.). *Charles the Bald, court and kingdom.* Oxford, 1981. (Brit. Arch. Reps., International Series, ci.)

Gwynn, Aubrey. Ireland and the Continent in the eleventh century. In *I.H.S.*, viii, no. 31 (Mar. 1953), pp 193–216. Reprinted in idem, *The Irish church in the eleventh and twelfth centuries*, ed. Gerard O'Brien (Dublin, 1992), pp 34–49.

——Some notes on the history of the Irish and Scottish Benedictine monasteries in Germany. In *Innes Review*, v (1954), pp 5–27.

Hammermayer, Ludwig. Zur Geschichte der Schottenabtei St Jakob in Regensburg. Neue Quellen aus schottischen Archiven. In *Zeitschrift für bayerische Landesgeschichte*, xxii (1959), pp 42–76.

——Neue Beiträge zur Geschichte des Schottenklosters St Jakob in Erfurt. In *Jahrbuch für den Bistum Mainz*, viii (1960), pp 205–33.

——Die irischen Benediktiner 'Schottenklöster' in Deutschland und ihr institutioneller Zusammenschluß vom 12. bis 16. Jahrhundert. In *Studien und Mitteilun-*

gen zur Geschichte des Benediktiner-Ordens und seiner Zweige, lxxxvii, Heft 3–4 (1976), pp 249–337.

Hennig, John. Irish saints in the liturgical and artistic tradition of central Europe. In *I.E.R.*, 5th ser., lxi (1943), pp 181–92.

——Irish monastic activities in eastern Europe. In *I.E.R.*, 5th ser., lxv (1945), pp 394–400.

——Ireland and Germany in the tradition of St Kilian. In *I.E.R.*, 5th ser., lxxvii (1952), pp 21–33.

——Irlandkunde in der festländischen Tradition irischer Heiliger. In Löwe, *Die Iren*, i, 686–96.

Horn, Walter, and Born, Ernest. *The monastery of St Gall*. 3 vols. Berkeley, 1989.

Ireland, Colin. Boisil: an Irishman hidden in the works of Bede. In *Peritia*, v (1986), pp 400–03.

——Aldfrith of Northumbria and the Irish genealogies. In *Celtica*, xxii (1991), pp 64–78.

Jacobsen, Peter Christian. Carmina Columbani. In Löwe, *Die Iren*, i, 434–67.

James, Edward. Archaeology and the Merovingian monastery. In Clarke & Brennan, *Columbanus*, pp 33–58.

——Ireland and western Gaul in the Merovingian period. In Whitelock, McKitterick, & Dumville, *Ire. in early med. Europe*, pp 362–86.

Jäschke, Kurt U. Kolumban von Luxeuil und sein Wirken im alemannischen Raum. In Arno Borst (ed.), *Mönchtum, Episkopat und Adel zur Gründungszeit des Klosters Reichenau* (Vorträge und Forschungen, xx; Sigmaringen, 1974), pp 77–130.

Kahl, Hans-Dietrich. Zur Rolle der Iren im ostlichen Vorfeld des agilolfingischen und frühkarolingischen Baiern. In Löwe, *Die Iren*, i, 375–99.

——Virgil und die Salzburger Slawenmission. In Dopsch & Juffinger, *Virgil von Salzburg* (Salzburg, 1985), pp 112–21.

Kerlouégan, François. Présence et culte de clercs irlandais et bretons entre Loire et Mons Jura. In J.-M. Picard (ed), *Aquitaine and Ireland in the middle ages* (Dublin, 1995), pp 189–206.

Koch, Margrit. *Sankt Fridolin und sein Biograph Balther: irische Heilige in der literarischen Darstellung des Mittelalters*. Zurich, 1959.

Koller, Heinrich. Die Iren und die Christianisierung der Baiern. In Löwe, *Die Iren*, pp 342–74.

Kottje, Raymond. Beiträge der frühmittelalterlichen Iren zum gemeinsamen europäischen Haus. In *Historisches Jahrbuch*, cxii (1992), pp 3–22.

Leonardi, Claudio. Gli irlandesi in Italia: Dungal e la controversia iconoclastica. In Löwe, *Die Iren*, i, 746–57.

Maestri, Annibale. *Il culto di San Columbano in Italia*. Piacenza, 1955.

Marenbon, John. Wulfad, Charles the Bald and John Scottus Eriugena. In M. Gibson and J. Nelson (ed.), *Charles the Bald, court and kingdom* (Oxford, 1981), pp 275–83.

Maror, Theodor. Die Anfänge der Reichenau. In *Zeitschrift für die Geschichte des Oberrheins*, ci (1953), pp 305–52.

Merdrignac, Bernard. Bretons et Irlandais en France du Nord—vi[e]–viiie siècles. In Picard, *Ire. & northern France*, pp 119–42.

Meyer-Sickendiek, Ingeborg. *Gottes gelehrte Vaganten: auf den Spuren der irischen Mission und Kultur in Europa*. Stuttgart, 1980.

Müller, Wolfgang. Der Anteil der Iren an der Christianisierung der Alemannen. In Löwe, *Die Iren*, i, 330–41.

Ní Mheara, Róisín. *In search of Irish saints: the peregrinatio pro Christo*. Dublin, 1994.

Ó Cróinín, Dáibhí. The Irish abroad in medieval Europe. In *Peritia*, v (1986), pp 445–51.

——The Irish missions. In Fabbri Bompani (ed.), *I Celti/ The Celts* (Venice, 1990), pp 659–62.

——The Irish as mediators of antique culture on the Continent. In P. Butzer and D. Lohrmann (ed.), *Science in western and eastern civilization in Carolingian times* (Basel, 1993), pp 41–52.

Ó Fiaich, Tomás. Virgils Werdegang in Irland und sein Weg auf den Kontinent. In Dopsch & Juffinger, *Virgil von Salzburg*, pp 17–26.

——Virgil's Irish background and departure for France. In *Seanchas Ardmhacha*, xi (1985), pp 301–17.

——*Gaelscrínte san Eoraip*. Dublin, 1986.

——and Connolly, Turlough. *Irish cultural influence in Europe, 6th to 12th century*. Dublin, 1967.

Ó Mara, Róisín. Die heilige Brigid und ihr Kult im Salzburger Land. In Dopsch & Juffinger, *Virgil von Salzburg*, pp 381–3.

Ó Néill, Pádraig P. Bonifaz und Virgil—Konflikt zweier Kulturen. In Dopsch & Juffinger, *Virgil von Salzburg*, pp 76–83.

——Irish cultural influence in Northumbria: the first thirty years, A.D. 635–664. In Benjamin T. Hudson and Vickie Ziegler (ed.), *Crossed paths: methodological approaches to the Celtic aspect of the European middle ages* (Lanham, Md., 1991), pp 10–23.

——An Irishman at Chartres in the twelfth century—the evidence of Oxford, Bodleian Library MS Auct.F. III. 15. In *Ériu*, xlviii (1997), pp 1–36.

Ó Riain-Raedel, Dagmar. Irish kings and bishops in the memoria of the German Schottenklöster. In Ní Chatháin & Richter, *Ire. & Europe*, pp 390–408.

——Spuren irischer Gebetsverbrüderungen zur Zeit Virgils. In Dopsch & Juffinger, *Virgil von Salzburg*, pp 141–6.

Prinz, Friedrich. *Frühes Mönchtum im Frankenreich. Kultur und Gesellschaft in Gallien, den Rheinlanden und Bayern am Beispiel der monastischen Entwicklung (4. bis 8. Jahrhundert)*. Munich, 1965.

——Monastische Zentren im Frankenreich: Entwicklungslinien und Forschungsprobleme. In *Studi Medievali*, xix (1978), pp 571–90.

——Columbanus, the Frankish nobility and the territories east of the Rhine. In Clarke & Brennan, *Columbanus*, pp 73–90.

——Die Rolle der Iren beim Aufbau der merowingischen Klosterkultur. In Löwe, *Die Iren*, i, 202–18.

——Papst Gregor der Große und Columban der Jüngere. In Ní Chatháin & Richter, *Ire. & Europe*, pp 328–37.

Rädle, Fidel. Die Kenntnis der antiken Literatur bei den Iren in der Heimat und auf dem Kontinent. In Löwe, *Die Iren*, i, 484–500.

Riché, Pierre. *Education and culture in the barbarian west, sixth through eighth centuries.* Translated from the 3rd French ed. by John J. Contreni. Columbia, S.C., 1976.

—— Columbanus, his followers and the Merovingian church. In Clarke & Brennan, *Columbanus*, pp 59–72.

—— Les irlandais et les princes carolingiens aux VIII<sup>e</sup> et IX<sup>e</sup> siècles. In Löwe, *Die Iren*, i, 735–45.

—— Les monastères hiberno-francs en Gaule du Nord—VII<sup>e</sup> et VIII<sup>e</sup> siècle. In Picard, *Ire. & northern France*, pp 21–6.

Richter, Michael. Der irische Hintergrund der angelsächsischen Mission. In Löwe, *Die Iren*, i, 120–37.

—— The young Willibrord. In G. Kiesel and J. Schroeder (ed.), *Willibrord, Apostel der Niederlande* (Echternach, 1989), pp 25–30.

—— England and Ireland in the time of Willibrord. In P. Bange and A. G. Weiler (ed.), *Willibrord, zijn Wereld en zijn Werk* (Nijmegen, 1991), pp 35–50.

—— The English link in Hiberno-Frankish relations in the seventh century. In Picard, *Ire. & northern France*, pp 95–118.

—— Neues zu den Anfängen des Klosters Reichenau. In *Zeitschirft für die Geschichte des Oberrheins*, cxliv (Stuttgart, 1996), pp 1–18.

—— *Ireland and her neighbours in the seventh century.* Dublin, 1999.

Schäferdiek, Knut. Columbans Wirkung im Frankenreich (591–612). In Löwe, *Die Iren*, i, 171–201.

Schaller, Dieter. Die siebensilberstrophen 'De mundi transitu'—eine Dichtung Columbans? In Löwe, *Die Iren*, i, 468–83.

Scherman, Katherine. *The flowering of Ireland: saints, scholars, and kings.* Boston and Toronto, 1981.

Schreiber, Georg. *Irland im deutschen und abendländischen Sakralraum: zugleich ein Ausblick auf St Brendan und die zweite Kolumbusreise.* Cologne, 1956.

Schrimpf, Gangolf. Der Beitrag des Johannes Scottus Eriugena zum Prädestinationsstreit. In Löwe, *Die Iren*, i, 819–65.

Semmler, Josef. Iren in der lothringischen Klosterreform. In Löwe, *Die Iren*, i, 941–57.

Spilling, Herrad. Irische Handschriftenüberlieferung in Fulda, Mainz und Würzburg. In Löwe, *Die Iren*, pp 876–902.

Strzelczyk, Jerzy. Irische Einflüsse bei den Westslawen im Frühmittelalter. In Ní Chatháin & Richter, *Ire. & Christendom*, pp 445–60.

Szövérffy, Josef. Köln und Dublin: Hirtenstab-Legende und politischer Rechtsanspruch im 12. Jahrhundert. In *Archiv für Kulturgeschichte*, xlii (1960), pp 267–79.

Tommasini, Anselmo. *Irish saints in Italy.* London. 1937.

Vaccari, Pietro, and others (ed.). *San Colombano e la sua opera in Italia: convegno storico colombaniano Bobbio 1–2 Settembre 1951.* Bobbio, 1951.

Van Berkum, A. Willibrord en Wilfried: een onderzoek naar hun wederzijdse betrekkeningen. In *Sacris Erudiri*, xxiii (1978-9), pp 347–415.

Vogel, Cyrille. *La discipline pénitentiale en Gaule des origines à la fin du vii<sup>e</sup> siècle.* Paris, 1952.

Vogt, Hermann J. Zur Spiritualität des frühen irischen Mönchtums. In Löwe, *Die Iren*, i, 26–51.

Waddell, Helen. *The wandering scholars*. London, 1927.

Wendehorst, Alfred. Die Iren und die Christianisierung Mainfrankens. In Löwe, *Die Iren*, i, 319–29.

Werner, Matthias. Iren und Angelsachsen in Mitteldeutschland: zur vorbonifatianischen Mission in Hessen und Thüringen. In Löwe, *Die Iren*, i, 239–318.

Wolfram, Herwig. Virgil als Abt und Bischof von Salzburg. In Dopsch & Juffinger, *Virgil von Salzburg*, pp 342–56.

——Virgil of St Peter's at Salzburg. In Ní Chatháin & Richter, *Ire. & Christendom*, pp 415–20.

Wood, Ian. A prelude to Columbanus: the monastic achievement in the Burgundian territories. In Clarke & Brennan, *Columbanus*, pp 3–32.

——The Vita Columbani and Merovingian hagiography. In *Peritia*, i (1982), pp 63–80.

——Pagans and holy men, 600–800. In Ní Chatháin & Richter, *Ire. & Christenheit*, pp 347–61.

Zagiba, Franz. Die irische Slavenmission und ihre Fortsetzung durch Kyrill und Method. In *Jahrbuch für Geschichte Osteuropas*, n.F., ix (1961), pp 1–56.

Zahn, W. Die Bauten der irischen Benediktiner in Deutschland. (Diss.Phil., Freiburg im Breisgau, 1967.)

## 7   Music

Abbott, T. K. *Catalogue of the Irish manuscripts in the Library of Trinity College, Dublin*. Dublin, 1900.

*Analecta hymnica medii aevi*. Ed. G. M. Dreves, C. Blume, and H. M. Bannister. 58 vols. Leipzig, 1886–1922.

Armstrong, E. C. R. *Irish seal matrices and seals*. Dublin, 1913.

Bates, R. S. Musical slates. In *Notes & Queries for Somerset and Dorset* xxii, pt 190 (Sept. 1936), pp 50–51, item 49. With comment by the Rev. S. H. A. Hervey.

Boydell, Barra (ed.). *Music at Christ Church to 1800: documents and selected anthems*. Dublin, 1999.

Brannon, Patrick V. The search for the Celtic Rite. The T.C.D. Sarum Divine Office manuscripts reassessed. In Harry White and Gerard Gillen (ed.), *Irish Musical Studies, ii: music and the church* (Blackrock, Co. Dublin, 1993), pp 13–40.

——Medieval Ireland: music in cathedral, church, and cloister. In *Early Music*, xxviii, no. 2 (May 2000), pp 193–2002.

Bromwich, Rachel. The keen for Art O'Leary, its background and its place in the tradition of Gaelic keening. In *Éigse*, v (1945–7), pp 236–52.

Brown, T. J. The oldest Irish manuscripts and their late antique background. In Ní Chatháin & Richter, *Ire. & Europe*, pp 311–27.

Buckley, Ann. Notes on the Tiompán in Irish literature. In *Studia Instrumentorum Musicae Popularis*, v (Stockholm, 1977), pp 84–90.

Buckley, Ann. What was the tiompán? A problem in ethnohistorical organology. Evidence in Irish literature. In *Jahrbuch für musikalische Volks- und Völkerkunde*, ix (1978), pp 53–88.

——Timpán/Tiompán. In *The new Grove dictionary of music and musicians* (London, 1980) and *The new Grove Dictionary of musical instruments* (London, 1986).

——A note on the history and archaeology of jew's harps in Ireland. In *N. Munster Antiq. Jn.*, xxv (1983), pp 29–35.

——Jew's harps in Irish archaeology. In *Second Conference of the ICTM Study Group on Music Archaeology*, ed. Cajsa S. Lund (Stockholm, 1986), pp 49–71.

——A ceramic signal horn from medieval Dublin. In *Archaeologia Musicalis*, i (1987), pp 9–10.

——A viking bow from 11th-century Dublin. In *Archaeologia Musicalis*, i (1987), pp 10–11.

——Musical instruments from medieval Dublin: a preliminary survey. In E. Hickmann and D. Hughes (ed.), *The archaeology of early music cultures: Proceedings of the Third International Conference of the Study Group on Music Archaeology* (Bonn, 1988), pp 145–62.

——Musical instruments in Ireland 9th–14th centuries: a review of the organological evidence. In *Irish Musical Studies*, i (Blackrock, Co. Dublin, 1990), pp 13–57.

——Sound tools from the Waterford excavations. Typescript, 1991.

——Harps and lyres on early medieval monuments of Britain and Ireland. In *Harpa*, vii (3/1992), pp 8–9, 15–21.

——An archaeological survey of musical instruments from medieval Ireland. In *Festschrift Tadeusz Malinowski* (Supsk–Pozna, 1993), pp 65–72.

——Music in medieval Irish society. In *Harpa*, xi (3/1993), pp 19–31.

——Music-related imagery on early Christian insular sculpture: identification, context, function. In *Imago Musicae/ International Yearbook of Musical Iconography*, viii (1991), pp 135–99.

——'And his voice swelled like a terrible thunderstorm…': music as symbolic sound in medieval Irish society. In *Irish Musical Studies*, iii (1995), pp 11–74.

——'A lesson for the people': reflections on image and habitus in medieval insular iconography. In *RIdIM/ RCMI Newsletter*, xx, pt 1 (spring 1995), pp 3–9.

——Music and manners: readings of medieval Irish literature. In *Bullán: an Irish Studies Journal*, iii, pt 1 (spring 1997), pp 33–43.

——Representations of musicians in John Derricke's *The image of Irelande* (1581). In Vjera Katalinić and Zdravko Blažeković (ed.), *Festschrift Koraljka Kos* (Croatian Musical Society; Zagreb, 1999), pp 77–91.

——Music and musicians in medieval Irish society. In *Early Music*, xxviii, no. 2 (May 2000), pp 165–90.

——Celtic chant. In *The new Grove dictionary of music and musicians* (London, 2000), pp 341–9.

——Representations of musicians in medieval Christian iconography of Ireland and Scotland as local cultural expression. In Katherine A. McIver (ed.), *Art and music in the early modern period: essays in honor of Franca Trinchieri Camiz* (Aldershot, 2003), pp 217–31.

——and Casey, Sara Gibbs. *Liturgical sources for the veneration of Irish saints: an annotated checklist.* 2 vols. In progress.

Byrne, Francis J. The Stowe Missal. In Liam de Paor (ed.), *Great books of Ireland* (Dublin, 1967), pp 38–50.

Carney, James. *Medieval Irish lyrics* with *The Irish bardic poet.* Portlaoise, 1985.

Casey, Sarah Gibbs. The Drummond Missal: a preliminary investigation into its historical, liturgical, and musicological significance in pre-Norman Ireland. (M.A. thesis, University of Pittsburgh, 1995.)

——The Sanctus chant of the Drummond Missal: a semiotic study. Unpublished typescript.

——'Through a glass, darkly': steps towards reconstructing Irish chant from the neumes of the Drummond Missal. In *Early Music*, xxviii, no. 2 (May 2000), pp 205–15.

*Catalogue of the manuscripts remaining in Marsh's Library, Dublin.* Compiled by John Russell Scott; ed. Newport J. D. White. Dublin, 1913.

Chambers, E. K. *The medieval stage.* 2 vols. Oxford, 1903.

Coens, Maurice. Les litanies bavaroises du *Libellus precum* dit de Fleury (Orléans MS 184). In *Anal. Bolland.*, lxxvii (1959), pp 373–91.

Coles, John M. Irish bronze age horns and their relations with northern Europe. In *Prehist. Soc. Proc.*, xxix (1963), pp 326–56.

——The archaeological evidence for a 'bull cult' in late bronze age Europe. In *Antiquity*, xxxix (1965), pp 217–19.

Colker, Marvin L. *Trinity College Library Dublin: descriptive catalogue of the medieval and renaissance Latin manuscripts.* With introduction by William O'Sullivan. 2 vols. Aldershot, 1991.

Connolly, Philomena, and Martin, Geoffrey (ed.), *The Dublin Guild Merchant roll, c.1190–1265.* Dublin, 1992.

Curran, Michael E. *The Antiphonary of Bangor.* Blackrock, 1984.

Czernin, Martin. Fragments of liturgical chant from medieval Irish monasteries in continental Europe. In *Early Music*, xxviii, no. 2 (May 2000), pp 217–24.

——*Die Musik der irischen Benediktiner in Wien.* Graz, 2002.

Derricke, John. *The image of Ireland; with a discoverie of woodkarne.* [1581]. Reprint with an introduction, transliteration and glossary by David B. Quinn. Belfast, 1985.

Dimock, James (ed.), *Giraldi Cambrensis opera.* London, 1867. (Rolls Series, v.)

Dobson, E. J., and Harrison, F. Ll. *Medieval English songs.* London, 1979.

Dolan, Diane. *Le drame liturgique de Pâques en Normandie et Angleterre au moyen âge.* Paris, 1975. (Publications de l'Université de Poitiers. Lettres et Sciences Humaines, xvi.)

Dumville, D. N. Liturgical drama and panegyric responsory from the eighth century? A re-examination of the origin and contents of the ninth-century section of the Book of Cerne. In *Journal of Theological Studies*, new ser., xxiii (1972), pp 374–406.

Egan-Buffet, Máire, and Alan J. Fletcher. The Dublin *Visitatio Sepulchri* play. In *R.I.A. Proc.*, xc (1990), sect. C, pp 159–241.

Fitzmaurice, E. B., and Little, A. G. (ed.), *Materials for the history of the Franciscan Province of Ireland* A.D. *1230-1450*. Oxford, 1920. (British Society of Franciscan Studies, ix.)

Fleischmann, Aloys. Die Iren in der Neumen und Choralforschung. In *Zeitschrift für Musikwissenschaft*, xvi (1934), pp 352–5.

——References to chant in early Irish manuscripts. In S. Pender (ed.), *Féilscríbhinn Tórna* (Cork, 1952), pp 43–9.

——Celtic rite, music of the. In *The new Grove dictionary of music and musicians*, iv (1980), pp 52–3.

——and Gleeson, Ryta. Music in ancient Munster and monastic Cork. In *Cork Hist. Soc. Jn.*, lxx, pt 2 (1965), pp 79–98.

Fletcher, Alan J. *Drama, performance and polity in pre-Cromwellian Ireland*. Cork, 2000.

Flood, W. H. Grattan. *History of Enniscorthy*. Enniscorthy, 1898.

——Irish organ-builders from the eighth to the close of the eighteenth century. In *R.S.A.I. Jn.*, xl (1910), pp 229–34.

——*A history of Irish music*. Dublin, 1905. Reprinted with introduction by Seóirse Bodley. Shannon, 1970.

Frere, Walter H. *Bibliotheca musico-liturgica*. I.1.2. (1894), II.1.2. (1932) London. Reprinted Hildesheim, 1967.

Gneuss, Helmut. *Hymnar und Hymnen im englischen Mittelalter: Studien zur Überlieferung, Glossierung und Übersetzung lateinischer Hymnen in England, mit einer Textausgabe der lateinischen-altenglischen Expositio Hymnorum*. Tübingen, 1968.

Gougaud, Louis. Celtiques [Liturgies]. In *The catholic encyclopedia*, iii (New York, 1908), pp 2969–3032.

——The remains of Irish monastic libraries. In *Féil-sgríbhinn Eóin Mhic Néill*, pp 319–34.

Grindle, W. H. *Irish cathedral music. A history of music at the cathedrals of the Church of Ireland*. Belfast, 1989. (Institute of Irish Studies, Q.U.B.)

Gushee, Marion S. Romanesque polyphony: a study of the fragmentary sources. (Ph.D. dissertation, Yale, 1964.)

——The polyphonic music of the medieval monastery, cathedral and university. In James McKinnon (ed.), *Antiquity and the middle ages from ancient Greece to the fifteenth century* (Basingstoke and London, 1990), pp 143–69.

Gwynn, Aubrey. The origins of the Anglo-Irish theatre. In *Studies*, xxviii (1939), pp 260–74.

——The first bishops of Dublin. In *Reportorium Novum*, i (1955–6), pp 1–26. Reprinted in Howard Clarke (ed.), *Medieval Dublin: the living city* (Blackrock, 1988), pp 37–61.

——The Irish Missal of Corpus Christi College, Oxford. In *Studies in Church History*, l (1964), pp 47–68.

——Anglo-Irish church life: fourteenth and fifteenth centuries. In Corish, *Ir. catholicism*, ii, fasc. 4 (1968).

Hand, Geoffrey. The psalter of Christ Church, Dublin (Bodleian MS Rawlinson G 185). In *Reportorium Novum*, i, pt 2 (1956), pp 311–22.

——Cambridge University Additional Manuscript 710. In *Reportorium Novum*, ii, pt 1 (1958), pp 17–32.

Harper, Sally. So how many Irishmen went to Glyn Achlach? Early accounts of the formation of *Cerdd Dant*. (Paper presented at the Fifth Conference of the Centre for Advanced Welsh Music Studies, University of Wales, Bangor, July 1999.)

Harrison, Frank Lloyd. *Music in medieval Britain*. London, 1963.

——Polyphony in medieval Ireland. In E. M. Ruhnke (ed.), *Festschrift Bruno Stäblein* (Kassel, 1967), pp 74–9.

——Celtic musics: characteristics and chronology. In Schmidt, *Celts*, pp 252–63.

——(ed.). *Motets of English provenance*. Text ed. and trans. Peter Lefferts. Monaco, 1980. (Polyphonic Music of the Fourteenth Century, xv.)

Hawkes, W. The liturgy in Dublin 1200–1500: manuscript sources. In *Reportorium Novum*, ii, pt 1 (1958), pp 33–67.

——Cashel MS 2: a thirteenth-century liturgical document in Dublin. In *Reportorium Novum*, iii, pt 1 (1962), pp 83–93.

Henry, Françoise. Remarks on the decoration of three Irish psalters. In *R.I.A. Proc.*, lxi (1960), sect. C, pp 23–40.

——and Marsh-Micheli, Geneviève. A century of Irish illumination. In *R.I.A. Proc.*, lxi (1962), sect. C, pp 101–66.

Hesbert, René-Jean. *Le tropaire-prosaire de Dublin: MS Add. 710 de l'Université de Cambridge (vers 1360)*. Rouen, 1966. (Monumenta Musicae Sacrae, iv.)

Heuser, Wilhelm. *Die Kildare-Gedichte*. Bonn, 1904. (Bonner Beiträge zur Anglistik, xiv.)

Hiley, David. Rouen, Bibliothèque Municipale, MS 249 (A.280), and the early Paris repertory of ordinary of mass chants and sequences. In *Music and Letters*, lxx, pt 4 (1989), pp 467–82.

Holmes, Peter. The manufacturing technology of the Irish bronze-age horns. In Michael Ryan (ed.), *The origins of metallurgy in Atlantic Europe: Proceedings of the Fifth Atlantic Colloquium* (Dublin, 1979), pp 165–81.

——*The evolution of player-voiced aerophones prior to 500 A.D.* Oxford, 1980. (Brit. Arch. Reps, xx.)

——and Coles, J. M. Prehistoric brass instruments. In *World Archaeology*, xii, pt 3 (1981), pp 280–86.

Huglo, Michel. Les instruments de musique chez Hucbald. In Guy Cambier (ed.), *Hommages à André Boutemy* (Collection Latomus, cxlv; Paris, 1976), pp 178–96.

——Organologie et iconographie médiévales. In *Annales d'Histoire et d'Arts et d'Archéologie* [Université Libre de Bruxelles], iii (1981), pp 97–113.

Huglo, Michel. L'Organum à Landévennec au IXe siècle. In *Études Celt.*, xxiii (1986), pp 187–92.

James, Montagu Rhodes. *A descriptive catalogue of the manuscripts in the library of Lambeth Palace*. Cambridge, 1930.

Karp, Theodore. A serendipitous encounter with St Kilian. In *Early Music*, xxviii, no. 2 (May 2000), pp 226–37.

Lehmann, Ruth P. M. Woman's songs in Irish, 800–1500. In John F. Plummer (ed.), *Vox Feminae: studies in medieval woman's songs* (Studies in Medieval Culture, xv, Medieval Institute Publications; Kalamazoo, 1981), pp 111–34.

Lipphardt, Walther. *Die Weisen der lateinischen Osterspiele des zwölften und dreizehnten Jahrhunderts.* Kassel, 1948.

——(ed.), *Lateinische Osterfeiern und Osterspiele.* Vols i–v. Berlin, 1975–6. Vol. vi. Berlin, 1981.

Long, Joseph. Dermot and the earl: who wrote 'The song'? In *R.I.A. Proc.*, lxxv (1975), sect. C, pp 263–72.

Messingham, Thomas. *Officii SS Patricii, Columbae, Brigidae.* Paris, 1620.

——*Florilegium insulae sanctorum.* Paris, 1624.

Meyer, Kuno (ed. and trans.), *Hibernica Minora, being a fragment of an Old Irish treatise on the Psalter with translation, notes and glossary and an appendix containing extracts hitherto unpublished from MS Rawlinson B 512 in the Bodleian Library.* Oxford, 1894.

Meyer, Wilhelm. Das turiner Bruchstück der ältesten irischen Liturgie. In *Nachrichten von der königlichen Gesellschaft der Wissenschaften zu Göttingen, phil.-hist. Kl.* (Göttingen, 1903), pp 163–214.

Mezey, László. Fragmentforschung im Schottenstift 1982–3. In *Codices Manuscripti: Zeitschrift für Handschriftenkunde*, ii, no. 10 (1984), pp 60–71.

Mills, James (ed.), *Account roll of the priory of Holy Trinity, Dublin, 1337–1346.* Dublin, 1890–91. Reprinted with introductions by James Lydon and Alan J. Fletcher. Dublin, 1996.

Murphy, T. A. The oldest eucharistic hymn. In *I.E.R.*, 5th ser., xlvi (1935), pp 172–6.

*Musik im mittelalterlichen Wien.* Vienna, 1986. (Historisches Museum der Stadt Wien, 103. Sonderausstellung, 18. Dezember bis 8. März 1987.)

Neary, Denise M. Organ-building in seventeenth- and eighteenth-century Dublin, and its English connections. In *The British Institute of Organ Studies: BIOS Journal*, xxxii (1997), pp 20–27.

Ní Riain, Nóirín. The female song in the Irish tradition. In Eiléan Ní Chuilleanáin (ed.), *Irish women* (Dublin, 1985), pp 73–84.

Nicholson, E. *Early Bodleian music*, iii. Oxford, 1913.

Nixon, Paul. Giraldus Cambrensis on music: how reliable are his historiographers? In Ann Buckley (ed.), *Proceedings of the First British-Swedish Conference on Musicology: Medieval Studies (11–15 May 1988)* (Stockholm, 1992), pp 264–89.

O'Conor, Charles. *Memoirs of the life and writings of the late Charles O'Conor of Belanagare.* Dublin, 1796.

O'Curry, Eugene. Of music and musical instruments in ancient Erinn. In *Manners and customs of the ancient Irish*, ed. with introduction and appendices by W. K. Sullivan (3 vols, London, 1873), iii, 212–409.

Ó Madagáin, Breandán. Irish vocal music and syllabic verse. In Robert O'Driscoll (ed.), *The Celtic consciousness* (Toronto, 1981), pp 311–32.

O'Meara, J. J. (ed. and trans.). *Gerald of Wales. The history and topography of Ireland.* Bungay, 1982.

O'Sullivan, William. Notes on the Trinity *Liber hymnorum*. In John L. Sharpe (ed.), *Roger Powell, the compleat binder* (Bibliologia, xiv; Turnhout, 1996), pp 130–35.

Partridge, Angela. Wild men and wailing women. In *Éigse*, xviii (1981), pp 25–37.

Polybius. *The histories*. With an English translation by W. R. Paton. 6 vols. London and Cambridge, Mass., 1967.

Rimmer, Joan. *The Irish harp*. Cork, 1984.

RISM [*Repertoire internationale des sources musicales*] B III⁴ *The theory of music, iv: manuscripts from the Carolingian era up to c.1500 in Great Britain and in the United States of America. Descriptive catalogue*. Pt i: Great Britain, by Christian Meyer. Pt ii: United States of America, by Michel Huglo and Nancy C. Phillips. Munich, 1992.

RISM B IV¹ Gilbert Reaney (ed.), *Manuscripts of polyphonic music, 11th–early 14th century*. Munich and Duisburg, 1966.

RISM B V¹ Heinrich Husmann, *Tropen- und Sequenzenhandschriften*. Munich and Duisburg, 1964.

Salmen, Walter. *Der Tanzmeister. Geschichte und Profile eines Berufes vom 14. bis zum 19. Jahrhundert. Mit einem Anhang 'Der Tanzmeister in der Literatur'*. Hildesheim, Zürich, and New York, 1997. (Terpsichore: Tanzhistorische Studien, herausgeben von Walter Salmen für das Deutsche Tanzarchiv Köln.)

Sanger, Keith. An Irish harper in an English graveyard? In *Harpa*, xxi (spring 1996), p. 17.

Schneiders, Marc. The origins of the early Irish liturgy. In Ní Chatháin & Richter, *Ire. & Europe* (1996), pp 76–98.

Schubiger, Anselm. *Die Sängerschule Sankt Gallens vom achten bis zwölften Jahrhundert. Ein Beitrag zur Gesanggeschichte des Mittelalters*. Einsiedeln and New York, 1858.

Shields, Hugh. Carolling at New Ross, 1265. In *Ceol*, iv, pt 2 (1973), pp 34–6.

——The walling of New Ross: a thirteenth-century poem in French. In *Long Room*, xii–xiii (1975–6), pp 24–33.

Stäblein, Bruno. *Hymnen*. Kassel, 1956. (Monumenta Monodica Medii Aevi, i.)

——Zwei Melodien der altirischen Liturgie. In Heinrich Hüschen (ed.), *Musicae Scientiae Collectanea. Festschrift für Karl Gustav Fellerer zum 70. Geburtstag* (Cologne, 1973), pp 590–97.

——*Schriftbild der einstimmigen Musik*. Leipzig, 1975. (Musikgeschichte in Bildern, iii, pt 1; general editor W. Bachmann.)

Stephen of Lexington. *Letters from Ireland, 1228–1229*. Trans. with introduction by Barry O'Dwyer. Kalamazoo, 1982.

Stevens, John. *Angelus ad virginem*: the history of a medieval song. In P. L. Heyworth (ed.), *Medieval studies for J. A. W. Bennett: aetatis suae lxx* (Oxford, 1981), pp 297–328.

Stevenson, Jane. Irish hymns, Venantius Fortunatus and Poitiers. In J.-M. Picard (ed.), *Aquitaine and Ireland in the middle ages* (Dublin, 1995), pp 81–110.

——Hiberno-Latin hymns: learning and literature. In Ní Chatháin & Richter, *Ire. & Europe* (1996), pp 99–135.

Ua Súilleabháin, Seán, and Donnelly, Seán. Music has ended: the death of a harper. In *Celtica*, xxii (1991), pp 165–75.

Van Schaik, Martin. The harp bag in the middle ages: an iconographical survey. In *The historical harp: proceedings of the International Historical Harp Symposium, Utrecht 1992* (Utrecht, 1994), pp 3–11.

Woods, Isobel. 'Our awin Scottis Use': chant usage in medieval Scotland. In *Journal of the Royal Musical Association*, cxii, pt 1 (1987), pp 21–37.

Woods Preece, Isobel. *'Our awin Scottis use': music of the Scottish church up to 1603*. Glasgow, 2000. (Studies in the Music of Scotland.)

Young, Karl. *The drama of the medieval church*. 2 vols. Oxford, 1933. Reprinted 1962.

## 8  *Science, medicine, theology, and philosophy*

Allard, Guy H. *Johannis Scoti Eriugenae Periphyseon*. Indices générales. Paris, 1983.

—— (ed.). *Jean Scot écrivain*. Montreal and Paris, 1986. (Actes du IVe Colloque International Montréal, 28 Aug.–2 Sept. 1983.) Includes articles by Werner Beierwaltes, C. Coallier, D. Descrosiers-Bonin, P. Dietrich and D. F. Duclos, G. D'Onofrio, Michael Herren, Édouard Jeauneau, Colette Jeudy, C. Leonardi, G. Madec, John J. O'Meara, Pádraig Ó Néill, Jean Pépin, G. Piemonte, and G. Touchette.

Beierwaltes, Werner. Eriugena. Aspekte seiner Philosophie. In Löwe, *Die Iren*, ii, 799–818.

Bergmann, Rolf. Dicuils 'De mensura orbis terrae'. In Paul Butzer and Dietrich Lohrmann (ed.), *Science in western and eastern civilization in Carolingian times* (Basle, 1993), pp 525–37.

Berschin, Walter. Griechisches bei den Iren. In Löwe, *Die Iren*, ii, 501–10.

Best, R. I. The St Gall incantation against headache In *Ériu*, viii (1916), p. 100.

—— Some Irish charms. In *Ériu*, xvi (1952), pp 27–32.

Bett, Henry. *Johannes Scotus Erigena*. Cambridge, 1925. New York, 1964.

Bieler, Ludwig. Some recent work on Eriugena. In *Hermathena*, cxv (1973), pp 94–7.

Binchy, D. A. The leech in ancient Ireland. In William Doolin and Oliver FitzGerald (ed.), *What's past is prologue* (Dublin, 1952), pp 5–9.

Bishop, T. A. M. Periphyseon: the descent of the uncompleted copy. In Whitelock, McKitterick, & Dumville, *Ire. in early med. Europe*, pp 281–306.

Blake, R. Marlay Folk-lore, with some account of the ancient Gaelic leeches and the state of the art of medicine in ancient Erin. In *Louth Arch. Soc. Jn.*, iv (1917), pp 217–25.

Bonser, Wilfrid. The dissimilarity of ancient Irish magic from that of the Anglo-Saxons. In *Folklore*, xxxvii (1926), pp 271–88.

Breen, Aidan. Iohannes Scottus, Periphyseon: the problems of an edition. In *R.I.A. Proc.*, cxi (1991), sect. C, pp 21–40.

Cappuyns, Maïeul. *Jean Scot Érigène, sa vie, son oeuvre, sa pensée*. Louvain, 1933. Reprinted, Brussels, 1964.

Carracedo-Fraga, J. *Liber de ortu et obitu patriarcharum*. Turnhout, 1996. (C.C.S.L., cviiiE.)

Conneely, Daniel. *St Patrick's letters: a study of their theological dimension*. Maynooth, 1993.

Davies, Wendy. The place of healing in early Irish society. In Ó Corráin, Breatnach, & McCone, *Sages, saints, & storytellers*, pp 43–55.

Draak, Maartje. A Leyden Boethius-fragment with Old-Irish glosses. In *Mededelingen der koninklijke Nederlandse akademie van Wetenschappen* (Afd. Letterkunde, N.R. Deel 11, no. 3; 1967), pp 113–27.

——Construe marks in Hiberno-Latin manuscripts. In *Mededelingen der koninklijke Nederlandse akademie van Wetenschappen*. Afd. Letterkunde, N.R. Deel 20, no. 10 (1957), pp 261–82.

——Virgil of Salzburg versus 'Aethicus Ister'. In *Dancwerc opstellen aangeboden aan D. Th. Enklaar* (Leyden, 1959), pp 33–42.

——The higher teaching of Latin grammar in Ireland during the ninth century. In *Mededelingen der koninklijke Nederlandse akademie van Wetenschappen*. Afd. Letterkunde, N.R. Deel 30, no. 4 (1967), pp 109–43.

Fontaine, Jacques. *Isidore de Séville et la culture classique dans l'Espagne Wisigothique*. 3 vols. Paris, 1983.

Hamlin, Ann. Some northern sundials and time-keeping in the early Irish church. In Rynne, *Figures from the past*, pp 29–42.

Hillgarth, J. N. The position of Isidorian studies: a critical review of the literature. In *Studi Medievali*, xxiv (1983), pp 817–905.

Holtz, Louis. *Murethach (Muridac) in Donati artem maiorem*. Turnhout, 1977. (C.C.C.M., xl. Grammatici Hibernici Carolini aevi, i.)

Jeauneau, Édouard. *Études Érigéniennes*. Paris, 1987.

——*Quatre thèmes érigèniennes*. Montreal, 1978.

Jones, Charles W. *Bede, the schools and the computus*. Ed. Wesley M. Stevens. Aldershot, 1994.

Kelly, Joseph F. T. Hiberno-Latin theology. In Löwe, *Die Iren*, 549–67.

Kristeller, Paul O. The historical position of Johannes Scottus Eriugena. In O'Meara & Naumann, *Latin script & letters*, pp 156–66.

Lapidge, Michael. Latin learning in Dark Age Wales: some prolegomena. In Evans, Griffith, & Jope, *Proc. 7th Congress*, pp 91–107.

MacArthur, William P. Some notes on old-time leprosy in England and Ireland. In *Royal Army Medical Corps Journal*, xlv (1925), pp 410–22.

——Famine fevers in England and Ireland: the Yellow Pestilence, pestis flava, or *buidhe chonaill*. In *Journal of the British Archaeological Association*, 3rd ser., ix (1944), pp 66–71.

——The identification of some pestilences recorded in the Irish annals. In *I.H.S.*, vi, no. 23 (Mar. 1949), pp 169–88.

——The pestilence called 'scamach'. In *I.H.S.*, vii, no. 27 (Mar. 1951), pp 199–200.

McCarthy, D. P. Easter principles and a fifth-century lunar cycle used in the British Isles. In *Journal of the History of Astronomy*, xxiv (1993), pp 204–24.

——The origin of the *latercus* paschal cycle of the Insular Celtic churches. In *Camb. Med. Celt. Studies*, xxviii (winter 1994), pp 25–49.

McCarthy, D. P. The lunar and paschal tables of *De ratione paschali* attributed to Anatolius of Laodicea. In *Archives for History of the Exact Sciences*, xlix, no. 4 (1996), pp 285–320.

—— and Breen, Aidan. Astronomical observations in the Irish annals and their motivation. In *Peritia*, xi (1997), pp 1–43.

—— An evaluation of astronomical observations in the Irish annals. In *Vistas in Astronomy*, xli (1997), pp 117–38.

—— and Ó Cróinín, Dáibhí. The 'lost' Irish 84-year Easter table rediscovered. In *Peritia*, vi–vii (1987–8 [1990]), pp 227–42.

Mac Conmara, Máirtín (ed.). *An léann eaglasta 1000–1200*. Dublin, 1982.
Includes articles by Frederic Mac Donncha, Dáibhí Ó Cróinín, Peadar Ó Duibhir, Seán Ó Duinn, Diarmuid Ó Laoghaire, and Pádraig Ó Riain.

Mac Mathúna, Liam. Irish perceptions of the Cosmos. In *Celtica*, xxiii (1999), pp 174–87.

McGrath, Fergal J. *Education in ancient and medieval Ireland*. Dublin, 1979.

Madec, G. *Jean Scot et ses auteurs. Annotations ériginiennes*. Paris, 1988.

Meurers, Joseph. Die geistige Situation der Naturwissenschaften zu Virgils Zeiten. In Dopsch & Juffinger, *Virgil von Salzburg*, pp 162–9.

Moran, Dermot. Nature, man and God in the philosophy of John Scotus Eriugena. In Richard Kearney (ed.), *The Irish mind* (Dublin, 1985), pp 91–106.

—— *The philosophy of John Scottus Eriugena. A study of idealism in the middle ages*. Cambridge, 1989.

—— Origen and Eriugena: aspects of Christian gnosis. In T. Finan and V. Twomey (ed.), *The relationship between Neoplatonism and Christianity*. (Dublin, 1995), pp 27–54.

—— Expounding Eriugena [review article]. In *I.H.S.*, xxxi, no. 122 (Nov. 1998), pp 247–58.

Ó Cróinín, Dáibhí. A seventh-century Irish computus from the circle of Cummianus. In *R.I.A. Proc.*, lxxxii (1982), sect. C, pp 405–30.

—— Mo-Sinnu moccu Min and the computus of Bangor. In *Peritia*, i (1982), pp 281–99.

—— *The Irish 'Sex Aetates Mundi'*. Dublin, 1982.

—— The Irish provenance of Bede's computus. In *Peritia*, ii (1983), pp 229–47.

—— Columbanus, the computistical writings. In M. Lapidge (ed.), *Columbanus: the Latin writings* (Woodbridge, 1997), pp 264–70.

O'Loughlin, Thomas. Unexplored Irish influence on Eriugena. In *Recherches de théologie ancienne et médiévale*, lix (1992), pp 23–40.

—— The earliest world maps known in Ireland. In *History Ireland*, i, no. 1 (spring 1993), pp 7–10.

—— *Celtic theology: humanity, world and God in early Irish writings*. London, 2000.

O'Meara, John J. *Eriugena*. Cork, 1969.

—— *Eriugena*. Oxford, 1988.

—— and Bieler, Ludwig (ed.). *The mind of Eriugena: papers of a colloquium, Dublin, 14–18 July 1970*. Dublin, 1973.
Includes articles by Guy-H. Allard, Jeanne Barbet, Werner Beierwaltes, Yves Christe, Marta Cristiani, M.-T. d'Alverny, Édouard Jeauneau, Hans Lie-

beschütz, Paul Meyvaert, Jean Pépin, René Rocques, Robert Russell, Gangolf Schrimpf, Jean Trouillard, and I. P. Sheldon-Williams.

Prinz, Otto. *Die Kosmographie des Aethicus Ister.* Munich, 1993.

Robins, Joseph. *Fools and mad: a history of the insane in Ireland.* Dublin, 1986.

Roques, René (ed.). *Jean Scot Érigène et l'histoire de la philosophie.* Paris, 1977. (Actes du Colloque International, dlxi.)

Shaw, Francis. Medieval medico-philosophical treatises in the Irish language. In *Féil-sgríbhinn Eóin Mhic Néill*, pp 144–57.

Shrewsbury, J. F. D. The Yellow Plague. In *Journal of the History of Medicine*, iv (1949), pp 1–47.

Smith, Brendan. Medicine in medieval Ireland. In *Retrospect*, [v] (1987), pp 13–17.

Smyth, Marina. Das Universum in der Kosmographie des Aethicus Ister. In Dopsch & Juffinger, *Virgil von Salzburg*, pp 170–82.

——The physical world in seventh-century Hiberno-Latin texts. In *Peritia*, v (1986), pp 201–34.

——Isidore of Seville and early Irish cosmography. In *Camb. Med. Celt. Studies*, xiv (winter 1987), pp 69–102.

——The earliest written evidence for an Irish view of the world. In D. R. Edel (ed.), *Cultural identity and cultural integration* (Dublin, 1995), pp 23–44.

—— *Understanding the universe in seventh-century Ireland.* Woodbridge, 1996.

Stevens, Wesley M. The figure of the earth in Isidore's 'De natura rerum'. In *Isis*, lxxi (June 1980), pp 268–77.

——Scientific instruction in early insular schools. In Herren, *Insular Latin studies*, pp 83–112.

—— *Cycles of time and scientific learning in medieval Europe.* Aldershot, 1995.

Tierney, J. J. *Dicuili 'Liber de mensura orbis terrae'.* Dublin, 1967. (Script. Lat. Hib., vi.)

Tristram, Hildegard L. C. Der homo octipartitus in der angelsächischen und frühen irischen Literatur. In *Z.C.P.*, xxxiv (1975), pp 119–53.

——Das Europabild in der mittelirischen Literatur. In Löwe, *Die Iren*, ii, 697–734.

——'*Sex aetates mundi': die Weltzeitalter bei den Angelsachsen und den Iren.* Heidelberg, 1985.

——Early modes of Insular expression. In Ó Corráin, Breatnach, & McCone, *Sages, saints, & storytellers*, pp 427–48.

Walsh, Katherine. Die Naturwissenschaften in Irland zur Zeit des hl. Virgil. In Dopsch & Juffinger, *Virgil von Salzburg*, pp 154–61.

Walsh, Maura, and Ó Cróinín, Dáibhí (ed.). *Cummian's letter 'De controversia Paschali' together with a related Irish computistical tract 'De ratione conputandi'.* Toronto, 1988. (Pontifical Institute of Medieval Studies; Studies and Texts, lxxxvi.)

Sheldon-Williams, I. P. Eriugena and Cîteaux. In *Studia Monastica*, xix (1977), pp 75–92.

——and Liebeschütz, Hans. Articles on Eriugena. In *Cambridge history of later Greek and early medieval philosophy* (Cambridge, 1967), pp 518–33, 576–86.

# INDEX

Place names are located, where possible, in terms of their modern setting: thus, 'Ard Ladrann, Co. Wexford' and 'Nice, France'. A name such as 'd'Exeter' is entered in that form but under 'E'.

The following abbreviations are used:

| | | | |
|---|---|---|---|
| abp | archbishop | O.Carm. | Order of Carmelites (friars) |
| bp | bishop | O.P. | Order of Preachers (Dominican friars) |
| cent. | century | O.F.M. | Order of Friars Minor (Franciscan friars) |
| kg | king | O.S.A. | Order of St Augustine (Augustinian friars) |

Aaron of Cologne, abp of Cracow, 886

Abbán, St, 193

abbots: administrative role, 621; hereditary succession, 319, 585–90, 608, 636, 642, 644–5; rules of, 605; marriage of, 319, 320, 587, 648; not in orders, 317, 648; property relationship of, 593–4; status of, lxxiii, lxxiv, 312, 590–91

abbreviations in MSS, 512

Aberdeen, Scotland, 968–69

Aberdeen Breviary, 778

Abermenai, Wales, 871

Abernethy church, Scotland, 674

Abhall Ceithernaig, treaty of (1133), 919

'Acallam na Senórach', 469, 489–91

Accius, poet, 390

Acgilberct, bp of Wessex, 383

Achill Island, 40

Aclea, battle of (851), 614

act of union (1801), 28–9

'Acta Lanfranci', 905, 912

'Acts of the council of Caesarea', 392

Adalbert of Bremen, 886

*adaltrach*, 314, 315

Adam of Bremen, 628

Adomnán, abbot of Iona (d. 704/5), 389, 607, 658, 882; *Cáin* (law of), 334–5, 337, 640, *see also* Cáin Adomnáin; church-building, 723, 734; 'De locis sanctis', 524; education of, 327; 'Law of the Innocents', 870; Life of Columba, *see* Columba (Colum Cille); poetry, 456; quoted in 'Hibernensis', 445; sketches of Jerusalem, 708; vocabulary of, 384

Aduar mac Echin, St, of Ossory, 583–4

adultery, 314, 315, 971

Áed, bp of Armagh (1088), 868

Áed, bp of Sletty, 606

Áed Allán mac Fergaile, of Uí Néill, high-kg (734–43), 211, 219–20, 227, 335n, 657, 658, 660, 664

Áed Dub mac Colmáin, bp of Kildare (d. 639), 197–8, 385, 673

Áed Dub mac Suibne, 210, 214

Áed Find, 'chief sage', 507

Áed Find mac Colmáin, 198, 673

Áed Findliath mac Néill, high-kg (d. 879), lxxx, 841, 857, 896

Áed in Gaí Bernaig, kg of Connacht (1046–67), 893

Áed mac Ainmerech, of Northern Uí Néill, high-kg (586–98), 199, 210, 217

Áed mac Brénaind, of Tethbae, 210

Áed mac Bréndain meic Maine, 208

Áed mac Bricc, 335n

Áed mac Cellaig, abbot of Kildare (d. 828), 673, 674

Áed mac Cennétig, *muire* of Clann Tairdelbaig, 876

Áed mac Colggen, kg of Leinster (715/28–738), 199–200

Áed Mac Crimthainn, abbot of Terryglass, 861, 865, 869–70

Áed mac Diarmata, kg of Uí Muiredaig, 198

Áed mac Domnaill, kg of Cenél nEógain (989–1004), 647

Áed mac Duib dá Chrích, abbot of Terryglass and Clonenagh, 615

Áed mac Echach, kg of Connacht (a.560/61–577), 229

Áed mac Néill meic Máel Shechlainn, 895–6

Áed mac Néill, of Uí Néill (855), 617

Áed mac Néill, kg of Cenél nEógain (1068–83), 902, 906

Áed Méránach, of Ulaid, 901, 902

Áed Oirdnide mac Néill, high-kg (797–819), 200–01, 657, 658, 659, 662, 663–4, 671, 895, 896

Áed Róin mac Beicc Bairrche, kg of Ulster (708–35), 194, 219, 637

1 (*above*). The massive orthostatic kerb around the base of the mound, Knowth, Co. Meath

2 (*left*). Mining maul from Ross Island, Co. Kerry

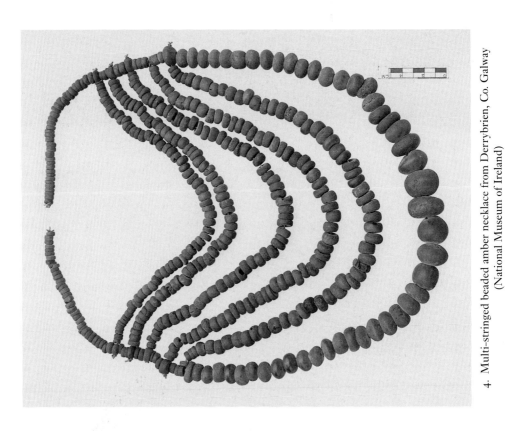

4. Multi-stringed beaded amber necklace from Derrybrien, Co. Galway (National Museum of Ireland)

3. Amber necklace of 116 beads from Garvagh, Co. Londonderry (Cork Public Museum)

5. Aerial photograph of earthen ringfort (rath), Lisnagade, Co. Down

6. Multivallate ringfort and crannog, Lisleitrim, Co. Armagh

7. Remains of wattle house, Deer Park Farms, Co. Antrim

8. Reconstruction of a ringfort, by Deiri Warner

9. Promontory fort, Dunseverick, Co. Antrim

10. Aerial photograph of stone houses near a stone ringfort or cashel, Ballynavenooragh, Co. Kerry

11. Aerial photograph of ringforts and fields, Ballybaun, Co. Clare

12. Cross of the Scriptures, Clonmacnoise, Co. Offaly: foot of east face; so-called 'Foundation scene'

13. The pilgrimage mountain of Croagh Patrick, Co. Mayo

14 (*left*). The Cathach (R.I.A., MS 12.R.33), f. 48r

15 (*below*). Cross-inscribed slab and tomb, Killabuonia, Co. Kerry

16. Beehive huts on Sceilg Mhichíl (Skellig Michael), Co. Kerry

17. Rotary quern beside the Crucifixion slab, Inishkea North, Co. Mayo

18. Clonmacnoise, Co. Offaly: aerial view of the monastic site

19. Codex Usserianus Primus (T.C.D., MS 55), f. 126v

20. The Cathach (R.I.A., MS 12.R.33), f. 36r

22. The Stowe Missal (R.I.A., MS D.II.3), p. 51

21. St Kilian's Gospel-book (Würzburg, Universitätsbibliothek, MS M.p.th.q.1a)

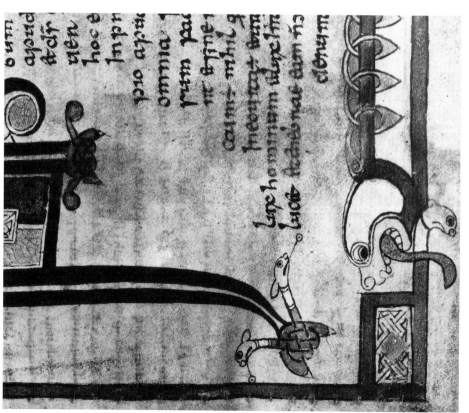

24. The 'Milan Basilius' (Milan, Biblioteca Ambrosiana, MS C 26 Sup.), f. 28r

23. St John's Gospel (bound as part of R.I.A., MS D.II.3), f. 1

25 (*right*). Wax tablet from Springmount Bog, Co. Antrim (National Museum of Ireland)

26 (*far right*). Milan, Biblioteca Ambrosiana, MS S 45 Sup., f. 19r

28. Willibrord's Calendar (Bibliothèque Nationale de France, Ms. lat. 10837), p. 39v, with marginal note in Willibrord's own hand

27. Milan, Biblioteca Ambrosiana, MS D 23 Sup., f. 2

30 (*above*). Durham Gospels (Durham Cathedral Library MS A.II.17), f. 66

29 (*left*). Augsburg Gospels (Augsburg, Universitätsbibliothek, Cod. 1.2.4°.2), f. 5r

31. Echternach book of the Prophets (Bibl. Nat., MS lat. 9382), f. 75

32. Bibl. Nat., MS lat. 10837, f. 32v

CRCUS euuangelista
di expeennbab
uismate piuusq: indiui
nosermone discipuussacendouim
misnahel agenssaeiindum connuen
leuita aduensus adpidemxpi eian
gelium iniraliascribsiu oscendens
ineoquid exgeneruisuodeberecca
xpo Naminuum principiumuoce

33. Book of Durrow (T.C.D., MS 57), f. 17r, introducing the argumentum for Mark in the
prefatory material

ores ibi eric plecus Gfor
muta autem sunt uoca
eleca ..
icabeunces pha
silum feceruhc
eum insermoue Guhia
apulos suos cumheroo

34. Book of Kells (T.C.D., MS 58), f. 96r

35. Garland of Howth (T.C.D., MS 56), f. 1v (p. 2)

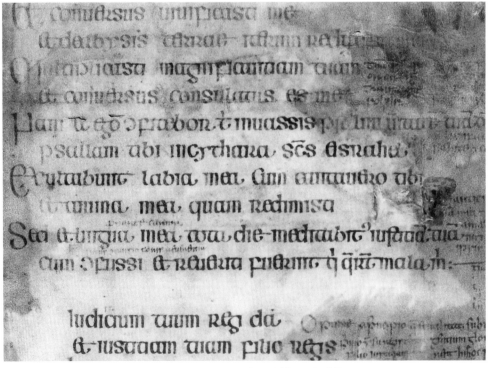

36. Double psalter (T.C.D., MS 1337), f. iiv

37 (*left*). Cormac Psalter (B.L., Add. MS 36929), f. 32r

38 (*above*). St Gall Gospels (St Gallen, Stiftsbibliothek, Cod. 51), p. 134

39. Book of MacRegol (Bodl., MS Auct. D.II.19), f. 2v

40. Antiphonary of Bangor (Milan, Biblioteca Ambrosiana, MS C 5), f. 10.

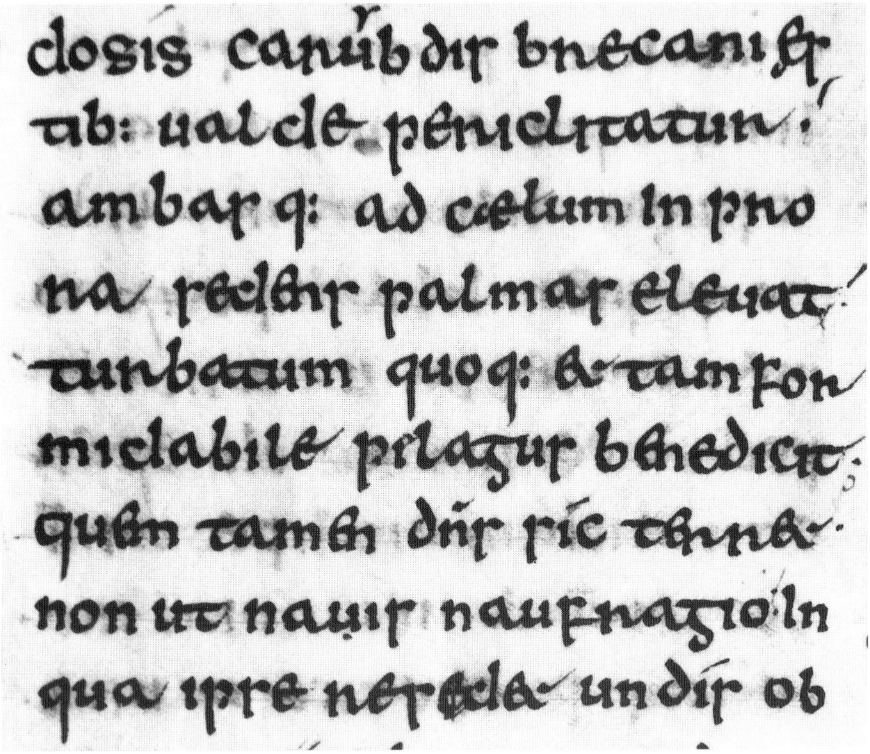

41. Adamnán's Life of St Columba, written by Dorbbéne (d. 713), abbot of Iona (Schaffhausen, Stadtsbibliothek MS Gen. 1), p. 17

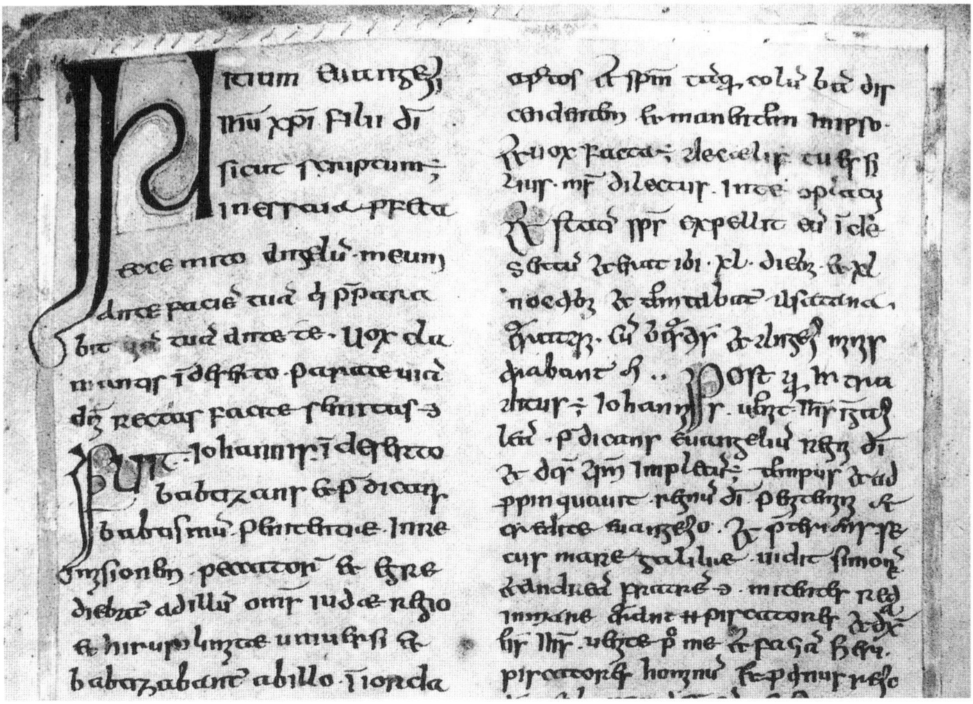

42. Book of Dimma (T.C.D., MS 59), p. 31

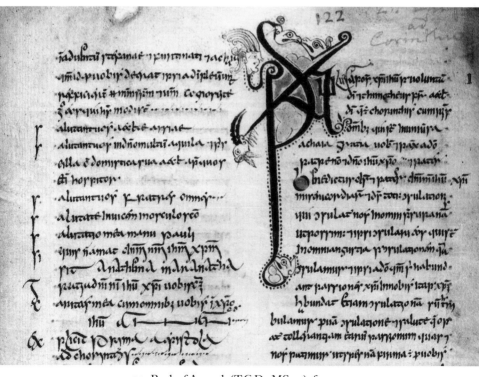

43. Book of Mulling (T.C.D., MS 60), f. 91v (formerly p. 182)

44. Book of Armagh (T.C.D., MS 52), f. 122r

mquidem

multi conati sunt ordi
nare narrationem que
innobis complete sunt re
rum sic ut tradiderunt no
bis qui abinitio ipsi uiderūt
& ministri fuerunt sermo
nis. Visum e & mihi adse
cuto aprincipio omnibus di
ligenter deinceps tibi scribere obeme
thsophile ut cognoscas eorum uerborum
dequibus erudit es e ueritatem : ·
Fuit in diebus herodis regis iude sacerdos
quidam nomine zacharias deuice abia & 
uxor illi de filiabus aaron & nomen eius
elizabeth. Erant aūt iusti ambo ante dm.
Incidentes in omnibus mandatis & iustificā
tionibus dm̄i sine querella. & non erat illis
filius eo quod esset helizabeth sterilis. &
ambo processissent in diebus suis. Factum e
aūt cum sacerdotio fungeretur in ordi

45 (*left*). MacDurnan
Gospels (Lambeth Palace
Library, MS 1370),
f. 117r

46 (*below*). Fragment
contained in Lambeth
Palace Library, MS 1229,
f. 7r

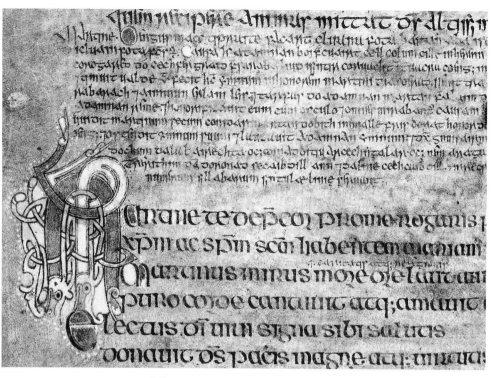

47. Liber Hymnorum (T.C.D., MS 1441), f. 8v

48. Liber Hymnorum (U.C.D., Franciscan House of Studies MS A1), f. 5v

49. Book of Deer (Cambridge University Library, MS I i.6.32), f. 2r

50. Edinburgh Psalter (Edinburgh University Library, MS 56), f. 46v

51. Gospels (B.L., Harl. MS 1023), f. 34v

52. Gospels (B.L., Harl. MS 1802), f. 87r

53. Drummond Missal (Pierpoint Morgan Library MS 627), f. 44

54. Schoolbook fragments from Glendalough (B.L., Eg. MS 3323), f. 18

55. Boethius, 'De arithmetica' (T.C.D., MS 1442), f. 5r

56. Stephen of Tournai, 'Summa super decretum Gratiani' (T.C.D., MS 1316/5), p. 89 (Lhuyd)

57. Latin translation (with glosses in Irish) of Chalcidius' commentary on Plato's 'Timaeus' (Bodl., MS Auct. F.3.15), f. 11r

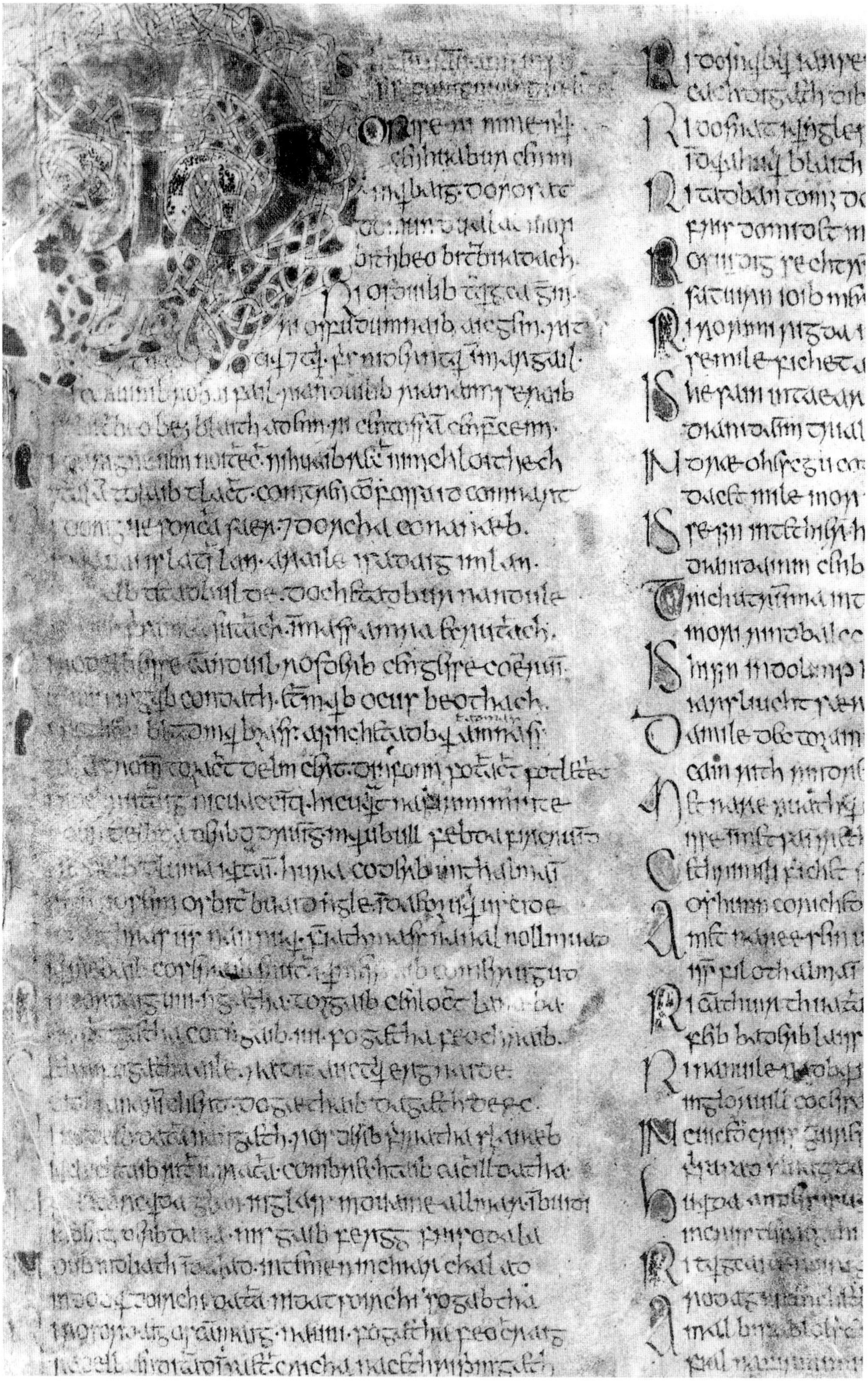

58. Opening section of 'Saltair na Rann' (Bodl., Rawl. B.502), f.19r.

59. Leabhar na hUidhre (R.I.A., MS 1229 (23.E.25), f. 11r

60. Section of the Annals of Tigernach (Bodl., Rawl. B.502), f. 11r

61. Book of Leinster (T.C.D., MS 1339), p. 17

62. Charter text of 1133, Book of Kells (T.C.D., MS 58), f. 6v

63. Cross of Muiredach, Monasterboice, Co. Louth: east face

64b. Detail of front: panels of gold filigree and amber borders

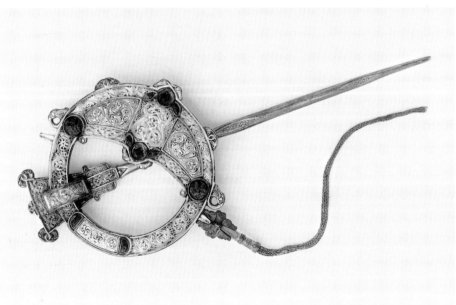

64a. Tara brooch, back (National Museum of Ireland)

65. Book of Kells (T.C.D., MS 58), f. 33r: eight-circle page or double-barred cross

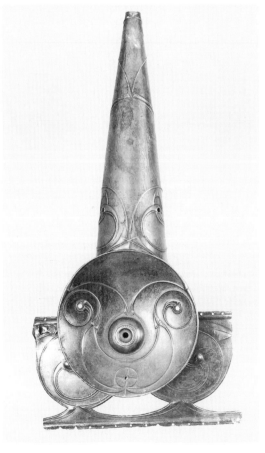

66a (*top*). Gold torc from Broighter, Co. Londonderry (National Museum of Ireland)

66b (*above*). Engraved slip of bone from Lough Crew, Co. Meath, *c*.second century A.D. (National Museum of Ireland)

66c (*left*). 'Petrie crown'; fragment of ceremonial or votive object (National Museum of Ireland)

67a. Newgrange, Co. Meath: main chamber; orthostat with triple spiral

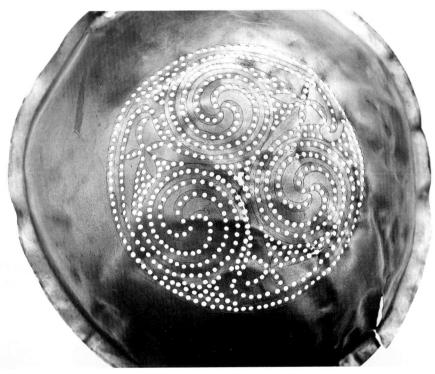

67b. Strainer from Moylarg crannog, Co. Antrim; detail of perforations arranged in spirals,
c.eighth century (National Museum of Ireland)

68. Lindisfarne Gospels (B.L., MS Cott. Nero D IV), f. 26v

69a. Cross of Muiredach, Monasterboice, Co. Louth: south side; panel of raised spirals

69b. Mullaghmast stone, Co. Kildare: unfinished pattern (National Museum of Ireland)

69c. Moylough belt-shrine: detail of front, adjoining buckle (National Museum of Ireland)

70a. Janus figure, Boa Island, Co. Fermanagh

70b. Statue from Tanderagee, Co. Armagh; Armagh cathedral

70c. Pillar carved with sundial, interlace, and fish, Clogher cathedral, Co. Tyrone

70d. Ballinderry gaming-board (National Museum of Ireland)

71a. The Ardagh chalice (National Museum of Ireland)

71b. Ardagh chalice: detail of applied decoration and inscription

72. Book of Kells (T.C.D., MS 58), f. 7v: detail, Virgin and Child with angels

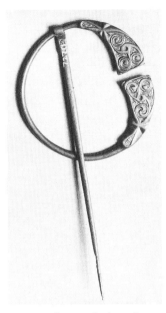

73a. Pennanular brooch
(Liverpool Museum)

73b. Cross of Muiredach, Monasterboice, Co. Louth: west
face; 'Ecce homo'

73c. Duvillaun slab, Co. Mayo: east face

74a (*above*). Hanging-bowl mount from Myklebostad, Norway (Bergen Museum)    74b (*right*). Book of Durrow (T.C.D., MS 57), f. 21v: symbol of St Matthew

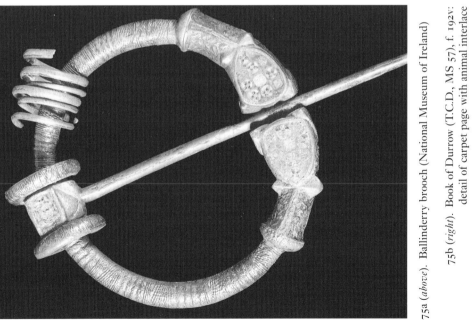

75a (*above*). Ballinderry brooch (National Museum of Ireland)

75b (*right*). Book of Durrow (T.C.D., MS 57), f. 192v: detail of carpet page with animal interlace

76. Book of Durrow (T.C.D., MS 57), f. 3v: carpet page

77a, 77b (*above*). Two sides of a finial from a large shrine (Musée des Antiquités Nationales, Saint-Germain-en-Laye)

77c (*left*). Hanging-bowl openwork mount, found in River Bann (Ulster Museum)

78. Shrine of St Patrick's Bell (National Museum of Ireland)

79a. Bronze mount from Aghaboe, Co. Laois (National Museum of Ireland)

79b. Carved pillar, Killadeas, Co. Fermanagh

79c. Carved figures, White Island, Co. Fermanagh

79d. Bronze bell from Bangor, Co. Down (Ulster Museum)

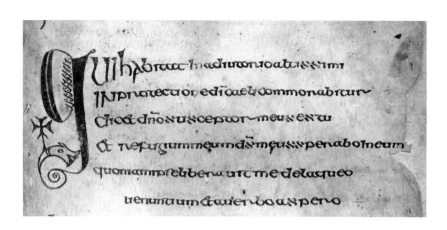

80a (*above*). The Cathach (R.I.A., MS 12.R.33), f. 48r: initial Q

80b (*left*). House-shaped shrine (Museo Civico Medievale, Bologna)

80c (*below*). Clonmore shrine: lower back plate (Ulster Museum)

81. Lichfield Gospels (Lichfield Cathedral Library): portrait of St Luke

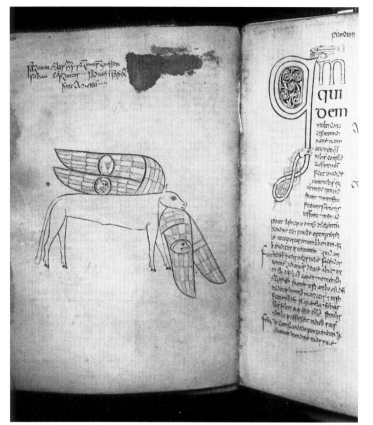

82a (*left*). Book of Armagh (T.C.D., MS 52), f. 68v and detail of f. 69r: symbol of St Luke and opening passage

82b (*below*). Door-handle from Donore, Co. Meath (National Museum of Ireland)

83. Book of Kells (T.C.D., MS 58), f. 34r: Chi-ro page, 'Christi autem generatio'

84a (*above*). Book of Kells, f. 48r (detail)

84b (*left*). Book of Dimma (T.C.D., MS 59), p. 30: portrait of St Mark

85a. Derrynavlan chalice (National Museum of Ireland)

85b. Derrynavlan paten (National Museum of Ireland)

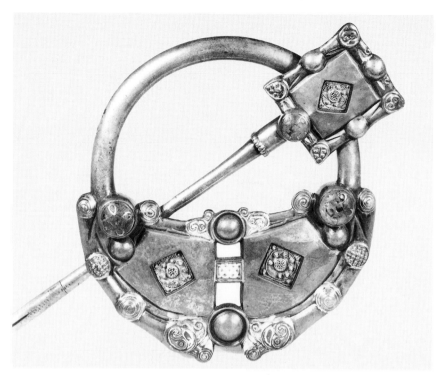

86a. Killamery brooch (National Museum of Ireland)

86b. Cavan or 'Queen's' brooch (National Museum of Ireland)

*(clockwise from top left)*

87a.  Kilnasaggart pillar, Co. Armagh

87b.  Cross-slab from Carrowntemple, Co. Sligo (National Museum of Ireland)

87c.  Small Chi-Ro cross (height 15 cm), from Inis Cealtra, Co. Clare

87d.  Grave-slab, Clonmacnoise, Co. Offaly, inscribed 'or [óit] do dainéil' (a prayer for Daniel)

88b. Cross and pillars, Carndonagh, Co. Donegal

88a. Cross-slab, Fahan Mura, Co. Donegal

89a. Cross of Patrick and Columba, Kells,
Co. Meath: west face

89b. Cross of Patrick and Columba, Kells,
Co. Meath: east face

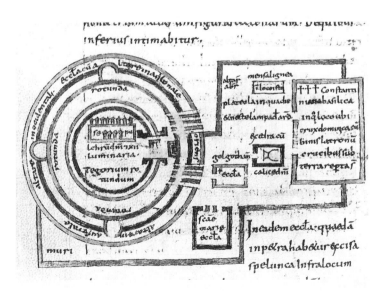

89c. Sketch of the church of the Holy Sepulchre and its surroundings,
from Adamnán, 'De locis sanctis' (Österreichische Nationalbibliothek,
Vienna, Cod. 458. f. 4v)

90b. St Martin's Cross, Iona

90a. North Cross, Ahenny, Co. Tipperary

91b. Cross of the Scriptures, Clonmacnoise, Co. Offaly

91a. Cross of Moone, Co. Kildare, scenes on base: Daniel, the sacrifice of Isaac, the fall of man

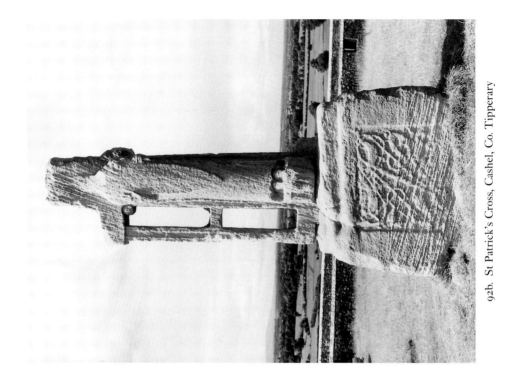

92b. St Patrick's Cross, Cashel, Co. Tipperary

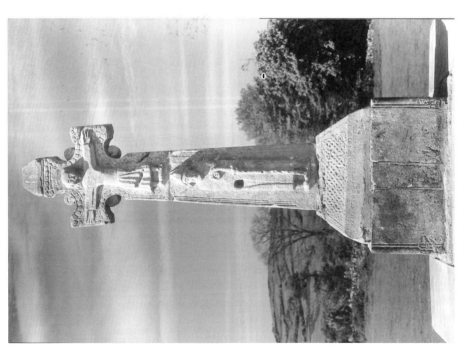

92a. Dysert O'Dea cross, Co. Clare

93a. Shrine of St Lachtin's arm (National
Museum of Ireland)

93b. Crosier found in Lismore Castle, Co.
Waterford (National Museum of Ireland)

94a. Shrine of Stowe Missal (National Museum of Ireland)

94b. Shrine of Stowe Missal: detail of side panel

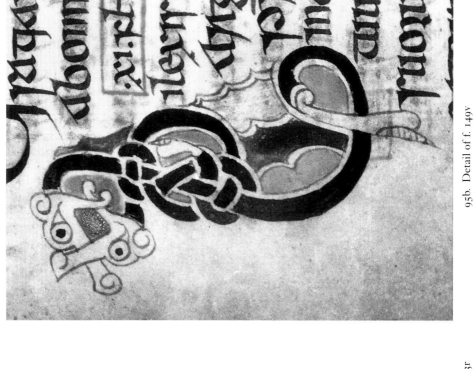

95b. Detail of f. 149v

95a. Missal (Corpus Christi College, Oxford, MS 282), f. 43r

96. The Cross of Cong (National Museum of Ireland)

97. Inishmurray, Co. Sligo: aerial view of the monastic enclosure

98. Clonmacnoise, Co. Offaly: ruins of the cathedral and (background) Temple Dowling; the Cross of the Scriptures was in front of the cathedral portal

100 (*above*). Muiredach's Cross, Monasterboice, Co. Louth: capstone in the form of a shrine or wooden church

99 (*left*). Book of Kells (T.C.D., MS 58), f. 202v: the temptation of Christ, showing church with ornate wooden roof

101. St MacDara's Island, Co. Galway: church prior to restoration. The stones of the roof give the impression of simulating shingles (wooden tiles)

102. Gallarus Oratory, Co. Kerry

103 (*left*). The so-called 'Church of St Columba', Kells, Co. Meath

104 (*below*). Early stone church at Fore, Co. Westmeath, with characteristic antae and lintelled doorway

105. Trinity Church, Glendalough, Co. Wicklow; interior, showing chancel

106. Temple Benén on Inismór, Aran Islands, Co. Galway; the walls formed from large slabs laid on their side

107. Round tower, Glendalough, Co. Wicklow; cap reconstructed in 1876

108. West façade of St Cronan's church, Roscrea, Co. Tipperary

109 (*left*). Carvings (c.1184)
on east window of Romanesque
arcading, Tuam cathedral,
Co. Galway

110 (*below*). Carved capitals
(c.1184) on chancel arch, Tuam
cathedral, Co. Galway

112. Romanesque portal, with tangent gable and carvings in thin relief, Killeshin, Co. Laois

111. Cormac's Chapel, Cashel, Co. Tipperary: exterior from south-west

114. Interior of chancel, Cormac's Chapel, Cashel, Co. Tipperary

113. North jamb of portal, with sculptured heads between patterns of 'Urnes' snake ornament, Killeshin, Co. Laois

115. Clonfert cathedral, Co. Galway; the most extravagant of the Romanesque portals of Ireland

116. Ardmore, Co. Waterford: monastic church with sculptured arcades (bottom left), dominated by late–twelfth–century round tower

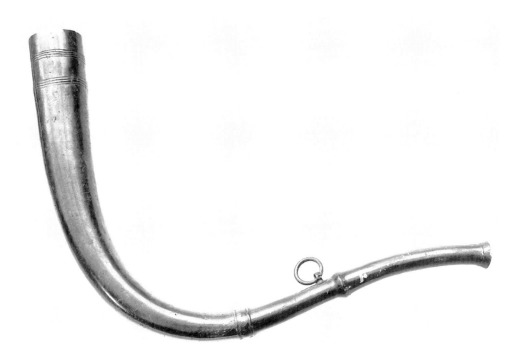

117. Bronze-age horn from Drumbest, Co. Antrim (National Museum of Ireland)

118. Horns and crotals from the late bronze-age (eighth–seventh century B.C.) hoard from Dowris, Co. Offaly (National Museum of Ireland)

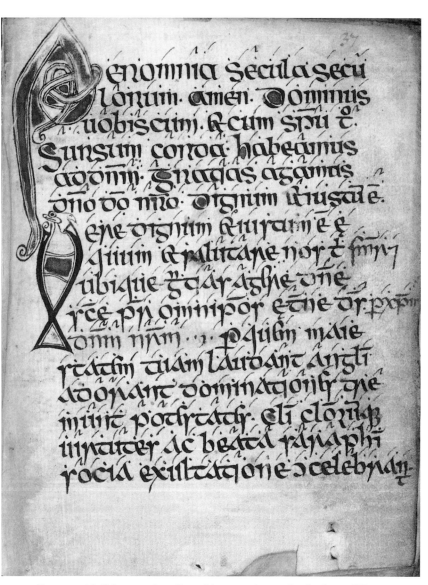

119. Responsorial dialogue and preface with neumatic notation in the twelfth-century
Drummond Missal (Pierpoint Morgan Library, MS M.627, f. 37r)

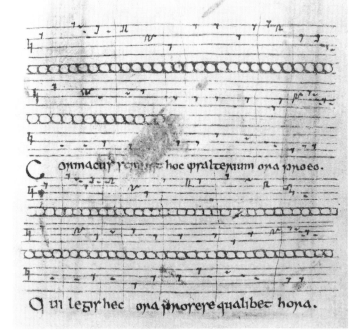

120 (*above*). Easter processional antiphon 'Dicant nunc Iudei', set for two voices in a twelfth- or thirteenth-century Irish gradual (Bodl., Rawl. MS C 892, ff 67–68r)

121 (*left*). Colophon set in three-part polyphony in an Irish psalter from the second half of the twelfth century (B.L., Add. MS 36929, f. 59r.)

122. The hymn 'Adest dies leticiae', in honour of St Brigid, in an Irish Divine Office antiphonal from the second half of the fifteenth century (T.C.D., MS 78, f. 139v)

123. Fragments of notation inscribed on one of four slates from Smarmore, Co. Louth, probably second half of the fifteenth century (National Museum of Ireland)

124. Detail from shrine of the Stowe Missal ('shrine of St Maelruain's Gospel'), eleventh century, depicting player of three-stringed plucked lyre, seated between two clerics (National Museum of Ireland)

125. Breac Maedóic ('shrine of St Mogue'), eleventh century, bearing the earliest Irish illustration of a trilateral harp, apparently with eight strings (National Museum of Ireland)

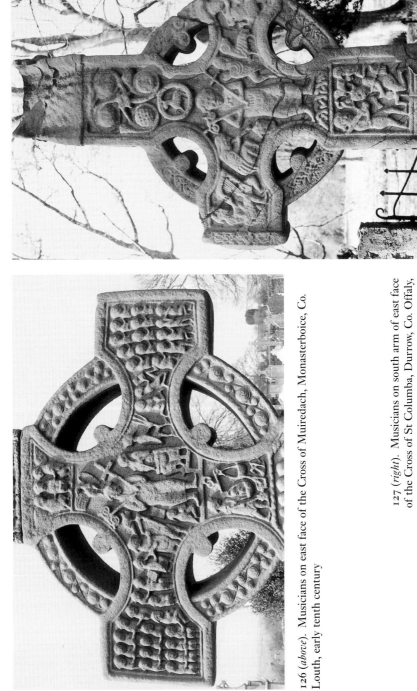

126 (*above*). Musicians on east face of the Cross of Muiredach, Monasterboice, Co. Louth, early tenth century

127 (*right*). Musicians on south arm of east face of the Cross of St Columba, Durrow, Co. Offaly, early tenth century

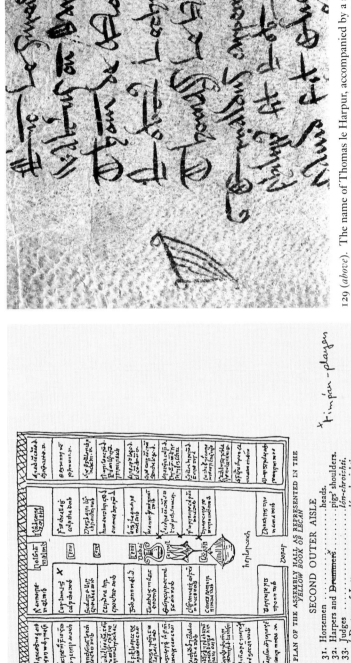

PLAN OF THE ASSEMBLY HALL AS REPRESENTED IN THE
YELLOW BOOK OF LECAN

SECOND OUTER AISLE

31. Horsemen . . . . . . . . . . . . . . . . . heads.
32. Harpers and Drummers . . . . . . . . pigs' shoulders.
33. Judges . . . . . . . . . . . . . . . . . . lón-chroichti.
34. { Doctors of Letters . . . . . . . . . . lón-chroichti.
      { Their nominated successors . . . . les-chroichti.
35. { Chief poets . . . . . . . . . . . . . . haunches.
      { Anruith (2d grade poets) . . . . . . cam-chnáim.
36. Hospitallers . . . . . . . . . . . . . . haunches.
37. { Master wrights and . . . . . . . . . pigs' shoulders.
      { their successors . . . . . . . . . . . cam-chnáim.
38. Soothsayers and Druids . . . . . . . . shin portions.
39. Builders and Wrights . . . . . . . . . fr-chroichti.
40. Horners and Pipers . . . . . . . . . . middle portion.
41. Engravers . . . . . . . . . . . . . . . . milgatan.
42. Cordwainers . . . . . . . . . . . . . . shoulder-fat.

65

timpán-player

129 (*above*). The name of Thomas le Harpur, accompanied by a sketch of a harp, in an entry for c.1200 in the Dublin Guild Merchant roll (c.1190–1265) (Dublin Corporation archives)

128 (*left*). Facsimile of reconstructed seating plan of Tech Midchúarda (the Hall of Tara) from the fourteenth-century Yellow Book of Lecan (T.C.D, MS 1318 (H.2.16), cols 243–4 (facsimile ed., p. 418))

130. Cross of the Scriptures, Clonmacnoise, Co. Offaly, showing lyre-player (central panel, south side of shaft) and player of the triple pipes (corresponding panel, north side), ninth or tenth century

131. Miracle of the loaves and fishes: figure with assymetrical lyre on west face of head of the ninth-century South Cross, or Cross of St Patrick and St Columba, Kells, Co. Meath

132. The only known medieval Irish representation of a bowed instrument: twelfth-century carving of lyre-player, from St Finan's church, Lough Currane, Waterville, Co. Kerry

133. Harper at Solomon's court, west wall of Ardmore cathedral, Co. Waterford

134 (*right*). Portrait of a musician from the Book of Kells, eighth or ninth century (T.C.D., MS 58, f. 292r): 'In principio' with stylised seated figure (letter 'i') holding letter 'c' as a stringed instrument.

135 (*below*). Woodcut (plate 3) from John Derricke's Image of Irelande (1583), representing a harper and reciter (and possibly a pair of crosáin to the right) performing at Mac Suibhne's feast, 1581

A    Now when into their fenced holdes, the knaues are entred in,
      To finite and knocke the cattell downe, the hangmen doe beginne.
      One plucketh off the Oxes cote, which he euen now did weare:
      Another lacking pannes, to boyle the flesh, his hide prepare.
C    These thecues attend vpon the fire, for seruing vp the feast:
B    And fryer smellfeast sneaking in, doth preace amongst the best.

3    who play'th in Romish toyes the Ape, by counterfetting Paull:
      For which they doe award him then, the highest roome of all.
      who being set, because the cheere, is deemed little worth:
      Except the same be intermixt, and lac'de with Irish myrth.
D    Both Barde, and Harper, is prepared, which by their cunning art,
      Doe strike and cheare vp all the gestes, with comfort at the hart.

(a)

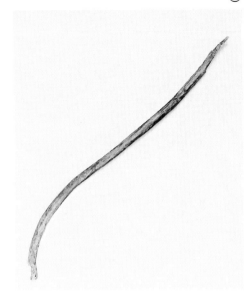

(b)

136 (*right*). Sword–dancing scene on fifteenth– or sixteenth–century book–cover bearing the arms of one of the FitzGeralds of Desmond (National Museum of Ireland)

137 (*far right*). (a) Fragment of wooden bow; (b) detail of terminal carved in Ringerike style, excavated from a mid–eleventh–century site in Christchurch Place, Dublin (National Museum of Ireland)

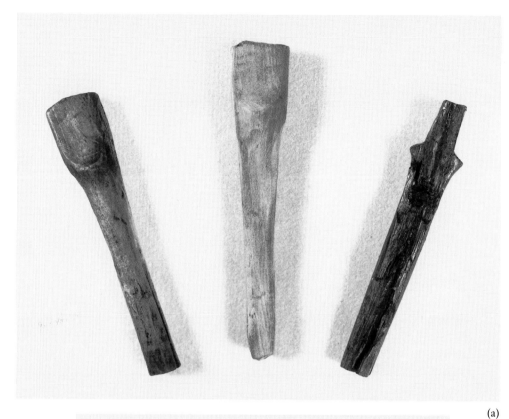

(a)

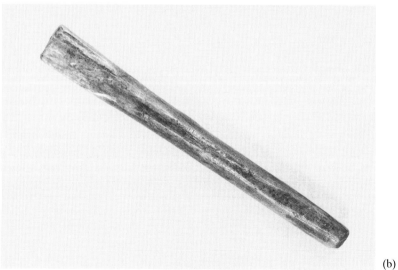

(b)

138. Tuning pegs made of yew: (a) shorter examples, probably from lyres, fiddles, or psalteries; (b) longer type, possibly from a harp (High Street; thirteenth century) (National Museum of Ireland)

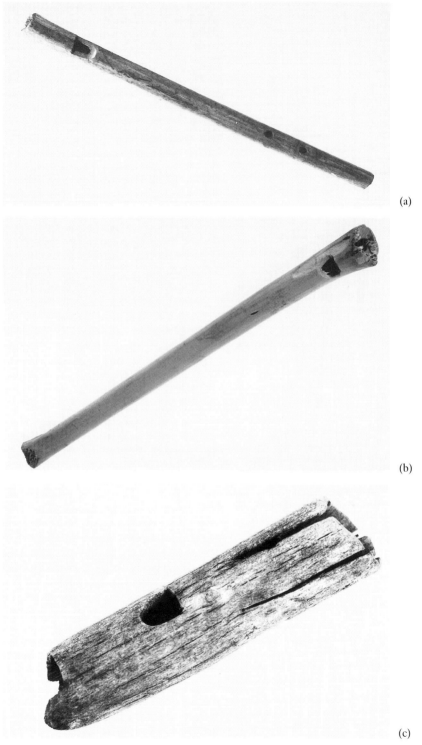

139. Flutes and flute fragments from excavations of medieval Dublin, left to right:
(a) bone flute with two fingerholes; (b) bone flute without fingerholes; and
(c) mouthpiece fragment of bone flute (all from High Street, thirteenth century)
(National Museum of Ireland)

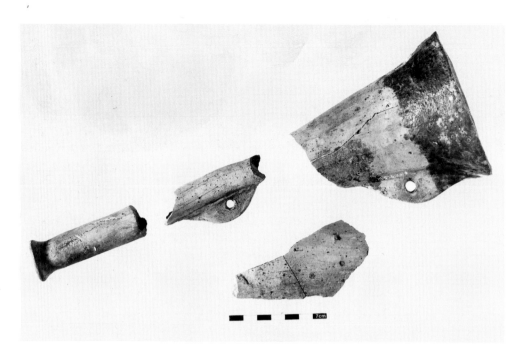

140a. Fragments of ceramic horn from Wood Quay, Dublin, thirteenth century (National Museum of Ireland)

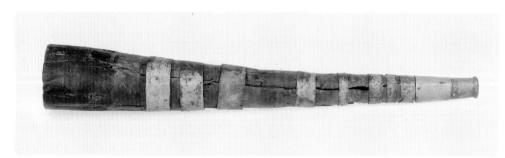

140b. Horn of yew with bronze mounts, eighth or ninth century, from Lough Erne, Co. Fermanagh (Ulster Museum)